Kontaktlinguistik
Contact Linguistics
Linguistique de contact

HSK 12.2

Handbücher zur
Sprach- und Kommunikationswissenschaft

Handbooks of Linguistics
and Communication Science

Manuels de linguistique et
des sciences de communication

Mitbegründet von
Gerold Ungeheuer

Herausgegeben von / Edited by / Edités par
Hugo Steger
Herbert Ernst Wiegand

Band 12.2

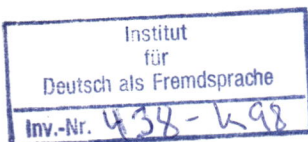

Walter de Gruyter · Berlin · New York
1997

Kontaktlinguistik
Contact Linguistics
Linguistique de contact

Ein internationales Handbuch zeitgenössischer Forschung
An International Handbook of Contemporary Research
Manuel international des recherches contemporaines

Herausgegeben von / Edited by / Edité par
Hans Goebl · Peter H. Nelde · Zdeněk Starý
Wolfgang Wölck

2. Halbband / Volume 2 / Tome 2

Walter de Gruyter · Berlin · New York
1997

∞ Gedruckt auf säurefreiem Papier, das die
US-ANSI-Norm über Haltbarkeit erfüllt.

Library of Congress Cataloging-in Publication Data

Kontaktlinguistik : ein internationales Handbuch zeitgenössischer
  Forschung / herausgegeben von Hans Goebl ... [et al.] = Contact
  linguistics : an international handbook of contemporary research /
  edited by Hans Goebl ... [et al.].
       p.   cm. − (Handbücher zur Sprach- und
  Kommunikationswissenschaft ; Bd. 12 = Handbooks of linguistics
  and communication science)
       German, English, and French.
       Includes bibliographical references and index.
       ISBN 3-11-013264-8 (alk. paper)
       1. Language in contact − Handbooks, manuals, etc.   I. Goebl,
  Hans. II. Series: Handbücher zur Sprach- und
  Kommunikationswissenschaft ; Bd. 12.
  P130.5.K66   1996
  410−dc20   96-20474
                                                                 CIP

Die Deutsche Bibliothek − CIP-Einheitsaufnahme

Handbücher zur Sprach- und Kommunikationswissenschaft /
mitbegr. von Gerold Ungeheuer. Hrsg. von Hugo Steger ;
Herbert Ernst Wiegand. − Berlin ; New York : de Gruyter.
  Früher hrsg. von Gerold Ungeheuer und Herbert Ernst Wiegand. −
  Teilw. mit Parallelt.: Handbooks of linguistics and communication
  science. − Teilw. mit Nebent.: HSK

Bd. 12. Kontaktlinguistik.
  Halbbd. 2. − (1997)

Kontaktlinguistik : ein internationales Handbuch
zeitgenössischer Forschung = Contact linguistics / hrsg. von
Hans Goebl ... − Berlin ; New York : de Gruyter.
  (Handbücher zur Sprach- und Kommunikationswissenschaft ; Bd. 12)

Halbbd. 2. − (1997)
  ISBN 3-11-015154-5

© Copyright 1997 by Walter de Gruyter & Co., D-10785 Berlin.
Dieses Werk einschließlich aller seiner Teile ist urheberrechtlich geschützt. Jede Verwertung außerhalb der
engen Grenzen des Urheberrechtsgesetzes ist ohne Zustimmung des Verlages unzulässig und strafbar. Das
gilt insbesondere für Vervielfältigungen, Übersetzungen, Mikroverfilmungen und die Einspeicherung und
Verarbeitung in elektronischen Systemen.
Printed in Germany
Satz und Druck: Arthur Collignon GmbH, Berlin
Buchbinderische Verarbeitung: Lüderitz & Bauer-GmbH, Berlin

Inhalt / Contents / Table des matières

2. Halbband / Volume 2 / Tome 2

Verzeichnis der Tabellen und Abbildungen / Index of Tables and Figures /
Index des tableaux et figures.................................... XXI

IX. Sprachkontakte in Nordeuropa
Language Contacts in Northern Europe
Contacts linguistiques en Europe du Nord

Norwegen / Norway / Norvège

116. Ernest Håkon Jahr, Norway *(Norwegen / Norvège)*............ 937
117. Geir Wiggen, Nynorsk-Bokmål 948
118. Nils Jernsletten, Norwegian-Saami
     (Norwegisch-Samisch / Norvégien-sami) 957
119. Anna-Riitta Lindgren, Norwegisch-Finnisch
     (Norwegian-Finnish / Norvégien-finnois) 961

Schweden / Sweden / Suède

120. Erling Wande, Sweden *(Schweden / Suède)* 966
121. Olavi Korhonen, Schwedisch-Samisch *(Swedish-Saami / Suédois-sami)* 976
122. Jarmo Lainio, Swedish-Finnish *(Schwedisch-Finnisch / Suédois-finnois)*.... 982

Finnland / Finland / Finlande

123. Heikki Paunonen, Finland *(Finnland / Finlande)* 993
124. Marika Tandefelt, Finnish-Swedish
     (Finnisch-Schwedisch / Finnois-suédois) 1007
125. Pekka Sammallahti, Finnish-Saami *(Finnisch-Samisch / Finnois-sami)*.. 1015

Dänemark / Denmark / Danmark

126. Frans Gregersen, Denmark *(Dänemark / Danmark)* 1020
127. Bent Søndergaard, Dänisch-Deutsch
     (Danish-German / Danois-allemand) 1033
128. Björn Hagström, Faroese-Danish *(Färöisch-Dänisch / Féroien-danois)* 1043
129. Michael Fortescue / Inge Kleivan, Greenlandic-Danish
     (Grönländisch-Dänisch / Grœnlandais-danois) 1049

Island / Iceland / Islande

130. Asta Svavarsdóttir, Iceland *(Island / Islande)* 1054

X. Sprachkontakte in Nordwesteuropa
Language Contacts in Northwestern Europe
Contacts linguistiques en Europe du Nord-Ouest

Großbritannien / Great Britain / Grande-Bretagne

131. Colin Baker, Great Britain *(Großbritannien / Grande-Bretagne)* 1059
132. Colin Williams, English-Welsh *(English-Walisisch / Anglais-gallois)* . . 1075
133. Wolfgang Viereck, Englisch-Gälisch
    (English-Scots Gaelic / Anglais-gaélique écossais) 1088

Irland / Ireland / Irlande

134. Pádraig Ó Riagáin, Ireland *(Irland / Irlande)* 1097

XI. Sprachkontakte in Westeuropa
Language Contacts in Western Europe
Contacts linguistiques en Europe de l'Ouest

Belgien / Belgium / Belgique

135. Albert Verdoodt, Belgique *(Belgien / Belgium)* 1107
136. Roland Willemyns, Niederländisch-Französisch
    (Dutch-French / Néerlandais-français) 1123
137. Rudolf Kern, Französisch-Deutsch
    (French-German / Français-allemand) 1130
138. Sonja Vandermeeren, Niederländisch-Deutsch
    (Dutch-German / Néerlandais-allemand) 1136

Niederlande / Netherlands / Pays-Bas

139. Cor van Bree / Jan de Vries, Netherlands *(Niederlande / Pays-Bas)* . . 1143
140. Durk Gorter, Dutch-West Frisian
    (Niederländisch-Westfriesisch / Néerlandais-frison occidental) 1152

Luxemburg / Luxemburg / Luxembourg

141. Harald Fröhlich / Fernand Hoffmann, Luxemburg
    (Luxemburg / Luxembourg) 1158

Frankreich / France / France

142. Jean-Baptiste Marcellesi / Foued Laroussi, France
    (Frankreich / France) 1172
143. Georg Kremnitz, Français-occitan
    (Französisch-Okzitanisch / French-Occitan) 1188
144. Domènec Bernardó / Georg Kremnitz, Français-catalan
    (Französisch-Katalanisch / French-Catalan) 1195

145. Jacques Thiers, Français-corse *(Französisch-Korsisch / French-Corsican)* 1201
146. Jean Chiorboli, Corse-italien *(Korsisch-Italienisch / Corsican-Italian)* .. 1214
147. Jean Petit, Français-allemand *(Französisch-Deutsch / French-German)* .. 1222
148. Bruno Callebaut / Hugo Ryckeboer, Français-néerlandais
   (Französisch-Niederländisch / French-Dutch) 1240
149. Yves Le Berre / Jean Le Dû, Français-breton
   (Französisch-Bretonisch / French-Breton) 1252
150. Jacques Allières, Français-basque
   (Französisch-Baskisch / French-Basque) 1260

XII. Sprachkontakte in Südwesteuropa
Language Contacts in Southwestern Europe
Contacts linguistiques en Europe du Sud-Ouest

Spanien / Spain / Espagne
151. Harald Thun, Spanien *(Spain / Espagne)* 1270
152. Francisco R. Rei, Espagnol-galicien
   (Spanisch-Galizisch / Spanish-Galician) 1285
153. Emili Boix / Lluís Payrató / F. Xavier Vila, Espagnol-catalan
   (Spanisch-Katalanisch / Spanish-Catalan) 1296
154. Gotzon Aurrekoetxea, Espagnol-basque
   (Spanisch-Baskisch / Spanish-Basque) 1303

Portugal / Portugal / Portugal
155. Jürgen Schmidt-Radefeldt, Portugal *(Portugal / Portugal)* 1310

XIII. Sprachkontakte in Südeuropa
Language Contacts in Southern Europe
Contacts linguistiques en Europe du Sud

Italien / Italy / Italie
156. Dieter Kattenbusch, Italien *(Italy / Italie)* 1318
157. Tullio Telmon, Italien-français (francoprovençal)
   *(Italienisch-Französisch (Frankoprovenzalisch) /
   Italian-French (Francoprovençal))* 1330
158. Carla Marcato, Italien-frioulan
   (Italienisch-Friaulisch / Italian-Friulan) 1337
159. Anna Cornagliotti, Italien-occitan
   (Italienisch-Okzitanisch / Italian-Occitan) 1344
160. Kurt Egger / Karin Heller, Italienisch-Deutsch
   (Italian-German / Italien-allemand) 1350
161. Mitja Skubic, Italien (frioulan)-slovène
   (Italienisch (Friaulisch)-Slowenisch / Italian (Friulian)-Slovenian) ... 1357

162. Walter Breu, Italienisch-Kroatisch *(Italian-Croatian / Italien-croate)* .. 1362
163. Mariateresa Colotti, Italien-grec
(Italienisch-Griechisch / Italian-Greek) 1366
164. Gabriele Birken-Silvermann, Italienisch-Albanisch
(Italian-Albanian / Italien-albanais) 1371
165. Rosita Rindler Schjerve, Sardaigne *(Sardinien / Sardinia)* 1376
166. Lois Craffonara, Ladinien *(Ladinia / Ladinie dolomitique)* 1383

Malta / Malta / Malte
167. Reinhold Kontzi, Malta *(Malta / Malte)* 1399

XIV. Sprachkontakte in Südosteuropa
Language Contacts in Southeastern Europe
Contacts linguistiques en Europe du Sud-Est

Jugoslawien / Jugoslavia / Yougoslavie
168. Gerhard Neweklowsky, Jugoslawien *(Jugoslavia / Yougoslavie)* 1407

Slowenien / Slovenia / Slovénie
169. Albina Nećak Lük, Slovenia *(Slowenien / Slovénie)* 1416

Kroatien / Croatia / Croatie
170. Milorad Pupovac, Croatia *(Kroatien / Croatie)* 1424

Bosnien-Herzegowina / Bosnia-Herzegovina / Bosnie-Herzégovine
171. August Kovačec, Bosnie-Herzégovine
(Bosnien-Herzegowina / Bosnia-Herzegovina) 1434

Makedonien / Macedonia / Macédoine
172. Victor A. Friedman, Macedonia *(Makedonien / Macédoine)* 1442

Albanien / Albania / Albanie
173. Raymond Detrez, Albanie *(Albanien / Albania)* 1451

Rumänien / Rumania / Roumanie
174. Wolfgang Dahmen, Rumänien *(Rumania / Roumanie)* 1458
175. Kurt Rein, Rumänisch-Deutsch
(Rumanian-German / Roumain-allemand) 1470
176. Gabriella Schubert, Rumänisch-Ungarisch
(Rumanian-Hungarian / Roumain-hongrois) 1478

Bulgarien / Bulgaria / Bulgarie
177. Grace Fielder, Bulgaria *(Bulgarien / Bulgarie)* 1487
     Ivan Duridanov, Annex *(Annex / Annexe)* 1496
178. Christina Kramer, Bulgarian-Macedonian
(Bulgarisch-Makedonisch / Bulgare-macédonien) 1498

179.	Birgit Igla, Bulgarisch-Türkisch *(Bulgarian-Turkish / Bulgare-turc)* . . .	1504
180.	Petya Assenova, Bulgare-grec *(Bulgarisch-Griechisch / Bulgarian-Greek)*	1510

Griechenland / Greece / Grèce

181.	Gunnar Hering, Griechenland *(Greece / Grèce)*	1515
182.	Charalambos Symeonides, Griechisch-Türkisch *(Greek-Turkish / Grec-turc)*	1525
183.	Wolfgang Dahmen, Griechisch-Aromunisch *(Greek-Arumanian / Grec-aroumain)*	1532
184.	Lukas D. Tsitsipis, Greek-Albanian *(Griechisch-Albanisch / Grec-albanais)*	1540
185.	Raymond Detrez, Grec-macédonien *(Griechisch-Makedonisch / Greek-Macedonian)*	1544
186.	Thomas Henninger, Griechisch-Bulgarisch *(Greek-Bulgarian / Grec-bulgare)*	1550

Europäische Türkei / European Turkey / Turquie d'Europe

187.	Johann Strauß, European Turkey *(Europäische Türkei / Turquie d'Europe)*	1554
188.	Johann Strauß, Turc-grec *(Türkisch-Griechisch / Turkish-Greek)*	1560
189.	Johann Strauß, Turkish-Judaeo-Spanish *(Türkisch-Judenspanisch / Turc-judéo-espagnol)*	1566
190.	Michael Job, Türkisch-Armenisch *(Turkish-Armenian / Turc-arménien)* .	1572

Zypern / Cyprus / Chypre

191.	Yvo J. D. Peeters, Cyprus *(Zypern / Chypre)*	1577

XV. Sprachkontakte in Mitteleuropa
Language Contacts in Central Europe
Contacts linguistiques en Europe Centrale

Polen / Poland / Pologne

192.	Jolanta Rokoszowa, Poland *(Polen / Pologne)*	1583
193.	Józef Wiktorowicz, Polnisch-Deutsch *(Polish-German / Polonais-allemand)*	1594
194.	Jerzy Treder, Polish-Kashubian *(Polnisch-Kaschubisch / Polonais-kachoube)*	1600
195.	Elżbieta Smułkowa, Polish-Byelorussian *(Polnisch-Weißrussisch / Polonais-biélorusse)*	1606
196.	Józef Marcinkiewicz, Polnisch-Litauisch *(Polish-Lithuanian / Polonais-lituanien)*	1614
197.	Janusz A. Rieger, Polish-Ukrainian *(Polnisch-Ukrainisch / Polonais-ukrainien)*	1622

198. Franciszek Sowa, Polish-Slovak
(Polnisch-Slowakisch / Polonais-slovaque) 1628
199. Janusz Siatkowski, Polnisch-Tschechisch
(Polish-Czech / Polonais-tchèque) 1634

Tschechien / Czechia / Tchèquie

200. Jiří Nekvapil, Tschechien
(Czechia / Tchèquie) 1641
201. Jiří Zeman, Czech-Slovak (Tschechisch-Slowakisch / Tchèque-slovaque) 1650
202. Jaromír Povejšil, Tschechisch-Deutsch
(Czech-German / Tchèque-allemand) 1656
203. Edvard Lotko, Tschechisch-Polnisch
(Czech-Polish / Tchèque-polonais) 1662

Slowakei / Slovakia / Slovaquie

204. Slavo Ondrejovič, Slowakei (Slovakia / Slovaquie) 1669
205. Gizela Szabómihály, Slowakisch-Ungarisch (Slovak-Hungarian / Slovaque-hongrois) 1678
206. Mária Papsonová / Ivor Ripka, Slowakisch-Deutsch
(Slovak-German / Slovaque-allemand) 1685
207. Slavo Ondrejovič / Sibyla Mislovičová, Slowakisch-Polnisch
(Slovak-Polish / Slovaque-polonais) 1692
208. Mikuláš Štec, Slowakisch-Ukrainisch
(Slovak-Ukrainian / Slovaque-ukrainien) 1695
209. Ivor Ripka, Slowakisch-Tschechisch
(Slovak-Czech / Slovaque-tchèque) 1702

Ungarn / Hungary / Hongrie

210. Miklós Kontra, Hungary (Ungarn / Hongrie) 1708
211. Regina Hessky, Ungarisch-Deutsch
(Hungarian-German / Hongrois-allemand) 1723
212. István Nyomárkay / Gabriella Schubert, Ungarisch-Serbokroatisch
(Hungarian-Serbo-Croatian / Hongrois-serbo-croate) 1731
213. Géza Szabo / Gabriella Schubert, Ungarisch-Slowenisch
(Hungarian-Slovenian / Hongrois-slovène) 1738
214. Anna Gyivicsán / Gabriella Schubert,
Ungarisch-Slowakisch (Hungarian-Slovak / Hongrois slovaque) 1744
215. Anna Borbély, Ungarisch-Rumänisch
(Hungarian-Romanian / Hongrois-roumain) 1749

Deutschland / Germany / Allemagne

216. Wolfdietrich Hartung, Deutschland (Germany / Allemagne) 1753
217. Bent Søndergaard, Deutsch-Dänisch
(German-Danish / Allemand-danois) 1769

218. Bo Sjölin, Deutsch-Nordfriesisch
(German-North Frisian / Allemand-frison septentrional) 1777
219. Alastair Walker, Dänisch-Nordfriesisch
(Danish-North Frisian / Danois-frison septentrional) 1782
220. Marron C. Fort, Deutsch-Ostfriesisch
(German-East Frisian / Allemand-frison oriental) 1786
221. Helmut Faßke, Deutsch-Sorbisch (German-Sorbian / Allemand-sorabe) 1790

Österreich / Austria / Autriche

222. Heinz Dieter Pohl, Österreich (Austria / Autriche) 1797
223. Heinz Dieter Pohl, Deutsch-Slowenisch
(German-Slovenian / Allemand-slovène) 1813
224. Gerhard Neweklowsky, Deutsch-Kroatisch
(German-Croatian / Allemand-croate)....................... 1821
225. Werner Holzer / Rainer Münz, Deutsch-Ungarisch
(German-Hungarian / Allemand-hongrois) 1828

Schweiz / Switzerland / Suisse

226. Jürg Niederhauser, Schweiz (Switzerland / Suisse) 1836
227. Heinrich Löffler, Deutsche Schweiz
(German-speaking Switzerland / Suisse alémanique).......... 1854
228. Pierre Knecht / Bernard Py, Suisse romande
(Französische Schweiz / French-speaking Switzerland) 1862
229. Marco Bischofsberger, Suisse italienne
(Italienische Schweiz / Italian-speaking Switzerland) 1870
230. Clau Solèr, Rätoromanische Schweiz
(Romansh-speaking Switzerland / Suisse rhéto-romane) 1879

XVI. Sprachkontakte in den westlichen GUS-Staaten
und im Baltikum
Language Contacts in the Western States of the CIS
and in the Balticum
Contacts linguistiques dans les Etats occidentaux de la CEI
et dans les Etats baltiques

Die westlichen GUS-Staaten / The Western States of the CIS /
Les Etats occidentaux de la CEI

231. Harald Haarmann, Die westlichen GUS-Staaten
(The Western States of the CIS / Les Etats occidentaux de la CEI) ... 1887

Estland / Estonia / Estonie

232. Mart Rannut, Estonia (Estland / Estonie).................. 1900

Lettland / Latvia / Lettonie
233. Ina Druviete, Latvia *(Lettland / Lettonie)* 1906

Litauen / Lithuania / Lituanie
234. Laima Grumadienė / Bonifacas Stundžia, Lithuania
(Litauen / Lituanie) 1912

Weißrußland / Byelorussia / Biélorussie
235. Sven Gustavsson, Byelorussia *(Weißrußland / Biélorussie)* 1919

Ukraine / Ukraine / Ukraine
236. Victor M. Britsyn, Ukraine *(Ukraine / Ukraine)* 1926

Moldawien / Moldavia / Moldavie
237. Harald Haarmann, Moldawien *(Moldavia / Moldavie)* 1933

XVII. Sprachkontakte des Jiddischen und Romani
Language Contacts of Yiddish and Romani
Contacts linguistiques du yiddish et du romani

238. Ronald Lötzsch, Jiddisch *(Yiddish / Yiddish)* 1942
239. Birgit Igla, Romani *(Romani / Romani)* 1961

Sprachenkarten / Linguistic Maps / Cartes linguistiques

Hans Goebl, Einleitende Bemerkungen / Introductory Remarks /
Remarques préliminaires............................ 1973

A Per Sture Ureland, Nordeuropa (Skandinavien und Island)
   *(Northern Europe (Scandinavia and Iceland) / Europe du Nord
   (Scandinavie et Islande))* 1981

B Edgar Schneider, Großbritannien und Irland
   (Great Britain and Ireland / Grande-Bretagne et Irlande) 1987

C Roeland van Hout/Ton Vallen, Benelux (Belgium, Netherlands,
   Luxemburg)
   *(Benelux (Belgien, Niederlande, Luxemburg) / Bénélux (Belgique,
   Pays-Bas, Luxembourg))* 1995

D Josef Felixberger, Frankreich *(France / France)* 2003

E Helmut Berschin, Spanien und Portugal
   (Spain and Portugal / Espagne et Portugal) 2013

F Dieter Kattenbusch, Italien *(Italy / Italie)* 2017

G Heinz Dieter Pohl, Slowenien, Kroatien, Bosnien-Herzegowina,
   Jugoslawien (Serbien und Montenegro), Makedonien und Albanien
   *(Slovenia, Croatia, Bosnia-Herzegovina, Jugoslavia (Serbia and
   Montenegro), Macedonia and Albania / Slovénie, Croatie, Bosnie-
   Herzégovine, Yougoslavie (Serbie et Monténégro), Macédoine et
   Albanie)* 2023

H	Klaus Steinke, Rumänien und Bulgarien *(Rumania and Bulgaria / Roumanie et Bulgarie)*	2027
I	Ekkehard W. Bornträger, Griechenland, Zypern und europäische Türkei *(Greece, Cyprus and European Turkey / Grèce, Chypre et Turquie d'Europe)*	2031
J	Baldur Panzer, Polen *(Poland / Pologne)*	2037
K	Michael Duschanek, Tschechien und Slowakei *(Czechia and Slovakia / Tchèquie et Slovaquie)*	2041
L	Michael Duschanek, Ungarn *(Hungary / Hongrie)*	2045
M	Baldur Panzer, Deutschland *(Germany / Allemagne)*	2049
N	Heinz Dieter Pohl, Österreich *(Austria / Autriche)*	2057
O	Michael Duschanek, Schweiz *(Switzerland / Suisse)*	2061
P	Peter Jordan, Weißrußland, Ukraine, westlicher Teil des europäischen Rußland, Baltikum (Litauen, Lettland, Estland) *(Byelorussia, Ukraine, Western Part of European Russia, Balticum (Estonia, Latvia, Lithuania) / Biélorussie, Ukraine, partie occidentale de la Russie d'Europe, Etats baltiques (Estonie, Lettonie, Lituanie))*	2065

Register / Indexes / Index

Autorenregister / Index of Authors / Index des auteurs 2069
Sachregister / Topical Index / Index des matières 2115

1. Halbband / Volume 1 / Tome 1

Verzeichnis der Tabellen und Abbildungen / Index of Tables and Figures /
Index des tableaux et figures. XXI
Vorwort. XXV
Preface XXX
Préface XXXV

I. **Bedingungsfaktoren der Kontaktlinguistik I:
Schwerpunkte der Forschungsgeschichte
Conceptual Prerequisites of Contact Linguistics I:
Central Issues of the History of Contact Linguistics
Facteurs constitutifs de la linguistique de contact I:
Antécédents historiques et conceptuels**

1. Els Oksaar, The History of Contact Linguistics as a Discipline
   (Wissenschaftsgeschichte der Sprachkontaktforschung / Histoire de la recherche sur les contacts linguistiques) 1

2. Michael Clyne, Sprache, Sprachbenutzer und Sprachbereich
   (Languages, Language User and Area of Usage / Langue, locuteur et domaine linguistique) 12

II. **Bedingungsfaktoren der Kontaktlinguistik II: Interdisziplinäre Wechselwirkungen**
    Conceptual Prerequisites of Contact Linguistics II: Interdisciplinary Framework
    Facteurs constitutifs de la linguistique de contact II: Le champ interdisciplinaire

3. Matthias Hartig, Soziologie und Kontaktlinguistik
   (Sociology and Contact Linguistics / Sociologie et linguistique de contact) 23

4. Josiane F. Hamers, Psychologie et linguistique de contact
   (Psychologie und Kontaktlinguistik / Psychology and Contact Linguistics) 31

5. Karmela Liebkind, Social Psychology and Contact Linguistics
   (Sozialpsychologie und Kontaktlinguistik / Psychologie sociale et linguistique de contact) 41

6. Daniel Véronique, Anthropologie et linguistique de contact
   (Anthropologie und Kontaktlinguistik / Anthropology and Contact Linguistics) 49

7. Michel Paradis, Neurologie et linguistique de contact
   (Neurologie und Kontaktlinguistik / Neurology and Contact Linguistics) ... 57

8. Colin H. Williams, Geography and Contact Linguistics
   (Geographie und Kontaktlinguistik / Géographie et linguistique de contact) ... 63

9. Selma K. Sonntag, Political Science and Contact Linguistics
   (Politikwissenschaft und Kontaktlinguistik / Politologie et linguistique de contact) 75

10. Piet van de Craen, Pédagogie et linguistique de contact
    (Pädagogik und Kontaktlinguistik / Education and Contact Linguistics) ... 81

11. Ludwig M. Eichinger, Literaturwissenschaft, Philologie und Kontaktlinguistik
    (Comparative Literature, Philology and Contact Linguistics / Critique littéraire, philologie et linguistique de contact) 89

III. **Bedingungsfaktoren der Kontaktlinguistik III: Kontaktfaktoren sprachlicher Ebenen**
     Conceptual Prerequisites of Contact Linguistics III: Levels of Linguistic Structure
     Facteurs constitutifs de la linguistique de contact III: Les catégories intralinguistiques

12. Lyle Campbell, Phonetics and Phonology
    (Phonetik und Phonologie / Phonétique et phonologie) 98

13.	Florian Coulmas, Orthographie und Graphemik *(Spelling and Graphemics / Orthographe et graphémique)*	104
14.	David P. Wilkins, Morphology *(Morphologie / Morphologie)*	109
15.	Pieter Muysken, Syntax *(Syntax / Syntaxe)*	117
16.	Madeleine Mathiot / Dorothy Rissel, Lexicon and Word Formation *(Lexik und Wortbildung / Lexique et formation des mots)*	124
17.	Felix Ameka / David Wilkins, Semantics *(Semantik / Sémantique)*	130
18.	Deborah Schiffrin, Discourse Analysis and Pragmatics *(Diskursanalyse und Pragmatik / Analyse du discours et pragmatique linguistique)*	138
19.	Bernd Spillner, Stilistik *(Stylistics / Stylistique)*	144

IV. Bedingungsfaktoren der Kontaktlinguistik IV: Sprachexterne Kontaktfaktoren
Conceptual Prerequisites of Contact Linguistics IV: External Research
Facteurs constitutifs de la linguistique de contact IV: Le champ extralinguistique

20.	Guy Héraud, Nation et Etat *(Nation und Staat / Nation and State)*	154
21.	Joseph-G. Turi, Législation linguistique *(Sprachgesetzgebung / Language Legislation)*	160
22.	Mónica Madera, Speech Community *(Sprachgemeinschaft / Communauté linguistique)*	169
23.	Ludo Melis, Frontières linguistiques *(Sprachgrenzen / Language Boundaries)*	175
24.	Konrad Ehlich, Migration *(Migration / Migration)*	180
25.	Foued Laroussi / Jean-Baptiste Marcellesi, Colonisation et décolonisation *(Kolonialisierung und Entkolonialisierung / Colonization and Decolonization)*	193

V. Grundbegriffe der Kontaktlinguistik
Basic Approaches to Contact Linguistics
Concepts de base de la linguistique de contact

26.	Claude Olivesi, Nationalismes *(Nationalismen / Nationalisms)*	200
27.	Silvo Devetak, Ethnicity *(Ethnizität / Ethnicité)*	203
28.	Normand Labrie, Territorialité *(Territorialität / Territoriality)*	210
29.	Harald Haarman, Identität *(Identity / Identité)*	218
30.	Georges Lüdi, Mehrsprachigkeit *(Multilingualism / Plurilinguisme)*	233
31.	Georg Kremnitz, Diglossie *(Diglossie / Diglossia)*	245
32.	Bernd Weisgerber, Mundart, Umgangssprache und Standard *(Dialect, Vernacular, Standard / Dialecte, koiné et langue standard)*	258

33. William F. Mackey, Langue première et langue seconde
(Erstsprache und Zweitsprache / First and Second Language) 271

34. Henning Wode, Erwerb und Vermittlung von Mehrsprachigkeit
(Language Acquisition and Teaching / Acquisition et enseignement de langues étrangères) 284

35. Walburga von Raffler-Engel, Nonverbal Communication
(Nonverbale Kommunikation / Communication nonverbale) 296

36. Joachim Raith, Religiöse Migration
(Religious Migration / Migrations religieuses) 311

37. George Lüdi, Migration und Mehrsprachigkeit
(Migration and Multilingualism / Migration et plurilinguisme) 320

38. Safder Alladina, Rural and Urban Migration
(Rurale und urbane Migration / Migrations rurales et urbaines) 327

39. Nancy Niedzielski / Howard Giles, Linguistic Accomodation
(Sprachliche Anpassung / Adaptation linguistique) 332

40. Erik Allardt, Dominant Autochthonous Groups
(Dominierende autochthone Gruppen / Groupes autochtones dominants) 342

41. Aureli Argemí / Oriol Ramon, Groupes autochtones dominés
(Dominierte autochthone Gruppen / Dominated Autochthonous Groups) 351

42. Armel Wynants, Droit à l'autodétermination
(Selbstbestimmungsrecht / Self-Determination of Language Groups . . . 357

VI. Forschungsansätze der Kontaktlinguistik
Central Issues in Contact Linguistics
Domaines majeurs de la linguistique de contact

43. Péter Bassola / Zsolt Lengyel, Altersgruppe I: Kinder
(Age Group I: Children / Catégorie d'âge I: enfants) 364

44. Kris van de Poel, Age Group II: Adults and the Elderly
(Altersgruppe II: Erwachsene und ältere Menschen / Catégorie d'âge II: adultes et personnes âgées) 370

45. Kurt Egger, Kleingruppe I: Familie
(Small group I: Family / Petit groupe I: famille) 379

46. Monica Heller / Laurette Lévy, Petit groupe II: Le couple
(Kleingruppe II: das Paar / Small Group II: Dyadic Relationships) . . . 385

47. Wolfgang W. Moelleken, Multilingualism in Religion
(Mehrsprachigkeit in der Religion / Plurilinguisme en matière de religion) 391

48. Selma K. Sonntag, Multilingualism and Politics
(Mehrsprachigkeit in der Politik / Plurilinguisme en matière de politique) 399

49. André Cyr, Plurilinguisme en matière d'administration
(Mehrsprachigkeit in der Verwaltung / Multilingualism and Public Administration) 405

50.	Theo Bungarten, Mehrsprachigkeit in der Wirtschaft *(Multilingualism and Economy / Plurilinguisme en matière d'économie)*	414
51.	Ulrich Ammon, Mehrsprachigkeit in Wissenschaft und Technik *(Multilingualism in Science and Technology / Plurilinguisme dans les sciences et la technique)*	421
52.	Oliver Boyd-Barrett / John Nootens / Anthony Pugh, Multilingualism and the Mass Media *(Mehrsprachigkeit in den Medien / Plurilinguisme et mass media)*	426
53.	George A. Barnett, Multilingualism in Telecommunication and Transportation *(Mehrsprachigkeit in Telekommunikation und Verkehr / Plurilinguisme en matière de télécommunication et transport)*	431
54.	François Grin, Plurilinguisme en matière de publicité *(Mehrsprachigkeit in der Werbung / Multilingualism and Advertising)*	438
55.	Josef Breu, Mehrsprachigkeit in der Toponymik *(Multilingualism and Toponymics / Plurilinguisme en matière de toponymie)*	444
56.	Werner Kallmeyer, Plurilinguisme dans les agglomérations urbaines *(Mehrsprachigkeit in der Großstadt / Multilingualism in Urban Areas)*	450
57.	Martine de Clercq / Normand Labrie, Plurilinguisme et belles-lettres *(Mehrsprachigkeit in der Literatur / Multilingualism and Literature)*	458
58.	Hugo Baetens Beardsmore, Education plurilingue en Europe *(Mehrsprachige Erziehung in Europa / Multilingual Education in Europe)*	465
59.	Jim Cummins, Education multilingue aux Etats-Unis d'Amérique et au Canada *(Mehrsprachige Erziehung in den USA und Kanada / Multilingual Education in the U.S. and in Canada)*	473
60.	Ernst F. Kotzé, Mehrsprachigkeitsmodelle in der „Dritten Welt" *(Approaches to Multilingualism in the "Third World" / Modèles d'éducation plurilingue dans le « Tiers Monde »)*	481
61.	Fred Genesee, Second Language Immersion Programs *(Zweitsprachen-Immersionsprogramme / Programmes d'immersion pour la seconde langue)*	493
62.	Herbert Christ, Tests de plurilinguisme *(Mehrsprachigkeitstests / Multilingual Proficiency Assessment)*	501
63.	Heinrich P. Kelz, Fachsprachenunterricht *(Instruction in Language for Special Purposes / Enseignement des langues de spécialité)*	507
64.	Alex Housen, Models of Second Language Acquisition *(Zweitsprachenerwerb / Acquisition d'une langue seconde)*	515
65.	Helmut Lüdtke, Changement linguistique *(Sprachwandel / Language Change)*	526
66.	Bates L. Hoffer, Borrowing *(Lehnvorgänge / Emprunt linguistique)*	541
67.	Wilhelm F. H. Nicolaisen, Language Contact and Onomastics *(Sprachkontakt und Onomastik / Contact linguistique et onomastique)*	549

68.	Michael Metzeltin, Lingua franca *(Lingua franca / Lingua franca)* ...	554
69.	Susan Gass, Transference and Interference *(Transferenz und Interferenz / Transférence et interférence)*	558
70.	Kenneth Hyltenstam / Christopher Stroud, Language Maintenance *(Spracherhalt / Maintien de la langue)*	567
71.	Kees de Bot, Language Loss *(Sprachverlust / Perte de la langue)*	579
72.	Susan Gal, Language Shift *(Sprachwechsel / Changement de langue)* ..	586
73.	Monica Heller / Carol W. Pfaff, Code-switching *(Codewechsel / Alternance de code)*	594
74.	Georg Bossong, Normes et conflits normatifs *(Standardisierung und Normenkonflikte / Standardization and Norm Conflicts)*	609
75.	Ludo Verhoeven, Literacy Programs *(Alphabetisierung / Alphabétisation)*	624
76.	Žarko Muljačić / Harald Haarmann, Distance interlinguistique, élaboration linguistique et « coiffure linguistique » *(Abstand, Ausbau und Überdachung / "Abstand", "Ausbau" and Language "Roofing")*	634
77.	Peter Mühlhäusler, Pidginization *(Pidginisierung / Pidginisation)*	642
78.	Albert Valdman, Créolisation *(Kreolisierung / Creolization)*	649
79.	Catherine Bereznak / Lyle Campbell, Defense Strategies for Endangered Languages *(Verteidigungsstrategien gefährdeter Sprachen / Stratégies de défense des langues menacées)*	659
80.	Tove Skutnabb-Kangas / Robert Phillipson, Linguicide and Linguicism *(Linguizid und Linguizismus / Linguicide et linguicisme)* ..	667
81.	Irène Fenoglio, Conscience linguistique *(Sprachbewußtsein / Linguistic Awareness)*	675
82.	Réné Dirven / Martin Pütz, Sprachkonflikt *(Language Conflict / Conflit linguistique)*	684
83.	Sonja Vandermeeren, Sprachattitüde *(Language Attitude / Attitudes linguistiques)*	692
84.	John Edwards, Language, Prestige and Stigma *(Sprachprestige und -stigma / Prestige et stigmate linguistiques)*	703
85.	John Baugh, Linguistic Discrimination *(Sprachliche Diskriminierung / Discrimination linguistique)*	709
86.	Alexandre Niculescu, Loyauté linguistique *(Sprachloyalität / Language Loyalty)*	715
87.	Janet Holmes, Sex and Language *(Geschlecht und Sprache / Sexe et langage)*	720

VII. Empirische Methoden und Verfahren
Empirical Methods and Procedures
Méthodes et techniques empiriques

88.	Hans-J. Hippler / Norbert Schwarz, Umfragen *(Surveys / Techniques d'enquête et de sondage)*	726
89.	Siegfried Gabler, Repräsentativität von Stichproben *(Representativeness of Sampling / Représentativité des échantillons)*	733
90.	Rolf Porst, Fragebogenerstellung *(Survey Design / Elaboration des questionnaires)*	737
91.	Charles L. Briggs, Interviewing *(Interviewtechniken / Technique de l'interview)*	744
92.	Erika Werlen, Teilnehmende Beobachtung *(Participant Observation / Observation participante)*	750
93.	Normand Labrie / Sonja Vandermeeren, L'analyse du profil de la communauté *(Gemeinschaftsprofilanalyse / Analysis of Community Profiles)*	764
94.	Jan de Vries, Language Demography *(Sprachdemographie / Démographie linguistique)*	771
95.	Wladyslaw Cichocki, Data Analysis *(Datenanalyse / Analyse des données)*	776
96.	Danielle Cyr, Ethnographie *(Ethnographie / Ethnography)*	788
97.	Rosita Rindler Schjerve, Domänenuntersuchungen *(Analysis of Domains / Analyse des domaines)*	796
98.	Li Wei, Network Analysis *(Netzwerkuntersuchungen / Analyse des réseaux)*	805
99.	Klaus J. Mattheier, Methoden der Sprachinselforschung *(Research Methods on Linguistic Islands / Méthodes de la recherche sur les îlots linguistiques)*	812
100.	Hannes Kniffka, Forschungsethik *(Research Ethics / Ethique de la recherche)*	819

VIII. Angewandte Kontaktlinguistik
Applied Contact Linguistics
La linguistique de contact appliquée

101.	Normand Labrie, Politique linguistique *(Sprachpolitik / Language Policy)*	826
102.	Björn H. Jernudd, Language Planning *(Sprachplanung / L'aménagement linguistique)*	833
103.	Harald Haarmann, Ökolinguistik *(Ecolinguistics / Ecolinguistique)*	842
104.	Ulrich Ammon, Sprachkontakt in multinationalen Betrieben *(Language Contact in Multinational Companies / Contacts linguistiques et entreprises multinationales)*	852

105.	Florian Coulmas, Language Contact in Multinational Organizations *(Sprachkontakt in multinationalen Organisationen / Contacts linguistiques et organismes multinationaux)*	858
106.	Mary E. McGroarty, Language Contact in Social Service Institutions *(Sprachkontakt in Sozialeinrichtungen / Contacts linguistiques et institutions sociales)*	865
107.	Christian Schmitt, Sprachpflege und Sprachreinigung *("Cultivation" of Language and Language "Purification" / Purisme et soins langagiers)*	871
108.	Otto Back, Plansprachen *(Artificial Languages / Langues artificielles)*	881
109.	Xavier Lamuela, Promotion et diffusion des langues *(Sprachförderung und Sprachverbreitung / Language Promotion and Propagation)*	887
110.	Iwar Werlen, Ausbau von Nationalsprachen *(Development of National Languages / Elaboration de langues nationales)*	893
111.	Joshua A. Fishman, Language Revitalization *(Sprachliche Revitalisierung / Revivification linguistique)*	902
112.	Braj B. Kachru, English as Lingua Franca *(Englisch als lingua franca / L'anglais comme « lingua franca »)*	906
113.	Albrecht Neubert, Übersetzen und Dolmetschen *(Translation and Interpretation / Traduction écrite et orale)*	913
114.	Konrad Ehlich, Interkulturelle Kommunikation *(Intercultural Communication / Communication interculturelle)*	920
115.	Joachim Raith, Forschungsorganisationen der Kontaktlinguistik in Europa *(European Research Organizations of Contact Linguistics / Organismes européens de recherche en matière de linguistique de contact)*	931

Verzeichnis der Tabellen und Abbildungen
Index of Tables and Figures
Index des tableaux et figures

2. Teilband / Volume 2 / Tome 2

Ernst Håkon Jahr, Norway
Fig. 116.1: The directions of influence between Norwegian, Sami and Finnish in northern Norway 945

Geirr Wiggen, Nynorsk-Bokmål
Tab. 117.1: The realization of *a* and *e* in B and N morphology 955
Tab. 117.2: B and N gender forms 955

Heikki Paunonen, Finland
Tab. 123.1: Population of Finland by language 1000

Marika Tandelfelt, Finnish-Swedish
Tab. 124.1: The Swedish-speaking population in Finland 1610–1990 1010

Pekka Sammallahti, Finnish-Saami
Fig. 125.1: North Saami phonemic inventory 1017
Fig. 125.2 North Finnish phonemic inventory 1017

Colin Baker, Great Britain
Tab. 131.1: Ethnic group composition in Britain 1066

Wolfgang Viereck, Englisch-Gälisch
Tab. 133.1: Gälisch- und nordischsprachige Gebiete in Schottland 1088
Abb. 133.1: Gälisch- und nordischsprachige Gebiete in Schottland im Mittelalter und der frühen Neuzeit (nach Withers 1979, 51 und 1984, 26) 1090
Abb. 133.2: Rückgang des Gälischen während der letzten 100 Jahre: Sprecher des Gälischen 1891 und deren prozentuale Verteilung (nach MacKinnon 1991, 522) 1092
Abb. 133.3: Sprecher des Gälischen 1991 und deren prozentuale Verteilung (nach 1991 Census 1993, 16) 1093
Tab. 133.2: Die Konstruktion be + after + Verb-ing 1094

Rudolf Kern, Französisch-Deutsch
Tab. 137.1: Sprachvarietäten: S1=Französisch, S2=niederfrk.-limburg. Mundarten, S3=moselfrk. Maa, S4=ripuarische Maa, S5=Hochdeutsch 1135

Sonja Vandermeeren, Niederländisch-Deutsch
Tab. 138.1: Befragte mit Dialektkenntnissen, die (fast) immer Dialekt im Umgang mit Gesprächspartnern mit Dialektkenntnissen sprechen 1140
Tab. 138.2 Befragte mit Dialektkenntnissen, die den Dialektgebrauch mit Gesprächspartnern mit Dialektkenntnissen als angemessen betrachten. ... 1141

Harald Fröhlich/Fernand Hoffmann, Luxemburg
Tab. 141.1: Bevölkerungsstruktur Luxemburgs von 1948 bis 1993. Quelle: Statec; Stand jeweils 1.1. (1981: 1.3.) 1159
Abb. 141.1: Luxemburg-Territorium und Gebietsveränderungen seit 1659 1160

Tab. 141.2: Alemannischer Einfluß im Lëtzebuergischen 1163
Tab. 141.3: Ripuarischer Einfluß im Lëtzebuergischen 1163
Tab. 141.4: Archaismen im Südwestlëtzebuergischen 1163
Tab. 141.5: Neuerungen im Ostlëtzebuergischen 1163
Tab. 141.6: Assimilation von Fremdwörtern im Lëtzebuergischen 1170
Tab. 141.7: Fremdwortdubletten im Lëtzebuergischen 1170
Tab. 141.8: Luxemburger Französisch 1170
Tab. 141.9: Luxemburger Deutsch 1171

Jean Petit, Français-allemand
Fig. 147.1: Carte linguistique d'Alsace-Lorraine. A partir d'un fond de carte publié dans: Notre avenir est bilingue. Zweisprachig: unsere Zukunft, Strasbourg 1968, René-Schickele-Kreis 1223
Fig. 147.2: Situation de l'Alsace et de la Moselle dans l'espace dialectal germanophone. (Carte établie d'après König, Werner (1978): dtv-Atlas zur dt. Sprache, Munich, 230–231) 1227
Fig. 147.3: Carte de la dialectophonie alsacienne: élèves de 3 à 12 ans. (Document établi par la Rectorat de Strasbourg à la rentrée scolaire de 1993) 1238

Bruno Callebaut/Hugo Ryckeboer, Français-néerlandais
Fig. 148.1: Le retrait du néerlandais dans le nord de la France. Source: Ryckeboer 1991, 169 (etiam in: Ryckeboer 1990, 243) 1241
Tab. 148.1: Connaissances active et passive du néerlandais à Hondschoote (d'après Ryckeboer/Maeckelberghe 1987) 1244
Fig. 148.2: Le substrat néerlandais dans le dialecte picard du Nord – Pas-de-Calais. Source: Ryckeboer 1991, 168 (d'après Carton/Lebègue 1989) 1247
Fig. 148.3: Les hétéronymes pour „menacer" dans le dialecte flamand de France. Source: Ryckeboer 1990, 265 (d'après Pée 1946) 1249

Yves Le Berre/Jean Le Dû, Français-breton
Fig. 149.1: Basse-Bretagne et Haute-Bretagne occidentale. Source: Balcou, Jean/Le Gallo, Yves (Eds.) (1987): Histoire littéraire et culturelle de la Bretagne, Paris/Genève, volume 1,3 1253

Harald Thun, Spanien
Tab. 151.1: Typologie der Sprachkontakte 1270
Tab. 151.2: Unter- und Sondergruppen bei Mauren und Christen 1274
Tab. 151.3: Domänenverteilung in den Autonomen Regionen 1277
Abb. 151.1: Entwicklung des Autonomisierungsprozesses in Spanien seit 1978 (nach: El País, 22.10.1994, S. 15) 1278
Abb. 151.2: Rückgang des Baskischen in der Neuzeit (nach: Echenique 1987, 109) 1279
Tab. 151.4: Funktionsverteilung von Kastilisch und Galegisch in Galicien früher (A) und heute (B) 1280
Abb. 151.3: Schichtung der vier Beherrschungsmodalitäten des Katalanischen (nach COM 1989, 41) 1281
Tab. 151.5: Die kleineren Regionalsprachen im Vergleich 1282

Francisco Fernández Rei, Espagnol-galicien
Fig. 152.1: Niveau de connaissance du galicien (les chiffres indiquent le pourcentage de la population) (IGE 1991,45) 1289
Fig. 152.2: Les pourcentages d'utilisation du galicien (IGE 1991, 45) 1289
Fig. 152.3: L'utilisation du galicien dans cinq villes. Les chiffres indiquent le pourcentage de chaque ville; les pourcentages résiduels se réfèrent aux réponses nulles (IGE 1991, 45) 1290
Fig. 152.4: Utilisation du galicien et du castillan d'après le *statut* social 1290
Fig. 152.5: Langue habituelle par générations (Monteagudo 1986, 77) 1291
Fig. 152.6: Rapport parents et grands-parents 1291
Fig. 152.7: Rapport des parents parmi eux 1291
Fig. 152.8: Rapport parents-enfants 1291

Tab. 152.1: (A) Langue habituelle des curés de la Galice. (B) Modèle idéal préféré par les séminaristes pour la prédication. (C) Distribution de messes d'après la langue employée (dans ce cas, les possibilités sont „galicien", „galicien et castillan" et „castillan") (López Muñoz 1989, 85, 92 et 157) 1293
Tab. 152.2: Exemples du *castrapo* 1294

Gotzon Aurrekoetxea, Espagnol-basque
Fig. 154.1: Aires bascophone, de contact et castillanophone en territoire basque (Euskaltzaindia 1979)................................. 1304

Tullio Telmon, Italien-français (francoprovençal)
Tab. 157.1: Vallées méridionales: données démographiques (d'après Telmon 1981, 59) . 1331
Tab. 157.2: Vallée d'Aoste: données démographiques (d'après Telmon 1981,38) 1331
Tab. 157.3: Traits linguistiques (d'après Telmon 1992,119)................... 1335

Kurt Egger/Karin Heller, Italienisch-Deutsch
Tab. 160.1: Stärke der drei Sprachgruppen in Südtirol 1991 (Astat 1992) 1350

Gabriele Birken-Silverman, Italienisch-Albanisch
Tab. 164.1. Spracherwerb und Sprachgebrauch der Kontaktidiome in den alb. Enklaven Nordkalabriens 1373

Rosita Rindler Schjerve, Sardaigne
Fig. 165.1: Classification des dialectes sardes (d'après Blasco Ferrer 1984a, 349) 1378

Lois Craffonara, Ladinisch
Tab. 166.1: Beschäftigungsverhältnisse in den Sellatälern 1386
Tab. 166.2: Bildungsniveau in den Sellatälern 1386
Tab. 166.3: Situation der Sellatäler laut Volkszählungen 1387

Albina Nećak Lük, Slovenia
Tab. 169.1. Population of Slovenia according to official censuses data 1419

August Kovačec, Bosnie-Herzégovine
Tab. 171.1: Les ressortissants de la Bosnie-Herzégovine d'après leur appartenance nationale (1949–1991) (Enc.Ju. 1982, 142; Bertić 1987, 228–230; Klemenčić 1993, 123)................................. 1436
Tab. 171.2: Les minorités nationales et ethniques en Bosnie (1981) 1437

Victor A. Frieman, Macedonia
Tab. 172.1: Language and ethnic groups in Macedonia 1445
Tab. 172.2: Districts with more than 10% non-macedonian population (1991) 1446

Wolfgang Dahmen, Rumänien
Tab. 174.1: Magyarismen und Germanismen im Rumänischen 1465
Tab. 174.2: Rumänismen im Deutschen und Ungarischen Rumäniens 1465
Tab. 174.3: Slavismen im Rumänischen 1467
Tab. 174.4: Neoromanismen im Rumänischen 1468

Grace Fielder, Bulgaria
Tab. 177.1: Ethnic composition of the population of Bulgaria 1490

Elżbieta Smułkowa, Polish-Byelorussian
Fig. 195.1: East slavic dialects in Poland 1607

Franciszek Sowa, Polish-Slovak
Tab. 198.1: Percentage of Slovak-Goral bilinguals 1630

Jiři Zeman, Czech-Slovak
Tab. 210.1: Numbers of Slovaks living in the CR 1651

Mikuláš Štec, Slowakisch-Ukrainisch
Tab. 208.1: Einwohnerzahl der Ukrainer in drei ostslowakischen Komitaten laut
offiziellen statistischen Angaben 1697

Miklós Kontra, Hungary
Tab. 210.1: Population figures for Hungarians and non-Hungarians in historic
Hungary (without Croatia-Slavonia), based on Dávid (1988, 343) 1709
Fig. 210.1: Ethnic Hungarian population of the Kingdom of Hungary in 1910 and of
partitioned Hungary after 1920. Reproduced from *Essays on World War I:
total war and peacemaking, a case study on Trianon*, B. K. Király/I. Sanders
(Eds.), New York, 1982 1710
Tab. 210.2: National and denominational distribution of Hungary's population around
1900 (Karady 1989, 287) 1713
Tab. 210.3: Changes from 1980 to 1990 of four minorities 1714
Fig. 210.2: Slovak parents' language socialization and their use of language to their
young children. N=600. Reproduced from Garami/Szántó (1991) 1716
Fig. 210.3: Parents' language socialization and their children's proficiency in Slovak.
N=600. Reproduced from Garami/Szántó (1991) 1717

Regina Hessky, Ungarisch-Deutsch
Abb. 211.1: Deutsche Mundarten in Ungarn 1729

Heinz Dieter Pohl, Österreich
Tab. 222.1 Statistik der nichtdeutschsprachigen Minderheiten Österreichs 1806

Werner Holz/Rainer Münz, Deutsch-Ungarisch
Tab. 225.1: Ungarisch in den Volkszählungen (Quellen: ÖSTAT 1993; Münz 1989) ... 1830
Tab. 225.2: Sprachkenntnisse im Burgenland 1990/91 (Quellen: Mikrozensus 1990;
Holzer/Münz 1993) 1830

Jürg Niederhauser, Schweiz
Tab. 226.1: Entwicklung der Wohnbevölkerung nach Sprachgruppen (Hauptsprache) in
absoluten Zahlen und in Prozent 1840
Tab. 226.2: Gegenwärtige Verteilung der Sprachgruppen in der Schweiz (Darstellung
der Wohnbevölkerung nach Hauptsprache und Staatszugehörigkeit gemäß
den Ergebnissen der Eidgenössischen Volkszählung 1990) 1841
Tab. 226.3: Ein- und Mehrsprachigkeit der Wohnbevölkerung, gestützt auf Fragen zur
Umgangssprache, d. h. Fragen nach den Sprachen, die im Alltag verwendet
werden (Ergebnisse der Daten der Volkszählung 1990) 1842

Pierre Knecht/Bernard Py, Suisse romande
Fig. 228.1: Géographie des cantons de la Suisse romande (avec indication des limites
linguistiques entre français et allemand et entre langue d'oïl et
francoprovençal 1863
Tab. 228.1: Distribution, pour 1990, des principales langues déclarées premières en
pourcentage. Ces chiffres prennent en compte les cantons unilingues
(Genève, Neuchâtel, Vaud) et les régions francophones des cantons
bilingues (Berne, Fribourg, Valais; à l'exclusion des villes bilingues Bienne,
Fribourg et Sierre) 1866

Clau Solèr, Rätoromanische Schweiz
Tab. 230.1: Sprachenverteilung in Graubünden 1881
Abb. 230.1: Strategie der Sprachwahl 1882
Tab. 230.2: Phasen der Spracherlernung (Willi/Solèr 1990, 456, erweitert) 1883
Tab. 230.3: Unterschiede zwischen Sursilvan und Vallader 1884
Tab. 230.4: Deutsche vs. bündnerromanische Phoneme 1884
Tab. 230.5: Traditionelle vs. heutige Aussprache 1884
Tab. 230.6: Konkreter vs. figurativer Sinn 1885
Tab. 230.7: Deutsch kontaminierte Wortstellung 1885

Harald Haarmann, Die westlichen GUS-Staaten
Tab. 231.1: Tendenzen des Sprachwechsels und der Zweitsprachenattraktion bei den
 Minderheiten in der Ukraine (nach Haarmann 1979b) 1891
Tab. 231.2: Eckwerte zur ethnischen Zusammensetzung der Bevölkerung Rußlands
 (nach *Social'noe razvitie* 1991) 1895
Tab. 231.3: Schriftreform im europäischen Teil der ehemaligen Sowjetunion 1897

Ina Druviete, Latvia
Tab. 233.1: Development of the population in the 20th century (Vēbers (Ed.) 1992,4) . . 1906
Tab. 233.2: Knowledge of Russian among Latvians (Čislennost' 1984, 71; Narodnoe
 [...] 1991, 77) 1908

Laima Grumadienė/Bonifacas Stundžia, Lithuania
Fig. 234.1: Sociolinguistic situation and boundaries of Lithuania 1914

Sven Gustavsson, Byelorussia
Tab. 235.1: Distribution of population of Belarusan SSR according to nationalities and
 their languages (1989). (Source: *Vestnik statistiki* 1990, 11) 1921

Victor M. Britsyn, Ukraine
Tab. 236.1: Aspects communicatifs de la diglossie entre ukrainien et russe 1929

Harald Haarmann, Moldawien
Abb. 237.1: Die ethnische Differenzierung der Bevölkerung Moldawiens (Haarmann
 1978,80). 1934
Tab. 237.1: Periodisierung der sowjetischen Sprachplanung und charakteristische
 Merkmale der moldauischen Standardsprache (Haarmann 1978, 259f) . . . 1938

IX. Sprachkontakte in Nordeuropa
Language Contacts in Northern Europe
Contacts linguistiques en Europe du Nord

116. Norway

1. Geography and demography
2. Territorial history and national development
3. Politics, economy and general cultural situation
4. Language contact
5. Critical evaluation of the sources and literature used
6. Bibliography (selected)

1. Geography and demography

Norway is the northwesternmost country on the Scandinavian peninsula. It is long and narrow, and stretches 1750 km in a straight line from the southernmost to the northernmost point on the mainland. It includes also the archipelago Svalbard (Spitsbergen) with the northernmost settlement in the world. The country covers (without Svalbard, which, by itself, has the size of Denmark) 323, 878 km^2; it is rocky and mountainous, and only a small percentage of the land can be used for agriculture. Most of northern Norway is situated above the Arctic circle. Norway has 4,233 mill. inhabitants (1991), about 0,5 mill. live in the capital Oslo, another 0,5 mill. in the surrounding region of the capital.

2. Territorial history and national development

Norway has common borders with Sweden, Finland and Russia. These borders are identical with the ones in 1814, when Norway regained political independence after having been in a union with Denmark for more than 400 years. In this union, Denmark was the dominant part, and Norway was more or less a Danish colony. The Old Norwegian language of the Middle Ages disappeared, and written Danish prevailed throughout the whole Dano-Norwegian kingdom. During the later half of the union, the contact between (spoken) Norwegian and (written) Danish yielded an interesting spoken variety among the upper-middle classes in Norway. Between 1814 and 1905, Norway shared king, defense and foreign policy with Sweden. Full national independence was obtained in 1905. During World War I, Norway successfully kept a neutral position and managed to stay out of the war, but between 1940 and 1945 the country was occupied by Nazi Germany. Norway joined the NATO alliance in 1949, and in 1972 a majority voted No in a referendum about joining the EC. This No was confirmed 1994 in a new referendum about joining the EU. Norway's historical background of union ties first with Denmark (till 1814) and then with Sweden (till 1905) gives some of the explanation why the population has been reluctant to join the EU (→ language map A).

3. Politics, economy and general cultural situation

Norway is a constitutional monarchy with a parliamentary democratic system. The constitution is from 1814, and at that time it was the most democratic constitution in Europe. The parliamentary system was introduced in 1884. Most national income derives from oil revenues, various industries and fisheries. About 90% of the population are members of the state church (Protestant/Lutherans). The national language is Norwegian which is found in two written standard varieties, *Bokmål* (the majority standard) and *Nynorsk* (the minority standard). Both written standards are taught in school. There is no officially codified or generally accepted spoken standard of Norwegian. Indigenous minority languages are Sami (Northern Sami and Southern Sami, together about 20 000 speakers, but estimates vary), Finnish (1500), and Romani (300). Immigrants with other languages total about 200 000. In the 1960s and 70s Norway received immigrants from southern Europe, Asia and Africa. In 1975 an immigration law was passed, prohibiting new labor permits for foreign citizens. Family reunions, however, are still allowed, as is the admission of those with expertise required by Norway. In spite of these regulations, Norway receives as many immigrants as before, but the majority are now from the Western part of the world and speak a European language. In addition, Norway accepts an annual quota of refugees. More than 80 different mother tongues are now registered among elementary school children in Norway. In 1990, the ten most frequent mother tongues in the elementary schools (other than Norwegian, Sami, Danish and Swedish) were: Urdu, Vietnamese, English, Spanish, Turkish, Arabic, Persian, Polish, German and Tagalog.

Since World War II there has been a major influx of Anglo-American culture and values, and English is understood and spoken by most people under 50. Foreign movies are never dubbed, but subtitled, and the high frequency of English and especially American films (and series on television) exposes the entire population to English on a massive scale. In 1991, the Norwegian Language Council (*Norsk språkråd*) launched a campaign against unnecessary use of English, of so-called "Anglo-Norwegian", especially in names of shops and various products and in advertising.

4. Language contact

In Norway, both diachronically and synchronically, it is possible to study a variety of language contact phenomena, situations and results. The following list provides a diachronic overview of the most important cases.

− Contact between Old Norwegian and Swedish in the 14th century, resulting in the mixed so-called "Birgittina-Norwegian" (cf. Sandvei 1938).
− Contact between Latin and Old Norwegian, resulting in stylistic influence from Latin on written Norwegian (cf. Seip/Saltveit 1971).
− Old and Middle Norwegian in contact with Low German in the Hansa period (especially the 14th and 15th centuries).
− Contact between Danish and Norwegian during the 400-year union, resulting in a mixed Dano-Norwegian variety.
− Contact between Norwegian (earlier: Proto Scandinavian) and Sami dating back almost two millenia, and between Norwegian and Finnish dialects from the 18th century onwards (both contact situations mainly in northern Norway − on contact between Southern Sami and Norwegian, cf. Bergsland 1992), resulting in linguistic admixture, language attrition and language shift.
− Contact between Sami and Finnish in northern Norway, resulting in linguistic admixture.
− Language shift yielding northern Norwegian dialects with grammatical generalization, and with ethnolectal features from Sami or Finnish.
− Contact between Norwegian (and probably also Sami and Finnish) and Russian resulting in the development of a pidgin, Russenorsk, in northern Norway from late 18th century till around 1920. The Norwegian−Russian contact also yielded a reduced Russian variety used by the class of merchants in Finnmark from about 1850.
− Parallel development with conflict and contact between the two modern Norwegian written standards, Bokmål and Nynorsk.
− Dialect contact, caused by migration from the south to various places in northern Norway, and in the town of Longyearbyen on Svalbard.

4.1. Low German−Norwegian contact

The only traditional Norwegian dialect with a two-gender-system instead of a three-gender-system is the city dialect of Bergen. Here, as is also the case with the Dano-Norwegian variety described below in 4.2, one can argue that the two-gender-system is due to language contact. For centuries the Hanseatic League had a major settlement in Bergen, with extensive contact between Norwegian and Low German as a result. This contact proved to be extremely important first for the development of the dialect of Bergen, then also for Norwegian in general. During the 14th and the 15th centuries, when the contact with Low German was most intense, Norwegian (together with the other Scandinavian languages) changed typologically from synthetic to an analytic structure. Whether this change in typology can be attributed mainly to the contact with Low German is disputed. There can be no doubt, however, that the contact between Low German and the Scandinavian Languages in the late Middle Ages at least contributed to the speed with which the typological transformation took place (cf. Jahr 1995a).

4.2. A Dano-Norwegian creoloid

An interesting result of contact between spoken Norwegian and (mainly) written Danish is the spoken idiom that developed among members of the educated upper-middle classes in Norway during the 18th and early 19th centuries, when Danish was the written medium throughout the whole Dano-Norwegian kingdom. Prosody, phonology and syntax were from spoken Norwegian, while word forms, morphology and vocabulary came from written Danish of the period. This special result of contact between Norwegian and Danish may perhaps be termed a *creoloid* (following Trudgill 1983, 102) since it from the very beginning had the status of being the mother tongue of its speakers (it never went through a period of reduction of functions like, say, a pidgin), it was intelligible to speakers of Danish and speakers of Norwegian dialects, and it exhibits some clear instances of phonological and grammatical simplification and levelling as well as admixture. In phonology, one salient example of levelling is the loss in this variety of the retroflex flap, /ɽ/, which is extremely frequent in spoken Norwegian (except in the western and northernmost dialects). This sound is used for Old Norwegian /l/ and (the cluster) /rd/, but in the upper-middle-class Dano-Norwegian variety it is substituted by /l/ and /r/ respectively, both sounds being clearly less marked than the retroflex flap.

In grammar, the general Norwegian three-gender system (m., f., n.) is reduced to two genders (comm., n.), like it is in Danish. This system has almost no gender distinctions in the plural. Also, in this variety, the conjugation of weak verbs shows both admixture (with Danish) and simplification (in comparison with other Norwegian varieties). The verb *kaste* 'throw' may serve as an example:

	inf.	past ts.	past part.
Old Norse:	kasta	kastaði	kastat
New Norw. dial.:	kasta/-e	kasta	kasta
Danish:	kaste	kastede	kastet
Dano-Norw. variety:	kaste	kastet	kastet

We observe here that the modern Norwegian system has the same ending in past tense and past participle (-*a,* -*a*), and that the Dano-Norwegian variety has adopted this simple system, but that it has taken the actual ending (-*et,* -*et*) from the Danish past participle. The verb *kaste* belongs to the largest weak verb category, and in the Dano-Norwegian creoloid this group has attracted a lot of other verbs which in other Norwegian varieties belong to various weak verb categories. This generalization too testifies to a strong tendency of morphological simplification in this variety. Another example of both simplification and admixture can be found in the pers. pronouns. For 3rd pers. pl. ('they') most Norwegian dialects have the same form for both nominative and oblique cases. (This system is reflected in Nynorsk: *dei* – *dei*). Danish, however, has different forms: *de* – *dem*. Here, then, the simplification process has yielded *de* – *de* [di:] in the mixed variety of the Norwegian upper-middle classes.

Even if this Dano-Norwegian creoloid-type of variety is a clear result of language contact it has always enjoyed the highest status of all spoken varieties in the Norwegian society, being as it was the mother tongue of the upper-middle classes. As will be apparent from the description in 4.3, the origin and history of this upper-middle-class variety has profound importance for the conflict in the 19th and 20th centuries between the two national standards Bokmål and Nynorsk.

4.3 The conflict between Bokmål and Nynorsk, sociolinguistic background

The sociolinguistic pattern of the conflict and contact between the two Norwegian standards cannot be fully understood or appreciated without taking into account the linguistic development of the country after 1814, i.e. in the period of the modern independent Norwegian state. What may at first look totally confusing and chaotic to most non-Norwegians (and to many Norwegians as well), can be satisfactorily accounted for in a description of the sociolinguistic history of Norwegian language struggle and language planning. Therefore, the following overview gives some basic interpretations and necessary historical premises for an understanding of the current sociolinguistic situation concerning the relationship between Bokmål and Nynorsk.

4.3.1. The nationalist period

The sociolinguistic situation around 1814 indicated two possible routes in developing a specific national language in Norway: one involved the elite or the upper classes in particular, and, more or less, excluded the lower classes; the other involved only the language of the lower classes, and excluded the spoken Dano-Norwegian creoloid variety of the elite. The first solution involved a "Norwegianization" of the written standard Danish inherited from the time of the Dano-Norwegian union. A consequence of this view was that the culture and language tradition of the upper classes, which had strong ties with Danish culture and values, and which originated and had developed during the time of the union, was defined and understood as genuinely *Norwegian*. Had this solution and view been the only one pursued, the sociolinguistic situation in Norway would — most probably — have developed to be very much the same as the one we find today in Sweden and Denmark: a strong and generally accepted standard written and spoken variety closely connected with the spoken idiom of the upper and educated classes, and with the lower classes using more or less low-status vernacular dialects, which in the course of time would have withdrawn to more remote rural areas leaving increasing geographical space to an expanding standard variety.

This, however, did not happen in Norway, since the question: *who* are the Norwegians, was answered also in this way: the real Norwegians are the dialect-speaking peasants, making up some 95% of the population in the early 18th century, and with dialects directly developed from Old Norwegian. The grammarian, dialectologist and language planner Ivar Aasen (1813—1896) demonstrated successfully the connection between Old Norwegian and the modern peasant dialects of the countryside. He did this by employing the comparative historical method developed by Rask, Grimm, Bopp and others. However, he disregarded every overt influence caused by the many centuries of language contact (with Low German and Danish, and especially with regard to vocabulary). The traditional purism in Nynorsk concerning loanwords from Low German and Danish has a more profound ideological importance than mere romantic puristic views, since it underlines the direct lines between Old Norwegian and the "unpolluted" peasant dialects (i. e. unpolluted by results of language contact). The idiom of the upper classes, however, was clearly a salient result of language contact. Regardless of its high social status in society, in Aasen's romantic view it had — because of its origin — to be disregarded as a candidate for a national language. To Aasen it represented Danish more than Norwegian, and as such it was totally unsuitable to serve as a national linguistic symbol. In the 1840s, Aasen collected dialect data from all the major dialect areas, and in 1853, he presented a written standard for these dialects, constructed as a common denominator. In 1885, Parliament decided to put this standard officially on a par with the other standard (Norwegianized Danish or "Dano-Norwegian"). This decision by Parliament implies that a view which suggested two competing cultures in Norway — one inherent and national, represented by the class of peasants, and one imported, unnational, represented by the educated upper-middle classes — now had been adopted by the political authorities, government and Parliament, after the introduction of parliamentary democracy in 1884. The Aasen standard was still unable to serve as a full-fledged written standard in society, but the political decision by Parliament in 1885 must be interpreted as an act which exploited the symbolic value of the Aasen standard ("the peasant's language") as a means to hit a blow at the still (culturally) dominant elite at their most important advantage: their cultural and sociolinguistic superiority.

The 1885 decision laid the ground for the language struggle up till 1917, a struggle between the two, now official, standards and with nationalistic more than social arguments. (These standards were termed *Riksmål* and *Landsmål* till 1929, from then on Bokmål and Nynorsk.)

In the second half of the 19th century the peasants' radical party pushed for a policy towards complete independence from Sweden, while the representatives of the elite and upper classes, in most cases, were more reluctant. This attitude gave rise to accusations that members of the elite were unnational in politics as they were — in the eyes of the peasants' party — in culture and language. However, in 1905, all ties between Norway and Sweden were severed, and in the following years accusations of being unnational were exclusively based on linguistic preference, and consequently more and more outdated. With the changes implemented in the major language reform of 1917, the time was definitely out for a view of the language situation based exclusively on a nationalistic interpretation involving "Norwegian" (represented by Aasen's Nynorsk standard) and "Danish" (represented by the — by now — quite Norwegianized Bokmål). This view is supported by an analysis of the protests in society brought about mainly because of the so-called "optional forms" introduced into written Dano-Norwegian in this reform (of 1917). These optional forms reflected popular, low status speech, and most of them were unknown to upper-middle class speech. In many school districts, the school board decided that these "optional" forms should be made obligatory in the school children's written essays. This decision caused a most fierce struggle in many parts of the country, especially in the south-east, where the traditional Dano-Norwegian Bokmål had its strongholds.

The sociolinguistic reaction to these optional forms in Bokmål, introduced and defended exclusively with nationalistic arguments by the language planners, showed that the language planning period in which nationalistic arguments could be employed, and succeed, was over. 1917 represents the end of the first — the nationalistic — period of Norwegian language planning. In this period, sociolinguistic issues had been of paramount importance, but the priority and basic rationale had been the question how to develop a national standard written variety. In 1917, this policy had resulted in not one, but two national standards, both with an obvious right to call itself Norwegian. (By now, books written in Bokmål started being translated into Danish for the first time. The separation of Danish and Dano-Norwegian Bokmål, caused by the Norwegianization process in Norway, had to be bridged by translation.)

4.3.2. The sociopolitical period

The reform of 1917 also represents the start of the second main period of Norwegian language planning, lasting till the 1960s, and with a definitive end in 1981 (with a reform of Bokmål that year). This second period could be called the sociopolitical period, because now the sociolinguistic perspective soon proved to have priority over the nationalistic. From about 1915 there was a majority in Parliament for a language planning policy aiming at a future fusion of the two competing standards. However, the main argument was based on the trivial linguistic differences between the two standards, not realizing that the sociolinguistic difference was far more important and excessively more difficult to bridge by a fused common standard "suitable for all Norwegians" as said in one slogan of that time. However, the reaction by the upper-middle classes to the (optional) low status dialect forms, which were included in the Bokmål standard in 1917 in order to "Norwegianize" the standard beyond the linguistic forms of the upper-middle class creoloid, proved beyond any doubt that a completely new language planning ideology or analysis of the situation was needed. In order to follow up the wish of the majority in Parliament to develop one amalgamated standard, the nationalist philosophy of the previous period was clearly insufficient. The new analysis was soon supplied by the growing social-democratic party, which adopted the view developed by the historian Halvdan Koht (1873—1965). In this analysis, a sociolinguistic understanding of the situation is the very basis, arguing that the only solution to the conflict situation is a sociopolitical one where the lower classes of workers and peasants conquer both written standards by gradually and simultaneously including more present-day low-status speech into them and thus, over time, move the standards towards a fusion. Halvdan Koht viewed the Nynorsk standard as too archaic, too removed from present-day speech, and Bokmål as too dependent on upper-middle class speech as well as on written Danish. By making Nynorsk linguistically more modern and, with the same linguistic means, making standard Bokmål more dependent on low-class speech, one could develop an amalgamated Common Norwegian standard. Such a sociolinguistically radical language planning policy could only be implemented by a strong political movement, consolidated and in agreement about both the analysis, the means and aims of the policy. Such total agreement was, however, never reached within the Labor party, although it adopted Koht's analysis in the 1930s and introduced a profound language reform in 1938. This reform dramatically reduced the importance of upper-middle class speech as the sole norm basis for Bokmål and consequently devalued this spoken variety sociolinguistically. The fierce post-war struggle over the Bokmål standard, culminating in the early 1960s and ending finally by a new reform in 1981, was clearly motivated by the sociolinguistic consequence of the 1938-reform. Adherents of the traditional, pre-1938 Bokmål (without the controversial "optional" forms introduced in 1917) which reflected upper-middle class speech almost totally, launched a massive campaign aimed at repairing, or better: reversing, the sociolinguistic impact of the 1938 reform. The leaders of this campaign were able to mobilize substantial support for their view also outside the rather restricted group of upper-middle class sociolectal speakers. Politically conservative leaders of business and commerce saw this language campaign as a means to weaken over time the overwhelming post-war Labor party majority in Parliament. Thus, the conservative language campaign in the 1950s never lacked financial support, and eventually it reached its goals. In the 1960s, the Labor government gave in and appointed a language commission aimed at finding a way to what was labelled "language peace". It should not surprise anyone that the only way suggested by this commission was to reverse the sociolinguistic experiment of the 1938 reform. With the 1981 reform, almost every linguistic form reflecting upper-middle class speech which had been taken out of standard Bokmål in 1938 was reintroduced into the standard.

The question remains, however, whether this action has also reinstalled upper-middle class speech, the Dano-Norwegian creoloid, at the overall high social level it enjoyed prior to the 1938 reform. This does not seem to be the case, since the official written Bokmål in its most frequently used variety since 1938 gradually has increased its importance as the norm also for normalized speech. At the same time upper-middle class speech — deviating in important and salient features from the official 1938 Bokmål standard — has been devalued as oral norm. To many people today, upper-middle class Oslo speech sounds a bit old fashioned and clearly marked socially. It is therefore not perceived any longer as a neutral unmarked standard variety, which it can be said to have been around 1917. Instead, this function has by now been taken over by a variety more close to the official written standard. This change in social status on the part of upper-middle class speech is a sociolinguistically interesting result of the language planning policy connected with the 1938 reform and Halvdan Koht's and the Labor party's analysis and linguistic program.

4.3.3. Success and failure in language planning

The first period of Norwegian language planning, up till 1917, must in most respects be viewed as successful. The main aim was to develop a national idiom different from the other Nordic languages. By 1917, Norwegians could choose between two written standards, both of which were clearly distinguishable from Danish and Swedish. However, the second period, in which the expressed aim was to solve the language question by getting rid of the two-standard situation, cannot be said to have been successful. There are still two standards of Norwegian, linguistically very close, but sociolinguistically very different. This difference goes back to the different sociolinguistic bases, or camps, on which the language planners of the 19th century relied when they developed their programs and language planning policies. Still today the difference between these two camps is very salient, even though the 1938 reform probably has resulted in a reduction of the overall social status of upper-middle class speech compared with the status it enjoyed prior to the 1938 reform. (Jahr 1989, 1992a).

4.4. Norwegian, Sami and Finnish

4.4.1. The multilingual situation in northern Norway

For about 2000 years there has been a situation of language contact in northern Norway. The first encounter between the Sami and Scandinavian speaking tribes can be dated by loanwords in Sami (Sköld 1979). Up till the present day this contact has prevailed, and other languages have also appeared on the scene. Norwegian, Sami, Finnish, Swedish, and Russian have all played major parts in forming the language contact situation that can be observed today, and which can be traced back some hundred years.

Many descriptions from travellers to the north testify to the multilingualism of northern Norway. Most of the travellers seem to be both astonished and overwhelmed by the cosmopolitical atmosphere in this remote part of Europe, created by the sound of many different languages. Beside Sami, Norwegian and Finnish, they could hear Swedish, Danish, Russian, English, German and French. Even a well-established pidgin language, Russenorsk, was in frequent use between late 18th and the two first decades of the 20th centuries. Thus, in this remote area of Europe one could observe a multitude of different language contact situations, some of which go back 2000 years. Arctic Norway is therefore an extremely interesting area for testing out hypotheses as to what linguistic and sociolinguistic effects can be expected from extensive and long-lasting language contacts: lexical and grammatical borrowings, grammatical reduction and generalization, language attrition, language shift, transference of features through language shifting, language birth, and language spread. – In the following, language contact more than language conflict will be discussed. The policy of the Norwegian authorities towards the Sami and Finnish speaking minorities, pursued up till the 1950s, and aiming at total assimilation of the minorities will therefore not be discussed here.

4.4.2. Norwegian–Sami

The overall socioeconomic and cultural differences were more pronounced between Norwegians and Sami than between Norwegians and the *Kvens*, i. e. the Finnish-speaking population, and this defined for generations the social framework within which the three languages could be influenced by one another. – A few loan words and some very few idioms and syntactic constructions are usually regarded as the product of Sami influence on Norwegian, but on the whole, Sami has not affected the traditional dialects of northern Norway to any appreciable degree. More important is the overwhelming Norwegian influence on Sami, most clearly seen in vocabulary and syntax, but today also noticeable in phonology. The syntactic influence of Norwegian on Sami varies according to context and the user's socio-cultural background and occupation. The oldest and consequently the best established influence is found in the religious use of the language. It dates back to the earliest translations of religious texts into Sami in the 18th century. Today, the influence is most apparent in the language used by Sami organizations and the media, and in terminology related to modern technology. The least important influence of Norwegian syntax on Sami is found in language related to traditional Sami occupations such as fishing, farming and reindeer herding. One phonological trait could be mentioned here, since up till now it has been exclusively Norwegian, but it is today spreading rapidly into Sami, namely the Norwegian retroflex phonemes, replacing clusters of /r/ + apical. Retroflex segments are common in eastern and northern Norwegian dialects, but were previously non-existent in Sami. This shows that Norwegian phonology today is also affecting Sami in addition to Norwegian vocabulary and syntax. Sami morphology has, however, not been exposed to Norwegian influence yet, and a Norwegian loan word in Sami must usually be brought into line with Sami phonotactic rules and Sami morphology.

4.4.3. Norwegian–Finnish

For a period of two hundred years the Finnish dialects of northern Norway have been strongly exposed to both Sami and Norwegian influence. This influence is most clearly seen in vocabulary and syntax. The syntax is affected most markedly by Sami, the vocabulary by Norwegian. Norwegian influence in Finnish phonology can be observed by the increasing tendency to accept initial consonant clusters, a Norwegian feature which is also observable in present-day Sami. Also, Finnish does not have a phoneme /f/, but we find /f/ in Norwegian loan words like *fini* (fine, adj., Norw. *fin*), *kaffi* (coffee, Norw. *kaffi*).

4.4.4. Sami Norwegian dialects

'Sami Norwegian' is not a uniform linguistic concept. Many Sami today have Norwegian as their first and only language, while a few, mostly old people, speak Norwegian only with great difficulty. The young Sami of the present generation are either bilingual or speak only Norwegian. Still it is possible to speak of specifically Sami Norwegians features. All of these are due to Sami substratum.

(a) Prosody. While accent 2 words in the northern Norwegian dialects have an even pitch on the stressed syllable, Sami Norwegian in general has falling pitch without any tonal distinction. This feature is due to the fact that Sami has no word tone opposition. Sami Norwegian sentence intonation is usually described as monotonous compared to other varieties of Norwegian. In a Sami sentence the word which is considered most important is assigned the highest pitch, and the intonation always falls at the end of every sentence. When this word and sentence intonation is used in Norwegian it lends the language one of the characteristic features of Sami Norwegian.

(b) Phonology. One of the most salient feature of Sami Norwegian phonology is due to the Norwegian opposition between the voiced and unvoiced plosives /b-p/, /d-t/ and /g-k/ in initial position, in particular when followed by the consonants /l/ or /r/. Sami has no opposition of voiced and unvoiced plosives in initial position; it also lacks the clear aspiration following the initial plosives found in Norwegian. In Sami, we only find unvoiced plosives without initial aspiration. These Sami features are reflected in Sami Norwegian, and popularly considered to be among the most salient traits of Sami Norwegian.

(c) Morphology. The most salient feature of Sami Norwegian morphology is perhaps the simplification of the Norwegian three-gender-system. This is obviously caused by the lack of grammatical gender in Sami. Also, Sami has no articles, while Norwegian has different articles for each of the three genders. In some places, this difference between Sami and Norwegian is reported to have resulted in the use of only one gender in Sami Norwegian. This simplification of the gender system is not, however, fully completed in most places, because the definite form singular seems to resist unification.

(d) Syntax. Sami Norwegian syntax is to a certain extent influenced by Sami syntax. Some places, the use of Sami illative and essive cases are reported to have been carried over to Sami Norwegian (Nesheim 1952, 128). Generalizations of Norwegian syntactic rules are also found. For example, in Norwegian a noun followed by a possessive pronoun has the definite form: *bilen min* ('car-the my'), *kua mi* ('cow-the my'), *huset mitt* ('house-the my'). But if the possessive pronoun precedes the noun, the noun has indefinite form: *min bil, mi ku, mitt hus*. In Sami Norwegian, this difference can be eliminated. The noun has definite form whatever the position of the possessive pronoun: *bilen min — min bilen* and so on. (Nesheim 1952, 127; Bull 1990).

Development within the Sami Norwegian dialects is rapid, and many of the most salient traits mentioned here will be most characteristic in the speech of older informants (cf. Bull 1992). The younger generations of Sami adapt more and more to the surrounding traditional Norwegian dialects, although Bull (1992) suggests that Sami Norwegian nevertheless constitutes separate ethnolects separate from the other northern Norwegian dialects.

4.4.5. Finnish–Norwegian

In spite of the long period of time during which Finnish has been used in northern Norway, the Norwegian dialect of, e. g., the town of Vadsø in Finnmark, one of the former strongholds of Finnish in Norway, shows no overt Finnish element today. However, there are some features of Vadsø speech where Finnish possible has had some influence. The whole area of east Finnmark, where Vadsø is situated, lacks the accent 2 word tone. This has usually been explained as a result of contact with the Finnish prosodic system, cf. that this lack of accent 2 is also manifested in Sami Norwegian. Finnish, like Sami, has no word tone opposition of the type we find in Norwegian. – The contact between Finnish and Norwegian may also have contributed to the tendency to morphological simplification and generalization which is observable in the Vadsø dialect and similar to the one we find in Sami Norwegian. Finnish, again like Sami, has no gender opposition. In Vadsø the opposition between the three genders is maintained in the singular (although not completely for the indefinite articles), but in the plural there is no difference in the declination. A similar tendency to simplification is also found in the verb morphology.

4.4.6. Sami and Finnish contact

For a period of two hundred years the Finnish dialects of northern Norway and Sami have been in close contact. However, it seems that Sami has had much more influence on the Finnish dialects than vice versa, especially concerning syntax. It appears that there has been an interesting general adstratum mechanism at work where Norwegian, being the dominant language, produced certain needs for syntactic changes in the Finnish speakers, and where Sami, being much closer to Finnish typologically, supplied the linguistic means to implement these changes (cf. Jahr 1982, 310 f).

As a conclusion of the discussion in section 4.4, the contact relationships between Norwegian, Sami and Finnish, and between Sami and Sami Norwegian and Finnish and Finnish Norwegian are shown in Figure 116.1.

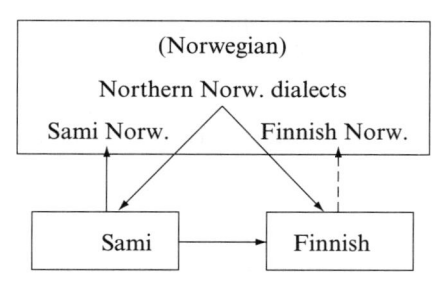

Figure 116.1: The directions of influence between Norwegian, Sami, and Finnish in northern Norway

4.5. Dialect contact

4.5.1. In northern Norway

An interesting field of research for contact linguists is dialect contact (Trudgill 1986). At several places in northern Norway we find descendants of immigrants from the southern part of the country who brought with them southern dialects into a northern dialect environment. The most important and largest area is inner Troms, which for 200 years has been a definite southern-dialect island in northern Norway. However, the long period of contact with northern dialects has resulted in both admixture and in levelling of certain marked forms. In principle, the processes one can observe with dialect contact resemble language contact processes to a large extent. (Jahr 1988.)

4.5.2. In Longyearbyen on Svalbard

A special case of dialect contact is found in Longyearbyen on Svalbard, situated on the 78th parallel. Since Svalbard has had a more or less permanent population only in the 20th century, Longyearbyen (about 1200 inhabitants) has no indigenous dialect, a fact which separates it from all other Norwegian towns and places (Mæhlum/Jahr 1986, Trudgill 1990). But a child who grows up in Longyearbyen nevertheless acquires a definite Norwegian variety. This variety, however, may differ considerably from the variety acquired by a child next door. While the first child may have a typical eastern Norwegian accent, the second may very well have a northern Norwegian one, and a third a western Norwegian one. The reason for this is that the population of Longyearbyen come from all over the Norwegian mainland, bringing with them all kinds of Norwegian dialects. A child will therefore be exposed to a multitude of different dialects without having a dominating indigenous dialect to focus towards. Although the dialect of the parents plays an important role for some children, a lot of others acquire varieties which have very little in common with the parental variety. Mæhlum (1992) has studied the linguistic strategies of the children in this diffuse linguistic situation. She was able to establish that both family-internal and family-external factors were involved, but also that several children opted for a kind of neutral linguistic variety in relation to the major Norwegian dialect areas, especially perhaps concerning prosody. It is evident that Longyearbyen offers a unique opportunity to study dialect contact processes involving many different varieties, and here without having to take into account the focusing impact of an indigenous dialect.

4.6. Russian

4.6.1. The pidgin Russenorsk

The arctic pidgin Russenorsk, now extinct, is one of the best known results of the longstanding language contact situation in the northern regions of the country. It was first described by O. Broch (1927), later by Lunden (1978), and by Broch/Jahr (1981, 1984). Russenorsk was created by Norwegian fishermen (i. e. Norwegians, Sami and Kvens) and Russian buyers of fish to overcome the communication barrier between Norwegian and Russian. A life span of about 150 years is attested for Russenorsk, i. e. from the second half of the 18th century up until shortly after the Russian Revolution in 1917.

4.6.2. Russenorsk compared to other pidgins

Russenorsk shows several interesting features compared to other pidgins. First, it was almost exclusively used in connection with the seasonal summer trade between Russians and Norwegians. Secondly, it was developed on the basis of two Indo-European languages, and thirdly, there was no social hierarchy between the two parties involved in the communication. The Russian traders and the Norwegian fishermen were on equal social terms. The oldest attested words in Russenorsk are from 1785 and 1807, and the language is first mentioned explicitly in written records between 1812 and 1814. Broch/Jahr (1984, 50) therefore suggest that Russenorsk developed during the second half of the 18th century. There exists some evidence of an

English-Russian pidgin in Archangel at the same time. This idiom, which was called "Solombala-English", exhibits the same verbal marker as Russenorsk (-*om*), and this fact indicates an early contact between these two pidgins. Which one of the two, Solombala English or Russenorsk, that first developed is, however, not possible to determine from available sources today. (Jahr 1995 b.) During the 19th century, the Russian trade in northern Norway attained a substantial scale. The 1870s and 1880s probably was the period when Russenorsk was most frequently used. In 1881, 470 vessels from the White Sea, with a total crew of 2287 men, sailed to the cities Vadsø, Vardø, Hammerfest and Tromsø in northern Norway. In the year 1900 the Russians delivered 4000 tons of flour and grain. If this amount is divided by the population of Finnmark and Troms, this is about 40 kg per person.

4.6.3. Reduced Russian in Finnmark

Up till about 1850 all Norwegians relied on Russenorsk in their contacts with the Russians. This also applied to the class of merchants, which constituted the local upper class. After 1850, however, the merchants tended to spend enough time with business colleagues in Russia, mostly in Archangel, so that they were able to speak better Russian. However, as shown by Lunden (1995), the Russian spoken by the local class of merchants in northern Norway was a radically reduced Russian, and as such a clear result of language contact. Language contact between Russian and Norwegian thus resulted in two distinct language varieties in northern Norway: the pidgin Russenorsk and the grammatically reduced Russian of the local upper class of merchants. Russenorsk was therefore, in the second half of the 19th century confined to the local fishermen, and subsequently despised and ridiculed by members of the local upper class who themselves took great pride in speaking their reduced variety of Russian, believing, of course, it to be Russian proper.

4.6.4. The decline of Russenorsk

Around the turn of the century the trade which was the basis both for Russenorsk and for the reduced Russian variety of the Finnmark merchants changed character from being basically a barter trade to becoming increasingly a cash-trade. On both sides the big merchants took over the trade and thus made the previous direct barter between the fishermen and the Russian buyers of fish superfluous. Presumably the ability to speak Russenorsk declined when the barter trade gradually disappeared. The Russian Revolution in 1917 then put a definitive end to this trade and consequently also to the pidgin Russenorsk.

4.6.5. Russenorsk, a short description

The Russenorsk texts which are available today consist of single words and isolated sentences, various wordlists of different lengths, and conversations in the form of dialogues. Almost all the texts come from the Norwegian side, only one comes from the Russian side. Unfortunately, we have no texts reflecting Sami use of Russenorsk, and only one small text from the Finnish side, although we know that many Sami and Finnish-speaking fishermen have been users of Russenorsk.

(a) Phonology. Today it is difficult to determine the pronunciation of Russenorsk; we have to work from written texts, most of which were written down by Norwegians. The spelling of individual words can vary from text to text, and we can establish that the pronunciation of Russenorsk has varied depending on the language and dialectal background of the individual speaker. In Russenorsk, phonemes which occur in only one of the source languages easily disappear. Since Russian lacks /h/, this sound became /g/ in Norwegian words used in Russenorsk, e. g. *gav* 'sea' < Norw. *hav*. Russian /x/, a phoneme which does not exist in Norwegian, becomes /k/ in Russenorsk, e. g. *klæba* 'bread' < Russ. *cleb*. Similarly, Russian consonant clusters are reduced to fit Norwegian phonotactic rules, e. g. *nogolo* 'many' < Russ. *mnogo li*, since Norwegian does not allow initial /mn-/.

(b) Morphology. Russenorsk morphology is very simple. The lexemes are as a rule uninflected. Nouns have a tendency to be marked by a final -a: *klæba, fiska, penga* ('bread', 'fish', 'money'). Russenorsk has a general verb marker (-*om*), but not all verbs are marked this way. The origin of the *om*-suffix is disputed, but it is quite obvious that there must be a connection between Russenorsk and Solombala-English on this point, since they both exhibit the same feature. There is no copula, and no verb to express possession. Frequent pronouns are *moja* 'I, my' and *tvoja* or *ju* 'you, your'. There is only one preposition: *po* 'on', and one question word, derived from Russian: *kak* 'what, etc.'. (Because of the frequent use of the pronouns mentioned, of *po* and of *kak*, Russenorsk has been referred to in different sources as "moja po tvoja-language"; "po-language" and "kak-speech"). Russenorsk shows different word-formation mechanisms: suffixation (*kral-om* 'steal' v., *kuk-mann* 'merchant'), compounding (*kua-sjorta* 'cow hide') and reduplication (*morramorradag* 'day after tomorrow'). The attested number of words in Russenorsk is around 400, half of which are hapax legomena. The core vocabulary therefore consisted of about 200 words, derived mostly from Norwegian and Russian, but also from Sami, Finnish, Swedish, English, Low German (or Dutch), French, and also one frequent word from an international nautical jargon (i. e. *skaffom* 'eat').

(c) Syntax. Russenorsk word order is normally SVO. Of syntactic rules exclusive to Russenorsk, one can distinguish at least two. In sentences containing an adverbial, the verb moves to final position; and if the sentence contains a negator it is always placed in second position. These two rules are not derivable from the two source languages Norwegian and Russian. The word *kak*, the general question word in Russenorsk, is also used as a subordinating conjunction. There are, however, only a few examples of dependent clauses in the Russenorsk corpus. Still, we must assume that the small size of the corpus is the reason why so few dependent clauses are attested. Once the word *kak* was introduced as a general conjunction, the language had clearly developed the grammatical apparatus necessary to mark subordination.

5. Critical evaluation of the sources and literature used

The description of language contact in Norway, especially northern Norway, is unfortunately still rather fragmentary. Except for studies of old Nordic loanwords in Sami (Qvigstad 1893), and O. Broch's 1927 paper on Russenorsk, language contact in Norway has attracted little interest among linguistic scholars. However, due mainly to the activity of linguists at the University of Tromsø (founded 1968) interest has increased considerably. In the past decade several influential publications have appeared (cf. Jahr/Lorentz 1990). Broch/Jahr 1981 (2nd ed. 1984) is the first monograph on Russenorsk. Most areas and aspects pertaining to language contact in northern Norway were outlined in Jahr 1982, cf. also Ureland 1987 (which covers northern Scandinavia in general). The process of language shift from Finnish to Norwegian was first mapped by Lindgren/Aikio 1979, cf. also Lindgren 1984 and Junttila 1990. For Sami, Jernsletten 1982 is a significant contribution, cf. also Martinussen 1989, Bergsland 1992, Jernsletten 1993, Jahr 1993. On Sami Norwegian, Nesheim 1952 is an early and important contribution, cf. also Lorentz 1982. Bull 1992 is an empirical study and discussion of certain surprising phonological features in Sami Norwegian. Bull suggests that these traits represent ethnolectal features in Sami Norwegian.

6. Bibliography (selected)

Bergsland, Knut (1992): "Language contacts between Southern Sami and Scandinavian." In: Jahr 1992b, 5–15.

Broch, Ingvild/Jahr, Ernst H. (1981): *Russenorsk — et pidginspråk i Norge*. (2nd. ed 1984), Oslo.

Broch, Ingvild/Jahr, Ernst H. (1984): "Russenorsk: a new look at the Russo-Norwegian pidgin in Northern Norway." In: *Scandinavian Language Contacts*, Ureland, P. S./Clarkson, I. (Eds.), Cambridge, 21–65.

Broch, Olaf (1927): "Russenorsk." In: *Archiv für slavische Philologie 41*, 209–262.

Bull, Tove (1990): "The influence of multilingualism on a northern Norwegian dialect." In: *Learning, keeping, and using language*, Halliday, M. A. K. et al. (Eds.), Amsterdam, 51–61.

Bull, Tove (1992): "A contact feature in the phonology of a northern Norwegian dialect." In: Jahr 1992b, 17–36.

Bull, Tove/Jetne, Kjellaug (Eds.) (1982): *Nordnorsk*, Oslo.

Jahr, Ernst H. (1982): "Language contact in northern Norway." In: *Die Leistung der Strataforschung und der Kreolistik*, Ureland, P. S. (Ed.), Tübingen, 307–320.

Jahr, Ernst H. (1988): "Dialektane i indre Troms – Baru og Målselv." In: *Ottar* 1988, No. 3, 39–44.

Jahr, Ernst H. (1989): "Limits of language planning? Norwegian language planning revisited." In: *International Journal of the Sociology of Language 80*, 33–39.

Jahr, Ernst H. (1992a): "Bokmål and Nynorsk: Norwegian majority and minority standards." In: *Minority Languages — The Scandinavian Experience*, Blom, G. et al. (Eds.), Oslo, 83–92.

Jahr, Ernst H. (Eds.) (1992 b): *Language Contact. Theoretical and Empirical Studies*, Berlin.

Jahr, Ernst H. (1993): "The Sami language in northern Scandinavia − a language maintenance perspective." In: *Language − A Doorway between Human Cultures* [Festschrift for Otto Chr. Dahl], Dahl, Ø. (Ed.), Oslo, 238−254.

Jahr, Ernst H. (Ed.) (1995 a): *Nordisk og lågtysk. Språksamfunn og språkkontakt i seinmellomalderen*, Oslo.

Jahr, Ernst H. (1995 b): "On the pidgin-status of Russenorsk." In: Jahr/Broch 1995.

Jahr, Ernst H./Broch, Ingvild (Eds.) (1995): *Language contact in the Arctic: Northern Pidgin and Contact Languages*, Berlin.

Jahr, Ernst H./Lorentz, Ove (Eds.) (1990): *Tromsø Linguistics in the Eighties*, Oslo.

Jernsletten, Nils (1982): "Språket i samiske samfunn." In: Bull/Jetne 1982, 107−117.

Jernsletten, Nils (1993): "Sami language communities and the conflict between Sami and Norwegian." In: *Language Conflict and Language Planning*, Jahr, Ernst H. (Ed.), Berlin.

Junttila, J. Hjulstad (1990): "Language use and language change in northern Troms." In: Jahr/Lorentz 1990, 196−202.

Lindgren, Anna-Riitta (1984): "What can we do when a language is dying?" In: *Journal of Multilingual and Multicultural Development 5*, 293−300.

Lindgren, Anna-Riitta/Aikio, Marjut (1979): "Finsk i Nord-Norge." In: *Språklig samling på folkemåls grunn*, Vikør, L./Wiggen, G. (Eds.), Oslo, 247−256.

Lorentz, Ove (1982): "Verknader av fleirspråklegheit på språket og språkbrukaren." In: Bull/Jetne 1982, 134−156.

Lunden, Sverdrup S. (1978): *Russenorsk Revisited. Meddelelser 15*, Slavic-Baltic Institute, University of Oslo.

Lunden, S. Sverdrup (1995): "The Vardø merchants' reduced Russian." In: Jahr/Broch 1995.

Martinussen, Bente (1989): "Språkskiftet på 1800-tallet." In: *Nordlyd: Tromsø University Working Papers on Language and Linguistics 15*, 123−132.

Mæhlum, Brit (1992): "Dialect socialization in Longyearbyen, Svalbard (Spitsbergen): a fruitful chaos." In: Jahr 1992 b, 117−130.

Mæhlum, Brit/Jahr, Ernst H. (1986): "Språklig variasjon i Longyearbyen." In: *Norsk Lingvistisk Tidsskrift 4*, 125−132.

Nesheim, Asbjørn (1952): "Samisk og norsk i Lyngen." In: *Sameliv, Samisk Selskaps Årbok 1951−1952*, Oslo, 129−129.

Qvigstad, Just (1893): *Nordische Lehnwörter im Lappisch*, Christiania [Oslo].

Sandvei, Marius (1938): "Birgittinernorsk." In: *Maal og Minne* 1938, 40−53.

Seip, Didrik A./Saltveit, Laurits (1971): *Norwegische Sprachgeschichte*, Berlin.

Sköld, Tryggve (1979): "The earliest linguistic contact between Lapps and Scandinavian." In: *Fenno-Ugrica Suecana 2*, 105−116.

Trudgill, Peter (1983): *On Dialect*, Oxford.

Trudgill, Peter (1986): *Dialect Contact*, Oxford.

Trudgill, Peter (1990): "Dialect contact and dialect mixture: the Svalbard perspective." In: *Forskning om mennesker på Svalbard*, Oslo, 103−108.

Ureland, P. Sture (1987): "Language contact research in northern Scandinavia." In: *Journal of Multilingual and Multicultural Development 8*, 43−73.

Ernst Håkon Jahr, Tromsø (Norway)

117. Nynorsk−Bokmål

1. Geography and demography
2. History
3. Politics, economy and general cultural and religious situation
4. Statistics
5. Sociolinguistic situation
6. Language political situation
7. General contactlinguistic portrait
8. Discussion within and between the two groups
9. Bibliography (selected)

1. Geography and demography

Synchronically, *Nynorsk* (N) [literally *New Norwegian*] and *Bokmål* (B) [literally *Book language*] are Norwegian language varieties. Diachronically, N is also the technical term covering the Norwegian spoken after about 1525. The term is used synchronically here. − Formally, B and N have an equal status as official standards. On the whole, their standardization applies to the written mode. Generally, spoken Norwegian is not standardized except for special purposes. Below, any notes concerning spoken B or N will be explicitly stated as such; otherwise, the presentation concerns B and N as the written language varieties they are in all essential respects. − The use of B and N is geographically restricted to Norway but for a few exceptions. Both standards are also being used in Nordic interrelations, as the mainland Scandinavian languages (Danish, Norwegian and Swedish) are interintelligible and one or more of them are being taught and learnt on the West Nordic islands. Moreover, both standards are being used in the U.S.A. by Norwegian immigrants and/or their descendants. — The social and geographical bases of B and N differ. Although both standards are well known to all Norwegians and belong to the cultural heritage of them all, they are being preferred differently in different parts of the country. Thus, N has its geographical basis in the southwestern and central parts of Norway and is least deep-rooted in southeastern and northernmost Norway. On a national level, B is the dominating variety with regard both to the extent and range of its use and to its normative influence on any variety of Norwegian, spoken or written. However, both varieties are exposed to each other every day in all parts of the country and are influenced by each other on various levels. The contact between B and N exists, then, nationally, regionally and locally on a societal level as well as inter- and even intraindividually.

2. History

Linguistically, B and N are not different languages. They both express the same language, viz. Norwegian. They have the bulk of their lexicon and grammar in common and are fully interintelligible. They do differ in some grammatical respects, however, above all in some crucial morphological categories and in certain lexical aspects, but even in some syntactical particulars, and they maintain different stylistic ideals and traditions. Their maintenance as separate and officially equal Norwegian standards despite their formal similarity and full interintelligibility is due to the historical and social connotations implied in and expressed by their formal differences and only to a lesser degree by their different relations to the existing spoken dialects of Norwegian. Here, only a brief outline of their historical background is given. For a more detailed outline → art. 116.

2.1. General background

Most Norwegians have been illiterates well into the 19th century. The ability to read (i.e. decode the script and acquire the content of) unknown written texts did not become general until the end of that century. During the 434 years during which Norway declined from being a kingdom united with Denmark to being a colony of that neighbouring country in every respect (1380—1814), the majority of the people maintained their popular dialects quite unmarked by Danish due to their illiteracy. Only in the minute circles of higher colonial civil servants and the clergy, whose privileges and education were given from and in Copenhagen, inclinations towards the use of a High variety of spoken Norwegian were noticeable from the first half of the 17th century onwards. That High variety was grammatically and lexically based on written Danish but phonologically modified by Norwegian. — Norway was cut loose from Denmark in 1814 as a result of Denmark's alliance with Napoleonic France and entered into a new alliance with Sweden later the same year. In that new alliance Norway had her status considerably raised and was able to enjoy domestic self-government in all matters but the ones concerning foreign policy until the final severance in 1905. Throughout the 19th century it seemed important to Norwegians under the influence of Romanticism to establish a Norwegian national language through which the Norwegian "folk spirit" (Germ. *Volksgeist*) might express itself. Since the only established written language in Norway was Danish, the Norwegians had to search elsewhere for a truly non-Danish as well as non-Swedish linguistic basis for establishing a uniquely Norwegian standard expression. That basis was found in the popular dialects.

2.2. Nynorsk

N was and is a written standard reflecting the general forms and structures of these popular dialects. It is based on the linguistic work of Ivar Aasen (1813—1896). During the 1840s he made empirical investigations into the popular dialects of the country. This study resulted in a grammar and a dictionary of these dialects in 1848 and 1850 respectively. He then experimented with various forms in different literary genres and was able to present a normative grammar in 1864 and a revised dictionary according to the established norms of grammar and word formation in 1873. This norm was called *Landsmål* [literally *the language of the country*]; N is its name since 1929. — Ivar Aasen's work and the standardization of N was motivated by educational, national and social considerations, above all the injustice laid on the peasants and their children to carry an extra burden when learning to read and write, viz. that of having to learn another language (Danish). N was meant to diminish the distance between the spoken mother tongue of most Norwegians and the language to be read and written, to connotate a Norwegian national adherence, and to lend a platform to the ordinary man and woman for the development of linguistic and cultural self-respect and social engagement beyond the local and private spheres. Politically, it represents an attempt to wrest the cultural hegemony from the ruling classes, i. e. the urban bourgeoisie and the civil servant elite. — Ivar Aasen's standard was maintained throughout the rest of the 19th century. It is not a standardization of one specific dialect, but rather a common denominator of general grammatical patterns and features in all popular dialects. In order to find historically and linguistically adequate forms representing the formal variation of the popular dialects, Aasen had chosen to standardize quite a few archaic forms. A purist, i. e. anti-Danish/-German, streak was also present in the derivational morphology. — N was taken up by some intellectuals and writers from the late 1850s. Its status of being an official standard equal to the "ordinary book language" of the time, i. e. Danish, was granted by the Parliament in 1885. A few years earlier, in 1878, the Parliament had laid down that the pupils should be free to use their dialectal mother tongues in speaking at school. Since 1892 the right to decide which standard to use as the main language of instruction at school has been delegated to the local communities and school authorities. As the main language of instruction at school (primary education) N was first and most solidly established in southwestern and central Norway, but even in many local communities elsewhere. The initial popularity and success of N made its opponents organize by the turn of the century, and N itself was reformed in 1901, 1910, 1917 and 1938 partly in order to accommodate to less archaic dialects, partly in compliance with the official policy from the beginning of the 1900s of bringing the two standards closer together in preparation of an eventual merger (*Samnorsk*, i. e. *Common Norwegian*). The implementation of such reforms necessitated the acceptance of both traditional and new grammatical and lexical forms within the standard; gradually, the older forms were exchanged with the new ones, which were previously substandard dialectal forms or forms borrowed from the alternative standard (B). Thus, each reform expanded the variational potential of the standard and gave support and identification to new dialectal and social groups, and N strengthened its position as the main language of instruction at school as well as of local and regional administrative bodies and the church by each reform. The peak of its expansion was reached in 1944, when 34,1% of all primary school pupils in Norway was taught in N. — Many local communities in Trøndelag and Northern Norway were won for N only after the reform in 1938. After World War II, N experienced a recession, loosing its grip in these most recently won districts first. Its position as the main language of instruction at school was gradually weakened by an average of 0,5% annually until it was stabilized in 1977. The decline was promoted by many factors, the most important of which are (i) a radical change in its connotation of national adherence and loyalty, which had been its privilege until the war, but which could no longer be denied B and its users and adherents after 1945; (ii) an enforced urbanization and a general centralization even in rural districts in Norway throughout the 1950s and 1960s; (iii) the impact of a general turn of interest from non-material cultural issues towards materialism and a consumer mentality following the establishment of mass production and the upsurge of a more uniformed mass culture in that connection throughout the Western world; and (iv) organizational weaknesses and tensions in the movements and bodies supporting the use of N. — Since 1977 the use of N has progressed somewhat. In 1993 it is the main language of instruction of 17% of all primary school pupils. The international "green wave" has contributed to that situation, but is by no means the sole or even main reason for that recent development. Both as a reaction to the indiscriminate use of English in present-day Norway and possibly anticipating new sentiments of nationalism, though most probably because of its connotations of nearness and domesticity, N has had a certain renaissance in some segments of commercial advertising, as has a similar use of local dialects. Furthermore, the position of N as the main language of instruction at school is being strengthened in regions where it already has a stronghold;

and N has begun to establish itself in urban areas. The latter is something quite new, and both the new urban establishments and the stronger regionalization of N give important clues to the future prospects of this variety.

2.3. Bokmål

The alternative to N when acknowledged as a national standard language in 1885, "det almindelige Bogsprog" [literally "the ordinary book language"], was little else than Danish. Only some very few orthographic and grammatical details, like the use of ⟨f⟩ for ⟨ph⟩ and the abandonment of capital letters in nouns and of separate plural forms of verbs, made it stand out from the Danish used in Denmark at the time. Only during the 1890s were changes made in the writing of this "ordinary book language" which made it reasonable to accept as something other than Danish, and the opponents of N rallied to defend it under the name of *Riksmål* [literally *the language of the state*]. An official reform of this standard in 1907 corroborated the actual changes that had taken place in text books and newspapers during the late 1800s and Norwegianized it further in grammar and lexicon. A second reform in 1917 brought it in harmony with the so-called "cultural speech" of the urban bourgeoisie and even opened it for optional dialectally based forms beyond that social basis. This gradual Norwegianization of Danish in Norway, resulting in Riksmål (from 1929 called *Bokmål*), rendered it necessary for Danes to translate Dano-Norwegian literature only after 1919. Some adherents of Riksmål did not accept any changes beyond the reflection of the "cultured speech" of the contemporary urban middle class and did neither accept the opening for dialectal forms in the 1917 reform nor the further Norwegianization of B in 1938 aiming at merging with N in a future Common Norwegian. These ultra-conservatives within the Dano-Norwegian tradition are still organized in a private organization called *Riksmålsforbundet* and a superstructural academy-like body of select members regulating the privately standardized Riksmål. The Riksmål movement was on the verge of relinquishing in 1940 but was forcefully revived after World War II. An extra-parliamentary opposition to the official Common Norwegian policy during the 1950s and early 1960s led to a new reform of B in 1981 granting the bulk of previously omitted Riksmål forms a place in the B standard.

Thus, the line of development since the beginning of the 20th century aiming at bringing B and N closer together through reforms every twenty-odd years, ending in a future Common Norwegian written language standard, was broken by the 1981 reform of B. A result of that new direction has been a polarization of the two varieties since 1981, strengthening the position of older, traditional forms in N as well.

3. Politics, economy and general cultural and religious situations

3.1. Politics

The official recognition of two standard varieties in 1885 occurred the year after the establishment of parliamentarism in Norway. Then, there were only two political parties, viz. *Høyre* (H) [i. e. *Right*] and *Venstre* (V) [i. e. *Left*]. H defended the traditional Civil Service government, opposed a policy of severance from Sweden and came to oppose the N movement. N was explicitly supported by V, the basis of which was the liberal small-towners and intelligentsia and, above all, the nation-wide peasants' movement. It was the V government that enforced parliamentarism in 1884 that secured the acknowledgement of N as an official standard as well. Later, when both parties split and new parties came up throughout the 20th century, N remained a cause for the bourgeoisie left and center parties (i. e. V itself and its splinter parties *Bondepartiet/Senterpartiet* (SP) [i. e. *The Farmers' Party*; 1920—] and *Kristelig Folkeparti* (KrF) [i. e. *Christian Popular Party*; 1934—]). H has remained a solid supporter for Riksmål and/or a conservative B variety. For some years during the first decades of the 20th century there was even a separate Riksmål party, and governments were very sensitive to the language questions of the time, so much so that a H prime minister had to resign after having attended a N meeting. Since the 1970s, H has gained access to the rural electorate in central and western Norway where the use of N prevails, and has had to pay due respect to N. On the whole, however, H is still marked by a conservative B adherence. A splinter party to the right of H, *Fremskrittspartiet* (FrP) [i. e. *the Progressive Party*], has gained some popularity since the 1970s partly on its extreme liberalist policy in economic matters, but mostly on a xenophobic anti-immigrant populist policy. This party is aggressively anti-N. – Initially, the labour movement parties were positively interested in the N movement. However, the dominating nationalist ideology and rhetoric of the N movement soon came to alienate the labour movement and its political parties, although the first leaders of *The Norwegian Communist Party* (NKP; 1923–) recognized the work of Ivar Aasen as a piece of cultural revolution compliant with its own revolutionary struggle. The leading, socialdemocratic *Arbeiderpartiet* (A) [i. e. the *Labour Party*] took up planned reforms of both B and N aiming at a future Common Norwegian written standard as its glottopolitical policy, and that party was the leading force in that direction from the 1930s until 1960, when it was dismissed from the party program. After 1970, A has not engaged much in traditional language politics. All the same, this party is represented by both N and B spokesmen in the Parliament, and due to the social connotations of the dialectal forms in B as "popular" (i. e. non-elitist/non-bourgeois) the B practised by Labour representatives have often been less conservative than the one practised by H representatives, although there is a noticeable tendency at the end of this century towards a more conservative usage altogether. In 1960 a new leftist socialdemocratic party, *Sosialistisk Folkeparti* (SF) [i. e. *Socialist Popular Party*] splintered from A on the question of Norwegian membership in NATO. From SF another faction splintered in 1968 forming a Maoist Marxist-Leninist party (AKP) which grew to be the largest one of its kind in all Western Europe during the 1970s. Both these new left wing parties have been and still are positive to the use of N and the dialectally based variants of B. SF merged in 1975 with a second splinter faction from the Labour Party after the referendum on EC membership in 1972 as well as with a much smaller splinter faction from the old NKP. This new party, *Sosialistisk Venstreparti* (SV) [i. e. *Socialist Left Party*] has grown to become one of the largest ones on a national level and is periodically breathing down the neck of both H and A. AKP, however, has been reduced to next to nothing during the latest decade and may be overlooked in this respect but for its daily newspaper which is read by quite a few because of its high-quality journalism, and which presents N and dialectally based B variants more than most dailies. – In sum: B is practised by members and representatives of all political parties as a function of its overwhelmingly dominant position in most quarters of society. The rightist parties H (ab. 25% on the Gallup polls in Spring 1993) and FrP (6–7%) tend to prefer and support the most conservative B variants and even the unofficial ultra-conservative Riksmål; FrP is even actively anti-N, which H is not. The largest labour party, A (28–30%), is no longer actively involved in the national language struggle but is represented in most administrative bodies (the government, the Parliament, regional and local administrative bodies) by users and spokesmen of both B and N. N has maintained its traditional party political stronghold of support and use in V (3–4%) and its splinter parties SP (10–12%) and KrF (6–7%), and is supported by the leftist socialdemocratic party SV (17–18%) and the Marxist-Leninist AKP (0.5–1%). What is more important: All parties represented in the Parliament, except FrP, are loyal to and defend the laws and regulations which have been passed to secure the position of and general opportunity to use both N and B in all their formal variation.

3.2. Economy

Since B and N are official standards, they both enjoy official economic support. In addition, the promotion of N is also supported by private funds as is the promotion of Riksmål and of the dialectally based variants of B. On the whole, though, B is not in need of private funding due to its dominant position in society. – Officially, B and N are supported economically in many ways which cannot be fully accounted for here. The support derives from the laws and regulations concerning the use of both varieties. Most importantly, school text books are to be available at the same time and at the same price in both standards for all pupils and schools to have a real choice, and publishers receive official means to secure that regulation. Also, all civil servants are bound by law to answer anyone turning to them in writing in the standard used by the individual writer. The skills in writing B and N should ideally be established during their general education, but if they prove inadequate, the official institution in question may spend means to update the relevant linguistic skills of their employees. Also, vital economic support is given to the many local, regional and national newspapers, both directly according to their circulation and indirectly through State advertisements which according to existing rules are being published in approximately 160 newspapers. N is mostly used in local and regional newspapers which are particularly sensitive to this kind of support. — Private funding in the form of advertising in Riksmål and N publications is also important. Traditionally, Riksmål is and has been supported in that way by wealthy parts of private enterprise. N is supported by organizations of which *Noregs Mållag* [i. e. the *Norwegian Language Association*] is the most influential one (ab. 20 000 fee paying members), and there are private funds donated by individuals for special purposes, e. g. literary prizes. Such funds also support the promotion of dialectally based B variants. Throughout the 20th century, moreover, the N movement has established an economic foundation in various types of real estate and business ownership and shareholding as well as in publishing houses and a few newspapers.

3.3. Cultural and religious situation

B and N are used in all quarters of cultural and religious life in Norway. Again, B is the dominating variety. More than in other sectors of society, however, N has acquired a solid position in literary art. Ever since the 1870s N has been the linguistic vehicle of many of the greatest authors and poets and still is. In this field it faces little criticism by its opponents. By a parliamentary decision, neither B nor N should be used in less than 25% of all verbal programs on the public service radio and television, but the quota of N rarely exceeds 20%. Standard spoken N is used only in manuscript-based emissions like news bulletins and announcements; in most programs the whole variety of Norwegian dialects are being used, maintaining interdialectal intelligibility and strengthening variational tolerance. B is the main language on stage. However, in Oslo the biggest and most modern and influential theatre uses only N, standardized or in dialectal varieties, and most regional theatres stage many of their pieces in dialectal adaptations. Nationally produced films are rarely linguistically standardized. Most films shown are foreign; they are subtitled, not dubbed, except films for the very young, and all subtitling is done in B. — Religious language use is generally conservative, and it took time for N to gain a foothold in that context. The Bible was not fully available in N until 1921, though the New Testament as well as collections of translated and original hymns had been published and used since the late 1800s. Today, the West Norwegian dioceses and many parishes beyond that region use N. Hymns are sung in N and B in all Norwegian churches irrespective of the main standard used in other contexts; since 1984 there has been a common B and N hymn book for the protestant churches. Norway is a predominantly protestant society with a Lutheran state church and many strong low church evangelic societies and missions besides quite a few nonconformist congregations; little more than one percent is catholic. The influential low church lay movement is historically connected with the Left party and has always been marked by much use of N. In the Norwegian Catholic church N is used more sparingly, almost exclusively in hymns, and in general both B and N is used in their most conservative variants, which reflects both the high church solemnity of catholic masses and the fact that this church is much of an immigrant church in Norway with little affinity to popular and especially rural cultural life.

4. Statistics

There are about 4 million users of Norwegian. All Norwegians are being taught to read and write both B and N at school, though one of the varieties is chosen as the main standard of instruction. It is chosen by the local electorate of each school district, but dissenting minorities of ten or more pupils have the right to be taught in the alternative standard if so wished. In 1993 17% of all primary school pupils had N as their main standard. This percentage has decreased since the mid 1940s, when it was 34,1%. A reasonable estimate of Norwegians using N today would be some 25%, though many individuals use both B and N depending on the context. Everyone is exposed to both varieties daily, though N is used little more than in 20% of the verbal programs on radio and television, likewise in official documents. — Norway has an indigenous minority of some 30 000 Samis. Most of them know Norwegian as a second language in its B variety; very few prefer N. The same applies to the very small indigenous Finnish-speaking minority. Some 200 000 people of non-Norwegian origin live in Norway. Immigrant children attend ordinary schools and learn both B and N with one of them as a main standard of instruction according to the choice of the local school community to which they belong. Adult immigrants, however, are so far being taught Norwegian only in the B variety due to lack of relevant teaching material in N.

5. Sociolinguistic situation

Despite their equal status as official written standards of Norwegian, B and N are unequally distributed both geographically and socially. That has to do with the social connotations and history of the two varieties. N is still linguistically closer to most of the popular dialects than B is. However, it has never properly gained access to the academic educational institutions although it is absolutely present there, and that is even more the case with the prestigious parts of private enterprise and of the military forces. So, while N so far has remained a variety associated with ordinary people, with rural Norway and, at that, especially with certain regions of it, economic and political power as well as the prestigeous advanced educational institutions are concentrated in urban areas where B prevails, and B has maintained those connotations of power and erudition previously adhering to Danish/Dano-Norwegian in the cultural and political elite of most local societies. These different connotations of power and powerlessness are, of course, contradicted in many cases, but on the whole the old stereotypes of B and N still survive and influence the attitudes to learning and using the two varieties, not least at school. Ridiculing N is a popular sport in B strongholds like the Oslo area and in socially upwards mobility circles elsewhere, and users of N are suffering under a continual pressure of negative attitudinal formation among the young as well as by repeated denials of linguistic rights. Legally and formally in other ways, however, the position of N is stronger than ever.

6. Language political situation

B and N are equally well represented in the Norwegian Language Council (NLC). NLC is an official body under the Department of Culture and is bound by law to advise official authorities as well as the public in language normative and political matters. NLC is also bound to look after the linguistic rights of the individual and pursue instances of legal violations. Also, NLC prepares major reforms of the B and N standards for the Parliament and may decide itself on minor adjustments of the standards. – The most active language political organizations are the N ones. There are academy-like as well as modern grassroot organizations defending the standard and promoting the use of N. The Riksmål movement is mostly active in publishing dictionaries and other prescriptive material. The Common Norwegian movement is the weakest language political position at the moment, active mostly in the academic field. – After 1972 much of the language political debate has been channelled into NLC, where all interested parties are represented. The conservative positions have grown stronger, especially in B but even in N, and the Common Norwegian policy has lost its impetus but is still maintained in the law of NLC as a long-term goal. – Outside NLC the traditional language struggle is still very much alive. Recently, however, an alliance across the traditional antagonist positions in the domestic struggle has fronted the inundation of Anglo-American language use in Norway. It has been official government policy since the late 1980s to counteract this contemporary tendency of Anglo-American usage and to inspire Norwegians to use Norwegian with self-respect and self-confidence in the ongoing process of internationalization.

7. General contactlinguistic portrait

7.1. B and N linguistic differences

The standardization of B and N concerns their orthography and their derivational and inflectional grammar. Syntax is not generally standardized except in a few particulars, nor is lexicon apart from what follows from the different rules of morphology. B and N have more in common than what is different. In addition, there are a series of optional forms within each standard, many of which overlap across the standards. In actual use this formal variation is practised more in N than in B, where the dialectally based variants are socially marked in a way they are not in N (cf. 2.). – Many differences between B and N reflect the fact that B historically is a Norwegian adaptation of Danish, whereas the raison d'être of N is to represent the forms and patterns of popular Norwegian dialects. That is the case in orthography and grammar where N retains the Old Norse diphthongs and B does not or does so only unsystematically; e. g. N *ein* – B *en* [i. e. *one*], but N *rein*

− B *rein/ren* [i. e. *clean*]. Similarly with N *au* − B *ø* and N *øy* − B *ø*. And that is so in all cases where N retains full vowels, above all *a* in grammatical morphemes, in accordance with the maintenance of such vowels in most Norwegian dialects, whereas B uses *e* in accordance with the reduction of such vowels to *schwa* in Danish and spoken Riksmål. Cf. Table 117.1. − There are several general orthographic differences. For instance, B generalizes the consonantal group *hv-* where N generalizes *kv-*, as in B *hva-* − N *kva* [i. e. *what*].

Tab. 117.1: The realization of *a* and *e* in B and N morphology

	Bokmål	Nynorsk
Masc. pl. indef.	-er	-ar
Masc. pl. def.	-ene	-ane
Fem. sg. def.	-en/-a	-a/-i
Fem. pl. indef.	-er	-er/-ar/-or
Fem. pl. def.	-ene	-ene/-ane-/one
Neut. pl. def.	-ene/-a	-a/-i
Nomina agentis	-er	-ar
Passive infin.	-es	-as(t)
Pres. ptc.	-ende	-ande
Pres. 1. cl. weak verbs	-er	-ar
Past (ptc.) 1. cl. weak verbs	-et/-a	-a
Comparative	-ere	-are
Superlative	-est(e)	-ast(e)

Likewise, B usually has a single *-t* after a diphthong, whereas N generalizes a double *-tt* in that position, e. g. B *greit* − N *greitt* [i. e. *simple; all right*]. − Most of the important differences are grammatical. Like standard Danish, B allows a two-gender system as optional to the Norwegian three-gender system. In practice, the three-gender system is used only haltingly. N generalizes the three-gender system. Cf. Table 117.2.

In B past participles of strong verbs end in *-et*. In N they end in *-e/-i*, as in B *båret* − N *bore/bori* [i. e. *carried*], again according to the patterns in Danish/spoken Riksmål and the

Tab. 117.2: B and N gender forms

	Bokmål	Nynorsk
Masculine (a − the man)	*en* mann − mann*en*	*ein* mann − mann*en*
Feminine (a − the woman)	*en/ei* kvinne − kvinn*en*/kvinn*a*	*ei* kvinne − kvinn*a*
Neuter (a − the house)	*et* hus − hus*et*	*eit* hus − hus*et*

popular dialects respectively. − The pronominal forms express the same system, but differ in many particulars. Particularly connotative of the B and N positions are the first person singular and the first and third person plural pronouns: B *jeg* − N *eg*; B *vi* − N *vi/me*; B *de* (nom.) and *dem* (obl.) − N *dei* (both nom. & obl.). Here N reflects West Norwegian dialectal forms, whereas B reflects partly East Norwegian dialectal forms, partly a Danish system. − Syntactico-stylistically, N reflects the right-branched verbal pattern typical of Norwegian dialectal usage. At that, syntagms are paratactic rather than hypotactic. B traditionally maintains more of the nominal and hypotactic syntax typical of German. However, style is not standardized, neither syntactically nor lexically, but the stylistic tradition of each variety plays a certain role. − To that tradition, but even affecting the prescriptive rules of each standard, belong different attitudes to non-Norwegian derivational affixes. N has a purist tradition in that respect, avoiding German and Danish affixes in particular, e. g. prefixes like *be-*, *an-* and *er-* and suffixes like *-heit*, *-else*, *-bar* and *-messig*. N allows a certain number of words derived by means of such morphemes, but they are alien to the N tradition although they are numerously present in the popular dialects. B has no inhibitions concerning the use of these derivational morphemes.

7.2. Reciprocal influences

If N had not been established, B would probably have remained little different from Danish. Its Norwegianization would hardly have gone further than the 1907 reform and certainly not beyond the most conservative variety of the 1917 reform. The establishment and increasing countenance to N up till World War II forced B to include many of the most typical Norwegian grammatical structures and forms. This historical opening of B to N forms and patterns also implies an opening to dialectal forms, though not as generally as the case is with N. The dialectal forms allowed in B today are predominantly East Norwegian. — During the latter 50 years the normative power has changed from N to B on the standardized levels of the written modes. B forms hardly ever yield to N forms in individual writing, but may well yield to forms that correlate with the dialects of the writer. Users of N, on the other hand, easily take up B forms in their writing, especially if those forms correlate with their dialectal forms too. Allomorphic differences, like the *a* — *e* opposition (cf. above), seem to be more liable to change than morphemic differences. Stylistically and lexically, though, N still exerts a certain influence on B usage. Style and lexicon seems not to be as socially connotative in the language political context as the lower levels of language. — The B and N standards themselves have polarized somewhat after the 1981 reform of B, which upgraded formerly omitted Dano-Norwegian forms. This return to more markedly different B and N forms is noticeable in practice, too, especially in official documents and in school text books, even in the fictional prose of the youngest generation. In newspaper usage, however, B seems to develop more in the direction of oral language models, incl. spoken language morphology and word formation.

8. Discussion within and between the two groups

Most Norwegians do not engage publicly in language politics. Most of those who do, accept the two-standard situation. During a couple of decades from the latter half of the 1960s, the policy of the N organizations was expressed in two slogans: *Nynorsk einaste riksmål i Noreg* [i. e. *Nynorsk as the only national language of Norway*] and *Tal dialekt, skriv nynorsk* [i. e. *Speak your dialect, write Nynorsk*]. While the latter was motivated by a social and pedagogical ideology and engagement and in turn motivated the maintenance of many optional forms within the N standard and a less purist attitude to loan words and derivational elements, the former was clearly unrealistic for any foreseeable future. Today, the youngest generations of N users and adherents attack the policy expressed by the latter slogan. Their ideology and engagement is a national(istic) one; they practise and advocate the most conservative N forms and criticize the large formal variation within the N standard as well as the pedagogical and social arguments for N having to be as representative of the popular dialects as possible. They upgrade the purist tradition of N. While their elders have pleaded their cause with reference to international variational sociolinguistics, they do not. — The defenders of dialectal forms and patterns in the B standard, i. e. the defenders of the Common Norwegian policy, also call upon international sociolinguistics for their support in opposition to the traditionalist and elitist Riksmål position. The adherents of Riksmål, however, invoke the academy-based standardization of languages and language societies like the French, Italian and German ones for their support. After having had most of their demands accepted by the 1981 reform of B, however, their cause has lost much of its impetus. Compared to the situation during the previous 20—30 years, the traditionalists and adherents of conservative forms and strict standards of both B and N are nonetheless in fair wind in the 1990s. Both inside and outside the Norwegian language Council they make a common cause in many cases. But overshadowing it all, B and N adherents stand together against the pressure of commercial Anglo-American influence everywhere in Norway at the moment.

9. Bibliography (selected)

Bull, Tove (1991): "Current issues in official Norwegian language planning". In: *New Language Planning Newsletter* 6:2, 1—3.

Gundersen, Dag (1977): "Successes and Failures in the Reformation of Norwegian Orthography". In: *Advances in the Creation and Revision of Writing Systems*, Fishman, J. A (Ed.), Haag, 247—265.

Haugen, Einar (1966): *Language conflict and language planning. The case of modern Norwegian*, Cambridge, Mass.

Jahr, Ernst Håkon (1992): "Bokmål and Nynorsk: Norwegian majority and minority standards". In: *Minority Languages. The Scandinavian Experience*, Blom, G. et al. (Eds.), Oslo, 83—92.

Vikør, Lars S. (1989): "The position of standardized vs. dialectal speech in Norway". In: *International Journal of the Sociology of Language* 80, 41—59.

Vikør, Lars S. (1993): *The Nordic Languages. Their Status and Interrelations*, Oslo.

Wiggen, Geirr (1986): "The role of the Affective Filter on the level of orthography". In: *New Trends in Graphemics and Orthography*, Augst, G. (Ed.), Berlin, 395–412.

Wiggen, Geirr (1989): "Norway". In: *Sociolinguistica* 3, 75–84.

Wiggen, Geirr (1995): "Norway in the 1990s: a sociolinguistic profile". In: *International Journal of the Sociology of Language* 115, 47–83.

Geirr Wiggen, Oslo (Norway)

118. Norwegian–Sami

1. Geography and demography
2. History, economy and general cultural situation
3. Sociolinguistic situation
4. Language political situation
5. Bibliography (selected)

1. Geography and demography

The Sami inhabitants of Norway live in an area stretching from the northern Sør-Varanger to Femund's Elgå, in the south (→ language map A). They constitute a highly heterogeneous population, possessing distinct cultural and linguistic traits. The southern Sami live in small, scattered clusters and families, and most of them have reindeer herding as their main livelihood. Reindeer herding has been an important factor for the creation of Sami unity in the southern areas.

In the fjord tracts, from Tysfjord and northward, there are still hamlets where the majority of the inhabitants are predominantly Sami. The Sami do not differ from the Norwegian population, however, when it comes to choice of occupation and industry. It is only in inner Finnmark that the Sami population is more dense than in other parts of the country. The Sami entail the majority of the population in the municipalities of Kautokeino, Karasjok, Tana and Nesseby. Hunting and fishing have been associated with the traditional Sami culture. Tame reindeer have been used by the Sami both as pack animals and hunting decoys, in the hunting of wild reindeer, for as long as the Sami people have been mentioned in historical accounts. This covers a period stretching over nearly two thousand years.

The distinctly modern reindeer herding prototype was developed during the 1600s. Less than 20 per cent of the population are engaged in reindeer herding among residents of the four largest Sami municipalitties in Finnmark. Only in the municipality of Kautokeino do the reindeer herding Sami constitute the largest section of the population. It is estimated that less than 10 per cent of all the Norwegian Sami are employed in reindeer herding. On the whole, however, reindeer herding is a central aspect of Sami society and culture. It is among this section of the population that traditional ways of working and related customs, societal patterns and the Sami language are most active. Reindeer herding is not only an occupation, but it is also something that constitutes a separate culture and way of life. On the whole, a distinct connection exists between the occurrence and maintenance of an active Sami culture and language, where reindeer herding, agriculture, fishing and trapping are to be found, and the presence of traditional industries. Here, accordingly, there are stable local communities that experience minimal social changes. The Sami language, too, is being upheld even though it has a low status in non-Sami society. The language is an integrated part of the social and cultural life of the local community.

The last Sami census in Norway was conducted in 1970, with both ethnic origin and language used as criteria. The census was based on reports by the Sami themselves and was only carried out in selected districts in North Norway. Thus the figures for 1970 are not comparable with earlier Sami censuses. In the 1970 census 10,535 individuals had Sami as their first language, 19,635 had at least one Sami-speaking parent or grandparent, but only 9,175 individuals considered themselves as Sami. This is probably due to the low status of Sami culture and language, especially in the fjord-areas. Social scientists have criticised this census for several reasons, and concluded that it is not reliable.

It is estimated that in Norway, Sweden and Finland there are a total number of about

50,000—70,000 Sami, of whom between 30,000 and 40,000 live in Norway, some 17,000 in Sweden and 5,700 in Finland (The Sami People, 1990).

2. History, economy and general cultural situation

Attitudes toward the Sami language have an historical background. Simultaneous with the development of national and political independence in Norway, an increasingly more conscious, and persistent, policy of Norwegian assimilation was enforced upon the Sami from the 1840s onward. The purpose was to turn the Sami into Norwegians, both culturally and linguistically.

Discriminating regulations led to the widespread attitude, among Sami who lived in mixed language communities, that Sami background and culture were inferior in relation to Norwegian values. The Sami language was looked upon as an obstacle in "the struggle for survival". In mixed language communities, schools and their ideology of Norwegianization worked together with other social pressures found in society. Schools administered knowledge of the Norwegian language, and this knowledge was essential when managing one's life. Knowledge of and skills in the Sami language, and way of life, were clearly not tolerated by the schools. To lessen societal and school pressures, the Sami had to learn how to suppress or hide such knowledge and skills outside of the home. Sami parents of the current generation living in mixed language communities, or in partially Norwegianized regions, are those who have suffered such adversities at school. This is why so many of them have not wanted to teach their children Sami at home.

In principle, the policy of Norwegianization in schools was to be completed in inner Finnmark in the same manner as in coastal regions. The Norwegian school, however, did not receive any favour or support from the inland Sami community. Norwegian settlement had not made much impression of any significance here. Within reindeer herding, the Sami had full control. Sami culture, together with a basis in traditional industries, followed a steady pattern of progression.

The Sami language had a natural role in this type of traditional Sami community. With the exception of more technical skills such as reading, writing and elementary mathematics, schools did not have anything to offer that was absolutely necessary for survival in the local community. Knowledge of Norwegian was something which a person could manage without. Merchants, on the contrary, had to learn Sami in order to carry on trade. The Sami people looked upon schools as something which aimed at alienating their children from Sami values in order to have them adopt Norwegian customs, language and mentality. The reindeer herding Sami are constantly complaining about how school takes precious time away from their children's training in the chores and way of life of the parents. In relation to Norwegianization, there were no societal pressures in inner Finnmark that the schools could utilize.

The history and the cultural situation of the Southern Sami is particularly interesting, in the light of the policy of Norwegianization. While individual coastal villages with a majority of Sami speakers could be Norwegianized in the course of a couple of generations, the Southern Sami have managed to preserve their language for many centuries. This they have done without any concentration of settlement possessing a normal Sami-language environment.

The reason for this, too, is that the language functioned in a society which had a traditional way of life and traditional industries. In more recent times, the culture of the Southern Sami has been almost wholly dependent upon reindeer herding. Conflicts could occur in a number of places between farmers and the Sami where both competed for the right to use outlying grazing grounds and mountain tracts. This often led to isolation of the Sami by the Norwegian villagers. Up to the 1950s, mixed marriages among the Southern Sami occurred relatively seldom for Norwegians and the Sami reindeer herding groups. Those Sami who married Norwegians were usually assimilated into a Norwegian environment. The Southern Sami population has, for this reason, remained at a statistically consistent level, a level adjusted to the possible number of people involved in reindeer herding in the area.

3. Sociolinguistic situation

When referring to a Sami language community, we must omit public institutions and administration. The exceptions are the school system and the church, where Sami at least has status as a supportive language. Schools give instruction in Sami when parents prefer this. And even though educational legislation has not authorized this earlier, instruction in Sami was offered from the early 1970s onward, in subjects other than the Sami language. The Norwegian Church has bilingual services in the Sami parishes of Nesseby, Tana, Karasjok, Kautokeino and occasionally in other parishes with Sami among the inhabitants.

If we disregard the official view of the linguistic situation, there are villages which can be characterized as monolingual Sami-language communities. Sami is the communicative language in all instances where the inhabitants themselves maintain control of the situation. Sami is spoken at work, in the stores, at the post office, the sports arena, and in different organizations. Even when Norwegian speakers are present, many of the discussions will continue in Sami. The children learn only Sami at home. Norwegian may be learned through their playmates and by watching TV. Most of them have a poor command of Norwegian when they begin at school. These children do strengthen their mother tongue, however, by their contact with the older generation. The children learn much of the vocabulary used in occupational activities of a traditional nature, such as cooking, "duodji" (needlework and handicrafts) and outside work. Traditional culture is passed on by the grandparents' generation: by stories, folk-tales and myths. TV and music cassettes do occupy some of the family's leisure time, but these kinds of cultural mediums do not seem to take up as much room among homogeneous Sami families as in Norwegian homes. Most family members are not completely bilingual. To them, Norwegian is a foreign language. This kind of monolingual Sami community is found in inner Finnmark. Similar Sami communities are located in the Finnish municipalities of Utsjoki and Enontekiö, and in Swedish Karesuando, situated in the Municipality of Kiruna.

Another reason that the Sami language has been preserved as the main means of communication in some Sami villages, is that the number of individuals is adequate to create a language community where the language can function in most situations. This is not the case in Sami regions further to the south. Sami settlement there is secured by its connection to reindeer herding. Grazing ground has nonetheless become so limited that the idea of an accumulated Sami settlement in any single region is not feasible.

As mentioned earlier, the Southern Sami live in small, dispersed family units. With the exception of family relations and their reindeer herding, the Sami people here must function as a part of the local Norwegian communities. The Sami groups are too small to create a separate language *community*. Sami is used here only as a means of communication within the family. Greater social gatherings, where the Sami from a larger region converge, are quite rare. In order to function in the local environs, the Sami must master Norwegian. The Sami have also become used to using Norwegian outside of the home, and among themselves, because of their minority status. This is the reason why the Southern Sami have mastered and used Norwegian as a means of communication for generations. Developments here are leading to the takeover of Norwegian as the language also of the domestic sphere. There are few young people who comprehend Sami well enough to use the language as an adequate means of communication. The cultural consciousness of the Southern Sami is expressed by an occupational pride in activities such as reindeer herding and *duodjii*, and by a conscious attitude toward Sami affairs.

In a fjord village one will now find a linguistic generation gap. Most of those of the grandparents' generation have Sami as their native language. This is the language that they learned at home and which they speak most fluently. Their Norwegian is, however, sufficient in daily affairs and relatively simple matters. Most of those who belong to the parental generation have also learned Sami as their mother tongue. But under various industrial and societal circumstances, they are used to thinking and speaking in Norwegian. This parental generation is therefore bilingual. The two languages are used according to situation and context.

It has become usual for the parents to teach their children only Norwegian at home. The domestic scene can therefore entail a mixed language situation: the parents speak Sami with the older generation, and Norwegian with the children. Many who are now between 20 and 30 years old have been raised in such multi-lingual homes, but they do not speak Sami. They cannot manage, they usually say, because they are not used to speaking Sami.

One characteristic of the assimilation process, in such a village, is that the Sami have felt impelled to curtail their Sami identity by Norwegian society. Based upon this fact, specific social roles have been developed in Sami society. There are, for instance, unwritten rules concerning where a person can speak Sami, and where he or she cannot (Eidheim 1971). All of the villagers know who is regarded as a Sami and who is considered to be Norwegian. If Norwegians are present in company, it is also looked upon as being "polite" to employ Norwegian customs and "etiquette". To simplify, one can conclude that the Sami language, as a result of these practices, is only utilized at home and in other situations which the Sami regard as private. When the Sami people go to the store, the post office, and other public utilities, they speak only Norwegian — even when there are only Sami speakers present.

An educational sociologist, Asle Høgmo, tells how tabooed Sami culture and language are in his own home district, a fjord region located in Finnmark: one does not mention it. To avoid talking about Sami language and culture is in itself a token of identity in the fjord village (Høgmo 1986).

In cases where the local Sami community became dependent upon a money economy that demanded capital, and which was administered in Norwegian centers, the process of assimilation was accelerated. The ethnographer Johannes Falkenberg explains how impoverished the Sami of the inner region of Laksefjord became during the transition to motorized fishing boats and a market economy in eastern Finnmark (Falkenberg 1941). Poverty was looked upon as a result of the Sami culture, which was not able to adopt to modern developments.

4. Language political situation

Official policies concerning the Sami and their culture have gradually changed from the time in 1963, when the Norwegian Storting debated the first report on the Sami language and culture, to the Sami Act of 1987, and the language provisions of the Sami Act that were passed in 1990. A consultative Sami Parliament was elected in 1989 according to the mandates of the Sami Act. The language provisions became effective in 1992.

The new regulations stipulate that Sami is to be put on an equal footing with Norwegian as an administrative language within a limited region. This allows the Sami people the right to use Sami when contacting the authorities and other public offices such as the judicial system, the welfare system and the church. This Sami administrative region encompasses the municipalities of inner Finnmark, where the Sami language already is secure, to the coastal municipalities of Porsanger, in Finnmark, and Kåfjord, in Troms. Outside of this area, one has the legal right to receive instruction in Sami.

The Sami Act's language provisions, and the "Sami Section" of the constitution, which was passed in 1988, are the results of a struggle that the Sami organizations have led since the Second World War. The right to receive adequate instruction in Sami, and the right to use the language in public transaction, has been an important aim during all this time. The existence of a strong cultural and linguistic core area (inner Finnmark) offers encouragement to the Sami who reside in areas dominated by Norwegians. One of the most effective methods utilized in attempts to Norwegianize the Sami was not to give information or knowledge of the Sami living outside of a person's own district. This also included a lack of history and culture. The Sami knew practically nothing at all concerning the Sami of other regions. They felt isolated and lost their self-esteem.

Simultaneous with the positive changes of official Sami policies, the younger generation of Sami living in the coastal regions has become more actively involved in preserving Sami cultural values. This applies to the language as well. Demand for Sami language courses, from Sami who have not learned Sami as their mother tongue, has increased greatly during the past ten years. Secondary schools located in Norwegian cities and towns must now offer instruction in Sami. The younger Sami need stamina if they wish to be taught Sami, and this is because the schools have done very little to offer permanent instruction in Sami. This must now be changed when it becomes a legal right to learn Sami.

One specific feature of the language situation is worth mentioning, which shows a changing attitude and greater sense of confidence regarding Sami in the larger Norwegian community. As late as the 1970s, it was usual in inner Finnmark that the parents in Sami-Norwegian mixed marriages only taught their children Norwegian. There are now many Sami-Norwegian parents, even in urban areas, who manage to use both Norwegian and Sami with their children so that the children will grow up as bilinguals. And these parents are very active when demanding Sami for their children in kindergartens and in schools.

What has been mentioned here indicates that the language provisions of the Sami Act and educational legislation can help arrest the Sami language's negative development in Norway. But the influences of Norwegian and English on TV and video programmes, music cassettes, etc., tend to stimulate the opposite development, since children and the younger generation hear very little Sami in the mass media.

5. Bibliography (selected)

Aarseth, Bjørn (1980): *Noen hovedtrekk i samfunnsutviklingen i samiske bosettingsomrader de siste årtier* [Some essentials of societal development in Sami settlement-areas in recent decades], Tromsø.

Aubert, Vilhelm (1978): *Den samiske befolkning i Nord-Norge. Artiklerfra Statistisk sentralhyrå nr. 107* [The Sami population of Northern Norway. Papers from the Central Statistical Bureau No 107], Oslo.

Bergsland, Knut (1945): "Det samiske slektskaps- og svogerskapssystem" [The Sami kinship and in-law system]. In: *Norsk Tidsskrift for Sprogvidenskap* 13, 148–198.

Eidheim, Harald (1971): "When ethnic identity is a social stigma". In: Eidheim, Harald: *Aspects of the Lappish minority situation, 5 Essays.* 50–67, Oslo.

Falkenberg, Johannes (1941): *Bosetningen ved Indre Laksefjord i Finnmark* [The settlement of Inner Laksefjord in Finnmark], Oslo.

Falkenberg, Johannes (1976): *Makt og kunnskap* [Power and knowledge], Oslo.

Falkenberg, Johannes (1986): "Det tredje alternativ" [The third alternative]. In: *Tidsskrift for samfunnsforskning* 27, 395–416.

Girji O. S, Davvi (1990): *The Sami People.*

Nils Jernsletten, Tromsø (Norway)

119. Norwegisch−Finnisch

1. Finnisch in Norwegen
2. Drei Minoritätengruppen
3. Die kvenische Kultur
4. Die Neuimmigranten
5. Sprachsoziologische Situation
6. Sprachpolitische Lage
7. Soziolinguistische Situation
8. Allgemeines kontaktlinguistisches Porträt
9. Bibliographie (in Auswahl)

1. Finnisch in Norwegen

In Norwegen kennt man drei Minoritäten finnischer Herkunft: Die sogenannten Waldfinnen in Mittel-Skandinavien, die Kvenen in Nord-Norwegen und neue Immigranten in verschiedenen Teilen des Landes. Die Kvenen haben drei Kontaktsprachen, Finnisch, Norwegisch und Samisch, die zwei anderen Minoritäten haben nur Finnisch und Norwegisch. Finnisch und Samisch gehören zu den finnisch-ugrischen Sprachen, Norwegisch zu den germanischen Sprachen.

2. Drei Minoritätengruppen

Die Waldfinnen in Mittel-Skandinavien stellen die älteste finnische Minorität in Norwegen dar. Sie stammen von Auswanderern aus Mittel-Finnland (in den Jahren 1570–1630) ab (Østberg 1978). Die Immigranten und ihre Nachkommen bauten eine finnische Landwirtschaftskultur in den schwedischen und norwegischen Grenzgebieten Värmland und Solør auf. Die finnische Sprache ist dort in den 1960er Jahren als Sprache des täglichen Umgangs ausgestorben.

Die zweite Minorität sind die sog. Kvenen in Finnmark und in Nord-Troms. Die Kvenen sind in historischen Dokumenten schon im Mittelalter genannt (Niemic 1995). Völkerbewegungen im 18. und 19. Jahrhundert stärkten den Anteil der Kvenen an der Bevölkerung. Sie kamen vornehmlich aus dem heutigen Nord-Finnland und dem schwedischen Tornedal. Diese Wanderung stellt die letzte Phase der finnischen bäuerlichen Expansion in das nördliche samische Gebiet bis zum Eismeer dar (Niemi 1978). Die Begegnung der Kvenen mit den anderen Bevölkerungsgruppen fiel in den verschiedenen Gebieten unterschiedlich aus. Im Inland (Guovdageaidnu und Kárásjohka) wurden die Kvenen früh samisiert, auf den Inseln norwegisiert. Eine lebendige kvenische Kultur entstand zwischen diesen Gebieten, auf den Küsten der Fjords und in den Flußtälern. Die Kvenen sind eine ethnische territoriale Minorität (Niemi 1995) und weisen auch Züge einer Grenzminorität auf (Seppola 1995).

Seit den sechziger Jahren sind neue Immigranten von Finnland nach Norwegen gekommen. Diese bilden einen Teil der gleichzeitigen Emigrationswelle von Finnland nach Schweden, wenn auch bedeutend weniger nach Norwegen gezogen sind. Die wichtigste Ursache bildet die Arbeitslosigkeit besonders in Nord-Finnland sowie die Arbeitsmöglichkeit in Norwegen. Ein Teil der Finnen hat in Norwegen nur saisonal gearbeitet, ein Teil hat sich dort fest niedergelassen. Diese Neuimmigranten können durchaus als Immigrationsminorität charakterisiert werden, obwohl ein Teil von ihnen in Nord-Norwegen in der Nähe der finnischen Grenze lebt (→ Sprachenkarte A).

3. Die kvenische Kultur

Das häufigste Gewerbe der traditionellen Kvenenkultur ist die Gesamtwirtschaft von Fischer-Bauern gewesen; sie besteht aus saisonalem Fischfang, bescheidener Landwirtschaft mit Viehzucht, Jagd, Sammeln von Waldbeeren und Handarbeit in verschiedenen Formen sowie im Westen auch Teerbrennen. Die Kvenen haben die Landwirtschaft in der Finnmark erweitert, und sie sind bekannt für ihre handwerklichen Fähigkeiten in Bauarbeiten und beim Teerbrennen. Kvenen sind auch in Bergwerken in Nord-Norwegen eingestellt gewesen. Die Kvenenkultur ist in erster Linie zu einer Kultur der Arbeiterklasse geworden, aber unter ihnen hat es auch schon früh Vertreter der Mittelschicht, z. B. Kaufleute gegeben. Zur Kvenenkultur gehörten sowohl wenig besiedelte Einöden, wie Dörfer unterschiedlicher Größe, als auch Stadtbezirke.

In den letzten Jahrzehnten hat sich im Zuge des allgemeinen Wandels im Norden auch die Gewerbestruktur der Kvenen geändert. Aus den auf dem natürlichen Umfeld basierenden Gewerben ist ein starker Wechsel zur Industrie sowie in Dienstleistungs- und andere mittelständische Gewerbe erfolgt. Hierzu gehört auch eine weitgehende Landflucht.

Die Religion der traditionellen Kvenengemeinschaften ist die laestadianische Sekte. Sie hat ihren Ursprung in den finnischen Gebieten von Nord-Schweden, in Norwegen kennt man sie vornehmlich als Glaube der nördlichen Minoritäten, der Kvenen und Samen.

Die Kultur der Kvenen kann man weder als finnisch noch als norwegisch charakterisieren. Sie enthält herkömmliche Züge aus beiden Richtungen, aber auch aus der samischen und der karelischen Kultur. Aus unterschiedlichsten Bestandteilen haben die Kvenen durch ihren schöpferischen Angleichungsprozeß ihre eigenartige Kvenenkultur geschaffen. Heute fühlen sich die Kvenen in Finnland als Ausländer. Die Kvenengemeinschaften bilden Inseln auf der bunten ethnischen Kulturkarte von Nord-Norwegen. Die wichtigsten Gemeinden, die die finnische Sprache bis heute beibehalten haben, sind von Westen nach Osten: Jyykeä (Samisch Ivgu, Norwegisch Lyngenfjord), Raisi (Ráisa, Nordreisa), Naavuono (Návuotna, Kvænangen), Alattio (Alaheadju, Alta), Porsanki (Porsanku, Porsangerfjord), Teno (Deatnu, Tana), Varanki (Várjjat, Varangerfjord) und Paatsjoki (Báhcaveadji, Pasvikdalen). Die Zahl der nach Norwegen immigrierten Kvenen wird auf 10 000 geschätzt (Niemi 1978). Die meisten Kvenen hat es in Vesisaari (Cáhcesuolu, Vadsø), der Hauptstadt der nördlichsten Fylke Finnmark, gegeben, wo die Kvenen Ende des 19. Jahrhunderts über die Hälfte der Bevölkerung ausmachten. Bei einer inoffiziellen Minorität ist es normalerweise schwierig, eine klare Grenze zwischen den zur Minorität gehörenden und den anderen Personen zu ziehen. In der Regel gibt es eine Kerngruppe, in der die Minoritätszugehörigkeit eindeutig ist, jedoch dazu marginale Gruppen, bei denen die Zugehörigkeit in der einen oder anderen Hinsicht unklar ist.

Die Zahl der Kvenen, die mit anderen Kvenen Finnisch sprechen, ist auf etwa 1500−2000 geschätzt worden (Aikio 1988). Diese stellen also eindeutig eine Kerngruppe dar. Sie bildete z. B. im Dorf Annijoki (Annejohka, Vestre Jakobselv) in Varangerfjord 42% der Bevölkerung, im Dorf Pyssyjoki (Bissojohka, Børselv) in Porsangerfjord 50% und in Yläraisi (norwegisch Øvre Reisadalen) in Nord-Troms 27% (Aikio 1988, Lindgren 1993). Dazu gibt es in den kvenischen Dörfern eine Bevölkerung, die Finnisch kann, aber es nicht mit anderen Kvenen benutzt, sondern nur mit Neuimmigranten und Finnen aus Finnland, und außerdem Kvenen, die Finnisch nicht sprechen, es aber verstehen und aufgrund ihrer Abstammung und Identität zu ihnen gehören. Wegen der allgemeinen Landflucht wohnt heutzutage ein bedeutender Teil der Kvenen außerhalb der traditionellen Kvenengemeinschaften. Insbesondere in Tromsø und Oslo wohnen offenbar viele vom Lande zugezogene Kvenen. Die Zahl der ethnischen Kvenen wird auf 20 000—30 000 geschätzt, von denen etwa 10 000—15 000 Finnisch mehr oder weniger beherrschen (Seppola 1995).

4. Die Neuimmigranten

Neuimmigranten findet man sowohl als Arbeiter als auch in mittelständischen Berufen. Eine markante Teilgruppe bilden die Arbeiter der Fischindustrie, eine zweite die mit Norwegern verheirateten finnischen Frauen. Die Kultur der Neuimmigranten entspricht der allgemeinen heutigen nordischen Kultur. Insbesondere lassen sich individuelle Verbindungen von norwegischen und finnischen Traditionen feststellen. Dies betrifft z. B. die Speisekultur und das Feiern der Festtage (Anttonen 1984).

Die Einstellung der Neuimmigranten zu Finnland und Norwegen wechselt. Wer als Erwachsener nach Norwegen kommt, hat eine andere nationale Identität als der, der im Kindesalter mit seinen Eltern gekommen ist, der in Norwegen als Kind finnischer Eltern geboren oder der in einer norwegisch-finnischen Ehe geboren ist. Finnen, die mit einem Norweger oder Kven eine Familie gebildet haben, sind in der Regel stärker in die norwegische Gesellschaft integriert als die anderen im Erwachsenenalter zugezogenen Immigranten. Anfang 1988 wohnten mit festem Wohnsitz in Norwegen etwa 3600 finnische Staatsbürger (Korkiasaari 1989). Außerdem gibt es in Norwegen eingebürgerte Finnen. Es wird geschätzt, daß etwa 3000—3500 Finnen zeitweilig in Norwegen arbeiten. Die Mehrheit der Neuimmigranten sind Frauen. Viele von ihnen (etwa 70%) sind mit Norwegern oder mit Kvenen verheiratet (Koskinen/Norman 1993). Die Kinder aus den norwegisch-finnischen Ehen bilden eine weitere zweisprachige Gruppe; die Gesamtzahl ist unbekannt.

Neuimmigranten wohnen meist in Nord-Norwegen, in Oslo und Umgebung sowie in Stavanger. In der Finnmark gibt es sie in allen Gemeinden, und obendrein auch in allen anderen norwegischen Fylken. Die Neuimmigration ist also nicht so regional beschränkt wie die Immigration der Kvenen und Waldfinnen in alten Zeiten.

5. Sprachsoziologische Situation

Finnisch war in Norwegen stets eine inoffizielle Minoritätensprache.

Die Sprachenkarte des traditionell kvenischen Gebietes unterliegt zahlreichen Schwankungen. Etwa bis zur Jahrhundertwende hat es dort manche überwiegend finnischsprachige Dörfer gegeben, in denen individuelle Einsprachigkeit verhältnismäßig häufig war. Dies ist typisch vor allem für die östlichen Teile der Finnmark gewesen, wo die Kvenen oft in eigenen Dörfern oder Stadtteilen gewohnt haben. In der mittleren und westlichen Finnmark sowie im nördlichen Troms hat es Gemeinschaften gegeben, für die Mehrsprachigkeit und enge Beziehungen zwischen den Sprachgruppen charakteristisch waren. Dort hat es finnisch-samische, finnisch-norwegische und auch dreisprachige Gemeinschaften gegeben.

Für viele Kvenen ist das Finnische eine nur mündlich verwendete Sprache, während ihre Schriftsprache das Norwegische ist. Die Fähigkeit, Finnisch zu lesen, wurde durch das Laestadianische unterstützt, weil das Finnische in dieser Sekte eine Sonderstellung einnahm. Andererseits läßt sich feststellen, daß für das Laestadianische im nördlichen Norwegen vor allem Mehrsprachigkeit typisch gewesen ist, sowie eine Praxis, die die Muttersprache eines jeden Teilnehmers achtet.

Das Finnische hat gewissermaßen die Stellung einer interethnischen Sprache eingenommen (Aikio 1988). Auch mit den Samen und Norwegern wurde in einigen Gemeinschaften in der Blütezeit der kvenischen Kultur verhältnismäßig viel Finnisch benutzt.

Im Laufe des 20. Jahrhunderts trat im kvenischen Gebiet eine starke Norwegisierung ein (Aikio/Lindgren 1982). Demzufolge machte sich in den Dörfern der östlichen Finnmark ein Übergang aus der Einsprachigkeit zu einer finnisch-norwegischen Zweisprachigkeit und in den samisch-finnischen Dörfern aus der Zweisprachigkeit zu einer sozial bestimmten Dreisprachigkeit bemerkbar (Triglossie). In allen kvenischen Gemeinschaften stellt sich das Finnische heutzutage vornehmlich als eine Sprache der älteren Generation dar. Unter den jüngeren Leuten sind zwar Kenntnisse des Finnischen vorhanden, aber untereinander wird gewöhnlich auf Norwegisch kommuniziert.

Die Neuimmigranten benutzen unter sich und mit Kvenen, die das Finnische beibehalten haben, regelmäßig nur Finnisch. Laut einer Untersuchung im nördlichen Norwegen gaben 40% der finnischen Mütter an, daß sie mit ihren Kindern immer finnisch sprechen, 44% finnisch und norwegisch und 16% nur norwegisch (von 319 Informanten; Koskinen/ Norman 1993). In der typischen Familie der Neuimmigranten mit einer finnischen Mutter und einem norwegischen Vater ist es recht üblich, daß die Hauptsprache der Kinder Norwegisch ist, jedoch sind sie zweisprachig. Es gibt nur eine kleine Minderheit von Familien, in denen beide Eltern Finnen sind.

6. Sprachpolitische Lage

Der norwegische Staat betrieb eine zielbewußte Politik der Norwegisierung von der späten Mitte des 19. Jahrhunderts bis zum zweiten Weltkrieg (Eriksen/Niemi 1981). Diese Politik wurde durch eine außenpolitische Angst motiviert. Sie richtete sich zuerst gegen Rußland, zu dem auch Finnland als autonomer Teil bis zum Jahre 1917 gehörte, und in der Zeit zwischen den Weltkriegen gegen das selbständige Finnland. Man befürchtete, daß die Kvenen in einer eventuellen Krisensituation zugunsten der Feinde Stellung nehmen würden; mithin war man bestrebt, sie zu norwegisieren. Dies führte wunschgemäß in wenigen Jahrzehnten zu einer weitgehenden Norwegisierung der Kvenen.

Nach den Kriegen herrschte in der norwegischen Minoritätenpolitik zunächst eine Phase des Stillstandes. Die in den vorangegangenen Jahrzehnten vorherrschende negative Einstellung lebte jedoch weiter. In den siebziger Jahren trat eine positivere Einstellung zu den Minoritätensprachen ein. Finnisch wurde als Fremdsprache in einigen Gymnasien eingeführt sowie auch an den zwei nördlichsten Hochschulen in Alta und Tromsø. Der nördliche Lokalradiosender führte regelmäßige finnischsprachige Programme ein. Die Einstellung gegenüber der kvenischen Kultur und der finnischen Sprache änderte sich sowohl unter den Kvenen als auch den Norwegern. Ende der siebziger und im Laufe der achtziger Jahre wurden viele Vereine sowohl von den Kvenen als auch von den Neuimmigranten gegründet sowie verschiedene kulturelle Veranstaltungen durchgeführt. Unter den Kvenen ist seit den achtziger Jahren eine gewisse Revitalisierung der Sprache und der Kultur erfolgt.

Die Schulsprache ist Norwegisch. Prinzipiell können die Immigrantenkinder in der Grundschule in der Heimsprache unterrichtet werden, aber nur etwa ein Drittel der Kinder der Neuimmigranten haben diesen Unterricht erhalten. Seit den achtziger Jahren haben die Kvenen in der Grundschule versuchsweise Finnisch als Zweitsprache an sieben Orten eingeführt. Obwohl dieser Versuch sehr erfolgreich war, hat das Unterrichtsministerium 1995 beschlossen, ihn einzustellen. Finnisch wird als Fremdsprache in Grundschulen unterrichtet (über 20 Schulen in Nord-Norwegen).

7. Soziolinguistische Situation

Die Kvenen sprechen Dialekte, die mit den finnischen Dialekten in Nordfinnland und im schwedischen Tornedal nahe verwandt sind. Ihr Abstand zur finnischen Hochsprache ähnelt dem anderer Varietäten des Finnischen, die in Gebieten des heutigen oder früheren Sprachenkontakts gesprochen werden, etwa die finnischen Dialekte im schwedischen Norrbotten, die südwestlichen Dialekte in Finnland und die „freiere" Schicht der Umgangssprache in der Hauptstadt Helsinki. Beim versuchsweisen Einsatz von Finnisch als Zweitsprache für kvenische Kinder wurde der Unterricht im heimischen Dialekt erteilt. Zwei Lehrer, die selbst Kvenen sind, stellten Unterrichtsmaterialien in ihrer Mundart her.

Die Neuimmigranten sprechen nicht dieselben nordfinnischen Dialekte wie die Kvenen, sondern bei ihnen finden sich verschiedene Formen der Umgangssprache. Die Variationen in ihrem Finnisch sind bisher nicht untersucht worden. Die am besten beherrschte Schriftsprache der im Erwachsenenalter von Finnland zugezogenen Immigranten ist die finnische Hochsprache.

8. Allgemeines kontaktlinguistisches Porträt

Die direkte Einwirkung anderer Sprachen auf die kvenischen Dialekte ist vornehmlich im Wortschatz untersucht worden. Dieser weist sowohl samische als auch norwegische Einflüsse in Form von verschiedenen Interferenzerscheinungen auf. Samische und skandinavische Lehnübertragungen hat es auch in den nordfinnischen Dialekten gegeben, die die Immigranten seinerzeit mitbrachten. Die Kontakterscheinungen stellen also eine Fortsetzung eines bereits vorhandenen Zustandes dar. Es hängt von der Thematik des jeweiligen Wortschatzes ab, ob der jeweilige kvenische Dialekt vornehmlich gemeinfinnische oder nordfinnische Wörter aufweist oder ob er von samischen oder norwegischen Interferenzen geprägt ist. Der Einfluß einer anderen Sprache ist stark in den Teilen des Wortschatzes, die solche Sachen und Dinge umfassen, die den Immigranten bei der Niederlassung an der norwegischen Küste neu waren. So gilt z. B. die Terminologie der Inlandgewässer zum größten Teil gemeinsam für die kvenischen und nordfinnischen Dialekte, während in der Meeresterminologie der samische Einfluß dominiert (Söderholm 1983). Die Benennungen der Hochseefische enthalten viel samischen und wenig norwegischen Einfluß, während der Wortschatz über die Fischgerichte und ihre Zubereitung vieles umfaßte, das auf norwegischem oder übers Norwegische auf internationalem Einfluß beruht (Andreassen 1989). Die allgemeine Modernisierung der Kultur hat besonders in der Zeit nach den Kriegen den kvenischen Dialekten viel internationales Wortgut hinzugefügt, das vom Norwegischen vermittelt wurde. Es scheint, daß ein mit den nordfinnischen Dialekten gemeinsamer Wortschatz und ein samischer Einfluß in den kvenischen Dialekten vor allem in Bereichen vorliegt, die mehr zur Natur und zur traditionellen Lebensweise gehören, während die allgemeine Modernisierung einen Strom von Wörtern aus dem Norwegischen mit sich bringt. Die Entlehnungen aus dem Samischen scheinen zu einer älteren kulturellen Schicht zu gehören; es gibt zwar auch bereits ältere norwegische Lehnwörter, dieser Einfluß ist jedoch stärker geworden und bildet den heutigen Hauptstrom.

In den kvenischen Dialekten gibt es in der Flexion einen direkten Einfluß des Samischen in einigen Ableitungstypen (Lindgren 1993). Eine bedeutendere Erscheinung als dieser direkte Einfluß ist die indirekte Einwirkung der Mehrsprachigkeit auf die Entwicklung des Flexionssystems. Die Art der Normativität einer Sprachgemeinschaft, ihre relative Toleranz Variationen gegenüber, wechselt. In den kvenischen Dialekten ebenso wie in einigen anderen Gebieten des Sprachkontakts ist die Normativität verhältnismäßig tolerant, und das führt dazu, daß morphologische Innovationen sich relativ leicht in der Sprache einbürgern. Dies hat zu einer ungewöhnlich schnellen morphologischen Entwicklung geführt. Der Änderungsprozeß an sich stellt jedoch eine natürliche morphologische Entwicklung dar (Lindgren 1993).

Phonologische und syntaktische Kontakterscheinungen in den kvenischen Dialekten sind kaum untersucht worden. Das gleiche gilt für Kontakterscheinungen in der Sprache der Neuimmigranten.

Das Norwegische in den kvenischen Gebieten kann als Ethnolekt bezeichnet werden, genauso wie die zweite Varietät des Norwegischen in Nord-Norwegen, nämlich das Norwegische der samischen Bevölkerung. Obwohl die norwegische Sprachpolitik in der Regel außerordentlich tolerant gegenüber Dialekten ist, sind diese Ethnolekte stigmatisiert worden.

Sowohl die schon ausgelöschten finnischen Dialekte im mittleren Skandinavien als auch die Sprache der Kvenen haben viele Ortsnamen in ihren traditionellen Wohngebieten hinterlassen. Etwas ähnliches ist bei den Neuimmigranten nicht festzustellen.

9. Bibliographie (in Auswahl)

Aikio, Marjut (1988): „Om to minoritetsspåk og flersprålighetsprofiler i Nord-Skandinavia" In: *Tredje nordiska symposiet om Nordskandinaviens historia och kultur.* Studia Historica Septentrionalia 14,2, 132−163. Gummerus, Jyväskylä.

Aikio, Marjut/Lindgren, Anna-Riitta (1982): „Den finske minoriteten i Nord-Noreg" In: *Nordnorsk. Språkarv og språkforhold i Nord-Noreg*, Red. Bull & Gjetne. Det norske samlaget. Oslo, 118−133.

Andreassen, Irene (1989): *Ordtilfang i kvenske fiskerihushold. En etnolingvistisk-dialektologisk analyse fra Vestre Jakobselv/Annijoki, Varanger.* Universitetet i Tromsø.

Anttonen, Marjut (1984): *Suomalaissiirtolaisten akkulturoituminen Pohjois-Norjassa.* Studies of the Ethnology Department of the University of Jyväskylä 18, Jyväskylä.

Eriksen, Knut-Einar/Niemi, Einar (1981): *Den finske fare. Sikkerhetsproblemer og minoritetspolitikk i nord 1860−1940*, Universitetsforlaget, Norge.

Helander, Kaisa Rautio (1990): *Yykeänperän vesistöappellatiivit*, Oulun yliopisto.

Junttila, Jorid Hjulstad (1988): *Språkval og språkbruk på Skibotn*, Universitetet i Tromsø.

Kvenene − en glemt minoritet? (1995) *Rapport fra seminaret 14. 11. 1994.* Universitetet i Tromsø, Informasjonsavdelingen.

Koskinen, Arja/Norman, Marjatta (1993): *Borte − men også hjemme. Rapport om finske kvinner i Nord-Norge*, Finnmark distriktshøgskole.

Korkiasaari, Jouni (1989): *Suomalaiset maailmalla*, Turku.

Lindgren, Anna-Riitta (1993): *Miten muodot muuttuvat. Ruijan murteiden verbitaivutus Raisin, Pyssyjoen ja Annijoen kveeniyhteisöissä*, Universitetet i Tromsø.

Livet på Finnskogen (1992). Heimebygsforeningen Finnetunet, Grue Finnskog.

Niemi, Einar (1978): „Den finske kolonisasjon av Nordkalotten − forløp og årsaker" In: *Ottar 103*, Tromsø, 49−70.

Niemi, Einar (1995): „Kvenene og staten − en historisk riss" In: *Kvenene − en glemt minoritet*, 13−29. Universitetet i Tromsø, Informasjonsavdelingen.

Norman, Marjatta (1990): „Finsknorske familiers tospråklighet − et kvinnespørsmål" In: *Flerspråklighet i och utanför Norden*. Herberts, K. Laurén, C. (Eds.), 239−250. Åbo Akademi. Åbo.

Seppolla, Bjørnar (1995): „Kortfattet informasjon om den kvenske befolkning" In: *Kvenene − en glemt minoritet*, 2−4, Universitetet i Tromsø.

Söderholm, Eira (1983): „Alattion murteen vesistöappellatiivit" In: *Sanajalka 25*, Turku, 43−62.

Söderholm, Eira (1992): „Lainastrategioita ja sanasemanttisia suhteita. Lapin vaikutus suomen pohjoismurteitten topografisiin appellatiiveihin" In: *Fennistica 10*, Åbo Akademi, Åbo.

Østberg, Kristian (1978): *Finnskogene*, Grue Finnskog.

Anna-Riitta Lindgren, Tromsø (Norwegen)

120. Sweden

1. Geography and demography
2. Territorial history and national development
3. Politics, economy and general cultural situation
4. Ethnoprofiles
5. Sociolinguistic situation
6. Language political situation
7. Presentation of language contact
8. Bibliography (selected)

1. Geography and demography

Sweden is situated on the Scandinavian paeninsula in northern Europe, bordering in the east on Finland and the Baltic, in the north on Norway, in the south on the Baltic and in the west on Norway, the North Sea and the Öresund passage, which separates it from its southwestern neighbour Denmark. The northernmost point of Sweden is located at the Three Country-mark, where the borders of Norway, Sweden and Finland meet, 69°4' north, the southernmost point is situated in the province of Skåne, at a latitude of 55°20' north. The length of the country is at most 1574 kilometres, the greatest width 499 kilometres. The length of the coast line with its archipelagoes in east and southwest is more than 7000 kms. The area is 486,661 km². The northernmost province, Norrbotten, forms about a fourth of the total area (→ language map A).

At the end of 1993 (Dec. 31) Sweden had 8,745,109 inhabitants. Population increased in 1993 by 53,096, whereas the increase ten years earlier had been only about 12,000. The number of foreign citizens and people with one or both parents born abroad was about 12 per cent of the total population. The vast majority of the foreign citizens have migrated to Sweden since World War II. Net immigration totalled 134,000 in the 1940's and 106,000 in the 1950's. During the 1960's Sweden experienced two major waves of immigration: the first, in the mid-1960's, consisted primarily of workers from Yugoslavia, Greece and Turkey, while during the period 1968−1970, a total of 166,000 foreign nationals came to Sweden, of whom 100,000 were from Finland. In the mid-1980's, annual immigration reached about 30,000. About two-thirds of these came from non-Nordic countries, as refugees or as relatives of immigrants already granted the right to stay in Sweden. For periods a substantial part of the immigrants have been members of the families of natives and of immigrant residents already in the country. Well known examples of this latter-mentioned phenomenon are migration from certain Saami or Finnish villages in northern Finland, from where practically whole villages moved to suburbs of Stockholm; "family tie" migration from Finland, Swedish regions in Ostrobothnia to southern Norrland, the district around the town Gävle; and chain migration from the Turkish Kulu-district in the central parts of Anatolia. Family tie migration was especially significant during the 70's, when it increased.

In 1991, 36,100 of the 43,900 foreign nationals who immigrated to Sweden were citizens of non-Nordic countries. A residence permit was granted to 18,700 of these (including children) on refugee or humanitarian grounds. About 15,000 aliens re-emigrated in the same year, resulting in a net immigration of 28,900 in 1991. Net immigration totalled 155,000 in the 1970's, and 163,000 in the 1980's.

At the end of 1991, about 484,000 foreign nationals were living in Sweden. The proportion of non-European immigrants were greater than that of Europeans. In addition, about 392,000 immigrants had become naturalized Swedish citizens. Around 40% of all foreign nationals in Sweden were from the Nordic countries (Denmark, Finland, Iceland and Norway).

During the most intense periods of immigration half or more than half of the immigrants came from the Nordic countries, and up to the beginning of the 1980's half of the total immigrant population was Finnish. Remigration to Finland has changed the proportion between Finns and others: Finns are now about 30 per cent of the total population of immigrants. In spite of this, persons of Finnish origin (including the second generation) are the largest migrant group in Sweden (301,651 in 1993). Other major groups of first and second generation immigrants in Sweden, by country or region of origin, are the following: Nordic countries (other than Finland) 13% (Former) Yugoslavia 6%, Germany 5%, Poland 4%, Iran 4%, Turkey 4%, Africa as a whole 3% and Chile 3%. Finns have, except for some decades in the 17th century, always been the biggest minority in Sweden.

During the postwar years the largest groups of refugees have been the following: 45,000 from the concentration camps 1945–1949, 8,000 Yugoslavs in the 1950's and 1960's, 13,000 Hungarians after 1956, 5,000 Czecho-Slovaks after 1968, 5,000 Greeks 1967–1974, 18,000 Chileans after 1973, 20,000 Assyrians/Syrians from Turkey and the Middle East after 1975, 12,000 Kurds, 9,000 Eritreans, 6,000 Palestinians, 23,000 Iranians after 1979 and 40,000 war refugees from the former Yugoslavia in the beginning of the 1990's.

The borders of today's Sweden were formed in the Peace Treaty of Hamina in Finland in 1809, after the war between Sweden-Finland and Russia, in which Finland was lost to Russia. Until that time Finland had for several hundred years formed part of Sweden (Sweden-Finland). The vast majority of the inhabitants were in 1809, as today, of Swedish origin and Swedish-speaking, with the peripheral and quantitatively small Saami and Tornedal Finns (Tornedalians) as the only exceptions. The Tornedalians and the Saami inhabited the northernmost parts of the country, the Saami also the westernmost parts in the Swedish mountains. These groups are both of Finno-Ugric origin. Since 1809 the Tornedalians have formed a Finnish-speaking or rather bilingual border minority, close to the Finnish–Swedish border along the Torne river and its affluents in the north.

Migration within the country, due to changes in economic and industrial life, causing unemployment in the regions of origin, has diminished the numbers of people in both groups sticking to their own language and culture. This change has been less drastic as a change of life style for the Tornedalians than for the Saami people, although it has meant for them also a move from rural to urban regions. Many of the Saami left the life connected with reindeer herding, now the livelihood of only a minor part of the Saami people (10%), while the culture of the Tornedalians was mainly formed by small scale farming and forestry, to a great extent of the same kind as that of their Swedish-speaking neighbours in other parts of northern Sweden or other thinly populated areas of the country.

Long-distance migration of the Tornedalians and the Saami has been directed to practically all industrial and urban centres of central and southern Sweden, the Stockholm area being the most important of these. Short-distance migration has been mostly directed to the industrial centres in the county of Norrbotten, namely the region around the town Luleå, the seat of the provincial government on the coast of the Gulf of Bothnia in the southern part of the region, and the mining areas north and northwest, around the towns Kiruna and Gällivare-Malmberget. In the mining districts Saami and Tornedalians met each other and during the last decades also many other new immigrants, especially from Finland. Migration to other parts of Sweden has meant for both of these autochtonous groups an absolute decrease of people speaking the original language and living within the traditional culture in the region of origin, although short distance migration sometimes means weekly commuting. In the Torne valley area (in Swed. *Tornedalen*, Finn. *Tornionlaakso*) the population is today about half of what it was in the 1950s. The population of the three Tornedal municipalities, Pajala, Övertorneå and Haparanda, amounts to about 25,500 (Dec. 31, 1993). All of these are not Tornedal Finnish-speakers, but on the other hand many of the inhabitants of the neighbouring mining municipalities, Kiruna and Gällivare, are of Tornedalian heritage and speakers of Tornedal Finnish or new migrants from Finland speaking Finland Finnish varieties. During the last century and until the postwar period Finnish speakers were concentrated in this area. Nowadays, when Finnish speakers are more frequent in Sweden than ever before, they are spread all over Sweden with concentrations in big cities and industrial areas of southern and central Sweden.

The Saami population amounts to approximately 15,000−20,000, depending on how Saami define themselves linguistically and ethnically. According to one definition, stated in an official report on the rights of the Saami (SOU 1989:41), a Saami is a person considering himself to be a Saami and credibly claiming 1. to have learned Saami as his first language, 2. that one of his parents or grandparents learned Saami as a first language, or 3. that one of his parents is or has been included on an electoral role for the *Sameting*.

From the middle of the 19th century until 1930, the earlier immigration patterns in Sweden were changed to one of emigration, primarily to America, but also to Australia. A smaller number of Swedes also moved to South America (esp. Misiones in Argentina). In the beginning of the 1930's Sweden became an immigrant country in the sense that immigration exceeded emigration.

Prior to World War II Sweden was an unusually homogeneous country, both ethnically and linguistically, the only exceptions being the indigenous minorities in the north. During and after World War II, refugees, most of them from the Baltic States, comprised the first modern immigrant flow to Sweden.

A characteristic of migration in the postwar period has been the movement from the periphery to center, or from rural areas to urban. This phenomenon was similar also for migration from Finland in the 1960's, but later many Finns who migrated to Sweden came from big cities.

The first labour migration from Italy and Yugoslavia to central Swedish towns was regulated by treaties between Swedish authorities and authorities in the countries involved. Migration within the Nordic countries has been free since the introduction of the common Nordic labour market in 1954, implying that citizens in Nordic countries can live and work in another Nordic country without special permission. No passport is needed for Inter-Nordic travel. In addition Nordic citizens are allowed to use their own language in contacts with authorities in the other countries.

2. Territorial history and national development

Sweden as a distinct geographical area started forming in the middle ages. In the 9th century the province of Uppland with the town Uppsala formed the centre of the emerging country. During this period Swedish Vikings, like their neighbours from the other Nordic countries, including Iceland, made vast robbery crusades especially eastwards, initially to Russia but also further down to the Mediterranean as well as other directions, including the British Isles and the European continent. The Swedish Vikings mostly originated from the coastal areas of Uppland, the co-called Ro[d]slagen, which according to some etymologists is the origin of the Finnish name for Sweden, *Ruotsi*, and, according to some archeologists may also be related to the terms *Russia* and *Russian*. Most of the Swedish runic stones originate from this period and represent the oldest documentation of Swedish language, often recounting the Viking crusades or other heroic events. Most frequently they can be found around Uppsala, in the Lake Mälar region and around Lake Vallentuna north of Stockholm.

Finland was conquered during three crusades to various parts of southern and Eastern Finland, namely Varsinais-Suomi, Häme and Carelia, during the 12th century. From that time on Finland formed part of Sweden (Sweden−Finland). The first border documented in an official treaty between Sweden−Finland and Russia was decided in the peace treaty of Pähkinäsaari (Swed. Nöteborg) in 1323. Gradually Sweden began expanding to the north and east, and in the peace treaties between Sweden and Russia in 1595 and 1617, Sweden acquired parts of Carelia.

In the middle ages, from 1389, Sweden formed a political union together with its Scandinavian neighbours Denmark and Norway. This was an attempt to unite Scandinavia politically, but it ended in 1523 with Sweden's proclamation of sovereignty with Gustav Vasa, who vanquished the Danes, as the new king. However, the borders between Sweden, Russia and Denmark–Norway were uncertain for centuries not only in the northernmost parts of Fenno-Scandinavia (the Northern Calotte) but also in West, South-West and East. The borders between Sweden and Russia were adjusted in several wars until they were finally decided as they are today in the peace treaty of 1809.

The territory of Sweden was at its largest after the 30 years war in Europe, when Sweden had the power in Finland, Ingermanland, Estonia, and parts of present-day Germany (Vorpommern-Stettin, Wismar, Bremen-Verden). Except in recent decades, Sweden has never been as multilingual and multicultural as during this period, in Swedish history called The Great Power Period. There were some 20 different languages spoken within the country. Multilingualism existed also at an individual level, which can be demonstrated by a short excerpt from the minutes of a meeting at the House of the Nobility in Stockholm in 1644:

"*Belefvedes alttså att de af den nederste skulle begynna.*
Joachim Transsehe: *Nach den guttern wie sie einbringen undt nach eines jeden Vermuegen.*
Jacob Steinberg: *Von sein (sic) Eigentthumb undt nach eines jeden Lohn und Lehnung.*
Lov. de Geer: *Nao den Paorden iss wol gutt maor beter nao Vermoegonheit.*
Jörgen Schildt: *Nach dem Rossdienst undt nach jeder Marck so erverrossdiensten muss.*"

Russia and Denmark (Denmark-Norway) are the countries Sweden has had the most war conflicts with as well as the most border conflicts. Sweden gradually lost its Great Power position in the Great Nordic War in the 18th century and the war against Russia in 1808–1809. The last war that Sweden was involved in as a combatant was fought against Denmark-Norway in 1814. From that time until 1905, Norway formed a fairly independent part of Sweden in a political union between the two countries.

Sweden was not directly involved in war incidents during either the first or the second World War. The country was a member of the League of Nations and is a member of the United Nations, with neutrality and independence as cornerstones of its foreign policy. Within the framework of European cooperation Sweden has achieved membership of EFTA and several other European and other international organizations, and became a member of the EU in 1995.

3. Politics, economy and general cultural situation

Sweden is a parliamentarily governed constitutional monarchy, where the monarch has merely a formal and representative function. The right to vote in parliamentary elections as well as the right to be proposed as a candidate or to be elected as a member of the Riksdag requires Swedish citizenship, and the right to vote in municipal elections is accorded to all who have lived in the country for at least three years. The unicameral Riksdag, the members of which are elected according to a direct and proportional system, has 349 members. Elections are held every three years. Voting and eligibility age is 18 years. Swedish citizenship can be acquired by citizens of other Nordic countries after two years of residence in Sweden, by others after five years. In 1991, Swedish citizenship was granted to 14,900 immigrants (including children). Aliens living in Sweden have the same rights as Swedish citizens as regards social benefits, education, etc.

On the whole, immigrants take part in political elections or are proposed as candidates proportionally to a much smaller extent than other Swedes, more in municipal political representations, though, than in elections to the Riksdag. The voting turnout among aliens has been between 40% and 60%, compared to around 90% among Swedish citizens. Few persons with immigrant backgrounds have been members of the Riksdag during the last two decades, three with Finnish backgrounds, representing the Social Democrats (2) and the Christian Democrats, and one of Greek background, representing the Communist Party. For higher appointments such as minister or other positions close to this level in the government or ministries, Swedish citizenship is also required. People with immigrant backgrounds have achieved high positions in various sectors of Swedish society e.g., as researchers, journalists, and social workers, but proportionally to a lower degree than people of Swedish origin. Highly educated immigrants, however, still often have difficulties in finding jobs corresponding to their education. On the whole, the typical immigrant jobs have been low-salary jobs like routine factory work, cleaning and the like. Unemployment, which during the last three years has grown from about 2,5% to 8−9%, is greater among immigrants than other citizens (in 1991, on average, 6,6% among immigrants). In 1991, the employment rate for foreign nationals was 66%, compared to 83% for the Swedish population. Compared to other immigrants, unemployment is lower among people from Nordic countries than from other parts of the world, and lower among male immigrants than female. Foreign nationals account for about 5% of the total workforce. As a rule as immigrants live longer in Sweden, their standard of living approaches that of the majority of Swedes.

With respect to the old minorities, the Saami and the Tornedalians, the situation is slightly different. There is no Saami representative elected to the Riksdag, although several Tornedalians are or have been. Both categories have succeeded fairly well in achieving high education and high positions elsewhere in the society. One Tornedalian, so far, has held the position of governor of Norrbotten.

Economically Sweden experienced rapid changes during the first half of this century. Population growth and maintenance problems in the end of the last century spurred industrial development, although emigration, mostly to America, lightened the maintenance burden within Swedish society. The industrial breakthrough was based on the natural wealth of the country: the forest industry, mining industry and water power. Sweden is now among the most highly industrialized countries in the world, with only 5% of the population employed in agriculture.

Old democratic traditions of the Swedish peasantry made development towards political democracy relatively easy. Industrial workers formed a new class of society, which very early developed a political consciousness. The official policy from the 1930's onwards was governed by a welfare ideology based on solidarity. Economic growth during the first post-war years was extremely rapid; workers were needed because of industrial expansions and the growth of service and public sectors. A considerable portion of immigrants to Sweden have been employed in the engineering industry, in companies like the car factories Volvo and Saab-Scania, Swedish Match, ASEA-Brown Boveri (ABB; energy industry) or Ericsson (telecommunications). Beside these industries female immigrants have often been employed in the textile industry and in public services like health care. Labour organizations have been strong and have had a great impact on immigrant policy and the working conditions of immigrants from the 1960's onwards.

Immigration policy before 1960 was characterized by assimilation, which obliged immigrants to attain the majority culture and language and to forsake their own. Attainment of the majority language was emphasized. There was no special instruction in Swedish organized for minority groups with a different mother tongue. However, Sweden never really has had a guest worker policy.

In the beginning of the 1960's the policy on immigrants could be characterized by the *melting pot* principle. In the 1960's, an intense, public debate on immigrant policy questions started in various mass media. Since the late 1960's pluralism and multiculturalism, including both linguistic and cultural differences, have made great strides, but Sweden has largely remained a monolingual country. Swedish as the only official language has never been questioned, but multiculturalism and multilingualism have existed and have been approved of in the sense that many languages are now spoken by members of Swedish society, with many cultures and ethnic groups existing side by side in the country.

A State Commission on Immigration was appointed in 1968 to investigate the problems facing immigrants and to propose different measures for their integration into Swedish society. As a part of this commission a special committee was appointed to investigate the needs of community interpreting for immigrants. The aims of immigrant policy formulated by the Commission were laid down by the Swedish Government in 1975. The goals were summarized in the three concepts of equality, freedom of choice, and partnership.

The goal of *equality* implies that immigrants should have the same opportunities, rights and obligations as ordinary citizens. Society should make an effort to create the necessary conditions for immigrants and their children to maintain their language, to pursue cultural activities, and to retain contact with their country of origin.

The goal of *freedom of choice* implies that society should create the necessary conditions for linguistic minorities living in Sweden to be able to choose to what extent they wish to retain and develop their original culture and linguistic identity. Measures to maintain contact with the culture and country of origin will also help the immigrant and her/his children to choose between remaining in Sweden and returning to the country of origin.

The goal of *partnership* implies cooperation between immigrant and minority groups and the majority population, based on mutual tolerance and solidarity. The goal of partnership also implies that immigrants become part of Swedish social and political life and take part in decisions directly related to their own situation.

One of the most important results of this commission's work was that the new policy was used as a basis for the so-called *Home Language Reform* of 1976, which gave children with a home language other than Swedish the right to receive home language instruction in school and pre-school.

Immigrants who arrived before the 1970's immigrated to entirely different circumstances with regard to official language policy and language instruction. Before the Home Language Reform, which had been preceded by experimental work and an intense debate on bilingualism, was implemented, the Swedish Government had formulated a goal for bilingualism, namely the principle of *active bilingualism*, a concept that has not been clearly defined but interpreted by some researchers as "double-sided first-language competence". Functional bilingualism is another, vaguely defined term used to describe this linguistic goal.

Originally home language training (in preschool) and home language instruction was given to all children whose home language was a "living feature of their domestic environment". In 1985 this was restricted to children whose language is a *daily means of communication at home*. Excepted from this restriction are the indigenous minorities, the Saami, the Tornedalians and the gypsies. Another recent restriction for home language instruction is that there must be at least five participants in the home language group and that home language teaching is not available after grade '7' in the comprehensive school. Finnish-speaking children are, however, excepted from this last-mentioned restriction, according to special rights emphasizing the exceptional position of the Finnish language in Sweden, proposed by the Government to the Riksdag on September 8, 1994 (the proposal is exceptional also formally, in that it is the first time in about 150 years that a governmental proposal to the Riksdag contains text in the Finnish language). The proposal suggests special rights for Finnish, motivated by the fact that Finnish always has been an indigenous (domestic) language, because of Finland's and Sweden's long, common history. The Government has declared that Finnish is part of the Swedish cultural heritage. The proposal does not consider a possible minority status for the Finnish-speaking group in Sweden. It is proposed that an official commission be set up to analyze further support to Finnish and Saami, possibly in accordance with the European treaty. A special state commission has also been proposed by the government (September 1994) to study the linguistic and cultural situation of the Tornedalians. For the Saami a State Commission in an official report (1989) recommended a special law on Saami conditions, a Saami Act, containing provisions concerning the promotion of Saami cultural and social life, above all through establishment of a representative Saami agency − a *Sameting* − elected by the Saami people. The first elections to the Sameting were held in 1993 and the same year it started its work (the official report contained summaries not only in English, as is common nowadays, but also in Saami). Since 1975 the Saami are members of the World Council of Indigenous Peoples (WCIP).

4. Ethnoprofiles

The Saami were most likely the first inhabitants of Northern Sweden and the mountain areas after the melting of the inland ice. The oldest archeological findings in the north are about 9000 years old. The southernmost parts of Sweden, the Skåne region and Västergötland, were probably inhabited from the European continent, with which they had a land connection. The oldest findings date 9500 years backwards in time. Central Sweden was the last part to be inhabited. Due to the inland ice pressure the Lake Mälar region lay below sea level until just a few thousand years ago.

The northern part of Sweden, called Norrland, covering 58 per cent of the territory of the country, has from prehistoric times had an orientation towards the world around it that has differed from that of the other parts of the country, Sveland (Central Sweden; Svear = 'Swedes') and Götaland (South Sweden). North Norrland especially has had cultural contacts with and been influenced by the east, probably by speakers of Slavic and Finno-Uric languages. Naturally Saami contacts have been frequent. As late as 1519, when the last Catholic archbishop of Sweden, Olaus Magnus, visited the yearly market of the town Tornio, situated at the northernmost part of the Gulf of Bothnia, multilingualism was a characteristic feature of the market. He stated enthusiastically:

"This town has an extremely beautiful and advantageous location and no other market place in the whole area up towards the North pole has more visitors than this Tornio. Here come Byelorussians, Lapps, Carelians, Bothnians, Finns, Swedes, Häme people and people from Hälsingland, and morover, passing the high mountains and vast wilds, also Norwegians come to visit this market place."

The Saami dialects in the north have been influenced by contacts with Finnish and Swedish also in recent times, as well as with Norwegian. Especially Jukkasjärvi Saami, spoken in the Kiruna area, has incorporated Finnish loans from practically all spheres of life, including bad language. Finnish has also been the *lingua sacra* for most Saami speakers in the northern parts of the province. This is due to the fact that Finnish was formerly the language of Læstadianism, a Low-Church revivalist movement that developed in the Finnish-speaking Torne Valley during the 19th century and spread over the Northern Calotte. The Norwegian contacts are associated with the former nomadic lifestyle characteristic of reindeer herding in these areas until a couple of decades ago, with herders moving from winter lands in the Swedish mountains to summer lands on the Norwegian coast. However, the Norwegian and on the whole older Scandinavian impact is stronger for the southern Saami dialects, from the Lule Saami area in the mountains of central Norrbotten, down to the South Saami speakers in northern Dalecarlia.

The Swedish Torne Valley was earlier mainly Finnish speaking. Contacts with Saami people have influenced terminology within reindeer herding also among Finnish speakers. In addition, many of the place names of the area apparently derive from old Saami names, although they may have been Finnicized or have parallel Saami and Finnish names, in some cases also a parallel Swedish name (e. g. Saami *Gieron*, Finn. *Kiruna/Kiiruna*; Swed. *Kiruna*, for the northernmost town of Norrbotten).

Contacts between Finnish speakers in the north and Swedish speakers from southern Norrland began developing on a larger scale approximately a thousand years ago.

Finnish or Finnish-based place names in the Kalix river valley indicate that Finnish settlement has been more widespread in this area than it is today. Finnish may have had an impact on the pronunciation of these Swedish dialects, but on the other hand, the Torne valley Finnish and Saami in northern Sweden have been influenced on almost all linguistic levels by Swedish, mainly Standard Swedish taught at school.

Standard Swedish and other Swedish dialects have also caused the development of new Swedish varieties in the mining districts (Kiruna and Gällivare-Malmberget), partly due to immigration of workers from southern Sweden to the mines, partly due to new settlement and contacts developed in connection with the building of the northern railways during the end of the last century.

Place names and other linguistic phenomena as well as cultural phenomena indicate that contacts have been directed east-west over the Gulf of Bothnia also in the province of Västerbotten and other provinces in Norrland. Further south, in Central Sweden, thousands of place names are reminiscent of Finnish settlement in the forest regions of Hälsingland, Dalecarlia and Värmland on the Norwegian border. Few Finnish words or other linguistic or cultural features have found their way into the Swedish language and Swedish culture, which, in turn, has had great impact on the Finnish, on the Finns and the Finnish settlement.

The close contacts with Norway and the fact that the provinces Jämtland and Härjedalen on the Norwegian border belonged to Denmark–Norway for several hundred years (until 1645) explain the fact that the Swedish dialects in these regions are linguistically very close to their neighbouring Norwegian dialects. This is also the case for Bohuslän on the Swedish west coast, north of Gothenburg.

The dialects of the southernmost provinces, Halland, Skåne and Blekinge, which belonged to Denmark until the middle of the 17th century, still have features in common with Danish, despite the conscious Swedicization of the language that was implemented in these provinces by the Swedish authorities in the period immediately following the conquest.

Swedish regional dialects preserved their regional features well until the levelling of dialects started with the development of mass media and communications some decades ago. School instruction has always had a strong emphasis on teaching of the Standard Language and has not been tolerant towards dialect speakers or the indigenous minority languages. There is an old tradition within the schools of linguistic uniformity, which is known also in other parts of Europe. In Sweden this trend started, after Latin had been replaced by Swedish as the language of religion in the 16th century, when Sweden turned Lutheran. Immigration during the postwar period has radically changed the linguistic reality of Sweden, towards a huge diversity replacing the strong linguistic homogeneity that had existed prior to World War II. There are people from at least 160 different countries representing 150 different languages in Swedish society today.

5. Sociolinguistic situation

Partly due to the fact that Standard Swedish was promoted not only as the written language of the school and in official contexts but also as the only spoken language, approved of officially in the school, in areas where minority languages were spoken, bilingualism or diglossia developed, as in the Torne valley or among Saami speakers. Areas with Swedish dialects, which are linguistically distant from the Standard and other Swedish dialects and not understandable to nonspeakers of these dialects, developed bidialectalism. Examples of these are the river valley dialects in North Sweden (Norrbotten and Västerbotten) and some dialects in Dalecarlia (Malung, Älvdalen).

Among the indigenous minority languages and Swedish, Swedish has the highest status, then Finnish and last Saami. Many people with Saami as their mother tongue have been trilingual and are partly still so. In addition to Saami, Finnish and Swedish, many Saami people also know Norwegian. Few Finnish speakers have known or know Saami and still fewer Swedish speakers know Saami or Finnish, although there have been, on the language border where Saami, Finnish, Swedish dialects and Standard Swedish meet in southern Norrbotten, exceptional cases of people being able to communicate in four languages or language varieties. Language development among Saami and Tornedal Finnish speakers has gone towards Swedicization since the end of the last century.

For new immigrants Swedish has often become a *lingua franca*. Swedish is also for them the high status language and they use their mother tongue mainly as a vernacular. As is the case for Saami and Tornedal Finnish, official varieties of these are emerging in the publishing of books and papers as well as in radio and TV, theatre and other cultural activities. The only languages besides Swedish that are used to a larger extent as written standards in Sweden are Saami and Finnish, which are the only languages besides Swedish that have their own language planning committees. There are, however, minor papers, radio broadcasts and public information in many of the other immigrant languages, e. g. Arabic, Turkish, Serbocroat, Greek and Polish. These languages are also used in religious activities. There is a government-subsidized newspaper for immigrants, which appears in eight languages. The ethnic press is entitled to the same kind of subsidies as the Swedish press. The government also subsidizes literature in various minority languages. Funds are made available for public libraries to purchase foreign literature. A special programme of government grants to national immigrant organizations has been introduced. There are about 50 national immigrant organizations with more than 1,000 local associations.

Approval of the minority and immigrant languages within the framework of home language teaching in school has improved their status to some extent.

Settlement in various parts of the country and, during the last few years, the establishment of refugee camps in all parts of the country have given Swedes new opportunities other than touristic to become acquainted with new cultures and languages. Refugees have been offered jobs and housing in municipalities all over the country. Many of them, however, prefer settling in big cities or other urban districts. Part of the reason for this has been family ties and better opportunities to get jobs. In some places this has led to conflicts between Swedes and immigrants. Sometimes these have been caused by religious ambitions, e. g. among Muslims who have wanted to build mosques. Seldom have the conflicts been apparently linguistic.

Two investigations were conducted, one in 1969 and one in 1987, on attitudes towards immigrants in Sweden. According to these, public opinions has undergone a considerable shift in favour of greater tolerance, greater generosity and greater understanding of cultural pluralism. The really big change occurred between 1969 and 1981, and opinion then appears to have levelled out until 1987. In recent years young people have not shown as favourable attitudes towards immigrants as older people have.

In Finnish or Finnish-Swedish bilateral companies in Sweden, the working language most often is English or Swedish — many Finland-Swedes (Swedish-speaking Finns) are employed in these companies — but some use Finnish as their internal working language. In companies like SAS (Scandinavian Airlines System), what characterizes language use, English excepted, is that Danes, Norwegians and Swedes use their own language but try to accommodate to some extent, mainly by using single words from the other language or by copying.

6. Language political situation

The above mentioned goals for immigrant policy presuppose that immigrants obtain the same educational opportunities as the rest of the population. Provisions have been made for the education of immigrants and their children at virtually all levels. These were implemented also with regard to the indigenous minorities, the Saami, the Tornedalians and the gypsies, but the measures were initiated due to the needs caused by the immigrant situation.

Pre-school home language support has been defined as an activity for children of pre-school age carried out in a minority language. It does not denote school instruction. There are different forms of language support:

a) *Home language group*: a group in pre-school in which all the children and the majority of the staff belong to the same linguistic and cultural minority, and the minority language is the common means of communication in the group. Some activities may be carried out in Swedish. b) *Composite group*: A group in pre-school in which about half of the children and staff members are of a linguistic minority, the remainder being Swedish speakers. Both the minority language and Swedish are used as means of communication. c) *Swedish-speaking group with home language support given by an itinerant home language teacher*: The means of communication is Swedish and children with a home language other than Swedish can have home language support from a home language teacher who comes a certain number of hours a week. Itinerant home language teachers usually provide home language support in several pre-schools for individual children or, sometimes, groups of children. d) *Family day care with a bilingual caretaker*: the caretaker speaks the common minority language with the child. e) *Family daycare with a Swedish-speaking caretaker and home language support given in an open pre-school*.

Quantitatively home language support has been best provided for children with Spanish, Finnish, Turkish and Greek as their first language. In 1984 the number of children in child daycare with a mother tongue other than Swedish was about 20,000, 60% of whom received home language support.

Compulsory schooling is provided in the following four types of classes: a) *Preparatory class*, when pupils with a variety of backgrounds receive short-term intensive instruction in their own language and in Swedish as a second language (Sw2), preparatory to attending a regular Swedish class. b) *Mother tongue class* (up to grade 6, except for Finnish-speaking children, who get it until grade 9): all the pupils have the same non-Swedish first language. Instruction in the first grade is almost entirely in the first language (L1), with several hours per week of Swedish as a second language (Sw2). Instruction in Swedish increases gradually in the higher grades. In practice education in this type of classes is bilingual. c) *Integrated class*: pupils with a particular L1 constitute about half of the class. They receive some instruction in their L1, some in Sw2 and some in regular instruction in Swedish. The rest of the class consists of Swedish pupils. d) *Regular Swedish class*, with about two lessons a week in the home language.

The majority of immigrant pupils in the compulsory school attend regular Swedish classes (89%), about 10% attend mother tongue classes and only about 2% integrated classes. As an average, about 60% of the immigrant pupils in compulsory school participated in some form of instruction in L1. Norwegian had the lowest attendance rate (7%) and Kurdish (Sorani) the highest (79%).

In autumn 1993, 11 per cent of the pupils in comprehensive school (102,280) and 6% in upper secondary school had a home language other than Swedish. The corresponding figures for 1992 were 12 and 6%, for 1986/1987 9% and 5%.

There were 125 different home languages in the Swedish schools in autumn 1993. The corresponding figure in 1986/1987 was 78. Finnish (23,100 pupils) was the most frequent language, followed by Arabic (12,150 pupils) and Spanish (11,840 pupils). In 32 of the languages there was no home language instruction. Mostly pupils with "odd languages" did not participate in the instruction. Reasons for this may be difficulties in finding teachers or problems of forming groups with at least 5 pupils, which is a new requirement.

In comprehensive school 57% of the pupils with home language other than Swedish attended home language instruction. The corresponding figure for upper secondary school was 41%. Compared to 1992 there has been no change in comprehensive school and a decrease in upper secondary school.

Swedish as a second language (Sw2) is obligatory for all immigrant children for whom the school regards it necessary. Sw2 instruction was attended by 55% of the pupils with home language other than Swedish in comprehensive school in 1993, the same amount as in 1986/1987. In upper secondary school the attendance was 24%, which means a slight increase (22% in 1986/1987). Compared to 1992, there has been a decrease in comprehensive school and a decrease in upper secondary school.

A new possibility of organizing school education, the so-called free schools, has given immigrants the possibility of starting their own schools with bilingual education. These schools are also subsidized by the state.

A large-scale programme of free Swedish language instruction was started in 1965. At present every newly arrived immigrant should receive an average of 700 hours of instruction in Swedish, and has the right to get off work for studying. This comprises an introduction to Swedish society. The municipalities are responsible for the instruction.

The local authorities are responsible for the interpreting service (community interpreting) provided by some 150 immigrants service offices around the country.

Since 1986 there has been an Ombudsman Against Ethnic Discrimination, whose task is to counteract ethnic discrimination both at work and within other areas of community life.

7. Presentation of language contact

The greatest impact of a foreign language on Swedish was probably that of the German language during the Middle Ages. This is due to a vast immigration of German merchants and shopkeepers especially to Stockholm, which was at that time a bilingual town. Also in many small towns Low German was a commonly used language. As an example of this may be mentioned that the heading of the report on legal proceedings of the South Swedish town Kalmar was written in Low German instead of Swedish: "Dit is des stades kalmeren denkebok". Both grammar and pronunciation were influenced by German, as well as vocabulary: words for the political organization of the towns, for trade, terms for professions, for household utensils and clothing. German was the *lingua franca* of Sweden during the Great Power Period. During the 18th century, on the other hand, French cultural impact was strong in Sweden, which also influenced vocabulary.

Despite the relatedness between the Danish and the Swedish spoken in the southern provinces, understandability between Danish and Swedish is no greater in these regions than elsewhere in the country: Danes understand Norrland Swedish dialects better than the dialects of the southern provinces. Danish-based Standard Norwegian (bokmål) is fairly well understandable for Swedes; the dialectally-based nynorsk (New Norwegian) is harder to understand, except for speakers of related dialects on the Norwegian–Swedish border (Jämtland, Härjedalen in middle Norrland and Värmland and Bohuslän further south). On the whole, Swedes from different parts of Sweden have difficulties in understanding the dialects of the southern provinces. This is apparently due to the uvular *r*-sound and the diphthongs and triphthongs used in these dialects. These features, on the other hand, make these dialects easier to understand for some foreigners, e. g. those with an Australian English background. The uvular *r*-sound of these dialects is obviously a phenomenon deriving from 17th century France, which has spread to various parts of Europe and in Sweden from south to the central parts of Götaland, where it stopped spreading some decades ago.

A recent phenomenon is the new varieties of Swedish emerging in the new neighbourhoods in the big cities and especially their suburbs, where immigrants from different countries live together, partly also with Swedes. Code-switching and borrowing of words create totally new language varieties, not least among the youth, with words and phrases from Swedish and several different immigrant languages.

8. Bibliography (selected)

Baudou, Evert (1992): *Norrlands forntid – ett historiskt perspektiv*, Förlags AB Wiken.

Den svenska historien (1966): Del I–III. Stockholm.

Den svenska historien (1967): Del IV–V. Stockholm.

Eriksson, Riitta (1994): *Biculturalism in Upper Secondary Education.* Studies in Comparative and International Education 31, Stockholm.

Extra, Guus/Verhoeven, Ludo (Eds.) (1993): *Immigrant Languages in Europe*, Clevedon.

Fact Sheets on Sweden (1992): Stockholm.

Finska i Sverige – ett inhemskt språk (1994): Rapport från Arbetsgruppen för stärkande av det finska språkets ställning. Utbildningsdepartementel, Stockholm.

Förteckning över kommunala Invandarbyråer och Flyktingsamordnare (1994): Stockholm.

Moberg, Lena (1989): *Lågtyskt och svenskt i Stockholms stads medeltida tänkeböcker*. Acta academiæ regiæ Gustavi Adolphi LVIII, Uppsala.

Nordberg, Bengt (Ed.) (1994): *The Sociolinguistics of Urbanization: The Case of the Nordic Countries*, Berlin.

Pamp, Bengt (1978): *Svenska dialekter*, Stockholm.

Samerätt och sameting (1989): Huvudbetänkande av samerättsutredningen. SOU 1989:41. Stockholm.

Sirén, Ulla (1991): *Minority Language Transmission in Early Childhood*. Studies in Comparative and International Education 21, Stockholm.

Statistics Sweden (1994): *Home language and home language instruction. Comprehensive school and integrated upper secondary school.* U 72 SM 9401, Stockholm.

Statistics Sweden (1994): *Population Statistics 1993*, Part 2, Stockholm.

Statistics Sweden (1994): *Population Statistics 1993*, Part 3, Stockholm.

Svanberg, Ingvar/Tydén, Mattias (1992): *Tusen år av invandring*, Stockholm.

Tema Invandrare (1991): Sveriges officiella statistik, Stockholm.

The Saami of Lapland (1988): Report No. 55, London.

Thelander, Mats (Ed.) (1982): *Talspråksforskning i Norden. Mål – material – metoder*, Lund.

Erling Wande, Stockholm (Sweden)

121. Schwedisch–Samisch

1. Geographie und Demographie
2. Geschichte
3. Politik, Wirtschaft und allgemeine kulturelle sowie religiöse Lage
4. Statistik und Ethnoprofile
5. Soziolinguistische Lage
6. Sprachpolitische Lage
7. Allgemeines kontaktlinguistisches Porträt
8. Bibliographie (in Auswahl)

1. Geographie und Demographie

1.1. Volks- und Landesbezeichnung

Die samischen Siedlungsgebiete im Norden der skandinavischen Halbinsel und der Halbinsel Kola in Rußland werden von den Samen selbst als *Sápmi* oder *Sámeeatnam*, 'Samenland' bezeichnet. Die schwedischsprachige Bevölkerung in Skandinavien benutzte früher das Wort *lapp* (Lappe).

In der englischen Literatur lebt *lapp* und *lappish* immer noch weiter, obwohl *sami* immer öfter erscheint. In Norwegen taucht das Wort *Finne* auf, das früher eine weit verbreitete Bezeichnung für *Same* war.

1.2. Der schwedische Teil Sápmis

Vor allem im Norden bilden die Flüsse eine deutliche zentrale Linie, von der die Nebenflüsse wie Äste von einem Baum abzweigen. Jeder dieser Äste ist eine sog. *Lappgemarkung*. In Schweden spricht man von Gebirgs- bzw. Waldsamendörfern. Die ersteren werden insbesondere durch weite Wanderungen zwischen den Grasweiden im Sommer und den Flechtengebieten im Winter charakterisiert. Bei den Waldsamengebieten sind die Entfernungen zwischen den Sommer- und Wintersiedlungen nie sehr groß. Waldsamendörfer gibt es heute nur noch in der Provinz Västerbotten und nördlich davon.

In wirtschaftlichen Notjahren für die Rentierwirtschaft war das Meer im Westen die Rettung. Dies ist einer der Gründe für die sprachliche und kulturelle Einheitlichkeit der samischen Siedlungen in Norwegen und Schweden (→ Sprachenkarte A).

Heute besitzen die Samen die ökonomischen und kulturellen Möglichkeiten einer modernen Gesellschaft, selbst wenn ein Sprachgesetz für die schwedischen Samen immer noch fehlt.

2. Geschichte

2.1. Regionalgeschichte

Das Auskommen der Samen in älterer Zeit gründete sich auf eine Kombination verschiedener gewerblicher Tätigkeiten. Dazu gehörten die Jagd und die Fischerei. Für den Transport besaß man eine kleine Anzahl zahmer Rentiere.

2.2. Die Herkunft der Samen

Die samische Sprache ist der westlichste Ausläufer der finnisch-ugrischen Sprachfamilie. Das Finnische steht dem Samischen am nächsten. Das Problem der sprachlichen Gleichheit und genetischen Ungleichheit in bezug auf die Finnen gab den Anstoß zu der Theorie eines Sprachwechsels zu altfinnischer Zeit (1500 und 1000 v. Chr.).

Man rechnet damit, daß in der Periode zwischen 1800 und 1500 v. Chr. die ersten Kontakte mit den Balten stattfanden, als baltische Lehnwörter in die Sprache kamen. Die ältesten germanischen Entlehnungen entstanden vor der Trennung des Samischen vom Finnischen. Auch nach ihrer Trennung beeinflußten sich die beiden Sprachen wechselseitig. Für die samische Geschichte im Norden ist der sprachliche Einfluß in altnordischer Zeit (etwa zwischen 200 und 800 n. Chr.) von großem Interesse.

Aus dem genannten Material kann die Ausbreitung der Samen während des ersten Jahrtausends v. Chr. grob bestimmt werden. Ihr dünn besiedeltes Gebiet soll zu dieser Zeit den Bereich vom Ladoga- und Onegasee, dem Weißen Meer und der Barentssee bis zu den südlichen und westlichen Teilen des heutigen Finnlands umfaßt haben.

2.3. Ursprung der Sprachkontakte

Wenn wir mit Hilfe der samischen Volksartbezeichnung die Vorgeschichte der Samen betrachten, muß das samische *dárru, dárrolaš* als nicht-samische Gebiets- und Personenbezeichnung genannt werden. Das finnische *taro* bedeutet 'Anbau, bewohnte Gegend (im Gegensatz zu Binnenland, Einöde)', was darauf hindeutet, daß sich das samische Wort ursprünglich auf die bewirtschafteten Gegenden im damaligen südlichen Sápmi bezog.

Im nördlichen und nordöstlichen Samisch finden wir *ruošša*, 'Russe'. Das Wort bezog sich ursprünglich auf die Waräger schwedischer Herkunft in den Gegenden des Ladogasees, die selbst die Samen *Lappen* nannten. Den Wortstamm findet man in dem Wort *Rus'* der frühen russischen Dokumente wieder, im Warägerreich der Wikingerzeit und im späteren Rußland.

3. Politik, Wirtschaft und allgemeine kulturelle sowie religiöse Lage

3.1. Politische Verhältnisse

Schon früh haben die schwedischen Samen z. B. durch die Herausgabe von Zeitungen oder in Form von Verbänden ihre Ansichten zu Problemen des politischen und kulturellen Lebens artikuliert. Im Jahre 1950 wurde der *Reichsverband schwedischer Samen* gegründet. Schon fünf Jahre zuvor hatte man die Kulturorganisation *Same-Ätnam* gegründet, die u. a. viel für das samische Kulturbewußtsein bedeutet hat. Seit 1973 haben die Samen in Finnland ein gemeinsames Organ, das sog. *Samenparlament*; Norwegen erhielt sein *Saamenthing* benanntes Gegenstück im Jahre 1989. In Schweden gibt es seit 1993 ein *Saamenthing* mit 31 Mitgliedern.

3.2. Wirtschaft und Erwerbstätigkeit

Nur ein geringer Teil der Samen in Schweden ist in der Rentierwirtschaft beschäftigt. In Schweden ist das Recht zur Rentierhaltung an die samische Abstammung gebunden. Die übrigen Samen sind in allen auch für andere schwedische Bürger üblichen Berufen tätig.

Im samischen Kunsthandwerk sind viele Samen beschäftigt. Dieser Gewerbezweig hat in Schweden durch die Einrichtung eines entsprechenden Ausbildungsgangs an der Samischen Volkshochschule in Jokkmokk eine hohe Verbreitung erreicht.

3.3. Kulturelle und religiöse Verhältnisse

Die samische Kultur wird von einem Konservatismus in dem Sinne geprägt, daß Teile der Kultur Züge aus sehr alter Zeit bewahrt haben. Gleichzeitig unterscheiden sich die Samen nicht von anderen Bevölkerungskreisen in der Benutzung moderner Hilfsmittel der

Gegenwart. Nennenswert sind die samische Erzählkunst und der samische Gesang, der Jojk (samisch *luohti* oder *juoiggus*). Heute besitzt der Jojk sehr oft lyrischen Charakter.

Die kirchlich-religöse Bewegung, die seit Ende des 19. Jahrhunderts einen kräftigen Zuspruch bei den Samen fand, ist der Laestadianismus, benannt nach seinem Begründer Lars Levi Laestadius, einem Geistlichen im nordsamischen Gebiet Schwedens.

4. Statistik und Ethnoprofile

4.1. Anzahl der Sprecher

Von der gesamten samischen Bevölkerung, etwa 60 000 Personen, lebten 1973 ca. 17 000 Samen in Schweden. Von diesen gehörten ca. 2400 Personen zu den Rentier züchtenden Haushalten. In der nördlichsten Provinz, in Norrbotten, wohnten ca. 47% der Samen, in Västerbotten ca. 17%. Erstaunlicherweise leben in Jämtland weniger Samen (etwa 7%) als im Großraum Stockholm mit 9%. In keiner schwedischen Gemeinde bilden die Samen die Bevölkerungsmehrheit.

4.2. Die samische Sprache und ihre Dialekte

Man teilt das Samische in drei Gebiete ein, nämlich in das *Ostsamische*, das *Mittelsamische* und das *Südsamische*. Das Ostsamische erstreckt sich bis nach Finnland. Das mittelsamische Gebiet mit dem größten Bevölkerungsanteil umfaßt die übrigen Teile Finnlands und die nördlichsten Gebiete Norwegens und Schwedens, wo das Samische alternativ auch als *Nordsamisch* bezeichnet wird. Südlich davon finden wir das *Lulesamisch* in der Lule-Lappgemarkung. Die Provinzen Västerbotten und Jämtland machen das im weitesten Sinne südsamische Gebiet aus.

4.3 Ethnolinguistische Verhältnisse

Auch bei Kontakten mit anderen Völkern waren die Samen ein beeinflussender Faktor. Viele samische Wörter für Gerichte, Kleidung und Schuhwerk, Jagd und Fischerei wurden in das Finnische und Nordschwedische entlehnt. Heute haben die Samen selbst in ihren Kerngebieten mit geringen Ausnahmen täglich Kontakt mit der schwedisch- oder finnischsprachigen Bevölkerung. Unter der heutigen samischen Elterngeneration haben die samischen Sprachkenntnisse abgenommen. Wenn einer der Elternteile kein samisch spricht, ist Schwedisch oft die erste Sprache der Kinder.

5. Soziolinguistische Lage

5.1. Sprachlicher Status und Einstellung

Charakteristisch ist eine starke samische Gruppenidentität und eine Hochschätzung der eigenen Sprachvarietät. Die Sprachkenntnisse innerhalb der Rentierhaltung treibenden Gruppe sind besser als bei den übrigen Samen. Voraussetzung für das Stimmrecht zum schwedischen und norwegischen Saamenthing und zum Samenparlament in Finnland sind eigene oder samische Sprachkenntnisse der Eltern und Großeltern.

5.2. Sprachkonflikte

Die staatliche Weigerung, das Samische als offizielle Sprache gesetzlich zu verankern, hat in der letzten Zeit viele Proteste aufkommen lassen. Der sehr deutlichen und negativen Haltung aus vergangenen Zeiten folgte zeitweise eine passive Einstellung, die sich besonders in den zuständigen staatlichen Entscheidungsgremien zeigte.

5.3. Sprachbeherrschung, Vielsprachigkeit

In der samischen Gesellschaft findet man heute alle sprachlichen Fertigkeiten, und zwar von Sprechern, die nur einzelne Worte oder Sätze beherrschen bis zu solchen, die alle alltäglichen Verhältnisse gut formulieren ausdrücken können. Im Kontakt mit Nachbarn, in der Schule und am Arbeitsplatz spricht man heute im allgemeinen Schwedisch. Die Sprache in der Rentierhaltung ist im Norden immer noch Samisch. Historisch gesehen ist samische Vielsprachigkeit eher die Regel als die Ausnahme.

6. Sprachpolitische Lage

Ein planmäßiges Zusammenwirken in der samischen Sprache in Skandinavien wird seit den fünfziger Jahren betrieben. Zu dieser Zeit wurde eine Orthographie geschaffen und im Laufe von einigen Jahrzehnten in Norwegen und Schweden eingeführt, jedoch mit dem 1978 gefaßten Beschluß über die derzeit gültige *gesamtskandinavische und nordsamische Rechtschreibnorm* revidiert. Für das Süd- und Lulesamische gibt es entsprechende anerkannte Orthographien.

6.1. Schulische Ausbildung, Institutionen

Es gibt sechs Samenschulen im nordschwedischen Binnenland und integrierten Sprachunterricht in kommunalen Schulen. Die Samische Volkshochschule in Jokkmokk betreibt

Erwachsenenbildung in samischer Sprache und Kunsthandwerk. Auf höherem Niveau gibt es nur wenige Spezialangebote, abgesehen von der samischen Fakultät an der Universität Umeå.

6.2. Verwaltung, Medien

Die schwedischen Samen besitzen seit 1919 eine eigene Zeitung, die sporadisch samischsprachige Artikel aufnimmt. Der Samenrundfunk hat kurze gesamtnordische Sendungen, und die übrigen Sendezeiten werden auf das Samisch der verschiedenen Gebiete verteilt.

6.3. Sprachplanung

Die Pflege der genuinen regionalen Sprachtraditionen steht in offensichtlichem Konflikt mit der Forderung nach rationeller Sprachplanung. In der Wahl zum 1. Saamenthing 1993 hat daher eine jugendliche Partei sich dafür ausgesprochen, eine einzige Schriftsprache anzustreben.

6.4. Standardisierung und Modernisierung

In den nördlichsten Gebieten Schwedens, Norwegens und Finnlands kann man von einer reellen Standardisierung des Samischen sprechen. Der Bedarf an neuen Termini in vielen modernen Tätigkeitsgebieten und Wissenschaften wächst. Für die Modernisierung der Sprache fehlt jedoch ein Sprachorgan mit entsprechenden Ressourcen.

6.5. Orthographien

Von den ersten gedruckten samischen Büchern (1619) bis zu den Erzeugnissen des beginnenden 19. Jahrhunderts war die Rechtschreibung sehr unsystematisch. Die damaligen Traditionen führten zu unseren heutigen Konsonantenzeichen c, č, đ, ŋ, š, ŧ und ž im Nordsamischen. Die Grapheme c und z, č und ž sowie š entsprechen den lule- und südsamischen ts, tj und sj (vgl. u.).

7. Allgemeines kontaktlinguistisches Porträt

Das Samische hat einen relativ synthetischen Charakter. Grammatische Kategorien werden oft durch Endungen indiziert, die an den Wortstamm angefügt werden. Die samische Wortstruktur ist sehr regelmäßig.

Wenn man die Konsonanten- (K) und Vokalstruktur (V) eines zweisilbigen samischen Wortes in seinem kleinsten und größten Umfang schematisch aufzeichnet, bildet sich folgendes Muster: K0-3 V1-2 K1-3 V1 K0-2.

7.1. Phonologie

Ein grundlegender Unterschied zwischen Nord- und Südsamisch ist, daß letzteres einen vereinfachten Konsonantismus besitzt. Das Südsamische hat hingegen einen viel komplizierteren Vokalismus.

7.2. Vokalismus

Die nordsamischen Vokalphoneme tauchen in drei Gruppen auf, die aus kurzen oder langen einfachen Vokalen und Diphthongen bestehen:

/i u   /i: u: /ie uo
e   o   e: o: ea   oa/
a/   a:/

Im Ost- und Südsamischen ist der Vokalismus komplizierter.

7.3. Konsonantismus

Die Zeichen č und ž im Nordsamischen ergeben den tsch-Laut (vgl. ch im englischen church), und c und z bezeichnen den nordsamischen ts-Laut. Die stimmhafte bzw. stimmlose Alternative des Dentalspiranten wird mit đ und ŧ geschrieben, ŋ ist das Zeichen für den ng-Laut und š für den sch-Laut, der im Samischen stimmlos sibilant ist.

Dieses System gilt in seinen Hauptzügen auch für das Lulesamische, in dem man jedoch ts, tj und sj statt c/z, č/ž und š verwendet. Der südsamische Konsonantismus ist unkompliziert. Das Wortende zeigt ursprüngliche Konsonanten auf und hat normalerweise auch Vokale in der dritten Silbe bewahrt.

Im Nordsamischen gibt es einen paradigmatisch bedingten Konsonantenwechsel, den Stufenwechsel, der Konsonanten zwischen betonter und unbetonter Silbe betrifft. Dabei unterscheidet man drei sog. *Stufen*.

7.4. Phonotax und Morphologie

Das Samische zeichnet sich u. a. dadurch aus, daß die Silbenstruktur eines Wortes die Substantivdeklination und die Verbkonjugation beeinflußt. Wo auf die betonte Silbe eines Wortes ein oder zwei unbetonte folgen, bilden sich zwei Arten von *Takten*. Die klare Struktur auf der Wortebene hat dazu geführt, daß sich die Grenzen für die traditionellen Wortklassen weitgehend verwischt haben.

Es fehlt die grammatische Kategorie des Genus, und wie dem Finnischen fehlen auch dem Samischen getrennte Pronomen für Femininum und Maskulinum. Das Samische unterscheidet auch nicht zwischen bestimmter und unbestimmter Form. Die nordsamische Grammatik rechnet mit sechs Kasus (Nominativ, Genitiv-Akkusativ, Illativ, Lokativ, Komitativ und Essiv), die syntaktische und semantische Funktionen haben.

Personalpronomen haben außer Kasus- auch Personenbeugung im Singular, Dual und Plural. Übrige Pronomen haben Numerus- und Kasusbeugung. In prädikativer Stellung ist ein Pronomen kongruent mit dem Substantiv außer im Illativ und Lokativ Singular; in attributiver Stellung ist es jedoch unbeugbar.

Die Segmentierung der Verben ist einfach. Die Infinitivbezeichnung ist -t, die bei gleichsilbigen Stämmen im Aktiv *a i u* in der zweiten Silbe haben. Verben werden nach Personen, drei Numeri und vier Modi konjugiert, nämlich Indikativ, Konditional, Potential und Imperativ.

Der Imperativ wird in allen Personen gebeugt (1. Pers. Sing. ist selten) und hatte ursprünglich zwei Formen für den kategorischen Imperativ und die höfliche Ermahnung.

7.5. Syntaktische Züge

Die Wortfolge des Samischen in neutralen Aussagesätzen ist Subjekt, gefolgt von Prädikat und Objekt (SPO), wobei das Attribut im allgemeinen vor seinem Bezugswort steht. Ein Fragesatz wird im Samischen nicht mit umgekehrter Wortfolge gebildet, sondern ein enklitischer Frageparktikel *-go* wird an das Wort angefügt, das im Satz hervorgehoben wird, *čállágo mánná?* 'Schreibt das Kind?'.

Ein positiver Antwortsatz beinhaltet eine Wiederholung dessen, was die Frage in erster Linie betraf, wobei das Nomen und das Verb entsprechend dem Kontext gebeugt werden, z. B. *geasa čálát* 'An wen schreibst Du?', *(čálán) áhččái* '(Ich schreibe) an den Vater'.

Dem Samischen fehlt ein Verb, das dem deutschen *haben* im Sinne von *besitzen* entspricht. In Aussagen, in denen ein konkretes oder abstraktes Besitzverhältnis ausgedrückt werden soll, steht der Besitz im Nominativ und der Besitzer im Lokativ.

7.6. Lexikalische Besonderheiten

Das Samische ist reich an Naturterminologie: Worte für Schnee und Eis, Bezeichnungen für Rentiere und andere Tiere. Schnee- und Eisbezeichnungen sind Beispiele für den Wortschatz, der das naturnahe Leben der Samen widerspiegelt. So war diese genaue Beschreibung der Landschaft in einer Zeit für das Überleben unabdingbar, in der es noch keine Massenkommunikationsmittel gab.

7.7. Lehnwörter und Neubildungen

Heute ist eine planmäßige Sprachentwicklung nötig, um den Bedarf abzudecken, den Gesellschaft und Verwaltung, Technik und Forschung an Ausdrücke in samischer Sprache stellen.

Da das Samische sich bei seinen Vorbildern für Wortentwicklungen oft in den Majoritätssprachen bedient, können Unterschiede zwischen Teilen des Sprachgebietes entstehen.

Das Ableitungssystem bietet große Möglichkeiten für Wortbildungen. Es gibt sowohl Präfixe (seltener) als auch Suffixe, *gulolaš* 'gehorsam' > *eahpegulolaš* 'ungehorsam' > *eahpegulolašvuohta* 'Ungehorsam'. Es gibt ungefähr hundert Ableitungssuffixe.

7.8. Interferenzphänomene, Codewechsel

Die langwährenden Kontakte zwischen verschiedenen Volksgruppen im Norden haben verschiedene Interferenztypen mit sich geführt. Das Samische und das Finnische haben viele gemeinsame Züge, die sie vom Schwedischen unterscheiden. Beiden Sprachen fehlt z. B. die Kategorie der bestimmten und unbestimmten Form, die Genusbeugung und verschiedene Pronomen für das Maskulinum und das Femininum.

Für den Samisch Sprechenden entstehen oft Schwierigkeiten bei der Wahl zwischen schwedischen Präpositionen. Das Samische hat Verben, auf die ein bestimmter Kasus folgt. Im Schwedischen verwendet man in solchen Fällen Präpositionalausdrücke, was auf eine andere Sichtweise hindeutet. Einige samische Verben führen Interferenzen mit sich, indem sie auf mehrere Arten übersetzt werden können.

Es gibt große Unterschiede in der Sprachbeherrschung bei der mehrsprachigen Bevölkerung. Die Rentierzucht treibenden Familien und ihre Kinder machen diejenige Gruppe aus, die die Sprache am besten bewahrt haben. Danach kommen Samen aus dem Binnenland. Ein reichlicher Gebrauch von schwedischen und finnischen Fremdwörtern kommt im ansonsten „guten" Samisch vor, wenn das Gesprächsthema Bereiche wie Politik, Gesellschaftsverhältnisse, Gewerbe u. ä. berührt.

Bedingt durch seine schwächere Stellung gegenüber dem Schwedischen und Finnischen wechseln Samen oft zu einer anderen Sprache über, wenn Sprecher, die das Samische nicht beherrschen, sich einer Gruppe anschließen. Dieser sozial bedingte Codewechsel hat eine lexikalische Entsprechung in Situationen, in denen der Bedarf nach einem modernen Terminus auftaucht.

7.9. Lexika, Grammatiken, Textbücher

Das Samische der norwegischen Provinz Finnmark ist in Konrad Nielsens Werk *Lapp Dictionary* (1932—1938, neue Auflage 1978) beschrieben worden. Ein modernes nordsamisch-finnisches Wörterbuch ist das von Pekka Sammallahti verfaßte *Sámi-suoma sátnegirji* (1989). In Harald Grundströms *Lulelapsk ordbok* (1946—1954) werden sechs Unterdialekte beschrieben (mit schwedisch/ deutscher Übersetzung). Für das Südsamische ist neulich ein umfassendes Wörterbuch herausgegeben worden, *Südlappisches Wörterbuch* (1981—1985) von Gustav Hasselbrink. Die Wörter in dem Buch *Lappischer Wortschatz* (1939) von Eliel Lagercrantz stammen aus vielen unterschiedlichen Gebieten.

Nielsen hat auch eine Grammatik, Übungsstücke und ein Vokabelverzeichnis (1926—1929) herausgegeben. In neuerer Zeit gibt es eine moderne Grammatik von Klaus Peter Nickels: *Samisk grammatikk* (1990).

In allen nordischen Ländern wird die samische Lehrbuchproduktion geplant und in einzelnen Projekten durchgeführt, die staatliche Mittel erhalten und von samischen Pädagogen geleitet werden.

8. Bibliographie (in Auswahl)

Aronsson, Kjell-Åke (1991): *Forest Reindeer Herding A. d. 1—1800*. Archaeology and Environment 10, Umeå.

Beach, Hugh (1981): *Reindeer-Herd Management in Transition. The Case of Tuorpon Saameby in Northern Sweden.* Uppsala Studies in Cultural Anthropology 3, Uppsala.

Bergsland, Knut (1967): *Lapp dialectal groups and problems of history. Lapps and Norsemen in old times*, Bergen.

Collinder, Björn (1949): *The Lappish Dialect of Jukkasjärvi*, Uppsala.

Grundström, Harald (1946—1954): *Lulelappisches Wörterbuch*. Schriften des Instituts für Mundarten und Volkskunde in Uppsala. Ser C. 1:1—4, Uppsala.

Hansegård, Nils E. (1967): *Recent Finnish Loanwords in Jukkasjärvi Lappish*. Studia Uralica et Altaica Upsaliensia 3, Uppsala.

Hasselbrink, Gustav (1981—1983): *Südlappisches Wörterbuch 1—3*. Schriften des Instituts für Dialektforschung und Volkskunde in Uppsala. Ser. C:4, Uppsala.

Itkonen, Erkki (1955): *Die Herkunft und Vorgeschichte der Lappen im Lichte der Sprachwissenschaft*. Ural-Altaische Jahrbücher 27, Wiesbaden.

Itkonen, Erkki (1960): *Lappische Chrestomathie mit grammatikalischem Abriss und Wörterverzeichnis*. Apuneuvoja suomalais-ugrilaisten kielten opintoja varten 7, Helsinki.

Itkonen, Erkki (1968): *Zwei Andenken an die Zeit von Karelien und Haalogaland im Lappischen*. Suomalais-ugrilaisen Seuran Toimituksia 145, Helsinki.

Korhonen, Olavi (1979): *Lappische Lehnwörter im ältesten Einödgebiet Finnlands*, Finnisch-ugrische Forschungen 43, Helsinki.

Lagercrantz, Eliel (1939): *Lappischer Wortschatz*, Helsinki.

Nielsen, Konrad (1932—1938): *Lapp Dictionary I—III*. Instituttet for sammenlignende kulturforskning B:XVII:1—3, Oslo.

Pehrsen, Robert (1957): *The Bilateral Network of Social Relations in Könkämä Lapp District*. Bloomington, Ind.

Pirak, Anta (1933): *En nomad och hans liv*. Skrifter utg. av Kungl. Hum. Vetenskaps-Samfundet i Uppsala 28:3, Uppsala.

Qvigstad, J. K. (1925): *Die lappischen Dialekte in Norwegen*. Oslo Etnografiske Museums skrifter 1, Hefte 1, Oslo.

Qvigstad, J. K./Wiklund, K. B. (1899): *Bibliographie der lappischen Litteratur*. Suomalais-ugrilaisen Seuran Toimituksia 13, Helsinki.

Ruong, Israel (1943): *Lappische Verbalableitung dargestellt auf Grundlage des Pitelappischen*, Uppsala.

Sammallahti, Pekka (1989): *A linguist looks at Saami prehistory*. Acta Borealia 2/1989, Oslo.

Schlachter, Wolfgang (1958): *Wörterbuch des Waldlappendialekts von Malå und Texte zur Ethnographie*. Lexica Societatis Fenno-Ugricae 14, Helsinki.

Sköld, Tryggve (1992): *Die Kriterien der urnordischen Lehnwörter im Lappischen I*, Uppsala.

Turi, Johan (1917): *Muittalus samid birra, en bog om lappernes liv. Utg. av Emilie Demant Hatt. Köpenhavn 1910*, Stockholm.

Whitaker, Ian (1955): *Social Relations in a Nomadic Lapp Community*, Samiska Samlinger 2, Oslo.

Wiklund, K. B. (1896): *Entwurf einer urlappischen Lautlehre I*, Helsinki.

Olavi Korhonen, Umeå (Schweden)

122. Swedish—Finnish

1. Geography and demography and ethnoprofile
2. History
3. Politics, economy and general cultural and religious situation
4. Sociolinguistic and language political situation
5. General contactlinguistic portrait
6. Bibliography (selected)

1. Geography and demography and ethnoprofile

1.1. The Tornedal Finnish minority

The Tornedal Finnish area is situated in the eastern Norrbotten province. In 1809 many Finnish-speakers and their villages in the Torne river valley remained on the Swedish side. Communication and 'cross-marriage' between northern Finland and Sweden have continued. The Finland Finnish (= FiFi) influence and the proportion of endogamy increased as a result of the Second World War.

Sweden does not allow language use census, but in a unique census (1930) there appeared to be 12,000 monolingual Finnish-speakers and 28,000 inhabitants who also understood or spoke Swedish and/or Sami. The monolinguals consisted of elderly people and small children.

Recent estimations — based on questionnaire data regarding listening habits of Finnish-speaking radio programs in the Norrbotten province in the 1960s — hover around 20,000—25,000 speakers of Tornedal Finnish (= ToFi). People understanding ToFi were estimated at about 40,000. The majority of Tornedal Finns live in smaller municipalities (e. g., Pajala, Korpilombolo, Haparanda, Övertorneå/Matarengi). A large number of Tornedal migrants live in northern regional centres (Kiruna, Luleå, Umeå) and in Stockholm (→ language map A).

The demolinguistic picture of Tornedal Finns is that of a language shifting minority: the top of the demographic pyramid is broad, the bottom is narrow. A fluent ToFi speaker is typically middle-aged or older. Children use Swedish as their main language, but older people may still use Finnish in various situations. Even children of all-Tornedal Finnish parents tend to become productively monolingual in Swedish. Urbanization has contributed to language shift: Finnish-speaking women escape the hardships of northern, countryside life, leaving unmarried men behind.

The post-war years were followed by regional and southern-bound migration especially to Stockholm. Later, the town of Haparanda on the Torne river turned into a target of immigration. The immigrants are mainly of Finland Finnish origin, moving from southern Sweden closer to Finland. Haparanda has the highest proportion in Sweden of people born in Finland: 34% (1989). Finnish-speaking Tornedal Finns should be added to this figure.

The northernmost towns of Sweden constitute specific language contact areas; ToFi, Swedish, FiFi varieties (non-standard, standard) are in contact. In addition, Sami languages coexist with these in periphery areas. Swedish spoken in Northern Sweden bears evidence of linguistic contact with Finnish and Sami.

The Tornedal Finns count themselves as Swedes by nationality and national identity, but also as a Finnish-speaking and bilingual population. Historical, linguistic and regional identities form essential parts of the increasing ethnic cohesiveness of Tornedal Finns. Tornedal Finnish has become a major cultural value for this process.

1.2. The Sweden Finnish minority

Immigration from Finland since the 1950s has resulted in an urban minority population. Scholars of history label all Finnish immigrants Sweden Finns, but the epithet is now generally used for Finnish-speaking post-war immigrants and their descendants. Immigration to Sweden was facilitated by the announcement of the common Nordic labour market and the abolition of passport control between the Nordic countries in 1954. Immigration reached a peak in 1969—1970, when 80,000 migrants arrived from Finland.

Finnish emigration was caused by high post-war birth-rates and restructurings of the agricultural and forestial labour markets in rural areas. No official 'guest worker' policy was adopted, but immigrants were seen as a temporary aid to Swedish industrial needs. Initial immigration was individual, later it turned into chain migration.

The origins of the Finnish immigrants have shifted from mainly northern, rural to southern and urban, especially after 1969–1970. Emigrants often experienced a multistage migration, with a shorter stay in an urban centre, e.g. Helsinki, Tampere, Turku or Oulu.

Ethnic revitalization resulted in regular minority activities among Sweden Finns in the late 1980s. This coincided with an improved socioeconomic status. Differences regarding material and social wealth have become smaller by the increasing average length of stay of Sweden Finns. Asocial isolation occurred initially among minor groups of Finns, caused by linguistic, social and cultural prejudice and differences. The educational level of the early immigrants was mainly that of an unskilled worker. Sweden Finns today constitute a socioeconomically and linguistically heterogeneous population.

There are 21 municipalities with more than 10%, or a total number of 3,000, of their inhabitants born in Finland (eight in the greater Stockholm area). There are 109 Swedish municipalities with more than 400 inhabitants born in Finland (24 in the province of Stockholm). Three out of 24 Swedish provinces do not contain any municipality fulfilling the mentioned demographic characteristics.

Finnish immigrants preferred central and southern Sweden, but immigration targeted all parts of Sweden. A pattern of four basic living environments evolved. Nine out of ten Sweden Finns live in various urban environments. About one third of all Sweden Finns live in the greater Stockholm area (78,000 people born in Finland in 1989). The three largest cities (Stockholm, Gothenburg, Malmö) account for about 45% of all Sweden Finns. The second type of milieu is the middle-size industrial towns, mostly situated in central Sweden, with a total population of around 100,000 (e.g., Södertälje, Eskilstuna, Norrköping, Borås, Västerås). Their proportion of inhabitants of Finnish origin is regularly five–ten per cent. The third type of milieu is made up of small towns and ironworks communities, which developed around one central industry, with the aid of external labour force. These areas have been hit by unemployment and outflow of inhabitants. The fourth area is the northern towns, many of which have needed labourers for the mining industry, and villages, where ToFi speakers lived before the arrival of the immigrants.

The four types of environments constitute different cultural, socioeconomic and linguistic settings, both for the maintenance of Finnish and the development of Swedish.

From the 1980s the first generation of Sweden Finns has reached the age of retirement. For many this has meant a re-Finnicization. Contacts with Swedes from the working sphere have not survived into the social networks of spare time life. A need to establish Finnish old-age care and medical care has developed. Medical, legal and social welfare occupations have become primary for women of immigrant background. The need for interpreters has thus partly been covered by bilingual persons, combining language knowledge with professional education in these fields. The Swedish society has generally not acknowledged the linguistic and cultural knowledge among immigrants as a formal merit.

In estimates of the number of Sweden Finns three aspects are involved: country of birth, citizenship and parental origin. The number of people born in Finland, living in Sweden was 220,497 (1989) (29% of all foreign-born in Sweden). The proportion of Finland Swedes among all Finnish immigrants in Sweden has been estimated at 25%.

About half a million Finns have moved to Sweden from the 1950s till the 1990s. Approximately one third has been estimated to have returned. The total amount of Finnish citizens, naturalized citizens, and descendant generations, would surmount to between 330,000 and 400,000.

The number of Finnish citizens (1989) was 123,867. Among the potential naturalizations of Finns, about 213,000 Finnish citizens were estimated to have received Swedish citizenship during the post-war years. About 170,000 earlier Finnish-speaking Finns were to be found among these.

In 1989 there were about 26,100 pupils with Finnish as a home-language at primary-school age. This accounts for 27% of all pupils with a home-language other than Swedish.

The 1980s has resulted in a return migration to Finland. Still, about 4,000–5,500 people move annually between the countries. If present-day trends persist, in twenty years no children of Finnish descent with a Finland-born mother will reach school age.

Finnish immigrants can identify either as Finns or Swedes, or both. Additionally, they can identify as Sweden Finns. First generation immigrants regularly retain their ethnic identity as (Finland) Finns. Some have become naturalized Swedes, also by self-classification. For the second generation growing up during the 1960s, the assimilationist policy often led to a forced acceptance of the majority Swedish identity. They and their parents have had difficulty in accepting their Finnish ancestry.

Second generation Finns growing up during the 1950s and 1960s did not receive any mother tongue tuition. Official and private pressure were directly aiming at fastest possible assimilation. Many early second generation Sweden Finns lack productive skills in Finnish. Second generation children who arrived during the 1970s and 1980s have to a high degree attended Finnish classes or home-language teaching on hour-basis. This has strengthened their bonds to a Finnish background. A Sweden Finnish identity is emerging, which seems to correlate with a high level of bilingualism.

2. History

Finland was the easternmost region of Sweden for seven centuries. West Finnish seasonal labourers have travelled to central Swedish farms, mines and as manual workers to Stockholm. Commerce and migration have been vivid between Stockholm and Turku. Stockholm has had a sizeable Finnish-speaking population for 600—700 years. The Finnish parish in the town was founded in 1533. Labourers have constituted the majority of emigrants from Finland, and innovative exploiters, administrators and officers the majority of immigrants to Finland. Finnish students have studied in Sweden for centuries.

Sweden lost Finland in the Swedish—Russian war (1808—1809). In northern Sweden, the Finnish-speaking population of the Torne river valley slowly turned into an ethnolinguistic minority. In 1809, Swedish mainland rural provinces counted thousands of Savo (eastern Finland) settlers' descendants, so-called forest or Värmland Finns. They had inhabited the inner forestial regions (in Sweden and Norway) since the 16th century, using their burn-beating agricultural methods.

Finns have escaped warfare and famine throughout history by emigrating, recurrently to Sweden. This has happened also in modern times. About 65,000 children were evacuated during World War II; 5,000 of these stayed permanently with their host families.

Today, two main sources of Finnish language contact with Swedish exist in Sweden: migrants, i. e., Sweden Finns, and an autochtonous population, Tornedal Finns. Värmland Finnish has been extinct since the late 1960s, when its last fluent speakers passed away.

Cultural and linguistic influence have merged into Finnish during more than half a millennium, both via socially dominant and equal status Swedish dialects. This concerns both the lexicon and grammar of Finnish in Finland. Migrants to Sweden have always had at their disposal a lexically and grammatically spiced language, prepared to incorporate new Swedish features. Finnish immigration has repeatedly offered fresh linguistic input to speakers of Finnish in Sweden.

Finnish impact on the Swedish language and culture in Sweden is, however, minimal. It can be summarized as a handful of lexical loans, e. g., Swe *pojke* Fi 'poika' Eng 'boy'; Swe *känga* Fi 'kenkä' Eng 'boot(s), shoe'; Swe (colloquial) *kola* Fi 'kuolla' Eng 'die'. Concentrations of place names are found in central and northern parts of Sweden. At the local level, especially in the Torne river area, both cultural and linguistic impact is extensive.

3. Politics, economy and general cultural and religious situation

Sweden has not signed international agreements regarding the fundamental rights of minorities other than Nordic recommendations. Tornedal Finns fulfil the criteria of a national minority, but the issue remains undecided by the Swedish government. Sweden Finns have been treated like any immigrant group, despite their long Swedish common history and various Nordic agreements.

Positive legal proposals and political rhetoric have often been in conflict with the executive power at local, administrator levels. Hansegård (1989, 140) uses a Sami expression to describe the attitudes of Swedish authorities in minority matters: *attii árjji dihte*, which can be translated as: 'he gave just so much that it was not possible to say that he had not given anything'. A change in the treatment of Sweden Finns has been promised at various occasions, both by former

Prime Minister Carl Bildt and the recent government. No public information is available about a progression in the matter thus far.

The ethnic revitalization in both Tornedalen and among Finnish immigrants started fairly late, in the 1980s. Public proponents of Sweden Finnish issues and ethnicity are on average more highly educated than the average Sweden Finn, and have better knowledge of policymaking; in addition, they have experience of administrative work at the terms of the majority. These characteristics are sometimes put forward as an argument against these proponents. In actual fact, they have approached the educational level of their majority opponents, who are not facing a similar criticism.

3.1. The Tornedal situation

The Swedish–Finnish geographical border reflects a cultural and linguistic border between Finland Finnish (FiFi) and Tornedal Finnish (ToFi). FiFi was re-codified and standardized in the 19th century. ToFi only followed the FiFi path for a short period after 1809. At the end of the century the FiFi impact was already reduced.

The Swedish authorities set out to assimilate Tornedalen politically and linguistically around the 1860s, when school politics were shifted into one of Swedicization. Only schools teaching in Swedish were given state support from 1888 and onward. This was justified by an inferred belief that the Finnish-speaking population would be Russified via neighbours and relatives in Finland. The assimilationist view was officially altered in 1975–1976, when the slogan 'equality, freedom of choice and partnership' was adopted, as a result of an Immigrant committee's recommendations. The new sensitivity to immigrants' needs and a softer transition to the Swedish society influenced also the Tornedal situation, resulting in an active revitalization and furthering of ethnolinguistic values.

A national association for Tornedalians was founded (Svenska Tornedalingars Riksförbund-Tornionlaaksolaiset (STR-T, 1981). Tornedalians now refer to their language as *Meän kieli* 'Our language', as in ethnic revitalization contexts elsewhere: 'we and ours', is stressed. The low esteem of ToFi both in Finland and in the Tornedal region was counterproductive to using ToFi in education and as a means of written communication until the mid-1980s. During the 1980s, fiction has been translated, educational programmes have involved FiFi and ToFi, dictionaries have been published, and an academy, Meän Akateemi / Academia Tornedaliensis, created in 1988. Writers and playwrights have recently published in ToFi, and theatre groups act in ToFi. The Gospel according to Mark has been translated from Greek into ToFi.

Religious activities in several branches of Laestadian Christianity (founded by the priest Lars Levi Laestadius (1800–1861)) were directly connected to the use of Finnish, but not all Tornedal Finns are Laestadians. Their meetings constituted social gathering events for large parts of the non-confessional community as well. By diminishing Laestadianism the amount of domains of Finnish-language use has shrunk. Clergymen in the Swedish state church in Tornedalen have regularly been required to know Finnish.

The most critical point in the process of language shift seems to have been during the adolescent generations of the 1940s and 1950s. Today, receptively monolingual Tornedal Finnish-speakers hardly exist.

3.2. The Swedish Finnish situation

Most post-war immigrants considered their stay temporary. This contributed to a low degree of motivation for integration and of organization of immigrants' social life. Despite this, many associations have celebrated their 40th and 50th anniversaries. The first Finnish association was founded in Stockholm in 1894. The national organization of Sweden Finnish associations (Ruotsinsuomalaisten yhdistysten keskusliitto, RSKL/SFFR) was founded in 1957. Initially, the associations had a social, get-together function. Later, they have become a channel for Swedish local and national authorities to communicate with Sweden Finns. Attempts to integrate younger association members have faced several conflicts: older members reluctantly accepted that Swedish be used in the associations, but the younger have avoided them, partly due to lack of skills in Finnish; an idealized perception of Finland among the older has further been disapproved of by second generation Sweden Finns.

There are national organizations for Sweden Finnish translators, teachers, journalists, students etc., most of which publish their own newsletters or weeklies.

Religious activity is low among Sweden Finns, especially the younger. Administrative and practical services of the parishes have been provided in Finnish. Finnish-speaking clergymen have been employed in many municipalities. Some parishes have arranged open and free pre-school activities for Finnish-speaking children.

A double shift from a majority rural to a minority urban environment has resulted in poor integration into the Swedish society for many. Decrease in power and status degradation has been greater for men than for women in the emigrational process to Sweden. First generation Sweden Finns have contributed comparatively little to public life and political discourse.

In 1976 Nordic citizens, as the first non-Swedes, were given the right to vote in local and provincial elections. The social democratic party has benefited most by Finnish immigrants. Finnish citizens retain their right to vote in Finnish elections. Sweden Finns show a lower frequency of voting than the Swedish and Finnish majorities.

The state support era, a result of the social democratic equality idea, resulted in identical solutions to problems of different immigrant groups. Reliance on the state and the hope to achieve common goals, and adherence to a non-conflict discourse, have partly been abandoned. One sign of this is that when the right-wing coalition changed the school funding system and made way for reduced home-language tuition, Finnish primary schools were founded, e.g. in Stockholm (two schools), Gothenburg, Eskilstuna and Borås. The present situation has accomplished a higher degree of self-reliance.

In spring 1992 Sweden Finnish national central organizations decided to declare Sweden Finns an ethnic minority. The declaration has received public support in Finland, but only minor publicity in Sweden, until the beginning of 1993. This may be seen as an example of increased group cohesiveness, and a preparation for the developing Swedish market-economy society.

4. Sociolinguistic and language political situation

4.1. The Tornedal Finnish situation

Nils-Erik Hansegård made his conclusion about double semilingualism on Tornedal Finnish circumstances. Follow-up studies regarding the Finnish and Swedish of Tornedal speakers did not confirm his hypotheses about competence. He later admitted that the description was not generally applicable to Tornedal Finns, but maintained that it was a regular phenomenon for the generations growing up during the 1940s and 1950s. Speakers themselves accepted the idea of semilingualism. The discussions had devastating effects on the sociolinguistic self-confidence of Tornedal speakers, and on one generation of immigrant children and their parents. The view of semilingualism still flourishes among Tornedalians. The belief is partly founded on the view that speaking a nonstandard variety, with a multitude of loan words, proves semilingualism to be present. The lay concept is based on a mixture of performance and competence skills. Labels such as 'deteriorated, vulgar and mixed' are still used to describe the ToFi variety, both by in-group and out-group members.

The progression of language shift has been somewhat halted. Since the 1950s the adolescent generation shifts language and introduces Swedish into the earlier monolingual Finnish-speaking homes. Adolescent speakers are mostly to be found among presumptive shifters to Swedish on a language shift continuum. However, whereas Swedish is being introduced in most private domains, ToFi has become used in some former High variety situations. There is thus no stable diglossia for ToFi.

Radio broadcasting in Finnish has been available to Tornedalians via Finland Finnish radio. Regional Finnish programs have been broadcast since the 1960s in the province of Norrbotten, and broadcasting in ToFi has been developed.

The main newspaper in the area, *Haparandabladet/Haaparannanlehti*, the only bilingual one in Sweden, includes writings in ToFi. In practice it suggests the Pajala dialect to become the standardized ToFi variety by frequency of use. A widespread opinion among Tornedal Finns about written ToFi is that it has no function to fill. ToFi is increasingly being used as a written medium. Since 1982 the trilingual (ToFi, FiFi, Swe) magazine *Met* has been published by the STR-T association. In 1990 a Tornedal Finnish publisher *Kaamos*, managed by STR-T, established itself. Among its published items are two dictionaries (Tornedal Finnish–Finnish–Swedish, and Gällivare Finnish–Finnish–Swedish).

The different social and political systems have caused diverging vocabulary developments in Tornedalen and Finland. The vocabulary of ToFi has become increasingly Swedicized since about the 1860s. The formation of Academia Tornedaliensis (1988) has created a forum for discussions on regional policy, identity and even standardization of ToFi. The publication of two dictionaries (1992) may have some prescriptive impact, though not intended as normative.

Tornedal Finnish dialectological traits were described in detail at the turn of the century. Present-day ToFi characteristics have been dealt with in three recent doctoral theses on its dialectal-lexical characteristics. Positive changes have lately been noted regarding its official status and prestige among both speakers and researchers.

Finnish as a subject has been taught in Tornedalen from time to time, and regularly since the 1950s. It remained limited until the 1970s. In 1976–1977 ToFi was first tried as a conscious medium of instruction, instead of FiFi. In the 1980s teaching in Finnish altogether decreased, but the 1990s has seen a slight increase in the teaching of Finnish in primary school. It is not known how much of this concerns ToFi, but teaching material in ToFi has been developed. At secondary level, fewer pupils than earlier take Finnish as a school subject. From 1993 the first school (in Kangos) has made ToFi obligatory for all in the first grade. The almost bilingual town of Haparanda has experienced several conflicts lately due to the growing Finnish influence. Conflicts have concerned the difficulty of monolingual Swedish-speaking pre-school children to find a regularly monolingual Swedish-speaking surrounding in Haparanda.

4.2. The Sweden Finnish situation

There are elderly and adult first generation immigrants with almost no productive and limited receptive skills in Swedish. Among infants there are children who have little or no productive knowledge of Swedish when entering the school system. Finnish day-care and pre-schools have existed in many municipalities. At the other end, there are second generation speakers with no productive knowledge of Finnish, especially among those who did not receive formal teaching in Finnish.

Many adults immigrated to environments where an existing basically Finnish-speaking network integrated them. Countrymen who had arrived earlier interpreted and assisted them in Swedish when necessary. Among the adults entitled to Swedish language tuition for immigrants, some never received their guaranteed hours of Swedish lessons. How widespread this was is not known.

Internal attitudinal factors may explain some cases of lacking Swedish skills. Attitudes regarding Swedish and Swedes have for historical reasons been juxtaposed to pro-Finnish attitudes, already in Finland. Stigmatization in Sweden may have reinforced the negative attitudes. The Finn in Sweden has carried the burden of a double stigma, both that of the historical and the immigrant underdog. Finnish national identity has been closely connected to language. Finnish has been a core value of national and cultural identity for Finns. Successful learning of Swedish was seen as a form of betrayal among first generation immigrants.

When the insight evolved that the immigrants would stay, the active immigration policy turned into one of straightforward assimilation. Later, in the mid-1970s, an integrational policy was adopted, which supported the cultural and linguistic heritage of immigrants, following European trends in immigration policies.

Second generation Sweden Finns have brought Swedish into their homes, as among Tornedal Finns. This can partly be explained by the assimilation policy: parents were officially instructed (e.g. by teachers, school nurses, doctors), and privately recommended (by neighbours, fellow workers etc.), that it was detrimental to teach Finnish to their children: they would not manage well in the Swedish society. Consequently, parents started using their language-learner Swedish. This was also a major opportunity for the parents to practise Swedish. According to some data, Swedish is used in 60% of cases among first-generation Finnish-speaking immigrants.

The question of identity among Sweden Finns contains several conflicts. Those who have become naturalized and/or assimilated, rarely identify as Sweden Finns, and they have often shifted to Swedish. Their average socioeconomic characteristics are more similar to those of the majority population. The low profile of these people has not supported an ethnic self-confidence. Groups of higher social prestige, such as white collar workers, teachers and journalists, have not willingly identified as Sweden Finns. Identifying as a Sweden Finn has until recently implied lower social and linguistic competence compared to Finland Finns and Swedes.

In highly urbanized areas mixed Finnish—Swedish marriages and marriage between Finnish and other immigrants are frequent. In the Stockholm area the combinations Finnish and Arabic, Finnish and Persian are common. These trilingual situations, with Swedish as a *lingua franca*, frequently seem to lead to abandonment of the third language (neither Finnish nor Swedish). Children do not receive double home-language teaching. Literacy skills are seldom developed in the third language. Trilingual familes have only recently been acknowledged in discussions regarding the fate of Sweden Finnish.

At the end of the 1970s, almost 90% were occupied within industry or production. During the 1980s both the statistical picture and the stereotype have changed. The level of education among second generation Sweden Finns has improved. The proportion of university students from Finnish immigrant background is still lower than for majority children. Contacts between Finns and Swedes have deepened, due to better language skills, and to the long-term integration process. Ironically, immigration of refugees with other racial backgrounds has — relatively speaking — improved the status of Finns.

Some Finnish companies took over large Swedish companies in the 1980s. This development showed Swedes a new type of Finn, the high position management representative. Occupations held by Sweden Finns presently include white-collar workers, such as teachers, journalists, lawyers, civil servants, health care staff and salespersons.

Ethnic revitalization did not reach Sweden Finns until the 1980s. The consensus-based cooperation with the majority has led to few serious conflicts between Swedes and Finns. Only within the language status sphere, represented by educational issues, has clear disagreement recurred. The question of educational programmes for the maintenance of Finnish, vs. transitional programs, has become the issue in which the practical implications of the Swedish slogans have been tested. Parents of children requiring Finnish classes or home-language teaching have occasionally gone on strike, to put pressure on local school boards and administrators.

The right to use the mother tongue in written and oral contacts with authorities has been settled in several Nordic agreements. These have not always been followed in practice in Sweden. The need to use interpreters has not decreased as was predicted; on the contrary, the demand for it has persisted. Training and funding of the use of Finnish-speaking interpreters have decreased during the 1980s.

In 1976 a Sweden Finnish language board, *Ruotsinsuomalainen kielilautakunta*, was founded. It has become the centre of vocabulary development, mainly for Finnish administrative terminology. Three dictionaries from different social fields have been published (School terminology, Social welfare terminology and Labour market terminology). The implementation of its proposals is the language board's largest practical problem. So far, lexical differences from FiFi is the only commonly acknowledged linguistic differentiation.

Only two of a handful of Sweden Finnish newspapers have managed to retain national coverage, *Ruotsinsuomalainen* (founded by RSKL in 1964) and *Viikkoviesti* (an informational weekly) founded by the state in 1967). A third major attempt was the private *Finn-Sanomat*, which was published in 1974—1985. Many regular Swedish newspapers have included minor writings and commercials in Finnish. This policy has been discontinued by most of them.

Finnish radio programmes have been broadcast since 1960, first as national tourist programs, later as news programmes. In 1968 Finland Finnish TV programs were broadcast once a week. Since 1969 the Finnish production studio of the Swedish Radio has been in operation. Since 1976 independent Finnish TV-programs of the Swedish state television are produced, and Finnish programs are broadcast via the local radio network. In 1988 Swedish Television started daily news programmes in Finnish. In 1993, a radio broadcasting reform concentrated broadcasting to regular working hours. Many listeners have lost the opportunity to listen to the programs live.

Most larger and mid-size municipality libraries have had Finnish books available. These libraries have often turned into cultural fora for Finns.

The Swedish immigrant policy contains no ethnic minority policy aspect: Sweden does not accept the concept of developing ethnic minorities. Crucial questions in a long-term perspective are: should programmes further integration, or maintenance of mother tongues and cultures? A turning point was the home-language legislation in 1975—1976. Support of the mother tongue was argued to have positive effects on the identity and language development of minority children. Swedish municipalities were required to arrange home-language (the official term for mother tongues other than Swedish) teaching for children with another language as a home-language. The educational programmes aim at fulfilling the objectives of active bilingualism. The amount of input has been clearly inadequate for this. The possibility to teach and give literacy training in the mother tongue in mother tongue classes has made the future perspective of bilingualism somewhat brighter. The so-called bilingual educational programmes imply functional language shift and integration via transition. The importance of the mother tongue was highlighted between 1975 and approximately 1985.

Three basic, voluntary educational programmes were introduced: 1) home-language hours (1−2 hours a week), 2) integrated classes, where a large proportion of a class has a mother tongue other than Swedish in common, and 3) mother tongue classes, with an increasing proportion of Swedish until most (or all) of the teaching takes place in Swedish in either grade four or seven. In addition, regular Swedish majority classes are offered. About one third of the pupils entitled to home-language teaching do not receive this. Each of the programmes has occasionally faced resistance at local school level and by Swedish parents. From the mid-1980s greater stress on teaching Swedish has recurred, now concerning Swedish as a second language. During 1991−1992, this kind of teaching too, has been drastically reduced. In 1989, 62% of the pupils entitled to teaching in Finnish participated in one of the three educational programmes including the mother tongue. The proportion has decreased from about 80% in 1980. A major change was the re-definition of who is entitled to home-language teaching. In 1978−1983 all who had *the language actively used in the child's local environment*, could receive home-language teaching. From 1985, those who had *the language actively used in the home environment on a daily basis* receive home-language teaching. The economic and administrative difficulties for arranging home-language teaching have also increased during the latter half of the 1980s. For 1992, more than one third of the funding given to home-language teaching was cancelled: classes either became larger or were cancelled.

Among the pupils who received home-language tuition (in 1989), ten per cent of the Finnish-speaking lacked knowledge in Swedish. The average for all home-language pupils was 17%.

No large-scale, national evaluations have been planned to study the pupils who followed the different educational options. It should be pointed out, that the models have in practice seldom been designed according to their theoretical intentions, due to local considerations.

Since 1990 another kind of bilingual schooling has become possible for Finnish-speaking children: Sweden Finnish primary schools. These are private, but indirectly state/municipality funded. The communities or the state do not direct their educational policies − but they generally follow the Swedish primary school curriculum. Their goal is active bilingualism, and teaching is done in Finnish, e. g., during 80% of the time, the rest in Swedish. Parents of children in these schools seem to differ slightly from the average social background of Sweden Finns. Families are often mixed, with one Finnish-speaking and one parent from a third country. Parents have been often studied at university level. Only positive reactions have been reported from these schools so far, from parents, teachers and children.

The continuum of language skills in Finnish among second generation Sweden Finns has come to range from fragmentary knowledge to a high level of academic and literate skills in Finnish. Skills in Finnish seem to become better than they were among earlier second generation speakers. Second generation speakers who have participated in a Finnish home-language programme show a good command of vernacular Finnish, but few seem to develop advanced written or standard Finnish skills, neither as a written nor as a spoken medium. Most second-generation speakers are orally fluent in Swedish and have developed Swedish literacy. Lack of training in and contact with written Finnish will ultimately make it difficult for them to pick it up again as a regular habit in adulthood.

Earlier, language shift appeared to be proceeding even faster than the three to four generations for overseas immigrants in North America. At present, the progression predicted by the development of the 1960s and 1970s has been halted. The functional division developing between spoken and written language does, however, not give cause to hope for better prospects in the future. Full-scale competence regarding the functional aspects of language use is normally not transferred to second and following generations of Sweden Finns.

5. General contactlinguistic portrait

5.1. Intralinguistic portrait of Tornedal Finnish

In the Swedish province of Norrbotten there are several Finnish dialects, among them ToFi. They all reflect more or less influence of Swedish and Sami. The further west and northwest one moves, the more obvious is the impact of Sami, especially within the vocabulary of topography, reindeer herding and features of the northern culture. Swedish impact is extensive within the administrative spheres, but it has also intruded into the every-day basic lexicon, e.g., ToFi *pappa* 'father', Swe 'pappa', Fi 'isä'; ToFi *mamma* 'mother' Swe 'mamma', Fi 'äiti'.

ToFi consists of several layers of older west and east Finnish dialects, as a result of several historical settler groups' linguistic sediment. This dialect impact concerns both grammar and the lexicon. The linguistic items retained from various dialects are often those that were not taken into use for the standard variety when east Finnish dialects enriched standard Finnish in the 19th century. This contributes to the impression of a high degree of nonstandardness in ToFi. There are also plenty of common grammatical structures and vocabulary in ToFi, dialectal and standard Finnish. One unique feature often referred to as typical of ToFi is the double metathesis of /h/ in some morphemes, e. g. for the illative case: *saarehen > saarheen > saahreen* '(in)to the island'.

The personal pronouns present the multidialectal origins. In the singlar they have east Fi (Karelian) *mie* 'I', *sie* 'you', and west Finnish *hän ~ hään* 'he/she', and in the plural, west Finnish *me(t)* 'we', *te(t)* 'you', *he(t)* 'they'. In oblique cases, all pronouns have west Finnish inflection. The accusative of the personal pronouns further has the west Fi *-n* case ending (east Fi and StFi have *-t*). In StFi the 3 p pl in the imperfect tense is *he anto + i + vat* 'they gave'. The morpheme *-vat* is lacking in (old) west Fi and ToFi: *het/net annoit*. In west Fi and StFi 3 p sg has no morpheme: (*hän*) *saa + ∅* 's/he gets'. ToFi and east Fi have (*hään*) *saa + pi*, with a separate morpheme *-pi* for 3 p sg after stressed syllables.

Some ToFi phonological features have been borrowed from Swedish. Two additional vowels are used in integrated loanwords containing /u/, based on the Swedish overrounded allophone of /u/, i.e. [ɯː], and [ɑː], a longer open, back *a*, based on Swedish differentiation between long and short /a/. Among consonants an allophonic stop feature, aspiration, has been added, which is lacking in FiFi. The age of a loanword may be inferred from the opposition of non-aspirated and aspirated stops: *talterikki* 'plate', StFi 'lautanen', Swe 'tallrik', is an older loan (non-aspirated /t/), whereas ToFi *tennis* 'tennis', StFi 'tennis', Swe 'tennis', is more recent (aspirated /t/). The aspiration in *tennis* reflects that it was taken from modern Swedish and not Finnish.

As an example of syntax, ToFi has finite verb forms of verbs expressing necessity (as in Swe), which in FiFi are impersonal/noncongruent:

mie   hääy + n   'I must',
1 p sg NOM + 1 p sg verb, vs.
minun   täytyy   'I must',
1 p sg GEN + 3 p sg verb.

In conclusion, Swe is evidently present at all grammatical levels, and above all in the vocabulary.

5.2. Intralinguistic portrait of Sweden Finnish

Little is *de facto* linguistically established about SweFi. Almost all FiFi varieties, nonstandard, standard, urban and rural, may be represented within the same Swedish municipality. In the early years most deviations from standard Finnish were labelled interference from Swedish. FiFi dialects have proved to contain much of the putative interference from Swedish. Typological changes in spoken FiFi further make statements of the origin of such features hazardous. SweFi has been referred to with various affective terms, such as 'vulgar, mixed, deteriorated, impure' and the like.

Also within lexicon borrowed from Swedish similar problems occur. Allophonic phonological features may distinguish a loan integrated already in FiFi from a freshly (re-) borrowed SweFi one, e.g., *viideo* Swe 'video' [ˈviːdeo], FiFi 'video' [ˈvideo]. 19th century Finnish in Finland contained thousands of cultural and every-day words borrowed from Swedish, such as *hantuuki* 'towel' Swe 'handduk', FiFi 'pyyheliina'; *universiteetti* 'university' Swe 'universitet' FiFi 'yliopisto'. Hitherto only the independent vocabulary consisting of loan translations created by the Sweden Finnish language board has been well described. Some of the recent innovations are not understood by Finland Finns, since they relate to Swedish cultural features.

Differences between first and later generations' Sweden Finnish await systematic studies. It has been observed that even those second generation speakers who show a remarkable fluency in both languages may reveal some vague grammatical and lexical usages differing from those of first generation immigrants and Finland Finns. Also in their Swedish, some quantitative differences seem to persist. The use of connectors (such as 'then; so') by bilingual Sweden Finnish children shows that variants which receive support in form and/or function from Finnish are preferred by bilingual Sweden Finnish adolescents. Such differences have little practical relevance, but may be sensed by monolinguals as undefinable and odd.

Tests of school-childrens' written language show influences from two main sources: spoken Finnish and Swedish. It is not clear what remains typical of their Finnish after primary school. Observations of spoken language in different settings by second generation adolescent speakers indicate monostylistic features and loss of complex morphology. Phonology and morphophonology seem to be acquired similarly to that of Finland Finns. Variation of sociolinguistic variants parallels that of informal language use of younger Finland Finns.

One study has described the internal variation of adults' Finnish in Sweden. Few obvious differences vis-à-vis FiFi corresponding dialects and superregional spoken Finnish have developed. Speakers seem to know what is going on in their own regional reference speech models. However, quantifications of phonological and morphological data indicated that a leveling is proceeding. Speakers of west Finnish, who traditionally have a higher over-all prestige in Finland, borrow from east Finnish dialects to a small extent and for some linguistic features. Speakers of east Finnish origin borrow from west Finnish speakers, differently from Finland Finns, and to a slightly higher extent than the west Finnish speakers borrow in the opposite direction. General characteristics observed in the process were: (1) variants being introduced by speakers into their dialect were identical to superregional variants in Finland, or, (2) they were supported by the standard variant, and (3) marked dialect features (in Finland) seem to vanish. Spoken SweFi seems to 'shadow' the FiFi development, contrary to what has been assumed. In comparison, American Finnish retains archaisms and one dialect has spread at the cost of others. Several reasons for this are probable: (1) most Sweden Finns retain regular contacts with Finland, (2) newcomers have continuously arrived from Finland, and (3) developments of change initiated already in Finland may continue in Sweden.

Extensive simplifications and generalizations of morphology and morphosyntax have not been attested among speakers of Finnish in Sweden. Simplification of the epenthetic vowel necessary to integrate loan words to Finnish morphology follows similar tracks to American Finnish. Most recent loan words with a final source language consonant receive an epenthetic vowel /i/ when integrated into Finnish morphosyntax, e.g. *rast + i* 'break', *termiin + i* 'semester' *insats + i* 'payment for condominium'. This is typical of FiFi as well as of ToFi.

In a code-switching study Sweden Finns were found to incorporate by integration to a higher extent than Swedish-Americans, who code-switch especially the terminology typical of Swedish society and non-existent in English. A widespread attitudinal resistance against code-switching seems to exist among Sweden Finns. This has been explained by a language purism tradition among Finns. The difference between Finnish- and English-speakers has been explained as a result of the long-established contacts between Swedish and Finnish and the extensive social networks among Sweden Finns. English and Swedish are genetically closer languages, but the continuous contacts between Swedish and Finnish have predisposed Finnish to incorporate Swedish linguistic items.

The question of retention of stylistic differentiation in Finnish is more complex than for Tornedal Finns, the latter of which have mainly had informal, spoken styles available as models. The restricted impact of standard Finnish on Sweden Finnish seems to become reinforced by the low degree of reading and listening to Finnish sound media among the younger. Though Finnish is both used as a medium and taught as a formal subject, it is not widely used among young people outside private domains.

The general use of standard Finnish has increased rather than decreased during the last two decades. This development, in which standard Finnish is gaining a wider field of usage, contributes to diminishing the former diglossic-like separation in function — Swedish as a High and Finnish as a Low variety — possibly for a restricted group of language users. The degree of bilingualism among Finns is increasing in parallel to this development, in which the monolingual use of Finnish is becoming more demanding. For the majority of descendants the future prospects regarding their Finnish most likely contain transmission of spoken language skills, but rather limited command of formal skills.

6. Bibliography (selected)

Airila, Martti (1912): *Äännehistoriallinen tutkimus Tornion murteesta*. Suomi 4:12, Helsinki.

Boyd, Sally (1985): *Language Survival: A study of language contact, language shift and language choice in Sweden*. Gothenburg Monographs in Linguistics 6. Department of Linguistics, University of Göteborg.

Eriksson, Riitta (1994): *Biculturalism in Upper Secondary Education*. Studies in Comparative and International Education 31. Stockholm University.

Hansegård, Nils-Erik (1968): *Tvåspråkighet eller halvspråkighet?* Stockholm.

Hansegård, Nils-Erik (1989): *Den norrbottensfinska språkfrågan*. Uppsala Multiethnic Papers 19, Uppsala.

Huss, Leena M. (1991): *Simultan tvåspråkighet i svensk–finsk kontext*. Acta Universitatis Upsaliensis. Studia Uralica Upsaliensia 21, Uppsala.

Hyltenstam, Kenneth (1989): "Svenska som andraspråk. Forskning och undervisning i Sverige". In: *Special Languages and Second Languages: Methodology and Research*, Nuopponen, A./Palmberg, R. (Eds.), 27–49. AFinLA Yearbook (1989), Vaasa.

Jaakkola, Magdalena (1983): *Finnish Immigrants in Sweden: Networks and Life Styles*. Research reports 30. Research Group for Comparative Sociology. University of Helsinki.

Lainio, Jarmo (1989): *Spoken Finnish in Urban Sweden*. Uppsala Multiethnic Papers 15. Uppsala.

Lainio, Jarmo (1993): "Sweden Finnish". In: *Immigrant Languages in Europe*, Extra, G./Verhoeven, L. (Eds.), Clevedon, Philadelphia & Adelaide, 21–53.

Loman, Bengt (Ed.) (1974): *Språk och samhälle 2. Språket i Tornedalen*, Lund.

Municio, Ingegerd (1987): "Hemspråksreformen – gräsrotsbyråkrater, makt och genomförande". In: *Nybyggarna i Sverige. Invandring och andrageneration*, Lithman, Y. (Ed.), Stockholm, 224–271.

Natchev, Eija/Sirén, Ulla (1987): *Goddag Hassan Heinonen. Förskolebarn med dubbelt minoritetsursprung*. (FoU-rapport nr 84.) FoU-byrån, Stockholm.

Peura, Markku/Skutnabb-Kangas, Tove (Eds.) (1994): *Man kan vara tråländare också ... Sverigefinnarnas väg från tystnad till kamp*. Sverigefinländarnas arkiv, Stockholm.

Popovic, Zvonimir (1993): *Finska språkets ställning i Sverige*, Norrköping.

Savolainen, Maija (1987): "Jag skäms inte för att jag är finne". In: *Nybyggarna i Sverige. Invandring och andrageneration*, Lithman, Y. (Ed.), Stockholm, 80–119.

SCB (1991): *Tema Invandrare/Focus on Immigrants*. Living conditions, Report no 69, Stockholm.

Sirén, Ulla (1991): *Minority Language Transmission in Early Childhood. Parental Intention and Language Use*. Studies in Comparative and International Education, 21. Stockholm University.

Sverigefinländarna år 2000 (1988): DEIFO. Arbetsmarknadsdepartementet, Stockholm.

Tarkianen, Kari (1990): *Finnarnas historia i Sverige 1. Inflyttarna från Finland under det gemensamma rikets tid*, Stockholm.

Tarkianen, Kari (1993): *Finnarnas historia i Sverige 2. Inflyttarna från Finland och de finska minoriteterna 1809–1944*, Helsingfors.

Thomas, George (1991): *Linguistic Purism*, London & New York.

Wande, Erling (1982): "Tornedalsfinskan och dess särdrag". In: *Finska språket i Tornedalen*, 40–73.

Wande, Erling (Ed.) (in press): *Finska varieteter utanför Finland*. Stockholm Studies in Finnish Language and Literature 8, Stockholm.

Winsa, Birger (1991): *Östligt eller västligt? Det äldsta ordförrådet i gällivarefinskan och tornedalsfinskan*. Acta Universitatis Stockholmiensis. Studia Fennica Stockholmiensia 2. Stockholm: Almqvist & Wiksell.

Winsa, Birger (1993): "Meän kieli ja torniolaaksolaisitten kakskielisyys: täälä plandathaan sprookit. *Virittäjä* 1, 3–33.

Jarmo Lainio, Stockholm (Sweden)

123. Finland

1. Geography and demography
2. Territorial history and national development
3. Politics and general cultural situation
4. Statistics and ethnoprofiles
5. Sociolinguistic situation
6. Language political situation
7. Language contacts and contact languages
8. Bibliography (selected)

1. Geography and demography

Finland is situated in Fennoscandia in the north of Europe between the Scandinavian peninsula and the lowlands of eastern Europe. Alongside Iceland it is the most northern country in the world, and lies entirely between 60 and 70 degrees latitude.

Although Finland officially is a bilingual country, it is at the same time one of the few countries in the world in which the majority language is overwhelmingly the mother tongue of the majority of the population. According to the language census for 1993, 93% of the population reported Finnish as their mother-tongue (see table 123.1, section 4). Inhabitants speaking Swedish, Sami or other languages are mainly to be found in the north (Lapland), along the coast (in the province of Ostrobothnia, in the Turku archipelago, in the province of Uusimaa where the capital Helsinki is situated, and in the Åland Isles) and in some bigger cities (→ language map A). In the inner parts of the country, especially in rural areas, contacts between people with different mother-tongues are rare.

2. Territorial history and national development

2.1. History of Finland

Finnish together with Karelian, Vepsian, Votian, Estonian and Livonian belongs to the most western branch of the Finno-Ugric languages, the languages of the Baltic Finns. Sami, the language of the Laplanders, and Hungarian are also Finno-Ugric languages as indeed are Mordvinian, Cheremis (Mari), Zyryan (Komi), Votyak (Udmurt), Ostyak (Khanty) and Vogul (Mansi). These languages are spoken by a total of some 20,000,000 people. Archeological finds would suggest that Finno-Ugric peoples have inhabited Finland and the Baltic region since shortly after the Ice Age, ca. 7,000 B.C. By 2,000–1,500 B.C. at the latest the Finns of the Baltic region had connections with both Baltic and Germanic peoples. Old Slavonic connections began 500–700 A.D. The Finnish words *pappi* ('priest'), *risti* ('cross') and *pakana* ('pagan'), so central to the Christian faith, are of Slavic origin. The earliest missionaries arrived in Finland from the east, from Orthodox Novgorod.

Finland's geographical position between Sweden and Russia has been reflected in her development as a nation and a state. In the early 11th century there was a struggle between Sweden and Novgorod over Finland and Karelia. The Swedes made three crusades into Finland: the first to the south-eastern coast in 1155, the second in 1249 to the province of Häme in the southern interior of the country, and the third to the eastern province of Karelia in 1293. The first crusade also marked the beginning of Swedish rule in Finland. The Swedish-speaking settlements on the Finnish coast date back at least thus far. The first border between Sweden and Novgorod was fixed in 1323. This border also meant that the most western Finnish tribes, the *(varsinais)suomalaiset* and *hämäläiset* came under Swedish rule, whereas Karelia was divided into two, and the central area of ancient Karelia remained on the Novgorod side of the border. This division had repercussions in religion: Those on the Swedish side became Roman Catholics, while the eastern Karelians became Christians of the Eastern Orthodox church.

At the time of the Scandinavian Union (1397–1521), Finland enjoyed a fairly independent position as a province. A rebellion led by the Swedish king Gustav Vasa removed Sweden from the League of Kalmar. On ascending to the throne Gustav Vasa devoted himself to concentrating the government on Stockholm. What was significant for Finland was that the state embarked on a deliberate policy of supporting the settlement of the province of Savo, which was directed towards the eastern and northern sides of the 1323 border. Between 1570 and 1595 Sweden and Russia engaged in a protracted border dispute in Finland. At the Peace Treaty of Täyssinä of 1595 the border between Sweden and Russia was drawn right up to the Arctic Ocean. At the Peace of Stolbova in 1617 a considerable part of Ladoga Karelia and Ingria, which had formerly belonged to Russia, was annexed to Finland. As a result of forceful attempts at Lutheranization a large part of the Orthodox Karelian population fled from the area to the interior of Russia, and the now vacant territory was settled by Lutheran Finns from Savo and the Karelian Isthmus. At the beginning of the 1700s in the Great Northern War Russia occupied the whole of Finland. While the war was still in progress Czar Peter I began work on the new Russian capital of St. Petersburg in Ingria, territory conquered from Sweden.

The fate of Finland for some considerable time to come was sealed in the war between Sweden and Russia 1808–1809. Under the terms of the Peace of Hamina of 1809 Finland was ceded to Russia. At the Diet of Porvoo held the same year Czar Alexander I assured Finland of the status of an autonomous Grand Duchy. Finland acquired her own government, central administration and national economy. The Czar undertook to uphold in Finland the laws made during the Swedish period. After the Peace of Hamina Finland also gained territory when those lands annexed to Russia in the 1700s, known as Old Finland, were reunited with the rest of Finland. At the same time the language situation in Finland changed significantly. At the end of the period of Swedish domination Finns had accounted for some 22% of the total population of the kingdom. In 1812 the population of Finland comprised some million souls, of which 87% were Finnish-speaking and 13% Swedish-speaking.

The diet convened after 1809 for the next time in 1863. In 1869 Czar Alexander II gave his assent to the order that caused parliament to convene regularly. In 1865 Finland renounced the Russian ruble and adopted the silver mark. At the end of the century, however, the position of Finland became threatened. In February 1899 Czar Nicolai II produced a manifesto according to which the laws appertaining to Finland which were of significance to imperial Russia as a whole were to be passed through the Russian legislative system. Russia's defeat at the hands of Japan, and the Great Strike, however, compelled Czar Nicolai II to abandon his manifesto in 1905. After the General Strike Finland changed in 1906 from a diet of estates to a single house of representatives with universal and uniform suffrage. A few years later came what is known as the second period of oppression. Under the terms of a law created in 1910 the legislation in all important matters pertaining to Finland was now transferred to the Russian parliament. The Russification of Finland, however, was disrupted by the outbreak of the First World War, and after the Russian Revolution the Finnish parliament approved the Finnish Declaration of Independence on 6 December, 1917.

Close on the heels of the Declaration of Independence came civil war in the winter of 1918. This ended in the defeat of the "Reds" who had espoused the socialist cause. During the 1920s and 1930s relations between Finland and Soviet Russia were tense. At the same time the inhabitants of the Åland Islands were anxious to sever their ties with Finland and annex themselves to Sweden. Sweden endeavoured to further this at the peace conference of Versailles and later at the League of Nations. In 1920 the Åland Islands declared their independence. The League of Nations in 1921 ruled that the group of islands belonged to Finland, but that Finland should ensure that they remained Swedish-speaking and allow the islanders extensive autonomy. The issue of the Åland Islands, however, continued to place a strain on relations between Sweden and Finland, and also influenced the internal strife in Finland on matters of language.

In October 1939 the Soviet Union issued demands as to territorial claims on areas of the Karelian Isthmus. When Finland refused to comply with such demands the Soviet Union declared war on Finland in November of that year. At the Peace of Moscow in March 1940 Finland ceded to the Soviet Union the Karelian Isthmus in its entirety, including the city of Viipuri, and also areas in the north of Finland. When Germany attacked the Soviet Union in 1941, partly by way of Finland, Finland was once again drawn into war. Finnish troops retook the areas ceded at the Peace of Moscow and advanced to eastern Karelia. In June 1944 the Soviet Army mounted a major offensive against the Finns. A truce was called in September 1944. Under the terms of the truce Finland ceded to the Soviet Union once again the areas agreed in the Peace of Moscow, and also Petsamo on the Arctic Ocean. The population of the ceded territories, a total of 420,000 persons moved *en masse* to be within the new boundaries of Finland. Since these wars Finnish foreign policy has been characterized by the effort to avoid conflict and to remain neutral.

2.2. National development and position of the Finnish language at different periods

In the 1300s and 1400s the uniting force of Finland was the Diocese of Turku, which at that time comprised the entire country. Although Latin was the language of the Roman Catholic church, by 1400 at the latest Finnish was also used in certain religious rites. It would appear that questions of language did not cause undue strife in the Middle Ages. In the 1500s the Finnish nobility was still using its own mother tongue. However, the concentration of administrative power in Stockholm, which began in the 1600s, had its effect in Finland. The language of administration was now Swedish. Simultaneously increasing numbers of administrative personnel speaking only Swedish were sent from Sweden to the Finnish provinces. There was as yet no overt Swedification of Finland.

During the 1500s the Nordic countries took unto themselves the Reformation in its Lutheran form. The reformation signalled the beginning of literature in the vernacular even in those countries where no medieval literary tradition existed. The first book in Finnish, the ABC book of Mikael Agricola, appeared in either 1542 or 1543. A Finnish translation of the New Testament in the name of Mikael Agricola appeared in 1548, and the whole Bible was published in Finnish in 1642. Hereafter and right up to the time of the end of Swedish domination the literature printed in the Finnish language was predominantly of a religious nature. Thus church and state came into a conflict of principles in their attitudes to the Finnish language. The position of the Swedish language in the fields of state administration, the law, the military and school grew stronger. The church, on the other hand, continued to be the champion of the Finnish language right up to the end of Swedish domination.

After the end of the 1600s Swedification tightened its grip on Finland. Many leading Swedish officials openly demanded the Swedification of Finland, supporting their claims with reasons of advantageousness. It was pointed out that it was impossible for Swedes to move to Finland because of the language, and that national unity demanded that the Finns adopt the Swedish language. Officially fear of Russia precluded any particularly radical Swedification measures. Swedification advanced in Finland in the 1700s on many fronts. Because a knowledge of Swedish was a prerequisite to professional advancement in the administration the Finnish gentry became almost completely Swedified in the 1700s. They were followed by the bourgeoisie. Thus two highly significant estates were completely Swedified.

The clergy, by contrast, remained Finnish-speaking. The church adhered consistently to the requirement that priests should have a knowledge of Finnish. In addition, other literature of an enlightening nature intended for the populace began to be published. The first Finnish newspaper was founded in 1776, but the following year it ceased to come out. As literacy spread, the more enlightened farmers of the Finnish peasantry repeatedly demanded of parliament in Stockholm that those appointed to administrational posts in the Finnish-speaking areas of Finland have a knowledge of the language so that the Finns could use their own language in their dealings with the officials. They also demanded arrangements for interpreting and translating in parliamentary proceedings.

In the parliament in Stockholm the position of the Finnish language was much discussed in the years 1746–1747, but the discussion did not progress to concrete action. Officialdom dared not risk embarking on radical measures for Swedification, but it would not comply with the Finns' demands. By the end of the 1700s language questions divided the Finns into two camps. The gentry and the bourgeoisie were completely Swedified, while the peasants and priests had retained their Finnish language. This division continued into the 1800s and was still apparent at the diet of 1897.

Although in the new Grand Duchy language conditions had changed to the clear advantage of Finnish, the Finnish requested at the diet of Porvoo in 1809 that Swedish be confirmed as the sole official language of the country. And so it became. During the period of autonomy the first goal was to create a national identity. It was for the Finns to demonstrate to the Czar their willingness to break away from Sweden. There was, however, the fear of Russification. In the course of the 1810s the political tenet crystallized into the slogan "We are not Swedes, we do not wish to become Russians, let us therefore be Finns!" In the first half of the nineteenth century national romantic thinking was reflected in a search for a Finnish identity. Among other things, a more systematic effort was made to collect Finnish folk poetry. In

1835 Elias Lönnrot published the *Kalevala*, which was based on the material collected. The influence of the *Kalevala* in the creation of a Finnish identity was decisive both within Finland and outside her boundaries.

As early as 1810 there was also writing which emphasized the significance of the Finnish language as the language of the majority. Demands were made that the élite of the country should also be able to speak Finnish. However, the actual age of national language and politics began only in the 1840s when J. V. Snellman became active. His national policy was greatly influenced by the thinking of Friedrich Hegel. Snellman claimed that the existence of a nation is justified only if its culture is alive. His slogan was "Culture for the nation and nationalism for the cultivated class!" Although Snellman's desire was for a monolingual Finland he demanded no abrupt changes. First, the Swedish-speaking élite were to become bilingual, while a new élite was to bred up out of the Finnish nation. Instead of a purely Swedish school system Snellman called for bilingual schools.

Snellman's programme has been described as *cultural fennomania*. He did not, however, insist on a rapid change in the official position of the Finnish language. *Political fennomania* with its more extreme views and demands only came into being in the 1850s. Its adherents demanded that the Finnish language and the Finnish speakers in the nation be rapidly assured of the same social rights as had the Swedish speakers. Instead of bilingual schools Finland was to have monolingual Finnish schools. The debate which raged in the 1850s about the Finnish grammar schools also marked the beginning of a political language struggle in Finland. For the Fennomanics the outcome was fortuitous; The first Finnish grammar school was founded in the town of Jyväskylä in 1858.

Next came the demand that the Finnish language be accorded official status. At the beginning of the 1860s the time appeared to be ripe for this. During the Crimean War the Finns had remained loyal to the Czar. Alexander II expressed his gratitude for this by allowing the diet to be convened in 1863. During the preparatory stage the issue of the position of the Finnish language came to the fore. The discussion centred particularly on the language to be used in the lawcourts. Although the committee of officials who worked on the question deemed the Finnish language to be not yet far enough developed to be used in the courts, Alexander reached a different decision. He issued a decree in 1863 to the effect that after a 20-year transitional period Finnish was to be accepted alongside Swedish as an official language in matters pertaining to Finns. Swedish was, however, still the only official language of the country, and the imperial decree did not extend to the language used in municipal government. Right until the turn of the century the position of Swedish remained strong, especially in the urban areas.

In second half of the last century the language question was a major bone of contention. The Fennomanics were opposed by the most ardent supporters of Swedish, the *Svekomanics*. The Fennomanic programme was one nation – one language. Their opponents demanded two nations – two languages. However, in both factions there existed a third, more compromising line calling for one nation – two languages. At first the balance tipped in favour of the supporters of Swedish, but at a Swedish party political meeting held at the end of the century the goal was for the preservation of Swedish in a position equal to Finnish. The issue was no longer that of recognising Finnish as being equal to Swedish, but rather of whether it was at all possible to maintain Swedish in an equal position with Finnish.

At the diet of 1897 there was heated debate as to the position of Finnish and Swedish in officialdom and in those municipalities with both languages. The diet was unable to reach a decision for the gentry and the bourgeoisie supported Swedish while the clergy and the peasantry supported the claims of the Fennomanics. The matter was laid before Czar Nicolai II, who in 1900 issued a decree on language according to which Russian was to be the language of higher officialdom. The ultimate end here was Russification. However, the General Strike which broke out in Russia in 1905 compelled the Czar to back down. The statute on language of 1906 restored the situation to what it had been in 1900. With the decrease in pressure from Russian the conflict between Swedish and Finnish flared up again.

The question of language became a major issue in the first parliamentary election of 1906. The dialogue was not, however, between Finnish and Swedish, but between two Finnish parties. Of these, the so-called "old Finns" were the ideological heirs of political Fennomania. Their goal was to be a "Finnish

Finland". The so-called "young Finns" had adopted a liberal view of society. This entailed the development of Finland's language conditions along bilingual lines. Swedish was to be recognized as a second domestic language even in Finnish-speaking Finland alongside the main national language, namely Finnish. The principles originating with these two factions continued to make themselves felt in the discussion on language held in the earliest days of Finnish independence.

After independence in 1917 speakers of Swedish felt that their position and future was threatened. This threat was accentuated by the Finns' conception of a national Finnish state. The idea had been evinced in Sweden as early as the 1910s that the Swedish-speakers resident in Finland were part of the Swedish nation. This view, where the Swedish-speaking population in Finland was called the eastern Swedes, fuelled the Swedish nationalist idea of setting up autonomous Swedish-speaking areas within Finland. As there was a desire for reconciliation in the Finnish faction the language issue was resolved in the constitution arrived at in 1919. Swedish was recognised as the second national language in Finland. In return the Swedish speakers relinquished all claim to autonomous Swedish-speaking areas on the Finnish mainland. The question of the Åland Islands was settled through separate legislation ensuring that this region retained considerable autonomy. The actual legislation which to this day governs the position and relation of the Finnish and Swedish languages is the Language Act of 1922.

The legislation undeniably took the edge off Swedish separatism and attempts at administrational isolation, but some speakers of Finnish believed that the law was over-generous to the Swedish-speakers. It was such individuals who formed the "Movement of the genuine Finns" in 1922 and declared that their goal was a monolingual Finnish state. The adherents of the movement took particular exception to the obligation to study Swedish in Finnish grammar schools and the language statute referring to the University of Helsinki. Although the "genuine Finns" did not actually form a political party of their own, their influence in Finnish domestic policy in the 1920s and 1930s was considerable. Their supporters were to be found notably in two important right-wing parties, the agrarian party and the conservative party. The social democrats did not consider language questions to be of any great significance. Towards the end of the 1930s those in charge of foreign policy endeavoured to improve relations with Sweden, thus divisive quarrels over language were best abandoned. The outbreak of the Second World War sent differences over language into oblivion in September 1939.

2.3. Principles for the further development of the Finnish language (1800–)

The implementation of the Fennomanic programme on language policy would not have been possible in the 1800s without a deliberate endeavour to develop the Finnish language. During the period of domination by Sweden secular writing consisted principally of booklets intended to enlighten the peasantry. There was a complete absence of literary writing, and legal language was decidedly underdeveloped. Those who researched the Finnish language in the 1800s were well aware that it had not reached the stage of development which would enable it to fulfill European requirements as a language of administration, teaching and culture.

Certain basic developmental trends in the work to upgrade the Finnish language can be discerned. Of these the most significant are those relating to the grammar, the vernacular and purism. These trends seldom surfaced entirely separately. The same cultivator of the language might call for different principles in different places. Moreover, the attitudes of the advocates of correctness varied when they were concerned with the written or spoken mode.

The notion of what was grammatical rested on the belief that there were comprehensive, "eternal" rules governing the life of the language. On the basis of these laws the researcher could direct and improve the language. The doctrine of the vernacular rested on what speakers of the language actually said. This reached its zenith in the 1820s and 1830s when an attempt was made to improve the old orthography of Finnish dating from the days of Swedish domination. The most significant of the prescriptive developmental trends was that relating to purism. It was directly connected to Snellman's Finnish national ideology. The aim on the one hand was to purge Finnish of all contamination from other languages, and on the other to make a cultural language. At the end of the nineteenth century the guiding principle for the further development of the Finnish language crystallized into a strict grammatical-purist view. In practice it meant that all words of foreign origin and dialect expressions were to be removed from the written language.

For the first fifty years of the nineteenth century the forms of the spoken language had consisted almost exclusively of dialects. The need to develop a spoken language suitable for the use of the cultivated class had been acknowledged at the beginning of the century. Until mid-century the view persisted that even cultured Finns should speak the dialect of their own region. Although in the development of the written language the grammar-purist principle had firmly entrenched itself by the 1850s, the course prescribed for the spoken language was still dominated by more liberal vernacular principles. The turning point was reached in 1863, when Finnish was accepted as a language of administration. At about the same time it began to be used increasingly as a language of instruction. Furthermore, the beginning of the 1860s saw the rise of the first cultivated homes where Finnish was used. There thus emerged a more concrete need for the development of both an official public language and for an unofficial spoken language suitable for cultivated speakers.

The solution arrived at was unusual but understandable in the light of the prevailing conditions in Finland. A deliberate initiative was taken so speak standard Finnish in official situations and in cultivated homes. One major factor in this was that in the capital there was no Finnish language background. Helsinki had been founded in a Swedish-speaking area. Moreover, many of the younger generation of cultivated Finns came from Swedish-speaking homes. They acquired their Finnish through textbooks and grammars, and this was the written variety. The third and deeper-going reason was the reservation of the cultivators of the language about dialect features in the written language. Because such were not to be tolerated in the written mode, they should also not occur in cultured speech. Thus the strict model of grammar-purism gained a firm hold in the spoken language. The standard language and the written language thus attained in spoken Finnish a superior position over the dialects. This was much apparent in the mother tongue teaching at school. One of the central aims was set in the 1900s as that of purging pupils' spoken and written language of dialect features.

3. Politics and general cultural situation

During the period of autonomy the quarrel between Fennomanics and Svekomanics had focussed on the language of the people of rank in particular. The Fennomanics wished to make the cultured classes Finnish-speaking, while the Svekomanics sought to keep the same people Swedish-speaking. In this the school system was in a crucial position. The development of a Finnish school system, however, was hampered by a shortage of qualified teachers. Thus a Finnish practice school was founded in Helsinki in 1867, but this was transferred in 1871 some 100 km inland to the town of Hämeenlinna at the insistence of the Swedish-speakers. In 1872 a collection was held throughout Finland with a view to founding in Helsinki a new Finnish grammar school. Some 100,000 individuals contributed to this, and on the proceeds this school began to function in Helsinki in 1873.

By the mid 1880s there were already 32 Finnish-language schools, and in the academic year 1877−1878 the percentage of pupils enrolled in Finnish schools was 24.4%. In the academic year 1895−1896 over half, 52.3% of all grammar school pupils were enrolled at Finnish schools. During the three-year period 1867−1870, of the 451 students enrolled at the University of Helsinki 94.5% had come from Swedish-language schools and 5.5% from Finnish-language schools. During the period 1888−1890 the proportion of those from Finnish schools was 50.4%, thus exceeding the number matriculating from Swedish schools. The data on language of instruction, however, do not yield very precise information as to what the students' mother tongue may have been, as a considerable proportion of the pupils at Finnish schools were from Swedish-speaking homes. For the academic year 1908−1909 almost three quarters (72.6%) were Finnish-speakers. This ratio remained roughly the same in the following decades.

The question as to the language of instruction in Finland's only university, which was moved to Helsinki from Turku in 1828, was not initially particularly problematic. The language of instruction at the university was Latin or then "some modern language understood by all". The regulation favoured Swedish, but also admitted the possibility of using Finnish as a lecturing language. A chair in the Finnish language was created in the University of Helsinki in 1850, and the first doctoral dissertation written in Finnish was examined in 1858. After 1872 an active knowledge of Finnish was required of those teaching in the theological and legal faculties and also of the professor of educational science. After 1894 all those applying for teaching posts at the university were required to demonstrate their ability to use Finnish, written and oral. At the diet of 1907 the "old Finns" made a proposal that the university be made completely Finnish. The proposal, however, had no chances of being adopted. The conflict over language issues in the University of Helsinki flared up again in the 1920s. In 1937, however, a compromise was arrived at. Under the terms of the legislation on the university enacted at that time Finnish was to be the only administrative language of the University of Helsinki, but 15 chairs were left to the Swedish-speakers. Furthermore, Swedish-speaking students were given the right to use Swedish in exercises and in oral and written examinations.

During the period of autonomy other foundations for a Finnish culture were laid. In 1834 the Finnish Literary Society was founded with the objective of developing the Finnish language and Finnish literature and of collecting Finnish folk tradition. The first significant Finnish author was Aleksis Kivi (1834–1872), whose works still rank among Finnish classics. The first Finnish theatre was founded in 1872. In 1850 there were only two Finnish newspapers and periodicals. In 1890 this number had risen to 36 newspapers and 50 periodicals. The oldest Finnish scientific societies are the Society for the Domestic Language (1876) and the Finno-Ugric Society (1886), whose objectives were the research and cultivation of Finnish and related languages. The Finnish Academy of Science was founded in 1908. Even until the 1930s, however, financial support for Finnish scientific and cultural life was scant. Among Finnish-speakers there were no foundations such as there were among Swedish-speakers. The most significant and enduring achievement in the "Movement of the genuine Finns" was the Finnish Cultural Fund, in 1937.

4. Statistics and ethnoprofiles

In 1993 the population of Finland was some 5,055,000. Of these approximately 93% spoke Finnish as their mother tongue (see Table 23.1). In October 1993 there were altogether 53,545 foreign nationals resident in Finland. At the end of 1991 there were 37,539 foreign nationals, whereas the corresponding figure for 1985 was only 16,765. This increase stems from the dissolution of the Soviet Union and the independence of the Baltic coutries. A considerable proportion of these foreign nationals have, however, Finnish as their mother tongue (18%) or then Swedish (10%). Such individuals are generally known as returnees who have not taken Finnish citizenship. They are chiefly from Sweden, Russia and Estonia.

The majority of those moving recently to Finland are either refugees or asylum seekers. Since 1989 the quota has been 500 per year. In October 1993 there were 6,400 refugees living in Finland, distributed over 111 municipalities throughout the country. Since the beginning of the 1990s the number of asylum seekers in Finland has grown rapidly. In 1988 there were only 64, while in 1992 there were 3,634. The largest group of refugees and asylum seekers originate from Somalia (2,559), Jugoslavia (1,957) and Vietnam (1,340).

At the beginning of 1993 almost 100 languages were spoken in Finland. Many of these, however, by a very small number of speakers. Table 123.1 provides an overview of those languages with at least 100 speakers in Finland on 1. 1. 1993.

The Sami are the indigenous people of Finland. There are at present in Finland some 6,000 ethnic Sami, of whom an estimated two thirds speak the Sami language. A total of 1,729 individuals have reported Sami as being their mother tongue. (For further information on the Sami see Pekka Sammallahti.) The Swedish-speaking Finns constitute Finland's largest language minority. (For further information see Marika Tandefelt.) The language rights of both groups are protected by law (see section 6). The number of those using sign language is not included in Table 123.1. They number some 5,000.

The other significant old minority groups in Finland include Romanies, Russians, Germans, Jews and Tartars. The language rights of these people are not specifically protected by law. They have assimilated to a considerable extent with Finnish- and Swedish-speakers. The emergence of such minorities as the Russians, Jews and Tartars in Finland relates to Finland's changed position: As an autonomous Grand Duchy Finland was for over 100 years part of the multi-ethnic Russian em-

Table 123.1: Population of Finland by language

Language	Population
Finnish	4 712 920
Swedish	296 435
Russian	9 335
Estonian	5 879
English	4 519
German	2 505
Vietnamese	2 146
Arabic	2 005
Somali	1 913
Sami	1 729
Chinese	1 500
Turkish	1 350
Spanish	1 096
Polish	1 070
French	813
Hungarian	687
Persian	666
Kurd	570
Thai	502
Italian	468
Norwegian	431
Bulgarian	357
Greek	342
Japanese	337
Dutch	333
Danish	296
Roumanian	279
Tagalog	269
Serbian	261
Bengali	254
Portuguese	230
Hebrew	222
Czech	203
Hindi	193
Punjabi	178
Albanian	174
Amharic	152
Urdu	131
Total	5 054 438

pire. What was decisive in the emergence of minorities was the Czar's edict of 1858 according to which all those who had served with the imperial army in Finland were entitled to remain in Finland with their families. In the 1800s the non-Finnish-speaking minorities in Finland tended to be concentrated in the cities, of which Viipuri and Helsinki were the most polyglot.

The Romanies (previously referred to as Gypsies) mostly came to Finland via Sweden, although some may have come via Russia. The oldest archive information on Romanies in Finland dates back to the 1500s. Their number in Finland is not great. Official statistics in 1895 put it at 1,551. Nowadays their estimated number is 6,000. The Finnish Romanies call themselves *kaale* (the word *kaale* goes back to the Romany adjective *kaló* 'black'). When speaking Finnish, they use either this word or the Finnish adjective *tumma* 'dark' of themselves. The most widespread Finnish word for Gypsy is *mustalainen* (derived from the Finnish word *musta* 'black'). Recently the term *romani* has become more common, and it is also used in official Finnish publications.

Right up to the present day the Romanies in Finland have preserved their original culture and habits, which is clearly seen in the traditional clothing they continue to use. The main language of the Romanies in Finland is Finnish. The Romany language spoken in Finland contains loanwords from both Finnish and Swedish. The phonology shows assimilation, but the morphology of Finnish Romany has preserved many old characteristics. At the end of the last century practically all the Romanies living in Finland had some knowledge of the Romany language. In the 1950s some 80% of the Romanies in Finland used only or mostly Finnish as their language of conversation. In 1954 some 70% of adult Romanies still knew the Romany language. However, it was used chiefly as a secret language. After this time the decline in the knowledge and use of Romany has been surprisingly rapid. This is attributed to its low prestige and the lack of teaching in school. Since the end of the 1980s, however, a conscious effort has been made in various directions to revive the Romany language: Instruction in the language is now being offered to Romany children at school. To promote material and spiritual conditions the Gypsy Mission was founded in 1904, and alongside it in 1967 the Finnish Gypsy Union. Since 1971 the Finnish Gypsy Union has published *Romano Boodos*, a magazine which includes articles written in Romany. As a written language, however, Finnish Romany is not firmly established.

At the beginning of this century there were some 1,000 Jews in Finland. They were registered with two Jewish congregations, in Helsinki and Turku. The earliest information on Jews in Finland goes back to the 1790s. Until 1858 there was legislation still in force from the days of Swedish rule forbidding Jews to settle in the Finnish cities. The first Jewish soldiers arrived in Finland with the imperial Russian army in the 1830s. In 1869 permission was granted to the Jews to engage in small-scale commerce in the Finnish cities.

The question of the national rights of Jews rose to prominence in the Finnish diet of 1872. At that time there were some 500 Jews in Finland. In 1890 Jews in Finland numbered rather more than 1,000. Numbers reached their peak in the 1930s. At that time there were some 1,300 Jews resident in Helsinki, with a further 500 in Turku and Viipuri. In 1918 they were granted citizens' rights.

The Jews who came with the imperial army to Finland originated in Russia, Lithuania and Poland. Their mother tongue was Yiddish. The men had also acquired some knowledge of spoken Russian in the army. The women and those children who were born in Finland knew less Yiddish. The Jews in Finland have never used Yiddish as their official language. Preaching in the synagogue has, however, sometimes been done in Yiddish. There have been indications of an attempt to change from Yiddish to the majority national language around the turn of the century. In Helsinki and Turku the Jews took to speaking Swedish, and in Viipuri to speaking Finnish. In 1918 a Jewish school was founded in Helsinki. Until 1933 the language of instruction was Swedish. Both Swedish and Finnish were used until 1942. Since then the school has been entirely Finnish-speaking. Hebrew is taught as an extra language. Finnish Jews over 60 years old are mostly bilingual in that they have Swedish as their first language. Jews between the ages of 40 and 60 are also bilingual, but their first language is Finnish. Jews under the age of 40 have largely become Finnish. Hebrew has appeared as a new mother tongue in the Jewish communities in Helsinki and Turku. It is spoken by younger Jews from Israel who have married in Finland.

Among the Russian troops placed in Finland after the 1830s there were also Tartars. However they did not remain in Finland when their term of service expired. The arrival of Tartar merchants in Finland began in the 1880s. Merchants who had come from the Kazan region to St. Petersburg began to infiltrate into Finland, initially Viipuri, but later the entire southern region. This immigration of Tartar merchants continued until 1917 and even later, both legally and illegally. The continuous nature of this immigration and the long period over which it took place were conducive to the preservation of both Tartar culture and language. Contacts with the Kazan region continue to flourish to this day. The Finnish law of 1925 on the freedom of religion made it possible to establish an Islamic congregation in Helsinki. A second congregation was established in the city of Tampere in 1943. Combined membership of these at the beginning of the century totalled 940. Efforts have been made to ensure that the congregations remain under Tartar control. Although other Muslims such as Arabs, Pakistanis and Iranians are entitled to take part in worship, they are not included in the congregation. The majority of the Finnish Tartars, some 700 souls, are concentrated in the Helsinki area.

The Finnish Tartars use several names to describe themselves – Tartars, Mishartartars, Finnish Turks, Northern Turks – these names are indicative of the identity problem of these people. Some see themselves as ethnic Tartars by origin, others have embraced the pan-Turkish ideology. The language is a Mishari Dialect of the Volga or Kazan. It is used in both the written and spoken modes. The Tartars' second language is most frequently Finnish. Since the early years of this century there has been a certain amount of teaching at school of the Tartar language. Between 1948 and 1969 a Finnish-Turkish junior school of four classes operated in Helsinki, and this was the first Tartar school in the West. Disputes involving the Turkish and Tartar languages, however, caused a reduction in the number of pupils and resulted in the closing of the school. Since the 1920s the Finnish Tartars have been active in publishing in their own language, initially only in Arabic letters, but subsequently in the 1930s in the Roman letters of modern Turkey. The teaching of children changed to Roman letters in the 1960s. Differences of opinion as to the letters to be adopted have been detrimental to the development of the written language, and it has not been possible to arrive at a consistent orthographic norm.

The Russians in Finland are of heterogenous origin. Diachronically three phases may be discerned: the minority originating from the days of autonomy, *emigrés* who remained in Finland after the Russian Revolution, and Russians who have immigrated to Finland in recent years. The first Russian minorities came into being in Old Finland in the 1700s. Merchants and businessmen moved to Viipuri and other towns in eastern Finland, mostly from the north of Russia. In the 1720s a considerable number of Russian serfs were transported to the village of Kyyrölä on the

Karelian Isthmus. In 1812, when Old Finland was united with the rest of Finland all the Russians in the area were granted full citizenship. Russian merchants subsequently began to move to other parts of the country, most notably to Helsinki. In 1850 some 40% of the Helsinki merchants were Russians. Moreover, Russian administrative personnel moved to Finland, likewise clergymen and military personnel and the camp-followers in the wake of the army.

In Helsinki in 1890 there were 3,878 Russians (12.1% of the population). The other focal point for Russians was the city of Viipuri, where in 1870 there were 3,257 (24.2% of the population). Throughout the period of autonomy Russian military divisions were stationed in Finland. In 1917 military personnel in Finland totalled 125,000. After the Russian Revolution there was an influx of people mostly from St. Petersburg. This peaked in 1921–1922, when their number was estimated at 20,000. In 1930 there were 7,682 Russian immigrants in Finland with Nansen passes, and the number of Russian-speaking Finnish citizens was 8,216. The majority of the immigrants also settled in the Helsinki and Viipuri areas.

By the 1870s many of the old Russian merchant families had begun to assimilate with the Swedish-speakers. They later also began to merge with the Finnish-speaking majority. Between 1940 and 1960 the number of Russians in Finland sank from 7,210 to 2,752. Those who had been born before the Second World War knew Russian, and those who were born after it did not. Another reason for the acceleration of assimilation was the loss of the old Russian centres on the Karelian Isthmus and in Viipuri. Yet another reason was fear of Russia. Indeed, Russia demanded that Finland hand over the leading figures of certain emigrant organizations. In recent decades a new type of Russian has immigrated increasingly to Finland. The majority of these are women who have married Finnish men working in the Soviet Union or Russia. At the beginning of 1993 there were 9,335 Russian-speakers in Finland, of whom 1,584 had acquired Finnish citizenship.

Until the late 1930s the Russian Orthodox congregation and Russian schools preserved Russian culture. The Russians in the area of Old Finland had eastern Orthodox congregations ever since the 1700s. The orthodox congregation in Helsinki came into being in 1808. During the period of autonomy the congregation was exclusively Russian-speaking. Nowadays it is bilingual. In the period of autonomy there were several Russian schools. In the 1920s and 1930s the *emigrés* had their own Russian schools which adhered to the Russian curriculum with an obligatory addition of 1–2 hours of Finnish per week. The last of the old Russian schools closed down in Helsinki in the 1950s due to lack of pupils. As one manifestation of Finnish-Russian postwar relations a Finnish-Russian school was founded in Helsinki in 1956 with the objective of teaching those Finnish pupils who wished to learn Russian at an early age.

The oldest roots of the German minority in Finland can be traced back to the days of the Hanseatic League. There were Germans living permanently in Viipuri ever since the turn of the 1500s and 1600s. The majority of the Germans in Viipuri, and later also in Helsinki originated from the north German commercial centres such as Lübeck and Hamburg. The German congregation in Viipuri was founded in 1743. Church services in German were first held in Helsinki in 1838. The German Lutheran congregation in Helsinki was founded in 1858. In 1870 there were 562 German-speaking residents in Helsinki (1.8% of the population of the city). Of these over half were of the gentry. As early as the 1800s the majority of the Germans took Swedish as their second language. The Germans were highly influential in Finnish economic life, notably in the further development of trade and commerce. The *Deutsche Schule* of Helsinki was founded in 1881. Today the school is bilingual. In 1993 there were 2,505 German-speaking residents in Finland, of whom 996 were Finnish citizens.

In recent years immigration to Finland has increased manifold. For those moving to Finland teaching in a second language has been organized. This second language has been Finnish or Swedish, depending on where the individual is settling. The majority of those arriving study Finnish as a second language. Immigrants are in unequal positions as regards instruction in Finnish. For refugees and asylum-seekers a fair amount of Finnish instruction is guaranteed, while other groups are compelled to obtain their studies largely at their own expense. Among the instruction given to adult refugees some 630–900 hours of Finnish has generally been included. For children intensive teaching in Finnish in their own groups is organized over a period of six months after which they are placed according to age and ability in classes together with Finnish children. They also receive a certain amount of coaching in Finnish. Children of all immigrant groups are entitled to teaching in their own mother tongue. In 1993 this teaching comprised one hour per week instead of the two hours which had previously been allotted. From 1994 the amount will be raised up to two or three hours again. In 1992 teaching was given in a total of 35 languages as the mother tongue. In the future curriculum Finnish as a second language and mother tongue of non-Finnish children will be taught in the comprehensive school (in Finland between ages 7–18). The objective is to further functional bilingualism. These new curricula are to be implemented as of autumn 1994.

5. Sociolinguistic situation

The attitude to the various forms of Finnish is characterized in the great respect in which the standard variety is held. This attitude originates in the 1800s when the standard variety was especially appreciated. The standard variety has been seen as the "good" and "correct" one, while the dialects, the urban colloquial variety and most notably slang have been seen as "bad" or "incorrect" language. The colloquial language used on radio and television in particular has frequently been the object of criticism.

Regional dialects, with fairly few changes, survived until the end of the 1930s. The main reason for this was that Finland was for a long time a primarily rural country. The loss of territory as a result of the Second World War and the increasing internal migration in the 1950s had the effect of reducing the likelihood that the old dialects would survive. Increased education and the ever-growing influence of the mass media, radio and television have also caused dialects throughout the country to draw nearer to the standard variety. Recent decades have seen the emergence of sociolects in Finland, but not nearly to such an extent as in the case of England. It is rather a matter of different urban colloquial varieties characterized by combinations of different components from the regional dialects, from the written and standard varieties. Formerly the most significant extra-linguistic parameters with bearing on colloquial speech were education and profession, and to some extent gender. Women with an academic education in particular spoke in a manner close to the written standard. Nowadays the most significant variable in colloquial speech is age.

The Finnish dialects have usually been divided into eight main groups. Differences between dialects are apparent chiefly in phonological and morphological features and in lexis. The differences are not so great as to render mutual comprehension impossible. The main dialectal divisions correspond to a considerable extent to the historical tribal divisions. Thus the dialects and those who speak them lend themselves to stereotyping. The people of Häme are said to be slow, the northerners are said to be level-headed and dignified, while the south-eastern (Finnish Karelian) people are said to be lively and conceivably unreliable. The dialects of Savo differ phonologically clearly from the standard variety, and through the 1900s a certain comic aspect has been attached to them, which has been exploited in Finnish plays and films. Those with the greatest reservations about dialect are the inhabitants of Helsinki, who associate dialect speech with rusticity. Elsewhere in Finland the dialects enjoy greater appreciation, while attitudes to urbanity and Helsinki dwellers are somewhat negative.

Language attitudes have also been coloured by the disputes between language groups. At the time when the language struggle between Finnish and Swedish was at its most intense there were frequent large-scale pitched battles between the sons of Finnish-speaking and Swedish-speaking gentlefolk. The Finnish-speaking schoolboys dubbed the Swedish-speakers *Sventuppe* ("Swedish roosters"), while the Swedish-speakers referred to the Finnish-speakers as *Finnkollo* ("stupid Finns"). At the beginning of the 1900s the fanatical Swedish press referred to the Finns as *Mongols*. The Finnish press in the 1920s used for the Swedish-speakers the pejorative term *Hurrit*. In recent years the term has found its way into the Swedish-speakers' own usage. Here it has acquired a distinctly positive connotation. For Finnish-speakers the term *hurri* may now refer to Swedish-speakers from Sweden, here it is still pejorative. Nowadays Swedish-speakers might call Finns *Ugrics*. At no point, however, has the dispute between speakers of the two languages pervaded the working classes. Working class speakers of the two languages lived side by side in the same apartment blocks and their children played together.

Relations with Russia were good until the end of the period of autonomy. However, the policy of oppression adopted by the Russians soon led to the growth of anti-Russian feeling, which manifested itself in tension between the language communities. Fights between schoolboys were common. Russians were dubbed *Ryssä* and attitudes were antagonistic. Anti-Russian feeling persisted into the 1950s, and this was of significance in the efforts of the Russian community to assimilate into Finnish society. Attitudes to other language communities, Jews and Tartars varied depending on the degree to which they were seen as rivals of the small businessmen of the Finnish- and Swedish-speaking communities. From the 1960s to the 1980s ethnic stereotypes in Finland remained very much beneath the surface. However, the rapid increase in the number of asylum seekers and refugees in the late 1980s has caused attitudes towards foreigners to become more tense. This has been exacerbated by the present economic recession in Finland which is significantly affecting the Finns' standard of living.

6. Language political situation

In Finland Finnish and Swedish stand on an equal footing as official languages. Their position is defined in the Finnish Constitution Act of 1919 and in the Language Act of 1922. Moreover, the position of the Sami language and the rights of the Sami people to use their own language have been defined in a separate law which came into force in 1922. (For further information see Pekka Sammallahti.)

The terms of § 14 of the Finnish constitution ensure the right of Finnish citizens to use their own mother tongue, either Finnish or Swedish, when conducting their own affairs in the lawcourts and with administrative officials. Laws and statutes, governmental proposals to parliament and parliamentary responses, proposals and other documents addressed to the government are to be written in both Finnish and Swedish. The state is further required to satisfy the cultural and economic needs of both the Finnish and Swedish language communities on the same principles. Those called up for military service also have the right to serve using their own mother tongue.

The Language Act of 1922 lays down in detail how the principles referred to in the constitution shall be applied. The law on language is to be applied to the courts of justice and civil servants, to municipal government and to the congregations of the evangelical Lutheran church. The law is not valid in the Åland Islands, whose exceptional position as regards language is provided for in the legislation on provincial self-government. The Language Act of 1922 reconciles two principles: the personal and the territorial principle. The personal principle ensures that every Finnish citizen has the right to use his or her own language, Finnish or Swedish, when conducting his or her own affairs in the courts of law or with other civil servants. This right extends throughout Finland.

The territorial principle involves the municipal level. The rights of inhabitants in relation to the local government depend on the linguistic status of the municipality. The municipality is bilingual if the Finnish- or Swedish-speaking minority exceeds 8% of the population or if there are over 3,000 speakers of the minority language. In respect of language classification the municipalities are divided into four groups: monolingual Finnish (399 in 1990), monolingual Swedish (26 including 16 in the Åland Islands), bilingual with Finnish the majority language (17), bilingual with Swedish the majority language (22). The language classification in the municipality determines what services (e. g. children's day care, schools, libraries, health care and social services) the municipality is to provide. The language classification is reviewed every ten years. Statistics are prepared on the basis of what the inhabitants have reported as being their mother tongue in the census. It should be noted that in a census Finnish citizens only give one language as their mother tongue. Thus it is not possible to draw conclusions from the census as to individual bilingualism in Finland.

In order to implement the terms of the legislation on language in Finland the language ability required of civil servants in central and local government are specifically defined. Several different standards are distinguished, the lowest being "ability to understand the minority language" and the highest being "perfect oral and written abilities". The higher the official position the more stringent the demands as to linguistic ability. The applicant must pass official language tests for the official post in order to be considered a competent applicant. However, once passed, a language proficiency test remains valid.

Since 1981 a Nordic language agreement ensures the rights of citizens of the Nordic countries (Finland, Sweden, Norway, Denmark and Iceland) to use their own language in all the Nordic countries when dealing with officials or other public bodies. In addition to the courts of law this right to one's own language extends to public bodies such as health care, social services, labour exchanges, taxation, police and school. The officials are obligated to ensure that individuals receive the translation and interpreting services they need in order to conduct their affairs. The agreement does not, however, extend to the Åland or Faroe Islands.

The supervision of the Finnish, Swedish and Sami languages is now an area of governmental responsibility. For purposes of language supervision The Finnish Literary Society established a committee for language problems already in 1928, and it was followed in 1945 by the Language Office, which came under governmental control in 1949, when a committee on language and a language office were set up under the aegis of the Finnish Academy. In 1976 these functions were merged into the Research Centre for Domestic Languages, whose mission it is to cultivate and plan not only Finnish but also Swedish and Sami. (For further detail on Swedish in Finland in this respect see Marika Tandefelt, for Sami see Pekka Sammallahti and for Finnish in Sweden see Jarmo Lainio.)

7. Language contacts and contact languages

7.1. Distinctive features of Finnish

Finnish is an agglutinative language, thus differing clearly from the Indo-European languages of Europe. It is characterized by an abundant exploitation of morphological devices. Several morphemes may be attached to the same stem, as in *talo+ssa+ni+kin* (house+in+my+too) 'in my house, too'. Finnish also differs from many Indo-European languages in that it has no grammatical gender and no system of articles. As many grammatical relations are expressed through morphological devices the syntactic word order of Finnish is fairly unrestricted. However, word order in Finnish does have a distinctive textual function.

There are 21 phonemes in Finnish: 8 for vowels (*a, o, u, ä, ö, y, e, i*) and 13 for consonants (*p, t, k, d, s, h, v, j, l, r, m, n, n*). The *d* phoneme is a late arrival in Finnish. The phonemes *b, g, f* and *š* may also occur in loanwords, but not all Finns can pronounce them. In old loanwords *b, d*, and *g* have been replaced by *p, t*, and *k*. In Finnish the consonants *p, t*, and *k* are pronounced without aspiration. Finnish is rich in diphthongs, but consonant clusters are infrequent. In initial position such clusters did not earlier occur at all.

Stress is always on the first syllable in the word. Length in Finnish is phonematically distinctive. The opposition concerns both consonants and vowels in all positions. The difference is also shown in the orthography, e.g. *tule* 'come!', (*ei*) *tuule* 'it is not windy', *tulee* 'he comes', *tuulee* 'it is windy', (*ei*) *tulle* 'he probably will not come', (*ei*) *tuulle* 'it is probably not windy', *tullee* 'he will probably come', *tuullee* 'it is probably windy'. The system of orthography is extremely phonematic, the principle being that of one phoneme per grapheme, and one grapheme per phoneme.

In Finnish the nominal has a paradigm comprising 14 oblique cases. Those of greater grammatical significance are the nominative (*kala+Ø* 'fish'), the genitive (*kala+n* 'of the fish') and the partitive (*kala+a* '(some) fish'), whose function it is to make clear the syntactic relations, subject and object. The genitive also expresses possession. There are six cases for expressing location. Three of these, the inessive (*talo+ssa* 'in the house'), the elative (*talo+sta* 'out of the house'), and the illative (*talo+on* 'into the house'), are known as internal cases, while the other three, the adessive (*kato+lla* 'on the roof'), the ablative (*kato+lta* 'off the roof'), and the allative (*kato+lle* 'onto the roof') are known as external cases. The case system demonstrates considerable overall symmetry. The inessive and the adessive answer the question *where*, the elative and ablative answer the question *whence*, and the illative and allative answer the question *where to*. Condition and change in that condition are shown by the essive (*sairaa+na* '(to be) ill') and translative (*sairaa+ksi* '(to become) ill'). In the modern language the comitative (*kaloi+ne+en* 'with his fishes'), abessive (*kala+tta* 'without fish') and instructive (*kaksi+n käsi+n* 'with both hands') are fairly unproductive and are not considered to belong to the paradigm. Prolative forms (*mai+tse* 'by land', *posti+tse* 'by post') are seen as adverbial.

The synthesizing nature of Finnish is also seen in suffixes denoting possession. Possession is expressed through the possessive suffix which corresponds to the possessive pronouns of many Indo-European languages: (*minun*) *kirja+ni* 'my book', (*sinun*) *kirja+si* 'your book', (*hänen*) *kirja+nsa* 'his/her book', (*meidän*) *kirja+mme* 'our book', (*teidän*) *kirja+nne* 'your book', (*heidän*) *kirja+nsa* 'their book'. There are also a lot of enclitic particles, which have a variety of semantic and pragmatic functions. These include *kin*, *ko* and *han*, *pa*, *s*. The *ko* suffix may be said to have the clearest function, that of making a statement interrogative, as in *Tulee+ko hän huomenna?* 'Will he come tomorrow?, *Huomenna+ko hän tulee?* 'Is it tomorrow that he is coming?', *Hän+kö tulee huomenna?* 'Is it he who is coming tomorrow?' The particle *kin* signifies 'too': *Hän+kin tulee huomenna.* 'He, too, will come tomorrow.' *Huomenna+kin hän tulee.* 'He will come tomorrow, too'. In keeping with this synthetic nature the use of derivatives is also very common, as in *maa* 'land, country, earth': *maa+lainen* 'peasant', *maa+llinen* 'earthly', *maa+sto* 'terrain', *maa+ton* 'landless', *maa+tu+a* 'to moulder', *maa+tta+a* 'to earth'.

7.2. Influence of other languages on Finnish

In the Finnish lexis it is possible to describe several eras in which borrowing has taken place. The phonology, morphology and syntax have also been subject to outside influences. On the other hand certain influences have been resisted owing to the typological nature and phonology, differing as they do from those of the neighbouring Indo-European languages. These have had a discouraging effect on the absorption of foreign influence. Moreover, ever since the 1800s those developing and guiding the language have deliberately sought to keep foreign elements out of Finnish.

Quantitatively most loanwords have come from Swedish. They entered the dialects and the written and spoken standard varieties both during the period of Swedish domination and thereafter. In the language of the populace the influence of Swedish has been most pronounced in the dialects of western Finland, notably in the vicinity of Swedish-speaking areas on the coast. At the beginning of the 1800s a conscious effort was made to finnicize the written standard. Finnish equivalents for elevated Swedish idioms and loanwords were sought. Although not all those in favour of Finnishness were fanatical purists, the view of those endeavouring to develop the language in the 1840s came to be that the vocabulary should be comprehensible to all and easy to pronounce. In keeping with this principle attempts were made to replace loanwords of foreign origin with Finnish derivatives or compound nouns. The 1800s saw the arrival of thousands of neologisms in standard written Finnish.

The principle of making the vocabulary Finnish continues to prevail. This does not, however, extend to professional and technical language whose terminology draws heavily on international roots. However, efforts to keep the basic vocabulary as Finnish as possible continue, as in the case of the Finnish word *puhelin* 'telephone', which is derived from the word *puhe* meaning speech/speaking. On other occasions Finnish equivalents have not been successful in ousting foreign originals; *radio* and *televisio* have taken their place in the Finnish language. Nowadays those concerned with preserving the language are more interested in combatting the anglicisms brought through Anglo-American than Swedish cultural influences. Words of foreign origin stand little chance of becoming widespread in Finnish owing to their very different pronounciation.

The influence of Swedish is at its most apparent in old Helsinki slang, which came into being in the bilingual working-class areas at the turn of the century. The main task of the old slang was to unite those Finnish- and Swedish-speaking boys who belonged within the same backyard or block. This slang sprang up for purposes of communication at the expense of community control and linguistic correctness. The main thing was that the message got across, not in what language it went. A third minor component in Helsinki old slang was Russian. There are also a few words which have been borrowed from German and English. A very few, notably in old slang, have also been taken from Romany and Yiddish. The Romany words have arrived by way of Stockholm underworld cant. Since the 1950s, the proportion of Swedish words in slang has clearly decreased. New expressions have been taken from British or American English slang.

The influence of languages other than Swedish on written and spoken standard Finnish has been much less. A certain number of Russian loanwords have infiltrated over the centuries into the eastern Finnish dialects. During the period of autonomy, however, the influence of Russian, particularly on colloquial Finnish, was more noticeable. Words were taken over from the language of the Russian merchants and soldiers. Only very few of these came into the written standard. Sami words have entered the standard written Finnish through the dialects of the Far North. They are mostly vocabulary referring to the living environment and natural phenomena which describe the Far North and Lapland.

8. Bibliography (selected)

Bradean-Ebinger, Nelu (1991): *Sprachkontakte und Zweisprachigkeit in Fennoskandinavien. Soziolinguistische Aspekte der Zweisprachigkeit im nördlichen Areal.* Studies in Modern Philology 8, Budapest.

Branch, Michael (1987): "Finnish". In: Comrie, B. (Ed.), *The World's Major Languages*, London.

Halén, Harry (1991): "Suomen tataariväestön kielellisestä sopeutumisesta". In: *Kielet kohtaavat.*

Harviainen, Tapani (1991): "Jiddišiä ja venäjää, ruotsia ja suomea – juutalaiset Suomessa". In: *Kielet kohtaavat.*

Herää Suomi. Suomalaisuusliikkeen historia. (1989): Kuopio.

Hämäläinen, Pekka K. (1968): *Kielitaistelu Suomessa 1917–1939*, Porvoo.

Jaakkola, Magdalena (1989): *Suomalaisten suhtautuminen ulkomaalaisiin ja ulkomaalaispolitiikkaan.* Siirtolaisuustutkimuksia 21, Helsinki.

Jaakkola, Magdalena (1991): *Suomen ulkomaalaiset. Perhe, työ ja tulot.* Työpoliittinen tutkimus 15, Helsinki.

Karlsson, Fred (1983): *Finnish Grammar*, Juva.

Kielet kohtaavat. Siirtolaisuus ja kielellinen sopeutuminen 1800-luvun Suomessa. (1991): Leif Nyholm (Ed.), Meddelanden från institutionen för nordiska språk och nordisk litteratur vid Helsingfors universitet. Serie B: 14, Helsingfors.

Klinge, Matti (1992): *A brief history of Finland*, Helsinki.

Klinge, Matti (1993): *The Finnish Tradition. Essays on structures and identities in the North of Europe*, Helsinki.

Korhonen, Mikko (1986): *Finno-Ugrian Language Studies in Finland 1828–1918.* The History of Learning and Science in Finland 1828–1918, Helsinki.

Leinonen, Marja (1992): "Language survival: Russian in Finland". In: *Slavica Tamperensia I*, Tampere.

Mitä laki sanoo kielellisistä oikeuksista (1992): Finlandssvensk rapport nr 22. Svenska Finlands folkting, Hanko.

Nuolijärvi, Pirkko (1990): "Suomen kielivähemmistöt 1990-luvulla". In: Almqvist, I./Cederhom, P.-E./Lainio, J. (Eds.) *Från Pohjolas pörten till kognitiv kontakt. Vänskrift till Erling Wande den 9 maj 1990.* Stockholm Studies in Finnish Language and Literature, Stockholm.

Nurmio, Yrjö (1947): *Taistelu suomen kielen asemasta 1800-luvun puolivälissä*, Porvoo.

Paunonen, Heikki (1993): "From a small Swedish town to a Finnish City". In: *Language Variation and Change.* Vol. 5, number 1.

Structure of Population (1991): Statistics Finland. Population 1992:11, Helsinki.

Torvinen, Taimi (1989): *Kadimah. Suomen juutalaisten historia*, Keuruu.

Vikør, Lars S. (1993): *The Nordic Languages. Their Status and Interrelations.* Nordic Language Secretariat. Publication no. 14. Oslo.

Vuorela, Katri/Borin, Lars (forthcoming): "About the Finnish Gypsies and Finnish Romani". In: Corrain, O. (Ed.) *Minority Languages in Scandinavia and the British Isles.*

Heikki Paunonen, Tampere (Finland)

124. Finnish–Swedish

1. Geography and demography
2. History
3. Politics, economy and general cultural and religious situation
4. Statistics
5. Sociolinguistic situation
6. Language political situation
7. General contactlinguistic portrait
8. Bibliography (selected)

1. Geography and demography

The Swedish-speakers in Finland live primarily along the coast and in a few cities not far from the coastline. Until the beginning of this century, the settled area was continuous, but today it is divided into a northern part (Ostrobothnia) and two southern parts one with Turku (in Swedish (Swe.) Åbo) and the other with Helsinki (in Swe. Helsingfors) as the centre.

The island province of Åland is entirely Swedish-speaking and, because of certain international and constitutional provisions, it is in an exceptional situation which means, among other things, that the position of the Finnish language can never become as strong as on the mainland.

A small part of the Swedish-speaking Finns also live in some cities (so called "language islands") in the inner and predominantly Finnish part of the country. This geographically dispersed area is called "Swedish Finland" (in Swe. Svenskfinland).

The Swedish-speakers in Finland are seen to be based both in the nation's centre as well as in the periphery. The group's strongest political, cultural and economic organisations are in the capital, where to a great extent bilingual Swedish-speakers work. On the other hand, the strongest popular and monolingual Swedish anchorage is to be found in Ostrobothnia (→ language map A).

When studying the minority's development one needs to differentiate between its urban and rural areas, since different factors have led to the decrease of the Swedish-speaking population in different parts of Swedish Finland.

The Swedish-speaking Finns have never consisted of more than a bare fifth of the country's population. A decrease in percentages, combined with an increase in absolute numbers, characterized the development up to World War II. Since then a decrease in absolute numbers may also be seen (see *statistics*).

There seem to be three reasons for the decrease of the Finland-Swedish population:

a) a lower birth rate, particularly during earlier periods as a result of the fact that Swedish-speaking Finns became more urbanised earlier than the Finnish-speaking Finns,
b) emigration (especially from rural areas, Ostrobothnia in particular) at the beginning of the century, especially to English-speaking countries but after WW II primarily to Sweden. An important reason for this has been an inadequate knowledge of Finnish, which in turn has meant reduced possibilities of the labour market in Finland,
c) Fennification in two different senses:
    i) the Fennification of previously monolingual Swedish or bilingual Swedish-dominated environments resulting from the large influx of Finnish-speaking people. This geographic mobility began in connection with the country's strong and late urbanisation at the end of the 19th century, which affected Greater Helsinki in particular. The changed balance between the language groups led to a fast growing bilingualism among the Swedish-speaking Finns. From bilingualism the step was not always very far to a new monolingualism in Finnish,
    ii) the Fennification of individuals as the result of marriage across the language border, which usually leads to the following generation growing up entirely with the majority language, Finnish. Exogamous marriages have been especially usual in the urban and principally bilingual environments, such as in the Greater Helsinki area (see part 5.).

2. History

For about 700 years Finland was part of Sweden, with the right to participate in the election of the King (from 1363) and then to send representatives to the Swedish Parliament. Finland was conquered by Russia in 1809 and then became a Grand Duchy under the Russian Tsar. For the Swedish-speaking inhabitants of Finland, this meant that they gradually began to identify themselves more and more with Finland.

In order to understand the position of the Swedish-speaking Finns in Finland, and to interpret the attitudes of the Finnish majority towards their cohabiting minority (see chapter 6.), it is important to know that the Swedish language, and not the Finnish, actually was the only official language of the country until 1863. It was not until the middle of the last century that the official position of the Finnish language gained strength through a series of decisions made by the Russian Tsar (see Heikki Paunonen's article).

The minority language (Swedish) was earlier the only usable language on the official level and is today one of the two national languages of the modern Finnish republic. In other words, earlier the Swedish language had a higher status than the Finnish language, and it has not actually lost that status, even though both languages are valued equally today. This has helped the minority to maintain its language.

As to historical roots, both Finnish- and Swedish-speaking Finns are mixed groups.

The distant roots of the Swedish-speaking Finns may be found not only in Sweden, but also in the area surrounding the Baltic Sea. Among the Swedish-speaking Finns, for example, the following lines of descent may be distinguished:

a) those whose ancestors came so long ago (e. g. through a spontaneous settlement of farmers and fishermen during the early Middle Ages) that their origin outside Finland cannot even be traced,
b) those whose ancestors moved to Finland as merchants, craftsmen, government officials or in the military service, especially during the 18th century,
c) those whose ancestors were Finnish-speaking but who became Swedish-speakers for example by schooling in Swedish, and as the result of the demand for Swedish on the public level. This shift from Finnish to Swedish took place primarily during the period between 1700–1850.
d) those whose ancestors emigrated to Finland and who were German-speaking in particular, but also Russian-speaking. Up until the 1920's foreigners who established themselves in Finland became Swedish speakers rather than Finnish speakers.

In other words, the ethnic background of the Swedish-speaking minority is varied and the only clear cultural element that binds them is their common language.

Conflicts between Swedish- and Finnish-speakers stirred at the turn of the century; real language strife can be spoken of during the thirties, though it was restricted to certain cities, particularly to Helsinki. During the Second World War and the years that followed, there was no language strife and the possibility of a worsened language climate in the future did not even seem possible (see 5. and 6.).

3. Politics, economy and general cultural and religious situation

The minority has some political institutions of importance: the Swedish Assembly of Finland is a cooperation body. There are 75 delegates to the Assembly and they represent six different political trends and cover the entire political scale, from right to left. The Assembly is convened every other year for a two-day session. The Assembly functions as a referral or investigative body having the task of looking after and forwarding the rights and interests of the Swedish-speaking population. The Assembly has three ombudsmen. One is the so-called Ombudsman for Language Protection and the two others are responsible for educational matters and information. The organisation also consists of an Assembly Secretary, an Assistant Secretary as well as office personnel.

The Swedish People's Party is a political party with 11 representatives in Parliament at present (1991–). The party is considered to be politically of the centre but undoubtedly has a greater breadth, both to the left and to the right, than a traditional centre party. The party has long been a Cabinet party and thus has held ministerial posts. In addition to these 11, there are 2 Swedish-speaking Social Democratic MP's, one who belongs to the Centre Party, one who represents the Finnish Christian League and one who represents the so-called Leftist Alliance. The province of Åland is always represented by an MP elected by the inhabitants of the Åland Islands.

The Swedish-speaking Finns also have several cultural organisations and foundations. There are foundations which give grants to artists, musicians and writers, and others that focus on scientific studies concerning e. g. the Swedish language, history, literature and folklore. There is also an association especially devoted to the cultivation of the Swedish language. Together all these organisations form a cultural network which also is of considerable economic importance. A number of local organisations complete the network of cultural organisations, that is of utmost importance for the Swedish-speaking minority.

The mass media that function in Swedish are also of importance. There is one national newspaper and seven more locally-oriented newspapers. There is also a national radio channel complemented by several local channels. There are national TV programs produced in Swedish, and it is also possible to watch programs produced in Sweden. The existence of the minority's own mass media guarantees that the members of the minority are able to keep in touch with what happens in different parts of the areas of Swedish-Finland and experience a feeling of a common group identity.

Novels, drama and poetry written and published in Swedish by Swedish-speaking Finns also contribute to a feeling of togetherness. The Finland-Swedish literature has always formed an important part of the national literature in Finland. The country's national poet actually only wrote in Swedish (in the 19th century).

However, it is easy to single out the most important guarantor of the Swedish-speaking minority's continued existence: the school supports the transfer of knowledge of the language and about the language group to younger generations.

A complete parallel school system exists for the minority, from primary school through secondary school, in which all subjects are taught in Swedish. Swedish is studied as a mother-tongue and Finnish as a foreign language (in practice taught on an advanced level to those pupils in bilingual or Finnish-dominated areas where language competence is high). In the Finnish majority schools, Swedish is similarly studied as a foreign language and Finnish as a mother-tongue.

With few exceptions all schools and universities in Finland are state owned and no tuition is charged. The administration within the school and education sector is divided on the basis of language — Swedish-speaking civil servants are responsible for education in Swedish at all levels.

It is also possible to continue studying in Swedish at various vocational institutes. Helsinki University is bilingual and Swedish-speaking students always have the right to use their own mother-tongue. The Åbo Academy University (in Swe. Åbo Akademi) in Turku is monolingually Swedish. In Helsinki there is a Swedish School of Economics and Business Administration (in Swe. Svenska handelshögskolan) which is monolingually Swedish too. The two last mentioned both have a small but significant number of Finnish-speaking students wishing to learn Swedish by studying solely in this language.

The Swedish-speaking Finns in general belong to the same church as the Finns. However, the Lutheran-Evangelical Church is divided according to language. There is a Swedish-language diocese with its own bishop, priests and other personnel.

4. Statistics

The most important reasons for the diminishing of the Swedish-speaking minority have been mentioned above (part 1.). The development in absolute numbers and in percentages is shown in table 124.1.

Table 124.1: The Swedish-speaking population in Finland 1610–1990

Year	Swedish-speaking Finns	%
1610	70 000	17.5
1749	87 200	16.3
1815	160 000	14.6
1880	294 000	14.3
1990	349 700	12.9
1920	341 000	11.0
1940	354 000	9.5
1960	330 500	7.4
1980	300 482	6.3
1992	296 435	5.9

Data about the citizen's mother tongue is collected in order to determine the linguistic status of the municipalities. Right now there are monolingual Swedish municipalities (10 + 16 on the Åland Islands), bilingual municipalities with a Finnish majority (17) and bilingual municipalities with a Swedish majority (22).

A municipality is considered monolingual if the entire population speaks the same language or if less than 8% speak the other official language of the country. If the minority is at least 8%, or numbers 3,000, the municipality is bilingual. A bilingual municipality does not become monolingual until the minority falls to 6% or lower. In special circumstances the Cabinet may decide to retain a municipality's bilingualism despite the fact that the minority has fallen below 6%.

The service a municipality is obliged to offer its inhabitants depends on how it is classified. In a monolingual municipality there is no obligation to uphold a day-care and a school system in the minority language. Neither is a civil servant obliged to pass a language test and to serve a minority member in his or her language. In a bilingual municipality, however, a speaker of the minority language in that municipality (Swedish or Finnish) has the right to demand service in his or her mother tongue (see also *sociolinguistic situation* and *language political situation*).

5. Sociolinguistic situation

The weakness of the Swedish-speaking Finns is their linguistic ingenuity. It was earlier mentioned (see 1.) that one reason for the decreasing number of Swedish-speaking Finns is "Fennification". This expression refers more specifically to the language shift which implies that the minority language is not passed on from one generation to another. This suggests that the exogamous families should be focused on since it is their actions, or rather lack of actions, that direct development.

A norm forbidding marriages across the language barrier has never existed. But earlier, exogamous marriages were not as frequent as they are today. Especially in the urban (and also more Finnish-dominated) parts of the area called Swedish Finland, more than half of the marriages contracted are exogamous.

When a child in a bilingual family does not grow up with two languages but rather with the majority language, it can seldom be explained as the result of the Finnish-speaking parent's negative attitude but rather as the result of the parents not being aware that they were faced with a choice.

Upbringing with two languages requires insight and information. Such information has been available for several years now through the Swedish Assembly of Finland, which distributes to all bilingual homes in Swedish Finland brochures about language upbringing and the choice of day-care and school language. The result of the information campaign is already noticeable in a greater interest in language questions, a decreasing distrust towards bilingual upbringing as well as in the greater number of children from bilingual homes being registered in the minority school.

As has been mentioned above, the Swedish-speaking Finns, in comparison to other linguistic minorities, do master their own language well and as a mother tongue. In Finnish-dominated environments this mother tongue proficiency is often coupled with such a high proficiency in Finnish that a Swedish-speaking Finn who speaks the majority language is not always identified as belonging to the minority. Since no visible cultural characteristics differentiate a Swedish-speaking Finn from a Finnish-speaking one, the minority may stay quite unnoticeable in the Finnish society. Thus, the assimilation process is easier and painless for the individual while at the same time it drains the group.

According to a study of attitudes conducted by several Canadian researchers in collaboration with the Finnish Gallup organisation, the minority's view of the majority is quite different from the majority's view of the minority. It seems, for example, that the Swedish-speaking Finns rank Finnish-speaking Finns considerably higher than they themselves are ranked by members of the majority.

An explanation of why Swedish-speaking Finns are so positive towards Finnish-speaking Finns, while they in turn feel more estranged perhaps even negatively inclined towards Swedish-speaking Finns, may be because the Finnish majority still maintains an image of their own language group as the earlier inferior language group of the country. Traces may be found in both groups of a language attitude which reflects a time long past. This results in a situation of latent conflict which may be activated in different situations. In some cases it may also lead to Swedish-speaking Finns abandoning their own group in order to avoid this slightly negative attitude.

6. Language political situation

An urban environment in southern Finland is often bilingual and usually clearly dominated by Finnish. The possibilities of getting the services in your mother tongue which local authorities are responsible for in a bilingual municipality vary in practice and are non-existent at times. Since a Swedish-speaking Finn who has grown up in a bilingual environment nearly always knows Finnish better than a Finnish-speaking civil servant knows Swedish, in practice any administrative matter is dealt with in the majority language. A rule of thumb says that the Swedish-speaking population must comprise ⅔ of the total population to be able to expect with much certainty that a Finnish civil servant will know Swedish.

Contact with authorities, or for example with health care personnel, occurring in Finnish, is seldom directly considered to be a problem by Swedish-speaking Finns who are bilingual enough to be able to cope in the majority language. This is mainly the case with people of working age who live in urban environments in southern Finland. On the other hand, children and old people are often not bilingual enough and thus require more service in their own language.

In the Ostrobothnian cities, on the other hand, it is mostly young people and younger middle-aged persons who know Finnish so well that they are not totally handicapped in the majority language. However, in the Swedish countryside, both in the North and in the South, access to service in your mother tongue is a must. For most people in the urban, bilingual centres, it is more a question of comfort and security.

It is difficult to get the Finnish-speaking majority to understand that there are Swedish-speaking Finns who know no Finnish at all or so little that their quality of life is impaired by lack of service in their mother tongue. The Finns usually consider it to be a duty to know the majority language. "In Finland you speak Finnish" is not an unfamiliar remark to a Swedish-speaking Finn living in a more or less Finnish-dominated area. Even highly educated bilingual Swedish-speaking Finns tend to ignore the fact that not every Swedish-speaking Finn feels comfortable using the Finnish language actively especially in more demanding contexts.

In other words, the regulations of the language law do not guarantee the availability of individuals with the language knowledge that the law presupposes. Neither does the language law in itself guarantee that Finnish-speakers with a knowledge of Swedish want to or dare to speak Swedish.

When the content of the language law lately has been questioned by the Finnish-speaking majority, it is primarily the Finnish-speaking civil servant's language requirement which is disputed. On the other hand, the minority's right to day-care and schools in their own language is never questioned. The Finnish-speaking majority may also perhaps point to the unfairness of there actually existing a proportionately greater number of study places in upper secondary schools and in higher education for Swedish-speakers than for Finnish-speakers. This is the result of the tradition of further education, beyond the compulsory schooling, having stronger foothold among the Swedish-speakers than among the Finnish-speakers.

As was mentioned above (see 2.) the language climate, compared to some other nations, has been harmonious. However, during the last 15 years some anti-Swedish sentiment has appeared. The result of this can be interpreted as a threat as well as being at the same time a conscience-raising warning. The abundant supply of study places in higher education has already been mentioned as an example of "injustice". Another one, according to certain Finnish-speakers, is the excessive number of Swedish-speaking Finns in leading positions in society. Naturally all of them use Finnish in the exercise of their profession, and their language proficiency has never been criticized. Judging by the letters-to-the-editor published in our Finnish-language newspapers, it is only protests against the compulsory study of Swedish in Finnish schools that have gained the greatest sympathy from the public.

Since 1970 all children who attend Finnish majority schools study Swedish as a foreign language for at least three years. If they choose Swedish as their first foreign language (instead of English, German, French or Russian) they study the language for seven years. In the Swedish minority school the situation is the opposite with Finnish as the first "foreign" language. This means that every schoolchild in the country has at least some knowledge in two languages besides his or her own mother tongue: the other national language and a foreign language. In the autumn of 1990 there was a vigorous debate in the Parliament concerning the obligatory teaching of Swedish in the majority school. A vocal minority among the MP's held the opinion that one foreign language (i. e. English) is enough in the compulsory school. The importance of knowing Swedish for cooperation with other Nordic countries was thereby severely underestimated. This debate still seems to be going on.

Among the Swedish-speaking Finns there have been no protests against the obligatory teaching of Finnish in Swedish schools and nobody has argued that there should be less than two obligatory languages in the compulsory schooling. As a matter of fact it is not very exceptional for a Swedish-speaking child with a fairly good knowledge in Finnish to study two foreign languages besides the other national language and the mother tongue. In upper secondary school (gymnasium) you may choose yet another foreign language and study that for three years if you want to.

It is difficult to assess justly how broad the support is today for the anti-Swedish line. On the other hand, it is easy to see that it could well be connected with other racist-inclined or anti-foreigner opinions which have been expressed in Finland. The language strife of today is more a verbal strife conducted through debates and in the press. It is more disagreeable than being directly dangerous for the Swedish-speaking minority. As long as it does not affect the language legislation or the Swedish school and day-care system the minority is quite safe.

7. General contactlinguistic portrait

Some research results show that both Swedish- and Finnish-speaking Finns represent the same spoken culture, i. e. the pattern for when to be silent and when to speak is the same regardless of the language. The sociocultural roles which steer language use may therefore be considered the same for Finns with a similar social background and who live within the same region, whether or not they speak Swedish or Finnish.

Finnish and Swedish are not related languages, but one could say that semantically they are close, as the result of having been in contact with each other for several hundreds of years. The fact that they are not related means that a Swedish-speaking Finn who must learn Finnish, or a Finn who must learn Swedish, has to learn many new things; and he or she has very few possibilities to fall back on earlier knowledge of or from his or her own language. In other words, the threshold is quite high for someone who has no natural contact with the other language in his or her own immediate environment.

The Swedish spoken in Finland — the so-called Finland-Swedish (in Swe. *finlandssvenska*) — is one of the regional varieties of the Swedish language. The language also has its own social and regional varieties, but what is referred to is a standard variety used in urbanized regions, in the Swedish-language mass media, generally at a Swedish theatre, and together with Swedes, Norwegians, Icelanders and Danes, in inter-Nordic contexts.

The difference between the Swedish in Finland and the Swedish in Sweden, if somewhat simplified, is comparable to the difference between American and British English. The norm for the written language is exactly the same as the norm in Sweden. Thus, we follow the same rules for spelling and writing, and we use the same dictionaries as in Sweden. It is primarily in speech that the characteristic features of the Finland-Swedish variety is noticeable. This means that a Swedish-speaking Finn always speaks Swedish with a characteristic accent but that a written text does not always reveal the writer's origin.

Many of the characteristic features of the Finland-Swedish language are quite old. The separate development is therefore not only the result of the separation of Finland from the kingdom of Sweden in 1809. The characteristic accent was e. g. mentioned in the middle of the 18th century.

Aside from the Finland-Swedish pronunciation — which differs from the Swedish variety primarily through the lack of the double tone — the variety also has smaller deviations in morphology and syntax. The Finland-Swedish vocabulary contains some words and expressions which no longer exist in the Swedish spoken in Sweden (so-called archaisms). Some of them are rooted in a Fenno-Swedish dialect, others are loan words from German or Russian. An ever-increasing group of loan words are those taken from Finnish (both as direct loans as well as through translation).

The number of Finland-Swedish characteristics found in the Swedish spoken in Finland, however, is so limited that non-solvable communication problems between a Swedish-speaking Finn and a Swede would not arise. If the text of a Swedish-speaking Finn were corrected, most likely it would often be the substitution of a specifically Finland-Swedish expression with another Swedish expression, which in no way would be unfamiliar to the Swedish-speaking Finn in question.

With the vastly-increasing number of bilingual families, the influence of Finnish on the Finland-Swedish language will also increase. There will also be more individuals who run the risk of growing up with an insufficient grasp of the minority language, Swedish. When more than one half of the pupils in a class come from bilingual homes, and in the greater Helsinki area and Turku practically all the pupils, consequences arise both regarding mother-tongue instruction (i. e. Swedish), as well as the teaching of Finnish. Many pupils feel more secure in Finnish than in Swedish when they begin in a Swedish-language school, which means that the school itself must take on a linguistic responsibility which it did not have earlier.

Language cultivation has long traditions in Finland, both as regards Swedish as well as Finnish (see Heikki Paunonen). This is connected with a common Nordic language cultivation tradition in which all the Nordic countries defend the right and obligation to develop, improve and strengthen their own national language or languages. At the turn of the century, the work of language cultivation also became a link in the struggle for the Finnish as well as the Swedish languages. In today's language cultivation of the Swedish spoken in Finland, there is considerable cooperation with experts of the Finnish language. Cooperation across the language boundaries is a necessary prerequisite, for example, for dictionary compilation.

The Research Institute for the Languages in Finland, established in 1976, functions as an instance in which cooperation regarding many different types of linguistic matters, across the language boundaries, could and should occur. Both a Finnish- and a Swedish-language section function at the research institute. These language sections answer questions related to language, posed both by professional language users as well as by the general public. Among other things, they each publish an information bulletin, arrange courses and are initiative-takers regarding language cultivation. A column related to language is published weekly in the national Swedish-language daily newspaper and some linguistic matters are dealt with on the national Swedish-language radio station.

The linguistic awareness, interest and responsibility of the Swedish language in Finland is no longer only confined to professional language preservers. A genuine interest in the Finland-Swedish language — the minority's unifying putty — also seems to exist among Swedish-speaking Finns in general.

8. Bibliography (selected)

Allardt, Erik/Miemois, Karl-Johan/Starck, Christian (1979): *Multiple and Varying Criteria for Membership in a Linguistic Minority, The Case of the Swedish speaking Minority in Metropolitan Helsinki*, Research Group for Comparative Sociology, University of Helsinki, Research Report 21.

Allardt, Erik/Starck, Christian (1981): *Språkgränser och samhällsstruktur. Finlandssvenskarna i ett jämförande perspektiv*, Lund.

Bergroth, Hugo (1917): *Finlandssvenska. Handledning till undvikande av provinsialismer i tal och skrift*, Helsingfors.

Finland i det svenska riket (1986): Kulturfonden för Sverige och Finland (red. S. Huovinen), Stockholm.

Finnäs, Fjalar (1986): *Den finlandssvenska befolkningsutvecklingen 1950–1980. En analys av en språkgrupps demografiska utveckling och effekten av blandäktenskap*. Skrifter utgivna av Svenska litteratursällskapet i Finland nr 533 (diss.), Helsingfors.

Fougstedt, Gunnar (1951): *Finlands svenska befolkning åren 1936–1945*. Bidrag till kännedom af Finlands natur och folk, utgifna af Finska vetenskaps-Societeten, H 15, Helsingfors.

Gambier, Yves (Ed.) (1989): *Le bilinguisme en Finlande. Pratiques et évaluations*, Cahiers de linguistique sociale 15, Université de Rouen.

Hämäläinen, P. K. (1968): *Kielitaistelu Suomessa 1917–1939*, Porvoo.

Klövekorn, Martin (1960): *Die sprachliche Struktur Finnlands 1880–1950. Veränderungen im sprachlichen Charakter der finnlandschwedischen Gebiete und deren bevölkerungs-, wirtschafts- und sozialgeographische Ursachen*. Bidrag till kännedom av Finlands natur och folk utgivna av Finska Vetenskaps-Societeten 105, Helsingfors.

Liebkind, Karmela (1984): *Minority Identity and Identification Processes: A Social Psychological Study*. Commentationes Scientiarum Socialium 22, Societas Scientiarum Fennica (diss.), Helsinki.

McRae, Kenneth D./Bennett, Scott E./Miljan, Toivo (1988): *Intergroup Sympathies and Language Patterns in Finland: Results from a Survey*, Suomen Gallupin julkaisusarja 16, Helsinki.

Modeen, Tore (1977): *Finlandssvenskarnas nationella grundlagsskydd I*. Acta Academiae Aboensis, ser. A Humaniora, vol. 54, nr 3, Åbo.

Reuter, Mikael (1992): "Swedish as a pluricentric language". In: *Pluricentric Languages. Differing Norms in Different Nations, Contributions to the Sociology of Language* 62, Clyne, M. (Ed.), Berlin.

Sandlund, Tom/Björklund, Kaj (1980): *Bilinguals in Finland*. Ethnicity and Mobility, report 5, Åbo Akademi, Åbo.

Tandefelt, Marika (1988): *Mellan två språk. En fallstudie om språkbevarande och språkbyte i Finland*. Acta Universitatis Upsaliensis, Studia Multiethnica Upsaliensia 3 (diss.), Uppsala.

Tandefelt, Marika (1989): "Deux langues sur un même marché: un peu d'histoire et changement en cours". In: *Cahiers de linguistique sociale* 15.

Tandefelt, Marika (1990): *Zweisprachigkeit in Finnland — gestern, heute und morgen*. Europa Ethnica, 47. Jg.

Tandefelt, Marika (1992): "The Finland-Swedes — the Most Privileged Minority in Europe?" In: *Minority Languages. The Scandinavian Experience. Papers read at the conference in Edinburgh 9–11 November 1990*, Blom, G./Graves, P./Kruse, A./Thorup Thomsen, B. (Eds.), Oslo.

Tandefelt, Marika (1994): "Urbanization and Language Shift". In: *The Sociolinguistics of Urbanization: The Case of the Nordic Countries*, Nordberg, B. (Ed.), Berlin, New York.

Vikør, Lars S. (1993): *The Nordic languages — their status and interrelations*, Oslo.

Marika Tandefelt, Helsinki (Finland)

125. Finnish—Saami

1. Geography and demography
2. History
3. General cultural and religious situation
4. Statistics
5. Sociolinguistic situation
6. Language political situation
7. General contactlinguistic portrait
8. Evaluation of the status of scientific discussions
9. Bibliography (selected)

1. Geography and demography

The Saami language (*sámegiella* in the vernacular) in Finland is traditionally spoken in an officially defined Saami home area which comprises the three northernmost parishes Enontekiö, Inari, and Utsjoki, as well as the Saami reindeer herding district in the Sodankylä parish (→ language map A). The number of Saami speakers in Finland varies between 1400 and 2650 according to the way data has been gathered: the smallest figures stem from self-announcement in censuses and the highest ones from survey interviews. The majority language in the Saami home area is Finnish which is the mother tongue of 80% of the inhabitants of the three northernmost parishes (cf. part 4.).

2. History

Finnish and Saami derive from the same protolanguage spoken about 4000 years ago. The split was brought about by Indo-Europeans who introduced primitive cattle herding and agriculture to the Pre-Finnish area on the coast of Finland. The Pre-Saami population continued subsisting on hunting, fishing, and gathering. The present sharp distinction between Finnish and Saami was brought about by the expansion of agricultural Finns to the north-east, assimilating the Saami south of the present Saami home area. As a result, the southern Saami idioms in Finland became extinct. To a certain extent, this assimilation process can be traced in historical documents.

When Finland became independent, the Russian-ruled Petsamo area was annexed to the former Grand Duchy of Finland. The inhabitants of Petsamo were mainly Greek Orthodox Skolt Saami, Finns, and Carelians. After World War II, Petsamo was ceded to the Soviet Union and the inhabitants were resettled mainly to the eastern parts of the Inari parish in Finland.

3. General cultural and religious situation

Traditionally, the Saami in Finland have been reindeer herders and fishers with hunting and berry-picking as important secondary livelihoods. In the present Saami area, dairy farming was introduced by the Finns in the 18th century. Cows were kept in many Saami households as an important secondary source of living up to the 1960's. At present, some Saami families along the upper Teno river in Utsjoki have dairy farming as their main source of livelihood. About 20% of the Saami households in Finland earn their living mainly from reindeer herding, but other occupations such as white-collar work are becoming more and more common. On the whole, Saami occupational profile is approaching the Finnish one.

The traditional occupation of the Finns in the Saami area has been dairy farming with fishing, and, in some cases, reindeer herding as secondary livelihoods. After World War II, state and parish administration, social services, educational system, and health care expanded causing an immigration of Finns from the south to the Saami area. This immigration added to the dominance of Finnish in most of the area and had a strong linguistic acculturating effect on the Saami.

Most of the Finns and Saami belong to the Lutheran state church. Some Finnish immigrants from the Petsamo area as well as the Skolt Saami originally from the same area are Greek Orthodox.

The Saami in Finland have a representational organ, the Saami Parliament, established in 1973. It is mainly an advisory body for the government in matters concerning Saami rights, language, and culture. It also has the right to propose amendments in legislation and administration regarding the Saami. Cooperation in Saami affairs across national borders is organized through different channels, the most important of which is the Nordic Saami Council, financed by the Nordic governments. The main Saami organizations meet in triennial Saami conferences, arranged by the Nordic Saami Council, to discuss ethnic rights and to decide on common lines of action.

4. Statistics

Saami speakers are in narrow majority in Utsjoki (population about 1500). Elsewhere Saami speakers are in minority, about 10% in Enontekiö (total population about 2400) and about 15% in Inari (total population about 7000). In Sodankylä the number of those speaking Saami as their mother tongue is diminishing rapidly with the passing of the generations born before World War II. In all areas, there is a small number of secondary Saami speakers who have acquired Saami outside of home, mostly in school where Saami is taught also as a second language. These secondary speakers are mostly people with some kind of Saami background.

Three out of the ten Saami regional variants, sometimes called dialects and sometimes languages, are spoken within the borders of Finland: North Saami, Inari Saami, and Skolt Saami. Inari Saami is spoken in the Inari parish by 300 individuals, and the number of Skolt Saami speakers (also in Inari after resettlement from Petsamo) is about 330. North Saami is spoken in Enontekiö by 250, in Inari by 350, and in Utsjoki by 800 individuals, totalling about 1400 speakers. In Sodankylä parish, the number of individuals speaking North Saami as their mother tongue is somewhat less than 100. The total number of Saami speakers is about 2100 in the Saami area and about 2500 in the whole country. In the whole country, there are about 2800 Saami with Finnish as their mother tongue; for the Saami area, the number is about 1500, out of which 200 in Utsjoki, 100 in Enontekiö, 1000 in Inari, and 200 in Sodankylä. Most of the Finnish-speaking Saami live in administrative centers where Saami-speakers are in minority as a norm.

5. Sociolinguistic situation

Practically all Saami speakers apart from very small children are bilingual in Saami and Finnish. Many Inari Saami are trilingual (Inari Saami − North Saami − Finnish), as well as some of the Skolts (Skolt Saami − North Saami − Finnish). Some Inari Saami are quadrilingual (Inari Saami − Skolt Saami − North Saami − Finnish). The Finns in the Saami area are normally monolingual, but the number of Finns with some command of Saami is increasing due to the inclusion of Saami in the curriculum of most schools in the area. The high number of monolingual Finns reflects majority attitudes towards minority languages.

6. Language political situation

According to the Saami language act in effect since 1992, a Saami person has the right to use his or her mother tongue when approaching authorities dealing with the Saami area. It is not mandatory for the officials to know Saami and in many cases, interpreters are used. Official documents are translated into Saami on demand, and both Finnish and Saami are the administrational languages in Utsjoki where official documents such as meeting records and agendas of administrational organs have to be produced in both languages. At present, the only official language in the Saami area is Finnish.

Practically all the schools in the Saami area have a Saami language program in the curriculum. In all the schools in Utsjoki, the pupils in the primary school (grades 1−6) can choose a Saami curriculum with Saami as the language of instruction and Finnish as a second language. In the upper grades (7−12), Saami is taught as the mother tongue subject, and, if teachers are available, other subjects can be taught in Saami as well. Compulsory education ends normally with grade 9. In the so-called Saami classes in other areas, Finnish is the dominant language of instruction, and Saami is taught as the mother tongue subject. In the high school graduation examination, Saami can be chosen for the written exam in the mother tongue, in which case an equivalent written exam will be taken in Finnish as well.

The Saami radio (a part of the Finnish General Broadcasting Corporation) has daily broadcasts in Saami, 4−5 hours on weekdays and 1 daily hour during the weekend. The language is mainly North Saami, but Inari and Skolt Saami have about one hour of weekly broadcasting time each. In addition, most of the Saami programs broadcast in Norway are transmitted on the Finnish side as well. In all, the programs in Saami run to some 30 hours weekly. The radio is by far the most important medium of information. There are no Saami newspapers in Finland, but two newspapers published twice a week in Norway write about Saami affairs in Finland as well; they also have reporters on the Finnish side of the border.

The standardization of Saami is taken care of by the Nordic Saami Language Board which has a sections for North, Inari, and Skolt Saami as well. Questions of development and planning are also discussed in the Saami Language Board in Finland, nominated by the Finnish department of education in the same manner as the language boards for Finnish and Swedish. Its recommendations are submitted to the Nordic Saami Language Board. The Saami Language Act has brought about a rapid development and standardization of new social terminology in Saami.

7. General contactlinguistic portrait

The three Saami languages in Finland have relatively complex segmental phonologies and regular morphophonologies. In contrast, Finnish segmental phonology is relatively simple and morphophonology contains many irregularities. North Saami has 28—36 consonant phonemes and 5—7 vowel phonemes depending on dialect, whereas the North Finnish dialects have 12 consonants and 8 vowels.

North Saami consonants						vowels	
b	z	d	ž	d'	g	u	i
m		n		ń	(ŋ)	o	e
M		N				(â) a (ä)	
p	c	t	č	t'	k		
(p')		(t')			(k')		
	f	s	ŧ	š	J	h	
	v		đ		j	(g)	
			l		l' r		
			L		R		

Fig. 125.1: North Saami phonemic inventory

(The western dialects lack at least those phonemes which have been placed between braces. The capital letters stand for voiceless sonorants; z and ž are voiced affricates; d', ń, t', l' are palatalized consonants; đ and ŧ are voiced and voiceless spirants, respectively.)

North Finnish consonants				vowels		
m	n		ŋ	u	ü	i
p	t		k	o	ö	e
	s			a		ä
v		j	h			
	l	r				

Fig. 125.2: North Finnish phonemic inventory

There is no Finnish interference in North Saami segmental phonology in the speech of fluent speakers in most of the area. The neutralization of some phonemic oppositions in the westernmost dialects is very likely due to Finnish influence (/s/ vs. /š/, /c/ vs. /č/ vs. /t/, /z/ vs. /ž/ vs. /d/, /đ/ vs. /r/, /ŧ/ vs. /s/).

North Saami has three distinctive quantities in stressed vowels in all the dialects (/pase/ '(does not) roast' vs. /vaa'se/ '(does not) go by' vs. /vaase/ 'vase') and, in the western dialects, in the following consonants (/čaaliih/ '(does not) let write' vs. /čaalliih/ 'to write' vs. /čaal'liih/ 'the writers'). In most of the cases, the eastern dialects have transferred the opposition between the double consonants to the preceding vowel (/čäälliih/ 'to write' vs. /čälliih/ 'the writers'). The opposition between long and short double phonemes (consonants and vowels) is not known in Finnish which only shows oppositions between single and double phonemes such as /pula/ 'need' vs. /kuula/ 'bullet' vs. /pulla/ 'bun' vs. /tuulla/ 'to blow'.

In morphology there is a number of prominent differences. The Saami declension has 6—9 cases (nominative*, genitive*, accusative*, illative*, locative*, comitative*, abessive, essive*, partitive; most North Saami dialects have those marked with an asterisk) whereas North Finnish shows 12 cases (or 13 if the accusative is regarded a separate case: nominative, genitive, accusative, partitive, essive, translative, illative, inessive, elative, allative, adessive, ablative, comitative). The main difference is the lack of the opposition between internal local cases (illative, inessive, elative) and external ones (allative, adessive, ablative) in Saami; the difference is compensated for with the use postpositions. This seems to account for the overuse (in comparison with the rest of the Finnish dialects) of local post-positions in the neighbouring North Finnish dialects: *vaaran päällä* 'on top of the hill' (cf. North Saami *vári alde* id.) vs. standard Finnish *vaaralla* id.

In addition to singular and plural found in both Finnish and Saami, Saami has dual forms for grammatical personal elements (possessive suffixes, personal verb endings and personal pronouns): *goahtán* 'my tent' vs. *goahtáme* 'the tent of the two of us' vs. *goahtámet* 'our tent', *boađán* 'I come' vs. *bohte* 'the two of us come' vs. *boahtit* 'we come', *mun* 'I' vs. *moai* 'the two of us' vs. *mii* 'we'. The opposition between the three numbers for personal elements is very persistent in Saami, although the age where a consistent opposition between dual and plural is acquired varies in bilingual children between 2 and 8 years.

Derivation is rich in both languages. On the whole, Saami verb derivation is more productive and in some cases comes at least close to an aspectual system: *Joavnna osttii heastta* 'John bought a horse' (completed action, basic verb *oastit*) vs. *Joavnna oastalii heastta* 'John was buying/about to buy a horse' (incomplete action, frequentative derivative *oastalit*).

The main source of syntactic interference is the fact that in Finnish, the subject, the predicative complement, and the object can be in the nominative or in the partitive (as well as the genitive and, if considered a separate case in nouns, in the accusative in certain cases), whereas in Saami, the subject and the predicative complement are in the nominative and the object in the accusative. For Finnish learners of Saami, a typical mistake is to use the genitive-accusative instead of the nominative in the predicative complement in cases like *viesut ledje alladat* (nom. pl.) 'the houses were high', c. f. Finnish *talot olivat korkeita* (part. pl.); Finnish partitive plural resembles the accusative plural in Saami, and both go back to the same proto-form. For Saami learners of Finnish, the selection between nominative-like accusative, genitive-like accusative singular and partitive for the object (and corresponding selection for the predicative complement) poses persistent difficulties as well as the choice between nominative and partitive for the predicative complement.

In the lexicon, Saami is characterized by a rich vocabulary for reindeer herding and natural milieu, and North Finnish has borrowed many lexical items from Saami such as *kermikkä* 'reindeer fawn in its first fall and winter' (< Saami, cf. North Saami *čearpmat*), *urakka* 'reindeer buck in its second year of age' (< Saami, cf. North Saami *varit*, Inari Saami *ooreeh*), *juovoa* 'to follow' (< Saami, cf. North Saami *čuovvut*), *suopunki* 'lasso' (< Saami, cf. North Saami *suohpan*, Inari Saami *suoppânj*), *kursu* 'ravine' (< Saami, cf. North Saami *gorsa*), *tunturi* 'field (area)' (< Saami, cf. North Saami *duottar*), *lompolo* 'river lake' (< Saami, cf. North Saami *luoppal*). The number of these loanwords runs to several hundreds.

There has also been a flow in the opposite direction from Finnish into Saami since the divergence of the languages, and the number of such loans can be estimated to run to several thousands. These contain such words as *ášši* 'matter, case' (< Finnish *asia*), *átnut* 'to ask to be forgiven' (< Finnish *anoa* 'to ask for, to beg'), *báhti* 'pot' (< Finnish *pata*), *báidnit* 'to color' (< Finnish *painaa* 'to weigh; to press; to color'), *beastit* 'to let go' (< Finnish *päästää*), *dáhkidit* 'to assure' (< Finnish *taata : takaa-*), *gásta* 'baptism' (< Finnish *kaste*), *haddi* 'price' (< Finnish *hinta*), *hápmi* 'form' (< Finnish *hahmo*), *ja* 'and' (< Finnish *ja*), *lávlut* 'to sing' (< Finnish *laulaa*), *miehkki* 'sword' (< Finnish *miekka*), *niitu* 'hay field' (< Finnish *niitty*), *oalga* 'straw' (< Finnish *olki*), *rámbi* 'lame' (< Finnish *rampa*), *sitkat* 'tough, gristly' (< Finnish *sitkeä*), *šaddat* 'to grow; to be born' (< Finnish *syntyä* 'to be born'), *váikkuhit* 'to influence' (< Finnish *vaikuttaa*) etc.

This flow of new Finnish words into Saami (and the corresponding flow of Swedish and Norwegian vocabulary on the Swedish and Norwegian side of the border) has been counterbalanced recently by indigenous words created for new concepts in modern society. These have been already introduced by the thousands and they are in constant use in the media and other sections of society. They contain such words as *čuovus* 'appendix', *dáidda* 'art', *dieđa* 'science', *dutkkus* 'exam', *juogus* 'section', *galba* '(road) sign', *fitnodat* 'company, enterprise', *máŋget* 'to (photo)copy, to duplicate', *máŋggus* 'mimeo, handout', *mielddus* '(photo)copy', *oadju* '(social) security' etc. In many cases, the corresponding Finnish word has served as a model by virtue of the similarity of the derivational system, as in *dáidda* 'art', Finnish *taide*.

After the orthography reform in 1979 uniting the North Saami area in the three Nordic countries, there has been an even flow of new literature in Saami. About 10 volumes of original Saami literature (mainly prose and poetry) have been published each year (mainly on the Norwegian side). A substantial body of the authors come from the Finnish side, especially from one school district in the Deatnu river valley in Utsjoki parish where there is a long tradition of Saami teachers. The most important writers on the Finnish side have been Hans Aslak Guttorm, Eino Guttorm, Rauni Magga Lukkari, Kirsti Paltto, Nils-Aslak Valkeapää, and Jouni-Antti Vest. In addition, literature is translated from various languages into Saami but the number of translations published annually is smaller. There is a Saami amateur theater group on the Finnish side staging plays written by Eino Guttorm.

For North Saami, there are two bilingual (Saami-Finnish) dictionaries (Sammallahti 1989, Sammallahti 1993) and some shorter vocabularies. There are two smaller dictionaries for Inari Saami (Sammallahti/Morottaja 1983 and 1993) as well as for Skolt Saami (Mosnikoff/Sammallahti 1988 and Sammallahti/Mosnikoff 1991), serving normative and practical purposes. There are no thorough Saami grammars written in Saami or Finnish, but the dictionaries contain adequate information on inflection (full sample paradigms and lists of inflectional types). In higher education, the North Saami grammar written in Norwegian by Nickel (1991) is used. The Nordic broadcasting corporations have produced two radio courses in North Saami as a joint effort, one for learners of Saami (Guttorm & Jernsletten & Nickel 1985–1987, 4 volumes, in Finnish, Norwegian and Swedish), the other for mother tongue instruction (Labba & Solbakk & Holmberg 1985–1986, 3 volumes, in Saami).

8. Evaluation of the status of scientific discussions

As much of the research on Saami has concentrated on questions of historical linguistics up to the 70's, there are almost no studies dealing with linguistic substance in a bilingual context in Finland; a number of sociolinguistic studies deal with the Saami language as a social object. The specific features of the Finnish language used by bilingual Saami has been studied by Fernandez 1982 (in French), but there are no studies on Saami linguistic substance. The most important of the sociolinguistic studies is Aikio 1988 (in Finnish) which deals with the language shift from Saami to Finnish, now practically completed, among the Sodankylä Saami during the present century. The historical information available on the Saami and their language south of the present Saami area has been summarized in Sammallahti 1982 (in Finnish). A number of shorter articles account for the social status of the Saami language in Finland (Marjut Aikio 1980, 1984, 1990, Aikio & Lindgren 1973, Samuli Aikio 1985, Asp 1980).

9. Bibliography (selected)

Aikio, Marjut (1980): "Saamen kielen asema ja käyttö Suomessa". In: *Congressus Quintus Internationalis Fenno-Ugristarum*. Pars III, Turku.

Aikio, Marjut (1984): "The Position and Use of the Sami Language: Historical, Contemporary and Future Perspectives, Second International Conference on Minority Languages, Turku 6.–12. June 1983". In: *Journal of Multilingual and Multicultural Development*, vol. 5, nos. 3, 4.

Aikio, Marjut (1988): *Saamelaiset kielenvaihdon kierteessä*. Kielisosiologinen tutkimus viiden saamelaiskylän kielenvaihdosta 1910–1980. Suomalaisen Kirjallisuuden Seuran Toimituksia 479, Helsinki. English Summary.

Aikio, Marjut (1990): "The Status of the Sámi language in the Nordic Countries; The Finnish Perspective". In: *Arctic Languages*, Collins, D. R. F. (Ed.), Paris.

Aikio, Marjut/Lindgren, Anna-Riitta (1973): "Kieliraportti". In: *Saamelaiskomitean mietintö*. Liite: Tutkimusraportit. Komiteanmietintä 1973:46, Helsinki.

Aikio, Samuli (1985): "Saamen kielen julkinen ja kirjallinen käyttö Suomessa". In: *Arsis* 1985, 4.

Asp, Erkki (1980): "Saamen kielen sosiaalinen asema ja merkitys". In: *Congressus Quintus Internationalis Fenno-Ugristarum*. Pars III, Turku.

Guttorm, Inga/Jernsletten, Johan/Nickel, Klaus P. (1985–1987): *Davvin* 1–4. Saamen kielen peruskurssi. Oy Yleisradio Ab, Helsinki.

Itkonen, Erkki (1986–1991): *Inarilappisches Wörterbuch* I–IV. Lexica Societatis Fenno-Ugricae XX,1–4, Helsinki.

Itkonen, T. I. (1958): *Koltan- ja kuolanlapin sanakirja*. Wörterbuch des Kolta- und Kolalappischen. I–II. Lexica Societatis Fenno-Ugricae XV, Helsinki.

Labba, Per S./Solbakk, Aage/Holmberg, Veikko (1985–1987): *Sámás* 1–3. Folkets Brevskole – Norsk Korrespondanseskole, Oslo.

Mosnikoff, Jouni/Sammallahti, Pekka (1988): *U'cc sää'm-lää'dd sää'nnkeârjaž*. Pieni koltansaame-suomi sanakirja, Jorgaleaddji Oy.

Nickel, Klaus P. (1990): *Samisk grammatikk*. Universitetsforlaget, Oslo.

Sammallahti, Pekka (1989): *Sámi-suoma sátnegirji*. Saamelais-suomalainen sanakirja. Jorgaleaddji Oy, Ohcejohka.

Sammallahti, Pekka (1993): *Sámi-suoma-sámi sátnegirji*. Saamelais-suomalais-saamelainen sanakirja. Girjegiisá Oy, Ohcejohka.

Sammallahti, Pekka/Mosnikoff, Jouni (1991): *Suomi-koltansaame sanakirja*. Lää'dd-sää'm sää'nnke'rjj. Girjegiisá Oy, Ohcejohka.

Sammellahti, Pekka/Morottaja, Matti (1983): *Säämi-suoma-säämi škovlasänikirje*. Inarinsaame-suomi-inarinsaame koulusanakirja. Ráidu 1. Ruovttueatnan gielaid dutkanguovddáža sámegiel doaimmahusat 1. Kotimaisten kielten tutkimuskeskus, Helsset.

Sammallahti, Pekka/Morottaja, Matti (1993): *Säämi-suomâ sänikirje*. Inarinsaamelais-suomalainen sanakirja. Girjegiisá Oy, Ohcejohka.

Pekka Sammallahti, Oulu (Finland)

126. Denmark

1. Geography and demography
2. Territorial history and national development
3. Politics, economy and general cultural and religious situation
4. Statistics and ethnoprofiles
5. Sociolinguistic situation
6. Presentation of language contact and contact languages not otherwise treated
7. Critical evaluation of the sources and the literature
8. Bibliography (selected)

1. Geography and demography

Denmark proper includes 43 093 square kilometers where 5 146 469 Danes live. Greenland includes 341 700 square kilometers, and 55 533 persons live there. Finally The Faroe Islands, which are also treated in a chapter of their own, include 1 398 square kilometers where 47 449 persons live. The figures are all of them as of January 1st 1991 (Danmarks Statistik 1992, 17).

As you can see from these figures the population density varies considerably as do the linguistic profiles of the three communities. Population density figures are: For Denmark proper 119,4 persons pr. square kilometer. The parallel figures for Greenland and the Faroe Islands are 0,2 and 33,9 respectively.

Geographically, Denmark is divided into the peninsula of Jutland (23 872 km^2) and the islands. Among these the most important are Sealand (7031 km^2), Funen (2984 km^2), Lolland (1242 km^2) and Falster (513 km^2). The capital of Denmark, Copenhagen is situated on Sealand and dominates the whole of the East coast of this island, the coast facing Sweden (→ language map A). The population density figure for the metropolitan area of and around Copenhagen is 598,8. This means that 1 713 736 of the slightly more than 5 million Danes have their abode in the Copenhagen area (Danmarks Statistik 1992, 17). This is a clue to the relatively important position within the Danish linguistic and political geography that Copenhagen occupies cf. below.

Demographically, Denmark is a stable society. The last twenty years have seen a slight growth in the metropolitan rural districts and in urban areas in Jutland while the rural areas proper both in Jutland and elsewhere witness a population loss of between 5 and 7% from 1970 to 1990. The Copenhagen region itself has a slight loss of 1,6%. This is all part of the same tendency of concentrating the Danes in large urban areas with a comparatively low density of housing since most Danes prefer to have their own house. 47,7% of the houses in Denmark are detached, undetached or semidetached one family houses and 52,4% of the households, i. e. 60,3% of the population live in this type of housing (Danmarks Statistik 1992, 76).

As of January 1st 1991 there were 160 641 foreign citizens in Denmark (equalling 3,1% of the population). Among these 35% are from the rest of Scandinavia, the EEC countries and North America, equalling 56 507 persons, while 37 428, equalling 23%, were refugees belonging to the most important nationalities: Iran, Palestine, Iraq, Sri Lanka, Poland, Vietnam, Lebanon, Afghanistan, Ethiopia (Tigre), and Chile. Finally 66 706 (42%) were immigrants coming from third countries, first and foremost Turkey, the former Yugoslavia and Pakistan (Bruun and Hammer 1991, 5). This makes Denmark a very homogeneous country and a country which has not welcomed large amounts of refugees, contrary to what is often believed.

Tabouret-Keller (1992, 269) describes Iceland as an exception since this is by far the country in Western Europe with the least amount of foreigners. Denmark, in his description, ranks with Luxembourg and Norway as countries in Europe with only slight amounts of immigrants. The Tabouret-Keller figure for Denmark of 120 000 immigrants seems, however, either to be too small (if you take all foreign citizens) or too big (if you only take those persons who are refugees and from third countries). Still, the point is well taken, Denmark is demographically and hence culturally homogeneous compared to a lot of Western European countries.

The most important cities in Denmark are: *Copenhagen*, founded at the close of the 12th century, the administrative and political capital of the realm and the only metropolis approaching European size. Copenhagen features a university founded in 1479, the National Museum, the Royal Library and the Royal theatre, opera and ballet. The Parliament and most of the governmental administration as well as the public service channels of the Danish State Radio and Television and the military headquarters are all situated within the metropolitan area. In the city of

Copenhagen there were as of January 1st 1992 464 566 inhabitants whereas the metropolitan area as a whole featured 1 718 805 inhabitants (Danmarks Statistik 1992 a, 19).

Århus may be seen as the regional capital of the Jutland peninsula. Founded in the middle ages around a harbour at the East Coast of Jutland facing the rest of Denmark, Århus now has 267 873 inhabitants (Danmarks Statistik 1992 a, 19). Århus since 1928 has had the second largest university in Denmark, the State Library is situated here and there is an opera and a regional TV station.

Odense is also a medieval town, it is the regional capital of Funen and its sphere of influence in some respects includes the Southern Jutland region as well. There is a newer university (founded in 1966) and the second Television channel which is partly financed by advertisements. There are 179 487 inhabitants in Odense proper (Danmarks Statistik 1992 a, 17).

2. Territorial history and national development

While comparable to the Netherlands in many respects Denmark is not a former colonial power in that the small territories in the third world which the Danish crown had captured during its expansive period in the 18th century have all been ceded without any enduring influence one way or the other. But Denmark has been and is a traditional power in the Nordic context. After 400 years of Danish rule in Norway this country was ceded to Sweden in 1814 only to become independent soon after.

The contemporary frontiers of both Sweden and Norway were formed during the 17th century. This has some relevance for the peculiar development of Copenhagen, a city which was originally placed in the middle of the realm, since to the West it had the rest of Sealand, Funen and Jutland and to the East it was bolstered by Scania. Scania became part of Sweden by the Roskilde treaty of 1658 and Copenhagen was left to expand west-, south- and northwards.

Iceland had been part of the Danish kingdom for centuries when during the second world war it declared itself independent (1944). When Iceland was part of the Danish realm a number of students were educated at Copenhagen University and thus a part of the academics became bilingual with Danish as their second language.

For the Faroe Islands and Greenland, things are a bit more complicated. Both of these parts of the realm have a certain amount of autonomy with the Faroes as the least connected with Denmark. I refer to the respective chapters focussing on them. As to the relationship with Germany, this has undergone various phases in the 20th century. Denmark lost the southernmost part of the Jutland peninsula to Germany in 1864. The two provinces Schleswig and Holstein thus became part of the German *Reich* though there was a sizeable body of Danes in Schleswig. By a referendum in 1920 the North of Schleswig voted to join Denmark and this reunion was much celebrated at the time as a victory for the principle of the right of popular self determination thus strengthening the ideology of one nation, one people, one language. The linguistic relationship is treated in a separate chapter.

By a referendum in 1972 Denmark became a member of the EEC. Several attempts at Nordic unions had failed and Britain was joining the EEC, so, the argument went, Denmark had to fall in line as well. The Norwegian population, on the other hand, rejected membership in 1972. The Norwegian government has renewed its application for full membership in 1992 but the referendum of 1994 affirmed the no. Denmark and Norway are both of them members of the NATO alliance. Not so with Sweden. Sweden, primarily for reasons of neutrality, never even thought of joining the EEC before they applied for full membership in 1992. This development has had the consequence that Denmark until 1994 has been the Nordic foothold, as it were, to the common market. If the two other Scandinavian countries and Finland were admitted to the EEC and if the populations had voted to accept the terms, the Nordic countries would for once have been united, this time as part of a more comprehensive political and economic alliance. The popular sentiment, in Denmark at least, is decidedly Nordic in its outlook. The Maastricht treaty which aims at developing a European union in various areas of government was rejected by the Danes at a referendum in June 1992. This led to the Edinburgh amendments adopted by the Council in December 1992. By May 1993 Denmark had a referendum on the Maastricht treaty with the Edinburgh amendments. To all intents and purposes the referendum decided the fate of

Denmark within the EEC in that the majority for a yes was slight. Denmark remains reluctant.

3. Politics, economy and general cultural and religious situation

In this chapter only those political, economical, religious and general cultural trends will be treated which have an effect on the linguistic scene. (For a reliable treatment of the general history cf. Oakley 1972).

The dominant religion in Denmark is the protestant National church. 88,9% of the population are members, this mean percentage covering significant variations between the figure of 77,4 for the city of Copenhagen and 92,7 for Jutland as a whole. Around 80 000 Danes belong to other religious denominations, the most prominent being the Roman Catholic Church numbering 30 000 Danes. Add to this that probably around 60 000 persons in Denmark are — non-registered — Muslims (as estimated by Bæk Simonsen 1990) and you get a picture of the most important religious movements in Denmark: Overwhelmingly Danes are protestants. The national Church is used for baptisms, confirmations and funerals whereas marriage is contracted by civil agreement to a significant extent. The impressive figures for membership of the National Church should not mislead the observer, though. Modern Denmark is a strongly secularized community.

By virtue of its contemporary profile and its history, Denmark is ideologically rather peculiar among the Western European nation states in that it is considered to be almost completely homogeneous linguistically. Since Denmark did not have any third world colonies like England, Belgium, Portugal or the Netherlands, or any substantial influx of immigrants and migrant workers like Sweden, the linguistic and cultural multiplexity so characteristic of at least the heavily urbanized parts of the modern nation state has come to Denmark only comparatively late and only comparatively feebly. This means that the romantic idea of one nation — one language has survived and thrives in Denmark. Compared to e. g. Norway, however, the Danish linguistic scene stands out as less tolerant towards varieties of Danish and less keen to accept equivalent forms altogether. The roots of this ideology lie at the beginning of the 19th century when under German influence the Danish romantic movement grew strong. Comparative Indo-European philology established as a fact that Danish was related to the Old Norse and in the course of the century when Denmark came under political pressure by Prussia and later on by the united Germany, a romantic ideology was forged whereby the Danish language became the hallmark of a separate Danish, Nordic identity. In the 20th century the nationalist thoughts have had a revival around the second world war when anti-German feelings were very strong and at various points in time when Germany has been felt to be a threat either politically, economically or both. Both in the public debate around the first campaign for or against joining the common market and again around the two referenda on the Maastricht treaty and its corollaries strong nationalist feelings have been prominent. This is not different from any other small nation feeling threatened by a stronger neighbour but in the case of Denmark, nationalism has been coupled with a strong linguistic and indeed cultural centralization. Since Copenhagen is a comparatively huge city dwarfing all other cities in the country and since up till 1928 all higher education at university level took place in this metropolis, Copenhagen has for a long time functioned as a melting pot where dialect features were lost at least to a certain extent. Conversely the linguistic features originally characteristic of the Copenhagen dialect gradually lose their geographical and social specificity only to become accepted as part and parcel of the standard language while the Copenhageners go on to develop new linguistic characteristics. This is an ongoing process.

The resulting linguistic centralization has gone hand in hand with a dialect levelling tendency commonly seen as being a natural development considering the country's size and geography (Brink and Lund 1975 and 1979, Normann Jørgensen 1984). It may be argued that the strong ideological commitment to the standard language sets Denmark apart from other countries where regional lects during the later half of the 20th century have had a revival.

Still, Danes, of course, notice and recognize the sexolects, sociolects, chronolects typical of various subgroups of the population as well as the dialect features which have survived. (For a comprehensive overview of the

Danish dialectological research effort, cf. Ejskjær 1993).

To any linguistically trained observer the intralinguistic Danish variation as well as the interlanguage variation within the speech community will, however, seem slight compared to the variation found in other Scandinavian countries and certainly compared to the multilingual and multicultural reality typical of the modern urbanized Western Europe. In Denmark all official business is carried out in Danish: Parliament sessions (including the speeches by members from the Faroe Islands and Greenland), trade union negotiations, military manoeuvers, court rulings are all in Danish only. In the court room, if necessary, an interpreter is called for, but it is considered highly improper for a Danish citizen not to be perfect in Danish.

For purposes of discussion of the language policy of Denmark it is necessary to distinguish sharply between the written and the spoken language. The written language in the schools and important parts of the administrative system is by law compelled to follow the standard spelling of the *Retskrivningsordbogen*. The first edition of this approbated normative spelling dictionary appeared in 1891 and the latest edition, which is substantially enlarged, appeared in 1986.

As to the spoken language there are several exclusively descriptive dialect dictionaries, including first and foremost the Jutish dictionary by Feilberg and the new Jutish dictionary four instalments of which have appeared 1970−1979. The dictionary of the Danish insular dialects was started in 1929 and the first and second volumes appeared in 1992 and 1994 (Ømålsordbogen 1992 ff). These dictionaries describe what is now a lost world, the dialect speaking Denmark of the second half of the 19th and the first half of the 20th century. The first two dictionaries of the pronunciation of modern Danish appeared in 1990 and 1991. Molbæk Hansen 1990 gives Standard pronunciations only whereas Brink et al. 1991 bring social and regional variants as well.

A strong sense of the national language as an important part of the national identity and a strong sense of the standard language as being the embodiment of the national language are dominant characteristics of the Danish speech community. This has had the effect of creating a rather indifferent attitude towards the many languages which have become a part of the linguistic scene by virtue of the influx of refugees from Hungary (1956), Poland (1969), Vietnam (1975), Iran (1984), Sri Lanka (1985), Iraq (1985), Palestine and Lebanon (1985) and lately from the former Yugoslavia and the trickling in of migratory workers from Turkey, Yugoslavia and Pakistan among other places. To a large extent the politics towards these groups has concentrated on inducing them to speak Danish. Thus the debate on integration and assimilation has tended to be a debate on how to teach the foreigners Danish. Researchers (Kampmann et al. 1992) have indeed speculated that too much is laid at the door of language in the day to day discussions among pedagogues about the *new Danes*.

It is vital in the discussions to distinguish sharply between first generation of male *migratory workers* who came to Denmark during the high tide of Danish industrial expansion, i. e. in the 1960's and 70's, and *the refugees* who have come to Denmark at various points in time depending on the crises in their home lands. The migratory workers came to work in Denmark, they took over the jobs which the Danes did not want and some of them in the 1980's settled here with their families. Most of them were at the time skilled or unskilled workers or peasants without any tradition for integration. Some of them still have close relations to their former country and some of them plan to go back. Some indeed go back. The refugees on the other hand have not chosen to go to Denmark. They have simply fled their former home land. Most of them plan to go back but the time perspective for this repatriation is evidently very uncertain. Most of them may in the end, however, prefer to stay because of their children.

Of course, this sharp distinction is analytical. Anne Holmen (personal communication) has pointed out that in a fair number of cases the distinction may become somewhat blurred, since e. g. the Kurds may have come to Denmark in order to escape political persecution even when they were classified as migratory workers. Before 1973 incoming Kurds would be classified as migratory workers, after the immigration stop in 1973 they may have come to Denmark as part of a family reunion programme whereas by 1992 they may be applying for asylum as political refugees.

The Ministry of education in 1992 estimated the number of pupils belonging to some linguistic minority in the Danish schools at about 5%. The ministry expects that the number will rise to 10% at the turn of the century. Since the new Danes are unevenly distributed geographically this makes it evident that some schools in the Copenhagen area come close to being multicultural and multilingual institutions – only they are never seen as such. They are seen as Danish schools with too few Danes in them.

The Danish school system has a compulsory nine years education. Whether the teaching is done in Danish or not is nobody's business as long as the pupils are able to pass Danish exams at the end. This makes room for free schools using a non Danish mother tongue as the medium of instruction. Some of the schools established for Muslims indeed have other languages as the medium of instruction and Danish as a second language. For regular pupils in the all Danish schools mother tongue courses are offered. The mother tongue offer comprises from three to five hours of study a week at the request of parents and is mostly placed outside of normal hours. It is in principle confined to non-Danish languages spoken at home. All languages, i. e. not only official languages, may be taught.

It is a prominent feature of the employment figures that the unemployment rates for the Norwegians, Swedes, British, German and American citizens in Denmark is at or below the national mean whereas the unemployment rates for the Turks, Yugoslavians, Pakistanis, Moroccans, Iranians, Sri Lankans, and the Polish immigrants is roughly from two to three times higher (Bruun and Hammer 1992, 48).

4. Statistics and ethnoprofiles

Any attempt at sketching a macrosociolinguistic description of the Danish speech community is hampered by the fact that Danish statisticians do not distinguish between the various languages. National statistics is concerned exclusively with nationalities. This is particularly misleading in the case of the Turkish community since this nationality includes – as do indeed the Iranian nationality and the Iraqui nationality – a number of Kurdish speaking persons. It is furthermore the case that the four Kurdish main dialects differ among themselves not only as such but also because of the use of different writing systems. Most of the Danish Kurds are migratory workers stemming from a place in Central Anatolia where they were forcefully resettled by the Turks. The complicated relationship between the Kurdish varieties, including the alphabets used, is certainly in evidence among the Kurds in Denmark as well, cf. Ağacanoğlu 1990.

Another obvious case of confusion is Yugoslavia. The migratory workers from the former Yugoslavia could until 1990 be described conveniently as belonging to the nationality of Yugoslavia and as speaking or at least understanding Serbo-Croatian most of them. In the 1990's this has become impossible.

In the absence of sound statistics we must follow a different route. This has to be the enumeration of, hopefully convergent, criteria for the isolation and description of speech communities within the larger speech community of Denmark.

The largest body of foreign residents in Denmark are those of Turkish nationality. As of January 1st 1991 there were 29 680 persons belonging to this category in Denmark. It is a community settled here for one generation. More than a third of them are below 14 years of age and since 30% of the Turkish citizens as a whole are born in Denmark (Bruun and Hammer 1992, 24) we may be reasonably sure that most of the children are born here. There are few naturalisations (only 1551 for the period 1980 to 1990) and very few of the Turks go to secondary or higher education institutions (Bruun and Hammer 1992, 31 and 42). The community of Turks are most severely drabbed by unemployment, only the Moroccans fare worse but they are far less numerous.

Geographically speaking, most of the Turks live in the Copenhagen metropolitan area but there are a few Turks in the other major cities and also in some of the provincial towns, e. g. Køge South of Copenhagen.

There is Turkish news a quarter of an hour every day broadcast by the public service State Radio since 1977 (Ditzel, personal communication). In a paper written in 1988 Leif Lønsmann of the Danish State Radio notes that there are local radio stations sending for a limited amount of time and for a limited audience in Turkish and Kurdish in the metropolitan area of Copenhagen, and in Western and Middle Jutland (only Kurdish). Several housing companies exploit satellite technology to receive Turkish television programmes which are then distributed to the customers by cable. Comparing Pakistani, Yugoslavian and Turkish nationalities speaking Kurdish, Turkish, Urdu, Panjabi, Serbo Croatian, Albanian and Macedonian, Jørgen Gimbel (1987) by way of introduction gives some figures relating to proficiency tests of Danish and the general evaluation by teachers of skills in Danish. This all adds up to the result that the Turks are rated to be the nationality least likely to succeed in learning Danish. The Turks themselves are overwhelmingly positive towards the, mostly Turkish, mother tongue courses offered by the Danish folk school as decided by law. In one commune in Sealand recent information shows that the mother tongue teaching offered is Turkish, even to Kurdish speaking children (Rosling 1992, 28). This seems to be general (Gimbel, personal communication, Normann Jørgensen, personal communication). In Just Jeppesen's investigation of the second generation of immigrants (Just Jeppesen 1989), the informants were asked what language they would speak to their parents, siblings, spouses and children. The options given were: the mother tongue, a mixture, presumably meaning code shift between the first language and Danish, and Danish pure and simple. The author documents that 92% of the young second generation Turks choose to speak their native language with their parents while only 43% of them stick to it in conversation with their brothers and sisters, 44% code shifting between the native language and Danish. The language loyalty of Turks and Kurds thus seems to be high but a functional diversification is beginning to make itself felt as witnessed by the fact that as many as 39% spoke both Danish and Turkish/Kurdish to their children (cf. Gimbel 1991, 68). Probably Just Jeppesen's remark that "it should be noted that the young parents speaking a language from their native country to their children do not always speak their own mother tongue. They will sometimes speak the official language of the native country in order to give their children the best chances ..." (Just Jeppesen 1989, 132) refers precisely to the group of Kurdish speaking Turks.

In the beginning of the 1980's both a Turkish-Danish dictionary and a Danish-Turkish dictionary were published.

On the whole the Turks, whether they are Kurds or Turkish speaking Turks, seem to be the least integrated or — looked at from another perspective — the most language loyal among the foreigners.

The second largest body of foreigners in Denmark are the Norwegians. Nothing is known about the language loyalty of the Norwegians — nor for that matter of the Swedish persons — in Denmark. We know that they as of January 1st 1991 were 10233 and 8158 respectively (Bruun and Hammer 1992, 12) and a fair guess is that they all adapt their native language slightly but do not shift altogether. A study of which features of Norwegian and Swedish are adaptable and which are not would be as interesting as a study of what features of the two other Scandinavian languages create most difficulties for Danes. The linguistic and cultural cooperation among the Nordic countries specifies that an introduction to spoken and written Norwegian and Swedish are an obligatory part of the teaching of Danish in schools, high schools and at the university. There is a common administrative structure, *Nordisk Språksekretariat*, making possible a certain amount of coordination of language planning in the Nordic countries (cf. Løland 1990 and Vikør 1993). The actual results have, however, been small and the teaching of the two neighbouring languages in Denmark is more notable for singular sparks of enthusiasm than for its overall efficiency.

There are some studies of interscandinavian communication, conveniently summarized in Ohlsson 1979 (cf. now Vikør 1993). They show that the pattern of comprehension is skewed: Danes on the whole understand Swedish much better than the Swedes understand Danish. Norwegian is the easiest language to understand for all Scandinavians, Danish being particularly difficult for the Swedes (Ohlsson 1979, 18). The interscandinavian comprehension figures are much higher for written language understanding, of course, one type of written Norwegian being virtually written Danonorwegian. Traditionally, i. e. before the advent of satellites and cable TV, Swedish television was an option for people living along the East coast of Sealand (i. e. including the Copenhagen metropolitan area) while Norwegian television was seen by some in the North of Jutland. Traffic by ferry connects Frederikshavn and other North Jutland towns with Norway and the North Sealand town of Elsinore with Swedish Helsingborg. In these commercial centres spoken Norwegian and Swedish are regularly heard and understood.

As for the British minority, including 10 226 persons as of January 1st 1991 (ibid.), the adults have no reason at all to abandon their native English since English has a very high prestige and is well understood in Denmark (cf. below, section 5.). Their children, of course, do learn Danish. Some of the British citizens are ethnically Pakistani, speaking Panjabi as their first language (Normann Jørgensen, personal communication).

The nationality of Yugoslavia has been for some time now a fiction since it includes Serbs, Croatians, Macedonians, Slovenians and Albanians as well as Turkish speaking former Yugoslavian citizens. The distribution and numbers are as yet totally unknown by the statisticians. The various groups differ also in that some of them came to Denmark as migratory workers from 1970 and onwards while recently Denmark has received a smaller amount of refugees from the Yugoslavian wars. This makes it almost impossible to say anything definite about the group, it is simply not one group linguistically. What we know is that they include a few Serbs, some Croatians, a fair number of Albanians (from Kosovo) and some Macedonians plus some Turkish speaking Muslims. The Yugoslavians have a conspicuously low rate of naturalisations (Bruun and Hammer 1992, 31). This is slightly surprising since we know from Just Jeppesen's investigation of the second generation of immigrants (Just Jeppesen 1989, 10) that the young Yugoslavians as a whole are much more prone to marry Danes than the Turks or the Pakistanis. 31% of the young Yugoslavian men and 24% of the young women are married to Danes. The Yugoslavians married to Danes are less religious, better educated, and more urban than the comparable groups of second generation immigrants (ibid.). Taken as a group the young Yugoslavians feel at home in Denmark and tend to identify themselves as Danish (Just Jeppesen 1980, 146). This is clearly a characteristic of the second generation and it would have been highly interesting to see a break up of these figures by ethnic lines. Results from Gimbel (1987, 52) suggest that the Albanian speaking Yugoslavians are much more like the Kurdish speaking Turks, in so far at least that they do significantly worse as to proficiency in Danish than their Serbo-Croatian speaking countrymen. The common label 'Yugoslavian' may be misleading in most cultural respects.

The State Radio broadcasts news in Serbo-Croatian every weekday for a quarter of an hour. The Copenhagen community offers mother tongue courses in all the Yugoslavian languages except Slovenian: Serbian, Croatian, Macedonian, Turkish, Albanian (Strandby, personal communication). There are no dictionaries for Albanian or Macedonian and only lists of words for interpreters of Serbo-Croatian.

The Iranian body of citizens in Denmark (8977 as of 1st of January 1991 (Bruun and Hammer 1992, 12)) are by far the best educated and the most prone to seek higher education among the refugees (Bruun and Hammer 1992, 42). Almost all of them came to Denmark between 1984 and 1990 (Bruun and Hammer 1992, 15 and 19). I know of no information on the languages of the refugees from Iran. Farsi is taught in Copenhagen as part of the mother tongue teaching effort and there is at least one local radio station in Copenhagen broadcasting in Farsi and one more in the county of Western Sealand. There are recent and research based dictionaries of Farsi and Danish.

The Palestinians number as of 1st of January 1991 7550 persons. In the statistics they are classified as being outside any nationality due to the complicated situation in the Middle East. Almost without exception they are refugees. Their first language is Arabic.

The Pakistani group includes 6231 persons as of 1st of January 1991 (Bruun and Hammer 1992, 12) but there are more former citizens of Pakistan in Denmark since the number of naturalisations for this group is rather high: 4071 Pakistani citizens have been naturalised during the period of time from 1980 to 1990 (Bruun and Hammer, 31).

The Pakistani group is special in that around 11% of them are classified as being independent in labour statistics, most of them presumably being shop owners. The first generation was much better educated and much more urban than the first Turks and Yugoslavians in Denmark (Just Jeppesen 1989, 45). This is particularly the case for the men. For the second generation pervasive sex differences are conspicuous if compared with the native Danes (but not if compared with the other immigrant groups). A fair percentage, viz. 22% of the young Pakistani men are students, a percentage far higher than the other immigrant groups except the Iranians. (The figures do not, however, agree with the figures in Bruun and Hammer 1991, 42).

The Pakistani are concentrated in Copenhagen and the Metropolitan area. Information from the office for the mother tongue courses in Copenhagen shows that at least Panjabi and Urdu are taught as mother tongues. Urdu is the language of at least one local radio station in Copenhagen. The Immigrant Library has a fair collection of books in Urdu and there are several orders for them although not nearly as many as the orders for Arabic books, cf. below. There are no dictionaries of Urdu and Panjabi in relation to Danish which presumably means that the Pakistani translate to Danish via English.

On the whole, the Pakistani seem to be pragmatic in their attitude towards Denmark apart from their views on gender related issues. The male members are consequently probably the best integrated among the traditional immigrant groups.

The rest of the foreigners in Denmark include a group of 5000 Tamils from Sri Lanka who came to Denmark from 1986 and onwards, a group of Poles numbering 4700, a group of Americans (circa 4500), 3700 Vietnamese, circa 3100 Lebanese (among them some Palestinians) and around 3000 from Morocco.

Some of these groups are linguistically active, notably the Tamil speaking group who have manned local radio stations in Århus and two other counties in Jutland. The Tamil group seem in addition to be very active readers as witnessed by the fact that the Immigrant Library which has a collection of 3400 books and audio visual material in Tamil had a total of 4000 orders for these books resulting in a mean of 103 days waiting, a figure far exceeding that of any other linguistic minority. A Danish-Tamil dictionary appeared in 1992.

The number of Arabic speakers in Denmark is, for reasons already mentioned, very difficult to estimate. A number of observations may be made, though. The immigrant library holds a total of 11 000 items in Arabic. Orders for these books etc. numbered in 1992 about 11 000 which makes the Arabic readers by far the most active. The comparative figure for the Turkish readers are 20 000 books etc. and 6800 orders. (Statistics from the Folkebibliotekernes Indvandrerbibliotek by courtesy of B. Kragh Schwarz).

The status of Arabic as a holy language, the language of the Koran, makes it obvious that religion has a bearing on the linguistic status of Arabic in Denmark. Bæk Simonsen 1990 has estimated that a total of 15 to 20% of the immigrant children in the Greater Copenhagen area regularly follow Koran school courses. These children come from Turkish, Yugoslavian, Pakistani, Moroccan, Arabic, Lebanese and Palestinian nationalities thus cutting right across the unit boundaries of current statistics. Dictionaries of Danish and Arabic exist for translation both ways.

The community of Danish Sign Language users is irrevocably Danish by nationality and yet a linguistic minority. Danish Sign Language is used by the group of deaf Danes numbering 3500. Some twenty years ago, Danish Sign Language had its official breakthrough as a medium of instruction in its own right and as worth interpreting to and from. In addition to the core group, around 1200 professional pedagogues, teachers and interpreters use Sign Language as a first or second language and probably there are 2 persons able to understand Danish Sign Language for every original user of it. The result is a community of circa 12 000 active or passive users.

For the Danish Sign Language user, written Danish is the first foreign language and with the advent of new technology such as writing phones, this second language has gained in importance as a means of every day communication. Since the communication modes diverge so sharply the analysis of interference or transfer from Danish Sign Language into Danish written language poses more problems than can be solved at the moment. Due to the pioneering work of Elisabeth Engberg-Pedersen Danish Sign Language is by far the most thoroughly studied of the minority languages (cf. e. g. Engberg-Pedersen 1993) although of course a lot still remains to be done.

5. Sociolinguistic situation

As noted in connection with the description of the various groups of foreigners there are only very few languages in Denmark spoken by enough people to make them more than home languages reserved for communication between next of kin and extended families. Some of these languages are backed up by social or religious activity among the various group members so that they may be kept alive as communication media for social interaction outside the family proper. Generally speaking, however, none of the languages in Denmark apart from Danish is sufficient for a citizen of Denmark. It is necessary to become bilingual in order for the foreigner to function as a member of the Danish community. A possible exception may be the Turkish first generation immigrants and their housewives. The Turkish minority in Denmark is probably the only one settled enough, geographically, focussed enough and, most importantly, numerous enough to sustain a life of their own linguistically.

This is only valid for a minority of the group, however, i. e. those of the first generation outside the labour force. Note that their children have to be educated for at least nine compulsory years and thus have to learn Danish well enough to pass the Danish exams. This means that the sociolinguistic situation of all other languages in Denmark is that they are confined to intra group communication and use inside the family, nuclear or extended as the case may be. There is however one very important exception to this statement, viz. English.

It is a commonplace in the language planning discussions in Denmark to note the extreme prestige accorded to English (Lund 1992). It is in fact the case that around 4000 copies of English or American newspapers are bought in Denmark every day, that any shop keeper in the Copenhagen area will be able to manage the rudiments of a trading session in English, that the Radio has news in English, that English since 1956 has been taught from the fifth grade in the Danish folk school, that the television shows undubbed, but subtitled, American films and television programs to an astonishing extent and that commercials are often in English, some of them even without Danish subtitles. All of these characteristics are valid first and foremost for the urban areas and the younger part of the population whose subculture is deeply influenced by the American way of life.

This has led Gregersen (1991) and Haberland et al. (1991) to suggest that the function of English in various domains for a substantial number of Danes threatens the use of Danish. This view is, however decidedly the view of a concerned minority. The official view is well presented by Hansen (1985) or Brink (1991) who both of them argue that Danish has the capacity to integrate an enormous amount of loan words and that the grammatical system is virtually unaffected. The apparent or real clash between the two views is at the same time a clash between two traditionally very different approaches to language contact phenomena.

One view holds that language contact leads to changes in the dominated language(s) so that loan words, first in the form of loan translations later on as the wholesale adoption of word forms adapted to the phonological and orthographical system of the dominated language infiltrate the lexicon, and finally that the penetration of the deeper levels of grammar by the dominant language leads to an approximation so that the two languages more or less merge.

Some of the phases in this process of influence by a dominant language over a dominated one have been witnessed by Danish in respect to Low German in the Middle Ages (Skautrup 1944—1946). Clearly the influence by English on Danish in this respect is not nearly as pervasive as that of Low German in the Hanseatic period (Brink 1991, Bojsen 1989, Lund 1989).

The other point of view takes as its point of departure the analysis of language use in a given speech community. If we divide the speech community according to strict principles of classification into its various spheres of activity, these spheres will themselves be constituted of various domains (Fasold 1984, 183 f). The domain analysis of a given speech community answers the simple question: What language(s) is(are) used for the transactions within the various domains? In this sense what is happening in Denmark is that a substantial part of the speakers begin to choose English instead of Danish for transactions within the domain of advertising and for scientific communication. Since the average Danish TV viewer is exposed to a massive amount of spoken English and since most younger Danes have been taught English at school, the comprehension competence for the urbanized part of the population is rather high.

On the one hand, then, Danish as a language system and a lexicon is not threatened by any outside influence whatsoever. On the other hand Danish as a medium of communication is losing ground in some important arenas.

6. Presentation of language contact and contact languages not otherwise treated

A list prepared by Anne Holmen and Jens Norman Jørgensen of the languages spoken in Denmark include apart from those already mentioned: Abkhazian, Amharic, Armenian, Assyrian, Azerbadjani, Bengali, Berberian, Bulgarian, Estonian, Fante, Frisian, Galla, Greek, Gujarati, Hausa, Hebrew, Hindi, Dutch, Belorussian, Igbo, Indonesian, Irish, Italian, Japanese, Cantonese, Catalonian, Khazak, Khmer, Mandarin, Chinese, Korean, Latvian, Lithuanian, Moldavian, Pashto, Portuguese, Romani, Rumanian, Russian, Sami, Sinhalese, Scots, Slovakian, Slovenian, Somali, Sorbian, Spanish, Swahili, Tagalog, Tartarian, Thai, Tigre, Tigrinyan, Czech, Twi, German, Ukrainian, Hungarian, Eskimo, Uzbekian, Welsh, Vietnamese, Yiddish (Holmen and Norman Jørgensen 1993). It must be understood that some of these languages are spoken as home languages by very small groups, some of them only by hundreds or even fewer. It is impossible to ascertain the precise nature of the linguistic diversity of Denmark as a speech community until the statisticians make up their mind to ask all migrants what language they speak (at home). Even then, one may have to supplement the figures with research efforts directed at mapping the macrosociolinguistic profile of the Danish speech community.

It is notable that the research on the acquisition of Danish as a second language has developed so late in Denmark – compared to e. g. Sweden, but this may be explained first and foremost by the small amount of foreigners and the strong tradition of focussing on Danish by the linguistic traditions in Denmark. It is even more notable that precisely this focus on the national mother tongue has had the unfortunate consequence of blinding the language planners to the obvious fact that Denmark is becoming more and more of a multicultural nation. The national debate has had a comparatively tedious ring of hatred and non-acceptance on the one hand and acceptance but discussion as to whether integration or assimilation of the foreigners should be the code word, on the other. The language planners of Denmark would do well to start a debate on what happens to the languages spoken by the foreigners when this is placed under the domination of the strong national norm of Danish and even better to initiate research on what happens to the speakers' attitudes towards their first language. To my knowledge there are as of March 1993 no studies published on the effect of Danish on say the Turkish of the Turks in Denmark nor of the language of any other group of foreigners.

If the development sketched here goes on and if Denmark gradually gets more deeply integrated into a larger multicultural European context, the traditional mental stereotype of the inveterate monolingual Dane must soon be replaced by an image of *the bilingual Dane* – irrespective of whether Danish is the first or the second language.

7. Critical evaluation of the sources and literature

The fact that Danish lives more or less happily with English as its competitor in some domains has not led to greater tolerance of or interest in the many exotic languages existing by virtue of the foreign citizens in Denmark. On the contrary it is an important fact about the sociolinguistic situation in Denmark that the research done on the languages of immigrants until the Køge project initiated in 1989 (Holmen 1991) has concentrated solely on how, and how well these non-Danes learn Danish. In recent years, this research has been intensified first and foremost due to the efforts of a small group of researchers, prominent among them Jørgen Gimbel, Anne Holmen, and Jens Normann Jørgensen all of them active at The Royal School of Educational Studies. Anne Holmen has recently taken up a post at Copenhagen University where research into Danish as a second language has been carried out since the middle of the 1980's.

The two most comprehensive and up to date reviews of the existing literature are those of Normann Jørgensen (1990) and Holmen (1991). What emerges from these overviews is a development from a focus on the second language learning via interlanguage analysis to research trying to come to grips with the interplay between first and second language in social interaction in natural settings. Intercultural communication rather than interlanguage has become the frame of reference. It is not possible to do justice to the many books and reports within the field of Danish as a second language. Suffice it here to make note of two important studies.

The only Ph. D. dissertation as yet is from Holmen (1990). Holmen was trained as a linguist and participated in the project led by Claus Færch on learner language a result of which is Færch et al. (1984). Holmen's background is thus a thorough knowledge of the results and methods practised by international research on foreign language learning. This is evident in that the thrust of the book is methodological and psycholinguistic rather than pedagogical or sociolinguistic. The informants are six learners of Danish, two Albanian speaking Yugoslavian citizens, both of them boys, one 15 years old and one 17 years old, two Vietnamese girls aged 16 and 15, and finally an American boy, 18, and an American girl, 17. The Americans were both of them exchange students and so likely to return to the USA relatively soon while the four others all of them had come to Denmark as part of the family reunion programme which is a right for children and spouses of everyone residing permanently in Denmark, including refugees and migrant workers.

If you compare these six learners the linguistic background whose is well known to be completely different typologically, the design may answer the question whether the acquisition of Danish follows the same broad lines irrespective of the mother tongue or whether the interlanguage at any given time in the acquisition process is more or less dependent on the L1.

The answer is a modified 'both and'. Pride of place in the dissertation is given to the description of the common main road to Danish, common to all of the learners. Holmen partly subscribes to the Givonian functional view but in the end finds that the model proposed by Rod Ellis (1985) is more valid. The universality of the model corresponds to its abstractness; the phases suggested are 1. the basic proposition in a fixed sequence, 2. syntax begins to creep in: the proposition now has more case roles expressed and the sequence of words begins to vary, 3. morphological systems are acquired, 4. sentences begin to be embedded and strung together (Holmen 1990, 34). This is precisely the sequence Holmen finds for her six learners (ibid. 196). On the other hand, Holmen also finds that there are interesting differences between the learners in their acquisition of Danish. This may or may not be explained by the characteristic features of their respective mother tongues, the important thing is to adopt a model (in this case Ellis') which allows for both universality and variation.

Another important study by the group affiliated to the royal School of Educational Studies is the study by Gimbel (1987). In the Danish debate the group of foreigners is most often taken to be uniform and is simply referred to as 'the strangers' or 'the foreign language speakers'. This is unhelpful since, as we have seen, the group of foreigners is in fact far from homogeneous, linguistically, culturally, religiously and with respect to their social position in Denmark.

Gimbel's sample includes 3 nationalities (64 Turkish persons, 48 Pakistani and 47 Yugoslavian persons), and 7 linguistic groups in that there are 18 Kurdish speakers, 57 Turkish speakers (11 of them being Yugoslavian by nationality), 24 Urdu speakers, 24 Panjabi speakers, 11 Serbo-Croatian speakers, 14 Albanian speakers and 11 Macedonian speakers. All of them are pupils, 78 being fourth grade and 81 sixth grade students. In addition 172 Danes were included as informants. Obviously, a study comprising so many persons cannot be carried out as a qualitative investigation of conversations but has to be based upon written data. The particular method employed is adapted from Hyltenstam 1978. It involves 72 sentences with a choice between two positions for a given item. What is tested is thus the acquisition of the rules of word order so characteristic of Danish.

The specific areas of syntax tested are the following: Negation in simple sentences, negation in subordinate sentences, inversion in yes/no questions, preposed adverbial in simple sentences, word order in interrogatory subordinate sentences, word order in declarative subordinate sentences, and the relative order of object and adverbial in simple sentences.

It is essential in the construction of a set of test sentences to investigate the grammaticality hierarchy involved. Thus a sentence like "Ved skolen __ Ole __ en ven" and a test item like "møder" lead to the two possible sentences:

(1) *Ved skolen Ole møder en ven* (By the school Ole meets a friend)
(2) *Ved skolen møder Ole en ven* (By the school meets Ole a friend).

Now the first sentence is seen by Gimbel as being ungrammatical in Danish (it is however fully grammatical in English) while the second one is fully grammatical in Danish (and completely unacceptable/ungrammatical in English). The interesting thing is whether you succeed in all cases to construct a set of test sentences where the choice between the two possibilities is psycholinguistically the same. I would accept *Ved skolen Ole møder en ven* as only vaguely ungrammatical and certainly not incomprehensible and in fact this particular sentence was deemed to be correct by 21 of the 159 foreigners. This result is awkward since it diverges sharply from the other 12 sentences supposed to tap precisely the same linguistic competence.

These methodological problems notwithstanding the results are as follows:

The order of acquisition seems to be the same for both Danes and immigrants and agrees very well with the Hyltenstam results for Swedish. The variation in results for the subgroups is conspicuous and may be explained by a combination of nationality and mother tongue:

"The subjects can be divided into 3 groups of increasing command of word order:

1. Turks speaking Kurdish and Yugoslavs speaking Albanian
2. Turks speaking Turkish and all Pakistani
3. Yugoslavs speaking Turkish, Serbo Croat or Macedonian" (Gimbel 1987, 107).

The author points out that the only explanation that seems to be valid for this particular scale of competence is the equivalent scale of status "... it is interesting that both of the two minority groups, who when combined constitute the weakest group in the study, are in fact groups of low status in their native countries. Apparently, the parents' social and educational status plays an important part." (Gimbel 1987, 110). This interpretation is valid as well for an interesting result of Holmen's, viz. that the Americans were significantly ahead and quicker in their acquisition of Danish despite their being only temporarily in Denmark (Holmen 1990, 197).

The question is whether the Gimbel results are in some ways an artefact of the method employed. It seems to be natural to expect an effect of the children's attitude to formal education precisely when employing the technique of filling out a prepared written test. This is not to say, however, that we would not find the same differences if we chose to investigate the Danish used in, say, conversation with Danish children. It may very well be the case that those pupils who come from a subculture least positive towards formal schooling are also prone to reject the integration into Danish mainstream culture which would presumably by and large lead to poor mastery of Danish.

9. Bibliography (selected)

Ağacanoğlu, Adnan (1990): "Kurdisk i Danmark". In: *Modersmålsundervisning i mindretalssprog*, Jørgensen, N./Holmen, A. (Eds.), Københavnerstudier i tosprogethed 13, Copenhagen, 63−72.

Bojsen, Else (1989): "Dansk under engelsk-amerikansk fortryllelse?" In: *Sprog i Norden/Språk i Norden*, Nordisk Språksekretariats skrifter 10, 39−46.

Brink, Lars (1991): "Nordens folkesprog i fare?" In: *Det danske sprogs status år 2001 − er dansk et truet sprog?*, Jørgensen, N. (Ed.), Københavnerstudier i tosprogethed 14, Copenhagen, 107−110.

Brink, Lars et al. (1991): *Den Store Danske Udtaleordbog*, Copenhagen.

Brink, Lars/Lund, Jørn (1975): *Dansk Rigsmål 1−2*, Copenhagen.

Brink, Lars/Lund, Jørn (1979): "Social factors in the sound changes of modern Danish". In: *Proceedings of the Ninth International Congress of Phonetic Sciences*, Vol. II, Copenhagen, 196−203.

Bruun, Inger/Hammer, Ole (1991): *Statistik om indvandrere og flygtninge 1991*, Dokumentation om INDVANDRERE, nr. 2, Copenhagen.

Bæk Simonsen, Jørgen (1990): *Islam i Danmark. Muslimske institutioner i Danmark 1970−1989*, Århus, Statens Humanistiske Forskningsråd.

Danmarks Statistik (1992): *Statistisk årbog/Statistical Yearbook 1992*, Copenhagen.

Danmarks Statistik (1992a): *Befolkningens bevægelser 1990/Vital Statistics 1990*, Copenhagen.

Dansk Sprognævn (1986): *Retskrivningsordbogen*, Copenhagen.

Ejskjær, Inger (1993): *Danish Dialect Research*, Copenhagen.

Ellis, Rod (1985): *Understanding Second Language Acquisition*, Oxford.

Engberg-Pedersen, Elisabeth (1993): *Space in Danish Sign Language*, Hamburg.

Fasold, Ralph (1984): *The Sociolinguistics of Society*, Introduction to Sociolinguistics, Volume 1, London.

Færch, Claus/Haastrup, Kirsten/Phillipson, Robert (1984): *Learner Language and Language Learning*, Copenhagen.

Gimbel, Jørgen (1987): *Indvandrerdansk er flere ting. Variationen i indvandrergruppers danskfærdighed belyst ved en undersøgelse af jugoslaviske, pakistanske og tyrkiske elevers beherskelse af dansk ledstilling i 4. og 6. klasse*. Under medvirken af: Jens Johansen og Svend Kreiner, Københavnerstudier i tosprogethed 3, Copenhagen.

Gimbel, Jørgen (1988): "Immigrant Danish − A Multitude of Languages". In: *Migracijske Teme* 4, no. 4, 469−476.

Gimbel, Jørgen (1991): "Magtsproget dansk". In: *Det danske sprogs status år 2001 − er dansk et truet sprog*, Jørgensen, N. (Ed.), Københavnerstudier i tosprogethed 14, Copenhagen, 53-76.

Gimbel, Jørgen (1991 a): "Tosprogede børns sproglige udvikling". In: *Håndbog om indvandrere og flygtninge*, Hammer (Ed.), Copenhagen, 246-259.

Gregersen, Frans (1991): "Dansk i 90'erne - et oplæg til diskussion". In: *Auditorium X, Dansk før, nu og i fremtiden?* Hansen, E. et al. (Eds.), Copenhagen, 230-251.

Haberland, Hartmut/Henriksen, Carol/Phillipson, Robert/Skuttnab-Kangas, Tove (1991): "Tak for mad! Om sprogæderi med dansk som livret". In: *Det danske sprogs status år 2001 - er dansk et truet sprog*, Jørgensen, N. (Ed.), Københavnerstudier i tosprogethed 14, Copenhagen, 111-138.

Hansen, Erik (1985): "La crise de la langue standard au Danemark". In: *La crise des langues*, Maurais, J. (Ed.), Québec, 295-301.

Holmen, Anne (1990): *Udviklingslinier i tilegnelsen af dansk som andetsprog - en kvalitativ, kvantitativ analyse*, Københavnerstudier i tosprogethed 12, Copenhagen (*English summary*).

Holmen, Anne (1991): "Forskning i dansk som andetsprog". In: *Nordens språk som andraspråk*, Axelsson/Viberg (Eds.), Stockholm.

Holmen, Anne/Norman Jørgensen, Jens (1993): *Tosprogede børn i Danmark*, Københavnerstudier: tosprogethed 17, Copenhagen.

Hyltenstam, Kenneth (1978): *Progress in Immigrant Swedish Syntax. A Variability Analysis*, Lund, Department of General Linguistics, University of Lund.

Just Jeppesen, Kirsten (1989): *Unge indvandrere. En undersøgelse af andengeneration fra Jugoslavien, Tyrkiet og Pakistan*, Copenhagen.

Just Jeppesen, Kirsten (1990): *Young Second Generation Immigrants in Denmark - An investigation of young people from Yugoslavia, Turkey and Pakistan who have resided in Denmark for at least 10 years*, Copenhagen.

Jysk Ordbog (1970 ff): *Jysk ordbog*, Bind I, Hæfte 1-4, Aarhus.

Kampmann, Jan/Moldenhawer, Bolette/Muschinsky, Lars J. (1991): *Nærvær og flygtighed. Om det flertydige i det flerkulturelle projekt*, Forskningsnoter nr. 9, Copenhagen.

Lund, Jørn (1989): "Tak for lån". In: *Sprog i Norden/Språk i Norden*, Nordisk Språksekretariats skrifter 10, Oslo/Copenhagen/Stockholm, 94-101.

Lund, Jørn (1992): "Drop it!" In: *Sprog i Norden/Språk i Norden*, Nordisk Språksekretariats skrifter 13, Oslo/Copenhagen/Stockholm, 76-83.

Løland, Ståle (Ed.) (1990): *Sprog i Norden/Språk i Norden*, Nordisk Språksekretariats skrifter 11, Oslo/Copenhagen/Stockholm.

Molbæk Hansen, Peter (1990): *Dansk udtale*, Copenhagen.

Normann Jørgensen, Jens (1984): "Societal Dialect Shift. A case study", In: *Sociolinguistic Papers*, 43-50.

Normann Jørgensen, Jens (1990): *Dansk som fremmed- og andetsprog i Danmark. En oversigt 1980-90*, Københavnerstudier i tosprogethed 11, Copenhagen.

Oakley, Stewart (1972): *The Story of Denmark*, London.

Ohlsson, Stig Örjan (1979): "Nordisk språkförståelse - igår, idag, imorgon". In: *Nordisk radio och television via satellit*, Kultur- och programpolitisk delrapport, Bilaga 6, København, Nordiska Ministerrådet NU A 1979: 6 Band 3.

Rosling, Marianne (1992): *Vilje til åbenhed! Oplæg til nye veje i Karlebo's integrationsarbejde for indvandrere*, Dokumentation om INDVANDRERE, nr. 4, Copenhagen.

Skautrup, Peter (1944 ff): *Det Danske Sprogs Historie* I-V, Copenhagen.

Tabouret-Keller, André (1992): "Some major features of the sociolinguistic situation in Europe and the European Charter". In: *Sociolinguistics Today. International Perspectives*, Bolton/Kwok (Eds.), London and New York, 266-280.

Vikør, Lars S. (1993): *The Nordic Languages*. Nordic Language Secretariat Publication no. 14, Oslo.

Ømålsordbogen (1992 ff): *Ømålsordbogen. En sproglig-saglig ordbog over dialekterne på Sjælland, Lolland-Falster, Fyn og omliggende øer*, Bind 1: A-bladlås, Copenhagen.

Frans Gregersen, Copenhagen (Denmark)

127. Dänisch—Deutsch

1. Geographie und Demographie
2. Geschichte
3. Politik, Wirtschaft und allgemeine kulturelle Lage
4. Statistik und Ethnoprofile
5. Soziolinguistische Lage
6. Sprachpolitische Lage
7. Allgemeines kontaktlinguistisches Porträt
8. Kritische Wertung
9. Bibliographie (in Auswahl)

1. Geographie und Demographie

1.1. Die sprachliche Kontaktzone zwischen Dänisch und Deutsch wird durch das alte Herzogtum Schleswig gebildet. Der nördliche Teil, Nordschleswig oder Sønderjylland, der administrativ Sønderjyllands Amt umfaßt und geographisch die Landschaft zwischen der Kongeå im Norden (welche die historische Grenze zwischen dem Königreich Dänemark und dem Herzogtum Schleswig darstellt) und der 1920 errichteten deutsch—dänischen Staatsgrenze im Süden einschließt, gehört heute zu Dänemark (→ Sprachenkarte A). Das Gebiet umfaßt ca. 3900 km² und hat ca. 250.000 Einwohner. Es gibt hier keine größeren Städte, und das Gebiet ist insgesamt recht wenig industrialisiert. Über diesen Landesteil verbreitet, aber mit der Tendenz zur Konzentration auf dessen südliches Gebiet, lebt eine deutsche Minderheit, die sich hinsichtlich der beruflichen Ausrichtung nicht entscheidend von der Mehrheit abhebt, auch wenn der Minderheit aus historischer Perspektive die Bezeichnung „gutbürgerlich" anhängt, da ihr ursprünglich viele Großbauern und wohlhabende Kaufleute in den Städten angehörten.

1.2. Es ist jedoch mit großen Schwierigkeiten verbunden, die Größe der Minorität mit angemessener Genauigkeit anzugeben, da in der öffentlichen Verwaltung keine Registrierung der Minderheitsmitglieder vorgenommen wird und auch die Minderheit selbst über kein zentrales Register verfügt (nur über Mitgliederverzeichnisse der verschiedenen Vereine und Organisationen).

Zahlenangaben über die mutmaßliche Größe der Minderheit liegen zwischen 15.000 und 25.000. Diese Unsicherheit geht indessen nicht nur auf die erwähnten Bedingungen zurück, sondern auch darauf, daß die eigentliche Definition über die Zugehörigkeit zur Minderheit unklar ist. Negativ formuliert läßt sich feststellen, daß von einer eigentlichen ethnischen Minderheit nicht die Rede sein kann. Weiterhin kann festgestellt werden, daß es sich nicht um eine sprachliche Minderheit in dem Sinne handelt, daß die gesamte Minorität eine andere Haussprache als die Majorität anwendet. Der größte Teil der hier lebenden Angehörigen beider Volksgruppen verwendet nämlich den dänischen Dialekt Sønderjysk. Auch im Hinblick auf die Lebensweise lassen sich kaum große Unterschiede zwischen Minderheit und Mehrheit beobachten. Die sprachlich-kulturellen Unterschiede der beiden Bevölkerungsgruppen sind eher graduelle als Wesensunterschiede, wodurch die Grenze zwischen ihnen fließend sein kann.

Zusammenfassend läßt sich sagen, daß es unmöglich ist, die deutsche Minderheit in Nordschleswig mit Hilfe objektiver Kriterien abzugrenzen. Cornett (1985—86) verwendet sogar die Bezeichnung „det usynlige mindretal" („die unsichtbare Minderheit"). Das einzige geltende Kriterium ist die subjektive Identifikation: Derjenige/diejenige gehört der Minderheit an, der/die sich als ihr zugehörig ansieht. Eine solche Definition ist jedoch so diffus, daß ein Forscher in der Praxis kaum mit ihr arbeiten kann.

Der Schlüsselbegriff zum Verständnis dieser Minderheit lautet Gesinnungsminorität. Es handelt sich um Dänen (= dänische Staatsbürger) mit einer deutschen Gesinnung, welches jedoch nicht unbedingt mit einer antidänischen Gesinnung einhergeht, indem viele dieser Menschen, besonders die jungen Leute, von einer deutsch—dänischen „Zweiströmigkeit" geprägt sind. Diese deutsche Gesinnung kann als eine emotionale Bindung zum Deutschsein bestimmt werden. Dies gilt primär für den sprachlich-kulturellen Bereich und sekundär für den geographisch-„gebietsmäßigen".

Vor diesem Hintergrund reicht es jedoch nicht aus, die deutsch-nordschleswigsche Minderheit allein als sprachlich-kulturelle Minorität in dem Sinne zu bestimmen, daß ihre Mitglieder — in einer mehr oder weniger stark ausgeprägten Weise — einen deutschen Bildungshintergrund aufweisen. Einige Angehörige der Majorität verfügen nämlich ebenfalls über eine hohe deutsche sprachlich-kulturelle Kompetenz, vornehmlich durch den intensiven Deutschunterricht sowie durch zahlreiche persönliche Kontakte mit Deutschland. Normalerweise ist bei diesem Personenkreis aber nicht von der oben erwähnten integrativen Haltung auszugehen, sondern eher von einer instrumentellen Auffassung. Ebenso wie viele deutschgesinnte Nordschleswiger ihre Form des Deutschseins als abweichend vom Selbstgefühl der Deutschen in der Bundesrepublik empfinden, können auch zugewanderte Deutsche Schwierigkeiten haben, sich mit dem Nordschleswiger „Deutschtum" zu identifizieren.

1.3. Das hier skizzierte deutsche Profil ist jedoch nicht bei allen Minoritätsangehörigen in gleicher Weise vorherrschend. Es gibt eine nicht besonders große Kerngruppe von sehr bewußt deutschgesinnten Individuen, umgeben von einer größeren Gruppe mit einem mehr oder weniger verblaßten Profil. In den letzten Jahren hat ein natürlicher „Abschleifungsprozeß" bei der Profilierung einiger Mitglieder stattgefunden, welches durch die innergesellschaftliche Entwicklung beschleunigt wurde. Eine nationale Gesinnungsminorität läßt sich am besten in einer statischen (überwiegend agrarischen) Gesellschaft mit geringer geographischer und sozialer Mobilität und mit beträchtlichen nationalen Spannungen zwischen Majorität und Minorität aufrechterhalten. Dieser Zustand war für die Situation der Minderheit in der ersten Jahrhunderthälfte nach der Grenzziehung von 1920 zutreffend, hat sich jetzt aber verändert. So sind beispielsweise viele der in der Region lebenden jungen Leute sowohl innerhalb der Minorität als auch der Majorität dazu gezwungen, den Landesteil zur Absolvierung einer Ausbildung oder zu Beginn ihrer Berufstätigkeit zu verlassen — es gibt keine Hochschulen in diesem Landesteil. Prozentual gesehen, kehren wenige zurück, vornehmlich wegen des Arbeitsplatzmangels. Diese Entwicklung trifft die Minorität stärker als die Majorität, da die jungen Angehörigen der Minderheit im Durchschnitt über eine höhere schulische Qualifikation verfügen als die Majorität. Das Phänomen *brain-drain* macht sich bemerkbar. Aber auch ganz andere Einflußfaktoren erschweren die Reproduktion der Minorität, z. B. die niedrige Geburtenrate und viele exogame Eheschließungen, die den Assimilationsvorgang fördern.

1.4. Betrachtet man die Entwicklung innerhalb der Minderheit seit Ende des Zweiten Weltkriegs bis heute aus der Vogelperspektive, zeichnet sich die Schwierigkeit ab, das Gleichgewicht zwischen einer freiwilligen Integration und einer freiwilligen Segregation zu finden, wobei der Ausgangspunkt 1945 von einer unfreiwilligen Segregation bestimmt war. Während ihres langen und zähen Kampfes um die volle Gleichstellung mit der Majorität wurde die Minorität immer stärker in die dänische Gesellschaft integriert, wodurch sich die Gefahr einer Assimilation erhöhte. Wirtschaftlich war die Minderheit schon immer integrierter Bestandteil der Gesellschaft. Ursprünglich stellte sie sich politisch als bewußt segregiert dar, aber gerade in diesem Bereich findet eine schrittweise Assimilierung statt. Im sprachlich-kulturellen Bereich versucht die Minderheit, eine gewisse Segregierung im Verhältnis zur Mehrheitsbevölkerung aufrechtzuerhalten — dies mit Hilfe eigener deutscher kultureller Einrichtungen.

2. Geschichte

2.1. Nach dem zweiten schleswigschen Krieg 1864 (den Dänemark gegen Preußen und Österreich verlor) gestaltete sich die nationalpolitische Situation in der Weise, daß ganz Schleswig (sowohl Nord- als auch Südschleswig) bis 1920 Preußen einverleibt blieb.

In den Grundzügen sah die sprachliche Situation folgendermaßen aus: Der überwiegende Teil der Bevölkerung, darunter die gesamte Landbevölkerung sprach *sønderjysk* (südjütisch), d. h. einen dänischen Dialekt, der insbesondere im Bereich des Wortschatzes stark vom Deutschen beeinflußt ist. (Der Dialekt weicht so stark von der standardisierten dänischen Sprache (Reichsdänisch) ab, daß es sich ausgehend von den gängigen Definitionskriterien um zwei verschiedene Sprachen handelt.) Doch gab es von alters her besonders in den Städten ansässige Nordschleswiger, die sich der deutschen Umgangssprache bedienten, vornehmlich innerhalb des gehobenen Bürgertums. Als Umgangssprache spielten dagegen weder Plattdeutsch noch Nordfriesisch in dieser Periode eine nennenswerte Rolle.

2.2. Nach 1864 nahm Preußen die schrittweise, aber mit zunehmender Härte durchgeführte Germanisierung der nordschleswigschen Bevölkerung vor, sowohl sprachlich als auch nationalpolitisch, ein Vorhaben, das Preußen in Mißkredit brachte, auch auf internationaler Ebene. Mit Unterstützung aus Dänemark wurde die dänischsprachige und dänischgesinnte Bevölkerung zur Zeit der preußischen Unterdrückungspolitik noch weiter zusammengeschweißt. Dadurch wurde eine ausgeprägte Sprachloyalität gegenüber der „vererbten" Sprache mobilisiert, die es für die deutschen Behörden unmöglich machte, durchgreifende Änderungen im täglichen Sprachgebrauch der Bevölkerung durchzusetzen, obwohl es in ihrer Macht stand, der Bevölkerung eine neue offizielle Sprache aufzuzwingen. In dieser zweiten Phase des dänisch–deutschen Sprachkampfes schlug der ihm zugrundeliegende „sprachliche Darwinismus" fehl. Das Hauptergebnis stimmte mit dem der ersten Phase des Sprachkampfes überein: Änderungsmaßnahmen hinsichtlich der Anwendung der offiziellen Sprache führen nicht zwangsläufig zu tiefergehenden Änderungen hinsichtlich der Umgangssprache.

2.3. Nach der Grenzziehung von 1920 kehrten die Behörden zu ihrer ursprünglichen Haltung zur Mehrsprachigkeit des Landesteils zurück, d. h. daß man sich von offizieller Seite nicht in die sprachlichen Verhältnisse einmischte, sondern sie dem freien Spiel der Kräfte überließ. Jetzt war Reichsdänisch die neue offizielle Sprache in Nordschleswig, und damit ging den Deutschsprachigen die Stütze verloren, die sie bisher durch den Status des Hochdeutschen als offizielle Sprache erhalten hatten.

Erst nach 1920 ist es sinnvoll, von einer deutschen Minderheit in der jetzigen Form zu sprechen. Diese war zunächst relativ groß, gut organisiert und verfügte deshalb über einen beträchtlichen politischen Einfluß. Das „Deutschtum" war in jeder Hinsicht ein wichtiger Machtfaktor in Nordschleswig in den 25 Jahren nach der Grenzziehung; und die nationalpolitischen Gegensätze zwischen Dänisch und Deutsch waren nicht zuletzt nach 1933 beträchtlich, als der Nationalsozialismus die Minderheit dominierte und auch auf die Mehrheitsbevölkerung Einfluß ausübte. Viele Menschen befanden sich in einem Loyalitätskonflikt zwischen „Herbergsstaat" und sprachlich-kulturellem „Mutterland". Vor diesem Hintergrund gestaltete sich die Abrechnung der Majorität mit der Minorität nach dem Zweiten Weltkrieg bitter. Die Stimmung war sehr deutschfeindlich, welches dazu führte, daß viele Menschen, die sich bislang zu ihrem Deutschsein bekannt hatten, die Minderheit verließen. Dies bedeutete jedoch nicht automatisch, daß sie prodänisch eingestellt waren, sondern es war üblich, daß sie *blakkede* wurden, d. h. nationalpolitisch neutral zwischen Dänisch und Deutsch standen — eine traditionelle Haltung im Landesteil. Die neue Entwicklung hatte auch die sprachliche Folge, daß einige Einwohner (der Klein- und Mittelstädte) vom Hochdeutschen zum Sønderjysk oder Südjütischen als Haussprache übergingen.

Diese Ereignisse führten zu einem Bruch im Nordschleswiger „Deutschtum". Das Deutsche hat die Stärke, die es in der Zeit vor dem Krieg gehabt hatte, nie zurückgewonnen, aber die Situation führte auch nicht den Untergang des „Deutschtums" herbei — so wie man es sich in Dänemark vorgestellt hatte. Bildlich gesprochen führte dieser Bruch zu einem „Blutverlust", nicht aber zum „Verbluten". Indessen war nicht nur der innere, sondern auch der äußere Verlust schmerzlich: Zwischen 700 und 800 junge Nordschleswiger fielen als freiwillige Soldaten in deutschen Heeren. Mehr als 3000 Minoritätsangehörige wurden von den dänischen Behörden interniert und mit rückwirkender Kraft verurteilt. Die deutschen Schulen wurden geschlossen und vom Staat beschlagnahmt.

Gerade die haßerfüllte antideutsche Stimmung in Verbindung mit dem harten Vorgehen der dänischen Behörden gegen die Minderheit schuf jedoch das psychologische Klima, das die überzeugten Deutschgesinnten wiederum zusammenschweißte. Bereits im November 1945 erklärte die Hauptorganisation der deutschen Minderheit, „Bund Deutscher Nordschleswiger", ihre absolute Loyalität gegenüber dem Herbergsstaat, und dies war der Beginn einer allmählichen Normalisierung des Verhältnisses von Majorität und Minorität. Auf dieser Grundlage gelang es der Minderheit, durch ihre zähe und zielbewußte Arbeit das notwendige Netzwerk der deutschen Vereine und Einrichtungen (wenn auch in verkleinertem Maßstab) wiederaufzubauen.

2.4. Zusammenfassend kann gesagt werden, daß es der Minorität und Majorität teilweise gelungen ist, den Grenzkampf früherer Zeiten durch eine vernünftige Form der Koexistenz abzulösen. Dies bedeutet jedoch nicht, daß diese gemeinsame Existenz problemfrei wäre. Die „glatte" Oberfläche (ohne größere sichtbare Konflikte) kann den uneingeweihten, von außen kommenden Beobachter leicht täuschen. Der teilnehmende Beobachter bemerkt jedoch, daß — eher auf der Mikro- als auf der Makroebene — Aggressionen, Ressentiments und negative Einstellungen lauern können, die sich leicht aktivieren lassen, sofern die kleinste Reibung entsteht.

Die Hauptursache für das relativ harmonische Verhältnis von Minorität und Majorität in Nordschleswig besteht darin, daß erstere ihr deutsches Profil gegenüber letzterer abdämpft, mitunter in einem Maß, das an Selbstverleugnung erinnert.

Das „Deutschtum" wird im wesentlichen in geschlossenen Kreisen innerhalb der Minorität gepflegt, vermutlich aufgrund einer nicht unbegründeten Angst davor, daß ein selbstbewußteres Auftreten negative Reaktionen in Teilen der Mehrheitsbevölkerung hervorrufen könnte. Auf der anderen Seite könnte man den deutschen Nordschleswigern mehr „Mut zum Bekenntnis" wünschen, weil weite Teile der Majoritätsbevölkerung einem Angehörigen der Minderheit, der sich klar zu seinem Deutschsein bekennt, mit Respekt begegnen würde.

3. Politik, Wirtschaft und allgemeine kulturelle Lage

3.1. Das Verhältnis zwischen Minorität und Majorität wird von den sog. Bonn-Kopenhagener Erklärungen aus dem Jahre 1955 geregelt: Hier wird u. a. festgelegt: „Das Bekenntnis zum deutschen Volkstum und zur deutschen Kultur ist frei und darf von Amts wegen nicht bestritten oder nachgeprüft werden." — „Angehörige der deutschen Minderheit und ihre Organisationen dürfen am Gebrauch der gewünschten Sprache in Wort und Schrift nicht behindert werden." — „Das besondere Interesse der deutschen Minderheit, ihre religiösen, kulturellen und fachlichen Verbindungen mit Deutschland zu pflegen, wird anerkannt." (Becker-Christensen 1992, 31 f).

Der die Sprache betreffende Teil der Bonn-Kopenhagener Erklärungen kann wie folgt zusammengefaßt werden: Die dänischen Behörden mischen sich nicht in die interne Sprachverwendung der Minderheit ein, wodurch die Wahl der jeweiligen Sprache innerhalb der eigenen Institutionen freigestellt bleibt. Die sprachliche Strategie der Minderheit zielt eindeutig darauf ab, die Anwendung des Deutschen innerhalb der Minderheit in hohem Ausmaß zu fördern. Da Dänemark offiziell jedoch ein einsprachiges Land ist, haben die Angehörigen der Minderheit keinen Anspruch darauf, die deutsche Sprache dänischen Behörden gegenüber in mündlicher oder schriftlicher Form verwenden zu können. Dies hätte wohl auch eher symbolische als praktische Relevanz, da die ansässigen Minderheitsangehörigen in der Lage sind, sich schriftlich in Reichsdänisch und mündlich in Sønderjysk und/oder Reichsdänisch auszudrücken. Auch in informellen Gesprächssituationen zwischen Angehörigen der Majorität und der Minorität wird Deutsch in keinem nennenswerten Umfang angewandt, obwohl dies theoretisch aufgrund der weit verbreiteten Deutschkenntnisse im Landesteil möglich wäre, eine solche Strategie würde aber von einem großen Teil der Mehrheitsbevölkerung als Provokation aufgefaßt werden.

3.2. Innerhalb des hier skizzierten Rahmens entfaltet die deutsche Minderheit in Nordschleswig weitverzweigte deutschsprachige Aktivitäten in einem Netzwerk von Institutionen und Vereinen politischer, kultureller, pädagogischer, sportlicher, sozialer und fachlicher Art. Ihre wichtigsten sollen kurz erwähnt werden.

Die Hauptorganisation der Minderheit nennt sich „Bund Deutscher Nordschleswiger" und hat etwa 4000 Mitglieder. Im Paragraph zur Zielsetzung der Organisation heißt es, daß man die geistigen und kulturellen Verbindungen zum deutschen Volk aufrechterhalten und verstärken will, ohne sich von Dänemark abzusondern. Die politische Partei des „Bundes Deutscher Nordschleswiger" nennt sich „Schleswigsche Partei" und verfügt über eins von 29 Mandaten in Sønderjyllands Kreistag und ist zusätzlich in 5 Stadträten Sønderjyllands vertreten, wenn auch meist nur mit bis zu 2 Mandaten. Doch hat eine starke politische Assimilation mit der Majorität stattgefunden. Bei der letzten Kreistagswahl erlitt die Partei 14% Stimmenverlust, d. h. erhielt nur noch ca. 4900 Stimmen; bei der letzten Kommunalwahl war ein Stimmenrückgang von 18% zu verzeichnen (ca. 4450 Stimmen für die Partei). Im Laufe der letzten drei Jahrzehnte hat die Partei erhebliche Rückschläge hinnehmen müssen, da einem Teil der Wähler andere als nationalpolitische Streitfragen relevanter erschienen.

In den letzten 25 Jahren hat die „Schleswigische Partei" nicht genügend Stimmen erhalten, um eine parlamentarische Repräsentanz im dänischen Parlament („Folketing") zu erhalten. Als Kompensation für diesen Umstand werden die landespolitischen Interessen der Minderheit von dem „Sekretariat der deutschen Volksgruppe in Nordschleswig" in der zentralen Verwaltung in Kopenhagen wahrgenommen.

Am bedeutendsten ist jedoch nicht der politische, sondern der sprachlich-kulturelle Zugriff, beispielsweise die Herausgabe der deutschsprachigen Tageszeitung „Nordschleswiger" mit einer Auflage von ca. 4000 Exemplaren täglich. In gleicher Weise ist das deutsche Bibliothekswesen, das im „Verband deutscher Büchereien" organisiert ist, von großer Bedeutung; es werden jährlich insgesamt ca. 290.000 Bücher ausgeliehen. Erwähnenswert ist auch die seit Jahrhunderten bestehende deutschsprachige Kirchentradition in Nordschleswig, wobei keine konfessionellen Gegensätzlichkeiten zwischen den deutschen und dänischen Gemeinden des Landesteils bestehen. Als Ergänzung soll angefügt werden, daß innerhalb der Minderheit eine umfassende Jugendarbeit unter der Leitung des „Deutschen Jugendverbandes für Nordschleswig" stattfindet, die dazu beiträgt, die jungen Leute auch über ihren Schulabschluß hinaus in der Minderheit zu halten.

4. Statistik und Ethnoprofile

4.1. Die deutsche Minderheit in Nordschleswig wird auf Dänisch *hjemmetyskere* („die Heimdeutschen") genannt. Die Bezeichnung enthält im Dänischen keine negativen Konnotationen, wird aber von der Minderheit normalerweise nicht geschätzt. Die Minderheit bezeichnet sich selbst als „Deutsche Volksgruppe in Nordschleswig". Indessen ist diese Bezeichnung begrifflich eigentlich nicht deckend, sofern man sich eine geschlossene Minoritätsgruppe vorstellt, die isoliert von der Mehrheitsbevölkerung lebt. Wie erwähnt, liegt eine hochgradige Integration vor, die die scharfen Konturen der beiden Bevölkerungsgruppen verwischt, die sich in vielen Bereichen „ähnlich sind" (dies auch in übertragener Bedeutung): Ihnen sind viele regional begründete Haltungen und Wertvorstellungen gemeinsam; das, was die Individuen der Minorität nicht mit der Majorität teilen, nämlich das „Deutschtum", behalten sie üblicherweise für sich und teilen es mit anderen Gleichgesinnten. Die deutschgesinnten Nordschleswiger sind auf diese Weise zutiefst davon geprägt, daß sie über Jahrhunderte hinweg Seite an Seite mit Dänischgesinnten im gleichen Landesteil gelebt haben. Viele Minoritätsmitglieder fühlen sich primär als Nordschleswiger, wenn auch mit einer besonderen deutschen Akzentuierung.

4.2. Es wurde bereits angesprochen, daß die deutsche Minderheit in Nordschleswig nicht generell die Minoritätssprache als tägliche Umgangssprache verwendet. Dies bedeutet gleichzeitig aber nicht, daß es keine Minderheitsangehörigen gäbe, die Deutsch als Haussprache hätten, es liegen jedoch keine umfassenden statistischen Untersuchungen über die Verteilung der Haussprache vor; Vieles weist darauf hin, daß die Anwendung des Codes so variabel ist, daß eine angemessene Beschreibung schwierig erscheint.

Die vorliegenden Untersuchungen der angewandten Haussprache machen alle eine Tendenz deutlich: Der überwiegende Teil der Minderheit (vielleicht ¾) spricht seit jeher zu Hause *sønderjysk* (vorherrschend oder ausschließlich), während ein kleinerer Teil deutsch spricht. Sønderjysk hat für viele Angehörige der Minderheit ein hohes Prestige, da dieser Code im Gegensatz zum Reichsdänischen eine ursprüngliche Anbindung an den Landesteil signalisiert; oft sprechen die Minderheitsangehörigen besser *sønderjysk* als die Mehrheitsbevölkerung, weil ihr Sprachcode weniger vom Reichsdänischen beeinflußt ist.

Bei einer Untersuchung dieses sprachlichen Ethnoprofils der Minderheit ist zwischen den endogamen und exogamen Ehen zu unterscheiden, besonders im Hinblick auf die Verteilung der Haussprache, da sich in den exogamen Ehen eine Verschiebung des Codes bemerkbar machen kann. Generell läßt sich feststellen: In einer ehelichen Verbindung zweier Nordschleswiger, in der der eine Ehepartner der Minderheit und der andere der Majorität angehört, ändert sich die Codeanwendung (im Verhältnis zu einer endogamen Verbindung) nicht unbedingt, da die Haussprache normalerweise „Sønderjysk" ist. Bei der Verbindung eines deutschen Nordschleswigers und eines dänischen Partners, der nicht aus dem Landesteil stammt, kann sich das Reichsdänische durchsetzen. Umgekehrt kann die deutsche Haussprache das Ergebnis einer Verbindung eines deutschen Nordschleswigers und eines deutschsprachigen zugewanderten Partners darstellen.

5. Soziolinguistische Lage

5.1. In Nordschleswig bestehen in bezug auf die mündliche Sprachanwendung drei Codes (Sønderjysk, Hochdeutsch, Reichsdänisch) und zwei standarisierte Schriftsprachen (Reichsdänisch und Hochdeutsch) nebeneinander. Viele ansässige Nordschleswiger verfügen über eine kommunikative Kompetenz in allen drei umgangssprachlichen Codes, wogegen sich die Beherrschung der jeweiligen Schriftsprachen unterschiedlich darstellt. Normalerweise können nur diejenigen Personen, die eine deutsche Schule besucht haben, sich in fließendem Deutsch schriftlich ausdrücken. Die älteste Generation (die die Schule besuchte, bevor der Landesteil 1920 dänisch wurde) hat zudem in ihrer Schulzeit niemals Dänischunterricht erhalten. Schließlich leidet ein Teil der mittleren und jüngeren Generation (gerade Absolventen der Minderheitenschulen) darunter, daß die Pflege der gesprochenen reichsdänischen Sprache früher an den Schulen nicht für wichtig erachtet wurde. Darüber hinaus spüren einige Menschen einen emotionalen Widerwillen gegen das Reichsdänische, da dieser Code für die Region fremd ist. Ein solches Defizit bedeutet Benachteiligung, da sie sich außerhalb Nordschleswigs sprachlich nicht durchsetzen können. In Dänemark gilt der gemeinhin akzeptierte Anspruch, daß alle Einwohner die offizielle Landessprache beherrschen sollten; und die übliche Haltung gegenüber einer dialektgefärbten gesprochenen Sprache ist ablehnend.

5.2. Das bisher Gesagte bedeutet jedoch nicht, daß die durchschnittliche Bevölkerung in Nordschleswig als trilingual im eigentlichen Sinne angesehen werden kann, d. h. mit einer der Muttersprache vergleichbaren Sprachbeherrschung der drei Codes. Diese Eigenschaft läßt sich nur einer kleinen Personengruppe innerhalb der Minderheit mit einem bestimmten Bildungsniveau zuschreiben.

In Søndergaard (1981) wird dargestellt, wie eine homogene Informantengruppe mit einer hohen trilingualen Kompetenz die drei Codes anwendet. Dies geschieht nicht willkürlich, sondern nach einem komplizierten Sprachmuster.

Zu Hause verwenden viele sowohl „Sønderjysk" als auch Deutsch, entweder personengebunden oder situationsabhängig. Außerhalb der Familie ist die Codeanwendung der mehrsprachigen Nordschleswiger flexibel und unverkrampft, indem sich die Wahl des Codes hauptsächlich danach richtet, welche Sprache in der gegebenen Situation oder der Person/den Personen gegenüber als am natürlichsten empfunden wird; hierbei werden nicht nur der Kommunikationsaspekt, sondern auch emotionale Aspekte berücksichtigt. Diese bewirken, daß Hochdeutsch nicht für die Kommunikation mit Majoritätsangehörigen verwendet wird; es liegen sogar Beispiele dafür vor, daß deutschgesinnte Nordschleswiger, die normalerweise deutsch untereinander sprechen, davon absehen, den Code zu verwenden, wenn Majoritätsmitglieder anwesend sind, weil sie hierauf negative Reaktionen erfahren haben. Auf diese Weise findet eine freiwillige Unterdrückung des Codes statt, auch wenn nicht bekannt ist, wie verbreitet dieses Phänomen ist. Diese sprachliche Strategie führt dazu, daß die Angehörigen der deutschen Minderheit die deutsche Sprache in einem verhältnismäßig geschlossenen Kontext der Minorität anwenden, in dem die Sprache als offizielle Sprache der Minderheit einen symbolischen Wert besitzt. Dadurch ist das Nordschleswiger-Deutsch im sprachlichen Alltag des Landesteils nur wenig sichtbar. Wenn die deutsche Sprache dennoch in einem gewissen Umfang „sichtbar gemacht" wird, ist dies vornehmlich den bundesdeutschen Einkaufs- und Ferientouristen zu verdanken. Hauptsächlich ihnen gegenüber wird die Mehrheitsbevölkerung dazu angehalten, ihre Deutschkenntnisse produktiv anzuwenden. In der untersuchten Informantengruppe wurde „Sønderjysk" meistens in informellen Gesprächssituationen angewandt, z. B. im Gespräch mit Nachbarn und Bekannten. Der Code wird tendenziell mit dem Volkstümlichen, Spontanen und Intimen assoziiert. Reichsdänisch wird dagegen hauptsächlich in Ämtern und Büros sowie in Geschäften verwendet, wenn man nicht voraussetzen kann, daß der Gesprächspartner „Sønderjysk" versteht/spricht. Die Untersuchung dokumentiert darüber hinaus, daß die Anbindung der Informantengruppe an die deutsche Kultur stark ist, wodurch gewisse Bereiche der „inneren Sprachanwendung" vom Deutschen dominiert werden, ohne daß jedoch die anderen Codes ausgeschlossen werden. Mit vollem Recht machte Willkommen (1975) darauf aufmerksam, daß die deutsche Sprache lebenswichtiger Bestandteil der ethnischen Identifikation der Nordschleswiger ist, aber es ist wichtig, diese Auffassung durch die von Byram (1986) gemachte Feststellung zu ergänzen, daß es nicht allein der Grad der deutschen sprachlich-kulturellen Kompetenz ist, der die Identität der deutschen Nordschleswiger ausmacht, sondern zusätzlich die Minoritätssozialisation, die in den deutschen Schulen stattfindet, da hier die emotionalen Bindungen an das „Deutschtum" etabliert werden.

5.3. Die Stellung der deutschen Sprache innerhalb der deutsch-nordschleswigschen Minderheit kann wie folgt zusammengefaßt werden: Deutsch hat sich nie als natürliche tägliche Umgangssprache durchsetzen können. Für viele blieb sie daher eine Art „Sonntagssprache", d. h. die offizielle Sprache der Minderheit, die Sprache der Kirche, Schule und Vereine. Hiermit stellt sie sich als Kultur- und Bildungssprache, nicht aber als Umgangssprache, Familiensprache und damit auch nicht als „Sprache des Herzens" dar.

6. Sprachpolitische Lage

6.1. Aus der bisherigen Darstellung geht hervor, daß (a) deutsche Sprache und Kultur eine zentrale Rolle für die deutschen Nordschleswiger spielen, (b) deren Vermittlung (in der Minorität als Ganzheit) primär nicht in den Familien geleistet wird. Dieser Aufgabe nehmen sich vornehmlich die minderheitsdeutschen Institutionen an, von denen die pädagogischen (Kindergärten und Schulen) eine so entscheidende Bedeutung haben, daß das jetzige sprachlich-kulturelle Profil kaum vorstellbar wäre ohne die intensive Sprach- und Kulturvermittlung, die hier stattfindet.

6.2. Die deutsche Minderheit verfügt über ein voll ausgebautes System von privaten Kindergärten und Schulen, die eine Alternative zum dänischen öffentlichen Schulsystem darstellen. Hierdurch wird ermöglicht, daß die Kinder von Beginn des Kindergartenalters (mit drei Jahren) während ihrer gesamten Schulzeit in diesem System verbleiben können, d. h. bis zum Abschluß der 9. Klasse, an die sich entweder ein freiwilliges 10. Schuljahr oder nach der 9. bzw. 10. Klasse der dreijährige Besuch des „Deutschen Gymnasiums für Nordschleswig" anschließen kann. Der gymnasiale Abschluß ist das „Deutsch-dänische Abitur", das die Studienberechtigung für Deutschland und Dänemark erteilt.

Die Minderheit verfügt über 24 Kindergärten mit ca. 600 Kindern (zwischen drei und fünf Jahren) und über 18 Schulen mit ca. 1200 Schülerinnen und Schülern. Es ist sehr problematisch, daß der Übergang vom Kindergarten zur Schule von fehlender „Schülerkontinuität" gekennzeichnet ist, da ca. 40% der Kinder, die einen deutschen Kindergarten besucht haben, nicht zur deutschen Schule gehen, wobei die Kindergärten (im Gegensatz zu den Schulen) viele Kinder aus der Mehrheitsbevölkerung anziehen, nicht so sehr aus sprachlichen, sondern aus allgemeinpädagogischen und rein praktischen Gründen. Die fehlende Kontinuität beim Übergang von der einen pädagogischen Einrichtung zur anderen sorgt für zahlreiche Probleme. Am auffälligsten ist der Schülermangel an den Schulen (9 Schulen haben weniger als 50 Schülerinnen und Schüler). Seit mehreren Jahren gehen die Schülerzahlen zurück, aus verschiedenen Gründen wie z. B. der niedrigeren Geburtenrate, der exogamen Ehen (als Assimilationsfaktor), der Übersiedlung der jungen Leute in andere Landesteile in Verbindung mit Ausbildung und Beruf.

Dieser Umstand bildet in den letzten Jahrzehnten den Hintergrund für einen pädagogischen Kampf zwischen den konservativen Kräften, die die deutschen Schulen als explizite „Volksgruppenschulen" erhalten, und progressiven Kräften, die diese zu modernen bilingualen und bikulturellen Schulen umwandeln wollen, damit diese auch für die Majorität attraktiv erscheinen können. Ein wesentliches Element dieses Kampfes ist mit der Plazierung der dänischen Sprache im Curriculum verbunden. In ihrer jetzigen Form sind die deutsch-nordschleswigschen Schulen nämlich eigentlich nicht bilingual, da Dänisch als ein Sprachfach isoliert angeboten wird, während Deutsch sowohl Sprachfach als auch Instrumentalsprache in allen anderen Fächern ist. An eine zeitgemäße bilinguale Schule wird dagegen der Anspruch gestellt, daß beide Hauptsprachen als *subject* und als *media of instruction* angewendet werden. Aus pädagogischer Sicht spricht nichts gegen eine solche Reformierung der Schulen, aber die emotionale Angst vor ihrer „Danisierung" ist groß. Diese Haltung wurde als „the emotional defence-at-all-costs of the German language" bezeichnet (Søndergaard und Byram, 1986). In einer späteren Arbeit (Byram 1992) wird es wie folgt ausgedrückt: „Among researchers there is a clear consensus that the current distribution of time and methods of teaching for Danish and German are unsatisfactory." Wie von Byram 1986 dargestellt, besteht eine Gefahr darin, die Schülerinnen und Schüler mit einer eingeschränkten sprachlich-kulturellen Kompetenz auszustatten — sowohl im Deutschen, so daß sie monolingualen (bundes)deutschen Gleichaltrigen in einem deutschen Ausbildungsgang unterlegen sind — als auch im Dänischen, so daß sie mit monolingual Dänischsprachigen nicht in vollem Maße konkurrieren können.

6.3. Zusammenfassend läßt sich sagen, daß eigene Kindergärten und Schulen unabdingbar für die deutsche Minderheit in Nordschleswig sind. Daher ist die Erhaltung eines vollständigen Schulsystems (einschließlich Gymnasium) von fundamentaler Bedeutung. Dieses kann langfristig durch sinkende Schülerzahlen bedroht werden, wodurch sich eine „pädagogische Modernisierung" als vordringliche Aufgabe darstellt.

7. Allgemeines kontaktlinguistisches Porträt

7.1. Wie erwähnt koexistieren in diesem Gebiet drei umgangssprachliche Codes:

(1) die gesamtdänische Reichssprache, die nur für wenige ansässige Nordschleswiger Haussprache ist, weshalb einige, besonders ältere Personen nur über eine beschränkte Kompetenz verfügen,
(2) „Sønderjysk" als die „Herzenssprache" des Landesteils, die von allen Ansässigen mit Ausnahme einiger Kinder und junger Leute in den Städten beherrscht wird,
(3) Hochdeutsch, das von der Minderheit nur in begrenztem Umfang als Haussprache angewendet wird.

Im folgenden wird das Augenmerk auf die letztgenannte Sprache gerichtet. Um die Sonderstellung dieser Sprache in Nordschleswig nachzuvollziehen, ist es wichtig festzuhalten, daß Nordschleswig-Deutsch nicht auf einem dialektalen Substrat aufbaut. Nissen (1985) charakterisiert sie treffend als „importierte Kunstsprache". Dies ist aber nicht gleichbedeutend mit einem „reinen" hochdeutschen Code, der im Gegenteil stark davon geprägt ist, daß er in einem sprachlichen Kontaktgebiet angewandt wird, in dem andere Codes, insbesondere „Sønderjysk", für Interferenzen sorgen. Nicht zuletzt in der gesprochenen Sprache muß das nordschleswigsche Idiom als Sonderform bezeichnet werden, nicht bloß im Verhältnis zu einer strikten hochdeutschen Norm, sondern auch im Verhältnis zu einem monolingualen Hochdeutsch, wie es südlich der Staatsgrenze gesprochen wird. Auffällig ist jedoch, daß es offenbar keine umfassende linguistische Beschreibung des Nordschleswig-Deutschen gibt, sondern nur kleinere Untersuchungen zur Intersprache (Uth 1968, Pedersen 1987).

Bei zugewanderten Angehörigen der deutschen Minderheit kann man mitunter herablassende Äußerungen über die sprachliche Qualität des Nordschleswiger Deutsch vernehmen. Eine solche Einschätzung verrät fehlendes Verständnis für die Grundbedingungen der Codes in einer sprachlichen Kontaktzone. Fragt man als Linguist einen sprachlich bewußten Bundesdeutschen danach, wie ein deutscher Nordschleswiger mit hoher Kompetenz deutsch spricht, kann man die Antwort erhalten: „Zwar gut, aber nicht perfekt." — Worin besteht nun das „Nicht-Perfekte"? Solange es keine wissenschaftlichen Beschreibungen zu diesem Thema gibt, kann die Frage nicht erschöpfend beantwortet werden. Vermutlich würden u. a. folgende Bereiche bei der Analyse zum Tragen kommen: (1) Hinsichtlich der Intonation ist Nordschleswig-Deutsch stark von „Sønderjysk" beeinflußt, daher hat der Code u. a. den sehr schwachen Nebendruck übernommen. (2) Die komplizierte morphologische Struktur des Deutschen im Vergleich zur einfachen Morphologie im Dänischen wird mitunter vereinfacht, z. B. die Unterscheidung zwischen Akkusativ und Dativ. (3) Ausgeprägte Interferenzen auf der Wortschatzebene sowie außerdem Codewechsel.

7.2. Eine linguistische Themenstellung, die wissenschaftlich (von Wieczerkowski) bearbeitet wurde, ist die Problematik des Wortschatzes bei zweisprachigen Nordschleswigern, die sich der Frage widmet: Weist der Wortschatz dieser Personen Defizite auf, und wenn ja, in einer oder in beiden „Hochsprachen" (Hochdeutsch und Reichsdänisch)? Es muß dabei jedoch hervorgehoben werden, daß es sich lediglich um intersprachliche Untersuchungen handelt. Ihre durchgehende Tendenz läßt deutlich werden, daß mit zunehmendem Alter eine wortschatzmäßige Annäherung der bilingualen an die monolingualen Sprecher stattfindet.

7.3. Es scheinen keine (über das Stadium der Intersprache hinausgehenden) linguistischen Analysen der schriftlichen Verwendung des Hochdeutschen in Nordschleswig vorzuliegen, obwohl es in großem Ausmaß angewendet wird. Die deutschsprachige Tageszeitung des Landesteiles wurde in Abschnitt 3. erwähnt. Darüber hinaus bedient man sich der Sprache u. a. in den regionalen periodischen Schriften: „Schriften der Heimatkundlichen Arbeitsgemeinschaft für Nordschleswig",

"Deutscher Volkskalender Nordschleswig", "Nordschleswig, ein Jahrbuch", auch wird eine sehr begrenzte deutschsprachige Belletristik verfaßt.

Solange keine linguistischen Analysen des Sprachgebrauchs vorliegen, ist es jedoch unmöglich zu entscheiden, inwieweit auch die schriftliche Sprachverwendung in Nordschleswig regionale Eigenheiten aufweist, die auf die spezifische Sprachkontaktsituation zurückgehen.

8. Kritische Wertung

8.1. Die deutsche Minderheit in Nordschleswig steht der Minoritätsforschung offen gegenüber. Auch wenn diesem Umstand zum Trotz eine sehr begrenzte moderne Minoritätsforschung auf wissenschaftlich angemessenem Niveau vorliegt, ist dies vermutlich primär auf die begrenzten wissenschaftlichen Ressourcen zurückzuführen. Die Minderheit ist so klein, daß sie schwerlich professionelle Forscher aus ihren eigenen Reihen hervorbringen und beschäftigen kann. Einige von ihnen (z. B. Cornett, Doege, Toft) haben eine Anbindung zur Minderheit. Andere Forscher (z. B. Wieczerkowski, Willkommen, Zeh) stammen aus der Bundesrepublik. Wiederum andere stehen als dänische Forscher außerhalb der Minorität (z. B. Becker-Christensen, Elklit, Pedersen, Søndergaard), wohingegen ein einziger Engländer ist (Byram). Unter diesen Bedingungen ist es schwierig, eine umfassende und thematisch zusammenhängende Forschung zu etablieren. Die vorliegenden Ansätze können als eher zufällig und fragmentarisch bezeichnet werden. Auseinandersetzungen mit größeren Themenkreisen liegen vor von Becker-Christensen, Doege und Rohweder. Außerdem lassen sich Ansätze zu einer modernen gesellschaftswissenschaftlichen Minoritätsforschung z. B. bei Cornett, Elklit, Toft finden. Im linguistischen Bereich mangelt es noch sehr an "Basisforschung". Ansätze hierzu werden z. B. von Pedersen, Søndergaard, Wieczerkowski und Willkommen geliefert. In den letzten Jahrzehnten wurden einige pädagogische Untersuchungen im Hinblick auf Zweisprachigkeit, vornehmlich von Byram und Søndergaard, durchgeführt. Eine interdisziplinäre Forschung, die das komplizierte Zusammenwirken der sehr unterschiedlichen Faktoren in diesem Problemkomplex aufzeigen kann, fehlt.

9. Bibliographie (in Auswahl)

Becker-Christensen, Henrik (1990): *Det tyske mindretal i Nordslesvig* (Mit dt. Zusammenfassung) Bd. I u. II. Apenrade.

Becker-Christensen, Henrik (1992): *The Danish—German Minority Arrangement — a Model for Others?*, Apenrade.

Byram, Michael (1986): *Minority Education and Ethnic Survival: Case Study of a German School in Denmark*, Clevedon.

Byram, Michael (1992): "Bilingual and Bicultural Education and the Case of the German Minority in Denmark". In: *European Models of Bilingual Education*, Baetens-Beardsmore, H. (Ed.), Clevedon.

Cornett, Andreas P. (1985/86): "Integration eller assimilation: Nationale mindretal i nutidens samfund". In: *Økonomi og politik 59/3*, 225—232.

Diercks, Willy/Walker, Alastair (1990): "Zur Bedeutung von Einstellungen und Vorurteilen gegenüber Minderheits-/Mehrheitssprachen. Perspektiven einer Untersuchung im Zusammenhang mit der Mehrsprachigkeit in der deutsch-dänischen Grenzregion". In: *Untersuchungen zu Attitüden und zum Sprachgebrauch im deutsch-dänischen Grenzgebiet*, Walker, A. (Ed.), Flensburg/Apenrade, 48—62.

Doege, Immo (1989): "Deutsche Schule in Nordschleswig". In: *25 Jahre Deutsches Gymnasium für Nordschleswig*, Doege, I./Nissen, H. J. (Eds.), Apenrade, 8—113.

Elklit, Jørgen et al. (1978): *Nationalt tilhørsforhold i Nordslesvig* (with an English summary), Århus.

Eriksen, Lars H. (1986): "Fall und Gegenfall. Ein Vergleich der Stellung und Sprache der deutschen Minderheit in Dänemark und der dänischen in Deutschland aus sprachenrechtlicher Sicht". In: *Europäische Sprachminderheiten im Vergleich*, Hinderling, R. (Ed.), Stuttgart.

Iwersen, Philipp (1989): "Deutsch in den Medien Nordschleswigs". In: *Deutsch als Umgangs- und Muttersprache in der Europäischen Gemeinschaft*, Kern, R. (Ed.), Brüssel, 209—216.

Kardel, Harboe (1970): "Die deutsche Volksgruppe in Dänemark". In: *Handbuch der europäischen Volksgruppen*, Straka, M. (Ed.), Wien.

Nissen, Hans J. (1983): "Die Situation der deutschen Volksgruppe in Nordschleswig im Jahre 1982". In: *Deutsche Volksgruppen in Europa*, Pelka, R. (Ed.), Sankelmark.

Nissen, Hans J. (1985): "Sprachigkeit und Sprachnotwendigkeit. Deutsche Sprachwirklichkeit in Nordschleswig": In: *Kolloquium zur Sprache und Sprachpflege der deutschen Bevölkerungsgruppen im Ausland*, Ritter, A. (Ed.), Flensburg, 131—141.

Nissen, Hans J./Pedersen, Karen M. (1988): *The German Language in Primary and Lower Education in Sønderjylland/Nordschleswig, Denmark*, Ljouwert/Leeuwarden.

Pedersen, Karen M. (1984): *Mødet mellem sprogene i den dansk-tyske grænseregion. En bibliografi*, Apenrade.

Pedersen, Karen M. (1985): „Kinder und Sprache in einer mehrsprachigen Region — Ergebnisse einer empirischen Untersuchung der sprachlichen Verhältnisse in Sønderjylland/Nordschleswig". In: *Kopenhagener Beiträge zur Germanistischen Linguistik 23*, 139—155.

Pedersen, Karen M. (1987): „German Minority Children in the Danish Border Region: Code-Switching and Interference". In: *Journal of Multilingual and Multicultural Development 8*, (1—2), 111—120.

Pedersen, Karen M. (1988): „Second Language Learners in the German Minority in Denmark". In: *Bilingualism and the Individual*, Holmen, A. et al. (Eds.), Clevedon.

Pedersen, Karen M. (Ed.) (1990): *Sprache und Unterricht in der deutschen, dänischen und friesischen Minderheit*, Apenrade.

Rohweder, Jürgen (1976): *Sprache und Nationalität. Nordschleswig und die Anfänge der dänischen Sprachpolitik in der ersten Hälfte des 19. Jahrhunderts*, Glückstadt.

Svalastoga, Kaare/Wolf, Preben (1969): „A Town in Danish Borderland". In: *Studies in Multilingualism*, Anderson, N. (Ed.), Leiden, 26—44.

Søndergaard, Bent (1980a): *Die Anfänge der bilingualen Forschung im deutsch-dänischen Grenzgebiet. Eine Bibliographie*. (Text auf dänisch, deutsch und englisch), Kopenhagen.

Søndergaard, Bent (1980b): *Sprogligt deficit. Sprogpædagogiske betragtninger over den dansk-tyske bilingualisme*. (Mit dt. Zusammenfassung), Apenrade.

Søndergaard, Bent (1981): „Tosprogethed med diglossi — højtysk, rigsdansk, sønderjysk i Nordslesvig". (Mit dt. Zusammenfassung) In: *Danske Studier 76*, 73—90.

Søndergaard, Bent (1983): „Öffnung ja — Identitätsverlust nein? Zur Problematik der deutsch—dänischen Minderheitenschulen". In: *Grenzfriedenshefte 2*, 84—89 u. *3*, 200.

Søndergaard, Bent (1987): „Die Buchzensur in den deutschen Schulen Nordschleswigs 1945 bis 1952 — eine Entmythologisierung". In: *Schriften der Heimatkundlichen Arbeitsgemeinschaft für Nordschleswig 55*, 9—74.

Søndergaard, Bent (1990a): „Problems of Pedagogical Continuity within a Minority". In: *Journal of Multilingual and Multicultural Development 11* (5), 421—433.

Søndergaard, Bent (1990b): „Die deutsche Schulpraxis in Nordschleswig aus der Sicht des Zweisprachigkeitsforschers". In: Pedersen (1990), 103—112.

Søndergaard, Bent/Byram, Michael (1986): „Pedagogical Problems and Symbolic Values in the Language Curriculum — the Case of the German Minority in Denmark". In: *Journal of Multilingual and Multicultural Development 7 (2—3)*, 147—167.

Toft, Gösta (1982): *Die bäuerliche Struktur der deutschen Volksgruppe in Nordschleswig*, Flensburg.

Toft, Gösta (1987): *Politische Grundhaltungen und Mediengewohnheiten — eine Pilotuntersuchung über die deutsche Volksgruppe in Nordschleswig*, Apenrade.

Uth, Manfred (1968): „Rechtschreib- und Stilfehler bei zweisprachigen Kindern". In: *Der deutsche Lehrer im Ausland 15*, 323—327.

Weitling, Günter (1990): *Die Heimdeutschen — Ursprung, Geschichte und Wesen*, Apenrade/Sonderburg.

Wieczerkowski, Wilhelm (1973): *Verbale Fertigkeiten bilingualer Schüler im deutsch-dänischen Grenzgebiet*, Hamburg. (unveröffentl. Manuskript).

Wieczerkowski, Wilhelm (1978): *Zum sprachlichen Können zweisprachiger Schüler in deutschen Schulen Nordschleswigs*, Hamburg. (unveröffentl. Manuskript).

Willkommen, Dirk (1975): „Zur Stellung der Kommunikation bei den Mitgliedern des Bundes Deutscher Nordschleswiger". In: *Beiträge zur Frage der ethnischen Identifikation des Bundes Deutscher Nordschleswiger*, Sievers, K. D. (Ed.), Sankelmark.

Zeh, Jürgen (1982): *Die deutsche Sprachgemeinschaft in Nordschleswig*, Stuttgart.

Bent Søndergaard, Flensburg (Deutschland)

128. Faroese—Danish

1. Geography
2. History
3. Ethnoprofiles
4. Sociolinguistic situation
5. Language political situation
6. General contactlinguistic portrait
7. Critical evaluation of the sources and literature used
8. Bibliography (selected)

1. Geography

The Faroe Islands are an archipelago of some 20 steep and rocky islands in the North Atlantic half-way between Shetland and Iceland. The total area is about 550 square miles. Tórshavn, the capital, lies in 62° N latitude and 6° 45'W longitude (→ language map A). The population numbers c. 45 000, a third of which live in the capital.

2. History

2.1. The first Nordic colonists probably settled in the Faroes about 800 A D. As Faroese dialects have most in common with those of south-western Norway, it has been suggested that the islands were populated mainly from that area. The 'Færeyinga saga' (composed in the 13th century) relates the history of the islands up to the middle of the 11th century. A thing was held in Tórshavn from about 900 A D., forming a kind of parliament for the Faroe Isles. In 1035 the Faroes became a tributary country under the Norwegian crown. As a result of the great Nordic union in the 1380's the islands from then on formed a part of the Dano-Norwegian kingdom. — The origin of Faroese—Danish language contact dates back to the late Middle Ages. Copenhagen was the capital of the kingdom, and the language of the royal chancellery was Danish. Subsequently the language of administration became Danish both in Norway and in the Faroes. Of major importance for the strengthening of the position of the Danish language in the Faroes was the introduction of the Danish Bible at the Reformation and with it Danish as the language of the church. From then on, Danish was the only written language in the Faroes. In this period the basis for *bilingualism* was laid. Although sprung from the same root (Common Scandinavian, before the Viking Age), West-Nordic Faroese and East-Nordic Danish were by now so different that Danish clergymen and officials could hardly understand spoken Faroese (no norm for written Faroese existed), and so the Faroese had to learn Danish to be able to communicate with the Danish-speaking officials and to understand what was said in church.

In the Middle Ages Bergen in Norway was the most important connection with the outer world for the Faroese. Already in the 13th century a trade monopoly was established. Two merchant ships a year were to supply the Faroes with those necessities of life the inhabitants could not raise themselves, above all grain. — For hundreds of years the islands seem to have counted 4000 to 5000 inhabitants, living in what has been characterized as "a stable peasant society" (West 1972, 11), where tradition was strong and changes few and slow. After the Reformation in the 1530's no considerable material, economic or social changes took place until well into the 19th century. In 1814 the Dano-Norwegian union was dissolved. The Faroes stayed under the Danish crown, and got the status of a Danish *amt* (county) in 1816. — In 1856 the trade monopoly was abolished. The opening of the islands to international commerce marked a turning-point in the history of the Faroes. The era of free trade brought about radical social and economic changes. People began to be more mobile, farm hands without property became professional fishermen, and the old agrarian society began to disintegrate. In the 1870's fishing on a large scale with ocean-going vessels started. That marked the beginning of the rapid progress of the Faroes to a modern welfare society. In 1948 there was once more a change in the political status of the islands. That year a Home Rule Act was passed in the Danish Parliament, and the Faroe Islands were now defined as "a self-governing community within the Danish kingdom". From then on the Danish state is represented by a resident state commissioner (Danish *rigsombudsmand*). Faroese was proclaimed as the chief language of the Faroes. Danish as well as Faroese may be used on all official occasions.

2.2. Material progress in the 19th century also brought about better conditions for a richer and more varied cultural life. In the

1870's there was a colony of Faroese students in Copenhagen. In their circle a patriotic movement arose under the inspiration of the Danish Folk High Schools, the Icelandic struggle for independence, and the Norwegian folk-language movement. The lyrical songs about the far-away homeland, which were the results of their literary activities, marked the birth of modern Faroese literature. — A prior condition for the growth of Faroese literature was a firm standard for the written language. At the end of the Middle Ages the spoken language of the Faroese had probably deviated considerably from Old Norse, and in the gap between spoken Faroese and written Old Norse all writing was taken over by Danish. Therefore, when the Faroese scientist and folklore recorder Jens Christian Svabo started to prepare a dictionary of Faroese and to write down ballads, in the 1770's, no documents written in his mother-tongue existed. Thus he had to construct his own orthography. In doing so, he chose the phonetic principle of writing. His aim was purely scientific and historical. Although Svabo had many followers, and the first books printed in Faroese in the 1820's (a ballad collection, 1822, and the Gospel of St Matthew, 1823) followed his spelling principles, it was not until the middle of the 19th century that an orthographic system for Faroese was put forth with the explicit aim to challenge Danish as the only written language of the Faroes. In 1846 a young Faroese theologian in Copenhagen, V. U. Hammershaimb, published a number of folklore texts in an entirely new orthography, which was based not on pronunciation, but on etymology. Contrary to Svabo's orthography, Hammershaimb's system bridged the dialectal differences in pronunciation. Hammershaimb's spelling system was soon accepted by his contemporaries, and to this day only slight revisions have been made.

3. Ethnoprofiles

3.1. The Faroese language is the mother-tongue of the great majority of the population. The Danish mother-tongue group is relatively small. (Exact figures can not be obtained, since both Faroese and Danes living in the Faroes are registered as 'Faroese'.) Most Danes in the Faroes have got there as adults, and many of them stay only for a short period (as administrators, medical officers, skilled workers, etc.). There are relatively more Danes in Tórshavn than in other towns and villages. Few Danes live in the smallest villages.

3.2. Up to recently the Danish-speaking clergy, officials and merchants belonged to another social level than the majority of the Faroese population, which consisted mainly of peasants and fishermen. This social difference, together with the fact that Danish was the language of the Church and the King, had the effect that Danish was considered the more prestigious language. As long as Faroese existed only as a number of spoken dialects, diglossia and widespread bilingualism were accepted by the Faroese as something imparted on them by Providence. Language conflicts and a Faroese language policy date back to the latter part of the 19th century, when the liberal impulses of the period reached Denmark, and Faroese students there applied ideas of cultural autonomy to the linguistic situation of their native islands. Now many Faroese became conscious of the oddity of speaking one language and writing another. A patriotic movement arose, the principal aim of which was to cultivate the Faroese language in speech and writing. — When the patriotic movement was transferred to the Faroes, it became more concerned with practical matters. From the 1880's to 1906, when the first political parties were formed, there was a period of growing national consciousness and political disturbance. As the Faroese language was felt to be the most important unifying symbol for the Faroese as a nation, linguistic patriotism was combined with political claims for self-determination. The language struggle has played an important role in Faroese politics. Up to the First World War the Unionist Party (Faroese *Sambandsflokkurin*) was the dominant force in Faroese political life. Their opponents were the Home Rule Party (Faroese *Sjálvstýrisflokkurin*), which aimed at Faroese autonomy and the acceptance of Faroese as the official language of the Faroes. — Although language conflicts have been many and violent during the last century, there is now, after the passing of the Home Rule Act, almost general acceptance of status quo.

4. Sociolinguistic situation

4.1. One aim of the national movement was to secure the Faroese language its rightful place in school, church and public life. Another was to cultivate the language. The two most important problems in the cultivation of the Faroese language have been how best to resist the constant Danish influence and how to develop a vocabulary to satisfy the demands of modern international culture. The principal trend in Faroese language cultivation has been to 'purify' the language, i. e. to replace Danish and international loanwords with native words. The puristic approach is evident in most periodicals edited in the Faroes. Of great importance was the first newspaper printed in Faroese, *Føringatíðindi*, which appeared, somewhat irregularly, as a monthly 1890—1906. Among more recent periodicals *Varðin* (1921—) is outstanding. In this magazine most Faroese authors up to this day have published stories, poems, and articles on various subjects in Faroese. — Important work in language cultivation has been done by Faroese lexicographers. The first dictionary printed was prepared by Jakob Jakobsen in 1891 and registered the vocabulary of Hammershaimb's Faroese Anthology and ballad collections. In 1927/8 M. A. Jacobsen and Christian Matras published a modern Faroese dictionary with pronunciation, grammatical information and translations into Danish, *Føroysk—donsk orðabók* (second enlarged edition 1961). The approach is puristic, common Danicisms being left out. Even more puristic are the dictionaries prepared by Jóhannes av Skarði, *Donsk—føroysk orðabók* (1967) and *Ensk—føroysk orðabok* (English—Faroese dictionary, 1984). — Since the Second World War there has been an increasing use of Faroese in scientific and scholarly matters. In 1952 *Fróðskaparfelag Føroya* (the Faroese Society for Higher Learning) was established. In its annual journal, *Fróðskaparrit* (1952—), articles on medicine, geology, philology, folklore, etc. are published in Faroese. In 1958 *Málstovnurin* was established (in 1985 reorganized as *Føroyska málnevndin*, i. e. the Faroese Language Committee), and since then the language cultivation programme has been in the hands of that institute. Without doubt Faroese language planners have been successful in their efforts to guide the development of the Faroese language in the puristic direction they have chosen. Faroese has shown its viability not only as a literary language, but also as a medium for all kinds of cultural and scientific purposes. Most authors accept the puristic trend and avoid Danicisms when writing. On the other hand, Danicisms are abundant in conversational Faroese, and there is often a wide gulf between the written and the spoken language. However, if the neologisms, created by puristic language planners, are sometimes felt to be 'highbrow' and 'difficult' at the beginning, they are often finally accepted as normal via the newspapers and the radio.

4.2. When estimating the degrees of bilingualism, several factors should be considered, viz. the proficiency in the two languages in listening, reading, speaking and writing, as well as the linguistic levels of phonology, grammar, vocabulary and semantics. — Among the Faroese population, competence in Danish varies considerably, depending on age, education and place of residence. Until recently most children grew up in next to unilingual surroundings and did not learn Danish until they began school. Today they as a rule hear Danish in TV-programmes, and thus get acquainted with Danish speech. All grown-ups are bilingual, most of them with good competence in Danish. Effective education in both languages, extended Faroese literacy, and increased use of Faroese in public life has favoured the development from diglossia to complete bilingualism.

A number of pressures force the Faroese to remain bilingual. For practical, cultural and political reasons they have to learn Danish. At the same time the Faroese language is felt to be an indispensible part of the Faroese cultural heritage and a symbol of national identity. — Unlike the Faroese mother-tongue group, the Danes in the Faroes are bilingual only to a small degree. Although some Danes acquire some listening and reading skill in Faroese, speaking and writing skills are rare. — The conclusion is that the burden of bilingualism is borne almost entirely by the Faroese mother-tongue group, while Danes can always expect to be addressed in their own language in all situations of intergroup communication. In this respect, however, attitudes have gradually changed during the last decades. While a generation ago it was considered downright rude to address a Dane in Faroese, bilingual conversations may be accepted today, viz. if people know each other well, and the Faroese knows that the Dane understands Faroese.

5. Language political situation

The functions of the Faroese and Danish languages in the Faroes, and the degrees of bilingualism, are determined by the historical and political background and the socio-cultural setting of language contact, as well as by the character of the two mother-tongue groups. The areas to be considered in relation to the functions of the two languages include all the media through which the languages are acquired and used, the most important ones being the home, the community, the school and the mass media.

5.1. In most Faroese homes, Faroese is the only language used in speech, contact with Danish being confined to reading and watching/listening to TV-programmes in Danish. In a small number of homes, Danish is the only language used. In mixed-married families there are as a rule two home languages. In such families there is a strong tendency among the Faroese-speaking members to switch between Faroese and Danish, depending on whom they are addressing, whereas the Danish-speaking member (often the wife) tends to use exclusively Danish.

5.2. Within the administration great linguistic changes have taken place in this century, particularly after 1948. Now the Faroese language is used both orally and in written communication within the sections of administration that have been taken over by the *løgting* (a publicly elected assembly with legislative powers) and the *landsstýri* (the local government). On the other hand Danish is the language used by the Danish administration in the Faroes. This means that Faroese employees in the departments of the Danish administration hear, speak, read and write Danish every day.

5.3. In 1823 a Faroese translation by J. H. Schrøter of the Gospel of St. Matthew was printed and distributed in the Faroes. Among later translators of the Holy Scripture Jákup Dahl (1878–1944) was the most prominent. A complete official Faroese Bible was published in 1961. A hymnbook appeared in 1960. The use of Faroese in church services was first permitted in 1903, but then only to a very limited degree. In 1939 a general ordinance was issued, which allowed the individual minister to use whichever of the two languages that came most natural to him. Today the whole divine service is as a rule conducted in Faroese.

5.4. The chief motivation for Hammershaimb, in 1846, to construct a universal Faroese orthography was a governmental proposal that compulsory schooling should be introduced in the Faroes. Since the Faroes had the status of a Danish *amt*, and there at that time was no officially accepted norm for written Faroese, it was taken for granted by the Danish authorities that the language of instruction as well as the 'mother-tongue' in the Faroese schools should be Danish. This proposal aroused vehement opposition from the Faroese, and gave rise to a lively debate of the whole linguistic situation of the country. The position of the Faroese language in education was a question of great importance, especially in the compulsory schools. However, not until 1912 was oral Faroese introduced as a special subject, and instruction in written Faroese was not compulsory until 1920. The Education Act of 1912 also allowed the teachers to use Faroese while instructing the younger pupils, "but in order to provide the required competence in the Danish language, it is necessary that the language of instruction in the various subjects is principally Danish, especially in the case of the older children". This very unpopular paragraph was in force till 1938. Today the language of instruction is Faroese on all stages of education, but all children must learn to read and write not only Faroese, but also Danish — for many children a foreign language —, which is studied from the third form. Thus bilingualism can be said to be codified through the Education Act.

5.5. Although Faroese literature is flourishing, and book production has been impressive in recent years, most books sold in the Faroes are imported from Denmark, as the Faroes form part of the Danish book-market — a consequence of the political status of the islands. As regards weekly magazines, the Danish dominance is overwhelming. Thus the Danish language has an important contact area in the printed word. Five Faroese newspapers are published, which means that most Faroese grown-ups read both Faroese and Danish almost every day. — Most copies of films shown in the Faroes are imported from Denmark and are subtitled in Danish, if they are not of Danish origin. If the language spoken is Danish, there are no subtitles. Up to recently foreign TV-programmes have as a rule been subtitled in Danish. Today more and more foreign programmes are subtitled in Faroese. The language used in the broadcasting programmes is principally exclusively Faroese.

6. General contactlinguistic portrait

6.1. As a consequence of incessant language contact Danish−Faroese, all types of linguistic borrowing and interference are found in present-day Faroese.

6.1.1. As might be expected, the Danish influence is strongest on the lexical level. Due to the relative isolation of the islands up to the middle of the 19th century, and to the diglossia, which was a result of the cultural and social stratification of the Danish−Faroese society, there were wide gaps in the Faroese vocabulary when modern civilization reached the islands. The genuine lexicon of Faroese is rich and varied within the areas of the old agrarian society, i. e. farming, fishing, sheep-breeding, topography, weather, folk culture, etc. On the other hand, Faroese was often lacking in words for administration, technology, the vast range of science, etc. Since the Faroese are bilingual, and have, at least in theory, the total vocabulary of the Danish language at their disposal, the gaps in Faroese vocabulary are easily filled with numerous loans from Danish. Common international words are as a rule transferred unanalyzed in their Danish form, which is gradually adjusted in accordance with the morphological and phonological structure of Faroese. Ex.: Danish *batteri, marmelade, sabotage* − Faroese *battarí* [bataˈruì], *marmuláta* [marmuˈlɔ̃ata], *sabotasja* [saboˈtaːša]. Loan translations are abundant. Of particular interest is the development of a semantic-morphological coding system: a combination of Faroese morphemes may refer to the equivalent combination of morphemes in Danish, independently of the meaning of the single morphemes in Faroese. Thus the Faroese, who for the first time hears or reads the words *skaðastova* and *vøggustova*, will probably at once understand their rather special meanings, because he knows Danish and identifies the Faroese compounds with the corresponding Danish ones: *skadestue* (casualty ward or emergency room) and *vuggestue* (day nursery, literally 'cradle room'). A third type of influence is the frequent occurrence of lexical interference in informal speech, where almost any Danish word may be used as Faroese, and pronounced and inflected as a Faroese word (Poulsen 1977, 100). Instead of *syrgin* (sad), *óneyðugur* (superfluous), *vanliga* (generally), one may hear *bedrøvaður, yvirflødigur, í almindeligheit* − from Danish *bedrøvet, overflødig, i almindelighed*.

6.1.2. Together with lexical loans a stock of affixes has been adopted, e. g. *be-, for-; -arí, -ilsi/-ulsi* from Danish *be-, for-; -eri, -else*. Ex.: *betala* (pay), *forferdiligur* (terrible), *bakarí* (baker's shop), *bangilsi* (fears). On the whole, however, the morphological system of Faroese is resistant to Danish influence. Foreign suffixes are as a rule transformed or substituted, if they do not accord with Faroese morphological structure. Loan-words ending in unstressed *-e* in Danish usually take *-a* and feminine gender (Clausén 1978, 62), e. g. *basilla*, *kapitalisma* from Danish *bacille, kapitalisme*. The choice of feminine *-a* in such nouns has a parallel in the correspondence between Danish *-e* and Faroese *-a* in the old common vocabulary: Danish *gave* (gift), *kone* (woman), *side* (side), Faroese *gáva, kona, siða*. An interesting case of suffix substitution occurs in Danish loan-words ending in *-er*, where several old suffixes have merged in Danish. In Faroese most of these words exchange *-er* for *-ari* or *-ur*. Only a few words keep *-er*, e. g. the names of the months, *september* (also *septembur*), etc. The derivational suffix *-ari* is especially productive in forming *nomina agentis*, e. g. *bakari* (baker). With such words as models, all words in Danish *-er* denoting persons get *-ari* in Faroese, e. g. *politikari* (politician), *fanatikari* (fanatic), *nekari* (negro) from Danish *politiker, fanatiker, neger*. Unlike words ending in *-ari*, genuine Faroese words in *-ur* with a radical *r* are often abstract, denoting qualities or conditions, e. g. *hungur* (hunger), *heiður* (honour), *myrkur* (darkness). Consequently, loan-words of these semantic categories exchange *-er* for *-ur*, e. g. *fepur* (fever), Danish *feber* (Hagström 1977, 45 ff). − The inflectional system of Faroese is not affected by Danish. Loan-words adopt Faroese endings throughout for gender, number, case, and definite article.

6.1.3. On the whole, the phonological system of Faroese is resistant to Danish influence. Loan-words are generally pronounced in accordance with Faroese phonology. There are, however, a few cases where the phonological system is affected by the impact of Danish, viz. the place of stress in loan-words, and the pronunciation of the letters *a* and *y* as [aː] and [yː] in some words. While in native Faroese words the first syllable has main stress, the stress in loan-words as a rule falls on the same syllable as in Danish. Thus the main stress lies on the second syllable in words like *studentur* (student), *romantiskur* (romantic), *politikari* (unlike Icelandic, where the first syllable of a word always has main stress). The pronunciation [a:] does not occur in genuine Faroese words (except in a few northern dialects for Old Norse *á*). In many common loan-words, however, the letter *a* is pronounced [a:], corresponding to the long Danish vowel spelt *a*. Ex.: *roman* (novel), *statur* (state), *tomat* (tomato). In some loan-words Danish *a* is pronounced [ɛ̃a], in others [ɔ̃a] (written *á*; *marmuláta*, etc. Poulsen 1977, 100). In a few recent loan-words Danish *y* is pronounced [y:], e. g. *typa* (Danish *type*), *typuhús* (standard house), *myta* (myth). The consonantism in Danish loan-words is regularly brought to harmonize with the phonological system of Faroese. This process may be exemplified with the treatment of Danish postvocalic *b*, *d*, *g*, which are identified as *p*, *t*, *k* in Faroese, as there is no opposition fortis:lenis in this position in spoken Faroese. This phonic substitution is also reflected in writing, e. g. Faroese *fepur* (fever), *fipur* (fiber), *putur* (powder), *tok* (train) from Danish *feber*, *fiber*, *pud(d)er*, *tog* (Hagström 1977, 33 ff).

6.2. In view of the socio-cultural situation, we can hardly expect a strong influence from Faroese on the mother-tongue of the Danish-speaking group. Since Danes can always use their own language in intergroup communication, their contact with Faroese is often superficial. However, a few Faroese loan transitions may appear in Danish, even in print, e. g. *østfald* and *vestfald*, from Faroese *eystfall* and *vestfall* (eastgoing and westgoing tidal currents).

7. Critical evaluation of the sources and literature used

Clausén 1978: This dissertation gives a survey of the linguistic situation of the Faroes, and is a comprehensive study of language planning, based on written as well as oral sources and personal contact with Faroese language planners. Considerable variation is found in the acceptance of neologisms for common Danicisms.

Debes 1982: A detailed study of the national revival up to 1906.

Hagström 1977: An investigation of how Danish loan-words in Faroese are gradually adjusted to harmonize with Faroese phonological and morphological structure.

Hagström 1984: A survey of Danish–Faroese language contact.

Poulsen 1977: A survey article, explaining the situation of the Faroese language.

Rasmussen 1987: A detailed examination, from a national and party political point of view, of how Faroese gradually came into use and was accepted as the language of the church.

Søndergaard 1986: A sociolinguistic investigation of attitudes to Danish and Faroese among Faroese students. The inquiry reveals that nowadays most students have rather unemotional attitudes to both Danish and Faroese, and that they feel motivated to learn both languages well.

Thomassen 1985: The conflicts and struggles leading to the acceptance and extended use of Faroese in the school are reported and analyzed.

8. Bibliography (selected)

Clausén, Ulla (1978): *Nyord i färöiskan. Ett bidrag till belysningen av språksituationen på Färöarna*, Stockholm.

Debes, Hans Jacob (1982): *Nú er tann stundin ... Tjóðskaparrørsla og sjálvstýrispolitikkur til 1906 við søguligum baksýni*, Tórshavn.

Føringatíðindi (1890–1906): (Offset reprint. Tórshavn 1969.)

Fróðskaparrit. Annales Societatis Færoensis, Tórshavn 1952–.

Hagström, Björn (1977): "'Hví hevur nekarin fepur?' Något om form, uttal och stavning av danska lånord i färöiskan". In: *Fróðskaparrit 25*, 26–56.

Hagström, Björn (1984): "Language contact in the Faroes". In: *Scandinavian Language Contacts*, Cambridge, 171–189.

Jacobsen, Mads A./Matras, Christian (1927/8): *Føroysk–donsk orðabók*, Tórshavn. (Second enlarged edition by C. Matras 1961.)

Lyngbye, Hans C. (1822) (Ed.): *Færöiske Quæder om Sigurd Fofnersbane og hans Æt*, Randers.

Poulsen, Jóhan H. W. (1977): "Det færøske sprogs situation". In: *De nordiska språkens framtid. Bidrag vid en konferens*, Sigurd, B. (Ed.), Lund, 90–102.

Rasmussen, Petur M. (1987): *Den færøske sprogrejsning med særligt henblik på kampen om færøsk som kirkesprog i national og partipolitisk belysning*, í Hoydølum.

Schrøter, Johan H. (1823) (trans.): *Evangelium Sankta Matthæussa*, Randers. (Offset reprint. Tórshavn 1973.)

av Skarði, Jóhannes (1967): *Donsk—føroysk orðabók*, Tórshavn.

av Skarði, Jóhannes (1984): *Ensk—føroysk orðabók*, Tórshavn.

Søndergaard, Bent (1987): *Unge uddannelsessøgende færingers holdninger til dansk og færøsk* (mimeographed), Tórshavn.

Thomassen, Arnfinnur (1985); *Færøsk i den færøske skole / Fra århundredskiftet til 1938*, Odense.

Svabo, Jens C. (1966—70): *Dictionarium Faroense. Farøsk—Dansk—Latinsk Ordbog I—II.* Faroensia VII. Matras, C. (Ed.), Copenhagen.

Varðin. Føroyskt tíðarskrift, Tórshavn 1921—.

West, John F. (1972): *Faroe — the emergence of a nation*, London/New York.

Björn Hagström, Stockholm (Sweden)

129. Greenlandic—Danish

1. Geography and demography
2. History
3. Politics, economy and general cultural and religious situation
4. Statistics and ethnoprofile
5. Sociolinguistic situation
6. Language political situation
7. General contactlinguistic portrait
8. Bibliography (selected)

1. Geography and demography

Greenland is the world's largest island with a total area of 2,175,600 square kilometers, of which 85% is covered by a permanent ice cap. As of January 1, 1994, the population of Greenland totalled 55,419 of whom 876 were living in North Greenland (Thule) and 3,448 in East Greenland. The capital of Nuuk is by far the largest town with 12,483 inhabitants of whom 3,243 were born outside Greenland. The number of Danes increased after the Second World War concurrently with the need for manpower in connection with the modernization of Greenland; their number has, however, diminished since 1989. The population is registered according to birthplace. As of 1994, the 13.3% born outside of Greenland includes primarily Danes but also foreigners working in Greenland and children born in Denmark of Greenlandic parents, e. g. studying in Denmark. Correspondingly, the group born in Greenland includes children born of Danish parents working in Greenland. Danes and foreigners in general only stay in Greenland for a few years. In about one fifth of marriages contracted in Greenland the husband only or (in most cases) the wife only was born in Greenland. — About 10,000 Greenlanders are living in Denmark, primarily students and women married to Danish men who have been working in Greenland.

2. History

The bearers of the Inuit Thule culture who immigrated ca. 1200 A. D. are the ancestors of the present Greenlanders. Ca. 1000 to 1500 A. D. Southwest Greenland was populated by farming settlers from Iceland but they do not seem to have had much contact with the Inuit. From the 16th century European explorers and from the 17th century European whalers as well occasionally visited Greenland. — The Danish-Norwegian colonization started in 1721. German Moravian missionaries lived in Southwest Greenland 1733—1900, but generally speaking Greenland was a closed country with a state monopoly with regard to both mission and trade up to 1950. Greenland became an integral part of Denmark in 1953; in 1979, however, Home Rule was established in Greenland.

3. Politics, economy and general cultural and religious situation

3.1. Politics

Greenland has its own Parliament and in addition two members of the Danish Parliament are elected in Greenland. The Home Rule Government is responsible for all aspects of government except foreign policy, defence, courts of justice and police. Greenland has chosen not to be a member of the EU even if Denmark is. Greenland is a member of ICC (Inuit Circumpolar Conference) together with Inuit from Canada, Alaska, and Siberia, but Greenland takes part also in cooperation between the Nordic countries.

3.2. Economy

The Greenlandic economy is weak and highly dependent on the transfer of block subsidies from Denmark. In the East and the North subsistence hunting and fishing are still important for a minority of the population, but the export-oriented fisheries have had serious problems in recent years.

3.3. General cultural situation

Literacy in Greenlandic has been high since the 19th century. There are nine years of compulsory education. Danish (Western) culture has made strong inroads into Greenland; Greenlandic cultural expressions in for example music, literature, art, kayaking as a sport, are, however, objects of ethnic pride. – Many Greenlanders have visited other countries, primarily Denmark, as students, patients at hospitals, participants in meetings, tourists, etc.

3.4. General religious situation

The church is part of the Danish National Evangelical Lutheran church but is administered by the Home Rule government. Other denominations are represented in Greenland but with very few followers.

4. Statistics and ethnoprofile

No precise statistics exist with regard to the language situation in Greenland. The great majority of Greenlanders have Greenlandic as their first language. Children who grow up in mixed families have varying knowledge of Greenlandic from nearly none at all to fluency. The tendency is that the knowledge of Greenlandic is increasing for this group (Langgård 1992). – The command of Danish by Greenlanders varies greatly, from fluency amongst the better educated to virtual no knowledge at all amongst children and old people, especially in the settlements. – The number of Danes who speak Greenlandic with any degree of fluency is very small. Some children in families where both parents were born outside Greenland, however, use Greenlandic as their second language, especially those living in settlements and smaller towns.

5. Sociolinguistic situation

5.1. Status and attitudes

Speaking Danish has high status because most well-paid jobs require an education where it is necessary to know Danish, but there is still greater status connected with being a fluent bilingual in Greenlandic and Danish.

5.2. Functions and diglossia

The Greenlandic language is used in homes, in the church, and also in Parliament, etc., but in most domains of society both languages are involved. Translation into and from Greenlandic is done on a large scale, both orally and in written form. It is not necessary for a Dane to know Greenlandic in order to function in Greenlandic society.

5.3. Stereotypes

It is a widespread stereotype that Danes cannot learn Greenlandic at all.

5.4. Bilingualism

Generally speaking Greenlanders are bilingual whereas Danes are monolingual (excluding their knowledge of other languages than Greenlandic). In the 1970s and later on the theory of double semilingualism was discussed in Greenland by teachers, parents and politicians and used to support the demand for more Greenlandic teachers.

6. Language-political situation

According to the Greenland Home Rule Act of 1978, "1) Greenlandic shall be the principal language. Danish must be thoroughly taught. 2) Either language may be used for official purposes". It is the aim of the Home Rule government to achieve a high degree of bilingualism in Greenlandic society with Greenlandic as the first language, Danish as the second language and English as a third language. Greenlandic cannot be considered a threatened language at present. The Greenlandic language is not only the most important symbol connected with Greenlandic ethnic identity (Kleivan 1969/1970), it is still supported by a strong popular will to use and develop the language.

6.1. Education

Education in Greenland has a long history of schooling with Greenlandic as the only or main language. A teachers' college was established in Nuuk in 1845, but many Danish teachers have been employed in Greenland since the 1950s due to a shortage of Greenlandic teachers. Danish teachers are only in exceptional cases able to teach in Greenlandic. In recent years their number has diminished compared with the number of Greenlandic teachers. It is the intention of the Home Rule Government that Greenlandic is going to be the main language at all levels of education. – Children with Danish as their first language are according to a recent decision by the Greenlandic Parliament gradually to be integrated into Greenlandic speaking classes within the folkeskole. At most educational institutions in Greenland the Danish language plays an important part. At Ilisimatusarfik, the university of Greenland, established in Nuuk in 1984, the students receive a higher education relevant for Greenlandic society. It has departments of Greenlandic Language and Literature, Culture and Society, and Administration.

6.2. Administration and the public sector

Because of the many Danes employed by the administration and the public sector the Danish language occupies a central position.

6.3. Religion

The language of the church has since the arrival of the first missionaries been Greenlandic. Greenlanders have replaced Danes as ministers except for two or three ministers who primarily function as ministers for Danes. Bilingual services are held on special occasions.

6.4. Media

Two bilingual newspapers published in Nuuk are read all over Greenland, Atuagagdliutit, inaugurated in 1861, which merged with the Danish language Grønlandsposten in 1952 to form a double-language periodical appearing three times a week, and the weekly Sermitsiaq, inaugurated in 1958. Besides some small local bilingual newspapers some cultural journals are published only in Greenlandic.

Radio Greenland is an independent public institution which includes both a radio and a television section. The majority of the radio programs are in Greennlandic, whereas the great majority of the television programs are re-transmissions from Radio Denmark in Danish or other languages. The number of radio and television programs in Greenlandic has increased in recent years.

A considerable number of books are published in Greenlandic. Besides the National Library in Nuuk there are libraries in towns and settlements.

Music is an important part of Greenland's cultural life and there exist many music groups. Recordings include modern rock, folk music, choir singing, and, to a small extent, traditional drumsongs. Song texts are nearly always in Greenlandic.

6.5. Standardization, orthography and language development

Written Greenlandic is based on the dialect spoken in the Nuuk area where the first missionaries settled and studied the language in the 1720s. Central West Greenlandic is considered to be the standard form of Greenlandic, even if several other dialects are still spoken. – A new phonemic orthography was introduced in 1973 after many years of discussion. – The Greenlandic Language Commission occasionally publishes lists of proposed neologisms within particular areas (e. g. technical and legal terms). Most of these words are native, but some of them are Danish loans. In fact there is little actual control and neologisms and loan words appear spontaneously in speech and in the writings of individual journalists and translators, etc.

7. General contactlinguistic portrait

The combined phonetic, morphosyntactic and lexical differences between Greenlandic and Danish are probably greater than those between any other two languages treated in this volume. This has no doubt contributed to the limited contact effects between them, as has sheer isolation.

7.1. Phonetics and phonology

Danish has a much larger inventory of phonemes than Greenlandic, especially as regards vowels, of which Greenlandic only has three. Moreover, consonants in clusters and in initial or final position are highly limited in Greenlandic. For Danes there are only a couple of 'difficult' sounds in Greenlandic, the uvular stop /q/ and voiceless geminate lateral /ll/. Typical phonetic and prosodic interference traits for the variety of Danish spoken by Greenlanders include the unaspirated pronunciation of Danish word-initial stops, the lack of Danish glottal 'stød', and a monotonous syllable-timed flow of speech (unlike 'stress-timed' Danish, Greenlandic lacks distinctive word-stress). Typical for Danes who speak Greenlandic is difficulty with distinctions of length in consonants and vowels (Greenlandic has both short and long and over-long syllables).

7.2. Morphosyntax

Morphosyntactic contact phenomena are more difficult to pinpoint and are largely limited to written Greenlandic. Some of these — such as relatively greater syntactic complexity of the written language, with widespread use of clausal nominalizations — have more to do with the transition from a purely oral language than with specific influence from Danish, although the latter of course supplied the model. Danish, a largely analytical language, is subject to strict syntactic ordering. By contrast, Greenlandic is highly polysynthetic, possessing a complex apparatus of productive and recursive suffixation but with relatively simple sentential syntax.

Some of the 'exotic' aspects of Greenlandic morphosyntax — apart from the sheer length of its words — are: lack of subordinating particles, verbal inflection being utilized instead; a wide range of bound verbalizing and nominalizing suffixes and, in general, productive derivation doing much of the work of external syntax in Danish; ergative clausal structure; fused inflections for verbal mood and person/number of both subject and object and for nominal number, case and personal possessor. None of these major structural differences have much direct bearing on contact phenomena, however. — The basic flexible SOV clause order of Greenlandic cannot be said to have been disturbed much by strictly SVO Danish either. However, in both literary works and administrative/journalistic/political texts, above all in translations from Danish, the ordering of successive clauses and phrases, e. g. the postposing of heavy object and adverbial clauses after the verb, often seems to reflect Danish norms. This was actually more apparent in translations from Danish in earlier times. — There are also gloss translations of Danish turns of phrase involving more than one word. Thus numerous metaphorical or 'poetic' expressions can be found in literary texts that are foreign to the spoken language, which makes very limited use of metaphor. Another matter entirely is the effect of Danish on the morphosyntax of young speakers in the capital Nuuk who come from mixed families or who have spent many years in Denmark. As can be expected, a greater preponderance of Danish-like constructions — frowned upon by elder speakers of standard Greenlandic — may be found in their speech. This applies too to the speech of Greenlanders living permanently in Denmark. — One area of interference from Danish that is spreading amongst younger speakers concerns the native pattern of replying to negative questions positively (with *aap* 'yes') if one agrees with the negation but with *naagga* 'no' if one wishes to assert the corresponding positive statement. The reverse Danish pattern, indicating 'logical' negation, can be heard more and more. This is also the case with 'negative raising' constructions based on Danish.

7.3. Lexicon

The area where contact phenomena are most apparent is the lexicon, though even here the number of direct loans from Danish into Greenlandic is relatively modest. There are also many native neologisms which one suspects of being gloss translations, especially of Danish compounds. Many of them are rather unwieldy 'explanations' rather than permanent new lexical forms, but such items as *inulluarit* 'goodbye' (literally 'live well', based on older Danish 'lev vel') have acquired a firm place in the language. Occasionally, also, one finds old words provided with a new, modern meaning in keeping with cultural introductions, thus *agiaq* 'violin' (originally 'shaman's rubbing stone').

Although Greenlandic has a relatively restricted number of lexical stems, its rich derivational morphology allows for the wholescale creation of new native words. This has been richly illustrated by R. Petersen (1976) from earliest contact times to the present. There is one area where native word-forming resources are highly restricted, however, and that is in the formation of nominal compounds, in which Danish, a typical Germanic language, abounds. There is no compounding as such at all in Greenlandic: all words, whether nominal or verbal, start with a single obligatory stem and end with an obligatory inflection, with any number of productive derivational suffixes in between. A few 'quasi-compounds', actually noun phrases containing a possessor noun, have made their way into the language under influence from Danish and are now treated as unitary lexicalizations as regards inflection, e. g. *ullo-

qeqqa 'midday' from *ullup qeqqa*, literally 'of the day, its middle'.

Greenlandic only has three word classes: nominals, verbs (actually verbal stems) and uninflected particles. The first two are each associated with their own sets of inflectional endings and the last comprises simple adverbials, interjections and conjunctions. Demonstratives (which refer to things or persons near/far/above/below/inside or outside/along the coast from the speaker) are a sub-class of nominal while qualitative verbal stems correspond to Danish adjectives. There are no gender distinctions and this can cause some difficulty for Greenlanders having to cope with both grammatical and natural gender when speaking Danish.

Derivational suffixes are not immune from Danish influence, note, even though Danish does not have equivalent suffixes in these instances. Thus the Greenlandic suffix *-sinnaa-* 'can' (expressing ability) can now be used in a modal sense of possibility like Danish *kan* and perfective aspectual/modal suffix *-sima-* can be used for past tense, corresponding to the Danish perfect. – The matter of lexical borrowing from Danish into Greenlandic is of considerable interest, since this has been going on for several centuries now. It is possible to stratify loan-words from different periods according to the degree of accommodation to Greenlandic phonology one finds in them. Thus the earliest ones, such as *palasi* 'priest' (Danish *præst*), show complete accommodation, somewhat later ones show less radical accommodation, and the most recent ones are in fact written in Danish to reflect the almost standard Danish pronunciation of such words by educated speakers.

Most loan-words are nouns, which can be rather easily integrated. Only a handful of verbs or adjectives have been borrowed. Recent Danish loan nouns may also become verbalized, as in *filmer-* 'see a film' (Danish noun *film*). Sometimes a loan will have a more restricted sense than in Danish, e.g. *dommeri* 'referee' from Danish *dommer* 'judge' (in the legal sense Greenlandic has its own native word *eqqortuussisoq*, lit. 'one who makes pronouncements about people').

One of the most important categories of loan-words is the numeral. The native system, based on finger and toe counting, went up to twenty, but today only the numbers up to twelve are used. Beyond that the Danish equivalents are found. In fact, in certain contexts the Danish numbers below that are used too, for example in combination with coinage, in dates, or in arithmetic.

Today many international words associated with new technological developments are entering the language, but still virtually always via Danish. Greenlanders generally accept that it is necessary to adopt loan-words for new phenomena when they are more succinct than native neologisms – as long, that is, as a perfectly usable native word does not already exist or can not easily be derived. The fate of such earlier native neologisms as *nalunaarasuartaat* 'telegraph', lit. 'means for conveying messages rapidly', is symptomatic: it has been largely superceded by Danish *telegraf*. It should be pointed out, however, that in certain lexical areas to do with modern academic, administrative and technical life native vocabulary is firmly in place – this includes basic legal and linguistic terminology, for example.

7.4. Prescriptive dictionaries and grammars

There have been several revisions of the standard Greenlandic-Danish dictionary and grammar, starting with those of Paul Egede (1750 and 1760), but the first that can really be called 'prescriptive' are those of Kleinschmidt (1851 and 1871), who with these works introduced the first consistent orthography. The rather abstract grammar appeared reworked in a more accessible guise in Rasmussen (1888). The language was undergoing important phonological changes in Kleinschmidt's time and he sometimes reconstructed underlying orthographical forms that were spurious, although they usually displayed historical insight. By the time of the introduction of the new orthography assimilation had rendered the learning of the 'old' orthography by children a difficult task. The latest in the line of Greenlandic-Danish dictionaries in the 'old' orthography was by Schultz-Lorentzen (1926). There is now also a Greenlandic-Danish dictionary in the new orthography, primarily for use in schools (Berthelsen et al. 1990). The latest Danish-Greenlandic dictionary (Bugge et al. 1960) consists as much of phrase-length explanations of Danish words as of actual lexical equivalents. The other two main dialects, East Greenlandic and Polar Eskimo, very much in the shadow of 'official' central West Greenlandic, each have thematically organized dictionaries, though there is as yet no official orthography and very little to read in these primarily spoken dialects. There are various practical text-books and other teaching aids for West Greenlandic, mainly written in Danish, but also a few in English and Greenlandic. Such works reflect changing norms, e. g. the simplification of nominal inflection types.

7.5. Literature

The long tradition of translation from Danish into West Greenlandic started with the first bible translations in the 18th century (the whole New Testament was published in 1766). Legends and myths of the oral tradition have been published (the earliest bilingual collection appeared in 1859—1863). Original Greenlandic written literature can be said to begin with the contributions to the journal *Atuagagdliutit* in the second half of the last century. Original poems, short stories, essays, plays and full-scale novels followed (the first Greenlandic novel was published in 1914). Most of this is not translated into Danish, though the best known writers such as Frederik Nielsen and Hans Lynge- have had a few of their works appear in translation. An anthology of Greenlandic literature with English translations can be found in Fortescue (1990).

There has not been so much original non-fiction (apart from the newspapers). Translations from Danish continue to predominate here. There is a tradition of short publications of an informative nature for the general public, however. Recent examples of somewhat more extensive non-fiction are a history of Greenlandic literature (Berthelsen 1994) and a series of local historical and geographical descriptions. There are also a good many original Greenlandic school books on most subjects taught in elementary and secondary school.

8. Bibliography (selected)

Berthelsen, Christian (1994): *Kalaallit atuakkiaat 1990 ilanngullugu*, Nuuk.

Berthelsen, Christian et al. (1990): *Oqaatsit Kalaallisuumiit Qallunaatuumut, Grønlandsk Dansk Ordbog*, Nuuk.

Bugge, Aage/Lynge, Kristoffer/Fuglsang-Damgaard, Ad./Nielsen, Frederik (1960): *Dansk Grønlandsk Ordbog*, Copenhagen.

Egede, Paul (1760): *Grammatica Grönlandica-Danica-Latina*, Havniæ.

Fortescue, Michael (1990): *From the Writings of the Greenlanders. Kalaallit atuakkiaannit*, Fairbanks.

Kleinschmidt, Samuel (1871): *Den grønlandske Ordbog omarbejdet*, Copenhagen.

Kleivan, Inge (1969/1970): "Language and Ethnic Identity: Language Policy and Debate in Greenland". In: *Folk* vol. 11—12, 235—285.

Langgård, Per (1992): "Grønlandssproget — tosproget — grønlandsksproget: nogle tendenser i det dansk-grønlandske sprogmøde blandt Nuuks skolebørn". In: *Grønlands kultur- og samfundsforskning 92*, 104—128.

Petersen, Robert (1976): "Nogle træk i udviklingen af det grønlandske sprog". In: *Tidsskriftet Grønland* nr. 5, 165—208.

Petersen, Robert (1979): "Danish influence on Greenlandic syntax". In: *Eskimo Languages, their present-day Conditions*, Basse, B./Jensen, K. (Eds.), Aarhus, 123—144.

Rasmussen, Chr. (1888): *Grønlandsk Sproglære*, Copenhagen.

Schultz-Lorentzen, C. W. (1926): *Den grønlandske Ordbog, grønlandsk-dansk*, Copenhagen, (English edition (1927): *A Dictionary of the West Greenlandic Eskimo Language*).

Michael Fortescue/Inge Kleivan, Copenhagen (Denmark)

130. Iceland

1. Geography and demography
2. Territorial history and national development
3. Politics, economy and general cultural and religious situation
4. Statistics and ethnoprofiles
5. Sociolinguistic situation
6. Language political situation
7. Presentation of language contact and contact languages
8. Evaluation of the status of research
9. Bibliography (selected)

1. Geography and demography

Iceland is an island in the North Atlantic with an area of 103.000 km². The nearest countries are Greenland, 287 km to the west, and the Faroe Islands, 420 km to the southeast. The climate is mild for the latitude, but the summers are short, the growing period hardly more than 4−5 months, and about ¾ of the island consists of glaciers and uninhabitable wasteland (→ language map A).

The population is about 260.000 and more than 60% lives in and around the capital, Reykjavík, in the southwest (cf. Landshagir 1992, 28). The population is increasing, but only a small part of this is due to immigration. There is, however, considerable migration, both internal and external (ibid. 22; 39). Some external migration results from the temporary residence of Icelanders abroad, which also partly explains why only about half of Icelanders born abroad are actually foreigners (ibid. 35). A great many foreigners living in Iceland, some of whom eventually gain Icelandic citizenship, probably marry into Icelandic families. Immigrant families are reportedly few in number.

2. Territorial history and national development

Iceland was settled in the 9th and 10th centuries by Norse immigrants who came mainly from Norway and the Norse settlements in Scotland and Ireland. There are no indications of an earlier population. The Icelanders bear some genetic resemblance to the Celtic population of Britain, e. g. in blood type, but the culture and the language are predominantly Nordic (Þorsteinsson/Jónsson 1991, 16 ff).

In 930 a free commonwealth was established and endured for more than three centuries. In 1262 Iceland came under the rule of the Norwegian king (ibid. 119). Later it became a colony of Denmark for more than five centuries. After a hard, though unarmed, struggle for independence during the 19th century, Iceland gained sovereignty in 1918, first in a royal union with Denmark, then as an independent republic from 1944 (ibid. 143−144; 359 ff; 409 f).

During the first centuries of Danish colonization, Iceland had considerable independence in domestic affairs, but the population lost it in 1662, when the absolute power of the monarchy was imposed (ibid. 223 ff), lasting for nearly two centuries.

Iceland has always been dependent on the import of necessities, e. g. cereal and wood, its main export being fishing products. In the beginning, most commerce went through Norway, but in the 14th and 15th centuries, foreign merchants, esp. from England and Germany, sailed to Iceland and traded directly with the inhabitants (ibid. 150 ff; 165 ff; 203 ff). In 1602 all trade with Iceland was monopolized and became confined to subjects of the Danish crown for 185 years (ibid. 209 ff; 256 ff). The rich fishing grounds around Iceland have attracted foreign fishing ships and whalers for centuries, e. g. from England, France, Spain and later Norway.

Iceland declared neutrality in both World Wars, but was occupied in 1940 by Great Britain. From 1941, US forces took part in the defence of Iceland. The last British troops left in 1945 but the United States has maintained a few military bases in the country to this day, beginning in 1951 under the auspices of NATO. These have caused disputes in Iceland for cultural as well as political reasons (ibid. 398 ff; 426 ff).

3. Politics, economy and general cultural and religious situation

Today, Iceland is a republic with a parliamentary democracy. Political and economic independence together with technological development, esp. in the fishing industries, has brought the nation a high standard of living (cf. Gíslason 1990, 54). However, the economy is unstable and vulnerable, as it relies mostly on one natural resource, marine products being 70−80% of exports (cf. Landshagir 1992, 121), and the cost of living is high.

Iceland has a long literary tradition and literacy has been general, at least since the 18th century (Þorsteinsson/Jónsson 1991, 237). Today, education is compulsory from the ages of 6 to 16, and over 60% of 19-year-olds attend school (cf. Landshagir 1992, 264). Schools at all levels are almost exclusively public schools. Other cultural institutions, e. g. radio and television stations and theaters, are run by the state or the largest municipalities. Numerous Icelandic books are published every year, as well as many papers and periodicals (ibid. 267).

More than 90% of the population belong to the State Lutheran Church (ibid. 38), but the participation of many people is limited to baptism, confirmation, marriage and funerals.

4. Statistics and ethnoprofiles

The population of Iceland is ethnically homogeneous. Foreigners, including those who have acquired Icelandic citizenship, make up scarcely more than 3−4% of the population. These are both immigrants and temporary residents and they are scattered throughout the country roughly in proportion with the native population. They are of many different nationalities, though mainly from Western Europe and the United States (ibid. 35), and they are too few and too scattered to form real minority groups.

5. Sociolinguistic situation

Icelandic is the native language of the entire nation. Only children of foreign parents are bilingual from the beginning. It is taken for granted that immigrants learn Icelandic within a reasonable time, but they receive little, though increasing, regular official support in their linguistic integration. Some language schools offer courses in Icelandic for foreigners.

Icelandic is spoken by less than 300.000 people, and even though it is the official and dominant language in Iceland, the nation is dependent on knowledge of other languages for communication with the outside world. This makes foreign language learning an extremely important part of general education. Most adults have at least some passive knowledge of one or more foreign languages. Danish and English are taught as part of compulsory education and many people learn at least one additional language, usually German or French.

During the long colonization of Iceland, Danish officials and merchants had little direct contact with most of the sparse and primarily rural population. The influence of Danish was greatest in the more densely populated areas near the centers of administration and commerce, esp. in later times, and it led the Danish philologist Rasmus Rask to predict, in 1813, that Icelandic would disappear in Reykjavík within 100 years and in the whole country within other 200 if nothing were done (cf. Ottósson 1990, 52), a prophecy that has yet to be realized. The struggle for independence was accompanied by strong nationalism and language reform on the model of the classical saga literature and the speech of the common rural people, considered to have preserved the language in its purest form (Halldórsson 1979, 79 ff).

The main source of linguistic influence switched from Danish to English during World War II. With the British occupation, the nation experienced extensive daily contact with a large group of foreigners for the first time; there was almost one soldier to every two natives in Reykjavík (cf. Landshagir 1992, 21; Tómasson 1983, 63). Since then, Anglo-American influence has been enormous, though perhaps in a more indirect way than during the war.

Dialectal variation is comparatively insignificant in Icelandic. It is primarily phonetic and lexical, much less morphological (Benediktsson 1961−1962, 74 ff). The existence of sociolects is a matter of debate (cf. Halldórsson 1979, 84; Pálsson 1979, 188 ff), and in the absence of any detailed research cannot be verified (see also Gíslason et al. 1988, 46−47).

6. Language political situation

The aim of Icelandic language policy is to keep the language system as intact and free from foreign influence as possible and to maintain the characteristics of the vocabulary by using native words and neologisms from native stems and affixes rather than loanwords (Halldórsson 1979, 84; B. Jónsson 1988, 5 f). Orthography is standardized, but there is no official standard of pronunciation. Laws on personal names include clauses to preserve Icelandic names and naming practises (cf. Kvaran/Jónsson 1991, 81 ff) differing from the neighbouring languages in the usage of patronymics, e. g. *Jónsson* and *Jónsdóttir*, 'son/daughter of John', rather than family surnames. Public institutions are expected to follow official language policy and standards, and the public mass media are required to be models of good language use.

Most people are exposed to foreign languages to varying degrees in their daily life. A large number of television programmes and the majority of films, both on television and in the cinemas, are foreign, mainly in English (cf. Árnason 1988, 4 f; Landshagir 1992, 273). Icelandic translations are obligatory, usually done by subtitles, though children's material is often dubbed. All radio broadcasting is in Icelandic, with the exception of lyrics to foreign music, a substantial part of the programming at many stations.

Most bookstores offer a variety of foreign books and magazines, and many people consult foreign reading material (textbooks, manuals, instructions, etc.) in their work.

7. Presentation of language contact and contact languages

Language contact in Iceland concerns Icelandic on the one hand and various foreign languages on the other, mainly English nowadays. Foreign influence on Icelandic is most extensive in vocabulary, via borrowing of words and other lexical entities, e. g. suffixes, as well as loan shifts and loan translations (J. H. Jónsson 1978, 356−359; 1988, 25 ff). Loan words from this century are e. g. *bíll* 'car' and *bleia* 'diaper' from Danish *bil* and *ble*, *jeppi* and *sjoppa* from English *Jeep* and *shop*, and *glögg* 'warm spiced wine' from Swedish *glögg*. Synonymous neologisms are sometimes used interchangeably with the loan words, often with some stylistic difference, e. g. *bifreið*, a more formal synonym of *bíll*. Other borrowings have a slightly different meaning from the original, e. g. *sjoppa* 'a small shop selling candy, tobacco, etc.'. Many native words have extended their meaning to include new concepts through loan shift, e. g. *skjár*, an old word for a window but now usually referring to a television or computer screen. The language also abounds with loan translations, e. g. *skýjakljúfur* 'skyscraper' and *fjölmiðill* 'mass medium'.

Icelandic is a highly inflected language and loan words usually undergo some morphological as well as phonological and orthographical adaptation. This means that nouns borrowed from English normally receive grammatical gender and are assigned to one of many declensional classes (Eiríksson 1975, 56 ff; Jónsson 1980, 63 ff). The degree to which particular loan words have been adapted depends on their age in the language and their status, old loans usually being more thoroughly adapted than new ones and words used in the written standard adapted to a higher degree than those mainly used in speech. The original form of words in the host language is also an important factor, as their adaptability can vary. Fairly recent borrowings, such as *poppa* (Eng. '(to make) pop(corn)*' and *rokk* (neuter; Eng. 'rock'), can therefore be just as familiar as the native *hoppa* 'to jump' and *brokk* 'trot (of horses)', though much older loan words have not lost their foreign appearance, e. g. *stúdent* 'student' and *organisti* 'organist'.

Instances of foreign influence in syntax are easily found, esp. in the collocation of words (Árnason 1988, 7 f; Fjalldal 1987, 118). They are most prominent in translations (Pálsson/Þráinsson 1988, 53 f), but it is not clear how far-reaching the syntactic influence is. External influence on phonology and inflection is minimal (Árnason 1988, 8).

8. Evaluation of the status of research

Contact between Icelandic and other languages and their influence of Icelandic are not very well studied. Loan words and other lexical borrowings have received the most attention, though mainly from a historical point of view, but there have been no systematic studies of foreign influence on other language levels. Observations and discussions on foreign influences on Icelandic are closely connected to language policy issues; most of the linguistic sources referred to above are reflections of this.

9. Bibliography (selected)

Árnason, Kristján (1988): "Ensk-amerísk áhrif á íslenskt mál". In: *Málfregnir 4*, 3−9.

Benediktsson, Hreinn (1961−1962): "Icelandic Dialectology: Methods and Results." In: *Lingua Islandica 3*, 72−113.

Eiríksson, Eyvindur (1975): "Beyging nokkurra enskra tökuorða í nútímaíslensku". In: *Mímir 23*, 55−71.

Fjalldal, Magnús (1987): "Leiðin frá helvíti til hi og bye". In: *Íslenskt mál og almenn málfræði 9*, 111−119.

Gíslason, Gylfi Th. (1990): *The Challenge of being an Icelander*, Reykjavík.

Gíslason, Indriði/Baldur Jónsson/Guðmundur B. Kristmundsson/Höskuldur Þráinsson (1988): *Mál og samfélag*, Reykjavík.

Halldórsson, Halldór (1979): "Icelandic Purism and Its History". In: *Word 30*, 76−86.

Jónsson, Baldur (1988): "Isländsk språkvård." In: *Språk i Norden*, 5−16.

Jónsson, Jón H. (1978): "Zur Sprachpolitik und Sprachpflege in Island". In: *Muttersprache 88*, 353−362.

Jónsson, Jón H. (1980): "Om skrivemåte og bøyning av fremmedord i islandsk". In: *Språk i Norden*, 61−67.

Jónsson, Jón H. (1988): "Tendenser og tradisjoner i islandsk orddannelse". In: *Språk i Norden*, 21−33.

Kvaran, Guðrún/Sigurður Jónsson (1991): *Nöfn Íslendinga*, Reykjavík.

Landshagir (1992): Statistical Abstract of Iceland. Reykjavík.

Ottósson, Kjartan G. (1990): *Íslensk málhreinsun. Sögulegt yfirlit*. Reykjavík.

Pálsson, Gísli (1979): "Vont mál og vond málfræði". In: *Skírnir 153*, 175−201.

Pálsson, Heimir/Höskuldur Þráinsson (1988): *Um þýðingar*, Reykjavík.

Tómasson, Tómas Þór. (1983−1984): *Heimsstyrjaldarárin á Íslandi 1939−1945*. I−II, Reykjavík.

Þorsteinsson, Björn/Bergsteinn Jónsson (1991): *Íslandssaga til okkar daga*, Reykjavík.

Ásta Svavarsdóttir, Reykjavík (Iceland)

X. Sprachkontakte in Nordwesteuropa
Language Contacts in Northwestern Europe
Contacts linguistiques en Europe du Nord-Ouest

131. Great Britain

1. The geography and demography of language contact in Great Britain
2. Territorial history and national development of contact languages
3. Political, economic, cultural and religious situation
4. Demographic and statistical situation
5. Sociolinguistic situation
6. The political situation of contact languages
7. Conclusions
8. Sources of information
9. Bibliography (selected)

1. The geography and demography of language contact in Great Britain

Language contact in Great Britian relates geographically to its rolling lowlands, high rise mountains and being surrounded on all sides by the ocean. Great Britain, constituting England, Northern Ireland, Scotland and Wales, contains a population of 54.9 million (1991 Census – see OPCS, 1992) of whom the greater percentage (estimated as between 95% and 98%) are monolingual in the English language. In the southern lowlands are the strongholds of the English language – dominating the language economy of Great Britain as it does in of many parts of the world. In these lowlands of Britain are the urban conglomerations where the newer, 'community' languages of Britain are to be found (e. g. Panjabi, Bengali, Greek, Turkish). In the north west highlands of Scotland, in the valleys and mountainous regions of Wales, and in Northern Ireland, the Celtic languages have survived. However, too tight a geographic stereotype is dangerous. While the Celtic languages tend to be relatively strong in the rural, low population density areas (e. g. the north-west of Scotland and the north-west of Wales), there are also culturally strong and sizable populations of Celtic speakers in large urban areas such as Cardiff and Swansea (Wales), Edinburgh and Glasgow (Scotland). In the same way, while urban areas such as London, Birmingham, Bradford and Coventry contain sizable proportions of the newer, community languages of England, language minority speakers are also to be found in scattered rural areas – the Chinese with their fast food businesses are a particularly strong example.

Being surrounded on all sides by the sea, there is little contact between the languages of Britain and the languages of neighbouring countries (e. g. France, Belgium, Netherlands; → language map B). Unlike various countries of Europe with migrant labour, guest workers and changing populations due to political and national change, Britain has relatively little in-migration or out-migration. (Historical tendencies in migration will be considered later in the chapter). The continuous coastline symbolises that language contact for most bilinguals and for language groups within the shores of Britain is internal and not external.

Apart from the Celtic languages and the newer, community Asian and European languages of Britain, there is also language contact among smaller, minority language groups. Manx Gaelic is spoken by a very few on the Isle of Man. The Lallans tongue is spoken in lowland Scotland. Norman French survives in the Channel Islands of Guernsey and Jersey (Spence 1984). In Cornwall, the Cornish language (Kernewek) died in the 19th century, but has been revived in recent decades. The British Roma, also called Gypsies or Traditional Travellers, probably originated in India, and moved across Europe from the fifth century, reaching Britain by the 15th century. Traditional prejudice against gypsies has tended to aid the maintenance of their separate language (Hancock 1984, 1985). Termed Anglo-Romani, the language of these people provides them with a sense of continued identity and installs boundaries from outsiders. British Sign Language is also regarded as a language of Britain (Alladina/Edwards 1991). A linguistic analysis of British Sign Language shows that it is complex and able to fulfil a wide range of communicative functions as other languages. British Sign Language was effective in deaf education in the 19th century but until recently has been regarded as a language that would not allow the integration of deaf children and adults into society. Parents have often been urged to use speech and not sign language with their deaf children. However, as Ladd (1991) has shown, British Sign Language has a history traceable to the 1500's and developed in deaf schools and deaf clubs in the Industrial Revolution of the 19th century. The British Sign Language community is estimated as between 50,000 and 100,000 strong. British Sign Language is used in deaf homes, as well as in clubs for deaf people and local community organisations. For many deaf children and parents, British Sign Language is their first language, and English is their second language. British Sign Language has regional variations and also an absence of a written form.

A threefold typology of language contacts in Great Britain is presented, with connections to varying status and power bases, demographic characteristics, historical antecedents, and use of survival arguments based on the territorial or personality principle, on collective, language group rights or individual 'freedom' rights:

(i) English with the better publicised Celtic languages (e. g. Scottish Gaelic, Welsh, Irish);
(ii) English with the newer 'community' languages of Britain (e. g. Panjabi, Bengali, Turkish);
(iii) English with the relatively less documented minority languages (e. g. Lallans, Romani, Sign Language, Manx, Cornish).

This third category cannot be considered in comparable detail in this chapter due to the paucity of reliable documentation. Romani is considered in article 239.

2. Territorial history and national development of contact languages

While the great majority of the population of Great Britain are native, monolingual speakers of English, and while those who are not native speakers mostly speak English relatively fluently as a second language, this has not always been the case. English was preceded in the British Isles by the Celtic languages (Milroy 1984). While English migrated from the northern European coast (between Jutland and north eastern France) around 400 A. D., it is likely that the Celts migrated to Britain during the Iron Age. In stark contrast, the newer, community languages of Britain mostly entered between the 1950's and 1980's.

The Celtic languages in Scotland, Ireland and Wales are presently short in numbers but long in history. The exact entrance of the Celtic languages into Britain is debated, but the Iron Age appears likely to mark Celtic settlement in the British Isles. Two forms of Celtic language began to appear. From the Brythonic or P-Celtic form of language derives modern Welsh, Cornish and Breton (see article 149 on Breton), and from the Goidelic or Q-Celtic branch of the language derives Irish and Scottish Gaelic. These two strands of the Celtic languages come from one family within the Indo-European group of languages. Edwards and Alladina (1991) describe the Celtic languages thus:

"Celtic languages draw on modes of grammatical organisation which are markedly different from the majority of Indo-European languages especially English. Thus, sentences are structured with the verb first, followed by the subject, object and the rest of the predicate; there is a system of prepositional pronouns where prepositions are marked for person; consonant mutations in the form, for instance, of lenition and nasalization, carry syntactic and semantic information" (page 31 and 32).

The history of the Celtic languages has tended to be one of decay and decline over many centuries, often in relationship to the parallel growth of the English language. The Angles, the Saxons, the Vikings and the Normans not only shaped the English language but also exerted influence on the form of Celtic spoken. The Roman Invasion, Norman settlers, the attempted destruction by the Tudors of the Celtic tongue, and the rejection of the native tongue by many of the natives themselves during the 19th century and 20th century, has led to a history of downward language shift. This is now considered in terms of individual nations.

In the history of Wales, English rule of the Celts was established in 1284. While the legal use of Welsh was retained, English law and English rule dominated. In the 16th century,

Acts of Union united England and Wales and excluded the Welsh language from official functions. In 1536, Wales was forcibly united with England and henceforth experienced a long and continuing period of economic, political, cultural and linguistic assimilation. The Welsh gentry were rapidly Anglicised and often moved across the border to reside in England.

A variety of historic factors have been given for the rapid decline of the Welsh (and Irish and Scottish Gaelic) language in their home heartlands during this century in particular. The rise of mass communications, radio, television, telephone and information technology have brought the pervading influence of the English language into almost every home. The spread of transport systems, railways, automobiles, aeroplanes and fast moving ocean liners have created ease of transport and movement of people (Baker 1985). While major highways into Wales have brought the promise of economic regeneration, they have also brought monolingual English inhabitants. Mobility of labour, allowing the highly educated and the highly entrepreneurial to seek affluence in London and other major trading centres, plus tourism and retirement homes in Wales, have all led to out-migration of Welsh speakers and in-migration of English monolinguals. Industrialisation in the twentieth century encouraged movement to large towns and cities. Such industrialisation and urbanisation has often meant English as the common denominator for new communities and new working relationships. The decline of religion within Welsh communities, decline in the power of the preacher and chapel conformity, has also been allied to decline in Welsh language support and usage. The Welsh language has tended to be subject to repression, sometimes through battles, sometimes through manifest or latent government policy and sometimes by Anglicised education. But what has helped the Welsh language to survive is often geological facts such as mountain lines, geographical marginalisation and rural isolation (Pryce 1986; Pryce/Williams 1988).

The Celts settled in Scotland around the 5th century, and by the 9th century, resided in much of Scotland that was not controlled by Norsemen in the Highlands. Norman families such as the Bruces, Stewarts and Comyns settled in the lowlands of Scotland some 300 years later. A division between the Gaelic speaking highlanders and the English speaking lowlanders gradually developed as English institutions gained a foothold in Scotland in the Early Middle Ages, with Scotland becoming part of Britain in 1707 (Thomson 1984). In Wales, the majority of the population were Welsh speaking until the turn of this century. In Scotland, Gaelic has not been the majority language since the 11th century. In Wales, there has never been the feeling that the native language is somewhat alien; but in much of Scotland, just such an attitude has prevailed, particularly in the more populated regions.

Historically, the Highlands of Scotland have been linguistically and culturally quite distinct, and before the 18th century, were relatively remote from central government control. In the middle of the 18th century, and during the 19th century, the Highlands began to become depopulated. During the 19th century, the school system was used for 'the teaching-out of Gaelic' and the attempted removal of Highland identity. In Scotland, there thus developed a divide between the Highlands and Lowlands. While there are cultural and linguistic differences, there is also a contrast between remote, sparsely populated areas in the Highlands and the urban areas of the Lowlands (Withers 1988).

It is sometimes customary to bracket together the Highlands and the Western Isles of Scotland when talking about the history of culture and language. However, they do differ in some important respects. The Western Isles, largely because of their remoteness, have resisted Anglicisation more successfully than the Highland mainland. That the Scottish Gaelic language has historically survived in the Western Isles is a bitter-sweet tale. The islands' inaccessibility, remoteness and scatteredness has tended to result in relatively little in-migration and much out-migration. Such remoteness has often left an aging and declining population.

In the Northern Isles of Scotland (Orkney and Shetland), there has not been a Celtic tradition. The people of the Northern Isles were Norse in origin. Indeed, Orkney and Shetland were part of the Kingdom of Norway until the 16th century when they were turned over in settlement of a debt. The people of the Northern Isles are still conscious of their separate identity and are almost as reluctant to be called Scots as the Scots are reluctant to be called English. But in the Northern Isles, there is no linguistic separation. The Norse dialects have died out and been replaced by a form of English. The founding of North Sea oil has meant prosperity for the Northern Isles. This has meant increased in-migration and Anglicisation.

Northern Ireland is known for its political and religious divides. The reign of the Stuarts in England during the 17th century saw a deliberate policy of Anglicising Celtic Ireland. Irish rebellions brought cruel repression, confiscation of land, and settlement by the British. A Roman Catholic country was invaded by the Protestant British. A high level of emigration in the 19th and 20th centuries (particularly to North America) followed the suppression. Repeated failure of the potato crop on which the impoverished, rural population depended, only fuelled the struggle for independence from Britain. The Easter Rising of 1916 plus guerrilla warfare led to the partition of Ireland in 1921. Northern Ireland remained part of Britain, but has constantly been the scene of militant activist fighting.

Much of Ireland, North and South, lives in relative peace and harmony. The Irish question is not simply about North versus South, or Protestant versus Catholic, convenient though it is for mass media and certain sectarians to present it in these terms. The conflict has its origins in the cultural divide between Irish natives and British settlers, symbolised to their adherence to Catholicism and Protestantism respectively. This in turn was the basis for partition. That there is political division and religious variation is obvious enough; such political and religious contention does not tell the whole story. Northern Ireland itself is not a purely Protestant area, but the area where Protestants are numerically dominant. Although many Northern Catholics do identify with the Republic, not all do so. By the same token, there are Protestants in the Republic who have no sympathy with Northern Unionism. Such Southern Protestants play an important and accepted role in Irish society. Although government policy in the South tends to be sympathetic to the Northern Catholics and to the reunification of Ireland, public support for the militant IRA is minute.

Ostensibly, the sectarian differences are about a Catholic preference for the reunification of Ireland, and the Protestant preference for remaining part of Britain. While the Irish language is undoubtedly found more amongst Republicans than Unionists in Northern Ireland, it is wrong to associate the Irish language with the republican movement. Many Northern Ireland Republicans, like their southern Irish colleagues, do not associate their political imperative with language insistence.

The Isle of Man, though at various times ruled by the Norse, Scots and English has been Celtic in population with a language closely related to Irish and Scots Gaelic. Written Manx did not appear until the 17th century, with spelling conventions based on English. Around the 1700's, English was not understood by about two-thirds of the islanders. But with the advent of schooling, English became the dominant language, so that by the mid 19th century, Manx was rarely used in the law courts and was ignored by the schools. Manx came to a formal conclusion with the death of the last native speaker of Manx in December 1974. However, there are current revivalist attempts.

The history of the community languages of Britain is short and recent, yet dynamic and developing. The newer, community languages include Arabic, Bengali, Cantonese, Gujerati, Greek, Hindi, Italian, Panjabi, Polish, Portuguese, Spanish, Turkish, Ukrainian and Urdu (Taylor 1981, 1985, 1987, 1988). The Linguistics Minority Project (1985) proposed a typology of recent migration to Great Britain. The typology makes the distinction between (i) in-migration because cheap labour was sought particularly in the 1950's and the 1960's, and (ii) political refugees who have migrated to Britain from the end of the Second World War to the present. In-migration for inexpensive labour tends to refer to speakers of Bengali, Panjabi, Gujerati, as well as to the Chinese and West Indians. Such a South Asian and West Indian group derive from the colonies of Britain. Other sources of migrant labour have come from Italy since the 1950's and also came from Portugal and Spain in the 1960's. Political refugees can be divided into the ex-colonial and the European groups. In the former group, there are, for example, East Africans and Vietnamese Chinese; in the latter group, for example, there are Polish and Ukrainians. That the typology cannot take in all cases is evident from those of Cypriot origin who can be regarded as both ex-colonial and of refugee status. Such a typology thus does not fully clarify the status and structural position of the linguistic minorities of England. It is also wrong to classify children of the newer languages in England as being in-migrants. The present children from language communities are often second or third or fourth generation British citizens. These are not migrant worker children nor immigrant children. They are not 'Gastarbeiter' or 'Wanderarbeiter'.

3. Political, economic, cultural and religious situation

As a generalisation, where the Celtic languages and the newer, community languages exist, there is relatively less affluence, less employment and less social and vocational mobility. The Celtic languages are often strong in small, scattered rural communities. The economy of such areas is often based in agriculture and not in new industry or technology. In the mountainous, lakeland areas of the Highlands and Islands of Scotland, relative inaccessibility makes it difficult to commence or develop vigorous new enterprises to create permanent, well-paid employment for Gaelic speakers. As with other Celtic regions, the remote, rural and lowly populated regions where the Gaelic language lies, means that attracting trade and business into the area is essential for retaining Gaelic language speakers. In the cwms (valleys) of South Wales, the decline in the coal mining industry has led to some new industrial initiatives, but a movement away from the greater linguistic homogeneity of communities found in the early decades of this century. While new business may mean the infiltration of English language and Anglophone culture, the Irish, the Welsh and the Scots are at one in realising the essential economic bases of the survival of different languages of different nations.

The economic situation of the community language groups is both similar and different to the Celtic economy. The difference is that employment is often in the factory based, less skilled industries (e. g. clothes factories) in highly populated urban areas. Unemployment is high among such communities, with comparatively poor housing and a failure to create equal job opportunities. The similarity between the Celtic and community languages is in the relative poverty and lower geographical, social and vocational mobility.

The Welsh speakers and the community language groups are also similar in the role of religion in language maintenance. That the Welsh language is still alive today is partly due to its strong historical links with literate, Protestant religion. What saved Welsh from decline on the scale suffered by other Celtic languages may be largely but not totally due to religion. A Welsh language Protestant religion was not a threat to the English rulers as was the Catholic Gaelic in Scotland or the Catholic Irish in Ireland. For the Scottish and Irish Celts, the attempted extinction of their Catholicism meant parallel attempted extinction of their language. The Protestantism of the Welsh was more acceptable. Hence, relatively speaking, was their language. Further, the nonconformist chapels were not particularly interested in politics or power, − more in the salvation of souls and that form of non-political society beyond the cemetery. Welsh was the language of the people, and there was much concern to save the people through their reading the Bible and becoming Christians than salvation through political or social change. A network of Sunday schools was effectively established to teach children and adults to read and discuss in Welsh. Around the middle of the 19th century, a fifth of the population were attending these Sunday schools. Literacy in Welsh became well established, supporting and reviving the language. Alongside such religious Welsh activity, a flourishing literary and musical culture grew up which was partly fostered in the chapels. Thus Welsh penetrated a person's whole way of life, even though there were pressures in the 19th and particularly in the 20th century to adopt the English language and culture. As social and vocational mobility required the English language, the language of salvation was not the language of prosperity. The success of literacy in Welsh and Welsh education often served to encourage immigration to richer and more prosperous parts − England and the U. S. in particular.

Religion is also important in the maintenance of British Community languages. That the British community languages are being reproduced is often due to their vitality in the temple, mosque, synagogue and church. Such religious institutions join with the nuclear and extended family in being a strong and vital institutional support for language survival. This is further considered in section five of this chapter.

The twentieth century has seen the rise of ethnic revivalists and language activists in Scotland and Wales, and also in Cornwall and the Isle of Man. The rise of the Welsh Nationalist Party and the Scottish Nationalist Party in recent decades, the rise of the militant Welsh Language Society after 1962, the rise of powerful parental pressure groups for bilingual education in Scotland and Wales, the clever alliance of powerful politicians, manoeuvring of mass media and Ghandi-like non-militant protests, has led to a rise in consciousness of the plight of the Gaelic and Welsh languages in particular. In Cornwall and the Isle of Man, small groups have sprung up to support a dead but resurrectable language. While Wales and Scotland have been ruled by England for many centuries, the twentieth century has seen a growing demand for devolution of power in both Scotland and Wales. The establishment of the Scottish Office and the Welsh Office has been a major symbol of a Welsh and Scottish nationhood. The desire for devolution of power to Scotland and Wales, while still a minority pursuit, nevertheless continuously raises the idea of different languages within different nations (Williams 1986; Williams/Raybould 1991).

Language has thus become a symbol of desired Celtic political devolution. The Welsh, Irish and Scots are Welsh or Irish or Scottish first, British reluctantly, and Europeans increasingly. The differences between Wales and England, and between Scotland and England, are more important than their similarities; the diversity is more important than solidarity. In contrast, for many English, the terms English and British are synonymous. There still exists a colonialist attitude of central government towards community languages in particular, and, at times, towards its Celtic inhabitants. The 19th century English colonialist preference for all Britain being English speaking areas, for bureaucratic convenience and colonialist supremacy, has thus often invited Celtic speakers to believe that the decline in their languages is more about English murder than Celtic suicide.

4. Demographic and statistical situation

In the 1991 Census, the population in Wales was counted as 2.8 million of whom 18.7% (530,000) described themselves as speaking Welsh (OPCS, 1992). The proportion of the 1991 population in Wales who were reported as Welsh speaking (18.7%) was a decrease of 0.3% from the 1981 Census. Thus the Welsh language appears to be holding steady — different from the dominant pessimistic view of Welsh language survival. However, such a 18.7% figure is bound to be contaminated by wide variations of fluency in the Welsh language, reflecting an attitude for or against the language on behalf of some groups, and representing a wide variety of actual usage in different and varying domains. For some of those who replied positively to the Census question, Welsh may be a language used only at school, or used only for a few functions (e. g. in chapel, with grandparents). For others, Welsh may be the language of school or workplace, of community life and of religion. While Welsh speakers are generally fluent in the English language, Welsh is less often used amongst those for whom it is a second language.

The decline of Welsh speakers in this century has become associated with age trends and Welsh illiteracy trends. Up until the 1971 Census, the tendency was for older rather than young people to be Welsh speaking. So, as older generations have died, newer generations failed to reproduce the Welsh language density in the population. The figures for the 1981 and 1991 Census, showing a considerable upturn in the 3—15 year olds speaking Welsh, is a reversal of age trends this century. The 1991 Census statistics show an increasing trend for younger people to be speaking Welsh. Of the 3—15 year old age group, 24.3% were reported to be Welsh speaking. In contrast, in the 16—40 year old age group, only 15.3% reported themselves as speaking Welsh. While the figure for young people may be inflated due to their speaking or learning Welsh in school, there is nevertheless the possibility of an upward trend in the Welsh language statistics in Wales. Further details are found in the succeeding chapter by Colin Williams.

Another factor predictive of language decline has been Welsh illiteracy. Where Welsh is spoken (by an individual or within a community) without the ability to read or write in Welsh, it has less functions, less status and less chance of survival in a technological global village. Such a situation is rather like historic British colonialism, where the vernacular language was used as a spoken language, and the English language was imposed as the system for reading and writing. Where oracy exists without literacy, the vernacular may be threatened (Baker 1985).

In Scotland, the 1991 Census indicated a population of 5.0 million people with 1.4%

speaking Gaelic (OPCS 1992). This represents a drop of 0.2% from the 1981 Scottish Gaelic Census. The age distributions in Scotland are not so optimistic as in Wales. Of 3−15 year olds, 0.9% reported speaking Gaelic, compared with 1.1% of 16−40 year olds and 2.2% of age 65 years and over. Thus, in Scotland, the trend appears to be towards Gaelic being the language of older rather than younger people with a threat to its future existence.

In the Scottish highlands and islands, migration of Gaelic speakers to Glasgow and Edinburgh, as well as to the north and south of England, has led to Scottish Gaelic declining from 5% of the population at the turn of the twentieth century to 1.4% in 1991. The threat of poverty and the pull of affluence has effected an eastward and southward movement from the highlands to the lowlands. Such outward migration from Gaelic speaking heartlands has, and still continues, to weaken the Gaelic population, and density of population, in such areas. In the lowlands of Scotland, half the population of Scotland lives in the district of Strathclyde, mostly in and around Glasgow. Glasgow, a city plagued in recent decades by overcrowding, urban decay, dying heavy industry and one of the highest rates of unemployment in Great Britain, also contains strong cells of Scottish Gaelic language and culture (MacKinnon 1991). While the Census figures are pessimistic, there is an optimism amongst many Gaelic language activists and Gaelic educationists that some kind of language reversal can be initiated through bilingual education.

Of a Northern Ireland population of around 1.6 million, 9% report being Irish speaking, and 5−6% as being literate in Irish. While in the 17th Century, the majority of the population of Ulster was Irish speaking, today the Irish language has no official status in the six counties of Northern Ireland. There are no official Northern Ireland forms in the Irish language (e. g. for registering children). Since 1937, the use of Irish has been illegal in Northern Ireland courts and could lead to imprisonment. While Irish on street names is illegal, nevertheless over 500 Irish language street names have been erected in recent years.

This is not to suggest that Irish is banned in Northern Ireland. It can be heard in particular communities and hostelries. Irish can also be heard in a few of Northern Ireland's schools. The Northern Ireland population can receive Irish language radio and television programmes from Eire. Since 1981, Radio Ulster has broadcast around two hours of programmes a week in Irish.

In the 1991 Census of Great Britain, nonwhite, ethnic minorities were found to number 3 million of the 55 million inhabitants of Great Britain (OPCS 1992). Not all of these ethnic minority groups will be bilingual (unfortunately, the Census of Great Britain does not ask a language question − except for the Celts). Thus, the number of speakers of languages other than English and the Celtic languages is unknown. If we were to assume (conservatively) that half of this ethnic minority group (i. e. about one and a half million people) spoke a mother tongue other than English, this would be three times the number who speak Welsh in Wales and some twenty times the number of people who speak Scottish Gaelic. As will be discussed later, Welsh in particular, but also Scottish Gaelic, tend to be given considerably more governmental consideration, status and power than the new languages of England. In contrast, in terms of absolute numbers, the language minorities of England far outnumber the language minority speakers in Celtic areas. It should also be noted that, of the 3 million ethnic minority population in Britain, only 100,000 live in Wales and Scotland (OPCS 1992). That is, the Celtic areas tend to house few of the in-migrants from India, Asia and Africa. Such language communities are found in towns such as Bradford with its Urdu and Panjabi speakers; in Peterborough where Panjabi and Urdu is joined by an Italian speaking community; in Haringey in North London where Greek and Turkish language communities − particularly from Cyprus − reside. In the east of London, there is a strong Bangladeshi community who speak Bengali, or rather Sylheti, a variety of Bengali.

While it is currently impossible to provide statistics for community language demographics, the 1991 Census data provides important information about the ethnic group composition in Britain.

Table 131.1, showing the ethnic composition of Britain in 1991, indicates that ethnic minorities account for 5.5% of the population. Mainland European and Celtic minorities are included by the Census figures under 'whites'. In Wales and Scotland, such 'nonwhite' ethnic minorities account for less than 1.5% of the population. The largest ethnic

Tab. 131.1: Ethnic group composition in Britain

Ethnic Group	British Population
Whites (including mainland European migrants)	51.8 million
Ethnic minorities	3.0 million
Black ethnic minorities	0.9 million
South Asian	1.5 million
Chinese	0.16 million
Other ethnic minorities	0.5 million
Total population	54.9 million

minority are the south Asians (Indian, Pakistani, Bangladeshi) who represent 2.7% of the British population. Census data shows that the ethnic minorities are largely concentrated in England's most populated and industrial areas. More than half the ethnic minority population of Great Britain lives in south east England. While the south east of England is the most highly populated region of Britain, the relative concentration of 'non-white' ethnic minorities in this region is greater than for white people. Greater London alone contains almost 45% of the ethnic minority population of Britain. The second largest concentration of the ethnic minority population is centred around Birmingham in the West Midlands. The West Midlands region accounts for more than 14% of the British ethnic minority population. Ethnic minorities are least well represented in the higher status growth areas and in the more rural parts of Britain. Between the 1981 and 1991 Census, there was a tendency towards increasing concentration of the ethnic minority population in the large urban settlements of Britain.

The 1987 Language Survey by the Inner London Education Authority found that almost of a quarter of London's children were using a language other than English as their mother tongue. The survey also revealed that there were 170 different languages spoken by children in the London area. While this figure is widely quoted to show the linguistic diversity of London and England, it fails to reveal that Bengali accounts for over 20% of bilingual children in London, with large numbers of Gujerati, Panjabi, Urdu, Turkish, Greek and Chinese speaking children in London. Of the 170 languages, 37 languages were spoken by one individual only.

Lallans, sometimes called Scots, is a vernacular language of Scotland and tends to reside in areas south and east of the Scottish Highlands. There is no Census or estimate of the number of speakers of Lallans. Any imputation that Lallans is a variety of English is hotly denied by its speakers. A visitor to Lowlands Scotland will tend to notice its differences rather than its resemblance to the English language. While the Lallans tongue has no legal status and no formal use in public administration, it is used in spoken communication. In 1985, the New Testament was translated into Lallans. There is no formal use in schools of the language but it is studied in Scottish universities and is included in the Scottish National Dictionary.

The Cornish language is a case of attempted language reversal starting from language death. The last native speaker of the Cornish language died in the 19th century. However, there has been a linguistic revival during this century with around a hundred people at present being able to converse reasonably fluently in the language. The language has no legal status, and has rare use in school. Attempts to learn the Cornish language tend to come through evening classes and a correspondence course. A six part introductory course to the Cornish language has been shown on television in the south west of England. Radio Cornwall, a local BBC radio station, runs a "First Steps in Cornish" course and there is a learner's magazine.

5. Sociolinguistic situation

While Great Britain has a strong central government preferring linguistic homogeneity, and while English is clearly the dominant language politically, economically and culturally, its regions and large conurbations hold considerable linguistic diversity. Yet that diversity is often hidden and enclosed. Geographic distances in Great Britain are not great; yet distances between the English language monolinguals, those speaking Celtic languages and the newer languages of Britain are many miles apart. Many English, living only a hundred to four hundred kilometres away from their Celtic cousins, may not be aware of the daily use or even of the existence of Irish, Scottish Gaelic or Welsh. Conversely, the Welsh speaker on the west coast of Wales, the Gaelic speaker in the remote Highlands or Islands of Scotland, tends to be unaware of the size and strength of the newer language minorities in urban England. Such Celts may combine together the inhabitants of England into one general category. The Turkish language in Haringey, Bengali in Bethnal Green or Urdu in Southall are distant, remote and often unknown to such Celts.

The status of minority languages in Britain needs to be defined with reference to the status and functions of English. The newer community languages of Britain tend to have restricted domains and restricted functions. As Martin-Jones (1984) indicates, English is the dominant language of literacy in education, in the media, in the workplace, in government and in all aspects of British life. "The ability to read and write Standard English is regarded as a crucial measure of educational performance, and as such it also serves as a means of discrimination in the labour market. Minority languages and literacies only have a legitimised place within minority institutions such as the home, the temple, church, mosque, or the local community association. They also have a place within the marginalised sectors of the economy, such as the 'rag' trade or in small family businesses: the corner shop or the fast food businesses" (Martin-Jones 1984, p. 427).

The newer, community languages tend to be found in four particular major domains. First, the new languages of England still have a place in home and extended family relationships. For example, many of the south Asian children only speak the mother tongue before going to school. Second, religious institutions provide an important contact for the maintenance of a heritage language. The mosque, the temple, the synagogue, the church or chapel and also a local community hall may be used for language teaching classes alongside religious worship. It is often argued that the Welsh language only survived due to chapel conformity and the considerable literacy tradition in Welsh chapels and churches. In parallel, contemporary maintenance for England's newer languages owes something to the role of the Muslim and Hindu religions and Orthodox Christianity, for example, within a persons' language life. Third, smaller and larger groups of language speakers sometimes come together for leisure, common interest and often for self preservation. In a local community hall, sometimes in homes, small groups of language speakers may interact, with language and cultural preservation being part of the implicit agenda. For example, Chinese families within a scattered community meet together, with Cantonese being the vehicle for conversation. Fourth, the newer languages of England have often being forced into marginalised sectors of the economy. Small clothing factories, small family businesses, fast food businesses and market stalls often provide both an occasion and a network for continued minority language usage.

It should be noted that school is excluded from this list of domains. While some children from language minority homes are allowed to speak their mother tongue for a year or two at the most, the pressure in the classroom, the canteen and the playground is normally towards English. The statutory British National Curriculum provides a detailed syllabus for each teacher, precluding use of a curriculum transmission medium other than English. National assessment which occurs at 7, 11, 14 and 16, has also increasingly put pressure on teachers to develop English-only skills within the school. Thus in England, schools usually work against the maintenance of the home language with attempted replacement of the home language by English (Baker 1988). The linguistic sovereignty of English is thoroughly attempted in its schools. Such sovereignty is joined to implicit messages about the superiority of a standard, received pronunciation of the English language and covert intolerance of linguistic and cultural diversity in English schools. The colonialist mentality is still embedded in attitudes to the newer minority languages from Africa and south and east Asia.

The religious affiliation of many language minorities in Britain also encourages biliteracy. Be it Urdu, Hindi written in the Devanagri script, Arabic, Spanish or Greek, religious or community provision through Saturday schools, Sunday schools or evening classes often enable a child to gain literacy in a language other than English. Such biliteracy may be highly significant in maintaining a language. In one of its pieces of research, the Linguistic Minorities Project (1984, 1985) found that of bilingual pupils in Bradford, Coventry, Haringey, Peterborough and Waltham Forest, around half had some degree of literacy in a language other than English. Apart from religion, language minority literacy may be encouraged by families, in personal correspondence and by community efforts.

There also exists an ethnic press, providing newspapers, magazines and booklets for the new language communities. Such linguistic minorities also have their own music, dance groups, programmes on local radio stations and programmes on national and satellite television. Video tapes and films in minority languages are also available to language communities. Sometimes through their own efforts, but also through imposed economic segregation and social apartheid, language communities use their own resources to provide entertainment and informal education. Despite poverty, racism and social marginalisation, such language communities often have vitality and integration (Taylor 1981, 1985, 1987, 1988).

Nevertheless, as in the United States, language shift in the newer language communities is also very evident. Second and third generations often lose the language of their ancestors. If employment and promotion, increasing affluence and social acceptance demands a movement towards English monolingualism, even monoculturalism, then second and third generation children are often found having made, or making, the transition. In white, monolingual British society, bilingualism and multilingualism is often seen as a disadvantage. Through compensatory English classes at school, through Anglo-American dominance in the media, language minority groups are under increasing pressure to shift towards English monolingualism (Baker 1988).

The English spoken by many bilinguals in England is often different to those who speak monolingual standard English. In the United States, it is possible to talk about Cuban-Americans, or Mexican-Americans. Such a label indicates that such bilingual/bicultural people are unlike the Mexicans living in Mexico and the Cubans living in Cuba, but are also unlike white American people. They are a mixture of Cuban or Mexican culture and American culture. In the same way, but relatively unspoken of in Britain, a Panjabi-English speaker is unlike the Panjabi people of India and Pakistan and unlike the English whites of England. It is also often invalid to talk about a dual identity or the idea of biculturalism as two separate parts to make a whole. Rather the Panjabi bilingual or the Turkish-English bilingual owns a new cultural and social reality. Such bilinguals will speak Panjabi differently from those in the Punjab, and Turkish unlike those in Turkey or Cyprus. Their linguistic reality belongs to a region of England, often with rulebound code switching skills. The language and culture of the community languages of England has adapted to new social networks and new patterns of working relationship.

Anglicisation of the Scottish lowlands and much of Wales and Northern Ireland over recent centuries has given the Celtic languages restricted sociolinguistic functions. The legal status of Scots Gaelic is, relative to Welsh, somewhat restricted. There is no right to use the Gaelic language in Scotland's courts as there is in using the Welsh language in Wales. Gaelic plays no part in national government and often tends to be used for tokenism in signs and adverts. While there are bilingual road signs in the Western Isles and in the Skye and Lochalsh district of the Highland region, it is the English language which dominates Scotland. The use of Gaelic in regional and district councils tends to be limited, although Western Island district councils do operate through Gaelic. In Wales, Welsh has a modicum of legal status, being used in law courts, for a range of bureaucratic purposes, is present throughout much of Wales on bilingual road signs and allocated prime time viewing on one of the four British TV channels. Currently, there are some 20 hours of Welsh language programmes per week on the Welsh Language television channel. These vary from general entertainment programmes, to nature and educational programmes. Some English medium broadcasts are also available through Teletext in English. European language programmes, football for example, are shown with a Welsh commentary dubbed onto the pictures. There are currently two national weekly newspapers in Welsh and two regional weekly newspapers, together with numerous monthly, religious and secular magazines written through the medium of Welsh. There are around 50 community newspapers (Papurau Bro) which operate on a voluntary basis throughout Wales. Thus, the Welsh language is supported by mass media, although audience preferences are often for the English medium channels.

Radio broadcasts are received in Gaelic in Scotland, with television broadcasts in Gaelic being one of the platforms where recent change is being successfully demanded by Gaelic language activists. Having seen the apparent success of Welsh medium television, there is pressure from Gaelic activists for their ancient language to have an identity in the all pervading mass media. However, it has become possible to assert Scottish identity without ownership or a feeling for the language.

Gaelic medium education is present in primary schools and exists also in pre-school playgroups. Within the Western Isles, primary schools use the Bilingual Education Project. Similarly, in Skye, in parts of the Highlands, Strathclyde and Tayside regions, there are particular primary schools which teach Gaelic as a second language. In the cities of Glasgow and Inverness, Gaelic-English bilingual primary schools have been instituted. Gaelic is taught to several thousand children in secondary schools in the north west of Scotland.

In Wales, the Welsh language is relatively strong in schools. Considered in detail in the next section, the Welsh language is taught as a first or second language to almost all pupils in schools. In most areas of Wales, Welsh medium education is available at Primary and Secondary level – and in Further and Higher education. As Baker (1993) has shown, bilingual education in Wales is regarded as a necessary but insufficient condition for the maintenance of the Welsh language. In Northern Ireland, it is estimated that 5% of primary children come into contact with Irish as a second language in school. There are two Irish medium primary schools, and in secondary schools, Irish can be taken as an examination subject at the age of 16 and 18.

In the life history of a language, attitudes play a crucial role in growth or decay, restoration or destruction of a language (Baker 1988, 1992). For any language policy to be successful, it has to accommodate the attitudes of the people, or seek to persuade those of different attitudes about the rightness of policy, since attitudes are both individual and social, individually held but derived and expressed through social discourse.

In Celtic regions, the dominant finding is that positive attitudes to the heritage language decline with age. For example, around 13 to 14 years of age, attitudes to Welsh tend to become less favourable and attitudes to English become more favourable. Research by Baker (1992) shows the key importance of engaging in a regular, participative Welsh speaking culture in order for attitudes not to decline as age increases. For the language to survive, people need to be actively involved in a participatory Welsh language culture. Such Welsh language participation occurred in chapels in days gone by, still on Eisteddfod fields for short periods of time, but also needs to be in weekly and daily social interaction in shop and school, on the street and screen.

Research in Scotland by MacKinnon in 1981 found marginally favourable attitudes towards the maintenance of Gaelic in Scotland. However, the attitudes towards Gaelic, and towards Irish in Ireland, tend to show that the public prefers to permit rather than be committed to the future of these minority languages. Attitudinal support towards Celtic languages may be towards language as a symbol of culture, heritage and identity. Generous attitudes towards survival of the language may not be translated into commitment at a personal level to the language. The Celtic languages are often seen as a symbol of ethnic identity and of cultural value. Yet there is often a pessimism in the attitude surveys, where the public feel that Government or voluntaryist revival attempts will not be successful, will not change the size of the language population, or create a viable minority language. While in Scotland, Ireland and Wales there tends to be, in such attitude surveys, evidence of growing support in attitude for minority language survival, this does not always appear to translate into active commitment and participation. There exist positive public attitudes but private skepticism. There exists interest in the survival of a minority language, but not in involvement in that language. As a symbol of ethnic history, heritage and national culture, the languages are valued. As a tool of widespread personal communication, as a medium of mass education, the languages may be less valued by the majority of the population. Even less positive attitudes are found towards Celtic minority language as of value in the workplace and in the economy. When the personal balance sheet includes employment and educational success, the credit of positive attitudes towards minority language is diminished by the costs of prior needs and motives. Goodwill stops when the personal payoff is not great. There is thus a difference between publicly stated attitudes and personal preferences, between symbolic and pragmatic attitudes.

6. The political situation of contact languages

The political terms used for British in-migrant language communities are highly symbolic. In the 1960's, the term was 'non-English speakers'; in the 1970's the term 'linguistic minorities' became more widespread amongst academics and liberal politicians; the academically preferred term is the 1980's and 1990's has been 'bilinguals' and 'language communities'. While liberal, academic labels have become less discriminatory, less compensatory and more concerned with potential than perceived deficiency, a white racist view, passively felt but sometimes actively expressed, tends to be a majority viewpoint. Britain therefore needs to be considered as a country with monolingual preferences and policies, and with a widespread apathy towards languages other than English. The implicit language of much political debate, although superficially moderate and liberal, is assimilationist and concerned with the melting pot of standard English. Welsh to a moderate extent, Scottish Gaelic to a lesser extent, Irish in Northern Ireland to an even lesser extent have some language rights at an individual level. For the newer languages of Britain, there is sometimes talk about language entitlement. However, the reality rather than the rhetoric is discriminatory towards the newer languages of Britain. Concerns about national unity, and nostalgia about the great British heritage, has led to central government preference for increasing the importance given to English (e. g. in schools) to create harmony, prosperity and nationhood.

The newer languages of Britain need to be seen as oppressed, not always by legislation or opposition, but often by lack of resources, lack of opportunity and the surrounding white supremacist culture that tends to leave pessimism and defeatism. That Britain does not have a language policy for the new community languages allows implicit ideologies and hidden agendas to operate. Any discussion of multilingualism in England tends to focus on duties and obligations of being a good British citizen; such discourse excludes questions about political power, economic opportunity and social access. The dominant ideology at best tolerates linguistic diversity in England, at the same time preferring national unity which is endangered by multilingualism. The dominant concept is that English provides cultural and linguistic self-sufficiency. Only very slowly are the economic, trading, cultural and social advantages of bilingualism beginning to be articulated.

The key question in the politics of languages in Britain is why there is a disparity of status between the Welsh language and the newer languages of England. The Welsh Language Acts of 1967 and 1993 provide some degree of equal validity to English and Welsh in Wales. For example, both languages are given equal status in legal proceedings. In Wales, children often have the opportunity to take most of their education through the medium of Welsh. Bilingualism in Wales is thoroughly encouraged by the British National Curriculum which makes Welsh a compulsory subject for almost all children. Monolingual English-speaking children in Wales are required by the British National Curriculum to learn Welsh from the age of 5.

The power, status and political leverage of the new 'community' languages of Britain is different from their Celtic neighbours. In Britain, a south Asian child is usually unable to use their home language in the curriculum at age 5. English primary schools occasionally follow a transitional bilingual education model, where the child is expected to move as quickly as possible from their home language to the English language (e. g. transition to English within one or two years). Children whose mother tongue is other than English normally only study their home language in the secondary school if a European language such as French and German is offered. It is clear therefore that a different status is given to the Welsh language in Wales, particularly in education, compared with the newer languages of England in English schools. This disparity is often explained by history and heritage, tradition and territory.

The political argument used strongly by the Welsh turns out to be a stab in the back for the newer languages of England. The argument for Welsh in Wales tends to be conducted on the territorial principle and collective rights. Geography is used to define group language rights and language provision (Stubbs 1991). Since Welsh is historically the language of Wales, a Welsh person, it is often argued, has the right to speak and use Welsh in schools, law courts and with bureaucracy in Wales. As soon as the Welsh speaker is in England, that territorial right disappears. This causes a problem for the newer languages of England. If Welsh is the natural indigenous language of Wales, what is the natural, indigenous language of England? The Welsh argument is that language belongs to a defined territory. If this is so, then the unfortunate resulting logic can be that English is the language of England. Since the newer languages of England (e.g. Panjabi, Hindi, Chinese) have geographical homes elsewhere, and have no 'historical' home in Britain, should such language communities become monolingual English? The argument from some right-wing English politicians has been that that community language speakers should either forget their non-English language, or return to their native country.

The territorial principle is also championed by Scottish Gaelic speakers, by Cornish revivalists, Manx speakers, Scots Lallans and Irish speakers in Northern Ireland. However, for the million and a half or more language minority speakers in England, the territorial principle as an argument weakens their position. The alternative for England's community languages is to argue on personality terms or in terms of individual language 'freedom' rights. Since language is an inherent part of their heritage and culture, of their colour and creed, destroying their language destroys part of their inner identity. If part of their cultural characteristic is taken away from them, then part of the individuality inherent in diversity would be lost. However logical the personality principle is as an argument to support the new 'community' languages of England, in British political terms, it appears to be a weaker argument than the territorial principle. The defence of the Celts unfortunately, and without intention, becomes an attack on England's language communities.

Liberal political movements do exist in British education to accommodate language minority children, although these tend to be towards multiculturalism and anti-racism rather than towards bilingualism. Within a thirty year period, the politics surrounding the education of children from community languages has evolved. In the 1960's, children of ethnic language minorities were placed in induction centres or language centres with 'English for Immigrants' programmes to teach English as fast as possible using a structurally based English as a Foreign Language model. In the 1970's, language minority children were often placed in remedial groups or withdrawal groups. Other times, such children were allocated to submersion classes with the intent of learning English as quickly as possible. Since the 1980's, language minority children have increasingly been placed in mainstream, regular, classes. With the ideology being to integrate such children as quickly as possible into regular classes, a teaching assistant from the local language community may work alongside the teacher in infant classrooms. However, the approach is transitional and not concerned with any form of maintenance of the home language. Thus, the movement in primary schools in England has been away from segregation in the 1960's to integration to the 1980's and 1990's (Reid 1988). While in the 1960's, such language minority children were often separated so that they would not have any effect on the achievement of majority, white English speaking children, the present system may be less discriminatory in terms of social relationships but not in terms of language. While separate provision has mostly disappeared, separation of languages is now in vogue.

Placed in a European context, the almost total absence in England of any 'strong' form of bilingual education is striking. While the MOTET project (Fitzpatrick 1987) illustrated that teaching infant children half through Panjabi and half through English was relatively effective and successful, heritage language education has been noticeably avoided in the English education system. Instead, resources (both human and material) go into teaching English as the second language. This leaves a paradox. While mother tongues are disparaged and discriminated against in education, trading languages such as French and German are encouraged in British schools. The paradox is that while bilingual education to support minority languages has tended to be depreciated in England, the current trend is to appreciate English speakers who learn a second language to ensure a continued influential role for the U.K. in world politics and the world economy. There is a tendency to value the acquisition of languages while devaluing the language minorities who have them. While integration and assimilation is still the dominant ideology in U.K. internal politics, external politics increasingly demand bilingual citizens, leaving a schizophrenic language policy. There is encouragement for the study of foreign languages for English monolinguals, at great cost and with great inefficiency. At the same time, the linguistic gifts that children from community language backgrounds bring to school are destroyed. Suppression of language minorities, particularly by the school system, may be seen as economic, social and cultural wastage. Instead, such languages can be viewed a natural resource to be exploited for cultural, spiritual and educational growth as well as for economic, commercial and political gain.

In England's schools, language communities and not mainstream schools are expected to preserve heritage languages. The newer languages of Britain are politically regarded as foreign languages rather than as home languages. Just as a French or German family living in Britain may retain its language by speaking in French or German to the children, so the Asian and European languages which have been resident in Britain for many decades and have some strength within language communities are expected to reproduce themselves without the institutional supports given to the Celtic languages. In the desire to establish common British identity, bilingual education for community languages is seen as divisive. At a voluntary level therefore, the new languages of England find their support. The provision for ethnic languages mostly derives from community rather than official sources. Evening classes, Saturday schools and Sunday schools have been set up to meet political, religious, cultural and linguistic goals. The instigators of such voluntary provision are sometimes religious bodies such as Orthodox churches, Synagogues, Mosques and Temples. Groups of parents or local community organisations sometimes rent premises, such as schools or community halls, for mother tongue classes. Tansley and Craft's (1984) survey found that at least 28 different languages were being taught in over 500 community or supplementary schools. Such languages were the Asian languages, such as Urdu, Hindi, Panjabi and Bengali; also European languages such as Greek and Italian, Spanish and Portuguese were being supported. Some local government authorities have provided financial support for bilingual assistants in classrooms or community resources to aid mother tongue maintenance. In areas such as Leicester, Peterborough, Nottingham, Coventry, Birmingham, Walsall, Manchester, Ealing, Brent, Haringey and Waltham Forest, there have been bilingual teachers, support services, materials, resources and special classes for such community language children. Tansley/Craft (1984) show that there is a wide gap between the needs of the population of bilingual children in England and support given to language communities and to education for mother tongue maintenance. However, Tansley/Craft (1984) also noted that teachers were becoming more enlightened. Instead of seeing such bilingual children as having problems and deficiencies, such bilingual learners were increasingly regarded as having certain linguistic resources not owned by monolinguals which they can bring to the school for the benefit of the whole class and school population.

In stark contrast to the politics surrounding the newer, community languages is the considerable support given to Welsh language education in Wales to reverse language shift. The growth of bilingual education from 1939 (the year of the first Welsh language primary school) and 1956 (the institution of the first Welsh language secondary school) has now mushroomed to a system which contains a wide variety of forms of bilingual education. The current statistics (Welsh Office, 'Statistics of Education', 1976—1990) show that: approximately one in every four primary school children in Wales are mostly or partly taught through the medium of Welsh. Under the National Curriculum, all children will be taught Welsh as a first or a second language. From Welsh being excluded from the curriculum in the early decades of this century, it has now become virtually compulsory in schools throughout Wales. There are 417 Welsh-speaking (bilingual) primary schools and 42 Welsh-speaking (bilingual) secondary schools in Wales. In terms of the total number of schools, this is respectively 24.1% of primary schools and 17.7% of secondary schools (Baker 1993).

In adult education classes, the learning of Welsh has been particularly sought by in-migrants to Wales as well as long standing residents. Over 4,000 adults each year learn Welsh through short or long classes, with the intensive ULPAN classes being particularly favoured. This remarkably strong language movement has included parents learning Welsh alongside their children, people learning Welsh to gain employment or gain promotion in employment, and it has also included those whose interests in learning Welsh are for integrative and cultural reasons. In this strong adult Welsh learning movement there is to be found, in deeds and symbolically, a strong tide of language optimism and a sense of rootedness among Welsh people. While Europeanization has led to increased interest in learning French and German, the concept of Europeanization and the global village appears to have led also to a movement to find local and regional roots, particularly located in the heritage language and culture.

7. Conclusions

Demographic trends and economic imperatives, together with hostility and sometimes direct repression towards both the newer, community and Celtic tongues have led to concerns about ethnic identity as well as language shift. The collapse of the political basis of Gaelic and Welsh societies has sometimes occurred through repressive legislation. Community languages face continued apathy, indifference and neglect by public and politicians alike. Where poverty and language co-exist, retaining heritage language and culture may be too high a price for an individual to pay against the temptations of increased prosperity. Where revivalist attempts exist, there is often pain and protest. A revival of a language cannot be a painless nor a peaceful process. Political protest has been joined in Wales by direct, sometimes violent action against property but not against people. While some protests have operated in the Martin Luther King non-violent mode, others have waged the struggle to reverse language decline through direct actions. While Basque-type militancy is not unheard of in Wales or Scotland, the majority of the people tend to have positive attitudes to revival but are less involved in action.

While militant action is constantly newsworthy, the future of Britain's language minorities is allied to a great deal of quiet and selfless activity by ordinary folk winning hearts and minds. For example, Urdd Gobaith Cymru, a Welsh language youth movement for 5–25 year olds, runs local and National Eisteddfodau, publishes magazines, runs summer youth camps and has weekly evening activities in almost all towns, cities and many villages of Wales. It encourages children to meet on a regular basis, using the Welsh language for a wide variety of activities, skiing to singing, folk dancing to folk festivals. Another example of quiet but effective attempts to reverse language downward shift is nursery school movements particularly found in Scotland and Wales. In many villages and towns of Wales, children of English speaking and Welsh speaking homes are encouraged to play together in Welsh in a community hall or chapel room before entering school. With Welsh introduced painlessly in such early nursery years, a fine foundation for Welsh language schooling is built.

Apart from economic, political and demographic trends often working against a major revival of the Celtic languages and a continued future for the community languages, there is another major obstacle to language minority maintenance. The strong position of English as a major international language has major consequences for the survival of the Celtic languages. Only a few extremists would argue against children being bilingual in English and a Celtic language. English is too obviously useful in a national and international context. British language minorities are always going to struggle in the world of science and international communications. But languages adapt. Welsh has gathered together an extensive vocabulary of scientific and technical terms. Just as English in its day borrowed extensively from French, Latin, Greek and other sources, so Celtic languages borrow and invent to produce a twentieth century version of their ancient language. Such revivalist attempts will always be a struggle; but in that struggle there is vitality and life.

8. Sources of information

Sources on language contact in Great Britain must be considered as a trickle rather than a flood. Until recently, the standard textbook has been Peter Trudgill's (1984) 'Language in the British Isles'. The book examines English in 14 chapters, the Celtic languages in six chapters, other languages (such as Romani) in 4 chapters with nine chapters on the sociolinguistic situation in the British Isles. The book is still regarded as authoritative and provides a comprehensive introduction to the topic. Ten years on, the place given to the new languages of England in Trudgill (1984) seems very meagre. Only in the sociolinguistic section are the newer minorities discussed with one further chapter on British Black English and West Indian Creoles. This imbalance has been partially corrected by Alladina/Edwards (1991) 'Multilingualism in the British Isles: the Older Mother Tongues and Europe'. This book provides a geolinguistic typology of non-English languages in the British Isles. The older mother tongues of the British Isles are authoritatively considered:

British Sign Language, Gaelic, Irish, Romani, and Welsh. The second classification is of Eastern European languages in Britain: Hungarian, Lithuanian, Polish, Ukrainian and Yiddish. The Mediterranean languages form the third category: Cypriots, Greek and Turkish communities, Italian and Portuguese communities, the Spanish and Moroccan speech communities. Expert and detailed, the book is scholarly and also assertive of the place of non-English languages in Britain. The tendency has been in literature to portray the Celtic languages as the key to understanding linguistic diversity in the British Isles. This important book tends to correct that misrepresentation. While including chapters on Celtic languages, it shows the strong European strand in British linguistic diversity.

An understanding of British linguistic diversity requires a thorough treatment of Asian languages. Bengali, Urdu, Gujerati, Chinese, Panjabi and Arabic, for example, need fuller treatment than is currently available. Alladina/Edwards (1991) provides the European side of British linguistic diversity; the Asian portfolio of languages requires fuller treatment. One key book on the Asian context is 'The Other Languages of England' (Linguistic Minorities Project, 1984, 1985). This covers the history and background of linguistic minorities in England, child and adult usage in selected parts, and identification of language support and language teaching projects in England. This book provides an extensive account of language use and mother tongue teaching provision in eleven different communities. It also discusses bilingualism and education within the British context. The meticulous work of Monica Taylor (1981, 1985, 1987, 1988) covers the origins and settlement, the culture and education of the newer, community languages. The scarcity of British writing and research on community languages currently serves to support the strong ideology against maintenance of minority languages in Britain.

9. Bibliography (selected)

Alladina, Safder/Edwards, Viv (1991): *Multilingualism in the British Isles*, Harlow, Essex.

Baker, Colin (1985): *Aspects of Bilingualism in Wales*, Clevedon, Avon.

Baker, Colin (1988): *Key Issues in Bilingualism & Bilingual Education*, Clevedon.

Baker, Colin (1992): *Attitudes and Language*, Clevedon.

Baker, Colin (1993): "Bilingual Education in Wales". In: *European Models of Bilingual Education*, Baetens Beardsmore, H. (Ed.), Clevedon.

Fitzpatrick, F. (1987): *The Open Door: The Bradford Bilingual Project*, Clevedon.

Hancock, Ian (1984): "Romani and Angloromani". In: *Language in the British Isles*, Trudgill, P. (Ed.), Cambridge.

Hancock, Ian (1991): "The Romani Speech Community". In: *Multilingualism in the British Isles*, Alladina, S./Edwards, V., Harlow, Essex.

Ladd, P. (1991): "The British Sign Language Community". In: *Multilingualism in the British Isles*, Alladina, S./Edwards, V., Harlow, Essex.

Linguistic Minorities Project (1984): "Linguistic Minorities in England". In: *Journal of Multilingual and Multicultural Development* 5, 4, 351−366.

Linguistic Minorities Project (1985): *The Other Languages of England*, London.

MacKinnon, Kenneth (1991): "The Gaelic Speech Community". In: *Multilingualism in the British Isles*, Alladina, S./Edwards, V., Harlow, Essex.

Martin-Jones, Marilyn (1984): *The Sociolinguistic Status of Minority Languages in England*, London.

Milroy, James (1984): "The history of English in the British Isles". In: *Language in the British Isles*, Trudgill, P. (Ed.), Cambridge.

Office of Population Censuses and Surveys (OPCS) (1992): The 1991 Census of Great Britain, HMSO.

Pryce, W. T. R. (1986): "Wales as a Culture Region: Patterns of Change 1750−1971". In: *The Welsh and Their Country*, Hume, I./Pryce, W. T. R., Llandysul, Dyfed.

Pryce, W. T. R./Williams, Colin H. (1988): "Sources and Methods in the Study of Language Areas: A Case Study of Wales". In: *Language in Geographic Context*, Williams, C. H. (Ed.), Clevedon, Avon.

Reid, E. (1988): "Linguistic Minorities and Language Education − the English Experience", In: *Journal of Multilingual and Multicultural Development* 9, 1 & 2, 181−191.

Spence, N. C. (1984): "Channel Island French", In: *Language in the British Isles*, Trudgill, P. (Ed.), Cambridge.

Stubbs, Michael (1991): "Educational language planning in England and Wales". In: *A Language Policy for the European Community*, Coulmas, F. (Ed.), Berlin.

Tansley, P./Craft, A. (1984): "Mother Tongue Teaching and Support". In: *Journal of Multilingual and Multicultural Development* 5,4, 367−384.

Taylor, Monica J. (1981): *Caught Between. A Review of research into the education of pupils of West Indian origin*, Windsor, Berks.

Taylor, Monica J. (1985): *The best of both worlds? A review of research into the education of pupils of South Asian origin*, Windsor, Berks.

Taylor, Monica J. (1987): *Chinese Pupils in Britain*, Windsor, Berks.

Taylor, Monica J. (1988): *Worlds Apart? A review of research into the education of pupils of Cypriot, Italian, Ukrainian and Vietnamese origin, Liverpool Blacks and Gypsies*, Windsor, Berks.

Thomson, R. L. (1984): "The History of the Celtic Languages in the British Isles". In: *Languages in the British Isles*, Trudgill, P. (Ed.), Cambridge.

Williams, Colin H. (1986): "Language Planning and Minority Group Rights". In: *The Welsh and Their Country*, Hume, I./Pryce, W. T. R., Llandysul.

Williams, Colin H./Raybould, W. H. (1991): *Welsh Language Planning – Opportunities and Constraints*, Cardiff.

Withers, Charles W. J. (1988): "The Geographical History of Gaelic in Scotland". In: *Language in Geographic Context*, Williams, C. H. (Ed.), Clevedon.

Colin Baker, Bangor (Great Britain)

132. English–Welsh

1. The geography and demography of language contact in Wales
2. Historical context
3. Political, economic, cultural and religious situation
4. Statistical profile
5. Sociolinguistic situation
6. The political situation of language in Wales
7. Conclusion
8. Bibliography (selected)

1. The geography and demography of language contact in Wales

Conventionally Wales is described as a peripheral and marginal appendage to its larger neighbour, England, to the east of Offa's Dyke. In strict geological and geographical terms Wales is a distinct region of the British mainland. It is characterised by a wide variety of rocks of different ages which provide not only the scenic basis for morphological and landscape features, but also endows Wales with a very rich resource deposit which has fuelled her diverse history of mineral extraction since pre-historic times. The physical core of Wales is an upland backbone running the whole length of the country comprised of Lower Palaeozoic rocks. To the north-east and south lie the coal measures which in recent times has been the most densely settled area. The third geographic region is the Lowland coastal belt which, though limited in its size, contains the richest farmland and most of the important towns which have acted as religious, strategic and commercial centres of life in Wales (→ language map B). In many ways this Upland-Lowland landscape divide has experienced a complementary relationship and provided the basis for Welsh agrarian development and mineral exploitation. In Feudal times Wales, unlike England, did not develop a network of important cities and the whole scale of the Welsh economic and social order is consequently more typical of the Sedentary-Pastoral regions of Western Europe such as the Celtic Fringe, Galicia, Euskadi and parts of Aquitaine, than it is of either elements of the Petty Commodity Zone or the Feudal Zone. Historically, patterns of inheritance, of landholding, of religious distinctiveness and of general social structure were markedly different in this Sedentary-Pastoral Zone. Undoubtedly physical location, combined with resource deposits and settlement distribution have played an important part in the interaction between speakers representing Celtic origins and those representing successive Latin, Scandinavian, Germanic and other peoples.

As Colin Baker, in article 131, has demonstrated, there has been a traditional interpretation of upland Britain being settled by Celts and lowland Britain being settled by those of Anglo-Saxon origin. This upland-lowland divide relates to such features as land holding, legal systems, inter-marriage patterns, military alliances and cultural development. However, to interpret Wales only in relation to her dominant neighbour, England, is to downplay the very long associations inhabitants of Wales have had with other Celtic lands such as Scotland, Brittany and most importantly Ireland and Cornwall. Since the age of the Celtic saints the Irish Sea and the western approaches to the Atlantic have been major routeways for the diffusion of pan-Celtic trade, culture, ideas and alliances and have remained a symbolic and material expression of the unity of Celtic lands, at least in the hearts and minds of a minority of Welsh people. In modern times these relationships have been overshadowed by the incorporation of Wales into an economic and political system controlled by England and by the large degree of out- and in-migration between the neighbouring countries which has accelerated since the Industrial Revolution. It is currently estimated that in the past decade, a million people were on the move between England and Wales, with Wales exporting her fecund well-educated youth searching for employment and better prospects in the wider market and importing predominantly aged, dependent retirees attracted by the slower pace of life and greater landscape attraction of coastal or rural, upland Wales. As we shall see below, this migration pattern is not without its difficulties for inter-community harmony and language/cultural tension often results from this imbalance.

2. Historical context

A general overview of the relations between English and other languages of the British Isles has been presented in 131.2 above. Here we may provide a quick summary of the key elements which facilitated the anglicisation of Wales. Wales was initially demarcated by the construction of a massive earthwork boundary by King Offa between A.D. 778 and 796, but it was not until the Edwardian conquest and settlement after 1282 A.D. that political and commercial authority was established and kept by a comprehensive network of formidable castles and garrison towns controlling the coastal reaches and the strategic valley route ways. Colonial control turned to a form of shared power with the accession to the English throne by the Welsh contender, Henry Tudor, who became Henry VII after the defeat of the Yorkist cause on Bosworth Field in 1485. His son, Henry VIII, enacted the Acts of Union 1536 and 1542 which formally incorporated Wales into the legal and political realm of England. In linguistic terms its principal clause was to expell Welsh from official life and institute a requirement that all public officialdom transacted in the 'Principality' be solely in English. The rationale was to develop an indigenous, anglicised ruling class which built upon the established practice of the Welsh gentry being incorporated within an hierarchical English stratification system. The practice of sending sons of the Welsh gentry to English public schools and of encouraging inter-marriage between landed families either side of the border accelerated this assimilation process. However, as Janet Davies has recently reminded us, "the process took at least 250 years and was virtually complete by the late eighteenth century. It had profound consequences. Linguistic differences reinforced class differences. Welsh culture, which had been essentially aristocratic, came into the guardianship of the peasantry and the 'middling sort of people'-craftsmen, artisans and the lower clergy. As the inhabitants of the gentry houses ceased to speak Welsh, the system of patronage which had maintained the Welsh poets over the centuries collapsed, and the standardised Welsh they had jealously defended came into peril of deteriorating into an assortment of mutually unintelligible dialects" (Davies 1993, p. 23). This denial of legal status since 1536 has had a critical influence on the relationship between the Welsh nation and the English, later British, state and has given rise to a number of theories and explanations which have variously interpreted the role of the 'English state' in Wales as either a 'murder machine' or as a liberation from a narrow, peasant-based traditional culture (Williams, C. H. 1990). The truth, of course, is somewhere in the middle of these positions, for there has been an historical dualism in the relationship between the state and the Welsh language. Having initially forbidden the use of Welsh for reasons of expediency and efficiency, the same Tudor state in 1588 authorised the translation of the Holy Bible and the Book of Common Prayer into Welsh under the supervision of Bishop William Morgan for exactly the same reasons, to secure the Welsh population in its Protestant base against Catholic incursions both at home, and more especially from Ireland. The Welsh Bible had a threefold impact on language reproduction. It provided a modern standardised, highly elegant, version of Welsh; it encouraged wider scholarship and publication of related literature; it provided the basis upon which a national network of Church-sponsored agencies developed a largely literate and involved population at an early stage compared with developments elsewhere in Europe. In the seventeenth century the development of new religious movements, such as the Independents (Yr Annibynwyr) and the Baptists (Y Bedyddwyr) heralded the way for non-Established religious affiliations with their own social organisations, networks and denominational presses. Despite discrimination and persecution, these groups flourished and encouraged a trans-Atlantic, Welsh-medium network of correspondents, journalists, teachers and interpreters of the scriptures and of radical change, which had widespread social and political influence. The next century was dominated by Calvinistic Methodism with its emphasis on order, sobriety, piety and learning and it soon became established as the dominant religious influence over vast parts of the countryside. However, it was in the great age of nonconformist dissent from the mid-eighteenth century to the period of Liberal Radicalism either side of the turn of the twentieth century that the lasting values of modern Wales were formed. During the latter part of the nineteenth century, rapid Anglicisation occurred as a result of industrialisation and urbanisation. For the first time in Welsh history bilingualism became a mass phenomenon and a new, if relatively unstable social pattern. New codes of worship, work, leisure and political beliefs were transmitted to an increasingly literate work force by a mass media created by print capitalism.

There is a smouldering debate in Wales as to whether or not mass industrialisation saved or threatened the Welsh language. The conventional view is that rural Wales suffered acute decline in the last century as a result of persistent out-migration to the industrial coalfields of South and North-East Wales, England and the overseas British Imperial possessions beyond. Massive out-migration weakened the Welsh Heartland and damaged the agricultural economies of the majority of Welsh counties. The opening up of the iron and coal industries, together with their dependent railway, port, service and urban-commercial functions, witnessed a huge increase in the non-Welsh born population as thousands of people flocked to the booming coalfield and coal-dependent new towns. This mélange of migrants quickly turned to the habitual use of English as the only official language of commerce and industry and thereby denied the separateness of Welsh culture in an increasingly Anglo-American dominated world economy. In contrast, Brinley Thomas (1959) argues that the Welsh language was saved in the nineteenth century by the redistribution of a growing population consequent to industrial expansion. G. Williams (1971) supports this thesis, arguing that, as industrialisation generated internal migration, the Welsh, unlike the Scots or the Irish, did not have to abandon their language and homeland for employment abroad, particularly in the New World. The large-scale rural-urban shift in Wales was capable of sustaining a new set of Welsh institutions, which gave a fresh impetus to the indigenous language and culture, institutionalising them within a new, modernising industrial domain. Geographical variations in the migration patterns of incoming Welsh and English migrants strengthened the threshold density of certain communities, making some valley communities, such as Cwm Rhymni, much more Welsh in speech and other coastal towns, such as Barry or Penarth, much more anglicised than hitherto.

Thomas's thesis portrays three periods of industrialisation. The first spans the formative period 1780–1800, where Wales was in the vanguard of the Industrial Revolution and exhibiting some of the traits that would come to full fruition a century later, namely religious dissent, cultural renaissance and political radicalism. The second act, which spanned the period 1800–1846, saw the beginning of a specifically Welsh urban form and culture epitomised by the growth of Merthyr Tydfil which boasted a population in 1846 of 33,000, 84% of whom were Welsh-born. They were overwhelmingly non-conformist in religion and experimenting with the construction of a working-class ideology and independent political action. The third act of the industrial trilogy, set in the period 1846–1900, is the crucial testing ground for the assertion that industrialisation did not necessarily accelerate language decline. It was a time when the twin forces of free trade economics and mineral exploitation combined to transform the coalfield regions into the foundry of empire, and the slate industry of North West Wales served to 'roof the world'. Not only was there a substantial rural-urban shift of Welsh speakers but there was also an appreciable natural increase in the burgeoning urban Welsh population. Added to this was the differential concentration of Welsh speakers within the valleys rather than the coastal towns and we see a pattern of a distinctly modern, industrial infra-structure set fair to sustain a more varied Welsh culture. Here were represented the great choral festivals, chapel-based social activities such as drama, poetry, self-education and public expression. In the wider industrial community were located the brass band tradition, miners' libraries, discussion groups, early national sporting federations. In short this 'cauldron of rebirth' gave rise to the popular image of industrial Wales, which was as much a redefinition of Welsh culture as it was the sharpening of a distinctly Anglo-Welsh identity and tradition best represented in the literature and poetry of Dylan Thomas, Gwyn Thomas and R. S. Thomas to choose only one popular surname for illustration. This duality of a Welsh and Anglo-Welsh popular culture growing and feeding from each other eventually influenced the nature and direction of Welsh-medium culture, for unlike rural Wales, such changes were operative within a set of formal, English-medium public sector and commercial domains.

3. Political, economic, cultural and religious situation

Thus at the beginning of this century English had become established as the dominant language in Wales. The principal agency of English transmission was the educational system at both school and college level. English was the sole language of education in state schools following the Education Act of 1870 and subsequent Acts such as the Welsh Intermediate Education Act of 1889 which introduced a new awareness of English values, culture and employment prospects and gave a most powerful institutional filip to the process of anglicisation.

The children of the Welsh masses, rural and urban alike, were exposed to overriding influences which sought to downgrade regional cultures and identification and exalted the culture of the dominant state core and its value system. How the masses welcomed this 'liberation' from traditionalism and conservatism is best evidenced by the wholesale generational language shift in the period 1914−1945 (Pryce, W. T. R. and Williams, C. H. 1988). English was perceived (and still is to a large extent) as the language of progress, of equality, of prosperity, of commerce, of mass entertainment and pleasure. As one of the world's most powerful languages, it is not surprising that it has penetrated every aspect of Welsh life throughout the course of this century. The wider experience of Empire-building, understandably, made acquisition of English a most compelling instrumental motivation, and the key to participation in the burgeoning British-influenced world economy.

Closer economic and administrative association with the rest of the U. K. followed the standardisation of education and local government. The whole modernisation process reinforced the dominance of English and saw the denigration of Welsh accompanied by a debased self-awareness on behalf of its speakers. Refusal to speak Welsh with one's children was a common enough reaction to the status differential which developed between the language groups. Added to this was the failure to use Welsh in the wide range of new speech domains which developed in all aspects of the formal and social life of the nation. Whether by policy choice or the habit of neglect, Welsh became increasingly marginalised. It lost ground especially among those groups most exposed to the opportunities of an improved standard of living in the urban culture of the south and north-east.

In addition to government policy one must consider the sociolinguistic effects of the developing infra-structure in Britain. A prime vehicle of modernisation was the rapidly expanding communication network which intensified in the late nineteenth century. Social communication theorists have long stressed the importance of both physical and social communication in the development of self-conscious nations and in the process of cultural reproduction and replacement. In Wales, geographic isolation had provided some basis for cultural differentiation both within and between linguistic communities. However, the development of an externally-derived communication system had served to reduce that isolation. Technology was to overcome the friction of distance. The critical factors influencing the development of the transport system were defence and commerce, in that it was designed to facilitate through traffic from England to Ireland via Wales. The main railway routes ran east-west through the centre and along the northern and southern coasts respectively, with branch lines penetrating the resource-rich hinterland allowing the exportation of slate, coal and iron and steel products. This had the effect of integrating South Wales economically with the Bristol region, the Midlands and London, and North Wales with the Lancashire conurbations focussed on Manchester and Liverpool. Wales's poorly developed internal road and rail system did not conduce to the creation of a nationally shared space and territorial identification and led to post-war economic initiatives being located either in better served British regions or attracted to Wales largely as a result of government subsidies and regional development grants.

As a consequence of both industrialisation and modernisation, political life in Wales reflected the radicalism of a largely working-class mass struggling for representation, equality of opportunity and decent working and living conditions for themselves and their dependents. At the turn of the century the overwhelming majority of males who exercised their freedom to vote supported the Liberal Party. It was a party dedicated to social justice, to the disestablishment of the Church of England in Wales, to Home Rule all round for the Celtic nations, particularly Ireland and to educational and health improvements under statutory regulation. In the Welsh-speaking parts of Wales it was the vehicle for cultural nationalism, for the development of a Nonconformist-influenced moral and social order. More prosaically, it was a mass movement which ordinary people could penetrate and use as a vehicle for their own, and their sub-group's upward social mobility. Its strength was its ability to represent marginalised people and places, particularly those drawn from the Celtic periphery and from the burgeoning urban settlements who were un- or under-represented in the Tory dominated shire counties and long established market towns.

During its periods of rule in the early part of this century, under its charismatic, Welsh-speaking Prime Minister, David Lloyd-George, the Liberal Party was perhaps the most influential political party on the world stage as a result of British Imperial power and interests. It was simultaneously the national party of Wales advocating self-government at home, whilst enslaving more and more indigenous people abroad in the name of God, King and Country. At the local level, the main conduit for spreading its message of social reform and democratic representation was the influential Free Church or Nonconformist Chapel System which pervaded almost every settlement in Wales. The spectacular growth of the Nonconformist denominations following on from the Great Religious Revival of 1905 not only made Wales an outwardly more Christian society than hitherto but also influenced nearly every aspect of public behaviour and private life. In architectural and urban design terms Wales is littered with the evidence of this great sea change of Liberal Nonconformity. Not only does one have the great denominational diversity of various chapels with their resplendent names of Siloam, Tabernacle, Hermon and Calfaria, but of course in an increasingly bilingual society the same denomination often provided a Welsh and an English-speaking place of worship, viz. the Congregationalists and the 'Welsh Independents' (Yr Annibynwyr), the Presbyterians (Calvinistic Methodists). In an increasingly secular society, Church closures and amalgamations have now decreased the impact of formal religion, whilst the surplus buildings are being used as nursery schools, youth clubs, cultural resource centers, houses, factories and garages etc. The Church and Chapel system has long been a pillar of support for Welsh cultural maintenance and its impact even today cannot be overestimated.

The early decades of this century witnessed a plethora of action groups and social movements who were concerned that English was becoming so all-powerful that it threatened to displace Welsh as a natural medium of communication for a significant proportion of the native population. Some of the heroes of the early language movement include Rev. Michael D. Jones, who led the small exodus to Patagonia to establish a wholly Welsh migrant community (Williams, G. 1992); Emrys ap Iwan, the first minster of religion to appear before a court of law and insist on the primacy of the Welsh language in legal proceedings in Wales; Dan Issac Davies, the HMI for Schools who advocated a greater use of Welsh-medium education; Thomas Gee, the publisher of such ambitious multi-volume Encyclopedias as 'Gwyddoniadur' and advocate of mass circulation periodicals in Welsh; and the most influential family of all, whom generations of Welsh youth learn to revere, O. M. Edwards, the university teacher, writer, publisher and first Chief HMI for schools in Wales, who tried to establish a more tolerant approach to bilingualism by attacking the injustice associated with the Welsh NOT within the school system (the practice, common in the 19th century, whereby teachers, at the request of parents and governors, punished pupils for using Welsh within the school). His son, Sir Ifan ab Owen Edwards, established Urdd Gobaith

Cymru (The Welsh League of Youth) in 1922 which has become the largest mass movement in Wales encouraging children and young adults to develop skills, competence and leadership qualities in a variety of contexts, principally community work, eisteddfodau (cultural festivals), and sporting achievements.

As a result of political and social action on behalf of the beleagured culture a number of national institutions were founded which have become the bedrock of Welsh public life today. Thus from 1883 onwards was established the University of Wales, a federal institution initially comprised of four constituent colleges at Aberystwyth, Cardiff, Bangor and Swansea and then expanded to incorporate the UWIST (now merged with University College, Cardiff), St David's University College, Lampeter, and the Welsh National School of Medicine at Cardiff. This federal university has been the single most important resource of the Welsh nation in terms of intellectual development, the formulation of social and cultural policy and in terms of reaching the masses in whose name the University was established. It continues to occupy a central and accessible position in Welsh life, although it is now joined by the Open University in Wales and the University of Glamorgan, together with a network of Higher and Further Education sector institutions providing a comprehensive educational service, though still vastly under-represented in terms of the Welsh-medium courses available. Even so, in Gwynedd and Dyfed there are interesting developments in the Further Education sector which use Welsh-medium courses in vocational training giving an additional economic value to language in the workplace.

In addition the National Library of Wales at Aberystwyth and the National Museum of Wales at Cardiff were established in 1907; the Church in Wales was created following the Act of Disestablishment in 1920 and a variety of cultural movements flourished such as Undeb Cenedlaethol Y Cymdeithasau Cymraeg (the National Union of Welsh Societies formed in 1913), and Urdd Gobaith Cymru in 1922. However, this impressive political-cultural infra-structure was still largely dependent upon external factors and sources of finance and elements within Wales soon concluded that the forces which militated against the reproduction of an indigenous Welsh culture could only be mediated by a form of genuine self-government or home-rule. Thus in 1925 Plaid Genedlaethol Cymru (The Welsh National Party) was formed by a small group of bourgeois intellectuals which included Saunders Lewis, a University lecturer and playwright, the Reverend Lewis Valentine, a Baptist Minister, and D. J. Davies, an economist. Their initial concerns were the preservation of Welsh cultural and spiritual values and forms, the maintenance of a small-scale, primarily rural, communitarian life-style, and to differentiate themselves from those political movements based upon either imperialist or social class appeals. Interestingly it was not until 1932 that self-government became part of the party's ideological and electoral platform (Butt Philip 1975). Since then its justification for advancing the cause of independence has widened considerably from the over-dominant language issue of the inter-war years to a more balanced and holistic view of Welsh problems in a broader British and European context (Williams, C. H. 1982; 1991). It currently returns four Members of Parliament, representing Heartland constituencies, and claims the political affiliation of about ten per cent of the Welsh electorate. Morally and intellectually it is still a 'focus for solidarity and motor for action' on the language issue as it was in the pre-war period, but it is currently joined by a large number of other agencies and movements engaged in the struggle for language survival and hence its leadership role has been diffused and overtaken somewhat as a co-ordinating body and fulcrum of resistance to anglicisation and centralism.

Chief among these alternative movements has been the vigorous development of Cymdeithas yr Iaith Gymraeg (The Welsh Language Society) formed in 1963 following Saunders Lewis' radio lecture, "Tynged yr Iaith" (The Fate of the Language). Often interpreted as the non-violent youth wing of Plaid Cymru, Cymdeithas yr Iaith has developed a style and a substance which serves to differentiate it quite markedly from the constitutional political party it so often berates for its slowness and lack of penetration. Initially concerned with single-issue campaigning in favour of such reforms as bilingual forms, tax and television licences, a separate Welsh-medium television channel and greater equality between Welsh and English in judicial affairs, 'Cymdeithas' has developed into a real force for sustained change in Wales. Over a thirty year period its members have engaged in a series of direct-action campaigns which may involve violence to property but never to persons. Its tactics include the vandalism of public property, inviting police action and prosecution, fines and imprisonment (Williams and Raybould 1991).

In essence it is both a direct-action pressure group and an unofficial language think-tank. It produces well-researched planning and policy documents in reasonable terms, which reflect a keen understanding of the nature of the political process and the barriers to full scale societal bilingualism. Its candour may be embarrassing at times to those who are embedded within the power structure of the central or local state, but its strategic aims are often prescient even if its methods do not always conduce. Its key contribution is awareness raising among both Welsh and English people. As a movement it can draw upon the good will and active involvement of a number of independent individuals and organisations which is another source of its collective strength. It is fair to say that in combination with other agencies, many of the language reforms we now enjoy in Wales are largely the result of the persistent campaigning of 'Cymdeithas' as a spearhead for the wider language movement, even if in any particular case we know that key decisions are often taken despite, not because of, the tactics of the movement.

However, real power in Wales during the latter half of this century has always rested with one of the two principal state-wide parties. Initially it was the Labour Party which developed the pioneering county council bilingual educational policies of Flint and Glamorgan. This developed into a modest, but significant Welsh-medium educational infra-structure epitomised by Ysgol Glan Clwyd and Ysgol Uwchradd Rhydfelen. In part this was a response to Nationalist pressure and also to Labour's commitment to satisfying the desires of parental pressure groups, organised bodies and the increased self-esteem of Welsh speakers. It is unfortunate that the language issue has become too closely identified with Plaid Cymru for that clouds the very real commitment of both Labour and Liberal politicians and activists to the creation of a more fully functional bilingual society in Wales, then as now. Even so, it would be less than honest not to also report that the greatest opposition to the development of Welsh-medium education and of language issues generally came from within Labour and Labour-affiliated ranks, an opposition which continues in some areas today.

Since 1979, of course, the U. K. has been governed by a Conservative administration. During the initial period of the century it is fair to say that the Tory Party and all that it represented were anathema to most Welsh people. They were the advocates of Unionism, of Centralism, of Anglicisation: the old religious and class-enemies of the Welsh masses, 'Y Werin', in popular mythology and political rhetoric. However, they have ruled over and indeed instituted several of the most far-reaching reforms that have hitherto influenced language choice and behaviour in Wales and are currently developing a new language planning framework as detailed in 131.6. The rationale for this unlikely support is subject to political and social interpretation. Being charitable it is possible to argue that this is a reflection of the government's commitment to satisfying consumer demands, with Welsh speakers representing a certain share of the market. Equally it is possible to argue that such reforms are designed to undermine the strength of Labour and nationalist opposition which has long fed on the Conservative's anti-Welsh culture image for political gain.

4. Statistical profile

Despite its many problems, which are well rehearsed in the literature, the decennial census returns are still the most comprehensive data source relating to language ability in Wales. The first language census in Wales was conducted in 1891 and it recorded that 898,914 spoke Welsh (54.4%). Ten years later in 1910 929,824 (49.9%) were so recorded.

At its census peak in 1911, the Welsh-speaking population numbered 977,366 (43.5%) of whom 190,300 were monoglot Welsh. Continuous decline throughout the century resulted in a 1981 population of 503,549 speakers, of whom 21,283 recorded themselves as monoglot. This figure should be regarded with caution for it is highly unlikely that many individuals aged five and over are unable to speak English in Wales (Williams, C. H. 1982). By 1991 the Welsh-speaking population had declined to 496,530, a fall of some 1.4% (Aitchison and Carter 1993). Care has to be taken in the recent decennial comparison 1981–1991 because the definition and treatment of absent households has changed in the intervening period. Thus if the population base used in the 1991 census is adopted, the Welsh-speaking population of Wales is 508,549, some 18.7% of the total population aged three and over of 2,723,623. In crude terms this suggests a proportional loss of 25%, down from 44% in 1911. It bodes well in that the long trend of decline has slowed, compared with the acute fall of 17.3% between 1961 and 1971, and the fall of 6.3% for the period 1971–1981. However, this certainly underestimates the total population of Welsh speakers on two counts. First, it excludes from the analysis the many thousands of Welsh speakers who reside outside Wales. Secondly, there is good evidence to suggest that many Welsh speakers interpret their self-assessed inadequacy to communicate effectively in 'standard Welsh' as sufficient reason not to claim an ability to speak, read and write Welsh on the official census. Conversely, of course, with any self-administered questionnaire there are also those who undoubtedly exaggerate their Welsh linguistic abilities. The true figure is probably nearer to 25% of the total population. But as the census question asks for ability not use it therefore provides a particular profile of the language community.

These recent figures are a welcome arrest of the pattern of decline and should be interpreted as a significant boost to halting language shift. A brief summary will confirm these structural adjustments. Geographically the recent census has observed the continued break up of 'Y Fro Gymraeg' (The Welsh Heartland) which has three types of consequence for language maintenance and language planning. First, it reduces the territorial dominance of Welsh as the unquestioned, 'traditional' 'normal' language of the north and west. Secondly, it reduces the cogency of territorial language planning schemes at the meso-scale. Thirdly, it throws into doubt the ability of local authorities to continue to advance ad hoc and reactive policies to promote Welsh anywhere within the country. With the advent of the strengthened Welsh Language Board it is likely that a new holistic approach to language in its widest social context will characterise the current attempts to influence language promotion. The weakening of the Heartland region will undoubtedly be a major focus for the WLB because this region has traditionally been the heart and the base of the Welsh speaking community.

A second trend confirmed by the 1991 census is the substantial increase in the numbers of Welsh speakers aged between 3 and 15 with all counties, save Gwynedd, recording absolute increases. The greatest growth was in the more Anglicised counties of Gwent, Powys and Mid Glamorgan and reveals a new geography of age-related development as in South Pembrokeshire where young speakers account for half of all speakers. Clearly we are dealing with relatively small populations, but even so the evidence suggests a reversal of the historical pattern of decline. One of the principal reasons for this growth is the development of formal bilingual nursery, primary and secondary schools which have acted as growth poles in the community radiating confidence, scholastic success and a form of Welsh infra-structure in restricted domains. Mudiad Ysgolion Meithrin (The Welsh Nursery Schools Movement), founded in 1971, has been exceptionally important as a means of language reproduction by feeding statutory bilingual education with 'good learners' who go on through the Welsh-medium educational system. In Anglicised areas they should be introducing new speakers into the Welsh speaking community. However, some of these children could be described as Welsh learners and not Welsh speakers in the community. Welsh is compulsory in the National Curriculum, creating vast numbers who can be said to speak Welsh (rudimentary skills) but do not speak Welsh in the playground or in the street. It may be asked in this context whether the Census question has become more of an attitude question as the Irish often interpret their national language census. Let us take one example to illustrate the age dimension in Welsh language reproduction. In 1991, the county of South Glamorgan, centered on Cardiff and its environs, reported that 29.1% of all females aged 5–15 were Welsh speaking and these constituted 30.3% of all Welsh speakers there. By contrast proportions of only 3.3% and 2.6% are recorded in several of the upper age cohorts, a dramatic testimony of the potential future for the language in comparison with its standing in the inter-war years when these older people were raised as monoglot Anglo-Welsh children. This is a general phenomenon in Anglicised areas and could be interpreted as a new base for an urban, bilingual population which is sharply differentiated from the Heartland region in a number of ways.

Encouraging though these figures are for the Anglicised parts of Wales one should not forget that a number of factors could reduce their impact on Welsh language reproduction in the next century. The development of mass tourism, seasonal employment patterns, out-migration, economic change and language of marriage partner will still influence rates of language loss and gain, but as each decennial census records higher and higher proportions in the younger age categories then the demographic future for Welsh seems brighter than at any other time since 1911. Whether the uses to which the language is put, or the particular form of Welsh expression, syntax and grammar are quite what the post-war cultural activists expected is quite another matter. In raw statistical terms the trends of the past two decades allow us to say that forecasts of the imminent death of the Welsh language were wildly exaggerated.

5. Sociolinguistic situation

Historically the hearth, the farm and the chapel have been the traditional domains which sustained a Welsh-medium network of agencies of language reproduction. This reached its zenith in the late nineteenth century when the institutions of Welsh nonconformity created a parallel 'social totality' which enabled Wales to cope with the huge upheaval of industrialisation and urbanisation, without losing its language or culture.

With the secularisation of society and the break-down of the relative homogeneity of rural communities an alternative, urban, formal set of domains has been constructed in the south and east. The principal instrument of language transmission in such environments is the Welsh medium school system which has done more than any other agency to promote the language and introduce it, and its related culture, to hitherto non-Welsh speaking families. Welsh-medium education across the curriculum now includes Maths and Science, Technology and Computing in addition to the conventional Humanities and Social Science subjects. The comprehensive, nation-wide network of primary, secondary and tertiary Welsh-medium institutions, are actively socialising a younger generation into anticipating living in a fully functional bilingual society.

The school's role is likely to increase following the reforms of the 1988 Education Act which insisted that Welsh be a core subject in the National Curriculum. It is now possible to teach a wide range of subjects including Maths and Science, Design and Computing through the medium of Welsh. From 1994, all save a few opt out schools in the secondary sector, were obliged to teach Welsh to the pupils in the lower forms. This, in turn, will expose a far greater number of Welsh youth to the language and culture of their homeland and will also require a huge investment in teachers and resources to be successful. In Higher Education circles also there is a wide range of vocational and non-vocational courses available to full and part-time students, but again we must emphasise that in all such developments the numbers involved within any particular course are small. Even so the trend and direction of change is significant for it extends both the domain use and practical utility of bilingualism in society.

There remains a crucial sociolinguistic question. If provision is increasing apace in most domains, what of the actual usage, status and application of bilingual skills in the market place?

Here again it is possible to over-exaggerate the significance of bilingualism as a daily phenomenon, for it depends a great deal upon what meaning one reads into various developments such as publishing.

The development of a lively and innovative publishing sector has contributed greatly to the enjoyment of written and read Welsh this century. By comparison with English the range and overall quality leaves much to be desired, although given the constraints which face any lesser-used language the output is remarkable. A third of all books are school texts or children's books, initially dealing with Welsh themes by Welsh authors, but increasingly translating the more popular English-medium stories, reference books and visually stunning discovery and factual/documentary guide books. Adult books are dominated by literary conventions which prize verse, prose, eisteddfodic competition winners and the like, reflecting the niche market of Welsh-medium publishing. Rarely would one find a Welsh translation of a highly popular English novel for it makes little economic sense. It is more probable that contemporary drama, rather than novels would be translated, in part because it is related to performance and in part to the probability of having been commissioned for television or radio. Broadcasting is one acid test of the social use and adaptability of Welsh culture. Radio paved the way with a limited range of Welsh medium transmissions in the fifties and sixties, largely devoted to religious, children or daily life issues. In 1977—1979 as a result of the development of VHF wavebands, an English-medium Radio Wales and a predominantly Welsh-medium Radio Cymru service was launched. The latter provides some 127 hours per week, ninety of which are in Welsh, and are of a high quality. One could almost describe this service as a 'friend of the family' to many Welsh speakers, for its presenters, such as Hywel Gwynfryn, are regular household names whose skill is to present musical and contemporary items in a manner which is simultaneously both intimate and professional. Thus Radio Cymru might be said to act like a national network for many, as it encourages audience participation to a far greater extent than do its far more diverse and hence specialist English counterparts.

The greatest boost to the popular and technical use of Welsh in this post-modern, international era was of course the inauguration of Sianel Pedwar Cumru on the 1st of November, 1982. It had been preceded by some thirty years of intermittent and gradually expanding television output in Welsh by the BBC, TWW, Teledu Cymru and Harlech TV which had demonstrated the potential for a sustained independent channel to serve the needs of a bilingual audience. The absence of such a channel had clear implications not only for language reproduction but also for sustained dissatisfaction on behalf of the unilingual English-speaking majority in Wales. Up to 1982 some ten percent of programmes were transmitted in Welsh, with the effect that those who preferred not to watch Welsh medium output had their television sets tuned permanently to English transmittors in the Mendips, Shrewsbury, Kidsgrove and Chester. In consequence one had the strange anomaly that very many households in Wales received their daily diet of regional news and accompanying programmes from a neighbouring region across the border. This also limited the appeal and impact of English-medium programmes produced in Wales, and of course, diminished the potential revenue derived from commercial advertising. Both sides of the 'linguistic divide' were thus profoundly unhappy with the situation. However, identifying the problem is one thing, acting to redress it is quite another, especially when there are huge political and financial implications. Nevertheless at a number of key turns in the seventies, it became obvious that there was a growing support in favour of a fourth channel being devoted in whole or in part to Welsh medium services. The 1974 Crawford Committee endorsed this view as did the Conservative manifesto pledge of 1979. However, within a few months of taking office the new administration withdrew their committment, preferring to improve the existing broadcasting arrangements. This policy change engendered the largest mass protests witnessed in post-war Wales, with a plethora of social movements, political parties, non-aligned interest groups campaigning in tandem to force the government to honour its pledge. The focus of this campaign was the May 5th, 1980 decision of Gwynfor Evans, a former leader of Plaid Cymru, to fast to death unless the government announced the creation of S 4 C. To the great relief of many, on 17th of September 1980 the government reversed its decision and Wales has enjoyed a decade or more of popular and varied Welsh-medium broadcasting. Over thirty out of 145 hours per week are transmitted in Welsh, mainly at peak time. They reach a relatively high percentage of their target audience and are facing the future with more confidence now. S 4 C is a commissioning rather than a production body, and in consequence has spawned a network of independent film makers, animators, creative designers, writers etc. who can turn their original Welsh language programmes into English or 'foreign' languages for sale in the international media market place. Cardiff ranks second to London as a media-production centre in the U. K. with all the technical, economic and post-production implications of a growing infra-structure in such a specialist industry. Three issues dominate the current TV debate viz., (1) financial self-sufficiency versus subsidy; (2) the relaxation of boundaries inside programmes between the use of Welsh and English; and (3) the multicultural nature of S 4 C which transmits European soccer and sport, repackaged documentaries, soaps, quizzes and a host of other material all dubbed into Welsh. In part this is to attract new viewers to the channel and in part it reflects S 4 C's participation in the European Broadcasting Union and commercial marketing of international television material.

At a more voluntary level there is a very active network of Eisteddfodau (competitive cultural festivals) which nurture school-based and community-based performances of Welsh plays, or plays in translation, of musical items, poetry, craft work, art and design and scientific projects. This network starts at the local level and the successful competitors progress through intervening stages to reach the National Eisteddfod and the Urdd National Eisteddfod. During the present century it was the Eisteddfod system which acted as a vehicle for national culture, setting both the themes and the standards of popular representation of Welshness. More recently the Urdd (The Welsh League of Youth) has reinterpreted traditional Welsh mass culture by adding go-karting, tenpin bowling, discos, and surfing 'in Welsh'. An additional voluntaristic element is the adult learning of Welsh through Ulpan and related schemes which are geographically widespread and well subscribed. These in turn often feed Welsh clubs and social centres which may have sport, folk dancing or music as their focus but offer a wider entrée into the indigenous culture. Their children, and those of in-migrants, may attend Language Centers for English only speakers, designed to speed up their integration into the local community. However, as in most unbalanced bilingual countries there are severe difficulties in reconciling the rights and obligations of indigenous citizens with those of incomers, many of whom are antagonistic or hostile to the requirement that their children attend a bilingual school. Thus Wales experiences grassroots parents movements in favour of extending bilingual education, and a lesser number, but often well organised, who oppose such an extension on the grounds that it limits their natural rights as British citizens.

6. The political situation of language in Wales

English has been the traditional state language since mediaeval times and, as we noted above, Welsh lost its formal role as a language of government and state affairs following the Acts of Union of 1536 and 1542. However, although there has not been a statutory obligation to recognise Welsh as an official language within Wales since the 16th century, clearly with a predominantly monolingual population until the past century and a half, agencies of the state and of the established Church did employ Welsh in a wide range of domains in the intervening period. However, it was not until the passing of the Welsh Courts Act of 1942 that the provisions prohibiting the use of Welsh by the Acts of Union were rescinded. Further legal recognition was given in the Welsh Language Act of 1967 which offered an initial and inadequate definition of equal validity of English and Welsh in Wales. This was related mainly to the greater provision of Welsh in the Courts of Law and in legal proceedings generally, but did not extend into the wider sphere of public administration and formal bilingual rights.

During the sixties and seventies a number of statutory and non-statutory bodies called for greater state support for the language. One initial response by the Welsh Office was the establishment in 1977 of the short-lived Cyngor yr Iaith Gymraeg (The Welsh Language Council). It also led to some limited financial support for Welsh language activities, both in the public arena and in education via specific provisions in two government acts passed during the latter part of the 1970s. Under section 26 of The Development of Rural Wales Act 1976, the Welsh Office provide support for Welsh language social activities, most importantly the work of Mudiad Ysgolion Meithrin (The Welsh Nursery Schools Movement, founded in 1971), Eisteddfod Genedlaethol Cymru (The National Eisteddfod of Wales), Cyngor Llyfrau Cymraeg (The Welsh Books Council) and via Menter a Busnes (Business and Enterprise), the promotion of a new spirit of enterprise in rural Welsh speaking communities.

Under section 21 of the 1980 Education Act, they provide grants to support specific activities in schools and colleges, such as the provision of additional staff and Welsh-medium teaching resources. As a result of the increased demand section 21 expenditure increased four-fold from £ 1 million in 1981 to £ 4 million in 1991. However, as Williams and Raybould 1991, p. 13 have noted such figures compare poorly with the level of support for teaching English as a second language in England and Wales. One LEA in England, for example, received £ 14 million in one year under section 11 of the 1980 Act.

A more purposeful educational planning body was established in February 1986 as a result of long-term political pressure. Pwyllgor Datblygu Addysg Gymraeg (PDAG, The Welsh Language Education Development Committee) was created by the authority of the Welsh Office, but it specified that it should function within the purview of the Welsh Joint Education Committee (CBAC, Cyd-Bwyllgor Addysg Cymru) as a Local Authority directed but Welsh Office and County Council funded agency. Its brief was to chart the anticipated needs of Welsh-medium education in the statutory sector, but it quickly enlarged this brief by tackling both the nursery and post-school provision, envisaging itself as a body concerned with all aspects of such education from the cradle to the grave. A pioneering body, it helped shape the priorities in the medium term, collated valuable experience and information, distributed government finances to support resource and learning development and generally acted as a mouth-piece for educational issues in Wales. As such, despite its small staff and budget is was an effective forerunner of what may become a more comprehensive national educational institute.

For the present its staff and role have been split between newly established government agencies which denies the cogency of its original justification, but is in keeping with current government thinking about replacing primarily local government agencies with central government quangos.

Within twelve months, continued calls for a new Welsh Language Act led to the establishment of a wholly government-appointed body to promote the use of Welsh in public life. The non-statutory Bwrdd yr Iaith Gymraeg (The Welsh Language Board) was established in July 1988. In its short, if controversial, life-span, the first Board had successfully raised the profile of Welsh in non-traditional language domains. It had been particularly active in encouraging former state-owned, now privately-owned corporations such as Gas, Electricity, Telephone and Water Companies to adopt visible bilingual advertising, customer enquiries, information packs, bilingual service points etc., all of which enable the language to be used in a larger number of formal settings than hitherto. It has also advised on needs, priorities and strategies for private industry to encourage bilingual practices and consumer relations such that in most Welsh towns and cities one can see far more bilingual service and information signs than ever, particularly in banks, large departmental stores and offices. Clearly this boosts not only the language equality argument but also defuses somewhat the traditional argument against Welsh, that it was a rural, small scale, traditional language out of place and out of sympathy with the modern, urban, post-industrial society. Of course, it is quite another issue as to what extent such symbolic bilingualism in the market place relates to customer usage or customer satisfaction, but nevertheless the public face of the power differential between English and Welsh is being addressed by the activities of the Welsh Language Board, and for Wales, at least, that is a novel experience.

In 1993 the British Parliament passed a new Welsh Language Act whose principal initiative was the establishment of a statutory Welsh Language Board. It has a developing remit to promote the formal acceptance of bilingualism as a societal norm in the public sector, to oversee the provision of Welsh-medium education in all sectors from the cradle to the grave, to oversee the language policy of major media institutions such as the BBC and S 4 C (Sianel Pedwar Cymru) to audit the financing and subscription levels of Welsh journals, to require Local Authorities to submit language plans detailing their policy and provision for meeting the needs of bilinguals in their authorities. All this forms part of the statutory, hence binding, remit of the W. L. B. Its role in the private sector will be to encourage the voluntaristic adoption of bilingual practices through W. L. B. joint-ventures and initiatives such as marketing the language, devising language courses for employees, preparing commercial documents and terminology to smooth the transition from English-only to bilingual working practices in some industries and regions. The establishment of the Welsh Language Board and its associated legal, research, educational and general language status divisions represents the single most important act of formal language planning ever experienced in Wales. It will surely act as a focus for a new holistic analysis of language in society and given its statutory powers will be able to influence social behaviour and in some part redress some of the grievances which have accumulated as a result of centuries of denial of language legitimacy and all its associated discriminatory implications for Welsh life.

7. Conclusion

Without doubt the inter-play between the forces promoting the spread of English and those perpetuating the resistance of Welsh in the past seven centuries captures the power, ambiguity, duality and opportunity inherent in any such relationship between neighbours. In strict logical terms it makes little sense that England's first and most successful colony should continue to resist incorporation and seek to re-establish its national identity through a language-led struggle. But then we do not live in a world dominated only by linguistic theories of competition and displacement. The search for an appropriate place for both English and Welsh in a bilingual Wales will continue apace, as will the attitudes towards Welsh in general. But the portents are more encouraging than ever that such a search will be continued in a non-violent, constitutional mode, emphasising the gradualist rather than the radical or reactionary approaches available. The public place of Welsh is beginning to be institutionalised, even if this necessitates greater dependence upon the local state as the source of both its legitimacy and finance. Having fought to obtain a semblance of equality for both languages in the post-war period, it is likely that the next generation's concerns will have far more to do with questions of economic development, environmental protection and conservation and holistic planning. This is particularly true for the Heartland region, for despite its relative decline as the source for initiative and social change, it is still the base and bedrock of a relatively autonomous Welsh culture. We may be attracted by the rapid development of bilingual networks in the burgeoning urban districts of the anglicised lowlands, but we neglect the northern and western base of Welsh culture at our peril, for its experience has taught that only when the language is a fully functional element in an integrated society will it prosper and please. No amount of formal language planning, however desperately needed, can substitute for the popular will to reproduce a language and culture, precisely because it is one's own and gives meaning and fulfillment in this life, which is a short sigh between two mysteries.

8. Bibliography (selected)

Aitchison, John/Carter, Harold (1993): "The Welsh Language in 1991". In: *Planet* 97, 3–11.

Butt Philip, Allan (1975): *The Welsh Question*, Cardiff.

Coupland, Niklas (Ed.) (1990): *English in Wales*, Clevedon, Avon.

Davies, John (1993): *The Welsh Language*, Cardiff.

Pryce, W. T. R./Williams, Colin H. (1988): "Sources and Methods in the Study of Language Areas: A Case Study of Wales". In: *Language in Geographic Context*, Williams, C. H. (Ed.), Clevedon, Avon.

Thomas, Brinley (1959): "Wales and the Atlantic Economy". In: *Scottish Journal of Political Economy* 6, 169–192.

Williams, Colin H. (Ed.) (1982): *National Separatism*, Cardiff.

Williams, Colin H. (1987): "Location and Context in Welsh Language Reproduction". In: *The Sociology of Welsh, International Journal of the Sociology of Language* 66, Williams, G. (Ed.), 61–68.

Williams, Colin H. (Ed.) (1991): *Linguistic Minorities, Society and Territory*, Clevedon, Avon.

Williams, Colin H. (1992): "Identity, Autonomy and the Ambiguity of Technological Development". In: *Globalization and Territorial Identities*, Mlinar, Z. (Ed.), Aldershot.

Williams, Colin H./Raybould, W. (1991): *Welsh Language Planning: Opportunities and Constraints*, Cardiff.

Williams, Glanmor (1971): "Language, Literacy and Nationality in Wales". In: *History* 56, 1–16.

Williams, Glyn (1991): *The Welsh in Patagonia*, Cardiff.

Williams, Glyn (Ed.) (1987): "The Sociology of Welsh". In: *International Journal of the Sociology of Language* 66.

Williams, Glyn (1992): *Sociolinguistics*, London.

Williams, Gwyn A. (1982): *The Welsh in their History*, London.

Williams, Gwyn A. (1985): *When was Wales?* London.

Colin Williams, Cardiff (Great Britain)

133. Englisch−Gälisch

1. Geographie und Demographie
2. Geschichte
3. Politik, Wirtschaft und allgemeine kulturelle sowie religiöse Lage
4. Statistik und Ethnoprofile
5. Soziolinguistische Lage
6. Sprachpolitische Lage
7. Allgemeines kontaktlinguistisches Porträt
8. Kritische Wertung der verwendeten Quellen und Literatur
9. Bibliographie (in Auswahl)

1. Geographie und Demographie

Schottland, der nördliche Teil der britischen Hauptinsel, umfaßt einschließlich der Hebriden, Orkney- und Shetland-Inseln 77 167 km², was einem knappen Drittel der Fläche des Vereinigten Königreichs von Großbritannien und Nordirland entspricht. Schottland ist im wesentlichen Gebirgsland. Die Horste der Highlands (Hochland) im Norden und der Southern Uplands (südschottisches Bergland) im Süden werden durch die Senke der Lowlands (mittelschottisches Tiefland) voneinander getrennt. Das Hochland und die Hebriden nehmen weit über die Hälfte der Fläche Schottlands ein. Die Hochflächen sind meist mit Heide und Moor bedeckt.

Die Bevölkerung Schottlands zählte bei der ersten Erhebung/Schätzung 1755 nur 1,26 Millionen. Bei der ersten offiziellen Volkszählung 1801 war sie auf 1,6 Millionen angestiegen. Danach wuchs sie rapide trotz starker Auswanderung vor allem nach Übersee um über 300% auf 5,23 Millionen (1971). Seither ist die Bevölkerungszahl leicht rückläufig; bei der Volkszählung 1991 betrug sie 4,96 Millionen. Deren Verteilung ist äußerst unregelmäßig, wie die Tabelle ausweist. Das karge Hochland entvölkerte sich insbesondere aus politisch-wirtschaftlichen Gründen zur Zeit der *Highland Clearances* und danach. Einen Überblick über die Bevölkerungsdichte in den einzelnen Verwaltungsbezirken aufgrund der Volkszählung von 1991 vermittelt Tab. 133.1.

Die Gebiete, in denen Gälisch in Schottland heute noch in nennenswertem Ausmaß gesprochen wird, sind die bei weitem am dünnsten besiedelten (→ language map B).

2. Geschichte

2.1. Gälisch, im Lateinischen bekannt unter der Bezeichnung 'Lingua Scotica', war die Sprache der Skoten (Scotti), einem keltischen

Tab. 133.1: Bevölkerungsdichte Schottlands (Stand 1991)

Gebiet	Bevölkerung über drei Jahre	Größe in km²	Bevölkerung pro 1 km²
Borders Region	103.311	4.672	22
Central Region	268.251	2.631	102
Dumfries & Galloway Region	147.732	6.370	23
Fife Region	340.138	1.307	260
Grampian Region	493.760	8.704	57
Highland Region	209.746	25.391	8
Lothian Region	724.107	1.755	413 (mit Edinburgh)
Strathclyde Region	2.219.110	13.537	164 (mit Glasgow)
Tayside Region	385.136	7.493	51
Orkney Islands	19.328	976	20
Shetland Islands	22.163	1.433	15
Western Isles	29.370	2.898	10

Volk aus Irland, das sich ca. 500 n. Chr. in Schottland, zunächst in Argyll, niederließ und dem Land seinen Namen gab. Es war damals *Common Gaelic*, denn vom irischen und schottischen Gälisch als zwei verschiedenen Sprachen kann man erst ab dem 13. Jahrhundert sprechen. Die Skoten trafen in Schottland auf die Pikten − ein Volk, dessen Sprache und Ursprung unklar bleiben −, mit denen sie jedoch 843 ein gemeinsames Königtum von Alban errichteten. Ferner siedelten vor den Angelsachsen ausweichende keltische Briten in Strathclyde. Um 850 weitete sich das Gälische in Schottland durch den Einfluß der Klöster (besonders auf Iona) aus. Bis zum 11. Jahrhundert war Gälisch die vorherrschende Sprache. Während der Regierungszeit Malcolms III. (1058–1093), der der letzte schottische König mit gälischer Muttersprache war, setzte die Anglisierung Schottlands ein. Malcolm, der selbst 15 Jahre in England im Exil gewesen war, hatte die westsächsische Prinzessin Margaret (Saint Margaret) geheiratet. Auf diese Weise konnte die englische Sprache und Kultur Eingang am schottischen Hof finden und auch die römisch-katholische Kirche mehr und mehr die Oberhand über die keltische Kirche der irischen Missionare gewinnen. Wichtig für die Anglisierung war die Einführung des anglonormannischen Feudalsystems unter Margarets jüngstem Sohn David I. (1124–1153). Es etablierte sich eine Verwaltung nach englischem Vorbild. Erwähnenswert ist nicht zuletzt auch die Errichtung von militärischen Standorten, den sogenannten *Burghs*, im 11. und 12. Jahrhundert, die sich alsbald zu örtlichen Handelszentren entwickelten und die die einheimische Bevölkerung mit Engländern und Normannen in Kontakt brachten.

Die Anglisierung der zentralen schottischen Lowlands setzte sich unaufhaltsam fort, ebenso die der tiefer gelegenen Gebiete entlang der Ostküste jenseits des Firth of Forth. Gälisch wurde zunehmend die Sprache der Unterschicht und der Landbevölkerung. Obwohl über den Rückzug des Gälischen im Mittelalter kein Zweifel besteht, erweist es sich indes als schwierig, den genaueren Grenzverlauf zwischen dem englisch- und dem gälischsprachigen Gebiet im 15. und 16. Jahrhundert festzustellen, weil hierzu die vorhandenen Beweisstücke nicht ausreichen. Karte 133.1 enthält in der Sekundärliteratur gemachte Vorschläge, beide Gebiete voneinander abzugrenzen. Jedoch können die verzeichneten Linien nur ungefähre Aussagen über den Grenzverlauf machen. Danach gab es im 16. Jahrhundert noch ein gälischsprachiges Gebiet in Galloway, dem Südwesten Schottlands, in dem sich Gälisch bis ins 17. Jahrhundert halten konnte. Ferner zeigt die Karte, daß das Gälische ab dem Ende des 16. Jahrhunderts im wesentlichen nur noch auf die Hochlandregion beschränkt war. Im Nordosten Schottlands war zu dieser Zeit noch das Nordische (Norse/Norn) verbreitet, was jedoch hier aus der Betrachtung herausfällt.

2.2. Im Südosten Schottlands ließen sich im 7. Jahrhundert Angeln aus Nordhumbrien nieder, die einen Dialekt des (Alt)englischen sprachen. Sie drangen bis nach Din Eidyn, dem heutigen Edinburgh, vor. Unter schottisch-englischen Dialekten ist bis ins 14. Jahrhundert der mit den nordenglischen Dialekten gleichförmige Dialekt zu verstehen – zunächst *Inglis*, seit der politischen Unabhängigkeit Schottlands 1328 *Scottis* genannt –, danach bis ins 17. Jahrhundert die darauf aufbauende Edinburgher Verwaltungssprache. Im Jahre 1603 erfolgte die *Union of the Crowns*. James VI. von Schottland zog als James I. von England mit seinem Hof nach London, was auch sprachliche Konsequenzen hatte. Die gebildete schottische Bevölkerung war fortan um das Standardenglisch bemüht – aufgrund schottischer Besonderheiten *Standard Scottish English* oder *Educated Scots* genannt. Wichtig in diesem Zusammenhang war die Einführung der englischsprachigen Bibel in Schottland, deren Übersetzung von James I. authorisiert worden war und die daher *Authorised Version* oder *King James Bible* genannt wurde.

2.3. Im 19. Jahrhundert haben Selkirk (1806, App. V), Walker (1808, 29), Murray (1873, 231 ff) und Ravenstein (1879, 592) die geographisch-sprachliche Grenze zwischen gälisch-sprachigen Highlands und anglisierten Lowlands beschrieben (zu deren Kriterien vgl. Thomson 1983, 109 f). Diese Grenze, die später auch als *Celtic Border* oder *Highland Line* (Hochlandlinie) bezeichnet wurde, verläuft vom Firth of Clyde im Südwesten in einem östlichen Bogen zum Moray Firth im Nordosten. In diesem Jahrhundert haben die Hochlandlinie Grant (1931, X ff), Catford (1957, 107) und Speitel (1981, 110) – letztere auf der Grundlage der Erhebungen des *Linguistic Survey of Scotland* – festzulegen versucht, allerdings mit dem wesentlichen Unterschied, daß sie seit Grant das Scots vom Englischen und nicht mehr vom Gälischen abgrenzt.

3. Politik, Wirtschaft und allgemeine kulturelle sowie religiöse Lage

Mit dem Zurückweichen des Gälischen in die Highlands entstand bald ein deutlicher Gegensatz zwischen den Lowlands einerseits und den Highlands andererseits, der nicht nur sprachlicher Natur war. Im 16. und frühen 17. Jahrhundert wurde das politische Leben Schottlands von den anglisierten Low-

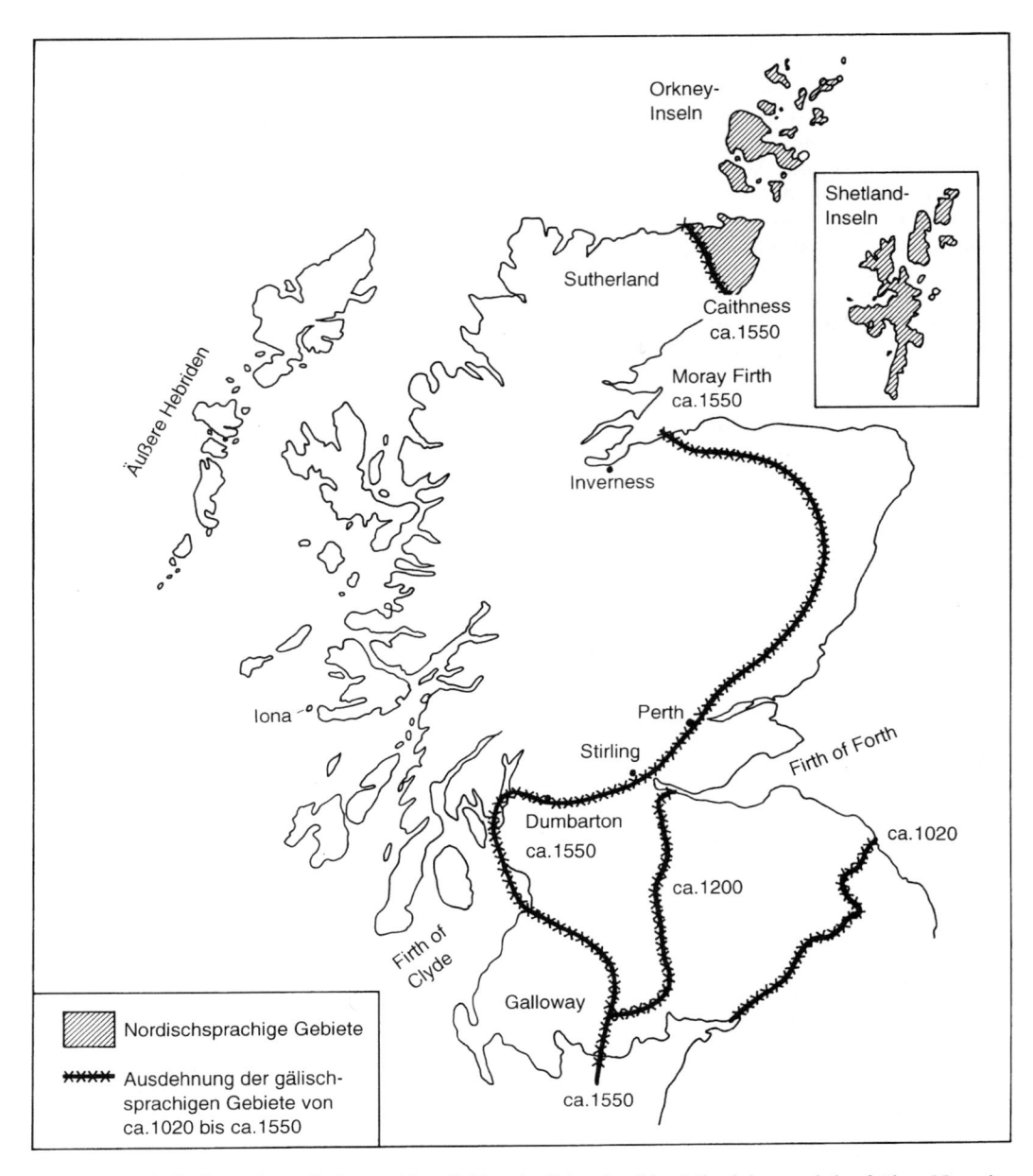

Abb. 133.1: Gälisch- und nordischsprachige Gebiete in Schottland im Mittelalter und der frühen Neuzeit (nach Withers 1979, 51 und 1984, 26)

lands bestimmt, was zu Spannungen mit den Bewohnern der Highlands führte. Zudem gab es Unterschiede in der Religion und der Sozialstruktur. Die Reformation, die sich anfangs in den Highlands kaum bemerkbar machte, setzte Gälisch gleich mit Unzivilisiertheit und dem letzten Rest des Papismus (vgl. auch 6.). Nichtsdestoweniger war Gä-

lisch Mitte des 16. Jahrhunderts auch noch außerhalb der Gaidhealtachd, also der Highlands und Western Isles, wie Griechisch, Latein und Hebräisch, aber im Gegensatz zu Englisch, eine Sprache der Gelehrsamkeit. Im Hochland spielten die Clans, keltische patriarchalische Stammesverbände, eine große Rolle. Die Geschichte des Clansystems ist sehr wechselvoll. Cromwell versuchte, die Macht der Clans zu brechen, aber nach der Wiederherstellung des Hauses Stuart festigte sich die alte Stammesverfassung aufs neue – zumindest bis zur Vertreibung des Hauses Stuart Anfang des 18. Jahrhunderts. Nach dem endgültigen Scheitern der Rebellion unter Prince Charles Edward (besser bekannt unter dem Namen Bonnie Prince Charlie) 1746 begann die bewußte Zerschlagung der gälischen Gesellschaftsstruktur. Während der berüchtigten *Highland Clearances* von 1782 bis 1853 wurden viele Highlander von den Großgrundbesitzern von ihrem angestammten Besitz vertrieben. Eine Person, die diesbezüglich in Sutherland tätig war, bemerkte, sie sei nicht eher zufrieden „until the Gaelic language and the Gaelic people would be extirpated root and branch from the Sutherland Estate; yes, from the Highlands of Scotland" (zit. nach Withers 1979, 48). Mit beginnender Industrialisierung zogen viele Gälen in die Städte der Lowlands (z. B. nach Glasgow) oder gingen nach Übersee. Die Folge war eine weitreichende Entvölkerung der Highlands und eine damit verbundene merkliche Schwächung des Gälischen.

4. Statistik und Ethnoprofile

Das Gälische ist in Schottland in den letzten 500 Jahren von 50% auf 1,4% im Jahre 1991 dramatisch zurückgegangen. Den Rückgang innerhalb des letzten Jahrhunderts belegen die Karten 133.2 und 133.3 eindrucksvoll. Seit 1981 ist ein Rückgang der gälischsprachigen Bevölkerung von 0,2% zu verzeichnen. Hinzu kommt, daß deren Altersverteilung wenig optimistisch ist. Insgesamt sprachen 1991 0,9% der 3–15jährigen, 1,2% der 16–44jährigen, 1,6% der 45–64jährigen, aber 2,2% der über 65jährigen gälisch. Dieser ungünstige Trend gilt auch für die beiden Regionen mit einem höheren bzw. hohen Anteil an Gälischsprechern. Sowohl in der Highland Region als auch auf den Äußeren Hebriden (den Western Isles) ist der Anteil an Gälischsprechern bei den über 65jährigen bei weitem am höchsten. Gälisch ist die Sprache der Älteren und Alten! Die pessimistischen Volkszählungszahlen sagen nichts über die Kompetenz der Befragten im Gälischen aus.

5. Soziolinguistische Lage

Wanderten Highlander in die englischsprachige Umgebung der Lowlands aus, überlebte das Gälische dort selten länger als zwei oder drei Generationen. Nach einer Phase der Zweisprachigkeit bedienten sich die Highlander ausschließlich des Englischen, der Sprache, mit der man es „zu etwas bringen" konnte und kann. Dies war auch das wichtigste Argument, mit dem junge Leute nach einem Aufenthalt in englischsprachigen Gebieten in die Highlands zurückkehrten und die Stellung des Gälischen dort unterminierten. Eine wesentliche Schwächung des Gälischen heutzutage auf den Western Isles ist nach MacKinnon (1991, 517) in dessen geringer Unterstützung durch junge Mütter bei ihren Kindern zu sehen. Selbst dort ist gälische Einsprachigkeit bereits ausgestorben, der Wechsel von Gälisch zu Englisch und umgekehrt jedoch noch recht häufig anzutreffen (vgl. Thomson 1983, 111 sowie 105 und die dort angegebene Literatur). Alle Anzeichen (vgl. auch die anderen Abschnitte) deuten heute darauf hin, daß, wenn nicht Einschneidendes sowohl im Bewußtsein der Bevölkerung als auch im Handeln des Staates passiert, Gälisch in Schottland dasselbe Schicksal erleiden wird wie Cornish und Manx, sicher noch nicht „before the end of the century", wie von Jackson (1958, 229) prophezeit, aber wohl nicht lange danach. Die Sprachenfrage war und ist in Schottland kein Politikum.

6. Sprachpolitische Lage

Im 17. Jahrhundert gab es Versuche, auf die gälischsprachige Bevölkerung einzuwirken. Die *Statutes of Iona* des Jahres 1609 und deren parlamentarische Ratifizierung im Jahre 1616 stellten den Versuch dar, durch die Errichtung eines auf dem Englischen gründenden Schulsystems das Gälische abzuschaffen. In dem Gesetz heißt es:

„Forsamekle as the Kingis Majestie haveing a speciall care and regaird that the new religion be advanceit and establisheit in all pairts of this Kingdome, and that all his Majesties subjectis, especially the youth, be exercised and trayned up in civilitie, godlines, knawledge and learning, that the vulgar Inglische toung be universallie plantit, and the Irische language (Gaelic), which is one of the chief and principal causes of the continewance of barbaritie and incivilitie amongis the inhabitants of the Iles and Heylandis, may be abolisheit and removit" (zit. nach Withers 1979, 44).

Als die Schulpflicht für Kinder von 5–13 Jahren 1872 eingeführt wurde, wurde in den Schulen ausschließlich das Englische verwen-

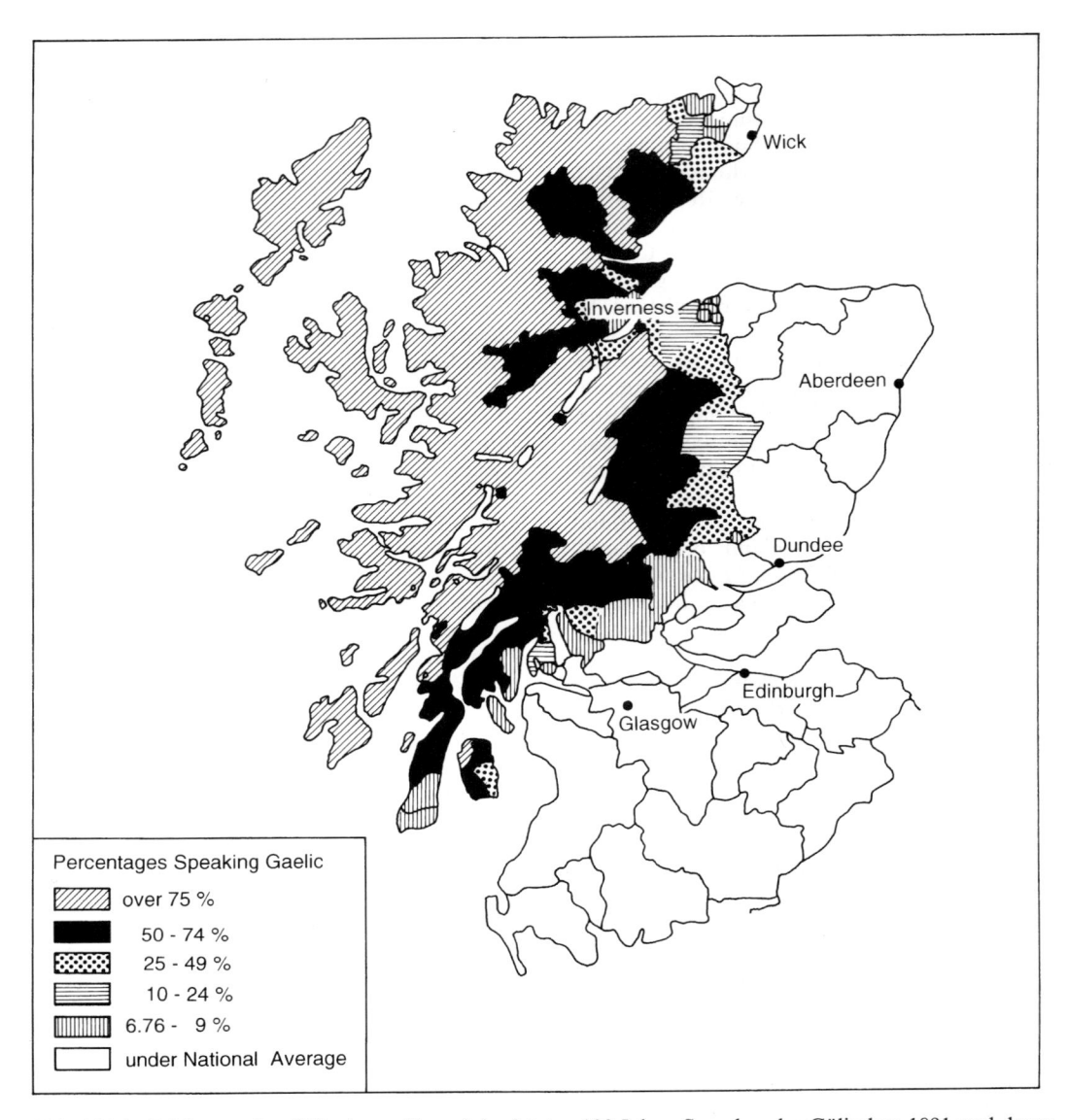

Abb. 133.2: Rückgang des Gälischen während der letzten 100 Jahre: Sprecher des Gälischen 1891 und deren prozentuale Verteilung (nach MacKinnon 1991, 522)

det. Gälisch wurde nicht geprüft. Es tauchte nur als Zugeständnis an die 2. und 3. Klasse auf. 1913 begegnen wir dem Konzept des *bilingual teaching*, um gälischsprachigen Kindern das Erlernen des Englischen zu erleichtern. Erst 1956 wurde Gälisch als Unterrichtsfach und Unterrichtssprache für andere Fächer an den Schulen zugelassen.

Heutzutage ist der rechtliche Status des Gälischen eingeschränkt. Es gibt z. B. kein Recht zur Verwendung des Gälischen in schottischen Gerichten. Die Western Isles, wo laut Volkszählung von 1991 mit 68,4% der bei weitem höchste Prozentsatz an Gälischsprechenden anzutreffen ist, sind seit 1975 ein eigener Verwaltungsbezirk. Regierungsamtliche Veröffentlichungen erscheinen hier in englischer und gälischer Sprache, so auch die über die Ergebnisse der Volkszählung: *1991 Census. Cunntas-sluaigh 1991: Monitor for Western Isles Islands Area. Paipear Comhairleachaidh Roinn nan Eilean an Iar.* General

133. English–Gälisch

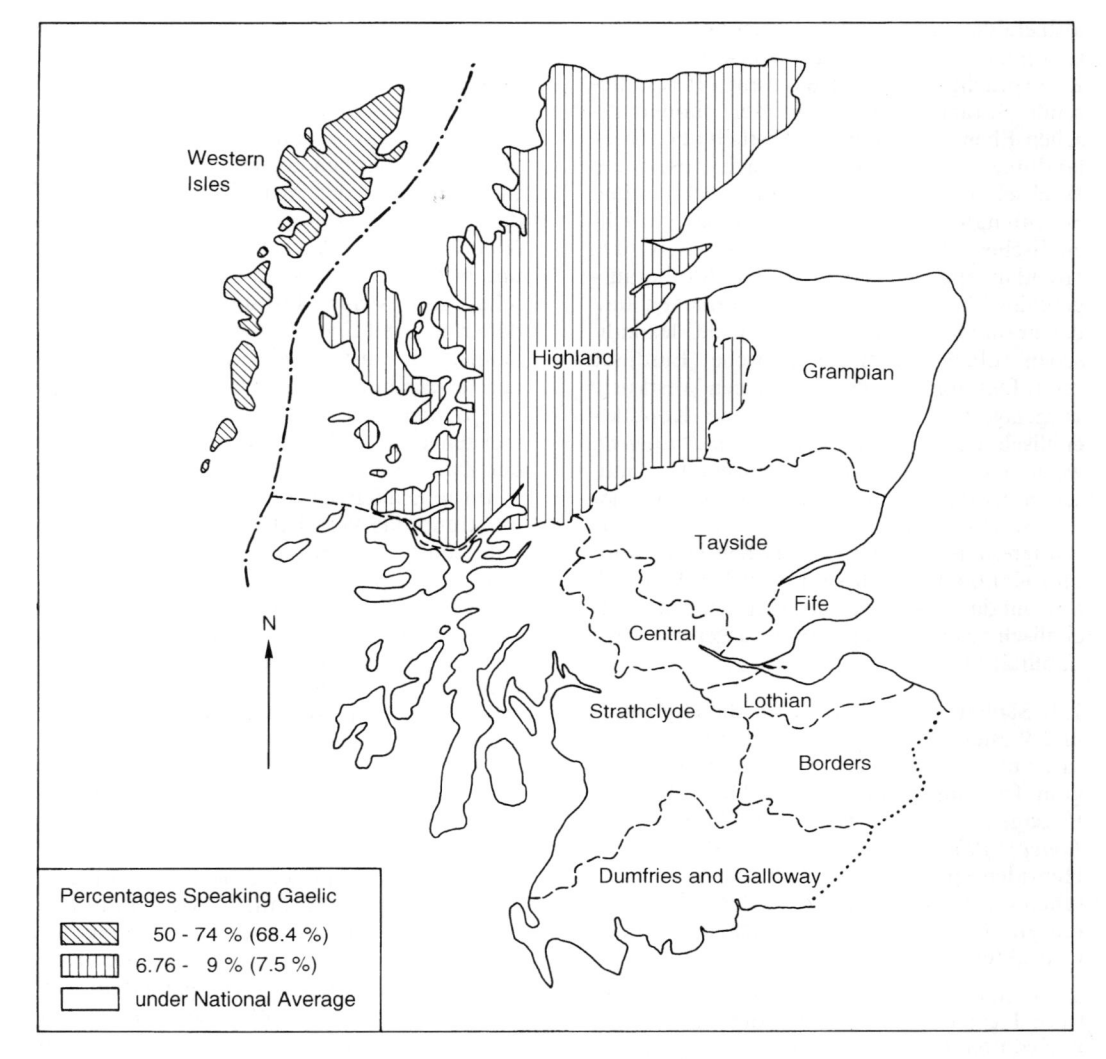

Percentages Speaking Gaelic
- 50 - 74 % (68.4 %)
- 6.76 - 9 % (7.5 %)
- under National Average

Abb. 133.3: Sprecher des Gälischen 1991 und deren prozentuale Verteilung (nach *1991 Census* 1993, 16)

Register Office Scotland. ARD-Oifis Claraidh Alba (1992). Das Gälische ist auf den Äußeren Hebriden und der Isle of Skye neben Englisch Unterrichtssprache in den Volksschulen (*Bilingual Schools*), andernorts in Schottland wird es in einigen Volksschulen (z. B. in Glasgow) als Zweitsprache unterrichtet. Während Radiosendungen in gälischer Sprache bereits überall in Schottland empfangen werden können, hat die britische Regierung erst Ende 1992 − viel − Geld für ein gälischsprachiges Fernsehprogramm zur Verfügung gestellt.

7. Allgemeines kontaktlinguistisches Porträt

7.1. Östlich der Hochlandlinie bildete sich einerseits ein Regionalstandard (schottisches Englisch oder *Standard Scottish English* oder *Educated Scots* genannt) und andererseits *Lowland* und *Insular Scots* heraus, also schottisch-englische Dialekte, die spätestens im 19. Jahrhundert reine Provinzdialekte geworden waren. Zwischen ihnen, besonders dem *broad Scots* und dem *Standard Scottish English* hat sich ein Dialekt − Standard-Kontinuum herausgebildet. Für den Nordosten des heutigen Grampian (Buchan) hat Wölck (1965) die Zweisprachigkeit und die daraus oft resultierende Sprachmischung auf der phonematischen Ebene beschrieben. Westlich der Hochlandlinie vollzog sich ziemlich rasch ein Wechsel vom Gälischen zum schulischen Schriftenglisch. Als Ergebnis dieses gälisch-englischen Sprachwechsels hat sich das Hochlandenglisch (*Highland English*) herausgebildet, das sowohl auf der lautlichen und der grammatischen als auch auf der lexikalischen Ebene deutliche gälische Einflüsse zeigt. Das auf den der schottischen Westküste vorgelagerten Inseln gesprochene Kontaktenglisch oder Inselenglisch (*Island English*) weist noch stärkere Interferenzen des Gälischen als das Hochlandenglisch auf, da hier der Sprachwechsel erst im 20. Jahrhundert erfolgte. Die Übergänge zwischen Hochland- und Kontaktenglisch sind natürlich fließend. Sowohl das Hochland- als auch das Kontaktenglisch zeichnen sich durch ausgeprägte Variabilität aus.

7.2. Sabban (1982, 14) hat für die Highlands und Western Isles festgestellt, daß in der Literatur mit sprachlichen Merkmalen dieser Region frei umgegangen wird. Die folgenden Passagen aus Lillian Beckwith, *The Hills is* (!) *Lonely* (1959) — einem Roman, der auf den Hebriden spielt — zeigen auf der grammatischen Ebene eine ganze Reihe der auf Interferenzen des Gälischen zurückzuführenden Charakteristika:

„Dear Madam, Its just now I saw your advert when I got the book for the knitting pattern I wanted from my cousin Catriona. I am sorry I did not write sooner if you are fixed up if you are not in any way fixed up I have a good good house stone and tiles and my brother Ruari who will wash down with lime twice every year. Ruari is married and lives just by. She is not damp. I live by myself and you could have the room that is not a kitchen and bedroom reasonable. I was in the kitchen of the lairds house till lately when he was changed God rest his soul the poor old gentleman that he was. You would be very welcomed. I have a cow also for milk and eggs and the minister at the manse will be referee if you wish such. Yours affectionately, Morag McDugan.
P. S. She is not thatched" (Beckwith 1988, 10)

„Surely its that quiet here even the sheeps themselves on the hills is lonely and as to the sea its that near I use it myself every day for the refusals" (Beckwith 1988, 11).

Folgende Erläuterungen seien zu den beiden kurzen Briefen angeführt: Die Wiederholung eines Adjektivs gilt im Gälischen als Intensivierung, daher *I have a good good house.* Im Gälischen steht das Adjektiv hinter dem Substantiv, das es qualifiziert, und nicht, wie im Englischen, davor, daher *bedroom reasonable.* Da es im Gälischen keinen unbestimmten Artikel gibt, geht der Artikelgebrauch im Brief durcheinander: *You could have the room that is not a kitchen.* Auch bezüglich der Genera unterscheiden sich beide Sprachen. Im Gälischen gibt es nur Maskulina und Feminina, daher im Brief *She* (*the house*) *is not thatched.* Schließlich weist das Gälische für alle Personen jeweils nur eine Verbform auf, daher *the sheeps themselves on the hills is lonely.* Die meisten dieser Merkmale dürften die Phase der Zweisprachigkeit kaum überdauern.

Im folgenden seien noch einige die Pronomina und das Verb betreffende Interferenzen aufgeführt: McArthur (1992, 470) zufolge sind „anticipatory pronoun constructions" typische Merkmale des Kontaktenglischen. Beispiele: *Who is he, the man?* oder *Did you see him, the minister?* In Anlehnung an das Gälische weichen Sprecher des Kontaktenglischen hinsichtlich des Tempusgebrauchs vom Standardenglischen ab. Da das Gälische zudem keine Verbform kennt, die den perfektiven Formen des Englischen in ihrer Bildungsweise entspricht, werden im Kontaktenglischen nicht-perfektive Verbformen zur Beschreibung einer in der Gegenwart fortbestehenden Situation gebraucht, wie z. B. in *I am a widower for five years* (Standardenglisch: *I have been a widower for five years*). Die Konstruktion *be* + *after* + Verb-*ing* ist ein typisches Merkmal des Kontaktenglischen, das eine Übernahme aus dem Gälischen darstellt (auch in Irland und in Wales belegt und sogar nach Neufundland ausgewandert ist). Das vollständige Paradigma sieht folgendermaßen aus:

Tab. 133.2: Die Konstruktion *be* + *after* + Verb-*ing*

Gälisch	Kontakt-englisch	Standard-englisch
tha e air bualadh	he is after striking	he has struck
bha e air bualadh	he was after striking	he had struck
bithidh e air bualadh	he will be after striking	he will have struck
bhitheadh e air bualadh	he would be after striking	he would have struck

Die beiden ersten Formen fand Sabban (1982, 162) in dem von ihr erhobenen Datenmaterial belegt, die beiden letzten in literarischen Darstellungen. Vgl. Sabban (1982, 54 ff und 1985, 125 ff) zu weiteren grammatischen Eigentümlichkeiten des Kontaktenglischen und zur Verwendung dieser Merkmale in der Literatur.

Als Beispiel dafür, daß sich manche Merkmale des Hochlandenglischen nicht so ausschließlich auf gälisches Substrat zurückführen lassen, wie manche Autoren es glauben machen wollen, sei Bähr (1974, 165) angeführt, der bezüglich des bestimmten Artikels kategorisch bemerkt: „Im Gälischen steht der Artikel bei Sprachen und Abstrakten. So sagt man *in the Gaelic* und *at the school* statt *in Gaelic* und *at school*". Zum einen ist der Artikelgebrauch hier sowohl im schottischen Englisch als auch in nordenglischen Dialekten weitverbreitet (zu letzterem Aspekt vgl. Viereck 1991, Karten S 5 und S 6), und zum anderen kann der bestimmte Artikel im Hochland- und Inselenglischen auch vor Krankheitsbezeichnungen stehen (*the headache, the toothache*), bei denen das Gälische diesbezüglich uneinheitlich verfährt. Auch hier ist eine englische Einflußquelle zu veranschlagen, die zumindest unterstützend gewirkt hat, denn der Artikelgebrauch ist sowohl im schottischen Englisch als auch in englischen Dialekten typisch, ein weiteres Zeugnis für die sprachgeschichtliche Gemeinsamkeit dieser Gebiete. Im letztgenannten Bereich ist die Angabe mit bestimmtem Artikel sogar am häufigsten belegt (vgl. Viereck 1991, Karten S 1 und S 2).

7.3. Da im Gälischen /b, d, g/ stimmlos sind, werden englische /b, d, g/ vielfach als /p, t, k/ gesprochen bzw. mißverstanden, was auch Schreibungen wie *pox* für *box* und *inteet* für *indeed* erklärt. Das Gälische hat keine stimmhaften Sibilanten. Daher werden englisch /z, ʒ, ʤ/ als [s, ʃ, tʃ] ausgesprochen, wobei die Oppositionen /s ≠ z/, /ʃ ≠ ʒ/, /tʃ ≠ ʤ/ verlorengehen. Schreibungen wie *chust* für *just* und *pleshure* für *pleasure* weisen darauf hin. Weitere Aussprachemerkmale des Hochland- und Kontaktenglischen sind Ersetzung von Englisch /θ/, /ð/ und /w/, die es im Gälischen nicht gibt, durch [s], [ts] für die beiden dentalen Frikative sowie [u]. Der englische Personenname *Macwatt* wird daher zu *Macouat* gälisiert. Die englische Opposition /θ/ ≠ /s/ fällt in /s/ zusammen, wodurch Homophone vom Typ /maus/ für *mouse* und *mouth* entstehen. Laut Wells (1982, 413 f) fallen im Gälischen /r/ plus /s/ in einem retroflexen Frikativ [ʂ] zusammen, was im Hochland- und Inselenglischen die Aussprachen [foʂ] *force*, [ˈmeʂe] *mercy* und [ˈpaʂls] *parcels* erklärt. Zu weiteren Aussprachemerkmalen des Hochland- und Kontaktenglischen vgl. McArthur (1992, 470) und Shuken (1985 a, 131 ff und 1985 b, 145 ff), zur Intonation vgl. McClure (1980, 201 ff).

7.4. Hinsichtlich des Wortschatzes des Hochlandenglischen bemerkt McArthur (1992, 470): „In general, vocabulary is the same as in Scottish English at large, and most people use such vernacular Scots words as 'bairn' (child), 'brae' (slope), 'greet' (weep), 'oot' (out), the negatives 'no' ('he is no in') and '-na' ('I canna say') and 'ay' (yes)". Im Kontaktenglischen fand Sabban (1982, 486 ff) nur wenige unverändert übernommene gälische Wörter. Diese hängen insbesondere mit gälischer Tradition und Lebensweise zusammen, wie *céilidh* 'gesellige Zusammenkunft' (allerdings mit englischem -*s* Plural). Auf gälisches Substrat zurückgehen dürfte das Anhängen der Diminutivform -*ag* als Koseform an Jungennamen wie z. B. *Tomag* und *Johnag*, die im Gälischen feminin ist und als Endung für Mädchennamen dient. Ein Merkmal, das als siedlungsgeschichtliches Indiz für die Wurzeln des in den amerikanischen Appalachen gesprochenen Englisch gilt, ist positives *anymore*, in der Bedeutung 'moreover, anyhow' wie in *The match is finished anymore*, das in anderen Varietäten des Englischen und natürlich im Standardenglisch nur in verneinenden und interrogativen Sätzen auftritt (vgl. Montgomery 1989, 241 f). Diese Verwendung geht zurück auf das gälische Adverb *tuilleadh*, das 'more, anymore, moreover' bedeutet und auch in positiven Sätzen gebraucht werden kann. Zu weiteren Beispielen, auch möglichen semantischen Entlehnungen aus dem Gälischen, vgl. z. B. Sabban (1982, 484 ff).

8. Kritische Wertung der verwendeten Quellen und Literatur

Scots, das in diesem Beitrag natürlich nicht im Vordergrund steht, ist sowohl in historischer als auch in gegenwartsbezogener regionalsprachlicher und soziolinguistischer Hinsicht sehr intensiv untersucht worden (vgl. z. B. MacLeod 1993 und Fenton/MacDonald

1994). Auch Orthographieprobleme und die Verwendung des Scots in der Literatur wurden oft behandelt. Für das Gälische gilt das in diesem Ausmaß noch nicht. Bereits seit langem liegen die drei Bände des *Linguistic Atlas of Scotland, Scots Section,* vor (vgl. Mather/Speitel 1975, 1977 und 1986), das Pendant der *Gaelic Section* wird 1996 unter dem Titel *Survey of the Gaelic Dialects of Scotland* (Dublin, 5 Bde.) erscheinen. Intensiver untersucht werden sollten die Faktoren und die Resultate der Infiltration des Gälischen durch das Englische, ein Bereich mit historischen, dialektalen und soziolinguistischen Dimensionen (vgl. Gillies 1980, 1 ff). So gibt es für das Gälische z.B. noch nichts Vergleichbares zu Parry-Williams (1923) und Piette (1973). Größeres Interesse erfuhren demgegenüber das Hochland- und Inselenglisch und hier besonders die Formen, die sich auf gälisches Substrat zurückführen lassen.

9. Bibliographie (in Auswahl)

Bähr, Dieter (1974): *Standard English und seine geographischen Varianten,* München.

Beckwith, Lillian (1988): „The Hills is lonely". In: *A Hebridean Omnibus,* Beckwith, L. London, 5–207.

Catford, John C. (1957): „The linguistic survey of Scotland". In: *Orbis* 6, 105–121.

Fenton, Alexander/MacDonald, Donald A. (Eds.) (1994): *Studies in Scots and Gaelic,* Edinburgh.

Gillies, William (1980): „English influence on contemporary Scottish Gaelic". In: *Scottish literary journal, Supplement* No. 12, 1–12.

Grant, William (Ed.) (1931): *The Scottish national dictionary,* Vol. I, Edinburgh.

Jackson, Kenneth (1958): „The situation of the Scottish Gaelic language and the work of the linguistic survey of Scotland". In: *Lochlann* 1, 229–234.

MacLeod, Iseabail (1993): „Some problems of Scottish lexicography". In: *English world-wide* 14, 115–128.

MacKinnon, Kenneth M. (1991): „Language-maintenance and viability in contemporary Gaelic communities: Skye and the Western Isles today". In: *Language contact in the British Isles,* Ureland, P. S./Broderick, G. (Eds.), Tübingen.

Mather, James Y./Speitel, Hans-Henning (Eds.) (1975, 1977, 1986): *The linguistic atlas of Scotland: Scots section,* London.

McArthur, Tom (Ed.) (1992): *The Oxford companion to the English language,* Oxford.

McClure, J. Derrick R. (1980): „Western Scottish intonation: a preliminary study". In: *The melody of language,* Waugh, L. R./van Schooneveld, C. H. (Eds.), Baltimore.

Montgomery, Michael (1989): „Exploring the roots of Appalachian English". In: *English world-wide* 10, 227–278.

Murray, James A. H. (1873): „Present limits of the Celtic in Scotland". Anhang von *The dialect of the southern counties of Scotland,* London, 231–237.

Parry-Williams, Thomas H. (1923): *The English element in Welsh,* London.

Piette, Jean R. F. (1973): *French loanwords in middle Breton,* Cardiff.

Ravenstein, Ernest G. (1879): „On the Celtic languages in the British Isles: A statistical survey". In: *Journal of the Royal statistical society* 42, 579–636.

Sabban, Annette (1982): *Gälisch-Englischer Sprachkontakt. Zur Variabilität des Englischen im gälischsprachigen Gebiet Schottlands. Eine empirische Studie,* Heidelberg.

Sabban, Annette (1985): „On the variability of Hebridean English syntax". In: *Focus on: Scotland,* Görlach, M. (Ed.), Amsterdam.

Selkirk, 5th Earl of (1806): *Observations on the present state of the Highlands of Scotland,* London.

Shuken, Cynthia R. (1985a): „Vowel systems in Hebridean English". In: *Scottish language* 5, 131–139.

Shuken, Cynthia R. (1985b): „Variation in Hebridean English". In: *Focus on: Scotland,* Görlach, M. (Ed.), Amsterdam.

Speitel, Hans-Henning (1981): „The geographical position of the Scots dialect in relation to the Highlands of Scotland". In: *So many people longages and tonges,* Benskin, M./Samuels, M. L. (Eds.), Edinburgh.

Thomson, Derick S. (Ed.) (1983): *The companion to Gaelic Scotland,* Oxford.

Viereck, Wolfgang, in collaboration with Heinrich Ramisch (1991): *The computer developed linguistic atlas of England 1,* Tübingen.

Walker, John (1808): *An economical history of the Hebrides and Highlands of Scotland,* Edinburgh.

Wells, John C. (1982): *Accents of English 2: The British Isles,* Cambridge.

Withers, Charles W. J. (1979): „The language geography of Scottish Gaelic". In: *Scottish literary journal. Supplement* No. 9, 41–54.

Withers, Charles W. J. (1984): *Gaelic in Scotland 1698–1981,* Edinburgh.

Wölck, Wolfgang (1965): *Phonematische Analyse der Sprache von Buchan,* Heidelberg.

1991 Census. Monitor for Scotland (1993) Edinburgh.

Wolfgang Viereck, Bamberg (Deutschland)

134. Ireland

1. Geography and demography
2. Territorial history and national development
3. Politics, economy and general cultural and religious situation
4. Statistics and ethnoprofiles
5. Sociolinguistic situation
6. Language political situation
7. Contactlinguistic portraits of Irish/English
8. Critical evaluation of the sources and literature used
9. Bibliography (selected)

1. Geography and demography

Ireland lies off the western coast of Europe and is part of the group of islands that include Great Britain. The island of Ireland is approximately 84,400 sq. km. The main features of its physical geography are a large limestone plain, containing considerable areas of bogland and many large lakes, in the centre of the island ringed almost completely by coastal highlands.

Politically, the major part of the island became an independent state in 1922, but the north-eastern region (Northern Ireland) is part of the United Kingdom. In 1841, the population of that part of the island comprising the present Irish state was 6.5 m, but widespread famines in 1846−47 caused a sudden decline to 5.1 m by 1851, due to death and emigration. Emigration − primarily to North America and Great Britain − continued to be the dominant demographic characteristic until 1961, when the population was only 2.6 m. Improved economic performance has, however, reversed these trends in recent decades and the present (c. 1991) population of the state is 3.6 m.

Nearly two-thirds of the population now live in towns and villages. The main towns are nearly all situated on the coast and originated as ports and trading centres. In general, the north-eastern, eastern and southern regions are the more urbanised and industrialised and they contain the larger towns. Dublin is the capital of the Republic (pop. 0.9 m), and the other large centres are Cork (0.15 m), Limerick (0.07 m), Galway (0.04 m) and Waterford (0.04 m).

By comparison with European patterns, a very high proportion of Ireland's population is concentrated in the younger age-groups. Nearly half the population is under 25 years.

2. Territorial history and national development

2.1. Early history

Evidence of human settlement in Ireland dating back to about 6,000 BC has been found, but the most important settlers − the Celts − came much later, in successive waves from about 600 BC to the time of Christ. They quickly dominated the earlier settlers and created a hierarchical political structure made up of a large number of local kingdoms nested with five provincial kingdoms. The island was not, however, politically unified but shared a common culture and language. Linguistically, the Celts belonged to the Indo-European family of languages. The economy was of a simple agrarian type, with society rigidly stratified into classes and regulated by an elaborate legal code.

Christianity was introduced into Ireland in the 5th century and it is from this period that written historical sources become available. The distinctive aspect of Irish Christianity was the central role played by monasticism. The great monasteries were centres of learning and culture and the largest of them may have functioned as towns, although due to their generally remote locations none developed as such into medieval times. The vitality of the monastic culture manifested itself in the period between the 6th and 9th centuries in (a) the establishment of monastic communities by Irish monks across a Europe recovering from the Dark Ages and (b) the production of an enormous range of elaborately designed ornamental jewellery, altar vessels and illuminated manuscripts. With some justification, this period is seen as the Golden Age of Irish history.

2.2. The Middle Ages

For two centuries, from around 800 to about 1000, Ireland experienced a series of invasions by the Vikings. Their attacks were initially directed at the wealth of the monasteries, but Vikings subsequently settled to establish trading centres around the Irish coast. Most of the larger towns were, in fact, founded by them. The political threat posed by the invasions eventually stimulated a measure of unity among the Irish kings which led to a comprehensive defeat of the Vikings in

1014. This military success seemed for a time to hold open the possibility of the development in Ireland of a strong centralised monarchy along European lines, but this was arrested in the 12th century by the arrival in Ireland of the Normans. While the Normans — with their superior military resources — quickly dominated three quarters of the island, and established the first political foothold for England in Ireland, they were not able to sustain their initial position. By the end of the 15th century, they had either been assimilated into the local population or pushed back, by successive counter-attacks, to a small area around Dublin on the east coast.

2.3. Early modern period

The Tudor monarchs sought to re-establish the Anglo-Norman dominance. A series of military campaigns over the 16th and early 17th centuries overthrew the native political system and established, for the first time, the dominion of England over all of Ireland. Religion was an added complication and divisive factor in the new political order. The new colonists were Protestant, the dispossessed Irish and old Anglo-Norman were Catholic. The persistence of this religious divide consolidated and sustained the cultural division between the relatively small Protestant ascendancy and the majority of the native population. To the political and religious barriers, a series of legal enactments were added in the 18th century which prevented Catholics from participating in economic or political affairs. The disaffected majority were, nonetheless, always a potential source of instability and, to minimise the dangers, in 1800 the Act of Union formally united Ireland and England.

2.4. Modern Ireland

The nineteenth century saw the gradual emergence of the Catholic majority as a powerful political force. The first half of the century was dominated politically by the struggle for Catholic Emancipation — which succeeded in 1829 in having virtually all the legal disabilities against Catholics removed — and the Great Famine in the 1840s. The second half of the century was dominated by campaigns for political independence and land reform. In the 1880s, both these struggles coalesced into a broad political movement for Home Rule. Although not successful, the following decades saw the growing emergence of the Irish nationalist movement. A military rising in 1916 was crushed, but the rebellion continued, and the sustained War of Independence in 1919—21 led to the Anglo—Irish Treaty of 1921 which conceded Free State status to 26 of the 32 counties of Ireland. The remaining six — Northern Ireland — remained within the UK.

The establishment of the Free State was followed by a civil war, which lasted until 1923. After this, the normal processes of democratic government were successfully established and maintained. Ireland remained neutral during the Second World War and in 1948 the Republic of Ireland Act was passed, removing the remaining constitutional link with Britain. In 1973, Ireland became a member of the European Communities (see Moody/Martin 1984, Graham/Proudfoot 1993 for a fuller historical treatment).

2.5. The origin and development of language contact

The history of language contact in Ireland is closely related to the political, social and economic interaction between the island and its nearest and more powerful neighbour, England. Even as late as the sixteenth century the Irish language was the sole or main language used in Ireland and the English monarchy had established only a modest and tentative foothold in eastern Ireland. But the political changes which began in the seventeenth century had profound long-term consequences for the spatial and social distribution of the two languages. The dispossession and dispersal of the Irish aristocratic families introduced relatively large number of native-born English to form a new landlord class.

While these developments within the upper class gave a decisive impetus to the process of language shift, the role of the towns, as the main locations of British military and administrative influence, was also significant. Over the eighteenth century the shift to English spread through the urban network, diffusing more slowly but relentlessly into the rural hinterland along a general east—west axis. The first Census of Population to include a question on language was undertaken in 1851. While difficulties of interpretation arise because of the nature of the data, it has been calculated that about 45% of the population were Irish-speaking during the last quarter of the eighteenth century, but this percentage had declined to just under 30% by the mid-nineteenth century.

Because the Great Famine was relatively more severe in western and poorer regions, most of those who died or emigrated were Irish-speakers. This not merely altered the demographic balance between the two language communities but the subsequent rise of large-scale emigration added a powerful new weight to the incentive to learn English.

However, as this linguistic shift entered an advanced phase, a movement for the preservation of Irish began to emerge. The most influential organisation of this type − the Gaelic League (est. 1893), in fact, took the offensive, aiming for the restoration of the vernacular language rather than just simply trying to preserve it. Although the movement started very slowly, within fifteen years after its foundation some 950 branches had been established throughout Ireland. Its influence was very considerable. (Lee 1989, Tovey et al. 1989)

In the early twentieth century the language movement was incorporated in the wider political independence struggle. While the Anglo−Irish War was still in progress (1917−1922), the Provisional Government established a Department of the National Language. Despite the well established dynamic of decline and the unpromising contemporary pattern of bilingualism − no more than 18% of the populations were Irish-speakers, the newly independent state in 1922 launched a comprehensive strategy to reverse the process of shift towards English and restore Irish as the national language. The crucial difference between the Irish case and the language policy of other European nation-states, of course, was the fact that by the beginning of the twentieth century, Irish was the language of a dominated, peripheral minority rather than an elite group.

To reverse the process of decline, therefore, the state itself had to try to create counter-pressures of sufficient persuasiveness. To this end it used its authority to change the structure of the language market prevailing in Ireland in order to enhance the symbolic, cultural and economic value attaching to competence to speak Irish. Some of the more significant policies sought to influence aspects of the operation of educational and labour market mechanisms.

3. Politics, economy and general cultural and religious situation

Although Ireland achieved political independence in 1922, it remained a dependent economy within the larger economic units of the British Isles and, since 1973, the EC. With several other states on the European periphery it shares the characteristics of a colonial past, a large agricultural sector, and weak industrial and urban infrastructure. The post-independence phase of development in the pattern of language contact cannot be understood except within this political and economic context. The traditional Irish-speaking areas on the western seaboard − collectively known as 'The Gaeltacht' − form an underdeveloped part of an economy and polity that is itself 'semi-peripheral'.

The development policies followed by the new state did not succeed in stabilising either the national economy or that of the western region which contained most Irish-speaking districts. Output in the agricultural sector did not grow between 1922 and 1960, and all rural areas suffered extensive out-migration. Substantial changes in economic policies in the 1960s reversed there trends and even rural areas − although somewhat later than their urban counterparts − enjoyed a measure of prosperity in the 1960s and 1970s. At this point, however, the social and regional structure of the state had been transformed. Agriculture was no longer the main occupation and the majority of the population lived in towns and cities. (Breen et al. 1990)

Even in the past few decades there have been some significant changes in the social and economic organisation of Irish society. Within the middle class occupations there has been substantial growth in skilled manual, service and professional employment, and a decline in public sector employment. Public sector employment had in the past been of great importance to the survival of Irish.

The political and social climate is now very different from that during which the original language strategy was formulated. The speed with which social change has occurred in Ireland, and the ambiguous feelings, inherited from colonial times, about Irish identity do not provide a secure ideological base for Irish language policy (see PAC 1988 for a fuller discussion).

4. Statistics and ethnoprofiles

Ireland's census language question provides one of the oldest continuous series of regularly collected, standard public statistics on any language in the world. Apart from two fifteen year intervals, it has been included every ten years in the national census of population since 1851. However, the question as put to census respondents, simply asks if they can speak Irish only or Irish and English. While, as a measure of language proficiency, the language question in the census is neither very precise nor informative, recent reserach has shown that the margin of error in census data does not invalidate its use for the purposes of analysis (O Riagáin 1988).

In 1981, some 1,018,413 persons (31% of the national population) were returned as Irish-speakers in the Census of Population. The ratio of Irish-speakers, as measured in the census, had increased steadily throughout the twentieth century from 18% in 1911. National percentages, however, hide some important regional variations. In 1911, the designated Irish-speaking areas on the west coast (collectively referred to as the Gaeltacht) contained 16% of the state's population but 57% of Irish-speakers. In 1981, following more than half century of continuous emigration from western rural areas and language shift within the residual population, they contained only 2.3% of the national population and 7.4% of Irish-speakers. Because the designated Irish-speaking areas, prior to their revision in 1956, were grossly inaccurate, these statistics overstate the rate of actual language shift. But on the census evidence it appears clear Irish was not maintained in its traditional core-area, although in 1981 these areas still contained 45% of Irish-speaking homes.

Thus, the increase in the national percentage of Irish-speakers, which can be observed across successive censuses of population, was due to a significant increase in the number of Irish-speakers in regions which were English-speaking in 1911.

5. Sociolinguistic situation

5.1. The incidence of bilingualism in society

Census data, of course, at best only measure the ability to speak Irish. More comprehensive and detailed research conducted since 1970 (CILAR 1975, O Riagáin/O Gliasáin 1994) clearly demonstrate that Irish is not extensively used in home, neighbourhood or work domains. Recent surveys would suggest that only about 5% of the national population use Irish as their first or main language. A further 10% use Irish regularly but less intensively in conversation or reading. In the state generally, these levels would appear to have remained stable over recent decades. As opposed to these relatively low ratios of spoken or active use of Irish, the ratios of passive use, primarily listening/watching Irish language radio and television programmes, are considerably higher. About 25% of the population watch some Irish language programme weekly.

In the Gaeltacht, where Irish has never ceased to be spoken, its use is very much higher than the national average. For example, in 1973, which is the last year in which a survey was conducted in all Gaeltacht areas, frequent and extensive home use of Irish was reported by about 60% of respondents (as compared to 5% nationally) and differences in work and social contexts are of the same order.

While in 1911, Irish-speaking families were predominantly found within the small farming sector in the western regions, by 1981 the urban professional, administrative and service classes had emerged as the groups with the highest relative and absolute proportions of Irish-speakers. While the current socio-economic status of the residents of the Gaeltacht areas reflects small farm and village occupations, in the urban areas Irish is now more likely to be used among higher socio-economic groups, particularly but not solely in the public sector. There is also a strong relationship between use of Irish and educational attainment. In survey data, there is a marked association between those with high levels of ability in Irish and those reporting intensive use of Irish. But in turn, high levels of competence in Irish are associated with high levels of education and not with the home. Therefore, bilingualism is more prevalent among the more highly educated groups.

5.2. Bilingual reproduction

The traditional Irish-speaking communities now account for less than 2% of the national population, they are very scattered and fragmented and a substantial minority of the residents in these areas do not use Irish frequently or, in many cases, at all.

Outside of the small Gaeltacht areas, only about one quarter of those who grew up in Irish language homes use Irish with the same intensity in their current homes. The marked variations in the ratios of Irish-speakers in different age-groups suggests a widespread discontinuity in use-patterns over the life-cycle of bilingual persons. Use of the language appears to be most intensive during schoolyears after which it is discontinued in the case of many individuals. These discontinuities are indicative of the weak position of bilingualism in Irish society generally. Except in Gaeltacht areas bilingualism in Ireland is based rather loosely on a thin distribution of family and social networks which have a degree of underpinning from a variety of state policies in education, work-place and media institutions (see below). But these networks are dispersed and weakly established and are very vulnerable to the loss of members over time as they are not sufficiently large or vibrant enough to easily attract and retain replacements.

However, it would also appear that a significant proportion of current users of Irish began to use the language in their adult years. This group did not have an Irish language home background, and did not appear to have had any strong association with Irish during their school years. How and why this group began to use Irish is not entirely clear from the research, but in the past it appears that Irish began to be used 'on marriage or on the establishment of their own households' (CILAR 1975). This group includes many of the small but growing minority of parents who have chosen Irish medium education for their children, and there is evidence to suggest that these schools help to establish or affirm home bilingualism and to introduce parents to Irish-speaking networks.

The existence of this last group of Irish-speakers, despite their small size, is evidence that Irish-speaking networks possess a capacity to recruit new members. This must be set against their overall inability to ensure an efficient reproduction of bilinguals.

5.3. Attitudes towards Irish

The strategy of reversing language shift, initiated by the language revival movement and state intervention has cut across a long-established decline, thereby generating a complex pattern of positive and negative attitudes. In the decades immediately following independence, the Romantic imagery which enveloped the Irish language greatly enhanced its status. But this perspective slowly waned, and the last couple of decades have seen a more sophisticated understanding of the cultural significance of Irish emerge in literary and intellectual circles. With a growing sophistication, however, has come a growth in uncertainty. While the process of rescuing the Irish language from its former metaphorical setting can be discerned in current debates, many of the older associations still retain a potency in the minds of sections of the population.

On the basis of large-scale national surveys of attitudes conducted in 1973, the Committee on Irish Language Attitudes Research (CILAR) observed that "the average person would seem to place considerable value on the symbolic role of the Irish language in ethnic identification and as a cultural value in and of itself. But while this would appear to be the central attitudinal element (and its strength is sufficient to support a desire to guarantee the transmission of Irish) it seems to be qualified by a generally pessimistic view of the language's future and a feeling of its inappropriateness in modern life". More recent surveys confirm the stability of this attitudinal pattern (O Riagáin/O Gliasáin 1994). If anything, the role of the Irish language in ethnic identification has strengthened slightly, but without any corresponding abatement in public pessimism about the language's future.

Although the Committee on Irish Language Attitudes Reseach appears to have established a relationship between the Irish language and ethnic identification, this finding is not without problems. It does not appear from its own analysis that this particular dimension of language attitudes is closely linked to actual personal behaviour supportive of Irish. Whereas these indicators serve to identify the extent to which Irish is seen to be a symbol of ethnic identification, it does not necessarily say anything about the vitality of ethnicity itself.

6. Language political situation

We turn now to the specifics of language policy. The language revival strategy formulated in the 1920s had three elements. The first was the maintenance of Irish as the spoken language in those areas where it was still the community language. As these areas were among the most impoverished and remote areas in the state, this dimension of the strategy quickly took on the character of a regional economic development programme. However, in 1926 the Irish-speaking areas contained only 16% of the national population. Elsewhere the objective was revival, for Irish-speakers were only a tiny scattered proportion of an almost entirely English-speaking population. Accordingly, the state looked to the educational system for an increase in the numbers of Irish-speakers in society. This was the 'Revival' part of the strategy, but it is not often enough noted that it was only part of a wider programme, which contained a substantial maintenance element as well. Both these dimensions of the strategy were serviced by a third, which was concerned with the provision of the necessary infrastructure for maintenance and revival dimensions alike (e. g. constitutional and legal status of Irish; standardisation and modernisation of the language etc.).

In the seventy years since the policy was first formulated, but particularly in the period up to about 1960, this strategy was implemented by the state with a substantial degree of commitment and vigour. There were, however, significant variations in the extent to which different age, regional and social groups supported individual policies.

However, with regard to the major policy areas, survey evidence would indicate that a majority of the population continue to support policies to maintain Irish in the Gaeltacht, to teach it in the schools, to provide Irish language services on the national television channels, to use Irish on public notices, to provide state services in Irish and officials who could speak Irish, to have one standard dialect in Irish and to support the voluntary Irish language organisations. Significantly, in all of these matters, there was an increase rather than a decrease in public support between 1973 and 1993 (CILAR 1975, O Riagáin/O Gliasáin 1994).

Space does not permit an examination of this strategy in detail, but the following sections deal with the most important components.

6.1. Irish-speaking areas

Because of its underdeveloped economy, the state has given the Gaeltacht priority treatment by comparison with other rural areas. Since 1926, when the policy was initially formulated, Gaeltacht policies have been better funded and more innovative. At every stage the theory and practice of national economic and social policy shaped discussions about Gaeltacht policy, affecting the way in which the problem was perceived, the search for possible solutions and the substance and style of state intervention. Thus in the decades immediately following independence the state's approach to the economic problems of the Gaeltacht were in keeping with the tenor of its generally very conservative development philosophy.

Land reorganisation, fishing and rural industries formed the core of state activity from about 1930 to about 1950. However, by 1950 the capacity for further re-settlement was limited, and in any case, this element of policy never came near to meeting the expectations of the government. Emigration had continued at unacceptable levels and there was evidence of further language shift within the Gaeltacht areas.

In the 1950s and 1960s, Gaeltacht policy was extensively re-orientated towards small-scale industry, forestry, fishing and tourism rather than agriculture. In recent decades this re-vamped policy has recorded some success. Emigration was halted in the 1970s and population levels again began to increase with the growth in employment opportunities outside of agriculture. However, the growth of employment has not been sufficient to absorb all of the outflow from agriculture and the entry into the labour market of school-leavers. Out-migration continues among the young adult age groups. More importantly, within the residual population the progressive language shift to English continues. This is related to the high level of in-migration and return migration which has accompanied the economic restructuring of the Gaeltacht.

Thus, 'the Irish Gaeltacht exemplifies the dilemmas of state management of both economic development and linguistic processes in a disadvantaged rural region. Economic change brings with it new contexts and social roles together with greater population mobility and heterogenity. The traditional agrarian economy is further marginalised from commercial agricultural progress. Established social networks are progressively incorporated into wider economic and social systems. Cultural autonomy and linguistic distinctiveness are substantially eroded'. (PAC 1988, O Riagáin 1992)

6.2. Irish in the schools

The teaching of Irish was made compulsory throughout the education system in the 1920s; the ultimate objective was to have *all* educational programmes taught through Irish. This policy was vigorously pursued by the state up to the 1950s at which point just over half the state's primary schools were offering an immersion programme of a full or partial type; i.e., programmes where the teaching medium was Irish. Subsequently, however, this pattern slowly yielded to the type of programme in which Irish was generally only taught as a subject and other subjects were taught through English. Furthermore, although the proportions of children receiving post-primary education increased rapidly in the period since 1960, the effect of this on acquisition of proficiency in Irish was countered by the discontinuation of the policy of making Irish a compulsory subject for state examinations in 1973.

All Irish children continue to learn Irish in both primary and post-primary schools as a subject, but despite some thirteen years experience in the case of the average child, these programmes do not generally produce highly competent active users of Irish. The speaking ability of the majority is only moderate or, in the case of a growing minority, negligible. (PAC 1986)

However, it must be noted that since 1970 there has been a revived interest in "all-Irish" or immersion-type programmes and some 50 schools have been established in English-speaking areas in this period in response to pressure from parents.

The age-specific language data in the census shows that the national increase in the proportion of Irish-speakers was primarily caused by a continual improvement — since the 1920s — in the proportion of young adult cohorts able to speak Irish. In 1981, 51% of the age-group between 15–19 years were returned as Irish-speakers in the census. As children do not begin schooling in Ireland until they have reached the age of four, the ratio of Irish-speakers in the young childhood cohort (3–4 years) is generally taken as a measure of the incidence of Irish-speaking homes. The percentage hardly moved from the 5% level since the 1920s. It is thus clear that the above average ratios of Irish-speakers in young adult groups is due to the schools rather than home or community bilingualism. Although over time the proportion of Irish-speakers in older adult cohorts also improved and continues to improve, the improvement is much smaller than the ratio of Irish-speakers in school-age cohorts would suggest. The constant 'slippage' from the relatively high levels of ability attained at school as the cohort moved into adulthood clearly reflects the low incidence of bilingualism in society.

Research findings show clearly that long-term ability levels and commitment to use Irish are related to the duration and intensity of Irish language programmes in the schools. (CILAR 1975, PAC 1986) Thus, those who received immersion-type teaching in their school years were ten times more likely to be now using Irish intensively than those who had studied Irish as a subject only. Apart from those who were exposed to immersion type courses, it is usually amongst those who stay in the system the longest and who take the academically most demanding syllabus that become proficient in Irish. In 1983, nearly three quarters of current users of Irish had post-primary schooling and nearly half had taken the higher level course in Irish.

Thus, notwithstanding the failure to sustain the immersion type programmes, it remains clear that if the schools had not continued to produce a small but committed percentage of bilinguals, the maintenance of urban-based Irish-speaking networks would long since have failed.

6.3. The work domain

As noted above, bilingual competence is a feature of the higher socio-economic groups. To be more exact, it is those fractions dependent on state employment that contain the largest proportions of competent and committed bilinguals. In fact some 60% of persons with a fluent competence in Irish are found in the middle and working class fractions dependent on state employment. By comparison, the percentages of such persons in other middle, working and farming fractions are much lower. However, among the public sector fractions themselves there are differences, with the upper middle and the working class fractions having the largest and the smallest proportion of competent bilinguals respectively. (O Riagáin 1992)

It would appear that Irish language policy, particularly in the period 1922–1960, temporarily changed the 'rules' of the social mobility process. State employment was particularly attractive to those sections of the middle classes whose levels of cultural capital were high but whose inherited economic capital was low. As recruitment to the state sector, until the early seventies, required a good competence in Irish, it followed that it was this sector of the middle-class that was most likely to be supportive of Irish.

These policies were not, however, comprehensive enough to affect all sectors of the economy, and therefore the impact was patchy. The private sector until recent decades required greater access to economic rather than cultural capital, and this left it to that extent untouched by state language policy. Furthermore, the acceleration of economic development since 1960, which occurred as a consequence of a series of development programmes, greatly modified the impact of the language policies. The growth of the private sector in this period made it possible, because of the expansion of white-collar occupations, for much larger numbers of well educated middle-class children to advance socially without the necessity of acquiring or maintaining a competence in Irish. (O Riagáin 1992, PAC 1986)

6.4. The media

Although television, and to a lesser extent radio, programmes in Irish attract a sigificant audience among Irish-speakers, the average Irish language output from the main state radio and television stations in the late 1980s was, with one exception, under 5% of total output. Furthermore, the bulk of Irish language television programming is carried on the second, and less popular, channel. In earlier decades the actual volume of Irish language programmes was much the same, but many of the television programmes were carried on the main, and at the time, only channel. The position of Irish language programming on the four national radio stations is different in only one case. In 1972 a radio station was set up to service the Irish-speaking areas along the west coast. This station broadcasts entirely in Irish, and it is primarily a local radio service whose reception was initially confined to those areas. But since the early 1980s it has been broadcast nationally on the VHF network. Apart from this, the other national stations carry very few Irish language programmes.

Thus the same pattern is visible on both radio and television. As the actual output of state services increased, the volume of Irish language material has also increased (or at any rate not declined), but the broadcasting source moved from the main station to one of the smaller, marginal operations. The trend has accelerated further in recent years with the advent of independent stations and consequent competition for audiences, and the outcome has been to further marginalise or eliminate Irish language programmes from the schedules of the main stations' programmes.

6.5. Language standardisation

The language policy of the newly independent state in 1922 placed immediate and enormous demands on the language itself. The policy of the state required the use of Irish in public administration, in law, in education and in the media. These were domains in which Irish had not been used for centuries. Because of the absence of a literary tradition in the immediately preceding centuries, many spelling and grammatical forms were archaic by comparison with the variants used in everyday speech. To compound the difficulties further, the surviving Irish-speaking districts were isolated from each other and dialect differences had developed. But while differences between the dialects were clearly in evidence, no one dialect had either the social or demographic weight to command respect as the standard.

The key body to undertake work on language reform was the Parliamentary Translation Office. This office was set up in 1922 to service parliament and, in practice, government departments generally when English documents were required in Irish translation. Initially, the main problem concerned the administrative need of sections of the Civil Service for a simplified and standardised spelling. In 1931, the Translation Section issued a memorandum showing how spellings were to be modified. The new spellings were in almost all cases shorter than the older spellings and represented the pronunciation of the modern dialects in a more systematic way. The simplifications were generally accepted, and their use consolidated by their adoption in all educational books and journals and particularly in the two major dictionaries, De Bhaldraithe's English/Irish dictionary (1959) and O Dónaill's Irish/English dictionary (1977).

The second phase of the standardisation process concerned the question of grammar. The Translation Service published its recommendations in 1958 and these were also widely adopted. A further important aspect of the cultivation of Irish in the last 60 years was the work of Terminology Committees which were set up for the creation and dissemination of specialised technical vocabularies.

On the basis of the publications that are available, in schools and elsewhere, and taking account of the more formal media events (e. g. news broadcasts), it would appear that the spelling and the grammatical reforms have been accepted and are used (O Baoill/O Riagáin 1990).

7. Contactlinguistic portraits of Irish/English

The two languages, Irish and English, have been in contact for many centuries. Not surprisingly, therefore, the structure of the languages themselves as spoken, and to a lesser extent as written, reveals the influence of the 'other' language. As the less widely spoken of the two languages, Irish has been particularly vulnerable. It will have been clear from the preceding sections that many current speakers of Irish are bilinguals whose mother-tongue is English. The Irish spoken by bilinguals reveals many grammatical, lexical, syntactic and pronunciation features that are due to the influence of English. Speakers and students of the Irish language are, of course, well provided with prescriptive grammars, textbooks and dictionaries (see O Murchú 1985). There are also research-based advanced courses designed to correct some of the most common non-standard grammatical and syntactical features found in written Irish. But in everyday speech, and in informal media events, it would appear that both native-speaker and learner alike tend to simplify grammatical structures more than the standard would allow. If Irish is to become a more generally used medium of communication, one can be almost certain that many of the contrasts now existing within the grammatical and phonological structure will be lost.

There is a considerable corpus of poetry, fiction and non-fiction prose in Irish extending back to early medieval times. The contemporary literary scene is very active and works of high quality are published every year. (MacCana 1980)

English is, of course, the language spoken by the vast majority of Irish people. While written English in Ireland adheres quite closely to Standard English, spoken varieties of English distinguish Irish-English as a mainstream dialect within the modern English-speaking world. There are recognisable and regular differences in pronunciation, grammar, syntax and vocabulary (O Muirithe 1977). Also of significance are regional and class variations. The linguistic repertoire of Irish society thus includes a substantial range of variation in English and some parts of this repertoire are more highly valued than others. In addition, the characteristics of the speakers and the contexts within which these varieties are used have changed even in recent decades. To-date very little of the necessary research into these issues has even begun.

There is little need to comment on the extensive and highly regarded corpus of poetry and prose written by Irish-born speakers of English. Many, including Wilde, Shaw, Joyce, Yeats, Beckett, have been absorbed into the main canon of English literature (Deane 1986).

8. Critical evaluation of the sources and literature used

Language contact research conducted prior to 1960 tended to rely mainly on census data. However, in the late 1960s and early 1970s, a number of studies began to use other official statistics in conjunction with the census data (Hindley 1990). The shortcomings of this phase of language-related research lie primarily in the limited value of the data themselves.

The modern phase of research in Sociology of Language in Ireland may be dated to the establishment, by the Minister of Finance, of the Committee on Irish Language Attitudes Research (CILAR) in 1970. Notwithstanding the Committee's terms of reference, it extended its research to also give attention to factors which could be hypothesized as 'intervening' between attitude and behaviour. Thus, a research design emerged which set out to establish patterns of language attitudes, use and ability and the relationships between these dimensions of the bilingual situation. The surveys carried out by the Committee between 1970–1975 included samples of the national population, primary and post-primary teachers, second-level pupils and civil servants, and in total they established a comprehensive base-line in bilingual research in Ireland which was, and still is, of international significance. ITE (The Linguistics Institute of Ireland) undertook the replication of some key surveys after ten years in 1983 and again in 1993; developed other data-sets (census, grants data, and examinations statistics) for research purposes; and, gradually developed a new research agenda independent of the CILAR research programme.

9. Bibliography (selected)

Bliss, Alan (1984): "English in the South of Ireland". In: *Language in the British Isles*, Trudgill, P. (Ed.), Cambridge.

Breen, Richard et al. (1990): *Understanding Contemporary Ireland: State, Class and Development in the Republic of Ireland*, Dublin.

(CILAR) Committee on Irish Language Attitudes Research (1975): *Report*, Dublin.

Deane, Seamus (1986): *A Short History of Irish Literature*, London.

Hindley, Reg (1990): *The Death of the Irish Language*, London.

Lee, Joseph (1989): *Ireland 1912–1985: Politics and Society*, Cambridge.

MacCana, Proinsias (1980): *Literature in Irish*, Dublin.

Ó Baoill, Dónall/Ó Riagáin, Pádraig (1990): "Reform of the Orthography, Grammar and Vocabulary of Irish". In: *Language Reform: History and Future*, Vol V, Fodor, I./Hagege, C. (Eds.), Hamburg.

Ó Muirithe, Diarmaid (Ed.) (1977): *The English Language in Ireland*, Cork.

Ó Murchú, Máirtín (1985): *The Irish Language*, Dublin.

Ó Riagáin, Pádraig (1988): "Bilingualism in Ireland 1973–1983". In: *International Journal of the Sociology of Language 70*, 29–53.

Ó Riagáin, Pádraig (1992): "Social Class, Education and the Irish Language". In: *Essays on Class and Culture in Ireland*, MacGrianna, S./Ua Conchubhair, P. E. S. (Eds.), Derry, 49–73.

Ó Riagáin, Pádraig (1992): *Language Maintenance and Language Shift as Strategies of Social Reproduction: Irish in the Corca Dhuibhne Gaeltacht 1926–86*, Institiuid Teangeolaiochta Eireann.

Ó Riagáin, Pádraig/Ó Gliasáin, Micheál (1979): *All-Irish Primary Schools in the Dublin Area: A sociological and spatial analysis of the impact of all-Irish schools on home and social use of Irish*, Dublin.

Ó Riagáin, Pádraig/Ó Gliasáin, Micheál (1984): *The Irish Language in the Republic of Ireland 1983: Preliminary Report of a National Survey*, Dublin.

(PAC) Planning Advisory Committee (1986): *Irish and the Education System: An Analysis of Examination Results*, Dublin.

(PAC) Planning Advisory Committee (1988): *The Irish Language in a Changing Society: Shaping the Future*, Dublin.

Tovey, Hilary/Hannan, D./Abramson, Harold (1989): *Why Irish? Irish Identity and the Irish Language*, Dublin.

Pádraig Ó Riagáin, Dublin (Ireland)

XI. Sprachkontakte in Westeuropa
Language Contacts in Western Europe
Contacts linguistiques en Europe de l'Ouest

135. Belgique

1. Géographie et démographie
2. Histoire territoriale et formation de l'Etat
3. Politique, économie, situations culturelle et religieuse en général
4. Statistiques et profils ethniques
5. Situation sociolinguistique
6. Etat de la politique linguistique
7. Présentation des contacts linguistiques
8. Examen critique de la bibliographie
9. Bibliographie (sélective)

1. Géographie et démographie

La Belgique est un pays de 30.521 km^2. Le sillon tracé par la Meuse et son affluent, la Sambre, la coupe en deux régions naturelles: à l'ouest s'étend une plaine à peine vallonnée; à l'est une région plus élevée, comprenant les Ardennes et les Hautes-Fagnes. Le climat est en général tempéré. L'ensemble est néanmoins assez diversifié, avec des plages de sable fin le long de la mer et des plateaux boisés à l'est.

Parallèlement à l'axe constitué par la Sambre et la Meuse court le sillon charbonnier; il est à l'origine de la première révolution industrielle sur le continent européen autour de Liège et de Charleroi. Aujourd'hui, le centre industriel et commercial a tendance à se déplacer vers l'ouest, notamment Bruxelles, Anvers et Gand. Bruxelles devient aussi une plaque tournante administrative et financière européenne. On y trouve la Commission européenne, le Conseil des ministres, le Secrétariat du Parlement européen et certaines de ses réunions, le Comité économique et social, l'OTAN, etc. Près de 300 organisations internationales y ont leur siège; les congrès y rassemblent 300.000 participants chaque année, de sorte qu'elle occupe en ce domaine la deuxième place parmi les villes du monde.

« La démographie (belge) est caractérisée par des degrés de fécondité et de mortalité tellement bas que le degré de croissance de la population est à peu près nul et que le vieillissement est croissant » (André 1990, 28). Au dernier recensement décennal de 1991, on comptait 9.978.681 d'habitants; cela représente une densité de 327 au km^2. Relevons que la population étrangère compte pour 9% dans ce total: on en trouve la grande majorité au sud et au centre du pays (cf. 4.1.). Voici les principaux pays d'origine: Italie (240.127), Maroc (142.098), France (93.363), Turquie (85.303), Pays-Bas (65.294), Espagne (51.318), Allemagne (27.924), Grande-Bretagne (23.129), Grèce (20.461), Portugal (16.528), Zaïre (11.828), Etats-Unis (11.502), Algérie (10.629), Tunisie (6.316), ex-Yougoslavie (5.872), Pologne (4.871), Luxembourg (4.646), autres (93.340). Il importe d'y ajouter un nombre indéterminé de résidents illégaux.

2. Histoire territoriale et formation de l'Etat

Jules César fut le premier à faire mention, dans son récit sur la guerre des Gaules, de la Belgique située entre la Seine et le Rhin. Conquise par les Romains au début de notre ère, elle fut latinisée et christianisée. A partir du 4e siècle, elle passa peu à peu au pouvoir des Francs mérovingiens dont les parlers germaniques s'imposèrent au nord du pays. En 843, par le traité de Verdun, la Belgique échut à Lothaire, petit-fils de Charlemagne. Son royaume couvrait un territoire situé entre la France et la Germanie. Il fut divisé administrativement en « pagi ». Au début du 8e siècle était déjà apparu le « pagus flandrensis » qui finit par couvrir la Flandre française actuelle, les provinces (belges de nos jours) de Flandre occidentale et orientale ainsi que la Flandre zélandaise (aux Pays-Bas maintenant). Vers la même époque apparurent la principauté épiscopale de Liège, les duchés de Brabant, du Limbourg et du Luxembourg et les comtés du Hainaut et de Namur. Progressivement, « la révolution des communes ouvrit la voie à une réelle autonomie politique et juridique. Les habitants des villes acquirent la liberté personnelle » (De Schrijver 1990, 59).

A la suite de mariages entre princes, d'achats ou de guerres, tous ces territoires, à l'exception de la principauté de Liège, passèrent à Philippe le Bon (1419−1467), duc de Bourgogne. Relevons que le comté de Hollande, à l'ouest des Pays-Bas, en faisait partie. Le centre du duché de Bourgogne se trouvait toutefois en Brabant, qui était partiellement roman, tout comme le comté de Flandre et les duchés de Limbourg et du Luxembourg, alors que le Hainaut et Namur étaient majoritairement romans. En 1477, le mariage de Marie de Bourgogne et de l'archiduc Maximilien fit passer la Bourgogne aux Habsbourg. Le petit-fils de Maximilien, Charles Quint (1519−1556), régna sur ce qu'on se remit à appeler la Belgique, mais gouverna aussi à partir de Bruxelles, l'Empire germanique, l'Espagne, l'Italie et les colonies. Cela ne dura guère. En effet, Guillaume, prince d'Orange, se révolta contre le fils de Charles Quint, le roi Philippe II, qui avait mécontenté les Belges, notamment par sa lutte farouche contre les Calvinistes. Le résultat ne se fit pas attendre: sept provinces du nord se séparèrent. Philippe II donna au sud une certaine autonomie sous le règne des archiducs Albert et Isabelle (1598−1633). A cette époque, les écoles des peintres Rubens et Van Dyck prospèrent à Anvers, Juste Lipse confirme la réputation de l'Université de Louvain, les Jésuites qui avaient donné naissance aux Bollandistes, entreprennent à Bruxelles le travail monumental des *Acta Sanctorum*, tandis qu'à Mons éclot le génie musical de Roland de Lassus.

Au 18e siècle, à la suite d'une guerre de succession en Espagne, le pays passa aux Habsbourg d'Autriche. L'impératrice Marie-Thérèse en respecta l'autonomie. Mais son fils, Joseph II, provoqua une révolution. Elle engendra la république des Etats belges unis (1789−1790). En 1794, la France annexa la Belgique, y compris la Principauté de Liège. Elle abolit tous les privilèges et divisa le pays en neuf départements, qui deviendront les neuf provinces belges en 1830. Après la défaite de Napoléon, le Congrès de Vienne (1815) décida, sans consultation des habitants, de ne pas redonner le pays aux Habsbourg mais au roi des Pays-Bas. Ce dernier commit des maladresses assez graves pour déclencher une révolte en 1830. Peu après, un Congrès national proclama l'indépendance de la Belgique. La couronne fut offerte à un prince saxon, vivant en Angleterre, de religion protestante. Il accepta de régner sur le jeune Etat, qui correspondait toutefois à une société civile fort ancienne. Mais le roi des Pays-Bas revint à la charge. Il ne s'inclina qu'en 1839, après le retour du duché du Limbourg et de l'est du duché du Luxembourg à la Confédération germanique; le roi des Pays-Bas en devint toutefois le duc.

Relevons ici que la Belgique reprit les frontières avec la France et la Prusse qui avaient été imposées par le Congrès de Vienne (1815). Ainsi se trouvaient confirmés la perte de la Flandre française, de l'Artois, de Thionville ainsi que le don fait à la Prusse des cantons d'Eupen, de Malmédy et de Saint-Vith. La Calamine (Kelmis) devint un condominium belgo-prussien et le restera jusqu'en 1919.

De 1914 à 1918, l'Allemagne occupa la majeure partie de la Belgique. Le gouverneur général allemand avantagea la langue néerlandaise en décrétant notamment que ce serait la langue d'enseignement à l'Université de Gand. Il favorisa aussi une séparation administrative entre le nord et le sud du pays. Ces dispositions furent abolies dès la défaite de l'Allemagne. A cette occasion, la Belgique acquit les cantons d'Eupen, de St-Vith et de Malmédy, dont six municipalités sur trente étaient à forte majorité wallonne. L'irrédentisme pro-allemand, encouragé par Berlin, s'y manifesta aussitôt.

De 1940 à 1944, l'Allemagne occupa à nouveau la Belgique. Elle reprit sa politique de sape de l'unité du pays. Ainsi elle libéra uniquement les sous-officiers et soldats faits prisonniers, qui pouvaient s'exprimer en néerlandais ou en allemand, mais maintint en captivité tous les autres pendant 5 ans. Elle ne tarda pas à déporter 300.000 travailleurs vers le Reich. Des 24.906 Juifs belges traînés en Allemagne, seulement 1.507 survécurent. En outre, elle annexa le secteur de Montzen-Welkenraedt ainsi que des parties de 6 villages du Luxembourg belge et les cantons d'Eupen, de Malmédy et de St-Vith. Dans tous ces endroits, elle imposa l'unilinguisme allemand, qui dura jusqu'à la nouvelle défaite de l'Allemagne. A ce moment, la Belgique récupéra tous ces territoires (→ carte linguistique C).

3. Politique, économie, situations culturelle et religieuse en général

3.1. Politique

Aux termes de la Constitution du 7 février 1831, la Belgique est une monarchie constitutionnelle. Avant les modifications récentes, le pouvoir exécutif appartenait au roi qui l'exerçait par l'intermédiaire et sous la responsabilité de ses ministres. Le pouvoir législatif appartenait collectivement au roi et au parlement (Sénat et Chambre des représentants).

La Constitution de 1831 visait surtout à protéger l'individu contre l'Etat. Aussi, se limite-t-elle à définir les droits politiques classiques. Toutefois le législateur belge a consacré ensuite par de simples lois la plupart des droits économiques, sociaux et culturels.

La Belgique était conçue comme un Etat unitaire, mais décentralisé en provinces et en communes. La révision constitutionnelle de 1970 stipule qu'il existe officiellement quatre régions linguistiques: la région de langue française, la région de langue néerlandaise, la région de langue allemande et une région bilingue de Bruxelles-Capitale (19 communes). Ces régions n'ont pas reçu de structure politique propre. Mais la réforme constitutionnelle de 1970 a aussi créé trois communautés: la française, la germanophone et une troisième dite flamande. Cette dernière appellation constitue un abus de langage, selon certains Brabançons néerlandophones (De Ridder 1989, 87) et des observateurs étrangers (Brugmans 1972, 60). Cette communauté englobe, en effet, non seulement les provinces de Flandre occidentale et orientale, mais aussi les provinces d'Anvers, du Limbourg et le nord du Brabant. La communauté française couvre les provinces du Hainaut, de Namur, du Luxembourg, de Liège et le sud du Brabant. La communauté germanophone couvre 9 communes à l'est du pays. A noter qu'en 1995, le nord et le sud du Brabant sont devenus des provinces distinctes; Bruxelles-Capitale ne fait plus partie d'aucune province.

Chaque communauté a reçu des compétences quasi exclusives au niveau culturel (arts, éducation, tourisme, etc.) ainsi que dans les domaines de l'aide aux personnes, de la politique de la santé et de la recherche scientifique appliquée. Chacune est dotée d'un conseil et d'un gouvernement dont les décrets ont force de loi.

En outre, la révision constitutionnelle de 1970 a créé trois régions économiques: la bruxelloise (19 communes), la «flamande» (au nord) et la «wallonne». Ce que nous avons signalé à propos de l'extension de la signification du terme «flamand» vaut aussi pour le terme «wallon», qui couvre ici non seulement la partie de la Belgique où l'on parle wallon, mais toute la partie romane du pays et même les 9 communes germanophones. Les territoires des régions ne coïncident donc pas avec ceux des communautés. Ces régions ont reçu, dans le domaine économique, de très larges pouvoirs et sont dotées d'un conseil et d'un gouvernement dont les décrets ont force de loi. Notons qu'au nord du pays, la communauté flamande et la région du même nom ont fusionné.

Il existe aussi des organismes de concertation et, en dernier ressort, un recours possible à une Cour d'arbitrage (cf. 6.3.).

Ces superstructures ne constituent toutefois pas les seules manifestations des différences entre Belges. Les divisions les plus importantes nous paraissent être liées aux trois grandes familles spirituelles: la catholique, la socialiste et la libérale. Elles se sont toutes trois dotées d'un réseau de sociétés d'assurance mutuelle, de syndicats, de coopératives, de journaux, de cliniques, d'hôpitaux, de mouvements éducatifs et, au moins dans la famille catholique, d'écoles de tous les niveaux. Ces organisations socio-économiques sont défendues respectivement par les partis sociaux chrétiens, les partis socialistes et les partis libéraux. On les appelle les partis traditionnels.

Il y a également des partis régionalistes. Mais ils ne parviennent généralement pas à se maintenir très longtemps, soit parce qu'ils ne s'entendent pas au niveau des choix de société, soit qu'ils ne disposent pas de tout le réseau d'œuvres dont sont entourés les trois partis traditionnels. D'ailleurs ces trois partis sont scindés linguistiquement; ils peuvent ainsi faire face aux partis régionalistes et reprendre une bonne partie de leur programme autonomiste.

Les gouvernements sont presque toujours des coalitions. En fait, à ce jour aucun parti francophone ou néerlandophone traditionnel n'est entré au gouvernement central sans être accompagné du parti homologue de l'autre langue. C'est dire l'importance persistante des divisions traditionnelles face aux linguistiques de date beaucoup plus récente.

Dans les années 80 est né un parti écologiste. Il est également divisé en deux ailes linguistiques.

Enfin, la révision constitutionnelle de 1993 a fédéralisé l'Etat. Elle a consacré les compétences des communautés et des régions et y a même ajouté le commerce extérieur, l'agriculture et l'ensemble de la politique scientifique. La compétence résiduelle, en attendant qu'on détermine la liste des compétences qui restent du ressort fédéral, est transférée en principe aux entités fédérées. Le sénat fédéral garde une composition proportionnelle au nombre d'habitants des régions économiques − à l'exception d'un siège qui est assuré à la communauté germanophone − mais devient essentiellement une chambre de réflexion.

3.2. Economie

La Belgique, en exportant 65% de sa production, dépasse actuellement tous les pays du monde en ce qui concerne la quantité de biens vendus à l'étranger par tête d'habitant. En revanche, ses frontières sont traditionnellement ouvertes à l'importation.

Le secteur primaire (agriculture, pêche, mines) est de plus en plus réduit. Ce sont des réacteurs nucléaires qui produisent 65% de l'énergie électrique. Le secteur secondaire (manufactures, constructions) subit une concurrence croissante. Cette dernière ne peut être soutenue que dans les industries de pointe (Pulinckx 1990, 240). Le secteur tertiaire (y compris les assurances et les services financiers) occupe 70% des travailleurs. Les transports publics et privés sont très développés; les autoroutes sont éclairées *a giorno*.

Le franc belge constitue de nos jours une monnaie stable; l'inflation dans le pays est la plus basse d'Europe. Par contre, la dette publique est énorme: 122% du produit national annuel (189,9 milliards de dollars).

Signalons que 70% des travailleurs sont syndiqués. Cependant 23% des ménages ne jouissent pas d'un revenu considéré comme décent (Deleeck 1990, 331). La misère est toutefois assez rare.

3.3. Situation culturelle et religieuse

Il existe un grand nombre de définitions de la culture. Prenons, parmi elles, celle de Linton (1986, 33): «La culture est la configuration des comportements acquis et des résultats de l'activité humaine dont les éléments sont transmis et partagés par les membres d'un groupe particulier». Cela paraît un point d'appui commode. Mais les difficultés surgissent au moment de s'en servir. Quand les comportements acquis et les résultats de l'activité humaine dans un même pays sont-ils à ce point différents qu'on peut parler de deux ou de plusieurs cultures? Il faudrait au moins s'entendre sur les indicateurs les plus typiques de la culture. Nous allons le tenter. Mais nous ne pouvons admettre au départ que deux langues coïncident nécessairement avec deux cultures. Deux langues aussi différentes que le finnois et le suédois sont soustendues en Finlande par une seule et même culture. En revanche, les Samis (Lapons) ont une autre langue et une autre culture. D'autre part, une même langue, par exemple l'anglais, peut se rencontrer dans plusieurs cultures.

Si nous considérons les arts en Belgique, nous constatons que leurs modes d'expression, assez éclectiques, sont loin de coïncider avec les groupes linguistiques. C'est vrai pour l'architecture, la peinture et la sculpture (Legrand 1990, 87), le théâtre, la danse et le cinéma (De Decker 1990, 508), la musique (Huys 1990, 514 et Wangermée 1990, 521). C'est même vrai pour la littérature de langue française (Sion, 1990, 463), de langue néerlandaise (Weisgerber 1990, 478) et de langue allemande en Belgique (Leonardy 1979, 241). Ces trois littératures présentent d'ailleurs certaines évolutions parallèles. Les courants artistiques en vogue chez les immigrants de la 2e génération ne sont pas non plus limités à un groupe linguistique (Lapiower 1992). Il est donc permis de conclure avec deux spécialistes de la vie culturelle (Liebaers et Robert-Jones 1990, 530): «Il a existé une tendance en Belgique visant à égaliser la langue avec la culture. Nous estimons que c'est une erreur de base. Les francophones belges ne sont pas des Français, les néerlandophones ne sont pas des Néerlandais et les germanophones ne sont pas des Allemands». Cela nous amène à jeter un coup d'œil sur l'ensemble des institutions au sens anthropologique du terme, c'est-à-dire «les moyens par lesquels l'influence spécifique de la société agit sur l'individu» (Kardiner 1969). Que nous prenions les institutions primaires (familles, écoles, mouvements de jeunesse) ou secondaires (religions, droit, économie, système politique), nous ne trouvons aucune étude démontrant une tendance fondamentalement différente au nord et au sud du pays. Au contraire, les enquêtes réalisées sur le plan européen par l'*European Value Systems Study Group* font ressortir clairement que «le facteur linguistique ne creuse pas entre les Belges une division aussi profonde que la lecture de l'actualité politique le laisserait entendre.

Quand nous comparons les néerlandophones aux Hollandais et les francophones aux Français, il apparaît qu'ils sont plus proches les uns des autres que de leurs voisins dont ils parlent la langue» (Rezsohazy et Kerkhofs 1984, 198, corroboré par Voyé et al. 1992, 12).

En ce qui concerne la vie religieuse, presque tous les habitants de nationalité belge sont baptisés dans l'Eglise catholique. Les protestants atteignent peut-être un pourcent de la population. Le calvinisme a cependant connu une heure de gloire. «C'est à Gand que, pendant plusieurs années, s'est trouvé leur noyau le plus dur. C'est à Nieuport qu'a eu lieu, en 1600, la victoire (...) la plus éclatante du Prince Maurice de Nassau (Brugmans 1972, 63)». Peu après 1600, les Calvinistes belges ont émigré vers la République des Provinces Unies. La Belgique est devenue les Pays-Bas catholiques, comme on la nomme sur les cartes de l'époque. Vers la même date, un certain nombre d'associations se mirent à défendre le sécularisme. Plus récemment, des immigrants albanais, maghrébins, turcs, etc. apportèrent la religion islamique.

Lors de l'occupation française à la fin du 18e siècle, les biens qui permettaient à l'Eglise de vivre furent presque tous nationalisés. Napoléon Bonaparte conclut en 1801 un concordat avec le Pape en vertu duquel les desservants des paroisses catholiques seraient rétribués par l'Etat français. C'était sa façon de compenser la nationalisation des biens ecclésiastiques. En 1830, la Belgique reprit cette disposition. En 1870, une loi étendit cette rétribution aux desservants anglicans, protestants et juifs; en 1974, une loi du même type fut votée en faveur de l'Islam; en 1985, ce fut le tour de la confession orthodoxe. Enfin en 1993, l'Etat prit à sa charge les traitements des délégués des organisations qui offrent une assistance morale selon une conception non confessionnelle. Précisions que la liberté des cultes ainsi que la liberté de manifester ses opinions sont assurées à tous les Belges (Art. 14 de la Constitution).

4. Statistiques et profils ethniques

4.1. Statistiques

Lors des premiers recensements – le tout premier remonte à 1846 – les questions concernant la langue ne parurent provoquer aucune passion. On s'accorde à reconnaître l'objectivité des réponses (Levy 1932 et Draye 1942). Mais une loi du 28 juin 1932 lia l'emploi des langues dans les communes du pays aux réponses données au recensement linguistique. Il semble que ce recensement a pris dès lors les allures d'un référendum en faveur du bilinguisme des écoles et des administrations communales.

Le recensement linguistique de 1947 fut particulièrement contesté («Geen talentelling» 1959). En 1959 quatorze spécialistes (statisticiens, sociologues et linguistes) furent invités par le gouvernement à trouver une formule acceptable par tous. La majorité des membres parvint à un accord. Son originalité consistait à multiplier les questions (en y incluant l'usage des langues régionales et de langues étrangères) dans l'espoir de provoquer moins de passion. Le rapport de cette Commission du recensement linguistique destiné à éclairer les parlementaires, n'a toutefois jamais été distribué. Le gouvernement social chrétien-libéral de l'époque décida de n'y donner aucune suite. Il s'orienta au contraire vers une fixation de la frontière des langues. Bon nombre de parlementaires estimaient qu'une étude scientifique ou un ultime recensement aurait dû être exécuté avant le clichage de la frontière des langues. Mais ils furent mis en minorité. Le 30 juillet 1963 le recensement linguistique fut supprimé, malgré le fait rassurant pour ses adversaires que le 8 novembre 1962 avait été votée une loi fixant la frontière linguistique. Ultérieurement, il fut décidé que tout changement dans ce clichage devait être adopté à la majorité des suffrages de chaque groupe linguistique de chacune des chambres, à la condition que la majorité des membres de chaque groupe se trouve réunie et pour autant que le total des votes positifs émis dans les deux groupes linguistiques atteigne les deux tiers des suffrages exprimés.

Pour pallier l'absence de recensement linguistique officiel, certains se livrent à des sondages. Révélons-en un de 1969, parce que réalisé sous la direction d'un professeur de la Vrije Universiteit Brussel, H. Vander Eycken: il s'agit de l'enquête Kluft-Van der Vorst (non publiée) qui nous semble présenter de sérieuses garanties scientifiques. Cette recherche ne porte que sur Bruxelles (19 communes). Elle relève que 17,6% des Bruxellois s'identifient subjectivement au groupe néerlandophone.

Pour l'ensemble du pays, on dispose des statistiques des langues choisies dans l'enseignement secondaire qui est de nos jours généralisé. Dans l'enseignement francophone où le choix est possible (c'est-à-dire en dehors de Bruxelles-Capitale, de la région germanophone et des communes malmédiennes et à facilités linguistiques), 60% suivent effectivement des cours de néerlandais. Dans l'enseignement néerlandophone où le choix est libre, 90% suivent effectivement des cours de français. Considérant que le nombre d'élèves est supérieur dans l'enseignement secondaire néerlandophone, cela donne une forte majorité à l'étude de la langue française.

Parmi les sondages relatifs au néerlandais, retenons ceux de Meeus (1979, 341). Il a découvert que dans la région de langue néerlandaise, 90% parlent en famille une langue régionale autre que le néerlandais. Cette dernière langue n'est parlée que par 2% à la campagne et par 20% dans les villes, si l'on ne considère que la classe ouvrière. Pour le sud du pays, il n'y a pas de sondages de cette envergure. On sait toutefois que les immigrants — surtout ceux de la première génération — n'ont généralement qu'une piètre connaissance du français.

On conçoit qu'en l'absence de tout recensement linguistique depuis 1947, il nous est impossible de nous prononcer sur le nombre de locuteurs des différentes langues officielles. Nous ne disposons que du nombre d'habitants de chacune des 4 régions linguistiques. C'est ainsi que l'Institut National de Statistique a relevé en 1991:

— dans la région bilingue de Bruxelles-Capitale: 954.045 habitants, dont 271.587 étrangers;
— dans la région officiellement de langue néerlandaise: 5.768.926 habitants, dont 258.848 étrangers;
— dans la région officiellement de langue française: 3.188.103 habitants, dont 360.760 étrangers;
— dans la région officiellement de langue allemande: 67.618 habitants, dont 9.660 étrangers.

Mais tout le monde sait qu'il y a, dans la région de langue néerlandaise, des dizaines de milliers de francophones, dont bon nombre de vieille date et de la classe aisée. Il y a beaucoup d'immigrants originaires du nord du pays dans la région de langue française, mais ils s'assimilent volontiers. Aussi, des politiciens du nord du pays continuent à s'opposer à toute espèce de recensement linguistique, officiel ou scientifique. Ils craignent la mise en question des mesures de contrainte qu'ils sont arrivés à faire prendre (cf. 6.3.). C'est le mythe de la paix par l'ignorance.

Quant aux locuteurs des langues régionales, divers comptages (Verdoodt 1989, 105−178) permettent les évaluations suivantes:

— pour les langues germaniques: 5.493.000, dont bas allemand (40.000), brabançon (2.400.000), bruxellois (100.000), flamand occidental (1.000.000), flamand oriental (1.300.000), limbourgeois (630.000) et luxembourgeois (23.000);
— pour les langues romanes: 1.872.000, dont champenois (4.000), lorrain (22.000), picard (450.000) et wallon (1.400.000).

Les locuteurs n'ayant qu'une connaissance passive sont inclus dans ces données. Ajoutons qu'en Belgique le lorrain est plus connu sous le nom de gaumais. Nous n'avons pas d'évaluation pour le francique-ripuaire.

Certains préfèrent appeler ces langues des *dialectes*. Mais cela peut prêter à confusion. Car les langues régionales germaniques et romanes peuvent apparaître ainsi comme des déformations d'une des langues officielles. Or, ces langues régionales sont plus anciennes que chacune des langues officielles.

Un argument parfois avancé contre les langues régionales est leur manque d'unité interne. En fait, aucune langue n'est strictement homogène. «Dans aucun essai de définition scientifique d'une langue, on ne trouve l'unité citée comme critère» (Bal 1990, 10). Finalement, ce qui fait une langue, c'est le plus souvent sa reconnaissance officielle. Or, ici nous pouvons renvoyer à la reconnaissance de sept d'entre elles par le Conseil de la Communauté française (cf. 6.2.).

Enfin, nous laissons au linguiste le soin de déterminer la distance linguistique qui sépare les diverses langues régionales. A la limite, une distance minime nous suffit. Il est bien certain qu'entre le bas-allemand et le limbourgeois il n'y a pas beaucoup de différences. L'important c'est de relever que la majorité des locuteurs du bas-allemand n'accepte pas que sa langue s'appelle le *limbourgeois*, même si elle lui est très semblable. Il en va de même pour le flamand oriental. Des experts (Weijnen 1966, 191) le classent avec le brabançon. La population toutefois estime qu'elle parle une forme de flamand.

En ce qui concerne les immigrants, les statistiques (cf. 1.) ne disent rien au sujet des langues maternelles ou usuelles. On sait cependant que parmi les Italiens, il y a un nombre indéterminé de germanophones (du Tyrol du Sud), de locuteurs d'albanais, de franco-provençal, de frioulan, de ladin, de piémontais, de sarde, de sicilien, de slovène et de vénitien. Pour les immigrants du Maroc, il y a un bon nombre de locuteurs de berbère; pour la Turquie, il y a des Araméens, des Arméniens et des Kurdes; pour la Grande Bretagne, des locuteurs de gallois et de gaélique; pour la Grèce, il y a des albanophones, des locuteurs d'aroumain, de pomak et de turc; pour l'Algérie, encore un bon nombre de locuteurs de berbère; pour l'ex-Yougoslavie, des locuteurs de serbe, de croate, de slovène, d'albanais, de macédonien, de hongrois, etc. Aucune de ces langues maternelles n'est enseignée en Belgique, sauf l'allemand. En effet, les enseignants des langues des immigrants sont généralement nommés et rétribués par les consulats. Les exceptions (constituées par quelques enseignants nommés et rémunérés par les communes) confirment la règle. On comprend dès lors que l'enseignement des langues pour les immigrants se limite en Belgique à l'arabe marocain, l'espagnol, le grec, l'italien, le portugais et le turc, c'est-à-dire à six langues officielles.

4.2. Profils ethniques

Selon l'inventaire conceptuel de Riggs (1985), l'ethnie peut se définir par la race, la langue, la religion, la culture ou une combinaison de ces facteurs. En Belgique, le facteur *race* ne joue que dans le cas d'immigrants. Nous y reviendrons. La langue ne constitue pas, à elle seule, un facteur ethnique; d'ailleurs la plupart des Belges sont plurilingues, surtout si l'on considère les langues régionales si répandues. L'opinion philosophique ou religieuse ne crée pas d'ethnie en Belgique, sauf pour certains Juifs de stricte observance à Anvers. En revanche, la culture paraît créer des groupes ethniques. Cela se manifeste notamment chez les immigrants qui restent fidèles à leurs associations et religions particulières. Ils privilégient souvent la langue de leur région d'origine comme langue de premier apprentissage de leurs enfants et une majorité souhaite que l'enseignement de leur langue d'origine soit assuré par l'école belge (Marques Balsa 1993, 87 sq). En revanche, la seconde génération d'immigrants choisit plutôt un type de vie belge. Mais cela ne va pas sans peine. « Le fait que beaucoup d'immigrants et leurs enfants s'assimilent de manière active est attaqué par certains groupes de pression autochtones ou des partis politiques pour dénoncer le caractère « abâtardi » de ces minorités: par l'emploi de symboles et d'expressions simplistes et de raisonnements qui reviennent de façon permanente dans toutes les situations où des groupes racistes entrent en action, on s'efforce de convaincre les autochtones (belges) que ces minorités doivent s'en aller. Les groupes minoritaires qui se distinguent phénotypiquement de la majorité sont surtout l'objet de ces campagnes. Les caractéristiques corporelles et génétiques sont, dans le discours raciste, confondues avec la culture ... de telle sorte que les « autres » sont rejetés dans leur totalité et cela sur base de ces caractéristiques « naturelles » que rien ne peut changer » (Roosens 1986, 175). Relevons ici l'hésitation de la plupart des partis politiques à reconnaître le droit de vote aux immigrants non-naturalisés. Mais l'Union européenne va imposer le droit de vote des immigrants des 15 pays membres au niveau communal. La région « flamande » demande déjà des exceptions.

« Quoi qu'il en soit, continue Roosens (1986, 176), ce qui se passe maintenant ne va ni dans le sens d'un retour massif au pays d'origine, ni vers une disparition sans réserve dans la majorité autochtone ... Un bon nombre de jeunes adultes italiens qui ont grandi en Belgique semblent disparaître dans la masse autochtone, du moins en ce qui concerne leur vie publique. En revanche, ils conservent un genre de vie italien, du moins partiel, dans leur vie privée ... D'autres jeunes italiens, qui pourraient aussi bien que ceux que nous venons d'évoquer, se tenir à l'arrière de la scène, ... se rendent au contraire éminemment visibles ... En aucun cas, ils ne peuvent revendiquer une forte continuité avec la culture objective de leurs parents ou avec leur région d'origine. Ils disposent sans doute de leur ascendance familiale, parfois de certaines caractéristiques phénotypiques et aussi de quelques éléments culturels ... Mais en général, ils ajoutent à cette continuité « objective » d'autres éléments de leur création ou empruntés à une tradition ou une expérience différente. Des jeunes d'origine sicilienne mentionneront comme faisant partie de leur « passé » ou de leur « culture » l'antiquité romaine, les grands auteurs ou les cinéastes italiens. Ainsi ils tenteront de s'élever au-dessus de la population autochtone. Et ils achèteront, en association, un morceau de terrain en Sicile et posséderont en commun une sorte de symbole fortement empreint d'émotion. En outre les chants martiaux qu'ils entonnent ne laissent subsister aucun doute: ils se forgent un passé en vue de se donner bonne figure ... Il est sans doute compréhensible qu'un membre de la seconde génération d'immigrants estime qu'il a été frustré d'une partie de sa culture dans et par le système scolaire autochtone, et que pas mal de choses seraient différentes si l'on avait respecté «l'identité culturelle» des enfants des immigrants».

Des recherches anthropologiques aussi précises manquent à propos de l'ethnogenèse des autres groupes d'immigrants et même des groupes autochtones. En revanche, des psychologues sociaux ont mené jadis quelques enquêtes relatives aux stéréotypes (McRae 1986, 91–109). Ce qui est certain, c'est que les Belges tolèrent mieux les immigrants qui proviennent d'un pays de l'Union européenne que ceux qui arrivent du Tiers-Monde (Bastenier 1992, 34). C'est ainsi qu'ils ne craignent généralement pas l'intégration européenne et leur soumission à des décideurs majoritairement étrangers. Mais les politiciens belges ne parviennent pas à accepter une hiérarchie des normes entre les lois fédérales belges et les décrets des entités fédérées (communautés, régions) (cf. 3.1.).

5. Situation sociolinguistique

5.1. Enseignement

L'enseignement en Belgique est confié à des instances officielles (communautés, provinces, communes), mais surtout à des institutions libres (la plupart catholiques). Ces écoles sont généralement subventionnées par la communauté. Le degré de scolarisation est le plus élevé de la Communauté européenne. Environ, 13% des jeunes de 18 ans sont inscrits à l'Université; en outre 40% fréquentent l'enseignement supérieur non-universitaire (Deleeck 1990, 330).

Les dispositions légales relatives à l'enseignement des langues seront passées en revue plus bas (cf. 6.3.). Relevons ici l'appréciation tantôt négative (p. ex. Hanse 1964, qui fait toutefois une exception en faveur de l'apprentissage précoce du wallon), tantôt positive du bilinguisme scolaire (Baetens-Beardsmore 1993, 6).

Dans les entreprises privées, on utilise sensiblement plus de langues que dans les services publics. Ces derniers sont souvent unilingues (cf. 6.3.). Au nord du pays, on y utilise le plus fréquemment, après le néerlandais, le français; l'anglais et l'allemand suivent. Au sud, la langue la plus utilisée est le français; puis viennent, dans l'ordre, le néerlandais, l'anglais et l'allemand (Verdoodt 1989, 70).

Les autorités de la région néerlandophone ont tendance à diminuer le nombre d'heures d'enseignement du français. Cela coûte cher à la communauté, parce que l'enseignement de promotion sociale pour adultes se voit maintenant obligé d'organiser de plus en plus de cours de français (Debrock 1991, 41).

5.2. Bilinguisme et diglossie

Nous définissons le bilinguisme comme étant une habilité individuelle à communiquer en deux langues (Van Overbeke 1970, 119). Nous ne pouvons ici entrer dans toutes les nuances. D'autant plus, qu'au point de vue social, l'autre notion, celle de diglossie, présente plus d'intérêt. Elle se rencontre quand, dans un milieu donné, certaines fonctions sociales sont généralement exercées dans une langue et d'autres fonctions en une (ou plusieurs) autre(s) langue(s) (Fishman 1971, 87). Le bilinguisme et la diglossie évoluent souvent de façon indépendante. Ainsi la Belgique du 19e siècle se caractérisait par un haut degré de diglossie et un bilinguisme limité. L'administration centrale et l'enseignement supérieur utilisaient le français; le peuple parlait principalement des langues régionales germaniques ou romanes. Puis certains philologues germaniques ont défendu l'idée qu'il fallait une langue commune à tout le nord du pays. Ils se trouvaient devant un choix: développer une langue propre ou prendre le néerlandais de l'ouest des Pays-Bas, qui s'était imposé au 19e siècle dans une grande partie de ce pays comme langue de communication. Bien qu'il n'y eut jamais de consultation de la population belge, on s'orienta vers le choix du néerlandais. La discussion continua à propos de la prononciation, du vocabulaire et même de la morphologie de cette langue importée en Belgique. Mais un argument économique influença à ce moment l'opinion d'une partie de la classe moyenne du nord du pays. «Considérant que les Pays-Bas avec leurs colonies constituaient un vaste marché et, qu'en outre, ce pays accusait un retard dans son industrialisation, les relations linguistiques offraient des chances au niveau économique» (Jaspaert et van Belle 1984, 73). De nos jours, cette aubaine économique a fortement diminué.

En outre, des enquêtes récentes montrent le désir de la population du nord de la Belgique de se démarquer par rapport au néerlandais de Hollande et de promouvoir une variété propre (Jaspaert 1984, 203). Le Brabant commence à fonctionner comme centre de convergence pour le néerlandais de Belgique (Deprez 1987, 101).

Le français de Belgique diffère sensiblement du pur parisien. L'allemand de Belgique présente également des déviations par rapport à la norme. Cela s'explique en partie par l'organisation politique, administrative et pédagogique propre à la Belgique. Mais cela semble encore davantage lié à des traditions différentes dans la prononciation et dans certaines parties du vocabulaire. Ainsi on trouve dans le français des différences dans le système de computation (p. ex. *septante*), la boulangerie-pâtisserie (p. ex. *pistolet* au lieu de *petit pain*) et le langage scolaire. En revanche, dans la langue écrite, le français et l'allemand sont assez proches de la variété utilisée par nos grands voisins. On notera toutefois que, pour le français, c'est encore le Brabant − surtout Bruxelles-Capitale et sa grande banlieue − qui fonctionne comme centre, car « beaucoup d'innovations dont la source est parisienne n'atteignent les provinces belges qu'après une escale bruxelloise » (Pohl 1979, 19).

6. Etat de la politique linguistique

6.1. Principes législatifs

Son principe de base est contenu dans l'article 23 de la Constitution belge de 1831: « L'emploi des langues usitées en Belgique est facultatif; il ne peut être réglé que par la loi, et seulement pour les actes de l'autorité publique et pour les affaires judiciaires ». Cette limitation doit toutefois être conciliée avec le droit reconnu en 1970 aux législateurs communautaires d'assurer la prééminence d'une langue dans les deux régions unilingues (cf. 3.1.). En revanche, à Bruxelles-Capitale et dans la région germanophone, seule l'autorité nationale est compétente pour y régler l'emploi des langues.

6.2. Législation relative aux langues régionales endogènes

Seule la Communauté française a légiféré à ce sujet. Le 14 décembre 1990, elle adoptait un décret reconnaissant l'existence, à côté du français, de langues régionales endogènes méritant protection et promotion.

En outre, le 19 mars 1991, l'exécutif (ou gouvernement) de la Communauté française instituait un *Conseil des langues régionales endogènes*. Ce Conseil est chargé de donner son avis sur les mesures aptes à protéger et à promouvoir l'usage de ces langues. Il est composé de 24 membres représentatifs des différents domaines liés aux langues régionales endogènes. Ces dernières sont, d'après la composition du Conseil, le *wallon*, le *picard*, le *lorrain*, le *champenois*, le *luxembourgeois*, le *bas-allemand* et le *bruxellois*. Notons que les quatre premières pouvaient déjà être enseignées à l'école, en vertu d'un décret paru au Moniteur belge du 15 mars 1983. (La Communauté germanophone et la Communauté flamande n'ont pas (encore) légiféré à ce sujet.)

Le Conseil des langues régionales a oublié le yiddish, parlé et imprimé en Belgique depuis le 16e siècle et le romani, la langue de migrants saisonniers depuis des siècles.

Relevons que la législation n'utilise pas le terme *dialecte* pour désigner les langues endogènes (cf. 4.1.).

6.3. Législation relative aux langues officielles

Le principe de la liberté linguistique fut consacré dans l'article 5 d'un arrêté du 16 novembre 1830 pris par le Gouvernement provisoire: « Les citoyens, dans leurs rapports avec l'administration sont autorisés à se servir indifféremment de la langue française, flamande ou allemande ». Cela vaut toujours pour l'administration centrale du pays. Mais le 30 juin 1981 un décret a réduit cette liberté dans la région néerlandophone, en vertu de la compétence que lui donne la révision constitutionnelle de 1970 (cf. 6.1.).

Le Bulletin officiel des lois fut publié depuis le 19 septembre 1831 dans les trois langues citées plus haut. Mais seul le texte français était officiel. En 1840, l'édition allemande fut supprimée, à la suite du retour à la Confédération germanique de l'est des provinces du Limbourg et du Luxembourg.

Il fallut ensuite plusieurs trains de lois pour arriver à une certaine égalité entre la langue française et la langue appelée alors *flamande* (maintenant *néerlandaise*). La langue allemande fut assez négligée au niveau national. La situation changea à la suite du rattachement des cantons d'Eupen, de Malmédy et de St-Vith après 1918. Elle ne deviendra favorable qu'en 1963.

On peut distinguer quatre ensembles de lois linguistiques: celles votées de 1873 à 1921, celles votées de 1930 à 1938, celles votées de 1961 à 1963 et celles votées depuis 1971. Nous n'évoquerons que les lois actuellement en vigueur. Elles datent fondamentalement de la période allant de 1930 à 1938; elles ont subi toutefois des adaptations territoriales et autres.

En matière administrative, ces lois, coordonnées le 18 juillet 1966, étaient nécessaires, notamment pour tenir compte de la suppression du recensement des langues (loi du 30 juillet 1963) et de la division du pays en 4 régions linguistiques. En effet, la loi antérieure en matière administrative (28 juin 1932, article 6) appliquait automatiquement un régime de facilités linguistiques lorsque le dernier recensement faisait apparaître une minorité atteignant trente pour cent. Désormais, l'emploi des langues dans les services locaux établis dans une région unilingue est limité, en principe, à la langue de cette région. Les conseils communaux des centres touristiques situés en région unilingue peuvent toutefois décider que les avis et communications aux touristes seront rédigés en au moins trois langues, jamais en deux.

Notons que la loi prévoit un régime linguistique spécial pour la région de langue allemande (9 communes), les 3 communes du pays de Montzen, les 2 communes malmédiennes, six communes périphériques de Bruxelles et une vingtaine de communes de la frontière linguistique situées en diverses provinces. A noter que ce régime spécial consiste en certaines facilités linguistiques dans les rapports administratifs avec les particuliers et pour l'organisation d'un enseignement primaire dans la langue minoritaire.

Dans les services unilingues, nul ne peut être nommé s'il ne connaît la langue de la région. Dans les services partiellement ou localement bilingues, il y a des dispositions spéciales.

Dans les services dont l'activité s'étend à tout le pays, les fonctionnaires d'un grade égal ou supérieur à celui de directeur sont répartis entre trois cadres: un français, un néerlandais et un bilingue. Ce dernier comporte 20 pour cent de l'effectif global des fonctions égales ou supérieures à celles de directeur.

Toute administration centrale est obligée de s'adresser dans la langue de la région aux services administratifs établis dans cette région, mais aussi aux entreprises industrielles, commerciales ou financières privées. Ce dernier point fut considéré comme allant à l'encontre de l'art. 23 de la Constitution. Mais il fut néanmoins voté. Il correspond à la loi du 2 août 1963 exigeant que tous les documents destinés au personnel de ces entreprises soient rédigés dans la langue de la région, sous peine de nullité. Une traduction peut y être jointe, si la composition du personnel le justifie. Le 19 juillet 1973, le *Conseil* (dit) *flamand* votait un décret étendant les dispositions de la loi aux « contacts verbaux, qui ont avec l'emploi un rapport direct ou indirect » (art. 3) et cela dans absolument toutes les entreprises situées au nord de la frontière linguistique. Ce décret a force de loi. Il est paru au Moniteur belge le 6 septembre 1973. C'est pourquoi certains l'appellent le *décret de septembre* (McRae 1986, 265).

La Cour d'arbitrage, qui constitue actuellement la seule juridiction belge dont le siège du jugement est, pour tous les litiges dont elle est saisie, composé de juges appartenant à des rôles linguistiques différents, a reconnu que ce décret était conforme aux compétences de la communauté (dite) flamande en vertu de la révision constitutionnelle de 1970.

Le Conseil d'Etat est essentiellement composé de chambres francophones et néerlandophones séparées. Il peut être appelé à donner un avis juridique aux pouvoirs législatif et exécutif.

Le *Conseil de la communauté française* a, de son côté, voté en 1978 un décret qui vise essentiellement à maintenir l'intégrité de la langue française en prohibant l'usage de termes étrangers dans les documents officiels ou d'intérêt public. Aucune sanction n'est prévue en cas d'infraction. C'est aussi le cas pour un décret de 1993 relatif à la féminisation des noms de métier.

Quant à l'allemand, il constitue de nos jours une langue nationale, à la suite d'un long processus amorcé en 1920 et qui n'a pas porté tous ses effets (Bergmans 1986, 80 et → art. 137).

Une *Commission permanente de contrôle linguistique* a pour mission de surveiller l'application des lois coordonnées en 1966. Elle est composée de cinq membres francophones, cinq néerlandophones et un germanophone (art. 60, § 1 et 2). Sa compétence n'est que consultative. En revanche, si on ne suit pas son avis, elle peut introduire un recours au Conseil d'Etat. L'accord gouvernemental de 1992 prévoit un élargissement de son pouvoir, quand les autorités sont défaillantes.

La loi sur l'emploi des langues à l'armée date du 30 juillet 1938. « L'instruction complète du soldat se donne dans sa langue (...) » (art. 19). Cette langue est présumée être celle de la commune où il est inscrit, sauf le droit pour l'intéressé de demander sa désignation pour un autre régime linguistique. Tout candidat désirant être admis à un cycle de formation d'officier de carrière, doit subir une épreuve approfondie de français ou de néerlandais et une épreuve de la connaissance élémentaire de l'autre langue ou de la langue allemande. S'il a subi l'examen sur la connaissance élémentaire de la langue allemande, il sera ensuite considéré comme appartenant au régime linguistique français ou néerlandais, suivant la langue pour laquelle il a subi l'épreuve sur la connaissance approfondie. A l'*Ecole royale militaire*, il y a une section française et une néerlandaise, mais certains cours y sont donnés dans l'autre langue. Les exercices sont commandés une semaine dans une langue, la semaine suivante dans l'autre.

Les candidats sous-officiers de carrière doivent, en obtenant au moins la moitié des points à un examen, donner la preuve de la connaissance de la langue de l'unité dans laquelle ils sont appelés à servir. A noter qu'il existe une unité de langue allemande. Un règlement spécial, respectueux des langues des sous-unités, est prévu pour les unités linguistiquement mixtes (art. 24).

Signalons ici l'existence d'une école primaire néerlandophone pour les enfants de militaires casernés au sud du pays et de deux écoles primaires françaises au nord, également pour de tels enfants.

En matière judiciaire. Ici aussi, la loi est déjà ancienne: elle date de 1935 (15 juin). Elle a été adaptée aux quatre régions linguistiques le 9 août 1963. Ici également la langue employée est, en principe, celle de la région linguistique. Et la procédure est poursuivie, s'il y a lieu, dans cette langue jusque devant la Cour suprême, appelée Cour de Cassation. Dans la région de Bruxelles, dans celle de langue allemande et dans les communes à facilités linguistiques, le choix de la langue est possible. En outre, devant les juridictions civiles et commerciales de première instance, lorsque les parties demandent de commun accord que la procédure soit poursuivie dans une langue autre que celle de la région, la cause est renvoyée à la juridiction de même ordre située dans une autre région linguistique (soit la plus proche, soit celle désignée par le choix commun des parties). En matière répressive, l'inculpé peut demander que la procédure se déroule dans sa langue. Toutefois, le tribunal peut décider qu'il ne peut faire droit à la demande du prévenu « à raison des circonstances de la cause » (art. 23). Si le prévenu n'a pas usé de cette faculté et qu'il se révèle qu'il ne connaît pas la langue de la procédure, le juge doit lui désigner un interprète aux frais de l'Etat.

La connaissance des langues par les magistrats, les avocats, jurés et greffiers est vérifiée selon les dispositions prévues aux articles 43 à 49 de la loi. Cela est important pour la région de langue allemande, où une loi du 23 septembre 1985 a créé un arrondissement judiciaire propre.

Relevons qu'il n'y a plus prééminence du texte français des lois sur le texte néerlandais ou allemand. Les divergences sont résolues suivant les règles ordinaires d'interprétation.

En matière d'enseignement. Rappelons d'abord que depuis 1830 l'enseignement primaire a été donné généralement dans la langue dominante de la région où l'école était située. Il n'y eu que 3% d'écoles primaires françaises au nord du pays (McRae 1986, 520). La loi du 30 juillet 1963 règle le régime linguistique des écoles. Elle ne contredit en rien l'art. 23 de la Constitution. Elle ne fait pas allusion à un enseignement dispensé en une autre langue (ou en d'autres langues) que celle de la région. Cela demeure toutefois possible, bien que les certificats qui y sont obtenus ne soient pas reconnus. Il y a lieu de présenter à nouveau les examens devant un jury appelé *jury central*. Ce dernier n'accorde en fait que 1% des diplômes homologués annuellement. Aucune subvention n'est allouée à cet enseignement par l'autorité publique. Ces écoles sont donc payantes, tandis que celles qui se conforment à la loi sont gratuites jusqu'à l'âge de 18 ans. Ces dispositions furent jugées discriminatoires par plusieurs groupes de parents. Ils introduisirent des requêtes devant la Commission, puis devant la Cour européenne des droits de l'homme. L'arrêt rendu ne fut pas défavorable à la loi du 30 juillet 1963, précisément parce que la liberté de dispenser un enseignement dans n'importe quelle langue était sauvegardée. Une seule disposition de la loi, qui n'avait pas été attaquée par les parents, mais qui apparut au cours du procès, fut trouvée discriminatoire. La loi empêche en effet des enfants francophones, dont les parents ne résident pas dans les six communes périphériques bruxelloises qui jouissent de facilités linguistiques, d'accéder aux écoles primaires francophones de ces communes, alors que les enfants néerlandophones domiciliés hors de ces communes, peuvent accéder aux écoles néerlandophones de ces six communes.

Dans les 19 communes bruxelloises ainsi que dans les communes «à facilités», la langue de l'enseignement primaire a été de 1932 à 1971, le néerlandais ou le français selon la langue maternelle ou usuelle de l'enfant. Cette langue était déterminée d'après une déclaration du chef de famille. Cette déclaration faisait l'objet d'un contrôle de l'inspection scolaire. En 1971, ce système fut supprimé à Bruxelles-Capitale et la liberté du chef de famille rétablie. Toutefois, les élèves qui ont commencé leurs études ailleurs et viennent habiter à Bruxelles-Capitale, doivent les continuer dans la langue dans laquelle ils les ont commencées. Pour eux, une inspection scolaire a été maintenue. Son contrôle très strict alimente régulièrement les écoles bruxelloises de langue néerlandaise (Swing 1980, 121). Ces dernières, très minoritaires, attirent aussi des enfants belges bilingues ou francophones, notamment parce que certains parents estiment qu'il y a trop d'immigrants dans les écoles bruxelloises francophones.

L'enseignement de la langue seconde dans *l'enseignement primaire* peut y être organisé à partir de la 5e année d'études. Toutefois, dans les communes de la région de langue allemande, celles de Bruxelles-Capitale, les communes malmédiennes et celles du pays de Montzen, cet enseignement peut être organisé à partir de la première année d'études et doit l'être à partir de la troisième.

La langue seconde sera, dans la région de langue néerlandaise, le français; dans la région de langue française, le néerlandais, l'allemand ou l'anglais; dans l'arrondissement de Bruxelles, ce sera le français dans les écoles de langue néerlandaise et le néerlandais dans les écoles de langue française; dans les écoles de la région germanophone, ce sera le français ou l'allemand. Il y a aussi absence de choix dans *les écoles secondaires* de Bruxelles-Capitale et de la région germanophone. Dans toutes les régions du pays, il faut étudier deux langues secondes parmi six possibles: français, néerlandais, allemand, anglais, italien et espagnol. Au *niveau universitaire*, tout le monde peut étudier dans la langue de son choix.

Enfin, relevons une *Directive obligatoire du Conseil des ministres des Communautés européennes en* date du 25 juillet 1977. Elle vise les enfants des travailleurs migrants soumis à l'obligation scolaire. Les ministres ont déclaré à cette occasion que la Directive s'applique aussi aux enfants des ressortissants qui ne sont pas du Marché commun. En son article 3, elle oblige les Etats membres à promouvoir un enseignement de la langue maternelle des enfants des travailleurs migrants. En Belgique, cette Directive se heurte à la loi du 30 juillet 1963. Néanmoins, quelques dizaines d'expériences ont été mises sur pied, dont une trentaine à Bruxelles-Capitale.

La même Directive, en son article 2, oblige les Etats membres à concevoir l'enseignement de la langue officielle aux immigrés comme celui d'une langue seconde. En outre, les enseignants qui l'assurent, recevront une formation initiale et continue dans cette perspective particulière. Ici aussi il y a lieu de signaler un certain nombre d'expériences.

En matière de presse, de radio et de télévision, il existe une liberté d'expression linguistique totale. La radiodiffusion et la télévision publiques sont subventionnées par les communautés et divisées en trois établissements selon leur langue. Il n'existe toutefois pratiquement pas de télévision belge de langue allemande. Il est à noter que les langues endogènes ont, en principe, accès aux trois établissements. Toutefois, la Radiodiffusion et la Télévision Belge de Langue Française (RTBF) est la seule à leur accorder régulièrement cette chance. Bon nombre de particuliers, notamment des immigrants, possèdent leurs propres postes de radiodiffusion.

En outre, la Belgique a installé sur presque tout son territoire une télévision par câble. Elle permet de capter non seulement les programmes nationaux et ceux des pays voisins, mais également ceux de la Grande-Bretagne, de l'Espagne, de l'Italie ainsi que CNN.

«Au niveau de la presse, il existe 17 quotidiens francophones, 14 néerlandophones et 1 germanophone. Pour survivre, la plupart de ces journaux se sont regroupés. Voici les tirages annoncés pour les principaux quotidiens:

— langue française:
Le Soir 517.300; groupe Vers l'Avenir 432.100; La Meuse/La Lanterne 335.000; groupe Nouvelle Gazette 315.300; La Dernière Heure/Les Sports 230.600; La Libre Belgique 192.600; Groupe Nord-Eclair 113.200, soit au total pour les 7 quotidiens les plus importants: 2.136.100.

— langue néerlandaise:
groupe De Standaard 334.665; groupe Het Laatste Nieuws 249.919; groupe Het Volk

186.610; groupe Gazet van Antwerpen 162.919; Het Belang van Limburg 91.693; groupe De Morgen 40.811; De Financieel-Ekonomische Tijd 23.811, soit au total pour les 7 quotidiens les plus importants: 1.072.428.
— langue allemande:
Grenz-Echo 12.600» (Beheydt et Jucquois 1992, 47). Récemment, des quotidiens de langue néerlandaise auraient augmenté leur tirage.

Standardisation, orthographe, élaboration linguistique.
Pour les langues endogènes belgo-romanes ainsi que le bruxellois, le bas-allemand et le luxembourgeois, c'est désormais le *Conseil des langues régionales endogènes* qui en est responsable. En dehors du bruxellois et du wallon, ces langues protégées sont aussi largement utilisées au-delà des frontières belges (le champenois, le lorrain et le picard en France; le brabançon et le limbourgeois aux Pays-Bas; le flamand en France et aux Pays-Bas; le luxembourgeois au Grand-Duché et en France, le bas-allemand en Allemagne), c'est le plus souvent dans ces pays qu'il faut chercher les centres de normalisation de ces langues. Pour le bruxellois, il existe une académie reconnue par la loi; elle organise des cours de langue, édite un dictionnaire, etc. Pour le wallon, l'orthographe standardisée de Jules Feller s'efforce de concilier les principes parfois contradictoires du phonétisme, de l'étymologie et de l'analogie avec le français. Pour le flamand, citons à titre d'exemple le manuel de Marteel (1992) paru ... en France.

Les langues officielles sont également utilisées beaucoup plus largement en dehors des frontières belges qu'à l'intérieur du pays. C'est en Allemagne, en France et aux Pays-Bas que ces langues sont normalisées. Pour les Pays-Bas, il y a toutefois une situation légale particulière. Ce pays a conclu avec la Belgique en 1980 un traité d'union langagière, en vertu duquel aucune réforme ne sera acceptée sans un accord conjoint du Parlement des Pays-Bas et du Conseil (dit) flamand. Il a donné lieu à la création d'un Secrétariat chargé de l'application des articles du traité relatifs au développement du néerlandais (cf. 5.2.).

7. Présentation des contacts linguistiques

7.1. Entre langues endogènes

Pour l'influence du bas-allemand sur le wallon liégeois, signalons Geschière (1950). En revanche, il y a eu des emprunts wallons dans le bas-allemand d'Eupen (Grondal 1955). Les parlers régionaux belgo-romans et germaniques ont échangé entre eux un certain nombre de termes (Grootaers 1924; Haust 1936, 431 sq); Carte linguistique C.

7.2. Entre langues endogènes et exogènes officielles

Attirons l'attention sur les influences du brabançon sur le français régional de Bruxelles (Baetens Beardsmore 1971, 45–56). Rappelons la thèse de Langhor (1933) visant à rattacher le secteur de Montzen et le canton d'Eupen au Limbourg et sa démonstration de la «superficialité» de l'allemand et du wallon dans ces endroits.

Enfin, il y a eu l'énorme bibliographie, aujourd'hui en déclin, relative à la chasse aux belgicismes (McRae 1986, 63): des philologues romans et des germanistes se plaignant de la percée du «substrat» régional dans les langues officielles (flandricismes, wallonismes) ou des interférences indues entre les langues officielles (p. ex. Haeseryn 1975, 1536–1551). Ces publications n'ont toutefois pas l'objectivité et la précision des études sur les régiolectes aux Pays-Bas.

7.3. Avec les langues étrangères

Pour l'italien, signalons l'enquête de Pivetta (1963); pour l'espagnol, relevons un travail collectif (Arguelles et al. 1979) et un article (García Macho 1986). Sur l'impact social des langues étrangères on pourra lire Costa (1983) et Verdoodt (1983 et 1984). Sur les interférences de l'arabe, du berbère, de l'espagnol, de l'italien et du turc à l'école, signalons Tassin (1981).

7.4. Langues pas traitées ailleurs

Il y a d'abord le latin et le grec classiques. Jusqu'en 1964, la filière gréco-latine était quasi la seule qui conduisait à l'Université. Pour ceux qui l'ont suivie et pour ceux qui la suivent encore, on peut déceler une influence bienfaisante sur la connaissance approfondie des langues modernes et un contact fécond avec les œuvres littéraires qui ont engendré notre civilisation. On peut affirmer en partie la même chose pour ceux qui étudient l'hébreu biblique et le judéo-araméen. Ces deux langues ne sont enseignées qu'au niveau universitaire.

Il y a enfin le latin d'église, l'arabe coranique, le grec ecclésiastique, le slavon, l'arménien, le copte, le syriaque, etc. A l'exception de l'hébreu et du latin, ces langues sont essentiellement liées aux religions des migrants. Elles partagent avec les autres langues spécialisées — y compris l'anglais commercial et scientifique — un sort peu enviable pour leur transmission: elles doivent être réapprises à chaque génération hors du cercle familial.

8. Examen critique de la bibliographie

De nombreux auteurs insistent sur la nécessité d'un consensus social par rapport à tout projet linguistique. Cela a même amené le créateur de l'expression « planification du langage » à revoir son concept et à inclure dans son modèle la notion d'*évaluation* (Haugen 1983, 275). La Belgique constitue, selon nous, un bon exemple de planification linguistique où l'évaluation des mesures prises fait singulièrement défaut.

Dans le domaine de l'aménagement du statut social de la langue, on aura remarqué l'insistance quasi exclusive sur les efforts des autorités politiques au plus haut niveau. Or, ce qui importe selon le simple bon sens, corroboré par les conclusions de la majorité des recherches, c'est la transmission de la langue d'une génération à la suivante. Il en résulte que les décrets relatifs à l'usage des langues dans l'enseignement ne peuvent pas à eux seuls assurer une telle transmission. D'abord, parce qu'en Belgique la plupart des enfants arrivent à l'école en parlant une langue autre que celle de l'école (cf. 4.1.). « Ensuite, parce que l'écart entre la fin de la scolarité et le commencement de la génération suivante est beaucoup trop long pour que l'école soit capable de combler toute espèce de lacune » (Fishman 1991, 373).

Une illusion de même nature règne à propos de l'influence des médias. Aucune étude ne peut la justifier. En conséquence, nous pouvons affirmer que « les médias sont insuffisamment interpersonnels, trop peu orientés vers l'enfant, trop dénués d'affectivité, pour obtenir la transmission effective d'une langue à la génération suivante » (Fishman 1991, 374).

Enfin, on a mis l'accent sur l'utilisation de la langue au travail et même sur une certaine autonomie régionale de l'économie. Cela aussi est aléatoire, étant donné la prédominance croissante des firmes et des relations internationales: 70% des 30.000 entreprises les plus importantes sont majoritairement étrangères.

Bien sûr, toutes les recettes que nous venons de citer paraissent contribuer au succès d'une politique linguistique. En fait, aucune n'est capable de convertir une langue non-maternelle en langue maternelle. C'est surtout l'œuvre de la famille, du voisinage et de toutes les relations primaires, c'est-à-dire vécues face-à-face. C'est parce qu'au nord de la Belgique, on a conservé au niveau de la famille et du voisinage les langues régionales qu'on a pu y introduire un enseignement, des médias, etc. en néerlandais et non l'inverse. Il en est de même au Luxembourg avec l'allemand, etc.

En outre, quand les locuteurs d'une langue maternelle ont tendance à trop diverger, « une première étape consiste à établir des normes communes au niveau de la grammaire, de la phonologie, de l'intonation et de la prosodie ... L'alternative consiste à adopter une variété historiquement inauthentique, qui n'est pas la variété régionale. Cela ne constitue pas un péché ..., mais a pour effet d'exposer un mouvement historique préoccupé d'authenticité ... à des accusations embarrassantes de manque d'authenticité » (Fishman 1991, 397). C'est le problème de la « nativisation » du néerlandais (Deprez 1991, 9; Doornaert 1993), mais aussi du français et de l'allemand (cf. 5.2.) en Belgique.

Considérant le grand nombre d'enfants qui arrivent à l'école en parlant une langue endogène non-officielle ou une langue étrangère, il est vital de tenir compte des mises-en-garde de Trudgill (1975, 80—83), un sociolinguiste anglais:

« Suggérer à un enfant que sa langue, et que celle des personnes auxquelles il doit son identité, est d'une certaine façon une langue inférieure, c'est supposer que l'enfant lui-même est inférieur. Cette attitude doit normalement conduire soit à une aliénation par rapport à l'école ..., soit au rejet du groupe dont il fait partie. Cette attitude constitue aussi une faute du point de vue social, parce qu'elle paraît impliquer que certains groupes ont moins de valeur que d'autres. Cela est particulièrement indésirable quand la langue stigmatisée est celle d'enfants de la classe ouvrière et que la langue prônée est celle d'instituteurs adultes de la classe moyenne. Enfin, et cela est peut-être le plus important, cette attitude est mauvaise au plan pratique, car elle ne produit pas et ne produira pas l'effet escompté. Apprendre une nouvelle langue constitue une tâche difficile ... et, en bien des cas, il est encore plus difficile d'apprendre une variante de sa propre langue, parce que ces deux langues sont si semblables et qu'il est particulièrement compliqué de les tenir séparées. Il faut aussi tenir compte du fait, qu'en bien de cas, un locuteur ne tient pas du tout à changer sa langue ... Les pressions liées à l'identification à son groupe ... sont très fortes. Les recherches linguistiques ont démontré que le groupe de référence adolescent (adolescent peer-group) constitue l'influence langagière la plus importante. Les enfants ne grandissent pas en s'entretenant comme leurs maîtres, leurs modèles sont ceux de leurs amis, de leurs pairs. En d'autres termes, c'est du temps perdu que d'essayer à l'école de tuer toute forme de langage non officiel. Si des enfants souffrent parce qu'ils utilisent de l'anglais non-standardisé, la solution ne consiste pas à éliminer les variétés non-standardisées. Bref, le problème n'est pas avant tout linguistique; il ne l'est même pas du tout. Tâchons donc, en tenant compte de ce qui précède, d'apprendre aux enfants à lire l'anglais normalisé. Mais en outre, tentons d'éduquer notre société à comprendre, à apprécier et à tolérer les variantes non-standardisées et à y reconnaître des systèmes complexes, valides et adéquats d'expression. Des critiques ont appelé cela utopique ... Néanmoins cela peut s'avérer plus simple ... que de transformer les modèles linguistiques de la majorité de la population. »

Cette mise-en-garde dramatique de Trudgill se trouve confirmée par une enquête-participation récente sur la petite communauté rurale de Lutrebois (Ardenne belge). Francard (1993, 13), analysant une situation de diglossie franco-wallonne, a constaté que les formes les plus vives d'insécurité linguistique n'avaient pas de rapport direct avec la pratique effective de la langue régionale, le wallon, mais paraissaient augmenter avec le nombre d'années de scolarisation. Ce serait l'institution scolaire qui générerait l'insécurité linguistique en développant à la fois la perception des variétés linguistiques et leur dépréciation au profit d'un modèle mythique ... (le français normé).

« Une réflexion sociologique construite à partir de la situation de la Belgique fait apparaître que l'Etat ne peut « contracter » avec la société qu'au travers des formes sociales, qu'on désigne parfois par le terme « société civile » et qui jouent un double rôle: permettre à la société, dans son hétérogénéité, de s'accommoder de la présence de la structure étatique et, à cette dernière, d'avoir une visibilité sociale » (Poche 1992, 43). Le système des trois familles spirituelles, la catholique, la libérale et la socialiste, constitue toujours l'interface fondamentale entre une société civile historiquement fragmentée et l'Etat. Mais un nouvel élément est intervenu: le doublet langue-territoire. Sa force est telle qu'il a tendance à casser en deux les familles spirituelles. Sans doute les organisations sociales qui les sous-tendent (syndicats, mutualités, coopératives) demeurent fondamentalement belges. Mais la famille spirituelle catholique a été amenée, sous la pression de l'Etat, à lâcher le principe de l'unicité de l'Université catholique de Louvain. Ce n'est qu'un des exemples les plus frappants du changement des structures. Et le transfert louvaniste s'est fait encore en bonne partie sous l'influence de quelques meneurs de la société civile, notamment de la presse. Mais qu'en sera-t-il des changements ultérieurs? N'auront-ils pas « pour effet de rendre presque inaudible la notion de régulation sociale non étatique. Si, du coup, l'Etat en face de ce réinvestissement du sociétal, entreprend de prendre directement en charge les notions correspondantes, il va tendre à les déplacer du domaine de la vie quotidienne au domaine rationnel/scientifique ... Cette tentative, selon nous, est vouée à un échec ... parce que les finalités qui s'y manifestent ne sont pas ... fonctionnalisables » (Poche 1992, 66). Néanmoins, les lois linguistiques en matière judiciaire et sur l'emploi des langues à l'armée fonctionnent bien depuis 60 ans. Il est vrai qu'elles laissent une porte ouverte à l'initiative personnelle. En revanche, les lois linguistiques relatives à l'administration et à l'enseignement (cf. 6.3.) engendrent des tensions; ces lois sont essentiellement territoriales. Les superstructures communautaires et régionales ont notamment pour effet de renforcer les polarisations. Quel que soit le processus d'intégration européenne, il y aura lieu de les dépasser.

Concluons donc avec le constitutionnaliste suisse M. Borghi (1993, 9 sq):

« Le principe de territorialité (linguistique) ... méconnaît la mobilité croissante de la population, en adoptant finalement une attitude guerrière et primitive de défense du territoire ... Une solution idéale ... pourrait être représentée par la création d'écoles bilingues ... Selon une initiative parlementaire déposée par la Conseillère nationale Lemi Robert et 27 cosignataires, l'encouragement à une éducation bilingue ... devrait être ancré dans la Constitution, qui devrait charger les cantons de cet encouragement ».

Une disposition constitutionnelle de ce type répondrait à la volonté de l'immense majorité des Belges (Verdoodt 1976).

9. Bibliographie (sélective)

André, Robert (1990): «Population». In: *Modern Belgium*, Boudart, M. et al. (Eds.), Palo Alto, 28—40.

Arguelles, M. et al. (1979): *Le bilinguisme et l'école. Enquête sur les enfants espagnols de Liège*, Liège.

Baetens Beardsmore, Hugo (1971): *Le français régional de Bruxelles*, Bruxelles.

Baetens Beardsmore, Hugo (1993): «Prolingua dans le contexte belge et européen» In: *Prolingua* 1, 6.

Bal, Willy (1990): «Langues régionales de Wallonie». In: *Conseil de la Communauté française*, 30 octobre, 8−11.

Bastenier, Albert (1992): «L'ethnicité visible à Bruxelles». In: *Revue Nouvelle* 11, 48−61.

Beheydt, Ludo/Jucquois, Guy (1992): «La Belgique, Trois langues, trois régions, trois communautés». In: *1992: Situations linguistiques dans les pays de la Communauté européenne*, Herreras, J. C. (Ed.), Valenciennes.

Bergmans, Bernhard (1986): *Le statut juridique de la langue allemande en Belgique*, Louvain-la-Neuve.

Borghi, Marco (1993): «Diversité et droit à la culture: l'exemple antinomique du système fédéraliste suisse». In: *Les droits culturels: une catégorie sous-développée des droits de l'homme*, Meyer-Bisch, P. (Ed.), Fribourg, 247−262.

Boudart, Marina/Boudart, Michel/Bryssinck, René (Eds.), (1990): *Modern Belgium*, Palo Alto.

Brugmans, Hendrik (1972): «Flamands et Hollandais: les complexes réciproques». In: *Septentrion* 1, 59−64.

Costa, Elisabeth (1983): *Necessidad en Bélgica de lenguas modernas extranjeras menos empleadas*, Louvain-la-Neuve.

D'Anfton, L. (1989): «La loi du 18 avril 1898 relative à l'emploi des langues dans les publications officielles». In: *Recueil des lois*, vol. 28.

Debrock, Mark (1991): «La situation actuelle du français en Flandre». In: *Septentrion* 20, 2, 40−50.

De Decker, Jacques (1990): «Theater, dance, and cinema». In: *Modern Belgium*, Boudart, M. et al. (Eds.), Palo Alto, 508−513.

Deleeck, Herman (1990): «The welfare system». In: *Modern Belgium*, Boudart, M. et al. (Eds.), Palo Alto, 324−335.

Deprez, Kas (1987): «Le néerlandais en Belgique». In: *Politique et aménagement linguistique*, Maurais, J. (Ed.), Québec, 200−250.

Deprez, Kas (1991): «Refenretiekader voor het Vlaams Nederlands». In: *De Standaard*, 29 oktober.

De Ridder, Paul (1989): «Préjugés antibruxellois des Flamands, vus par un Bruxellois (N)». In: *Toudi* 3, 87−91.

De Schrijver, Reginald (1990): «Belgium until World War I». In: *Modern Belgium*, Boudart, M. et al. (Eds.), Palo Alto, 54−72.

Doornaert, Mia (1993): «Koningin Paola hoeft geen Vlaams te leren». In: *De Standaard*, 18 august.

Draye, Hendrik (1942): *De studie van de Vlaamsch-Waalsche taalgrens in België*, Louvain.

Fishman, Joshua (1971): *Sociolinguistique*, Bruxelles.

Fishman, Joshua (1991): *Reversing language shift*, Clevedon.

Francard, Michel (Ed.) (1993): *L'insécurité linguistique en Communauté française de Belgique*, Coll. «Français et Société», n° 6, Bruxelles.

Garcìa Macho, Maria Lourdes (1986): «Inventaire du degré et du mode d'utilisation de l'espagnol en Belgique». In: *Recherches sociologiques* 27, 2, 200−212.

Geschiere, Louis (1950): *Eléments néerlandais du wallon liégeois*, Amsterdam.

Grootaers, L. (1924): «Quelques emprunts entre patois flamands et wallons». In: *Leuvensche Bijdragen* 16, 43−64.

Grondal, G. (1955): «Le canton d'Eupen». In: *Bulletin de la société verviétoise d'archéologie et d'histoire* 42, 7−82.

Haeseryn, René (1975): «Taal en Vlaamse Beweging». In: *Encyclopedie van de Vlaamse Beweging*.

Hanse, Joseph (1964): *Maîtrise de la langue maternelle et bilinguisme scolaire*, Liège.

Haugen, Einar (1983): «The implementation of corpus planning: Theory and practice. In: *Progress in language planning*, Cobarrubias, J. (Ed.), Berlin.

Haust, Jean (1936): «Eléments germaniques du dictionnaire liégeois». In: *Bulletin de toponymie et de dialectologie* 10, 431−470.

Huys, Bernard (1990): «Music in Flanders». In: *Modern Belgium*, Boudart, M. et al. (Eds.), Palo Alto, 514−520.

Jaspaert, Koen (1984): *Statuut en struktuur van standaardtalig Vlaanderen*, Louvain.

Jaspaert, Koen/van Belle, William (1989): «The evolution of the diglossic system in Flanders (1850−1914)». In: *Language and intergroup relations in Flanders and in the Netherlands*, Deprez, K./Van Belle, W. (Eds.), Dordrecht.

Kardiner, Abram (1969): *L'individu dans la société*, Paris.

Langohr, Jozef (1933): *Le Nord-Est de la province de Liège et le canton d'Eupen. Terre belge flamande, superficiellement allemandisée et romanisée*, Bruges.

Lapiower, Alain (1992): «Le rap, culture d'immigration». In: *Revue Nouvelle* 11, 85−93.

Legrand, Francine-Claire (1990): «Architecture, painting and sculpture». In: *Modern Belgium*, Boudart, M. et al. (Eds.), Palo Alto, 487−507.

Leonardy, Ernst (1979): «Die deutschsprachige Literatur im ostbelgischen Raum». In: *Deutsch als Muttersprache in Belgien*, Nelde, P. H. (Ed.), Wiesbaden, 241−251.

Levy, Paul M. G. (1932): « Le recensement des langues en Belgique ». In: *Revue de l'Institut de sociologie* 3, 507–570.

Liebaers, Herman/Robert-Jones, Philippe (1990): « Conclusion ». In: *Modern Belgium*, Boudart, M. et al. (Eds.), Palo Alto, 530–532.

Linton, Ralph (1986): *Les fondements culturels de la personnalité*, Paris.

Marques, Balsa, Casimiro (1993): « Vitalité et stratégies de transmission des langues au sein des communautés étrangères en Belgique ». In: *International Journal of the Sociology of Language* 104, 87–112.

Marteel, Jean-Louis (1992): *Het Vlaamse dan men oudders klappen*, Dunkerque.

McRae, Kenneth (1986): *Belgium*, Waterloo (Ontario).

Meeus, Baudewijn (1979): « A diglossic situation: standard vs dialect: the case of Dutch in Belgium ». In: *Trends in Linguistics*, Mackey, W. et al. (Eds.), The Hague, 335–344.

Nelde, Peter H./Weber Peter J. (1995): « Les trois identités linguistiques en Belgique – des particularismes culturels? ». In: *Sociolinguistica* 9, Tübingen, 88–95.

Pivetta, Marie-Louise (1963): *Le parler des Italiens de Merlemont*, Liège.

Poche, Bernard (1992): « La Belgique entre les piliers et les mondes linguistiques ». In: *Recherches sociologiques* 23, 3, 150–200.

Pohl, Jacques (1979): *Les variétés régionales du français*, Bruxelles.

Pulinckx, Raymond (1992): « Manufacturing and construction industry ». In: *Modern Belgium*, Boudart, M. et al. (Eds.), Palo Alto, 238–246.

Rezsohazy, Rudolphe/Kerkofs, Jan (1984): *L'univers des Belges*, Louvain-la-Neuve.

Riggs, Fred (1985): *Ethnicity*, Hawaii.

Roosens, Eugeen (1986): *Micronationalisme. Een antropologie van het ethnisch reveil*, Louvain.

Sion, Georges (1990): « French-language literature ». In: *Modern Belgium*, Boudart, M. et al. (Eds.), Palo Alto, 463–477.

Swing, Elisabeth (1980): *Bilingualism and linguistic segregation in the schools of Brussels*, Québec.

Tassin, M. (1981): *Et vous, si vous étiez à l'école à Ankara, Rabat, Rome, Madrid?*, Bruxelles.

Trudgill, Peter (1975): *Sociolinguistics*, Harmondsworth.

Verdoodt, Albert (1976): « Les problèmes communautaires belges à la lumière des études d'opinion ». In: *Courrier hebdomadaire du CRISP*, 742, 1–21.

Verdoodt, Albert (1983): *Enquête relative aux besoins généraux en langues dans les entreprises et les services publics*, Louvain-la-Neuve.

Verdoodt, Albert (1984): *Enquête relative aux besoins généraux en langues du personnel académique et scientifique et des étudiants des universités*, Louvain-la-Neuve.

Verdoodt, Albert (1989): *Les langues écrites du monde. Volume 3. Europe occidentale*, Québec.

Verdoodt, Albert (1989a): « L'unilingue, cet analphabète du XXIe siècle ». In: *Diagnostics; enjeux sociaux et politiques en Belgique*, Rezsohazy, R. (Ed.), Louvain-la-Neuve, 150–175.

Voyé, Liliane et al. (1992): *Belges, heureux et satisfaits*, Bruxelles.

Wangermée, Robert (1990): « Music in Wallonia and Brussels ». In: *Modern Belgium*, Boudart, M. et al. (Eds.), Palo Alto, 521–526.

Weijnen, Antoon (1966): *Nederlandse dialectkunde*, Assen.

Weisgerber, Jean (1990): « Dutch-language literature ». In: *Modern Belgium*, Boudart, M. et al. (Eds.), Palo Alto, 478–486.

Geen talentelling (1959): Bruxelles (Vlaams aktiekomitee Brussel en taalgrens).

Albert Verdoodt, Louvain-la-Neuve (Belgique)

136. Niederländisch–Französisch

1. Geschichte
2. Soziolinguistische Lage
3. Allgemeines kontaktlinguistisches Porträt
4. Bibliographie (in Auswahl)

1. Geschichte

1.1. Im Gebiet des heutigen Belgien hat es die Kontaktsituation zwischen der niederländischen und der französischen Sprache immer gegeben. Die romanisch-germanische Sprachgrenze, die ungefähr um das 11. Jahrhundert den jetzigen Verlauf eingenommen hat (Draeye 1942), teilt Belgien in zwei Teile.

Historische Linguisten sehen als Beweis für frühe Kontakte z. B. die Palatalisierung von altgemeingerman. /u/ und die Vokalisierung von /l/ in der Sequenz „a, o + l + Dental" an. Die Gebersprache soll der pikardische Dialekt, d. h. der Grenzdialekt in Nord-frankreich, gewesen sein. Vor allem die am engsten benachbarten (west-)flämischen Dialekte sollen als Vermittler für den romanischen Einfluß auf das übrige Niederländisch fungiert haben (Gysseling 1960). Obwohl später in diesem Artikel vor allem von Interferenz als Folge des Sprachkontaktes zwischen Flamen und Wallonen die Rede sein wird, sieht man hier, daß auch der französische Nachbar, und zwar nicht nur im Mittelalter, oft einen nicht unbeträchtlichen Einfluß ausgeübt hat.

Im Laufe der Jahrhunderte hat sich der Verlauf der Sprachgrenze kaum verändert, dagegen jedoch oft der Status der Kontaktsprachen (Willemyns 1994). Heute ist die Sprachgrenze eine offizielle Binnengrenze, die beide Landesteile trennt und den Kontakt zwischen den beiden belgischen Sprachgruppen auf ein Mindestmaß reduziert hat. Bis vor kurzem jedoch fiel die Sprachgrenze nie völlig mit den politischen Grenzen zusammen. Sowohl zu Flandern als auch zu Brabant und zu Lüttich haben immer niederländisch- und französischsprachige Gebiete gehört (→ Sprachenkarte C).

1.2. Von Anfang an wurde der Kontakt mit der französischen Sprache noch dadurch intensiviert, daß die Grafschaft Flandern ein Lehen des französischen Königs war. Ältere niederländ. literarische Texte waren sehr oft Bearbeitungen von (alt)französischen Vorlagen, und in der ganzen alten niederländ. Schriftsprache machte sich der französische Einfluß bemerkbar (De Vries/Willemyns 1993). Salverda de Grave (1906) zeigt, daß viele Wörter schon im 12. Jahrhundert entlehnt wurden.

Nach der (überall eintretenden) Ersetzung von Latein als Amtssprache hat zuerst eine Zeitlang Französisch die frühere Funktion des Lateins übernommen, d. h., daß viele der nicht-adligen Intellektuellen zweisprachig waren. In Brabant, das dem „Heiligen Römischen Reich Deutscher Nation" zugehörig war, war der französische Einfluß bei den Adligen geringer und in der Verwaltung kaum vorhanden.

1.3. Während der burgundischen Zeit (ab 1369) war zuerst Französisch nicht nur die Hof-, sondern auch die Verwaltungssprache. Obwohl allmählich das Niederländische seinen angestammten Platz wieder eroberte (Armstrong 1965), markierte jedoch die Burgunderzeit die allgemeine Durchsetzung der Zweisprachigkeit (bei den höheren Schichten) in den Niederlanden (Willemyns 1995).

Nach dem Tod Karls V. brach während der Regierung seines Sohnes Philipp II. der achtzigjährige Krieg aus, der zur Spaltung der Niederlande führte (die Folgen für die Sprachentwicklung werden u. a. in Willemyns/Van de Craen [1988] besprochen). De facto wurden Nord und Süd 1585 nach dem „Fall von Antwerpen", de jure erst 1648 durch den „Westfälischen Frieden" getrennt.

1.4. Die nördlichen Gebietsteile erlangten ihre Unabhängigkeit, der Süden jedoch blieb fest in spanischer Hand, wurde „rekatholiziert" und erlebte einen ökonomischen Niedergang, dem ein Exodus der Mehrheit der wirtschaftlichen, politischen, wissenschaftlichen und kulturellen Oberschicht vorangegangen war. Im zurückgebliebenen Süden schloß sich die sich allmählich neu heranbildende Oberschicht der französischen Orientierung des flämischen und brabantischen Adels an. Während des Regimes der Spanier und im folgenden der Österreicher (ab 1714) standen die südlichen Niederlande unter französischem (und damit fremdem) Kultureinfluß. Dementsprechend wurde die gesamte Oberschicht und ein Teil der nach Aufstieg strebenden Mittelschicht französisiert (Deneckere 1954).

1.5. Als 1794 das spätere Belgien von Frankreich annektiert wurde, erreichte der französische Einfluß in Flandern seinen Höhepunkt. Gesetzlich wurde der Gebrauch jeder anderen Amtssprache als Französisch in der gesamten Republik untersagt. Die Französischkenntnisse waren jedoch sozial determiniert: je höher die Sozialschicht, desto mehr war zweisprachige Kompetenz vorhanden, die es auch mehr in den Städten als auf dem Lande gab. Am Ende der französischen Zeit (1814) war das Niederländische eine völlig prestigelose Sprache, der kaum noch offizielle Funktionen geblieben waren, die kaum noch gedruckt wurde und nur in Dialektform weiterlebte, und zwar als Kommunikationsmittel der Unterschicht. Die Wiedervereinigung der nördlichen und der südlichen Niederlande in einem „Vereinten Königreich der Niederlande" (1814−1830) war zu kurz, um Grundlegendes zu ändern.

1.6. Der echte „Sprachenkampf" aber, der so lange das politische Leben Belgiens bestimmen sollte, hat erst 1830 richtig eingesetzt, in jenem Jahr, in dem Belgien politisch „unabhängig" wurde. Eine kleine herrschende Schicht kontrollierte alle Verwaltungsfunktionen. Sie beherrschte das gesellschaftliche Leben, die Wirtschaft und die Staatsverwaltung. Und sie sprach Französisch (Ruys 1982, 46). Am 26. 11. 1830 wurde Französisch zur einzigen Verwaltungssprache erklärt.

1.6.1. Eine sogenannte „Flämische Bewegung" (EVB 1973—75) versucht von Anfang an, für die kulturellen und sprachlichen Rechte der unmündigen Bürger (von 3,5 Millionen Einwohnern waren nur 46 000 wahlberechtigt) zu kämpfen. Das Volk war in hohem Maße ungebildet. Der Volksschulunterricht, der weiter in der (niederländ.) Volkssprache erteilt wurde, stand auf einem niedrigen Niveau. An allen weiterführenden Schulen, auch den Berufs- und Handwerkerschulen, wurde ausnahmslos in der französischen Sprache unterrichtet (Ruys 1981, 46). 1877, bzw. 1883 wurde die Möglichkeit eingeräumt, in Gerichtshöfen und im Oberschulwesen Niederländisch (neben Französisch, versteht sich) zu verwenden, und erst 1889 wurde das sogenannte „Gleichheitsgesetz" verabschiedet, nach dem Französisch *und* Niederländisch zu den beiden offiziellen Sprachen des belgischen Staates erklärt wurden. Schließlich wurde im Jahr 1930 die Universität von Gent „niederlandisiert".

1.6.2. Danach beschleunigte sich die Entwicklung. 1932 wurde mittels der sogenannten „Sprachgesetze" der niederländische Charakter Flanderns offiziell festgelegt. Da die Wallonen eine allgemeine Zweisprachigkeit im gesamten belgischen Raum ablehnten, wurden beide Teilgebiete einsprachig, und so war die Voraussetzung für eine konsequente Handhabung des Territorialitätsprinzips geschaffen. Später haben die Belgier mittels Grundgesetzänderungen von 1970, 1980, 1988 und letztlich 1993 das sogenannte „Sprachenproblem" gelöst, indem sie die frühere zentralistische Struktur des Landes in eine föderale umgewandelt haben. Die Grenzen zwischen den vier Gebieten (dem niederländischsprachigen Flandern, der französischsprachigen Wallonie, dem zweisprachigen Brüssel und den deutschsprachigen „Ostkantonen") wurden endgültig bestimmt und durch ihre Eintragung ins Grundgesetz quasi unveränderlich gemacht.

2. Soziolinguistische Lage

2.1. Charakteristisch für die linguistische Situation in Flandern ist ein Sprachkontinuum, das vom Dialekt bis zur Hochsprache reicht. Der *Dialekt* wird von einer langsam kleiner werdenden, aber immerhin noch sehr großen Gruppe von Flamen für die alltägliche und informelle Kommunikation benutzt. In etwas formelleren Situationen kann eine *regionale Umgangssprache* verwendet werden, eine durch erhebliche Dialektinterferenz gekennzeichnete Mischform, deren sozialer Gebrauchswert auch immer mehr auf die weniger gebildete Schicht der Bevölkerung beschränkt wird. In semi-formellen Situationen bedienen sich immer mehr Flamen einer Sprachvarietät, die als *belgische Kultursprache* gekennzeichnet werden kann („Belgisch Beschaafd" wird sie oft genannt). Obwohl sie zweifellos eine standardsprachliche Funktion erfüllt, fehlen ihr wichtige Charakteristiken, die normalerweise eine Standardsprache auszeichnen, wie z. B. eine allgemein akzeptierte Norm. Auch weist eben diese Varietät eine viel größere Zahl von „Belgizismen" auf, darunter die noch zu besprechenden „Gallizismen". An der Spitze des Kontinuums befindet sich die *allgemeine Standardsprache*, die gemeinsame Hochsprache der Niederlande und des niederländischen Belgien. Obgleich sowohl von den Flamen als auch von den Niederländern eine rigide Normierung angestrebt wird, kann man auf Grund bestimmter Faktoren (z. B. Intonation und Rhythmus) meistens den Unterschied zwischen einer nördlichen und einer südlichen Realisierung der Standardsprache hören (Willemyns 1987). Ähnliche wie die für Flandern genannten Sprach- und Registerunterschiede gibt es auch im französischsprachigen Teil Belgiens, obwohl da angeblich der Dialektgebrauch weniger als in Flandern verbreitet ist. Genaue Angaben fehlen hier aber, da über die Sprachsituation in der Wallonie bislang nur sehr wenige soziolinguistische Studien erschienen sind (Pohl 1979).

2.2. Wie man der historischen Übersicht entnehmen kann, war in den Gebieten des jetzigen Belgiens Französisch jahrhundertelang die Prestigesprache. Die Situation hat sich in den letzten Jahrzehnten allmählich geändert und zwar auf Grund verschiedener extralinguistischer Faktoren.

Seit dem Ende der 50er-Jahre hat sich das Zentrum der ökonomischen Entwicklung und Macht in Belgien allmählich von der Wallonie nach Flandern verlagert. Hier hat ein großer wirtschaftlicher Aufschwung dafür gesorgt, daß diese vorher vorwiegend agrarische Region sich in ein hochindustrialisiertes Gebiet umwandelte, welches das politische, soziale und ökonomische Leben Belgiens weitgehend beherrscht. Fast zur gleichen Zeit passierte in der Wallonie genau das Umgekehrte: ihre veraltete industrielle Struktur brach zusammen, und das führte zu einer tiefgehenden und andauernden Wirtschaftsrezession.

Die Kombination dieser Ereignisse hat dafür gesorgt, daß die Machtstruktur völlig umgeworfen wurde, auch im kulturellen und linguistischen Bereich. Das hat den Flamen ermöglicht, in den letzten Jahrzehnten mehr von ihren sprachlichen und kulturellen Forderungen zu verwirklichen, als dies während des letzten Jahrhunderts der „flämischen Bewegung" möglich war. Das Niederländische, das schon immer die Mehrheitssprache war, hat allmählich auch den Status der Prestigesprache des Landes erlangt (Willemyns 1992). Das zeigt sich u. a. auch daran, daß sich auch die Zweisprachigkeitsverhältnisse geändert haben. Die Flamen, die früher immer gezwungenermaßen diejenigen waren, die die andere Landessprache zu beherrschen versuchten und zu verwenden verpflichtet waren, kümmern sich heutzutage immer weniger darum, während umgekehrt die Französischsprachigen sich immer mehr Mühe geben, Niederländisch zu lernen und zu verwenden. So sieht man, daß Fishmans Maxime „The weak are always more likely to be bilingual than the strong" auch hier zutrifft.

3. Allgemeines kontaktlinguistisches Porträt

3.1. Niederländisch − Französisch

3.1.1. Das erste „echte" Sprachpflegebuch handelt von der französischen Sprache: Poyart 1811 analysiert „Flandrizismen, Wallonismen und andere Sprachfehler". Bei vielen der angegebenen und verpönten Beispiele hat man es viel mehr mit übersetztem Niederländisch als mit Französisch zu tun. Einige Beispiele:

− nicht „je *suis* gagné" (Nl. „ik *ben* gewonnen")
sondern „j'*ai* gagné" [ich habe gewonnen]
− nicht „il est *la demi d'une heure*" (Nl. het is *half een*]
sondern „il est *midi et demi*" [es ist halb eins]

Poyart steht damit am Anfang einer Tradition, die bis heute andauert. Bestimmte Bücher von Sprachpflegern wie Doppagne (1979), Hanse et al. (1987), sind immer noch Bestseller, die vor sog. Belgizismen warnen. Davon stellen die sog. Flandrizismen die Mehrheit dar und werden auch häufig von Leuten verwendet, die gar kein Niederländisch können. Umgekehrt ist, wie wir weiter sehen werden, in Flandern von „Gallizismen" die Rede, und in vielen Fällen hat man es mit dem kombinierten Einfluß von einerseits der peripheren Lage des Sprachgebiets bezüglich des Standardisierungsschwerpunktes der Sprache (Bister/Willemyns 1988) und andererseits dem Sprachkontakt zu dem anderssprachigen Nachbarn zu tun.

3.1.2. Manchmal ist von lexikalischen Elementen die Rede (d. h. Lehnwörtern bzw. Lehnübersetzungen), von denen wir hier nur einige bekannte Beispiele anführen, wie *bloquer* [büffeln], *bourgmestre* [Bürgermeister], *brosseur* [Schwänzer], *couque* [Plätzchen, Kuchen], *drève* [Allee], *kermesse* [Kirmes], *polders* [Polderlandschaft], *potiquet* [Töpfchen], *spéculaus* [Spekulatius], *wassingue* [Aufnehmer].

Daß diese Erscheinungen kein Einzelfall sind, zeigen u. a. die systematischen Analysen von Wind (1960) und Baetens Beardsmore (1971). Im ersten Fall ist das belgische Französisch im allgemeinen, im zweiten vor allem das Brüsseler Französisch der Untersuchungsgegenstand.

3.1.2.1. Wind (1960, 10) weist darauf hin, daß die unten angeführten Beispiele mehr als nur linguistische Kuriositäten sind. Daß die genannten Konstruktionen auch zum normalen Sprachgebrauch gehören − sogar bei Sprechern, die selber nicht mehr Niederländisch können − zeigt, wie weitreichend diese Einflüsse des Bilinguismus sind:

− Die zweisprachigen Flamen haben die Auslautverhärtung auch auf das (belgische) Französische übertragen, und sie ist im belgischen Französischen charakteristisch geworden: [lank] = langue; [roop] = robe. Wie im Niederländischen „hebben − ik [hep]", hat man im belgischen Französisch „tomber − je [tomp]"
− Wahrscheinlich kommt durch niederländischen Einfluß die progressive Assimilation,

die normalerweise im Französischen eher selten auftritt, in Belgien oft vor. Gemäß dem niederländischen Muster „ontfangen; ontsien" spricht man „achfer (achever); échfin (échevin):
- „*Jef sa tante*" nach dem niederländischen Muster „*Jan z'n hoed*";
- In Belgien hört man „*cet homme n'est pas à fier, Mr. n'est pas à causer*".

Wahrscheinlich liegt hier niederländischer Einfluß vor, wo genau diese Konstruktion bei bestimmten intransitiven Verben möglich ist. Auch die syntaktische Konstruktion: „*mon mari est déjà cinq ans mort*" ist nur vom Niederländischen aus zu erklären. Andere Beispiele solcher syntaktischen Lehnübersetzungen sind:

- „Qu'est-ce que c'est que cela *pour* un homme" (Nl. wat is dat voor een man) [was ist das für ein Mann];
- „Tu dois tirer fort *pour l'avoir dehors*" (Nl. je moet hard trekken om het eruit te krijgen) [man muß sehr ziehen, um es herauszukriegen];
- „Je n'ai *rien* besoin" (Nl. ik heb niets nodig) [ich brauche nichts];
- „*ça* je veux bien" (Nl. dat wil ik wel) [das will ich schon gern].

3.1.2.2. Baetens Beardsmore (1971) betont, daß eine Analyse von Syntax und Morphologie klar zeigt, „wie sehr das Brüsseler Französisch bis in die innere Struktur von niederländischen Elementen geprägt" wird. „Der größte Einfluß" so meint er (1971, 435), „stammt daher, daß oft ein Zweisprachiger in der einen Sprache denkt, aber in der anderen redet". Eben dadurch, erklärt er, bleibt auch „die interne Struktur der Sprache nicht unbetroffen, weil die Besonderheiten der einen Sprache auch auf die andere übertragen werden und zwar in beiden Richtungen. Das Niederländische übernimmt vom Französischen vor allem lexikalische Elemente, die Morphologie und die Syntax sind dagegen weniger betroffen. Das Französische wird vor allem auf phonetischer Ebene vom Niederländischen beeinflußt. Aber auch die Syntax, die Morphologie und die Semantik unterliegen gewissen niederländischen Einflüssen" (Baetens Beardsmore 1971, 48—49). Als Beispiele der niederländischen Interferenz im Französischen von Brüssel nennt Baetens Beardsmore u. a.:

- Adjektive werden vor dem Nomen verwendet „une propre chemise" (Nl. een schoon hemd) [ein sauberes Hemd];
- das Adverbium „assez" wird, wie „genoeg" im Nl. am Satzende verwendet: „pas bon assez" (niet goed genoeg) [nicht gut genug];
- Nach niederländischem Muster werden Possessiva verwendet, wo im Französischen der Artikel steht: „il a mal à sa jambe" (Nl. hij heeft pijn aan zijn been) [das Bein tut ihm weh];
- „ça" wird mit „être" verwendet wie Niederländisch „dat" mit „zijn": „ça est bon"; (Nl. dat is lekker [das ist lecker]);
- Bestimmte Modalverben werden in der niederländischen statt in der französischen Bedeutung verwendet: „savoir" statt „pouvoir": „je ne sais pas te le dire" [ich kann es dir nicht sagen];
- Verwendung von Modalpartikeln, die Lehnübersetzungen aus dem Niederländischen sind und/oder auf Französisch nicht existieren: „dites-moi *une fois*" (Nl. vertel mij *eens*) [erzähl' mir mal];
- Präpositionen werden als Adverbien verwendet: „vous avez fini *avec*?" (Nl. ben je *daarmee* klaar?) [bist Du damit fertig?].

3.2. Französisch-Niederländisch

3.2.1. Im lexikalischen Bereich (wo die Interferenz am beträchtlichsten ist) unterscheidet man meistens drei Kategorien, die auf Interferenz beruhen und somit als Gallizismen betrachtet werden. Allerdings hat in der Sprachpflegetradition im niederländischen Sprachraum der Begriff „Gallizismus" mit mehr zu tun als nur mit Sprachkontakt. Obwohl es im gesamten niederländischsprachigen Raum französischen Einfluß gibt, werden als „Gallizismen" *stricto sensu* meistens nur solche Wörter betrachtet, die zwar häufig im belgischen Niederländisch auftreten, in der (auf nördlicher Grundlage normierten) niederländischen Standardsprache aber nicht verwendet werden. Es ist Tradition in der niederländischen Sprachpflege, daß alle Wörter, die nur regionale Verwendung finden (z. B. nur in Belgien) immer als regelwidrig und folglich nicht als zur Standardsprache gehörend empfunden werden (Willemyns 1986). Trotzdem ist es auffällig, daß im maßgebenden niederländischen Wörterbuch *Van Dale* ziemlich tolerant über flämische Regionalismen geurteilt wird: „(...) dat de aanduiding 'Zuidnederlands' geen discriminatie, geen brandmerk inhoudt (...) Er is geen sprake van afkeuring" [... daß die Markierung 'Südniederländisch' keine Diskriminierung, kein Brandmal beinhaltet. Von Ablehnung ist hier nicht die Rede]. Sofort wird auch hinzugefügt „tenzij het een gallicisme is" [Es sei denn, es handelt sich um einen Gallizismus].

3.2.2.
Von den drei lexikalischen Kategorien, die allgemein als Gallizismen betrachtet werden, gibt es zwei „normale" und eine „besondere". Die normalen sind:

3.2.2.1. Lehnwörter
(a) unverändert übernommen
autostrade (Nl. autoweg; [Autobahn]); *chauffage* (Nl. verwarming; [Heizung]); *mazout* (Nl. stookolie; [Heizungsöl]) *pistolet* (Nl. broodje; [Brötchen]).
(b) dem Niederländischen angepaßt
mutualiteit (Fr. mutualité; Nl. ziekenfonds; [Krankenkasse]); *nonkel* (Fr. oncle; Nl. oom; [Onkel]); *solden* (Fr. soldes; Nl. koopjes; [Angebote]).

3.2.2.2. Lehnübersetzungen
dagorde (Fr. ordre du jour; Nl. agenda; [Tagesordnung]); *kroon* (Fr. couronne; Nl. krans; [Kranz]); *schrik hebben* (Fr. avoir peur; Nl. bang zijn; [Angst haben]); *wachtzaal* (Fr. salle d'attente; Nl. wachtkamer; [Wartesaal]); *zakencijfer* (Fr. chiffre d'affaires; Nl. omzetcijfer; [Umsatzzahlen]).

3.2.2.3. „Purismen"
Die dritte Kategorie ist besonderer Art, da es sich hier um *indirekten* Einfluß handelt. Die Flamen, die sich — vor allem aus sprachpolitischen Gründen — gerne gegen französischen Einfluß wehren (allerdings nicht immer erfolgreich), haben eine Reihe von französischen Lehnwörtern, die sie in ihren Dialekten kennen, für die hoch- oder umgangssprachliche Verwendung „übersetzt". Da diese Übersetzungen aber in der Standardsprache fehlen, werden sie als regelwidrig angesehen. Solche Hyperkorrektionen werden auf Niederländisch als „purismen" eingestuft: *duimspijker* (Nl. punaise; [Heftzwecke]); *koetswerk* (Nl. carrosserie; [Karosserie]); *regenscherm* (Nl. paraplu; [Regenschirm]); *uurwerk* (Nl. horloge; [Uhr]); *voetpad* (Nl. trottoir; [Bürgersteig/Fußweg]); *wisselstukken* (Nl. reserveonderdelen; [Ersatzstücke]).

3.2.3.
Selbstverständlich gibt es Gallizismen auch außerhalb des lexikalischen Bereichs. Sie werden seltener erwähnt, auch weniger als solche erkannt und deshalb auch hier nicht weiter besprochen.

3.2.4.
In dieser Übersicht wurde nur auf die Hochsprache und Umgangssprache Rücksicht genommen. Französischen Einfluß gibt es aber auch in den niederländischen Dialekten, so wie es auch niederländischen in den französischen Dialekten gibt.

3.3. Sprachpflege
Der niederländische Einfluß auf das Französische ist vor allem im belgischen Französisch bemerkbar. Umgekehrt reicht der französische Einfluß auf das Niederländische weit über die belgische Grenze hinaus (Frijhoff 1991). Allerdings ist der Einfluß des Französischen in Flandern noch viel größer und zeigt sich deutlich sowohl in den flämischen Dialekten und in der südlichen Umgangssprache als auch in der belgischen Varietät der niederländischen Hochsprache. Eine Erklärung ergibt sich aus der in unter 2. beschriebenen historischen Entwicklung. Im 19. Jahrhundert hatte die Unterdrückung des Niederländischen in Belgien einen Höhepunkt erreicht. Der zeitgenössische Sprachpfleger H. Meert schreibt:

„Wie könnte der Flame, dem ein ungenügender Unterricht in seiner Muttersprache vermittelt wurde, der also nur mangelhaft die allgemeine Standardsprache beherrscht, wie könnte der einwandfreies Niederländisch verwenden? Täglich werden wir vom französisch Lesen beeinflußt und so viele französische Ausdrücke haben sich in unserem Kopf eingenistet, mit deren niederländischen Gegenstücken wir nicht vertraut sind und die wir also unbewußt übersetzen" (Meert 1899, 21).

Ähnliche Klagen finden sich bei seinem Kollegen W. de Vreese (1899). Aus dem Buch des Sprachpflegers C. Peeters *Woordenboek van Belgicismen* geht hervor, daß sich auch 1930 die Situation nicht wesentlich geändert hatte. Peeters hat seine Absicht, wie folgt, formuliert:

„In unserem Wörterbuch werden, in alphabetischer Reihenfolge, die wichtigsten südniederländischen Abweichungen der Hochsprache aufgezeichnet und erklärt und die normgerechten hochsprachlichen Termini angegeben. Ausgangspunkt ist, was am vertrautesten ist, d. h. die sprachliche Varietät so, wie sie bei uns üblich ist, (einschließlich aller Provinzialismen, Barbarismen, französischen Ausdrücke usw.). Nach deren Erklärung gilt es das weniger Vertraute zu vermitteln, d. h. die korrekte hochsprachliche Form".

Bis auf den heutigen Tag erscheinen nicht nur Bücher, sondern auch regelmäßig Zeitungsartikel, in denen aus der gleichen Perspektive versucht wird, den niederländischen Sprachgebrauch der Flamen von Belgizismen und anderen Sprachfehlern zu „säubern". Eine Zeitlang wurde ähnliches auch mittels Radio- und Fernsehsendungen angestrebt. Diese Sprachplanungskampagne und inwieweit sie ihre Ziele erreicht hat, wird in Willemyns (1988) ausführlich beschrieben.

4. Bibliographie (in Auswahl)

Armstrong, C. A. J. (1965): „The Language Question in the Low Countries; The Use of French and Dutch by the Dukes of Burgundy and Their Administration". In: *Europe in the Late Middle Ages*, Hale, J. R./Highfield, J./Smalley, B. (Eds.), London, 386—409.

Baetens Beardsmore, Hugo (1971): *Le français régional de Bruxelles*, Brüssel.

Bister, Helga/Willemyns, Roland (1988): „Perifere woordenschat in woordenboeken van het Duitse, Franse en Nederlandse taalgebied". In: *De Nieuwe Taalgids 81*, 417—429.

Deneckere, Marcel (1954): *Histoire de la langue française dans les Flandres (1770—1823)*, Gent.

De Vreese, Willem (1899): *Gallicismen in het Zuidnederlandsch. Proeve van taalzuivering*, Gent.

De Vries, Jan/Willemyns, Roland/Burger, Peter (1993): *Het verhaal van een taal: Negen eeuwen Nederlands*, Amsterdam.

Doppagne, Albert (1979): *Belgicismes de bon aloi*. Brüssel.

Draeye, Henri (1942): *De studie van de Vlaamschwaalsche taalgrens in België*, Brüssel.

EVB. *Encyclopedie van de Vlaamse Beweging*. Tielt, 1973—75 (zwei Bände).

Frijhoff, J. Willem (1991): „Bastertspraek en dartele manieren. De Franse taal in Nederlandse mond". In: *Jaarboek van de Maatschappij der Nederlandse letterkunde te Leiden 1989—1990*, 13—25.

Gysseling, Maurits (1960): „Schets van het ontstaan van de Frans-Nederlandse taalgrens". In: *Wetenschappelijke Tijdingen 20*, 433—438.

Hanse, Joseph/Doppagne, Albert/Bourgeois-Gielen, Hélène (1987): *Chasse aux Belgicismes*. 12e édition, Brüssel.

Lorwin, Val (1972): „Linguistic Pluralism and Political Tension in Modern Belgium". In: *Advances in the Sociology of Language II*, J. A. Fishman (Ed.), Den Haag, 386—412.

Meert, Hypoliet (1899): *Onkruid onder de tarwe*, Gent.

Peeters, Constant H. (1930): *Nederlandsche Taalgids. Woordenboek van Belgicismen met verklaring, en opgave van de overeenkomstige woorden en uitdrukkingen in het algemeen Nederlandsch*, Antwerpen.

Pohl, Jacques (1979): *Les variétés régionales du français: études belges (1949—1977)*, Brüssel.

Poyart, N. (1811): *Flandricismes, Wallonismes et expressions impropres dans la langue française (...) par un ancien professeur*, Brüssel (deuxième édition).

Ruys, Manu (1981): *Die Flamen. Ein Volk in Bewegung, eine werdende Nation*, Tielt.

Salverda de Grave, J. J. (1906): *De Franse woorden in het Nederlands*, Amsterdam.

Willemyns, Roland (1986): „Regionalismen in het Nederlands". In: *Verslagen en Mededelingen van de Koninklijke Academie voor Nederlandse Taal- en Letterkunde*, 108—131.

Willemyns, Roland (1987): „Norm en Variatie in Vlaanderen". In: *Variatie en Norm in de Standaardtaal*, de Rooij, J. (Ed.), Amsterdam, 143—164.

Willemyns, Roland (1988): „Language Planning as an Indicator of Linguistic Change". In: *Georgetown Roundtable on Languages and Linguistics*, 349—357.

Willemyns, Roland (1992): „Linguistic Legislation and Prestige Shift". In: *Status Change of Languages*, Ammon, U./Hellinger, M. (Eds.), Berlin/New York, 3—16.

Willemyns, Roland (1994): „Patterns of Linguistic Fluctuation along the Romance-Germanic Language Border in France and in Belgium". In: *Contrastive Sociolinguistics*, Ammon, U./Hellinger, M. (Eds.), Berlin/New York.

Willemyns, Roland (im Druck): „Taalpolitiek in de Bourgondische tijd". In: *Versagen en Mededelingen van de Koninklijke Academie voor Nederlandse Taal- en Letterkunde*.

Willemyns, Roland/Van de Craen, Pete (1988): „Growth and Development of Standard Dutch in Belgium". In: *Sociolinguistica. 2*, 117—130.

Wind, Bartina H. (1960): „Nederlands-Franse taalcontacten". In: *Neophilologus 44*, 1—11.

Roland Willemyns, Brüssel (Belgien)

137. Französisch—Deutsch

1. Geographie und Demographie
2. Geschichte
3. Wirtschaft und Kultur
4. Statistik und Ethnoprofile
5. Soziolinguistische Lage
6. Sprachpolitische Lage
7. Allgemeines kontaktlinguistisches Porträt
8. Forschungslage
9. Bibliographie (in Auswahl)

1. Geographie und Demographie

1.1. Geographie

Seit Gründung des Staates 1830 werden in Belgien von einer bodenständigen Bevölkerung drei Sprachen gesprochen: Französisch, Niederländisch und Deutsch. Die deutsch-französischen Sprachkontakte in Belgien sind somit so alt wie der belgische Staat selbst. Zwei territoriale Verschiebungen haben jedoch die Geographie und Demographie der Deutschsprachigen verändert: (a) eine erste 1839, als durch die Abtretung eines gerade in Besitz genommenen Teils Luxemburgs an das Großherzogtum Luxemburg auch ein großer Teil der deutschsprachigen Bevölkerung wieder aus dem belgischen Staatsverband ausschied — der verbliebene Teil wird in der Literatur üblicherweise „Altbelgien" genannt — und (b) eine zweite 1920, als sich infolge der durch den Versailler Vertrag bestimmten Angliederung der ehemals deutschen (preußischen) Gebietsteile um Eupen und Malmedy das belgische Staatsgebiet durch das Gebiet des sog. „Neubelgien" auf seine heutige Ausdehnung wieder vergrößerte. Diese beiden Ereignisse bilden zusammen mit dem kurzen, aber folgenschweren Gebietswechsel von 1940 bis 1945 (Rückangliederung Neubelgiens, Nordaltbelgiens und anderer Teile an das Deutsche Reich) die äußeren Gliederungsmarken für die allgemein geschichtliche und damit auch sprach- und kontaktgeschichtliche Entwicklung des deutschen Sprachgebiets. Eine Darstellung, die die deutsch-französischen Sprachkontakte allein auf das heute gesetzlich festgelegte Territorium („Neubelgien", abzüglich Malmedy und Weismes) beschränkte, wäre folglich höchst unzureichend, da sie nicht nur die sprachhistorischen Tatbestände Altbelgiens ausschlösse, sondern sich auch der Möglichkeit beraubte, die heutige soziolinguistische Wirklichkeit unterhalb der Gesetzesebene in eben diesem Gebiet wahrzunehmen.

Uneinheitlichkeit besteht in unserem Untersuchungsgebiet jedoch nicht nur in geschichtlicher Hinsicht, auch geographisch bildet es trotz seiner relativ bescheidenen Ausdehnung kein zusammenhängendes Ganzes. Neben dem im Osten des Landes, an der belgisch-deutschen Staatsgrenze liegenden und durch die Gebirgsschranke des Hohen Venns in einen nördichen (Eupener Land) und südlichen Teil (St. Vither Land) getrennten schmalen Gebietsstreifen des deutschsprachigen Neubelgiens können, diesem vorgelagert, drei weitere Teilgebiete unterschieden werden, die man in der Terminologie von P. Nelde (1979, 7 ff) als *Altbelgien-Nord* (Montzener Land, von den Frankophonen „Welkenraedter Gegend" genannt), *Altbelgien-Mitte* (Bocholz, mit den Dörfern Deifeld, Urt und Watermal) und, weiter abgesetzt und an der belgisch-luxemburgischen Staatsgrenze liegend, als *Altbelgien-Süd* (Areler Land) zu bezeichnen pflegt (→ Sprachenkarte C).

1.2. Demographie

Was die demographische Struktur der Gebiete betrifft, so hat nach der Staatswerdung der Zuzug vorwiegend wallonischer oder französischsprachiger Amtspersonen zum schnellen Wachstum vor allem der städtischen Bevölkerung in Altbelgien beigetragen (in Arel z. B. hat sich nach 1830 in weniger als einem Jahrzehnt die Bevölkerung versechsfacht). Aber auch nach Eupen-St. Vith sind Zuwanderungen aus Innerbelgien und Wallonien, jedoch auch aus Altbelgien und dem Großherzogtum Luxemburg erfolgt. Die neuere, von Mobilität der Arbeits- und Lebenswelt (Pendlertum, Gastarbeitertum, Tourismus, Mischehenpraxis usw.) geprägte Zeit hat, wie auch andernorts, die alten Gesellschaftsformationen weiter aufgelockert. Das Bevölkerungswachstum der letzten Jahrzehnte hat sich insgesamt jedoch kaum nennenswert verändert (3% im Eupener Gebiet in den letzten 40 Jahren, Nullwachstum in St. Vith, s. Benrath 1994, 4).

2. Geschichte

2.1. Altbelgien

Die unmittelbar nach der Unabhängigkeit Belgiens verkündete sog. Sprachenfreiheit — „Die Bürger dürfen sich in ihren Beziehungen mit der Verwaltung frei der französischen, flämischen oder deutschen Sprache bedienen" (Erlaß v. 16. Nov. 1830, Art. 5; bekräftigt durch Art. 23 der Verfassung) — fand, ebenso wie die Verfügung, den Gesetzen und Erlassen im deutsch-belgischen Gebiet eine deutsche Übersetzung beizufügen, schon bald nach 1839 keine praktische Anwendung mehr. Verwaltungssprache und Gerichtssprache waren in Deutschbelgien fortan fast ausschließlich Französisch. Bezüglich des Unterrichtswesens legte ein Gesetz vom 25. Sept. 1842 fest, daß der Primarschulunterricht neben Rechnen, Schreiben, Lesen usw. „notwendigerweise und je nach den Bedürfnissen der Ortschaften auch die Grundbegriffe der französischen, flämischen oder deutschen Sprache zu umfassen hatte" (Bull. Off. Nr. LXXXIII, Art. 6). Weitergehend regelte dann Art. 15 des Gesetzes vom 19. Mai 1914, „daß der Unterricht in den Gemeindeschulen auf allen Stufen in der Muttersprache der Kinder zu erteilen ist". Allerdings belegen zahlreiche Klagen aus jener Zeit, daß auch hier Gesetzeswirklichkeit und Schulwirklichkeit oft auseinanderklafften. Der Sekundarschulunterricht erfolgte weiterhin auf Französisch, eine leichte Besserung des Zustandes trat erst 1932 ein.

Die während des 1.Weltkrieges von der deutschen Besatzung getroffenen Verordnungen zur rechtlichen Besserstellung der deutschen Sprache im Amtsverkehr wurden am Ende des Krieges sofort wieder aufgehoben. In der Sprachgesetzgebung der Zwischenkriegszeit fand das Deutsche kaum oder gar keine Berücksichtigung mehr. Nach dem Einmarsch deutscher Truppen in Belgien wurden durch die Erlasse Hitlers vom 18. und 23. Mai 1940 außer dem Gebiet von Eupen-Malmedy auch neun nordaltbelgische Gemeinden sowie Bocholz (Altbelgien-Mitte) dem Deutschen Reich angegliedert. Bis 1945 galt dort deutsche Gesetzgebung, d. h. deutsche Einsprachigkeit in Verwaltung, Gerichtswesen, Schule usw. Diese Maßnahmen wurden nach Rückführung dieser Gebiete nach Belgien wieder außer Kraft gesetzt. Der offiziellen Ächtung der deutschen Sprache schloß sich zahlreicher persönlicher Verzicht auf deren Gebrauch auch im inoffiziellen Bereich an. Schließlich mußte das Deutsche auch noch aus Schule und Kirche weichen, wo es sich noch bis zuletzt halten konnte, nachdem es schon lange aus dem administrativen und judiziären Bereich verschwunden war. Damit hatte das Deutsche als Kultur- und Schriftsprache in Altbelgien ausgespielt. Seitdem existiert es dort nur noch als „Volkssprache" im Rückzugsbereich der häuslichen und dörflichen Sphäre, und zwar fast ausschließlich in der mundartlichen Sprachform.

2.2. Neubelgien

Für das durch den Versailler Friedensvertrag mit Wirkung vom 10. Januar 1920 Belgien zugesprochene bisher deutsche (preußische) Gebiet Eupen-Malmedys, Neutral-Moresnets sowie einiger kleinerer, später hinzugekommener Teile wurde — außer für Neutral-Moresnet, das gleich der Provinz Lüttich zugeteilt wurde — zunächst ein mit voller gesetzgeberischer und ausführender Gewalt ausgestattetes Übergangsregime unter Gouverneur General Henri Baltia eingerichtet. Man beauftragte ihn mit der Einführung der belgischen Gesetzgebung und der Organisation der Verwaltungs- und Gerichtsstrukturen. Mit Dekret vom 30. Sept. 1920 wurden alle reichsdeutschen Bestimmungen, die den ausschließlichen Gebrauch der deutschen Sprache vorschrieben, abgeschafft, und das Französische neben dem Deutschen als gleichwertige Amtssprache bestimmt. An den Primarschulen wurde der Unterricht in der Regel in der Muttersprache erteilt; der obligatorische Unterricht der Zweitsprache Französische begann, analog zur Regelung im altbelgischen Gebiet von Montzen und Arel, im deutschsprachigen Neubelgien bereits im ersten Jahr, der Zweitsprachenunterricht Deutsch in den wallonischen Schulen Malmedys erst vom 5. Jahr an. In den Sekundarschulen Eupens und, seit 1926, St.Viths „liefen Deutsch und Französisch als Unterrichtssprachen der unteren Klassen parallel; in der Oberstufe wurde nur noch französischer Unterricht erteilt" (Pabst 1979, 26). Diese Sprachenregelung in Gerichtswesen, Verwaltung und Schule blieb über das Ende des Übergangsregimes (1925) hinaus im großen und ganzen bis 1940 gültig. Nach Rückangliederung der bereits erwähnten, 1940 an Deutschland abgetretenen Gebiete, setzte 1945 eine breite Repression gegen die Bevölkerung ein, der die erzwungene Sezession als „ziviler Ungehorsam" ausgelegt wurde. Den „wiedergewonnenen Kantonen" wurde vom Innenminister ein strenges Anpassungsprogramm verordnet:

„Die Aufgabe, die der Regierung in den Ostkantonen obliegt, besteht in ihrer Reassimilierung an die belgische Lage in kürzester Zeit. Es sollte berücksichtigt werden, daß vor den Ereignissen von

1940 diese Assimilierung nicht vollständig war und daß die jetzige Lage ein Klima und Voraussetzungen geschaffen hat, die es auszunutzen gilt..." (Bergmans 1986, 24)

In diesem Sinne setzte auch eine breite sprachliche „Reassimilierung" ein, die insbesondere das Schulwesen betraf, um den Rückstand des Französischen möglichst bald aufzuholen. Nach gründlicher Säuberung der Lehrerschaft war in den 50er Jahren etwa folgender Stand erreicht: „In der Grundschule hatte zwar Deutsch als Unterrichtssprache vielerorts noch eine Vorrangsposition behalten, in den Mittelschulen und Gymnasien jedoch mußte die deutsche Sprache zusehends dem Französischen als Unterrichtssprache, als Fach- und Lehrsprache weichen" (Jenniges 1992, 6). Diese Assimilierungsphase war noch vollauf im Gange, als in den 60er Jahren ein politischer Umschwung eintrat, der zu einem neuen Abschnitt in der Geschichte der drei Sprachengruppen in Belgien führen sollte. Unter dem massiven Druck der Flamen, der sich gegen den vorwiegend französisch dominierten Zentralstaat richtete, wurde eine kulturelle Föderalisierung geschaffen, die auch den deutschsprachigen Neubelgiern zugute kam: sie erhielten − wie die beiden anderen Sprachengruppen − ein auf dem Territorialitätsprinzip beruhendes und mit einer sprachlich-kulturellen Autonomie ausgestattetes, eigenes, geographisch genau umgrenztes „deutsches Sprachgebiet" − wobei nach belgischer Rechtsterminologie unter „Sprachgebiet" nicht ein Gebiet zu verstehen ist, in dem eine bestimmte Sprache gesprochen wird, sondern ein Gebiet, in dem und gegenüber dem diese Sprache öffentlich benutzt werden muß. Die nicht nachlassenden Forderungen nach noch stärkerer Dezentralisierung leiteten schließlich einen umfassenden Staatsumbau ein. An die Stelle zentralstaatlicher Gewalt treten jetzt neue föderale Strukturen mit genau abgegrenzten Vollmachten. So besitzt der „Rat der deutschsprachigen Gemeinschaft" seit 1980 gesetzgeberische Vollmachten in allen sprachlich-kulturellen Angelegenheiten, einschließlich des Unterrichtswesens, und sogar in einigen darüberhinausgehenden Bereichen (z.B. im Sozialwesen). Er fungiert wie ein Gebietsparlament, ist direkt von der Bevölkerung gewählt und wählt seinerseits seit 1984 eine aus drei Personen („Ministern") bestehende „Exekutive", die die Gebietsregierung darstellt. Der entscheidende neue Artikel 1 der revidierten belgischen Verfassung lautet jetzt: „Belgien ist ein Föderalstaat, der sich aus Gemeinschaften und Regionen zusammensetzt." Während die deutschsprachigen Neubelgier als „deutschsprachige Gemeinschaft" eine der drei belgischen „Gemeinschaften" bilden, sind sie in den „Regionen", den zweiten konstitutiven Bestandteilen des Föderalstaates, denen die Wahrnehmung wichtiger, v. a. wirtschaftspolitischer Befugnisse obliegt, als eigenständiger Partner nicht vertreten; sie sind vielmehr in die „wallonische Region" integriert, in der auch die Altbelgier ihren Platz haben.

Amtssprache in dem Gebiet der „deutschsprachigen Gemeinschaft" ist nach dem vom Staatsrat festgelegten Prinzip grundsätzlicher Einsprachigkeit und Homogenität von „Sprachgebieten" de jure allein Deutsch. Da dieses Gebiet jedoch zugleich ausnahmslos ein Gebiet mit weitgehenden Spracherleichterungen zugunsten der französischen Sprache ist, kann man sagen, daß de facto Französisch zweite Amtssprache ist. Unterrichtssprache in den Schulen ist in der Regel (mit Ausnahmen) Deutsch, in den französischen Schulen bzw. Schulklassen Französisch. Auch die Sprache der Kirche ist Deutsch. Ebenso wird in den nichtöffentlichen Domänen das Deutsche, sei es in hochsprachlicher, umgangssprachlicher oder mundartlicher Form, gebraucht.

3. Wirtschaft und Kultur

3.1. Wirtschaft

Das Wirtschaftsbild Neubelgiens hat sich gegenüber früheren Zeiten insgesamt erhalten: der Norden in und um Eupen ist stärker industrialisiert, das südliche St.Vither Land mehr landwirtschaftlich geprägt. Im einzelnen hat sich aber die wirtschaftliche Infrastruktur z. T. erheblich verändert. An die Stelle der einst blühenden Textilindustrie (Eupen) oder Kalksteingewinnung (Kelmis) sind neue Produktionszweige getreten, darunter die Metallverarbeitung, mit dem Kabelwerk in Eupen als größtem Wirtschaftsunternehmen des Gebietes. Eupen beherbergt Dienstleistungsunternehmen und Gewerbebetriebe, es ist wirtschaftlicher Mittelpunkt und zugleich Verwaltungszentrum mit Sitz des Gebietsparlaments und der Gebietsregierung. Sonst herrscht das Kleinunternehmertum vor. Während im Süden die Landwirtschaft in den letzten Jahren stark zurückgegangen ist (30% innerhalb von acht Jahren), entwickelten sich Tourismus und gastronomisches Gewerbe zu neuen, wichtigen Wirtschaftsfaktoren. Die Arbeitslosenrate (1990: 7,5%) liegt weit unter der in Wallonien oder in Gesamtbelgien. Ein nicht unbedeutender Teil der Bevölkerung (± 4.000) arbeitet im benachbarten Aachener Raum und im Großherzogtum Luxemburg; nicht bezifferbar ist die Zahl wallonischer Pendler im deutschen Sprachgebiet. (Benrath 1994, 5ff; Jenniges 1991, 15f) Was das Gebiet Altbelgiens betrifft, so ging auch hier der Anteil der in der Landwirtschaft tätigen Personen stark zurück. Ein Ausgleich wird oft außerhalb des Gebietes gesucht, im Norden in Lüttich, im Süden im benachbarten Luxemburg.

3.2. Kultur

Das Kulturleben in Neubelgien war eigentlich zu allen Zeiten lebendig. Neben lokalen Vereinigungen der Volkskultur (Gesangsvereinen, Karnevalsgesellschaften usw.) gibt es auch Vereine mit wissenschaftlichem (Geschichtsvereine) oder künstlerischem Anspruch (Theatergruppen, Literaturzirkel). Durch das Vorhandensein deutschsprachiger Medien (einer Tageszeitung, eines ganztägig Deutsch sendenden Rundfunks, eines Fernsehens im Versuchsstadium) wird auch auf die Kultur außerhalb des Gebietes geblickt und Kulturaustausch begünstigt. In Altbelgien dagegen kann von einem deutschen Kulturleben längst keine Rede mehr sein. Nur noch in wenigen Nischen existiert alte Volkskultur fort. Am auffälligsten wohl in Form der in den letzten Jahren neubelebten Mundarttheater, die sich sowohl im nördlichen wie im südlichen Teil großer Beliebtheit erfreuen. Im Areler Land nimmt sich seit 1976 eine Kulturvereinigung („Arelerland a Sprooch") der Erhaltung der Volkssprache und des Kulturerbes an (Kern 1983, 78ff), in Altbelgien-Nord und Altbelgien-Mitte fehlen vergleichbare Initiativen.

4. Statistik und Ethnoprofile

4.1. Ethnolinguistik

Die niederfränkischen, ripuarischen und moselfränkischen Mundarten Alt- und Neubelgiens stellen historisch gewachsene Altmundarten dar, die sich sprachgeographisch gut voneinander abgrenzen lassen: so haben das Montzener Land und der westliche Teil des Eupener Landes niederfränkisch-ostlimburgische, der östliche Teil des Eupener Landes und der nördliche Teil des St.Vither Landes ripuarische, das restliche St.Vither Land, Bocholz und das Areler Land im Süden moselfränkische Mundarten. Weil die deutsche Schrift- und Kultursprache in Altbelgien seit 1945 durchgängig durch Französisch ersetzt ist, ist es üblich geworden, sowohl die niederfränkischen Mundarten des Montzener Landes als auch die moselfränkischen Mundarten des Areler Landes mit Hilfe der Terminologie von Kloss als „dachlose" deutsche Mundarten zu bezeichnen − im Gegensatz zu den entsprechenden „überdachten" Mundarten des westlichen Eupener Landes bzw. des St.Vither oder auch Bitburger-Prümer Landes. (Kramer 1984, 129ff) Die Ähnlichkeit des im Montzener und westlichen Eupener Land gesprochenen Dialekts mit dem Niederländischen hat jedoch Anlaß gegeben, die geolinguistische Zuweisung dieses Dialekts zum Deutschen in Zweifel zu ziehen. Solche am Anfang des Jahrhunderts aufgekommene und in den 20er und 30er Jahren verstärkte und von politische Nebenabsichten nicht freie Versuche („Glottotomie") sind allerdings ohne Erfolg geblieben und gelten heute als überholt. (Pabst 1979, 29; Nelde 1979, 23) Ebenso hat ein anderer Versuch, diese Dialekte lieber „kontinentalwestgermanisch" zu nennen, schon wegen des viel zu weiten Bedeutungsumfangs dieser Bezeichnung keinen Anklang gefunden. Im Unterschied dazu ist für den moselfränkischen Dialekt des Areler Gebiets neben die älteren Bezeichnungen „Luxemburgerdeutsch", „Arelerdeutsch", ja sogar (fälschlich) „Plattdeutsch", neuerdings, d. h. seit der gesetzlichen Anhebung des luxemburgischen Dialekts zur „Nationalsprache" des Großherzogtums Luxemburg 1984, die verkürzende Selbstbezeichnung „Luxemburgisch" (ähnlich wie „Elsässisch" für „Elsässerdeutsch") jetzt in allgemeineren Gebrauch gekommen.

4.2. Statistische Angaben

4.2.1. Neubelgien

Als Neubelgien zu Belgien kam, zählte es rund 60.000 Einwohner, von denen etwa 50.000 Deutsch bzw. deutsche Mundarten und etwa 10.000 Französisch bzw. wallonische Mundarten sprachen. „Während es frankophone Bürger in den deutschsprachigen Gemeinden so gut wie nicht gab, wohnten in den französischsprachigen Gemeinden um Malmedy − infolge Zuzuges und Einheirat − etwa 30% Deutschsprachige." (Kramer 1984,

143) Deren heutiger Anteil (bei 16.242 Einwohnern 1990) wird von Héraud (1989, 31) auf 20%, von Jenniges (1991, 18) auf 25% geschätzt. Das offiziell deutschsprachige Gebiet von Eupen und St.Vith zählte am 31.12.1990: 67.584 Einwohner, davon 40.278 im Eupener und 27.306 im St. Vither Bezirk. Der Anteil der zugezogenen Französischsprachigen beträgt gegenwärtig nach Héraud (1989, 32) insgesamt etwa 5%, nach Jenniges (1991, 18) im Eupener Raum 5%, im St.Vither Raum 1%.

4.2.2. Altbelgien

Die Zahl der deutschsprachigen Altbelgier belief sich 1830 auf ungefähr 250.000, 1839 auf rund 50.000, d. h. weniger als 1% der Gesamtbevölkerung (Bischoff 1941, 35). Die amtliche belgische Statistik nennt für die kommenden Jahrzehnte folgende Zahlen: 1846: 34.060, 1906: 36.344, 1910: 77.395, 1920: 42.063 Altbelgier; im belgischen Parlament sprach man um die Jahrhundertwende von 14.635 und zugleich 112.000 deutschsprachigen Belgiern (Pabst 1979, 22; Nelde 1979, 28). Wie diese, sind auch Zahlen aus späterer Zeit verwirrend und unzuverlässig. Zwei Forscher haben daher, nach Einstellung der offiziellen Sprachenzählungen in Belgien 1947, durch eigene Felderhebungen den tatsächlichen Sprachenstand aufzuklären versucht: Der erstere, A.Verdoodt (1968, 5f), kommt für ganz Altbelgien (bei 47.000 Bewohnern im Areler und 17.500 im Montzener Gebiet) auf 30.000 bis 50.000 deutschsprechende Personen; der zweite, P. Nelde (1979, 52f, 73), mit verfeinerten Untersuchungsmethoden arbeitend, gibt den Anteil der deutschen Mundartsprecher für das Montzener Land mit 70%, für Altbelgien-Mitte mit 77,5% und für das Areler Land mit 66% an. Legt man diese kontaktlinguistisch erhobenen Angaben zugrunde, kommt man auf rund 42.000 deutschsprachige Altbelgier (± 30.000 im Areler, ± 12.000 im Montzener Raum). Danach dürfte die deutschsprachige Bevölkerung Belgiens heute insgesamt rund 100.000 Personen umfassen (= weniger als 1% der Gesamtbevölkerung).

5. Soziolinguistische Lage

In Altbelgien besitzt das Deutsche keinen legalen Status mehr. Das Französische hat als offizielle Sprache auch voll die Funktion der Schrift- und Kultursprache übernommen und dient auch als Leitsprache im mündlichen Sprachverkehr. Das Deutsche, nur noch geschwächt in mündlicher Sprachform vorhanden, ist in seiner Verwendung auf den Bereich des Dorfes, des Familien- und Bekanntenkreises eingeschränkt. Die Mundart ist (und war immer) typische Volkssprache, ihr Gebrauch setzt heute aber Bekanntheit mit dem Gesprächspartner und lokale Umgebung voraus. In Neubelgien ist Deutsch in hochsprachlicher Form in allen offiziellen und inoffiziellen Bereichen verwendbar; in mündlicher Kommunikation tritt oft mundartlicher oder umgangssprachlicher Gebrauch an die Stelle der Standardsprache.

Die Einstellungen und Haltungen der altbelgischen Mundartsprecher gegenüber ihrer Sprache sind widersprüchlich: zum einen wird diese, vor allem bei den aktiven Benutzern, als wertvolles und erhaltenswertes Kulturgut geschätzt; zum anderen löst die Mundart, teils wegen ihres geringen Nutzwertes, teils auf Grund einer verbreiteten Abwehrhaltung gegenüber dem Dialekt insgesamt, negative Gefühle aus. Das sprachliche Einstellungsprofil der Neubelgier ist geprägt durch die Gespaltenheit ihrer gleichzeitigen Zugehörigkeit zum belgischen Staat und zur deutschen Sprach- und Kulturnation. Das wache Wissen um diesen Doppelcharakter ihrer Existenz steuert das sprachliche Handeln des einzelnen wie der Gruppe. Unbedingter Staatstreue und großer Zuneigung zu französischer Sprache und Kultur, die im Norden stärker in Erscheinung tritt als im Süden, steht ein Festhalten an der Muttersprache gegenüber, das an ein oft zwiespältiges Verhältnis zu deutscher Ethnizität und Geschichte gekoppelt ist, woraus mancherlei Identitäts- und Kontinuitätsbrüche resultieren. Charakteristisch dafür ist die freiwillig gewählte neue Selbstbezeichnung „deutschsprachige Belgier" sowie die skrupulöse Ersetzung des Wortes „deutsch" durch „deutschsprachig" in allen offiziellen Denominationen, worin sich ein ethnischer Bruch mit dem angestammten Deutschtum ausdrückt — ein einmaliger Vorgang, der, außer bei den Elsaß-Lothringern, sonst bei keiner anderen, selbst durch erheblichen Muttersprachenverlust geschwächten deutschen Volksgruppe in Europa zu beobachten ist.

Gemäß dem Prinzip homogener und einsprachiger Sprachgebiete gibt es weder in Alt- noch in Neubelgien institutionelle Zweisprachigkeit, wohl aber individuelle Diglossie und Triglossie, d. h. Mehrsprachigkeit je nach dem „Kontext" (Sprachbereichen, Sprechsituationen, Vertraulichkeitsgrad der Sprecher usw.). Altbelgien zeigt, von wenigen Ausnahmen abgesehen, ein diglossisches (Französisch — Mundart), Neubelgien ein triglossisches Bild (Mundart — Hochdeutsch — Französisch). Schematisch läßt sich das heutige Sprachprofil der Deutschsprachigen in Alt- und Neubelgien etwa wie in Tab.137.1 darstellen.

Tab. 137.1: Sprachvarietäten: S1 = Französisch, S2 = niederfrk.-limburg. Mundarten, S3 = moselfrk. Maa, S4 = ripuarische Maa, S5 = Hochdeutsch

	offiz. Spr.	tatsächl. Sprachverwendung
AB: Nord (Montzen)	S1	S1 + S2
Mitte (Bocholz)	S1	S1 + S3
Süd (Arel)	S1	S1 + S3
NB: Nord (Eupen)	S5	S2/S4 + S5 + S1
Süd (St. Vith)	S5	S3 + S5 + S1
	Einsprachigkeit	Diglossie in AB Triglossie in NB

6. Sprachpolitische Lage

Die frühere, auf Assimilierung gerichtete Sprachenpolitik des belgischen Zentralstaates hat mit der Verabschiedung der Sprachgesetze von 1962—63 ihren Abschluß gefunden. Deren Ergebnis war eine Teilung des deutschen Sprachgebiets in ein gesetzlich anerkanntes deutsches Sprachgebiet (Neubelgien), das mit seiner die „deutschsprachige Gemeinschaft" bildenden Bevölkerung dank der Föderalisierung des Staates jetzt weitgehende sprachlich-kulturelle Selbstverwaltung genießt, und andererseits in ein Gebiet (Altbelgien), das durch die Zuweisung zum französischen Sprachgebiet heute nur noch als „dachloses" deutschsprachiges Reliktgebiet existiert.

Die bislang entwickelte Sprachpolitik der Gebietsregierung der „deutschsprachigen Gemeinschaft" erscheint angesichts der vorhandenen Möglichkeiten als teils restriktiv, z. B. in bezug auf die Unterstützung der deutschen Sprache in Altbelgien, teils expansiv, z. B. in bezug auf die Tolerierung der illegalen französischen Schulen bzw. Schulklassen oder die Zweisprachigkeitsbeschriftungen im Eupener Raum. Die allgemeine Tendenz geht dahin, durch verstärkte Förderung der französischen Sprache eine durchgehende individuelle Zweisprachigkeit im Gebiet herzustellen.

7. Allgemeines kontaktlinguistisches Porträt

Es liegt auf der Hand, daß das Zusammentreffen zweier Sprachen über einen längeren Zeitraum nicht ohne nachhaltige Wirkung auf die dominierte Sprache bleiben kann. So wurden nicht nur die Volksmundarten, sondern auch das in Belgien gebrauchte Hochdeutsche von starkem französischem Einfluß erfaßt. Die Beeinflussungen betreffen alle Ebenen des Sprachsystems: die Syntax (z. B. Wortstellungsbesonderheiten), Morphologie (Abweichungen bei Präfigierungen, Rektion und Valenz der Verben), weniger die Phonetik, vor allem aber den lexikalisch-semantischen Bereich (*Garage* für Werkstatt, *Mazout* für Heizöl usw.). Auf letzteren haben aber auch Niederlandismen (*anwesig* für anwesend, *anbefohlener Preis* für empfohlener Preis) und selbst im Binnendeutschen ungebräuchliche Anglizismen (*Parking* für Parkplatz, *Self Service* für Selbstbedienung) sowie intralinguale Wortbildungen eingewirkt. Zusammenfassend kann man sagen, daß von allen äußeren Einflüssen die französischen am stärksten sind und daß gerade sie, zusammen mit den anderen Faktoren, dem in Belgien verwendeten Deutsch ein gewisses sprachliches Eigenprofil verleihen, wodurch sich dieses sog. Belgiendeutsch von dem Deutsch des benachbarten Rheinlandes abhebt (Nelde 1973—4, 113 ff; Kern 1979, 123 ff).

8. Forschungslage

Im Unterschied zu dem insgesamt besser erforschten Sprachgebiet Neubelgiens stellt das heutige Altbelgien ein soziolinguistisch noch wenig erschlossenes Untersuchungsgebiet dar. Nach den wegbereitenden Anfängen von A. Verdoodt (1968) waren es fast ausschließlich die von der Brüsseler Forschungsstelle für Mehrsprachigkeit unter Leitung von P. Nelde ausgehenden Feldforschungen, die Aufschlüsse über die sprachlichen und damit zwangsläufig kontaktsprachlichen Verhältnisse dieses Raumes gebracht haben. Aber selbst diese Untersuchungen liegen bereits 15 Jahre zurück. Angesichts des fortschreitenden Rückgangs der Volkssprache wäre es wünschenswert, die sprachlichen Kontaktbeziehungen innerhalb dieses Reliktgebietes in einem erneuten Anlauf umfassend zu untersuchen.

9. Bibliographie (in Auswahl)

Benrath, Josef (1994): „Wirtschafts- und sozialpolitische Entwicklung der deutschsprachigen Gemeinschaft Belgiens". In: *Kolloquien zur Kultur der deutschsprachigen Bevölkerungsgruppen im Ausland*, Flensburg.

Bergmans, Bernhard (1986): *Die rechtliche Stellung der deutschen Sprache in Belgien*, Neulöwen.

Bischoff, Heinrich (1941): *Geschichte der Volksdeutschen in Belgien*, Aachen.

Héraud, Guy (1989): „Deutsch als Umgangs- und Muttersprache in der Europäischen Gemeinschaft. Syntheseberricht". In: *Deutsch als Umgangs- und Muttersprache in der Europäischen Gemeinschaft*, Kern, R. (Ed.), Brüssel.

Jenniges, Hubert (1991): „De huidige situatie van het Duitstalig gebied in België", unveröf. Vortragsmanuskript.

Jenniges, Hubert (1994): „Effektivität und Defizite — die kulturelle Autonomie der deutschen Sprachminderheit in Belgien". In: *Kolloquien zur Kultur der deutschsprachigen Bevölkerungsgruppen im Ausland*, Flensburg.

Kern, Rudolf (1979): „Schriftliche Ausdrucksschwierigkeiten deutschsprachiger Belgier an der französischsprachigen Universität zu Löwen". In: *Deutsch als Muttersprache in Belgien*, Nelde, P. (Ed.), Wiesbaden, 123—131.

Kern, Rudolf (1983): „Zur Sprachsituation im Arelerland". In: *Mehrsprachigkeit und Gesellschaft*, Jongen, R. et al. (Eds.), Tübingen, 70—87.

Kramer, Johannes (1984): *Zweisprachigkeit in den Benelux-Ländern*, Hamburg.

Nelde, Peter H. (1973): „Zum gegenwärtigen Zeitungsdeutsch in Ostbelgien". In: *Cahiers de l'Institut de Linguistique de Louvain* II, 3, 113—139.

Nelde, Peter H. (1979): *Volkssprache und Kultursprache*, Wiesbaden, 9—38.

Pabst, Klaus (1979): „Politische Geschichte des deutschen Sprachgebiets in Ostbelgien bis 1944". In: *Deutsch als Muttersprache in Belgien*, Nelde, P. (Ed.), Wiesbaden, 9—38.

Verdoodt, Albert (1968): *Zweisprachige Nachbarn*, Wien — Stuttgart.

Rudolf Kern, Neulöwen (Belgien)

138. Niederländisch—Deutsch

1. Einleitung
2. Demographie und wirtschaftliche Lage
3. Geschichte
4. Sprachpolitische Lage der Kontaktsprachen
5. Spaltung der Vurener Bevölkerung
6. Soziolinguistische Lage der Kontaktsprachen
7. Sprachkontakt auf linguistischer Beschreibungsebene
8. Bibliographie (in Auswahl)

1. Einleitung

Im Osten Belgiens trennt die amtliche niederländisch-französische Sprachgrenze das Vurgebiet (offiziell niederländischsprachig) vom sogenannten Altbelgien-Nord (offiziell französischsprachig). Der Schein dieser territorialen Einsprachigkeit trügt jedoch. Erstens entspricht diese sprachpolitische Grenze fast völlig der von Philologen festgestellten niederländisch-deutschen Kultursprachgrenze (mit den Vurener Dörfern und dem offiziell französischsprachigen Aubel-Zentrum auf der niederländischen Seite und den nordaltbelgischen Dörfern und dem auch offiziell französischsprachigen Aubel-Klause auf der deutschen (vgl. Goossens 1975, 1164f). Da die deutsche Kultursprache seit dem Zweiten Weltkrieg in Altbelgien-Nord vom Französischen verdrängt wurde, ist die niederländisch-deutsche Sprachgrenze zu einer theoretischen geworden. Zweitens bedient sich ein Teil der Vurener Bevölkerung der niederländischen Kultursprache, der andere der französischen, und drittens sprechen sowohl die Vurener als auch die Nordaltbelgier ein und dieselbe südniederfränkische Mundart.

2. Demographie und wirtschaftliche Lage

Das Vurgebiet mit einer Länge von etwa 16 km und einer Breite von 0,5 bis 6 km (ca. 50 km²) und ca. 4100 Einwohnern besteht aus insgesamt sechs Dörfern: Moelingen, 's Gravenvoeren, St-Martens-Voeren, St-Pieters-Voeren, Remersdaal und Teuven. Altbelgien-Nord mit den Orten Baelen, Gemmenich, Kapell, Homburg, Membach, Montzen, Moresnet, Sippenaken und Welkenrat hat eine Fläche von ca. 163 km² (dreimal größer als das Vurgebiet) und zählt ca. 19 800 Einwohner. Das an das Vurgebiet und an Altbelgien-Nord grenzende Aubel hat 3680 Einwohner (→ Sprachenkarte C).

Die Bevölkerungsstatistik weist in diesem Grenzgebiet einen verhältnismäßig hohen Anteil von Ausländern auf. Die neuesten Zahlen des Nationalen Instituts für Statistik von 1992 zeigen für Altbelgien-Nord eine Konzentration von 5,4% Deutschen und eine niedrigere von Niederländern (ca. 2,5%). In den sechs Vurgemeinden zusammen liegt der Gesamtanteil der Niederländer bei 14%, der der Deutschen bei kaum 0,5%. Von den Einwohnern Aubels sind dagegen nur 1,3% Niederländer und 0,25% Deutsche.

Die landwirtschaftliche Struktur wird in dieser Gegend von der Viehhaltung und in geringerem Maße vom Obstanbau dominiert. Die in der Landwirtschaft tätige Bevölkerung hat jedoch drastisch abgenommen. Aus Mangel an Arbeitsplätzen im landwirtschaftlichen Sektor suchten stets mehr Vurener, Nordaltbelgier und Aubeler Arbeit in den Lütticher Ballungsgebieten. Parallel zur Abnahme der bäuerlichen Bevölkerung reduzierte sich die dortige Einwohnerzahl übrigens insgesamt.

3. Geschichte

Vom 10. bis zum Ende des 13. Jahrhunderts bildete das Herzogtum Limburg die einzige große politische Einheit im heutigen nordostbelgischen Gebiet. Die Ost-Orientierung des Herzogtums Limburg auf die Stadt Köln verkehrte sich unter der brabantischen (ab 1288) und darauffolgenden burgundischen Herrschaft (1384—1482) immer stärker in eine West-Orientierung auf Brüssel und Löwen (Bertha 1988, 64). Daraus entstand für das heutige Altbelgien-Nord bis um 1800 eine Dreisprachigkeit: das Brabantische (eine Vorform des Niederländischen) als Verwaltungssprache, das Hochdeutsche als Schul- und Kirchensprache wegen der alten kirchlichen Verbindung nach Aachen und die südniederfränkische Mundart als Volkssprache.

Unter französischer Herrschaft (1795—1814) fiel das limburgische Kerngebiet an das Urtdepartement (Département Ourthe) mit dem Verwaltungssitz Lüttich. 1814 wurde das westliche Limburg auf dem Wiener Kongreß dem Königreich der Vereinigten Niederlande zugeteilt. Die Situation war paradox. Einerseits versuchte die niederländische Behörde, das Französische zugunsten des Niederländischen zurückzudrängen, andererseits bedeutete das Beibehalten der administrativen Verbindung des limburgischen Grenzgebietes mit der französischsprachigen Provinz Lüttich (Urtdepartement), daß es auch in der Zeit nach der französischen Vorherrschaft vom niederländischen Sprachraum (Niedermaasdepartement) administrativ abgeschnitten war. Um der Niederlandisierung den Boden zu bereiten, sollte auch das Deutsche im alten Limburg allmählich dem Niederländischen weichen. Die katholische Geistlichkeit leistete der protestantischen niederländischen Behörde jedoch demonstrativ Widerstand, indem sie zunehmend Hochdeutsch sprach. Auch im Schulunterricht behielt das Deutsche in den nordaltbelgischen Gemeinden weiterhin seine Position (Pabst 1979, 20 f; Schärer 1978, 23).

Als 1839 die Grenze zwischen den Niederlanden und dem 1830 geschaffenen Belgien endgültig festgelegt wurde, verblieb das benachbarte Maastrichter Gebiet — administrativ gesehen — bei den Niederlanden. Diese Trennung vom ethnischen und sprachlichen Hinterland förderte nicht gerade die Ausbreitung des Niederländischen als Kultursprache im Vurgebiet, aber wegen des sprachbewahrenden Einflusses der niederländischsprachigen Institutionen Schule und Kirche wurde sie auch nicht verhindert.

Schon nach dem Ersten Weltkrieg ging die Verbreitung der deutschen Sprache in Altbelgien-Nord zurück. Nach den Feindseligkeiten des Zweiten Weltkriegs wurde dann im nordaltbelgischen Gebiet, das Deutschland 1940 zusätzlich zu den 1919/20 verlorenen Kreisen Eupen und Malmedy mitannektiert hatte, erst recht die antideutsche Einstellung sichtbar: Französisch wurde Verwaltungs-, Schul- und Kirchensprache. Während bei der Volkszählung von 1930 noch 37,33% der Nordaltbelgier behauptet hatten, immer oder meistens Deutsch zu sprechen (54,96% Französisch und 3,20% Niederländisch), erklärten 1947 nur noch 11,76%, deutschsprachig zu sein (76,44% französischsprachig und 5,35% niederländischsprachig).

Im 19. Jahrhundert wurde in Klause (einem Weiler von Aubel) das Niederländische durch das Deutsche in Kirche und Schule ersetzt. Schon seit dem letzten Viertel des vorigen Jahrhunderts hat jedoch allmählich das Französische diese Bereiche übernommen;

auch in Aubel-Zentrum war dies der Fall, wo das Niederländische die Stellung hatte halten können (Cajot 1989, 311 f). Ergiebig sind hier die Ergebnisse der Volkszählungen von 1930 und 1947: 85,78% bzw. 90,67% französischsprachige Aubeler.

Auch im Vurgebiet hat seit Beginn des 20. Jahrhunderts das Französische des wallonischen Hinterlandes an Einfluß gewonnen, und zwar vor allem durch intensivere Kontakte mit der französischen Sprache im Berufsleben. Mit der Pendelarbeit drang das Französische des industrialisierten wallonischen Hinterlandes in die einst geschlossene agrarische Gemeinschaft ein. Außerdem war die Vurener Jugend auf die wallonischen Sekundarschulen angewiesen.

4. Sprachpolitische Lage der Kontaktsprachen

4.1. Amtssprache

Für das Vurgebiet gilt seit der Sprachgrenzfestlegung 1963 ein besonderer sprachpolitischer Status. Es ist zwar offiziell niederländischsprachig, aber den französischsprachigen Einwohnern wird ein sprachlicher Minderheitenschutz gewährt. Dieser Minderheitenschutz besteht aus dem Recht, in allen Verwaltungsangelegenheiten in Französisch bedient zu werden, und der Möglichkeit, Schulen mit Französisch als Unterrichtssprache einzurichten.

Die Vurgemeinden waren und sind die umstrittensten Sprachgrenzgemeinden. Seit 1963 war das Statut der Vurgemeinden ein regelmäßig wiederkehrender Punkt in den Programmen der aufeinanderfolgenden belgischen Regierungen. Drei Kabinette haben wegen des Vurproblems zurücktreten müssen und unzählige Koalitionen sind durch die Vurfrage gefährdet worden. Die Bemühungen der Regierungen in den siebziger und achtziger Jahren, eine Lösung für das Vurproblem zu finden, lassen sich mit einer dauernd ansteigenden Spannung um das Vurgebiet in Verbindung bringen (bei Kundgebungen frankophoner und flämischer Gruppierungen kam es oft zu schweren Zwischenfällen). Alle neu ausgedachten Regelungen für das Vurgebiet wurden jedoch verworfen, so daß die Sprachgrenze und die Sprachengesetze von 1962 bis jetzt unangetastet geblieben sind.

Für Altbelgien-Nord gibt es seit der Sprachgrenzfestlegung auch ein Spezialstatut des Minderheitenschutzes. Das Sprachengesetz von 1962 schreibt für dieses Gebiet die französische Einsprachigkeit vor. Es wird jedoch laut Artikel 56 den Gemeinden die Möglichkeit geboten, den Minderheitenschutz für ihre nicht französischsprachigen Einwohner zu beantragen (der Gesetzgeber hat Aubel nicht in diese Liste aufgenommen). Bisher hat keine einzige Gemeinde in diesem Gebiet diese vom Gesetz gebotene Möglichkeit genutzt (Bertha 1989c, 252). Die Sprache, die für den mündlichen Kontakt zwischen Verwaltung und Einwohnern und als Schulsprache in Frage kommen würde, wird im Gesetz nicht angegeben. Es kann sich also sowohl um Deutsch als eventuell auch um Niederländisch oder irgendeine andere Sprache handeln.

4.2. Schulsprache

Alle Nordaltbelgier werden seit 1945 auf französisch unterrichtet, die Aubeler schon seit Ende des 19. Jahrhunderts. In den meisten Dorfschulen des Gebiets werden ab dem vierten Schuljahr ein paar Deutschstunden gegeben. In der Sippenakener Dorfschule wird Niederländisch oder Deutsch (je nach Anzahl deutsch- und niederländischsprachiger zugezogener Schüler in einer Klasse) als Zweitsprache angeboten. Im vierten Schuljahr werden zwei, im fünften und sechsten Schuljahr drei Wochenstunden erteilt.

Die Vurener Jugendlichen verteilen sich auf französischsprachige und niederländischsprachige Schulen. In der niederländischsprachigen Schule werden im dritten und vierten Schuljahr drei Wochenstunden Französisch gegeben und im fünften und sechsten Schuljahr wöchentlich fünf Stunden. Niederländischunterricht erhalten die Kinder der französischsprachigen Schule ab dem dritten Schuljahr mit vier Stunden in der Woche, ab dem fünften Schuljahr mit acht Wochenstunden.

4.3. Kirchensprache

Nach dem Zweiten Weltkrieg hat sich in Altbelgien-Nord das Französische in der Kirche verstärkt durchgesetzt. Als einzige Pfarren haben Moresnet, Gemmenich und Membach zweisprachige (deutsch-französische) Pfarrblätter. Zu Weihnachten kann es hier gelegentlich deutsche Lieder und eine kurze Homelie in deutscher Sprache geben (Bertha 1988, 99). Bis 1986 wurde in Sippenaken im Gottesdienst Französisch (für die Mitteilungen an die Pfarrkinder) und Mundart (für die

Predigt) gebraucht. Jetzt (1995) hat der Ort einen Pfarrer ohne Dialektkenntnisse, der die Mitteilungen und auch eine Kurzfassung der Predigt auf niederländisch gibt (Bertha 1989a, 207).

Für die Vurgemeinden (außer Remersdaal) läßt sich der Sprachgebrauch im kirchlichen Bereich folgendermaßen beschreiben. Die Gottesdienste am Wochenende und an Werktagen werden auf niederländisch gehalten. Die Liturgie bei Taufen und Trauungen wird sprachlich auf die Wünsche der betreffenden Familie abgestimmt. Die Hauptliturgie bei Beerdigungen ist niederländischsprachig. Neben dem Niederländischen kann auf Wunsch auch das Französische für die sich eher auf die Familie (und nicht auf die ganze Kirchengemeinde) beziehenden gottesdienstlichen Handlungen (z. B. Gebete auf dem Friedhof) verwendet werden. Auf diese Weise gewährt die kirchliche Behörde den Französischsprachigen eine Art Minderheitenschutz im kirchlichen Bereich.

5. Spaltung der Vurener Bevölkerung

Die wirtschaftlich bedingten Französierungsansätze verwandelten sich ab 1962 in eine bewußte Assimilation derjenigen Vurener, die gegen die Eingliederung Vurens in die flämische Provinz Limburg waren. Das Hauptmerkmal dieser Französierung ist eine deutliche Gruppenidentifikation, die als eine Gesinnung betrachtet werden kann, weil die Entwicklung der Sprachloyalität dem Französischen gegenüber und die wallonischgesinnte politische Mobilisation viel schneller voranschritten als die objektive sprachliche Assimilation. Die sprachliche Identität der jüngeren Generation, die genausogut Französisch wie die Wallonen spricht — mit denen sie dieselben Schulen besucht hat —, ist vom politischen Engagement ihrer Eltern und Großeltern geprägt worden, deren Französisch nur einfachsten Kommunikationsbedürfnissen genügte.

Der Assimilierungswille war bereits nach dem Zweiten Weltkrieg erkennbar. Bei der Volkszählung von 1930 hatten noch 76,31% der Vurener Gesamtbevölkerung erklärt, niederländischsprachig zu sein, während 17,88% angaben, immer oder meistens Französisch zu sprechen. Bei der nächsten Volksbefragung nach dem Zweiten Weltkrieg im Jahre 1947 ergab sich jedoch eine umgekehrte sprachliche Zuordnung: 51,83% der Vurener fühlten sich französischsprachig und nur 38,97% niederländischsprachig. Die Prozentzahlen haben sich im Vergleich zu denen von 1930 so schlagartig geändert, weil ein Teil der Vurener Bevölkerung demonstrativ gegen die sprachpolitischen Konsequenzen der Sprachenzählung von 1930 reagieren wollte. Laut Sprachengesetz vom 28. Juni 1932, das die Sprachgemeinschaftszugehörigkeit der Gemeinden an der Sprachgrenze von alle zehn Jahre abzuhaltenden Volksbefragungen abhängig machte, wurde nämlich das Vurgebiet in die flämische Sprachgemeinschaft eingegliedert.

Die kriegsbedingten antideutschen Emotionen haben 1947 zweifellos auch die Sprachloyalität beeinflußt. Die von wallonischer Seite stark betonte Kollaboration flämischgesinnter Belgier hatte zu antiflämischen Gefühlen geführt (Deprez/Wynants 1987, 707). Zudem schien es sozial opportun zu sein, das prestigeträchtige Französisch zu sprechen, ob man es nun gut konnte oder nicht.

Hermans und Verjans (1983, 9 f) zufolge betrachte die flämische Bewegung ohne triftigen Grund die französischsprachige Elite Vurens als die Vorreiter der Französierung. Sie seien es ja gewesen, die gegen den Provinzwechsel vom französischsprachigen Lüttich zum niederländischsprachigen Limburg opponiert haben, aber die Mehrheit der Vurener Bevölkerung sei ihnen aus freier Wahl gefolgt.

In den siebziger und achtziger Jahren wurde deutlich, daß die Vurener Gemeinschaft sich zunehmend polarisiert hat. Auf der einen Seite gibt es die flämischgesinnte Partei „Voerbelangen"; sie erhielt 1989 bei den letzten Gemeindewahlen 40,2% Wahlstimmen. Auf der anderen Seite gibt es die wallonischgesinnte Partei „Retour à Liège", die den Status der offiziellen Zweisprachigkeit anstrebt und 59,8% der Stimmen erhielt. Der Kampf des wallonischgesinnten Bürgermeisters und seiner gleichgesinnten Gemeinderatsfraktion gegen eine von der Zentralregierung verordnete amtliche niederländische Einsprachigkeit macht ab und zu Schlagzeilen. Im dörflichen Alltag ist dieser Konflikt jedoch nur latent zu spüren, da die Funktion der Mundart als lingua franca zwischen den beiden Gemeinschaften die aufgeworfenen Gräben teilweise wieder zuschüttet.

Die Vurener Gemeinschaft hat sich jedoch auch in dem Sinne gespalten, daß Wallonischgesinnte und Flämischgesinnte zum Teil getrennte soziale Netzwerke haben. Die Flämischgesinnten frequentieren „flämischgesinnte", die Wallonischgesinnten „wallonischgesinnte" Kneipen. In gleicher Weise sind auch die Vereine strukturiert. Seit der Sprachgrenzfestlegung schicken Flämischgesinnte ihre Kinder nicht mehr in die französischsprachigen Schulen Walloniens und gehen die Kinder der Wallonischgesinnten nicht mehr in die niederländischsprachigen Grundschulen des Vurgebiets (vgl. Wynants 1980, 472).

6. Soziolinguistische Lage der Kontaktsprachen

Gesprächspartnerbezogene Fragen nach dem Sprachgebrauch haben bei einer 1990 durchgeführten Fragebogenerhebung im Vurdorf Teuven und im nordaltbelgischen Sippenaken (Vandermeeren 1992) größere Unterschiede im Sprachgebrauch und in den Spracheinstellungen im Bereich der Kindererziehung und im Umgang mit anderen Dorfbewohnern ans Licht gebracht.

6.1. Sprachgebrauch

Tab. 138.1: Befragte mit Dialektkenntnissen*, die (fast) immer Dialekt im Umgang mit Gesprächspartnern mit Dialektkenntnissen sprechen

	Fl	Sip	Wal
im Umgang mit Kindern	85%	50%	55%
(gleichgesinnten) anderen Dorfbewohnern	100%	80%	60%
dem Ehepartner	95%	65%	65%
Freunden und Bekannten	100%	75%	70%
Geschwistern	95%	70%	75%
Eltern	100%	80%	80%
andersgesinnten Dorfbewohnern	100%	–	90%

* 95% der Fl(ämischgesinnten), 80% der Sip(penakener) und 75% der Wal(lonischgesinnten)

Von den Antwortverteilungen der Flämischgesinnten bezüglich des Dialektgebrauchs mit Gesprächspartnern innerhalb von Familie, Freundeskreis und Dorfgemeinschaft weist nur die Variable „Dialektgebrauch im Kontakt mit den Kindern" einen niedrigeren Anteil als 95 oder 100% für „(fast) immer" auf, nämlich 85%. Der Dialektgebrauch der Wallonischgesinnten dagegen ist in starkem Maße gesprächspartnergebunden. Mit Kindern (55%), Gleichgesinnten (60%) und Ehepartner (65%) sprechen sie weniger Mundart als mit Freunden und Bekannten (70%), Geschwistern (75%), Eltern (80%) und Andersgesinnten (90%). Im Vergleich zu den Sippenakenern zeigt für die Wallonischgesinnten nur die Variable „Dialektgebrauch im Kontakt mit anderen (gleichgesinnten) Dorfbewohnern" einen niedrigeren Anteil von „(fast) immer"-Antworten auf (60 versus 80%).

Schulsprache und Sprachwechsel im Kontakt mit den Kindern können nicht voneinander getrennt werden. Um den Kindern den Eintritt in eine französischsprachige Schule zu erleichtern, sprechen manche wallonischgesinnten Vurener und altnordbelgischen Eltern Französisch mit ihnen. Sie schätzen nämlich die Mundart als hemmend für den Erwerb des Französischen ein. Weil die französische Standardsprache einen höheren „sozialen" Status als die Mundart hat, sehen sie die Änderung des Sprachgebrauchmusters im Kontakt mit den Kindern, denen sie den sozialen Aufstieg garantieren wollen, als eine Investition in deren Zukunft. In der ehepartnerlichen Interaktion wird dadurch, daß mit den Kindern mehr Französisch gesprochen wird, im allgemeinen automatisch auch mehr Französisch gesprochen. Hinzu kommt, daß die Kinder in der Schule das Französische als prestigeträchtigere Sprache kennenlernen und demnach zu Hause mehr Französisch sprechen (vgl. Wynants 1980, 472).

Bei ungefähr der Hälfte der nach der Sprachgrenzfestlegung 1962 geborenen Kinder von Wallonischgesinnten ist das Französische zur Erstsprache geworden. Sie haben überhaupt keine oder nur mehr rudimentäre Dialektkenntnisse, im Gegensatz zu den vor 1962 Geborenen, die alle noch gute Dialektkenntnisse haben. Für die Sippenakener setzt die Tendenz zur hochsprachlichen Erziehung zur gleichen Zeit (Anfang der siebziger Jahre) ein, als die Flämischgesinnten anfangen, ihre Kinder in der Hochsprache zu erziehen. Für die Flämischgesinnten ist die Tendenz zur Hochsprache-Erziehung jedoch viel schwächer als für die Sippenakener und die Wallonischgesinnten.

Flämischgesinnte Vurener sprechen mit vertrauten Personen in der Regel Mundart.

Auch die Sippenakener behaupten, — abgesehen von der Kindererziehung — in den sich auf Dorf und Familie beziehenden Bereichen überwiegend Mundart zu sprechen. Zu der Annahme, daß in Sippenaken — sowie in Gemmenich und Membach — im Vergleich zu den anderen nordaltbelgischen Gemeinden die Mundart nur in geringem Maße gefährdet ist, kommt auch Nelde (1979a, 61—65) aufgrund einer in Altbelgien-Nord durchgeführten Umfrage. Als äußerst gefährdet gilt nach dieser Umfrage die Mundart in Baelen, Kapell und Aubel-Klause. Für Aubel-Zentrum zeigt sie, daß dort bis auf wenige Restbestände die Mundart weitgehend aus dem öffentlichen und privaten Leben verdrängt worden ist.

Der Sprachgebrauch der wallonischgesinnten Teuvener mit gleichgesinnten Teuvenern unterscheidet sich in markanter Weise vom Sprachgebrauch der Sippenakener mit anderen Sippenakenern. Dieser Mehrgebrauch des Französischen läßt sich darauf zurückführen, daß das konstituierende Merkmal der wallonischgesinnten Gruppenzugehörigkeit ja die französische Sprache ist. Es liegt auf der Hand, daß gerade im Umgang mit Gleichgesinnten das Gefühl der Gruppenzugehörigkeit sprachsteuernd wirkt.

Die Polarisierung der beiden Vurener Gemeinschaften, die die Gefährdung der Mundart heraufbeschworen hat, garantiert aber zur gleichen Zeit ihre Bewahrung, weil sie als einzige Sprache für die Kommunikation zwischen Flämisch- und Wallonischgesinnten in Frage kommt. Die Mundart spielt eine Schlüsselrolle in der Kommunikation zwischen Wallonisch- und Flämischgesinnten, weil beide Kultursprachen zu sehr stigmatisiert sind. Die Wallonischgesinnten betrachten die niederländische Kultursprache als die ihnen von der Sprachpolitik aufgezwungene Amtssprache. Die Flämischgesinnten betrachten die französische Sprache als ein Symbol der Illoyalität gegenüber der flämischen Abstammung der Gesamtbevölkerung.

6.2. Spracheinstellungen

Alle Befragten bejahen das Prinzip der standardsprachlichen Erziehung mehr, als sie es in Wirklichkeit umsetzen. Was die anderen Gesprächspartner betrifft, hängt der erwünschte Sprachgebrauch der Sippenakener vom Öffentlichkeitsgrad der Gesprächssituation ab. Im Kontakt mit Familienmitgliedern (80%) tolerieren Sippenakener eher den Mundartgebrauch als mit anderen Dorfbewohnern (60%). Die Haltung der wallonischgesinnten

Tab. 138.2: Befragte mit Dialektkenntnissen*, die den Dialektgebrauch mit Gesprächspartnern mit Dialektkenntnissen als angemessen betrachten

	Fl	Sip	Wal
im Umgang mit Kindern	45%	25%	10%
Familienmitgliedern	95%	80%	40%
Freunden und Bekannten	95%	70%	40%
(gleichgesinnten) Dorfbewohnern	90%	60%	40%

* 95% der Fl(ämischgesinnten), 80% der Sip(penakener) und 75% der Wal(lonischgesinnten)

Teuvener ist unterschiedlich. Erstens tolerieren sie den Mundartgebrauch weniger als die Sippenakener, zweitens betrachten sie ihn im Kontakt mit allen vom Fragebogen erfaßten Gesprächspartnern in demselben Maße als unerwünscht (40%) und drittens markieren sie die Mundart als dominierender in ihrem Sprachgebrauch, als sie sie in ihrem erwünschten Sprachgebrauch darstellen.

Zusammenfassend läßt sich sagen, daß beide Gruppen eine jeweils andere positive Einstellung zum Dialekt haben. Für die Sippenakener ist die Spracheinstellung in ihrer mehrsprachigen Identität eingebettet. Bei den Wallonischgesinnten handelt es sich um eine gewohnheitsbedingte positive Einstellung, die in fast schizoglossischer Weise (Nelde 1986, 117) von ihrer wallonischgesinnten Identität verneint und verdrängt wird. Die Wallonischgesinnten haben somit eine doppelte Loyalität: eine gewohnheitsbedingte zur Mundart und eine normbedingte zum Französischen, das im Gegensatz zur Mundart — sprachpolitisch gesehen — zu ihrer frankophonen, wallonischgesinnten Identität paßt. Für die Flämischgesinnten gehört ihre positive Einstellung zur Mundart zu ihrer lokalen und flämischen — sich auf die Abstammung berufenden — Identität.

7. Sprachkontakt auf linguistischer Beschreibungsebene

7.1. Auf phonologischer Ebene

Wynants (1975, 614—616) untersucht, inwieweit sich der Einfluß des südniederfränkischen Dialekts auf die französische Kultursprache bei Zweisprachigen in St-Martens-Voeren nachweisen läßt. Es stellt sich heraus, daß diese Sprachberührung auf phonologischer Ebene nur in beschränktem Maße sichtbar wird. So wird zwar das französische /g/ von den Zielpersonsen als /ɣ/ ausgesprochen, und ihr Fanzösisch zeigt den typisch südniederfränkischen Schleifton oder Trägheitsakzent; aufs Ganze betrachtet unterscheidet sich das Untersuchungsmaterial jedoch nicht wesentlich von dem im wallonischen, ostbelgischen Hinterland gesprochenen Französisch. Ganz wichtig erscheint in dem Zusammenhang die weitgehende phonologische Konvergenz zwischen dem ostbelgischen Französisch und dem Südniederfränkischen. Daß diese Übereinstimmung das Ergebnis einer gegenseitigen Beeinflussung beider Kontaktsprachen ist, kann demnach nicht ausgeschlossen werden. Synchron betrachtet, sprechen die französischsprachigen Vurener und Nordaltbelgier das Französische, das sie von und mit ihren wallonischen Nachbarn in der Schule und am Arbeitsplatz gelernt haben.

7.2. Auf lexikaler Ebene

Cajot (1989, 305) beschreibt die Grenze zwischen dem Vurgebiet und Altbelgien-Nord als eine Hemmschwelle für die Expansion deutschen Sprachguts aus dem Osten und niederländischen Sprachguts aus dem Westen.

In der Vurgegend zeigt seit der Sprachgrenzfestlegung der Dialektgebrauch der Flämischgesinnten niederländischen Einfluß, der hauptsächlich französische Lehnwörter beseitigt oder niederländische Translate (Lexeme) für neue Begriffe einführt. Bei den Wallonischgesinnten nimmt andererseits der schon große Anteil französischen Wortschatzes weiter zu (Cajot 1989, 307).

Vom Vurgebiet unterscheidet sich Altbelgien-Nord dadurch, daß — weil hier das Deutsche Kirchen- und Schulsprache war — mehr deutsche Transferenz entstanden ist. Französische Translate stellen in Altbelgien-Nord bei Variabilität der Bezeichnung jedoch die jüngere Sprachschicht dar und überlagern dabei sowohl deutsches als auch niederländisches Sprachinventar. Der niederländische Einfluß spielt in Altbelgien-Nord kaum noch eine Rolle. Nur einige der im letzten Jahrhundert aufgekommenen Begriffe haben in den westlichen Orten Sippenaken und Homburg eine Bezeichnung, die dem Niederländischen und nicht dem Französischen oder dem Deutschen entspricht (Cajot 1989, 287, 289, 308).

Im Vergleich zum Vurgebiet hat Aubel-Zentrum weniger niederländische Translate und im Vergleich zu Altbelgien-Nord weniger deutsche Translate, dafür aber die meisten französischen Lehnwörter. Dies ist nicht verwunderlich, da ja das Französische schon 1874 das Niederländische in der Volksschule als Unterrichtssprache verdrängt hat (Cajot 1989, 310).

8. Bibliographie (in Auswahl)

Amian, Werner (1979): „Die Interdependenz linguistischer und politischer Faktoren im Sprachgrenzbereich am Beispiel Altbelgien-Nord". In: *Deutsch als Muttersprache in Belgien*, Nelde, P. H. (Ed.), Wiesbaden, 95−100.

Beaufays, Jean et al. (1985): *La problématique fouronnaise*, Lüttich.

Bertha, Alfred (1988): „Die Stellung des Deutschen im Montzener Land". In: *Deutsch als Umgangs- und Muttersprache in Belgien*, Jenniges, H. (Ed.), Brüssel/Eupen, 63−72.

Bertha, Alfred (1989a): „Zum Deutschunterricht und zur Stellung der deutschen Sprache im Montzener Land". In: *Deutsch als Umgangs- und Muttersprache in der Europäischen Gemeinschaft*, Kern, R. (Ed.), Brüssel, 145−151.

Bertha, Alfred (1989b): „Deutsch in den Medien des Montzener Landes". In: *Deutsch als Umgangs- und Muttersprache in der Europäischen Gemeinschaft*, Kern, R. (Ed.), Brüssel, 205−208.

Bertha, Alfred (1989c): „Zum Gebrauch des Deutschen in den öffentlichen Diensten des Montzener Landes". In: *Deutsch als Umgangs- und Muttersprache in der Europäischen Gemeinschaft*, Kern, R. (Ed.), Brüssel, 252−254.

Bertha, Alfred (1989d): „Deutsch in den Sozialbeziehungen des Montzener Landes". In: *Deutsch als Umgangs- und Muttersprache in der Europäischen Gemeinschaft*, Kern, R. (Ed.), Brüssel, 289−292.

Cajot, José (1989): *Neue Sprachschranken im 'Land ohne Grenzen'? Zum Einfluß politischer Grenzen auf die germanischen Mundarten in der belgisch-niederländisch-deutsch-luxemburgischen Euregio*, Wien.

Cajot, José/Beckers, Hartmut (1979): „Zur Diatopie der deutschen Dialekte in Belgien". In: *Deutsch als Muttersprache in Belgien*, Nelde, P. H. (Ed.), Wiesbaden, 151−218.

CRISP (1979): *Le problème des Fourons de 1962 à nos jours* (CRISP Courrier Hebdomadaire 859).

Deprez, Kas/Wynants, Armel (1987): „Voeren: onmogelijk op te lossen?". In: *Kultuurleven* 54, 701−721.

Deprez, Kas/Wynants, Armel (1988): „De grond, de macht en het geld. Het communautaire hoofdstuk van het regeerakkoord". In: *De Nieuwe Maand* 31, 42−48.

Deprez, Kas/Wynants, Armel (1989a): „Voeren/Fourons". In: *Historische Sprachkonflikte*, Nelde, P. H. (Ed.), Bonn, 95−105.

Deprez, Kas/Wynants, Armel (1989b): „La Révolution Française et le conflit linguistique en Belgique". In: *Zeitschrift für Phonetik, Sprachwissenschaft und Kommunikationsforschung* 42, 601–607.

Fontaine, José (1987): „De Voerkwestie: uiteindelijk een belangrijk probleem". In: *Kultuurleven* 54, 219–221.

Fonteyn, Guido (1983): *Voeren, een heel Happart verhaal*, Antwerpen.

Fonteyn, Guido (1987): „Voeren, rariteit uit België". In: *Jaarboek Vlaamse Beweging*, 81–86.

Goossens, Jan (1975): „Overmaas". In: *Encyclopedie van de Vlaamse Beweging* II, 1164–1165.

Hermans, Michel/Verjans, Pierre (1983): „Les origines de la querelle fouronnaise". In: *CRISP Courrier Hebdomadaire* 1019.

Kern, Rudolf (Ed.) (1989): *Deutsch als Umgangs- und Muttersprache in der Europäischen Gemeinschaft*, Brüssel.

Klinkenberg, Jean-Marie (1988): „Les Fourons: un laboratoire sociolinguistique". In: *Présence francophone* 33, 61–78.

van Laar, Hans (1988): *Voeren. Een politiek-cultureel antropologische studie van de tweespalt in 's-Gravenvoeren*, Brüssel.

Nelde, Peter H. (1979a): *Volkssprache und Kultursprache. Die gegenwärtige Lage des sprachlichen Übergangsgebietes im deutsch-belgisch-luxemburgischen Grenzraum*, Wiesbaden.

Nelde, Peter H. (1979b): „Zur volkssprachlichen Situation in einer germanisch-romanischen Übergangszone". In: *Deutsch als Muttersprache in Belgien*, Nelde, P. H. (Ed.), Wiesbaden, 67–84.

Nelde, Peter H. (1984): „Sprachökologische Überlegungen am Beispiel Altbelgiens". In: *Spracherwerb – Sprachkontakt – Sprachkonflikt*, Oksaar, E. (Ed.), Berlin/New York, 167–179.

Nelde, Peter H. (1986): „Volkssprache oder Kultursprache. Sprachliche Polarisierung in Altbelgien". In: *Kolloquium zur Sprache und Sprachpflege der deutschen Bevölkerungsgruppen im Ausland*, Ritter, A. (Ed.), Flensburg, 49–72.

Pabst, Klaus (1979): „Politische Geschichte des deutschen Sprachgebiets in Ostbelgien bis 1944". In: *Deutsch als Muttersprache in Belgien*, Nelde, P. H. (Ed.), Wiesbaden, 9–38.

Schärer, Martin R. (1978): *Deutsche Annexionspolitik im Westen. Die Wiedereingliederung Eupen-Malmedys im Zweiten Weltkrieg*, Bern.

Stassen, Albert (1987): „La situation des dialectes dans les Fourons". In: *Europa Ethnica* 44, 185–188.

Vandermeeren, Sonja (1992): *Spracheinstellungen links und rechts der Sprachgrenze. Eine kontaktlinguistische Umfrage im Vurgebiet und in Altbelgien-Nord* (Plurilingua 14), Bonn.

Verjans, Pierre (1985): „Les Fouronnais imaginaires. Conditions sociales du militantisme régional dans une commune symbole de la frontière linguistique en Belgique". In: *La problématique fouronnaise*, Beaufays, J. et al. (Eds.), Lüttich.

Voercolloquium 21.11.1980. Herckenrode, Marnixring Limburg. Aufsätze von J. Cajot, W. Van den Steene und A. Wynants.

Wynants, Armel (1975): *Taalcontacten in de Voerstreek*, Diss., Lüttich.

Wynants, Armel (1980): „Taalovergang en taaltrouw in de Voerstreek sinds de aansluiting bij de provincie Limburg". In: *Sprachkontakt und Sprachkonflikt*, Nelde, P. H. (Ed.), Wiesbaden, 467–473.

Sonja Vandermeeren, Duisburg (Deutschland)

139. Netherlands

1. Demography
2. Territorial history and national development
3. Politics, economy and general cultural and religious situation
4. Statistics and ethnoprofiles
5. Sociolinguistic situation
6. Language political situation
7. Language contact and contact languages
8. Evaluation of literature
9. Bibliography (selected)

1. Demography

On 1 January 1992, the Kingdom of the Netherlands ("Holland") had a population in excess of 15 million people almost half of whom lived in the *Randstad*, an area of densely populated urban agglomerations in the west of the country. In 1979 heavy immigration accounted for 42% of population growth, and by 1992 non Dutch of many different nationalities formed 4% of the total population (in May 1947 this was only 1,1%). As well as the criterion of nationality, there is also that of ethnicity on which basis ethnic minorities are distinguished as relatively stable groups with an originally foreign culture. Members of these groups may have Dutch nationality. This applies particularly to the groups mentioned under 2. and 3.

The largest ethnic minorities are:

(1) Turks, Kurds (with Turkish nationality), Moroccans and other Mediterranean groups. Legally and sometimes illegally, these people came to the Netherlands after 1960 as migrant workers to perform a range of unskilled jobs. By 1 January 1992, partly attributable to family reunion, marriage and births, there were some 450,000 Mediterraneans living in the Netherlands of which 215,000 Turks, including Kurds, and 165,000 Moroccans. Less significant groups which will not figure further in this discussion are: Spanish (15,000), Portuguese (10,000), Cape Verdeans (10,000), Italians (20,000), former Yugoslavians (14,000) and Greeks (4,000).

(2) Surinamese originating from the former Dutch colony of Suriname in South America (an estimated 210,000 in 1991). They belong to a diversity of ethnic groups (see 4.2.). Migration to the Netherlands by these people was motivated by poor economic conditions and fear of ethnic tensions in their own country.

(3) Antillians, peoples from the Dutch Antilles (Curaçao, Bonaire, Aruba, Saint Martin, Saba, and Saint Eustatius), former colonies which now form part of the kingdom (an estimated 70,000 in 1991). They are predominantly migrant workers. Arubans are considered to be a separate group as their country has had political autonomy since 1986.

(4) Moluccans, the people from a number of islands in eastern Indonesia including Ambon (approximately 35,000). The Moluccans were originally soldiers who came to the Netherlands in 1951 after the formation of the Republic of Indonesia and the disbanding of the Dutch colonial army because they did not wish to live under Indonesian rule.

(5) Chinese (not officially recognised as a minority group). Prior to 1988 their numbers were estimated at around 45,000. The majority originate from China or Hong Kong. Many of these Chinese work in the restaurant industry.

Smaller groups (to which no further attention will be paid) are gypsies and political refugees. Of the earliest group of immigrants, the Jews, only a small number remain largely as a result of the holocaust.

The Indo-Dutch (Eurasians) form a special group. They are the descendants of marriages between Europeans and the indigenous people of the former Dutch East Indies, who came to the Netherlands after Indonesian independence. It is difficult to estimate their numbers since they hold Dutch nationality, but there are certainly several hundred thousand of them living in the Netherlands (→ Language Map C).

2. Territorial history and national development

The beginnings of the Kingdom of the Netherlands as an independent nation date from the sixteenth century when the northern states (including Friesland), until that time part of the Spanish-Habsburg Empire, formed a free Union, while the southern Netherlands (roughly speaking modern-day Belgium: → art. 135) remained subject to Spanish-Austrian rule. The economic, political and cultural heart of the republic came to lie in the west, in Holland, and therefore it was here that from the sixteenth century a standard language developed, initially as a written language. In the wake of the French Period (from 1813) the Netherlands were united with Belgium to form one kingdom. The northern and southern Netherlands, however, had grown too far apart and consequently after a brief struggle Belgium became an independent kingdom in 1830. As a result of these political developments the Dutch language area or, in other words, the area where standard Dutch is dominant and dialects closely related to it are spoken, is divided across two nations. The border with Germany is at the same time the eastern border of the language area defined above. As far as dialect is concerned, this border transects (what was originally) a continuum.

3. Politics, economy and general cultural and religious situation

The Netherlands is a parliamentary democracy. Democratic rights, however, do not apply to immigrants unless they hold Dutch nationality. Residents without Dutch nationality may vote in local elections if they have resided legally in the Netherlands for a continuous period of five years. In the case of the Mediterranean immigrants, the Dutch government had always assumed that their stay would be temporary. In recent years the government has aimed at greater integration of these people into Dutch society, although there is no consensus on the degree of integration and acculturation.

The social position of immigrants (with the exception of the Indo-Dutch) is generally weak. Despite greater integration, this also applies to the Surinamese, Antillians and Arubans. Immigrants usually perform unskilled, low status work and live in the older working class areas of large cities. Characteristic of the Moluccans is that they were originally housed in camps and are today concentrated in certain neighbourhoods. Unemployment amongst all groups is high. Amongst the *Restaurant Chinese* unemployment is probably also high, but the extent is largely concealed owing to the closed nature of this community.

Like the Dutch, all immigrants enjoy complete religious freedom. Particularly as a result of immigration from Morocco and Turkey, 3% of the Dutch population is Moslem.

4. Statistics and ethnoprofiles

4.1. Dialect and standard language

From the west, standard Dutch was spread across an increasing number of regions and social groups. This has led to standard language and dialect existing together. In a large area of the province of Friesland the situation is complicated further by use of a form of standard Frisian as well as dialects, some resembling Dutch and some resembling Frisian. In Holland, the region where the standard language originated, dialects (sub-standard forms) are not clearly distinct. Rather, they form a continuum with the standard language. Because they are strongly associated with particular social levels, they are also called sociolects. In other areas, especially peripheral areas of the language region, standard language and dialect still form distinct language systems. Even in the experience of dialect speakers there is a form of diglossia. The degree to which dialect is maintained depends on the region, town or village. In the south of the province of Limburg, for example, dialect has a firmer foothold than in the province of Groningen, while within Limburg there is a difference between Maastricht (very conscious of dialect) and Heerlen (with more migration from the west).

4.2. Dutch and other languages

The majority of migrants from Turkey (over 90%) speak standard Turkish, the official language of Turkey, as well as mutually intelligible Turkish dialects (belonging to the Altaic language family). A minority of around 10% speaks a Kurdish dialect belonging to the Indo-European Iranian language family together with standard Turkish. Kurdish is not taught in Turkish schools. The language has only little written tradition. The Kurds form a separate group in the Turkish community with its own identity. Turks and Kurds are both followers of Islam. They live mainly in the *Randstad*.

Of the Moroccans, 70% speak Berber and the remainder a Moroccan-Arabic language. Although Moroccan and Berber bear no linguistic relation, the influence of Islam has led to a cultural relationship which is particularly evident in the lexicon. Berber, a language not taught at school in Morocco, has little written tradition since the Berber culture is an oral one. Berbers are competent in Moroccan-Arabic, but Berber is not spoken outside their own group. Through (religious) education Moroccans have a basic command of classical Arabic or standard Arabic. Moroccans live in the *Randstad*, especially in Rotterdam.

Surinamese speak a diversity of mother tongues besides Dutch and Suriname-Dutch (more about this later). The two largest groups are the Hindustanis and the Creoles. Creoles, descendants of slaves transported from Africa to Suriname, speak Sranan, an English-based creole language which also has a written form. They have their own cultural identity stemming from Surinamese plantation culture, a blend of African, Indian and European Christian elements. Creoles are for the most part Protestants (Moravians). The Hindustanis, descendants of contract labourers recruited from British India in the nineteenth century and comprising 80% Hindus and 20% Moslems, speak Sarnami (Surinamese-Hindi), which is seldom written, but also Hindi (by Hindus) or Urdu (by Moslems), two very closely related languages belonging to the Indo-European language group. A smaller group of Surinamese are the Javanese, descendents of contract labourers recruited around 1900. Suriname Javanese speak a language which exists mainly in oral form. The majority are Moslems and as a rule they remain true to Javanese culture. Other groups are: Indians, the indigenous people of Suriname, belonging to a diversity of tribes, with their own languages; Bush Negroes or Maroons, descendants of escaped Negro slaves whose purely oral creole languages are influenced by Portuguese or by English; Hakka-Chinese, descendants of contract labourers from Northern China; and finally Jews of Portuguese and Eastern European origin, Portuguese from Madeira, and Lebanese. Surinamese in the Netherlands are chiefly concentrated in the *Randstad* (25% in Amsterdam) and form an integrated group with its own cultural identity, despite differences between Creoles and Hindustanis.

The majority of Antillians come from Curaçao and Bonaire and like the Arubans speaks Papiamento, a creole language based on Portuguese-Spanish. The language has a written form and is a medium of formal instruction in island schools. Small numbers come from Saint Martin, Saba and Saint Eustatius, where an English-based creole language is spoken. On all the islands Dutch is the official language and many are competent in it. Most Antillians and Arubans are Roman Catholics and maintain an identity which is distinctly different from that of the Surinamese.

The Moluccans, most of whom are Christian but a small number of whom are Moslem, not only speak Dutch and a language more or less obsolescent in the Moluccas these days, but also Malay, an Austronesian language which is closely related to Indonesian. Malay is the language used on official occasions in the Moluccan community, the language of the church and the media. The Moluccans form a close community with its own identity, strengthened by their ideal of returning to their homeland.

The Chinese, with the exception of the Chinese from Suriname and Indonesia who have undergone complete acculturation, form a number of close communities rather than one close community. The largest group comes from southern China, just above Hong Kong, and has Cantonese, the language of Hong Kong city culture, as its mother tongue. Chain migration after the Second World War has caused an increase in the population of these *Restaurant Chinese*. The same applies to another group of Chinese, the Zhejiangs from the Wenzhou area south of Shanghai. Their mother tongue is the Wu dialect, but unlike the Cantonese they also speak standard Chinese or Mandarin, a language understandable to all educated Chinese. The Zhejiangs and the Cantonese consider themselves sejourners, temporary foreign guests who eventually will (or want to) return to China.

Some Indo-Dutch consider themselves to belong to a group with its own identity, of which the feeling of having two homelands is a fundamental factor. This identity is reinforced by the diversity of languages used in their own circles.

5. Sociolinguistic situation

5.1. Dialect and standard language

Diglossia in (peripheral) dialect regions is unstable by nature: an increasing number of people only speak the standard language as a result of migration or background, and there is also loss of function of the dialect whereby upbringing and home environment play a role. Furthermore, social rather than regional factors now determine dialect to an increasing extent. Loss of function leads to loss of structure and this loss of structure leads to a form of dialect which is both simplified and heavily influenced by the standard language. It is particularly vocabulary (content words) which is affected by this. Aspects of sound, syntax, including grammar words, are much better immune. A form of semi-dialect does carry certain advantages. Not only does it solve the problem of bilingualism, it also enables a compromise in attitude between community loyalty and loyalty to society as a whole. Another advantage is that increased contact between communities has caused the disappearance of most local language characteristics. For this reason one can speak of regiolects. As mentioned in 4.1. the extent of loss of function and loss of structure is strongly dependent on region. The rate, however, is slower than expected. Complaints about the *degeneration* of dialect date from the nineteenth century. Conversely, under the influence of regional dialects, varieties (*accents*) of the standard language have arisen. Regional loyalty may play a role in this, but often it is a question of speech characteristics which are difficult to shed.

In reaction to the processes described above there has been a revival of interest in dialect: there are institutes, societies and projects whose goal is to preserve and study old dialects, in general regional history and culture. The use of old dialect in daily speech situations, however, is hardly affected by this. It is possible that an archaic form of dialect will remain in existence which is artificially preserved for cultural purposes and which also may be written.

Within the Dutch language community there is generally a more positive reaction to dialects which are markedly different from the standard language and to regional standard accents than to (western) sociolects with their strong associations with the lower classes. As a result of covert prestige, however, the latter appear to be deeply rooted in the Netherlands. Attitudes towards dialect are various: the dialect of the capital Amsterdam is more prestigious than that of Leiden, and it seems that in the evaluation of dialects outside the *Randstad* the degree of understandability plays a role. In all respects the standard language enjoys highest prestige.

5.2. Dutch and other languages

To Turks, Kurds and Moroccans, Dutch is a second language with high prestige used particularly in formal situations (public life) and informal situations where speakers do not share a common mother tongue. For young people, especially those born in the Netherlands, Dutch is gaining importance as the home language during the period they attend primary school, even in communication with their parents. Turkish is prestigious amongst Turks. It remains the language for interaction with compatriots. The attitude of Kurds towards their own language, strictly a language used in the domestic situation, is mixed. On the one hand, they are uneasy about projecting their own identity and language (attitudes brought with them from Turkey), while on the other hand, there appears to be resurgence of pride in their own identity. Turkish continues to play a role in this community, particularly as a written language. Arabic, the language of Islam, is highly esteemed by Moroccans. Both Moroccan-Arabic and Berber have prestige as home languages. In most cases, however, it would be true to say that the home languages of these communities are coming under increasing influence from Dutch.

To the Surinamese, Dutch, especially Suriname-Dutch (which will be discussed below), a language taught and commanded from a young age, has high prestige in both formal and informal situations. Existing alongside this is Sranan, the language of Surinamese identity for the non-Hindustani population in particular. Sarnami, the home language of the Hindustanis, has little prestige (unlike Hindu or Urdu), although in the Netherlands the status of Sarnami is increasing. It is also used as a written language. Amongst Hindustanis, however, there is no consensus about which language reinforces their identity: Hindu/Urdu or Sarnami.

Dutch has high prestige in the eyes of Antillians and Arubans, but from birth they are generally less competent in it than the Surinamese. Amongst this group Papiamento is held in equally high regard, especially amongst young people, as an informal home language or medium for communication with friends.

To Moluccans, Dutch is the language of public life and often also the home language, especially in the interaction of young people. In addition to this, Malay is the language of their own identity: the language of religious life, the language of Moluccan public life and often the home language as well.

For the majority of Chinese it is true that Dutch has high status, but this is mainly because it is the language of the (temporary) guest country and as such is mastered no more than necessary. Young people, however, have a better command of Dutch. In the Cantonese speaking group Cantonese is the language held in high esteem. It is considered the proper medium for communication between group members (at home a Cantonese dialect will be spoken) and it also facilitates participation in the Chinese city culture of Hong Kong (videos). Outside this group as well Cantonese is used increasingly as the general day-to-day language of Chinese communication even amongst the Zhejiangers who remain truest to standard Chinese as the language of Chinese culture (often an old-fashioned language in the eyes of young people) and prefer to use this language in their contacts with other Chinese. Their mother tongue, a Wu dialect, functions as the home language. The status of Cantonese can be expected to decline in favour of standard Chinese when Hong Kong becomes part of China.

For the Indo-Dutch, Dutch is the language for all situations. Only for informal use in their own circles is Indo-Dutch used.

6. Language political situation

6.1. Dialect and standard language

In public life and also in the media, dialects play an insignificant role. There is no question of attempts at standardisation. Limited financial support is sometimes provided by local governments: the province of Groningen, for example, employs a dialect official. Although the law permits dialect to be used as a medium of formal instruction at primary school, little use is made of this provision.

6.2. Dutch and other languages

Netherlands law requires compulsory education for children from minority groups and so these children learn Dutch as a second language at school. Basic education for adult migrants with an emphasis on Dutch language acquisition is still in its early stages.

In the 1980's, with the support of government, clear form was given to the idea that ethnic minorities should be integrated into society with acculturation as the end result. Education in their own language and culture was deemed necessary to enable the eventual return of migrants to their country of origin and to maintain their own cultural identity. A maximum of two and a half hours of regular schooltime a week is allotted for mother tongue education and culture. Out of schooltime, moreover, two and a half hours of subsidised education can be given. Especially Turks, Moroccans and Moluccans benefit from this. The accent is on learning the official language of the country of origin. Kurdish and Berber are not taught. Antillians, Arubans and Surinamese are unable to benefit from these provisions because Dutch is the official language of their homeland. There have been a few experiments with bilingual education. At some secondary schools foreign pupils are able to follow lessons in their own language, even to examination level (not available to Dutch pupils). It is not uncommon for Chinese, especially those from the Cantonese-speaking community, to organise several hours a week of education in their own language, in many cases unsubsidised (all Chinese prefer where possible to send their children to China for several years). The Chinese do not have official minority status and generally do not wish this in view of the dependence on the government which it involves. Some Arabic courses are given for Islamic foreigners in the context of religious education.

Radio and television provide programmes on culture for minorities in languages including Berber and Kurdish. On a small scale, newspapers and magazines as well as folk and pop music are available in Turkish, Arabic and Chinese (especially Cantonese). The availability of books in minority languages other than Sranan and Papiamento is very limited.

Language norms are derived from the norms in the homeland. An exception to this is the Malay of the Moluccans where the spelling is based on the spelling of Malay developed by the Dutch and diverges from official Indonesian spelling. Although standardisation of (Moluccan)-Malay is desired by the Moluccan community, it has yet to be realised.

7. Language contact and contact languages

7.1. Dialect and standard language

There are considerable differences in the dialects found in the Netherlands or, to be more accurate, the Dutch language area, and as a result dialects are often unintelligible to other Dutch speakers. In general, the linguistic distance between dialect and standard language increases the further one travels from the *Randstad*. Dialects in the east are related to those of Germany. Going from west to east, for example, we find an increase in the use of the umlaut: e.g. with the plural of the substantive, some present tense forms and diminutives. This is illustrated well by comparing the dialect of the Twente region in the east with standard Dutch: *greun/groen* ("green"), *deupen/dopen* ("to baptise"), *hee slöp/hij slaapt* ("he is sleeping"), *boom-beumke/boom-boompje* ("tree/little tree"). Dialects in the north-east are more closely related to those in Northern Germany. For example, the present tense plural ends in -*t* in the case of verbs compared with the standard language -*e(n)*: *wij maakt/wij make(n)* ("we make"). The dialects of the south-east form a continuum with those in the German Rhineland. They are characterised by such things as contrastive tones and by forms which have undergone the High German Sound Shift (*ich, mich* etc.). The dialects of the south are closely related to those of Dutch-speaking Belgium. This explains why one finds the construction *ik heb geen boek bij* ("I haven't got a book with me") (standard language *bij me*) in both the Dutch province of North Brabant and the Brabant region over the border.

The penetration of dialect into standard language resulting in standard accents has particular affect on peculiarities of pronunciation. A well known example is the *zachte 'g'* ("soft" 'g') as it is called (clearly a voiced fricative) which is characteristic of the southern region including Belgium. In the *Randstad* this phoneme is pronounced without voicing and often with a scraping sound. A further example is the pronunciation of the vowels in *heel* ("whole"), *groot* ("big"), *neus* ("nose"). In the west these are clear diphthongs (as in English), in the east monophthongs (as in German). Moreover, syntactic peculiarities (including grammar words) frequently penetrate from dialect into standard language. An example is the Brabant construction cited above.

7.2. Dutch and other languages

Foreign migrants have learnt Dutch as a second language to various levels of proficiency. A continuum of interlanguages from mother tongue to Dutch are spoken. Variants which are more or less stable have not developed in the Netherlands to any degree.

An exception to this is Melaju-Sini, the Malay that is spoken by younger Moluccans in informal situations. Structurally, this language can be considered as a somewhat simplified Malay and lexically, to a large extent, as Dutch: *trein-trein vertraging* has the structural characteristics of Malay (doubling of the substantive and the omission of the copula verb), but the words are Dutch.

In the former Dutch East Indies comparable mixed languages developed (compare also the now extinct creole language *Negerhollands* of the Virgin Islands), especially when foreign women who did not speak Dutch cohabited with Dutch men in or around army barracks, for example. The structural basis is a form of Malay or another Austronesian language, but the vocabulary is for the main part borrowed from Dutch. The language would then be passed on to children born as a result of the concubinage or marriage and they, in turn, spread the language in the streets. In Batavia (now Jakarta), for example, Pecok came to be used as an informal street language and language between friends. In the Netherlands this language, disdained in the former colony, became the expression of an own identity for a number of Indo-Europeans. It has even been used as a literary medium.

In the former colonies of Dutch East India and Suriname varieties of Dutch also developed which were brought to the Netherlands. Both varieties of Dutch are by no means homogenous. Suriname-Dutch forms a continuum ranging from the standard Dutch that is spoken by educated Surinamese to varieties with many deviations from the standard language, spoken by the Creole working class. We limit ourselves to the varieties which are spoken by the educated and which have general acceptance. Besides a number of borrowings and peculiarities of pronunciation such as a bilabial *w*, Surinam-Dutch is characterised by the use of *gaan* ("go") as an auxiliary of tense (*ik ga naar Amsterdam gaan/ik ga naar Amsteram* – "I'm going to Amsterdam"), the passive meaning of active verb forms (*ik ga mijn haar knippen/ik laat mijn haar knippen* – "I'm going to have my hair cut") and the omission of a reflexive pronoun (*ga baden/ga je baden* – "bathe yourself"). Indo-Dutch is characterised by a number of Malay borrowings and pronunciation features such as a bilabial *w*, a rolled dental *r* and a tense *b* and *d*.

8. Evaluation of literature

8.1. Literature and standard language

Although the rise of modern sociolinguistics (Labov) has also led to studies of urban languages in the Netherlands, it would seem that attention, certainly from around 1980, has been focused on the relationship and the mutual influence of dialect and standard language. An earlier pioneering study on the problems of bilingualism in the village of Borne in Twente is Nuijtens (1962). A significant study during the Seventies is the Kerkrade Project which investigated the problem of dialect in primary school education in the Limburg town of Kerkrade. This research resulted in practical recommendations. For a general summary see Hagen (1989) and for further research see also Cheshire et al. (1989).

Studies concerning dialect and standard language make use of sociolinguistic methods. Connections are established between the processes of change (loss of function and loss of structure) and style, socio-economic position, gender and/or age group (research into language change in apparent time). The language disciplines focused on – phonology, morphology, syntax and/or lexicon – vary according to the study. Attitudes are also considered: attitudes to dialect, dialect use and dialect change. A general overview is given by Hagen and Giesbers (1988).

From Nijmegen, research is currently underway in the regions of Limburg and East

Brabant (Maastricht, Sittard, Ubach over Worms, Ottersum, Venray, Nijmegen; Deurne) led by Anton M. Hagen. Hagen (1986) provides a summary of this. See further for Maastricht, Münstermann (1989); for Ottersum and Nijmegen compared to Bonn and the surrounding area, see Hagen (1986a); and for Ubach over Worms, see Hinskens (1992). A comprehensive study of urban dialectology carried out in Nijmegen city itself is Van Hout (1989). A study of code-switching in Ottersum is Giesbers (1989). Research in Venray concentrated on the question to what extent young standard language speakers in a dialect speaking environment acquire dialect (see Vousten 1995).

Research is also being carried out from other centres. In Groningen, Cor Hoppenbrouwers deserves mention. It was Hoppenbrouwers who introduced the concept of *regiolect*. His research (in the east of the province of North Brabant) and that of his students (in the province of Groningen), which focuses specifically on loss of structure, has revealed implicational ordering in the continuum between standard language and dialect. This is summarised in Hoppenbrouwers (1990) (see also Hoppenbrouwers 1982 and 1987). In Leiden Cor van Bree can be mentioned. Van Bree's research, conducted in a number of locations in Twente, concentrates chiefly on loss of structure with particular reference to the stability of global language aspects: lexicon, morphology, syntax etc. The influence of dialect on standard language is also examined. Van Bree (1992) provides an overview. Camiel Hamans carried out research in the city of Roermond in Limburg (see Hamans 1985) into the question in how far certain morphological processes in dialect are still productive. Under his supervision an investigation was carried out in the town of Katwijk aan Zee in the province of South Holland (where a characteristic dialect is still spoken) into the influence of commuting on loss of dialect (see Wald 1984). An interesting area of research was chosen by Harry Scholtmeijer: the *IJsselmeerpolders*, drained areas of the old *Zuiderzee* where immigrants with very different dialect backgrounds came into contact (Scholtmeijer 1992). For the convergence of dialect and standard language see Stroop 1992. Recent publications are Cornips 1994 (about the regional variety of Dutch spoken in the Limburg town of Heerlen) and Voortman 1994 (about regional variation in language use of dignitaries in three towns: Middelburg, Roermond and Zutphen). For further recent research see Van Hout and Huls 1991.

Worthy of mention is research that is being carried out on dialects on both sides of the Dutch-German border. For the influence which these dialects have undergone from standard Dutch and standard German see Kremer (1991) (and the literature mentioned herein). For the south-east (including parts of Belgium, Germany and Luxembourg) see Cajot (1989). For the influence of the Dutch-Belgium border on standard language and dialect see Taeldeman 1991 and Van Bree and Van Scherpenzeel 1993 and the literature mentioned herein. For recent research see Van Hout and Huls 1991.

The research of language use of ethnic minorities is mainly focused on temporal and structural aspects (in correlation with social-economic and social-psychological factors) of the acquisition of Dutch as a second language, especially by children of Turkish and Moroccan origin: a general overview is given by Extra (1990); see also Extra and Vallen (1985 and 1988), Appel (1984), Lalleman (1986), Vermeer (1986), and Verhoeven (1987a). Less attention is devoted to the acquisition by adults (Broeder et al. 1986) and to the acquisition of phonetic aspects (Van Boeschoten 1989). Much research is carried out within the framework of a European Science Foundation project, focusing on the acquisition of second, dominant languages in five Western European countries; Guus Extra of the Catholic University of Brabant is the supervisor of this project in the Netherlands (see Perdue 1984).

Less attention is also devoted to the acquisition of minority languages by children in the Netherlands and to the use, the maintenance (or the loss) of minority languages. An overview is given by De Ruiter (1991) and Extra (1993); for Surinamese see also Charry et al. (1983), for Melaju-Sini Tahitu (1989), and for an overview of Indo-Dutch De Vries (1993). Boeschoten and Verhoeven (1985 and 1986) investigated the acquisition of Turkish by Turkish children, and Verhoeven (1987b) the acquisition of Turkish and Dutch vocabulary by Turkish children. For language loss see Jaspaert et al. (1986).

9. Bibliography (selected)

Appel, R. (1984): *Immigrant children learning Dutch. Sociolinguistic and psycholinguistic aspects of second-language acquisition*, Dordrecht.

Boeschoten, Hendrik/Verhoeven, Ludo (1985): "Integration niederländischer lexikalischer Elemente ins Türkische. Sprachmischung bei Immigranten der ersten und zweiten Generation". In: *Linguistische Berichte 98*, 347–364.

Boeschoten, Hendrik/Verhoeven, Ludo (1986): "First language acquisition in a second language submersion environment". In: *Applied Psycholinguistics 7*, 241–255.

Broeder, Peter et al. (1986): "Acquiring the linguistic devices for pronominal reference to person. A crosslinguistic perspective on complex tasks with small words". In: *Linguistics in the Netherlands*, Beukema, F./Hulk, A. (Eds.), Dordrecht-Providence, 27–40.

Cajot, José (1989): *Neue Sprachschranken im 'Land ohne Grenzen'? Zum Einfluß politischer Grenzen auf die germanischen Mundarten in der belgisch-niederländisch-luxemburgischen Euregio*, Bd. I: Text, Bd. II: Karten und Tabellen, Wien.

Charry, Eddy/Koefoed, Geert/Muysken, Pieter (Eds.) (1983): *De talen van Suriname*, Muiderberg.

Cheshire, Jenny et al. (Eds.) (1989): *Dialect and education: some European perspectives*, Clevedon–Philadelphia.

Cornips, Leonie (1994): *Syntactische variatie in Het Algemeen Nederlands van Heerlen*, IFOTT, Amsterdam.

De Ruiter, Jan J. (Ed.) (1991): *Talen in Nederland*, Groningen.

De Vries, Jan W. (1993: "The language of the Indo-Dutch". In: *The Low Countries: multidisciplinary studies: Publications of the American Association for Netherlandic Studies 4*, Bakker, M. (Ed.), Lanham, New York and London.

Extra, Guus (1990): "Processes of language change over time: A linguistic prespective on ethnic minority research in the Netherlands". In: *Contemporary Dutch Linguistics*, Aarts, F./van Els, T., Washington.

Extra, Guus (Ed.) (1993): *Community languages in the Netherlands*, Amsterdam.

Extra, Guus/Vallen, Ton (Eds.) (1985): *Ethnic minorities and Dutch as a second language*, Dordrecht.

Extra, Guus/Vallen, Ton (1988): "Language and ethnic minorities in the Netherlands". In: *International Journal of the Sociology of Language 73*, 85–110.

Giesbers, Herman (1989): *Code-switching tussen dialect en standaardtaal*, Amsterdam.

Hagen, Anton M. (1986): *Dialectverlies en dialectbehoud*, themanummer *Taal en Tongval*.

Hagen, Anton M. (1986a): "Dialekt und Standardsprache. Zur heutigen Situation im niederländischen Grenzgebiet". In: *Rheinische Vierteljahresblätter 50*, 287–297.

Hagen, Anton M. (1989): "The Netherlands". In: *Sociolinguistica 3: Dialekt und Schule in den europäischen Ländern*, Ammon, U. et al. (Eds.), Tübingen, 61–74.

Hagen, Anton M./Giesberg, Herman (1988): "Dutch sociolinguistic dialect studies". In: *International Journal of the sociology of language 73*, 29–44.

Hamans, Camiel (1985): "Achteruitgang van het dialect?". In: *Dialect, standaardtaal en maatschappij*, Taeldeman, J./Dewulf, H. (Eds.), Leuven–Amersfoort, 115–135.

Hinskens, Frans (1992): *Dialect levelling in Limburg. Structural and sociolinguistic aspects*, Nijmegen (diss.).

Hoppenbrouwers, Cor (1982): *Language change; a study of phonemic and analogical change with particular reference to S. E. Dutch dialects*, Groningen (diss.).

Hoppenbrouwers, Cor (1987): "The instability of peripheral /e./. /ø./ and /o./ in Dutch lects". In: *Papers from the VIIth International conference on historical linguistics (Pavia, 9–13 september 1985)*, Ramat, A. G./Carruba, O./Bernini, G. (Eds.), Amsterdam, 285–295.

Hoppenbrouwers Cor (1990): *Het regiolect. Van dialect tot algemeen Nederlands*, Muiderberg.

Jaspaert, Koen/Kroon, Sjaak/van Hout, Roeland (1986): "Points of reference in first-language loss research". In: *Language attrition in progress*, Weltens, B./de Bot, K./van Els, Th. (Eds.), Dordrecht–Providence, 37–49.

Kremer, Ludger (1991): "Zur Entwicklung der Diglossie beiderseits der niederländisch-deutschen Staatsgrenze". In: *Jahrbuch des Vereins für niederdeutsche Sprachforschung 114*, 134–150.

Lalleman, Josien A. (1986): *Dutch language proficiency of Turkish children born in the Netherlands*, Dordrecht–Providence.

Münstermann, Henk (1989): "Dialect loss in Maastricht attitudes, functions and structures". In: *Language and Intergroup Relations in Flanders and in The Netherlands*, Deprez, K. (Ed.), Dordrecht, 99–128.

Nuijtens, Emiel (1962): *De tweetalige mens. Een taalsociologisch onderzoek naar het gebruik van dialect en cultuurtaal in Borne*, Assen.

Perdue, Clive (Ed.) (1984): *Second language acquisition by adult immigrants. A field manual*, Rowley Mass.

Scholtmeijer, Harm (1992): *Het Nederlands van de IJsselmeerpolders*, Kampen.

Stroops, Jan (1992): "Towards the end of the standard language in the Netherlands". In: *Dialect and Standard Language, Dialekt und Standardsprache, in the English, Dutch, German and Norwegian Language Areas*, Van Leuwensteijn, J. A./Berns, J. B. (Eds.), Amsterdam etc., 162–177.

Taeldeman, Johan (1991): "De belgisch-nederlandse rijksgrens als dialectgrens". In: *De kracht* van het woord. 100 jaar germaanse filologie aan de RUG (1890–1990), Taalkunde, Studia Germanica Gandensia 24, Demoor, M. (Ed.), 65–90.

Tahitu, Egbertus (1989): *Melaju Sini. Het Maleis van Molukse jongeren in Nederland,* Leiden (diss.).

Van Boeschoten, Joost A. (1989): *Verstaanbaarheid van klanken in het Nederlands gesproken door Turken, in context van woord en zin,* Leiden (diss.).

Van Bree, Cor (1992): "The stability of language elements, in present-day eastern Standard-Dutch and eastern Dutch dialects". In: *Dialect and Standard Language, Dialekt und Standardsprache, in the English, Dutch, German and Norwegian Language Areas,* van Leuvensteijn, J. A./Berns, J. B. (Eds.), Amsterdam etc., 178–203.

Van Bree, Cor/Van Scherpenzee, Marianne (1994): "Contact en nationaliteit. Bewustzijn omtrent flamingismen bij inwoners van Baarle-Nassau en Baarle-Hertog en naburige nederlandse en belgische plaatsen". In: *Leuvense Bijdragen 83* (1994), 317–341.

Van Hout, Roeland (1989): *De structuur van taalvariatie. Een sociolinguïstisch onderzoek naar het stadsdialect van Nijmegen,* Dordrecht.

van Hout, Roeland/Huls, Erica (Eds.) (1991): *Artikelen van de Eerste Sociolinguïstische Conferentie,* Delft.

Verhoeven, Ludo (1987a): *Ethnic minority children acquiring literacy,* Dordrecht–Providence.

Verhoeven, Ludo (1987b): "Lexical development in ethnic minority children". In: *Belgian Journal of Linguistics 2,* 75–91.

Vermeer, Anne (1986): *Tempo en structuur van tweede-taalverwerving bij Turkse en Marokkaanse kinderen,* Tilburg (diss.).

Voortman, Berber (1994): *Regionale variatie in Let taalgebruik van notabelen. Een sociolinguïstisch onderzoel in Middelburg, Roermond en Zutphen.* IFOTT, Amsterdam.

Vousten, Rob (1995): *Dialect als tweede taal. Linguïstische en extra-linguïstische aspecten van de verwerving van een Noordlimburgs dialect door standaardtalige jongeren,* Nijmegen–Amsterdam (diss.).

Wald, Alfred (1984): "Forenisme en taalverandering". In: *Taal en Tongval 36,* 143–161.

Cor van Bree/Jan de Vries, Leiden (Netherlands)

140. Dutch–West Frisian

1. Geography and demography
2. History
3. Politics, economy and general cultural and religious situation
4. Statistics and ethnoprofile
5. Sociolinguistic situation
6. Language political situation
7. General intralinguistic portrait
8. Critical evaluation of the sources and scientific discussions
9. Bibliography (selected)

1. Geography and demography

The province of Friesland (Fri. *Fryslân*) is located in the northwestern part of the Netherlands. The landscape is characteristically flat and the largest part of the province is below sea-level. The total population is 600,000 which is equal to 179 inhabitants per km² (cf. The Netherlands: 15.1 million inhabitants; 446 per km²). The capital is Leeuwarden (Fri. *Ljouwert*), with 85,000 inhabitants. Four Waddensea islands are part of the province. A dense pattern of some 300 small villages (population less than 1,500) and only a few larger towns is typical for Friesland. The administrative borders of the province coincide well with the geographic area in which the Frisian language is spoken today.

In 1830 the population of Friesland (205,000) comprised almost 8% of the total population of the Netherlands. By 1950 the absolute number of inhabitants had more than doubled (468,000), but it had sharply decreased relatively (only 4.6%). Today it is less than 4% of the total population of the Netherlands.

According to age, the youngest group (below 19 years) and the oldest group (over 65 years) are slightly overrepresented in Friesland compared to the Netherlands. In terms of educational level and income the population of Friesland is below average.

Migration is an important factor. During the early 1950s there was massive emigration from Friesland. From 1960 till today the number of persons leaving the province every year has remained fairly constant, averaging ± 25,000. However, the number of newcomers has fluctuated from just over 20,000 in 1960, going up to a high point of almost 35,000 in 1974, decreasing to 22,000 in 1984 and settling at almost 27,000 in 1991. The outcome has been a surplus of immigrants between 1971 and 1982 and a negative departure balance in most other years. Additionally, there were internal migration flows from the countryside to the towns and from some larger towns to the surrounding commuter villages. As will be clear, the effect of an annual relocation of some 8–12% of the total population on the distribution of the language has been substantial. Both processes of migration made geographic, language related differences less distinct.

An additional factor is the operation of a 'dual labour market': (lower class) workers are recruited mainly on a regional (or local) scale, but (middle and upper class) staff is selected from the Netherlands as a whole (in particular from the neighbouring northern provinces). This process strengthens the social position of Dutch, and is consequently negative for Frisian (→ Language Map C).

2. History

The Frisians were first identified as a separate people in Roman historical sources in 12 B.C. The origin of the name 'Frisii' is still disputed. Their living area was then much larger (*Frisia Magna*), but the current province of Friesland was always about in the centre. In the early Middle Ages Frisians were an important sea-faring and trading people. For example, in those times the current North Sea was also called the Frisian Sea. Except for a few scattered runic inscriptions, the oldest written texts in (Old-)Frisian date back to the early 13th century. Old-Frisian consists of a relatively one-sided corpus: mainly legal documents. Of importance is the legendary idea of 'Frisian freedom', a privilege supposedly granted by Charlemagne. The period of 'Frisian freedom' ended in 1498 with the investment of foreign rule, but the idea continued to play an important role in the Frisian historical consciousness. In 1579 (The Union of Utrecht) Friesland was incorporated as one of the seven autonomous provinces of the federal Republic of the United Netherlands (Friesland then ranked second in economic and political importance).

The Frisians had already realized for a long time that they are a separate people. This consciousness was reinforced during the 19th century when, under the influence of Romanticism, the beginnings of an organized Frisian movement were laid. Those developments led to a renewed interest in the Frisian language, culture and history. For some it included emphasizing the heroic past with legendary medieval Frisian kings and glorification of the idea of 'Frisian freedom'.

The founding of the united Kingdom of the Netherlands (1813) with its centralistic structure led among other things to increased language contact. The standard variety of Dutch – which came into prominence during the 19th century – also became gradually more important in Friesland, in particular through education, religion and the printed media. During the first half of the 20th century compulsory primary education and the introduction of new means of communication (telephone and radio) and transport (railways and bicycles) further increased the number of contacts of Frisian speakers with the Dutch language. Finally, after WW II, television, the automobile, migration and tourism, i.e. new possibilities for communication and transport, created a situation where even in the most remote corners of the countryside every Frisian speaker is confronted daily with Dutch as a spoken and as a written language. Consequently, the monolingual Frisian speaker, in a strong sense, has ceased to exist.

The history of Friesland and the Frisians during the 19th and 20th centuries is determined to a large extent by being part of the Netherlands. In particular its different linguistic and cultural situation give it a special place.

3. Politics, economy and general cultural and religious situation

The authority of the Province of Friesland as an administrative body is limited in the Netherlands. The state (as law-making body) and the municipalities (execution of specific tasks) are more important and the province is a weak in-between layer with tasks of control and supervision.

In political terms the same parties are active in Friesland as in the rest of the Netherlands and the 'political landscape' is not all that much different from that in other provinces: christian-democrats, social-democrats, liberals, democrats, some small right-wing (religious) and a small left-wing (green) party. There is one exeption, however: the Frysk

Nasjonale Partij (FNP), which only takes part in elections at provincial and municipal level. The FNP attracts some 5% of the votes and currently has three seats (of 55) in the Provincial Council.

In the economy of Friesland the agricultural sector is traditionally strong (in particular dairy-farming and growing seed potatoes). Today the financial service sector (banking and insurance) and tourism are of increasing importance.

The general cultural situation has become more and more similar to the rest of the Netherlands. Still, some typical forms of cultural expression, folklore and traditional sports have remained. Typical traditional sports include pole-vaulting (*fierljeppen*), barge-sailing (*skûtsjesilen*) and jeu-de-pelote (*keatsen*).

Another cultural example is the form of musical expression found in brass-bands and (church) choirs. During the last few years several Frisian (hard) rock groups have obtained growing popularity. Amateur theatre groups in the Frisian language are flourishing in almost all villages, although there is only one professional theatre group.

Frisian literature offers a rich diversity in products, with over 100 new books published every year; many are translations (children's books) and some are original Frisian creations (most poetry and novels). Publishing in Frisian is stimulated by the Provincial government and professional counsel is available through the Frisian Literary Museum and the Foundation for the Frisian Book. An annual promotional campaign for Frisian books is carried out by means of door-to-door sales by volunteers; the books are carried in wheelbarrows through the neighborhoods and villages.

The educational system in Friesland is the same as in the rest of the Netherlands. The only exception involves a number of provisions for the teaching of Frisian in primary and secondary schools.

In religion the population of Friesland is predominantly Protestant (± 44%), a small proportion is Catholic (± 8%) and there are a number of smaller denominations. Due to a process of on-going secularisation the non-religious part of the population is growing (± 43%).

4. Statistics and ethnoprofile

No census data are available on the Frisian language (nor on Dutch). From representative sample surveys we know that ± 73% can speak Frisian (Fri. *Frysk*). This implies approximately 400,000 speakers. A substantial part of them are second language learners, as 55% report having learned Frisian as the first language as a child. Also just over half of the population currently speak Frisian in the home. From the same survey (Gorter et al. 1984) it is known that approximately 94% of the population can understand Frisian, 65% can read it and only 10% can write it. Except for a slow decline in speaking proficiency those percentages have been relatively stable over more than a decade. The historical contrast between towns and countryside is reflected in the spread of the Frisian language: it still has its strongest base today in the countryside. In the villages the figure for Frisian as the home language is around 70% and in the larger towns (over 10,000 inhabitants) it is only 40%, which is a reflection of a former, much stronger contrast between countryside and towns.

Predominantly during the 17th century a separate linguistic system came into being in the towns: so-called "city-Frisian" (*Stedfrysk*). On three Waddensea islands a number of separate dialects can be found. The area of It Bildt in the northwestern part of the province was reclaimed from the "Middle-sea" in the 16th century and was then settled by farmers from the province of Zuid-Holland. Up until today a separate dialect (*Bilts*) has been in use in that municipality. In a small area in the province of Groningen — neighbouring to the eastern border of Friesland — Frisian is also spoken. In two southeastern municipalities, East- and West-Stellingwerf, a Saxon dialect (*Stellingwerfs*) is spoken by about one-third of the inhabitants.

5. Sociolinguistic situation

The Frisian language is officially recognized as the second language of the Netherlands. That formal recognition has, however, hardly entailed active promotion of the language by the state. Outside the province of Friesland people are often barely aware of the developments concerning Frisian. There the status of the language is relatively low, even though it may be held in high regard inside the province of Friesland. In the domains of the family and the neighbourhood Frisian holds a relative strong position as a majority of the population habitually uses Frisian there and then. Its use in the domains of education, media, public administration and law is limited. The social and the linguistic position of Frisian has been characterized as in between a vernacular and a standard language.

There is a wide variety of attitudes towards Frisian. Frisian speakers seem to be basically positively predisposed toward their language. They express a certain emotional attachment and there is widespread agreement on the 'beauty' and 'value' of Frisian. At the same time they can wholeheartedly oppose certain specific measures to promote the use of Frisian, e. g. for education or public administration.

Language conflicts are part and parcel of daily life in Friesland, but only on a small scale at the level of individual interaction. There is no large-scale social conflict over the use of the language. An exception was the introduction of Frisian place-names in 1989 when organized resistance by small entrepreneurs made it very difficult to effectuate the measure.

Stereotypes about Frisian are two-faced: on the one hand there is praise for the old respectable language worthy of survival; on the other hand there is scorn for the peasant language as something from the past not fit for 'modern' society. That Janus face can be found among speakers themselves and among the population outside Friesland.

The degree in which there exists a diglossic relationship between Frisian and Dutch is subject to some intellectual debate. It is clear that older stricter 'divisions of functions' between the two languages have given way to new patterns, where Dutch enters into and cannot be kept out of the intimate spheres of the home, friends and family and where at the same time Frisian seeks to conquer some of the 'higher' domains of education, media and public administration. Frisian as a written language has remained marginal so there is a sharp diglossic distribution between spoken and written language functions.

Individual and social bilingualism are the rule in Friesland as three-quarters of the population can speak (at least some) Frisian and Dutch. Many claim to have some active command of languages such as English, German and French as well. Increased contacts with speakers of other languages (immigration of guest-workers, refugees, international exchanges, tourism and media) make the use of such languages more than just a potential, theoretical issue.

Inhabitants of Friesland very much live in an increasingly multilingual environment where contact, albeit often passive, with many languages is rather frequent.

6. Language political situation

There exists an official language policy framework in the form of a contractual agreement between the state and the provincial government. In a slow process of legal codification certain provisions for the use of Frisian in dealings with the government have been made. Over half of the 31 municipalities indeed have a formal, documented language policy. In education efforts were undertaken as early as 1907 to teach Frisian (then outside regular school hours). After 30 years, in 1937, Frisian obtained a modest place inside the curriculum as a 'living regional language'. From the early 1950s a process began of introducing the teaching of Frisian. In 1980 the language became an obligatory part of the curriculum of all primary schools (with a few exceptions in areas where less Frisian is spoken). In 1993 Frisian has also obtained a modest place in the first three grades of secondary school. Teacher training for Frisian is taken care of by departments in two large colleges for higher vocational training in Leeuwarden. There is no university in Friesland; at university level Frisian is taught in Amsterdam, Groningen and (part-time) Leiden. Even if Frisian has only a very modest place in the educational system, this domain is considered one of the spearheads of language policy.

In scientific research Frisian has hardly any place at all, except for the *Fryske Akademy*. Since its foundation in 1938 the Akademy has occupied itself with research about the Frisian language, history and society. Important projects regard lexicography (*Larger Dictionary of the Frisian Language*), history and social science. The latter not only just concerning the sociology of language or European minority languages, but also economic labour market research and political science studies on regionalism and decentralization. There is a staff of some seventy and almost two thirds carry out scholarly work. Since its beginning the Akademy has published almost 800 books.

In the public sector Frisian has a minor role as written language of commerce and industry. At the workplace Frisian will be spoken freely by Frisian speakers among each other, but a switch to Dutch will almost automatically take place in the presence of non-Frisian speakers. The management level is dominated by Dutch speakers, so the language of almost all interaction will be Dutch, even among Frisian speakers.

Every Sunday a number of church services are conducted through the medium of Frisian (< 5%). An organization of Frisian pastors has a policy aimed at increasing that number. Once a year a 'Frisian Sunday' is organized to have Frisian sermons delivered in the maximum number of services. There are Frisian versions of the Bible and the Book of Hymns available.

The two major daily newspapers have limited amounts of Frisian texts every day (< 3%), and a special Frisian page every week. Local papers generally follow this pattern; here and there some have more. There is one all-Frisian monthly magazine (circulation 5,500, formerly a weekly), a few literary journals and one monthly magazine for education. Of recent there are two special 'youth magazines' aiming at the age category under 18.

The Fryske Akademy publishes a quarterly magazine and a scientific journal (although the latter is only partly in Frisian; both circulate at ± 3,000). The number of hours broadcasted by the regional radio station has gone up quite considerably over the last few years, to approximately 50 hours a week. Frisian television remained very modest for a long time at less than one hour a week, including school TV programs. Starting in 1994 there is one hour every day (excluding rerunning of programs).

Spelling for Frisian was established by private initiative in 1879; after a reform by the Fryske Akademy in 1946, a new slight reform was officially authorized by the provincial government in 1980.

Also in 1980 a Language Bureau (*Taalburo*) was established at the Fryske Akademy to develop new terminology for domains where Frisian was introduced, in particular for public administration and law. There is no official body for language standardization but the dictionaries published by the Fryske Akademy have a normative effect. To some extent the language norm of the AFUK (an organization for adult language courses and children's books) has some influence as well.

7. General intralinguistic portrait

Frisian and Dutch are both Germanic languages, but they differ linguistically in a number of respects.

Phonetically Frisian is characterized by a larger number of vocals than Dutch, with a number of distinct diphthongs.

On the morphosyntactic level Frisian and Dutch are quite close. Some typical differences are in affixes, formation of the diminutive and the order of verbs in dependent clauses and infinitive constructions.

It is particularly on the lexical level that Frisian and Dutch are most conspicuously different. Also on the lexical level the most obvious interferences take place. Dutch lexical items are incorporated into Frisian quite easily, sometimes to create new concepts, but quite often also superseding the older Frisian word. There is a difference between spoken and written language, the latter being more conservative and sticking closer to established language norms.

No recent prescriptive grammar is available in Frisian. There is, however, an English reference grammar (Tiersma 1985). For language courses there are several textbooks on all levels and there are desk dictionaries for Dutch-Frisian and Frisian-Dutch. Of the scientific larger Frisian dictionary some 10 volumes (of ± 23) have been published; a Frisian-Frisian desk dictionary (1999) and a Frisian-English dictionary (1998) are currently being written.

Every year several new books (mainly original novels and poetry) are published. The number of non-fiction books in Frisian remains relatively small. For example over the last 45 years only 10 doctoral dissertations have been written in Frisian.

8. Critical evaluation of the sources and scientific discussions

There are several articles in English offering a general, mostly introductory overview of the social and linguistic position of the Frisian language (e. g. Feitsma 1981, Gorter 1985, 1987, Jelsma 1983, Zondag 1984, Ytsma and De Jong 1992). Those can be considered reliable as first introduction. However, the serious student of the contact-situation between Frisian and Dutch should preferably at least have passive reading command of Frisian in order to gain access to the many articles and books written in Frisian on all kinds of aspects of Frisian.

In that way it will be possible to evaluate the different points of view in a number of discussions that have dominated the field of Frisian studies in the last decades. Those discussions include topics such as the change of the spelling-system (until it was settled in 1980), the teaching of Frisian in particular in primary school, the usefulness and results of language planning (mainly by the provincial government), the role of the Frisian movement (today, but also e. g. during WW II), the linguistic norm for Frisian (flexible or strict: allowing more or less Dutch forms and/or dialectic variation), the issues of Frisian identity and ideology, etc.

9. Bibliography (selected)

Extra, Guus (1989): "Ethnic minority languages versus Frisian in Dutch primary schools". In: *Journal of Multilingual and Multicultural Development* 10, 59–73.

Feitsma, Anthonia (1981, 1991^2): "Why and how do the Frisian language and identity continue?" In: *Minority Language Today*, Haugen, E. et al. (Eds.), Edinburgh, 163–176.

Feitsma, Anthonia (1984): "Interlingual communication Dutch-Frisian, a Model for Scotland?" In: *Scottish Language and Literature, Medieval and Renaissance*, Strauss, D./Drescher, H.W. (Eds.), Frankfurt, 55–62.

Fishman, Joshua A. (1991): *Reversing Language Shift*, Clevedon.

Gorter, Durk et al. (1984): *Taal yn Fryslân*, Ljouwert/Leeuwarden (English summary separately published in 1988).

Gorter, Durk (1985): "Bilingualism in Friesland and sociolinguistic Research". In: *Sociolinguistics* 15, 42–52.

Gorter, Durk (Ed.) (1987): *The Sociology of Frisian* (International Journal of the Sociology of Language 64), (with an overview of sociolinguistic research into several aspects of Frisian).

Gorter, Durk/Jonkman, Reitze J. (1995): *"Taal yn Fryslân – op 'e nÿ besjoen"*, Ljouwert.

Gorter, Durk/Ytsma, Johannes (1988): "Social Factors and Language Attitudes in Friesland". In: *Language Attitudes in the Dutch Language Area*, van Hout, R./Knops, U. (Eds.), Dordrecht, 59–71.

Haan, Germ de (1990): "Grammatical borrowing and language change: the Dutchification of Frisian". In: *Fourth International Conference on Minority Languages, vol. 1: General Papers*, Gorter, D. et al. (Eds.), Clevedon.

Hoekstra, Jarich/Tiersma, Pieter (1994): "Frisian". In: *The Germanic Languages*, van der Auwera, J./König, E. (Eds.), London.

Jelsma, Gjalt H. (1983): "The former and present social situation of the Frisian language". In: *Friserstudier III*, Odense, 49–63.

Khleif, Bud B. (1985): "Issues of Theory and Methodology in the Study of Ethnolinguistic Movements (the case of Frisian Nationalism in the Netherlands)". In: *New Nationalisms of the Developed West*, Tiryakian, E.A./Rogowski, R. (Eds.), Boston, 176–199.

Mahmood, Cynthia (1989): *Frisian and free: a study of an ethnic minority of the Netherlands*, Prospect Heights (Illinois).

Plank, van der Pieter (1984): "Ethnicity in Friesland". In: *Sociolinguistcs in the low countries*, Deprez, K. (Ed.), Philadelphia, 319–333.

Sikma, Jantsje A./Gorter, Durk (1991): *European Lesser used languages in Primary Education (inventory and proceedings of the colloquy)*, Ljouwert.

Tiersma, Pieter M. (1985): *Frisian Reference Grammar*, Dordrecht.

Ytsma, Jehannes/de Jong, Sijjo (1993): "Frisian". In: *Community Languages in the Netherlands*, Extra, G./Verhoeven, L. (Eds.), Amsterdam, 29–49.

Ytsma, Jehannes (1995): *"Frisian as First and Second Language"*. Ljouwert.

Zondag, Koen (1984): "Acid rain: a description of bilingual Friesland". In: *Journal of Multilingual and Multicultural Development* 5, 339–349.

Zondag, Koen (Ed.) (1993): *Bilingual Education in Friesland (facts and prospects)*, Ljouwert.

Durk Gorter, Leeuwarden (Netherlands)

141. Luxemburg

1. Geographie und Demographie
2. Territorialgeschichte und Staatsbildung
3. Politik, Wirtschaft und allgemeine kulturelle sowie religiöse Lage
4. Statistik und Ethnoprofile
5. Soziolinguistische Lage
6. Sprachpolitische Lage
7. Bibliographie (in Auswahl)

1. Geographie und Demographie

Das Großherzogtum Luxemburg liegt am Westrand Mitteleuropas, hat eine Gesamtfläche von 2586 km^2 und gehört der Europäischen Union an, deren kleinster Mitgliedsstaat es ist. Es grenzt an folgende Nachbarländer:

Im Westen: Königreich Belgien (Provinzen Luxembourg und Liège/Lüttich), Grenzlänge 148 km, Grenzverlauf zu etwa ¾ mit der romanisch-germanischen Sprachgrenze übereinstimmend, zu etwa ¼ mit der Ostgrenze des ehemals zu Luxemburg gehörigen, nunmehr belgischen Areler Landes;

im Osten: Bundesrepublik Deutschland (Bundesländer Rheinland-Pfalz und Saarland), Grenzlänge 135 km, im wesentlichen entlang der Flüsse Our, Sure/Sauer und Moselle/Mosel;

im Süden: Republik Frankreich (Départements Meurthe-et-Moselle und Moselle), Grenzlänge 73 km, Grenzverlauf unmittelbar südlich der Industriestandorte Esch-sur-Alzette und Dudelange.

Luxemburg läßt sich in zwei natürliche Landschaften teilen: das im Norden gelegene Ösling, geologisch handelt es sich um Ausläufer der Ardennen (32% der Gesamtfläche), und das flachere Gutland/Bon Pays (68% der Gesamtfläche).

Administrativ zerfällt Luxemburg in 3 Distrikte, 12 Kantone und 126 Gemeinden. Zum im Norden gelegenen Distrikt Diekirch gehören die Kantone Clervaux/Clerf, Diekirch, Redange/Redingen, Wiltz und Vianden. Im östlichen Distrikt Grevenmacher liegen die Kantone Echternach, Grevenmacher und Remich. Der Distrikt Luxemburg umfaßt die Kantone Capellen, Esch-sur-Alzette, die Stadt Luxemburg und Mersch.

Die demographische Struktur ist durch einen traditionell hohen Ausländeranteil geprägt. Dieser betrug bereits im Jahre 1948 10%, stieg 1981 erstmals über ein Viertel der Gesamtbevölkerung (26%) und liegt zur Zeit (1993) bei 30,3%. Zur nachfolgenden tabellarischen Übersicht (Tab. 141.1), die neben den Daten der alle zehn Jahre erfolgenden Volkszählungen auch jene Zahlen der letzten beiden Jahre sowie von 1948 enthält, die durch die statistische Zentralstelle in Luxemburg (Statec) genannt wurden, sind die folgenden differenzierenden Bemerkungen notwendig (vgl. zu allen demographischen Daten Statec 1993): Die zahlenmäßig stärksten Gruppen – Italiener und Portugiesen – wurden seit Beginn der sechziger Jahre überwiegend als billige Arbeitsmigranten ins Land geholt und werden vor allem in Bauwirtschaft und Gastronomie beschäftigt. Der seit 1981 bei den Italienern beobachtbare Rückgang dürfte eher durch bessere Integration vor Ort (Naturalisation), als durch effektive Rückwanderung bedingt sein; so wurden etwa 1986 insgesamt 3330 Einbürgerungen von Minderjährigen mit luxemburgischer Mutter und ausländischem Vater durchgeführt, wobei gleichzeitig allein die Zahl der italienischen Staatsangehörigen seit der letzten davor erfolgten Volkszählung von 1981 um 1.600 Personen sank. Die soziale Integration der Portugiesen scheint schon aufgrund des starken Wachstums dieser Gruppe problematischer zu sein.

Die weiteren quantitativ starken Gruppen umfassen die im Großherzogtum ansässigen Angehörigen von Anrainerstaaten, also Belgier, Deutsche und Franzosen. Sie sind vor allem in solchen Bereichen der Wirtschaft und der Politik tätig, die eine ausgeprägte Internationalität aufweisen. Dadurch ergibt sich für die beiden Ausländergruppen ein stark unterschiedliches soziales Prestige.

In der Tab. 141.1 werden die Beamten der Europäischen Gemeinschaft nicht getrennt aufgeführt. Sie stellen – über ethnische Abgrenzungen hinweg – eine eigene Gruppe im oberen sozialen Bereich dar. Erwähnenswert scheinen an dieser Stelle auch die insgesamt 43.300 Pendler (Stand 1992, immerhin 21,5% aller Arbeitnehmer), davon allein 22.200 Franzosen, 13.600 Belgier und 7.500 Deutsche.

2. Territorialgeschichte und Staatsbildung

Die Lage des heutigen Großherzogtums auf basilektal germanischem Boden ist das Resultat einiger Gebietsverkleinerungen im Laufe

Tab. 141.1: Bevölkerungsstruktur Luxemburgs von 1948 bis 1993. Quelle: Statec; Stand jeweils 1.1. (1981: 1.3.); Einheit = 1000; Ausländer auch in %; • = keine Daten verfügbar.

	1948	1961	1971	1981	1991	1992	1993
Gesamt	291,0	314,9	339,8	364,6	384,6	389,8	395,2
Luxemburger	261,9	273,4	277,3	268,8	269,3	275,1	275,5
Ausländer (in %)	29,1 (10%)	41,5 (13%)	62,5 (18%)	95,8 (26,3%)	115,3 (30,0%)	114,7 (29,4%)	119,7 (30,3%)
Belgier	3,6	5,2	6,5	7,9	7,9	9,7	10,0
Deutsche	7,5	7,9	7,8	8,9	8,9	8,8	8,8
Franzosen	3,7	5,0	8,5	11,9	13,2	13,1	13,3
Holländer	0,1	1,8	2,5	2,9	3,4	•	•
Italiener	7,6	15,7	23,4	22,3	19,1	19,8	19,9
(Ex-)Jugoslawen	•	0,2	0,5	1,5	2,2	•	•
Portugiesen	•	•	5,8	29,3	39,3	40,4	42,7
Spanier	•	•	2,2	2,1	2,5	•	•
US-Amerikaner	0,1	0,4	0,7	0,7	1,2	•	•
Übrige	•	•	4,6	8,3	15,2	•	•

seiner Geschichte (vgl. dazu und im folgenden Margue 1978, Thill 1983, Trausch 1977 und 1981). Ausnahmen stellen nur noch zwei kleine Ortschaften (Doncols und Soller/Sonlez) an der belgisch (wallonisch)-luxemburgischen Grenze und ein Dorf (Lasauvage) an der französisch (frz.)-luxemburgischen Grenze dar, in welchen sich basilektal romanische Spuren finden lassen oder bis vor einiger Zeit noch nachweisen ließen (vgl. Atten 1980, Doppagne 1971). Ursprünglich lag das Land, welches frühestens seit dem Wiener Kongreß (1815) als zumindest theoretisch eigenständiges Staatsgebilde gelten und seit damals „Luxemburg" im heute gebräuchlichen Sinn genannt werden kann, zu beiden Seiten der Grenze zwischen den beiden Sprach- und Kulturgroßräumen Romania und Germania. Die erste namentliche Erwähnung erfolgt in einer Urkunde des Jahres 963, in der von einem in den Ardennen beheimateten Graf Sigfrid die Rede ist, der das frühere Römerkastell Lucilinburhuc (> Lützelburg, „kleine Burg" > Luxemburg) kaufte. Den Ardennern folgte 1136 das westlich orientierte Haus Namur nach, was eine starke Bindung Luxemburgs an Frankreich nach sich zog. Unter Johann dem Blinden erfolgt im Jahre 1340 eine Teilung des Besitzes in zwei administrative Sektoren, das *Quartier allemand* und das *Quartier wallon*. Dies kommt einer offiziellen Anerkennung der sprachlichen Besonderheit des romanischen Teils des Herzogtums gleich, da bis zu diesem Zeitpunkt amtliche Schriftstücke für das gesamte Verwaltungsgebiet mehrheitlich in regionalem Mittelhochdeutsch verfaßt worden waren. Nach der Übernahme des Landes (durch Kauf) durch die Burgunder (1443−1477) avancierte jedoch das Französische (Frz.) zur offiziellen Landessprache. Dieser Zustand blieb auch aufrecht − zumindest im Hinblick auf die äußere Amtssprache −, als das Herzogtum Luxemburg in der Folge mehrfach den Besitzer wechselte. Von 1477−1684 gehörte es zum Herrschaftsbereich der (ab 1521 spanischen) Habsburger; 1659 wurden Teile des luxemb. Südens (Sédan, Montmédy, Marville, Mont St.Martin, Damvillers und Thionville; vgl. Abb. 141.1) im Pyrenäenfrieden an Frankreich abgetreten; 1684−1697 gehörte das gesamte Land zu Frankreich, 1697−1714 erneut zu Spanien, wobei zwischen 1701 und 1704, im Spanischen Erbfolgekrieg, der Besit-

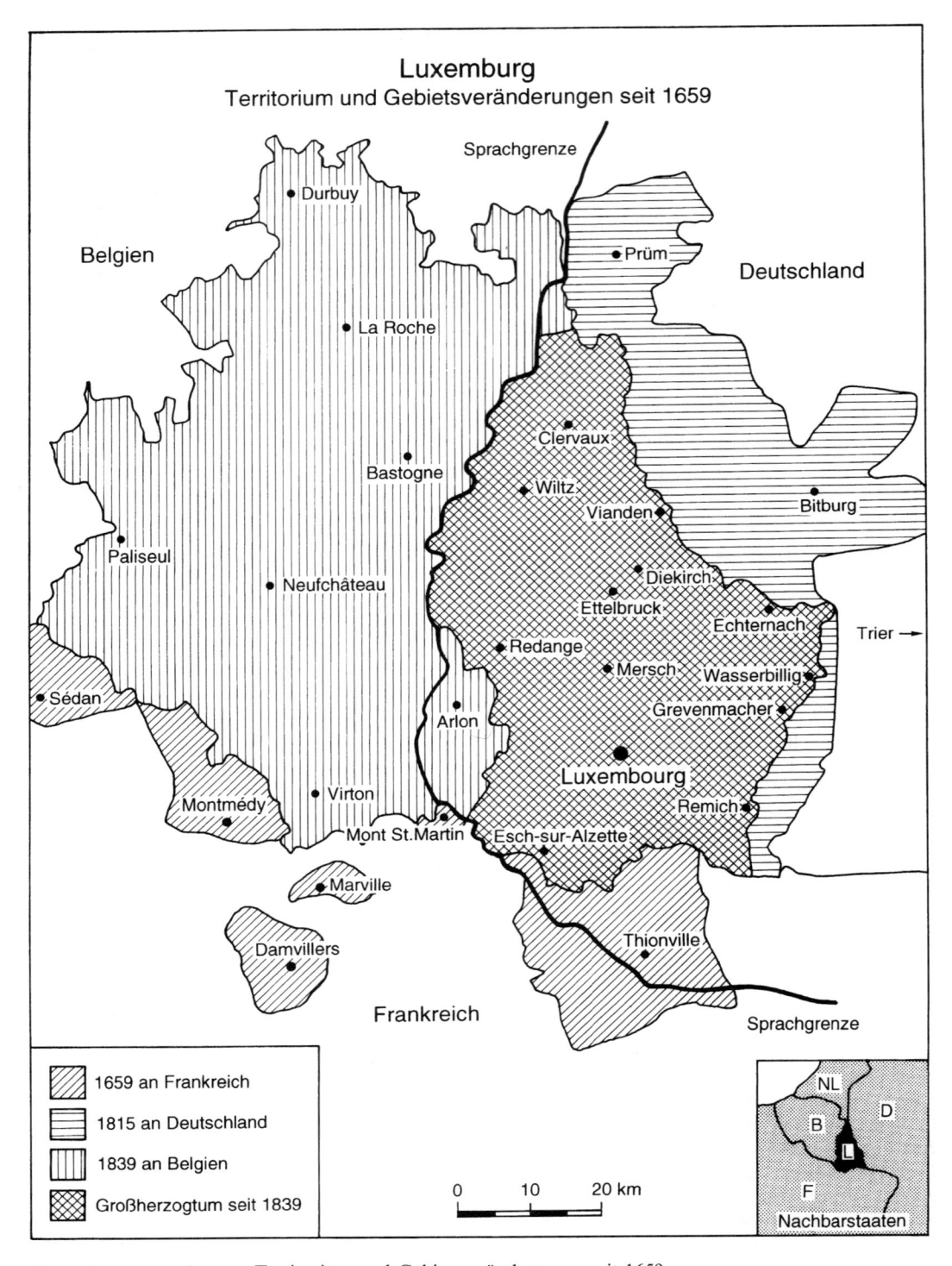

Abb. 141.1: **Luxemburg** – Territorium und Gebietsveränderungen seit 1659
Fette Linie: französisch-deutsche Sprachengrenze

zer mehrfach wechselte; 1714—1795 war das Herzogtum wiederum habsburgisch; 1795 wurde das Territorium von frz. Truppen besetzt und auf drei frz. Departements aufgeteilt. Auf dem Wiener Kongreß (1815) erfolgte einerseits die Erhebung zum Großherzogtum, andererseits, nach Verlust der östlich von Our, Sauer und Mosel gelegenen Gebiete an Deutschland (vgl. Karte), aber die Zuteilung des übrigen Landes zum persönlichen Besitz des niederländischen Königs Wilhelm I. von Oranien. Gleichzeitig wurde Luxemburg Mitglied des Deutschen Bundes. Aus dieser Tatsache erklärt sich auch die Bevorzugung des Frz. als Amtssprache von Luxemburg durch die Niederlande, da auf diese Weise deutscher Einfluß abgeschwächt werden sollte. Nach 1830 verbleibt nur die Stadt Luxemburg bei den Niederlanden, das übrige Luxemburg schließt sich der Belgischen Revolution an und gehört bis zu deren Ende (1839) faktisch zu Belgien. In der Stadt Luxemburg wird im übrigen der amtliche Gebrauch des Hochdeutschen erstmals 1830 zugelassen, als die sich frankophon artikulierenden belgischen Sezessionsbestrebungen zu einer ernsthaften Bedrohung der Niederlande wurden. Am Ende der Belgischen Revolution (1839) wird Luxemburg geteilt: Das ehemalige *Quartier wallon* und das basilektal germanophone Gebiet um Arlon/Arel kommen zu Belgien, der verbleibende Rest des *Quartier allemand* wird wieder in Personalunion mit den Niederlanden verbunden, erhält aber erstmals politische Unabhängigkeit. 1848 bekommt das Großherzogtum seine erste demokratische Verfassung, 1867 tritt es aus dem Deutschen Bund aus und beschließt seine immerwährende Neutralität. 1890 endet die niederländisch-luxemburgische Personalunion aus erbrechtlichen Gründen, Adolf von Nassau wird erster luxemburgischer Großherzog. Im Ersten Weltkrieg wird Luxemburg vom Deutschen Reich besetzt, die luxemb. Regierung bleibt aber weiterhin im Amt. Ein herausragendes politisches Ereignis bilden im Jahr 1939 die Feierlichkeiten zum 100. Jahrestag des Londoner Vertrages (1839), in welchem die politische Unabgigkeit beschlossen worden war. Unter dem Motto „100 Jahre unabhängiges Luxemburg" wurde bewußt versucht, Nationalgefühl und Patriotismus in der gesamten luxemb. Bevölkerung zu stärken bzw. überhaupt erst zu begründen. Die Notwendigkeit nationaler Abgrenzung nach Osten schien umso dringlicher, als damals nationalsozialistische Expansionsgelüste die Eigenständigkeit des Landes bedrohten. Die Besetzung erfolgte dann tatsächlich 1940 unter der Parole der „Heimholung ins Reich" und dauerte bis zum Einmarsch amerikanischer Einheiten 1944. Die flankierenden Maßnahmen der geplanten kulturellen und sprachlichen Gleichstellung mit NS-Deutschland erlitten allerdings im Jahre 1941 eine schwere Niederlage, als — nach einer Serie von sprachpolitischen Verordnungen zugunsten des Deutschen (Dt.) — eine großangelegte *Personenstandsaufnahme* mit Fragen nach Staatszugehörigkeit, Volkszugehörigkeit und Muttersprache abgebrochen werden mußte, da eine überwältigende Mehrheit der stimmberechtigten Luxemburger auf die Fragen nicht dreimal die suggerierte Antwort „Deutsch", sondern „driemol lëtzebuergesch" (— so die ausgegebene Parole —) anführte. 1948 wurde die Verfassung revidiert, die immerwährende Neutralität aufgehoben; 1949 trat Luxemburg der NATO bei.

3. Politik, Wirtschaft und allgemeine kulturelle sowie religiöse Lage

Seit 1964 steht Jean de Luxembourg an der Spitze des Großherzogtums, welches derzeit (1993) von einer Koalition aus Christlich-Sozialen (CSV) und Sozialisten (LSAP) unter Jacques Santer (CSV) regiert wird. Die Wahlen 1989 brachten für das 60 Sitze umfassende Parlament (Chambre des Députés) das folgende Ergebnis: CSV: 22 Sitze, LSAP: 18 Sitze, Liberale (DP): 11 Sitze, Aktionskomitee 5/6: 4 Sitze, Grüne: 4; Kommunisten (KPL): 1 Sitz. Im Laufe des Wahlkampfes waren vereinzelt ausländerfeindliche Parolen zu vernehmen. Die dafür verantwortlichen Gruppen konnten sich damit aber in keiner Weise auf der politischen Szene etablieren. Luxemburg ratifizierte die Maastrichter Verträge im Juli 1992, setzte aber eine Klausel zur Gewährung des Kommunalwahlrechtes nur für solche EG-Ausländer durch, die schon mindestens sechs Jahre im Land gelebt haben. 1992 lag der Anteil der wahlberechtigten EG-Ausländer in 59 der 132 Gemeinden Luxemburgs bereits über 20%, die Wahlrechtsbeschränkung ist demnach als direkte Maßnahme zur Wahrung der nationalen, im besonderen der lokalen Identität zu interpretieren. Ausländer stellen seit Anfang der 90er Jahre etwa 45% der Arbeitnehmer im Großherzogtum, wobei dieser Prozentsatz nach Schätzungen der OECD weiter ansteigen wird.

Gemessen am Bruttosozialprodukt pro Kopf ist Luxemburg nach der Schweiz das zweitreichste Land der Welt. Den Löwenanteil der Wirtschaftsleistung erbringt der Dienstleistungssektor (1992: über ⅔ der Gesamtleistung, Tendenz steigend); einen traditionell wichtigen Wirtschaftszweig stellt die Stahlindustrie im Süden des Landes (1992: 22%, Tendenz fallend) dar. Die Rohstahlproduktion pro Kopf (1990) erreicht dabei z. B. das Achtfache der belgischen und sogar das Fünfzehnfache der deutschen Produktion. Durch eine auch für Ausländer günstige Finanzgesetzgebung entstand zudem eine Konzentration von internationalen Banken, Investment- und Versicherungsunternehmen, so daß das Land zu einer Drehscheibe des europäischen Geldmarktes wurde. Die Banken beschäftigen immerhin 15.000 Arbeitnehmer und erwirtschaften 15% (1990; vgl. 1970: 3,4%) des Bruttoinlandprodukts.

Die luxemb. Bevölkerung gehört in überwiegendem Maße der Römisch-Katholischen Kirche an (1970: 97%), bei den Ausländern liegt dieser Prozentsatz nur um weniges tiefer (1970: 90%). Die 1870 gegründete Diözese Luxemburg ist in 15 Dekanate und 273 Pfarreien unterteilt, wobei dazu noch eine 274. nicht territoriale, „europäische" Pfarrgemeinde kommt.

4. Statistik und Ethnoprofile

Die Ethnoprofile der betroffenen Kontaktsprachen bzw. von deren Sprechern sind in Luxemburg insofern nur unter besonderen Vorzeichen darstellbar, als die Verwendung der auf luxemb. Territorium hauptsächlich gesprochenen und geschriebenen Sprachen nicht primär als Merkmal der einen oder anderen ethnischen Gruppe gelten kann. Eine statistische Teilung der Bevölkerung läßt sich, wie unter 1. dargestellt, nur nach den Kategorien „autochthone Luxemburger" vs. (temporär) ansässige „ausländische Staatsangehörige" vornehmen, wobei Rückschlüsse auf die verwendeten Sprachen nur in eingeschränktem Maße zulässig sind. Die autochthone Gruppe, also die quasi-Gesamtheit der luxemb. Staatsangehörigen, erlernt als Muttersprache das auf moselfränkischer, somit germanischer, Grundlage entwickelte *Lëtzebuergesch (Lëtz.)*. Früher wurden im Lëtz. auch *Lëtzebuerger Däitsch* und *Eis Sprooch*, „unsere Sprache", als pan-luxemburgische Sprachennamen verwendet. Im Dt. existiert parallel zu *Lëtzebuergesch* die Bezeichnung *Luxemburgisch*. Bereits ab der Primärschule erwerben die Luxemburger aber auch *Standarddeutsch* (lëtz. *Däitsch, Héidäitsch*) und *Französisch* (lëtz. *Franséisch*).

Die solchermaßen erworbene, je nach Bildungsniveau mehr oder weniger gut ausgebaute dreisprachige Kompetenz bildet einen konstitutiven Teil der kollektiven (=nationalen bzw. ethnischen) Identität der Luxemburger (vgl. Christophory s. a.). Die allochthonen Gruppen sind territorial nicht eingrenzbar, allenfalls lassen sich Wohngebiete mit verstärkten Ausländeranteilen feststellen. Die ethnolinguistische Situation, wie z. B. die Stellung und Entwicklung der „mitgebrachten" Muttersprachen, dürfte sich ähnlich wie in anderen europäischen Industriestaaten verhalten. Studien dazu liegen derzeit noch nicht vor. Statistisch lassen sich die Kontaktsprachen wie folgt darstellen (vgl. COF 1985: 4, Statec 1993):

Lëtz. war 1985 die Muttersprache von 75,2% der Gesamtbevölkerung, Portugiesisch von 8,4%, Frz. und Italienisch von jeweils 6,3% und Dt. von 3,1%. Die *grosso modo* damit vergleichbaren (und so zumindest eine Entwicklung andeutenden) demographischen Daten von 1993 weisen 69,7% der Bevölkerung als Luxemburger aus, 10,8% sind Portugiesen, nur mehr 5% Italiener und 2,2% Deutsche. Der momentane Anteil der frankophonen Muttersprachler ist nicht genau zu eruieren, da die offizielle Bevölkerungsstatistik zwar die Franzosen mit 3,3% ausweist, aber die frankophonen Belgier nicht als eigene Kategorie aufführt. Der Gesamtanteil der belgischen Staatsbürger beträgt derzeit 2,5%. In dieser Gruppe sind einerseits frankophone und niederlandophone, andererseits aber auch ein gewisser Prozentsatz zumindest in Resten basilektal luxemburgophoner Personen enthalten, die aus dem an Luxemburg angrenzenden Areler Land stammen.

Die von der autochthonen Bevölkerung im Kontakt mit allochthonen Personen einsetzbare mehrsprachige Kompetenz ist im Hinblick auf interethnische Verständigungsprobleme unter dem Aspekt der europäischen Integration geradezu vorbildhaft. Dabei kommt wegen der überwiegend romanophonen Herkunft der Einwanderer das Frz. als „Lingua franca" naturgemäß stärker zum Einsatz als das Deutsche. Diese beiden Sprachen haben auch außerhalb der Kommunikation mit Fremden einen hohen Stellenwert für die luxemb. Bevölkerung, da sie die Aufgabe der

Bildungs- und Kulturvermittlung zur Gänze übernehmen. Lëtz. bildet zwar ein wesentliches Instrument der luxemb. Identität, wie dies seine Erhebung per Gesetz in den Rang einer Nationalsprache im Jahr 1984 deutlich dokumentiert (vgl. 6.2.), doch bleiben Dt. und Frz. unverzichtbare Bestandteile des luxemb. Sprachalltags. Die in vielfacher Hinsicht erfolgreiche Anwendung von mehrsprachiger Kompetenz hat in dieser an der Grenze zwischen zwei großen europäischen Sprach-, Kultur- und früher auch Wirtschaftsräumen gelegenen Region eine durchaus jahrhundertelange Tradition. Der Verlust frankophoner Gebiete nach der Belgischen Revolution (1830–1839) führte dabei keineswegs zur Schwächung des Frz., welches zu diesem Zeitpunkt als Gesetzessprache längst voll etabliert war. Das Dt. hat zwar durch die NS-Episode beträchtlich an Prestige und öffentlicher Verwendbarkeit eingebüßt, bleibt aber – auch wegen seiner linguistischen Nähe zum Lëtz. – nach wie vor ein wichtiges Instrument der Bildungs- und Kulturvermittlung. Die Luxemburger erleben den Zustand der Dreisprachigkeit, und damit den dadurch ermöglichten direkten Kulturkontakt, als durchaus typisch und erhaltenswert (vgl. Fröhlich 1992).

Neben der im Mittelpunkt dieses Artikels stehenden Koexistenz des Lëtz. und der luxemb. Varianten des Hochdeutschen und des Standardfranzösischen sei auf die zusätzlich vorhandene inner-luxemb. Sprachvariation und deren identitätsstützende Funktion hingewiesen. Die dialektale Kammerung des luxemb. Sprachraumes ist anhand ausgewählter phonetischer Merkmale deutlich aufzeigbar.

Im Süden macht sich innerhalb des Lëtz. ein deutlicher alemannischer Einfluß bemerkbar, für den vor allem die Palatalisierung von „s" vor dentalem Okklusiv charakteristisch ist (siehe Tab. 141.2).

Tab. 141.2: Alemannischer Einfluß im Lëtz.

Bp.Nr.		Lëtz.	Deutsch
1	Fest	[fescht]	[fest]
2	Rest	[rescht]	[rest]

Dieser alemannische Einfluß nimmt in nördlicher Richtung ab und ist im Ösling nicht mehr vorhanden. Kennzeichnend hingegen für die Mundarten des mittleren und nördlichen Öslings ist ein starker ripuarischer Einfluß, erkennbar z. B. am Velarverschluß vor Dental (siehe Tab. 141.3, Bp. 3, 4) und nach Nasal (siehe Tab. 141.3, Bp. 5, 6).

Tab. 141.3: Ripuarischer Einfluß im Lëtz.

Bp.Nr.	Zentrallëtz.	Ostlëtz.	Nordlëtz.	Deutsch
3	Leit	Lett	Leckt	Leute
4	haut	hett	heckt	heute
5	Wäin	Wain	Weng	Wein
6	schéin	schinn	sching	schön

Der Einfluß wird nach Süden hin immer schwächer und ist vor Ettelbruck ganz verschwunden. Der Westen, vor allem der südliche, weist als eine dialektal stark konservierende Zone eine Reihe alter Luxemburgismen auf, wie z. B. die Palatalisierung von anlautendem [k] zu [ç] (ich-Laut) (siehe Tab. 141.4).

Tab. 141.4: Archaismen im Südwestlëtz.

Bp.Nr.	Südwestlëtz.	Lëtz. Koiné	Deutsch
7	Chaunt	Kand	Kind
8	Chaulef	Kallef	Kalb

Der luxemb. Osten ist gekennzeichnet durch das Vordringen „trierischer" Neuerungen vom Rhein her, die zum großen Teil aber nicht über die Hänge des linken Moselufers hinauskommen (siehe Tab. 141.5).

Tab. 141.5: Neuerungen im Ostlëtz.

Bp.Nr.	Westlëtz.	Ostlëtz.	Deutsch
9	Brudder	Brouder	Bruder
10	gutt	gout	gut

Entlang der Mosel-Sauer-Our-Achse gelangen ost-luxemb. Lautungen allerdings auch bis ins östliche Nordösling.

Die Lokal- und Regionalmundarten werden überdacht von einer überregionalen, im ganzen Großherzogtum gesprochenen und verstandenen Koiné, die generell einen Ausgleich zwischen allen Varietäten darstellt, sich dabei aber primär auf die Mundart im Tal der Alzette zwischen Dommeldange, einem Vorort nördlich der Hauptstadt und Schieren bei Ettelbruck stützt. Die Koiné dient im allgemeinen der überregionalen inner-luxemb. Kommunikation, wobei sich neuerdings, im Zuge der Rückbesinnung auf ihre regionale Identität, die jüngeren Generationen verstärkt auch der lokalen und regionalen Varianten bedienen. Dabei können, bei entsprechender Distanz, durchaus Kommunikationsschwierigkeiten zwischen Luxemburgern auftreten.

Die Öslinger Mundarten gelten gemeinhin als „bäuerisch", und zwar in stärkerem Maße als dies für die Mundarten an der Mosel im Osten gilt. Das Ösling ist die ärmste Landschaft in Luxemburg. Dort wohnten bis zum Beginn der industriellen Erschließung des Landes am Ende des 19. Jahrhunderts vor allem Kleinbauern und Tagelöhner, während bei den Weinbauern an der Mosel immer schon größerer Wohlstand geherrscht hatte. Luxemburger Autoren benutzen die Öslinger Mundarten gerne zur Erzielung komischer Effekte.

Die Mundarten des Südens gelten gemeinhin als „breit, grob und häßlich". Der Süden ist industrielles Ballungsgebiet mit einer Bevölkerung von vorwiegend Metallarbeitern und Stahlkochern.

Das höchste Ansehen genießt zweifellos die Koiné, die schon deshalb oft als das „klassische" Lëtz. angesehen wird, weil auch die Nationaldichter Dicks (Edmond de la Fontaine, 1823—1891) und Michel Lentz (1820—1893) sie benutzten. Als „schön" gelten zudem die der Koiné nahestehenden Varianten des flachen Landes um die Hauptstadt. Im luxemb. Mundarttheater werden diese Statusunterschiede nicht selten zur sozialen Differenzierung der Charaktere verwendet.

5. Soziolinguistische Lage

5.1. Allgemeines

In einer mehrsprachigen Gesellschaft wie der in Luxemburg wird die Handhabung soziolinguistischer Unterschiede zu einem wichtigen Bestandteil des sozialen Lebens überhaupt. Kennzeichnend für Luxemburg ist, daß die lëtz.-dt.-frz. Dreisprachigkeit von den Betroffenen als im wesentlichen konfliktfrei empfunden wird.

Um jedoch den domänenspezifischen Gebrauch der drei Sprachen präzise darlegen zu können, muß zunächst festgehalten werden, daß in allen soziolinguistisch relevanten Bereichen die Strukturen des mündlichen Sprachengebrauchs deutlich von denen der schriftlichen Sprachenverwendung abweichen (vgl. dazu und im folgenden Hoffmann 1979 et passim, Kramer 1984 et passim, Kloss 1986 und → Sprachenkarte C).

Lëtz. ist zwar in den meisten Fällen und ohne thematische Beschränkungen die einzige Sprache, die ein Luxemburger zur Kommunikation mit anderen Luxemburgern verwendet. Doch erfordert der hohe Prozentsatz an Ausländern, die zudem gegenüber dem Lëtz.-Erwerb wenig aufgeschlossen sind, regelmäßig den spontanen Wechsel zu Frz. oder Dt. Dies betrifft die Domäne Arbeitsplatz, aber auch die anderen Sektoren des öffentlichen und des sozialen Lebens.

Geschrieben wurden und werden in überwiegendem Maße Dt. und Frz., wobei generell dem letzteren ein höheres Prestige anhaftet, das Dt. aber allgemein als verständlicher gilt. In den letzten Jahrzehnten kam es zudem zu einer Erweiterung der schriftsprachlichen Anwendungen des Lëtz. Das bereits erwähnte Sprachengesetz schuf zusätzliche Anreize, so daß die Sprachenverteilung dadurch zugunsten des Lëtz. in Bewegung gekommen ist.

Unter Rückgriff auf die soziolinguistischen Konzepte *Diglossie* und *Bilinguismus* sowie unter der Voraussetzung, das Lëtz. unter Berücksichtigung seiner breiten Verwendbarkeit als *Sprache* zu definieren, kann die luxemb. Sprachenlage wie folgt beschrieben werden:

Der mündliche Bereich der inner-luxemb. Kommunikation ist einsprachig, wobei für die verschiedenen Teile des Sprachgebietes unterschiedlich stark ausgeprägte diglossische Verhältnisse von jeweiligem Dialekt und Koiné anzusetzen sind. In der Kommunikation mit Nicht-Luxemburgern ist die alltagssprachliche Realität aber als zumindest tri- bzw. tetraglossisch ([lëtz. Dialekt-lëtz. Koiné]-Dt.-Frz.), wenn nicht sogar, in Abhängigkeit vom Bildungsniveau der jeweiligen Sprecher, als trilingual (Lëtz.-Dt.-Frz.) plus diglossisch (Dialekt-Koiné) anzusehen. Der schriftliche Bereich weist dagegen stärker voneinander abgegrenzte Funktionsbereiche auf und ist im wesentlichen als triglossisch zu bezeichnen. Für die Nicht-Luxemburger (Immigranten etc.) ergeben sich in der Regel di- oder triglossische Verhältnisse (Muttersprache-Frz.-Dt.), wobei die jeweiligen Erst- bzw. Muttersprachen, sofern es sich nicht um Frz. oder Dt. handelt, in starkem Maße auf die

141. Luxemburg

betreffenden Privatbereiche beschränkt sind und in den öffentlichen Domänen kaum zum Tragen kommen.

5.2. Sozialprestige und Mehrsprachigkeit

Trotz der universellen Einsetzbarkeit des Lëtz. in allen sozialen Bereichen und auf allen thematischen Gesprächsebenen ist der gesellschaftliche Aufstieg in Luxemburg ohne Zweifel an gute Kenntnisse des Frz. und des Dt. gebunden, da die (schulische) Vermittlung sowohl allgemeiner wie auch spezieller Bildung und Kultur in diesen beiden Hochsprachen erfolgt. Dabei steigt der Anteil des Frz. in den höheren Stufen des Bildungswesens spürbar an. Im Bereich der Stadt Luxemburg gilt die Verwendung des Frz. ohnehin als elegant bzw. als Markenzeichen der sozialen Elite (vgl. Hartmann 1986). Das Standarddeutsche erlitt zwar während der NS-Zeit den erwähnten Prestigeverlust, stellt aber gerade für Luxemburger ohne höhere Schulbildung das einzige von Grund auf erlernte schriftliche Kommunikationsmittel dar und ist schon deshalb für das Funktionieren der Gesellschaft unverzichtbar. So können gesellschaftliche Positionen insofern mit der linguistischen Situation in Verbindung gebracht werden, als die für das gesamte Land theoretisch nachweisbare gesellschaftliche Dreisprachigkeit nur bei denjenigen Sprechern realiter vorhanden ist, die einen entsprechend hohen Bildungsgrad aufweisen. Dies ändert natürlich nichts an dem Faktum, daß jeder Luxemburger ungeachtet seiner tatsächlichen sprachlichen Fähigkeiten im Alltag mit allen drei Sprachen konfrontiert wird und damit auch irgendwie zurechtkommen muß.

5.3. Domänenspezifische Funktionen der Kontaktsprachen

5.3.1. Familie und Freundeskreis

Solange dem engeren Privatbereich eines Luxemburgers keine nicht-luxemb. Personen angehören, bleibt die mündliche Kommunikation einsprachig lëtz. Dabei ist es jedoch nicht ungewöhnlich, daß je nach Gesprächsthema fremdsprachige Begriffe, etwa aus einer speziellen Terminologie, die im Lëtz. nicht zur Verfügung steht, spontan übernommen werden. Schriftliche Äußerungen können in jeder der drei Sprachen erfolgen, die Wahl hängt dabei stark vom Bildungsgrad des Schreibers, aber auch vom Adressaten ab. Die mangelnde Kenntnis der Orthographie des Lëtz. hindert viele Luxemburger an dessen verstärktem Gebrauch, z. B. für private Briefe. Einladungen oder Urlaubsgrüße werden aber häufig, auch wegen der damit verbundenen Signalwirkung, auf Lëtz. verfaßt.

5.3.2. Gesellschaftsleben, Medien, Kunst und Kultur

Je weiter sich der Durchschnittsluxemburger aus seinem engeren Familien- und Freundeskreis entfernt, je stärker er also am gesellschaftlichen Leben teilnimmt, desto häufiger wird er mit der Notwendigkeit, seine diversifizierten Sprachkenntnisse einzusetzen, konfrontiert. Dies bedeutet aber nicht, daß das Lëtz. an sich thematischen Beschränkungen oder sozialen Stigmatisierungen unterworfen wäre, ganz im Gegenteil.

Eine simple Bestellung in einem Café oder Restaurant erfolgt häufig in Frz. (vgl. Christophory 1992, 169), beim anschließenden Kinobesuch wird ein Film, nach belgischem und frz. Vorbild, in der Originalfassung konsumiert, wobei als Verständnishilfe je nach Ausgangssprache frz., dt. und/oder niederländische, keinesfalls aber lëtz. Untertitel angeboten werden.

Dem Theaterbesucher bietet sich eine Palette von deutsch- und französischsprachigen Veranstaltungen, lëtz. Übersetzungen von dramatischer Weltliteratur kommen nicht zur Aufführung.

Das Pressewesen ist prinzipiell mehrsprachig, wird aber eindeutig vom Dt. dominiert. Die größte Tageszeitung, das *Luxemburger Wort*, enthält im redaktionellen Teil in überwiegendem Maße deutschsprachige, daneben im Kulturteil oder Feuilleton auch einzelne frz. Artikel. Lëtz. wird in wachsendem Ausmaß für Leserbriefe, Kleinanzeigen, Werbung oder sonstige private und persönliche Mitteilungen (Heiratsanzeigen etc.) gebraucht. Auffällig ist die bewußte Integration des Lëtz. in das mehrsprachige äußere Erscheinungsbild der Titelseiten vieler in Luxemburg erzeugter Zeitungen und Zeitschriften. So nennt sich etwa eine dt. und frz. redigierte Wochenzeitschrift im Haupttitel *d'Letzeburger Land*, eine dt. gehaltene Programmzeitschrift heißt *Revue, d'lëtzebuerger illustréiert,* und dem *Luxemburger Wort* wird wöchentlich eine Beilage angefügt, die sich *Die Warte, Perspectives, Vue hebdomadaire sur les Arts et les Idées, Kulturelle Wochenbeilage des „Luxemburger Wort"* [sic] nennt. Jahrgang und Faszikelnummer sind frz., Tag und Erscheinungsdatum dt. vermerkt. Die Ausgabe vom 27. Januar 1994 etwa bringt auf der ersten Seite einen Beitrag zum Projekt eines neuen luxemb. Wörterbuchs, der einen lëtz. Titel (*Een neie lëtzebuergeschen Dixionär*), einen dt. Untertitel (*Prolegomena zu einem neuen Wörterbuch der luxemburgischen Sprache*), ein nicht übersetztes englisches Zitat am Beginn und daran anschließend einen dt. Haupttext mit lëtz., dt. und ebenfalls nicht übersetzten frz. Zitaten enthält. Die drei Kapitelüberschriften (*Das Gesetz von 1984, Die Commission du Dictionnaire et de l'Orthographe, Den neien Dixionär*) sind ebenfalls mehrsprachig (vgl. Reisdoerfer 1994).

Neben einheimischen Erzeugnissen wird im Großherzogtum ein breites Angebot dt. und frz. Presseprodukte verkauft. Die einzige völlig frz. gehaltene Tageszeitung für Luxemburg wird in Frankreich erzeugt und berichtet auch über die angrenzenden frz. Regionen.

Der Buchmarkt ist ebenso mehrsprachig, dt. Literatur wird wie die frz. oder belgische im Original gelesen. Luxemb. Autoren schreiben vorrangig in Dt. oder Frz., aber auch in Lëtz. (vgl. Hoffmann 1964/1967, 1979, 1981, Christophory 1978).

Das mediale Angebot war in Luxemburg schon immer besonders groß, da bereits vor der Epoche der Unterhaltungssatelliten der problemlose Zugriff auf belgische, bundesdeutsche und frz. Radio- und Fernsehprogramme möglich war. Eine private Gruppe betreibt sowohl den kommerziell orientierten dt. Sender *RTL*, als auch den frz. Sender *Télé Luxembourg*, der täglich auch lëtz. Sendungen anbietet. Im Rundfunk wird von *RTL* ein komplettes lëtz. Programm auf einer eigenen Sendefrequenz angeboten.

Katholische Messen werden heutzutage großteils auf Lëtz. gelesen. Daneben kann für einzelne Abschnitte der Liturgie das Dt., in der Hauptstadt auch das Frz. zum Einsatz kommen. In der Predigt ist jedoch Lëtz. die vorherrschende Sprache.

5.3.3. Privatwirtschaft

Die luxemb. Wirtschaft ist voll in die Europäische Union integriert und schon deshalb verstärkt auf internationale Kontakte ausgerichtet. Dabei bedient man sich zur Abwicklung der Geschäfte naturgemäß des Dt. und des Frz., je nach Erfordernis auch einer anderen Fremdsprache (Englisch, Spanisch etc.). Lëtz. spielt dabei eine untergeordnete Rolle, ja verliert in diesem Bereich sogar seine Bedeutung als ausschließliche Arbeitssprache zwischen Luxemburgern (vgl. Fröhlich 1992).

Im Schriftverkehr überwiegt das vom Prestige her höher eingeschätzte Frz., jedoch wird die Wahl einer Sprache zunächst von deren kommunikativer Effizienz abhängig gemacht. Auf jeden Fall sind sich die Luxemburger dabei der Vorteile ihrer Mehrsprachigkeit bewußt.

5.3.4. Behörden, Gerichte, Parlament, Öffentlichkeit

Bei luxemb. Behörden wird mit Inländern selbstverständlich nur lëtz. gesprochen. Dies gilt nicht für den Parteienverkehr mit Ausländern (vgl. Hoffmann 1979, 60—65, Kramer 1984, 207—209).

Schriftstücke des behördeninternen Schriftverkehrs werden bevorzugt frz. verfaßt (vgl. zur Geschichte des Frz. als Amtssprache in Luxemburg bes. Houdremont 1897). Allerdings ist es nicht außergewöhnlich, wenn Dienststellen der untergeordneten Verwaltungsebenen auch auf Dt. miteinander verkehren. Mitteilungen an die luxemb. Staatsbürger erfolgen zumeist frz., jedoch sind Formulare — v. a. der Finanzbehörden — immer zweisprachig, also dt. und frz., abgefaßt. Als Rechtfertigung dafür hört man, daß das Frz. als „schwierig" gilt, während das Dt. als leichter verständlich eingestuft wird (vgl. Fröhlich 1992, 195 f). Seit der Verabschiedung des Sprachengesetzes im Jahre 1984 (vgl. 6.2.) ist auch die Verwendung des Lëtz. für Verwaltungsakte oder kommunale Verordnungen zulässig. Dem Bürger wurde die Möglichkeit zugestanden, Anfragen an die Behörden (auch) in Lëtz. zu schreiben, die Beamten sind jedoch nur insofern zur Benützung der in der Anfrage verwendeten Sprache verpflichtet, als sie sich dazu auch in der Lage fühlen. Derzeit fehlt aber eine lëtz. Verwaltungsterminologie. Detaillierte Studien liegen dazu (noch) nicht vor.

Vor Gericht besitzt das Frz. als Sprache der luxemb. Gesetzgebung die volle und ausschließliche juristische Gültigkeit. Verfahrenstechnisch hat sich jedoch vor allem für Strafprozesse die Verwendung aller zur Verfügung stehenden Sprachen als günstig erwiesen (vgl. Hoffmann 1979, 52). Mit einem luxemb. Angeklagten wird nur lëtz. gesprochen, wobei allein der Richter an ihn das Wort richtet. Beisitzer, Staatsanwälte und Verteidiger äußern sich in der Verhandlung nur frz. und nur gegenüber dem Richter, der ihnen ebenso frz. antwortet und etwaige Fragen auf lëtz. an den Angeklagten weitergibt. Strafantrag sowie Plädoyer des Verteidigers erfolgen ebenfalls auf Frz. Dieses Procedere soll einerseits den Beklagten in die Lage versetzen, die an ihn gestellten Fragen zur Gänze zu verstehen, andererseits ist es so den Juristen möglich, sich ausschließlich des Frz., welches in diesem Fall als Fachsprache fungiert, zu bedienen. Die Verkündung des Urteils erfolgt auf Dt., ebenso wird auf Dt. protokolliert. In Zivilprozessen wird grundsätzlich frz. verhandelt und plädiert. Auch das Urteil wird auf Frz. verkündet. Luxemb. Zeugen werden, wie in Strafprozessen, durch den Richter auf Lëtz. befragt.

Im luxemb. Parlament, der Abgeordnetenkammer (Chambre des Députés), werden die meisten Debatten auf Lëtz. geführt, nur standardisierte Redeteile, wie Worterteilungen durch den Kammerpräsidenten, geschehen auf Frz.; das Dt. hat seinen Rang als Diskussions- und Protokollsprache fast völlig eingebüßt, bleibt aber die Sprache der regelmäßig an die Haushalte verschickten Zusammenfassungen der Debatten.

Bedingt durch die historischen Ereignisse v. a. seit dem Wiener Kongreß war das Großherzogtum immer wieder gezwungen, sich durch Abgrenzung nach außen zu definieren. In der zweiten Hälfte des 20. Jahrhunderts zeigt sich diese Haltung unter anderem in einer bewußten Distanzierung vom dt. Kulturraum. Das äußere Erscheinungsbild des Landes — genannt sei die sprachliche wie optische Gestaltung von Verkehrsschildern, Hinweistafeln, Straßenmarkierungen, Firmenschildern, Briefköpfen, Aufschriften oder auch Denkmalbeschriftungen — scheint bewußt an die westlichen Nachbarstaaten angelehnt, bzw. bewußt im Gegensatz zum östlichen Nachbarn konzipiert zu sein. Die dt. Sprache ist aus dieser Domäne verschwunden, die optische Dominanz des Frz. wird aber durch die zunehmende Verwendung des Lëtz. gebrochen.

5.3.5. Schulen

Angesichts der hohen kommunikativen Anforderungen an die luxemb. Gesellschaft ist das staatliche Erziehungswesen bemüht, in der Schule den Unterricht des Dt. und des Frz. so effektiv wie möglich zu gestalten. Lëtz. fungiert im ersten Schuljahr als informelle Kommunikationshilfe und wird in den ersten sieben Schuljahren im Ausmaß von nur einer Wochenstunde unterrichtet. Wurde dieser Lëtz.-Unterricht seit seiner Einführung im Jahre 1912 hauptsächlich zur Pflege der Heimatliteratur benützt, so wird derzeit ein verstärktes Augenmerk auf Grammatik und Orthographie gelegt. Den Lehrplänen zufolge ist die eigentliche Unterrichtssprache der Primärschule allerdings das Dt. Der Deutschunterricht umfaßt zunächst vier, dann acht Wochenstunden, ab dem zweiten Halbjahr des zweiten Schuljahres wird Frz. im Ausmaß von ebenfalls acht Wochenstunden gelehrt. Das Dt. bleibt auch in der Unterstufe der Gymnasien (7.–9. Schulstufe) wichtigste Unterrichtssprache; allerdings wird Mathematik auf Frz. vermittelt, welches dann in der Oberstufe (10.–13. Schulstufe) die offizielle Unterrichtssprache für alle Fächer außer Dt., Englisch und Kunst- und Musikerziehung wird (vgl. Projet de loi 2535/4, 14).

6. Sprachpolitische Lage

6.1. Rechtliche Regelungen des Sprachengebrauchs bis 1984

Wie unter 2. ausgeführt, erfolgt im Jahre 1340 durch die verwaltungstechnische Teilung in ein *Quartier wallon* und ein *Quartier allemand* die erste amtliche Zurkenntnisnahme der sprachlichen Gegebenheiten des damaligen Herzogtums. Die Amtssprache Dt. behält ihren Status bis 1443, als die Burgunder das Frz. als offizielle Sprache einführen. Bis 1795, dem Datum der frz. Besetzung, bleibt das Frz. äußere und erste Amtssprache; die unteren Verwaltungsebenen erhalten ihre Instruktionen jedoch, wenn nötig, auf Dt. Die Franzosen machen das Frz. ab 1795 auch im *Quartier allemand* zur alleinigen Amtssprache. Nach dem Wiener Kongreß benutzt Wilhelm I. zunächst das Frz. als Gegengewicht gegenüber dt., ab 1830 das Dt. gegenüber belgischen (= frankophonen) Einflüssen. Dies führt 1830 zur erstmaligen, 1834 zur wiederholten Dekretierung der Wahlfreiheit zwischen Dt. und Frz. im amtlichen Gebrauch (vgl. Projet de loi 2535/1, 7–8, Hommes 1985, 15–17).

Nach dem Verlust der frankophonen Gebiete am Ende der Belgischen Revolution (1839) kann das Frz. im verkleinerten Großherzogtum seine traditionelle Position ungeschmälert behaupten: Es bleibt einerseits Gesetzes- und Verwaltungssprache und fungiert andererseits als elitäres Bildungssymbol des Großbürgertums. Die Verfassung von 1848 verankert die Wahlfreiheit zwischen Dt. und Frz. für den öffentlichen Bereich.

1896 versucht der sozialistische Abgeordnete Caspar-Matthias Spoo, seine Antrittsrede im Parlament auf Lëtz. zu halten, was einen handfesten Skandal auslöst. Obwohl der Sprachenwahl Spoos eigentlich sozialpolitische Absichten zugrundeliegen — es ging ihm im wesentlichen um die Stärkung des Arbeiterstandes —, kommt es dadurch zur ersten öffentlichen sprachpolitischen Debatte in der luxemb. Geschichte. Spoo verteidigte sich hauptsächlich mit patriotischen Argumenten, die ihm widersprechenden Abgeordneten führten sprachästhetische Ansichten ins Feld. Die Diskussion wurde durch ein für das Lëtz. klar negatives Votum beendet (vgl. Hoffmann 1987 a).

Lëtz. wird erst ab dem Zeitpunkt entscheidend gestärkt, als es den Luxemburgern dazu dient, sich gegen nazideutsche Einflüsse zu wehren. 1939, im Jahr der Feierlichkeiten zur 100jährigen Unabhängigkeit, wird eine Verordnung erlassen, die die Beherrschung des Lëtz. als Voraussetzung für eine Einbürgerung nennt. Ab 1940, als dt. Truppen das Land besetzen, sind die Luxemburger einer radikalen sprachlichen Germanisierungspolitik ausgesetzt. Frz. wird durch eine Reihe von Verordnungen in jeglicher Erscheinungsform verboten (vgl. die Facsimile-Abdrucke von Plakaten der *Zivilverwaltung* und der *Volksdeutschen Bewegung* in Hoffmann 1992, 161—163). Frz. Schilder, Aufschriften, Bücher, Zeitschriften, ja sogar Vor- und Familiennamen müssen entfernt bzw. germanisiert werden. Der Gebrauch von frz. Fremdwörtern in lëtz. Gesprächen wird ebenfalls untersagt (vgl. Hommes 1985, 23—30).

In dieser Situation erleichtert das von den Machthabern nicht verbietbare „germanische" Lëtz. zumindest die sprachliche Abgrenzung. Die als abschließender Beweis der Zugehörigkeit der Luxemburger zum Deutschtum geplante *Personenstandsaufnahme* des Jahres 1941 wird zum sprachpolitischen Fiasko für die Deutschen, da die Bevölkerung auf den Erhebungsformularen nicht nur sich selbst, sondern auch ihre Sprache als „luxemburgisch" und nicht als „deutsch" deklariert.

In der Verfassungsrevision von 1948 wird die bereits 1848 festgelegte Regelung der prinzipiellen Sprachenfreiheit beibehalten, da eine Amtssprachendebatte politisch nicht opportun erscheint: Dt. hat stark an Prestige verloren, kann aber als Amtssprache aus pragmatischen Gründen nicht abgeschafft werden. Frz. als alleinige Amtssprache festzulegen, widerspräche den sprachlichen Tatsachen. Lëtz. hat an Prestige gewonnen, ersetzt das Dt. mündlich im Parlament, ist aber als Amtssprache noch zu wenig ausgebaut.

Die bisher größte sprachpolitische Debatte wird im Jahre 1980 entfacht, als sich die rechtsextreme Presse der Bundesrepublik Deutschland für Luxemburg zu interessieren beginnt (vgl. Projet de loi 2535/4, 6; Reisdoerfer 1994, Fn. 1). Unter dem Titel *Luxemburgs Selbstverleugnung. Flucht des Miniaturstaates aus der deutschen Identität* versuchte die *Deutsche Nationalzeitung* (Nr. 10 vom 7.3.1980, 5) in einer Reaktion auf Hoffmann (1979) das Deutschtum der Luxemburger zu beschwören:

„(...) Ist das Luxemburgische eine separate Schriftsprache? An antideutschen Komplexen leidende Kreise wollen den im Großherzogtum beheimateten deutschen Dialekt zu einer solchen hochstilisieren. (...) Die Bevölkerung aber redet deutsch und liest deutsch. Die luxemburgischen Kinder werden in Deutsch unterrichtet, müssen aber schon ab dem zweiten Schuljahr Französisch büffeln, damit sie als Untertanen die Sprache der Obrigkeit verstehen (...)".

Die luxemburgische Empörung über Töne, die mit Recht an die Zeit der Naziherrschaft denken ließen, führte in der Folge, und angetrieben durch Agitationen des luxemb. Sprachpflegevereins *Actioun Lëtzebuergesch*, zu einer eingehenden Auseinandersetzung mit der Frage nach einer definitiven Amtssprachenregelung (vgl. Projet de loi 2535/0—7), die im Beschluß des Sprachengesetzes im Jahre 1984 enden sollte.

6.2. Das Sprachengesetz von 1984 und seine Problematik

Am 24. Februar 1984 wird das Lëtz. zur *Nationalsprache* erhoben, das Dt. und das Frz. werden zu gleichberechtigten *Amtssprachen*, das Frz. darüber hinaus zur *Sprache der Gesetzgebung* (vgl. Loi (...) 1984). Die terminologische Unterscheidung von *Amts*- und *National*sprachen, die der Schweizer Situation nicht unähnlich ist — Dt., Frz. und Italienisch sind dort *Amts*sprachen, Rätoromanisch ist *National*sprache —, sollte dazu dienen, den Status des Lëtz. per Gesetz zu erhöhen, ohne dabei die Positionen der beiden anderen Sprachen unnötig in Frage zu stellen:

Loi du 24 février 1984 sur le régime des langues
Art. 1.: Langue nationale
La langue nationale des Luxembourgeois est le luxembourgeois.

Art. 2. Langue de la législation
Les actes législatifs et leurs règlements d'exécution sont rédigés en français. Lorsque les actes législatifs et réglementaires sont accompagnés d'une traduction, seul le texte français fait foi. Au cas où des règlements non visés à l'alinéa qui précède sont édictés par un organe de l'Etat, des communes ou des établissements publics dans une langue autre que la française, seul le texte dans la langue employée par cet organe fait foi. Le présent article ne déroge pas aux dispositions applicables en matière de conventions internationales.

Art. 3. Langues administratives et judiciaires
En matière administrative, contentieuse ou non contentieuse, et en matière judiciaire, il peut être fait usage des langues française, allemande ou luxembourgeoise, sans préjudice des dispositions spéciales concernant certaines matières.

Art. 4. Requêtes administratives
Lorsqu'une requête est rédigée en luxembourgeois, en français ou en allemand, l'administration doit se servir, dans la mesure du possible, pour sa réponse de la langue choisie par le requérant.

Art. 5. Abrogation
Sont abrogées toutes les dispositions incompatibles avec la présente loi, notamment les dispositions suivantes:

— Arrêté royal grand-ducal du 4 juin 1830 contenant des modifications aux dispositions existantes au sujet des diverses langues en usage dans le royaume;

— Dépêche du 24 avril 1832 à la commission du Gouvernement, par le référ. intime, relative à l'emploi de la langue allemande dans les relations avec la diète;

— Arrêté royal grand-ducal du 22 février 1834 concernant l'usage des langues allemande et française dans les actes publics.

Die gesetzliche Regelung des amtlichen Sprachengebrauchs in Luxemburg, die seit 1948 ausstand, war unbedingt notwendig. Ob allerdings der Schritt, den man nach fast 150 Jahren endlich tat, gleich zu einem Sprung ins Ungewisse hätte ausarten müssen, ist eine andere Frage. Dem, worum es den meisten Luxemburgern im Grunde genommen ging, nämlich der offiziellen Anerkennung ihrer Muttersprache, wäre auch Genüge getan gewesen, wenn man das Lëtz. nur zur *Nationalsprache*, und nicht gleichzeitig zur dritten *Amtssprache* gemacht hätte. Durch Art. 4 des Gesetzes wurde nämlich ein Idiom ohne verbindliche lexikalisch-semantische und morpho-syntaktische Normen, das seit 1975 mit einer sehr widerspruchsvollen offiziellen Orthographie ausgestattet ist, in diese Rolle gedrängt (zu Negativprognosen hinsichtlich der Zukunft des Lëtz. vgl. Hartmann 1976; Hoffmann 1974, 67—69, 76—81; Schaus 1983; Treinen 1986). Es gibt zwar eine summarische und rein deskriptive Grammatik von Robert Bruch (Bruch 1968) und ein fünfbändiges Wörterbuch (vgl. Luxemburger Wörterbuch 1950); doch hat letzteres keinerlei normativen Charakter. Verstärkte Sprachplanung und Normierung wären, sollte mit dem für den amtlichen Gebrauch unabdingbaren Ausbau des Lëtz. wirklich ernst gemacht werden, die erste conditio sine qua non. Trotz der im Land zur Verfügung stehenden Fachkräfte erhebt sich allerdings die Frage, ob der zu erwartende personelle und finanzielle Aufwand zu verantworten wäre. Auch schiene die Einführung des Lëtz. als Vollfach in der Primärschule dann nicht mehr abwendbar, womit sich automatisch die Frage der Gewichtung der Sprachenfächer stellen würde und solcherart womöglich, aus Rücksicht auf den Stundenplan und die Belastung der Kinder, der Status des Frz. im Primärunterricht gefährdet wäre. Damit käme eine andere Säule der von den Aktivisten in Sachen Lëtz. immer wieder beschworenen nationalen Identität ins Wanken: der äquilibrierte dt.-frz. Bilinguismus.

Ob die verschiedenen Sprachregionen den in der Koiné realisierten pragmatischen Ausgleich auch noch hinnehmen würden, wenn er einmal offizialisiert würde, ist fraglich. Wahrscheinlich würde es keine Region dulden, daß ihr Sprachgebrauch von Amts wegen in eine Randzone gedrängt würde. Hier scheint der sprachliche Landfrieden gefährdet. Den Luxemburgern könnte ein Sprachenkampf ins Haus stehen.

6.3. Gegenseitige Beeinflussungen der Kontaktsprachen

Das in Luxemburg gesprochene Moselfränkische weist starke romanische Einflüsse auf. Es sind verschiedene diachronisch gestaffelte Schichten zu unterscheiden (vgl. Bruch 1953):

1. Relikte aus der Zeit der Zugehörigkeit zum Imperium Romanum,
2. salisch-fränkische Impulse, zunächst durch nach Westen gerichtete Wanderungen der salischen Franken bis an die Somme, besonders aber durch deren Rückwanderung aus dem Pariser Becken nach Osten im 6. Jh.n.Chr.,
3. frz. Einflüsse, bedingt durch die Nachbarschaft Frankreichs und Walloniens,
4. Einflüsse, die auf die Vormachtstellung des Frz. im amtlichen Bereich und seine Bedeutung in der Schule zurückgehen.

Lëtz. ist durchsetzt mit teils assimiliertem, teils nicht integriertem Fremdwortgut. Dabei fällt auf, daß frz. Wörter (siehe Tab. 141.6, Bp. 11−13) schneller assimiliert werden als hochdeutsche (siehe Tab. 141.6, Bp. 14−16); vgl. Hoffmann 1981, 70−75; 1987b, 129− 140; weitere Bp. bei Pletschette 1935, Southworth 1954, Kramer 1992).

Tab. 141.6: Assimilation von Fremdwörtern im Lëtz.

Bp.Nr.	Deutsch	Lëtz.	Französisch
11	Becher	*Gubbeli*	*gobelet*
12	Regenschirm	*Präbbeli*	*parapluie*
13	Getriebe	*Buatt*	*boîte*
14	*Kupplung*	*Kupplung*	embrayage
15	*Messer*	*Messer*	couteau
16	*Staubsauger*	*Staubsauger*	aspirateur

Daneben kommt es durch doppelte Beeinflussung des Lëtz. zu Fremdwortdubletten (siehe Tab. 141.7).

Tab. 141.7: Fremdwortdubletten im Lëtz.

Bp.Nr.	Deutsch	Lëtz.	Französisch
17	*Flieger*	*Flieger Avion*	*Avion*
18	*Bleistift*	*Bläisteft Crayon*	*Crayon*
19	*Fernsehen*	*Fernseh Televisioun*	*télévision*

Es gibt Sprachpfleger, die den frz. Einfluß als sprachschädigend ansehen, andere indessen raten dort, wo der Sprachausbau durch Neologismen nicht zu vermeiden ist, jeweils das frz. Wort zu übernehmen, eben weil es vom Lëtz. besser assimiliert werden kann. Die an und für sich germanische Syntax des Lëtz. ist ebenso romanisch beeinflußt, wie sich z. B. anhand der fehlenden Nominativ-Akkusativ-Markierung zeigen läßt. Das Resultat ist ein starres Satzschema, weil, um Mißverständnisse zu verhindern, das Subjekt immer in Kopfstellung stehen muß und keine Inversion möglich ist, vgl. dt. *Der Löwe zer-* *reißt den Hasen, Den Hasen zerreißt der Löwe*; lëtz. *De(n) Léiw frësst den Hues*; frz. *Le lion dévore le lièvre*.

Natürlich wirkt sich der Sprachkontakt auch in den beiden anderen Sprachen aus. In den luxemb. Schulbüchern für den Französischunterricht gibt es ganze Listen von „Luxemburgismen". Diese sind oftmals als Belgizismen zu identifizieren (siehe Tab. 141.8, Bp. 20−22; weitere Beispiele bei Doppagne 1971, Kramer 1992), andere sind auf dt. Einfluß zurückzuführen (siehe Tab. 141.8, Bp. 23−25; vgl. dazu Kramer 1992, 210; weitere Beispiele bei Noppeney 1959).

Tab. 141.8: Luxemburger Französisch

Bp.Nr.	Deutsch	Luxo-Frz.	Französisch
20	Imbißstand	*friture*	*friterie*
21	Ansichtskarte	*carte vue*	*carte postale illustrée*
22	Akademiker	*académicien*	*diplomé d'université*
23	*frei haben*	*avoir libre*	*avoir congé*
24	Komponist	*componiste*	*compositeur*
25	*Fremdenzimmer*	*chambre d'étrangers*	*chambre à louer*

Das in Luxemburg verwendete Hochdeutsch ist durch eine Reihe von Sonderentwicklungen bzw. Transferenzen aus dem Lëtz. gekennzeichnet (siehe Tab. 141.9, Bp. 26, 27). Bp. für Gallizismen stehen in Tab. 141.9, Bp. 28−30 (weitere Beispiele bei Hommes 1985, 68−84 und Magenau 1964).

Ebenso häufig ist im luxemb. Hochdeutsch die Verwechslung von Nominativ und Akkusativ, die Genitivbildung durch ein präpositionales Attribut oder ein Possessivpronomen und die Bildung des Passivs mit *geben* als Hilfsverb (*Dem Vater seinen Hut gibt von der Mutter gebürstet. Das Dach von dem Haus brach ein*).

Was die Phonetik anbelangt, so gibt es im Lëtz. keinen Knacklaut (*glottal stop*). Statt dessen existiert eine starke intervokalische Lenisierung, die bewirkt, daß Luxemburger die Verschlußlaute nicht scharf gegeneinander absetzen und das Hochdeutsche viel weicher aussprechen als Bundesdeutsche. Auch wird gewöhnlich, ähnlich wie im Lëtz., die Stimme am Ende eines Satzes nicht gesenkt,

Tab. 141.9: Luxemburger Deutsch

Bp.Nr.	Deutsch	Luxo-Dt.	Französisch
26	Gebäude	Gebäulichkeit	
27	ohne	sonder (lëtz: sonner)	
28	Personenbeschreibung	Signalement	signalement
29	Damenmannschaft	Damenequipen	équipe de femmes
30	ernst nehmen	als ernst nehmen	prendre pour sérieux

sondern gehoben. Dies führt zu der in Luxemburg typischen Schaukelmelodie im gesprochenen Hochdeutsch.

7. Bibliographie (in Auswahl)

Atten, Alain (1980): *Le wallon frontalier de Doncols-Sonlez*, Luxemburg.

Berg, Guy (1993): „Mir wëlle bleiwe wat mer sin". *Soziolinguistische und sprachtypologische Betrachtungen zur luxemburgischen Mehrsprachigkeit*, Tübingen.

Bruch, Robert (1953): *Grundlegung einer Geschichte des Luxemburgischen*, Luxemburg.

Bruch, Robert (1968): *Précis populaire de grammaire luxembourgeoise. Luxemburger Grammatik in volkstümlichem Abriß*, Luxemburg.

Bruch, Robert (1969): *Gesammelte Aufsätze*, Luxemburg.

Christophory, Jules (1978): *The Luxembourgers in their own words. Les Luxembourgeois par eux-mêmes*, Luxemburg.

Christophory, Jules (1992): „Angewandte Linguistik in einem Luxemburger Kulturinstitut". In: Dahmen, 165–187.

Christophory, Jules (s. a.): *Luxembourgeois, qui êtes-vous? Echos et chuchotements*, Luxemburg.

COF (Commission ministérielle chargée de définir les objectifs de l'enseignement du français) (1985): *Enquête sur les habitudes et les besoins langagiers au Grand-Duché de Luxembourg. Rapport.*

Dahmen, Wolfgang et al. (Eds.) (1992): *Germanisch und Romanisch in Belgien und Luxemburg* (Romanistisches Kolloquium VI), Tübingen.

Doppagne, Albert (1971): „Le Français au Grand-Duché de Luxembourg. Considérations sociologiques et linguistiques". In: *Centre d'étude des arts, traditions et parlers populaires. Institut de Sociologie de l'Université libre de Bruxelles. Document de travail No.11*, Brüssel, 2–21.

Fröhlich, Harald (1989): „Dreisprachiges Luxemburg – Sprachkontakt ohne Sprachkonflikt?" In: *Germanistische Mitteilungen 30*, 105–116.

Fröhlich, Harald (1992): „Hierarchisierung und Kategorisierung im sprachrelevanten Alltagswissen. Anmerkungen zur soziolinguistischen Situation Luxemburgs". In: Dahmen, 188–202.

Harenberg Länderlexikon '93/94, Dortmund 1993.

Hartmann, Claudia (1976): „Luxemburgisch, eine zum Tode verurteilte Sprache?". In: *d'Letzeburger Land (Luxemburg) 23*, No.18, 8–9.

Hartmann, Claudia (1986): „Französisch hebt das Sozialprestige. Wer spricht in Luxemburg wann und wo mit wem welche Sprache?". In: *Süddeutsche Zeitung (München) 19.2.1986*, 45.

Hoffmann, Fernand (1964/1967): *Geschichte der Luxemburger Mundartdichtung*, 2 Bände, Luxemburg.

Hoffmann, Fernand (1974): *Standort Luxemburg*, Luxemburg.

Hoffmann, Fernand (1979): *Sprachen in Luxemburg*, Wiesbaden.

Hoffmann, Fernand (1981): *Zwischenland*, Hildesheim/New York.

Hoffmann, Fernand (1987a): „Spoo und die Folgen". In: *Galérie. Révue culturelle et pédagogique (Differdange) 5*, No. 1, 40–61.

Hoffmann, Fernand (1987b): „Pragmatik und Soziologie des Lëtzebuergeschen". In: *Aspekte des Lëtzebuergeschen*, Goudaillier, J.-P. (Ed.), Hamburg, 91–194.

Hoffmann, Fernand (1988): „Luxemburg". In: *Sociolinguistics – Soziolinguistik*, Ammon, U./Mattheier, K. J./Dittmar, N. (Eds.), Berlin/New York, 1334–1340.

Hoffmann, Fernand (1992): „1839–1989: Fast 150 Jahre amtlicher Zwei- und privater Einsprachigkeit in Luxemburg. Mit einem nationalsozialistischen Zwischenspiel". In: Dahmen, 149–164.

Houdremont, Alphonse (1897): „Histoire de la langue française comme langue administrative du pays de Luxembourg". In: Athenée de Luxembourg, Ecole industrielle et commerciale de Luxembourg (Ed.): *Programme de l'année scolaire 1896–1897*, Luxemburg, 3–60.

Hommes, Brigitte (1985): *Entwicklung und aktueller Stand des Sprachengebrauchs im Großherzogtum Luxemburg*, Köln, Magisterarbeit.

Kloss, Heinz (1986): „Der Stand der in Luxemburg gesprochenen Sprachen beim Jahresende 1984". In: *Germanistische Mitteilungen 24*, 83–94.

Kramer, Johannes (1983): „La situation linguistique au Grand-Duché de Luxembourg". In: *Europa Ethnica 40*, 195–202.

Kramer, Johannes (1984): *Zweisprachigkeit in den Benelux-Ländern*, Hamburg.

Kramer, Johannes (1986): „Gewollte Dreisprachigkeit — Französisch, Deutsch und Lëtzebuergesch im Großherzogtum Luxemburg". In: *Europäische Sprachminderheiten im Vergleich. Deutsch und andere Sprachen*, Hinderling, R. (Ed.), Wiesbaden, 229—249.

Kramer, Johannes (1992): „Einige Bemerkungen zum Französischen in Luxemburg". In: Dahmen, 203—223.

„Loi du 24. février 1984 sur le régime des langues". (1984) In: *Mémorial, Journal officiel du Grand Duché de Luxembourg — Amtsblatt des Großherzogtums Luxemburg. Recueil de législation, vol. A, Nos. 1—115 (1984)*, Luxembourg, 196—197 (und in: *Europa Ethnica 41 (1984)*, 97).

Luxemburger Wörterbuch (1950—1977), 5 Bände, Luxemburg.

Magenau, Doris (1964): *Die Besonderheiten der deutschen Schriftsprache in Luxemburg und in den deutschsprachigen Teilen Belgiens*, Mannheim.

Margue, Paul (1978): *Luxemburg in Mittelalter und Neuzeit*, Luxemburg.

Noppeney, Marcel (1959): *Le Complexe d'Esope*, Luxemburg.

Pletschette, Nikolas (1935): „Fremde Klänge im Luxemburger Dialekt". In: *Jonghemecht* (Luxemburg), 13—16, 65—67, 107—110, 158—163, 192—200.

Projet de loi sur le régime des langues. Documents parlementaires (Luxembourg) No. 2535, 17.11.81 — No. 2535/7, 11.01.84.

Reisdoerfer, Joseph (1994): „Een neie lëtzebuergeschen Dixionär. Prolegomena zu einem neuen Wörterbuch der luxemburgischen Sprache". In: *Die Warte (Luxemburg)*, 27.01.1994; 03.02.1994.

Schaus, Emile (1983): „Die große Not unserer Nationalsprache". In: *Luxemburger Wort 136*, No. 196, 4; No. 201, 13; No. 206, 4.

Southworth, F. C. (1954): „French Elements in the Vocabulary of the Luxemburg Dialect". In: *Bulletin Linguistique et Ethnologique (Luxembourg) 2*, 1—20.

Statec (Service central de la statistique et des études économiques) (1989—1993): *Luxembourg en chiffres 1989 [1990, 1991, 1992, 1993]*, Luxemburg.

Statec (Service central de la statistique et des études économiques) (1990): *Statistiques Historiques 1839—1989*, Luxemburg.

Statec (Service central de la statistique et des études économiques) (1993): *Annuaire statistique du Grand-Duché de Luxembourg 1992*, Luxemburg.

Thill, G. (1983): *Vor- und Frühgeschichte Luxemburgs*, Luxemburg.

Trausch, Gérard (1977): *Le Luxembourg sous l'Ancien Régime*, Luxemburg.

Trausch, Gérard (1981): *Le Luxembourg à l'époque contemporaine*, Luxemburg.

Treinen, Jean Michel (1986): „Vun Ziipe, Schècksen a Geliits. Jugendsprache in Luxemburg". In: *Lëtzebuerger Almanach*, 378—385.

Harald Fröhlich, Salzburg (Österreich)
Fernand Hoffmann, Luxemburg (Luxemburg)

142. France

1. Apparences et réalités: lente émergence du français
2. La francisation d'un espace, origine de la superposition des langues
3. L'idéologie du français, langue de la citoyenneté
4. La rupture récente
5. Situations actuelles
6. Effets de la symbiose
7. Les langues et l'immigration
8. Les langues non-territorialisées
9. Les langues déterritorialisées
10. Langue(s) et identité(s)
11. L'école
12. L'alternance de langues
13. Les emprunts réciproques
14. Les créations ethno-lexicales
15. Conclusion
16. Bibliographie (sélective)

1. Apparences et réalités: lente émergence du français

Un simple coup d'œil à la carte linguistique de la France (→ carte D) fait ressortir une double spécificité: l'illusion fréquente selon laquelle la France est un pays très unifié linguistiquement et la richesse linguistique originelle du territoire: les marges présentent une langue non indo-européenne (le basque) et trois familles des langues indo-européennes:

celtique (breton), germanique (flamand et alsacien-lorrain), latine sous trois branches: ibéro-roman (catalan), italo-roman (corse) et enfin gallo-roman (français et occitan).

2. La francisation d'un espace, origine de la superposition des langues

Ce dernier se présente en tant que langue(s) d'oïl (français et variétés gallo-romanes de la moitié Nord du pays), langue(s) d'oc ou occitan et, pour ceux qui en admettent l'autonomie, francoprovençal.

L'étude du contact des langues est donc inséparable de l'examen de l'espace occupé par ce pays et de son expansion. En outre la présence en France des langues dites « territoriales » (Marcellesi 1975, 6−7) comme celle des langues immigrées est en rapport avec l'histoire. Géographiquement, la France métropolitaine occupe, avec la Corse, 551.500 km^2 et est l'un des pays des plus étendus d'Europe (après la Russie et l'Ukraine). Les frontières actuelles sont celles que le royaume de France a atteintes à la fin du XVIIIe siècle.

Le rapport de cet ensemble avec les questions linguistiques a nécessairement varié: il y a longtemps que l'ancienne Gaule connaît une situation linguistique complexe. Si l'on peut penser qu'à l'exception sans doute d'une partie de l'Armorique, les langues celtiques ont disparu de Gaule à l'époque des invasions germaniques, la substitution linguistique ne s'est pas faite au profit du latin des lettrés ou de l'Eglise mais au profit de variétés qui sont nées du contact entre latin et celtique (même si les mots gaulois sont très peu nombreux eux-mêmes) et de l'adoption de ces « créoles » par les peuples germaniques romanisés et chargés de protéger la Gaule romaine avant de s'en emparer. Ces créoles au second degré sont couramment désignés par le terme « roman » qu'il faut entendre comme un générique s'appliquant à tout ce qui, dans l'ancienne Gaule, n'est ni le latin des clercs ni le « tudesque » (lat. médiéval *theodiscus*), terme générique pour désigner un ensemble de diverses variétés germaniques encore utilisées à l'époque. L'émergence politique du « roman », dans les Serments de Strasbourg de 842, se fait donc après quatre siècles (au moins) de plurilinguisme (germanique/roman) et de diglossie (latin/roman). Il faudra encore plus d'un siècle pour que l'ancienne Gaule ait un souverain de la nouvelle dynastie des Capétiens ignorant le « tudesque » (Hugues Capet accède au trône de France en 987).

Balibar (1985, 1.1), à juste titre, a mis en évidence le caractère symbolique de la prestation de serment − à Strasbourg, en 842, − de Louis le Germanique en roman, reconnaissant ainsi les locuteurs de cette langue comme sujets de son frère Charles II dit le Chauve, à qui on réservait ainsi la partie occidentale du pays des Francs, « la Francia Occidentalis » délimitée par le « roman ». Les foyers nationaux de ce qui allait devenir la France et l'Allemagne, étaient ainsi posés par la différence de langue.

Paris et sa langue d'Ile-de-France (« francien » des linguistes, puis « français ») n'ont la prééminence qu'à partir de l'avènement de la dynastie d'Hugues Capet. Il va falloir cinq siècles encore pour que le « domaine royal » (où en principe le roi était le maître) et le « royaume » coïncident. Cinq siècles pour l'émergence de la langue, cinq siècles pour la superposition domaine royal/royaume/langue française (ce qui nous conduit au XVIe siècle et à François I, 1515−1547).

Cette longue durée a vu progressivement le domaine royal s'étendre à la partie nord du royaume. Mais seule l'extension du domaine royal rendait la prééminence de la langue du royaume sur les autres variétés de roman effective. La grande plaine du bassin parisien (des Vosges à l'Armorique) s'est prêtée à cette première expansion alors que le Sud du royaume, morcelé par le relief, a maintenu plus longtemps l'autonomie des feudataires, et a permis l'éclosion de foyers linguistiques gallo-romans (langue(s) d'oc), nettement différents de ceux du nord (langue(s) d'oïl). La mainmise royale sur les Etats de langue(s) d'oc se fera progressivement de l'annexion du Comté de Toulouse au domaine royal (après la croisade contre les Albigeois au XIIIe siècle) jusqu'au rattachement définitif de Nice à la France au XIXe siècle sous le Second Empire.

Le Duché de Bretagne (avec sa partie bretonnante) (suivant les terres d'oc déjà passées dans le domaine royal) avait donné lieu, en 1532, à l'entrée dans le domaine royal d'une langue non-romane, *celtique*. Avec l'arrivée sur le trône de France de Henri IV (1598−1610) la France acquiert (sans désormais la reconnaître) une 3ème langue de France: le *basque* (langue non indo-européenne, contrairement aux autres).

Le XVIIe siècle voit le royaume pousser ses frontières vers le Sud (acquisition, en 1659, du Roussillon de langue *catalane*, 4ème langue de France chronologiquement), vers le Nord, si bien qu'un district de langue *flamande* (ou néerlandaise) (5ème langue de France) entre dans le royaume (annexion d'une partie de la Flandre avec Dunkerque), vers l'Est avec la mainmise sur l'Alsace (1648) et Strasbourg (1681), d'où l'entrée de *l'allemand* comme 6ème langue de France. De nouveaux problèmes linguistiques se poseront également lors de l'annexion du reste de la Lorraine (1766). En 1768, le royaume de France annexe la Corse. La 7ème des langues de France, le *corse*, (dont on croyait que c'était simplement de l'italien) s'ajoutait à la panoplie linguistique du royaume.

Il est à noter ici que les nommer c'est déjà prendre parti. Dire *allemand* ou *germanique* ou *alsacien* pour la langue autochtone d'Alsace et de Lorraine thioise, *néerlandais* ou *flamand* ou *flamand du Westhoek* pour la variété d'origine de la région de Dunkerque, c'est prendre une certaine position.

3. L'idéologie du français, langue de la citoyenneté

Un point important de cette histoire est la stratégie glottopolitique suivie jusqu'à une date récente par les régimes successifs et dont sans doute les meilleures illustrations se trouvent dans les débats qui ont suivi le déclenchement de la Révolution française de 1789. Certes le pouvoir royal avait proclamé légitime la langue française mais ne s'était guère préoccupé de la faire apprendre ou de la répandre dans le pays. En revanche la Révolution française s'est préoccupée tout de suite (1) de former des citoyens (Giacomo 1975, 16−19), (2) d'unifier le pays, (3) de faire reculer l'ignorance.

Une tendance très centralisatrice se faisait jour à la fois dans les textes sur l'école (projets Talleyrand, Lanthenas) et dans l'enquête linguistique de l'abbé Grégoire (1790−1794). Ce dernier, protagoniste de l'abolition de l'esclavage et désireux de mettre les Français à même d'être de véritables citoyens, s'était donné pour tâche de faire «extirper» les «patois» (terme qui pouvait englober pour lui les langues régionales ou minoritaires) et répandre le français des lettres. D'où son enquête, à questionnaire très orienté, qui a réussi à faire ressortir l'urgence de mesures (puisque, selon lui, seul 1 Français sur 7 savait vraiment le français).

Tout le XIXe siècle et la première moitié du XXe siècle ont vécu, pour ce qui est de la politique linguistique française, sur les conceptions de l'abbé Grégoire appliquées non seulement à toute la France mais aussi à l'empire colonial que le pays s'est constitué. Les nouvelles colonies, contrairement à la plupart des anciennes conçues comme des terres de peuplement (Canada, Louisiane), se sont vu appliquer les mêmes principes glottopolitiques que les départements français, mais en outre ont constitué des réservoirs de migrants vers la France (dont le flux continue encore aujourd'hui).

Le gouvernement de Vichy, dépendant de l'occupant nazi de 1940 à 1944, a ménagé une brèche dans l'omnipotence du français, en préconisant un certain enseignement des dialectes (compte tenu de ce qui lui restait comme territoire à administrer): il s'agissait de langue(s) d'oc (ou occitan), de catalan, de corse. Assez curieusement, l'esprit de la Libération souffla dans le même sens... Mais il s'est agi d'abord du basque et du catalan, notamment pour faire pièce à Franco qui interdisait ces langues chez lui (Giacomo 1975). On y ajouta le breton et, in extremis, l'occitan. Ce fut la Loi Deixonne de 1951 (cf. Gardin 1975, Giacomo 1975) du nom du député rapporteur de la commission parlementaire chargée de ce dossier. Le résultat était que les quatre langues (basque, breton, catalan, occitan) pouvaient être prises en épreuve facultative au bac (comptant donc uniquement pour la mention) (Gardin 1975, 31−32). De même, la spécificité française était (par exemple par rapport à l'Italie) que seuls étaient admis les systèmes linguistiques qui n'étaient pas rattachés à la langue officielle d'un pays étranger (d'où l'exclusion des langues dites allogènes, du corse, considéré alors comme de l'italien, de l'alsacien, considéré comme de l'allemand, et du flamand, considéré comme du néerlandais). Ce cadre a duré vingt ans: l'esprit en a été modifié par l'admission du corse dans le club des langues régionales (1974), mais officiellement aucune nouvelle loi ne s'est substituée à la loi Deixonne qui, officiellement, est encore valide.

4. La rupture récente

Les années 80 ont marqué, dans la pratique, la rupture avec le principe de l'exclusivité linguistique du français. Diverses mesures ont considérablement élargi l'application de la loi

Deixonne. Ces mesures réclamées par divers mouvements revendicatifs ont trouvé une légitimation dans le rapport Giordan (1982) commandé par le ministre de la Culture. Ce texte faisant ressortir la richesse linguistique du pays, mettait en avant le principe du *droit à la différence*, soutenait la *dialectique de l'un et du multiple* tant pour le rapport entre français et *autres langues de France* qu'entre les variétés intérieures à chaque langue (Laroussi/Marcellesi 1990, 57—58). Les circulaires Savary ont permis d'utiliser les activités d'éveil pour la sensibilisation aux langues régionales. La notion même de *langues régionales* a été intentionnellement laissée dans le vague, ce qui a permis, sur le terrain, là où les conditions sociopsychologiques étaient réunies, de faire bénéficier certains dialectes d'oïl eux-mêmes de la loi.

Dans la partie orientale de la Bretagne le gallo, proclamé par ses défenseurs «langue gallèse», a pu profiter ainsi de la volonté d'affirmation identitaire en face du breton, langue celtique.

Le retour au pouvoir des socialistes, en 1990, s'est accompagné de mesures plus nettement orientées vers les sept langues (basque, breton, catalan, corse, néerlandais, allemand, occitan). L'ouverture de sections de CAPES (Certificat d'Aptitude Pédagogique à l'Enseignement Secondaire, concours qui confère au reçu un poste de titulaire) a été adaptée à la revendication et à la spécificité des situations. Le CAPES de breton entre dans les «langues régionales» alors que le corse a fini par donner lieu à une section particulière «corse» et que le catalan était l'objet d'un concours du type des Langues Vivantes Etrangères. Ces CAPES ont donné lieu à des expériences intéressantes rompant, en pratique (pour le breton par exemple) ou de manière explicite dans les textes pour le corse, avec les conceptions normatives de la langue. D'où la théorisation de concept de «langues polynomiques» (cf. Marcellesi 1983) élaboré d'abord pour le corse et dont le colloque de Corte de 1990 a pu montrer la validité pour d'autres systèmes (Chiorboli 1991).

5. Situations actuelles

L'état général de la pratique linguistique est difficile à établir. Toutes les recherches convergent pour affirmer que le monolinguisme total de la langue régionale est négligeable sur le plan quantitatif. Les chiffres font ressortir que le pourcentage des bilingues actifs des langues régionales doit approcher les 10%. Les causes de cette francisation progressive de l'espace sont diverses; on peut toutefois considérer que l'école a été le premier vecteur, notamment à partir de la scolarisation de masse, à la fin du XIXe siècle (lois scolaires de Jules Ferry). L'acquisition du français étant une condition nécessaire à la promotion sociale, notamment par l'administration, les mesures de refoulement des langues régionales (usage du *signum*, objet qu'on repassait à l'école à quelqu'un qui parlait une langue ou un dialecte régional) ont trouvé un terrain favorable et provoqué *l'aliénation linguistique* — ou *l'auto-odi* —, sentiment par lequel on accepte ou on justifie l'écrasement de sa propre langue. Le déplacement des populations vers les villes (francisées en premier lieu), les deux guerres mondiales (le français a été la langue constante de communication à l'armée) ont fait le reste. Même dans les régions où la résistance culturelle paraît la plus forte (Corse, par exemple), la transmission de la langue comme *première* ou *maternelle* est de plus en plus rare. D'où l'acceptation ou la revendication que l'école supplée cette non-transmission par la famille.

Ce qui est vrai à des degrés divers pour les sept langues régionales, est encore plus vrai pour les systèmes plus proches du français, le *francoprovençal* et les *dialectes d'oïl*. Le premier serait encore parlé de manière active par 60.000 locuteurs, et la disparition du dernier locuteur du francoprovençal en France (car en Italie, dans le Val d'Aoste, la résistance est encore plus forte) n'est guère prévisible, selon Tuaillon (1988a) avant la fin du XXIe siècle.

Plus proches du français, plus tôt soumises à l'administration directe du roi, les variétés de langues d'oïl autres que le français couvrent un domaine plus vaste. Selon Lefebvre (1988), ces systèmes ont fourni longtemps des langues littéraires qui ont pu, à certaines époques, concurrencer le français. Si, dans beaucoup de régions, elles ne sont plus pratiquées à l'heure actuelle que dans certains îlots villageois ou dans la famille avec parfois l'occultation de la barrière entre français et langue locale, il faut noter que le *picard* (sous la forme du «chtimi») a pu se développer comme variété urbaine encore vivante, notamment en milieu ouvrier. De même, sous diverses variétés, le picard est encore écrit et sert à diverses compositions en prose et en vers.

De son côté, le *gallo* a pu donner lieu, d'en haut, à un effort de lettrés pour le promouvoir en tant que « langue romane ». Les enjeux glottopolitiques de cet effort se manifestent par l'existence de quatre systèmes graphiques différents (Lefebvre 1988, 274—275) qui d'une manière ou d'une autre traduisaient, comme pour le picard, une « réification du patois », face à celle du français, aux dépens de la « langue réellement parlée par les couches sociales peu scolarisées » (Lefebvre 1988, 278).

D'une manière générale la disparition des dialectes d'oïl ne se fait pas par la simple substitution du français au système local mais par l'apparition d'une langue intermédiaire (« français régional ») qui ne fait disparaître de la variété autochtone que certains traits phonétiques ou morphologiques spécifiques.

6. Effets de la symbiose

Le français régional parlé dans chaque région a ses schèmes intonatifs spécifiques (cf. Carton 1987) liés à l'articulation caractéristique de la langue régionale, à un vocabulaire emprunté partiellement au substrat linguistique (cf. Tuaillon 1988 b) et à une syntaxe calquée, pour certains points, sur la grammaire du système local. Ces particularités peuvent être repérées par les locuteurs et éventuellement alors donner lieu à stigmatisation. Mais elles peuvent être aussi considérées comme étant du français courant, tant la barrière entre l'un et l'autre est parfois insaisissable. C'est ainsi que le français régional peut avoir une structure phonologique nettement différente du français. Le linguiste normand R. Lepelley a décrit l'étonnement qui l'avait saisi dans sa jeunesse quand il avait lu que le français ignorait l'opposition *longue*/*brève* dans le système vocalique. Un ensemble de tests d'orthographe et de discrimination auditive et de prononciation lui a permis plus tard de constater que le Normand ne prononçait pas de la même manière le masculin et le féminin, le singulier et le pluriel des participes passés et les distinguait à l'audition. La lecture de textes tapés par des secrétaires d'origine normande permet de constater que l'opposition /e/ vs /ɛ/ tend à être neutralisée au profit de /ɛ/, si bien que sur les é et les è du français central, l'accent grave devient, à l'écrit, signe passe-partout.

Le vocabulaire s'enrichit de termes locaux, assez rarement reconnus comme tels par les locuteurs originaires de Normandie comme *pouque* ou sa variante française *pouche* (grand sac à pommes ou à pommes de terre), *banette* (corbeille à papier), *dalle* (évier). Pour ce dernier, un étudiant de doctorat enquêtant à Yerville (Seine-Maritime) s'est entendu répondre par un locuteur qui n'a jamais quitté la région et pratiquait quotidiennement le cauchois, son dialecte normand, que *dalle* (dans ce sens) était le vrai mot français et qu'*évier* était un mot local. Même sur le plan du signifié, les écarts peuvent être importants. En zone rurale, P. Brasseur, enquêteur de l'*Atlas Linguistique et Ethnographique de la Normandie*, a pu constater qu'en Pays de Caux le pommier n'était pas inclus mais opposé à l'ensemble des arbres, si bien que l'énoncé « il y a dix arbres et cinq pommiers » est fort possible. De la même manière, M.-R. Simoni-Aurembou a constaté, en faisant l'*Atlas linguistique de l'Ile-de-France et de l'Orléanais* que la *couleuvre* et la *vipère* n'entraient pas, pour les locuteurs natifs, dans l'ensemble des serpents, car il n'y a de serpents qu'en Afrique, dans la jungle.

Il est nécessaire d'ajouter ici une remarque sur le « français ». On entend souvent exposer une conception schématique (qui n'est pas sans doute innocente) selon laquelle le français serait le produit direct du dialecte de l'Ile-de-France, à peu près au même titre que les autres langues de France sont les produits de leurs formes médiévales. En réalité le français (que, justement à ce titre, les linguistes distinguent du « francien », dialecte de l'Ile-de-France) est une langue superposée, résultant non seulement de l'évolution de ses formes médiévales mais aussi, et sans doute surtout, des processus politiques dans lesquels elle s'est trouvée impliquée. A être devenue langue de tout le royaume, puis langue nationale, la langue française est le produit complexe d'une histoire complexe et là encore l'image d'une filiation linguistique linéaire est mystificatrice. Sans doute les états anciens du français ont joué un grand rôle dans l'élaboration de ses états les plus récents, mais les listes de mots originaires des autres régions sont longues, la syntaxe et la prononciation ont considérablement changé et personne ne peut imaginer que, à évoluer toute seule, la langue française serait à peu de chose près devenue ce qu'elle est devenue.

On peut prendre comme argument le système phonologique des lycéens parisiens décrit par A. Lefebvre (1988). Avec seulement 13 phonèmes vocaliques (10 oraux et 3 nasales) et 18 phonèmes consonantiques, c'est-à-dire 31 unités distinctives, il n'est pas conforme au modèle du français de l'école. Ainsi en fin de mot, le jeune Parisien ne peut choisir entre /o/ et /ɔ/. Il utilise toujours un phonème qui se réalise /o/ et de ce fait *paume* et *pomme* se confondent phonétiquement. Cela conduit à délimiter les notions de « français populaire » et de « français régional ». « Parmi les variantes linguistiques du français, il y en a qui sont communes à toutes les régions: ce sont les variantes populaires ou argotiques » (Tuaillon 1988 b, 291). En revanche « seules constituent le français régional les variantes qui peuvent se délimiter géographiquement, de telle manière que leur aire d'emploi s'oppose au reste du domaine français (...) » (idem). Mais toute forme de français régional se trouve en présence du français de référence. Dans la mesure où on a le sentiment de leurs différences, les couches aspirant à l'ascension sociale (les "middle classes" de W. Labov) essaient d'adopter la langue de référence sans pouvoir toujours y arriver entièrement. Si bien que le français régional, variété interne au groupe, parlée au travail, à l'atelier, à l'usine, garde une fonction identitaire et est ainsi « la langue populaire » d'une zone déterminée. Le français régional peut être moins riche en phonèmes (7 voyelles orales seulement chez certains locuteurs lillois) ou plus riche (en Franche-Comté comme en Normandie, avec la multiplication des phonèmes vocaliques oraux grâce à l'opposition *longue*/*brève*).

L'interaction entre le français de Paris et le français régional peut être illustrée sur le plan phonétique et sur le plan de la syntaxe. On constate en effet dans la capitale (Walter 1988, 300) que si les Provinciaux arrivant à Paris, perdent l'opposition /ɛ̃/ vs /œ̃/ (*brin* vs *brun*) que Paris n'avait plus depuis longtemps, les Parisiens, sous l'influence des Provinciaux, perdent l'opposition /a/ vs /ɑ/ qui était bien installée à Paris et qui permettait de distinguer *patte* et *pâte*. De même la restitution de l'articulation du « e » dit « muet » qu'on constate à Paris, correspond bien à la prononciation méridionale où « e » caduc est généralement articulé. C'est vrai pour la première syllabe des mots comme *belote*, *semelle*, *menu* mais aussi en finale où on voit même un « e » d'appui apparaître dans certaines circonstances après des mots ayant une terminaison consonantique comme *but* prononcé /bytə/ et *bac* prononcé /bakə/. En ce qui concerne la syntaxe, on entend également se répandre chez les Parisiens la construction avec accord du participe passé suivi de l'infinitif (je l'ai *faite* marcher où « l » représente un féminin alors que dans la forme correcte je l'ai *fait* marcher « l » représente un masculin ou un féminin). Il est à noter que cette forme est typique, à l'origine, du substrat occitan. Mais en outre, au XVIe siècle, le manifeste de la Pléiade (*Défense et illustration de la langue française*, 1549) a recommandé l'emprunt systématique aux dialectes et langues de France autres que le français (à l'époque uniquement dialectes d'oïl, langue d'oc et éventuellement breton). Tous les mots en -*ade*, par exemple, sont dus à cette pratique de l'emprunt aux systèmes méridionaux et bien des mots comme *abeille* ont pu s'imposer en français à la place d'anciennes formes oïliques (p. ex. *è*, *avette*, *mouche à miel*). Certes, cette stratégie d'enrichissement linguistique a été abandonnée par la suite. En face d'un Montaigne (1533−1592) déclarant qu'il choisissait des mots ou des membres de phrases gascons (que le gascon « y aille » si « le français ne peut »), Malherbe (1555−1628) a restauré la prééminence parisienne affirmée au Moyen Age (« il n'est bon bec que de Paris ») et toute la période classique l'a suivi.

En revanche, bien des variantes restent pour l'essentiel liées à une région. Tuaillon (1988 b, 393) signale ainsi que la prononciation /lui/ pour /lyi/ (écrit *lui*) caractérise les Lillois, « vingt » sous la forme /vɛ̃t/, avec un « t » articulé en dehors de toute liaison, est typique de l'Est; le « r » roulé, de la Bourgogne et du Berry; les « a » vélaires de la Picardie; la prononciation de /œ/ en /o/, de la région de Lyon. De même la présence d'un pronom sujet tonique devant l'infinitif dans les propositions infinitives de but (*pour moi manger* au sens de *pour manger* ou *pour que je mange*) reste le lot de l'Est et du Nord, alors que la construction du complément d'objet direct avec un *à* (*regarde à Dominique*) est typiquement méridionale (de même que, en cas de pronominalisation, *s'il me cherche, à moi, il va me trouver*).

Ainsi le français central et les français régionaux vivent en état d'interaction. Si l'école tend à diffuser la norme traditionnelle de même que majoritairement les journaux et autres médias, les français régionaux ne sont pas sans influencer sur bien des points le français central. Cette symbiose a du reste été théorisée par Gardy et Lafont (1981) qui notent que: « s'il existe bien une langue dominée (langue B) et une langue dominante (langue A), celles-ci n'interviennent jamais en tant que telles, mais l'une relativement à l'autre, l'une face à l'autre. La langue *dominée* ne peut exister que dans et par la relation de subordination qui la lie à la langue *dominante*, alors même que cette dernière est absente; et, inversement, la langue *dominante*, quelle que soit la situation de parole, suppose la langue *dominée*. Toute performance occitane s'effectue sous le contrôle du français, et, en dernière analyse, sur les marges de celui-ci.»

7. Les langues et l'immigration

On estime à environ quatre millions d'individus la population étrangère vivant en France. Il faut noter à cet égard l'imprécision de ces chiffres due à l'ambiguïté du terme «étranger» et à l'existence d'un grand nombre d'immigrés clandestins. Mais en l'absence de recensement linguistique (aucun organisme de sondages ou de statistiques n'a encore inclus dans ses questionnaires une rubrique relative aux langues maternelles), nous ne pouvons aborder la question des langues maternelles des populations migrantes (cela vaut surtout pour les ressortissants d'Afrique Noire et du Maghreb) que par l'analyse socio-géographique des locuteurs en question.

Historiquement, dans la première moitié du XIXe siècle, il s'agissait surtout d'Italiens (dans le Sud), de Polonais et de Belges (dans les bassins miniers du Nord et de Lorraine) puis d'Espagnols fuyant la dictature franquiste (dans le Sud-Ouest).

A partir des années 60, on assiste à une nouvelle vague de migrants: Espagnols, Portugais et surtout Maghrébins auxquels s'ajoutent des Africains (Afrique Noire), des Turcs et, plus récemment, des migrants venant d'Asie du Sud-Est. Cette population immigrée est inégalement répartie sur le territoire français: elle est nombreuse surtout en région parisienne et un peu moins dans les zones de l'Est et du Sud-Est.

Une grande partie des immigrés non-européens viennent de ce qui a été l'empire colonial français. Cela concerne les langues d'Asie du Sud-Est bien représentées en France et les diverses langues d'Afrique (aussi bien Afrique Noire que Maghreb). Mais selon la date de départ de leur pays, les statuts peuvent différer. Avant 1989/90, les causes de l'immigration récente des ressortissants des pays de l'Est étaient plus souvent en réalité *économiques* (comme le montrent la continuité actuelle et le renforcement même du flot) autant que *politiques*. Pour ce qui est des ressortissants des départements et territoires d'outre-mer (DOM-TOM), il s'agit d'une transplantation purement *économique*.

On peut aussi constater que certaines de ces langues peuvent avoir, hors de France, un espace où elles sont installées comme langues autochtones et où, même, elles sont officielles. Quand les locuteurs émigrent on dit que, dans le pays d'accueil, leurs langues sont «déterritorialisées». Mais d'autres langues pour des raisons diverses peuvent n'avoir aucun espace de ce genre ailleurs au monde: on dit alors qu'elles sont «non-territorialisées». Il s'agit d'un côté des groupes de Juifs venus de divers pays: Europe centrale (langue(s) yiddish), Afrique du Nord (langues judéo-arabes) et d'autres venus d'Espagne soit directement soit par l'Afrique du Nord (ladino ou langue judéo-espagnole) et dont l'arrivée en France est surtout liée à des raisons politiques (antisémitisme, décolonisation en Afrique du Nord). Il s'agit aussi de nomades (souvent citoyens français depuis longtemps et descendants de citoyens français), appelés «Tsiganes», «Bohémiens» ou «Gitans».

8. Les langues non-territorialisées

8.1. Les langues des sociétés juives: judéo-espagnol et judéo-arabe

Il s'agit de langues mixtes nées du contact de l'espagnol (judéo-espagnol) et l'arabe (judéo-arabe) avec la langue sacrée des Juifs, l'hébreu, réduite souvent à peu de chose dans la communauté avant sa réinstallation, d'abord artificielle, comme langue d'Israël. De toutes les langues minoritaires de France, le judéo-espagnol et le judéo-arabe sont probablement «les plus atteints dans leurs structures linguistiques profondes» (Sephiha 1988). Il y a actuellement à peu près 80.000 locuteurs judéo-espagnols et 150.000 locuteurs judéo-arabes en France (Sephiha 1988, 305). L'enseignement et la diffusion du judéo-espagnol en France sont assurés par des cours communautaires et universitaires, des activités culturelles et des associations diverses. Quant au judéo-arabe, enseigné, lui aussi, à l'université, il n'a pas encore connu, en France, le regain d'intérêt populaire que connaît le judéo-espagnol.

8.2. Le yiddish

En France, on estime que le yiddish est la langue de la communication courante d'environ 60.000 à 80.000 personnes et la langue maternelle de 150.000 (Ertel 1988, 332). Le yiddish est une des langues parlées par les Juifs en diaspora. Née de cinq composantes essentielles (hébreu, araméen, allemand, roman, slave), le yiddish tient une place particulière par sa diffusion et par le statut qu'il avait fini par acquérir en Europe centrale en tant que langue orale, littéraire, populaire et savante (Weber 1987 et → art. 238).

L'importance de la culture yiddish en France remonte à l'entre-deux-guerres et dépasse de loin l'importance numérique du groupe (Ertel 1988). La vie associative reste probablement la marque la plus caractéristique de la communauté juive originaire d'Europe orientale installée en France. Toutes sortes de cercles d'intérêts sont organisés. La bibliothèque Medem est la plus grande bibliothèque yiddish d'Europe.

8.3. Les langues tsiganes

On pense généralement aujourd'hui que la langue tsigane (la langue *romani* ou le *romanès*) dérive de l'indo-iranien proche parent du sanskrit et de langues, encore parlées aujourd'hui, de l'Inde centrale ou de la région de l'Indus (→ art. 239). Cette langue s'est enrichie dès les premières migrations vers l'Ouest (XIIIe siècle): des termes ont été empruntés à l'iranien, à l'arménien, puis, dans une forte proportion, au grec. Plus tard, par suite de la dispersion dans toute l'Europe, plusieurs dialectes se sont constitués. Beaucoup de noms leur ont été donnés: *Tsigane* (du grec byzantin *Atsinkanos* par référence à une secte orientale de magiciens et de devins); le nom d'*Egyptiens* a longtemps prévalu (dans la Grèce médiévale, les voyageurs occidentaux avaient remarqué une de leurs colonies en un lieu dit «Petite-Egypte»: d'où, en espagnol, *Egitanos, Gitanos*); *Bohémiens* (car ils présentaient au XVe siècle des passeports du roi de Bohême). Répandus dans la plupart des nations du monde, les Tsiganes sont presque les seuls nomades qui ne soient ni pasteurs ni conquérants. Même lorsqu'ils sont sédentaires de gré ou de force, sous divers noms et avec une structure plus ou moins tribale, ils demeurent profondément marqués par le nomadisme ancestral. Il est difficile de les dénombrer. En France, on estime leur nombre de 150.000 à 250.000 individus dont plus de 90% environ sont de nationalité française et dont les ⅔ sont sédentaires (d'après le recensement de 1989). Au contact de peuples différents, en Europe, la langue tsigane a évolué d'une manière qualifiée par Williams (1988, 381) d'«arborescente». Il serait donc plus approprié aujourd'hui de parler des langues tsiganes au pluriel. Les Tsiganes empruntent du vocabulaire, des tournures syntaxiques, des manières de prononcer aux différents peuples (en particulier chez les *Gadjé* (non Tsiganes)) qu'ils croisent et qu'ils côtoient. «Les langues que parlent les Tsiganes — écrit Williams (1988, 382) — sont nées de la rencontre entre un idiome venu de l'Inde et une multitude d'idiomes européens».

En France, on distingue aujourd'hui quatre groupes principaux: les *Manouches* qui venaient des frontières franco-germaniques (leur dialecte est très influencé par l'allemand), les *Sinte* (piémontais), les *Gitans* (le terme désigne, en France, à la fois le groupe des Tsiganes venus d'Espagne et les Tsiganes en général avec toutefois des connotations péjoratives), les *Rom*, les plus traditionalistes, arrivés assez récemment des pays de l'Est. Chez les *Manouches*, la maîtrise de la langue est inégalement partagée (Williams 1988).

Quant aux *Yenisches* (d'origine germanique, en Europe occidentale), ce sont des nomades, mais non pas des Tsiganes. Les Yenisches de France ont perdu leur propre idiome. Beaucoup parmi eux ne se déterminent plus que comme *Voyageurs* ou parfois même comme *Manouches*.

9. Les langues déterritorialisées

9.1. Le vietnamien

Le vietnamien est une langue monosyllabique à tons parlée sur tout le territoire du Vietnam où elle est la langue maternelle des ⅚ de la population. Installée en France surtout depuis 1945, la colonie vietnamienne est hétérogène: elle est formée de rapatriés d'Indochine ayant suivi l'armée et l'administration française au moment de la décolonisation, d'intellectuels, de fonctionnaires et d'étudiants. On ne peut évaluer le nombre de cette population de manière précise (250.000 selon l'INSEE, 1990); il sont répartis aujourd'hui sur l'ensemble du territoire français mais constituent des groupes relativement plus importants dans la région parisienne et la région Provence−Côte d'Azur.

9.2. Le khmer

Le nombre des ressortissants cambodgiens en France est moins important que celui des Vietnamiens et d'installation plus récente. Leur langue, le khmer, est parlée en France surtout par des étudiants cambodgiens. On peut dater de 1975 leur véritable installation. Le nombre des Cambodgiens de France est de 36.880 (INSEE 1989).

9.3. Le lao

Le lao (langue officielle de l'Etat lao, parlée comme langue maternelle par la majorité des citoyens de ce pays) appartient à la famille des langues thaï, et il est parlé aussi en Thaïlande. La répartition des Laotiens entre Lao et autres ethnies du Laos est difficile à faire. Installés pour la plupart dans la région parisienne et dans les grandes villes de province, ils se composent de Lao, Hmong, Yao et Khmer avec une proportion chinoise difficile à évaluer. Les Laotiens de France comptent 37.904 personnes au recensement de 1989.

9.4. Le hmong

Les Hmong, qu'ils soient ressortissants laotiens ou vietnamiens, forment, en France, une petite communauté urbaine qui a suivi le départ des Français d'Indochine. Ils sont employés dans leur quasi-totalité comme manœuvres dans l'industrie et constituent des groupes de travailleurs immigrés souvent sans projet de retour et au statut juridico-politique de réfugié (cf. Hassoun 1988a). Leur langue, le hmong, est une des principales langues de famille miao, elle-même principale composante de l'ensemble ethno-linguistique miao-yao. Le hmong est une langue à tons et monosyllabique.

9.5. Le chinois

Les Chinois de France ne comptent que 8.175 individus au recensement de 1989. Une partie de cette population est venue directement de Chine. Une autre partie était installée à Saigon et a suivi le départ de l'administration française. Le «chinois», terme recouvrant à l'oral des langues très différentes, a une place relativement importante dans certains quartiers de grandes villes. Majoritairement installés dans la région parisienne, les Chinois s'inscrivent dans une dynamique marquée par une scolarisation, en français, des plus jeunes et par l'ouverture linguistique qu'elle implique (Hassoun 1988b).

9.6. Les langues du Maghreb

La présence des langues du Maghreb est liée à l'importance de la colonisation française en Afrique du Nord (130 ans en Algérie, 80 ans en Tunisie et 40 ans au Maroc). Les Algériens ont même eu la nationalité française. L'immigration dans le sens Maghreb−France continue et est la cible principale des discours démagogiques présentant fallacieusement les immigrés comme responsables du chômage en France.

9.6.1. L'arabe

L'arabe (avec, éventuellement diverses qualifications, c'est-à-dire *algérien*, *marocain* ou *tunisien*) est la langue maternelle d'un bon nombre de ressortissants des pays du Maghreb. Il est très difficile de donner un chiffre précis quant à leur nombre, compte tenu des nombreuses personnes qui ne sont pas arabophones (cf. 9.6.2.) et parce que de nombreux Français d'origine maghrébine sont bilingues, parlant arabe et/ou berbère. Cependant, selon les chiffres de l'INSEE de 1989, le nombre des Maghrébins en France est de 1.509.578 ressortissants des trois pays: Algérie, Maroc et Tunisie: soit 725.049 Algériens, 558.799 Marocains et 227.530 Tunisiens. La langue *officielle* (qui n'est en aucun cas la langue *maternelle*) de ces pays est l'arabe littéraire moderne, appelé aussi «arabe standard». Cependant chaque communauté parle son arabe maternel et l'utilise dans la communication quotidienne. Les jeunes arabophones issus de parents immigrés vivent quotidiennement une situation fort complexe: d'une part, ils évoluent en France dans un environnement non arabisé qui généralement ne leur permet pas d'opérer des échanges dans leurs langues maternelles respectives; d'autre part, à l'école, (sous la tutelle des ambassades de leurs pays respectifs), ces enfants peuvent apprendre l'arabe standard moderne qui, généralement, n'est pas parlé par leurs parents et qui présente des différences importantes avec les différentes variétés maternelles (tunisien, algérien, marocain) tant au niveau lexical que morphosyntaxique.

9.6.2. Le berbère

Le berbère est très répandu au Maghreb: l'Algérie (20%) et le Maroc (45%) comptent le plus de berbérophones. Ces deux pays ayant fourni la plus grande partie de la population d'origine maghrébine en France, les berbérophones constituent, en France, une communauté d'origine étrangère des plus importantes. Confondus dans l'ensemble de l'immigration maghrébine, les berbérophones ou leurs descendants sont rangés par l'opinion courante dans la population dite « arabe » (Chaker 1988). Ainsi le berbère se présente-t-il comme une langue toujours « occultée » (idem) aussi bien au Maghreb qu'en France. Parmi les berbérophones, les locuteurs algériens du kabyle représentent actuellement le groupe qui revendique le plus son identité sociolinguistique.

9.7. Les langues d'Afrique Noire

L'implantation de la population d'Afrique Noire en France est relativement récente; elle s'est produite après l'indépendance des pays en question (vers 1960). Il est difficile de dresser un tableau exhaustif des comportements linguistiques de ces populations compte tenu de la diversité de leurs origines, de leur installation en France, de leur situation familiale. La grande majorité des ressortissants d'Afrique Noire, résidant dans la région parisienne, vient de l'Afrique de l'Ouest (Mauritanie, Mali, Sénégal, Guinée, Côte d'Ivoire) et, en moins grand nombre, de la Guinée Bissau, du Niger, du Bourkina Faso ou du Cameroun.

Il est préférable de donner l'inventaire de ces populations en tenant compte non pas des pays (d'où viennent les personnes) mais des diverses ethnies en nous référant, sur cette question, au classement (en ordre décroissant) établi par S. Platiel (1988, 10): les Sooninkés (Mauritanie, Sénégal), les Peuls (Mauritanie, Mali, Sénégal, Guinée, Niger, Cameroun), les Bambaras (Mali), les Malinkés regroupant divers parlers plus ou moins intercompréhensibles (Sénégal, Mali, Guinée, Guinée Bissau), les Dioulas (Mali, Côte-d'Ivoire), et une multitude d'autres ethnies moins représentées: Sérère (Sénégal), Touaregs (Mali, Niger), Mousis (Bourkina Faso), Douala et Bamilékés (Cameroun), etc. Dans cette multiplicité d'ethnies, on observe une mosaïque de comportements linguistiques allant de l'utilisation presque exclusive du français (intellectuels, étudiants ou autres) à l'ignorance quasi-totale de celui-ci. Beaucoup d'individus issus de tradition exclusivement orale, sommairement alphabétisés en français (le cas de la plupart des immigrés de la première génération), ont des difficultés d'accès à la culture française. Ainsi sur la base de ce seul critère, on peut répertorier les migrants originaires d'Afrique Noire installés en France en deux groupes: (1) Les individus ayant poursuivi des études de niveau élevé: ce sont généralement des intellectuels qui ont préféré s'installer en France plutôt que de retourner dans leurs pays. Ces personnes ont appris le français bien avant qu'elles soient venues en France et se sont habituées à le pratiquer quotidiennement. Cette familiarité avec le français implique-t-elle pour autant l'abandon de leur propre langue? Si l'individu appartient à une ethnie majoritaire (ce qui est le cas le plus fréquent), il est rare qu'il choisisse de ne plus parler sa langue d'origine quand l'occasion se présente. En général, ces individus conservent la pratique des deux langues. D'une manière générale, ils pratiquent un français très normé, désignent, sous l'effet de l'idéologie coloniale, leur(s) langue(s) nationale(s) comme « dialecte(s) », et si on leur parle de bilinguisme, ils pensent uniquement au bilinguisme français—anglais occultant ainsi fondamentalement le leur. (2) Les individus n'ayant pas fait d'études en français. Ils représentent la majorité des immigrés d'Afrique Noire (dits de la « première génération »). Ces personnes parlant peu ou pratiquement pas le français sont restées très attachées à leurs langues et cultures d'origine; le français ne représente pour elles qu'un outil de communication qu'elles utilisent en fonction de leurs besoins. La superposition des langues aboutit chez elles au développement d'un français rudimentaire (« petit nègre »).

9.8. Les langues des Départements et Territoires d'Outre-Mer (DOM-TOM)

L'installation des langues des DOM-TOM en France est étroitement liée à l'histoire des territoires et, plus précisément, aux guerres et traités qui se déroulaient en Europe du XVIIe au XIXe siècle. L'arrivée des Français s'est faite dans la plupart des territoires au XVIIe siècle (Tessonneau 1988, 165). Les périodes d'occupation française sont entrecoupées de périodes d'occupation anglaise ou portugaise. Des îles considérées aujourd'hui comme des ex-colonies britanniques (Saint-Vincent, la Dominique, Sainte-Lucie et Tobago) ont été des zones neutres occupées par quelques familles françaises avant d'être l'objet de conflit entre la France et la Grande-Bretagne. La Guadeloupe, la Martinique, la Guyane et la Réunion sont devenues des Départements d'Outre-Mer (DOM) par la loi du 19 mars 1946 mise en application le 1er janvier 1948. Il y a en France, en 1989, environ 175.000

individus originaires des DOM, principalement de la Martinique (72.000), de la Guadeloupe (60.000), de la Réunion (40.000) et avec un nombre moins important de Guyanais (3.000). L'arrivée de cette population (DOM) s'est faite généralement avant 1960, avec des étudiants, des militaires de carrière ou des fonctionnaires en congé administratif. A partir de 1960, l'armée a proposé aux jeunes gens du service militaire la possibilité de suivre une formation en France après leur service. Certains d'entre eux s'y installeront. A partir de 1973, le BUMIDOM (Bureau des migrations pour les DOM) freine la migration à cause de la situation économique de la France. Pour ce qui est du créole parlé en France, nous nous contenterons de dire que les variétés du créole parlées en France s'inscrivent dans une dynamique de *continuum* avec le français.

9.9. Les langues d'Europe

Bien sûr, toutes les langues d'Europe sont représentées en France: si nombre d'entre elles (anglais, allemand, néerlandais, tchèque, slovaque, langues scandinaves) ne sont pas mentionnées ici, c'est parce que leurs locuteurs sont généralement peu nombreux et dispersés ou en partie assimilés. On peut néanmoins en dresser un tableau provisoire.

9.9.1. L'espagnol

L'immigration espagnole en France est l'une des plus importantes du point de vue du nombre (352.232 au recensement de 1989). Elle se situe aujourd'hui à la quatrième position derrière les immigrations portugaise, algérienne et italienne. Cette immigration est souvent qualifiée aujourd'hui d'immigration « sans problème » (Taboada Leonetti 1988, 194). C'est une population discrète qui ne suscite apparemment pas beaucoup d'intérêt de la part des chercheurs. L'assimilation de cette population ne pose pas de problème majeur, cette dernière étant aujourd'hui en voie de disparition en tant que groupe distinct.

9.9.2. Le grec

Comptant 8.169 ressortissants en 1989, la communauté hellénique de France est composée, d'une part, de petits commerçants et artisans provenant surtout d'une immigration antérieure à celle de 1967 (putsch des colonels) et, d'autre part, d'une catégorie d'universitaires et de cadres supérieurs qui sont arrivés après 1967. Les ressortissants grecs sont organisés essentiellement autour de la « Communauté hellénique de Paris ». Cette association a la responsabilité du fonctionnement des écoles grecques en France. Celles-ci calquent leur programme sur le modèle des écoles en Grèce (Androussou 1988).

9.9.3. L'italien

Jusqu'à une date très récente, l'image des Italiens a été indiscutablement négative dans l'opinion française (ressemblant à celle des Maghrébins actuellement). La communauté d'origine italienne en France est l'une des plus importantes au point de vue du nombre (378.339 en 1989).

A partir d'une « répression douce », l'« italophonie honteuse » (Vegliante 1988, 224), risque d'aboutir à l'impasse de la langue maternelle « morte ».

9.9.4. Le polonais

La répartition des Polonais en France dans l'entre-deux-guerres correspond aux besoins du marché du travail. Dès leur arrivée, les populations migrantes, en particulier les « Westphaliens » (qui sont des Polonais d'origine prussienne ayant vécu longtemps en Westphalie) créent de multiples associations locales. Partiellement, à côté de l'apprentissage du français, l'enfant polonais suit souvent des cours de langue maternelle à l'école.

Les lois scolaires de Jules Ferry (1881–1883) avaient mis l'accent sur la diffusion des valeurs françaises aux dépens des langues et cultures régionales. Avant les Polonais, aucune communauté étrangère « n'avait cherché à entamer ce monopole » (Ponty/Masiewicz 1988, 269). En dehors du cadre scolaire, un certain nombre d'organisations proposent des cours de polonais: la bibliothèque polonaise du quai d'Orléans à Paris, l'Association France–Pologne, le Centre de Civilisation Polonaise, rattaché à l'Université de Paris IV, etc.

9.9.5. Le portugais

D'après le recensement de l'INSEE (1989), la communauté portugaise compte 846.499 individus. Avec un tel chiffre, cette population est devenue la plus importante communauté étrangère de France depuis 1975. En général, dans cette communauté, la langue d'origine est maintenue, et le français est relativement acquis oralement par les adultes. Selon Villanova (1988, 293–294), la nécessité de réussir l'insertion entraîne une « survalorisation » de la société d'accueil et une « dévalorisation » de la langue maternelle, associée à une situation familiale difficile qui, par amalgame, connote négativement la culture d'origine.

9.9.6. Les langues des immigrés turcs

La langue *turque* elle-même appartient au groupe des langues dites « ouralo-altaïques », et plus précisément à la branche altaïque turco-tartare. Cependant beaucoup d'immigrés turcs en France parlent des langues différentes: le *kurde*, qui est une langue indo-européenne de la branche iranienne, est présent, en France, dans ses deux variétés les plus importantes: le *zaza* et le *sorani* (Petek-Salom 1988, 305). Souvent privés d'accès aux différents éléments médiateurs, comme la presse, la radio, la télé, les échanges, les rencontres sur le lieu de travail et surtout l'échange socio-verbal avec les Français, les immigrés turcs, dans leur grande majorité de foi musulmane, s'emmurent dans la « quête de valeurs propres » ou se tournent vers d'autres « véhicules d'identifications » (idem). A noter toutefois les activités importantes des militants culturels kurdes.

9.9.7. Le serbe, le croate et les autres langues de l'ex-Yougoslavie

En France, la majorité de la population provient de la Serbie, mais on y trouve aussi une minorité importante de ressortissants d'autres régions. Leur nombre atteint, en 1989, environ 68.809 personnes. L'immigration de la population de l'ex-Yougoslavie est ancienne avec un grand nombre de naturalisés et de personnes nées en France. Pour la grande majorité des jeunes, le français devient progressivement leur langue dominante, alors que la langue des parents perd son poids et son caractère fonctionnel dans beaucoup de situations.

9.9.8. L'arménien

Considérée comme l'un des groupes d'origine étrangère les mieux intégrés à la vie sociale française, la communauté arménienne de France a été marquée à l'origine par les conditions de son arrivée en France (génocide des Arméniens en Turquie, 1915–1917). Cette population est touchée aujourd'hui par « les mouvements de revendication identitaire qui traversent les autres minorités ethniques de ce pays » (Andesian/Hovanessian 1988, 60). Installés principalement dans les grandes villes — Paris, Lyon, Marseille — les personnes d'origine arménienne sont pour la plupart des citoyens français, le reste étant composé de réfugiés ou d'immigrés de différentes nationalités. La détermination de la communauté arménienne de France à affirmer son identité est remarquable.

10. Langue(s) et identité(s)

Les débats médiatico-politiques actuels montrent que l'émergence d'une génération issue de l'immigration pose à la société française une série de questions. La répartition par nationalité fait apparaître comme largement majoritaires, dans l'immigration, les jeunes Portugais (28,5%) et Algériens (27,4% de l'ensemble de la population immigrée), suivis des Marocains (10,5%), des Espagnols (7,5%) et des Italiens (6%) (cf. Dabène/Billiez 1987, 63).

Notre propos est de décrire, ici, surtout la condition identitaire des Maghrébins, Espagnols et Portugais. La plupart des chercheurs précisent que chez ces jeunes, l'identité linguistique est fortement corrélée à l'identité ethnique.

En déclarant que l'arabe ou le berbère est sa langue réelle et véritable, le jeune maghrébin manifeste le désir d'appartenir à cette communauté, même si l'expérience a montré que cette identité ne correspond pas souvent à des pratiques effectives de la langue. C'est ainsi que la langue d'origine (prétendue parlée, voir maîtrisée par le locuteur) acquiert une valeur symbolique importante. Dabène/Billiez (1987, 65) ont montré, à travers l'analyse d'entretiens réalisés auprès de jeunes issus de l'immigration algérienne, portugaise et espagnole, que la langue d'origine « est la trace des racines ». Les personnes veulent la conserver en soi et souhaitent « la transmettre aux générations suivantes ». Les jeunes Espagnols « se représentent la langue comme un élément génétiquement constitutif de l'individu au même titre que le sang et la chair » (idem).

S'agissant des pratiques langagières en langue d'origine, Dabène/Billiez (1987, 67) distinguent quatre situations: (1) « les pratiques intenses »: le locuteur déclare parler sa langue d'origine avec ses parents ou lors du retour dans son pays d'origine; (2) « la pratique moyenne »: la personne affirme avoir recours à l'alternance de langues, c'est-à-dire à la commutation entre sa langue d'origine et le français selon les situations de communication dans lesquelles elle se trouve; (3) « la pratique non réciproque »: le sujet répond qu'il ne parle pas sa langue d'origine avec ses parents mais qu'il la comprend; (4) « la pratique nulle »: le locuteur affirme que l'usage de la langue d'origine est totalement absent du milieu familial.

Dabène/Billiez précisent que les jeunes Algériens, à une exception près, se situent dans les deux dernières catégories, à savoir une pratique non réciproque ou nulle de la langue d'origine. Quant aux sujets ibériques, ils reconnaissent une pratique moyenne, dans la mesure où, dans la majorité des cas, ils ont maintenu des liens étroits avec les pays d'origine.

Même si les comportements langagiers de ces individus ne peuvent être saisis de façon homogène, il semble qu'il s'agit d'une répartition fonctionnelle des langues. La langue d'origine, même en cas d'une mauvaise maîtrise, est réservée à l'usage informel, intime, aux échanges familiaux en direction des parents ou de la famille élargie lors des contacts fréquents avec le pays d'origine. Quant au français, il représente le code (social et linguistique) majoritaire, parlé en dehors du cadre familial, dans la rue ou en contact avec les institutions.

11. L'école

L'école constitue le milieu d'acquisition principal de la langue d'accueil. Il n'est certes pas le seul, mais il est celui qui met en contact l'enfant immigré avec la norme standard du français. Cette norme essentiellement représentée par l'écrit sera diversement intériorisée en fonction de la plus ou moins grande docilité sociale du sujet et de sa famille. Les problèmes spécifiques rencontrés par l'enfant issu de parents immigrés dans son parcours scolaire ne doivent pas être analysés en termes de déficit mais plutôt en termes d'organisation différente du répertoire linguistique (au sens gumperzien du terme) et de difficulté à passer d'une composante à l'autre; oraliser, par exemple, sur la base de l'écrit et vice-versa.

Un autre aspect de l'école est celui de l'enseignement des langues d'origine. En effet, la plupart des jeunes migrants fréquentent des cours parallèles dispensés généralement à l'initiative des Consulats. Ces cours, imposés par les parents, et presque toujours mal acceptés par les enfants pour des raisons diverses (éloignement du domicile, horaires peu propices, etc.), ne semblent pas avoir eu de résultats très appréciables d'un point de vue strictement linguistique. Néanmoins, ils représentent, pour ce public scolaire, un moment de contact avec la norme de la langue d'origine dont les pratiques langagières au sein de la famille sont très éloignées. Dans la majorité des cas, on n'enseigne pas, aux enfants maghrébins, par exemple, leurs langues *maternelles*; il s'agit plutôt de la langue *officielle* du pays dont les parents sont originaires.

12. L'alternance de langues

Un des phénomènes les plus caractérisants du parler du jeune issu de l'immigration est celui de l'alternance de langues (*code switching* → art. 73). Ce phénomène n'est possible qu'entre des locuteurs bilingues et de fait c'est surtout dans le milieu familial qu'on observe le plus ce type de phénomène. Les chercheurs, qui ont travaillé sur cette question, distinguent, par rapport aux comportements langagiers des bilingues, deux types d'alternance de langues:

– l'alternance de langues « d'incompétence » qui permet au bilingue de pallier ses insuffisances dans une langue en faisant appel à une autre.
– l'alternance de langues de « compétence » qui témoigne chez le sujet bilingue de la possibilité d'utiliser tantôt une langue tantôt l'autre pour répondre à ses besoins expressifs.

Nous pouvons avancer avec réserve, qu'en France, les migrants de la première génération sont caractérisés par le premier type d'alternance alors que chez les générations suivantes, c'est le second type d'alternance qui prévaut. Pour Dabène/Billiez (1987, 74), il y a alternance de langues « toutes les fois que le locuteur remet en cause un choix de langue qu'il a lui-même antérieurement effectué ». Nous l'avons déjà écrit (Laroussi 1991) que ce type de discours n'est pas toujours l'indice d'une mauvaise compétence dans la langue étrangère mais qu'il peut s'agir d'une stratégie communicationnelle souvent « stylistique » que la situation de communication appelle et dont dispose le locuteur pour mieux gérer une interaction fort hétérogène.

L'alternance de langues pourrait être interprétée comme l'adhésion à un certain contexte et revêtir aussi une fonction emblématique. Par ailleurs, l'usage de l'alternance de langues peut servir à des fins totalement opposées: il permet au locuteur, par exemple, de prendre du recul vis-à-vis des propos de son interlocuteur. En tant que stratégie de distanciation, l'alternance peut être considérée comme un marqueur d'identité qui pose ainsi sa cohésion par rapport au groupe monolingue dominant. Un Maghrébin qui parle français en émaillant ses propos de segments ou de phrases arabes ou berbères marque ainsi sa connivence et une certaine solidarité avec son interlocuteur: « je sais que tu comprends, donc je peux le dire » (fonction emblématique).

Il y a encore d'autres phénomènes qui caractérisent le parler du migrant: il s'agit des « marques transcodiques » (Lüdi 1985). On peut, par exemple, citer le cas de *l'emprunt*, c'est-à-dire la présence, dans un énoncé en langue A, d'un item (généralement lexical) appartenant à une langue B. Pour ce qui est du transfert (ou calque), le terme conserve sa racine lexicale dans une langue mais adopte les marques morphologiques d'une autre: par exemple, la *banque* deviendra, en arabe, « lba:nka ».

13. Les emprunts réciproques

Nous présenterons, ici, l'emprunt (le plus souvent sous forme d'un item lexical) comme une alternance qui s'est généralisée et qui se trouve totalement intégrée dans le système morphosyntaxique de la langue Y (langue d'arrivée).

Il est bien connu que le contact interlinguistique ne produit pas des effets à sens unique; d'où la richesse potentielle d'une telle situation de plurilinguisme.

En ce qui est des comportements langagiers des Maghrébins arabophones, on entend souvent employer, dans des discours tenus en arabe, des termes tels que *marši* (marché), *minitel* (fr. minitel), *tjersi* (tiercé), *šomoeur* (chômeur), ou *mšoemir* (par addition d'affixes). D'autres emprunts constituent même le paradigme de conjugaison: le nom (français) « téléphone » a donné (en arabe tunisien) *telefu:n* qui a donné à son tour *ytalfan* (il téléphone) ou *telfnu:* (ils ont téléphoné). D'autres procédés de calque ou de métaphorisation peuvent être signalés. Prenons par exemple le verbe « blanchir » (en français) qui, on le sait, peut avoir différentes significations (« rendre blanc, recouvrir d'une matière blanche » ou « disculper » « innocenter »). Il m'était arrivé d'entendre un jeune tunisien résidant en France employer le verbe *ybaidh* (l'équivalent de « blanchir » en arabe tunisien) dans le sens de « disculper » ou « innocenter » alors que le verbe arabe ne connaît pas ce sens-là. Dans le cadre des emprunts entre français et arabe, il est souvent difficile de savoir si ces emprunts sont issus de l'immigration ou s'ils résultent d'une situation antérieure, celle du contact des deux systèmes linguistiques en Afrique du Nord pendant la période de la colonisation. Dans le sens arabe — français, les francophones (surtout dans un registre familier) ont emprunté des termes tels que *chouia*, *bled*, *kif-kif*, etc.

Concernant le contact entre le français et le polonais, selon Ponty/Masiewicz (1988, 274), l'influence française la plus facilement repérable se manifeste sur le plan lexical. Les auteurs distinguent deux types d'emprunt, les « mots français non assimilés » et « ceux qui ont subi une intégration morphologique ». Même si les auteurs ne considèrent pas le premier type d'« emprunts véritables », ces emprunts « se trouvent souvent dans la même phrase à côté du mot polonais, tantôt comme un équivalent absolu » (ibid.). Les auteurs affirment que ces derniers emprunts se manifestent beaucoup chez les personnes dites de « première génération ». En voici quelques exemples: *aksy'dan* (accident), *ekono'mik* (économique), *paty'sry* (patisserie). Quant aux emprunts « véritables » introduits dans le vocabulaire de la diaspora polonaise, ils sont « polonisés soit à l'aide d'une désinence, soit par l'adjonction d'affixes polonais ». Voici deux exemples: *ten aperytif* « cet apéritif », *ten asuras* « cette assurance ». On peut aussi avancer le cas des noms qui ont été adaptés au paradigme de dérivation polonaise: *na arbazu* « dans l'herbage », *nie bierz aspiratora* « ne prends pas l'aspirateur », ou *jedzie kamionem* « il roule en camion », etc.

Les dérivés dont le mot français constitue la base complétée par un affixe polonais, représentent le deuxième groupe d'emprunts intégrés: par exemple, des créations nominales ayant reçu les suffixes suivants: — dans *kesa* (caisse), *szena* (chaîne (de télévision)), *-ka* très productif en polonais comme diminutif: *kamionetka* (camionette), *marmazelka* (mademoiselle), etc. Hérédia (1987, 112) a qualifié d'« hybrides » les termes issus du contact linguistique dont une partie appartient à une langue et l'autre à l'autre langue. Par exemple, le contact entre le français et le portugais fait ressortir chez les immigrés portugais l'emploi des termes tels que le *courdeur* < pg. *corredor* «couloir», *la fite* < pg. *fita* «ruban».

14. Les créations ethno-lexicales

Comme l'a signalé Gumperz (1989, 61), lorsque l'idéologie politique et les normes sociales changent, les attitudes à l'égard des parlers minorés peuvent changer également; les locuteurs se mettent alors à les revendiquer comme partie intégrante et composante essentielle de l'identification. L'auteur donne l'exemple du «pocho ou calo» qui était en Californie et ailleurs dans le Sud-Ouest américain «un terme péjoratif» désignant l'espagnol des Chicanos. Mais «de par l'éveil de la conscience ethnique et de la fierté des traditions folkloriques locales» le pocho ou calo est devenu «le symbole des valeurs ethniques chicanos» et est «employé de plus en plus et de manière efficace dans la poésie et dans la prose chicanos modernes (...)». Pour revenir en France, on peut par exemple citer, dans le domaine de la musique, le Rap en tant que musique contestataire (*to rap*: frapper, *to rap out an oath*: lâcher un juron), qui témoigne d'une volonté d'affirmer son originalité et sa différence. En France, ce courant est représenté surtout par les Africains mêlant, sur le plan strictement linguistique, langues africaines et français.

Dans le même domaine, on peut citer des chanteurs tels que Chab Khaled ou Najat Atabou combinant intentionnellement différentes langues dans leurs chansons. Najat Atabou «n'arrivant plus à endurer les difficultés de l'immigration», a chanté par exemple: *ana zi:t, ana zi:t* «je suis revenue, je suis revenue», *j'ani marre* «j'en ai marre», *wahha* «oui», *j'ani marre*. Pour finir, on peut considérer aussi que la chanson en immigration a beaucoup servi la revendication berbère.

15. Conclusion

Nés et scolarisés en France, les jeunes issus de l'immigration peuvent à juste titre être considérés comme des *francophones*. Toutefois cette qualification doit être nuancée car elle ne rend compte que partiellement de la complexité du répertoire verbal de ceux-ci. Le rôle de la famille, les relations souvent maintenues avec les pays d'origine, le sentiment d'appartenance ethno-culturel «ont entraîné chez eux le développement d'une forme de bilinguisme qui leur est spécifique et qu'il serait regrettable de voir disparaître avec la génération suivante au profit d'un monolinguisme sans nul doute appauvrissant» (Dabène/Billiez 1987, 77). Leur déchirement ne serait-il pas proportionnellement lié au regard porté par la société française sur eux? Celle-ci tantôt les considère comme des Français *de fait*, tantôt elle en fait des Français *pas comme les autres*, puisqu'ils sont aussi «immigrés», «maghrébins», «arabes», «beurs», «jeunes de deuxième génération»...

Si l'on fait le compte des locuteurs effectifs ou virtuels de diverses langues de France (langues régionales ou autres, langues non-territorialisées, langues déterritorialisées), on s'aperçoit que le bilinguisme hérité de la famille ou qu'on désire récupérer, est un phénomène massif. On est même étonné que d'aucuns se soient tellement évertués à prôner le bilinguisme alors qu'il est là constamment sous les yeux. Mais pour comprendre le bilinguisme et le langage, il faut s'y faire et ne pas passer à côté de l'essentiel parce qu'on s'est mis ou laissé mettre des œillères.

16. Bibliographie (sélective)

Andesian, S./Hovanessian, M. (1988): «L'arménien. Langue rescapée d'un génocide». In: Vermes, tome 2, 60–84.

Androussou, A. (1988): «Le grec. Son image dans une petite communauté». In: Vermes, tome 2, 218–233.

Balibar, Renée (1985): *L'institution du français: essai sur le colinguisme des Carolingiens à la République*, Paris.

Balibar, Renée/Laporte, Dominique (1974): *Le français national*, Paris.

Brunot, Ferdinand (1972): *Histoire de la langue française des origines à nos jours*, Paris, 13 tomes (réédition).

Carton, Fernand (1987): «Les accents régionaux». In: Vermes/Boutet, tome 2, 29–49.

Chaker, S. (1988): «Le berbère. Une langue occultée, en exil». In: Vermes, tome 2, 145–164.

Chiorboli, Jean (Ed.) (1991): *Les langues polynomiques*, Corte (PULA 3/4).

Dabène, L./Billiez, J. (1987): «Le parler des jeunes issus de l'immigration». In: Vermes/Boutet, tome 2, 62–77.

De Certeau, Michel/Julia, Dominique/Revel, Jacques (1975): *Une politique de la langue. La Révolution française et les patois*, Paris.

Ertel, R. (1988): «Le yiddish. Entre élection et interdit». In: Vermes, tome 1, 332−359.

Gardin, B. (1975): «Loi Deixonne et langues régionales: représentation de la nature et de la fonction de leur enseignement». In: *Langue Française 25*, 29−36.

Gardy, Philippe/Lafont, Robert (1981): «La diglossie comme conflit: l'exemple occitan». In: *Langages 61*, 75−87.

Giacomo, Mathée (1975): «La politique à propos des langues régionales: cadre historique». In: *Langue Française 25*, 12−28.

Giordan, Henri (1982): *Démocratie culturelle et droit à la différence: rapport au ministre de la culture*, Paris.

Gumperz, John (1989): *Sociolinguistique interactionnelle*, Paris.

Hassoun, J. P. (1988a): «Le hmong. Une langue en absence d'écriture et une petite communauté». In: Vermes, tome 2, 120−131.

Hassoun, J. P. (1988b): «Le chinois. Une langue d'émigrés». In: Vermes, tome 2, 132−144.

Hérédia (de), C. (1987): «Du bilinguisme au parler bilingue». In: Vermes/Boutet, tome 2, 93−129.

Laroussi, Foued (1991): *L'alternance de codes arabe dialectal−français: étude de quelques situations dans la ville de Sfax (Tunisie)*, Thèse de doctorat, Rouen, 2 tomes.

Laroussi, Foued/Marcellesi, Jean-Baptiste (1990): «Le français et les langues en France». In: *La Pensée 277*, 45−61.

Lefebvre, Anne (1988): «Les langues du domaine d'oïl. Des langues trop proches». In: Vermes, tome 1, 261−290.

Lüdi, Georges (1985): «Aspects lexicaux du parler bilingue de migrants suisses-alémaniques à Neuchâtel». In: *Actes du XVIIe Congrès International de Linguistique et Philologie romanes*, Aix-en-Provence, vol. 7 (Contacts de langues, discours oral), 28−47.

Madray, F./Marcellesi, Jean-Baptiste (1981): «Langues de France et nation». In: *La Pensée 221/222*, 18−31.

Marcellesi, Jean-Baptiste (1975): «L'enseignement des 'langues régionales'». In: *Langue Française 25*, 3−11.

Marcellesi, Jean-Baptiste (1984): «La définition des langues en domaine roman; les enseignements à tirer de la situation corse». In: *Actes du XVIIe Congrès de Linguistique et Philologie Romanes*, Aix-en-Provence, vol. 5 (Sociolinguistique), 307−314.

Marcellesi, Jean-Baptiste (1985): *Pour une politique démocratique de la langue*, Ajaccio.

Petek-Salom, G. (1988): «Le turc. Une langue en ghetto». In: Vermes, tome 2, 301−316.

Platiel, S. (1988): «Les langues d'Afrique Noire en France». In: Vermes, tome 2, 9−30.

Ponty, J./Masiewicz, A. (1988): «Le polonais. Immigré depuis trois générations». In: Vermes, tome 2, 263−282.

Sephiha, A. (1988): «Le judéo-espagnol. Une langue sans interlocuteur. Le judéo-arabe: le parler arabe d'une communauté». In: Vermes, tome 2, 305−331.

Taboada Leonetti, I. (1988): «L'espagnol. Langue nationale de référence». In: Vermes, tome 2, 194−217.

Tessonneau, A. (1988): «Le créole en métropole. Point d'ancrage de l'identité DOM». In: Vermes, tome 2, 165−193.

Tuaillon, Gaston (1988a): «Le franco-provençal. Langue oubliée». In: Vermes, tome 1, 188−207.

Tuaillon, Gaston (1988b): «Le français régional. Formes de rencontre». In: Vermes, tome 1, 291−300.

Vegliante, J. C. (1988): «L'italien. Une italophonie honteuse». In: Vermes, tome 2, 234−262.

Vermes, Geneviève (Ed.) (1988): *Vingt-cinq communautés linguistiques de la France*, Paris, 2 tomes; tome 1: *Langues régionales et langues non-territorialisées*; tome 2: *Les langues immigrées*.

Vermes, Geneviève/Boutet, Josiane (1987): *France, pays multilingue*, Paris, 2 tomes; tome 1: *Les langues en France, un enjeu historique et social*; tome 2: *Pratiques des langues en France*.

Villanova (de), R. (1988): «Le portugais: Une langue qui se ressource en circulant». In: Vermes, tome 2, 283−300.

Walter, Henriette (1988): *Le français dans tous les sens*, Paris.

Weber, M. H. (1987): Le Yiddish. In: *Cahiers de Linguistique Sociale 10* [Rouen, Greco-Ired].

Williams, P. (1988): «Langue tsigane. Le jeu 'romanès'». In: Vermes, tome 1, 381−413.

Jean-Baptiste Marcellesi/Foued Laroussi, Rouen (France)

143. Français—occitan

1. Géographie et démographie
2. Histoire
3. Politique, économie, situations culturelle et religieuse en général
4. Statistiques et profils ethniques
5. Situation sociolinguistique
6. Etat de la politique linguistique
7. Portrait général des contacts linguistiques
8. Examen critique de la bibliographie
9. Bibliographie (sélective)

1. Géographie et démographie

L'espace où l'on parle aujourd'hui occitan (oc.) couvre à peu près 200.000 km² et compte ainsi parmi les grands domaines linguistiques en Europe. Il se trouve à peu d'exceptions près à l'intérieur de l'Etat français. Dans une certaine mesure, il s'agit d'un espace fictif, étant donné que partout l'oc. est aujourd'hui en coexistence avec le fr.; l'on pense qu'il n'y a plus de locuteurs monolingues. Le domaine géographique de l'oc. couvre *grosso modo* le tiers méridional de la France. Au sud, il faut en enlever la partie occidentale du département des Pyrénées Atlantiques qui fait partie du domaine basque (*Iparralde* ou *Euskadi-Nord*) et le département des Pyrénées Orientales qui est de langue catalane (sauf le Fenouillet, qui est considéré comme oc.; il s'agit en réalité d'une zone de transition qui couvre la zone la plus méridionale de l'oc. et la plus septentrionale du catalan). Au nord, la limite linguistique avec les variétés les plus méridionales du fr. se trouve d'abord sur les rives de la Gironde pour ensuite se tourner vers le nord, laissant à l'oc. le Limousin et l'Auvergne, avec une zone de transition au nord, appelée le *croissant*. Plus à l'est, la limite descend vers le sud, laissant Saint-Etienne juste en domaine francoprovençal, traverse le Rhône au nord de Valence et atteint la frontière italienne après un parcours assez accidenté, laissant Grenoble en domaine francoprovençal. L'on sait qu'une partie des hautes vallées alpines en Italie est de langue oc. Il y a quelques enclaves historiques: françaises surtout à l'ouest (les Gavacheries), italiennes à l'est (Monaco). Pour plus de détails cf. Ronjat (1930—1941, vol. I, 10 sq) et Bec (⁵1986, 8 sq). Des îlots de langue oc. se trouvent en Catalogne (Val d'Aran; → art. 151) et Italie (Calabre; → art. 159); autrefois il y en avait aussi en Allemagne du Sud et même en Amérique (Argentine); → cartes linguistiques D et F.

Il n'y a pas de recensements linguistiques, étant donné que tous les Français sont censés parler le fr. Cela rend illusoire toute indication précise du nombre des locuteurs de l'oc. L'on sait qu'environ 12,5 millions de personnes vivent dans les régions de langue oc. Mais certaines parties du domaine oc. sont des terres d'immigration, d'autres ont connu, au moins dans le passé, une émigration importante. Il faudrait par conséquent compter p. ex. Paris et Lyon parmi les grandes villes oc. (on sait qu'il s'y trouve toujours des foyers d'occitanité), alors que certaines villes en domaine oc. sont aujourd'hui presque entièrement désoccitanisées. Ce processus s'est accentué, à certains endroits, pendant les dernières vingt-cinq années. La Région du Languedoc-Roussillon a récemment fait faire un premier sondage selon les méthodes modernes de démoscopie. Les résultats, qui semblent en gros fiables, indiquent que près de 50% de la population de la partie oc. de cette région (environ 1 750 000 personnes représentées) comprennent l'oc., que 28% savent parler la langue, que 9% la parlent souvent, que 13% savent la lire et que seuls 6% sont capables de l'écrire (Média Pluriel 1991, 10). Ces résultats sont meilleurs pour l'oc. que l'on ne pouvait craindre, la désoccitanisation ayant fait des progrès considérables depuis la reprise économique du sud, il y a quinze ans. L'implantation de la langue oc. est la plus forte dans les petites communes agricoles et parmi les personnes âgées, donc dans des zones résiduelles, et tous les indicateurs montrent que le mouvement de substitution continue. L'on ne sait pas, si ces résultats se laissent extrapoler à d'autres régions oc. Si on le fait, avec beaucoup de précaution, on peut supposer que près de trois millions de personnes savent (peut-être) parler la langue et qu'un million la parle effectivement de façon plus ou moins régulière (pour d'autres estimations et calculs, cf. Kremnitz 1981, 11 sq). Toute indication supplémentaire relèverait de la pseudo-exactitude.

2. Histoire

Le rattachement des terres oc. au domaine des rois de France a été un processus multiséculaire. Il commence par l'héritage des terres des Comtes de Toulouse (1271), à la suite de la croisade contre les Cathares (1209–1229). Cette croisade marque la fin de la civilisation médiévale (trobadoresque) oc. et de l'essor des premiers grands centres urbains ou de ce que l'on a appelé parfois « l'accélération » de ces régions. A partir de ce moment-là, l'oc. est virtuellement en situation de dépendance, même si les conditions pour une politique linguistique ne sont pas encore réunies. D'autres étapes importantes seront l'acquisition définitive d'une grande partie de la Gascogne (appelée alors Guyenne) à la suite de la bataille de Castillon et de la fin de la guerre de Cent Ans (1453/1455), l'héritage de la Provence en 1481 après la mort de René d'Anjou, dernier roi de Provence, et l'annexion du Béarn (royaume de Navarre) en 1607. D'autres terres oc. qui appartiennent à diverses familles royales, passent peu à peu sous l'influence directe des rois de France. Pendant la Révolution, Avignon et le Comtat Venaissin sont rattachés à la France. En 1860 c'est finalement le tour du Comté de Nice.

Ce rattachement successif aux terres des rois de France crée les conditions pour le contact ultérieur des deux langues. Le manque d'unité politique du domaine oc. empêche cependant que les relations panoccitanes, existantes dans la période des trobadors, soient maintenues voire élargies à d'autres couches sociales et que le sentiment d'unité linguistique devienne très profond. Après l'annexion du Comté de Toulouse il n'y avait plus de pouvoir oc. de quelque durée, capable de maintenir voire de créer un développement culturel indépendant. Dorénavant, l'histoire de l'Occitanie (ou des terres occitanes appartenant à la France) se confond avec l'histoire de la France.

3. Politique, économie, situations culturelle et religieuse en général

Sur le plan politique, il n'y a — de nos jours — aucune entité territoriale qui corresponde au domaine oc. L'unité territoriale de base continue à être le département; or, le sol oc. est couvert par une bonne trentaine de départements, parfois les limites linguistiques et les limites politiques ne coïncident pas. Ces départements forment en gros les régions d'Aquitaine, Midi-Pyrénées, Languedoc-Roussillon (moins les Pyrénées Orientales), Provence-Côte d'Azur, Limousin, Auvergne plus une partie de Rhône-Alpes. Pendant longtemps, les régions oc. votaient majoritairement pour la gauche, mais depuis les élections régionales de 1990 toutes les régions sont dirigées par la droite, et la majorité, parfois écrasante, de la gauche (occitane) à l'Assemblée Nationale n'existe plus depuis 1993. Il faudra voir si, sur le plan communal, la gauche pourra sauver sa prépondérance qui d'ailleurs remonte souvent à la fin du XIXe siècle. Trois des régions commencent à mener, depuis quelques années, une politique active de soutien à la langue et à la culture oc.: Languedoc-Roussillon, Midi-Pyrénées et Provence-Côte d'Azur; une quatrième, Aquitaine, semble se diriger vers une attitude comparable. Bien que cette politique reste dans des limites relativement étroites, elle signifie une rupture profonde avec la politique nationale antérieure qui avait pour but explicite la disparition des langues minoritaires du sol français (cf. Kremnitz 1992).

Il ne paraît pas possible de donner une description quelque peu complète de la situation économique du domaine oc.: avec plus de 200 000 km^2 il est plus grand que bien des Etats indépendants. Longtemps connu pour le maintien d'une agriculture parfois archaïque (viticulture et élevage), l'espace oc. est aujourd'hui caractérisé par son extrême diversité: des restes d'un secteur primaire parfois peu rentable subsistent, surtout dans des zones de montagne, mais la viticulture languedocienne p. ex. s'est profondément modernisée après la crise des années 60/70. Des villes comme Montpellier, Toulouse ou Bordeaux comptent aujourd'hui parmi les centres d'innovation économique en France. De ce point de vue, la régionalisation mitterandienne, amorcée au début des années 80, a certainement déjà porté ses fruits. Entre ces points d'attraction la désertification des campagnes s'accentue, difficilement neutralisée par le développement du tourisme, autre activité importante. Le déchirement interne des terres d'oc. n'a pas pris fin.

L'on sait qu'un des points de départ de la minorisation du sud était la différence religieuse, le catharisme; il était suivi par la présence d'autres religions ou confessions dissidentes sur le sol oc. Des intellectuels oc. ont voulu en tirer une « essence » hétérodoxe des Occitans (surtout René Nelli, cf. 1968); il faut se méfier de telles interprétations qui dégénèrent facilement en idéologie. Mais il convient de rappeler que dans une France essentiellement catholique, certaines régions de langue oc. ont une tradition calviniste, comme le

Béarn, les Cévennes et certaines parties du sud-ouest, et que d'autres ont un passé valdéiste. Même parmi les catholiques, il y a eu des scissions qui ont parfois duré longtemps (notamment sous la Révolution). Ce n'est pas d'hier qu'on assiste, dans le domaine spirituel, à une polarisation de la société entre une laïcisation accrue et un intégrisme religieux accentué, mais également entre différents groupes religieux. La deuxième religion, quant au nombre des fidèles, est aujourd'hui l'islam, comme partout en France.

4. Statistiques et profils ethniques

Tous les habitants du Tiers Sud de la France parlent fr.; un pourcentage qui pourrait approcher celui que je viens d'indiquer (cf. 1.), parle également oc. L'absence de statistiques ne laisse d'autre choix que d'extrapoler avec beaucoup de précaution les résultats de recherches ponctuelles. Il faut distinguer entre deux catégories de locuteurs de l'oc.: les locuteurs primaires qui ont appris la langue naturellement, dans l'interaction familiale, et pour lesquels elle a une fonction pratique, et les locuteurs secondaires qui ont appris la langue à la suite d'une décision consciente, le plus souvent à l'école ou à l'université, et pour lesquels elle a commencé par avoir une fonction symbolique (cf. Schlieben-Lange 1971, 43−45; Kremnitz 1974, 345). On ne trouve pratiquement plus de locuteurs ne parlant pas fr., et même ceux qui le parlent difficilement sont très rares. Actuellement, les locuteurs primaires commencent à disparaître: ceux qui meurent ne sont plus remplacés par des jeunes. Il suffit de rappeler, à titre d'exemple, que, parmi 1000 élèves interrogés vers 1983, il y en avait 0,7% qui ont indiqué avoir appris le fr. et l'oc. en même temps (Rogge 1987, 89). Cela veut dire que le degré de compétence linguistique collective baisse, mais en même temps que son profil se redessine: les locuteurs secondaires dont le nombre augmente lentement, ont en général une compétence relativement élevée dans les domaines de la lecture et de la compréhension passive, tandis qu'ils s'expriment plus difficilement que les locuteurs primaires. Même s'ils savent écrire l'oc., ils acquièrent rarement un degré supérieur de compétence. Cela veut dire que souvent leur manque de pratique orale les fait éviter les entretiens en oc. Il est impossible d'appuyer ces observations, faites pendant les dernières vingt-cinq années, par des données statistiques.

On trouve le plus grand nombre de locuteurs primaires parmi les agriculteurs et parmi ceux qui travaillent dans le secteur primaire, c'est-à-dire parmi les couches socialement défavorisées. Le degré de compétence est le plus élevé parmi les personnes âgées, en général davantage chez les hommes que chez les femmes. Ces catégories de personnes se trouvent surtout dans des villages. S'ils ont peu quitté leur lieu de naissance, il en résulte souvent une compétence encore plus élevée. Ces données valent souvent pour des régions de montagne avec des réseaux de transport peu développés. A partir de ces données statistiques, il serait possible de dresser un portrait-fantôme des meilleurs locuteurs de l'oc.

Si la dénomination *occitan* semble aujourd'hui être acceptée dans les milieux scientifiques, parce qu'elle ne prête pas à confusion, il n'en est pas ainsi parmi les usagers. A côté du terme d'oc., on trouve toujours des dénominations particularisantes comme *provençal* ou *gascon*. Ceci est dû en partie à l'histoire qui n'a guère favorisé le développement d'une conscience collective panoccitane, en partie aussi à la lutte que les pouvoirs fr. ont longtemps menée contre les langues minoritaires. Sur le terrain, on trouve également le terme de *patois* qui s'emploie couramment pour désigner des variétés locales (et qui par conséquent est localiste et néglige par là l'appartenance d'une variété locale à un ensemble plus grand), souvent avec une nuance péjorative (qui peut cependant avoir des connotations affectives dans la bouche de certains locuteurs). Le terme d'*oc.* est cependant en progrès, également parmi les locuteurs. Après 1945, il y avait une opposition très nette entre les défenseurs du terme d'*oc.*, en général proches de l'Institut d'Etudes Occitanes (fondé en 1945, issu de la Résistance, politiquement orienté plutôt à gauche), et ceux qui préféraient des termes tels que *provençal*, surtout dans les milieux proches du Félibrige (fondé en 1854, en majorité proche du régime de Vichy); cette opposition idéologique existe toujours, mais elle s'est nettement affaiblie.

5. Situation sociolinguistique

Le fr. est toujours la seule langue à avoir un statut officiel en France; l'ajout récent à la constitution a, une fois de plus, précisé cette situation. Néanmoins, le temps de la « chasse aux patois » est terminé, les langues minoritaires ont presque disparu du sol français. Cette disparition a privé la France d'un certain nombre d'atouts, même du point de vue commercial et politique si bien qu'on peut leur concéder maintenant un petit espace public. La *loi Deixonne* de 1951 qui a un peu ouvert les portes de l'école à certaines langues minoritaires, a entériné l'existence légale de l'oc. pour la première fois. Suivant la loi Haby de 1975, les langues régionales peuvent être enseignées pendant toute la scolarité. Les derniers amendements du statut de l'oc. datent de la circulaire Savary (1982) qui a amélioré les conditions de l'enseignement. Les mesures que le rapport Giordan (Giordan 1982) a préconisées pour offrir aux langues de France une «réparation historique» n'ont jamais trouvé de réalisation. En 1985, le gouvernement Fabius a créé un *Conseil National des Langues et Cultures Régionales* qui n'a jamais vraiment fonctionné. Le statut de l'oc. reste précaire (cf. Rouquette 1987). Au début des années 80, la région du Languedoc-Roussillon a déclaré coofficiels l'oc. et le catalan, mais cette mesure est restée symbolique.

Ce statut précaire de l'oc. explique pourquoi il ne remplit guère de fonctions formelles. Il y a bien sûr les occitanistes (ou provençalistes) convaincus qu'ils l'emploient pour toutes les fonctions, mais en général, il reste confiné aux emplois informels. Les emplois publics, écrits ou oraux, et la production littéraire existent, certes, mais leur impact reste limité.

La situation de contact entre fr. et oc. est une situation clairement diglossique (emplois différents, différemment connotés, une partie des locuteurs seulement parlant la langue dominée). C'est pourquoi la sociolinguistique oc. a fait siennes les analyses catalanes du *conflit linguistique* (cf. Gardy/Lafont 1981). Les éléments conflictuels, très vivaces, il y a vingt ans, sont moins nets aujourd'hui. Cela est dû à la disparition progressive des locuteurs primaires, à la reconnaissance partielle et timide des années 80, qui a toutefois satisfait un certain nombre de demandes et réintégré dans une certaine mesure les langues minoritaires de France. Un des facteurs pour l'amélioration de leur situation est sans doute l'immigration avec ses conséquences linguistiques. Tous ces facteurs ont contribué à faire disparaître, dans une large mesure, la conscience «patoisante» des locuteurs, sans que les attitudes plus positives envers l'oc. aient vraiment changé le comportement linguistique (R. Lafont, 1967, a jadis proposé le terme d'*aliénation* ethnique et linguistique, R. Ninyoles, 1969, celui de *auto-odi*, haine de soi). Certaines images qui marquaient autrefois le locuteur oc. mènent toutefois une vie souterraine dure et réapparaissent facilement. Cela résulte entre autres des expériences que Markhof a faites: face à une image assez positive de l'oc. qui ressort de son enquête (1987, 264 sq), un test opérant selon les techniques du *matched guise* montre que les préjugés anciens (arriéré, vieillot, etc.) reviennent facilement. Ces résultats sont confirmés par plusieurs travaux publiés dans la revue *Lengas* (Montpellier).

6. Etat de la politique linguistique

6.1. Emploi public (normalisation)

Le fr. étant l'unique langue officielle en France, la reconnaissance de l'oc. ne dépasse pas des limites légales très étroites. Parfois, on trouve sur des affiches, sous le nom français, le nom occitan des communes, (p. ex. à Orange ou dans plusieurs villes de l'Aude), parfois les noms des rues sont marqués dans les deux langues (p. ex. à Montpellier ou à Béziers). Ni l'administration, ni la justice n'utilisent l'oc., même si à partir de 1981 son emploi en justice n'est plus puni.

L'oc. a pu se tailler une certaine place dans l'enseignement. Cela a commencé par la *loi Deixonne* en 1951 dont la portée a été améliorée par plusieurs circulaires ministérielles. Cette loi a donné une place facultative à l'oc. au lycée mais non pas dans le primaire où, vers 1951, il y avait encore des enfants qui au début de leur scolarisation ne parlaient pas français. Le nombre des participants à l'épreuve facultative du baccalauréat monte de 236 (1952) à environ 9000 (vers 1980). La circulaire Savary de 1982 inclut l'oc. dans le nombre des langues *étrangères* (sic!) au programme. Au milieu des années 80, il y avait selon des statistiques officielles 66 000 élèves dans les classes d'oc., dont 13 000 dans le secondaire. Les classes bilingues, admises suivant la loi, sont toujours peu nombreuses, bien que dans certains départements des enseignants convaincus aient beaucoup fait pour les promouvoir. Il y a également un mouvement d'écoles privées, appelées *Calandretas*, important surtout au niveau des maternelles et du primaire. Mais dans l'ensemble, le nombre des élèves bénéficiant d'un enseignement de l'oc. reste très bas. Même la nomination des premiers professeurs titulaires du CAPES en été 1992 ne change rien à cette situation; c'est une nouvelle victoire symbolique qui signifie l'intégration de l'oc. dans les matières scolaires, pas plus (cf. pour le rôle de l'oc. à l'école les travaux de Rogge 1987, Markhof 1987, Cichon 1988).

Dans les médias, presque entièrement privatisés, la place de l'oc. reste modeste. Dans les chaînes régionales de télévision, l'oc. a droit à quelques minutes d'émission, avec des différences notables entre les stations (à Toulouse et Montpellier, une émission hebdomadaire d'une demi-heure, à Marseille également, dans les autres stations pas d'émissions régulières; parfois des émissions spéciales). Il semble que la situation est meilleure en ce qui concerne la radio. Surtout quelques stations locales semblent s'engager pour l'emploi de la langue. On observe cependant des changements considérables, étant donné que l'engagement oc. des stations est souvent lié à l'engagement personnel de certains leaders culturels. Il semble que ces émissions suivent souvent des conceptions modernes et essayent de rendre compte de la vie actuelle; c'est important puisqu'elles contribuent ainsi à libérer l'oc. de sa réputation passéiste. Elles ne peuvent cependant proposer que des fragments de civilisation oc. à leurs auditeurs.

Quant à la presse écrite, l'impression est contradictoire. Il n'y a pas de périodique paraissant à intervalles brefs en oc. (à l'exception d'un hebdomadaire depuis 1995). Il y a quelques mensuels qui ne permettent pas de saisir vraiment l'actualité. En plus, ils ont des tirages restreints et une mauvaise distribution. Ce manque n'est compensé que partiellement par le fait que des quotidiens de langue fr., p. ex. à Toulouse, Bordeaux, Montpellier ou Marseille, publient régulièrement ou de temps en temps des textes en oc. Dans ce domaine encore la situation est peu stable.

Après 1968, parmi les facteurs les plus importants pour une audience plus large des revendications oc., c'est la chanson qui a pu attirer de larges publics (une trentaine de chanteurs sur disque, parmi eux: Martí (Carcassonne), Mans de Breish (Carcassonne), Patric (Montpellier), Jacmelina (Montauban), Eric Fraj (Toulouse), etc.), et les troupes de théâtre (surtout le *Teatre de la Carrièra*, près d'Arles). Mais ces deux activités n'ont pas su se renouveler suffisamment, leur audience a diminué et l'on ne peut pas prévoir, si une certaine reprise se prépare (cela semble être le cas pour le théâtre). Le cinéma occitan se limite à quelques succès éphémères; il n'y a pas de production cinématographique régulière.

6.2. Formes linguistiques de référence (normativisation)

Un des grands problèmes de l'oc. consiste dans le fait que ses locuteurs n'ont pas pu établir un consensus en ce qui concerne le système graphique à employer, ni en ce qui concerne la (ou les) forme(s) référentielle(s) de la langue. Le premier problème discuté (historiquement) a été celui de la graphie à employer. A la cohérence graphique (relative) des textes médiévaux a succédé la perte presque complète des traditions scriptologiques de l'oc. médiéval (Bec parle de «déstandardisation postmédiévale»). A partir de 1550 au plus tard, les textes sont écrits selon des normes graphiques empruntées avec plus ou moins de bonheur au fr. Le mouvement renaissantiste, au XIXe siècle, a reposé la question à laquelle le système de Frédéric Mistral et du Félibrige a été une première réponse. Ce système est, grosso modo, une régularisation et application à l'oc. des conventions graphiques fr.; les traditions graphiques oc. ne s'y retrouvent guère. Implicitement, ce système, appliqué au parler bas-rhodanien de Mistral, suggérait l'emploi de cette variété de la langue comme référentielle. C'est probablement la similarité visuelle entre la graphie mistralienne et l'orthographie fr. qui a provoqué les oppositions les plus vives. Ces dissensions aboutissent finalement à la grammaire de Loïs Alibert (1935) qui tente de combiner les traditions médiévales avec le système mistralien et celui du catalan, alors récemment élaboré par Pompeu Fabra. Alibert a conçu son système (tout comme Mistral et Roumanille d'ailleurs) d'abord pour un groupe dialectal donné, le languedocien; mais après 1945, dans une situation historique différente, sa grammaire a été déclarée référentielle pour l'ensemble des variétés de l'oc., par l'Institut d'Etudes Occitanes. Des tentatives de réforme du système alibertin n'ont guère contribué à décanter la situation; elles ont au contraire augmenté les insécurités des usagers. Aujourd'hui, la plupart des Occitans qui écrivent leur langue utilisent le système alibertin alors qu'en Provence le système mistralien garde toujours une importance considérable (il n'a pratiquement pas subi de modifications). D'autres systèmes existent, mais n'ont qu'une valeur marginale (dans ce sens, l'entrée limitée de l'oc. à l'école a quelque peu clarifié les choses). Un certain nombre d'écrivains oc. continuent à employer des systèmes personnels (cf. Kremnitz 1974, 1991; Bernal/Bernal 1984; Holtus/Metzeltin/Schmitt 1991).

A partir de la renaissance du siècle dernier, l'oc. a été employé pour des catégories nouvelles de textes. Il en résulte une certaine activité novatrice *de fait*, les nouveaux textes nécessitant parfois de nouvelles terminologies et de nouvelles stratégies textuelles (qui n'ont pas toujours réussi entièrement; la première thèse universitaire écrite en oc., celle de l'abbé Aurouze, 1907, donne une impression des difficultés). Alibert et à sa suite un certain nombre d'autres occitanistes, ont systématiquement essayé de créer des terminologies modernes, surtout scientifiques. Dans ce domaine, le bilan est carrément positif (cf. Kremnitz 1974, 320 sqq.).

7. Portrait général des contacts linguistiques

L'on ne parlera pas du fr. ici. L'oc. est une langue romane, voisine du fr., du catalan, du castillan, des variétés septentrionales de l'italien et du francoprovençal. Sa parenté génétique est particulièrement étroite avec le catalan (selon la terminologie de Kloss ces deux variétés se distinguent par leur *Ausbau*). Ronjat (1930, 6–7) et à sa suite Bec (^{5}1986, 23 sq) ont tenté d'établir la spécificité linguistique de l'oc. à l'aide de 19 traits qui l'opposent aux langues romanes citées ci-dessus. Il convient toutefois d'ajouter que, si pour le linguiste l'unité de l'oc. est facile à saisir, le grand nombre de variétés dialectales rend cette unité moins évidente pour le commun des mortels (de là un des préjugés contre la langue). Cette variation dans l'espace s'explique par plusieurs raisons: d'une part, toute langue naturelle se diversifie dans l'espace, si des forces centripètes ne s'y opposent. Cette tendance s'accroît, si la géographie est accidentée (montagnes). Dans le cas de l'oc., l'on constate les conséquences néfastes de l'absence d'un centre politique ou culturel autochtone qui aurait pu neutraliser les effets du pouvoir fr. qui, lui, avait centralisé les voies de communication sur Paris tout en accentuant ainsi les développements divergents des variétés oc. Le manque de culture *occitane* de la plus grande partie des locuteurs, dû à l'absence prolongée de l'oc. dans les écoles, augmente l'incertitude face à des variétés linguistiques pourtant peu différentes les unes des autres. Plus accentuées sont les différences du gascon par rapport aux autres variétés. Néanmoins, la grande majorité des renaissantistes a toujours considéré le gascon comme une forme de l'oc.

La coprésence des deux langues, fr. et oc., entraîne des influences mutuelles. Elles ont attiré l'intérêt des chercheurs depuis longtemps, d'abord sous la dénomination de *français régional*. Les domaines étudiés sont la phonétique, la phonologie et surtout le lexique (p. ex. Brun 1931, Séguy 1951, Gebhardt 1974). Le terme de fr. régional, appliqué également à d'autres régions, doit mettre en évidence le mode d'importation secondaire du français; il se substitue à l'oc. Des chercheurs oc. se sont appliqués à saisir plus profondément les particularités de ces influences en proposant le terme de *francitan* (Couderc 1975, cf. maintenant Boyer 1991, 144 sq) pour désigner le continuum que l'on peut observer entre deux points extrêmes (et virtuels), à savoir le « fr. neutre » et « l'oc. référentiel ». Les influences dans les deux langues ne sont pas symétriques: les traits oc. en fr. sont avant tout phonétiques, phonologiques et lexicologiques, beaucoup moins syntaxiques, tandis que les traits fr. en oc. relèvent avant tout du lexique et de la syntaxe (Kremnitz 1981, 3–6). Le francitan assourdit, comme l'oc., de consonnes finales; on rencontre parfois un *r apical* (« roulé »); on prononce tous les *e instables* du fr. ce qui donne une tout autre allure à la phrase et l'allonge en même temps. Le nombre des particularités lexicales du francitan est très élevé, il faut renvoyer aux lexiques spécialisés. Les traits les plus saillants de la syntaxe du francitan sont des différences d'emploi en ce qui concerne les *adjectifs possessifs*, la valence beaucoup plus étendue de l'auxiliaire *être*, le *dativus ethicus* et d'autres phénomènes dans le domaine verbal. Il y a des différences de détail entre les régions oc. Pour la plupart des locuteurs du francitan, le fr. constitue la langue cible; par conséquent, ils « améliorent » souvent leur discours oc. par des éléments fr. Les traits oc. en fr. jouissent en général de peu de prestige. De là des configurations très changeantes du discours francitan. Il va de soi que les influences sont plus fortes dans l'oral que dans l'écrit.

Pour les ouvrages de référence – linguistiques, grammaticaux, littéraires, etc. – cf. la bibliographie.

8. Examen critique de la bibliographie

Cette présentation rapide a dû négliger beaucoup de détails; elle s'est appuyée sur un choix des travaux de recherche les plus solides. Il convient de constater que la recherche sur le domaine oc. a atteint un niveau sérieux bien qu'à côté des travaux cités, il y ait un nombre considérable d'écrits que l'on ne peut consulter qu'avec beaucoup de précaution. Pour les divergences idéologiques cf. les chapitres précédents. On manque actuellement entre autres de grammaires descriptives modernes capables de donner une vue d'ensemble des variétés de l'oc. et de synthèses de la production culturelle, surtout littéraire (l'histoire de Lafont/Anatole a 25 ans et est aujourd'hui dépassée dans les détails).

9. Bibliographie (sélective)

Alibert, Loïs (^{2}1976): *Gramatica occitana, segon los parlars lengadocians*, Montpelièr (^{1}1935).

Alibert, Louis (1965): *Dictionnaire occitan–français d'après les parlers languedociens*, Toulouse (^{2}1977).

Armengaud, André/Lafont, Robert (Eds.) (1979): *Histoire d'Occitanie*, Paris.

Aurouze, Joseph (1907): *Lou prouvençau à l'escolo*, Vilo-Diéu/Avignon: Roumanille (thèse secondaire).

Bec, Pierre (^{5}1986): *La langue occitane*, Paris.

Bernal Bernal, Chesús Gregorio (1984): *La gramática de Alibèrt y la normalización moderna del occitano*, thèse non publiée, Zaragoza.

Blanchet, Philippe (1986): *Le français régional de Provence; étude phonétique, phonologique, lexicale et syntaxique. Analyse du substrat provençal*, Lille.

Boyer, Henri (1991): *Langues en conflit. Etudes sociolinguistiques*, Paris.

Brun, Auguste (1931): *Le français de Marseille*, Marseille.

Cichon, Peter (1988): *Spracherziehung in der Diglossiesituation: Zum Sprachbewußtsein von Okzitanischlehrern*, Vienne.

Couderc, Yves (1975): «Francitan». In: *Occitània passat e present* (Antibes) 3, 24–27 et 4, 34–37.

Garavini, Fausta (1970): *La letteratura occitanica moderna*, Florence/Milan.

Gardy, Philippe/Lafont, Robert (1981): «La diglossie comme conflit: l'exemple occitan». In: *Langages* 61, 75–91.

Gebhardt, Karl (1974): *Das okzitanische Lehngut im Französischen*, Berne/Francfort.

Giordan, Henri (1982): *Démocratie culturelle et droit à la différence*. Rapport au ministre de la Culture, Paris.

Holtus, Günter/Metzeltin, Michael/Schmitt, Christian (Eds.) (1991); *Lexikon der Romanistischen Linguistik, Band V, 2: Okzitanisch, Katalanisch*, Tübingen, 1–126.

Kremnitz, Georg (1974): *Versuche zur Kodifizierung des Okzitanischen seit dem 19. Jahrhundert und ihre Annahme durch die Sprecher*, Tübingen.

Kremnitz, Georg (1981): *Das Okzitanische. Sprachgeschichte und Soziologie*, Tübingen.

Kremnitz, Georg (Ed.) (1981): *Entfremdung. Selbstbefreiung und Norm. Texte aus der okzitanischen Soziolinguistik*, Tübingen.

Kremnitz, Georg (1988): «La recherche (socio-)linguistique en domaine occitan». In: *Bulletins de l'Association Internationale d'Etudes Occitanes*, no. 2 et 3.

Kremnitz, Georg (1991): «Die Kodifikationen des Okzitanischen im Spannungsfeld zwischen Autonomie und Dependenz». In: *Zum Stand der Kodifizierung romanischer Kleinsprachen*, Dahmen, W. et al. (Eds.), Tübingen 171–184.

Kremnitz, Georg (1992): «Veränderungen im Status der Minderheitensprachen in Frankreich». In: *Le français aujourd'hui. Mélanges offerts à Jürgen Olbert*, Dorion, G. et al. (Eds.), Francfort/Main, 211–216.

Lafont, Robert (1967): «Sur l'aliénation occitane». In: *Le Fédéraliste* IX, 107–138.

Lafont, Robert (1974): *La revendication occitane*, Paris.

Lafont, Robert (1979): «La diglossie en pays occitan, ou le réel occulté». In: *Bildung und Ausbildung in der Romania, Akten des Romanistentages in Gießen 1977*, Kloepfer, Rolf (Ed.), Munich, vol. II, 504–512.

Lafont, Robert (1989): «Trente ans de sociolinguistique occitane (sauvage ou institutionnelle)». In: *Lengas* 25, 13–25.

Lafont, Robert (1991): *Temps tres. Petites passejades històriques per als escamarlats de la frontera*, Perpignan.

Lafont, Robert/Anatole, Christian (1970/1971): *Nouvelle histoire de la littérature occitane*, Paris, 2 vol.

Markhof, Wolfgang (1987): *Renaissance oder Substitution? Eine soziologische Untersuchung zur Stellung des Okzitanischen im Département Cantal*, Genève.

Média Pluriel (Ed.) (1991): *Occitan: pratiques et représentations dans la Région Languedoc-Roussillon*, Montpellier.

Nelli, René (1968): *Dictionnaire des hérésies méridionales et des mouvements hétérodoxes ou indépendants apparus dans le Midi de la France depuis l'établissement du christianisme*, Toulouse.

Ninyoles, Rafael Lluís (1969): *Conflicte lingüístic valencià*, Valence.

Pic, François (1977): *Bibliographie des sources bibliographiques du domaine occitan*, Béziers.

Rogge, Waltraud (1987): *Aspekte des Sprachwissens von Jugendlichen im Bereich der französisch-okzitanischen Diglossie. Aspekte einer empirischen Untersuchung in Albi, Bédarieux, Mende und Montpellier*, Trèves.

Ronjat, Jules (1930–1941): *Grammaire istorique* [sic] *des parlers provençaux modernes*, Montpellier, 4 vol.

Rouquette, Rémy (1987): *Le régime juridique des langues en France*. Thèse non publiée, Paris/Nanterre.

Schlieben-Lange, Brigitte (1971, ²1973): *Okzitanisch und Katalanisch. Ein Beitrag zur Soziolinguistik zweier romanischer Sprachen*, Tübingen.

Séguy, Jean (1951, ³1978): *Le français parlé à Toulouse*, Toulouse.

Teulat, Roger (1972): *Grammaire de l'occitan de référence (les sons, les mots, les formes)*, Villeneuve-sur-Lot.

Georg Kremnitz, Vienne (Autriche)

144. Français—catalan

1. Géographie et démographie
2. Histoire
3. Politique, économie, situations culturelle et religieuse en général
4. Statistiques et profils ethniques
5. Situation sociolinguistique
6. Etat de la politique linguistique
7. Portrait général des contacts linguistiques
8. Examen critique de la bibliographie
9. Bibliographie (sélective)

1. Géographie et démographie

La partie septentrionale de l'aire linguistique catalane correspond à l'actuel département français des Pyrénées-Orientales. Le département des Pyrénées Orientales a une population de 369 476 habitants pour une superficie de 4143 km². Il est divisé en plusieurs « comarques » très différenciées (côte, basse plaine, grandes vallées, zones de moyenne et haute montagne). La plaine draine aujourd'hui la majeure partie des ressources du pays et plus de la moitié de la population est rassemblée sur Perpignan et les villages des environs. Une agriculture caractérisée par une prédominance de la petite propriété à exploitation directe et axée sur les fruits et légumes (primeurs, cultures sous serres), une production viticole de qualité et, à un moindre degré, l'élevage, constituent l'activité principale traditionnelle. Elle a su se moderniser et faire face à de nombreuses difficultés, mais une part de moins en moins importante de la population active s'y trouve directement ou indirectement impliquée. Le tissu industriel, en grande partie archaïque, est en pleine décomposition et le secteur du bâtiment et des travaux publics, après une période de prospérité, connaît lui aussi de graves difficultés. Le tourisme, quant à lui, est en passe de devenir l'activité la plus importante. Les demandeurs d'emploi représentent environ le cinquième de la population active.

Des mouvements de population récents ont modifié la structure du peuplement — alors que les flux successifs plus anciens — politiques et économiques — issus de la Catalogne espagnole avaient contribué au maintien de la catalanité. Un exode massif des jeunes s'est accompagné de plusieurs vagues d'immigration (rapatriés d'Afrique du Nord, retraités et pré-retraités du Nord de la Loire des années 1960–1970) s'ajoutant aux flux continu de diverses immigrations étrangères (belges, hollandais et britanniques — travailleurs maghrebins, andalous et portugais). Tandis que la tendance générale était à une diminution de la mobilité résidentielle, la Catalogne française — tout comme le Languedoc — a connu une nouvelle vague d'immigration qui fait que, tout en ayant un dynamisme démographique propre nul, elle a un solde migratoire positif (qui s'est trouvé multiplié par 2,6 de 1975 à 1982, de +17 460 à +44 467). Les nouveaux arrivants des années 1980 sont plus jeunes, avec des enfants en cours de scolarité et un niveau de qualification supérieur à la moyenne. La population autochtone a pu intégrer — sinon assimiler — certaines fractions des vagues antérieures. L'opinion générale était plutôt pessimiste en ce qui concerne les flux les plus récents mais certaines données d'enquête (sondage Média

Pluriel de 1993; cf. infra 5.) tendraient à prouver que cette capacité s'est plus ou moins maintenue.

2. Histoire

Le Traité des Pyrénées (1659) qui institutionalise l'annexion par le royaume de France des comtés catalans septentrionaux, constitue une date de référence. Ce repère historique a surtout un caractère symbolique: déjà avant 1659, la société nord-catalane connaissait des problèmes glottopolitiques, avec la pénétration du castillan; par contre, la plupart des problèmes linguistiques découlant de ces changements géopolitiques du XVIIe siècle n'apparaîtront qu'au XIXe ou même au XXe siècle.

Le processus de francisation peut être décomposé en trois phases principales:

(1) une francisation horizontale et sélective qui permet à certains groupes sociaux de maintenir leur position hégémonique: coupées du Sud par l'annexion, les classes dominantes ne peuvent préserver leurs intérêts qu'en s'intégrant à l'appareil d'Etat français et en occupant des charges publiques (processus facilité par la non-vénalité des charges en Roussillon); des politiques répressives sont développées à plusieurs reprises mais elles ne sont pas caractéristiques de cette étape;

(2) la francisation devint ensuite descendante et spontanée: les classes intermédiaires tentent de se franciser à l'image des classes dominantes — notamment la grande bourgeoisie devenue leur groupe de référence; quatre situations pourront se présenter:

(a) mobilité sociale sans changement linguistique: une grande partie des individus économiquement ascendants se trouve dans l'impossibilité de réduire rapidement la distance sociale; la langue servant à renforcer les barrières de classe, le processus de francisation s'en trouvera retardé et il y aura, souvent pendant fort longtemps, décalage entre situation de classe et statut;

(b) mobilité sociale et changement linguistique: tout un dispositif, basé notamment sur de nouvelles écoles religieuses françaises, permet la réussite d'une francisation complète qui se limitera à certaines fractions de la moyenne bourgeoisie;

(c) ni mobilité sociale ni changement linguistique: c'est le cas des classes populaires;

(d) changement linguistique sans mobilité sociale: il s'agit là d'une attitude compensatoire affectant divers sous-groupes et qui se traduit par une recherche de statut fictif;

(3) la francisation se fera de plus en plus coercitive dans la mesure où ce dernier processus d'imitation à distance est relativement lent. C'est l'appareil éducatif qui assurera, pour l'essentiel, cette mission — surtout à partir des lois scolaires de Jules Ferry (à la fin du XIXe siècle, la francisation ne touchait encore qu'un quart des enfants). C'est l'ère du «Soyez propres, parlez français». L'intégration au marché national et la participation à deux guerres mondiales viendront consolider ce processus de substitution.

La période actuelle peut être appréhendée en termes de *stabilisation* (cf. infra).

3. Politique, économie, situations culturelle et religieuse en général

Le terme de «déliquescence» a été récemment utilisé par un haut fonctionnaire pour rendre compte de la situation régnant dans le département des Pyrénées Orientales. La nature et l'origine des réactions provoquées par ce jugement sans nuance et diverses «affaires» ultérieures ont confirmé la validité de cette analyse.

Longtemps considéré comme «de gauche», ce département a progressivement glissé à droite, sinon à l'extrême droite (dont il constitue l'un des bastions électoraux). Les mouvements migratoires — notamment l'arrivée des rapatriés d'Afrique du Nord — et le vieillissement de la population (28% de plus de soixante ans en 1990), combinés à un clientélisme de notables locaux — avec toutes les dérives qu'implique un tel système — sont généralement avancés pour expliquer ce phénomène. Toutes les organisations politiques assument d'une manière ou d'une autre (démagogie, folklorisation, double discours, clientélisme) le fait catalan, mais peu ont tenté d'y réfléchir sérieusement (P.S.U. puis P.C.F. dans la période 1968−1978). Le catalanisme politique, après une phase groupusculaire, a su se structurer et même s'il demeure électoralement marginal, il s'est trouvé, au début des années 1990, tout comme le mouvement écologiste, en position d'arbitre et s'est intégré à diverses coalitions (Liste Perpignan-Oxygène, par exemple, aux élections municipales de 1993) − ce qui lui permet de disposer désormais d'un certain nombre d'élus.

La problématique religieuse se limite à l'affrontement traditionnel entre catholiques et anti-cléricaux — les pratiques religieuses connaissant la même régression que dans le reste de l'Etat français. Sur le plan linguistique et culturel, l'Eglise a joué un rôle ambigu: elle a longtemps conservé la langue catalane (sermons, chants), a maintenu ou a fait revivre des lieux et des manifestations emblématiques et a fourni de nombreux érudits impliqués dans le mouvement culturel catalan, tout en participant activement au processus d'acculturation au travers des écoles religieuses et de la catéchèse.

Dans un environnement culturel marqué — comme dans la plupart des régions périphériques de l'Etat français — par son provincialisme, le mouvement culturel nord-catalan, né au XIXe siècle et fort, aujourd'hui, d'une centaine d'associations, a joué un rôle fondamental. Il a su former un public, a favorisé une création littéraire et artistique considérable et a permis une ouverture sur la vie culturelle sud-pyrénéenne. Les activités associatives constituent, en outre, depuis les années 1980, un domaine stratégique d'emploi de la langue vernaculaire.

La Catalogne française présente toutes les caractéristiques d'un espace rentier (cf. Solans 1993). L'état critique de l'économie nord-catalane résulte de cette culture rentière et de sa dérive actuelle. Acculturation et diglossie pourraient permettre, en dernière instance, d'expliquer les comportements des acteurs économiques et leur incapacité à saisir les opportunités offertes par la proximité de la métropole barcelonaise.

4. Statistiques et profils ethniques

L'analyse démolinguistique se heurte à de nombreuses difficultés:

— d'importants noyaux de populations mixtes sont apparus à la suite du développement des mouvements migratoires et de la régression de l'endogamie, mais en l'absence de travaux sociolinguistiques sur les couples mixtes ou les familles composites, il n'est pas possible de traiter convenablement les données du recensement et de l'état civil;
— le critère de naissance utilisé pendant longtemps n'est plus fiable (retour des Nord-Catalans de l'émigration économique nés à l'extérieur — enfants nés en Catalogne française des nouveaux venus non intégrés);
— les formes d'identité évoluent et les enquêtes les plus récentes mettent en évidence l'émergence d'une nouvelle catalanité caractérisée par la connaissance et l'utilisation de la langue catalane et l'enracinement;
— plusieurs groupes n'assument pas leur catalanité («pieds-noirs» d'origine sud-catalane, par exemple);
— certains sous-groupes roussillonnais ont une conception très restrictive de la catalanité et rejettent les Sud-Catalans (qualifiés d'«Espanyols»).

Toute opération de dénombrement destinée à pallier l'absence de données ethnolinguistiques collectées dans le cadre des recensements de population officiels s'avère difficile. Les réponses données aux items d'identification ne sont pas fiables, plusieurs pré-enquêtes ayant prouvé que de multiples facteurs, comme l'origine de l'enquêteur, par exemple, affectent l'information collectée dans ce domaine, les mêmes enquêtes pouvant aller jusqu'à donner des réponses diamétralement opposées. Si l'on se contente des données linguistiques, environ une personne sur deux (48%) déclare parler catalan, deux personnes sur trois (63%) déclarent comprendre le catalan (sondage Média Pluriel 1993). Compte tenu du fait qu'une partie (non encore évaluée) de la population de souche est décatalanisée, que les enquêtes des années 1970 mettent en évidence un taux d'intégration avancée (avec un début d'apprentissage de la langue) d'environ 15% chez les nouveaux-venus, et que les mouvements de population de ces quinze dernières années ont porté sur plus de la moitié de la population totale, il est possible d'analyser la situation actuelle en terme de *stabilisation*. L'évolution classique monolinguisme B — diglossie sans bilinguisme — bilinguisme et diglossie — monolinguisme A a été freinée.

Le nombre de personnes possédant une bonne compétence linguistique augmente avec l'âge (16% des 18—24 ans, 35% des 25—44, 55% des 45—64 et 73% des plus de 65 ans); il faut cependant prendre en compte les conditions de l'apprentissage qui déborde souvent sur l'âge adulte (études supérieures, formation continue, cours pour adultes) ainsi que l'impact des cours d'adultes chez les décatalanisés et les nouveaux arrivants du troisième âge. La proportion de personnes sachant parler catalan est sensiblement la même chez les hommes et les femmes.

La catalanophonie demeure caractérisée par son hétérogénéité: outre des groupes très particuliers comme les gitans catalanophones sédentaires, il existe plusieurs sous-ensembles nettement différenciés tant par leur situation économique, sociale et culturelle que par leurs pratiques langagières. C'est ainsi que les processus à l'œuvre chez les dialectophones ruraux — notamment les petits propriétaires fonciers de la plaine du Roussillon qui ont constitué un bastion d'endogamie — sont totalement différents de ceux qui affectent les couples mixtes urbains issus de mariages entre Catalans du Nord et du Sud, qui constituent un noyau particulièrement dynamique auquel se sont agrégés des éléments originaires des cantons frontaliers et des roussillonnais recatalanisés.

5. Situation sociolinguistique

Un sondage réalisé en 1993 à la demande du Conseil Régional du Languedoc-Roussillon (sondage Média Pluriel) fournit les données clés suivantes sur la situation de la langue vernaculaire en Catalogne française:

— deux personnes sur trois comprennent le catalan (63%);
— une personne sur deux sait parler catalan (48%);
— un tiers des enquêtés le parle quotidiennement ou très souvent (66% des catalanophones);
— les ¾ des locuteurs déclarent savoir lire (dont 40,7% sans aucune difficulté, soit rapporté à la population locale, une personne sur quatre);
— parmi les personnes qui déclarent savoir lire, 21,6% savent écrire (mais ils sont 40% parmi celles qui lisent facilement);
— 55,7% de l'ensemble se déclarent attachés à la langue catalane (83% dans le sous-groupe des locuteurs) — avec une légère dominante masculine; 35,5% des personnes qui ne comprennent pas le catalan se déclarent aussi attachées à cette langue;
— les personnes qui parlent catalan perçoivent majoritairement leur pratique comme restant stable (60,6%) ou en augmentation (18,6%); c'est à Perpignan et dans les hauts cantons que l'on trouve le plus grand nombre de personnes estimant que leur pratique personnelle augmente (30% et 26%).

Les idéologies linguistiques de la francisation ont pratiquement disparu, comme l'«auto-odi» (selfhatred), ou sont en régression (idéologies diglossiques). Reste le thème conflictuel de l'unité de la langue, réactivé par le sécessionisme linguistique valencien. Les résultats de certaines enquêtes récentes reposent sur des approches méthodologiques discutables (question confuse «parle-t-on la même langue dans votre département et à Barcelone, Valence, en Andorre et aux Baléares?», avec 67% de réponses négatives dans le sondage Média Pluriel — insuffisance des premiers traitements qui laissent cependant apparaître que plus de la moitié des locuteurs ont donné une réponse positive). Le problème mériterait une analyse plus rigoureuse, lorsque les résultats d'autres travaux en cours seront connus; → cartes linguistiques D et E.

6. Etat de la politique linguistique

Les normes de l'Institut d'Estudis Catalans ont été adoptées en Catalogne française, non sans provoquer quelques polémiques plus ou moins vives — les intellectuels localistes prenant des positions très divergentes allant de l'adhésion critique à l'opposition systématique. La question semble avoir été définitivement réglée dans le courant des années 1970.

L'absence, en France, d'une véritable législation linguistique a provoqué diverses revendications limitées, dans un premier temps, à la présence et au statut de la langue catalane dans le secteur éducatif. Ces revendications ont pris un caractère plus global à la suite de l'officialisation de cette langue à différents niveaux (autonomies espagnoles, institutions européennes et internationales).

Les moyens de communication de masse (presse régionale, radio et télévision publiques, radios locales) accordent une place marginale à la langue catalane, avec une nette évolution positive de la part de Radio-France-Roussillon (programmation, formation linguistique du personnel). Les catalanophones disposent par ailleurs d'une radio associative (Radio Arrels) (quatre fréquences F. M. — 168 heures de programmation hebdomadaire, dont 50 heures de production propre) et d'un hebdomadaire (El Punt, tirage de 4000 exemplaires), et ont pour la plupart, la possibilité de recevoir les chaînes de télévision sud-catalanes (TV3, Canal 33, TVE2 canal català). Selon le sondage Média Pluriel de 1993, un habitant sur trois déclare écouter régulièrement ou occasionnellement des émissions de radio en langue catalane (un sur deux dans les cantons frontaliers) et un sur deux regarde les émissions de télévision de langue catalane (France 3: 55%, TV3: 43%, TVE2: 14%, Canal 33: 11,4%).

La langue catalane est présente dans la vie publique, depuis l'intervention dans le débat politique, dans les années 1970, d'organisations utilisant le catalan comme langue véhiculaire. Ultérieurement, le développement de relations administratives avec des entités sud-catalanes (municipalités, autorités provinciales, administration du Gouvernement Autonome) a largement contribué à réintroduire la langue vernaculaire dans un domaine qui lui était interdit depuis plus de deux siècles — avec un impact certain sur les idéologies linguistiques même si ces pratiques demeurent généralement limitées aux seules initiatives transfrontalières (réunions de travail, colloques, manifestations culturelles, expositions ...). Le cadastre et les cartes I. G. N. sont en cours de révision (recatalanisation des toponymes). Dans le domaine controversé de la signalétique, le sondage de 1993 fait apparaître que deux personnes sur trois sont favorables à l'existence de panneaux bilingues.

L'utilisation professionnelle de la langue s'est développée hors de ses bastions traditionnels (agriculture, bâtiment et travaux publics, transports) sous l'effet de la diversification sociale du mouvement de loyalisme linguistique et de la prise en compte des réalités administratives et économiques sud-pyrénéennes. La compétence en langue catalane commence à apparaître dans le profil de certaines offres d'emploi et des actions de formation continue de personnels bilingues régulièrement programmées depuis 1992.

La situation dans le domaine éducatif est donc, à bien des égards, exceptionnelle:

— la population scolaire concernée est relativement importante:

– écoles pré-élémentaires: 57; 3746 élèves; 94 maîtres;
– écoles primaires: 84; 5093 élèves; 154 maîtres;
– collèges: 19; 1325 élèves; 23 professeurs;
– lycées: 11; 532 élèves; 11 professeurs;
– Université: 210 étudiants spécialistes et 250 étudiants non-spécialistes (enseignement optionnel) (données 1991–1992);

— la couverture pédagogique dans les secteurs public et privé sous contrat d'association est complète depuis l'enseignement pré-élémentaire jusqu'à l'enseignement supérieur (avec un cursus spécialisé complet — D. E. U. G., Licence, Maîtrise, préparation au CAPES, D. E. A., Doctorat — à l'Université de Perpignan); par ailleurs, quatre écoles et un collège de langue catalane des associations La Bressola et Arrels accueillent un peu plus de deux cents enfants. Un réseau relativement dense de cours d'adultes complète ce dispositif.

— l'environnement est favorable tant sur le plan international où le fait d'être adossé à une communauté particulièrement dynamique d'une dizaine de millions de personnes constitue un atout indéniable, que sur le plan local — avec un début de normalité (média, vie publique), une utilité socio-économique certaine (deux personnes sur trois pensent qu'apprendre le catalan est un facteur d'intégration professionnelle) et l'attitude positive de la société civile (une grande majorité de population — 83% — est favorable à ce qu'existe pour tous la possibilité d'apprendre le catalan à l'école).

L'actuel processus de récupération linguistique repose cependant sur la seule mobilisation du mouvement de loyalisme linguistique. Le traitement institutionnel amorcé (Plan Académique, concours de recrutement de professeurs, conventions avec les écoles catalanes) demeure inadéquat et en retrait par rapport à d'autres aires linguistiques (Pays Basque, Alsace) comme pour le développement des écoles de langue vernaculaire ou des expériences de filières à orientation bilingue de l'enseignement public.

7. Portrait général des contacts linguistiques

Il conviendrait de compléter les informations classiques par les trois points suivants:

(1) variétés dialectales: la dialectologie distingue un «catalan septentrional» ou «roussillonnais» qui n'a plus aucune existence sociale sur le terrain (sinon une existence résiduelle) pour plusieurs raisons, notamment:

— les mouvements de population (mais rien n'a été fait sur la langue parlée et transmise (quand c'était le cas) par des couples de locuteurs originaires de «comarques» différentes):
— l'apprentissage différé, dans lequel l'appareil éducatif joue un rôle aussi (sinon plus) important que la famille;

(2) quelques observations sur le français régional dit « méridional »:

— il n'est plus le fruit d'interférences massives avec le catalan (phonologiques dont l'une des plus notables était le traitement de [R], lexicales et morpho-syntaxiques: « la machine, elle me s'est cassée ... »); il s'agirait plutôt d'un sous-standard régional semblable à celui de Montpellier, Marseille ou Toulouse;

— il paraît être en régression (effets des moyens de communication de masse?) avec d'importants noyaux de résistance;

— autre variété: le français « pied-noir » (un peu plus de 10% de la population).

(3) les interférences:

— en français: cf. supra;
— en catalan: pas d'étude disponible; stables ou en extension (alors qu'elles régressent en français);
  — morphosyntaxiques: très limitées;
  — phonologiques: massives chez une minorité de locuteurs (surtout des recatalanisés des années 60−70); très limitées chez les autres (développement de l'enseignement, normalisation des relations avec le Sud, mariages entre Catalans du nord et du sud);
  — lexicales: massives et en extension (deux Etats, avec leurs institutions propres − néologie française productive, par exemple dans le domaine technologique − informatique − alors que la tendance péninsulaire (castillan et catalan) est aux américanismes).

8. Examen critique de la bibliographie

Les problèmes rencontrés par la recherche sociolinguistique en domaine nord-catalan sont relatifs à la collecte et à l'archivage des données et à la définition de problématiques adéquates.

8.1. Le matériel collecté − de qualité inégale (enquêtes associatives, travaux universitaires de tous niveaux) − est relativement important mais il n'a souvent fait l'objet que d'un traitement limité ou partiel, avec une diffusion ponctuelle des résultats, et demeure donc peu connu et difficilement accessible. C'est pour remédier à cette situation qu'a été récemment créé dans le cadre de la Maison des Pays Catalans de l'Université de Perpignan un « Observatori Sociolingüistic del Pirineu Català ».

Pour répondre aux demandes de décideurs politiques − notamment du Conseil Régional du Languedoc-Roussillon − et des grands organismes de recherche, deux enquêtes portant sur l'ensemble de la population nord-catalane ont été réalisées aux débuts des années 1990:

— un sondage de Média Pluriel, financé par le Conseil Régional, portant sur cinq cents personnes (échantillonnage par quotas);
— une enquête plus complète (entretien directif, questionnaire et évaluation linguistique), sur deux cent soixante dix-huit personnes (échantillon aléatoire stratifié) à la charge du Centre de Recherches et d'Etudes Catalanes (C. R. E. C.) de l'Université de Perpignan.

La forte médiatisation des premiers résultats, avec toutes les dérives qu'elle peut comporter, amène à émettre un certain nombre de réserves qui viennent s'ajouter aux critiques classiques formulées à l'encontre des sondages − à moins de faire de cette médiatisation un analyseur, éventuellement construit, de la situation sociolinguistique. Un programme d'enquêtes ciblées − comme celui de l'Observatoire Sociolinguistique − paraît constituer une approche méthodologique plus satisfaisante.

8.2. Les recherches de terrain et le traitement des données collectées sont affectés par les insuffisances des problématiques retenues. Le bilinguisme lecteur, par exemple, demeure sous-estimé ou ignoré − l'item relatif à la compréhension écrite étant ainsi généralement réservé aux seuls locuteurs de langue catalane, comme dans l'enquête Média Pluriel.

Les problématiques démolinguistiques demeurent de type traditionnel (majorité/minorité) alors que les mouvements migratoires récents et l'expérience des acteurs sociaux (stratégie du « noyau dur ») appellent des modèles plus complexes.

Au delà de ces déficiences partielles, l'absence de problématique d'ensemble est particulièrement significative. Alors que la situation méridionale, avec les enjeux valenciens, a fait l'objet de nombreuses analyses mettant clairement en évidence les processus à l'œuvre, les enjeux septentrionaux demeurent mal perçus. Il semble pourtant que l'avenir de la langue catalane se joue autant au centre que sur la périphérie, notamment dans l'ensemble incluant la Catalogne française, l'Andorre et les zones occitanes limitrophes. L'étude de ce « repte [= défi] septentrional » constitue l'un des axes de recherche privilégiés de l'Observatori Sociolingüístic del Pirineu Català.

9. Bibliographie (sélective)

Les sources bibliographiques sont de deux ordres:

— la «littérature grise» (enquêtes, travaux universitaires, monographies) dont la majeure partie est archivée par l'Observatoire Sociolinguistique des Pyrénées Catalanes de l'Université de Perpignan;
— les articles scientifiques consacrés à la situation sociolinguistique nord-catalane, généralement publiés dans la revue *Treballs de Sociolingüística Catalana* (les autres publications faisant l'objet, dans cette même revue ainsi que dans le bulletin de l'Observatoire Sociolinguistique, d'un compte-rendu ou d'une fiche signalétique).

Arrels (1992): *Qui són els Catalans del Nord*, Perpignan/Perpinyà.

Bernardó, Domènec (1988): «La problématique nord-catalane». In: *Vingt-cinq communautés linguistiques de la France*, Vermes, G. (Ed.), Paris, vol. I, 133—149.

Dossier «Catalunya del Nord» (1993). In: *Crònica d'Ensenyament 52*, 24—37.

Média Pluriel Méditerranée (1993): *Catalan — pratiques et représentations dans les Pyrénées Orientales*, Montpellier.

Solans, Henri (1993): *Essai sur l'économie des Pyrénées Orientales*, Perpignan.

Domènec Bernardó, Perpignan (France)
Georg Kremnitz, Vienne (Autriche)

145. Français—corse

1. Géographie et démographie
2. Histoire
3. Politique, économie et situation culturelle
4. Statistiques linguistiques
5. Le discours épilinguistique
6. Education
7. Administration, vie publique, politique
8. Religion
9. Médias
10. Orthographe
11. Portrait général des contacts linguistiques
12. Examen critique de la bibliographie
13. Bibliographie (sélective)

1. Géographie et démographie

L'île de Corse est située dans la mer Tyrrhénienne, à 200 km de Nice, à 90 de Livourne et à 10 de la Sardaigne. Avec 1822 km², 183 km de long et 83 de large, 1000 de côtes en falaises ou en plages, des chaînes élevées (Cintu à 2710 m), elle est «une montagne dans la mer». La mer est présente partout, jamais à plus de 40 km à vol d'oiseau, d'un quelconque point de l'île. Pourtant les Corses, à l'exception des populations du Capicorsu, ont généralement tourné le dos à la mer. La flore (plus de 2000 espèces) est très variée et dominée par le maquis. Un sillon central sépare la partie schisteuse et la partie granitique, division qui a déterminé l'histoire et a abouti à une partition administrative en deux départements. L'unité traditionnelle de la vie économique et sociale, de type surtout agro-pastoral, était la *pieve*, ensemble de communautés villageoises dont la structure a fortement marqué la culture et les mentalités insulaires. Depuis le début du 19ème siècle, la démographie a connu un développement irrégulier, avec une période d'accroissement (162.000 hs en 1801 — 276.000 en 1884), une grave crise démographique (170.000 hs en 1955) et une reprise (240.000 hs en 1982). Cette évolution résulte d'une forte émigration vers le continent français et du vieillissement de la population causé par l'exode des jeunes, suivis d'une immigration importante en provenance des anciennes colonies françaises d'Afrique du Nord. Ce mouvement se poursuit aujourd'hui par les arrivées du continent français. L'intérieur se dépeuple régulièrement au profit des villes du littoral. La statistique des composantes de la population alimente des polémiques car cette question est un enjeu du discours politique. Les services officiels (INSEE 1986) donnent, pour 1982, 214.132 Français (sans distinguer entre Corses et continentaux) et 25.880 Non-français (dont 4.576 Italiens et 15.848 Maghrébins); → cartes linguistiques D et F.

2. Histoire

La présence de l'homme en Corse remonterait au 9ème millénaire av. J. C. L'histoire de l'île est une succession ininterrompue de résistance aux invasions (Phocéens, Romains, Vandales, Byzantins, Papauté, Pise, Gênes, Aragon, Banque de Saint-Georges, France, Gênes à nouveau, puis France depuis 1768). A retenir deux épisodes lourds de signification politique: en 1358, la création de la *Terra di u Cumunu* contre les féodaux et en 1729, contre le pouvoir génois, le début des révolutions de Corse qui aboutissent en 1755 à la création d'un Etat corse indépendant sous le généralat de *Pasquale Paoli*. Celui-ci met en place des institutions inspirées des «lumières» et la Corse fait figure auprès des philosophes européens de première organisation démocratique. Le traité de Versailles entre la France et Gênes met fin à cette expérience originale, car la France, qui a reçu en gage la Corse, écrase les milices de Paoli à Ponte Novu (1769). Comme les Etats-Unis d'Amérique et plus tard le Risorgimento italien, la Révolution française reconnaîtra un précurseur en Paoli qui sera rappelé en Corse en 1790, mais devant la lutte des clans et les péripéties révolutionnaires, la Corse fera sécession pendant le royaume anglo-corse (1794–1796). Les armées de la République reprendront alors l'île et commencera pour elle une période de difficultés et de révoltes durement réprimées. A partir de 1815, la Corse, pacifiée militairement mais difficilement administrable, entrera progressivement dans l'orbite française, mais en conservant jusqu'à nos jours de fortes spécificités qui expliquent le présent de la question insulaire. Gérée sur le mode colonial et largement abandonnée au pouvoir des clans locaux, l'île ratera son entrée dans la modernité et connaîtra le sous-développement et l'exil (on estime à 600.000 personnes la diaspora corse vivant aujourd'hui de par le monde du fait de cette émigration séculaire). L'effondrement démographique et économique s'accentue après la première guerre mondiale avec 35.000 Corses tués au combat (chiffres controversés) et la pénurie de main d'œuvre agricole. Occupée en 1942 par les armées de Mussolini, la Corse sera le premier département français libéré en septembre 1943. L'histoire actuelle est marquée par la montée du nationalisme corse qui ne cesse de progresser depuis les années 1970 et par les problèmes d'une société en crise.

3. Politique, économie et situation culturelle

La politique centraliste de la France n'a jamais tenté de réduire une structure politico-culturelle spécifique, les clans, dont elle s'est servie et se sert encore pour administrer une île aux fortes particularités qui ont forcé l'Etat à concéder par deux fois (1982 et 1992) un statut particulier à la Corse.

3.1. Le clan

Structure de défense et d'entraide à l'origine, le clan est devenu une organisation politico-culturelle superposée aux structures et aux partis politiques français. Le noyau de base est localisé dans la commune et a pour enjeu les élections municipales. Qui est élu maire s'assure une position déterminante dans la vie locale et favorise ses partisans, souvent au détriment de l'intérêt général. Le chef du clan apporte son appui à un candidat à l'élection cantonale, est souvent président du conseil général du département et peut ainsi favoriser les communes qui servent ses intérêts. Souvent aussi, il est député, sénateur ou ministre et apporte ainsi, en échange de l'appui électoral, son aide au niveau local, régional et auprès des administrations et services tant en Corse qu'à Paris. Le service rendu est à la base du système qu'il maintient en garantissant la solidarité de tous les membres de cette association qui a su traverser les bouleversements anciens et récents. Témoin sa mainmise sur la nouvelle Assemblée de Corse élue en mars 1992 où il détient la majorité régionale par un jeu d'alliances qui disqualifie la répartition des étiquettes gauche–droite dans les partis français, après avoir combattu vivement la loi portant organisation du statut particulier de la Corse et malgré le score important des nationalistes à ces élections.

3.2. Les nationalistes

Il existe plusieurs groupes: *Corsica Nazione* (les autonomistes de l'*Unione di u Populu Corsu* (UPC), les écologistes *I Verdi Corsi*, les nationalistes de la *Cunsolta Naziunale*), l'*Accolta Naziunali* (ANC) et le *Muvimentu Corsu per l'Autodeterminazione* (MPA). A ces mouvements publics il faut ajouter les clandestins du *Fronte di Liberazione Naziunale di a Corsica* (FLNC), lui-même divisé sur la stratégie de la lutte armée, et d'autres mouvements plus éphémères. Les idées nationalistes ont aussi pénétré depuis 1985 le monde des associations et syndicats du travail avec le *Sindicatu di i Travagliatori Corsi* qui bénéficie d'une audience sans cesse élargie, à côté des représentants locaux des grandes organisations françaises. Malgré ses dissensions, le mouvement nationaliste représente pour la vie politique insulaire une alternative, bien qu'il soit traversé par une crise profonde.

3.3. Economie

Tous les indicateurs économiques révèlent une situation de crise profonde. Pour donner une idée de l'état de faiblesse économique, il suffira ici de citer quelques chiffres officiels concernant l'emploi et le chômage: le taux d'activité régional est le plus faible de France aussi bien pour la population totale (36,8% contre 43,4%) que pour la population des 16 à 59 ans (59,9% contre 70%). Le taux d'activité des hommes est inférieur à la moyenne française et celui des femmes extrêmement bas (21,5% contre 34,6% et, pour les femmes de 16 à 59 ans, 37,6% contre 57,7%!). Le taux du chômage en Corse est supérieur à la moyenne nationale (11,5% contre 10,5%).

3.4. Culture et société

La lente déculturation subie depuis deux siècles a implanté en Corse un mode de vie, des habitudes et des besoins qui sont ceux de l'ensemble de la population française et, plus généralement, de la société de consommation, avec les graves problèmes que celle-ci entraîne (marginalisation, criminalité, drogue, etc.). Pourtant ces influences n'ont pas supprimé l'influence de structures traditionnelles comme la solidarité familiale ou le sentiment d'appartenance communautaire. S'ensuit dans les pratiques de vie (et plus souvent dans les mentalités) la permanence de valeurs collectives comme l'attachement à la terre et à la culture corse, majoritairement définie non comme une culture ethnique, mais comme l'héritage d'une histoire où la terre insulaire a fondu dans le même creuset culturel la population native et les apports externes (cette idée de la «communauté de destin» est d'ailleurs la base du programme politique nationaliste). Les mariages, les enterrements, les fêtes patronales et religieuses, le football et les foires sont l'occasion de manifester la cohésion communautaire aux différents niveaux (familles, villages, pieve, Corse), mais c'est surtout autour des thèmes de la protection de la nature et du patrimoine, de la langue et du chant que s'affirme et se maintient le sentiment de l'identité corse. Cette cristallisation identitaire a provoqué un mouvement important depuis une vingtaine d'années surtout et les réalisations ne sont pas négligeables (cf. Ettori 1982), bien que les mécanismes de la déculturation ne paraissent pas pouvoir être enrayés sans une intervention puissante des moyens politiques et publics.

4. Statistiques linguistiques

La difficulté de l'enquête de démographie linguistique est celle des situations minorées. La tentative de l'INSEE (1982) a produit des résultats surprenants: sur 166 600 personnes d'origine corse 96% comprendraient le corse et 86% le parleraient couramment; sur 33 600 personnes d'origine continentale ⅓ comprendraient le corse et 1 personne sur 9 le parlerait; sur 39 800 personnes d'origine étrangère ½ le comprendraient et ¼ le parleraient. La réalité de la corsophonie est bien inférieure à ces chiffres. Quant au contact français—corse, on peut affirmer qu'il touche peu ou prou l'ensemble de la population (quand il s'agit du français de Corse) et l'ensemble des corsophones (quand il s'agit du corse).

5. Le discours épilinguistique

La manière dont les Corses jugent les langues qu'ils parlent, la valeur et le statut attribués aux composantes linguistiques insulaires, permet d'interpréter le phénomène qui relie la conscience linguistique au sentiment de l'identité corse. Or on constate que ce discours ne reflète pas des comportements réels, car il ne mentionne que trois langues: le *corse*, le *français* et *l'italien*. Quand sont évoquées les autres langues parlées par les groupes plus restreints (variétés arabes, italiques, sardes, portugaises) ou acquises à l'école (anglais, allemand, espagnol, etc.), elles ne paraissent en rien concerner l'identité des Corses. Quant au contact des langues et à celui des variétés dialectales corses, il rend perplexes les membres de la communauté qui s'accordent à y voir un symptôme majeur de l'érosion de leur culture. Sur ce triptyque, le corse fait figure de *langue maternelle*. On lui prête généralement un fort coefficient identitaire du fait des racines et de l'histoire. Cette valeur nourrit un réel désir de maintenir vivante «la langue des ancêtres», «la langue du cœur» dotée d'une chaleur particulière. Après le corse, le français qui est considéré comme la *langue du citoyen*, non celle de l'identité culturelle, même lorsqu'il est indéniablement la première langue pratiquée par la personne interrogée. L'opinion paraît unanime pour dire qu'il est «la langue du pain». L'italien arrive en dernière place, affecté d'une *valeur culturelle* d'échange avec le corse, en souvenir de l'ancien couple corse—toscan. Les processus symboliques à l'œuvre dans ce système de représentations opèrent un tri dans le foisonnement identitaire du réel pour le reformuler dans des termes conformes au système d'images dont se nourrit le discours sur l'identité corse.

5.1. La langue et la culture françaises sont placées hors de l'identité culturelle. Quant aux références à l'histoire elles ne retiennent d'implantations françaises que coloniales qui de ce fait font figure d'intrus. Pour ce qui est de la littérature corse en français, elle déroute les personnes interrogées car son existence remet en cause le statut purement économique et juridique attribué à la langue française. Par ailleurs, lorsque les locuteurs sont mis en présence de ce qu'il est convenu d'appeler « le français régional de Corse » (désormais *f.r.c.*) et qui est plutôt un ensemble de phénomènes et de tendances de l'hybridation linguistique qu'une variété régionale de français nettement caractérisée, ils manifestent la même gêne. Le f.r.c. est en effet si répandu dans toutes les couches de la société que, s'il peut représenter un obstacle pour l'apprentissage de la norme scolaire, joue aussi un rôle ambigu d'identification à la Corse. Les Corses répugnent à reconnaître l'extension de ce langage hybride parce que la conscience identitaire se refuse à authentifier le mélange des langues qui à toute époque et en toute société passe pour une des manifestations premières de l'Impur.

5.2. L'italien dont il s'agit ici n'est que très rarement ce que Berruto (1987, 19) appelle « l'italiano contemporaneo », car l'opinion des Corses relève en effet d'un jugement épilinguistique qui remonte au 19ème siècle et qui a été repris sans interruption jusqu'à l'époque de l'entre-deux-guerres. Ce préjugé fait du « dialecte corse » un trait de pure toscanité archaïque conservé par l'insularité alors que dans la péninsule le contact des langues et les invasions entachaient la pureté originelle de ce langage. On voit alors se profiler, dans la référence épilinguistique corse à « l'italien », un autre enjeu: l'historicité et la dignité du corse, quelque chose comme le pendant linguistique et culturel d'une souveraineté qui ne peut être revendiquée explicitement, vu les conditions historiques et l'allégeance du sujet corse à l'officialité française. Cet état de la conscience collective en relation avec l'histoire linguistique et culturelle italiennes s'est trouvé profondément bouleversé par l'émergence d'un Etat-nation italien et par les rapports que celui-ci a entretenus avec la France.

Naguère encore on répugnait à reconnaître la parenté génétique des systèmes italien et corse, à cause du traumatisme né de la montée du fascisme mussolinien et de l'occupation italienne de la Corse (1942−1943). Aujourd'hui cette parenté ne semble plus hypothéquer l'autonomie sociolinguistique du corse, même si certains linguistes observateurs des tendances actuelles de « l'élaboration » du corse ont mis en lumière l'action persistante des normes de l'italien standard, influence d'autant plus pernicieuse qu'elle se produit à l'insu même des « codificateurs » du corse (cf. Chiorboli 1991, 90). Il convient donc d'interpréter différemment la référence à l'italianité selon l'époque et les opinions considérées. Aussi poserons-nous d'emblée l'identité et la langue corses comme procédant d'une *construction d'histoire* qu'il convient d'élucider par le recours à l'analyse proprement sociolinguistique.

5.3. L'analyse de la *diglossie*: Pour comprendre le rapport de ces images du discours épilinguistique avec les comportements individuels et collectifs, nous engageons aussi les concepts de la sociolinguistique des conflits, et en particulier ceux des sociolinguistes catalans et occitans et de la praxématique. Ainsi sont mis en évidence les fonctionnements diglossiques qui posent la diglossie non comme le cadre social distribuant les usages linguistiques entre langue(s) dominante(s) et langue(s) dominée(s) selon les leçons de Ferguson et de Fishman, mais comme l'intériorisation du conflit des langues et des cultures par le locuteur-sujet social et psychanalytique dont le langage révèle, en actes de discours et d'interaction verbale, un travail difficultueux de la signifiance, dans un environnement où les sommations idéologiques et sociales sont la plupart du temps vécues sur le mode de la contrainte et de la sujétion. L'idéologie diglossique repose sur un schéma dichotomique dont les termes concurrents s'excluent l'un l'autre. Elle engendre la nostalgie d'un âge d'or mythique de l'identité culturelle, entrave l'intellection du présent et interdit la maîtrise du pluralisme linguistique et culturel (Thiers 1987, 140). Nous avons complété cet édifice conceptuel en donnant corps au discours épilinguistique et en le posant comme l'observatoire des mouvements idéologiques et sociaux à l'œuvre dans la communauté ainsi que du processus par lequel ils sont réfractés dans l'imaginaire des sujets qui la composent (Thiers 1988, 433 sq).

La « triglossie » corse: quelques mots sur l'histoire de la diglossie corse pour expliquer dans quelle mesure et à quelles conditions on peut aujourd'hui analyser la forme du discours identitaire corse comme celle d'un discours issu de la diglossie. Disons sommairement que dans son histoire moderne (datons arbitrairement à partir des années 1800) la Corse est marquée par une sorte de triglossie. Avant la francisation de l'île, les deux langues en présence étaient « l'italien » et le corse, tous deux dialectes de la même aire linguistique italo-romane. Ces deux langues étaient perçues comme deux modalités différentes n'entretenant aucun conflit, comme deux niveaux hiérarchisés d'un seul et même système linguistique et culturel *italique* dont la représentation visible et pour ainsi dire l'icône était *l'italien écrit*. Lorsque, après la pénétration du français, l'italien eut reculé dans la pratique des Corses, les deux langues désormais en présence étant génétiquement différentes, le conflit devint patent. Le français avait pris la place qu'occupait auparavant la référence italienne, sans toutefois effacer complètement le souvenir de l'ancienne association. C'est pourquoi nous retrouvons aujourd'hui, dans le discours identitaire des Corses, la mention presque obligée de ces trois langues. Les Corses d'aujourd'hui retiennent le souvenir de l'ancienne diglossie corso-toscane et lui attribuent le caractère d'une cohabitation sereine et bénéfique alors qu'ils considèrent que le contact du corse et du français ne peut se conclure sans disparition du corse comme langue parlée, à plus ou moins brève échéance. De ces trois pôles entre lesquels circule la conscience linguistique, découle un sentiment identitaire éclaté, dominé très souvent par l'angoisse devant l'avenir, par l'impression aiguë de la perte du patrimoine et par l'envahissement de la nostalgie. Les jugements émis à propos du corse, du français et de l'italien nous informent donc sur les tendances contradictoires de la conscience identitaire actuelle. Les réticences manifestées à propos du français s'expliquent sans aucun doute par un mécanisme de compensation symbolique. En discours, le français devient tout court la langue de la citoyenneté politique et s'oppose au corse qui définit le sujet ethnique. Ce fonctionnement s'étend jusqu'aux personnes d'origine non corse désireuses de s'intégrer à la communauté du peuple corse.

5.4. Corse « hérité » et corse « élaboré »: Il serait trop long de décrire par le menu le débat qui anime une conscience culturelle particulièrement attentive au devenir de la langue corse, tant du point de vue de sa vitalité que des évolutions imprimées à la forme linguistique par le contact des langues et l'adaptation aux contextes d'emploi hier impensables pour un vernaculaire soumis à la fonctionnalisation diglossique. Ce débat est, dans sa substance, celui qui se développe dans toutes les situations où cohabitent — et s'opposent — des variétés promues au rang de langues officielles et d'autres hypothéquées par leur situation de langues minorées. Les représentations sociales liées à la langue et à la culture corses font apparaître un faisceau d'attitudes contrastées où l'attachement au corse « hérité » le dispute à l'acceptation du corse « élaboré ». Le premier n'est autre que la nostalgie d'un état exclusivement patrimonial et dialectal de la langue qui recoupe aussi l'aire d'un isolat culturel centré sur la cellule familiale dans un environnement de préférence rural. Le second implique l'assomption hardie des évolutions imprimées à la société corse et la gestion raisonnée d'un présent composite, dans un contexte où les déterminations géographiques sont remises en cause par les moyens de communication, l'information, le contact des cultures et les nouveaux langages informatiques et télématiques. Il n'est pas rare que l'affrontement des idéologies politiques se nourrisse des phénomènes liés à l'apparition d'un corse « élaboré ». Les adversaires déclarés du mouvement nationalitaire corse prennent souvent prétexte d'un simple mot pour se prévaloir du titre de champion de l'identité culturelle patrimoniale. Les acteurs de l'élaboration linguistique sont alors suspectés de sympathie pour les séparatistes clandestins et les néologismes interprétés comme des indices d'appartenance idéologique (Thiers 1986, 70). Les exemples ne manquent pas. Caractéristique est l'évolution d'un néologisme apparu dans les années 1970: *oghjincu*, d'abord créé à partir de l'adverbe *oghje* (« aujourd'hui »), pour ajouter au traditionnel *mudernu* (« moderne ») une connotation particulière: *oghjincu* voulait ainsi dire « qui concerne une vision moderne » de la Corse. Cet adjectif a d'abord pris une acception socio-culturelle et sociopolitique: « qui concerne les luttes de la corsitude », « militant ». Il semble aujourd'hui avoir perdu une partie de sa charge idéologique dans certains cas, comme dans son acception substantivée (*un oghjincu* peut désigner « un journal quotidien »), mais il l'a conservée dans le verbe qui en est dérivé (*ughjincà* c'est «moderniser, adapter selon l'esprit de la Corse actuelle et militante»).

6. Education

(1) Cadre général: On peut considérer, malgré les évaluations pessimistes de l'opinion militante, que la Corse est, parmi les régions de France, celle qui a tiré le meilleur parti d'une application tardive (1974) des textes réglementaires. L'enseignement de la «langue et de la culture corses» (LCC) est ainsi passé du militantisme à une professionnalisation accrue et les élus corses ont officiellement accepté l'existence de cet enseignement. L'article 53 de la loi n° 91-428 du 13 mai 1991 dispose que «l'Assemblée (de Corse) adopte un plan de développement de l'enseignement LCC, prévoyant notamment les modalités de l'insertion de cet enseignement dans le temps scolaire. Ces modalités font l'objet d'une convention conclue entre la collectivité territoriale de Corse et l'Etat». La politique commune en matière de langue corse est définie à l'intérieur du contrat de plan Etat-région qui prévoit: un plan de formation des enseignants, la création de laboratoires de langue, d'ateliers de langue corse dans les écoles, l'édition de manuels scolaires pour tous les niveaux et une banque de données informatique en langue corse.

(2) Enseignement primaire: En 1990-1991, 586 instituteurs (42%) ont déclaré dispenser un enseignement LCC à 11 749 élèves, mais seuls 14% des maîtres déclarent faire 3 heures de corse par semaine. Le contrat de plan 1990-1993 prévoit de former 540 instituteurs.

(3) Enseignement secondaire: Les chiffres sont plus précis: De 1983 à 1992, l'effectif est passé de 1485 élèves à 5105 élèves.

(4) A l'Université existe un cursus complet d'études corses, du DEUG au doctorat. En outre, le corse est présent obligatoirement dans toutes les filières (1 h ou 1 h 30 par semaine). La préparation professionnelle des futurs maîtres comprend un enseignement de corse. Il existe également un concours de recrutement national spécifique des professeurs, le CAPES de corse; 28 enseignants ont été recrutés en 1991 et 1992).

(5) Editions pédagogiques: Le CRDP de Corse et l'Assemblée ont édité plusieurs ouvrages didactiques pour le corse.

7. Administration, vie publique, politique

La place du corse dans la vie administrative et officielle est pratiquement inexistante. Un timide progrès se fait jour dans la signalétique de la toponymie, mais avec bien des réticences. Dans la vie politique le statut apparent du corse ne reflète pas les potentialités de cette langue et des compétences du personnel politique, surtout au niveau communal et cantonal, la plupart des élus locaux et régionaux étant de compétence bilingue. Les réunions courantes des conseils municipaux dans les petites communes rurales se déroulent souvent en corse, réservant au français la lecture des textes officiels et la rédaction des actes. Dans les situations formelles la place du corse est exiguë, mais de plus en plus souvent quelques conseillers régionaux font un usage partiel du corse lors des sessions de l'Assemblée de Corse, notamment lorsque les thèmes de l'identité culturelle, du patrimoine et de la protection de l'environnement sont engagés. Cette pratique sporadique relaie un état antérieur ou, par auto-censure et réflexe idéologique, la majorité des élus abandonnait la revendication linguistique et l'usage public du corse à certains des hommes politiques autonomistes et nationalistes. D'ailleurs ceux-ci se sont contentés généralement, par impréparation ou par stratégie, d'émailler leurs déclarations de quelques phrases en corse. Cette pratique du discours nationaliste, qui contredit le programme affirmé (revendication d'officialité pour le corse), suscite une critique interne de la part de militants qui voudraient en voir réduire l'ampleur. Aussi peut-on juger globalement que l'emploi public et officiel du corse est objet de débat plutôt que de pratique, même si l'on sent dans ce domaine sensible l'amorce d'une évolution du fait de l'accroissement des compétences régionales et de la présence grandissante des élus nationalistes.

8. Religion

La Corse est majoritairement catholique par tradition culturelle plus que par esprit religieux. Bien que la plupart des prêtres soient corsophones, ce qui permettrait une généralisation du corse dans la liturgie, l'expression publique de la foi reste francophone. Il faut voir dans cette situation l'effet contemporain d'une politique déterminée de la formation cléricale depuis la deuxième moitié du 19ème siècle menée de pair avec la francisation de l'école. On ne connaît pas aujourd'hui d'opposition déclarée à l'expression religieuse en langue corse: une initiative diocésaine qui remonte à ces vingt dernières années a permis la traduction en corse et l'adoption du rituel de la messe, *Messa nustrale* («Messe de chez nous»). Une traduction de la Bible vient d'être entamée, dont la première étape sera la traduction des évangiles (l'été 1994: les textes de Matthieu et de Luc devraient être publiés dans quelques mois). Quelques offices sont périodiquement célébrés en langue corse, à l'initiative de prêtres qui font figure de militants culturels ou à la demande expresse de particuliers ou d'associations. Pourtant ces célébrations restent occasionnelles et l'on ne sent pas de la part des autorités religieuses une quelconque volonté de généraliser l'emploi de la langue corse. Dans ce domaine comme dans d'autres le principal obstacle à l'extension de l'emploi public du corse paraît être l'action des fonctionnements diglossiques repérables dans l'ensemble de la société insulaire; peut-être la moyenne d'âge élevée des ecclésiastiques explique-t-elle en partie l'attitude conservatrice d'un clergé peu enclin à bouleverser l'ordre des choses existant, dans un contexte où la revendication linguistique s'est accompagnée ces dernières années d'un fort coefficient idéologique.

9. Médias

A partir de 1982, le corse a fait son entrée dans les médias publics, mais aujourd'hui, seule R.C.F.M., station régionale de Radio-France, fait un usage courant du corse, en particulier avec la diffusion quotidienne d'un journal d'informations locales, nationales et internationales entièrement en langue corse, véritable laboratoire pour l'élaboration linguistique (cf. Thiers 1989, 89 sq).

10. Orthographe

La codification est un fait remarquable, car elle est quasiment achevée sans intervention académique ni autoritaire (Geronimi/ Marchetti 1971; Ettori 1981, 31 sq), mais elle suscite sporadiquement des résistances d'arrière-garde. Quoi qu'il en soit, après des décennies d'incertitudes et de querelles, l'accord sur l'essentiel paraît s'être réalisé par la pratique empirique de l'écriture: à preuve le questionnaire mis au point par un chercheur autrichien (Klaus Hofstätter, Salzbourg) pour une enquête en cours et dans lequel on ne relève comme hésitations notables que quelques problèmes de transcription portant sur:
— la forme du verbe «être» à la 3ème personne du singulier de l'indicatif présent: *hè* vs *è* («il est») — la forme de l'adjectif démonstratif «ce»: *issu* vs *ssu* vs *su* vs *'su* — l'utilisation de l'accent grave pour rendre compte de la régulation de sandhi: ex: *e fiare* («les flammes»), *focu è fiare* («du feu et des flammes»); *a sera* («le soir»), *dumane à sera* («demain soir»). Du fait de l'absence d'accent grave les pratiques d'écriture en cours ne permettent pas toujours de distinguer la nature différente de *e*, de *a* (articles) et de *è* (conjonction) ou *à* (préposition) — l'enclise du pronom: *dammilu* vs *dà mi lu* («donne-le moi»). Ainsi la plus grande partie de la variation dans les pratiques d'écriture ne tient pas aux incertitudes de l'orthographe en cours mais à la variation dialectale (ex: *imbernu, inguernu, invernu, inguarnu* («hiver») sont autant de graphies correspondant à des articulations dialectales). Ce n'est donc pas sur les pratiques scripturales que porte l'incertitude actuelle, mais bien plutôt sur l'état de la conscience identitaire qui n'est pas encore totalement acquise aux phénomènes qu'engendre l'élaboration linguistique.

11. Portrait général des contacts linguistiques

Si le contact français—corse est une réalité immédiatement reconnaissable, sa caractérisation scientifique pose des problèmes de définition et de description. Jusqu'à une date récente, les Corses traitaient ces phénomènes uniquement par la dérision, ou sous l'angle de la réaction puriste (cf. Alfonsi 1926). Quant à Bottiglioni (1939—1941), il se contentait de déplorer de nombreux gallicismes. Quant à Colombani (1968), il voit le contact français—corse comme une variété en phase de constitution, mais on perçoit dans l'appellation «u francorsu» la même dérision. Les premiers essais de description scientifique ne datent que des années 1980, avec le début des études sociolinguistiques à l'Université de Corti. Dans toute la période précédente, l'évocation du contact s'est faite dans la passion et la polémique. Ce fut le cas de la synthèse prononcée par P. Marchetti au Congrès International de Bastia sur le Bilinguisme en 1984. Celui-ci distingue «u francorsu» et «u corsancese»: «MM. Thiers et Fusina ont parlé l'un et l'autre du «francorse» ou «francorsu» (...). Or le francorse ne saurait être que du français parlé à la corse. Mais ce que nous entendons trop souvent, autour de nous, n'est point du français parlé à la corse; c'est du corse parlé à la française. Je propose donc le terme de «corsancese» pour désigner ce langage» (C.C.E.C.V. 1986, 169 sq). Depuis cette date, l'étude s'est quelque peu affinée, en particulier avec Comiti (1992) et surtout Filippi (1992) que nous citerons souvent ici. Quant à nous, nous préférons définir les effets du contact en les éclairant par les pratiques langagières effectives observables au quotidien: dans cette optique, il faut parler de continuum et d'interaction plutôt que de variétés bien caractérisées. On voit alors se dessiner des pôles référentiels sollicités alternativement ou par des phénomènes d'hybridation plus ou moins importants selon le contexte, l'enjeu de l'échange, les rôles et les compétences des locuteurs. Il y a dans la Corse actuelle une situation langagière complexe à propos de laquelle nous ne possédons pas encore de description d'ensemble. C'est donc par commodité de langage que l'on peut alléguer, comme ensembles *in fieri* ou *in posse*, les variétés que l'on a pris l'habitude de nommer: le f.r.c. ou «le francorse» d'une part, «u corsancese» ou «u francorsu» d'autre part.

11.1. Problématique du français

Solidement inclus au répertoire linguistique, le français constitue désormais, associé au corse, la base de l'accès au langage et à la socialisation. Cette évidence doit éclairer l'étude du contact.

11.1.1. Francorse ou français régional de corse (f.r.c.)

L'impression générale est que le f.r.c. comprend une zone commune de traits attribuables à l'influence du substrat corse agissant dans la compétence linguistique individuelle, mais que certains groupes font de cet hybride un usage ludique et identitaire qui l'apparente dans certains contextes à un métalangage et/ou à une langue spéciale de connivence. Sans doute le retard des études sur ce point repose-t-il sur une réticence inconsciente à donner corps, par une analyse systématique, à une évidence que l'on veut ignorer. Il existe depuis longtemps une veine satirique qui caricature les *Corsi inpinzutiti* («les Corses francisés») en leur reprochant de parler (mal!) le français. Mais il ne s'agit plus de ce qui était appelé naguère *u francese strappatu* («le français écorché») dont il suffira sans doute de citer cet exemple éloquent rappelé par F. Ettori: *Le dimanche je porte ma femme à sentir la musique des soldats* où les verbes *porte* et *à sentir* traduisent le corse *purtà* et *à sente*. Ces faits relèvent de l'interlangue plus que de l'affectation. Les énoncés que l'on considère aujourd'hui comme relevant du f.r.c. sont fréquents même chez ceux qui ne connaissent pas le corse et semblent parfois renvoyer à une fonction psychosociale de contact des langues. Témoin ces paroles échangées aujourd'hui par des jeunes gens: *On a scrouqué une bagnole, et puis, en face de l'Arinella, elle a spatsé, spatsé ... de peu on se charbe* et surtout marquées, entre autres contaminations, par les calques *scrouquer, spatser* et *se charber* où se lit l'influence du corse *scruccà, spazzà, scialbassi*. Les mots français correspondants («voler», «déraper», «heurter un obstacle») étant connus par ces locuteurs, force est de voir dans cet usage un langage de connivence. L'hybridation joue donc dans ce cas un rôle sociolinguistique (reconnaissance des membres de la communauté dans la communication francophone, intégration partielle des non-Corses, substitut du corse lorsque la compétence active en langue corse n'est pas suffisante chez tel ou tel des interlocuteurs (cf. Thiers 1988, 277 sq).

Si l'on veut distinguer entre francorse et f.r.c., on peut dire comme Filippi (1992) que le f.r.c. représente la réalisation corse du standard français, à côté d'une variété d'hybridation plus grande, le «francorse», relativement éloignée de ce standard. D'autres n'établissent pas le même distinguo (cf. Comiti 1992, 246). Cette définition du f.r.c. s'étend en effet jusqu'au recours au code-switching. Ce n'est pas le cas de Filippi (1992) qui identifie le f.r.c. parmi les variétés suivantes: *Je dis que Pierre frappa Paul* (français soutenu) – *Je dis qu'il y a Pierre qui a frappé Paul* (français usuel) – *Je dis que Pierre il a mis une rouste à Paul* (français populaire) – *Je dis que Pierre, à Paul, il l'a frappé* (f.r.c.) – *Je dis que Pierre il a donné une concie à Paul/ Je dis que Pierre il a chaqué une tchibe à Paul* (francorse) – *A Paul, je te le dis, Petru l'hà datu una concia* (code-switching) – *Petru hà datu una concia à Paulu/Petru hà minatu à Paulu* (corse). On doit donc conclure que la définition du f.r.c. est extensible, et cette extension dénote la labilité d'un phénomène qu'on ne saurait isoler en variétés bien formées.

11.1.2. Traits caractéristiques du f.r.c.

Quelques exemples: – *ils sont à Strasbourg*: réalisation apicale de [r], chez de nombreux locuteurs âgés, par opposition au [R] vélaire de la norme d'usage du français; – e instable articulé par tous les locuteurs: *je te le donne* [ə]; – opposition é fermé/è ouvert; – emploi des temps et des modes: *quelle heure il sera maintenant?* (futur à valeur hypothétique); *si c'était moi, je me présentais encore* (ind.impft. *présentais* au lieu du cond. prés. *présenterais* en français standard); – extension au f.r.c. du *chì* corse polyvalent: *viens que mon père attend*; – accusatif prépositionnel: *je les aime à tous*; – emploi de certains outils grammaticaux: *ils avaient sa* (adj.poss.sing. au lieu du pluriel) *maison chaque* (adj.ind. au lieu de pronom).

C'est surtout à l'étude sociolinguistique qu'il appartient d'éclairer la véritable fonction de l'emploi de très nombreux calques et emprunts conscients tels que *chapper* ou *scapper* pour «s'échapper», *stoumaguer* pour «dégoûter». La conversation quotidienne et souvent aussi des prises de parole plus formelles se présentent donc comme une réalité langagière qui circule entre le français et le corse. C'est le lieu d'élection de l'alternance linguistique (les locuteurs passant sans cesse du corse au français), des calques plus ou moins conscients, des interférences et des ratés du discours. On serait donc tenté de parler d'un langage en état de dysfonctionnement permanent si certains indices ne laissaient supposer que ces formes du contact jouent aussi un rôle convivial. Au niveau éducatif ces phénomènes posent un problème qui n'a pas encore été abordé et que la structure officielle d'enseignement ignore au prétexte que ces effets du contact linguistique disparaissent avec l'acquisition du bon usage français à l'école, alors que tous les travaux menés dans ce domaine démontrent qu'en ignorant les langues dites «locales» et les variétés régionales du français, l'école aggrave le handicap linguistique. Il existe une analogie certaine entre le francorse/f.r.c. et le francitan de l'Occitanie. Pourtant, alors qu'en Occitanie le francitan peut constituer la base d'un processus de reconquête d'occitanité (cf. Lafont 1984, 21), processus pouvant aller «jusqu'au besoin de construction de la langue identitaire» (Guespin/Marcellesi 1986, 11), le francorse/f.r.c est aujourd'hui ressenti et analysé exclusivement comme un handicap: il n'est donc que stigmatisé par tous les locuteurs, corsophones ou non-corsophones.

11.2. Problématique du corse

Le corse ne se présente plus sous la forme d'un reflet vernaculaire de structures sociales archaïques. Travaillé par les mouvements de la population à travers l'île, les phénomènes transdialectaux et l'élaboration, le corse s'est ainsi profondément modifié pour devenir apte à l'expression de l'universel et des contraintes socio-techniques de la modernité. Mais cette adaptation s'est souvent faite par l'intégration d'emprunts, au français surtout, dans un contexte de domination peu favorable à la sollicitation systématique des moyens spécifiques du corse. Une telle évolution provoque souvent l'inquiétude des locuteurs qui y lisent une perte d'identité à cause de la rapidité des changements et de l'absence du statut glottopolitique qui permettrait d'en contrôler les effets (co-officialité, bilinguisme officiel, enseignement obligatoire sont des revendications soutenues dans la population). Le mouvement, qui affecte aussi la forme des productions orales et écrites dans de nouveaux registres et domaines d'emploi (Thiers 1988, 459 sq), peut dérouter des locuteurs accoutumés aux usages dialectaux. C'est dans ce climat de créativité fébrile et d'insécurité linguistique que l'on a vu apparaître une foule de phénomènes linguistiques fortement marqués par le contact et rangés sous des étiquettes rien moins que scientifiques: «u francorsu» et «u corsancese».

11.3. U corsancese

L'évolution, commencée au XIXème siècle, s'est intensifiée et aggravée à partir des années 1960 selon Marchetti (1989, 248 sq). Cet auteur distingue des emprunts «absorbés tels quels» comme *briquet, garage, restaurantu*, et «une série de mots français déformés, dialectalisés» comme *uvrieru, quaffore, greva, sciansa, mascina* (fr.: «ouvrier, coiffeur, grève, chance, machine»). S'appuyant sur d'autres publications (cf. Colombani 1968) et sur l'observation directe, Marchetti cite successivement: *orosu, malorosu, duiesimu, eppisseria, bulansgeria, busceria, settadire, cuà, lappini, cursgette, cassà a crutta, melansgià*, calques du français «heureux, malheureux, deuxième, épicerie, boulangerie, boucherie, c'est-à-dire, quoi, lapins, courgettes, casser la croûte, mélanger» au lieu des traditionnels *beatu, disgraziatu, secondu, buttea, panatteru, macellu, vene à dì, cumu!, cunigli, zucchini, rompe u dighjunu, mischià*. Marchetti déplore que par l'enseignement et la médiatisation « les plus choquantes corruptions » soient passées de la langue parlée à la langue écrite ou médiatisée. Il mentionne: — des attractions par ressemblance: la préposition *da* («par») remplacée par *per* qui en corse veut dire «pour»; la préposition *da* («de» marquant la provenance) remplacée par *di*; — des calques sur des particularités du français; — des calques morphologiques: *mubilisazione*, au détriment de la forme corse *mubilizazione*; — l'intrusion de l'article partitif français: *d'altri dicenu* («d'autres disent») au détriment de *altri dicenu*; — la tendance à garder une forme française à ce qui est référence universelle: *issu zitellu, simile a u Juif Errant*; — «l'épineux problème des néologismes»: parmi ceux-ci il distingue les «gallicismes d'une extrême pauvreté» comme *rivitalizà l'interiore* (auquel il préfère *ridà vita à l'internu* ou mieux *rinvivisce l'aldinentru*) et ceux qui marquent un progrès comme *vittura* de préférence au «passe-partout» *macchina*. Concluant sur la glottophagie en cours, il montre l'action de la langue dominante sur le corsancese en citant un grand nombre d'exemples.

Cet intérêt pour le contact n'inspire que stigmatisation et déploration de la perte d'identité linguistique subie par le corse hérité. Il est vrai que ces phénomènes sont observables dans toutes les productions orales et écrites, en contexte informel ou formel. L'exemple du journal quotidien en langue corse de R.C.F.M. est significatif de ces réticences qui alimentent le discours sur les effets néfastes du contact. Des termes tels que *emissione, mudernisazione, riaffirmà, spirà, espluattazione, busgià, tavula ritonda, pulitica di rigore, fà greva* («émission, modernisation, réaffirmer, inspirer, exploitation, bouger, table ronde, politique de rigueur, faire grève») sont ressentis soit comme des emprunts inévitables soit comme une trahison du corse authentique. Il est remarquable que ce sentiment soit partagé par les journalistes eux-mêmes qui tentent alors de réagir, de manière plus désordonnée que raisonnée, en recherchant des formulations plus authentiques ou qu'ils croient telles. En voici quelques exemples: — généralisation (parfois trop systématique) de l'ordre verbe + sujet, fréquent en corse: on a donc *hà annunziatu erisera Bagdad...* («Bagdad a annoncé hier soir...»);

— préférence pour l'emploi de prépositions qui permettent un écart par rapport à l'emploi français: *u ministru sarà in Corsica à studià i prublemmi* («le ministre sera en Corse pour étudier les problèmes») où *à* permet une distanciation plus grande que *da* ou *per*, tous deux possibles selon l'usage courant; — recherche d'écarts divers: *nomina, ingagiu*, par réaction contre les termes courants *numinazione, ingagiamentu* dont le suffixe paraît trop proche du français «nomination, engagement»; *regulà parte* («régler une partie»), avec suppression de l'article; généralisation de l'emploi de structures idiomatiques, même au prix d'une complexité peu conforme aux habitudes de réception du public: *smessusi* («qui s'est démis de ses fonctions»), participe passé réfléchi alors que l'emploi ordinaire est une relative (*chì s'hè smessu* ou *chì hà demissiunatu*). Comme cet effort d'élaboration et d'authenticité linguistique ne bénéficie pas d'une norme instituée, il aboutit quelquefois à des erreurs sémantiques: c'est le cas de *voce ferrata* là où le lexique français—corse de Lingua corsa et Ceccaldi (1968) donnent pour «voie ferrée»: *strada ferrata*: *voce ferrata*, qui procède d'une confusion entre «voie» et «voix» s'explique donc par une erreur psycholinguistique.

Ce qu'il est convenu d'appeler «le corse élaboré» pourrait donc être considéré comme relevant du «corsancese». Cette variété (j'inclinerai plutôt pour un «ensemble de variétés») qui se développe surtout depuis les années 1970, est la conséquence de l'effort généralisé de l'*ausbau* dans des milieux culturels et sur les médias radiophoniques. Or ce développement doit beaucoup à la démarche empirique: hormis quelques études ponctuelles (l'effort le plus constant et le plus programmé est celui de l'Association pour le Développement des Etudes du Centre-Est de la Corse (A.D.E.C.E.C.), c'est au niveau de la créativité individuelle que se dessine le mouvement. L'observateur natif peut attester la diffusion dans la communauté d'un nombre important de néologismes et de procédés relevant de ce mouvement, mais nous ne disposons, là non plus, d'aucune description achevée. Ainsi, contrairement à ce que l'on pourrait supposer, si dans le «corsancese», c'est-à-dire le corse soumis au contact du français, le contact se joue certes au détriment de la langue dominée, il assure aussi, de manière empirique ou plus construite, les avancées de cette même langue dominée par l'accession à de nouveaux domaines d'emploi. On doit en effet insister sur un fait important: l'élaboration (*ausbau*) klossienne du corse ne peut se faire et ne se fait en réalité qu'au prix de larges emprunts au français, qu'on accepte cet état de choses ou qu'on puisse regretter que l'absence d'une politique linguistique favorable ne permette pas de solliciter plus largement d'autres ressources moins périlleuses pour l'identité linguistique du corse. C'est pourquoi il nous faut conclure ce rapide panorama en constatant que les enjeux du contact français–corse sont à étudier dans la situation psycho-sociale et socio-politique.

12. Examen critique de la bibliographie

Nous avons dit (cf. 11.) que les phénomènes relevant du contact français–corse n'ont retenu l'attention des études scientifiques qu'avec l'apparition d'une sociolinguistique *corse*. Les premières confrontations d'expériences – avec notamment les études *occitanes*, *catalanes* et *créoles* – datent du Symposium International de Glottopolitique de Rouen (cf. Winter 1987). Le Colloque International des Langues Polynomiques (Corti90), coorganisé par le Centre de Recherches Corses, l'URA « Etudes sociolinguistiques, sociolittéraires et sociodidactiques en domaine occitan » (Univ. de Montpellier) et l'URA SUDLA (« Sociolinguistique, Usage et Devenir de la Langue », Univ. de Rouen) a élargi l'échange, mais c'est surtout au sein de l'URA SUDLA que l'étude du contact français–corse s'est développée. Elle y a trouvé, en y apportant sa propre contribution, un large front conceptuel où les traits typiques du contact s'éclairent de notions et de procédures d'investigation et d'interprétation connexes. Les termes de « glottopolitique, épilinguistique, individuation sociolinguistique » (et son contraire, la « satellisation ») constituent l'environnement notionnel et le prolongement de l'étude du contact. Les termes « fonctionnements diglossiques, fable d'identité », le couple « bilinguisme/diglossie », « autonomie linguistique » et « coofficialité » en élargissent la perspective par l'engagement de la sociolinguistique du bilinguisme et la problématique du conflit des langues. La sociolinguistique corse sollicite également les concepts de « volonté populaire » et d'« élaboration linguistique », empruntés à la standardologie comparée fondée par Heinz Kloss et vulgarisée par H. Goebl et Ž. Muljačić (1986, 53 sq).

12.1. Les langues polynomiques

Cependant le pilier central de cet édifice épistémologique est la théorie des *langues polynomiques* (Marcellesi 1991, 331 sq). Le concept définit des langues « dont l'unité est abstraite et résulte d'un mouvement dialectique et non de la simple ossification d'une norme unique, et dont l'existence est fondée sur la décision massive de ceux qui la parlent de lui donner un nom particulier et de la déclarer autonome des autres langues reconnues ». Cette proposition règle plusieurs problèmes, en particulier celui de la diversité dialectale, que l'on croyait contraire à l'expansion sociale du corse. Car la division en deux grandes aires insulaires (Nord et Sud) adoptée par commodité de langage et de présentation avait fini par occulter le continuum interdialectal et accréditer l'idée que corsophones du nord et du sud ne se comprenaient pas.

Or dans la perspective polynomique, la diversité dialectale n'est plus une entrave à l'unité du corse. On peut aussi inclure dans cette optique les phénomènes du contact avec l'italien et le français, apports exigés par la néologie lexicale particulièrement importante aujourd'hui du fait de l'élaboration linguistique. Le bilan corse de la langue polynomique peut être considéré comme positif, car dans la première période de sa diffusion il est venu entériner ce que la volonté populaire sait intuitivement: point n'est besoin d'unifier les langues pour les déclarer majeures et les doter des attributs institutionnels et véhiculaires généralement accordés à cet état. Les tenants de la langue polynomique ont graduellement étendu leur réflexion à l'éducation bilingue et, sans abandon de leur loyauté linguistique, à une problématique langagière ouverte sur une large compétence de communication.

Une telle modification de la visée ne va pas sans problèmes ni conflits. Les fonctionnements liés à l'idéologie diglossique trouvent un aliment nouveau dans cet effort de rationalisation du réel langagier et du discours sur la langue minorée. Au début, l'attitude polynomiste a pu passer aux yeux de certains pour une trahison de l'idéal militant, mais il semble qu'aujourd'hui soit reconnue majoritairement sa véritable finalité: situer la revendication et l'action en faveur du corse parmi les enjeux réels et maîtriser intellectuellement les conditions objectives de son maintien et de son extension comme langue de communication assumant entièrement sa vocation véhiculaire. La corsité polynomique vise à privilégier la communication tout en ménageant la fonction identitaire de la langue tenue pour « maternelle » en dépit de son recul dans la pratique. Elle induit un modèle théorique à variables qui exclut toute hiérarchisation parmi les variétés internes au corse, qu'il s'agisse des dialectes hérités et des traits transdialectaux.

Dans la mesure où la poussée de l'élaboration linguistique rend nécessaire le recours au français et à l'italien pour enrichir le code corse, elle inclut aussi une partie des effets du contact des langues, au niveau identitaire. La problématique du contact des langues se contente en effet souvent d'enregistrer les zones d'interpénétration des systèmes. Or le contact linguistique entraîne le conflit parce que l'interprétation du processus est induite par l'existence des descriptions de la norme des langues dominantes (c'est le cas pour le français et l'italien, parlés ou connus par la majorité des corsophones) ou d'un discours sur la norme de la langue dominée (c'est le cas du corse, dont la norme insuffisamment décrite mais constamment alléguée a une prégnance fortement fantasmatique). Les risques réels ou supposés de *glottophagie* (par le français) ou de *satellisation* (par l'italien) condamnent le chercheur à se détourner de la réalité vivante au profit d'une recherche, certes utile et déontologiquement confortable, mais à notre sens de plus en plus éloignée de son objet.

Nous sommes donc conduit à souligner l'intérêt du concept de « langue polynomique » dans la situation corse et à en étendre la pertinence de la perspective interne (rapport entre dialectes du corse) à l'option interlinguistique (phénomènes de contact du corse avec le français et, dans une moindre mesure, avec l'italien). Il faut alors opérer une conversion épistémique en considérant que les normes respectives de ces langues en contact avec le corse changent de nature lorsqu'elles se trouvent sollicitées par un locuteur corsophone s'exprimant en langue corse dans une interaction verbale réelle. Car lorsqu'il s'agit d'actes langagiers et non de réflexion métalinguistique, on peut théoriquement poser que, par la force de l'individuation des indicateurs linguistiques toujours présents malgré le contact, s'opère la transformation de la norme de la langue étrangère (norme d'extériorité) en norme d'interaction (norme d'intériorité fonctionnant en relation dialectique avec la charge symbolique des indicateurs linguistiques de corsité qui sont de véritables fétiches identitaires). L'acceptation complète de la conception polynomique nous paraît donc conditionner étroitement l'avenir même de la corsité linguistique.

12.2. Divergences

Le courant polynomiste est actuellement en interaction avec deux autres tendances. (1) La corsité *satellite* semble attirée par une réintégration du corse à l'italien. Elle se prévaut des indéniables parentés génétiques entre le corse et les variétés de l'aire italo-romane. Si elle se développait explicitement dans un groupe productif, elle pourrait constituer un risque de satellisation, en rupture avec l'affirmation de l'autonomie linguistique du corse obtenue notamment lors de ces vingt dernières années. Le développement le plus achevé de cette position se trouve dans Marchetti (1989). Bien qu'elle ne se manifeste par aucune production en langue corse et n'ait aucun effet visible sur les pratiques langagières, elle peut ramener au repliement nostalgique et au refus de l'élaboration actuelle la fraction des locuteurs encore hésitants devant les nécessités de l'évolution du corse. (2) La corsité de *distanciation* juge pour sa part qu'il est possible d'atteindre à un niveau moderne et universel d'expression à partir des ressources exclusives du corse hérité. Elle a flirté un temps avec une vision mythique de l'âge d'or de la langue; elle se défend aujourd'hui d'être puriste et inspire des productions de qualité. Emus par le recul du corse parlé et par les effets du contact, les Corses sont hantés par la nostalgie de la « langue pure » et tentés par les stratégies de la distanciation (Thiers 1988, 567 sq). Or la « corsité de distanciation » se donne comme résolument appuyée sur l'oral traditionnel, mais repose en réalité sur la recherche de l'écart maximum avec le français. C'est ainsi que, par exemple, les grammaires normatives prescrivent pour l'irréel du présent l'emploi du subjonctif imparfait dans la subordonnée de condition (*s'o vulissi*) parce que la forme orale traditionnelle emploie l'indicatif imparfait (*s'o vulia*) comme le français (« si je voulais »). On entend aussi rejeter des emprunts au français pourtant intégrés depuis longtemps: *differenza* et *abbunamentu*, par exemple, sont stigmatisés au profit de *sfarenza* et *arrugamentu*, sans doute parce qu'ils rappellent « différence » et « abonnement ». Pour ce courant, le but est de « retrouver la langue des aïeux », mais en réalité le produit de cet effort souvent inquiet est une construction d'identité normative actuellement peu susceptible de diffuser largement dans les pratiques langagières des masses. Chacun des traits linguistiques allégués comme définissant le système de « la langue corse pure », est effectivement attesté dans les usages réels; aussi la prétention normative de cette tendance se masque-t-elle d'une idéologie de naturel. Ce qui est en cause, ce n'est donc pas l'authenticité de ces traits, mais la volonté de les réunir intégralement dans une structure systémique serrée, excluant la possibilité d'insérer tout contact, ne tolérant qu'une variation minime et présentée comme la reprise à l'identique d'un usage oral ancien, vision qui oblitère les phénomènes historiquement reconnus du contact et du conflit des langues en Corse et peut-être l'histoire elle-même. Ainsi ce qui paraît contestable, ce ne sont pas les prescriptions de la norme prises une à une, mais *l'attitude idéologique qui*, en se prévalant d'une norme fantasmatique, prétend assurer à des constructions écrites récentes — d'ailleurs littérairement très estimables! — la fonction de régir et de censurer dogmatiquement la parole vivante. Le dialogue est permanent entre cette orientation et les études sociolinguistiques corses (cf. *Kyrn*, numéros 217, 218, 219, 221, Aiacciu, 1988 et *Rigiru* 1989). Cette interaction de tendances nous paraît salutaire car, quels que soient les choix linguistiques actuels et à venir, l'existence de ces trois directions est susceptible d'éclairer la masse des locuteurs sur le rapport d'une logique exclusivement métalinguistique aux concessions qu'imposent les besoins langagiers réels dans la communauté corse contemporaine. Il est remarquable que le mouvement de l'élaboration s'accomplisse sans qu'on ait vu apparaître le préalable d'une unification du corse ni le rejet des influences que celui-ci reçoit en puisant, pour se moderniser, dans le corpus des langues au contact desquelles l'a mis l'histoire dominée du peuple corse.

13. Bibliographie (sélective)

Alfonsi, Tommaso (1926): *Una filza di francesismi colti nelle parlate dialettali corse*, Ajaccio.

Berruto, Gaetano (1987): *Sociolinguistica dell'italiano contemporaneo*, Rome.

CCECV (1986): *Cungressu Internaziunale nantu à u bislinguisimu/Congrès International sur le bilinguisme (Bastia 1984)*, Conseil de la Culture de l'Education et du Cadre de Vie (Ed.), Bastia.

Ceccaldi, Mathieu (1968): *Dictionnaire corse–français de la pieve d'Evisa*, Paris.

Chiorboli, Jean (1991): »Polynomie corse et glottopolitique«. In: *Corti90*, 69–74.

Colombani, Ignaziu (1968): *Francorsu*, Bastia.

Comiti, Jean-Marie (1992): *Les Corses face à leur langue*, Aiacciu.

Corti90: *Actes du Colloque International des Langues Polynomiques (17–22 septembre 1990)*, Publications Universitaires de Linguistique et d'Anthropologie (PULA), n° 3/4, Corti.

Ettori, Fernand (1981): *Langue corse: incertitudes et paris*, Ajaccio.

Ettori, Fernand (1982): « Le sursaut d'une culture menacée ». In: *Le Mémorial des Corses*, tome 5, Ajaccio, 334–385.

Filippi, Paul (1992): « Le français régional de Corse », thèse de doctorat, Université de Corse, Corti.

Geronimi, Dominique Antoine/Marchetti, Pascal (1971): *Intricciate è cambiarine. Manuel pratique d'orthographe corse*, Nogent-sur-Marne.

Guespin, Louis/Marcellesi, Jean-Baptiste (1986): « Pour la glottopolitique ». In: *Langages 83*, 5–34.

INSEE (1986): *Tableaux de l'économie corse*, Ajaccio.

Lafont, Robert (1984): « Pour retrousser la diglossie ». In: *Lengas 15*, 5–36.

Marcellesi, Jean-Baptiste (1991): « Polynomie, variation et norme ». In: Corti90, 331–336.

Marchetti, Pascal (1989): *La Corsophonie, un idiome à la mer*, Paris.

Muljačić, Žarko (1986): « L'enseignement de Heinz Kloss (modifications, implications, perspectives) ». In: *Langages 83*, 53–64.

Thiers, Jacques (1986): « Epilinguisme, élaboration linguistique et volonté populaire: trois supports de l'individuation sociolinguistique corse ». In: *Langages 83*, 65–74.

Thiers, Jacques (1987): « Idéologie diglossique et production de sens ». In: *Peuples méditerranéens 38–39*, 139–152.

Thiers, Jacques (1988): *Epilinguisme et langue polynomique: l'exemple corse*, thèse de doctorat (linguistique), Université de Haute-Normandie, Mont-Saint-Aignan.

Thiers, Jacques (1989): *Papiers d'identité(s)*, Levie.

Winter, Alexandre (Ed.) (1987): *Problèmes de glottopolitique*, Cahiers de Linguistique Sociale 7, Publications de l'Université de Rouen, Rouen.

Jacques Thiers, Corti (France)

146. Corse—italien

1. Remarques préliminaires: histoire, sociolinguistique
2. Niveaux du contact linguistique corse-italien
3. Péripéties du discours scientifique
4. Bibliographie (sélective)

1. Remarques préliminaires: histoire, sociolinguistique

Jusqu'à la 2ème guerre mondiale, le contact entre italien et corse est un phénomène fréquent. En ce qui concerne la compétence passive en italien, on peut supposer qu'elle est le fait de l'ensemble de la population corse, ce qui dans une certaine mesure est encore le cas aujourd'hui quand il s'agit d'italien populaire (cela est exclu pour les autres variétés: technique et scientifique, bureaucratique, etc.: voir «l'architecture» de l'italien telle qu'elle est représentée par Berruto (1987)). Toujours à la même époque, l'italien est employé comme langue écrite quasi exclusive par les Corses instruits, c'est-à-dire par une faible minorité qui a également, mais à un degré moindre, une compétence active orale dans cette langue. En l'absence de données concrètes et fiables, nous avons tendance à remettre fortement en question la thèse, encore très répandue aujourd'hui, que les Corses non seulement écrivaient mais parlaient couramment l'italien avant les progrès de la francisation (voir Thiers 1977). Il faut ici évoquer «l'idéologie culturelle italienne véhiculée par les élites» (Fusina 1991, 195 indique qu'au XIXème siècle elle a une emprise encore très forte), mais surtout la réalité des pratiques langagières recouverte par le terme «italien» quand il est employé pour qualifier le moyen exclusif d'expression des Corses (le «peuple», surtout celui de «l'intérieur» évoqué par le rapport Mottet par exemple dans les années 1820). Aux témoignages qui parlent de «l'italien de Corse», on pourrait opposer ceux qui évoquent ou montrent des documents mettant en scène le «dialecte» ou «l'idioma corso» utilisé dans certaines circonstances.

Le niveau de compétence des Corses en langue italienne ne peut être évalué indépendamment de la situation d'alphabétisation (les données quantitatives précises manquent); dans la Sardaigne toute proche la compétence en italien est faible vers 1900 pour les locuteurs peu scolarisés (il y a 88% d'analphabètes en 1871: Sotgiu in Loi Corvetto 1992, 910). Quant aux Corses alphabétisés, ils écrivent souvent un italien émaillé d'interférences corses (voir Chiorboli 1978 et Nesi 1992).

Dans la deuxième moitié du XXème siècle la Corse bascule totalement dans le champ de communication français. Pour l'ensemble des Corses, le français domine les échanges dans toutes les situations de communication, et la coupure avec l'italien vivant est totale. Dans le domaine de l'enseignement, on note qu'en 1992 38% seulement d'élèves étudient l'italien (en 1ère, 2ème ou 3ème langue); les chiffres sont encore plus faibles pour la 1ère langue (en 1991–1992, 137 élèves corses ont choisi l'italien en 1ère langue, contre 11 439 pour l'anglais). Dans l'enseignement supérieur on note l'ouverture tardive d'un cursus d'italien à l'Université de Corse (160 étudiants en 1993). La naissance récente de *A Viva Voce*, revue corse en langue italienne créée par des «intellectuels bastiais fidèles à l'antique italianité de la ville», a suscité des réactions diverses («de peur de nous noyer dans la Seine faut-il que nous nous jetions dans l'Arno et le Tibre?»; de Zerbi in *Kyrn* 11/1992), de même que l'annonce par le Recteur de la Corse (Septembre 1993) d'une «section méditerranéenne» où le corse et l'italien seraient à la fois matières et instruments d'enseignement. Quant au rôle des médias italiens en Corse (RAI notamment), il semble jusqu'à présent limité dans ses effets de masse, contrairement à ce qui se passe dans d'autres pays méditerranéens où la télévision italienne a eu des effets linguistiques importants: «non sembra che qualcosa di analogo si verifichi in Corsica dove le sorti declinanti dell'italiano non ricevono soccorso dai programmi della televisione italiana» (Bruni 1992, XX). Certains auteurs au contraire, considérant que Corses et Italiens parlent «essentiellement» la même langue, s'étonnent de voir que «la télévision régionale [corse] éprouve le besoin de traduire en voix off, en corse ou en français, les propos tenus en italien» (Dalbera-Stefanaggi 1989, 128).

2. Niveaux du contact linguistique corse-italien

2.1. Attitudes et idéologies métalinguistiques

Afin de débusquer dans la masse de productions linguistiques concrètes les faits qui relèvent de l'interférence entre deux systèmes il faut au préalable les avoir caractérisés. Nous n'insisterons pas ici sur la difficulté de l'entreprise. La variété d'italien qui fonde la caractérisation est d'ordinaire l'italien «moderne, commun, standard, etc.» (Ineichen 1993 b, 2265) malgré l'imprécision des termes. Quant au corse, notre caractérisation est basée sur les traits linguistiques communs à l'ensemble des variétés corses, ce qui nous permet de donner un contenu au concept de «corse commun» que nous utiliserons.

Nous choisissons ici de n'alléguer que certains traits caractérisants (par rapport aux langues autres, ici surtout l'italien) et communs à l'ensemble des dialectes (sans pour autant exclure du corse commun les autres traits ou variantes locales, spécifiques ou non, allogènes ou autochtones, nécessaires au fonctionnement du système).

Si le contact du corse avec le français a été maintes fois abordé et condamné, le contact avec le toscan a été surtout évoqué pour démontrer que le corse (autrefois différent du toscan-italien) est devenu de l'italien à la suite de sa toscanisation. Rares sont ceux qui ont évoqué des influences «in senso opposto» (Da Pozzo in Nesi 1992, 933) ou des échanges dans les deux sens (Acquaviva 1982); on se réfère dans tous les cas à des époques anciennes. Pour l'époque moderne (disons, après 1861), la question des emprunts du corse à l'italien semble devenue un sujet tabou. Si le terme «gallicisme» a au moins une occurrence dans toute étude consacrée au corse, «l'italianisme» est rarement évoqué.

Les productions linguistiques corses actuelles comprennent cependant un certain nombre de variantes et de normes empruntées à l'italien officiel. Ces emprunts ne sont pratiquement jamais le résultat d'interférences (le bilinguisme corse/italien n'existe pas en tant que phénomène social) mais procèdent d'innovations individuelles et volontaires, savantes ou semi-savantes, qui ont un impact variable sur l'usage (un degré d'acclimatation variable). Ce type d'emprunt est dû la plupart du temps à une idéologie linguistique diffuse qui recherche plus *l'écart maximum* par rapport à la norme du français que la *convergence* avec l'italien. De tels emprunts, de luxe ou de nécessité, sont diffusés par les agents glottopolitiques qui en occultent systématiquement l'origine italienne. Ils sont accueillis comme des formes authentiquement corses («sputiche») par les usagers moyens du corse élaboré, incapables de déceler la convergence avec une norme italienne qu'ils ignorent en grande partie. Le résultat est l'intégration rapide d'un nombre considérable d'emprunts qui, s'ils sont majoritairement lexicaux, concernent également les autres niveaux linguistiques, syntaxe comprise.

Les italianismes dans le corse actuel ont le même statut que les latinismes dans les langues romanes: le corse *disoccupatu* «chômeur» est calqué sur le modèle italien (*disoccupato*) de la même façon que le français *infarctus* ou l'italien et l'espagnol *infarto* sont formés au XIXème siècle sur le modèle latin *infarctus*.

S'agissant du corse et de l'italien, il faudrait parler non pas de contact de *langues*, mais de contact de *modèles*. L'italien est considéré par un certain nombre de codificateurs comme un réservoir de formes et de normes disponibles pour le corse. Les formes et les normes italiennes empruntées ne sont pas déduites le plus souvent de l'usage vivant ni même de la compétence des codificateurs, mais des grammaires prescriptives, des manuels d'enseignement et des ouvrages lexicographiques italiens.

Il est à noter qu'il s'agit d'une norme italienne restrictive et datée, basée sur une variété littéraire peu ouverte sur l'usage contemporain. Le modèle pratiquement exclusif est la grammaire didactique italienne pour francophones, qui tend à réduire la variation par la condamnation d'un des deux termes (par exemple le premier dans des couples comme *comprendere/capire*, *attendere/aspettare*, *arrivare/riuscire*, *forzare/obbligare*, *branca/ramo*) indépendamment de toute prise en considération de fréquence ou de spécialisation sémantique.

S'intéresser aujourd'hui au contact entre corse et italien c'est observer l'intervention savante sur la langue. L'analyse de l'idéologie linguistique qui détermine l'action glottopolitique est partie intégrante de la description pour le linguiste, observateur-acteur dans sa communauté même s'il s'abstient de tout jugement moralisateur.

Une caractérisation typologique poserait un autre type de problèmes d'ordre scientifique, en raison notamment de l'absence de modèle théorique général.

Il serait intéressant par exemple de noter la coexistence en corse de traits qui selon certaines règles typologiques romanes s'excluent mutuellement. Le corse, qui accepte (comme l'italien) le passif périphrastique (*un omu hè statu tombu*) et l'article partitif (*ci sò i sbagli ind'è ssu libru*), devrait exclure l'accusatif prépositionnel («périphérique et méridional»: Ineichen 1993 b, 2273, mais aussi corse *chjamu à Petru*). L'accusatif prépositionnel est aussi considéré comme incompatible avec l'accord du participe parfait passif (Körner in Ramat 1984, 149) mais le corse possède l'un et l'autre (*à elle e cunnoscu*/*l'aghju viste passà*).

Notre tâche consistera donc ici essentiellement à repérer et à évaluer dans l'activité normative corse et dans l'usage ce qui est à imputer au modèle italien (tel qu'il est perçu et véhiculé par les agents glottopolitiques corses).

2.2. Phonologie/graphie

La variation automatique des consonnes initiales est considérée comme un des phénomènes romans les plus importants et les plus complexes; ses modalités corses ont un caractère spécifique et emblématique (Tekavčić 1972, 225), notamment en ce qui concerne la lénition (certaines modalités sont pancorses; sonorisation de /f/ et spirantisation de /v/ en position intervocalique, initiale ou interne).

La fusion de V et B latins (bétacisme) est un phénomène pancorse bien que l'influence toscane (via la Sardaigne) ait abouti en Corse du Sud à la phonologisation de /v/ (*vinu* [vinu]) qui n'a pas touché la Corse du Nord. L'orthographe note d'ordinaire la consonne étymologique qui «coiffe» des réalisations différentes (*vinu* pour [vinu] au Sud et [binu] au Nord). Cependant la tendance étymologisante (ou italianisante) a parfois comme résultat d'introduire des oppositions graphiques qui occultent une même réalisation pancorse: malgré la graphie on a /b/ ([b]) initial dans *banditu* comme dans *valisgia* (Muntese 1985; cf. *balicia* en calabrais notamment).

La fusion de V et B après liquide est pancorse et correspond au latin vulgaire (*alveus* non *albeus*: Appendix Probi); les codificateurs (surtout du Nord) oscillent cependant entre v (dû sans doute au modèle italien) et b: *nervu, serve*/*corbu, cerbellu* (Romani 1990, 57); *corvu, nervu*/*ciarbellu* (Marchetti/Geronimi 1971, 37).

L'affricatisation de /s/ postconsonantique (*corsu* [kortsu] en Corse du Sud) est la plupart du temps considérée comme typique du Mezzogiorno (Rohlfs 1966, 267) ou de l'italien centro-méridional (à l'exclusion de la Toscane). Cependant l'affricatisation de /s/ après /l/ concerne toute la Corse; la réalisation [s] est donc exclue après /l/ (réalisé [l] ou [r] selon les variétés, malgré les fluctuations graphiques (s/z) fréquentes: *falsu, salsa, imbalsamatu, polsu*/*falzu, salza, imbalzamatu, polzu*.

Le retour vers l'étymologie (ou l'italien) semble caractériser les ouvrages plus récents: la variante *falsu* apparaît dans Muntese 1985 alors que Muntese 1960 ne proposait que *falzu*.

Au plan de l'évolution du système orthographique corse, après l'alignement initial sur l'italien et la distanciation marquée par Marchetti/Geronimi 1971 dans les années 70, on note un retour au modèle italien ou un refus des innovations divergentes (parfois abandonnées par leurs promoteurs initiaux). Nous citerons la graphie des formes pronominales (*canta la*/*cantala*); le verbe «être» à la 3ème personne (*hè*/*è*); les prépositions ou adverbes complexes (*à cantu*/*accantu*; le modèle italien peut servir de référence explicite ou implicite: cf. Multedo in ADECEC 1986, 16: «u talianu hà risoltu u prublemu mettendu duie *d*» [dans *abbastanza*], è u corsu hà seguitatu avendu listessa ortografia chè u talianu»).

2.3. Morphosyntaxe

Dans les langues romanes, les noms correspondant à des étymons masculins en -*a*, -*ma*, -*ta*, en -*is* (généralement féminins), ou -*ista* (masc. et féminin) peuvent soit subir une adaptation populaire (*gramma* > corse *grammu*, italien *grammo*), soit conserver ou acquérir une finale savante (*poeta* > corse *pueta*, italien *poeta*; mais les deux langues connaissent ou ont connu des variantes du type *puetu*/*poeto*).

En corse on note un accroissement récent des finales savantes. C'est l'italien littéraire qui fournit le modèle. La réfection savante corse épargne en effet — pour l'instant — les rares formes issues de -*is* qui présentent en italien une évolution populaire. On aurait pu avoir par exemple en corse *dosi comme *sintassi* (*dosis, syntaxis*; cf. espagnol *dosis, sintaxis*). C'est sans doute l'absence de finale savante dans l'italien *dose* qui fait que le correspondant corse *dosa* (Muntese 1985) conserve sa finale, avec comme résultat une différence de traitement entre *sintassi* et *dosa* parallèle à celle de l'italien (*sintassi*/*dose*; *dosa* est attesté au XIIème s. et encore aujourd'hui dans le Mezzogiorno). Une étape ultérieure est franchie lorsque *fasa*, qui gardait sa finale «populaire» malgré le même étymon en -*is*, est concurrencé non pas au profit du «lecte possible » (Berrendoner/Le Guern/Puech 1983) étymologisant *fasi*, mais au profit de *fase* (Muntese 1985) qui correspond exactement au modèle italien « standard ».

Dans le domaine qui nous occupe l'évolution récente en corse, prévisible, peut être résumée comme suit: apparition de nombreuses finales savantes à côté des finales populaires déjà en usage: *pilotu, fascistu* (Muntese 1960−1967) / *pilota, -u, fascista, -u* (Muntese 1985); élimination de la variante populaire: *dramu, -a, tesi, -a* (Muntese 1960−1967) / *drama, tesi* (Muntese 1985).

On assiste aussi à la généralisation hypercorrecte de la finale savante (divergente par rapport à l'étymologie et/ou à l'italien standard): *u tomu* (Muntese 1985) / *u toma II*; U Ribombu 8/7/1988) et à des transformations diverses dues à l'insécurité linguistique (qui bien entendu n'épargne pas les codificateurs eux-mêmes): *a calma* (Ceccaldi 1968) / *u calma* (U Ribombu 27/9/1991).

On soulignera que la normativisation actuelle tend à suivre l'italien élaboré moderne, jusque dans ses choix anti-étymologiques. Alors que Muntese 1960−1967 propose par exemple *stratega, -u*, Muntese 1985 ne retient que *stratega*, c'est-à-dire la forme italienne aberrante quant à l'étymologie.

Le résultat de la réfection corse savante détermine également un flottement de l'accent (l'accent grec s'oppose souvent à l'accent latin et donc corse). On a ainsi comme équivalent du français *analyse* (au moins) 4 formes: *analìsa* (Ceccaldi 1968, évolution populaire quant à la finale -*a* et le schéma paroxyton), *anàlisi* (Muntese 1985, évolution savante quant à la finale et au schéma proparoxyton), *analisi* (Muntese 1960−1967) et *anàlisa* (*RCFM* 2/4/93; évolution semi-savante comme le précédent, croisement des 2 premières formes). De même le locuteur corse moyen va chez le *radiològu*, le *cardiològu* (tendance populaire à la paroxytonie soutenue par le contact avec le français) alors que les doctes vont consulter le *radiòlugu*, le *cardiòlugu*; cf. italien *radiòlogo, cardiòlogo*). On a, même dans les variétés élaborées, des oppositions entre mots accentués sur le premier élément du composé (*francòfunu* ou *francòfubu*: Muntese 1985) et mots accentués sur le deuxième (*cursofònu* « corsophone », *spichjafònu* « télévision »: Marchetti 1983, Marchetti 1974; il s'agit ici de cas particuliers dans la mesure où le même auteur applique en général le schéma savant: *lissicògrafi* Marchetti 1983, 433).

L'usage contemporain permet d'observer une fluctuation du genre de certains noms (*seguitu/seguita; minutu/minuta*, etc.). On notera que ce type de fluctuations en corse est relevé lorsque s'opposent les normes française et italienne. Tout se passe comme si dans de tels cas la norme de l'italien servait de révélateur et de déclencheur potentiel pour un conflit de normes en corse.

Le substantif *fronte* est féminin en italien et dans les dictionnaires corses; il est souvent masculin dans l'usage courant corse (de même qu'en sarde, en ligurien, en italien méridional conformément à l'étymologie latine; Rohlfs 1966, 391, 183). On notera que le genre masculin est limité au sens militaire en italien (influencé par le français au cours de la première guerre mondiale: Battisti/Alessio 1975) comme en corse.

Comme d'habitude, le conflit de normes entraîne hypercorrections, hybridations et insécurité linguistique. L'italien *(la) percentuale* s'est imposé en corse quant à la forme mais pas quant au genre (corse *u percentuale* « le pourcentage », Muntese 1985).

Le correspondant corse de « art » (masculin en français, féminin en italien) est masculin dans l'usage courant mais varie en genre dans le même dictionnaire (*arte goticu/arte roza*) ou dans le même article (*e bell'arti/arti meccanichi*).

Les dictionnaires donnent tous le masculin pour l'équivalent corse de *courant* (français *le courant* / italien *la corrente*) avec parfois (pour Muntese 1985) des variations (« *seguità u (ou a) currente* ») accompagnées de notations curieuses (« à noter qu'en Balanin le courant d'air est resté féminin, de même qu'à Bastia le courant marin »).

En ce qui concerne l'emploi de l'article défini, l'usage courant omet l'article avec l'indication de l'année (peut-être aussi grâce à la pression du français): *simu in 1993*. Cependant la fréquence de la construction avec l'article s'accroît et l'usage varie, parfois chez les mêmes auteurs. Dans ce cas, c'est toujours pour abandonner la construction sans article; sans doute avons-nous, ici aussi, la solution habituelle du conflit entre les modèles français et italien (*in ondeci*, Geronimi in *Rigiru* 7/1975, 26; *in lu 75*, Geronimi in *Rigiru* 5/1976, 32).

Il ne fait pas de doute que l'emploi (rare) de l'article avec l'indication de l'heure dans certains ouvrages normatifs (*chi ora sarà? Saranu e sette*; Yvia-Croce 1972, 142) s'explique par la pression du modèle italien (officiel, car le type *sò sett'ore* généralisé dans l'usage courant corse moderne est normal en italien archaïque ou poétique).

L'évolution de la morphologie verbale corse a conduit à une généralisation de l'infixation: *minà: mengu; impruvisà: impruviseghju*. On pourrait donc formuler une règle selon laquelle l'infixation est la règle et l'absence d'infixation l'exception (Chiorboli 1993, 50). Cette particularité importante du corse est d'ordinaire tue ou minimisée par les grammaires normatives.

Certaines prescriptions normatives tendent à restreindre l'emploi de l'infixe corse issu de *-idiare* (et à exclure par exemple *ringrazieghja* ou *studieghja* au profit de *ringrazia* et *studia*: Marchetti 1984, 34) ce qui a comme conséquence objective de réduire la distance par rapport à l'italien.

Le corse est aussi caractérisé par l'exclusion de *-ando* comme désinence de gérondif: *cantà: cantendu* (cf. italien *cantare: cantando*). Aucune variété corse ne connaît de gérondif en *-andu* malgré la variation (écrite) *cantandu/cantendu* qui ne recouvre aucune différenciation interne (l'opposition phonologique existant par ailleurs: *tandu* «alors»/*tendu*: «je tends»). Ici la persistance du modèle italien introduit une incohérence dans le système (graphique) corse, et occulte un trait corse (et sarde notamment; Chiorboli 1933) qui n'est d'ordinaire pas relevé.

De même le corse exclut *-amus* à l'indicatif présent au profit de *-emu/-emi* (*cantemu, -i*) et *-unt* au profit de *-enu/-ini* (*vendenu, -ini; dormenu, -ini, finiscenu, -ini*). La préférence marquée du corse pour *-e-* dans les adjectifs issus du participe présent (*luccichente/lucciante*) ou dans le subjonctif imparfait (*cantessi/cantassi*) vont dans le même sens et contribuent à définir un système qui s'oppose à l'italien et a fondé l'identification d'une zone intertyrrhénienne (Lüdtke 1956) qui constitue selon nous un cadre satisfaisant pour caractériser le corse (Chiorboli 1989).

2.4. Syntaxe

Les grammaires ont tendance à réprimer de nombreuses particularités syntaxiques qui opposent le corse à l'italien officiel, comme l'irréel du présent du type *si habebam, dabam* (*s'ell'avia u pane, u ti dava* «s'il avait du pain, il te le donnerait»).

L'emploi de l'indicatif est condamné par toutes les grammaires corses qui considèrent que la structure est d'origine italienne et préconisent à sa place l'emploi du subjonctif. (En sarde où l'on a la même variation qu'en corse l'appréciation est inverse: le subjonctif est imputé à l'influence toscane alors que l'indicatif est considéré comme autochtone.)

Les structures caractéristiques du corse qui ont le tort de s'opposer à la fois à la «concordance des temps» et à la norme italienne sont totalement ignorées: c'est le cas par exemple de la structure pancorse et très fréquente qui fait dépendre un subjonctif imparfait d'une principale au *présent (hè megliu ch'ellu falessi)*.

Quant à l'expression du futur, dans le passé, si certaines grammaires tolèrent l'emploi du conditionnel présent (*sapia ch'ellu vinaria*) d'autres considèrent qu'il est «plus élégant» d'employer un temps composé (*sapia ch'ellu saria vinutu*, Yvia-Croce 1972; cf. italien *sapeva che sarebbe venuto*).

Le gérondif précédé de *in*, très fréquent en corse à l'oral et employé même à l'écrit (*l'aghju vistu in passendu* «je l'ai vu en passant = alors que le passais») fait l'objet d'une condamnation unanime de la part des grammairiens. Le développement des études linguistiques, notamment romanistiques, est peut-être à l'origine d'une amorce de réhabilitation; sa présence en italien ancien – chez Dante par ex.: *in camminando* – a pu le faire inclure parmi les phénomènes de «paléosyntaxe» (Marchetti 1989, 43) qui, abandonnés par l'italien moderne, tendent aujourd'hui à se généraliser en corse sous l'influence française.

Le corse connaît l'emploi de *esse* au lieu de *stare* dans certaines périphrases (autre trait qui trouve corse et sarde en opposition avec l'italien): forme «progressive» (*un discorsu che t'eri priparendu*, Mambrini in *Corse-Matin* 7/8/90) et futur proche (*hè per more*; Chiorboli 1989). Si d'autres constructions sont possibles en corse (notamment *esse in traccia di*, soutenu par le *français* «être en train de»), la «forme progressive» préconisée par certaines grammaires (*stava scrivendu quandu tu hai picchiatu*, (Yvia-Croce 1972, 139) est calquée sur l'italien et sans écho notable au niveau de l'usage (Chiorboli 1993).

Le corse emploie des formes différentes pour l'interrogatif animé (*quale, -i?*) et le relatif sans antécédent (*à chì*) alors que toutes les langues romanes (selon B. Pottier) connaissent la même forme pour les deux emplois (cf. corse *quale a sàlà chì colla à chì fala* et italien *chi lo sa/chi scende e chi sale*). La force du modèle italien est telle que les ouvrages normatifs corses proposent des exemples (type *chi è chi picchia à a porta?*, Muntese 1985) qui sont exclus de l'usage vivant (l'interrogatif *chì* est en corse réservé aux non animés: *à chì pensi* «à quoi penses-tu?»; *à quale pensi?* «à qui penses-tu?»; Chiorboli 1987).

Le pronom personnel sujet est obligatoire avec les verbes au subjonctif et facultatif (bien que très fréquent) avec les verbes à l'indicatif (*hè megliu ch'ellu falghi dumane / sò chì fala dumane*) alors qu'en italien le pronom n'est jamais obligatoire. La pronominalisation est également obligatoire pour les relatifs complément d'objet qui sont ainsi formellement distincts des formes sujet (*l'omu chì chjama / l'omu ch'ellu chjama*; cf. italien *l'uomo che chiama / l'uomo che (egli) chiama*). En corse l'opposition sujet/objet repose obligatoirement sur l'expression du pronom, et non sur l'opposition /ki/- /ke/ comme l'indiquent les grammaires (par ex. Paganelli 1975, 45) sans doutes influencées par l'opposition qui/que dans le modèle français.

D'où la nécessité, pour la linguistique générale et la typologie, de se méfier des sources d'orientation normative, qui peuvent fausser les conclusions ou tout au moins restreindre leur validité.

2.5. Lexique

Avant le XXème siècle, les emprunts à l'italien arrivent de manière pratiquement exclusive par la voie littéraire, et sont l'œuvre d'écrivains corses qui puisent chez leurs modèles l'inspiration en même temps que certaines formes qui fonctionnent comme des variables stylistiques et de registre.

Certaines de ces formes connaissent une fortune telle que leur qualité d'emprunt n'apparaît plus qu'aux historiens de la langue. D'autres sont des variantes individuelles, parfois des hapax, mais sont cependant répertoriées dans les ouvrages lexicographiques, en raison surtout de leur rareté. Il s'agit de formes d'origine latine ou même de latinismes, présents dans la plupart des langues romanes littéraires.

Un exemple nous permettra d'illustrer ce propos.

Pour les divers sens du français «rester» les dictionnaires corses enregistrent *restà (ristà, ristà si)* et *rimane (à* côté de *firmà si)* et *stà (stà si)*. Malgré leur fréquence faible ou nulle dans l'usage vivant, *restà* et *firmà* apparaissent plausibles en corse en raison de l'existence de formes correspondantes dans la plupart des langues romanes.

Un contingent récent d'emprunts à l'italien, fréquents surtout à partir des années 70, est dû à la situation d'élaboration, c'est-à-dire à la nécessité d'adapter la terminologie corse aux besoins nés de l'accession à de nouveaux domaines et à un statut d'une certaine officialité.

Le résultat de la normativisation ne procède sans doute pas systématiquement d'une volonté délibérée de s'aligner sur l'italien standard. Simplement dans un domaine où l'équipement linguistique du corse est nécessaire, le recours au dictionnaire italien représente la solution de facilité, surtout quand l'idéologie linguistique dominante refuse la tendance populaire à l'adaptation pure et simple du français.

Dans le «corse coofficiel» récent on peut ainsi relever quantité de termes empruntés à l'italien (nous renonçons à indiquer les références pour ne pas alourdir le texte): *altu, bassu* «grand, petit»; *assegnate* «attribuées», *vendita à l'asta* «vente aux enchères»; *audiuvisivi* «audiovisuels»; *cantente* «chanteur»; *circa e direzzioni* «en ce qui concerne...»; *compitu* «tâche, devoir»; *equipaggiamentu idraulicu* «équipement hydraulique»; *ghjuria* «jury»; *incartamentu* «dossier»; *incrisciosa* «fâcheuse»; *neguziati* «négociations»; *pressu à pocu* «à peu près» (c'est l'expression recommandée par Muntese 1985 qui note que *a pocu pressu* est un gallicisme: ce qui est vrai); *genitori* «parents» (*parenti* est considéré comme un gallicisme; *parenti* pour *genitori* caractérise cependant aussi l'italien régional de Sardaigne; *postu* «place» (préféré à *piazza*); *à puntate* «(roman) feuilleton»; *messe à saccheghju* «mises à sac»; *sanità* «santé (*organizazione mundiale di a sanità*)»; *u vertice* «le sommet»; *scattà* «prendre (une photo)»; *surteggiu, surteghju* «tirage au sort»; *bau bau* «ouah ouah»; *bancu di dati* «banque de données»; *agenzie* «agences»; *l'aeriu* «l'avion»; *metri quadri* «mètres carrés»; *macchina da scrive* «machine à écrire»; *a dumanda (= a quistione) di i rapporti USA/Libia* (la tendance à préférer *dumanda* «question (poser une question)» à *quistione* entraîne une généralisation abusive); *macchia* «tâche» (italianisme proposé pour remplacer *tacca* considéré comme un gallicisme mais connu en toscan ancien, sarde, catalan, génois: Rohlfs 1979, 66).

3. Péripéties du discours scientifique

Au plan de la normativisation corse, les choix glottopolitiques sont étroitement liés à la situation de contact linguistique. L'idéal de la langue standard peut se fonder sur l'usage interne (l'idéologie de type *endo*normatif implique des choix indépendants de modèles autres) ou bien sur l'usage externe (le standard *exo*normatif pourrait calquer ses choix sur l'italien — c'est aujourd'hui le cas le plus fréquent — ou sur un autre modèle comme le français).

En ce qui concerne la Corse, nous avons vu que l'attitude est plutôt exonormative (l'italien conserve son prestige parmi de nombreux agents glottopolitiques et la pression du français est combattue avec plus ou moins de succès), mais les effets linguistiques objectifs sont divers et souvent originaux: la distance par rapport au modèle reste grande en raison de la faible disponibilité de ce même modèle.

Si les aspirations à la langue standard sont fortes, le champ corse a cependant permis de donner une nouvelle pertinence, d'ordre surtout glottopolitique, au concept de *polynomie*. A la polynomie comprise comme la pluralité observable des normes qui caractérisait par exemple les idiomes romans médiévaux, les groupes universitaires rouennais et cortenais (sous l'impulsion de Marcellesi 1984) intègrent la dimension essentielle de l'intertolérance et l'absence de hiérarchisation sociale liée à la différenciation linguistique interne.

Si l'on en juge par le nombre et la variété impressionnants des langues représentées au colloque international sur les langues polynomiques de Corti (voir les Actes: Chiorboli 1991), le concept tel qu'il a été (re)défini est applicable à de nombreuses langues modernes.

L'abandon de l'idée de langue standard unifiée est considéré comme nécessaire si l'on veut comprendre quelque chose à la phase initiale des langues romanes (cf. Ineichen 1993c, 88). Il semble que de tels types de langues « présentant peu de sélectivité grammaticale et lexicologique et dont le phonétisme était variable selon les dialectes » (Ineichen 1993c, 88) pourraient correspondre assez bien aux langues polynomiques modernes.

De la même façon qu'on pourrait donner une définition caractérisante (sommaire) en disant que « l'italien est la langue qui possède la préposition *da* » (Ineichen 1993b, 2266), on pourrait définir le corse comme la langue qui possède l'adverbe affirmatif *iè* (Giacomo 1983) ou qui innove en créant *tandu* « alors » (ce trait, caractéristique aussi du Mezzogiorno, oppose le corse au toscan et à l'italien standard).

Concernant l'idéologie linguistique et les thèses en présence, on peut distinguer une thèse « catastrophiste » (le corse est malade à cause de la contamination du français qui n'épargne aucune variété du répertoire: Marchetti 1989) et une thèse « relativiste » (seul le corse « élaboré » est francisé, le corse « hérité » lui est bien vivant et guère pénétré par le français: Dalbera-Stefanaggi 1989). Les deux thèses se rejoignent pour considérer que *l'italianité* du corse est évidente, ce qui exclut toute prétention à l'autonomie linguistique.

La thèse de *l'italianité* du corse trouve une formulation radicale dans un ouvrage en préparation qui fait des Corses des Italiens « par définition » (« I Corsi, proprio perché sono Corsi, *sono* italiani »; Vignoli à paraître, 9). L'auteur cité se déclare étonné et affligé par les affirmations selon lesquelles « les Corses sont corses et non italiens » (Acquaviva 1982).

La thèse de *l'indépendance linguistique* a été récemment affirmée pour réclamer l'enseignement obligatoire du corse qui a « dignité de langue autonome nettement distincte de tout dialecte italien ou français » (pétition au Parlement Européen de la FEDER-MEDITERRANEO, 19/7/1993).

Quant à l'état actuel de la « Question linguistique », un article de Nesi (1988) constitue à ce jour la synthèse la plus complète des diverses définitions et classifications antérieures; il apporte quelques nouveaux résultats et surtout une perspective (relativement) nouvelle qui intègre le corse dans un « areale tirrenico » (Corse, archipel tyrrhénien) aux caractéristiques originales (surtout lexicales pour l'auteur) et conçu comme « partiellement indépendant des pressions toscanes » (ce point de vue rejoint celui d'une aire « intertyrrhénienne » définie comme un nouveau cadre possible pour la classification du corse à partir de traits morphosyntaxiques: Chiorboli 1989 et → art. 145).

Les travaux cités ne remettent pas en cause les « indéniables parentés entre le corse et les variétés de l'aire italo-romane » (Thiers 1992, 232) mais la référence exclusive à la Toscane (continentale, marginale, ou périphérique) qui a pu faire passer beaucoup de traits corses pour des convergences exclusives avec le toscan (archaïque, ancien, moderne) alors qu'on les retrouve en latin ou aux quatre coins de l'aire italo-romane, et même en dehors (les exemples sont innombrables; voir notamment Chiorboli 1989, Chiorboli 1993).

Pour les institutions françaises le corse est une des « langues de France » et n'a donc pas à justifier un classement parfaitement convenable pour les auteurs (Marcellesi/Thiers 1988), le seul préalable théorique étant l'acceptation du concept de langue polynomique. Dans cette perspective il s'agit de mesurer — à la suite d'enquêtes — le degré d'autoconscience linguistique en évaluant un certain nombre de faits linguistiques (indicateurs de corsité pancorses mais le plus souvent régionaux) du point de vue de l'attachement symbolique des usagers et sans préjuger du fonctionnement linguistique dans le système.

Nous assumons quant à nous une perspective sociolinguistique dans la mesure où elle intègre la description et la caractérisation linguistique. Nesi (1988, 802) note en citant notre contribution aux *Sessione Universitarie* de 1983 (Chiorboli 1984) que la « classification sociolinguistique » trouve un cadre théorique dans l'application du concept de diasystème attribué au corse. Dans ce travail nous avions défini la langue corse comme un « diasystème composé d'un certain nombre de membres, c'est-à-dire de dialectes » en y intégrant l'absence de hiérarchisation entre les variantes coexistantes (Chiorboli 1983, 37). La perspective polynomique (Marcellesi 1984), qui met en valeur la notion *d'intertolérance*, constitue donc pour nous un cadre théorique satisfaisant, même si elle ne se prononce pas sur les modalités du fonctionnement linguistique. Elle nous semble de nature à concilier des perspectives théoriques diverses, récentes ou traditionnelles, et donne une nouvelle épaisseur au concept d'« hétérogénéité ordonnée » en faisant apparaître une sorte « d'ordre social » compatible avec l'instabilité consubstantielle des systèmes linguistiques, ordre lui-même instable parce que résultant de rapports de forces variables.

4. Bibliographie (sélective)

A Viva Voce (depuis 1992): *Trimestrale di cultura*, Bastia.

Acquaviva, Sabino (1982): *La Corsica. Storia di un genocidio*, Milan.

ADEDEC (1986): *A scrittura di a lingua corsa*, Cervioni.

Battisti, Carlo/Alessio, Giovanni (1975): *Dizionario etimologico italiano*, Florence, 5 vol.

Berrendoner, Alain/Le Guern, M./Puech, G. (1983): *Principes de grammaire polylectale*, Lyon.

Berruto, Gaetano (1987): *Sociolinguistica dell'italiano contemporaneo*, Rome.

Bruni, Francesco (Ed.) (1992): *L'italiano nelle regioni. Lingua nazionale e identità regionali*, Turin.

Ceccaldi, Mathieu (1968): *Dictionnaire corse–français. Pieve d'Evisa*, Paris.

Chiorboli, Jean (1978): « Reflets de la langue corse dans un manuscrit du XVIIème siècle ». In: *Etudes corses 10*, 155–176.

Chiorboli, Jean (1984): « A sesta fonica di u corsu ». In: Università di Corsica/F.A.L.C.E. 1984: *Atti di e Sessione Universitarie d'estate 83*, Corti.

Chiorboli, Jean (1985): *La langue corse entre l'usage et le code. Fonctionnement et tendances de l'évolution*, thèse de 3ème cycle, Université de Rouen.

Chiorboli, Jean (1986): « Fondements linguistiques dans le processus d'individuation de la communauté corse ». In: Marcellesi/Thiers, 1–18.

Chiorboli, Jean (1987): « Traits morphosyntaxiques du corse ». In: *Etudes corses 28*, 77–109.

Chiorboli, Jean (1988): « Le laboratoire corse: la codification ». In: PULA 0, 23–57.

Chiorboli, Jean (1989): « L'individuation corse dans la Romania intertyrrhénienne ». In: PULA 1, 61–88.

Chiorboli, Jean (Ed.) (1991): *Les langues polynomiques*, Corti (PULA 3/4).

Chiorboli, Jean (1993): *La langue des Corses. Notes linguistiques et glottopolitiques*, Bastia.

Corse-Matin, Nice.

Dalbera-Stefanaggi, Marie-José (1989): « Corse: réalité dialectale et imaginaire linguistique du cœur de l'Italie aux marges de la France ». In: Centre d'Etudes Corses: *L'île Miroir*, Actes du Colloque d'Aix-en-Provence, Ajaccio, 121–131.

Etudes corses 20–21 (1983): *Hommage à Fernand Ettori*, Ajaccio.

Fusina, Jacques (1991): « L'italien de Corse. Sur l'appréhension ambiguë des situations de langue en Corse au XIXème siècle ». In: Chiorboli, 194–201.

Giacomo-Marcellesi, Mathée (1983): « Le temps de la langue d'iè ». In: *Etudes corses 20–21*, 163–166.

Giacomo-Marcellesi, Mathée (1988): « Histoire du corse ». In: Holtus/Metzeltin/Schmitt, 820–828.

Goebl, Hans (1988): « Korsisch, Italienisch und Französisch auf Korsika ». In: Holtus/Metzeltin/Schmitt, 829–835.

Holtus, Günter/Metzeltin, Michael/Schmitt, Christian (1988): *Lexikon der Romanistischen Linguistik (LRL)*, vol. 4, Tübingen.

Ineichen, Gustav (1993 a): « Pour une caractérisation typologique de l'italien ». In: *Actas do XIX Congreso Internacional de Lingüística e Filoloxía Románicas*, Lorenzo Ramón (Ed.), A Coruña, vol. V (Gramática Histórica e Historia da Lingua), 249–254.

Ineichen, Gustav (1993 b): « Per una nuova caratterizzazione tipologica dell'italiano ». In: *Omaggio a Gianfranco Folena*, Padoue, vol. III, 2265–2273.

Ineichen, Gustav (1993 c): « L'apparition du roman dans les textes latins ». In: *Le passage à l'écrit des langues romanes*, Selig, Maria/Frank, B./Hartmann, J. (Eds.), Tübingen, 83—90.

Kyrn, Bastia.

La Corse, Ajaccio.

Loi Corvetto, Ines (1992): « La Sardegna ». In: Bruni, 875—917.

Lüdtke, Helmut (1956): « Das Präsenssystem der südlichen und südwestlichen Romania ». In: *Vox Romanica 15*, 39—53.

Marcellesi, Jean-Baptiste (1983): « Identité linguistique, exclamatives et subordonnées: un modèle syntaxique spécifique en corse ». In: *Etudes corses 20—21*, 399—424.

Marcellesi, Jean-Baptiste (1984): « La définition des langues en domaine roman; les enseignements à tirer de la situation corse ». In: *Actes du XVIIème Congrès de Linguistique et Philologie Romanes*, Aix-en-Provence, vol. 5 (Sociolinguistique), 307—314.

Marcellesi, Jean-Baptiste/Thiers, Jacques (1986): *L'individuation sociolinguistique corse*, Corti/Mont-Saint-Aignan (A.T.P., C.N.R.S. 91 1164).

Marcellesi, Jean-Baptiste/Thiers Jacques (1988): « Korsisch: Soziolinguistik/Sociolinguistique ». In: Holtus/Metzeltin/Schmitt, 809—819.

Marchetti, L. F. (1984): *Ancu di grazia ...*, Santu Niculaiu.

Marchetti, Pascal (1974): *Le corse sans peine*, Paris.

Marchetti, Pascal (1983): « Acquisti è pruspettive di lissicugrafia corsa ». In: *Etudes corses 20—21*, 425—442.

Marchetti, Pascal (1989): *La corsophonie. Un idiome à la mer*, Paris.

Marchetti, Pascal/Geronimi, D. (1971): *Intricciate è cambiarine*, Nogent-sur-Marne.

Migliorini, Bruno (1957): *Saggi linguistici*, Florence.

Muljačić, Žarko (1988): « Norma e standard » In: Holtus/Metzeltin/Schmitt, 286—304.

Muntese (1960—1967): *Lexique français-corse*, Bastia, 4 vol.

Muntese (1985): *Dizziunariu corsu francese*, Levie (Corse), 4 vol.

Nesi, Annalisa (1988): « Corso. Evoluzione del sistema grammaticale ». In: Holtus/Metzeltin/Schmitt, 799—908.

Nesi, Annalisa (1992): « La Corsica ». In: Bruni, 918—940.

Paganelli, J. (1975): *Les règles grammaticales du parler sartenais*, Corti.

PULA: Publications Universitaires de Linguistique et d'Anthropologie, Université de Corse, Corti.

Ramat, Paolo (1984): *Linguistica tipologica*, Boulogne.

RCFM = Radio Corsica Frequenza Mora, Bastia.

Rigiru, Lopigna (Corse).

Rohlfs, Gerhard (1966—1972): *Grammatica storica della lingua italiana e dei suoi dialetti*, Turin, 3 vol.

Rohlfs, Gerhard (1972): *Studi e ricerche su lingua e dialetti d'Italia*, Florence.

Rohlfs, Gerhard (1979): « Toscana dialettale delle aree marginali ». In: *Studi di lessicografia italiana*, 1, 83—262.

Romani, G. (1990): *Le corse à l'école. Orthographe*, Ajaccio.

Tekavčić, Pavao (1972): *Grammatica storica dell'italiano*, 1972—1974, Bologne, 3 vol.

Thiers, Jacques (1977): « Aspects de la francisation en Corse au cours du XIXème siècle ». In: *Etudes corses 9*, 5—40.

Thiers, Jacques (1989): *Papier(s) d'identité*, Levie (Corse).

Thiers, Jacques (1992): « La Méditerranée dans le discours corse ». In: *La Mediterranée et ses cultures*, Berriot-Salvadore, E. (Ed.), Paris, 225—238.

U Ribombu, Bastia.

Vignoli, G. (à paraître): « Corsica ». In: *I territori italofoni non appartenenti alla Repubblica Italiana: agraristica*, parte seconda, 2—16.

Yvia-Croce, Hyacinthe (1972): *Grammaire corse*, Ajaccio.

Jean Chiorboli, Corti (France)

147. Français—allemand

1. Géographie et démographie
2. Histoire
3. Evolution linguistique et sociolinguistique
4. Interférences linguistiques
5. Développements récents et perspectives
6. Bibliographie (sélective)

1. Géographie et démographie

Aire primitivement germanophone de 11.300 km², située aujourd'hui en territoire français (fr.) et abritant la minorité de langue allemande (ald.) la plus importante d'Europe

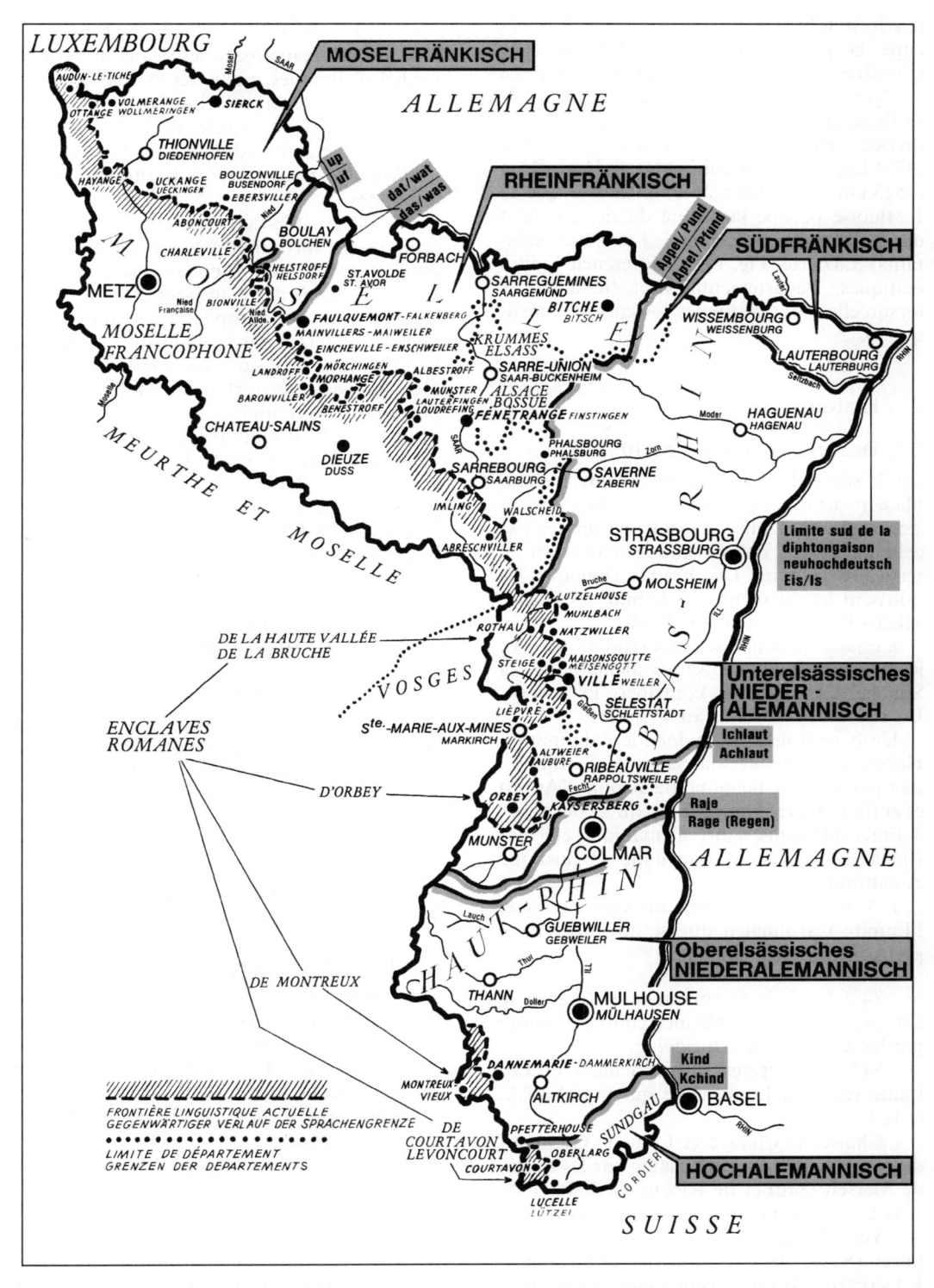

Fig. 147.1: Carte linguistique d'Alsace-Lorraine. (A partir d'un fond de carte publié dans: Notre avenir est bilingue. Zweisprachig: unsere Zukunft, Strasbourg 1968, René-Schickele-Kreis). Adaptation cartographique: H. Kneidl (Ratisbonne).

(environ 1.200.000 dialectophones). Elle occupe la presque totalité de l'Alsace (A.) (Elsaß) et la partie de la Lorraine (L.) appelée L. germanophone ou thioise (Deutsch-Lothringen). Administrativement, l'A. est divisée en 2 départements: Bas-Rhin (4755 km², 938.000 habitants) et Haut-Rhin (3525 km², 662.000 habitants) tandis que la L. thioise occupe la moitié du département de la Moselle (6216 km², 1.000.000 habitants). La carte (Fig. 147.1) différencie limites étatiques, départementales et linguistiques lorsqu'elles sont distinctes; → carte linguistique D.

2. Histoire

2.1. De l'époque romaine au 10e siècle

Au 3e siècle de notre ère, les Alamans s'établissent sur le sol alsacien (als.), alors possession romaine. Leur expansion est limitée par celle de Francs qui s'installent eux aussi en territoire romain. Les Francs ripuaires repoussent les Alamans vers le Sud, les Francs saliens les repoussent vers l'Est.

L'espace alémanique comprend alors: l'A., le Pays de Bade, la Suisse alémanique, la Souabe, l'Allgäu et le Vorarlberg autrichien. Il s'adjoindra le Valais au 9e siècle.

L'espace francique englobe le Palatinat, la Hesse, la Franconie, la Sarre, la L. thioise, une partie de la Belgique (la région d'Arlon) et enfin le Luxembourg. Bien qu'à cheval sur 4 Etats différents, l'aire alémanique et l'aire francique présentent une unité linguistique et culturelle.

L'A. et la L. participent aux vicissitudes de l'Empire Carolingien que se disputent les 3 petits-fils de Charlemagne:

— 842: Louis le Germanique et Charles le Chauve scellent leur alliance contre Lothaire par les *Serments de Strasbourg*.
— 843: les 3 frères se réconcilient et Lothaire reçoit la Lotharingie qui englobe l'A. et la L.
— Charles le Chauve et Louis le Germanique se partagent la Lotharingie par les traités de Mersen (870) et de Ribemont (880). L'A. et la L. sont rattachées au royaume de Louis.
— Vers 900 constitution de duchés héréditaires (Saxe, Bavière, Souabe, Franconie et L.) s'octroyant une certaine indépendance.
— 959: division du duché de L. en duché de Basse-L. et duché de Haute-L. Rattachement de l'A. au duché de Souabe.

2.2. Du 10e siècle au Traité de Westphalie

L'A. et la L. connaissent les fléaux du monde médiéval: famines, peste, lèpre, massacres et pillages de la Guerre de 100 Ans.

Au début du 13e siècle, le duc de L. crée une nouvelle entité administrative: le *baillage d'Allemagne*, pour gérer ses territoires germanophones.

Du 14e au 16e siècle, l'A. connaît un essor économique (artisanat, négoce, art gothique, agriculture) et est progressivement intégrée aux possessions des Habsbourg.

La Réforme s'y propage rapidement, sauf dans les territoires administrés par les Habsbourg. Strasbourg est conquise par les idées nouvelles et sert même de refuge aux protestants fr. et anglais persécutés. La cathédrale accueille le culte protestant!

Au début du 16e siècle, la révolte des paysans als., les *Bundschuhe*, est férocement réprimée par le duc de L.

Lorsque la Guerre de 30 Ans s'achève par le Traité de Westphalie (1648), l'Alsace-Lorraine (A.-L.) a perdu près de la moitié de ses habitants et ses villes sont saccagées. Seules Strasbourg, Mulhouse et Colmar ont réussi à échapper à la dévastation.

2.3. De 1648 à la Révolution Française

Le Traité de Westphalie transfère à la France (F.) les titres et possessions territoriales des Habsbourg en A. Le reste de l'A. demeure dans le *Saint-Empire Romain Germanique*. Mais le *Roi Soleil*, insatiable, annexe Colmar en 1673 et investit Strasbourg en 1681.

Mulhouse, alliée aux cantons suisses depuis 1515, ne sera rattachée à la F. qu'en 1798, sous le Directoire.

2.4. De la Révolution Française à 1870

Un certain nombre d'Als. et de Lorrains (Lor.) adhèrent à la Révolution Fr. Mais pendant la Terreur, 40.000 artisans et paysans quittent le pays. L'anticléricalisme détourne lui aussi de la Révolution une part importante de la population qui héberge les prêtres et pasteurs traqués.

Sur le plan social et politique, le bilan est positif: des milliers de paysans sont devenus propriétaires. Libérés des droits seigneuriaux et des dîmes, ils ont payé leurs dettes. La bourgeoisie profite des nouveaux débouchés (administration, justice, enseignement). La suppression des péages, l'introduction du système métrique et décimal relancent l'économie. Les jeunes générations ont épousé l'idéal de liberté, fraternité et égalité. C'est de cette époque que date le rattachement de cœur de l'A.-L. à la F.

Sous Napoléon, l'A. et la L. fournissent 55.000 hommes à la Grande Armée: certains y font carrière, mais beaucoup tombent sur les champs de bataille.

Apport positif du régime napoléonien: le Concordat de 1801 qui reconnaît les églises catholique et luthérienne comme églises d'Etat.

L'administration napoléonienne améliore les routes et favorise l'agriculture. L'A.-L. connaît alors un réel essor économique. Mais dans la 2e moitié du 19e siècle, la poussée démographique amène les Als.-Lor. à participer à la conquête coloniale ou à émigrer (Russie, Etats-Unis).

2.5. L'Alsace-Lorraine dans l'Allemagne wilhelminienne (1871–1918)

Aux termes du traité de Francfort (mai 1871), le Bas-Rhin et le Haut-Rhin sont regroupés avec 5 arrondissements de la L. et forment le *Reichsland Elsaß-Lothringen*, administré depuis Berlin par un ministère. Un mouvement autonomiste naît alors et son influence croît rapidement. Sous sa pression, le ministère d'A.-L. est transféré à Strasbourg. En 1879 est créé le *Landesausschuß*, parlement régional votant les lois et le budget. Les libertés de réunion, d'association, d'expression, très réduites après l'annexion, sont réintroduites à partir de 1900. En 1911, le *Reichstag* octroie à l'A.-L. une constitution: le *Landtag* élu vote les lois et le budget, mais le gouvernement est nommé par Berlin. La L. manifeste plus de réticence que l'A. à se couler dans ce moule. Elle considère aussi les mouvements autonomistes avec méfiance: ici comme là, elle est en position d'infériorité numérique.

L'activité économique recule d'abord. Les débouchés fr. se ferment: il faut s'adapter au marché ald. La croissance reprend en 1895 et c'est sous le drapeau ald. que l'A.-L. entre dans l'ère de l'industrialisation et de l'urbanisation (bassin minier lor.).

Lorsqu'éclate la guerre de 1914, 220.000 soldats du *Reichsland* sont incorporés dans l'armée du Kaiser, mais 3.000 mobilisables passent les frontières vosgienne et helvétique pour ne pas endosser l'uniforme ald. La population subit bombardements, rationnements, réquisitions et exactions. Dans la zone des combats, les Als.-Lor. sont suspectés par les 2 belligérants et souvent internés.

2.6. L'entre-deux-guerres (1918–1940)

L'enthousiasme qui accueille les armées fr. en 1918 fait vite place à la déception. L'économie als. et lor. se heurte aux mêmes difficultés qu'en 1871. Elle doit cette fois se réorienter vers le marché fr. Elle surmonte cette crise en 1922 et connaît une certaine prospérité jusqu'en 1929.

Mais la F., incurablement centralisatrice, ignore l'autonomie qu'ont connue les 2 provinces sous le régime ald. Les *Altdeutsche* sont expulsés ou émigrent. La gestion de l'ancien *Reichsland* est confiée à un Commissaire Général assisté d'un Conseil Supérieur d'A.-L. dont les membres sont nommés par Paris. Originaires pour la plupart d'autres régions de F., les nouveaux dirigeants ne connaissent pas les problèmes locaux et s'y adaptent mal.

Le malaise als-lor. qui se développe alors comporte une forte composante linguistique. Il culmine en 1924: Edouard Herriot veut pratiquer en A. une politique d'assimilation rapide et dénoncer le Concordat. Il recule devant la résistance rencontrée.

Le mouvement autonomiste exige une certaine indépendance dans la République Française, le maintien du statut religieux et scolaire et la reconnaissance du droit au bilinguisme. Des groupes séparatistes apparaissent dans quelques centres ruraux protestants, encouragés secrètement par l'Allemagne (All.). La F. réagit brutalement. Les autonomistes arrêtés sont inculpés de complot contre la sûreté de l'Etat et traduits devant la Cour d'Assises de Colmar en 1928. Les peines prononcées sont légères, mais l'affaire soulève une émotion énorme.

A partir de 1929, l'A. et la L. sont frappées par la crise économique mondiale.

En 1936, le Front Populaire l'emporte en F., mais pas en A. où l'union n'a pu se faire.

2.7. L'Alsace-Lorraine sous le Troisième Reich (1940–1944)

Le 10 mai 1933, les œuvres de René Schickele sont brûlées, avec celles des grands écrivains ald., dans les *autodafés* organisés par les hordes hitlériennes. En 1940, l'A. et la Moselle sont annexées au Troisième Reich.

La propagande nazie se déploie et la délation est mise en place. Les Als.-Lor. francophiles sont expulsés.

Les jeunes sont embrigadés (*Hitlerjugend, Bund Deutscher Mädchen*). 13.000 Als.-Lor. sont incorporés de force dans la *Wehrmacht*. Un camp de rééducation est ouvert à *Schir-*

meck, un camp d'extermination au *Struthof*. Des milliers de déportés y sont gazés ou meurent d'épuisement. Leurs cadavres alimentent en matériel anatomique la Faculté de Médecine de Strasbourg.

Le délire antisémite s'applique aussi à l'A. et à la L. Les synagogues sont anéanties et 8.000 Juifs (un dizième de la population juive d'A.-L.) sont envoyés dans les camps de la mort. Les autres fuient.

2.8. De 1945 à nos jours

La libération s'accompagne d'une explosion de joie. Mais en 75 ans (1870–1945), l'A.-L. a changé 4 fois d'appartenance politique et le bilan de la 2e guerre mondiale est lourd pour elle: plus de 60.000 victimes par faits de guerre et de déportation. Des tensions apparaîssent entre les Als. restés sur place et ceux qui ont fui, ont été déportés ou engagés de force. La dénazification, bien acceptée dans son principe, conduit, dans son application, à de graves abus. Le malaise général qui en résulte ne se dissipera qu'avec les lois d'amnistie en 1951 et 1953.

3. Evolution linguistique et sociolinguistique

3.1. De l'époque romaine au 10e siècle

3.1.1. Genèse de l'allemand

Au moment où les tribus germaines envahissent l'empire romain (5e siècle) s'amorce au sud de l'aire germanophone la *2e mutation consonantique*. Elle scinde le germanique primitif en *Hochdeutsch* (subissant la mutation) et en *Niederdeutsch* (ne la subissant pas). Le *Hochdeutsch* se divise géographiquement en *Mitteldeutsch*, parlé en All. moyenne, et en *Oberdeutsch*, parlé en All. du Sud (cf. fig. 147.2). Dans le temps, le *Hochdeutsch* se décompose en *Althochdeutsch* (de 900 à 1150), *Mittelhochdeutsch* (de 1150 à 1250) et *Neuhochdeutsch* (de 1250 à nos jours).

La 2e mutation consonantique affecte pour l'essentiel les occlusives sourdes [p t k], du germanique:

— en position postvocalique, derrière une sonante ou une liquide, ces occlusives se transforment en fricatives doubles [ff ss χχ], vite réduites à des fricatives simples après voyelle longue en finale: germanique *dorp, *up, *dat, *ik → althochdeutsch dorf, uf, das, iχ. Cette transformation affecte au 5e–6e siècle tous les parlers *hochdeutsch*, à l'exception du francique mosellan et du francique ripuaire pour la transformation [t → s] et à l'exception du francique ripuaire et d'une partie du francique mosellan pour la transformation [p → f] (cf. figures 147.1 et 147.2);

— en initiale absolue ou derrière consonne, ces occlusives se transforment en affriquées [pf, ts, kχ]: germanique *appla, *ti:d, *kind → althochdeutsch apful, zi:t, hochalemannisch kχind. La transformation [t → ts] est la plus précoce et la plus générale: elle se produit au 5e–6e siècle et affecte la totalité de l'espace *hochdeutsch*. La transformation [p → pf] se propage plus tardivement (6e–7e siècle) et ne touche que l'aire *Oberdeutsch* (*Alemannisch, Bairisch-österreichisch, Ostfränkisch*; cf. carte 147.2). La mutation [k → kχ] est encore plus tardive (7e–8e siècle) et plus limitée. Elle est réduite au *Hochalemannisch* et à la partie méridionale de l'espace *Bairisch-österreichisch*.

L'articulation linguistique des parlers als.-lor. apparaît sur les cartes 147.1 et 147.2. L'A. comporte:

— à son extrémité méridionale, *une aire haut-alémanique*, le *Sundgau*, délimitée par l'isophone Kind/Kchind;

— plus au Nord, *une aire bas-alémanique* (de *Altkirch* jusqu'au-delà de *Haguenau*). Les isophones Ichlaut/Achlaut et Raje/Rage (Regen), orientés Sud-Ouest/Nord-Est et encadrant la ville de *Colmar*, séparent *unterelsässisches* et *oberelsässisches Niederalemannisch*.

— dans sa partie septentrionale, *2 aires sud-franciques*. L'aire orientale est fermée vers le Sud par la rivière *Seltzbach* qui coïncide avec l'isophone Eis/Is, limite méridionale de la diphtongaison *neuhochdeutsch* (celle-ci se propage à partir du 12e siècle depuis l'aire bavaroise). Ces 2 aires sud-franciques sont d'appartenance *Oberdeutsch*, parce que situées à l'Est de l'isophone Apel, Pund/Apfel, Pfund (*Speyerer Linie*) dont le point de départ est *Lutzelhouse*.

— *Le francique rhénan de Moselle*, limité à l'Ouest par l'isophone dat, wat/das, was (*Hunsrückbarriere*) qui passe près de *Faulquemont* et de *Saint-Avold*.

— La limite supérieure du *francique mosellan* se situe hors de F.: elle est marquée par l'isophone dorp/dorf orienté Sud-Ouest/Nord-Est. L'aire francique mosellane est en outre traversée par l'isophone up/uf (*Trierer Linie*) qui passe à l'Est de *Boulay* et de *Bouzonville*. La géographie linguistique de la L.

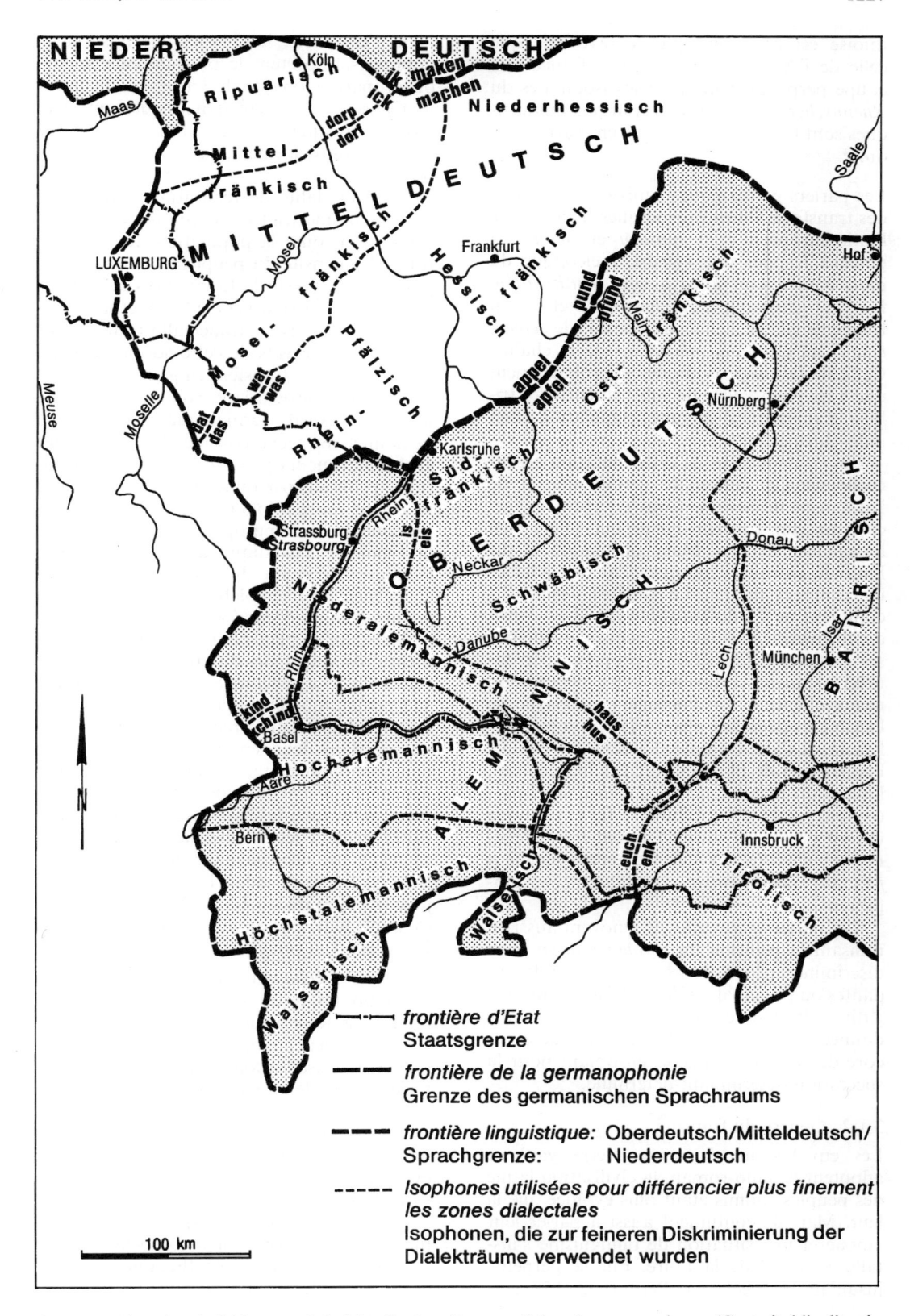

Fig. 147.2: Situation de l'Alsace et de la Moselle dans l'espace dialectal germanophone. (Carte établie d'après König, Werner (1978): dtv-Atlas zur deutschen Sprache, Munich, 230−231). Cartographie: H. Kneidl (Ratisbonne).

thioise est nettement plus défavorable que celle de l'A.: en L., la frontière franco-ald. coupe perpendiculairement les isophones du *Rheinischer Fächer* et les variations linguistiques sont très importantes sur une surface réduite.

Les parlers germaniques subissent également des transformations prosodiques. L'accent de l'indo-européen était *musical* et *mobile*: il pouvait frapper une syllabe quelconque du mot, contribuant ainsi à son *identification*. L'accent germanique est *dynamique* et *fixe*: il frappe la syllabe *initiale* du vocable, le *démarquant* des éléments précédents de la chaîne. Cette mutation prosodique est probablement due à un phénomène de substrat entre les tribus germaniques et une population non indo-européenne.

Les conséquences de cette mutation accentuelle sur l'évolution du germanique et de l'ald. sont immenses. Contrairement à l'accent musical, l'accent dynamique tolère bien les syllabes fermées. Mais son placement sur l'initiale entraîne l'amuïssement des syllabes inaccentuées finales. Le système désinentiel complexe de l'indo-européen est ainsi considérablement réduit et des marqueurs préposés (articles, prépositions, pronoms personnels) viennent compenser cette déperdition morphologique. La typologie synthétique de l'indo-européen fait place à la typologie analytique de l'ald. En outre l'accent ald. évolue: l'apparition de préfixes verbaux inaccentués, l'ingestion massive de vocabulaire latin paroxytonique et de vocabulaire fr. oxytonique le font passer du statut d'accent *fixe* à *fonction démarcative* au statut d'accent *mobile* à *fonction identificative* (<u>um</u>fahren ~ um<u>fahren</u>).

Les parlers germaniques innovent aussi en utilisant la position du *verbum finitum* pour discriminer propositions assertives indépendantes ou principales (*Zweitstellung*), interrogatives alternatives (*Spitzenstellung*) et subordonnées (*Endstellung*). Ils se distinguent encore des langues romanes en optant pour la succession déterminant-déterminé.

3.1.2. Genèse du français

Les envahisseurs francs en terre gauloise adoptent le gallo-roman, la civilisation latine des peuples soumis étant plus évoluée que la leur. Mais ils continuent aussi à parler leur langue et une situation de bilinguisme s'installe au Nord de la Loire. Elle se perpétue jusqu'au 11ᵉ siècle (cf. Petit 1992, 158 sqq).

Dans l'ensemble, les Francs devenus romanophones respectent le positionnement par- ou proparoxytonique de l'accent latin, mais ils réalisent cet accent dynamiquement, à la mode francique (cf. Petit 1987, passim) et non pas musicalement, selon l'usage galloroman.

Cette modalité de réalisation accentuelle, perçue comme trait d'identité du vainqueur, s'impose à toute la population du royaume franc. La densité du peuplement franc (proportion de 20% sur la Loire, croissant vers le Nord et décroissant vers le Sud), et la longévité du bilinguisme franc/gallo-roman sont des facteurs décisifs de cette adoption. L'accent dynamique transféré en gallo-roman, lamine le fond lexical latin comme il a laminé le fond lexical germanique. Le système flexionnel se trouve considérablement réduit et des marqueurs préposés (articles, prépositions, pronoms personnels) viennent combler ce déficit morphologique. La typologie synthétique de l'indo-européen est remplacée par la typologie analytique du fr. En ce sens, l'évolution menant du *germanique* au *Neuhochdeutsch* est semblable à celle menant du *gallo-roman* au *fr. moderne*.

Mais, sur le plan phonologique et notamment prosodique, des différences subsistent et s'accusent. La rencontre de l'accent d'intensité germanique et de la tendance à l'ouverture syllabique, qui caractérise les langues romanes dans leur ensemble, constitue une conjonction délétère: elle provoque non seulement la disparition des syllabes inaccentuées mais aussi la dissolution du consonantisme fermant les syllabes accentuées subsistantes. Cette érosion est donc plus dévastatrice en fr. qu'en ald. (cf. tu joues [ty'ʒu], il joue [il'ʒu] ~ du spielst [du'ʃpʰiːlstʰ], er spielt [ˀeːʁ'ʃpʰiːltʰ]). Elle est aussi sans égale dans la Romania. Les principales étapes en sont:

— 4ᵉ-5ᵉ siècle: réduction des géminées latines ll, pp, bb, tt, dd, ff, vv, ss (conservées par l'italien) à des consonnes simples;
— 10ᵉ siècle: élimination de la consonne nasale avec nasalisation compensatoire de la voyelle précédente en finale syllabique: latin *plan-ta-re* → fr. planter [ã];
— 11ᵉ siècle: vocalisation du [l] antéconsonantique avec, en finale, amuïssement d'une éventuelle consonne subséquente: latin *falsus* → fr. faux;
— 12ᵉ siècle: chute du [s] dans le groupement [st] avec allongement compensatoire de la voyelle précédente, prothétique (*scola* → escola → école) ou non (*hostis* → hôte);

- 15ᵉ siècle: apocope frappant le [s] du pluriel, de la 2ᵉ personne du singulier et tout le consonantisme terminal.

L'allergie consonantique ainsi développée en finale syllabique se double d'une propension à initialiser la syllabe plutôt par une consonne (C) que par une voyelle (V). Plusieurs phénomènes convergents (éviction de l'hiatus, élision, liaison) contribuent alors à la prolifération du schème CV.

Diminués de leur syllabe finale inaccentuée, les paroxytons latins deviennent des oxytons; les proparoxytons subissent le même sort, soit par amputation des 2 dernières syllabes inaccentuées, soit par déplacement de l'accent sur l'avant-dernière syllabe et amputation de la dernière. Le schème oxytonique se trouve ainsi généralisé et sa fonction *démarcative* consacrée par là-même. En outre, à partir du 13ᵉ siècle, cet accent perd son caractère dynamique. Il est aujourd'hui très peu marqué et réalisé par un abaissement fréquentiel et/ou par une élongation des segments. Il a tendance à disparaître dans le groupe et à démarquer ainsi non plus des éléments isolés, mais les groupes eux-mêmes: il est de nature syntaxique et syntagmatique, non lexicale et paradigmatique.

La base articulatoire très individualisée du fr. l'oppose à toutes les autres langues de la Romania. Exposées de façon plus modérée à l'accent d'intensité germanique, elles n'ont transformé en oxytons que quelques paroxytons du fonds latin. Elle ont ainsi adjoint le schème oxytonique aux schèmes par- et proparoxytonique et développé un accent *mobile* dont la fonction *identificative* préserve la netteté et la force dans le groupe.

Mais c'est avec les langues de la Germania *lato sensu* et surtout avec l'ald. que l'opposition est maximale: ces langues affectionnent les syllabes fermées par une et même par plusieurs consonnes. Elles présentent des schèmes syllabiques de tout type. Enfin, leur accent à forte composante *dynamique* est *mobile* et sa fonction *identificative* empêche sa disparition dans les groupes.

L'opposition acoustique entre fr. et ald. est considérable: la phrase fr. se développe d'une seule coulée avec ses accents de groupe tempérés et ses liaisons feutrées; la phrase ald. déploie un relief tourmenté de montagne alpine avec ses crêtes intensives et les failles de ses coups de glotte.

3.1.3. La fixation de la frontière germano-romane

Charlemagne, l'empereur trilingue (francique, latin, gallo-roman) accorde une attention particulière à l'A. et à la L. Le centre administratif de l'empire se situe en terre francique (Köln, Aachen). Les abbayes als. sont florissantes et Otfried von Weißenburg écrit dès 860 (près de 7 siècles avant la Bible de Luther) une Histoire Sainte en *Althochdeutsch*.

Les *Serments de Strasbourg* (842) font date dans l'histoire linguistique. Rédigés non plus en latin, mais en langue vulgaire (en *roman* par et pour les représentants de Charles le Chauve; en *tudesque* par et pour les représentants de Louis le Germanique), ils marquent le déclin du latin, l'accession des langues populaires à l'écriture et officialisent l'existence de 2 cultures d'expression différente: romane et germanique.

C'est à partir du traité de Ribemont que s'installe, entre les parlers romans et les parlers germaniques, la frontière linguistique que nous avons définie. Quelques poches romanophones en Moselle et en montagne vosgienne sont réduites au 11ᵉ siècle. Les modifications intervenues depuis sont négligeables et la stabilité de cette démarcation est impressionnante, mise en regard avec les bouleversements politiques qui ont affecté le pays. Elle atteste l'équivalence des cultures et langues impliquées.

3.2. Du 10ᵉ siècle au Traité de Westphalie

Au 10ᵉ siècle, le centre de gravité du Saint-Empire se déplace de l'aire francique vers l'aire alémanique et l'A. connaît alors un premier âge d'or avec les *Minnesänger*. Les œuvres de Reinmar von Hagenau (1160–1210) et de Gottfried von Straßburg (...1210...) rayonnent sur la totalité du territoire germanique.

A partir du 14ᵉ siècle, le pôle de la culture germanophone se déplace vers l'Est, vers la Bavière. La puissance politique des Habsbourg unifie la langue parlée d'Augsbourg à Vienne et d'Innsbruck à Nuremberg: le *gemeines Deutsch*. La cohésion de cette zone s'oppose à l'émiettement linguistique qui règne à l'Est et au Sud-Ouest et elle explique la diffusion, à partir de la Bavière, des phénomènes de diphtongaison et d'apocope qui vont être adoptés par le *Neuhochdeutsch*. Dessaisie de son rôle de mentor linguistique, l'A. n'en reste pas pour autant inactive: le prédicateur strasbourgeois Johannes Tauler contribue, 2 siècles avant Luther, à l'élaboration d'un vocabulaire abstrait traduisant les états et les mouvements de l'âme.

Avec la Renaissance, l'A. connaît un 2e âge d'or culturel: développement de l'imprimerie (Gutenberg passe 10 ans de sa vie à Strasbourg), de l'enseignement, floraison artistique (Hans Baldung Grien, Tobias Stimmer), abondance de prédicateurs (Geiler von Kaysersberg), d'historiens (Jakob Wimpfeling), de narrateurs (Wickram von Colmar) et d'auteurs satiriques. Le plus illustre de ceux-ci est Sebastian Brant (1457−1521): *Sa Nef des fous* (*Das Narrenschiff*), rédigée en ald. et imprimée à Bâle en 1494, est traduite dans toutes les langues du continent et même en plattdeutsch et en latin. C'est la première œuvre obtenant un succès européen. Elle représente aussi le 3e apport als. constitutif d'une langue littéraire ald., encore et toujours avant la traduction de la Bible par Luther (1522−1534).

La Réforme entraîne un nouvel affaiblissement de la position culturelle et linguistique de l'aire alémanique, au profit cette fois de l'aire *ostfränkisch* et *ostmitteldeutsch*. La Bible de Luther connaît une diffusion foudroyante. Luther n'y crée pas une langue nouvelle, mais utilise le parler *Ostmitteldeutsch* (thuringien et saxon), intermédiaire entre *Oberdeutsch* et *Niederdeutsch*. Lorsque les formes *ostmitteldeutsch* lui semblent trop particulières, il n'hésite pas à les remplacer par des formes *oberdeutsch* (il adopte la mutation de [p] en [pf]).

Dès 1525, les imprimeurs als. cessent d'utiliser leur parler alémanique pour adopter le nouvel ald. littéraire qui devient leur langue écrite.

L'arrivée en A. des réfugiés fr. fuyant l'intolérance religieuse (7−8% de la population als.) constitue par ailleurs la première amorce d'une vocation bilingue de la région.

La vie culturelle connaît une grave récession pendant la Guerre de Trente Ans. Mais c'est malgré tout dans l'aire francique et alémanique qu'œuvrent les rares écrivains de cette époque, tous inspirés par la guerre: Moscherosch, Balde et Grimmelshausen.

3.3. De 1648 à la Révolution Française

Lors de son annexion par la F., l'A. est une terre d'expression orale alémanique et francique depuis 12 siècles et d'expression écrite *neuhochdeutsch* depuis 123 ans. Le Traité de Westphalie coupe ce territoire de la sphère culturelle germanophone. Quant à l'als. luimême, il porte ombrage au *Roi Soleil*. Un arêt du Conseil d'Etat (1685) ordonne l'emploi exclusif de la langue fr. dans les actes publics.

Par le jeu des mariages, Stanislas Leczcynski, le roi polonais en exil, devient duc de L. en 1738. En 1748, il exige l'usage exclusif du fr. dans les documents officiels.

A la mort de Stanislas en 1766, le duché de L. est rattaché à la F. En L. thioise, l'annexion linguistique a donc précédé l'annexion politique, contrairement à ce qui s'est passé en A.

La francisation ne s'effectue que progressivement: elle prend la forme d'une infiltration rampante. La connaissance du fr. accélère la carrière dans l'armée et l'administration, mais l'ancien régime est plus préoccupé de luttes politiques et religieuses que de questions linguistiques.

Au 18e siècle, Strasbourg demeure foncièrement germanophone et, en 1789, le nombre des Strasbourgeois parlant le fr. ne dépasse pas 300 ... C'est donc tout naturellement à Strasbourg que Goethe rencontre Herder en 1770 et y pose avec lui les fondements du *Sturm und Drang*.

Les écrivains als. de ce 18e siècle: Pfeffel, Schoepflin, l'abbé Grandidier sont d'ailleurs tous de langue ald. Mais, si l'expression orale et écrite demeure germanophone, l'on ne peut que constater le dépérissement qualitatif et quantitatif de la création littéraire, conséquence de la Guerre de Trente Ans qui a mis à sac non seulement l'A. et la L., mais aussi l'All., leur arrière-pays: la vie culturelle y connaît un siècle de régression et de stagnation.

La F., épargnée par cette Guerre, est au contraire florissante. L'unification politique précoce, réalisée autour du royaume de l'Ile-de-F., a entraîné la diffusion de la langue d'oïl. Depuis l'Edit de Villers-Cotterêts (1539), le fr. a remplacé le latin dans les textes administratifs et juridiques. Dès le 17e siècle, il est devenu la langue des traités scientifiques. Le succès des armes fr. a favorisé l'exportation des œuvres de Corneille, Racine et Molière. Le fr. jouit ainsi au 17e−18e siècle d'un prestige considérable dans toute l'Europe. Il est la langue de la cour en Russie et surtout en Prusse (Frédéric II et Voltaire). Il est aussi la langue de la diplomatie et la langue étrangère de prédilection dans les familles européennes éclairées et non francophones.

Au 18e siècle, le fr. poursuit, par son prestige, sa pénétration non dans les milieux populaires, mais dans les milieux nobles et bourgeois d'A.-L. Mais ces mêmes milieux n'en rejettent pas pour autant les dialectes et l'ald. standard qui en constitue la forme écrite. Ils deviennent bilingues et l'A. affirme sa vocation à être le foyer du bilinguisme fr.-ald. et le trait d'union entre les cultures romane et germanique.

3.4. De la Révolution Française à 1870

Les révolutionnaires jacobins perpétuent la politique linguistique de la royauté absolue, mais lui communiquent une justification et une virulence nouvelles. Pour eux, le fr. ajoute une prétention universaliste à celles qu'il avait déjà: il devient la langue de la liberté, de la déclaration des droits de l'homme et du citoyen. Il convient d'éradiquer tous les autres idiomes parlés sur le territoire national. L'abbé Grégoire est le représentant marquant de cette idéologie. Il impulse une véritable croisade contre les patois. L'alémanique et le francique sont particulièrement visés: ils rendent la population suspecte de connivence avec l'ennemi et sont considérés comme contre-révolutionnaires. Dès 1793, l'utilisation du fr. devient obligatoire à Strasbourg pour toutes les inscriptions publiques et les habitants sont sommés de renoncer à leurs costumes germaniques. Les départements de la Moselle, de la Meurthe et du Bas-Rhin sont tracés sans considération de la frontière linguistique. Des mesures de déportation pour rééducation linguistique sont même envisagées!

Mais la fébrilité théorisante de la Révolution ne débouche sur aucune réalisation pratique. Les mesures législatives restent inopérantes: la Révolution Fr. a manqué de temps, de moyens financiers et d'enseignants compétents. En outre, toutes les tentatives de diffusion du fr. se sont heurtées à l'opposition irréductible de l'Eglise pour qui cette langue reste celle de l'antireligion.

Le régime napoléonien ne reprend pas à son compte l'intolérance linguistique de la Révolution, mais la participation aux guerres et à l'administration du Premier Empire fait progresser la francisation de l'A. et de la L. germanophone. C'est surtout dans le domaine scientifique que le fr. gagne alors du terrain. Les Eglises qui n'ont pas encore oublié les persécutions de la Révolution, résistent clandestinement ou ouvertement à la francisation.

Avec le développement de l'enseignement primaire (loi Guizot, 1833) et la multiplication des écoles normales francophones (Strasbourg 1810; Colmar et Metz 1833), la question linguistique se pose avec une acuité nouvelle. Les campagnes et les villes parlent le dialecte. La langue véhiculaire de l'école est l'ald. Le fr. est parfois enseigné comme langue vivante, mais selon les méthodes d'enseignement des langues mortes et les résultats demeurent décevants. Quand les dialectes sont exceptionnellement pris en compte par l'enseignement (à Saint-Avold par exemple), l'on planifie leur remplacement progressif par le fr.

C'est à Strasbourg qu'apparaissent les premières réflexions sur l'efficacité de la didactique des langues vivantes. Vivien, directeur de l'école normale, prône l'utilisation de la méthode naturelle, déjà pratiquée par les familles aisées dans l'antiquité gréco-latine, pour installer chez leurs enfants un bilinguisme gréco-latin. Vivien apparaît ainsi comme le précurseur méconnu de la *méthode directe*.

En 1853, le fr. étant promu langue d'enseignement, l'enseignement *en* ald. devient *ipso facto* enseignement *de* l'ald., à raison de 45 minutes par jour. En 1865, il sera supprimé totalement en Moselle.

L'exacerbation de la francisation de 1850 à 1870 s'explique par l'évolution de la situation politique ald. Les nationalistes y ont retourné le principe jacobin *une nation, une langue* en *eine Sprache, eine Nation*. Il s'agit donc pour la F. de ruiner le fondement juridique de cette revendication par une politique linguistique à grande échelle dont l'école est l'instrument. Les jardins d'enfants ouverts sous la monarchie de juillet 1830 répondent à cette intention et ont une efficacité remarquable. En 1870, l'ald. standard n'est plus représenté en A.-L. que sous forme écrite.

Pourtant, à la veille de la guerre, l'A. et la L. thioise sont loin d'être totalement francophones. L'obligation scolaire n'existant pas encore — elle ne sera introduite qu'en 1882 par la loi Jules Ferry —, la population enfantine n'est affectée qu'à 60% par l'enseignement. Les vieux maîtres ignorent les nouvelles instructions et continuent à travailler à l'ancienne. Les jeunes n'ont pas toujours une connaissance suffisante du fr. pour l'enseigner valablement. La grande bourgeoisie a adopté le fr., mais son expression demeure gauche et marquée par l'accent régional. Dans les couches moyennes cultivées (prêtres, pasteurs, médecins, avocats, employés), le fr. est la langue de la formation, mais alterne avec le dialecte et l'ald. dans l'exercice de la profession. La langue véhiculaire des paysans et des ouvriers, reste le dialecte. La langue liturgique utilisée dans les sermons, les prêches, les prières et les cantiques, demeure l'ald.

A côté d'une littérature de langue ald. (Stoeber), et d'une littérature de langue fr. (Edouard Schuré, Erckmann et Chatrian), l'on voit naître une littérature dialectale qui produit des œuvres lyriques et théâtrales (Arnold, Lustig, Stoskopf). La présence du fr. en A.-L. préserve, à ce moment de l'évolution, les dialectes d'une assimilation par la *Hochsprache*, telle qu'elle se produit dans de nombreuses régions d'All. (menace *endogène*). Mais dans le même temps, le dialecte est tellement pénétré par des éléments lexicaux fr. que l'on s'inquiète pour sa survie (menace *exogène*).

Quant au multilinguisme, il apparaît de plus en plus comme une marque identitaire de l'A.-L. et commence à être revendiqué avec insistance.

3.5. L'Alsace-Lorraine dans l'Allemagne wilhelminienne (1871−1918)

L'annexion provoque des mouvements de population: de 1871 à 1872, 128.000 ressortissants de la bourgeoisie (autochtones bilingues et Fr. de l'intérieur) quittent l'A.-L. Ils sont remplacés par un nombre équivalent de *Altdeutsche*. Dans les villes de garnison et les centres industriels (Metz et Strasbourg) la proportion de ces immigrés dépasse 40% et le *Hochdeutsch* réapparaît comme langue parlée. Le service militaire dans l'armée ald. favorise cette réimplantation.

La politique linguistique de l'All. vise à éliminer le fr. L'ald. devient langue obligatoire dans la vie publique. Cette mesure soulève des protestations véhémentes des populations qui, après 2 siècles de vie commune avec la F., réclament un statut particulier pour le fr. et même un enseignement bilingue. Des dispositions transitoires (traductions) sont alors prises pour les régions francophones. Elles seront abrogées ou très réduites après 1889.

En 1873, l'école devient obligatoire en A.-L. L'ald. est dès lors la langue exclusive de l'enseignement, le fr. n'est plus toléré que facultativement et provisoirement à raison de 4 heures en *Mittel-* et *Oberstufe*. En 1888 l'on n'en trouve plus trace à l'école primaire. L'enseignement bilingue que les Als.-Lor. revendiquent dès 1873, leur est refusé. Cependant, le Kaiser tolère le bilinguisme dans les régions à majorité francophone: l'ald. y est enseigné à raison de 5 heures hebdomadaires, mais le fr. y reste langue véhiculaire jusqu'en 1880 et l'on enregistre alors, pour la première fois dans l'histoire scolaire de l'A.-L., « ein befriedigendes Nebeneinander der Sprachen » (Hartweg 1958, 1985). A partir de 1880 toutefois, calcul, géographie et chant seront abordés en ald.

Sur le plan didactique l'on expérimente diverses techniques et l'on découvre ainsi la primauté de l'oral sur l'écrit. Initialement bannis au profit de l'ald., les dialectes seront autorisés dans le primaire par 2 décrets (juin 1890, janvier 1891).

Dans le second degré, l'enseignement du fr. est réduit et l'on tente d'utiliser les dialectes pour renforcer l'ald.

La mission linguistique de l'école devient un enjeu politique: la question est débattue avec passion dans le *Landesausschuß*, au *Landtag* et dans la presse de 1875 à 1887 et de 1908 à 1912. Tablant sur la résistance des milieux ecclésiastiques à la francisation, les autorités ald. espéraient bénéficier du soutien de l'Eglise dans leur politique de germanisation. Mais le *Kulturkampf* amène les catholiques à changer de camp et à défendre le fr. dans leurs écoles tout en y maintenant l'enseignement de la religion en ald. Le protestantisme als.-lor. est plus conciliant et renforce ses liens avec l'All.

En 1914, la fonctionnalité des langues en présence est bien établie: affaibli par l'émigration et par son élimination de l'école primaire, le fr. perd du terrain dans les couches inférieures de la population. Mais dans les couches supérieures, qui maintiennent le contact avec la F., il est utilisé comme signe de culture et manifestation de particularisme et d'opposition au nouvel ordre établi. En 1902, la suppression de la censure permet le développement de la presse d'opinion et d'une propagande fr. et francophone. Le code-switching ald.-fr. ou dialecte-fr. commence à se manifester: il est pratiqué par les autochtones pour narguer les *Altdeutsche* ou se démarquer d'eux! L'ald. est la langue de l'école, du service militaire, des relations avec les autres *Reichsländer*. Il est maîtrisé oralement par les *Altdeutsche* et dans sa forme écrite par toute la population (obligation scolaire). Il règne seul dans la liturgie et acquiert aussi une réelle importance littéraire avec Ernst Stadler (1883−1914) et René Schickele (1883−1940). Le dialecte demeure la langue véhiculaire de la vie quotidienne et familiale, sauf dans les milieux bilingues où il est évincé par le fr. Le contact rétabli avec le standard ald. fait ressurgir la menace endogène. Quant à l'écriture d'expression dialectale, elle poursuit un essor pris dès le début du 19e siècle et s'épanouit dans le théâtre.

Le début de la guerre 1914−1918 est marqué en A. et surtout en L. par une précipitation de la germanisation: interdiction de parler fr. sous peine de prison, traduction en ald. des noms de rues, inscriptions publiques et toponymes. La déportation des populations est même envisagée. Les quelques sympathies que s'étaient acquises les *Altdeutsche* en 40 ans de patience et de prudence sont perdues. L'autonomie complète, octroyée en octobre 1918, arrive trop tard pour réparer les erreurs commises.

3.6. L'entre-deux-guerres

Du jour au lendemain, le fr. devient langue de l'administration et de la justice, l'ald. est interdit. Dans leur majorité, les fonctionnaires fr. nommés en A. pour remplacer les fonctionnaires ald. émigrés ou expulsés sont purement francophones. Ils marginalisent les fonctionnaires als. dont l'expression est mal assurée en fr. et dont la promotion se trouve freinée ou bloquée. Dans le primaire, le fr. devient langue unique à compter de janvier 1920 et les maîtres als.-lor. sont astreints à effectuer des stages dans la F. de l'intérieur. De nombreux enseignants et inspecteurs, originaires de régions francophones, sont mutés dans les 2 provinces. La méthode imposée pour l'enseignement du fr. est la méthode directe excluant le recours à la langue autochtone. Mais les maîtres chargés de l'appliquer ne maîtrisant pas le fr., leurs élèves ne maîtrisent eux-mêmes ni l'une ni l'autre des 2 langues et constituent la *génération perdue*.

Seul l'enseignement religieux continue à jouir d'un statut spécial et est dispensé en ald. ou en als., à raison de 4 heures hebdomadaires. En 1919, l'administration fr. tente de supprimer totalement l'enseignement de l'ald., mais doit reculer devant le mécontentement suscité. A compter de 1924, l'ald. est même enseigné obligatoirement à raison de 3 heures hebdomadaires à partir de la 4e année primaire.

Dans le second degré, l'ald. perd tout statut particulier après une très courte période transitoire: il est traité comme une langue *étrangère* parmi d'autres.

En 1927, la Troisième République tolère 2 heures d'enseignement de la lecture en ald. dans le dernier semestre de la 2e année primaire (décret Poincaré-Pfister) et assouplit les instructions relatives à la mise en œuvre de la méthode directe.

Mais en 1936, le gouvernement Léon Blum envisage une prolongation de la scolarité pour la seule A.-L. afin d'y rattraper le retard entraîné par l'enseignement de la religion et de la langue ald. Devant la vivacité de la réaction, Blum renoncera, mais il ne pourra empêcher une nouvelle poussée autonomiste et même séparatiste.

Dans ce climat tourmenté, la littérature als. continue à se développer: l'expression dialectale est représentée par Albert et Adolphe Matthis, Marie Hart et Nathan Katz, poète du Sundgau. Sur la scène, l'interdiction de l'ald. induit l'apparition de pièces traduites en dialecte, le fr. restant encore inaccessible à un nombreux public. Mais les pièces écrites directement en dialecte se multiplient elles aussi et connaissent un vif succès. En 1933, le théâtre de Strasbourg est autorisé à entretenir une troupe germanophone.

La création en ald. est illustrée par Albert Schweitzer (1875−1965) − qui est bilingue mais écrit en *Hochdeutsch* −, la création en fr. par Dadelsen et Naegelen. La création bilingue fr.-ald. est elle aussi représentée par Alexandre, Goll et Arp, fondateurs du *dadaïsme*.

Dans le domaine des médias, les quotidiens d'expression ald. ou bilingues demeurent majoritaires jusqu'en 1939. Radio Strasbourg est largement bilingue et consacre des soirées entières à des émissions en dialecte.

La période de l'entre-deux-guerres aura donc été marquée linguistiquement par une politique d'assimilation systématique. Ignorant complètement la dialectophonie familiale, elle crée des situations d'*acquisition maternelle contrariée* qui installent dans les classes moyennes et populaires un *bilinguisme soustractif*, i. e. une possession imparfaite des 2 langues. Pour ces couches de population, le dialecte demeure encore la langue orale dominante et l'ald. la langue écrite imparfaitement tandis que le fr. est compris, mais mal parlé et mal écrit.

3.7. L'Alsace-Lorraine sous le Troisième Reich (1940−1944)

Les vainqueurs interdisent le fr., *langue décadente* («*Raus mit dem welschen Plunder!*»). Les livres fr. sont brûlés. Noms de rues, d'entreprises, toponymes, inscriptions funéraires, noms de famille et prénoms sont germanisés.

Les dialectes als.-lor. sont traités comme les autres dialectes ald.: ils doivent être supplantés par le *Hochdeutsch*.

3.8. 1945–1990: La francisation à grande vitesse

Après la libération:

— Les affiches françaises «Raus mit dem Schwowe Plunder» remplacent les affiches nazies «Raus mit dem welschen Plunder!». Le fr. redevient la seule langue officielle. L'ald. et le dialecte sont tolérés pour quelques années (domaine juridique et fiscal, sécurité sociale, postes et télécommunications). Pour les opérations électorales, le bilinguisme fr.-ald. demeure la règle.
— Domaine scolaire: dans le primaire il est «*provisoirement*» interdit d'utiliser l'ald. comme langue véhiculaire et même de l'enseigner. Cette situation durera 8 ans! Envers les dialectes, l'Education Nationale pratique la *pédagogie de rupture*: elle les dénigre ou les ignore.
— Les crimes perpétrés par le régime nazi ont terni l'image de l'ald., *Sprache des Feindes*, dans la population. L'efficacité des mesures linguistiques prises pour la vie publique et l'enseignement s'en trouve accrue.
— Nouveau recul de l'ald. en Lor. dans les années 60: concurrencées par des sources d'énergie plus rentables, les houillères entrent en récession: 3.000 Sarrois qui venaient y travailler trouvent maintenant à s'employer dans l'All. du *Wirtschaftswunder*.
— Les dialectes souffrent des mutations socio-économiques intervenues dans les nations industrialisées européennes après la 1re et surtout la 2e guerre mondiale: croissance économique, modernisation et restructuration de l'agriculture, exode rural, urbanisation, disparition de métiers traditionnels, mobilité accrue des travailleurs, employés et fonctionnaires, extension de la presse écrite et des médias audio-visuels, efficacité accrue de l'enseignement. Ces facteurs accélèrent la propagation des langues officielles. En F. cette évolution a affaibli les grandes langues régionales (breton, basque, catalan, occitan). C'est pourquoi les dialectes als.-lor. n'ont jamais été menacés par les dialectes romans du voisinage mais seulement par le fr. standard. Ayant échappé à l'action nivelante du système éducatif fr. de 1870 à 1918, les dialectes als.-lor. s'étaient bien maintenus jusqu'en 1939. Mais en 1945, ils sont vulnérabilisés par leur ascendance germanique. Présentés comme une entrave à la réussite, ils perdent leur prestige et leur fonctionnalité et *disparaissent de la vie familiale* en 3 générations (*Dreigenerationenmodell*):
— Les grands-parents sont dialectophones ou bilingues dialecte-fr. Ils parlent le dialecte entre eux, mais ne le transmettent plus à leurs enfants.
— Les parents comprennent encore le dialecte mais ne le parlent plus et ne peuvent donc le transmettre.
— Les petits-enfants sont francophones monolingues. Leur connaissance du dialecte se borne à savoir que les grands-parents l'utilisent encore.
— Une autre récession se produit dans les années 60 *sur les lieux de travail*. L'intégration linguistique des travailleurs étrangers s'était effectuée jusque-là par le dialecte. Mais après 1960, la proportion des sujets exclusivement francophones venus de F. ou du Maghreb s'accroît jusqu'à 30% de la population. Les Sarrois abandonnant le bassin minier lor. sont souvent remplacés par des Nord-Africains. L'intégration des travailleurs migrants ne s'effectue plus alors par le dialecte, mais par le fr. Le fr. devient aussi la langue dans laquelle l'on s'adresse à une personne inconnue et il supplante le dialecte sur ce point. Pour des dialectophones parlant des dialectes différents, le fr. assume enfin le rôle d'une κοινή, bien que les différences en question ne constituent pas une entrave véritable à la communication.
— Vie religieuse: L'église catholique abandonne son principe du catéchisme et de la messe «*in der Muttersprache*». L'ald. conserve une place plus importante dans l'église protestante.
— La presse bilingue est soumise dès 1945 à une réglementation sévère: toutes les informations pour la jeunesse doivent être rédigées en fr. Ces dispositions sont abrogées en 1984, mais les éditions continuent à respecter les normes de 1945. *Das Metzer Freie Journal*, rebaptisé *France Journal* en 1945, arrête sa parution en 1989. En A., les 2 quotidiens bilingues, *L'Alsace* et *Les Dernières Nouvelles d'Alsace*, sont en recul.
— Le studio *Radio France-Alsace* ne fait qu'une part réduite aux émissions en ald. et en dialecte. *FR3-Alsace* diffuse 8h 35 hebdomadaires d'émissions télévisées en fr., 2h 20 seulement en dialecte et ignore l'ald. Mais dans les régions proches de la frontière, 50% des foyers reçoivent les émissions télévisées de la Belgique, du Luxembourg et de l'All.

– Dans l'ensemble, le fr. s'est installé dans une position de dominance totale et nous sommes en présence d'un changement de langue (*Sprachwechsel*).

Mais une évolution se manifeste aussi en sens contraire:

– La langue ald. est peu à peu dissociée des crimes nazis et Albert Schweitzer trouve la consécration en All., dans le monde et même en F. (1951: *Friedenspreis des deutschen Buchhandels*; 1952: prix Nobel de la paix; 1954: distinction *Pour le mérite*).
– La réconciliation franco-allemande devient réalité et la République Fédérale entreprend sa *Vergangenheitsbewältigung*.
– Son économie florissante emploie des travailleurs als. et lor. (En 1989, 9500 pour la seule Moselle.) Ceux-ci sont ainsi replongés dans la culture et la langue ald., mais leur insuffisance linguistique les confine dans des emplois subalternes.
– Le Conseil Général du Bas-Rhin se saisit de la question du bilinguisme als. dès 1946 et y revient presque annuellement par la suite. Celui du Haut-Rhin lui emboîte le pas en 1950. Les 2 Conseils Généraux débattent même du problème en réunion commune (1971, 1980, 1982). Ils se sentent soutenus dans leur revendication par l'opinion publique als.: un sondage, réalisé en 1953 par les autorités académiques auprès des familles, révèle qu'elles sont favorables à 84% à l'enseignement de l'ald. dès l'école primaire! D'autres sondages, effectués par des instituts spécialisés dans les années suivantes, fourniront des résultats analogues.
– Mais la spécification linguistique de l'A. continue à être ignorée par l'Etat fr. La *loi Deixonne* (1951) autorise l'enseignement facultatif des langues régionales. Corse, flamand, lor. et als. sont toutefois exclus, en tant que *variantes locales de langues exogènes*. En 1953, le décret André Marie autorise tout de même les instituteurs als. volontaires à enseigner l'ald. 1 heure hebdomadaire dans les 2 dernières années du primaire. Mais la mesure, insuffisante et mal appliquée, reste inopérante.
– 1968: le mouvement de réhabilitation des langues et cultures régionales s'affirme en F., impulsé par des associations privées: *Seaska* au Pays Basque, *La Bressola* en Roussillon, *Diwan* en Bretagne. En Als. est créé le *Cercle-René-Schickele* pour défendre et promouvoir la culture bilingue. L'opinion publique als. prend conscience de l'identité régionale.

Cette évolution est catalysée par le dramaturge Germain Muller et par des auteurs comme Eugène Philipps, Adrien Finck et André Weckmann, qui rattachent la préservation du patrimoine culturel als. aux préoccupations écologiques et revendiquent le droit au bilinguisme.
– Ce consensus finit par ébranler l'Education Nationale qui lance la «*réforme Holderith*»: 30 classes als. de 5ᵉ année reçoivent à partir de 1972 une initiation à l'ald. Misant sur la parenté entre als. et *Hochdeutsch*, l'on pense ranimer le bilinguisme à peu de frais: 4 à 5 séances hebdomadaires d'une ½ heure. Mais l'enseignement ne doit être confié qu'à des maîtres volontaires et les germanophones se font rares; quant aux élèves, la plupart n'ont plus du dialecte qu'une connaissance passive et le transfert espéré ne s'effectue pas.
– Au début des années 80, le succès des institutions *Seaska, La Bressola* et *Diwan* oblige l'Education Nationale à prendre en compte les langues et cultures régionales et à autoriser des «*classes expérimentales bilingues*». Les premières maternelles publiques bilingues sont alors ouvertes au Pays basque fr. et en Bretagne en 1983.
– Les Conseils Généraux réclament en 1982 la reconnaissance de l'association *dialecte als.-lor. parlés + ald. standard* (norme de référence écrite) comme *langue régionale* de France. Mais il n'existe pas en A.-L. de secteur scolaire associatif pour l'enseignement bilingue et l'Education Nationale se borne à de simples déclarations d'intention: le Recteur de Strasbourg en 1985 et celui de Nancy-Metz en 1990 adoptent l'argumentation juridique des Conseils Généraux. En 1985, des instructions réservent une place au dialecte dans les écoles maternelles et, dans le second degré, l'enseignement de l'ald. est invité à utiliser la base dialectale.
– En 1984–1985 est mise en place en F. une option *Langue et Culture régionales* à partir de la 3ᵉ année de collège. Appliquée en A.-L., la mesure est trop modeste pour être efficace.

4. Interférences linguistiques

Les contacts prolongés entre les dialectes germaniques d'A.-L. et le fr. ont déclenché des interférences.

4.1. Phonologie

Dans la mesure où les parlers primitivement installés étaient les dialectes, le transfert a joué vers le fr. Ces interférences ont été ensuite adoptées par la génération suivante comme traits de langue constitutifs du fr. régional. Ce mécanisme a fonctionné 2 fois dans l'histoire de l'A.-L.: une 1re fois au 18e siècle, avant 1870, et une 2e fois après 1918.

La prosodie du fr. parlé en A.-L. est de type germanophone. L'accent de mot est déplacé vers l'initiale dans les bisyllabiques et les trisyllabiques, ce déplacement s'accompagnant d'une élongation de la voyelle accentuée si celle-ci est suivie d'une consonne sonore: broder → ['pro:de]; aborder → ['ʔaborde]. En fr. standard, l'accent de mot est peu marqué et réalisé par un abaissement du fondamental laryngé, accompagné d'une légère élongation des segments subtoniques. En fr. als.-lor., l'accent de mot est très marqué et réalisé par une élévation du fondamental, accompagnée d'une forte élévation d'intensité.

Les transferts phonématiques sont difficiles à décrire en termes généraux par suite de la variabilité du tissu dialectal. En alémanique et en francique rhénan, l'on constate:

— qu'à l'initiale [b d g] ~ [p t k] sont réalisés comme [p t k] ~ [pʰ tʰ kʰ] devant voyelle: beau → [po:]; peau → [pʰo:]; cette réinterprétation phonologique évite l'homophonie. Mais devant consonne l'opposition est neutralisée et l'on prononce donc *crocs* comme *gros*: [kro:];

— qu'en finale ces mêmes [b d g v] sont assourdis en [p t k f], cette neutralisation n'aboutissant toutefois pas à l'homophonie: il se produit en effet un allongement compensatoire de la voyelle précédant l'occlusive: vide → [vi:t] ~ vite → [vit]; grive → [kri:f] ~ griffe → [krif]. Il s'agit encore de la réinterprétation phonologique d'un trait purement phonétique: en fr. standard, les voyelles suivies d'une consonne sonore sont plus longues que les voyelles suivies de la forme sourde de cette même consonne;

— que les oppositions [z] ~ [s] et [ʒ] ~ [ʃ] sont neutralisées en [s] et [ʃ] avec maintien de la disphonie: rose → [ro:s] ~ rosse → [ros]; cage → [kʰa:ʃ] ~ cache → [kʰaʃ];

— que les timbres vocaliques du fr. subissent des altérations très variables, l'opposition [ɔ] ~ [ø] étant toutefois généralement neutralisée au profit de [ɔ] en toutes positions et non pas seulement en finale comme en fr. standard;

— que les voyelles nasales sont purement et simplement dénasalisées ou rendues par la succession *voyelle pure* + [ŋ]; que les voyelles placées en finale absolue sont généralement allongées comme en dialecte et en *Hochdeutsch*.

Depuis 1945, un transfert phonologique en sens inverse se manifeste. Il est dû à l'immigration massive de ressortissants francophones et à la dominance très marquée du fr. dans la vie publique. Il se traduit par un glissement de l'accent de mot vers la finale et par un affaiblissement de son caractère dynamique. Au niveau segmental, l'on note une atténuation du souffle des occlusives sourdes [pʰ tʰ kʰ], ainsi qu'un affaiblissement du coup de glotte [ʔ] et du *Hauchlaut* [h], pouvant aboutir à une disparition totale de ces 2 phonèmes.

4.2. Lexique

Trois siècles d'immersion des dialectes als. et lor. dans la civilisation fr. ont conduit ces parlers à adopter, dès l'époque napoléonienne, un nombre considérable de termes fr. dans les domaines les plus divers. Il s'agit surtout de substantifs, assimilés phonologiquement pour la plupart, si bien qu'ils ne sont plus reconnus par un francophone à première audition. Ils ont trait à la politesse (*bonjour, salut, au revoir, bonsoir, adieu, merci; salutiere, derangiere, regrettiere*), aux imprécations (*numdebibb* = nom d'une pipe, *num de die* = nom de Dieu), à la nourriture, à l'habillement, à l'habitation, aux transports, à la santé ...

Certains de ces emprunts, réalisés indirectement par l'intermédiaire de l'ald.: *Ade, Banane, Kaffee, poussieren*, etc. ont encouragé des emprunts directs formés parfois sur le même modèle: *ambetiere, exküsiere, sich debrujiere, sich demärdiere*. Positif lorsque le mot emprunté comble une lacune sémantique de la langue emprunteuse (*Banane, Garage*), l'emprunt lexical est alarmant lorsque le terme emprunté vient supplanter un terme déjà existant dans la langue emprunteuse sans apporter d'enrichissement sémantique ou stylistique (*ami, crayon, timbre, vélo*, etc.).

Les éléments lexicaux empruntés par le fr. à l'als. sont rares. Ils se rapportent au domaine culinaire et sont assimilés phonologiquement: *choucroute* (*Sauerkraut*), *Kirsch, Kouglof* (*Kugelhupf*), *Schnaps*.

4.3. Sémantique et syntaxe

Dans ce domaine aussi, le transfert jouait surtout jusqu'ici des dialectes vers le fr. régional et se manifestait:

— dans les mécanismes de *word order*: *Il faut ça aussi écrire* (= Il faut écrire ça aussi; induit par l'agencement: *Man muß das auch schreiben*); *Je donne aux vaches du foin* (= Je donne du foin aux vaches; dans les dialectes alémaniques et franciques, comme en ald. standard, le complément indirect (datif) apparaît avant le complément direct (accusatif): *Ich gebe den Kühen Heu*);
— dans des *décalques* de lexèmes ou locutions: *cartes à vue* (= cartes postales; induit par *Ansichtskarten*); *donner du gaz* (= accélérer; induit par *Gas geben*);
— dans des (ré)interprétations germaniques de vocables ou de mots-outils fr.: *C'est lui qui cuit* (= C'est lui qui fait la cuisine; induit par le sens du verbe *kochen*; également attesté en L. et en Belgique); *une tasse de thé de camomille* (= *une infusion de camomille*; induit par: *Kamillentee*);
— dans des constructions ou régimes déviants: *s'intéresser pour quelque chose* (= s'intéresser à quelque chose; induit par: *sich interessieren für*).

Les transferts sémantiques et syntaxiques en sens inverse se sont multipliés depuis 1945. Les exemples ci-dessous ont été recueillis en A. (sauf indication contraire):

— *Er het zehn Johr* (= Er ist zehn Jahre; induit par: *Il a 10 ans*); *Unser Junger hadd 25* (= Unser Junge ist 25; induit par: *Notre garçon a 25 ans*; observé en Moselle);
— *Er isch krànk gefàlle* (= Er ist krank geworden; induit par: *Il est tombé malade*);
— *Diss isch siner Fähler* (= Er ist schuld daran; induit par: *C'est sa faute*);

4.4. Le *code-switching* alsacien-lorrain

Un autre phénomène d'interaction est le *code-switching* als.-lor. Il consiste à truffer une conversation menée en dialecte de vocables fr. et/ou de locutions fr., ou même, à la limite, à alterner dans une même conversation des séquences en dialecte et des séquences en fr.: *Am lundi isch Ecole*; *Ich brüch a hüffe Biecher ùn Hefter, a pààr Protäschkajee, e Stilo, e Kreju-Spitzer un e neji Truss, denn miner àlt Plümje isch kàpütt* (= Lundi, il y a école; il me faudrait beaucoup de livres et de cahiers, quelques protège-cahiers, un stylo, un taille-crayons et une nouvelle trousse, car mon vieux plumier est fichu). L'exemple suivant a été recueilli en L.: *Ben, ils vont prendre une chambre. Sie gehen ins Hotel schlafen*. Le *code-switching* est un phénomène essentiellement urbain et beaucoup plus féminin que masculin. Ses premières manifestations écrites en A. remontent à 1902, mais il s'est considérablement répandu depuis 1945, au point d'être abusivement considéré comme une particularité als. et lor. (Il était couramment pratiqué au 18e siècle, à la cour du roi de Prusse).

Le *code-switching* als.-lor. possède plusieurs fonctions parfois contradictoires: marque identitaire, jonglerie de bilinguisme accompli … ou signe de faiblesse d'un bilinguisme imparfait. Aujourd'hui il est un symptôme de déclin (Hartweg 1985, 1973, passim; Petit 1993, 30). Il déclenche des mécanismes de rapprochement phonologique des 2 langues: affaiblissement articulatoire et diminution du souffle des occlusives sourdes [p^h t^h k^h], flottement dans la réalisation du *Hauchlaut* à l'initiale. Il suscite enfin de nouveaux emprunts lexicaux.

5. Développements récents et perspectives

La situation, déjà préoccupante en 1990, s'est encore aggravée:
— Sur le plan médiatique, l'ald. standard n'est plus représenté que sous forme écrite et dans la presse religieuse, protestante surtout. La part des émissions télévisées régionales en dialecte a été réduite en 1990 à 1h 30. Les programmes pour enfants n'existent plus. Les émissions radio dialectales sur modulation de fréquence ont été totalement supprimées en 1992.
— Malgré une certaine restauration de l'image des dialectes, le *Dreigenerationenmodell* continue à fonctionner. En se fondant sur les indications fournies par les enseignants des écoles maternelles et primaires en 1993, le Recteur de Strasbourg dresse une carte de la dialectophonie des enfants de 3 à 12 ans (fig. 147.3): le dialecte est en récession rapide en milieu urbain, plus lente en milieu rural. Le Nord (43 à 62%) résiste mieux que le Sud (moins de 10%).
— L'élimination externe du dialecte se double d'un travail de démolition de sa structure linguistique: sur le plan phonologique, transformation respective des proparoxytons et paroxytons en paroxytons et oxytons. Sur le plan lexical, multiplication d'emprunts redondants au fr.; sur le plan syntaxique, neutralisation de l'opposition locatif ~ directif (*Ich liege im Bett* ~ *Ich gehe ins Bett*). Le code-switching a pris des proportions telles

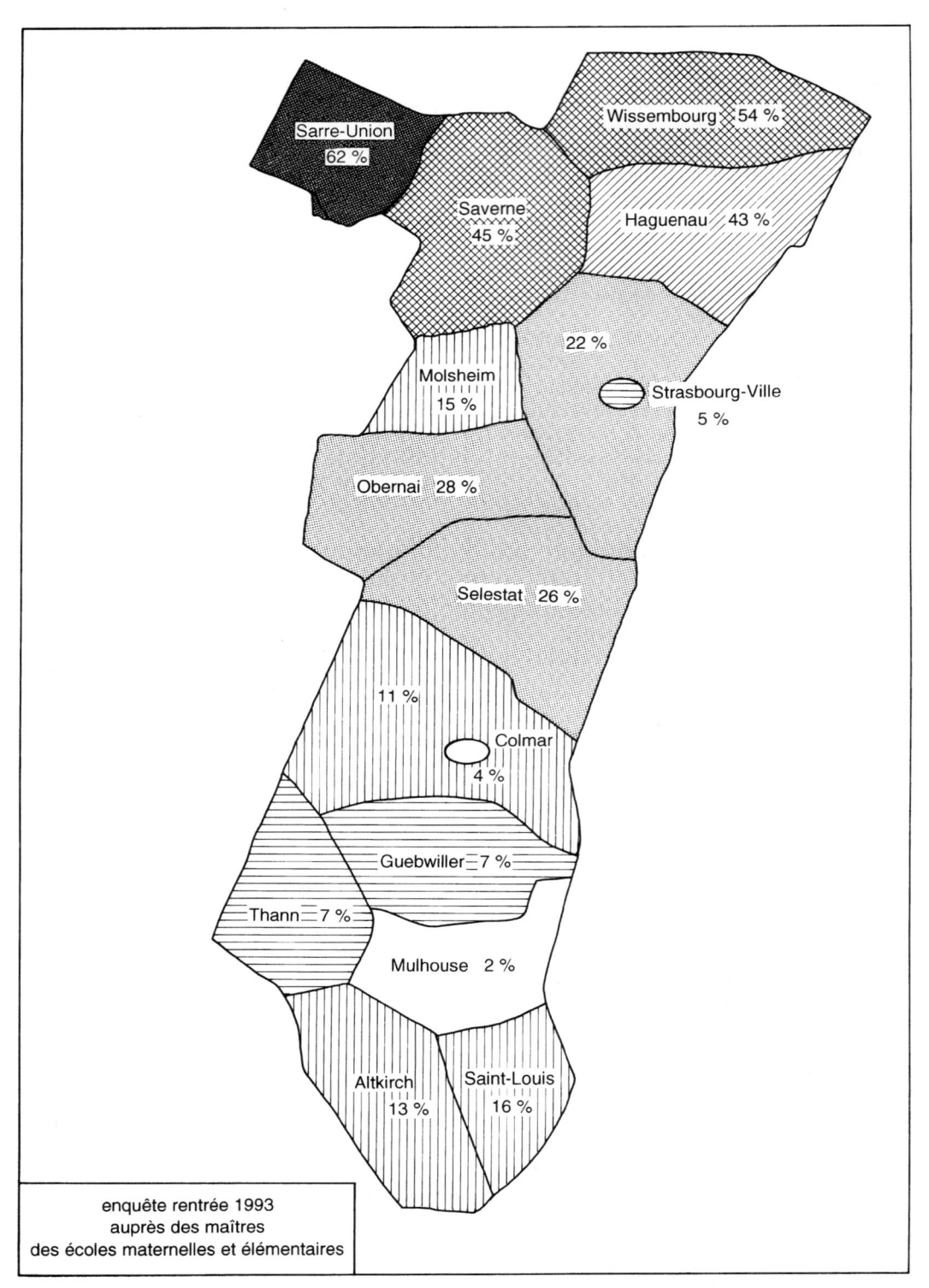

Fig. 147.3: Carte de la dialectophonie alsacienne: élèves de 3 à 12 ans. (Document établi par le Rectorat de Strasbourg à la rentrée scolaire de 1993).

qu'il devient la forme de remplacement du dialecte disparu. Sur le plan culturel, le théâtre als. constitue un dernier bastion de résistance.

Mais la réaction est vigoureuse:

— Créé en 1990, le *Haut Comité de référence pour la Langue et la Culture Alémanique et Francique*, alerte l'opinion.
— Devant le refus de l'Education Nationale et l'attitude négative du syndicat des instituteurs, des parents d'élèves et des enseignants du Haut-Rhin fondent en novembre 1990 l'*Association pour le Bilinguisme en Classe dès la Maternelle* (*ABCM*). Elle se propose d'ouvrir des filières bilingues là où la demande en sera formulée par la population. Prenant le conseil de spécialistes, elle opte pour la parité horaire des 2 langues (fr./ald.-dialecte) et pour le *principe de Ronjat*: un enseignant — doté d'une compétence de *native speaker* — pour chaque langue.

En septembre 1991, *ABCM* ouvre 3 classes maternelles. Le Conseil Régional, les Conseils Généraux des 2 départements et la *CEE* octroient les subsides nécessaires.

En septembre 1991 s'engage « *la bataille de Pulversheim* » (cf. Petit 1993, 43—44), querelle juridique entre la Préfecture et *ABCM* … pour une question de locaux. *ABCM* perd le procès en août 93. L'affaire fait grand bruit: la classe est désormais hors la loi, la rentrée 92—93 approche, les parents sont atterrés. Le Maire, fin lettré nourri aux sources des 2 cultures, fait front: « *Und wenn es sein muß, gehe ich eben ins Gefängnis* » (*Frankfurter Allgemeine Zeitung*). La F. se trouve à quelques semaines du referendum sur les accords de Maastricht … L'incohérence est flagrante, la position intenable. Un accord intervient *in extremis* entre les autorités académiques et la Municipalité de Pulversheim: la classe est intégrée dans l'Education Nationale avec son statut bilingue et son personnel enseignant.

En 1993, le Président du Conseil Général du Haut-Rhin, et le Ministre de l'Education Nationale signent une charte prévoyant la participation financière du département pour l'ouverture de maternelles bilingues dans l'enseignement public.

Rentrée 1993: le Recteur de Strasbourg envisage la création, dans chaque secteur de collège, de filières bilingues complètes de la maternelle à l'université.

A la rentrée 1994:

— l'on dénombre 41 classes bilingues paritaires dans le secteur public, 12 dans l'association *ABCM* et 4 dans le secteur privé confessionnel.
— l'*Office régional du Bilinguisme*, créé en 1993, diffuse un *Guide de l'enseignement bilingue précoce à parité horaire*. Il porte les signatures du Président du Conseil Régional, du Recteur de Strasbourg et des Présidents des 2 Conseils Généraux.
— une circulaire remarquable du Recteur de Strasbourg présente les modalités d'ouverture des classes bilingues et les principes psycho- et sociolinguistiques sur lesquels se fondent leur didactique.

La dynamique semble irréversible: l'A. devient une région pilote en matière de bilinguisme institutionnel.

Une préoccupation demeure: le recrutement et la formation de maîtres en quantité et en qualité suffisantes.

L'on déplore enfin qu'en 1995 la F. se refuse toujours à signer la charte des langues régionales ou minoritaires, qui considère comme «*imprescriptible*» le droit de pratiquer ces langues dans la vie privée ou publique et qui a déjà été adoptée par 23 des 27 Etats siégeant au Conseil de l'Europe.

Mais, si les classes bilingues associatives et publiques continuent à se développer en A.-L. et si elles atteignent leur objectif, il n'est pas impossible que l'on assiste à une renaissance du bilinguisme fr.-ald. par insémination institutionnelle, sans pose de bombes ni bain de sang.

6. Bibliographie (sélective)

Beyer, Ernest/Matzen, Raymond (1969): *Atlas linguistique et ethnographique de l'Alsace*, vol. 1, Paris.

Bothorel-Witz, Arlette/Philipp, Marthe/Spindler, Sylvane (1985): *Atlas linguistique et ethnographique de l'Alsace*, vol. 2, Paris.

Cercle-René Schickele-Kreis (1968): *Notre avenir est bilingue. Zweisprachig: unsere Zukunft.* Strasbourg.

Gardner-Chloros, Pénélope (1985): « Le code switching à Strasbourg ». In: *Le français en Alsace*. Etudes recueillies par Gilbert-Lucien Salmon, Paris/Genève, 51—60.

Hartweg, Frédéric (1983): « Tendenzen in der Domänenverteilung zwischen Dialekt und nichtdeutscher Standardsprache am Beispiel des Elsaß ». In: *Dialektologie. Ein Handbuch zur deutschen und allgemeinen Dialektforschung*, Besch, Werner/Knoop, Ulrich/Putschke, Wolfgang/Wiegand, Herbert Ernst (Eds.), Berlin/New York, vol. 2, 1428–1443.

Hartweg, Frédéric (1985): «Die Entwicklung des Verhältnisses von Mundart, deutscher und französischer Standardsprache im Elsaß seit dem 16. Jahrhundert». In: *Sprachgeschichte. Ein Handbuch zur Geschichte der deutschen Sprache und ihrer Erforschung*, Besch, Werner/Reichmann, Oskar/Sonderegger, Stefan (Eds.), Berlin/New York, vol. 2, 1949–1977.

Hoffmeister, Walter (1977): *Sprachwechsel in Ost-Lothringen. Soziolinguistische Untersuchung über die Sprachwahl von Schülern in bestimmten Sprechsituationen*, Wiesbaden.

Ladin, Wolfgang (1982): *Der elsässische Dialekt museumsreif? Analyse einer Umfrage*, Strasbourg.

Levy, Paul (1929): *Histoire linguistique d'Alsace et de Lorraine*, 2 tomes, Paris.

Matzen, Raymond (1985): «Les emprunts du dialecte alsacien au français». In: *Le français en Alsace*. Etudes recueillies par Gilbert-Lucien Salmon, Paris/Genève, 61–70.

Petit, Jean (1987): *Acquisition linguistique et interférences*, Paris.

Petit, Jean (1992): *Au secours, je suis monolingue et ... francophone*, Reims.

Petit, Jean (1993): *L'Alsace à la reconquête de son bilinguisme*, Nancy.

Pfister, Charles (1890): «La limite de la langue française et de la langue allemande en Alsace-Lorraine». In: *Bulletin de la Société de Géographie de l'Est* 12.

Philipp, Marthe (1967): «La prononciation du français en Alsace». In: *La Linguistique* 1, 63–74.

Philipp, Marthe/Bothorel, Arlette/Levieuge, Guy (1977): *Atlas linguistique et géographique de la Lorraine germanophone*, vol. 1, Paris.

Philipps, Eugène (1975): *Les luttes linguistiques en Alsace jusqu'en 1945*, Strasbourg.

Stroh, Cornelia (1993): *Sprachkontakt und Sprachbewußtsein. Eine soziolinguistische Studie am Beispiel Ostlothringens*, Tübingen.

Tabouret-Keller, Andrée/Luckel, Frédéric (1981): «La dynamique sociale du changement linguistique: quelques aspects de la situation rurale en Alsace». In: *International Journal of the Sociology of Language* 29: Regional Languages in France, Tabouret-Keller, Andrée (Ed.), 51–70.

Toussaint, Maurice (1955): *La frontière linguistique en Lorraine. Les fluctuations et la délimitation actuelle des langues françaises et germaniques de la Moselle*, Paris.

Vogler, Bernard (1993): *Histoire culturelle de l'Alsace*, Strasbourg.

Weckmann, André (1981): *Plaidoyer pour une zone bilingue franco-allemande/Plädoyer für eine deutsch-französische Bilingua-Zone*, Strasbourg.

Jean Petit, Reims (France)

148. Français–néerlandais

1. Géographie et démographie
2. Histoire
3. Statistiques et profil ethnique
4. Situation sociolinguistique
5. Etat de la politique linguistique
6. Portrait général des contacts linguistiques
7. Bibliographie (sélective)

1. Géographie et démographie

La zone étudiée de contacts entre le néerlandais (vu comme diasystème) et le français (aussi dans sa variante locale, le picard) se situe géographiquement le long de la partie occidentale de l'actuelle frontière franco-belge, à l'ouest de Tourcoing et de Mouscron, au point où frontières linguistiques et nationales se recoupent. Cette frontière politique a été tracée dans la deuxième moité du XVIIe siècle, quand Louis XIV s'empara de territoires importants dans les Pays-Bas espagnols, et fut fixée par la Paix de Nimègues en 1713. Pour les zones de contact linguistique à l'est de celle décrite ici, notamment dans l'actuelle Belgique: → art. 135 et 136. Quoique beaucoup d'aspects historiques et systématiques en soient certainement communs, les contacts linguistiques dans l'actuelle région Nord, Pas-de-Calais méritent un traitement particulier: déjà par les particularités de l'évolution depuis l'annexion à la France, il y a 300 ans, de territoires longtemps néerlandophones, mais aussi pour les différences dans l'évolution linguistique des zones traitées dès avant cette annexion (→ cartes linguistiques D et C).

La politique menée par les premiers comtes de Flandre et par leurs successeurs a réuni pendant des siècles les territoires au nord de la Somme et à l'ouest de l'Escaut, politiquement, religieusement, économiquement et socioculturellement. Cela ne pouvait manquer de susciter des contacts et des échanges intenses entre les deux communautés linguistiques de l'ancien comté des Flandres, la Flandre wallingante et la Flandre flamingante, et des zones voisines.

1.1. Conditions démographiques du contact linguistique

L'actuelle zone de contact linguistique dans le Nord de la France se situe principalement dans deux régions. D'abord, il y a l'arrondissement de Dunkerque, où entre la frontière linguistique et la frontière belge, seules les générations âgées et habitant les campagnes, parlent encore le dialecte flamand (voir fig. 148.1).

La deuxième région qui a connu des conditions de contact linguistique au cours des derniers 150 ans, est la vaste région lilloise. L'industrialisation intense de la deuxième moitié du XIXe siècle et du début du XXe siècle — surtout dans l'industrie textile florissante — autour des villes de Lille, Tourcoing et Roubaix, a attiré un flux très important d'ouvriers et de petits commerçants belges, pour la plupart flamands, qui s'y sont établis de façon durable (Lentacker 1974, Vandenbroeke 1993). Lentacker (1974, 239) s'exprime ainsi: « La Belgique a fourni pendant le XIXe siècle au département du Nord un apport démographique sans lequel le doublement de son chiffre de population de 1851 à nos jours n'eût pas été possible ». L'influence de la langue familiale flamande de la première (et parfois de la deuxième) génération d'immigrés sur le français régional de l'agglomération lilloise a été considérable, mais n'a pas encore fait l'objet d'études assez poussées. Il faut peut-être englober dans cette zone le Hainaut français occidental (zone du rouchi de Valenciennes), qui est solidaire de la région lilloise économiquement et sans

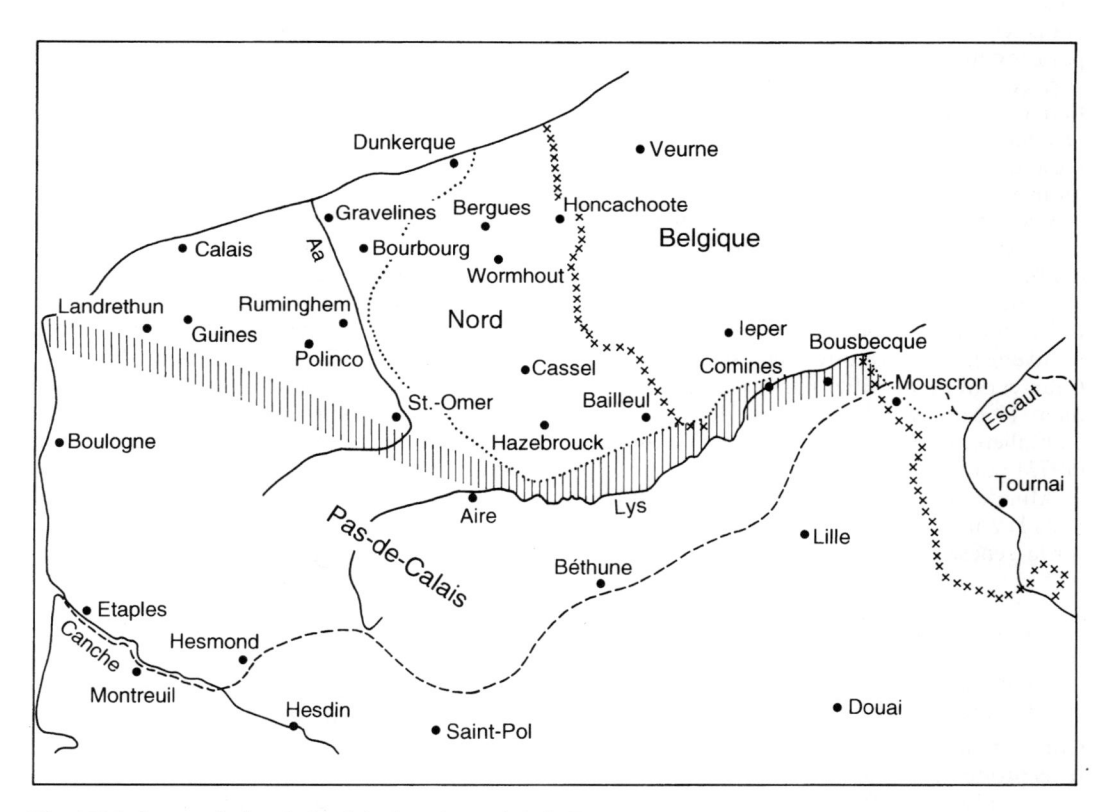

Fig. 148.1: Le retrait du néerlandais dans le nord de la France.
Source: Ryckeboer 1991, 169 (etiam in: Ryckeboer 1990, 243).

Légende: – – – – La frontière linguistique (approximative) aux VIIIe et IXe siècles, selon Gysseling 1976.
| | | | | | | La zone de frontière linguistique présumable vers 1300, selon Gysseling 1976.
.... La frontière linguistique actuelle selon Pée 1946.

doute aussi, dans une moindre mesure, sur le plan des migrations. Le témoignage des dictionnaires du rouchi (Dauby 1968 et déjà Hécart 1833) montre certainement une solidarité linguistique, et les mêmes traces de contacts linguistiques (peut-être par diffusion de traits intrapicards). Qui plus est, durant le XIXe et dans la première moitié du XXe siècle, des ouvriers agricoles saisonniers partirent chaque année, et cela pendant des décennies, de la Flandre belge vers les grandes exploitations du Nord de la France. Ils ont sans doute pu y introduire quelques éléments de leur jargon (v. la répartition de *pik(é)* sur la carte de la « sape », carte 120 dans Carton/ Lebègue 1989). La stagnation démographique en France du début du siècle ainsi que les effets de la première guerre mondiale ont attiré beaucoup d'agriculteurs flamands dans ce pays; ils se sont établis surtout dans les départements de l'Aisne, Oise et Somme ainsi qu'en Normandie. Dans certains villages, ils constituaient même la majorité des résidents. Dans les variations locales du français parlé par ces communautés rurales, on constate encore çà et là la survivance de quelques mots flamands, mais à notre connaissance, cela n'a pas encore fait l'objet d'études détaillées. Ce n'est que depuis quelques décennies que le mouvement s'inverse et actuellement 50 000 ouvriers du Nord de la France travailleraient dans des entreprises de la Flandre belge (Vandenbroecke 1993, 158).

Il est donc évident que les fluctuations de la conjoncture économique ont causé des mouvements migratoires en sens opposé. Ceux-ci ont pu modifier parfois considérablement le caractère linguistique de la région frontalière, comme l'a démontré Duvosquel (1973) pour la ville de Comines.

Afin de mieux situer le contact linguistique dans la zone discutée, il s'impose d'en esquisser la genèse et l'histoire.

2. Histoire

2.1. Genèse de la frontière linguistique dans le nord de la France

Contrairement à ce que l'on pourrait penser, le territoire de langue néerlandaise ne s'est jamais confiné aux frontières occidentales du comté de Flandre, notamment l'Aa (voir la carte 148.1), mais s'est aussi étendu au nord du comté d'Artois et au Boulonnais et Calaisais. L'aire où l'on parle encore le flamand de nos jours, au nord et à l'est de la frontière linguistique, comme elle est tracée par Pée en 1936−1938 (Pée 1946), n'est que le vestige de ce qui était dans le haut Moyen Age un territoire beaucoup plus vaste de langue néerlandaise au nord de la France.

En effet, à la suite des invasions germaniques du Ve siècle au nord de la Gaule romanisée, s'est constitué un pays où l'on utilisait tant le roman que le germanique. C'est exactement par l'effet de ce superstrat germanique que l'ancien français est devenu une langue différente du latin vulgaire (von Wartburg 1969). Mais pendant les trois siècles suivants, cette situation de bilinguisme et de diglossie a évolué vers un équilibre plus ou moins stable, qui a abouti à la formation d'une frontière linguistique au sud de laquelle le roman était en usage et au nord le germanique. On désigne ce germanique parfois par les termes historiques « francique » ou « thiois ». En tout cas, c'est un parler précurseur du moyen-néerlandais et du néerlandais moderne qui a pu se développer dans les zones limitrophes, quoiqu'il eût sans doute des affinités particulières avec l'ancien anglais. En effet, le Boulonnais a connu pendant les VIIe et VIIIe siècles une forte immigration de Saxons venant de l'Angleterre, ce qui se reflète entre autres dans le grand nombre de toponymes en *-t(h)un* dans le Boulonnais (Vanneufville 1979). Se basant sur le développement respectivement roman ou germanique des toponymes de la région, Gysseling (1976) trace cette frontière linguistique au VIIIe−IXe siècle a partir de l'embouchure de la Canche par Montreuil, Fruges, Béthune, puis allant au nord de la cité de Lille vers Mouscron (en Belgique). Tandis que la prolongation de cette frontière linguistique en Belgique n'a subi que des modifications mineures depuis lors, l'aire du néerlandais au nord de la France s'est par contre rétrécie progressivement au cours des onze siècles suivants en faveur du picard et du français.

2.2. Recul du néerlandais dans le Pas-de-Calais

Pendant les IXe et Xe siècles, la romanisation semble avoir atteint la Lys et affecté la région à l'ouest d'Aire. A partir du XIIe siècle, les toponymes accusent une romanisation progressive de la région entre Saint-Omer et Boulogne et en même temps, ils indiquent qu'au XIIIe siècle le néerlandais n'y est pas encore disparu. Plus au nord-est, le néerlandais résiste plus longtemps. On peut le considérer au XIVe siècle comme langue vernaculaire sur un territoire situé au nord d'une ligne approximative qui part du Cap Gris-Nez, passe en dessous de Guines, Ardres, Eperleques et Saint-Omer, pour se prolonger sur la Lys à l'est d'Aire. La romanisation a certainement commencé dans les villes, si tant est que le roman n'y a pas persisté parmi une certaine couche de la population. La ville de Boulogne était encore bilingue au XIIe siècle. A Saint-Omer, la bourgeoisie semble avoir adopté le français à partir de la deuxième moitié du XIIIe. Ceci n'empêche que les classes inférieures y ont continué à parler le flamand jusqu'au XVIIe et dans les deux hameaux occidentaux de Hautpont et de Lysel jusqu'au début du XXe (Derville 1981, 84). Les nombreuses interférences de mots néerlandais dans les règlements latins des échevins de la ville de Calais en 1293 et l'anthroponymie démontrent clairement que la langue usitée par les artisans et surtout par les pêcheurs y était le néerlandais au moins jusqu'au XIVe siècle. La période de la romanisation définitive de la ville reste encore à fixer. En tout cas, dans les villages ruraux entre Calais, Gravelines et Saint-Omer, le flamand se maintient jusqu'au XVIIe ou XVIIIe, et à Ruminghem et à Watten jusqu'au début du XXe siècle. Le recul millénaire du néerlandais dans le Pas-de-Calais et sa substitution par le picard implique un contact de langues (bilinguisme et diglossie) dont il est très difficile de retracer l'histoire (Poulet 1987, 33−34). En effet, à quelques exceptions près − qui ont d'ailleurs une valeur documentaire très importante pour le vieux néerlandais (voir le fameux « Hebban olla vogala nestas hagunnan ... », équivalent néerlandais des Serments de Strasbourg) − le français y est devenu la seule langue écrite à partir du XIIIe siècle.

Dans la partie flamingante du Comté de Flandre, donc à l'est de l'Aa, le latin en tant que langue administrative locale a généralement été remplacé au XIIIe siècle par le néerlandais. Néanmoins, au début le français semblait l'emporter sur le néerlandais aussi dans la partie occidentale de la Flandre flamingante dans certaines villes, surtout à Ypres où le magistrat de la ville − dominé par des familles d'origine arrageoise − a utilisé le français pendant près d'un siècle, avant de passer au néerlandais (Mantou 1972). Cela prouve que l'usage de la langue écrite ne donne en soi aucune indication sûre de celui de la langue vernaculaire, et en même temps que dans tout le Comté de Flandre le français a toujours été la langue de prestige, parlé par la haute noblesse et utilisé dans l'administration comtale à partir du XIIe siècle. Cette tradition a subsisté sous la domination des ducs de Bourgogne, puis sous celle des Habsbourg espagnols et autrichiens. La langue des administrations locales par contre, tout comme la langue littéraire, était le néerlandais partout dans le nord du comté de Flandre et dans les autres principautés des Pays-Bas situées au nord de la frontière linguistique.

Cette intégration totale dans la culture de langue néerlandaise ne fut interrompue, pour la région de Bourbourg, Dunkerque, Cassel, Hazebrouck et Bailleul, qu'à partir de la soumission politique de ces villes à Louis XIV entre 1659 et 1678. Quelques ordonnances royales limitaient l'usage du néerlandais comme langue officielle en général, et dans les villes de garnison de Gravelines, Bourbourg et Dunkerque, l'on introduisit des écoles françaises. C'était le début d'une francisation superficielle qui n'eut que très peu d'impact jusqu'à la fin de l'Ancien Régime (voir les chapitres sur la vie intellectuelle dans Coornaert (1970). A la veille de la Révolution, le néerlandais jouait toujours son rôle de langue culturelle et de langue d'enseignement, comme le confirmait P. Andries, professeur au collège de Bergues, dans sa réponse à l'enquête de l'abbé Grégoire sur les patois en France en 1790 (de Certeau et al., 1975, 231−243).

3. Statistiques et profil ethnique

Dans les années 1970 et 1980, quelques sondages sociolinguistiques ont été menés qui nous permettent d'en avoir une idée approximative (Ryckeboer 1976). Röhrig (1987) a d'abord voulu démontrer les caractéristiques diglossiques du contact linguistique. Pour cela, il n'a interrogé que des informateurs plus ou moins bilingues. Ainsi les gens qui ont plus de cinquante ans, constituent une part démesurée dans le total de ses interrogés. Comme les unilingues parlant uniquement le français n'ont pas été pris en compte, ses chiffres concernant le nombre de flamandophones ne sont pas entièrement fiables. Une enquête réalisée en 1984 à Hondschoote, petite bourgade frontalière, nous montre qu'une conversion linguistique (*language shift*) presque totale s'est produite pendant les trois dernières générations (Ryckeboer/Maeckelberghe 1987). D'après les données provenant de l'enquête sur les élèves d'Hondschoote, les grands-parents de ces derniers parlent ou parlaient entre eux pour 36% le français, 38% le néerlandais et 26% les deux langues. La génération des parents, née entre 1932 et 1952, emploie pour 75% le français comme seule langue au foyer. Dans le quart restant, on parle aussi le néerlandais à côté du français, mais presque jamais avec les enfants. Les élèves eux-mêmes ne parlent, à une rare exception près, que le français. La maîtrise des langues est à l'avenant. Quand on leur demande quelle langue ils parlent le plus couramment, 97% des jeunes indiquent le français, 1% le néerlandais et 2% disent maîtriser les deux langues de la même manière. 78% des parents parlent mieux le français, 7% mieux le néerlandais et 15% pensent maîtriser les deux langues de la même façon. La connaissance passive du néerlandais serait encore meilleure. Un quart des élèves prétend comprendre le néerlandais, de même que la moitié des parents. Mais que faut-il penser de cette connaissance? Le tableau 148.1 donne le pourcentage des réponses à des questions plus précises:

Tab. 148.1: Connaissances active et passive du néerlandais à Hondschoote (d'après Ryckeboer/Maeckelberghe 1987)

Réponses	Connaissance active (en %)				Connaissance passive (en %)			
	1	2	3	4	1	2	3	4
Elèves	61,7	28,2	12	4,7	69,5	49,5	24,5	9,2
Pères	67	56	51	48	74,4	67	58	50
Mères	50	50	36	33	70	58,3	45	60,5

1 = quelques mots, 2 = quelques phrases, 3 = une conversation facile, 4 = tout
(Comme on a prévu plusieurs possibilités, le pourcentage total peut dépasser 100%.)

De ces données, on peut facilement déduire que la connaissance du néerlandais est considérablement plus faible parmi les femmes adultes que parmi les hommes, et surtout que très peu de jeunes sont encore familiarisés avec le néerlandais. Cela est directement lié aux attitudes des parents, dont 82% estiment que cela ne vaut plus la peine de transmettre le dialecte néerlandais à la génération suivante. Mais nombre de jeunes pensent exactement l'inverse! Une telle attitude est assez caractéristique d'une situation dans laquelle la mort d'une langue est imminente.

Néanmoins, le bilinguisme existe toujours dans la région et les contacts frontaliers, qui gagneront certainement en importance dans le contexte européen à venir, entraînent un vif intérêt pour l'enseignement du néerlandais, la langue standardisée des voisins belges et néerlandais à laquelle le dialecte local est étroitement apparenté.

4. Situation sociolinguistique

Durant le XIXe siècle, le néerlandais a graduellement perdu sa fonction de langue de culture par le fait qu'il était exclu complètement de l'enseignement secondaire et supérieur par la loi Montalivet de 1833. Le néerlandais, dans une variante pourtant très dialectale, continua néanmoins à fonctionner quelque temps comme langue intermédiaire à côté du français. On peut le déduire entre autres d'un livre scolaire de Cavry: *Dialogues Flamands-Français entre un cultivateur et son domestique*, édité à Wormhout en 1848. Lorsque en 1880 l'enseignement primaire est rendu obligatoire pour tous les Français (lois scolaires de Jules Ferry), le français gagne lentement du terrain dans toutes les couches de la population, aussi dans les classes les plus basses de la société (Pée 1957 a donné une bibliographie raisonnée des publications traitant de ce recul). Seule l'Eglise catholique, en dépit d'interdictions officielles, persistera à enseigner en néerlandais («flamand») le catéchisme jusqu'au début de la première guerre et à prêcher occasionnellement en flamand même jusqu'au début de la deuxième guerre mondiale.

Pée (1946) constate que l'habitude de parler le français avec les enfants s'est généralisée dans la plupart des familles dans la période de l'entre-deux-guerres. Beaucoup de ces jeunes ont quand même appris le flamand dans la rue ou lors des travaux à la campagne. Cela n'était plus le cas ni dans les petites villes ni pour la plupart des filles à la campagne, qui ici comme ailleurs se sont montrées les plus sensibles à la langue de prestige. Le recul très rapide du flamand après la deuxième guerre mondiale a été documenté par Vanneste (1982), indiquant comme causes les plus importantes, l'explosion de la population dans les villes par une forte immigration de non-autochtones, la stagnation ou même la régression de la population dans les petites communes rurales constituant les derniers bastions du flamand, ainsi que la scolarisation générale. Ces facteurs interviennent d'ailleurs aussi dans le recul du dialecte picard pour l'ensemble du Nord de la France (Carton 1981). Les générations nées pendant et après la guerre ont définitivement accepté le français comme langue véhiculaire, et beaucoup d'entre elles ont même perdu la connaissance passive du flamand.

Une analyse sociolinguistique globale de la situation linguistique en Flandre française est donnée par Willemyns (1994).

5. Etat de la politique linguistique

L'enseignement des langues (y inclus de celle considérée comme langue maternelle) se situe dans le contexte historique d'une politique globalement négative à l'encontre des langues minoritaires sur le territoire français (v. Calvet 1974, de Certeau et al. 1975 et pour la zone étudiée surtout Van Goethem 1987). Celle-ci s'inspirait d'une méfiance jacobine envers les allophones, soupçonnés d'un manque de loyauté envers la République, alors que dans la pratique c'est cette politique même qui a suscité des frustrations, voire une hostilité envers l'Etat central chez une minorité d'activistes ethniques. A la lumière de tout ceci, il est significatif que l'allemand en Alsace-Lorraine et le néerlandais étaient exclus des facilités qu'offrait la loi Deixonne (de 1951) à l'enseignement des langues minoritaires. Toutes les demandes antérieures d'un rétablissement de l'enseignement dans la langue maternelle (voir pour un aperçu historique et une bibliographie Wood 1980 et Ryckeboer 1990) ne purent aboutir, étant suspectes aux yeux des autorités françaises, entre autres par leur motivation prétendument trop nationaliste ou à cause d'implications glottopolitiques, parmi lesquelles l'appui de l'Allemagne pendant la deuxième guerre mondiale. Cela n'a changé dans le Nord que dans les années 1970, sous l'impulsion d'un mouvement régionaliste-écologiste de tendance gauchisante. En ce qui concerne l'enseignement de la langue, ce mouvement fixait, à juste titre, comme premier objectif de décomplexer l'usage de la langue néerlandaise. Le manuel de Sepieter *Vlaemsch Leeren* (Dunkerque 1978) a eu un succès inattendu. Cela fut accompagné par une action continue et tenace en faveur d'un émetteur libre: la *Radio Uylenspiegel*. Celle-ci s'est vue légaliser depuis; elle émet en partie en néerlandais, a donné au début des cours de dialecte flamand et plus tard aussi de néerlandais, la langue standard. A côté de ses activités musicales, l'Association *Het Reuzekoor* à Dunkerque a commencé en 1980 un cours de flamand, dont l'auteur a publié un manuel remarquable (Marteel 1992). Le cours du Reuzekoor est un cours libre. Il n'a donc jamais fait partie des cours de langue et culture néerlandaises qui ont été instaurés — à l'instigation de l'association *Tegaere Toegaen* — dans les collèges de Grande-Synthe, Steenvoorde, Hondschoote, Wormhout, Bourbourg et Cassel, suite à la circulaire Savary de 1982. Après un succès considérable au début, ces cours semblent vivoter depuis, tandis que l'enseignement du néerlandais gagne du terrain.

Cette évolution reflète une lutte assez remarquable entre particularistes, prônant l'enseignement du *dialecte flamand*, et ceux qui prônent l'enseignement du *néerlandais*. Une telle controverse, à relents politiques, est nourrie par un manque d'information. Cette ignorance est favorisée par l'absence totale d'intérêt scientifique, par exemple du département de néerlandais à l'Université de Lille, et du monde scientifique français en général, pour la présence historique du néerlandais en France. Pour tirer profit des occasions offertes par la circulaire Savary et des initiatives développées à sa suite par le gouvernement socialiste, les propagandistes de l'enseignement du flamand ont essayé de présenter le flamand de France comme une langue différente du néerlandais. Ils ont par exemple rédigé un dictionnaire, dont la valeur scientifique est fort douteuse, ainsi qu'une grammaire du même niveau en appendice (Fagoo et al. 1985), et publié sur le rapport du flamand de France avec le néerlandais des informations qui ne résistent pas à la critique scientifique (Sansen 1988). De la même façon, Marteel (1992) s'arrête surtout au statut sociolinguistiquement particulier du dialecte flamand en France, et en minimise la parenté linguistique avec le néerlandais. L'épilogue de son livre, intitulé *Etude comparative du Flamand du Westhoek et du Néerlandais* (de la main d'Eric Duvoskeldt) constitue une tentative méritoire de nuancer cette prise de position. Mais toute cette littérature illustre une ignorance impardonnable des acquis de la dialectologie et des études historiques sur les stratifications linguistiques dans l'aire néerlandophone.

Néanmoins, depuis 1976 le néerlandais peut être choisi comme filière majeure à Lille III, mais le manque de débouchés dans l'enseignement et peut-être l'inadéquation de cet enseignement face à la situation de contact linguistique spécifique, font que le néerlandais n'y jouit pas de l'intérêt qu'il méritait.

D'autre part, depuis les années 1950, le *Komitee voor Frans-Vlaanderen* (Comité (belge) pour la Flandre française) a soutenu une propagande active pour l'enseignement du néerlandais standard dans l'école primaire et secondaire dans la région flamandophone et a organisé des cours libres. Cette action a contribué à faire proposer le néerlandais comme matière facultative dans beaucoup d'écoles secondaires du Nord de la France. Une expérience d'enseignement bilingue a commencé à l'école primaire de la ville frontalière Wervicq-Sud en 1985. Cette expérience a connu un succès considérable et par la suite elle a été étendue vers l'enseignement secondaire de la même ville et aussi de la ville frontalière de Bailleul (Belle), où la municipalité s'efforce depuis des années d'installer l'enseignement du néerlandais. Cet enseignement fait partie d'un programme d'échanges entre la France, les Pays-Bas et la Flandre belge. Il aura sa pleine valeur dans la perspective de l'Europe sans frontières. Tous les intéressés espèrent qu'il pourra passer du stade expérimental au stade institutionnel (Halink 1991 et van Hemel/Halink 1992).

6. Portrait général des contacts linguistiques

6.1. Les interférences du néerlandais/flamand en français régional (emprunts lexicaux)

L'indice le plus frappant d'une influence linguistique, consécutive ou non à un contact direct entre langues, est bien sûr l'emprunt lexical. Les emprunts faits au néerlandais par le français sont assez bien décrits par Valkhoff (1931). Il montre que la voie la plus importante pour cette influence a été le commerce, très intense au Moyen Age entre le Nord de la France et les Pays-Bas méridionaux, surtout par la mer (Valkhoff 1931, 8−34). Guiraud (1968) souligne que les Pays-Bas sont avec l'Italie le principal foyer d'irradiation d'emprunts durant le haut Moyen Age. Les emprunts des dialectes du Nord de la France aux parlers germaniques limitrophes ont été présentés par Weijnen 1964/1965, avec des cartes et des commentaires, basés sur l'*Atlas linguistique de la France* de J. Gilliéron.

Certaines hypothèses erronées ont continué à se maintenir à cause de l'absence, jusqu'il y a peu, de matériaux lexicaux dialectaux dûment localisés. Nous sommes mieux renseignés depuis la parution des ouvrages de Poulet 1987, Carton/Lebègue 1989 et Carton/Poulet 1991.

Le recul du néerlandais dans le nord du Pas-de-Calais se vérifie dans la densité des lexèmes néerlandais recueillis dans Carton/Lebègue 1989. Plus la picardisation ou la francisation des localités est récente, plus on y trouve de lexèmes néerlandais (voir la carte: fig. 148.2 reprise de Ryckeboer 1991 a). Pour cette carte, certains mots n'ont pas été pris en compte, parce que leur répartition va très loin au delà de la frontière linguistique. Il s'agit d'emprunts anciens au francique: *ram* (bouc), *gat* (chèvre), *èk(é)* (barrière), *étrik* (étriche), ou des mots du domaine de l'agriculture, qui ont été diffusés probablement dans un passé récent par des ouvriers belges ou par le commerce: *pik* (sape), *brak* (houe), *rap* (navet). Poulet (1987, 366−367) mentionne par ailleurs que 37,5% du vocabulaire qu'elle a recueilli dans le triangle entre Calais, Saint-Omer et Gravelines (et qui est aussi en partie du français commun), est d'origine germanique. Pour ce qui est des lexèmes proprement picards, 27,40% en seraient typiquement flamands ou néerlandais. Poulet a tort de se baser ici uniquement sur les indications du FEW de von Wartburg, dont les dénominations «germanique», «francique», «anglo-saxon» ou «allemand» seraient à remplacer souvent dans l'aire de recherche en question par «néerlandais» ou «flamand», en vue d'une linguistique de contact des langues. Très instructif à cet égard est aussi le Lexique du picard d'Oye, Gravelines et Loon, des localités où le dialecte flamand ne disparut qu'au cours des XVIIIe et XIXe siècles (Dupas 1980). L'interférence à partir du néerlandais/flamand dans le vocabulaire dialectal ou dans le français régional n'est pourtant guère décrite de façon satisfaisante dans ces ouvrages, ni d'ailleurs dans des lexiques plus anciens ou dans le FEW. Il est urgent de développer à cet effet une étude de la stratigraphique historique des contacts de langues des deux côtés de la frontière linguistique franco-néerlandaise à partir de matériaux lexicaux récemment recueillis dans le Nord de la France. Ryckeboer (1995) en donne maints exemples repris de Carton/Lebègue (1989).

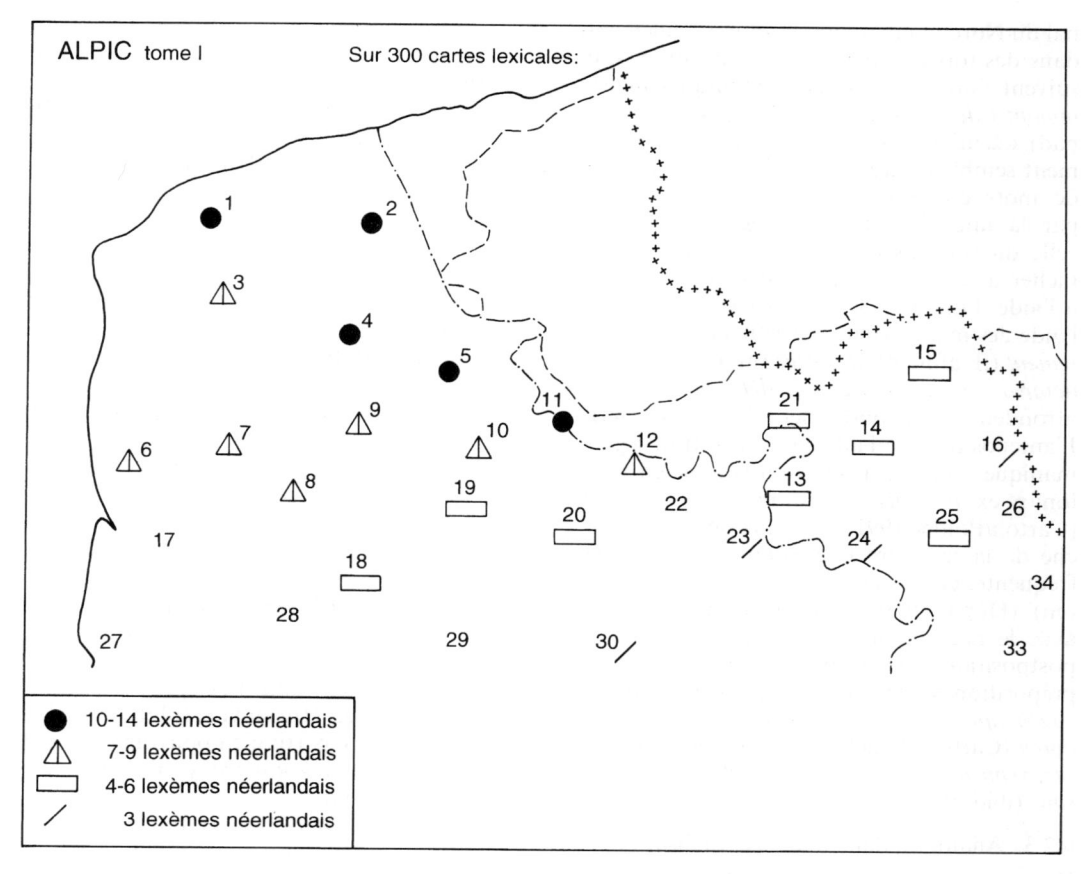

Fig. 148.2: Le substrat néerlandais dans le dialecte picard du Nord – Pas-de-Calais.
Source: Ryckeboer 1991, 168 (d'après Carton/Lebègue 1989).

6.2. Les correspondances linguistiques des deux côtés de la frontière linguistique

6.2.1. Correspondances phonologiques

Certains auteurs ont cru pouvoir déceler toutes sortes de correspondances linguistiques des deux côtés de la frontière linguistique dans le Nord de la France. On en trouve un aperçu chez Weijnen 1964 et van Hoecke 1978. L'explication de ces correspondances peut différer d'après la nature du phénomène. Pour certaines, on peut penser à la rencontre fortuite d'évolutions universelles ou internes aux langues en question (cf. van Hoecke 1988); d'autres ne s'expliquent que par une situation de contact des langues. On peut alors relever la possibilité d'un substrat ou d'un superstrat germanique en territoire roman ou d'un superstrat roman en territoire germanique. Vu la chronologie indiquée dans le paragraphe 2.1., il faut donc postuler pour le nord du Pas-de-Calais un substrat néerlandais et non pas un superstrat.

L'analyse de ce substrat lexical néerlandais n'éclaire pas seulement l'évolution du patois local, picard ou français. Elle jette aussi une lumière sur les stades les plus anciens des variantes de l'ancien néerlandais de l'extrême sud-ouest et sur la parenté de ce dernier avec l'ancien ou moyen anglais. Par exemple, la forme *écraper* dans le Boulonnais et à Berck et Montreuil (Carton/Poulet 1991, 47) indique clairement une parenté avec l'anglais *scrape* et le néerlandais littoral (hollandais) *schrapen*, alors que le régionalisme *écrêper* se rapproche de la forme flamande à apophonie vocalique *schrepen*.

6.2.2. Emprunts grammaticaux

A côté des correspondances phonétiques et lexicales, il y a celles situées sur le plan morphologique et syntaxique. Le français régional du Nord connaît ainsi — et non seulement dans des toponymes — des compositions qui suivent l'ordre des mots germaniques *déterminant / déterminé*, p. ex. *piedsente* (nl. voetpad) «sentier pédestre». Les verbes notamment semblent être formés d'après le modèle de mots composés néerlandais et accusent par là une fréquence d'usage supérieure à celle du français commun: p. ex. *afiker* (attacher avec une épingle), *ablouker* (attacher à l'aide d'une boucle), *agriper* (s'accrocher à l'aide des mains) (Dupas 1980); *défaire un vêtement* (fl. afdoen), *déparler* (nl./fl. afzeggen), *détaper* (nl./fl. afslaan), *détourner* (nl./fl. afronden) (Carton/Poulet 1991, 43—44). L'antéposition de l'adjectif, autre trait «germanique», est fréquente tout comme en wallon: p. ex. *du frais café, un grand fort homme* (Carton/Poulet 1991, 53). Plus on se rapproche de la frontière linguistique plus elle est fréquente, cfr. *les court-tours* (fl. de korte keren) (Dupas 1980, 54). Autre parallélisme avec le néerlandais: les expressions en construction absolue, de la postposition, de la préposition ou de l'adverbe: p. ex. *crier après, courir après, la nuit après, rien après, le reste après* (Carton/Poulet 1991, 18); *pas long assez, venir avec, avoir avec*, etc. (ibid. 20); *faire sans* (ibid. 97).

6.2.3. Analogies dans la conceptualisation

Dans tous ces cas, il s'agit de calques évidents du néerlandais. Un cas bien connu *à la maison* (nl./fl. thuis) pour *chez soi* est illustré par Weijnen (1964/1975, 161) avec une carte basée sur ALF 267. Un examen plus détaillé montre que ces calques ou flandricismes foisonnent dans le français régional du Nord, surtout dans des expressions figées, lexies, etc. On les rencontre couramment dans l'aire encore actuellement bilingue, où les locuteurs bilingues pratiquent souvent le *code switching*, mais aussi dans le français de Dunkerque et dans le dialecte picard d'Oye, Gravelines, Loon, Clairmarais et Rumingham, localités où le dialecte néerlandais était encore parlé il n'y a guère qu'un siècle, ainsi que dans le français de l'agglomération Lilloise, surtout à Roubaix. Mais tout le Nord en est affecté, même le picard ou plutôt le français régional du Hainaut français, tous les deux déjà plus éloignés de la frontière linguistique. Un petit choix d'exemples:

- dire son cœur tout droit dehors (fl. *zijn hart recht uit spreken*) = dire ce qu'on pense (à Dunkerque, Carton/Poulet 1991, 35)
- il veut comme pleuvoir (fl. *het wil (ge)lijk regenen*) = on dirait qu'il va pleuvoir (ibid. 35)
- rester droit (fl. *recht(e) blijven*) = rester debout (ibid. 45)
- encore toujours (nl./fl. *nog altijd*, cfr. aussi le français de Belgique) = toujours (ibid. 48)
- frayeux (nl./fl. *kostelijk*) = dispendieux (ibid. 54)
- goûter (nl./fl. *smaken*) = plaire au goût (ibid. 57)
- goûteux (nl./fl. *smakelijk*) = qui plaît au goût (ibid. 57)
- grandier (fl. *groots*) = fier, hautain (ibid. 57)
- il ne faut pas être honteux (fl. *je moet niet beschaamd zijn*) = il ne faut pas être timide (ibid. 62)
- tenir (nl./fl. *houden*) = conserver, garder (ibid. 102)
- faire une vie (fl. *een leven maken*) = crier très fort, faire beaucoup de bruit (ibid. 107)
- courir en voie (nl./fl. *weglopen*) = s'en aller, s'esquiver; être en voie (nl./fl. *weg zijn*) = partir, être parti; n'en pouvoir voie (nl./fl. *niet meer weg kunnen*) = n'en pouvoir plus (ibid. 108)
- pourlire (fl. *overlezen*) et lire en bas (fl. *aflezen*) = conjurer, guérir par la prière (Dupas 1980, 99)
- ver (fl. *worm*) = larve quelconque, ver intestinal, ver de terre, etc. (ibid. 119)
- ainsi! (nl./fl. *zo!*) = ce n'est pas possible! — exclamation d'étonnement (ibid. 123)

Très caractéristique est aussi l'usage analogue de quelques prépositions, p. ex. sur l'rue (*op de straat*) = à/dans la rue (Dauby 1968).

Pour beaucoup des parallélismes cités, la direction du mouvement d'emprunt n'est pas décelable: du français régional au flamand ou vice versa? Il ne reste alors qu'à faire la constatation d'une conceptualisation analogue des deux côtés de la frontière linguistique. Par exemple:

- tomber dans le beurre (fl. *(met zijn gat) in de boter vallen*) = avoir de la chance (Carton/Poulet 1991, 25)
- faire sa commission (fl. *zijn commissie doen*) = aller aux WC (ibid. 35)
- moineau sans tête (fl. *vogel zonder kop*) = tranche de viande roulée et farcie (ibid. 77)
- tirer son plan (aussi en Wallonie — fl. *zijn plan trekken*) = se tirer d'affaire (ibid. 86)

- pois de sucre (fl. *suikerbonen*) = haricots verts (ibid. 86)
- quand vous voudrez (fl. *als ge wilt*) = formule de congé qui accompagne l'au revoir (ibid. 89)
- aller servir (fl. *gaan dienen*) = aller en pèlerinage dans un sanctuaire (ibid. 98)
- acater [avec phonétique picarde] un enfant (fl. *een kind kopen*) = mettre un enfant au monde (Dauby 1968).

Dans quelques cas l'emprunt au flamand ou au néerlandais est quand-même hors de doute:

- devenir tout drôle (fl. *helegans aardig komen*) = se sentir mal (Carton/Poulet 1991, 45)
- bou(r)ler court (fl. *te kort bollen*) = épuiser sa matière avant d'avoir fini (ibid. 27)
- je ne sais plus ni quoi ni qu'est ce (fl. *ik weet niet meer wien(e) is welk*) = je ne sais plus où j'en suis (ibid. 79)
- oui mais non! (nl./fl. *ja maar nee!*) = ah non! (ibid. 81)
- saisi (fl. *gepakt*) = ahuri (ibid. 97)
- tête pressée (fl. *geperste kop*) = charcuterie faite de déchets bouillis (ibid. 102).

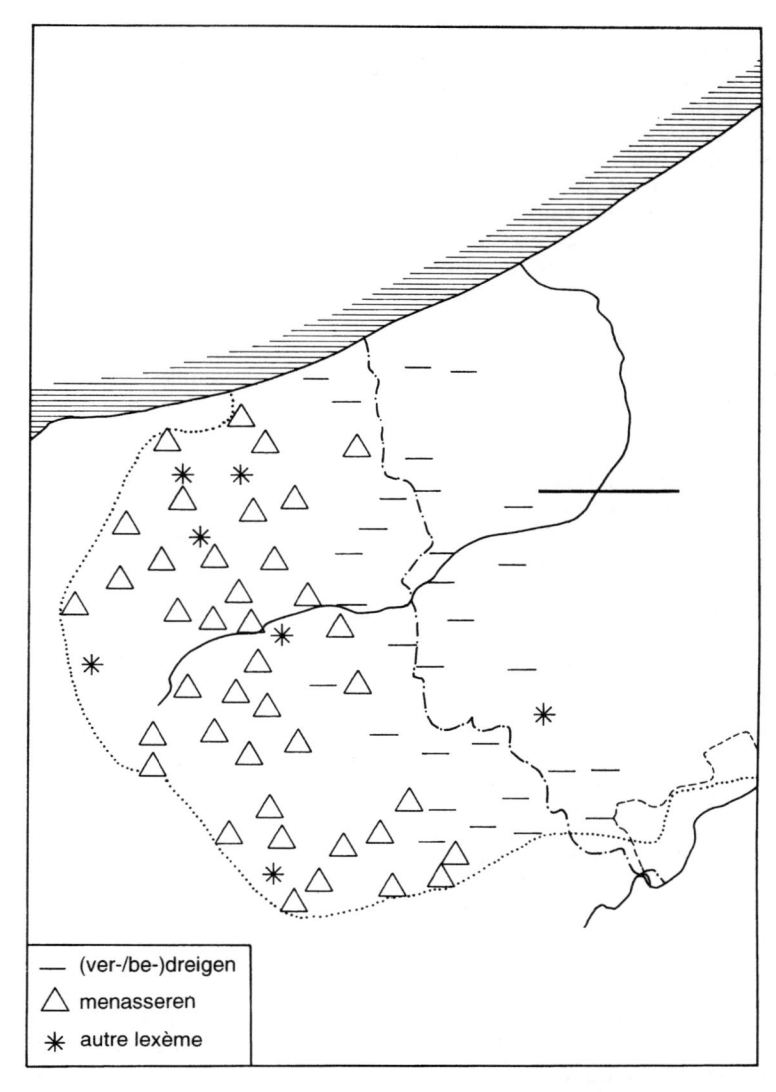

Fig. 148.3: Les hétéronymes pour «menacer» dans le dialecte flamand de France.
Source: Ryckeboer 1990, 265 (d'après Pée 1946).

6.3. Interférences du français dans le néerlandais/flamand avoisinant

Il est évident que l'influence du picard et du français sur les dialectes néerlandais limitrophes a également été considérable. Les emprunts lexicaux au latin, au roman et au français/picard sont particulièrement nombreux, surtout dans les dialectes de la Flandre occidentale. On peut y parler de la présence d'un superstrat très important, à cause du prestige dont a joui le français, aussi dans sa variante picarde, et cela dès le Moyen Âge (v. aussi supra). Weijnen 1967/1975 donne une analyse stratigraphique des transferts latins et/ou romans en néerlandais et dans les dialectes néerlandais. Comme le constate aussi van Hoecke (1980, 102), des études spécifiques concernant la zone bilingue de l'arrondissement de Dunkerque manquent. Pourtant non seulement les dialectologues mais aussi les locuteurs natifs signalent que l'un des traits les plus marquants du flamand du Nord de la France est son ouverture aux emprunts au français. Déjà en 1713, Andries Steven de Cassel, auteur d'un manuel scolaire, le *Nieuwen Nederlandschen Voorschriftboek*, se plaignait de l'altération et de la francisation de la langue maternelle, et en 1886 un instituteur d'Armboutscappel, près de Dunkerque, qualifiait son flamand de « jargon souvent affreux, [ou un] mélange de flamand-français ». Comme vers 1920 le bilinguisme gagnait aussi les campagnes flamingantes et que les occasions de *code-switching* devenaient de plus en plus fréquentes, les interférences à partir du français s'intensifiaient. Pée (1946) cite 69 mots de son corpus qui sont remplacés uniquement en Flandre française par des mots français. Il s'agit non seulement de mots ayant trait à des réalités contemporaines, mais aussi de mots courants du vocabulaire de base, avec toutefois une prédominance des mots abstraits. Cela s'illustre bien dans la carte pour *dreigen* « menacer » (fig. 148.3), reprise de Ryckeboer 1990). On peut y voir que seules les communes limitrophes de la Belgique ont conservé le mot autochtone *(ver/be)dreigen*, remplacé partout ailleurs par la forme hybride *menasseren*. Des enregistrements faits dans les années soixante révèlent que le nombre des mots français usités uniquement dans le flamand de France augmente considérablement surtout chez les locuteurs les plus jeunes (Ryckeboer 1977, 55). Une première étude systématique des interférences françaises dans le dialecte flamand a été faite à partir de ce corpus d'enregistrements par Vandenberghe (1995).

6.4. Conclusion

Les études dans le domaine des contacts linguistiques pour l'aire étudiée souffrent encore de certaines carences. Il importe de promouvoir les recherches dans les directions suivantes:

(1) la rédaction d'un inventaire des flandricismes dans les dialectes et dans le français régional du Nord de la France, comme on a déjà commencé à le faire pour le français de Belgique;
(2) l'analyse de cet inventaire par un groupe de recherche mixte, composé de spécialistes des deux domaines linguistiques impliqués;
(3) l'institutionnalisation de la recherche scientifique sur tous les aspects de la présence historique du néerlandais dans le Nord de la France pour assurer la formation de chercheurs et pour aboutir ainsi à une meilleure information du public sur le patrimoine linguistique et historique de cette région.

7. Bibliographie (sélective)

Calvet, Louis-Jean (1974): *Linguistique et colonialisme*, Paris.

Carton, Fernand (1981): « Les parlers ruraux de la région Nord-Picardie: situation sociolinguistique ». In: *International Journal of Sociology of Language* 29, 15−28.

Carton, Fernand/Lebègue, Maurice (1989): *Atlas linguistique et ethnographique du Picard*, tome I, Paris.

Carton, Fernand/Poulet, Denise (1991): *Dictionnaire du français régional du Nord − Pas-de-Calais*, Paris.

Coornaert, Emile (1970): *La Flandre française de langue flamande*, Paris.

Dauby, J. (1968): *Lexique rouchi−français*, Amiens.

de Certeau, Michel/Julie, Dominique/Revel, Jacques (1975): *Une politique de la langue. La Révolution française et les patois*, Paris.

Derville, Alain (Ed.) (1981), *Histoire de Saint-Omer*, Lille.

Dupas, Georges (1980): *Le Vieux Parler à Oye − Gravelines − Loon*, Dunkerque.

Duvosquel, Jean-Marie (1973): « L'emploi des langues à Comines et Warneton du Moyen Age à nos jours ». In: *Le Patois Picard de Comines et de Warneton, Mémoires de la Société d'Histoire de Comines et de la région*, Bourgeois, H. (Ed.), Tome III, Comines.

Fagoo, Arthur/Sansen, Joël/Simon, Philippe (1985): *Dictionnaire Flamand/Français, Français/Flamand*, Dunkerque.

FEW: von Wartburg, Walther (1928 sqq): *Französisches Etymologisches Wörterbuch. Eine Darstellung des galloromanischen Sprachschatzes*, Bonn.

Guiraud, Pierre (1968): *Les mots étrangers*, Paris.

Gysseling, Maurits (1976): « Ontstaan en verschuiving van de taalgrens in Noord-Frankrijk » [Genèse et déplacement de la frontière linguistique dans le nord de la France]. In: *De Franse Nederlanden – Les Pays-Bas français I*, 70–85. (La version française aussi dans: *Bulletin du Comité flamand de France 19*, 1974).

Halink, Ruud (1991): « Nederlands leren: hoe jonger hoe beter » [Apprendre le néerlandais: aussi tôt que possible]. In: *De Franse Nederlanden – Les Pays Bas français 16*, 35–50 (avec résumé français), Rekkem.

Hécart, G. A. J. (1833): *Dictionnaire Rouchi–Français*, Valenciennes.

Lentacker, Firmin (1974): *La frontière franco-belge. Etude géographique des effets d'une frontière internationale sur la vie des relations*, Lille (thèse).

Mantou, Reine (1972): « Actes originaux rédigés en français dans la partie flamingante du comté de Flandre (1250–1350). Etude linguistique ». In: *Mémoires de la Commission Royale de Toponymie et de Dialectologie 15*, Bruxelles.

Marteel, Jean-Louis (1992): *Cours de Flamand. Het Vlaams dan men oudders klappen. Méthode d'apprentissage du dialecte des Flamands de France*, Lille.

Pée, Willem (1946): *Dialect-Atlas van West-Vlaanderen en Fransch-Vlaanderen* [Atlas dialectologique de la Flandre occidentale et de la Flandre française], Antwerpen (Reeks Nederlandsche Dialect-Atlassen 6).

Pée, Willem (1957): *Anderhalve eeuw Taalgrensverschuiving en Taaltoestand in Frans-Vlaanderen* [Le déplacement de la frontière linguistique et la situation linguistique pendant un siècle et demi en Flandre française]. (Bijdragen en Mededelingen van de Koninklijke Akademie van Wetenschappen te Amsterdam 17), Amsterdam.

Poulet, Denise (1987): *Au contact du Picard et du Flamand: parlers du Calaisis et de l'Audomarois*, Lille.

Röhrig, Johannes W. (1987): *Die Sprachkontaktsituation im Westhoek. Studien zum Bilinguismus und zur Diglossie im französisch-belgischen Grenzraum*, Gerbrunn bei Würzburg.

Ryckeboer, Hugo (1976): « De behoefte aan een taalsociologisch onderzoek in Frans-Vlaanderen » [La nécessité d'une recherche sociolinguistique dans la Flandre française]. In: *De Franse Nederlanden – Les Pays-Bas français 1*, 156–168.

Ryckeboer, Hugo (1977): « Het Nederlands van de Franse Westhoek, situatie en situering » [Le néerlandais du Westhoek français, situation sociolinguistique et topolinguistique]. In: *Taal en Tongval 29*, 50–66.

Ryckeboer, Hugo (1990): « Jenseits der belgisch-französischen Grenze: der Überrest des westlichen Kontinentalgermanischen ». In: *Germanistische Linguistik 101–103*, 241–271.

Ryckeboer, Hugo (1991): « Le flamand de Busbecq et ses interférences avec le gotique de Crimée ». In: *Sur les traces de Busbecq et du Gotique*, Rousseau, André (Ed.), Lille, 167–178.

Ryckeboer, Hugo/Maeckelberghe, Frank (1987): « Dialect en standaardtaal aan weerszijden van de rijksgrens in de Westhoek » [Dialecte et langue standard des deux côtés de la frontière dans le Westhoek]. In: *De Franse Nederlanden – Les Pays-Bas français 12*, Rekkem, 129–151.

Ryckeboer, Hugo (1995): « Frans-Nederlands taalcontact in het noorden van Frankrijk » [Contact linguistique français–néerlandais dans le nord de la France]. In: *Artikelen van de tweede sociolinguistische Conferentie*, Huls, Erica/Klatter-Folmer, Jetske (Eds.), Delft, 507–521.

Sansen, Joël (1988): « Le flamand. Une langue-frontière mal connue ». In: *Vingt-cinq communautés linguistiques de la France, tome I: Langues régionales et langues non territorialisées*, Vermes, Geneviève (Ed.), Paris, 169–187.

Valkhoff, M. (1931): *Etude sur les mots français d'origine néerlandaise*, Amersfoort.

Vandenberghe, Roxane (1995): *Het Frans-Vlaamse dialect: Morfologische integratie van de Franse lexicale outleningen en syntactische kenmerken* [Le dialecte flamand de France: intégration morphologique des emprunts lexicaux français et caractéristiques syntaxiques]. Mémoire de licence inédite, Université de Gand.

Vandenbroeke, Chris (1993): « Migraties tussen Vlaanderen en Noord-Frankrijk in de negentiende en twintigste eeuw » [Migrations entre la Flandre et le Nord de la France aux XIXe et XXe siècles]. In: *De Franse Nederlanden – Les Pays-Bas français 18*, 157–168 (avec résumé français et bibliographie).

van Goethem, Herman (1987): « Eén volk, één taal. Nationalisme en taalwetgeving in Frankrijk vanaf 1670, en in de geannexeerde Zuidelijke Nederlanden (1795–1813) » [Un peuple, une langue. Nationalisme et législation linguistique en France depuis 1670 et dans les Pays-Bas méridionaux annexés (1795–1813)]. In: *Wetenschappelijke Tijdingen 46*, 57–86 et 129–147.

van Hemel, Hedwig/Halink, Ruud (1992): « Belle: hartje van onderwijs Nederlands in Frans-Vlaanderen » [Bailleul: le centre de l'enseignement du néerlandais en Flandre française]. In: *De Franse Nederlanden – Les Pays-Bas français 17*, 60–74 (avec résumé français).

van Hoecke, Willy (1978): « De wisselwerking tussen Romaans en Germaans in Noord-Frankrijk. 1. De streektalen » [L'interaction entre roman et germanique dans le Nord de la France. 1. les dialectes]. In: *De Franse Nederlanden – Les Pays-Bas français 3*, 85–108 (avec résumé français).

van Hoecke, Willy (1979): « De wisselwerking tussen Romaans en Germaans in Noord-Frankrijk. 2. De Franse standaardtaal » [L'interaction entre roman et germanique dans le Nord de la France. 2. La langue française standard]. In: *De Franse Nederlanden – Les Pays-Bas français 4*, 43–68.

van Hoecke, Willy (1980): « De wisselwerking tussen Romaans en Germaans in Noord-Frankrijk. 3. De Nederlandse standaardtaal » [L'interaction entre roman et germanique dans le Nord de la France. 3. La langue standard néerlandaise]. In: *De Franse Nederlanden – Les Pays-Bas français 5*, 86–116.

van Hoecke, Willy (1988): « Parallèles phonétiques des deux côtés de la frontière linguistique franco-néerlandaise: la diphthongaison de [ə] entravé ». In: *Distributions spatiales et temporelles, Constellations des Manuscrits,* van Reenen, Pieter/van Reenen-Stein, Karin (Ed.), Amsterdam/Philadelphia, 187–202.

Vanneste, Alex (1982): « Le français et le flamand en Flandre française: essai sur le recul de la frontière linguistique ». In: *Sprachen in Kontakt – Langues en Contact*, Caudmont, Jean (Ed.), Tübingen 17–35.

Vanneufville, Eric (1979): *De l'Elbe à la Somme. L'espace saxon-frison des origines au Xe siècle*, Amiens.

von Wartburg, Walther (1969): *Evolution et structure de la langue française*, Berne.

Weijnen, Antoon (1964/1975): « Fonetische en grammatische parallellen aan weerszijden van de taalgrens » [Parallèles phonétiques et grammaticaux des deux côtés de la frontière linguistique]. In: *Tijdschrift voor Nederlandse Taal- en Letterkunde 80*, 1964, 1–25. (Aussi dans: *Algemene en vergelijkende Dialectologie*, Amsterdam 1975.)

Weijnen, Antoon (1976/1975): « Leenwoorden uit de Latinitas, stratigrafisch beschouwd » [Les emprunts du latin/roman, une vue stratigraphique]. In: *Verslagen en Mededelingen van de Koninklijke Vlaamse Academie voor Taal en Letterkunde*, 1967, 365–480. (Aussi dans: *Algemene en vergelijkende Dialectologie*, Amsterdam 1975.)

Willemyns, Roland (1994): « Taalcontact en erosie: het geval Frans-Vlaanderen » [Contact de langues et érosion: le cas de la Flandre française]. In: *Neerlandica Wratislaviensia VII (Acta Universitatis Wratislaviensis No 1640)*, 249–266.

Wood, Richard (1980): « Language Maintenance and External Support: The Case of the French Flemings ». In: *International Journal of Sociology of Language 25*, 107–119.

Bruno Callebaut, Valenciennes (France)
Hugo Ryckeboer, Gand (Belgique)

149. Français–breton

1. Géographie et démographie
2. Histoire
3. Politique, économie, situations culturelle et religieuse en général
4. Statistiques et profil ethnique
5. Situation sociolinguistique
6. Etat de la politique linguistique
7. Portrait général des contacts linguistiques
8. Examen critique de la bibliographie
9. Bibliographie (sélective)

1. Géographie et démographie

1.1. La Bretagne bretonnante ou Basse-Bretagne couvre la totalité du département du Finistère et la partie orientale du Morbihan et des Côtes-d'Armor. La limite linguistique est l'aboutissement de l'expansion séculaire des parlers romans ruraux de Haute-Bretagne au détriment du celtique. La double incurvation de son tracé s'explique au nord par l'influence de la ville de Saint-Brieuc, gagnée au français au cours des derniers siècles, au sud par la résistance de la ville de Vannes, longtemps demeurée bretonnante. Sa population est d'environ 1 500 000 d'habitants (2 800 000 dans la région administrative), dont les trois cinquièmes sont regroupés sur une frange côtière d'une vingtaine de kilomètres de largeur; → carte 149.1 et carte linguistique D.

1.2. La Bretagne a été longtemps une région à forte natalité. Depuis le début du XIXème siècle sa population a augmenté de façon régulière en dépit d'une émigration constante des jeunes. Les guerres mondiales et l'accroissement de l'émigration ont provoqué une baisse de la population. Un redressement démographique s'est effectué après 1946 pour aboutir dans les années 1968–1974 à un bilan migratoire positif. Puis la crise a entraîné une reprise des départs, tan-

149. Français–breton

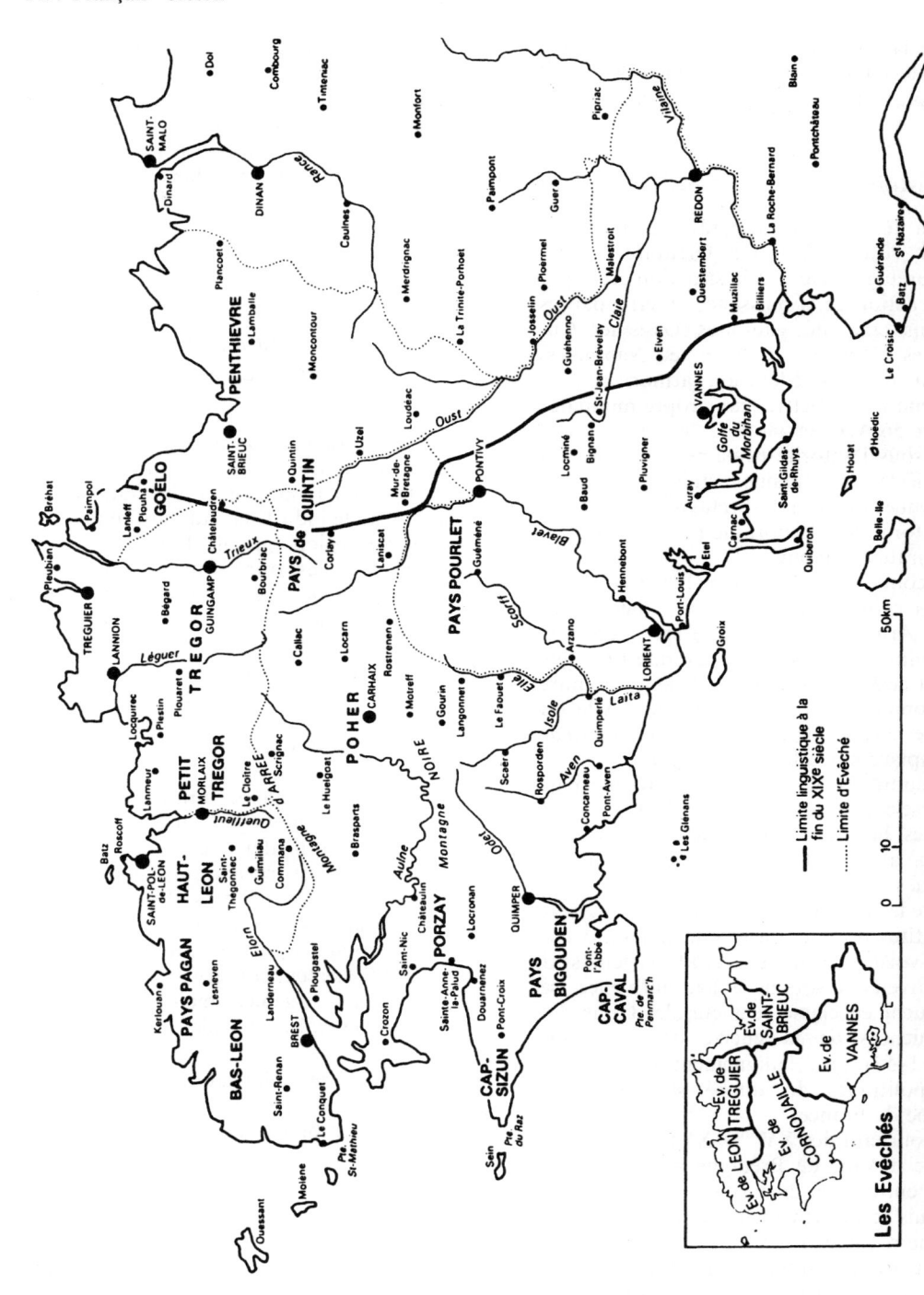

Fig. 149.1: Basse-Bretagne et Haute-Bretagne occidentale.
Source: Balcou, Jean/Le Gallo, Yves (Eds.) (1987): *Histoire littéraire et culturelle de la Bretagne*, Paris/Genève, volume 1, 3.

dis que la natalité s'aligne sur les tendances nationales. L'intérieur de la Basse-Bretagne est en plusieurs points en voie de désertification.

2. Histoire

Une entité politique apparaît au début du premier siècle A.C. sur le territoire de l'actuelle Bretagne. Devant la situation créée par la destruction de la puissance arverne par les Romains, cinq cités gauloises (Ossismes, Curiosolites, Vénètes, Redones et Namnètes) forment une confédération armoricaine et commencent à émettre leur propre monnaie.

Entre 56 A.C. et 486 P.C. les Armoricains vivent sous l'autorité romaine. Au cours du IVème siècle, les Romains installent des garnisons venues de Grande-Bretagne sur le pourtour littoral de l'Armorique pour la protéger de la piraterie saxonne.

Au cours des VIème et VIIème siècles, les Bretons acquièrent une position hégémonique en Armorique. Leur nombre augmente: l'instabilité politique de la Grande-Bretagne conduit certaines familles de l'île à rejoindre leurs compatriotes sur le continent. A la fin de cette période, le nom même d'*Armorique* est remplacé par celui de *Bretagne*.

Au cours du IXe siècle un *royaume* parvient à se constituer à la faveur de dissensions entre les héritiers de Charlemagne. Il disparaîtra au début du Xème siècle sous les coups des Normands.

Entre le XIème et le XVème siècle, un Duché se constitue dont les dirigeants, alliés aux dynasties voisines (Capétiens et Plantagenêts) et alternativement soumis à leur influence, se constituent en classe seigneuriale. L'une des conséquences de la guerre de Cent Ans (1339−1453) sera l'alignement des institutions politiques du duché sur celles du royaume de France.

Au tournant des XVème−XVIème siècles, le mariage d'Anne de Bretagne avec le roi de France entraîne la disparition de la cour ducale, puis le rattachement de la province au domaine royal en 1532.

Jusqu'à la révolution de 1789, la Bretagne aura le statut de « pays d'Etat ». Administrée directement par le personnel royal, elle conserve néanmoins un parlement, dominé par la noblesse et le haut clergé, dont les prérogatives limitent en principe le pouvoir royal.

En 1790, la province est partagée entre cinq départements: Finistère, Morbihan, Côtes-du-Nord, Ille-et-Vilaine et Loire-Inférieure. La Bretagne ne possédera plus aucune institution politique propre jusqu'en 1956.

Reconstituée alors comme région administrative et économique − à l'exception de la Loire-Atlantique, rattachée aux Pays-de-Loire − elle sera dotée en 1974 d'un Conseil formé de représentants des collectivités locales et territoriales, puis en 1986 d'une Assemblée élue au suffrage universel.

3. Politique, économie, situations culturelle et religieuse en général

3.1. La Basse-Bretagne est une région essentiellement agricole. Son agriculture a connu à partir des années 1950 une transformation radicale qui l'a fait passer de l'autosubsistance au stade industriel. Aujourd'hui elle est la première région agricole de France.

Le paysage s'est transformé: réseau routier et habitat modernisés, remembrement des surfaces agricoles qui entraîne la disparition du bocage, création de zones industrielles. Cependant, en raison de la crise, l'industrialisation régresse, tandis que la pêche devient marginale. En outre, la Bretagne est la deuxième région touristique de France.

3.2. La Basse-Bretagne rurale, de tradition catholique, n'est homogène ni dans ses pratiques religieuses ni dans ses comportements politiques. Elle est traversée par une « diagonale contestataire » (Flatrès 1986, 14) nord-est/sud-ouest, peu pratiquante, voire anticléricale, et votant à gauche, entourée de deux zones politiquement conservatrices. La population urbaine, largement majoritaire, suit les tendances générales des villes françaises.

3.3. Le taux de scolarisation de la Bretagne est l'un des plus élevés de France, et la région fournit de nombreux cadres à l'ensemble du pays.

4. Statistiques et profil ethnique

4.1. Si l'on excepte les immigrés récents d'origine maghrébine, portugaise ou turque (dont la proportion est inférieure à 1% de la population totale), les habitants de la Bretagne ne se considèrent pas comme ethniquement différents des autres Français. On a toujours observé en Basse-Bretagne comme ailleurs en France des divergences politiques entre les citoyens. Mais rares étaient les moments où ces oppositions ont été exprimées en termes de minorité nationale. Pour les Bretonnants comme pour tous les Français, le plein exercice de la citoyenneté va de pair avec l'usage de la langue française. La question du contact entre les diverses langues pratiquées dans la région n'est donc pratiquement jamais l'expression métonymique d'un contact entre populations de natures ou de cultures différentes.

4.2. Devenus au cours des cent dernières années minoritaires dans des espaces sur lesquels ils régnaient presque sans partage depuis la fin du haut Moyen Age, les dialectes d'origine celtique (à l'ouest) et ceux d'origine romane (à l'est) ont cessé de se transmettre dans les années 1960.

4.3. Du fait de leur éloignement génétique du roman, les dialectes celtiques ont longtemps été le mode de communication obligé entre la population et diverses institutions, particulièrement l'Eglise et la Justice. De cette pratique institutionnelle sont nés au cours du Moyen Age et à l'époque moderne des standards subrégionaux globalement appelés 'breton'. Tous les textes constituant la littérature du breton sont écrits dans ces standards qui ne sont jamais la simple inscription des parlers vernaculaires. Dans l'usage courant, ces deux aspects de la réalité linguistique sont toutefois confondus sous le nom de 'langue bretonne'.

4.4. L'apogée historique du nombre des locuteurs du breton a été atteint dans les premières années du vingtième siècle après la révolution démographique. Estimé pour cette époque à un million et demi d'individus, il n'a depuis cessé de décroître: autour d'un million dans les années 1930, environ un demi-million aujourd'hui. Seules quelques dizaines de milliers de personnes font encore usage du breton comme langue de communication quotidienne: ruraux, âgés, socialement peu actifs, bénéficiant d'un niveau d'instruction élémentaire. S'il leur arrive d'écrire, c'est toujours en français. Autour de ce noyau de résistance déclinant, entre trois et quatre centaines de milliers de personnes comprennent encore le breton, sont parfois capables de le parler, éventuellement de l'écrire. Dispersés dans les villages, les bourgs et les villes de Bretagne, ayant parfois quitté la région pour des raisons liées à la recherche du travail, ils n'ont en pratique que rarement l'occasion d'exercer leur compétence linguistique.

4.5. Les parlers *romans* de la Haute-Bretagne, génétiquement apparentés à ceux du bassin de la Loire, ont longtemps été désignés de façon indéfinie du nom de 'patois'. Relativement plus proches linguistiquement du français normé, ils n'ont pas connu à la fin du Moyen Age d'élaboration institutionnelle sous forme de standards. Depuis une vingtaine d'années, un mouvement de défense et de promotion culturelle lié au *revivalism* rejette le mot 'patois', connoté péjorativement, et lui préfère celui de 'gallo' (ou 'langue gallèse'), par lequel les bretonnants désignaient traditionnellement les romanophones habitant le long de la frontière linguistique du breton (de *gall* 'gaulois', c'est-à-dire — paradoxalement — 'personne parlant une langue romane'). Il est scientifiquement impossible d'estimer le nombre des locuteurs de ces parlers, la norme du français et les traits du vernaculaire étant désormais toujours mêlés dans leur discours, bien que dans des proportions très variables. Leur profil sociologique est très semblable à celui des locuteurs du breton.

5. Situation sociolinguistique

5.1. L'image du bretonnant est connotée dans l'imaginaire national. Il représentait traditionnellement le rustre ignorant le français:
— *baragouiner*, c'est-à-dire parler de façon inintelligible, viendrait du breton *bara* 'pain' et *gwin* 'vin'. Une autre image s'est superposée à l'ancienne depuis la révolution agricole des années 1960, celle du Breton entreprenant et contestataire.

5.2. Le long de la limite linguistique, la population est très consciente de l'opposition entre bretonnants et patoisants. Les premiers s'appellent eux-mêmes et sont appelés par leurs voisins 'bretons'. Pénétrer en zone bretonnante, c'est aller 'en Bretagne' pour les Haut-Bretons, qui ne se désignent eux-mêmes comme bretons que pour se différencier des Français des autres provinces.

5.3. Depuis les années 1970, propagé par quelques pamphlets militants, l'intérêt pour la langue bretonne et la civilisation préindustrielle, qui n'avait été jusque-là le fait que d'un cercle très restreint d'intellectuels, se répand en Bretagne comme dans toutes les régions périphériques de France et même au-delà, ainsi qu'en témoigne le succès du livre de P. J. Hélias *Le cheval d'orgueil*. On fait porter à l'école de la République la responsabilité de l'affaiblissement de la place du breton dans la société. On stigmatise par exemple l'usage ancien du *symbole*, objet passant de main en main chez les élèves surpris à faire usage de la langue vernaculaire. Des cours d'initiation à la langue sont créés, principalement dans les villes. Ce courant s'affaiblit considérablement au cours des années 1980, mais en même temps, paradoxalement, il s'institutionnalise du fait de la régionalisation.

Une littérature abondante et largement répandue en France comme à l'étranger tend à présenter le changement de langue en Basse-Bretagne sous l'aspect d'un conflit intercommunautaire. Ce discours revendicatif, volontiers agressif, voire nationaliste, émane majoritairement de citadins débretonnisés depuis des générations, voire d'étrangers à la région. Imperméables à ce discours, les bretonnants héritiers de la langue bretonne se considèrent comme des citoyens de la République et non pas comme les membres d'une communauté distincte. La langue bretonne a longtemps constitué le pôle familier d'un couple diglossique avec le français. Une génération transitoire a certainement souffert psychologiquement du remplacement rapide de ce pôle par le français, d'où des réactions de rejet du breton considéré comme un obstacle au progrès. Les générations suivantes se désintéressent du breton, même si certains l'évoquent, comme le passé qu'il représente, avec une certaine nostalgie. Au-delà de tout clivage politique, la langue française représente à leurs yeux l'instrument incontournable du progrès individuel et social: il suffit de voir la puissance de la mobilisation des Bas-Bretons en faveur de la défense de leur école quand ils estiment qu'elle est menacée.

6. Etat de la politique linguistique

6.1. Il n'existe pas en France d'institution officielle spécifiquement chargée d'appliquer une politique linguistique. Du point de vue légal, le monopole de fait de la langue française vient tout juste d'être officialisé par une inscription dans la Constitution en 1992.

6.2. La langue bretonne n'a jamais servi de langue de l'administration. Le français est devenu la langue des chartes en Basse-Bretagne entre 1250 et 1280, seulement quelques années après qu'il eût remplacé le latin dans la Loire moyenne, l'Anjou, la Touraine et le Berry.

6.3. Le breton a été longtemps auprès du latin la seule langue de l'église catholique en Basse-Bretagne. Après 1918, le français s'est répandu progressivement comme langue du *catéchisme*, tandis que la *prédication* se poursuivait en breton. On a donc constaté un décalage d'une génération dans le processus d'adoption du français par l'Eglise, qui s'est achevé vers 1950. Le breton est désormais absent des églises en dehors de quelques cantiques. Signalons pour mémoire une tentative d'évangélisation par des pasteurs méthodistes gallois au XIXème siècle, qui avaient dans certains secteurs implanté des écoles en langue bretonne calquées sur les *circulating schools* du Pays-de-Galles. Leur succès a été limité et éphémère.

6.4. Un timide début d'enseignement a été amorcé au moment de l'adoption de la loi Deixonne en 1951. Depuis une quinzaine d'années, cet enseignement s'est étendu dans le secondaire, qui dispose maintenant d'un corps spécifique de professeurs de breton (8 titulaires en 1992) recruté par un CAPES (Certificat d'aptitude pédagogique à l'enseignement secondaire). Le breton est matière d'examen (deuxième langue vivante). Environ 1000 élèves subissent bon an mal an une épreuve optionnelle de breton au baccalauréat. Dans le primaire, à côté des écoles privées *Diwan* (environ 800 élèves), on a opté pour le développement — tout relatif — des classes bilingues qui en 1992 touchent entre 400 et 500 enfants. On peut considérer que 10 000 enfants environ (2% des élèves de l'Académie de Rennes) sont touchés au moins par une initiation à la langue bretonne dans la seule Education nationale.

La langue bretonne est enseignée dans les Universités de Brest et de Rennes à tous les niveaux (DEUG, licence, maîtrise, DEA, doctorat). L'Université de Brest dispose d'un important centre de documentation, le *Centre de recherche bretonne et celtique*.

6.5. Une radio de langue bretonne a été créée pendant l'Occupation à Rennes, sous la direction de Roparz Hemon (et avec la participation du celtisant allemand Leo Weisgerber). Supprimée à la Libération, elle fut remplacée par une émission hebdomadaire de *radio-Quimerc'h* dans le Finistère. Destinée au public bretonnant des campagnes, elle fut longtemps réalisée par l'écrivain Per-Jakez Hélias et par Per Trépos, professeur de celtique à l'Université. La place du breton s'est étendue par la suite, et aujourd'hui on dispose d'une série d'émissions hebdomadaires à la télévision (1h20 en tout) et d'une dizaine d'heures par semaine sur *Radio Bretagne Ouest* (RBO), antenne décentralisée de *Radio France*.

6.6. Après la mise en place des institutions décentralisées, une *Charte Culturelle* fut proposée par le Président de la République, Giscard d'Estaing, à Ploërmel en 1977. Cette Charte déboucha en 1981 sur la création d'un *Institut Culturel de Bretagne*, dont l'une des tâches est de favoriser la création et la publication d'ouvrages en langue bretonne.

7. Portrait général des contacts linguistiques

7.1. Au dix-neuvième siècle, le grammairien Le Gonidec est le créateur d'une orthographe « philosophique », essayant pour la première fois de faire coïncider graphie et prononciation. Il est l'introducteur de l'usage des *k* et *g* durs remplaçant *qu* et *gu* du français, écrivant désormais *keginer* « cuisinier » au lieu de *queguiner*. D'autres innovations ne seront jamais utilisées pour des raisons typographiques. Ce système et ceux qui le suivront, surtout utilisés à des fins militantes ou littéraires, ne sortiront guère de quelques cénacles érudits. Basé sur la prononciation, reflétant en même temps une conception puriste de la langue, il rend très difficile la transcription des emprunts, et même leur utilisation. Les auteurs, membres du clergé écrivant en direction du peuple, adopteront certaines des innovations de Le Gonidec. Son disciple La Villemarqué, créant une langue épurée et normalisée était soucieux de rendre la langue bretonne « plus propre à instruire le peuple (...) de développer les bons instincts des classes laborieuses (...) Ils [les hommes éclairés] se servent de la langue bretonne comme du seul instrument à leur portée, car le peuple n'en comprend pas d'autre, et, tant qu'ils n'en auront pas un plus adapté aux besoins populaires, ils croiront devoir l'employer » (La Villemarqué 1847: LXV; réed. 106).

Les principes généraux de la purification sont bien connus: rejet de ce qui ressemble au français, adoption de mots de la langue galloise (considérée comme sœur aînée, plus prestigieuse, du breton), création de néologismes.

L'essai d'imposition au clergé de ces règles n'a pas eu de suite, et a même provoqué un profond rejet.

Une codification des standards départementaux est entreprise dans des cercles d'intellectuels en 1908.

Ce n'est qu'avec l'apparition du nationalisme breton après 1920 que naîtront, sur la base des principes élaborés au siècle précédent, deux normes fictives. D'une part, la norme KLT, créée par François Vallée et René Le Roux et imposée dans les milieux nationalistes par Roparz Hemon (professeur d'anglais au lycée de Brest, il créa et dirigea de 1925 à 1944 la revue *Gwalarn*, qui publiait des textes inédits et surtout de nombreuses traductions destinées à forger une norme bretonne). De l'autre, la norme du vannetais, répandue par Loeiz Herrieu (Le *barde-laboureur* dirigea la revue *Dihunamb* de 1904 à 1944: s'adressant au début à la paysannerie, elle dériva progressivement vers un public petit-bourgeois). Leur fusion ne devait − et ne pouvait − se réaliser, dans l'esprit de ses promoteurs, que dans un futur Etat breton. Les standards, qualifiés de « jargon mixte » reflétant à leurs yeux l'état de sujétion du peuple breton, étaient rejetés en bloc.

La pseudo-normalisation s'achèvera sous l'Occupation avec l'absorption du standard vannetais dans la norme générale du breton. Le 8 juillet 1941, pour diverses raisons, en particulier pour faciliter l'édition de manuels de breton eut lieu à l'initiative du celtisant Leo Weisgerber, responsable allemand de la politique culturelle en Bretagne, une réunion d'écrivains destinée à mettre sur pied une orthographe superunifiée de la langue bretonne. On décida entre autres la fusion symbolique du KLT et du vannetais en introduisant le digraphe *zh*: « chat » s'écrit *kaz* en KLT et *kah* en vannetais: on écrira donc *kazh*, d'où le fameux sigle *BZH* représentant une abréviation de *Breiz/Breih*, écrit *Breizh* « la Bretagne ».

La création des régions administratives sous Vichy et celle d'un enseignement optionnel de la langue bretonne (arrêté du 24 décembre 1941) lui fournissaient un cadre institutionnel favorable. Cette norme ne fut pas agréée par le rectorat de Rennes (circulaire du Recteur d'Académie du 6 novembre 1943).

En conséquence du vote de la loi Deixonne de 1951, une commission mit sur pied l'orthographe universitaire de la langue bretonne qui renouait pragmatiquement avec les anciens standards. Approuvé en 1955 par le Ministre de l'Education nationale, ce système ne fut jamais accepté par les milieux nationalistes.

Un essai d'unification fut tenté entre 1970 et 1975: il se termina par la création d'une troisième graphie dite 'interdialectale'.

7.2. Le français des bretonnants est plus ou moins fortement marqué par la phonétique et la syntaxe du breton selon l'âge et le niveau social. Pour le Finistère et les Côtes d'Armor, un accent d'intensité portant sur la pénultième (en Morbihan, l'accent se rapproche de celui du français), l'assourdissement des sonores en finale absolue (*rouche* pour 'rouge') et la sonorisation des sourdes en position interne et de sandhi devant voyelle et les consonnes l, m, n et r (*des vêd'ments* pour 'des vêtements'; *touz ensem* pour 'tous ensemble'. Les calques sont de même plus ou moins nombreux, dans les mêmes conditions. Les plus rémanents sont l'usage de la préposition 'avec' dans des phrases du type *J'ai eu des sous avec ma mère* pour 'Ma mère m'a donné de l'argent' et l'emploi du verbe *envoyer* pour 'mener, conduire, porter, expédier', etc.

Les générations actuelles ne conservent presque plus rien des traits du breton, si ce n'est quelquefois l'intonation, des faits comme la sonorisation des sourdes devant l, m, n et r et quelques rares traits de vocabulaire.

7.3. Le breton est une langue mixte. Si son vocabulaire grammatical est massivement d'origine celtique, son vocabulaire lexical est partagé à peu près également entre le celtique et le roman. A l'instar de l'anglais, il est pénétré de mots issus du latin et du français de toutes les époques.

Depuis le *Catholicon* breton/latin/français de 1499 — qui est à la fois le premier dictionnaire breton et le premier dictionnaire français — un nombre impressionnant de dictionnaires, lexiques, glossaires a été publié. Des manuels pour l'étude du français par le breton ont paru au début du vingtième siècle. Le plus important d'un point de vue sociolinguistique est la longue série des *Dictionnaires et colloques français et breton* parus à partir de 1626, destinés en priorité à « plusieurs personnes de qualitéz, ayant des affaires en ce pays de basse Bretagne, qui n'ont l'intelligence de son vulgaire breton (…) », et qui ont en fait servi de manuels de français aux Bretonnants (plusieurs dizaines d'éditions jusqu'en 1914).

7.4. Les manuels d'initiation sont également très nombreux. Ils ont dans les premiers temps servi à l'apprentissage de la langue par les prédicateurs jésuites au moment de la Contre-Réforme pour aboutir de nos jours à l'enseignement scolaire de la langue.

7.5. Les ouvrages de type scientifique, peu nombreux, n'ont été publiés qu'à titre d'exemples au vingtième siècle, pour démontrer la capacité du breton à tout dire. L'existence d'écoles bilingues induit la parution de manuels spécifiques.

8. Examen critique de la bibliographie

8.1. Dans le *Petit Larousse* on lisait encore en 1948 au mot *bretonnant*: « Se dit de la partie de la Bretagne et des Bretons qui ont conservé leur ancien langage, leurs mœurs primitives ». Tenant compte de l'évolution moderne du sens de primitif, les éditions ultérieures ont remplacé les derniers mots par « qui ont conservé leur langue ».

Le mot 'primitif' du Larousse renvoyait à la notion d'antériorité. En France, le gaulois a commencé dès la Renaissance à supplanter l'hébreu comme langue des origines nationales. Or la langue bretonne figurait dans l'imaginaire national comme le descendant direct du gaulois: « Chose étonnante, cette Langue si ancienne est celle que parlent encore aujourd'hui les Bretons de France, & les Galois d'Angleterre » affirme en 1703 dom Pezron, dans son *Antiquité de la nation et de la langue des Celtes autrement appelés Gaulois*. Ce courant celtomane, qui a été jusqu'à avancer la filiation gauloise de la langue française – « notre françois n'est rien autre chose que le gaulois des vieux Druides » – lit-on dans *l'Encyclopédie* de Diderot et d'Alembert – culmina en 1804 avec la création de l'*Académie Celtique* pour perdre avec lui tout crédit en 1814. N'ayant plus de support politique, scientifiquement contestées par le développement de la romanistique – niant toute filiation du gaulois au français – et les travaux d'historiens comme La Borderie, ces théories furent enterrées par le linguiste Joseph Loth. Dans sa thèse (Loth 1883), il imposa l'idée que le breton était une langue importée de toutes pièces par des immigrants venus de Grande-Bretagne dans une Armorique entièrement romanisée à l'instar du reste de la Gaule. Cette conception, exaltée par le courant bretoniste, faisait de cette vieille province, préservée du matérialisme bourgeois, le point de départ du renouveau catholique de la France. Reprise par le nationalisme breton, la théorie insulaire est longtemps demeurée une idée reçue. Ce n'est que depuis quelques décennies, avec en particulier les travaux de F. Falc'hun (Falc'hun 1962), que commence à se répandre l'idée que le breton est la forme moderne du gaulois armoricain, revigoré depuis la fin de l'occupation romaine par des vagues successives d'immigrants d'Outre-Manche parlant des langues très voisines. La frontière linguistique actuelle représente donc la limite extrême orientale du recul du celtique devant le roman.

8.2. Si un nombre non-négligeable de travaux universitaires concernent la langue ou la littérature bretonnes (plus d'une trentaine soutenus en France ou à l'étranger de 1973 à 1990), peu de chercheurs se sont penchés de façon scientifique sur la situation sociolinguistique de la langue bretonne. Des remarques — souvent intéressantes — dans les introductions des ouvrages de dialectologie et un petit nombre d'articles y sont consacrés. Cette lacune vient d'être comblée par la publication de la thèse de F. Broudic (Broudic 1995). On y trouve la somme des références touchant de près ou de loin à ce problème au cours de l'histoire. On trouve par ailleurs des constats de type revendicatif dans des publications militantes qui n'ont guère leur place ici. La monumentale *Histoire Littéraire et Culturelle de la Bretagne* ne traite pratiquement pas du problème au vingtième siècle.

9. Bibliographie (sélective)

Ambrose, John (1980): « Micro-scale Language Planning: an Experiment in Wales and Britanny ». In: *Discussion Papers in Geolinguistics 2*, 51 p., ill.

Balcou, Jean/Le Gallo, Yves (Eds.) (1987): *Histoire littéraire et culturelle de la Bretagne*, Paris/Genève.

Berger, Maria Renate (1988): *Sprachkontakt in der Bretagne: Sprachloyalität versus Sprachwechsel*, Tübingen.

Broudic, François (1985): « La pratique du breton aujourd'hui: approche méthodologique des problèmes d'évaluation ». In: *La Bretagne Linguistique 1*, 73—80.

Broudic, François (1995): *La pratique du breton de l'Ancien Régime à nos jours*, Rennes.

Dauzat, Albert (1922): « Le breton et le français ». In: *La Nature 2717*, 273—278.

Dressler, Wolfgang/Wodak-Leodolter, Ruth (1977): « Language preservation and language death in Brittany ». In: *International Journal of the Sociology of Language 12*, 33—44.

Eggs, Ekkehard (1980): « Sprache, soziale Konflikte und Geschichte. Zur bretonischen Bewegung ». In: *Lendemains 17—18*, 62—82.

Falc'hun, François (1958): « Langue bretonne ». In: *Orbis 7*, 516—533.

Falc'hun, François (1962): « Le breton, forme moderne du gaulois ». In: *Annales de Bretagne 64*, 413—428.

Falc'hun, François (1969): « Essai sur la minorité linguistique de Basse-Bretagne ». In: *Lingual Minorities in Europe*, Oslo, 109—117.

Flatrès, Pierre (1986): *La Bretagne*. Paris.

Floc'h, Guillaume (1981): « Emploi du breton et vente du poisson en Bretagne-Sud ». In: *International Journal of the Sociology of Language 29*, 29—50.

Hélias, Pierre-Jakez (1975): *Le cheval d'orgueil — Mémoires d'un Breton du pays bigouden*, Paris.

Humphreys, Humphrey Ll. (1991): « The Geolinguistics of Breton ». In: *Linguistic Minorities, Society and Territory*, Williams, Colin (Ed.), Clevedon/Philadelphie, 96—119.

La Villemarqué (1847): « Essai sur l'histoire de la langue bretonne ». Rééd. critique in: Tanguy, Bernard: *Aux origines du nationalisme breton*, 1977, Paris, vol. 1.

Le Dû, Jean (1980): « Sociolinguistique et diglossie: le cas du breton ». In: *Sociolinguistique: approches, théories, pratiques*, Gardin B./Marcellesi, J. B. (Eds.), Paris, 153—162.

Le Dû, Jean/Le Berre, Yves (1987): « Contacts de langues en Bretagne ». In: *Travaux du Cercle Linguistique de Nice 9*, 11—33.

Le Dû, Jean (1990): « Langue nationale unique ou retour de la différence? » In: *Wiss. Zeitschr. der Karl-Marx-Univ. Leipzig 39*, 380—387.

Le Dû, Jean/Le Berre, Yves (1990): « Le contact français—breton: un pseudo-conflit ». In: *ABLA papers 14*, Bruxelles, 115—123.

Le Dû, Jean/Le Berre, Yves (1991): « Langues et Institutions: à propos du breton ». In: *Publications Universitaires de Linguistique et d'Anthropologie 3/4*, Corte 292—304.

Le Floc'h, Jean-Louis (1985): « Controverses sur la langue bretonne dans le clergé finistérien au XIXe siècle ». In: *Bulletin de la Société Archéologique du Finistère 114*, 165—177.

Lemarchand-Unger, Brigitte (1981): « Die Verwendung der bretonischen Sprache unter soziolinguistischem Aspekt». In: *Kulturelle und sprachliche Minderheiten in Europa*, Ureland, P. S. (Ed.), Tübingen 201–218.

McDonald, Maryon (1989): *We are not French! Language, Culture and Identity in Brittany*, London/New York.

Sébillot, Paul (1886): « La langue bretonne, limites et statistiques ». In: *Revue d'Ethnographie 5*, 1–29.

Timm, Lenora A. (1980): « Bilingualism, Diglossia and Language Shift in Brittany ». In: *International Journal of the Sociology of Language 25*, 29–41.

Timm, Lenora A. (1983): « The Shifting Linguistic Frontier in Brittany ». In: *Essays in honor of Charles Hockett*, Agard F. B./Kelley, B. (Eds.), Leyde 443–447.

Van Rijn, Gerard/Sieben, Cees (1987): « The Effects of Regionalist Ideas on Public Policy. Some Developments in Language Policy in Wales, Brittany and Friesland ». In: *International Journal of the Sociology of Language 64*, 47–57.

Williamson, Robert C./Virginia, L./Van Eerde, John A. (1983): « Language Maintenance and Shift in a Breton and Welsh Sample ». In: *Word 34*, 67–88.

Yves Le Berre/Jean Le Dû, Brest (France)

150. Français–basque

1. Géographie et démographie
2. Histoire
3. Politique, économie, situations culturelle et religieuse
4. Contacts linguistiques
5. Situation sociolinguistique
6. Etat de la politique linguistique
7. Portrait général des contacts linguistiques
8. Examen critique de la bibliographie
9. Bibliographie (sélective)

1. Géographie et démographie

Le Pays basque « nord » ('Iparralde') couvre aujourd'hui avec ses 3094 km² un peu moins de la moitié du département des Pyrénées-Atlantiques; les anciennes provinces qui le composent sont, d'O en E: le Labourd (777 km²; 200 000 hab.), la Basse-Navarre (1500 km², 29 000 hab.) et la Soule (817 km², 16 000 hab.); → carte linguistique D. De tout temps, la règle traditionnelle de l'« aînesse intégrale » lors des héritages a entraîné l'expatriation de nombreux puînés contraints d'aller trouver fortune loin du pays, particulièrement en Amérique; mais beaucoup reviennent nantis et fondent de nouveaux foyers.

2. Histoire

Le pays bascophone constitue au nord de la frontière naturelle le résidu non romanisé des populations que César désigne sous le nom d'« Aquitains », et auxquelles il attribue « une langue, des coutumes et des lois » différentes de celles des Gaulois – les autres Aquitains, romanisés, devenant les futurs Gascons. L'hémotypologie confirme aujourd'hui l'appartenance de ces populations à un groupe spécifique, de forte concentration au Pays basque et dans certaines vallées pyrénéennes (à l'ouest du col de Port), et allant se diluant jusqu'au cours de la Garonne. Le premier idiome auquel *l'euskara* s'est trouvé confronté fut naturellement le latin, que les Romains y avaient implanté à la suite de la conquête. Selon toute vraisemblance, c'est effectivement un « proto-basque » que parlaient les Aquitains de ce triangle Pyrénées–Garonne–Océan, langue qui, lorsque la majorité d'entre eux l'abandonna au profit de la langue des conquérants, imprima à cette dernière des traits spécifiques liés à leur propre idiome, et qui fit du gascon un parler roman nettement différent du languedocien voisin. Après avoir éventuellement emprunté des mots au latin – auparavant, il n'est pas exclu que, des deux côtés de la chaîne, quelques termes celtiques soient également passés au basque –, les Basques n'ont vraisemblablement jamais perdu le contact avec leurs frères romanisés, auxquels ils ont donc continué à effectuer des emprunts, revêtus désormais d'un habit proprement *gascon*, cependant que le gascon local intégrait naturellement des « euskarismes ». Le *français*, venu s'imposer progressivement sur l'ensemble du territoire selon un processus séculaire que la Révolution et l'Empire ont considérablement accéléré, n'est donc que la forme la plus récente du superstrat dû à la conquête romaine, forme qui offre cette particularité d'être née bien loin du Pays basque, en Ile-de-France, et de présenter dès lors un vêtement phonétique souvent totalement étranger au basque, ce qui n'était réellement le cas ni du latin, ni du gascon — ni du castillan vers lequel l'euskara, même sous ses variétés septentrionales, n'a jamais cessé de se tourner. Mais tout n'est pas aussi simple, et il est très souvent bien malaisé, sinon impossible, de faire le départ entre ces diverses sources d'emprunt.

3. Politique, économie, situations culturelle et religieuse

Les Basques ont été longtemps perçus comme fort différents des populations voisines, cependant de même souche mais sans doute affinés, «acculturés» par la séculaire romanisation. Leur indépendance et leur hostilité aux hiérarchies féodales sont devenues proverbiales, et l'on peut considérer que leurs structures sociales et les assemblées égalitaires qu'ils réunissaient à date régulière pour gouverner, constituèrent un embryon bien réel de démocratie en plein Ancien Régime. Leur économie était fondée sur l'élevage, l'agriculture, l'exploitation des minéraux et des forêts soit pour la construction des charpentes ou des navires, soit pour la production de charbon de bois destiné aux forges, et enfin la pêche, en rivière ou en haute mer, jusqu'à Terre-Neuve en particulier — d'autres marins célèbres servirent du reste le roi comme corsaires. Culturellement, les traditions n'étaient pas très différentes de celles qui prévalaient dans la Gascogne voisine, mais on note toutefois une plus longue persistance des croyances et des pratiques païennes à peine christianisées — la sorcellerie y jouait un rôle important, et les procès de Bayonne instruits au XVIIe siècle par Pierre de Lancre ont mené au bûcher des dizaines de malheureuses. Le clergé a toujours occupé une place majeure, proche du peuple et exerçant une autorité d'autant plus grande qu'il représentait autant le savoir que la conscience et la morale collectives: il fut un élément essentiel pour la sauvegarde de la langue. On ne saurait oublier les jeux et les fêtes chez ce «peuple qui chante et qui danse au pied des Pyrénées» comme dit Voltaire: les premiers ont popularisé la «pelote», à partir du «jeu de paume» de l'Ancien Régime, les secondes, liées aux rites populaires, se perpétuent aujourd'hui avec les «mascarades» souletines à l'époque du Carnaval. Egalement souletines sont les «pastorales», théâtre populaire sur tréteaux, interprété — en basque, bien entendu — de façon très conventionnelle par les habitants des villages eux-mêmes, et illustrant des événements historiques très variés. Egalement populaire est la tradition des *bertsulari*, improvisateurs qui, à deux, rivalisent d'adresse et d'esprit lors des cérémonies collectives (repas de fêtes, etc.).

4. Contacts linguistiques

On a vu plus haut de quelle façon le latin, devenu le roman (*gascon* en ce qui nous concerne), s'est surimposé au basque: cette langue est longtemps demeurée l'idiome unique des masses populaires; le gascon voisin est connu sur toute la périphérie, où le bilinguisme est la règle, et pénétra également sous cette forme le long de la côte atlantique (toponymes gascons à St-Jean-de-Luz («chemin de Chibau») et jusqu'au «Cabo Higuer» («figuier») au S de la frontière. Le gascon fut la première langue administrative sous l'Ancien Régime, tôt relayée par le français, qui resta longtemps le moyen d'expression des classes sociales privilégiées, de la petite bourgeoisie et des fonctionnaires, particulièrement dans les villes et les bourgades importantes, et sur la côte fréquentée par des «étrangers».

5. Situation sociolinguistique

La synthèse des résultats obtenus par le biais d'une enquête réalisée en 1991 (Héguy 1991) fait apparaître que sur les 236 963 habitants que compte la partie «basque» du département des Pyrénées-Atlantiques, 56% étant bascophones, 54,7% de ceux-ci ont une «bonne» connaissance du basque, 24% une connaissance «imparfaite», le déficit affectant bien plus la côte labourdine (42,5% de bascophones, dont 24,9% entrant dans la seconde catégorie, 17,6% seulement dans la première), tandis que le Labourd intérieur (76,8% de bascophones, 1e catég. 54,4%, 2e catég. 22,4%) le dispute tout autant à la Basse-Navarre (resp. 77,3%, 64,5%, 12,8%) qu'à la Soule (resp. 78,7%, 54,7%, 24%) pour l'emploi de la langue traditionnelle; une enquête plus poussée nous indique que dans cette population scolaire le nombre des individus qui comprennent et parlent «un peu» le basque atteint 23%, proportion appréciable à côté de ceux qui le comprennent (38,9%) et le parlent (33,2%) bien — et de ceux qui ni ne le comprennent (37,9%) ni ne le parlent (43,9%). Les pourcentages diminuent sensiblement s'il s'agit de le *lire* (bien 28,4%, un peu 16,6%) ou de l'*écrire* (bien 19,9%, un peu 17,2%). Cet état de choses explique bien que le Basque ne soit pas suffisamment conscient du «poids» linguistique de l'idiome et ne se rende donc pas très bien compte des influences qu'il peut exercer sur son français, souvent du reste tout aussi mal perçu puisque parlé selon des habitudes locales que l'école ne parvient pas à extirper. Sans doute l'écoute des radios locales — 4 émettant du «Nord», 1 du «Sud» — est-elle naturellement fonction de la compétence préalable de l'auditeur, car on n'écoute volontiers que si l'on comprend bien ... Mais il reste que près de 70% des élèves n'écoutent *jamais* d'émissions en basque! Ce «medium» ne paraît donc pas assez contraignant pour obtenir l'impact souhaité. La lecture n'est pas meilleure, puisque 88,9% de la population bascophone ne lit jamais d'ouvrage en basque ... Les Basques sont néanmoins conscients de ce déficit et souhaitent à plus de 50% (jusqu'à 70% dans certains cas) que des mesures soient prises afin de conforter ou restaurer l'usage du basque — reste à savoir si la politique linguistique du «Sud» et ses modalités (diffusion exclusive du «batu») conviennent à des bascophones fiers de la qualité de leur langue et peu enclins à l'infléchir dans le sens — discutable — préconisé par ceux du «Sud».

5.1. L'enseignement

Dès 1969, les *ikastola* l'assuraient à titre privé au niveau maternel puis élémentaire; leur intégration dans l'enseignement public, réclamée en 1982, s'effectue l'année suivante; les classes bilingues se multiplient alors, aboutissant en 1986 à la fondation de l'association de parents d'élèves *ikas bi* «deux apprentissages»; parallèlement, l'enseignement privé ouvre une classe en 1968–1969, puis d'autres en Labourd jusqu'en 1986, date à laquelle des contrats sont passés avec l'Etat, ce qui favorise depuis une progression continue jusqu'à la signature en 1992 d'un accord-cadre avec l'Education nationale, prévoyant une future intégration. Cet enseignement offre trois filières possibles: la première consiste à donner un enseignement facultatif de trois heures hebdomadaires assuré par un instituteur «itinérant», formule qui, à son apogée il y a dix ans et appliquée du Labourd à la Soule avec un maximum en Basse-Navarre, décline depuis au profit des classes bilingues. La seconde partage l'enseignement en deux moitiés égales, matières professées en français et matières professées en basque ou en français selon les élèves; le nombre des élèves «bilingues» est passé en 10 ans de 17 à 1189 dans le «public», et a doublé dans le «privé» depuis 1989 — l'implantation de cette filière est surtout sud-labourdine, avec deux «esquisses» en Basse-Navarre (Baïgorry-Cize) et en Soule (Mauléon). Dernière filière: tout en basque en maternelle avec introduction progressive du français en enseignement élémentaire; le nombre d'élèves inscrits est ici passé de 8 en 1969–1970 à 916 en 1992–1993, avec une implantation majeure au Labourd méridional. Pour corriger une image qui peut paraître excessivement optimiste, rappelons toutefois que le pourcentage des élèves inscrits en maternelle et en école élémentaire hors de ces filières, donc sans aucune référence au basque, atteint 85% ...

L'enseignement du basque et en basque connaît donc un réel succès, qui est allé croissant. Son implantation, néanmoins, se trouve circonscrite à des zones «privilégiées», qui d'ailleurs enregistrent aussi une croissance démographique sensible. Il est à souhaiter qu'une action positive soit tentée, sous des formes adéquates, pour homogénéiser au Pays Basque «nord» l'accession des jeunes générations à cette langue ethnique et à cette culture éminemment originales et authentiquement «européennes». Un problème est celui du matériel d'enseignement, manuels et exercices à divers niveaux; tandis que le Pays basque «sud» développe toute une politique éditoriale, aidée par les moyens considérables que lui offrent l'économie d'une région autonome relativement riche et l'attitude volontariste et centralisatrice (le «batu») des pouvoirs publics, le «Nord» balance entre un recours systématique à ces publications du «Sud», que la nature de la «koiné» proposée rend quelque peu suspecte dans un milieu linguistique fier de sa tradition dialectale plus proche du basque «classique» et plus fidèle au génie de la langue, et l'élaboration d'un autre «batu» de meilleur aloi, nécessairement plus coûteuse et entraînant une certaine cassure de l'unité souhaitable. Le choix n'est pas encore fait.

6. Etat de la politique linguistique

Tandis que longtemps seul le clergé eut, avec quelques hauts fonctionnaires, hommes de loi ou grands bourgeois le privilège de l'écriture, l'enseignement obligatoire institué par la République imposa le français; la situation ne change réellement, à cet égard, que depuis très peu, sous nos yeux pourrait-on dire, comme en témoignent les données qui suivent: l'introduction du basque à l'école fut d'abord l'affaire de l'enseignement privé (avec les « ikastola », classes maternelles où le basque est seul parlé), mais depuis la seconde guerre mondiale le renouveau des cultures populaires aboutit au vote de la fameuse « Loi Deixonne » qui en 1951 officialise et « laïcise » l'enseignement des langues « régionales ». Depuis une dizaine d'année, un nouvel élan est donné, et tout récemment (1994) le gouvernement français a pris de nouvelles mesures en ce sens. Pour dresser un bilan récent de l'« impact » de cette politique en Pays basque, nous avons consulté deux sources: d'abord une enquête réalisée en 1991 par Txomin Héguy, directeur de l'Institut Culturel Basque, sur les conditions d'emploi de l'euskara dans les provinces septentrionales (Iparralde), ensuite un bilan dressé deux ans plus tard (1993) par Francis Jauréguiberry (CNRS) sur « Le basque à l'école maternelle et élémentaire » dans cette même zone.

7. Portrait général des contacts linguistiques

Les interférences concernent au premier chef l'impact du basque sur le français régional; si nous faisons également état de celui qu'il exerce sur le gascon, dans une population partiellement bilingue en ce sens depuis des siècles, on aurait tout intérêt à mesurer aussi inversement l'influence des deux langues romanes sur le basque local, en comparaison d'autres zones dialectales. Mais l'entreprise serait aventureuse et ne s'adresserait qu'à d'authentiques spécialistes.

Un mot préalable du statut socio-linguistique de ces interférences, notamment en ce qui concerne les emprunts lexicaux, les seuls dont le locuteur puisse avoir spontanément une conscience claire: pour ce qui touche les échanges entre basque et français, la situation peut varier entre des emprunts réellement socialisés et codifiés par la « norme » locale du français parlé au Pays basque ou dans sa périphérie immédiate, et, chez les bilingues, des réflexes ponctuels et occasionnels, que le locuteur est prêt à corriger en fonction d'une certaine norme plus ou moins consciente s'il vient à s'en rendre compte, et que nul ne songerait à faire entrer dans l'écrit — mais ceci vaudrait évidemment bien plus pour le basque, dont les usagers ne peuvent se référer à un modèle depuis longtemps standardisé et imposé à l'instar du français, que pour ce dernier. Il n'en va pas de même des rapports entre le basque et le gascon, tous deux idiomes perçus comme « mineurs » et également dépourvus du prestige que confèrent au français l'écriture, l'administration et l'enseignement.

Les interférences peuvent affecter ici *tous les registres de l'idiome*, de la phonétique et la phonologie au lexique en passant par la morphosyntaxe, et leur statut socio-linguistique peut varier avec l'acuité de la perception que l'on en a. D'autre part, on se gardera d'oublier que le français auquel le basque se trouve confronté, assez éloigné de la variété parisienne de référence, a largement subi l'action du substrat gascon, ou du moins de la variété de gascon en usage dans les Pyrénées-Atlantiques, ce qui ne rend pas particulièrement aisée l'identification des causes et des effets.

Les matériaux sur lesquels nous avons appuyé notre recherche sont relativement pauvres, et de nature aussi diverse qu'inégale. Outre notre expérience personnelle, nous nous référerons essentiellement, pour l'influence exercée par le basque sur le français, (1) au mémoire inédit consacré à ce sujet en 1959 par une étudiante bascophone originaire de Bayonne, Marie-Monique Capdevielle, intitulé *Le français parlé au Pays basque*, complété par les études de phonologie du français régional publiées par Henriette Walter, (2) au mémoire également inédit rédigé en 1965 par Etienne Ithurria, fils de pêcheurs luziens et professeur à l'Université de Toulouse, sur *Le vocabulaire de la pêche et le parler du milieu pêcheur à Saint-Jean-de-Luz*, (3) à la partie française du bref dialogue trilingue entre conjoints que nous avons enregistré à Labastide-Clairence, localité située à la lisière septentrionale de la Basse-Navarre, texte publié en 1978 dans la revue *Via Domitia* (Toulouse), (4) enfin à la saynète comique également luzienne intitulée *Les cascarotes au commissariat*, et mettant en scène des bohémiennes de la côte labourdine au parler savoureux et fort évocateur.

7.1. Impact du basque sur le gascon
7.1.1. Phonétique et phonologie
7.1.1.1. Vocalisme

Le système phonologique des voyelles toniques gasconnes est illustré par la c. 2210 du vol. VI de l'*ALG*, dont on pourra rapprocher la c. 1609 du vol. V consacrée au vocalisme utilisé en morphologie verbale. Toute une zone côtière occidentale incluant les Landes et la Gironde y apparaît comme caractérisée par un système à trois degrés d'aperture au lieu de quatre (du moins en ce qui concerne la série palatale — c'est le cas dans le reste de l'Occitanie). Cette substitution occidentale d'un timbre moyen [ᴇ] à la paire de phonèmes [e] [ɛ], rééquilibrant du reste un système qui n'avait déjà qu'un degré moyen [o] du côté vélaire, rend le vocalisme gascon occidental semblable à celui du basque, qui ne possède que trois degrés d'aperture vocalique — comme le castillan, ce qui n'est certainement pas fortuit. Outre ce phénomène, nous avions noté (*ALG* V c. 1809—1810) une certaine réticence du gascon local à fermer [ɔ] en position prétonique dans la flexion verbale, ce qui est contraire à la règle commune et conforme en revanche au phonétisme euskaro-castillan.

7.1.1.2. Consonantisme

On ne trouve rien d'important à signaler dans ce domaine, car le système du gascon occidental (Béarn, Landes) correspond globalement à celui du basque, avec des faits locaux intéressants comme (*ALG* VI c. 2214) la répartition géographique des variantes [ʒ] et [j] du phonème correspondant à *j* des graphies occitane et basque: à sa réalisation occidentale [ɟ] («*d* mouillé») ou [j] répond le [j] béarno-landais, tandis que le [ʒ] souletin est identique au [ʒ] des vallées gasconnes limitrophes d'Ossau, Aspe et Barétous.

7.1.2. Morphosyntaxe

Comme nous sommes en présence, à ce niveau, de deux «univers» distincts, les interférences ne peuvent être que mineures. Néanmoins on peut se demander si l'absence d'un Prétérit dans le système verbal du gascon landais (*ALG* V c. 1698) ne prolonge pas directement, par contact ou par l'effet d'interférences plus anciennes et plus profondes, l'absence en basque d'un tiroir simple exprimant le passé ponctuel, que les deux idiomes rendent par un Plus-que-Parfait. Peut-être pourrait-on également invoquer dans le même sens la concentration maximale dans le sud-ouest de la Gascogne des thèmes de Futur et Conditionnel sans syncope de la voyelle thématique à la cl. II, soit les types *averà, venerà* ou *diserà* pour *aurà* «il aura», *vendrà* «il vendra», *dirà* «il dira», ce rejet d'une multiplicité de thèmes correspondant à une flexion d'esprit moins «roman». Enfin, on signalera la tournure béarnaise *que s'a crompat pomas de las maduras* «il a acheté des pommes mûres», écho peut-être de l'emploi fréquent en basque souletin du partitif pour les adjectifs épithètes: *bi berset dolorusik* dit le poète Etchahun, «deux couplets (des) douloureux»...

7.1.3. Lexique

Ici, la cueillette est plus riche. Mais on constate à confronter les enquêtes basque et gasconne de Labastide-Clairence que l'impact du gascon (et du français, souvent malaisée à distinguer de la précédente) sur le basque est infiniment plus important que celui du basque sur le gascon et le français: à 200 «romanismes» environ — dont, du reste, 25 gallicismes seulement! — notés en basque dans toute l'enquête correspondent une vingtaine d'«euskarismes» apparents en gascon, dont une majorité de calques. C'est très peu. Citons quelques exemples: à la carte 15 de l'ALG «sanglier», le gascon *pòrc sauvatge* correspond au basque *urde basa*, tandis que les alentours emploient le gallicisme *sanglièr*; de même, la c. 180 «capitules de la bardane» donne *volurs* (gallicisme, comme bsq. *ohoinak*, tout autour *gats/gahèts*; pour la c. 309 «bêcher», gasc. *virar* «(re)tourner» comme bsq. *itzuli*, tout autour *hòder/palaherrar* ... etc.

7.2. Impact du basque sur le français régional

Ici, les interférences sont mieux connues, pour les raisons évoquées plus haut.

7.2.1. Phonétique et phonologie

7.2.1.1. Vocalisme

Nous retrouvons dans ce français régional le système à trois degrés d'aperture évoqué ci-dessus, qui confond les voyelles moyennes ouvertes [ɛ] [œ] [ɔ] et moyennes fermées [e] [ø] [o], les neutralisant sous un timbre plutôt ouvert, tandis que le [ɑ] reste inconnu et que [ə] rejoint le [œ] susdit lorsqu'il ne se délabialise pas en [e]—à moins qu'en finale il ne s'efface, particulièrement après un [ʀ] (souvent articulé comme un (x]), contrairement aux habitudes «méridionales» et rejoignant de la sorte le français normatif; les timbres les plus fermés [i] [y] [u] se réalisent eux aussi plus ouverts qu'en français standard, comme en basque (où seul le souletin connaît un [y]). On note d'autre part la nasalité intense des voyelles nasalisées — ainsi que la tendance de [ɛ̃ŋ] à se diphtonguer dans certains cas: [bjẽẽŋ] «bien», [mẽintənɹ] «maintenir» —; or on sait que le souletin possède de telles voyelles, et que le «nasillement» propre au gascon voisin de la région d'Orthez prolonge l'aire souletine; mais on ignore où se situe le point de départ du phénomène, qui paraît être commun aux deux domaines.

7.2.1.2. Consonantisme

On ne trouve que peu de particularités frappantes. Comme dans tout le Midi — et ailleurs —, un *e* prosthétique vient «soutenir» un *s* suivi d'occlusive: *estylo, estatue* ..., comme l'occitan dit *espirala* «spirale» et le basque *eztera* «stère». Le souffle [h] est souvent émis avec force, mais ce trait est aussi un gasconnisme, et l'«aspiration» est ignorée du labourdin, surtout côtier. Si les géminées, inconnues du basque comme du gascon, sont absentes, en revanche l'[r] à plusieurs battements, qui s'oppose phonologiquement à [ɾ] simple, se réalise en général [ʁ] (sonore) ou [x] (sourd). Quant aux sifflantes et chuintantes, comme le basque possède un [s] dorsoalvéolaire, noté *z*, à côté d'une sifflante rétroflexe [ʂ], notée *s*, et d'une chuintante palatale [ɕ] notée *x*, le français régional prononce l'*s* «à la française» et non «à la castillane», apico-alvéolaire; la sonore [z], ignorée du basque, s'articule de même.

7.2.1.3. Faits suprasegmentaux

Si la mélodie de la phrase paraît ici plus «linéaire» et monotone que dans d'autres régions de France (région parisienne, Provence ...), le Basque donne néanmoins à ses énoncés, en basque ou en français, une importante tonalité affective, qui l'amène à employer les mêmes moyens suprasegmentaux que les autres francophones de France, mais selon des schémas souvent différents: il allongera volontiers la voyelle porteuse d'un accent d'insistance, accentuera le mot important sur l'initiale, fera monter la mélodie de sa phrase tant affirmative qu'interrogative ou exclamative. L'accent d'insistance pourra déclencher une intonation descendante-montante, un peu à la façon du 4e ton chinois; mais la phrase se déroulera néanmoins sans pause sensible jusqu'à son terme, simplement scandée par des allongements vocaliques expressifs et des modulations spécifiques.

7.2.2. Morphosyntaxe et structure de l'énoncé

7.2.2.1. Rythme de phrase et jonctures

On soulignera ici l'emploi constant des liaisons banales «et» (basque *eta*, très fréquent et souvent «suspensif» en fin d'énoncé), «et puis» (basque *eta gero*, assez fréquent dans l'usage de certains bascophones pour déclencher chez l'interlocuteur une reprise narquoise en écho, *hotz eztenean bero!* «lorsque ce n'est pas froid, [c'est] chaud!»), «alors» (*orduan*). On pourrait également soupçonner le basque sous-jacent d'être à l'origine d'un emploi courant de «que» pour renforcer un énoncé simplement affirmatif; or un tel emploi caractérise aussi l'ensemble du gascon: cela permet-il de soutenir qu'il s'agit d'un effet de substrat attribuable au proto-basque? La langue actuelle n'offre pas de formule unique lui correspondant, mais les préfixes *ba-* (affirmation), *bait-* (explication) et le suffixe *-la* de «complétif» employé absolument, très fréquents, s'en rapprocheraient sans conteste: *ba-* précédé en basque *da* «il est» pour dire «il y a»: *bada norbait hemen* «il y a quelqu'un ici», *du* «il a» pour préciser «il possède»: *badu etxe bat* «il possède une maison», *doa* «il va» dans *badoa* «il s'en va», *daki* «il (le) sait» dans *badaki* «idem»; on cite la phrase *baietz* («que oui»), *izanen dukala!* «que oui, que tu l'auras!», où le complétif en *-la* reste «en l'air». En revanche, la fréquence relativement grande de «hé» [ɛ] ponctuant les phrases comme pour prendre l'interlocuteur à témoin n'a pas de base précise dans la langue autochtone, qui l'emploie de la même façon.

7.2.2.2. Procédés de renforcement

Pour insister sur une affirmation ou une négation, le Basque aime aussi à faire suivre immédiatement, sans pause, le mot essentiel, souvent (mais pas forcément) placé en fin d'énoncé, d'un «oui», «non» calquant l'emploi en basque de *ba(i), ez*: «Il viendra *oui*!» *jinen da ba*, «Il ne (le) sait pas *non*!» *eztaki ez*; on cite des phrases telles que «Elle ne vient plus; elle a toujours une raison *oui*», «A Arnéguy, il n'était pas tendre *non*, le douanier», «il va leur enseigner *oui* ça», «Oh tè, ils vont rester *oui* sans doute», «Les cotèles (cf. occitan *costèla* «côtelette») de porc il faut les acheter *oui*». Cette reprise insistante de l'affirmation ou de la dénégation, réduplication que l'on constate aussi avec les pronoms — «je l'ai vu *oui moi*», «je le connais (à) *lui*» — se double de l'emploi très fréquent d'adverbes-adjectifs tels que «pareil» — basque *(ba) berdin* — au sens de «de la même façon», «bien sûr» (*segur*); on remarquera le sémantisme très large du dernier mot, énergique, dans la phrase «ils dansaient mal, ils suivaient pas la musique, *rien*!». C'est la recherche permanente d'expressivité par les moyens élémentaires d'une rhétorique « de base ». On peut citer dans le même registre *Cascarotes* « Il se serait léché les doigts *et puis tout* ».

7.2.2.3. Ordre des mots

Cette liberté prise avec les « règles » du discours français répond sans aucun doute aux structures du basque, langue à déclinaisons où les fonctions sont indiquées par des suffixes; ici donc, excepté la règle d'or qui, une fois le sujet posé, place à la fin de l'énoncé le prédicat précédé de toutes ses expansions, et commande toujours l'ordre complément-complété, bien des libertés sont permises — comme en latin —, et le français local se débarrasse volontiers, par analogie, du carcan stylistique traditionnel: l'objet est posé en début d'énoncé — « *Un livre* j'ai acheté hier » *Liburu bat erosi nuen atzo* —, l'adverbe ou l'expansion précèdent le prédicat — « C'est le pays le plus beau parce que *là* je suis né » *Herri ederrena da han sortu nintzalakotz* —, « *En basque* il faut que je dise? » *Euskaraz erran behar dut?* —, et cela même, par une sorte de prolepse, après un subordonnant dans l'exemple suivant — mais on rappelle qu'en basque tout complément précède le prédicat: « Il nous a dit *dix mille francs* que ça s'était vendu » *Erran dauku hamar mila libera saldu izan zela;* Casc. « *Marié* vous êtes? » *Ezkondua zare?*

7.2.2.4. Economie morphologique et structures singulières

Assez remarquablement aussi, comme sa langue inclut dans le verbe des indices personnels correspondant aux divers participants de l'action, le bascophone tend à faire l'économie d'un anaphorique des 3ᵉ-6ᵉ personnes — économie qui touche aussi l'indéfini « en » qu'ignore le basque —: « On va (le) faire », « Y en a pas beaucoup de mon âge qui n'ont (= « ne l'ont ») pas fait ici dans le pays », « Moi aussi j'(en) ai », « On ne va pas (les) faire dedans non », « Oui ils sont venus aujourd'hui (la) chercher », Casc. « C'est plein » p. « C'*en* est plein ». Ecarts entre les syntaxes respectives, « raccourcis » et calques lexicaux combinés suscitent d'assez étonnantes formulations, aussi insolites que cocasses pour le témoin non averti: nous citerons pêle-mêle « un billet va-t'en-venir » (= « aller et retour », basque *joan-jin*), « un crayon pour guiser » (= « un aiguise-crayon », régime avant le verbe en basque), dit par un paysan « Bon ou mauvais, il faut porter » (= « [Qu'il fasse] bon au mauvais, il faut porter [le lait au laitier] », bsq. *On ala tzar, ekarri behar da*), « Papa *et puis* sont là » (= « Papa et les autres sont là », bsq. *Aita (e)ta hor dira*), « On est allés au marché, Papa *et les deux* » (= « Papa et moi nous sommes allés au marché », bsq. *Merkaturat joan gara, aita ta biak*), « Pour aller on a, mais pour revenir derrière on aura? » se demandent deux paysannes allant à la foire voisine (bsq. *Joaiteko badugu, bainan gibelat itzultzeko izanen dugu?*). Signalons enfin les fréquentes *onomatopées* incluses dans les énoncés français comme dans leurs modèles basques: « Ils s'en allaient *ttur ttur ttur* (pron. [ṭur ṭur ṭur], avec une dentale palatale), tranquillement », « les bidons qui *parrapatapam* », etc. On rapprochera enfin la question « Qui où cinquante mille? » (il s'agissait d'une prime accordée à qui permettrait la capture d'un contrebandier), avec deux interrogatifs juxtaposés, du sigle *Nor nun*, litt. « qui où? », choisi comme titre de l'*Annuaire International des Basques* (notoires): c'est là un « euskarisme » courant.

7.2.2.5. Le genre grammatical; les prépositions

Les erreurs de genre chez les usagers d'une langue qui ignore cette catégorie sont fréquentes; si les exemples mettant en jeu des pronoms personnels — « on touche presque rien, l'organisation *il* touche tout là-dedans! », « Maman *il* a porté le pain », « l'autre voiture *il* arrivait par derrière » — peuvent se comprendre partant de l'absence en basque de pronom-affixe, les choses deviennent plus graves avec des substantifs: on peut entendre dans les conversations des tours comme « *tous* les maisons du village », tandis qu'un enseignant conseillera à un élève « N'utilisez pas les barres *transversaux* » … Egalement Casc. « *du* couenne ». Autre problème: les fréquentes confusions relevées entre prépositions courantes reposent aussi sur l'inadéquation mutuelle de deux systèmes, dont l'un est fondé sur l'emploi exclusif de prépositions, l'autre sur l'usage complémentaire de suffixes de déclinaison et de « postpositions » juxtaposées au substantif ou gouvernant certains cas. Autre phénomène: comme en basque seul l'« indéterminé » (ni singulier ni pluriel) possède un partitif (à suffixe *-ik*), on ne s'étonnera pas de voir employée la combinaison *de* + article à la place de la préposition seule: « Il faut donner moins *du* charbon », dans la bouche d'un quinquagénaire, ou « Il y avait beaucoup *de l'*eau», dans celle d'une fillette, ou encore Casc. «Il avait beaucoup de *la* peine». On a noté aussi − mauvaise perception du système ou confusion entre substantifs et adjectifs, peu distincts en basque − «se mettre colère».

7.2.3. Le lexique

Le lexique, qu'on le considère ou non comme un système, occupe une place à part dans la langue: les phénomènes qui le touchent sont les plus propres à émerger dans la conscience linguistique, et l'on sait aussi que c'est généralement sur la base de références lexicales que les dialectophones opposent les parlers entre eux. Dans le cas du français parlé au Pays basque, les interférences sont constantes, dans les deux sens évidemment − la francisation du lexique basque est toujours combattue par les puristes, qui ne l'empêchent guère de sévir dans l'usage quotidien, mais là n'est pas notre propos. Pour donner une idée de cette interprétation, nous nous référerons essentiellement d'abord aux *Cascarotes* pour le langage familier, ensuite au travail déjà cité d'Etienne Ithurria pour une langue déjà quelque peu technique. Mais il faut d'entrée préciser les conditions dans lesquelles ces emprunts «fonctionnent»; les adaptations se font d'autant plus naturellement que les phonétiques respectives du basque et du français local sont proches: pas d'accent tonique en basque, pas de phonèmes insolites non plus. Comme premier exemple, citons l'exlamation de cette fillette de Labastide-Clairence, s'écriant en regardant le ciel d'orage «Quelle dembore!», transposant le basque *Zer dembora!* «Quel temps!» Les «cascarotes» émaillent aussi leurs propos d'exclamations, «oh *nola*?» = «oh, comment?», «qu'est-ce que tu me dis *gaxua* [gaɕua]?» «... (ma) pauvre?», «*hori* tu es comme les vaches maintenant» «tiens (litt. «cela»; très fréquent) ...», ou de mots basques simplement plaqués dans le discours français: «un tour dans le *barne*» «... l'intérieur», «s'ils (les enfants) t'ont fait tout dans les *xatar*?» «... dans les langes?», «... mal aux *ixter*» «... aux cuisses», «l'*eltzekaria* qui brûle» «le potage (?) ...», expressions parfois traduites: «du vin chaud comme ça, *berotua*» «... chauffé»; en alternant «toujours, *beti bezala*, toujours» «... comme toujours ...»; parfois la forme est faussement «francisée»: «faire les *xuriket(s)*» «... les lessives (*xuriketak*, pl. de *-keta*)»; des expressions onomatopéiques: «je l'ai pris bien *ttinko-ttinko* contre moi» «... bien serré ...», «j'étais comme ça *tilintalan*» «... traînant»; signalons pour finir un trait morphosyntaxique avec l'absence d'article partitif et de liaison dans «je leur ai porté *bouillon légumes*», basque *baratzeki-salda* ekarri nioten. Dans la langue plus technique des pêcheurs de Ciboure, les mots basques s'intègrent tels quels dans le discours français, sous leur vêtement le plus simple, sauf adaptations minimales, comme «bolade», b. *bolada* «réaction favorable, bon mouvement, bonne humeur» (origine romane), «bolinche», b. *bolintxa* «filet rond d'origine espagnole», «camagne», b. *kamaña* «lit de paille», «cracade», b. *krakada* «repas copieux» (gasconnisme), «liste», b. *lista* «planche fine et étroite» (castillanisme?), «padère», b. *padera* «poêle à frire» (gascon), etc. Mais d'autres mots terminés en -*a* s'intègrent tels quels: «il (le bateau) a fait keñada», b. *keñada* cf. *keñu* «signe», c'est-à-dire que le bateau a viré de cap pour aller vers le banc qu'il a repéré; «avec ce zurda ([surda]), il n'y a pas de gros thon qui va nous manquer (litt.!)», basque *zurda* «crin de pêche», la phrase signifiant «avec ce crin, même un gros thon n'emportera pas la ligne». On pourrait multiplier les exemples, le travail cité contenant une soixantaine de tels «euskarismes» d'emploi quotidien chez les pêcheurs de Ciboure, et se référant à toutes les situations, emprunts qui peuvent être des formes déclinées, comme «j'ai vu un thon uberan», basque *ubera* «reflux, sillage», donc «dans le sillage» (inessif sing.), ou encore «il (certain oiseau de mer) a fait atzaparkan», cf. basque *atzapar* «griffe» + -*ka*- suffixe adverbial + -*n* d'inessif, expression qui signifie que cet oiseau vient de frapper l'eau de ses pattes, faisant rejaillir l'écume et révélant ainsi la possible présence du poisson. Des enquêtes menées dans d'autres milieux apporteraient certainement une foule de telles tournures calquées sur le basque, et seraient précieuses pour l'ethnolinguistique du domaine en question.

Pour corriger ce genre de «déviation», il n'existe pas, à notre connaissance, d'ouvrages du type de «ne dites pas, mais dites» ou des fameux *Gasconnismes corrigés* de Desgrouais, tandis qu'en sens inverse les Basques du «sud» font depuis longtemps la chasse aux «erderismes» − castillanismes −, afin de préserver la pureté (?) de la langue (cf. dès 1929 *Erderismos* de Severo Altube, publié par l'*Euskaltzaindi*). Sans doute pense-t-on au «Nord» qu'il n'y a qu'à prêcher d'exemple en évitant de donner du français régional, dans de tels ouvrages, une image peu édifiante ... C'est assurément une erreur, car mieux vaut prendre conscience des «fautes» si l'on désire les corriger. A l'égard du gascon, le problème ne saurait se poser — du moins pour le moment.

8. Examen critique de la bibliographie

Nous pensons avoir tout dit dans ce qui précède. Pour les généralités, cf. la bibliographie contenue dans la contribution proposée par ceux du «Sud» (→ art. 154). Pour le basque d'«Iparralde», la meilleure grammaire est toujours sans conteste possible celle du chanoine Pierre Lafitte, *Grammaire basque (navarro-labourdin littéraire)*, IKAS, Bayonne, fruit d'une connaissance profonde tant du parler quotidien que des œuvres littéraires de toute espèce, pleine de conseils judicieux et modérés vers un respect de la tradition du bon basque, exemple d'excès, d'artifices ou de laxismes regrettables, et prolongeant la leçon des grands écrivains classiques; le meilleur dictionnaire «de version» est celui du Père Pierre Lhande, *Dictionnaire basque—français* («*et français—basque*», non réalisé), Paris 1962, et de «thème» le *Lexique français—basque* d'André Tournier et Pierre Lafitte (Bayonne 1954), dont la qualité est garantie par le nom du second auteur. La contribution du «Sud» (→ art. 154) indiquera la bibliographie du «batu»: c'est là un autre problème.

9. Bibliographie (sélective)

ALG: Séguy, Jean (1954—1974): *Atlas linguistique et ethnographique de la Gascogne*, 6 vol., Matrices dialectométriques, Paris.

Allières, Jacques (1979): «Les versions basque, gasconne et française d'un même dialogue à Labastide-Clairence (Pyrénées-Atlantiques), point 691-0 de l'ALG». In: *Hommage à Jean Séguy* [Numéro spécial de: *Via Domitia*, Toulouse], vol. 2, 3—19.

Allières, Jacques (1987): «Gascón y euskera: afinidades e interrelaciones lingüísticas». In: *Pirenaico navarro-aragonés, gascón y euskera.* (V curso de verano en San Sebastián), Cierbide Martinena, R. (Ed.), s. l., 181—198.

Altube, Severo (1929): «Erderismos». In: *Euskera 10* (réimpression: 1975), Bilbo/Bilbao.

Bonaparte, Louis-Lucien (1864, 1869): *Le verbe basque en tableaux*, Londres.

Bouda, Karl (1948): «Romanische syntaktische Einflüsse im Baskischen». In: *Indogermanische Forschungen 59*, 186—204.

Broca, Paul (1875): «Sur l'origine et la répartition de la langue basque [Basques français et Basques espagnols]». In: *Revue d'Anthropologie 1*, 1—54.

Capdevielle, Marie-Monique (1959): *Le français parlé au Pays Basque*, Toulouse [Mémoire de Maîtrise].

Desgrouais, J. (1766): *Les Gasconnismes corrigés*, Toulouse.

Etxeberria, P./Hurch, B./Oñederra, M. L. (1988): «Loanwords in Basque: phonetics and phonology». In: *Euskara Biltzarra/Congreso de la lengua vasca/Congrès de la Langue Basque/Conference on the Basque Language*, Gasteiz/Vitoria, 157—162.

Etxepare, Bernard (1545/1987): *Linguae Vasconum Primitiae (Edizio kritikoa)*, Altuna, P. (Ed.), Bilbo/Bilbao.

Euskaltzaindia: *Euskal Herriko Hizkuntz Atlasa* (= EHHA) [Atlas linguistique basque], Aurrekoetxea, G./Videgain, X. (Eds.), Bilbo/Bilbao (en préparation).

Goyheneche, Eugène (1979): *Le pays basque: Soule-Labourd-Basse Navarre*, Pau.

Haase, Martin (1992): *Sprachkontakt und Sprachwandel im Baskenland: Die Einflüsse des Gaskognischen und Französischen auf das Baskische*, Hambourg.

Haase, Martin (1993): *Le gascon des Basques. Contribution à la théorie des substrats*, Hambourg.

'Haize Garbia' (1972/1975): *Dictionnaire basque pour tous. 2 vol.: 1. Basque—Français, 2. Français—Basque*, Saint-Sébastien/Hendaye.

Haritschelhar, Jean (1970): *L'œuvre poétique de Pierre Topet-Etchahun [Texte — Traduction — Variantes — Notes]*, Bilbao.

Héguy, Txomin (1991): *Enquête sur les conditions d'emploi de l'euskara dans les provinces septentrionales (Iparralde)* s. l.

Ithurria, Etienne (1965): *Le vocabulaire de la pêche et le parler du milieu pêcheur à Saint-Jean-de-Luz*, Toulouse [Mémoire de Maîtrise].

Jauréguiberry, Francis (1993): *Le basque à l'école maternelle et élémentaire dans les provinces septentrionales (Iparralde)* s. l.

Lafitte, Pierre (1979): *Grammaire basque (Navarro-Labourdin Littéraire)*, Donostia/Saint-Sébastien.

Lafon, René (1951): «La langue de Bernard Dechepare». In: *Boletín de la Real Sociedad Vascongada de los Amigos del País 6*, 309—338.

Lafon, René (1962a): «La frontière linguistique du basque et du gascon». In: *Actes du XVe Congrès d'études régionales tenu à Peyrehorade les 5 et 6 mai 1962, Bulletin de la société de Borda*, 7—11.

Lafon, René (1962b): «Sur la voyelle ü en basque». In: *Bulletin de la Société de Linguistique (Paris) 52*, 83—102.

Lhande, Pierre (1962): *Dictionnaire basque—français*, Paris.

Meyer-Lübke, Wilhelm (1924): «Romanobaskisches». In: *Revue internationale des Etudes Basques 14*, 463—485.

Mujika, Urdangarin, Luis Maria (1982): *Latina eta erromanikoaren eragina euskaran (Euskal lexikoaren azterketa bideetan)*. [L'influence du latin et du roman sur le basque d'après le lexique], Donostia/Saint-Sébastien.

Rohlfs, Gerhard (1970): *Le gascon. Etudes de philologie pyrénéenne*, Tübingen.

Sánchez Carrión «Txepetx», José Maria (1991): *Un futuro para nuestro pasado. Claves de la recuperación del Euskara y teoría social de la Lengua*, Donostia/Saint-Sébastien (2ème édition).

Schuchardt, Hugo (1893): *Baskische Studien. Über die Entstehung der Bezugsformen des baskischen Zeitworts*, Wien.

Séguy, Jean (1952): «Basque et gascon dans l'Atlas linguistique de la Gascogne». In: *Orbis 1*, 385—391.

Tournier, André/Lafitte, Pierre (1954): *Lexique français—basque*, Bayonne.

Txillardegi, P. et al. (1987): *Euskal dialektologiaren hastapenak,* [Débuts de la dialectologie basque], s. l.

Videgain, Charles (1983): «Alokutiboa Lopez-engan (1782)», [L'allocutif chez Lopez (1782)]. In: *Iker 2*, 625—649.

Walter, Henriette (1977): *La phonologie du français*, Paris.

Jacques Allières, Toulouse (France)

XII. Sprachkontakte in Südwesteuropa
Language Contacts in Southwestern Europe
Contacts linguistiques en Europe du Sud-Ouest

151. Spanien

1. Einleitung
2. Vorrömische Zeit
3. Römische Periode
4. Germanische Reiche
5. Arabische Epoche
6. Reconquista und kastilische Expansion
7. Sprach(en)kontakt im modernen Spanien
8. Zusammenfassung
9. Bibliographie (in Auswahl)

Tab. 151.1: Typologie der Sprachkontakte

Phasen	Richtungen
A. Von den Anfängen bis ca. 1500 n. Chr.	I. Binnenkontakte II. Von außen nach innen getragene Kontakte
B. Ab ca. 1500 bis heute	III. Von innen nach außen getragene Kontakte

1. Einleitung

Die geographische Lage Spaniens auf der Iberischen Halbinsel, die es sich heute nur mit Portugal, der Kleinstrepublik Andorra und der britischen Besitzung Gibraltar teilen muß, erleichtert Sprachkontakte aller Art sehr: die Küsten sind offen, die Flüsse, Binnengebirge und die Pyrenäen überwindbar. Von alters her hat die Iberische Halbinsel jene Völker, die sich später dort niederließen, angezogen: so schon die vorrömischen Kelten, die periodisch wiederkehrten, so auch die phönizisch-karthagischen Kaufleute oder die modernen Touristenmassen. Demographische Transitbewegungen (wie jene der Vandalen im 5. Jahrhundert oder die der marokkanischen Gastarbeiter heute) sind seltener und als Sprachkontakt kaum erkennbar.

Mit Beginn der auch von ihm selbst eingeleiteten Neuzeit hat Spanien durch imperiale Ausdehnung nach Amerika, Süditalien, den Niederlanden, ferner nach Afrika (Kanarische Inseln, Marokko, Río de Oro) und Asien (Philippinen) die Sprachkontakte enorm vermehrt. Die Geschichte des Sprachkontakts gliedert sich für den spanischen Raum grob in zwei Phasen (A, B) und nach drei Richtungen (I—III) der Kontaktwirkung:

Der Richtungstyp III eröffnet mit den Entdeckungsfahrten und Eroberungen einen eigenen sehr großen Untersuchungsbereich der Folgen (z. B. Amerikanismen) dieser Außenkontakte auf den Binnenbereich. Der Richtungstyp II wird, je näher wir unserer Gegenwart kommen, desto mehr, von der physischen Begegnung miteinander sprechender Menschen (*face to face-communication*) unabhängig. Wie überall tragen die Medien fremdsprachliche Elemente in den hispanophonen Raum hinein und auch hinaus. Dieser Fernkontakt ist in der Regel unidirektional.

Hinsichtlich der Binnenkontakte (Richtungstyp I) läßt sich das neuzeitliche Spanien (Phase B) mit Frankreich vergleichen. Hier wir dort werden im Zuge der staatlichen Einigung die Kontaktzonen an die Peripherie verschoben und dabei verkleinert. Aber stärker als in Frankreich organisiert sich heute die Peripherie (v. a. Katalonien, Baskenland, neuerdings auch Galicien), wodurch Mehrsprachigkeit und Sprachkontakt ins Bewußtsein der Bevölkerung eintreten und politisch brisant werden.

Man muß den Sprachkontakt aus dem Blickwinkel *aller* in Spanien vorkommenden Varietäten untersuchen: Es sind das: Dialekte, Soziolekte, Stile, Fach- und Sondersprachen, die zum Spanischen gerechnet werden, ferner nichtspanische Regionalsprachen (Katalanisch, Baskisch, Galegisch, → Art. 152, 153, 154 und Karte E), die lusischen

Sprachinseln entlang der Grenze mit Portugal (→ Art. 155), die englische Enklave Gibraltar, die an der marokkanischen Küste gelegenen Exklaven Ceuta und Melilla, sowie die weniger durch Ortsfestigkeit oder zeitliche Kontinuität gekennzeichneten Sprachen der Minderheiten (*gitanos*), der Immigranten und der Touristen (darunter auch die Ruheständlerkolonien etwa auf den Kanaren, mit ihrer extremen generationellen Disproportion zwischen Einheimischen und Zugereisten). Wir besprechen zunächst die Sprachkontakte der Standardsprache (bzw. ihrer Grundlage und Vorstufe, des kastilischen Dialekts) und gehen dabei auch auf deren Frühphasen ein. Die chronologische Gliederung innerhalb der Phasen A und B (cf. Tabelle 151.1) lehnt sich an die Sprachgeschichten an (z. B. Lapesa 1980) und betrachtet den Sprachkontakt historisch-typologisch sowie als Kollektivphänomen.

2. Vorrömische Zeit

Schon für die ersten namentlich bekannten Völkerschaften (alle nicht-indoeuropäisch) — Tartesser/Turdetaner im Süden, Iberer im Zentrum und Nordosten, Basken im Norden — ist Einwanderung wahrscheinlich, ohne daß die sprachlichen Spuren ausreichen, das Herkunftsgebiet zweifelsfrei zu lokalisieren. Ab ca. 1000 v. Chr. besiedeln die semitischen Phönizier-Karthager, meistens in Faktoreien, den Südosten und verdrängen griechische Kaufleute an die nordöstliche Küste. In den Nordwesten (später Galicien), den Westen (Portugal) und ins Zentrum wandern die indoeuropäischen Kelten ein. Der überlieferte Name „Keltiberer" bezeugt ethnischen und sprachlichen Kontakt durch Bevölkerungsmischung. Iberer und Basken waren für Wilhelm von Humboldt dasselbe, d. h. er hält die Basken für Nachfolger der Iberer. Dagegen nimmt man heute meist ethnische Verschiedenheit an und führt die im ganzen auf wenige Elemente (z. B. iberisch *ili*-, baskisch *iri*- „Stadt" in Ortsnamen wie *Ilerda* > *Lérida*, cf. Tovar 1977) gegründete Sprachähnlichkeit auf Arealkontakt zurück.

Da die Sprecher der vorrömischen Sprachen den Sprachwechsel zum Lateinischen vollziehen, betrachtete diese die ältere Sprachwissenschaft als „Substratsprachen". Nur die Basken sind bis heute nicht in ihrer Gesamtheit zum Romanischen (Spanisch, Französisch, roman. Dialekte) übergewechselt, wenngleich ihre Sprache zunächst stark latinisiert und dann romanisiert worden ist. Vielleicht hat sogar ein Baskolatein als Mischsprache existiert (cf. Echenique 1987). In älterer Terminologie ist Baskisch daher bis heute „Adstrat" des Kastilischen und zugleich Substrat in den entbaskisierten Gebieten.

Das Griechische tritt ebenfalls, aber diskontinuierlich, in Kontakt: zunächst punktuell und direkt durch die griechischen Faktoreien (Sprachspuren sind Ortsnamen wie *Ampurias* < *Emporion*, „Handelsplatz"), dann vermittelt durch die Gräzismen des Lateinischen (besonders zahlreich sind christenlateinische Gräzismen: *Angelus*, *Episcopus*, etc.) und des Arabischen. Gräzismen entstehen ferner durch die byzantinische Rückeroberung Südspaniens im 7. Jahrhundert, und dann durch den Humanismus (meist Internationalismen, wie *termodinámica*).

3. Römische Periode

Die Römer eroberten die Iberische Halbinsel in ihren Kriegen mit Karthago. Die Latinisierung ist in den sechs Jahrhunderten der politischen Herrschaft (ca. 200 v. Chr.–450 n. Chr.) nicht vollendet worden. Noch aus der Westgotenzeit wird von Landbewohnern berichtet, die des Lateinischen nicht mächtig waren. Die Latinisierung bzw. Romanisierung seit der Herausbildung romanischer Volkssprachen (spätestens im 8. Jahrhundert) ist wegen des erwähnten sprachlichen Widerstands der Basken sogar bis heute nicht abgeschlossen.

Der politische Zwang, unter dem auf der Iberischen Halbinsel großräumige Sprachkontaktsituationen hergestellt werden (durch militärische Eroberung, Befriedungsfeldzüge in unruhigen Provinzen, planmäßige Ansiedlung von Veteranen, die einheimische Frauen heiraten), steht in bemerkenswertem Gegensatz zur offensichtlich von staatlichem Zwang freien Einführung des Lateinischen. Dieses verbreitet sich durch *soziale* (Aufstieg im römischen Staatsapparat verlangt Beherrschung des Lateinischen), durch *rechtliche* (lat. Bürgerrecht für die „hispanici" schon 70 n. Chr.) und *materielle* Faktoren (röm. Friedensordnung statt Stammeskriege, großer Wirtschaftsraum). Mit der Latinisierung wird die Iberische Halbinsel zugleich in den die ganze Mittelmeerwelt umspannenden lat. Sprachkontaktraum eingebunden. Den gleichen großräumigen Außenkontakt eröffnet später das Christentum, das in der Kaiserzeit über die Infrastruktur des heidnischen Staates in den Provinzen Fuß faßt.

Über die Vorstufen des Sprachwechsels sind wir schlecht unterrichtet. Anzunehmen sind progressiver Bilinguismus vor allem auf Seiten der Unterworfenen und Diglossie mit nachfolgendem Verlust der ursprünglichen L_1. Im langen Kontaktprozeß sind diatopisch und diastratisch bedingte Unterschiede nachweisbar. Diatopisch vollzog sich die Latinisierung auf zwei Wegen: von der Baetica (später: Andalusien) durch das Land der keltischen Lusitanier (später: Portugal) ins heutige Galicien, sowie vom heutigen Katalonien in nordöstlicher Richtung den Ebro hinauf. Diastratisch läßt die südliche Latinisierung ein städtisches sowie aristokratisch-konservatives Sprachverhalten erkennen, die nördliche hingegen ein bäuerlich-soldatisch-innovatorisches. Schon die antiken Autoren erkannten diese soziale Differenzierung. Strabon (58 v. Chr.–25 n. Chr.) bemerkt, daß sprachliche Nähe (Keltisch und Lateinisch), ähnliche soziale Organisation (städtische Lebensweise im Süden) und ethnische Mischung (durch römische Kolonien) den Sprachwechsel und zugleich die kulturelle Assimilation fördern. Während zur Zeit Augustus' (30 v. Chr.–14 n. Chr.) die Turdetaner in der Baetica schon zu *togati* (Togaträgern) geworden waren und „ihre Lebensweise in eine völlig römische verwandelt und selbst ihre eigene Sprache vergessen hatten" (Strabon, 3. Buch, III, 15), mußten zur gleichen Zeit die Asturer und Cantabrer erst militärisch befriedet werden, wobei ihnen vermutlich ein eher substandardhaftes Latein vermittelt wurde. Diatopische Differenzierung auch auf römischer Seite behauptet die besonders von Menéndez Pidal (1980) vertretene, sehr kontroversielle „osko-umbrische Hypothese", die aufgrund sprachlicher (v. a. lautlicher Parallelen), bestimmter onomastischer (*Huesca* < *Osca*) sowie zeitgenössischer Hinweise annimmt, daß die nordöstlichen Iberer mit süditalienischen Truppenteilen in Kontakt gekommen sind.

Die betreffenden sprachlichen Merkmale (wie Metaphonie, Konsonantenreduktion *mb* > *m*, *palumba* > *paloma* „Taube") sind zwar nicht exklusiv osko-umbrisch, aber ihr gemeinsames Auftreten ist auffällig. Wissenschaftsgeschichtlich ist diese Hypothese bereits eine Art Sprachkontaktforschung „avant la lettre".

Ab dem 1. Jahrhundert n. Chr. bis in die Spätantike stammen viele Staats- und Kirchenmänner sowie Künstler aus Hispanien: 5 Kaiser (darunter Trajan (98–117) und Hadrian (117–138)), zahlreiche Dichter und Schriftsteller (wie Martial (43–104), Quintilian (ca. 40–ca. 115)), viele Märtyrer und Heilige und auch ein Papst (Damasus). Gleichwohl wirken noch im 2. Jahrhundert in Hadrians „bäurischer Aussprache" kontaktsprachliche Artikulationsgewohnheiten nach.

Die Rekonstruktion der nicht-lateinischen Kontaktsprachen ist schwierig. Nur wenige Eigennamen (Personen-, Stammes-, Orts-, Gewässernamen) können den Tartessen/Turdetanern, Phöniziern und vorrömischen Griechen zugeschrieben werden. Auch die unsichere Kenntnis des Iberischen macht die Identifikation von Kontaktspuren dieser Sprache schwierig. Einige sehr gebräuchliche spanische Wörter wie *perro* „Hund", *manteca* „Butter", *silo* „Silo", *lama* „Schlamm" sind vermutlich vorrömisch. Man schreibt sie besser mit Lapesa (1980) einer nicht näher bestimmbaren vorröm. Kontaktsprache („Substrat") zu. Größere Sicherheit herrscht bei Keltismen und Baskismen. Keltisch und Baskisch haben mit lautlichen, morphologisch-syntaktischen und lexikalischen Interferenzen das moderne Kastilische (betrifft Keltisch und Baskisch), und auch alle ibero-romanischen Varietäten (betrifft Keltisch) stark beeinflußt.

Keltismen: phonetisch: Sonorisierung der intervokalen Verschlußlaute (z. B. *vita* > *vida* „Leben"), -kt- > tš (z. B. *nocte* > *noche* „Nacht"), vielleicht auch Umlaut e > i (*féci* > *hice* „ich machte"). Morphologisch: ein heute unproduktives Suffix *-iego* < *-aikol aeku* (z. B. *mujeriego* „Schürzenjäger"); morphosyntaktisch: Bevorzugung des Nominativ Plural *-os* statt *-i* durch keltische Parallele. Lexikon: regionales Sondervokabular wie *légamo* „lehmiger Schlamm", *abedul* „Birke", *puerco* „Schwein", *toro* „Stier", *colmena* „Bienenkorb", *gorar* „brüten", *tranzar* „flechten". Dazu kamen zahlreiche Ortsnamen, bei denen oft lat.-kelt. Hybridbildungen (wie *Caesarobriga*, heute Talavera) vorkommen. Zu den baskischen Interferenzen (deren Chronologie schwieriger zu bestimmen ist) cf. hier 5. und Art. 154.

4. Germanische Reiche

Der Kontakt zwischen Hispaniern und Germanen vollzieht sich in drei Stufen: (1) Einströmen germanischen Wortgutes in das Lateinische, mit dem die Germanen seit dem 1. Jahrhundert v. Chr. als römische Soldaten und als Siedler auf Reichsgebiet in enge Berührung gekommen sind; (2) Sporadische Germaneneinfälle seit der Mitte des 3. Jahrhunderts, die abgewehrt werden; (3) dauerhafte Landnahme. Letztere gelingt nur den *Sueben* (Galicien und nördliches Portugal, ab 409) und *Westgoten* (ab 466), allerdings nicht den *Alanen* (418 vernichtet) und *Vandalen* (429 Abzug nach Nordafrika). Zunächst wird der Kontakt durch die folgenden Faktoren behindert: (a) Religionsverschiedenheit (Arianismus der Westgoten und Sueben verhindert Heiraten mit den athanasischen Hispaniern), (b) soziale Distanz (die germanischen Eroberer bilden eine Krieger- und Herrenkaste), (c) Rechtsverschiedenheit (germanisches versus römisches Recht), (d) getrennte Siedlungen (die nicht mehr als ca. 200 000 Westgoten besiedeln nur ein relativ kleines zentralspanisches Kerngebiet, wo Ortsnamen wie *Godos* und *Romanos* die Trennung beider Bevölkerungsgruppen anzeigen). Diese Bedingungen machten einen erneuten Sprachwechsel der autochthonen Hispanier unmöglich. Vielmehr latinisierten sich die zugewanderten Germanen, vor allem nach dem Übertritt zum athanasischen Katholizismus (Westgoten: 587/589). Der Wechsel zum Lateinischen wird durch den vorherigen langen Aufenthalt im Römischen Reich (Westgoten fast 100 Jahre in Dakien, dann über 150 Jahre in Westgallien) erleichtert. Im 7. Jahrhundert scheint der Sprachwechsel der Westgoten vollzogen; das Westgotische ist damit zu einem echten „Superstrat" geworden. Der Mangel an Schriftquellen, die Nähe der betreffenden germanischen Sprachen zueinander und die großräumige Verbreitung der Germanismen im Römischen Reich erschweren die Identifikation der spezifisch *westgotischen* bzw. *suebischen* Kontaktspuren. Bedeutsame Reste in Phonetik und Morphosyntax, die bei langer Zweisprachigkeit und Diglossie zu erwarten wären, sind nicht zu erkennen. Phonetische Interferenz liegt bei Lexemen gotischer Herkunft vor, bei denen die Sonorisierung nicht stattfindet: z. B. *espeto* < *spitus* „Spieß", statt **espedo*. Das Suffix *-engo* (< *-ing*) und das Substantiv *guisa* (< *wisa* „Weise") bilden Hybridformen (*realengo* „königlich", *fiera guisa* „wild"). Die zahlreichen lexikalischen Translate bezeugen erwartungsgemäß Besonderheiten der Germanen (Rechtswesen: *werra* > *guerra* ersetzt lat. *bellum* „Krieg"; *ban* cf. span. *bandido*; *raupa* > *ropa* „Geraubtes", „Kleidung"; Gefühl: *orgôli* > *orgullo* „Stolz"; Soziales: *gasalia* > desubst. *agasajar* „bewirten"). Die bis heute häufigen Personennamen germanischen Ursprungs (*Álvaro*, *Gonzalo*, *Rodrigo*) belegen das Prestige der gotischen Oberschicht. Das gilt auch für die durch germanische Interferenz verstärkten, ursprünglich aber vorrömischen Patronymika auf *-ez* (*González*). Die Goten- und Suebenherrschaft beschleunigen die peninsulare sprachliche Eigenentwicklung und die innere Differenzierung durch Verringerung der Innen- und Außenkontakte. Bemerkenswert ist bis heute die positive Identifikation der Hispanier mit ihren germanischen Bezwingern (wo auch die Reconquista mitspielt). Dies bestätigen indirekt die ironische Bezeichnung der Festlandspanier als *godos* auf den Kanarischen Inseln und die Verwendung dieses Volksnamens als Schimpfwort für die Spanier im lateinamerikanischen Unabhängigkeitskrieg. − Ein gewisser germanischer Fernkontakt (vermittelt durch Soldaten, Kaufleute, rückkehrende spanische Gastarbeiter und einreisende Touristen aus „germanischen" Ländern; Richtungstyp II) ist seither nie abgerissen.

5. Arabische Epoche

Die Araberherrschaft und die von Kastilien dominierte christliche Rückeroberung (Reconquista) bestimmen die Geschichte der Iberischen Halbinsel für fast 800 Jahre. Zum Vergleich: ca. 700 Jahre dauerten die Römer- und Westgotenzeit; ca. 500 Jahre die europäische Präsenz in Amerika. In diesen 800 Jahren wurden die bis heute bestehenden Sprachverhältnisse auf der Iberischen Halbinsel festgelegt. Es entstehen und vergehen − gesteuert vom Faktor Religion − eigenartige Sprachkontaktkonstellationen zwischen islamischer und christlicher Bevölkerung. „Die islamische Welt war mächtiger und weiter vorangeschritten in Kriegswesen, Wissenschaften und Künsten als die christliche, so konnte sich ihre Herrschaft in Spanien für lange Zeit festigen" (übersetzt aus Menéndez Pidal 1980, 415). Durch die rasche arabische Eroberung (mit Ausnahme der nordspanischen Gebirge, von wo aus die christlichen Kleinreiche die Reconquista beginnen) kommen Araber und Hispanier (Hispanogoten) sehr plötzlich in einen großräumigen Kontakt. Abfolge von Kriegs- und Friedensperioden, wechselnde Bündnisse, Christen in muslimischen und Muslime in christlichen Diensten, sprachliche bzw. religiöse Intoleranz und Toleranz (letztere meist durch Tribute erkauft) sowie Fanatismus erleichtern oder erschweren ihn, bis dann 1609 – 117 Jahre nach dem Ende der politischen Herrschaft der Araber – Philipp III. (1598–1621) ihn durch Vertreibung der christianisierten Araber (*moriscos*) beendet. Dabei kommt erstmals ein ethnisches Kriterium zur Geltung (cf. Boase 1990).

Der Sprachkontakt bekam, vor allem im Süden, auch eine ethnische Basis durch Mischehen zwischen arabisch-berberischen Invasoren und einheimischen Frauen. In den getrennt wohnenden Gesellschaften der *moros* und *cristianos* bilden sich spiegelbildliche Strukturen, die von Kultur- und Sprachkontakt geprägt sind, wie das auch die arabisch-hispanischen Bezeichnungen ausdrücken:

Tab. 151.2: Unter- und Sondergruppen bei Mauren und Christen

MOROS		CRISTIANOS
mozárabes		mudéjares
muladíes	enaciados	moriscos
renegados		
judíos		judíos

Die *mozárabes* (< arab. *mustá'rib* „der sich den Arabern angleicht") bewahren christliche Religion und roman. Sprache und entwickeln eine eigene Literatur (*jarchas*, arabisch verschriftet). Die *muladíes* (< arab. *muwalladîn* „Adoptierte") sind zum Islam übergetretene Christen, aus christlicher Sicht also „Renegaten". Die *mudéjares* (< arab. *mudággan* „dem erlaubt wurde zu bleiben" in Andalusien; aber *tagarinos* < arab. *tagarí* „Grenzbewohner" im Königreich Aragón), sind Mauren unter christlicher Herrschaft, die ihre Religion bewahren; die *moriscos* zum Christentum Konvertierte. Die *judíos* (Juden), die bekannte mehrsprachige Gelehrte und eine eigene judeo-hispanische Literatur hervorgebracht haben, entwickeln mit dem *judéo-español* eine eigene, schwer lokalisierbare roman. Varietät. Die *enaciados* (< arab. *nâzi'* „Überläufer" x *nâzih* „Vertriebener") sind christliche oder arabische Überläufer, durch Zweisprachigkeit zu Spionagediensten geeignet. Neben verbreiteter individueller Mehrsprachigkeit (z. B. im religiösen Bereich) und vereinzeltem Sprachwechsel hat der lange Kontakt bei den Arabern ein besonderes „hispano-árabe" erzeugt. Es war das ein stark arabisch unterlegtes Kastilisch, wohl eine Mischsprache, die von den Kastiliern *aljamía* (< arab. *'aǧamîya* „fremde Sprache"), von den Arabern auch *romance* (d. h. roman. Volkssprache) genannt und noch im Theater des 17. Jahrhunderts den *moriscos* in den Mund gelegt wurde.

Die Kontaktspuren sind im Kastilischen sehr zahlreich. Die (ca. 4000) lexikalischen Arabismen stellen das zweitstärkste Kontingent nach dem lat. Grundwortschatz dar; es sind überwiegend Substantive, die zentrale Bereiche der arabischen Kultur bezeichnen. Viele sind, über Italien vermittelt, zu Internationalismen geworden (*Alkohol*, *Zucker*). Viele dieser Arabismen stammen ihrerseits aus anderen Sprachen (z. B. *ajedrez* „Schach", Sanskrit; *jazmín*, pers.; *arroz* „Reis", griech.; *alcázar* „Burg", < lat. *castrum*). Griechische Philosophie und Wissenschaft wurden durch die Araber der christlichen Welt wieder zugänglich gemacht. Groß ist der arabische Einfluß in der Toponymie (Ortsnamen: *Alcalá* „die Burg", *Medina* „Stadt", Hybridbildungen: *Almonaster*, Choronyme: *la Mancha*, Hydronyme: wie *Guadalajara* „Steinfluß"). Typisch sind die regelmäßige Bewahrung des arabischen Artikels im Spanischen und Portugiesischen, sein häufiger Abfall im Katalanischen und der konsequente Verlust auf Sizilien (cf. Spanien *azúcar*, it. *zucchero*). Als Vermittler des arabischen Artikels werden die an der Eroberung zahlreich beteiligten Berber angenommen. Sie hätten den arabischen Artikel nicht erkannt und ihn als vermeintlichen Wortbestandteil mit dem Wort an die Mozaraber weitergereicht („Berberthese" Elcocks, 1975, 293).

Seit dem 17. Jahrhundert wird die Zahl der Arabismen durch Obsoletwerdung und semantische Aushöhlung laufend kleiner: z. B. *almófar*, Teil der mittelalterlichen Rüstung; Ersetzung durch Romanismus: *sastre* statt *alfayate*; semantische Verschlechterung: *alguacil* „Gouverneur" → „Gerichtsdiener"). Selten werden alte Arabismen wiederbelebt: cf. wie *azafata* („Stewardess", in Konkurrenz zu *aeromoza*). Man kann die Arabismen nach Gebrauchsfrequenz und grammatischer Gestalt klassifizieren. Während schon Adjektive (cf. *baladí* „wertlos"), Adverbien (z. B. die Hybridform *en balde* „vergebens"), Verben (wie *halagar* „schmeicheln"), grammatische Partikel (Präposition *hasta* „bis", Proform *fulano* „Herr X"), Wortbildungsmorpheme (relationales Suffix -*í*, z. B. in *alfonsí* „zu Alfonso gehörend") selten entlehnt wurden, gilt dies noch mehr für Phonetik und Semantik, wofür der kollektive Bilinguismus offenbar zu gering war. Die als Interferenzen identifizierbaren Fälle sind zudem umstritten. So kann sich s > š [> χ] (sapone > χabon [Lautwert š], heute jabón „Seife") durchaus auch ohne arabischen Einfluß entwickelt haben (cf. Lapesa 1980). Was für die einen ein semantischer calque aus dem Arabischen ist, hat für andere eine roman. Basis (so hidalgo, ojo de agua „Quelle", anochecer en „die Nacht verbringen in"; cf. Coseriu 1961).

6. Reconquista und kastilische Expansion

6.1. Externe Expansion

Die Linien, entlang derer heute der Sprachkontakt zwischen den Sprachen Spaniens verläuft, sind durch die militärische, politische, wirtschaftliche und kulturelle Dominanz Kastiliens während der Reconquista entstanden. In der 1. Phase der Reconquista (8.–10. Jahrhundert) ist ein kollektives Bewußtsein für die Existenz der romances (roman. Volkssprachen), für deren reziproke Divergenz und Distanz zum Lateinischen (das in funktioneller Diglossie für alle offiziellen und kirchlichen Zwecke benutzt wurde) entstanden. Entscheidend für dieses frühe Diglossie-Bewußtsein dürfte das Zusammenspiel zweier Phänomene gewesen sein: (a) die karolingische Lateinreform (cf. Lüdtke 1964, Wright 1982), die zuerst von der fränkisch-spanischen Mark (Grafschaft Barcelona, Katalonien) ausstrahlte und später (11. Jahrhundert) durch die cluniazensische Reform verstärkt wurde; (b) die Existenz von lateinisch-romanischen Interlekten (von den Mozarabern als „latinum circa romanicum" bezeichnet und vom für sie schwer verständlichen „latinum obscurum" geschieden, cf. Lapesa 1980, 163). Vermutlich hat Arealkontakt des aragonesisch-navarresischen romance mit dem Baskischen (einer vom Lateinischen total verschiedenen Varietät) die Entstehung der ältesten hispanoromanischen Texte begünstigt (Glossen aus den Klöstern San Millán und Silos, um 1000). — In die mittlere Phase der Reconquista fällt der Ausbau des Kastilischen zur Literatur- (Cantar de Mío Cid, Mitte 12. Jahrhundert) und Wissenschaftssprache (Alfons der Weise, 1252–1282, und seine Toledaner Übersetzungsanstalt, 2. Hälfte 13. Jahrhundert). Die hispanischen romances treten durch Internationalisierung der Reconquista (Teilnahme französischer und okzitanischer Ritter; Pilgerströme nach Santiago de Compostela) v. a. in Kontakt mit dem Französischen (frühe Gallizismen wie homenaje „Ehrung", mesón „Gasthaus").

In der letzten Phase der Reconquista wird mit der Vereinigung der Königreiche Kastilien und Aragón (einschließlich Kataloniens) im Jahr 1479 der gesamte Norden der Iberischen Halbinsel der Kastilianisierung geöffnet (Asturien-León bereits im 11. Jahrhundert, Galicien im 13. Jahrhundert mit Kastilien vereinigt, Navarra ab dem 15. Jahrhundert kastellanisiert). Im Zentrum hat das nach Süden keilförmig vordringende Kastilische („la cuña castellana", Menéndez Pidal) die lokalen ibero-romanischen romances gespalten und durch seine Expansion nach Südwesten und Südosten die zunächst eigenständigen Reconquistas Asturien-Leóns, Navarras und Aragón-Kataloniens gehemmt. Nur die galicisch-portugiesische Reconquista konnte ungehindert die Algarve erreichen. Nach Abschluß der Reconquista (1492: Eroberung des Königreichs Granada) wird durch Vertreibung der Juden der dortige Sprachkontakt abrupt beendet („judéo-español" wird Außendialekt im osmanischen Reich), nachdem schon vorher durch Ghettoisierung der Mauren die Kontaktsituationen stark eingeschränkt worden sind. Ähnliches erfolgte auch im 16. Jahrhundert mit den moriscos.

Die relativ große sprachliche Homogenität in den wiedereroberten und planmäßig wiederbesiedelten Regionen Zentralspaniens erklärt sich durch Dialektausgleich mit Dominanz des Kastilischen unter den Neusiedlern. Die Sprachentwicklung im Süden wird heute kontrovers beurteilt. Nach älterer Ansicht vollzog sich ein Varietätenwechsel: Die während der Araberherrschaft geschwächten Mozaraber hätten weitgehend das Kastilische der Eroberer angenommen, aus dem durch relativ geringen mozarabischen Einfluß ein sogenannter sekundärer Dialekt (Coseriu 1981) entstanden ist. Von andalusischer Seite wird dagegen behauptet, das Andalusische sei ein ebenso primärer Dialekt wie das Kastilische, Asturisch-Leonesische oder Navarresische, es sei lediglich sekundär kastellanisiert worden (Mondéjar 1986). — In den Außenzonen der asturisch-leonesischen Reconquista (Extremadura) und der aragonesisch-katalanischen Reconquista (Königreich Murcia) werden durch die zunächst gemeinsame Reconquista und Besiedlung, dann durch laterales Vordringen des Kastilischen erst Mischvarietäten, dann schließlich regionale Varietäten des Kastilischen herausgebildet. — Das in der Zeit der Reconquista sehr dynamische Kastilische hat sich so über die Iberische Halbinsel verbreitet, wobei seine Hauptcharakteristika aus dem Arealkontakt mit dem Baskischen herrühren. Von allen noch heute auf der Iberischen Halbinsel bestehenden Sprachkontakten ist der zwischen Kastilisch und Baskisch immerhin der älteste: er entstand im Ausgangsgebiet der kastilischen Reconquista (Altkastilien, Hauptort Burgos). Für Bilinguismus, vielleicht sogar Sprachmischung, spricht außer lexikalischer Entlehnung (wie *izquierdo* „links") v. a. eine Reihe lautlicher Merkmale, die zu den Innovationen des Kastilischen zählen und seine Sonderstellung in der Iberoromania bedingen: lat. F > h → Ø (FOLIA > *hoja*; Verlust von anlautendem V zugunsten von b; frikative Varianten der stimmhaften Okklusiva B, D, G; prothetisches a vor R- (*arrepentir*); Reduktion der lat. Nexus PL-, CL-, FL- (und Palatalisierung, z. B. *flamma* > *llama*) und das einfache Vokalsystem haben baskische Analogien und sind in ihrer Bündelung auffällig (cf. Echenique 1987).

6.2. Interne Expansion

Der externen Expansion des Kastilischen folgt zeitverschoben die interne Expansion im Königreich Kastilien, und zwar in die Domänen des Lateinischen, des zur Minderheitensprache gewordenen Arabischen und des Galegischen als Sprache der lyrischen Dichtung. Die Ablösung des Lateinischen durch das Kastilische vollzieht sich über Jahrhunderte. Im Rechtswesen herrscht zunächst pragmatische Funktionsteilung: Lateinisch für die rechtsgültige Version, Kastilisch (oder andere *romances*) für solche Texte, die von dem sich ständig vergrößernden Kreis der Lateinunkundigen verstanden werden sollten (Tilander 1967). Ab der Mitte des 13. Jahrhunderts überwiegt das Kastilische in offiziellen Dokumenten. Die Vorstellung, das Kastilische sei im Mittelalter zu einem bestimmten Zeitpunkt durch Gesetz zur offiziellen Sprache des Rechts erklärt worden, scheint eine Projektion der Renaissance nach rückwärts zu sein (González Ollé 1978). Im Unterrichtswesen und in der Wissenschaft wird das Lateinische zu Gunsten des Kastilischen vorsichtig durch Philipp II. (1583 und 1588) eingeschränkt, aber erst 1813 offiziell per Dekret durch das Kastilische ersetzt. Dagegen versucht im kirchlichen Bereich die Inquisition seit ca. 1550, das Kastilische durch das Lateinische zurückzudrängen, freilich ohne dauerhaften Erfolg.

In der durch Inquisition und Türkengefahr angeheizten Atmosphäre des 16. Jahrhunderts werden die *moriscos* ihrer zunächst garantierten religiösen, rechtlichen und auch sprachlichen Sonderrechte (Gebrauch des Arabischen) beraubt. Dabei werden erstmals in der spanischen Geschichte Gesetze zum Verbot einer Minderheitensprache erlassen (1526; Vorspiel zur Vertreibung der *moriscos*). Sicher waren politische und nicht national-staatliche Gründe dafür ausschlaggebend (wie im 19. Jahrhundert) (cf. Eberenz 1992, 370 f). Doch wird A. Nebrijas Maxime „siempre la lengua fue compañera del imperio" (in seiner *Gramática castellana*, 1492, der ersten vollständigen Grammatik einer roman. Sprache überhaupt) als Rechtfertigung der Instrumentalisierung der Sprache durch die Herrschaft gedeutet. Nicht nur „hat die Sprache immer die Herrschaft begleitet" (dazu Asensio 1960), sie darf von dieser — ganz wie ab dem 19. Jahrhundert — auch gegen andere Sprachen verwendet werden. — Als Musterfall von Diglossie in der schönen Literatur gilt die Verwendung des Galegischen bzw. Galegisch-Portugiesischen in der Lyrik durch kastilische Autoren im Hochmittelalter. Ab Ende des 14. Jahrhunderts dringt das Kastilische massiv in diese Domäne ein, nachdem schon vorher das Kastilische mit nur mehr stereotypen Lusismen(Galegismen dekoriert worden war (Lapesa 1953, Vázquez Cuesta 1981).

6.3. Normierung und Sprachpolitik

Interne und externe Expansion des Kastilischen werden zweifelsohne gestützt durch das Prestige, das seine Literatur ab dem 15. Jahrhundert gewinnt. Hinzu kommt gegenüber den zurückgedrängten Dialekten und Regionalsprachen ein zeitlicher Vorsprung in Normierung und Kodifizierung (durch Grammatiken, Orthographielehren, Gründung der Real Academia Española 1713; 1726—1736 deren einflußreiches *Diccionario de Autoridades*). Demgegenüber ist neuerdings behauptet worden, daß nicht das „reine" Kastilische, sondern eine Koiné auf kastilischer Basis mit substantiellen Beiträgen aus den Randsprachen alltägliches Verständigungsmittel an der Peripherie gewesen sei. Erst seit der aggressiven Sprachpolitik der Bourbonen (2. Hälfte des 18. Jahrhunderts) sei das bislang friedliche

Vordringen der Ausgleichskoiné „español" durch einen Bewußtseinswandel der zum sprachlichen Widerstand entschlossenen Peripherie aufgehalten worden (López García 1985). Die Annahme, daß die *formelle* Kastellanisierungspolitik ihre Gegner gestärkt habe und deshalb auf lange Sicht ein „Fehler" gewesen sei, klingt plausibel. Sie verdeckt aber den wohl wichtigsten Vektor der Kastilianisierung, nämlich die vom Zentrum ausgehende sozioökonomische Modernisierung der Peripherie, die ab dem 19. Jahrhundert zur Landflucht und zur Kastellanisierung besonders des städtischen Bürgertums führt (vor allem in Galicien, Navarra, Valencia). Umgekehrt fördert heute die wirtschaftliche Kraft der bürgerlichen Schichten Kataloniens und des Baskenlandes den Widerstand gegen den Kastellanisierungsprozeß.

Von Karl III. (1768) bis Franco (1945) versucht eine lange Reihe von Sprachgesetzen, dem Kastilischen Exklusivität in immer neuen Domänen zu verschaffen, nicht nur in vom Staat kontrollierten Bereichen wie Schule und Universität, Verwaltung und Rechtswesen, sondern auch in der öffentlichen Mündlichkeit, so schon 1801 im Theater. Zuletzt wird unter dem Galicier Franco ab 1938/1939 der Gebrauch des Katalanischen — Hauptgegner des Kastilischen — in der Öffentlichkeit überhaupt untersagt. Dabei soll durch Verbot nichtkastilischer *Firmen-*, *Marken-*, *Schiffs-*, *Orts-* und sogar der *Vor*namen der Einzelne in seiner wirtschaftlichen Tätigkeit, seinem Lebensraum und in seiner sprachlichen Identität zwangskastellanisiert werden (cf. Benet 1979, Ferrer 1986). Die ideologische Begründung dafür hatte schon der Diktator Primo de Rivera (1923—1930) in seinem Appell an die Katalanen, Basken und Galicier geliefert, das Kastilische als „einziges Mittel, die rassischen und geistigen Grundlagen Großspaniens zu stärken und zu erweitern" anzunehmen (cf. Morales et alii 1976, 160). Die Dauer des Kastellanisierungsprozesses, seine Steigerung unter den Frankisten sowie die mehrmalige Wiederholung vieler Gesetze (besonders im Schulbereich) zeigen aber auch den sich verhärtenden Widerstand der Peripherie dagegen auf.

7. Sprach(en)kontakt im modernen Spanien

7.1. Verfassungsrechtliche Regelungen

Ähnlich wie die republikanische Verfassung von 1931 erklärt die jetzige Verfassung (1978, Art. 3 der Präliminarien) den Reichtum Spaniens an sprachlicher Vielfalt zum schützenswerten „patrimonio cultural", bekräftigt den Status des „castellano" als offizielle Sprache des Staates, die jeder Bürger kennen müsse („deber de conocer") und gebrauchen dürfe („derecho de usar"), verleiht den übrigen Sprachen Spaniens („las demás lenguas españolas") koffiziellen Status in den Autonomen Regionen („Comunidades Autónomas", s. Abb. 151.1) und überläßt deren Verfassungen die Einzelregelungen. Letzteres betrifft v. a. die Entscheidung, was weitere „lenguas españolas" oder „modalidades lingüísticas" (interpretierbar als Oberbegriff, als „Mundart" oder sogar als „Ausdrucksweise") seien und welche Rechte und Funktionen jede Varietät habe. Das Spannungsfeld zwischen Kastilisch und Regionalsprache repräsentiert sich heute wie in Tabelle 151.3 dargestellt.

Tab. 151.3: Domänenverteilung in den Autonomen Regionen

	offiz. Domänen	nicht-offiz. Domänen (berufl., private)
Kastilisch	Status geschützt, muß maximale symmetr. Aufteilung der Domänen akzeptieren	Status geschützt, auf Verlangen des Individuums
Regionalsprache	kann jede Domäne besetzen, muß Kopräsenz des Kast. dulden	Status geschützt, muß als Minimum passive Kenntnis des Kastilischen beim Individuum dulden

Konsequenzen für das Kastilische: keine formelle Zwangskastellanisierung, keine Exklusivität in offiziellen Domänen (Kopräsenz), aber zumindest obligatorischer asymmetrischer Bilinguismus beim Sprecher. Konsequenzen für die Regionalsprache: keine Exklusivität in offiziellen Domänen, kein regionalsprachlicher Monolinguismus beim Sprecher. Anders als in der Verfassung von 1931 bleibt aber offen, ob die Kenntnis der Regionalsprache obligatorisch gemacht werden kann, bzw. ob kastilischer Monolinguismus bewahrt werden darf.

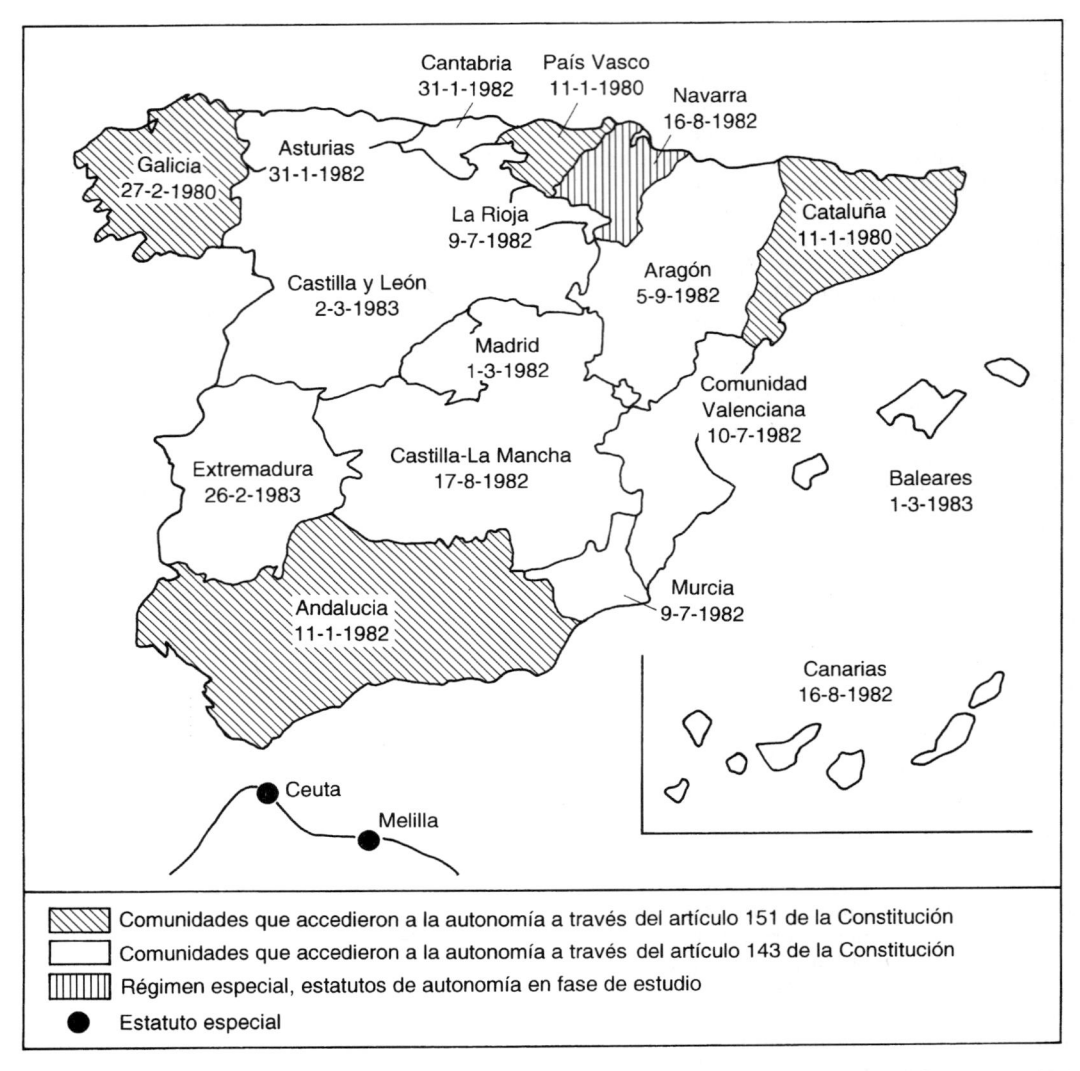

Abb. 151.1: Entwicklung des Autonomisierungsprozesses in Spanien seit 1978 (nach: El País, 22. 10. 1994, S. 15)

7.2. Die größeren Regionalsprachen

7.2.1. Baskisch

Abb. 151.2 verdeutlicht den kontinuierlichen Rückgang des Baskischen in der Neuzeit. Wilhelm von Humboldts Prophezeiung (*Die Vasken*, 1801), Spanisch und Französisch werden bis 1900 das gesprochene Baskisch verdrängt haben, hat sich nicht erfüllt. Aber durch baskische Emigration, kastellanophone Immigration, Kastellanisierung der Basken, Sprachverbot am Ende des Bürgerkrieges, Prestigeverlust bei den Sprechern selbst, drohte das Baskische zur Minderheitensprache zu werden. Dem wird seit Anfang des 20. Jahrhunderts gegengesteuert: Zunächst — beflügelt vom ausländischen wissenschaftlichen Interesse am Baskischen — durch Zeitschriften, Kongresse, Vereinigungen, Akademie (1919) und lexikographische sowie grammatische Darstellungen, dann — 1936 bis 1939 — durch politisch-rechtliche Maßnahmen, ab den 50er Jahren erneut durch Förderung von Kultur und Literatur, ab den 60er Jahren durch praktischen Schulunterricht (*ikastolas*, oft gestützt von Priestern), ab 1968 mittels Normativisierung auf allen Sprachebenen (durch die Baskische

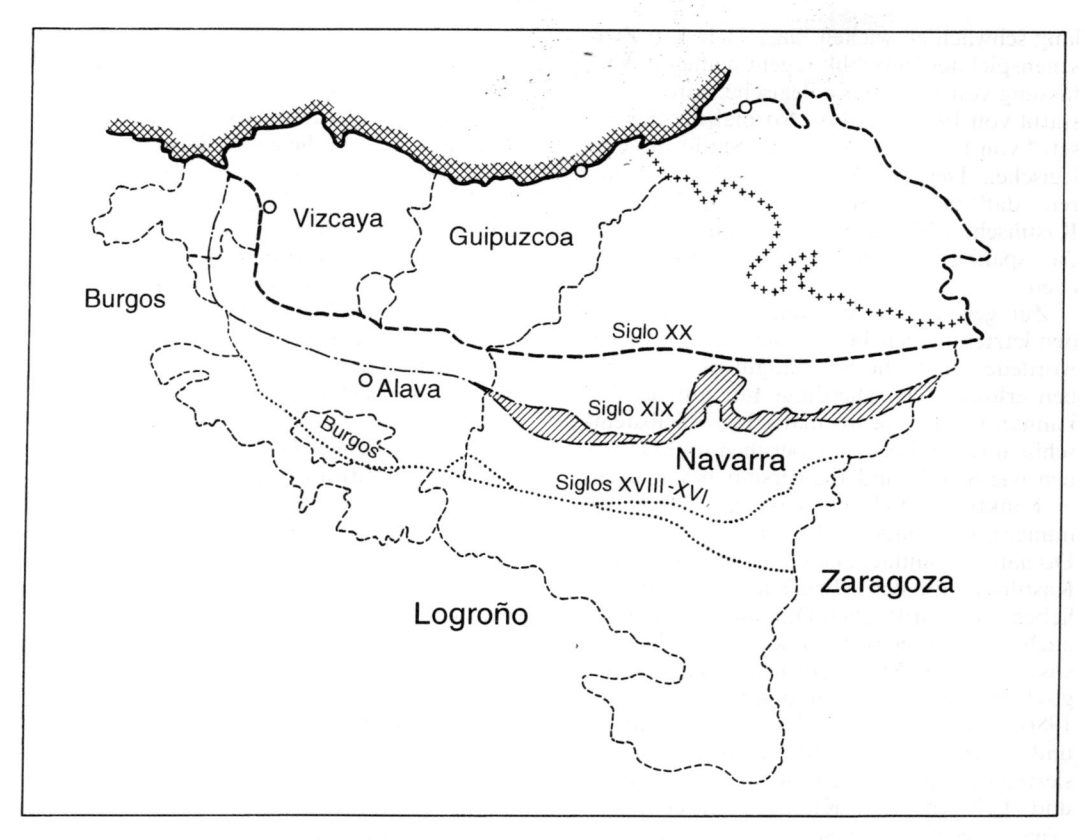

Abb. 151.2: Rückgang des Baskischen in der Neuzeit (nach: Echenique 1987, 109)

Akademie *Euskaltzaindia*) und Schaffung einer vereinheitlichten Sprache (*euskera batua*, „gesammeltes/vereinigtes Baskisch"), schließlich ab 1979 durch das neue Autonomiestatut (cf. Überblick bei Echenique 1987). Ob *euskera batua* im dialektal stark zerklüfteten Baskenland als Standardsprache angenommen wird (auch im französischen Baskenland), ist noch nicht entschieden. Anders als das Katalanische muß sich das Baskische die ihm jetzt offenstehenden offiziellen Domänen (Verwaltung, Rechtswesen) nicht *wieder-*, sondern *erstmals* erobern. Wenn die kastilischen Interferenzen beseitigt werden sollten, müßten sie zunächst umfassend und systematisch erfaßt werden (Forschungsdesiderat). Den neueren Sprachstand beschreibt ein von der baskischen Regierung 1986 herausgegebenes soziolinguistisches Kartenwerk. Zur weiteren Information → Art. 150 und 154.

7.2.2. Galegisch

Das moderne Galegisch (analog zur Selbstbezeichnung *galego*; statt *galicisch* zur besseren Unterscheidung vom slav. *galizisch* „westukrainisch") ist durch starke diglossische Einengung, Sprachmischung und gleichzeitige Bindung an zwei Standardsprachen (Portugiesisch und Kastilisch) in einer schwierigeren Lage als das Baskische oder Katalanische. Als sprachliche Individualität wird ein Galegisch-Asturisch zu Beginn der Reconquista im Königreich Asturien erkennbar. Nach Gründung der Grafschaft Portugal (1095) innerhalb Galiciens, dann des Königreiches Portugal (nach 1139) und seiner Ausbreitung in der Reconquista entsteht durch Kontakt mit dem Mozarabischen ein „neogallego" (Coseriu 1987), nämlich das Portugiesische, das die mittelalterliche literarische Tradition des Galegischen fortsetzt und eine eigene Standardsprache ausbildet. Das Galegische bleibt bis ins 14./15. Jahrhundert im literarischen und religiösen Gebrauch und wird dann vom Kastilischen abgelöst. Nach ca. 500jähriger Unterbrechung beginnt 1863 mit Rosalías de Castros *Cantares gallegos* die neugalegische Literatur, die sich aber — besonders im Vergleich zur katalanischen — bislang schwach entwickelt hat. Nach dem Zwischenspiel der Republik regeln heute die Verfassung von 1978, das galegische Autonomiestatut von 1981 und das „Normalisierungsgesetz" von 1983 den rechtlichen Status des Galegischen. Der Zwangsbestimmung des letzteren, daß in der Schule Galegisch (neben Kastilisch) obligatorisch sei, hat allerdings die spanische Zentralregierung widersprochen.

Zur gegenwärtigen Sprachlage hat die in den letzten beiden Jahrzehnten sehr aktiv gewordene galegische Soziolinguistik Stichproben erhoben, die allerdings nur auf der bekanntermaßen problematischen Selbsteinschätzung der Befragten beruhen und Domänen wie Schule und Universität bevorzugen. — Funktional-diglossisch ist das Galegische immer noch weitgehend Sprache der privaten Domänen (Familie, Nachbarn, Freunde), das Kastilische die der offiziellen, formell-mündlichen und schriftlichen Domänen. So bleiben auch die Printmedien i. a. kastilisch; die akustisch-visuellen Medien öffnen sich dem Galegischen (*Radio Galega* und *Televisión Galega*, 1986). Die größten Erfolge hat die amtliche und durch Privatinitiative gestützte Galegisierungskampagne vermutlich bei Schülern und Lehrern. Die Kirche dagegen bleibt „Agent der Kastellanisierung" (Monteagudo/Santamarina 1993, 143).

Der Varietätenkontakt ist nach Monteagudo/Santamarina (1993, 143) nach einer jahrhundertelangen stabilen Funktionsverteilung (A) heute komplex und konfliktreich geworden (B) (Tab. 151.4).

A	B	
Kastilisch	Standard-kastilisch	Standard-galegisch
→	↓	↓
Populäres Galegisch	Regional-kastilisch	Populäres Galegisch
	↔	

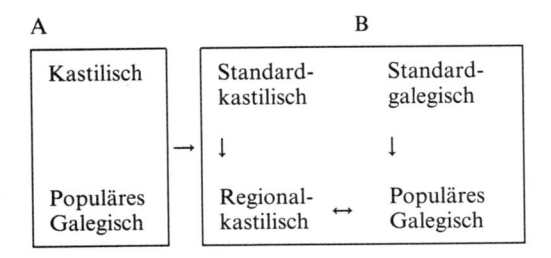

Tab. 151.4: Funktionsverteilung von Kastilisch und Galegisch in Galicien früher (A) und heute (B)

„Standardkastilisch": gesprochen von den monolinguen jüngeren Angehörigen der städtischen oberen mittleren und höheren Schicht. „Regionalkastilisch": gesprochen von städtischer Mittel- und Unterschicht und von ländlicher Mittelschicht; meist beherrschen diese Sprecher auch populäres Galegisch. „Standardgalegisch", das heute ausgebaut wird und dem Standardkastilischen seine Domänen streitig machen soll, wird erst von wenigen aktiv beherrscht. Das populäre Galegisch umfaßt die ganze Breite der dialektalen Variation (von denen der neue *Atlas Lingüístico Galego* ein genaueres Bild gibt) und wird v. a. von den ländlichen und städtischen Schichten gesprochen.

In der gegenwärtigen Sprachplanung des Standardgalegischen stehen sich vor allem zwei Richtungen gegenüber. Es eint sie die Abgrenzung gegen das Kastilische, es trennt sie der Grad der Annäherung ans Portugiesische. Ein puristisches, sich am mittelalterlichen literarischen Galegisch orientierendes „galego identificado" propagieren die *Real Academia Galega* und das *Instituto da Lingua Galega*. Ihre *Normas ortográficas e morfolóxicas do idioma galego* (1982) sind offizialisiert. Im Gegensatz zu diesen „Autonomisten" wünschen die besonders von portugiesischer Seite geförderten „Reintegrationisten" (organisiert in der *Associaçiom Galega da Lingua*) die sprachliche Annäherung ans Portugiesische. Das Galegische würde nach Ansicht der Autonomisten „satelizado". Im Standardgalegischen sollten Konvergenzen mit dem Portugiesischen bevorzugt werden. Extremisten dieser Richtung wollen sogar das Portugiesische als Standardvarietät in Galizien einführen, womit das eigentliche Gallego zum ländlichen Dialekt des Portugiesischen würde. Dies entspricht sicher nicht dem wachsenden Eigensprachlichkeitsgefühl der Bevölkerung Galiziens. Wie das Schicksal des Galegischen in Brasilien lehrt, könnte allzu große Nähe zur Dachsprache zum Sprachentod führen. Die Einführung des Portugiesischen würden außerdem weder der spanische Staat noch die gerade in den hispanophonen Ländern sehr aktiven Auslandsgalegos dulden (Coseriu 1987).

7.2.3. Katalanisch

7.2.3.1. Revisionserfolge

Unter den Regionalsprachen Spaniens haben die katalanischen Revisionsbemühungen den größten Erfolg (cf. Strubell i Trueta 1993, 175). Als günstige Voraussetzungen für das Wiedereinrücken in die alten Funktionen gelten: (a) die geringe dialektale Differenzierung des Katalanischen (traditionell zweigeteilt in Ostkatalanisch mit Nord-, Zentralkatalanisch, Balearisch und Algheresisch — in der nordwestsardischen Stadt L'Alguer/Alghero

— sowie Westkatalanisch mit Nordwestkatalanisch und Valenzianisch); (b) die ab 1978 wiedererrungene Ko-Offizialität in den autonomen Regionen Katalonien, Valencia und Balearen (einzige offizielle Sprache ist Katalanisch in Andorra; nicht offiziell ist das nordkatalanische Rossellonesisch im französischen Département Pyrénées-Orientales; das betrifft auch das Katalanische in Ostaragón, Murcia und Alghero); (c) die zunehmende literarische Produktivität seit der *Renaixença* im 19. Jahrhundert, heute auch bei der Sachliteratur und wissenschaftlichen Werken; (d) die traditionelle Unterstützung der Kirche; (e) die auch zur Zeit der Bourbonen und Francos nie ganz aufgegebene Verwendung in offiziellen Domänen (z. B. in Verhandlungen lokaler Organisationen); (f) das Engagement bekannter Soziolinguisten, Sprachplaner, Philologen, unterstützt durch ausländisches Interesse; (g) umsichtige Kodifikation einer Standardnorm (*normativització*, vor allem dank Pompeu Fabra, gefördert vom einflußreichen Institut d'Estudis Catalans (Barcelona) und von den katalanischen Behörden; (h) staatlich unterstützte Statusplanung (*normalització*) zwecks Akzeptanz- und Domänenerweiterung besonders in der Schule und in den Print- und audio-visuellen Medien.

7.2.3.2. Hindernisse

(a) Immigration: Nach den verfügbaren Daten erreicht in den wirtschaftlich aktivsten Zonen (Industrie, intensive Landwirtschaft, Tourismus; cf. Karte in COM 1989, 35) die Immigration kastellanophoner Sprecher Anteile bis 50% an der Bevölkerung. Oftmals konzentriert in kompakten Gruppen wohnend (wie im Industriegürtel um Barcelona) regeln die Immigranten ihre Außenkontakte mit Katalanophonen auf Kastilisch (Bastardes 1987, 156). Zur Zeit der intensivsten Einwanderung (60er Jahre) bestand noch keine Möglichkeit, die Immigranten über die Schule zu katalanisieren. Trotz oftmals positiver Einstellung der Immigranten zu Katalanisch (Strubell i Trueta 1993, 192) ist es weiterhin ungewiß, ob aus diesen Kreisen neue Sprecher des Katalanischen zu gewinnen sind (skeptisch Lüdtke 1991, 241). Statt Spontansprecherkompetenz scheint am ehesten passiver Bilinguismus (Verstehen des Katalanischen, zum Teil auch Lesen) bei den Immigranten erreichbar. Trotz des Katalanischunterrichts in der Schule ist in Gebieten mit hoher Immigration (Barcelona, Cornellà) bei Grundschülern die Rate der Katalanisch*leser* immer noch höher als die der Katalanisch*sprecher*, was als „Latinisierung" oder „Irlandisierung" des Katalanischen Anlaß zur Sorge gibt (COM 1989, 41).

(b) Progressive Kastellanisierung: Dieser Prozeß (bis hin zum Sprachwechsel) schreitet, soweit aus den Daten erkennbar, auch bei ursprünglich katalanophonen Einheimischen voran, v. a. in Valencia, Alacant/Alicante, Eivissa/Ibiza, Formentera und Mallorca (Stadt). Dort geht auch bei Schulkindern selbst das Verstehen des Katalanischen zurück. Weniger dramatisch ist die Lage in ländlichen Gegenden, wo (wie in Xátiva/Játiva, südlich von Valencia) Verstehen und Sprechen des Katalanischen auch bei Schülern besser entwickelt sind, die Lese- und Schreibfertigkeiten aber stagnieren. Allgemein, besonders außerhalb der katalanischen Kerngebiete, ist ungewiß, ob das durch schulische Katalanisierung erreichte Sprechvermögen zu einem effektiven Spontangebrauch im Normalalltag führt.

(c) Beschränkung auf Mündlichkeit: Die „alte Gewohnheit der Katalanen, kastilisch zu schreiben" (Bastardes 1987, 156) — vergleichbar mit dem Gebrauch des Lateinischen für schriftliche Zwecke in früherer Zeit — ist trotz der gegenwärtigen katalanischen Schulpolitik noch nicht bereinigt worden. Für alle katalanisch-sprachigen Gebiete (ohne Roussillon und Alghero) zeigt die aus COM 1989, 41, adaptierte Abbildung 151.3, daß das Katalanische mehrheitlich eine gesprochene Sprache ist.

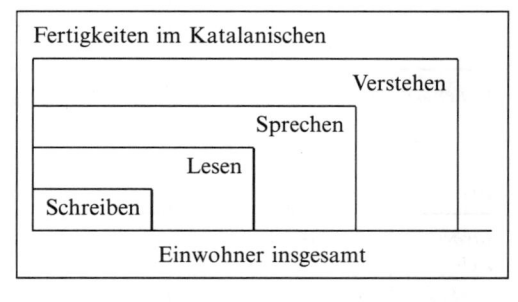

Abb. 151.3: Schichtung der vier Beherrschungsmodalitäten des Katalanischen (nach COM 1989, 41)

(d) Partikularismus: Einer effektiven Rekatalanisierung stehen Koordinationsmangel zwischen den katalanischen Regionen und ein gewisser Sprachseparatismus, v. a. in Valencia, entgegen (cf. Lüdtke 1991, 241). — Ob unter diesen Voraussetzungen funktionales

Gleichgewicht zwischen Katalanisch und Kastilisch erreichbar ist, bleibt abzuwarten. Ein radikaler Sprachwechsel zugunsten des Katalanischen scheint illusorisch und auch nicht mit den Interessen der Sprecher vereinbar.

7.2.3.3. Sprachkontaktfolgen

Auf die vielfältigen alten Sub- und Superstrateinflüsse und die neueren frz., okz., engl. (Menorca) und it./sard. (Alghero) Adstratkontakte sei hier nochmals hingewiesen. Der kastilische Einfluß ist überall am bedeutendsten. Innerhalb des Katalanischen ist er wie folgt gestaffelt: höher in der gesprochenen Sprache, in den städtischen Varietäten, in der Lexik; weniger in der geschriebenen Sprache, auf dem Lande und in der Grammatik. Die lexikalischen Interferenzen (cf. Bruguera 1986, Colón, 1976) können chronologisch geordnet werden. (Bsp.: *amo* „Herr", *boda* „Hochzeit", 14. Jahrhundert; *apoiar* „unterstützen", *burro* „Esel", Siglo de Oro; *túnel*, *vacuna* „Impfung", 19./20. Jahrhundert etc.). Sie betreffen alle technische (etc.) Innovationen, die aus dem oder über das Kastilische kamen (z. B. Amerikanismen wie *gautxo* „Gaucho"). Doch sprechen für die relative Vitalität des Katalanischen Nachbildungen („calques", wie *finestreta* nach *ventanilla* „Schalterfenster") und semantische Veränderungen katalanischer Wörter unter kastilischem Einfluß. Oft stehen umgangssprachliche Kastilianismen (wie *buscar*) literarischen Katalanismen (wie *cercar*) gegenüber. Im *Atlas Lingüístic de Catalunya* (Griera 1923) finden sich zahlreiche ältere Kastilianismen (marginal: *espejo* „Spiegel", statt kat. *mirall/espill*; weitere Verbreitung: kast. *servilleta*/frz. *servieta* „Serviette" statt angestammtem *tovalló/tocaboques*).

Grammat. Kastilianismen: Konstruktion des direkten pers. Objekts mit *a*: *busca a Joan* „er sucht Johann" (Badia i Margarit 1991, 147); *anar a* + Inf. (nach kast. *ir a* + Inf.) in der Bedeutung eines nahen Futurs (Lüdtke 1984, 78). Die Katalanismen im Kastilischen sind auch sehr zahlreich und zum Teil überaus gebräuchlich (cf. *faena* „schwere Arbeit", *papel* „Aufgabe", „Rolle", *pólvora* „Pulver", *añoranza* „Sehnsucht"; Colón 1976, → Art. 153).

7.3. Die kleineren Regionalsprachen

7.3.1. Übersicht

(Siehe Tabelle 151.5.)

7.3.2. Erläuterungen

Unbehandelt bleiben Kanarisch, Extremeño (in Extremadura), Andalusisch und Murcianisch, da sie von den Sprechern selbst als Varietäten des Kastilischen betrachtet und für

Tab. 151.5: Die kleineren Regionalsprachen im Vergleich

	amtl. Bezeichnung	Ko-offiziell	Normierung (Kodifiz.)	Normalisierung (Domänenerweiterung)	Sprachbewußtsein	Sprachkonflikt	digloss. Hauptfunktion	Hauptkontaktsprache
Aranesisch	Sprache	+	begonnen	begonnen	hoch	–	Heimsprache	Kast./(Kat.)
Aragonesisch	„Modalität"	–	versucht	gefordert	schwach	kaum	Heimsprache	Kast.
Navarresisch	nicht erwähnt	–	–	–	–	–	(Regionalvarietät des Kast.)	Kast.
Leonesisch	nicht erwähnt	–	–	–	–	–	Heimsprache	Kast.
Asturisch	nicht spezifiziert	–	begonnen	gefordert	zunehmend	beginnend	Heimsprache	Kast./Galeg.
Regionalsprache in Gibraltar	–	–	–	–	hoch	–	Heim- u. Verkehrssprache	Engl.

sie, wie im Falle des Andalusischen, unseres Wissens keine organisierten linguistischen Forderungen nach Statusverbesserungen, Normierung oder Normalisierung erhoben werden. Kontaktfolgen ließen sich allerdings aufzeigen, besonders im Verhältnis Andalusisch-Kastilisch (cf. Mondéjar 1992, 504 f). Das gilt auch für das früh kastilianisierte Leonesische und noch mehr für das Navarresische, die hier als Beispiele für „primäre Dialekte" stehen. Beide sind durch Kontakt mit dem Kastilischen zu einer Art „Substrat"-sprachen geworden. Das andalusisch geprägte Regionalspanische in Gibraltar koexistiert friedlich mit dem Englischen, der offiziellen Sprache. Lexikalische Interferenz in beide Richtungen ist häufig (cf. Cavilla Ote 1978). — Am günstigsten ist innerhalb Spaniens die Situation des Aranesischen, einer Außenvarietät des Gaskognischen, gesprochen im Val d'Aran (span. Valle de Arán, Hauptort Vielha/Viella: ca. 6000 Einwohner, politisch zu Katalonien gehörend; cf. Winkelmann 1989). Im katalanischen Autonomiestatut als „llengua aranesa" bezeichnet, ist sie 1987 in ihrem Gebiet für den Verkehr mit der katal. Regierung und für den talinternen mündlichen und schriftlichen Verkehr in allen Domänen offizialisiert und als optionales Schulfach etabliert worden. Aranesisch ist Heimsprache von fast 60% der einheimischen, v. a. älteren Bevölkerung und steht in Kontakt mit Kastilisch (Amtssprache und Sprache von fast 30% der Bevölkerung, die alle Immigranten sind); Französisch (und Okzitanisch) fungieren als Verkehrssprachen (ca. 4%), ebenso Katalanisch (weniger als 9%). Ein *Centre de Normalisacion lingüística dera Val d'Aran* hat für die Orthographie des Aranesischen entsprechende Normen veröffentlicht.

Das Aragonesische, dessen „verschiedene sprachliche Modalitäten" das Autonomiestatut schützt, wurde vom *Consello d'a Fabla aragonesa* (1987) außeramtlich und ohne wissenschaftlichen Begleitschutz zur (aragonesischen) Sprache (*lengua aragonesa*) erklärt. Die literarische Produktion ist noch bescheiden, die Kodifizierung steht am Anfang. In Hocharagón herrscht größte dialektale Zersplitterung (cf. Saralegui 1992).

Das Autonomiestatut des *Principado de Asturias* verleiht zwar der einheimischen Varietät, dem *bable*, keinen besonderen Status, doch werden für dessen lokale Formen Schutz sowie der Gebrauch in Medien und Schule zugesagt. Neuere Schätzungen nennen 350 000 Sprecher, besonders im ländlichen Raum (cf. García Arias 1992). Binnenmigration in die städtischen Industriezentren und kastellanophone Zuwanderung verstärken die Kastellanisierung und erschweren die Kodifizierung einer Standardsprache auf der Basis einer vom Kastilischen möglichst weit entfernten Subvarietät. Normierung, Normalisierung und Schärfung des Sprachbewußtseins betreiben unter anderem der private *Conceyu Bable* (*Normes Ortográfiques del Bable* 1978) und die *Academia de la Llingua Asturiana* (*Gramática Bable* 1976).

8. Zusammenfassung

Insgesamt begünstigt die Verfassung von 1978 die Bewahrung der Sprachkontaktsituationen in allen Domänen und ermöglicht in den zweisprachigen Regionen einen individuellen und kollektiven symmetrischen Bilinguismus. Damit wird ein jahrhundertelanger Reduktionsprozeß (Sprachwechsel, Sprach(en)tod) zumindest verlangsamt, für einige Varietäten vielleicht sogar umgekehrt. — Positives Recht der Regionalsprachen auf Expansion, unklare nationale Regelungen, die regionale Initiativen herausfordern, intensive Politisierung der Sprachenfrage an der Peripherie, wo man die eine eigene Identität durch Eigensprachlichkeit stützen will und auch vor Separatismus nicht zurückschreckt, sowie rechtliche Besitzstandsgarantie für das Kastilische und demographischer Druck der Kastilischsprecher in fast allen Regionen haben in neuerer Zeit die sprachliche Situation Spaniens wieder stark dynamisiert und dieses Land zu einem interessanten Beobachtungsfeld der Sprachkontakt-, Sprachkonflikt- und Sprachplanungsforschung sowie der Sozio- und Psycholinguistik gemacht, worin nicht selten die Linguisten selber zu Akteuren werden.

9. Bibliographie (in Auswahl)

Alvar, Manuel (Ed.) (1986): *Lenguas peninsulares y proyección hispánica*, Madrid.

Asensio, Eugenio (1960): „La lengua compañera del Imperio. Historia de una idea de Nebrija en España y Portugal". In: *Revista de Filología Española 43*, 399—413.

Badia i Margarit, Antoni (1991): „Art. 349. Katalanisch: Interne Sprachgeschichte I. Grammatik. Evolución lingüística interna I. Gramática". In: *LRL V, 2*, 127—152.

Bastardes, Albert (1987): „L'aménagement linguistique en Catalogne au XXe siècle". In: *Politique et aménagement linguistiques*, Maurais, J. (Ed.), Québec/Paris.

Benet, Josep (1979): *Catalunya sota el règim franquista*, vol. 1, Barcelona.

Boase, Roger (1990): „The morisco expulsion and diaspora: an example of racial and religious intolerance". In: *Cultures in contact in medieval Spain. Historical and literary essays presented to Leonard P. Harvey*, Hook, David/Taylor, B. (Eds.), 9–28, London.

Bruguera, Jordi (1986): *Història del lèxic català*, Barcelona.

Cavilla Ote, Manuel (1978): *Diccionario Yanito*, Gibraltar.

Colón, Germán (1976): *El léxico catalán en la Romania*, Madrid.

COM ensenyar el català als adults, suplement núm. 6, desembre 1989. Publicació del Gabinet de Didàctica (1989), Barcelona.

Coseriu, Eugenio (1961): „¿Arabismos o romanismos?". In: *Nueva Revista de Filología Hispánica 15*, 4–22.

Coseriu, Eugenio (1981): „Los conceptos de 'dialecto', 'nivel' y 'estilo de lengua' y el sentido propio de la dialectologìa". In: *Lingüística española actual 3*, 1–32.

Coseriu, Eugenio (1987): „El gallego y sus problemas. Reflexiones frías sobre un tema candente". In: *Lingüística española actual 9*, 127–138.

Eberenz, Rolf (1992): „Art. 384. Spanisch: Sprache und Gesetzgebung. Lengua y legislación". In: *LRL VI, 1*, 368–378.

Echenique Elizondo, Maria T. (²1987): *Historia lingüística vasco-románica*, Madrid.

Elcock, William Denis (²1975): *The Romance Languages*, London.

Eusko, Jaurlaritza/Gobierno, Vasco (1986): *Soziolinguistikazko Mapa 1986. Urteko erroldaren arberako Euskal Autonomi elkarteka azterketa demolinguistiko/Mapa sociolingüístico. Análisis demolingüístico de la Comunidad autónoma Vasca derivado del padrón de 1986*, Vitoria/Gasteiz.

Ferrer i Gironès, Francesco (⁴1986): *La persecució política de la llengua catalana*, Barcelona.

García, Constantino (1976): „Interferencias lingüísticas entre entre gallego y castellano". In: *Revista española de lingüística 6*, 329–343.

García, Constantino (1985): *Temas de lingüística galega*, La Coruña.

García, Constantino et al. (1990ff): *Atlas lingüístico Galego*, Santiago.

García Arias, Xaver Luís (1992): „Art. 408. Asturianisch: Externe Sprachgeschichte. Evolución lingüística externa". In: *LRL VI, 1*, 681–693.

González González, Manuel (1994): „Art. 413. Galegisch: Soziolinguistik/Sociolingüística". In: *LRL VI, 2*, 46–66 [auf galegisch].

González Ollé, Fernando (1978): „El establecimiento del castellano como lengua oficial". In: *Boletin de la Real Academia Española BRAE 58*, 229–280.

Griera, Antoni (1923ff): *Atlas Lingüístic de Catalunya*, Barcelona.

Lapesa, Rafael (1953): „La lengua de la poesía lírica desde Macías hasta Villa-sandino". In: *Romance Philology 7*, 51–59.

Lapesa, Rafael (⁸1980): *Historia de la lengua espanola*, Madrid.

López García, Angel (1985): *El rumor de los desarraigados*, Barcelona.

LRL: Holtus, Günter/Metzeltin, Michael/Schmitt, Christian (Eds.) (1988ff): *Lexikon der romanistischen Linguistik*, Tübingen, 1988ff.

Lüdtke, Helmut (1964): „Die Entstehung der romanischen Schriftsprachen". In: *Vox Romanica 23*, 3–21.

Lüdtke, Jens (1984): *Katalanisch. Eine einführende Sprachbeschreibung*, München.

Lüdtke, Jens (1991): „Art. 356. Katalanisch: Externe Sprachgeschichte/Histoire externe de la langue". In: *LRL V, 2*, 232–242.

Menéndez Pidal, Ramón (⁹1980): *Orígenes del español. Estado lingüístico de la Península Ibérica hasta el siglo XI*, Madrid.

Mondéjar, José (1986): „Naturaleza y status social de las hablas andaluzas". In: *Lenguas peninsulares y proyección hispánica*, Alvar, Manuel (Ed.), 143–149.

Mondéjar, José (1992): „Art. 394. Spanisch: Arealinguistik II. Andalusisch/Areas lingüísticas II. Andalucía". In: *LRL VI, 1*, 504–521.

Monteagudo, Henrique/Santamarina, Antón (1993): „Galician and Castilian in Contact: historical, Social and Linguistic Aspects". In: *Trends in Romance Linguistics and Philology. Vol. V: Bilingualism and Linguistic Conflict in Romance*, Posner, Rebecca/Green, John N. (Eds.), 117–173.

Morales, Francisco/Díez, Miguel/Sabín, Angel (1976): *Las lenguas de España*, Madrid.

Posner, Rebecca (1992): „Language Conflict or Language Symbiosis? Contact of Other Romance Varieties with Castilian". In: *Essays in Spanish Linguistics presented to Frederick William Hodcroft*, MacKenzie, David/Michael, Jan (Eds.), Oxford, 1–18.

Posner, Rebecca/Green, John N. (Eds.) (1993): *Trends in Romance Linguistics and Philology. Vol. V: Bilingualism and Linguistic Conflict in Romance*, Berlin/New York.

Saralegui, Carmen (1992): „Art. 360. Aragonesisch/Navarresisch: Externe und interne Sprachgeschichte/Evolución lingüística externa e interna". In: *LRL VI, 1*, 37–54.

Steiger, Arnald (1967): „Arabismos". In: *Enciclopedia Lingüística Hispánica II*, 93–126.

Strubell i Trueta, Miguel (1993): „Catalan : Castilian". In: *Trends in Romance Linguistics and Philology. Vol. V: Bilingualism and Linguistic Conflict in Romance*, Posner, Rebecca/Green, John N. (Eds.), 175–207.

Tilander, Gunnar (1967): „Fuentes jurídicas". In: *Enciclopedia Lingüística Hispánica II*, 447–461.

Tovar, Antonio (1977): *Einführung in die Sprachgeschichte der Iberischen Halbinsel*, Tübingen (spanisch 1968).

Vázquez Cuesta, Pilar (1981): „O bilinguismo castelhano-português na época de Camoes". In: *Arquivos do Centro Cultural Português XVI*, 807–827.

Vázquez Cuesta, Pilar/Mendes da Luz, Maria Albertina (^{3}1971): *Gramática portuguesa. Tercera edición*, Madrid, 2 vols.

Winkelmann, Otto (1989): *Untersuchungen zur Sprachvariation des Gaskognischen im Val d'Aran (Zentralpyrenäen)*, Tübingen.

Wright, Roger (1982): *Late Latin and Early Romance in Spain and Carolingian France*, Liverpool.

Harald Thun, Kiel (Deutschland)

152. Espagnol–galicien

1. Géographie et démographie
2. Histoire
3. Politique, économie, situations culturelle et religieuse
4. Statistiques
5. Situation sociolinguistique
6. Etat de la politique linguistique
7. Portrait général des contacts linguistiques
8. Bibliographie (sélective)

1. Géographie et démographie

Le territoire linguistique du galicien actuel comprend la Galice administrative (29 434 km^2) – située au NO de la Péninsule Ibérique –, et les régions voisines de la Terra Navia-Eo (Asturias), du Bierzo occidental (León) et des Portelas (Zamora). Les formes sans diphtongue *pedra* et *porta* et *canciois* et *ter* sans -N- latin intervocalique séparent le galicien oriental de l'asturien occidental, qui présente *piedra, puerta, canciones* et *tener*; l'absence des voyelles nasales et des sifflantes sonores en galicien et leur présence en portugais permettent d'ailleurs d'établir la frontière linguistique avec le portugais septentrional (Fernández Rei 1990 a, 18–30).

D'après les renseignements du IGE (1991, 45) dans la Galice administrative, il y a presque 2 800 000 habitants (pour les pourcentages de connaissance, écriture et utilisation cf. 4.1.). Dans les régions limitrophes de la Galice, il y a plus de 70 000 habitants (50 000 à la Terra Navia-Eo, 20 000 au Bierzo occidental et 2 500 aux Portelas). Du point de vue démographique, la population galicienne est distribuée en 31 894 communes qui correspondent presqu'à la moitié de celles de l'Espagne. Parmi celles-ci, seulement sept sont des villes importantes (Ferrol, A Coruña, Santiago de Compostela, Pontevedra, Vigo, Lugo et Ourense), auxquelles il faut ajouter un grand nombre de villes (de quelques centaines ou milliers d'habitants) et un grand nombre de villages.

Hors de la Galice, il y a actuellement plus de 550 000 Galiciens adultes nés en Galice (200 000 en Espagne, 180 000 en Europe et 175 000 en Amérique), selon les résultats d'une recherche inédite faite par M. Monteagudo Romero, dans laquelle les taux d'émigration, de mortalité et des retournés sont pris en considération. Entre 1860 et 1910, 500 000 Galiciens émigrèrent en Amérique du Sud, et une quantité comparable entre 1915 et 1930. Entre 1946 et 1965, ce chiffre descend à 350 000. Plus récemment, l'émigration s'est dirigée, fondamentalement, vers les zones industrialisées d'Europe, avec 200 000 émigrants entre 1960 et 1977 (Sixirei 1988).

2. Histoire

2.1. Le Moyen Age

Dans l'histoire de la Galice, la *découverte* du tombeau de l'Apôtre Saint-Jacques au début du IXe siècle constitue un événement de toute première importance; d'où un renforcement de l'idéologie de la reconquête chrétienne qui favorisera l'essor politique, économique et culturel de Saint-Jacques-de-Compostelle. Peu à peu, les villes prennent de l'importance si bien qu'au XIIe siècle se produit le premier soulèvement des bourgeois de Compostelle contre l'archevêque Xelmírez. Mais la bourgeoisie urbaine galicienne perd son importance politique depuis le règne de Fernando III (1230–1253), qui avait attaqué le pouvoir des villes et qui avait envoyé des étrangers pour gouverner la Galice.

En ce qui concerne la situation linguistique, le latin, que le peuple ne comprenait plus, avait été la langue littéraire et religieuse et aussi celle des actes juridiques et administratifs, pendant une grande partie du Moyen Age dans toute la Péninsule Ibérique. En Galice, ce bilinguisme culturel s'est maintenu jusqu'au XIIe siècle où l'on a trouvé les premiers textes totalement écrits en galicien.

Les XIIe–XIVe siècles ont constitué une étape de splendeur pour le galicien, qui est devenu la langue lyrique par excellence de la Péninsule ce dont témoignent le très important corpus lyrique médiéval formé par les *cantigas de amigo, de amor, de escarnio e maldicir* de même que la collection des miracles des *Cantigas de Santa María* du roi Afonso X le Savant. Concernant la prose, au Moyen Age on a écrit quelques œuvres historiques, didactiques ou littéraires autour des grands thèmes de la littérature européenne de l'époque, généralement traduites du castillan ou du latin.

A cette époque, le galicien était une langue d'utilisation normale pour toute la population, et on s'en servait aussi dans les actes judiciaires et administratifs. Jusqu'au milieu du XVIe siècle, c'est toujours en galicien qu'on rédige les procès-verbaux et les contrats des conseils municipaux et des corps de métiers, des testaments, des actes de procès et d'affaires légales. Mais la pénétration du castillan qui avait commencé durant le règne de Fernando III (XIIIe s.) deviendra plus forte à partir du XIVe siècle après la lutte pour la couronne de Castille entre Pedro I et Henrique II. Avec la victoire de ce dernier, la noblesse galicienne vaincue commence à être substituée par des nobles castillans (Chacón 1979). Ce processus sera achevé pendant le règne des Rois Catholiques (XVe s.) quand les postes principaux de l'administration et de l'église seront occupés par des étrangers utilisant exclusivement le castillan. La noblesse et le clergé galiciens suivent les voies tracées par la noblesse castillane qui s'est installée en Galice et qui devient le *noyau diglossique assimilé* (Monteagudo Romero 1985, 105).

2.2. Du XVIe au XVIIIe siècle

Après la Renaissance européenne le galicien disparaît complètement au niveau de l'écrit et reste circonscrit au monde rural et familier, tandis que d'autres langues romanes s'affermissent en tant que langues d'Etat; il continuait à être parlé par la majeure partie de la population, alors que le castillan était la langue d'une minorité influente qui détenait le pouvoir économique, politique et culturel en Galice; le fait que pendant les XVIe et XVIIe siècles seulement 2% des magistrats de l'Audience Royale du Royaume de la Galice étaient des Galiciens en est une bonne preuve; ce pourcentage était monté jusqu'à 15% au XVIIIe siècle (Villares 1984, 100 sq). L'Audience Royale représentait un office du Gouvernement de la Monarchie centrale, avec des attributions administratives, gouvernementales et judiciaires.

L'église catholique a joué un rôle très négatif pour le développement du galicien puisqu'elle l'a exclu des pratiques religieuses. On utilisait le castillan dans l'administration des sacrements et dans les prières collectives, de même que dans les prières quotidiennes de dévotion personnelle qui, toutes, étaient enseignées dans cette langue; et les choses n'ont pas changé depuis. Il faut ajouter à tout cela le fait que pendant ces siècles le système d'enseignement dépendait de l'église, laquelle utilisait le latin et le castillan pour l'éducation religieuse d'un peuple qui parlait en galicien. Ceci s'explique par le fait que presque tous les postes ecclésiastiques étaient occupés par des gens d'origine non galicienne. Les données sur la castillanisation de la hiérarchie ecclésiastique en Galice sont très éloquents: entre 1500 et 1830, il n'y a eu que deux évêques galiciens dans tout le diocèse de Lugo, un dans celui de Tui, deux à Mondoñedo, cinq à Ourense et encore cinq à Saint-Jacques (Vázquez Cuesta 1980, 707).

Dans les *siècles obscurs*, lorsque le galicien perd son prestige social, il y a pourtant une tradition revendicative (et qui lui apporte du prestige) chez les classes les plus instruites du pays (Monteagudo 1991). A la fin du XVIe siècle, le chapitre de Compostelle avait protesté parce qu'on accordait les meilleurs bénéfices à tous ceux qui ne savaient pas parler le galicien. Au XVIIe siècle, quelques écrivants composaient de la poésie en galicien. Durant le siècle des Lumières apparaissent les premiers signes d'un intérêt pour l'étude et la récupération de la conscience idiomatique du galicien. Le Père Sarmiento, lequel dénonce dans ses œuvres la situation marginale du galicien et critique le fait qu'il ne soit pas utilisé comme langue d'alphabétisation, de l'administration et de l'église, en constitue un exemple. Son œuvre marque le début de la linguistique galicienne scientifique.

Pendant ces siècles de décadence, les traits fondamentaux qui caractérisent le galicien en face du portugais s'affermissent; les deux langues avaient eu une étape commune pendant le Moyen Age. Le Portugal, avec ses propres institutions politiques et muni d'un centre politique et culturel, a répandu une norme idiomatique unique dans le territoire de son Etat, tandis qu'en Galice, la langue du pays a continué son évolution naturelle tout en gardant les formes archaïques, en introduisant des innovations particulières et en subissant la pression constante du castillan.

2.3. Le XIXe siècle: le *Rexurdimento*

L'invasion et la conquête de la Péninsule Ibérique par les troupes de Napoléon (1808—1810), qui avait provoqué des soulèvements populaires anti-français, a entraîné un collapsus de l'Etat centralisateur. En 1808, on a formé l'Assemblée Souveraine du Royaume de la Galice, qui appelle à la révolte contre les Français. Les pamphlets et les brochures écrits en galicien, par lesquels on invitait la population à participer à la résistance, constituèrent l'un des moyens d'agitation les plus populaires. La « Guerre de l'Indépendance » marque avec l'expulsion des Français la fin de l'Ancien Régime en Espagne et le début des Temps Modernes; le nouveau régime cependant ne s'instaure pas pleinement puisque le XIXe siècle est une période de grande instabilité politique, avec des luttes entre les conservateurs (traditionalistes) et les libéraux (progressistes).

A partir de la troisième décennie de ce siècle, le nouveau régime sera consolidé, sous la forme d'un Etat monarchique autoritaire, avec la prédominance des libéraux et des conservateurs, mais aussi avec une forte militarisation et centralisation. Parmi les mesures centralisatrices, il faut noter la création des provinces en substitution des anciennes régions (comme le Royaume de la Galice) et aussi la création d'un enseignement indépendant de l'Eglise Catholique, lequel comptait parmi ses objectifs celui de l'unification linguistique de l'Etat entier, avec l'imposition du castillan et le refoulement des langues de la périphérie (galicien, catalan et basque). Un Décret Royal de 1902 qui interdit d'utiliser ces langues à l'école, confirme la même politique, qui continue avec plus ou moins d'intensité, et presque sans interruption, jusqu'à la promulgation de la nouvelle Constitution Espagnole de 1978 (García Negro 1991, 207—239).

Dans la seconde moitié du XIXe siècle, comme réaction contre le centralisme uniformisateur de l'Etat, un mouvement idéologique (le *galeguismo*) se fait jour. Ce mouvement s'est développé en deux temps: le *provincialismo* (de 1840 à 1885) et le *rexionalismo* (de 1885 à 1915). Le *galeguismo* aboutira, dans le premier tiers du XXe siècle, au *nacionalismo*. Dans la seconde moitié du XIXe siècle, c'est la renaissance et la résurrection du galicien comme langue littéraire (Hermida 1992), avec la publication de *Cantares Gallegos* (1863) de Rosalía de Castro (1837—1885). Cette poétesse et aussi les poètes Eduardo Pondal (1835—1917) et M. Curros Enríquez (1851—1908) représentent les « trois couronnes » de ce *Rexurdimento*. A cette époque, on peut trouver aussi les premières grammaires et les premiers dictionnaires du galicien, dont notamment la grammaire de X. A. Saco Arce et le dictionnaire de Marcial Valladares. C'est aussi à cette époque que se font les premiers appels à la création d'une académie de la langue galicienne, qui sera fondée en 1906 sous la devise *Colligit, expurgat, innovat* (« (Elle) collecte, épure, innove »).

3. Politique, économie, situations culturelle et religieuse

3.1. Du *Posrexurdimento* au Statut de 1936

Pendant les 90 dernières années, de grands changements économiques et sociaux se sont produits. Selon le recensement de 1900, 88,7% de la population galicienne étaient d'origine rurale et 6% d'origine urbaine, et seulement quelque 4,7% habitaient les petites villes (entités moyennes entre la ville et le village). Actuellement, plus de la moitié de la population habite les villes ou leurs aires d'influence.

Les ressources économiques de la Galice au début du XXe siècle étaient presque toutes agricoles, avec une agriculture presque féodale qui ne produisait que pour l'autoconsommation et le paiement des *foros* ('rentes foncières'). L'industrialisation presque inexistante se limitait à la fabrication de tabacs et à l'industrie des conserves, très importante pour la Galice, et où l'on n'employait presque que des femmes. Il y avait aussi la fabrication du fil, du cuir, du papier, de la poterie, etc. La faiblesse de l'industrie explique la faiblesse des mouvements ouvriers (CNT, UGT), en contraste avec la puissance des organisations d'agriculteurs, grâce auxquelles les rentes foncières ont pu être supprimées entre 1910 et 1930. Ceci provoque un grand changement social, parce que les rentes foncières étaient un obstacle pour le développement de l'agriculture.

L'année 1916 est très importante dans l'évolution du *galeguisme*, avec la formation des *Irmandades da Fala* ('Confréries de la Langue') lesquelles, bien qu'elles formulent des objectifs fondamentalement culturels (la défense et la diffusion du galicien à travers son emploi systématique), finiront par s'occuper aussi de la politique (Ière Assemblée Nationaliste de Lugo, 1918). Ceci a abouti à la fondation du *Partido Galeguista* en 1931, l'année de la proclamation de la IIe République Espagnole. Ce nouveau parti politique a été un instrument très important pour l'obtention d'un Statut d'Autonomie de la Galice (1936), où l'on reconnaissait le galicien et le castillan comme langues officielles. Dans l'activité culturelle et politique de la Galice des années 20 et 30, les intellectuels de la *Xeración Nós* ('Génération Nous') qui n'utilisent que le galicien dans leurs écrits littéraires, scientifiques ou politiques, jouent un rôle fondamental. L'activité de ces intellectuels constitue un grand pas vers l'élaboration du galicien moderne. Les membres du *Seminario de Estudos Galegos* (1923), l'entreprise scientifique et culturelle la plus remarquable avant 1936, rédigent des mémoires scientifiques sur l'ethnographie, la géographie, l'archéologie, la préhistoire et sur les sciences naturelles et appliquées.

3.2. De l'après-guerre à nos jours

La Guerre Civile (1936−1939) constitue un retard, voire une rechute, dans le processus de modernisation, parce que le changement socio-économique a été bloqué jusqu'aux années 60, tandis que progressivement on a remplacé l'agriculture traditionnelle de subsistance (polyculture) par une agriculture spécialisée, développée surtout dans le secteur de l'élevage. Dans le secteur industriel, on peut bien constater des innovations dans la construction d'usines de transformation des produits agraires, dans la croissance de l'industrie navale à Vigo et à Ferrol, et dans les installations de groupes monopolistes qui cherchent en Galice des matières premières d'exploitation facile, de l'énergie à bon marché et de la main-d'œuvre abondante. Pourtant, économiquement, la Galice des années 60 et 70 est encore en retard par rapport au reste de l'Espagne: en 1975, seulement 22% de la population active galicienne étaient employés dans le secteur secondaire (l'industrie et la construction), tandis que dans le reste de l'Etat ce chiffre montait jusqu'à 36% (Santamarina/Fernández Rei 1992, 25). Vers le milieu des années 70, il y a une crise de croissance provoquée par la chute de la demande pour les secteurs primaires. Cette crise s'accroîtra vers la fin des années 80 avec la reconversion industrielle qui touchera lourdement le secteur naval; la même chose vaut pour l'entrée de l'Espagne dans la CEE, qui touche la pêche, l'agriculture et l'élevage.

En ce qui concerne la situation linguistique, l'extension de la scolarisation et des mass média modernes, avec de nouvelles valeurs culturelles, diffuse peu à peu le castillan dans tous les coins du pays. Avant les années 60, parmi les faibles signes de résistance contre la *castillanisation* accélérée de la Galice, il faut mentionner la fondation de la maison d'édition Galaxia (1950). Pendant les années 60, la vie culturelle est ravivée avec la création d'un réseau d'associations culturelles dans les principaux centres urbains et dans les petites villes, lesquelles ont comme objectif principal la défense du galicien. L'activité politique clandestine des forces démocratiques s'est réanimée; parmi celles-ci le Parti Communiste occupe une place de choix, qui créera en 1968 une organisation autonome pour la Galice. Il faut également citer les deux tendances de la gauche nationaliste, le Parti Socialiste Galicien (1963) et l'Union du Peuple Galicien (1964), qui emploieront publiquement le galicien. Le nationalisme politique et syndical sera, pendant les années 70, le *moteur* de la normalisation de l'utilisation du galicien (Fernández Rei 1990 b, 1994).

4. Statistiques

4.1. Les niveaux de connaissance et d'utilisation de la langue

Pendant les années 80, surtout après la promulgation de la Loi de Normalisation Linguistique (1983), on a commencé à faire des études démolinguistiques plus amples que celles des années 70, toujours dans des secteurs spécifiques (l'école, l'université et l'église); mais nous n'avons pas de renseignements complets et généraux pour toute la Galice, ni d'informations sur la connaissance et l'utilisation de la langue parce que de telles questions n'ont pas été posées lors du Recensement officiel de la Population et du Logement (1991), réalisé par l'Etat lui-même auprès de la population totale de la Galice.

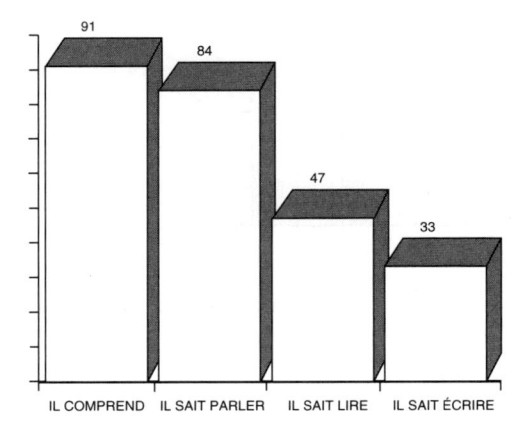

Fig. 152.1: Niveau de connaissance du galicien (les chiffres indiquent le pourcentage de la population) (IGE 1991, 45)

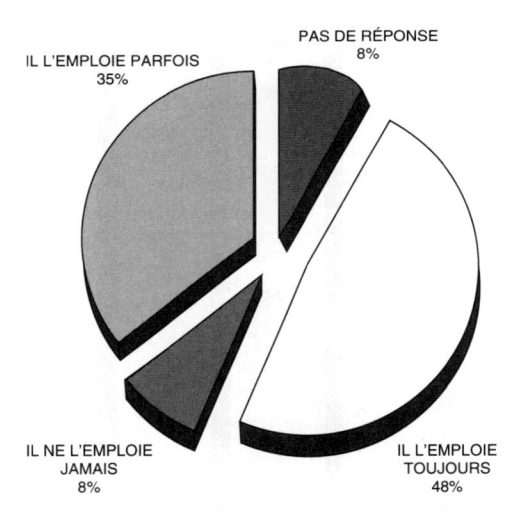

Fig. 152.2: Les pourcentages d'utilisation du galicien (IGE 1991, 45)

Des figures 152.1 et 152.2, on peut déduire que toute la population comprend le galicien et qu'elle est capable de le parler; en revanche, moins de la moitié sait lire en galicien et seulement un tiers déclare savoir l'écrire. Concernant la pratique de la langue, presque la moitié de la population donne la préférence au galicien dans la conversation quotidienne, tandis que plus d'un tiers des Galiciens sont bilingues actifs et effectifs, puisqu'ils savent parler les deux langues et les utilisent fréquemment. La proportion des Galiciens monolingues en castillan n'arrive pas à un sur dix. Ceci nous donne une impression générale de la situation sociolinguistique galicienne: le galicien est la langue de la plus grande partie de la population. Sur le plan oral, c'est la langue la plus employée, mais ce n'est pas le cas pour la langue écrite. Le bilinguisme passif est généralisé, tandis que le bilinguisme actif ne comprend qu'un tiers des Galiciens (Monteagudo/Santamarina 1993, 126−137). En ce moment, l'Académie Royale Galicienne est en train d'éditer une carte sociolinguistique de la Galice (Fernández Rodriguez/Rodriguez Neira 1994, 1995).

4.2. L'habitat: le rural et l'urbain

L'enquête de l'IGE (1991) fournit des renseignements sur la connaissance et l'utilisation du galicien dans les villes principales: voir la figure 152.3.

Dans toutes les villes, le pourcentage de bilingues effectifs monte considérablement par rapport à ce que nous montre la figure 152.2. Les deux villes les plus grandes (A Coruña et Vigo) présentent le taux le plus élevé de bilinguisme; les pourcentages de monolingues effectifs sont cependant un peu plus hauts pour le castillan que pour le galicien.

Les centres urbains ont été les lieux privilégiés de la pénétration du castillan à travers les principaux organismes de l'Etat et les institutions de l'éducation; en plus, la bourgeoisie, à qui on doit le dynamisme de l'économie urbaine de la Galice, était pour la plupart étrangère. De cette façon, l'ambiance linguistique des villes, et surtout celle des zones centrales habitées par les cadres les plus aisés, a exercé une forte pression en faveur du castillan, ce qui a engendré dans la conscience sociale l'idée que le galicien n'est qu'une langue rustique, associée au retard économique et social, tandis que le castillan est une langue urbaine, associée à la modernité et au progrès.

5. Situation sociolinguistique

Une étude réalisée en 1984 parmi des élèves de l'enseignement primaire s'occupe du rapport entre la langue maternelle des élèves et le *statut* social de leurs parents. La stratification en résultant est visualisée dans la figure 152.4.

De la figure 152.4 il ressort clairement que le castillan est lié aux professions urbaines

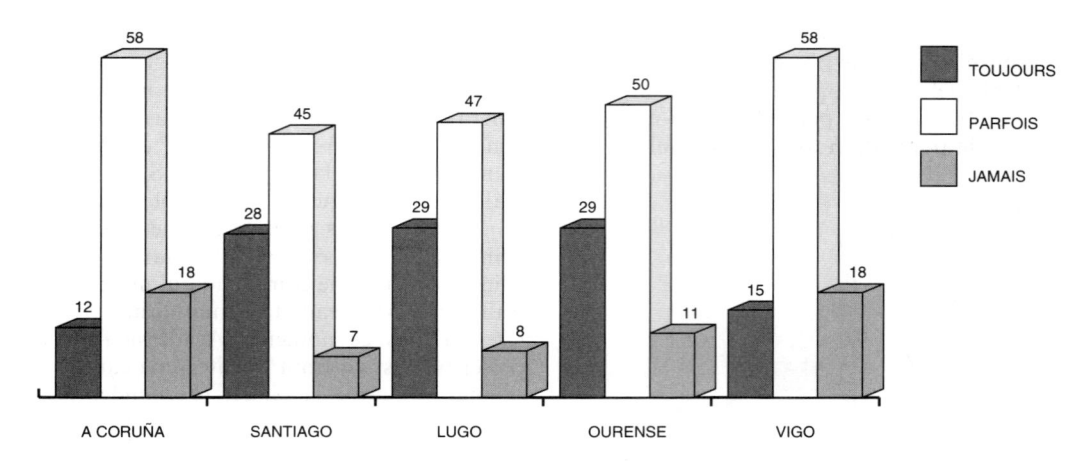

Fig. 152.3: L'utilisation du galicien dans cinq villes. Les chiffres indiquent le pourcentage de chaque ville; les pourcentages résiduels se réfèrent aux réponses nulles (IGE 1991, 45).

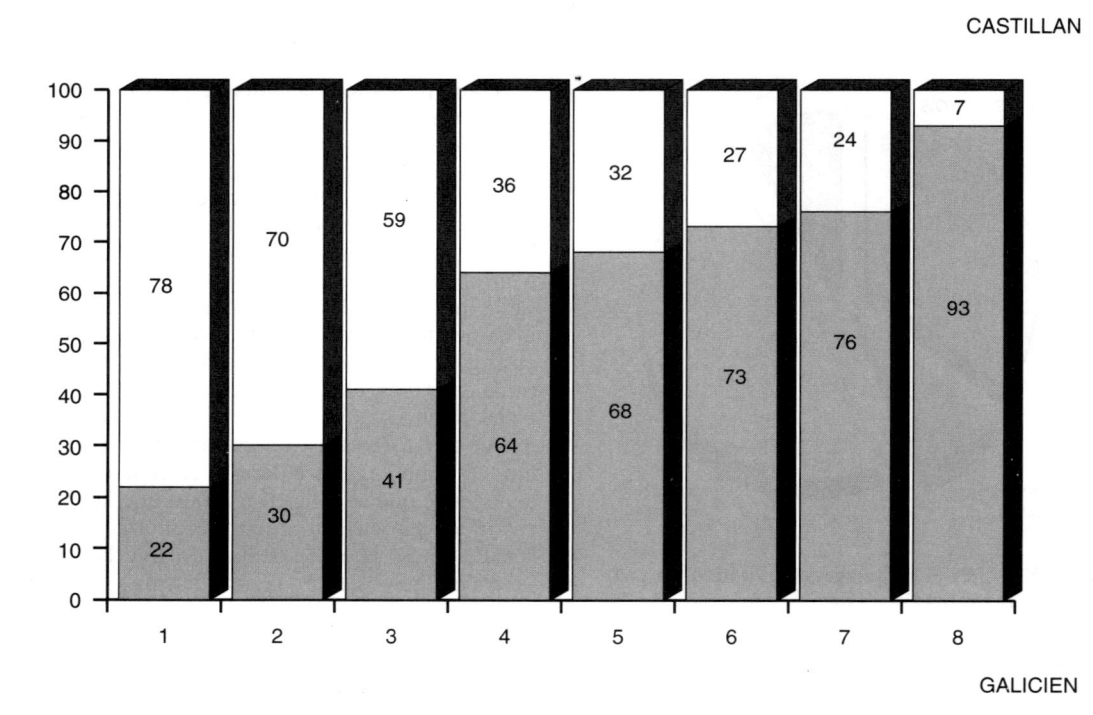

Fig. 152.4: Utilisation du galicien et du castillan d'après le *statut* social.

Les chiffres renvoient aux catégories sociales suivantes: 1. − Les professionnels avec des études supérieures, les enseignants, les artistes; 2. − Les hauts fonctionnaires, les directeurs et les directeurs généraux d'entreprise; 3. − Les fonctionnaires moyens, administratifs, etc.; 4. − Les ouvriers qualifiés; 5. − Les petits et moyens employés, commerçants, etc.; 6. − Le personnel subalterne de l'administration, des entreprises et du commerce; 7. − La population inactive (au chômage, à la retraite); 8. − Les agriculteurs, les éleveurs, les pêcheurs (Monteagudo 1986, 55).

ayant un *statut* supérieur, soit qu'il correspond à une instruction plus avancée, soit qu'il est associé aux bénéfices économiques cités plus hauts, soit qu'il est mis en rapport avec les postes les plus importants dans les institutions et les entreprises. Encore une fois, la distribution du galicien et du castillan produit dans la conscience populaire l'image que le castillan est l'apanage du bonheur matériel et de l'instruction supérieure, tandis que le galicien est la tare des couches les plus basses et des moins instruites. C'est pour cela que la plupart des Galiciens considèrent que le castillan favorise la promotion sociale et que le galicien en est plutôt un obstacle.

5.1. La famille: le procès de *dégalicisation*

Le déclin du galicien dans les trois dernières générations est spectaculaire, comme le démontre la figure 152.5.

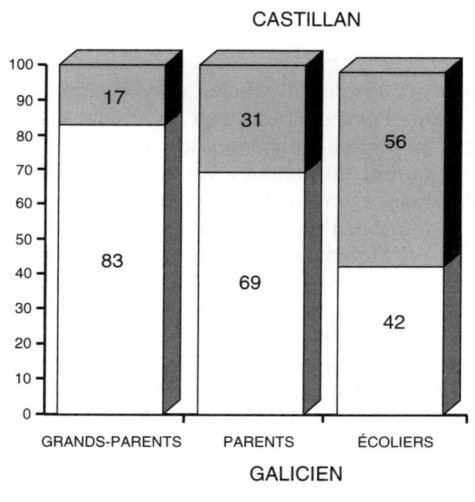

Fig. 152.5: Langue habituelle par générations (Monteagudo 1986, 77).

Dans les villes, quelques grands-parents et un grand nombre de parents qui pratiquent le castillan comme langue habituelle, ont eu comme langue première le galicien. Dans la génération des grands-parents (il y a environ 60 ans), la langue galicienne était majoritaire en Galice, et dans la génération des parents (il y a environ 30 ans), le galicien était beaucoup plus utilisé qu'aujourd'hui. Le comportement linguistique à l'intérieur des familles fait voir la tendance substitutive typique du bilinguisme en Galice, c'est-à-dire qu'il reflète la transition vers la castillanisation complète.

Pour le comportement linguistique dans les relations entre les diverses générations à l'intérieur de la famille, voir les figures 152.6–152.8.

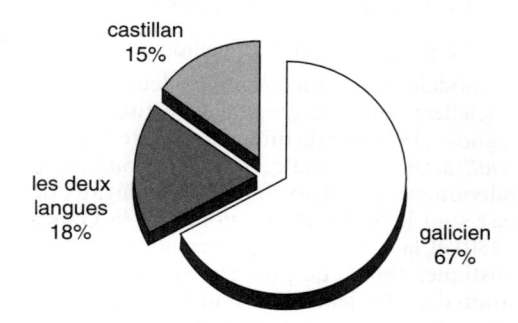

Fig. 152.6: Rapport parents et grands-parents

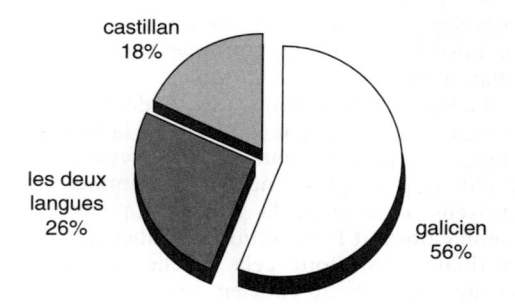

Fig. 152.7: Rapport des parents parmi eux

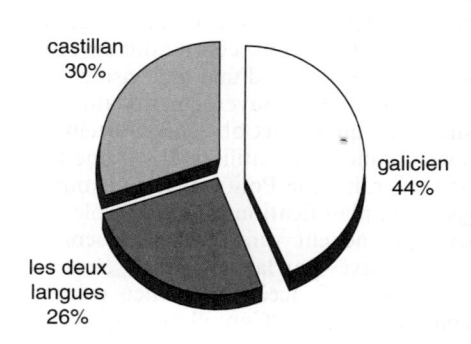

Fig. 152.8: Rapport parents-enfants

La situation de la Galice constitue un exemple de bilinguisme substitutif, avec une nette diglossie chez beaucoup de Galiciens. Il s'agit d'une *diglosia de adscripción* (Rojo 1981, 270 sq.; 1982, 94 sq.), bien qu'on soit déjà entré dans une situation de *diglossie conflictuelle* nette (Fernández 1978, 390). Or il existe une réaction sociale qui réclame un redressement de cette situation pour donner au galicien la place qui lui appartient en tant que langue maternelle de la Galice.

6. Etat de la politique linguistique

6.1. Le galicien langue officielle

Le modèle de *coofficialisation* (deux langues officielles) consacré dans la Constitution espagnole (1978) ne distingue pas entre la *coofficialisation* territoriale et la *coofficialisation* individuelle. Les deux autres textes légaux de base sont le Statut d'Autonomie de la Galice (1980) et la LNL (Loi de Normalisation Linguistique, 1983). Le premier stipule l'instauration d'un Parlement et d'un Gouvernement autonomes, tous les deux fortement galicisés dans leurs publications officielles et dans la langue utilisée publiquement par les responsables politiques. Dans les organismes officiels dépendants de l'Etat, la langue d'utilisation normale en Galice continue à être le castillan, malgré la *coofficialisation*.

Le Statut d'Autonomie (art. 5) déclare que le galicien est la langue naturelle de la Galice, engage les pouvoirs publics à le favoriser et établit le principe de ne pas discriminer les citoyens à cause de la langue. La LNL a comme objectif l'égalisation du galicien et du castillan, c'est pour cela qu'elle établit la pleine officialité du galicien: toute procédure administrative ou judiciaire sera valable et produira ses effets quelle que soit la langue officielle employée. La LNL a constitué un progrès considérable dans le domaine légal et institutionnel. Les effets cependant en sont restés limités à cause d'une indécision gênante de la part des gouvernements autonomes successifs quant aux objectifs à atteindre et quant aux moyens à utiliser. Il y a une Direction Générale de la Politique Linguistique, chargée de la planification et du contrôle des mesures qui mènent vers l'accomplissement des objectifs fixés par la LNL, mais c'est un organisme peu efficace, étant conçu comme un département de la 'Consellería de Educación' (l'équivalent d'un ministère dans le gouvernement galicien), donc sans aucun pouvoir hors du domaine éducatif. D'autre part, cette Direction Générale manque de personnel qualifié ayant une bonne formation sociolinguistique.

6.2. L'enseignement

Dans l'enseignement, il y a eu des initiatives positives, mais l'absence de planification en réduit l'efficacité énormément. En peu d'années, on est passé de l'enseignement facultatif (1979) à l'enseignement obligatoire (1983) de la langue dans l'ensemble de l'enseignement primaire et secondaire; plus tard (1987), il est prévu l'emploi du galicien comme langue véhiculaire dans les premières années de l'enseignement primaire et, en plus, son utilisation dans les cours de *Sciences Sociales* (2e de l'enseignement primaire). On a d'ailleurs prévu son emploi comme langue véhiculaire dans deux matières obligatoires de l'enseignement secondaire. Cependant cet objectif n'a pas été atteint à cause du manque de prévision, d'appui et de contrôle des autorités. A l'Université, on peut dire que seulement l'administration est galicisée, avec l'utilisation presque exclusive du galicien. Au sujet de l'emploi du galicien dans les différents secteurs de l'enseignement, on a publié récemment des rapports détaillés (Rubal/Rodríguez Neira 1987, Rodríguez Neira/López Martínez 1988, Rubal/Veiga/Arza 1992, Rodriguez Neira 1993).

6.3. Les mass media

L'absence totale du galicien dans ces moyens pendant l'étape franquiste et l'analphabétisme en langue galicienne des adultes constituent autant de facteurs qui créent des difficultés pour l'emploi du galicien dans la presse écrite. Aujourd'hui, il n'y a qu'un hebdomadaire d'information politique entièrement écrit en galicien (*A Nosa Terra*) et quelques publications périodiques de diffusion régionale ou locale. Il y a ensuite des revues culturelles de périodicité plus espacée (*Grial, Encrucillada, A Trabe de Ouro*). Avant l'apparition de *O Correo Galego* (janvier de 1944) – le premier journal de l'histoire de la Galice écrit complètement en langue galicienne –, dans la presse quotidienne, l'utilisation du galicien était presque nulle et se réduisait à quelques petites contributions des commentateurs, à des collaborations littéraires et à la politique galicienne et locale.

C'est en 1985 qu'est entrée en fonction la chaîne de Radio-Télévision de la Galice. Elle dépend de l'administration autonome; la radio émet toujours en galicien, tandis que la TVG dispose actuellement d'environ 90 heures par semaine avec une programmation entièrement en galicien. La première chaîne de la TV espagnole en Galice commença ses brèves émissions en galicien autour de 1975. Actuellement, elles ont une durée d'environ une heure par jour avec quelques annonces aussi en galicien au long de la journée.

Tableau 152.1: (A) Langue habituelle des curés de la Galice. (B) Modèle idéal préféré par les séminaristes pour la prédication. (C) Distribution de messes d'après la langue employée (dans ce cas, les possibilités sont 'galicien', 'galicien et castillan' et 'castillan') (López Muñoz 1989, 85, 92 et 157).

		Galicien	+Galicien	+Castillan	Castillan
A.	Curés	73%	12%	12%	3%
B.	Séminaristes	37%	41%	15%	5%
C.	Messes	7%	23%		70%

6.4. L'église

On a déjà dit (2.2.) que l'église galicienne était un agent puissant de castillanisation, aussi bien parmi les élites distinguées que parmi la population normale. Quand, dans les années 60, le Concile Vatican II imposa la célébration des rites dans les langues vernaculaires, c'est le castillan qui a été choisi en Galice; et en fait, la version officielle en galicien du Missel Romain (1987) et celle de la Bible (1989) sont très récentes. Quant aux pratiques et aux attitudes linguistiques du clergé galicien voir le tableau 152.1.

6.5. La *codification* du galicien

La norme la plus complète du galicien standard a été élaborée par le ILG-RAG (1982) et a été officialisée en 1982 même. On y considère que le galicien est une langue autonome alors que AGAL (1983) l'envisage comme variante du portugais. Sur le *statut* et la planification du corpus du galicien cf. Fernández Rei (1993), Herrero Valeiro (1993), Monteagudo (1993, 1995) et Santamarina (1994).

La *Gramática* de Alvarez Blanco/Regueira/Monteagudo (1986), trois chercheurs de l'ILG, constitua un progrès considérable dans la description et la formalisation des règles grammaticales fondamentales du galicien. Quant à l'établissement du lexique et à son épuration, l'apport le plus important est celui du *Vocabulario ortográfico da lingua galega* (inédit), coordonné par Santamarina et González González, eux-aussi chercheurs de l'ILG. Ce vocabulaire groupe environ 50 000 mots. L'ILG et la RAG ont publié un *Diccionario da Lingua Galega* (1990) qui ne dispose que de 12 000 entrées. Il y a encore d'autres dictionnaires monolingues (galicien–galicien), comme p. ex. Alonso Estravís (1986, 1995), Ares Vázquez (1986), Feixó Cid (1986) et Xove Ferreiro (1995); il y a en plus des dictionnaires bilingues galicien–castillan, comme p. ex. Monteagudo Romero/García Cancela (1988) et aussi en sens invers (castillan–galicien), comme p. ex. Navaza Blanco (1990) avec plus de 35 000 entrées.

7. Portrait général des contacts linguistiques

L'interférence du galicien sur le castillan de la Galice est très évidente dans le domaine de l'intonation qui présente des tonèmes propres du galicien. Elle se fait également jour dans l'utilisation des voyelles ouvertes ou fermées au degré moyen, et dans le *n* vélaire là où le castillan présente un son alvéolaire (*con aquella*). Dans la morphologie, le système verbal est le plus interféré, avec l'absence des temps composés, comme p. ex. *llegué, llegara* (gal. *cheguei, chegara*; cast. *llegué* et *he llegado, había llegado*) ou avec l'utilisation des périphrases ayant la même valeur que les pendants galiciens, comme p. ex. *no doy acabado* (gal. *non dou acabado*, cast. *no consigo acabar*), *hube de caer* (gal. *houben caer*, cast. *estuve a punto de caer* et non pas *tuve que caer*) ou *he de hacerte un regalo* (gal. *heiche facer un agasallo*, cast. *te haré un regalo* et non pas *tengo que hacerte un regalo*). Il y a beaucoup de traits syntaxiques galiciens dans le castillan de la Galice, comme p. ex. l'emploi du pronom dit de *solidarité* (*aquí te hace calor, Brais no le vino*; cast. *aquí hace calor, Brais no ha venido*; gal. *aquí faiche calor, Brais non che veu*) ou l'utilisation d'une préposition après quelques verbes transitifs (*llaman por ti, tira con ese palo*; cast. *te llaman, tira ese palo*; gal. *chaman por ti, tira con ese pau*) (García 1976).

Dans le lexique, les champs sémantiques les plus interférés sont ceux relatifs à la vie familière et domestique, à la caractérisation physique ou psychologique des personnes, aux animaux et plantes naturelles du pays et, en général, au lexique de la campagne et de la mer. Pour quelques exemples du castillan *galicisé*, appelé dépréciativement *castrapo*, voir le tableau 152.2.

Tableau 152.2: Exemples du *castrapo*

Castillan	Castillan coloré à la galicienne	Galicien
colcha, manta	*cobertor*	*cobertor*
olla	*pota*	*ola, pota*
tapadera	*tiesto*	*testo*
aplastar	*esmagar*	*esmagar*
regazo	*colo*	*colo*
barbilla	*queso*	*queixo*
bobo, -ada	*parvo, -ada*	*parvo, -ada*
goloso	*lambón*	*lambón*
reyezuelo	*carrizo*	*carrizo*
urraca	*pega*	*pega*
zarzal	*silvera*	*silveira*
aulaga	*tojo*	*toxo*
jurel	*jurelo*	*xurelo, chicharro*
mújol	*muje*	*muxe*
muro	*valo, muro*	*valo, muro*
roca	*con*	*con, pena*
pan *duro*	pan *reseso*	pan *reseso*

L'influence du castillan sur le galicien populaire (dépréciativement dit *chapurrado* et même *castrapo*) se manifeste surtout dans le lexique. Quelques mots castillans qui appartiennent également au galicien populaire (*Dios, Iglesia, pueblo, siglo* au lieu de *Deus, Igrexa, pobo, século*) sont déjà documentés au Moyen Age. D'autres plus récents (p. ex. *pareja, conejo, juez*) peuvent s'adapter à la phonétique du galicien (*parexa, conexo, xuez* au lieu de *parella, coello, xuíz*), soit avec l'élimination totale de la forme autochtone, soit avec la coexistence de tous les deux mais avec une spécialisation sémantique (González Seoane 1994, Graña Nùñez 1993 et Noia Campos 1984).

Parmi les interférences morphosyntaxiques du castillan, typiques surtout du galicien des gens qui ont le castillan comme langue maternelle, il faut mentionner l'altération du genre, comme p. ex. *a sal, a leite, o auga* (gal. *o sal, o leite, a auga*; cast. *la sal, la leche, el agua*) et celle des formes verbales, comme p. ex. *anduven, supen, había feito* (gal. *andei, souben, fixera*; cast. *anduve, supe, había hecho*). Signalons encore l'emploi proclitique du pronom atone, comme p. ex. *llo digo, te chamei* au lieu de gal. *dígollo, chameite* (cast. *se lo digo, te llamé/te he llamado*).

L'influence du castillan est évidente dans quelques modèles phonétiques des mass media sonores qui emploient le galicien (Regueira 1994).

8. Bibliographie (sélective)

AGAL [Asociaçom Galega da Língua] (1983): *Estudo crítico das normas ortográficas e morfológicas do idioma galego*, Coruña.

Alonso Estravís, Isaac (dir.) (1986): *Dicionário da língua galega*, 3 vols., Madrid.

Alonso Estravís, Isaac (1995): *Dicionário da língua galega*, Santiago de Compostela.

Alvarez, Rosario/Regueira, Xosé Luís/Monteagudo, Henrique (1986): *Gramática galega*, Vigo.

Ares Vázquez, M. C. et al. (1986): *Diccionario Xerais da lingua*, Vigo.

Chacón, Rafael (1979): «Diglosia e historia». In: *Grial* 93, 349–364.

Feixó Cid, Xosé C. (coord.) (1986): *Diccionario da lingua galega*, 3 vols., Vigo.

Fernández, Mauro (1978): «Bilingüismo y diglosia». In: *Verba* 5, 375–391.

Fernández Rei, Francisco (1990 a): *Dialectoloxía da lingua galega*, Vigo.

Fernández Rei, Francisco (1990 b): «Nacionalismo e dignificación da lingua galega no período 1972–1980». In: *A Trabe de Ouro* 1, 43–71.

Fernández Rei, Francisco (1993): «La place de la langue galicienne dans les classifications traditionnelles de la Romania et dans les classifications standardalogiques récentes». In: *Plurilinguismes 6. Sociolinguistique Galicienne*, Rodríguez Yáñez, X. P. (Ed.), 89–120.

Fernández Rei, Francisco (1994): «Contribución das organizacións políticas á normalización da lingua galega (1963–1989)». In: *Actas do XIX Congreso Internacional de Lingüística e Filoloxía Románicas Universidade de Santiago de Compostela (1989)*, Lorenzo, R. (Ed.), 51–74.

Fernández Rodríguez, Mauro A./ Rodríguez Neira, Modesto A. (Ed.) (1994): *Lingua inicial e competencia lingüística en Galicia*. Real Academia Galega. Seminario de Sociolingüística.

Fernández Rodríguez, Mauro A./Rodríguez Neira, Modesto A. (coords.) (1995): *Usos lingüísticos en Galicia. Compendio do II volume do Mapa Sociolingüístico de Galicia*. Real Academia Galega. Seminario de Sociolingüística.

García, Constantino (1976): «Interferencias lingüísticas entre gallego y castellano». In: *Revista Española de Lingüística* 6, 327–343.

García Negro, Mª Pilar (1991): *O galego e as leis. Aproximación sociolingüística*, Vilaboa.

García Negro, Mª Pilar (1993): «La législation concernant la langue galicienne (la légalité vs la nécessité)» In: *Plurilinguismes 6. Sociolinguistique Galicienne*, Rodríguez Yáñez, X. P. (Ed.), 155−179.

Gonzales Seoane, Ernesto (1994): «Variedade e empobrecemento do léxico». In: *Cadernos de Lingua* 10, 89−102.

Graña Núñez, Xosé (1993): *Vacilacións, interferencias e outros «pecados» da lingua galega*, Vigo.

Hermida, Carme (1992): *Os precursores da normalización. Defensa e revindicación da lingua galega no Rexurdimento (1840−1891)*, Vigo.

Herrero Valeiro, Mário J. (1993): «Guerre des graphies et conflit glottopolitique: lignes de discours dans la sociolinguistique galicienne». In: *Plurilinguismes 6. Sociolinguistique Galicienne*, Rodríguez Yáñez, X. P. (Ed.) 181−209.

IGE [Instituto Galego de Estatística] (1991): *Censos de Poboación e Vivendas 1991. Avance de resultados*, [Santiago].

ILG-RAG [Instituto da Lingua Galega − Real Academia Galega] (1982): *Normas ortográficas e morfolóxicas do idioma galego*, Vigo (12ª edición revisada, Maio 1995).

López Muñoz, Daniel (1989): *O idioma da Igrexa en Galicia*, Santiago.

Monteagudo Romero, Henrique (1985): «Aspectos sociolingüísticos do uso do galego, castelán e latín na Idade Media en Galicia». In: *Revista de Administración Galega* 1, 85−108.

Monteagudo, Henrique et al. (1986): *Aspectos sociolingüísticos do bilingüismo en Galicia segundo os alumnos da 2ª etapa de EXB*, [Santiago de Compostela].

Monteagudo Romero, Henrique/García Cancela, Xermán (Eds.) (1988): *Diccionario normativo galego-castelán*, Vigo.

Monteagudo, Henrique (1991): «As leis, as letras e a lingua galega. Breve ollada retrospectiva». In: *Contos da xustiza*, Monteagudo, H. et al. (Eds.), Vigo, 5−31.

Monteagudo, Henrique (1993): «Aspects of corpus planning in Galician». In: *Plurilinguismes 6. Sociolinguistique Galicienne*, Rodríguez Yáñez, X. P. (Ed.), 121−153.

Monteagudo, Henrique (Ed.) (1995): *Estudios de sociolingüística galega. Sobre a norma do galego culto*, Vigo.

Monteagudo, Henrique/Santamarina, Antón (1993): «Galician and Castilian in contact: historical, social and linguistic aspects». In: *Trends in Romance Linguistics and Philology 5: Bilingualism and Linguistic Conflict in Romance*, Posner, R./Green, J. N. (Eds.), Berlin/New York, 117−173.

Navaza Blanco, Gonzalo (Ed.) (1990): *Diccionario Xeral castelán-galego de usos, frases e sinónimos*, Vigo.

Noia Campos, Mª Camino (1984): «Contribución ó estudio do léxico dos bilingües». In: *Verba* 11, 181−195.

Regueira, Xosé Luís (1994): «Modelos fonéticos e autenticidade lingüística». In: *Cadernos de Lingua* 10, 37−60.

Rodríguez Neira, Modesto A. (1993): «Análisis de la situación sociolingüística del gallego desde el ámbito escolar». In: *Plurilinguismes 6. Sociolinguistique Galicienne*, Rodríguez Yáñez, X. P. (Ed.), 55−87.

Rodríguez Neira, Modesto/López Martínez, M. Sol (1988): *O galego na Universidade*, Santiago.

Rojo, Guillermo (1981): «Conductas y actitudes lingüísticas en Galicia». In: *Revista Española de Lingüística* 11, 269−310.

Rojo, Guillermo (1982): «La situación lingüística gallega». In: *Revista de Occidente* 10−11, 93−110.

Rubal Rodríguez, Xosé/Rodríguez Neira, Modesto (1987): *O galego no ensino público non universitario*, Santiago.

Rubal Rodríguez, Xosé/Veiga Martínez, Daniel/Arza Arza, Neves (1992): *A lingua do alumnado e profesorado nas franxas occidentais de Asturias, León e Zamora*, Santiago.

Santamarina, Antón/Fernández Rei, Francisco (1992): «Dinamismo económico e identidade en Galicia». In: *A Trabe de Ouro* 9, 21−33.

Santamarina, Antón (1994): «Galegisch: Sprachnormierung und Standardsprache. Norma y standard». In: *Lexikon der romanistischen Linguistik VI, 2*, Holtus, G./Metzeltin, M./Schmidt, Ch. (Eds.), Tübingen, 66−79 (Reproducido en Monteagudo (Ed.) (1995), 53−98).

Sixirei Paredes, Carlos (1988): *A emigración*, Vigo.

Vázquez Cuesta, Pilar (1980): «Literatura gallega». In: *Historia de las literaturas hispánicas no castellanas*, Díaz Borque, J. M. (Ed.), Madrid, 621−896.

Villares, Ramón (1984): *A historia*, Vigo.

Xove Ferreiro, Xosé (1995): *Diccionario da lingua galega*, Vigo.

*Francisco Fernández Rei,
Saint-Jacques-de-Compostelle (Espagne)*

153. Espagnol—catalan

1. Géographie et démographie
2. Histoire
3. Politique, économie, situations culturelle et religieuse
4. Statistiques et profils ethniques
5. Situation sociolinguistique
6. Etat de la politique linguistique
7. Portrait général des contacts linguistiques
8. Examen critique de la bibliographie
9. Bibliographie (sélective)

1. Géographie et démographie

Le territoire de la langue catalane s'étend principalement à l'est de la Péninsule Ibérique. Du point de vue administratif, il correspond aux communautés autonomes de Catalogne, Valence (ou Pays Valencien) et des Iles Baléares et à la région orientale de l'Aragon (Franja de Ponent) en Espagne; à la co-principauté d'Andorre; au Département des Pyrénées-Orientales (Catalogne-Nord) en France; et à la ville de L'Alguer (Alghero) en Sardaigne. Il n'existe pas un nom unique généralement accepté pour désigner cet ensemble, bien que la question, souvent reprise, ait donné lieu à plusieurs propositions, entre autres à celle du terme de *Pays Catalans*, que nous allons employer par la suite (L'Alguer reste habituellement exclu de cet appellatif). L'ensemble des Pays Catalans occupe 64 437,1 km², dont 31 895,1 km² correspondent à la Catalogne, 23 005,3 km² au Pays Valencien; 4 952 km² aux Baléares; 4 116 km² à la Catalogne-Nord; 468 km² à l'Andorre (Cardús 1992); → carte linguistique E.

Le contact entre catalan et espagnol (ou castillan) se produit principalement en Espagne et Andorre. Nous n'allons pas nous occuper ici des autres territoires malgré l'existence historique de contacts entre ces langues aussi en Catalogne-Nord et à L'Alguer (cf. Veny 1983, 71, 117).

En 1991, la population des territoires étudiés était de 6 006 245 h. en Catalogne; 3 898 241 h. au Pays Valencien; 739 501 h. aux Baléares (Censo de población 1991, 17) et de 59 048 h. en Andorre (Govern 1992). La population, concentrée sur le littoral, est surtout urbaine, avec quelques grands centres: les agglomérations de Barcelone et de Valence et les concentrations de Palma de Mallorca, de Tarragona-Reus et d'Alacant-Elx (Alicante-Elche).

La présence de citoyens étrangers dans les Pays Catalans espagnols est très minoritaire (moins de 1%, à majorité communautaire, marocaine et latino-américaine en 1991 (Anuario 1992, 82); ce chiffre reste fort approximatif, car il n'inclut pas les nombreux immigrants (illégaux), toujours en hausse); par contre, les étrangers forment 82,39% du recensement d'Andorre (1989), dont 47,5% sont des citoyens espagnols (la plupart d'entre eux des Catalans), 10,29% des Portugais, 7,44% des Français, etc. (Govern 1992). Les Pays Catalans espagnols connaissent une proportion très élevée de citoyens nés dans d'autres communautés de l'Espagne (26,38%, dont 31,18% en Catalogne, 20,37% en Valence et 19,38% aux Baléares; Anuario 1993). Il s'agit là d'immigrés arrivés surtout pendant les années 50—70 dans les grands centres urbains.

2. Histoire

La population pré-romaine des Pays Catalans fut presque totalement latinisée entre le deuxième siècle avant Jésus-Christ et le cinquième siècle après Jésus-Christ, et celle-ci assimila à son tour culturellement les peuples germaniques arrivés à l'époque de la chute de l'Empire Romain. Les Arabes conquirent la Péninsule Ibérique (au VIIIe siècle), provoquant l'intervention des Francs, ce qui aboutit à l'apparition de ce que l'on a appelé la Marche Hispanique, qui donna naissance à la Catalogne. Les comtés héritiers de la Marche, devenue très tôt (XIe s.) un ensemble presque indépendant sous l'hégémonie du comte de Barcelone, formèrent une confédération avec le Royaume d'Aragon et effectuèrent une première expansion au sud de la Gaule. La croisade française contre les Albigeois marqua la perte des territoires occitans et réorienta l'expansion catalane vers le sud. La conquête des royaumes de Majorque (1229) et de Valence (1232—1244) préluda à l'expansion militaire et commerciale vers la Sardaigne, Sicile, Naples et même la Grèce (XIVe—XVe s.). Les Baléares furent entièrement repeuplées par des Catalans, tandis qu'au Royaume Valencien, qui reçut des populations d'origine diverse mais à majorité catalane, les autochtones, islamisés et arabophones, ne furent expulsés qu'en 1609.

Aux XVᵉ, XVIᵉ et XVIIᵉ siècles, les Pays Catalans connurent la crise économique, le désarroi social et des guerres civiles, ainsi que les guerres contre la Castille. Malgré l'union des monarques catalano-aragonais et castillan (1492), les Pays Catalans continuèrent à jouir d'un haut degré d'indépendance.

La défaite catalane dans la Guerre de Succession d'Espagne (1701−1714) aboutit à l'annexion formelle à la Castille et marqua le début de la persécution progressive de la langue catalane (depuis le Decreto de Nueva Planta), pendant tout le XVIIIᵉ siècle et le siècle suivant. Dans la deuxième moitié du XIXᵉ siècle, on a tenté de récupérer les libertés politiques perdues aux Pays Catalans. Ces tentatives s'intensifièrent avec l'industrialisation de la Catalogne et son essor économique.

Au XXᵉ siècle, la puissance du mouvement nationaliste de la Catalogne fut freinée par la dictature de Primo de Rivera en 1924−1931. Pendant la deuxième République Espagnole (1931−1936/1939), la Catalogne regagna une part de son autonomie politique (1932), mais la dictature de Franco (1936/1939−1975) essaya à nouveau d'anéantir la langue catalane. L'immigration massive de castillanophones, attirés par le développement industriel et touristique, l'extension de la scolarisation obligatoire et le développement des médias − tous en espagnol −, mirent en contact, pour la première fois, et de façon généralisée, la population catalane avec la langue castillane. La transition politique et le processus de démocratisation à partir de 1975 ont permis l'instauration des régimes d'autonomie.

Andorre, resté un Etat indépendant, a connu un essor économique très remarquable grâce au tourisme, au commerce et à l'activité bancaire et vient de se doter, en 1993, d'une constitution moderne.

3. Politique, économie, situations culturelle et religieuse

Après 1978, les territoires espagnols de langue catalane ont reçu un certain degré d'autonomie politique de la part de l'Etat espagnol. Cette autonomie est considérable en Catalogne, plus restreinte en Valence, et encore plus limitée aux Iles Baléares et en Aragon. Andorre constitue une co-principauté parlementaire souveraine, bien que, du point de vue économique, elle dépende entièrement de l'extérieur. En 1991, 51,1% de la population des Pays Catalans − avec la Catalogne-Nord et sans la *Franja* d'Aragon − travaillaient dans le secteur tertiaire (surtout dans le tourisme et le commerce tant en Andorre qu'aux Baléares), 9,6% dans la construction, 29,9% dans l'industrie (textile, métallurgie, chimie, alimentation, surtout en Catalogne et Valence) et 5,4% dans l'agriculture, surtout au Pays Valencien et en Catalogne-Nord (Cardús 1992, sqq). Ces territoires présentent un bilan commercial positif par rapport au reste de l'Espagne, mais négatif du point de vue fiscal et financier, étant de plus en plus dépendants du capital extérieur. L'activité économique se concentre sur la côte méditerranéenne, dans les agglomérations urbaines de Barcelone, Valence, Tarragona-Reus, Alacant-Elx (en esp. Alicante-Elche) et Palma, où il y a beaucoup d'immigration, mais elle reste faible à l'intérieur qui se dépeuple.

Plus de la moitié de la population se reconnaît catholique, sans être pourtant pratiquante. La sécularisation se répand progressivement, particulièrement en Catalogne: le nombre d'indifférents, d'agnostiques et d'athées augmente. Les clivages religieux ne coïncident pas avec les clivages linguistiques (González/González 1990, 38 sq).

4. Statistiques et profils ethniques

En 1991, les pourcentages de la population − la *Franja* et Andorre exclues − déclarant *comprendre*, *parler*, *lire* et *écrire* le catalan étaient les suivants: la Catalogne (93,7%, 68,3%, 67,6% et 39,9%), Valence (77,1%, 49,4%, 24,3% et 7%, y compris les territoires historiquement de langue espagnole), Iles Baléares (88,7%, 66,7%, 54,9% et 25,9%) (Censos 1992). On peut dire que, dès l'enfance, presque la totalité de la population maîtrise l'espagnol. En Andorre, en 1989, 44,5% de la population avaient le catalan comme première langue, 37,3% l'espagnol, 7% le portugais et 6,7% le français (Martínez et al. 1989). Un recul lent du catalan comme langue familiale se produit au Pays Valencien, tandis qu'en Catalogne la situation est stable (Strubell 1989, 103 sqq). En Aragon, le catalan n'est qu'une langue parlée, avec quelque 60 000 locuteurs (Marí 1992, 92). En 1990, dans la région de Barcelone, 35% des 4 millions d'habitants avaient le catalan comme langue première et 60% l'espagnol, tandis que dans le reste de la Catalogne les catalanophones sont en majorité. Dans la région de Barcelone, le nombre des bilingues familiaux augmente sans cesse: 17% de la population entre 18 et 21 ans (Subirats et al. 1992, 37). Tandis qu'en Catalogne les catalanophones se concentrent dans les catégories sociales supérieures et moyennes (aussi bien urbaines que rurales), en Valence ils se concentrent dans les couches moyennes et basses. C'est dans ces domaines, par conséquent, que le catalan subit le contre-coup d'attitudes et de préjugés négatifs (*auto-odi*, « haine de soi-même ») qui contribuent à sa substitution. L'effet combiné des migrations de populations castillanophones et la castillanisation d'une partie des autochtones — surtout en Valence et parmi les élites, numériquement réduites mais influentes, aux Baléares et en Catalogne — fait que la diffusion récente de la connaissance scolaire du catalan ne favorise pas sa diffusion comme langue familiale.

5. Situation sociolinguistique

La vitalité du catalan est très variable selon les territoires. Dans l'ensemble des Pays Catalans, le catalan est encore la langue habituelle pour les rapports interpersonnels parmi les catalanophones, tandis que l'espagnol est la langue d'usage dans les relations avec les autres groupes linguistiques. En ce qui concerne les fonctions instrumentales, l'espagnol est la langue la plus répandue et la plus nécessaire dans le secteur du travail, même si la connaissance et l'usage du catalan augmentent dans le secteur public, surtout dans l'administration locale et régionale. La loyauté linguistique face au catalan se manifeste dans les réseaux de relations interpersonnelles, mais très peu dans les activités instrumentales et économiques.

En dehors de la Catalogne, les glottonymes du catalan se réfèrent à des régions (*valencien, majorquin* ...). En Valence, cette diversité onomasiologique repose sur une tradition particulariste assez puissante. Selon une enquête de 1992, 50% des Valenciens considéraient que leur parler faisait partie de l'ensemble du catalan, tandis que 42% le considéraient comme une langue indépendante (*Servei*, 1992).

6. Etat de la politique linguistique

La Constitution espagnole de 1978 (art. 3) oblige tous les citoyens à connaître le castillan, langue officielle de l'Etat, et leur reconnaît le droit à s'en servir partout. Elle reconnaît aussi l'officialité « des autres langues » en accord avec les statuts d'autonomie de chaque communauté territoriale.

Il n'existe aucune obligation constitutionnelle de connaître le catalan. Les constitutions régionales de la Catalogne (art. 3) et des Iles Baléares (art. 3) déclarent le catalan *langue propre* (*llengua pròpia*) de chaque communauté et le rendent officiel à côté du castillan. Dans la Communauté de Valence, on considère le *valencien* — appellation locale du catalan — comme langue officielle à côté du castillan (art. 7). L'Aragon se limite à reconnaître les variétés linguistiques, sans faire du catalan une langue officielle (art. 7). Il y a donc deux concepts fondamentaux: (1) la *double officialité* ou l'officialité pleine de chaque langue qui exclut le recours à l'autre, par opposition à la *co-officialité*, qui exigerait la présence générale des deux langues (comme à Bruxelles, cf. Witte et al. 1984); (2) la notion de *langue propre*, qui permettrait de favoriser l'usage de la langue de la communauté dans les institutions (Puig Salellas 1989).

L'analyse de la situation sociolinguistique et le processus d'aménagement linguistique s'appuient aux Pays Catalans sur le concept de *normalisation linguistique* (*normalització lingüística*) (Aracil 1982). On entend par là l'inversion du processus de substitution linguistique (qui avait créé le *conflit linguistique*) au moyen de la création et de l'extension sociale de normes d'usage pertinentes. Mis à part l'Aragon, les trois communautés catalanes en Espagne ont approuvé des « Lois de normalisation linguistique » (Catalogne et Valence en 1983; Baléares en 1986) visant à surmonter les effets néfastes de trois siècles de persécutions linguistiques. Les problèmes de fixation de la norme linguistique ont été réglés entre 1918 (grammaire officielle) et 1932 (dictionnaire normatif et adoption de la norme officielle au Pays Valencien; cf. 7.). Dans le domaine de la planification du corpus, il ne reste aujourd'hui que des questions mineures à résoudre, notamment des questions stylistiques et relatives à la terminologie scientifique surtout (cf. 8.).

L'aménagement du statut linguistique offre par contre de nombreux déséquilibres, nés d'un côté des propres contradictions internes de chaque Pays Catalan et de leur ensemble (la Catalogne mène la politique la plus active, alors qu'en Aragon, rien où presque n'a été fait), et, de l'autre, du fait que l'Etat espagnol n'a jamais renoncé à une politique linguistique en faveur du castillan dans tous les domaines.

Les effets de *normalisation* ont touché principalement l'enseignement: le catalan est matière obligatoire à l'école primaire et secondaire, au même niveau que le castillan, sauf en Aragon, où il est facultatif. Le catalan est objet d'étude dans toutes les universités des Pays Catalans. La *catalanisation* (ou adoption du catalan comme langue véhiculaire habituelle) de l'école, par contre, est le privilège de la seule Catalogne, où depuis 1983 toutes les écoles doivent l'employer comme moyen de communication pour un minimum d'un ou deux cours selon le niveau éducatif, et où la méthode d'immersion en catalan est appliquée à des dizaines de milliers d'élèves castillanophones. Comme résultat, durant l'année scolaire 1989—1990, 36% des écoles primaires en Catalogne avaient adopté le catalan comme langue d'enseignement et 40% étaient en train de le faire, tandis que 24% employaient le catalan et le castillan en proportions diverses. Il ne restait qu'un seul pourcent à ne jamais utiliser le catalan comme langue véhiculaire (Vial 1990).

Le domaine des médias reflète les contradictions des différents pouvoirs: les gouvernements autonomes possèdent deux chaînes de télévision en catalan en Catalogne (TV3 et Canal 33) et une chaîne bilingue en Valence (Canal 9). La télévision publique espagnole produit aussi des programmes en catalan. Cependant, le gouvernement central a obligé les chaînes privées à desservir tout le territoire espagnol les forçant ainsi à émettre en castillan. Il en est de même de la télévision par satellite. Le gouvernement espagnol entrave en outre la réception des télévisions de la Catalogne et de Valence en dehors de leurs territoires respectifs. Le déséquilibre en faveur du castillan se répète encore pour la radio (Institut 1992) et devient écrasant dans le domaine du cinéma, de la vidéo et de la presse, malgré l'existence de plusieurs journaux, magazines, etc. Par contre, il faut remarquer l'expansion de l'édition de livres en catalan, qui, en 1992, a déjà dépassé le nombre de 5000 titres par an. Notons en outre le succès massif des groupes de pop-rock en catalan. Le théâtre utilise surtout le catalan (Institut 1992).

Ce n'est qu'en Catalogne qu'on a promu le catalan dans bien d'autres domaines. Ainsi, pendant les premières années d'aménagement linguistique, les pouvoirs publics ont encouragé le changement des attitudes et comportements individuels en faveur du *bilinguisme passif*. On entend par là un comportement linguistique consistant à utiliser le catalan même quand l'interlocuteur n'est que bilingue réceptif dans cette langue. Cette attitude volontariste fut fort critiquée; aujourd'hui le processus de normalisation s'adresse avant tout aux communications institutionnelles (Bastardas 1990, Marí 1992).

7. Portrait général des contacts linguistiques

Bien qu'il n'y ait pas d'études basées sur des chiffres concrets, le contact linguistique entre l'espagnol et le catalan est généralement caractérisé par un déséquilibre manifeste dans la direction et le poids des influences interlinguistiques, qui sont très marquées de l'espagnol sur le catalan et très superficielles dans la direction inverse. Cet état de choses n'a rien de surprenant si on tient compte, d'un côté, des différentes masses démographiques correspondant à chaque langue et, de l'autre côté, des vicissitudes historiques et culturelles que le catalan a traversées.

7.1. La perspective historique

Les premiers emprunts lexicaux de l'espagnol sont documentés en catalan depuis le XIVe siècle, tout particulièrement dans la deuxième moitié, mais ils sont alors encore très rares. Au XVe siècle, ils sont déjà plus nombreux, et le chiffre augmente au cours des siècles suivants (XVIe et XVIIe: Colón 1976, 182 sq; 354 sq; Bruguera 1986, 66 sq). L'interdiction de l'usage officiel de la langue catalane à partir du XVIIIe siècle, et le poids de l'immigration espagnole pendant le XXe siècle, contribuent à un accroissement encore plus notable de l'influence espagnole sur le lexique du catalan. L'espagnol, en plus, sert comme langue de pont par laquelle le catalan adopte des emprunts qui proviennent d'autres langues. En échange, mais à une échelle moindre, le catalan a fait aussi le pont vers l'espagnol pour des mots d'origine occitane et italienne. Quant aux catalanismes lexicaux de l'espagnol, on peut suivre leur trace depuis le XIVe siècle jusqu'au XXe (Colón 1967; Bruguera 1986, 72 sq; Solà 1991, 57 sq). Bien que le total des catalanismes de l'espagnol soit considérable (numériquement et qualitativement), il est de loin inférieur à celui que l'on observe dans la direction inverse. En définitive, l'influence de l'espagnol sur le catalan constitue historiquement une interférence par emprunt (surtout lexical), typique d'une langue dominante sur une langue récessive dans un processus de substitution linguistique (Argente/Payrató 1991, 469 sq). Pour l'espagnol, l'interférence du catalan représente, mis à l'écart les emprunts lexicaux incorporés par la langue commune, une interférence par substitution (surtout phonique) qui, à l'instar d'un effet de substrat, caractérise la variété spécifique de l'espagnol utilisé par des locuteurs dont la première langue est le catalan.

7.2. Variétés actuelles

Aucune variété intermédiaire n'est apparue comme résultat de l'hybridation entre les deux langues. Les locuteurs bilingues actifs pratiquent l'alternance des langues spécialement en fonction de la sélection de l'interlocuteur et de la situation conversationnelle en question.

Il n'y a pas d'études qui offrent des données quantitatives sur les interférences actuelles en fonction des registres utilisés (oraux/écrits, formels/informels, génériques/techniques), ni en fonction des variétés sociales et selon les générations. Quelques variétés géographiques du catalan ont reçu une attention spéciale, tel le valencien (Montoya 1989, Blas 1993) et le roussillonnais (Veny 1978, 155 sq), mais la majorité des études fournissent des données relatives aux dialectes centraux ou à l'ensemble de la langue catalane (Solà 1977; Payrató 1985). Le niveau linguistique le plus étudié est celui du lexique (cf. les travaux cités ci-dessus et Cerdà 1983; Colón 1989).

L'influence espagnole se manifeste surtout dans les parlers catalans urbains, spécialement dans ceux des villes avec beaucoup d'immigrés (agglomérations de Barcelone et Valence). Quant au catalan de locuteurs catalans d'origine (les catalanophones), les interférences castillanes sont surtout lexicales et syntaxiques: dans le lexique, ceci concerne les emprunts et les calques, et aussi les vocabulaires techniques ou spécialisés (*acús de rebut* 'accusé de réception', *àmbar* 'ambre', *bòveda* 'voûte', *catarata* 'cataracte', *cauce* 'lit', *membret* 'entête') et le lexique familier (surtout dans la phraséologie et dans beaucoup de dénominations ordinaires et argotiques: *de repent* 'soudain', *nada menos* 'rien de moins', *posar pegues* 'trouver à redire'; *alfombra* 'tapis', *bandeja* 'plateau', *nòvio/-a* 'fiancé/-e', *novato* 'bleu', *xupar* 'sucer'; *estar fet pols* 'mort de fatigue', *al.lucinar per un tubo* 'halluciner, s'étonner'); dans la syntaxe, ceci vaut aussi surtout pour les connecteurs (prépositions et conjonctions: *hasta* 'jusque', *pel matí* 'le matin', *degut a què* 'par Suite de', *pero* 'mais', *pues* 'donc', *doncs* 'donc' causal). L'influence est bien visible aussi au niveau discursif: ceci à cause de l'utilisation (non normative) très fréquente de quelques marqueurs discursifs espagnols dans les variétés orales (*bueno*, *pues*, *vale*). La phonétique et la morphologie sont plus à l'abri de l'influence de l'espagnol, bien que quelques phénomènes attendent des études plus approfondies, qui devraient élucider leur caractère, situé à cheval entre le déroulement spontané et le changement induit, ce qui vaut aussi pour certains phénomènes syntaxiques (comme l'usage des prépositions *per* et *per a*, 'par' et 'pour'), lexicaux (verbes *ser* et *estar*, 'être') et pragmatiques (perte progressive du traitement de *vós* 'vous' en faveur de *tu* 'tu' et *vostè* 'vous'). Sur le plan phonique, l'introduction du son [χ] a été l'objet de controverses (Veny 1991), bien qu'il s'agisse d'un son satellite plutôt que d'un nouveau phonème de la langue (Payrató 1985, 99 ss).

Ce sont les interférences phoniques dans le catalan des locuteurs castillanophones (d'origine) qui sont très remarquables, avec réductions vocaliques (e/ɛ → e, *set* ['set]; o/ɔ → o, *bo* ['bo]; a/ə → a, *cara* ['kara]), assourdissements généralisés (z → s, *casa* ['kasə]; z → ʃ, *boja* ['bɔʃə]) et [l] non vélarisé (*mal* [mal]). De même dans l'espagnol des catalanophones, avec les phénomènes inverses: hyperdifférentiation vocalique (*cielo* ['θjɛlo], *rosa* ['rɔsa], *vida* ['biðə]), sonorisations indues (*las amigas* [laz a'miɣas]) et [l] vélarisé (*fatal* [fa'taɫ]). Dans cette dernière variété, moins étudiée, les calques sémantiques et les emprunts lexicaux (quelques-uns répandus aussi parmi les populations castillanes des Pays Catalans) sont également fréquents (*explicar* 'raconter', *sentir* 'entendre'; *paleta* 'maçon', *plegar* 'finir', *vaga* 'grève'), et, quant aux aspects grammaticaux, il faut remarquer les calques syntaxiques et la réduction à deux degrés du système des déictiques: *a más a más* 'en plus', *¿que se puede?* 'peut-on entrer?', *todo y que* 'quoique'; *aquí/ahí/allí* (-*á*) — *aquí/allí*(-*á*) 'ici/là', *este/ese/aquel* — *este/aquel* 'celui-ci/celui-là' (voir Moll 1961; Badia 1964, 145 sq; 1980; Marsá 1986; Solà 1991, 57 sq; Tusón/Payrató 1991).

8. Examen critique de la bibliographie

Malgré le nombre croissant des données sur la sociologie des langues dans les Pays Catalans (cf. 4., 5., 7.), il reste encore des lacunes notables à propos de la situation sociolinguistique, notamment en ce qui concerne l'usage spontané. Ce déficit rend difficile l'évaluation de l'impact des politiques linguistiques et celle de l'évolution du contact linguistique entre le castillan et le catalan.

Le nombre d'études portant sur les conséquences linguistiques du contact (voir 7.) est réduit, surtout si on fait abstraction des travaux relatifs au discours prescriptif qui, eux, représentent un grand nombre de pages. Beaucoup d'ouvrages normatifs officiels et une large collection de manuels de diffusion sous la forme de dictionnaires d'incorrections ou « barbarismes » (voir Solà 1977, 1991; Payrató 1985) s'inscrivent dans cette tradition. Dans la perspective diachronique, la vision de la grammaire historique traditionnelle de la romanistique est toujours en place (Colón 1967, 1976, 1989; Veny 1978; Coromines 1980−1991; Casanova 1991; Colomina 1991). Elle vient d'être complétée cependant par des études plus récentes avec une perspective carrément sociolinguistique qui s'intéresse au changement linguistique diachronique (Montoya 1986, Gimeno/Montoya 1989). Pour les aspects synchroniques, nous renvoyons aux nombreuses études présentées au *IX Col.loqui Internacional de Llengua i Literatura Catalanes* (Alacant-Elx, sept. 1991), dont l'approche linguistique était centrée sur le contact des langues. Il manque encore des corpora représentatifs de toutes les variétés en contact, aussi bien qu'une intensification de l'analyse contrastive (voir Payrató 1988), et des études (et décomptes) des types et des degrés de l'interférence (aussi dans une perspective contrastive avec attention spéciale aux variétés contextuelles et aux standards). De même, seules des analyses contrastives approfondies, et qui incorporent une dimension historique, pourront éclairer les phénomènes de l'évolution spontanée (mais logiquement parallèle) de deux langues étroitement apparentées et les résultats de l'évolution induite par l'influence interlinguistique. En revanche, il faut souligner les recherches sur le choix et l'alternance des langues (Calsamiglia/Tuson 1980; Woolard 1987, 1990, 1992; Boix 1993), ainsi que la théorie portant sur les concepts du conflit linguistique, de la substitution et de la normalisation linguistiques, de la diglossie et du bilinguisme (cf. Vallverdú 1980; Aracil 1982; Argente (Ed.) 1991, Pueyo 1992).

9. Bibliographie (sélective)

Anuario de migraciones (1992/1993): Madrid, Ministerio de Trabajo y Seguridad Social, Dirección General de Migraciones.

Aracil, Lluís Vicent (1982): *Papers de sociolingüística*, Barcelone.

Argente, Joan A. (Ed.) (1991): *Debat sobre la normalització lingüística*, Barcelone.

Argente, Joan A./Payrató, Lluís (1991): « Towards a Pragmatic Approach to the Study of Languages in Contact: Evidence from Language Contact Cases in Spain ». In: *Pragmatics 1*, 465−480.

Arnau, Joaquim et al. (1992): *La educación bilingüe*, Barcelone.

Badia, Antoni Maria (1964): *Llengua i cultura als Països Catalans*, Barcelone.

Badia, Antoni Maria (1980): « Peculiaridades del uso del castellano en las tierras de lengua catalana ». In: *Actas del I Simposio para Profesores de Lengua y Literatura Españolas*, Madrid, 11−31.

Bastardas, Albert (1990): « L'extensió de l'ús del català: fonaments teòrics per a una nova etapa ». In: *Revista de Catalunya 38*, 13−23.

Blas, José Luis (1993): *La interferencia lingüística en Valencia (dirección: catalán − castellano). Estudio sociolingüístico*, Castelló.

Boix, Emili (1993): *Triar no és trair. Identitat i llengua en els joves de Barcelona*, Barcelone.

Bruguera, Jordi (²1986): *Història del lèxic català*, Barcelone.

Calsamiglia, Helena/Tuson, Empar (1980): « Ús i alternança de llengües en grups de joves d'un barri de Barcelona: Sant Andreu de Palomar ». In: *Treballs de Sociolingüística Catalana 3*, 11−82.

Cardús, Salvador (1992): *Estadístiques dels Països Catalans*, Barcelone.

Casanova, Emili (1991): « Evolució i interferència en el sistema demostratiu català ». In: *IX Col.loqui AILLC,* Alacant (sous presse).

Censo de población 1991. Avance de resultados (1992). Madrid, Instituto Nacional de Estadística.

Censos de població i habitants 1991. Resultats provisionals (1992), Valence.

Cerdà, Ramon (1983): « Diglosia y degradación semántica en el habla de Constantí (Campo de Tarragona) ». In: *Philologica Hispaniensia in Honorem Manuel Alvar*. Madrid, vol. I, 137−158.

Colomina, Jordi (1991): « La llengua catalana a Múrcia ». In: *IX Col.loqui AILLC*, Alacant (sous presse).

Colón, Germà (1967): « Catalanismos ». In: *Enciclopedia Lingüística Hispánica*, Madrid, vol. II, 193−238.

Colón, Germà (1976): *El léxico catalán en la Romania*, Madrid.

Colón, Germà (1989): *El español y el catalán, juntos y en contraste*, Barcelone.

Coromines, Joan (1980−1991): *Diccionari etimològic i complementari de la llengua catalana (DECLC)*, Barcelone.

Direcció General de Política Lingüística (1991): *Estudis i propostes per a la difusió de la llengua catalana*, Barcelone.

Gimeno, Francesc/Montoya, Branli (1989): *Sociolingüística*, Valence.

González Blasco, Pedro/González-Anleo, Juan (1992): *Religión y sociedad en la España de los 90*, Madrid.

Govern d'Andorra (1992): *Estadístiques. Any 1991*.

Institut de Sociolingüística Catalana (1992): *La llengua catalana en l'actualitat*, Barcelone.

Marí, Isidor et al. (1992): *La llengua catalana als països catalans*, Barcelone.

Marí, Isidor (1992): *Un horitzó per a la llengua. Aspectes de la planificació lingüística*, Barcelone.

Marsá, Francisco (1986): «Sobre concurrencia lingüística en Cataluña». In: Víctor García de la Concha et al.: *El castellano actual en las comunidades bilingües de España*, Salamanca, 93−104.

Martínez, Gerard et al. (1989): *Recull estadístic general d'Andorra*, Andorra la Vella.

Moll, Francesc de Borja (1961): «El castellano en Mallorca». In: *Homenaje ofrecido a Dámaso Alonso*, Madrid, vol. II, 469−475.

Montoya, Brauli (1986): *Variació i desplaçament de llengües a Elda i a Oriola durant l'edat moderna*, Alacant.

Montoya, Brauli (1989): *La interferència lingüística al sud valencià*, Valence.

Payrató, Lluís (1985): *La interferència lingüística. Comentaris i exemples català − castellà*, Barcelone.

Payrató, Lluís (1988): «L'anàlisi contrastiva català − castellà: història i futur». In: *On Spanish, Portuguese, and Catalan Linguistics*, John J. Staczek (Ed.), Washington, 226−239.

Pueyo, Miquel (1992): *Llengües en contacte en la comunitat lingüística catalana*, Valence.

Puig Salellas, Josep Maria (1989): *La situació jurídica de la llengua catalana, avui*, Barcelone.

Servei d'Estudis i Investigació Sociolingüística (1992): *Unitat i nom de la llengua*, Valence.

Solà, Joan (1977): *Del català incorrecte al català correcte*, Barcelone.

Solà, Joan (1991): *Episodis d'història de la llengua catalana*, Barcelone.

Subirats, Marina et al. (1992): *Enquesta de la Regió Metropolitana 1990, Vol. 4. Educació, llengua i hàbits culturals*, Barcelone, Institut d'Estudis Metropolitans.

Strubell, Miquel (1989): «Evolució de la Comunitat Lingüística». In: *El nacionalisme català a la fi del segle XX*, Barcelone, 103−140.

Tusón, Amparo/Payrató, Lluís (1991): «El español en contacto con el catalán. Interferencias y alternancia de lenguas en el español hablado en Cataluña». In: *1st International Conference on Spanish in Contact with other Languages*, Los Angeles (manuscrit).

Vallverdú, Francesc (1980): *Aproximació crítica a la sociolingüística catalana*, Barcelone.

Veny, Joan (1978): *Estudis de geolingüística catalana*, Barcelone.

Veny, Joan (1991): *Els parlars catalans*, Palma de Mallorca.

Veny, Joan (1991): «Problemes d'interferència en català». In: *IX Col.loqui AILLC*, Alacant (sous presse).

Vial, Salvador (1990): «Comparació de la situació sociolingüística a l'escola primària a Catalunya entre els cursos 1986−1987 i 1989−1990». In: *Notícies del SEDEC*, 4−7.

Webber, Jude/Strubell, Miquel (1991): *The Catalan Language Today. Progress towards Normalization*, Sheffield.

Witte, Els et al. (1984): *Le bilinguisme en Belgique. Le cas de Bruxelles*, Bruxelles.

Woolard, Kathryn A. (1987): «Code switching and comedy in Catalonia». In: *Papers in Pragmatics 1*, 106−122.

Woolard, Kathryn A. (1990): *Double Talk. Bilingualism and the Politics of Ethnicity in Catalonia*, Stanford.

Woolard, Kathryn A. (1992): *Identitat i contacte de llengües a Barcelona*, Barcelone, version catalane revisée.

Emili Boix/Lluís Payrató/F. Xavier Vila, Barcelone (Espagne)

154. Espagnol−basque

1. Géographie et démographie
2. Histoire
3. Politique, économie et situation culturelle
4. Statistiques et profils ethniques
5. Situation sociolinguistique
6. Etat de la politique linguistique
7. Aspects intralinguistiques des langues en contact
8. Examen critique de la bibliographie
9. Bibliographie (sélective)

1. Géographie et démographie

1.1. Géographie

Les Basques désignent par *Euskal Herria* [Pays Basque] le territoire où l'on parle la langue basque, situé sur les deux versants des Pyrénées occidentales, sur les bords du golfe de Biscaye, dans les Etats espagnol et français: dans la partie péninsulaire d'une étendue de 17 682 km^2, au nord des Pyrénées d'une étendue de 2 982 km^2 (Gómez Piñero/Ochoa/Gandarillas/Villanueva 1979, 80).

Pays de contrastes malgré sa dimension réduite: de climat océanique sur le versant septentrional, avec prés et pâturages abondants; de climat méditerranéen sur le versant méridional, riche en céréales et vins; pays industriel autour de Bilbao et des petites villes industrielles; pays de pêcheurs avec les ports de Ondarroa, Bermeo, etc.; pays de tourisme avec Saint-Sébastien (Donostia), Zarautz, Biarritz. A un habitat rural très dispersé des fermes du versant Nord, répondent sur le versant Sud des noyaux urbains resserrés.

Dans l'Etat espagnol, la langue basque est parlée dans la CAV (= Comunidad Autónoma Vasca), dans les localités situées au nord du territoire d'Alava, en Biscaye sur tout le territoire à l'exception de la partie occidentale à partir de Bilbao (Bilbo) et dans le Guipuzcoa en entier. En Navarre, le basque s'étend sur le versant Nord et jusqu'à la région de Pampelune.

1.2. Démographie

La CAV compte 2 104 081 habitants et la Navarre 521 940 selon le recensement de 1991. « Le fait immigratoire est le facteur démographique le plus caractéristique de la période et celui qui comporte aussi les plus graves conséquences pour le processus historique de la langue basque » (Euskaltzaindia 1977, 276). Le rythme d'immigration a été particulièrement accéléré dans les années 1961−1965 puisque 90 000 personnes ont immigré vers la seule Biscaye (Rotaetxe 1987a, 167). Depuis 1975, l'immigration s'est progressivement tarie et elle est négative aujourd'hui (Gobierno Vasco 1989, 16).

2. Histoire

2.1. Histoire régionale

Au Moyen Age, la communauté qui parle le basque est structurée en différents territoires indépendants rattachés à des entités politiques distinctes. Ces territoires sont régis par les *fors* (ordonnancement juridique propre dont se sont dotées les communautés basques).

Les « guerres carlistes » (1833−1839, puis 1872−1876), fomentées autour de la succession au trône du roi Ferdinand VII, opposent un secteur traditionaliste, rural, contre le libéralisme centralisateur en plein développement. « Les guerres carlistes supposent la fin du système traditionnel d'autonomie quant au juridique, à l'administratif et à l'économique en Pays Basque » (Argüeso 1991, 17).

Dans ce contexte surgit le mouvement nationaliste basque sur le thème de « *Euzkadi* est la patrie des Basques ».

Le triomphe du général Franco en 1939 amène pour le nationalisme basque une répression sans précédent. Dans les années 50 naît l'organisation ETA, *Euskadi Ta Askatasuna* [Pays Basque et liberté] « une organisation socialiste, révolutionnaire, basque, de libération nationale » (Haritschelhar 1983, 446) qui pratique la lutte armée. Après la mort de Franco (survenue en 1975) la dictature laisse place à une nouvelle organisation juridique avec l'approbation de la nouvelle Constitution espagnole (en 1978) et la formation d'un régime d'autonomie au sein de l'Etat espagnol.

2.2. Historique du contact linguistique

Le basque a été en contact avec d'autres langues depuis une période très ancienne à l'intérieur même de son territoire. C'est que les classes les plus influentes ont utilisé une autre langue que le basque comme véhicule de communication; le basque est demeuré l'idiome de la communauté rurale essentiellement. Louis-Lucien Bonaparte (1813−1891), père de la dialectologie basque, affirmait que la grande majorité des localités du Pays Bas-

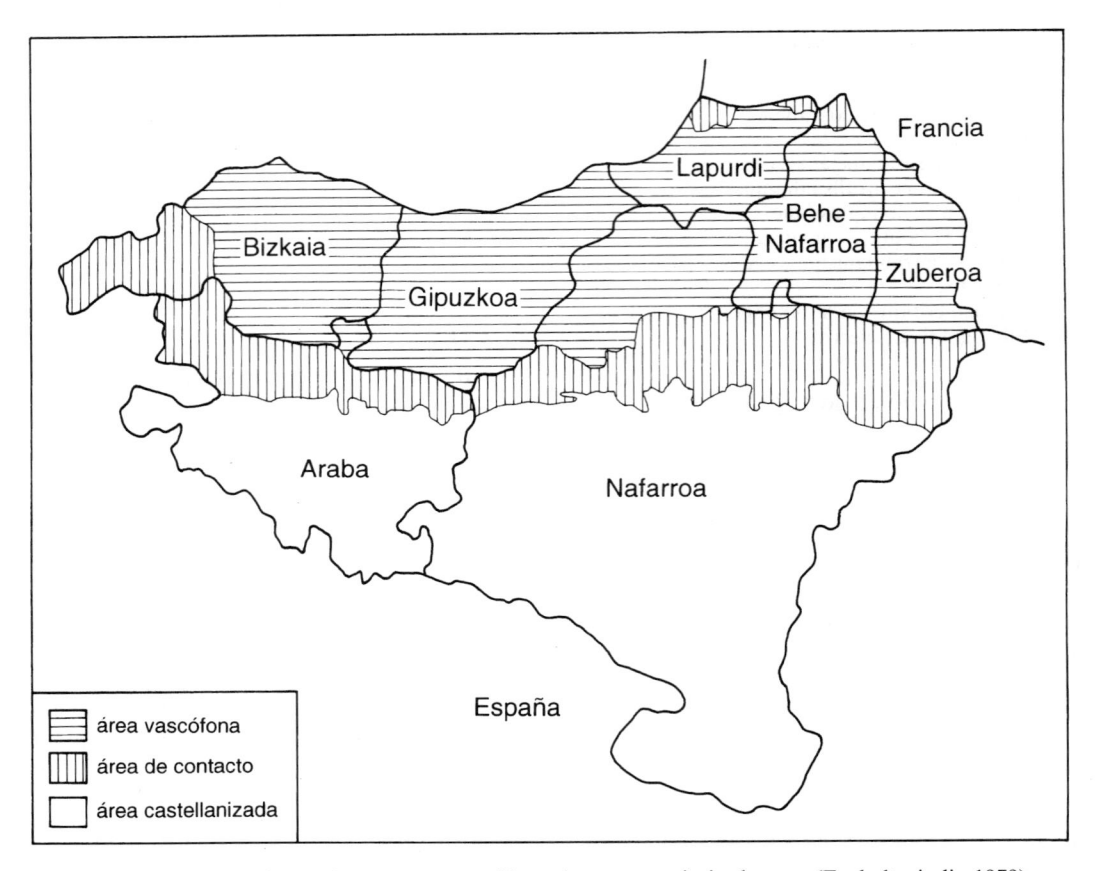

Fig. 154.1: Aires bascophone, de contact et castillanophone en territoire basque (Euskaltzaindia 1979)

que étaient mixtes du point de vue de la langue. Le contact linguistique entre euskera et espagnol date donc de fort longtemps: c'est pourquoi tout le territoire de langue basque est zone de contact linguistique.

Certes, dans un travail élaboré par la société SIADECO pour l'Académie de la langue basque (Euskaltzaindia 1979), trois types d'aires sont distingués: zone bascophone, zone de contact et zone non bascophone. Mais ce même document met en doute l'exactitude de cette distinction pour deux raisons: l'espagnol est généralisé dans l'aire bascophone et le basque est présent en zone non bascophone grâce aux *ikastola* [écoles en basque] et aux cours du soir d'apprentissage de la langue (voir la fig. 154.1).

3. Politique, économie et situation culturelle

3.1. Situation politique

«La nation basque existe. Prenons le mot dans sa signification étymologique qui évoque l'appartenance à un groupe soudé par des liens de naissance, habitant un territoire défini, parlant une langue commune» (Haritschelhar 1983, 443).

Ce territoire est aujourd'hui divisé en deux Etats différents et en trois zones administratives. Dans l'Etat français, la communauté basque vivant dans une partie du département des Pyrénées-Atlantiques ne constitue aucune entité politique propre. Dans l'Etat espagnol, la Constitution proclame «l'indissoluble unité de la Nation espagnole (...) et reconnaît et garantit le droit à l'autonomie des nationalités et régions qui la constituent». L'autonomisation de l'Espagne a pourtant entraîné la division du Pays Basque péninsulaire en deux communautés autonomes: la Communauté Autonome Basque (CAV) et la Communauté Forale de Navarre.

3.1.1. Communauté Autonome Basque (CAV)

Le Statut d'Autonomie de la CAV fut approuvé fin 1979. Administrativement, il se divise en trois territoires historiques: Biscaye avec Bilbao pour capitale; Guipuzcoa avec Saint-Sébastien pour capitale et Alava, avec pour capitale Vitoria-Gasteiz.

Le siège du Gouvernement Basque est situé à Vitoria-Gasteiz. Son président est actuellement (1993) J. A. Ardanza, du Parti Nationaliste Basque, qui gouverne en coalition avec le Parti Socialiste Espagnol.

3.1.2. Communauté Forale de Navarre

Le statut d'autonomie de Navarre intitulé « Loi organique d'Intégration et Amélioration du Régime Foral de Navarre » fut promulgué en 1982. Le parlement navarrais siège à Pampelune. Le président du gouvernement est à ce jour J. C. Alli (de l'Unión del Pueblo Navarro — UPN).

3.2. Situation économique

Le Pays Basque longtemps tenu pour une place forte sur le plan économique, subit aujourd'hui une sévère récession. Le taux de chômage est un des plus élevés d'Europe: à la fin de 1992: 22,1% dans la CAV et 12% en Navarre selon les statistiques de l'Institut National de Statistique.

3.3. Situation culturelle

La langue basque est le facteur le plus important dans l'identification de la culture et la construction du sentiment d'être basque. La renaissance culturelle basque remonte au début du XXe siècle.

Les premiers essais d'introduction de l'enseignement en basque, étouffés par la guerre de 1936 à 1939, ont resurgi dans les années 60, quand naissent clandestinement les *ikastola*: écoles non officielles, illégales jusqu'en 1968, et dont la langue d'enseignement est le basque. Le mouvement s'est intensifié depuis lors jusqu'à toucher 50 000 élèves en 1977—1978, soit 9% des enfants scolarisés dans les deux communautés (Garagorri 1983, 10). En 1981—1982, ils étaient déjà 70 000 élèves.

4. Statistiques et profils ethniques

4.1. Nombre de locuteurs

En 1975, la société SIADECO a estimé à 632 000 le nombre des bascophones dans tout le Pays Basque, dont 496 660 pour la CAV et 53 340 pour la Navarre (Euskaltzaindia 1979, 68).

Pour la seule CAV, nous pouvons nous référer à des chiffres plus récents du Gouvernement Basque (Gobierno Vasco 1992, 27). Les parlants basques sont passés de 21,5% en 1981 à 24,4% en 1986 et 26,7% en 1991. Les castillanophones qui étaient 64% en 1981 ont été réduits à 53,8% en 1991. En valeur absolue, on compte 548 100 bascophones en 1991, soit 100 000 de plus en 10 ans de communauté autonome. A partir de ces chiffres, Mme Garmendia (Gobierno Vasco 1992, 45), secrétaire générale de la Politique Linguistique au Gouvernement Basque, déclare que « gaurko egoerak ez duela inolako antzik duela hamar urtekoarekin. Guzton ahaleginaz euskararen egoerari buelta ematea lortu dugu: etengabe galtzetik irabaztera pasa gara » [la situation actuelle ne ressemble en rien à celle d'il y a 10 ans. Par l'effort de tous, on a réussi à renverser la situation du basque: d'un recul continuel, on est passé à un gain]. Siguan (1992, 233) exprime la même opinion à partir de données de 1986. Mais il faut tenir compte du fait que le basque ne dispose pas d'individus monolingues basques et qu'il est en contact avec des monolingues hispanophones. En Navarre, de 11% de bascophones en 1975, on est passé en 1986 à 10% (50 989) (Gobierno de Navarra 1989, 11).

Il faut aussi compter sur le phénomène des néo-bascophones, appelés *euskaldunberri*. Dans la CAV, ils représentent 3,57% de la population, soit 10,97% des bascophones (56 063 en valeur absolue). On ne dispose pas de données pour la Navarre.

4.2. Situation ethnique

Le basque, seul survivant des langues pré-indoeuropéennes en Europe, est la langue du groupe ethnique basque. Le Basque désigne sa langue du nom d'*euskara*, se désigne lui-même comme *euskaldun*, c'est-à-dire comme celui « qui possède l'euskara ». Le terme opposé est « erdara » qui désigne toute autre langue étrangère.

5. Situation sociolinguistique

5.1. Statut des langues en contact

Le castillan, langue dominante dans ses relations avec le basque depuis fort longtemps est maintenu dans cette position par la Constitution espagnole qui stipule le devoir pour tout citoyen de connaître l'espagnol, tandis que les autres langues, officielles dans leurs territoires respectifs, ne sont marquées par aucun caractère obligatoire (Rotaetxe 1987 b, 162).

Avec la création du Gouvernement Basque, la langue basque reçoit pour la première fois un appui institutionnel. Dans la CAV, la langue basque a, avec le castillan, caractère de langue officielle. En Navarre, le basque a aussi caractère de langue officielle mais seulement dans les zones bascophones.

5.2. Fonction des langues en contact

Le foyer est le lieu où l'on parle le plus en basque: ainsi le font 74% des bascophones de naissance et 47% des personnes ayant appris le basque (Gobierno Vasco 1983, 117).

Selon une étude récente sur le Guipuzcoa, la publicité commerciale se faisait pour 85,6% exclusivement en espagnol. De façon plus générale, analysant le rôle de l'euskara dans la vie publique, l'auteur déclare que le basque, outre sa valeur symbolique, accomplit aussi des fonctions d'ornement et de décoration. Seulement 25% des habitants pratiquent le basque parlé, alors que 55% le connaissent. Ceci fait réfléchir l'auteur dans le sens que le processus de substitution de la langue est très avancé et consolidé même dans cette province (Larrañaga 1986, 371−374).

5.3. Attitudes et conflits linguistiques

Rappelons les termes de Sánchez Carrión (1972, 190) sur l'état dans lequel a vécu la langue basque pendant longtemps: «L'individu se voit enfermé dans son village, réduit à une aire de langage de plus en plus petite, et quand il en sort, la moquerie, les plaisanteries, le mépris sont les attitudes par lesquelles est généralement reçue son ignorance du castillan. C'est alors que son lien à la langue se transforme en mépris et qu'il essaie de ne pas la transmettre à son fils».

Selon l'étude de SIADECO de 1975, 90% des bascophones tenaient pour nécessaire l'introduction de la langue basque dans le système éducatif et 75% estimaient absolument nécessaire l'éducation en basque. 91% étaient favorables au basque dans l'administration et les moyens de communication (Euskaltzaindia 1979, 123−131). Dans la population de langue castillane, les chiffres sont comparables.

Enfin, selon une enquête de 1991 du Secrétariat de la Politique Linguistique sur l'attitude quant à la promotion du basque dans la CAV, 89% pensent que l'Administration Publique doit stimuler l'emploi du basque et 44% estiment que peu a été fait en 10 ans de politique linguistique (Gobierno Vasco 1992, 11).

L'attitude des bascophones se manifeste aussi dans l'administration locale; le mouvement en faveur du basque développé par l'organisme populaire *Euskal Herrian Euskaraz* [au Pays Basque en basque] a amené une vingtaine de municipalités à se déclarer monolingues (basques).

5.4. Diglossie et bilinguisme

La diglossie du Pays Basque est un fait assumé par tous les sociolinguistes qui s'occupent de la question.

Selon SIADECO, 12,7% seulement utilisent les deux langues avec la même aisance. Mais 63,1% reconnaissent qu'il leur est plus facile de lire en espagnol (12% lisent dans les deux langues avec facilité).

L'enquête du Gouvernement Basque (1983, 112−117) révèle que 44% des bascophones de naissance ont plus d'aisance en basque qu'en espagnol, mais 65% d'entre eux parlent basque; seulement 26% des personnes ayant appris le basque le parlent; 10% ne le parlent jamais. Dans une étude plus récente (Larrañaga 1986), on a mesuré l'utilisation du basque en Guipuzcoa. Le basque est présent dans les lieux publics pour 25%; l'espagnol seul pour 61%.

Selon les données de 1991, 39% des bilingues fonctionnels parlent plus facilement le basque, 26% les deux langues et 35% l'espagnol (Gobierno Vasco 1992, 10). On ne peut qu'ajouter avec Rotaetxe (1987a, 170): «le drame du basque, c'est justement de n'exister qu'en situation diglossique».

6. Etat de la politique linguistique

6.1. Politique linguistique

La CAV et la Navarre possèdent un Secrétariat Général de la Politique Linguistique chargé d'émettre les directives principales en matière de politique linguistique et de surveiller l'application des lois relatives à la langue basque. Dans la CAV, la «Loi de Base de Normalisation de l'Utilisation du basque» fut approuvée en 1982. Cette politique linguistique se base sur quatre piliers: administration, enseignement, mass media et vie sociale. Dans la Communauté Forale de Navarre, la «Loi Forale du basque» fut approuvée en 1986: elle découpe le territoire en trois zones différentes: zone bascophone dans laquelle le basque est langue officielle au même titre que le castillan; une zone mixte et une zone non bascophone dans lesquelles le basque n'est pas officiel. Selon Atxa (1990, 105), on ne peut parler d'un plan de « normalisation » de la langue basque. La loi n'est pas conçue en fonction de la réussite d'une normalisation linguistique.

6.1.1. Education

La politique linguistique du Gouvernement Basque dans l'éducation a été formulée dans le « Décret du bilinguisme », en 1983, qui établit trois modèles de centres scolaires selon le rôle accordé à la langue basque: (a) modèle A: enseignement en espagnol avec enseignement du basque comme discipline; (b) modèle B: enseignement de certaines disciplines en espagnol et d'autres en basque; (c) modèle D: enseignement en basque avec enseignement de l'espagnol comme discipline; (d) modèle X: enseignement exclusivement en espagnol, modèle destiné à disparaître. Si l'on compare les chiffres entre les années 1982−1983 et 1992−1993, on constate: (1) en préscolaire, le modèle A est passé de 54% à 27%, le modèle B de 23% à 35% et le modèle D de 23% à 38%; (2) dans le primaire, le modèle A a diminué de 18%, tandis que les modèles B et D passent à 51%; (3) dans le secondaire, 75% des élèves suivent le modèle A, 2% le modèle B et 23% le modèle D (Gobierno Vasco 1992, 30). Selon des données du Conseil d'Education dans l'ensemble de l'enseignement non universitaire, 57% suivent le modèle A, 24% le modèle D et 18% le modèle B en 1992−1993.

L'Université du Pays Basque est récente. Les études de philologie basque datent de 1979. L'Université a créé différents organes pour réussir la normalisation: le Vice-Rectorat de basque, le Cabinet Technique de basque et la Commission de basque (Osa 1990, 127). Selon Kintana, directeur du Cabinet Technique, en 1992−1993, 23% des cours ont lieu entièrement ou en partie en basque, soit 144 cours et 1128 élèves. 34% des disciplines sont données en basque.

En Navarre, la loi change selon la zone: (a) en zone basque sont appliqués les trois modèles existant dans la CAV; (b) en zone mixte l'implantation de l'enseignement *du* basque et *en* basque dépend de l'administration; (c) en zone non bascophone l'enseignement en basque est impossible. On ne dispose pas de données officielles sur la scolarisation en Navarre. Quant aux *ikastola*, le nombre d'élèves a augmenté de 4% entre 1991 et 1992.

6.1.2. Administration

La « Loi de Base de Normalisation de l'Utilisation du Basque de la CAV » définit l'emploi du basque dans l'Administration. Cette loi se concrétise dans les décrets postérieurs. En 1979 est créé l'Institut Basque de l'Administration Publique dans le but de former des fonctionnaires bilingues et de renforcer la normalisation du basque dans l'Administration. Un décret de 1989 précise la planification de la normalisation de l'emploi du basque et détermine quatre profils linguistiques dans l'Administration.

Très souvent, il a été fait appel devant le Tribunal Supérieur contre les décisions prises par l'administration locale en faveur de la prise en compte du basque dans le recrutement d'employés.

6.1.3. Vie publique

Le quatrième chapitre de la « Loi de Base (…) » traite de l'usage social du basque. Aussi a-t-il été créé en 1981 l'organisme HABE pour l'alphabétisation et l'enseignement du basque chez les personnes adultes dans la CAV. Un autre organisme, non gouvernemental, AEK, s'occupe également, dans tout le Pays Basque, de l'enseignement du basque aux adultes depuis une vingtaine d'années.

6.1.4. Mass media

En 1982 a été créée dans la CAV la « Radio-télévision Basque » qui possède plusieurs chaînes de radio (dont l'une exclusivement en basque) et deux chaînes télévisées, dont l'une est en basque. La télévision basque (ETB) a été considérée comme un pas de géant pour la normalisation du basque. En Navarre, Télé-Navarre consacre seulement 5 heures par semaine à la langue basque (Atxa 1990, 101−102).

Dans la presse écrite, il n'existe pas que le quotidien basque *Euskaldunon egunkaria* [Journal des Basques] issu d'une initiative populaire. Il ne bénéficie d'aucun appui des institutions publiques qui se dispensent même de lui confier la publicité officielle.

6.2. Standardisation linguistique

6.2.1. Unification linguistique

L'unification de la langue constitue un labeur attendu depuis longtemps. La naissance de Euskaltzaindia-Académie de la Langue Basque en 1918 répond, parmi d'autres objectifs, au désir des Basques de se doter d'une norme commune. Ce désir est exprimé dans le premier article de ses statuts. Il a fallu cependant attendre jusqu'en 1968 pour que s'effectuent les premiers pas de l'unification de la langue écrite quant à l'orthographe et à la morphologie. Les travaux publiés dans *Euskera*, organe officiel de l'Académie, exposent les différentes étapes: emprunts lexicaux, composition et dérivation, etc. Une grammaire normative est en train de s'achever.

6.2.2. Modernisation linguistique

Le basque souffre d'une carence terminologique dans les domaines scientifiques et administratifs, puisqu'il a été longtemps exclu de certains champs du savoir. De nos jours, tous les efforts sont concentrés pour combler ces lacunes et pour faire avancer le processus de modernisation (Etxebarria 1988, 335).

L'Académie n'est pas seule à œuvrer à la modernisation du lexique. UZEI, organisme indépendant, s'occupe de l'élaboration de dictionnaires spécialisés des différentes terminologies techniques.

7. Aspects intralinguistiques des langues en contact

« Le basque n'est aucunement une langue romane, mais il a vécu dans une telle symbiose avec elles depuis de nombreux siècles que son histoire et sa préhistoire ne peuvent être étudiées (...) que par une connaissance non superficielle de la linguistique romane » (Michelena 1964, 116).

7.1. Caractérisation phonologique des langues en contact

7.1.1. Système vocalique

Le système vocalique du basque et de l'espagnol comptent tous les deux cinq phonèmes. Il y a cependant une divergence dans les deux systèmes: si l'espagnol admet les diphtongues croissantes, le basque s'y refuse sauf dans des emprunts romans.

7.1.2. Système consonantique

Le basque ne possède pas la fricative interdentale sourde [θ]. L'espagnol, par contre, ne connaît pour les sifflantes que les sons fricatif [ś] et affrique [č] alors que le basque possède une sifflante fricative apicale [ś], une dorsale [s] et une prépalatale [š], sans compter les trois sifflantes affriquées correspondantes: [ć], [c] et [č] (Txillardegi 1980, 127). En outre, le basque préfère l'occlusive sonore à l'initiale alors qu'en espagnol l'opposition est claire: *gauza, denbora, bake, dorre* (esp.: *cosa, tiempo, paz, torre*). Le basque admet difficilement la vibrante initiale, qui est fréquente en espagnol. Dans les emprunts, la prothèse des voyelles « a » ou « e » est normale: *arratoi, arrazoi, arrosario (errosario), errefrau, errege, errezibu, erromeria, erregu* (esp.: *ratón, razón, rosario, refrán, rey, recibo, romería, ruego*). Le son [f] est d'introduction relativement récente en basque mais on peut le considérer comme intégré: *afari, frakak (prakak), fraile (praile)* (fr.: *dîner, pantalon, moine*), mais lat. *fortis* > basq. *bortitz*. Après « n », « l », « r » en basque les sifflantes sont affriquées, phénomène inconnu de l'espagnol: *bertso, pultsu, pentsatu, deskantsu, saltsa* (esp.: *verso, pulso, pensar, descanso, salsa*).

7.2. Caractérisation morphosyntaxique des langues en contact

De ce point de vue, les deux langues en contact sont extrêmement différentes. Selon la typologie traditionnelle, le basque est une langue agglutinante avec des morphèmes qui s'ajoutent à la base.

La construction ergative du basque est inconnue des langues voisines (Rotaetxe 1987 b, 221).

Les problèmes de configurationalité apparaissent aussi en syntaxe dans la relation entre syntagme nominal et syntagme verbal (ibidem).

7.3. Caractérisation lexicale des langues en contact

Malgré son caractère de langue non indoeuropéenne, le basque a recouru fréquemment au fonds gréco-latin pour enrichir son lexique: *lege* (< legem), *eliza* (< ecclesiam), *eskola* (< scholam), *diru* (< denarium), *lore* (< florem), *estrata* (< stratam), *gaztelu* (< castellum). De tels emprunts sont courants aussi de nos jours pour les termes relatifs à la technique: *telefono, telebista, radar, periskopio*. La dérivation et la composition sont cependant mises à contribution en développant le fonds autochtone: *neska-mutilak* 'enfant' (fille-garçon), *harreman* 'relation' (*hartu* 'prendre' + *eman* 'donner'), *argibide* 'information, renseignement' (*argi* 'clair' + *bide* 'chemin'), *aldagela* 'vestiaire' (*alda(tu)* 'changer' + *gela* 'chambre') ... (Azkarate 1990).

8. Examen critique de la bibliographie

Le thème du contact entre le basque et l'espagnol ne se limite pas au champ scientifique mais déborde amplement sur le domaine de la politique, et non pas seulement celui de la politique linguistique, mais aussi celui de la politique en général.

La langue basque n'est plus alors un simple patrimoine culturel à sauvegarder mais devient un objet de lutte permanente entre ceux qui défendent son existence et ses détracteurs, généralement castillanophones.

Il est très difficile d'être objectif et impartial en Pays Basque: toujours est-il que les défenseurs de la langue mettent l'accent sur la situation réelle dans la vie quotidienne (Atxa, Argüeso, Euskaltzaindia, Larrañaga), demandent des mesures urgentes et proposent une étude scientifique des faits (Azkarate, Txillardegi).

9. Bibliographie (sélective)

Argüeso, Mª Angeles (1991): *El euskara en Bilbao (situación y perspectivas)*, Bilbao.

Atxa, Jesus (1990): «Euskararen egoera Nafarroan» [La situation de la langue basque en Navarre]. In: *Jakin 56*, 74–106.

Azkarate, Miren (1990): *Hitz elkartuak euskaraz* [La composition en basque], Saint-Sébastien.

Etxebarria, Maitena (1988): «Normalización y uso del euskera en la administración». In: *Revista española de Lingüística 18*, 331–341.

Euskaltzaindia (1977): *El libro blanco del euskara* (édition bilingue), Bilbao.

Euskaltzaindia (1979): *Conflicto lingüístico en Euskadi* (édition bilingue), Bilbao.

Garagorri, Xabier (1983): «Ikastoletako irakaskuntzaren garapena eta egoera» [Situation et développement de l'enseignement dans les ikastola]. In: *Jakin 28*, 1–68.

Gobierno de Navarra (1989): *El euskara en la enseñanza de Navarra*, Pampelune.

Gobierno Vasco (1983): *La lucha del euskera: encuesta básica: conocimiento, uso y actitudes* (édition bilingue), Vitoria.

Gobierno Vasco (1989): *Mapa sociolingüístico. Análisis demolingüístico de la Comunidad Autónoma Vasca derivado del padrón de 1986* (édition bilingue), Vitoria.

Gobierno Vasco (1992): *Comparecencia, a petición propia, de la secretaria general de Política Lingüística ante la Comisión de Instituciones e Interior del Parlamento Vasco*, Vitoria.

Gobierno Vasco (1995): *Euskararen Jarraipena/La continuidad del Euskara/La continuité de la langue basque*, Vitoria.

Gómez Piñero, Francisco/Ochoa, E. M./Gandarillas, Maria A./Villanueva, Maria Dolores (1979–1980): *Geografía de Euskal Herria*, Saint-Sébastien.

Haritschelhar, Jean (Ed.) (1983): *Etre Basque*, Toulouse.

Larrañaga, Iñaki (1986): «Euskararen erabilpen erreala Gipuzkoan: leku publikoetan, udal erakundeetan, gizarteko zerbitzuetan» [Emploi réel de la langue basque en Guipuzcoa dans les lieux publics, l'administration locale, les services sociaux]. In: *Sociología de lenguas minorizadas*, Ruiz Olabuenaga/Ozamiz, J. A. (Eds.), Saint-Sébastien.

Michelena, Luis (1964): *Sobre el pasado de la lengua vasca*, Saint-Sébastien.

Michelena, Luis (1985): «Normalización de la forma escrita de una lengua: el caso vasco». In: *Lengua e historia*, Madrid, 213–228.

Osa, Eusebio (1990): «Universitat del País Basc». In: *Normalització Lingüística Universitària*, Alemany, R. (Ed.), Alicante.

Rotaetxe, Karmele (19787a): «L'aménagement linguistique en Euskadi». In: *Politique et Aménagement linguistiques*, Maurais, J. (Ed.), Paris.

Rotaetxe, Karmele (1987b): «La norma vasca: codificación y desarrollo». In: *Revista Española de Lingüística 17*, 219–244.

Ruiz Olabuenaga, J. Ignacio/Ozamiz, J. A. (Eds.) (1986): *Sociología de lenguas minorizadas*, Saint-Sébastien.

Sánchez Carrión, José Mª (1972): *El estado actual del vascuence en la provincia de Navarra (1970)*, Pampelune.

Sánchez Carrión, José Mª (1981): *El espacio bilingüe*, Saint-Sébastien.

Siguan, Miquel (1992): *España plurilingüe*, Madrid.

Txillardegi (1980): *Euskal Fonologia*, Saint-Sébastien.

Gotzon Aurrekoetxea, Bilbao (Espagne)

155. Portugal

1. Geographie und Demographie
2. Territorialgeschichte und Staatsbildung
3. Politik, Wirtschaft und allgemeine kulturelle sowie religiöse Lage
4. Formen des Sprachkontakts
5. Forschungsdefizite und Perspektiven
6. Bibliographie (in Auswahl)

1. Geographie und Demographie

Portugal, ein geographisches Rechteck im Südwesten der iberischen Halbinsel, grenzt im Süden und Westen an den Atlantik, im Norden und Osten an Spanien; seine kontinentale Landfläche beträgt 88.000 km², die Einwohnerzahl insgesamt 9.853 Mill. Einwohner (1991). Die Azoren und Madeira (*Ilhas adjacentes*) mit 3131 km² und 489.700 E. (1991) gehören ebenso zur Republik Portugal. Alle überseeischen Provinzen (*ultramar*) haben sich von Portugal gelöst, was in den letzten Jahren zu einer Bevölkerungsrückwanderung von ca. 700.000 Flüchtlingen (*desalojados* bzw. *retornados*) geführt hat. Anfang der 90er Jahre leben 94.000 Ausländer (d. h. 0,9% der Bevölkerung) in Portugal; die Zahl der Gastarbeiter in Portugal beläuft sich auf 30.000 (d. h. 0,6% der Erwerbstätigen); 100.000 Farbige sind aus den port. Überseeprovinzen nach Portugal eingewandert.

Portugal ist in 20 Verwaltungsdistrikte (18 auf dem Festland, 2 autonome Regionen auf den Inseln) gegliedert, von denen Beja die größte Fläche einnimmt (10.240 km²); die größten städtischen Agglomerationen sind die Hauptstadt Lissabon (830.500 E. /1988/ mit Umland 1,7 Mill. E.) und Porto (350.000 E. mit Umland 1,4 Mill. E.); mittelgroße ländliche Distrikte sind Braga, Sétubal, Santarém, Coimbra und Viseu. Binnenwanderungsprozesse (Weber 1980, 226) finden vom Land in die städtischen Zentren statt (Landflucht), vor allem in die Regionen von Lissabon, Sétubal, Porto und die Algarve (Faro); → Sprachenkarte E.

Die Emigrationsschübe sind für Portugal ein dauerhaftes Problem; seit Ende des 19. Jahrhunderts findet ein „enormer Bevölkerungsverlust" (Weber 1980, 228) statt: vor der Jahrhundertwende bis zum Ersten Weltkrieg und gleich nach dem Weltkrieg verließen bis zu 80.000 Portugiesen jährlich das Land mit dem Ziel Nordamerika. Weitere Schübe nach dem Zweiten Weltkrieg bis 1974 hatten als Auswanderungsziele Venezuela und Brasilien, Kanada und die U.S.A., zuletzt dann Frankreich und auch Deutschland. Zwischen 1964 und 1988 kamen ca. 229.000 Portugiesen in die BRD, 181.500 kehrten im selben Zeitraum nach Portugal zurück. Portugal verlor 3.543.170 E. durch Auswanderung von 1875–1974. Sofern man für diese hundert Jahre eine Verdoppelung der Bevölkerung Portugals von 4 auf 8 Mill. E. ansetzen kann, heißt das, „der natürliche demographische Zuwachs ist fast zur Hälfte durch die Auswanderung abgezogen worden" (Weber 1980, 229).

Das portugiesische Volk weist große ethnische Einheitlichkeit auf; es gründet auf einer lusitanisch-keltiberischen Schicht, die romanisiert wurde. Hinzu kamen von Nord nach Süd regional geringe germanische, arabisch-berberische Populationen, die voll integriert wurden, in der letzten Neuzeit auch überseeische Mischpopulationen.

Amtssprache ist Portugiesisch.

2. Territorialgeschichte und Staatsbildung

Portugal ist seit 1143 unabhängiges Königreich auf der Grundlage des Vertrags von Zamora (Lehnseid von Afonso Henriques (1139–1185) gegenüber dem Papst). Bereits 1254 gab es ein Ständeparlament (Cortes), in dem das städtische Bürgertum als dritter Stand zugelassen war. Die Cortes verloren ihre Macht aufgrund monarchistischer Zentralisierung (Manuel I, 1495–1521), durch Einführung des römischen Rechts und sozialer Veränderungen, die durch Überseebesitztümer hervorgerufen wurden. Portugal hatte im 13. und 14. Jahrhundert eine erstaunlich moderne Sozialstruktur (z. B. Aufhebung der Leibeigenschaft). Das Territorialgebiet der port. Monarchie wurde – in den bis heute bestehenden Grenzen – mit dem Vertrag von Alcañiz (Teruel, Spanien) 1297 gegenüber Spanien vollendet. Die Dynastie Burgund (1128–1385) begründete den Staat Portugal in der Reconquista gegen die Mauren und im Abgrenzungskampf gegen Spanien. Nach diversen Übergriffen Spaniens wie auch portugiesischen Ansprüchen auf Galicien (Fernando 1369/70) kam es 1411 zu einem Friedenspakt zwischen Spanien und Portugal.

155. Portugal

Auf der Suche nach starken Bündnispartnern schloß Lissabon mit London 1386 einen Vertrag, der bis heute gültig ist.

Die Dynastie Avis (1385–1580) begann mit einer Finanzkrise, entwickelte dann jedoch ab 1415 (Eroberung von Ceuta) bei großem Einsatz von Mitteln die überseeischen Unternehmungen und Entdeckungen. Die geographische Randlage in Europa, die ständige Bedrohung durch Spanien, die Sicherheitskontakte zu England und Frankreich waren existentielle Gründe für die Orientierung Portugals nach Übersee: zuerst entlang der afrikanischen Westküste, um das 'Kap der Stürme' (1498) bis Timor (1516) und Japan (1542) führten die Entdeckungsfahrten; westwärts wurden Grönland und der St. Lorenz-Strom (1472), Labrador (1492) und Brasilien (1500) entdeckt. Die Bevölkerungsziffer belief sich auf ca. eine Million in dieser Zeit, nachdem sie vor der Zeit der Entdeckungen schon 2 Mill. gezählt hatte.

In Afrika und Asien wurden lediglich Faktoreien errichtet, die transatlantischen Inseln und Brasilien jedoch wurden in umfassendem Sinne kolonisiert, und zwar durch Portugiesen sowie, über mehrere Jahrhunderte hinweg, durch Sklavenimporte aus Schwarzafrika. Mit dem Aussterben der Dynastie Avis in Portugal übernahm der Habsburger Filipe I. (II.) (1581–1598) von Spanien in Personalunion legal die Oberhoheit über Portugal („spanisches Interregnum" 1580–1640). Portugiesisch blieb zwar Landessprache, doch kam es zu einem Bilingualismus: „Pratiquement, c'est seulement vers la fin du XVIIe siècle que le bilinguisme luso-espagnol cesse d'exister." (Teyssier 1994, 466). Die port. Armada ging 1588 – zusammen mit der spanischen – gegen England verloren. Portugal verlor sein universales Handelsimperium sukzessive im 17. Jahrhundert. Als allerletztes wird Macao (chines. Territorium von 18 km² unter port. Verwaltung) ab 1999 an die VR China übergehen: von den 373.900 E. (1992) in Macao sind ca. 12.000 E. Portugiesen und Mischlinge.

Mitte des 16. Jahrhunderts suchte Portugal unter der Dynastie Bragança (1640–1910) militärische Hilfe gegen Spanien bei Frankreich, 1703 schloß es einen Handelsvertrag mit England (Methuen-Vertrag).

Im span. Erbfolgekrieg stand Portugal auf Seiten Englands, am Ende der Französischen Revolution mit England und Spanien gegen Frankreich (1792/93); nachdem Spanien jedoch aus dem Bündnis ausgetreten war, waren sich Spanien und Frankreich nach der Besetzung Portugals im Okt. 1807 durch frz. Truppen (Napoleonische Kriege) einig, die Dynastie Bragança abzusetzen und das Land aufzuteilen. Der portugiesische Hof flüchtete nach Brasilien, Portugal wurde erst 1811 durch ein britisches Heer befreit. Nach vielen innenpolit. Unruhen in der ersten Hälfte des 19. Jahrhunderts brachte dann die *Regeneration* ab 1851 ruhigere Zeiten, in denen sich drei Parteien (die konservative Regenerationspartei, die historische und die progressive Partei) friedlich ablösten. Portugal blieb ein rückständiges Agrarland. Am 5. Okt. 1910 wurde die Republik ausgerufen.

Der Beginn der *parlamentarischen Republik* brachte von 1911 bis 1926 einen ständigen Wechsel von insgesamt 44 parlamentar. Regierungen, die letzte wurde durch eine militär. Revolte aus dem Amt getrieben, das Parlament aufgelöst, die Verfassung aufgehoben.

General Fragoso Carmona wurde von 1928 bis 1951 Präsident. Er berief A. de Oliveira Salazar zum Finanzminister, der die Staatsfinanzen in Ordnung brachte, dann Ministerpräsident wurde und dem Land ab 1933 (Estado Novo) eine ständisch-autoritäre Staatsform gab; nur eine Partei (União Nacional) war zugelassen, die Opposition wurde mit Hife der PIDE (Geheime Staatspolizei) unterdrückt.

Aus Furcht vor notwendigen sozialen Veränderungen blieb der Lebensstandard niedrig, die sozialen Unterschiede waren groß, die Inflationsrate gering, der Analphabetismus unverändert, Industrie und Wirtschaft blieben ohne nennenswerte Entwicklung.

Als letztes europäisches Land wollte Portugal seine Überseeprovinzen mit Gewalt halten und gab noch 1951 den Bürgern in den Kolonien die Staatsbürgerschaft. Es verlor dann aber 1961 Goa, Damão und Diu an Indien; in Angola, Mosambik und Guinea wurde der Kampf gegen die Befreiungsbewegungen für Portugal immer aufwendiger. Die Revolution vom 25. April 1974 („Revolution der Nelken") wurde durch die „Bewegung der Streitkräfte" unblutig durchgeführt und brachte grundlegende Veränderungen der Sozialstruktur. Großbetriebe, Banken, Versicherungen und Großgrundbesitz (insbesondere im Alentejo im Hinblick auf eine Agrar-Reform) wurden enteignet. Politiker wie Mário Soares (Sozialisten) und Alvaro Cunhal (Kommunisten) kehrten aus dem Exil zurück, die parlamentarische Republik entstand neu (Verfassung vom 2. April 1976). Die letzten Überseeprovinzen wurden in die Unabhängigkeit entlassen (Guinea-Bissau 1974, Mosambik, die Kapverden, São Tomé und Príncipe, Angola 1975 und Portugiesisch-Timor 1976 (Anschluß an Indonesien).

3. Politik, Wirtschaft und allgemeine kulturelle sowie religiöse Lage

Das heutige politische System der Republik Portugal ist demokratisch, parlamentarisch, präsidentiell. Der *Staatspräsident* (seit 1986 Mário Soares, 1991 wiedergewählt) wird für 5 Jahre vom Volk gewählt, er ernennt den Premierminister und auf dessen Vorschlag die Minister; er kann das Parlament auflösen und Neuwahlen einberufen. Der *Revolutionsrat* hat neben gesetzgeberischen Befugnissen im militärischen Bereich die Aufgabe eines Hüters der Verfassung „im Geiste der portugiesischen Revolution vom 25. April 1974" und berät den Staatspräsidenten bei allen staatspolitischen Entscheidungen. Der Revolutionsrat wird nicht in allg. und freier Wahl gewählt, was konstitutionellen Prinzipien wie Gewaltenteilung und Volkssouveränität widerspricht. Der *Premierminister* (seit 1985 Cavaco Silva) mit seinem Ministerrat bildet die *Regierung*; er wird vom Staatspräsidenten nach Anhörung des Revolutionsrates sowie der im Parlament vertretenen Parteien auf der Grundlage der Wahlergebnisse ernannt und ist dem Staatspräsidenten gegenüber politisch verantwortlich. Das *Parlament* (250 Abgeordnete) ist die Versammlung der Republik (Assembleia da República). Die Abgeordneten werden alle 4 Jahre in allg., freien, gleichen und geheimen Wahlen nach dem Verhältniswahlrecht gewählt. Der Staatspräsident kann das Parlament nur auflösen, wenn im Parlament dreimal das Programm einer Regierung abgelehnt wurde. Das Parlament muß aufgelöst werden, wenn es dreimal innerhalb einer Legislaturperiode die Regierung durch Verweigerung des Vertrauensvotums oder durch Mißtrauensvotum gestürzt hat. Die Assembleia hat die Gesetzgebungskompetenz und autorisiert die Regierung zur Gesetzesvorlage; sie hat nicht das Recht, den Premierminister zu wählen. In der Wahl vom 6. 10. 1991 gewann die PSD (Partido Social Democrático) 135 Sitze, die PS (Partido Socialista) 72, die PCP (Partido Comunista de Portugal) 17, die PP (Partido do Centro Democrático Social) 5 und sonstige Parteien je einen Sitz.

Portugal ist seit 1986 Mitglied der EG.

Das Bruttosozialprodukt pro Kopf lag Anfang der 90er Jahre bei 3115 Ecu (EG-Durchschnitt: rund 12.439 Ecu), die Arbeitslosenquote der letzten Jahrzehnte durchschnittlich bei 7,6%, das Wirtschaftswachstum bei 2,5%. Portugal hat große Handelsdefizite (4,3 Milliarden Ecu) und ist zu 88,2% von Energie-Importen abhängig. Die Wirtschaftssektoren verteilen sich wie folgt: Landwirtschaft (7,5%), wobei Portugal eine 50%ige landwirtschaftliche Nutzfläche aufweist, Industrie (37,9%) und Dienstleistungen (54,6%). In der Zeit von 1960—1974 verließen fast 1 Mill. Erwerbspersonen, vor allem aus dem primären Wirtschaftssektor, das Land.

Hinsichtlich des Bildungsniveaus ist festzustellen, daß 72% der über 15jährigen vor dem 15. Lebensjahr die Schule verlassen. Portugal verwendet 4,1% des BSP auf Bildung und Erziehung, 0,34% des BSP auf Forschung und Entwicklung.

Nach dem gegenüber Spanien so frühen Abschluß der Reconquista konnte Portugal das erste Land mit territorialer Einheit werden, dessen feste Grenzen zu großer Homogenität (gerade auch in der Standardisierung der Sprache) und konservativer Abgeschlossenheit beitrugen (Berschin 1994, 371). Die Regierungszeit von Dom Dinis (1279—1325) brachte die erste kulturelle Blüte mit internationalen Handelskontakten. Die erste Universität wurde in Lissabon 1290 gegründet (Transferierung nach Coimbra 1307). Der manuelinische Stil im Anschluß an die Hochgotik ist eine eigene Stilrichtung Portugals (Kloster Batalha, Hieronymitenkloster und Turm von Belém in Lissabon), Zisterzienserkloster wie Alcobaça und das Kloster des Christusordens Tomar sind europäische Kulturleistungen. Die „azulejos" (Kacheln) finden sich nicht nur im Rokokoschloß Queluz, sondern in vielen Kirchen und öffentlichen Gebäuden.

Die galicisch-portugiesische Minnelyrik (13.—14. Jahrhundert) ist ein europäischer Höhepunkt der Literatur. Das nationale Epos der port. Entdeckungen sind „Os Lusiadas" (1572) von Luís de Camões (1524—1580). Portugal hat sich den kulturellen Einflüssen Spaniens, Frankreichs und Englands nie entziehen können, jedoch immer wieder eigene Entwicklungen und Strömungen versucht (Crónicas, religiös-didaktische Prosa, *saudosismo*, *modernismo*). Der wohl bedeutendste Dichter Portugals im 20. Jahrhundert ist Fernando Pessoa (1888—1935).

Wenngleich das Bildungswesen allgemeine Schulpflicht (7 bis 13 Jahre) vorschreibt, ist die Analphabetenquote noch relativ hoch (1970 bei 30%). Das Bildungsniveau ist in den letzten zwei Jahrzehnten nach der Nelkenrevolution merklich gestiegen und die Schulsituation hat sich erheblich verbessert; Indiz dafür ist auch, daß viele neue Universitäten (Aveiro, Braga, Évora, Faro, Funchal, Vila Real) zu jenen in Lissabon, Coimbra und Porto hinzugekommen sind.

Der größte Teil der Bevölkerung Portugals (über 90%) sind Katholiken, hinzu kommen Protestanten (ca. 38.000), Muslime (15.000) und Juden (2.000); Kirchenaustritte und Atheismus haben steigende Tendenz. Die Altersgruppen in Portugal verteilen sich Anfang der 90er Jahre auf 21,3% unter 15 Jahren, 12,7% über 65 Jahren. Portugal hat gegenüber Mitteleuropa und auch Übersee immer wieder eine kritische Distanz eingehalten, was sich im 20. Jahrhundert grundlegend geändert hat.

4. Formen des Sprachkontakts

4.1. Kontaktformen

Für Portugal und das Portugiesische lassen sich grundsätzlich vier Arten von Sprachkontakt aufzeigen, von denen die beiden ersten lokal determiniert sind, die beiden anderen wesentlich (jedoch nicht ausschließlich) den medialen Sprachkontakt im 20. Jahrhundert kennzeichnen: einerseits entweder aufgrund von regional oder temporär begrenztem Zusammenleben mit anderen Völkerschaften (etwa an den Landesgrenzen zu Galicien, zu León, zur span. Extremadura), aufgrund von territorialer Besetzung (wie durch Goten, Mauren, Spanier oder Franzosen) oder aufgrund von eingewanderten Sprachminderheiten (Stadt- und Landregionen), − andererseits durch medial vermittelte Kultur- und Sprachimporte (Hellenismen, Italianismen [z. B. *cicerone, diletante, fiasco, influenza, lazarone, piano, cantata, ópera* u. a. Musikbegriffe], Latinismen [vgl. Messner 1990], Germanismen [z. B. *lumpenproletariado, apfelstrudel* oder *guerra relâmpago*], Anglizismen und Französismen [s. u.], Mediterraneismen [vgl. Simões 1972−1978] sowie die alten Importe aus den Bantu-Sprachen [z. B. *batuque, macaco, carimbo*], aus asiat. Sprachen [*canja, chá, champana, junco*], aus dem karibisch-mexikanischen Raum [*canoa, cacique, condor, tomate, alpaca*] oder die alten und neuesten Brasilianismen [z. B. durch die 'telenovelas' vermittelt *esquentar a cabeça, estar grilado*] [Messner 1990, Simões 1972−1978]).

Das grundlegende Sprachsystem (Phonemsystem, Morphosyntax) des Portugiesischen wurde durch Sprachkontakte kaum verändert, im Gegensatz zum Lexikon.

Die prähistorischen, lokal determinierten Sprachrelikte der kantabrisch-pyrenäischen, lusitanischen, keltiberischen Völker haben nur bruchstückhaft Substrate hinterlassen, vor allem Orts-, Fluß- und Flurnamen (z. B. *Laccobriga* [Lagos], *Caetobriga* [Sétubal], *Conimbriga, Bracara* [Braga]), Suffixe (z. B. *-antia, -entia, -ace, -ice, -oce, -asco, -briga*) und eine beschränkte Anzahl von Lexemen (z. B. *barro, bezerro, carrasco, mina, saia, sapo, veiga*).

Lexikalisch erfaßt sind demgegenüber die german. Adstrate (Sueben, Westgoten) des 5. bis 7. Jahrhundert (z. B. Lexeme wie *banco, elmo, espora, guarda, guerra, roubar*) und die arabischen/mozarab. Adstrate des 8. Jahrhunderts bis 1249 (Reconquista von Faro) sowie danach; letztere sind jedoch im Vergleich zum Kastilischen geringer zu veranschlagen.

Die maurischen Adstrate sind aus einem gelebten Sprachkontakt (s. o.) hervorgegangen, z. B. *alcachofa, alcatra, aldeia, alface, alfama, alfândiga, alfarroba, alferes, alfinete, algarismo, algodão, almofada, armazém, azeite, azenha, chafariz, lezira* (oder *leziria*).

Differenziert müssen hier nicht nur lokale Schwerpunktbildungen des Sprachkontakts erarbeitet werden („mozárabes fugitivos fizeram de Coimbra un foco contribuindo para a importância desta cidade", Messner 1990, 26), sondern es gilt auch, die sozialen Lebensbereiche der notwendig gewordenen Bezeichnungen im Zusammenhang mit den überlieferten Texten und Textsorten zusammen zu sehen.

4.2. Galego-Portugiesisch

Die sprachliche Minderheit Galicien im Königreich Spanien umfaßt heute ca. 2,5 Mill. Sprecher; schicksalhaft an León gebunden, fiel es 1071 an die spanische Krone. Das Altgalicische ist historisch die Wurzel des Portugiesischen. Der schwelende Sprachkonflikt zwischen Kastilisch und Galicisch machte sich erfolglos im 15. Jahrhundert Luft, erstarkte dann patriotisch Mitte des 19. Jahrhunderts bis zu Beginn der Zweiten Weltkriegs („Rexurdimento") und hat in seiner letzten Phase nach 1940 einen großen Aufschwung zur Konsolidierung genommen

(Sprachnormierung, Orthographie, Belletristik). Die spanische Verfassung von 1978 (besonders im Art. 2) sichert neben dem offiziellen Kastilisch auch den anderen Sprachen des Staatsgebiets Lebensraum und Protektion als „patrimonio cultural" zu. Wie sich in diesem diglossalen Gebiet der Sprachkontakt, -konflikt, die Sprachplanung und -politik entwickeln werden, ist offen (Kastilisch als *lengua superior*, Galicisch als *lengua inferior*). Die regionale Identität muß konsolidiert, der partiell vorhandene sprachliche Minderwertigkeitskomplex muß kompensiert werden, um ein gleichberechtigtes ausgewogenes Nebeneinander des Kastilischen und Galicischen in allen Lebensbereichen zu garantieren (→ Art. 152). Der Sprachkontakt und Sprachkonflikt wird gegenwärtig von mindestens 5 unterschiedlichen Positionen aus betrachtet, wobei der reintegrativen, revitalisierenden, lusitanistischen Position nach Azevedo Filho (1990, 395–398) die größten Chancen eingeräumt werden („se o galego é um dialeto rural do português, a sua norma culta só pode ser a portuguesa", ibid. 398). Das Galicische muß als eine *Varietät* „dentro do mesmo domínio (ou diasistema ...) galego-português" (Elia 1992, 134) gesehen werden. Eine Monographie des galego–leonesisch–kastilischen Sprachkontakts ist ein Desiderat (Henríquez Salido 1993).

4.3. Spanisch-portugiesische Sprachkontakte

Sprachkontakt zwischen den beiden Nachbarländern Portugal und Spanien ist durch alle Jahrhunderte nachweisbar.

Besonders in der Zeit eines verbreiteten Bilingualismus zwischen dem 15. und 17. Jahrhundert schrieben viele portugiesische Schriftsteller auf spanisch (vgl. *Cancioneiro Geral* [1516], Gil Vicente, Sá de Miranda, Camões sowie der Polyhistor des 17. Jahrhundert Francisco Manuel de Melo), manche konvertierten sogar ganz ins Spanische (z. B. Jorge de Montemayor, Manuel de Faria e Sousa). Der Sprachkontakt und die Einflußnahme waren wechselseitig, beide Sprachen standen einander sehr viel näher als heute (Teyssier 1994, 466–467): es finden sich Hispanismen im Portugiesischen (z. B. *bobo, à frente, cavalheiro, fandango, picaresco, sequidilha, zarzuela, quixotesco*) wie auch Lusismen im Kastilischen (z. B. *ir buscar* anstatt *ir a buscar, agradeço* anstatt *agradezco*). Der spanisch–portugiesische Sprachkontakt ist durch alle Jahrhunderte nachweisbar, weniger in der portugiesischen Morphosyntax, mehr im portugiesischen Wortschatz.

Sprachgrenzkontakte bzw. *falares fronteiriços/hablas fronterizas* zwischen Portugal und Spanien wurden bereits 1901 von Leite de Vasconcelos beschrieben. Im äußersten Nordosten wurde sogar ein Trilingualismus von Leonesisch, Galicisch und Portugiesisch bis zum Ersten Weltkrieg in Rio de Onor festgestellt („coexistência de três idiomas em Rio de Onor" (Dias/Herculano de Carvalho 1954): die Varietät des *rionorês*, das ein größeres Spektrum von Vokalen, Diphthongen und Triphthongen aufwies, besonders Diminutiva (*rapacico, Manulico, cafelito*), morphologische Spezifika (*rapaça* „Mädchen") und lexikalische Eigenentwicklungen. Nach dem spanischen Bürgerkrieg hat sich das Kastilische seinerseits voll durchgesetzt, ebenso in den anderen alten Dialekten von Guadramil, Petisqueira und Deilão (Moura Santos 1967, 138). Der *dialecto mirandês* der Terra de Miranda mit 15.000 Sprechern weist demgegenüber größte Vitalität auf, wird als Alltagssprache von allen Altersgruppen gesprochen; das Portugiesische (*fala grabe, fala politica*) besitzt allerdings das höhere Prestige. Das Leonesische im nördlichen Teil des Concelho de Miranda do Douro hat sich neben dem Mirandesischen und Portugiesischen halten können (Trilingualismus bei einem Fünftel der Bevölkerung), in östlichen Dörfern herrscht echter Bilingualismus (Moura Santos 1967, 132). Der *dialecto mirandês* hat sich in oralen Traditionen (christliche Legenden etc.) volkstümlicher Literatur erhalten, so daß Herculano de Carvalho (1984, 95) schreibt: „o *mirandês*, isto é, o leonês falado em Terra de Miranda, constitui presentemente uma ilha linguística encravada entre o *português*, de um lado – na sua variedade transmontana –, e o *castelhano*, de outro lado". Das Bewußtsein der Bewohner, auf einer Sprachgrenze zu leben, drückt sich in den Bezeichnungen „fala atrabessada", „fala raiana" aus. Die Interferenzen zwischen den Idiomen beeinträchtigen die Kommunikation kaum. Das Standardportugiesische prädominiert gegenüber dem Kastilischen in der transmontanischen Region; rückkehrende Emigranten stärken zudem vermehrt das Standardportugiesische.

Ein weiterer Sprachgrenzkontakt mit „geordnetem Bilingualismus" (Weinreich) liegt in der Region um La Alamedilla und Xalma vor (port. Beira-Mundart, span. Leonesisch-Kastilisch), die soziale und sprachliche Orientierung geht zunehmend nach Spanien (Kirche, Schule, Medien), jüngere Sprecher sind monolingual kastilisch.

In dem weiter südlich anschließenden Sprachkontaktdistrikt (gleichfalls eine „fronteira viva", cf. Azevedo Maia 1977) von Campo Maior, Elvas, Alandroal, Olivenza ist die Situation jener von Galicien vergleichbar; das Kastilische ist *lengua superior*, der Dialekt des Alentejano *lengua inferior*; soziale Aufstiegschancen bietet der Jugend nur das Kastilische. Die port. Mundart gilt als niederes „chaporreo" (Matias 1984, 96), was zugleich auf die frühere Umsiedlung dieser Bevölkerung aus Galicien zurückweist. Diese Region eines „habla de tránsito" kann als hochgradig potentiell bilingual bezeichnet werden: „o camponês pela manhã fala espanhol e à noite português" (Matias 1984, 88), der „yeísmo" ist bei Älteren und Analphabeten verbreitet.

Der südlichste Teil der Sprachkontaktgrenze zwischen Portugal und Spanien (Rosal de la Frontera, Beja, Huelva) ist areallinguistisch bisher kaum beschrieben (Simões da Silva Lopes 1975–1978, 274–279).

4.4. Kontakte mit dem Provenzalischen und Französischen

Nach frühen Kontakten über das Galicische Ende des Mittelalters (13./14. Jahrhundert Literatursprache der *Cancioneiros* und *Cantigas*), durch die auch einige Provenzalismen ins Altportugiesische gelangten (z. B. *sen* [senso], *cor* [coraçon], *prez* [preço], *gréu* [grave, „schwierig"]), erlangte vor allem das Französische als Kultursprache die Rolle der Vermittlung nach Europa nördlich der Pyrenäen (insbesondere auch für frühe Anglizismen). Mitte des 18. Jahrhunderts wurde der Einfluß des Französischen derart prädominant (z. B. über das *teatro de cordel*), daß als Gegenreaktion sogar eine puristische Bewegung entstand (Luís de Sequeiro Oliva kritisierte 96 Französismen, von denen heute noch 49 im Gebrauch sind; vgl. Teyssier 1994, 469). Im portugiesischen Wortschatz wurden Französismen wie die folgenden völlig adaptiert: *arranjar, assemblea, audacioso, detalhe, egoismo, etiqueta, equipagem, finanças, garantir, justeza, mancar, nuanças, ponto de vista, sentimental, suportar, taxa, tratamento* u. a. m. Dieser Sprachkontakt wurde im 19. Jahrhundert durch Reisebewegungen, Literatur- und Kulturkontakte (Eça de Queirós u. a.), durch Französischkenntnisse im Volk verstärkt, was weitere Importe aus dem frz. Wortschatz zur Folge hatte: *abandonar, blusa, boné, chalé, chefe, cheque, chique, convém, coquete, debutar, ducha, equipa, importa, musse, tarte* und Wendungen wie *pedir perdão, fazer a honra, fazer greve, de maneira a*).

4.5. Angloamerikanische Kontakte des Portugiesischen

Nachdem in früheren Jahrhunderten Arabismen, Italianismen, Kastilianismen, Anglizismen, Gallizismen und Exotismen unterschiedlichster Provenienz auf direktem oder indirektem Wege in das Portugiesische gelangten (dazu Messner 1990), sind seit Mitte des 19. Jahrhunderts und zunehmend nach dem Zweiten Weltkrieg die Anglizismen zu nennen, oft über das Französische vermittelt.

Chronologisch läßt sich der Einfluß des Englischen grob in drei Phasen gliedern: eine Frühphase Ende des 19. Jahrhunderts und um die Jahrhundertwende, dann die Zeit zwischen den Weltkriegen und schließlich nach 1945; in einem Anglizismus-Wörterbuch wird dieses auch durch das Beleg-Korpus der Einträge deutlich (Schmidt-Radefeldt 1994; Schmidt-Radefeldt/Schurig 1995). Die Frühphase der Anglizismen im Portugiesischen ist durch „the English way of life" geprägt (Politik, Sport, Umgangsweise): z. B. *bife, bluff, bote, clube, dandi, desporte, espline, futebol, jockey, lanche, match, pique-nique* (offensichtlich über das Französische), *pudim, punch, recorde, revólver, repórter, sanduíche, tramway, uiste, yacht* und *luta pela vida*. Die neueste Kontaktphase als Überflutung des Portugiesischen durch Anglizismen findet vor allem in den Bereichen Technik, Mode, Musik, Medien u. a. statt: *fast-food, feed-back, mini-saia, pop, scanner, top, video-clube* etc. (Schmidt-Radefeldt/Schurig 1995).

Nach einer Auswanderungswelle vor und nach der Jahrhundertwende in die U.S.A. (zuerst nach Hawaii, Kalifornien), in den dreißiger Jahren dann vornehmlich an die amerikanische Atlantik-Küste (Massachusetts, New York, Pennsylvania, New Jersey und Connecticut) kamen die Auswanderer später wiederum nach Madeira und den Azoren zurück; das Portugiesische dieser Inseln wurde durch das gesprochene Angloamerikanische im Lexikon und in der Idiomatik zeitweilig stark geprägt (Gonçalves 1956, Pap 1949, Schmidt-Radefeldt 1986).

5. Forschungsdefizite und Perspektiven

Ein grundlegendes Defizit in der Sprachkontaktforschung zu Portugal ist darin zu sehen, daß die linguistischen Folgen der sozialen Migration der port. Minderheiten in europäische Länder wie Frankreich und Deutschland — mit unterschiedlichem Sprachverhalten durch zwei (bzw. drei) Generationen hindurch — bisher nur in ersten Ansätzen erforscht sind (Brauer-Figueiredo 1993, 1993 a). Sprachkontakt und Spracherwerb würden die Sozio- und Psycholinguistik in ihrer interdisziplinären Verschränkung herausfordern und neue Beschreibungsverfahren, -modelle und -bewertungen erforderlich machen.

Analog dazu gilt es, die sprachliche und soziale Reintegration der Rückwanderer aus den früheren Überseeprovinzen nach Portugal und den Kontakt ihrer Varietät mit dem Standardportugiesischen zu beschreiben; bisher sind in diesem Bereich kaum Forschungen initiiert worden.

Zu den Sprachkontakten Portugals in Übersee liegen detaillierte Studien vor, die jedoch in Mitteleuropa oft schwer erhältlich sind; allerdings fehlen umfassende Monographien zum Sprachkontakt mit der brasil. Variante und in den ehemaligen Überseeprovinzen (port. Minderheiten gegenüber den dortigen Landessprachen).

6. Bibliographie (in Auswahl)

Azevedo Filho, Leodegário A. de (1990): „Questões do Galego-Português". In: *Actas. II Congresso internacional da língua Galego-Portuguesa na Galiza 1987*, A Corunha, 387—398.

Azevedo Maia, Clarinda de (1977): *Os falares fronteiriços do Concelho de Sabugal e da vizinha região de Alma e Alamedilla*, Supl. Revista Portuguesa de Filologia, Coimbra.

Azevedo Maia, Clarinda de (1986): *História do Galego-Português. Estado linguístico da Galiza e do Noroeste de Portugal desde o século XIII ao século XVI*, Coimbra.

Baldinger, Kurt (1958/1963): *La formación de los dominios lingüísticos en la península ibérica*, Madrid.

Berschin, Helmut (1994): „Diglossie und Polyglossie". In: *LRL VI,2*, 367—381.

Boivert, Georges (1983/1985): „Guerra às palavras afrancesadas! Une polémique linguistique dans la presse lisbonnaise en octobre 1812". In: *Bulletin des Etudes Portugaises et Brésiliennes 44/45*.

Borges, Naír Odete de Câmara (1960): *Influência anglo-americana no falar da ilha de S. Miguel (Açores)*, Coimbra.

Brauer-Figueiredo, M. Fátima V. (1993): „Apresentação de um projecto de investigação sobre o português falado por emigrantes da 2a geração em Hamburgo". In: *Actas do Terceiro congresso da Associação Internacional de Lusitanistas*, Lissabon, 787—805.

Brauer-Figueiredo, M. de Fátima (1993a): „Sprachkontakt: Wie redet die zweite Generation der Immigranten in Hamburg Portugiesisch?" In: *Studia Hispanica. Akten des Deutschen Hispanistentages Göttingen*, Strosetzki, C. (Ed.), Frankfurt, 307—327.

Cortes y Vásquez, L. (1950): „Dos textos dialectales de Riohonor y dos romances portugueses de Hermisende". In: *Boletim de Filologia 11*, 388—403.

Dias, Jorge/Herculano de Carvalho, José G. (1954): *O falar de Rio de Onor* (Biblos vol. 30), Coimbra.

Elia, Sílvio (1992): „A posição de galego no domínio des línguas ibéricas". In: *Actas. III Congresso internacional de lingua galego-portuguesa na Galiza 1990*, do Carmo, M./Salido, H. (Ed.), A Corunha, 113—135.

Goebl, Hans (1986): „Problems and Perspectives of Contact Linguistics from a Romance Scholar's Point of View". In: *Proceedings of the Working Groups 12 and 13 at the XIIIth International Congress for Linguists. August 29—September 4, 1982*, Tokyo, Nelde, P. H./P. St. Ureland/I. Clarkson (Eds.), Tübingen, 125—150.

Gonçalves, Carlos Lélis de Câmara (1956): *Influência inglesa na Ilha de Madeira. Contributo para um estudo linguístico e histórico*, Diss. Universidade de Coimbra.

Herculano de Carvalho, José G. (1952): „Porque se falam dialectos leoneses em Terra de Miranda?" In: *Revista Portuguesa de Filologia 5*, 265—280; ebenso in: id., *Estudos linguísticos 1*, Coimbra 1984, 71—92.

Herculano de Carvalho, José G. (1984): „Elementos estranhos no vocabulário mirandês". In: id., *Estudos linguísticos 1*, Coimbra, 93—110.

Herculano de Carvalho, José G. (1984a): „Moçarabismo linguístico ao Sul do Mondego". In: id., *Estudos linguísticos 1*, Coimbra, 159—170.

Henríquez Salido, Maria de Carmo (1993): „O uso do Galego-Português na perspectiva de Europa Comunitária". In: *O uso das linguas na perspectiva da Europa Comunitária*, Associço Galega da Lingua (Ed.), A Corunha, 101—120.

Krüger, Fritz (1925): *Die Gegenstandskultur Sanabrias und seiner Nachbargebiete*, Hamburg.

Krüger, Fritz (1965): „Aportes a la fonética dialectal de Sanabria y de sus zonas colindantes". In: *Revista de Filología Española 48*, 251—282.

Leite de Vasconcelos, José (1902): „Linguagens fronteiriças". In: *Revista Lusitana 7*, 133—145.

Leite de Vasconcelos, José (1933): „Português dialectal da região de Xalma (Hespanha)". In: *Revista Lusitana 31*, 164—270.

Leite de Vasconcelos, José (1936): „Guadramil e Riodonor". In: *Revista Lusitana 34*, 291−292.

Lorenzo, Ramón (1968): *Sobre cronologia do vocabulário Galego-português*, Vigo.

LRL = Holtus, Günther/Metzeltin, Michael/Schmitt, Christian (Eds.) (1988 f): *Lexikon der Romanistischen Linguistik*, Tübingen.

Machado, José Pedro (1991): *Vocabulário português de origem árabe*, Lissabon.

Mermet, Gérard (1991): *Die Europäer. Länder, Leute, Leidenschaften. Mit zahlreichen Karten, Tabellen und Abbildungen*, München.

Messner, Dieter (1990): *História do léxico português (com a origem das palavras citadas)*, Heidelberg.

Metzeltin, Michael (1978): Besprechung zu: Moura Santos 1967. In: *Vox Romanica 37*, 378−379.

Moura Santos, Maria José de (1967): *Os falares fronteiriços de Trás-os-Montes*, Coimbra.

Moura Santos, Maria José (1980): „Importação lexical e estruturação semântica, os arabismos na língua portuguesa". In: *Biblos 56*, 573−598.

Pap, Leo (1949): *Portuguese-American Speech: An Outline of Speech Conditions among Portuguese Immigrants in New England and elsewhere in the United States*, New York.

Paufler, Hans-Diether (1985): „Bilinguismus und Diglossie in Galicien". In: *Wissenschaftliche Zeitschrift der Humboldt-Universität zu Berlin 4*, 297−302.

Rezende Matias, Fátima de (1984): *Bilinguismo e niveis sociolinguísticos numa região Luso-espanhola* (Supl. Revista Portuguesa de Filologia), Coimbra.

Rezende Matias, Fátima de (1986): „Português e espanhol em contacto em Olivença". In: *Revista galaico-portuguesa de Cultura 2/3*, 7−30.

Santamarina, Antón (1988): „Efectos do contacto lingüístico na toponimia galega". In: *Homenagem a Joseph M. Piel por ocasião de seu 85° aniversario*, Kremer, D. (Ed.), Tübingen, 87−96.

Schmidt-Radefeldt, Jürgen (1986): „Anglicisms in Portuguese and Language Contact." In: *English in Contact with other Languages. Studies in Honour of Broder Carstensen on the Occasion of his 60th Birthday*, Viereck, W./Bald, W.-D. (Eds.), Budapest, 265−285.

Schmidt-Radefeldt, Jürgen (1990): „Aspectos da interferência linguística. O exemplo do galego. Anotaçom de A. Gil Hernández". In: *Agália. Revista da Associaçom Galega da Lingua 22*, 143−159.

Schmidt-Radefeldt, Jürgen (1991): „Problemas com anglicismos e germanismos no registo das entradas de um dicionário de português". In: *Terminologie et Traduction* (Bruxelles) *1*, 211−230.

Schmidt-Radefeldt, Jürgen (1994): „Adaptionsphänomene der Anglizismen. Zur Konvergenz und Divergenz in romanischen Sprachen". In: *Romanistisches Kolloquium VIII. Konvergenz und Divergenz in den romanischen Sprachen*, Dahmen, W. et al. (Eds.), Tübingen 1995, 191−203.

Schmidt-Radefeldt, Jürgen / Dorothea Schurig (1995): *Dicionário dos anglicismos e germanismos na língua portuguesa*, Frankfurt.

Simões de Silva Lopes, Ana Maria (1972−1978): „O vocabulário marítimo português e o problema dos mediterraneísmos". In: *Revista Portuguesa de Filologia 16* (1972−1974), 29−284; *17* (1975−1978), 211−337.

Teyssier, Paul (1994): „Histoire externe de la langue portugaise". In: *LRL VI,2*, 461−472.

Weber, Peter (1980): *Portugal. Räumliche Dimension und Abhängigkeit*, Darmstadt.

Weinreich, Uriel (1953/1976): *Sprachen in Kontakt*, München.

Woll, Dieter (1994): „Portugiesisch: Sprachnormierung und Standardsprache". In: *LRL VI,2*, 382−398.

Jürgen Schmidt-Radefeldt, Rostock (Deutschland)

XIII. Sprachkontakte in Südeuropa
Language Contacts in Southern Europe
Contacts linguistiques en Europe du Sud

156. Italien

1. Geographie und Demographie
2. Territorialgeschichte und Staatsbildung
3. Politik, Wirtschaft und allgemeine kulturelle sowie religiöse Lage
4. Statistik und Ethnoprofile
5. Soziolinguistische Lage
6. Sprachpolitische Lage
7. Sonstige Sprachkontakte/Kontaktsprachen
8. Kritische Wertung der verwendeten Quellen und Literatur
9. Bibliographie (in Auswahl)

1. Geographie und Demographie

Die italienische Republik (Repubblica Italiana) grenzt im Norden an Frankreich, die Schweiz, Österreich und Slowenien. Italien erstreckt sich über eine Länge von rund 1300 km und hat eine Landfläche von 294.050 km². Innerhalb des ital. Staatsgebietes liegen die „unabhängigen Staaten" San Marino (60,6 km²) und Vatikanstaat (Stato della Città del Vaticano; 0,44 km²). Die Küstenlänge beträgt 7456 km. Rund 80% Italiens sind Gebirgsland. Bevölkerung 1991: rund 57,8 Mio. (1971: 54,1 Mio.; 1981: 56,6 Mio.; Bev.-wachstum im Zeitraum 1971−1981: 4,5%, 1981−1991: 2,2%; Bev.-dichte 1991: 191,9 E./km²). Hinzu kommen rund 11 Mio. Auslandsitaliener (v. a. in den europ. Industriestaaten, aber auch in den USA, Südamerika und Australien). Am stärksten besiedelt sind die stark industrialisierten Regionen Lombardei (373,5 E./km²), Ligurien (318,8) und Venezien (238,8) sowie die Ballungsräume von Rom und Neapel, während die Alpengebiete (Aostatal: 35,3 E./km², Südtirol: 65,1) und die mittel- und südital. Regionen Umbrien (97,0), Molise (75,6), Basilicata (62,4) und Sardinien (68,8) nur schwach besiedelt sind. 1981 wohnten 54% der Bev. in Städten mit mehr als 20.000 E., 28% in Städten mit 100.000 oder mehr E.

1990 lebten 68,9% in Städten. Lebenserwartung bei Geburt: Frauen 78,9, Männer 72,4 (Durchschnitt 1985−1990). Analphabeten 1985: 3,0% (1971: 6,1%).

Von 1984−1988 wanderten knapp 308.000 Italiener aus, davon rund 247.000 in andere europ. Länder, rund 38.000 nach Amerika (in dieser Zeit ca. 302.000 Rückwanderer). Die Zahl der Auswanderer ist gering im Vergleich zu den rund 3,6 Mio. Italienern, die zwischen 1876 und 1914 (¾ davon nach der Jahrhundertwende) ausgewandert sind. Der Grund für die erste Auswanderungswelle war vor allem die hohe Geburtenrate bei gleichzeitig schlechten Beschäftigungsmöglichkeiten besonders im industriearmen Süden und auf den Inseln. Wegen der verstärkten Industrialisierung des Nordens Italiens (v. a. in den Ballungsräumen von Mailand, Genua und Turin) nach dem Zweiten Weltkrieg wurde die Auswanderung zunehmend durch eine Binnenwanderung ersetzt, wodurch sich das wirtschaftliche und soziale Gefälle zwischen dem Norden und dem Süden verschärfte (gegensätzliche Beschäftigungsstruktur; hohe Arbeitslosigkeit im Süden − hohe Bevölkerungsdichte im Norden); → Sprachenkarte F.

2. Territorialgeschichte und Staatsbildung

„Italia" ist seit dem 6./5. vorchr. Jahrhundert belegt als Name der Griechen für die kalabrische Halbinsel; er wird im 4. Jahrhundert auf ganz Süditalien ausgedehnt, von den Römern übernommen und ab Mitte des 3. Jahrhunderts v. Chr. für die ganze Apenninenhalbinsel bis zu den Alpen verwendet. Bis zur polit. Einigung 1860 bleibt „Italia" weitgehend ein geographischer und kultureller Begriff. Erst mit der Errichtung mehrerer abhängiger Republiken im Norden durch die Franzosen und der Umbenennung der *Cisalpinischen Republik* 1802 in *Italienische Republik* (Lombardei, Modena, Brescia, Bergamo, Veltlin, Herzogtum Massa Carrara, Romagna) bekommt der Name in der Folge zunehmend auch eine politische Bedeutung. Die *Ital. Republik* wird nach Napoleons Erhebung zum Kaiser (1804) in *Königreich Italien* (Regno d'Italia) umbenannt, zu dessen König er sich 1805 krönt und das in den Jahren 1806—1810 progressiv um Venetien, die Marken, Trient und Teile Tirols erweitert wird. Die nicht zum Ital. Königreich gehörenden Gebiete Nord- und Mittelitaliens werden zwischen 1800 und 1808 von Frankreich annektiert (Piemont, Ligurien, Parma, Toskana, Umbrien, Latium). 1806 werden die Bourbonen aus dem Königreich Neapel vertrieben. Triest, Istrien und Dalmatien sowie Westkärnten und die Krain kommen 1809 zu Frankreich („illyrische Provinzen").

Nach dem Zusammenbruch der napol. Herrschaft in Italien (1814/15) und dem Wiener Kongreß werden der Kirchenstaat, die Königreiche Neapel-Sizilien (Königreich beider Sizilien), Piemont-Sardinien (mit Genua) und das Großherzogtum Toskana wiederhergestellt. Österreich erhält die Lombardei und Venetien. Die auf die napol. Zeit zurückgehende Hoffnung auf nationale Selbstbestimmung bleibt unter den Intellektuellen Italiens lebendig. Sie mündet in die als *Risorgimento* bekannten Einigungsbestrebungen der nächsten Jahrzehnte (1815—1870). Widerstand gegen die Fremdherrschaft formiert sich im Adel und im gehobenen Bürgertum. Es entstehen freimaurerähnliche Geheimbünde (Carbonari). Aufstände in verschiedenen Städten (Neapel, Piemont 1820/21, Modena, Romagna 1830/31). 1831 gründet Mazzini die Gesellschaft *La Giovine Italia* (Ziel: Schaffung eines republikanischen und demokratischen Italiens). Von ihm organisierte Aufstände (Piemont 1833/34, Bologna 1843, Kalabrien 1844, Rimini 1845) scheitern. Waren die Erhebungen der Mazzinianer noch isolierte Aktionen einer intellektuellen Elite, so kam es 1848 unter dem Eindruck von Hunger und Arbeitslosigkeit und als „Ausdruck der ungeduldigen Fortschrittshoffnungen der bürgerlichen Schichten und der Intelligenz" (Procacci 1989, 255) auch in Italien zur Revolution. Carlo Alberto von Piemont setzt sich an die Spitze der Freiheitsbewegung, unterliegt aber im Freiheitskrieg 1848 gegen die Habsburger und dankt 1849 zugunsten seines Sohnes Vittorio Emanuele II. ab. Eine *Römische Republik* unter Mazzini und Garibaldi besteht nur kurz (Febr. 1849 — Juli 1849). Die 48er Revolution scheitert zwar, doch ist der Wille nach Einheit und Unabhängigkeit inzwischen zu stark, als daß sie noch verhindert werden könnten. In Piemont, dem einzigen konstitutionellen Staat Italiens, kommt 1852 Cavour an die Macht, der entscheidend zur ital. Einheit beiträgt. Er gewinnt Napoleon III. als Verbündeten gegen Österreich, das in den Schlachten von Magenta (4. 6. 1859) und Solferino (24. 6.) unterliegt und im Frieden von Zürich die Lombardei an Napoleon abtritt, der sie an Piemont weitergibt. Piemont annektiert die Toskana, Modena, Parma und die Emilia-Romagna und tritt Savoyen sowie Nizza an Frankreich ab (1860). Garibaldi landet im Mai 1860 auf Sizilien, erobert zunächst die Insel, dann ganz Süditalien; Neapel-Sizilien, Umbrien und die Marken schließen sich Piemont an. Vittorio Emanuele II. nimmt den Titel „König von Italien" an (17. 3. 1861); Hauptstadt wird Turin, 1865 Florenz. Italien beteiligt sich auf preußischer Seite am Krieg gegen Österreich (alle militär. Aktionen scheitern), das 1866 im Frieden von Wien Venetien an Frankreich abtritt, welches es an Italien weitergibt. Nach Abzug der frz. Truppen besetzen ital. Truppen am 20. 9. 1870 Rom. Anschluß des Kirchenstaates, Rom wird Hauptstadt.

1877 gründet Imbriani-Poerio die Vereinigung *Italia irredenta* (unerlöstes Italien), die sich die Gewinnung der „unerlösten" Gebiete mit ital.-sprach. Bevölkerung, die nach der Einigung noch unter österr.-ungar. Hoheit verblieben sind (Trient, Triest, Istrien, dalmatische Küste), zum Ziel setzt. Schon vor 1914 geht der Irredentismus über seine ursprünglichen Ziele hinaus und fordert für Italien die natürlichen Grenzen: die Wasserscheide in den Alpen und in Dalmatien. Hinter dem irredent. Gedanken stehen Organisationen wie die Gesellschaft *Dante Alighieri*, die Vereinigung *Pro Patria*, die *Lega Nazionale*, die *Nazione Italiana*. Führer der trentinischen Irredenta ist ab 1890 Cesare Battisti. — Bei Ausbruch des Ersten Weltkrieges 1914 erklärt Italien seine Neutralität (trotz des 1882 geschlossenen, von den Irredentisten abgelehnten, Dreibundes zwischen Deutschland, Österreich-Ungarn und Italien). Im Londoner Geheimvertrag (26. 4. 1915) wird Italien die Brennergrenze zugesichert, vorausgesetzt, es tritt an der Seite der Alliierten gegen den bisherigen Verbündeten Österreich in den Krieg ein, was am 23. Mai 1915 geschieht.

Aufgrund des Friedensvertrages von Saint-Germain-en-Laye (10. 9. 1919) erhält Italien Südtirol bis zum Brenner, Trient, das Küstenland (Görz, Gradisca, Istrien, Triest) sowie Zara (Zadar) mit deutsch-, ladinisch- und slawischsprachigen Minderheiten.

Mit der Machtübernahme der Faschisten beginnt für die in Italien lebenden ethnischen Minderheiten eine schwere Zeit. Besonders die Deutsch-Südtiroler haben unter dem Regime zu leiden. Der dt.-ital. Vertrag vom 25. 10. 1936 begründet die *Achse Berlin-Rom.* Mussolini und Hitler schließen ein Abkommen über die Aussiedlung der dt. und lad. Bevölkerung in Südtirol (21. 12. 1939), die bis Ende 1940 abgeschlossen sein soll, aber wegen der Kriegsereignisse nur zum Teil durchgeführt wird. Italien erklärt Frankreich und Großbritannien am 10. Juni 1940 den Krieg. Nach schweren Niederlagen gegen Griechenland und Großbritannien in Nordafrika (1940/41) und wegen der Unfähigkeit der italienischen Regierung, das Bündnis mit Deutschland zu lösen, wird Mussolini 1943 gestürzt und verhaftet. Neuer Ministerpräsident wird Badoglio, der vor den nach Süden vorrückenden deutschen Truppen nach Süditalien flieht. Von deutschen Fallschirmjägern am Gran Sasso befreit, gründet Mussolini in Norditalien die *Italienische Soziale Republik (Repubblica Sociale Italiana)* mit „Hauptstadt" Salò (Gardasee). 28. 4. 1945: Mussolini wird von Partisanen erschossen. 2. Mai: Inkrafttreten der Kapitulation der deutschen Streitkräfte in Italien.

Infolge des Zweiten Weltkrieges verliert Italien − seit dem 18. 6. 1946 Republik − seine Kolonien. Die vorwiegend slawischsprachigen Gebiete an der Ostgrenze kommen zu Jugoslawien; Triest wird zunächst Freistaat (Pariser Friedensvertrag 10. 2. 1947), aufgrund des Abkommens vom 5. 10. 1954 zwischen Italien, Jugoslawien, Großbritannien und den USA aber wieder Italien zugeschlagen. Das Aostatal und Südtirol erhalten 1948 ein Autonomiestatut, ebenso Sizilien (1946), Sardinien (1948) und Friaul-Julisch Venetien (1963).

3. Politik, Wirtschaft und allgemeine kulturelle sowie religiöse Lage

3.1. Politik

Italien ist eine parlamentarisch-demokratische Republik (Verfassung 1. 1. 1948). Der Staatspräsident (auf 7 Jahre vom Parlament sowie Vertretern der Regionen gewählt) vertritt Italien völkerrechtlich und ernennt die Regierung. Das Parlament besteht aus Senat (315 auf 5 Jahre gewählte Senatoren; je Region mindestens 7 Senatoren, Aostatal 1 Senator) und Abgeordnetenhaus (630 auf 5 Jahre gewählte Mitglieder). Möglichkeit des Volksentscheids sowie der Einleitung von Gesetzgebungsverfahren durch Volksbegehren. In Italien herrscht ein Vielparteiensystem; Parteien der Mitte:

− Democrazia Cristiana (DC), seit 1993 Partito Popolare Italiano (PPI);
− Partito Liberale Italiano (PLI);
− Partito Repubblicano Italiano (PRI);
− Partito Socialista Democratico Italiano (PSDI).

Traditionell zweitstärkste Partei ist der Partito Comunista Italiano (PCI), seit 1992 umbenannt in Partito Democratico di Sinistra (PDS); zur viertstärksten Partei rückte bei den vorgezogenen Parlamentswahlen vom 5./6. April 1992 die rechte Lega Nord auf (in Norditalien zweitstärkste Partei), deren Ziel die Verhinderung der vermeintlichen Umverteilung des Wohlstands aus dem Norden in den wirtschaftlich rückständigen Süden ist; zu nennen sind außerdem − neben einigen weiteren kleineren bzw. nur regional antretenden Parteien (wie z. B. Südtiroler Volkspartei, Union Valdôtaine, Partito Sardo d'Azione): Movimento Sociale Italiano (MSI; Neofaschisten); Partito Radicale (PR; vertritt Bürgerrechts- und Minderheitsbewegungen); Partito Socialista Italiano (PSI); Verdi (Grüne).

Bei den Wahlen von 1992 erhielten die seit Kriegsende in verschiedenen Bündnissen regierenden Christdemokraten erstmals weniger als 30%.

Italien befindet sich nach den politischen und Bestechungsskandalen der letzten Jahre im politischen Umbruch. Nachdem die meisten führenden Politiker der DC (ebenso wie des PSI) mit Gerichtsverfahren zu rechnen haben, hat sich die Partei auf einem Kongreß im Juli 1993 aufgelöst und unter dem Namen *Partito Popolare Italiano* neu gegründet. Bei den administrativen Wahlen im Juni 1993 erreichte die DC in den Gemeinden über 15.000 Einwohnern lediglich 18,8%. Die Parlamentswahlen 1994 ergaben eine Mehrheit für ein Rechtsbündnis aus Lega Nord, Alleanza Nazionale (ehem. MSI) und der erst wenige Monate vor der Wahl gegründeten Partei Forza Italia.

3.2. Wirtschaft

Obwohl arm an Rohstoffen, hat Italien nach dem Zweiten Weltkrieg einen Wandel vom Agrar- zum Industriestaat vollzogen, begünstigt durch den Rückgang der landwirtschaftlichen Produktivität während des Krieges auf 65% (gegenüber 10% Rückgang bei der industriellen Produktivität). Betroffen war vor allem der agrarisch ausgerichtete Süden. Dieses Ungleichgewicht hat sich in den folgenden Jahrzehnten verstärkt. Während 1987 das Gesamtwachstum des Nationaleinkommens 3,1% betrug, kam der gering industrialisierte – teilweise noch durch Großgrundbesitz geprägte – Süden nur auf 1,6%. Die Landwirtschaft war zu Beginn der 80er Jahre nur noch mit 5,8% am Bruttosozialprodukt beteiligt. Von den 1990 knapp 22 Mio. Erwerbstätigen in Italien waren nur 8,7% in Land- und Forstwirtschaft und Fischerei tätig (1971: 17,2%). Eine in den 60er Jahren geplante Industrialisierung des Südens wurde nur zum Teil durchgeführt. Bei den über 20 mit staatlicher Hilfe im Süden gegründeten Unternehmen handelt es sich vorwiegend um hochautomatisierte Teilfertigungsbetriebe, es fehlt jedoch die weiterverarbeitende Industrie. Während landesweit die Arbeitslosenquote 1990 bei 11% lag, betrug sie in Süditalien 20,7% (Norden 5,2%, Mittelitalien 9,8%). Die Binnenwanderung nach Norden hält bis heute an, der Zuzug in die großen Industriestädte des Nordens hat sich jedoch verlangsamt. Stattdessen setzt sich die Wanderung in die Provinzhauptstädte des Südens unvermindert fort. Unter den ital. Exportgütern standen 1990 Maschinen und Fahrzeuge an erster Stelle (37,4% des ges. Ausfuhrwertes). Wichtigster Wirtschaftszweig ist der Tourismus (1989: 55 Mio. Auslandsgäste, Deviseneinnahmen 12 Mrd. US-$). Auch hier bildet der Süden das Schlußlicht: Molise 277.000, Basilicata 454.000 Übernachtungen gegenüber 26,3 Mio. in Trentino-Südtirol, 24 Mio. Emilia-Romagna.

3.3. Kultur

Italien ist seit dem Altertum eine Stätte intensivsten kulturellen Schaffens im weitesten Sinn. Davon zeugen unzählige historische Bauwerke, Ausgrabungsstätten, Museen und Galerien. Italien, seit dem 15. Jahrhundert bereits ein kultureller Begriff, wird ab Mitte des 18. Jahrhunderts beliebtes Ziel europäischer Künstler, Schriftsteller und Dichter. Heute zieht es jährlich Millionen von „Kulturtouristen" an (1983 über 25 Mio.). Ein Problem stellt die Instandhaltung der Kulturgüter dar; nur 0,2% der öffentlichen Ausgaben sind für Kulturgüter vorgesehen.

Bildungswesen: Schulpflicht (8 Jahre): Scuola Elementare (Grundschule, 5 J.), Scuola Media Unica (Einheitsmittelschule, 3 J.); danach wahlweise Besuch des Istituto Tecnico (technische Schule, 5 J.), des Istituto Magistrale (Lehrerbildungsanstalt, 4 J.), des Liceo Classico/Scientifico/Artistico (Humanist./Mathemat.-Naturwissen./Musisches Gymnasium, 5 J.) oder der Scuola Professionale (Berufsschule, 2–3 J.). 49 Hochschulen bieten die Möglichkeit eines Studiums (1988/89). – 1985 3,0% Analphabeten; auch hier deutliches Nord-Süd-Gefälle. Probleme im Bildungswesen v. a. aufgrund unzureichender Schulgebäude und mangelhafter Organisation.

Presse: Die auflagenstärksten nicht parteigebundenen Tageszeitungen, die in ganz Italien Verbreitung finden, sind: Corriere della Sera (Mailand): 633.000, La Stampa (Turin): 553.000, La Repubblica (Rom) 503.000 (1985).

Rundfunk/Fernsehen: Bis 1976 praktisch staatliches Monopol; seither zahlreiche Privatsender. Italien ist in Europa führend im „Fernsehkonsum": 99,2% (BRD 97%) aller Haushalte besitzen einen Fernsehapparat (1991). Die tägliche durchschnittliche Fernsehdauer von 3 Stunden und 17 Minuten pro Person wird nur übertroffen von Großbritannien, Portugal und Irland. Ausgaben für Fernsehwerbung 1990 mehr als 3 Mrd. US-$.

3.4. Religion

Die zwischen dem Königreich Italien und dem Vatikan am 11. 2. 1929 geschlossenen Lateranverträge legten den Katholizismus als Staatsreligion fest. 12. 2. 1984: Konkordat zwischen dem Vatikan und Italien: Katholizismus ist nicht mehr Staatsreligion. 83,2% der ital. Bevölkerung bekennen sich zum römisch-katholischen Glauben, 13,6% gehören keiner Religion an; 2,6% Atheisten, 0,6% gehören einer anderen Bekenntnisgruppe an; 180.000 Protestanten; 35.000 Juden. Der Katholizismus hat Kultur und Geschichte stark beeinflußt, jedoch heute – vor allem im hoch industrialisierten Norden – an Einfluß verloren, was sich u. a. in den Volksentscheiden über die Ehescheidung (1974: 59,1%) und den Schwangerschaftsabbruch (1981: 67,9%) ausdrückt.

4. Statistik und Ethnoprofile

4.0. Kulturadstrate

Das Ital. hat seit dem Mittelalter zahlreiche Wörter aus verschiedenen anderen europäischen Sprachen entlehnt. Eine besondere Rolle kam dabei dem Frz. zu, das jedoch in jüngster Zeit als Kultur- bzw. Bildungsadstrat zunehmend vom Englischen verdrängt wird, was vor allem in den Medien und in den Unterrichtsplänen der Schulen seine Wirkung zeigt. Eine wesentlich geringere Bedeutung als Kulturadstrat hat das Deutsche (v. a. in den Printmedien tauchen gelegentlich Entlehnungen wie z. B. *ostpolitik* auf).

4.1. Albanisch

Albanische Sprachinseln sind über ganz Süditalien verstreut. Ursprünglich 100 albanische Orte, heute noch 49 Ortschaften und Weiler (44 Gemeinden, vgl. Karte F mit Kommentar), v. a. in Kalabrien. Schätzungen der Sprecherzahl des Italo-Alb. in Süditalien schwanken erheblich. Realistisch ist eine Zahl von 80–100.000; hinzu kommen einige Tausend in die nord-ital. Industriestädte abgewanderte Italo-Albaner (ca. 15.000 in Mailand).

4.2. Deutsch

4.2.1. Südtirol

67,99% dt., 27,65% ital., 4,36% lad., Gesamtbevölkerung: 422.851 (1991). Gemeinden mit mehrheitlich ital.-sprachiger Bevölkerung: Bozen/Bolzano 73%, Branzoll/Bronzolo 60%, Leifers/Laives 69%, Salurn/Salorno 61%, Pfatten/Vadena 58%. Die Interessen der meisten Deutschsüdtiroler und Ladiner in Südtirol werden vertreten durch die *Südtiroler Volkspartei* (SVP).

4.2.2. Deutsche Sprachinseln

4.2.2.1. Val d'Aosta

Walsersiedlungen (Sprache „Ditsch") Gressoney La Trinité, Gressoney St. Jean/Greschôney (1991 zusammen 1048 E.), Issime/Eischeme (1990 365 E.);

4.2.2.2. Piemont

Sesiatal (Alagna/Im Land, Rima/Rimmu, Rimella/Rèmmallju), Anzascatal (Macugnaga/Makana, hier kennt die Jugend die Mundart kaum noch);

4.2.2.3. Trentino

- Fersental: Frassilongo/Gereut (mit Eichleit), Fierozzo/Florutz (mit St. Franz und St. Felix), Palù/Palai; 1985: 1165 E.;
- Luserna/Lusern (1981: 401 von 415 E. = 96,6%; 1993 noch 375 E.);

4.2.2.4. Veneto

- Tredici Comuni (Prov. Verona): 1971 noch 2,2% Sprecher (nur noch Giazza/Ljetzan: 257 von 563 Einwohnern = 45,6%); diese absolute Zahl sagt jedoch nichts über die aktive Kompetenz der Sprecher aus;
- Sette Comuni (Prov. Vicenza): 1981 noch 1,2% Sprecher (nur noch Roana/Rowan mit Mezzaselva: 227 von 3.597 E. = 6,3%);
- Sappada (Pladen);

4.2.2.5. Friuli-Venezia Giulia

- Timau (Tischlwang), Sauris (Zahre);
- Kanaltal: 7986 E. (1992), davon 1533 Einheimische, davon 47% deutschsprachig.

4.3. Frankoprovenzalisch

4.3.1. Val d'Aosta

Ca. 116.000 E. (1991), 80.000 Emigranten in Paris. Autonomiestatut: kooffizielle Sprachen Frz., It. Ca. 35–40.000 Aostaner sprechen Frankoprovenzalisch, wesentlich mehr verstehen es. Frz. wird von der bodenständigen Bevölkerung bereits als Fremdsprache empfunden; politische Vertretung der frankophonen Minderheit: *Union Valdôtaine*.

4.3.2. Piemont

Alpentäler nordwestlich von Turin: Val di Susa (ca. 10.000 Sprecher, ca. 23% der Bevölkerung), Val Soana (990 Sprecher, ca. 59%), (Val Cenischia 990 Sprecher, ca. 58%) sowie in weiteren Tälern, insgesamt rund 22.000 Sprecher (ca. 28% der ansässigen Bev.);

4.3.3. Apulien (Prov. Foggia)

Faeto, Celle San Vito: ca. 1200 Sprecher (galloromanische Sprachinsel seit dem 13. Jahrhundert).

4.4. Friaulisch

(Vorwiegend linguistische Kriterien, ca. 500.000 Sprecher): Friuli-Venezia Giulia; Timau (Tischelwang), Sauris (Zahre): dt./friaulisch; Kanaltal: it./dt./slow./friaul.; Grado, Triest, Monfalcone venedisch; Grenzgebiet zu Slowenien slow.; Erto ladinisch; im Westen der Region sowie im Südosten des Veneto friaul.-vened. Übergangszone; in den größeren Städten Friauls sowie in deren näherer Umgebung immer stärkere Verbreitung einer venedischen Koiné als Basilekt; → Sprachkarte F.

4.5. Griechisch

4.5.1. Kalabrien (Prov. Reggio Calabria)

Nur in Chorio di Rogudi/Chorio tu Roghudiu (700 E.) und Galliciano (350 E.) wird üblicherweise Griechisch gesprochen; in Bova/

Vua (Bova Superiore 2000 E.) nur von Erwachsenen. In Condofuri und Amendolea/Amiddalia nur noch wenige Griechischsprecher.

4.5.2. Apulien (Prov. Lecce)

Calimera, Sternatia, Martano, Zollino, Castrignano dei Greci, Corigliano d'Otranto. Praktisch ausgestorben ist das Griechische in Martignano, Soleto und Melpignano. – Sprecherzahl nach Spano 1965: Sternatia 74,9%, Corigliano 71,1%, Martano 59,8%, Zollino 59,4%, Martignano 56,8%, Castrignano dei Greci 52,4%, Calimera 51,5%, Melpignano 17,4%, Soleto 11% (Einwohnerzahlen nach Karanastasis: Calimera 7000, Sternatia 4000, Corigliano 5000, Martignano 2000, Zollino 3000, Martano 9000). Nach Informationen des Centro Studi „Chora Ma" in Sternatia (Brief vom 29. 9. 1992) sprechen in Sternatia von 3000 Einwohnern 60% sowohl Griechisch als auch Ital., 10% verstehen Griech., 30% sprechen nur Ital. In Soleto, Melpignano, Calimera und Zollino sprechen nur noch 20% Griechisch, in Martignano, Martano, Castrignano dei Greci und Corigliano sind es 35% (→ Art. 163).

4.6. Katalanisch

Alghero (kat. *L'Alguer*; Sardinien, Prov. Sassari) 45.000 E., davon ca. 45% Kat.-sprecher.

4.7. Kroatisch

Molise: Acquaviva Collecroce (Zivavoda Brdodokriz/Kruč), San Felice del Molise (Sti Filič), Montemitro (Mundimitar). Rund 2000 der 2449 Einwohner (1981) sprechen Kroatisch.

4.8. Ladinisch

4.8.1. (Sella-)Ladinisch

Gadertal, Gröden, Fassa, Buchenstein, Ampezzo. Ladiner in Gadertal und Gröden 1991: 15.468 von 15.880 Ansässigen (laut Sprachzugehörigkeitserklärung). Fassa 1991 8.621, Buchenstein und Colle Santa Lucia zusammen 1918 Ansässige; in Ampezzo lebten am 31. 12. 1991 7070 Personen.

Nach Gubert 1976 gaben sich in Fassa nur 64% der Befragten als Ladiner aus, was einer absoluten Zahl von rund 5000 entspräche. Heute kann man davon ausgehen, daß sich im Fassatal rund 80% als Ladiner empfinden. Die Schätzungen für die lad.-sprachige Bevölkerung von Ampezzo schwanken zwischen 30 und 50%. Eine absolute Zahl von etwa 2500 Ladinern ist realistisch.

Insgesamt beträgt die Zahl der in den drei betreffenden Provinzen lebenden Ladiner (unter Berücksichtigung einer nicht genau feststellbaren Zahl weiterer Ladiner in den Prov. Trient und Belluno, jedoch ohne Comelico) rund 30.000.

4.8.2. Comelianisch

(Ladinisch nach linguistischen Kriterien; geringes Sprachbewußtsein): Candide, Casada, Comèlico, Costa, Costalissoio, Costalta, Danta, Dosoledo, Pàdola, Santo Stefano, Valle; ca. 10.000 Sprecher.

4.9. Provenzalisch

4.9.1. Piemont (Prov. Torino)
Alpinokzitanisch

Chisonetal, Pellicetal; 1974 rund 46.000 Okz.-Sprecher, Tendenz abnehmend.

4.9.2. Kalabrien (Prov. Cosenza)

Guardia Piemontese 1992 449 E., davon 341 Okz.-Sprecher, sowie Guardia Marina 50 Okzitanophone.

4.10. Sardisch

Ganz Sardinien außer z. T. Alghero (45% Katalanisch), Carloforte und Calasetta (genuesische Sprachinseln). Von den rund 1,6 Mio. E. sprechen ca. 80% Sardisch. Das Sassaresische und das Galluresische im Norden sind stark vom Korsischen beeinflußt.

4.11. Slowenisch

Region Friuli-Venezia Guilia: in den Prov. Trieste (ca. 8%), Gorizia (ca. 12%) und Udine (ca. 28%) gibt es, insgesamt rund 50.000 Sprecher. Zahlen basieren auf Volkszählungen, werden aber sowohl von der Minderheits- als auch von der Mehrheitsbevölkerung angezweifelt. Neben Standardslow. zahlreiche Mundarten. Mehrheitlich slowenische Gemeinden:

– Prov. Udine: Resia/Rezija, Taipana/Tipana, Lusévera/Brdo;
– Prov. Gorizia: S. Floriano del Collio/Števerjan, Savogna d'Isonzo/Sovodnje ob Soči, Doberdò del Lago/Doberdob;
– Prov. Trieste: Sgonico/Zgoník, Monrupino/Repentabor, S. Dorligo della Valle/Dolina.

5. Soziolinguistische Lage

In Italien liegt weitgehend eine binnensprachliche Diglossie Dialekt vs. Hochsprache (prestigeärmere *L[ow]*-Varietät und prestigereichere *H[igh]*-Varietät) vor. Führt diese Situation bereits häufig zu Konflikten, so ist die Kontaktsituation im Falle der nichtitalienischen Sprachen besonders konfliktbeladen, da hier sogar eine Triglossiesituation vorliegt: ethnische Sprache, ital. Hochsprache, ital. (Regional)dialekt. In einzelnen Gebieten treten sogar vier oder mehr verschiedene Varietäten in Kontakt: in den okz. Tälern im Piemont: ältere Generation: Ital., Frz., Prov.; jüngere Generation: Ital., Prov., Piemontesisch; im Aostatal: Frz., Frankoprov., Ital., Piemont. sowie in einigen Orten *Titsch* (Walserdeutsch), im Falle des Ladinischen in Südtirol: als Muttersprache erlernte Talvarietät des Lad., lad. Varietäten der Nachbartäler, dt. Hochsprache (als Schriftsprache), Ital., (beide als Unterrichtssprachen), dt. Dialekt (bairisch). Grundsätzlich ist davon auszugehen, daß die Diglossie- bzw. Bilinguismussituation (im Fall der Minderheitensprachen liegt Bilinguismus + Diglossie im Sinne Fishmans 1971 vor) langfristig instabil ist, solange die Muttersprache (L1) nur auf den oralen Verwendungsbereich beschränkt bleibt. Bestand in der Vergangenheit (bis in unser Jahrhundert hinein) kaum Notwendigkeit, das Ital. (L2) mündlich und schriftlich zu beherrschen, so hat sich durch die politischen und wirtschaftlichen Verhältnisse die Situation grundlegend geändert. Die L1 läßt sich dauerhaft nur erhalten mit Hilfe eines Prestigezuwachses bzw. einer Erweiterung des Verwendungsradius. Für die kleinen nichtital. Gruppen in Süditalien, die nur ein bis drei Gemeinden umfassen (Provenzalen in Guardia Piemontese, Frankoprovenzalen in Faeto und Celle San Vito, Kroaten im Molise), scheint das so gut wie unmöglich zu sein. Hier bleibt der Verwendungsradius der Sprache zwangsläufig auf den örtlichen Rahmen beschränkt (an eine überregionale Kommunikation mit den prov. bzw. frankoprov. Tälern in Nordital. bzw. mit Kroatien ist kaum zu denken). Ein − wenn auch geringer − Prestigezuwachs wäre bereits durch die Einführung der Sprache als Unterrichtsfach an den örtlichen Schulen zu erreichen, hierzu fehlt es aber an Lehrmaterialien und Lehrern, außerdem sind die betreffenden Lokolekte nicht kodifiziert. Ähnlich verhält es sich mit den germanophonen Streusiedlungen und den griechischsprachigen Gemeinden. Hier könnte man zwar einerseits auf das Hochdt., andererseits auf das Neugriech. als Normvarianten zurückgreifen, was für die Sprecher jedoch hieße, eine weitere Fremdsprache lernen zu müssen, da die lokalen Varietäten sich von den jeweiligen Schriftsprachen strukturell sehr stark unterscheiden. − Eine relativ hohe sprachliche Affinität besteht zwischen dem Katalanischen von Alghero und dem Normkat. in Katalonien. Alghero besitzt eine eigenständige teils ital.-, teils kat.-sprachige Literatur. Die Sprache ist in mehreren Grammatiken festgehalten, weitgehend kodifiziert und kann sich zudem auf die Norm Barcelonas stützen. Dennoch ist ihr Weiterbestand in hohem Maße gefährdet: bereits 1980 erfolgte die Primärsozialisation der Kinder nur noch in 7,3% der Fälle auf Kat. (→ Art. 165).

Das Problem der fehlenden überdachenden Norm besteht auch für die Italoalbaner. Die italoalb. Varietäten unterscheiden sich zum einen untereinander erheblich, zum anderen besteht ein deutlicher Unterschied zur Sprache Albaniens. Hinzu kommt, daß zwischen den weiter voneinander entfernten albanophonen Ortschaften so gut wie kein Kommunikationsbedarf besteht, der Verwendungsradius also auch bei Schaffung einer Dachsprache auf die nähere Umgebung beschränkt bliebe.

Kompaktere Sprachgebiete bilden die prov. und frankoprov. Täler in Nordwestitalien. Aber auch hier stellt sich die Frage nach der Verwendbarkeit der Sprache; zwar gehören die jeweiligen Varietäten zu in den Nachbarstaaten weiter verbreiteten Sprachen, dieselben befinden sich jedoch ihrerseits in einer Minderheitensituation und sind vom ständigen Rückgang bedroht (Okz./Prov. in Frankreich; Frankoprov. in Frankreich und der Schweiz). Während sich die Provenzalen in den Alpentälern Piemonts auf eine für die Zwecke ihrer (bescheidenen) Literatur ausreichend kodifizierte Sprache stützen können, ist das Frankoprov. so gut wie nicht kodifiziert, zudem ist im Aostatal nicht das Frankoprov., sondern das Frz. − neben dem Ital. − Amts- und Bildungssprache. Zu Beginn der 80er Jahre sprachen in den okz. Tälern nur noch 29% der Kinder Okz. (Bonini 1983, 170).

Ein ebenfalls kompaktes Sprachgebiet wird vom Sard. besetzt. Zwar müßten die Insellage und die hohe Zahl von Muttersprachlern (rund 80% der 1,6 Mio. Sarden sollen Sard. sprechen) den Erhalt der Sprache begünstigen, doch herrscht auch auf Sardinien eine instabile Diglossiesituation, die immer öfter zum Sprachwechsel (aufgund von italophoner Primärsozialisation der Kinder sardophoner Eltern) zugunsten eines ital. Monolinguismus führt, da das dialektal zersplitterte Sard. (ohne Standardnorm) kaum (noch) in der Lage ist, prestigeträchtige Domänen zu besetzen.

Bei all den bisher genannten Sprachen scheinen erhebliche Stützungsmaßnahmen notwendig zu sein, will man ihr Überleben langfristig sichern, d. h. − den Willen der Sprachgemeinschaft vorausgesetzt − sie als vollwertiges Kommunikationsmittel tradieren. Eine wesentlich bessere Ausgangsposition haben (heute) die übrigen sog. Minderheitensprachen in Italien. Die stärkste Position nimmt zweifellos die dt. Sprache in Südtirol ein. Die zahlenmäßig drittgrößte nicht italophone Sprechergemeinschaft kann sich auf eine seit Jahrhunderten kodifizierte Kultursprache stützen, die sowohl über ein hohes Prestige als auch einen großen Verwendungsradius verfügt und sämtliche Domänen besetzen kann. Außerdem bestehen umfassende sprachpolitische Regelungen zum Schutz der Sprache. Letzteres gilt für die lad. Sprache in der Prov. Bozen und seit 1994 in ähnlichem Umfang auch in der Prov. Trient. Aufgrund eines Gesetzes zur Förderung der Minderheiten in der Region Veneto vom 23. Dezember 1994 kommen auch die Ladiner der Provinz Belluno in den Genuß einer (wenn auch vorerst eher bescheidenen) Förderung. Es fehlen jedoch nach wie vor einheitliche Regelungen zum Schutz der Sprache für alle Ladiner sowie eine überdachende Hochsprache. Ein erster Schritt in diese Richtung war die Normierung der Orthographie. Stark ausgeprägt ist jedoch das Zusammengehörigkeitsgefühl der Ladiner. − Gute Voraussetzungen unter dem Aspekt der Größe und der Kompaktheit des Gebiets der Sprachgruppe haben auch Friauler und Slowenen. Hier müßten jedoch weitreichende Schutzmaßnahmen ergriffen werden, um die schleichende sprachliche Assimilierung zu stoppen.

Die Unzufriedenheit der Minderheiten mit ihrer Situation hat sich in den letzten Jahrzehnten immer wieder in legalen und illegalen Aktionen geäußert: Das Spektrum reicht von Gesetzesvorschlägen über das Beschmieren von Ortstafeln bis hin zu Bombenanschlägen auf staatliche Einrichtungen.

Die Mehrheit der ital. Bevölkerung steht den sprachlichen Minderheiten heute eher indifferent gegenüber. Forderungen nach gesetzlichen Regelungen zu deren Schutz werden eher argwöhnisch beurteilt. Es darf nicht übersehen werden, daß die politisch und kulturell führenden Schichten Italiens teilweise noch einem risorgimentalen Gedankengut verhaftet sind, das sich u. a. in antislawischen Ressentiments (mit bürokratischen Schikanen und Aktionen gegen slowenische Aufschriften im Raum Triest und Görz) und plakativ vorgetragenen Einheitsparolen äußert.

6. Sprachpolitische Lage

Die ital. Verfassung gehört zu den wenigen europäischen Verf., die den Minderheitenschutz in ihren Grundprinzipien berücksichtigen:

Art. 3: „Tutti i cittadini hanno pari dignità sociale e sono eguali davanti alla legge, senza distinzione di sesso, di razza, di lingua, di religione, di opinioni politiche, di condizioni personali e sociali."

Art. 6: „La Repubblica tutela con apposite norme le minoranze linguistiche."

Die ersten Autonomieregelungen nach dem Zweiten Weltkrieg resultierten jedoch weniger aus den Bestimmungen der Verf. als vielmehr aus internat. Vereinbarungen (das Autonomiestatut für Trentino-Südtirol aus dem Abkommen zwischen Österreich und Italien − Gruber-De Gasperi-Abkommen 5. 9. 1946) bzw. kamen aufgrund internationalen Drucks zustande (das Autonomiestatut für das Aostatal aus Angst vor Annexion durch Frankreich). Es dauerte noch Jahrzehnte, bis die in den Autonomiestatuten verbrieften Rechte auch in die Tat umgesetzt wurden: Aostatal Ende der 70er Jahre, Südtirol 1992 (Streitbeilegungserklärung vor der UNO zwischen Österreich und Italien nach weitgehender Umsetzung des im 2. Autonomiestatut von 1972 beschlossenen Maßnahmenpakets).

Die wenigen Maßnahmen zum Schutz der Slowenen in Friuli-Venezia Giulia gehen auf die alliierte Militärregierung zwischen 1945 und 1954 zurück (in dieser Zeit war das Gebiet um Triest, die sog. Zone A, zunächst unter amer. Besatzung, ab 1947 Freistaat unter UNO-Aufsicht; 1954 kam Triest mit einem Großteil der Zone A an Italien, die Zone B im Süden von Triest zu Jugoslawien) und wurden nach 1954 vom ital. Gesetzgeber bestätigt: z. B. die Regelungen über den Gebrauch des Slow. in örtlichen Gremien in der Prov. Triest oder slow. Schulen in den Prov. Triest und Görz. Die vom Artikel 8 des Vertrags von Osimo zwischen Jugoslawien und Italien (1975, von Italien ratifiziert am 14. 3. 1977, Vertrag zur Regelung der Grenzstreitigkeiten zwischen Jugoslawien und Italien; der Vertrag regelt — nach dem Zerfall Jugoslawiens — auch die Beziehungen zwischen Slowenien und Italien) vorgesehenen Maßnahmen zum Schutz der slow. Minderheit wurden bisher nicht umgesetzt.

Staatlicherseits sind nach wie vor nur die Art. 3 und 6 der Verfassung sowie die Sonderstatuten der autonomen Regionen rechtskräftig. *De facto* genießen einen gewissen Schutz von seiten des Zentralstaates nur die Frankophonen (und seit 1993 auch die Walser) im Aostatal, die Dt.-sprachigen und Ladiner in der Region Trentino-Südtirol und die Slowenen in Friuli-Venezia Giulia.

Der bereits auf die 70er Jahre zurückgehende Entwurf eines 18 Artikel umfassenden Gesetzes (Disegno di legge n. 612), das den Schutz der sprachlichen Minderheiten regeln soll, wurde am 20. 11. 1991 von der Abgeordnetenkammer angenommen, muß aber noch vom Senat verabschiedet werden.

Einzelne regionale gesetzgeberische Initiativen zugunsten von Minderheiten werden immer wieder unter Berufung auf Art. 117 der Verfassung blockiert, wonach der Schutz sprachlicher Minderheiten Sache des Staates sei. Besonders Initiativen zugunsten der Verwendung von Minderheitensprachen in der Schule sind immer wieder an bürokratischen Hindernissen gescheitert. Maßnahmen zur Erhaltung der Sprache als kultureller Wert sind in jüngerer Zeit in die Kompetenz von Region bzw. von kleineren Verwaltungseinheiten verlagert worden.

7. Sonstige Sprachkontakte/ Kontaktsprachen

7.1. Interne Migration

Während über das Sprachverhalten und die Entwicklung der Muttersprache italophoner Auswanderer zahlreiche Studien vorliegen (vgl. *Studi emigrazione* N. 96, anno 26 [1989] und N. 104, anno 28, [1991]: *Rassegna bibliografica sull'emigrazione e sulle comunità italiane all'estero dal 1975 ad oggi*), sind die individuell unterschiedlich, z. T. kompliziert ablaufenden Stadien von Bilinguismus und/oder Diglossie im Verlauf der sprachlichen Akkulturation im Fall von interner Migration, wobei verschiedenste Varietäten (dialetto locale und italiano regionale sowohl der Ausgangsregion als auch der Zielregion, italiano popolare, italiano „formale") in Kontakt treten, bisher nur vereinzelt untersucht worden (z. B.

Pautasso 1969, Tempesta 1978, Sobrero s. a. und 1982, Berruto 1982). Einen extremen Fall von Sprachkontakt weist die von Pautasso 1969 untersuchte Gemeinde Pettinengo (Prov. Vercelli, Piemont) auf, wo 1967 59% der ansässigen Bevölkerung (1334 von 2225 Einwohnern) Zuwanderer aus anderen ital. Regionen bzw. — in geringer Zahl — Ausländer waren. Die Untersuchung zeigt, daß ein großer Teil der Zuwanderer den lokalen Dialekt versteht, jedoch nicht in der Lage ist, die meisten einer Reihe von vorgegebenen Sätzen in den Dialekt zu übersetzen. Offensichtlich haben Aufenthaltsdauer, Alter zum Zeitpunkt der Zuwanderung, Beschäftigungsart, Herkunftsregion u. a. Faktoren einen erheblichen Einfluß auf die erreichte dialektale Kompetenz. Zuwanderer aus nördlichen Regionen fällt es leichter, den Dialekt zu verstehen und zu erlernen, als Zuwanderern aus Apulien, Kalabrien und der Basilicata.

7.2. „Zingari"

Ital. *zingaro* stammt aus dem Griech. (Αδίγγανι) und bedeutet dort 'unberührbar' bzw. bezeichnet die Mitglieder einer Ketzersekte (Soravia 1977, 50); es kann ebenso diskriminierend verwendet werden wie das dt. Wort *Zigeuner*, wird aber von Vertretern der Ethnie selbst benutzt. Korrekter wäre das Sanskrit-Wort *Rom* (Plur. *Roma*) 'Mann, Ehemann' und *Romani* für die von den Roma gesprochene (indoeuropäische) Sprache. *Romani* ist eine vornehmlich mündlich verwendete Sprache, die sich in vier Dialekte gliedern läßt (Olmi 1986, 142). Die Zingari sind in Norditalien vornehmlich Nomaden, in der Region Abruzzo und im Umland von Rom Halbnomaden. Seßhaft sind sie in zahlreichen Ortschaften des Südens, wo sie einer fortschreitenden kulturellen und sprachlichen Assimilierung ausgesetzt sind. Von staatlicher Seite bestehen keinerlei gesetzliche Regelungen zum Schutz der Zingari.

Die Interessen der Zingari werden vertreten von *Opera nomadi* (1963 zunächst auf regionaler Ebene — Trentino-Südtirol — gegründete, 1965 auf ganz Italien ausgedehnte und 1970 als Ente morale [juristische Person, Körperschaft] anerkannte Gesellschaft [DPR 347 vom 26. 3. 1970]). Opera nomadi setzt sich in erster Linie ein in den Bereichen

— Verbesserung der Lebensbedingungen (Wohnungssituation);
— Schule und Unterricht;
— Schutz von Sprache und Kultur.

Die Zahl der Zingari und Viaggianti wird von Opera nomadi auf rund 80 bis 100.000 geschätzt, wobei seit den 70er Jahren und besonders in jüngster Zeit ein starker Zustrom von Roma und Sinti aus Ex-Jugoslawien (v. a. Kroatien und Bosnien-Herzegowina) zu verzeichnen ist.

Ein gezielter Schutz von Sprache und Kultur (im weitesten Sinne) von staatlicher Seite würde aufgrund der nur geringen Seßhaftigkeit auf besondere Schwierigkeiten stoßen. In einigen Regionen bestehen gesetzliche Regelungen zugunsten der „minoranza zingara" (Veneto, Lazio, Trentino, Sardegna, Emilia-Romagna, Toscana, Friuli-Venezia Giulia, Lombardia).

Nach Angaben des ital. Unterrichtsministeriums besuchten im Schuljahr 1988/89 2054 „Zingari" und 3358 „Nomadi" (eine willkürliche, nicht ethnisch zu begründende Einteilung in seßhafte und nicht seßhafte Zingari) ohne ital. Staatsbürgerschaft ital. Schulen, davon 1658 bzw. 2858 die scuola elementare. Unter Berücksichtigung derjenigen Roma, die die ital. Staatsbürgerschaft besitzen, ergäben sich weit höhere Zahlen. Ein geringer Teil der Kinder und Jugendlichen kommt in den Genuß eines regelmäßigen Unterrichts, wobei dieser erschwert wird durch geringe Kenntnis der ital. Normsprache (Verwendung des regionalen mit Romaniwörtern durchsetzten Dialekts, geringer Gebrauch von Präpositionen und Konjunktionen, Schwierigkeiten beim Gebrauch der Verben etc.; (vgl. *Romano Lil Scuola*, giugno 1992, 18).

Zahlreiche v. a. lexikalische Elemente sind in verschiedene *gerghi italiani* eingedrungen, wie z. B. *čuččastra* 'donna di malaffare' (Palermo) < *čuči* 'mammella' (Plur. *čuča*) oder *divia* 'prostituta giovane e bella' (Neapel) < *divio* 'cattivo'. Desgleichen treten in den heutigen Dialekten des Romani zahlreiche Entlehnungen aus dem Ital. bzw. seinen Dialekten auf, z. B. *áldə* 'alto', *čerəsə* 'ciliegia', *prikókkə* 'pesca', *kwítə* 'zitto'.

An Periodika sind zu nennen: *Romani Lil* (Circolare dell'Opera nomadi, Via dei Barbieri, 22 – 00186 Roma), *Lacio Drom* (Buon cammino).

7.3. Einwanderung aus Staaten der „Dritten Welt"

War Italien in den vergangenen rund 100 Jahren ein Auswanderungsland, so ist es seit Mitte der 70er Jahre in zunehmendem Maße zu einem Einwanderungsland geworden. Bislang gibt es keine zuverlässigen Daten über die Zahl der – z. T. illegalen – Zuwanderer. Schätzungen gehen bis zu 1,6 Mio. für das Jahr 1987 (Ispes). In der Presse verbreitete Zahlen liegen sogar über 2 Mio. Nach einer auf ital. Daten beruhenden Studie von *isoplan* (Institut für Entwicklungsforschung, Wirtschafts- und Sozialplanung, Saarbrücken) lebten 1988/89 rund 645.000 Ausländer regulär in Italien, davon 30% aus den hochindustrialisierten Staaten Europas und Amerikas (40% aus Ländern mit hohem Pro-Kopf-Einkommen, d. h. Ländern mit einem Pro-Kopf-Bruttosozialprodukt von mehr als 6.000 US-$). Nach Angaben des ital. Innenministeriums stieg die Zahl der Zuwanderer aus Drittweltländern in den 80er Jahren überdurchschnittlich (die Zahl der Afrikaner von 1981 bis 1987 beispielsweise um 162%). Für 1987/88 wird die Zahl illegaler Einwanderer in Italien auf 850.000 geschätzt; Tendenz steigend. Die illegalen Einwanderer stellen in Italien die Mehrheit der Ausländer dar (schätzungsweise 55%). Abgesehen von Einflüssen auf den Arbeitsmarkt und Folgen für die soziale Struktur u. a. in den Großstädten ist die Situation der Immigranten natürlich auch unter kontaktlinguistischen Gesichtspunkten interessant. Hierzu liegen – von Ansätzen abgesehen – jedoch bisher keine grundlegenden Untersuchungen vor. Es scheint jedoch festzustehen, daß die Immigranten beim Erlernen des Ital. als L2 im allgemeinen nicht über das Stadium eines *italiano pidginizzato* bzw. des *baby talk* oder *foreigner talk* hinauskommen (vgl. Vedovelli 1981, 1989; Banfi 1983, 1986, 1988; Giacalone Ramat 1988, Orletti 1988). So treten beispielsweise morphologische Generalisierungen auf, wie **il orario*, **il lingua*, Verwendung des Verbs ausschließlich im Infinitiv bzw. im Indikativ: **quando venire n'italia loro aiutato* 'quando sono arrivato in Italia, loro mi hanno aiutato' etc. (vgl. Banfi 1986). Die erreichte Sprachkompetenz ist zweifellos höher, wenn es sich bei den L2-Lernern um Studenten bzw. um die Kinder von Eingewanderten handelt, sofern letztere regulär eingeschult werden. Im Schuljahr 1988/89 besuchten 5609 „extraeuropei" die verschiedenen ital. Schultypen, davon 2648 die *scuola elementare* (vgl. Todisco 1990, 310). Von den ausländischen Schülern in den staatlichen Schulen erzielte rund ein Viertel schlechtere Noten als die ital. Mitschüler, was auf eine geringere sprachliche Kompetenz in der L2 zurückgeführt werden kann. Fast alle ausländischen

Schüler haben bei der Einschulung Sprachprobleme. Bei den nicht aus Europa kommenden Immigranten handelt es sich zum großen Teil um Analphabeten, so daß ein Erlernen des Ital. durch fehlende Schreib- und Lesekompetenz erschwert wird. Vorbildcharakter beim Überwinden dieser Schwelle hat zweifellos ein Alphabetisierungsprojekt für Einwanderer aus Nicht-EG-Staaten, das 1981 in Mailand angelaufen ist. Am dortigen Liceo Volta wird hauptsächlich erwachsenen Immigranten aus Nicht-EG-Ländern (1986/87 von 121 Teilnehmern 52 Äthiopier, 36 Chinesen) eine Alphabetisierung sowohl in der L2 als auch in der L1 ermöglicht (Favaro 1988). Während für die Einwanderer selbst die Erlernung der ital. Sprache das Hauptproblem darstellt, erfolgt bei den in Italien geborenen Kindern der Einwanderer häufig eine Beeinträchtigung der Kenntnis der Muttersprache, die meistens nur in der Familie bzw. im engeren privaten Umfeld verwendet wird, was durch das Fehlen muttersprachlichen Unterrichts beschleunigt wird. Sprechen beide Elternteile dieselbe Sprache, so sprechen die Kinder diese Sprache oder verstehen sie zumindest. Sprechen die Eltern unterschiedliche Sprachen bzw. stark voneinander abweichende Varietäten derselben Sprache, so lernen die Kinder gewöhnlich nur Ital., wie im Fall der chinesischsprachigen Einwanderer in Mailand beobachtet wurde (Giambelli 1986, 779).

8. Kritische Wertung der verwendeten Quellen und Literatur

Recht zahlreich sind die Publikationen, die sich seit Mitte der 70er Jahre ausschließlich oder teilweise mit den „minoranze linguistiche" in Italien befassen. Ihre Positionen reichen von *für die Minderheit Stellung beziehend* — sehr zum Unwillen der politischen Rechten — (Salvi 1975, Olmi 1986) über *neutral informierend* (Arbeitsgemeinschaft Alpen-Adria 1990) bis hin zu *polemisch-diskreditierend* (z. B. Pellegrini 1986, 1991 bezüglich der Stellung der Ladiner).

Verschiedene Autoren oder Autorenkollektive beschäftigen sich mit den Minderheiten einzelner Regionen (so z. B. Piromalli 1981, Arbeitsgemeinschaft Alpen-Adria 1990), nicht alle Publikationen sind jedoch von gründlicher Sachkenntnis geprägt, vgl. z. B. die Kritik von Birken-Silverman 1993 an Bellinello 1991; Kattenbusch 1987 an Pellegrini 1986.

Zur sozioling. Situation einzelner Minderheiten liegen verschiedene grundlegende Untersuchungen vor (vgl. z. B. Rindler Schjerve 1987 zum Sardischen). Behandelt werden Sprachkontakte bzw. Probleme von Minderheiten auch in Publikationen, die das Phänomen in einem überstaatlichen Rahmen betrachten, so z. B. Bochmann 1989; mit einem erheblichen Informationsdefizit jedoch: Commissione delle Comunità europee (Ed.) 1985. Zu rechtlichen Fragen (v. a. zu Südtirol, aber auch zur allg. Situation der Minderheiten) s. die zahlreichen Arbeiten von Pizzorusso (zuletzt 1993). Zum Verhältnis von Kirche und Minderheiten: Mauri 1981.

Zahlreiche — zum Teil leider nicht veröffentlichte — vornehmlich linguistische Untersuchungen zu einzelnen Minderheitensprachen gehen auf Sprachkontaktphänomene (Interferenzen) ein, so zum Beispiel Profili 1983 (Griech. in Apulien, unveröff.), Kattenbusch 1982 (Frankoprov. in Apulien), Birken-Silverman 1989 (Albanisch auf Sizilien).

Aktualisierte Daten und Informationen zur Situation der Minderheiten in Beiträgen verschiedener Kongreßakten, z. B. Albano Leoni (Ed.) 1979, Perini (Ed.) 1988, Kattenbusch (Ed.) (1995).

9. Bibliographie (in Auswahl)

Albano Leoni, Federico (Ed.) (1979): *I dialetti e le lingue delle minoranze di fronte all'italiano. Atti dell'XI Congresso Internazionale di Studi, Cagliari, 27–30 maggio 1977*, Rom.

Arbeitsgemeinschaft Alpen-Adria (1990): *Die Minderheiten im Alpen-Adria-Raum*, Klagenfurt.

Banfi, Emanuele (1983): „Problemi linguistici delle 'nuove minoranze'. Osservazioni sulla competenza dell'italiano spontaneamente acquisito come codice scritto da lavoratori eritrei immigrati in area milanese". In: *Annali della Pubblica Istruzione 29*, 5, 591–595.

Banfi, Emanuele (1986): „Elementi di italiano semplificato pidginizzato appreso spontaneamente da arabofoni immigrati in area milanese". In: *Italiano & oltre 5*, 231–234.

Banfi, Emanuele (1988): „Osservazioni sulla sintassi dell'italiano spontaneamente acquisito da parlanti arabofoni". In: Giacalone Ramat (Ed.), 127–141.

Bechert, Johannes/Wildgen, Wolfgang (1991): *Einführung in die Sprachkontaktforschung*, Darmstadt.

Bellinello, Pier Francesco (1989): „Le colonie dei „Cimbri" in Italia". In: *Le minoranze etniche e linguistiche. Atti del 2° Congresso Internazionale,*

Piana degli Albanesi, 7/11 settembre 1988, Palermo 751–776.

Bellinello, Pier Francesco (1991): *Minoranze etniche nel Sud*, Cosenza.

Berruto, Gaetano (1982): „Langue et dialectes en contact dans les villes industrielles de l'Italie du Nord: bilinguisme et migrations italiennes". In: *Travaux neuchâtelois de linguistique 4*, 111–146.

Birken-Silverman, Gabriele (1989): *Phonetische, morphosyntaktische und lexikalische Varianten in den palermitanischen Mundarten und im Sikuloalbanischen von Piana degli Albanesi*, Wilhelmsfeld.

Birken-Silverman, Gabriele (1992): „Phasen des Rückgangs einer Sprache am Beispiel des Albanischen in Italien". In: *Zeitschrift für Balkanologie 28*, 1–22.

Birken-Silverman, Gabriele (1993): Rez. zu Bellinello 1991. In: *Europa Ethnica 50*, 151–153.

Bochmann, Klaus (1988): „Italienisch: Diglossie und Polyglossie". In: *LRL IV*, 269–286.

Bochmann, Klaus (1989): *Regional- und Nationalitätensprachen in Frankreich, Italien und Spanien*, Leipzig.

Bonini, Giuseppe Fausto (1983): „Le valli occitane italiane". In: Freddi (Ed.), 152–175.

Bornträger, Ekkehard W. (1993): „Le popolazioni alloetniche e la loro tutela". In: *Rivista di Studi Politici Internazionali 60*, 189–225.

Carrozza, Paolo (1992): „Situation juridique des minorités en Italie". In: *Les minorités en Europe*, Giordan, Henri (Ed.), Paris, 215–232.

Chiellino, Carmine/Marchio, Fernando/Rongoni, Giocondo (^{2}1989): *Italien*, München.

Commissione delle Comunità europee (Ed.) (1985): *Le minoranze linguistiche nei paesi della Comunità europea*, Luxemburg.

Clauss, Jan Ulrich (1982): *Sprachminderheiten in den EG-Staaten am Beispiel von acht Fallstudien aus Italien und Belgien*, Diss. Europ. Hochschulinstitut, Badia Fiesolana/Florenz.

Favaro, Graziella (1988): „Immigrazione e formazione linguistica: il progetto del Liceo Volta a Milano". In: *Dal Terzo Mondo in Italia. Studi e ricerche sulle immigrazioni straniere*, Melotti, Umberto (Ed.), Mailand, 79–88.

Ferguson, Charles A. (1959): „Diglossia". In: *Word 15*, 325–340.

Fishman, Joshua A. (1971): „Bilinguism with and without Diglossia; Diglossia with and without Bilinguism". In: *Journal of Social Issues 23*, 29–38.

Frau, Giovanni (1984): *I dialetti del Friuli*, Udine.

Freddi, Giovanni (Ed.) (1983): *L'Italia plurilingue*, Bergamo.

Furlani, Silvio/Wandruszka, Adam (1973): *Österreich und Italien. Ein bilaterales Geschichtsbuch*, Wien/München.

Giacalone Ramat, Anna (Ed.) (1988): *L'italiano e le altre lingue: strategie di acquisizione*, Bologna.

Giambelli, Rodolfo (1986): „Strategie produttive e riproduttive nella comunità cinese a Milano". In: *Milano e il suo territorio*, Della Peruta, Franco/Leydi, Roberto/Stella, Angelo (Eds.), Mailand (= *Mondo Popolare in Lombardia 13*), 771–792.

Gubert, Renzo (1976): *L'identificazione etnica. Indagine sociologica in un'area plurilingue del Trentino – Alto Adige*, Udine.

Istituto Geografico De Agostini (1987): *Grande Atlante d'Italia De Agostini*, Novara.

Karanastasis, A. (s. a.): „Lo stato in cui si trovano oggi i dialetti neogreci dell'Italia meridionale". In: *Bilinguismo e diglossia in Italia*, s. l. [Pisa], 23–27.

Kattenbusch, Dieter (1982): *Das Frankoprovenzalische in Süditalien*, Tübingen.

Kattenbusch, Dieter (1987): Rez. zu G. B. Pellegrini, Minoranze e culture regionali, Padua 1986. In: *Ladinia 11*, 247–252.

Kattenbusch, Dieter (Ed.) (1995): *Minderheiten in der Romania*, Wilhelmsfeld.

Kloss, Heinz (^{2}1978): *Die Entwicklung neuer germanischer Kultursprachen seit 1800*, Düsseldorf.

Kommission der Europäischen Gemeinschaften (1991): *Die Einwanderung aus Drittstaaten in die südlichen Mitgliedsländer der Europäischen Gemeinschaften*, Luxemburg (= *Soziales Europa*, Beiheft 1/91).

Landesinstitut für Statistik der Autonomen Provinz Bozen/Südtirol (1992): *Statistisches Jahrbuch für Südtirol 1992*.

Lill, Rudolf (^{4}1988): *Geschichte Italiens in der Neuzeit*, Darmstadt.

Loi Corvetto, Ines (1979): „Il sardo e l'italiano: interferenze lessicali". In: Albano Leoni (Ed.), 133–146.

LRL = Holtus, Günter/Metzeltin, Michael/Schmitt, Christian (Eds.): *Lexikon der Romanistischen Linguistik*, Tübingen. Bd. III: *Die einzelnen romanischen Sprachen und Sprachgebiete von der Renaissance bis zur Gegenwart. Rumänisch, Dalmatisch/Istroromanisch, Friaulisch, Ladinisch, Bündnerromanisch*, 1989. Bd. IV: *Italienisch, Korsisch, Sardisch*, 1988.

Mauri, Marco (1981): *Nelle case del Padre. Chiesa e minoranze etniche in Italia*. Brescia.

Olmi, Massimo (1986): *Italiani dimezzati. Le minoranze etnico-linguistiche non protette*, Neapel.

Orletti, F. (1988): „L'italiano dei filippini a Roma". In: Giacalone Ramat (Ed.), 143–159.

Pautasso, Mariella (1969): *Dialetto, lingua e integrazione linguistica a Pettinengo*, Turin.

Pellegrini, Giovan Battista (1986): *Minoranze e culture regionali*, Padua.

Pellegrini, Giovan Battista (1991): *La genesi del retoromanzo (o ladino)*, Tübingen.

Perini, Nereo (Ed.) (1988): *Isole linguistiche e culturali. Atti del 24° Convegno dell'A.I.M.A.V., Udine 13−16 maggio 1987*, Udine.

Piromalli, Antonio (1981): *Inchiesta attuale sulle minoranze etniche e linguistiche in Calabria*, Cosenza.

Pizzorusso, Alessandro (1993): *Minoranze e maggioranze*, Turin.

Procacci, Giuliano (1989): *Geschichte Italiens und der Italiener*, unv. Nachdr. der 1. Aufl. 1983, München.

Profili, Olga (1983): *Le parler grico de Corigliano d'Otranto*, Thèse, Université des Langues et Lettres de Grenoble.

Rindler Schjerve, Rosita (1987): *Sprachkontakt auf Sardinien. Soziolinguistische Untersuchungen des Sprachwechsels im ländlichen Bereich*, Tübingen.

Salvi, Sergio (1975): *Le lingue tagliate. Storia delle minoranze linguistiche in Italia*, Mailand.

Salvi, Sergio (1973): *Le nazioni proibite*, Florenz.

Sobrero, Alberto (s. a.): „Il cambio linguistico nell'acculturazione dell'immigrato: nuovi problemi di glottodidattica". In: *Bilinguismo e diglossia in Italia*, s. l. [Pisa], 137−148.

Sobrero, Alberto (1982): „Aspects linguistiques des migrations internes en Italie". In: Dittmar, Norbert/Schlieben-Lange, Brigitte (Eds.): *Die Soziolinguistik in den romanischsprachigen Ländern*, Tübingen, 153−162.

Soravia, Giulio (1977): *Dialetti degli Zingari Italiani*, Pisa (= Profilo dei dialetti italiani 22).

Spano, B. (1965): *La grecità bizantina e i suoi riflessi geografici nell'Italia meridionale e insulare*, Pisa.

Statistisches Bundesamt (1992): *Länderbericht Italien*, Wiesbaden.

Steinicke, Ernst (1992): „Das viersprachige Kanaltal − seine ethnogeographische Sonderstellung im Friaulischen Gebirge". In: *Europa Ethnica 49*, 185−203.

Telmon, Tullio (1982): „La minoranza di parlata provenzale". In: *Sociologia della comunicazione I*, 2, 17−32.

Tempesta, Immacolata (1978): *Lingua ed emigrazione. Indagine sul comportamento sociolinguistico degli emigranti salentini*, Lecce.

Todisco, Enrico (1990): „La scolarizzazione degli immigrati stranieri in Italia". In: *Studi emigrazione 99*, 306−348.

Vedovelli, Massimo (1981): „La lingua degli immigrati stranieri in Italia". In: *Lingua e nuova didattica 10*, 3, 17−23.

Vedovelli, Massimo (1989): „Gli immigrati in Italia: note sociolinguistiche". In: *Studi emigrazione 93*, 68−94.

Virdis, Maurizio (1988): „Sardisch: Areallinguistik. Aree linguistiche". In: *LRL IV*, 897−913.

Wurzer, Bernhard (1977): *Die deutschen Sprachinseln in Oberitalien*, Bozen.

Dieter Kattenbusch, Gießen (Deutschland)

157. Italien−français (francoprovençal)

1. Géographie et démographie
2. Histoire
3. Politique, économie, situations culturelle et religieuse
4. Statistiques et profils ethniques
5. Situation sociolinguistique
6. Etat de la politique linguistique
7. Portrait général des contacts linguistiques
8. Problèmes ouverts et perspectives
9. Bibliographie (sélective)

1. Géographie et démographie

Aux régions francoprovençales (frpr.) de la France, qui vont du Grésivaudan et du Forez, au Sud, jusqu'à la Franche-Comté au Nord et à celles de la Suisse (Jura, Vaud, Neuchâtel et Valais), correspond du côté italien une série de vallées parallèles à partir de la Vallée de Suse jusqu'à la Vallée d'Aoste.

L'ensemble du territoire comprenait au total 187 799 habitants (recensement du 1981), distribués en 127 communes, avec une population active de 71 461, dont 10 490 agriculteurs et 60 971 employés dans les secteurs industriels et dans les services. Tout le territoire a une configuration uniformément montagneuse. Plusieurs éléments sociologiques, sociolinguistiques, démographiques et administratifs contribuent néanmoins à distinguer assez nettement la Vallée d'Aoste (VA) de tout le reste du domaine frpr. Premièrement, parce que celui-ci fait partie de la province de Turin, tandis que la VA jouit du statut spécial de Région autonome; deuxièmement, parce que la VA a connu une augmentation constante de sa population, tandis que la population des autres vallées a diminué sensiblement à partir de 1951; et enfin, parce que les parlers frpr. jouissent, en VA, d'une vitalité considérable, tandis que dans les autres vallées, les patoisants n'atteignent pas les 30%. L'ensemble de ces remarques nous amène à considérer séparément les deux secteurs du territoire frpr. d'Italie. Les vallées de la province de Turin sont disposées horizontalement et orientées d'Ouest en Est. La plus méridionale est la Val Sangone; suivent la Vallée de Suse avec la vallée latérale du torrent Cenischia, les trois Vallées de Lanzo (Val de Viù, Val d'Ala, Val Grande), la Vallée de Locana et la Val Soana. L'ensemble du territoire a une configuration vaguement trapézoïdale: la limite occidentale est très bien représentée par la frontière d'Etat entre la France et l'Italie, et la limite septentrionale est également bien représentée par la limite entre la province de Turin et la VA; en revanche, au Sud, la séparation face aux parlers occitans et gallo-italiens piémontais n'est pas si nette, tout comme la délimitation, face à ces derniers, aux débouchés orientaux des vallées. Ce territoire comprend 53 communes avec 78 907 habitants, situées à une hauteur moyenne de 742 m au-dessus du niveau de la mer. Présentées par vallées, les données sont exposées dans le tableau 157.1.

Tableau 157.1: Vallées méridionales: données démographiques (d'après Telmon 1981, 59)

Vallée	Comm.	Habitants	Patoisants	%	Altitude
Sangone	3	13.708	2.760	20,13	632
Suse	22	45.136	10.450	23,46	507
Cenischia	3	1.618	990	58,09	1.056
Viù	4	3.246	1.700	52,37	913
Ala	5	4.045	1.650	55,05	952
Grande	6	4.585	2.100	45,80	734
Locana	6	4.868	1.470	30,19	1.054
Soana	4	1.692	990	58,51	977
Total	53	78.907	22.060	28,44	742

Les communes de la VA sont au nombre de 74, pour une population globale de 112 353 habitants (1981). Le tableau 157.2 montre la croissance ininterrompue au cours de ce dernier demi-siècle:

Tableau 157.2: Vallée d'Aoste: données démographiques (d'après Telmon 1981, 38)

Année	Habitants	Croiss.	Id. %	Croiss. tot.
1951	94.890			
1961	100.959	+6.069	+6,39	
1971	108.892	+7.933	+8,36	14.002=14,7
1981	112.353	+3.461	+2,93	17.463=17,7

Cette augmentation constante en VA ne concerne pas seulement la population (+6,39% entre 1951 et 1961; +8,36% entre 1961 et 1971; +2,93% entre 1971 et 1981), mais aussi le nombre des communes qui ont connu une croissance démographique dans l'un des recensements successifs à celui de 1951, ce qui est nettement supérieur à celui du reste de l'aire frpr., soit en valeurs absolues, soit en pourcentage. Il s'agit en effet de 38 communes, dont 15 en progression constante et continue, avec des pointes atteignant jusqu'à 79,18% à Courmayeur (→ carte linguistique F).

2. Histoire

C'est l'histoire la plus récente qui explique la différence entre les deux régions: avant la deuxième guerre mondiale, en effet, les destins des deux côtés semblaient se confondre dans la rapide et inexorable décadence de l'économie agricole, et en particulier de celle des pays alpins. L'après-guerre, au contraire, a réservé des traitements différents aux deux territoires: du côté piémontais la décadence a continué sans cesse; du côté valdôtain, l'obtention de l'autonomie a permis d'aménager la région en favorisant les aires les plus faibles à l'aide d'activités économiques plus florissantes (tourisme, industrie de la plaine d'Aoste, Casino de Saint-Vincent, commerce). L'histoire de l'unité linguistique, au contraire, est très ancienne, puisqu'elle remonte à l'époque de la romanisation de l'Italie celtique et de la Gaule. Les peuplades celtiques avaient évidemment les mêmes langues d'un côté et de l'autre de la chaîne alpine, ceci malgré la subdivision administrative en *provinciae* différentes. Tout en étant assez présente pour convaincre tout le monde de l'importance d'apprendre sa langue, Rome était trop éloignée pour diffuser ses innovations linguistiques jusque dans le territoire gaulois. Le modèle linguistique fut celui de la classe dirigeante latinophone de Lugdunum (Lyon), la capitale de la Gallia Lugdunensis et, au Moyen Age, des marchands francophones de Lyon dont l'importance et le rayonnement ne firent que croître au cours des siècles. En ce qui concerne le côté italien, par ailleurs, il ne faut pas oublier que la frontière située bien en aval de la ligne de partage des eaux, aux débouchés des vallées, avait encore une importance non négligeable à l'époque où Charlemagne défit les Lombards, en 774. Quant à la séparation face à la haute vallée de la Doire Ripaire, occitane, il faut tenir compte du fait qu'en amont de Suse, et précisément à Gravere, passait jusqu'en 1713 (Traité d'Utrecht) la limite entre la couronne de France (Haute Vallée) et le Duché de Savoie. Un exemple: les deux villages de Bardonnèche et de Modane, aujourd'hui unis par une dizaine de kilomètres d'autoroute ou de chemin de fer, sont linguistiquement occitan et frpr., respectivement. L'explication dérive du fait, plutôt ironique, que Bardonnèche (it. Bardonecchia), aujourd'hui italienne, a appartenu à la France jusqu'en 1713, alors que Modane (en Maurienne), aujourd'hui française, a appartenu aux ducs de Savoie jusqu'en 1861, date du passage de cette région à la France.

3. Politique, économie, situations culturelle et religieuse

Passons à la description des faits économiques et sociaux. Revenons donc aux vallées de la province de Turin: il s'agit, on l'a vu, de 53 communes distribuées dans huit vallées alpines. La morphologie du sol explique la densité assez faible de la population: 41 communes sur 53 ont moins de 100 habitants par km^2; 16 communes (c'est-à-dire 30% du total) ont moins de 25 habitants par km^2. L'évolution démographique révèle une situation dramatique: en vingt ans, le nombre des communes ayant moins de 500 habitants a doublé, alors que les villages avec une population comprise entre 1000 et 2000 habitants ont connu une évolution opposée. Si l'on considère par ailleurs les communes où la tendance est inverse, on constate que les six communes dont la population s'est accrue, se trouvent dans la basse Vallée de Suse, plus industrialisée et aussi plus proche de la VA. De plus, cette tendance inverse s'est arrêtée assez rapidement au cours des dernières années, avec la fermeture de presque toutes les usines. Ce qui est remarquable, c'est que 38 communes sur 53 ont subi une baisse démographique supérieure à la moyenne, atteignant un maximum à Ingria, dont la population a diminué de 71,16%. On sait par ailleurs que le secteur qui a été le plus affecté par la diminution est celui de la population active. Ce qui frappe encore plus, c'est l'effondrement qui menace le secteur agricole. Ce dernier, qui déjà en 1961 connaissait des pourcentages assez faibles (23,52% contre 76,46% pour les employés de l'industrie), a vu se réduire ultérieurement le nombre de ses employés de plus de 40%: les villages typiquement agricoles ont complètement disparu, et même les villages de montagne, dépourvus soit d'usines soit de ressources touristiques, sont réduits à la fonction de villages-dortoirs pour les travailleurs employés dans les villes de la plaine piémontaise. Le tableau qu'on vient de brosser fait très bien comprendre les conditions auxquelles est soumise la culture locale. Au déracinement des montagnards partis vers la ville, s'ajoute le vieillissement de la population restée sur place, et surtout le mépris avec lequel les valeurs anciennes sont perçues par les nouvelles générations, qui les assimilent à la misère tout court.

Pour la VA, on assiste à une tendance contraire. D'un côté, on constate que la population des nombreuses communes situées dans l'aire urbaine du chef-lieu et bénéficiant du développement industriel et surtout commercial de celui-ci, a augmenté; d'autre part, au développement industriel du fond de la vallée, répond l'essor touristique des villages situés au dessus de 1200 m, parmi lesquels une quinzaine ont vu augmenter leur population. La différence la plus importante, du point de vue juridique et administratif, entre les vallées piémontaises et la VA, est le statut d'autonomie régionale dont jouit cette dernière, et qui a permis des interventions économiques avec des programmes et des buts précis. Ce qui a eu comme conséquence d'atténuer l'effet de la crise de l'agriculture dont les emplois ont diminué dans des proportions moins catastrophiques qu'ailleurs. Les mouvements migratoires des villages alpins de la VA, dépourvus de tourisme, s'arrêtent aujourd'hui à l'intérieur de la région, tandis qu'ailleurs ils se dirigent vers les noyaux industriels extérieurs, situés dans la plaine du Piémont.

4. Statistiques et profils ethniques

4.1. Les vallées méridionales

Les caractéristiques linguistiques des quelque 22 000 patoisants de la province de Turin sont très bigarrées, pour des raisons à la fois géographiques et sociolinguistiques. Ces parlers ont en effet une tendance à développer des particularités presque municipales (il suffit de voir le grand nombre d'aboutissements modernes du suffixe latin *-are* (cf. Telmon 1978, 43 sq)) dans le traitement de certains phénomènes qui sont souvent cités comme typiques du frpr. Le fait que l'on se trouve dans une zone marginale de l'aire frpr., exposée par conséquent aux influences provençales et piémontaises, explique par ailleurs que le caractère frpr. des parlers soit nuancé. La présence d'au moins trois systèmes linguistiques différents (frpr., piémontais, italien) sur tout le territoire nous autorise à parler d'un trilinguisme effectif pour presque tous les habitants. En effet, même dans les localités où le parler frpr. est désormais totalement remplacé par une variété de piémontais, les locuteurs sont capables de distinguer leur nouveau code piémontais du turinois, et d'utiliser les deux codes dans leur discours d'une façon tout à fait consciente. Les aires les plus menacées sont les entrées des vallées: ceci vaut aussi pour les vallées basses, surtout si, comme c'est le cas pour la Vallée de Suse, elles sont sujettes à un trafic commercial et une industrialisation intenses. Avec l'altitude moyenne très basse des communes, ce sont les facteurs économiques qui expliquent la remarquable réduction des patoisants frpr., justement dans la Vallée de Suse et dans le Val Sangone. Depuis le début du siècle, ces vallées ont été par ailleurs touchées de vagues immigratoires massives provenant de l'Italie nord-orientale et du Sud et, en même temps, de fortes émigrations d'autochtones vers la France, la Belgique, l'Allemagne et, plus récemment, aussi vers Turin. Malgré cela, de l'examen des traits linguistiques qui caractérisent le frpr., on peut tirer deux conclusions prudentes. La première est que tous ces parlers restent encore fortement individualisés par rapport aux dialectes dont le type n'est pas galloroman; la deuxième, qu'ils présentent tous, à des dégrés plus ou moins forts, l'un ou l'autre des traits frpr. souvent cités dans les classifications dialectologiques. Le résultat est donc une variété bien intégrée dans le cadre du frpr., sans parler de leur variabilité géographique dans le temps; elle fait voir en outre une certaine adaptation de ces parlers au modèle turinois.

4.2. La Vallée d'Aoste

En ce qui concerne la VA, sa condition de minorité linguistique a abouti à la concession de l'autonomie régionale (cf. Bétemps 1979, 5 sq). La vallée tout entière est en effet frpr., avec beaucoup de différences internes, à l'exception toutefois d'une enclave linguistique alémanique à Gressoney-La-Trinité, à Gressoney-Saint-Jean et à Issime, où les parlers sont alémaniques de type suisse-valaisan (walser). L'extrapolation des données d'une étude réalisée en 1974 et son adaptation aux chiffres du recensement de 1981 (population totale 112 353 (+ 2,93%); active 47 575 (42,34%); agriculture 3 911 (8,22%); industrie 16 979 (35,69%); commerce 9 561 (20,10%); transports et communications 2 485 (5,22%); crédit et assurances, services, etc. 1 709 (3,59%); administration et services publics et privés 10 620 (22,32%)) nous amène à évaluer à environ 68 000 les patoisants frpr. et à 1 000 le nombre des dialectophones alémaniques. En plus, plusieurs familles de la moyenne et de la haute bourgeoisie ont maintenu la tradition de l'enseignement du français comme langue maternelle — langue officielle et langue de la culture jusqu'à la période du fascisme (1922—1945) (cf. Adler 1980, 223 sq). Ces francophones (un millier environ) sont concentrés surtout dans la ville d'Aoste, dont la population (37 194) comprend un tiers d'indigènes et deux tiers d'immigrés (moitié valdôtains et moitié italiens, surtout vénitiens et méridionaux).

5. Situation sociolinguistique

Du tableau qu'on vient de tracer on peut assez bien déduire les caractéristiques sociolinguistiques des deux volets du territoire frpr. Du côté piémontais, le frpr. ne jouit d'aucune forme de protection officielle. Il a été menacé d'abord par le piémontais et ensuite par l'italien qui constituent actuellement les codes les plus prestigieux et socialement plus élevés, ce qui ne laisse aux patois frpr. que des fonctions de plus en plus limitées (familiales, «langue de grand-papa» et parfois même «langue de la mémoire»). L'interruption des activités agricoles a souvent entraîné l'abandon du dialecte. Celui-ci commence par le déplacement de la population du village vers les pôles industriels (de langue italienne ou piémontaise), et finit par l'apprentissage de la langue de l'usine de la part des travailleurs émigrés. Vient ensuite un effort conscient, visant à camoufler les connotations linguistiques maternelles — typique de celui qui est amené à avoir honte de ses propres origines. L'étape suivante sera la nécessité de communiquer avec les personnes étrangères et de suppléer à l'insuffisance de situations de communication interpersonnelle affective. A travers les stades successifs de diglossie avec prévalence du patois, de bilinguisme avec parité des deux codes, de diglossie avec marginalisation du patois, une masse toujours croissante de dialectophones finit par abandonner son propre patois pour adopter l'italien.

Du côté valdôtain, la connaissance et l'emploi des patois montrent au contraire beaucoup plus de vitalité, bien que la plupart des patoisants frpr. soient bi- ou trilingues (cf. Berruto 1983, 78 sq), étant donné qu'ils emploient, en plus de leurs patois, l'italien (dans les rapports avec l'administration publique) et le français (dans les rapports avec l'administration régionale et avec les institutions culturelles non scolaires). Une bonne partie de la population, surtout dans la basse vallée, connaît et parle aussi un dialecte piémontais.

6. Etat de la politique linguistique

Le statut réel dont bénéficient les patois en VA dépasse celui des autres vallées frpr. au Sud du seul point de vue pratique; d'un point de vue théorique, cependant, le frpr. demeure quelque chose de très vague. Le statut de langue n'est attribué en effet qu'à l'italien et au français: c'est ce dernier qui partage avec l'italien les horaires scolaires, et c'est en français qu'on lit les enseignes des magasins ou les panneaux de signalisation. Et partout, on l'a déjà dit, les patois sont très florissants, surtout si on les compare à la situation du Piémont ou à celle, encore pire, de la France. Après une première phase, pendant laquelle une poussée plutôt exclusive vers la francophonie était évidente, l'action de l'administration régionale a en effet presque toujours favorisé la conscience de l'individualité et des particularités linguistiques et culturelles du frpr. Certaines initiatives ont contribué à la naissance d'une certaine fierté des Valdôtains à l'égard du patois: citons, à titre d'exemple, la constitution de plusieurs groupes de théâtre dialectal, précédés par le célèbre *Charaban* d'Aoste (cf. Corgnier 1988, 37 sq), la création de nombreuses bibliothèques dans presque tous les hameaux, avec des activités d'animation culturelle parfois très intenses et les contacts ininterrompus avec les patoisants frpr. de la Savoie et du Valais, soit à l'occasion de fêtes soit par des rencontres. Même à l'intérieur de l'école, bien qu'avec plus de difficultés, les parlers frpr. ont trouvé une place et des domaines d'expression dans le *Concours Cerlogne*, une espèce de grande festivité scolaire des écoliers valdôtains, que la Région organise, une fois par an, dans des endroits toujours différents. Ce concours comporte des expositions de travaux scolaires et de recherches qui ont été effectués tout au long de l'année scolaire, relatifs à des sujets de la culture matérielle et de la sphère de la vie populaire (religieuse, ludique, etc.). En outre, un *Centre d'Etudes francoprovençales* a été créé, il y a plus de vingt ans. Ce centre a son siège soit à Saint-Nicolas, auprès du musée dédié au poète dialectal Jean Baptiste Cerlogne (1826−1910), soit à Aoste, auprès du *Bureau Régional pour l'Ethnologie et la Linguistique* (BREL). Ce sont justement le Centre de Saint-Nicolas et le BREL qui coordonnent toutes les activités relatives de près ou de loin à la diffusion et à l'étude du patois et qui organisent périodiquement des cours de recyclage pour les instituteurs. L'ensemble de ces activités a contribué à un rétablissement de l'emploi, même quotidien, du patois: les importantes variations diatopiques mentionnées ci-dessus n'empêchent pas par ailleurs une bonne compréhension réciproque et n'obstruent pas la conscience d'une homogénéité typologique de tous les parlers frpr. de la VA.

La situation dans les autres vallées frpr. est tout à fait différente: les quelques groupes qui de leur propre gré essaient d'encourager des recherches et des études sur leurs parlers et sur leur culture sont, dans la plupart des cas, dépourvus de possibilités économiques ou d'organisation, et ne jouissent d'aucune assistance scientifique et technologique, ce qui les force à vivoter péniblement et ne leur permet pas d'exercer une influence positive sur les populations des vallées. L'administration a souvent réuni les zones gallo-romanes avec les zones linguistiquement piémontaises du Canavese ou de la plaine, ce qui a contribué à réduire non seulement l'emploi du patois frpr. mais aussi la conscience de la diversité linguistique et culturelle. Les exemples de patoisants frpr. ne manquent pas qui croient parler piémontais. Même là où la volonté d'employer et de valoriser le patois se manifestent clairement, les difficultés dues à l'absence d'une orthographe unifiée, désormais résolues en VA, constituent un obstacle insurmontable. Il faut par ailleurs ajouter que l'école des vallées en question dépend directement de l'administration centrale à Rome, centrée évidemment sur l'italophonie la plus absolue, et censurant toute manifestation des dialectes locaux et même de toute inflexion dialectale.

En ce qui concerne l'usage linguistique dans l'administration et dans les institutions publiques, il y a des différences très nettes entre la VA et les autres vallées. Le bilinguisme officiel italo-français de la VA a augmenté la tolérance linguistique: même si les patois continuent à ne pas être présents dans l'usage officiel, ils ne sont pas soumis à des sanctions négatives dans le cas d'emploi oral dans les bureaux de l'administration régionale. Il faut préciser toutefois que la plupart des efforts des institutions visent plutôt à sauver la langue française, symbole de l'élite et de la culture. Il faut préciser aussi qu'auprès de certaines administrations (postes, chemins de fer, impôts, etc.) la présence d'une majorité de travailleurs immigrés, rend impossible l'utilisation du français et du patois frpr. Dans les autres vallées, il est pratiquement impensable que, dans les rapports avec l'administration publique, l'on fasse appel à une langue autre que l'italien. Très rarement, il arrive que le patois (mais aussi le piémontais) soit employé durant les délibérations des conseils communaux des villages de montagne (même si les procès-verbaux sont écrits en italien). Les moyens de communication de masse les plus répandus se servent presque exclusivement de l'italien, à l'exception de la VA, où néanmoins l'alternative est représentée par le français plutôt que par les parlers frpr.: pour la télévision francophone, mentionnons les programmes français de la Deuxième chaîne de la télévision et, pour la presse en français, les journaux suivants: « Le peuple valdôtain », « La ville d'Aoste », « Rassemblement valdôtain », qui appartiennent tous à des mouvements politiques locaux. Dans les autres vallées frpr., les journaux les plus répandus sont les quotidiens de Turin. Il y a en plus un certain nombre d'hebdomadaires locaux, gérés pour la plupart par l'église catholique, dans lesquels l'on traite quelquefois des arguments concernant la langue ou la culture locales. Il arrive parfois que des associations « piémontésistes » organisent les cours de langue piémontaise, ou bien des fêtes et des rencontres à l'intérieur des vallées frpr., ce qui contribue également à l'affaiblissement des patois frpr.

7. Portrait général des contacts linguistiques

Les traits linguistiques qui distinguent les parlers frpr. des parlers occitans, du français, de l'italien et des parlers piémontais, sont désormais bien connus. Tout d'abord, il y a la palatalisation de *A* tonique latin: l'occitan alpin, l'italien et le piémontais (sauf dans l'infinitif de la première conjugaison) ne connaissant pas la palatalisation, le français ne connaît que la palatalisation, tandis que le frpr. palatalise la voyelle uniquement après une consonne palatale (cf. Ascoli 1878, 63). Dans la forme lat. *pratu*, par exemple, la voyelle tonique *a* se palatalise en français (*pré*) et se conserve tant en occitan qu'en frpr. (*pra*, *prat*), tandis que pour la forme lat. *capra* se sont les seuls patois provençaux alpins qui conservent la voyelle *a* malgré la palatalisation de la consonne initiale (*tšabro*), le français et le frpr. aboutissent à des voyelles palatales (*chèvre*, *tśirva*, etc.). De plus, les parlers frpr. n'ont pas participé aux évolutions phonétiques qui ont abouti, dans les parlers d'oïl, à la chute de la voyelle finale de mot, à l'oxytonie généralisée qui en résulte (cf. Tuaillon 1972b, 336), à la palatalisation de la voyelle U latine (cf. Tuaillon 1968, 100 sq), à l'harmonisation analogique des formes des trois premières personnes de l'indicatif présent des verbes de la 2ème et 3ème conjugaison (cf. Martin 1983, 32 sq), etc. Le tableau 157.3 nous donne une vue synoptique de ces traits dans les parlers gallo-romans (o., fp., fr.), en italien (it.) et en piémontais (p.).

Tableau 157.3: Traits linguistiques (d'après Telmon 1992, 119)

Trait	fr.	fp.	o.	p.	it.
lénition forte	+	+	−	+	−
diphtongaison	+	+	−	+	−
pron. suj. obligatoire	+	+	−	+	−
conservation voy. fin.	−	+	+	+	+
palatalisation de CA-	+	+	−	−	−
palatalisation de Ū	+	−	−	+	−
double aboutiss. de A	−	+	−	−	−
oxytonie généralisée	+	−	−	−	−
1#2#3 vs. 1=2=3 dans le prés. indicatif des verbes de la 2ème et 3ème conjugaison	−	+/−	+	+	+

Quant aux contacts linguistiques, le frpr. est le code le plus concerné: les parlers frpr. reçoivent les emprunts de tous les autres codes. Les emprunts les plus anciens viennent du français, suivis des interférences du piémontais et de l'italien (Grassi 1971); l'effet inverse est beaucoup plus rare.

On a déjà dit qu'il n'y a pas d'orthographe officielle pour le frpr.: le peu d'usage qu'on fait du frpr. pour l'écrit est en général le fruit d'essais personnels, surtout dans les vallées méridionales, où il n'existe aucune norme graphique, tandis qu'en VA on dispose de plusieurs modèles: citons celui de J. B. Cerlogne, qui remonte au siècle passé, et la graphie recommandée par le Centre d'Etudes francoprovençales de Saint-Nicolas (Schüle 1980, 1 ss.). Ce centre a beaucoup de mérite aussi pour l'édition et la diffusion, en patois frpr., des belles-lettres et de la littérature populaire: on compte déjà plusieurs dizaines de livres de poésie, de prose et d'histoire locale rédigés par les écoliers, publiés tous par les soins du Centre. Les travaux sur la langue sont aussi — si l'on excepte les travaux scientifiques rédigés par des spécialistes — le produit des efforts faits à l'intérieur de la VA même: citons, à ce propos, la première grammaire des patois valdôtains (Cerlogne 1893, 1 sq), restée sans succession jusqu'à nos jours; puis le dictionnaire de J. B. Cerlogne (1907). C'est toujours en VA que l'action infatigable d'Aimé Chenal et de Raymond Vautherin a abouti d'abord au grand Vocabulaire des patois valdôtains (Chenal/Vautherin 1962—1982) et ensuite au vocabulaire bilingue français—patois (Chenal/Vautherin 1984).

8. Problèmes ouverts et perspectives

En dépit d'une créativité linguistique intense déployée depuis la fin du XIXe siècle, beaucoup de problèmes restent ouverts. Sans avoir la prétention d'être exhaustif, nous citerons ici, par exemple:

(1) la question du nom de cette pléiade de patois qu'est le francoprovençal: un problème qui a beaucoup troublé des générations de linguistes et qui n'est pas encore clos, dans la mesure où il touche aussi les problèmes de la genèse de cet idiome (cf. Tuaillon 1972b).
(2) la subdivision géolinguistique (Keller 1958, 5 sq; Müller 1974, 7 sq; Schmidt 1974, 31 sq). Il y a, on vient de le voir, de très bonnes raisons sociologiques pour séparer la VA du reste du territoire frpr. italien. La différence des répertoires justifie cette attitude même du point de vue sociolinguistique: nous devons donc vérifier si ce découpage sociolinguistique se réalise aussi au niveau (intra)linguistique, et s'il correspond avec les hypothèses de découpage formulées pour les domaines français et suisse.
(3) le problème des contacts linguistiques avec l'italien, le piémontais et l'occitan alpin, qui soulève des questions relatives aux limites, aux aires intermédiaires et aux interférences (Tuaillon 1964, 127 sq; Escoffier 1958, 1 sq; Grassi 1971, 79 sq; Telmon 1974, 1 sq): ces problèmes restent toujours actuels, surtout parce que les limites socio- et géolinguistiques se modifient sans cesse sous la poussée des codes les plus puissants.
(4) la syntaxe, qui — comme on le sait — est un secteur plutôt négligé de la dialectologie en général, pourrait — aussi en territoire frpr. — apporter des réponses géolinguistiques très intéressantes.
(5) Au niveau de la morphologie et de la phonologie, des études pourraient encore être entreprises, par exemple, sur la chronologie de la palatalisation du $\bar{U}$ latin (Tuaillon 1968, 100 sq); d'autres études pourraient porter sur le déplacement de l'accent vers la syllabe finale, trait qui caractérise aussi certains parlers piémontais (cf. Tuaillon 1972a, 377; Rossebastiano Bart 1984, 391 sq).
(6) Sur le plan sociolinguistique, la discussion relative à la fragmentation dialectale du territoire pourrait rejoindre celle portant sur la typologie des répertoires linguistiques des locuteurs. On pourrait également envisager une recherche complémentaire relative à la conscience métalinguistique des sujets, concernant soit la dimension historique (croyances sur l'origine des patois, et sur leurs filiations génétiques, hypothèses sur les emprunts, etc.), soit la dimension synchronique (images subjectives des similitudes dialectales, expériences vécues d'intercompréhension ou de manque de compréhension entre patois de villages contigus, les blasons populaires, les «shibboleths», etc.).

9. Bibliographie (sélective)

Adler, Winfried (1980): «La politica del fascismo in Valle d'Aosta». In: *Bollettino storico-bibliografico subalpino 78*, 223—275.

Ascoli, Graziadio Isaia (1878): «Schizzi francoprovenzali». In: *Archivio Glottologico Italiano 3*, 61—120.

Berruto, Gaetano (1983): «Aspetti e problemi del plurilinguismo in Valle d'Aosta». In: *L'educazione plurilingue in Italia*, Di Iorio, Francesco (Ed.), I Quaderni di Villa Falconieri, 2, 77−101, Frascati.

Bétemps, Alexis (1979): *Les Valdôtains et leur langue*, Aoste.

Chenal, Aimé/Vautherin, Raymond (1962−1982): *Nouveau dictionnaire de patois valdôtain*, 13 vol., Aoste.

Chenal, Aimé/Vautherin, Raymond (1984): *Nouveau dictionnaire de patois valdôtain. Dictionnaire français−valdôtain*, Aoste.

Cerlogne, Jean-Baptiste (1893): *Petite grammaire du dialecte valdôtain*, Aoste.

Cerlogne, Jean-Baptiste (1907): *Dictionnaire du patois valdôtain. Précédé de la petite grammaire*, Aoste.

Corgnier, Giselle (1988): *Le théâtre populaire valdôtain: l'œuvre de René Willien*, Saint-Nicolas.

Escoffier, Simone (1958): *La rencontre de la langue d'oïl, de la langue d'oc et du francoprovençal entre Loire et Allier. Limites phonétiques et morphologiques*, Paris.

Grassi, Corrado (1971): «Francoprovençal et Italie du Nord». In: *Actes du Colloque de dialectologie francoprovençale*, Marzys, Zygmunt (Ed.), Neuchâtel/Genève, 79−92.

Keller, Hans-Erich (1958): *Etudes linguistiques sur les parlers valdôtains*, Berne.

Martin, Jean-Baptiste (1983): «Le francoprovençal». In: *Nouvelles du Centre d'études francoprovençales ‹ René Willien › 8*, 28−45.

Müller, Bodo (1974): «La structure linguistique de la France et la romanisation». In: *Travaux de linguistique et de littérature XII, 1*, 7−29.

Rossebastiano Bart, Alda (1984): «Isoglosse francoprovenzali nelle parlate rustiche piemontesi del Canavese: progressione e regressione d'accento». In: *Corona Alpium, Miscellanea di studi in onore di Carlo Alberto Mastrelli*, AA.VV. (Eds.), Florence, 391−405.

Schmitt, Christian (1974): «Genèse et typologie des domaines linguistiques de la Galloromania». In: *Travaux de linguistique et de littérature 12, 1*, 31−83.

Schüle, Ernest (1980): *Comment écrire le patois? (Principes et conseils pratiques)*, Saint-Nicolas.

Telmon, Tullio (1974): *Microsistemi linguistici in contatto in Val di Susa: l'articolo determinativo*, Pise.

Telmon, Tullio (1978): «Une analyse grammaticale: les verbes réguliers dans la Vallée d'Aoste». In: *L'Atlas des patois valdôtains. Etat des travaux 1978*, Schüle, Ernest/Schüle, Rose-Claire/Telmon, Tullio (Eds.), Aoste, 39−51.

Telmon, Tullio (1981): «Per un atlante delle parlate galloromanze in territorio piemontese». In: *Bollettino dell'Atlante Linguistico Italiano*, III serie, 3−4, 58−71.

Telmon, Tullio (1982): «La minoranza di parlata francoprovenzale». In: *Sociologia della comunicazione I, 2*, 33−45.

Telmon, Tullio (1992): *Le minoranze linguistiche in Italia*, Alessandria.

Tuaillon, Gaston (1964): «Limite nord du provençal à l'est du Rhône». In: *Revue de linguistique romane 28*, 127−142.

Tuaillon, Gaston (1968): «Aspects géographiques de la palatalisation u > ü, en gallo-roman et notamment en francoprovençal». In: *Revue de linguistique romane 32*, 100−125.

Tuaillon, Gaston (1972a): «Frontière linguistique et cohésion de l'aire dialectale». In: *Studii şi cercetări lingvistice 4*, 367−396.

Tuaillon, Gaston (1972b): «Le francoprovençal. Progrès d'une définition». In: *Travaux de linguistique et de littérature 10, 2*, 293−339. Réédité sous le même titre par le Centre d'Etudes francoprovençales, Saint-Nicolas, 1983.

Tullio Telmon, Turin (Italie)

158. Italien−frioulan

1. Géographie et démographie
2. Histoire
3. Politique, économie et situation culturelle
4. Statistiques et profils ethniques
5. Situation sociolinguistique
6. Etat de la politique linguistique
7. Portrait général des contacts linguistiques
8. Etat des discussions
9. Bibliographie (sélective)

1. Géographie et démographie

1.1. Le Frioul fait partie de la Région autonome à statut spécial (instituée en 1963) «Friuli-Venezia Giulia», située au nord-est de l'Italie aux frontières de l'Autriche et de la Slovénie. Le Frioul comprend les territoires des provinces d'Udine, de Pordenone et de Gorizia (Gorice) (7633 km^2), tandis que

Trieste est située en Vénétie Julienne (211 km²). Trieste est le chef-lieu administratif régional, alors qu'Udine — ville située au centre de la région — est le chef-lieu culturel du Frioul (→ carte linguistique F).

1.2. Le Frioul actuel correspond grosso modo au Frioul historique (cf. 2.) et il est peuplé de plus d'un million de personnes. Selon les sondages du dernier recensement qui remonte à 1981, le Frioul compte 947 350 habitants tandis que la province de Trieste en compte 282 579.

1.3. Le Frioul, surtout la zone de la montagne, a toujours été caractérisé par une forte émigration. La période de la plus grande émigration va de 1881 à 1915. En 1890, le nombre des émigrants est de quelque 40 000 personnes. Dans les années suivantes, le nombre des émigrants est environ de 20 000; à partir de 1957, le chiffre tombe jusqu'à 2 500 en 1979. Seulement une partie retourne au Frioul.

1.4. La carte physique du Frioul est divisée en trois parties: l'on distingue, au sud, une ample bande de plaine qui s'étend jusqu'à la mer (Bassa friulana), puis une zone de collines qui s'étend le long de la frontière de la Slovénie (Collio), et une zone septentrionale montagneuse (Alpes Carniques et Juliennes).

2. Histoire

2.1. A l'époque préromaine, le Frioul était surtout habité par des tribus de Carniens (faisant partie des Celtes), et par quelques Vénètes dans la plaine, qui était sans doute dépeuplée ou presque. La conquête romaine commence par la fondation d'Aquileia (181 av. J.-C.), puis de Forum Iulii (aujourd'hui Cividale), de Iulium Carnicum (aujourd'hui Zuglio) et de Concordia. Le territoire entier, qui comprenait ces quatre *municipia* romains, fut affecté, à l'époque de l'empereur Auguste, à la Xème Regio «Venetia et Histria». Les anciennes frontières romaines réapparaissent souvent dans les subdivisions diocésaines, mais ce n'est pas le cas de Iulium Carnicum, de Forum Iulii et d'Aquileia dont les territoires sont déjà réunis au VIIIème siècle.

Le territoire du diocèse de Concordia, qui comprend la zone située entre les fleuves Tagliamento et Livenza, reste à part. La scission entre les diocèses d'Aquileia et de Concordia joue un rôle déterminant dans la constitution de certains types de frioulanité (le «frioulan d'Aquileia» et le «frioulan de Concordia»).

2.2. Les Lombards s'installent dans l'ancien Forum Iulii en 568 et en font la capitale du Duché lombard dont la superficie correspond grosso modo au Frioul historique. Ensuite c'est le tour des Francs qui transforment le Duché en une Marche orientale, qui deviendra un Comté et sera assigné par l'empereur germanique Henri IV aux Patriarches d'Aquileia en 1077. A partir de cette date, l'histoire du Frioul se confond plus ou moins avec l'histoire du Patriarcat d'Aquileia. L'Etat patriarcal correspond au territoire qui s'appelait déjà à la fin du XIème siècle «Patria Fori Iulii». Le Patriarcat passe, en 1420, sous la domination de la République de Venise alors que le Frioul oriental reste sous la domination des comtes de Gorice (Gorizia) (d'origine tyrolienne et carinthienne) et suit, de 1500 jusqu'en 1918, le sort de la Maison d'Autriche.

2.3. C'est durant la longue période patriarcale, et plus particulièrement entre le IXème et le Xème siècle (ou, selon une autre évaluation, entre le XIème et le XIIIème siècle) que s'effectue l'ethnogenèse frioulane, même si des préludes significatifs de ce processus peuvent déjà être notés auparavant (cf. Francescato/ Salimbeni 1976, Menis 1991). De toute façon, il est certain qu'à l'époque patriarcale se créent les conditions favorables pour un développement autonome de la culture frioulane. Celle-ci se caractérise, entre autres, par un isolement progressif et une certaine distance face aux courants culturels de la péninsule. Tous ces éléments sont indispensables pour une bonne compréhension de la naissance de l'identité frioulane.

2.4. Le Frioul actuel reflète le Frioul historique, c'est-à-dire les territoires occupés par les circonscriptions romaines de Concordia, d'Aquileia, de Forum Iulii et de Iulium Carnicum (dont il ne reste de nos jours que la Carnia avec la vallée du Fella). Autrefois lié à Concordia, le district de Portogruaro a été séparé du Frioul en 1838 et fait partie, de nos jours, de la province de Venise. Certaines régions qui appartenaient jadis à Iulium Carnicum ont été affectées, par la suite, à des provinces non frioulanes: c'est ainsi que le Cadore, le Comélico et la partie haute du Cordévole font depuis longtemps partie de la province de Belluno, et la Pusteria de la province de Bolzano (cf. Frau 1984, 4–5).

2.5. Tout en appartenant au Frioul historique, certaines zones marginales ne sont pas de langue frioulane (comme la zone de Sacile à l'ouest, et les localités maritimes de Grado et de Marano, ainsi que le territoire de Monfalcone). D'autres le furent dans le passé, par exemple le district de Portogruaro ou la ville de Pordenone. Trieste et Muggia (de par les variétés du «tergestino» et du «muglisano») faisaient autrefois partie de la frioulanité. Au nord, en Carnie, se trouvent deux îlots linguistiques d'origine germanique (Sauris/Zahre et Timau/Tischelwang) et à l'est d'autres d'origine slave (Val Resia, Val Natisone). Dans les principaux centres de la région (Udine, Gorizia, Cividale, Latisana, etc.) on trouve, à côté du frioulan, un mésolecte de type vénitien qui s'est imposé grâce au prestige de Venise. L'adoption des innovations linguistiques vénitiennes, favorisée par l'hégémonie de Venise, se manifeste déjà dans les documents de la *scripta* frioulane du Haut Moyen Age: le vénitien est alors considéré, surtout par les citadins et les bourgeois, comme un parler plus civil, plus distingué. Le vénitien s'infiltre donc, au cours des siècles, très lentement, dans les amphizones vénitiennes et frioulanes occidentales sous l'apparence du vénitien oriental de Trévise («liventino»). Dans les campagnes cependant, le frioulan se maintient avec beaucoup de vitalité.

2.6. Les rapports du Frioul avec la culture italienne et avec le toscan sont au début plutôt rares, soit à cause de l'isolement géographique de cette région, soit à cause du fait que les classes dominantes à l'époque du Patriarcat sont d'origine germanique dont la langue maternelle et la culture de référence sont germaniques (cf. Francescato 1991, 203—205); évidemment la langue écrite est, comme partout en Europe centrale et occidentale, le latin. Il ne faut pas oublier que jusqu'en 1250 les Patriarches sont presque exclusivement d'origine germanique, ce qui retarde l'ouverture de la «Patria Fori Iulii» à la culture italienne. En plus, la culture et la langue germaniques n'intéressent presque exclusivement que les couches sociales élevées, la noblesse et le clergé. Malgré cela le frioulan subit une certaine influence au niveau lexical où il enregistre un nombre discret d'emprunts germaniques.

Dans la *scripta*, l'impact du toscan est très limité par rapport à celui de la *koiné* vénitienne. Le toscan et le vénitien interfèrent également avec les systèmes du latin et du frioulan. Au XVIe siècle, les milieux littéraires frioulans finissent par s'orienter vers le toscan littéraire et la diffusion de l'italien se réalise à travers la diffusion des livres. Même le clergé adopte parfois l'italien dans les prédications. A ce propos, il faut souligner que les patriarches d'Aquileia recommandent la prédication en dialecte frioulan (prescriptions de 1660 ratifiées en 1703) refusant ainsi de recourir à un moyen important pour la diffusion de l'italien. Cette langue, qui a déjà pénétré dans les couches les plus hautes des centres urbains (où l'on parle surtout le vénitien), ne se répand parmi les couches les plus basses et dans les campagnes frioulanophones que dans la seconde moitié du XIXe siècle avec l'introduction de la scolarisation (pour la pénétration de l'italien au Frioul, cf. Morgana 1992). L'on sait que l'annexion du Frioul central et occidental à l'Italie remonte à 1866 et celui du Frioul oriental à 1918/19.

3. Politique, économie et situation culturelle

3.1. La région «Friuli-Venezia Giulia» est une Région autonome à statut spécial et peut légiférer au niveau local. Mais pour mieux comprendre cet état de choses, il est bon de souligner que l'identité culturelle frioulane, dont la langue est le facteur le plus important, est encore solidement ancrée dans la population. Elle a connu d'ailleurs un moment de renouveau après le tremblement de terre de 1976. La présence au Frioul d'une conscience autonomiste, bien que d'une manière assez modérée, s'exprime par un vif sentiment de «frioulanité». La frioulanité se manifeste à travers des initiatives politiques et culturelles visant à conserver des valeurs considérées comme caractéristiques par les habitants, telle que la langue, les traditions, etc. Sur le plan politique, citons le «Movimento Friuli» (créé à la fin des années 60) dont l'objectif est la revendication du caractère frioulan dans le cadre de la Région et surtout vis-à-vis de Trieste, chef-lieu de la Région autonome. Il ne s'agit pas seulement d'une valorisation culturelle mais aussi d'une revendication socio-économique. Comme le retard économique a pu être comblé depuis lors (le Frioul occupe aujourd'hui une position de choix dans les statistiques nationales), ce mouvement est aujourd'hui en perte de vitesse. Quant aux revendications autonomistes, elles sont aujourd'hui exprimées surtout par la «Lega Nord».

3.2. Dans le domaine économique, il faut souligner que le développement industriel du Frioul s'est effectué d'une façon plus lente que dans les autres régions italiennes. C'est pourquoi le phénomène de la croissance urbaine est peu considérable; seules des agglomérations comme Pordenone et Udine ont été affectées d'une immigration interne. En général, il s'agit de petites et moyennes industries qui cohabitent avec une économie basée sur l'agriculture. C'est ainsi que l'on constate très souvent une économie mixte où l'ouvrier qui travaille à l'usine, gère aussi une petite entreprise agricole. Malgré le développement de l'industrie, le flux migratoire des zones de montagnes, bien que fort réduit par rapport à celui du passé, ne s'est pas arrêté; il se dirige de préférence vers des pays européens et extra-européens. On remarque également, dans cette région, une immigration d'employés du tertiaire provenant d'autres zones italiennes, notamment du Centre-Sud.

4. Statistiques et profils ethniques

4.1. Il n'existe pas de relevés précis du nombre de frioulanophones. On pense qu'il s'agit d'environ 700 000 personnes vivant dans les provinces d'Udine, de Gorizia et de Pordenone, et de 300 000 émigrés frioulans disséminés dans le monde (cf. Francescato 1989, 601).

4.2. Les frioulanophones parlent tous, en plus du frioulan, un italien régional de type septentrional. L'italien qui est la langue maternelle de certains milieux sociaux (surtout celle des immigrés provenant d'autres régions), se répand de plus en plus chez les personnes nées dans la région.

4.3. Dans certaines zones du Frioul, les frioulanophones parlent aussi le vénitien, en général une variété particulière de celui-ci (cf. 2.5.) mais son usage est en train de s'affaiblir, comme on peut le remarquer à Udine.

4.4. Même si les données quantitatives sur les parlants sont rares et d'ampleur limitée, les recherches sociolinguistiques, surtout dans des endroits spécifiques, ne manquent pas (Francescato 1956, 1981 etc.; Del Toso 1978). Nous signalons en particulier les nouvelles recherches menées par l'ISIG (Istituto di Sociologia Internazionale di Gorizia).

4.4.1. Dans une recherche concernant toute la région qui date de 1977−1978, des échantillons statistiques comprenant tous les résidants entre 18 et 65 ans ont été pris en considération (cf. De Marchi 1980 auquel nous nous référons). L'échantillonnage comprend 4 zones (frioulane, vénitienne, allemande, slovène, hormis le slovène des provinces de Gorizia et de Trieste) et un total de 1 500 individus. En ce qui concerne les données recueillies à l'aide d'un échantillon purement frioulan (385 unités), on peut remarquer une baisse du frioulan chez les générations les plus jeunes; ce phénomène est diamétralement opposé à l'évolution de l'italien qui est en hausse. On observe que les parlants conservent l'usage du frioulan lorsqu'ils rencontrent des interlocuteurs avec lesquels ils parlaient frioulan durant leur enfance. Tous ceux qui ont parlé frioulan avec leurs parents et leurs frères durant leur enfance, continuent de le faire aussi après. On assiste cependant à un changement de code en faveur de l'italien chez des parents qui, pour des raisons d'utilité ou de prestige, parlent entre eux frioulan, mais italien avec leurs enfants. L'emploi du frioulan (mais aussi des autres parlers minoritaires) diminue au profit de l'italien, tandis que celui-ci, encouragé par l'école, s'impose surtout dans les villes. Le frioulan est employé surtout par les gens d'un même village (81%), entre amis (73%), avec le curé (62,9%). Son usage fléchit beaucoup parmi les employés des bureaux publics (28,6%), parmi les instituteurs et les professeurs (17,4%). On note, en outre, une plus forte « frioulanophonie » chez les hommes que chez les femmes (78,9% et 71%).

4.4.2. Une autre enquête de l'ISIG (Istituto di Sociologia Internazionale di Gorizia) − limitée au frioulan − a été effectuée en 1985 dans la province d'Udine (cf. Strassoldo 1986 et 1991). Cette enquête a été lancée par la province d'Udine qui à l'époque avait chargé le catalan Xavier Lamuela de codifier le frioulan. Cela s'est passé au début des années 80 lorsqu'il semblait que la loi pour la sauvegarde des langues minoritaires, étayée par le consensus de toutes les forces politiques régionales, allait devenir une réalité. La recherche de l'ISIG se fixait quatre objectifs: (1) d'analyser les tendances socio-économiques et démographiques des différentes zones de la province de Udine, (2) de sonder l'opinion sur un échantillon d'environ 150 individus entre 18 et 65 ans, (3) d'enquêter auprès d'un groupe de 223 administrateurs locaux sur la loi pour la sauvegarde des langues minoritaires, (4) d'enquêter sur un échantillon représentatif de 316 enseignants. Les résultats confirmèrent ceux de l'enquête précédente. Ils montraient que l'emploi du frioulan diminuait avec l'augmentation du niveau des études scolaires. Cette diminution n'empêche point que presque la moitié des personnes instruites pratique régulièrement le frioulan même si cet usage diminue aussi avec l'âge. Il est intéressant de noter que le frioulan cesse d'être la langue de la famille pour devenir la langue de la rue (de la « piazza », du bistrot, du travail, de la « communauté »). La majorité des personnes interviewées, qui appartenaient à toutes les catégories sociales, se sont déclarées favorables à l'introduction du frioulan à l'école. Seulement 15% des interviewés a exprimé un avis contraire. A noter encore le décalage entre la connaissance active et passive du frioulan: 75% de la population de la province d'Udine parlent régulièrement le frioulan, 10% le parlent occasionnellement ou rarement, presque tous le comprennent.

5. Situation sociolinguistique

5.1. Le frioulan constitue un ensemble de variétés linguistiques relativement homogènes qui remontent — selon Francescato 1989, 602 — « agli sviluppi differenziati di un unico schema strutturale (diasistema) ». De recherches récentes sur le frioulan, il appert que les variétés internes sont plus accusées que ce que l'on avait cru auparavant (cf. Francescato 1966, Frau 1984). Celles-ci ne compromettent cependant pas l'inter-compréhension entre les frioulanophones.

5.2. Le frioulan est plus répandu au fur et à mesure que l'on s'éloigne des centres les plus importants (ceux-ci ont accueilli le vénitien et l'italien comme parlers véhiculaires). Comme on peut l'imaginer, le frioulan est plus conservateur dans les zones périphériques. Du point de vue social, on constate que plus le milieu socioculturel des parlants est modeste, plus le frioulan est original. Le frioulan se maintient le mieux dans les zones de collines et de montagnes, ainsi que chez les paysans et les ouvriers. Ces derniers continuent à parler frioulan même s'ils résident dans des zones urbaines. Ce comportement linguistique s'explique par le fait qu'il s'agit de classes sociales renouvelées continuellement par des éléments qui proviennent des couches paysannes (cf. Francescato 1989, 602). L'emploi diversifié du frioulan à la campagne et dans la ville dépend aussi de la présence, dans les centres urbains, d'un contexte culturel différent de celui de la campagne, et des exigences communicatives de certaines couches de la population pour lesquelles le frioulan n'offre pas de solution linguistique adéquate (cf. Francescato 1989, 603). En plus des différences géographiques et socio-économiques, il existe également des différences générationnelles (voir sous 4.; l'abandon du frioulan de génération en génération a déjà été souligné par Francescato 1956 dans une recherche concernant la ville d'Udine).

5.3. La situation linguistique frioulane oscille entre des conditions de diglossie et de bilinguisme. Le contexte frioulan révèle une opposition diglossique entre l'usage « familier » des variétés locales et l'usage « conventionnel » (littéraire et parfois même technique) (cf. Francescato 1989, 608). Mais le cas le plus fréquent est constitué par la diglossie entre l'italien et le frioulan: l'italien est réservé aux usages conventionnels, littéraires, techniques, etc., le frioulan par contre à l'usage familier. La « lingua-guida » du frioulan est ainsi l'italien. Le rapport italien-frioulan ne produit pas de véritables conditions de bilinguisme mais un bilinguisme avec diglossie, étant donné que le frioulan n'est pas à même d'entrer en compétition avec les usages fonctionnels de l'italien. Le bilinguisme est possible surtout parmi les nouvelles générations qui s'expriment parfaitement en italien sans renoncer à l'usage du frioulan.

5.4. De nos jours, le frioulan est en crise, surtout parce qu'il n'est pas en mesure de répondre aux exigences communicatives actuelles en offrant un modèle standard, universellement accepté. L'absence d'un frioulan hautement standardisé, d'une véritable *koiné*, représente « uno dei fattori negativi che non può non pesare sulla condizione generale del friulano in Friuli » (Francescato 1989, 608). Il n'existe qu'une koiné *littéraire*, basée sur le frioulan central, dont l'emploi est limité.

5.5. L'italien est la « lingua-guida » du frioulan; il a le même rôle d'ailleurs pour tous les parlers de l'« italoroman », appelés communément « dialectes italiens ». Considérer le frioulan comme une « langue » est au Frioul un stéréotype courant (alors que le vénitien, par exemple, est considéré comme un dialecte). C'est la conséquence d'une attitude ethnocentrique de fermeture, voire de repli, que l'on remarque souvent au sein de la société frioulane. Vue de l'extérieur, celle-ci semble compacte, mais, de fait, elle se compose de petites communautés locales imprégnées, chacune, d'un vigoureux esprit de clocher. Néanmoins, le sens d'une « frioulanité » est encore fort robuste. Il est significatif que le frioulanophone qui décide de parler en frioulan avec ses enfants et non pas en italien, ne le fait presque jamais pour des raisons pratiques, mais parce qu'il désire conserver sa culture locale, signe d'unité et de distinction de son groupe culturel, ou pour un besoin expressif voire affectif (ce sont les réponses de l'enquête de 1977—1978 citée précédemment: cf. De Marchi 1980, 32—33).

6. Etat de la politique linguistique

6.1. Le frioulan est de nos jours caractérisé par une certaine vitalité sociolinguistique (cf. Morgana 1992, 307). Vu la situation sociale actuelle (1993) du Frioul, la sauvegarde et la valorisation du patrimoine linguistique semblent être un problème culturel qui intéresse plutôt les chercheurs que les profanes (cf. Strassoldo 1991). Cela est dû, semble-t-il, à l'apaisement du mouvement frioulaniste surgi après le tremblement de terre de 1976. Les initiatives pour la conservation du patrimoine culturel sont cependant nombreuses. Il faut d'abord citer la loi régionale du 2 juillet 1969 n° 11 qui prévoit des interventions de la part du gouvernement de la Région en faveur d'activités culturelles. La loi reconnaît à la Società Filologica Friulana (SFF: fondée en 1919) une fonction spéciale sur le plan culturel. La SFF publie des textes sur et en frioulan et organise des cours d'apprentissage du frioulan. A l'Université d'Udine (créée en 1978) incombe le devoir de « divenire organico strumento di sviluppo e di rinnovamento dei filoni originali della cultura, della lingua, delle tradizioni e della storia del Friuli ».

6.2. D'autres initiatives importantes sont à la charge des nombreuses associations culturelles locales. Souvent, il s'agit de projets linguistico-culturels tels que la promotion de l'emploi du frioulan dans les écoles, dans les médias, des traductions en frioulan, et aussi des activités folkloriques. Citons à ce propos l'association « Clape Cultural Acuilee », qui s'occupe surtout de la traduction d'auteurs classiques étrangers. Toutefois il manque une certaine coordination et il n'existe aucun organisme politique en mesure d'assumer cette tâche. Aucun programme global d'interventions politico-administratives n'a été réalisé, malgré la multiplication de bonnes intentions. Tout cela prélude à une proposition de loi de l'Etat pour la sauvegarde des parlers minoritaires qui est encore *in itinere*. Il semble que seule une intervention de la part de l'Etat puisse surmonter toutes les difficultés et tous les problèmes liés à l'écriture (orthographe), à la normalisation et à la standardisation du frioulan.

6.3. Malheureusement, ces difficultés entravent l'introduction de l'enseignement du frioulan dans les écoles et rendent vaines les tentatives de l'association « Scuele libare furlane ». Ils font échouer également les programmes détaillés d'éducation bilingue organisés dans le cadre des activités du « Bureau Européen pour les Langues moins répandues » (voir Schiavi Fachin 1991). Il va de soi que l'enseignement du frioulan serait capital pour la conservation de la langue.

Dans ce but, il faut citer l'excellente grammaire descriptive du frioulan de Marchetti, publiée en 1952 et basée sur la koiné littéraire, ainsi que d'autres matériaux didactiques très utiles comme *Marilenghe* de Nazzi Matalon (1977) ou *Il libri di furlan* de Lelo Cjanton (1988) (cf. Marcato 1989). Il manque cependant une véritable grammaire normative du frioulan moderne. L'enseignement du frioulan nécessiterait également l'analyse préalable d'autres problèmes, comme l'adaptation linguistique des non-frioulanophones, le choix de la variante de frioulan à enseigner, etc.

7. Portrait général des contacts linguistiques

7.1. L'absence d'un vrai bilinguisme italien/frioulan, les fréquents changements de code et le mixilinguisme favorisent les interférences entre les deux codes. Il s'avère toutefois que l'impact de l'italien, qui est la langue de prestige, est beaucoup plus fort sur le frioulan que vice versa, tant à l'oral, qu'à l'écrit. Il n'est pas rare de trouver des textes écrits en frioulan qui ont été conçus en italien et traduits par la suite. Le parler local apparaît donc influencé par l'italien. Il n'est authentique que dans certaines situations et pour des domaines bien déterminés (cf. Francescato 1989). La typologie de contact linguistique au Frioul se complique encore par la présence du dialecte vénitien dans les villes.

7.2. L'italianisation du frioulan ne concerne pas seulement le lexique mais aussi la structure du système: en font preuve par ex. les réductions de certaines oppositions phonématiques, la simplification des règles morphologiques, les ajustements analogiques (cf. Vanelli 1991).

7.3. Mais le frioulan influence aussi l'italien. Il en résulte un registre linguistique défini «italien régional». C'est une variété structurée de manière moins rigide qui se caractérise notamment par des faits d'intonation, par l'allongement des voyelles et par l'effacement des pronoms atones (cf. Orioles 1985; Scalco 1986).

7.4. Tandis que pour l'italien il existe une tradition grammaticale consolidée, soit descriptive, soit prescriptive, une grammaire prescriptive du frioulan n'existe pas, même si des descriptions grammaticales et d'autres instruments didactiques ne manquent pas (cf. 6.). La situation sur le plan lexical est meilleure (cf. Marcato 1989). Citons la publication du dictionnaire italien—frioulan de Nazzi en 1993 et aussi celle de dictionnaires frioulan—italien.

7.5. La production écrite en frioulan (très souvent dans un frioulan approximatif) est de caractère soit publiciste soit littéraire (il faut citer aussi une activité de traduction d'œuvres de la littérature mondiale en frioulan).

8. Etat des discussions

8.1. On remarque aujourd'hui une tendance à la «défrioulanisation» linguistique (face à quelques symptômes de «refrioulanisation» chez certaines élites politico-culturelles) et la présence d'un sens de «frioulanité» très vif chez les Frioulans. Il est évident que des interventions appropriées sont indispensables pour protéger le frioulan et pour en revigorer l'emploi fonctionnel (cf. Perini 1991). A ce but, une loi linguistique adéquate est absolument indispensable. Cependant les discussions nationales relatives aux langues minoritaires n'ont pas encore abouti à des résultats concrets. Cela est dû à la désinformation et aux préjugés stéréotypés qui affectent la notion de «minorité linguistique», ainsi qu'aux rapports tendus entre langue nationale et variétés linguistiques locales.

8.2. Il faudrait surtout mettre au point une norme pan-frioulane et en assurer l'enseignement scolaire pour rééquilibrer le rapport de prestige entre frioulan et italien. Des recherches relatives à ce sujet sont également urgentes.

8.3. Il faudrait aussi multiplier les recherches consacrées à la description des conditions linguistiques et sociolinguistiques du frioulan et approfondir l'étude de l'italien régional du Friuol, qui jusqu'à ce jour n'a été l'objet d'aucune analyse exhaustive.

9. Bibliographie (sélective)

Del Toso, Luciana (1978). «Un esempio della situazione sociolinguistica in Friuli: Mortegliano [Un exemple de la situation sociolinguistique au Frioul: Mortegliano]» In: *Studi Goriziani 48*, 33—49.

De Marchi, Bruna (1980): «La condizione linguistica del Friuli-Venezia Giulia: analisi degli aspetti teorico-metodologici e dei risultati di una ricerca [La condition linguistique du Frioul-Vénétie Julienne: analyse des aspects théoriques et méthodologiques et des résultats d'une recherche]». In: *Studi Goriziani 51—52*, 13—40.

Francescato, Giuseppe (1956): «Saggio statistico sul friulano a Udine [Essai statistique sur le frioulan d'Udine]». In: *Ce fastu? 32*, 39—59.

Francescato, Giuseppe (1966): *Dialettologia friulana* [Dialectologie frioulane], Udine.

Francescato, Giuseppe (1981): «Il friulano a Maniago: due «vitalità» a confronto [Le frioulan à Maniago: confrontation de deux vitalités]». In: *Maniago. Pieve, feudo, comune*, Maniago, 133—159.

Francescato, Giuseppe (1989): «Friaulisch: Soziolinguistik. Sociolinguistica». In: *Lexikon der Romanistischen Linguistik, III*, Holtus, G./Metzeltin, M./Schmitt, C. (Eds.), Tübingen, 601—610.

Francescato, Giuseppe (1991): *Nuovi studi linguistici sul friulano* [Nouvelles études linguistiques sur le frioulan], Udine.

Francescato, Giuseppe/Salimbeni, Fulvio (1976): *Storia, lingua e società in Friuli* [Histoire, langue et société au Frioul], Udine.

Frau, Giovanni (1984): *Friuli* [Frioul], Pise.

Marcato, Carla (1989): «Friaulisch: Grammatikographie und Lexikographie. Grammaticografia e lessicografia». In: *Lexikon der Romanistischen Linguistik, III*, Holtus, G./Metzeltin, M./Schmitt, C. (Eds.), Tübingen, 637—645.

Marchetti, Giuseppe (1952): *Elementi di grammatica friulana* [Eléments d'une grammaire frioulane], Udine.

Menis, Gian Carlo (1991): «Etnogenesi friulana: stato delle ricerche [Ethnogenèse frioulane: état de la recherche]». In: *Innovazione nella tradizione: Problemi e proposte delle comunità di lingua minoritaria*, Perini, N. (Ed.), Udine, 169—179.

Morgana, Silvia (1992): «Il Friuli-Venezia Giulia [Frioul-Vénétie Julienne]». In: *L'italiano nelle regioni*, Bruni, F. (Ed.), Turin, 282—315.

Nazzi, Gianni (1993): *Dizionario pratico italiano—friulano* [Dictionnaire pratique italien—frioulan], Udine.

Orioles, Vincenzo (1985): «L'interazione friulano—italiano [L'interaction frioulan—italien]». In: *Identità 13*, 108—115.

Perini, Nereo (1991): «Introduzione al dibattito: «Alle soglie del 2000 — continuità e mutamento nella identità friulana» [Introduction au débat: au seuil de l'an 2000: continuité et changement de l'identité frioulane]. In: *Innovazione e tradizione: Problemi e proposte delle comunità di lingua minoritaria*, Perini, N. (Ed.), Udine, 161−167.

Scalco, Laura (1986): «Lingua italiana nel Friuli: aspetti morfologici [La langue italienne au Frioul: aspects morphologiques]». In: *Ce fastu? 62*, 121−134.

Schiavi Fachin, Silvana (1991): «Bilinguismo scolastico in Friuli [Bilinguisme scolaire au Frioul]». In: *Innovazione e tradizione: Problemi e proposte delle comunità di lingua minoritaria*, Perini, N. (Ed.), Udine, 235−240.

Strassoldo, Raimondo (1986): «La tutela del friulano in provincia di Udine: una ricerca sociologica [La protection du frioulan dans la province d'Udine: une recherche sociologique]». In: *Ladinia 10*, 133−164.

Strassoldo, Raimondo (1991): «La lingua e i parlanti: alcune ricerche sociologiche sul caso friulano [La langue et les locuteurs: quelques recherches sociologiques sur le cas frioulan]». In: *Innovazione e tradizione: Problemi e proposte delle comunità di lingua minoritaria*, Perini, N. (Ed.), Udine, 187−197.

Vanelli, Laura (1991): «Friulano e italiano: aspetti contrastivi [Frioulan et italien: aspects contrastifs]». In: *Scuola, lingue e culture locali*, Perini, N. (Ed.), Codroipo, 227−240.

Carla Marcato, Udine (Italie)

159. Italien−occitan

1. Géographie et démographie
2. Histoire
3. Politique, économie, situations culturelle et religieuse
4. Statistiques et profils ethniques
5. Situation sociolinguistique
6. Etat de la politique linguistique
7. Portrait général des contacts linguistiques
8. Examen critique de la bibliographie
9. Bibliographie (sélective)

1. Géographie et démographie

Une vaste zone du Piémont, plus étendue que l'aire francoprovençale, mais moins peuplée, est actuellement de langue occitane. Elle comprend les vallées de Coni et de Saluces (Vermenagna, Gesso, Stura di Demonte, Grana, Maira, Varaita, Po), de Pignerol (Pellice, Germanasca, Chisone) et la haute vallée de Suse (au-dessus de Gravere). Il y a presque trente ans, on a découvert comme occitanes trois vallées au sud du Piémont (vallées du *kyé* = «je»: Pesio, Ellero, Corsaglia), fait qui démontre que la zone de l'occitan forme une nappe cohérente de l'ouest au sud-est. Il faut encore ajouter deux communes: Briga Alta (vallée du Tanaro) e Olivetta San Michele (province d'Impéria, Ligurie). Le territoire que l'on vient de définir comprend 78 communes avec une population comptant, il y a dix ans, environ 80 000 âmes dont ceux qui connaissent un patois occitan et sont encore en état de le parler ne constituent à peine que la moitié. La situation démographique est carrément négative, à cause d'un continuel flux migratoire vers la ville de Turin ou vers les petites villes des parties basses des vallées. Le mouvement inverse est pratiquement inexistant sur le plan statistique. Par contre, certaines vallées (p. e. la vallée de Suse) ont enregistré un fort accroissement de leur population dû au tourisme.

Outre les terres occitanes du Piémont, il existe encore une commune occitane en Calabre, Guardia Piemontese (province de Cosenza). Elle comptait, il y a dix ans, presque 500 habitants et 200 autres à Guardia Marina, parlant tous un patois occitan défini «guardiolo». Il s'agit de la seule commune vaudoise ayant survécu parmi les seize qui jadis existaient en Calabre (→ carte linguistique F).

2. Histoire

La zone occitane du Piémont forme un *continuum géographique* avec les territoires occitans transalpins même si, du point de vue politique, une partie dépendait du Duché de Savoie, une autre du Marquisat de Saluces, une autre encore du Dauphiné. Les variations du *statut politique* y ayant trait n'ont presque jamais altéré la couche occitane.

Quant à l'origine du patois de Guardia Piemontese, elle a été fort discutée: Morosi (1890−1892) considérait le Val Pellice comme lieu d'origine des Vaudois calabrais, tandis que Genre (1986), sans exclure le noyau originaire du Val Pellice, estime que le «guardiolo» est maintenant une langue composite, résultant de la fusion de colons des zones limitrophes, qui se réunirent à Guardia Piemontese après le massacre perpétré par l'Inquisition en 1561, et de groupes occitans transalpins réfugiés ensuite. Jusqu'à l'époque de la Réforme, la communauté vécut en toute tranquillité, fidèle à sa croyance religieuse et à ses moeurs traditionnelles, tâchant de ne pas révéler sa diversité à l'extérieur. Son isolement socioculturel fut favorisé par la position géographique presque inaccessible de Guardia.

3. Politique, économie, situations culturelle et religieuse

L'économie des zones occitanes reproduit fidèlement la situation géographique: au Piémont, il s'agit d'une économie de type agropastoral et, en Calabre, de type agricole et de pêche. Dans les deux domaines, la situation économique n'est pas prospère, surtout au Sud, à cause de la pénible condition de misère et d'isolement. En ce qui concerne la religion, il faut remarquer que le Val Pellice et les colonies calabraises pratiquent le culte vaudois, tandis que le reste professe la religion catholique. Au Synode de Chanforan (1532), les Vaudois piémontais décidèrent d'abandonner l'occitan en faveur de l'italien ou du français. Au siècle passé, en 1832, l'impression des textes bibliques en occitan ne fut pas bien accueillie par les pasteurs vaudois qui, habitués à l'emploi de l'italien ou du français dans un état de bilinguisme complet, considéraient le recours à l'occitan pour le culte peu convenable. Encore en 1931, les traductions en patois occitan ont été considérées comme indignes d'être utilisées à cause de la prétendue grossièreté de leur langue et du danger du ridicule. Cette attitude de refus se maintient jusqu'aux années récentes: en effet, en 1978 la traduction de l'Evangile de St-Marc réalisée par le linguiste Arturo Genre, en principe appréciée du point de vue linguistique, continue à susciter les réserves des pasteurs.

4. Statistiques et profils ethniques

Il est très difficile d'évaluer le nombre de locuteurs, car les données rapportées par les spécialistes sont très variables. Je citerai donc les chiffres présentés par ceux parmi les experts que je considère comme les plus sérieux. Tullio Telmon (1982) précise qu'en 1974, quand il réalisa une enquête pour le Bureau de la Présidence de la Chambre des Députés, le nombre des habitants était de 81 515, dont 56,57%, c'est-à-dire 46 115, parlaient encore occitan. Mais comme, dans ces vallées, la population active diminue tous les dix ans de plus de 20%, il faut réduire de beaucoup les données statistiques de 1974, si l'on veut aboutir à une estimation fiable des locuteurs encore occitanophones en 1995. En tout cas, il faudrait distinguer entre les locuteurs actifs et passifs, opération presque impossible.

Pour ce qui est de la communauté calabraise, en 1992 Arturo Genre comptait à Guardia 449 habitants dont 76%, c'est-à-dire 341, étaient occitanophones (locuteurs actifs) et 24%, c'est-à-dire 108, locuteurs passifs. A Guardia Marina, les occitanophones étaient au nombre de 50.

5. Situation sociolinguistique

Il faut remarquer que dans les vallées occitanes du Piémont les principales caractéristiques sociolinguistiques ne se présentent pas partout de la même manière: dans la plupart des cas, on peut constater l'existence de trois langues ou codes: occitan, italien et piémontais dans un état de bilinguisme avec diglossie. Mais pour certaines vallées (Pellice, Germanasca et une partie de la vallée du Cluson (Chisone) et de Suse), un quatrième code est présent, le français, mais sans diglossie. La variabilité diatopique du code occitan est considérable tant sur le plan de la phonétique que de la morphosyntaxe et du lexique. Les locuteurs sont en général très attentifs à ces variations diatopiques, peut-être plus qu'aux caractères communs. Il n'existe pas de koiné alpino-occitane qui unisse les patoisants occitans, bien qu'ils soient parfaitement conscients de représenter un groupe linguistique particulier par rapport à l'italien et plus encore aux dialectes piémontais. Il faut ajouter que le piémontais employé par les Occitans est de type standard, ainsi que l'italien, et est exempt de particularités locales susceptibles de dénoncer l'allophonie de ses locuteurs. Les questions posées par les enquêteurs aux patoisants ont démontré que la plupart d'entre eux considèrent leur propre patois comme le code le plus employé dans le village et comme le plus apparenté au provençal de France (= occitan de Provence), ensuite au piémontais ou au français, jamais à l'italien. A l'intérieur de la famille, on remarque, même si les parents sont tous les deux patoisants, la tendance à employer l'italien liée à la conscience d'appartenir à la nation italienne ou à la conviction que ce fait faciliterait la formation scolaire des enfants. C'est pourquoi les jeunes ne connaissent souvent que de façon passive le patois qu'ils entendent parler par les parents ou par les grands-parents entre eux. Actuellement on n'a pas encore établi une graphie commune qui puisse satisfaire les exigences de tous les occitanophones, malgré les efforts des mouvements culturels ou politiques pourtant très actifs.

La situation sociolinguistique de Guardia apparaît comme tout à fait particulière. Le « guardiolo » ne s'est jamais trouvé dans une position concurrentielle avec d'autres langues. Il s'est conservé grâce au fait d'être un code complètement atypique, avec très peu de rapports avec l'italien. L'interdiction des autorités ecclésiastiques d'employer l'occitan n'a pu que fortifier le « guardiolo », au point que la personne non occitane qui entrait dans une famille occitane se voyait obligée d'apprendre le nouveau code. L'isolement a donc constitué un moyen de conservation et de défense contre toute innovation, au moins jusqu'à la deuxième Guerre Mondiale. Pour le moment, malgré la forte pression exercée par les dialectes calabrais et surtout par l'italien, Guardia est encore une île occitane très vivante.

6. Etat de la politique linguistique

Jusqu'à présent, l'on doit constater que la politique de l'Etat italien n'a pas beaucoup fait pour la conservation des patrimoines linguistiques locaux. Ceci vaut également pour l'occitan. Les minorités occitanes en Italie ne jouissent d'aucun traitement de faveur, sauf les libertés indiquées dans les articles 3 et 8 de la Constitution italienne de 1947. L'article 6 qui prévoit expressément des mesures de sauvegarde pour les minorités, n'a apporté aucune prérogative aux communautés occitanes. En plus, si l'on considère l'article 9 qui impose aux organismes intéressés d'encourager le développement de la culture et de défendre le patrimoine historique et artistique (et on ne peut nier que la langue fait partie du patrimoine culturel), l'on constate qu'il a été bien souvent violé. Après deux lois régionales pour la sauvegarde du patrimoine linguistique et culturel du Piémont, du 20.6.1979 et du 15.11.1982, on est arrivé, avec la loi du 10.4.1990 (qui remplace les précédentes), à une réglementation pour la « sauvegarde, valorisation et promotion de la connaissance du patrimoine linguistique original du Piémont », dont les articles 3, 4, 5, 6 et 8 se réfèrent à la conservation des langues minoritaires. La structure scolaire en Italie vise généralement à réprimer le plus possible l'emploi du patois, et à favoriser l'usage de l'italien, la seule langue universellement acceptée. Il y a des exceptions là où l'instituteur ou le professeur possède le même code minoritaire que les élèves et là où les élèves sont dans une situation linguistique homogène. Mais dans la majorité des cas, l'occitan se limite à la vie familiale ou aux jeux. Telmon (1982) a observé qu'il y a trois phases dans la vie des patoisants dans lesquelles l'emploi du patois se fait plus fort: (1) entre 8 et 14 ans, phase des jeux, où le patois est librement utilisé; (2) après 16 ans, phase de groupe, où le patois devient souvent une sorte de marqueur pour pouvoir s'insérer dans la société des adultes; (3) période du service militaire, où les soldats provenant de la même localité emploient le patois comme langue secrète. Signalons le fait bien documenté que l'école semble nuire à la survivance du patois, et plus particulièrement au milieu culturel dans lequel le patois vit: ceci arrive par la transmission de la civilisation italienne entendue comme civilisation monolithique, qui s'accorde mal avec la situation complexe et multiculturelle des personnes de religion vaudoise. L'italien prédomine solidement et l'occitan est donc en danger de disparition, menacé de plus en plus par d'autres codes. Dans les années 60, la prise de conscience de posséder un patrimoine important du point de vue culturel a provoqué chez les locuteurs une reprise spontanée dont le premier fruit fut la création de deux associations: *L'Escolo dóu Po,* créée le 14 août 1961, et peu après du *Coumboscuro* avec son journal homonyme. Depuis 1968 d'autres associations sont nées, parfois avec un but politique clairement marqué ou dans un esprit d'opposition régionaliste.

7. Portrait général des contacts linguistiques

7.1. Traits caractéristiques de l'occitan piémontais

On ne peut indiquer que très sommairement les phénomènes linguistiques qui opposent l'occitan à l'italien et au piémontais, étant donné la grande variabilité des différents patois. Ces phénomènes relient d'ailleurs l'occitan du Piémont à celui de France. Sous l'aspect phonétique on remarquera:

– la diphtongaison de *o* accentué libre et entravé:
fuék (*fŏcus*), puérk (*pŏrcus*), fuéio (*fŏlia*), nuéč (*nŏx*)
– le passage de *-a* atone finale à *-o*:
térro (*tĕrra*), fénno (*femina*), kužíno (**cŏcína*), vən démo (*vindemia*)
– la conservation de *-au-* primaire, tonique ou non:
áuro (*aurum*), ráuć (*raucus*), ərpáus (*riposare*)
– la palatalisation de *ca-* et *ga-*:
ćábro (*capra*), ćamp (*campus*), ćat (*cattus*), ǵál (*gallus*),
contre-carrée souvent par la conservation de la vélaire ou d'autres issues sous l'influence du piémontais;
– la sonorisation de *-p-* intervocalique:
abéịo (*apĭcula*), abríl (*aprilis*), cubérto (**cooperta*)
– l'évolution palatale du nexus *-tr-* > ir:
páire (*patre*), réire (*retro*), péiro (*petra*)
– la conservation des groupes consonantiques *pl* et *bl*:
plúmo (*pluma*), blánk (*blancus*), plátto (*plattus*), blá (*blaw*)

Les traits suivants opposent occitan à l'italien, mais non pas au piémontais:

– la conservation de *au* secondaire:
auzár (**ausare*)
– le passage de *ct* > ć:
dréć (**dirictus*), laćúo (*lactuca*), fáćo (*factus*).

Pour ce qui est de la morphologie, l'*s* morphématique du pluriel apparaît seulement lorsque le mot est suivi d'une voyelle:

laz érba (sg. *l'érbo*/*e*), *la fénna* (sg. *la fénno*/*e*), *louz aráires* (sg. *l'aráire*), *lou líbre* (sg. *lou líbre*).

Dans la conjugaison verbale le morphème *-en* de la première personne du pluriel de l'indicatif s'oppose à *-iámo* de l'italien comme à *-úma* du piémontais. Citons encore la survivance éphémère de *habueram* et *fueram* avec des fonctions différentes de celles du latin classique. Parmis les particularités lexicales, qui sont nombreuses, on trouve les formes suivantes:

ambúrsá 'fraise', *trúfas* 'pommes de terre', *sęba* 'oignon', *kịavél* 'clou', *alümęto* 'allumette', *dəịo* 'faux', *santána* 'juillet', *blię* 'février', *tzalénda* 'noël', *nęsá* 'nièce', *nébịa* 'nuage'

7.2. Traits caractéristiques de l'occitan calabrais

A Guardia, la situation phonétique est plus compliquée à cause de l'interférence avec des phonèmes calabrais qui ont pénétré dans l'occitan:

– la finale *-ə*:
rítə (*rēte*)
– la diphtongue ye < *ĕ*/*ŏ*:
prýest (*praesbyter*), fýekə (*fŏcus*), pýett (*pĕctus*), pịérk (*pŏrcus*)
– la ḍ vélaire < *-ll-*, *-tl-*:
kaváḍḍə (*caballus*), spáḍḍə (*spatula*), aḍḍórə (*ad illam horam*)

Dans la morphologie on remarque la survivance du parfait périphrastique *vado* + *infinitif* (vo annárə) désormais disparu dans l'occitan du Piémont.

La position de l'adjectif, placé après le substantif, dénonce l'influence calabraise.

Pour le lexique citons:

arribiná 'labourer pour la deuxième fois', *júkku* 'juchoir', *maịúrsula* 'fraise', *múttə*/*mút* 'motte de terre', *vrizá* 'briser', *alivíncu* 'aubier', *tóra* 'chenille', *ścrirúolu* 'écureuil', *bárbə* 'oncle', *avúnt* 'où', *tuttavịə* 'toujours'.

8. Examen critique de la bibliographie

8.1. Instruments de recherche

Il y a quelques dictionnaires et grammaires dédiés à l'une ou à l'autre des variétés patoisantes occitanes: outre le volume de Pons (1973), il vaut la peine de signaler les œuvres de Bruna Rosso (1973), Vignetta (1981), Perron (1984), Baccon Bouvet (1987), Bologna (1991), Massajoli/Moriani (1991).

Le monde occitan piémontais fut l'objet de recherches approfondies depuis le début du siècle (Merlo 1901), tandis que des études dédiées à des microsystèmes avaient été conduites déjà bien avant la fin du siècle passé, si l'on songe à l'œuvre consacrée au vaudois de Calabre par G. Vegezzi Ruscalla en 1862. L'ALF en 1902 avait compris parmi ses enquêtes trois localités occitanes du Piémont: Oulx (972), Maïsette di Perrero (982), Bobbio Pellice (992). L'AIS avait réalisé en 1928 huit enquêtes: Rochemolles Bardonecchia (140),

Sauze di Cesana (150), Pramollo (152), Pontechianale (160), Ostana (161), Pietraporzio (170), Valdieri (181), Limone Piemonte (182). Il faut encore ajouter Giaglione (84) dans l'ALJA e La Brigue (76) de l'ALP. Ugo Pellis avait accompli pour l'ALI une dizaine d'enquêtes: Ruà di Pragelato (46), Ghigo di Praly (47), Serre d'Angrogna (55), Bertines di Casteldelfino (62), Gilba di Brossasco (63), Villar d'Acceglio (72), Pietraporzio e Bersezio dell'Argentera (78), Perdioni di Demonte (79), Vernante (87), Briga Marittima (94). L'Université de Turin possède les enquêtes suivantes de la CDI (Carta dei dialetti italiani): Bardonecchia (T022), Les Arnauds di Bardonecchia (T022/1), Melezet di Bardonecchia (T022/2), Millaures di Bardonecchia (T022/3), Rochemolles di Bardonecchia (T022/4), Bousson di Cesana (T074/1), Savoulx di Oulx (T075/3), Chiomonte (T080), Ramat di Chiomonte (T080/1), Exilles (T0100), Inverso Pinasca (T0122/1), Perosa Argentina (T0124), Dubbione di Pinasca (T0190/1), Eclause di Salbertand (T0232/1), San Germano Chisone (T0242), San Secondo di Pinerolo (T0254), Sestriere (T0263), Villar Perosa (T0307). L'entreprise la plus importante qui donnera les meilleurs fruits est sans doute l'ALEPO (Atlante linguistico ed etnografico del Piemonte occidentale), né de la collaboration entre la Région du Piémont et le Dipartimento di Scienze del Linguaggio de l'Université de Turin. L'ALEPO fut conçu dans les années 80 et est actuellement en cours d'exécution. Les principales zones d'enquête du secteur occitan, du nord au sud, sont les suivantes: Val di Susa, Bardonecchia (Millaures), Chiomonte; Val Chisone, Pramollo, Sestriere (Borgata); Val Germanasca, Perrero (San Martino); Val Pellice, Villar Pellice; Val Po, Oncino; Val Varaita, Bellino, Sampeyre; Val Maira, Canosio, Cartignano; Val Grana, Monterosso Grana (Santo Lucio di Coumboscuro); Valle Stura di Demonte, Argentera (Bersezio), Aisone; Val Gesso, Entraque; Val Vermenagna, Limone (Limonetto); Val Pesio, Chiusa Pesio; Val d'Ellero, Frabosa Soprana (Fontane); Valle Tanaro, Briga Alta (Upega). On prévoit même une enquête à Guardia (P. 760 de l'AIS). Le questionnaire de l'ALEPO comprend 7000 questions et a été conçu explicitement pour un milieu alpin. En ce moment, à la fin des 42 enquêtes principales (qui s'occupent naturellement aussi du francoprovençal), on dispose d'environ 300 000 réponses dialectales, sans parler du matériel ethnographique (dessins et photos). Un répertoire bibliographique relatif à l'occitan alpin est en chantier.

8.2. Conclusion

Grassi (1993) a cité trois raisons qui, à son avis, ont causé un certain retard dans l'individuation et le traitement scientifique des patois occitans: (1) l'absence d'études d'ensemble comparables à celles effectuées pour le ladin ou le francoprovençal; (2) l'utilisation de données occasionnelles et assez divergentes entre elles pour les descriptions; (3) l'importance exagérée attribuée au seul vaudois qui s'explique par la présence d'une littérature religieuse considérable.

Grassi a aussi relevé certaines erreurs dans les travaux dialectologiques de Morosi (1890−1892), tout en lui accordant le mérite d'avoir reconnu, à l'intérieur du système occitan, la pénétration du piémontais. Morosi avait également mis au point la différence de l'occitan des deux versants des Alpes. Grassi a précisé que hors du Piémont les patois vivent dans un rapport de diglossie avec la langue nationale, tandis qu'au Piémont, les Occitans connaissent et pratiquent le piémontais sans que l'on puisse exactement définir cette situation comme relevant de la diglossie ou du bilinguisme. Une prise de conscience plus lucide eut lieu dans les œuvres de Jaberg (1919) et de Terracini (1922) qui tentèrent d'examiner les voies et les effets de la pénétration du piémontais et la résistance de l'occitan au milieu d'un contexte sociolinguistique pluridimensionnel. On a pu observer une sorte d'homogénéité (toute relative d'ailleurs) dans les patois occitans du Piémont qui va du nord au sud alors que les vallées ont une direction géophysique de l'ouest à l'est. Il semble que cette cohérence soit due aux passages alpins qui les unissent à leur hinterland provençal. Pour ce qui est de la pénétration du piémontais, on en a distingué deux types: l'un, rustique, s'est lentement emparé de la partie basse des vallées par simple contact linguistique; l'autre, plus urbain, s'est installé dans les localités principales pour des motifs commerciaux et touristiques.

9. Bibliographie (sélective)

AIS: Jaberg, Karl/Jud, Jakob (1928−1940): *Sprach- und Sachatlas Italiens und der Südschweiz*, Zofingen, 8 vol.

ALI: *Atlante Linguistico Italiano*, en rédaction auprès de l'Université de Turin, Institut de l'ALI.

ALJA: Martin, Jean Baptiste/Tuaillon, Gaston (1972−1982): *Atlas linguistique et ethnographique du Jura et des Alpes du Nord (Francoprovençal Central)*, Paris, 4 vol.

ALP: Bouvier, Jean Claude/Martel, Claude (1975−1986). *Atlas linguistique et ethnographique de la Provence*, Paris, 3 vol.

Baccon Bouvet, Clelia (1987): *A l'umbra du cluchí Salbertand. Patuà e vita locale attraverso i tempi*, Turin.

Bert, Paul (1907): *Le patois de la haute Vallée du Cluson. Essai de philologie romane*, Mortara.

Bologna, Piero (1991): *Dizionario della lingua brigasca*, Rome.

Bruna Rosso, Pietro A. (1973): *Piccolo dizionario del dialetto occitano di Elva*, Coni (Cuneo).

CDI: Carta dei Dialetti Italiani, matériaux recueillis dans les Archives du l'Université de Turin, copie des fascicules conservés à l'Université de Turin, Institut de l'ALI.

Clivio, Gianrenzo/Gasca Queirazza, Giuliano (Eds.) (1978): *Lingue e dialetti nell'arco alpino occidentale. Atti del Convegno Internazionale di Torino (12−14 aprile 1976)*, Turin.

Ettmayer, Karl (1905): «Die provenzalische Mundart von Vinadio». In: *Bausteine zur romanischen Philologie. Festgabe für A. Mussafia*, Halle, 211−223.

Genre, Arturo (1986): «A proposito degli studi sulla parlata e l'origine dei calabro-valdesi». In: *Bollettino dell'Atlante Linguistico Italiano 8−10*, 5−25.

Grassi, Corrado (1969): «'parla du kyé': un'isola linguistica provenzale nelle valli monregalesi». In: *Protimesis. Scritti in onore di V. Pisani*, Lecce, 129−138.

Grassi, Corrado (1993): «Bilancio degli studi e delle ricerche torinesi sulle parlate occitaniche cisalpine moderne». In: *Atti del Secondo Congresso Internazionale dell'AEIO (Association Internationale des Etudes Occitanes), Turin, 31/8−5/9 1987*, Gasca Queirazza, Giuliano (Ed.), Turin, 1015−1033.

Greco, Anna R. (1993): «Aspetti fonetici e morfosintattici della parlata guardiola». In: *Atti del Secondo Congresso Internazionale dell'AEIO (Association Internationale des Etudes Occitanes), Turin, 31/8−5/9 1987*, Gasca Queirazza, Giuliano (Ed.), Turin, 721−724.

Griset, Ilia (1966): *La parlata provenzaleggiante di Inverso Pinasca (Torino) e la penetrazione del piemontese in Val Perosa e in Val San Martino*, Turin.

Hirsch, Ernst (1978): *Provenzalische Mundarttexte aus Piemont*, Tübingen.

Jaberg, Karl (1919): «Notes sur l's final libre dans les patois provençaux et francoprovençaux du Piémont». In: *Bulletin du Glossaire des Patois de la Suisse Romande 10*, 1−31.

Massajoli, Pierleone/Moriani, Roberto (1991): *Dizionario della cultura brigasca − Disiunari da cultura brigasca, I. Lessico*, Alessandria.

Morosi, Giuseppe (1890−1892): «L'odierno linguaggio dei Valdesi del Piemonte». In: *Archivio Glottologico Italiano 11*, 309−415.

Perron, Piero (1984): *Sul ban d'la chapelle. Grammatica del patois de Jouvençaux*, Bra.

Pons, Teofilo (1973): *Dizionario del dialetto valdese della Val Germanasca*, Torre Pellice.

Salvioni, Carlo (1907): «Il dialetto provenzaleggiante de Roaschia (Cuneo)». In: *Mélanges Chabaneau*, 525−539.

Talmon, Alberto (1922): «Saggio sul dialetto di Pragelato». In: *Archivio Glottologico Italiano 18*, 1−104.

Telmon, Tullio (1974): *Microsistemi linguistici in contatto in Val di Susa: l'articolo determinativo*, Pise.

Telmon, Tullio (1982): «La minoranza di parlata provenzale». In: *Sociologia della comunicazione 1*, 17−32.

Telmon, Tullio (1993): «La variété des parlers provençaux à l'est des Alpes d'après quelques données de l'ALEPO». In: *Atti del Secondo Congresso Internazionale dell'AEIO (Association Internationale des Etudes Occitanes), Turin, 31/8−5/9 1987*, Gasca Queirazza, Giuliano (Ed.), Turin, 979−1003.

Terracini, Benvenuto (1922): «La varietà nel parlare di Usseglio». In: *Archivio Glottologico Italiano 18*, 105−186.

Vegezzi Ruscalla, Giovenale (1862): «Colonia piemontese in Calabria». In: *Rivista Contemporanea 31*, 161−193.

Vignetta, Andrea (1981): *Patuà. Grammatica del dialetto provenzale alpino della media Alta Val Chisone*, Pignerol (Pinerolo).

Anna Cornagliotti, Turin (Italie)

160. Italienisch—Deutsch

1. Geographie und Demographie
2. Territorialgeschichte und Regionsbildung
3. Politik, Wirtschaft sowie kulturelle und religiöse Situation
4. Ethnoprofil
5. Soziolinguistische Situation
6. Sprachpolitische Situation
7. Die Kontaktsprachen
8. Bibliographie (in Auswahl)

1. Geographie und Demographie

Ein enger Kontakt zwischen Deutsch und Italienisch als Muttersprachen besteht in den südlichen Teilen Südtirols seit Jahrhunderten, in ganz Südtirol seit dem Jahr 1919, als Südtirol von Italien annektiert wurde.

Südtirol liegt an der Südseite der Zentralalpen, ist 7.400 km² groß und hat 438.269 Einwohner (Volkszählung 1991). Südtirol ist ein Teil des historischen Tirol und gehörte bis 1919 zu Österreich. Politisch ist Südtirol eine italienische Provinz mit Sonderstatut. Die offizielle Bezeichnung lautet: Autonome Provinz Bozen/Südtirol — Provincia Autonoma di Bolzano/Alto Adige; → Sprachenkarte F.

2. Territorialgeschichte und Regionsbildung

Als Grenzgebiet hat Südtirol eine wechselvolle Geschichte hinter sich. Die Römer eroberten das Gebiet 15 v. Chr. und romanisierten die ursprünglich „rätische" Bevölkerung. Nach dem Niedergang Westroms (476) drangen germanische Stämme in das Gebiet ein, vor allem die Bayern vom Norden her, und das Gebiet wurde nach und nach eingedeutscht.

Mit dem Friedensvertrag von Saint Germain (1919) wurde das historische Tirol zerschlagen, der nördliche und östliche Teil Tirols blieben bei Österreich, Südtirol wurde von Italien annektiert. Der Faschismus (1922—1943) versuchte, durch Entnationalisierung der Südtiroler (Verbot der deutschen Sprache, Verbot deutscher Schulen und Ortsnamen, Auflösung der deutschen Vereine usw.), durch Massenansiedlung von Italienern (besonders in der Industriezone von Bozen) und Aussiedlung der Südtiroler (als Folge des 1939 geschlossenen Abkommens zwischen Hitler und Mussolini, mit der sogenannten „Option") das Südtirolproblem zu lösen.

Im Pariser Vertrag (1946/47) verpflichtete sich Italien gegenüber Österreich, durch besondere Maßnahmen die Erhaltung des Volkscharakters sowie die wirtschaftliche und kulturelle Entwicklung der deutschen Sprachgruppe zu gewährleisten. Dieser besondere Schutz hat seinen Niederschlag im Autonomiestatut von 1948 und in dessen Neufassung von 1972 gefunden.

3. Politik, Wirtschaft sowie kulturelle und religiöse Situation

3.1. Bei den italienischen Volkszählungen, die im Abstand von zehn Jahren durchgeführt werden, wird in Südtirol auch die *Sprachgruppenzugehörigkeit* erhoben (Tabelle 160.1).

Tab. 160.1: Stärke der drei Sprachgruppen in Südtirol 1991 (Astat 1992)

	Absolut	%
Italiener	116.914	27,65
Deutsche	287.503	67,99
Ladiner	18.434	4,36
Insgesamt	422.851	100,00

Im Jahre 1910 hatte der Anteil der Deutschen 92,2%, der Italiener 3,0%, der Ladiner 4,0% betragen (Südtirol-Handbuch 1987, 178). Die während des Faschismus bewirkte Veränderung der Bevölkerungsstruktur geschah vor allem durch Zuwanderung von Italienern in die öffentliche Verwaltung und in die Industrie.

3.2. Da Südtirol im Rahmen des italienischen Staates eine autonome Provinz ist, in der die deutschsprachige Bevölkerung die Mehrheit bildet, hat die deutschsprachige Bevölkerung die Möglichkeit, viele Entscheidungen in Wirtschaft, Politik und Kultur in Absprache mit der italienischen und ladinischen Sprachgruppe selbständig zu entscheiden. Südtirol ist aber nicht nur durch die Autonomie geschützt, es hat auch als Schutzmacht Österreich, das infolge des Pariser Vertrags legitimerweise die Interessen der deutschen Minderheit in den internationalen Beziehungen vertreten kann. Dieser Funktion als Schutzmacht ist Österreich vor allem ab 1960 bei den Verhandlungen der Südtiroler Frage vor der UNO und bei den Verhandlungen über das neue Autonomiestatut vom Jahr 1972 nachgekommen.

3.3. Die deutsche Sprachgruppe ist in der Lage, ein eigenständiges kulturelles Leben zu führen. Sie hat eine Vielzahl von Verbänden und Vereinen mit sozialer und bildungspolitischer Bedeutung. Es besteht ein großes Angebot an Presseerzeugnissen aus dem In- und Ausland, eigene Radio- und Fernsehsendungen werden vom Sender Bozen ausgestrahlt. Als wichtigster Faktor der Kultur- und Sprachbewahrung wird die Schule angesehen (siehe 6.2.).

3.4. Die deutschsprachige Bevölkerung Südtirols gehört (wie übrigens auch die übrigen Bevölkerungsanteile) fast vollständig der katholischen Kirche an. Während des Faschismus war die katholische Kirche eine der stärksten Stützen der deutschen Minderheit; heute geht ihr Bemühen vor allem dahin, das friedliche Zusammenleben der Sprachgruppen zu fördern. Außer der katholischen Kirche gibt es kleine evangelische Gemeinden in Bozen und Meran und eine kleine israelitische Kultusgemeinde in Meran.

3.5. Die Stärke der deutschen Minderheit in Südtirol kommt sicher auch daher, daß sie politisch mit einer einzigen Stimme spricht. Seit dem Zweiten Weltkrieg hat die christlichdemokratisch orientierte „Südtiroler Volkspartei" bei allen politischen Wahlen den überwiegenden Anteil der Stimmen der deutschsprachigen Südtiroler erhalten.

4. Ethnoprofil

Das Ethnoprofil der deutschen Sprachgruppe wird geprägt durch das Autonomiestatut (siehe 6.), durch die demographische Stärke (siehe 3.1.) sowie durch die Siedlungsform.

4.1. Alle drei Sprachgruppen in Südtirol, die deutsche, die italienische und die ladinische, werden durch die Autonomie gefördert. Im Alltagsgespräch nennen sich die Angehörigen der Sprachgruppen „Deutsche", „Italiener" und „Ladiner". Die deutschen Südtiroler nennen ihre Sprache „Deutsch" und machen gewöhnlich keinen Unterschied, ob sie damit die Hochsprache oder die Mundart meinen.

4.2. Die in Südtirol ansässigen italienischen Staatsbürger sind gehalten, bei der Volkszählung ihre *Sprachgruppenzugehörigkeit* zu erklären. Diese Erklärung bildet die Grundlage für die Anwendung der Proporzbestimmungen bei der Aufnahme in den öffentlichen Dienst und für den sozialen Wohnungsbau (siehe 6.1.).

Infolge der Proporzbestimmungen wird der Bevölkerungsentwicklung in Südtirol besondere Aufmerksamkeit geschenkt. Von einer gewissen Bedeutung für die Entwicklung des Sprachgruppenverhältnisses in Südtirol sind die sprachlich gemischten Ehen. Die Volkszählung von 1981 zeigte, daß bei 6,9% der Familien in Südtirol ein Ehepartner der deutschen, der andere der italienischen Sprachgruppe angehört (Egger 1985, 21).

4.3. Zum Kontakt zwischen den Sprachgruppen und zur Verbreitung der Zweisprachigkeit trägt auch die Siedlungsform bei. Nur die Ladiner wohnen in einem sprachlich homogenen Gebiet. Vereinfachend könnte man sagen, daß die deutsche Sprachgruppe im städtischen und ländlichen Bereich, die italienische Sprachgruppe vorwiegend im städtischen Bereich lebt. Die Städte und viele größere Orte sind dadurch zweisprachig.

5. Soziolinguistische Situation

Im allgemeinen ist die sprachliche Situation Südtirols gekennzeichnet durch Diglossie und Mehrsprachigkeit.

5.1. Domänen des Sprachgebrauchs

Für die sozio-linguistischen Gesamtbeschreibungen der Sprachsituation in Südtirol wurde vor allem die Domänenanalyse verwendet. Es gibt eine ganze Reihe von diesbezüglichen Überblicksdarstellungen (Francescato 1975, Egger 1977, Gubert 1978, Eisermann 1981, Kramer 1981, Astat 1986, Gubert/Egger 1990). Insgesamt geben diese Analysen ein eher positives Bild der Entwicklung der Sprachgruppen in Südtirol, im Unterschied etwa zu den vor allem politisch begründeten Klagen über die schwierige Position von Minderheiten.

Zudem gibt es zu allen speziellen Domänen, die man seit Fishman gewöhnlich in fünf große Bereiche zusammenfaßt, auch zur Südtiroler Sprachsituation Untersuchungen: Zweisprachige Familien (Egger 1985 und Weber Egli 1992), frühe Zweisprachigkeit (L'apprendimento precoce 1983), Nachbarschaft, Bekannte, Freunde (Buson 1992), Kirche (Capraro 1991), Schule (Deutsches Schulamt 1992), Sprache im öffentlichen Dienst (SVP-Fraktion 1987).

Insgesamt kann festgestellt werden, daß die deutsche Sprache in den letzten vierzig Jahren viele Bereiche zurückgewonnen hat. Es gibt nun kaum einen Bereich des öffentlichen Lebens (wenigstens der Rechtslage nach), in dem nicht auch das Deutsche verwendet werden kann; es gibt eine Reihe von Domänen, in denen auch die Italiener Deutschkenntnisse besitzen müssen. Freilich werden einige Domänen, vor allem Politik und öffentliche Verwaltung, weil viele Italiener nicht zweisprachig sind, auf einige Jahre hinaus noch von Zweisprachigkeit gekennzeichnet sein (Egger 1990, 85).

5.2. Kenntnis der Zweitsprache

Der Zweitsprachunterricht in den Schulen, der Kontakt zwischen Deutschen und Italienern durch die Siedlungsstruktur, der Kontakt am Arbeitsplatz und die Medien in verschiedenen Sprachen tragen zur Kenntnis der Zweitsprache bei. Wer in den öffentlichen Dienst eintreten will, muß den Nachweis von Zweitsprachkenntnissen erbringen. Die Ergebnisse der Zweisprachigkeitsprüfungen zeigen, daß die Ladiner am stärksten mehrsprachig sind, gefolgt von den Deutschsprachigen; die Italiener haben den geringsten Grad an Zweisprachigkeit. 90% der Deutschen, 67% der Italiener und fast alle Ladiner sagen, daß sie Deutsch und Italienisch sprechen bzw. verstehen (Buson 1992, 103). Freilich reduziert sich die Anzahl der Zweisprachigen, wenn es darum geht, problemlos ein Gespräch in der anderen Sprache zu führen. Dies können 15% der Italiener und 36% der deutschsprachigen Südtiroler; die Hälfte der Ladiner hingegen kann ein Gespräch sowohl auf Deutsch als auch auf Italienisch führen, sie sind also dreisprachig (Astat 1986, 145).

5.3. Die deutschen Sprachinseln in Italien

Die deutschen Sprachinseln in Italien befinden sich am Südrand der Alpen. Es handelt sich um relativ kleine Sprach- und Siedlungsgemeinschaften in einem anderssprachigen größeren Gebiet.

5.3.1. Soziolinguistische Situation

Zusammenfassend sollen einige Merkmale genannt werden, die auf alle deutschen Sprachinseln in Italien zutreffen.

Fast alle Sprachinseln sind im 12. und 13. Jahrhundert als Folge von Wanderbewegungen entstanden.

Es handelt sich heute um relativ kleine Gruppen: Walser 1100 Sprecher (Fazzini Giovannucci 1978, 8−29); Pladen (Sappada) 1000−1500 (Hornung 1986, 13); Zahre (Sauris) 250 (Hornung 1986, 15); Fersental (Val dei Mòcheni) 950 (Gubert 1990, 279); Lusern (Luserna) 550 (Hornung 1986, 8); 7 und 13 Gemeinden: Roana (Rovan) und Giazza (Ljetzan) 5−50 (Hornung 1986, 9); Kanaltal (Val Canale) 850 (Steinicke 1984, 102); Tischelwang (Timau) 600 (Hornung 1986, 17).

Sprachverschiebung und eventuell Sprachtod hängen mit der sozialen und rechtlichen Lage von Minderheiten zusammen. Die Erschließung der Täler, die wirtschaftlichen Veränderungen, der Tourismus, die Abwanderung von Arbeitskräften und der Zuzug von italienischen Familien, die Medien und die Schule förderten zunächst die Zwei- und Mehrsprachigkeit und führten dazu, daß das Italienische immer größere Bedeutung gewann. Abgesehen von den Bestimmungen für Südtirol, Aosta und die Slowenen fehlt in Italien ein Minderheitenrecht für die kleineren Sprachminderheiten, obwohl es auf lokaler Ebene einzelne Bestimmungen dazu gibt.

Hinsichtlich der Sprachdomänen in diesen Sprachinseln gilt: Die deutsche Mundart wird in der Familie erlernt und gesprochen; Schulsprache ist das Italienische. In mehreren dieser Sprachinseln wird zudem noch ein italienischer Dialekt gesprochen. Die Erhaltung der deutschen Sprache und ihr Nutzen wird nun auch in einem größeren Zusammenhang gesehen, und zwar als Beitrag zu einem vielsprachigen Europa. Der Deutschunterricht in der Schule, der Kontakt mit dem deutschen Sprachraum und die Tätigkeit der Kulturinstitute tragen dem Rechnung.

5.3.2. Das Interesse der Sprachforscher

Die Bedeutung dieser Sprachinselmundarten für die Sprachwissenschaft liegt in der Altertümlichkeit der Sprache, die Rückschlüsse auf den binnendeutschen Sprachstand zur Zeit der Aussiedlung erlaubt; in der Sonderentwicklung der Sprache aufgrund des Sprachkontakts und der Interferenzen; in der Verarmung der Sprache aufgrund der Isolation (Hornung 1965, 278, 285−287; Hornung 1988). Charakteristika dieser Mundarten sind die Archaismen, die der Muttermundart ähnlichen autochthonen Entwicklungen, die Eigenentwicklungen und die Beeinflussung durch das Italienische (Matzel 1989, 79−83).

5.3.3. Sprachverfall/Sprachtod

„Der Tod einer Sprache (...) bleibt in seinem Verlauf und in den Konstellationen, die ihn bedingen, immer ein einmaliger Akt" (Matzel 1989, 85). In der Forschung werden viele Merkmale der sprachlichen Desintegration beschrieben. Diese betreffen „sowohl den Strukturverfall des sprachlichen Systems, der nicht mehr kompensiert wird, als auch die Funktionseinschränkung der Sprache im sozialen Bereich und nicht zuletzt den Normenverlust bei den Sprechern" (Rindler Schjerve 1989, 12). Wer sich mit kleinen Minderheitensprachen beschäftigt, die Anzeichen von Desintegration zeigen, scheint eine gewisse Scheu davor zu verspüren, vom Sprach*tod* zu sprechen. Viele Forscher und Forscherinnen, die sich mit den deutschen Minderheiten in Italien befassen, haben ein ausgesprochenes Interesse, diese Sprachen zu bewahren.

5.3.4. Die Walsersiedlungen

Die Walsersiedlungen liegen im Nordwesten Italiens, in der Region Aosta und in der Provinz Novara. Sie entstanden am Anfang des 13. Jahrhunderts. Die Herkunft der (höchstalemannische Dialekte sprechenden) Kolonisten aus dem deutschsprachigen Wallis ist wissenschaftlich gesichert. Nach Fazzini Giovannucci (1978, 6—31) ist das Deutsche in Alagna und Macugnaga unter starkem Druck, in Rima und Rimella nicht mehr vorhanden; günstiger ist die Lage in Gressoney, Formazza und Issime.

Die „Möglichkeiten einer Rettung" werden von Fazzini Giovannucci (1978, 48) eher pessimistisch beurteilt. Auch Zinsli (1986, 390) weist darauf hin, daß es vor allem ein gestärktes walserdeutsches Sprachbewußtsein braucht.

5.3.5. Südbairische Sprachinseln

In Nordostitalien (heute wird dieses Gebiet in italienischen Veröffentlichungen mit dem vorläufigen Namen „Nord-Est" bezeichnet) gibt es mehrere deutsche Sprachinseln, die vom bairischen Sprachraum aus besiedelt wurden (vgl. vor allem Hornung 1986).

Das Fersental/Valle di Fèrsina (auch: Val dei Mòcheni) in der Provinz Trient wurde aus verschiedenen Tälern Tirols zwischen 1250 und 1320 besiedelt. Die Fersentaler werden von den Italienern Mòcheni genannt (aus dem häufig gebrauchten Zeitwort „mâchn"/ „machen"); dieser Spitzname ist auch in der Verbindung „mòcheno-cimbro" in Dokumenten vorzufinden (vgl. Identità 1991, Nr. 4). Zur Zeit wird die Mundart auch im Kindergarten benutzt und Deutsch als Zweitsprache in der Schule unterrichtet. Im Jahre 1987 wurde das „Istituto culturale mòchenocimbro" errichtet, und für Kindergärtnerinnen gibt es seit 1991 eine Bescheinigung, wenn sie Kenntnisse der einheimischen Mundart nachweisen (Identità 1991, Nr. 4).

Lusern/Luserna — an der alten Grenze zwischen Österreich und Italien, aber noch im Trentino gelegen — um 1650 angelegt, ist eine jüngere Sprachinsel, die bis zum Ersten Weltkrieg besonders gute Verbindungen zum deutschen Sprachgebiet hatte. Die deutsche Schriftsprache hat Südtiroler Färbung, die rechtliche Position der deutschen Sprache ist ähnlich wie im Fersental (Identità 1991, Nr. 4).

Die 7 Gemeinden (Sette Comuni) in der Provinz Vicenza wurden um 1100 von deutschen Siedlern aus Tirol gegründet; um 1280 erfolgte mit einem weiteren Zuzug aus dem Ötztal die Gründung der 13 Gemeinden (Tredici Comuni) in der Provinz Verona. Die Sprache der 7 und 13 Gemeinden wird auch als „Zimbrisch" bezeichnet, nach dem 101 v. Chr. von Marius bei Vercellae besiegten germanischen Stamm; dies ist aber eine volkstümliche Erklärung, die vermutlich auf ital. Humanisten des 16. Jahrhunderts zurückgeht. In den 7 und 13 Gemeinden finden wir nur noch Reste der deutschen Sprache, die durch mehrere Institutionen gefördert wird (→ Art. 156).

Die Besiedlung von Pladen/Sappada in der Provinz Belluno erfolgte um 1270 aus dem Osttiroler Pustertal. Die deutsche Schriftsprache ist durch zeitweisen Unterricht und durch Medien verbreitet. Der Gebrauch der Mundart hat durch wissenschaftliche Untersuchungen (z. B. Hornung 1972) Auftrieb erhalten. Die Region Venetien hat durch Gesetz (Nr. 51/1984 und Nr. 8/1987) einige Bestimmungen zugunsten der Pladener und der 7 Gemeinden erlassen.

Zahre/Sauris in der Provinz Udine wurde um 1250 aus dem Osttiroler Pustertal gegründet. In der Zahre werden drei Sprachen gesprochen: Friaulisch, Italienisch und Deutsch, wobei das Deutsche besonders für informelle Gelegenheiten benutzt wird (Denison 1979, 29) und als die „eigene" Sprache angesehen wird (De Marchi 1983, 22).

Tischelwang/Timau, Provinz Udine, an der österreichisch-italienischen Grenze, wurde um 1200 von Kärnten her besiedelt. Seit 1866 gehört Tischelwang zu Italien. Die Bewohner von Tischelwang beurteilen die Zukunft der deutschen Mundart positiver als die Bewohner der Zahre (De Marchi 1983, 22).

Das Kanaltal/Val Canale, an der österreichisch-italienischen Grenze bei Tarvis, gehörte bis 1918/20 zu Kärnten und hatte damals, ähnlich wie heute noch Unterkärnten, eine gemischtsprachige deutsch-slowenische Bevölkerung mit Einflüssen der umgebenden Romania. Was heute wie eine „Sprachinsel" aussieht, gehörte zum Kontinuum der bairisch-slowenischen Ansiedlung. Im Kanaltal leben germanische, slawische und romanische Sprachgruppen neben- und miteinander. Die Kontakte mit dem deutschen Sprachraum werden zur Zeit verstärkt; das Deutschtum hatte vor allem durch die Abwanderung im Zug der Aussiedlung nach 1939 („Option") gelitten. Es besteht jedoch ein Gegensatz zwischen den beiden kleinen Minderheiten dieses Gebietes, den Slowenen und den Deutschen, so daß die Förderung der einen Gruppe jeweils als Bedrohung der anderen empfunden wird (vgl. Steinicke 1984, 80/81).

6. Sprachpolitische Situation

Grundlage der Sonderrechte der deutschen Sprachminderheit in Südtirol ist der 1946 zwischen Italien und Österreich abgeschlossene Pariser Vertrag (Ratifizierung erst 1947). In diesem Vertrag wird der „deutschen Minderheit die volle Gleichberechtigung mit den italienischen Einwohnern im Rahmen besonderer Maßnahmen zum Schutz der volklichen Eigenart und der kulturellen und wirtschaftlichen Entwicklung" zugesagt. Im Anschluß an diesen Vertrag wurde im Jahre 1948 das erste Autonomiestatut erlassen. Die wesentlichen autonomen Befugnisse lagen jedoch bei der Region Trentino/Südtirol, in der Region waren die Südtiroler Minderheit. Die Unzufriedenheit mit der politischen Lage, die sich auch in Attentaten (verstärkt ab 1961) äußerte, führte zu neuen Verhandlungen zwischen Österreich und Italien, wie auch zwischen der Römischen Zentralregierung und der deutschen Minderheit. Diese Verhandlungen führten 1972 zum neuen Autonomiestatut, gewöhnlich „Paket" genannt. Die wichtigsten Bestimmungen des Autonomiestatutes seien im folgenden kurz beschrieben (in Klammer wird auf die Artikel des Autonomiestatuts von 1972 verwiesen).

6.1. Die Stellung der deutschen Sprache

Die deutsche Sprache ist in der Region Trentino/Südtirol der italienischen Sprache gleichgestellt (Art. 99−101). Seit Mai 1993 gelten die Bestimmungen, daß der Bürger das Recht auf einen Prozeß in der eigenen Muttersprache hat, und daß Prozesse und Urteile, die gegen diese Bestimmung verstoßen, ungültig sind.

Aufgrund der Proporzbestimmungen (Art. 15, 61, 89 und Durchführungsbestimmungen DPR Nr. 752 vom 26. Juli 1976) muß die Besetzung der Stellen im öffentlichen Dienst im Verhältnis zur zahlenmäßigen Stärke der Sprachgruppen vorgenommen werden. Der Proporz gilt auch für die Zuweisung der Wohnungen im sozialen Wohnungsbau. Insgesamt unterliegen ca. 21.500 Stellen den Proporzbestimmungen (Peterlini 1980, 136).

Bei den allgemeinen Volkszählungen Italiens wird in Südtirol die Zugehörigkeitserklärung zu einer der drei Sprachgruppen abgegeben. Die Erklärungen bilden u. a. die Grundlagen des Proporzes.

Voraussetzung für die Aufnahme in den öffentlichen Dienst ist die „angemessene Kenntnis" der italienischen und deutschen Sprache (Art. 1 des Proporzdekretes). Die Kenntnis der beiden Spachen wird seit 1977 durch die „Zweisprachigkeitsprüfung" festgestellt.

6.2. Schulunterricht in der Muttersprache

Aufgrund des Autonomiestatutes (Art. 19) „wird der Unterricht in den Kindergärten, Grund- und Sekundarschulen in der Muttersprache der Schüler, d. h. in italienischer oder deutscher Sprache, von Lehrkräften erteilt, für welche die betreffende Sprache ebenfalls Muttersprache ist" (Art. 19). Die Sprachgruppen in Südtirol haben also jeweils ihr eigenes Schulsystem. Kinder der deutschen und italienischen Sprachgruppe können vom Kindergarten bis zur Reifeprüfung die Schule in ihrer Muttersprache besuchen. In den ladinischen Tälern sind − bei geringer Berücksichtigung des Ladinischen − Italienisch und Deutsch die Schulsprachen. Aufgrund geschichtlicher Erfahrungen mißt die deutsche Sprachgruppe in Südtirol der Schule in der eigenen Muttersprache eine ganz besondere Bedeutung bei. Das Verbot der deutschen Schulen zur Faschistenzeit wird auch heute noch wegen der damit verbundenen psychologischen und ethnopolitischen Folgen als ein besonders schweres Unrecht angesehen.

7. Die Kontaktsprachen

Die Sprachsituation in Südtirol ist gekennzeichnet durch den Kontakt von Mundart und Hochsprache und durch den Kontakt von Deutsch, Italienisch und Ladinisch.

7.1. Mundart und Hochsprache

Die deutschsprachigen Südtiroler sprechen in alltäglichen Lebenssituationen untereinander Dialekt. Angesichts der Grenzziehung von 1919, wodurch Südtirol von Gesamttirol abgetrennt und Italien angeschlossen wurde, könnte man meinen, daß es einen „Südtiroler Dialekt" gebe, der sich vom Dialekt Nord- und Osttirols unterscheidet. Die einschlägige Forschung und insbesondere die Karten des Tiroler Sprachatlasses zeigen, daß es wohl verschiedene Dialekte in Südtirol gibt, nicht aber einen „Südtiroler Dialekt", der sich als Einheit von einem „Nordtiroler Dialekt" abheben würde (Lanthaler/Meraner 1985).

Umstritten ist in der Forschung, ob es in Südtirol zwischen Hochspache und Mundart eine Umgangssprache gibt. Während in früheren Publikationen das Fehlen einer modernen Umgangssprache behauptet wurde (Riedmann 1972, 31) und von einem eventuellen Ausbau der Umgangssprache eine Stärkung der deutschen Sprache in Südtirol insgesamt erwartet wurde (Egger 1977, 10), wird in neuerer Zeit am Vorhandensein einer solchen Umgangssprache nicht mehr gezweifelt, ja es wird die Forderung nach dem Ausbau von „umgangssprachlichen Registern", vor allem durch den schulischen Deutschunterricht, erhoben (Moser 1982, 87 f).

Der deutschen Hochsprache wird besondere Bedeutung beigemessen, weil sie den Kontakt mit dem gesamten deutschen Sprach- und Kulturraum ermöglicht, was für eine Sprachminderheit besonders wichtig ist.

7.2. Die italienische Sprache

Da die Italiener aus verschiedenen italienischen Provinzen zugewandert sind, war es für die erste Generation notwendig, untereinander die Hochsprache zu verwenden. Francescato (1975, 32) hat das in Südtirol von den Italienern gesprochene Italienisch als ein „neutrales" Italienisch bezeichnet. Neuere Untersuchungen zeigen, daß es ein „italiano regionale bolzanino" (Mioni 1990, 27) gibt, das etwas stärker standardisiert ist als das anderer oberitalienischer Städte. Das Italienisch in Südtirol kennt fast keine lexikalischen Interferenzen aus dem Deutschen.

7.3. Die ladinische Sprache

Bei der Volkszählung 1991 haben sich 4,36% der Südtiroler als Angehörige der ladinischen Sprachgruppe bezeichnet. Die in Südtirol liegenden ladinischen Gebiete (Gadertal und Gröden) werden durch Sonderbestimmungen geschützt. Das Ladinische wird vor allem in den Familien und im Alltag gesprochen. Es wird aber immer mehr auch bei offiziellen Anlässen verwendet und ist seit 1989 obligatorische Amtssprache in den ladinischen Tälern neben Deutsch und Italienisch (→ Art. 166).

7.4. Interferenzforschung

Die deutsche Sprache in Südtriol ist sehr häufig in bezug auf Interferenzen aus dem Italienischen untersucht worden. Wenn z. B. unter dem Einfluß des Italienischen der Führerschein „Patent", das Autokennzeichen „Targa" oder der kleine braune Kaffee „Macchiato" (= gefleckt) genannt werden, so sind das sprachwissenschaftlich leicht erklärbare Phänomene, es kann darin aber auch ein Problem der Sprachloyalität gesehen werden. Indem sich die Interferenzforschung mit der Frage beschäftigt: „Wie rein erhält sich die Sprache?" hat sie eine wichtige Aufgabe für das Selbstverständnis einer Gruppe. So ist es nicht verwunderlich, daß gerade dieser Aspekt des Sprachkontakts in Südtirol besonders und mit Erfolg erforscht worden ist (Moser 1982, Pernstich 1984). Durch die Interferenzforschung wurde das in den frühen siebziger Jahren recht pessimistische Urteil über die Qualität und Überlebenschancen der deutschen Sprache in Südtirol erheblich korrigiert.

7.5. Ausblick

Die Südtiroler gehören sicher zu den rechtlich am wenigsten benachteiligten Minderheiten in Europa. Anderseits verlangt aber die historische Erfahrung (vor allem die Erinnerung an Faschismus und Option) von der Minderheit eine große Wachsamkeit. Von Außenstehenden (vgl. Kramer 1981) wird das oft nicht verstanden. Insgesamt suchen die politischen, gesellschaftlichen und kirchlichen Kräfte einen Ausgleich zwischen den Sprachgruppen, damit die Autonomie allen Sprachgruppen zugute kommen kann.

8. Bibliographie (in Auswahl)

Astat — Landesinstitut für Statistik (1988): *Sozialer Survey 1986: Meinungen, Werte und Lebensformen in Südtirol*, Bozen.

Astat (1989): *Sozialprodukt und Wirtschaftsentwicklung in Südtirol 1980–1987*, Bozen.

Astat (1992a): *Statistisches Jahrbuch für Südtirol*, Bozen.

Astat (1992b): *Interethnische Beziehungen: Leben in einer mehrsprachigen Gesellschaft*, Bozen.

Bacher, Josef (1905, Neuauflage 1976): *Die deutsche Sprachinsel Lusern*, Wien.

Bertoldi, Maria B. (1983): *Luserna: una cultura che resiste*, Trient.

Buson, Ornella (1992): „Bilinguismo, relazioni interetniche e formazione: risultati dell'indagine Astat 1991". In: *Interethnische Beziehungen: Leben in einer mehrsprachigen Gesellschaft*, Bozen, 101–115.

Capraro, Giuseppe (1991): „Die Religiosität der achtziger Jahre in Südtirol". In: *Beiheft zum Konferenzblatt 3/1991*.

Craffonara, Lois (1981): „Die kulturelle und politische Situation der Sellaladiner". In: *Kulturelle und sprachliche Minderheiten in Europa*, Ureland, P.S. (Ed.), Tübingen, 8–108.

Cusanus-Akademie (1987): „Zusammenleben der Sprachgruppen in Südtirol". In: *Konferenzblatt für Theologie und Seelsorge 4*, 210–241.

Das neue Autonomiestatut (1981). Sonderdruck zur Informationsschrift des Landtages und der Landesregierung, Bozen.

De Marchi, Bruna (1983): „Uso linguistico e atteggiamenti verso le parlate locali nelle isole linguistiche del Friuli-Venezia Giulia, Sauris e Timau". In: *Terra Cimbra XIV*, 21–26.

Denison, Norman (1979): „Zur Triglossie in der Zahre". In: *Standardsprache und Dialekte in mehrsprachigen Gebieten Europas*, Ureland, P.S. (Ed.), Tübingen, 27–37.

Die Schule in Südtirol (1992): Informationsschrift des deutschen Schulamtes, Bozen.

Egger, Kurt (1977): *Zweisprachigkeit in Südtirol. Probleme zweier Volksgruppen an der Sprachgrenze*, Bozen.

Egger, Kurt (1985): *Zweisprachige Familien in Südtirol: Sprachgebrauch und Spracherziehung*, Innsbruck.

Egger, Kurt (1990): „Zur Sprachsituation in Südtirol: Auf der Suche nach Konsens". In: *Deutsche Sprache 1*, 76–88.

Egger, Kurt (1992): „Sprachforschung in Südtirol 1972–1992. Ein Überblick". In: *Schlern 66*, 764–779.

Eisermann, Felix (1981): *Die deutsche Sprachgemeinschaft in Südtirol*, Stuttgart.

Ermacora, Felix (1984): *Südtirol und das Vaterland Österreich*, Wien.

Fazzini Giovannucci, Elisabetta (1978): *Die alemannischen Dialekte im westlichen Norditalien*, Wiesbaden.

Fontana, Josef et al. (Eds.) (1985–1988): *Geschichte Tirols*, Bd. 1–4, Bozen/Innsbruck/Wien.

Francescato, Giuseppe (1975): „Analisi di una collettività bilingue: Le condizioni attuali del bilinguismo in Alto Adige". In: *Quaderni per la promozione del bilinguismo 7/8*, Brescia, 6–16, 23–37.

Geyer, Inge (1984): *Die deutsche Mundart von Tischelwang in Karnien (Italien)*, Wien.

Gruber, Alfons (1974): *Südtirol unter dem Faschismus*, Bozen.

Gubert, Renzo (1978): *La città bilingue. Indagine sociologica sulla domanda di bilinguismo degli italiani di Bolzano*, Bozen.

Gubert, Renzo (1990): „Volksgruppen deutschen Ursprungs in der Provinz Trient". In: *Die Minderheiten im Alpen-Adria-Raum*, Klagenfurt, 279–286.

Gubert, Renzo/Egger, Kurt (1990): „Die deutsche Volksgruppe in Südtirol". In: *Die Minderheiten im Alpen-Adria-Raum*, Klagenfurt, 249–264.

Hornung, Maria (1965): „Die Bedeutung der Sprachinselkunde für die Erforschung der mundartlichen Verhältnisse im binnendeutschen Raum". In: *Zeitschrift für Mundartforschung 32*, 274–288.

Hornung, Maria (1972): *Wörterbuch der deutschen Sprachinselmundart von Pladen/Sappada in Karnien (Italien)*, Wien.

Hornung, Maria (1988): „Aspekte sprachlicher und kultureller Erosion am Beispiel der deutschen Sprachinseln in Ostoberitalien". In: *Isole linguistiche e culturali*, Udine, 75–88.

Hornung, Maria und Herwig (1986): *Deutsche Sprachinseln aus Altösterreich*, Wien.

Identità. Notiziario trimestrale dell'Istituto Culturale Mòcheno Cimbro.

Innerhofer, Josef (1982): *Die Kirche in Südtirol*, Bozen.

Kramer, Johannes (1981): *Deutsch und Italienisch in Südtirol*, Heidelberg.

Kühebacher, Egon (Ed.) (1986): *Amtlicher Gebrauch des geographischen Namensgutes*, Bozen.

Lanthaler, Franz (Ed.) (1990): *Mehr als eine Sprache. Zu einer Sprachstrategie in Südtirol. Più di una lingua. Per un progetto linguistico in Alto Adige*, Meran.

Lanthaler, Franz/Meraner, Rudolf (1985): „Die Tiroler Mundarten". In: *Dialekt – Hochsprache als Unterrichtsthema*, Saxalber-Tetter, A. (Ed.), 157–161.

L'apprendimento precoce della seconda lingua (1983), Provincia Autonoma di Bolzano, Bozen.

La Valle del Fersina e le isole linguistiche di origine tedesca nel Trentino (Atti del Convegno) (1978), S. Orsola.

Kranzmayer, Eberhard (1981): *Laut- und Flexionslehre der deutschen zimbrischen Mundart*, Wien.

Matzel, Klaus (1989): „Der Untergang deutscher Sprachinseln in Norditalien (Sette comuni e Tredici comuni)". In: *Germanische Rest- und Trümmersprachen*, Beck, H. (Ed.), Berlin/New York, 69–86.

Mioni, Alberto M. (1990): „Bilinguismo intra- e intercomunitario in Alto Adige/Südtirol: Considerazioni sociolinguistiche". In: *Mehr als eine Sprache. Zu einer Sprachstrategie in Südtirol. Più di una lingua. Per un progetto linguistico in Alto Adige*, Lanthaler, F. (Ed.), Meran, 9–29.

Moser, Hans (1982): „Zur Untersuchung des gesprochenen Deutsch in Südtirol". In: *Zur Situation des Deutschen in Südtirol*, Moser, H. (Ed.), 75–90.

Moser, Hans (Ed. unter Mitwirkung von Oskar Putzer) (1982): *Zur Situation des Deutschen in Südtirol. Sprachwissenschaftliche Beiträge zu den Fragen von Sprachnorm und Sprachkontakt*, Innsbruck.

Quattrocchi, Luigi/Putzer, Oskar (1982): *Prove di bilinguismo: analisi e valutazione*, Bolzano.

Pernstich, Karin (1984): *Der italienische Einfluß auf die deutsche Schriftsprache in Südtirol*, Wien.

Peterlini, Oskar (1980): *Der ethnische Proporz in Südtirol*, Bozen.

Putzer, Oskar (1982): „Italienische Interferenzen in der gesprochenen Sprache Südtirols – Faktoren der Variation". In: *Zur Situation des Deutschen in Südtirol. Sprachwissenschaftliche Beiträge zu den Fragen von Sprachnorm und Sprachkontakt*, Moser, H. (Ed.), 141–162.

Riedmann, Gerhard (1972): *Die Besonderheiten der deutschen Schriftsprache in Südtirol*, Duden-Beiträge 39, Mannheim.

Rindler Schjerve, Rosita (1989): „Sprachverschiebung und Sprachtod: Funktionelle und strukturelle Aspekte". In: *Germanische Rest- und Trümmersprachen*, Beck, H. (Ed.), Berlin/New York, 1–14.

Rowley, Antony R. (1982): *Fersentaler Wörterbuch*, Hamburg.

Rowley, Antony R. (1982): *Fersental (Val Fèrsina bei Trient/Oberitalien). Untersuchung einer Sprachinselmundart*, Tübingen.

Saxalber-Tetter, Annemarie (Ed.) (1985): *Dialekt – Hochsprache als Unterrichtsthema*, Bozen.

Steinicke, Ernst (1984): *Das Kanaltal/Val Canale. Sozialgeographie einer alpinen Minderheitenregion*, Innsbruck.

Stolz, Otto (1927): *Die Ausbreitung des Deutschtums im Lichte der Urkunden*, Bd. 1–4, Oldenburg.

Südtirol-Handbuch (1987), hrsg. von der Südtiroler Landesregierung, Bozen.

SVP-Fraktion im Südtiroler Landtag (1987): *Die deutsche Sprache in Südtirols öffentlichem Dienst*, Bozen.

Weber Egli, Daniela (1992): *Gemischtsprachige Familien in Südtirol/Alto Adige. Zweisprachigkeit und soziale Kontakte. Ein Vergleich von Familien in Bozen und Meran*, Meran.

Wiesinger, Peter (1983): „Deutsche Dialektgebiete außerhalb des deutschen Sprachgebietes". In: *Dialektologie. Ein Handbuch zur deutschen und allgemeinen Dialektforschung*, Besch, W. et al. (Eds.), Berlin/New York, Bd. 2, 900–930.

Wurzer, Bernhard (1977, 4. Aufl.): *Die deutschen Sprachinseln in Oberitalien*, Bozen.

Zelger, Peter (1988): „Seelsorge in Südtirol seit 1918". In: *Theologisch-praktische Quartalzeitschrift 136*, 159–167.

Zinsli, Paul (1986, 5. Aufl.): *Walser Volkstum in der Schweiz, in Vorarlberg, Liechtenstein und Piemont*, Chur.

Kurt Egger, Bozen (Italien)
Karin Heller, Innsbruck (Österreich)

161. Italien–slovène

1. Géographie et démographie
2. Histoire
3. Politique, économie, situations culturelle et religieuse
4. Statistiques et profil ethnique
5. Situation sociolinguistique
6. Etat de la politique linguistique
7. Interférences linguistiques
8. Problèmes de rigueur scientifique
9. Bibliographie (sélective)

Le titre n'épuise pas la matière: sur le territoire qui nous occupe se trouvent, en réalité, deux langues romanes, l'italien et le frioulan: c'est pourquoi il convient de parler, souvent, de relations romano-slovènes.

1. Géographie et démographie

Dans son extrême nord-est, dans trois provinces de la Région de Frioul-Vénétie Julienne (Trieste, Gorizia, Udine), la République italienne compte parmi ses citoyens des gens de nationalité et langue slovènes.

Dans la province d'Udine, il y a des Slovènes dans le nord, dans trois villages de la Valcanale. Dans cette vallée, entrent en contact les mondes roman, germanique et slave, ce qui représente un cas unique. Encore faut-il ajouter que le monde roman y est représenté par le frioulan et par l'italien. De plus, si le slovène et l'allemand datent du haut Moyen

Age, la présence des deux langues romanes dans cette vallée est récente; elle est la conséquence de migrations d'Italiens et de Frioulans survenues le plus souvent au cours de et après la deuxième guerre mondiale, dues à des accords politiques entre l'Allemagne et l'Italie. Toujours dans la province d'Udine, l'ethnie slovène se trouve dans la vallée de Résia et dans les hautes vallées de la rivière de Natisone et de ses affluents (cette contrée est appelée par les Italiens *Slavia veneta* ou *Slavia friulana* et *Benečija* ou *Beneška Slovenija* par les Slovènes) et dans la vallée de la rivière de Torre/Ter.

Dans la province de Gorizia, l'ethnie slovène vit dans la banlieue de Gorizia (slov. Gorica) et sur les collines au-dessus de la ville, nommées justement Collio/Brda.

Enfin, il existe une minorité slovène à Trieste, surtout dans les communes rurales autour de la ville; → carte linguistique F.

2. Histoire

2.1. Les ancêtres des Slovènes, les Slaves des Alpes orientales, arrivèrent sur le territoire occupé de nos jours par les Slovènes vers la fin du VIe siècle, après que les Langobards eurent abandonné la Pannonie (v. Paul Diacre, Historia Langobardorum, I,7). Dans la zone de contact, les Slaves prirent possession des collines et des hautes vallées: la toponymie, à commencer par le nom slovène *Gorica* 'colline couverte de vignes', en est la preuve.

2.2. Les Slaves ne s'installèrent pas sur un territoire vide. Ils y trouvèrent des Celtes et des Illyres romanisés. La romanisation, toutefois, ne semble pas avoir été profonde. En outre, l'histoire nous renseigne qu'il y a eu des migrations de populations romanes vers le midi, vers l'Istrie. Néanmoins, il y a des éléments latins dans le lexique actuel slovène, témoins du contact entre les envahisseurs slaves et la population autochtone, romane ou romanisée. Ce sont d'une part des toponymes latins ou prélatins, comme *Ptuj* de *Poetovio*, et d'autre part des appellatifs, comme *račun* 'compte' de *rationem* ou *kmet*, *kumet* 'paysan' de *comitem*. De plus, le latin est resté pendant des siècles un inépuisable réservoir pour la terminologie technique. Une influence analogue, dans le domaine lexical, est propre aussi à l'italien: on la trouve dans le lexique des arts, lettres, théâtre, musique et aussi dans des secteurs de l'activité humaine moins sublimes comme les finances ou l'art de la guerre.

2.3. Sensiblement plus forte est la contribution linguistique romane aux dialectes slovènes occidentaux en Italie. Il convient de mettre en relief quelques périodes historiques particulièrement importantes. – Le Frioul, y compris le territoire où vit l'ethnie slovène, formait sous les patriarches d'Aquilée un important Etat féodal. Cependant, à partir de l'an 1420, la partie centrale et occidentale (y compris la *Slavia friulana*) fait partie de la République de Venise, tandis que les territoires autour de Gorizia forment un comté indépendant. La frontière fut établie sur la rivière de Iudrio. Quand la famille des comtes de Gorizia s'éteint (1500), l'empereur Maximilien obtient, par des négociations et par les armes, le droit d'adjoindre à la couronne autrichienne tout le Frioul oriental et les parties slovènes du comté. La ville de Trieste, elle, s'était donnée à la maison de Habsbourg dès 1382.

Cette division a duré (à l'exception du bref intervalle napoléonien et de la période suivante du Royaume lombardo-vénitien) jusqu'à la première guerre mondiale. Alors, l'Italie a réussi à obtenir, outre les territoires linguistiquement et ethniquement italiens et frioulans, aussi une partie du territoire ethniquement slovène. Les traités conclus après la deuxième guerre mondiale ont rectifié, partiellement, les partages précédents erronés. Le Mémorandum de Londres (1954), puis les Accords d'Osimo (1972) ont réglé, plus ou moins définitivement, la question des frontières entre l'Italie et la Yougoslavie, et partant la Slovénie, qui est depuis 1991, pour la partie qui la regarde, l'héritière légitime de l'ex-Yougoslavie.

3. Politique, économie, situations culturelle et religieuse

3.1. Certaines parties de l'actuelle Région de Frioul-Vénétie Julienne ont toujours été économiquement importantes et par conséquent relativement riches. La ville de Trieste, devenue sous l'empereur Charles VI (1719) port libre, était le port le plus important de l'Europe centrale. Pour l'Italie par contre, Trieste est seulement un de ses ports et ne compte certainement pas parmi les plus importants. La ville connut une émigration économique, comme, quoique moins prononcée, toute la

Région de Frioul-Vénétie Julienne dans la période après la dernière guerre mondiale. Certes, l'émigration, moins forte peut-être, mais certainement plus tragique, s'est vérifiée dans la zone montagneuse parmi les Slovènes qui ont émigré vers les mines de Belgique, vers la France, aux Etats-Unis ou en Australie. Le Frioul de ces dernières décennies, il est vrai, ne connaît plus d'émigration: l'industrie offre assez de possibilités de travail. Toutefois, pour les villages dans les montagnes ce réveil économique est venu trop tard: les jeunes avaient opté, depuis longtemps, soit pour l'émigration soit pour un travail dans la plaine. Souvent, ce ne sont que les vieux qui sont restés au pays.

3.2. La minorité slovène a une vie culturelle intense, surtout à Trieste (centre culturel, théâtre, bibliothèque d'études, institut de recherches, maison d'édition, publications périodiques dont un journal, radio); à Gorizia il y a un centre culturel, à Cividale une maison de la culture.

3.3. La population slovène est de religion catholique. Elle est répartie entre les diocèses de Trieste, Gorizia et Udine. Dans l'histoire le rôle du patriarcat d'Aquilée (Aquileia) a été de toute première importance pour la christianisation des Slovènes. Le siège du patriarcat, juridiquement toujours domiciliée à Aquilée, a été transféré d'abord à Cividale, ensuite à Udine. Suite aux insistances diplomatiques de l'impératrice Marie-Thérèse, le pape déclara déchu le patriarcat d'Aquilée et institua les archevêchés de Gorizia et d'Udine (respectivement en 1752 et 1753).

4. Statistiques et profil ethnique

Il y a donc trois ethnies en contact: l'ethnie slovène, l'ethnie frioulane et l'ethnie italienne. Et trois langues: le slovène, le frioulan et l'italien; ce dernier aussi dans sa variante vénitienne. En ce qui concerne le nombre de locuteurs, il faut dire que les statistiques officielles sont souvent fallacieuses. D'ailleurs, les recensements sous le régime fasciste n'admettaient guère une déclaration de nationalité: officiellement, il n'y en avait qu'une, la nationalité italienne. Pour les décennies après la 2e guerre mondiale, il faut tenir compte du fait que toute déclaration de la propre slovénité linguistique et/ou culturelle était automatiquement soupçonnée de soutenir de fantomatiques prétentions territoriales de la part de la Yougoslavie «communiste». Et puis, le triste sort des minorités, probablement de toute minorité, est celui de l'assimilation silencieuse: plus l'individu monte sur l'échelle sociale dans un milieu qui n'est pas le sien, plus il est en danger de perdre son identité linguistique et nationale, même s'il utilise sa langue dans la vie intime, en famille. Pour toutes ces raisons, Salvi (1974, 209) estime judicieusement que le nombre approximatif de Slovènes dans toute la Région est de cent mille personnes.

5. Situation sociolinguistique

Il faut bien le dire: les Slovènes en Italie, dans la Région de Frioul-Vénétie Julienne où ils forment une ethnie autochtone, ne cessent d'être des citoyens de second ordre.

5.1. La Constitution de la République italienne (de 1947) parle, il est vrai, de la défense et des droits des minorités (art. 3 et 6). En réalité, la situation juridique de la population slovène et le statut sociolinguistique de la langue slovène sont différents dans chacune des trois provinces. Pour Trieste, l'Italie est liée par un contrat international: théoriquement, le slovène est une langue ayant tous les droits. En pratique, les choses sont loin d'être ainsi. Les Slovènes ont certes un système d'éducation public très bien élaboré (écoles élémentaires, lycée, école magistrale, école de musique, écoles de formation professionnelle); ils ont, en outre, d'importantes institutions culturelles. Mais, dès que la langue slovène cherche à pénétrer dans la vie publique, les choses changent radicalement. Chaque tentative de réclamer, pour le slovène, des droits hors du milieu strictement slovène peut provoquer, et le fait souvent, à Trieste, pour être juste et précis, dans les milieux politiquement extrémistes, de violentes protestations. Seul le tribunal respecte scrupuleusement la Constitution: l'accusé a le droit d'être convoqué et de se défendre dans sa propre langue.

Il faut dire que le Statut de la Région n'est ni clair ni généreux. La comparaison avec les statuts des autres régions autonomes (Aoste, Trentin-Haut Adige) est très instructive (v. Paladin, 1969, 17 ss.). L'article 3 du Statut stipule que le citoyen ne peut pas être poursuivi par la loi pour avoir employé sa propre langue. Ceci semble aller de soi; néanmoins, par rapport à la situation de l'entre-deux-guerres, la disposition de la loi représente un progrès considérable. L'auteur de ces lignes se souvient encore de l'inscription lue à la gare de Trieste, en 1936 ou 1937, qui disait carrément: *Qui si parla solo italiano*.

A Gorizia, de tradition plus libérale que Trieste, la situation est néanmoins fort semblable à celle de Trieste. Quant à la province d'Udine par contre, elle y est catastrophique: Là, pour l'Italie officielle, les Slovènes, tout simplement, n'existent pas; tout comme les Frioulans, d'ailleurs.

5.2. Ecole et église: Sans une connaissance du cadre extralinguistique il serait difficile de comprendre l'état sociolinguistique du slovène dans la Région. Il faut ici mettre en relief deux aspects: l'école et l'église.

5.2.1. D'après Salvi (1974, 33) une langue se conserve si elle est enseignée à l'école; mieux encore, si, à l'école, l'enseignement se fait *dans* cette langue.

Les villages slovènes de l'actuelle province d'Udine n'ont jamais connu d'école slovène sauf pendant une très brève période (1943—1945) au cours de la deuxième guerre. Tout récemment, une école privée, bilingue, a commencé a fonctionner à S. Pietro al Natisone. Par contre, à Trieste et à Gorizia, la situation scolaire avant la guerre de 1914—1918 avait été toute différente. Et même après la guerre: pour l'année scolaire 1919/1920 le territoire de l'ancien comté de Gorizia comptait encore 59 écoles slovènes avec 13 000 écoliers. Mais, la soi-disant *Riforma Gentile*, d'après le nom du ministre de l'Instruction publique du premier gouvernement Mussolini, le philosophe Giovanni Gentile, un libéral(!) indépendant, rendue publique par le décret royal le 1ᵉʳ octobre 1923 et entrée en vigueur le jour même de sa publication dans la « Gazzetta Ufficiale », éliminait de l'enseignement dans les premières classes des écoles primaires toute autre langue que l'italien. Le décret-loi concernait tous les territoires acquis par l'Italie à la fin de la guerre. Dans les années suivantes, ce décret-loi s'étendra progressivement aux classes supérieures. En réalité, le fascisme, ayant aboli les institutions démocratiques (janvier 1925), précipita aussi la disparition de tout ce qui sentait l'étranger. C'est dans ce sens que s'est faite l'italianisation forcée des noms et des prénoms (cf. Parovel 1985).

5.2.2. Le seul refuge de la langue slovène restait l'église. On y prêchait en slovène. Certes, la *Riforma Gentile* était valable aussi pour le catéchisme à l'école publique; mais les curés, dans les petits villages au moins, continuaient à enseigner le catéchisme dans la langue des écoliers au presbytère.

Cependant, en 1933, l'archevêché d'Udine émit l'interdiction formelle de prêcher en slovène. La langue slovène était donc bannie de l'église. Ce ne fut pas le cas du diocèse de Gorizia. La forte personnalité de l'archevêque Margotti avait su tenir tête aux autorités civiles et, certes, aussi ecclésiastiques, lesquelles par suite des Accords de Latran de 1929 tenaient à de bonnes relations avec le régime fasciste. Avec la fin de la guerre, les choses se sont normalisées. Toutefois, pour l'archevêché d'Udine, il a fallu attendre l'an 1976 pour que l'actuel archevêque ait formellement levé l'interdiction imposée en 1933 par son prédécesseur.

5.3. Il est donc compréhensible que le slovène et l'italien, sociolinguistiquement, ne sont pas sur un pied d'égalité. Autrement dit, pour les Slovènes, l'italien a été et est toujours la langue du registre haut. Le frioulan, d'ailleurs, n'est pas en meilleure position parce qu'il se heurte contre une langue de la même famille.

Après la guerre, l'Italie démocratique a pansé beaucoup de blessures, mais pas toutes. Les Slovènes attendent toujours la loi globale de protection de la minorité qui devrait conférer au slovène des droits dans la vie publique. Certes, tous les Slovènes, à quelques exceptions près, ont une bonne connaissance de l'italien et sont plus ou moins bilingues. Le contraire n'est pas vrai: un nombre infime d'Italiens et de Frioulans apprennent le slovène et s'en servent. Il s'ensuit que dans les contacts directs on parle l'italien. Nous avons donc affaire à un type d'assimilation silencieuse qui peut être tout aussi dangereuse qu'une assimilation imposée, brutale. La tragédie des membres d'une minorité est qu'ils sont constamment obligés de s'interroger sur l'utilité de leur langue.

Dans les milieux ruraux, montagnards, unilingues, la langue de la minorité semblerait moins menacée. Là, le danger est le dépeuplement.

5.4. L'assimilation, et en dernière instance la disparition d'une langue et d'une ethnie, est donc une menace constante. Un certain bilinguisme est inévitable, toujours de la part du plus faible. Certes, l'idéal d'un bilinguisme équilibré dans un territoire biethnique, serait que je parle dans ma langue et que mon voisin me comprenne; que lui, à son tour, me parle dans la sienne et que moi, je le comprenne. Une telle situation, si jamais elle a existé sur le territoire qui nous concerne, n'existe certainement pas de nos jours.

6. Etat de la politique linguistique

Les dialectes slovènes font partie intégrante du diasystème de la langue slovène. Il va de soi que la Slovénie cherche à maintenir des contacts aussi étroits que possible avec les zones slovénophones du Frioul. Cela renforce la conscience nationale et crée la nécessité et le désir de maîtriser la langue littéraire qui devrait s'imposer comme norme. En même temps, cela comporte certains sacrifices pour la langue parlée qui subit, immanquablement, l'intrusion d'éléments de la langue standard.

Les parlers de la vallée de Résia, qui constituent des dialectes slovènes très conservateurs, ont donné lieu à un curieux débat scientifique dont la politique s'est emparée sans scrupules. Une vieille tradition voudrait que les habitants de la vallée ne soient pas des Slovènes, mais les descendants d'un ancien peuple slave, russe ou plus ancien encore. L'orgueilleuse confusion est due à une mauvaise interprétation de l'enseignement du linguiste polonais Jean Baudouin de Courtenay et à la méconnaissance de la dialectologie slovène (cf. Ramovš 1935, 31 ss.).

7. Interférences linguistiques

Dans le jeu des interférences entre les trois langues qui se partagent le territoire, une réciprocité n'est pas imaginable: le slovène a reçu beaucoup plus que ce qu'il n'a pu donner aux deux langues romanes. D'autre part, les interférences que l'on constate dans les parlers slovènes de la Slavia Veneta ne sont pas toutes nécessairement dues à l'influence romane.

7.1. Ni l'apparition de l'article défini, ni du pronom démonstratif, *ta parwa zviezda* 'l'étoile du berger', ni l'emploi du pronom-sujet avec les verbes exprimant des conditions atmosphériques *to lampa* 'il fait des éclairs' ne sont complètement inconnus en slovène. La perte du neutre et la perte du duel ne sont pas étrangers aux dialectes slovènes centraux. Par contre, la construction de la phrase, surtout l'ordre des éléments de la subordonnée, ou bien la formation de l'impératif négatif *ni dešiderat!* contre l'italien *non desiderare!* ou le frioulan *no dešiderâ!* ne peuvent être que des calques syntaxiques d'après les modèles romans.

7.2. Les emprunts lexicaux sont nombreux et, par leur aspect phonique, étymologiquement hors de doute. Ils appartiennent à des champs sémantiques très variés: vêtements, nourriture, maison, vie sociale, politique, travaux champêtres, métiers, occupations de toute sorte, outils. Ils sont fréquents aussi dans la sphère abstraite. De plus, on trouve parmi les emprunts des adjectifs, des verbes, des adverbes, des particules, des interjections, des jurons, ce qui témoigne de l'étroite symbiose entre les deux ethnies. L'image phonique peut être précieuse: les emprunts *planta* 'plantation' par la conservation du groupe initial PL-, et *čamra* 'chambre', de par le sort de l'occlusive vélaire devant la voyelle *a*, confirment leur provenance frioulane.

8. Problèmes de rigueur scientifique

De la part des intéressés, il est toujours difficile d'avoir une vision impartiale. Une preuve nous est offerte par les dictionnaires régionaux. Le seul dictionnaire du dialecte triestin digne de foi est celui de Doria (1987). Dans les autres, le nationalisme domine ou prédomine ce qui leur enlève toute crédibilité. Voir, pour citer un exemple convaincant, Rosamani (1958) qui oublie trop souvent, quand il s'agit d'un vocable slave, d'en indiquer la provenance: *otava* (715) 'le regain', de provenance slave certaine, n'a rien à voir avec le numéral ordinal *octavus*; et pourtant, dans ce sens le mot se trouve inséré entre *otava de Pasqua* 'dimanche de Quasimodo' et *otava* 'la huitième division de l'hôpital (de Trieste)'; ou bien, *osmiza* (p. 712), du slovène *osem* 'huit' 'débit de vin provisoire, où le viticulteur, pendant *huit* jours, vendait du vin de sa propre production, sans payer les impôts': Rosamani n'en indique pas la provenance, pourtant incontestable.

9. Bibliographie (sélective)

Dapit, Roberto (1995): *La Slavia friulana*. Lingue e culture. Resia, Torre, Natisone/Beneška Slovenija. Jezik in kultura. Rezija, Ter, Nadiža, Bibliografia ragionata/Kritična bibliografija, Cividale (Čedad)/ San Pietro al Natisone (Špeter).

Doria, Mario (1987): *Grande dizionario del dialetto triestino*, Trieste.

Paladin, Livio (1964): *Commento allo Statuto della Regione Friuli-Venezia Giulia*, Udine.

Parovel, Paolo (1985): *L'identità cancellata*, Trieste.

Pellegrini, Gian Battista (1972): «Contatti linguistici slavo-friulani». In: *Saggi sul ladino dolomitico e sul friulano*, id. 420–438, Bari.

Ramovš, Fran (1935): *Historična gramatika slovenskega jezika*, VII, Ljubljana.

Rosamani, Enrico (1958): *Vocabolario giuliano*, Bologna.

Salvi, Sergio (1975): *Le lingue tagliate*, Milan.

Steenwijk, Han (1992): *The Slovene dialect of Resia*, Amsterdam/Atlanta.

Mitja Skubic, Ljubljana (Slovénie)

162. Italienisch–Kroatisch

1. Geographie und Demographie
2. Territorialgeschichte und Einwanderung
3. Politik, Wirtschaft und allgemeine kulturelle sowie religiöse Lage
4. Eigenbezeichnung, Statistik
5. Soziolinguistische Lage
6. Sprachpolitische Lage
7. Allgemeines kontaktlinguistisches Porträt
8. Gegenwärtiger Forschungsstand
9. Bibliographie (in Auswahl)

1. Geographie und Demographie

Heute bestehen noch drei kroatischsprachige Dörfer im südlichen Italien, genauer in der Region Molise, Provinz Campobasso, ca. 30 km von der Adriaküste entfernt, im hügeligen Hinterland zwischen den Flüssen Biferno und Trigno gelegen. Die drei Dörfer, *Kruč*, italienisch (ital.) Acquaviva Collecroce, *Filič*, ital. San Felice del Molise, und *Mundimitar*, ital. Montemitro, liegen nur wenige Kilometer voneinander entfernt und bilden ein geschlossenes Areal. Sie sind umgeben von italienischsprachigen Dörfern, mit teils beträchtlichen Dialektunterschieden, wobei aber besonders intensiver Kontakt zu denen in Küstenrichtung hin besteht, von denen einige selbst früher kroatischsprachig waren. Nur durch das ital. Palata von Acquaviva getrennt ist ein weiterer Ort mit nichtitalienischsprachiger Bevölkerung, das albanische Montecilfone. Als städtisches Zentrum spielt die mehr als 50 km im Inland gelegene Provinzhauptstadt Campobasso eine geringere Rolle als die Adriastädte Termoli und Vasto (Abruzzen); → Sprachenkarte F.

2. Territorialgeschichte und Einwanderung

Die Moliseslaven sprechen einen štokavisch-ikavischen kroatischen Dialekt. Aufgrund weiterer sprachlicher Besonderheiten wurde ihre ursprüngliche Heimat auf das Gebiet östlich der mittleren Neretva in der Hercegovina festgelegt, von der Adriaküste durch das Gebirgsmassiv des Biokovo getrennt, vgl. Ivić (1958, 262–268). Die Auswanderung erfolgte unter dem Druck der vordringenden Türken vor ca. 500 Jahren, wobei das Molisekroatische (Mkr.) keine Turzismen aufweist. Die Zusammensetzung der Kolonisten bei ihrer Flucht über das Meer dürfte nicht einheitlich gewesen sein, da sich im Mkr. auch küstenländische Čakavismen nachweisen lassen. Es ist nicht klar, inwieweit sich die Molisekroaten auch noch in Italien mit bestehender slavischer Bevölkerung mischten, da schon seit dem frühen Mittelalter, insbesondere aber seit dem 12. Jahrhundert, im südlichen Italien slavische Besiedlung urkundlich nachweisbar ist und noch heute viele Ortsnamen bis in die Abruzzen hinein auf eine ehemals weiter verbreitete slavische Teilbevölkerung hinweisen, vgl. Rešetar (1911, 17–50). Nach Ausweis der Lehnwörter ist schon für die älteste Zeit nach der Einwanderung intensiver Sprachkontakt mit ortsansässiger ital. Bevölkerung wahrscheinlich. Der wissenschaftlichen Welt sind die Slaven des Molise erst seit der Mitte des 19. Jahrhunderts bekannt.

3. Politik, Wirtschaft und allgemeine kulturelle sowie religiöse Lage

Die drei mkr. Dörfer bilden selbständige Gemeinden. Traditionell beschäftigten sich die Einwohner so gut wie ausschließlich mit Landwirtschaft auf oft sehr kleinen Parzellen, was seit den 50er Jahren verstärkt zu Auswanderung führte. Heute ist Haupterwerbslandwirtschaft auf relativ wenige Familien beschränkt, während viele Einwohner in Industriebetrieben Termolis (Fiat) sowie im Handel und in der kommunalen Verwaltung tätig sind. Hierdurch hat der Sprachkontakt stark zugenommen. Jedes der Dörfer ist auch kirchlich selbständig. Die Bewohner sind von Alters her römisch-katholisch, so daß sich anders als bei den ursprünglich orthodoxen Albanern von daher kaum Unterschiede zu den Italienern des Umlands ergaben. Mischheiraten waren und sind deshalb häufig. Wie in jedem Dorf der Umgebung gibt es besondere Feste und Prozessionen zu Ehren des jeweiligen Dorfheiligen, und die Hochzeiten spielen eine wichtige Rolle. In letzter Zeit wurde mehrfach versucht, vollständig untergegangenes „slavisches" Brauchtum wiederzubeleben. Davon scheint sich vor allem der Umzug der *Pagliera* (einer überdimensionalen, reichgeschmückten Strohfigur) am 1. Mai als Touristenattraktion wieder durchgesetzt zu haben, vgl. Neri (1987, 34).

4. Eigenbezeichnung, Statistik

In ital. lautet die Eigenbezeichnung der Molisekroaten *slavo*, älter *schiavone*, vgl. Rešetar (1911, 108), in mkr. *slav*, älter *šklavun*, d. h. es bestehen nur Entlehnungen. Ihre Sprache nennen sie ital. *lo slavo*; in ihrem eigenen Dialekt lautet die Sprachbezeichnung *naš jezik* 'unsere Sprache' bzw. (adverbiell) *na našu*. Die Einwohnerzahl in den drei Dörfern belief sich nach offiziellen Statistiken 1991 für Acquaviva auf 882, S. Felice 910, Montemitro 576. Das entspricht für Acquaviva mehr als einer Halbierung gegenüber 1951 (2250 Einw.), in S. Felice und Montemitro ist der Rückgang nicht ganz so stark (1951: 1727 Einw. bzw. 906). In den vierzig Jahren vorher waren nur kleinere Abnahmen eingetreten, wie die Zahlen für 1911 zeigen (Acq. 2243, S. Fel. 1641, M. 1017), vgl. Neri (1987, 65). Die schon stark reduzierte Einwohnerzahl ist hinsichtlich der tatsächlichen Sprecher des Mkr. weiter zu relativieren. So ist der Prozentsatz der slavisch Sprechenden in S. Felice nur mehr sehr gering, im Gegensatz zu Acquaviva und insbesondere zu Montemitro. Allerdings entsprechen in allen drei Dörfern die angegebenen Einwohnerzahlen schon deshalb nicht der Realität, als viele Familien infolge ihres Haus- und Grundbesitzes noch offiziell gemeldet sind, sich tatsächlich aber den größten Teil des Jahres entweder als Gastarbeiter v. a. in Norditalien, Deutschland und der Schweiz aufhalten oder gar nach Argentinien oder Australien ausgewandert sind und sich mehr oder minder regelmäßig nur noch im Sommerurlaub in ihrer alten Heimat einfinden.

5. Soziolinguistische Lage

Früher galt, daß eingeheiratete Italiener(innen) grundsätzlich sprachlich assimiliert, d. h. zweisprachig wurden. Unter den Slaven selbst waren v. a. die Männer, die in der Regel Außenkontakte hatten, zweisprachig, während die Frauen nur Mkr. beherrschten. Angesichts der vielen Mischehen dürfte in vielen Familien auch der ital. Dialekt eine gewisse Rolle gespielt haben. Die Sprache des privaten und öffentlichen Lebens innerhalb der Dörfer und im Kontakt miteinander war dagegen slavisch. Daran hatte auch der standardital. Schulunterricht nichts geändert. Kinder aus gemischten Familien erhielten auf jeden Fall durch Gleichaltrige beim Spiel auf der Straße ihre slavische Prägung. Diese Situation einer prinzipiellen Zwei- oder Dreisprachigkeit (slavisch, ital. Dialekt, ital. Standard) mit einheitlichem Gebrauch des Slavischen im Alltag hat sich erst in den letzten 20 bis 30 Jahren mit Intensivierung des Schulunterrichts, der größeren Mobilität (Termoli, Norditalien) und dem Eindringen der Medien verändert. Der von Rešetar (1911, 235) prognostizierte unmittelbar bevorstehende Sprachtod ist zwar auch nach fast einem Jahrhundert noch nicht eingetreten. Kinder sind allerdings öfter nur noch einsprachig ital., normale Verständigungssprache unter Kindern und Jugendlichen ist auf der Straße das Ital. Das Slavische wird in der jüngeren Generation mehr und mehr zur Haussprache und zum Verständigungsmittel unter engeren Bekannten zurückgedrängt. Da die Eltern großen Wert auf das Fortkommen ihrer Kinder und auf ihre schulischen Leistungen legen, wird der Gebrauch des Ital. auch im häuslichen Bereich, mit Ausnahme ausgesprochen konservativer Familien, gefördert. Dabei ist die Einstellung zum ererbten Dialekt nicht etwa negativ. Er wird nur als etwas Selbstverständliches angesehen, mit dem man sich nicht weiter zu beschäftigen braucht.

6. Sprachpolitische Lage

Der ital. Staat erkennt ethnische oder sprachliche Minderheiten in Süditalien nicht an. Auf regionaler und lokaler Ebene gibt es aber starke Bestrebungen zur Förderung sprachlicher und kultureller Besonderheiten der Minoritäten. War eine entsprechende Gesetzgebung in den früheren Jahren durch Rom immer blockiert worden, so scheinen einzelne Regelungen nun doch in die Realität umsetzbar. Traditionell ist der Schulunterricht allein ital., und das (Serbo)kroatische konnte auch nicht als Wahlfremdsprache an der Scuola Media gelehrt werden. Nach halblegalen Versuchen mit zweisprachigem Unterricht im Kindergarten soll nun in Acquaviva mit Hilfe des neuen Gemeindestatuts kroatischer Unterricht auch in der Schule eingeführt werden, vgl. die in Breu (1992, 95, Anm. 95) abgedruckten sprachrelevanten Passagen. Öffentliche Aufschriften und Wegweiser werden seit einiger Zeit teilweise zweisprachig angebracht, wobei, was das Slavische angeht, eine Mischung aus Mkr. und Standardkroatisch verwendet wird. Grundsätzlich gibt es unter denjenigen Intellektuellen, die den schriftlichen Gebrauch des Kroatischen fördern wollen, zwei Richtungen. Die eine strebt eine Verschriftlichung des Lokaldialektes an, möglichst unter Vermeidung auffälliger Italianismen und mit einer gemischten Orthographie, die andere ist für eine Übernahme des kroatischen Standards. Der Normalbevölkerung sind diese Bestrebungen sowieso gleichgültig, da sie in der Regel keinerlei Schwierigkeiten mit ital. geschriebenen Texten haben, im Slavischen aber „Analphabeten" sind. Zusammenhängende kroatische Texte, in welcher Sprachform auch immer, wurden bisher nur äußerst selten veröffentlicht. Eine Ausnahme ist etwa Genova (1990). Zur Förderung des Interesses auch in Laienkreisen an der mkr. Situation hat der historisch-kulturelle Führer von Neri (1987) beigetragen. Versuche mit Periodica, die wenigstens teilweise in Kroatisch geschrieben wurden, z. B. *Naš Jezik* oder *Naš Život*, sind mangels Kaufinteresse bisher stets wieder eingestellt worden. Kirchensprache ist ausschließlich Ital. Für die Geistlichen hat der Ortsdialekt zu wenig Prestige, das Standardkroatische ist wegen seiner eingeschränkten Verständlichkeit inbesondere auch angesichts der Gemischtheit der Bevölkerung untauglich. Fernsehen, Rundfunk, Presse sind italienisch.

Um dem Sprachverfall entgegenzuwirken, wird verstärkt auf die Förderung der Beziehungen zum Mutterland gesetzt. Die Mkr. erhalten sehr billige Urlaubsangebote in Dalmatien, können an Sprachkursen teilnehmen oder an der Universität Zagreb studieren. Es wurde neuerdings eine Satellitenanlage zum Empfang des kroatischen Fernsehens aufgebaut, kroatische Filmteams machen Vorführungen, die Reisen von Lokalpolitikern nach Kroatien und kroatischer Diplomaten und Bischöfe in den Molise sind an der Tagesordnung. Dadurch wird eine neue Mehrsprachigkeit mit der kroatischen Standardsprache vorangetrieben, aber nur bei einer kleinen Schicht.

7. Allgemeines kontaktlinguistisches Porträt

Als präskriptive Grammatik des Mkr. besteht nur Vidov (1974), der sich aber in seiner Standardisierung stark an das Serbokroatische anlehnt. Ebenso wie das kleine Wörterbuch von Vidov (1972) hat es außerdem keinen praktischen Wert, da es vor Ort nicht zu haben ist. In den vergangenen Jahrhunderten stand das Mkr. vor allem in Kontakt mit dem ital. Dialekt der Umgebung. Seit ca. einem Jahrhundert ist das Standardital. als Kontaktsprache hinzugekommen. Während im ersteren Fall nur mündlicher Kontakt vorliegt, kommt im letzteren Fall auch der schriftliche Einfluß hinzu. Es ist aber davon auszugehen, daß sich die kontaktbestimmten Charakteristika des Mkr. fast ausschließlich bereits zur Zeit des alleinigen dialektalen Einflusses herausgebildet hatten.

7.1. Das wird, abgesehen von dem starken Einfluß im Bereich lexikalischer und phraseologischer Entlehnungen, die auch heute noch in jeder Sphäre des Alltagslebens − nicht nur im bäuerlichen Wortschatz − eine wichtige Rolle spielen, besonders im lautlichen Bereich deutlich, wo auslautende Vokale einer starken qualitativen und quantitativen Reduktion unterworfen sind, so daß sie für das ungeschulte Ohr oft kaum zu hören sind. Auch die unbetonten Binnenvokale weisen analog zur dialektalen ital. Aussprache qualitative Veränderungen auf, insbesondere eine starke Öffnung der Vokale mittlerer Höhe und, hierdurch bedingt, tendenziellen Zusammenfall mit a. Bei den Konsonanten sind kontaktbedingt Clustervereinfachungen festzustellen. Andererseits werden Geminaten innersprachlich vereinfacht. Aufgrund solcher nach wie vor produktiver Prozesse ist es schwer, bei Lehnwörtern, deren potentielle Quellwörter sich nur im Vokalismus oder in geminierten Konsonanten unterscheiden, zwischen molisanisch-dialektaler und standardsprachlicher Herkunft zu differenzieren. Es sei denn, es kommen noch andere lautliche Kriterien hinzu, die eine solche Unterscheidung ermöglichen, z. B. bei ˈban(a) 'Seite' ← molis. *bbannə* (vs. ital. *banda*), *h'en* 'Heu' ← molis. *h'iènə* (vs. ital. *fieno*) oder *lejit* 'lesen' ← molis. *lèjjə* (vs. ital. *leggere*).

7.2. Im formalmorphologischen Bereich zeigt das Mkr. beim Verbum eine Verminderung der Stammklassen und eine analogische Angleichung der Endungsreihen, so daß man im Endeffekt von nur mehr zwei Konjugationsreihen ausgehen kann, gegenüber fünf im Standard. Die beiden dominanten Klassen sind dabei diejenige mit Infinitiv auf *-a(t)* und die auf *-i(t)*, die in gewisser Hinsicht der auch in ital. Dialekten der Gegend üblichen Reduktion der vier lateinischen Klassen auf *-a(re)* und *-i(re)* entsprechen. Die Verminderung der Stammklassen kann durch die Lehnverbintegration initiiert worden sein, da aus naheliegenden Gründen nur in diese Klassen integriert wurde. Angesichts der so herbeigeführten alleinigen Produktivität dieser beiden Klassen werden auch jüngere Lehnverben aus dem Standardital., das noch vier Klassen aufweist, nur in die *-a(t)*- (← *-are*) und *-i(t)*-Klasse (← *-ire, -ere, -ére*) integriert. Die alte Lehnwortschicht und damit indirekt der ital. Dialekt wirken somit als Filter für die Integration aus der Standardsprache. Der über Verbpaare ausgedrückte slavische Verbalaspekt ist erhalten geblieben, wobei auch Lehnverben, in der Regel perfektiv integriert, durch Suffigierung ein imperfektives Partnerverb herausbilden. Beispiel: ital. *decidere* → *dečidit* (pf.) / *dečidivat* (impf.) 'entscheiden'. Beim Substantiv geschieht die Lehnwortintegration in der Regel nach dem ital. Genus, wobei Maskulina in die 1. Klasse (∅-Endung im Nominativ), die Feminina in die 2. Klasse (*a*-Endung) integriert werden. Auch hier dürfte das Lehnwortintegrationsverfahren in alter Zeit die Reduktion der slavischen Deklinations- und Genusklassen verursacht haben. Die Neutra des Erbwortschatzes sind zu den Maskulina übergetreten. Die Substantive der 3. Deklination des Standards (Feminina) haben sich — häufig entsprechend ihrem Genus im Ital. — auf die beiden produktiven Deklinationsklassen verteilt. Adjektive zeigen natürlich ebenfalls nur noch zwei Genera.

7.3. Im morphosyntaktischen Bereich ist beim Verbum analog zum ital. Kontaktdialekt eine deutliche Umstrukturierung festzustellen. So ist der alte Aorist, der in den Dialekten des Auswanderungsgebietes noch erhalten ist, durch das analytische Perfekt ersetzt, während das Imperfekt weiterbesteht. Diese Anpassung an den Kontaktdialekt widerspricht einer sonst im gesamtslavischen Dialektraum feststellbaren diachronen Konstante, nämlich dem Schwund des Imperfekts vor dem Aorist. Als neue Kategorie tritt ein kontaktinduziertes HABEN-Futur auf, das das ererbte WOLLEN-Futur in den Bereich eines Wahrscheinlichkeitsfuturs abdrängt, während es selbst eine eindeutig obligative (nezessitative) Komponente enthält. Neu ist auch die Herausbildung aspektueller Verbalperiphrasen (etwa entsprechend der englischen Verlaufsform), wobei nur mkr. *stoim za* + Infinitiv genau ital. *sto per* + Infinitiv entspricht, während die Umfunktionierung des Adverbs *sa* (< *sada* 'jetzt') zur Aspektpartikel nur als indirekte Nachkonstruktion für ital. *sto* + Gerund zu werten ist. Beim Substantiv ist die prinzipielle Erhaltung der Deklination angesichts ihres völligen Fehlens in der Kontaktsprache auffällig. Lediglich die Zahl der Kasus wurde durch den Verlust von Vokativ und Lokativ reduziert. Außerdem ist bei den Feminina der Dativ mit dem Akkusativ zusammengefallen. Schließlich wird im Instrumental und Genitiv zusätzlich zur Kasusendung obligatorisch eine Präposition gesetzt. Wo erhalten wir etwa *s nožem* 'mit dem Messer' bzw. *do žene* 'der Frau'. Die im Genitiv verwendete Präposition *do* hat dabei eine „doppelte Etymologie", insofern als hier slavisch *do* 'bis, hin zu' mit ital.-dial. *də* 'von' zu mkr. *do* 'von' kontaminiert wurde. Das Adjektiv weist ebenfalls Erhaltung der Kasusflexion auf, allerdings nur bei Stellung vor dem Substantiv. Die Komparation hat sich an den analytischen ital. Typ angepaßt (it. *più grande* = mkr. *veča velik*). Nur die Komparative *bolje* 'besser' und *gorje* 'schlechter', die im Ital. ebenfalls synthetische Entsprechungen haben (*meglio, peggio*), sind erhalten geblieben. Die Stellung des attributiven Adjektivs relativ zum Substantiv richtet sich nach dem ital. Muster, insofern die ererbte Voranstellung durch allgemeine Nachstellung verdrängt wurde, außer in den Fällen, wo auch im Ital. beide Möglichkeiten bestehen. Wie im Ital. werden Pronomina vor das Substantiv gestellt. Dabei werden sie stets dekliniert.

Das Mkr. hat keinen der Kontaktsprache entsprechenden determinierten Artikel entwickelt.

8. Gegenwärtiger Forschungsstand

Als Standardwerk für die Beschreibung des Kroatischen im Molise muß immer noch Rešetar (1911) gelten, der die komplexe Forschungsgeschichte und die damals aktuelle außersprachliche Situation darstellt und dazu eine Dialektbeschreibung unter Einschluß der Besonderheiten des Sprachkontakts, umfangreiches Textmaterial sowie ein Glossar bringt. In der Folgezeit hat Reichenkron (1934) auf der Basis von Rešetars Material mehrere Hypothesen zum romanischen Einfluß im grammatischen Bereich aufgestellt. Innerhalb Italiens haben sich seit den 50er Jahren mehrere (ungedruckte) Dissertationen mit den Molisekroaten befaßt, aus denen sowohl Muljačić als auch Vidov die Daten für ihre Arbeiten bezogen haben. Innerhalb der Slavistik gilt das Mkr. seit Duličenko (1981) als „Mikroliteratursprache", wobei aber die äußerst geringe Zahl von mkr. Publikationen wie überhaupt der ungelöste Status einer verschrifteten Variante des Minderheitendialekts eine solche Klassifikation zumindest als fraglich erscheinen läßt. In Breu (1990) wurde eine Bestandsaufnahme der bisherigen Forschung sowie eine allgemeine sprachkontaktorientierte Beschreibung der Situation der Molisekroaten und ihrer Sprache gegeben, in Breu (1992) wird die Restrukturierung des Verbsystems untersucht, und Breu (im Druck) beschäftigt sich mit dem Vergleich der italienisch-kroatischen und der italienisch-albanischen Sprachkontaktsituation im Molise.

9. Bibliographie (in Auswahl)

Breu, Walter (1990): „Sprache und Sprachverhalten in den slavischen Dörfern des Molise (Süditalien)". In: *Slavistische Linguistik 1989*, Breu, Walter (Ed.), München, 35–65.

Breu, Walter (1992): „Das italokroatische Verbsystem zwischen slavischem Erbe und kontaktbedingter Entwicklung". In: *Slavistische Linguistik 1991*, Reuther, Tilmann (Ed.), München, 93–122.

Breu, Walter (im Druck): „Italoslavo ed italoalbanese nella zona di contatto linguistico del Molise". In: *Atti del 3° Convegno Internazionale di Studi sulla Lingua albanese 1991*, Del Puente, Patrizia/ Landi, Addolorata (Eds.), Salerno.

Duličenko, A. D. (1981): *Slavjanskie literaturnye mikrojazyki* [Slavische Mikroliteratursprachen], Tallinn.

Genova, Angelo (1990): *Ko jesmo... bolje: ko bihmo?!*, Vasto.

Ivić, Pavle (1958): *Die serbokroatischen Dialekte*, Band I, Den Haag.

Muljačić, Žarko (1973): „Su alcuni effetti del bilinguismo nella parlata dei croati molisani". In: *Bilinguismo e diglossia in Italia*, Cortelazzo, Manlio (Ed.), Pisa, 29–37.

Neri, Pierino (1987): *I Paesi Slavi del Molise*, Campobasso.

Reichenkron, Günter (1934): „Serbokroatisches aus Süditalien". In: *Zeitschrift für Slavische Philologie 11*, 325–339.

Rešetar, Milan (1911): *Die serbokroatischen Kolonien Süditaliens*, Wien.

Vidov, Božidar (²1974): *Grammatica del dialetto ikavo-štokavo delle località dell'isola linguistica croata nel Molise*, Toronto (Grottaferrata ¹1968).

Vidov, Božidar (1972): *Vocabolario in dialetto dell'isola linguistica croata nel Molise*, Toronto.

Walter Breu, Konstanz (Deutschland)

163. Italien–grec

1. Géographie et démographie
2. Histoire
3. Politique, économie, situations culturelle et religieuse
4. Statistiques et profil ethnique
5. Situation sociolinguistique
6. Etat de la politique linguistique
7. Portrait général des contacts linguistiques
8. Littérature dialectale
9. Bibliographie (sélective)

1. Géographie et démographie

Il y a en Italie deux îlots intéressés par le contact italien-grec: une enclave de 144 km² comprenant neuf villages dans le Salente (Calimera, Corigliano d'Otranto, Martano, Castrignano dei Greci, Zollino, Sternatia, Martignano, Melpignano, Soleto), avec 35.911 habitants, et un territoire de 233 km² avec cinq villages (Bova Superiore, Rochudi, Condofuri, Roccaforte, Chorio) dans le massif de l'Aspromonte et, dans la vallée de l'Amendolea, avec 12.979 habitants (Istat, 1992); → carte linguistique F.

2. Histoire

Il est difficile, parce qu'on ne possède aucune documentation pré-médiévale acceptable (Battisti 1927), d'établir l'époque d'arrivée des populations grecques dans des régions que la latinisation même ne réussit pas à rendre homogènes: une première date (*thèse dorique* ou *archaïsante*) est celle du VIIIe siècle av. J.-C., coïncidant avec l'établissement dorique en Italie du Sud (Rohlfs 1934); au contraire, la *thèse modernisante* soutient une colonisation byzantine − non antérieure à 588 pour la Calabre, non postérieure à 878 pour le Salente − née des grandes migrations monastiques du VIIe siècle (Spano 1965, ch. 3).

3. Politique, économie, situations culturelle et religieuse

Récemment, des événements négatifs ont caractérisé la vie de ces enclaves, la région salentine étant influencée par des épisodes de *nouvelle mafia* et la Calabre par le phénomène de la *'ndrangheta*, qui, elle, est déterminée par une politique malsaine. Le chômage y a été très élevé, d'où des migrations massives (1951−1961) vers le nord. L'économie du Salente repose sur le tertiaire et l'agriculture; mais récemment, les habitants ont accentué les activités industrielles et agro-alimentaires et celles liées au bâtiment et au commerce. Les conditions générales de la région ont déterminé la misère économique de l'îlot linguistique de la Calabre (cf. 4.3.), toujours caractérisé par l'exode. L'alphabétisation (Istat 1981 indiquait 1.464 analphabètes pour la zone grecque de la Calabre, 2.806 pour celle du Salente) s'est diffusée rapidement ces dernières années. Le rite orthodoxe, jadis la religion incontestée de ces zones, a cédé le pas au rite catholique (Cassoni 1934−1937) depuis le XVIe siècle.

4. Statistiques et profil ethnique

4.1. Mis à part des chiffres démesurés de *grécophones*, fournis par les municipalités et servant l'amour-propre des indigènes, aujourd'hui (Istat 1992) la population du contact compte à *Calimera* 7.321 habitants, à *Castrignano* 3.985, à *Corigliano* 5.628, à *Martano* 9.591; *Martignano* en a 1.846, *Melpignano* 2.155, *Soleto* 356, *Sternatia* 2.808 et *Zollino* 2.291.

Bova Superiore, situé à 827 mètres, capitale du grecanico, compte 603 habitants: *Bova Marina*, en aval de *Bova*, localité dont la réelle participation à l'îlot linguistique est plutôt récente, 4.361 habitants. *Roccaforte*, situé à 935 mètres, compte 1.215 habitants, *Condofuri* 5.299, *Rochudi* 1.501. Ces chiffres concernent non seulement les centres historiques et les communes mais aussi les hameaux isolés dans la campagne: le village de *Chorio de Rochudi*, plusieurs fois évacué, et *Gallicianò*.

4.2. Il est désormais normal d'appeler *grico* (*gríko*) ou *grec salentin* le parler des villages du Salente, pour le distinguer du *grec* ou *grecanico* de Calabre: cette distinction, qui n'est pas l'apanage des locuteurs mêmes, a souvent été employée par les linguistes (cf. Alessio 1975, 11). Dans la zone du *grecanico*, on signale par le terme *bovese* la variété de la capitale, et par celui de *amendolese* la variété du territoire traversé par l'*Amendolea* (cf. 5.3.). Finalement, les tenants de la thèse dorique préfèrent le terme *grecanico*, et ceux de la thèse byzantine-romanisante le terme *romaico* (cf. 7.6.2.).

4.3. Le Salente constitue un paysage plat, sans cours d'eau, avec quelques dénivellements qui ne dépassent pas les 200 mètres: les villages du contact sont reliés entre eux et le reste du Salente par un excellent réseau routier. En ce qui concerne le climat, l'irrégularité des pluies influence négativement le développement de l'agriculture. Le massif de l'Aspromonte, en Calabre, est marqué par un isolement géographique hermétique, ce qui, depuis toujours, a imposé une économie carrément archaïque; de plus, les crues et les tremblements de terre ont renforcé cet isolement.

4.4. La vision pangrecque, qui épouse la thèse archaïsante, ne s'affirme que rarement et avec difficulté; le seul ouvrage moderne (Miranda, SLI 1980, 34) qui traite ce sujet, montre, à travers l'examen des coutumes, rites, chants populaires relatifs au printemps et à la mort et d'un certain nombre de cérémonies, la profonde *unitarieté culturelle* de la région salentine, qui ne se subdivise donc pas en sous-aires grecques et romanes.

5. Situation sociolinguistique

5.1. Il s'agit ici de la coexistence des dialectes romans et de la langue italienne (avec ses variétés), avec le grec. Les grands-parents se servent d'un grec 'romanisé' dans toutes les situations, mais — avec leurs enfants — ils préfèrent parler le dialecte salentin ou calabrais: ils ont une maîtrise très réduite de l'italien au niveau actif et assez limitée au niveau passif. La génération des parents parle rarement le grec, en possède néanmoins à 45% une maîtrise passive, utilise surtout le dialecte roman et cherche à parler italien avec ses enfants: c'est donc la couche sociale la moins favorisée, au moins lorsqu'elle n'a pas effectué un recyclage professionnel ce qui la rapproche de la génération des jeunes gens, qui utilise le dialecte grec dans des contextes exclusivement familiaux et amicaux, alors que l'italien standard et littéraire prédomine à l'école (Karanastasis 1974): une fonction cryptolalique du grico est signalée dans SLI 1980 (339).

5.2. Le *grico* et le *grecanico*, langues de paysans isolés, ont donc reculé devant les parlers romans employés dans les villages voisins, et devant l'italien.

5.3. Dans les neuf communes du Salente, on considère la variété de Martano comme la plus pure et la plus correcte (Parlangèli 1953, 50), tandis qu'en Calabre, on préfère le *bovesien* alors que l'*amendolese* est considéré comme étant grossier. En général, on peut constater que le grec est jugé 'inférieur' et 'pas fonctionnel parce que marginal'. On enregistre en plus une grande défiance à son égard, à laquelle font face une certaine valorisation du dialecte roman et l'adhésion idéologiquement bien ancrée à la langue italienne.

5.4. Il s'agit donc d'une situation plus compliquée que celle d'une simple diglossie, qu'on peut signaler pour la troisième génération seulement (cf. 5.1.): c'est même un cas de triglossie, car, finalement, il y a trois langues qui s'affrontent dans des contextes sociaux différents (italien, dialecte roman, grico).

6. Etat de la politique linguistique

6.1. Auprès de l'AIDLCM (Association Internationale pour la Défense des Langues et Cultures Menacées) la délégation des Italo-Grecs de Calabre est toujours active et, en 1970, les deux aires se sont réunies dans l'*UGIM, Union des Grecs de l'Italie méridionale*. En 1976, on décida, dans le Salente, de réaliser un enseignement expérimental du grec dans les écoles et de rédiger, dans les *Centres Sociaux d'Education Permanente des adultes*, des textes populaires et d'organiser des représentations religieuses. C'est en 1978 que fut créé à Castrignano un *Comité Permanent pour la sauvegarde des Intérêts Culturels de la Grecia*: citons, parmi les manifestations des dernières années, les *Alcyoniadi* (22−26 octobre 1992) et les *Dionisia*, rencontres de poètes grecs et italo-grecs; le *Kieme* grec et les *Assessorats de la Culture* des municipalités favorisent ces activités, et, tous les ans, 250−300 participants se déplacent de part et d'autre des deux rives de l'Adriatique. En Calabre, l'organisme le plus intéressé à la diffusion de la langue est *'La Jonica'*, née en 1968 à Reggio de Calabre. Là aussi, on a essayé de renouer les contacts avec la Grèce: parallèlement, le gouvernement grec, à travers l'envoi de livres, de cassettes, et de disques, a encouragé ces efforts. Malgré beaucoup de problèmes, les revues et les associations survivent: *Zoì ce glossa* ('Vie et langue') à Gallicianò; *Cinurio Cosmo* ('Le Nouveau Monde') à Bova Marina, *Apodiafazi* ('Le soleil se lève') à Bova.

6.2. Les médias et la télévision surtout ont fortement contribué à la résurrection du grec, dénonçant la condition d'infériorité de la génération des grands-parents. Récemment les radios locales *Radio Bova, Radio Melito, Radio S. Paolo* à Reggio ont commencé à émettre *en* grec et à parler *du* grec.

6.3. Tout cela a suscité des activités de standardisation et des manifestations de loyauté linguistique face à l'ancien idiome. Mais il s'agit là d'opérations réalisées surtout au niveau de l'écrit, et rarement au niveau oral, toujours flottante à cause du contact avec l'italien et les dialectes romans environnants.

6.4. Ces dialectes sont transcrits, par les chercheurs locaux, moyennant les caractères utilisés aussi pour la langue italienne, sans respecter la réalité articulatoire des sons:

quant aux linguistes de métier, ils utilisent rarement la transcription de l'IPA et préfèrent la transcription rohlfsienne (c'est à dire celle de l'EWuG, cf. 7.5.).

7. Portrait général des contacts linguistiques

Tendance vers l'iotacisme, gémination de /λ/, qui donne toujours /ḍḍ/ et qui se retrouve également en Grèce (Colotti 1977), emploi du futur et des formes périphrastiques pour le présent (Tsopanakis 1968): tels sont les phénomènes les plus importants du *gríco* et du *grecanico*. Plusieurs de ceux-ci ont déjà disparu sous le coup du contact avec les parlers romans environnants.

7.1. Le vocalisme du grecanico demeure inaltéré, tandis que la situation des consonnes grecques, que le roman ne connaît pas, est différente; par ex., les aboutissements de la fricative interdentale θ sont au nombre de 3: à Bova, nous avons χorò 'je vois' < θεωρῶ, à Rochudi θorò, à Gallicianò forò. On peut alléguer aussi, pour caractériser la fragmentation interne du système, le traitement du nexus [kt]: le grico réalise ce nexus soit par amuïssement, soit par *f*, soit par assimilation régressive (*tt*): le verbe 'ἀνοίγω, ἀνοίκτω' 'j'ouvre', par ex., donne dans le grico les résultats *anio, enío, nío, nífto, nítto* — alors qu'en Calabre on trouve [ft], [θt], [st] — cf. le nom μάκτρα, 'pétrin', avec ses variantes [*máfta, mátra, mástra, máttra*]. Cette oscillation, qui affecte également les groupes /pt/, /ps/, /ks/, /kn/, s'est généralisée dans les assimilations /tt/, /zz/, /zz/, /nn/, surtout dans le Salente, moins en Calabre: δίψα, 'soif' donne *díttsa, títtsa* dans les villages du Salente, mais *díspa, víspa* en Calabre.

Dans les parlers romans du Salente l'on constate la persistance d'un polymorphisme phonétique hérité du grec autochtone. Il s'agit de variations phonétiques entre occlusives sourdes et sonores, le plus souvent dans des mots d'origine grecque et en position initiale: p. ex. à Otrante: *táfini/dafini* « laurier », *dánato/tánato* « mort », *céma/jéma* « sang ». Des oscillations similaires affectent aussi le stock latin du lexique des dialectes salentins. L'on y constate, en effet, des alternances telles que *ddispiéttu/tispiéttu* « dispetto » ou *ddíttu/títtu* « detto ».

7.2. Les interférences touchent toutes les catégories grammaticales; cela engendre une instabilité surtout phonétique et lexicale: l'osmose avec les parlers romans a créé des possibilités d'échange: dans le lexique, on enregistre la présence massive du dialecte roman et de l'italien (p. ex.: dédoublement de l'adjectif: à Bova *nan azzári méga méga*, 'un très grand poisson'), tandis que la syntaxe grecque maintient ses particularités (emploi du génitif et de l'accusatif, refus du futur, période hypothétique toujours avec l'indicatif), mis à part quelques calques morphosyntaxiques sur le roman, comme, p. ex., les infinitifs régis par un verbe qui, contrairement à la syntaxe classique qui ne les connaît pas, s'infiltrent aussi bien dans le *gríco* que dans le *grecanico* (cf. Rohlfs 1977, 190−192). Les emprunts à l'italien et aux dialectes romans sont nombreux. Ils s'expliquent surtout par la perte de la conscience linguistique et par l'usage limité d'un lexique lié aux objets de la vie de tous les jours. Dans l'élocution libre d'une bilingue gríca de 53 ans, j'ai calculé que les emprunts romans touchent plus de 20% des mots. Des doublets dus au prestige du dialecte roman et de l'italien sont omniprésents: les gricophones connaissent, certes, le verbe *azzemolò*, 'se confesser', mais ils lui préfèrent le substantif *kunfessiúna* 'confession' à la place de *azzemolóisi*; cela concerne aussi le domaine des adjectifs où les doublets gríco/romans sont fréquents: *macréo/lungo*, 'long', *aníttο/aperto*, 'ouvert', et les adverbes qui souvent sont des semi-emprunts: it. *divers-a-ménte* et grico *aḍḍ-a-ménte*, 'différemment'. Le lexique de la parenté, des sentiments, des maladies, des travaux des champs est d'origine grecque, alors que celui de la maison est italo-roman. Le 'cru' et l'alimentation en général sont grecs, mais non pas le 'cuit' et le lexique du commerce. Le nombre des calques gréco-romans est également très important: gríco *istéo*, italien (it.) *stare*, 'être, se trouver, rester': *ísteki*, 'il est'; gríco *strata kánnonta*, salentin *stráta faciéndu*, it. *strada facendo*, 'chemin faisant'.

Dans le *grecanico*, le contact linguistique affecte surtout les substantifs, selon la typologie déjà signalée; la morphologie verbale résiste, mais le thème verbal peut être emprunté: à la place de διακρίνω, it. *distinguere*, 'distinguer', on retrouve l'it. *scoprire*, 'découvrir' dans l'emprunt σκουπερέω; φατιγέω, 'je travaille', est un calque du verbe it. *faticare* (Karanastasis 1974, 16). Les doublets étymologiques sont fréquents (*bbirgognéugomai*, it. *vergognarsi*, vit à côté de *andrépomai* < ἐντρέπομαι, 'j'ai honte'; à côté de *sceré-*

nome < ξεραίνω, 'je sèche', on trouve *assughéo*, it. *asciugo*). Ceci vaut également pour les adverbes temporels italiens (*dópou*, it. *dópo*, 'après'; *fína*, it. *fino*, 'jusqu'à').

7.3. Mis à part Morosi 1870 et 1878 (Colotti 1979), la seule grammaire vraiment scientifique est celle de Rohlfs 1950 (1977) (à consulter également les compléments de Kapsomenos 1953, Tsopanakis 1981). Des renseignements plutôt sommaires se trouvent dans Tondi 1935, Cassoni 1937, Scott 1979 et Profili 1984—1985.

7.4. Pour la querelle relative à l'histoire de ces zones, voir Rohlfs 1934, Karatzas 1958, Battisti 1927 et Parlangèli 1953. Le livre de Spano 1965 est richement documenté.

7.5. Citons, pour la lexicologie, l'ouvrage fondamental de Rohlfs, *Etymologisches Wörterbuch der unteritalienischen Gräzität (EWuG)* (1964) (voir aussi Alessio 1932). Récemment Karanastasis a terminé son Ἱστορικὸν Λεξικὸν τῶν Ἑλληνικῶν Ἰδιωμάτων τῆς κατῶ Ἰταλίας (1992).

7.6. Quant à la passionnante querelle sur la genèse des îlots grecs, elle concerne les noms les plus illustres de la linguistique européenne, en commençant par Schwitzer, en passant par Ascoli et Meyer-Lübke, pour finir avec Rohlfs et Battisti. Il s'agit d'ailleurs d'une discussion qui a toujours suscité l'intérêt de tous les romanistes.

7.6.1. *De 1870 à 1960*. Depuis les travaux de Witte 1830, Pott 1865, Kind 1858, Comparetti 1866, Morosi 1870, 1878 et Pellegrini 1880 (cf. Colotti 1979, 335), deux thèses s'affrontent en ce qui concerne l'origine: la première a prévalu jusqu'aux innombrables travaux de G. Rohlfs (1924, 1930, etc.) qui toujours a plaidé en faveur de la genèse paléo-grecque des deux îlots linguistiques. Les thèses de Rohlfs (Colotti 1988), contestées tant en Italie (Battisti 1927, Alessio 1932) qu'en France (Pernot 1936), avaient pourtant été favorablement reçues par A. Meillet et J. Vendryès, et soutenues par tous les linguistes grecs, qu'ils appartiennent au siècle passé (Hatzidakis) ou au siècle présent. C'est en 1953 que Parlangèli lança une attaque véhémente contre Rohlfs, refusant tout archaïsme. Une date historique pour la thèse rohlfsienne est cependant l'année 1958 quand Karatzas à l'aide du *Dictionnaire Historique de l'Académie d'Athènes*, allégua des données en sa faveur, en signalant la présence d'archaïsmes de type dorien (par ex. γᾶς ἔντερον, 'ver de terre', τάμισος 'présure') susceptibles de démontrer la continuité de la colonisation dorienne dans ces îlots. Une troisième thèse (Franceschi, Hubschmid) qui admet une byzantinisation pour le Salente et une grécité non interrompue quant à la Calabre, ainsi qu'une quatrième (Kapsomenos) qui soutient la superposition de colons byzantins à l'ancienne colonisation, ne connurent que peu de succès.

7.6.2. *De 1960 jusqu'aujourd'hui*. Evidemment la description diachronique des phonèmes, du lexique (cfr. Karanastasis 1974, Falcone 1971, Colotti 1977) et la récolte d'archaïsmes ou de byzantinismes n'ont jamais cessé. Plus récemment, les recherches prennent en compte les phénomènes du contact (SLI 1980).

8. Littérature dialectale

La littérature locale, pourtant forte et très consistante dans le passé, a malheureusement subi des revers à cause de déchirements idéologiques intrinsèques. La littérature *gréco-salentine* est souvent l'œuvre d'une élite intellectuelle qui se sert du grec à des fins plutôt personnelles (je renvoie aux noms des poètes, écrivains et «hellénistes» suivants: V. D. Palumbo, P. Lefons, M. Cassoni, P. Stomeo, etc.: cf. Colotti 1979; SLI 1980, 352). Pour la *Calabre* citons des auteurs tels que E. Capialbi, L. Bruzzano, A. Nocera, F. Mosino et L. Borrello (Rossi-Taibbi 1959).

9. Bibliographie (sélective)

Alessio, Giovanni (1932, 1933): «Aggiunte e correzioni al 'Lessico Etimologico dei grecismi nei dialetti dell'Italia meridionale' di G. Rohlfs». In: *Archivio Storico per la Calabria e la Lucania 2*, 261—273; *3*, 138—152.

Alessio, Giovanni (1975): «Grecità e romanità nell'Italia meridionale». In: *Byzantino-Sicula 2*, 11—43.

Battisti, Carlo (1927): «Appunti sulla storia e la diffusione dell'Ellenismo nell'Italia meridionale». In: *Revue de Linguistique romane 3*, 1—3.

Cassoni, Mauro (1930): *Hellás otrantina o disegno grammaticale*, Grottaferrata.

Cassoni, Mauro (1934—1937): «Il tramonto del rito greco in Terra d'Otranto». In: *Rinascenza Salentina 2*, 1—15; *3*, 71—80; *4*, 73—83; *5*, 234—250.

Colotti, Mariateresa (1976): «Tre lettere di Morosi a Comparetti, con note di linguistica grika, Problemi di morfosintassi dialettale». In: *Atti dell'XI Convegno del CSDI*, Pisa, 53−61.

Colotti, Mariateresa (1977): *Il problema delle geminate nei dialetti neogreci del Salento*, Bari.

Colotti, Mariateresa (1979): «Carteggio Morosi-Ascoli-Comparetti». In: *Lares 45*, 335−345.

Colotti, Mariateresa (1988): «Gerhard Rohlfs». In: *Lares 54*, 629−633.

Falcone, Giuseppe (1971): «Ipotesi di lavoro per una ricerca organica (storico-linguistica) sulla crisi del bovese». In: *Studi linguistici Salentini 4*, 53−96.

Kapsomenos, Stavros G. (1953): «Beiträge zur historischen Grammatik der griechischen Dialekte Unteritaliens». In: *Byzantinische Zeitschrift 46*, 320−348.

Karanastasis, Anastasios (1974): «I fattori che hanno contribuito al regresso dei dialetti neogreci dell'Italia meridionale». In: *Dal dialetto alla lingua*, Pisa, 5−18.

Karatzas, Stavros C. (1958): *L'origine des dialectes néo-grecs de l'Italie méridionale*, Paris.

Parlangèli, Oronzo (1949): «Due note grike. I. il nome *grico*. II. *plonno*». In: *Aevum 23*, 170−176.

Parlangèli, Oronzo (1953): *Sui dialetti romanzi e romaici del Salento*, Milan.

Pernot, Hubert (1936): «Hellénisme et Italie méridionale». In: *Studi Italiani di Filologia Classica 13*, 161−182.

Profili, Olga (1984−1985): «Description du système phonétique et phonologique du parler gríco de Corigliano d'Otranto». In: *Studi Linguistici Salentini 14*, 9−117.

Rohlfs, Gerhard (1934, 1974): *Scavi linguistici nella Magna Grecia*, Galatina.

Rohlfs, Gerhard (1950, 1977): *Historische Grammatik der unteritalienischen Gräzität*, Munich. Trad. it.: S. Sicuro: *Grammatica storica dei dialetti italo-greci* (Calabria, Salento), Munich.

Rohlfs, Gerhard (1961): «Oskisch **grécus (*grícus)*, lat. *graecus?*». In: *Glotta 39*, 268−273.

Rohlfs, Gerhard (1964²): *Etymologisches Wörterbuch der unteritalienischen Gräzität*, Tübingen.

Rossi-Taibbi, Giuseppe/Caracausi, Girolamo (Eds.) (1959): *Testi neogreci di Calabria*, Palerme.

Scott, Stan (1979): *Grammatica elementare del greco di Calabria*, Paleon Faliron.

SLI [Società di Linguistica Italiana] (1980): *I dialetti e le lingue delle minoranze di fronte all'italiano*, Rome.

Spano, Benito (1965): *La grecità bizantina e i suoi riflessi geografici nell'Italia meridionale e insulare*, Pise.

Tondi, Domenicano (1935): *Glossa. La lingua greca nel Salento*, Noci.

Tsopanakis, Agapitos (1968): «I dialetti neogreci dell'Italia meridionale rispetto a quelli greci». In: *Italia Dialettale 31*, 1−23.

Tsopanakis, Agapitos (1981): «Contributo alla conoscenza dei dialetti greci dell'Italia meridionale». In: *Italia Dialettale 64*, 233−282.

Mariateresa Colotti, Bari (Italie)

164. Italienisch−Albanisch

1. Geographie und Demographie
2. Geschichte
3. Politik, Wirtschaft und allgemeine kulturelle sowie religiöse Lage
4. Statistik und Ethnoprofil
5. Soziolinguistische Lage
6. Sprachpolitische Lage
7. Allgemeines kontaktlinguistisches Porträt
8. Kritische Wertung der verwendeten Quellen und Literatur
9. Bibliographie (in Auswahl)

1. Geographie und Demographie

Das Kerngebiet des ital.-alb. Sprachkontakts umfaßt heute 49 von ursprünglich mehr als 100 über das gebirgige Landesinnere Süditaliens verstreuten Sprachinseln (z. T. mit Tochterkolonien), mit Schwerpunkt in Kalabrien (65,3%) (Prov. Cosenza 25, Catanzaro 7), ferner in Lukanien (Prov. Potenza 5), Abruzzo-Molise (Prov. Campobasso 4, Pescara 1), Sizilien (Prov. Palermo 4), Apulien (Prov. Foggia 2, Tarent 1), Kampanien (Prov. Avellino 1). Die von wachsendem Bevölkerungsschwund gekennzeichneten, ethnisch gemischten Siedlungen bilden z. T. Fraktionen italophoner Zentren. Hinzu kommen heute Agglomerationen in Nachbarstädten und u. a. den Industriemetropolen des Nordens (Turin, Mailand). Im Hauptareal des Sprachkontakts, dem nordkalabrischen (nkal.) Cratital, beträgt der ethnische Proporz 65,9% alb., 15,9% kalabrischer (kal.) und 18,1% gemischter Abstammung (Birken-Silverman, i.Vorb.); → Sprachenkarte F.

2. Geschichte

Der ital.-alb. Sprachkontakt geht auf die Gründung alb. Militär- und Flüchtlingskolonien in Süditalien infolge der politischen Ereignisse des 15./16. Jahrhunderts zurück, die zu einer engen Beziehung zwischen Albanien und Italien beitrugen. Der Kampf Alfons I. von Aragon gegen den anjoutreuen Adel im Königreich Neapel führte 1448 zur Anwerbung alb. Hirtenkrieger unter Führung Demetri Reres und zur dauerhaften Niederlassung in Militärkolonien. Um 1470, 1480 und 1534 wurden durch die türkische Eroberung des Balkans drei Flüchtlingswellen ausgelöst, deren Diaspora in Italien durch die guten Beziehungen Gjergji Kastriota Skanderbegs, des erstmals die alb. Stämme einigenden Heerführers, zur Republik Venedig, zum Königreich Neapel und zum Kirchenstaat begünstigt wurde. Die auf den Exodus um 1470 und 1480 zurückgehenden Kolonien (Neugründungen, Anschluß an italophone Gemeinden oder Repeuplierung) führten v. a. gr.-orth. Südalbaner heterogener Herkunft zusammen (Çamëria, Labëria, Bregdeti), während nach 1534 (Fall der venez. Kolonie Korone auf dem Peloponnes) alb. Oberschichtangehörige vom Peloponnes gemeinsam mit Griechen in bereits bestehende alb. Orte zuzogen und als letzte Kolonie 1744 Villa Badessa gründeten. Daraus resultierten plurilektale Dorfgemeinschaften mit schichtenspezifischem alb.-gr. Bilinguismus. Insgesamt ist von 20.000 Emigranten sowohl aus dem Adels- als auch aus dem Bauernstand sowie Soldaten auszugehen, die z. T. nach längerer Migration durch verstreute Ansiedlung auf dem Land weltlicher und geistlicher Feudalherren (Basilianerklöster, röm.-kath. Kirche) in das südital. Feudalsystem integriert wurden. Die Dynamik des Bilinguismusprozesses verläuft in drei Phasen: Isolation, wirtschaftliche Autarkie und weitreichende Selbstverwaltung stützen Sprache, Religion und Traditionen dort, wo das alb. Element nicht binnen kurzer Zeit von der südital. einheimischen Bevölkerung absorbiert wird. Generell spielen zu jener Zeit die sprachlichen Differenzen eine weit geringere Rolle als die religiösen zwischen *Greci* einerseits und *Latini* andererseits. Nach anfangs nur sporadischen Sprachkontakten zur umgebenden dialektophonen ital. Ethnie erfolgte Mitte des 16. Jahrhunderts eine Intensivierung im religiösen und wirtschaftlichen Bereich mit Erweiterung des sozialen Netzwerks. Zum einen bewirkten kirchliche Mißstände, Inquisition und Anschluß an röm.-kath. Bistümer nach Loslösung vom gr.-orth. autokephalen Erzbistum Ohrid (1564) eine Schwächung bzw. örtlich sogar den Verlust des Alb. und Gr. als Kirchensprache; zum anderen öffneten sich die alb. Enklaven Italienern, die jedoch zumeist assimiliert wurden. Diese Entwicklungsphase der interethnischen Kontakte ist gekennzeichnet durch Interaktion zwischen entsprechenden männlichen Rollenträgern wie Hirten und durch einen von der größeren Einheit, dem Lehen, zum Dorf und zur Kirchengemeinde fortschreitenden Bilinguismusprozeß mit Diglossie, wie das Zeugnis des Kalabresen Marafiotti (1595) belegt: „(...) tra di loro parlano secondo l'uso della loro natiua lingua, ma con noi parlano secondo 'l nostro vso (...)". Die heute allgemeine Zweisprachigkeit der Alb. reflektiert die kulturelle, soziale, wirtschaftliche und technische Entwicklung: Schulpflicht, soziale Differenzierung, Exogamie, Mobilität, Massenmedien, Erweiterung des Kommunikationsradius, höhere Frequenz interethnischer Kommunikation. Dabei eröffnet erst die Durchsetzung der Schulpflicht den Zugang zu den bis dahin der Landbevölkerung weitgehend unbekannten Normen des Standardital., so daß dieses im Vergleich zu den dialektalen Varietäten das Sprachsystem kaum beeinflußte, wohl aber als Prestigeidiom die heutige Primärsozialisation. In den Fällen eines jungen Sprachwechsels (z. B. Cervicati) bezeugen Substratspuren noch die einstige Sprachtradition.

3. Politik, Wirtschaft und allgemeine kulturelle sowie religiöse Lage

Waren die Italoalbaner ebenso wie die mit ihnen im Kontakt lebende ital. Ethnie z. Zt. des Feudalismus politisch weitgehend rechtlos, so gehörten sie nach seiner Abschaffung zu den engagiertesten Verfechtern der Einigung Italiens (u. a. der Staatsmann F. Crispi) und verstehen sich bis heute als loyale ital. Staatsbürger alb. Ethnie. Die sozioökonomische Situation entspricht i. a. der rückständigen Agrarstruktur des Mezzogiorno mit hoher Analphabetenquote (Kalabrien 40%) und starker Emigration. Trotz partieller Akkulturation hat sich die Kultur der Alb. in der Diaspora besonders entwickelt und ihre Charakteristika bewahrt, die als objektive Minderheitskategorien die ethnische Identität bestimmen: neben Sprache und Brauchtum die Literatur mit mündlicher Überlieferung (*Kalimere*, Märchen), frühem religiösem Schrifttum (erste alb. Katechismusübersetzung 1592) und romantischer Dichtung (G. De Rada, A. Santori, G. Serembe). Die wesentlichste sprachstützende Funktion kommt m. E. der sprachpflegerisch engagierten unierten Kirche (Anerkennung des Papstes) mit i. a. trilingualer Liturgie (Alb./Gr./It.) zu. Geistige Zentren bilden die Bischofsitze Piana degli Albanesi auf Sizilien (seit 1937), dem 1960 auch die lat. Pfarreien der sikuloalb. Orte unterstellt wurden, und Lungro in Kalabrien (1919).

4. Statistik und Ethnoprofil

Differierende Sprachstatistiken schätzen die Größe der Außengruppe der alb. Sprechergemeinschaft, der *Arb(ë)reshe* mit den großen Untergruppen der Kalabro- und Sikuloalb., auf 80.000–200.000 Sprecher. Der Grad der koarealen Mehrsprachigkeit differiert von Ort zu Ort je nach geographischer Lage (Ballungsräume alb. Enklaven vs. Isolation), Verwaltungsstruktur und Ritus. Für den Siedlungsschwerpunkt im nkal. Cratital ergibt sich ein Anteil von 70% Albano- und 30% Italophonen bei örtlichen Schwankungen zwischen 22,2% und 100%, während Rother 1966 die Gesamtquote der Alb.-Sprecher in den Enklaven auf 82,2% beziffert. Vergleiche mit früheren Sprachstatistiken zeigen für 1861–1901 eine Zunahme der Alb.-Sprecher um 3,9%, von 1901–1966 einen Rückgang von 10,5%, von 1861–1992 (bez. L1 Alb.) um 11,5%. Es handelt sich bei der primär mit den ital. Mundarten und sekundär mit dem *ital. regionale/popolare* in Kontakt stehenden Idiom, dem *Arb(ë)resh* (Arb.), um 49 dachlose, nicht kodifizierte und geolinguistisch schwer klassifizierbare Ortsmundarten, die mündlich tradiert werden.

5. Soziolinguistische Lage

Die Sprachsituation in den alb. Enklaven ist durch generations- und geschlechtsspezifisch variierenden Plurilinguismus mit schichtenspezifischer Diglossie charakterisiert. Angesichts des Fehlens umfassender soziolinguistischer Studien und örtlich stark divergierender Verhältnisse seien in Tabelle 164.1 die 1990–1992 in 22 Enklaven in Nkal. bei 504 Informanten ermittelten Daten (in %) aufgeführt (Birken-Silverman, i. Vorb.):

Tab. 164.1: Spracherwerb und Sprachgebrauch der Kontaktidiome in den alb. Enklaven Nordkalabriens

Code	Arb.	Kal.	It.	Arb.+It.Var.
L1	65.9	17.9	3.8	10.9
L2	7.9		61.5	
Kompetenz	Arb.	Kal.	It.	Arb.+It.Var.
passiv	91.2	86.5	95.8	
aktiv	84.2	57.0	94.3	80.4
Männer	85.4	62.0	96.8	83.4
Frauen	81.9	48.4	90.4	74.0
über 50 J.	87.6	59.3	87.0	79.1
über 25. J.	83.1	54.7	99.5	82.6
bis 25. J.	81.0	56.9	97.1	78.8
Untersch.	88.0	50.8	89.0	81.1
Mittelsch.	79.5	63.4	98.2	78.3
Obersch.	94.3	45.3	100.0	94.3
Frequenz	Arb.	Kal.	It.	
täglich/oft	77.4	28.0	62.1	
manchmal	6.8	29.6	32.5	
nie	15.9	42.5	5.4	
Domäne	Arb.	Kal.	It.	Arb.+It.Var.
Großeltern	67.8	21.9	8.3	1.2
Eltern	66.8	18.7	9.3	3.4
Geschwister	72.4	12.2	9.0	5.1
Ehepartner	63.3	14.2	13.9	4.2
Kinder	61.9	9.3	14.4	8.3
Enkel	53.8	9.1	30.3	6.8
Arbeit	27.9	9.6	30.1	29.4

Das Arb. erfüllt damit die Funktion einer Heimsprache, während das Ital. bzw. Gebrauch beider Codes die Domäne Arbeit charakterisiert. Grundsätzlich ist die interethnische Kommunikation angesichts der Massenmehrsprachigkeit hochgradig multilingual, die Sprachwahl i. a. von der Kompetenz des Partners abhängig — ausgenommen die offizielle Domäne Schule, die das Ital. vorschreibt, sowie die Verwaltung (Schriftverkehr).

Die Sprachattitüde gegenüber dem Arb. ist insgesamt zu über 70% positiv, bei L1 Ital./Kal. jedoch nur zu ca. 50%, wobei letztere in hohem Maße (20%) unentschieden sind. Positive Bewertung gründet auf den Kriterien Bildungswert und ethnische Identität, negative auf geringem Nutzen und Nachteilen bei Erwerb als L1.

6. Sprachpolitische Lage

Da der ital. Staat den Arb. als *minoranza di insediamento antico* die Zuerkennung eines Minderheitenstatus versagt, ist in offizieller Funktion als Amts- und Schulsprache nur Ital. zulässig, abgesehen von zweisprachiger Ortsbeschilderung und sporadisch angebotenem fakultativem Unterricht. Infolge des ethnischen *risveglio* in den 60er Jahren entstanden zahlreiche Kulturzirkel, etliche größtenteils auf Ital. verfaßte Zeitschriften (*Zjarri*/*Il fuoco, Katundi Ynë*/*Il nostro paese, Lidhja*/*L'Unione*), private Radiosender und ein wöchentliches standardalb. TV-Nachrichtenmagazin, denen es indessen an Kontinuität und Koordination mangelt. Abgesehen von der Rechtslage erweist sich als Hauptproblem bei der Sprachplanung die fehlende Kodifizierung und Erfassung der Arb.-Mundarten sowie die typologische Distanz zum Standardalb., das der Mehrzahl der Arb.-Sprecher wenig verständlich ist.

7. Allgemeines kontaktlinguistisches Porträt

Die Sprachkontaktsituation impliziert die jeweiligen diatopischen Varianten des Arb. und des Ital. auf verschiedenen diachronischen Stufen, welche allein — im Unterschied zum *ital. popolare*/*standard* — für die starke Interferierung des Arb. maßgebend sind. Die Arb.-Mundarten stellen eine spätmittelalterliche Variante des Alb. auf südwesttoskischer Basis dar. Trotz der unterschiedlichen genealogischen Zugehörigkeit der Kontaktsprachen — Alb. als eigenständiger Zweig des *Indogerm.*, die südital. Mundarten als *ostrom.* Varietä-ten — existieren eine Reihe von historisch bedingten Konkordanzen: Übereinstimmungen zwischen dem den südital. Dialekten zugrundeliegenden Lat. und dem des Illyricums in der *Romania submersa* mit 650 Latinismen im Alb., gemeinsames gr. Sub-/Adstrat, frühe ital. Lehnwörter im Alb. von venez. und südital. Herkunft.

Wegen des Problems des Kontakts der im einzelnen stark divergierenden, lokal begrenzten Subsysteme seien hier stellvertretend die im heutigen Kernareal des alb.-ital. Sprachkontakts, d. h. im nkal. Cratital, in Kontakt stehenden Systeme vorgestellt.

7.1. Phonetik

Das Nkal. kennt 8 Vokale (/a/, /i/, /u/, /ẹ/, /ę/, /ë/, /ọ/, /ǫ/), das Arb., das die einst phonetisch relevante Opposition von 3 Längengraden weitgehend aufgegeben hat, 6 (ohne /ẹ/, /ọ/). Die Konsonanteninventare stimmen überein in /b/, /v/, /p/, /f/, /d/, /t/, /s/, ṣ/, /ts/, /dṣ/, š/, /tš/, /dš/, /j/, /g/, /g'/, /k/, /k'/, /m/, /n/, /ŋ/, /n'/, /l/, /l'/. Hinzu kommen im Kal. die Kakuminale (/ṛ/, /d(ṛ)/, /ṭṛ/, /ṣṭṛ/) sowie /gu̯/, /ku̯/, /β/ und Geminaten, im Arb. *th* (/ϑ/), *zh* (/ʓ/). Lokal begrenzte Konkordanzen liegen bei /h'/, /χ/, /δ/, /γ/, /r/ vor. Über das Lautinventar hinaus bestehen Unterschiede in bezug auf die Postion, z. B. im Arb. i. a. Desonorisierung der Auslautkonsonanten im Sandhi, während konsonantischer Auslaut sekundär auch in nkal. Mundarten auftritt und dort ebenso entsprechend dem ursprünglich weitgehenden Fehlen unbetonter Anlautvokale im Arb. unter best. Bedingungen anlautende Konsonantencluster auftreten.

7.2. Morphosyntax

(1) Im Gegensatz zu der Präposition des det. Artikels im Ital. hat das Alb. Postposition. Der Form nach entspricht der det. Art. Sg. des Alb. (m.-*i*/-*u*, f. -*(j)a*) ital. Genusmorphemen, so daß substantivische Entlehnungen problemlos integriert werden können: kal. indet. *mašcu* 'Käseform' — arb. det. *mashku*, indet. *mashk*; kal. indet. *meta* 'Heuhaufen' — arb. det. *meta*, indet. *met*; kal. *zimmuni* 'Schweinestall' — arb. det. *cimbuni*, indet. *cimbun*.

Im Gegensatz zum Ital. kennt das Alb. einen Gelenkartikel.

(2) Ggü. den zwei Genera des Kal. (m., f.) existiert im Arb. ferner ein Neutrum.

(3) Die Deklination des Arb. mit Zusammenfall von Gen./Dat. zeigt ggü. dem Ital.

stärkere synthetische Züge: arb. *ljopët e tatës* — ital. *le vacche del padre*.

(4) Das Arb. kennt drei Konjugationen mit teils synthetischer, teils analytischer Temporabildung: *qumështit ngrohet* (3. Sg. Pr. Pass.) 'il latte viene riscaldato'. Das Futur wird mit „wollen" gebildet (*do të martohemi* 'ci sposeremo'); der Infinitiv fehlt (*mund të pi* 'puoi bere'). Ital. Entlehnungen werden nach den örtlichen morphologischen Regeln integriert: arb. *ncitárin*, 3. Sg. Pr. 'pfropfen' < kal. *nzitari*, Inf.

7.3. Lexik

Die Lexik umfaßt ein althergebrachtes Inventar (autochthone Elemente, hoher Bestand an Gräzismen, einige Slawismen, die auch für die Toponymie gelten) und einen hohen Anteil von Transferenzen aus den ital. Mundarten, die phonetisch kaum adaptationsbedürftig sind, morphologisch i. a. in das Arb. integriert werden.

7.4. Graphie

Die seit 1958 gültige Graphie des Alb., die sich in 17 Graphemen vom Ital. unterscheidet, aber nicht für alle Phoneme des Arb. Zeichen besitzt, spielt für den Sprachkontakt keine Rolle, da die Allgemeinheit über keine Lese- und Schreibkompetenz verfügt. Die Arb.-Literatur weist unter Orientierung an den zu verschiedenen Zeiten geltenden alb. Alphabeten je nach Epoche starke Heterogenität und Individualität der jeweiligen Graphie auf.

7.5. Interferenzen

Trotz ausgeprägter unilateraler Interferierung durch südital. Mundarten kann von einer „Mischsprache" nicht die Rede sein, da nur vereinzelt in Fällen starken Rückgangs des Arb. Auswirkungen auf Phonetik und Morphosyntax (z. B. Deklinationsverfall) vorliegen. Zu erwähnen sind jedoch bes. intensive Beeinflussung der Lexik, zurückzuführen auf das Fehlen einer Norm, auf Massenmehrsprachigkeit und den großen Anpassungszwang an den Kommunikationspartner, ferner verbreitetes *switching* und *mixing* der Codes sowie innerlinguistische Gründe wie der bereits vor der Einwanderung hohe gemeinsame Lexembestand (Latinismen des Alb., Gräzismen in Süditalien, nur 600 autochthone Wörter im Alb.).

Bedingt durch die Situation einer Streuminderheit besitzen Beispiele für Transferenzen nur in bezug auf einzelne Ortsmundarten Gültigkeit. Im phonetischen Bereich tritt der Fall der Erweiterung des alteinheimischen Lautsystems durch Übernahme ital. (mundartlicher) Phoneme selten auf (z. B. in Falconara Rezeption von /ḍ/), häufiger hingegen zeigt sich eine Tendenz zur Substitution alb. Laute und Nexus unter dem Einfluß ital. (mundartlicher) Aussprachegewohnheiten.

Lexikalische Transferenzen manifestieren sich (1) als Import von Fachwortschatz und Spezialterminologie aus den Mundarten zwecks Auffüllen vorhandener Systemlücken aufgrund ursprünglicher kultureller Differenzen zwischen Albanern und Italienern (z. B. im Bereich Arbeit und Gesellschaft), (2) als Importe standardital. bzw. regionalital. Neologismen (z. B. moderne Technik), (3) als Verdrängungsmechanismen in Wortschatzbereichen, die kulturellem Wandel unterliegen. Bewahrt wurde weitgehend der kulturspezifische und naturverbundene Grundwortschatz, bes. alb. Lexeme, die durch das Gr. und/oder ital. Mundarten gestützt werden (z. B. alb. *mandra*, det. 'Pferch; Herde', gr. μάνδρα, kal. *mandra*).

8. Kritische Wertung der verwendeten Quellen und Literatur

Der alb.-ital. Sprachkontakt ist bislang kaum Forschungsobjekt gewesen, da das Interesse der Eigengruppe sich primär auf die Literatursprache richtet und erst in jüngster Zeit auf empirische Dokumentationen mit diagnostisch-prognostischen Zielen.

Erst in letzter Zeit ist die Sprachkontaktsituation von Mitgliedern der Eigengruppe in einer Reihe von — häufig pseudowissenschaftlichen — Untersuchungen nicht nur unter linguistischen, sondern auch unter ethnographischen und pädagogischen Aspekten ansatzweise dokumentiert worden, deren Nutzen jedoch z. T. wegen wissenschaftlicher Mängel, z. T. wegen Nichtveröffentlichung der Ergebnisse begrenzt ist.

9. Bibliographie (in Auswahl)

Altimari, Francesco/Bolognari, Mario/Carrozza, Paolo (1986): *L'esilio della parola*, Pisa.

Birken-Silverman, Gabriele (1992): „Phasen des Rückgangs einer Sprache". In: *Zeitschrift für Balkanologie 28*, 1—22.

Birken-Silverman, Gabriele (i. Vorb.). *Die italienischen Lehnwörter in den kalabroalbanischen Mundarten des Cratitals.* (Habilschr.)

Breu, Walter/Glaser, Elvira (1979): „Zur sprachlichen Situation in einer italoalbanischen Gemeinde". In: *Münchner Zeitschrift für Balkankunde 2*, 19–50.

Camaj, Martin (1974): „Bilinguismo nelle oasi linguistiche albanesi". In: *Bilinguismo e diglossia in Italia*, Centro di Studio per la Dialettologia Italiana (Ed.), Pisa, 5–13.

Çabej, Eqrem (1933): *Italoalbanische Studien*, Wien.

Glaser, Elvira (1987): „Lexikalische Entlehnungen im Italoalbanischen". In: *Balkan-Archiv N. F. 12*, 167–182.

Guzzetta, Antonino (Ed.) (1983): *Etnia albanese in Italia*, Palermo.

Guzzetta, Antonino (1989): *Le minoranze etniche e linguistiche*, Palermo.

Rohr, Rupprecht (1981): „Sprachliche Minderheiten in Europa am Beispiel des Kalabro-Albanischen". In: *Kulturelle und sprachliche Minderheiten in Europa*, Ureland, P.S. (Ed.), Tübingen, 53–58.

Rohr, Rupprecht (1983). „Zum Problem des semantischen Feldes in der etymologischen Forschung". In: *Ziele und Wege der Balkanlinguistik*, Reiter, N. (Ed.), Berlin, 177–190.

Rohr, Rupprecht (1984): „Beiträge zur kalabro-albanischen Lautlehre". In: *Zeitschrift für Balkanologie 20*, 192–204.

Rother, Klaus (1968): „Die Albaner in Süditalien". In: *Mitteilungen der Österreichischen Geographischen Gesellschaft 110*, 1–20.

Solano, Francesco (1984): *I dialetti albanesi dell'Italia meridionale*, Castrovillari.

Gabriele Birken-Silverman, Mannheim (Deutschland)

165. Sardaigne

1. Détails géo-économiques et démographiques
2. Histoire
3. Aspects ethnolinguistiques
4. Etat de la politique linguistique
5. Bilan
6. Bibliographie (sélective)

1. Détails géo-économiques et démographiques

Avec une superficie de 24 000 km², la Sardaigne a environ 1,6 million d'habitants et est la deuxième île italienne de la Méditerranée. Cagliari et Sassari sont avec leurs 100 000 habitants les deux plus grandes villes de l'île. Géologiquement, l'île se scinde en deux macro-régions dont l'économie est traditionnelle: les régions montagneuses du nord se concentrent sur la production de bétail et de pâturage, les plaines du Sud sur l'agriculture. Une répartition inégale des terres (cf. Salvi 1973, 588), des structures économiques et sociales archaïques (cf. Le Lannou 1979), de même que les revendications des autonomistes du mouvement sarde de la fin du 19ème siècle et de la Ière Guerre Mondiale (Brigata Sassari) (cf. Del Piano 1975; Melis 1979) ont contribué à faire reconnaître la Sardaigne, en 1948, comme région autonome. Cette autonomie avait pour but une réforme agraire et une meilleure utilisation des ressources naturelles qui devaient entraîner une restructuration sociale de la région (cf. Francioni 1979, 4). Mais la réforme agraire des années 50 fut un échec. Dans le cadre du « Piano di Rinascita Sarda » (cf. Pala 1974), des raffineries pétrolières ont été installées en 1962 pour traiter le pétrole importé d'Afrique du Nord, moyen par lequel on espérait endiguer le chômage croissant et l'émigration (cf. Vargiu 1979). L'industrialisation forcée entraîna un exode rural et une restructuration démographique accompagnés d'une urbanisation des campagnes. Beaucoup de Sardes perdirent alors leurs attaches aux us et coutumes traditionnels, ce qui se refléta aussi dans leur comportement linguistique: ils se détournèrent du sarde pour recourir à l'italien, qui devint ainsi le symbole du progrès et de l'ascension sur l'échelle sociale.

2. Histoire

La cohabitation de deux langues remonte en Sardaigne à une ancienne tradition résultant de bouleversements divers et de dominations étrangères qui ont marqué l'histoire sarde depuis la période préchrétienne. Plus tard, après la chute de l'Empire romain (476), la Sardaigne tomba sous la domination des Vandales et fut prise en 534 par les Byzantins. Jusqu'au 9ème siècle, les Sardes conservèrent une relative autonomie qui aboutit à la formation des judicats de Cagliari, Arborea, Torres et Gallura. L'expansion de la domination arabe en Afrique du Nord au 11ème siècle eut pour conséquence des incursions de Sarrasins sur les côtes de Sardaigne; c'est pourquoi les Sardes appelèrent à leur secours des soldats de Gênes et de Pise; c'est ainsi que les Génois et les Pisans établirent des comptoirs de commerce et finirent par contrôler l'île entière. Des luttes intestines entre les judicats et la concurrence entre Gênes et Pise pour la domination de la Sardaigne marquèrent les siècles suivants jusqu'à la prise de l'île par les Aragonais en 1326. Ceux-ci, vassaux du Pape Boniface VIII, soumirent en 1297 les judicats de Gallura, Torres et Cagliari. Quant au judicat d'Arborea qui était à son apogée politique et culturelle sous Mariano et plus tard sous Eleonora, il résista avec force. Cependant, en 1478, la bataille de Macomer fit passer définitivement la Sardaigne sous la domination aragonaise (cf. Carta Raspi 1977, 701 s). Le catalan devint la langue administrative et culturelle, tandis que le sarde commença à dégénérer en dialecte. Selon Wagner (1950, 138 s), le catalan était particulièrement répandu dans le sud et pratiquement inexistant dans le nord à l'exception de la ville d'Alghéro où les Aragonais avaient installé des Catalans après en avoir chassé la population sarde en 1354.

La Sardaigne passa ensuite à l'Espagne en 1479 à la suite de l'union des Maisons d'Aragon et de Castille, mais le catalan ne fut remplacé qu'au 17ème siècle par l'espagnol qui devint la langue officielle. Cette dernière, toutefois, était parlée par l'aristocratie et le clergé, le peuple continuant à parler le sarde. Un parlement installé à Cagliari d'après le modèle ibérique régnait sur l'île et l'administrait, tandis que la ville de Sassari conservait son autonomie et s'administrait d'après ses propres statuts; quant à la population rurale, elle était gouvernée d'après les lois fixées par Eleonora d'Arborea dans la «Carta de Logu» (1395) qui, en 1421, devint la «loi nationale des Sardes» (cf. Carta Raspi 1977, 668 s). Après la paix d'Utrecht, la Sardaigne passa à la Maison de Savoie en 1720. C'est en 1764 que l'italien fut déclaré langue officielle. En 1827, la vieille loi des Sardes, la «Carta de Logu» fut définitivement abrogée. Mais ce n'est qu'avec l'insertion de la Sardaigne dans le «Regno d'Italia» (1860) que l'italien, petit à petit, a initié son essor comme langue officielle.

3. Aspects ethnolinguistiques

D'après les estimations de la CE, les Sardes avec environ 1,6 million de locuteurs forment la plus grande minorité linguistique officiellement non reconnue en Italie (cf. Clauss 1983). Environ 80% de la population insulaire parlent sarde; les 20% restants englobent la population italianisée, les immigrés et les habitants de San Antioco et San Pietro qui, eux, parlent un vieux dialecte ligure, et aussi les Catalans d'Alghéro.

3.1. Sarde : Italien

Les romanistes considèrent le sarde comme langue romane autonome (cf. Ascoli 1882—85; Meyer-Lübke 1920; Wagner 1950; Contini/Tuttle 1982; Blasco Ferrer 1984a, 1986; Blasco Ferrer/Contini 1988; Loi Corvetto 1988), même s'il ne dispose pas d'une langue standard codifiée. Le sarde se compose de deux grandes koinés, du logoudorien aux variétés dialectales diversifiées (dans le nord de l'île) et du campidanien aux variétés dialectales moins marquées (dans le sud) (voir fig. 165.1). Il est difficile d'attribuer les parlers septentrionaux, le gallurien et le sassarien, soit au sarde soit à l'italien (cf. Wagner 1950; Pittau 1975; Sanna 1975; Blasco Ferrer 1984b; Contini 1987). La fragmentation dialectale, les barrières de communication interdialectale et les différences de prestige dont jouissent les diverses variétés sardes, ont déclenché une crise linguistique interne à la Sardaigne concernant la fixation de la norme d'une langue standard (cf. Lavinio 1977); il faut ici remarquer que le logoudorien se trouve en haut de l'échelle du prestige sociolinguistique en raison de sa tradition littéraire (cf. Sanna 1976, 130) et de son conservatisme linguistique; ceci vaut avant tout pour le logoudorien central. Jusqu'à ce jour «la questione della lingua sarda» n'a pas été résolue (cf. Rindler Schjerve 1991). Les tentatives récentes pour établir une grammaire sarde tiennent compte du logoudorien ainsi que du campidanien, mais laissent de côté le sassarien et le gallurien (cf. Blasco Ferrer 1986).

La renaissance linguistique du sarde atteignit son apogée dans les années 70; on s'est efforcé de planifier tant le *corpus* que le *statut* de la langue sarde en la codifiant (cf. Rindler Schjerve 1991), en lui conférant de nouveaux domaines d'application sociale dans les médias (cf. Brigaglia 1978; Cossu 1982) et dans les Prix littéraires (cf. Tola 1978).

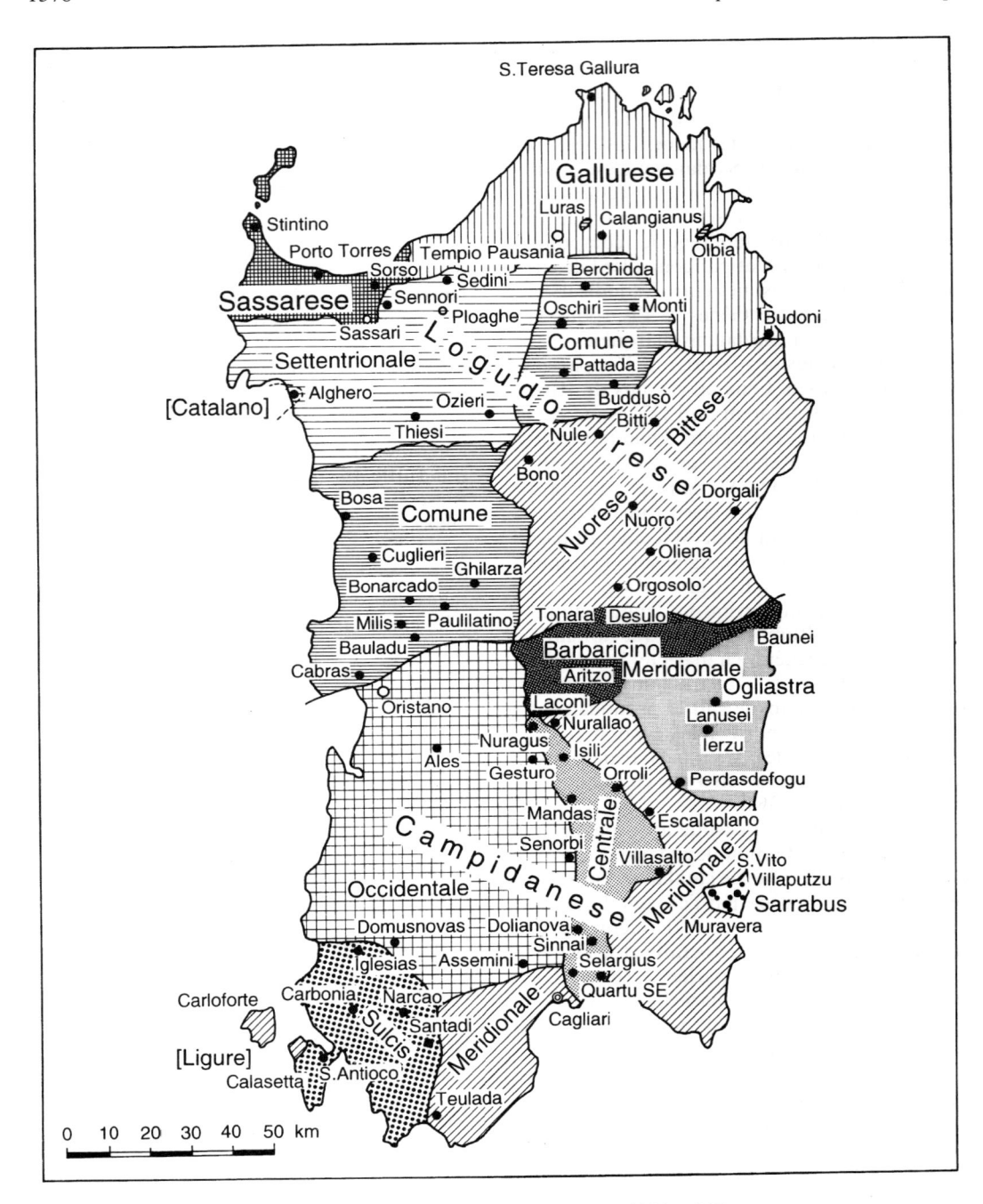

Fig. 165.1: Classification des dialectes sardes (d'après Blasco Ferrer 1984a, 349).

C'est aux 16ème et 18ème siècles qu'apparurent les premiers textes littéraires, surchargés d'intentions puristes et qui incitèrent à l'élaboration du sarde littéraire basé sur le logoudurien (cf. Sanna 1957, 24s). Les premiers livres de grammaire et de vocabulaire sardes furent publiés au 19ème siècle (cf. Porru 1811, 1832; Spano 1840, 1851). Beaucoup de chercheurs étrangers poursuivirent ces travaux; ici il faut mentionner avant tout les recherches de Wagner (1941, 1950, 1960−64) à partir desquelles on a cherché à unifier l'orthographe (cf. Pittau 1978), le lexique (cf. Loi Corvetto 1988) et la grammaire du sarde (cf. Dettori 1988), dans ces dernières décennies.

La subordination sociolinguistique du sarde à l'italien résultant de la situation juridique officielle, a eu pour conséquence la dégradation du sarde en patois italien. Actuellement, il règne une diglossie bilingue instable avec de nettes tendances vers un changement de code au profit de l'italien. Des sondages récents (cf. Mercurio Gregorini 1980; Sole 1981, 1982, 1988; Rindler Schjerve 1987) confirment cette régression du sarde dans les villages et les villes des provinces de Nuoro, d'Oristano et de Sassari. Tous les résultats des sondages effectués vont dans la même direction: en général, les femmes favorisent l'italien plus que les hommes; les jeunes Sardes préfèrent parler italien dans le privé; les parents parlent de plus en plus italien à leurs enfants; et enfin le sarde est en recul aussi dans les couches sociales moins cultivées. Les résultats des sondages d'Oristano semblent montrer que le changement dans l'utilisation des deux langues se fait très vite (cf. Sole 1988), tandis que les études détaillées d'Ottava et de Bonorva (Province de Sassari) mettent en évidence que l'italianisation à la campagne est freinée par le manque de mobilité sociale et par la pression normative du réseau sardophone campagnard (cf. Rindler Schjerve 1987). Contrairement aux sondages d'Oristano qui ont été faits à l'aide de questionnaires, ceux de Bonorva ont été réalisés par l'observation directe du comportement linguistique dans des réseaux communicatifs variés. Il en résulte que les jeunes femmes socialisent leurs enfants en italien mais que, en revanche, elles utilisent le sarde autant que les locuteurs plus âgés en raison de leur immobilité sociale et de leur intégration dans le réseau sardophone (cf. Rindler Schjerve 1987, 223−288); au cours de la campagne politique en faveur du sarde, un changement d'attitudes de la part des locuteurs a eu lieu, faisant du sarde le symbole d'une identité ethnique particulière dont on était fier et qui permettait de se démarquer des Italiens de la péninsule. Quant à l'italien, il était accepté comme langue écrite de culture tout en restant une langue étrangère. Des études sur le changement linguistique dans la socialisation première de la famille sarde montrent les résultats suivants: depuis le début des années 70, les enfants ont été élevés dans la langue italienne sous la pression de l'école tout en vivant dans un milieu sardophone; ceci entraîne un conflit potentiel pour les parents qui n'atteignent que rarement une socialisation primaire en langue italienne à un niveau avancé (cf. Wodak/Rindler Schjerve 1985; Rindler Schjerve 1987, 268s; Rindler Schjerve 1990). Une analyse plus récente concernant le *code-switching* sarde-italien dégage de nouveaux aspects de l'interpénétration de facteurs sociaux, socio-psychologiques et linguistiques qui, tous, sont responsables de la régression du sarde comme langue minoritaire (cf. Rindler Schjerve 1993 b). Actuellement, il est impossible de fournir des données plus détaillées à défaut d'analyses précises sur le changement linguistique italosarde. D'après un sondage sommaire (cf. Coveri 1986), 54,2% des familles sardes parlent encore la langue autochtone ce qui a motivé les enseignants des langues à revendiquer la reconnaissance du sarde dans les écoles et à promouvoir le développement d'un enseignement contrastif (cf. Lavinio 1989).

Ces dernières décennies, la régression de la langue autochtone va de pair avec l'italianisation croissante de la communauté linguistique sarde. C'est ainsi qu'est née une variété régionale de l'italien (cf. Loi Corvetto 1983). Les analyses sociolinguistiques de Rindler Schjerve (1983; 1987; 329 s.) ont montré que cet italien régional surgit des interférences de l'italien et du sarde; ces interférences sont marquées socialement, c.-à-d. qu'elles concernent avant tout les couches culturelles et sociales défavorisées, où l'italien, le plus souvent, est parlé selon le modèle structurel du sarde; p.ex.

sarde: A bi enis?
　　　　Pesada tinne ses?
　　　　Appo saludadu a Mariu.
ital. rég.: A ci vieni?
　　　　Alzatati sei?
　　　　Ho salutato a Mario.
ital.: Vieni? (fr.: Tu viens?)
　　　　Ti sei alzata? (fr.: tu t'es levée?)
　　　　Ho salutato Mario. (fr.: J'ai salué Mario.)

3.2. Catalan: sarde : italien

Les Catalans d'Alghéro, un port de quelque 40 000 habitants au nord-ouest de l'île, forment une minorité linguistique au sein de la minorité sarde. La langue d'Alghéro fait partie des dialectes catalans orientaux; elle possède une littérature particulière qui est codifiée, soit dans la graphie catalane officielle, soit dans une graphie italianisante. La prise de conscience linguistique des Catalans d'Alghéro a été sensiblement renforcée par la renaissance du catalan dans la deuxième partie du 19ème siècle; c'est à cette époque que parurent les premières études sur le catalan d'Alghéro (cf. Guarnerio 1886; Morosi 1886; Toda 1888). Plus tard, les premières grammaires furent publiées (cf. Palomba 1906; Pais 1970; Blasco Ferrer 1983). Dans le cadre des Prix littéraires sardes, on accorde souvent une place particulière à la langue d'Alghéro dont le statut de langue minoritaire est également reconnu dans le projet de loi relatif à l'introduction du bilinguisme en Sardaigne.

La situation d'Alghéro est triglossique car, en raison des fluctuations démographiques, le catalan est entré en contact avec le sarde et l'italien. Du point de vue sociolinguistique, le catalan d'Alghéro conserve malgré sa régression dans la vie quotidienne une certaine vitalité; les Catalans d'Alghéro, séparés de la patrie catalane, se considèrent comme autonomes d'un point de vue ethnolinguistique (cf. Grossmann 1991). Le catalan est employé dans la communication informelle, c'est-à-dire dans la famille, entre les amis, etc., mais il cède de plus en plus devant l'italien; la même chose vaut pour le sarde qui avait été introduit à Alghéro par les immigrés sardophones ces dernières décennies. Les résultats du sondage sociolinguistique réalisé par Grossmann/Lörinczi Angioni (1980) montrent bien que le catalan est en régression dans le domaine familial et avant tout dans la socialisation première des enfants (il ne reste que 7,3% de socialisés en catalan). Selon cette analyse (cf. aussi Grossmann 1983), l'italien est employé dans 36,8%, le catalan dans 28,1% et le sarde dans 6,3% des cas; dans 28,8% des cas, l'utilisation triglossique dépend de la situation (cf. Grossmann/ Lörinczi Angioni 1980, 234).

4. Etat de la politique linguistique

Malgré les multiples avatars de la domination étrangère, les rapports linguistiques entre les différentes langues dominantes et le sarde sont restés plutôt stables jusqu'à nos jours. Ceci signifiait que l'élite dirigeante dans les villes utilisait la langue dominante de l'époque, tandis que la population rurale continuait de parler le sarde (cf. Sanna 1957, 24). Ce n'est qu'au début du 20ème siècle que l'italien s'imposa dans les villes comme seule langue administrative et culturelle. Après la Deuxième Guerre mondiale et à la suite d'une campagne massive contre l'analphabétisme, l'école fut rendue obligatoire et contribua à la diffusion de l'italien comme langue véhiculaire suprarégionale. On peut donc dire que les fonctions communicatives du sarde et de l'italien ont été distinctes jusque vers 1955 et qu'il régnait une diglossie stable: l'italien était presque exclusivement limité aux domaines publics de l'administration, de la culture officielle et de la religion, tandis que le sarde prévalait dans tous les autres domaines de la communication quotidienne. Le fait que les générations anciennes présentent aujourd'hui des lacunes dans leurs connaissances de l'italien, prouve que cette langue n'a pu s'imposer dans les familles paysannes sardes que depuis peu.

Les rapports diglossiques changèrent fondamentalement au cours de la restructuration économique et sociale au début des années 60: le passage à des formes de production moderne, l'ouverture industrielle et touristique de l'île et les multiples efforts d'imitation du modèle culturel panitalien ont accéléré la pénétration de l'italien dans les domaines sociaux dominés auparavant par le sarde. A la fin des années 60, la population urbaine et avant tout la couche bourgeoise de cette dernière, était pour la plupart italianisée; et même dans les milieux ruraux on se mit à parler aux enfants en langue italienne.

Ce fut le moment où la bourgeoisie intellectuelle sarde commença à remettre en question l'intégration socio-économique de la Sardaigne dans l'Etat italien unifié; il en résulta une crise d'identité ethnique et aussi une déperdition de la langue sarde. Au début des années 70, le mouvement autonomiste néosarde (cf. Salvi 1978; Melis 1979; Satta 1971−72; Murru Corriga (Ed.) 1977) a inclus dans ses revendications politiques le règlement de la question linguistique sarde qui n'avait pas été traitée dans le statut d'autonomie de 1948.

Le statut particulier de la Région de Sardaigne avait pris en compte seulement les particularités *socio-économiques*, mais non pas les particularités *ethnolinguistiques*, et cela en violation flagrante de l'article 6 de la Constitution italienne qui prévoit expressément la protection des minorités. Ce fut la résolution prise par l'Université de Cagliari en 1971 qui a hissé le problème de la renaissance du sarde au niveau politique: elle réclamait au Gouvernement de la Sardaigne et à l'Etat italien la reconnaissance des Sardes comme *minorité ethnolinguistique* ainsi que celle de la langue sarde comme *langue nationale* du *peuple sarde* (cf. Satta 1971−72, 664). En 1975, le PSd'A (Parti d'Action Sarde) prépara un projet de loi demandant à la Région de mettre au même niveau le sarde et l'italien (cf. Partito Sardo d'Azione 1977). En 1977, on créa le premier forum de discussions pour organiser un référendum concernant le bilinguisme; en 1978, le Comitau Limba Sarda présenta au Conseil régional une proposition de loi signée par 15 499 Sardes exigeant de reconnaître les Sardes comme minorité linguistique et de traiter la langue sarde sur un pied d'égalité avec la langue italienne, − et de garantir en même temps la protection des dialectes corso-toscans de la Gallura et de Sassari, des idiomes ligures de San Antioco et de San Pietro, ainsi que du catalan d'Alghéro. En 1980, deux projets de loi y furent ajoutés; le second a été finalement approuvé par le Conseil régional au printemps 1981. Mais jusqu'à maintenant, aucune décision relative à ce projet de loi n'a été prise à l'Assemblée Nationale de Rome.

5. Bilan

La politisation de la question linguistique survenue dans les années 70, a largement favorisé les recherches sur le sarde. Des linguistes sardes et étrangers se sont penchés sur les implications sociopolitiques de ce conflit linguistique. L'application de méthodes interdisciplinaires en a fait voir les graves conséquences sociales et psychologiques pour la communauté sardophone. Ces recherches ont fait avancer l'étude du sarde en tant que langue minoritaire, et ont poussé en avant nos connaissances des phénomènes de diglossie instable, du changement de langue, de l'italianisation croissante et du recul du sarde, sans oublier les nombreuses tentatives de codification (cf. Rindler Schjerve 1987; 1991; 1993 a). En même temps, l'étude linguistique systématique du sarde s'est fortement intensifiée (cf. Blasco Ferrer/Contini 1988; Dettori 1988; Loi Corvetto 1988; Virdis 1988) si bien que le sarde compte parmi les langues romanes mineures les mieux analysées.

Malgré tout, il faut reconnaître qu'il est difficile d'évaluer le degré réel de la vitalité ethnolinguistique du sarde ainsi que sa convergence avec l'italien du point de vue fonctionnel et structurel. Et pourtant, le sarde, malgré sa régression évidente, reste une langue ethnique romane vitale. Son avenir pourrait être assuré, si l'Etat italien acceptait enfin de lui reconnaître un statut autonome.

6. Bibliographie (sélective)

Ascoli, Graziadio I. (1882−85): «L'Italia dialettale». In: *Archivio glottologico italiano II/1*, 111−160.

Blasco Ferrer, Eduardo (1983): *Grammatica storica del catalano e dei suoi dialetti con speciale riguardo all'algherese*, 2 vol., Tübingen.

Blasco Ferrer, Eduardo (1984a): *Storia linguistica della Sardegna*, Tübingen.

Blasco Ferrer, Eduardo (1984b): «Sull'italianità linguistica del gallurese e del sassarese». In: *Revue roumaine de linguistique 29*, 339−413.

Blasco Ferrer, Eduardo (1986): *La lingua sarda contemporanea. Grammatica del logudorese e del campidanese*, Cagliari.

Blasco Ferrer, Eduardo/Contini, Michel (1988): «Sardisch: Interne Sprachgeschichte I. Grammatik». In: *Lexikon der romanistischen Linguistik IV*, Holtus, G./Metzeltin, M./Schmitt, Ch. (Eds.), Tübingen, 836−853.

Brigaglia, Manlio (1978): «Qualche riflessione sull'editoria in Sardegna». In: *La grotta della vipera 10−11*, 64−67.

Carta Raspi, Raimondo (1977): *Storia della Sardegna*, Milan.

Clauss, Jan U. (1983): «Regional authorities and linguistic minorities in Italy». In: *Centres et périphéries: le partage du pouvoir*, Meny, I. (Ed.), Paris, 127−148.

Contini, Michel (1987): *Etude de géographie phonétique instrumentale du sarde*, 2 vol., Alessandria.

Contini, Michel/Tuttle, Edward F. (1982): «Sardinian». In: *Trends in Romance Linguistics and Philology 3: Language and Philology in Romance*, Posner, R./Green, J. (Eds.), La Hague/Paris/New York, 171−188.

Cossu, Antonio (1982): «Lingua e cultura sarda nella stampa periodica». In: *La grotta della vipera 22−23*, 67−74.

Coveri, Lorenzo (1986): «Chi parla dialetto in Italia?» In: *Italiano e oltre 5*, 198−202.

Del Piano, Lorenzo (1975): *Le origini dell'idea autonomistica in Sardegna (1861−1914)*, Sassari.

Dettori, Antonietta (1988): «Sardisch: Grammatikographie und Lexikographie». In: *Lexikon der romanischen Linguistik IV*, Holtus, G./Metzeltin, M./Schmitt, Ch. (Eds.), Tübingen, 913−935.

Francioni, Federico (1979): «Storia dell'idea di 'nazione sarda'». In: *La Sardegna-Enciclopedia*, Cagliari, 165−183.

Grossmann, Maria (1983). *Com es parla a l'Alguer? Enquesta sociolingüística a la població escolar*, Barcelone.

Grossmann, Maria (1991): «Katalanische Soziolinguistik». In: *Lexikon der Romanistischen Linguistik V, 2*, Holtus, G./Metzeltin, M./Schmitt, Ch. (Eds.), Tübingen, 166−191.

Grossmann, Maria/Lörinczi Angioni, Marinella (1980): «La comunità linguistica algherese. Osservazioni sociolinguistiche». In: *I dialetti e le lingue delle minoranze di fronte al l'italiano*, Albano Leoni, F. (Ed.), Rome, 207−235.

Guarnerio, Pier E. (1986): «Il dialetto catalano d'Alghero». In: *Archivio glottologico italiano 9*, 261−364.

Lavinio, Cristina (1977): «La questione della lingua in Sardegna: alcune considerazioni». In: Murru Corriga (Ed.), 99−119.

Lavinio, Cristina (1989): «Cultura e varietà linguistiche sarde nel curricolo di educazione linguistica». In: *La grotta della vipera 46*, 13−24.

Le Lannou, Maurice (1979): *Pastori e contadini di Sardegna*, Cagliari.

Loi Corvetto, Ines (1983): *L'italiano regionale di Sardegna*, Bologne.

Loi Corvetto, Ines (1988): «Sardisch: Interne Sprachgeschichte II». In: *Lexikon der romanistischen Linguistik IV*, Holtus, G./Metzeltin, M./Schmitt, Ch. (Eds.), Tübingen, 854−867.

Melis, Guido (1979): «Dal sardismo al neosardismo: crisi autonomistica e mitologia locale». In: *Il Mulino 28*, 418−440.

Mercurio Gregorini, Rimedia (1980): «L'italiano e il sardo nelle scuole elementari». In: *I dialetti e lingue delle minoranze di fronte all'italiano*, Albano Leoni, F. (Ed.), Rome, 527−554.

Meyer Lübke, Wilhelm (1920): *Einführung in das Studium der romanischen Sprachwissenschaft*, Heidelberg.

Morosi, G. (1886): «L'odierno dialetto catalano di Alghero». In: *Miscellanea di filologia e linguistica in memoria di N. Caix e A. Canello*, Florence, 312−333.

Murru Corriga, Giannetta (Ed.) (1977): *Etnia lingua cultura: un dibattito aperto in Sardegna*, Cagliari.

Pais, J. (1970): *Gramàtica algueresa*, Barcelone.

Pala Pietro (1974): *La Sardegna in cammino*, Sassari.

Palomba, G. (1906): *Grammatica del dialetto algherese odierno*, Sassari.

Partito Sardo d'Azione (1977): «Pruposta de leze rezonale de inissiativa pubulare». In: Murru Corriga, G. (Ed.), 188−205.

Pittau, Massimo (1975): *Problemi di lingua sarda*, Sassari.

Pittau, Massimo (1978): *Pronunzia e scrittura del sardo-logudorese*, Sassari.

Porru, Vissentu (1811): *Saggio di grammatica sul dialetto sardo meridionale*, Cagliari.

Porru, Vissentu (1832): *Nou dizionariu universali sardu-italianu*, Cagliari (réimpression: Boulogne 1976).

Rindler Schjerve, Rosita (1983): «Zum italiano regionale sardo». In: *Varietätenlinguistik des Italienischen*, Holtus, G./Radtke, E. (Eds.), Tübingen, 69−83.

Rindler Schjerve, Rosita (1987): *Sprachkontakt auf Sardinien. Soziolinguistische Untersuchungen des Sprachenwechsels im ländlichen Bereich*, Tübingen.

Rindler Schjerve, Rosita (1990): «Sprachenwechsel in bilingualen Minderheiten». In: *Language conflict and minorities*, Nelde, P. H. (Ed.), Bonn, 223−235.

Rindler Schjerve, Rosita (1991): «Sardisch». In: *Zum Stand der Kodifizierung romanischer Kleinsprachen*, Dahmen, W. et al. (Eds.), Tübingen, 119−137.

Rindler Schjerve, Rosita (1993a): «Sardisch: Italienisch». In: *Trends in Romance Linguistics and Philology 5, Bilingualism and Linguistic Conflict in Romance*, Posner, R./Green J. (Eds.), Berlin/New York/Amsterdam, 271−294.

Rindler Schjerve, Rosita (1995): «Code-switching in bilingualen Kontexten am Beispiel des Sardisch-Italienischen». In: *Wiener Linguistische Gazette 55−56* (à paraître).

Salvi, Sergio (1973): *Le nazioni proibite*, Florence.

Salvi, Sergio (1975): *Le lingue tagliate*, Milan.

Salvi, Sergio (1978): *Patria e matria*, Florence.

Sanna, Antonio (1957): *Introduzione agli studi di linguistica sarda*, Cagliari.

Sanna, Antonio (1975): *Il dialetto di Sassari (e altri saggi)*, Cagliari.

Sanna, Antonio (1976): «La situazione linguistica e sociolinguistica della Sardegna». In: *Archivio sardo del movimento operaio, contadino e autonomistico 6−7*, 127−138.

Satta, Antonio (1971−72): «Lingua sarda e subnazione italiana». In: *Studi sardi 22*, 642−690.

Sole, Leonardo (1981): «Sardegna: bilinguismo e cultura di frontiera». In: *Quaderni per la promozione del bilinguismo 29−30*, 2−47.

Sole, Leonardo (1982): «La Sardegna tra bilinguismo e diglossia». In: *Sociologia della communicazione 1.2*, 123−135.

Sole, Leonardo (1988): *Lingua e cultura in Sardegna*, Milan.

Spano, Giovanni (1840): *Ortografia sarda nazionale ossia grammatica della lingua logudorese paragonata all'italiana*, 2 vol. (réimpression: Cagliari 1974).

Spano, Giovanni (1851): *Vocabolariu sardu-italianu e italianu-sardu*, Cagliari (réimpression: Cagliari 1972).

Toda, E. (1888): Un poble català d'Italia: l'Algher, Barcelone.

Tola, Salvatore (1978): «I premi di poesia nella cultura sarda d'oggi». In: *La grotta della vipera* 12–13, 66–78.

Vargiu, Luciano (1979): «Intervento». In: *Questione Sarda. Materiali per il dibattito. Tonara 1978*, Cagliari, 60.

Virdis, Maurizio (1988): «Sardisch: Areallinguistik». In: *Lexikon der romanistischen Linguistik IV*, Holtus, G./Metzeltin, M./Schmitt, Ch. (Eds.), Tübingen, 897–913.

Wagner, Max L. (1941): *Historische Lautlehre des Sardischen*. Halle.

Wagner, Max L. (1950): *La lingua sarda*, Berne.

Wagner, Max L. (1960–64): *Dizionario etimologico sardo*, 3 vol., Heidelberg.

Wodak, Ruth/Rindler Schjerve, Rosita (1985): *Funktionen der Mutter beim Sprachwechsel – Konsequenzen für die Primärsozialisation und Identitätsentwicklung*. Wiesbaden.

Rosita Rindler Schjerve, Vienne (Autriche)

166. Ladinien

1. Sprachgebiet
2. Geschichte
3. Politik, Wirtschaft, kulturelle und religiöse Situation
4. Statistik und Ethnoprofile
5. Selbst- und Fremdeinschätzung sowie die Nachbarn in der Sicht der Ladiner
6. Sprachliche Situation
7. Sprachkonflikte
8. Plurilinguismus
9. Sprachkontakte
10. Bibliographie (in Auswahl)

1. Sprachgebiet

Die vom zentralen Sellamassiv (Dolomiten) ausgehenden Täler:

Nördliche Täler: Gadertal/Val Badia (mit dem großen Seitental Enneberg/Mareo) bis zur Talenge von Peraforada; Gröden/Gherdëina bis zur Talenge von Pontives;
Südliche Täler: Fassa/Fascia und die Ortschaft Moena (im obersten Fleimstal); Buchenstein/Fodom und die Ortschaft Colle S. Lucia/Col.

Nicht einbezogen: das im Boitetal gelegene, heute bereits sehr stark italienisch geprägte Cortina d'Ampezzo, dessen einheimische Mundart zum Cadore-Ladinischen gehört, aber dessen autochthone Bevölkerung sich aufgrund ihrer langen Zugehörigkeit zu Österreich (1511–1918, mit einer Unterbrechung zur napoleonischen Zeit) mit den Sellaladinern verbunden fühlt. Das nach dem Zweiten Weltkrieg noch deutlich spürbare Sprach- und Nationalbewußtsein dieser Ortschaft wurde von den sozioökonomischen Begleiterscheinungen, v. a. der Olympischen Winterspiele 1956, zurückgedrängt. Diese Tendenz setzt sich bis heute fort. Nicht einbezogen werden auch einige an Buchenstein (und Ampezzo) anschließende, innerlinguistisch betrachtet stark ladinisierende Ortschaften, weil dort aus sozialpsychologischer Sicht weder eine ladinische Sprachlandschaft noch eine ladinische Volksgruppe existiert. Die Sprachscheide zwischen Buchenstein und etwa Laste und Rocca Pietore ist dialektologisch gesehen minimal, aber die sozialpsychologische und pragmalinguistische Identitätsdimension hat auf beiden Seiten eine ganz andere Relevanz, so daß man mit H. Goebl von einem „Basel-Lörrach-Syndrom" sprechen kann. Auch die Enqueteure des ALD I bestätigen das (Mitteilung von H. Goebl); → Sprachenkarten F und N.

2. Geschichte

15 v. Chr.: Eroberung durch die Römer und Romanisierung des Gebietes; um 600 n. Chr.: Vordringen der Bajuwaren über den Brenner und Beginn der Germanisierung Südtirols; 1027 Entstehung des bischöflichen Fürstentums Brixen; mit dem Zuwachs der Grafschaft Pustertal 1091 unterstehen die Sellatäler zur Gänze dem Kirchenfürsten; ca. 1150: Entdeckung der Erzvorkommen in Fursil bei Colle (Schmelzöfen in Buchenstein, Caprile und später auch im Gadertal mit den dazugehörigen Hammerwerken); durch Belehnung verliert der Bischof im 13. Jahrhundert Gröden (mit Colfosch im Gadertal) an die Grafen von Tirol; Erlassung eigener Statuten für

die ladinischen Gerichte Buchenstein (1541), Thurn an der Gader (1550), Fassa (1550) und Enneberg (ca. 1565) [nach damaliger Terminologie das heutige Enneberg-Mareo und die gesamte rechte Seite des Gadertals]; 1603–1788: Gadertal, Buchenstein und Fassa im kirchlichen Dekanat „Cis et ultra montes" zusammengefaßt; seit Errichtung des Brixner Priesterseminars (1609) immer mehr einheimische Geistliche; 1697 verliert der Bischof die Oberhoheit über das Gericht Enneberg an die Grafschaft Tirol. De facto ist aber inzwischen das ganze bischöfliche Gebiet bereits mehr oder weniger ein Teil des seit 1363 zu Österreich gehörenden Tirol geworden; 1755 Schließung des Bergwerks Fursil; 1803 Säkularisierung: das Gebiet wird unmittelbar Tirol bzw. der österreichischen Regierung unterstellt; 1806 Abtretung Tirols an das Königreich Bayern; 1809 Beteiligung der Ladiner aller Täler an den Tiroler Freiheitskämpfen; 1810 Angliederung von Buchenstein und Fassa an das napoleonische Königreich Italien; 1813 Rückgliederung aller ladinischen Täler an Österreich; 1817 Anschluß Fassas an den Amtskreis Trient; 1818 Fassa und Gröden der Diözese Trient unterstellt; 1833 erster Versuch seitens des Gadertaler Geistlichen Micurá de Rü (= Nikolaus Bacher) zur Schaffung einer einheitlichen Schriftsprache; 1868 eigene Bezirkshauptmannschaft (die einzige ganz ladinischsprachige) für Ampezzo, Buchenstein und Colle; 1870: die ladinischen Theologiestudenten am Brixner Priesterseminar gründen den Verein „Naziun ladina" mit sprachpflegerischen Zielsetzungen; nach 1870 von außen gesteuerte Germanisierungsversuche („Enneberger Schulstreit") und in den südlichen Tälern Italianisierungsbestrebungen (v. a. in Fassa); 1905 Gründung der „Uniun ladina" in Innsbruck (ab 1912 „Union dei Ladins"); 1915–1917 Weltkriegsfront mitten durch die Sellatäler: große menschliche und materielle Verluste, Evakuierung der Einwohner von Buchenstein; 1918 Ladiner verlangen vergeblich das Selbstbestimmungsrecht; 1919 gegen den Willen der Bevölkerung Angliederung des Gebietes an Italien (Provinz Trient); 1921 Italianisierung der Schule auch in den nördlichen Tälern: 1922 Machtergreifung durch die Faschisten: kein Platz für ladinische Identität; Sprache von den Staatsbehörden als „italienischer Dialekt" behandelt; 1923/1927 verwaltungsmäßige Aufteilung des Gebietes: Buchenstein mit Colle zur Provinz Belluno (1923); Gadertal und Gröden zur neugeschaffenen Provinz Bozen (1927); Fassa zu Trient; 1939 Option für das nationalsozialistische Reich (Gröden 81%, Buchenstein 40%, Gadertal 31%, Colle 20%) oder das faschistische Italien; die Ladiner (mit Ausnahme der Fassaner) werden als „allogeni" zur Auswanderung gedrängt; Umsiedlung durch Zusammenbruch der Diktaturen gestoppt; 1946 Gründung der kurzlebigen politischen Bewegung „Zent Ladina Dolomites"; Großkundgebung auf dem Sellajoch gegen die immer noch bestehenden faschistischen Verwaltungsgrenzen und für die Vereinigung von Fassa, Buchenstein und Colle (sowie Ampezzo) mit der Provinz Bozen; Gründung der „Union Generela di Ladins dla Dolomites"; Pariser Abkommen zwischen Italien und Österreich: Ladiner darin nicht erwähnt; 1947 Verfassung der Republik Italien hält an der faschistischen Aufteilung des Gebietes fest; 1948 Sonderstatut für Region Trentino-Tiroler Etschland [= Südtirol]: es wird nur allgemein vom Ladinischunterricht in den Volksschulen, von der ladinischen Toponomastik und Kultur gesprochen. Die Ladiner der Provinz Bozen erhalten die paritätische Schule, in der Italienisch und Deutsch zu gleichen Teilen für den Unterricht der Fächer verwendet werden (Immersionsunterricht), Ladinisch eine Wochenstunde (gesetzliche Regelung erst 1973); 1951 Ladiner der Provinz Bozen als eigene Sprachgruppe gesetzlich anerkannt; Beginn von mehr oder weniger regelmäßigen Radiosendungen; 1964 Angleichung der Diözesangrenzen an die politischen Verwaltungsgrenzen: Gröden kehrt zur ursprünglichen Diözese – nun Bozen-Brixen genannt – zurück, Buchenstein mit Colle (und Ampezzo) wird gegen den Willen der Bevölkerung an das Bistum Belluno abgetreten; Fassa weiterhin bei der Diözese Trient; 1972 „Paket" (= das neue Autonomiestatut für die Region Trentino-Südtirol): verschiedene Schutzbestimmungen für die Ladiner der Region (bessere Behandlung der Ladiner der Provinz Bozen als jener der Provinz Trient); 1975 eigenes Ladinisches Schulamt für Gröden und das Gadertal; Ladinisches Kulturinstitut „Majon di Fascegn" für Fassa; 1976 eigene Talgemeinschaft (Comprensorio) für Fassa; Ladinisches Kulturinstitut „Micurá de Rü" für Gadertal und Gröden (Beginn der Tätigkeit Herbst 1977); 1983 Gesetz der Region Veneto zur Finanzierung kultureller Tätigkeiten der Buchensteiner, Colleser und Ampezzaner, sowie von „altri gruppi ladini del Veneto"; 1987 Ladinisches Pädagogisches Institut für die Ladiner der Provinz Bozen; 1988 regelmäßige Fernsehsendungen (zweimal wöchentlich 10 Minuten, zusätzlich eine halbstündige Sendung alle drei Wochen) und Ausweitung der Radiosendungen (werktags 20 und 25 Minuten) seitens der RAI für die Ladiner der Provinz Bozen und Trient sowie Empfang des TV- und Radioprogramms der Rätoromanen Graubündens für das Gadertal und Gröden; 1989 Ladinisch neben Italienisch und Deutsch obligatorische mündliche und schriftliche Verwaltungssprache in den Ämtern des Gadertals und Grödens mit Dreisprachigkeitszulage für die Gemeindebeamten; 1993 zwei wöchentliche Ladinischstunden in den Volksschulen des Gadertals und Grödens gesetzlich vorgeschrieben; Gesetzesdekret zum Schutz der Ladiner der Provinz Trient (Ladinisch Amtssprache neben Italienisch, Pflichtfach in der Pflichtschule, Vorrang für ladinischsprachige Lehrer und öffentliche Beamte in Fassa; Recht auf Sprachzugehörigkeitserklärung bei Volkszählung).

Für die Bildung eines eigenen Sprach- und Volksbewußtseins der Selladiner mögen v. a. folgende historische Gegebenheiten ausschlaggebend gewesen sein:

(1) die lange politische und kirchliche Ausrichtung nach Norden, gegeben
(a) durch die Einbindung des Bistums Säben (dann Brixen) in die Kirchenprovinz Salzburg,
(b) durch die — letztendlich in die Besitzübernahme mündende — Hegemonie der seit 1363 habsburgischen Grafschaft Tirol über die früher bischöflichen Gebiete;
(2) die im großen und ganzen einheitlichere innere politische Ordnung bei teilweise vorhandenen talübergreifenden rechtlichen und wirtschaftlichen Strukturen;
(3) häufige gemeinsame Aktionen im Laufe der Geschichte zur Gebietsverteidigung: z. B. im 14. Jahrhundert gegen die Agordiner, im 15. Jahrhundert gegen die Venezianer, 1809 gegen Napoleon, zuletzt im Ersten Weltkrieg gegen Italien (Verteidigung der Dolomitenfront).

Auch in innersprachlicher Hinsicht haben diese Faktoren — v. a. die Nordorientierung — ihre Auswirkungen gehabt: In unserem Gebiet wurde die Romanität (ähnlich wie in Graubünden und Friaul) von der südapenninischen sprachlichen Ausstrahlung, die die ursprünglich unserem Gebiet nahestehende Padania immer mehr beeinflußt und umgemodelt hat, lange Zeit nur marginal erreicht, so daß sich das bestehende System zunächst in relativer Ungestörtheit entsprechend den strukturellen Rahmenbedingungen weiterentwickeln konnte. Man denke z. B. an die bereits früh eingetretene Delabialisierung von *kwalgwa* (< *qualgua*), wodurch die Palatalisierung von *čalǧa* (<*calga*) schon Ende des ersten Jahrtausends phonologisiert worden ist (vgl. Craffonara 1979). Man denke aber auch an die nicht wenigen deutschen Lehnübernahmen, über die später ausführlich gesprochen wird.

Auch in neuester Zeit gab es hierfür einige Stimuli. So hat z. B. der vor fast einem Jahrhundert begonnene und politisch motivierte Versuch bestimmter italienischen Kreise, die ladinischer Täler zu einem italienischen Dialektgebiet zu erklären, v. a. bei den ladinischen Intellektuellen Gegenreaktionen ausgelöst. Im Zusammenhang mit dem gestärkten ladinischen Sprachbewußtsein darf man auch die Vorbildfunktion der deutschen Südtiroler nicht unterschätzen, deren aktives Engagement für die Erhaltung ihrer Sprache und Kultur sich sicher fördernd auf die ladinische Bewegung ausgewirkt hat. Erwähnenswert ist auch die Einführung des paritätischen Schultyps in den nördlichen Tälern, der durch die paritätische Anbindung an beide Nachbarsprachen die Besonderheit der Ladiner unterstreicht und der Assimilierung in die eine oder andere Richtung entgegenwirkt. Und nicht zuletzt hat der in den letzten Jahrzehnten durch den Tourismus erreichte Wohlstand das Selbstbewußtsein der Ladiner gestärkt.

3. Politik, Wirtschaft, kulturelle und religiöse Situation

3.1. Politik

Die vier Sellatäler sind auf zwei Regionen (Trentino-Südtirol und Veneto) und drei Provinzen (Bozen, Trient und Belluno) aufgeteilt. Im Gegensatz zum Veneto ist Trentino-Südtirol eine autonome Region.

Die Ladiner Südtirols (Provinz Bozen) wurden bisher politisch in erster Linie von der „Südtiroler Volkspartei" (SVP) vertreten, die von der Mehrzahl der Gadertaler und Grödner gewählt wird. In letzter Zeit macht sich jedoch ein Abwärtstrend der SVP bemerkbar; besonders starke Stimmverluste gab es bei den Regionalratswahlen 1993: die SVP ist zwar prozentual immer noch die stärkste

Tab. 166.1: Beschäftigungsverhältnisse in den Sellatälern

	Provinz Bozen		*Prov. Trient*	*Prov. Belluno*
	Gadertal	Gröden	Fassa	Buchenstein
Landwirtschaft	20,19%	3,28%	6,51%	18,66%
Industrie und marktbest. Dienstleistung	60,46%	80,26%	77,93%	68,22%
öffentl. Verwaltung, öffentl. Dienste etc.	19,33%	16,45%	15,58%	13,11%

Tab. 166.2: Bildungsniveau in den Sellatälern

	Provinz Bozen		*Provinz Trient*	*Provinz Belluno*
	Gadertal	Gröden	Fassa	Buchenstein
Doktorat	69 − 0,79%	97 − 1,22%	96 − 1,16%	22 − 1,03%
Reifeprüfung	350 − 4,00%	580 − 7,28%	579 − 7,01%	100 − 4,70%
Mittelschulabschluß	2132 − 24,39%	2551 − 28,25%	2260 − 27,41%	527 − 24,78%
Grundschulabschluß	3825 − 43,76%	2821 − 35,41%	3882 − 47,08%	1196 − 56,22%

Partei der beiden Täler, hat aber infolge des inzwischen eingeführten Mehrheitswahlrechts die politische Vertretung an die neugegründete Partei „Ladins" abgeben müssen.

In Fassa (Provinz Trient) wählten die meisten Ladiner bei den Parlamentswahlen bisher DC. Bei den Regionalratswahlen 1983 ging die „Union Autonomista Ladina" eine Listenverbindung ein und konnte zum ersten Mal einen ladinischen Landtagsabgeordneten und bei den Parlamentswahlen 1992 einen Senator stellen.

3.2. Wirtschaft

Charakteristisch für die Sellatäler sind ausgedehnte Wälder, weite Almflächen und ein ausgeprägter Reichtum an Naturschönheiten. Jahrhundertelang lebte die Bevölkerung fast ausschließlich von einer viehzuchtorientierten Landwirtschaft. Die klimabedingte karge Ertragslage zwang zum Nebenerwerb und ließ typische Talgewerbe entstehen, etwa die Holzschnitzerei in Gröden, die Tischlerarbeit im Gadertal, das Malergewerbe in Fassa u. a. m. Verdienstmöglichkeiten bot früher auch die bereits erwähnte Erzverarbeitung in Buchenstein und im Gadertal. In unserem Jahrhundert verschob sich das Schwergewicht immer mehr auf die Tourismusindustrie, so daß sich heute in den einzelnen Wirtschaftszweigen folgende Aufteilung der Berufstätigen ergibt (nach Valentin 1987) (s. Tab. 166.1).

Der Tourismus und die damit verbundene wirtschaftliche und soziale Umstrukturierung haben eine umfangreiche Abwanderung der ländlichen Bevölkerung verhindert. Dazu kommt noch, daß in den Tälern der Provinz Bozen aufgrund der Einrichtung des sog. „geschlossenen Hofes" (der als unteilbare Einheit vererbt wird) der Bauer auch als solcher zumindest leichter sein Auskommen findet.

Der Tourismus hat einen mehr oder weniger gleichmäßig verteilten Wohlstand gebracht und das Selbstbewußtsein der Ladiner gestärkt, die sich nicht mehr als Bürger zweiter Klasse gegenüber den „reichen" deutschsprachigen Nachbarn fühlen müssen. Die negativen Begleiterscheinungen eines so rapiden wirtschaftlichen und sozialen Aufschwungs sind allgemein bekannt.

3.3. Kultur

Die Übersicht (Tab. 166.2) veranschaulicht den Bildungsgrad der Bevölkerung (nach Valentin 1987; die Prozentanteile beziehen sich jeweils auf die Gesamtbevölkerung).

3.4. Kirche

Die Sellaladiner bekennen sich − mit wenigen Ausnahmen − zur römisch-katholischen Kirche. Die diözesane Zugehörigkeit folgt

Tab. 166.3: Situation der Sellatäler laut Volkszählungen

	Gesamtbevölkerung				Erklärte Ladiner			
	1961	1971	1981	1991	1961	1971	1981	1991
Gadertal	7148	8042	8741	9229	6800	7788	8367	8591
Gröden	7085	8758	9338	9580*	5175	6558	7663	7650*
Fassa + Moena	6974	7759	8246	8620				
Buchenstein + Colle	2503	2321	2127	1926				

*) Wegen einer Neuerung anläßlich der letzten Volkszählung (1991) ist es nicht mehr möglich, die Situation in den ladinischen Fraktionen der ansonsten deutschsprachigen Gemeinde Kastelruth zu erfassen. Die angegebenen Zahlen sind somit als zu gering zu betrachten.

seit 1964 den Provinzgrenzen. Im Gadertal und in Gröden wirken fast ausschließlich ladinische Geistliche. Die ladinische Sprache ist in den meisten Kirchen des Gadertals neben Italienisch und Deutsch mehr oder weniger präsent, in Gröden nur bei besonderen Anlässen, in Fassa und Buchenstein nur in Ausnahmefällen. Laut einer 1978 in der Diözese Bozen-Brixen gemachten Erhebung besuchten 84,9% der Gadertaler und 69,4% der Grödner regelmäßig die Sonntagsmesse. Inzwischen ist dieser Prozentsatz gesunken, besonders bei der Jugend.

4. Statistik und Ethnoprofil

Die Zahl der Sellaladiner beträgt heute schätzungsweise 27 000–28 000 (mit Ampezzo etwa 30 000) Personen. Amtliche Ergebnisse liegen nur aus der Provinz Bozen vor: 1971: 15 456 (= 3,7%); 1981: 17 736 (= 4,21%); 1991: 18 434 (= 4,36%) − erfaßt auf Provinzebene, so daß auch jene Ladiner mitgezählt sind, die sich auch nach ihrer Abwanderung noch als solche bezeichnen. Wenn man gelegentlich in der Fachliteratur die Zahl der Sellaladiner zwischen 12 000–15 000 angegeben findet (z. B. Haarmann 1973, 150), dann liegt wahrscheinlich eine Verwechslung mit früheren Volkszählungsergebnissen der Provinz Bozen vor. Mit Ausnahme von Buchenstein weisen die Sellatäler im Durchschnitt eine gesunde Altersstruktur auf.

Bekanntlich entsprechen amtliche Erhebungen in mehrsprachigen Gebieten nicht immer ganz der Wirklichkeit, vor allem in konfliktgeladenen sprachlichen Kontaktzonen oder in Gebieten, in denen politische oder sozioökonomische Gegebenheiten der Minderheit einen Nachteil oder Vorteil bringen. In Südtirol sind die außerhalb ihres Tales lebenden Ladiner infolge der Proporzregelung bei der Besetzung öffentlicher Stellen im Nachteil. So haben sich z. B. anläßlich der Volkszählung 1991 lange nicht alle in Bruneck lebenden Ladiner als solche erklärt; in Gröden hingegen, wo die Ladiner durch den Proporz begünstigt werden, haben sich 79,63% als ladinischsprachig erklärt, obwohl der Prozentsatz der tatsächlich Ladinischsprechenden auf alle Fälle viel niedriger liegt.

Die Ladiner der Provinzen Trient und Belluno hatten bei den letzten Volkszählungen keine Möglichkeit, sich als Ladiner zu erklären. Gadertal, Gröden und Fassa haben einen kontinuierlichen Bevölkerungsanstieg zu verzeichnen, teils auch durch Zuzug von außen. Der Rückgang der Buchensteiner geht auf das Fehlen von Beschäftigungsmöglichkeiten im eigenen Tal zurück. Was die effektive Verwendung des Ladinischen im täglichen Leben angeht, steht das Gadertal an der Spitze (sicher über 95%; auch viele Zugewanderte lernen und verwenden die Sprache), gefolgt von Buchenstein und − mit einem beachtlichen Abstand − von Gröden und Fassa.

5. Selbst- und Fremdeinschätzung sowie die Nachbarn in der Sicht der Ladiner

Der Ladiner nennt sich selbst bzw. seine Sprache *ladin (< latinu)*, eine Bezeichnung, die nicht nur im unteren Gadertal heimisch war, wie immer wieder seit Gartner fälschlich zu lesen ist (zuletzt noch im EWD und in Telmon 1992, 107). Der Enneberger nennt sein Ladin auch *mareo*, der Obergadertaler *badiot*, der Grödner *gherdëina*, der Buchensteiner *fo-*

dóm, der Fassaner *fascian*, wobei er zusätzlich zwischen *cazet* (im oberen Tal) und *brach* (im unteren Tal) unterscheidet, und der Moenate *moenat*. Der Italiener hieß früher gewöhnlich *Lombert/Lumbert* (negativ konnotiert), heute *Talian*, die deutschen Nachbarn *Todësc/Tudësc*, wobei die Pustertaler bei den Gadertalern gelegentlich noch *i Bodois* (d. h. 'die Birken', angeblich wegen ihres harten Schädels) genannt werden. Die Ladiner und ihre Sprache werden von den Deutschsüdtirolern oft mit dem von den Ladinern als abwertend empfundenen Ausdruck *Krautwalsch* (bereits zu Beginn des 19. Jahrhunderts für die vier Sellatäler bezeugt) bezeichnet. Im übrigen betrachten die Deutschsüdtiroler die Ladiner als Tiroler. Die südlichen Nachbarn im Agordino sowie die Trentiner sprachen und sprechen von den Sellaladinern als den *todesc*, den 'Deutschen'. Die Faschisten betrachteten das sellaladinische Gebiet als „una macchia grigia che deve essere grattata via" (Ettore Tolomei); bei der geheimen Volkszählung vom 23. 6. 1939 wurden die Ladiner zu den *allogeni* (= Fremdstämmigen) dazugezählt und mußten sich (mit Ausnahme der Fassaner) für oder gegen „Heim ins Reich" entscheiden. Heute empfinden noch manche Italiener trotz der zumindest teilweise offiziellen Anerkennung der ladinischen Sprachgruppe deren Selbsteinschätzung fast wie einen Staatsverrat. Doch scheint die schroffe „Siamo-in-Italia-Mentalität" immer mehr einer verständnisvolleren Haltung Platz zu machen, sicher auch dank einiger italienischer Autoren oder touristischer Erfahrungen. Nachzuhinken scheinen noch immer bestimmte italienische philologische Kreise, vgl. zuletzt Telmon 1992, 107 ff: „(...) con questa denominazione [scil. Ladini] non si intende né un'etnia né una 'nazione' (...)". Wenn es 1918 in einem gemeinsamen Aufruf der sellaladinischen Gemeinden u. a. heißt: „Wir sind keine Italiener, wollten von jeher nicht zu ihnen gezählt werden und wollen auch in Zukunft keine Italiener sein! Ein selbständig Volk, das seine Geschicke selber bestimmt!", so ist dieses klare Bekenntnis keinesfalls ein Nebenprodukt der Sprachwissenschaft (Pellegrini 1972 a, 102: „(...) è veramente singolare il caso che la coscienza di tale nazionalità *è unicamente la conseguenza di ricerche glottologiche* attuate nella seconda metà del secolo passato e dovute sopratutto al nostro Ascoli") oder ein von der Presse geschürtes Nationalgefühl (laut Kramer 1981, 149 f soll gar die 1905 erschienene und nach drei Nummern eingestellte Zeitung *L'Amik di Ladins* die „Zurückbesinnung" auf die nationale Besonderheit ins Gadertal getragen haben!). Bereits ein Jahrhundert früher, als 1810 auch die zwei nördlichen Täler dem napoleonischen Königreich Italien zugeschlagen werden sollten, begründeten die Gemeindevorsteher des Gadertals ihre Petition für den Verbleib bei Bayern u. a. wie folgt: „(...) aus Besorgnis, daß (...) die italienische Mundart vielleicht auch dem Gerichte Enneberg [im damaligen Sprachgebrauch nach der Säkularisation = das gesamte Gadertal] und dessen Bewohnern zugemuthet werde, und daher dieses Gericht das Loos des Etschkreises treffen könnte [der Etschkreis wurde nämlich zu Italien geschlagen] (...). Ganz irrig würde man daran seyn, wenn man den Bewohnern des Gerichts Enneberg die italienische Sprache zumuthen wollte (...); (...) die sogenannte Badiotten-Sprache, eine Sprache, die einzig in ihrer Art ist, und die, wie es allgemein bekannt ist, der Italiener ebensowenig versteht, als die Kundigen dieser Sprache den Italiener" (Stolz 1927 ff, Bd. 4, 255 f). Ähnlich die drei für Gröden zuständigen Richter: „(...) und obschon in dem Thale Gröden und in dem Gerichte Wolkenstein eine sowohl von der deutschen als italienischen ganz abweichende (nämlich die ladinische) Sprache gesprochen wird, so werden doch daselbst alle Gerichtsgeschäfte in deutscher Sprache verhandelt (...). (...) daß die Grenzlinie zwischen Südbaiern [= damalige Bezeichnung für Tirol] und Italien alldort gezogen werde, wo physische Lage und Sprache dieselbe auf die deutlichste Weise verzeichnen" (Stolz 1927 ff, Bd. 3, I. Teil, 268). Aus vorascolianischer Zeit sei hier noch (stellvertretend) der Gadertaler Micurá De Rü (= Nikolaus Bacher) erwähnt, der in seiner 1833 verfaßten *Deutsch-ladinischen Sprachlehre* klar zwischen ladinischer Sprache und ihren Mundarten, und zwischen ladinischer Sprache einerseits und italienischer Sprache andererseits unterscheidet (vgl. S. VII und IV). Auch von Andersprachigen aus nah und fern wurde die sprachliche und kulturelle Sonderstellung der Sellaladiner schon lange vor Ascoli anerkannt, so z. B. vom Trentiner Historiker Giangrisostomo Tovazzi O. S. F. (1731—1816). Er schreibt über die Gadertaler, die sich wegen besserer Arbeitsmöglichkeiten im Trentino aufhielten, daß sie „et lingua et habitu et moribus neque Germani neque Itali sunt". 1869 lesen wir bei Gustav Laube u. a.: „(...) ihre Abneigung gegen die Wälschen

[= Italiener] geht deutlich genug aus der Geringschätzung hervor, mit welcher sie von ihnen sprechen, und aus der Art und Weise, wie sie sich gegen die Ansicht, sie selbst seien Wälsche, zu vertheidigen suchen. Es ist ihr Stolz, Ladiner zu sein, und gerade dieses Nationalgefühl ist vielleicht das einzige noch, was sie vor dem Aufgehen in einer oder der anderen brandenden Nation schützt". Unter Österreich-Ungarn wurden die Ladiner bei den vier Volkszählungen (1880, 1890, 1900 und 1910) und in den darauf beruhenden Veröffentlichungen der K. K. Statistischen Zentralkommission nicht gesondert gezählt, sondern — trotz zahlreicher Proteste — unter dem globalen Verwaltungs-Glottonym „italienisch-ladinisch" erfaßt. Bei der unter Italien 1921 durchgeführten Volkszählung gab es hingegen für Italiener und Ladiner getrennte Spalten (18 253 Ladiner; für Colle und Ampezzo — je 1 Ladiner! — besteht begründeter Verdacht auf amtliche „Revision" der Daten, wie sie auch anderswo nachgewiesenermaßen stattgefunden hat).

Ein nicht zu übersehender Wandel vollzieht sich seit Jahrzehnten im Zugehörigkeitsgefühl der Sellataler zu Tirol, wie es z. B. im oben zitierten Aufruf 1918 noch klar zum Ausdruck gekommen ist („Tiroler sind wir und Tiroler wollen wir bleiben!"). Vor allem bei der Jugend hat das „Tirolersein" oft an Aktualität verloren. In Südtirol interpretiert man sich eher historisch als „Urtiroler", während in den südlichen Tälern das Tirolergefühl gelegentlich fast schon als Verrat an der ladinischen Identität empfunden wird (s. auch Born 1992 b, 166 u. 274 ff). Sehr aufschlußreich war diesbezüglich das negative Ergebnis des Präreferendums in Buchenstein (1992) zwecks Durchführung einer Volksbefragung über eine eventuelle Angliederung an die Provinz Bozen.

6. Sprachliche Situation

Jedes Tal schreibt bis heute die eigene(n) Variante(n). Allerdings kristallisieren sich im Gadertal (wo es nicht weniger als sechs Mundarträume gibt), in Gröden und ansatzweise auch in Fassa im schriftlichen Sprachgebrauch anstelle der Lokolekte eigene Talschaftskoineen heraus. Seit 1988 wird an der Schaffung einer gemeinsamen sellaladinischen Schriftsprache, dem „Ladin dolomitan", gearbeitet. Offiziell unterrichtet werden die jeweiligen Talvarianten im Gader- und Grödental (Pflichtschule, Sprachenlyzeum) sowie in Fassa (Volksschule und demnächst auch Hauptschule).

Während früher kaum die Notwendigkeit bestand, Italienisch und Deutsch gut zu beherrschen — intellektuelle Berufe ausgenommen — und man sich mit den mageren Schulkenntnissen bzw. dem üblichen Dienstjahr bei deutschen Nachbarn begnügte, hat sich die Lage aufgrund der politischen, wirtschaftlichen und sozialen Umwälzungen unseres Jahrhunderts schlagartig geändert.

In Buchenstein und Fassa wird heute das Ladinische fast nur im mündlichen und informellen Bereich verwendet (in Fassa müßte sich das in Hinkunft ändern, s. oben), doch genügt die Anwesenheit eines Nichtladiners, um in das Italienische überzuwechseln. Das geschriebene ladinische Wort beschränkt sich im Mittel auf 1 (Buchenstein) bzw. 2—3 (Fassa) Zeitungsseiten wöchentlich, einige Kinderbücher, Gedichtbände, Theaterstücke, die Texte für die fassanischen Radio- und Fernsehsendungen und den Briefverkehr zwischen kulturellen Institutionen und einzelnen Aktivisten. In den nördlichen Tälern findet das Ladinische viel mehr Verwendung (v. a. im Gadertal): abgesehen von der institutionalisierten Präsenz in Schule und Verwaltung sind wöchentlich in der Presse 7—8 mittlere Zeitungsseiten pro Tal zu lesen, die literarischen Werke sind seit dem Zweiten Weltkrieg immer zahlreicher geworden und reichen von der Lyrik bis zum Roman, vom Kinderbuch bis zur Sach- und wissenschaftlichen Prosa (im Gegensatz zu den aus der Luft gegriffenen Behauptungen von Telmon 1992, 113). Im Gadertal ist das Ladinische zudem in der Liturgie und im privaten Briefverkehr immer mehr im Kommen.

Die Einstellung vieler Ladiner der nördlichen Täler zu ihrer Sprache hat sich in den letzten Jahrzehnten merklich verbessert. Man fühlte sich zwar auch früher als Ladiner, zweifelte aber am praktischen Wert der Sprache. Inzwischen ist die Sprache in vielen offiziellen Bereichen präsent (sogar als Amtssprache), und ihre Kenntnis kann sogar wirtschaftliche Vorteile bringen (Vorzug bei Punktegleichheit in der Stellenbesetzung der Lehrer, Dreisprachigkeitszulage für das Verwaltungspersonal der Gemeinden u. a. m.). Borns Bemerkung (1992 b, 163), daß mit zunehmender Altersstufe eine stärkere Identifikation mit dem Ladinischen einhergehe, stimmt sicher für die südlichen Täler; für die nördlichen Täler habe ich die gegenteilige Erfahrung gemacht. Allerdings stimmt noch vielfach der von Born (1992 b, 163) zitierte Satz: „Ladinisch ja, ist ja unsere Muttersprache, aber nicht übertreiben!", wobei „übertreiben" sehr variabel interpretiert wird.

7. Sprachkonflikte

In der Vergangenheit kam es mehrmals zu Sprachdiskussionen und -konflikten. So entstand z. B. ein Predigtstreit in der 2. Hälfte des 18. Jahrhunderts, als ein deutschsprachiger Arzt, der sich in Wolkenstein/Sëlva niedergelassen hatte, wegen der ladinischen Predigten und Christenlehren Protestschreiben an die Kurie richtete (vgl. Wolfsgruber/Richebuono 1986). Bereits im darauffolgenden Jahrhundert wurde die Kirchensprache — soweit sie nicht lateinisch war — immer mehr Italienisch (vgl. Gartner 1879, IX) und dann immer häufiger Deutsch (bessere Fremdsprachenkenntnisse infolge der Einführung der Pflichtschule). 1906 verbreitete Franz Moroder, Mitglied des Gemeinderates von St. Ulrich/Urtijëi, die Flugschrift *Warnung* gegen die Verdeutschung in Gröden. 1911 veröffentlichte er eine fünfseitige Schrift, *Das Deutschtum in Gröden*, in der wir u. a. lesen, die Grödner sollen im eigenen Interesse die deutsche Sprache zwar fleißig üben, aber die Muttersprache als ein Heiligtum betrachten. 1912 forderte schließlich Moroder in einer weiteren Schrift, auch den Religionsunterricht — wie überall — in der Muttersprache zu halten, unter Zuhilfenahme des italienischen Katechismus.

Im Gadertal ist uns bis in die 2. Hälfte des vorigen Jahrhunderts nichts von derartigen Sprachkonflikten bekannt. Ende der 60er Jahre setzten jedoch von den Behörden gewollte Germanisierungsbestrebungen ein. 1868 fragte ein besorgter Gadertaler in den „Tiroler Stimmen" (Nr. 68): „Warum soll die ladinische Sprache getödtet werden?" Als Österreich dann tatsächlich die deutsche Unterrichtssprache einführte, kam es zum sog. „Enneberger Schulstreit" (1873—1895), angeführt von der lokalen Geistlichkeit, die dabei nicht nur gegen die Germanisierung kämpfte, sondern v. a. auch um die Erhaltung und Ausweitung des Italienischunterrichts, worin sie nicht nur ein Mittel zu einem effizienteren Religionsunterricht sah (der damals auf Ladinisch mit Zuhilfenahme von italienischen Lehrbüchern durchgeführt wurde), sondern auch ein Bollwerk gegen das damalige deutsch-liberale Gedankengut. Dagegen strebten die österreichischen Behörden im Staatsinteresse und unter Vorgabe wirtschaftlicher Vorteile mit der Einführung des Deutschen eine sanfte Germanisierung an. Über 20 Jahre lang dauerte der Konflikt, in dem die Geistlichkeit und die Gemeinden immer wieder Eingaben an die Schulbehörden und an das Unterrichtsministerium richteten sowie Proteste an die Presse schickten und den Bischof um Intervention baten. Schließlich wurde 1894/95 die Einführung von 5 Italienischstunden in allen Schulstufen gewährt. So blieb es bis 1916, als die Regierung den Italienischunterricht einstellte.

Unter italienischer Herrschaft wurden die Ladiner — trotz Berücksichtigung bei der Volkszählung 1921 — gleich als Italiener tout court behandelt und erhielten eine rein italienische Schule (1921/22). Proteste mehrerer Gemeinden Grödens und des Gadertals beim Staatsrat wurden zurückgewiesen. Das Ladinische wurde in der Schule nicht einmal mehr als Hilfssprache (wie unter Österreich) geduldet. Nach dem Zusammenbruch der Diktatur (1943 bzw. 1945) standen die meisten Ladiner allem Italienischen ablehnend gegenüber. Nach dem Krieg begann in Gröden und im Gadertal ein Schulkampf, bei dem sich der größte Teil der Bevölkerung für ein deutschladinisches Modell aussprach. Als Rom 1947 die italienische Schule (bei geduldeter stärkerer Präsenz des Ladinischen in der ersten Klasse und ab der zweiten Klasse mit 1 Wochenstunde Ladinisch und 1 täglichen Deutschstunde) vorschrieb, erklärten die meisten ladinischen Eltern ihre Kinder als Angehörige der deutschen Volksgruppe. Als Kompromiß wurde 1948 der paritätische Schultyp eingeführt, der sich inzwischen bewährt hat und in der Bevölkerung große Zustimmung findet.

8. Plurilinguismus

Im Gadertal und in Gröden sind die mittlere Generation und, nach Abschluß der Pflichtschule, auch die junge Generation dreisprachig, wobei zum Hochdeutschen nicht selten noch eine mittelmäßige Kenntnis des Deutschtiroler Dialekts hinzukommt. Die ältere Generation hingegen, die während des Faschismus die einsprachige italienische Schule besucht hat, kann sich in der Regel nur gebrochen auf deutsch (gewöhnlich in Tiroler Mundart) ausdrücken.

In den südlichen Tälern kommt zum Ladinischen und der italienischen Hochsprache gelegentlich auch eine trentinische (Fassa) oder bellunesische (Buchenstein) Nachbarmundart hinzu. Bedingt durch den Tourismus sind allerdings auch hier einige wenige Sprecher mehr oder weniger des Deutschen mächtig.

9. Sprachkontakte

Bis nach dem Ersten Weltkrieg standen die ladinischen Täler jahrhundertelang v. a. mit dem deutschsprachigen Gebiet in Verbindung: Fassa und Gröden mit dem Eisacktaler und Bozner Raum, das Gadertal und Buchenstein mit dem Pustertal sowie (v. a. das untere Gadertal) mit den seit dem späten Mittelalter eingedeutschten Eisacktaler Seitentälern von Lüsen, Afers und Villnöß.

Nicht so eng waren damals die Kontakte mit dem Süden (unmittelbar angrenzende Ortschaften ausgenommen). Hier ist vor allem der vom Bergwerk Fursil ausgehende Erzhandel zu erwähnen, der auch regelmäßige wirtschaftliche Beziehungen mit dem Agordino (v. a. mit Caprile), dem Zoldotal (über den Staulanzapaß) und mit Teilen des westlichen Cadore (mit Selva, Pescul und — über den Foradapaß — mit Borca) brachte. Sie dauerten vom ausgehenden 12. Jahrhundert bis in die Mitte des 18. Jahrhunderts und betrafen Buchenstein, aber auch das Gadertal. Nach der Schließung des Bergwerks suchten v. a. viele Obergadertaler Arbeit im Trentino (Trient, Rovereto und Riva). Saisonbedingte Kontakte ergaben sich durch den starken Zustrom von Bettlern aus dem Agordino (v. a. aus Alleghe, San Tomaso und Cencenighe) ins untere Gadertal (Buchenstein und das obere Gadertal waren wegen ihrer beträchtlichen Höhenlage selber arm) und nach Enneberg/Mareo (Declara 1884; Pellegrini 1987, 290 f). Auch die im vorigen Jahrhundert tätigen Krämer aus dem Trentino — v. a. aus der Val Sugana — sorgten für Kontakte mit dem Süden. Somit ist mit Parachutage-Elementen aus diesen Gegenden, wie auch umgekehrt von den ladinischen Tälern in Richtung Süden, zu rechnen.

Die Grödner Frauen begannen bereits in der ersten Hälfte des 18. Jahrhunderts mit ihrem Klöppelwarenhandel außerhalb ihres Tales und die Männer um die Mitte desselben Jahrhunderts mit dem internationalen Spielzeugvertrieb, der sie von Palermo bis Lissabon, von Rom bis Brüssel führte. Die Fassaner Möbel- und Stubenmaler arbeiteten während der Wintermonate in Österreich, Bayern und in der Schweiz.

Unser Jahrhundert hat neue wirtschaftliche und kulturelle Orientierungen gebracht: Vor allem die verwaltungsmäßige Aufteilung unter dem Faschismus hat Ladinien eine Mehrfachausrichtung gegeben.

Früher erfolgte die Kommunikation mit den nicht-ladinischen Nachbarn wohl ausschließlich auf dialektaler Ebene, heute dagegen immer mehr auf der Ebene der beiden Hochsprachen.

Sprachkontakteinflüsse schlagen sich bekanntlich am leichtesten im lexikalischen Bereich nieder. Wenn wir vom Sprachausbau der letzten Jahrzehnte absehen, fällt beim „alten" Wortschatz der relativ starke Anteil der Entlehnungen aus dem Deutschen auf. „Von den 6454 Wörtern, die das grödnische Wörterbuch von A. Lardschneider verzeichnet, stammen 845, das sind 13%, aus dem Deutschen. Von diesen 845 sind 82 vor dem 13. Jahrhundert, davon 32 vor dem 12. Jahrhundert, und davon wieder 6 vor dem 9. Jahrhundert entlehnt", schreibt Kuen (1978, 39). Niedriger ist der deutsche Anteil im Wortschatz des Gadertals, bedeutend niedriger in Buchenstein und noch niedriger in Fassa. „Von den ca. 270 deutschen Lehnwörtern des Buchensteinischen sind (...) über 50 in alter Zeit [= vor Ende des 16. Jh.s] übernommen worden. Das sind natürlich weniger als die über 70 als alt erkennbaren deutschen Lehnwörter des Gadertalischen und die über 90 des Grödnischen, doch immerhin mehr als die von Elwert S. 238 ff als „ahd." aufgezählten 26 Wörter und die 10 mit Sicherheit als alt erkennbaren „mhd.", also an die 40 alten fassanischen Entlehnungen aus dem Deutschen" (Kuen 1985 b, 694). Bei den älteren deutschen Entlehnungen handelt es sich hauptsächlich um Wörter, die das Handwerk betreffen oder z. T. auch mit der bäuerlichen Kultur zu tun haben.

Auch die Lehnprägungen nach deutschem Muster sind zahlreich, seien es nun Lehnbedeutungen (z. B. gad. *aldí* 'hören' < *audire* erhält zusätzlich die Bedeutung von 'sich gehören, sich geziemen': *astílete sciöch' al alda!* 'benimm dich, wie es sich gehört!') oder Lehnbildungen. Letztere sind Lehnübersetzungen, die in den allermeisten Fällen die ladinischen syntagmatischen Regeln beachten (z. B. gad. *aurelacörta* nach dt. Kurzweil, mit nachgestelltem Eigenschaftswort), gelegentlich aber auch Morph-für-Morph-Übersetzungen (z. B. dieselbe Lehnübersetzung im gröd. *curtaurela*, mit unerwarteter Vorausstellung des Eigenschaftswortes). Weitere Beispiele: gad. *cüüf d(a)l tonn*, gröd. *ciof dal tëune* oder *tëunesc* (Pl.; *tonn/tëune* 'Donner' = Ableitung von *tonare*) 'Alpenrose' nach dtir. *tondərpuschn*; gröd. *fever*, fass. *faure* (< *fabru*) 'Schnellkäfer' nach dtir. *schmîd* 'dasselbe'; altgad. *poms de tera* (heute *soni*), oberfass. *pomes de tera* nach dt. Erdäpfel, u. a. m.

Als ein klassisches Beispiel deutscher Interferenz wird in der Literatur immer wieder die im Sellaladinischen übliche Verb-Adverb-Periphrase angeführt, z. B. gad. *assié jö/suié jö*, gröd. *suië jü*, buch. *suié jú*, fass. *sièr jú/siar jú* 'abtrocknen' usw. Bei der Mehrzahl der Beispiele handelt es sich auch tatsächlich um deutsche Lehnübersetzungen, allerdings — und das wird in der Regel vergessen — nach einem typischen romanischen Schema, das wir — wie v. a. Gsell (1982) dargelegt hat — in den Zentral- und Ostalpen sowie in deren voralpinen Zonen (bis Mailand, Brescia, Belluno) vorfinden, gefolgt von einer an Intensität des Phänomens abnehmenden Zone (Rest der Lombardei, Emilia, der Großteil des Veneto und Friaul) und einer Zone mit nur geringer Präsenz (Romagna, Osttoskana, ein Großteil Umbriens und der Marche, letzte Ausläufer in Latium und in den Abruzzen). Gelegentlich kann diese Struktur aber auch im Portugiesischen, Spanischen, Französischen (lassen wir den Sonderfall des Französischen und der wallonischen Mundarten in Belgien beiseite) und im Rumänischen vorkommen, ja wir finden sie auch schon bei den frühen lateinischen Autoren (z. B. bei Plautus). Diese beachtliche Ausdehnung des Phänomens zwingt geradezu, an eine ursprünglich autochthone Entstehung zu denken (das ist auch der Grund, weswegen dieses Phänomen hier und nicht unter der Syntax behandelt wird). Daß aber dieses romanische Modell für sehr viele Lehnübersetzungen aus dem Deutschen gedient hat, ist unbestreitbar. Allein die Tatsache, daß es in Buchenstein und v. a. in Fassa viel weniger Verwendung findet als in den nördlichen Tälern, weist klar darauf hin. Es muß aber auch daran erinnert werden, daß das Sellaladinische besonders im Gadertal und in Gröden nicht selten über das Deutsche hinausgeht, sowohl bei Idiomatisierung der beiden Komponenten (z. B. gad. *s'la dormí ia* [< *via*] 'verschlafen', gröd. *judé davën* [< *a(d)iutare + de ab inde*] 'zum Schaden sein') als auch bei fakultativer redundanter Beifügung des Adverbs (z. B. gad. *destachè* 'ausschalten' = *destachè fòra* [< *foris*]). Bei der Frage Lehnübersetzung aus dem Deutschen oder nicht ist auch der deutsche Wortschatz früherer Jahrhunderte in Betracht zu ziehen: z. B. gad. *scuté sö*, gröd. *scuté sú*, buch. *scouté sú* (< *ascultare + susu*) 'zuhören' findet im mhd. *auflosen* eine Entsprechung (Gsell 1982). Allgemein ist bei Periphrasen mit *sö/sú*, *jö/jú*, *fòra/òra* und *ia/via*, die auch im Süden sehr häufig (teilweise sogar häufiger) vorkommen, bei der Herkunftsbestimmung Vorsicht geboten, obwohl damit nicht behauptet werden soll, daß jede parallele Bildung mit dem Süden eine Lehnübersetzung nach deutschem Muster ausschließt.

Ascoli spricht in solchen Fällen von „materia romana con ispirito tedesco". Bei der Entstehung solcher Lehnbildungen war sicher der Umstand ausschlaggebend, daß die phonologische und morphologische Struktur des Deutschen für eine einfache Wortentlehnung zu verschieden war.

Der lexikalische Einfluß aus dem Süden scheint in früheren Epochen nicht sonderlich groß gewesen zu sein. Es muß allerdings bedacht werden, daß frühe Entlehnungen aus dem Süden infolge der Systemverwandtschaft phonetisch wie morphologisch oft voll integriert werden konnten. Später jedoch hat sich der Einfluß aus dem Süden bedeutend verstärkt, vor allem in den südlichen Tälern. Eine diesbezügliche Quantifizierung ist noch nicht vorgenommen worden. Besonders wirkte er sich im Bereich der Religion und der Abstrakta aus: z. B. gad. *capiun*, gröd. buch. *capion* 'Aschermittwoch' aus agord. *capiuni* (< *caput ieiunii*); gad. gröd. buch. fass. *calonia* 'Pfarrhof' aus agord. *calonega* (vgl. it. *canonica*); *fede* 'Glaube' usw. Infolge der Systemverwandtschaft haben wir es mit Wortentlehnungen und nicht mit Lehnprägungen zu tun.

Sogenannte „Luxuslehnwörter" aus beiden Nachbarsprachen sind keine Seltenheit, z. B. gad. *mistier*, gröd. *mestier*, buch. *mestier*, fass. *mistiér* 'Handwerk' (statt *ert/ert*); gad. *ghenau* 'genau' (statt *avisa*), *dòncscenn* 'danke schön' (statt *dilan*); gad. *iô* 'ja' (statt *scê, scescê, aé, ê, hei, hê, poa, pô, popô*); gröd. *bàiter* 'weiter' (statt *inant*), *ònchel* und *tante* (statt *berba/bera* und *anda*); fass. *zio* und *zia* (statt *berba/barba* und *ámeda*), *primavera* (statt *aisciuda*), usw. Vor allem in den großen Tourismuszentren besteht die Tendenz, in Fällen, bei denen das Ladinische lexikalisch differenzierter ist oder die Semanteme im

Deutschen und/oder Italienischen unterschiedlich abgegrenzt sind, das einheimische Vokabular der (den) Nachbarsprache(n) anzugleichen. So unterscheiden Gröden und das Gadertal ursprünglich zwischen *crëier/crëie* 'Glauben schenken, gläubig sein, glauben an, glauben' — *ratè/aratè* 'vermuten, glauben' — *miné* 'meinen, glauben'; heute verwenden viele Grödner, aber auch manche Obergadertaler fast nur mehr *crëier/crëie*, z. B. *ie crëie de messëi (ti) la zedeliö crëii da messëi (ti) la zede* 'ich glaube, es aufgeben zu müssen' (statt *ie rateliö arati ...*); ähnlich bei 'brauchen' (nicht im Gadertal): gröd. *duman adroves permò da levé dala diesc* 'morgen brauchst du erst um 10 Uhr aufzustehen' (statt *duman es permò drë de ...*); für 'heute abend' und 'gestern abend' werden in Gröden immer mehr *encuei da sëira* und *inier da sëira* (statt *ensnuet* und *ensëira*) verwendet. Unter dem Druck der Neuerung verschwindet nicht selten das ältere Wort, wie es v. a. in Fassa bei vielen Erbwörtern geschehen ist: z. B. *ègher* 'sauer' < > gad. *aje*, gröd. buch. *eje* (< *acidu*); *vardèr/vardár* 'schauen' < > gad. *ćiarè*, buch. *ćialé*, gröd. *cialé* (< *calare*); *volintiéra* 'gern' < > enneb. *ienn*, gad. *ion/gën*, gröd. buch. *gën* (< ?; vgl. bündn. *jent, gugent*); *smilsa* 'Milz' < > gad. *splënja*, gröd. *splëngia*, buch. *splënjia* (< *splenia*); *setemëna* (buch. *setemána*) 'Woche' < > gad. *édema*, gröd. *éna* (< *hebdoma*); *spala* (= buch.) 'Schulter' < > gad. gröd. *sciabla* (< *scapula*); *fascína* (= buch.) 'Reisigbündel' < > gad. *(v)ancëi*, gröd. *vencëi* (< *vinciliu*); u. a. m. Ein Beispiel aus Buchenstein: beim Personalpron. 1. u. 2. Pers. Sg. Nom. ist das südl. *mi, ti* 'ich, du' eingedrungen und hat die Nachfolger von lat. *ego, tu*, die noch in den übrigen Tälern vorhanden sind, verdrängt.

Heute sind noch weitere Faktoren in Betracht zu ziehen: (a) die interladinische Beeinflussung (Medien, persönliche Kontakte), z. B. gröd. *jadins* 'Schlittschuhe' (auf lautmalerischer Basis in den 50er Jahren entstanden) hat auch im Gadertal Fuß gefaßt; gad. *audanza* 'Glückwunsch' (zu Beginn der 60er Jahre aus *audè* 'wünschen' < *advotare* entstanden) setzt sich auch in Gröden immer mehr durch; u. a. m. b) die bewußte Wortübernahme aus Graubünden und aus Friaul, z. B. *scolina* 'Kindergarten' < engad. *scoulina*, gad. *paslunch*, fass. *paslench* (gröd. hingegen *pudejé*) 'Langlauf' < bündn. *passlung*, gad. gröd. *cendrin* 'Aschenbecher' < engad. *tschendrin*, oder — mit Suffixwechsel — gröd. *cudejel* 'Heft' < sursilv. *cudischet* 'Broschüre',

gad. *belijia* 'Juwel' < friaul. *belisie* 'Schmuckstück', u. a. m.

Der gegenwärtige Sprachausbau (bisher hauptsächlich vom Istitut Cultural Ladin „Micurá de Rü" getragen) basiert in erster Linie auf dem internationalen romanischen Vokabular, versucht aber auch, entweder aus eigenem Material Neuprägungen zu schaffen, oder aus Graubünden und Friaul solche zu übernehmen. Diesem Sprachausbau widersetzt sich nicht selten ein historisch-retardierend orientierter Purismus, wobei eine — sicher ehrlich gefühlte — Angst vor dem „Verwelschtwerden" mitschwingt, oder aber — und das scheint v. a. in gewissen Grödner Kreisen der Fall sein — eine antiquierte Vorstellung vom Ladinischen als reiner Stubensprache.

Buchenstein scheint vom lexikalischen Ausbau bisher am wenigsten berührt worden zu sein (keine Radio- und Fernsehsendungen, kein Ladinischunterricht und kein Ladinisch in der öffentlichen Verwaltung).

Obwohl wir im Rahmen dieser Darlegung von ad-hoc-Entlehnungen abgesehen und uns auf bereits etablierte Elemente beschränkt haben, muß hier doch erwähnt werden, daß in größeren Tourismuszentren häufig zur unkontrollierten lexikalischen Mischrede tendiert wird, z. B. (von einem Gadertaler gehört): *sëise os la Frau de chël Ding da Longega?* 'sind Sie die Frau von dem Dingsda aus Zwischenwasser?' Nicht selten kann man v. a. in Gröden und Fassa Leute hören, die mehr oder weniger nur mehr die „cola", d. h. 'den Leim' — wie es spöttisch heißt — auf ladinisch bringen: Artikel, Pronomina, Hilfs- und Modalverben, Präpositionen sowie die einfachsten Wörter des Alltags; ja manchmal kommt sogar ein halber Satz in der anderen Sprache.

Morphosyntaktische und phonetische Interferenzen sind seltener anzutreffen.

In Gröden begegnet man nicht selten der Konstruktion *fé* + (meist dt.) Inf. nach dtir. *tian* 'tun' + Inf.: *fejs'a sën telephonieren?* 'telephonierst du jetzt?' — dtir. *túesche iatz telefonirn?*; auch in Fällen, bei denen es im Deutschtirolischen nicht möglich wäre: *ie vede a fé telephonieren* 'ich gehe (zu tun) telephonieren'.

Die Angaben der Zwischenuhrzeiten in den nördlichen Tälern: während die vollen Stunden, die man durch die alte Sonnen-, Wasser- und Sanduhr bestimmen konnte, allgemein auf ladinisch ausgedrückt werden (gad. *la öna, les döes,* (...), gröd. *la un, la doi* [an sich würde man *la una, la doves* erwarten]), werden die Zwischenzeiten, die man erst nach dem Aufkommen der mechanischen Uhr angeben konnte, nach deutschem Muster bezeichnet: gad. *n chert passè les cinch* 'Viertel nach 5 Uhr', *la mesa d(a)les cater* 'halb 4 Uhr', *i trëi cherć d(a)les set* 'drei Viertel 7 Uhr', *cin menüć dô les dódesc* 'fünf Minuten nach 12 Uhr', *diesc menüć dan les nü* 'zehn Minuten vor 9 Uhr'. Ähnlich in Gröden; dagegen gilt in den südlichen Tälern das italienische Muster (*e — meno*): buch. *le úndesc y mesa* 'halb 12 Uhr', *le cinch y trei cherć* 'drei Viertel 6 Uhr', *(l) mánćia diesc a le set* 'zehn vor 7 Uhr'. Diese Formen sind in ähnlicher Art auch in Fassa zu finden.

Als Folge der vielen entlehnten deutschen Berufsbezeichnungen auf *-er* (*pinter* 'Faßbinder', *tis(t)ler* 'Tischler', *slosser* 'Schlosser', *capuziner* 'Kapuziner', *petler* 'Bettler' usw.) kommt es zur hyperkorrekten Ausweitung des Lehnsuffixes *-er;* z. B. gad. gröd. buch. fass. *scizer* 'Schütze', gad. gröd. *musiconter* 'Musikant', gröd. *cumedianter* 'Komödiant', gröd. *u(r)glister* 'Orgelist (= Organist)'.

Nach deutschem Vorbild können in den nördlichen Tälern die Konsequenz eines Wenn-Satzes (*wenn—so*) und ein mit Unwillen bzw. Nachdruck formulierter Imperativ (*so*) mit *sce* eingeleitet werden: gröd. *scemía mei che te posses, sce vie!* 'Wenn du nur irgendwie kannst, so komm!', gröd. *sce va pu!* 'so geh' doch!' Ähnlich im Gadertal, v. a. in Enneberg/Mareo. Allerdings wird diese noch zu Beginn unseres Jahrhunderts häufig belegte Konstruktion neuerdings immer seltener verwendet.

Deutscher Einfluß beginnt sich in Gröden (v. a. in St. Ulrich/Urtijëi und Pufels/Bula) in der Negation verstärkt zu zeigen, z. B. *fé n cunfront (...) ie per de plu rejons belau nia puscibl* 'einen Vergleich anzustellen, ist aus mehreren Gründen fast nicht möglich' (entnommen aus einem 1994 vorgestellten Programm „per lo sviluppo del ladino delle Dolomiti"; man würde eine gedoppelte Verneinung erwarten: *(...) ne ie (...) nia (...)*, oder zumindest die Verneinung vor dem Verb: *(...) ne ie (...))*.

Deutscher und italienischer Einfluß können dazu beigetragen haben, die überkomponierten Tempora immer mehr abzubauen. Heute hört und liest man sie nur noch selten und fast ausschließlich in temporalen Nebensätzen: buch. *spoche nos on bú mané*, gad. *dô ch'i ún albü menè*, gröd. *do che on abú mandá* (< **habumus habutu mandatu*) 'nachdem wir gesendet hatten', usw.

In den nördlichen Tälern stehen die qualitativen Adjektiva nach dem Substantiv, und nur bei einer relativ kleinen Gruppe von alltäglichen Eigenschaftswörtern — meist Gegensatzpaaren (z. B. *gran* 'groß' — *pice* 'klein', *pros* 'brav' — *rî* 'böse', *bun* 'gut' — *stlet* 'schlecht', *maiú* 'größer' — *ménder* 'kleiner', usw.) — haben wir Voranstellung. Die Toponomastik belegt jedoch, daß früher auch diese Gruppe nachgestellt wurde: vgl. gad. *Miribun* < *meridie + bonu, Taibun* < **taliu + bonu, Valbuna* < *valle + bona, Terabona, Costamaiú* < *costa + maiore* usw. In den nördlichen Tälern dürfte der Positionswechsel (i. e. Voranstellung) wohl hauptsächlich unter deutschem Einfluß eingetreten sein, in den südlichen Tälern, wo die Stellung des Adjektivs im allgemeinen etwas freier gehandhabt wird, hauptsächlich unter italienischem Einfluß. Heute werden in den nördlichen Tälern — v. a. von Radio-Journalisten — gelegentlich auch „neumodische" Eigenschaftswörter dem Hauptwort vorangestellt, z. B. gröd. *la tradiziunela festa*, gad. *la tradizionala festa* 'das traditionelle Fest' (statt *la festa tradiziunela/tradizionala*), wobei sowohl Deutsch als auch Italienisch Pate gestanden haben können.

Italienischer Einfluß liegt vor bei der Setzung des Dativ- und Akkusativpronomens nach dem Infinitiv im Fassatal (kaum in Moena): statt oberfass. *va a les comprèr!* 'geh sie kaufen!' hört man heute fast ausschließlich *va a comprerles!;* statt unterfass. *vae a me comprar na ciameija* 'ich gehe, mir ein Hemd zu kaufen', hört man *vae a comprarme (...)*. Das gilt auch für die Setzung des bestimmten Artikels beim attributiven Possessivum. Wie in anderen romanischen Sprachen und im Deutschen entfällt ursprünglich im Selladinischen vor dem attributiven Possessivum der Artikel. In Buchenstein ist allerdings die Verwendung des Artikels praktisch verallgemeinert worden und hat auch das obere Gadertal und v. a. Fassa schon bis zu einem gewissen Grad erfaßt: buch. *la nosta ćesa* 'unser Haus' (allgemein), fass. *la noscia val* (oft), neben *noscia val* 'unser Tal', obergad. *la mia roda* 'mein Fahrrad' neben heute wieder häufigerem *mia roda*.

In den zusammengesetzten Zeiten der reflexiven Verba unterscheidet sich das Selladinische (und mit ihm Romanischbünden, Teile des Veneto u. a. m) von der heutigen italienischen Schriftsprache durch die Verwendung des Hilfszeitwortes avëi/aér 'haben' und des unveränderten Partizips, z. B. gad. ëll/ëra s'á lavè 'er/sie hat sich gewaschen'. Heute kann man in allen Tälern gelegentlich auch Konstruktionen mit ester/vester/esser 'sein' und Übereinstimmung des Partizips nach italienischem Muster hören (v. a. in Lehrerkreisen).

Wahrscheinlich zur Vermeidung der semantischen Ambiguität der Konstruktion *sum laudatus* (Vorgang und Resultat/Zustand) hat sich bei der Passivbildung — ähnlich wie in Graubünden — das Bewegungsverb *venire* (in wenigen Fällen auch *ire*) als vorgangsbezeichnendes Hilfsverb etabliert: z. B. *la blâ é gnüda venüda bun* (neben *(...) é jüda venüda (...)*) 'das Getreide ist gut verkauft worden'. Obwohl gad. *gní*, gröd. *uní*, buch. *vegní* auch 'werden' im Sinne von 'entstehen' bedeuten, dürfte wohl kaum deutsche Interferenz den Ursprung des Phänomens darstellen. Sie hat die romanische Struktur wohl höchstens nur gestützt (*venire* kommt bekanntlich auch im Italienischen in den einfachen Zeiten neben *essere* vor). In Buchenstein werden heute in der Regel nur die einfachen Zeiten mit *vegní* gebildet, die zusammengesetzten fast ausschließlich mit *ester*; in Fassa verwendet man — ähnlich wie im Italienischen — sowohl *esser* (Betonung der *Resultate*) als auch *vegnir* (Betonung des *Vorgangs*). In beiden Tälern liegt wohl italienische Interferenz vor, auch wenn bereits 1833 der Gadertaler N. Bacher (M. de Rü) in seiner Grammatik — die nach Möglichkeit alle Täler berücksichtigt — beide Formen gelten läßt. Auch in Gröden und im oberen Gadertal kann man bei zusammengesetzten Zeiten gelegentlich *vester* bzw. *ester* hören.

Wird der Satz durch ein Objekt oder eine Umstandsbestimmung eröffnet oder geht dem Hauptsatz der Nebensatz voraus, haben wir in den nördlichen Tälern — ähnlich wie im Bündnerromanischen und Deutschen — Inversion sowohl des substantivischen als auch des pronominalen Subjekts: gad. *(in)doman vëgn le perel(in)doman vëgnel*, gröd. *duman vën l perel/duman vënel* 'morgen kommt der Vater/kommt er'. In Anbetracht der Tatsache, daß Inversion des pronominalen Subjekts auch im Venezianischen oder des substantivischen Subjekts im Toskanischen des späten Mittelalters (letzteres heute nur mehr ein impressionistisches Stilmittel) — vom Alt- und Mittelfranzösischen ganz zu schweigen — belegt ist, könnte es sich ursprünglich wohl um eine fakultative romanische Struktur gehandelt haben, die in der Folge sowohl in Ladinien als auch in Graubünden durch die parallele Struktur des Deutschen konsolidiert und verallgemeinert worden ist. In den südlichen Tälern scheint inzwischen keine Spur mehr davon vorhanden zu sein: buch. *davò marëna l pere l á dit/davò marëna dël l á dit*, oberfass. *do marena l pere l á dit/do marena el l á dit* 'nach dem Mittagessen hat der Vater gesagt/hat er gesagt'. Aber auch bei einzelnen Grödnern und Obergadertalern ist bei substantivischem (kaum bei pronominalem) Subjekt die Inversion verloren gegangen, wobei der Einfluß aus dem Süden evident ist.

Die nördlichen Täler verwenden häufig die unpersönliche Konstruktion (vgl. Gsell 1984): gad. *al plöi*, gröd. *l pluev* 'es regnet', gad. *al s'un va la löm*, gröd. *l se n va la lum* 'es geht das Licht aus', gad. *mëssel ester?*, gröd. *muessel (pa) vester?*, 'muß es sein?' gad. *ël gnü le zumpradú?*, gröd. *iel (pa) uní l zumpradëur?* 'ist der Zimmermann gekommen?' Da z. T. ähnliche Strukturen noch im Venezianischen des ausgehenden Mittelalters vorkommen, ist wohl an spontane romanische Genese des Phänomens zu denken, das aber in der Folge von den ähnlichen südbairischen Gegebenheiten gestützt werden konnte. In Norditalien ist das Phänomen unter dem Druck der italienischen Hochsprache weitgehend aufgesogen worden. Dieser südlichen Entwicklung hat sich Fassa fast gänzlich angeschlossen (oberfass. *ven un temporel* 'es kommt ein Gewitter', neben *el piev* 'es regnet'), und Buchenstein folgt in einem gewissen Abstand. Aber selbst in Gröden tendieren einzelne Sprecher immer mehr in diese Richtung, z. B. *ulache vën fates prupostes* 'wo Vorschläge gemacht werden' (belegt im oben erwähnten Programm „per lo sviluppo del ladino delle Dolomiti"; man würde erwarten: *ulache l vën fat prupostes!*).

Seltener sind Interferenzen im morphologischen Bereich festzustellen:

Italienische Interferenz liegt wohl sicher beim selladinischen Futur (Periphrase mit Inf. + *habeo*) vor, das bereits in den ersten stark italienisierenden Dokumenten aus dem 17. und 18. Jahrhundert bezeugt ist und die ältere Periphrase mit *(ve)gní + a + Inf.* in der ersten Hälfte des vorigen Jahrhunderts (zumindest im Gadertal) gänzlich verdrängt hat. Bereits Ettmayer (1920, 17) spricht von indirekten Argumenten, die uns zu einer solchen Annahme führen. Die Grammatik von Bacher (1833) kannte er (wie auch der ihn kritisierende Elwert 1943, 152) noch nicht, die die ältere neben der neuen (und schon zu Bachers Zeit dominierenden) Form mehrmals verzeichnet, z. B. S. 88: „Künftige Zeit: *Jeu serà* oder *vëgne a estr*, ich werde seyn", S. 101: „Künftige Zeit: *Jeu amerà*" neben S. 102: „*Che jeu vëgne a amè*, daß ich lieben werde", usw. Die Periphrase auf *venire + ad* (vgl. die unmittelbare Zukunft in franz. *je vais chanter*) kann aber wohl nicht, wie Kuen (1978, 43) es für die analoge Form in Graubünden annimmt, auf deutsche Interferenz zurückgeführt werden, denn im Rätoromanischen hat man es mit einem *Bewegungsverb* zu tun, im Deutschen hingegen — wo sich *werden + Inf.* zur Bezeichnung des Futurs erst im späten Mittelhochdeutschen allmählich durchsetzt — mit einer zunächst *inchoativen* Aktionsart.

Italienische Interferenz liegt ferner vor bei der Entsigmatisierung des Fem. Pl. in Buchenstein (im 17. Jh. ist die sigmatische Endung noch vorhanden) und im unteren Fassatal (mit Moena). Das gilt auch für die 2. Pers. Sg. u. Pl. des Verbs in beiden Tälern, in Fassa noch mit zusätzlicher Änderung der Endung der 2. Pl.: buch. *le porte* 'die Türen', *(ti) te ćiante* 'du singst', *(vos) ćiantei* 'ihr singt'; unterfass.: *le porte, (tu) tu ciante, vo ciantade*, gegenüber oberfass. und gröd. *la portes*, oberfass. *tu te ciantes, vo ciantede*, gröd. *tu ciantes, vo ciantëis*, gad. *les portes, tö (te) ćiantes, os ćiantëis*.

Ein Fall von Hyperkorrektur gegenüber dem Italienischen — oder vielleicht einfach von Einfluß des Bündnerromanischen — dürfte hingegen in dem v. a. im Gadertal, aber auch in Gröden immer häufiger zu hörenden und zu lesenden sigmatischen Plural bei rezenten Nomina auf *-l* vorliegen: *locals* 'Lokale', *retils* 'Reptilien', usw. (statt *locai*, *retii*).

Im phonologischen Bereich sind relativ wenige Interferenzerscheinungen festzustellen:

Eindeutig deutsche Interferenz liegt bei der im vorigen Jahrhundert in Gröden bereits vollzogenen, im Gadertal erst beginnenden Integrierung des *[h]* als Phonem vor: gad. *rehl* 'Reh' ~ *rerl* 'Backrohr', gröd. *huza* 'Baumknollen' ~ *l puza* 'er stinkt'.

Während die Angleichung des Sibilantensystems von Colle an jenes des Agordino sicher auf südlichen Einfluß zurückzuführen ist, ist der fast totale Umbau desselben Teilsystems des Moenatischen nicht so eindeutig zu erklären. Doch haben wohl systeminterne Schwachstellen unter Einwirkung fleimstalischer Gegebenheiten zum heutigen Resultat geführt: **s > ts, *z > dz, *š > s, ts = ts* (vgl. Heilmann 1980).

Das Fassanische unterscheidet sich seit etwa einem Jahrhundert von der übrigen sellaladinischen Umgebung in der Behandlung der lateinischen Verbindungen Konsonant + L *(pl, bl, fl, cl, gl)*. In allen Fällen — mit Ausnahme von *cl-*, das zu *chi- [ki]* und nicht zu *[ĉ]* geworden ist *(clamèrl-ar > chiamèrl-ar)* — hat es sich an das Oberitalienische angeglichen.

10. Bibliographie (in Auswahl)

ASTAT (1988 ff): *Statistisches Jahrbuch für Südtirol — Annuario Statistico della provincia di Bolzano*, Bozen.

Battisti, Carlo (1931): *Popoli e lingue nell'Alto Adige*, Florenz.

Battisti, Carlo (1941): *Storia linguistica e nazionale delle valli ladine*, Florenz.

Belardi, Walter (1991): *Storia sociolinguistica della lingua ladina*, Roma/Corvara/Selva.

Beninca, Paola (1985—1986): „L'interferenza sintattica: Di un aspetto della sintassi ladina considerato di origine tedesca". In: *Quaderni Patavini di Linguistica 5*, 3—17.

Born, Joachim (1983): „Domänen und Attitüde in den ladinischen Dolomitentälern". In: *Theorie, Methoden und Modelle der Kontaktlinguistik*, Nelde, P. H. (Ed.), Bonn, 259—272.

Born, Joachim (1992a): „Soziolinguistisches von den Rätoromanen. Über die Vergleichbarkeit der sprachlichen Situation in Graubünden und in den Dolomiten anhand zweier Befragungen". In: *Beiträge zur sprachlichen, literarischen und kulturellen Vielfalt in den Philologien*. Festschrift für Rupprecht Rohr zum 70. Geburtstag, Birken-Silverman, G./Rössler, G. (Eds.), Stuttgart, 316—328.

Born, Joachim (1992b): *Untersuchungen zur Mehrsprachigkeit in den ladinischen Dolomitentälern. Ergebnisse einer soziolinguistischen Befragung*, Wilhelmsfeld.

Calafiore, Giovanni (1985): „La geografia delle minoranze: i Ladini". In: *Mondo ladino 9*, 11—40.

Chiocchetti, Fabio (1980): „Primi risultati di un' indagine tipologica sulle interferenze ladino — italiano. Val di Fassa, anno scolastico 1979/1980". In: *Mondo ladino. Quaderni 3*, 19—33.

Craffonara, Lois (1979): „Zur Palatalisierung von CA und GA in den Sellatälern". In: *Ladinia 3*, 69—93.

Craffonara, Lois (1981): „Die kulturelle und politische Situation der Selladiner (Frühjahr 1981)". In: *Kulturelle und sprachliche Minderheiten in Europa.*

Aspekte der europäischen Ethnolinguistik und Ethnopolitik. Akten des 4. Symposions über Sprachkontakt in Europa, Ureland, P. St. (Ed.), Mannheim 1980, 81—110.

Declara, Janmatî (1884): *Valgunes recordanzes ladines.* Ms.

Elwert, W. Theodor (1943): *Die Mundart des Fassatals,* Heidelberg.

Ettmayer, Karl (1920): „Vorläufiger Bericht über Phonogramm-Aufnahmen der Grödner Mundart". In: *Akademie der Wissenschaften in Wien,* Sitzungsberichte, 191. Bd., Wien, 1—95.

EWD: Kramer, Johannes (1988 ff): *Etymologisches Wörterbuch des Dolomitenladinischen,* Hamburg.

Fontana, Josef (1978): „Der Enneberger Schulstreit". In: *Ladinia 2,* 75—88.

Fontana, Josef (1981): „Die Ladinerfrage in der Zeit 1918 bis 1948". In: *Ladinia 5,* 151—200.

Gartner, Theodor (1879): *Die Gredner Mundart,* Linz.

Goebl, Hans (1979): „Glottonymie, Glottotomie und Schizoglossie. Drei sprachpolitisch bedeutsame Begriffe". In: *Ladinia 3,* 7—38.

Goebl, Hans (1982 a): „Johannes Kramer: Deutsch und Italienisch in Südtirol. (...) Heidelberg (...) 1981 (...)." [Rez.]. In: *Ladinia 6,* 223—249.

Goebl, Hans (1982 b): „Kulturgeschichtliche Bedingtheiten von Kontaktlinguistik. Bemerkungen zum gegenwärtigen Stand der 'Questione ladina'". In: *Die Leistung der Strataforschung und der Kreolistik. Typologische Aspekte der Sprachkontakte.* Akten des 5. Symposions über Sprachkontakt in Europa, Ureland, P. St. (Ed.), Mannheim 1982, Tübingen, 155—169.

Goebl, Hans (1984): „Sprachklassifikationen im Spannungsfeld zwischen Politik und Wissenschaft". In: *Das Romanische in den Ostalpen,* Messner, Dieter (Ed.), Wien, 207—244.

Goebl, Hans (1989): „Regionale Identität aus sprachwissenschaftlicher Sicht. Vier Fallbeispiele aus dem Bereich der Romania". In: *Regionalwissenschaftliche Forschung. Fragestellungen einer empirischen Disziplin,* Aufhauser, E./Giffinger, R./ Hatz, G. (Eds.), Wien, 404—418.

Goebl, Hans (1990): „Methodische Defizite im Bereich der Rätoromanistik. Kritische Bemerkungen zum Stand der soziolinguistischen Diskussion rund um das Dolomitenladinische". In: *Sociolinguistica 4,* 19—49.

Gsell, Otto (1982): „Las rosas dattan ora — les röses da fora — le rose danno fuori. Verbalperiphrasen mit Ortsadverb im Rätoromanischen und Italienischen". In: *Fakten und Theorien. Festschrift für Helmut Stimm zum 65. Geburtstag,* Heinz, S./ Wandruszka, U. (Eds.), Tübingen, 71—85.

Gsell, Otto (1984): „Unpersönliche Konstruktion und Wortstellung im Dolomitenladinischen". In: *Ladinia 8,* 67—98.

Gsell, Otto (1989 a ff): „Beiträge und Materialien zur Etymologie des Dolomitenladinischen". In: *Ladinia 13,* 143—164; *14,* 121—160; *15,* 105—165; *16,* 129—162.

Gsell, Otto (1989 b ff): Besprechungen neuer Bände des EWD. In: *Ladinia 13,* 278—286 (EWD I); *14,* 351—369 (EWD II); *16,* 223—240 (EWD III).

Haarmann, Harald (1973): *Soziologie der kleinen Sprachen Europas.* Bd. I: Dokumentation, Hamburg.

Heilmann, Luigi (1980): „La didattica del ladino nel quadro delle interferenze ladino-italiano". In: *Mondo ladino — Quaderni 3,* 65—86.

Heilmann, Luigi (1988): „Individuo, etnia, Stato. A proposito di pianificazione linguistica nella comunità ladina dolomitica. Considerazioni di 'ecologia del linguaggio'". In: *Mondo ladino 12,* 23—37.

Heilmann, Luigi/Plangg, Guntram A. (1989): „Ladinisch: Externe Sprachgeschichte". In: *Lexikon der Romanistischen Linguistik,* Holtus, G./Metzeltin, M./Schmitt, Chr. (Eds.), Bd. III, 720—733.

Heller, Karin (1976): „Zentralladinische Verba im romanisch-deutschen Spannungsfeld". In: *Der Schlern 50,* 406—416.

Kattenbusch, Dieter (1986): „Raetia antiqua et moderna. W. Theodor Elwert zum 80. Geburtstag. (...), Holtus, G./Ringger, K. (Eds.), Tübingen 1986". [Rez.]. In: *Ladinia 10,* 179—201.

Kattenbusch, Dieter (1987): „Giovan Battista Pellegrini: Minoranze e culture regionali, Padova 1986". [Rez.]. In: *Ladinia 11,* 247—252.

Kramer, Johannes (1981): *Deutsch und Italienisch in Südtirol,* Heidelberg.

Kramer, Johannes (1986): „Äußere Sprachgeschichte, Eigensprachlichkeitsbewußtsein und Sprachnormierungsversuche bei den Dolomitenladinern". In: *Raetia antiqua et moderna. W. Theodor Elwert zum 80. Geburtstag,* Holtus, G./Ringger, K. (Eds.), Tübingen, 581—615.

Kuen, Heinrich (1978): „Der Einfluß des Deutschen auf das Rätoromanische". In: *Ladinia 2,* 35—49.

Kuen, Heinrich (1981): „Verfeinerung des Werkzeugs zur gedanklichen Erfassung der Wirklichkeit durch Sprachkontakt in der Mundart". In: *Sprachkontakt als Ursache von Veränderungen der Sprach- und Bewußtseinsstruktur,* Meid, W./Heller, K. (Eds.), Innsbruck, 141—147.

Kuen, Heinrich (1985 a): „Deutsch-ladinische Sprachkontakte in alter und neuer Zeit". In: *Ladinia 9,* 19—29.

Kuen, Heinrich (1985 b): „Die deutschen Lehnwörter in der ladinischen Mundart von Buchenstein (Fodóm, Livinallongo) und ihre chronologische Schichtung". In: *Stimmen der Romania. Festschrift für W. Theodor Elwert zum 70. Geburtstag,* Schmidt, G./Tietz, M. (Eds.), Wiesbaden, 681—696.

Laube, Gustav (1869): „Die Ladiner in Tirol". In: *Mitteilungen der Geographischen Gesellschaft in Wien 12*, 161−166.

Mair, Walter N. (1989): „Ladinisch: Soziolinguistik". In: *Lexikon der Romanistischen Linguistik*, Holtus, G./Metzeltin, M./Schmitt, Chr. (Eds.), Bd. III, Tübingen, 697−704.

Muljačić, Žarko (1984): „Der Stellenwert der „alpenromanischen" Ausbausprachen in einem soziolinguistischen Modell". In: *Das Romanische in den Ostalpen*, Messner, D. (Ed.), Wien, 133−146.

Palla, Luciana (1986): *I Ladini fra Tedeschi e Italiani. Livinallongo del Col di Lana: una comunità sociale 1918−1948*, Venedig.

Palla, Luciana (1988): „Processi di tedeschizzazione e di italianizzazione dei Ladini dolomitici nel periodo della grande guerra e dell'annessione all'Italia". In: *Ladinia 12*, 159−189.

Pellegrini, Giovan Battista (1972 a): „A proposito di 'ladino' e di 'Ladini'". In: Pellegrini, G. B.: *Saggi sul ladino dolomitico e sul friulano*, Bari, 96−130.

Pellegrini, Giovan Battista (1972 b): „Il confine ladino-veneto nel bacino del Cordevole". In: Pellegrini, G. B.: *Saggi sul ladino dolomitico e sul friulano*, Bari, 49−95.

Pellegrini, Giovan Battista (1972 c): „Osservazioni sul confine del ladino centrale". In: Pellegrini, G. B.: *Saggi sul ladino dolomitico e sul friulano*, Bari, 11−48.

Pellegrini, Giovan Battista (1981): „Considerazioni sociolinguistiche sul ladino centrale". In: *Logos Semantikos 5*, 339−348.

Pellegrini, Giovan Battista (1986 a): *Minoranze e culture regionali*, Padua.

Pellegrini, Giovan Battista (1986 b): „Considerazioni sui rapporti lessicali del fassano". In: *Mondo ladino 10*, 359−373.

Pellegrini, Giovan Battista (1987): „The Sociolinguistic Position of Central-Rhaeto-Romance (Ladin)". In: *Romance Philology 40*, 287−300.

Plangg, Guntram A. (1980): „Le interferenze linguistiche: tedesco−ladino". In: *Mondo ladino − Quaderni 3*, 89−100.

Plangg, Guntram A. (1981): „Sprachliche Interferenzen im Ladinischen des Gadertals". In: *Sprachkontakt als Ursache von Veränderungen der Sprach- und Bewußtseinsstruktur*, Meid, W./Heller, K. (Eds.), Innsbruck, 187−194.

Plangg, Guntram A. (1983): „Venedisches im Dolomitenladinischen". In: *Linguistica e dialettologia veneta. Studi offerti a Manlio Cortelazzo dai colleghi stranieri*, Holtus, G./Metzeltin, M. (Eds.), Tübingen, 259−269.

Richebuono, Bepe (1982): „La presa di coscienza dei Ladini". In: *Ladinia 6*, 95−154.

Runggaldier, Heidi (1981): „Zum Problem der sprachlichen Interferenz im Grödnerischen". In: *Sprachkontakt als Ursache von Veränderungen der Sprach- und Bewußtseinsstruktur*, Meid, W./Heller, K. (Eds.), Innsbruck, 203−217.

Runggaldier, Heidi (1982): „Das Ladinische in Südtirol". In: *Innsbrucker Beiträge zur Sprachwissenschaft. Germanistische Reihe 13*, 215−228.

Sanguin, André-Louis (1993): „Les Ladins des Dolomites, une minorité dans la minorité". In: *Les minorités ethniques en Europe*, Sanguin, A.-L. (Dir.), Paris, 177−193.

Siller-Runggaldier, Heidi (1985): „La negazione nel Ladino Centrale". In: *Revue de Linguistique Romane 49*, 71−85.

Stolz, Otto (1927 ff): *Die Ausbreitung des Deutschtums in Südtirol im Lichte der Urkunden*, Bd. I−IV, München.

Telmon, Tullio (1992): *Le minoranze linguistiche in Italia*, Alessandria.

Valentin, Hugo (1987): *Sozioökonomische Aspekte in Dolomitenladinien*. Referat gehalten anläßlich der 12. Tagung der sprachlichen Minderheiten der Nachbarländer am 16. Oktober 1987 (Typoskript).

Valentini, Erwin (1977): „Ladinische Kultur oder Kultur der Ladiner?" In: *Ladinia 1*, 1−38.

Vanelli, Laura (1984): „Il sistema dei pronomi soggetto nelle parlate ladine". In: *Das Romanische in den Ostalpen*, Messner, D. (Ed.), Wien 147−160.

Wolfsgruber, Karl/Richebuono, Bepe (1986): „Predigten auf Grödnerisch. Ein 200 Jahre altes Dokument". In: *Ladinia 10*, 41−45.

Lois Craffonara, Bruneck (Italien)

167. Malta

1. Geographie und Demographie
2. Geschichte
3. Politik, Wirtschaft, Kultur und Religion
4. Soziolinguistische Lage
5. Herausbildung und Entwicklung des Maltesischen
6. Arabisch-italienisch-englischer Sprachkontakt
7. Kritische Wertung einiger Termini
8. Bibliographie (in Auswahl)

1. Geographie und Demographie

Die Republik Malta hat eine Gesamtfläche von 315,6 km². Davon entfallen 245,7 km² auf die Hauptinsel Malta, 67,1 km² auf die Insel Gozo (*Għawdex*) und 2,8 km² auf Comino (*Kemmuna*). Die Einwohnerzahl beträgt 358 000 (Statistisches Bundesamt, Länderbericht Malta 1992, 13 f). Nach Norden ist Sizilien 93 km entfernt; nach Tunesien im Westen sind es 288 km. In Malta gibt es weder Gebirge noch Flüsse. Von mehreren natürlichen Häfen ist der „Große Hafen", (*Il-Port il-Kbir*) bei der Hauptstadt Valletta der wichtigste; → Sprachenkarte F.

2. Geschichte

In historischer Zeit waren Phönizier/Punier, Römer und wahrscheinlich auch Byzantiner Siedler oder Besatzer auf Malta (Blouet 1989, 32 ff). Die Araber besetzten 870 Malta von Sizilien her. Von dort wurde Malta auch 1090 von den Normannen erobert. Für mehrere Jahrhunderte hatten Sizilien und Malta dieselben Machthaber, bis Karl V. 1530 Malta dem Johanniterorden übertrug. Von der Normannenzeit bis zum Ende der Ordensherrschaft im Jahre 1798 bestand enge Verbindung mit Sizilien.

1798 besetzte Napoleon Malta und vertrieb den Orden. Bald erhoben sich die Malteser gegen die Franzosen und riefen die Engländer zu Hilfe, denen im Frieden von Paris 1814 die Inseln zugesprochen wurden. Die Engländer beherrschten Malta bis 1964. Der Kampf der Malteser um Selbstbestimmung entfachte sich immer wieder an der Sprachenfrage (5.3.1.). Im Zweiten Weltkrieg wurde Malta von den Achsenmächten heftig bombadiert. 1964 wurde Malta unabhängig und gab sich eine eigene Verfassung (Großjohann 1989, 115 ff).

3. Politik, Wirtschaft, Kultur und Religion

Malta ist eine parlamentarische Republik mit einem Präsidenten als Staatsoberhaupt. Das Parlament wird von 69 Mitgliedern gebildet. Es besteht ein Zweiparteiensystem. Die regierende Partei ist derzeit die *Nationalist Party (Partit Nazzjonalista)* mit 35 Sitzen im Parlament. Die Oppositionspartei ist die *Malta Labour Party (Partit tal-Ħaddiema)* mit 34 Sitzen. Diese führte 1971−1987 Reformen durch, die die politische Macht der Kirche und der traditionellen Eliten brachen (Großjohann 1989, 123). 1987 gewann die Nationalistische Partei die Wahlen und ist seitdem an der Macht.

Die heimische Landwirtschaft produziert Getreide, Gemüse, Obst und Wein. Eine große Rolle spielt der Fischfang. Aber ein Großteil Maltas ist bebaut oder landwirtschaftlich nicht nutzbar. Malta verfügt über keine Bodenschätze. Seine Wirtschaft basiert auf vielen Säulen: In den Trockendocks werden Schiffe gebaut und repariert; es gibt viele kleine und mittlere Betriebe, der Tourismus floriert. Eine finanzielle Stütze des Staates ist auch das *Offshore Financial and Trading Centre*. Diese verschiedenen Aktivitäten verschaffen Malta genügend Einnahmen und Arbeit (Großjohann 1989, 136 ff − Department of Information 1992, 16 f).

97% der Malteser sind katholisch (Baratta 1992, 456). „Trotz aller säkularen Tendenzen bleiben die Malteser ein tief religiöses Volk" (Großjohann 1989, 168).

Malta entfaltet ein reiches kulturelles Leben. Seit 1769 hat es eine Universität. In dem 1732 eingerichteten Teatro Manuel wird heute noch gespielt. Daneben gibt es moderne Theatergruppen. Es gibt eine Rundfunk- und eine Fernsehstation und interessante Museen. Kulturelle Veranstaltungen werden von verschiedenen Seiten organisiert. Jährlich wird eine Buchmesse abgehalten. Malerisch sind die Feste aus religiösen Anlässen, bei denen die Dorfkapellen (*baned*) eine große Rolle spielen.

4. Soziolinguistische Lage

4.1. Status

Seitdem das Maltesische kodifiziert ist (cf. 5.3.2.), hat es den Status einer Standardsprache (Ammon 1987, 243). Außerdem hat es nach der Verfassung den Status der *Nationalsprache* und der *Amtssprache* (5.3.1.). Auch das Englische ist Amtssprache (Department of Information 1975, 2).

4.2. Funktion

Die Verwendung des Englischen als Amtssprache nimmt ab (Mazzon 1992, 25 ff). Bei allen offiziellen Anlässen wird Maltesisch gesprochen. Parlamentsdebatten werden auf Maltesisch gehalten und auch so veröffentlicht. Das Amtsblatt der Regierung, Gesetzestexte und Schriftstücke bei Gericht sind zweisprachig. Daneben besteht bei den Behörden im Schriftverkehr noch die Tendenz, eher das Englische zu benutzen.

Englisch wird auch bevorzugt in Formularen der Banken und der Krankenhäuser, in Verträgen und in Anschlägen der Ämter und der Schulen. Im Geschäftsleben werden sowohl Maltesisch als auch Englisch verwendet. Praktische Faktoren bestimmen die Wahl der Sprache. Im Verkehr mit dem Ausland und im Kontakt mit Ausländern benutzt man Englisch. Aber auch auf Malta bedient man sich im Geschäftsleben weithin des Englischen.

Zuweilen werden die Sprachen diglossisch verwendet. Man schreibt Englisch, wenn der Formalitätsgrad hoch ist (Mazzon 1992, 30 f). In Geschäften spricht man mit Touristen Englisch, während die Verkäufer unter sich und mit einheimischen Kunden Maltesisch verwenden. Spricht ein maltesischer Kunde Verkäufer auf Englisch an, wird er als „reich und snobistisch" betrachtet (Mazzon 1992, 32). Von Maltesern wird als Zeichen der Solidarität Maltesisch erwartet.

Auch die Presse zeigt uns, daß Malta eher zweisprachig als diglossisch ist. Täglich erscheinen eine englische Zeitung und zwei maltesische. Betrachtet man die Tageszeitungen und die Sonntagsausgaben zusammen, erkennt man, daß das Publikum einer stärkeren schriftlichen Einwirkung des Maltesischen ausgesetzt ist (Mazzon, 1992, 34 ff).

In über 20 Verlagen erscheint ein Teil der Bücher in Maltesisch, ein großer Teil auch in Englisch.

Was das gesprochene Wort in den Massenmedien angeht, sendet „Television Malta" nach den Erhebungen von Mazzon (1992, 44 f) wöchentlich 20 Stunden in Maltesisch und 24 Stunden in Englisch. Von besonderer Relevanz ist ferner das italienische Fernsehen. Es wirkt besonders stark auf die Kinder. Manche Eltern sagen, daß diese, vom Fernsehen angeregt, unter sich Italienisch sprechen (Mazzon 1992, 46).

Auf Malta gibt es 183 staatliche und 90 Privatschulen. Schon von der Grundschule an sind Maltesisch und Englisch Pflichtfächer. In den Privatschulen wird viel mehr Wert auf das Englische gelegt. Bis vor 15/20 Jahren war das Maltesische aus diesen Schulen verbannt. Aber heute drängen die Eltern auf mehr Maltesisch-Unterricht, denn zum Eintritt in die Universität werden Zeugnisse über Maltesisch-Kenntnisse verlangt (Mazzon 1992, 52). Aus Befragungen ergab sich, daß 73,4% der Schüler unter sich Maltesisch sprechen und 5,5% Englisch (die anderen wechseln — Mazzon 1992, 56).

An der Universität sprechen die Studenten unter sich überwiegend Maltesisch. Schriftliche Arbeiten liefern sie auf Englisch ab. Vorlesungen werden auf Englisch gehalten. Der Lehrkörper hält seine Beratungen auf Maltesisch ab, aber die Protokolle erscheinen auf Englisch. Die Verwaltungssprache der Universität ist Englisch (schriftliche Auskunft des Dekans der Theologischen Fakultät vom 31. 3. 1993).

Auf religiösem Gebiet wird normalerweise Maltesisch gebraucht. Dies gilt für Messen, Gebete und Gesänge. Gesangbücher, liturgische Bücher und Literatur über religiöse Themen sind maltesisch.

In der privaten Domäne ergab sich aus Umfragen von Lydia Sciriha unter Schülern, daß 96% der Mütter und 97% der Väter mit ihren Kindern Maltesisch sprechen (Borg, Mifsud, Sciriha 1992, 11).

Nach Erhebungen von Mazzon für die private Domäne (Mazzon 1992, 60−74) ist in älteren Generationen Maltesisch verbreiteter als in den jüngeren. Doch überwiegt in allen Fällen Maltesisch.

Wenn Jugendliche beim anderen Geschlecht Eindruck machen wollen, wird von ihnen in nur 46,5% der Fälle Maltesisch gebraucht. Kennen sie sich näher, wird in 60% der Fälle Maltesisch verwendet. Zuerst will man sich also mit dem prestigereichen Englisch als gebildet darstellen. Später benutzt man zum Zeichen der Vertrautheit eher die einheimische Sprache (Mazzon 1992, 71).

4.3. Attitüde

Die reservierte Haltung mancher Malteser gegenüber Englisch in der Kolonialzeit ist überwunden. Man will nun, frei aller politischen Zwänge, Englisch als Instrument benutzen, d. h. als *Language of Wider Communication*

(Mazzon 1992, 24). Die heutige Lage ist ausgedrückt in „facciamo parte dell'Europa" und in „ormai non dipendiamo più del Regno Unito" (Mazzon 1992, 101). Die integrative Motivation gilt nun voll für das Maltesische. Die Benutzung des Maltesischen symbolisiert die Solidarität mit der maltesischen Nation. Englisch wird wegen seines Nutzens und wegen seines Prestiges verwendet. Doch ist in der letzten Zeit die Prestigewirkung des Englischen ambivalent geworden. Einerseits wird Englisch von vielen gerade in formellen Situationen benutzt. Andererseits werden zuweilen Anglophone als Snobs, ja geradezu als Verräter gebrandmarkt (Mazzon 1992, 103).

4.4. Konflikt

Die heutige Lage wird von Albert Borg 1992, 5) wie folgt charakterisiert: „(...) we have to think of Maltese and English with their different roles no longer als languages in conflict but as languages in harmonious contact". Dann haben die Malteser „(...) a national language which distinguishes them from all others, and an international language which binds them to the rest of the world."

Gegenüber dem Italienischen sind die Aversionen aus der Kriegszeit verschwunden. Als neuer Faktor ist das italienische Fernsehen aufgetreten, das die Rolle eines „Italienisch-Lehrers" einnimmt (Mangion 1992, 72). Es hat eine gewisse Rückkehr des Italienischen bewirkt, so daß Mazzon (1992, 107) vermutet, daß Italienisch eines Tages zu einer ernsthaften Konkurrenz für Englisch werden könnte.

4.5. Diglossie – Bilinguismus

Es gibt heute in Malta 5 Varietäten: die maltesische Standardsprache, Englisch (*British English*), die maltesischen Dialekte, die *Sprache von Sliema*, und das *maltesische Englisch*. Es gibt auf Malta sowohl Zweisprachigkeit als auch Diglossie. Das Englische britischer Ausprägung wird nur von auf Malta ansässigen Engländern sowie von solchen Maltesern gesprochen, die in Großbritannien studiert haben. Das *Maltese English* ist die maltesische Ausprägung der New Englishes, die sich im britischen Empire herausgebildet haben. Das Standard-Maltesische sowie Englisch gehören zu den High-Languages in Malta. Sie können in der Regel von allen Maltesern gebraucht werden. Sie sind die Varietäten der Zweisprachigkeit und zugleich die High-Languages der Diglossie im Sinne von Ferguson (1959, 327). Die Sprache von Sliema sowie die maltesischen Dialekte sind die prestigeärmeren Varietäten, die Low-Languages der Diglossie.

Die Sprache von Sliema genießt kein großes Ansehen bei den Maltesern. Wer diese Sprache spricht, gilt als snobistisch. Aquilina nennt sie *kawlata* („gemischte Gemüsesuppe"), *Sliema Jargon* oder *Pidgin Maltese* (Aquilina nach Huber 1982, 96). Albert Borg bezeichnet sie als *Mixed Maltese English* (Alb. Borg nach Huber 1982, 97). In der Tat liegt eine Code-Mischung vor, bei denen die Proportionen der Mischung von Fall zu Fall verschieden sind, wie z. B. in dem Satz [allura taparsi jiġi jara allura ai hav tustei hi:ə a zgur] „et alors il vient voir *je dois rester ici*, bien sûr" (Huber 1982, 99).

Eine im Parlament, in der Schule und in der Kirche verwendete Sprache kann nicht als L-Language eingestuft werden. Aber einige Domänen sind vom Englischen besetzt, z. B. an der Universität und in der Geschäftswelt. Es besteht also auf Malta eine Kombination von Bilinguismus und Diglossie.

5. Herausbildung und Entwicklung des Maltesischen

5.1. Herausbildung und Kontaktsituationen

Die Araber brachten ab 870 das Maghrebinische nach Malta, das rasch von den Bewohnern angenommen wurde. Nach 1090 kam Malta in intensiven Kontakt mit Sizilien. Von dort wirkte das Italienische stark auf die Sprache Maltas ein, zuerst in der sizilianischen Varietät, später in der toskanischen. Arabisch-maghrebinische Dialekte und das Sizilianisch-Toskanische zusammen konstituieren das Maltesische. Zum Kontakt zwischen der einheimischen Sprache und dem Italienischen kam es in der Hafenzone, d. h. in den „Drei Städten" Senglea (*L'Isla*), Cospicua (*Bormla*) und Vittoriosa (*Birgu*), später auch in Valletta. Hier wanderten Menschen aus Sizilien und Süditalien ein, was sprachliche Innovationen bewirkte. Hier bildete sich eine Koiné heraus, als Basis für die spätere maltesische Standardsprache (Brincat 1991, 91–109). Diese Sprache wurde jahrhundertelang nicht für formelle Zwecke verwendet. Maltesisch war nur Low-Language. High-Languages waren das Latein und Italienisch (Wettinger 1990–1993, 151 f).

5.2. Die Triglossie unter den Engländern

Die Engländer trachteten von Anfang an danach, Italienisch durch Englisch zu ersetzen (Huber 1982, 57). Die Malteser leisteten jedoch Widerstand und hielten an „ihrer" Sprache fest, und das war für die Elite Maltas das Italienische (Frendo 1988, 187). Der gebildete Malteser kam gar nicht auf den Gedanken, daß er sich für die Sprache des eigenen Volkes einsetzen könnte, die ja nur gut war für „Küche und Tenne" (Sammut 1990, 16). Man hielt sie für einen arabischen Dialekt, der keine einheitliche Orthographie hatte, und von dem es nichts Geschriebenes von Bedeutung gab. So entstand eine Triglossiesituation. Die beiden Hochsprachen waren Englisch und Italienisch (Mazzon 1992, 98). Maltesisch war die Umgangssprache, die Low-Language.

Doch das Maltesische hatte auch Fürsprecher. Um 1850 begannen viele Intellektuelle „die Würde der maltesischen Sprache und die Nützlichkeit der Annahme des Englischen zu verkünden" (Mazzon 1992, 6f). Das Ringen um die Durchsetzung des Maltesischen dauerte bis in den Zweiten Weltkrieg hinein.

5.3. Die Normalisierung des Maltesischen

Die Vorkämpfer wollten Maltesisch auf das Niveau einer Standardsprache erheben, d. h. sie wollten seine Normalisierung. Eine Sprache ist dann normalisiert, wenn in jeder formellen oder informellen Situation ihr Gebrauch ohne Diskriminierung möglich ist (Ferro 1984, 183; s. auch Kremnitz 1990, 34). Die Anhänger des Maltesischen wollten ihr Ziel durch drei Mittel erreichen: (1.) durch politisches Wirken, (2.) durch die Kodifizierung (Normativierung) und (3.) durch den Ausbau des Schrifttums (Kloss 1978, 46—55).

5.3.1. Politisches Wirken

Die Vorkämpfer des Maltesischen führten einen politischen Kampf gegen die eigenen Landsleute, die „Nationalisten", die sich paradoxerweise nicht für die Sprache ihrer Nation einsetzten, sondern für die italienische Sprache und Kultur. Der Kampf entbrannte an der Frage der Sprachen in der Schule. Die Befürworter des Maltesischen erfuhren Hilfe von den Briten, denn „merkwürdigerweise wollten die Engländer Maltesisch an den Schulen fördern, um damit (...) allmählich Italienisch zu verdrängen" (Frendo 1975, 24). Der Keenan-Report (1880), der die Verdrängung des Italienischen beinhaltete, führte zu einem die maltesische Gesellschaft jahrzehntelang spaltenden politischen *Sprachenstreit*. Erbitterter wurde der Kampf, als Mussolini in Italien die Macht ergriff und die Faschisten Einfluß bei den Italophilen gewannen. Zweimal wurde wegen des Sprachenstreits die Verfassung geändert (Bartholy 1992, 199 ff). Schließlich regelten die Engländer per Dekret die Sprachenfrage endgültig in ihrem Sinne. 1933 wurde Maltesisch Gerichtssprache anstelle des Italienischen. 1934 wurden Englisch und Maltesisch zu Amtssprachen erklärt. Italienisch wurde in der Grundschule nicht mehr unterrichtet. Die Hochsprachen waren nun Englisch und die maltesische Standardsprache, während die maltesischen Dialekte die prestigeärmeren Varietäten darstellten (Huber 1982, 81 ff; 148). Die schrecklichen italienischen Bombenangriffe während des Zweiten Weltkrieges gaben der italienischen Sprache auf Malta den Gnadenstoß (Mangion 1992, 70). Aus dem Zweiten Weltkrieg ging das Englische gestärkt hervor. Freilich wurde es immer noch als die Sprache der Kolonialherren empfunden. In der Verfassung des unabhängigen Maltas wurde die Sprachenfrage klar geregelt. Dort steht in § 5: „Das Maltesische ist die Nationalsprache Maltas. Maltesisch und Englisch (...) sollen die Amtssprachen Maltas sein" (Department of Information 1975, 2). An allen Schulen muß Maltesisch gelehrt werden, und zum Teil wird auch in Maltesisch unterrichtet. Zur weiteren Stärkung des Maltesischen legte der Erziehungsminister im Oktober 1989 einen Gesetzentwurf „zur Festigung des Status der maltesischen Sprache" vor (Suppliment tal-Gazzetta tal-Gvern ta' Malta, Nru 15, 188, Malta 1989, 1176—1180), doch ist dieser Entwurf noch nicht Gesetz geworden.

Die „*International Academy of Language Law*" veranstaltete 1992 in Malta ein Treffen von Fachleuten, um der maltesischen Sprachplanung Anregungen zu geben.

Sprachpolitisch aktiv ist auch die „*Akkademja tal-Malti*" („Maltesische Akademie"). Sie hat 1924 schon den *Tagħrif* (5.3.2.1.) entwickelt und ist in den letzten Jahren wieder sehr engagiert. So gab sie 1987 die *Żieda* heraus und 1992 das *Aġġornament* (5.3.2.1.).

5.3.2. Kodifizierung (Normativierung)

Damit eine Sprache von der Bevölkerung als Standardsprache angenommen wird, müssen feste Regeln vorliegen, die dem Sprachbenutzer helfen, mit ihr sicher umzugehen. Ein Alphabet muß geschaffen und Orthographieregeln erstellt werden, ferner eine Grammatik für die Morphosyntax formuliert werden. Es müssen Wörterbücher geschrieben und Anleitungen zu gutem Stil geliefert werden (Kloss 1978, 37).

5.3.2.1. Orthographie

Annähernd 40 Orthographievarianten wurden vorgeschlagen, bis man im Jahre 1924 die endgültige Lösung fand (Aquilina 1970, 75 – 101 b). So schrieb man Maltesisch mit arabischen Buchstaben, dann mit einer Kombination von lateinischen und arabischen Buchstaben, oder man versah das lateinische Alphabet mit Sonderzeichen. Lange schrieb man Maltesisch in Anlehnung an das Italienische. Es bestanden über einen längeren Zeitraum mehrere Systeme nebeneinander. 1921 gründeten einige Gelehrte die *Għakda tal Chittieba tal-Malti* „Vereinigung maltesischer Schriftsteller", die sich die Pflege der maltesischen Sprache zur Aufgabe machte. Sie ließ eine kohärente maltesische Orthographie ausarbeiten, die 1924 mit dem Titel *Tagħrif fuq il-Kitba Maltija* „Bekanntmachung zum Maltesischschreiben" veröffentlicht wurde. In diesen Orthographieregeln löste man sich völlig von der italienischen Schreibweise. Die neue, 1934 offiziell anerkannte Orthographie ist heute allein üblich. 1987 fügte die Maltesische Akademie unter dem Titel *Żieda mat-Tagħrif* „Zusatz zu der Bekanntmachung" neue Regeln hinzu, die die eingebürgerten italienischen und englischen Wörter auch in der Schreibweise inkorporierten. 1991 beschloß die Akademie weitere Verbesserungen, die unter dem Titel *Aġġornament tat-Tagħrif fuq il-Kitba Maltija* „Aktualisierung zur Bekanntmachung zum Maltesischschreiben", 1992 in *Il-Malti* veröffentlicht wurden.

5.3.2.2. Grammatik

Ninu Cremona verfaßte eine leicht zu verstehende Grammatik, die unter dem Titel *Tagħlim fuq il-Kitba Maltija* „Unterweisung zum Maltesischschreiben" 1934 – 1936 in zwei Bänden erschien.

5.3.2.3. Wörterbücher

Erin Serracino-Inglott schrieb unter dem Titel *Il-Miklem Malti* (9 Bände, 1975 – 1989) ein einsprachiges Wörterbuch. Das *Maltese-English Dictionary* von Aquilina dient auch als etymologisches Wörterbuch.

Es gibt zahlreiche Hilfsmittel zum Erlernen der maltesischen Grammatik und eines guten Stils. Maltesisch ist heute standardisiert.

5.3.3. Ausbau des maltesischen Schrifttums

5.3.3.1. Belletristik

Von der Mitte des 19. Jahrhunderts erschienen immer öfter literarische Texte auf Maltesisch. Romane, Novellen, Theaterstücke und Gedichte bewiesen, daß man Maltesisch schreiben kann. Seitdem erschließt sich das Maltesische neue Literaturgattungen.

5.3.3.2. Sachprosa

Für die Erhaltung einer kleinen Sprache ist weniger eine hochspezialisierte Literatur denn die generelle Existenz von Geschriebenem notwendig. Dies gilt u. a. für die Sachprosa (Kloss 1978, 28; 38; 40 ff). Sie ist auf Maltesisch in großer Zahl vorhanden (Kochrezepte, Kirchenblätter, Gesetzestexte). Dennoch sind in den Buchhandlungen viel mehr Texte auf Englisch zu finden.

5.3.3.3. Fachprosa

In der Fach- oder Forscherprosa ist Maltesisch noch wenig vertreten. Hier gibt es auf Maltesisch vor allem Schriften, die das Eigene betreffen: die eigene Sprache, Literatur, Religion, Geschichte und Natur (Kloss 1978, 47 f).

Abschließend kann man sagen: die maltesische Standardsprache hat sich politisch durchgesetzt. Sie ist kodifiziert und hat ein vielfältiges Schrifttum entwickelt.

6. Arabisch-italienisch-englischer Sprachkontakt

Maltesisch ist eine Mischsprache, die entstanden ist durch den intensiven Kontakt mit dem Maghrebinischen und dem Sizilianischen. Später traten Hochitalienisch und Englisch hinzu.

6.1. Interferenzen von seiten des Italienischen

Das italienische Element wirkte sich besonders stark im Lautsystem aus. Im morphosyntaktischen Bereich waren die Einflüsse geringer. Im Lexikon waren sie dagegen sehr zahlreich.

6.1.1. Interferenzen im Lautsystem

Infolge des Sprachenkontakts wurden arabische Phoneme aufgegeben und italienische Phoneme übernommen.

Das Vokalsystem des maghrebinischen Arabisch ist zumindest in seiner tunesischen

Variante zweistufig (Singer 1984, 64), während das des Maltesischen dreistufig ist. Krier führt dies auf die Einwirkung des Sizilianischen zurück (Krier 1976, 20 f).

Das Konsonantensystem wurde unter dem Einfluß des Italienischen stark verändert. Typisch arabische Züge im hinteren Artikulationsraum wurden z. T. aufgegeben, und es kam durch Phonemzusammenfall zu Reduzierungen. So fielen die Phoneme /ḥ/ und /ḫ/ unter /ḥ/ zusammen. Ebenso wurde aus ʿAyn und Ġayn zunächst ein einziges Phonem (geschrieben ⟨ ġħ ⟩), das aber heute als Konsonantenphonem ausgefallen ist und nur in der Längung (plus Laryngalisierung) des benachbarten Vokals weiterlebt. Von den typisch arabischen Phonemen sind nur /ʾ/, /ḥ/ und /w/ erhalten. Das Maltesische hat auch die Reibelaute /ṯ/ und /ḏ/ zugunsten der Verschlußlaute /t/ und /d/ aufgegeben. Diese Veränderungen führten zu Phonemzusammenfällen und -ausfällen, die uns das folgende Schema zeigt: d, ḍ, ḏ, ẓ > d ⟨d⟩; t, ṭ, ṯ > t ⟨t⟩ s, ṣ > s ⟨s⟩; ḥ, ḫ > ḥ ⟨ħ⟩; h > O ⟨h⟩; ʿ > O ⟨għ⟩; ġ > O ⟨għ⟩.

Durch diese Phonemzusammenfälle sind im Maltesischen viele Homonyme und Homophone entstanden, z. B.: malt. xagħar [šār] „Haar" < ar. šaʿr neben malt. xahar [šār] „Monat" < ar. šahar. Durch den Einfluß des Italienischen haben sich die maltesischen Phoneme weitgehend entarabisiert.

Maltesisch hat aus dem Italienischen die Phoneme /p/, /v/, /ts/, /dz/, /č/ und /g/ übernommen (Krier 1976, 15 ff; Kontzi, im Druck).

So liegt ein Mischsystem vor, in dem eine Reihe von arabischen Phonemen aufgegeben wurden und in das italienische Phoneme eingedrungen sind.

6.1.2. Morphosyntax

In der stark arabisch bestimmten Morphosyntax finden wir auch italienische Züge, die sich mit dem arabischen Element mischen. So werden z. T. italienische Nomina nach arabischem Muster in den Plural gesetzt. Zu *forma* „Form" gehört der Pl. *forom*.

Bei der Konjugation setzt sich auch bei italienischen oder englischen Verben das arabische Muster durch. So heißt z. B. „er nimmt an" (it. *accetta*) auf malt. *jaċċetta* mit dem Präfix *j-* für die 3. Pers. Sing. In der Flexion des Verbes erscheinen auch italienische Formen. Zu dem Verb arabischer Herkunft *emmen* „glauben" gehört das Part. Perf. *emmnut* mit dem Suffix *-ut* < ital. *-uto*.

Nach italienischem Vorbild kann das Passiv auch mit *ġie* (= *venire*) + Part. Perf. gebildet werden. Wo bei S. Pellico der italienische Text lautet *Fui chiamato alla continuazione* übersetzt der Malteser *Ġejt imsejjaħ biex jissoktaw*.

6.1.3. Lexikon

6.1.3.1. Ausdrucksseite

Den Mischcharakter des Maltesischen sieht man am deutlichsten am Lexikon. Zuerst drangen Wörter aus Sizilien ein. Das zeigen uns Wortformen wie *ċar* „klar". Später wurden Ausdrücke der italienischen Hochsprache ins Maltesische übernommen.

Italienisch und Maltesisch können sich auch in einem Wort mischen, z. B.: *sakranazz* „betrunken" < ar. *sakrān* + ital. Pejorativsuffix *-azzo*.

Italienische Interferenzen haben arabische Wortfamilien und deren ursprünglich homogene etymologische Strukturen aufgerissen. Die Grundbedeutung eines Wortes wird im Arabischen durch die Wurzel ausgedrückt, die bei allen Ableitungen die gleiche Grundidee beinhaltet. Z. B. ist KTB die Wurzel für „schreiben", und so finden wir nicht nur *kataba* „schreiben, er schrieb", sondern auch *kitāb* „Buch", *kātib* „Schriftsteller", *maktūb* „Geschriebenes, Brief", *maktab* „Büro", *maktaba* „Bibliothek". Zwar sagt man im Maltesischen für „schreiben" *kiteb*, für „Buch" *ktieb* und für „Schriftsteller" *kittieb*, aber durch das Italienische kamen für „Büro" *uffiċċju*, für „Brief" *ittra* und für „Bibliothek" *librerija* herein.

6.1.3.2. Semantische Strukturen

Durch italienische Interferenz wird zuweilen der arabische Ausdruck mit den Bedeutungsstrukturen des entsprechenden italienischen Wortes gefüllt. Malt. *mess* leitet sich von ar. *massa* „berühren" ab. In dieser Bedeutung lebt es auch im Maltesischen weiter. Aber in Luk. 15,12 steht in maltesischer Übersetzung: *Missier, agħtini s-sehem li jmissni mil-wirt*, wo die Bedeutung „berühren" nicht paßt. Es ist zu übersetzen „Vater gib mir das Erbteil, das mir zusteht". Im Italienischen steht da *Padre, dammi la parte che mi tocca*. Das malt. *mess* hat die Bedeutung von ital. *toccare* = „berühren" + „zustehen" übernommen.

6.2. Interferenzen vonseiten des Englischen

Das Englische ist in die Lautstrukturen des Maltesischen weniger tief eingedrungen als das Italienische. Noch mehr gilt das für die

Grammatik. Jedoch auf lexikalischem Gebiet sind die englischen Elemente außerordentlich zahlreich.

6.2.1. Lautliche Interferenzen

Das Konsonantenphonem /ž/ wurde durch Englisch ins Maltesische eingebracht, z. B. in *divixin* < engl. *division*. welches [diviž ən] ausgesprochen wird (Aġġornament, 17).

6.2.2. Morphosyntax

Die englischen Wörter werden, wie im Englischen selbst, im Plural meist mit -s versehen. Zu *brejk* „Bremse" gehört der Plural *brejks*. Der Plural kann auch durch das Suffix *-ijiet* (< ar. *-āt*) gebildet werden. So gibt es zu *brejk* auch den Plural *brejkijiet* (Alexander Borg 1978, 335).

6.2.3. Lexikon

Besonders häufig sind englische Wörter auf allen Gebieten des modernen Lebens (E. Fenech 1978, 80—147). Z. B. ist *fjuż* „(elektrische) Sicherung".

6.3. Zusammenwirken von Italienisch und Englisch

Bei manchen Ausdrücken sehen wir, daß sowohl das Italienische wie das Englische auf die Sprache Maltas einwirken. So wurde in dem Wort für „Bibliothek" das arabische *maktaba* ersetzt durch das italienische *librerija*, das die Bedeutung des englischen *library* angenommen hat.

6.4. Zusammenwirken von Arabisch, Italienisch und Englisch

In dem Ausdruck *swiċċ b'żewġ modi* (Joseph Borg 1974, 7) „Schalter, der auf zwei Weisen bedient werden kann", entstammen *swiċċ* dem Englischen (< *switch*), *b'żewġ* dem Arabischen (< *bi-zawġ*) und *modi* dem Italienischen.

7. Kritische Wertung einiger Termini

Der Begriff *Ausbau* wird bei Kloss in doppelter Weise verwendet. Er benutzt ihn für die „Umwandlung" von bislang mündlich gebrauchten Sprachvarianten in Schriftsprachen" (Kloss 1978, 37). Und er verwendet ihn für die Kodifizierung und für die Ausweitung im schriftlichen Gebrauch (Kloss 1978, 46). Daß die Verwendung des Terminus *Ausbau* nicht eindeutig ist, sieht man bei Ammon, der von „Ausbau im engeren Sinn" spricht (Ammon 1987, 243). Daher benutze ich als übergeordneten Begriff für die Entwicklung des Maltesischen zur Schriftsprache das Wort *Normalisierung*. Sie umfaßt (1) das *politische Wirken*, (2) die *Kodifizierung* (*Normativierung*) und (3) den *Ausbau*, den ich nur auf die Erweiterung des Schrifttums anwende. Ich ziehe auch den Terminus *Kodifizierung* dem der *Normativierung* vor, um lautliche Ähnlichkeiten zu vermeiden (5.3.). Für die Entwicklung des Begriffes *Normalisierung* weise ich auf die katalanischen Soziolinguisten hin (Kremnitz 1979, 23 ff; Aracil bei Kremnitz 1979, 139—147).

8. Bibliographie (in Auswahl)

„Aġġornament tat-Tagħrif fuq il-Kitba Maltija (1924)" (1992): *Il-Malti*. Edizzjoni Speċjali.

Ammon, Ulrich (1987): „Funktionale Typen/Statustypen von Sprachsystemen". In: *Sociolinguistics/ Soziolinguistik*, Ammon, Ulrich/Dittmar, Norbert/ Mattheier, Klaus (Eds.), Berlin/New York, 230—263.

Aquilina, Joseph (1970): *Papers in Maltese Linguistics*, Malta.

Aquilina, Joseph (1987—1990): *Maltese-English Dictionary*, 2 vol., Malta.

Baratta, Mario von (Ed.) (1992): *Der Fischer Weltalmanach*, Frankfurt/M.

Bartholy, Heike (1992): *Sprache, kulturelle Identität und Unabhängigkeit dargestellt am Beispiel Malta*, Weiden.

Blouet, Brian (1987): *The Story of Malta*, Malta.

Borg, Albert/Mifsud, Manwel/Sciriha, Lydia (1992): *The position of Maltese in Malta*, Manuskript eines während der Sitzung der „Laqgħa ta' Esperti dwar il-Pjanifikazzjoni Lingwistika" gehaltenen Referates, Valletta.

Borg, Alexander (1978): *A historical and comparative phonology and morphology of Maltese*, Diss. Jerusalem.

Borg, Joseph (1974): *Is-sengħa tad-dawl*, Valletta.

Brincat, Joseph M. (1991): „Language and Demography in Malta". In: *Malta. A Case Study in International Cross-Currents*, Fiorini, Stanley/Mallia-Milanes, Victor (Eds.), Amsterdam.

Cachia, Mons. Lawrenz (1994): *L-Ilsien Malti: Il-Bierah u l-Lum* [Die maltesische Sprache, gestern und heute], Malta.

Camilleri, Antoinette (1995): *Bilingualism in Education. The Maltese Experience*, Heidelberg.

Cremona, A. (1970): *Tagħlim fuq il-Kitba Maltija. L-Ewwel Ktieb*, 3. Aufl., Malta.

Cremona, A. (1973): *Tagħlim fuq il-Kitba Maltija. It-Tieni Ktieb*, 10. Aufl., Malta.

Department of Information (1975): *Constitution of the Republic of Malta*, Valletta.

Department of Information (1992): *Malta Information*, Valletta.

Fenech, Edward (1978): *Contemporary Journalistic Maltese. An Analytical and Comparative Study*, Leiden.

Ferguson, Charles A. (1959): „Diglossia". In: *Word 15*, 325–340.

Ferro Ruibal, Xesús (1984): „O Acordo Ortográfico e Morfolóxico de 1982". In: *I Encontros Labaca. Ponencias*, A Coruña/La Coruña.

Frendo, Henry (1975): „Language and Nationality in an Island Colony: Malta". In: *Canadian Review of Studies in Nationalities 3*, 22–33.

Frendo, Henry (1988): „Maltese Colonial Identity: Latin Mediterranean or British Empire?" In: *The British Colonial Experience 1800–1964: The Impact on Maltese Society*, Mallia-Milanes, Victor (Ed.), Msida, 185–214.

Großjohann, Wilfried (1989): *Malta. Ein politisches Reisebuch*, Hamburg.

Huber, Cécile (1982): *Variation linguistique dans le cadre du bilinguisme maltais. Linguistische Variation im Rahmen der Zweisprachigkeit auf Malta*, Diss. Graz.

Hull, Geoffrey (1993): *The Malta Language Question. A Case Study in Cultural Imperialism*, Valletta.

Kloss, Heinz (1978): *Die Entwicklung neuer germanischer Kultursprachen seit 1800*, 2. Aufl., Düsseldorf.

Kontzi, Reinhold (im Druck): „Das Maltesische". In: *Lexikon der Romanistischen Linguistik VII*, Holtus, G./Metzeltin, M./Schmitt, Chr. (Eds.), Tübingen (im Druck).

Kremnitz, Georg (Ed.) (1979): *Sprachen im Konflikt. Theorie und Praxis der katalanischen Soziolinguisten. Eine Textauswahl*, Tübingen.

Kremnitz, Georg (1990): *Gesellschaftliche Mehrsprachigkeit: Institutionelle, gesellschaftliche und individuelle Aspekte. Einführender Überblick*, Wien.

Krier, Fernande (1976): *Le maltais au contact de l'italien. Etude phonologique, grammaticale et sémantique*, Hamburg.

Mangion, Giovanni (1992): *Studi Italo-Maltesi*, Malta.

Mazzon, Gabriella (1992): *L'inglese di Malta*, Neapel.

Sammut, Frans (1990): „What future the mother tongue? A historical background". In: *Society 6*, 16–19.

Serracino-Inglott, Erin (1975–1989): *Il-Miklem Malti*, 9 vol., Malta.

Singer, Rudolf (1984): *Grammatik der arabischen Mundart der Medina von Tunis*, Berlin/New York.

Wettinger, Godfrey (1990–1993): „Plurilinguism and cultural change in Medieval Malta". In: *Mediterranean Language Review 6–7*, 144–160.

„Żieda mat-Tagħrif". In: *Il-Malti* 1987, I–VIII.

Reinhold Kontzi, Stuttgart (Deutschland)

XIV. Sprachkontakte in Südosteuropa
Language Contacts in Southeastern Europe
Contacts linguistiques en Europe du Sud-Est

168. Jugoslawien

1. Geographie und Demographie
2. Territorialgeschichte und Staatsbildung
3. Politik, Wirtschaft und allgemeine kulturelle sowie religiöse Lage
4. Statistik und Ethnoprofile der Kontaktsprachen
5. Soziolinguistische Lage
6. Sprachpolitische Lage der Kontaktsprachen
7. Darstellung von Sprachkontakten bzw. Kontaktsprachen
8. Kritische Wertung der verwendeten Quellen und Literatur
9. Bibliographie (in Auswahl)

1. Geographie und Demographie

Die Bundesrepublik Jugoslawien besteht heute (1996) aus den beiden früheren jugoslawischen Teilrepubliken Serbien (88.361 km^2) und Montenegro (13.812 km^2), zusammen 102.173 km^2. Bis 1990 bestanden innerhalb Serbiens die beiden autonomen Provinzen Vojvodina (21.506 km^2) und Kosovo (10.887 km^2) (Engeres Serbien 55.968 km^2). Serbien ist relativ dicht besiedelt, dennoch bestehen innerhalb des Landes große Unterschiede: Kosovo hat die größte Bevölkerungsdichte mit 200 Ew. pro km^2 (geschätzt), das Engere Serbien weist 104,3 Ew. pro km^2 auf, Montenegro ist mit 46,3 Ew. pro km^2 dünn besiedelt (Rehder 1992, 604, 429). Nach der Volkszählung von 1991 hat Serbien 9,8 Mio Ew., Montenegro 615.000, zusammen 10,4 Mio. Da die Volkszählung teilweise boykottiert wurde, dürfte die Zahl der Ew. in Wirklichkeit etwas höher liegen, vor allem gibt es mit Sicherheit mehr Albaner.

In Serbien sieht die nationale Zusammensetzung so aus: Serben 65,8%, Albaner 17,2%, Ungarn 3,5%, Jugoslawen 3,2%, Muslime 2,4%, Montenegriner 1,4%, Roma (Zigeuner) 1,4%, Kroaten 1,1%, Slowaken 0,6%, Makedonier 0,4%, Rumänen 0,4%, Bulgaren 0,3%, Bunjewatzen 0,2%, Ruthenen (Russinen) 0,2%, Walachen 0,2%, Türken 0,1%. In Montenegro machen die Montenegriner 61,8%, die Muslime 14,6%, die Serben 9,3%, die Albaner 6,6%, die Jugoslawen 4,0% aus (Daten nach Seewann 1993, 80). Genaueres unten 4.

Die wichtigsten Bevölkerungsverschiebungen waren durch die Ausdehnung des Türkischen Reiches seit dem späten Mittelalter bedingt. Die folgenschwerste Migration innerhalb des heutigen Serbiens war die Auswanderung der Serben aus ihrem Kernland Raszien (heute Kosovo und Sandžak Novi Pazar) 1690 unter dem Patriarchen Arsenije Crnojević in die heutige Vojvodina. Andererseits konnten die Albaner in die nun menschenleeren oder dünner besiedelten Gebiete nachrücken. Die türkische Minderheit im Kosovo sowie die (serbokroatischsprachigen) Muslime des Sandžaks gehören zum Erbe des türkischen Reiches. Die Ungarn und Rumänen in der Vojvodina sowie die Bulgaren im Engeren Serbien schließen an die Siedlungsgebiete der jeweiligen Staaten an, während die Voraussetzungen für die Einwanderung der Slowaken und Russinen der Vojvodina, teils auch der Rumänen, in der Abwanderung der Türken aus Pannonien im Zuge der Kriege des ausgehenden 17. Jahrhunderts gegeben waren. Auch die Bunjewatzen sind Zuwanderer; sie sprechen den jüngeren štokavisch-ikavischen Dialekt, der sonst in der westlichen Herzegowina und Dalmatien gesprochen wird (zu ihrer Herkunft s. Sekulić 1986, 41–58); → Sprachenkarte G.

2. Territorialgeschichte und Staatsbildung

Nach der Teilung des Römischen Reiches kam der östliche Teil der Balkanhalbinsel unter byzantinische Herrschaft. Im 6. Jahrhundert drangen die Slawen über die Karpathen und die Donau vor. Erste Staatsbildungen entstanden unter Županen („Gaufürsten") in Hum (Herzegowina), Duklja (Diocleia, Montenegro) und Raška (Raszien, Altserbien). Im 12. Jahrhundert gelang es dem Großžupan Stefan Nemanja (regierte bis 1196), die Macht zu übernehmen. Sein Sohn Stefan der Erstgekrönte wurde 1217 erster serbischer König (vom Papst gekrönt). Sein zweiter Sohn Rastko, der spätere Heilige Sava, gründete das autokephale serbische Erzbistum und wandte sich ganz der Orthodoxie zu. Zum Zentrum des serbischen Geisteslebens wurde das Kloster Hilendar auf dem Athos. Die größte Macht erlangte das mittelalterliche Serbien unter dem Zaren Stefan Dušan dem Mächtigen. Unter ihm wurde 1346 das serbische Patriarchat gegründet.

Das Vordringen der Türken begann nach der Mitte des 14. Jahrhunderts. Von schicksalhafter Bedeutung war die Schlacht auf dem Amselfeld 1389, in der die Serben unterlagen. Ein serbischer Vasallenstaat (die Despotovina) bestand noch bis 1459 (Fall von Smederevo). Die Türkenherrschaft brachte dem Land die Isolierung vom Westen, bis es im 17. Jahrhundert zu den türkisch-österreichischen Kriegen kam (Friede von Karlowitz 1699). Im 18. Jahrhundert bildete sich in der heutigen Vojvodina ein serbisches Schrifttum heraus, zunächst auf russischer und russisch-kirchenslawischer Grundlage, später unter immer mehr Beimengungen der Volkssprache (slawenoserbisch), bis in der ersten Hälfte des 19. Jahrhunderts Vuk Karadžić die serbische Volkssprache als Schriftsprache durchsetzte.

Erst die serbischen Aufstände (1804–1813) unter Karađorđe (dem „Schwarzen Georg") und Miloš Obrenović (1815–1817) brachten die Unabhängigkeit. Das Fürstentum Serbien wurde 1830 von den Türken anerkannt. Zwischen den Dynastien Obrenović und Karađorđević herrschte ständig Rivalität, das Königreich wurde 1882 unter Milan Obrenović errichtet.

Montenegro bewahrte seine Unabhängigkeit nach dem Zerfall des Serbischen Zarenreiches bis 1499. Ab 1700 sicherten sich die Bischöfe aus dem Stamm Njegoš die Herrschaft (Neffennachfolge). Der bekannteste ist der montenegrinische Dichterfürst Petar II. Petrović Njegoš (gest. 1851). Die Fürstentümer Serbien und Montenegro wurden auf dem Berliner Kongreß 1878 anerkannt. Der Sandžak („Provinz") von Novi Pazar blieb bei der Türkei (Korridor zu Bosnien-Herzegowina), ebenso das heutige Albanien. Makedonien und Kosovo wurden nach dem Balkankrieg 1912/13 an Serbien angegliedert.

Die Spannungen mit Österreich-Ungarn entluden sich 1914 in der Ermordung des Thronfolgers Franz Ferdinand und seiner Gemahlin in Sarajevo, die den Ersten Weltkrieg auslöste. Nach dem Zusammenbruch der Mittelmächte wurde 1918 das Königreich SHS („Königreich der Serben, Kroaten und Slowenen") gebildet. Die nationalen Zwistigkeiten waren jedoch vorprogrammiert und führten 1929 zur Diktatur von König Alexander (seit jener Zeit besteht der Name Jugoslawien); sie führten 1934 zu seiner Ermordung. Jugoslawien schloß sich dem Balkanpakt an. 1937 wurden die Gegensätze zu Italien und Bulgarien beigelegt. Als 1941 Jugoslawien dem Dreimächtepakt beitrat, wurde der König (Peter II.) gestürzt; er ging ins Exil. Kroatien entstand unter Einschluß Sirmiens, Bosniens und der Herzegowina als Vasallenstaat Deutschlands; Serbien wurde unabhängig. Ein großer Teil der Küste und der Inseln fiel an Italien, Teile der Vojvodina an Ungarn, Montenegro wurde unter italienisches Protektorat gestellt, der Rest aufgeteilt (zwischen Deutschland, Italien, Bulgarien).

Nach dem Sieg der Partisanen gründete Josip Broz-Tito 1945 die Föderative Volksrepublik Jugoslawien (Verfassungsänderungen 1953, 1963). Nach der Verfassung von 1974 erhielten Kosovo und die Vojvodina weitgehende Autonomie innerhalb Serbiens. Nach dem Tod Titos 1980 nahmen die innenpolitischen Repressionen zu, es kam zu Unruhen im Kosovo. Ab 1988 setzte der Zerfall Jugoslawiens ein. Nach der Verfassung Serbiens von 1990 wurde Kosovo zu einer „territorialen Einheit" erklärt und seiner Autonomie wieder weitgehend beraubt. Seit jener Zeit finden Schulstreiks statt.

Die Konflikte des neuen Jugoslawien mit seinen Nachbarstaaten Kroatien und Bosnien-Herzegowina sind bekannt. Mit Bulgarien stand es jahrzehntelang in Streit wegen Makedonien. Die Unabhängigkeitserklärung Makedoniens 1991 hat den Konflikt auf Makedonien selbst verlagert. Ungarn fühlt sich als Schutzmacht der Ungarn in der Vojvodina, und die Spannungen mit Albanien wegen Kosovo schwelen seit Jahrzehnten. Lediglich mit Rumänien gibt es derzeit keine aktuellen Spannungen; die rumänische Minderheit in der Vojvodina ist relativ klein.

3. Politik, Wirtschaft und allgemeine kulturelle sowie religiöse Lage

Nach den bekannten kriegerischen Auseinandersetzungen seit 1991, Volksabstimmungen (Slowenien, Kroatien, Bosnien-Herzegowina, Krajina) und internationalen Anerkennungen einer Reihe von Republiken, blieben nur noch Serbien und Montenegro, die die Bundesrepublik Jugoslawien bilden. Die Albaner riefen 1990 eine Republik Kosovo aus, die von Serbien aber nicht anerkannt wurde. Serbien und Montenegro haben einen gemeinsamen Staatspräsidenten; die kommunistische Partei organisierte sich als Sozialistische Partei um, Oppositionsparteien sind zugelassen.

Trotz der Bodenschätze, der Wasserkräfte, der Wälder, des Weide- und teilweise fruchtbaren Ackerlandes steht der Staat vor dem Bankrott: hohe Auslandsverschuldung und galoppierende Inflation mit (Juni 1993) 200% pro Monat. Dazu kommt das internationale Handelsembargo seit 1992, das die Wirtschaft empfindlich trifft. Am besten entwickelt ist die Vojvodina mit ihren großen Agrokombinaten; dort gibt es auch Erdgas und Erdöl. Von den Wasserkraftwerken ist Đerdap am Eisernen Tor zu nennen. Serbien besitzt reiche Buntmetallbergwerke (Kupfer, Blei, Zink) im Serbischen Erzgebirge und im Kosovo (z. B. Trepča), wo auch große Braunkohlelager sind. Dennoch gehört Kosovo zu den unterentwickelten Regionen, ebenso Montenegro, das kaum natürliche Resourcen besitzt.

Im kommunistischen Jugoslawien waren Staat und Religion streng voneinander getrennt. Durch den aufkommenden Nationalismus haben auch die Religionen einen neuen Stellenwert erhalten. In kaum einem anderen Land sind Nationalität und Religion so eng miteinander verbunden wie in den Nachfolgestaaten Jugoslawiens: die Serben und Montenegriner sind orthodox, ebenso die Minderheiten der Makedonier, Rumänen, Bulgaren, die Albaner sind Muslime, zu einem kleinen Teil auch katholisch, moslemische Serben leben im Sandžak, die Ungarn und Kroaten sind Katholiken, die Slowaken größtenteils Kalviner, die Russinen und Ukrainer Griechisch-Unierte. Oberhaupt der autokephalen serbisch-orthodoxen Kirche ist der serbische Patriach, Oberhaupt der Muslime ist der Reis-ul-Ulema in Sarajevo (derzeit Neuordnung).

4. Statistik und Ethnoprofile der Kontaktsprachen

Die letzte Volkszählung in der SFR Jugoslawien fand im März 1991 statt. Die Ergebnisse aus Serbien: Einwohner 9,791.475, davon: Serben 6,428.420, Albaner 1,686.661, Ungarn 345.376, Jugoslawen 317.739, Muslime 237.358, Montenegriner 140.024, Roma (Zigeuner) 137.265, Kroaten 109.214, Slowaken 67.234, Makedonier 47.577, Rumänen 42.386, Bulgaren 25.214, Bunjewatzen 21.662, Russinen (Ruthenen) 18.339, Walachen 17.557, Türken 11.501, Slowenen 8.340, übrige 46.788, unbekannt 61.278 (Seewann 1993, 80, und *Politika* vom 20. Dez. 1991). In der *Politika* werden auch 992 „Schokatzen" (katholische Serben) angeführt.

Die Volkszählung wurde von den Albanern im Kosovo boykottiert, die angegebene Zahl ist eine Schätzung des Statistischen Provinzamtes Kosovo. Die Zahlen für den Kosovo lauten (*Politika* vom 6. Dez. 1991): 335.650 Ew. (in Wirklichkeit über 2 Mio.), davon Serben 195.301, Muslime 57.408, Roma 42.806, Montenegriner 20.045, Türken 10.838, Albaner 8.593, Kroaten 8.161, Ägypter 5.984, Jugoslawen 3.070, andere 3.444.

Die Bunjewatzen und Schokatzen leben in der Vojvodina. Die Ägypter sind als Roma (Zigeuner) zu verstehen. Die „separatistische Führung der Albaner" (*Politika* vom 6. Dez. 1991, 16) rechnet mit rund drei Mio. Albanern in Serbien, hauptsächlich im Kosovo. Nach der Volkszählung von 1981 hatte Kosovo noch 1,58 Mio. Ew. (77,4% Albaner). Die Geburtenrate der Albaner ist die höchste in Europa (6,6 Kinder pro Familie). Heute ist der Anteil der Albaner auf über 90% gestiegen, der Anteil der Serben und anderer Völker weiter gefallen. Bei der Volkszählung 1961 zählten die Albaner nur 647.000 und die Serben noch 227.000 (Bender 1984, 8 ff, Bogdanović 1986, 252).

Die Zahlen für Montenegro: 615.276 Ew., davon Montenegriner 380.484, Muslime 89.932, Serben 57.176, Albaner 40.880, Jugoslawen 25.845, übrige und unbekannt 14.963 (Seewann 1993, 80).

Insgesamt fällt im Vergleich zu 1981 das starke Anwachsen des albanischen Teils um fast 30% (in Wirklichkeit noch mehr) im Kosovo und um 8% in Montenegro auf, ferner das Anwachsen der Zahl der Muslime in Serbien um 10%, in Montenegro um 15% und die Zunahme der Zahl der Roma um 24% in Serbien. Die Zahl der in anderen Republiken beheimateten Völker ist zurückgegangen (Kroaten, Slowenen, Makedonier, Montenegriner), ebenso die Zahl der Jugoslawen (um 28% in Serbien, um 17% in Montenegro, ein Zeichen für die nationale Polarisierung); in Montenegro ist die Zahl der Montenegriner gefallen (6%), weil sich viele von ihnen als Serben deklariert haben, in Serbien ist die Zahl der Serben um fast 4% gestiegen, die Zahl der anderen Volksgruppen aber gefallen (Ungarn um 11,25%, Slowaken 8%, Rumänen 21%, Bulgaren 24%, Ruthenen 7%, Walachen 31%, Türken 17%).

Sprachnamen: Unter der serbokroatisch sprechenden Bevölkerung bezeichnen die Serben und Montenegriner ihre Sprache als Serbisch, die Muslime im Sandžak nennen sie Bosnisch (bošnjački), die Kroaten bezeichnen sie als Kroatisch (daneben aber auch als Bunjewatzisch). Das Albanische wird von den Albanern selbst *shqiptar* (Skipetarisch) genannt, von den Serben offiziell als *albanski*, vielfach aber auch als *šiptarski* (mit pejorativem Beigeschmack); daneben bestehen auch die alten Bezeichnungen *arbanaški* und *arnautski* (letzteres aus dem Türkischen).

Zur territorialen Verteilung der genannten Sprachen siehe Sprachenkarte G, ferner die Karte in Enciklopedija Jugoslavije, 2. Ausg. (Bd. 6, 243).

5. Soziolinguistische Lage

Durch den Zerfall Jugoslawiens haben die jahrzehntelangen Diskussionen um den gemeinsamen Namen der Sprache der Serben, Kroaten, Montenegriner und Muslime und die Variantenproblematik, die die jugoslawische Linguistik und Sprachpolitik beherrscht haben, ein Ende genommen. Bis 1990 wurde die Sprache in Serbien und Montenegro serbokroatisch genannt, seither offiziell serbisch. Die Variantenproblematik bleibt im Neuen Jugoslawien insofern erhalten, als die serbische Standardsprache in Serbien und Montenegro nicht identisch ist. Allerdings geht es nicht mehr um eine östliche und eine westliche Variante (Belgrad − Zagreb), zu der manche eine dritte, die bosnische, hinzufügen (Okuka 1991, 274−277), sondern es geht um zwei serbische (östliche) Varianten, die sich sprachlich vor allem durch den Reflex des Jat als *e* (Ekavisch) oder *jelije* (Jekavisch) unterscheiden (*mleko : mlijeko, reka, rečica : rijeka, rječica*). Beide Varianten sind gleichberechtigt. Dies drückt sich in der Presse so aus, daß namentlich gezeichnete Beiträge sprachlich nicht vereinheitlicht werden.

Eine offizielle Staatssprache gibt es in den Republiksverfassungen Serbiens und Montenegros nicht (zumindest gab es sie nicht im Rahmen der SFRJ, vgl. Brborić 1984, 282−285, 291−298), es gibt jedoch zwei dominante Sprachen: Serbisch und Albanisch. Serbisch dient als Mutter- und Zweitsprache im engeren Serbien, in der Vojvodina und in Montenegro, offiziell auch im Kosovo, wo es aber praktisch durch Albanisch verdrängt worden ist. Die serbokroatische Sprache ekavischer Variante kann als Verkehrssprache angesehen werden, da sie sehr viele Angehörige anderer Sprachgemeinschaften beherrschen. Von einer kollektiven Zweisprachigkeit der Nichtserbokroatischsprachigen kann aber keine Rede sein. Sprecher der kleineren Amtssprachen oder der in der Verfassung nicht genannten Sprachen sind oft dreisprachig (Türken im Kosovo, die auch Albanisch und Serbisch können, Slowaken und Rumänen in der Vojvodina, die neben ihrer Muttersprache auch Ungarisch und Serbisch sprechen; auch viele Roma sind sprachgewandt und können sich in verschiedenen Sprachen ihrer Umgebung ausdrücken).

Einen Sonderfall stellt die bulgarische Minderheit dar. In der alltäglichen Kommunikation spricht sie die gleichen südserbischen Mundarten wie ihre serbischen Nachbarn, als Standardsprache bedienen sich aber die einen der bulgarischen, die anderen der serbischen Sprache. Die bulgarischen Gemeinden kamen nämlich zu einer Zeit zu Serbien, als sich bei ihnen schon ein bulgarisches nationales Bewußtsein herausgebildet hatte.

Die Walachen, deren Sprache wie die der Rumänen in der Vojvodina ein dakorumänischer Dialekt ist, leben im nordöstlichen Serbien als Viehzüchter und Ackerbauern, gebrauchen ihre Sprache nur als Haussprache; sie wird weder als Kirchen-, Schul- oder Publizistiksprache verwendet. National deklarieren sie sich vielfach als Serben (Kovačec 1990, 73 ff).

Nach der jugoslawischen Verfassung und den Republiksverfassungen waren auch die beiden Schriften der serbokroatischen Sprache (lateinisch, kyrillisch) gleichberechtigt. Im Engeren Serbien und Montenegro (zu diesem Mićović 1984) überwiegt die kyrillische Schrift, in der multinationalen Vojvodina aber die Lateinschrift (Antonić 1987); für das Russinische ist die kyrillische Schrift (ukrainischen Typs) obligatorisch. Die kyrillische Schrift war im öffentlichen Leben seit den 70er Jahren immer mehr zurückgetreten, heute dringt sie wieder vor.

Bezüglich des Sprachgebrauchs in der Vojvodina bestehen zahlreiche Untersuchungen (zum Unterschied vom Kosovo). Nach Mikeš (1989, 222 ff) reicht die Bandbreite im Gebrauch der Muttersprache von 97% (Russinen in Ruski Kerestur im Umgang mit anderen Russinen) bis 43% (Ungarn in Novi Sad/Neusatz mit serbischer Schulbildung im Verkehr mit anderen Ungarn). Beim Gebrauch der Zweitsprache stehen wieder die Ungarn von Neusatz an erster Stelle mit 89% (Serbisch im Umgang mit Anderssprachigen), an letzter Stelle die untersuchten Serben, die nur zu 19% im Umgang mit Anderssprachigen Ungarisch verwenden.

6. Sprachpolitische Lage der Kontaktsprachen

Außer Serbisch, Ungarisch und Albanisch werden in der Verfassung als Amtssprachen noch genannt: Slowakisch, Rumänisch, Russinisch in der Vojvodina (Međeši 1984, 151 f) und Türkisch im Kosovo. Auf Gemeindeebene ist auch Bulgarisch Amtssprache. Sprachen ohne Status einer Amtssprache sind Romanes (das aber eine gewisse Unterstützung genießt), Walachisch mit einer relativ großen Sprecherzahl, Deutsch, Ukrainisch, Tscherkessisch u. a.

Während der Elementarunterricht in den Sprachen der Volksgruppen abgehalten wird, gilt dies für die Gymnasien und anderen mittleren Schulen schon mit einer gewissen Einschränkung, noch mehr für die Höheren Schulen und Universitäten. In Subotica wird z. B. nach den Angaben in Babin 1984, 207 f (neuere Daten waren mir nicht zugänglich) an der Pädagogischen Akademie der Unterricht zur Gänze zweisprachig (ungarisch, serbisch) geführt, während an der Höheren Technischen Lehranstalt der Unterricht im wesentlichen serbisch gehalten wird. In Wirtschaft und Bauwesen wird serbisch, teilweise allerdings auch ungarisch unterrichtet. − In der Vojvodina werden große Anstrengungen unternommen, die Schulbücher und Lektüre in allen Amtssprachen zur Verfügung zu stellen. Alle Gesetzestexte und Verlautbarungen werden regelmäßig in allen Amtssprachen veröffentlicht. Rundfunk und Fernsehen sind verpflichtet, alle Zuhörer und Zuseher in allen Amtssprachen zu bedienen. Wie zu erwarten, ist der Anteil der serbokroatischsprachigen Hörer und Seher, die anderssprachige Sendungen konsumieren, gering, während die zwei- und dreisprachigen Angehörigen der kleinen Völker viel aufgeschlossener sind (Turčan 1984, 229 f).

Im Kosovo entstanden die ersten albanischen Schulen während der italienischen und deutschen Besatzungszeit des Zweiten Weltkriegs. 1958/59 wurde die Pädagogische Hochschule und 1970 die Universität in Priština eingerichtet, mit Albanisch und Serbokroatisch als Unterrichtssprachen. 1990 wurde im Zuge der Aufhebung der Autonomie der serbische Lehrplan an den Schulen eingeführt; die Zahl der Albaner, die an die Gymnasien und die Universität aufzunehmen seien, wurde drastisch beschränkt. Seither gibt es kein geregeltes Unterrichtswesen mehr (Kohl/Libal 1992, 130−135).

7. Darstellung von Sprachkontakten bzw. der Kontaktsprachen

Die Kontakte sind außerordentlich mannigfaltig. Im Zentrum des Kontaktgebietes steht die Sprache der Serben und Montenegriner, die Kontaktzonen befinden sich dagegen größtenteils an der Peripherie. Jedoch ist auch die serbokroatische Sprache auf diesem Gebiet nicht einheitlich; ihre südöstlichen Gebiete gehören zum Areal der Balkansprachen (vgl. Sandfeld 1930). Mit anderen Worten: In den Kontaktgebieten der Vojvodina wird serbisch „slawischen" Typs gesprochen, während das Serbische des Kosovo einem stärker „balkanischen" Typ angehört. Die Sprache Montenegros liegt dazwischen, aber näher dem ersten als dem zweiten Typ. Die auftretenden Kontakte betreffen meist auf der einen Seite Serbisch, auf der anderen Seite aber Sprachen, die dem Serbischen unterschiedlich nahe verwandt sind, und zwar: (a) andere slawische Spachen (Russinisch, Slowakisch), (b) eine romanische Sprache (Rumänisch), (c) Albanisch, (d) eine ugrische Sprache (Ungarisch), (e) eine germanische (Deutsch), (f) eine Turksprache (Türkisch). Zu den genannten Kontakten kommen noch Beziehungen zwischen Ungarisch und Slowakisch, Albanisch und Türkisch, in Einzelfällen auch zwischen Türkisch und Tscherkessisch, Slowakisch und Deutsch, Ungarisch und Deutsch u. a. Die Roma siedeln verstreut und befinden sich − sofern sie ihre Sprache bewahren — mit der oder den Sprachen der Umgebung (→ Art. 239) in Kontakt.

Die Kontakte zwischen Ungarisch und Serbokroatisch in der Vojvodina setzen sich jenseits der Grenzen im südlichen Ungarn (Branau mit Fünfkirchen, Batschka mit Frankenstadt, zahlreiche Sprachinseln) fort (→ Art. 212, Genc 1985).

7.1. Russinisch (ruthenisch)

Die russinische Sprache ist eine eigene Literatursprache, die in der Vojvodina (Zentrum Ruski Kerestur) gesprochen wird. Historisch gesehen handelt es sich um einen aus den Karpaten stammenden ostslowakischen Dialekt mit ukrainischen und polnischen Beimengungen. Die Zuwanderung in die heutigen Wohnsitze in serbischer Umgebung erfolgte ab der Mitte des 18. Jahrhunderts. Die Entstehung der Schriftsprache ist mit dem Namen Havrijil Kostel'niks, der 1923 die erste Grammatik verfaßte, verbunden.

Die Transferenzen gehen nur in eine Richtung, vom Serbokroatischen zum Russinischen, und sind auf allen Ebenen der Grammatik zu finden. Sie sind am offenkundigsten in der Morphologie, vgl. das Eindringen der Endung -a des Gen. sg. der Deklination statt -u (Barić 1986, 36f), den Lok. sg. der Mask. auf -u (neben -e) (na hrobu/hrobe „am Grab", Barić 1985, 31), ferner im Gebrauch der Präpositionen; serbokroatisch za und od haben vielfach die Funktion übernommen, die den russinischen na und zos/zoz zukommt, z. B. paljivo za žimu „Brennholz für den Winter" (statt na žimu), sok od jahodox „Saft aus Erdbeeren", oder ohne Präposition nach serbokroatischem Vorbild roboti privedzeni koncu „zu Ende geführte Arbeiten" statt (hu koncu) (Barić 1985, 31).

Serbokroatischer Einfluß ist im Gebrauch der Konjunktion da (statt naj, oder statt des Infinitivs) zu spüren, z. B. statt čekaj ljem naj vežnjem bateriju „warte, daß ich die Taschenlampe einschalte" hört man da vežnjem, statt idzem še zmic „ich gehe mich waschen" sagt man idzem da še zmijem (Barić 1985, 32). Charakteristisch ist auch der Gebrauch der serbokroatischen Konjunktion pa(k) statt al ta „und", des Pronomens isti „derselbe", ferner die Entlehnung serbokroatischer Modalwörter wie ipak „dennoch, aber", dabo(h)me „freilich", dakle(m) „also", zapravo „eigentlich" (Barić 1986, 35).

Zahlreich sind die serbokroatischen lexikalischen Übernahmen: družtvo „Gesellschaft", zastava „Fahne", majmun „Affe", maharec „Esel", ladja „Schiff", korisc „Nutzen" usw. usw. (Barić 1986, 36).

7.2. Slowakisch

Die in der Vojvodina gesprochenen slowakischen Mundarten gehören größtenteils dem mittel-, zu einem kleineren Teil dem westslowakischen Typ an (Štolc 1968, Karte vor S. 297). Die Slowaken sind gewöhnlich zwei- oder mehrsprachig und benützen die slowakische und/oder die serbische Standardsprache (Mijavec 1985, 116f). Diese ist die Geber-, Slowakisch die Nehmersprache (Dudok 1977, 229f). Die Situation des Slowakischen ist die einer Sprachinsel, getrennt vom kompakten slowakischen Sprachgebiet.

Die slowakischen Dialekte sind phonetisch von den serbokroatischen Dialekten der Umgebung relativ wenig berührt. So wird z. B. die typisch slowakische Sonorisierung der Obstruenten an der Wortgrenze bewahrt (peď injekciou < peť „fünf Injektionen", čamedz e < čamec „das Boot ist", brad mój < brat „mein Bruder") (Štolc 1968, 90f). Nach den Dialektbeschreibungen (Dudok 1972, Štolc 1968) ist auch die Morphologie wenig vom Serbokroatischen beeinflußt. Die Kontakte sind am deutlichsten in der Lexik und Phraseologie, aber auch bei den Funktionswörtern und in der Syntax vorhanden. Aus dem Serbokroatischen sind die Präpositionen posl'e und preko übernommen, der Funktionsbereich von za wird gemäß dem serbokroatischen Vorbild erweitert und ersetzt slowakische Präpositionen. Beispiele: posl'e tejto vojńe „nach diesem Krieg", za mńa „für, um mich" (statt o), st'e počul'i za doktora „habt ihr vom Doktor gehört" (statt o), čo za seba zarobí „was er für sich verdient" (statt pre), pohár za vodu „Wasserglas" (statt na) (Štolc 1968, 175, 178). In der Lexik und Phraseologie können wir alle Erscheinungen beobachten, die sich beim Kontakt zwischen nahe verwandten Sprachen ergeben. Die morphologische Adaptierung macht dabei keine Probleme. Einige typische Sphären lexikalischer Entlehnungen sind (a) Administration und Recht (kazna „Strafe" neben slow. trest, pokuta; molba „Gesuch" neben slow. žiadost), (b) Wirtschaft, Finanzen (blagájna „Kasse" neben pokladńa; kamata „Zinsfuß" neben úrok), (c) Politik (odbor „Ausschuß" neben víbor; sávet, vét'e „Rat, Versammlung" neben rada), (d) Gesundheitswesen (bólnica „Krankenhaus" neben špitál, ńemocńica; pritisak „Blutdruck" neben tlak), (e) Militär (armija neben *armáda; bárut* „Schießpulver"), (f) Berufe (*čuvár, stražár, redár* „Wächter" neben *strážńik; stručńák* „Fachmann" neben *odborńík*), (g) Gegenstände, Geräte (*autopút* „Autobahn" neben *autocesta, autostráda; dizalica* „Kran" neben *žeriau̯, vint; prikoľica* „Anhänger" neben *vľečka*). Durch die nahe Verwandtschaft der beiden Sprachen kommt es zu Bedeutungserweiterungen und -einengungen nach serbokroatischem Vorbild, z. B. *mišľenie* slow. „Denken", aber auch „Gutachten", *dodeliť* „austeilen", aber auch „zuteilen, zuweisen". Noch auffälliger sind die Bedeutungsübernahmen, wenn die Lautketten zwar zusammenfallen, die Semantik aber eine ganz verschiedene ist, z. B. *baňa* serbokroatisch „Bad", slowakisch „Bergwerk", *koristʼ* serbokroatisch „Nutzen", slowakisch „Beute", usw. (Dudok 1977, 231 ff).

7.3. Rumänisch

Zu den bekannten Sprachkontakten zwischen Serbokroatisch und Rumänisch gehört der Austausch von Lexemen, die die beiden Sprachen als ganze betreffen. Hier wollen wir nur von den regional beschränkten Kontakten in der Vojvodina sprechen. Im Banat sind diese Kontakte sehr intensiv und gehen über die lexikalische Ebene hinaus.

Unter serbischem Einfluß kommt es in den rumänischen Mundarten zur Entstehung von neuen Phonemen wie /ń/ /ľ/ /j/, zur Monophthongisierung von *oa* zu *o*, zur Aussprache von *â* als *e*, im Diphthong *ua* wird *v* als Hiatustilger eingefügt. Man sagt, daß ein Viertel des Banaterrumänischen Wortschatzes aus dem Serbischen übernommen worden ist; es bestehen zahlreiche Lehnprägungen (Enciklopedija Jugoslavije, 1. Ausg., Bd. 7, 117, Flora 1962, 144). Die Lexik ist stark serbisch beeinflußt, wobei das Serbische auch als Mittler für Wörter anderssprachiger Herkunft dienen kann; einige Beispiele aus dem bäuerlichen Milieu: *avlíje < avlija* „Hof", *kâpíje < kapija* „Tor", *glavíie < glavica* „Kopf (Zwiebel)", *ruótka < rotkva* „Radieschen", *mîrkuóv* „Karotte", *pâsúľe < pasulj* „Bohnen" usw. (Flora 1962, 143). Ähnliches gilt für die Phraseologie (*a chema la răspundere* „zur Verantwortung ziehen" nach serbokroatisch *pozvati na odgovornost*) (Magdu 1980, 248), für den Gebrauch der Präpositionen u. a.

Andererseits sind auch serbische Mundarten rumänisch beeinflußt. So hat sich in der Gegend von Vršac der Akzent auf der vorletzten oder letzten Silbe festgesetzt (*krompír,* *furúna, paprika*); durch rumänischen Einfluß ist die Nichtunterscheidung zwischen /č/ und /ć/, /dž/ und /đ/ hervorgerufen, ferner die Erweichung des /l/ vor /i/ (*ľivada* „Wiese"), die Diphthongisierung von *o* zu *uo* (*kuoliba* „Hütte"), die Bewahrung des /h/. In der Morphologie ist der Gebrauch des Akkusativs statt des Lokativs oder Instrumentals auffällig; auch die Wortstellung kann übernommen werden (*ne se vraća* „er kehrt nicht zurück"; *se može* „man kann"). Im Banat ist die Übernahme rumänischer Lexeme im Bereich der Hirtensprache typisch, z. B. *brindza* „Brimsenkäse", *galʼata* „Gefäß zum Melken der Schafe", *čuonka* „Schaf mit gebrochenem Horn", *čukule/čukale* „Ruf zum Locken der Schafe", *frula/flura* „Flöte" usw. (Enciklopedija Jugoslavije, 1. Ausg., Bd. 7, 117, Flora 1962, 25, 148 f, 151 f). Über rumänische Lehnwörter im Bereich des Fischereiwesens, die von engen Sprachkontakten zeugen, berichtet Gamulescu 1982 (z. B. die Fischnamen *florečika, fuca, gimpuš, murga* u. a.).

7.4. Deutsch

Im Vorkriegsjugoslawien betrug die Zahl der Deutschen etwa 500.000 (Vojvodina und Slawonien), unmittelbar nach dem Zweiten Weltkrieg gab es noch 200.000, 1948 noch 55.337, bis diese Zahl 1981 auf 8.712 absank, davon in der Vojvodina 3.808 (Enciklopedija Jugoslavije, 2. Ausg., Bd. 6, 245). Sie siedeln nicht mehr geschlossen, so daß man heute kaum noch von einer Kontaktsituation sprechen kann.

Die Ansiedlung der Deutschen erfolgte unter Kaiser Karl VI., Maria Theresia und Josef II. seit 1722 aus dem Deutschen Reich, besonders aus dem Bezirk des Ober-Rheins (Schwaben), aber auch aus anderen Gegenden (Steiermark, Tirol, Böhmen, Hessen, Rheinpfalz). Die deutsche Sprache beeinflußte alle Kontaktsprachen unseres Raumes. Deutsche Lexeme wurden aus den Bereichen Militär, Schule, Gerichtswesen, Handel, Eisenbahnen, Maschinen usw. übernommen, und zwar hauptsächlich während der Zeit der Banater Militärgrenze (1764—1873) unter deutscher Kommandosprache, aber auch seit Beginn der Kolonisierung. Beispiele für Rumänisch: *púcer* „Offiziersdiener", *ľenunk* „Löhnung", *šilbuók* „Schildwache", *grumbúk* „Grundbuch", *priefúnk* „Prüfung", *givít (givíkt)* „Gewicht", *firáng* „Vorhang", *verštát* „Werkstatt", *vínglu* „Winkel", *àizimbán* „Eisenbahn" usw. (Flora 1962, 128—133). Andererseits haben auch die deutschen Dialekte

Lehngut aus den verschiedenen Kontaktsprachen übernommen. Einige Beispiele für Weißkirchen (Bela Crkva) aus dem Serbischen: *ráki* „Schnaps" < *rakija*, *kátšihozn* „Unterhose" < *gaće*, *kolá:č(n)* „Kuchen" < *kolač*, *pétjar* „Taugenichts" < *bećar*, aus dem Ungarischen *ra:mpaš* „neuer Wein" < *rámpás*, *köpənek* „Schafpelzmantel" < *köpenyeg*, *ra:daš* „Zugabe beim Verkauf" < *ráadás*, aus dem Rumänischen: *pašók traim* „Witze machen" < *badjoc* „auslachen", *nubún* „Taugenichts" < *nui bun* „nicht gut" (Weifert 1975, 86 f).

7.5. Albanisch

Das Albanische gehört zu den Balkansprachen, die einander seit Jahrhunderten beeinflußt und so eine konvergente Entwicklung auf allen sprachlichen Ebenen genommen haben. Häufig ist die albanische Sprache insgesamt vom Slawischen beeinflußt. Die albanischen Dialekte des Kosovo und Montenegros gehören dem gegischen Dialekt an, der auch die Grundlage für die im Kosovo bis 1968 gebrauchte Variante der Schriftsprache war. Seither sind auch die Albaner des Kosovo zur vereinheitlichten Schriftsprache (Toskisch) übergegangen.

Aus der dialektologischen Literatur sind kleinräumigere Kontaktzonen (zweisprachige Gebiete) bekannt, in denen bestimmte serbokroatische Dialektmerkmale durch albanischen Einfluß erklärt werden (vgl. Omari 1989 mit Literatur, bes. 46—51, Pižurica 1984, 88—91, Popović 1960, 574—577, 600 ff): In der Phonetik werden der Verlust des musikalischen Akzents und die Kürzung unbetonter Längen genannt. In Montenegro hat der Übergang des beweglichen Vokals *a* in *šva* (*novac* > *novəc* „Geld") seine Parallele im Albanischen (*gëzim* < *gazim* „Freude"). Die Monophthongierung von *ije* > *i* oder *e* (*snijeg* > *snig* oder *sneg*) hat ihr Vorbild im Albanischen, ebenso wie der Übergang von unbetontem *a* in *o* (*anamo* < *onamo* „dorthin"). Zu den durch das Albanische hervorgerufenen Lautveränderungen gehören noch die Verwechslung von /l/ und /l'/, /n/ und /ń/, das Auftreten der Affrikata /dz/, die Palatalisierung der Velare *g, k* zu *g', k'* vor *e i*, der Zusammenfall von *č* und *ć*, die Desonorisierung der stimmhaften Obstruenten am Wortende. Als Lehnübersetzung kann man das Beispiel *tavaj* < *eto ovaj* „dieser" nach albanisch *qaj* < *qe + aj* betrachten. Zu den syntaktischen Merkmalen gehört der Gebrauch des Akk. statt des Lok., z. B. *živim u selo* statt *u selu* „ich lebe im Dorf", ferner die Verdoppelung des Personalpronomens beim Objekt (*mene mi se čini* „es scheint mir") und die balkanische Wortstellung.

Einige Beispiele für Übernahmen aus dem albanischen Wortschatz, die regional begrenzt sind: *ćafalćava* „Hügel" < *qafë*, *dorza* „Handgriff am Pflug" < *dorëzë* „Sterz" (zu *dorë* „Hand"), *dreteza* „Himbeere" < *dreth ëzë*, *asal* „Winterweide" < *hasëll*, *asull*, *ashtull*, *kuce* „Mädchen" < *kocë*, *gocë*, *dreza* „Schraubenzieher" < *dredhë* (zu *me dredh* „zudrehen"), *drmjet* „mitten" < *(m)dërmjet*, *ljajka* „Betrug" < *lajkë* „Liebkosung" (Popović 1960, 600 f).

7.6. Türkisch

Während das Osmanisch-Türkische nicht als Balkansprache bezeichnet werden kann, haben die türkischen, westrumelischen Dialekte der Balkanhalbinsel balkanische konvergente Tendenzen mitgemacht. Die Situation des Türkischen im Kosovo ist die einer Sprachinsel, getrennt vom kompakten türkischen Sprachgebiet.

Unter den phonetischen Merkmalen des Westrumelischen, die auf Sprachkontakte zurückgehen können, werden genannt (Friedman 1982, 38—44): (a) das Fehlen des Phonems /ö/ und sein Übergang in /ü/ oder /o/ ([ö] fehlt in allen Balkansprachen, [ü] ist im Albanischen fest verankert), z. B. *güz* „Auge" < *göz*, *dort* „vier" < *dört*, im Dialekt von Prizren *dert* (Sureja 1987, 35), (b) Fehlen des Phonems /h/, ein gemeinsames Merkmal der serbischen und albanischen Dialekte des Kosovo (Beispiele *Asan, Amet, Mamut* statt *Hasan, Ahmet, Mahmut*) (s. auch Sureja 1987, 63), (c) Palatalisierung von *k, g* vor *e, i* und arabischem „hellem" *a*, z. B. *duçan* „Geschäft, Laden" (= *dükkân*), *celdi* „er kam" (= *geldi*); sie konnte dort auftreten, wo die Laute *k', g'* nicht vorhanden waren und substituiert wurden (Sureja 1987, 56 ff), (d) Verletzungen der Vokalharmonie, Typ *buldi* statt *buldu*, *kapi* „Tor" statt *kapı*. Sie kommt in allen türkischen Dialekten des Kosovo vor und ist in der Morphologie und Wortbildung durch Versteinerung einer der Morphemvarianten begünstigt, z. B. *celdilar* statt *geldiler* (Sureja 1987, 48—53).

In der Wortbildung hat sich im Einklang mit den Nachbarsprachen die Tendenz zur Bezeichnung des natürlichen Geschlechts von Lebewesen mit Hilfe des Suffixes *-ka* entwickelt, z. B. *koyşika* „Nachbarin" (Sureja 1987, 87). Lexikalische Übernahmen aus dem Serbokroatischen sind in der gesprochenen

Sprache häufig, in der geschriebenen selten. Unter den syntaktischen Merkmalen fällt die Inversion der Ezafetkonstruktion auf, z. B. *familiasi adamın* statt *adamın familiası* „die Familie des Mannes" (Friedman 1982, 43), ferner Konstruktionen mit Modalverben, Lehnübersetzungen, Wortstellung.

8. Kritische Wertung der verwendeten Quellen und Literatur

Die Aufgabe, die mit der Abfassung dieses Artikels gestellt wurde, war ausgesprochen schwierig. Mit dem Embargo gegen Jugoslawien sind auch die wissenschaftlichen Kontakte 1992 unterbrochen worden. Informationen müssen über private Kanäle beschafft werden. Für die nichtlinguistischen Daten ist ein hervorragendes Nachschlagewerk Rehder 1992 (berücksichtigt auch die neueste Entwicklung), dazu ergänzend für Kosovo Kohl/Libal 1992. Sehr wichtige Daten, auch linguistischer Natur, bieten die zwei Ausgaben der Enzyklopädie Jugoslawiens. Die zweite (lateinschriftige) Ausgabe ist bis zum 6. Band (bis K) gediehen. Für die soziolinguistischen und sprachpolitischen Fragen, besonders der Vojvodina, ist die Zeitschrift Sveske (Sarajevo) eine hervorragende Quelle (allerdings waren mir die letzten Bände nicht zugänglich), dagegen sind Arbeiten zu den Sprachen des Kosovo kaum zu finden. Für die linguistischen Fragestellungen ist noch immer Sandfeld 1930, bei dem die konvergente Entwicklung der Balkansprachen dargestellt wird, ein Klassiker. Ein hervorragendes Werk, das auch die meisten Kontaktsprachen unseres Raumes berücksichtigt, ist Popović 1960, einen Überblick über die wichtigste Literatur und die Forschungsmethoden zum Bilinguismus in Jugoslawien bieten Bugarski/Mikeš 1985.

9. Bibliographie (in Auswahl)

Antonić, Ivana (1987): „Upotreba ćirilice i latinice u osnovnim i srednjim školama u Novom Sadu" [Gebrauch der kyrillischen und lateinischen Schrift in Volks- und Mittelschulen von Novi Sad/Neusatz]. In: *Prilozi proučavanju jezika 23*, 129−152.

Babin, Radomir (1984): „Ostvarivanje jezičke ravnopravnosti u obrazovanju na području severne Bačke" [Verwirklichung der sprachlichen Gleichberechtigung auf dem Gebiet der nördlichen Batschka]. In: *Sveske II 5−6*, 205−212.

Barić, Eugenija (1985): „Rusinski jezik u štokavskom okruženju" [Die russinische Sprache in štokavischer Umgebung]. In: *Hrvatski dijalektološki zbornik 7*, 29−36.

Barić, Eugenija (1986): „Hrvatsko-srpski elementi u djelima Havrijila Kosteljnika" [Kroato-serbische Elemente in den Werken von Havrijil Kosteljnik]. In: *Fililogija* (Zagreb) *14*, 31−39.

Bender, Rainer Joha (1984): „Die Krisenprovinz Kosovo". In: *Zeitschrift für Balkanologie 20/1*, 4−24.

Bogdanović, Dimitrije (1986): *Knjiga o Kosovu* [Das Buch über Kosovo], Belgrad.

Brborić, Branislav (1984): „Srpskohrvatskijezik u svjetlu ustavnopravnih i sociolingvističkih određenja" [Die serbokroatische Sprache im Licht verfassungsrechtlicher und soziolinguistischer Bestimmungen]. In: *Sveske II 5−6*, 255−303.

Bugarski, Ranko i Melanija Mikeš (1985): „Pregled tipova i metoda istraživanja višejezičnosti u Jugoslaviji" [Überblick über Untersuchungstypen und -methoden der Mehrsprachigkeit in Jugoslawien]. In: *Sveske III 9*, 79−86.

Dudok, Daniel (1972): *Nárečie Pivnice v Báčke* [Die Mundart von Pivnica in der Batschka], Martin.

Dudok, Daniel (1977): „Neke karakteristične pojave u govoru Slovaka u Jugoslaviji kao rezultat kontakta slovačkog jezika sa srpskohrvatskim jezikom" [Einige chrarakteristische Erscheinungen in der Sprache der Slowaken in Jugoslawien als Ergebnis des Kontaktes der slowakischen mit der serbokroatischen Sprache]. In: *Naučni sastanak slavista u Vukove dane 6/1*, 225−237.

Enciklopedija Jugoslavije (1955−1971), 1. Ausgabe (Lateinschrift), 1−8, Zagreb.

Enciklopedija Jugoslavije (1980-), 2. Ausgabe (Lateinschrift), bisher 6 Bände, Zagreb.

Flora, Radu (1962): *Dijalektološki profil rumunskih banatskih govora sa vršačkog područja* [Das dialektologische Profil der Banaterrumänischen Mundarten des Werschetzer Gebiets], Neusatz.

Friedman, Victor A. (1982): „Balcanology and Turcology: West Rumelian Turkish in Yougoslavia as reflected in prescriptive grammar". In: *South Slavic and Balkan Linguistics*, Barentsen, A. A./Sprenger, R./Tielemans, M. (Eds.), Amsterdam, 1−77.

Gamulescu, Dorin (1982): „Termes serbocroates du vocabulaire de la pêche empruntés au roumain". In: *Zbornik za filologiju i lingvistiku 25/2*, 21−36.

Genc, Lajoš (1985): „Psihološka ispitivanja mađarsko-srpskohrvatske dvojezičnosti u Vojvodini" [Psychologische Untersuchungen der ungarisch-serbokroatischen Zweisprachigkeit in der Vojvodina]. In: *Sveske III 9*, 119−126.

Sureja, Jusuf (1986): *Prizrenski turksi govor* [Der türkische Dialekt von Prizren], Priština.

Kohl, Christine von/Libal, Wolfgang (1992): *Kosovo: gordischer Knoten des Balkan*, Wien/Zürich.

Kovačec, August (1990): „Jezici etničkih skupina u SFRJ" [Die Sprachen der ethnischen Gruppen in der SFRJ]. In: *Jezička politika i planiranje jezika u Jugoslaviji*, Vasić, V. (Ed.), Neusatz, 69−80.

Magdu, Lia (1980): „Influenţe sîrbocroate în limba româna din Voivodina" [Serbokroatische Einflüsse in der rumänischen Sprache der Vojvodina]. In: *Kontrastivna jezička ispitivanja*. Simpozijum, Berić, V. et al. (Eds.) Neusatz, 247−252.

Međeši, Helena (1984): „Ustavna načela o jezičkoj ravnopravnosti naroda i narodnosti Vojvodine i ostvarivanje ravnopravnosti jezika i pisama u praksi organa i organizacija uprave u SAP Vojvodini" [Verfassungsgrundlagen zur sprachlichen Gleichberechtigung der Völker und Volksgruppen der Vojvodina und die Verwirklichung der Gleichberechtigung der Sprachen und Schriften in der Praxis der Verwaltungsorgane und -organisationen in der SAP Vojvodina]. In: *Sveske II 5−6*, 151−155.

Mićović, Veljko (1984): „Ravnopravnost pisama u sredstvima javnog informisanja, izdavačkoj djelatnosti i administrativnoj praksi u SR Crnoj Gori" [Die Gleichberechtigung der Schriften in den Medien, bei der Publikationstätigkeit und in der Verwaltungspraxis in der SR Montenegro]. In: *Sveske II 5−6*, 375−382.

Mijavec, Marija (1985): „O kontaktu slovačkog jezika u Vojvodini sa srpskohrvatskim" [Über den Kontakt der slowakischen Sprache der Vojvodina mit der serbokroatischen]. In: *Sveske III 9*, 111−118.

Mikes, Melanie (1989): „Language contacts in multilingual Vojvodina". In: *Yougoslav general linguistics*, Radovanović, M. (Ed.), Amsterdam/Philadelphia, 203−225.

Okuka, Miloš (1991). „Theorien zur serbokroatischen Standardsprache". In: *Wiener slawistischer Almanach 28*, 271−280.

Omari, Anila (1989): „Ndikime të gjuhës shqipe në të folmet jugore të Serbishtes" [Einflüsse der albanischen Sprache auf den südserbischen Dialekt]. In: *Studime filologjike 43 (26)/1*, 43−61.

Pižurica, Mato (1984): „Tragovi međujezičkih dodira u govorima Crne gore" [Spuren der intersprachlichen Berührungen in den Mundarten Montenegros]. In: *Crnogorski govori*, Milović, J.M. (Ed.), Titograd, 83−95.

Popović, Ivan (1960): *Geschichte der serbokroatischen Sprache*, Wiesbaden.

Rehder, Peter (Ed.) (1992): *Das neue Osteuropa von A−Z*, München.

Sandfeld, Kristian (1930): *Linguistique balkanique. Problèmes et résultats*, Paris.

Seewann, Gerhard (1993): „Die Ethnostruktur der Länder Südosteuropas aufgrund der beiden letzten Volkszählungen im Zeitraum 1977−1992". In: *Südost-Europa. Zeitschrift für Gegenwartsforschung 42/1*, 78−82.

Sekulić, Ante (1986): *Narodni život i običaji bačkih Bunjevaca* [Volksleben und Bräuche der Bunjewci in der Batschka], Zagreb.

Štolc, Jožef (1968): *Reč Slovákov v Juhoslávii, I. Zvuková a gramatická stavba* [Die Sprache der Slowaken in Jugoslawien, I. Lautliche und grammatische Struktur], Bratislava.

Turčan, Jaroslav (1984): „Praćenje radio i televizijskog programa na nematernjim jezicima u višejezičnoj Vojvodini" [Der Konsum des nichtmuttersprachlichen Radio- und Fernsehprogramms in der mehrsprachigen Vojvodina]. In: *Sveske II 5−6*, 227−234.

Weifert, Ladislaus (^{2}1975): *Die deutsche Mundart von Weißkirchen*, Salzburg.

Gerhard Neweklowsky, Klagenfurt (Österreich)

169. Slovenia

1. Geography and demography
2. History and national development
3. Political, economic and cultural situation
4. Statistics and ethnoprofiles
5. Sociolinguistic situation
6. Language political situation
7. Language contacts
8. Conclusion
9. Bibliography (selected)

1. Geography and demography

The Slovene ethnic territory and hence the area of Slovene language contacts extends well beyond the actual state border of the Republic of Slovenia and encompasses a significant proportion (about 10%) of the Slovene-speaking autochthonous population in the neighbouring countries of Austria, Croatia, Italy, and Hungary. Owing to migration waves in different periods, Slovene communities also live in other European countries, in the USA, Canada, South America, and Australia. Thus, according to unofficial estimates, up to 20% of the total Slovene population lives outside the actual Slovene state borders.

The territory of the Republic of Slovenia covers 20,256 km^2, and population density reaches 97.5 people per km^2. In the 1991 census, 87.55% of the total population defined themselves as Slovenes (cf. table 169.1). − In the Republic of Slovenia the Slovene language is in contact with several languages. Most of these contacts are sporadic. Of 24 ethnic categories registered during the 1991 census, only three exceed 1% of the total population, and none attains 3%. Most groups attain barely some hundred speakers. A more detailed inspection of the absolute numbers shows that only in six cases are there more than 2000 (Italians, Hungarians, Albanians, Macedonians, Montenegrins, Romanies) and in three cases more than 20,000 persons of the same ethnic group (Croats, Serbs, and Muslims). Nevertheless, due to a substantial concentration of populations of diverse ethnic origin in some districts and due to historical reasons, the language contact situations constitute a socially relevant phenomenon.

Because of the imbalanced structural development of the Slovene economy, migrations from other parts of Yugoslavia to Slovenia and the emigration of Slovenes to other European countries, the concentration of the non-Slovene population has steadily risen, especially in centers where it ranges from 10% to 23% of the population. With the collapse of Yugoslavia and the creation of nation states on its territory, the previously official term "the Serbo-Croatian language", which was often exposed to ardent professional and political discussions, lost its basis. In this article, the abbreviation "SRC" shall be used to denote both the Serbian and the Croatian languages and their varieties.

Slovene-SCR language contacts, however, have an additional dimension: until 1992 Slovenia was a part of Yugoslavia in which the regulation of the status and function of the languages of the individual ethnic groups had been a potential source of conflict since the very creation of a common state in 1918 (→ Language Map G).

2. History and national development

Slovene is in contact with German in the north, with the Romanic language groups (Italian and Frioulan) in the southwest, Hungarian in the northeast (since the 9th century), and Croatian in the southeast.

2.1. The first Slovene early feudal state of Karantania (7th to 11th centuries) soon had to avow supremacy of Franks and Bavarians retaining, nevertheless, the right to perform the rites of the enthronement of their dukes in the Slovene language. From that point, German influence was predominant in the majority of Slovene territories for centuries to come.

Until the beginning of the 20th century, diglossia was a characteristic feature of the Slovene ethnic territory. German functioned as high language in certain formal domains even in territories where the population was predominantly Slovene. The exceptions were Venetian Slovenia and the Slovene part of Istria where Italian occupied the majority of formal domains, and Prekmurje where Hungarian functioned as the high language. Some documents, however, prove that Slovene was also used for in-group communication among the non-Slovene nobility and bourgeoisie. The influence of Italian and Hungarian respectively was augmented by the legal status of these languages accorded to them by Austro-Hungarian Empire.

2.2. In the history of the Slovene people, language has been one of the very central issues. Two major factors determined Slovene language planning throughout history: (1) The relationship of Slovene to genetically unrelated languages (German, Italian, Hungarian), the central issue being functional expansion of Slovene; (2) the relationship of Slovene to the genetically-related South Slav languages, the central issue being structural delimitation of Slovene from these languages.

The first documents that mention the existence of a specific ethnic group (Karantani and later Slovenes) and their state reach back to the 9th century. In the 16th century when Primož Trubar (1508−1586), a Slovene Protestant priest, translated about twenty religious and encyclopedic texts into the language of his village, a central Slovene dialect, the Slovene language planning process started and the ethnogenesis of the Slovene nation proceeded along with it. In spite of foreign political and consequently foreign language dominance, Slovene as the language of culture (literature and religion) developed steadily. However, owing to the unstructured speech networks, the use of Slovene in certain domains was limited. Frequently, Slovene was considered a language of the common man. Nevertheless, its elaboration process continued, and after the era of educational and legislative reforms (during Enlightened

Absolutism in the 18th century) the Slovene language functionally expanded substantially, particularly in terminology. In spite of the tendency to promote the status of German, the Austro-Hungarian Empire had to concede to other languages, Slovene among them, in some speech domains, namely in the areas of legislation, education, and later on even in the army.

Until the 19th century, the cultivation of the Slovene language was oriented towards the education of the simple man. With Romanticism, literary production focused on the social and cultural elite. At this stage the process of national integration of the Slovene people acquired a political dimension. The United Slovenia program (1848) was the first act of political emancipation. This act was persistently repeated in all the States in which the Slovenes tried to find their national self-realization until 1991.

The first demarcation line between South Slavic languages was set by Trubar: he established that Slovene was a language per se and that its speakers belonged to the European Latin cultural realm. This orientation was later confirmed by the Enlightenment and especially by Romanticism. Nevertheless, other options were also advanced: Illyrism supported by the Pan-Slavic movement in the 19th century strove for the cultural as well as the linguistic unification of the South Slav peoples, including Slovenes. Although linguistic fusion was rejected by prominent Slovenian intellectuals (France Prešeren, 1800–1848, Janez Bleiweis, 1808–1881) leaning on South Slav relatives seemed appropriate when political issues were considered. This approach contributed to the emergence of Yugoslavia in 1918.

2.3. In 1918, Slovenes joined with Serbs and Croats in the common state which in 1929 was renamed the Kingdom of Yugoslavia (the First Yugoslavia, 1918–1941). However, due to international agreements, a substantial part of the Slovene population was left outside the borders of Yugoslavia. Within the new state the Slovenes were confronted with new social and cultural circumstances. On the one hand, the status of Slovene changed with regard to German and Hungarian that became minority languages. On the other hand the official Yugoslav language policy tried to create a single "Yugoslav" language of Serbs, Croats, and Slovenes. Threats to the Slovene language autonomy that had been repeated in several periods throughout the existence of Yugoslavia were countered by insistent puristic efforts in Slovenia.

3. Political, economic and cultural situation

During the 1980's the resistance against the centralization efforts of Belgrade augmented in Slovenia. With the multiparty elections in 1990, aspirations to transform the Slovene society in concordance with principles of the parliamentary democracy gained solid ground. Following the referendum demands (December 23, 1990) independence of the Republic of Slovenia was declared (June 25, 1991). After the subsequent "Ten Day War" against the Yugoslav federal army all its units left Slovenia by October 26th, in concordance with the Brioni Agreement (July 7). In 1992 Slovenia became a full member of the CSCE and of the UN, and in 1993 a full member of the Council of Europe. With the transformation of Slovenia to a market economy, inflation was held to 1% monthly; the new national currency, the Tolar, became relatively stable and convertible. However, the loss of Yugoslav markets and the privatization problems caused the economic situation to deteriorate. Thus ever rising unemployment (ca 13% in 1992) together with the influx of refugees from Bosnia provides fertile grounds for nationalistic tensions, one of the major issues being the assignment of Slovene citizenship to non-Slovene nationals from ex-Yugoslav republics.

The economic crisis is reflected in several fields of language and culture related activities; e. g. since 1991 the number of books issued in Slovenia has decreased by 14% and the number of newspapers and periodicals by 7,5% (2136 books and 641 newspapers and periodicals published in 1992).

Freedom of religious activities for all groups is guaranteed in article 7 of the Constitution. According to the 1991 Census ca 23% of the population are either atheists or declined to declare their creed, 71% belong to the Catholic Church, less than 1% are Protestants (Slovenes and Hungarians, mostly in the North East of the country). Migrants from other ex-Yugoslav republics are either Catholic, Orthodox or Muslim. The Catholic clergy is active in the so-called "reconciliation" process between the two opposing sides in WWII, the anticommunist collaborationist homeguard militia and the partisan movement guided by communists, which fought together with the Allies. The Church has become an important factor in the society; nevertheless, there is still much controversy about its role in public life, especially in education.

4. Statistics and ethnoprofiles

An overview of the available data gathered in population censuses in the First Yugoslavia and in the SFRY is given in table 169.1. The official tendency to merge Yugoslav nations into one was demonstrated by the 1931 census statistical category of "mother tongue" where the Slovene and the Serbocroatian language figured as one item.

The drastic decline in numbers of Hungarians and Germans in the 1931 Census was attributed on the one hand to the expression of national consciousness by Slovenes in border areas who again reported their original nationality, and on the other to the attempts of the Hungarians and Germans who had concealed their ethnic origin attempting to get a share of the land distributed in the process of the agricultural reform. Throughout the censuses, two characteristic trends can be observed in the case of the German minority: a steady drop in the category of ethnic origin (a turn upwards is evident in 1991), and the huge discrepancy between adherence to German nationality and to the German mother tongue. While a trend of stagnation or a drop in the number of members of autochthonous minorities is evident and the Slovene group is not very prolific either, the growth rate of migrant groups (speakers of SCR) is rather high. The first two population censuses after WWII reflect the unresolved border question with Italy, the drop in 1953 being due to the Italians who opted for Italy. After the Memorandum of Understanding (London 1954), the number of Italians increased because part of the district of Koper then belonged to Slovenia. Since 1961 the number has stabilized except for a drop in 1981 which remains to be fully explained (it has been largely attributed to the statistical procedures used).

4.1. The autochthonous Hungarian minority is settled in the area along the Slovene-Hungarian border in the easternmost part of the Prekmurje region. This five-to-eight-kilometer-wide strip of predominantly hilly country includes 33 towns and villages with mixed Slovene and Hungarian populations in two

Table 169.1: Population of Slovenia according to official censuses data*

Ethnic origin Mother tongue	Total	Slovene	Hungarian	Italian	SCR	German	Austrian	Romani
1921 E. O.	1,054.919	980.222	14.429	701	11.898	41.514	–	–
M. T.	–	–	–	–	–	–	–	–
1931 E. O.	–	–	–	–	–	–	–	–
M. T.	1,144.298	1,101.815	7.961	–	–	28.998	–	–
1948 E. O.	1,391.873	1,350.149	10.579	1.458	23.817	1.824	–	46
M. T.	–	–	–	–	–	–	–	–
1953 E. O.	1,466.425	1,415.448	11.019	854	32.176	1.617	289	1.663
M. T.	1,466.425	1,419.294	11.445	805	28.699	2.597	–	996
1961 E. O.	1,591.523	1,522.248	10.498	3.072	59.671	732	254	158
M. T.	–	–	–	–	–	–	–	–
1971 E. O.	1,727.137	1,624.029	9.785	3.001	75.131	422	278	977
M. T.1	1,727.137	1,627.462	10.562	3.471	76.801	1.322	–	969
1981 E. O.	1,891.864	1,712.445	9.496	2.187	140.712	380	180	1.435
M. T.	1,891.864	1,726.604	10.114	2.901	151.274	1.189	–	1.428
1991 E. O.	1,965.986	1,727.018	8.503	3.064	145.668	546	199	2.293
M. T.	1,965.986	1,727.360	9.240	4.009	155.013	1.543	–	2.847

districts (22 in Lendava and 11 in Murska Sobota). As with earlier censuses, in the 1991 census the label "Hungarian" varies as to ethnic origin and mother tongue (table 169.1).

4.2. The autochthonous Italian population is settled in three coastal districts where 23 towns and villages have the status of ethnically-mixed territories (9 in Koper/Capodistria, 1 in Izola/Isola, 13 in Piran/Pirano). In the 1991 census, 3063 inhabitants of Slovenia (0.16%) reported themselves as Italian. Again the number of persons who declared Italian as their mother tongue is higher (4003).

4.3. Proceeding from the actual ethnodemographic data, one can hardly speak about Germans in Slovenia as a group phenomenon. In the 1991 census, 546 persons (0.03%) declared themselves as German and 182 (0.01%) as Austrian. They live scattered throughout Slovenia. The numbers regarding German as their mother tongue are higher (1544 persons), but again their dispersion is great: some ten persons in individual districts with the exception of Maribor where 290 persons declared German as their mother tongue. Whether they are descendants of the German speaking population who became an ethnic minority with the breakdown of the Austro-Hungarian Empire or migrated to Slovenia later remains to be analyzed. In any event, during the last two years there has been an evident effort on part of their representatives as well as on the part of the Austrian authorities to treat Germans in Slovenia as an ethnic minority again.

4.4. A small island of autochthonous Serbian population lives in some villages near the Croatian border. Their number hardly exceeds a hundred. — The three most numerous groups registered in the 1991 census (Croats, Muslims and Serbs) together with Montenegrins and individuals who declared themselves as Yugoslavs (this census category did not indicate an ethnic identity but rather an uncertainty in this respect: usually persons from mixed marriages resorted to it) belong to either the Serbian or Croatian language groups. Migrants from other linguistic regions (Albanians, Macedonians, etc.) should be mentioned in this context since they also use SRC in Slovenia as their *lingua franca*.

4.5. Data about the Romany ethnic group whose status and special rights are regulated in article 65 of the Constitution reflect the course of social development and attitudes toward members of this group. In the 1961 census they resorted to the newly introduced Yugoslav affiliation, but the 1991 census figures point to the reinforced ethnolinguistic vitality of this group.

5. Sociolinguistic situation

When speakers of German, Hungarian, and Italian became minorities in Slovenia (after 1918 and 1945 respectively), the three languages in contact with Slovene had a higher status due to the historical development. In the new circumstances their legal status changed but as these were languages of established nations with developed cultural and state traditions, their prestige hardly diminished. The fact that diglossia with bilingualism was characteristic for Slovene territory at the beginning of the 20th century — the Slovene population being bilingual while among Germans, Hungarians, and Italians this was rarely the case — illustrates the language status relations at the end of the Austro-Hungarian Empire. Today still, the influence of the higher international status of German and Italian is evident: although for some years immediately following WWII a kind of mental distance toward everything connected with the attribute "German" was apparent, this attitude gradually changed and German began to figure as the second most frequently chosen foreign language in primary and secondary schools (English being the first), especially in areas near the Austrian border. The case of Italian was similar in spite of the fact that it was imposed on the Slovene population in the Trieste and Littoral regions during WWII and that under Fascist Italy and during WWII plans were made to abolish the use of the Slovene language in this area. The perception of Hungarian as a language of higher prestige which predominated in the Prekmurje region in the First Yugoslavia gradually lost ground.

After a decade of expressly centralistic rule in the second Yugoslavia (1950–1960) the delimitation of functions between SCR and Slovene in the territory of Slovenia and in communication with federal authorities became an ardent issue. Ever more frequent were requests to implement the language equality principle in practice: the language of an individual nation was supposed to function as the official language in the territory of the respective republic while all languages were supposed to have equal status as means of communication at the federal level. No language was thus accorded the status of (federal) state language. In Slovenia, however, SCR persevered in several domains: in the mid-1960s SCR was largely used on television programs and figured as the only language of the daily news, instructions for medical and other products, and it was the language of communication in foreign affairs, in the army, etc. Gradually during the 1960's and 1970's, the Slovene language occupied most of these domains, and the equality principle was regulated by the 1974 federal constitution. SCR, however, remained the language of command in the army. Still, in most instances of communication at the federal level SCR was used as a *lingua franca*, in spite of the translation services available. This was due to accommodation on the part of the Slovenes who acquired some proficiency in SCR in school where SCR figured as obligatory subject in the 5th grade of the primary school curriculum until 1993. Due to military service Slovene — SCR bilingualism was more frequently the case among Slovene men than women. — Today still, there is a regular supply of daily and periodical newspapers in SCR; television and radio programs as well as books and manuals are available in SCR; several professional domains (transport and trade services) are occupied by SCR native speakers with poor proficiency in Slovene. In order to promote the Slovene language cultivation and to influence patterns of language behaviour a Council for the promotion of the Slovene language in public use functioned during 1980—1990. The task of one of its sections, named the "language court", was to expose the most blatant cases of abuse of regulations on the Slovene language status and to point to the most frequent contact-induced mistakes.

6. Language political situation

The Constitution of Slovenia specifies: "The official language of Slovenia shall be Slovene. In those areas where Italian or Hungarian ethnic communities reside, the official language shall also be Italian or Hungarian" (1991 Constitution, article 11).

6.1. Two models of bilingual education are practiced in the ethnically-mixed areas. A bilingual educational system has operated in the Prekmurje region since 1959. All children, regardless of their ethnic background, attend mixed Slovene and Hungarian classes from kindergarten onwards. Both languages, Slovene and Hungarian, are languages of instruction used concurrently during lessons in all subjects of the curriculum. Pupils can use their mother tongue with all subjects. The bilingual school syllabus is adapted to the specific ethnic circumstances, contents from Hungarian history, geography, and culture being added to the syllabus of Slovene schools. School administration and documents, public announcements and instructions are bilingual. In 1991/92 there were 1.408 pupils in 10 bilingual primary schools; the bilingual secondary school was attended by 318 pupils. At the university level Hungarian can be studied in Maribor (teacher training) and in Ljubljana. Cooperation with the school authorities of the Republic of Hungary is also well established. At the moment the bilingual school model has become an issue of conflict. Some Slovene parents are opposed to it, claiming that the right of the Slovene children to instruction in their mother tongue has been violated by compulsory bilingual school.

In accordance with the Special Statute (Annex to the London Memorandum) regulations, Italian minority children attend preschool institutions and primary and secondary schools with Italian as the language of instruction. Slovene is an obligatory subject. Italian is the language of oral and written communication in school as well as with parents. In the ethnically-mixed area, Italian is an obligatory subject in educational institutions with Slovene as the language of instruction from kindergarten onwards. In many instances, Slovene children enroll in secondary schools with Italian as the language of instruction. In 1991/92 there were 9 Italian primary schools attended by 516 pupils and 3 Italian secondary schools attended by 233 pupils.

6.2. The unhindered use of the minority language in public communication is supported by "institutional bilingualism". In accordance with the statute of the commune, the work of public institutions, administrative agencies, and public services must be organized in such a way that written and oral communication in the language of the party (client) concerned is guaranteed (e. g. bilingual topographic signs, street names, names of firms, public announcements and warnings, forms, invitations, decrees, regulations, and documents such as identity card, matrimonial documents, passports in both languages). While in the Slovene-Italian area institutional bilingualism is a matter of course, bilingual personal documents cause some tension in the Slovene-Hungarian area. In practice, the right to use one's mother tongue is fulfilled to varying degrees in individual institutions. As a rule, bilingual communication is better provided for in the courts of law and at the level of communal administration, political assemblies, and public signs while it is not so satisfactory in public and private enterprises and factories. Employees in administrative agencies and schools who according to the job requirement should be proficient in Italian or Hungarian in addition to Slovene are awarded a supplement to their salary, which is often a source of dispute.

6.3. The weekly *Népújság* has been published in Hungarian since 1956. Collections of prose and poetry written by Hungarian minority members are published together with translations of the Slovenian litterature in cooperation with the Hungarian publishing house Europa. Local radio has been broadcasting also in Hungarian since 1958, while TV programming in Hungarian is broadcast once per week on TV Ljubljana.

The Italian minority in Slovenia publishes printed media in the Italian language together with the Italians living in Croatia. The daily newspaper *Voce del Popolo* has been published since 1944, and there are several periodical publications for children and adults. For 40 years now the publishing house EDIT has been publishing belletristics and professional litterature, textbooks and manuals in Italian. On Radio Koper Italian-language programs (since 1949) are available for 13 hours per day while TV programming in Italian is broadcast on TV Koper for 7 hours per day, some of the items being subtitled in Slovenian. Lately, attempts to augment the presence of Slovene in RTV programs in Koper have been a source of tension.

An important share of cultural activities in Hungarian and Italian is executed by local cultural associations (amateur theatre, literary clubs, choruses and folklore dance clubs, etc.) as well as by visiting professional and amateur theater groups from Italy and Hungary.

6.4. In the ethnically mixed areas religious services in Slovenian and Italian or Hungarian are available. Children can attend religious instruction in either language, and the choice of language is practiced with other ceremonies (baptism, wedding, funeral).

6.5. While group rights are guaranteed to both autochthonous minorities, individual rights are guaranteed to individuals of any nationality, namely the free identification of each person with a national grouping or ethnic community and the fostering of one's culture and use of one's own language and script (articles 61 and 62 of the Constitution). The SCR-speaking population (and others) can resort to this regulation in the exercise of their language rights. However, such interest is seldom expressed, and only one primary school in the SCR language operates in Ljubljana.

With the establishment of the association "Freiheits Brücke" (1991), questions on the rights of the German minority in Slovene Styria have become a matter of political and professional discussion.

7. Language contacts

Centuries of contact of Slovene with the neighbouring languages influenced all layers of the Slovene language structure. As the language of a relatively small, non-dominant group Slovene less frequently penetrated the other languages. Situated on the crossroads of Slavic, Germanic, Romanic and Hungarian world, Slovene abundantly adopted foreign language elements. At the same time strong puristic tendencies, especially with regard to the South Slavic languages but also with respect to other languages, are characteristic for the Slovene language cultivation process. Due to wide exposure to SCR its influence is evident in vocabulary and syntax of Slovene. The relationship among languages in the former Yugoslavia is manifested in the domain of Slovene political terminology which is derived from the SCR substratum. Most foreign influence, both in colloquial and standard Slovene, is due to the contact with German on the lexical as well as on the structural level.

Italian influence is evident mostly in terminology of fine arts and literature. In the majority of the western Slovene dialects loanwords and calques (denoting time) from Italian are regular phenomena. Italian influence is felt also on the syntactic level (word order, conditional sentence construction, etc.). In Italian some geographical terms (denoting Karst phenomena) are of Slovene origin. Widespread use of the imperfect in colloquial Venetian may be contact induced.

A substantial part of the Hungarian lexicon is of Slavic origin, Slovene influence being evident especially in political, religious and agricultural terminology. Excepting some lexical items, Hungarian influence is absent in standard Slovene; it is felt mostly in the northeastern Slovene dialects, especially in terminology related to state administration matters.

In the past all minority languages were sources of interference in the Slovene language. Today the influence is reverse, on account of two social factors: (1) Owing to weakened contacts with the mainstream language, both minority languages exhibit certain archaic features. A trend toward either simplification (omission of double consonants in Hungarian, e. g. *foras* < *forras*) or hypercorrection can be observed. Especially in Hungarian but also in Italian, differentiation along age and educational status is evident. Lack of variety has been noticed in verbal behaviour of Italian and Hungarian native speakers, e. g. monotonous, reduced vocabulary, uncertainty as to syntax patterns and use of tenses. Examples of the shift or omission of consonants and syllables in Italian (cf. *cittadina* : *cittadella*, *precisione* : *precisazione*, *capricci* : *cappricci*) may point to the language shift. In Hungarian, the shift of /ó/ to /u/, /ő/ to /ü/, and /e/ to /ö/, as well as the pronouncing of the grapheme /ly/ as /l/ instead of /j/ may be considered contact induced. (2) New political terminology constructed in Yugoslavia was introduced also into the minority languages, adapted to the phonological and morphological characteristics of the respective language. Many Slovene terms are transferred into colloquial Italian or Hungarian in their original form, adapted to the syntax or word formation rules of the language (e. g. Italian: *la položnica* 'postal order', *la skupščina* 'an assembly', Hungarian: *skupščinabol* 'from the assembly').

8. Conclusion

Several research institutions in Slovenia are engaged in discussion on language contact issues. In addition to the linguistic departments at the Faculty of Arts, the Institute for Ethnic Studies and Institute of Educational research should be mentioned. Intercultural communication appears to be one of the most prominent research topics at the moment as well as the historical destiny of the German minority after WWII. In the past ten years joint research by scholars from Italy and Hungary on language contact issues, as well as other topics concerning interethnic relations, has become a frequent practice.

9. Bibliography (selected)

Biber, Dušan (1966): *Nacizem in Nemci v Jugoslaviji 1933−1941* [Nazism and Germans in Yugoslavia 1933−1941], Ljubljana.

Devetak, Silvo (1986): "Aspects of Linguistic Equality in Slovenia". In: *Slovene Studies 2*, 53−63.

Devetak, Silvo (Ed.) (1987): *Madžari in Slovenci − Sodelovanje in sožitje ob slovensko-madžarski meji* [Hungarians and Slovenes − Cooperation and coexistence along the Slovene-Hungarian border], Ljubljana.

Dular, Janez (1988). "Med jezikovno politiko in jezikovno kulturo" [Between language policy and language culture]. In: *XXIV. Seminar slovenskega jezika, literature in kulture*, Ljubljana, 31−47.

Klopčič, Vera/Stergar, Janez (Eds.) (1993): *Ethnic Minorities in Slovenia*, Ljubljana.

Lük, Albina (1976): "Kontaktna madžarsko-slovenska in italijansko-slovenska področja" [Contact Hungarian-Slovene and Italian-Slovene Areas]. In: *Jezik u društvenoj sredini*, Bugarski, R./Ivir, V./Mikeš, M. (Eds), Novi Sad, 91−102.

Nećak Lük, Albina (1990): "Raziskovanje dvojezičnosti v jugoslovanskem prostoru" [Research on bilingualism in the Yugoslav areas]. In: *Jezik in književnost*, (Trst), 1, 31−41.

Nećak Lük, Albina/Štrukelj, Inka (Eds.) (1984): *Bilingualism − Individual and Societal Issues*, Ljubljana.

Novak Lukanovič, Sonja (1992): "Jezik manjšine in izobraževanje" [Minority language and education]. In: *Razprave in gradivo*, (Ljubljana), 26−27, 118−124.

Orožen, Martina (1989): "Prekmurski knjižni jezik" [The Prekmurje standard language]. In: *XXV. Seminar slovenskega jezika, literature in kulture*, Ljubljana, 37−60.

Pogorelec, Breda (Ed.) (1983): *Slovenščina v javnosti* [The Slovene language in public communication], Ljubljana.

Pogorelec, Breda (1988): "Delež jezika umetnosti in znanosti za slovenski knjižni jezik" [The importance of the language of arts and science for standard Slovene]. In: *XXIV. Seminar slovenskega jezika, literature in kulture*, Ljubljana, 19—29.

Population Census in Republic of Slovenia, Final Data (1992). In: *Statistical Informations*, No. 181, Ljubljana.

Rotar, Janez (1992): "Narodnokonstitutivni pojmi začetnih obdobij slovenske narodne integracije" [Nation-constituent conceptions in early periods of the Slovene national integration]. In: *XXVIII. Seminar slovenskega jezika, literature in kulture*, 123—148.

Rumpler, Helmut/Suppan, Arnold (Eds.) (1988): *Geschichte der Deutschen im Bereich des heutigen Slowenien 1848—1941*, Wien.

Rupel, Dimitrij (1986): "The Maintenance of National Language in a Socialist Setting: Slovene in Yugoslavia". In: *Slovene Studies, Journal of the Society for Slovene Studies 2*, 43—52.

Slovenščina v javnosti [The Slovene language in public communication] (1978). In: *Jezik in slovstvo 23, 6*, (Ljubljana), 165—284.

Štrukelj, Inka (Ed.) (1987): *Minority Languages and Mass Communication*, Ljubljana.

The Constitution of the Republic of Slovenia (1992), Ljubljana.

Toporišič, Jože (1990): "40 let povojnega jezikoslovja slovenskega jezika" [40 years of the postwar linguistics of the Slovene language]. In: *Jezik in književnost 1*, (Trst), 7—30.

Toporišič, Jože (1991): *Družbenost slovenskega jezika* [Societal issues of the Slovene language], Ljubljana.

Zgodovina Slovencev [History of the Slovenes] (1979), Ljubljana.

Albina Nećak Lük, Ljubljana (Slovenia)

170. Croatia

1. Geography and demography
2. Territorial history and national development
3. Politics, economy and general cultural and religious situation
4. Statistics and ethnoprofiles
5. Sociolinguistic situation
6. Language political situation
7. Bibliography (selected)

1. Geography and demography

The Republic of Croatia, one of the republics of the former Yugoslavia, officially recognized in 1992, covers a territory of 56,538 sq.km., and is horse-shoe shaped. This horse-shoe consists of three main regions. Its northern and eastern arm is Peripannonial and Pannonial in the smaller part. Its western and southern arm is Adriatic, i. e. Mediterranean, while its third, central part, to be found between the latter two, is *karstic* in its largest part. Since the beginning of its history, the Pannonial and the Adriatic regions have been of vital importance to Croatia, demographically, politically and economically. Due to this fact, Croatia has been and has remained throughout its history a Pannonial and Mediterranean country. At the same time, because of its central *karstic* part, it has been a link among the Pannonial, Mid-European and Mediterranean parts of Europe. Croatia is also a link between Europe's north-west and south-east, not only because of its waterways (Danube, Sava and Drava, as well as the Adriatic Sea) but also because land roads pass through the Sava river basins and along the Adriatic coast.

1.1. This geographic complexity makes Croatia, geolinguistically, a complex territory composed of Mid-European, Mediterranean and Balkan linguistic communities. Its Adriatic section belongs predominantly to the Mediterranean circle of languages, highly influenced by the Romance languages, primarily Italian. Its Peripannonial and Pannonial part belongs mostly to the Mid-European circle with a significant German and Hungarian influence. The central part of Croatia, for the most part, belongs to the Balkan language community, while its marginal parts also belong to the Mediterranean and Mid-European circle.

1.2. According to the census released in 1991, Croatia had a population of 4,601,469. The most populated part of Croatia is its Peripannonial region (113 people per sq.km.), followed by the Adriatic region, while the least populated area is its central region (only 19 people per sq.km.). Croatia has an unfavourable age structure, especially in its central region and on the islands. This is due to the fact that its natural population increase is minimal, even decreasing, and also because the rate of emigration is high. Sixty percent of Croatian municipalities are considered depopulated and as many as 73% are registered as emigrational. Since the Second World War, the agricultural population decreased from 62% to only 15%, while the percentage of the illiterate population over 10 years of age decreased from 20% to 5,6%. However, the percentage of illiterate population is still high in the municipalities of central Croatia, about 10% to 22%. Fifty-three percent of the total Croatian population lives in towns. The highest stage of urbanization is to be found at the north coast. Here, ⅔ of the population live in towns. The level of education, as a whole, is still considerably low. Expressed in percentages, it is as follows: 8,9% without primary schooling, over 36% without secondary schooling, while only 6,4% of the total population have college and university education. The Republic of Croatia is a multinational community, with the following national structure: Croats, Serbs, Italians, Czechs, Hungarians, Slovaks, Romanies, Muslims, Slovenians, Ruthenians, Ukrainians, Macedonians, Montenegrins, Albanians, etc.

1.3. As also characteristic for the whole of the Balkans, Croatia is a very migrational territory. It is to the very high percentage of migrations that have occurred during the past five centuries that Croatia owes the present characteristics of its sociolinguistic picture. The most significant migration moves were the result of Turkish conquests. From the present central Croatia, Dalmatia and Slavonia, but especially from central Croatia, people moved towards the north (Burgenland, Austria), to the east (Baranja and Transylvania) and to the south (Molise, Italy). These emigrations occurred from the 15th to the 17th centuries. A great deal of the migrants belonged to the Chakavian dialect, but there were also many who came from Bosnia, Herzegovina and Montenegro to Dalmatia, central Croatia and Slavonia, who spoke the Štokavian dialect. The most significant consequence of these immigrations was the formation of the Military Krajina, a protective buffer zone between the Turkish and Austro-Hungarian Empires, which was formed almost exclusively of Serbs and Valachs, orthodox Romanian population, which was soon integrated into the Serbian nation. At the beginning of this century, which was characterized by hunger and economic crises, Croatia lost many of its population to Australia, and South and North America. Due not only to war losses but also to war refugees, the Second World War caused yet another considerable migration. After the war, many people from central Croatia and north and south Dalmatia moved to Slavonia and Vojvodina. Rapid industrialization increased inner migration, especially from villages to towns, and from central Croatia to the Adriatic and Peripannonial regions. From 1991 to the present time, because of war circumstances, over 500,000 people have been registered as either refugees or displaced persons. With regard to the character of this war, over 250,000 ethnic Croats have emigrated from the central parts of Croatia (mainly from Slavonia and Krajina) and are now in its other parts (Dalmatia, Istria and north Croatia) or abroad. About 100,000 to 200,000 ethnic Croats arrived from Bosnia and Herzegovina, as well as from FR Yugoslavia. During this war, 250,000 ethnic Serbs have either emigrated or have been registered as displaced. Most of them went to FR Yugoslavia, while some left for the part of Bosnia and Herzegovina controlled by the Serbs, and the others settled down in UNPAs (United Nations Protected Areas), e. g., Krajina. One part of them, probably several tens of thousands, is in a third country. The war has greatly changed the ethnic and the social structure of Croatia. As a result of this, many towns have been inhabited by recently suburban and village populations (→ Language Map G).

2. Territorial history and national development

In the process of the great Slavic migration of the 7th century, the Croats came to the Adriatic Sea, moving as far as Istria, mixing with Illyrians, and in the background of the Romanian, Roman and Dalmatian towns they formed their territorial core, the core of their future country. During the 9th and 10th centuries this territory spread from the river Cetina in the south towards Istria in the west and as far as the river Una in the north. It is from this time and territory that the Trpimirović dynasty originates, which ruled from 852 to 1120 (Lord Trpimir, *dux croatorum*). Although under partial Byzantine and French domination, the Croatia of that time was gradually given the right to rule over the

Dalmatian towns (King Petar Krešimir IV). At the beginning of the 11th century and under this very throne, Croatia became an independent country, but at the end of the same century lost its independence when after the conflict with the Arpáds, the Hungarian dynasty, King Zvonimir made a *pacta conventa* with them. From that time on and until the Austro-Hungarian Empire was formed and gradually destroyed, certain parts of what today is Croatia were under their domination. With exceptions of occasional periods of Byzantine influence, the Dalmatian coast and Istrian region were almost constantly under Venetian domination. Turkish penetration to the West, the fall of Bosnia in the 15th century and the defeat of the Hungarian army in the 16th century were fatal for Croatia. Because a large part of its territory today falls under the domination of Turkey, Croatia became *reliquiae reliquiarum*. At that time, i. e. in the 16th century, the territory of Croatia, as indeed the complete territory of former Yugoslavia, was split among the Venetian republic, Hungary and Turkey. Until the beginning of the 19th century the Republic of Dubrovnik, i. e. the area around Dubrovnik, had the status of a free town-republic. At the beginning of the 19th century, under the ruling of Napoleon's marshal Marmount, Illyric provinces started to form. They consisted of Dalmatia, Istria, Civil Croatia and Military Krajina. The first half of the 19th century was marked by the Illyric renaissance (led by Ljudevit Gaj), which was the beginning of a new, modern Croatian nation, and a unique standard Croatian language in community with the other Yugoslav nations and with the Serbian national and linguistic movement. The 19th century was also marked by the merging of Ban's Croatia with other Croatian countries, first with Slavonia, followed by Military Krajina and lastly with Dalmatia. This unification had many positive things to say, not about the modern civil Croatian class but also about Croatian-Serbian national coalitions, i. e. Serbs in Croatia. After the fall of the Austro-Hungarian Empire in 1918, a new, shared country was formed: the Kingdom of Serbs, Croats and Slovenians. Slovenians, Croats and Serbs who lived under Austro-Hungarian domination united with the Kingdom of Serbia into one country. After numerous constitutional and political crises and efforts to solve the so-called Croatian question, an agreement was made between the president of the leading Croatian party (the Peasant party), Vlatko Maček, and the President of Yugoslavia to form a new republic, Ban's Croatia, in fact a Republic of Croatia within the Kingdom of Yugoslavia. The Second World War, occupation of Croatia by Nazi Germany and fascist Italy, as well as the creation of a puppet state of Ustashis, prevented the stabilization and further definition of the future of the Ban's Croatia. An antifascist movement under the leadership of communists and antifascist, democratic coalitions reestablished Yugoslavia within which Croatia was one of the Republics. In 1992, Croatia, a former Republic of Yugoslavia, became independent by the acknowledgment of the UN.

3. Politics, economy and general cultural and religious situation

According to its present constitution, the Republic of Croatia is a unitary national state with strong central power and a semipresidential system. It is a young state which arose from the liberated national emotions of the Croatian people. Such constitutional characteristics run counter to the aspirations of the Serbian minority in Krajina who would like to keep the constitutional status they have had for the past 150 years, as well as to the aspirations of some other regions, such as Istria and Dalmatia, who wish to have more power in relation to the central government. The newly liberated national enthusiasm of the majority of the Croatian people, as indeed that of the Serbian minority, caused the radical historicism and traditionalism of their national identities, not only linguistic but cultural and political as well. In the time that awaits us, these problems − Croatia as a complex and decentralized country, renewal of the modern national identity of the Croatian majority and the Serbian minority − will have to be settled within Croatian politics. Of course, this will not happen without some effect on the characteristics and development of linguistic policy in Croatia.

3.1. The Croatian economy is based on three sectors: industry, agriculture and tourism. The most developed among the industrial sectors are metal production and the chemical industry. In the last three decades, tourism has represented one of the three basic economic sectors. The economy is not developed equally in Croatia, so there is a great difference among its regions. The most developed of them are the northern parts of Croatia, industry and agriculture, and Istria and the coastal regions because of tourism and shipbuilding. The next is a region of Dalmatia, in which tourism contributes mostly to economic growth. The most underdeveloped part of Croatia is its central region and that is what Krajina is today. In the whole territory of the former Yugoslavia, only Kosovo has a lower level of development.

3.2. Croatia is a multicultural society. Observed diachronically, it is composed of Mideuropean, Mediterranean and Balkan influences. From a synchronic aspect, it belongs to semideveloped industrial and postindustrial cultures. Indicators of the cultural standard (for 1983 and 1984), also relevant as possible indicators of the communication standard, are: libraries – 374 professional (scientific) and 294 national; books and brochures – number of titles: 2,333; theaters – professional: 14, for children: 15, and 17 amateur; cinemas – 309; no. of TV-subscribers – 987,000; no. of newspapers – 686, and magazines – 370.

3.3. There are more than twelve different religious communities in Croatian society. Nevertheless only three of them are significant by number of members: Roman Catholic (76,6% of the total population), Orthodox (11,1%), and Islamic (1,1%). Protestants are divided into small groups among which Adventists and Evangelists are the largest and most influential groups. The Jewish community is quite small, numbering only about 630 people.

Following the collapse of communism, religion and church plays an important role in the social life of Croatia. This is caused also by the fact that religious differences represent a significant factor of ethnic identities and differences in Croatian society. The consequent "religionization" of everyday life of the society contributes to a certain intransparency in distinguishing between religious, state, and ethnic-national affairs.

The renewal of the role of religion is related to a renewal of the distinctive power of script differences. The distinction between Latin and Cyrillic has become an important factor of national identity. Latin is linked to Croat (Catholic) ethnicity, Cyrillic to Serb (Orthodox) ethnicity.

4. Statistics and ethnoprofiles

There are 23 ethnic and language communities in the Republic of Croatia: Albanian, Austrian, Bulgarian, Czech, German, Greek, Hungarian, Italian, Jewish, Macedonian, Montenegrin, Muslim, Polish, Romanian, Romany, Ruthenian, Russian, Slovak, Slovenian, Serbian, Turkish, Ukrainian, and Valachian. This does not include the ethnic communities with fewer than 1,000 speakers, which translates as 0,02% of the total population.

There are 12,032 reported Albanian speakers in Croatia. It is plausible to assume that the real number of speakers is larger, but most of them do not have regular citizenship status, so they could not be included in the official census. Although the term *šiptarski* for the Albanian language is not so widespread in Croatia, it still exists in colloquial use. The Albanian speakers live on the whole in Croatian territory, especially in the large towns and along the Adriatic coast. They are mainly economic migrants who arrived in Croatia in the last 30 years. Their language functions exclusively for intraethnic communication.

There are 9,724 Montenegrins in Croatia. They use the national name for their language rarely; their language identity is not quite clear in Croatia. They consider their language variously as Serbo-Croatian (the language identification of the majority until 1990), as Serbian, as Montenegrin, or as Croatian. They are dispersed in the large towns. They are mainly economic migrants within the former Yugoslavia. Except for the function of intraethnic communication, their language does not have other developed functions.

There are 12,953 Czechs in Croatia. They and their language are locally called *Pemac* and *pemački*, respectively. The Czech-speaking population are located in west Slavonia – mostly in Daruvar, Grubišno Polje, Garešnica and Končanica. The Czech language is one of intraethnic communication, not only in private but also in public spheres: primary education, magazines, a short radio- and TV-programme. The Czechs immigrated to Croatia during the Austro-Hungarian monarchy. The influence of Czech on Croatian and Serbian is significant, not only because of direct language contact (numerous surnames have remained: *Krivanek, Haluža, Halonja, Šafarik*) but also because of words that were borrowed on purpose at the beginning of this century (*naklada, naslov, obzor, odraz, pojam, povod, slog, stroj, tlak, uloga, ustav, važnost, zbirka, živalj*), when the Czech language was a model for developing a standard and for exemption from influences of borrowings.

There are 3,922,725 speakers of Croatian in Croatia. During the last 150 years, except for the term *Croatian*, the terms *Croato-Serbian* and *Croatian* or *Serbian* have often been used. This language is used over the entire Croatian territory, but due to the war and a great number of refugees and exiles, the number of speakers of Croatian has decreased drastically in regions under UN protection, e. g. in Krajina, so it is *de facto* a minority language there (used by maybe a few thousand people).

There are a little over 1,000 Istria-Romanian-speaking people. They are called *Ćići* and their language *ćićarijski*. This language is spoken on the Istrian Peninsula – north (Ćićarija) and south-west of the Učka mountain (Čepićka dolina). The Istria-Romanian speaking population are descendants of Balkan Valachians who immigrated to the Istrian region during the 15th century. This is one of the four basic dialects of the Romanian language.

Some 6,280 Macedonian-speaking people are dispersed in the large towns in Croatia. Most of them are economic migrants within the former Yugoslavia. Macedonian is the language of interpersonal communication.

There are 43,369 *Bošnjak*-Muslims in Croatia. (The number could well be much higher because of the refugees from Bosnia and Herzegovina, and people without citizenship status.) Until 1990, they spoke either Croatian, or a Bosnian-Herzegovinian version of Croato-Serbian, i. e. Serbo-Croatian. Today their language identity is not clear and varies between the old form and a possible new identity which could be either Croatian or *Bošnjak*. The communicative function of their language is restricted to intraethnic communication with some public use (newspapers). Like other Yugoslav people, *Bošnjak*-Muslims came to Croatia as economic migrants in the past thirty years. Although the influence of the Turkish language on the dialects of Bosnian Muslims is considerable, the same influence is important also for Croatian and the Serbian. Thus, Turkisms such as these are often found in these languages: *dućan* (Tur. *dükkjan*) "trgovina", *juriš* (Tur. *jürüjüš*), *pendžer* (Tur. *pendžere*) "prozor", *du-han* (Tur. *dühan*), *kavga* (Tur. *kavga*) "svađa", *jarak* (Tur. *jarak*) "prokop, kanal", *boja* (Tur. *bojali*), *top* (Tur. *top*).

There are 2,635 German-speaking people in Croatia, mostly in Slavonia. German functions as a language of interpersonal communication. Due to the fact that German as the language of public communication exerted influence on Croatian and Serbian for centuries, Germanisms still exist in these languages: *frišak* (Ger. *frisch*), "svjež", *gebis* (Ger. *Gebiß*) "zubalo", *gemišt* (Ger. *mischen*) "mješavina, vino pomiješano s mineralnom vodom", *šnajder* (Ger. *Schneider*) "krojač", *pekar* (Ger. *Bäcker*), *urar* (Ger. *Uhr*), *logorovati* (Ger. *Lager*). Besides, a great deal of Croatian words are in effect calques from German: *časopis* (Ger. *Zeitschrift*), *potpisati* (Ger. *unterschreiben*), *zastupnik* (Ger. *Vertreter*), *zrakoplov* (Ger. *Flugzeug*).

There are 6,695 Romani speakers in Croatia. They live in western Slavonia and in other large towns of Croatia. This number could well be larger. Their dialects are strongly influenced by Croatian and Serbian. The communication function of Romani is restricted exclusively to interpersonal communication.

There are 3,253 Ruthenian-speaking people. They live mostly in eastern Slavonia (Vukovar, Vinkovci). Today many of them live elsewhere as refugees or have the status of displaced persons. Until the war, Ruthenian was the language of intraethnic communication with limited public use (elementary schools, magazines and shorter radio programmes).

There are 5,606 Slovaks. They live in eastern Slavonia (Vukovar) and in the region of Našice. The use of Slovak is similar to that of Ruthenian. Like Czechs, Slovaks immigrated to Croatia during the Austro-Hungarian monarchy.

There are 22,376 people in Croatia who speak the Slovenian language. They live in the north-west parts of Croatia. Slovenian is used for interpersonal communication.

About 688,000 people in Croatia speak the Serbian language. Up to 1990, this language was commonly known as Serbo-Croatian, and also Serbian or Croatian. It is spoken: in UNPA regions, e. g., Krajina, in all the larger towns like Zagreb, Rijeka, Osijek, Karlovac, Split, Zadar and Sisak, and in more or less ethnically compact enclaves, for example in some areas of Gorski Kotar and west Slavonia. In the UNPAs, the Serbian language has become the majority language since the war caused a big ethnic movement of the population, while in large towns in Croatia, where most of the Serbs lived, the use of the Serbian language has drastically decreased.

There are approximately 23,000 users of the Hungarian language in Croatia, while the number of Hungarians is 25,439. Most Hungarian speakers live in the region of eastern Slavonia, or more precisely, at Beli Manastir (today UNPA's Sector East) and Osijek. During this war many emigrated to Hungary, or moved to other towns in Croatia. Hungarian is the language of intraethnic communication with limited public use (elementary schools, magazines, radio and TV broadcasts). Although Hungarian and Croatian share 900 years of direct contact, Hungarian influence on Croatian is not as strong as, for example, the influences of German, Italian or Turkish. Some Hungarian words are in use in Croatian and Serbian: *džak* (H zsak) "vreća", *(h)alas* (H. halas) "ribar", *gazda* (H. gazda) "gospodar", *gumb* (H. gumb) "dugme", *gulaš* (H. gulya – govedo, krdo), *salaš* (H. szallas).

There are about 25,000 Italian-speaking people in Croatia. This language is spoken in the Istrian Peninsula, in towns like Rijeka, Rovinj, Pula, Opatija, Poreč, Labin, Kopar and Buje. It is also spoken in the area of Pakrac and Lipik, as well as in Zadar, and on the island of Cres. Italian functions as the language of municipal and regional communication, in official and public spheres. Its influence on southern Croatian and south-western Serbian dialects, which was obvious through the centuries, left highly visible traces: *diletant* (It. diletante) "nestručnjak, nevješt", *izolacija* (It. isolare), *kala* (calle) "ulica", *pasati* (It. passare) "proći", *maškara* (It. maschera), *nobil, Nobilo* (It. nobile) "plemić, aristokrat", *terakota* (It. terra cotta) "pečena glina", *zakantati* (It. cantare) "zapjevati".

There are 2,494 Ukrainian language users. They live in Slavonia, i. e. Vukovar and Slavonski Brod. At present many of them are living elsewhere with refugee status. With respect to the development of communication functions, Ukrainian is similar to Slovak and Ruthenian.

5. Sociolinguistic situation

Taking into account status and function, we can differentiate two language groups in Croatia, as we could see from the previous section. The first group includes Croatian, Serbian and Italian, while the second includes the remaining languages. The first group is characterized by either real official language status and use in public communication, or by such status in process whether on a state or a substate, regional level. Accordingly, the Croatian language (and Latin alphabet) have the status of an official language and it is obligatory throughout Croatia. The Serbian language and Cyrillic alphabet, according to the present statutory regulations, would have the status of an official language only in self-governing local units, where Serbs form a majority, but the Croatian language and Latin alphabet must be used nevertheless. In fact, the reality is much different because throughout the areas under UN protection, Serbian has the status of the only official language. Serbian outside of this area has the same status practically as the languages in the second group. On the basis of existing practice and agreement between the two countries, Italian also has the status of official language in some autonomous localities where a significant number of Italian language users live. Istrian authorities insist that, according to their understanding of the agreement and the opinion of the majority of the population in this region, that region is to be, in an official sense, bilingual. The second group characterizes the status of intraethnic or interpersonal communication. Languages of the newly formed minorities, e. g. Macedonian, Slovenian or *Bošnjak*-Muslims and the languages of the nonrespected minorities such as Romanies and Albanians, have the status of intraethnic and even more interpersonal communication. Languages of the so-called autochthonous minorities, like Czech, Hungarian, Slovakian and German, have favoured intraethnic communication status, while some of them, Czech first of all, have the potential status of an official language on the municipal level.

Only Croatian, Serbian and Italian among the languages mentioned function as languages of public communication: Serbian in UNPAs, and Italian in the Istrian region and the coast.

The strongest attitudes about language, mainly negative, are between users of Croatian Serbian. The negative attitude of the Croatian language users toward the Cyrillic alphabet was because the script became one of the means for Serbian national homogenization before and during the war, and words became recognized as Serbisms (*pavlaka, supa, hljeb, hiljada*). Serbian language users exhibit a less negative attitude towards the Latin alphabet, but they have a negative, almost mocking attitude towards the results of the Croatization of the Croatian language, especially towards archaisms (*glede, postaja, vrhovnik*) and neologisms (*računalo, rednik,* "kompjutor", *zrakomlat, uvrtnjak,* "helikopter"). Italian and German, but especially Italian in Istria and on the coast, are accepted as the second language in the region, not only by Italian speakers but also by the Croatian population. Speakers of other minority languages, especially Romany, Albanian and *Bošnjak*-Muslim, are not positively accepted. It is interesting that within Serbian and Croatian there are significant differences in language consciousness. The southern Dalmatian Croatian areas traditionally are more conscious of their regional idiom (Chakavian-Ikavian dialect and regional Štokavian dialect) than in other regions, and consequently their distance towards the new Croatian language identity is much greater. Language loyalty of the Krajina's Serbs to Croatian as the official language of the country practically does not exist at all.

There are two kinds of bilingualism in Croatia, the usual minority bilingualism (minority uses the majority language next to its own minority language) and less frequent majority bilingualism (majority speaks minority language besides the respective majority language) as well as the rejection of either. The usual minority bilingualism characterizes all minority language communities in Croatia, while minority bilingualism is very rare and limited. Majority bilingualism is frequent among the Croats in Istria in relation to the Italian language; it is not only the result of a historical domination of the Italian language in this area, but it also desires from the international role of the Italian language. Croato-Hungarian majority bilingualism is attested in eastern Slavonia. As for Croato-Serbian bilingualism, since until recently, the Croatian- and Serbian-speaking population communicated in the same language, with different standard variants, and since even today they can communicate without any difficulties, Croato-Serbian bilingualism can be discussed only in the symbolic sense as bilingualism of two standard languages. In this sense, the Serbs living in large towns in Croatia are bilingual with the Croatian language. The Serbs in the UNPAs, e. g. Krajina, refuse such bilingualism. Similarly, Croats in Croatia refuse bilingualism with the Serbian language. A good example of this is the fact that the Cyrillic alphabet is no longer in use in Croatian schools nor is the Latin alphabet taught in schools in Krajina, except for the purpose of teaching foreign languages.

Elements of possible diglossia in Croatia started to appear since the discussion about reconstruction of standard variants of Croatian and Serbian began. Radical puristic reconstruction of vocabulary, word formation and syntactic constructions in the Croatian language distanced the standard variety of Croatian from most of the non-standard Croatian varieties allowing for possible diglossic tendencies in the Croat speech community. In the UNPAs, Serbian, on the other hand, has made Ekavian, instead of Iekavian, as its official and often public speaking base, followed by changes of formation and vocabulary, again creating preconditions for possible diglossia (for example: *Nisi trebao ići u općinu prije nego konzultiraš svoje savjetnike > Nije trebalo da ideš u opštinu pre nego konsultuješ svoje savetnike*).

6. Language political situation

There are three main language policy questions in Croatia: possible principles of language policy; language identity of the Croatian and Serbian languages; status and relation of international and regional communication language.

6.1. Like most newly formed states in Europe, Croatia has no adequate relation between the existing principles of language policy and the actual language situation. Although Croatian society is multilingual, regionalized and polyvalent from the view of different cultures and national values, present language policy does not leave much space for articulation of such characteristics. Language unity is more important than language differences, centralism and the symbolic function of language is much more important than its communicative function, and linguistic interventionism is more important than linguistic realism. Nevertheless, the language conflict between the Croatian and the Serbian languages, and the conflicts concerning the type and level of bilingualism in certain parts of Croatia, will most probably contribute to a more realistic language policy.

6.2. Certainly the most significant problem of language policy and language planning, i. e. language standardization, in Croatia as well as in the entire former Croato-Serbian language territory, is the problem of language identity. After over 150 years of language unity, the Croats and the Serbs started to form separate languages. Thus, like most European nations, they are trying to establish links between national and language identities. They differ from most European nations because they are doing this *post festum*, after national identity has already been formed on the other grounds: religion, tradition, culture, awareness of particularity. Croats and Serbs thus deduce their language identity from their national identity, not inversely. Although this is not the only case of language split and revision of language identity, it is rather interesting to see the genesis of the problem.

6.2.1. Croatian and Serbian in the territory of Croatia went through three naming phases. During the early phases of regional written languages, in the 17th, 18th and 19th centuries, national Slavic names were in frequent use: *slovinski, slavjanski ilirski* (Illyrian). In the second phase (19th century and the beginning of the 20th), i. e. the phase of national movements and liberation from domination of other nations, national names like *Croatian, Serbian*, or double-national as *Croato-Serbian, Croatian or Serbian*, were in use. During the 1960's and 1970's, national names for languages were renewed, so discussions concerning it have presented the main language policy topics until the time when the national and language names were finally established: since 1990 not only variants (in the case of Croatia), but languages have got national names: Croatian and Serbian.

6.2.2. The other significant element of identity, not only of language but also of the Croatian and Serbian nations, is the script. Since the 11th century Croats and Serbs have used *glagoljica*, as the first Slavic literary script, and from 12th century the Cyrillic alphabet, as the second and mostly widespread Slavic script. Nevertheless, it was from the 14th century, when the Latin alphabet became usual in most Croatian regions, that the difference between Croats and Serbs with regard to writing system originated: gradually, the former used Latin, and the latter Cyrillic. Although this difference has not been strictly observed up until the present time, because many Croats used the Cyrillic (at least as an alternate system) and the great majority of Serbs used Latin as a first alphabet, still most Croats and Serbs perceived the difference between these alphabets as features of their national identities. At the beginning of the 20th century (during the unification of Yugoslavia), there were attempts from both Croatian and Serbian intelligentsia to make some kind of language-policy compromise: Serbs should have to adopt Latin script and Croats, Ekavian. However, these attempts did not succeed, and the writing systems still had a role as a means of national identification, which culminated especially during the crash of Yugoslavia.

6.2.3. In the first half of the 19th century, when Croats and Serbs decided to adopt the most widespread and common Štokavian dialect, instead of Kaikavian or Chakavian, as a basis for their standard language, and in the middle of the same century, when they established grounds for an unique orthography (Vienna Agreement), they actually moved towards the creating of an unified language standard. However, this mutual language standardization was variant from the very beginning: Croats and the western parts of the Croato-Serbian regions (this includes Serbs in Croatia and those in Bosnia) developed their standard on the grounds of Novoštokavian-Iekavian, while the Serbs in Serbia developed a Novoštokavian-Ekavian type. With the exception of the period from 1941 to 1945, when a separated and artificial Croatian language with etymological orthography was created in the Independent State of Croatia, these differences were interpreted up to the sixties as variants of not only one language, but also of one standard. Sometimes they were called the Zagreb variant and the Belgrade variant, or west and east variants. From the sixties, i. e. from the Declaration on behalf of Croatian literary language, these variants were understood as separate standard languages within the one language − or a diasystem. Since this kind of understanding of variants did not imply national standard languages but rather languages of a republic (in the sense of federal unit), and since the unified language of Croats and Serbs was still accepted, these changes within Croatia did not cause significant reactions. However, the most significant changes were those that occurred in 1990, when the Croats proclaimed that Croatian is not only a separate form of standard language but a separate language with specific features, which had been suppressed during the language unity and which should now be renewed. At that time the Serbs in Croatia, those in Krajina, moved towards identification of their national and language identity, and they proclaimed Serbian. At that moment they had two options: to use the standard form which was the common language until yesterday, or to adopt the standard form which was in use in Serbia. On the level of proclamation, the former occurred, but on the level of communication the latter appeared. As for Serbs outside of the UNPAs, they are "bilingual": they use Croatian with its innovations and they perceive the previous common standard to be their own language. Nevertheless, neither Croats nor Serbs have completed the process of reconstruction of their standards and we can merely say that there is still no significant linguistic distinction of the Croatian and the Serbian languages on the horizon.

6.2.4. As in the case of standardization, it is also possible to follow discussions on the common and separate orthography of the Croatian and the Serbian languages. At the end of the 19th century phonetic orthography replaced the etymological, as advocated by some Croat linguists. But this did not mean that all orthographic rules were balanced. Differences appeared in punctuation (Croatian was "grammatical", and Serbian was "logical"), in different ways of writing the forms of the future tense (Cro. *radit ću*, Srb. *radiću*) and in transcription (Cro. *Washington*, Srb. *Vošington*). After the achievement of independence, discussions started in Croatia about abandoning the phonetic principle and adopting the etymological principle of orthography. These discussions are still under way, but "etymologists" almost gave up even though "phoneticians", who are dominant, made some minor concessions. In Krajina, there are two orthographies in use: the previously common orthographic solutions, and orthography which is in use in Serbia.

6.2.5. During all the years of language unity between Croats and Serbs, certain words have appeared as words of difference:

Croatian	Serbian	
tisuća	*hiljada*	"a thousand"
kruh	*hljeb/hleb*	"bread"
vlak	*voz*	"train"
plin	*gas*	"gas"

Many words served only as doublets without symbolic function, as previous:

Croatian	Serbian	
dopustiti	*dozvoliti*	"to permit"
sudjelovati	*učestvovati*	"to participate"
stvaralac	*kreator*	"creator"
uspješan/ djelotvoran	*efikasan*	"efficacious"

In the Croatian language, derived forms were also accepted, except many words were recognized as variantly or nationally marked in their basic forms:

Serbian	Croatian
talas, "wave"	*val*, but: *talasati se*, "to wave"
krst, "cross"	*križ*, but: *krstiti*, "to cross"
voz, "train"	*vlak*, but: *voziti se*, "to drive"

However, in the last four years, an effort to eliminate all so-called "Serbisms" has been evident in Croatia. These efforts are so intense that even words not marked as "Serbisms" or as doublets have been replaced by Croatian words:

s obzirom na	>	*glede*
opasnost	>	*pogibelj*
propaganda	>	*promidžba*
stanica	>	*postaja*
disciplina	>	*stega*
omladina	>	*mladež*

In Krajina and among the Serbs in general, there has been no real increase of negative sensitivity towards the words that are not recognized as Serbian enough, but there is an increase of absorption of words, served as doublets, which were much more in use in the eastern variant (*bezbedonosan*, *fudbal*, *mangup*).

6.2.6. As words, some morphemes of word formation have had a distinct function. Their number in Croatian has greatly increased in the past four years. Thus many words received new derivational morphemes:

čita-lac	>	*čita-telj*
sa-općenje	>	*pri-općenje*
izvješ-taj	>	*izvješ-će*
upotreba	>	*uporaba*

The Serbs in Croatia still use doublets for word formation, while those in Krajina in this case, as in the case of words, use the eastern solutions much more (*ignorirati* > *ignorisati*, *općina* > *opština*, *surađivati* > *sarađivati*).

Summarizing, the process of creating new language identities for Croatian and Serbian is still open. At this moment it is impossible to predict to what extent it will remain a symbolic-linguistic process, as it is now, or will develop in the communicative-linguistic direction. The only certainty for the time being is that Serbs and Croats *speak* in different languages, but from a linguistic point of view, they *understand* each other without any difficulties.

6.3. The Croatian territory has traditionally been a crossroads of different worlds and regional languages. Even today this territory is witnessing encounters of quite a few languages. First of all, there is English as the language of a wide range of international communication. Following English there is German as the language which once had the status of a means of regional, Mid-European communication, and which today is holding this position again. Finally, there is Italian as the language of subregional Mediterranean communication, which, like German, is renewing its functions in some parts of Croatia. As such, these languages represent a significant element in the sociolinguistic frame of Croatia.

7. Bibliography (selected)

Anić, Vladimir (1991): *Rječnik hrvatskog jezika*, Zagreb.

Babić, Stjepan (1986): *Tvorba riječi u hrvatskom književnom jeziku*, Zagreb.

Babić, Stjepan/Finka, Božidar/Moguš, Milan (1971): *Hrvatski pravopis*, Zagreb.

Brozović, Dalibor (1970): *Standardni jezik*, Zagreb.

Brozović, Dalibor (1978): "Hrvatski jezik, njegovo mjesto unutar južnoslavenskih i drugih slavenskih jezika, njegove povijesne mijene kao jezika hrvatske književnosti". In: *Hrvatska književnost u evropskom kontekstu*, Flanker, A. and Pranjić, K. (Eds.), Zagreb.

Brozović, Dalibor/Ivić, Pavle (1988): *Jezik srpskohrvatski, hrvatskosrpski, hrvatski ili srpski*, Zagreb.

Ivić, Pavle (1956): *Dijalektologija srpskohrvatskog jezika*, Novi Sad.

Ivić, Pavle (1971): *Srpski narod i njegov jezik*, Beograd.

"Jezici naroda i narodnosti Jugoslavije" (1989). In: *SOL, Lingvistički časopis* 8, Vol. 4, 85−144.

Jonke, Ljudevit (1971): *Hrvatski književni jezik 19. i 20. stoljeća*, Zagreb.

Kašić, Jovan (1972): *Govor Srba u Hrvatskoj i njihov odnos prema književnom jeziku*, Novi ljetopis Srpskog kulturnog društva Prosvjeta, broj 2, Zagreb.

Katičić, Radoslav (1970): *Jezikoslovni ogledi*, Zagreb.

Katičić, Radoslav (1986): *Novi jezikoslovni ogledi*, Zagreb.

Katičić, Radoslav (1986): *Sintaksa hrvatskoga književnog jezika*, Zagreb.

Korać, Stanko (1979): *Književna hrestomatija*, Zagreb.

Kovačec, August (1988): "Balkanski jezični savez". In: *SOL, Lingvistički časopis* 6, Vol. 3, 21−52.

Maretić, Tomo (1931): *Gramatika hrvatskoga ili srpskoga književnoga jezika*, Zagreb.

Moguš, Milan (1993): *Povijest hrvatskoga književnoga jezika*, Zagreb.

Petrović, Dragoljub (1978): *Govor Banije i Korduna*, Novi Sad/Zagreb.

Pravopis hrvatskosrpskog književnog jezika (1960), Zagreb/Novi Sad.

Pupovac, Milorad (1994): *Jezička politika i jezik Srba u Hrvatskoj*, Zagreb.

Pupovac, Milorad (1994): *Language Policy in the Newly Established States of Europe*. Paper presented at the International Conference on Language and Law, Freiburg, Sept. 14−17. 1994.

Škiljan, Dubravko (1988): *Jezična politika*, Zagreb.

Veliki geografski atlas Jugoslavije (1987), Zagreb.

Vince, Zlatko (1978): *Putovima hrvatskoga književnog jezika*, Zagreb.

Milorad Pupovac, Zagreb (Croatia)

171. Bosnie-Herzégovine

1. Géographie et démographie
2. Histoire territoriale et développement national
3. Politique, économie et situations culturelle et religieuse en général
4. Statistiques et profils ethniques
5. Situation sociolinguistique
6. Etat de la politique linguistique
7. Présentation des contacts linguistiques
8. Examen critique de la bibliographie
9. Bibliographie (sélective)

1. Géographie et démographie

1.1. Entre 1944 et 1992, la Bosnie-Herzégovine a été l'une des Républiques constitutives de la Fédération Yougoslave. La proclamation de son indépendance, en 1992, a servi de prétexte pour l'insurrection des Serbes autochtones et pour une guerre atroce qui finit par opposer entre eux les Serbes, les Musulmans et les Croates. Les frontières actuelles du pays correspondent approximativement aux frontières telles qu'elles se sont fixées entre le 17e et le 19e siècle, sous la domination ottomane (Enc. Ju. 1982, 179−180). Par leur position géographique centrale, la vallée située entre les villes de Sarajevo et de Zenica et les régions voisines ont représenté une aire vers laquelle ont depuis toujours convergé les voies de communication. C'est cette partie du pays qui a été le noyau de presque toutes les formations politiques les plus durables.

1.2. D'après le recensement de 1991, la Bosnie-Herzégovine a eu 4.364.574 habitants sur une superficie de 51.129 km². Plus de 97,5% de la population appartenaient aux quatre groupes ethniques ou 'nationaux' (Musulmans, Serbes, Croates, Yougoslaves; v. les statistiques, ch. 4.). Si le groupe national des *Musulmans* est aujourd'hui le plus nombreux, avant 1971 la plupart des adeptes de l'Islam se déclaraient comme *Croates*, *Serbes* ou *Yougoslaves*. Depuis le Moyen Age, le territoire de la Bosnie-Herzégovine a été le théâtre de nombreuses migrations provoquées soit par des causes économiques soit par des conflits politiques, religieux et ethniques. Parmi les populations des bergers, la transhumance a été un phénomène assez fréquent. Pendant l'industrialisation socialiste de l'après-guerre, un grand nombre des habitants des régions rurales est venu s'établir dans les villes. A la fin des années 40, un déplacement particulièrement important a été la migration des Serbes des régions pauvres vers la Vojvodine en Serbie ainsi que vers la Slavonie et la Baranja en Croatie. Au cours des années 60 commence une migration économique vers l'Europe occidentale (Allemagne, Suisse, Autriche, Suède) et vers les pays d'outre-mer (EUA, Canada, Australie). L'exode touche surtout les Musulmans, les Serbes et les Croates, mais l'émigration croate a été, proportionnellement, la plus importante. Dans la période de l'après-guerre, beaucoup de Croates, en tant qu'élément ethnique anathématisé et indésirable, ont abandonné la Bosnie pour s'établir en Croatie (→ carte linguistique G).

2. Histoire territoriale et développement national

2.1. Dès le milieu du 6e siècle, les Slaves commencèrent à pénétrer sur le territoire de la Bosnie-Herzégovine qui, à cette époque, faisait partie de l'Empire byzantin. Ils y trouvèrent des populations romanes ou illyriennes romanisées, qu'ils allaient assimiler par la suite (Enc. Ju. 1982, 225). Ce n'est qu'au 12e s. qu'une partie de la Bosnie centrale et orientale a acquis une certaine indépendance. Vers la fin du 12e s., sous le ban Kulin, la Bosnie joue un rôle important dans la région et se lie à l'Eglise de Rome. Dès le commencement du 13e s. s'est répandue en Bosnie une hérésie (*bogumili*) qui, pour presque trois siècles, sera la cause de luttes intestines et de confrontations avec l'Eglise de Rome et la papauté. En 1377, le ban Tvrtko s'est fait sacrer roi de Bosnie, mais peu après cet événement commence une pénétration systématique des Turcs. La chute de la place forte de Jajce entre les mains des Turcs, en 1463, marquera l'écroulement de l'Etat de Bosnie. A la suite de ces événements, une partie de la population s'est peu à peu islamisée, tandis qu'un bon nombre de la population catholique s'est exilé en Croatie ou dans d'autres pays (Peroche 1992, 67−68). Dans les régions dévastées par les guerres et dépeuplées, les Turcs ont amené et installé des bergers serbes et valaques (les uns et les autres orthodoxes; Enc. Ju. 1982, 176−177; Peroche 1992, 86−87). C'est sous la domination ottomane, jusqu'à la fin du 18e s., que se sont formées les principales aires ethniques (nationales et confessionnelles). La domination austro-hongroise (1878—1918) a amélioré les conditions économiques, sociales et culturelles, mais elle n'a pas réussi à neutraliser les conflits ethniques et religieux qui ne feront que s'aggraver après 1918 quand la Bosnie-Herzégovine fut intégrée dans l'Etat Yougoslave. La création de la *Banovina Hrvatska* en 1939 semblait avoir apaisé les conflits, mais l'éclatement de la guerre en 1941 mit fin à cette solution. La terreur instaurée par différentes milices nationales et par les armées occupantes pendant la Deuxième Guerre mondiale n'a fait qu'aggraver les hostilités entre les Croates et les Musulmans d'un côté et les Serbes de l'autre. La proclamation, par les partisans, de la Bosnie-Herzégovine comme un des Etats dans le cadre de la Fédération Yougoslave (1943) a pu sembler une solution acceptable pour tous. Cependant, une fois la guerre terminée, la politique centraliste (à dominance serbe) reprit avec le but de reléguer à l'arrière-plan tout particularisme ethnique, culturel ou linguistique.

2.2. Les autorités ottomanes faisaient la distinction entre plusieurs communautés 'nationales' (ethniques) sur la base de leur appartenance religieuse (*millet*): musulmans, orthodoxes (*Rum-milleti, Srb-milleti*), catholiques (*Katolik-milleti*), juifs. Ce n'est au 19ᵉ s. que les orthodoxes se sont identifiés avec les Serbes, et les catholiques avec les Croates. Jusqu'à la fin des années 60, les musulmans se déclaraient tantôt comme Croates (de leur nationalité) tantôt comme Serbes. En 1968, les autorités politiques de la Yougoslavie ont reconnu aux musulmans le statut de *peuple* (*Musulmans*), et par conséquent le statut du troisième peuple constitutif de l'Etat de Bosnie-Herzégovine. Bien que le nombre des Yougoslaves ethniques soit resté toujours assez élevé parmi les membres des trois confessions, la plupart des adeptes de l'Islam se déclarent, depuis cette époque, comme Musulmans (v. ch. 4.; Brozović 1982, 352).

3. Politique, économie et situations culturelle et religieuse en général

3.1. Dans une situation du chaos provoqué par une guerre (depuis 1992) sans fin prévisible, où toutes les valeurs humaines et civiques sont menacées, il est difficile de se prononcer sur la politique et l'économie, sur les relations culturelles et religieuses. D'après la Constitution, la Bosnie-Herzégovine est une République démocratique parlementaire. Cependant, il faut souligner que dans les élections libres de 1990 ce sont trois partis nationaux qui ont gagné la majorité des voix. Surtout après la Déclaration de l'indépendance, les partis mettent au premier plan les intérêts particuliers de leur propre peuple. C'est en accord avec cela que se sont cristallisées trois conceptions d'un Etat de Bosnie-Herzégovine. Les Serbes ont plaidé en faveur d'une Bosnie-Herzégovine faisant partie de la Yougoslavie, avec un minimum d'autonomie. Au commencement, les Musulmans ont défendu la conception d'une Bosnie comme unité fédérale de la Yougoslavie, pour pouvoir conserver la communication avec la population musulmane de Serbie et du Monténégro. Depuis que la guerre civile a éclaté en Bosnie (1992), les Musulmans plaident plutôt pour une Bosnie indépendante mais unitaire, pour un «Etat des citoyens». Les Croates défendent la conception d'une Bosnie-Herzégovine organisée comme Etat indépendant, mais un Etat où les trois peuples constitutifs bénéficieraient de droits égaux et d'une autonomie territoriale là où ils représentent la majorité de la population. Les divergences concernant l'organisation future de l'Etat représentent l'une des causes des conflits armés entre les Croates et les Musulmans à partir de 1993.

3.2. Les trois communautés confessionnelles, culturelles et nationales (musulmane, serbe orthodoxe et croate catholique) se sont développées l'une à côté de l'autre et se sont influencées réciproquement, mais elles sont restées nettement distinctes. Jusqu'en 1992, les mass media étaient imprégnés d'un esprit «yougoslave» qui avait de la répugnance pour tout particularisme ethnique, culturel ou linguistique. La législation de la République Socialiste de Bosnie-Herzégovine n'admettait pas l'existence de sociétés ou associations culturelles ou professionnelles basées sur le principe ethnique. L'esprit national ne se manifestait que par l'intermédiaire des associations et publications de caractère religieux (avant tout islamique et catholique) (Enc. Ju. 1982, 333). Le rôle des organismes religieux a considérablement augmenté depuis les élections de 1990. La petite communauté juive a joué un rôle très important dans la vie culturelle et intellectuelle du pays; mais ce n'est que de temps à autre qu'on publiait un recueil de folklore en judéo-espagnol moribond. Il n'y avait pas de publications dans les langues des autres minorités, sauf quelques manuels pour l'enseignement de l'ukrainien dans les écoles primaires (Strehaljuk 1984, 189).

4. Statistiques et profils ethniques

4.1. Les Croates, Serbes, Musulmans et Yougoslaves constituent plus de 97% de la population de la République. Les rapports numériques entre les communautés nationales pour la période après la Deuxième Guerre mondiale sont représentés dans le tableau 171.1.

Comme il ressort du tableau, le seul groupe à connaître un accroissement démographique régulier et très dynamique, au cours des deux dernières décennies, a été le groupe musulman. Bien que la population, au point de vue ethnique et confessionnel, soit mixte sur toute l'étendue de la République, il y a quelques aires géographiques plus ou moins «pures» ou à prédominance d'un seul peuple. L'extrême nord-ouest des deux côtés de la rivière Una est une zone à forte majorité musulmane (ville principale Bihać) et à minorité serbe et croate. Au sud-est de cette région et parallèlement avec elle, principalement à l'ouest et à l'est du cours inférieur de la rivière Vrbas (ville principale Banja Luka), se trouve une vaste zone à majorité ethnique serbe, mais avec d'importantes enclaves de Musulmans et de Croates. Ces deux zones constituent ce que les historiens appellent la *Croatie turque*. Des deux côtés du cours inférieur de la Bosnie habite une population à majorité croate (villes principales Bosanski Brod, Derventa, Orašje), mais avec un pourcentage assez élevé de Serbes et de Musulmans. Une autre aire à population croate compacte, et avec un certain nombre de Musulmans, se trouve en Herzégovine occidentale, à l'ouest de la Neretva, et en Bosnie centrale à l'ouest du cours supérieur de la rivière Bosna. La Herzégovine de l'Est a une majorité serbe, un certain nombre de Musulmans et un petit nombre de Croates. Le long du cours moyen et à l'est du cours supérieur de la Bosna, la population est en majorité musulmane mais aussi avec un pourcentage discret de Croates et de Serbes. Entre les rivières Bosna et Drina habitent surtout les Musulmans, de petits groupes de Croates et d'importantes et compactes enclaves serbes.

4.2. Les minorités ethniques et linguistiques sont représentées par un nombre réduit de personnes (moins de 40.000 personnes, moins de 1% de la population). D'après le recensement de 1981 (Enc. Ju. 1982, 142; Kovačec 1990, 243−245), les minorités de Bosnie-Herzégovine se répartissent comme l'indique le tableau 171.2.

Les Slovènes, les Macédoniens, les Monténégrins et les Albanais représentent une immigration récente (après 1945); ils ne disposent pas d'un «territoire à eux» et vivent dispersés sur le territoire de la République toute entière, avant tout dans les centres urbains. En 1993, la République de Slovénie a fait évacuer une bonne partie des Slovènes de Bosnie.

La présence des Tsiganes est attestée en Bosnie depuis le 15e s. (Enc. Ju. 1982, 232). La première colonie de Juifs espagnols (Sephardim) s'est constituée à Sarajevo dès le milieu du 16e s.; c'est à la fin du 18e et au cours du 19e s. que se sont formées des colonies juives aussi dans d'autres villes de la Bosnie-Herzégovine (Enc. Ju. 1982, 232; Kovačec 1968, 163, 165−166; 1987, 157). Les Ukrainiens, les Tchèques, les Slovaques, les Polonais, les Ruthènes, les Italiens, etc. se sont établis dans les parties septentrionales de

Tableau 171.1: Les ressortissants de la Bosnie-Herzégovine d'après leur appartenance nationale (1949−1991) (Enc. Ju. 1982, 142; Bertić 1987, 228−230; Klemenčić 1993, 123)

Année du recensement	1949	1953	1961	1971	1981	1991
Musulmans	788.403	−	842.248	1.482.430	1.630.033	1.905.829
Serbes	1.135.147	1.264.045	1.406.057	1.393.148	1.320.738	1.369.258
Croates	614.123	654.227	711.665	772.491	758.140	755.895
Yougoslaves	−	891.798	275.883	43.796	326.316	239.845
Autres	25.635	37.389	42.095	54.246	89.029	93.747
Total	2.563.308	2.847.459	3.277.948	3.746.111	4.124.256	4.364.574

Tableau 171.2: Les minorités nationales et ethniques en Bosnie (1981)

Minorités 'autochtones'	
Tsiganes	7.251
Ukrainiens	4.502
Ruthènes	111
Slovaques	350
Tchèques	690
Polonais	609
Italiens	616
Juifs	343
Au total	14.391

Minorités d'origine récente	
Monténégrins	14.114
Macédoniens	1.892
Slovènes	2.755
Albanais	4.394
Au total	23.155 (ou 0,65%)

la Bosnie sous la domination autrichienne à la fin du 19ᵉ s. (Enc. Ju. 1982, 232).

Les Tsiganes, les Sephardim, les Italiens, les Ukrainiens, les Ruthènes, les Tchèques, les Slovaques, les Polonais vivent dans des communautés plus ou moins compactes (leurs communautés habitent des villages, des parties de villages, des parties de villes). Les Bulgares (180 personnes), les Roumains (302), les Turcs (277), les Russes (295), les Allemands (460), les Hongrois (945) ne constituent plus que des groupes exigus bien que, jusqu'à la période de l'après-guerre (i. e. après 1945), les Allemands et les Hongrois firent partie du groupe des minorités autochtones.

5. Situation sociolinguistique

5.1. Jusqu'en 1992, la langue officielle de Bosnie-Herzégovine a été la « langue des trois peuples », désignée le plus souvent par le nom *serbocroate* (*srpskohrvatski*) (Brozović et Ivić 1990, 49, 87; Kovačec 1990, 242). On insistait sur le fait qu'il s'agissait d'une variante de la langue standard de Serbie, de Croatie et du Monténégro (Janković 1984, 50; Okuka 1984, 134–135), surtout dans des déclarations officielles. C'est de cette manière qu'on voulait rester fidèle aux principes promus par l'*Entente littéraire de Vienne* (*Bečki književni dogovor*; v. Vince 1990, 275–281), signée en 1850 par quelques écrivains et philologues serbes, croates et slovènes. La langue standard de Bosnie-Herzégovine est basée sur le dialecte štokavien (ou, plus précisément, néoštokavien) de l'Herzégovine de l'Est, et la prononciation est (en principe) « ijekavienne ». (Dans les parlers sud-slaves occidentaux, la voyelle protoslave *ě* (dont le correspondant paléoslave était la voyelle notée par la lettre *ѣ*, appelée « iat ») a abouti à trois résultats différents: *ije*, *e*, *i* (*tělo* « corps »: *tijelo*, *telo*, *tilo*); c'est en tenant compte de ces évolutions que les parlers štokaviens se divisent en *ije*kaviens, *e*kaviens ou *i*kaviens; les parlers de Bosnie-Herzégovine sont presque exclusivement *ije*kaviens ou *i*kaviens.) Au moins du point de vue formel, l'écriture latine et l'écriture cyrillique ont bénéficié du même statut. Dans la plupart des écoles, on accordait une importance particulière à l'apprentissage et à l'usage de l'alphabet cyrillique, tandis que dans les principaux journaux les textes en caractères cyrilliques alternaient presque obligatoirement et régulièrement avec ceux en caractères latins. Cependant, l'alphabet latin a été beaucoup plus employé que l'alphabet cyrillique, même parmi les Serbes.

Après 1945, la politique officielle tâchait d'unifier la langue de Bosnie en imposant le vocabulaire et les terminologies de type serbe (Brozović 1992, 358). On admettait un certain nombre de caractéristiques typiques de la langue des Musulmans, mais on procédait, en même temps, à un nettoyage des mots démarqués comme croates (*kazalište* « théâtre », *općina* « commune », *odvjetnik* « avocat », *nogomet* « football », *siječanj* « janvier », *tjedan* « semaine », etc. ont été remplacés, dans la langue des communications publiques et officielles, par les mots *pozorište*, *opština*, *advokat*, *fudbal*, *januar*, *nedjelja*, etc., mots caractéristiques de la norme serbe). L'introduction de la « Nouvelle orthographe » en 1960 (dès 1954, à Novi Sad) a imposé une orthographe commune au serbo-croate. Au moins en apparence, les Musulmans acceptaient cette orthographe, tandis que les Croates (toute résistance ouverte était impossible) se sont très souvent servis de deux sortes de langue: du serbocroate officiel dans les contacts et communications officiels et publics, et d'une forme plutôt croate dans les communications de type privé. Dans les communications de tous les jours, la plupart des Croates et une bonne partie des Musulmans se servent de la variété ikavienne du dialecte štokavien, tandis que presque tous les Serbes emploient la variété ijekavienne (Brozović 1992, 356, 358). Les parlers serbes sont généralement innovateurs et accusent plusieurs traits balkaniques, tandis que les parlers des Musulmans et des Croates sont très souvent conservateurs (prosodie, consonantisme, etc.). Après les élections libres en 1990, les Serbes désignent leur langue standard le plus souvent par le nom *serbe* (*srpski*), tandis que les Croates emploient, pour désigner leur propre langue, le glottonyme *croate* (*hrvatski*). Surtout ces derniers temps, les Musulmans désignent leur langue par le nom *bosniaque* (*bosanski, bošnjački jezik*; Isaković 1992, 26; Hadžiefendić 1993, 24−25; v. aussi Brozović 1992, 352).

5.2. Les langues des minorités ethniques sont parlées, généralement, par un nombre réduit de personnes vivant en petits groupes. Exception faite, partiellement, des Ukrainiens et des Tsiganes, ainsi que dans une moindre mesure des Tchèques et des Italiens, ces minorités ne disposent pas d'institutions et de mécanismes sociaux (école, église, une tradition folklorique à part, un mode de vie particulier, etc.) qui se servent de leur langue et qui soient capables de contribuer à sa conservation (Kovačec 1990, 247). Tous les membres des communautés minoritaires sont obligatoirement bilingues depuis la plus tendre enfance et ils parlent la « langue du pays », le plus souvent, sans accent. Malgré un enseignement rudimentaire en ukrainien, en italien et en tchèque jusqu'à 1992 (Strehaljuk 1984, 191), les Ukrainiens aussi bien que les Tchèques, les Polonais ou les Italiens ont parfois des difficultés à s'exprimer en leur propre langue dès qu'ils sont obligés de traiter de sujets plus sophistiqués (cf. Strehaljuk 1984, 189). Il faut noter aussi que, jusqu'en 1992, le judéo-espagnol n'a été parlé que par quelques dizaines de personnes plutôt âgées (Kovačec 1990, 245), et dans des circonstances plutôt exceptionnelles. Aujourd'hui, les derniers locuteurs du judéo-espagnol de Sarajevo se sont réfugiés en Israël, en Espagne, en Croatie (Split, Zagreb). Si pour les peuples de Bosnie-Herzégovine il existe une diglossie plus ou moins prononcée, elle consiste dans l'emploi de la langue standard alternant, chez les mêmes locuteurs, avec différentes formes régionales, sociales, confessionnelles, etc. du dialecte štokavien; le bilinguisme proprement dit ne concerne que les petites communautés des Ukrainiens, Tsiganes, Italiens, Tchèques, Sephardim, Polonais. Cependant, si l'on tient compte du nombre très restreint des situations où l'on peut se servir de l'ukrainien, de l'italien, du judéo-espagnol, etc., ainsi que du fait que les locuteurs des langues minoritaires n'ont pas de possibilité de se servir, sauf à l'école, des formes standard des langues en question, les idiomes des petites enclaves pourraient être envisagés comme 'dialectes' fonctionnels de la langue du pays.

6. Etat de la politique linguistique

6.1. La politique et l'aménagement (planification) linguistiques en Bosnie-Herzégovine ont été centrés, au moins jusqu'en 1992, sur les problèmes relatifs à la langue standard et officielle du pays, qui devait satisfaire les besoins des trois peuples. Ils suivaient généralement les grandes lignes de la politique linguistique conçue par le parti communiste et dirigée par les autorités fédérales de Belgrade. C'est en partant de l'« unité du serbo-croate », érigée en principe politique, qu'on voulait aboutir à l'unité linguistique des trois peuples de la Bosnie-Herzégovine. On se proposait de combattre tout « particularisme » linguistique, et cela aboutissait, dans la pratique de tous les jours, à l'élimination des éléments linguistiques relevant de la tradition croate et parfois aussi de celle des Musulmans. Dès les classes inférieures, l'enseignement se faisait sur des textes à empreinte serbe prononcée, les premières leçons de l'écriture commençaient par l'alphabet cyrillique (même dans les régions à majorité ethnique croate ou musulmane). C'est sur le modèle de l'orthographe serbe aux caractères cyrilliques, qui rend les noms propres romans et germaniques sous une forme phonique approximative, qu'on a basé la translittération latine de noms propres telsque *Šekspir, Gete, Igo, Bodler, Bokačo,* etc. pour *Shakespeare, Goethe, Hugo, Baudelaire, Boccaccio,* etc. Dans la syntaxe, on favorisait l'emploi du génitif aux dépens des autres cas obliques et des adjectifs relationnels, on évitait l'emploi de l'infinitif (typique pour l'usage croate) en le remplaçant par une proposition subordonnée (comme dans les langues balkaniques). La terminologie a été, bien entendu, de type serbe (cf. aussi Brozović 1992, 365−374). A côté de ces tendances unificatrices officielles, il faut relever trois types sous-jacents d'élaboration linguistique qui étaient (et le sont encore) les plus manifestes dans les publications religieuses. 1) Le type serbe a été le plus proche de la langue officielle, mais il puisait largement aussi aux sources lexicales du vieux-slave ecclésiastique et du russe et admettait d'une façon considérable l'emprunt. 2) Le type musulman évite les emprunts aux langues occidentales et favorise les dérivés à partir des éléments autochtones ainsi que les emprunts à l'arabe et au turc (cf. Isaković 1984, passim). 3) Quant au type croate, il est légèrement archaïsant (il ne faut pas oublier que, dès le 17ᵉ s., ou deux siècles avant la réforme de V. S. Karadžić, les franciscains de Bosnie ont élaboré une langue littéraire croate sur la base du dialecte štokavien; cf. Vince 1990, 43—46), il réduit au minimum les emprunts aux langues étrangères, admet largement le calque lexical et syntaxique (sur le latin, l'allemand, etc.), exploite les possibilités internes de la dérivation, tâche de suivre les normes linguistiques en vigueur en Croatie. Malgré le fait que les trois types d'élaboration se basent sur le même type structural de la langue (le dialecte štokavien), les différences réelles entre eux sont parfois considérables, surtout en ce qui concerne le vocabulaire et les terminologies (cf. Isaković 1992, 26). Néanmoins, ce qui compte le plus c'est la volonté de ces trois communautés nationales de se démarquer aussi par la langue: les idées concernant le statut linguistique de chaque communauté et les rapports entre elles sur le plan linguistique sont devenues une réalité dont toute politique linguistique devra tenir compte (cf. Isaković 1992, 26) et aussi, faut-il le souligner, toute recherche sociolinguistique.

6.2. La politique linguistique concernant les langues des minorités se proposait de protéger les droits des enclaves linguistiques (ukrainienne, tchèque, polonaise, italienne, tsigane), mais elle n'a pas apporté de résultats spectaculaires, très probablement à cause du fait qu'il s'agit de communautés minuscules. Le projet d'un enseignement en tsigane (Kovačec 1990, 246) a échoué faute d'une forme normalisée de cette langue (sur un total de 7.250 Tsiganes en Bosnie, il y a 1.360 personnes dans la commune de Bjeljina; la plupart des Tsiganes de Bosnie parlent le dialecte gurbet; Brozović 1989, 227). Ce ne sont que les Ukrainiens (dans les communes de Prnjavor, Banja Luka et Laktaši, 2.750 Ukrainiens vivaient dans des communautés plus ou moins compactes) qui ont bénéficié de ces efforts. Jusqu'en 1992, les Ukrainiens organisaient un enseignement régulier de leur langue dans plusieurs écoles primaires et, en collaboration avec les Ukrainiens et les Ruthènes de Croatie, des cours d'été de langue et de culture ukrainiennes. Dans quelques écoles des communes de Prnjavor et de Prijedor on organisait un enseignement du tchèque et de l'italien (dans le village de Štivor, commune de Prnjavor, 400 personnes parlent un dialecte trentin) pour un petit nombre d'élèves. Il n'y a pas eu de solutions semblables pour les Polonais (162 personnes dans la commune de Prnjavor), pour les Slovaques, les Allemands, etc. (Strehaljuk 1984, 191). La guerre qui a commencé en 1992 a supprimé ce type d'enseignement. Même avant 1992, la communauté judéo-espagnole a été réduite à quelques dizaines de personnes âgées de plus de 60 ans.

7. Présentation des contacts linguistiques

7.1. Depuis plusieurs siècles, les Croates, les Serbes et les Musulmans vivent mêlés dans de vastes zones de Bosnie-Herzégovine, parfois dans les mêmes agglomérations, et les influences réciproques entre trois traditions et trois types d'élaboration linguistiques à l'intérieur du même système social étaient inévitables. Les éléments lexicaux de provenance turco-arabe sont la conséquence de la domination ottomane en Bosnie-Herzégovine pendant plus de quatre siècles. Encore aujourd'hui, les Serbes et les Croates empruntent des éléments lexicaux d'origine orientale par l'intermédiaire de la langue des Musulmans. Si les Croates et les Serbes admettent un certain nombre d'éléments lexicaux (et de dérivation) d'origine turque et arabe, les Musulmans s'en servent largement, surtout quand il s'agit de sujets relatifs à la vie religieuse ou au mode de vie typique pour le monde islamique (Isaković 1992, 26; Hadžiefendić 1993, 25). La norme linguistique serbe de Bosnie se sert de nombreux mots provenant du vieux-slave ecclésiastique et du russe (il ne s'agit parfois que d'éléments caractérisés par un phonétisme particulier), et beaucoup de ces éléments sont acceptés aussi par les Musulmans (*uopšte* « en général », *opšti* à côté de *opći* « commun », *dejstvovati* « agir », *vinovnik* « coupable; instigateur », etc.). Au lieu de l'emprunt, l'usage croate préfère la dérivation à l'aide d'éléments autochtones et le calque lexical. L'usage d'éléments croates dans la « langue standard commune » (jusqu'en 1992) a été sujet à différentes sanctions (interventions des 'lecteurs' officiels des maisons d'édition ou des rédactions des mass-media); l'usage des mots typiquement croates (p. ex. *rujan* « septembre », *kolodvor* « gare », *tijekom* « au cours de » au lieu de *septembar*, *stanica*, *tokom*, etc.) équivalait, dans certains milieux, à un discrédit politique et social. Néanmoins, la tradition linguistique des Croates a laissé d'importantes traces surtout dans la langue écrite des Musulmans. Si l'on prend en considération aussi les lexiques techniques, les différences entre le vocabulaire des Croates et des Serbes, des Serbes et des Musulmans, des Croates et des Musulmans remontent à plusieurs milliers de paires (Isaković 1992, 26; Hadžiefendić 1993, 24−25), dont quelques centaines d'un usage courant. Ce type d'échanges « intralinguistiques » est dynamique, mais il est nécessaire de souligner qu'il varie d'un milieu à l'autre, d'un groupe social à l'autre, d'un locuteur à l'autre et il reste toujours assez flou. Les emprunts de ce genre jouent un grand rôle surtout dans la langue littéraire et dans le style des écrivains.

7.2. Les langues des minorités linguistiques sont exposées à une influence très forte de la langue du pays, principalement à cause du bilinguisme général (obligatoire) et actif de leurs locuteurs. C'est à cause des affinités structurales et lexicales entre les langues slaves que l'ukrainien, le ruthène, le tchèque et le polonais de Bosnie (la même chose vaut pour le slovène et le macédonien) utilisent un nombre important d'emprunts à la langue officielle du pays, un certain nombre de calques lexicaux et parfois même des éléments morphologiques (désinences de cas) ou structures syntaxiques (une subordonnée remplaçant l'infinitif) sur le modèle de la langue officielle (Barić 1986, 32, 35).

7.3. Le judéo-espagnol a laissé quelques traces dans la langue parlée des habitants non-juifs de Sarajevo. Ils désignent le judéo-espagnol par le nom *španjolski* (d'après *(e)spañól*, *(e)špañól* au lieu du plus courant *ǧidyó*, *léngua ǧudíya* dans la langue des Sephardim), pour le distinguer de *španski* « espagnol (d'Espagne) » (terme de provenance serbe). Jusqu'il y a peu, en voyant passer un Juif on se servait d'une expression partiellement tautologique *nálduga* « le voilà » (en judéo-espagnol *náldu* « le voilà », *nálda* « la voilà », etc. et *-ga* pron. pers. « le », du štokavien). Dans la langue populaire de Sarajevo on se sert parfois encore de l'expression *kayádu* pour dire « silence! » ou « en silence ». Si la guerre a dispersé les derniers locuteurs du judéo-espagnol de Sarajevo, l'histoire culturelle et économique de Bosnie gardera le souvenir de cette communauté aussi grâce à de nombreux noms de famille (*Abinun, Albahari, Alevi, Altarac, Baruh, Danon, Eškenazi, Finci, Gaon, Kabiljo, Kalderon, Katan, Konforti, Montiljo, Pardo, Perera*, etc.; Kovačec 1968, 174).

7.4. Bien que de date assez récente (Kovačec 1987, 158−159), l'influence de la langue slave de Bosnie sur le judéo-espagnol est plus importante du point de vue linguistique. Il faut signaler tout d'abord un grand nombre d'emprunts lexicaux, le plus souvent des termes techniques: *yagóda* « fraise » (štok. *jagoda*), *kobíla* « jument » (štok. *kobila*), *k(r)umpír* « pomme(s) de terre » (štok. *krumpir/krompir*, d'origine allemande), *snupítyos/snupíćos* « petites gerbes » (štok. *snop*, diminut. *snopić*), *ćumúr/tyumúr* « charbon de bois » (štok. *ćumur*, d'origine turque), *učitél* « instituteur » (štok. *učitelj*), etc. (Stankiewicz 1967, 77, 84−85, 88−89; Kovačec 1968, 175−176). Le terme *grahítas* « petits pois » (štok. *grašak*; à côté de *fávas*, qui a aussi la signification « fèves ») est en même temps un emprunt (*grah-* « haricot rouge ») et un calque approximatif (*grašak* est interprété et traduit comme diminutif de *grah: grahíta*). En judéo-espagnol de Sarajevo les calques lexicaux sont assez fréquents: *ambizadóra* « institutrice » (štok. *učiti* « enseigner » = j.-e. *ambizár*), *kái lúvya* « il pleut » (traduction litt. du štok. *pada kiša*, litt. « /il/ tombe la pluie »), *yevár kúdyo* (ou *kúydo*) « prendre soin de, s'occuper de » reproduit mot-à-mot l'expression štokavienne *voditi brigu* (litt. « mener soin ») (Kovačec 1987, 159). Bien que le système grammatical du judéo-espagnol reste assez stable devant l'influence slave, il faut signaler la formation des adverbes de manière en *-o* (*yorár dolorózo* « pleurer douloureusement », *entéro ótros* « complètement différents »), où le morphème štokavien *-o* a la fonction de l'esp. *-mente*. Dans la syntaxe, il faut signaler la perte progressive du subjonctif parce que le štokavien n'a pas de subjonctif (le judéo-espagnol de Sarajevo ne conserve que le subjonctif du présent et du passé composé; le subjonctif de l'imparfait n'apparaît que dans les romances et les dictons). Très souvent, on trouve un indicatif (comme en štokavien) là où l'on s'attendrait à un subjonctif (*kéru ki vyénis* « je veux que tu viennes», à côté du traditionnel *kéru ki véngas*). Le manque de la «concordance des temps» romane s'explique par l'influence štokavienne (*él mandó ki li digámus la vardá* «il /nous/ a ordonné de lui dire la vérité» comme en štok. *on je naredio da mu kažemo istinu*). Comme dans les langues balkaniques, l'infinitif tend à être remplacé par une proposition subordonnée (*él kéri ki vénga* «il veut venir» au lieu/à côté de *él kéri venír*, comme en serbe on *hoće da dođe*; *káli ke si fága* «il faut faire» au lieu/à côté de *káli fazér*, comme en serbe *treba da se učini*). Pour terminer, nous signalons aussi le fait que le judéo-espagnol de Bosnie a introduit, dans son système consonantique, les phonèmes palataux /ṯ, ḏ/ ou /ć, đ/ tout probablement sous l'influence du štokavien qui distingue /ć, đ/ et /č, ǧ/ (Kovačec 1987, 166–168). La langue tsigane de Bosnie utilise un grand nombre de mots empruntés au štokavien. Il semble qu'elle a adopté plusieurs traits grammaticaux du type balkanique (anticipation du complément d'objet par un pronom personnel, article postposé, formation du futur à l'aide de l'auxiliaire signifiant «vouloir», etc.) même avant l'arrivée des Tsiganes en Bosnie (Uhlik 1973, passim et → art. 239).

8. Examen critique de la bibliographie

8.1. Dans la République Socialiste de Bosnie-Herzégovine on attribuait, aux problèmes de la langue standard, une importance plutôt politique et sociale que strictement linguistique. La preuve en est le fait que dans une publication périodique de renommée internationale comme le sont, par exemple, les «Annales de l'Académie des Sciences et des Arts de Bosnie-Herzégovine» (*Godišnjak Akademije nauka i umjetnosti Bosne i Hercegovine*) on n'a presque rien publié à propos de ce sujet; la majorité des études traitant des problèmes de la langue standard de Bosnie ont été publiées dans des revues dédiées aux questions socio-politiques ou à la culture en général (p. ex. «Sveske», «Odjeci», etc.). D'autre part, les études traitant des langues standard des quatre républiques ex-yougoslaves ont à peine effleuré la question linguistique de Bosnie; on procédait le plus souvent comme si le problème de la langue standard de Bosnie pouvait se résoudre automatiquement par la fusion du serbe et du croate (cf. même Brozović et Ivić 1990). Les contributions qui, en partant d'un niveau théorique, ont tenu compte des réalités sur le terrain (Janković 1984; Okuka 1984) se réfèrent à la Bosnie-Herzégovine plutôt par allusion que d'une manière explicite. Rares sont les études (Brozović 1992) qui, en étudiant les langues standard du type štokavien, prêtent une attention nécessaire aussi à la langue standard de Bosnie. Du côté musulman on a dénoncé, au début, le fait que la politique linguistique officielle a complètement négligé la composante musulmane de la langue (Isaković 1984) pour empêcher la constitution de la «troisième variante du serbo-croate». Ces dernières années, les Musulmans ont réagi à cette politique d'une manière violente et parfois intransigeante (cf. Isaković 1992; Hadžiefendić 1993).

8.2. Exception faite du judéo-espagnol, on a peu étudié les idiomes des minorités de Bosnie. Il n'y a, que nous sachions, aucune étude linguistique consacrée au tchèque, au polonais ou au ruthène de Bosnie; pour l'italien (trentin) cf. Rosalio 1979. Sur l'ukrainien et le tsigane on a publié plusieurs articles traitant des questions de détail. Sauf pour le judéo-espagnol, l'ukrainien et le tsigane, nos assertions sur les idiomes des minorités se basent sur des informations orales ou puisées dans la bibliographie. Pour la linguistique de contact, l'étude de ces enclaves linguistiques représente un grand intérêt tant du point de vue structural que sociolinguistique.

9. Bibliographie (sélective)

Barić, Eugenija (1986): «Hrvatsko-srpski elementi u djelima Havrijila Kosteljnika» [Les éléments croato-serbes dans les œuvres de Havrijil Kosteljnik]. In: *Filologija 14*, 31–39.

Baruch, Kalmi (1930): «El judeo-español de Bosnia» [Le judéo-espagnol de Bosnie]. In: *Revista de filología española 17*, 115–151.

Bertić, Ivan (Ed.) (1987): *Veliki geografski atlas Jugoslavije* [Grand Atlas Géographique de la Yougoslavie], Zagreb.

Brozović, Dalibor (1984): «O nazivu jezika Srba, Hrvata, Muslimana i Crnogoraca» [A propos du nom de la langue des Serbes, des Croates, des Musulmans et des Monténégrins]. In: *Sveske 5–6*, 351–356.

Brozović, Dalibor (1989): «Sociolingvistički aspekti periodizacije romskog jezika» [Les aspects sociolinguistiques relatifs à la périodisation de la langue tsigane]. In: *Međunarodni naučni skup Jezik i kultura Roma / International Symposium on Romani Language and Culture ... (Sarajevo, 9—11. VI 1986)*, Šipka, M. (Ed.), 223—238.

Brozović, Dalibor (1992): «Serbo-Croatian as a pluricentric Language». In: *Pluricentric Languages. Differing Norms in Different Nations*, Clyne, M. (Ed.), Berlin/New York, 347—379.

Brozović, Dalibor/Ivić, Pavle (1990): «Jezik, srpskohrvatski/hrvatskosrpski, hrvatski ili srpski» [Langue, serbocroate/croatoserbe, croate ou serbe]. In: *Enciklopedija Jugoslavije*, Sirotković, J. (Ed.), Tome 6, Zagreb, 48—94.

Enc. Ju., 1982 = *Enciklopedija Jugoslavije*, Cecić, Ivo (Ed.), Tome 2, Zagreb, 108—375 (s. v. Bosna i Hercegovina; par un groupe d'auteurs; avec une bibliographie exhaustive par chapitres).

Hadžiefendić, R. (1993): «Jezik savršena kontinuiteta» [Une langue à une continuité parfaite]. In: *Behar II, 7*, 24—25.

Isaković, Alija (1984): «Leksika muslimanskih pisaca i naši pravopisi» [Le lexique des écrivains musulmans et nos manuels d'orthographe]. In: *Sveske 5—6*, 329—341.

Isaković, Alija (1992): «Bosanski jezik» [La langue bosniaque]. In: *Behar I, 3*, 26.

Janković, Srđan (1984): «Nacija i standardnojezička varijanta» [La nation et la variante de la langue standard]. In: *Sveske 5—6*, 49—60.

Klemenčić, Mladen (Ed.) (1993): *A concise Atlas of the Republic of Croatia and of the Republic of Bosnia and Herzegovina*, Zagreb.

Kovačec, August (1968): «Les Sephardim en Yougoslavie et leur langue». In: *Studia Romanica et Anglica Zagrabiensia 25—26*, 161—177.

Kovačec, August (1987): «Sobre el valor de las unidades [t] y [d] en el judeo-español de Sarajevo y Dubrovnik» [Sur la valeur des unités [t] et [d] dans le judéo-espagnol de Sarajevo et Dubrovnik]. In: *Studia Romanica et Anglica Zagrabiensia 32*, 157—169.

Kovačec, August (1990): «Jezici naroda, narodnosti i etničkih skupina u SFRJ» [Les langues des peuples, minorités nationales et groupes ethniques de la RSF de Yougoslavie]. In: *Enciklopedija Jugoslavije*, Sirotković, J. (Ed.), Tome 6, Zagreb, 241—249.

Pluka, Miloš (1984): «Jezička politika i vidovi njenog ispoljavanja u nas» [La politique linguistique et les aspects de ses manifestations chez nous]. In: *Sveske 5—6*, 133—137.

Peroche, Gregory (1992): *Histoire de la Croatie et des nations slaves du Sud*, Paris.

Rosalio, Maria Rita (1979): *Studi sul dialetto trentino di Štivor* (Bosnia), Florence.

Stankiewicz, Edward (1967): «Balkanski i slovenski elementi u judeo-španskom jeziku Jugoslavije» [Les éléments balkaniques et slaves dans la langue judéo-espagnole de Yougoslavie]. In: *Jevrejski almanah 7*, 84—91.

Strehaljuk, Vaso (1984): «Jezici narodnosti u našoj školi» [Les langues des minorités nationales dans l'enseignement scolaire de chez nous]. In: *Sveske 5—6*, 185—194.

Uhlik, Rade (1973): «Govori južnoslovenskih Cigana u okviru balkanskog jezičkog saveza» [Les parlers des Tsiganes yougoslaves dans le cadre de la ligue linguistique balkanique]. In: *Godišnjak Akademije nauka i umjetnosti Bosne i Hercegovine, Knjiga X, Centar za balkanološka istraživanja*, Knjiga 8, 53—108.

Vince, Zlatko (1990): *Putovima hrvatskoga književnoga jezika. Lingvističko-kulturno-povijesni prikaz filoloških škola i njihovih izbora. Drugo, dopunjeno izdanje* [En suivant les chemins d'évolution de la langue littéraire croate. Présentation linguistique, culturelle et historique des écoles philologiques et de leurs choix. Deuxième édition, augmentée], Zagreb.

August Kovačec, Zagreb (Croatie)

172. Macedonia

1. Geography and demography
2. Territorial history and national development
3. Politics, economy, general cultural and religious situation
4. Statistics and ethnoprofiles
5. Sociolinguistic situation
6. Language political situation
7. Language contact
8. Sources and discussion
9. Bibliography (selected)

1. Geography and demography

1.1. The Republic of Macedonia, which from 1944 to 1991 was an administrative unit within Yugoslavia, became officially independent on 17 November 1991. Except for the account of events prior to the partition of 1913 and observations on conflicts with neighboring countries (paragraph 2), the remainder of this discussion refers to the Republic of Macedonia as *Macedonia*. The Republic's boundaries with Albania, Serbia, Bulgaria, and Greece run along Mounts Jablanica, Korab, Šar, Skopska Crna Gora, Kozjak, Osogovo, Maleševo, Belasica, Kožuf, Nidže, and Lakes Ohrid and Prespa.

1.2. The current majority group, who call themselves *Makedonci* 'Macedonians', are descended from the Slavs who settled in the Balkan peninsula from north of the Carpathian range circa 550−630 A.D. Albanians claim autochthonous descent from the Illyrians, but evidence suggests that their language may be descended from a dialect of Dacian or Thracian that was pushed ahead of the invading Slavs (cf. Hamp 1982, 77 f). The Aromanians (Vlahs) claim to be descended of Romanized non-Greek or pre-Greek inhabitants of Macedonia, although it is also claimed that they are descended of Roman colonists or Romanized Dacians who migrated from north of the Danube. The Turkish dialects spoken in Macedonia are descended from Ottoman. Greeks claim that Ancient Macedonian was a dialect of Greek and that therefore the original (Indo-European) inhabitants of Macedonia were Greek, but evidence indicates that Ancient Macedonian was linguistically separate from what later became Greek (cf. Hamp 1990, 15; Ilievski 1993, 241 ff). Jews are known to have come to the region in ancient times but their modern language, Judezmo, descended from the Spanish spoken by Jews exiled from the Iberian peninsula in 1492. The Roms (Gypsies), who entered the Balkans no later than the late medieval period, emigrated from India some centuries before. Since World War II there has been a general shift of population from villages to towns and from both towns and villages to the capital. According to Velkovska (1991, 6), more than a quarter of the population (563, 301) lives in the Skopje region. There is also a tradition of men going abroad to earn a living. Serbs moved to northern Macedonia after World War I, and there was an influx of Macedonian and Vlah Christians from Aegean Macedonia in the wake of the Greek Civil War in 1948. Many Muslims, regardless of language, emigrated to Turkey after World War II. Since the uprising of 1981 in Kosovo, many Albanians have moved to Macedonia. Finally, since mid-1991 thousands of Serbo-Croatian-speaking victims of the Yugoslav war have fled to Macedonia (estimates vary from 60 000 to 150 000); → Language Map G.

2. Territorial history and national development

2.1. At the time of the Slavic invasions, the territory of Macedonia was part of the Byzantine Empire, after which it shifted between Greek and Slavic domination until the end of the fifteenth century, when it was incorporated into the Ottoman Empire. It remained there until the First Balkan War (1912), when Greece, Serbia, and Bulgaria pushed Turkey to its present location in Europe. In 1913 the allies fought the Second Balkan War over their conflicting territorial claims and partitioned Macedonia under the Treaty of Bucharest. During World War II, Yugoslav Macedonia was partitioned between Bulgaria and Albania. It was established as a Republic in 1944 (see 1.1.).

2.2. Modern Macedonian national consciousness has its origins in the nineteenth century. Under Ottoman rule, national identity was determined by *millet* 'religiously defined community'. The two principal *millets* of Macedonia were *Türk* 'Turkish', meaning 'Muslim' and *Rum* 'Greek', meaning 'Greek Orthodox Christian'. During the first third of the nineteenth century, Hellenizers, who used religion as a vehicle to impose Greek language, competed with Slavic activists, who sought to establish Slavic ethnic identity on the basis of language. The Slavic authors of this period in both Macedonia and Bulgaria called their vernacular language *Bulgarian*. As major centers of literary activity coalesced in northeastern Bulgaria and western Macedonia a rift between Macedonians and Bulgarians arose. The establishment of the Bulgarian Exarchate in 1870 marked the recognition of the Bulgarians as a distinct *millet*, but the definition was still religious. The earliest published statement of Macedonian identity dates from 1875; the first concrete proposal for a Macedonian literary language dates from 1903. References to Macedonian as a separate language by outsiders date to the beginning of this century (see Friedman 1985a, 32−35; 1993, 162 ff; Lunt 1986, 729 ff). It should be noted that the South Slavic dialects form a continuum along which there is no bundle of isoglosses so thick that mutual incomprehensibility results at two contiguous points. Thus the definition of the boundaries of a South Slavic *language* rely on geographic or other criteria. Macedonia was also the site of the Albanian Alphabet Conference of 1908 (held in Bitola), where the official adoption of the Latin alphabet (versus Arabic or Greek) was a crucial step in uniting Albanian national consciousness on the basis of language rather than dividing Albanians on the basis of religion (approximately 70% were Muslim, 20% Eastern Orthodox and 10% Catholic).

2.3. Following the partition of 1913, Macedonians and other ethnic groups were denied linguistic rights and pressured to assimilate to Greek, Bulgarian, or Serbian language and nationality. After the establishment of Macedonia as a republic within Yugoslavia in 1944, Macedonian was recognized as a language and ethnicity in Yugoslavia, Albania, and Bulgaria (in 1946), but with the Tito-Stalin break of 1948 Bulgaria repudiated the legitimacy of the Macedonian language, and later of Macedonian nationality. Bulgaria recognized the Republic of Macedonia in 1992 but continues to deny the existence of Macedonian nationality and to insist that Macedonian is a Bulgarian dialect. Greece has always officially denied the existence of Macedonian language and nationality, although a Macedonian primer was printed in Athens in 1925 in accordance with article 9 of the Treaty of Sèvres concerning minority language education. The book was never used and most copies were destroyed (Friedman 1993, 174). As of 1993, Greek persecution of Macedonians on its territory and crossing its borders and Greek harassment of Macedonia on the international scene are sources of tension. Relations between Macedonia and Serbia, while good during the post-1944 period, have grown increasingly strained. In 1988 there were polemics in the mass media (collected in Kosteski 1990) concerning the relationship of Serbo-Croatian to Macedonian: benign bilingualism or imposed assimilationism. Since then extremist Serbian politicians, who represent the second most powerful force in Serbian politics as of 1993, have publicly denied the legitimacy of Macedonian language and nationality and demanded a reabsorption of Macedonia into Serbia. Macedonia's relations with Albania have varied. Although teachers from the Republic of Macedonia were expelled and schools closed following the 1948 Tito-Stalin break, Albania did not repudiate the recognition of its Macedonian minority and there were a few schools through grade four. Relations were good in the 1970's but broken off following the Kosovo uprising of 1981 and then gradually reestablished. Albania officially recognized Macedonia in 1993. Some Macedonian Albanians declared an autonomous republic called *Ilirida* (from *Illyria* and *Dardania*) in western Macedonia in 1992, but this declaration remains moot.

3. Politics, economy and general cultural and religious situation

Macedonia is a parliamentary democracy. The numerous political parties can be characterized as belonging to two general types: ethnic-nationalist and reform-pluralist. Macedonia was the only republic in which ethnic-based parties did not win a majority in the 1990 Yugoslav elections (Mirčev 1992, 7). Language rights are a major concern of all political parties (cf. 6.1.). The combination of embargo against Serbia and Greek harassment have severely damaged Macedonia's economy and disrupted privatization. Although the poorest of the six former Yugoslav republics, Macedonia can meet basic food and energy needs through its own agricultural and coal resources. Because language-oriented institutions are government subsidized, Macedonia's economic situation has a direct impact on language policy and subsequently on inter-ethnic relations. Weak economy has impeded cultural activities. Lack of paper prevents publications and lack of funding prevents productions. The National Theater produces drama in Macedonian, the Theater of the Nationalities puts on productions in Albanian and Turkish. There have also been productions in Romani. There are folklore groups in various towns and places of work for all the ethnicities of Macedonia. The situation as reflected in the number of individual publications by language in Macedonia for 1987 was the following (*SGJ* 1988, 600): Macedonian (789), Serbo-Croatian (55), Albanian (51), Turkish (21), Slovenian (4), Hungarian (2), other languages (31). Most publications in other languages are in English, French, German, and Russian, although works in Vlah or Romani are occasionally published. During the 1980's cultural censorship, e. g. the forbidding of "nationalist" songs, was directed at Albanians in connection with the expansion of Serbia's Communist party policies into Macedonia (cf. 6.1.). Tension has also been occasioned by the public performance of Serbian nationalist songs. The majority of Macedonians belong to the Macedonian Orthodox Church. A minority of Macedonian-speakers are Muslims, some of whom identify with the Muslim nationality (see paragraph 4). The majority of Albanians, Turks, and Roms are Muslim, while Vlahs and Serbs are Orthodox Christian. There are also a few Catholics (mostly Albanian) and Protestants. Almost all Jews were deported and killed by the Nazis in 1943. Freedom of religion is guaranteed in article 19 of the Constitution and discrimination on the basis of religion is prohibited in article 54. The rise of multiparty politics has led to a resurgence of religious feeling and ecclesiastical power, including attempts at censoring performances deemed blasphemous. Macedonian nationalist politicians have come into conflict with Muslims over the use of Christian symbols as national.

4. Statistics and ethnoprofiles

4.1. The correspondence between declared ethnic group and language is not one-to-one because a member of one ethnic group may delcare a different language as mother tongue and the Muslim ethnic group is based on religion. The Census conducted on 31 March 1991 was boycotted by most Albanians, who believed that they would not be counted fairly. Some Albanian political groups now claim that Albanians constitute 40% of the population while the official statistics are based on projections. While the 1981 Yugoslav census gave figures for 24 ethnic groups and 26 mother tongues, the statistics available from the 1991 Macedonian census only distinguish 5 ethnic groups and do not give data on declared mother tongue. Table 172.1 gives the available figures for those languages and ethnic groups in Macedonia with populations over 5000 from the amended 1981 census (*SGJ* 1988, 441–42) and the preliminary results of the 1991 census (Velkovska 1991, 6).

According to Petrović (1992, 8), Muslim mother tongues in 1981 were the following: Serbo-Croatian (41.3%), Macedonian (38.1%), Albanian (12.6%), Turkish (5.6%). The remaining 2.4% probably had Romani.

Table 172.1: Language and ethnic groups in Macedonia

	1981 group	language	1991 group
Total	1909136	same	2033964
Macedonian	1279323	1334524	1328187
Albanian	377208	391829	441987
Turkish	86591	64907	77080
Romani	431125	37780	52103
Serbian	44468	63350	42775
Muslim	39513	–	31356
Vlah	6384	5931	7764
Remaining	32524	10815	52712

The 1981 figure for Serbo-Croatian mother tongue includes Croats and Montegrins, and the 1981 ethnic category 'Remaining' includes Yugoslavs, regionals, undeclared nationality, and unknown. The remaining languages recorded for the 1981 census included Bulgarian (1419), Greek (647), and 19 others.

4.2. There are a number of ethnolinguistic divisions that do not figure into census statistics, e. g. a group of Albanian-speakers called *Egipḱani/Eǵupci (Ǵupci)* who appear to be people of Romani descent, but who identify as a separate ethnic group and claim Egyptian descent. The majority of Macedonian Albanians are Gegs (North Albanians), but south of a line running between Struga and Debar they are Tosks (South Albanians). There are about sixty Turkish-speaking villages in southeastern Macedonia whose inhabitants identify as *Juruk* (Turkish *yürük* 'Janissary foot-soldier, nomad'). They are descended from Ottoman soldiers and other immigrants from Anatolia and form a distinct ethnos from other Turks in the area, whom they call *čitak* ('quarrelsome, vulgar' in Anatolian dialects) and whom they consider to be descended from earlier non-Turkish local populations. Linguistically, the Juruk dialects do not belong to the West Rumelian group, to which all the other Macedonian Turkish dialects belong, but form their own group closer to the dialects on which Standard Turkish is based. (Jašar-Nasteva 1986, 139; Friedman 1982, 71). There are a number of Romani-speaking groups, of whom the largest are the Arlija (Turkish *yerli* 'local'), Džambaz (Turkish *cambaz* 'horse-dealer, acrobat'), Burgudži (Turkish *burgucu* 'gimletmaker') and Gurbet (Turkish *gurbet* 'emigra-

Table 172.2: Districts with more than 10% non-Macedonian population (1991)

	Mac.	Alb.	Turk.	Rom.	Serb.	Other
Brod	68.01	0.30	21.39	0.13	0.20	9.87
Gostivar	16.89	62.70	10.75	1.81	0.32	7.53
Debar	11.98	43.97	21.13	4.90	0.20	15.82
Kičevo	39.30	45.92	7.69	1.20	0.53	5.36
Kruševo	57.77	7.61	12.80	0.52	0.38	20.92
Kumanovo	50.28	34.47	1.71	4.06	7.96	1.53
Radoviš	82.51	0.10	15.67	0.90	0.42	0.40
Resen	69.84	12.38	13.87	0.48	0.41	3.03
Skopje	61.84	17.61	4.08	5.28	3.86	7.23
Struga	52.66	42.85	1.64	0.84	0.17	1.84
Tetovo	22.09	71.10	2.81	1.46	0.73	1.80
Valandovo	78.30	0.40	13.14	0.08	2.45	2.63

tion'). Among the Vlahs, two linguistic groups can be distinguished: The Aromanians proper, who call themselves *Armîn*, and the Megleno-Romanians of the Gevgelija region, who number about 2000 in the Republic of Macedonia and call themselves *Vla* (pl. *Vlaš*) (Atanasov 1990, 4; Gołąb 1984a, 5−27).

4.3. According to the 1981 and 1991 censuses, there are Macedonians, Turks, Serbs, Muslims, and Roms in all thirty districts (*opština* 'commune') of Macedonia, Albanians in all but two districts (Probištip and Vinica), and Vlahs in all but 7 districts. Table 172.2 gives the percentages for those districts with more than 10% non-Macedonian population in 1991.

5. Sociolinguistic situation

5.1. According to the preamble of the Macedonian Constitution, Macedonians constitute a people (*narod*), other groups are nationalities (*narodnosti*), i. e. national minorities. The groups specifically mentioned are Albanians, Turks, Vlahs, and Roms. Other groups are subsumed under the term "others". Article 7 of the Constitution establishes Macedonian and its Cyrillic alphabet as official but allows for the additional official use of other languages in units of local self-government with a majority or „considerable number" of members of a nationality. Article 48 guarantees the protection of language rights of the nationalities. From an attitudinal point of view Romani and Vlah are at the bottom of the linguistic hierarchy, and all adults are multilingual. For Christians, Macedonian forms the next level, while for Muslims there is an intermediate level comprising Albanian and Turkish. Until recently, Turkish had higher status than Albanian. With the increased demographic and political importance of Albanian, however, this situation is generally reversed. Until 1991, Serbo-Croatian was above Macedonian as the dominant language in Yugoslavia. Macedonian has a peculiar status not described in sociolinguistic literature, namely that of 'threatened dominant language'. Due to Bulgarian, Greek, and right-wing Serbian propaganda combined with Albanian and Turkish linguistic demands backed by Albania and Turkey, respectively, many Macedonians perceive themselves as linguistically and culturally beleaguered in their own country and threatened with extermination outside of it. Moreover, when Macedonia was part of Yugoslavia, Macedonian was subordinate to Serbo-Croatian on the federal level and in various ways even in the republic (cf. Tollefson 1991, 188−99; but also Naylor 1992, 82).

5.2. Albanian political parties are demanding that Albanian be elevated to the status of *narod* alongside Macedonian. Serb political parties object to the fact that Serbs are not specifically named in the Constitution, while Macedonian nationalists object to what they perceive as linguistic threats from both Serbo-Croatian and Albanian. Remaining linguistic conflicts concern the implementation of educational and other official policies (cf. paragraph 6.). Moreover, conflicts that are essentially economic in nature fragment along ethnic lines. As a result, inter-ethnic stereotypes are for the most part negative, especially between Macedonians and Albanians, who perceive themselves as each threatened by the other. The Turks, who were perceived as the oppressors during the Ottoman period, are now looked on with nostalgia by Macedonians in comparison with the perceived Albanian threat. It is felt that the Turks encouraged multilingualism and that in Macedonian towns Turks spoke Macedonian just as Macedonians spoke Turkish. The Albanians, however, are perceived as relatively recent arrivals who refuse to learn Macedonian. The ethnic composition of Western Macedonia prior to World War II is the subject of considerable debate, and Macedonians for the most part do not learn Albanian.

5.3. Macedonian, Albanian and Turkish all have diglossic situations as do the Serbian dialects of Pehčevo in Eastern Macedonia spoken by refugees from Gallipoli settled there in 1922, and non-standard Serbian elsewhere in Macedonia. Literary Macedonian is based on the West-Central dialects but combines enough features from the Eastern dialects that all speakers have both literary and colloquial registers. Literary Albanian is based on the Tosk dialect of Korçë in Southern Albania with numerous elements from Geg and other Tosk dialects. In Macedonia, Albanians use their dialects in all but formal situations such as school, the mass media, and public speaking. The Turkish dialects of Macedonia differ significantly from the standard language, and the literary Turkish of Macedonia differs from standard Turkish (see 6.2.). Romani and Aromanian are both written languages in Macedonia, but they are not codified and as yet not taught in schools. Until 1991, all Yugoslav males learned Serbo-Croatian in the army, and the subject was compulsory in schools. In principle, then, monolingualism is only possible among older Macedonian, Albanian, and Turkish women in rural areas, but no study has been done on the number of functional monolinguals. Because of the position of Serbo-Croatian within Yugoslavia, Serbs in Macedonia could also be functionally monolingual (cf. Lunt 1984, 86). It should be emphasized, however, that Macedonia is at the heart of the Balkan contact zone and that multilingualism has been a fact of everyday life for many people for centuries (cf. Hamp 1989a, 44f; Gołąb 1984a, 10−16).

6. Language political situation

6.1. Article 48 of the Constitution guarantees the right to instruction in nationality languages in primary and secondary education and requires the study of Macedonian. The chief conflict revolves around the number of minority language classes available, the quality of Macedonian instruction in minority language schools, and the question of mother tongue versus national identity. During the 1980's, the number of Albanian and Turkish language classes was reduced. In 1983 it became obligatory for non-Macedonian schools to keep all records, public notices, etc. in Macedonian as well as any other language, and in 1989 a law was passed permitting only Macedonian in school records. The 1982 ruling requiring the use of Macedonian toponyms in minority language texts and media (e. g., *Skopje* for Albanian *Shkup*, Turkish *Üsküp*) is also a source of tension. Another problem is that some Macedonian-speaking Muslims are demanding Albanian or Turkish language schools for their children. This problem also arose at the end of World War II (Risteski 1988, 430−31) and is the result of religion taking precedence over language as the source of ethnic identification: Macedonian is associated with the Macedonian Orthodox Church and Albanian/Turkish with Islam. Moreover, this belief is being reinforced by the contention that Macedonian-speaking Muslims are not Islamicized Slavs but rather Slavicized Albanians/Turks. The available data does not support this, however. There has been no move to establish Aromanian classes or schools, but the Ministry of Education has begun efforts to introduce Romani as a language of study at the elementary and high school levels with the goal of eventually opening a university department. In 1989 Turkish and Albanian each had an hour and ten minutes of weekly TV programming. By early 1993, Romani and Vlah each had 25 minutes of weekly TV time and Albanian and Turkish TV air-time had each increased to about six hours a week. Before independence much air-time was devoted to foreign shows and to programs from other Yugoslav republics. Since independence there has been considerable increase in Macedonian-language programming. The mass media publication situation is illustrated by the fact that Skopje has two Macedonian-language dailies while the main Turkish and Albanian newspapers are tri-weekly. There is an irregular newspaper in Aromanian, and thus far Romani has been used in posters and books but not in mass media publications. Serbo-Croatian and Albanian publications from outside Macedonia are available in reduced numbers since the Yugoslav war began.

6.2. Romani is in the process of official standardization. The current proposal is that the base be Arlija but with morphological and lexical enrichment from other dialects. Prior to World War II, Geg had emerged as the basis of a Literary Albanian, and after the War this base continued to be elaborated in Yugoslavia while a Tosk-based standard was promulgated in Albania. In 1968, however, Albanian intellectuals in Yugoslavia voted to adopt the Tosk-based standard of Albania for the sake of ethnic unity (see Byron 1985, 60). In the case of Turkish, the main standardization problem is that puristic reforms which were later rejected in Turkey continue in use in Macedonia (Tanasković 1992, 157 f). Orthographically, Macedonian is differentiated from the other languages of Macedonia by the use of Cyrillic as opposed to a Latin alphabet. At times this becomes an issue of identity, since a Yugoslav Latinization is also used for Macedonian and objections have been raised to Macedonian public signs in Latin orthography rather than Cyrillic. Examples of mixing, e. g. Macedonian-language signs using Turkish orthography, occurred in some commercial neighborhoods, but are no longer to be seen. In 1993 a new Latinization using an acute accent where Yugoslav Latinization has ⟨j⟩ was introduced for international documents. Albanian and Turkish both use the standard orthographies for their languages. Romani is generally written in a Yugoslav Latin orthography, although there is an international, supradialectal orthography proposed at the Fourth World Romani Congress in Warsaw, 1990. Vlah is written with both Yugoslav and Romanian based orthographies.

7. Language contact

The Indo-European languages of Macedonia share a variety of structural and lexical features that result from centuries of contact in the Balkan *Sprachbund*. Exemplary are absence of an infinitive, analytic future with an invariant particle from the verb 'will', reduced case systems, analytic comparison of adjectives, morphological expression of definiteness, and loanwords and calques from Turkish. Even the Turkish dialects of Macedonia (except Juruk) display Balkan structural features, e. g. the use of the optative-subjunctive instead of the infinitive as in *Lâzımdır calışalım* for *Calışmamız lâzım* 'We need to work'. Modern contact phenomena reflect different types of dominance and intimacy. The tendency to pronounce Macedonian clear /l/ as palatal /l'/ results from Serbo-Croatian dominance aided by the fact that the Cyrillic grapheme for the Serbo-Croatian sound (љ) is identical to the grapheme for Macedonian clear /l/ (except before a front vowel). Similarly, use of interdental fricatives in Greek loanwords among the older generation of Megleno-Romanian speakers and substitution of dental stops in the younger generation represents a shift in dominance from Greek to Macedonian. On the other hand the shift of /ö/ to /e/ or /o/ in west Macedonian Turkish or of /ü/ to /i/ in the Albanian of northwest Macedonia result from intimate contact or possibly language shift (cf. 4.2.). The loss of /h/ in Albanian, Macedonian and Turkish (but not Vlah and Romani) dialects in western Macedonia may also be contact induced, as is probably the fixed antepenultimate accent of west Macedonian. On the morphological level, Macedonian has influenced Romani and Vlah in the formation of the superlative (the prefix *naj-* 'most'), Turkish has supplied productive derivational affixes to all the Balkan languages (e. g., *-dži* 'nomen actoris'), Macedonian and Vlah have mutually influenced one another in perfect formation (Macedonian calqued the Vlah construction in 'have', Vlah calqued a Macedonian construction using 'be'; see Gołąb 1984a, 135). Syntactically, the tendency to separate the subordinating clitic *da* 'that, to' from the verb phrase to which it is bound in Macedonian, especially in technical writing, is a result of Serbo-Croatian dominance. Turkish dialectal word order head-genitive (e. g. *annesi sultanın = majka mu na carot = nëna e mbretit* 'the mother of the king' versus standard Turkish *sultanın annesi*) has been calqued from Macedonian and Albanian through intimacy, while the colloquial Macedonian order genitive-head (*na carot majka mu*) is from previous Turkish dominance. All the contact languages have borrowed from one another lexically. In general Turkish, Greek and Slavic have penetrated the other languages in all types of vocabulary as the politically, culturally or numerically dominant languages for centuries, although the fact that Macedonian is now dominant in all spheres is reflected in current sociopolitical terminology and the reduction of many Turkisms and Hellenisms to colloquial, dialectal, archaic or ironic status. Pastoral terminology is often of Vlah origin, while Albanian and Romani have contributed significantly to Macedonian secret languages, e. g. the vocabularies used by members of certain trades and professions for carrying on private conversations in the presence of outsiders (see Jašar-Nasteva 1970). Slavic influence on Albanian is often from Serbo-Croatian due to its former position, its continued imposition in Kosovo, and the influence of Kosovar Albanian on that of Macedonia, e. g. *bauk i komunizmit* 'the bogeyman of communism' (versus Macedonian *bauč*, Albanian *gogol*).

8. Sources and discussion

8.1. Because questions of language are so intimately bound up with politics (see paragraphs 3 and 6), discussions of language contact are frequent in the mass media. The Macedonian, Albanian, and Turkish language press in Macedonia frequently carry articles about topics such as correct literary usage, the influence of contact languages, demands for minority language schools, and the use of minority languages in public arenas. Such publications are thus important sources of information on language contact and even when incorrect (e. g. confusing the Balkan Albanians with the Caucasian Albanians, the homonymy of whose ethnonyms is sheer coincidence) nonetheless reflect attitudes within Macedonia. On the scholarly level, publications such as *Makedonski jazik* and the *Prilozi* of the Macedonian Academy of Arts and Sciences also treat questions of contact phenomena. International scholarly discussion is marred by the fact that most Bulgarian and Greek scholars are incapable of separating politics from science. As a result, their publications on Macedonia reflect political agendas rather than serious studies, e. g. attempts to "prove" that Macedonian is a Bulgarian dialect, that Aromanians are really Greeks, etc. (see Lunt 1984, 87−95).

8.2. The items in the bibliography are selected for their recency and contain references to earlier works. Studies of language contact in Macedonia often place it in the context of the Balkan *Sprachbund*, although older studies and even some modern ones fail to distinguish Macedonian from Bulgarian and/or Serbian (see 2.3. and 8.1.). The classic study is Sandfeld (1930); Joseph (1992) gives a recent survey of the basic literature. Joseph (1983) represents the kind of detailed single-problem study combining diachronic and synchronic analysis that is needed for all the phenomena generally considered in the context of Balkan language contact. Koneski (1965, 170 ff; 1983, 50 ff, 78 ff, 97 ff) and Koneski, Vidoeski, and Jašar-Nasteva (1968) address contact issues specifically for Macedonian. Tomić (1991) treats verbal systems in Macedonian, Serbo-Croatian, Aromanian, Albanian, Turkish, Greek and Bulgarian. Macedonian-Vlah contact is covered by Gołąb (1984 b, 5−27; 1984 b) and Atanasov (1990, 240 ff), Macedonian-Turkish (and also Albanian-Turkish) by Jašar-Nasteva (1992) and Friedman (1986, 36−49, 56−58), Romani in Macedonia has been treated by Friedman (1985 b) and Boretzky (1989), Albanian in Macedonia is discussed by Ismajli (1991, 342 ff), Jašar-Nasteva (1970), and Jašar-Nasteva, Koneski and Vidoeski (1990); Serbian-Macedonian contact is treated in Korubin (1986, 40 ff) and Kosteski (1990).

Since this article was written, the final 1991 census figures have been published (Antonovska 1994), Egipḱani were recognized as a separate category (3307 in 1991), an extraordinary census was held in 1994 (preliminary results are being published), and there has been an increase in mass communications in all the minority languages. The Albanian newspaper is now a daily, a Romani newspaper has appeared sporadically, and there are numerous private sources of mass communication.

9. Bibliography (selected)

Antonovska, Svetlana et al. (1994): *Statistički godišnik na Republika Makedonija 1993* [Statistical yearbook of the Republic of Macedonia], Skopje.

Atanasov, Petar (1990): *Le mégleno-romain de nos jours*, Hamburg.

Boretzky, Norbert (1989): "Zum Interferenzverhalten des Romani". In: *Zeitschrift für Phonetik, Sprachwissenschaft und Kommunikationsforschung* 42, 357−74.

Byron, Janet (1985): "An overview of Language planning achievements among the Albanians of

Yugoslavia". In: *International Journal of the Sociology of Language* 52, 59–92.

Friedman, Victor A. (1982): "Balkanology and Turcology: West Rumelian Turkish in Yugoslavia as Reflected in Prescriptive Grammar". In: *Studies in Slavic and General Linguistics* 2, 1–77.

Friedman, Victor A. (1985a): "The Sociolinguistics of Literary Macedonian". In: *International Journal of the Sociology of Language* 52, 31–57.

Friedman, Victor A. (1985b): "Problems in the Codification of a Standard Romani Literary Language". In: *Papers from the Fourth and Fifth Annual Meetings: Gypsy Lore Society, North American Chapter*, Grumet, Joanne (Ed.), New York, 56–75.

Friedman, Victor A. (1986): "Turkish Influence in Modern Macedonian: The Current Situation and Its General Background". In: *Festschrift für Wolfgang Gesemann, Band 3, Beiträge zur slawischen Sprachwissenschaft und Kulturgeschichte*, Schaller, Helmut (Ed.), Munich, 85–108.

Friedman, Victor A. (1993): "The First Philological Conference for the Establishment of the Macedonian Alphabet and the Macedonian Literary Language: Its Precedents and Consequences". In: *The Earliest Stage of Language Planning: The "First Congress" Phenomenon*, Fishman, Joshua (Ed.), Berlin, 159–80.

Gołąb, Zbigniew (1984a): *The Arumanian Dialect of Kruševo in SR Macedonia SFR Yugoslavia*, Skopje.

Gołąb, Zbigniew (1984b): "South Slavic *da* + Indicative in Conditional Clauses and its General Linguistic Implications". In: *Papers for the V. Congress of Southeast European Studies*, Shangriladze, Kot K./Townsend, Erica W. (Eds.), Columbus, 170–98.

Hamp, Eric P. (1982): The Oldest Albanian Syntagma. In: *Balkansko ezikoznanie* 25, 77–79.

Hamp, Eric P. (1989a): "Postscriptum on *Ohrid*". In: *Zeitschrift für Balkanologie* 25(1), 42–43.

Hamp, Eric P. (1989b): "Yugoslavia – a Crossroads of Sprachbünde." In: *Zeitschrift für Balkanologie* 25(1), 44–47.

Hamp, Eric P. (1990): "The Need to Know an Answer before Starting a Comparison". In: *Papers from the 26th Regional Meeting on the Chicago Linguistic Society*, Ziolkowski, Michael/Noske, Manuela/Deaton, Karen (Eds.), Chicago, 9–24.

Ilievski, Petar H. (1993): "The Position of Ancient Macedonian." In: *Balkan Forum* 1(2), 241–54.

Ismajli, Rexhep (1991): "Mbi statusin e shqipes standarde në RSF të Jugosllavisë" [On the status of Standard Albanian in SFR Yugoslavia]. In: *Gjuhë dhe etni*, Prishtina, 327–368.

Jašar-Nasteva, Olivera (1970): "Za makedonskite tajni jazici" [On Macedonian secret languages]. In: *Godišen zbornik na Filozofskiot fakultet na Univerzitetot vo Skopje* 22, 553–69.

Jašar-Nasteva, Olivera (1986): "Prilog kon proučuvanjeto na Jurucite od Radoviško" [A contribution to the study of the Yuruks of the Radoviš region]. In: *Etnogenezata na Jurucite i nivnoto naseluvanje na Balkanot*, Krum Tomovski et al. (Eds.), Skopje, 125–146.

Jašar-Nasteva, Olivera (1992): "Soziolinguistische Aspekte des Makedonischen und der anderen Sprachen der Republik Makedonien". In: *Die Welt der Slaven* 37(16), 188–210.

Jašar-Nasteva, Olivera/Koneski, Blaže/Vidoeski, Božidar (1990): "Kontaktet e të folmeve maqedonase me të folmet shqipe" [Contacts of Macedonian dialects with Albanian dialects]. In: *Gjurmime albanologjike* 19, 55–63.

Joseph, Brian (1983): *The synchrony and diachrony of the Balkan infinitive*, Cambridge.

Joseph, Brian (1992): "Balkan Languages". In: *International Encyclopedia of Linguistics*, vol. 1, Bright, William (Ed.), Oxford, 153–55.

Koneski, Blaže (1965): *Istorija na makedonskiot jazik* [History of the Macedonian language], Skopje.

Koneski, Blaže (1983): *A Historical Phonology of the Macedonian Language*, Wiesbaden.

Koneski, Blaže/Vidoeski, Božo/Jašar-Nasteva, Olivera (1968): "Distribution des balkanismes en macédonien". In: *Actes du premier congrès international des études balkaniques et sud-est européens*, vol. 6, Gălăbov, I./Georgiev, V./Zaimov, J. (Eds.), Sofia, 517–546.

Korubin, Blagoja (1986): *Jazikot naš denešen* [Our language of today], Skopje.

Kosteski, Nikola (Ed.) (1990): *Zboruvame li makedonski?* [Do we speak Macedonian?], Ohrid.

Lunt, Horace (1984): "Some Sociolinguistic Aspects of Macedonian and Bulgarian". In: *Language and Literary Theory*, Stolz, Benjamin et al. (Eds.), Ann Arbor, 83–127.

Lunt, Horace (1986): "On Macedonian Language and Nationalism". In: *Slavic Review* 45, 729–34.

Mirčev, Dimitar (1992): "Ethnic Strife and the Disintegration of a National Elite", Paper presented at the conference Regime Transitions, Elites and Bureaucracy, Bamberg University, 23–25 April, 1992.

Naylor, Kenneth E. (1992): "The Sociolinguistic Situation in Yugoslavia, with Special Emphasis on Serbo-Croatian". In: *Language Planning in Yugoslavia*, Bugarski, Ranko/Hawkesworth, Celia (Eds.), Columbus, 80–92.

Petrović, Ruža (1992): "Nacionalni sastav stanovništva, 1991" [National composition of the population 1991], *Jugoslovenski pregled* 36, 3–22.

Risteski, Stojan (1988): *Sozdavanjeto na sovremeniot makedonski literaturen jazig* [The creation of the Macedonian literary language], Skopje.

Sandfeld, Kristian (1930): *Linguistique balkanique*, Paris.

SGJ (1988): *Statistički Godišnjak Jugoslavije* [Statistical yearbook of Yugoslavia], Vol. 35, Belgrade.

Tanasković, Darko (1992): "The Planning of Turkish as a Minority Language in Yugoslavia". In: *Language Planning in Yugoslavia*, Bugarski, Ranko/Hawkesworth, Celia (Eds.), Columbus, 140–61.

Tollefson, James W. (1991): *Planning language, planning inequality*, New York.

Tomić, Olga Mišeska (1991): "Contrastive reflexes in contact linguistics", *Languages in Contact and Contrast*, Ivir, Vladimir/Kalogjera, Damir (Eds.), Berlin, 451–67.

Velkovska, Vera (Ed.) (1991): *Broj i struktura na naselenieto vo Republika Makedonija po opštini i nacionalna pripadnost: Sostojba 31.03.1991 godina* [The number and structure of the population of the Republic of Macedonian according to district and national membership: Situation as of 31.03.1991], Skopje.

Victor A. Friedman, Chicago (USA)

173. Albanie

1. Géographie et démographie
2. Histoire
3. Situations politique, économique, culturelle et religieuse
4. Majorité et minorité ethnolinguistiques
5. Situation sociolinguistique
6. Situation politique des langues en contact
7. Contacts albano-grec, -macédonien et -aroumain
8. Evaluation critique de la bibliographie
9. Bibliographie (sélective)

1. Géographie et démographie

1.1. L'Albanie (albanais: *Shqipëri*) est située à l'ouest de la péninsule balkanique. Au nord, elle est limitée par la Serbie, et plus exactement par l'ancienne province autonome albanaise de Kosovo (*Kosovë*). A l'est, elle voisine avec la République de Macédoine, et au sud avec la Grèce. A l'ouest, elle est bordée par l'Adriatique et la mer Ionienne. Le canal d'Otranto, dont la largeur est de 75 km, sépare l'Albanie de l'Italie. La superficie du pays est de 28 748 km². 335 km séparent le nord de l'Albanie du sud et 150 km en séparent l'ouest de l'est.

Plus de trois quarts de la surface de l'Albanie sont couverts par de hautes montagnes qui dépassent 2000 mètres et qui font partie des Alpes Dinariques. Le long de la côte s'étend, du nord à Vlorë, une longue plaine, qui à la hauteur de Shkodër, Tiranë et Elbasan s'enfonce profondément dans les montagnes. Cette plaine, irriguée par de nombreux torrents, est humide (parfois marécageuse) et fertile.

Le sous-sol albanais est riche en chrome, ferro-nickel, bitume, pétrole et cuivre. Ceux-ci forment la base de l'industrie albanaise et en constituent les produits d'exportation les plus importants (centres: Tiranë, Ballsh, Kukës, Fier et Durrës, qui est en même temps le port principal). Outre la capitale Tiranë, les villes de Shkodër, Krujë, Elbasan, Berat, Korçë, Gjirokastër et Vlorë représentent les centres historiques et culturels les plus importants (→ carte linguistique G).

1.2. La population de l'Albanie s'élève à 3 180 000 habitants (avril 1989). Le pourcentage de l'accroissement naturel de la population est parmi les plus élevés d'Europe; il atteint 2,1% (seul le pourcentage des Albanais de Kosovo dépasse ce chiffre). Du point de vue ethnique et linguistique, la population de l'Albanie est assez homogène: selon le recensement de 1989, la population de la république est à 98% albanaise (Rehder, 1992, s. 14). Le reste se compose de minorités nationales ou ethniques, qu'elles soient grecque, macédonienne, monténégrine, italienne, arménienne, juive, valaque ou tzigane. Les recensements fiables font défaut et il est probable que les chiffres exagèrent le nombre d'Albanais ethniques au détriment des minorités (cf. 4.).

2. Histoire

2.1. Le territoire de l'Albanie actuelle était habité, dans l'antiquité, par les Illyriens, qui sont, comme l'admettent généralement les archéologues et les linguistes, les ancêtres des Albanais. Dès 168 av. J.-C., leur territoire fut incorporé dans la province romaine d'Illyricum, qui comprenait toute la partie occidentale de la péninsule balkanique. Après le partage de l'empire romain par Théodose en 395, la future Albanie fit partie de l'empire byzantin. Au cours des siècles, elle fut dévastée successivement par les Wisigoths, les Huns et les Avars. Des tribus slaves s'établirent dans les Balkans aux 6ᵉ et 7ᵉ siècles. Ils slavisèrent définitivement la partie septentrionale de l'ancienne Illyrie (la Yougoslavie) et modifièrent radicalement la composition ethnique des régions méridionales (Epire, Macédoine). Durant les siècles suivants, l'Albanie fut conquise et perdue par la Byzance et la Bulgarie, par les Normands (fin 11ᵉ−12ᵉ siècle), les Anjou (fin 13ᵉ−début 14ᵉ siècle) et les Serbes sous Stefan Dušan (1331−1355). Dans le même temps, des féodaux albanais autochtones tentaient en vain d'obtenir l'indépendance. Après l'invasion ottomane à la fin du 14ᵉ siècle, ils formèrent une alliance sous la direction de Gjergj Kastrioti−Skanderbeg (1405−1468) et furent ainsi en mesure de défendre leur liberté jusqu'en 1479. Sous la domination ottomane, une certaine forme d'autonomie put être maintenue par les Albanais.

2.2. A la suite de l'invasion slave, le territoire qu'occupèrent des masses compactes d'Illyriens/Albanais se reduisit à la moitié septentrionale de l'Albanie actuelle. Ils ne disparurent cependant pas complètement dans les régions limitrophes. Durant la période ottomane, la population albanaise connut une expansion considérable vers le Kosovo, la Macédoine et l'Epire. L'Albanie proprement dite restait assez hétérogène du point de vue ethnique. Des enclaves grecques et slaves pénétraient loin dans son territoire. La présence de semi-nomades valaques était également importante. Au cours des siècles, ces populations furent en grande partie albanisées.

2.3. Bien qu'il y eût des indications d'une prise de conscience nationale albanaise dès les années trente du 19ᵉ siècle, les historiens considèrent la fondation de la Ligue de Prizren, en 1878, comme le point de départ du mouvement national albanais. Cette Ligue, qui rassemblait des intellectuels et des notables albanais, avait pour but de défendre l'intégrité de la zone ethnique albanaise à l'intérieur des frontières de l'empire ottoman, et de lutter contre les revendications territoriales des pays voisins, dont les frontières furent tracées au Congrès de Berlin (juin 1878). Jusqu'à la veille des Guerres balkaniques (1912−1913), les Albanais ne cessèrent de réclamer au sultan l'autonomie des provinces albanaises. Durant la Première Guerre balkanique (1912−1913), le projet élaboré par le Monténégro, la Serbie, la Grèce et la Bulgarie pour se répartir le territoire albanais fut déjoué suite à la proclamation de l'indépendance albanaise le 28 novembre 1912. Le Traité de Londres (mai 1913) marqua la reconnaissance de l'Albanie par les puissances européennes. Néanmoins, une grande partie de la zone ethnique albanaise, notamment le Kosovo, où vivait un tiers des Albanais, fut attribuée à la Serbie. D'autre part, l'Epire du Nord fut rattachée à l'Albanie, bien qu'il y vécût une population grecque considérable. La Serbie, le Monténégro et la Grèce, ne pouvant se résigner à l'existence de l'Albanie ni à ses frontières, voulurent à nouveau se répartir le territoire albanais pendant la Première Guerre mondiale. Après celle-ci, en 1921, les anciennes frontières furent restaurées, à l'exception de quelques corrections mineures. L'un des territoires cédés par la Grèce à l'Albanie était la région à l'ouest du lac de Prespa, habitée principalement de Macédoniens. La Grèce ne reconnut les nouvelles frontières, y compris le rattachement de l'Epire du Nord, qu'en 1923. La Yougoslavie n'y consentit qu'en 1926.

2.4. Dans la période d'entre-deux-guerres, l'Albanie, gouvernée par le roi Zog, mena une politique de centralisation, qui aspirait à consolider la nation albanaise au détriment des minorités. Elle devint de plus en plus dépendante, politiquement et économiquement, de l'Italie. En 1939, l'armée italienne occupa le pays. En 1940, Mussolini lança son attaque contre la Grèce au départ de l'Albanie. Mais les forces italo-albanaises furent repoussées et la Grèce occupa l'Epire du Nord, avec l'intention de s'y installer définitivement. Après leur capitulation en avril 1941, les Grecs furent forcés d'abandonner la région; en outre, les Italiens confièrent l'administration de l'Epire du Sud − territoire grec peuplé par une minorité albanaise assez importante − au gouvernement albanais semi-autonome. A la suite de la capitulation de la Yougoslavie en 1941, qui précédait de quelques jours celle de la Grèce, le Kosovo fut également rattaché à l'Albanie. Ainsi tous les territoires habités par des Albanais étaient réunifiés.

2.5. Après la guerre, les anciennes frontières albanaises furent restaurées, mais la Yougoslavie et la Grèce émirent à nouveau quelques réticences. Les maquisards communistes albanais, qui avaient emporté la victoire sur les nazis, installèrent un régime stalinien, dominé depuis la fin de la guerre jusqu'à sa mort en 1985 par Enver Hoxha. L'Albanie collabora, au début, avec la Yougoslavie; puis, après la rupture entre Staline et Tito en 1948, elle opta pour l'Union Soviétique. En 1961, elle prit ses distances d'avec l'Union Soviétique pour s'allier à la Chine et ce jusqu'en 1978. Le projet (yougoslave) d'incorporer l'Albanie réunifiée au Kosovo à la fédération yougoslave, à titre de septième république, fut abandonné en 1948. L'Albanie, prenant le parti de Staline, secoua la tutelle de Belgrade, mais dut abandonner le Kosovo à la Yougoslavie. Athènes et Tirana ne conclurent formellement la paix qu'en 1987. A cette occasion, la Grèce renonça officiellement à ses revendications territoriales sur l'Epire du Nord.

3. Situations politique, économique, culturelle et religieuse

Jusqu'en 1990, l'Albanie était une dictature communiste du type stalinien. Le Parti du Travail d'Albanie exerçait un contrôle absolu dans tous les domaines de la vie politique, économique, sociale et culturelle. La propriété privée était défendue; les usines et les coopératives agricoles étaient nationalisées, les activités économiques centralisées et planifiées. Sur le plan culturel aussi, l'Albanie se modelait sur l'Union Soviétique stalinienne. L'ensemble du pays était complètement isolé. En 1967, la religion fut officiellement abolie. Prêtres et imams furent l'objet de persécutions, les églises et mosquées furent fermées ou détruites. En fait, le but était d'effacer les distinctions religieuses afin de créer une société albanaise homogène. Plus que marxiste, le régime de Hoxha était farouchement nationaliste, ce qui aggrava la situation des minorités.

1990 vit l'effondrement du système communiste albanais. Les minorités en profitèrent pour créer leurs propres organisations et avancer leurs propres revendications nationales (Pettifer 1994, 72−74). Les Grecs constituèrent même leur propre parti, le *Konkord* (en grec *Omonia*, « concorde »), qui fut rebaptisé *Union pour les Droits de l'Homme* en 1992, lorsque le gouvernement albanais interdit les partis « ethniques ». A l'heure actuelle, les minorités ethniques peuvent parler leur propre langue en public sans être importunées par la police; la nationalité des membres des minorités peut être indiquée dans leur passeport, s'ils le désirent; ils ont le droit de se rassembler et de se réunir, la liberté de presse et le droit de voyager à l'étranger et d'y établir des contacts culturels, commerciaux et autres. D'autre part, le pluripartisme a encore renforcé les réflexes nationalistes, albanais et grecs. Les partis de droite albanais veulent limiter les droits culturels et civils de la minorité grecque. Simultanément, l'irrédentisme grec à l'égard de Epire du Nord, resurgi, nourri surtout par le clergé et parfois soutenu par des Grecs de l'Albanie, pèse sur les relations entre l'Albanie et la Grèce, et sur celles entre les Albanais et les Grecs en Albanie même. En avril 1993, l'archevêque de l'Eglise orthodoxe albanaise, citoyen grec, fut accusé d'avoir propagé le séparatisme et fut obligé de quitter le pays. En outre, la situation économique du pays, catastrophique, ne permet pour le moment ni l'amélioration de l'enseignement, ni la subvention de publications dans les langues minoritaires, ni l'élévation du niveau de vie en général. Quelques centaines de milliers d'Albanais (grecs et albanais) ont cherché et trouvé, souvent clandestinement, du travail en Grèce. Le fait que le consulat préfère donner des visas aux membres de la minorité grecque a amené même des Albanais musulmans à se faire passer pour des Grecs. A la suite du séjour prolongé de milliers d'Albanais, surtout mâles, comme travailleurs en Grèce, la connaissance de la langue grecque en Albanie s'est répandue considérablement.

4. Majorité et minorité ethnolinguistiques

4.1. Les Albanais, qui s'appellent eux-mêmes *shqiptarë* (sing. *shqiptar'*), parlent l'albanais (*shqipe*), une langue indo-européenne qui, selon toute probabilité, dérive de l'illyrien antique. L'albanais se partage en deux groupes de dialectes: le guègue (*gegërishte*), parlé au nord de la rivière Shkumbin (y compris dans le Kosovo), et le tosque (*toskerishte*), parlé dans le sud (cf. 7).

Sur le plan religeux, 70% des Albanais, des Guegues surtout, sont musulmans; 17% sont chrétiens orthodoxes (tosques) et 10% sont catholiques (des Guègues de la région de Shkodër) (Poulton 1991, 193). Il s'agit ici, bien entendu, d'affiliations religieuses plutôt historiques que réelles, bien qu'à présent, les religions en Albanie soient en train de se rétablir. En profitent aussi les bektachi, secte islamique qui a toujours été très répandue en Albanie.

4.2. La minorité grecque, la plus répandue de l'Albanie, comptait en 1989 officiellement 59 000 personnes (1,9% de la population), un chiffre qui, sans aucun doute, est inférieur à la réalité. Aux élections parlementaires en 1992, le parti grec remporta 54 000 voix, ce qui suggère, comme l'ont admis les autorités albanaises mêmes, que la minorité grecque compte au moins 100 000 personnes (Austin/ Engelbrekt/Perry 1994, 19). Partant des résultats du recensement organisé par la Société des Nations en 1922, et tenant compte de l'accroissement naturel de la population, on arrive à un nombre de 200 000 personnes d'origine grecque (ce qui ne dit rien, évidemment, de leur conscience nationale ni de leur connaissance de la langue albanaise). Par ailleurs, le nombre de 400 000 que donnent les associations des émigrés grecs de l'Epire du Nord, ainsi que l'Eglise grecque, semble exagéré, incorporant manifestement comme grecs tous ou en tout cas la plupart des croyants orthodoxes d'Albanie, même s'ils sont d'expression albanaise. Les Grecs sont tous orthodoxes.

La minorité grecque habite le sud de l'Albanie, notamment la région de Korçë (grec Korytsa), de Gjirokastër (grec Argyrokastro), de Himarë (grec Himara) et de Saranda (grec Agii Saranda). Elle se concentre surtout dans la région de Dropull, qui s'étend de Gjirokastër vers le sud, ou il y a une centaine de villages grecs, homogènes ou à population mixte albanaise-grecque. Les centres urbains les plus importants sont Sofratikë et Vrisera.

4.3. La minorité slave en Albanie est représentée par des Monténégrins dans la région de Shkodër (serbe Skadar), dans le nord du pays, et par des Macédoniens (appelés «Bulgares» dans la littérature ancienne) dans le sud-est du pays.

4.3.1. Le nombre des Monténégrins est inconnu. Au début de 1991 se constitua à Vraka une association monténégrine, qui rassemble plus de 1000 membres, un chiffre qui n'est qu'une vague indication de leur nombre total.

4.3.2. Concernant le nombre des Macédoniens, on ne dispose pas de chiffres officiels sûrs. Ceux fournis par d'autres sources sont assez divergents. Dans son discours devant le 7e Congrès du Parti du Travail Albanais en 1975, le leader albanais Enver Hoxha faisait mention de 3000 à 4000 Macédoniens, installés dans neuf villages de la région de Prespa. Selon le recensement de 1983, il y avait 11 000 Macédoniens (0,4% de la population); en 1989, ils n'étaient plus que 6000 (0,2%), chiffre qui comprenait en outre les Valaques, les Tziganes et les autres minorités à l'exclusion des Grecs. Popovski (1981, 247) évalue leur nombre à 45 000. Des observateurs neutres estiment que leur nombre va de 10 000 à 20 000 (Poulton 1991, 201).

Les Pomaks (Macédoniens islamisés), dont le nombre est probablement plus élevé, sont considérés et traités comme des Albanais par le gouvernement. Etant donné que les Pomaks en Bulgarie et en Grèce ont tendance à s'assimiler assez facilement à la population islamique environnante (turque), il n'est pas exclu que les Pomaks albanais se soient de leur côté assimilés aux Albanais islamiques déjà avant la guerre.

Les Macédoniens habitent quatre régions voisines, mais non liées entre elles: la large région entre Debar (en albanais Dibër), en République Macédoine, Peshkopi et Elbasan (environ 25 villages); la région de Korçë (presque 20 villages); la région de Pogradec, à la rive occidentale du lac d'Ohrid (environ 15 villages à population mixte); la région de Prespa (environ 15 villages, dont 10 macédoniens et 5 mixtes) (Popovski 1981, 240−242). Ce n'est que dans cette dernière région que la population macédonienne est encore compacte et relativement bien conservée. Les Macédoniens dispersés dans les villes se sont albanisés.

4.4. Les Valaques, un peuple souvent confondu avec les Albanais ou les Tziganes dans les sources anciennes, parlent une langue romane, l'aroumain, parente du roumain. Voici quelques générations, les Valaques menaient encore une vie semi-nomade, appelée *transhumance*: ils passaient les hivers dans leurs maisons dans les vallées et les étés en errant dans les montagnes avec leurs troupeaux (→ art. 183). La fermeture des frontières et la nationalisation de l'économie ont mis fin à ce mode de vie traditionnel. Selon le recensement de 1983, il y avait en Albanie 14 000 Valaques; en 1989 leur nombre était ramené à quelques milliers. Cependant, selon les experts, il y en aurait encore environ

35 000. On les trouve dispersés dans les villes situées surtout au sud de l'Albanie. La population est relativement dense dans la région de Kolonja, au sud-est du pays (Winnifrith 1987, 35).

Au 17ᵉ et au 18ᵉ siècles, les Valaques sédentaires formaient une communauté nombreuse et riche, dont le centre culturel était Voskopojë, mieux connu sous le nom grec Moschopolis. (Les Valaques utilisaient le grec comme langue culturelle). Au cours du 19ᵉ siècle, la plupart d'entre eux furent assimilés par la population albanaise environnante.

4.5. Le nombre de Tziganes est estimé à 5000 environ, mais quelques spécialistes donnent le chiffre de 50 000 (Gronenmayer, Rakelman 1988, 207), ce qui est plus vraisemblable, vu le nombre de Tziganes dans les pays limitrophes.

4.6. Le nombre de Juifs et d'Arméniens ne surpasse pas quelques centaines. Après l'effondrement du communisme, presque tous les Juifs ont quitté l'Albanie pour Israël.

5. Situation sociolinguistique

5.1. Avant la Deuxième Guerre mondiale, les deux (groupes de) dialectes albanais, le tosque et le guègue, avaient le même statut social et culturel, le guègue étant peut-être plus lié avec les centres culturels catholiques du nord et avec les Albanais musulmans, le tosque avec les orthodoxes du sud. Les deux dialectes s'utilisaient comme langue littéraire. Après la guerre, le guègue a été supplanté par le tosque, devenu la langue standardisée, mais il semble exister une grande tolérance sur le plan de la langue parlée.

5.2. Dans le passé, le grec était la langue liturgique des Albanais orthodoxes et la langue de la couche sociale supérieure de commerçants grecs ou grécisés dans les villes. Le grec était aussi la langue obligatoire de l'instruction parmi les Albanais orthodoxes. Au 19ᵉ siècle, à la suite de l'immigration massive de villageois albanophones, les villes furent progressivement albanisées. Aujourd'hui, les Grecs ne sont plus majoritaires dans les villes; en outre, les Grecs citadins sont bilingues. La plus grande partie de la population grecque de l'Albanie est rurale. Bien que dans les régions grecques les Grecs soient majoritaires dans la plupart des villages, surtout à Dropull, des villages grecs homogènes sont plutôt rares. Seulement des gens âgés (et surtout des femmes) ne parlent que le grec.

5.3. Bien que les minorités nationales et ethniques soient reconnues et leurs droits garantis par la Constitution de 1946, l'Albanie, en tant qu'Etat national du peuple albanais, a toujours aspiré à créer une nation albanaise homogène. Sous le prétexte marxiste de « la lutte contre les préjugés religieux », lancée en 1967, se cachait une politique de dénationalisation. Ainsi, en 1975, les noms géographiques (de villes, villages, rivières, montagnes, etc.) à caractère religieux, ainsi que les noms propres et les noms de famille religieux, furent « albanisés ». Cette mesure touchait surtout la minorité grecque, la foi orthodoxe étant la pierre angulaire de sa conscience nationale.

Dans une large mesure, la situation des minorités et de leurs langues dépendait des relations que Tirana entretenait avec leurs « patries » respectives. Ainsi, l'enseignement en grec s'améliora dans une certaine mesure dans les années quatre-vingts, lorsque le gouvernement socialiste de Papandhreou normalisa les relations entre la Grèce et l'Albanie. Les relations avec les Slaves (et avec les Monténégrins en particulier) furent toujours plus tendues. Entre 1945 et 1948, alors que l'Albanie et la Yougoslavie étaient toutes deux membres du bloc communiste et collaboraient étroitement, les Albanais encouragèrent l'enseignement en macédonien dans 13 villages de la région de Prespa. Des manuels en macédonien furent importés de Yougoslavie; des instituteurs macédoniens furent invités à donner des cours en Albanie. Après la résolution anti-yougoslave de Staline en juillet 1948, l'enseignement en macédonien fut tout à coup supprimé. Dans les années soixante, l'enseignement en macédonien fut réintroduit sur une échelle beaucoup plus modeste. Il n'est pas exclu que, dans les années quatre-vingts, le traitement imposé aux Slaves en Albanie fût implicitement lié à celui qu'imposèrent les Serbes aux Albanais au Kosovo.

6. Situation politique des langues en contact

6.1. L'albanais est la seule langue officielle en Albanie: langue de l'administration, de la justice, de l'enseignement, des medias, etc. A l'heure actuelle, ses normes orthographiques et grammaticales sont bien fixées. Au 19ᵉ siècle, l'albanais s'écrivait en caractères arabes, grecs ou latins, selon les convictions religieuses des auteurs. Il existait aussi nombre d'orthographes personnelles, aux caractères souvent fantastiques. L'alphabet de Naim Frashëri dit « d'Istanbul » de 1879 − fondamentalement latin, mais contenant quelques caractères grecs et originaux − introduisait le principe phonématique. L'alphabet albanais « définitif », latin, accepté au Congrès de Manastir (Bitola) en 1908, contenait deux caractères à signe diacritique (ë et ç) et neuf digrammes (*dh, gj, ll, nj, rr, sh, th, xh, zh*). Le Congrès orthographique de 1972 y apportait des améliorations mineures. Le même congrès fixa également les normes grammaticales de la « langue littéraire nationale ». Celle-ci fut basée sur le tosque − la langue de la plupart des leaders politiques d'après-guerre − mais elle emprunta nombre d'éléments lexicaux et grammaticaux au guègue, la langue des missions catholiques dans la région de Shkodër, très actives au 19ᵉ et au début du 20ᵉ siècle dans le domaine de l'éducation et de la littérature, qui avait une tradition littéraire plus longue et riche que le tosque.

6.2. Bien que l'albanais soit la seule langue officielle, les langues minoritaires sont officiellement reconnues. Leur pratique, cependant, est limitée; en fait, elles sont devenues des langues vernaculaires. Le plus haut degré d'institutionnalisation est atteint par le grec. Ceci est dû à la présence importante de Grecs en Albanie et à leur conscience nationale très développée, ainsi qu'aux interventions diplomatiques grecques en leur défense. Sous la domination ottomane, les écoles grecques étaient fréquentées également par des Albanais orthodoxes qui n'étaient pas autorisés à avoir leurs propres écoles. Après l'Indépendance, les écoles grecques devinrent des écoles minoritaires. En 1922, il y en avait encore 36 (Poulton 1991, 199). En 1993, une loi ordonna la fermeture de toutes les écoles grecques privées. (Des écoles grecques d'Etat continuèrent à exister.) Sur la demande de la Grèce, la Société des Nations força l'Albanie à abroger sa décision. Après la Deuxième Guerre mondiale, l'enseignement albanais fut nationalisé. L'enseignement en grec n'était organisé que dans la région de Dropull où la minorité grecque est la plus dense. Jusqu'en 1992, les cours en grec se limitaient aux quatre premières années de l'école primaire; dans les quatre années suivantes, la langue de l'instruction était obligatoirement l'albanais; les cours de langue grecque se limitaient à quelques heures par semaine. En 1992, suite à des protestations de l'*Union pour les Droits de l'Homme* et du gouvernement grec, les autorités albanaises ont consenti à augmenter le nombre des années scolaires, pendant lesquelles tous les cours peuvent être donnés en grec, de quatre à cinq. L'*Union pour les Droits de l'Homme* a exigé également que la littérature et l'histoire grecques soient enseignées. L'institut pédagogique (c.-à-d. l'école normale) de Gjirokastër héberge une section de philologie grecque, qui prépare les enseignants grecs. Depuis 1945 paraît à Gjirokastër, deux fois par semaine, le journal *Laiko Vima* (Tribune populaire), entièrement rédigé en grec. Dans les écoles des villages macédoniens de la région de Prespa, des cours sont donnés en macédonien dans les quatre premières années de l'école primaire. Edités à Tiranë, les manuels, qu'on y utilise, sont rédigés dans le dialecte local et non pas dans le macédonien standard de la République de Macédoine.

On enseigne en aroumain dans les deux premières années des écoles primaires dans quelques villages valaques aux environs de Gjirokastër, Saranda et Korçë (Winnifrith 1987, 35). Cependant, mis à part les manuels, on ne note aucune publication en macédonien ou en aroumain.

L'existence minimale d'un enseignement dans les langues minoritaires n'a pas empêché le gouvernement communiste de poursuivre une politique d'assimilation conséquente − et efficace. Cet enseignement ne fut organisé que là où l'ensemble de la population du village était grec, macédonien ou valaque. En même temps, on « encouragea » les Albanais à s'établir dans les villages des minorités, alors que les membres de ces mêmes minorités furent systématiquement mis au travail loin de leur terre natale et où ils étaient tenus de parler l'albanais. L'utilisation des langues minoritaires en public fut découragée, parfois même défendue. Avant 1990, les Macédoniens ne pouvaient se rendre dans la République (yougoslave) de Macédoine, et encore moins en importer des livres en macédonien. Les Valaques non plus n'avaient l'autorisation d'entrer en contact avec les Valaques des pays voisins. Ainsi, l'isolation culturelle qui pesait sur tous les citoyens de l'Albanie avait surtout pour les minoritées macédonienne et valaque un effet concomitant d'assimilation.

7. Contacts albano-grec, -macédonien et -aroumain

7.1. L'albanais appartient à l'union linguistique balkanique: il partage avec le grec, le macédonien, l'aroumain (et les autres langues balkaniques) la tendance à l'analytisme, l'emploi de l'article défini adjoint (pas en grec), des éléments morpho-syntaxiques, etc. En ce qui concerne l'albanais même, il existe, comme nous l'avons déjà mentionné, deux (groupes de) dialectes, le tosque et le guègue. Les différences, mineures mais nettes, sont d'ordre phonologique surtout: la préservation des anciennes voyelles nasales en guègue, perdues en tosque, le développement de /n/ intervocalique en /r/ en tosque (rhotacisme tosque), la préservation de la voyelle /ə/ (écrit *ë*) en position non-accentuée et des consonnes sonores finales en tosque, etc. Sur le plan morphologique et syntaxique, le tosque semble avoir plus de traits typiquement « balkaniques », p. ex. le futur périphrastique composé de particule + verbe conjugué (*do të punoj*) « je travaillerai », là où le guègue préfère une construction avec le verbe *habeo* + infinitif (*kam me punue*), du type roman; l'emploi, dans la langue parlée, de l'aoriste en tosque au lieu du parfait en guègue; l'emploi d'une construction hypotactique en tosque là où le guègue préfère l'infinitif (substantif verbal), etc.

7.2. Les contacts linguistiques albano-grecs en Albanie n'ont pas fait l'objet d'une étude approfondie. Hamp (1967, 664−665) a attiré l'attention sur quelques particularités des dialectes albanais méridionaux qui s'expliquent par la proximité du grec: la neutralisation de l'opposition *y* /ü/ et *i*; l'emploi de l'imparfait (morphologique) de *jam* (être) et *kam* (avoir) pour exprimer l'aoriste, pendant que les autres dialectes albanais possèdent des formes distinctes de l'aoriste de *jam* et *kam*.

7.3. Les contacts linguistiques albano-macédoniens ont été étudiés du point de vue diachronique et de manière comparative, dans le cadre de l'étude de l'union linguistique balkanique. Les données de caractère sociolinguistique récentes sont rares. On dispose, cependant, du livre de A. M. Seliščev (1931), qui a étudié en détail les phénomènes récursifs des contacts entre l'albanais et le macédonien (qu'il appelle « bulgare »); nombre d'entre eux sont encore en vigueur. Les dialectes albanais de l'Albanie du Sud contiennent des éléments lexicaux spécifiques, qui ne s'expliquent que parce que ces dialectes sont parlés par une population d'origine slave, qui, après une période de bilinguisme, s'est finalement albanisée. Comme Courthiade (1988, 152) a pu constater, ce processus est encore en plein déroulement. L'albanais a emprunté au slave des noms qui désignent des objets nouveaux (surtout dans le domaine de l'agriculture); d'autre part, de nombreux mots albanais se virent attribuer un doublet d'origine slave, doté d'une valeur affective spécifique. C'est ainsi qu'une partie de la terminologie sexuelle de l'albanais est empruntée au slave (Seliščev 1931, 193−195).

7.4. Il n'y a pas d'informations sur les contacts socio-linguistiques albano-aroumains.

8. Evaluation critique de la bibliographie

La description synchronique la plus exhaustive de la langue albanaise est sans aucun doute Buchholz et Fiedler (1987). Hamp (1967) a étudié les relations linguistiques de l'albanais avec les autres langues balkaniques. Vatasescu (1979) a étudié des mots aroumains dans les argots albanais professionnels. Exception faite de la littérature grecque irrédentiste et plutôt pamphlétaire sur la minorité grecque d'Albanie du Sud, les sources concernant les autres populations minoritaires d'Albanie sont rares. La littérature albanaise minimalise leurs nombres et essaie de nous convaincre que celles-ci bénéficient de tous leurs droits minoritaires, et aussi que la sauvegarde de leurs langues serait garantie. D'autre part, les pays voisins qui ont des minorités en Albanie ont tendance à dépeindre d'une manière tendancieuse le sort auquel ces minorités étaient soumises, en expliquant immuablement l'oppression, propre à la dictature communiste, en termes de tensions ethniques et d'assimilation forcée. Les deux points de vue sont souvent influencés par le type de relations existant entre les deux pays concernés. Ainsi, la critique qu'émet la Grèce sur le traitement de la minorité grecque fut très atténuée sous le gouvernement de Papandhreou (1981−1989), qui voulait à tout prix normaliser les relations gréco-albanaises.

Pourtant, la situation des Grecs ne s'améliora qu'à peine et le grec continua à être dénigré. De son côté, le gouvernement albanais admit à cette époque implicitement que la minorité grecque en Albanie était plus importante qu'il ne l'avait prétendu.

Signalons encore que les historiens et linguistes bulgares considèrent les dialectes slaves, parlés en Albanie, comme étant bulgares.

9. Bibliographie (sélective)

Austin, Robert/Engelberkt, Kjell/Perry, Duncan M. (1994): «Albania's Greek Minority». In: *RFE/RL Research Report*, 3, No 11, 19–24.

Buchholz, Oda/Fiedler, Wilfried (1987): *Albanische Grammatik*, Berlin.

Byron, Janet I. (1976): *Selection among alternates in language standardization: the case of Albanian*, La Haye.

Byron, Janet I. (1979): «Language planning in Albania and in Albanian-speaking Yugoslavia». In: *Word* 30, 15–44.

Courthiade, Marcel (1988): «Les derniers vestiges du parler slave de Boboščica et Drenovøne (Albanie)». In: *Revue d'Etudes Slaves* LX, No 1, 139–157.

Fjalori enciklopedik shqiptar [Dictionnaire encyclopédique albanais] (1985), Tiranë.

Hamp, Eric (1967): «La langue albanaise et ses voisins». In: *Actes du Premier Congrès International des Etudes balkaniques et sud-est européennes*, 6 Linguistique, Sofia, 663–668.

Horak, Stephan M. (1985): «National Minorities in Albania». In: *East European National Minorities: 1919–1980*, Horak, S. M. (Ed.), Colorado, 309–313.

Pettifer, James (1994): *Albania. Blue guide*. Londres/New York.

Popovski, Tošo (1981): *Makedonskoto nacionalno malcinstvo vo Bugarija. Grcija i Albanija* [La minorite nationale macédonienne en Bulgarie. Grèce et Albanie], Skopje.

Poulton, Hugh (1991): *The Balkans. Minorities and States in Conflict*, Londres.

Rehder, Peter (Ed.) (1992): *Das neue Osteuropa von A–Z*, Munich.

Seliščev, Afanasi M. (1931): *Slavjanskoe naselenie v Albanii* [La population slave d'Albanie], Sofia.

Tamas, André (1938): «La Roumanie et la minorité roumaine en Albanie». In: *Voix des Peuples Minoritaires* 5, 79–89.

Vatasescu, Cătălina (1979): «Macedo-Romanian words in Albanian slangs». In: *Revue des Etudes sud-est européennes* 17, 409–16.

Weigand, Gustav (1888): *Die Aromunen*. Leipzig (2 vol.).

Winnifrith, Tom J. (1987): *The Vlachs. The history of a Balkan people*, Londres.

Raymond Detrez, Louvain (Belgique)

174. Rumänien

1. Geographie und Demographie
2. Territorialgeschichte und Staatsbildung
3. Politik, Wirtschaft und allgemeine kulturelle sowie religiöse Lage
4. Statistik und Ethnoprofile
5. Soziolinguistische Lage
6. Sprachpolitische Lage
7. Sonstige Sprachkontakte
8. Wertung der Quellen und Literatur
9. Bibliographie (in Auswahl)

1. Geographie und Demographie

Rumänien ist ein in Südosteuropa gelegener mittelgroßer Staat (Gesamtfläche: 237 500 km^2), der in seiner heutigen Gestalt eine Ausdehnung von etwa 500 km in nord-südlicher und 600 km in west-östlicher Richtung hat. Im Norden und Nordosten stößt das Land an die Ukraine und Moldova (im Dt. auch Moldawien genannt), also Nachfolgestaaten der ehemaligen UdSSR, im Süden an Bulgarien, im Südwesten und Westen an (Rest-)Jugoslavien und Ungarn. Im Osten ist auf rund 250 km Länge das Schwarze Meer die Landesgrenze. Rumänien liegt somit an einer Schnittstelle zwischen Mittel-, Ost- und Südeuropa, so daß das Land von alters her von wichtigen Handelswegen durchzogen wurde. Geographisch wird Rumänien beherrscht vor allem vom Karpatenbogen, der das hügelige Siebenbürgische Becken (Transsilvanien) als zentralen Raum umschließt. Den Karpaten, deren höchste Erhebungen 2500 m erreichen, vorgelagert sind größere Hügelländer oder Ebenen – im Nordosten die Moldauische Platte, im Süden und Südosten die Walachische Ebene, an die sich der Mittelgebirgshorst der Dobrudscha anschließt, im Westen schließlich grenzt an die Munţi Apuseni das Pannonische Becken an. Insgesamt ergibt sich ungefähr eine Dreiteilung zwischen Gebirgsregionen (30%), Hügelland (37%) und Tiefebenen (33%) (Blanc 1973, 10−26).

Nach der Volkszählung von 1992 hat Rumänien 22 760 449 Einwohner (statistische Angaben zur Bevölkerungsstruktur nach Baratta 1993, ältere Vergleichszahlen nach Jackson/Happel 1977), was eine Bevölkerungsdichte von 96 pro km² ergibt; damit gehört das Land − wie auch die anderen Staaten Südosteuropas (zum Vergleich etwa: Bulgarien 81, (Rest-)Jugoslawien 102) − zu den weniger dicht besiedelten Ländern Europas. Bedeutend ist aber der Bevölkerungsanstieg in Rumänien seit dem Ende des Zweiten Weltkriegs: Von 1948 bis 1992 ist die Bevölkerungszahl um fast die Hälfte von 15,9 auf 22,8 Mill. angestiegen (im Vergleich dazu ist etwa in Bulgarien die Bevölkerung im gleichen Zeitraum nur um gut 20% gewachsen). Neben der deutlichen Senkung der Kindersterblichkeitsrate von 14,3% auf 3,3% sind hierfür vor allem bevölkerungspolitische Maßnahmen während der Ceauşescu-Ära (1965−1989) verantwortlich. Dies zeigt sich auch darin, daß der Anteil der Kinder (bis 14 Jahre) an der Gesamtbevölkerung mit 23,1% ungewöhnlich hoch ist (zum Vergleich Deutschland: 16,2%). Tiefgreifende wirtschaftliche Veränderungen haben bewirkt, daß bei der letzten Volkszählung der Anteil der städtischen Bevölkerung erstmals mehr als die Hälfte der Gesamtbevölkerung betrug (53%; im Vergleich dazu 1948 nur 23,4%).

Nach der Verfassung vom 8.12.1991 ist Rumänien eine Republik. Das Parlament (*Marea Adunare Naţională*) besteht aus zwei Kammern, der Deputiertenversammlung sowie dem Senat. Administrativ ist das Land in 40 Kreise (*judeţe*) sowie das Municipium Bukarest gegliedert (→ Sprachenkarte H).

2. Territorialgeschichte und Staatsbildung

Innerhalb Europas gibt es keinen Großraum, in dem die Verbindung von Volk und Staat so komplex ist wie gerade in Südosteuropa. Analog zu den meisten anderen Staaten dieser Region ist Rumänien ein junges Gebilde, das seine Entstehung letztendlich den Verwerfungen im Gefolge des Niedergangs des Osmanischen Reiches und dem aufkommenden Nationalismus im Balkanraum verdankt.

Wie in mehreren Nachbarländern sind damit aber auch Keime für spätere − zumeist ethnisch begründete − gewalttätige Auseinandersetzungen zwischen verschiedenen Volksgruppen gelegt, die im Laufe der letzten 100 Jahre noch für territoriale Veränderungen gesorgt haben. Die Beschäftigung mit der jüngeren Geschichte Rumäniens darf aber nicht den Blick darauf verbauen, daß die verschiedenen territorialen Einheiten (Moldau, Walachei, Siebenbürgen, Dobrudscha, Bukowina, Bessarabien) seit dem ausgehenden Mittelalter entweder gemeinsam oder eigenständig oder als Teil eines fremden Herrschaftsgebiets eine wichtige Rolle gespielt haben, wobei ethnische Probleme meist von großer Bedeutung waren.

2.1. Die rumänische Ethnogenese

Die rumänische Ethnogenese ist ein bis auf den heutigen Tag umstrittenes und vielfach auch politisiertes Problem. Indirekt ist damit nämlich die Frage verbunden, ob Ungarn oder Rumänen früher in Siebenbürgen siedelten, was als Argument bei Auseinandersetzungen häufig benutzt wurde (noch heute werden in rumänischen Publikationen Ungarn und Deutsche in Siebenbürgen gerne als „Einwanderer" bezeichnet).

Nachdem die Römer schon seit geraumer Zeit Teile des Gebiets südlich der Donau besetzt hatten, gelang es ihnen erst mit den Feldzügen Trajans in den Jahren 105/106, das nördlich der Donau liegende Dakien zu erobern und dem Imperium Romanum einzugliedern. Die Herrschaft der Römer über die norddanubischen Gebiete dauerte jedoch nur knapp 170 Jahre, denn bereits 271 mußte Kaiser Aurelian die römischen Truppen wieder auf das südliche Ufer zurückziehen und die Provinz Dacia aufgeben. Die Frage ist nun, ob es eine Kontinuität des romanischen Elementes im Gebiet des heutigen Rumänien seit der Zeit der römischen Herrschaft gegeben hat (was vor allem von rumänischen Forschern vehement vertreten wird) oder ob die romanisierte Bevölkerungsschicht nach der Aufgabe der römischen Provinz in die Gebiete südlich der Donau zog, wo sie sich mit der dortigen − ebenfalls romanisierten − Bevölkerung vermischte. Erst später habe dann eine (Rück-) Wanderung von den südlich der Donau gelegenen Gebieten in die nördlichen stattgefunden. Für diese Migrationsthese, die vor allem außerhalb Rumäniens (Ungarn, Deutschland, Frankreich) Anhänger fand, sprechen mehrere Argumente:

— spätrömische Geschichtsquellen des 4. Jahrhunderts (Flavius Vopiscus, Eutropius, Sextus Rufus) sprechen davon, daß Aurelian bei der Aufgabe der Provinz die „Römer" in die süddanubischen Gebiete umgesiedelt hätte. Hiergegen läßt sich allerdings einwenden, daß zum einen die Autoren keine Zeitzeugen waren und daß zum anderen damit nicht unbedingt gemeint sein muß, daß wirklich die gesamte romanisierte Bevölkerung die Gebiete nördlich der Donau verlassen hat.
— Schwerwiegender ist das Argument des „Schweigens der Jahrhunderte": Erst byzantinische Chronisten des 11./12. Jahrhunderts erwähnen eine romanisierte Bevölkerung (*Vlachen*, Βλάχοι) nördlich der Donau; auch fehlen Toponyme, die auf die römische Epoche zurückgehen.
— Die starken Gemeinsamkeiten, die das Rumänische mit den anderen Balkansprachen („Balkansprachbund"), vor allem mit dem Albanischen und dem Bulgarischen, aufweist, legen nahe, daß das Rumänische nicht nur mit dem Bulgarischen, sondern früher auch mit dem Albanischen in unmittelbarem Kontakt gelebt hat. Wenn man auch davon ausgehen kann, daß das Albanische nicht an der Adriaküste, wo es heute verbreitet ist, entstanden ist, sondern weiter im Innern der Balkanhalbinsel, so wird man doch die Urheimat der Albaner nicht nördlich der Donau suchen. Auch die Existenz der drei süddanubischen Varietäten des Rumänischen (Aromunisch, Megleno- und Istrorumänisch) legt nahe, daß die Urheimat der Rumänen südlich der Donau zu suchen ist.

In sprachgeographischen Untersuchungen auf der Basis der Materialien der rumänischen Sprachatlanten wurde später versucht, einen Mittelweg zwischen Kontinuitäts- und Migrationstheorie zu gehen, indem die Existenz mehrerer Kerngebiete nördlich und südlich der Donau postuliert wurde, und neuerdings schlug Niculescu (1992) eine „continuité mobile" vor, in der die traditionelle Lebensweise der Rumänen als Hirtenvolk Berücksichtigung findet.

2.2. Die rumänischen Territorien bis zur Vereinigung der Donaufürstentümer

Die angedeutete Lücke in den Quellen verhindert es, präzisere Angaben zur Geschichte des heutigen Rumänien in der Zeit zwischen dem 4. und 10. Jahrhundert zu machen, doch darf man wohl davon ausgehen, daß es keine staatliche Autorität gab, sondern mehr oder weniger autonome „communités rurales" (Castellan 1984, 8). Gepiden, Hunnen und Awaren zogen durch das Gebiet des heutigen Rumänien, bevor sich seit dem 6. Jahrhundert Slaven ansiedelten. Aus der darauf folgenden langen romanisch-slavischen Kontaktsituation sind zahlreiche Slavismen des Rumänischen zu erklären. Die Gründung eines rumänischen Staates wurde zunächst verhindert durch die übermächtigen Nachbarn: im Nordosten das Tatarenreich, im Süden Byzanz bzw. das Zweite Bulgarische Reich, im Westen das Königreich Ungarn, das seine Eroberungen in Siebenbürgen u. a. durch die systematische Ansiedlung von Deutschen ab dem 11./12. Jahrhundert zu sichern versuchte. Erst im 14. Jahrhundert gelingt es dem Voivoden Basarab I., in der Walachei das erste selbständige rumänische Fürstentum aufzubauen, rund 50 Jahre später folgt die Moldau als zweiter rumänischer Staat. Mit dem Erstarken des Osmanischen Reiches kündigt sich dann aber schon bald das Ende der Zeit der rumänischen Eigenständigkeit an. Ab der ersten Hälfte des 16. Jahrhunderts geraten sowohl die Walachei wie auch die Moldau in immer größere Abhängigkeit von der Pforte, unterbrochen lediglich durch kurze Phasen wie etwa die Regierungszeit Michaels des Tapferen (Mihai Viteazul, 1593—1601), dem es gelingt, Walachei, Moldau und Siebenbürgen kurzfristig zu vereinen. Ein besonderes Kapitel stellt die Zeit von 1711 bis 1821 dar, als die beiden Fürstentümer von griechischen Statthaltern, den Phanarioten (benannt nach dem Stadtteil Phanar in Konstantinopel), verwaltet wurden, was einen starken Einfluß des Griechischen zur Folge hat.

Im Gegensatz zur Walachei und zur Moldau bleibt Siebenbürgen bis zum Ende des 17. Jahrhunderts (abgesehen von dem kurzen Intermezzo der Herrschaft Michaels des Tapferen) in den Händen einheimischer ungarischer Fürsten. 1691 schließlich fällt Siebenbürgen als Kronprovinz an das Haus Habsburg, das sich schon bald mit massiven Forderungen der rumänischen Bevölkerungsgruppe nach Gleichstellung mit den „nationes" der Magyaren, Sachsen und Szekler (Angehörige eines magyarisierten Turkvolks, die die Grenzen vor allem in den Ostkarpaten sichern sollten), die seit der „unio trium nationum" (1437) privilegiert waren, konfrontiert sieht. Sichtbaren Ausdruck finden diese Bemühungen in der Bittschrift „Supplex Libellus Valachorum transsylvaniensium"

(1791), in der u. a. die Kontinuität des rumänischen Volkes in Siebenbürgen seit der Antike als Argument angeführt wird.

Das 19. Jahrhundert ist geprägt durch den Kampf um die Gründung eines rumänischen Nationalstaates, der am Ende des Jahrhunderts (1878) dann auch tatsächlich erreicht wird. Wichtige Komponenten in diesem Kampf sind der Latinismus der Siebenbürger Schule (*școala ardeleană*) sowie die starke Orientierung an Frankreich in der Walachei und Moldau. Die Phanariotenherrschaft findet 1821 nach einem erfolgreichen Aufstand ihr Ende, nunmehr herrschen rumänische Fürsten unter osmanischer Oberhoheit in der Walachei und Moldau. 1859 wird Alexander Ion Cuza nacheinander zunächst zum Fürsten der Moldau, dann zum Fürsten der Walachei gewählt — die Union der beiden rumänischen Fürstentümer ist damit perfekt.

2.3. Rumänien seit der staatlichen Einigung

Die volle Souveränität erhält Rumänien, das seit 1866 von der Hohenzollerndynastie (Karl von Hohenzollern-Sigmaringen) beherrscht wird, mit dem Berliner Kongreß 1878, wobei Rumänien allerdings Südbessarabien an Rußland abtreten muß. In Siebenbürgen hingegen werden den Rumänen nach dem „Ausgleich" zwischen Österreich und Ungarn mit dem ungarischen Nationalitätengesetz von 1868 zuvor gewährte Rechte wieder genommen. Dies führt zu irredentistischen Strömungen unter den Rumänen Siebenbürgens, wobei die orthodoxe Kirche eine bedeutende Rolle spielt.

Der Erste Weltkrieg, in dem sich Rumänien lange neutral verhält, bevor es 1916 Österreich-Ungarn den Krieg erklärt, beschert dem Land mit dem Zugewinn nicht nur Siebenbürgens, sondern auch Bessarabiens, der Bukowina und der Süddobrudscha eine beträchtliche Vergrößerung: Im Vergleich zu 1913 wachsen sowohl das Staatsgebiet als auch die Bevölkerungszahl jeweils um mehr als das Doppelte. Hinzu kommt durch die Zugewinnung von Rohstoffquellen und Industriegebieten eine völlig veränderte sozioökonomische Struktur des Landes (Huber 1973, 111), durch die Einbeziehung fremder Nationalitäten jedoch auch eine Quelle latenter Unruhe. Der Zweite Weltkrieg, in dessen Verlauf Rumänien territoriale Zugewinne (im Osten) wie Verluste (im Westen) zu verzeichnen hat, revidiert einen Teil der Ergebnisse (Abtretung Bessarabiens und der Bukowina an die UdSSR, der Süddobrudscha an Bulgarien), beläßt dem Land, das von 1947 bis zum Sturz Ceaușescus unter kommunistischer Herrschaft steht, aber eine hohe Zahl von ethnischen Minoritäten.

3. Politik, Wirtschaft und allgemeine kulturelle sowie religiöse Lage

Die Machtübernahme durch die Kommunistische Partei im Gefolge des Zweiten Weltkriegs ließ Rumänien zuerst zu einer Volksrepublik, dann zu einer Sozialistischen Republik werden, die alle Merkmale eines zentralistisch regierten kommunistischen Staatssystems aufwies, allerdings auch einige Besonderheiten hatte: Eine betont nationalistische Politik wurde — besonders im westlichen Ausland — lange als eigenständiger Weg Rumäniens interpretiert, wobei weitgehend übersehen wurde, daß im Innern und vor allem gegenüber den ethnischen Minderheiten ein äußerst rigides Regiment geführt wurde (Ceaușescu auf dem 11. Parteitag 1974: „Es wird in absehbarer Zukunft in Rumänien keine Nationalitäten mehr geben, sondern nur noch eine sozialistische Nation"); auch nahm im Lauf der Zeit der Personenkult um den „Führer" (*Conducător*) Nicolae Ceaușescu immer bizarrere Formen an. Der Sturz und die Hinrichtung Ceaușescus im Dezember 1989 haben dieses System nur partiell verändert, da im Gefolge der Revolution eine „innerparteiliche Gruppierung" (Hösch 1993, 272) um den späteren Staatspräsidenten Ion Iliescu die Macht übernahm, die nicht einen so radikalen Wandel verfocht wie die neuen Regierungen in den anderen ehemals kommunistisch regierten Staaten Ost- und Südosteuropas. In den darauffolgenden Wahlen (1990 und 1992) wurde Iliescus „Demokratische Front der nationalen Rettung" bestätigt, doch erzielten in Siebenbürgen und im Banat die Vertreter des „Demokratischen Verbandes der Ungarn Rumäniens" nicht nur bei Kommunalwahlen, sondern auch bei den Parlamentswahlen 1992 beachtliche Ergebnisse (Deputiertenversammlung: 7,5%; Senat: 7,6%). In der Verfassung vom Dezember 1991 ist zwar eine gewisse Dezentralisation und Lokalautonomie vorgesehen, doch gibt es in der Praxis nach wie vor eine zentralistische Struktur nach französischem Vorbild.

Die wirtschaftliche Lage Rumäniens, das durchaus über reiche Ressourcen verfügt, hatte sich in den letzten Jahren der Ceaușescu-Ära katastrophal verschlechtert: Der

Hauptgrund hierfür war der Versuch, eine weitgehende wirtschaftliche Autarkie zu erreichen und das Land von seinen Auslands-(devisen)schulden zu befreien (was auch weitgehend gelang: 1991 betrug die Auslandsverschuldung Rumäniens nur 1,6 Mrd. $; zum Vergleich etwa: Bulgarien: 11,4 Mrd. $; Ungarn: 22,7 Mrd. $). Dadurch aber wurden die einheimischen Ressourcen in einem unverantwortlichen Maße geplündert, so daß der Lebensstandard in Rumänien in dramatischer Weise sank. Auch nach dem Ende der Ceaușescu-Diktatur hat sich die wirtschaftliche Lage nicht entscheidend verbessern können, da durchgreifende wirtschaftliche Reformen ausblieben und sich westliche Investoren deutlich zurückhielten. Selbst wenn man berücksichtigt, daß sich die ökonomische Lage in den meisten der ehemals kommunistisch beherrschten Staaten Ost- und Südosteuropas momentan nicht eben rosig präsentiert, so sind die wirtschaftlichen Daten Rumäniens doch besonders erschreckend (1991/92: Inflationsrate: 210%; Rückgang der Brutto-Industrieproduktion um 22,1%; Rückgang des Realeinkommens um 15%).

Nach den letzten Angaben (Baratta 1993, 574) bekennen sich in Rumänien 87% zur rumänisch-orthodoxen Kirche, 5% sind römisch-katholisch, 3,5% gehören den reformierten Kirchen (kalvinistisch, lutheranisch) an, 1% sind griechisch-orthodox, 0,5% Baptisten; hinzu kommen noch 55 000 Muslime und 18 000 Juden. Schon diese Zahlen zeigen die Sonderstellung der rumänisch-orthodoxen Kirche, die praktisch die Kirche des rumänischen Bevölkerungsteils ist, während die anderen Religionsgemeinschaften die verschiedenen Minoritäten vertreten. Die rumänisch-orthodoxe Kirche genießt dabei zahlreiche Privilegien. Bereits zu Zeiten Ceaușescus hatte sie einen Status, von dem Religionsgemeinschaften in den anderen sozialistischen Staaten nur träumen konnten: Der Grund hierfür liegt vor allem darin, daß die rumänisch-orthodoxe Kirche eine positive Rolle bei der Ende der sechziger Jahre von Ceaușescu propagierten eigenständigen Außenpolitik gerade gegenüber dem westlichen Ausland spielen sollte (Suttner 1977, 469−472). Hinzu kommt, daß die traditionell ausgesprochen national gesinnte rumänisch-orthodoxe Kirche in vielen Dingen mit der Staatspartei gemeinsame Sache machte: bestes Beispiel hierfür ist der Beitritt der rumänisch-orthodoxen Kirche zur Front der Sozialistischen Einheit im Jahre 1974.

Die anderen christlichen Glaubensgemeinschaften (mit Ausnahme der griechisch-orthodoxen, die eine Sonderstellung einnimmt) haben als Kirchen der nicht-rumänischen Bevölkerungsgruppen hingegen mit mehr oder weniger großen Schwierigkeiten (Verweigerung der Rückgabe enteigneter Grundstücke, Gebäude, Bibliotheken; Nicht-Zulassung kirchlicher Schulen etc.) zu kämpfen: Gerade in jüngster Zeit sind in der Presse vermehrt anti-katholische Artikel zu finden. Die Ungarn sind zumeist römisch-katholisch oder kalvinistisch, die Deutschen vorwiegend lutheranisch. Durch den massiven Exodus der deutschen Bevölkerungsgruppe ist dabei die Zahl derer, die sich zum evangelisch-lutherischen Glauben bekennen, in den letzten Jahren stark zurückgegangen. Zudem stellt sich hier teilweise das Problem der seelsorgerischen Betreuung, da auch viele Pfarrer das Land verlassen haben.

Das Ende der Ceaușescu-Diktatur brachte den Minderheiten, vor allem den Ungarn und Deutschen, im kulturellen Bereich zunächst deutliche Verbesserungen, die aber später teilweise wieder in Frage gestellt wurden: So wurden etwa die Fernsehsendungen in Ungarisch und Deutsch, die 1985 eingestellt worden waren, Anfang 1990 wieder aufgenommen, später aber unter Hinweis auf den Zwang zum Energiesparen wieder eingeschränkt (Kendi 1992, 150). Wichtig ist aber vor allem, daß die Möglichkeiten der Unterstützung der jeweiligen Volksgruppen durch Ungarn und Deutschland erweitert wurden, so daß beispielsweise in Ungarn erschienene Bücher und Zeitungen, deren Import in den letzten Jahren der Ceaușescu-Diktatur wegen angeblich antisozialistischer und antirumänischer Hetze der ungarischen Presse verboten worden war (Kendi 1992, 81), auch in Rumänien angeboten werden können.

4. Statistik und Ethnoprofile

4.1. Statistik

In Rumänien werden seit 1930 in unregelmäßigen Abständen Volkszählungen durchgeführt. Gefragt wurde teilweise nach Volkszugehörigkeit und Muttersprache, teilweise nur nach der Muttersprache. Die letzte Zählung (1992) ergab folgende Zahlen:

Rumänen   89,4%
Ungarn   7,1%
Sinti/Roma   1,8%
Deutsche   0,5%

Ukrainer	0,25%
Serben	0,16%
Juden	0,11%
Tataren	0,11%
Türken	0,11%
Russen	0,10%
Slowaken	0,10%
Bulgaren	0,05%
Lippowaner	0,05%
Tschechen	0,04%
Griechen	0,03%
Kroaten	0,03%
Polen	0,02%
Armenier	0,01%
Aromunen	0,01%
Ruthenen	0,01%
Slowenen	0,01%

Es fehlen in dieser Aufstellung die Csángó, die in rumänischen Quellen stets als Rumänen geführt werden. Es handelt sich dabei um eine magyarische Volksgruppe, die in der Moldau siedelt und deren Sprache − bedingt durch die lange Trennung − manchen Archaismus aufweist (→ Art. 176). Heute spricht die Mehrheit der Csángó, die römisch-katholisch sind, rumänisch.

Vergleicht man die Zahlen von 1992 mit den Ergebnissen der früheren Zählungen (Zach 1982, 58−59; Kendi 1992, 18−20), so zeigt sich ein deutlicher Rückgang bei den Minoritäten und analog eine Zunahme des prozentualen Anteils der Rumänen, die 1930 (allerdings im ethnisch noch bunteren Großrumänien) 71,8% und 1948 85,7% der Gesamtbevölkerung ausmachten. Drei Faktoren können hierfür vor allem verantwortlich gemacht werden (Zach 1982, 60−62): Industrialisierung und damit verbunden Urbanisierung, Assimilation und schließlich Emigration. Nicht in diese Tendenz paßt die Entwicklung der größten Minderheitengruppe, der Ungarn, deren prozentualer Anteil von 1948 bis 1992 zwar von 9,4% auf 7,1% gesunken ist, deren absolute Zahl jedoch von 1,5 Mill. auf 1,62 Mill. gestiegen ist (in Ungarn geht man − sicherlich nicht ganz zu Unrecht − u. a. durch Zuzählung der Csángó ohnehin von mehr als 2 Mill. Ungarn in Rumänien aus). Hier spielen Assimilation und Emigration keine Rolle, Binnenwanderung in die größeren Städte ist zwar auch bei den Ungarn zu beobachten, doch ziehen sie zumeist in die größeren Städte Siebenbürgens, die ohnehin eine lange ungarische Tradition besitzen wie etwa Cluj (Kolozsvár, Klausenburg). Neben den Ungarn sind Sinti und Roma die einzige Minorität, deren Zahl nach dem Zweiten Weltkrieg angestiegen ist. Dies liegt sowohl an der hohen Geburtenrate als auch daran, daß Sinti und Roma sich häufig selbst gerne als Rumänen ausgegeben haben, da sie zum Teil starken Diskriminierungen ausgesetzt waren und sind. Emigration ist der Hauptgrund des Rückganges des Anteils der Deutschen, der sich in zwei Schüben vollzog: zum einen während und unmittelbar nach dem Zweiten Weltkrieg (Umsiedlungen, Deportation in die Sowjetunion, Abwanderung zusammen mit der abziehenden Wehrmacht), zum anderen während der kommunistischen Diktatur, verstärkt nach dem Abkommen zwischen der Bundesrepublik Deutschland und Rumänien von 1978, das die Ausreise von jährlich 11 000 Menschen vorsah, und nach dem Umsturz 1989 (Schreiber 1993). Besonders stark ist auch der Rückgang der jüdischen Bevölkerungsgruppe. Von den ehemals etwa 800 000 Juden in Großrumänien vor dem Zweiten Weltkrieg (wobei anzumerken ist, daß gerade in den von Rumänien dann an die Sowjetunion abgetretenen Gebieten Bessarabiens und der Nordbukowina viele Juden wohnten) überlebte nur etwa die Hälfte Holocaust und Zweiten Weltkrieg. Durch die (erlaubte) Emigration nach Israel schrumpfte die Zahl der Juden dann bis heute auf etwa 20 000.

4.2. Wohngebiete

Ungarn und Deutsche hatten in Siebenbürgen traditionell festumrissene, in sich mehr oder weniger kompakte Wohngebiete, denen noch jeweils verschiedene Sprachinseln zuzurechnen sind (Karte bei Illyés 1981, 21). Nach der Volkszählung von 1992 sind Ungarn lediglich in zwei Kreisen (*judeţe*) die Mehrheit der Bevölkerung, und zwar in Harghita (84,6%) und Covasna (Kovászna) (75,2%), also im Gebiet der früheren Ungarischen Autonomen Region (cf. 6.). Daneben stellen Ungarn nur noch im Kreis Satu Mare (35%) mehr als 10% der jeweiligen Bevölkerung.

Dies bedeutet, daß mehr als 2/3 der ungarischen Bevölkerung Rumäniens auf der administrativen Ebene des Kreises in der Minderheit gegenüber den Rumänen sind. Die massive Auswanderung der deutschen Bevölkerung in den letzten Jahren hat es mit sich gebracht, daß bei der jüngsten Volkszählung der Anteil der Deutschen in keinem Kreis mehr als 4% betrug: Die höchsten Anteile wurden im Banater Kreis Timiş (Temesch) mit 3,8% (1977 noch 14,1%) sowie im Kreis Sibiu (Hermannstadt) mit 3,7% (1977: 20,0%) erreicht.

Die meisten der in Rumänien vertretenen slavischen Volksgruppen leben in den direkt an das jeweilige Sprachgebiet angrenzenden Regionen. Die Existenz von Slaven, die nicht in einem solchen unmittelbaren Kontakt zu ihrem Heimatland leben (wie etwa Slowaken, Tschechen, Polen), erklärt sich aus der früheren Zugehörigkeit der entsprechenden Siedlungsgebiete (vorwiegend Südbukowina) zum habsburgischen Vielvölkerstaat. Bei den Lippowanern handelt es sich um eine aus Rußland stammende Bevölkerungsgruppe, die ihre Heimat im 17. Jahrhundert aus religiösen Gründen verließ und sich im Donaudelta ansiedelte (Zinovieff/Thual 1980, 48—49).

Zahlenmäßig nur noch von geringer Bedeutung in Rumänien sind die Angehörigen von Turkvölkern. Es gibt Tataren, die die Nachkommen einer Gruppe sind, die 1784 die Krim vor den anrückenden russischen Truppen verließ, um sich zunächst in Bessarabien, dann schließlich in der Dobrudscha niederzulassen, weiterhin osmanische Türken, von denen viele nach dem zweiten Weltkrieg emigriert sind. Bekannt ist etwa die Aussiedlung der türkischen Bevölkerungsgruppe, die bis Ende der sechziger Jahre auf der in der Donau am Eisernen Tor gelegenen Insel Ada Kaleh gelebt hatte, die durch den Bau des Donaustaudamms dann überflutet wurde. Nicht in der Statistik taucht die Gruppe der Gagausen auf, die noch ein Dorf in der Dobrudscha bewohnen (Zach 1982, 56).

Ebenfalls in der Dobrudscha leben die meisten Aromunen; hierbei handelt es sich um die Nachkommen von Emigranten aus Griechenland, die zwischen den beiden Weltkriegen, der rumänischen Propaganda folgend, ihre angestammten Siedlungsgebiete verlassen hatten, zunächst in der Süddobrudscha angesiedelt wurden und dann nach der Abtretung dieses Gebiets an Bulgarien in die Norddobrudscha zogen (Saramandu 1972).

Auf die Gründe für den starken Rückgang der jüdischen Bevölkerungsgruppe wurde bereits hingewiesen. Während Siebenbürgen und die Walachei sephardisch geprägt waren und dort das Judenspanische gebräuchlich war, lebten in der Moldau und der Bukowina vor allem Ashkenasim. Heute leben Juden noch in einigen größeren Städten, doch gibt es auch noch vereinzelt jüdisch geprägte Dörfer wie etwa das bukowinische Dorohoi, das gerne als „letztes Städtel der Welt" bezeichnet wird (Judentum ... 1982).

Ein zusammenhängendes Siedlungsgebiet der traditionell nur bedingt ortsansässig lebenden Sinti und Roma, die nach den Ungarn inzwischen immerhin die zahlenmäßig stärkste Minderheit sind, gibt es nicht; Presseberichten ist allerdings zu entnehmen, daß sie in neuester Zeit verstärkt in von Deutschen verlassenen Gegenden angesiedelt werden, was verschiedentlich bereits zu Spannungen geführt hat.

5. Soziolinguistische Lage

Die Ausdehnung des Rumänischen auf Kosten der Minderheitensprachen in den letzten Jahren hat auch Konsequenzen auf die mit ihm in Kontakt lebenden Sprachen gehabt, wobei zu unterscheiden ist zwischen dem Deutschen und Ungarischen einerseits und den anderen Minoritätensprachen, die bereits von ihrem sprachpolitischen Status (cf. 6.) her von weniger großer Bedeutung sind, andererseits. Im Verhältnis Ungarisch-Rumänisch bzw. Deutsch-Rumänisch ist in gewisser Weise eine Umkehrung in der Gewichtung festzustellen. Jahrhundertelang waren in Siebenbürgen das Ungarische und das Deutsche die Sprachen der Oberschicht mit hohem Prestige, während das Rumänische geringeres Ansehen genoß. Das Ungarische und das Deutsche (sowie das Lateinische, dessen man sich gerade in Siebenbürgen lange gerne bediente) garantierten zudem die Verbindung zur mitteleuropäischen Kulturwelt, während das Rumänische, das bis 1860 im kyrillischen Alphabet geschrieben wurde, eher die Verbindung zur byzantinisch geprägten Welt Südosteuropas symbolisierte. Aus diesem Grunde findet sich im Wortschatz des Rumänischen eine ganze Reihe von Lexemen aus dem Ungarischen und Deutschen, die sich auf die „staatliche Organisation und die materielle Kultur" (Crößmann-Osterloh 1985, 37), vor allem die traditionellen Handwerksbezeichnungen, beziehen.

Seit der Eingliederung Siebenbürgens in den rumänischen Staat hat nunmehr umgekehrt das Rumänische als Nationalsprache in starkem Maße auf das Ungarische und Deutsche eingewirkt, so daß sich seitdem in diesen beiden Sprachen — neben zahlreichen weiteren Sprachkontaktphänomenen (Art. 175 und 176) — Entlehnungen aus dem Rumänischen gerade im Bereich der Terminologie der Administration finden (Márton/Péntek/Vöő 1977, 7; Rein 1979, 134 f).

Tab. 174.1: Magyarismen und Germanismen im Rumänischen

rumän. Wort	Bedeutung	entlehnt aus	Bedeutung
oraş	Stadt	ung. *város*	Stadt
mişaráş	Fleischer	ung. *mészáros*	Fleischer
vamă	Zoll	ung. *vám*	Zehent, Zoll
chelner	Kellner	dt. *Kellner*	
şpalt	Druckspalte	dt. *Spalte*	
şvaiţui	schweißen	dt. *schweißen*	

Tab. 174.2: Rumänismen im Deutschen und Ungarischen Rumäniens

Sprache	Bedeutung	entlehnt aus rum.	Bedeutung
ung. *zsudec*	Kreis	*judeţ*	Kreis
dt. *Schudetz*	Kreis	*judeţ*	Kreis
ung. *primar*	Dorfrichter, Bürgermeister	*primar*	Bürgermeister
dt. *Primar*	Notar, Bürgermeister	*Primar*	Bürgermeister
ung. *grenicser*	Grenzsoldat	*grănicer*	Grenzsoldat
dt. *Granitscher*	Grenzsoldat	*grănicer*	Grenzsoldat

Heute ist davon auszugehen, daß die ungarische und die deutsche Minderheit in Rumänien in einer Situation der Zweisprachigkeit leben, in der das Ungarische bzw. Deutsche immer mehr in den Rang einer L-Varietät mit dem vorwiegenden Verwendungsbereich Familie/Kirche zurückgedrängt wird (Krefeld/Schmitt 1989, 236). Dieser Prozeß hat sich für das Deutsche durch die massive Auswanderung in den letzten Jahren immer mehr verstärkt und ist deutlich weiter vorangeschritten als beim Ungarischen. Noch sehr viel ausgeprägter ist diese Situation der ungleichgewichtigen Funktionalität der Sprachen natürlich bei den Sprechern der kleineren Minoritätensprachen, die – nicht nur auf diese Weise – einem noch stärkeren Assimilationsdruck ausgesetzt sind als Ungarn und Deutsche.

6. Sprachpolitische Lage

Wenn man die Sprachpolitik Rumäniens gegenüber den Minderheiten beurteilen will, muß man zunächst unterscheiden zwischen den völkerrechtlichen Verpflichtungen, die der rumänische Staat eingegangen ist, sowie den innerstaatlichen Rechtsvorschriften. Daneben ist aber zu berücksichtigen, daß nicht immer Anspruch bzw. Vorschrift und Wirklichkeit deckungsgleich sind.

Nach den großen territorialen Zugewinnen im Gefolge des Ersten Weltkriegs ging Großrumänien – vor allem auf Druck der Westmächte – in mehreren Verträgen (Einzelheiten bei Kendi 1992, 24–30) Verpflichtungen zum Schutz der nunmehr auf seinem Boden lebenden Minderheiten ein. Diese Verpflichtungen sind jedoch genauso wie die Bestimmungen des Friedensvertrags, den die Siegermächte des Zweiten Weltkriegs 1947 in Paris mit Rumänien schlossen und in dem allen Menschen Rumäniens „without distinction as to race, sex, language or religion" (Kendi 1992, 31) u. a. das Recht auf freie Meinungsäußerung, Religionsausübung sowie Pressefreiheit zugestanden wurde, nicht korrekt eingehalten worden: Rumänien wurde deshalb 1950 von der UN-Vollversammlung verurteilt, der Internationale Gerichtshof stellte sogar den Bruch des Friedensvertrags fest.

Die innerstaatlichen gesetzlichen Regelungen, die seit dem Ende des Zweiten Weltkriegs in Rumänien gegenüber den Minoritäten getroffen wurden, zeichnen sich dadurch aus, daß es wenig Kontinuität gibt, daß vielmehr ein weitgehend ideologisch bedingtes Vor und Zurück zu konstatieren ist, wobei, insgesamt gesehen, aber sicherlich eher eine negative Bilanz zu ziehen ist.

In den ersten Jahren des kommunistischen Rumänien wurde – parallel zur damaligen Politik Stalins – eine weniger nationalistische und damit relativ minderheitenfreundliche Politik verfolgt. Davon profitierten vor allem die Ungarn, da sie zum einen die zahlenmäßig stärkste Gruppe waren, zum anderen, weil Rumänien es sich zu diesem Zeitpunkt mit dem sozialistischen Bruderland Ungarn nicht verderben wollte. Sichtbarsten Ausdruck fand diese Politik in der Gründung der *Ungarischen Autonomen Region* im Jahre 1952 mit dem Verwaltungszentrum Tîrgu Mureş (Marosvásárhely, Neumarkt). Seit dem Ungarnaufstand 1956 sind dann aber die in der Verfassung von 1952 garantierten Rechte immer mehr abgebaut worden: Zunächst gab es 1960 eine administrativ-territoriale Neugliederung, durch die sich das Verhältnis der ungarischen zur rumänischen Bevölkerung innerhalb der *Autonomen Region* von 77%:20% auf 62%:35% verringerte (Illyés 1981, 135), 1968 schließlich wurde die *Autonome Region* im Zuge einer territorialen Neugliederung Rumäniens ganz aufgelöst. Parallel dazu wurde durch sprachpolitische Maßnahmen u. a. im Schul- und Hochschulbereich der Assimilationsdruck erhöht: Hier ist etwa die Verschmelzung der traditionsreichen ungarischen *Bolyai*- mit der erst nach dem Zweiten Weltkrieg gegründeten rumänischen *Babeş*-Universität in Cluj (Klausenburg) im Jahre 1959 zu nennen, was praktisch das Ende der ungarischen Universitätsausbildung in Rumänien bedeutete.

Mit dem Ende der *Ungarischen Autonomen Region* endet auch der territorialrechtliche Minderheitenschutz in Rumänien, es verbleibt der personalrechtliche. In den Verfassungen von 1952 und 1965 (mit späteren Modifikationen) sowie in den nachgeordneten Gesetzen galten die Minoritäten als „mitwohnende Nationalitäten" (*naţionalităţi conlocuitoare*), denen verschiedene Rechte auf Gebrauch ihrer Sprache garantiert wurden. So hieß es in Artikel 22 der Verfassung von 1965 (in der Fassung von 1986):

„In der Sozialistischen Republik Rumänien werden den mitwohnenden Nationalitäten der freie Gebrauch der Muttersprache sowie Bücher, Zeitungen, Zeitschriften, Theater und der Unterricht aller Stufen in ihrer eigenen Sprache gesichert. In den territorialen Verwaltungseinheiten, in denen außer der rumänischen Bevölkerung auch Bewohner anderer Nationalität leben, bedienen sich alle Organe und Institutionen mündlich und schriftlich auch der Sprache der betreffenden Nationalität und setzen Beamte aus deren Reihen oder aus den Reihen anderer Bürger ein, die die Sprache und Lebensart der örtlichen Bevölkerung kennen." (Kendi 1992, 181 f).

In der Praxis konnte im Verkehr mit den Behörden die jeweilige Minderheitensprache (*de facto* ohnehin nur Ungarisch oder Deutsch) allerdings nur mündlich gebraucht werden, da der Beamtenapparat trotz dieser Vorschriften fest in der Hand von Rumänen war. Ähnliches gilt auch für den Bereich der Kultur, wo die den Minderheiten zugesicherten Rechte im Laufe der Zeit, vor allem als das Verhältnis zum Nachbarland Ungarn sich mehr und mehr verschlechterte, zum Teil unter Hinweis auf die schlechten wirtschaftlichen Bedingungen wie Papiermangel immer stärker abgebaut wurden, so daß etwa die Zahl der in den Minoritätensprachen publizierten Bücher, die teilweise sehr beachtlich gewesen war, immer mehr zurückging: Im Bukarester Kriterion-Verlag, der 1969 als Verlag der Minderheiten gegründet worden war, waren von 1970 bis 1982 immerhin 1300 Titel in ungarischer, 400 in deutscher, 150 in serbokroatischer, 115 in ukrainischer, 38 in jiddischer und jeweils einige Titel in slowakischer, bulgarischer, türkischer und tatarischer Sprache erschienen (Kendi 1992, 78).

Die „post-revolutionäre" Verfassung vom 8. 12. 1991 garantiert den Minderheiten ähnliche Rechte wie die früheren, etwa das Recht auf Unterricht der und in der Muttersprache (Art. 32), mindestens ein Mandat je Volksgruppe in der Deputiertenkammer (Art. 59) oder das Recht auf einen kostenfreien Dolmetscher vor Gericht (Art. 127). Andererseits betont die Verfassung aber auch deutlich die Einheit des Staates: so ist im Art. 1 vom „einheitlichen Nationalstaat" die Rede, in Art. 2 wird als Träger der Souveränität das „rumänische Volk" (nicht etwa „das Volk Rumäniens") genannt. Rumänisch ist nach der Verfassung die Staatssprache, eine Regelung über die Verwendung von Minderheitensprachen als Amtssprache gibt es nicht. Weitere Regelungen sind Nachfolgegesetzen vorbehalten, an denen teilweise noch gearbeitet wird. So ist ein Nationalitätengesetz vorgesehen, die Einrichtung eines Minderheitenrates ist von der rumänischen Regierung bereits beschlossen. Man wird abwarten müssen, in welcher Form sich nunmehr Anspruch und Wirklichkeit zueinander verhalten werden.

7. Sonstige Sprachkontakte

Neben den hier behandelten Kontakten des Rumänischen mit dem Deutschen (→ Art. 175) und dem Ungarischen (→ Art. 176) gibt es natürlich auch wechselseitige Beeinflussungen durch die Berührungen des Rumänischen mit den anderen auf dem Staatsgebiet gesprochenen Sprachen, vor allem im Wortschatz. Hier ist in der Regel das Rumänische als Staatssprache die dominante Form, die die Minderheitensprachen beeinflußt. Wenn auch detailliertere Untersuchungen zu dieser Problematik weitgehend fehlen, so vermitteln doch die entsprechenden Aufnahmepunkte der Sprachatlanten Rumäniens, die die wichtigsten Minderheitensprachen berücksichtigen (Kramer 1993, 14f), schon einen ersten Eindruck.

Von großer Bedeutung für das Rumänische ist ferner der (freilich indirekte) Kontakt mit dem Französischen. Zur genaueren Erklärung dieser auch heute noch wichtigen Beziehung muß ein kurzer Blick in die Sprachgeschichte geworfen werden. Über Jahrhunderte hinweg war das Rumänische einem intensiven Sprachkontakt mit slavischen Sprachen ausgesetzt gewesen: An den mittelalterlichen und frühneuzeitlichen Höfen der Bojaren im Gebiet des heutigen Rumänien war das Slavische in einer eigenständigen, dem Mittelbulgarischen nahestehenden Form (zumeist als „Slavonisch" oder „Dako-Slavisch" bezeichnet) die Sprache der Oberschicht gewesen, derer man sich auch schriftlich (das erste schriftliche Zeugnis des Rumänischen stammt erst aus dem Jahre 1521) bediente, während das Rumänische das Odium einer Hirten- und Bauernsprache besaß. In gewisser Weise hatte das Slavische für das Rumänische in dieser Zeit eine Funktion, die das Lateinische für die anderen romanischen Sprachen innehatte. Somit ist das Rumänische vor allem (aber durchaus nicht ausschließlich) im Wortschatz in starkem Maße vom Slavischen geprägt (Gălăbov 1980).

Ein radikaler Wandel vollzieht sich nun ab dem Ende des 18., verstärkt im 19. Jahrhundert. Parallel zu den Bemühungen um die nationale Einheit (cf. 2.2., 2.3.) wird versucht, Anschluß an die westliche Romanität zu gewinnen. Dabei orientieren sich die siebenbürgischen Rumänen vorwiegend an Rom (mit dem Hinweis auf die Abstammung von den Römern konnte man seine Herkunft im Vergleich zu Ungarn und Deutschen gewissermaßen „adeln"), die der Walachei und der Moldau, wohin zahlreiche Franzosen aus unterschiedlichen Gründen gekommen waren, überwiegend an Frankreich. Im 19. Jahrhundert findet eine bewußte (Re-)Romanisierung des Rumänischen beispiellosen Ausmaßes statt, durch die — parallel zum Prozeß der Erlangung der politischen Unabhängigkeit vom osmanisch-balkanischen Einfluß — eine Annäherung an die übrige romanische Welt

Tab. 174.3: Slavismen im Rumänischen

rumän. Wort	Bedeutung	entlehnt aus slav.	Bedeutung
graniţă	Grenze	slav. *granica*	Grenze
prieten	Freund	slav. *prijateli*	Freund
drag	lieb	slav. *dragŭ*	lieb, wertvoll
sfînt	heilig	slav. *svętŭ*	heilig
iubi	lieben	slav. *ljubiti*	lieben
omorî	töten	slav. *umoriti*	töten

erreicht werden soll („reintegrare a poporului român şi a culturii sale în lumea modernă, dar, în primul rînd, între popoarele şi culturile neolatine" [das rumän. Volk und seine Kultur in die moderne Welt zu re-integrieren, vor allem aber in die romanischen Völker und Kulturen], Ivănescu 1980, 664). Damit verbunden ist natürlich die (auch sprachliche) Abgrenzung von den wenig geliebten Nachbarn. Die Hauptquelle, aus der bei diesem Prozeß geschöpft wird, ist dabei das Französische (daneben — in geringerem Umfang — das Latein, was die Vertreter der Siebenbürgischen Schule propagierten, sowie das Italienische, für das vor allem der Schriftsteller Ion Heliade-Rădulescu plädierte). Die rumänische Sprache hat auf diese Weise im 19. Jahrhundert ein deutlich anderes Aussehen bekommen (Schroeder 1989, 353–355).

Die Annäherung an das Französische beschränkt sich aber durchaus nicht auf diese Zeit, vielmehr ist es bis auf den heutigen Tag in vielerlei Hinsicht Vorbild für das Rumänische geblieben, so daß die französische Sprache noch immer die größte Quelle für Entlehnungen darstellt. Statistische Untersuchungen zum rumänischen Wortschatz beweisen die Dominanz des Französischen sehr deutlich: So hat Macrea (1982, 56f) festgestellt, daß bei den rund 50 000 Wörtern des *Dicţionar limbii române moderne* (1958) die aus dem Französischen stammenden mit 38,42% deutlich überwiegen vor dem lateinischen Erbwortschatz mit 20,02% und den Entlehnungen aus dem Altslavischen mit 7,98% (jeweils

Tab. 174.4: Neoromanismen im Rumänischen

rumän. Wort	Bedeutung	entlehnt aus	Bedeutung	Erstbeleg (nach Tiktin/Miron 1986–89)
bursă	Börse	frz. bourse	Börse	1826
elev	Schüler	frz. élève	Schüler	1800
jurnal	Zeitung	frz. journal	Zeitung	1787
amical	freundschaftlich	frz. amical	freundschaftlich	1832
deposeda	enteignen	frz. déposséder	enteignen	1862
comerciant	Kaufmann	it. commerciante	Kaufmann	1805

einschließlich dazu gebildeter innerrumänischer Ableitungen; man muß allerdings anmerken, daß sich die Relationen verändern, wenn man nicht nur *types* sondern auch *tokens* berücksichtigt, da die „Strukturwörter" vor allem lateinische Erbwörter sind). Bei den heutigen Neologismen (untersucht am Neologismenwörterbuch von Dimitrescu 1982, das Lexeme der Jahre 1960 bis 1980 umfaßt) liegen unter den aus Fremdsprachen entlehnten Wörtern die aus dem Französischen stammenden gemeinsam mit den Anglizismen an erster Stelle; dahinter folgen – mit deutlichem Abstand – Entlehnungen aus dem Deutschen und Italienischen, erst dann – noch einmal mit klarem Abstand – solche aus dem Russischen (Elwert 1986, 166). Hierin spiegelt sich u. a. die Fremdsprachenpolitik Rumäniens wider: Auch nach dem Zweiten Weltkrieg hat das Französische seine Position als erste Fremdsprache in Rumänien halten können, Französisch ist ebenso die Sprache der wissenschaftlichen wie auch der literarischen Kommunikation (man denke an Autoren wie etwa Ionesco, Istrati etc.); Frankreich galt bei allen ideologischen Gegensätzen in vielem (etwa in der Territorialadministration) nach wie vor als Vorbild. So ist es kein Wunder, daß es noch immer mit dem Englischen als der Sprache, aus der natürlich zahlreiche Entlehnungen aus dem Bereich der modernen Technik stammen, mithalten kann. Nur auf den ersten Blick erstaunlich ist der geringe Anteil von Entlehnungen aus dem Russischen. Während noch in den fünfziger Jahren zahlreiche Termini aus dem Bereich des sozialistischen Gesellschafts- und Wirtschaftssystems aus dem Russischen ins Rumänische eingedrungen waren, spiegelt sich in dem Material von Dimitrescu die zunehmende politische wie ökonomische Distanzierung von der UdSSR wider.

8. Wertung der Quellen und Literatur

Die Besonderheit der Literatur, die sich mit den vielfältigen Sprachkontakten in Rumänien beschäftigt, ist darin zu sehen, daß häufig nicht getrennt wird zwischen seriöser wissenschaftlicher Untersuchung und tendenziöser Darstellung der zugegebenermaßen komplexen Situation, so daß linguistische und historische Argumente herhalten müssen, um (manchmal zweifelhafte) politische Entscheidungen zu legitimieren. Mehr noch als in anderen Staaten, in denen versucht wird, die Existenz von Minderheiten durch rechnerische, terminologische oder auch geschichtsverfälschende Manipulationen zu banalisieren, ist in Südosteuropa, das eine ethnische Vielfalt zeigt, die in Europa ihresgleichen sucht, in den relativ jungen, zumeist mit der Idee eines Nationalstaats gegründeten Ländern eine historisierende Denkweise verbreitet, die häufig wenig Raum für objektive Darstellungen läßt (Troebst 1993). Für denjenigen, der sich mit Fragen des Sprachkontakts in Südosteuropa beschäftigt, besteht demnach die erste Aufgabe darin, die Seriosität der Quellen und Literatur zu prüfen. Es ist so auch nicht weiter verwunderlich, daß eine moderne Sprachkontaktforschung für den rumänischen Sprachraum nur in Ansätzen vorhanden ist (etwa Rein 1980, 1983). Die vorliegende sprachwissenschaftliche Literatur beschäftigt sich bevorzugt mit historischen Erscheinungen des *multi-* („Balkansprachbund": Sandfeld 1930, Schaller 1975, Solta 1980) oder auch *bi*lateralen (etwa Arvinte 1971, Bakos 1982, Crößmann-Osterloh 1985, Márton/Péntek/Vöö 1977, Petrovici 1957, Schubert 1982) Sprachkontakts, wobei die traditionelle Lehnwortforschung im Vordergrund steht.

9. Bibliographie (in Auswahl)

Arvinte, Vasile (1971): *Die deutschen Entlehnungen in den rumänischen Mundarten (nach den Angaben des Rumänischen Sprachatlasses)*, Berlin.

Bakos, Ferenc (1982): *A magyar szókészlet román elemeinek története* [Geschichte der rumänischen Elemente des ungarischen Wortschatzes], Budapest.

Baratta, Mario von (Ed.) (1993): *Der Fischer Weltalmanach 1994*, Frankfurt a. M.

Blanc, André (1973): *La Roumanie, Le fait national dans une économie socialiste*, Paris/Brüssel/Montréal.

Brunner, Georg/Lemberg, Hans (Eds.) (1994): *Volksgruppen in Ostmittel- und Südosteuropa*, Baden-Baden.

Cadzow, John F./Ludanyi, Andrew/Elteto, Louis J. (Eds.) (1983): *Transylvania: The Roots of Ethnic Conflict*, Kent, Ohio.

Castellan, Georges (1984): *Histoire de la Roumanie*, Paris.

Crößmann-Osterloh, Helga (1985): *Die deutschen Einflüsse auf das Rumänische, Probleme — Kriterien — Anwendungen*, Tübingen.

Dicţionarul limbii române moderne [Wörterbuch der modernen rumänischen Sprache] (1958), Bukarest.

Dimitrescu, Florica (1982): *Dicţionar de cuvinte recente* [Wörterbuch der Neologismen], Bukarest.

Elwert, W. Theodor (1986): „Entwicklungstendenzen bei der Erweiterung des neurumänischen Wortschatzes". In: *Rumänistik in der Diskussion*, Holtus, G./Radtke, E. (Eds.), Tübingen, 164—176.

Gălăbov, Ivan (1980): „Languages in Contact — ein typischer Fall: das Rumänische". In: *Sprachkontakte. Zur gegenseitigen Beeinflussung romanischer und nicht-romanischer Sprachen*, Werner, R. (Ed.), Tübingen, 17—28.

Hartl, Hans (1982): „Nationalitätenpolitik und Nationalismus in Rumänien". In: *Nationalitätenprobleme in der Sowjetunion und Osteuropa*, Brunner, G./Meissner, B. (Eds.), Köln, 151—164.

Hösch, Edgar (²1993): *Geschichte der Balkanländer: Von der Frühzeit bis zur Gegenwart*, München.

Huber, Manfred (1973): *Grundzüge der Geschichte Rumäniens*, Darmstadt.

Illyés, Elemér (1981): *Nationale Minderheiten in Rumänien. Siebenbürgen im Wandel*, Wien.

Ivănescu, G. (1980): *Istoria limbii române* [Geschichte der rumänischen Sprache], Iaşi.

Jackson, Marvin R./Happel, Stephen K. (1977): „Population Structure". In: *Rumänien*, Grothusen, K.-D. (Ed.), Göttingen, 426—457.

„Judentum in Rumänien heute" (1982). In: *Europa Ethnica 39*, 232.

Kendi, Erich (1992): *Minderheitenschutz in Rumänien. Die rechtliche Normierung des Schutzes der ethnischen Minderheiten in Rumänien*, München.

Kramer, Johannes (1993): „Sprachatlanten des Rumänischen". In: *Stand und Perspektiven der romanischen Sprachgeographie*, Winkelmann, O. (Ed.), Wilhelmsfeld, 3—20.

Krefeld, Thomas/Schmitt, Christian (1989): „Rumänisch: Diglossie und Polyglossie". In: *Lexikon der Romanistischen Linguistik (LRL)*, Holtus, G./Metzeltin, M./Schmitt, Ch. (Eds.), vol. III, Tübingen, 229—239.

Macrea, D. (1982). *Probleme ale structurii şi evoluţiei limbii române* [Probleme der Struktur und Entwicklung der rumänischen Sprache], Bukarest.

Márton, Gyula/Péntek, János/Vöö, István (1977): *A magyar nyelvjárások román kölcsönszavai* [Rumänische Lehnwörter in den ungarischen Mundarten], Bukarest.

Niculescu, Alexandru (1992): „Le daco-roumain — Romania antiqua, Romania nova et la continuité mobile. Une synthèse". In: *Actes du XVIIIe Congrès International de Linguistique et de Philologie Romanes, Université de Trèves (Trier) 1986*, Kremer, D. (Ed.), vol. 1, Tübingen, 86—108.

Petrovici, Emil (1957): *Kann das Phonemsystem einer Sprache durch fremden Einfluß umgestaltet werden? Zum slavischen Einfluß auf das rumänische Lautsystem*, Den Haag.

Rein, Kurt (1979): „Neuere Entwicklungstendenzen der deutschen Sprache in Rumänien". In: *Standardsprache und Dialekte in mehrsprachigen Gebieten Europas*, Ureland, P. S. (Ed.), Tübingen, 125—147.

Rein, Kurt (1980): „Diglossie und Bilinguismus bei den Deutschen Rumäniens". In: *Sprachkontakt und Sprachkonflikt*, Nelde, P. H. (Ed.), Wiesbaden, 263—269.

Rein, Kurt (1983): „Didaktische Probleme aus Diglossie und Bilingualismus bei deutschsprachigen Schülern in Südosteuropa". In: *Vergleichbarkeit von Sprachkontakten*, Nelde, P. H. (Ed.), Bonn, 141—152.

Sandfeld, Kr. (1930): *Linguistique balkanique. Problèmes et résultats*, Paris.

Saramandu, Nicolae (1972): *Cercetări asupra aromânei vorbite în Dobrogea* [Forschungen über das Aromunische in der Dobrudscha], Bukarest.

Schaller, Helmut Wilhelm (1975): *Die Balkansprachen. Eine Einführung in die Balkanphilologie*, Heidelberg.

Schramm, Gottfried (1985—1987): „Frühe Schicksale der Rumänen. Acht Thesen zur Lokalisierung der lateinischen Kontinuität in Südosteuropa". In: *Zeitschrift für Balkanologie 21*, 223—241; 22, 104—125; 23, 78—94.

Schreiber, Wilfried E. (1993): „Demographische Entwicklungen bei den Rumäniendeutschen". In: *Südosteuropa Mitteilungen 33*, 204—211.

Schroeder, Klaus-Henning (1989): „Rumänisch. Etymologie und Geschichte des Wortschatzes". In:

Lexikon der Romanistischen Linguistik (LRL), Holtus, G./Metzeltin, M./Schmitt, Ch. (Eds.), vol. III, Tübingen, 347–357.

Schubert, Gabriella (1982): *Ungarische Einflüsse in der Terminologie des öffentlichen Lebens der Nachbarsprachen*, Wiesbaden.

Solta, Georg Renatus (1980): *Einführung in die Balkanlinguistik mit besonderer Berücksichtigung des Substrats und des Balkanlateinischen*, Darmstadt.

Suttner, Ernst Chr. (1977): „Kirchen und Staat". In: *Rumänien*, Grothusen, K.-D. (Ed.), Göttingen, 458–483.

Tiktin, H./Miron, Paul ([2]1986–1989): *Rumänisch-deutsches Wörterbuch*, Wiesbaden.

Troebst, Stefan (1993): „Aufgaben und Ziele vergleichender historischer Forschung zur ethnischen Struktur und zu den Nationalismen Osteuropas". In: *Südosteuropa Mitteilungen 33*, 146–156.

Zach, Krista (1982): „Rumäniens kleine Minderheitengruppen nach 1945". In: *Europa Ethnica 39*, 49–62.

Zinovieff, Maurice/Thual, François (1980): *Le paysage linguistique de la Roumanie*, Paris.

Wolfgang Dahmen, Jena (Deutschland)

175. Rumänisch–Deutsch

1. Geographie und Demographie
2. Geschichte
3. Politische und sozioökonomische Lage
4. Statistik
5. Soziolinguistische Lage
6. Sprachpolitische Lage
7. Allgemeines kontaktlinguistisches Porträt
8. Zum Diskussionsstand
9. Bibliographie (in Auswahl)

1. Geographie und Demographie

Kontakte zwischen Deutsch und Gallo-, Italo-, Räto-, ja sogar Hispano-Romanisch sind weitaus bekannter als die mit der östlichsten romanischen Sprache, Rumänisch; und doch gibt es sie, und zwar:

(a) *indirekte Kontakte* zwischen den beiden Ethnien in Mitteleuropa und auf dem Balkan, die schriftlich-literarisch oder durch Vermittlung der dazwischenliegenden Sprachen Ungarisch und z. T. Polnisch zustande kamen; aber auch

(b) *direkte Kontakte* in Rumänien selbst mit Angehörigen der deutschen Minderheitengruppen.

1.1. Distanz zwischen den Verbreitungsgebieten

Die Distanz zwischen den geschlossenen Verbreitungsgebieten ermöglicht keine Direktkontakte über den allgemeinen Schrift- und Kulturaustausch; und zwar herrschte bei der West-Ost-Wanderung der (west)europäischen Zivilisation im allgemeinen ein starkes Ungleichgewicht, das Heitmann (1986, 23) so formuliert:

„Nicht nur geographisch gesehen hingen hingegen die unter türkischer Souveränität stehenden Fürstentümer Moldau und Walachei vom Interesse der deutschsprachigen Welt weiter ab. (...) Anlässe zur Beschäftigung aus der Ferne mit den Rumänen in den Donaufürstentümern bot die große internationale Politik (...) als Schauplätze von Türkenkriegen bzw. als Teile des osmanischen Imperiums. Später verfolgte man dort den nationalen Emanzipationsprozeß der Rumänen, wenngleich das Interesse der deutschsprachigen Öffentlichkeit mehr der sogenannten orientalischen Frage galt."

Er konstatiert auch später einen „verhältnismäßig geringen Rang der Rumänen in der Wichtigkeitshierarchie der Völker für Deutsche und Österreicher"; was erkläre, „warum deren Bild nicht so reichhaltig ausgeführt und nicht in derselben Weise profiliert wirkt wie das bestimmter unmittelbarer Nachbarn und ständiger Kontrahenten der deutschsprachigen Welt in neuer Zeit".

1.2. Kontakte und Einflüsse unterhalb der Hochsprachen

Ist der Vergleich der Hoch- oder Schriftsprachen auch negativ, so zeichnet sich unser Kontaktbeispiel dadurch aus, daß es – bezieht man auch die jeweiligen Regional- oder Fach- und Sondersprachen beider Sprachen in die vergleichende Betrachtung mit ein – intensive, philologisch interessante Kontakt- bzw. Interferenzphänomene aufweist.

1.3. Kontakte in den deutschen Sprachinseln (SI)

Die deutschen Enklaven stellen regional begrenzte, aber intensive rumänisch-deutsche (rum. dt.) Kontaktzonen dar, die ihren Niederschlag offenbar früh im Sprachlichen gefunden haben und auch zum bevorzugten Studienobjekt rumänisch-deutscher Linguistik gehören (Kelp 1990). Diese rumänisch-deutschen Sprachkontaktzonen am NW-Rand des rumänischen Sprachgebiets werden z. T. überlagert durch solche mit dem Ungarischen (Kroner 1975) sowie Ukrainischen im Norden und dem Serbischen im Westen. Die drei wichtigsten deutschen SI sind:

1.3.1. Die Sprachinseln der Siebenbürger Sachsen

Sie sind seit Beginn des 12. Jahrhunderts — mit rd. 225 000 Sprechern im Jahre 1920 heute ca. 50 000 — gegliedert in:
Nordsiebenbürgen um Bistritz/Bistriţa (ca. 40 Orte) und
Südsiebenbürgen, verteilt auf das Burzenland (12 Orte) um Kronstadt/Braşov und das größere Altland zwischen Kokel und Alt mit dem kirchlichen und politischen Zentrum der ganzen Gruppe in Hermannstadt/Sibiu (Bergel 1989).

1.3.2. Die Sprachinseln der Banater Schwaben

Sie befinden sich in den Bezirken Times und Caran Sebes um deren Zentrum Temeswar/Temeschburg/Timişoara. Die Ansiedlung der Deutschen erfolgte hier seit der Rückeroberung dieses Gebietes durch Österreich Ende des 17./Anfang des 18. Jahrhunderts. Ihre Zahl betrug 1920 ca. 270 000; heute vielleicht nur noch ein Fünftel (Petersen 1933, 207—286; Nebel 1985 und Kühnel 1988).

1.3.3. Die Sprachinseln der Bukowinadeutschen

(Petersen 1933, 611—644; Lang 1961) In dem 1774 erst von den Türken befreiten und zum Kronland „Bukowina" erhobenen Nordteil der Moldau wurden durch die österreichischen Militärbehörden bald Deutsche südlich der Hauptstadt Czernowitz angesiedelt. Die bei ihrer Umsiedlung 1940 knapp 100 000 Deutschen zerfielen in

(1) die meist bäuerlichen „*Schwaben*" im Südosten des Landes,
(2) die *Zipser* in den ehemaligen Bergwerksorten des Südwestens und
(3) die bairisch/österreichischen *Deutschböhmen* und Österreicher in den Städten.

Trotz ihres geringen Anteiles von nur 10% der je zur Hälfte rumänischen bzw. ukrainischen Gesamtbevölkerung hatten die Deutschen eine führende Rolle, weil das Kronland verwaltungsmäßig Wien direkt unterstand und Deutsch bis 1918 Amtssprache war; dazu kam, daß auch die gebildeten Juden aufgrund ihres guten Zugangs von ihrem als mittelhochdeutsche Mundart anzusehenden Jiddisch sich des Deutschen bedienten. Das erhielt eine über die Zahl der Deutschen weit hinausgehende Bedeutung als Zweit- oder Fremdsprache und diente Ukrainern, Rumänen und Serben als Koiné bzw. als Vehikel für den Anschluß an die westliche Zivilisation (Rein 1975, 145 ff; Rein 1990) (→ Sprachenkarte H).

2. Geschichte

2.1. Kontakte seit dem Mittelalter

Direkte Kontakte sind anfänglich wohl nur durch Reisende und Kaufleute (Weczerka 1960) entstanden; aber auch deutsche Ärzte, Beamte und Bojaren (Valjavec 1953, 202 ff) gab es später in Bukarest und Jassy. Obgleich die Rumänen auch als Mitstreiter gegen die Türken interessant für die Deutschen wurden (Heitmann 1986, 22 ff), zeigen diese frühen Kontakte keinen sprachlichen Niederschlag im Deutschen (Knobloch 1976, 479 f) — sieht man von dem vom Volksnamen zur Tierbezeichnung gewordenen „Wallach" oder der Kenntnis von freilich nicht nur rumänischen Titeln wie *Bojar, Woiwode* etc. ab.

2.2. Direktkontakte mit deutschen Einwanderern

2.2.1. Die Ansiedlung in Siebenbürgen

Sie erfolgte unter den ungarischen Königen Geisa II. und Andreas II. Mitte des 12. Jahrhunderts und führte zur Gründung von rund 250 städtischen und dörflichen deutschen Siedlungen (Klein 1963).

2.3. Neuzeitliche Kontakte

(a) *Indirekt* ab dem 18. Jahrhundert in Form sich intensivierender Rezeption deutscher Bildung und Literatur (Munteanu 1986),
(b) aber dann höchst *direkt* durch die neuzeitliche deutsche Einwanderung ins Banat und in die Bukowina.

2.3.1. Kulturkontakte ab dem 18. Jahrhundert

Sie sind Teil des Interesses der Gebildeten für die Geistesströmungen des Westens, insbesondere seit der Aufklärung (Turczynski

1985). Der Einfluß des Deutschen nimmt trotz der Vorliebe für das sprachverwandte Französisch beim rumänischen Adel, der in Deutschland und Österreich studierte, und beim Bürgertum noch zu. Als Folge beherrscht das Deutsche im 19. Jahrhundert z. B. weithin die entstehenden Fachsprachen in der Wissenschaft oder dem Bildungsbereich (Oprea 1986, 89 ff).

2.3.2. Neuzeitliche Direktkontakte
2.3.2.1. Österreichische Ansiedlung im Banat

Nach der Zurückdrängung der Türken auch aus dem Raum zwischen Donau und dem Siebenbürger Karpatenland organisierte die österreichische Militärverwaltung ab 1716/18 die Neubesiedlung des größtenteils entvölkerten Landes durch Deutsche aus Süd-West-Deutschland. Diese Kolonisation erfolgte in drei Wellen: beginnend unter Karl VI., ab 1744 unter Maria Theresia (hauptsächlich katholische Banater) und ab 1782 unter Joseph II. (auch Protestanten) (Petersen 1933 s. v.).

2.3.2.2. Banat-„Schwäbisch" — eine neue (Ausgleichs-)mundart

Die Anpassung unter den heterogenen (Petersen 1933, 220 ff), im wesentlichen südwestdeutschen Siedlern bzw. ihren Heimatmundarten führte zunächst zu relativ homogenen Ortsmundarten und über weitere „Ausgleichsvorgänge" (Schwob 1971) schließlich zu einer Banater Regionalmundart, die aufgrund der Wiener Kanzleitradition „Schwäbisch" (Rein 1961, 8—13 und 1962, 30—34) genannt wurde (obgleich sie in der Mehrheit der Merkmale eher westmitteldeutsch-pfälzisch ist); analog dazu entstand der Name „Donauschwaben" für diesen deutschen Neustamm (Scherer 1973, 169—73) in Direktkontakt mit dem Rumänischen.

2.4. Kontakte der Hochsprachen

In der wechselvollen weiteren Geschichte — ab 1867 übernahm Ungarisch viele Funktionen des Deutschen als Amtssprache — nach dem Ersten Weltkrieg mit dem Anschluß an Großrumänien wurde Rumänisch die Staatssprache. Es gab auf allen sozialen Ebenen intensive Kontakte zwischen Rumänen und Deutschen, und trotz der z. T. kurzen Kontaktzeit sind zahlreiche Interferenzen in beiden Sprachen nachzuweisen: zuerst deutsche im Rumänischen (besonders der Gebildeten), dann nach 1918 und vollends ab 1944 auch rumänische im Deutschen.

3. Politische und sozioökonomische Lage

Die heutige Situation der Rumäniendeutschen, im Alltag die deutschen Partner dieses Sprachkontakts, gibt nur noch ein schwaches Abbild jener jahrhundertealten alltäglichen Kontaktsituation, die wir aufgrund der jeweiligen Transferenzen als intensiv bezeichnen können.

Dies ist auf die Entwicklung in den letzten 50 Jahren zurückzuführen (Kotzian 1991, 243 ff). Nach einer ersten Statusminderung von der — in der Bukowina uneingeschränkten — Staats- zur Minderheitensprache nach 1918 und einer Anpassungsphase in der Zwischenkriegszeit geriet die deutsche Sprache nach dem hier bereits am 23. August 1944 mit dem Sturz Antonescus beendeten Zweiten Weltkrieg in den Strudel des Niedergangs alles Deutschen.

4. Statistik

4.1. Die Entwicklung seit dem Zweiten Weltkrieg

Der Rückgang der vor dem Krieg etwa 750 000 Rumäniendeutschen auf weniger als die Hälfte erfolgte durch:

(1) Umsiedlung z. B. der Bukowinadeutschen: 1940 wurden als Auftakt aller nachmaligen „ethnischen Säuberungen" die fast 100 000 Buchenlanddeutschen zusammen mit den Bessarabiendeutschen und anderen deutschen Splittergruppen im deutsch-sowjetischen Interessensraum „heim ins Reich" umgesiedelt und bis zur erneuten Vertreibung 1945 in den polnischen Westgebieten angesiedelt (Jachomowski 1984).

(2) Evakuierung der Nordsiebenbürger: Ein ähnliches Schicksal hatte ein Teil der Siebenbürger, die im Herbst 1944 aus dem seit dem Wiener Schiedsspruch 1940 zu Ungarn gehörigen Nordsiebenbürgen von der deutschen Wehrmacht nach Österreich evakuiert wurden und nach dem Krieg nicht mehr in ihre Heimat zurückkonnten.

(3) Arbeitsdeportation und Familienzusammenführung nach 1944: Infolge Entlassung der zur deutschen Wehrmacht Eingezogenen sowie der Arbeitsdeportierten aus der Gefangenschaft in der UdSSR nach Deutschland ergab sich die Möglichkeit zu einer Zusammenführung im Westen. Dies wirkte als permanenter Auswandererstrom. Bei der ersten Volkszählung nach dem Kriege 1948 lebten

343 919 Deutsche auf dem Gebiete der Volksrepublik Rumänien — je zur Hälfte Siebenbürger Sachsen und Banater Schwaben.

4.2. Die jüngste Entwicklung seit 1989

Die Zahl der Deutschen wurde nochmals reduziert, als nach den revolutionären Ereignissen von 1989 die Auswanderung freigegeben wurde und die Deutschen als „Spätaussiedler" davon regen Gebrauch machten. Neuere Schätzungen von 1992 nennen noch 110 000 Deutsche in Rumänien.

5. Soziolinguistische Lage

5.1. Ältere Sprachkontakte 16.—19. Jahrhundert

Trotz der bis 1870 geltenden Standes- und „Nations"verfassungen mit ihren die nationalen Siedlungsgebiete scharf trennenden Niederlassungsbeschränkungen scheinen die Kontakte recht intensiv gewesen zu sein und dies nicht nur in den Bereichen Vieh-, besonders Schafzucht, Pflanzen, Nahrungsmittel. Wie die früh entlehnten Termini in der orthodoxen Kirche oder den rumänisch-fürstlichen Verwaltungsämtern etc. belegen, sind Sozialkontakte auch noch früher nachweisbar (Klaster-Ungureanu 1958, 197—219).

5.2. Intensivierung der Sprachkontakte und des Bilingualismus ab 1918

Bereits im 19. Jahrhundert setzte eine weitere Kontaktintensivierung in vielen anderen Lebensbereichen ein. Der Anschluß an Rumänien 1918 bringt eine Gleich-, ja Vorrangstellung des Rumänischen und führt zu — zumindest sozialem — Bilingualismus (Rein 1979a, 124—147). Die rumänischen Entlehnungen nehmen auch in der deutschen Umgangssprache zu und zeigen neben abstrakten Begriffen auch Vorliebe für solche aus dem emotionalen Bereich.

5.3. Ab 1944 — individueller Bilingualismus

Mit der Halbierung der deutschen Minderheit und dem Verbot ihrer kulturellen Organisationen trat auch ein nahezu vollständiger Zusammenbruch des bisherigen Kommunikationsnetzes für Deutsch ein, das auf die Bereiche Familie und Kirche beschränkt wurde.

5.4. Bilingualismus und Diglossie

Die Zweisprachigkeitssituation der Rumänien-Deutschen wird durch eine durchgängige Diglossie noch zusätzlich kompliziert (Rein 1980, 263 ff).

5.4.1. Diglossie bei den Siebenbürgern

Ihr „Sächsisch" genannter archaischer Dialekt zeigt die lautlichen Merkmale des Moselfränkisch-Ripuarischen im Nordwesten des deutschen Sprachgebiets (z. B. ripuarischer Verschiebungsstand, rheinische Schärfung, typischer Wortschatz). Das an Luxemburgisch anklingende Idiom zeigt beträchtliche sprachliche Distanz zum Hochdeutschen. Die Ortsmundarten unterhalb dieser Regionalvarietäten zeigen eine noch größere, insbesondere lautliche Vielfalt (Klein/Schmidt 1961; Rein/Hildebrandt 1979).

Durch die Verwendung des Hochdeutschen als Kirchensprache der Sachsen ist dessen Kenntnis bei diesen bis zur Schulzeit hin zusätzlich gesichert und ermöglicht so einen muttersprachlichen Schulunterricht in deutscher (Hoch)Sprache (König 1988, 129 ff).

5.4.2. Die Diglossiesituation bei den Banater Schwaben

Deren „Schwäbisch" zeigt eher pfälzisch-rheinfränkischen Lautstand (s. 2.3.2.2.), aber besonders im Wortschatz auch bairisch-österreichische Züge. Die der Schriftsprache näherstehende banatschwäbische Regionalmundart wird in Temeschburg durch eine süddeutsch-bairische Hochsprachvarietät überdacht, so daß gleichfalls Muttersprachenunterricht stattfinden kann (Wolf 1975).

5.4.3. Tendenzen zum Abbau von Diglossie und Bilingualismus

Unter dem Druck der Staatssprache entstand eine Tendenz zur Aufgabe dieser Triglossie zugunsten einer diglossie-ähnlichen Zweier-Kombination. Je nach Bildung des Sprechers wird entweder die Hochstufe (H) oder Tiefstufe (T) in der Erstsprache aufgegeben:

A: Aufgabe der Muttersprachenhochstufe H_1
Durch Hinzutritt des Rumänischen (als H_2) entsteht: H_2 (rum. H) + T_1 (dt. Dial.)

B: Aufgabe der Muttersprachentiefstufe T_1 (dt. Dialekt)
Durch Hinzutreten des Rumänischen: H_1 (dt.) + H_2 (rum.)

Lösung A entspricht der im Elsaß, d. h.: alte Mundart und neue Hochsprache, Lösung B der unter Baltendeutschen, d. h.: alte Hochsprache + neue Hochsprache (unter Aufgabe jeden Dialekts!).

Letzteres führt zu stärkerer Öffnung der Erstsprache L_1 für — vor allem lautliche — Interferenzen aus L_2 und schließlich zu Aufgabe/Verlust von L_1 (Rein 1980, 263 ff).

6. Sprachpolitische Lage

Sie ist schwer zu beurteilen und erlaubt nur sehr vorläufige Aussagen.

Die schulpolitische Situation besteht bei den noch immer relativ liberalen Minderheitengesetzen heute vor allem in Organisationsproblemen, um die vom rumänischen Staat und aus dem deutschen Sprachgebiet großzügig angebotenen Bildungsmöglichkeiten den wenigen im Lande verbliebenen deutschen Schülern zugänglich zu machen. Dies erfordert u. a. die Öffnung der traditionell guten deutschen Minderheitenschulen im Lande für alle Schüler, die Deutsch lernen wollen; es bedeutet auch einen Wandel von der Mutter- zur Zweitsprachendidaktik mit allen methodischen Implikationen und verbesserten Lehrmittelangeboten (Rein 1983, 141 ff).

7. Allgemeines kontaktlinguistisches Porträt

7.1. Asymmetrie des Kontaktverhältnisses

Nach den Transfererscheinungen herrschte lange Asymmetrie hinsichtlich Richtung und Intensität der Beeinflussung: Während sich im deutschen Lexikon so gut wie keine Wörter rumänischer Herkunft finden, sind solche in der rumänischen Hochsprache „stärker nachzuweisen als bisher angenommen" (Crößmann-Osterloh 1985). Zahlreicher sind deutsche Wortentlehnungen in den rumänischen Mundarten, wenn auch meist nur in den Regionen mit deutschen Bevölkerungsanteilen.

7.2. Rumänische Interferenzen im Deutschen

Umgekehrt zeigen sich bei den deutschen Mundarten — wie auch bei der insgesamt etwas archaischen und österreichisch beeinflußten rumäniendeutschen Variante des Hochdeutschen — starke, seit 1944 rapide zunehmende Interferenzen aus dem Rumänischen. Diese zunächst an der Lexik als der offensten — und für Entlehnungen anfälligsten — Sprachebene festzumachende Aussage läßt sich auch für die anderen Sprachebenen bestätigen (Jumuga 1986, 41 ff; Kottler in: Kelp 1990, Anmerkungen 151 ff).

7.2.1. Rumänische Interferenzen im Siebenbürgischen

Die folgenden Beispiele entstammen der bislang systematischsten Untersuchung zu „rumänischen Transferenzen in die Siebenbürgisch-Sächsischen Ortsmundarten" von K. Ney (1984). Ihr Befund (S. 210) lautet u. a.:

(1) „Isolierte rumänische Phonemrealisationen sind nicht in das Siebenbürgen-Sächsische übernommen worden."
(2) „Analytische, isolierte Übernahme von rumänischen Morphemen tritt nur sehr selten auf."
(3) Dagegen ist „der syntaktische Transfer bedeutender als bisher in der Forschung angenommen". Das gilt „besonders (für) Verbstellung, Präpositionssetzung wie überhaupt Satzbaupläne".

Ohne auf die Strukturkontraste zum Rumänischen näher einzugehen, seien als besonders typisch hier nur herausgehoben: (1) die Tendenz zur Ausklammerung — die aber auch bei den wesentlich kürzer dem Rumänischen ausgesetzten Banater und Bukowiner Mundarten anzutreffen ist und selbst in binnendeutschen Mundarten zunimmt, (2) die Stellung der Negation direkt vor dem Verb beim Imperativ: z. B. „Nicht fürchte Dich!" (Florea 1986, 47—53) (auch ungarisch, z. B. ne fély!).

7.2.2. Sonderfall: semantische Entlehnung

Wesentlich schwerer erkennbar ist die fremde Beeinflussung bei schon länger übernommenem Lehngut. Nach den Untersuchungen von G. Richter (1960) ist das im Siebenbürgischen besonders oft der Fall bei:

(1) *Lehnübersetzungen*, bei denen ein „rumänischer Begriff aus sächsischem Wortgut" nachgebaut wird, z. B.: „Hundsholz" — sächsisch für „Faulbaum", Holunder (Rein/Hildebrandt 1979), wörtlich aus rumänisch „lemnul ciinelor".
(2) *Bedeutungswandel* eines sächsischen Worts unter rumänischem Einfluß, z. B. „machen" i. S. v. „gebären" — „sie hat ein Kind gemacht = geboren" (Richter 1960, 6).
(3) *Übersetzung ganzer Wendungen:* Hier kann das Kernwort rumänisch bleiben, z. B. „Geh in die Pustie" (= „Wüste, Weite"), oder auch übertragen werden, wodurch eine rein deutsche Wendung, aber mit durchscheinender rumänischer Semantik entsteht.

Alle diese Beispiele fügen sich in das von R. Post (1982, 11) formulierte Schema, wonach sich die Interferenzanfälligkeit von Sprachebenen umgekehrt zum Grad der Strukturierung verhält; d. h. am resistentesten sind die stark strukturierten Phonemsysteme der Sprachen, während das umfangreiche und weniger strukturierte lexikalische System besonders anfällig für Interferenzen aus anderen Sprachsystemen ist.

7.2.3. Problem der Bewertung von Interferenzen: Entlehnung oder Fehler?

Die Beurteilung, ob es sich um (a) „usuelle" Verwendung mehrerer Sprecher = „Regionalismus des Deutschen" handelt oder um (b) „okkasionelle" Bildung = Lapsus eines/mehrerer Sprecher, macht den Transfer zu einem im Deutschunterricht zu bekämpfenden (Interferenz-) „Fehler". Dies ist das Hauptproblem der Sprachpflege und -erhaltung, welches in der bisherigen Schulgeschichte und Literatur eine eher untergeordnete Rolle spielt, aber in der nächsten Zeit entscheidende Bedeutung gewinnen wird.

7.3. Deutscher Einfluß auf das Rumänische

7.3.1. Interferenzen in der Hochsprache

Sie gelten als selten, in den rumänischen Mundarten häufiger, besonders in den ehemals österreichischen Nordwestregionen (die ja auch die deutschen Minderheiten beherbergen). Mit exakten Zahlen kann Crößmann-Osterloh (1985) jedoch erstmals belegen, daß es mit 2% „nicht so wenige" sind. Diese derzeit beste Untersuchung weist für Schriftsprache wie Mundart selbst in den stabileren Bereichen Phonetik und Morphologie deutsche Einflüsse nach (Crößmann-Osterloh 1985, 228 ff). Sie bestätigt die bekannte regionale Verbreitung für die in älterer Zeit aufs Sächsische, in neuerer Zeit aufs Österreichische zurückzuführenden Germanismen, kann aber vor allem erstere auch weit darüber hinaus im Altreich und in der Schriftsprache belegen. Ebenso erweitert sie die bisher bekannten Sachbereiche — „sowohl volkstümlich-handwerkliche" als auch „technisch-wissenschaftliche" —, die je nach Popularität des Fachs auch über ihren fach- oder sondersprachlichen Randstatus hinaus in die rumänische Gemeinsprache vordrangen.

Trotz ihrer Einschränkung, daß „aus sprachlichen Erscheinungen keineswegs alle kulturellen Einflüsse zu erfassen" sind, wagt sie dann weittragende Aussagen über die rumänisch-deutschen Kontakte: sie seien „nicht beschränkt auf Sachkultur und handwerkliches Können (...) geistige Einflüsse können zumindest im Sachbereich der Philosophie" und „im Vokabular und vor allem in Denkmustern der Publikationen westlicher Landesteile noch in der ersten Hälfte dieses Jahrhunderts gesehen werden".

Sie geht so weit, deutsche „praktische und theoretische Einflüsse in der Sprachprogrammierung" und damit „in der Förderung der eigensprachlichen Entwicklung" zu sehen, wie sie dann bei der Reromanisierung und „Eliminierung der sprachlichen Überfremdung" (Crößmann-Osterloh 1985, 234) — also auch der Zurückdrängung gerade des deutschen Spracheinflusses — wirksam wurden.

7.3.2. Der deutsche Einfluß auf die rumänischen Mundarten

Die aus den Karten des „Atlasul lingvistic român" (ALR) ablesbaren Einflüsse gehen meist auf die ehemalige deutsche Verwaltungssprache und auf Direktkontakte mit den Deutschsprechern im Lande selbst zurück. (Vgl. Vasile Arvinte 1971, dessen rund 50 Wortkarten die jeweils größeren Verbreitungsgebiete deutscher Lehnwörter im modernen Rumänisch belegen.)

8. Zum Diskussionsstand

Wie kontrovers das Thema ist, zeigt Crößmann-Osterlohs (1985, 237) Schlußfeststellung, daß es „nicht darum gehe, die deutschen Einflüsse größer zu machen, als sie sind", sondern „um eine objektive Beurteilung" (auch: Munteanu 1986, 227 ff). Bereits die zweite Arbeit zu diesem Thema (Mandrescu 1904) kommt im Gegensatz zum Vorgänger (Borcia 1904, 138—253) zu weit weniger deutschen Belegbeispielen und auch zu einer strittigen Bewertung dieses deutschen Einflusses: Mandrescu sieht diesen als „gefährlich", insbesondere für das Rumänische im „austro-ungarischen Imperium" an und will diesen Einfluß „nicht weiter vordringen lassen, sondern ihn zum Verschwinden bringen" (Zit. n. Crößmann-Osterloh 1985, 93).

Diesen emotionalen Anfängen folgten nach 1918 objektivere Detailuntersuchungen über Fachsprachen und nach der Fertigstellung des ALR (1938 ff) der systematische Einbezug der Dialekte in diese Forschung.

Im sozialistischen Rumänien war unsere Frage in den Hintergrund des ansonsten regen Linguisteninteresses getreten. Das Standardwerk dazu entstand im Westen: in der kritisch die umfangreiche Literatur sichtenden Dissertation von Helga Crößmann-Osterloh, die wohl die abschließende, auch methodisch befriedigende Darstellung ist. In jüngster Zeit erschienen in Corbeas „Jassyer Beiträgen" (1986) Einzelbeiträge zu dieser insbesondere im Literaturbereich wieder aufgegriffenen Interferenzthematik. Analoges läßt sich umgekehrt bei der Untersuchung rumänischer Interferenzen unter den Rumäniendeutschen beobachten, die etwa zur gleichen Zeit mit Brenndörfers ungarisch geschriebener Untersuchung begann (1903). G. Kisch und A. Schullerus, die damals kompetentesten siebenbürgisch-sächsischen Philologen, wiesen an vielen Beispielen nach, daß Brenndörfer „mehr aufgenommen hat, als wissenschaftlich verantwortet werden kann" (Korrespondenzblatt 1903, Nr. 5, 65 ff und Nr. 1, 1 ff) und insbesondere die altromanischen Lehnwörter aus der rheinischen Urheimat der Siebenbürger (Hudler 1966, 162 ff) nicht kannte. Die frühe Arbeit von E. Grigorovitza (1901, 14 ff) gar kann Kisch nur als „amüsant, aber wissenschaftlich wenig fördernd" abtun.

In den Zwischenkriegsjahren war die Siebenbürger Dialektforschung zu sehr mit der Herkunftsfrage beschäftigt, als daß man sich mit der Frage des rumänischen Einflusses befaßt hätte. In den erst nach 1944 wieder einsetzenden Untersuchungen zur rumänisch-deutschen Interferenz läßt sich eher eine gegenteilige Tendenz zu dessen Überbewertung feststellen. G. Richters (1960, 1−56) erste umfassende Arbeit zeichnet sich durch eine mit zahlreichen Beispielen belegte Gliederungssystematik der semantischen Entlehnungen aus, die eine Fülle von kleineren Beiträgen auslöste. Auch hier liegt die abschließende Darstellung in der Dissertation von Karin Ney (1984) vor.

So können Geschichte und Bedeutung der Kontakte der rumänischen wie der deutschen Sprache − ungeachtet weiterer Untersuchungen zu Detailproblemen − als im wesentlichen bekannt und erforscht angesehen werden.

9. Bibliographie (in Auswahl)

Arvinte, Vasile (1971): *Die deutschen Entlehnungen in den rumänischen Mundarten* (nach den Angaben des Rumänischen Sprachatlasses), Berlin.

Bergel, Hans (1989): *Siebenbürgen*, Wien.

Borcia, Ion (1904): „Deutsche Sprachelemente im Rumänischen". In: *Zehnter Jahresbericht des Instituts für rumänische Sprache* (Rumänisches Seminar) zu Leipzig, Weigand, G. (Ed.), Leipzig, 138−253.

Brenndörfer, Johann (1903): „Román (Oláh) elemek az erdélyi szász nyelvben [Rumänische Elemente in der siebenb.-sächs. Sprache]". In: *Korrespondenzblatt des Vereins für siebenbürgische Landeskunde*, XXVI. Jahrg., Heft 2−3, Schullerus, A. (Ed.), Hermannstadt, 36 ff.

Corbea, Andrei/Nicolae, Octavian (Eds.) (1986): *Interferențe culturale româno-germane/Rumänisch-deutsche Kulturinterferenzen*, Jassy.

Crößmann-Osterloh, Helga (1985): *Die deutschen Einflüsse auf das Rumänische. Probleme − Kriterien − Anwendungen*, Tübingen.

Dicționarul limbi romîne moderne (1958): Bukarest.

Florea, Ion A. (1986): „Elemente de origine germana in Bucovina de Nord". In: Corbea/Nicolae (Eds.), 47 ff.

Heitmann, Klaus (Ed.) (1986): *Rumänisch-deutsche Interferenzen. Akten des Bukarester Kolloquiums über Literatur- und Geistesbeziehungen zwischen Rumänien und dem deutschen Sprachraum vom 13.−15. Oktober 1983*, Heidelberg.

Hudler, Ingeborg (1966): „Altromanisches Lehnwortgut im Westen und Südosten". In: *Luxemburg und Siebenbürgen*, Klein, K. K. (Ed.), Graz, 162 ff.

Jachomowski, Dirk (1984): *Die Umsiedlung der Bessarabien-, Bukowina- und Dobrudscha-Deutschen*, München.

Jumuga, Margareta-Sigrid (1986): „Rumänische Einflüsse in den deutschen Siedlungsmundarten und in der deutschen Umgangssprache der Bucovina". In: Corbea/Nicolae (Eds.), 41 ff.

Kelp, Helmut (1990): *Germanistische Linguistik in Rumänien 1945−85. Bibliographie*, SOKW München.

Kisch, Gustav (1903): „Rumänische Elemente im Siebenbürgisch-Sächsischen". In: *Korrespondenzblatt des Vereins für siebenbürgische Landeskunde*, XXVI. Jahrg. Nr. 5, Schullerus, A. (Ed.), Hermannstadt, 13 ff.

Klaster-Ungureanu, Grete (1958): „Wirtschaftliche und gesellschaftliche Beziehungen zwischen Rumänien und Sachsen im Spiegel des siebenbürgisch-sächsischen Wortschatzes". In: *Revue Roumaine de Linguistique* 3, 197−219.

Klein, Karl K./Schmitt, Ludwig E. (Ed.) (1961 ff): *Siebenbürgisch-Deutscher Sprachatlas, bearb. v. K. Rein, Band I: Laut- und Formenatlas, 1 u. 2, Band II: Wortatlas*, Marburg.

Klein, Karl K. (1963): *Transsylvanica. Gesammelte Abhandlungen und Aufsätze zur Sprach- und Siedlungsforschung der Deutschen in Siebenbürgen*, München.

Knobloch, Johann (1976): "Ein rumänisches Lehnsuffix in der österr. Umgangssprache". In: *Sprachwissen 1*, 479 f.

König, Walter (1988): "Muttersprachlicher Unterricht bei durchgehender Zweisprachigkeit. Zur Situation der deutschsprachigen Schulen und Abteilungen in Rumänien". In: *Kolloquium zum Deutschunterricht und Unterricht in deutscher Sprache bei den deutschen Bevölkerungsgruppen im Ausland*, Flensburg, 129–152.

Kotzian, Ortfried (1991): "Die Deutschen in den Aussiedlungsgebieten – Herkunft und Schicksal". In: *Modellversuch Aussiedler, Band II*, Dillingen.

Kroner, Michael (1973): *Interferenzen rumänisch-ungarisch-deutscher Kulturbeziehungen*, Cluj/Klausenburg.

Kühnel, Horst (1988): *Die Donauschwaben*.

Lang, Franz (1961): *Buchenland. 150 Jahre Deutschtum in der Bukowina*, München.

Mândrescu, Simion C. (1904): *Influența limbei germanei supra limba române*, Jassy.

Munteanu, Romul (1986): "Rumänische Aufklärer über Erziehung, Kultur und Fortschritt. Die Auswirkungen des Josephinismus". In: *Rumänisch-deutsche Interferenzen: Akten des Bukarester Kolloquiums über Literatur- und Geistesbeziehungen zwischen Rumänien und dem deutschen Sprachraum vom 13.–15. Oktober 1983*, Heitmann, Klaus (Ed.), Heidelberg, 11–19.

Nebel, Jeanne J. (1985): *The Danube Swabians*, Gersheim.

Ney, Karin (1984): *Rumänische Transferenzen in vier siebenbürgisch-sächsischen Ortsmundarten des Kreises Hermannstadt/Rumänien*, Marburg.

Oprea, Ioan (1986): "Rolul limbii germane la formarea terminologiei filosofice românești". In: Corbea/Nicolae (Eds.), 89 ff.

Petersen, Carl u. a. (Ed.) (1933): *Handwörterbuch des Grenz- und Auslandsdeutschtums*, Breslau, 1933, 611–644.

Post, Rudolf (1982): *Romanische Entlehnungen in den westmitteldeutschen Mundarten*, Wiesbaden.

Rein, Kurt (1961): "„Sächsisch" und „Schwäbisch" als Stammesbezeichnung im Südostdeutschtum". In: *Südostdt. Semesterblätter 7*, 8–13, und 9, 1962, 30–34.

Rein, Kurt (1975): "Die Germanistik an der Universität Czernowitz". In: *Alma mater Francisco Josephina*, Wagner, R. (Ed.), 145–179.

Rein, Kurt (1979): "Neuere Entwicklungstendenzen der deutschen Sprache in Rumänien". In: *Standardsprache und Dialekte in mehrsprachigen Gebieten Europas*, Tübingen, 124–147.

Rein, Kurt/Hildebrandt, R. (Eds.) (1979 c): *Siebenbürgisch-Deutscher Sprachatlas, Band II*: Wortatlas, Marburg.

Rein, Kurt (1980): "Diglossie und Bilingualismus bei den Deutschen Rumäniens". In: *Sprachkontakt und Sprachkonflikt*, Nelde, P. H. (Ed.), Wiesbaden, 263–269.

Rein, Kurt (1983): "Didaktische Probleme aus Diglossie und Bilingualismus bei deutschsprachigen Schülern in Südosteuropa". In: *Vergleichbarkeit von Sprachkontakten*, Nelde, P. H. (Ed.), Bonn, 141–152.

Rein, Kurt (1990): "Politische und kulturgeschichtliche Grundlagen der deutschsprachigen Literatur in der Bukowina". In: *Die Bukowina. Studien zu einer versunkenen Literaturlandschaft*, Goltschnigg, D./Schwob, A. (Eds.), Tübingen, 27–47.

Richter, Gisela (1960): "Zur Bereicherung der siebenbürgisch-sächsischen Mundart durch die rumänische Sprache". In: *Forschungen zur Volks- und Landeskunde 7*, Hermannstadt/Rumänien.

Scherer, Anton (1973): "50 Jahre Stammesname Donauschwaben". In: *Südostdeutsche Vierteljahresblätter 22*, 169–173.

Schwob, Anton (1971): *Wege und Formen des Sprachausgleichs in neuzeitlichen ost- und südostdeutschen Sprachinseln*, München.

Turczynski, Emanuel (1985): *Von der Aufklärung zum Frühliberalismus. Politische Trägergruppen und deren Forderungskatalog in Rumänien*, München.

Valjavec, Fritz (1953): *Geschichte der deutschen Kulturbeziehungen zu Südosteuropa*, München.

Weczerka, Hugo (1960): *Das mittelalterliche und frühneuzeitliche Deutschtum im Fürstentum Moldau*, München.

Wolf, Johann (1987): *Kleine Banater Mundartenkunde*, Bukarest.

Kurt Rein, München (Deutschland)

176. Rumänisch—Ungarisch

1. Geographie und Demographie
2. Geschichte
3. Ethnoprofile
4. Soziokulturelle Rahmenbedingungen des Sprachkontakts
5. Allgemeines kontaktlinguistisches Porträt
6. Forschungsstand
7. Bibliographie (in Auswahl)

1. Geographie und Demographie

1.1. Demographie

1992 habe der Anteil der ungarischen Minderheit an der Gesamtbevölkerung Rumäniens (22,76 Mio.) nach rumänischen statistischen Angaben 7,1% bzw. 1,62 Mio. und damit um 5,5% weniger als 1977 betragen, während der Anteil der rumänischen Mehrheit von 88,1% im Jahre 1977 bis 1992 um 7,1% auf 89,4% (20,35 Mio.) gestiegen sei (România 1992, 5). Von ungarischer Seite wird die Zahl der in Rumänien lebenden Ungarn auf über 2 Mio. geschätzt (Kendi 1992, 21). Zu dieser Diskrepanz trägt u. a. bei, daß die moldauischen Csángós von rumänischer Seite nicht als Magyaren anerkannt und daher nicht zur ungarischen Minderheit gezählt werden (vgl. dazu unter 1.2.2. und 3.) (→ Sprachenkarte H).

1.2. Kontaktzonen

1.2.1. Siebenbürgen

(ung. *Erdély*, rum. *Transilvania* [lat.] bzw. *Ardeal* (< ung. *Erdély*): Region des von den Karpaten umschlossenen historischen Siebenbürgen; in einem weiteren Sinne auch das gesamte, 1920 an Rumänien abgetretene Gebiet der einstigen ungarischen Reichshälfte der Österreichisch-Ungarischen Monarchie, i. e. die Region des historischen Siebenbürgen sowie das Banat (rum. *Banat*, ung. *Bánát*) und das Partium: das Kreischgebiet (rum. *Crişana*, ung. *Kőrösvidék*) und die Marmarosch (rum. *Maramureş*, ung. *Máramaros*).

Hier leben ca. 90% der ungarischen Minderheit: davon ca. 60% in relativ geschlossenen Siedlungen:

(a) im Szeklerland (Székelyföld) im südöstlichen Teil Siebenbürgens. Bei der Volkszählung von 1977 war der Anteil der ungarischen Bevölkerung an der Gesamtbevölkerung im Kreis Harghita 85%, in Covasna 78,1% und in Mureş 43,9% (vgl. Eisenburger 1978). Hier bilden sie in Orten wie Odorhellen (Odorheiu Secuiesc, Székelyudvarhely), Sankt Georgen (Sfîntu Gheorghe, Sepsiszentgyörgy), Neumarkt (Tîrgu Mureş, Marosvásárhely), Szeklerburg (Miercurea Ciuc, Csikszereda) die absolute Mehrheit;

(b) im Nordwesten Siebenbürgens. Das hier bis zum 17. Jahrhundert einheitliche Sprachgebiet zwischen Großwardein (Oradea, Nagyvárad), Zalău (Zilah) und Sathmar (Satu Mare, Szatmár) wurde durch Dörfer mit überwiegend rumänischer Bevölkerung zerteilt. Eine ungarische Mehrheit finden wir hier in Sathmar, Marghita (Margitta), Karol (Carei, Nagykároly), Trestendorf (Tăşnad, Tasnád), Şimleu Silvaniei (Szilágysomlyó), Großwardein und Salonta (Nagyszalonta). Etwa 30% leben zwischen diesen beiden Gebieten, in der Mitte Siebenbürgens, in kleineren Dörfern rings um Klausenburg (Cluj, Kolozsvár), um Huedin (Bánffyhunyad), südlich von Thorenburg (Torda, Turda) und östlich von Neuschloß (Gherla, Szamosújvár) sowie Dees (Dej, Dés).

Die zahlenmäßig größte Gruppe ungarischer Muttersprachler (110 000) lebt in Klausenburg, Neumarkt (82 000), Großwardein (100 000) und Sathmar (65 000) (Angaben von 1985; Kocsis 1990, 10).

1.2.2. Moldau

Etwa 10% der ungarischen Minderheit, die *Csángós* (vgl. unter 3.), leben in äußeren Sprachinseln oder in einer emigrationsähnlichen Diaspora außerhalb der Karpaten:

(a) westlich des Flusses Sereth (Siret), in den heutigen moldauischen Kreisen Bacău (ung. *Bakó*) und Neamţ (ung. *gyimesi csángók*), sowie östlich von Kronstadt (Braşov, Brassó), in Siebendörfen (Şapte sate, Hétfalu) (ung. *hétfalusi csángók*);

(b) Eine kleine Siedlung von Csángós, die aus der Bukowina stammen, gibt es noch um Diemrich (Deva, Déva), Kreis Hunedoara (Hunyad).

Die genaue Zahl der Csángós ist nicht bekannt; Kendi (1992, 21) schätzt sie auf 200 000 (vgl. dazu auch unter 3.).

1.2.3. Bukarest

In der Hauptstadt Bukarest lebt gegenwärtig ebenfalls eine größere Gruppe von Ungarn.

2. Geschichte

2.1. Entstehung des Sprachkontakts

Die Geschichte ist mit dem Problem der Urheimat der Rumänen verbunden. Hierzu gibt es zwei entgegengesetzte Standpunkte: (1) die „Kontinuitätstheorie", seit dem 18. Jahrhundert von Historikern und Sprachwissenschaftlern wie Thunmann, Šafařík, Mommsen, Ranke, besonders aber von rumänischen Wissenschaftlern (wie Hașdeu, Densușianu, Pușcariu, Iorga, gegenwärtig u. a. von Pascu und Condurachi) vertreten. Sie betrachtet die Rumänen von heute als Abkömmlinge jener dakischen Bevölkerung, die nach der Eroberung Dakiens durch Kaiser Trajan (101–106 n. Chr.) romanisiert wurde und in der Dacia Trajana ununterbrochen seßhaft geblieben ist; (2) die „Wandertheorie", Ende des 18. Jahrhunderts von Sulzer und etwas später von Engel begründet, im 19. Jahrhundert von namhaften Sprachwissenschaftlern (u. a. Miklosich, Kopitar, Tiktin, Jireček, Roesler), besonders aber von ungarischen Historikern und Sprachwissenschaftlern (wie Alföldi, Makkai, Gáldi, Tamás und Kniezsa) vertreten. Diese wiederum lokalisiert die Heimat der Rumänen in Süddanubien, von wo sie in der Zeit vom 9.–13. Jahrhundert in mehreren Wellen in das heutige Rumänien eingewandert, zum Teil auch planmäßig angesiedelt worden seien (hierzu u. a. Kocsis 1990, 4). Die „Wandertheorie" stützt sich in erster Linie auf die Ereignisse von 271 n. Chr., als Kaiser Aurelian Dakien aufgab und die römischen Truppen auf das rechte Donauufer zurückzog. Römische Quellen berichten hierzu, der Kaiser habe mit den Truppen die gesamte Stadt- und Landbevölkerung nach Mösien umgesiedelt. Beide Theorien vertreten einseitige Standpunkte, die relativierende Sichtweisen ausschließen. Solche sind jedoch angebracht. Einerseits erscheint die restlose Umsiedlung eines Volkes unrealistisch und ist es eher vorstellbar, daß Teile der Landbevölkerung auch nach 271 in Siebenbürgen verblieben sind. Andererseits ist auch die Ansicht, nach welcher Siebenbürgen die Wiege der Rumänen ist, unhaltbar. Es dürfte vielmehr eines von mehreren rumänischen Kerngebieten gewesen sein; weitere befanden sich sehr wahrscheinlich nördlich und südlich der Donau und im serbisch-bulgarischen Grenzland, von wo Rumänen im späten 12. und 13. Jahrhundert nach Siebenbürgen eingewandert sind (hierzu u. a. Brătianu 1942, Schubert 1982 a, 70 f). Die Ausschließlichkeit beider Theorien ist jedoch mit dem politischen Rechtsanspruch auf dieses Gebiet motiviert. Die Frage nach der Priorität in Siebenbürgen wurde daher zum konfliktträchtigen Politikum in den rumänisch-ungarischen Beziehungen. Hieraus folgend kann der früheste Zeitpunkt der rumänisch-ungarischen Sprachkontakte nicht mit Sicherheit genannt werden; es kann sie in Siebenbürgen bereits unmittelbar nach der ungarischen Landnahme gegeben haben.

2.2. Regionalgeschichte

Im 10./11. Jahrhundert wurde Siebenbürgen von den Ungarn eingenommen. Zur Sicherung dieses Gebietes gegen Einfälle von außen legte der ungarische König an strategisch wichtigen Punkten Grenzfestungen an, siedelte als Grenzwächter Szekler (vgl. unter 3.) an und verlieh ihnen Privilegien.

Gegen Ende des 12. Jahrhunderts siedelten sie im Komitat Bihar (Bihor), 1210 in der Gegend um Hermannstadt (Szeben, Sibiu) und 1222 im Karpatengebiet des Aranyos-Tals (Arieș). Von hier aus überschritten sie gemeinsam mit den von Andreas II. (1204–1235) nach Siebenbürgen gerufenen Deutschrittern und ungarischen Truppen die Berge, drangen ins damalige Kumanien vor und gründeten als Gruppe der *Csángós* mehrere Dörfer im Südwesten der Moldau (Bákó/Bacău, Roman, Putna) sowie einen Szeklerkreis in der Walachei.

Das erste „walachische Knezentum" (ung. *kenézség*) ist in ungarischen Urkunden auf dem Gebiet des heutigen Muntenien erwähnt. In der „Goldenen Bulle" von 1222, im „Sächsischen Freibrief" und im „Privilegium Andreanum" von 1224 wurde in Siebenbürgen ein Nebeneinander von privilegierten „nationes receptae" bzw. „populi", z. B. Ungarn, Szekler und Sachsen, und der unterprivilegierten „plebs", z. B. Rumänen, Ruthenen und Slowaken, bestätigt. Ein vom ungarischen König ernannter Wojewode leitete als königlicher Vertreter die siebenbürgische Komitatsverwaltung. Die Ungarn bildeten im historischen Siebenbürgen die Mehrheit. Sie bewohnten vor allem das siebenbürgische Hochland (Podișul Transilvaniei). Eine Ausnahme bildeten die als Grenzwächter eingesetzten Szekler, die wegen des Zuzugs der Sachsen im 13. Jahrhundert an den Fuß und in das von ihnen auch heute bewohnte Vorland der Ostkarpaten umgesiedelt worden waren. Im 14. Jahrhundert kam es zu größeren planmäßigen Ansiedlungen von Rumänen in Siebenbürgen, vor allem im Gebirge und in der Nachbarschaft der Ungarn am Bergfuß, von wo sie im 15. Jahrhundert in die ungarischen Dörfer des Hochlandes und auch in die deutschen Siedlungen des Sachsenlandes im Süden abwanderten. Dennoch stellten die Ungarn am Ende des 15. Jahrhunderts im historischen Siebenbürgen noch die Mehrheit der Bevölkerung.

Seit 1421 häuften sich osmanische Überfälle auf Siebenbürgen. 1442 wurden die Osmanen vom siebenbürgischen Fürsten und Feldherrn Hunyadi nur für kurze Zeit gestoppt. Nach ihrem Sieg bei Mohács/Mohatsch (1526) und der Einnahme Ofens (ung. Buda) wurde Siebenbürgen ein von Ungarn getrenntes, gegenüber dem osmanischen Sultan halbsouveränes Vasallenfürstentum mit einem eigenen Landtag der drei „Nationen" und einem von diesem gewählten Fürsten. Unter Stephan IV. Báthory (1571–1586) und Gábor Bethlen (1613–1629) erlebte Siebenbürgen eine wirtschaftliche und kulturelle Blüte. 1568 deklarierte der Landtag in Thorenburg (Torda, Turda) den Angehörigen der vier anerkannten Konfessionen (Katholiken, Lutheraner, Reformierte und Unitarier) freie Religionsausübung; 1581 wurde in Klausenburg (Kolozsvár, Cluj) eine Universität gegründet. Angriffe durch Türken und Tataren zwischen 1657 und 1661 führten zu Verwüstungen ungarischer Siedlungen zwischen dem Szeklerland (Székelyföld) und den Komitaten Bihar (Bihor) und Szatmár (Satu Mare). Hier ließen sich Rumänen nieder und bildeten bald eine Mehrheit. Nach der Befreiung Ungarns mußte Fürst Michael Apafi 1686 die habsburgische Oberhoheit anerkennen. 1692 war Siebenbürgen von den Osmanen befreit; seit 1699 gehörten Ungarn und Siebenbürgen zum Habsburgerreich. Siebenbürgen wurde mit weitgehender Autonomie als eigenes Großfürstentum von einem Gubernium in Hermannstadt (Szeben, Sibiu) und in der Siebenbürgischen Hofkanzlei in Wien verwaltet. Im 17. und 18. Jahrhundert stieg der rumänische Anteil an der Gesamtbevölkerung Siebenbürgens kontinuierlich: 1590: 31%, 1721: 49%, 1761: 56% (Kocsis 1990, 5, Tab. 2). 1850 betrug der Anteil der Rumänen an der Gesamtbevölkerung (1,87 Mio.) 58%, während jener der Ungarn nur noch 26% betrug. (ebd., Tab. 1). 1848–1849 wurde Siebenbürgen für kurze Zeit mit Ungarn vereinigt; nach dem österreichisch-ungarischen Ausgleich (1867) kam es wieder zu Ungarn. Gegen die zunehmende Magyarisierung ab 1876 wehrten sich die Sachsen und Rumänen Siebenbürgens (hierzu vgl. unter 4.1.). 1892 wandten sie sich in einem „Memorandum" an Kaiser Franz Joseph I. Im Frieden von Trianon (1920) mußte Ungarn Siebenbürgen mit 5,2 Mio. Einwohnern, von denen nach Kocsis (1990, 6) 1910 54% Rumänisch, 31,7% Ungarisch und 10,5% Deutsch als Muttersprache hatten, an Rumänien abtreten. Zwischen 1918 und 1924 flohen 197 000 Ungarn aus Siebenbürgen nach Ungarn (vgl. ebd., 6). Durch Zuwanderung von Rumänen aus der Moldau und der Walachei ging in den Städten der Anteil der Ungarn weiter zurück. 1930 waren von den 3 218 000 Einwohnern Siebenbürgens nach offiziellen rumänischen Angaben 57,6% Rumänen und 29,1% Ungarn (neben 7,9% Deutschen und 2,4% Juden) (Enciclopedia României I, 147–149). 1940 verlor Rumänien Nordsiebenbürgen und weitere angrenzende Gebiete an Ungarn. Durch den Friedensvertrag von Paris (1947) wurde der Vorkriegsstand wiederhergestellt. Auf beiden Seiten kam es gegenüber der jeweiligen Minderheit zu Übergriffen und Vertreibungen. 1947 wurde Rumänien „Volksrepublik", 1965 „Sozialistische Republik"; seit 1989 ist die Staatsbezeichnung wieder „Rumänien".

3. Ethnoprofile

Gegenwärtig bildet die ungarische Minderheit in Siebenbürgen ein weites Spektrum sozialer und regionaler Gruppierungen. Im Szeklerland (in den Bezirken Covasna, Harghita und Mureș) besitzen die relativ geschlossenen und in Abgeschiedenheit siedelnden Szekler sprachlich wie kulturell ein eigenes Gepräge. Über den Ursprung der Szekler (ung. *székely*, ungarländisch-lat. *siculus*) gibt es keine gesicherten Erkenntnisse (hierzu z. B. Györffy 1942). Möglicherweise gehörten sie zur militärischen Vorhut der landnehmenden ungarischen Stämme auf ihrem Weg nach dem Karpatenbecken. Aus der Szeklerschrift, die mit türkischen Kerben die ungarische Sprache wiedergibt, geht hervor, daß sie zu dieser Zeit Ungarisch sprachen. Seit der Grenzziehung von 1920 verstärkte sich die regionale Eigenart des von den Szeklern gesprochenen Ungarisch; sie ist auf den ständigen Kontakt mit dem Rumänischen zurückzuführen, das ebenfalls Spuren dieses Kontakts aufweist (vgl. hierzu unter 5.2.). Im heutigen Ungarn werden die Siebenbürger Szekler vielfach als Vertreter eines unverfälschten „Urmagyarentums" angesehen. Aus ihrer Reihe gingen bedeutende Schriftsteller wie z. B. András Sütő (geb. 1927) hervor.

Die moldauischen Csángós sind römisch-katholischer Konfession; in Sprache und Alltagskultur haben sie sich seit dem 17. Jahrhundert mehr und mehr an ihre rumänische Umgebung akkulturiert, besonders in den Städten. In den Dörfern ist ihre kulturelle Authentizität etwas stärker. Hier sprechen sie weiterhin Ungarisch, jedoch stark mit dem Rumänischen gemischt (vgl. auch unter 5.2.). Der Sprechername *csángó* hängt möglicherweise mit einem veraltet-ungarischen *csáng* „herumschweifen" zusammen; dies ist ein von den Siebenbürger Ungarn gegenüber ihren migrierenden Landsleuten verwendeter Spitzname. Gegenwärtig wird um die Csángós eine heftige Kontroverse geführt; von rumänischer Seite wird die These vertreten, daß es sich bei ihnen um ehemals in Siebenbürgen siedelnde und zwangsmagyarisierte Rumänen handele. Budapest dagegen betrachtet die Csángós als einen magyarischen Volksstamm (hierzu u. a. Ghermani 1986, Tschangos 1987).

Das interethnische Zusammenleben in Siebenbürgen wird u. a. durch stereotype Vorstellungen von den jeweils Anderen belastet. Den Ungarn wird von rumänischer Seite unterstellt, sie würden die Ablösung dieser Provinz und ihre Wiedereingliederung in den ungarischen Staat betreiben. Damit verbinden sich immer wieder Hinweise auf die nomadische, „asiatische" Herkunft der Ungarn und Klischees über ihre vermeintliche Jähzornigkeit, Streitsüchtigkeit und Unzuverlässigkeit. Umgekehrt prägt das Bild der Ungarn von den Rumänen die stereotype Vorstellung von der „Primitivität" des „schwerfällig-langsamen" walachischen Wanderhirten; *oláh* „Walache" hat in diesem Zusammenhang, mit wechselnden Epitheta versehen, pejorative Konnotation. Dennoch entwickelten sich im Zusammenleben von Ungarn und Rumänen auch zahlreiche Gemeinsamkeiten und Interferenzen in verschiedenen Lebensbereichen. Solche entstanden durch ständige Interaktion auf Wochen- und Jahrmärkten, in Handel und Handwerk (etwa in der Töpferei, Kerbschnitzerei), aber auch auf anderen Gebieten der Alltagskultur: in Siedlungsformen (pannonische Straßendörfer), auf dem Gebiet des Bauens und Wohnens (Gehöfttyp; Inneneinrichtung des Hauses; vgl. in diesem Zusammenhang rum. *sobă* 1. „Zimmer" (Siebenbürgen), 2. „Ofen" (Moldau, Walachei) < ung. *szoba* „Zimmer"), in den Eßgewohnheiten und in der Kleidungsgestaltung. Bis zur Mitte des 18. Jahrhunderts waren in der Kleidung ungarische Vorbilder maßgeblich: Männer trugen z. B. die weite ungarische Männerhose (vgl. rum. *gaci* „weite Hose" < ung. *gatya*) und den reich verzierten Hirtenmantel *szűr*. Beliebt waren auch ungarische Verzierungstechniken wie das „geschriebene" (ung. *írásos*) Muster, vor allem an Ärmelrüschen; vgl. rum. *fodori* „Rüsche" (zu ung. *fodor*). In einzelnen Dörfern um Huedin (ung. Bánffyhunyad) konnte man die Rumänin kaum von einer Ungarin unterscheiden. Umgekehrt verbreiteten sich bei den Ungarn der rumänische Hirtenmantel *glugă*, rumänische Sticktechniken, Stick- und Webmuster. Rumänischen Vorbildern sind in der Kleidung am meisten die moldauischen Csángós gefolgt (hierzu Dunăre/Treiber-Netoliczka 1978).

4. Sozio-kulturelle Rahmenbedingungen des Sprachkontakts

4.1. Ungarische Minderheiten- und Sprachpolitik bis 1918

Bis zum Beginn des 20. Jahrhunderts war das Ungarische in Siebenbürgen die Sprache einer privilegierten „Nation" und die Herrschaftssprache. Sie setzte die Norm für alle Bereiche des öffentlichen Lebens (hierzu Schubert 1982b). Zwar war in Ungarn anfangs die offizielle Verwaltungssprache Latein, doch hat sich in Siebenbürgen bereits im 16. Jahrhundert auch das Ungarische als Amtssprache durchgesetzt. Nur so ist es zu erklären, daß bereits vor Beginn der Magyarisierungswelle so viele Termini des öffentlichen Lebens ins Rumänische entlehnt wurden. Die ungarischen Elemente der rumänischen Literatursprache haben ein eindeutiges Übergewicht gegenüber den rumänischen Elementen des Ungarischen (vgl. hierzu unter 5.1.1., 5.1.2.).

Bis zum Sprachendekret Kaiser Josephs II. (1784) und dem Aufkommen des ungarischen Sprachnationalismus verlief das rumänisch-ungarische Miteinander ohne offene nationale Konflikte; die Druckerei der Universität in Pest versorgte z. B. auch die Moldau und die Walachei mit rumänischsprachigen Büchern; 1825 erschien hier das erste größere Wörterbuch in rumänischer Sprache: „Lexicon Budense", kurz darauf in Ofen die erste rumänische Zeitschrift „Biblioteca Românească".

Die Wende in diesen Beziehungen wurde durch das Sprachendekret Josephs II. 1784 eingeleitet, mit dem das Deutsche als Amtssprache in der Habsburgischen Monarchie eingeführt wurde. Den ungarischen Beamten wurde eine Frist von drei Jahren gewährt, um das Deutsche zu erlernen. Bei den Ungarn rief dies eine Welle des Protestes und ein Aufflammen nationaler Bestrebungen hervor, die dann schließlich in der Magyarisierungswelle gegenüber den ungarländischen Minderheiten mündete. Nach 1867, als Siebenbürgen an Ungarn angegliedert wurde, leitete Ungarn mit dem Minderheitengesetz von 1868 eine Phase rücksichtsloser Assimilierungspolitik ein. Sie war begleitet von Gesetzen, die die ungarische Sprache zur alleinigen Behörden-, Gerichts- und Schulsprache erhoben (1879, 1883). 1898 wurde per Gesetz der Gebrauch ungarischer Ortsnamen in amtlichen Schriftstücken verordnet. Ende des Jahrhunderts wuchs die Zahl der Bevölkerung mit ungarischer Muttersprache infolge erhöhter Geburtenrate und sprachlicher Assimilation von Juden, Deutschen, Armeniern und Roma. Die Rumänen spielten im politischen Leben keine Rolle mehr; während vier- bis fünftausend ungarischsprechende Székler einen Abgeordneten ins Parlament nach Budapest entsandten, entfiel auf 500 000 – 600 000 Rumänen lediglich ein Abgeordneter (Kann 1964, 316). Die Hoch- und Mittelschulen waren fast vollständig magyarisiert. Die Rumänen gründeten darauf 1891 in Bukarest eine rumänische kulturelle Liga. Die „Lex Apponyi" (1907) weitete die staatliche Kontrolle und den Unterricht in ungarischer Sprache in den Gemeinde- und Konfessionsschulen aus. Erst jetzt begann sich eine starke rumänische Opposition gegen die verschärfte Magyarisierungspolitik des ungarischen Parlaments zu formieren. Der rumänische Widerstand führte im Ersten Weltkrieg 1916 dazu, daß Rumänien Österreich-Ungarn den Krieg erklärte. Mit dem Zerfall der Habsburger Monarchie wuchs die Aktivität der Rumänen. Ungarische Zugeständnisse in letzter Minute blieben wirkungslos; im Dezember 1918 erklärte der neu gewählte „Consiliu Dirigent" den Anschluß Siebenbürgens an Rumänien.

4.2. Rumänische Minderheiten- und Sprachpolitik von 1918–1994

Zum Ausgleich für die ihnen früher widerfahrene Diskriminierung waren die Rumänen im neuen Nationalstaat Rumänien von dem Wunsch getragen, einen national einheitlichen Staat zu schaffen. Im November 1918 versprach die rumänische Nationalversammlung in den „Karlsburger Beschlüssen" „die volle nationale Freiheit für alle mitwohnenden Völker" des neuen Staatsverbands, für die Minderheiten Unterrichts-, Verwaltungs- und Rechtspflege in der eigenen Sprache, ferner Beteiligung an der Landesregierung. Zu einer Umsetzung dieser Beschlüsse kam es jedoch nicht. Da mit der neuen Provinz Siebenbürgen eine geschlossene ungarische Minderheit übernommen wurde, die vor allem in den Städten die Mehrheit bildete, sollte dieses Verhältnis durch Kolonisierung und Schaffung von „Kulturzonen" verändert werden.

In der Zwischenkriegszeit gab es Ansätze zu einem interethnischen Dialog in allen Bereichen, so im öffentlichen und wirtschaftlichen Leben, im Bildungs- und Pressewesen (vgl. u. a. Szegedi 1992, 310 ff); diese hatten jedoch keine größeren Auswirkungen. 1923 wurde in der Verfassung Groß-Rumäniens das Königreich Rumänien zu einem einheitlichen und unteilbaren Nationalstaat und die rumänische Sprache zur offiziellen Landessprache erklärt. Die frühere Schul- und Kirchenautonomie der Szekler und Siebenbürger Sachsen blieben unberücksichtigt. Die Verfassung enthielt für die Minderheiten lediglich individuelle, jedoch keine kollektiven Rechte. Nach 1931 verbesserten sich die interethnischen Beziehungen. 1933 wurden die Karlsburger Beschlüsse wieder angenommen. Der rumänisch-ungarische Dialog wurde im Geiste eines toleranten Transilvanismus vorangetrieben. Die Annäherung der Kulturen wurde zum Grundsatzprogramm erhoben (vgl. die Jahrgänge der Zeitschrift „Erdélyi Helikon" bis 1940). Dieser Dialog blieb jedoch wiederum in seinen Ansätzen stecken. 1933 wurde die staatliche Unterstützung für Konfessionsschulen gestrichen; radikal-rechte politische Strömungen kamen unter den Rumänen auf. Die Verfassung von 1938 war bereits ethnozentrisch konzipiert. Der Wiener Schiedsspruch von 1940 schuf durch die Verschiebung der Grenzen zugunsten Ungarns neue Minderheiten. 1944 wurde die Grenzverschiebung wieder rückgängig gemacht. Im Minderheitenstatut von 1945 wurde in Rumänien die rumänische Sprache als Amtssprache festgelegt. Den „mitwohnenden Nationalitäten" wurde jedoch der freie Gebrauch ihrer Muttersprache in allen Bereichen des privaten, wirtschaftlichen und kulturellen Lebens zugesichert.

Unter dem Druck Stalins, der die Ungarn für den Verlust Nordsiebenbürgens zu „entschädigen" trachtete, verfolgte das kommunistische Rumänien in den Nachkriegsjahren bis etwa 1957 gegenüber der ungarischen Minderheit eine relativ liberale Politik. Es entstand eine Autonome Ungarische Region im Südosten Siebenbürgens; Verwaltungszentrum wurde Neumarkt (Tîrgu Mureș/Marosvásárhely) mit einem ungarischen Bevölkerungsanteil von 73,8% (1956). Im Zusammenhang mit dem Volksaufstand im November 1956 in Ungarn ging Bukarest jedoch zu einer zunehmend repressiven Nationalitätenpolitik über, der auch die Autonome Ungarische Region schrittweise zum Opfer fiel. Ende 1960 wurde hier die ethnische Relation zugunsten der Rumänen durch die Umstrukturierung des in Autonome Ungarische Region Mureș umbenannten Gebietes verändert, indem der südliche, mehrheitlich ungarische Teil abgetrennt und im Westen ein mehrheitlich rumänisches Gebiet angeschlossen wurde. 1950/51 gab es noch 20 ungarische Fakultäten; bis 1958/59 wurden sie auf neun Fakultäten und drei Abteilungen mit ungarischer Unterrichtssprache reduziert, dann allmählich aufgelöst, so daß nur noch einige Veranstaltungen an den Universitäten in Klausenburg und Neumarkt auch in ungarischer Sprache angeboten wurden. 1959 wurden die getrennten ungarischen und rumänischen Fakultäten der Bólyai-Universität in Klausenburg unter rumänischer Leitung zwangsvereinigt und in Babeș-Bólyai-Universität umbenannt. Zwischen 1957 und 1961 wurden ungarische mit rumänischen Schulen zusammengelegt. 1968, drei Jahre nach Ceaușescus Machtübernahme, wurde die Region Mureș aufgelöst. Rumänien führte die Gliederung des Staatsgebiets in Kreise wieder ein. Ceaușescu proklamierte die volle Gleichberechtigung aller Bürger, ungeachtet ihrer Nationalität. Die Entwicklung nahm jedoch einen entgegengesetzten Verlauf. Seit Beginn der 70er Jahre wurde die Assimilierung der ethnischen Minderheiten an das staatstragende Rumänentum forciert vorangetrieben. Weitere ungarische Hochschulen und Lyzeen wurden geschlossen. Presse, Rundfunk, Fernsehen, Theater und Buchproduktion der Ungarn erfuhren Einschränkungen (Kendi 1992, 81). Für alle Bereiche des öffentlichen Lebens wurde, auch in rein ungarischen Gemeinden, die Verwendung des Rumänischen verordnet. Im Zuge einer forcierten Industrialisierung und Urbanisierung wurden zahlreiche gewachsene ungarische Dorfkulturen und Kulturgüter zerstört, Bewohner ganzer Regionen „umgeschichtet" und damit kulturell entwurzelt. Diese Maßnahmen zogen die Auswanderung vieler ungarischer Intellektueller nach Ungarn oder in andere Länder nach sich.

Nach dem politischen Umbruch von 1989 gab es zunächst eine Bereitschaft zum Dialog. Es entstanden Vereine wie „Gruppe für Sozialen Dialog", „Liga Pro Europa" oder die Zeitschriften „Puntea" und „22", die sich den interethnischen Dialog zum Ziel setzten. Bald jedoch kam es wieder zu Spannungen zwischen Rumänen und Ungarn. Im März 1990 kam es im Zusammenhang mit den Forderungen der ungarischen Minderheit nach kultureller Autonomie, Anerkennung von Zweisprachigkeit im öffentlichen Leben, Wiedereinführung von rein ungarischen Bildungsanstalten sowie der Bólyai-Universität in Klausenburg in Neumarkt zu blutigen Straßenschlachten mit mehreren Toten und Hunderten von Verletzten (hierzu u. a. Socor 1990). Seitdem hat es zwar Änderungen gegeben, die auch die Situation der ungarischen Minderheit verbesserten, doch bleibt die Lage gespannt. Ein Minderheitengesetz wird verzögert; der Minderheitenschutz beinhaltet nur individuelle Rechte. Der Gebrauch der Minderheitensprache ist im öffentlichen Leben nicht durchzusetzen.

5. Allgemeines kontaktlinguistisches Porträt

5.1. Bis 1918

5.1.1. Ungarische Elemente im Rumänischen
Viele Magyarismen sind über das ganze dakorumänische Sprachgebiet verbreitet. Einige Entlehnungen aus dem Ungarischen erscheinen bereits in slavischen Urkunden Siebenbürgens und der mittelalterlichen rumänischen Fürstentümer: vgl. z. B. rum. *a cheltui* „ausgeben" < ung. *költ* (+ *ui* in Anlehnung an slav. *-ovati*; zuerst 1432 belegt). In solchen Urkunden findet man auch den Severiner Banatsvorsteher als „banus" des ungarischen Königs erwähnt. Von jenen Münzen, die vom Banus hier in Umlauf gebracht wurden, leitet sich die heute im Rumänischen allgemein verbreitete Bedeutung „Geld" für *bani* her.

Während der ungarischen Herrschaft über Siebenbürgen verbreiteten sich im Rumänischen zahlreiche ungarische Begriffe des öffentlichen Lebens (hierzu u. a. Schubert 1982 b):

(a) Bezeichnungen der Verwaltung: z. B. rum. *hotar* „Grenze" (ung. *határ*); *oraş* „Stadt" (*város*); *îngădui* „gestatten, zulassen" (*enged*); *pecetlui* „Stempeln" (*pecsétel*);
(b) des Gerichtswesens: z. B. rum. *birău* „Schulze, Dorfrichter" (ung. *bíró*); *referălui ~ referelui* „referieren" (*referál*); *celuşag* „Betrug" (*csalság*); *chezeş* „Bürge" (*kezes*);
(c) des Geldverkehrs, Zoll- und Steuerwesens: z. B. rum. *a cheltui* „ausgeben" (ung. *költ*); *vamă* „Zoll" (*vám*);
(d) des Wirtschaftslebens und Handwerks: z. B. rum. *gazdă* „Wirt, Gastwirt, Hausherr, Herberge" (*gazda*); rum. *holdă* „Morgen" (*hold*); *marfă* „Ware" (*marha* „Vieh"); *meşteşug* „Kunst, Handwerk" (*mesterség*).

Auch viele ungarische Begriffe des Alltagslebens (neben Substantiven auffallend viele Verben) verbreiteten sich im Rumänischen: vgl. u. a. rum. *a băsădi* „plaudern", *dărab* „Stück", *a alcătui* „bilden", *a bîntui* „heimsuchen", *belşug* „Überfluß", *a chibzui* „überlegen", *a lăcui* „wohnen" (1418), *a mântui* „erretten", *beteag* „krank"; ebenso Lehnübersetzungen wie rum. *a face destul* zu ung. *eleget tenni* „Folge leisten", *de multe feluri* „vielerlei" nach ung. *sokféle*, *a scris sus* „er hat aufgeschrieben" zu ung. *felírni*.

Bis 1840 bezeichnete *neam* „Nation, Volk" < ung. *nem* „Geschlecht, Volk, Sippschaft" als Synonym für *naţie* die Rumänen der Fürstentümer (*neamul Românesc* − bezogen auf die Walachei; *neamul Moldovenesc* − bezogen auf die Moldau); zur Kennzeichnung des einfachen Volkes diente ung. *nép* (~ dial. *níp*) „Volk"; vgl. rum. *nip* „Volk".

Neben Nomina und Verba wurden ungarische Suffixe mit einheimischen Bezeichnungen verknüpft, hier vor allem *-ş, aş, -eş, -auş* < ung. *-s*; vgl. *ceteraş, chipeş*, rum. *-ău* < ung. *-ó*, vgl. z. B. *nătărău*, rum. *-işag, -şug, -şig* < ung. *-ság, -ség*; vgl. z. B. rum. *furtişag, beteşug, eftinşig*. Dieser Prozeß setzt sich heute weiter fort.

Im siebenbürgischen Rumänisch sind Diffusionsgrad und Gebrauchshäufigkeit der ungarischen Lehnwörter sehr viel höher als in den übrigen rumänischen Regionen. Nach Puşcariu (1943, 399) finden sich solche Lehnwörter auch in einsprachig rumänischen Gegenden; sie seien von den Städten ausgestrahlt und haben sich aus den Kreisen der Ungarn oder in ungarischen Schulen aufgewachsenen Beamten und Intellektuellen in vertikaler Richtung verbreitet. Zu den „Ardelenismen" gehören auch Latinismen, die besonders die Sprache der gebildeten siebenbürgischen Schichten prägten; vgl. z. B. *conscribălui* „konskribieren" (18. Jh.) < lat. und ungarländisch-lat. *conscribere* (hierzu u. a. Puşcariu 1943, 520).

5.1.2. Rumänische Elemente des Ungarischen

Diese bilden im Ungarischen eine relativ kleine Gruppe: Die frühesten stammen aus der Terminologie des walachischen Wanderhirtentums und sind im umgarischen Schrifttum bereits zu Beginn des 14. Jahrhunderts belegt: z. B. ung. *cserge* „Decke, grobes Wollgewebe" (rum. *cergă*), *furulya* „Hirtenflöte" (*fluerá*), *csobán* „Schäfer" (*cioban* < osm.-türk. *çoban*). Ferner finden sich im Ungarischen einige rumänische, aus dem Vulgärlatein stammende Begriffe wie z. B. ung. *ficsor* (< aung. *ficsúr*) „Bursche, Kerl" < rum. *fecior, ficior*.

5.2. Ab 1918

In den mehrheitlich von Ungarn besiedelten Gebieten Rumäniens ist Rumänisch Amts- und Fachsprache; Ungarisch Umgangssprache. Die Kompetenz des Ungarischen ist am größten unter jenen Ungarn, die in größeren Gruppen zusammenleben (siehe unter 1.2.1.); sie nimmt ab unter den Bewohnern von Sprachinseln und Streusiedlungen (s. ebd.). Am geringsten ist sie unter den Csángós jenseits der Karpaten.

Seit 1920 hat sich die Zahl der Rumänismen in der Sprache der siebenbürgischen Ungarn erhöht. Sie betreffen nicht mehr nur Bezeichnungen, die mit der rumänischen Herrschaft zusammenhängen (vgl. *siguráncia* zu *siguranţa* „Schutzpolizei", *lej* „Leu" zu *lei* − Pl. zu *leu* „rum. Münzeinheit"), Lehnübersetzungen und -konstruktionen wie z. B. *régiség* „Dienstzeit" zu rum. *vechime*, sondern auch die Alltagssprache, die eine Mischsprache ist: *látni fogom a norokot* zu rum. *am sa văd norocul* „ich werde das Glück sehen" oder *kékek* „Auberginen" − wörtlich „Blaue" zu rum. *vinete* bzw. *patlagele vinete* „Auberginen". Auffällig sind ferner unter dem Einfluß der Zweisprachigkeit Strukturveränderungen des Ungarischen wie z. B. der Infinitiv-Verlust; vgl. *kell hogy megyek* „es ist nötig, daß ich gehe, ich muß gehen" statt *mennem kell* − nach rum. *trebuie să merge* „ds.". Interferenzen zeigen sich auch in der Wortfolge (z. B.: Objekt steht vor dem Prädikat), in dem vom Ungarischen abweichenden Gebrauch des Plurals nach Zahlwörtern, von Flexionsendungen nach Präpositionen.

Zu den Interferenzerscheinungen gehören auch einige isophonische Erscheinungen: Bei den Ungarn, mit Ausnahme des Szeklerlandes, werden die ungarischen Vokale *ë* und *o* offener (z. B. *azak* "jene", *vagyak* "ich bin" statt *azok*, *vagyok*), die kurzen Vokale dagegen länger (z. B. *múlat* "sich unterhalten" statt *mulat*) als allgemein üblich ausgesprochen. Umgekehrt sprechen die Szekler und Csángós den Vokal im Akk. Pl. geschlossener als in der Gemeinsprache (z. B. *házakot* "die Häuser" statt *házakat*). Ferner verkürzen sie die langen Vokale *í*, *ű*, *ő*. Besonderheiten weist — möglicherweise unter dem Einfluß des Ungarischen — auch das Siebenbürger-Rumänische auf: u. a. die gedehnte Aussprache der Monophthonge, wodurch es insgesamt langsam und schwerfällig wirkt; ferner die Monophthongierung von *-oa* zu *[å]* (z. B. *[câs:ə]* für *coasă* "Sense").

Fast alle Mischungsverhältnisse zwischen Ungarisch und Rumänisch kommen vor. Selten ist eine gleichgewichtige Zweisprachigkeit bzw. eine Sprachsituation, in der die beiden Sprachen oder Idiome in gleicher Weise und Funktion gebraucht werden. Vielmehr handelt es sich meistens um eine asymmetrische Zweisprachigkeit, in welcher die Staatssprache, d. h. das Rumänische, dominiert; lediglich im Szeklerland kommt es vor, daß das Ungarische die gemeinsame Kommunikationsbasis darstellt, jedoch auch hier nicht durchgängig. Die Ungarn in Siebenbürgen, besonders Intellektuelle, sind zweisprachig; in gemischten Dörfern sind dies auch Rumänen, jedoch seltener. Die Kompetenz des Ungarischen der Csángós ist zugunsten der des Rumänischen stark zurückgegangen; ähnlich verhält es sich bei den in kleineren Sprachinseln lebenden Ungarn (hierzu Márton/Péntek 1977).

Die ungarisch-rumänischen Lehnbeziehungen sind in Siebenbürgen häufig wechselseitig; vgl. z. B. ung. *ardéj* "Paprika" < rum. *ardei* im Szeklerland, aber rum. *popricǎ* "ds." < ung. *paprika* in Marmarosch; ung. *fuszulyka* "Bohne" im Szeklerland < rum. *păsúlă*; ebenso ung. *kozsék* "Pelzjacke" < rum. *cojoc*, aber rum. *bundă* "Pelzmantel" < ung. *bunda*.

6. Forschungsstand

Viele Arbeiten zu den rumänisch-ungarischen Sprachbeziehungen entstanden vor dem Hintergrund der ungarisch-rumänischen Auseinandersetzungen um die Besiedlungspriorität in Siebenbürgen; sie entbehren daher vielfach der Objektivität. In der rumänischen Forschung des vergangenen Jahrhunderts waren die Magyarismen des Rumänischen vor allem als zu vermeidende "Barbarismen" von Interesse (so z. B. Budai-Deleanu; Rădulescu 1847). Auf ungarischer Seite hingegen war das Interesse gegenüber dem ungarischen "Einfluß" auf das Rumänische aus guten Gründen groß: er sollte die längere Ansässigkeit der Ungarn in Siebenbürgen und ihre kulturelle Superiorität gegenüber den Rumänen evident machen (vgl. z. B. bei Hunfalvy 1894; Gáldi 1943). Diese Ansicht vertritt — bis etwa 1944 — selbst Tamás (dezidiert 1943, 27 f).

Die erste größere Sammlung ungarischer Lehnwörter (etwas über 500 Lexeme) enthält Bd. II des von A. Cihac 1879 veröffentlichten Dakorumänischen Etymologischen Wörterbuchs; viele von ihnen werden fälschlicherweise dem Ungarischen zugeschrieben. Von ungarischer Seite beschäftigte sich — sehr unvollkommen — Alexics 1888 mit diesem Thema. 1892 erschien von Mândrescu eine etwas differenziertere Arbeit hierzu. Einen beachtlichen Aufschwung erfuhr die Erforschung der rumänisch-ungarischen Sprachbeziehungen nach dem Ersten Weltkrieg; u. a. haben Gáldi und Tagliavini Magyarismen in den von ihnen publizierten Wörterbüchern zusammengetragen. Seit 1930 profilierte sich Tamás (alias Treml) auf dem Gebiet der ungarisch-rumänischen Kultur- und Sprachbeziehungen. Das von ihm 1966 publizierte historisch-etymologische Wörterbuch der ungarischen Elemente im Rumänischen enthält 2800 Wortartikel. 93% von ihnen sind mundartlich — dabei stehen die siebenbürgischen Mundarten im Mittelpunkt. Die verbleibenden 7% (195 Lexeme) sind gemeinrumänisch. Neuere Untersuchungen zu ungarisch-rumänischen Sprachbeziehungen stammen u. a. von Reichenkron, Schubert (vgl. unter 7.). Mit den rumänisch-ungarischen sprachlichen Interferenzen der Gegenwart beschäftigen sich u. a. Márton/Péntek/Vöö (vgl. ebd.). Zur neuesten rumänisch-ungarischen Diskussion um die Csángós vgl. Ghermani 1986, Tschangos 1987.

7. Bibliographie (in Auswahl)

Alexics, György (1888): *Magyar elemek az oláh nyelvben* [Ungarische Elemente in der walachischen Sprache], Budapest.

Bakos, Ferenc (1982): *A magyar szókészlet román elemeinek története* [Geschichte der rumänischen Elemente des ungarischen Wortbestands], Budapest.

Brătianu, Gheorqhe I. (1942): *Ein Rätsel und ein Wunder der Geschichte: Das rumänische Volk* (Die Dacia-Bücher), Bukarest, Reprint München 1968.

Budai-Deleanu, Ion: *Lexicon Românesc-nemțesc* [Rumänisch-deutsches Wörterbuch]. MSSE Romîne 3728−3731. Biblioteca Academiei R. S. R.

Cihac, Alexandre de (1879): *Dictionnaire d'étymologie dacoroman. Elements slaves, magyars, turcs, grecs-moderne et albanais*, Frankfurt am Main.

Dunăre, Nicolae/Treiber-Netoliczka, Luise: „Rumänische, sächsische und ungarische Beziehungen auf dem Gebiete der Volkskunde". In: *Zur Interethnik. Donauschwaben, Siebenbürger Sachsen und ihre Nachbarn*, Weber-Kellermann, I. (Ed.), Frankfurt am Main, 240−274.

Eisenburger, Eduard (1978): *Egalitate reală − participare activă* [Echte Gleichberechtigung − aktive Partizipation], Bukarest.

Gabanyi, Anneli Ute (1990): *Die unvollendete Revolution. Rumänien zwischen Diktatur und Demokratie*, München.

Gáldi, László (1943): „Ungarisch-rumänische Kulturbeziehungen". In: *Siebenbürgen und seine Völker*, Mályusz, E. (Ed.), Budapest, 231−255.

Ghermani, Dionisie (1986): „Die historische Legitimierung der rumänischen Nationalitätenpolitik". In: *Südost-Europa* 35, 352−354.

Győrffy, György (1942): „Der Ursprung der Szekler". In: *Ungarische Jahrbücher 22*, 129−151.

Hunfalvy, Pál (1894): *Az oláhok története* [Geschichte der Walachen], 2 Bde., Budapest.

Kann, Robert A. (^{2}1964): *Das Nationalitätenproblem der Habsburgermonarchie* Bd. I: *Das Reich und die Völker*, Graz−Köln, 309−321 (zur nationalen Frage der Rumänen in Siebenbürgen).

Kendi, Erich (1992): *Minderheitenschutz in Rumänien. Die rechtliche Normierung des Schutzes der ethnischen Minderheiten in Rumänien*, München.

Klein, Samuelis (1944): *Dictionarium Valacho-Latinum*, Gáldi, L. (Ed. und Einleitung), Budapest.

Kocsis, Károly (1990): *Atlas Ost- und Südosteuropa. Aktuelle Karten zu Ökologie, Bevölkerung und Wirtschaft*. Österreichisches Ost- und Südosteuropa-Institut, Wien.

Koepeci, Béla (Ed.) (1990): *Kurze Geschichte Siebenbürgens*, Budapest.

Márton, Gyula/Péntek, János/Vöő, István (1977): *A magyar nyelvjárások román kölcsönszavai − Imprumuturile românești ale dialectelor maghiare − Rumänische Lehnwörter in den ungarischen Mundarten*, Bukarest.

Pascu, Ștefan/Ștefănescu, Ștefan (Ed.) (1987): *Das gefährliche Spiel der Geschichtsfälschung*, Bukarest.

Pușcariu, Sextil (1943): Die rumänische Sprache. Ihr Wesen und ihre volkliche Prägung. Dt. Übers. von H. Kuen, Leipzig, insbes. 395−401.

Rădulescu, I. E. (1847): *Vocabularu de vorbe streine în limba romană adica: slavone, ungurescĭ, turcescĭ, nemțescĭ, grecescĭ etc.* [Vokabular der fremden Wörter im Rumänischen, und zwar slavischer, ungarischer, türkischer, deutscher, griechischer usw.], Bukarest.

Reichenkron, Günter (1959): „Methodisches zu den ungarischen Lehnwörtern im Rumänischen". In: *Ural-Altaische Jahrbücher 31*, 319−335.

România: Recensamîntul populației și locuințelor. Rezultate preliminare [Rumänien: Einwohner- und Wohnungszählung. Vorläufige Ergebnisse]. Conferință de presă, Comisia Națională pentru Statistică, Bukarest, 29. Mai 1992.

Simonyi, Siegmund (1907): *Die ungarische Sprache. Geschichte und Charakteristik*, Straßburg.

Schubert, Gabriella (1982 a): „Ungarn und Rumänen. Zu den ungarisch-rumänischen Sprachbeziehungen". In: *Ural-Altaische Jahrbücher N. F. Bd. 2*, 63−89.

Schubert, Gabriella (1982 b): *Ungarische Einflüsse in der Terminologie des öffentlichen Lebens der Nachbarsprachen*, Berlin.

Socor, Vladimir (1990): „Forces of Old Resurface in Romania: The Ethnic Clashes in Tîrgu-Mureș". In: *Report on Eastern Europe* vol. I, No. 15, 13. 4. 1990, 36−43.

Szegedi, Edith (1992): „Ansätze zum interethnischen Dialog in Rumänien 1918−1940 und 1990". In: *Minderheitenfragen in Südosteuropa*, Seewann, G. (Ed.), München, 1992, 309−326.

Tagliavini, Carlo (1930): *Il „Lexicon Marsilianum". Dizionario latino-rumeno-ungherese del sec. XVII.* [Das „Lexicon des Marsigli". Lateinisch-rumänisch-ungarisches Wörterbuch des XVII. Jh.s], Bukarest.

Tamás, Lajos (1943): *Ungarn und Walacho-Rumänen*, Budapest.

Tamás, Lajos (1966): *Etymologisch-historisches Wörterbuch der ungarischen Elemente im Rumänischen*, Budapest.

Tschangos (1987): „Der rumänische Ursprung der Tschangos. Argumente der rumänischen Sprache". In: Pascu, Șt./Ștefănescu, Șt. (Eds.): s. o., 266−297.

T. Szabó, Ádám (1991): „A Hungarian University in Transylvania". In: *The New Hungarian Quarterly 123/32*, 103−107.

Gabriella Schubert, Berlin (Deutschland)

177. Bulgaria

1. Geography and demography
2. Territorial history and national development
3. Politics, economy and general cultural and religious situation
4. Statistics and ethnoprofiles
5. Sociolinguistic situation
6. Language political situation
7. Other language contacts
8. Critical evaluation of the sources and literature used
9. Bibliography (selected)

1. Geography and demography

1.1. The Republic of Bulgaria [hereinafter referred to as Bulgaria] borders on Romania to the north, Turkey and Greece to the south, Macedonia and Serbia to the west and the Black Sea to the east. The Danube River forms the northern boundary as far as the Danube port of Silistra, at which point the border veers east to the Black Sea (including the southern portion of the Dobrudža Tableland). The Black Sea forms the eastern border as far as the Turkish border at the Rezovska River. The southern border runs along the Strandža Mountains bordering Turkey, and the Rhodope Mountains and Pirin Mountains bordering Greece.

1.2. The current majority group, who call themselves *Bŭlgari* (Bulgarians), are descended from Slavs who came from north of the Carpathian mountains in the wake of the Avars around 575—625 and settled in the Balkan peninsula, and from the Bulgars, a Turkic people who entered the lower Danube in 679 but were eventually assimilated by the Slavs. The Macedonians are also descended from the Macedo—Bulgarian group which settled in the southeastern portion of the Balkans (→ art. 172). In the early part of the 20th century thousands of Macedonians living in Aegean Macedonia in present-day Greece were transferred to Bulgaria in accordance with the Treaty of Neuilly and then were resettled in those areas along the Black Sea formerly settled by Greeks. In 1912—13 many Macedonians left Vardar Macedonia in the present-day Republic of Macedonia for Pirin Macedonia in present-day Bulgaria to escape Serbian domination. Ethnic Turks are descended from the Turkish Ottomans, as opposed to the Pomaks who are generally held to be ethnic Bulgarians who have converted to Islam. The ethnic Turk population is concentrated mainly in the south in the Arda river basin and in the northeast in Dobrudža, with scattered communities in the central and eastern Balkan Mountains and in the Rhodope Mountains. The Pomaks live primarily in the Rodope Mountains and Loveč area. In the 20th century, there have been substantial migrations of ethnic Turks; first in 1950 and 1951 and more recently in 1989 when between 250—300,000 Turks emigrated to Turkey (although almost 120,000 of these are said to have returned). Additionally, there are reports concerning a new wave of emigration of nearly 70,000 in the summer of 1992).

The origin of the Aroumanians or Vlachs has been attributed to either Romanized Illyrians, Romanized Dacians from north of the Danube who thus represent the branch which split off to the south of the Danube, or descendants of Roman colonists (Gołąb 1984). After the Slavic migrations most remained in the area as shepherds. While the largest Aroumanian population is located in Vardar Macedonia (in present-day Macedonia) and Aegean Macedonia (in present-day Greece), there are also Vlachs in Pirin Macedonia. A number of Vlachs, apparently émigrés from these areas of Macedonia, now live in the Dobrudža region and the coastal areas around Varna. There are no available statistics for a Romanian population, due mainly to the population transfers in the 20th century whereby Bulgarians left Northern Dobrudža for Southern Dobrudža and the Romanian population moved South to North. While Jews were present in the region in ancient times, primarily in cities along the Black Sea, the largest emigration to the Balkans stemmed from the exile of the Sephardic Jews from the Iberian peninsula in 1492. Their language, Ladino (or Judezmo), is a form of Spanish written in Hebrew characters with Hebrew, Aramaic and Balkan elements. The Romany, or Gypsies, came from India to Europe probably prior to the 14th century. There has been a significant and longstanding Armenian presence particularly in the area of Plovdiv which dates from the sixth century when Armenians emigrated from Byzantine-controlled eastern Anatolia and settled in northern Thrace. Greek peoples were predominant along the Black Sea, but the population transfers following World

War I have reduced the Greek population in Bulgaria significantly and left them mainly in Sofia, Plovdiv and Varna (→ Language Map H).

2. Territorial history and national development

2.1. Following the settlement of the Slavs in the Balkans, the Bulgars in 681 established the First Bulgarian Khanate after having brought the Slavs under their control. The Bulgars, however, were completely assimilated by the Slavs so that by the 9th century the Bulgarian Empire was a Slavic state. Between the 9th and 10th centuries the boundaries had expanded north of the Danube to include the Transylvanian Basin and the Hungarian Plain to the west, and to southern Thrace, as well as the Aegean port of Salonika and east across Vardar Macedonia and Albania to the Adriatic. By 1014 the First Bulgarian Empire became part of the Byzantine Empire, until 1185—86 when the Second Bulgarian Empire (characterized as being "of the Vlachs and Bulgars") emerged under the leadership of the Vlach brothers Ivan and Petŭr Asen. The Second Bulgarian Empire was gradually weakened by the Mongol invasion of 1242, internal factions and invasions by Byzantium and Hungary—Croatia. Its western territories were lost to Serbia, and Dobrudža became an independent territory. By 1396 Bulgaria ceased to exist as an independent entity having gradually lost territory to the Ottoman Turks and remained an Ottoman territory until 1878. In 1878 Russia and the Ottoman government signed the Treaty of San Stefano which called for an independent state of Bulgaria. This new state would have included not only the territory north and south of the Balkan mountains (= Eastern Rumelia), but also parts of Thrace, including the port of Salonica, and almost all of what is currently the Republic of Macedonia. The subsequent Congress of Berlin (1878), which was attended by Russia, Britain, France, Germany, Italy, Austria—Hungary and the Ottoman Empire, established Bulgaria as an autonomous tributary state of the Ottoman Empire with boundaries equivalent to those of today north of the Balkan mountains. Eastern Rumelia became a semi-autonomous province, while Thrace and Macedonia remained under Ottoman rule. In 1885 East Rumelia was united with Bulgaria, and in 1908 Bulgaria became independent. One of the factors leading to World War I was the belief of Bulgaria in its rights to those borders established by the Treaty of San Stefano. In particular the dispute over Macedonia as belonging to Bulgaria, Serbia, or Greece caused persistent disagreements. Following the Balkan Wars (1912—13), Bulgaria was given the port of Dedeagač and the Struma basin. Romania received southern Dobrudža and Macedonia, except for the Struma basin, and Pirin went to Serbia and Greece. World War I and World War II essentially saw Bulgaria's attempt to regain those territories to which it felt entitled by the Treaty of San Stefano, but in both cases it was on the losing side. Following World War I and the Treaty of Neuilly, Bulgaria lost those portions of western Thrace acquired in the Balkan Wars to Greece, the Strumica basin (and other western territories) to Serbia, and southern Dobrudža, annexed by Bulgaria during the Balkan Wars, to Romania. Following World War II and the Treaty of Paris in 1947, Bulgaria was forced to return all its wartime acquisitions, except for southern Dobrudža. See Jelavich 1983 for a full discussion of territorial issues.

At present Bulgaria has relatively stable relations with its Balkan neighbors. In the past Bulgaria's relations with Romania have varied according to specific issues, e. g., a low point occurred in the 1980's amidst mutual accusations of environmental pollution in the area of Ruse. Currently, Bulgaria's relations with Greece are relatively comfortable (Greece is now the major source of imports for Bulgaria), although there continues to be some tension over the issue of Macedonia. Relations with Turkey are on the mend with the cessation of assimilationist policies against the Turkish minority. Bulgaria's relations with Yugoslavia were strained after the 1948 Tito—Stalin split and remain so with the Republic of Macedonia, which it has recognized as a state, but not a nation.

2.2. National Development. Because Bulgaria was under strong Ottoman rule, organization was by religious millet: the Orthodox millet, under Constantinople with an autocephalous church in Ohrid (in present-day Macedonia) and the Muslim millet, as well as Georgian Armenian, Catholic and Jewish millets (and in 1905, a Vlach millet; cf. Brailsford 1906, 189). With the abolishment of the Archbishopric of Ohrid in 1767, the Bulgarian Christian population fell completely under the jurisdiction of Constantinople. This resulted in the dominance of the Greek language in education and religious services, with Greek also at that time the language of commerce. While Greek was the language of secular schools, Church Slavic was used in lower level education in churches and monasteries. As in other Balkan areas, a cultural revival (the Bulgarian Renaissance in the 18th–19th centuries) led to the development of a sense of national identity and a perceived need for a standard literary language that would unite the Bulgarians. Gradual economic prosperity, centered mainly in the northeast, combined with active resistance to a southwest influence, gave precedence to the northeastern dialects in the formation of a standard language. The most opposition to the developing standard language came not from the Ottoman Empire, but from the Hellenizing influence of the Greek church. The main item of contention was the degree to which the standard literary language should reflect Church Slavic versus the spoken vernacular. At this point there was a Macedonian–Bulgarian Unity of sorts, which saw a mutual advantage in breaking away from Greek domination. In fact with the establishment of the Bulgarian Exarchate in 1870, the Macedonian Slavs identified themselves with the Bulgarians as opposed to the Greeks, but it needs to be stressed that this was a religious identification (see Friedman 1975 for further discussion). This uneasy alliance between Bulgaria and Macedonia gradually eroded over time and after 1948 with the Tito–Stalin split, Bulgaria denied Macedonian first as a separate language and later as a separate nationality. It is important to note that, generally speaking, it is difficult to make an unambiguous distinction between languages in the South Slavic linguistic territory. The South Slavic dialects constitute more of a continuum than a strict division, thus creating a situation whereby the mutual intelligibility among speakers varies more or less in proportion to their geographic proximity.

3. Politics, economy and general cultural and religious situation

3.1. After the November 1989 fall of the Communist regime (first established in September 1945), Bulgaria made a transition to a parliamentary democracy. The first multi-party elections took place in June 1990. The major parties that emerged are the Bulgarian Socialist Party (BSP, a reform communist party) and the Union of Democratic Forces (UDF), with the Movement for Rights and Freedoms (MRF), a predominantly ethnic Turkish party, allying itself first with UDF after the October 1991 elections, then with BSP after October 1992, at which time it helped bring down the Dimitrov UDF coalition government. In the beginning of 1993 a non-party government led by Prime Minister Lyuben Berov was formed. The popularly elected president is Zhelyu Zhelev who has suffered a growing loss of support by the UDF (cf. Engelbrekt 1994 for a summary of these political events). In the current political situation, all parties try to exploit ethnic identity issues and tend to be identified with particular groups, but the predominantly Turkish MRF remains a powerful force due to its broad ethnic power base and its ability to avoid the constitutional restriction on parties with a religious, racial or ethnic basis. In March 1993 UDF dissenters split off and formed a separate caucus, the New Union for Democracy (NUD). Manush Romanov, of the Democratic Union of Gypsies (ROMA), which represents about 50,000, was elected to parliament in the 1990 election, but ROMA was not allowed to participate in the 1991 elections since it was denied the status of a political party due to the current constitutional prohibition against parties with a racial, ethnic or religious basis. There are various other nationalist parties, including the Bulgarian National Radical Party and the Fatherland Party of Labor, to which this restriction apparently does not apply. Troxel 1992 provides a discussion of the political situation of Bulgaria's Roma. Special interest groups, such as the Antifascist Union, Macedonian Revolutionary Organization-Union of Macedonian Associations (IMRO-UMA), which is a Bulgarian nationalist movement as opposed to the Ilinden which supports recognition of ethnic Macedonians, and the Bulgaria Kingdom monarchist movement have come into being in the new political climate.

3.2. A formerly rich agricultural economy has been undermined by industrialization under Communism. The exodus of Turks in 1989 to Turkey particularly weakened agriculture, as well as certain industries. The shift to a market economy has often resulted in economic chaos, which has caused massive migration from rural areas to urban areas. Bulgaria's largest trade partners are Russia, Germany and Greece. In fact, fully half of the goods imported by Bulgaria are from Greece (Engelbrekt 1993). While Bulgaria is eager to join the EU, this is not likely in the near future. The embargo due to the conflict in Bosnia has badly hurt the Bulgarian economy, and the railroad strike in Romania effectively cut off Bulgaria from Europe during summer of 1993. The worsening economic situation has also had the effect of intensifying nationalistic hostilities.

3.3. The two primary religions are Christianity (Bulgarian Orthodoxy) and Islam, both of which have seen increased participation since religious freedom was guaranteed by the new constitution. The 1992 census (which is problematic, cf. 4.1.) shows that 87% identify themselves as Christian (86% Orthodox, less than 1% Catholic and Protestant) and 12.7% as Moslem (12 Sunni Muslim, less than 1 percent Shiite). There are more than 25 registered faiths in Bulgaria (Helsinki Report on Human Rights and Democratization in Bulgaria 1993). Like other formerly communist countries, Bulgaria has become the target of aggressive missionary activity by various religious groups, including among others the Mormon Church and the Church of Reverend Moon, as well as a number of non-Christian groups. The increased missionary activity has resulted in a pronounced concern regarding the influence of cults on the part of many Bulgarians.

4. Statistics and ethnoprofiles

4.1. The preliminary results of the 1992 census give a total population of 8,472,724 (which shows a decrease of 5.3% since the 1985 census, most probably due to emigration). The official figures are: Bulgarians 85.8%, Turks 9.7% and Roma 3.4%, with all other minorities below 1%. However, Ilchev and Perry 1993 estimate ethnic and religious minorities to constitute about 20−25% of the current population, rather than the 14.2% of the 1992 census. The reliability of the 1992 census is in question for several reasons, not the least of which were boycotts by a number of minority groups and the absence of certain categories; see Nikolaev 1993 for a discussion of the various problems. One example Nikolaev gives is that a group calling themselves the Association of Vlachs in Vidin filed a protest because they were not listed as a separate ethnic group on the census. In keeping with Bulgaria's official position that Macedonians are Bulgarians, there was also no separate listing for them (Article 178 suggests 2.5% as a possible figure). Additionally, it is believed that some Roma have identified themselves as either Turks or Bulgarians for various reasons, including those of religion and language, but also because of the low social status of Roma. There is also reason to believe that some Pomaks (Bulgarian Muslims) have also reported themselves as Turks for similar reasons. The problems presented by the 1992 census are further complicated by the fact that post−1956 statistics are not reliable due to the assimilationist policies of the Communist government toward minorities. In the 1985 census, for example, questions on ethnic affiliation, native language and religion were omitted. Magocsi 1993 provides the following "informed estimates" for 1985 (where 0% = less than 0.1%), which are supplemented by the estimates given by Ilchev and Perry 1993 in parentheses.

Table 177.1: Ethnic composition of the population of Bulgaria

	Number	Percent
Bulgarians	6,219,000	69.7
Pomaks	269,000 (250−300,000)	3.0
Turks	578,000 (800−1,000,000)	15.0
Gypsies	577,000 (550−600,000)	6.5
Macedonians	250,000	2.8
Romanians	1,000	0
Jews	5,000	0
Armenians	20,000	0.2
Russians	10,000	0.1
Greeks	8,000	0
Tatars	5,000	0
Germans	1,000	0
Vlachs	200,000	2.2
Albanians	10,000	0.1
Other	4,000	0.0
Total	8,950,000	

In comparing Magocsi's estimates for 1985, the wave of Turkish emigrations should be considered to have reduced that portion of the population by approximately 270,000.

4.2. Due to the problems with the 1992 census and the policy of assimilation by the communist regime, it is difficult to assess the status of the other contact language speakers, in terms of the actual number of speakers who identify with a given group. For example, it has been generally assumed that the Vlachs have been for the most part assimilated, yet there is little concrete evidence for or against this assumption. While those Vlachs cited by Nikolaev 1993 as protesting the census are probably Daco-Romanians (cf. Nestorescu 1971), the fact that such a group is asserting its ethnic identity is perhaps indicative of a new trend. The Jewish organization "Shalom", based in Varna, published a cookbook of Sephardic cuisine in 1993 and plans one of Ashkenazic cuisine, a fact which indicates an increased visibility for an assimilated group. Karpat 1990 mentions a 1938 study by Manov which supports the existence of non-assimilated Gagauz, Christianized Turkish Moslems settled around Varna. The question of to what extent less numerous minority groups have indeed been assimilated remains unresolved at this time.

5. Sociolinguistic situation

A discussion of the nature and role of standard literary Bulgarian is necessary for an understanding of the sociolinguistic situation. The official language for Bulgaria has been Bulgarian since 1878 (with the exception of 1940–58, when Macedonian was also an official language for the Pirin region), thus most contact language speakers can be assumed to be at least bilingual. Church Slavic (the Old Bulgarian variant) was established in the ninth century as a literary language and used as the official state and church language. The Turkish conquest at the end of the fourteenth century put an end to its development, although it continued to be used in its archaic form, despite its competition with Greek. Meanwhile, however, the Bulgarian dialects continued their own development which eventually resulted in a diglossic situation. It is also generally agreed that during this time, most Bulgarians were bilingual speakers of their own dialect and Turkish, which resulted in a strong influence of Turkish on Bulgarian (cf. Grannes 1987). When the need for a literary language identified with a Bulgarian nation emerged during the Bulgarian Renaissance in the 19th century, Bulgaria was confronted with the same problems of language planning that faced other European nations, particularly Slavic. Thus, the discussions centred mainly on to what extent the new literary language should reflect the traditional norms (i.e. Church Slavic) versus the vernacular (i.e. the dialects). The various positions were played out in the literature of that time and by the second half of the 19th century the modern Bulgarian literary language actually in use reflected the main features of certain dialects, rather than the older norms. As is typical for most emerging European nations in the 19th–20th centuries, the codified standard Bulgarian language represented a means of unification and identification with the nation. This political significance is reflected in the tendency on the part of most Bulgarian linguists to overemphasize the codified language at the expense of the language actually used by speakers (cf. Aronson 1982, Fielder 1993). Since the codified variant of standard literary Bulgarian does not represent any existing dialect, but is based largely on the northeastern dialects, although with a mixture of features from other dialects, there is a marked difference between the standard language as codified and the variant spoken by educated speakers. Thus the political significance of a supra-national literary language spoken by all citizens has often taken precedence over sociolinguistic reality in linguistic descriptions, i.e. changes and developments in the standard language itself are often ignored. This attitude is reflected in the numerous grammar handbooks used in the school system which are aimed at eliminating "mistakes" which result from the influence of dialects (e.g., Bojadžiev et al. 1987) and the archaic character of the current Bulgarian Academy of Sciences Grammar (a reprint from 1983) which cites as the norm forms and constructions often felt to be archaic by contemporary educated speakers and excludes others in everyday use. This tendency, however, has started to change, as evidenced by recent sociolinguistic studies such as Videnov 1990 and Bajčev and Videnov 1988. At the same time the influence of the standard language has been spreading due to the processes of urbanization, education, and social and political pressure for the "correct" use of the codified language. The dominant role of the standard language intensified during the 20th century and culminated in the 1980's with the official position that only Bulgarians lived in Bulgaria, i.e. differences in ethnic identity, native language and religion were not officially recognized, and were both unofficially and officially discouraged. This led to the situation where the contact speaker's native language was spoken primarily at home and among other speakers of the contact language, but not in public. It is therefore not unusual for a bilingual speaker to be reluctant to admit knowledge of a language other than Bulgarian. In Sofia, the large influx of the population from the countryside to the city has resulted in what some linguists have called an interdialect, the speakers of which are viewed with some disdain by the (relatively) long-time resident population. A somewhat ironic development in the Bulgarian language today is that while in the process of purifying Bulgarian from Greek and Turkish elements, Russian served as an important source for Slavic elements. Currently, however, Bulgarian is undergoing a purification from Russian elements (yet at the same time borrowing intensively from English).

6. Language political situation

6.1. Since the codification of the Bulgarian standard literary language in the 19th century it has served as the official language of Bulgaria, the study of which is compulsory in schools. Since language is regarded as an integral defining characteristic of a nationality, assimilation policies have often targeted language. One example is the refusal of Bulgaria to recognize Macedonian as a language. The official Bulgarian position (both pre- and post-1989) is most clearly articulated in *Edinstvoto na bŭlgarskija ezik v minaloto i dnes* [The Unity of the Bulgarian Language in the Past and Today] originally published in 1980 as an article in the journal *Bŭlgarski ezik* and subsequently translated into a number of Western European languages. Lunt 1984 provides a detailed and thorough rebuttal to this position. See also the relevant articles in this handbook. Generally speaking, the pre-1989 official policy has been the assimilation of minority groups into a single homgenous Bulgarian nation-state. Following the 1878 liberation, the 1879 Tŭrnovo Constitution made elementary education compulsory and the study of Bulgarian mandatory (although this was not strictly enforced). Nonetheless, minority languages were still taught in private schools.

Rudin and Eminov 1993 in their discussion of the history of Turkish language policies in Bulgaria provide a picture of minority language education in Bulgaria. They cite the 1959 study by Negencov and Vanev which illustrates the status of minority language education in Eastern Rumelia, prior to its annexation by the Kingdom of Bulgaria. In 1882–83, there were 866 Bulgarian schools, 771 Turkish schools, 3 Greek schools, 13 Jewish schools, and 4 Armenian schools. In 1945, schools were nationalized and the study of Bulgarian was again pronounced to be compulsory, although, for example, Turkish still remained the language of instruction in Turkish schools until the 1970's. While there had been attempts to assimilate minorities before, in 1969 large-scale plans for assimilating and Slavicizing the largest minority groups were adopted and implemented among the Roma, the Pomaks, and the Turks until the fall of the Communist regime in 1989. Assimilation policies included the closing of minority language schools, forcible resettling, forcible changing of names, the closing of minority language publishing houses, and the prohibition against public use of any language other than Bulgarian. While the July 1991 Constitution now protects the rights of individuals, minority rights *per se* are not explicitly protected and, as stated above, political parties with an ethnic, racial, or religious basis are prohibited. Thus, minority groups have restricted access to political power as minority groups. At the same time, the assimilation policies of the previous regime are essentially a thing of the past and overall minorities enjoy a wider range of freedom to express their identities. In 1991 the government approved a plan to introduce minority languages into the optional school curriculum, including Hebrew, Turkish, Armenian and Romany, but this remains to be implemented as education reform is proceeding slowly. The growing nationalistic sentiment in Bulgaria coupled with the worsening economic situation continues to complicate the transition to pluralism and tolerance. Other contact languages are discussed below.

6.2. The Roma have historically been a target of discrimination in Europe, and the Balkans have not proved the exception. While the 1992 census reports that Roma constitute approximately 3.4% of the population, many Roma apparently identified themselves as either Turks or Bulgarians (Nikolaev 1992) due to the low social status of Roma. Higher estimates put the figure at somewhere between 5% and 11% (Troxel 1992). As elsewhere in Europe, the Roma have a low level of education and economic stability and typically exist on the periphery of mainstream society. Since the 1950's the government attempted to assimilate the Roma by means of forced resettlement and name-changing (Simonov 1990). As a result the Roma have had to live in ghettos in the larger cities (Sliven, Sofia, Varna and Plovdiv) in substandard living conditions, and until 1989 they were unable to organize themselves freely for cultural or political purposes. Although numerous cultural and political organizations have since been formed, they still lack political representation due to the above-mentioned constitutional restrictions. Thus the two main political parties, the Independent Democratic Socialist Association of Gypsies and the Roma Democratic Union, do not have parliamentary representation. Overall the government has taken measures to raise the educational and living standards. One of the difficulties facing the Roma is their own internal diversity: between 50%–75% of Roma are Muslim (which leads to potential identification with the Turkish community), and Kenrick 1993 estimates that there are more than 30 Romany dialects spoken throughout Bulgaria (and about 300,000 speakers). They have not had formal schooling in their own language and are undoubtedly all bilingual. Their overall lack of education and low position in society has caused them to suffer extremely high levels of unemployment, and even when employed, they are generally on the lowest rung of the economic ladder. Roma, like most economically underprivileged groups, are typically considered to be dirty, ignorant and basically criminally-inclined. Reported incidences of discrimination and violence against the Roma have been on the rise in recent years in Bulgaria (as elsewhere in Europe).

6.3. The Pomaks are generally acknowledged to be ethnic Bulgarians who speak Bulgarian, but who have converted to the Islamic religion and have adopted Islamic customs. Eminov 1990 and Karpat 1990 suggest that Pomaks were originally Turkish (perhaps Cumans), but if in fact they were Bulgarian, then the conversion was voluntary. Gandev 1972 is representative of the official Bulgarian view that conversion was a forcible attempt at "debulgarizing" the population. Hupchick 1968 attempts a synthesis of the evidence. Pomaks live primarily in the Rhodope Mountains, along the Mesta valley in Pirin (around Goce Delčev), and in the area of Loveč north of the Balkan Mountains. While they are estimated to constitute approximately 3% of the population (Magosci 1993), the 1992 census lists them at less than 1%. This is probably due to the fact that many identify with the Turkish population because of the various assimilation campaigns begun in 1948 which reached a peak in the 1970's (Poulton 1991). Originally only those whose names had been changed after 1984 (i.e. ethnic Turks) were allowed to change them back, but eventually the government granted this right to all Turks and Pomaks. It is noteworthy that Turkey has not been amenable to accepting Pomaks as immigrants and has administered language tests to distinguish them from ethnic Turks, thus limiting their emigration.

6.4. The Vlachs, nomadic pastorals who speak a form of Aroumanian and live in the mountainous areas of the Balkan peninsula, are a problematic group, due to the lack of any reliable statistics (Poulin 1991, Nikolaev 1992 and Eminov 1990). Much that is known about them is anecdotal and is complicated by the fact that they are often confused with other pastoral nomads, particularly with the Sarakačani or Sarakatsani (called Karakačani in Bulgaria) who share a number of customs. The Sarakatsani, however, are Greek-speaking transhuments who live primarily in highland Greece, but are scattered in the mountainous areas of Bulgaria. While a group identifying themselves as Vlachs currently live in the northwest of Bulgaria, mainly in the city of Vidin, these are probably Daco-Romanians. Winnifrith 1987, who found few Vlachs in Bulgaria (most of them more recent arrivals), discusses the various problems of identifying Vlachs in Bulgaria and throughout the Balkans.

6.5. There are no reliable statistics for Romanians in Bulgaria. One would presume that Romanian-Bulgarian contact must have taken place at the very least among the populations in Dobrudža, which went back and forth between Bulgaria and Romania and which was the site of large population transfers. One would also expect contact speakers to be located in areas in the north along the Danube. Indeed, Romanian linguists have published on this topic, specifically, Nestorescu 1971 and 1973 on southern Dacian-Romanian dialects in Vidin, and Nestorescu and Petrişor 1970 on Romanian dialects in Bregovo. There is also a group of Albanian speakers in the village of Mandrica near Ivailovgrad.

6.6. In 1990 there were some 40,000 guestworkers, 60% of whom were Vietnamese, but such arrangements have been discontinued and the workers presumably have left. According to the 1993 Helsinki Report the treatment of Armenians, Jews and other small minorities is positive and they have received few reports of discrimination or antisemitism. Bulgaria continues to take pride in its role in saving Bulgarian Jews during the Holocaust.

7. Other language contacts

Bulgaria is located in the linguistic area known as the Balkan league which is the result of language contact. It shares with the other members (Albanian, Greek, Balkan Romance and Balkan Slavic) a number of common features such as the stressed mid-central vowel, a postposed article (*kniga* 'book', *knigata* 'the book'), the reduction of case distinctions (while most Slavic languages distinguish six or seven cases, Bulgarian has lost case endings and uses prepositional constructions to express these relations), the replacement of the infinitive by a finite construction (the particle *da* plus a conjugated form of the verb), and reduplicated object pronouns (*Nego go znaja* 'I see him'). For a more complete discussion of these shared features, and the languages of the Balkans, see Joseph 1992 and Sandfeld 1930. While some scholars claim that Balkanisms are due to a substratum of ancient Balkan languages such as Thracian and Illyrian (Katičić 1976), others attribute it to a Romance substratum (Gołąb 1973). Moreover, Gołąb 1973 characterizes Slavic-Romance contact as bi-directional: the Slavicization of an Aroumanian (Vlach) population south of the Danube and the Romanization of an old Slavic population north of the Danube (Daco-Romanian).

8. Critical evaluation of the sources and literature used

Reliable source material on contact speakers is difficult to locate, primarily because of the pre-1989 position that all people living in Bulgaria spoke Bulgarian and were Bulgarian (and even if they spoke another language or were descended from another ethnic group, they supposedly still felt themselves to be Bulgarian). This attitude is changing at least somewhat as a Rusanov's 1992 publication on sociolinguistic issues attests. Poulton 1991 provides a fairly complete discussion of minority issues in the Balkans. The historical atlas of Magosci 1993 provides a particularly clear picture of the fluctuating borders and migrations in the Balkans. Gołąb 1973 discusses the Romance−Slavic influence in the Balkans. Sandfeld 1930 is generally acknowledged to the classic discussion of Balkanisms; for additional details and bibliography of the Balkan Sprachbund, see Joseph 1987 and 1992. The problems involved in the development of the Bulgarian literary language are discussed in detail in articles by Dell'Agata 1984, Dinekov 1985, and Pinto 1980, as well as monographs by Georgieva et al. 1989, Gyllin 1991, and Venediktov 1990. Grannes 1987 deals specifically with the influence of Turkish on Bulgarian. Romanian dialects in Bulgaria are discussed by Nestorescu 1971 and 1973 (for the city of Vidin), and Nestorescu and Petrişor 1970 (for the city of Bregovo). The Albanian dialect spoken in Mandrica is discussed in Desnickaja 1968, Hamp 1965, Shuteriqi 1965 and is the subject of Sokolova's 1983 monograph. Simeonov 1970 describes the phonological system of the Karakačan dialect in Berkovica. Gilliat-Smith 1915−16 discusses Romany tribes in northeastern Bulgaria, while Bojadžiev 1972 and Igla, Konstantinov and Alhaug 1991 treat the specific Romany dialects. Winnifrith 1987 is the most recent account of the Vlach population in the Balkans.

9. Bibliography (selected)

Aronson, Howard (1982): "On 'naturalness' and structure in the contemporary standard Bulgarian literary language." In: *International Journal of Slavic Linguistics and Poetics* XXV/XXVI, 51−63.

Bŭlgarska Akademija Na Naukite (1983; reprinted 1993): *Gramatika na suvremennija bŭlgarski knižoven ezik* [Bulgarian Academy of Sciences: Grammar of the Contemporary Bulgarian Language], Vols. I−III, Sofia.

Bajčev, Bojan/Videnov, Mixail (1988): *Sociolingvističesko proučvane na grad Veliko Tŭrnovo* [A Sociolinguistic Study of the city Veliko Turnovo], Sofija.

Bojadžiev, Todor (1972): *Govorŭt na s. Sŭčanli, Gjumjurdžinsko* [The Dialect of Sučanli, Gjumjurdžinsko], Sofia.

Bojadžiev, Todor/Radeva, Vasilka/Mladenov, Maksim Sl. (1987): *Meždu dialektnoto i knižovnoto* [Between the Dialect and the Literary Standard], Sofia.

Brailsford, Henry Noel (1906): *Macedonia: its races and their future*, London.

Dell'Agata, Giuseppe (1984): "The Bulgarian language question from the Sixteenth to the Nineteenth century." In: *Aspects of the Slavic language questions*, Vol. 1, Picchio, Ricardo/Goldblatt, Harvey (Eds.), New Haven, 157—188.

Desnickaja, Agniia V. (1968): *Albanskij jazyk i ego dialekty* [The Albanian Language and its Dialects], Leningrad.

Dinekov, Petur (1985): "Aspects of the history of the Bulgarian literary language in the Eighteenth and Nineteenth centuries." In: *The Formation of the Slavonic literary languages*, Stone, G./Worth, D. (Eds.), Columbus, Ohio, 125—131.

"Edinstvoto na bŭlgarskija ezik v minaloto i dnes." (1978). In: *Bŭlgarski Ezik* XXVIII, 1. English Translation: "The Unity of the Bulgarian language in the past and today," 1980, Sofia.

Eminov, Ali (1990): "There are no Turks in Bulgaria." In: *The Turks of Bulgaria: The history, culture and political fate of a minority*, Karpat, K. (Ed.), Istanbul, 202—222.

Engelbrekt, Kjell (1993): "Greek-Bulgarian Relations: A disharmonious friendship." In: *RFE/RL Research Reports*, Vol. 2, 28, 28—32.

Engelbrekt, Kjell (1994): "Bulgaria: Balkan 'Oasis of Stability' facing drought?" In: *RFE/RL Research Report*, Vol. 3, 1, 106—110.

Fielder, Grace (1993): *The Semantics and pragmatics of verbal categories in Bulgarian*, Lewiston, New York.

Friedman, Victor (1975): "Macedonian language and nationalism during the Nineteenth and early Twentieth centuries." In: *Balkanistika* 2, Columbus, Ohio, 83—98.

Georgieva, Elena/Žerov, Stojan/Stankov, Valentin (Eds.) (1989): *Istorija na novobŭlgarskija knižoven ezik* [History of the Modern Bulgarian Language], Sofia.

Gilliat-Smith ['Petulengro'] (1915—16): "A Report on the Gypsy Tribes of North-East Bulgaria — 2". In: *Journal of the Gypsy Lore Society*, 2nd ser. 9, 65—109.

Gołąb, Zbigniew (1973): "On the Mechanism of Slavic-Romanian Linguistic Interference in the Balkans." In: *Bulgaria Past & Present*, Butler T. (Ed.), Columbus, Ohio, 296—308.

Gołąb, Zbigniew (1984): *The Origins of the Slavs: A linguist's view*, Columbus, Ohio.

Grannes, Alf (1987): "Turkish Influence on Bulgarian." In: *Folia Slavica*, Vol. 8, 2—3, 224—249.

Gyllin, Roger (1991): *The Genesis of the modern Bulgarian Literary Language*, Uppsala.

Helsinki Commission on Security and Cooperation in Europe (September, 1933): *Human Rights and Democratization in Bulgaria*, Washington, D.C.

Hamp, Eric (1965): "The Albanian Dialect of Mandres." In: *Die Sprache* 9, 1/2, 137—54.

Hupchick, Dennis (1983): "Seventeenth century Bulgarian Pomaks: forced or voluntary converts to Islam." In: *Society in Change*, Steven B. (Ed.), Boulder, Colorado, New York.

Igla, Birgit/Konstantinov, Yulian/Alhaug, Gulbrand (1991): "Some Preliminary Comments on the Language and Names of the Gypsies of Zlataritsa (Bulgaria)." In: *Tromsö University Working Papers on Language & Linguistics*, vol. 17, 118—34.

Ilchev, Ivan/Duncan, Perry (1993): "Bulgarian ethnic groups: politics and perceptions." In: *RFE/RL Research Reports*, Vol. 2, 12, 35—401.

Jelavich, Barbara (1983): *History of the Balkans. Vols. I and II.* Cambridge (UK).

Joseph, Brian D. (1987): "A Fresh Look at the Balkan Sprachbund: Some Observations on H. W. Schaller's Die Balkansprachen." In: *Mediterranean Language Review*, vol. 3, 105—114.

Joseph, Brian D. (1992): "Balkan languages." In: *International Encyclopedia of Linguistics*, Vol. 1, Bright, W. (Ed.), Oxford, 153—155.

Katičić, Radoslav (1976): *Ancient languages of the Balkans*, vol. 1 (Trends in linguistics: state-of-the-art reports 4), The Hague.

Karpat, Kemal (1990): "Introduction: Bulgarian way of nation building and the Turkish minority." In: *The Turks of Bulgaria: The history, culture and political fate of a minority*, Karpat, K. (Ed.), Istanbul, 1—22.

Karpat, Kemal (Ed.) (1990): *The Turks of Bulgaria: The history, culture and political fate of a minority*, Istanbul.

Kenrick, Donald (1993): "Romani at the crossroads." In: *Immigrant Languages in Europe*, Extra, G./Verhoeven, L. (Eds.), Clevedon, England, 285—295.

Lunt, Horace (1984): "Some sociolinguistic aspects of Macedonian and Bulgarian." In: *Language and Literary Theory*, Stoltz, B./Titunik, I. R./Doležel, L. (Eds.), Ann Arbor, Michigan, 83—132.

Magosci, Paul Robert (1993): *Historical Atlas of East Central Europe*, Volume 1, Seattle.

Manov, Atanas I. (1938): *Potekloto na Gagauzite i texnite običai i nravi v dve časti* [The Origin of the Gagauz and Their Customs and Manners] Cited in Karpat 1990.

Nestorescu, Virgil (1973): "Diftongul ea in graiurile românilor din regiunea Vidin (R.P. Bulgaria)" [The Dipthong "ea" in the Local-Dialect of Vidin Romanians (R.P. Bulgaria)]. In: *Limba Româna*, vol. 22, 161—66.

Nestorescu, Virgil (1971): "Stadiul actual al palatalizarii labialelor în graiurile româneşti din regiunea Vidin (R.P. Bulgaria)" [The Actual Stage of Labial Phoneme Palatalization in the Romanian Regional Dialects from the Vidin Area (R.P. Bulgaria)]. In: *Studii si Cercetari Lingvistice*, vol. 22, 41−50.

Nestorescu, Virgil/Petrişor, Marin (1970): "Graiul românilor din Bregovo (R.P. Bulgaria). Cîteva particularităti fonetice" [The Regional Dialect of the Romanians from Beregovo (R.P. Bulgaria). Some Phonetic Peculiarities]. In: *Actele celui de-al XII-lea congres international de linguistica si filologie romanica*, Rosetti, A./Reinheimer-Ripeanu, S. (Eds.), Vol. II, Bucharest, 997−1002.

Nikolaev, Rada (1993): "Bulgaria's 1992 Census: Results, Problems, and Implications." In: *REF/RL Research Report*, Vol. 2, 6, 58−62.

Petrov, Petur (1987): *Po sledite na nasilieto: dokumenti i materiali za nalagane na isljama* [On the Trail of the Coercian: Documents and Materials on the Imposition of Islam] Sofia. (Summaries in English, French and Russian).

Pinto, Vivian (1980): "Bulgarian." In: *The Slavic literary languages: formation and development*, Schenker, A./Stankiewicz, E. (Eds.), New Haven, 37−51.

Rusanov, Valeri (Ed.) (1992): *Aspekti na etnokulturnata situatsija v Bŭlgarija* [Aspects of the Ethnocultural Situation in Bulgaria] Vols. 1 and 2. Sofia.

Poulton, Hugh (1991): *The Balkans: Minorities and states in conflict*, London.

Rudin, Catherine/Eminov, Ali (1993): "Bulgarian nationalism and Turkish language in Bulgaria." In: *Balkan Studies*, Vol. 1, *Language Contact − Language Conflict*, Kramer, C./Fraenkel, E. (Eds.), 43−71.

Sandfeld, Kristian (1930): *Linguistique balkanique*, Paris.

Simeonov, Boris (1970): "Fonologičeskaja sistema karakačanskogo dialekta Berkovicy/Veršeca" [The Phonological System of the Karakačan Dialect of Berkovica/Veršeca]. In: *Linguistique Balkanique*, Vol. XIV, 2, 41−53.

Simonov, Simon (1990): "The Gypsies: a re-emerging minority." In: *Report on Eastern Europe*, 21.

Shuteriqi, Dhimitër S. (1965): "Fshati shqiptar i Bullgaris, Mandrica. Studim dhe tekste" [The Albanian Village of Bulgaria, Mandrica. Study and Texts]. In: *Studime filologjike* 1, 103−141.

Sokolova, Boika Borisova (1983): *Die albanische Mundart von Mandrica*, Wiesbaden.

Sokolova, Boika Borisova (1979): *Albanski vuzroždenski pečat v Bulgarija* [Albanian Renaissance Press in Bulgaria], Sofia.

Stojkov, Stojko (1968): *Banatskijat govor* [The Banat Dialect], Sofia.

Troxel, Luan (1992): "Bulgaria's Gypsies: Numerically Strong, Politically Weak." In: *RFE/RL Research Report*, 6 March 1992, 58−61.

Varon, Matilda (Ed.) (1983): *Evrejska Sefaradska kuxnja: comidas judias* [Jewish Sephardic Cuisine: Jewish Cuisine], Varna.

Venediktov, Grigorij (1990): *Bolgarskij literaturnyj jazyk poxi vozroženija* [The Bulgarian Literary Language during the Renaissance], Moscow.

Videnov, Mixail (1990): *Bulgarska sociolingvistika* [Bulgarian Sociolinguistics], Sofia.

Winnifrith, Tom J. (1987): *The Vlachs: The history of a Balkan people*, London.

Grace Fielder, Tucson/Arizona (USA)

Annex: Die „mazedonische Frage" in der Sprachwissenschaft

Die neubulgarische Sprache als Standardsprache entwickelte sich im Laufe des 19. Jahrhunderts, d. h. während der „Bulgarischen Wiedergeburt", deren führende Vertreter aus dem Osten und Westen des bulgarischen ethnolinguistischen Territoriums stammten. Der Begründer der „Bulgarischen Wiedergeburt", Otec Paisij Hilendarski, gebürtig aus Bansko (Pirin-Mazedonien, das westliche bulgarische ethnolinguistische Territorium), schrieb in seinem berühmten Werk *Istorija slaveno-bolgarskaja* (1762): „Du, Bulgare, laß dich nicht verführen, lerne deinen Stamm und deine Sprache kennen, und lerne in deiner Sprache!" Der Autor der ersten bulgarischen Grammatik, *Bolgarska gramatika* (1835), Neofit Rilski stammte ebenso aus Bansko. 1861 veröffentlichten die Brüder D. und K. Miladinov ihre Sammlung mit bulgarischen Volksliedern unter dem Titel *Bŭlgarski narodni pesni* in Zagreb.

In der „Bulgarischen Wiedergeburt" war eine ganze Reihe mazedonischer Lehrer und Schriftsteller führend, die sich „Bulgaren" nannten und ihre Sprache ausdrücklich als „Bulgarisch" bezeichneten (R. Žinzifov, Parteni Zografski, J. Hadži-Konstantinov-Džinot, Gr. Părličev, Kuzman Šapkarev u. a.). Mit vollem Recht sagt der große russische Slawist A. M. Seliščev: „Mazedonien ist die Wiege des alten und des neuen bulgarischen Schrifttums. Mazedonien ist die Wiege der Bulgarischen Wiedergeburt. Von hier sind die frühen Aufklärer des bulgarischen Volkes gekommen" (Seliščev 1918, 283).

Für viele Slawisten (seit A. Leskien, V. Jagić, V. Oblak) galt stets der bulgarische Charakter der mazedonischen Dialekte als unwiderlegbar. Es gilt als wissenschaftlich gesichert, daß alle diese Dialekte die für bulgarische Sprachen typischen Züge zeigen, namentlich die fundamentalen Züge des Balkansprachbunds: (1) Verfall der Deklination (die Kasusbeziehungen werden durch Präposition + allgemeine Form ausgedrückt). (2) Ein postpositiver Artikel. (3) *Da* − Nebensätze statt Infinitiv-Konstruktion (*iskamda pija* 'Ich möchte trinken' − altbulg. *choštǫ piti*). (4) Bildung des Futurs mit dem Hilfsverb *šte*. (5) Analytische Steigerung der

Adjektive (*dobăr* – 'gut', *po-dobăr* – 'besser', *naj-dobăr* – 'der beste'). (6) Verdoppelung des Objektes.

Demnach kann es vom linguistischen Standpunkt aus problematisch sein, von „bulgarisch-mazedonischen" Sprachkontakten zu sprechen. Diese können dieser Sichtweise folgend nur in geographisch-politischem Sinn verstanden werden. Es handelt sich im diesem Gebiet demnach wohl eher um bulgarische Dialekte. So kann weder in der Vergangenheit noch in der Gegenwart eine isoglossisch festgelegte Sprachgrenze nachgewiesen werden (vgl. Georgiev 1979).

Für die Klärung der „mazedonischen" Frage in soziolinguistischer Sicht sind noch folgende Tatsachen in Betracht zu ziehen:

Im Laufe von zwei Jahrhunderten, bis in die neueste Zeit, demonstrierte die mazedonische intellektuelle Schicht unentwegt ihr bulgarisches Nationalbewußtsein. Zwischen den beiden Weltkriegen kämpfte sie in Mazedonien, das in den Grenzen des ehemaligen Jugoslawien blieb, für ihr Recht, sich als Bulgaren zu bestimmen und die bulgarische Sprache zu verwenden.

Es gab jedoch bereits am Anfang des 20. Jahrhunderts einen Versuch eines mazedonischen Intellektuellen, sich von der bulgarischen Nationalität abzuwenden: 1903 erschien in Sofia eine Broschüre unter dem Titel *Za makedonckite raboti* (Über die mazedonischen Angelegenheiten) von Krăste Misirkov, in welcher der Verfasser versuchte, die wesentlichen Elemente einer mazedonischen Literatursprache zu formulieren. Dieser separatistische Versuch mißlang, denn er fand wenig Unterstützung bei der mazedonischen intellektuellen Bewegung, weder in Bulgarien noch in Jugoslawien. Ganz unbeachtet blieb dieser Versuch bei der *Inneren Mazedonischen Revolutionären Organisation* (VMRO), deren Führer (Goce Delčev u. a.) die bulgarische Standardsprache verwendeten.

Dreißig Jahre später wurde diese Frage wieder angeschnitten: die Führer der Kommunistischen Internationale beschlossen im Jahr 1934, eine „mazedonische" Nation zu schaffen (Palešutski 1985, 223). In Übereinstimmung mit diesem Beschluß wandte sich das Auslandsbüro der Bulgarischen Kommunistischen Partei an bekannte Slawisten in Moskau und Kiew mit der Bitte, einen Plan zur Schaffung einer mazedonischen Literatursprache zu entwerfen (ibid., 224). Dieser Plan wurde erst nach 1944 realisiert, als der „Mazedonismus" sich in eine Staatspolitik im Rahmen Nachkriegs-Jugoslawiens verwandelte. So wurde nach 1944 sofort damit begonnen, in Skopje Literatur auf Mazedonisch herauszugeben (Belletristik, wissenschaftliche Bücher) und Lehrbücher zu verfassen. Wie weit die Bemühungen der Philologen aus Skopje gegangen sind, kann man aus den Ergebnissen einer Umfrage vor einigen Jahren ersehen, in deren Schlußfolgerungen folgendes zu lesen ist: „Der Sprachausdruck der zur Prüfung kommenden Schüler dieser Gruppe stellt am häufigsten eine Mischung der Heimatmundart und jener Sprachen dar, in denen sie die Ausbildung erworben haben"; und weiterhin: „Den Lehrern wird vorgeworfen, daß sie nicht imstande sind, sich von ihren Heimatmundarten zu befreien, daneben unterlagen sie dem Einfluß anderer Sprachen, besonders der serbokroatischen (Minova-G'urkova 1989, 92).

Zusammenfassend kann man folgendes sagen. Die „mazedonische Frage" entstand nach dem Berliner Kongreß (1878), als Mazedonien in den Grenzen des Osmanischen Reiches verblieb. Sie entstand als politische Frage und ist bis heute weitgehend ungelöst.

Die „mazedonische Frage" wurde – nach diesem Verständnis unberechtigt – in die Linguistik eingeführt, ohne ausreichende Rücksicht auf zahlreiche in der Slawistik seit dem Anfang des 19. Jahrhunderts erstellten Forschungsarbeiten.

Literatur (in Auswahl)

Georgiev, Vladimir (Ed.) (1979): „Edinstvoto na bălgarskija ezik v minaloto i dnes" [Die Einheit der bulgarischen Sprache in Vergangenheit und Gegenwart]. In: *Bălg. ezik 28,1* (Sonderdruck).

Minova-G'urkova, Liljana (1989): „Makedoncite denes za jazikot" [Die Mazedonier heute über die Sprache]. In: *Godišen zbornik. Filol. fak. na Univerzitetot – Skopje 15*, Skopje.

Palešutski, Kastadin (1985): „*Jugoslavskata komunisticeska partija i makedonskija văpros 1919–1945*" [Die kommunistische Partei Jugoslawiens und die mazedonische Frage 1919–1945), Sofia.

Palešutski, Kastadin (1992): „Genezis i razvitie na idejata za avtonomija na Makedonija" [Genese und Entwicklung der Idee für eine Autonomie Mazedoniens]. In: *Aspekti na etnokult. situacija v Bălgarija i na Balkanite 2*, 168–184.

Seliščev, Matreevič M. (1918). *Ocerki po makedonskoj dialektologii* [Ein Abriß der mazedonischen Dialektologie], Kazan'.

Velčeva, Borjana/Mladenov, Maksim (1992): „Problemăt za ezika v 'makedonskija văpros'" [Das Problem der Sprache in der 'mazedonischen Frage']. In: *Aspekti na etnokult. situacija v Bălgarija in Balkanite 2*, 202–213.

Ivan Duridanov, Sofia (Bulgarien)

178. Bulgarian−Macedonian

1. Geography and demography
2. Territorial history and national development
3. Politics, economy, and general cultural and religious situation
4. Statistics and ethnoprofile
5. Sociolinguistic situation
6. Language political situation
7. General contactlinguistic portrait
8. Critical evaluation of sources and literature used
9. Bibliography (selected)

1. Geography and demography

Bulgaria's population as of December 1992 was 8,472,729. Since according to the first official reports of the Bulgarian 1992 census there are no Macedonians in Bulgaria, figures on the Macedonian population are taken from the *Encyclopedia Brittanica World Book 1992* even though these figures are based on a high estimate of total population. The Macedonian population makes up 2.5% of the population estimated at 9,005,000 people. Furthermore, the *World Book* gives the following figures for mother tongue in Bulgaria: Bulgarian 7,680,000; Turkish 770,000; Macedonian 230,000; Romany 230,000; Armenian 30,000; Russian 20,000; other 50,000.

The territorial definition of Macedonia is generally not disputed. Macedonia covers a geographic region divided into three parts following the Balkan wars of 1912−1913 including: The Republic of Macedonia (Vardar Macedonia, formerly a republic of Yugoslavia), much of northern Greece (Aegean Macedonia) and the southwestern corner of Bulgaria (Pirin Macedonia). The Pirin Region of Bulgaria is located in the southwest corner of Bulgaria and includes the Struma and Mesta river valleys. Major towns and cities in the region include Blagoevgrad (formerly Gorna Džumaja), Goce Delčev (formerly Nevrokop), Petrič, Sandanski and Razlog. While this discussion will focus on the Pirin (Blagoevgrad district, formerly Gorna Džumaja) region, there is also a large Macedonian population in the capital city Sofia and there are Macedonians living in other parts of Bulgaria as well.

Bulgarians and Macedonians were part of the migration of Slavs into the Balkan peninsula in the sixth and seventh centuries AD. The Macedo-Bulgarians have occupied this south-eastern corner of the Balkans since. The exact borders between Greek and Slav territory as well as between Macedonian and Bulgarian territory have been the subject of much antipathy in the region. The most significant modern migrations of Macedonians into Bulgaria include the exchange of population with Greece during the early part of this century when, in accordance with the Treaty of Neuilly, thousands of Macedonians were resettled in Bulgaria. Another notable migration into Bulgaria took place in 1912−1913 when Macedonians left Vardar Macedonia to escape Serbian domination (→ Language Map H).

2. Territorial history and national development

There is little to be said about contact between Macedonian and Bulgarian prior to the codification of the modern standard languages in the nineteenth and early twentieth centuries. It has been remarked elsewhere (for example Lunt 1959, 21, 1984, 92, Friedman 1975, 89) that there is no clear linguistic boundary between Bulgarian and Macedonian. Rather, dialects shade into one another as one moves from Macedonian north into Serbo-Croatian linguistic territory or east into Bulgarian linguistic territory. The modern history of contact between Bulgarian and Macedonian can be said to begin during the nineteenth century with the awakening of nationalist feeling amongst the south Balkan Slavs and the concomitant debate over the codification of a standard language. During the nineteenth century the question of standardizing a written language arose. As Friedman (1975, 91) argues, at this time the Macedonians sought common ground with the Bulgarians in a unified struggle against the use of Greek. Macedonian intellectuals envisioned a compromise between various Macedonian and Bulgarian dialect features in the creation of a Macedo-Bulgarian language. The most frequently cited problems in such a unified language were those of understanding between speakers of Macedonian and eastern Bulgarian dialects. The newspaper *Pravo* in 1869 (v. Venediktov 1993, 154) wrote that Macedonian Bulgarians understood Danubian Bulgarians and vice versa worse than either understood Church Slavonic; as a result there was no consensus on the choice of dialect base for a joint standard language.

By the early 1870s with the establishment of the Bulgarian exarchate the Bulgarians had fully rejected a linguistic compromise and they "publicly adopted the attitude that Macedonian was a degenerate dialect and that Macedonians should learn Bulgarian" (Friedman 1975, 88). Macedonians such as Shapkarev publicly espoused a linguistic compromise but published textbooks based on purely Macedonian features. The most comprehensive statement for the codification of the Macedonian language was written by Krste Misirkov and published in Sofia in 1903. Most of the volumes were destroyed but the work remains as evidence of an active debate beginning in the nineteenth century leading to the codification of a standard Macedonian language.

Events of the early twentieth century solidified the development of a separate Macedonian language. At the close of the second Balkan war the Treaty of Bucharest (10 August 1913) partitioned Macedonia among Bulgaria, Greece and Serbia. This treaty thwarted all attempts at Macedonian linguistic and cultural unity. Rossos (1991, 282) emphasizes that this event resulted in the division of the region which had, since the era of warring dynastic states in the Medieval Balkans, comprised an economic and ethno-cultural union. The linguistic result was that the Macedonian language continued to develop in Vardar Macedonia, while it was cut off from further development in both Pirin and Aegean Macedonia. Although the Serbs permitted the publication of so-called dialect literature in Macedonian (v. Friedman 1975, 90) the official language in Vardar Macedonia was Serbian which was used in all official spheres of public life, including schooling, which led the local population to become clear in the view that they were not Serbs (Lunt 1984, 112).

In the late twenties the Balkan Communist Parties recognized the separateness of the Macedonians but it was not until 1934 that the Comintern ruled that the Macedonians had a right to exist as a separate people with a separate language, a policy which led ultimately to the recognition of the Macedonian standard language. In April 1941, however, the Bulgarian royal government was allowed by Hitler to occupy most of Macedonia. At first the local population welcomed the Bulgarians as their liberators from the Serbs.

Nevertheless, the liberators were soon seen as new colonial oppressors and the Partisan movement gained strength in Macedonia.

In December 1943 a document was issued by the Bulgarian Communist Party (BCP) which seemed to call for a return to the Comintern line of the mid-twenties, i. e. for an independent Macedonia within a Balkan federation. The Macedonian People's Republic was proclaimed with Macedonian as the official language on August 2, 1944. The Macedonian Literary language was thus codified after nearly a century of debate and was not, as suggested in Bulgarian scholarship, the result of a language born by proclamation and developed artificially by committee.

From 1944 through 1946 governments of Yugoslavia and Bulgaria and the respective Communist Parties discussed the possible unification of Macedonian territories. In 1946 the Bulgarian government headed by Georgi Dimitrov, both of whose parents were Macedonian, recognized Macedonian as a separate ethnicity with a separate language. This recognition is reflected in newspaper articles and scholarly works of the period.

With the new political reality began more serious steps for the affirmation of the Macedonian literary language in Pirin Macedonia. In 1947 Macedonian language, literature and national history were taught in all elementary schools and gymnasia in Pirin, in which there were approximately 32,000 students enrolled. Teachers and student exchanges were carried out between Pirin and Vardar Macedonia. Ninety-six teachers were sent from Vardar Macedonia and 148 students were sent to Skopje to study. Also in 1947 the first Macedonian bookstore opened in Gorna Džumaja followed by the opening of bookstores in Petrič and Nevrokop. The book stores sold Macedonian literary works, magazines, readers, and school books. The newspaper *Nova Makedonija* sold more than 2,000 copies, *Mlad Borec* 2,500, and *Pionerski Vesnik* 7,200 (*Nova Makedonija*, May 29, 1990, p. 4). The first Macedonian regional theatre opened in Gorna Džumaja in 1947 with the play *Pečalbari*. In 1949 a Macedonian amateur theatre opened with the same play in Sofia.

By the end of 1947 all attempts to solve the Macedonian question through a Yugoslav-Bulgarian federation broke down. Stalin declared that the time was not right to change the status quo. The cultural exchanges and the development of Macedonian as an official language in Pirin Macedonia came to an end with the Tito-Stalin break in 1948 which led to the deterioration of relations between Bulgaria and Macedonia. While some recognition of a separate Macedonian language and ethnicity persisted through 1956, as seen in the census figures for that year, Bulgarian policy returned to its earlier denunciation and campaign against the language. This situation continues to the present with the Želev (Zhelev) government which has explicitly stated that while it recognizes a politically independent state of Macedonia, it does not recognize a separate language and ethnicity.

3. Politics, economy and general cultural and religious situation

In September 1946 Bulgaria was declared a People's Republic and by 1948 the Bulgarian Communist Party (BCP) was completely in control. The BCP remained in complete control until late 1989 when events in the Soviet Union and elsewhere in eastern Europe swept into Bulgaria. In December 1989 the Mladenov government voted to reverse Živkov's policy of assimilation. While some degree of recognition was granted to the Turkish minority, the ongoing political shifts did not change the official government view that there was no ethnic Macedonian minority. Despite the official attitude of party leaders, Macedonian political activity in Pirin continued. In 1989 the Macedonian organization *Ilinden*, claiming to represent 250,000 ethnic Macedonians, organized a rally in Sofia demanding cultural and national autonomy. Further evidence of political activity in Pirin was documented in a series of articles in the Macedonian newspaper *Nova Makedonija* in 1990 entitled "Among the Macedonians in Pirin Macedonia". The articles focused on individual lives touched by Macedonian-Bulgarian relations as well as a general profile of the region. There were reports of imprisonment and of discrimination in employment against Macedonians. Many of those interviewed stated that democratic processes sweeping Bulgaria did not have relevance for the Macedonians of Pirin and for their organization *Ilinden*. The United Macedonian Organization Ilinden continues to agitate for recognition of ethnic Macedonians. The Bulgarian government views this activity as Skopje intervention in its national affairs.

What may be a representative example of this conflict was the attempt by Macedonians in the spring of 1993 to lay a wreath at the grave of the revolutionary hero Jane Sandanski (1872–1915) and the subsequent crackdown by police.

The Orthodox Church represents another battle ground for ethnic loyalties between Macedonians and Bulgarians. Recent figures on religious affiliation in Bulgaria may not be accurate, but figures from 1982 were as follows: 64.5% atheist; 26.7% Orthodox; 7.5% Moslem; 0.7% Protestant; 0.5% Roman Catholic. Bulgarians and Macedonians belong to the Orthodox Church, but the Bulgarian exarchate does not recognize the authority of the Macedonian autocephalous church. The archbishop recently claimed he would recognize the authority of that church when the Serbian archbishop did so — an event not likely to take place.

4. Statistics and ethnoprofile

In order to approximate the numbers of ethnic Macedonians in Bulgaria it is helpful to look at statistics from several different censuses. The population figures for the 1946 census were never made public by the Bulgarian authorities but several works attempt to provide this data. Poulton (1991, 107), noting the conflicting figures in successive censuses, gives the following figures of the 1946 census taken from Yugoslav sources. In 1946 252,908 people claimed themselves to be Macedonian. This population lived predominantly in the Pirin region as reflected in the data from Kiselinovksi (1987, 101) who gives the following percentages for Macedonians by region: Petrič 85–90% Macedonian; Sveti Vrac 80–85%, Nevrokop 60–65%, Razlog 55–60%, Gorna Džumaja 45–50%. A document containing a survey of schools, pupils and teachers in Pirin Macedonian from 1946–1947 cited in *The Historical Truth* also reflects a high number of Macedonian students, for example in the survey there were 32 399 Macedonian students enrolled, 3074 Bulgarians, 383 Turks, 581 Romanies, 32 Jews, 3753 Macedonian Mohammedans, 61 other.

The following figures are from the 1956 census: Pirin Macedonia had 281,015 inhabitants. Of this 178,862 persons or 63.7% declared themselves to be of Macedonian nationality.

According to the 1956 census, Macedonians also lived in the Varna region (423), in the Plovdiv region (1,955), in the Pleven region (326), and in the Sofia region (4,046).

In the 1965 census according to Poulton (1991, 107) the number of people declaring themselves to be Macedonian dropped to 8750 and in the Blagoevgrad district less than 1% claimed to be of Macedonian ethnicity. For other estimates compare section 1 above.

5. Sociolinguistic situation

During the nineteenth century codifiers of an eastern-dialect-based Bulgarian standard language spoke of Macedonian dialects with derision. Almost no Macedonian features were adopted, the most notable exception being the gerund in -*jki* (Lunt 1984, 89). Lunt points out that the Bulgarians adopted a particularly narrow view of state. They sought to become a homogeneous, monolingual state by denying the linguistic rights of minorities. Minorities were not recognized and with the exception of limited instruction in Turkish (see Eminov/Rudin 1993, 45) there has been almost no mother-tongue instruction in minority languages. During the late 1940s Macedonian became, along with Bulgarian, official in Pirin. During this period Macedonian was used in many social and cultural functions. Books were published, journals and newspapers were circulated, cultural events were staged in Macedonian and the standard language was taught in the schools (v. Kiselinovski 1987). Macedonian retained this de facto official status until 1958 when the Bulgarian Communist Party changed its policy. Although there were political changes involving the Macedonian question in the years 1948–1958, the BCP continued to recognize the Macedonian name and language as can be seen in the census figures of 1956 in which 63.7% of the population in Pirin declared itself Macedonian.

After 1958 Macedonian lost its official status and in Pirin again became a language restricted to use only in the home. Since the late fifties Bulgarian influence has spread and become, particularly through the influence of schools and mass media, the second family language. This pervasive linguistic influence, according to Kiselinovski (1987, 110), erodes both the language and ethnicity of Macedonians in Pirin. However, Macedonian is still spoken within the home. Kiselinovski (1987, 110) cites an article from *Rabotničko delo* 30. 10. 1987:

"The carriers of the traditional local dialect are the oldest people in the village (…) School-aged children also switch to the local dialect when speaking among themselves (…) During breaks between classes, in the same classrooms, in the school yard, in the corridors, conversations begin which are interwoven with dialect words or are carried on completely in dialect. In the family, between parents, acquaintances, friends, i. e. outside of school, the percentage of dialect words used by the students in conversation is growing (…)"

The Bulgarian scholarly community considers all Macedonian dialects to be Bulgarian. As Lunt (1984, 90) and others have pointed out, linguistic factors are readily available to support this ideology. Since both Macedonian and Bulgarian shared in developments separating them from the rest of the Slavic languages, including the loss of declension and infinitive, the development of a post-posed article, the restructuring of the comparative, and certain morphological developments of the verb, Bulgarian linguists have claimed that all dialects with these features are de facto Bulgarian.

The Macedonian literary language is referred to in scientific literature as a written regional variant. This view, expressed most completely in the 1978 publication of the Bulgarian Academy of Sciences (BAN), republished as a separate booklet in English in 1980, has not changed in recent years. A collection of articles on various aspects of nationalism in the Balkans, *National Problems in the Balkans* (1992), gives the most complete recent statement concerning the status of Macedonian which given the attitudes of the Želev government is unlikely to change soon (cf. 8).

6. Language political situation

Various governments since 1878, and especially during the Živkov regime, attempted to achieve cultural homogeneity through assimilation of minorities (see Eminov/Rudin 1993, 45). Language policies have reflected this view. Bulgaria has had various official attitudes toward the Macedonian language and the recognition of a separate Macedonian ethnicity. It does not now recognize Macedonian ethnicity although it has in the past particularly in the years between 1946 and 1956. The official Bulgarian censuses have shown ever decreasing numbers up to the 1992 census when questions of ethnicity were addressed, but Macedonian was not recognized as a separate ethnicity.

The Bulgarian census of December 1992 asked questions concerning ethnicity for the first time since 1965. Bulgarian nationalists protested that this was divisive and would lead to a splintering of the nation along ethnic lines (Nikolaev 1993, 59). Despite these fears, the census contained questions concerning ethnicity, but Macedonian was not one of the allowable choices. The Želev government recognizes the independent state of Macedonia, but continues to deny the existence of a separate Macedonian ethnicity.

The ethnic Macedonian organization *Ilinden* in Pirin complained to a number of international organizations over the Bulgarian refusal to include Macedonian as a separate ethnicity. *MAKNEWS* (a listserv news service covering news from the Republic of Macedonia, published by MILS News bureau of the Australian Macedonian Society, Inc.) stated that in early reporting in the region of Petrič and Sandanski up to 30% of the population declared themselves as Macedonian and it was reportedly announced on Bulgarian television that 20−30% of the population in Sandanski and Petrič declared themselves on the census as Macedonians. On *MAKNEWS* #238 (Feb. 3, 1993) the Bulgarian president was reported to have told *Nova Makedonija* that there were problems with the census in the Pirin region saying that tens of thousands had stated they were another nationality. Želev did not say what that other nationality was. Other incidents have been reported from Pirin where, for example, on 4 December 1992 police arrested an activist of *Ilinden* as he put up a poster calling on Bulgarian Macedonians to declare themselves as an ethnic unit distinct from Bulgarian.

It is unlikely that official Bulgarian policy will change soon. Bulgarian recognition of an independent Macedonia may provide, however, a base for eventual recognition of Macedonian as well. There have been meetings between government and cultural delegations. Želev, for example, went to Skopje in early 1993 to participate in the launching of the Macedonian translation of his memoirs.

7. General contactlinguistic portrait

There have been no studies to my knowledge on language contact between Bulgarian and Macedonian in Bulgaria for obvious political reasons. There has been one article on Bulgarisms in Macedonia by Ugrinova in *Makedonski Jazik* 1968, another by Todor Dimitrov in *Literaturen Zbor* (1968) and brief mention is given in Kiselinovski (1987, 111). This situation may change now that some students from Pirin Macedonia are studying at the University of Kiril and Metodij in Skopje. It is clear that dialect speakers in Bulgaria, while knowing standard Bulgarian, continue to use non-standard dialect speech in certain situations as evidenced by the Rabotničko Delo article cited above.

Further evidence of the persistent use of dialect can be gleaned from works prepared for teachers of standard Bulgarian to detect non-standard usage amongst their students. These handbooks which strive to teach prescriptive norms provide telling evidence of the types of interference most likely to occur from inter-language contact. All of these cited errors could serve as the basis for a more formal study of language contact in the Pirin region.

In one such handbook the teachers say that dialect forms are more evident in spoken than written work. Of all the errors in class VII in the Blagoevgrad region 61% of errors in written work are dialectal based. This percentage drops to 42% by Class VIII. The following were cited as the most common types of interference from local dialect (data reported by teachers in the Blagoevgrad region). Approximately 90% of students make mistakes in the definite form of masculine nouns. Students made errors in the realization of syllabic l and r, for example in place of standard Bulgarian *pŭrvi* 'first', *cŭrkvi* 'church' and *vŭlci* 'wolves' students use *pruvi*, *crukvi*, *vluci*. Standard Macedonian has a syllabic liquid in these words: *prvi*, *crkvi*, *vlci*.

There is evidence of the loss of initial *x* in both native words and words of Turkish origin, a feature widespread in Bulgarian dialects as well as in standard Macedonian, for example: *leb* 'bread', *ubavo* 'beautiful', and *ajde* 'come on!' for standard: *hljab*, *hubavo*, *hajde*.

Bulgarian has shifting stress whereas standard Macedonian has fixed ante-penultimate stress. Differences in accent are mentioned in the following verb forms. In all instances the dialect form has antepenultimate or, in bisyllabic words, penultimate, where standard Bulgarian has final stress. The following were examples cited: *chEta/chetA*, *bEra/berA*, *nApiša*, *dOnesa*, imperative *pIši*, *kAži*.

Morphological interference includes the use of the Macedonian future particle *ke* instead of *šte*.

The most frequently studied area of interference has been in the lexicon. According to Kiselovski, Macedonians try to preserve the purity of their dialect and will point out Bulgarisms to Macedonian speakers. Nonetheless, according to Kiselovski, there are numerous lexical borrowings, for example Bulgarian *zaxar* 'sugar' for Macedonian *šeḱer* and *botuš* 'boot' for Macedonian *čizmi* (see Kiselinovski 1987, 110 f for additional examples).

There are no grammars of Macedonian written in Bulgaria. Macedonian is mentioned but only as a dialectal variant of standard Bulgarian in numerous works, for example the dialect atlas of Bulgarian published by the Bulgarian Academy of Sciences as well as numerous handbooks on standard Bulgarian. These works include all regions of Macedonia in the dialect descriptions of Bulgarian. There is one Macedonian-Bulgarian dictionary published in Skopje. Otherwise, there is little work which looks at the two languages from either a contact or comparative aspect.

One should give special mention to a number of authors who are claimed by both Bulgaria and Macedonia as national writers. These include all nineteenth-century writers who wrote in Macedonian such as Dimitar and Konstantin Miladinov and Žinzifov, as well as the twentieth-century writers Venko Markovski who defected to Sofia and Nikola Vapcarov, president of the Macedonian Literary Circle in Sofia. Although Markovski was on the one hand hailed by the Bulgarians as an example of Bulgarian nationalist writers, on the other he was criticized for translating his works into 'Macedonian dialect' since he claimed his countrymen would not understand him if he wrote in Bulgarian (Ristovski 1989).

8. Critical evaluation of sources and literature used

The works by Lunt and Friedman on the sociolinguistics of Macedonian and the history of its codification are the most comprehensive works in English on these questions. There has been an ongoing exchange between Bulgarian and Macedonian scholars on various questions, much of which is treated by the aforementioned authors. Recent articles include the works cited below in *National Problems in the Balkans*. The work by Venediktov on the history of the codification of Bulgarian contains many citations by a wide variety of nineteenth-century Slavic intellectuals and so places the discussion in historical context. The emigré community itself is divided on the issue. The Newspaper *Macedonian Tribune*, a publication of the MPO, the pro-Bulgarian Macedonian Political Organization in the United States, contains two articles on the Macedonian language in the Jan. 28, 1993 issue. One article, published in both English and Bulgarian, emphasizes the separateness and distinctness of the Macedonian language. A different article restates the Bulgarian view that Macedonian was created by decree in 1944 and was imposed by terror and force.

Given the current level of debate it seems unlikely that a careful study of language contact can be carried out. It seems likely that speakers of Macedonian in Bulgaria know standard Bulgarian as well as their native Macedonian. A careful study of the ways in which the languages interact would be of significant research interest.

9. Bibliography (selected)

BAN. Bulgarska akademija na naukite (1978): "Edinstvo na bălgarskija ezik v minaloto i dnes". In: *Bălgarski ezik 28*, 3–43 [published in English *The Unity of the Bulgarian Language in the Past and Today*].

Bojadžiev, Todor (1987): *Meždu dialektnoto i knižovnoto* [Between the dialectical and literary], Sofia.

Čašule, Vanga (1970): *Od priznavanje do negiranje* [From Recognition to Repudiation], Skopje.

Crvenkovski, Dušan/Pendovski, Branko (Eds.) (1983): *The Historical Truth*, Skopje.

Cvetkovski, Victor (1990): "Meǵu Makedoncite vo Pirin" [Among the Macedonians in Pirin]. In: *Nova Makedonija*, Skopje.

Dimitrovski, Todor/Koneski, Blazhe/Stamatoski, Trajko (Eds.) (1978): *About the Macedonian Language*, Skopje.

Eminov, Ali/Rudin, Catherine (1993): "Bulgarian Nationalism and Turkish Language in Bulgaria". In: *Language Contact – Language Conflict*, Fraenkal, E./Kramer, Ch. (Eds.), New York.

Fine, John (1983): *The Early Medieval Balkans*, Ann Arbor.

Friedman, Victor (1975): "Macedonian Language and Nationalism During the Nineteenth and Early Twentieth Centuries". In: *Balkanistica 2*, 83–98.

Friedman, Victor (1985): "The Sociolinguistics of Literary Macedonian". In: *International Journal of the Sociology of Language 52*, 31–57.

Friedman, Victor (1989): "Macedonian: Codification and Lexicon". In: *Language Reform History and Future*, Fodor, I. (Ed.), Hamburg.

Friedman, Victor (1993): "Language Policy and Language Behaviour in Macedonia: Background and Current Event". In: *Language Contact-Language Conflict*, Fraenkal, E./Kramer, Ch. (Eds.), New York.

Kabasonov, Staiko (1966): *Za obučenieto na literaturen bălgarski ezik v dialektna sreda* [For the instruction of literary Bulgarian Language in a dialect area], Sofia.

Kiselinovski, Stojan (1987): *Statusot na makedonskiot jazik vo Makedonija (1913–1987)* [The Status of the Macedonian language in Macedonia], Skopje.

Korobar, Pero/Ivanoski, Orde (Eds.) (1983): *The Historical Truth: The Progressive Social Circles in Bulgaria and Pirin Macedonia on the Macedonian National Question 1896–1956*, Skopje.

Lunt, Horace (1952): *A Grammar of the Macedonian Literary Language*, Skopje.

Lunt, Horace (1959): "The Creation of Standard Macedonian: Some Facts and Attitudes". In: *Anthropological Linguistics 1* (5), 19–26.

Lunt, Horace (1984): "Some Socio-Linguistic Aspects of Macedonian and Bulgarian". In: *Language and Literary Theory in Honor of Ladislav Matejka. Papers in Slavic Philology 5*, 83–132.

Lunt, Horace (1986): "On Macedonian Nationality". In: *Slavic Review*, 729–734.

Misirkov, Krste P. (1903): *Za Makedonickite raboti* [On Macedonian Matters], Sofia Reprint (1974), Skopje.

Mladenov, Maxim (1992): "Language and the National Problem". In: *National Problems in the Balkans*, Sofia, 72–84.

Nikolaev, Rada (1993): "Bulgaria's 1992 Census: Results, Problems, and Implications". In: *RFE/RL Research Report* Vol. 2, 6,5.

Poulton, Hugh (1991): *The Balkans*, London.

Pribichevich, Stoyan (1982): *Macedonia Its People and History*, University Park, Pennsylvania.

Ristovski, Blaže (1989): *Portreti i profili* [Portraits and Profiles] (three volumes), Skopje.

Rossos, Andrew (1991): "The Macedonians of Aegean Macedonia: A British Officer's Report, 1944". In: *The Slavonic and East European Review*, Vol. 69, Number 2, 282–309.

Stavrianos, Leften S. (1958): *The Balkans since 1453*, New York.

Stojkov, Stojan/Bernstein, Samuil R. (1964): *Bălgarski dialekten atlas* [Bulgarian dialect atlas], Sofia.

Stojkov, Stojan (1971): *Upatvane za proučvane leksikata na mesten govor* [Towards the study of the lexicon of regional dialects], Sofia.

Strašimir, Dimitrov (1992): "Ethnoreligions and ethnocultural aspects of the National Problem in the Balkans". In: *National Problems in the Balkans*, Sofia, 58–72.

Ugrinova, Rada (1968): "Bugarizmite vo sovremeniot makedonski jazik" [Bulgarisms in the contemporary Macedonian language]. In: *Makedonski jazik 19*, 111–137.

Venediktov, Grigorii K. (1990): *Bolgarskij literaturnij jazik epoxi vozroždenija* [The Bulgarian Literary Language during the Period of the Bulgarian Revival], Moscow.

Christina Kramer, Toronto (Canada)

179. Bulgarisch–Türkisch

1. Geographie und Demographie
2. Geschichte
3. Politik und allgemeine kulturelle Lage
4. Ethnoprofil
5. Soziolinguistische Lage
6. Sprachpolitische Lage
7. Allgemeines kontaktlinguistisches Porträt
8. Wertung der Literatur
9. Bibliographie (in Auswahl)

1. Geographie und Demographie

Die türkischsprachige Bevölkerung Bulgariens bietet unter ethnischen und religiösen Aspekten ein vielschichtiges Bild: die mit Abstand größte Gruppe stellen die Türken, Nachfahren von Kolonisten in osmanischer Zeit. Nach den Ergebnissen der Volkszählung von 1992 beträgt der Anteil der Türken, der größten Minderheit des Landes, an der Gesamtbevölkerung 9,7% (gegenüber 8,6% 1956), während der Anteil der Moslems, zu denen neben Türken und Zigeunern auch die bulgarischsprachigen Pomaken zählen, 12,7% der Gesamtbevölkerung ausmacht. Ballungsgebiete türkischer Bevölkerung sind das Deliorman (Ludogorie) in Nordostbulgaren (Varna, Šumen, Razgrad, Silistra) und die östlischen Rhodopen (Haskovo, Kărdžali), wo die Türken in einzelnen Orten über 80% der Bevölkerung stellen. Die gleichfalls im Nordosten siedelnden türkischsprachigen christlichen Gagausen, von denen der größte Teil im 18. und 19. Jahrhundert nach Bessarabien ausgewandert ist, und die als ethnischreligiöse Minderheit nicht ausdrücklich erfaßt werden (vgl. Troebst 1990, 474), muß man unter den 1,1% Türken christlicher Konfession vermuten. Wenig zuverlässig sind die Daten der letzten Volkszählung hinsichtlich der Pomaken und Zigeuner, weil sie entweder gar nicht erfaßt werden oder sich − zum einen der traditionellen, aus osmanischer Zeit ererbten Gleichsetzung von Moslem und Türke, Christ und Bulgare folgend, dann auch im Nachklang der repressiven Minoritätenpolitik in kommunistischer Zeit − als „Türken" ausgegeben haben. Die Anzahl der von der Krim stammenden muslimischen Tataren, die im 19. Jahrhundert von den Türken in Nordostbulgarien angesiedelt wurden, beläuft sich heute auf ca. 6000.

Unter der Herrschaft der seit 1944 etablierten kommunistischen Partei kam es wiederholt zu Massendeportationen/Emigrationen in die Türkei: 1950−1951 verließen 155.000 Moslems das Land, zwischen 1968−1978 130.000. Schwere Zusammenstöße zwischen der türkischen Minderheit und den staatlichen Autoritäten infolge der zwangsweisen Bulgarisierung türkischer Namen (vgl. 4.6.) führten um die Jahresmitte 1989 zu einem Massenexodus von über 300.000 Türken, von denen seitdem über die Hälfte nach Bulgarien zurückgekehrt ist (→ Sprachenkarte H).

2. Geschichte

Der Kontakt zwischen slavischen Bulgaren und Turkvölkern gliedert sich in mehrere Phasen: Die erste Staatsgründung erfolgte im 7. Jahrhundert (681) durch die (Wolga-) Bulgaren (heute im Kontext der bulgarischen Geschichte meist: „Protobulgaren" oder „Urbulgaren"), ein Turkvolk, das die slavische Bevölkerung südlich der Donau unterworfen hatte. Bis zum 9. Jahrhundert waren die Turkbulgaren von der beherrschten slavischen Bevölkerung sprachlich assimiliert worden; seit dieser Zeit wurde der Name „Bulgare" auch für die slavische Bevölkerung verwendet. Das Ethnonym ist das wichtigste sprachliche Vermächtnis des türkischen Eroberervolkes: im heutigen Bulgarischen finden sich nur wenige Lexeme, die auf die Sprache der Wolgabulgaren zurückgehen. Auch die Petschenegen und Kumanen, die im 11. Jahrhundert in Bulgarien einfielen, wurden assimiliert, ohne Spuren in der bulgarischen Sprache zu hinterlassen. Von ungleich größerer Bedeutung für die Geschichte des Landes wie für die Entwicklung der bulgarischen Sprache war die fast fünfhundertjährige Zugehörigkeit des Landes zum osmanischen Reich (1396−1878). Die Kolonisationen durch anatolische Türken während dieser Zeit haben die heutige Bevölkerungsstruktur Bulgariens entscheidend mitgeprägt.

3. Politik und allgemeine kulturelle Lage

Die Türken Bulgariens sind nach der Konfession mehrheitlich sunnitische Moslems, in Nordostbulgarien gibt es auch Anhänger des Schiitentums. Der Islam ist für die Türken Bulgariens neben der Sprache das wichtigste identitätsstiftende Moment.

In der Sozialstruktur bestehen große Diskrepanzen zwischen der türkischen Minorität und der Gesamtbevölkerung. Zur Veranschaulichung einige Daten (nach Troebst 1990, 479): Über 80% der Türken leben auf dem Land, der Anteil der Genossenschaftsbauern lag 1975 mit 29% weit über dem Landesdurchschnitt (6,7%), von den Arbeitern (64%) war der größte Teil ebenfalls in der Landwirtschaft tätig (56,1%), während die Angestelltenquote mit 4,9% eklatant unter dem Landesdurchschnitt (26,7%) lag.

Die politischen und kulturellen Rechte der türkischen Minderheit waren seit 1958 immer stärkeren Restriktionen ausgesetzt. Die strikt assimilatorische Politik, die auf der Definition Bulgariens als mononationalem Staat beruhte (→ Art. 177, 3.6.), leugnete die Existenz nationaler/ethnischer Minderheiten und rechnete die Türken unter die Bezeichnung *bălgarski mohamedani* („bulgarische Moslems") dem bulgarischen Staatsvolk zu. Seit der Gründung der *Dviženie za pravi i osvobodi* (DPS − „Bewegung für Rechte und Freiheiten"), im Volksmund auch „türkische Partei", hat die türkische Bevölkerung eine eigene Interessenvertretung, die bei den Wahlen im Oktober 1991 7,6% der Stimmen erhielt und seitdem im Parlament vertreten ist.

4. Ethnoprofil

Nicht endgültig geklärt ist die Ethnogenese einzelner Teile der türkischsprachigen Bevölkerung Bulgariens: so rechnet man für die

Türken des Deliorman damit, daß es sich um schon vor Beginn der osmanischen Herrschaft türkisierte Slaven handelt (Kowalski 1933, 3 f, 10 f). Für die These, daß die christlichen Gagausen, die heute in der Gegend um Varna ansässig sind, Nachfahren vorosmanischer Turkvölker seien (Kowalski 1933), welche später sprachlich „osmanisiert" wurden, ergeben sich aus der Untersuchung der synchronen Struktur des Gagausischen keine Anhaltspunkte (vgl. Hazai 1978, 116). Unter den Gagausen ist eine starke Tendenz, das Türkische aufzugeben und zum Bulgarischen zu wechseln, festzustellen (Boev 1968, 177). Die oft durch die dunklere Hautfarbe auffallenden moslemischen Roma (Zigeuner), die das Romani durch Türkisch als Muttersprache ersetzt haben, geben als Eigenbezeichnung „Türken" an, während die Türken auf Abgrenzung bestehen und sie in Übereinstimmung mit der offiziellen Terminologie als *turski cigani* („türkische Zigeuner") oder einfach *cigani* bezeichnen.

5. Soziolinguistische Lage

Mit dem Ende der osmanischen Herrschaft 1878 hatte das Türkische in Bulgarien unter der nicht-islamischen Bevölkerung seinen vormaligen Status einer Prestigesprache eingebüßt. Noch bis zum Zweiten Weltkrieg waren in den kompakten Siedlungsgebieten der Türken viele Frauen und Kinder Monolinguale (vgl. Rudin/Eminov 1990, 149), während die in diesen Gebieten als regionale Minderheiten lebenden Bulgaren neben ihrer Muttersprache auch Türkisch sprachen (Kowalski 1933, 4). Die Assimilationsmaßnahmen im Schulsystem, aber auch die durch die gestiegene Mobilität der ländlichen Bevölkerung verstärkten Beziehungen zwischen Türken und Bulgaren und der Einfluß der Medien haben während der letzten Jahrzehnte dazu geführt, daß die Bulgarischkenntnisse unter der türkischen Minderheit allenthalben gestiegen sind. Die Auswirkungen auf das Türkische – verstärkte Interferenzen, Schwinden der schriftlichen, teilweise Zurückgehen der mündlichen Kompetenz – werden von Rudin/Eminov (1990) in einer zwar knappen, dennoch sehr aufschlußreichen Studie behandelt.

Der traditionelle Einfluß des Osman- bzw. Türkeitürkischen hat schon beizeiten zu einer Nivellierung der regionalen Mundarten geführt; am stärksten von der Standardsprache beeinflußt sind die nordostbulgarischen Dialekte. Da die türkischen Dialekte Bulgariens nie eine eigenständige Schriftnorm entwickelt, sondern sich immer am Türkeitürkischen orientiert haben, war für die westlichen, strukturell wie geographisch weiter vom Istanbuler Standard entfernten Dialekte immer eine Tendenz zur Diglossie bzw. einer vom Bildungsgrad der Sprecher abhängigen Varietätenbildung vorhanden. Nach Németh (1965, 6) ist die sprachliche Situation in Vidin durch die Existenz dreier Sprachformen gekennzeichnet: (a) das Türkische der Zigeuner, (b) die osmanisch geprägte, in der Schule erlernte Gemeinsprache und (c) die Vidiner Volkssprache, eine archaischere Mundart. Untersuchungen darüber, ob die Einschränkungen im Bildungswesen während der letzten Jahrzehnte Tendenzen zur Nivellierung der Dialekte rückgängig gemacht haben, stehen noch aus.

6. Sprachpolitische Lage

Nach 1944 erfuhr das vorher lediglich tolerierte Minderheitenschulwesen zunächst starke staatliche Unterstützung. Es galt, die allgemeine Schulpflicht, die für die Minderheiten lediglich auf dem Papier bestand, durchzusetzen und die Analphabetenrate, die vor allem unter den Türken größer war als in der übrigen Bevölkerung, zu senken. Mit der Wende in der Nationalitätenpolitik seit 1958 (s. Troest 1990, 487 ff) wurde auch das türkische Schulwesen schrittweise abgebaut. Nach der Einführung von Bulgarisch als obligatorischem Unterrichtsfach verlor das zweistufige türkische Schulsystem seine Selbständigkeit und wurde in das bulgarische Schulsystem integriert; schließlich wurde das Türkische zu einem Wahlfach herabgestuft, um 1974 vollständig aus den Lehrplänen gestrichen zu werden (vgl. Bachmeier 1990, 496). Im Zuge der Assimilationspolitik wurde auch die Anzahl der türkischen Zeitungen erst 1959, dann erneut 1968 stark reduziert (vgl. Troebst 1990, 479). Die Assimilationspolitik kulminierte 1984/85 in einer Kampagne, mit der die türkische Minderheit zur Ersetzung ihrer türkisch-islamischen Vor-, Vaters- und Familiennamen durch bulgarisch-christliche gezwungen wurde. Von dieser Maßnahme waren in der Geschichte des Landes andere islamische Minderheiten (Pomaken, Zigeuner) schon früher, zuletzt 1971–1974, betroffen. Im Dezember 1989 beschloß das ZK der Kommunistischen Partei, die Maßnahmen zur Zwangsassimilation der islamischen Minoritäten aufzuheben. Seit Ende des kommunistischen Regimes zeichnet sich eine radikale Wende im Bereich der Medien und im Bildungswesen ab und inzwischen wird das Türkische wieder als fakultatives Unterrichtsfach gelehrt.

7. Allgemeines kontaktlinguistisches Porträt

Mit Bulgarisch und Türkisch treffen zwei typologisch unterschiedlich strukturierte Sprachen aufeinander: während das Bulgarische eine zur Familie der slavischen Sprachen gehörige indoeuropäische Sprache mit stark flektierenden Zügen ist, gehören die auf dem Balkan gesprochenen türkischen Dialekte („rumelische Dialekte") wie das Türkeitürkische zum (west-)oghusischen Zweig der Turksprachen (vgl. Doerfer 1990, 19), in denen agglutinierende Züge überwiegen. Das Bulgarische weicht in wesentlichen Strukturmerkmalen von den übrigen slavischen Sprachen ab; es handelt sich vor allem um solche Züge, die für den sogenannten Balkansprachbund charakteristisch sind (→ Art. 172, 7.): nachgestellter Artikel, Infinitivverlust, Ersatz flexivischer durch periphrastisch gebildete Kasusausdrücke, Doppelsetzung des Objekts u. a.

Németh (1956) hat die balkantürkischen Dialekte nach vorwiegend phonetischen Kriterien, insbesondere Unterschieden im Vokalismus, in ost- und westrumelische Mundarten gegliedert; die durch Übergangsdialekte gekennzeichnete Grenze zwischen den beiden Dialektgruppen verläuft durch das bulgarische Sprachgebiet, wo sie mit einer wichtigen bulgarischen Dialektgrenze, der sogenannten jat-Grenze (nach dem Reflex von altbulgarisch ě als e bzw. ja, vgl. ostbulg. *njama* „er hat nicht/es gibt nicht" (vs. westbulg.-makedonisch *nema*) zusammenfällt. Das wichtigste morphologische Merkmal in Némeths Katalog der Unterschiede zwischen ost- und westbalkanischen türkischen Dialekten ist das *y*-Präsens in westlichen vs. *yor*-Präsens in östlichen Dialekten (und im Türkeitürkischen) vgl. *isteyim* vs. *istiyorum* „ich möchte". Detailliertere Gliederungsvorschläge der balkantürkischen Dialekte wurden von Hazai (1964) und Mollova (1970) unterbreitet; Mollova diskutiert auch das Zusammentreffen slavischer und türkischer Dialektgrenzen.

Der historische Einfluß des Osman-Türkischen auf das Bulgarische ist bis heute im Lexikon, der Phraseologie und einigen Wortbildungssuffixen zu erkennen. Außerdem wird die Entstehung des Narrativs (Inferential) sowie der Erhalt des reichen Tempussystems mit türkischen Einfluß erklärt (vgl. Mirčev 1978, 94, Conev III, 1940, 94). Seit dem Ende der osmanischen Herrschaft in Bulgarien 1878 hat sich die Einflußrichtung zwischen dem Türkischen und dem Bulgarischen in Bulgarien umgekehrt; der Anteil der Turzismen im Bulgarischen ist seitdem — auch im Ergebnis puristischer Sprachpolitik — stark zurückgegangen. Der synchron festzustellende bulgarische Einfluß auf die türkischen Dialekte des Landes ist am augenfälligsten in der Syntax, umfaßt aber auch Lexikon, Phonetik und die Morphologie/Morphosyntax, u. zw. jeweils in unterschiedlicher Ausprägung in den Einzeldialekten. Generalisierungen sind daher nur in bezug auf vorhandene Tendenzen zu treffen.

Die unter 7.1—7.3 aufgeführten Beispiele folgen der in den jeweiligen Quellen verwendeten Orthographie.

7.1. Phonetik

Für die westlichen Dialekte sind Durchbrechungen der Vokalharmonie in großem Umfang zu verzeichnen, vgl. für Küstendil *söylerlar* „sie sagen" (Kakuk 1961, 307), Vidin *başlarler* „sie beginnen" (Németh, 1965, 45) gegen Türkeitürkisch (ttk.) *söylerler* und *başlarlar*. Kontaktsprachlichen Einfluß auf die Phonetik nimmt Németh (1965, 8, 64) allerdings nur für die Entlehnung von *c* [ts] an, welches jedoch auf bulgarische Lehnwörter beschränkt bleibt. Kowalski (1933, 23) führt die Durchbrechung der im standardsprachlichen Türkisch durchgängigen Paroxytonese in nordostbulgarischen Dialekten, wo die Akzentstelle auf die Paenultima oder Antepaenultima vorgezogen werden kann, auf den Einfluß der Kontaktsprache zurück. Für den türkischen Dialekt von Vidin konnte Németh (1965, 77) keine grundsätzlichen Abweichungen der Akzentverhältnisse von der (türkeitürkischen) Standardsprache feststellen.

7.2. Morphologie und Morphosyntax

Anfänge einer — dem Türkischen fremden — Genusdistinktion sind in der Sexusunterscheidung bei Belebten mithilfe des entlehnten Suffixes *-ka* zu erkennen, vgl. für Vidin *koy-qa* „Dorfbewohnerin" zu *koy* (ttk. *köy*) „Dorf" (Németh 1965, 80), gagausisch *padišax-ka* „Königin" (Kowalski 1933, 23) zu *padišah* „König", Westrhodopen *mitarka* „Frau des Dorfvorstehers" zu ttk. *muhtar* „Gemeindevorsteher" (Mollov/Mollova, 1966, 123). Im letztgenannten Dialekt finden sich einige weitere Beispiele für sonst auf *-ka* beschränkte Entlehnung von Wortbildungsmorphemen: So die Deminutivsuffixe *-čo*, *-ička*, *-ica*; die Vokativendung *-ko* bei Feminina und sogar der im Bulgarischen für Feminina charakteristische Ausgang *-a* in kadän-a „Frau" gegen ttk. *kadın* u. a.

Für die westrhodopischen Dialekte sind unter typologischen Aspekten äußerst bedeutsame Fälle von Umstrukturierung von Kategorialausdrücken belegt: Anstelle der standardsprachlich mithilfe von Suffixen ausgedrückten Verbformen werden periphrastische Ausdrücke verwendet. Für den Nezessitativ, der im Türkischen mit dem Affix *-malı-/ -meli-* gebildet wird, verwendet der Rhodopendialekt das Adverb *l'azăm* (ttk. *lâzım*) „nötig, erforderlich" mit dem Optativ bzw. Konjunktiv, vgl. türk. *al-malı-yım* „ich muß nehmen" gegen dial. (*ben*) *l'azăm alajăm* „dass.". Der Ausdruck ist parallel zu Bulgarischen *trjabva da vzema* mit unflexivischem *trjabva* „nötig sein" und dem Konjunktiv (= *da* + Präsens) von „nehmen" konstruiert. An der Kontaktsprache orientiert ist auch eine Futurbildung mit *var* „es gibt" bzw. *yok* „es gibt nicht" in der negierten Form. Im Bulgarischen wird das Futur dialektal mit dem Verb *ima* „haben" (schriftsprachlich mit der aus „wollen" herzuleitenden Partikel *šte*) und dem Konjunktiv gebildet. Das Türkische, das kein Verb für „haben" besitzt, drückt Possession durch eine Konstruktion mit den unflektierbaren *var* und *yok* aus, die hier parallel zu bulg. *ima* bzw. *njama* als Futurmarker dienen; vgl. (*ben*) *var alajăm* wörtl. „es gibt – ich nehme", dazu die negierte Form (*ben*) *jok alajăm* „es gibt nicht – ich nehme" (Mollov/Mollova 1966, 126) mit dem Optativ (in der 3. Person mit dem Imperativ) des Verbs „geben" gegen das standardtürkische Futur *al-acağ-ım* „ich werde nehmen" mit dem Futurmarker *-acak-* (*-ecek-*).

In demselben Dialekt sind auch bulgarische Objektspronomina entlehnt worden, vgl. *jazdăm gu* „ich habe es geschrieben" (bulg. dialektal *gu* < *go*, Personalpronomen 3. sg. akk.). Der parallele Gebrauch türk. und bulg. Pronominalformen dürfte bulgarischen Konstruktionen mit doppeltem Objekt nachgebildet sein, für welche dem Türkischen, das nur eine Form des Objektspronomens hat (gegenüber einer betonten und einer unbetonten im Bulgarischen), die Ausdrucksmittel fehlen, vgl. *ben onu* (tk.) *vermisim gu* (bulg. „ich es gab es" (Mollov/Mollova 1966, 125).

7.3. Syntax

Während die oben behandelten Interferenzphänomene auf den Dialekt der Westrhodopen beschränkt sind, sind Umstrukturierungen in Wort- und Satzgliedstellung weiter verbreitet. Abweichend von der im Standardtürkischen ziemlich konsequent gehandhabten Anordnung SOV liegt in den türkischen Dialekten Bulgariens eine eher freie, von pragmatisch-kommunikativen Faktoren gesteuerte Stellung vor. Zum Gagausischen hält Kowalski (1933, 23) fest: „Les phrases gagaouzes font souvent l'impression d'une traduction littérale d'une langue étrangère, dont la syntaxe serait entièrement différente de la syntaxe turque." Németh (1965, 113) über den Dialekt von Vidin: „Es kommen (...) die kühnsten Inversionen vor, und zwar nicht nur ausnahmsweise, wir finden die Regeln der gewöhnlichen osmanischen Wortfolge (...) auf Schritt und Tritt übergangen." Während im von Németh behandelten Dialekt die standardtürkische Wortstellung bei allen Abweichungen noch vorherrschend ist, konstatieren Mollov/Mollova umgekehrt für den Dialekt der Westrhodopen, daß die Wortstellung im Satz nur ausnahmsweise von der des Bulgarischen abweiche: „L'ordre des mots dans la phrase suit celui de la phrase bulgare. (...) Parfois l'ordre des mots ne se soumet pas à celui de bulgare" (1966, 128).

In den Texten aus türkischen Dialekten Bulgariens findet man abweichend von der in der türkischen Schriftsprache geltenden Regel für die Wortfolge innerhalb der NP, nach der das Determinans vor dem Determinatum steht, invertierte Konstruktionen, in denen der lexikalische Kopf (head) an erster Stelle steht, vgl. die Stellung des attributiven Adjektivs in *elma altın* „Apfel – goldener" vs. ttk. *altın elma*. Entsprechend die Anordnung der Glieder beim possessiven Genitiv, vgl. *baba-si qız-in* (Vater-POSS Tochter-GEN) „der Vater des Mädchens" (Németh 1965, 114) gegen ttk. *kızın babası*.

Die Anordnung der Satzglieder weicht stark vom Türkischen ab: das Prädikat kann satzinitial stehen, Objekte am Anfang oder Ende einer Phrase. Stellungstypologisch sind also starke Einbrüche gegenüber der Ausgangssprache zu verbuchen, die zweifellos dem Einfluß der Kontaktsprache zuzurechnen sind. Anstelle von türkischen Nominal-

und Gerundialfügungen werden in den türkischen Dialekten Bulgariens hypotaktische Konstruktionen mit finiten Verbformen verwendet. Wenn die Nebensätze durch Konjunktionen eingeleitet werden, steht das Verb in der Regel im Indikativ; bei uneingeleiteten Nebensätzen, die bulgarischen Nebensätzen mit *da* entsprechen, stehen die 1. und 2. Person im Optativ-Konjunktiv, die 3. hingegen im Imperativ. Nach *istemek* „wünschen, wollen" und einigen anderen Verben steht ein finites Verb anstelle des Infinitivs, vgl. den Satz „ich möchte essen" mit Infinitiv im Türkeitürkischen (1), dem abhängigen Verb in finiter Form, d. h. Zweifachmarkierung der Person sowohl im Dialekt von Küstendil (2) als auch im Bulgarischen (3):

(1) ye-mek   isti-yorum
    ess-INF woll-1.PRÄS

(2) iste-yim   ye-yim
    woll-1.PRÄS   ess-1.OPT

(3) iskam   da   jam
    woll:1.PRÄS daß ess:1.PRÄS

Das Bulgarische unterscheidet wie die übrigen Balkansprachen finale (mit *da* eingeleitete) und nicht-finale (mit *če* eingeleitete) Objektsätze. Türkische Dialekte Bulgariens lassen eine ähnliche Differenzierung erkennen, die allerdings weniger konsequent durchgeführt zu sein scheint. Im finalen Satz steht ein konjunktionsloser Nebensatz mit dem Prädikat im Konjunktiv, vgl. *söylerlar čobana gütürsin* (...) (Kakuk 1960, 251) „sie sagten dem Schäfer, er solle (...) bringen" (bulg. *kazaxa na ovčarja da donese*). Der nicht-finale Satz wird durch *ki* eingeleitet: *söyle-ki girmiš kendisi* (Kakuk 1960, 250) „sie sagt, daß er von selbst hereingekommen sei" (bulg. *kazva če e vljazol sam*).

Einer im Bulgarischen umgangssprachlich weit verbreiteten Konstruktion nachgebildet sind temporale und konditionale Nebensätze mit interrogativer Verbform in der Protasis. Die Funktionsbreite des Interrogativsuffixes *-mi*, in seiner Primärfunktion eine Entsprechung zu der bulgarischen Fragepartikel *li*, ist nach dem Muster des Bulgarischen ausgeweitet worden. Dieser Nebensatztyp ist in den türkischen Mundarten weit verbreitet, vgl. für den Dialekt von Küstendil: *eve geldimi* (...) Kakuk 1961, 321) „als er nach Hause kam (...)" und bulg. *počne li da vali* „wenn/sobald es zu regnen beginnt..."

8. Wertung der Literatur

Eine kurze Darstellung der Geschichte der Balkanturkologie findet man in Hazai 1978; ausführlicher ist Tryjarski 1990 — beide mit reichlich bibliographischen Angaben. Unter den Arbeiten, die sich auf den bulgarischen Raum beziehen, nimmt die Monographie von Németh 1965 noch immer eine hervorragende Position ein. Während über die Einflüsse des Türkischen auf das Bulgarische und die übrigen Sprachen Südosteuropas eine reichhaltige Literatur existiert — zu bibliographischen Angaben sei auf Hazai 1961 sowie auf Tietze 1990 verwiesen — ist die entgegengesetzte Einflußrichtung eher stiefmütterlich behandelt worden: zu Unrecht, wie die kurzen Studien von Kakuk 1960, Mollov/Mollova 1966 sowie Rudin/Eminov 1990 zeigen.

9. Bibliographie (in Auswahl)

Bachmeier, Peter (1990): „Schulsystem". In: *Südosteuropa-Handbuch VI*, Grothusen, K. D. (Ed.), Göttingen.

Boev, Emil (1968): „Za bălgarsko-tjurskite ezikovi vrăski" [Über die bulgarisch-türkischen sprachlichen Beziehungen]. In: *Izvestija na Instituta za bălgarski ezik* 16, 177—183.

Conev, Benjo (1940): *Istorija na bălgarski ezik I—III* [Geschichte der bulgarischen Sprache I—III], Sofia.

Doerfer, Gerhard (1990): „Die Stellung des Osmanischen im Kreise des Oghusischen und seine Vorgeschichte". In: *Handbuch der türkischen Sprachwissenschaft*, Hazai, Gy. (Ed.). Wiesbaden/Budapest.

Erimer, K. (1970): „Anadolu ve Rumeli ağızları üzerinde bir bibliyografya denemesi" [Versuch einer Bibliographie der Mundarten Anatoliens und Rumeliens]. In: *Türk dili araştırmaları yıllığı belleten 1970*, 211—236.

Grannes, Alf (1989): „Turkish Influence on Bulgarian." In: *International Journal of Turkish Studies* 4, 223—239.

Hazai, György (1961): „Remarques sur les rapports des langues slaves des Balkans avec le turc-osmanli". In: *Studia Slavica* 7, 97—138.

Hazai, György (1964): „O nekotoryx aktualnyx voprosax issledovanija balkano-tureckix dialektov" [Zu einigen aktuellen Fragen der Untersuchung der balkantürkischen Dialekte]. In: *Balkansko ezikoznanie* 9,1, 57—69.

Hazai, György (1978): *Kurze Einführung in das Studium der türkischen Sprache*, Wiesbaden.

Höpken, Wolfgang (1987): „Modernisierung und Nationalismus: Sozialgeschichtliche Aspekte der bulgarischen Minderheitenpolitik gegenüber den

Türken". In: *Nationalitätenprobleme in Südosteuropa*, Schönfeld, R. (Ed.), München.

Johanson, Lars (1992): *Strukturelle Faktoren in türkischen Sprachkontakten.* (Sitzungsberichte der wissenschaftlichen Gesellschaft an der Johann Wolfgang Goethe-Universität Frankfurt am Main), Frankfurt am Main.

Kakuk, Zsuzsanna (1960): „Constructions hypotactiques dans le dialecte turc de la Bulgarie Occidentale". In: *Acta Academiae Scientiarium Hungaricae* 11, 249–257.

Kakuk, Zsuzsanna (1961): „Die türkische Mundart von Küstendil und Michajlovgrad". In: *Acta Linguistica Academiae Scientiarum Hungaricae* 11, 301–385.

Kowalski, Tadeusz (1933): *Les Turcs et la langue turque de la Bulgarie du Nord-Est*. (Mémoires de la Commission Orientaliste de l'Académie des Sciences de Cracovie 16), Krakau.

Mirčev, Kiril (1978): *Istoričeska gramatika na bălgarski ezik* [Historische Grammatik der bulgarischen Sprache], Sofia.

Mollov, Riza/Mollova, Mefküre (1966): „Parlers turcs des Rhodopes de l'ouest au point de vue slavistique". In: *Balkansko Ezikoznanie* 11,1, 121–136.

Mollova, Mefküre (1970): „Coïncidence des Zones Linguistiques Bulgares et Turques dans les Balkans". In: *Actes du Xe Congrès International des Linguistes, Bucarest 1967*, Bukarest.

Németh, György (1956): *Zur Einteilung der türkischen Mundarten Bulgariens*, Sofia.

Németh, György (1965): *Die Türken von Vidin. Sprache, Folklore, Religion*, Budapest.

Pundeff, Marin (1990): „Churches und Religious Communities". In: *Südosteuropa-Handbuch VI: Bulgarien*, Grothusen, K.-D. (Ed.), Göttingen.

Rudin, Catherine/Eminov, Ali (1990): „Bulgarian Turkish: The Linguistic Effects of Recent Nationality Policy". In: *Anthropological Linguistics* 32, 1–2, 149–162.

Tietze, Andreas (1990): „Der Einfluß des Türkischen auf andere Sprachen. (Veröffentlichungen seit etwa 1950)". In: *Handbuch der türkischen Sprachwissenschaft*, Hazai, Gy. (Ed.), Budapest.

Troebst, Stefan (1990): „Nationale Minderheiten". In: *Südosteuropa-Handbuch VI: Bulgarien*, Grothusen, K.D. (Ed.), Göttingen.

Tryjarski, Edward (1990): „Balkan Dialects". In: *Handbuch der türkischen Sprachwissenschaft*, Hazai, Gy. (Ed.), Budapest.

Birgit Igla, Sofia (Bulgarien)

180. Bulgare–grec

1. Géographie et démographie
2. Histoire
3. Situation sociale et culturelle
4. Situation ethnolinguistique
5. Situation sociolinguistique
6. Politique linguistique
7. Portrait général des contacts linguistiques
8. Etudes sur le grec en Bulgarie
9. Bibliographie (sélective)

1. Géographie et démographie

Les locuteurs grecs en Bulgarie appartiennent à deux groupes d'origine différente. Les héritiers des colonistes grecs de l'Antiquité sont concentrés dans les vieux quartiers (situés sur de petites péninsules) des villes du littoral de la Mer Noire – Sozopol et Nessèbre (partiellement à Pomorié). La seconde communauté d'expression grecque est formée par les Karakatchans (*Ks*) qui sont installés dans les localités montagneuses au pied de la Stara planina: Mihailovgrad, Berkovica, Vărsec, Sopot, Karlovo, Kazanlăk, Sliven (et les villages voisins), Karnobat (et les villages voisins); et au pied de la montagne Rila: Dupnica, Samokov (et les villages voisins).

Une diminution sensible de la population grecque en Bulgarie est due aux émigrations après les conflits bulgaro-grecs de 1906 et après la Deuxième Guerre balkanique (1913), mais surtout après l'accord «Mollov-Caphandaris» de 1927. Si le nombre de la population parlant le grec comme langue maternelle, selon le recensement de 1900 était 70.887 (1,89%), en 1926 ce nombre est déjà 12.787 (0,23%). Selon le recensement de 1956 les Grecs comptent 7.437 (y compris les réfugiés politiques après la guerre civile de 1949 qui se sont rapatriés dans les années 1970–1980) et les Ks – 2.085 personnes. Les données du recensement de 1992 montrent: 8.000 personnes parlant le grec comme langue maternelle, 4.930 Grecs (dont 4.517 ayant le grec comme langue maternelle), 5.144 Ks (dont 2.891 ayant le grec comme langue maternelle); → carte linguistique H.

2. Histoire

Les contacts linguistiques bulgaro-grecs datent de l'époque de l'installation des ancêtres slaves des Bulgares dans les Balkans, c.-à-d. sur le territoire de l'Empire byzantin (VIe–VIIe siècle). La christianisation adoptée de Byzance (864) et les traductions des livres ecclésiastiques du grec en vieux bulgare (IXe siècle) engendrent les contacts littéraires entre les deux langues. Pendant la période de la domination byzantine en Bulgarie (1018–1186) ces contacts se renforcent.

Après la chute de la Bulgarie sous le joug ottoman (1396), les autorités turques ayant délégué à la Patriarchie de Constantinople les droits de représenter tous les chrétiens, les Bulgares sont soumis à une grécisation intense qu'ils attaquent tout le long du XIXe siècle et la rejettent en 1870 quand l'indépendance de l'Eglise bulgare fut proclamée. La restriction du nomadisme des Ks après la formation des nouveaux Etats balkaniques au cours du XIXe siècle et l'orientation vers une vie sédentaire en Bulgarie, les mettent en contact avec les Bulgares. Les grandes migrations du XXe siècle ont limité les contacts linguistiques bulgaro-grecs dans les îlots de population mixte en Bulgarie.

3. Situation sociale et culturelle

Les communautés linguistiques grecques en Bulgarie confessent la religion chrétienne orthodoxe. Ils prennent une part active à la vie sociale en Bulgarie. Ces deux faits contribuent à l'intégration des héritiers des colons grecs (surtout des habitants des grandes villes industrielles Varna et Bourgas) au milieu bulgare. Les Ks qui exercent leur métier traditionnel — élevage de moutons — conservent bien leur identité ethnique et culturelle, grâce à la manière d'habiter en masse compacte et de pratiquer le mariage endogame. Après 1989 deux organisations de locuteurs grecs sont créées: l'une englobe des Grecs et des Bulgares hellénophiles, l'autre — des Ks. Toutes les deux communautés linguistiques sont très actives dans le domaine culturel.

4. Situation ethnolinguistique

Les ancêtres des grécophones habitant le littoral occidental de la Mer Noire s'y sont installés à partir du VIIIe siècle av. J.-C., mais surtout après l'invasion des Cimmériens et des Scythes en Asie Mineure en 650 av. J.-C. (Bérard 1960, 100). Deux villes — Mégare dorienne et Milet ionienne — fondent d'une façon directe ou indirecte toutes les colonies grecques du Pont-Euxin: Apollonie (Sozopol), Messembria (Nessèbre = *Ns*), Odessos (Varna), Anchialos (Pomorié), Navlochos (Obzor), Bizoné (Kavarna), Pyrgos (Bourgas = *Bs*). Les Slaves ont peuplé la côte de la Mer Noire au début du VIIe siècle. Les colonies grecques sont annexées à l'Etat bulgare à partir du VIIIe siècle et au début du IXe siècle. Le caractère mixte — bulgare et grec — des villes du littoral Achtopol, Sozopol, Anchialos, Messemvria, Bourgas et Varna est attesté dans des documents du XVIIIe et XIXe siècle (Nikov 1932, 29–37; Eneholm 1938, 122–125).

Les grécophones du littoral emploient l'ethnonyme *Grekós, Grekiá*. A l'intérieur de la Bulgarie le grec fut parlé dans les villes Plovdiv, Assenovgrad (jusqu'en 1934 Stanimaka) et Melnik. La population grecque de Melnik qui résulte d'une immigration de Byzance de la fin du XIIIe siècle, a quitté la ville après le « Traité de Bucarest » de 1913. Les (vraies) familles grecques de Plovdiv et d'Assenovgrad n'étaient pas nombreuses, mais elles possédaient le pouvoir économique, politique et spirituel et ont grécisé une bonne partie des Bulgares. Vers la fin du XVIIIe siècle et le début du XIXe siècle l'élément grec dans la région commence à fondre (Genčev 1981, 70–73) pour disparaître après les échanges de population entre la Bulgarie et la Grèce (1919, 1927).

Il y a deux grandes hypothèses sur l'origine des Ks: 1) c'est une population grecque dont le nomadisme date de l'Antiquité (ou bien du XIVe siècle); 2) c'est une population aroumaine grécisée (Antonijević 1975, 206–211 et les auteurs qui y sont cités). Une supposition qu'ils seraient héritiers des Thraces est exprimée par des anthropologues (Boev 1972, 263). L'ethnonyme avec lequel les Ks se nomment eux-mêmes est en gr. *Vláhos, Vláha*, le parler *vláhika* et en bulg. *Karákačánin, Karákačánka*, le parler *karákačánski*.

5. Situation sociolinguistique

Actuellement, il n'y a plus de bilingues parmi les Bulgares. Mais au début du XIXe siècle les Bulgares érudits, ayant reçu leur éducation en grec, étaient bilingues additifs (dialecte bulgare + grec littéraire).

Les deux communautés linguistiques grecques en Bulgarie pratiquent un bilinguisme bulgaro-grec collectif et subordonné. (En 1967 j'ai constaté des cas isolés de monolingues parmi les femmes karakatchanes.) Bien que le grec soit la première langue à apprendre, son fonctionnement est limité au cadre familial. C'est le bulgare qui a le rôle primordial dans la communication au niveau social. Les jeunes gens maîtrisent mieux le bulgare que leur dialecte maternel (ils ne se servent que du bulgare par écrit). Cette diglossie bulgaro-grecque dissimule la tendance vers un monolinguisme bulgare: parmi la jeune génération des héritiers des colons grecs et des Ks il y a déjà des monolingues bulgares.

6. Politique linguistique

Vers la fin du XVIIIe siècle et le début du XIXe siècle, sous l'influence du Réveil national en Grèce, les communautés grecques en Bulgarie ont ouvert leurs premières écoles: à Plovdiv en 1780, à Pomorié en 1790, à Melnik en 1813, à Sozopol au début du XIXe siècle, à Bourgas en 1844, à Assenovgrad en 1844, à Varna en 1845. Certaines informations confirment l'existence d'écoles grecques au XVIIe siècle. Etant donné qu'elles étaient les premières écoles laïques en Bulgarie, beaucoup d'écoliers bulgares les fréquentaient. L'éducation en grec, au moins jusqu'aux années 40, quand apparaissent les écoles bulgares, a joué le rôle principal pour la formation des premiers hommes de lettres bulgares (Alexieva 1979, 158).

Au cours de la première moitié du XIXe siècle le grec a cédé, dans les églises et dans les écoles des Bulgares, devant leur langue maternelle. Les écoles des communautés grecques ont cessé d'exister après le début des grandes émigrations vers la Grèce (à Bourgas et à Pomorié en 1906, à Assenovgrad en 1913).

7. Portrait général des contacts linguistiques

Appartenant à l'union linguistique balkanique, le bulgare et le grec (avec le roumain et l'albanais) montrent un rapprochement de leurs structures surtout au niveau de la morphosyntaxe: tendance vers l'analytisme, syncrétisme du datif et du génitif, *ubi = quo*, redoublement de l'objet, isomorphisme des constructions remplaçant l'infinitif, des formes du futur et du conditionnel, etc. Le grec ne possède pas la voyelle moyenne balkanique *ə* et la postposition de l'article défini.

L'influence grecque sur le bulgare est de caractère littéraire et concerne le lexique et la syntaxe. Les dialectes bulgares du Sud-Est et du Sud-Ouest contiennent des emprunts lexicaux faits au grec qui y ont pénétré par voie orale (Mirčev 1978, 75). L'influence bulgare sur le grec se manifeste dans le lexique des dialectes de l'Epire et de la Thessalie.

Les parlers des deux communautés d'expression grecque en Bulgarie appartiennent aux dialectes grecs septentrionaux et partagent leurs traits spécifiques.

7.1. Phonétique

La réduction des voyelles *e > i* et *o > u* forme une continuité géographique embrassant les dialectes grecs du Nord et les dialectes bulgares de l'Est. L'élision des *i, u* atones est généralisée dans le parler des Ks, par ex. *ts màna t kurčù < τῆς μάννας τοῦ κοριτσιοῦ* 'à la mère de la fille', et restreinte dans les parlers de Melnik et du littoral, par ex. *màna s < μάννα σου* 'ta mère', mais *spìti* 'maison'.

Les consonnes *š, ž, tš, dž* qui resultent de la palatalisation de *s, z, ts, dz* devant *e, i, t', k'* dans le parler de Ks, par ex. *dhiavaš < διαβάζει* 'il lit', restent inconnues dans le parler du littoral.

Le parler du littoral va de pair avec les autres dialectes grecs du Nord où la sonorisation des groupes nasaux *mp, nt, nk* aboutit aux consones *b, d, g*, par ex. *àdras < άντρας* 'homme, mari', *abèli < αμπέλι* 'vignoble'. Le parler des Ks garde la nasale, y compris dans les cas où les groupes *mp, nt, nk* apparaissent simplifiés en grec commun, par ex. *mbalònu < μπαλλώνω* [balóno] 'raccomoder', *ndrépundan < ντρέπονταν* [drépondan] 'ils ont honte'.

La règle de l'accent fixe sur l'antépénultième n'est plus respectée ni dans le parler du littoral, par ex. *pàndrepsane* 'ils se marièrent'; ni dans le parler des Ks, par ex. *pérasaman* 'nous passâmes'. On peut croire que ce phénomène, observé aussi en Thessalie (Newton 1972, 198), est renforcé par l'influence bulgare.

Les systèmes phonétiques des deux parlers ont subi des changements identiques sous l'influence du bulgare: le phonème *l* a perdu sa caractéristique grecque dorso-apicale et ne diffère pas du *l* bulgare coronal; la voyelle moyenne *ъ* apparaît dans les emprunts faits au bulgare, par ex. *gə̀rna* (Ks), *gə̀rnè* (Ns) 'seau' et comme résultat de la réduction de l'*a* dans le parler des Ks, par ex. *èraftъn* 'ils cousaient'.

7.2. Morphosyntaxe

Les deux parlers partagent la prédilection des dialectes grecs du Nord vers l'analytisme. L'expression casuelle de l'objet indirect, par ex. *Dhoki t kavalar'* 'Donne au brave!', alterne avec la construction analytique σε + acc. (plus souvent dans le parler des Ks), par ex. *STU kalò tu kurič' na tu dhòši* [à + art.acc. − belle − art.acc. − fille-que-le-donne] 'Qu'il le donne à la belle fille'. La même construction est valable pour l'expression des rapports possessifs (au lieu du gén.) dans le parler des Ks, par ex. *i màna STU pidhì m* [art. − mère − à + art.acc. − fils mon] 'la mère de mon fils', mais aussi *ta škl'a t adherfu m* 'les chiens de mon frère'. Le parler des Ks a reduit le nombre des oppositions casuelles des noms aussi sur le plan paradigmatique: la forme du nom. est généralisée au pl., au sg.f., sg.n.; il n'y a que deux formes casuelles − nom./cas oblique − au sg.m. Il est possible que l'analytisme bulgare ait influencé le développement du parler des Ks dans ce sens, mais il ne faut pas oublier le rôle conservateur de la tradition littéraire qui a manqué à cette population nomade.

Le parler du littoral a développé la forme plus ancienne du conditionnel (employée par la katharévoussa (→ Art. 181) et dans certains dialectes): *volo* (impf.) + inf., en remplaçant l'infinitif par le conjonctif. De cette façon la forme coïncide avec la structure de la forme conditionnelle en bulgare (=*fut.-praet.*): *ìthili na ìni i dhiò eftihizmèni* (Bs) 'Ils seraient tous les deux heureux' où *ìthili na ìni* correspond au bulg. *šteše da sa* (*vouloir*, 3. p. sg. impf. − conjonction − conjonctif, *être*).

Le parler des Ks se sert du conditionnel du grec commun θα + impf., quand la condition est nettement formulée dans l'apodose (1), et d'un pendant structurel et sémantique de la construction ci-dessus, pour exprimer un *fut. praet.* non réalisé (2): (1) *An dhèn iha piaštì, THA NÀ-PEFTA* [*Si-ne-saisir*, plqprf. − *tomber*, cond.] 'Si je n'avais pas trouvé d'appui, je serais tombée'; (2) *Ònda ìmun mikrì THALÀ PÈSU stu rèma* [*Quand-j'étais-petite-tomber-dans* + art. *−rivière*] 'Quand j'étais petite, j'allais tomber dans la rivière'.

7.3. Calques faits sur le bulgare

L'interférence dans la langue se manifeste par les emprunts lexicaux, mais aussi par les calques syntaxiques, morphologiques et sémantiques. Les expressions impersonnelles de sens volitif dans le parler de Melnik reproduisent littéralement le modèle bulgare: *mi pìniti = mi se pìe* 'J'ai envie de boire' (litt. 'il se boit à moi') gr. διψώ. Le même parler ne fait pas la différence grecque entre la négation générale όχι et la négation préverbale δεν et n'emploie que la dernière (Andriotis 1989, 23), juste comme en bulgare *ne*.

A la manière bulgare le parler du littoral emploie des adverbes de quantité dans une fonction attributive au lieu des adjectifs, par ex. *I perisòtero* (gr. περισσότεροι) *ìni sti Thesalonìki.* (Bs) 'La plupart sont à Salonique'. La rection du verbe γεμίζω από est changée − *jomàto me* ('avec') *ikònes* (Ns) 'plein d'icônes' sur le bulg. *pòlen s* ('avec'). L'expression *vrèhi vrohì* (Ks) au lieu de βρέχει 'il pleut' imite le bulg. *valì dъžd* 'la pluie tombe'.

Les calques morphologiques faits sur le bulgare remplacent des lexèmes grecs de dérivation différente: par ex. *dhiàvenane* pour gr. έφευγαν 'ils partirent' (Vafiadou 1974, 123) reflète les morphèmes de bulg. *za-mìna* 'partir'; *Àspri thàlasa* pour gr. Αιγαίον 'Mer Egée' correspond au bulg. *B'àlo morè* «Mer Blanche»; *dhòsimo* pour gr. φόρος 'impôt' (Andriotis 1989, 41) dérive du verbe δώσω 'donner' comme le bulg. *dànъk* 'impôt' < *dam* 'donner'.

Dans le but inconscient d'aligner la sémantique du lexème grec sur celle du lexème bulgare correspondant, le bilingue emploie par ex. *hartì* 'papier' dans le sens de βιβλίο 'livre' sous l'influence du bulg. *knìga* qui unit les deux sens.

7.4. Mélange des codes

Le milieu bilingue rend possible le passage naturel de l'une des deux langues à l'autre dans le cadre d'une même phrase, souvent sans que le locuteur ne s'en rende compte, par ex. (la composante bulgare est en majuscule). *Anhìelos ìtan piò KULTÙREN CÈNTъR ap tu Pìrγu.* (Bs) 'Pomorié était un centre culturel plus important que Bourgas'.

Les éléments syntaxiquement indépendants − clichés, exclamations, interjections, particules expressives, certains adverbes, etc. − s'adaptent mieux au mélange des codes, par ex. *Halasi i hara VEČI ...* (Ks) 'Les noces se sont déjà terminées'. L'apparition d'éléments bulgares syntaxiquement indépendants et de noms propres insère dans le texte grec d'autres mots bulgares. Dans les exemples suivants le mot provoquant le mélange des codes est souligné: *I zui* VEČI SЪ OBMEN'A NAPЪ LNO (Ks) 'la vie change complètement déjà'; *Konda tu* MARINKEVITE HAMBARI BEŠE NEGOVA KЪŠTA (Bs) 'il avait une maison tout près de Marinkevite hambari'.

La restriction du mélange des codes dans les groupes des mots syntaxiquement reliés n'agit pas toujours — le mélange apparaît souvent dans le groupe attributif, par ex. *Istira* CALITI *himonis* VEČI *šti Vulgaria ...* (Ks) 'plus tard, des hivers entiers déjà — en Bulgarie ...'; et dans le groupe prédicatif, par ex. *I zui itan puli* TRUDNA (Ks) 'La vie était très difficile', *Itane* SЪ DRUŽNICI (Bs) 'Ils étaient associés'.

8. Etudes sur le grec en Bulgarie

Une description détaillée de l'ethnographie, de la culture matérielle et du parler des Ks de Thessalie et d'Epire est faite dans Höeg 1925, 1926. La phonologie du parler des Ks en Bulgarie est discutée dans Bidwell 1964 et Simeonov 1970. Des observations sur les contacts bulgaro-grecs dans le parler des Ks sont exposées dans Assenova 1976, 1984.

L'étude ethnographique de Vafiadou 1974 sur Sozopol est précédée d'une brève description (116—122) des particularités du parler de la ville par rapport au grec commun. L'abondance de textes originaux rend possibles des conclusions objectives. Le livre d'Andriotis 1989 décrit le lexique du parler de Melnik (enregistré après l'installation de sa population en Grèce) et fournit des observations grammaticales.

9. Bibliographie (sélective)

Alexieva, Afrodita (1979): «Grăckata prosveta i formiraneto na bălgarskata văzroždeska inteligencija [L'instruction grecque et la formation de l'intelligentsia bulgare]». In: *Studia balcanica* 14, 156—180.

Andriotis, Nicolaos P. (1989): *To glôssiko idiôma tou Melenikon* [Le dialecte de Melnik], Thessalonique.

Antonijević, Dragoslav (1975): «Sarakacani» [Les Sarakatsans]. In: *Balcanica* 6, 201—233.

Assenova, Petja (1976): «Les contacts linguistiques sur la péninsule Balkanique reflétés dans le parler des Karakatchans de Bulgarie». In: *Linguistique balkanique* 19, 4, 9—21.

Assenova, Petja (1984): «Observations sur les interférences entre le grec et le bulgare dans le parler des Karakatchans en Bulgarie». In: *Bmori българо-гръцки симпозиум*, 18—22 IX 1980, Sofia, 160—165.

Bérard, Jean (1960): *L'expansion et la colonisation grecque jusqu'aux guerres médiques*, Paris.

Bidwell, Charles E. (1964): «On Karakatsan Phonology». In: *Papers in Memory of George C. Pappageotes. Supplement to Word vol.* 20, 3, 7—16.

Boev, Petăr (1972): *Die Rassentypen der Balkanhalbinsel und der ostägäischen Inselwelt und deren Bedeutung für die Herkunft ihrer Bevölkerung*, Sofia.

Eneholm, Gerhard (1938): «Notice sur les villes situées au-delà des Balkans occupées par les Troupes Russes pendant la glorieuse campagne de 1829 (St-Petersburg 1830) (traduction en bulgare S. Boyadžiev)». In: *Archives des établissements humains Ière année, 1 fasc.*, 121—129.

Genčev, Nikolaj (1981): *Văzroždenskijat Plovdiv* [Plovdiv à l'époque du Réveil national], Plovdiv.

Höeg, Carsten (1925): *Les Sarakatsans, une tribu nomade grecque, t. I*, Paris.

Höeg, Carsten (1926): *Les Sarakatsans, une tribu nomade grecque, t. II*, Paris.

Mirčev, Kiril (1978): *Istoričeska gramatika na bălgarskija ezik* [Grammaire historique de la langue bulgare], Sofia.

Newton, Brian (1972): *The Generative Interpretation of Dialect. A Study of Modern Greek Phonology*, Cambridge.

Nikov, Peter (1932): «Eine unbekannte Beschreibung der bulgarischen Küste des Schwarzen Meeres aus dem XVIII. Jahrhundert». In: *Annuaire de l'Université de Sofia. Faculté historico-philologique*, t. 28, 3, 3—60.

Simeonov, Boris (1970): «Fonologičeskaja sistema karakačanskogo dialekta Berkovicy/Veršeca» [Le système phonologique du dialecte des Sarakatsans de Berkovica et Văršec]. In: *Linguistique balkanique* 13, 2, 41—53.

Vafiadou, Valasia (1974): «Ethe kai ethema Sôzopoleôs» [Les us et les coutumes des habitants de Sozopol]. In: Λαογραφια 29, 115—226.

Petja Assenova, Sofia (Bulgarie)

181. Griechenland

1. Geographie und Demographie
2. Territorialgeschichte und Staatsbildung
3. Statistik und Ethnoprofile
4. Soziolinguistische Lage
5. Sprachpolitische Lage
6. Sonstige Sprachkontakte
7. Kritische Wertung
8. Bibliographie (in Auswahl)

1. Geographie und Demographie

In den Grenzen Griechenlands von 1832 lebte nur ein Teil der Griechen. 1864 trat England die Ionischen Inseln ab, vom Osmanischen Reich erwarb Griechenland 1881 Thessalien und Arta, 1913 Nordgriechenland, Kreta und Samos, von Bulgarien 1918 Gebiete östlich des Nestos und von Italien 1947 die Dodekanes. Infolge dieses Gebietsgewinns, des Bevölkerungswachstums, der Rückwanderung aus alten Diasporagemeinden im 19. Jahrhundert sowie infolge des Bevölkerungsaustauschs mit Bulgarien 1919 und mit der Türkei 1923 lebt heute die Mehrheit der Griechen in Griechenland (9,7 Mill. Einwohner); rund 500 000 Griechen bilden die Bevölkerungsmehrheit (ca. 80%) der Republik Zypern. Große Kolonien bestehen in den Auswandererländern USA und Kanada (1–1,25 Mill., davon 350 000–450 000 in der 3. und 4. Generation), Australien (1981 über 420 000), Südafrika (1992: 30 000). 1955–1977 reisten 758 351 Griechen als Gastarbeiter in europäische Länder, davon 630 177 1960–1977 allein nach Deutschland. Die griechische Wohnbevölkerung im europäischen Ausland umfaßte 1992 etwa 650 000, in Deutschland allein 346 000 Personen. 200 000 Auslandsgriechen in Europa, überwiegend in Großbritannien, sind Zyprioten (Chasiotis 1993; Sauerwein 1976; *Population du Royaume ...* 1962, 1972; jährlich erscheint: *Statistical Yearbook of Greece*). Die vertraglich geschützte Minderheit in der Türkei (Istanbul, Imbros, Tenedos) ist infolge diskriminierender Behandlung zusammengeschrumpft. In Istanbul dürften heute ca. 4000, auf Imbros und Tenedos weniger als 1000 Griechen leben. Im Zusammenhang mit dem Zypernkonflikt kam es 1964/1965 zur Massenausweisung griechischer Staatsbürger aus Istanbul. Eine starke Minderheit lebt in Südalbanien (kontroverse Angaben zwischen 60 000 und 250 000), in Bulgarien sollen mindestens 7500 Griechen wohnen. Bei der jugoslawischen Volkszählung von 1971 bestand die Möglichkeit der Deklaration griechischer Nationalität unter „übrige Nationen und Nationalitäten", praktisch war dieses Bekenntnis unerwünscht. Außerdem existieren noch Reste alter Siedlungen in Unteritalien (Kalabrien, Terra d'Otranto); → Sprachenkarte I.

2. Territorialgeschichte und Staatsbildung

2.1. Geschichte

Seit dem Altertum entstanden griechische Kolonien im Mittel- und Schwarzmeerraum. In einigen Fällen läßt sich eine durch periodische Zuwanderung gestärkte Siedlungskontinuität nachweisen, neuere Forschungen zeigen auch diskontinuierliche Koloniebildungen am selben Ort. Griechisch war im östlichen Mittelmeerraum als Bildungs- und Verkehrssprache, als Sprache der orthodoxen Kirche weit verbreitet, in Byzanz verdrängte es das Latein als Verwaltungssprache. Infolge der Errichtung „fränkischer" Herrschaften 1204, der Ausbreitung der venezianischen Herrschaft im 13. Jahrhundert und schließlich der Expansion des Osmanischen Reiches seit dem 14. Jahrhundert ergaben sich neue Sprachkontakte und Rezeptionsprozesse in beiden Richtungen. Im venezianischen und im osmanischen Herrschaftsgebiet entstanden Sprachkontakte des Griechischen mit der venezianischen bzw. osmanischen Verwaltungssprache. Auf Chios schrieben griechische Katholiken ihre Sprache mit lateinischen Lettern („Frankochiotisch"). Andererseits hatte das Griechische als Sprache der griechisch-orthodoxen Kirche, zu der auch die Serben, Bulgaren, Aromunen und Albaner im Jurisdiktionsbereich des Patriarchats von Konstantinopel gehörten, weiters als Verkehrs- und Bildungssprache in der Türkei große Bedeutung. Seit dem 16. Jahrhundert bildeten sich hier griechischsprachige und kulturell griechisch orientierte soziale Eliten heraus, die großen Einfluß in den autonomen Fürstentümern Moldau und Walachei gewannen; das Griechische fand dort Eingang in Verwaltung und Bildungsinstitutionen. Türkische Texte mit griechischen Lettern (sog. Karamanlidika) dürften schon im 14./15. Jahrhundert entstanden sein und wurden im

18. Jahrhundert gedruckt. In einzelnen Regionen (Jannina, Kreta) sprachen Türken bis zum Beginn des 20. Jahrhunderts auch oder überwiegend Griechisch, sie übersetzten den Koran ins Griechische und schrieben auf Griechisch mit arabischen Schriftzeichen islamische Hymnen. Kinder aus Ehen muslimischer Väter mit Griechinnen erlernten meistens auch die Sprache der Mutter. Nach der Niederlage Griechenlands im Kleinasienkrieg wurde 1923 mit der Türkei der obligatorische Bevölkerungsaustausch nach dem Religionsbekenntnis vereinbart. Griechenland nahm über 1,1 Millionen orthodoxe Christen aus der Türkei auf, von denen ein Teil hauptsächlich oder ausschließlich Türkisch sprach; in die Türkei mußten rund 470 000 Muslime, überwiegend Sprecher des Türkischen, abziehen (Pentzopoulos 1965). Muslimische Sprecher des Griechischen blieben in der Türkei, islamisierte Meglenorumänen wurden nach Kleinasien umgesiedelt. Vom Austausch ausgenommen waren die Muslime in West-Thrazien und die Orthodoxen in Istanbul sowie auf Imbros und Tenedos. Außerdem bestehen heute noch regionale griechisch-türkische Sprachkontakte auf Zypern.

Für Sprachkontakte auf der Ebene der Verwaltung und der kulturellen Rezeption kommen weiters das Englische (britisches Protektorat über die Ionischen Inseln 1815–1864, Herrschaft über Zypern 1878–1960), das Deutsche (bayerische Regentschaft in Griechenland 1833–1835), das Italienische (Dodekanes 1912–1947) und schließlich die Staatssprachen der Nachfolgestaaten des Osmanischen Reiches mit griechischen Minderheiten (Türkei, Albanien, Bulgarien, Serbien bzw. Jugoslawien) in Betracht. Während der Besetzung Griechenlands im Zweiten Weltkrieg verwendeten die Okkupationsbehörden in ihren jeweiligen Okkupationszonen das Deutsche, das Italienische und das Bulgarische als Verwaltungssprache.

Weiters haben fünf langfristige demographische Vorgänge zu intensiven Sprachkontakten geführt: (1) infolge von Wanderungsbewegungen bildete sich eine ethnischsprachliche Gemengelage im Balkanraum heraus (Sprachkontakte mit den Sprechern des Türkischen, Aromunischen, Meglenorumänischen, Albanischen, Judenspanischen und südslawischer Dialekte); (2) griechische Kaufmanns- und Händlerkolonien entstanden in Italien (Venedig, Livorno, Neapel, Ancona, Triest), in Wien und Leipzig, im serbischen Siedlungsraum, in Ungarn, Polen, Rumänien, Frankreich (Marseille, Paris), in den Niederlanden und England, verfielen aber im Laufe des 19. Jahrhunderts. Dagegen wuchs die griechische Kolonie in Ägypten im 19. Jahrhundert stark an. (3) Rund 250 000 Griechen lebten nach 1917 in Zentral- und Südrußland (Chasiotis 1993). (4) im 19./20. Jahrhundert folgten die Wellen der Auswanderung nach Übersee, politisch bedingte Fluchtbewegungen und schließlich die Wanderung von Gastarbeitern seit den 1950er Jahren vornehmlich in die Bundesrepublik Deutschland.

Kontakte ergaben sich sodann mit den Umgangssprachen anderssprachiger Ortsansässiger, Händler, Geistlicher usw. im eigenen Siedlungsraum, ferner bei überregionaler Kommunikation (Binnenwanderungen, Handel, Wallfahrten, Schiffahrt, Transportgewerbe, innerkirchliche Kommunikation) mit den Sprachen in den Korrespondenzräumen. Als wichtigste Kontaktsprachen kommen hier in Betracht: italienische Dialekte, Aromunisch, südslawische Sprachen, Albanisch, Russisch, Rumänisch, Judenspanisch, Französisch, seit dem 18. Jahrhundert auch Deutsch, Türkisch, Arabisch, Persisch, Armenisch.

Die orthodoxen *Aromunen* waren im griechischen Siedlungsraum seit dem 19. Jahrhundert größtenteils zweisprachig. Die horizontal mobilen, d. h. zwischen Sommerweiden und Winteraufenthaltsorten wandernden „Walachen" der Fernweidewirtschaft nahmen im Transportgewerbe, im Fernhandel, in der kommerziellen Gastlichkeit sowie im städtischen Handwerk eine starke Position ein. Im 18./19. Jahrhundert traten viele von ihnen als Träger griechischer Kultur, im 19. Jahrhundert auch als Anwälte der griechischen Nationalbewegung hervor. In den Donaufürstentümern und in den Kaufmannskolonien in Ungarn, in denen sie mit Rumänen in Kontakt kamen, differenzierten sich die nationalaromunisch bzw. rumänisch gesinnten Aromunen von den gräzisierten. Im griechischen Siedlungsraum hatte die nationalaromunische Bewegung geringere Wirkungen. Die Kompetenz in der griechischen Kultur- und Verkehrssprache blieb hier Voraussetzung horizontaler Mobilität sowie sozialen Aufstiegs. Zur Verschriftung des Aromunischen wurde das griechische wie nach rumänischem Vorbild das kyrillische Alphabet empfohlen. Das seit dem Ende des 18. Jahrhunderts wachsende Sprachbewußtsein der Aromunen hatte keine antigriechische Färbung. Die aromunische Inschrift in der Apostelkirche von Klinovo aus dem letzten Viertel des 18. Jahrhunderts, ein frühes Zeugnis der Verschriftung des Aromunischen, ist mit griechischen Lettern geschrieben; auch das erste aromunische Alphabetarium von K. Oukoutas (1797), der die Aromunen zum Gebrauch ihrer Sprache ermuntern wollte, hat das griechische Alphabet zur Grundlage. Hingegen vertraten rumänische Politiker, Publizisten und Wissenschaftler die Auffassung, die Aromunen bildeten den „südlichen Zweig des rumänischen Volkes" (Capidan 1925—1936, 1932), der seine Nationalität „verloren" habe. Die aromunische Nationalbewegung, als deren Führer Margaritis hervortrat, fand jedoch keinen Massenanhang. 1878 sagte die osmanische Regierung den Schutz der Aromunen in den Vilayets Monastir, Saloniki, Jannina zu. 1870 gestattete das bulgarische Exarchat, 1889 auch das Patriarchat den Gebrauch des Aromunischen bzw. Rumänischen in den von den Aromunen errichteten Kirchen. In den blutigen Nationalitätenkämpfen zwischen Griechen und Bulgaren in Mazedonien zu Beginn des 20. Jahrhunderts wurden auch Aromunen Opfer von Gewalttaten beider Seiten. Dabei kam es auch zu Konflikten zwischen nationalaromunisch und griechisch orientierten Aromunen. 1905 anerkannte die osmanische Regierung die Aromunen als eigene Korporation (millet) mit dem Recht auf eigene Schulen und den Gebrauch der eigenen Sprache. Durch die irredentistischen Bestrebungen Rumäniens ist die Verschriftung des Aromunischen zugunsten der Einführung des Dakorumänischen an den von Rumänien geförderten Schulen und Kirchen aufgegeben worden. Im Anschluß an den Frieden von Bukarest 1913 wurden rumänische Schulen und Kirchen in den neuerworbenen griechischen Gebieten zugelassen. Italienische und rumänische Versuche, im Zweiten Weltkrieg diese Bevölkerungsgruppe für die Eigenständigkeit zu gewinnen, schlugen fehl.

Griechisch-albanische Sprachkontakte ergaben sich mit südtoskischen Mundarten verschiedener Entwicklungsstufen. Im epirotischen Überschneidungsbereich des griechischen und albanischen Siedlungsraums kamen Sprecher des Griechischen und des çamischen Dialektes in Kontakt. Dagegen hat der Zustrom von Albanern nach Mittelgriechenland, den Inseln des Saronischen Golfs, den Kykladen, den Nördlichen Sporaden und der Peloponnes im 14.—16. Jahrhundert zur Lösung dieser Sprecher vom albanischen Sprachraum und in der Abgeschiedenheit zur Herausbildung eigenständiger, durch die Bewahrung archaischer Elemente des Albanischen geprägter Mundarten („Arvanitisch") geführt. 1770 wurden zur Niederschlagung eines Aufstands noch einmal 10 000—15 000 muslimische Albaner aus Albanien in die Peloponnes gebracht, die jedoch keinen Kontakt zu den arvanitischen Altsiedlern aufnahmen. Im 19. Jahrhundert wuchs das Interesse griechischer Gelehrter und Politiker an den christlichen Albanern. Auffassungen von der gleichen Abstammung oder engen Verwandtschaft von Griechen und Albanern gewannen an Boden, man hoffte auf eine politische Interessengemeinschaft gegenüber südslawischen irredentistischen Bewegungen, ja sogar auf eine griechisch-albanische Föderation. Griechische Philologen und Publizisten gaben zur Frage der Verschriftung des Albanischen durch das lateinische, das griechische oder ein gemischtes Alphabet unterschiedliche, auch vom Kalkül der leichteren Hellenisierung beeinflußte Stellungnahmen ab. In der zweiten Hälfte des 19. Jahrhunderts erschienen gelegentlich arvanitische Zeitungsartikel, Wahlaufrufe u. dgl. in griechischer Schrift. 1859 kam die Monatszeitung „Pelasgos ke Fthiotis" im ersten Teil mit dem Untertitel „Vorläufer der Albanischen oder Helleno-Pelasgischen Bibliothek", im zweiten Teil mit einem albanischen Untertitel heraus.

Intensive *griechisch-bulgarische* Sprachkontakte hatten bis zur Mitte des 19. Jahrhunderts zur Rezeption griechischer Kultur durch die Bulgaren geführt. Zu wachsenden Spannungen zwischen Griechen und Bulgaren, die auch die Sprachkontakte teils deformierten, teils unterbrachen, kam es, als die bulgarische Nationalbewegung schon in der ersten Hälfte des 19. Jahrhunderts die Einführung des Altkirchenslavischen als Kirchensprache in bulgarischen Sprengeln und andere Reformen forderte. Die Konflikte um die Errichtung und den Jurisdiktionsbereich des bulgarischen Exarchats und die blutigen griechisch-bulgarischen Bandenkämpfe in Mazedonien-Thrazien zu Beginn des 20. Jahrhunderts, der 2. Balkankrieg gegen Bulgarien 1913 und die Gegnerschaft in den beiden Weltkriegen führten zu lang anhaltender Entfremdung und leisteten auf beiden Seiten nationalistischen Ressentiments Vorschub. Der Gebrauch slawischer Mundarten wurde während der Metaxas-Diktatur (1936—1941) unterdrückt. Im Bürgerkrieg bildete die kommunistische Seite eigene makedo-slawische

Formationen, deren Angehörige 1949 vor den Regierungstruppen flohen. Die irredentistische Propaganda der jugoslawischen Republik Mazedonien gab Anlaß zur weiteren Diskriminierung der südslawischen Mundarten in Griechenland. Zu neuen Sprachkontakten kam es infolge der Auswanderung nach Nordamerika und Australien, aus Zypern nach Großbritannien und seit den 1950er Jahren infolge der Massenabwanderung von Arbeitskräften in europäische Länder.

Ein spezifischer Faktor der Sprachkontakte ist die Universitätsbildung. Bis ins 18. Jahrhundert studierten Griechen fast ausschließlich an der Universität Padua in den Kontaktsprachen Latein und Venezianisch, erst später auch an anderen west- und mitteleuropäischen Universitäten. Sprachkontakte ergaben sich dadurch mit dem Französischen, Deutschen, Italienischen, Englischen, für eine geringere Zahl von Studierenden mit dem Russischen, Tschechischen, Ungarischen und Rumänischen. In Athen und Thessaloniki bestehen deutsche, englische und französische Gymnasien. Über die Realisierung des seit 1836 für die Sekundarstufe vorgeschriebenen fremdsprachlichen Unterrichts in der Provinz liegen keine zuverlässigen Untersuchungen vor. An Universitäten sind deutsche, englische, französische und italienische Philologie sowie turkologische Studien etabliert.

2.2. Recht

Griechenland ist seit 1974 eine parlamentarische Demokratie. Das allgemeine Männerwahlrecht hat Griechenland als erster europäischer Staat (*de facto* 1844) auf Dauer eingeführt; Frauen wählen seit 1956. Seit 1844 bzw. 1864 sind die Bürgerrechte durch die Verfassung garantiert. Staatssprache ist Griechisch, allerdings erst seit 1975 nicht mehr die Katharevousa, wie dies in der Verfassungsrevision von 1911 sowie in der Verfassung von 1952 verankert war. Traditionell ist die Orthodoxie Staatsreligion, zu ihr bekennen sich bis auf die türkischsprachigen Muslime und die Armenier alle Sprachminoritäten. In Griechenland genießt jeder In- und Ausländer den Schutz des Lebens, der Ehre und der Freiheit ungeachtet seiner Nationalität, Rasse, Sprache, seiner Religion und seiner politischen Überzeugungen (Art. 5.2 der Verfassung). Griechenland hat die Europäische Menschenrechtskonvention und ihr Zusatzprotokoll ratifiziert. Publikationen jeder Art können bis zum Gerichtsentscheid u. a. dann konfisziert werden, wenn sie die christliche „oder jede andere bekannte Religion" beleidigen oder sich gegen die territoriale Integrität des Staates richten. Schul- und Hochschulbildung ist unentgeltlich. Obwohl Konflikte mit Nachbarstaaten, insbesondere mit der Türkei und Mazedonien, nationalistische Emotionen hervorrufen, erhebt keine Partei Gebietsansprüche; die Förderung des Friedens und der Freundschaft unter den Völkern ist seit 1975 Verfassungsgebot. Völkerrechtsregeln sind unmittelbar geltendes Recht.

3. Statistik und Ethnoprofile

Bürger ohne griechische Sprachkenntnisse bilden heute eine marginale Gruppe, am ehesten sind sie unter Türken anzutreffen. Präzise offizielle Daten über die Sprachverwendung sowie empirische Untersuchungen des Sprachverhaltens liegen nicht vor. Zum letzten Mal wurde in der Volkszählung von 1951 die Muttersprache erfaßt (*Apotelesmata tis apografis ... 1951*); es fehlen jedoch differenzierende Angaben zur Mehrsprachigkeit. Statistische Erhebungen und Schätzungen lassen jedenfalls die Entwicklungstendenz erkennen: Von 1928 bis 1951 erhöhte sich der Anteil der griechischsprachigen Staatsbürger von 92,8 auf 95,6%, der Anteil der Muslime an der Bevölkerung ging in diesem Zeitraum von 2 auf 1,4% zurück.

Die Verwendung des Aromunischen, Arvanitischen oder Makedoslawischen in der täglichen Kommunikation geht vor allem in der jüngeren Generation zurück. Die Aromunen (Eigenbezeichnung: Armânii; griechisch: Βλάχοι, Κουτσόβλαχοι): haben ihre traditionellen Wohngebiete im Pindosgebirge, in Mazedonien und Thessalien. Meglenorumänen (Selbstbezeichnung: Vlasi) wohnen im griechisch-jugoslawischen Grenzbereich. Eine eigene kleine Gruppe von Walachen bilden die Albanisch sprechenden Farscheroten (Selbstbezeichnung: rramańi, griech.: Arvanitovlachi). Von rumänischer Seite wurden übertriebene statistische Angaben über die aromunische Bevölkerung propagiert. In der Zwischenkriegszeit und nach dem Bürgerkrieg sind Aromunen nach Rumänien abgewandert; die Zahl der Meglenorumänen ist seit dem Ende des Ersten Weltkriegs stark gesunken, da die Muslime 1923 in die Türkei abziehen mußten und ca. 600 Familien damals in die rumänische Dobrudscha auswanderten. Bei der Volkszählung von 1951 wurden knapp 39 855 „Walachen" verzeichnet

(*Apotelesmata tis apografis* ... 1961), jedoch ist dieser Wert zu niedrig, da sich viele Aromunen, wie Averof (1948) behauptet, wegen ihres nationalen Bekenntnisses auch sprachlich als Griechen deklariert haben.

Die Arvaniten: (Eigenbezeichnung: arva'ɲít (Pl. —ə); ältere Stammesbezeichnung: arbër; griech. ’Αρβανίτης; Sprachbezeichnung: arvaníte, arvaníst, griech. ἀρβανίτικα). Arvaniten leben in Böotien, in Phokis, Phthiotis, Attika, in Ortschaften der Nordpeloponnes, weiters auf Süd-Euböa und Ägäis-Inseln (Karte: Ciampi; Haebler 1965, 15). Hahn schätzte die Zahl der Arvaniten 1854 auf 173 000—200 000, korrigierte aber diesen Wert selbst nach unten (158 000; Überblick über ältere Schätzungen bei Mpires 1960, 334 ff). Bei der Sprachzählung von 1951 gaben 22 736 Personen Albanisch als Muttersprache an (*Apotelesmata tis apografis* ... 1961); die Zahl der Personen arvanitischer Herkunft und Sprache ist für 1951 erheblich höher anzusetzen. Im griechisch-albanischen Grenzbereich dürften heute allenfalls einzelne Albanischsprachige leben. In großer Zahl halten sich jetzt albanische Gastarbeiter (größtenteils illegal) in Griechenland auf.

Der größte Teil der jüdischen Bürger (1928: 72 791, 1940: 67 662) waren sephardische Sprecher des Judenspanischen in Thessaloniki. Die Juden in anderen Ortschaften waren seit langem gräzisiert. Einige Juden verfügten über Hebräischkenntnisse und schrieben Hebräisch mit griechischen Lettern. Fast 60 000 Juden wurden in Deutschland ermordet, 10 000—12 000 überlebten. Bei der Volkszählung von 1951 deklarierten 1339 Personen Spanisch, 853 Jiddisch als Muttersprache (*Apotelesmata tis apografis* ... 1961).

Bei der letzten Erhebung der Sprecherzahlen 1951 wurden in ganz Griechenland (einschl. Rhodos und Kos) 179 895 Türkischsprachige gezählt (hierzu und zum folgenden: *Apotelesmata tis apografis* ... 1961; Mionotites stin Ellada 1992; The European Bureau for Lesser Used Languages 7, 1990/1991). Die muslimische Minderheit in den thrazischen Präfekturen Xanthi, Rhodopen und Evros zählt rund 120 000 Personen (Gesamtzahl der Einwohner Thraziens 1971: 329 582). Ca. 27 000 Muslime sind Pomaken (Sprecher des Bulgarischen) und überwiegend in der Rhodopen-Präfektur ansässig, ca. 20 000 Zigeuner. Bei der Volkszählung von 1951 hatten 18 671 Personen „Pomakisch" als Muttersprache angegeben. Es gibt Ortschaften mit einer sprachlich gemischten Einwohnerschaft sowie andere, die fast ausschließlich oder überwiegend Griechen, Türken oder Pomaken bewohnen. Viele Pomakendörfer stehen seit Ende des Zweiten Weltkriegs unter militärischem Sonderstatus, der trotz der griechisch-bulgarischen Entspannung nicht aufgehoben ist.

Etwa 250 000 Menschen südslawischer Muttersprache hatten nach den Balkankriegen 1912/1913 und dem Ersten Weltkrieg das Land verlassen, ca. die Hälfte von ihnen im Rahmen des griechisch-bulgarischen Bevölkerungsaustauschs von 1919. Bei der Erhebung von 1951 wurden nur noch 41 017 Sprecher slawischer Dialekte in Nordgriechenland erfaßt. Im Raum von Florina scheint das Bewußtsein sprachlicher und kultureller Eigenständigkeit noch immer stark verwurzelt zu sein.

Die nichtchalkedonensischen Armenier sind heute in Athen-Piräus und Saloniki konzentriert. 1928 lebten in Griechenland 33 634 Sprecher des Armenischen, deren Zahl bis 1951 vor allem infolge der Auswanderung nach Armenien zurückging. 1951 gaben nur mehr 8 990 Personen Armenisch als Muttersprache an.

4. Soziolinguistische Lage

In den Jahrhunderten der osmanischen und venezianischen Herrschaft war Mehrsprachigkeit weit verbreitet, außerdem bildete sich die intragriechische Diglossie weiter aus: Neben den Lokaldialekten gab es mehr oder weniger archaisierende Varianten, die man in der überregionalen Kommunikation und besonders in der Verwaltung und der Kirche verwendete. Die gesprochene Sprache war die Grundlage der in die byzantinische Zeit zurückreichenden demotischen schriftsprachlichen Tradition („Dimotiki"). Der Gebrauch der Fremdsprachen war funktional differenziert, doch zeigt z. B. die Inhaltsanalyse des neugriechisch-aromunisch-bulgarisch-albanischen Lexikons des Daniil Moschopolitis ein breites Spektrum der Sprachkontakte: 27,7% der erfaßten Wörter stammen aus dem Bereich Gesellschaft, die übrigen Einträge betreffen in der Reihenfolge ihrer Häufigkeit: Beschäftigung und Arbeit, Natur, Religion, Gesundheit, Wirtschaft und Familie. Nach der Errichtung südosteuropäischer Nationalstaaten im 19. Jahrhundert, in denen jeweils die Sprache eines Volkes zur Staatssprache erklärt wurde, erhielten die anderen Sprachen den meistens nicht gesicherten Status von „Minderheitssprachen" und wurden z. T. diskriminiert. Der Gebrauch des Türkischen in Schulen und Institutionen der Muslime ist in Griechenland seit 1923 rechtlich gesichert. Darüber hinaus wird das Türkische bzw. das Arabische bei der Regelung familien- und zivilrechtlicher Angelegenheiten der Muslime nach islamischem Recht verwendet. Lokale Radiosender strahlen türkischsprachige Sendungen aus; in Thrazien erscheinen türkische Zeitungen und Zeitschriften. Staatssprache ist jedoch allein das Griechische; der Gebrauch des Türkischen bei griechischen Behörden ist nicht möglich. Auch im Wohngebiet der Minorität gibt es keine zweisprachigen Ortstafeln. Ehen zwischen Muslimen und Christen sind äußerst selten: Vor der Einführung der Zivilehe 1985 waren sie nur unter der Voraussetzung der Bekehrung des muslimischen Ehepartners zur Orthodoxie möglich. Die städtische Bevölkerung rechnet Sprecher des Aromunischen und Arvanitischen eher der bäuerlichen Welt zu und verwendet insbesondere das Wort Βλάχος, Walache = Aromune, im weiteren Sinn: Viehzüchter, häufig pejorativ zur Bezeichnung unkultivierter Menschen. Das Arvanitische war im 19. Jahrhundert in den Wohngebieten der Arvaniten durchweg in Gebrauch, die Verwaltung mußte manchmal Dolmetscher in Anspruch nehmen, Bekanntmachungen, Wahlaufrufe und Zeitungsartikel erschienen gelegentlich arvanitisch mit griechischen Lettern. Zwischen den Weltkriegen verstanden noch viele Frauen auf Andros, Böotien und in abgelegenen Dörfern kein Griechisch.

Das Armenische wird nicht diskriminiert oder negativ bewertet, kulturelle Aktivität (Sprachpflege, Vereinsbildung u. dgl.) nicht behindert. In der Gesellschaft genießen die Armenier Sympathien wegen der gemeinsamen Frontstellung gegen die osmanische Herrschaft.

Nach Übersee ausgewanderte Sprecher südslawischer Idiome haben die rapide Gräzisierung der letzten Jahrzehnte nicht mitgemacht, sondern sprechen neben ihrem Dialekt Englisch. Daher bestehen in diesem Milieu günstige Voraussetzungen für die nationalmazedonische Option und nationalistische Propaganda. Bei Verwandtenbesuchen in Griechenland erleben die Sprecher des Makedoslawischen in der Heimat, daß ihrem Dialekt Prestige im Ausland zukommt. Ähnliche Wirkungen haben auch Radiosendungen aus der Republik Mazedoniens, doch wird deren standarisierte Sprache nicht überall leicht verstanden.

Von den bulgarisch gebildeten Einwohnern, die vor 1912 Schulen des bulgarischen Exarchats und später in geringerer Zahl bulgarische Sekundarschulen oder die Universität Sofia besucht haben, leben nur noch wenige.

Einige griechische Autoren erklären die Erhaltung der aromunischen, arvanitischen und südslavischen Dialekte damit, daß das Neugriechisch wegen des Reichtums der Grammatik und des Wortschatzes schwer zu erlernen sei; die Griechen hingegen, an kommerziellen Beziehungen mit Sprechern dieser Sprachen interessiert, hätten die Kompetenz in Kontaktsprachen leichter erworben. Diese Erklärung ist jedoch nicht stichhaltig, weil für die sprachliche Assimilation nicht das archaisierende Hochgriechisch, sondern in erster Linie die (dialektal gefärbte) Umgangssprache der Nachbarn im Dorf und sonstiger Kommunikationspartner in Betracht kam. Im übrigen war die Masse der Aromunen und Arvaniten im 20. Jahrhundert zweisprachig. Die genannten Sprachen dürften sich bis ins 20. Jahrhundert deshalb erhalten haben, weil ihre Sprecher entweder in einem größeren zusammenhängenden Raum oder in schwer zugänglichen, isolierten Rückzugsgebieten lebten und mit der Außenwelt nicht intensiv kommunizierten; einige Aromunendörfer wurden erst 1982 elektrifiziert. Außerdem war die Schulpflicht nicht überall durchgesetzt: Noch 1951 waren 11% der männlichen und 35% der weiblichen Einwohner über 10 Jahre Analphabeten. Somit fehlte eine entscheidende Voraussetzung sprachlicher Gräzisierung.

Eine Reihe von Faktoren, deren relative Bedeutung nicht systematisch untersucht wurde, bewirken heute den Untergang der nichtstandardisierten und rechtlich nicht geschützten Sprachen (wie auch der griechischen Dialekte). (1) Im Zuge wirtschaftlich-technischer Veränderungen verschwindet mit alten Handwerksbranchen, mit ihren Fertigkeiten und Geräten der einschlägige Wortschatz. Über eine normierte Terminologie für neue Technologien und Güter verfügt nur das Türkische. (2) Die Einbeziehung auch entlegener Landstriche in überlokale und überregionale Kommunikationsnetze, der Ausbau der Verkehrswege, Urbanisierung und Motorisierung, die Durchsetzung der Schulpflicht und damit der Alphabetisierung, ferner Ausbildung und Erwerbstätigkeit führen zum Rückgang der Zahl der Sprecher des Aromunischen und Arvanitischen. (3) Der Militärdienst trägt erheblich zur Gräzisierung junger Männer vor allem aus ländlichem Milieu bei. (4) Die Sprecher des Aromunischen und Arvanitischen haben ein Sprach- und Regional-, aber kein konkurrierendes Nationalbewußtsein und wollen sich von den Griechen nicht so abgrenzen wie Türken, Pomaken oder Armenier. Der Gebrauch des Griechischen als Staats-, Verkehrs- und Bildungssprache ist für sie selbstverständlich. Sprecher des Arvanitischen beschreiben ihre jeweilige lokale Mundart als stärker gräzisiert und halten Elemente, die sie als stark „albanisch" empfinden, für Eigenheiten von Mundarten anderer Dörfer (Tsitsipis 1984, 124). (5) Die Sprecher des Arvanitischen haben die Beurteilung ihrer Sprache und ihrer Gruppe durch die Umwelt („rückständig", „unintelligent", „schwerfällig") rezipiert und genieren sich für ihre Sprache. Erst seit 1977 wächst das Interesse junger Menschen an der Sprache ihrer Vorfahren. 1981 wurde der Arvanitische Verein von Griechenland gegründet. Auch erscheinen Schriften, allerdings von zweifelhaftem Wert.

Eine eigene Problematik bilden die Sprachkontakte der griechischen Auswanderer. In Griechenland hat der Kontakt mit den westeuropäischen Sprachen die Übernahme von Wörtern stark gefördert. Traditionell wurden Vokabeln übernommen, deren Gebrauch die Vertrautheit mit europäischem Lebensstil signalisiert; dabei legt der Gebildete bzw. der Angehörige der Oberschicht auf die korrekte Aussprache Wert. Zweitens werden Elemente des politischen Vokabulars, drittens Begriffe für neue Konsumgüter, schließlich termini technici aus Wissenschaft und Technologie übernommen.

5. Sprachpolitische Lage

Griechenland anerkennt nur Religions- und Sprach-, aber keine nationalen Minderheiten. Die einzige rechtlich fixierte und gesicherte Sprechergruppe bilden die türkischsprachigen Muslime auf Grund von Art. 45 des Vertrags von Lausanne 1923, der dieser Minderheit dieselben Rechte zuerkennt, die nach Art. 37—44 der orthodoxen Minderheit in der Türkei zustehen (Rechtsgleichheit, Freiheit der Gründung und Aktivität wohltätiger, religiöser und sozialer Institutionen, Schulen und Bildungsinstitute, Freiheit des Sprachgebrauchs und des Kultus). In den fünfziger Jahren stützte Athen die (nach dem Staatsgründer der modernen Türkei, Kemal Atatürk, als „Kemalisten" bezeichneten) Modernisierer in der deshalb konsequent als „türkisch" bezeichneten Minderheit. In jüngster Zeit läßt der Staat, um den Einfluß der Türkei einzudämmen, nur die Bezeichnung „muslimisch" zu; Parlamentsabgeordnete der Minderheit wurden wegen ihres Bekenntnisses zur türkischen Nationalität scharf gerügt — dem entspricht die Haltung der türkischen Behörden gegenüber der griechischen Minorität. Der muslimischen Minderheit in Thrazien stehen 163 vom Staat unterhaltene Schulen mit über 474 muslimischen Lehrern zur Verfügung, die ca. 11 000 Schüler besuchen; in Thessaloniki besteht eine Pädagogische Akademie für Volksschullehrer. Außerdem bestehen Koranschulen. Die griechische Minderheit in Istanbul unterhält 15 Schulen mit 90 Lehrern, jedoch ist durch die Abwanderung zumal der jüngeren Menschen die Schülerzahl auf 390 Schüler zurückgegangen; eine Reihe von Schulen und Institutionen der Minderheit dürfte in absehbarer Zeit schließen.

Die arvanitische Sprache genießt keinerlei Förderung, doch werden das aufkommende Interesse von Arvaniten und Aromunen an ihrer Sprache und ihren Überlieferungen sowie die Beschäftigung von Publizisten und Forschern mit diesen Gruppen nicht behindert.

Ein großer Teil von Menschen südslawischer Muttersprache hatte das Land seit 1913 und am Ende des Bürgerkriegs 1949 verlassen. Die Rückkehr der slawischen Bürgerkriegsflüchtlinge wird behindert. Auf Grund von Art. 111.6 der Verfassung ist der Entzug der Staatsbürgerschaft von nicht volkszugehörigen Griechen, die das Land ohne Rückkehrabsicht verlassen haben, möglich. Der Staat erkennt keine makedoslawische Minderheit an; griechische Forscher bestreiten die Existenz einer slavomazedonischen Sprache und betrachten das in Griechenland und in der Republik Mazedonien gesprochene Südslawisch als bulgarische Mundarten bzw. als bulgarisch-serbischen Übergangsdialekt. Griechische Makedoslawen, die im In- und Ausland für ihre Gruppe eintraten, wurden wegen „Verbreitung falscher Nachrichten" gerichtlich belangt. Die „Stätte der Mazedonischen Kultur" mußte schließen. Die Sprecher makedoslawischer Dialekte haben keine Möglichkeit des Sprachunterrichts; der Gebrauch ihrer Sprache in der Öffentlichkeit, besonders in den Schulen, ist unerwünscht; die Behörden versuchen, selbst die Aufführung von Volksmusik und -tänzen dieser Gruppe zu unterbinden. Wohngebiete der bulgarischsprachigen Pomaken in der Präfektur Xanthi gehören z. T. auch heute zum militärischen Sperrgebiet auf Grund von Gesetzen der Metaxas-Diktatur 1936, die sich gegen den „inneren Feind" (= nationale Minderheiten) richteten.

Nichtgriechische Ortsnamen wurden in mehreren Purifikationswellen durch (z. T. neuerfundene) griechische ersetzt. Auch in Thrazien dürfen nur die griechischen Ortsnamen verwendet werden.

Mit Ausnahme der Diktaturen (1936–1941 und 1967–1974) sowie der deutsch-italienisch-bulgarischen Okkupation besteht in Griechenland Pressefreiheit. Ausländische Zeitungen und Zeitschriften werden in den Städten, Touristenzentren und bei Nachfrage vertrieben.

Das Neugriechische wird in den Nachbarstaaten, in denen die Kontaktsprachen dominieren, sprachpolitisch unterschiedlich behandelt. Entweder ist es als Lokaldialekt geduldet (Italien), oder seine Sprecher werden nicht als Griechen anerkannt (Mazedonien); neben Fällen zwischenstaatlicher Vereinbarungen über den Minoritätenschutz (Griechenland – Türkei). In Albanien hing die Anerkennung als Grieche von der früheren Registration unter kommunistischer Herrschaft ab.

6. Sonstige Sprachkontakte

Von den Kontaktsprachen, mit denen Sprecher des Griechischen im griechischen Hauptsiedlungsraum in Kontakt gekommen sind, haben das Türkische, Bulgarische, Makedoslawische, Albanische, Italienische und Armenische neben lokalen Mundarten wie das Griechische selbst eine standarisierte Variante als Verkehrssprache. Dagegen sind Aromunisch und Arvanitisch dialektal aufgesplittert und verfügen weder über eine schriftsprachliche Tradition noch über eine wissenschaftliche, technische und administrative Terminologie. Bemühungen um Sprachausbau und -unterricht sind nicht festzustellen; die Sprecher dieser Sprachen sind daran auch nicht interessiert. Sie verlieren Kompetenz im Wortschatz und erlernen auch die Grammatik (im Arvanitischen z. B. den Gebrauch des Gerundiums, des Subjunktivs und der Hypotaxe) nicht mehr richtig (Beispiele: Tsitsipis 1984, 126 ff).

7. Kritische Wertung

Über Sprachkontakte zwischen Griechisch und anderen Sprachen werden keine systematischen Forschungen betrieben, Kontaktlinguistik ist in Griechenland als Disziplin der Sprachwissenschaft nicht etabliert. Für kontaktlinguistische Forschungen kommen in erster Linie Untersuchungen zum Wortschatz des Griechischen und der Kontaktsprachen in Betracht. Die Arbeiten von Andriotis, Dangitsis, Koukkidis und Tsopanakis sind hier an erster Stelle zu nennen. Die Grundlage der Lehnwortforschung schuf Miklosich; Ch. Meyer, G. Pascu, A. Tietze, Ch. Symeonidis (→ Art. 182) und Ch. Tzitzilis haben diese Richtung konsequent und mit bemerkenswerten Ergebnissen weitergeführt. Die Bedeutung der Sprachkontakte für diese Sprachen steckt allerdings noch in den Anfängen. Zum Sprachkontakt mit dem Türkischen sind seit Miklosichs Grundlagenstudie (1884) rund 70 Bücher und über 400 Aufsätze erschienen, die für kontaktlinguistische Studien interessant sind (Forschungsstand bis 1983: Tietze 1983). Systematische Forschungen werden dadurch behindert, daß es kein abgeschlossenes etymologisches Lexikon des Türkischen gibt; auch steht die türkische Dialektologie noch in den Anfängen. Für das Albanische und Arvanitische zeigen griechische Forscher und Publizisten seit dem 19. Jahrhundert Interesse. Albanologische Forschungen sind zunächst durch Mitkos, Koulouriotis und Christoforidis (zum Teil dilettantisch) betrieben worden. C. H. T. Reinholds Sammlung zum Arvanitischen (Texte, Grammatik, Wörterverzeichnis) von 1855/1856 bildet die frühe Grundlage der arvanitischen Studien. Die Stationen der Forschung markieren die Arbeiten von G. Weigand (1926, jedoch auf unzureichender Materialgrundlage), Fourikis, Haebler und Sasse.

Zu den Desideraten der Forschung gehören auch die Sprachkontakte mit den Pomaken, zu denen nur disparate Einzelbefunde vorliegen.

Vielversprechend sind inhaltsanalytische Untersuchungen von Lehrbüchern, Textsammlungen und Hilfsmitteln. So hat sich z. B. gezeigt, daß die mehrsprachigen Lexika (Griechisch-Kontaktsprachen) des 18./19.

Jahrhunderts dem Sprachkontakt auf unterschiedlichen Ebenen dienten. Von den 1170 Wörtern des dreisprachigen und den 800 des viersprachigen Lexikons sind nur 296 gemeinsam; Kavalliotis' Werk enthält mehr Abstrakta wie Opfer, Ruhm, Friede, Geschichte, Gesetz, Nation, Volk.

8. Bibliographie (in Auswahl)

Averof, Evangelos A. (1948): *I politiki plevra tou koutsovlachikou zitimatos* [Der politische Aspekt der Kutsowalachenfrage], Athen.

Alexandris, A. (1992): *The Greek Minority of Istanbul and Greek-Turkish Relations, 1918–1974*, Athen.

Anastasiadis, G. I. (1948): „Chaï-Chouroum (armenoglossoi Ellines)" [Armenischsprachige Griechen]. In: *Mikrasiatika Chronika 4*, 37–46.

Andriotis, Nikolaos (1951): *Etymologiko lexiko tis kinis ellinikis* [Etymologisches Lexikon der neugriechischen Koiné, Athen.

Apotelesmata tis apografis tou plithismou tis 7 Apriliou 1951 (1961): [Ergebnisse der Volkszählung vom 7. April 1951], Bd. 1, Athen.

Aravantinos, Panajotis (1905): *Monografia peri Koutsovlachon* [Monographie über die Koutsowalchen], Athen.

Bornträger, Ekkehard W. (1989): „Die slawischen Lehnwörter im Neugriechischen". In: *Zeitschrift für Balkanologie 25/1*, 8–25.

Bunis, David M. (1981): *Sephardic Studies: A Bibliography*, New York.

Capidan, Theodor (1925–1936): *Meglenoromânii* [Die Meglenorumänen], 3 Bde., Bukarest.

Capidan, Theodor (1932): *Aromânii* [Die Aromunen], Bukarest.

Caracausi, Girolamo (1990): *Lessico greco della Sicilia e dell'Italia meridionale*, Palermo.

Chasiotis, Ioannis K. (1993): *Episkopisi tis istorias tis neoellinikis diasporas* [Übersicht über die Geschichte der neugriechischen Diaspora], Thessaloniki.

Cortelazzo, M. (1970): *L'influsso linguistico greco a Venezia* [Griechischer Spracheinfluß in Venedig], Bologna.

Coutelle, Louis (1971): *Le Greghesco*, Thessaloniki.

Christoforidis, Konstantinos (1882): *Grammatiki tis Alvanikis Glossis kata tin toskikin dialekton syntachtheisa* [Grammatik der albanischen Sprache nach dem toskischen Dialekt verfaßt], Konstantinopel.

Christoforidis, Konstantinos (1977): *Lexikon Alvano-Ellinikon* [Albanisch-griechisches Lexikon], Prishtinë.

Cutsumbis, M. N. (1970): *A Bibliographical Guide on Greeks in the United States 1890–1968*, Staten Island, N. Y.

Dawkins, R. M. (1916): *Modern Greek in Asia Minor*, Cambridge.

Dawkins, R. M. (1937): „The Pontic Dialect of Modern Greek in Asia Minor and Russia". In: *Philological Society's Transactions*, 15–52.

Exarchos, Giorgis S. (1986): *Vlachi. Mnimia zois enos politismou pou chanete* [Die Walachen. Denkmäler einer Kultur, die untergeht], Athen.

Fourikis, Petros A. (1932, 1933): „I en Attiki ellinoalvaniki dialektos" [Der griechisch-albanische Dialekt in Attika]. In: *Athina 44*, 28–76; *45*, 49–181.

Füves, Ödön (1965): *I Ellines tis Oungarias* [Die Griechen Ungarns], Thessaloniki.

Giochalas, Titos (1980): *To ellino-alvanikon lexikon tou Markou Botsari* [Markos Botsaris' griechisch-albanisches Lexikon], Athen.

Haebler, Claus (1965): *Grammatik der albanischen Mundart von Salamis*, Wiesbaden.

Hering, Gunnar (1987): „Die Auseinandersetzungen um die griechische Schriftsprache". In: *Sprachen und Nationen im Balkanraum. Die historischen Bedingungen der Entstehung der heutigen Nationalsprachen*, Hannick, Christian (Ed.), Köln/Wien, 125–194.

Hill, Peter (1990): „Mehrsprachigkeit in Südosteuropa". In: *Zeitschrift für Balkanologie 26/2*, 123–141.

Jochalas, Titos (1971): „Über die Einwanderung der Albaner in Griechenland". In: *Dissertationes Albanicae 13*, 89–106.

Karakasidou, Anastasia (1993): „Politicizing Culture: Negating Ethnic Identity in Greek Macedonia". In: *Journal of Modern Greek Studies 11*, 1–28.

Karanastasis, Anastasios (1984–1988): *Istorikon lexikon ton ellinikon idiomaton tis Kato Italias* [Historisches Lexikon der griechischen Idiome Süditaliens], 3 Bde., Athen.

Katsougiannis, Tilemachos M. (1964): *Peri ton Vlachon ton ellinikon choron* [Über die Walachen der griechischen Gebiete], 2 Bde., Thessaloniki.

Kavalliotis, Theodoros (1770): *Lexikon Ellinikon Aploun ke Vlachikon ke Alvanitikon* [Neugriechisches und Walachisches und Albanisches Wörterbuch], Moschopolis 1760–1770, Venedig.

Konstantakopoulou, Aggeliki (1988): *I elliniki glossa sta Valkania (1750–1850). To tetraglosso lexiko tou Daniil Moschopoliti* [Die griechische Sprache in den Balkanländern 1750–1850. Das viersprachige Lexikon des Daniil Moschopolitis], Ioannina.

Koulouriotis, Anastasios I. (1882): *Alvanikon Alfavitarion kata to en Elladi omiloumenon alvanikon idioma* [Albanisches ABC nach dem in Griechenland gesprochenen albanischen Idiom], Athen.

Lazarou, Achillefs G. (1976): *I Aromouniki* [Das Aromunische], Athen.

Lazarou, Achillefs, G. (1986): *L'Aroumain et ses rapports avec le Grec*, Thessaloniki.

Lienau, Cay (1989): *Griechenland*, Darmstadt.

Manousakas, Manousos I. (1973, 1980): „Vivliografia tou Ellinismou tis Venetias" [Bibliographie des Griechentums in Venedig]. In: *Thesaurismata 10*, 7−87; *17*, 7−21.

Margaritis, Apostolos (1886): *Les Grecs, les Valaques, les Albanais et l'Empire ottoman par un Valaque du Pinde*, Brüssel.

Meyer, Gustav (1893): „Die griechischen und romanischen Bestandteile im Wortschatze des Osmanisch-Türkischen". In: *Sitzungsberichte der Kaiserl. Akademie der Wissenschaften zu Wien, Phil.-hist. Kl. 128*, 1−96.

Michailidis, Evangelos (1966): *Vivliografia ton Egyptioton Ellinon* [Bibliographie der ägyptischen Griechen], Alexandria.

Miklosich, Franz (1870): *Die slavischen Elemente im Neugriechischen*, Wien.

Miklosich, Franz (1884ff): „Die türkischen Elemente in den südost- und osteuropäischen Sprachen". In: *Denkschriften der Kaiserl. Akademie der Wissenschaften zu Wien, Phil.-hist. Kl. 34*, 239−338; *35*, 105−192, QQ.

Mionotites stin Ellada (1992): [Minderheiten in Griechenland], 1, Athen.

Mitkos, Evthymios (1878): *Alvaniki Melissa* [Albanische Biene], Alexandria.

Moskos, Ch. (1989): *Greek Americans*, New Brunswick, N. J.

Mpiris, Kostas (1960): *Arvanites. I Doriis tou neoterou Ellinismou* [Arvaniten. Die Dorer des neueren Griechentums], Athen.

Mpogkas, Evangelos Ath. (1964, 1966): *Ta glossika idiomata tis Ipirou* [Die sprachlichen Idiome von Epirus], 2 Bde., Ioannina.

Papadrianos, Ioannis A. (1993): *I Ellines apodimi stis giougkoslavikes chores (18os−20os e.)* [Die griechischen Auswanderer in den südslawischen Ländern (18.−20. Jh.)], Thessaloniki.

Pascu, George (1924): *Rumänische Elemente in den Balkansprachen*, Genf.

Pentzopoulos, Dimitri (1965): *The Balkan Exchange of Minorities and its Impact upon Greece*, Paris/Den Haag.

Peyfuss, Max Demeter (1974): *Die aromunische Frage*, Wien/Köln/Graz.

Population du Royaume de Grèce (1962): D'après le recensement du 19. 3. 1961, Athen.

Population du Royaume de Grèce (1972): D'après le recensement du 14. 3. 1971, Athen.

Reinhold, Carl Heinrich Theodor (1855, 1856): *Noctes Pelasgicae*, Athen [Ergänzungen aus dem Nachlaß (1896) hsg. v. Gustav Meyer: *Albanesische Studien 5*].

Reiter, Norbert (1984): „Sprachenstreit auf dem Balkan als Ausdruck gesellschaftlicher Gegensätze". In: *Zeitschrift für Balkanologie 20*, 173−191.

Rohlfs, Gerhard (1924): *Griechen und Romanen in Unteritalien. Ein Beitrag zur Geschichte der unteritalienischen Gräzität*, Genf.

Rohlfs, Gerhard (1930): *Etymologisches Wörterbuch der unteritalienischen Gräzität*, Halle.

Rohlfs, Gerhard (1964): *Lexicon Graecanicum Italiae inferioris*, Tübingen.

Sarantis, Theodoros K. P. (1975): *I vlachofoni tou ellinikou chorou* [Die Walachophonen des griechischen Raumes], Ioannina.

Sasse, Hans-Jürgen (1991): *Arvanitika: Die albanischen Sprachreste in Griechenland*, Bd. 1, Wiesbaden.

Sauerwein, Friedrich (1976): *Griechenland, Land − Volk − Wirtschaft in Stichworten*, Wien.

Studemund, M. (1975): *Bibliographie des Judenspanischen*, Hamburg.

Symeonidis, Charalambos (1971/1972): „Lautlehre der türkischen Lehnwörter im neugriechischen Dialekt des Pontos". In: *Archeion Pontou 31*, 19−234.

Symeonidis, Charalambos (1973): „Griechische Lehnwörter im Türkischen". In: *Balkan Studies 14*, 167−200.

The European Bureau for Lesser Used Languages: Contact (1990/1991): Bd. 7, Nr. 3: Multilingualism in Greece (verfaßt von Miquel S. Siguan).

Tietze, Andreas (1983): „The Present State of the Study of Turkisms in the Languages of the Mediterranean and of the Balkan Peninsula". In: *Mediterranean Language Review 1*, 15−26.

Trudgill, Peter/Tzavaras, George (1977): „Why Albanian-Greeks are not Albanians: Language Shift in Attica and Biotia". In: Giles, H. (Ed.), *Language, Ethnicity, and Intergroup Relations*, London/New York, 171−184.

Tsitsipis, Lukas D. (1984): „Functional Restriction and Grammatical Reduction in Albanian Language in Greece". In: *Zeitschrift für Balkanologie 20/1*, 122−131.

Tsopanakis, Agapitos G. (1970/1971): „Eléments lexicaux étrangers en Chypre et à Rhodes". In: *Epetiris Kentrou Epistimonikon Erevnon Lefkosias 4*, 133−208.

Türkiye'de halk ağzindan derleme söziüğü (1963−1976), 12 Bde., Ankara.

Türkiye'de halk ağzindan söz derleme dergisi (1939−1951), 4 Bde., Istanbul.

Tzitzilis, Christos (1987): *Griechische Lehnwörter im Türkischen*, Wien.

Tzitzilis, Christos (1988): „Beiträge zur aromunischen Wortschatzforschung". In: *Zeitschrift für Balkanologie 24/2*, QQ-199.

Tzitzilis, Christos (1989): „Zu den griechisch-türkischen Sprachbeziehungen". In: *Academie Bulgare des Sciences Linguistique balkanique 32/3−4*, 185−197.

Vakalopoulos, Apostolos E. (1974−1976, 1968−1988): *Istoria tou neou Ellinismou* [Geschichte des neueren Griechentums], Bd. 1−2, Bd. 3−8, Thessaloniki.

Wagner, Max L. (1925): „Los dialectos judeo-españoles de Karaferia, Kastoria y Brusa". In: *Homenaje ofrecido a Menéndez Pidal 2*, 193−203.

Weigand, Gustav (1888): *Die Sprache der Olympo-Walachen*, Leipzig.

Weigand, Gustav (1891): *Vlacho-Meglen*, Leipzig.

Weigand, Gustav [1895, 1894]: *Die Aromunen. Ethnographisch-philologisch-historische Untersuchungen über das Volk der sogenannten Makedo-Romanen oder Zinzaren*, 2 Bde., Leipzig.

† Gunnar Hering, Wien (Österreich)

182. Griechisch−Türkisch

1. Geographie und Demographie
2. Geschichte
3. Wirtschaft und allgemeine kulturelle sowie religiöse Lage
4. Statistik und Ethnoprofile
5. Soziolinguistische Situation
6. Sprachpolitische Situation
7. Allgemeines kontaktlinguistisches Porträt
8. Stand der Kontaktforschung
9. Bibliographie (in Auswahl)

1. Geographie und Demographie

Nach dem Austausch der griechischen und türkischen Bevölkerung im Jahre 1922 aufgrund der Religionszugehörigkeit sind zahlreiche Türken in Griechisch-Thrakien sowie eine große Zahl von Griechen in Konstantinopel geblieben. Nachdem sie 1956 aus ihrem alten Wohnsitz vertrieben wurden, leben heute nur noch etwa 2000 von ehemals 150000 Griechen in Konstantinopel (Istanbul). In Griechisch-Thrakien leben heute ca. 80000 Moslems in Xanthi und Komotini. Auf Zypern lebten die griechischen und türkischen Gemeinden gemischt bis zum Jahr 1974, als die Insel durch die türkische Invasion in Nord-Zypern, wo heute fast ausschließlich Türken wohnen, und in Süd-Zypern, wo die griechischen Zyprioten wohnen, geteilt wurde (→ Sprachenkarte I).

2. Geschichte

Erste Kontakte zwischen Griechisch und Türkisch bzw. den türkischen Stämmen in den östlichen Grenzen des Byzantinischen Reiches und seinen griechisch sprechenden Bürgern fallen in die Zeit Ende des 11. Jahrhunderts. Die sprachliche und kulturelle Berührung der beiden Völker ist in den nächsten Jahrhunderten durch die Eroberung Konstantinopels durch die Osmanen (1453) stärker geworden und dauerte bis in die 20er Jahre des 20. Jahrhunderts an, als 1922 der Austausch der Bevölkerung zwischen beiden Staaten auf Grund der Religionszugehörigkeit stattgefunden hat. Sie hinterließ ihre Spuren in beiden Sprachen, die sich seitdem gegenseitig beeinflußt haben. Dies gilt besonders für Thrakien und Zypern, wo der Kontakt zwischen beiden Sprachen nie abgebrochen ist. Griechisch wird immer noch in einigen Dörfern in den Gebieten von Ofis und Tonja, aber wahrscheinlich auch in anderen Gegenden Kleinasiens von Griechen gesprochen, die zum Islam übergetreten sind und heute beide Sprachen beherrschen. Dies sind Nachfahren der sogenannten Kryptochristen, die nach außen hin Moslems, in Wirklichkeit aber Christen waren und doppelte Namen, einen christlichen und einen moslemischen trugen (*Michael-Mehmet, Helene-Emine* usw.). Schon vor der Eroberung Konstantinopels, aber vor allem danach, haben sich viele christliche Griechen unter Zwang, aber auch freiwillig, um ihr Eigentum und sich von der türkischen Willkürherrschaft zu retten, zum Islam bekannt. Diese Kryptochristen sind je nach Gebiet unter verschiedenen Namen bekannt; sie hießen *Klostoi* (Pontos), *Linovambakoi* (Zypern), *Tourkokretes* (Kreta), *Valaades* (Makedonien) usw. Zum Thema Kryptochristen siehe ausführlich die Arbeit von Photiadis (1988).

3. Wirtschaft und allgemeine kulturelle sowie religiöse Lage

Da Griechenland ein Agrarland mit wenig Industrie ist, lebt sowohl die griechische als auch die türkische Gemeinde des Kontaktgebiets hauptsächlich von der Landwirtschaft. Die Haupteinnahmequelle der Einwohner ist der Tabak. Das kulturelle Niveau beider Gemeinden entspricht dem der griechischen Provinz, die sich nur langsam entwickelt. Die Gründung der neuen Demokritos-Universität in Komotini verspricht jedoch viel für die kulturelle Entwicklung des Gebiets. In Griechenland herrscht Religionsfreiheit. Das Land ist Zentrum des christlich-orthodoxen Glaubens. Die Moslems können ihren Glauben praktizieren und verfügen über Moscheen und andere Religionseinrichtungen.

4. Statistik und Ethnoprofile

In Griechisch-Thrakien leben heute etwa 80000 griechische Bürger moslemischen Glaubens, die offiziell Moslems, sonst aber im alltäglichen Sprachgebrauch einfach Türken heißen. Sie sind Nachfahren der Türken, die während der türkischen Herrschaft (1453–1921) im heutigen Griechisch-Thrakien wohnten. Die ältere Generation spricht fast ausschließlich Türkisch, die jüngere aber auch Griechisch. Von diesen sind die Pomaken desselben Gebiets zu unterscheiden, die einfach zu den Türken gezählt werden, weil sie neben ihrem slawischen Dialekt gewöhnlich auch Türkisch beherrschen, Moslems sind und türkische Eigennamen tragen. Die Griechen Griechisch-Thrakiens sind entweder direkte Nachfahren der Byzantiner oder Einwanderer aus Kleinasien und Bulgarien. Die meisten Griechen (vor allem die älteren) der Kontaktgebiete beherrschen die türkische Sprache oder haben passive Türkischkenntnisse.

5. Soziolinguistische Situation

Obwohl die offizielle und die herrschende Sprache das Griechische ist, wird das Türkische bei den Moslems als Muttersprache gesprochen. Die ältere moslemische Generation hat nur beschränkte Möglichkeiten, sich auf Griechisch zu äußern. Die jüngere Generation ist dank der überall verbreiteten griechischen Schulen im allgemeinen des Griechischen mächtig. Im täglichen Gespräch werden beide Sprachen benutzt, je nach Sprecher und sprachlicher Situation. Für die Moslems ist das Türkische die Familiensprache, das Griechische die Prestigesprache, womit man sich in die griechische Gesellschaft besser integrieren kann. Für die Griechen ist das Türkische die Sprache des Nachbarn, die zum besseren Verständnis und zum Handel treiben mit Moslems führt, die nicht Griechisch sprechen können.

6. Sprachpolitische Situation

Obwohl das Türkische eine Minoritätensprache ist, hat es seitens des Staats und der Gesellschaft die gleiche Berechtigung wie das Griechische. Der griechische Staat gibt seinen moslemischen Bürgern die Möglichkeit, in Schulen rein griechischer Ausrichtung oder moslemischer Ausrichtung Unterricht in türkischer Sprache und Kultur zu erhalten. Die moslemische Gemeinde verfügt über eine eigene Presse und einen Rundfunk. Zahlreiche Schulbücher werden aus der Türkei für die Bedürfnisse der türkischen Gemeinde importiert. In speziellen moslemischen Schulen, die von der türkischen Gemeinschaft beaufsichtigt werden, werden die Imame ausgebildet. In der Mohammedanischen Hochschule von Thessaloniki werden die Lehrer für den Islam ausgebildet, zugleich aber auch für den türkischen Sprachunterricht. Im allgemeinen kümmert sich der griechische Staat um Ausbildungschancen für seine Bürger moslemischen Glaubens.

7. Allgemeines kontaktlinguistisches Porträt

7.1. Griechischer Einfluß auf das Türkische

Perioden und geographische Verteilung der Entlehnungen. Wenn man die Tatsache berücksichtigt, daß gewisse anatolische Formen auf heute nicht mehr belegbare griechische Dialektformen zurückgehen, muß man annehmen, daß manche Entlehnung schon sehr alt ist, obwohl die Nicht-Belegbarkeit einer griechischen Dialektform nur zufällig sein kann; so scheint türkisch *gudalis* nicht direkt auf spätgriechisch κώταλις „Mörserkeule, Stößel", sondern auf einer entsprechenden griechisch-pontischen Form zu beruhen, die im Pontischen nicht mehr belegt ist. Der beste Beweis jedoch, daß manche türkischen Entlehnungen auf eine frühere Periode zurückgehen, liefert uns der Codex Cumanicus

(13. Jh.), wo eine ganze Reihe von griechischen Lehnwörtern zu finden ist: *chiras* < κεράσι, *mangdanus* < μακεδονήσι, *uskuli* < σκουλί usw. Was die geographische Verteilung angeht, so zeigen die Dialektbeispiele eine große Mannigfaltigkeit; es gibt nämlich aus dem Griechischen entlehnte Wörter, die mehr oder weniger in allen Gebieten des Landes vorkommen, während andere Wortgruppen nur für einen bestimmten Teil des Landes typisch sind, was auf wirtschaftsgeographische Gründe zurückzuführen ist. So sind z. B. griechische Lehnwörter für Fische und andere Seetiere, Geräte für die Seefahrt und die Fischerei vorwiegend an der kleinasiatischen Küste zu finden. In manchen Gebieten häufen sich die griechischen Lehnwörter der verschiedensten Sachgebiete auffallend, was z. B. in den pontischen Gebieten der Fall ist, weil der Anteil von Griechen an der Bevölkerung ziemlich hoch war (s. Symeonidis 1976, 16 f, Tietze 1955, und Tzitzilis 1987, 149 f).

7.1.1. Phonologie

Die griechischen Lehnwörter bleiben nur in der Schriftsprache möglichst unverändert. Sonst werden sie in den Dialekten, aber auch in der Schriftsprache, verschiedenen Veränderungen unterworfen, die die Phonomorphologie und Struktur des türkischen Wortes betreffen, von denen hier nur die Vokalharmonie und Vokalanaptyxe im Anlaut hervorzuheben sind (vgl. Symeonidis 1976, 31 ff, 99 f).

Vokalharmonie. Von den drei Arten der Vokalharmonie in den Turksprachen, nämlich der Palatalharmonie (innerhalb eines Wortes können nur hintere Vokale — *a, ı, o, u* — oder nur vordere — *ä, i, ö, ü* — erscheinen: *at* „Pferd", *atlar* „Pferde", *ev* „Haus", *evler* „Häuser"), der Labialharmonie (nach einem runden Vokal — *o, ö, u, ü* — der vorgehenden Silbe ist der Bindevokal ebenfalls rund: *bol* „viel", *bolluk* „eine Menge"; nach einem breiten Vokal — *a, ä, e, ı* — ist der Bindevokal ebenfalls breit: *at* „Pferd", *atlı* „Reiter" usw.) und der Labialattraktion (der auf einen runden Vokal folgende Vokal ist stets rund: *göz* „Auge", *gözlör*, statt *gözler*, „Augen"; besteht nur in einigen Turkdialekten), gibt es zahlreiche Phänomene der Palatalharmonie.

(a) Weist ein griechisches Lehnwort zufällig nur Vokale der türkischen hinteren oder vorderen Vokalreihe auf, so wird es ins Türkische unverändert übernommen: μάλαμα „Gold" > mundartlich türkisch *malama* „Pfund (Geld)", κάβανος „Holz- oder Tonkrug" > türkisch *kavanos* „irdener Topf", κόφα „Korb" > mundartlich türkisch *kofa*, κουκούλα „Kapuze, Kappe" > mundartlich türkisch *kukula, gugula*; δικέλι „zweizinkige Hacke, Karst" > mundartlich türkisch *dikel, dikkel, tikel*, νηνί „kleines Kind, Pupille" > mundartlich türkisch *nini, ninni* usw.

(b) Weist ein griechisches Lehnwort Vokale sowohl der vorderen als auch der hinteren Vokalreihe auf, so wird es in vielen Fällen dem Gesetz der Palatalharmonie unterworfen: αυλή „Hof" > mundartlich türkisch *avli, avlu*, καδί „Eimer" > mundartlich türkisch *kadı* „kleines Fäßchen", ζευγάρι „Gespann, das Ochsenpaar vor dem Pflug" > mundartlich türkisch *zıvgar, çıvgar* „Wagen mit vier Pferden"; εκκλησία „Kirche" > türkisch *kilisa, kilise*, λυχνάρι „Öllämpchen" > mundartlich türkisch *ilkmen, ilikmen*, βασιλικόν „Basilikum" > türkisch *fesligen, fesliyen*, σανίδι „Brett" > mundartlich türkisch *senid, senit* „Teigbrett".

(c) Während des Prozesses der Palatalharmonie bei einem griechischen Lehnwort, das Vokale der beiden Reihen aufweist, kann die palatalharmonische Anpassung gleichzeitig entweder an die vordere oder an die hintere Vokalreihe stattfinden: παχνί „Futterkrippe" > mundartlich türkisch *pehni, behni* oder aber *pahna, bahna*, πίσσα „Pech" > mundartlich türkisch *pise, pusa*, γούφαινα „eine Fischart" > mundartlich türkisch *köfene*, türkisch *kofana* usw.

Vokalanaptyxe. Auffallend bei den griechischen Lehnwörtern des Türkischen ist die Vokalanaptyxe (das Erscheinen eines Sproßvokals im An- und Inlaut eines Wortes aus phonologischen Gründen: griechisch καπνός „Rauch" > türkisch *kapinoʒ*; griechisch κλαδευτήρι „Gartensichel" > türkisch *girifteri* „ds.".) im Anlaut, die folgendermaßen stattfindet:

(a) Vor Konsonantenverbindungen, die den türkischen Sprachen überhaupt fremd sind (Räsänen, 1949, 51, Caferoğlu, 1959, 247): σκελετός „Skelett, Gerippe" > türkisch *iskelet*, σμέουρο „Himbeere", Pl. σμέουρα > türkisch *ızmaola, ızmaola, ızmavula*. Die Erscheinung wird zum ersten Mal in spätgriechischen Inschriften aus Kleinasien belegt.

(b) Vor den Konsonanten *l, r*, denen in den griechischen Lehnwörtern ein Vokal vorgeschoben wird (weil die echten türkischen Wörter ursprünglich mit allen Konsonanten außer *l, r, n, v* beginnen können, Caferoğlu,

1949, 247, Kowalski, 1931, 1000, § 28, Räsänen, 1949, 51): λάχανα „Kohl" > mundartlich türkisch *lahana, ilahana, ilahna*, mittelgriechisch λιμένιον „Hafen" > türkisch *liman, iliman*, ρόκα „Spinnrocken" > mundartlich türkisch *roka, röke, höreke*, ρυμός „Deichsel" > mundartlich türkisch *iramas, iremas*, Ρωμιός „Grieche" > mundartlich türkisch *Urum*.

Es ist festzustellen, daß kein griechisches Phonem in die türkische Schriftsprache oder in die türkischen Dialekte eingedrungen ist und auch kein griechisches morphologisches Element wie z. B. Präfix, Suffix usw. im Türkischen produktiv geworden ist. Im Gegensatz dazu haben sich türkische Phoneme und Suffixe im phonologischen und morphologischen System des Griechischen eingebürgert (s. unter 7.2.1. und 7.2.2.).

7.1.2. Morphologie

Da das Türkische kein grammatisches Genus kennt, wird das Genus der griechischen Wörter nicht berücksichtigt. Die Ausgangsbasis für die türkischen Lehnwörter ist in vielen Fällen nicht der Nomin. Singularis, sondern der Akkusativ Singularis (mittelgriechisch παπαγᾶς „Papagei", Akk. παπαγᾶν > türkisch *papağan*) oder sogar Pluralis, der die Bedeutung des griechischen Sing. im Türkischen trägt (φασούλι „Bohne", Pl. φασούλια > türkisch *fasulya, fasulye* „Bohne"), d. h. die gebräuchlichsten Kasus des Griechischen. Die griechischen Wörter und Wortelemente scheinen eine geringe Produktivität im Türkischen zu haben. Türkische Verbalbildungen auf Grund von griechischen Substantiven sind selten: ἐμπίς „Pinzette" > mundartlich türkisch *imbiz* „Stachel", *imbizlemek* „den Ochsen mit dem Stachel antreiben"; φηλί „Schlüsselloch" > mundartlich türkisch *fili, filli* „Türschloß, Riegel", *fillemek* „verriegeln" usw.

7.1.3. Lexik

Den größten Prozentsatz des dem Griechischen entlehnten Sprachgutes stellen Substantive dar; Adjektive, Verben und Adverbien sind in sehr beschränktem Umfang entliehen. Das griechische Lehngut des Türkischen bezieht sich vorwiegend auf das materielle Leben der Türken im Gegensatz zu den griechischen Lehnwörtern in den europäischen Sprachen, die das geistige Leben zum Ausdruck bringen. Die griechischen Lehnwörter bezeichnen Pflanzen und Tiere, Werkzeuge und Geräte, Behälter und Gefäße, sind Begriffe des Ackerbaus, der Bienenzucht und Termini der Landwirtschaft, was auf wirtschaftliche und soziale Entwicklungen im Leben der Türken zurückzuführen ist (Wechsel Nomadentum—seßhaftes Leben) (vgl. Tzitzilis 1987, 144).

Türkisches Argot. Der Anteil der griechischen Lehnwörter im Istanbuler türkischen Argot, der neben den einheimischen Elementen noch zigeunerische, armenische, kurdische und italienische Lehnwörter aufweist, ist relativ stark. Die griechischen Lehnwörter erscheinen hier mit ihrer Haupt- oder metaphorischen Bedeutung: μεθυσμένος „betrunken" > *matizmenos, matiz* „ds.", τακτικός „Polizist" > *tahtakoz* „ds.", κορόιδο „Gegenstand des Spottes, dumm" > *koroydo* „ds."; σμαρίδα „Art Kleinfisch" > *izmarid* „Zigarettenstummel", σπίνος „Fink" > *ispinoz* „geschwätzig, Schwätzer", αναφόρι „geweihtes Brot (in der christlichen Kirche)" > *anafor* „gratis". Phrasen: αυτός ποιος είναι, „wer ist das?" > *aftospiyoz* „unwürdig, unfähig", εβδομήντα κόφτε „Schneide von dem, was er erzählt, 70% ab" > *eftaminta kofti* „Lüge", σα πανώρια „als ob sie sehr schön wäre" > *sapanorya* „häßlich". Türkische Ableitung auf Grund griechischer Basis: *erketeci* „Person, die vor der Ankunft von Polizisten warnt" < ἔρχεται „er kommt" + *-ci*, *klefteci* „Dieb" < κλέφτης „Dieb" + *-ci*.

Griechische Rückentlehnungen aus dem Türkischen. Ein interessantes Kapitel der griechisch-türkischen Sprachbeziehungen bilden jene griechischen Wörter, die entweder unmittelbar oder durch arabische und persische Vermittlung ins Türkische einst eingedrungen und dann mit einer neuen Form und Bedeutung wieder ins Griechische rückentlehnt wurden: πόλτος „Brei" > türkisch *pelte* „Fruchteis" > πελτές „Gelée, Marmelade"; ποντικόν (d. h. κάρυον) „pontische Nuß, Haselnuß" > türkisch *fındık* „ds." > φουντούκι „ds."; σεμίδαλις „feinstes Weizenmehl" > arabisch *sämid* „bestes Mehl" > türkisch *simid* „Weißbrot" > σιμίτι „kleine Sesambrezel"; προφαντά, τα „Erstlingsfrüchte" > neupersisch *terwende* „ds." > türkisch *turfanda, trofanda* „ds." > τροφαντά, τρουφαντά „ds.". Mittelgriechisch διφθέριον „Haut, Leder" > persisch-arabisch *tefter* „Geschäftsbuch, Register" > τεφτέρι „ds.".

7.2. Türkischer Einfluß auf das Griechische

Nach der Reinigung des gesprochenen Griechisch von fremden Elementen, vor allem türkischen und italienischen Ursprungs, im

Zuge der Befreiung Griechenlands (1830 ff) ist der türkische Einfluß heute auf eine geringe Zahl von Wörtern beschränkt. In der Schriftsprache werden Türkismen vermieden (vgl. Dizikirikis 1975). Einige türkische Lehnwörter haben sich vor allem durch den Einfluß der Sprache von griechischen Schriftstellern, die aus Kleinasien und den anliegenden Inseln stammten, als poetische Wörter in der neugriechischen Literatursprache eingebürgert: ρουμάνι „Wald" (orman), (μ)πεσκέσι „Geschenk" (peškeš), ντορής „rotbraunes Pferd" (dorı), κονάκι „Wohnstätte" (konak), κρεμεζί „rot" (kırmızı), κιοτής „Feigling" (kötü) usw.

Karamanlı-Literatur. Am stärksten hat aber das Türkische die neugriechischen Dialekte Kleinasiens (besonders das Kappadokische und teilweise das Pontische) beeinflußt. In gewissen Gebieten Kleinasiens (Kayseri, Nevşehir, Niğde, Konya usw.) hat sogar das Türkische das Neugriechische völlig ersetzt. Die griechisch-orthodoxe Bevölkerung dieser Gebiete hat die eigene Sprache (nicht aber ihren Glauben) vergessen und das Türkische übernommen. Aus diesem Grund haben sich griechische Gelehrte die Aufgabe gestellt, ausgewählte Texte der Bibel und Bücher christlich-orthodoxen Inhalts sowie kulturgeschichtliche Werke gewöhnlich aus dem Griechischen und seltener aus anderen europäischen Sprachen ins Türkische zu übersetzen, um ihren Landsleuten zu helfen, wenigstens ihren Glauben nicht zu vergessen und ihre eigene Kultur zu pflegen. Auf diese Weise ist eine mit griechischem Alphabet geschriebene türkischsprachige Literatur entstanden, die Karamanlı/Karamanlidika heißt. Eine analytische Bibliographie zu den Karamanlı-Veröffentlichungen, die meistens in Konstantinopel (Istanbul) erschienen sind, haben S. Salaville und E. Dalleggio (1966) übernommen. Eckmanns (1964) Ansicht, es gehe hier nicht um christliche Griechen, sondern um Seldschuken, die sich zum Christentum bekannt hätten, ist nicht haltbar.

7.2.1. Phonologie

Von den türkischen Phonemen scheint nur *ı* im Pontischen und Kappadokischen einen Phonemwert bekommen zu haben; türkisch c [dž] ist neben dem italienischen g [dž] vielleicht für die Entstehung des gemeinneugriechischen τζ [dz] verantwortlich, das in ursprünglich griechischen Wörtern nicht erscheint.

Vokale. Von den türkischen Vokalphonemen hat (dumpfes, ungerundetes) *ı* seinen Phonemwert nur im Pontischen und Kappadokischen sicher bewahrt: pontisch αρτιρεύω „steigern" < türkisch artırmak, kappadokisch μπαγιρδού „schreien" < türkisch bağırmak; Spuren des türkischen Phonems sind auch anderswo (z. B. in nordgriechischen Mundarten μπακιρένιος „aus Kupfer gemacht, kupfern" < türkisch bakır) selten zu finden. Sonst wird türkisch *ı* im übrigen Neugriechischen durch [i, u, e] wiedergegeben: lâkırdı „Geschwätz" > λιακιρντί, hızmet „Dienst" > χουσμέτι, kaldırım „Steinpflaster" > καλντερίμι.

Konsonanten. Die türkischen Affrikata š, ç und c [dž] erscheinen in den neugriechischen Dialekten Kleinasiens und teilweise in gewissen neugriechischen Mundarten unverändert. Im Gemeinneugriechischen und in den meisten Dialekten sind sie in *s, ts* und *dz* übergegangen, haben also ihre Affrikation verloren: šerbet „Fruchtsaft, Sorbet" > pontisch σερπέτιν, neugriechisch σερμπέτι, çardak „auf vier Säulen oder Pfosten ruhendes Dach" > pontisch kappadokisch τσαρντάχ, neugriechisch τσαρντάκι/τσαρδάκι, ciğer „Lunge, Leber" > pontisch τζιγέρ', neugriechisch τζιγέρι. Durch Entlehnung von türkischen und italienischen Wörtern ins Neugriechische in neuerer Zeit, die den dž-Laut aufweisen, ist ein neues Phonem im Neugriechischen entstanden, das im Altgriechischen anscheinend überhaupt nicht existiert und im Mittelgriechischen selten als fremdes Phonem (z. B. der Eigenname Τζιμισκής) erscheint.

7.2.2. Morphologie

Obwohl zur Zeit keine wissenschaftliche exakte und fundierte Arbeit zur Morphologie der türkischen Lehnwörter im Griechischen zur Verfügung steht, ist Folgendes festzustellen:

Anpassung an das neugriechische Deklinationssystem. Weist ein türkisches Lehnwort zufällig in der Endsilbe den Vokal *-a* oder *-i* (-ı, -ü, -u) auf, dann kann es dem neugriechischen Deklinationssystem als Femininum oder Neutrum ohne weiteres angepaßt werden: çanta „Ledertasche" > η τσάντα, cami „Moschee" > τζαμί, çarşı „Markt" > τσαρσί, koru „Wald" > κουρί, örtü „Bedeckung, Mantel" > mundartlich (Megara) γιουρδί „eine Art Mantel". Sollte aus einem türkischen Lehnwort, das auf einen Vokal endet, ein neugriechisches Maskulinum gebildet werden, so wird das türkische Wort im Neugriechischen um ein -s erweitert: *balta* „Axt" > *ο μπαλτάς*, *bekri* „Trunkenbold" > *ο μπεκρής*, *nârgile* „Wasserpfeife" > *ο ναργκιλές*, *kötü* „schlecht" > *ο κιοτής*. Bemerkenswert ist die Bildung von Verben im Gemeinneugriechischen, die aus dem türkischen Aoriststamm + neugriechischem Suffix *-ίζω* gebildet werden: *boyamak* „färben", *boyadı* „er färbte" + neugriechisch *-ίζω* > *μπογιαντίζω* „färben", *kullandırmak* „benützen" > *κουλαντρίζω*, *bayılmak* „ohnmächtig werden" > *μπαϊλντίζω*, *kavurmak* „rösten" > *καβουρντίζω* usw.

Suffixe. Von den türkischen Suffixen sind *-cı*, *-cık*, *-lı*, *-lık* und *-î* sowohl im Gemeinneugriechischen als auch in den Dialekten produktiv geworden. Bei der Bildung der neugriechischen Berufsnamen auf *-cı* wird die diesbezügliche türkische Regel (*-cı* nach Vokalen und stimmhaften Konsonanten, aber *-çı* nach stimmlosen Konsonanten) streng angewandt: *παλια-τζής* „Händler von alten Waren", *καταφερ-τζής* „geschickt" gegenüber *παοκ-τσής* „Anhänger des Vereins P. A. O. K.", *γιαουρτ-τσής* „Verkäufer von Joghurt". Nach *kavga-cık* „kleiner Streit", *para-cık* „kleine Münze" usw. sind *λαου-τζίκος* „armes Volk" und *φουκαρα-τζίκος* „armer, sympathischer Mann" (obwohl ein türkisches *fıkaracık* möglich ist) gebildet. Türkisch *-lı* und *-lık* werden als *-λής* und *-λίκι* auf griechische Wurzeln zur Bildung von Adjektiven und Substantiven hinzugefügt: *μουστακαλής* „mit Schnurrbart", *μπεσαλής* „treu, zuverlässig", *υπαλληλίκι* „Beruf des Beamten", *υπουργιλίκι* „Amt des Ministers", *προεδριλίκι* „Amt des Präsidenten" usw. Die türkische Produktivendung *-î*, womit Adjektiva von beliebigen Substantiva gebildet werden können, darunter auch Farbadjektiva, hat sich im Neugriechischen auf die Bildung von Farbadjektiva beschränkt und spezialisiert; nach *fıstıkî* „pistaziengrün" (> neugriechisch *φιστικί*), *limonî* „zitronengelb" (> neugriechisch *λεμονί*) usw. werden im Neugriechischen von einem beliebigen farbenbezeichnenden Substantiv entsprechende Farbadjektiva gebildet: *κεραμιδί* „ziegelrot" zu *κεραμίδα* „Ziegel", *λαδί* „dunkelgrün" zu *λάδι* „Öl", *ουρανί* „himmelblau" zu *ουρανός* „Himmel", *σταχτί* „aschenfarbig" zu *στάχτη* „Asche" usw.

7.2.3. Syntax

In bezug auf die Syntax scheint das Türkische keinen bedeutenden Einfluß auf das Gemeinneugriechische ausgeübt zu haben. Nur in der neugriechischen Phraseologie ist die Struktur gewisser Phraseologismen sicher türkisch: *έρχεται στο νου μου* < *aklıma geliyor* „an etwas denken", *έρχεται από το χέρι μου* < *elimden geliyor* „können", *βάζω μπελά στο κεφάλι μου* < *başıma belâ komaklalmak* „Ärger haben", *βγάζω στο μεϊντάνι* < *meydana çıkarmak* „an den Tag bringen, enthüllen" usw.

Zahlreiche syntaktische Strukturen nach türkischem Vorbild sind im Pontischen und besonders im Kappadokischen zu finden: pontisch *εγώ απ' εκείνον μεγάλος είμαι* < *ben ondan büyük im* „ich bin älter als er" = kappadokisch *απού μεν μικρός* < *benden küçük* „jünger als ich" (Vergleich ohne Komparativ), pontisch *έπαρ' ας ελέπομεν* < *al bakalım* „nimm' mal", *κ' έξερα αοίκον δουλείαν ντο θα εποίνεν* < *boyle iş yapacağını bilmiyordım* „ich wußte nicht, daß er eine solche Arbeit machen würde", *πολλά ψηλά πη τερεί* < *çok yüksek bakan* „wer von der Höhe schaut" usw., kappadokisch *να πάω ήτον* < *gidecek idim* „ich würde gehen", *σπιτιού το σκυλί* < *evin köpeği* „der Hund des Hauses", *τομό 'ναι δεϊ πήρεν το* < *benim dir dey aldı* „er nahm es, als ob es ihm gehöre", *δράνσε κι, έρχονται* < *gördü ki, geliyorlar* „er sah, daß sie kommen" usw. usf.

7.2.4. Lexik

Hier sollte man zwischen dem türkischen Einfluß auf die neugriechische Sprache, wo er heute nur noch gering ist, und dem auf die neugriechischen Dialekte vor allem Kleinasiens, wo er am stärksten gewesen ist, unterscheiden. Wir beschränken uns auf die türkische Lexik im Gemeinneugriechischen. Der türkische Lehnwortschatz beschränkt sich auf ein paar hundert Wörter, von denen die meisten türkische Begriffe für Lebensmittel, Küche etc. sind (die türkische Küche ist ja auf dem ganzen Balkan verbreitet):

(a) Küche: *dolma* „mit Reis oder Hackfleisch gefüllte Weinblätter" > *ντολμάδες*, *ντολμαδάκια*, *yuvarlak* „kleine Fleisch- oder Reisklöße" > *γιουβαρλάκια*, *imambayıldı* „Art Speise aus Auberginen" > *ιμάμ-μπαγιλντί*, *türlü* „Art Speise aus verschiedenen Gemüsearten" > *τουρλού*, *köfte* „Fleischklößchen, Frikadelle" > *κεφτές*, *kıyma* „Hackfleisch" > *κιμάς*, *turşu* „in Essig eingelegte Gurken, Tomaten usw." > *τουρσί*, *yufka* „Art Teigblätter" > *γιουφκάς*, *baklava* „Art süße Mehlspeise" > *μπακλαβάς*, *kadayıf* „Art Mehlspeise" > *κανταΐφι*, *halva* „Art Sü-

ßigkeit" > χαλβάς, lokma „Art Teigspeise" > λουκουμάς usw.
(b) Orientalische Kultur: vakıf „religiöse Stiftung" > βακούφι, yaşmak „Schleier" > γιασμάκι, tellâl „öffentlicher Ausrufer" > τελάλης/δελάλης, derviš „Derwisch" > δερβίσης, kaldırım „Steinpflaster" > καλντερίμι, kilim „Kelim" > κιλίμι, minder „Sofa" > μιντέρι, nârgile „Wasserpfeife" > ναργκιλές, paša „Pascha" > πασάς, πασιάς, cami „Moschee" > τζαμί, halı „Teppich" > χαλί usw.
(c) Kleinere Gruppen von türkischen Lehnwörtern können sich auf die verschiedensten Gebiete des materiellen Lebens der Griechen beziehen. Beachtenswert sind diejenigen türkischen Lehnwörter, die im täglichen Gespräch gebräuchlicher sind als ihre semantischen Partner griechischer Herkunft (vgl. Dizikirikis 1975): εργένης „Junggeselle" (ergen) oder μπεκιάρης „ds." (bekâr), sonst άγαμος; ρουσφέτι „Bestechung" < rüšvet, sonst δωροδοκία; τεμπέλης „Faulenzer" < tembel, sonst οκνός/οκνηρός; ζόρι „Gewalt" < zor, sonst βία; χαρτζιλίκι „Taschengeld" < harclık, sonst μικροέξοδα; σεργιανίζω „bummeln" < seyran (etmek), sonst βολτάρω. Es gibt Fälle, wo gewisse türkische Lehnwörter bevorzugt werden, weil sie expressiver sind als ihre Entsprechungen griechischer Herkunft: ραχάτι „Bequemlichkeit" < rahat (= ησυχία); τζερεμές „Geldstrafe" < cereme (= πρόστιμο); λουφές „Belohnung" < ulüfe (= αμοιβή); νταλγκάς „große Liebe" < dalga (= έρωτας); ζαβαλής „unglücklich, bedauernswert" < zavallı (= δυστυχισμένος); ρεζίλι „Blamage" < rezil (= εξευτελισμός); χουβαρντάς „großzügig" < hovarda (= γενναιόδωρος) usw.

8. Stand der Kontaktforschung

8.1. Auf dem Gebiet des griechischen Einflusses auf das Türkische haben G. Meyer und A. Tietze bedeutende Beiträge geliefert. Meyers Werk (1893) beruht auf Sprachmaterial, das türkischen Wörterbüchern und literarischen Quellen entnommen ist, und aus diesem Grund enthält seine Arbeit ausschließlich Wörter der Gelehrtensprache. Im Gegensatz dazu werden bei Tietze (1955 und 1962) nur Wörter der Volkssprache behandelt, die im wesentlichen aus Veröffentlichungen der „Türkischen Sprachwissenschaftlichen Gesellschaft" (Türk Dil Kurumu) gesammelt sind. Meyer und Tietze ergänzen sich gegenseitig und geben uns einen ersten Eindruck des griechischen Einflusses sowohl auf die türkische Schriftsprache als auch auf die türkischen Mundarten Kleinasiens (sonst anatolische Dialekte). Tietzes Arbeiten zum fremden Einfluß auf das Türkische waren in der Erforschung der fremden Elemente im Türkischen und in der türkischen Etymologie bahnbrechend. An Tietze knüpfen die Arbeiten von Symeonidis (1973) und Tzitzilis (1987) an, die neue griechische Wörter und Wortformen vor allem in den anatolischen Dialekten untersuchen. Es scheint, als ob das griechische Wortmaterial, das in den anatolischen Dialekten vorhanden ist, noch nicht gründlich genug erforscht worden ist.

Alle erwähnten Arbeiten beziehen sich hauptsächlich auf die Lexik, und nur gelegentlich gibt es Bemerkungen zur Grammatik. Für das Thema Vokalismus der griechischen Lehnwörter im Türkischen ist die Arbeit von Symeonidis (1976) relevant. Es fehlen noch Arbeiten zur Morphologie (vor allem zu türkischen Suffixen, die im Griechischen produktiv geworden sind) und Phraseologie (besonders in Fällen, wo türkische Phraseologismen von entsprechenden griechischen Vorbildern abhängig sind).

8.2. Was den türkischen Einfluß auf das Griechische Griechenlands anbelangt, so beschränkt sich die diesbezügliche Forschung hauptsächlich auf Arbeiten, die die türkischen Lehnwörter im Griechischen zu bestimmen versuchen (vgl. Ronzevalle 1911, Koukkidis 1959). Einen guten Eindruck von der Lautlehre der türkischen Lehnwörter im Griechischen bekommen wir bei Georgiadis 1974. Es fehlen noch Arbeiten zur Morphologie und vor allem zur Phraseologie, wo das Türkische eine bedeutende Rolle in allen Balkansprachen zu spielen scheint. Auf die neugriechische Grammatik hat das Türkische keinen wesentlichen Einfluß ausgeübt. Hier bilden die griechischen Dialekte Kleinasiens, das Pontische und besonders das Kappadokische eine Ausnahme; beide sind in bezug auf alle Sprachebenen, vor allem aber in bezug auf Lexik und Syntax, stark vom Türkischen beeinflußt worden.

9. Bibliographie (in Auswahl)

Bogas, Evangelos (1951): „Ta eis ten Tourkiken, Persiken kai Araviken daneia tes Hellenikes" [Die griechischen Lehnwörter im Türkischen, Persischen und Arabischen]. In: *Athena 55*, 67–113.

Caferoğlu, Ahmet (1959): "Die anatolischen und rumelischen Dialekte". In: *Philologiae Turcicae Fundamenta I*, Deny, J./Grønbech, K./Scheel, H./Togan, Z. V. (Eds.), Wiesbaden.

Devellioğlu, Fuat (1945): *Türk argosu* [Das türkische Argot], Konstantinopel.

Dizikirikis, Jakovos (1975): *Na ksetourkepsoume te glossa mas* [Wir sollten unsere Sprache enttürkisieren], Athen.

Eckmann, Janos (1964): "Die karamanische Literatur". In: *Philologiae Turcicae Fundamenta II*, Bazin, L./Bombaci, A./Deny, J./Gökbilgin T./İz, F./Scheel, H. (Eds.), Wiesbaden.

Georgiadis, Pavlos (1974): *Die lautlichen Veränderungen der türkischen Lehnwörter im Griechischen*, München.

Kahane, Henry und Renée/Tietze, Andreas (1958): *The Lingua Franca in the Levant. Turkish Nautical Terms of Italian and Greek Origin*, Urbana.

Koukkidis, Konstantinos (1959): "Lexilogion hellenikon lexeon paragomenon ek tes Tourkikes" [Vokabular griechischer Wörter türkischer Herkunft]. In: *Archeion tou thrakikou laographikou kai glossikou thesaurou 24*, 281–312, 25 (1960), 121–200.

Kowalski, Tadeus (1931): "Osmanisch-türkische Dialekte". In: *Enzyklopädie des Islams 4*, Leiden.

Maidhof, Adam (1920): "Rückwanderer aus den islamitischen Sprachen im Neugriechischen (Smyrna und Umgebung)". In: *Glotta 10*, 1–22.

Meyer, Gustav (1893): "Türkische Studien I. Die griechischen und romanischen Bestandteile im Wortschatze des Osmanisch-Türkischen". In: *Sitzungsberichte der Kaiserlichen Akademie der Wissenschaften zu Wien, Phil.-hist. Kl.*, Bd. 128, 1–96.

Papadopoulos, Anthimos A. (1932): "Ta ek tes Hellenikes daneia tou Tourkikes" [Die griechischen Lehnwörter des Türkischen]. In: *Athena 44*, 2–27.

Photiadis, Kostas (1988): *Oi eksislamismoi tes Mikras Asias kai oi kryptochristianoi tou Pontou* [Die Islamisierungen von Kleinasien und die Kryptochristen des Pontos], Thessaloniki.

Räsänen, Martti (1949): "Materialien zur Lautgeschichte der türkischen Sprachen". In: *Studia Orientalia 15*.

Ronzevalle, Louis (1911): "Les emprunts turcs dans le grec vulgaire de Roumélie et spécialement d'Adrinople". In: *Journal Asiatique 18*, 69–106, 257–336, 405–462.

Salaville, Sévérien/Dalleggio, Eugène (1966): *Karamanlidika. Bibliographie analytique d'ouvrages en langue turque imprimés en caractères grecs*, Bd. 1 [1584–1850] und 2 [1851–1865], Athen 1958 u. 1966.

Symeonidis, Charalambos (1973): "Griechische Lehnwörter im Türkischen". In: *Balkan Studies 14*, 167–200.

Symeonidis, Charalambos (1976): *Der Vokalismus der griechischen Lehnwörter im Türkischen*, Thessaloniki.

Tietze, Andreas (1955): "Griechische Lehnwörter im anatolischen Türkisch". In: *Oriens 8*, 204–257.

Tietze, Andreas (1962): "Einige weitere griechische Lehnwörter im anatolischen Türkisch". In: *Nemeth Armağanı* (Ankara), 373–388.

Tzitzilis, Christos (1987): *Griechische Lehnwörter im Türkischen (mit besonderer Berücksichtigung der anatolischen Dialekte)*, Wien.

Charalambos Symeonidis, Thessaloniki (Griechenland)

183. Griechisch–Aromunisch

1. Geographie und Demographie
2. Geschichte
3. Die kulturelle und religiöse Situation
4. Der Name der Aromunen
5. Soziolinguistische Lage
6. Sprachpolitische Lage
7. Allgemeines kontaktlinguistisches Porträt
8. Kritische Wertung der verwendeten Quellen und Literatur
9. Bibliographie (in Auswahl)

1. Geographie und Demographie

Eine aromunische Bevölkerung ist im Gebiet des heutigen Griechenland seit dem 10. Jahrhundert durch verschiedene byzantinische Geschichtsschreiber bezeugt. Im Mittelalter gab es vermutlich zwei größere Siedlungsgebiete der Aromunen, nämlich das Pindusgebirge sowie die Gegend im heutigen östlichen Albanien bis zum Gebirgszug des Grammos. Zwischen dem 16. und 18. Jahrhundert bildete sich eine von Aromunen getragene städtische Kultur vor allem im Gebiet des heutigen Albanien heraus. So gab es in Voskopojë (Moschopolis), das in seiner Blütezeit angeblich 12 000 Häuser zählte, eine Akademie sowie eine bedeutende Druckerei. Die weitgehende Zerstörung dieser städtischen Zentren durch zumeist mohammedanische Albaner in der zweiten Hälfte des 18. Jahrhunderts bewirkte eine Flucht der Aromunen nach Norden und Osten, wo man sich teilweise direkt in oder zumindest in der Nähe von schon bestehenden aromunischen Orten, teilweise aber auch in bislang von Griechen oder Slaven bewohnten Gegenden ansiedelte. Die traditionelle Lebens- und Wirtschaftsweise der Aromunen mit einem regelmäßigen Wechsel zwischen Sommer- und Winteraufenthaltsorten (Transhumanz) hat ein weiteres dazu getan, daß man bis auf den heutigen Tag Aromunen in vielen Gegenden der Balkanhalbinsel verstreut findet.

Den regionalen Schwerpunkt der Aromunensiedlungen im heutigen Griechenland bildet nach wie vor das Pindusgebirge, in dem es etwa 70 — zu einem großen Teil aber nur im Sommer bewohnte — aromunische Orte gibt. Des weiteren finden sich aromunische Wohngebiete im Vermiongebirge, am Fuß des Olymps und im Piniostal, in der Nähe der Stadt Volos sowie an der nordwestlichen Küste nördlich und südlich von Igoumenitsa. Außerdem leben Aromunen, öfters auch in gemeinsamen Wohnvierteln, natürlich in allen größeren griechischen Städten, die sie dann häufig im Sommer verlassen, um in ihre Heimatdörfer in den Bergen zurückzukehren.

Die genaue Zahl der Aromunen anzugeben, ist unmöglich, denn abgesehen von den definitorischen Unklarheiten (nach welchen Kriterien kann bestimmt werden, wer Aromune ist?) existieren keinerlei zuverlässige Zählungen, da gerade in Griechenland jeder dort Lebende auch als Grieche gilt. So verwundert es nicht, daß die Schätzungen weit auseinandergehen: während griechische Quellen nur auf wenige Zehntausend kommen (Angelopoulos 1979, 131, zählt 40 000), gehen Exilaromunen von bis zu einer Million aus (Barba 1987, 3). Als einziger hat Weigand (1894—1895, Bd. 1, 278—300) die Kriterien seiner Berechnungen genau dargelegt: Er kommt dabei für die Zeit des ausgehenden 19. Jahrhunderts auf 150 000, „die sich ihrer Muttersprache noch bedienen", wobei er einen drastischen Rückgang seit der Zerstörung der städtischen Zentren am Ende des 18. Jahrhunderts konstatiert und eine noch stärkere Abnahme im 20. Jahrhundert prognostiziert. Letzteres ist allerdings zweifellos nicht eingetreten, so daß es realistisch erscheint, für die heutige Zeit von etwa 200 000—300 000 Aromunen auszugehen (→ Sprachenkarte I).

2. Geschichte

Die Frage nach der Herkunft der Aromunen ist eng verknüpft mit dem sehr umstrittenen Problem der rumänischen Ethnogenese und dem Verhältnis der vier großen Varietäten des Rumänischen (Dakorumänisch, Aromunisch, Megleno- und Istrorumänisch) zueinander. Es gibt gute Gründe für die Annahme, daß die Urheimat der Aromunen in Südserbien liegt, von wo sie zwischen dem 6. und dem 10. Jahrhundert in ihre heutigen Siedlungsgebiete gelangt sind (Kramer 1992). Seit diesem Zeitpunkt hat das Aromunische keinen direkten Kontakt mehr mit den übrigen drei Varietäten.

Während die Aromunen im Mittelalter teilweise eigene Staatsgebilde errichten konnten (vor allem die „Große Walachei" in Thessalien und die „Kleine Walachei" in Acharnien und Ätolien), gingen sie nach dem Untergang des Byzantinischen Reiches wie auch die anderen Völker der Balkanhalbinsel in den großen Vielvölkerstaat des Osmanischen Reiches auf. Für die Aromunen erwies sich dies insofern als nicht ungünstig, als sie den Handel auf dem Balkan weitgehend in ihren Händen hatten und zahlreiche Herbergen an den bedeutenden Routen führten.

Mit dem allmählichen Zusammenbruch des Osmanischen Reiches werden auch die Aromunen ein Faktor in dem sich nun entwickelnden nationalistischen Puzzlespiel in Südosteuropa. In der zweiten Hälfte des 19. Jahrhunderts bildet sich — mehr und mehr von Bukarest beeinflußt — eine aromunische Nationalbewegung heraus, deren Ziel es zunächst ist, eine weitgehende Autonomie zu erreichen, die dann später aber auch nach einem eigenen Staat strebt. Der bedeutendste Erfolg ist die Anerkennung der Aromunen als *millet* im Jahre 1905, die auf Betreiben von Deutschland, Italien, Österreich-Ungarn und Rußland erfolgt, die aber gleichzeitig zu großen Spannungen zu Griechenland führt, das eine offizielle Anerkennung der Aromunen verhindern möchte. So sind aus der Folgezeit zahlreiche Greueltaten griechischer Banden gegen nationalgesinnte Aromunen bekannt (Peyfuss 1974, 97 f).

Die Balkankriege und der Friede von Bukarest (1913) machen dann jedoch den weitreichenden Hoffnungen der Aromunen ein Ende: Es wird kein eigener aromunischer Staat etwa in den Grenzen der mittelalterlichen „Großen Walachei", wie es in Rumänien gefordert wurde, errichtet; aus aromunischer Sicht schlimmer noch ist die Tatsache, daß die Aromunen ihre nationale Einheit verlieren und nunmehr auf mehrere Staaten aufgeteilt werden, womit auch die traditionellen Wanderbewegungen zumindest teilweise unterbunden werden. In einem Notenwechsel im Anschluß an den Friedensvertrag von Bukarest, in dem die Aromunen gar nicht erwähnt sind, verpflichten sich Bulgarien, Serbien und Griechenland zwar zur Respektierung der kirchlichen und schulischen Autonomie in den von Aromunen bewohnten Gebieten, doch erweist sich dies schon bald als eine leere Versprechung: Serbien etwa schließt bereits 1918 wieder die aromunischen Schulen, in Griechenland bestehen sie zwar bis zum Bürgerkrieg Ende der vierziger Jahre weiter, doch werden hier nach und nach den Aromunen wichtige Rechte entzogen, ja teilweise wird der Gebrauch des Aromunischen als „antigriechische Aktivität" geahndet (Peyfuss 1974, 97).

Heutzutage spielen die Aromunen offiziell überhaupt keine Rolle mehr in Griechenland, sie sind auch nicht als Minderheit anerkannt, und es kann passieren, daß das Aromunische in sich seriös gebenden Publikationen als (alt-)griechischer Dialekt auftaucht (als Beispiele etwa Κεραμόπουλλος 1939, Παπαζήσης 1976, Κολτσίδας 1976) und Sprachwissenschaftler, die Aufnahmen bei den Aromunen machen wollen, wegen „Anschlags auf die Einheit des griechischen Staats" angeklagt werden (Rolshoven 1989, 190).

3. Die kulturelle und religiöse Situation

Ein eigenständiges kulturelles Leben gibt es bei den Aromunen in Griechenland heutzutage praktisch nicht mehr. Die städtischen Zentren, die einstmals Kristallisationspunkte der aromunischen Kultur waren (cf. 1. und 2.), gibt es nicht mehr. Die einzige größere aromunische Siedlung in Griechenland, die eine solche Rolle wenigstens ansatzweise spielen könnte, ist Metsovon, das etwa 4 000 Einwohner zählt.

Es gibt heutzutage kein tiefergehendes aromunisches Selbstbewußtsein in Griechenland. Auf die Frage nach der Nationalitätenzugehörigkeit erhält man in der Regel die Antwort, man sei Grieche. Zur Begründung hierfür lassen sich mindestens zwei Faktoren anführen: zum einen die mehr oder weniger offizielle Staatsdoktrin, daß jeder in Griechenland lebende Bürger auch Grieche ist; zum anderen aber auch die Tatsache, daß jede Annäherung an das Rumänische und vor allem an den Staat Rumänien bei den Aromunen heute sehr verpönt ist. In den meisten aromunischen Ortschaften gibt es Familien, die Verwandte in Rumänien haben, die zwischen den beiden Weltkriegen den Versprechungen des rumänischen Staates geglaubt und ihre angestammte Heimat verlassen hatten (vgl. 2.); von diesen Auswanderergruppen bzw. ihren Nachfahren aber hören die Aromunen in Griechenland nun nicht sehr viel Gutes über deren Schicksal in Rumänien, so daß alles, was mit Rumänien zu tun hat, zunächst mit Mißtrauen betrachtet wird.

Die Aromunen bekennen sich in der Regel zur orthodoxen Kirche. Zwar gab es bei Teilen der aromunischen Nationalbewegung Sympathien für eine Vereinigung mit Rom, um sich damit dem Einfluß des griechischen Klerus zu entziehen, doch konnten sich diese Kreise nicht durchsetzen (Peyfuss 1974, 59—65).

4. Der Name der Aromunen

Die wissenschaftliche Bezeichnung der Aromunen, die sich in analoger Form auch in den meisten anderen Sprachen findet (frz. *Aroumains*, engl. *Arumanians*, rum. *Aromâni*), geht auf eine Prägung Gustav Weigands (1894—1895, Bd. 2, VII—VIII) zurück, der damit die Selbstbezeichnung der Aromunen (je nach dialektaler Herkunft *Armîn*, *Arämän* etc. < lat. *romanus*) aufgreift. Dieser Terminus hat ältere und unpräzisere Ausdrücke wie *Mazedo-Romanen*, *Südrumänen*, *Pinduswalachen* etc. weitgehend, wenn auch nicht vollständig, verdrängen können. Von den Griechen werden die Aromunen in der Regel Βλάχοι genannt, was letzten Endes auf germ. *walhos zurückgeht und womit anfangs ein u. a. bei Caesar als *Volcae* erwähnter keltischer Stamm bezeichnet wurde. Mittlerweile haben die Aromunen selbst diesen Namen auch als Eigenbezeichnung übernommen. Daneben existieren Namen, die den Aromunen von den Nachbarvölkern gegeben wurden, und die ursprünglich eine pejorative Konnotation besaßen, wie etwa Κουτσόβλαχοι oder Цинцари, die aber vereinzelt auch in die wissenschaftliche Terminologie Einzug halten konnten (etwa dtsch. *Kutzowlachen*, *Zinzaren*).

5. Soziolinguistische Lage

Parallel zu den geschilderten Veränderungen nach dem Zusammenbruch des Osmanischen Reiches (cf. 2. und 3.) hat sich im Laufe des 20. Jahrhunderts auch die soziolinguistische Situation des Aromunischen in Griechenland deutlich verändert. Man muß heute davon ausgehen, daß es keine einsprachigen Aromunen mehr gibt, daß vielmehr alle auch das Griechische (die Sprache des Staates, der Schule und Kirche) beherrschen. Einen interessanten Wandel hat es dabei vor allem bei der Rolle gegeben, die die aromunischen Frauen spielen. Récatas (1934, 18−28) hatte festgestellt, daß gerade die aromunischen Frauen Garantinnen für die Bewahrung des Aromunischen waren, da sie praktisch keinerlei Außenkontakte hatten: Auch nach dem Besuch der Schule waren die Mädchen normalerweise nicht in der Lage, sich auf Griechisch zu verständigen. Im Alter von etwa 15 Jahren verlobten sich die jungen Mädchen (bzw. sie wurden verlobt) und durften dann bis zur Heirat mit etwa 18 Jahren keine Kontakte zu anderen Personen außer den engsten Familienangehörigen haben. Auch gingen nur verheiratete Frauen zur Kirche, wo sie allerdings von der griechischen Liturgie so gut wie nichts verstanden. Die Männer waren hingegen auch schon zur Zeit der Untersuchung von Récatas zum größten Teil zweisprachig, da sie − bedingt vor allem durch den Handel − auf griechische Sprachkenntnisse angewiesen waren. In der Familie aber wurde nur aromunisch gesprochen. In der heutigen Zeit hat sich nun gerade das Sprachverhalten der aromunischen Frauen stark geändert. Sie sind nicht mehr die Bewahrerinnen des Aromunischen: Da sie zu der Überzeugung gelangt sind, daß für ihre Kinder die Beherrschung des Griechischen unabdingbar für ein gesellschaftliches Weiterkommen ist, sprechen gerade sie mit ihren Kindern häufig bewußt griechisch, das sie spätestens in der Schule erlernt haben und mit dem sie etwa durch Radio und Fernsehen auch täglich konfrontiert werden. Untereinander sprechen allerdings auch die jüngeren Frauen vorwiegend aromunisch, während der Sprachgebrauch der Männer häufig vom Thema abhängt: Diskussionen über geschäftliche Dinge sowie über Politik oder Sport werden eher auf Griechisch als auf Aromunisch geführt (Wild 1981, 10−11).

Die Verwendung des Aromunischen ist heutzutage vor allem von zwei Faktoren abhängig, dem Alter und dem Wohnort (Kramer 1987, 137−138). Die älteste Generation verwendet fast ausschließlich noch das Aromunische; die mittlere Generation der Vierzig- bis Fünfzigjährigen, die die Sprache noch perfekt beherrscht, spricht sie vorwiegend mit den Älteren, während man in der Konversation mit den Jüngeren schon auf das Griechische umsteigt, so daß bei den Jugendlichen heutzutage häufig nur noch passive Sprachkenntnisse anzutreffen sind. Der zweite wichtige Faktor ist die Lage des Wohnortes: Hier gilt, daß das Aromunische umso besser erhalten ist, je abgeschiedener der Ort liegt. Vereinzelt dient das Aromunische aber auch als Identifikationsmerkmal zur Dorfgemeinschaft bzw. der Einheimischen gegenüber zugezogenen Fremden. Eingeheiratete Ehepartner werden heutzutage sprachlich in der Regel nicht assimiliert, d. h. man spricht mit ihnen Griechisch und erwartet auch nicht, daß sie das Aromunische erlernen.

Ein Eigensprachlichkeitsbewußtsein ist bei den Aromunen in Griechenland nicht vorhanden. Häufig hört man die Einschätzung, daß das Aromunische keine „richtige" Sprache sei, da man es nicht schreiben könne. Nicht selten findet man die (von pseudowissenschaftlichen Werken − cf. 2. − noch unterstützte) Meinung, das Aromunische sei ein verderbtes bzw. regional gefärbtes oder archaisches Griechisch. In der älteren Generation, die noch die rumänischen Schulen sowie die rumänische Propaganda erlebt hat, trifft man auf die Kenntnis, daß das Aromunische etwas mit dem (Dako-)Rumänischen zu tun hat, doch ist dies in den Augen der meisten Aromunen nicht gerade ein positiver Aspekt (cf. 3.).

6. Sprachpolitische Lage

In der heutigen Zeit besitzen die Aromunen in Griechenland das, was man zu elementaren Rechten einer sprachlichen Minderheit rechnen darf (Schulen, Kirchen, Zugang zu Massenmedien etc.), nicht. Dies ist einerseits vom griechischen Staat, der schon die bloße Existenz der Aromunen gerne verschweigt, eindeutig gewollt. Andererseits muß man sagen, daß die Aromunen selbst in Griechenland keine übermäßigen Anstrengungen unternehmen, um an dieser Lage etwas zu ändern.

Nur ein vorübergehender Erfolg war den Bemühungen beschieden, das Aromunische (bzw. sogar das Dakorumänische) als Liturgiesprache einzuführen und den Aromunen einen eigenen Bischof als geistliches Oberhaupt zu gewähren, wobei viele der Geistlichen, die den Gottesdienst in aromunischer Sprache feierten, starkem Druck von seiten der griechischen Hierarchie ausgesetzt waren und teilweise angeblich sogar gefoltert wurden (Peyfuss 1974, 66). Auch muß man betonen, daß diese Versuche einen weiteren Keil zwischen die nationalistisch eingestellten und die gräkophilen Aromunen trieb. Mit der bereits erwähnten schrittweisen Verschlechterung der Lage der Aromunen nach dem Frieden von Bukarest (cf. 2.) geht der Gebrauch des Aromunischen als Kultsprache jedoch immer mehr zurück, so daß heute die Aromunen Griechenlands den Gottesdienst nur in griechischer Sprache feiern können: Auch dies ist zweifellos ein wichtiger Grund dafür, daß das Aromunische gerade auch in den Augen vieler Aromunen selbst ein soviel geringeres Prestige besitzt als das Griechische.

Eng verknüpft mit dem Versuch, das Aromunische als Liturgiesprache einzuführen, war der Aufbau eines eigenen aromunischen Schulsystems. Die erste aromunische Schule wurde 1864 in Tirnovo bei Bitola (Monastir) gegründet, dank tatkräftiger finanzieller Unterstützung durch den rumänischen Staat folgten rasch weitere Gründungen, so daß am Anfang des 20. Jahrhunderts mehr als 100 aromunische Schulen mit insgesamt über 4 000 Schülern und fast 300 Lehrern bestanden (genauere Zahlen bei Peyfuss 1974, 106, und Dahmen 1991, 32 f). Auch dies aber trug zu einer Spaltung der aromunischen Bevölkerung bei, denn während die eher nationalistisch Gesinnten ihre Kinder auf diese an Bukarest ausgerichteten Schulen schickten, tendierten andere zu den griechischen Lehranstalten: Vor allem die sozial besser gestellten Schichten wie etwa die einflußreichen Kaufleute bevorzugten für ihre Kinder, namentlich für die Jungen, das griechische Gymnasium, da man sich vom Griechischen weit mehr versprach als vom Aromunischen bzw. Dakorumänischen (Weigand 1897, 53 f).

In der Zwischenkriegszeit ging der Einfluß der aromunischen Schulen in Griechenland, die im Gegensatz zu denen in Albanien und Serbien weiterbestanden, immer mehr zurück, da der rumänische Staat seine finanzielle Unterstützung weitgehend einstellte zugunsten einer gezielten Werbung, mit der man Aromunen zur Umsiedlung nach Rumänien locken wollte. Die letzten aromunischen Schulen wurden dann während des Griechischen Bürgerkriegs (1946—1949) endgültig geschlossen. Seitdem gibt es in Griechenland keinerlei Unterricht in aromunischer Sprache mehr.

Versuche, das Aromunische aufzuwerten, werden heutzutage vor allem von Exilaromunen gestartet. Sie haben sich in mehreren Vereinigungen zusammengeschlossen und versuchen u. a., eine Kodifizierung des Aromunischen zu erreichen. Dabei können sie auf frühere Erfahrungen zurückgreifen, denn bereits seit dem 18. Jahrhundert gibt es Bestrebungen, das Aromunische als Schriftsprache zu verwenden. Im wesentlichen lassen sich zwei Epochen unterscheiden:

(a) Am Ende des 18. und zu Beginn des 19. Jahrhunderts erscheinen mehrere Werke, in denen eine grammatische und orthographische Normierung des Aromunischen versucht wird. Das bedeutendste Werk ist hierbei die später mehrfach wieder aufgelegte Sprachlehre von Bojadschi (1813), die bis auf den heutigen Tag eigentlich die beste Grammatik des Aromunischen geblieben ist. Dieses Werk ist von griechischer Seite stets als Bedrohung empfunden worden: So hat angeblich der Patriarch nicht nur Bojadschi als Häretiker verflucht, weil er gegen die Sprache sei, in der Gott gesprochen habe und spricht, sondern auch alle, die diesem Glauben schenkten (Peyfuss 1974, 27).

(b) Aus der Zeit der rumänischen Schulen bei den Aromunen datiert eine ganze Reihe von Publikationen in aromunischer Sprache: Natürlich gibt es vor allem Schulbücher, daneben aber auch belletristische Werke sowie mehrere Zeitungen und Zeitschriften, die allerdings teilweise nur kurzfristig existierten. Allen diesen Werken ist eines gemeinsam: ihre Ausrichtung auf Rumänien, wo sie auch entstanden waren. Dies zeigt sich deutlich in der Orthographie, die sich am Dakorumänischen orientierte, ja in einzelnen Werken wird *expressis verbis* gesagt, daß man eine gemeinsame Schriftsprache für das Dakorumänische und Aromunische schaffen will.

Die aktuellen Bemühungen der exilaromunischen Vereinigungen zur Propagierung einer aromunischen Schriftsprache stoßen jedoch auf mehrere Probleme: Zunächst stellt sich die Frage, welches Alphabet verwendet werden soll. Die Herausgeber dieser Publikationen haben sich allesamt für das lateinische entschieden, womit sie sowohl der Tradition der bisherigen Versuche treu bleiben als auch den immer wieder besonders betonten romanischen Charakter des Aromunischen hervorheben können. Damit aber stellt sich der Verbreitung dieser Schriften in Griechenland schon von vornherein ein großes Hindernis in den Weg, denn abgesehen von der Tatsache, daß zweifellos viele Aromunen lateinische Buchstaben gar nicht zu lesen vermögen, gilt das griechische Alphabet in Griechenland geradezu als sakrosankt und der Gebrauch einer anderen Schrift als der griechischen läßt bereits Zweifel an der Loyalität gegenüber dem Staat aufkommen.

Die Frage nach einer einheitlichen Orthographie des Aromunischen wurde auf den seit 1985 (in Mannheim und Freiburg) durchgeführten aromunischen Kongressen immer wieder heftig diskutiert.

7. Allgemeines kontaktlinguistisches Porträt

Wie in 5. dargelegt, ist davon auszugehen, daß die Aromunen heutzutage völlig zweisprachig (je nach Staatszugehörigkeit aromunisch—griechisch / albanisch / mazedonisch) sind, so daß es nicht selten ist, daß ein Aromune mitten im Gespräch, gegebenenfalls mitten im Satz einen Wechsel der Sprache vornimmt. Diese Form des Bilinguismus mit der jeweiligen Staatssprache hat nun u. a. als Konsequenz, daß das Aromunische sich gerade im Wortschatz, vor allem im Bereich der Bezeichnungen für technische Neuerungen, auseinanderentwickelt, so daß sich Divergenzen zwischen dem Aromunischen Griechenlands, Albaniens und des ehemaligen Jugoslawien ergeben. Im folgenden sollen nun einige ausgewählte Beispiele für den Einfluß des Griechischen auf das Aromunische vorgestellt werden. Der umgekehrte Prozeß (also die Beeinflussung der griechischen Dialekte durch das Aromunische) ist bislang nicht untersucht worden. Man darf aber wohl davon ausgehen, daß die jahrhundertelange Kontaktsituation auch zu Beeinflussungen des Griechischen (wie analog auch des Bulgarischen bzw. Mazedonischen) durch das Aromunische geführt hat, wenn diese auch aufgrund des unterschiedlichen Prestiges der Sprachen bestimmt geringer sind als umgekehrt. Nicht weiter ausgeführt werden hier die Erscheinungen, die als Merkmale des „Balkansprachbundes" bekanntgeworden sind, da es sich hier ja nicht um Besonderheiten des griechisch—aromunischen Sprachkontakts handelt, sondern eben um Phänomene, die sich in mehreren Balkansprachen finden.

7.1. Phonetik und Phonologie

Das phonologische System des Aromunischen kennt drei Phoneme, die aus dem Griechischen entlehnt sind: die beiden interdentalen Laute /δ/ und /θ/ und das velare /γ/, so daß die Frikativreihe im Aromunischen vollständig ist und jedem Okklusivlaut ein frikativer entspricht: /d/–/δ/, /t/–/θ/, /g/–/γ/ (Minimalpaare bei Caragiu Marioţeanu 1968, 42—44). Diese Laute sind mit der Übernahme entsprechender Wörter aus dem Griechischen ins Aromunische gedrungen: *δáskal* 'Lehrer' (griech. δάσκαλος), *θimó* 'Wut' (griech. θυμός), *γíftu* 'Zigeuner, Schmied' (griech. γύφτος). Wie stark diese Phoneme aber bereits im Aromunischen verhaftet sind, zeigt die Tatsache, daß vereinzelt auch lateinische Erbwörter diese Laute aufweisen können, wie beispielsweise *θeámină* 'weiblich' (< lat. *femina*).

Die vom Griechischen wenig beeinflußten nördlichen Mundarten des Aromunischen im ehemaligen Jugoslawien (vor allem die Dörfer Gopeš und Malovište) kennen diese Laute nicht; an ihrer Stelle finden sich in den aus dem Griechischen entlehnten Wörtern — sofern sie in diesen Mundarten überhaupt bekannt sind (cf. 7.3.) — /d/ oder /v/ für /δ/, /t/, /f/, /s/ für /θ/ und /g/ für /γ/ (Beispiele bei Saramandu 1984, 432).

Neben diesen direkten Entlehnungen griechischer Phoneme findet sich aber noch eine andere Besonderheit, die mit dem griechischen Einfluß erklärt werden kann: Das Aromunische hat *ts* und *dz* aus lat. *c, g* + *e, i* im Gegensatz zum Dakorumänischen, wo sich — wie etwa auch im Italienischen — č und ğ finden. Da ältere Belege des Aromunischen auch diese Formen aufweisen, liegt die Vermutung nahe, daß *ts* und *dz* Weiterentwicklungen aus früherem č und ğ unter griechischem Einfluß sind, da das Griechische diese Laute nicht kennt.

7.2. Morphosyntax

In der Verbalmorphosyntax fällt ein weitgehender Parallelismus zwischen dem Aromunischen und dem Griechischen auf: Dies betrifft etwa den Gebrauch des „historischen Perfekts" („Perfectu simplu": *kîntáį* 'ich sang / ich habe gesungen'), das es zwar im Dakorumänischen auch gibt, das dort aber heute ungebräuchlich ist, während es im Aromunischen — analog zum griechischen Aorist — sehr vital ist. Ebenfalls aus dem griechischen Adstrateinfluß zu erklären sein dürfte die Bildung des Plusquamperfekts im Aromunischen, die — wie im Griechischen — analytisch mit Hilfe der konjugierten Form des Verbs 'haben' geschieht (*aveámᵘ skrisắ* 'ich hatte geschrieben'), während die im älteren und regionalen Dakorumänischen neben der synthetischen Form existierenden analytischen Bildungen vom Typ *am fost scris* sind (Kramer 1981, 100—103).

Weitere Besonderheiten des Aromunischen, die aus dem Kontakt zum Griechischen zu erklären sein dürften (Kramer 1981, 97—99, 104 f), sind etwa der präpositionslose Gebrauch von Ortsangaben nach Verben der Bewegung und des Sichbefindens (*mi dúkᵘ Sắrúnắ* 'ich gehe / fahre nach Saloniki', *ésku Sắrúnắ* 'ich bin in Saloniki', analog zu πάω / εἶμαι Σαλονίκη), die Verwendung des bestimmten Artikels bei männlichen und weiblichen Vornamen sowie der Gebrauch von *áre* ohne ein weiteres Ortsadverb in der Bedeutung 'es gibt' (analog zu ἔχει): *áre o̜ámiń ̜ ţi...* 'es gibt Männer, die...'.

7.3. Wortschatz

Die stärkste Beeinflussung des Aromunischen durch das Griechische zeigt sich naturgemäß im Wortschatz. Der allgemein verbreitete Bilinguismus der Aromunen (cf. 5.) führt dazu, daß griechische Lexeme häufig unadaptiert übernommen werden, so daß man in der Regel von einem potentiellen Nebeneinander von griechischem und aromunischem Wortmaterial ausgehen muß, bei dem die momentane Sprechsituation darüber entscheidet, welcher Form man sich bedient.

In einer statistischen Auswertung der ersten Auflage des aromunischen Wörterbuches von Papahagi (1963) hat Caragiu Marioţeanu (1975, 256—264) 2534 Wörter griechischer Herkunft ermittelt (gegenüber 1628 lateinischen, 1620 türkischen, 577 slavischen, 350 albanischen und 300 italienischen Ursprungs). Schon diese Zahl, in der freilich auch eine kleine Zahl von Wörtern enthalten ist, die zu einer so frühen Zeit entlehnt wurden, daß sie auch in den anderen Varietäten des Rumänischen auftauchen, zeigt deutlich die große Bedeutung des griechischen Einflusses auf den aromunischen Wortschatz. Auch hier gibt es aber natürlich regionale Unterschiede, viele dieser Wörter sind bei der nördlichen Gruppe der Aromunen nicht bekannt (eine Liste von Wörtern, die in allen Unterdialekten vorkommen, gibt Saramandu 1984, 469; die ausführlichste Darstellung des griechischen Elements im Aromunischen ist die heute allerdings in manchem veraltete Arbeit von Geagea 1931—1932; cf. auch Capidan 1932, 155—169).

Der griechische Einfluß im Wortschatz macht sich aber natürlich nicht nur in den direkten Übernahmen bemerkbar: Es gibt auch Veränderungen des semantischen Gehalts von Wörtern unter griechischem Einfluß wie etwa *fudzí* (< lat. *fugere*), das die Bedeutung 'abreisen' (nach griech. φεύγω) bekommen hat. Auch gibt es „hybride" Wortbildungen: *kuţubeá* 'ein wenig trinken', zusammengesetzt aus griech. κουτσο- 'wenig' + arom. *beá* (< lat. *bibere* 'trinken'), *aɣrukáprắ* 'Wildziege' (< griech. ἀγριο- 'wild' + arom. *káprắ* 'Ziege').

8. Kritische Wertung der verwendeten Quellen und Literatur

Von den drei süddanubischen Varietäten des Rumänischen ist das Aromunische sicherlich die am besten erforschte (cf. Bibliografie macedo-română 1984, Carageani 1986). Der Sprachkontakt mit den anderen in diesem traditionell multilingualen Raum gesprochenen Sprachen (vor allem Griechisch, Albanisch, Mazedonisch und bis 1912 auch Türkisch) ist dabei durchaus berücksichtigt worden, allerdings muß man gewisse Einschränkungen machen: Die Untersuchungen hatten vor allem den Einfluß dieser Sprachen auf das Aromunische, nicht aber den des Aromunischen auf die anderen Sprachen zum Gegenstand. Auch ist eine deutliche Konzentration auf den Bereich des Wortschatzes festzustellen. Es fehlen neuere Arbeiten zur Soziolinguistik etwa in den Bereichen der Sprachverwendung sowie der Einstellung zur und des Wissens über die Sprache, die über die eher impressionistischen Eindrücke, die bei dialektologischen Untersuchungen für den Aromunischen Sprachatlas (Dahmen/Kramer 1985—1994; Kramer 1987) gewonnen wurden, hinausgingen. Zu bedauern ist vor allem, daß die, die zu solchen Arbeiten am besten geeignet wären, d. h. griechische oder aromunische Sprachwissenschaftler, offensichtlich fehlen, bzw. nicht in der Lage sind, ohne ideologische Scheuklappen eine solche Aufgabe anzugehen.

9. Bibliographie (in Auswahl)

Angelopoulos, Athanasios (1979): „Population Distribution of Greece Today According to Language, National Consciousness and Religion". In: *Balkan Studies 20*, 123−132.

Barba, Vasile (1987): „Über die Aromunen, ihre Sprache und Kultur". In: *Die Aromunen. Sprache − Geschichte − Geographie*, Rohr, R. (Ed.), Hamburg, 1−14.

Bibliografie macedo-română [Mazedorumänische Bibliographie] (1984), Freiburg.

Bojadschi, Michael G. (1813): *Romanische, oder Macedonowlachische Sprachlehre*, Wien.

Capidan, Theodor (1932): *Aromânii. Dialectul aromân. Studiu lingvistic* [Die Aromunen. Der aromunische Dialekt. Linguistische Studie], Bukarest.

Carageani, Gheorghe (1986): „Intorno alla pubblicazione della 'Bibliografia macedoromena'" [Zur Publikation der „Mazedorumänischen Bibliographie"]. In: *Balkan-Archiv, Neue Folge 11*, 245−278.

Caragiu Marioțeanu, Matilda (1968): *Fonomorfologie aromână* [Aromunische Phono-Morphologie], Bukarest.

Caragiu Marioțeanu, Matilda (1975): *Compendiu de dialectologie română* [Handbuch der rumänischen Dialektologie], Bukarest.

Dahmen, Wolfgang (1991): „Der Stand der Kodifizierung des Aromunischen". In: *Zum Stand der Kodifizierung romanischer Kleinsprachen*, Dahmen, W., et al. (Eds.), Tübingen, 29−39.

Dahmen, Wolfgang/Kramer, Johannes (1985−94): *Aromunischer Sprachatlas*, 2 Bde., Hamburg.

Geagea, Christea (1931−1932): „Elementul grec în dialectul aromân" [Das griechische Element im aromunischen Dialekt]. In: *Codrul Cosminului 7*, 205−432 (Separatdruck: Cernăuți 1932).

Keramopoullos, Antonios (1939): *Ti einai oi Koutsoblachoi?* [Wer sind die Kutzowlachen?], Athen.

Koltsidas, Antones (1976): *Oi Koutsoblachoi* [Die Kutzowlachen], Bd. 1, Thessaloniki.

Kramer, Johannes (1980): „De tweetaligheid der Aromoenen in Griekenland" [Die Zweisprachigkeit der Aromunen in Griechenland]. In: *Sprachkontakt und Sprachkonflikt*, Nelde, P. H. (Ed.), Wiesbaden, 255−261.

Kramer, Johannes (1981): „Griechische Konstruktionen im Aromunischen". In: *Balkan-Archiv, Neue Folge 6*, 95−105.

Kramer, Johannes (1987): „Soziolinguistische Eindrücke bei Sprachaufnahmen bei den Aromunen Griechenlands und Gedanken zu einer aromunischen Schriftsprache". In: *Die Aromunen. Sprache − Geschichte − Geographie*, Rohr, R. (Ed.), Hamburg, 132−144.

Kramer, Johannes (1989): „Rumänisch: Areallinguistik II. Aromunisch". In: *Lexikon der Romanistischen Linguistik (LRL)*, Holtus, G./Metzeltin, M./Schmitt, Ch. (Eds.), Bd. III, Tübingen, 423−435.

Kramer, Johannes (1992): „La romanità balcanica. Introduzione" [Die balkanische Romanität. Einführung]. In: *Actes du XVIIIe Congrès International de Linguistique et de Philologie Romanes*, Kremer, D. (Ed.), Bd. I, Tübingen, 58−75.

Papahagi, Tache (1963, 1974): *Dicționarul dialectului aromân general și etimologic* [Allgemeines und etymologisches Wörterbuch des aromunischen Dialekts], Bukarest.

Papazeses, Demetrios Triantaphyllos (1976), *Blachoi (Koutsoblachoi)* [Wlachen (Kutzowlachen)], Athen.

Peyfuss, Max Demeter (1974): *Die aromunische Frage. Ihre Entwicklung von den Ursprüngen bis zum Frieden von Bukarest (1913) und die Haltung Österreich-Ungarns*, Wien/Köln/Graz.

Récatas, B. (1934): *L'état actuel du bilinguisme chez les Macédo-Roumains du Pinde et le rôle de la femme dans le langage*, Paris.

Rolshoven, Jürgen (1989): *Eine selbstlernende generativ-phonologische Grammatik*, Tübingen.

Saramandu, Nicolae (1984): „Aromâna" [Das Aromunische]. In: *Tratat de dialectologie românească*, Rusu, V. (Ed.), Craiova, 423−476.

Schlösser, Rainer (1985): *Historische Lautlehre des Aromunischen von Metsovon*, Hamburg.

Weigand, Gustav (1894−1895): *Die Aromunen. Ethnographisch-philologisch-historische Untersuchungen über das Volk der sogenannten Makedo-Romanen oder Zinzaren*, 2 Bde, Leipzig.

Weigand, Gustav (1897): „Die nationale Bewegung unter den Aromunen (Rumänen der Türkei)". In: *Globus 71*, 53−55.

Wild, Beate (1981): „Dialektologische Forschungen bei den Aromunen im Frühjahr 1980 und im Sommer 1980: Reisebericht und Angaben zu den besuchten Orten I: Frühjahr 1980". In: *Balkan-Archiv, Neue Folge 6*, 7−17.

Wolfgang Dahmen, Jena (Deutschland)

184. Greek—Albanian

1. Geography and demography
2. History
3. Politics, economy, general cultural and religious situation
4. Statistics and ethnoprofile
5. Sociolinguistic situation
6. Language political situation
7. General contactlinguistic portrait
8. Critical evaluation of the sources
9. Bibliography (selected)

1. Geography and demography

Albanian speakers are presently enclaved in various geographical regions mainly in south-central Greece and the nearby islands of the Aegean. The appearance of the Albanian-speaking element on what is now Greek national territory is the result of several migratory waves that took place in the late Byzantine period, mostly induced and encouraged by the emperors of that period. Although the 14th and the 15th centuries are generally accepted as the most likely time that the migrations happened, scholars of various historical persuasions have frequently pushed the migratory movements back in time (Tsitsipis 1981, 1—6).

Albanian speakers occupied territories appropriate for agriculture, which traditionally constituted the one major economic occupation of the immigrants, the other being military activities mostly serving the needs of the heavily decentralized, feudally structured empire.

Today, and particularly after the decline of state communism in Albania, new waves of migrants from this country have made their appearance in Greece, a complex social phenomenon that remains to be settled.

2. History

The major historical trajectory in terms of contact linguistics suggests that Greek and Albanian speech communities have coexisted peacefully for most of the time. Shared Christian faith has been certainly a powerful contributing factor. The basic agricultural character of the political-economic profile of the Albanian-speaking element kept Albanians on Greek territory mostly confined in peasant areas and on the periphery of the major urban centers during most of medieval and modern history. Such a socio-geographic situation strongly contributed to the long relative isolation of Albanians and the consequent survival of their language. As part of the Balkan resistance to Ottoman rule, Albanians participated in the Greek national rising against the Ottoman yoke in the crucial years around 1821.

In the formative years of Greek nationalism in the 19th century, Albanian was to follow the route of minoritization along with other languages spoken in Greece, although not necessarily through formal means of ideological compartmentalization.

3. Politics, economy, general cultural and religious situation

Economically, Albanians in Greece have been primarily agricultural populations and craftsmen. This confinement to the periphery of modernizing technological and commercial activities — which also characterizes other peasant Greek-speaking populations — has been decisive for linguistic isolation of Albanians as well. It has also somehow influenced the political position and ideological choices of the Albanian-speaking element. In earlier decades a considerable portion of the peasant populations in Greece had developed a royalist political ideology, a condition that promoted the view among non-Albanian speakers that Albanians were conservative. However, this ethnostereotypically constructed political feature did not prevent the rather smooth mutual adjustment of Greek- and Albanian-speaking segments of the population. The common Balkan cultural background and the same religious faith, as well as the common religious ceremonial activities within the Orthodox Christian denomination, promoted this process.

In recent and current socio-political and economic processes at the state and national level, Albanians who trace their ancestry back to the early immigrants (cf. 1.) are not obviously differentiated from other Greek citizens regardless of local ideological and ethnic considerations.

4. Statistics and ethnoprofile

The variety of Albanian spoken in Greece is known as *Arvanítika* and the people are called by Greek monolinguals and call themselves *Arvanítes* (sing. masc. *Arvanítis*, sing. fem. *Arvanítisa*). The indefinite grammatical form of the language name is *Arvanít* and is morphologically and lexically kept apart from the name *Alvanónjet* "The Albanians" and *Alvanjiká* "the Albanian language", both Greek terms used by Arvanítes. The Albanian language name *shqip* is little known and unpredictably used by the Albanians in Greece.

Arvanítika belongs to the Tosk, i. e. to the southern major dialect of the Albanian language, the northern being the Geg dialect. In fact, the very dialect classification of Arvanítika attests to the regions of origin of the Arvanítika populations of Greece, that is, the southern parts of what is now Albania. (For dialectological and similar issues see Gjinari 1966, 31–50; 1970; Hamp 1972; 1978, 155–164).

Although Arvanítika ethnic identity is locally recognized, no link with Albanians from Albania is generally felt to exist. True, due to information from scholars and intellectuals as well as to the massive penetration of illegal Albanian immigrants into Greece over the last several years, Arvanítes are discovering their historical and ethnolinguistic relation to the Albanian ethnic core, vaguely so however. As Greek citizens Arvanítes fought as patriotic elements in some of the Greek nation's independence wars (for instance, World War II against the Italian and the Nazi invasion of the country, 1940 to 1944).

Statistics of various censuses concerning Arvanítes and their language are not particularly reliable as to the criteria used for the counting of languages and ethnic groups. Thus, according to whatever statistical information is available, Arvanítes have been found to number around 22,000 (see Tsitsipis 1981, 77–82 for a critical presentation of earlier censuses and statistics).

Arvanítika communities are mostly clustered around the main urban centers of south and east central Greece and due to various internal migrations and mixed ethnic marriages Arvanítika people are scattered all over the national territory. They are engaged in agriculture, wage labor, and other urban, semi-urban, and rural activities. Prominent figures in various literary, political, and scientific fields have been of Arvanítika origin.

5. Sociolinguistic situation

Arvanítika speakers are bilingual; they speak Modern Greek and Arvanítika. It is almost a myth that one can find a monolingual Arvanítika speaker today. We are dealing, however, not with a coordinate or stable bilingualism in which the two languages are functionally specialized. No doubt there has been and still is some functional specialization of the two codes: Greek serves communicative needs having to do with contacts with the official state services, bureaucracy, and administration, whereas Arvanítika is used exclusively in the social context of the local communities.

An earlier state of rather stable bilingualism has given way gradually and through complex processes to a situation in which Arvanítika, fully subordinated to Greek sociolinguistically, is facing attrition and death. Various factors such as the official linguistic ideology of the Greek state, modernization through extension and complication of economic networks, schooling, and modern transportation routes have caused Arvanítika to become a threatened language. Although this is a case of gradual shift and replacement, the process was accelerated during the 1950's due to the nation's rapid modernization after the end of World War II and the civil war (1949). The direction the language has taken towards attrition is obvious synchronically in the internal profiles of the communities. Thus crucial differences in linguistic competence as well as actual language use of Arvanítika separate older speakers from younger ones. The former are *fluent speakers*, and the latter I call *terminal speakers*. The older and middle-aged people are in the majority fluent speakers of Arvanítika, they use the language in their domestic communication and control grammatical and lexical resources of the language well, even though their communication is filled with conversational switches to Greek. Grammatical as well as lexical competence of terminal speakers has, in comparison to that of fluent speakers, considerably diminished, and the social context in which they use Arvanítika is far more restricted. They use Arvanítika only in an interlocutor-bound context, that is, when they communicate with members of the grandparental generation, when they want to tease or test outsiders, or when they intend to offer tokens of short narrative genres like anecdotes which filter a particular ideological discourse directed against fluent-speaker linguistic habits (Tsitsipis 1989, 117–137; 1991, 153–173).

The idea that Arvanítika is a deficient code, deficiently structured and lexically impoverished, stems from linguistic stereotypes connected with the dominance of the Greek culture and language. This idea has penetrated also the Arvanítes' view of themselves, leading to a process of *self-deprecation*. Older and middle-aged speakers frequently express ambivalent attitudes towards their language switching from praising the unifying function of the Arvanít language (i. e. Arvanítika is shared by members of the community) to demoting it to the status of an inadequate code. The Greek monolingual speech community is captive to the negative stereotypes concerning Arvanítika people and their language (*ethnic slurs* or *blasons populaires*, Dundes 1975, 93−103). The Arvanítes themselves associate older times with a certain moral order and the use of the local language, but Greek is taken to be the medium that triggers an opening to the modern world with opportunities in material and symbolic capital (Tsitsipis 1988, 61−86 for a discussion of narratives revealing these ideological points).

6. Language political situation

Arvanítika is not a written language and has never been recognized as part of sociolinguistic variation. The school system, which in the past promoted the romantic ideal of one language − one nation − one culture, has discouraged the use of Arvanítika at school or on the playground, as older informants claim. This official attitude seems to be indicated also by the unsystematic way population censuses have treated non-Greek language and ethnic groups (cf. the discussion of statistics by the National Statistic Service of Greece in section 4. above). Nevertheless, due to the peaceful integration of the Arvanítika element into society, no social cleavages or upheavals with regard to this issue have ever been reported. On the other hand, the negative attitude of the state towards minority languages has certainly contributed to the fact that there has not been any movement for a revival of Arvanítika or its becoming a literary means of communication.

7. General contactlinguistic portrait

Greek as the sociolinguistically dominant language has left its mark on Arvanítika more pervasively than vice versa. Only a few lexical borrowings from Albanian into Greek are reported whereas Arvanítika has absorbed many lexical borrowings from Greek. Lexical loans are generally adapted to Albanian morphophonology. This regular process of the adaptation of foreign linguistic material to native morphophonology holds primarily true for fluent speakers of Arvanítika, whereas terminal speakers (Tsitsipis 1984, 122−131) exhibit symptoms of an almost unpredictable morphological variation (i. e. agrammatisms in the sense of Sasse 1990). Thus the plural form of "men" *njérez* (definite form: *njéreztë*) would be expressed by the terminal speaker as *njerézite, njérezute, njérite*, etc. On the other hand agrammatisms are frequent in the speech of terminal speakers not only in Greek borrowings but also in the way they use indigenous Albanian means of expression. It is prominent namely in those parts of the Arvanítika language system which do not have a support in similar structuring of the Greek language. Thus the system of concordial particles that connect members of the Noun Phrase of a syntagm which does not have an exact structural equivalent in Greek has been skewed markedly in terminal Arvanítika speech. In phonology also sounds that either do not exist in Greek or do not function as members of regular phonemic pairs are produced irregularly and unsystematically by terminal speakers, or not at all. For instance, the distinction between /e/ and /ë/ − the second being the shwa − is not regularly observed by terminal speakers in naturally produced speech. Thus, an expression such as *dúa të vesh edhé të vësh potíri në trapézi* "I want you to go and put the glass on the table" would be rendered by terminal speakers without the distinction of /e/ vs. /ë/ which is phonemic in Arvanítika. Such facts constitute the most dramatic symptoms of Arvanítika language death. Terminal speech deviates in these and similar instances from the fluent-speaker norm immensely.

Changes that set apart terminal from fluent speech are of two kinds, *discontinuous changes* and *complete changes*. Discontinuous changes concern phenomena such as morphological leveling, loss of suppletive variants, and neutralization of phonemic oppositions (for similar phenomena in East Sutherland Gaelic language death cf. Dorian 1981). In the terminal morphosyntactic system, for example, a frequent confusion between the future marker *do* and the subjunctive subordinator *të* shows up. Thus, the expression "I want you to write" *dúa të shkrúash* is often rendered as *dúa do shkrúash*. This is due to the gradual disappearance of the social contexts in which the class of terminal speakers would/could use complex syntactic constructions.

There are, on the other hand, changes that concern the communities as sociolinguistic and linguistic wholes. These are the *completed changes* including, for instance, the loss of the Albanian admirative mood and the loss of the productivity of the optative which can be attributed to Greek influence.

But the intralinguistic portrait includes more than just structural changes, losses, and adjustments. Broader socio-cultural phenomena are complexly reflected in the local communities and affect also the ways the languages are used pragmatically. Thus fluent speakers use what I would call an *integrative code-switching*, that is, a meaningful alternation of Greek and Arvanítika, in their daily interactions, as when they offer a word-by-word translation from one language to the other in order to foreground a message or to evaluate the central point of a narrative (Tsitsipis 1988, 61–86).

The use of Greek and Arvanítika by terminal speakers is also far from mechanical. Through anecdote-telling and spontaneous performance of tokens of other short genres they become pragmatically creative. In their discourse younger speakers embed social-ideological commentaries concerning the Arvanítika language and the fluent speakers as a social group. Thus for instance a young terminal speaker may end an anecdote by asking a metalinguistic question with a slightly ironic undertone: "How do you call x in katharévusa Arvanítika?" The ironic undertone is produced by the contrast between traditionality and the historically high status of katharévusa ("katharévusa" – as opposed to "dimotiki" – usually refers to a puristic code of Greek, cf. Art. 187) and the lower social status of Arvanítika in comparison to Greek.

8. Critical evaluation of the sources

Arvanítika has been occasionally the focus of scientific as well as popular discussions primarily in Greece. The Arvanítika philologist Furíkis (1932, 28–76) produced extremely accurate descriptions of the structure and dialectological status of the language and also provided information on folklore and customs. His works constitute respectable pieces of scholarly endeavor given the context of the time. Contributions by E. Hamp (1972, 1626–1692; 1978, 155–164) have brought the linguistic and dialectological study of Albanian in general and of Arvanítika in particular to the center of scholarly discourse touching on historical linguistics, structural-descriptive linguistics, and migration issues. A detailed monograph on sociolinguistic change among Arvanítika speakers of Greece has been written by Tsitsipis (1981). This work has embedded the study of Arvanítika in the research context of language obsolescence making the Arvanítika case comparable to other cases studied by linguists and ethnographers.

Within the Arvanítika communities themselves there is occasional interest in Arvanítika language and culture in contact with Greek, usually in the form of local festivals or popular conferences. The major ethnolinguistic and ideological point emerging from this concern is the tendency to search for the roots of Arvanítika in Greek antiquity which is the result of the long hegemonical process of embedding the communities into the mainstream of modern Greek society. This kind of ideological process has somehow neutralized potential conflicts along ethnic and linguistic lines. It remains, of course, to be seen how the Arvanítika element of Greece will respond to the recent waves of Albanian immigrants.

9. Bibliography (selected)

Dorian, Nancy C. (1981): *Language Death: The Life Cycle of a Scottish Gaelic Dialect*, Philadelphia.

Dundes, Alan (1975): "Folk Ideas as Units of Worldview". In: *Toward New Perspectives in Folklore*, Paredes, A./Bauman, R. (Eds.), Austin, 93–103.

Furikis, Petros A. (1932): "I en Attikí Ellinoalvanikí Diálektos" [The Greek-Albanian Dialect of Attica]. In: *Athiná 44*, 28–76.

Gjinari, Jorgji (1966): "Essai d'une Démarcation Dialectale de la Langue Albanaise". In: *Studia Albanica 2*, 31–50.

Gjinari, Jorgji (1970): *Dialektologjia Shqiptare*, Prishtinë.

Hamp, Eric P. (1972): "Albanian". In: *Current Trends in Linguistics 9*, Sebeok, T. (Ed.), Paris, 1626–1692.

Hamp, Eric P. (1978): "Problems of Multilingualism in Small Linguistic Communities". In: *International Dimensions of Bilingual Education*,

Alatis, J. E. (Ed.), *Georgetown Round Table on Languages and Linguistics*, Washington, D. C., 155−164.

Sasse, Hans-Jürgen (1990): *Theory of Language Death and Language Decay and Contact-induced Change: Similarities and Differences*. Arbeitspapier No. 2 (Neue Folge), Institut für Sprachwissenschaft, Universität zu Köln, Köln.

Tsitsipis, Lukas D. (1981): *Language Change and Language Death in Albanian Speech Communities in Greece: A Sociolinguistic Study* (Ph. D. Dissertation), Department of Anthropology, University of Wisconsin.

Tsitsipis, Lukas D. (1984): "Functional Restriction and Grammatical Reduction in Albanian Language in Greece". In: *Zeitschrift für Balkanologie* 20, 122−131.

Tsitsipis, Lukas D. (1988): "Language Shift and Narrative Performance: On the Structure and Function of Arvanítika Narratives". In: *Language in Society 17*, 61−86.

Tsitsipis, Lukas D. (1989): "Skewed Performance and Full Performance in Language Obsolescence: The Case of an Albanian Variety". In: *Investigating Obsolescence: Studies in Language Contraction and Death*, Cambridge (UK), 117−137.

Tsitsipis, Lukas D. (1991): "Terminal-fluent Speaker Interaction and the Contextualization of Deviant Speech". In: *Journal of Pragmatics 15*, 153−173.

Lukas D. Tsitsipis, Thessaloniki (Greece)

185. Grec−macédonien

1. Géographie et démographie
2. Histoire territoriale et formation de l'Etat
3. Situations politique, économique, culturelle et religieuse en général
4. Statistiques et langues en contact
5. Situation sociolinguistique
6. Situation politique des langues en contact
7. Portrait général des contacts linguistiques
8. Evaluation critique de la bibliographie
9. Bibliographie (sélective)

1. Géographie et démographie

1.1. La Macédoine se définit comme une entité géographique, limitée, au nord, par les chaînes du Char, du Rila et des Rhodopes, par la rivière le Nestos (slave Mesta) à l'est, la mer Egée, l'Olympe et la chaîne du Pindhos au sud, et les lacs d'Ohrid et de Prespa à l'ouest. En 1913, le Traité de Bucarest divisa la Macédoine en trois parties: la Macédoine serbe (yougoslave), à présent la République ex-yougoslave de Macédoine, appelée aussi *Macédoine* (de la rivière) *du Vardar* (grec Axios); la Macédoine bulgare ou *Macédoine* (de la chaîne) *du Pirin*; la Macédoine grecque ou *Macédoine de l'Egée*.

1.2. La Macédoine grecque, qui couvre une surface de 34.356 km² au nord du pays, est une région montagneuse, traversée de rivières, dont les avals ont créé de vastes plaines qui, par leur humidité, font de la Macédoine l'une des régions les plus fertiles de la Grèce. Celle-ci pourvoit le marché grec de légumes et de fruits; la culture de tabac apporte des revenus considérables. Le port de Salonique (slave Solun), capitale de la Macédoine, avec ses industries et son arrière-pays bulgare et ex-yougoslave, est d'un intérêt économique et stratégique énorme.

1.3. Du point de vue ethnique, la Macédoine grecque est à présent une région relativement homogène, habitée par une majorité de Grecs et des minorités slave, valaque (aroumaine), albanaise et autres, ne constituant que quelques pourcentages de la population totale. La grande majorité des Grecs n'est pas autochtone: la plupart sont les descendants d'immigrés grecs d'Anatolie, qui se sont établis massivement en Macédoine dans les années vingt. La plupart des Slaves de la Macédoine grecque, et plus particulièrement de l'ouest de l'Axios, se disent *Macédoniens* (*makedonci*) ou *autochtones* (*dopii*). Ils sont également considérés comme *macédoniens* dans la République de Macédoine. En Bulgarie, par contre, les Slaves macédoniens sont considérés comme Bulgares. En Macédoine grecque et surtout à l'est de l'Axios, les Macédoniens âgés appellent leur langue *vulgarika* (bulgare), ce qui ne semble pas toujours impliquer une conscience nationale bulgare (Cowan 1990, 39). Quelques slavisants étrangers partagent le point de vue bulgare, quoique la plupart ait accepté l'idée d'un peuple macédonien particulier. Les Grecs utilisent les termes *Grecs slavophones* ou *bulgarophones* ou *bilingues*, indiquant ainsi qu'il s'agit là d'une minorité à conscience nationale grecque mais d'expression slave. Certains historiens et linguistes serbes sont tentés de concevoir les Macédoniens comme des Serbes. Nous désignerons ici les membres de la minorité slave de la Macédoine grecque par le terme *Macédoniens*, qui est le plus répandu et généralement accepté à l'heure actuelle.

1.4. A la suite de l'urbanisation plus rapide des Grecs, la position démographique des Macédoniens dans les villages est devenue plus solide qu'elle n'était dans le passé (Drettas 1981, 154); → carte linguistique I.

2. Histoire territoriale et formation de l'Etat

2.1. Dans l'antiquité, la Macédoine était habitée par des tribus dominées par une classe entièrement hellénisée. A partir du 2ième siècle av. J.-C. jusqu'en 395, elle fit partie de l'Empire romain. Aux 4ième et 5ième siècles, la Macédoine, byzantine, fut dévastée par les Goths, les Huns et les Slaves. Ces derniers s'y établirent définitivement vers la fin du 6ième siècle. Comme en témoignent de nombreux toponymes, la Macédoine fut profondément slavisée (Zaimov 1967), bien que dans les villes et sur la côte, la population autochtone se soit maintenue. Salonique ne fut jamais envahie. Au cours des siècles suivants, l'élément grec s'imposa progressivement, en assimilant les immigrés slaves. Cependant la Macédoine demeura une zone de transition, avec une majorité slave au nord et grecque au sud. Son territoire fut continuellement disputé par Byzance et la Bulgarie. Sous le règne de Stefan Dušan (1331—1355), toute la Macédoine, à l'exception de Salonique, fut rattachée au royaume serbe. Vers la fin du 14ième siècle, la Macédoine tomba entre les mains des Ottomans. Salonique fut conquise en 1430.

2.2. Les Turcs (et des autochtones turquisés et islamisés) composèrent bientôt un tiers de la population, tout comme les Grecs et les Slaves. La fondation d'une communauté autonome de croyants orthodoxes de toutes nationalités, où la liturgie et l'enseignement étaient confiés à des grécophones, contribua à l'hellénisation de la population slave, urbaine surtout. La langue grecque se développa comme la *lingua franca* des commerçants balkaniques, slaves y compris. L'usage du grec, considéré comme une marque d'appartenance à la bourgeoisie aisée, exerçait un grand pouvoir de séduction. Au cours du 18ième siècle, la population macédonienne rurale, qui avait échappé à l'influence hellénisante, fut attirée par les emplois créés par l'économie manufacturière, et émigra massivement vers les villes, en (re)slavisant celles-ci. Cette «ruralisation des villes» inaugura une lutte acharnée entre Grecs et «grécomanes» d'une part et Slaves de l'autre pour le contrôle de l'église et de l'enseignement. Cette lutte aboutit en 1870 à la création, par la Porte, de l'Exarchat. Cette église *nationale* bulgare élargit progressivement son territoire: son statut prévoyait l'adhésion de nouveaux diocèses là où ce fut revendiqué par les deux tiers de la population. A la veille de la Première Guerre balkanique (1912), les «exarchistes» avaient, en Macédoine grecque, des représentants temporaires à Kastoria (slave Kostur), Florina (slave Lerin), Edhessa (slave Voden), Salonique, Kilkis (slave Kukuš), Serre (slave Sjar) et Drama (slave idem). Ils y financèrent plus de 200 écoles.

2.3. Après le Traité de Berlin (1878), la Bulgarie, devenue indépendante, la Grèce et la Serbie commencèrent une guerre de propagande irrédentiste, menée par l'église et l'enseignement et qui devait convaincre les Macédoniens à être bulgares, grecs ou serbes, respectivement. Dès le tournant du siècle, la guerre de propagande s'accompagna d'une guerre de bandes armées, qui terrorisaient la population. De plus en plus, une partie des Macédoniens se considérait un peuple slave particulier.

Les statistiques de Hilmi Paşa, considérées généralement comme les plus véridiques, donnent, pour l'année 1904, dans la province de Salonique (qui ne comprenait pas les régions au nord-ouest de ce qui serait la Macédoine grecque où la population slave est la plus dense), 207.317 Bulgares (exarchistes uniquement) sur 373.227 Grecs (patriarchistes non-grecs y compris) et 487.555 «musulmans» — ce qui donne une idée de la proportion slave dans l'ensemble de la population à cette époque (Lithoxoos 1990, 43—44).

2.4. Le Traité de Bucarest (1913), qui mit fin aux Guerres balkaniques, divisa la Macédoine entre la Bulgarie, la Grèce et la Serbie. Pendant la Première Guerre mondiale, la Bulgarie tenta en vain de conquérir toute la Macédoine. Le Traité de Neuilly (1919) restaura les anciennes frontières. Afin de décourager tout mouvement irrédentiste, le Traité imposa une «émigration volontaire» ou «échange de minorités» entre la Bulgarie et la Grèce. 60.000 à 80.000 Macédoniens quittèrent la Macédoine, plus en particulier la région orientale de Serre, Drama et Kilkis. Peu après, 600.000 Grecs environ, qui avaient été forcés de quitter la Turquie à la suite de l'échange des populations grecque et turque, prévu par le Traité de Lausanne (1923), furent implantés en Macédoine. En 1928, la population slave y est passée de presqu'un tiers de la population totale, avant les guerres, à quelques pourcentages. En outre, les immigrés reçurent (trop) des terres, abandonnées par les musulmans, ce qui aboutit à des tensions sociales entre les autochtones slaves et les nouveaux venus grecs. Ceux-ci dominent les structures sociales et politiques locales jusqu'à présent.

La Grèce appliquait, dans les territoires macédoniens acquis, une politique d'assimilation forcée. En 1924, sous la pression de la Société des Nations, le gouvernement grec reconnut officiellement, par le Protocole bulgaro-grec Kalfov-Politis (1924), l'existence d'une «minorité bulgare» et promit d'installer des écoles primaires slaves. En 1925, un *Abécédaire*, en caractères latins et basé sur le dialecte macédonien de Bitola et Florina, fut imprimé. Mais à la suite de protestations serbes contre la reconnaissance d'une minorité *bulgare*, et de protestations bulgares contre l'enseignement d'une autre langue que le bulgare standard, la Grèce abandonna avec soulagement le projet (Kofos 1964, 49). En 1913 déjà, les écoles slaves furent supprimées. Dans les églises, les services religieux ne se faisaient qu'en grec; les inscriptions slaves furent enlevées. En 1926, les noms géographiques slaves furent interdits et remplacés par des noms grecs. Ceux qui parlaient le macédonien en public ou même chez eux, étaient condamnés à des peines humiliantes et parfois même à l'emprisonnement ou l'exil. Ces mesures furent appliquées avec plus de rigueur encore sous la dictature de Metaxas (1936–1939). Les seuls à défendre les intérêts nationaux des Macédoniens étaient les communistes qui s'engagèrent, entre 1924 et 1935, pour une Macédoine autonome dans une fédération balkanique. En témoigne leur journal *Rizospastis* (le «Radical»), qui au début des années trente publiait des articles en macédonien en caractères grecs. L'*Organisation Révolutionnaire Interne Macédonienne* (unie) aspira à l'union des «trois Macédoines». A Florina, elle publia son journal *Zemjodelsko zname* (Drapeau de l'agriculteur) en macédonien.

2.5. Pendant la 2ième Guerre mondiale, la Macédoine grecque fut occupée par l'Axe et son allié bulgare. Après la fondation, en 1943, du *Front Slavo-Macédonien de Libération Nationale* (SNOF), qui faisait partie de l'*Armée Populaire de Libération Nationale* (ELAS) des communistes et anti-fascistes grecs, les Macédoniens participèrent en grand nombre à la résistance. Dans les territoires contrôlés par le SNOF, les autorités ouvrirent des écoles macédoniennes et firent imprimer des manuels scolaires en macédonien; une dizaine de journaux macédoniens sortirent à Kastoria, Moglena (slave Meglen) et Florina; le macédonien fut reconnu comme langue officielle, à côté du grec (Popovski 1981, 211–218).

2.6. Après l'accord de Varkiza (février 1945), qui restaura la situation d'avant-guerre, le gouvernement grec supprima les droits nationaux que les Macédoniens avaient acquis. Suspectés d'avoir aspiré à la création d'une Macédoine autonome, ils furent considérés comme des traîtres. Pendant la guerre civile (1946–1949), les Macédoniens réussirent à ouvrir 180 écoles et à éditer leurs journaux, mais après la défaite des communistes en 1949, la situation d'avant-guerre fut rétablie. Les Macédoniens étaient persécutés et terrorisés: 35.000 personnes environ se virent obligées d'émigrer (Kofos 1964, 186). Un décret de 1953 interdit les patronymes macédoniens; les fonctionnaires d'Etat d'origine macédonienne furent licenciés. La situation empira encore sous la dictature nationaliste des colonels (1967–1974). Par après, le régime policier se relâcha, surtout sous le gouvernement socialiste de Papandhreou (1981–1989), et la situation politique et culturelle de la minorité macédonienne s'améliora un peu.

3. Situations politique, économique, culturelle et religieuse en général

3.1. Les Macédoniens de Grèce, n'étant pas reconnus comme minorité, ne possèdent pas de droits nationaux. Ils n'ont aucun représentant au parlement de Grèce, ni dans aucune institution ou organisation politique. Les fonctions-clés dans l'administration locale sont occupées par des Grecs. Il n'existe aucune institution culturelle macédonienne, l'expression de l'identité nationale macédonienne étant interdite. Il n'existe qu'une culture populaire, folklorique plutôt, semi-clandestine. La pratique des coutumes ancestrales non-orales est tolérée, mais la police empêche l'interprétation de chansons macédoniennes, la commémoration des événements historiques, etc. (Exceptionnellement, un festival de chansons macédoniennes eut lieu à Edhessa en 1992.). Ceux qui s'opposent à cette politique (les membres du Comité Central de l'Organisation pour des Droits Humains Macédoniens et le Mouvement des Droits Humains et Nationaux des Macédoniens de la Macédoine grecque, qui se sont plaints au Centre pour les Droits Humains de l'ONU à Genève et au Conseil de l'Europe) ont eu de sérieux ennuis tout comme les rédacteurs du journal *Ta Moglena*, édité à Edhessa et rédigé entièrement en grec, qui défendent les intérêts minoritaires des Macédoniens.

4. Statistiques et langues en contact

4.1. Le dernier recensement officiel, qui nous fournit des chiffres à propos de la population « slavophone » en Grèce, date de 1951. Elle fait mention de 41.017 Macédoniens (chiffres officiels antérieurs: 81.984 en 1928, 84.751 en 1940.). Dans des rapports confidentiels de 1927, les autorités grecques supposaient qu'il y avait environ 200.000 « bulgarophones », dont 80.000 à 90.000 « sans conscience nationale grecque » (Mavrogordatos 1983, 247). Lithoxoos (1992, 61) estime que le nombre réel des Macédoniens est deux ou trois fois et demi plus élevé que celui donné par les recensements officiels. Le nombre de 200.000 que donnent les historiens à Skopje (Popovski 1981, 193), semble être exagéré. Une estimation de 100.000 à 150.000 paraît acceptable, bien que beaucoup dépende des critères qu'on applique (origine, maîtrise de la langue, conscience nationale). Quoi qu'il en soit, les Macédoniens ne forment qu'une petite minorité par rapport au million de Grecs environ qui habitent la Macédoine.

4.2. La population macédonienne se concentre dans le nord-ouest de la Macédoine grecque, dans les villages, souvent homogènes, de la région de Kastoria, Florina et Edhessa. A Salonique, il y a un nombre considérable d'immigrés d'origine rurale.

4.3. Les Macédoniens appellent leur langue *makedonski* ou *ta dopika* (la ‹langue› autochtone), rarement *bulgarski* (qui était plus usuel avant la guerre). En Bulgarie, le macédonien est considéré comme un dialecte bulgare, ce qui est, du point de vue linguistique, tout à fait raisonnable. Avant la guerre, les Grecs parlaient de la langue *bulgare*, mais ils utilisaient parfois, dans des documents administratifs, le terme de *makedhonikon glossikon idhioma* (idiome linguistique macédonien). A l'heure actuelle, les Grecs n'ont aucun nom approprié pour désigner la langue de la minorité slave: ils parlent de *dialecte slavophone* ou de *slave* tout court. La langue officielle de la République de Macédoine est appelée par les Grecs *le patois de Skopje*, cela pour éviter le mot *macédonien*, mais ce terme n'est jamais utilisé en rapport avec le macédonien en Grèce, étant donné qu'il évoque un lien de parenté entre les deux populations.

5. Situation sociolinguistique

5.1. Pendant la période ottomane, le slave était la langue usuelle en Macédoine (à l'exception des villes et des régions méridionales). Il était parlé par la population macédonienne et compris par les autres groupes ethniques, la langue officielle étant le turc ottoman. Le grec, que les slaves urbanisés connaissaient, était la « katharévoussa », la langue puriste ou savante qu'ils avaient apprise à l'école s'ils n'avaient pas fréquenté les écoles slaves. Les Grecs parlaient aussi la « dhimotiki », la langue commune ou langue parlée, ou un de ses dialectes, qui était leur langue maternelle (→ art. 181). Cette particularité permettait de distinguer nettement les Macédoniens hellénisés des Grecs ethniques (Weigand 1924, 76). Après le rattachement de la Macédoine méridionale à la Grèce et l'interdiction de l'enseignement slave, le grec « katharévoussa » devint la langue officielle et la seule à être enseignée. Après les changements démographiques des années vingt, le macédonien devint une langue minoritaire ou langue parlée en famille, la langue dominante étant le dialecte pontique des immigrés qui ignoraient le macédonien. A l'heure actuelle, la génération des Macédoniens qui ne connaissent que leur langue maternelle, s'est éteinte. Les mères et grand-mères, qui étant illettrées et n'ayant reçu aucune formation en grec, autrefois, conservaient et transmettaient le mieux les traditions culturelles et linguistiques, à présent exigent que leurs enfants parlent le grec pour leur éviter des difficultés avec les autorités, bien que la présence d'une grand-mère semble toujours favoriser l'usage du macédonien (Drettas 1981, 154). Un autre facteur correspond aux mariages mixtes (homme grec/femme macédonienne), plus fréquents depuis les années soixante-dix: le macédonien cède toujours devant le grec qui s'impose comme «langue maternelle». Le facteur le plus important est l'influence de l'enseignement très normatif, du service militaire et des medias. Néanmoins, ces dernières années, on a pu constater chez les jeunes le réveil d'une conscience macédonienne, phénomène qui s'exprime par des protestations contre les traitements réservés aux Macédoniens et par un usage plus audace du macédonien en public. Ce phénomène s'explique par la libéralisation politique après 1981 et l'influence des idées européennes sur les droits des minorités.

6. Situation politique des langues en contact

En Grèce, la seule langue officielle, celle de l'administration, de la justice, etc. est le grec. Il n'y a point d'enseignement en macédonien. Les enfants qui parlent le macédonien à l'école pendant la récréation, sont punis. Il y a en Macédoine relativement plus de crèches qu'ailleurs en Grèce: les autorités veulent que les enfants macédoniens apprennent le grec le plus tôt possible. Jusqu'en 1986, les Macédoniens (et Grecs) avaient la possibilité de faire leurs études à l'Université de Skopje; depuis, Athènes ne reconnaît plus les diplômes parce que la langue de l'enseignement qui y est donné, ne serait pas reconnue par la communauté internationale. Il n'existe aucune publication en macédonien. En principe, les journaux, revues et livres, publiés dans la République de Macédoine, sont confisqués à la frontière par la douane grecque bien qu'il ne soit pas interdit d'en posséder. L'importation et la vente, à échelle commerciale, ne sont pas tolérées. Les émissions de radio et de télévision à Skopje sont pour les Macédoniens grecs la seule possibilité de contact passif, avec le macédonien comme langue culturelle ou littéraire. Malgré les mesures de répression prises par les autorités, il semble y avoir, dans la vie quotidienne, une certaine tolérance, aussi de la part du clergé (Drettas 1981, 148).

7. Portrait général des contacts linguistiques

7.1. Tous les Macédoniens sont bilingues, mais les personnes âgées ou moins instruites parlent le grec avec un accent: les interdentales spirantes *th* et *dh* sont prononcées comme *t* et *d* et la gutturale spirante vélaire *g* comme une occlusive vélaire (Drettas 1981, 151). Pour les jeunes qui ont joui d'une éducation grecque, la langue de leurs grands-parents est devenue une langue secondaire, étrangère, qu'ils comprennent à peine et qu'ils parlent avec un accent grec, prononçant les chuintantes macédoniennes *č*, *š*, *ž* comme *ts*, *s* et *z*.

7.2. La coexistence du grec et du slave en Macédoine, pendant de longs siècles, s'est accompagnée d'interférences plus radicales qui ont abouti à un nombre de traits communs en phonétique, morphosyntaxe et au lexique. La grande majorité de ces correspondances appartiennent aux «balkanismes»; on les retrouve dans toutes les langues balkaniques. Néanmoins, il y a aussi des particularités propres aux seuls dialectes macédoniens et grecs de la Macédoine grecque (et aux dialectes albanais et aroumains parlés dans la région qui fait partie, dans le cadre de l'union linguistique balkanique, d'une zone de contacts linguistiques très intenses).

7.3. Il s'agit d'abord, sur le plan phonétique, de la réduction des voyelles atones *e* et *o*, qui deviennent *i* et *u* (comme en bulgare) ou disparaissent complètement − phénomène typique des dialectes grecs septentrionaux et des dialectes macédoniens du sud-est. Il est probable que la palatalisation des consonnes *g*, *k*, *l* et *n*, suivies de voyelles antérieures, et la prononciation de la liquide *l*, suivie de voyelles postérieures, comme *l* vélaire, s'expliquent, elles aussi, par le contact avec le slave.

7.4. Le plus frappant, sur le plan morphosyntaxique, est la formation du parfait, composé du verbe *avoir* et du participe passé aoriste neutre singulier en -*meno*: grec *echo grammeno*, macédonien *imam napišano* (j'ai écrit), la forme courante en grec étant *echo grapsi*. Ce qui est typique du grec et du slave de la Macédoine grecque est le maintien de l'opposition sémantico-fonctionnelle entre l'aoriste et le parfait, avec cependant une nette préférence pour l'aoriste. En macédonien, comme en grec, le conditionnel de l'irréel est formé par une particule préverbale et un verbe à l'imparfait: grec *tha egrafa*, macédonien *ke pišev* (j'aurais écrit). (Le bulgare préfère *štjah da piša*, dont le correspondant macédonien *kev da pišuvam* est désuet.)

7.5. Sur le plan lexical, le macédonien, comme toutes les langues des peuples orthodoxes, a emprunté au grec un grand nombre de termes religieux et liturgiques. En outre, le macédonien contemporain, tel qu'il est parlé en Macédoine grecque, a repris, entre autres choses, la terminologie judiciaire et administrative grecque. L'infiltration de ces termes grecs en macédonien est due au fait que, dans leurs contacts avec les représentants de l'Etat grec, les Macédoniens sont obligés de parler le grec, et que la terminologie macédonienne correspondante, usuelle dans la République de Macédoine, leur est inconnue. Les jeunes Macédoniens bilingues connaissent mieux le grec que le macédonien et ont recours au vocabulaire grec chaque fois que le mot macédonien leur échappe.

L'apport macédonien au vocabulaire grec est plus modeste: les emprunts se limitent à la vie rurale et agricole: grec *i stani* (la bergerie), macédonien *stan* (le logement); grec *i tsouska*, macédonien *čuška* (le poivron).

8. Evaluation critique de la bibliographie

8.1. Les publications grecques sur la minorité slave en Macédoine sont extrêmement rares et généralement tendancieuses et polémiques. Le plus souvent, l'existence des Macédoniens est niée ou tue, sauf dans la précieuse étude de Drettas (1981). Quelques études d'ethnographes amateurs locaux nous donnent également des informations utiles (Ioannou 1989; Koufis 1990). La langue macédonienne est considérée comme un dialecte oscillant entre le serbe et le bulgare ou, qui pis est, comme un charabia, et cela non seulement par l'homme de la rue, mais aussi par les intellectuels et même par certains scientifiques (Andriotis 1991). Pour les Grecs, le terme *macédonien* appartient au patrimoine historique et culturel grec et ne peut être appliqué à un peuple ou une langue slave. En outre, la reconnaissance de la minorité macédonienne et de sa langue pourrait favoriser, d'après les Grecs, l'irrédentisme de la République de Macédoine. Pour des raisons pareilles, les Grecs évitent de considérer la langue de leur minorité slave comme véritablement serbe ou bulgare.

8.2. Les Bulgares considèrent la population slave de la Macédoine grecque et sa langue comme bulgares. Bien que leurs arguments historiques et linguistiques ne manquent pas de pertinence scientifique, les Bulgares continuent à être aveugles au fait qu'à l'heure actuelle, la grande majorité de la population à conscience slave se déclare *macédonienne* et non pas *bulgare* (→ art. 172, 177). En étudiant la langue des immigrés macédoniens de Bulgarie, les dialectologues bulgares ont fourni de remarquables descriptions des dialectes slaves de la Macédoine grecque (Ivanov 1972, Mladenov 1977, Šklifov 1973, e. a.).

8.3. Les historiens et linguistes macédoniens de leur côté, font une entorse à la vérité en voulant « macédoniser » à tout prix une réalité historique et linguistique qui ne peut être séparée de l'héritage bulgare. Malgré cela les études macédoniennes ont elles aussi une valeur scientifique indéniable. Dans les recherches linguistiques, la controverse bulgaro-macédonienne est avant tout une question de définitions (dialectes *bulgares* ou *macédoniens*, particularité régionale *bulgare* ou trait spécifique de la langue *macédonienne*, etc.), dont le scientifique peut facilement déceler toute la portée.

9. Bibliographie (sélective)

Abecedar (1985): *Abecedar. Jubilejno izdanie* [L'abécédaire. Édition jubilaire] 1925–1985, Skopje.

Andriotis, Nicholas P. (1991): *The Federative Republic of Skopje and its language*, Thessalonique.

Asenova, Petya (1989): *Balkansko ezikoznanie* [Linguistique balkanique], Sofia.

Boeschoten, Riki van (1993): *Minority Languages in Northern Greece. Study Visit to Florina, Aridea*, (Report to the European Commission, Brussels).

Cowan, Jane K. (1990): *Dance and the Body Politic in Northern Greece*, Princeton.

Drettas, Georges (1981): « Tant que les grands-mères parlent ». In: *Epitheorisi Kinonikon Erevnon*, Athènes, 143–157.

Ioannou, K. (1989): *Koleda babo koleda* [Noël, grand-mère, Noël], Florina.

Ivanov, Jordan (1972): *Bulgarski dialekten atlas. Bulgarski govori ot Egejska Makedonija* [Atlas dialectologique bulgare. Dialectes bulgares de la Macédoine de l'Egée], Sofia (2 vols.).

Karakasidou, Anastasia (1991): *Politicizing Culture. Negating Ethnic Identity in Greek Macedonia*. A paper prepared for the Modern Greek Studies Association Symposium in Gainesville, Florida.

Kiselinovski, Stojan (1987): *Statusot na makedonskiot jazik vo Makedonija 1913–1987* [Le statut de la langue macédonienne en Macédoine 1913–1987], Skopje.

Kofos, Evangelos (1964): *Nationalism and Communism in Macedonia*, Thessalonique.

Koufis, Pavlos (1990): *Alona Florinas* [Alona ‹de la région› de Florina], Athènes.

Kondosopoulos, Nikolaos (1981): *Dhialekti ke idhiomata tis neas ellinikis* [Dialectes et idiomes du grec moderne], Athènes.

Lithoxoos, Dhimitris (1990): *Mionotika zitimata ke ethniki synidhisi stin Elladha* [Questions de minorités et conscience ethnique en Grèce], Athènes.

Lithoxoos, Dhimitris (1992): «I mitriki glossa ton katikon tou ellinikou tmimatos tis Makedhonias prin ke meta tin antallagi ton plithysmon» [La langue maternelle des habitants de la partie grecque de la Macédoine avant et après les échanges de populations]. In: *Theseis* 38, 39–66.

Mavrogordatos, George Th. (1983): *Stillborn Republic. Social Coalitions and Party Strategies in Greece, 1922–1936*, Berkeley.

Mladenov, Maksim (1977): «Beležki po govora na s. Kufalovo, Solunsko» [Notes sur le dialecte du village de Kufalovo, région de la Salonique]. In: *Bâlgarski ezik* 27, 6, 472–485.

Papadhopoulos, Anthymos (1927): *Grammatiki ton vorion idhiomaton tis neas ellinikis glossis* [Grammaire des dialectes septentrionaux de la langue grecque moderne], Athènes.

Popovski, Tošo (1981): *Makedonskoto nacionalno malcinstvo vo Bugarija, Grcija i Albanija* [La minorité nationale macédoine en Bulgarie, Grèce et Albanie], Skopje.

Poulton, Hugh (1995): *Who are the Macedonians*, Londres.

Šklifov, Blagoj (1973): *Kosturskijat govor* [Le dialecte de Kastoria], Sofia.

Weigand, Gustav (1924): *Ethnographie von Mazedonien*, Leipzig.

Zaimov, Jordan (1967): *Zaselvane na bûlgarskite slavjani na balkanskija poluostrov. Proučvane na žitelskite imena v bûlgarskata toponimija* [Recherches sur les noms des lieux habités dans la toponymie bulgare], Sofia.

Raymond Detrez, Louvain (Belgique)

186. Griechisch–Bulgarisch

1. Geographie und Demographie
2. Jüngere Geschichte
3. Wirtschaft, politische Lage, Religion
4. Ethnoprofile
5. Soziolinguistische und sprachpolitische Lage der Kontaktsprachen
6. Sprachliche Interferenzen
7. Kritische Bewertung der Literatur
8. Bibliographie (in Auswahl)

Slavische Bevölkerung in Griechenland findet man in zwei Provinzen, Thrakien (Thr.) und Makedonien (Mak.). Die Trennung zwischen Slaven (Sl.) in Thr. und Mak. steht mit einer größeren dialektischen Unterschiedlichkeit in Verbindung und drückt sich auch soziolinguistisch aus, da die Sl. in Mak., im Gegensatz zu denen in Thr., auch als Makedonier und ihre Sprache als Makedonisch identifiziert werden. Artikel 185 untersucht die Frage der Makedonier (Sl. in Griechisch-Mak.), während sich dieser Artikel auf Sl. in Thr. konzentriert.

1. Geographie und Demographie

1.1. Geographie

Die griechische (gr.) Provinz Thr., mit einer Fläche von 8.586 km², grenzt im Osten an die Türkei mit dem Grenzfluß Evros und im Westen an den Fluß Nestos; im Süden liegt das Ägäische Meer, und im Landesinneren besteht ein großer Teil aus den südlichen Ausläufern des bulgarischen (bg.) Rhodopengebirges vom Norden her. Klimatisch ist dies ein Übergangsgebiet zwischen dem kontinentalen Klima im Inneren und dem mediterranen Klima an der nordägäischen Küste.

1.2. Demographie

Traditionell war die Bevölkerung Thr.s gr.-, bg.- und türkischsprachig, ohne daß eine dieser Gruppen je eine klare Mehrheit dargestellt hätte. Der einst relativ bedeutende bg. Teil der Bevölkerung Thr.s ist jetzt infolge umfassender Völkerschaftsverschiebungen in den zwei Balkankriegen von 1912–1913 und im Ersten Weltkrieg sowie besonders eines Völkerschaftsaustausches nach dem Ersten Weltkrieg stark reduziert.

1913 im 2. Balkankrieg flohen etwa 70.000 Griechen aus Thr. vor der bg. Armee, während 47.000 Bulgaren im Rahmen eines Austauschvertrages aus Thr. auswanderten (Djordjević 1989, 116 f). Nach der bg. Besetzung Thr.s im Ersten Weltkrieg (1916) wurden etwa 46.000 Griechen nach Bulgarien (Bg.) deportiert und weitere 16.000 flohen vor den Bulgaren in andere Teile Griechenlands (Gr.); daraufhin zogen 39.000 bg. Siedler nach Thr. (Djordjević 1989, 118). Nach dem Waffenstillstand von 1918 fand eine entsprechende Gegenwelle von Migrationen statt, als etwa 51.000 Griechen in ihre thrakische Heimat zurückkehrten (Djordjević 1989, 118). Nach dem Ersten Weltkrieg wurde 1919 unter dem Abkommen von Neuilly zwischen Gr. und Bg. ein Völkerschaftsaustausch auf freiwilliger Basis vereinbart. Die Auswanderer wurden hauptsächlich entlang der jeweiligen Grenzgebiete angesiedelt, was diese stabilisierte. Der Völkerschaftsaustausch erhöhte drastisch den Anteil an Griechen in Thr.; stellten die Griechen in Thr. 1913 nur 17% der Bevölkerung, so war diese Zahl 1924 auf 62% gestiegen (Woodhouse 1976, 8). Jene Sl., die nach dem Völkerschaftsaustausch in Thr. blieben, mußten die gr. Staatsangehörigkeit annehmen. Als Bg. im Zweiten Weltkrieg 1941 wiederholt u. a. das gr. Thr. besetzte, flohen wieder viele Tausende von Griechen aus diesem Gebiet oder wurden in andere Teile Gr.s vertrieben; gleichzeitig wurden etwa 122.000 Bulgaren in Thr. (und Ostmak.) angesiedelt (Kostanick 1963, 43). Die Abwanderung vieler Griechen und die Ansiedlung bg. Familien veränderten zeitweilig die ethnische Zusammensetzung dieser Gegend; nach dem Waffenstillstand mit Bg. im Oktober 1944 wurden diese Bulgaren jedoch in ihre Heimat zurückgebracht, und viele Griechen kehrten nach dem Zweiten Weltkrieg nach Thr. zurück (→ Sprachenkarte I).

2. Jüngere Geschichte

2.1. 1912−1913

Im 1. Balkankrieg von 1912 wurde u. a. Thr. von Bg. erobert. Nach der Niederlage im 2. Balkankrieg von 1913 mußte Bg. nach dem Bukarester Friedensvertrag vom August 1913 den Großteil seiner Eroberungen an Gr. abtreten, durfte jedoch Thr. mit seinem Ausgang zur Ägäis und dem Hafen von Dedeagač behalten, einem 120 km langen schlechten Küstenstreifen zwischen den Mündungen des Nestos und des Evros. Thr. war seit einem abortiven Versprechen im Vertrag von San Stefano 1878 Ziel bg. Aspirationen gewesen.

2.2. 1916−1924

Im Ersten Weltkrieg besetzten 1916 bg. Truppen Thr. und versuchten, die Einwohner dieser Gebiete, die in der Mehrzahl keine Sl. waren, zu entnationalisieren. Als Bg. 1918 den Krieg verlor, mußte es nach dem Vertrag von Neuilly 1919 den Ausgang zur Ägäis wieder aufgeben. Thr. wurde nach einer kurzen Periode internationaler Verwaltung an Gr. zurückgegeben. Der Hafen von Dedeagač wurde in Alexandrupolis umbenannt. Der Vertrag von Neuilly von 1919 hatte die wirtschaftliche Konzession dieses Hafens in Form einer Dauerpacht vorgesehen, was aber bulgarischerseits zurückgewiesen wurde. Auf der Konferenz in Lausanne 1922−1923 war Gr. weiterhin bereit, Bg. Transportmöglichkeiten und die Nutzung einer Freizone in einem ägäischen Hafen zu gewähren. Die bg. Seite forderte jedoch autonome Verwaltung für Thr. mit Nutzung von Alexandrupolis, was nicht zugelassen wurde. 1924 sah zwecks weiterer Schlichtung ein vom Völkerbund aufgesetzter gr.-bg. Vertrag die Abtretung eines schmalen gr. Streifens an Bg. und das Recht auf Errichtung eines bg. Hafens in Alexandrupolis unter Aufsicht des Völkerbundes vor, was nochmals an dem bg. Anspruch auf völligen Besitz eines dafür vorgesehenen Korridors scheiterte. Gr. war nun zu keiner territorialen Abtretung mehr bereit (Mylonas 1947, 140).

2.3. 1941−1944

1941 besetzte die bg. Armee, ähnlich wie im Ersten Weltkrieg, u. a. das gr. Thr. Die Bulgaren verwalteten dieses Gebiet als souveränes Territorium, vertrieben jedoch mehr als die Hälfte der dortigen gr. Bevölkerung und arbeiteten mit systematischem Terror und erheblichen Lebenseinschränkungen für die verbliebene gr. Bevölkerung, so daß weiterhin ein großer Teil zur Flucht in andere Teile Gr.s gezwungen war. Da in dem besetzten Gebiet nur wenige Sl. waren, trachteten die Behörden danach, so viele Griechen wie möglich zwangsweise zu bulgarisieren oder sie durch bg. Siedler zu ersetzen. In kultureller Hinsicht wurden gr. Schulen im besetzten Gebiet geschlossen und die Lehrer vertrieben; gr. Priester wurden durch bg. ersetzt; auch die gr. Sprache wurde stark unterdrückt und sogar gr. Grabaufschriften verunstaltet. Nach dem Friedensvertrag mit Bg. im Oktober 1944 wurde Thr. sofort an Gr. zurückgegeben.

3. Wirtschaft, politische Lage, Religion

Thr. nimmt eine wichtige strategische Lage in der Ägäis ein und hat auch wirtschaftlichen Wert. Alexandrupolis ist der einzige wichtige

Handelshafen. Die Ebenen entlang der ägäischen Küste sind ein wertvoller Erzeuger von Weizen, Tabak, Baumwolle und Weintrauben. Die politische und religiöse Lage der Sl. in Thr. ist mit denen im gr. Mak. weitgehend identisch. Unter der bg. Minderheit in Thr. findet man keine Spuren der bg. autokephalen Kirche.

4. Ethnoprofile

4.1. Griechen

In Gr. sprechen heute etwa 97% der Bevölkerung Griechisch als Muttersprache. Historisch gesehen verlief die gr. Sprachgrenze nördlich der Insel Korfu nach Nordosten bis etwa zehn km südlich von Kastoria, von da etwas südlich und bog dann wieder nach Norden bis nach Verria und weiter bis zur Mündung des Axios im Golf von Thessaloniki. Die Gegend um Thessaloniki war von Sl. bewohnt. Griechisch tauchte dann wieder südöstlich davon auf und erstreckte sich weiterhin auf die Chalkidische Halbinsel und große Teile der ägäischen Küste bis nach Istanbul (Sandfeld 1930, 16). Seit den 20er Jahren dieses Jahrhunderts hat sich diese Situation im Sinne einer Gräzisierung der nördlichen Teile geändert.

4.2. Bulgaren und Makedonier

Gr.-bg. Sprachkontakte im Gebiet des heutigen Gr. findet man praktisch nur in den nordgr. Provinzen Mak. und Thr. Man muß hier eine Trennungslinie zwischen den zwei sl. Sprachen Bulgarisch und Makedonisch (mak.) ziehen, die in dem Gebiet östlich von Thessaloniki, etwa ab dem Fluß Strimon und somit in Ostmak. verläuft. Das ostmakedonische Gebiet zwischen Thessaloniki und dem Nestos wird traditionell als nicht zu Mak. zugehörig betrachtet. Diese sozusagen historische Abgrenzung vom eigentlichen Mak. ist auch in der mak.-bg. Sprachgrenze ausgedrückt.

4.3. Bulgarische Mundarten in Thrakien

Global gesehen werden die bg. Dialekte in ein westliches und ein östliches Areal eingeteilt, wobei das Hauptkriterium die Realisierung des alten Phonems „jat" (-ě-) als hauptsächlich *ja* (im Osten) oder *e* (im Westen) ist. Die Jat-Grenze verläuft in einer breiten Isoglosse, in der die östlichen Mundarten allmählich in die westlichen übergehen. Im Süden, auf heute gr. Territorium, verläuft diese Übergangsisoglosse im Gebiet von Serres, Sidhirokastro(n), Nea Zighni, und Thessaloniki. Bis zum 16. Jh. verlief diese Isoglosse viel weiter südwestlich. Die sl. Dialekte in Griechisch-Thr. (und Türkisch-Thr.) werden unter die südöstlichen bg. Dialekte eingeordnet, die Teil des ostbg. Areals sind. Im engeren Sinne gehören sie zu den südthrakischen Mundarten der östlichen Gruppe der südöstlichen Dialekte. Die südöstlichen Dialekte weisen phonetisch starke Palatalität der Konsonanten, weiche Zischlaute und teilweise eine aspirierte Variante des *h* z. B. *храна* 'Speise') auf. Morphologisch findet man Kasusreste bei Personennamen, eine Aoristendung auf *-ъх* anstatt *-ох*, eine Präsensendung auf *-овам*, eine Imperativendung für den Plural auf *-ume*, und Iterativendungen auf *-ицам*. Als bg. definierbare (und makedonischerseits nicht beanspruchte) Mundarten findet man auch im östlichen Teil von Griechisch-Mak. zwischen dem Nestos und dem Strimon. Diese gehören zu einer westlichen Gruppe der südöstlichen Dialekte. Ein Großteil davon befindet sich in der Übergangsisoglosse (Kočev 1986, Bojadžiev 1984).

5. Soziolinguistische und sprachpolitische Lage der Kontaktsprachen

Die soziolinguistische und sprachpolitische Situation des Bulgarischen in Gr. ist mit der des Makedonischen vergleichbar, mit der Ausnahme, daß die Existenz einer bg. Sprache griechischerseits anerkannt wird und sogar im Balkanischen Institut von Thessaloniki unterricht wird, (→ Art. 185). Abgesehen von der offiziellen gr. Haltung, die sl. Minderheit u. a. in Thr. als „slavophone Hellenen" zu bezeichnen, wird offiziell keine weitere Unterscheidung zwischen Bulgaren und Makedoniern gemacht. Bulgarisch wird heute nicht als Sprache einer Minderheit in Gr. anerkannt und wird entsprechend nicht in Schulen gelehrt, geschweige denn als offizielle Sprache verwendet. Die bg. Sprache in Thr. wird ausschließlich im engeren Familienkreis oder bg. sozialen Umfeld verwendet. Es liegen keine konkreten Statistiken vor.

6. Sprachliche Interferenzen

6.1. Bulgarisch und Griechisch allgemein

Bulgarisch ist eine südsl. Sprache innerhalb des großen Zweiges der sl. Sprachen, während das Griechische genetisch nicht mit dem

Bulgarischen verwandt ist. Beide Sprachen haben sich jedoch aus dem Indogermanischen entwickelt, wobei das Griechische seinen eigenen Zweig bildet. Etwa in den letzten 800 Jahren haben die auf dem Balkan gesprochenen Sprachen verschiedene gemeinsame Besonderheiten entwickelt, die zu der Idee einer „Balkansprachbundes" führten. Sowohl das Griechische als auch das Bulgarische gehören zu verschiedenen Ausmassen diesem Sprachbund an.

6.2. Slavisch-bulgarischer Einfluß

Von der Zeit der großen Slaveninvasion in Gr. ab dem 6. Jh., infolge derer sich viele Sl. in Gr. niederließen, jedoch spätestens bis zum 15. Jh. assimiliert waren, ist u. a. eine stattliche Anzahl von sl. geographischen Namen bezeugt. So findet man z. B. in Thr. 9 sl. Ortsnamen im Gebiet von Xanthi (Vasmer). In Mak. und Thr. hielt sich das sl. Element praktisch bis heute. Sl.-bg. Einfluß auf die gr. Sprache findet man praktisch nur in der Lexik. Die Anzahl sl. Lehnwörter im Griechischen ist relativ gering und beträgt nur ca. 300 Wörter. Der größere Teil dieser Entlehnungen sind Tier- und Pflanzenbezeichnungen oder Begriffe aus dem Hirtenwesen, mit nur sehr wenigen Verbalentlehnungen. Einige dieser sl. Lehnwörter sind älter und wurden zwischen dem 6. bis 15. Jh. übernommen. Nur wenige davon sind in der modernen gr. Volkssprache in normalem Gebrauch, z. B: σανός 'Heu' < altbg. сѣно, sowie das sl. Deminutivsuffix -ίτσα. Den größeren Teil dieser älteren Entlehnungen findet man in den nordgr. Dialekten von Mak. und Thr., Epirus und Thessalien. Lehnwörter aus jüngerer Zeit sind auf die Dialekte Thr.s und Mak.s beschränkt, wo jahrhundertelang Zweisprachigkeit bis in die Neuzeit geherrscht hat; dies zeigt sich auch in gewissen hybriden gr.-bg. Ausdrücken. Eine jüngere Entlehnung ist z. B. βίδρα 'Otter' < видра in einem gr. Idiom aus der Gegend von Dhidhimotichon (Kampasakalis 1991 gibt eine Liste von 57 Wörtern bg. Herkunft); diese Wörter sind alle voll in die morphologischen Paradigmata des Griechischen integriert. In den nordgr. Dialekten findet man, ähnlich wie in den ostbg. Dialekten, eine Vokalreduzierung $o > u$, $e > i$ und $a > ă$ sowie den Ausfall unbetonter Vokale (Asenova 1989, 21).

6.3. Griechischer Einfluß

Auch der auf das 9. Jh. zurückgehende gr. Einfluß auf die bg. Sprache hat sich hauptsächlich im Wortschatz ausgedrückt. Jedoch ist dieser Einfluß viel bedeutender als umgekehrt und hat sich praktisch in allen Lebensbereichen sowohl in den Mundarten als auch der Literatursprache gezeigt. Man kann unterscheiden zwischen solchen Entlehnungen, die gesamtbg. in Gebrauch sind, z. B. молив 'Bleistift' < μολύβι; volkssprachlichen oder dialektalen Elementen in den südlicheren Gebieten, die auf Kontakten mit gr. Bevölkerung beruhen, z. B. матима 'Lehrstunde' < μάθημα. Schließlich gibt es Entlehnungen an der südlichen Peripherie des bg. Sprachgebiets, die das Ergebnis jahrhundertelanger Zweisprachigkeit sind, z. B. плескуда 'Haarzopf' < πλεξούδα (Filipova-Bajrova 1969, Teil 2). Dieses letzte Beispiel ist typisch für die bg. Mundarten in Xanthi und Komotini in Thr., jedoch sind die meisten gr. Entlehnungen an der Peripherie nicht nur auf ein Gebiet beschränkt. Im Rahmen des kulturell führenden Griechentums entstanden, sind sie spezifischer als die Masse der gr. lexikalischen Elemente in den nördlicheren bg. Dialekten. Ein großer Teil der volkssprachlichen gr. Elemente im Bulgarischen reflektiert phonetische Züge der nordgr. Dialekte. Allgemeinbg. ist ein produktives gr. wortbildendes Element, -s-, mit dem gr. Verbalentlehnungen in das bg. System integriert werden; allgemeinbg. ist auch ein gr. Suffix für Abstrakta, -ija. Die gr. Entlehnungen wurden im allgemeinen an bg. Paradigmata phonetisch und morphologisch angeglichen.

7. Kritische Bewertung der Literatur

Zu diesem spezifischen Thema besteht nur eine begrenzte historische und linguistische Literatur. Im geschichtlichen Zusammenhang werden die Bulgaren in Thr. lediglich in Gesamtbetrachtungen erwähnt, die auch Mak. einbeziehen und konkrete Abgrenzungen kaum möglich machen. In der linguistischen Literatur gibt es eine gewisse Anzahl von dialektologischen Untersuchungen des Bulgarischen in Thr. Evenso gibt es ältere Untersuchungen über bg. Bräuche und Folklore in Thr. Es fehlt eine zusammenfassende Monographie über historische und dialektologische Aspekte der Bulgaren in diesem Gebiet sowie eine soziolinguistische und sprachpolitische Betrachtung dieser Minderheit nach dem Zweiten Weltkrieg. Untersuchungen über die aktuelle Lage der Bulgaren in Thr. werden durch eine höchste obstruktive Politik der griech. Behörden erschwert.

8. Bibliographie (in Auswahl)

Asenova, Petja (1989): *Balkansko ezikoznanie. Osnovni problemi na balkanskija ezikov săjuz* [Balkanische Sprachwissenschaft. Grundlegende Probleme des Balkansprachbundes], Sofia.

Bojadžiev, Todor (1984): *Pomagalo po bălgarska dialektologija* [Handbuch für bulgarische Dialektologie], Sofia.

Djordjević, Dimitrije (1969): „Migrations during the 1912−1913 Balkan Wars and World War One". In: *Migrations in Balkan History*, Tasić, N./Stošić, D. (Eds.), Belgrad, 115−129.

Filipova-Bajrova, Marija (1969): *Grăcki zaemki v săvremennija bălgarski ezik* [Griechische Lehnwörter in der heutigen bulgarischen Sprache], Sofia.

Kampasakalís, Dimităr J. (1991): „Bălgarski zaemki v săvremennija ezikov idiom na Amarion, rajon na Didimotika, Zapadna Trakija" [Bulgarische Lehnwörter im heutigen Sprachidiom von Amarion, Gebiet von Didimotika]. In: *Relations et influences réciproques entre Grecs et Bulgares XVIIIe−XXe siècle*, Institut für Balkanstudien (Eds.), Thessaloniki, 241−253.

Kočev, Ivan (1986): „Bălgarskite dialekti" [Die bulgarischen Dialekte]. In: *Uvod v izučavaneto na južnoslavjanskite ezici*, BAN (Eds.), Sofia, 296−315.

Kostanick, Huey Louis (1963): „The Geopolitics of the Balkans". In: *The Balkans in Transition (Essays On the Development of Balkan Life and Politics Since the Eighteenth Century)*, Jelavich, Charles/Jelavich, Barbara (Eds.), Berkeley, Neudruck 1974, 1−55.

Mylonas, George E. (1947): *The Balkan States. An Introduction to Their History*, 2. Aufl., Saint Louis.

Sandfeld, Kristian (1930): *Linguistique balkanique. Problèmes et résultats*, 2. erweit. Aufl., Paris.

Vasmer, Max (1941): *Die Slaven in Griechenland*, Berlin; phototyp. Neudruck, Ditten, H. (Ed.), Leipzig, 1970.

Woodhouse, Christopher Montague (1976): *The Struggle for Greece 1941−1949*, London.

Thomas Henninger, London (Großbritannien)

187. European Turkey

1. Geography and demography
2. History
3. Politics, economy and general cultural and religious situation
4. Statistics and ethnoprofiles
5. Sociolinguistic situation
6. Language political situation
7. Other language contacts
8. Critical evaluation
9. Bibliography (selected)

1. Geography and demography

1.1. European Turkey (T. *Trakya* − "Thrace" or *Doğu Trakya* − "Eastern Thrace") is one of the eight geographical regions of Turkey, and with an area of 2,300 square kilometers, it forms approximately 3% of the territory of the Republic of Turkey (T. *Türkiye Cumhuriyeti*). By Turkish standards, the area is relatively densely populated: according to the census of 1990 there are 5,975,449 inhabitants (GNS 1991, 3). Its major urban centres are, apart from Istanbul, Edirne (102,345), Tekirdağ (80,442), Çorlu (74,681), Lüleburgaz (52,384) and Kırklareli (43,017). Istanbul, the ancient capital of the Ottoman Empire, has seen an extraordinary population increase during the last decades (from 1,182,256 inhabitants in 1955 to 4,734,857 in 1990, excluding the Asian suburbs).

1.2. Unlike the population in neighbouring territories of Bulgaria and Greece, the population of Eastern Thrace is nowadays ethnically and linguistically more or less homogeneous. As a result of the Balkan wars (1912−1913), deportations during World War I, and the exchange of minorities between Greece and Turkey (Treaty of Lausanne, 1923), as well as other minor population movements, the area (with the exception of Istanbul) has lost almost the whole of its former considerable Greek, Armenian, Bulgarian and Jewish population (for figures cf. McCarthy 1990). In exchange, large numbers of Muslim immigrants (T. *muhacir*) from the Balkans have been settled there. Even before the latest exodus of Bulgarian Turks (1989), some of the cities of Eastern Thrace had the highest ratio of immigrants in Turkey (cf. Keleş 1985, 485); → Language Map I.

2. History

2.1. (Thrace) The territory of Eastern Thrace is the last remnant of what was once the European part of the Ottoman Empire (T.

Rumeli). It was among the first territories conquered by the Ottoman Turks, almost a hundred years before the fall of the capital of the Byzantine Empire. In 1352 the Ottomans made their first territorial gains in Europe. The city of Adrianople (T. *Edirne*) was the capital of the Empire until the conquest of Constantinople (1453). As a result of a massive influx of Turkish settlers, the toponomy of Eastern Thrace was thoroughly Turkified. Elements reminiscent of former non-Muslim inhabitants have been further eliminated in more recent times (cf. Kreiser 1975, XXXV). The present-day borders of Turkey in Europe date back to 1923. They were not drawn along ethnic or linguistic lines. During the Balkan wars (1912/13) Edirne fell into the hands of the Bulgarians but was eventually retaken by the Turks after an occupation lasting 117 days (1913). As a result of the Treaty of Sèvres (1920), concluded after Turkey's defeat in World War I, almost the whole of Eastern Thrace (with the exception of Istanbul and the adjacent areas) was awarded by the Allies to Greece and was occupied by the Greek army (July 1920 – November 1922). However, after the victory of the nationalists under the leadership of Mustafa Kemal (later Atatürk) in Anatolia the area was restored to Turkey under the Treaty of Lausanne.

2.2. (Istanbul) The conquest of Constantinople (T. *Istanbul*) in 1453 also radically transformed the cultural and demographic structure of the population. Apart from a few neighbourhoods along the city walls, which continued to be inhabited by the indigenous population, the former capital of the Byzantine Empire became a Turkish-dominated town. However, the Greek-Orthodox community, as well as the smaller Armenian and Jewish communities already present in the city at the time of its conquest, were to be continuously replenished and grew in size as time went by. After the City was captured, Sultan Mehmed II appointed the Greek scholar and priest, George Scholarius (Gennadius II), patriarch in 1454. He was invested with civil and ecclesiastical authority over his coreligionists, i. e., over the entire Greek Orthodox population of the Empire (including the large non-Greek-speaking communities). After the Greeks, the Armenians and Jews were given their own special position within the system of largely autonomous religious communities known as the *millet*-system (cf. Braude/Lewis 1982). This system survived until 1919. In the second half of the 19th century, most of the discriminatory regulations to which the non-Muslim communities had been subjected under Islamic Law were abolished. The effects of the reforms known as *Tanzimat* (1839 – 1876) were particularly tangible in the cosmopolitan capital, Istanbul. All the minorities came under strong Western influence. Numerous schools and prestigious institutions of higher education were founded. In addition to ethnic languages (Greek, Armenian, Bulgarian etc.) French was widely taught and used as language of instruction at some institutions. French was to become the *lingua franca* between the communities. However, the position of non-Muslims was at times severely shaken by 19th century nationalism: the Greek-Orthodox Patriarch was hanged at the outbreak of the Greek Revolution in 1821, massacres of Armenians occurred in 1896, etc. Despite these temporary setbacks, Greeks, Armenians and – to a lesser extent – Jews from Istanbul played an important role in all spheres of public, economic and even political life during this period (cf. Çark 1953, Alexandris 1983, 28 – 32, Shaw 1991).

The Balkan Wars and especially the first World War brought many hardships for the non-Muslim communities in Istanbul but those in Thrace or in the Anatolian provinces suffered infinitely more. During the "Years of the Armistice" (T. *Mütareke yılları*, 1918 – 1922), on the other hand, when Istanbul was occupied for the first time in history by foreign armies, the minorities in Istanbul, especially Greeks and Armenians, enjoyed a privileged position. This created considerable resentment among the Turkish population, the effects of which can still be felt today.

3. Politics, economy and general cultural and religious situation

The situation for the non-Muslim communities in Istanbul changed considerably with the foundation of the Turkish Republic in 1923. They were granted privileges unknown to any other ethnic or linguistic group in Turkey by Articles 38 – 42 of the Treaty of Lausanne, but they were now isolated. Both the government and public opinion tended to regard them as foreign elements despite their political status as Turkish citizens. Members of the minorities were gradually removed from government posts. However, non-Muslims from Istanbul, and notably Greeks, continued to dominate economic life. This led to calls for the replacement of non-Muslims in commerce by Turks. The discriminatory capital levy (T. *Varlık Vergisi*) of 1942 was the most determined attempt by the Turkish authorities to break this dominance.

The far-reaching powers of the former heads of the *millets*, the Œcumenical and Gregorian Patriarchs and the Chief Rabbi, were curtailed. They were accepted by the government solely as the religious authority for the relevant religious community in Istanbul. The participation of non-Muslims in the political life of Turkey came to an end in the early sixties when their last deputies were elected to the National Assembly.

Today, the Greek community has almost disappeared from sight and the Armenian community generally keeps a low profile. The Jewish community, on the other hand, though much reduced in size since 1948, is still very present in public life: its members include a number of well-known university teachers, journalists and businessmen (cf. Shaw 1991, 264 f). Since neither territorial claims nor historical antagonism trouble their relations with the Turks or the Turkish state, the quincentenary of the expulsion of the Jews from Spain and their migration to Ottoman lands was commemorated in 1992 with many public events highlighting the harmonious relations between Turks and Jews. In some respects, the climate has also improved for other minorities in recent times. For many Istanbul Turks the loss of the cosmopolitan character of their city has become a matter of concern. Nostalgia for the good old days is widespread, especially among intellectuals, and books and pamphlets written on this topic (sometimes by members of the minorities themselves) find a large readership. A recent publication on Armenian literature by an Istanbul Armenian, the first such publication since 1912, was widely welcomed by the Turkish literary community (Tuğlacı 1992).

4. Statistics and ethnoprofiles

4.1. The main language of European Turkey is now Turkish (T. *Türkçe, Türk dili*). It is mother tongue to the overwhelming majority of the inhabitants of the area. According to the 1965 census (the last indicating religion and language), 35,097 Greek-speakers among the 47,207 Orthodox Christians and 29,479 Armenian-speakers (Andrews 1989, 128, 143) were registered in Istanbul. The census figures for Jews have always been somewhat puzzling since many of them have — sometimes quite wrongly — considered Turkish as their native language (cf. Şaul 1983, 347, Murphy 1986, 186). Thus, only a quarter of the 30,831 members of the community declared *Yahudice* as their mother tongue in 1965 (Shaw 1991, 259). Due to emigration, and also, as in the case of the Jews, to language shift, the number of speakers of the ethnic languages has decreased in all communities since then. The decline has been most dramatic in the case of the Greek speakers whose numbers are estimated today at 2000—3000 individuals. In terms of demography the Armenian community is better off (some 60,000 according to Murphy who collected his data 1977—1981 (Murphy 1986, 178)) thanks to the steady influx of migrants from Anatolia. Almost all of them, however, are monolingual speakers of Turkish. Thus, only half of the community in Istanbul is supposed to have an active command of the language. The official Jewish figure for the size of the community (including Yiddish or French-speaking Ashkenazic Jews) is 20,000, but this figure is disputed (cf. Shaw 1991, 259).

4.2. The languages used by members of the officially recognised minorities are Greek, Armenian and Judaeo-Spanish. Istanbul Greeks who normally designate themselves as *Ellines* or *Romií* (T. *Rumlar*) usually refer to their first language as *ellinika*, but the older term *roméika* (T. *Rumca*) is still popular. The ethnic language of the Istanbul Armenians (in Armenian: *Hayer*) is Armenian (*hayerên, hai lezu*; T. *Ermenice*) in its Western variant. Judaeo-Spanish, the ethnic language of the Sephardic Jews of Istanbul, is referred to by its speakers as *espaniól* (Şaul 1983, 328) or *cudeo-espanyol* (Benbanaste 1988, *passim*) (T. *Yahudice* "Jewish" or (*Cudeo-*) *İspanyolca*). Both Greeks and Armenians use their own traditional scripts, whereas the Hebrew-based *Raši*-script, formerly used for Judaeo-Spanish, has been gradually replaced by the Latin alphabet in its Turkish version since 1928.

4.3. More detailed data on the present living areas of the minorities are only available for

Jews (→ art. 189). The non-Muslim communities, once scattered in many neighbourhoods on both sides of the Golden Horn, now live predominantly on the Galata side, particularly around Beyoğlu ("Péra") and the adjacent neighbourhoods (Şişli, Kurtuluş etc.) which are more European in style. Only the Armenians have retained a centre in Old Istanbul in the *Kumkapı* neighbourhood where the Patriarchate and the administration of the community is based. On the Asian shore, one can still find them in some cosmopolitan neighbourhoods like Kuzguncuk or Kadıköy. On the once predominantly Greek Princes' Isles (T *Adalar*: Burgaz, Büyük Ada, Kınalıada, Heybeliada), Greeks have been replaced by Jews to some extent. The minority groups usually remain selfcontained. While members of the Armenian and Jewish community may occasionally marry Turks, such mixed marriages are considered unthinkable by the Greek community.

4.4. Due to demographic developments (the small Greek Catholic and Protestant communities are now almost extinct) little remains today of the often fierce antagonism that existed between the different rites (Greek-Orthodox, Armenian Apostolic ("Gregorian") versus Catholic Uniates and Protestants). There are, however, no differences in the liturgical languages, excepted the case of the "Turkish Orthodox Church" (→ art. 188) which uses Turkish.

5. Sociolinguistic situation

5.1. Although Turkish has been the official language and the language of the majority, it is fair to say that until the second half of this century, the concept of Turkish as a "dominant language" would have made little sense. Many members of the minorities were plurilingual and used to speak the languages of other minorities fluently (including the Levantine variety of French), but they were unable to speak proper Turkish. Among the minority languages, Greek enjoyed the highest prestige and was widely spoken by Armenians and Jews, occasionally even by Muslims in neighbourhoods inhabited by minorities (cf. Scognamillo 1990, 70 f). A very high proportion of Armenians have traditionally been bilingual in Turkish and Armenian and monolingual speakers of Armenian seem to have been the exception.

5.2. Psychological pressure, applied steadily from the late twenties onwards to promote the use of Turkish among non-Muslim Turkish citizens (under the slogan: "Citizen, speak Turkish" (*Vatandaş Türkçe konuş!*)) had relatively little impact in the Greek and Levantine community and hardly affected the bilingual Armenians. Thanks to some active proponents of cultural integration (A. Galanté, Tekinalp) it eventually proved very successful with the Sephardic community (Şaul 1983, 339). Turkish family names, introduced by law in 1934, were not made compulsory for the minorities. Cases of the voluntary adoption of a Turkish family name were extremely rare among Istanbul Greeks. They seem to have occurred more frequently with the Armenians. Since their patronyms are frequently of Turkish origin, they become unrecognizable if the characteristic *-yan* ending is dropped (e. g. *Tuğlacı* instead of *Tuğglaciyan*) or replaced with the Turkish suffix *-oğlu-* "son of". Many Jewish males even had their Hebrew forenames translated into Turkish, or appended to their real name, whereas many women continued to be given French names (Şaul 1983, 346).

5.3. A considerable change in the attitude of the minorities occurred after World War II. (cf. Şaul 1983, 347, Alexandris 1983, 297). Today the younger generation is 100% bilingual and in the case of the Sephardic Jews, the linguistic shift to Turkish is now complete: only the older generation still speaks Judaeo-Spanish, whereas children have become monolingual speakers of Turkish (Séphiha 1991, 79, → art. 189).

5.4. Among the Turcophone population none of the minority languages seems to have ever enjoyed any particular prestige. The slang of Istanbul, however, contains numerous elements from all minority languages, including Gypsy (cf. Aktunç 1990). For educated speakers, Armenian influences, namely in pronunciation (T *Ermeni şivesi*, i. e. the shortening of vowel length in loan words from Arabic or Persian) and lexicon have been a matter of major concern (cf. Steuerwald 1964, 126, 128, 137, Banarlı 1986, 145). The conspicuously defective pronunciation of Turkish by members of the non-Muslim minorities in Istanbul was until recently an inexhaustible source of popular humour.

5.5. The written varieties of the minority languages in Istanbul have long been characterised by conservatism and purism. All of them have been very reluctant to admit Turkish loanwords (cf. Kočar 1981, 6, Séphiha 1986, 77, → art. 188). *Diglossia* (in Ferguson's sense) was particularly noticeable in the Greek community in Istanbul where the formal variety (*katharevousa*) had some of its most ardent supporters. In the Armenian community, *diglossia* was overcome in the nineteenth century and the new literary standard language which replaced Classical Armenian (*grabar*) was based to a large extent on the dialect of Istanbul. A "mild form" (Şaul) of *diglossia* still exists in Judaeo-Spanish whose written variety used for religious purposes (*Ladino*; see art. 189) has preserved some archaic features and is strongly influenced by Hebrew syntax.

6. Language political situation

6.1. In principle, all of the languages used by the aforementioned minorities in Istanbul enjoy the same status: "(...) no restriction shall be imposed on the free use by any Turkish national of any language in private intercourse, in commerce, religion, in the press, or in publications of any kind or at public meetings. Notwithstanding the existence of the official language, adequate facilities shall be given to Turkish nationals of non-Turkish speech for the oral use of their own language before the Courts." (Article 39) "[The minorities shall also] have an equal right to establish, manage and control at their own expense (...) schools and other establishments for instruction and education, with the right to use their own language (...)" (Art. 40 of the Treaty of Lausanne 1923). Not all of these regulations have actually been implemented (the minority languages have never been admitted in the courts). Of the once flourishing press in the minority languages (Greek, Armenian, Judaeo-Spanish and French) only two Greek papers and four Armenian periodicals are left. The Jewish weekly *Şalom* has been published since 1984 in Turkish and contains only one page in Judaeo-Spanish. The last Jewish paper in French, *Le Journal d'Orient* (founded in 1917), ceased its publication in 1971 (Benbanaste 1988, 61).

6.2. Since the minority languages are used neither in the administration nor in the modern electronic media, those schools where the principal language of instruction is one of the officially recognized minority languages play a key role for language maintenance. Whereas both Greeks and Armenians lost no time in exercising their linguistic rights, the Jews renounced them on the assumption that the equality of all citizens, irrespective of race or creed, guaranteed by the Turkish Constitution, made such rights redundant (cf. Shaw 1991, 287 f). As a result Judaeo-Spanish is not taught in the two Jewish minority schools, but classes in Hebrew are offered.

6.3. The written variety of Greek taught in minority schools by teachers sent from Greece using textbooks printed in Greece does not differ from the standard language of Greece. The situation is more complex for the Armenians since Western Armenian, unlike Modern Eastern Armenian, is a diaspora language. It is not subject to any control by academic or similar institutions (→ art. 190). The written variety of Judaeo-Spanish is undoubtedly the least standardized of these languages. It varies, according to the preferences of the writer, between Hispanicized and Gallicized varieties. The Istanbul variety (*Şalom*) is termed *judéo-fragnol* by Séphiha. It is the Turkish language, however, which has undergone the most considerable changes in this century. The "Language Reform" (T. usually *Dil Devrimi* "Language Revolution"), starting in the early Thirties, was intended "to free the Turkish language from the yoke of foreign languages" (Atatürk 1930). It was dominated by purism, one of its main objectives being the elimination of the Arabic and Persian elements in the older language (termed as *Osmanlıca*). Thanks to the active support of governments, schools and many intellectuals, the language reform proved highly successful, although opponents still regularly voice their complaints (for a more recent assessment see Brendemoen 1990). Members of the minorities in general have shown little if any interest in the language reform. Their Ottoman scholars usually remained very attached to the older language. One exception is, however, the Armenian Agop Martayan who was given the Turkish family name "Dilâçar" ("Tongue-opener") by Atatürk himself. Dilâçar (1895−1979), who became a member of the Turkish Linguistic Society (*Türk Dil Kurumu*), wrote numerous works on the Turkish language and was even a fervent supporter of the "Sun-language theory" (T. *Güneş-Dil Teorisi*) (Türkay, 1982).

7. Other language contacts

7.1. There can be no doubt that many other languages are still spoken in European Turkey today as first or second languages, especially in the "melting pot" of Istanbul. Former official population records used to list up to 20 "mother-tongues" (T. *anadil*) from Abkhazian (T. *Abaza*) to "Jewish" (*Yahudice*) (cf. Keleş 1985, 476). Although some of these languages are used mainly by communities located in Anatolia, almost all of them are also spoken by sections of the present population of Istanbul as a first or second language. The list of languages is, however, neither accurate nor exhaustive since some languages were not listed separately, and some terms (like *Yahudice*) are misleading. There is also the puzzling case of the Levantine community whose ethnolinguistic profile is extremely difficult to establish. The principal languages used by its members are French, Italian and Greek, but there are others (cf. Murphy 1986, Scognamillo 1990).

7.2. New non-Muslim communities have emerged due to the influx of Christian migrants from eastern Anatolia, like members of the Syrian Orthodox Church (T. *Süryani*) studied by Murphy (Murphy 1986; for figures see Andrews 1989, 161 f). Immigrant settlers from the former Soviet Union or Chinese Turkestan (Sinkiang) also form relatively compact communities in present-day Istanbul. However, none of the aforementioned languages are used as the medium of instruction in schools, and it is probable that their speakers will eventually shift to Turkish.

8. Critical evaluation

8.1. Despite the fascinating prospects it offers for research, Istanbul is still to a large extent *terra incognita* for studies on linguistic contacts. Even major reference works hardly ever refer to the situation in Istanbul. As to the officially recognized minority languages which are dealt with in articles 188, 189, 190, there is a large amount of literature on the situation of Sephardic Jews and their ethnic language (Şaul 1983, Séphiha, Shaw 1991), but apart from Murphy's short article (Murphy 1986), almost no further data are available on the present situation of speakers of Armenian and Greek.

9. Bibliography (selected)

Aktunç, Hulki (1990): *Türkçenin Büyük Argo Sözlüğü (Tanıklarıyla)* [Dictionary of Turkish Slang with References], Istanbul.

Alexandris, Alexander (1983): *The Greek Minority in Istanbul and Greek-Turkish Relations 1918–1974*, Athens.

Andrews, Peter Alford (Ed.) (1989): *Ethnic Groups in the Republic of Turkey*, Wiesbaden.

Banarlı, Nihat Sami (1986): *Türkçenin sırları* [The Secrets of the Turkish language], 9th edition, Istanbul (1st edition 1972).

Benbanaste, Nesim (1988): *Örneklerle Türk Musevi Basının Tarihçesi* [History of the Jewish Press in Turkey with Examples], Istanbul.

Braude, Benjamin/Lewis, Bernard (Eds.) (1982): *Christians and Jews in the Ottoman Empire. The Functioning of a Plural Society*, 2 vols., London.

Brendemoen, Bernt (1990): "The Turkish Language Reform and Language Policy in Turkey". In: Hazai, 454–493.

Çark, Rh. Y. (1953): *Türk Devleti Hizmetinde Ermeniler 1453–1953* [Armenians in the service of the Turkish State, 1453–1953], Istanbul.

GNS 1991: Genel Nüfus Sayımı. İdari bölünüş. 1990 Census of Population. Administrative Division, Ankara.

Grothusen, Klaus-Detlev (Ed.) (1985): *Handbook on South Eastern Europe, Volume IV: Turkey*, Göttingen.

Hazai, György (Ed.) (1990): *Handbuch der türkischen Sprachwissenschaft. Teil I.*, Wiesbaden.

Keleş, Ruşen (1985): "Population Structure". In: Grothusen (1985), 472–495.

Kočar, Meri Račievna (1981): *Turetskie elementy v yazyke konstantinopol'skikh arm'an* [Turkish elements in the language of the Armenians of Constaninople], Erevan.

Kreiser, Klaus (1975): *Die Ortsnamen der europäischen Türkei nach amtlichen Verzeichnissen und Kartenwerken*, Freiburg.

McCarthy, Justin (1990): "The Population of Ottoman Europe before and after the Fall of the Empire". In: *IIIrd Congress on the Social and Economic History of Turkey*, Lowry, H.W./Hattox, R.S. (Eds.), Istanbul-Washington-Paris, 275–298.

Murphy, Richard A. (1986): "Observations on Language Usage Among Bilingual Communities in Istanbul". In: *Osmanlı Araştırmaları* V, 175–193.

Şaul, Mahir (1983): "The Mother Tongue of the Polyglot: Cosmopolitism and Nationalism Among the Sepharadim of Istanbul". In: *Anthropological Linguistics* 25/3, 326–358.

Scognamillo, Giovanni (1990): *Bir Levantenin Beyoğlu Anıları* [A Levantine's Souvenirs of Beyoğlu], Istanbul.

Séphiha, Haïm Vidal (1986): *Le Judéo-Espagnol*, Paris.

Séphiha, Haïm Vidal (1991): *L'agonie des Judéo-espagnols*, 3rd edition, Paris.

Shaw, Stanford J. (1991): *The Jews of the Ottoman Empire and the Turkish Republic*, New York.

Steuerwald, Karl (1963): *Untersuchungen zur türkischen Sprache der Gegenwart*, 3 vols., Berlin 1963—1966.

Tuğlacı, Pars (1992): *Ermeni Edebiyatından Seçkiler* [Selections from Armenian Literature], Istanbul.

Türkay, Kaya (1982): *A. Dilâçar*, Ankara.

Johann Strauß, Freiburg i. Brg. (Germany)

188. Turc—grec

1. Géographie et démographie
2. Histoire
3. Politique, économie et situations culturelle et religieuse
4. Répartition géographique, statistique et questions de religion et d'ethnicité
5. Situation sociolinguistique
6. Politique linguistique
7. Les parlers grecs et le contact linguistique
8. Critique des sources et de la bibliographie
9. Bibliographie (sélective)

1. Géographie et démographie

1.1. Conformément à l'article 2 de la « Convention concernant l'échange des populations grecques et turques » signée le 30 janvier 1923 à Lausanne, la présence d'une communauté « de religion grecque orthodoxe » dans la Turquie d'Europe (et en même temps dans la Turquie entière) devrait se limiter aux habitants « déjà établis avant le 30 octobre 1918 dans les circonscriptions de la préfecture de la ville de Constantinople » dont trois se trouvaient sur la rive asiatique du Bosphore. Les habitants grecs des îles de Imbros (G. *Ímvros*; T. *İmroz*; depuis 1970: *Gökçeada*) et de Ténédos (G. *Ténedos*; T. *Bozcaada*) à l'entrée des Dardanelles (aujourd'hui dans la province de Çanakkale) ont été également exemptés de l'échange lorsque ces territoires, occupés par la Grèce depuis la première guerre balkanique (1912), ont été restitués à la Turquie en septembre 1923 (Alexandris 1980, 15).

1.2. Jusqu'en 1922, la région qui comprend la Turquie d'Europe (Thrace orientale) (T. *Trakya*, G. *Anatolikí Thráki*) avait compté parmi ses habitants aussi un taux considérable de populations de foi grecque-orthodoxe (T. *Rum*) (cf. art. 187). Ces populations (comprenant 1,177 personnes après le départ des troupes grecques en 1922; Pallis 1925, 329) ainsi que ceux parmi les habitants d'Istanbul et d'Imbros et Ténédos qui émigrèrent par la suite pour une raison ou une autre, se sont établis en majorité en Grèce. D'autres repartirent pour l'étranger (3,500 Imbriotes aux Etats-Unis en 1970; Alexandris 1980, 30). (Sur les immigrés turcophones → art. 187); → carte linguistique I.

2. Histoire

Tandis que la Thrace orientale figure parmi les premiers territoires byzantins soumis à la domination ottomane (→ art. 187), Constantinople (T. *İstanbul* < εις την πόλη; G. *Konstantinúpolis* ou simplement *i Póli*) ne tombera qu'en 1453, suivie par Imbros et Ténédos en 1455—1456. L'arrivée massive de populations turcophones en Thrace après la conquête se reflète dans la toponymie rurale qui a été dans une large mesure turquisée (→ art. 187). (A Imbros, par contre, des toponymes turcs n'ont été introduits que dans la période républicaine.) Istanbul perdit une grande partie de sa population indigène à la suite de la conquête, et l'élément turc-musulman allait y dominer (→ art. 187). Devenus minoritaires et sujets à certaines formes de discrimination, les habitants grecs-orthodoxes n'ont pourtant pas été exposés à une assimilation religieuse ou linguistique. La position du clergé orthodoxe s'améliora même, grâce aux privilèges accordés par le sultan au patriarche œcuménique. Ce dernier fut reconnu officiellement comme chef et responsable du *Rum milleti*, c'est-à-dire de la communauté des Grecs-orthodoxes qui comprenait aussi des communautés non-grécophones (slaves, albanaises, roumaines, arabes, *karamanlıs* [voir 4.4.], etc.). Par la suite, les Grecs-orthodoxes devaient toujours garder une position privilégiée par rapport aux autres communautés non-musulmanes et c'est à des Grecs d'Istanbul (« Phanariotes »), que furent alors réservés les postes les plus élevés accessibles à de non-musulmans (Grands dragomans de la Porte, voïvodes de Moldavie et de Valachie, 1711–1821).

Quand la Révolution grecque éclata en 1821, la communauté grecque d'Istanbul se trouva dans une situation très précaire (exécution du patriarche et de nombreux Phanariotes). Mais les réformes entreprises à partir de 1839, la protection des Etats européens (notamment la Russie) et le soutien moral et matériel de la Grèce indépendante lui ont permis un redressement remarquable. De nombreux établissements scolaires, des sociétés savantes et littéraires (comme le célèbre *Syllogos*, 1861–1922), des imprimeries, des journaux, etc. fondés pendant cette période formèrent la base d'un renouveau que l'on a appelé la « rehellénisation » (Clogg 1982, 197) des communautés grecques-orthodoxes de l'Empire, de l'Anatolie aussi bien que de la Thrace. Les membres de cette nouvelle élite occupèrent des postes très importants dans l'administration ottomane (diplomates, ministres des affaires étrangères, gouverneurs généraux (Samos (1834–1912); Crète (1878–1889), etc.). L'incontestable prédominance grecque dans l'économie, mais aussi dans certaines professions libérales, a créé l'idée très répandue dans le monde grec, selon laquelle les banquiers, entrepreneurs, industriels et hommes d'affaires grecs sont les « éducateurs des Turcs » (*dáskali ton Túrkon*) (cf. Sarris 1991, 21).

3. Politique, économie et situations culturelle et religieuse

3.1. Après la déroute de l'armée grecque en Asie Mineure (1922), peu s'en fallut que la communauté grecque d'Istanbul ne partage le sort de ses compatriotes d'Anatolie et de la Thrace Orientale qui furent échangés contre les Musulmans de Grèce (à l'exception de ceux installés en Thrace occidentale; → art. 182). Les stipulations négociées à Lausanne semblaient perpétuer les privilèges accordés auparavant aux *millets*, mais il s'est avéré très vite que ces privilèges étaient de moins en moins compatibles avec l'esprit du nouvel Etat turc, républicain, laïque et nationaliste. Malgré les quelques périodes de calme et de prospérité — coïncidant en général avec un rapprochement gréco-turc (1930–1940, 1946–1954, 1959–1964) —, l'histoire de la communauté grecque à Istanbul (de même qu'à Imbros et Ténédos) dans le nouvel Etat turc s'inscrit dans un déclin continuel et irréversible.

3.2. Sur le plan économique, la communauté grecque réussit à garder sa position forte pendant les premières décennies de la République. Mais dans le cadre d'une politique de nationalisations, le gouvernement turc commença à décréter des restrictions frappant en particulier les ressortissants helléniques. Pendant la guerre, le prélèvement sur les fortunes (T. *Varlık Vergisi*) a mené à des conditions très défavorables pour de nombreuses entreprises commerciales grecques. La période de calme de l'après-guerre se termina avec l'éclatement de la crise de Chypre (incidents du 5 au 6 septembre 1955), crise qui se solda avec l'effondrement de la communauté (sur les aspects économiques, cf. Sarris 1991, 22).

3.3. La participation des Grecs d'Istanbul à la vie politique, qui depuis 1876 avaient eu des députés au parlement, s'est achevée dans les années 60 (voir Alexandris 1983, 276).

3.4. L'emprise de l'Etat n'a pas épargné les institutions éducatives. Dans une ville comme Istanbul, qui avait été encore au début du siècle un des centres des activités scientifiques et de l'érudition du monde grécophone, on n'imprime plus de livres en grec et tout ce qui reste de la presse grécophone — jadis florissante — sont deux quotidiens à quatre pages, *Apoyevmatiní* (fondé en 1926) et *Ihó* (fondé en 1976).

3.5. Vu l'attitude peu loyale de la hiérarchie ecclésiastique pendant les « Années de l'Armistice » (→ art. 187), la permanence du Patriarche œcuménique à Istanbul a été mal vue par les négociateurs turcs à Lausanne. Dans les années vingt, deux patriarches ont été expulsés. Par la suite, des questions concernant la nationalité, le statut et les fonctions de ce dignitaire, allaient provoquer d'interminables discussions. De même, les activités de « Papa Eftim » (i. e. Paul Euthymios Karahisaríðis, 1884–1968), prêtre anatolien d'origine *karamanlı*, qui fut créateur d'une église « turque orthodoxe » (Jäschke 1964), ont envenimé pendant longtemps les rapports du patriarcat avec les autorités turques.

4. Répartition géographique, statistique et questions de religion et d'ethnicité

4.1. Vu la vie secrète de cette communauté, il est difficile de la repérer dans le tissu urbain aujourd'hui. Nous savons toutefois qu'elle s'est pratiquement éteinte dans le vieux Stamboul et même à Galata. On rencontre encore des grécophones à Beyoğlu (G. *Péra* ou *Stavroδrómi*) (où se trouvent aussi les lycées du Zápion et Zográfion fondés respectivement en 1857 et 1890, et les églises de la Ayía Triáδa et de la Panayía) et à Kurtuluş (G. *Tatáula*), autrefois le seul quartier d'Istanbul exclusivement grécophone. D'autres restes se trouvent aux Îles des Princes (→ art. 187) et à certains endroits sur les rives européennes et asiatiques du Bosphore. Dans les anciens faubourgs situés au sud d'Istanbul comme Bakırköy (*Makriköy*; G. *Makrohóri*) qui ont connu une poussée démographique extraordinaire (1,5 millions en 1990), les minorités traditionnelles ont été littéralement noyées au sein de la population turcophone.

4.2. En 1927 (premier recensement indiquant les langues maternelles), 91,902 personnes se déclaraient grécophones à Istanbul dans une communauté grecque-orthodoxe de 100,214 âmes, en plus de 26,419 avec un passeport grec (Alexandris 1983, 142). En 1965 (dernier recensement indiquant les langues maternelles) on n'enregistre plus que 47,207 Grecs-orthodoxes, dont 35,097 grécophones (Andrews 1989, 143). Pour la période après 1965 il n'y a que des estimations. Murphy donne encore un chiffre de 9,000 – 12,000 individus (Murphy 1986, 181), chiffre qui s'est réduit à 2,000 – 3,000 âmes entretemps (Sarris 1991). A Imbros, le nombre de grécophones est estimé à 1,000 personnes (Meinardus 1985, 57).

4.3. A la suite du processus de rehellénisation déjà évoqué, les termes *elliniká*, *ellinikí γlóssa* pour la langue et *Ellines* pour ceux qui la pratiquent, a remplacé dans une grande mesure les termes traditionnels de *roméika* («roméique») et de *Romií* (*Roméi*) (utilisés encore presqu'exclusivement par les auteurs phanariotes du XVIIIe siècle). Ces termes jouissent cependant toujours d'une certaine popularité et s'emploient avec une valeur affective ou sentimentale. Notons qu'une confusion semblable règne aujourd'hui dans la langue turque où le terme traditionnel de *Rumca* («grec») tend de plus en plus à être remplacé par *Yunanca* (à l'origine «grec ancien»).

4.4. La communauté grécophone d'Istanbul est aujourd'hui presqu'exclusivement de religion grecque-orthodoxe, les communautés catholiques et protestantes s'étant apparemment éteintes. Parmi les Orthodoxes turcophones (T. *Karamanlı*, G. *Karamanlíδes*) installés à Istanbul depuis le XVIe siècle, l'usage du turc (en caractères grecs) dans leurs écrits était très courant. («Papa Eftim» l'introduisit même dans la liturgie). Mais étant en grande partie bilingues, beaucoup de *Karamanlıs* s'étaient déjà hellénisés au cours du XIXe siècle. D'ailleurs, il y a eu toujours des individus d'origines ethniques différentes (slaves en particulier) au sein de la communauté grecque-orthodoxe. Les nationalismes surgis au XIXe siècle (schisme bulgare de 1870) et la rehellénisation menèrent toutefois à une différenciation plus nette. Signalons cependant qu'en 1927 encore un groupe d'Albanais orthodoxes à Istanbul demanda la séparation (Alexandris 1983, 172). Les membres de la petite communauté grecque-orthodoxe arabophone d'Istanbul, pour la plupart originaires de la province de Hatay (l'ancien Sandjak d'Alexandrette), ignorent en général le grec, fournissent cependant aujourd'hui les gardiens de nombreuses églises.

5. Situation sociolinguistique

5.1. Dans le Traité de Lausanne (→ art. 187) l'Etat turc reconnut la permanence de la minorité linguistique grécophone, mais pas sur un pied d'égalité avec la langue officielle. Les droits linguistiques dont elle devait jouir, se limitaient à un nombre restreint de prérogatives, surtout dans le domaine de la culture et de l'éducation (→ art. 187). Du reste, la politique était restrictive: C'est ainsi que les affiches, les publicités et les enseignes en grec ont disparu à Istanbul depuis la fin des années vingt. En 1964, l'importation de périodiques de la Grèce a été interdite. Pour mieux comprendre ce changement, il faut le comparer à la situation d'avant 1912, où le grec jouissait d'un statut *de facto* semi-officiel: à cette époque, la plupart des textes de lois et de codes étaient disponibles aussi dans une version grecque, la gazette officielle de la province d'Edirne parut aussi dans une version grecque et les habitants d'Imbros et Ténédos faisaient leur correspondance avec la capitale en grec (Alexandris 1980, 17).

5.2. L'attitude des grécophones d'Istanbul envers leur langue a été assez différente de celles des autres minorités linguistiques. Aux yeux de ceux qui la pratiquaient, le grec (en effet plutôt sa variété savante, la *kaθarévusa*) était une des langues les plus prestigieuses du monde avec un glorieux passé littéraire, qui, en plus, était enseignée dans les écoles de l'Occident. Jusqu'en 1922, l'idée d'une mission civilisatrice de la langue grecque pour tout l'Orient était bien implantée au sein de ce qu'on appelait la « Grande Idée » (Μεγάλη Ἰδέα) (Clogg 1982, 197). C'était aussi le grec qui jouissait du plus grand prestige chez les autres minoritaires d'Istanbul (→ art. 187). Un sens de supériorité culturelle même vis-à-vis des habitants de la Grèce métropolitaine (les « *Paleoelladítes* »), se fait d'ailleurs remarquer chez les Grecs d'Istanbul jusqu'à nos jours (cf. Kazazis 1970, 117). En ce qui concerne l'attitude des grécophones d'Istanbul envers la langue turque, elle rangeait en général entre l'indifférence et l'hostilité. L'introduction du turc dans le programme des écoles grecques a été accueillie à l'époque avec beaucoup de réserves. Les écoliers y réagissaient avec des propos comme: « Qu'est-ce que je ferai avec le turc? A quoi cela me sert? » (Τὶ θὰ κάμνω τὰ τουρκικά; τὶ μὲ χρειάζεται; Konstantinidis 1873, 11). Rien n'indique que cette attitude ait beaucoup changé par la suite. A en croire certains auteurs, l'antagonisme gréco-turc empêchait les grécophones même d'employer certains turquismes, qui étaient pourtant populaires dans la langue commune (cf. Dizikirikis 1975, 51). Notons qu'un contact plus intime avec les turcophones était pratiquement superflu, vu la ségrégation des communautés ethniques et religieuses dans la ville (cf. Laskaridou 1987, 35).

5.3. Un changement dans l'attitude culturelle et linguistique de la communauté ne s'est produit qu'après la guerre. L'intensification de l'étude du turc dans le programme des écoles minoritaires a certainement contribué dans une large mesure à ce que la génération née après 1950 était « devenue réellement bilingue et parlait couramment le turc » (Alexandris 1983, 297). La maîtrise du turc qui s'est généralisée dans la jeune génération, n'a cependant jamais risqué de déboucher sur le monolinguisme (cf. Murphy 1986, 187).

5.4. La « Question de la langue » (Γλωσσικόν Ζήτημα), à savoir le conflit entre la langue vulgaire, le démotique (*δimotikí*), et la langue écrite, archaïsante et puriste (*kaθarévusa*; cf. Mackridge 1985, 6−11), troublait les Grecs d'Istanbul beaucoup moins que ceux de la métropole; comme ailleurs, il y en avait qui se moquaient des excès de purisme (« *ellinikúres* »; cf. Dizikirikis 1975, 119). Mais grâce à l'influence des membres de la hiérarchie ecclésiastique et des sociétés savantes, des professeurs et des journalistes, la position de la *kaθarévusa* ne fut jamais mise en doute (cf. Dizikirikis 1975, 17). Un dernier reflet de cette attitude est l'*Apoyevmatiní* qui utilise jusqu'à nos jours une variété très proche de la *kaθarévusa*.

6. Politique linguistique

Le grec enseigné aux écoles d'Istanbul, depuis 1954 aussi par des professeurs venant de Grèce (Alexandris 1983, 249) et avec des manuels imprimés en Grèce, ne s'est jamais écarté du grec standard (GS). Le turc standard (TS) est la langue d'instruction obligatoire pour des matières comme l'histoire et la géographie. Il ne manque d'ailleurs pas d'observateurs à remarquer que la situation des écoles grecques (pour des statistiques voir Alexandris 1983, 287) est devenue désormais des plus précaires.

Depuis les années soixante, aucun dictionnaire bilingue n'a vu le jour à Istanbul, à l'exception de l'édition pirate d'un ouvrage datant de 1962 (et dont l'auteur fut un instituteur grec de la Thrace occidentale) en 1989. Notons cependant que depuis quelques années, le grec moderne est enseigné à titre de langue étrangère à l'Université d'Ankara.

Intéressée en premier lieu à garder le status quo linguistique, la communauté grecque n'a pas pris une part active dans l'élaboration de la nouvelle langue turque (→ art. 187). Le cas de l'avocat Theologos Anthomelidis (« *Teologos Gülbağlıoğlu* ») qui donnait dans les années 30 des conférences sur la Réforme de la langue aux « Maisons du Peuple » (T. *Halkevleri*) (Alexandris 1983, 193), est tout à fait exceptionnel.

7. Les parlers grecs et le contact linguistique

7.1. Les variétés de grec parlées dans la Turquie d'Europe se divisent en trois groupes bien distincts: (a) les parlers grecs d'Imbros et Ténédos, (b) les parlers de la Thrace orientale (GT) (qui ne survivent que chez les émigrés) dont les traits dialectaux sont assez saillants (cf. Ronzevalle 1911): en phonétique, c'est en particulier la substitution de /i/ et /u/ à /e/ et /o/ en syllabe atone. (c) le parler d'Istanbul (GI). Ce dernier, tout en partageant certains traits caractéristiques des dialectes grecs septentrionaux « ne diffère guère de la langue parlée commune » (Georgiadis

1974, 63; sur quelques particularités voir Kazazis 1970).

7.2. Au niveau du code écrit, l'influence du turc ne se manifeste que dans la langue commune, encore moins, quand il s'agit du style puriste de la *kaθarévusa*. Rappelons cependant l'emploi obligatoire de toponymes turcs (*Istambúl* au lieu de G *Konstantinúpolis*, etc.), qui a été décrété par le gouvernement dans les années trente. Au niveau du code oral, on avait observé jadis en GT l'emploi d'éléments turcs (mots, phrases) «dans des proportions vraiment extraordinaires» (Ronzevalle). Le GI, par contre, semblait avoir subi à un degré sensiblement moindre cette influence. En effet, les éléments turcs en GI qu'on peut relever dans la littérature (glossaires, romans, etc.) se rencontrent pour la plupart aussi dans la langue commune (du moins dans le vocabulaire passif) ou dans les parlers d'autres régions de la Grèce (cf. Koukkidis 1959). Comme en GS, quelques suffixes empruntés au turc sont devenus productifs, d'autres, comme *-siz* «sans» n'apparaissent que dans les emprunts (GI *hairsízis* < T *hayırsız* «vaurien»; GT *hairsï'is* et *hairsïž'kus*). Le statut de ces turquismes est, comme d'ailleurs dans toutes les langues balkaniques, assez instable (cf. Kazazis 1972). En GT aussi bien qu'en GI un bon nombre de termes et de phrases semblent être employés en premier lieu pour des motifs d'expressivité, d'ironie, ou simplement dans l'intention d'imiter les Turcs. A la différence des emprunts grecs en TS, les éléments turcs en GI (et aussi GT) sont souvent employés concurremment avec des synonymes relevant de la langue parlée (p. ex. *haiváni* — < T *hayvan* «animal, bête» — «imbécile» à côté de *zóo*, GT *zúo*, etc.) ou, dans le domaine des termes techniques, de la langue savante et liturgique.

7.3. En ce qui concerne l'adaptation phonétique des éléments turcs, le GT a adopté les voyelles turques /ï/, /ö/ et /ü/ étrangers au GS, tandis que le GI les remplace par les sons les plus proches. L'adaptation des phonèmes consonantiques turcs inconnus en GS a été relativement facile en GT, puisque ceux-là faisaient déjà partie de son système. En GI, par contre, beaucoup de locuteurs éprouvent des difficultés à prononcer les chuintantes /š/ et /ž/ et les palatales /dž/ et /č/ et les remplacent par /s/ et /z/ ou /dz/ et /ts/, un trait qui est caractéristique de l'accent traditionnel *Rum*.

Morphologiquement, en GI aussi bien qu'en GT les éléments turcs ont été parfaitement adaptés au système. (Pour les substantifs cf. Newton 1963, 26.) Des adjectifs à base turque — plutôt rares en GI, mais très nombreux en GT — sont formés à l'aide de suffixes (*-ikos*; *-iδikos*, GT *-iθ'kus*; *-énios*; etc.; de même que des verbes; surtout par *-dizo*: *kavurdízo*, < T *kavur-mak*, «fricasser, rôtir»), également assez rares en GI.

7.4. Il existe en GS et TS de nombreuses expressions idiomatiques parallèles (étudiées souvent dans le cadre de la linguistique balkanique; cf. Kazazis 1972, 96—98) que l'on pourrait aussi considérer comme des calques sémantiques. En ce qui concerne des interférences, on peut en détecter dans la phrase stambouliote (communiquée par P. Georgiadis) suivante: «*páo na playáso* (GS: «faire coucher») *hrímata stin bánka* (< T; GS *trápeza*)» — «Je vais déposer de l'argent à la banque», car elle reflète l'expression turque *para yatırmak* (T *yatırmak* 1. faire coucher; 2. déposer).

7.5. Du côté turc les effets d'un contact linguistique se sont manifestés surtout au niveau de l'argot de l'ancienne capitale, où les éléments empruntés au grec étaient autrefois particulièrement nombreux. Parfois l'élément grec emprunté — un impératif, un participe, une phrase, etc. — a été aussi incorporé dans un verbe phraséologique (avec *etmek* «faire») comme dans *kitakse etmek* — < G *kítakse* «regarde!» — «regarder, observer», *piyastos etmek* — < G *piastós* (part.) «pris, attrapé» — «attraper», ou même *kopsi kefali etmek* «couper la tête; circoncire». Certaines de ces expressions sont entrées dans la langue commune des Turcs. On les rencontre non seulement dans des traductions de romans policiers, mais ils figurent aussi dans les dictionnaires. Il y en a qui ont été popularisées par des auteurs comme Sait Faik (Abasıyanık; 1906—1954), alors que d'autres sont tombées en désuétude (cf. Aktunç 1990, 357—359).

8. Critique des sources et de la bibliographie

Par rapport au nombre toujours croissant d'études consacrées à la situation linguistique en Anatolie, la recherche sur les contacts linguistiques turco-grecs dans la Turquie d'Europe se trouve encore à un stade peu avancé. Pour les parlers de la Thrace orientale, nous disposons d'excellents articles du P. Ronzevalle datant du début du siècle et de quelques publications — à valeur très inégale — du

Ἀρχεῖον τοῦ θρακικοῦ λαογραφικοῦ καὶ γλωσσικοῦ θησαυροῦ. Sur le développement récent à Imbros et Ténédos nous ne savons rien. D'après Alexandris, il n'est pas rare d'entendre des jeunes parler en turc entre eux dans les quartiers des émigrés d'Istanbul à Athènes (Alexandris 1983, 297). Vu le développement démographique actuel, la recherche sur les contacts linguistiques devra donc commencer là-bas.

Je tiens à remercier M. Paul Georgiadis (Munich) et M. Basile Photiadis (Methymni/Lesbos) des renseignements qu'ils ont bien voulu me fournir.

9. Bibliographie (sélective)

Aktunç, Hulki (1990): *Türkçenin Büyük Argo Sözlüğü (Tanıklarıyla)*, Istanbul.

Alexandris, Alexandros (1980): «Imbros and Tenedos: A Study of Turkish Attitudes Towards Two Ethnic Greek Island Communities Since 1923». In: *Journal of the Hellenic Diaspora* VII/1, 5–31.

Alexandris, Alexandros (1983): *The Greek Minority in Istanbul and Greek-Turkish Relations 1918–1974*, Athènes.

Andrews, Peter Alford (Ed.) (1989): *Ethnic Groups in the Republic of Turkey*, Wiesbaden.

Clogg, Richard (1982): «The Greek *Millet* in the Ottoman Empire». In: Braude, Benjamin/Lewis, Bernard (1982): *Christians and Jews in the Ottoman Empire*, Londres, I., 185–207.

Dizikirikis, Giakovos S. (1975): *Na xetourkepsôme tê glossa mas* [Déturquifions notre langue!], Athènes.

Georgiadis, Pavlos (1974): *Die lautlichen Veränderungen der türkischen Lehnwörter im Griechischen* (thèse), Munich.

Jäschke, Gotthard (1964): «Die Türkisch-Orthodoxe Kirche». In: *Der Islam 39* (1964) 95–129; *45* (1969), 317–323.

Kazazis, Kostas (1970): «The Relative Importance of Parents and Peers in First-Language Acquisition: The Case of some Constantinopolitan Families in Athens». In: *General Linguistics 10*, 111–120.

Kazazis, Kostas (1972): «The status of Turkisms in the present-day Balkan languages». In: *Aspects of the Balkans: Continuity and Change*, H. Birnbaum/S. Vryonis (Eds.), La Haye/Paris, 87–116.

Konstantinidis, Alexandros (1873): *Theôrêtikê kai praktikê methodos pros ekmathêsin tês othômatikês glôssês* [Méthode théorique et pratique pour l'apprentissage de la langue ottomane], Constantinople.

Koukkidis, Konstantinos (1959): «Lexikologion hellênikôn lexeôn paragomenôn ek tês tourkikês glôssês» [Glossaire de mots grecs d'origine turque]. In: *Archeion tu thrakiku laografiku kai glôssiku thêsauru* XXIV/1959, 281–312; XXV/1960, 121–200.

Laskaridou, Aikaterini D. (1987): *Dekapente hiliades meres stên Kônstantinoupolê tên patrida mou* [Quinze mille jours à Constantinople, ma patrie], Athènes.

Mackridge, Peter (1985): *The Modern Greek Language. A Descriptive Analysis of Standard Modern Greek*, Oxford.

McCarthy, Justin (1990): «The population of Ottoman Europe before and after the Fall of the Empire». In: *IIIrd Congress on the Social and Economic History of Turkey*, Lowry, S./Hallox, R. S. (Eds.), Istanbul/Washington/Paris, 275–298.

Meinardus, Ronald (1985): «Die griechisch-türkische Minderheitenfrage». In: *Orient 26*, 48–60.

Murphy, Richard A. (1986): «Observations on Language Usage Among Bilingual Communities in Istanbul». In: *Osmanlı Araştırmaları 5*, 175–193.

Newton, Brian (1963): «The Grammatical Integration of Italian and Turkish Substantives into Modern Greek». In: *Word 19*, 20–30.

Pallis, A. Alexandros (1925): «Racial migrations in the Balkans during the years 1912–1924». In: *Geographical Journal 66*, 315–331.

Ronzevalle, P. Louis (1911): «Les emprunts turcs dans le grec vulgaire de Roumélie et spécialement d'Andrinople». In: *Journal Asiatique*, 10ᵉ sér., 18, pp. 69–106, 257–226, 405–461.

Sarris, Neoklis (1991): «Thesmikê plaisiosê tôn meionotêtôn me basê tên Synthêkê tês Lôzanês» [Le cadre légal des minorités d'après le Traité de Lausanne]. In: *Dikaiôma*, (recueil édité par l'Association des émigrés grecs d'Imbros, d'Istanbul, de Ténédos et de la Thrace orientale en Thrace [grecque]), Komotini, 20–28.

Johann Strauß, Freiburg i. Br. (Allemagne)

189. Turkish—Judaeo-Spanish

1. Geography and demography
2. History
3. Politics, economy and general cultural and religious situation
4. Statistics and ethnoprofile
5. Sociolinguistic situation
6. Language political situation
7. General contactlinguistic portrait
8. Critical evaluation of the sources and bibliography used
9. Bibliography (selected)

1. Geography and demography

In European Turkey, Judaeo-Spanish (JS) speaking Sephardic Jews are presently concentrated in the former capital of the Ottoman Empire, Istanbul (JS *Estanbol*; old: *Konstan(dina)*). Other communities that existed until recently in Eastern Thrace (Edirne, Tekirdağ, Kırklareli etc.) are now almost extinct (cf. Epstein 1989, 522; for figures on communities in Anatolia, cf. Andrews 1989, 157, Séphiha 1991, 78). The number of Jews living in European Turkey, estimated at some 70,000 persons before the Balkan wars (for statistics cf. Gilmer 1986, Appendix A, Shaw 1991, 273 f), has dwindled mainly as a result of emigraton. After the creation of the state of Israel, a large number of Jews from Turkey left for that state where they form the largest Sephardic community after that of Turkey itself. It is well organized and has retained close ties with Turkey. Periodicals in JS published there (*La Luz de Israel*, *Aki Yerushalayim*) have also readers in Turkey (cf. Séphiha 1991, 74). Other sizable emigrant communities from Turkey exist in South America, the US and in France (for figures see Séphiha 1991). More than 5000 Jews from Turkey are said to have returned from Israel to their home-country between 1948 and 1965 (Shaw 1991, 258); → Language Map I.

2. History

The Sephardic Jews in European Turkey owe their presence in these parts to the expulsion of their ancestors from the Iberian peninsula at the end of the 15th century. The majority of these forced emigrants eventually settled in the Ottoman Empire where they were to form compact communities in the major urban centres. The dynamic Sepharadim also absorbed the older, Greek or Slavic-speaking Jewish communities and became, with a few exceptions, the dominant element both in the Balkans and in Anatolia. In Istanbul, a Greek-speaking Jewish community (termed *Romaniotes* or *Gregos* by the newcomers), some Ashkenazic Jews and a number of Karaites were already present at the time of the arrival of the Sephardic Jews. After the conquest of Constantinople (1453) the Jews had become part of the Ottoman *millet*-system (→ art. 187) and the Grand Rabbi (T *hahambaşı*) Moses Capsali had been recognized by Sultan Mehmed II as the spiritual and administrative leader of the Istanbul Jewish community in 1456. The Spanish (or Portuguese) speaking Sepharadim arrived in Istanbul under Mehmed's successor Bayezid II (1481—1512). Until the second half of the 17th century, the Ottoman Jews played a very important role in the economy of the state as bankers, traders, tax-farmers etc. In 1493 already, the newcomers from the Iberian peninsula had established the first Hebrew Printing Press in Istanbul (which was also the first press in the Ottoman Empire). This period is therefore regarded as the "Golden Age of Ottoman Jewry" (Shaw). The following decline is largely due to internal struggles. The activities of Shabbetai Zevi from Izmir (1625—1676), the "False Messiah", led to an internal division and to the emergence of a new community of Crypto-Jews (T *Dönme* "Turncoats"). Furthermore, the Jews faced increasing competition with the other non-Muslim communities (Greeks, Armenians) who, moreover, would eventually enjoy the special protection of foreign powers. Despite the tolerance of the Ottomans in religious matters, Jews (like the other non-Muslim communities) suffered from discrimination. Also their relations with other minorities were often strained. In the 19th century, the situation of the community in Istanbul (and elsewhere) is described by many in rather sombre colours. First attempts of Westernization met with strong resistance from the conservative religious leadership which was supported by the majority of the community.

The turning point came when the *Alliance Israélite Universelle* (founded in 1860) started its activities. The first modern school founded by the *Alliance* in Istanbul (in the Hasköy neighbourhood) dates from 1874. In the *Alliance*-schools, French was the primary language of instruction. French was subsequently to become the second (or even first) language of the educated members of the community. There was a flourishing press, mainly in JS and French and occasionally also in Turkish (sometimes in Hebrew characters) or Hebrew. In Istanbul, the first periodical in JS, *Or Israel* "The Light of Israel" appeared in 1853 (cf. Benbanaste 1988). In the field of literature, the record is less impressive. Mainly popular novels were published in Judaeo-Spanish, most of them translated from French or Hebrew. A few Jewish poets like Isaac Ferera (1883–1933) and Avram Naon (İbrahim Nom; 1878–1967) even used Ottoman-Turkish as a medium of literary expression.

3. Politics, economy and general cultural and religious situation

In the Turkish Republic (founded in 1923), the fate of the Jewish community was quite different from that of Greeks and Armenians. Zionism had not troubled the relations of the community with the Turks. It had relatively few active supporters among the Istanbul community. During the "Years of the Armistice" (1918–1922), the Jewish community refused to cooperate with the Greeks and the Armenians and some of its members actively supported the National Movement under Mustafa Kemal (later Atatürk). This loyalty has also been gratefully acknowledged by many Turks (cf. Yetkin 1992, *passim*). Jews did not suffer from territorial restrictions, as did the Greeks and Armenians, but in 1934, the Turkish authorities had all Jews forcibly removed from the strategically sensitive zones of Edirne and the Straits. Certain privileges (including linguistic rights) granted by the Treaty of Lausanne to the former *millets* (→ art. 187) were renounced by the community in 1925 (Shaw 1991, 246). It was hit very hard financially by the 1942 *Varlık Vergisi* (→ art. 187). Also the events of September 1955, whose victims had been the Greek population, gave a new impetus to emigration. In the '80s, the community came under attack by Arab terrorists. However, except for participation in political life (which came to an end in the early sixties; see Shaw 1991, 265), Jews have been very conspicuously present in all spheres of public life in the last decades. There are prominent Jewish industrialists, businessmen, journalists and university teachers and even writers (J. H. Gerez). Since the emigration movement had primarily affected the poorer section of the population, the present community is generally well-off. It is well organized. There are actually twenty-six synagogues in Istanbul and a number of social and service organizations (including hospitals, sports clubs etc.) are run by the community (cf. Kastoryano 1992). Intermarriage with Muslim Turks is still frowned upon (cf. Malinowski, 1982, 13). It is, however, estimated by some as high as eight to ten percent a year (Shaw 1991, 267). The Fifth Centennial of the expulsion from Spain was commemorated in 1992 (as had been the fourth in 1892) with a number of public events. Prominent members of the Jewish community in Istanbul, for which Turkey had provided a safe haven during the Holocaust, have repeatedly stressed their loyalty to the Turkish Republic and that they bear no grudge against Turkey either for the *Varlık Vergisi* or any other calamity that had befallen it in this century (cf. Yetkin 1992, 271 f (interview with Jak Kamhi)).

4. Statistics and ethnoprofile

4.1. No official statistics have been available for the Jewish population in Istanbul since 1965. At that time, a total of 30,831 Jews were registered in Istanbul from which only a quarter declared "Jewish" (T. *Yahudice*) as their mother tongue (→ art. 187). The present figures speak of some 20,000 Jews in Istanbul (Shaw, 259). As to the number of speakers of JS, there are only conjectures.

4.2. There have been several internal migration movements among the Jewish population of Istanbul in this century (cf. Kastoryani 1992, 257 ff). Old Jewish neighbourhoods like Balat and Hasköy on the shores of the Golden Horn with their ancient synagogues are now in a desolate state and very few Jews still live there. A survey of Istanbul Jewry carried out in February 1987 and published in the *Şalom* newspaper found that the bulk of Istanbul Jewry was living in the area north of Taksim square, in the Şişli (31%), Gayrettepe (25%), Nişantaş (17%), and Kurtuluş (6%) areas, while most of the remainder live in the Anatolian suburbs of Göztepe (with an important community centre) (5%), Caddebostan (5%) and Suadiye (3%), and the remaining 13 percent live elsewhere (cf. Shaw 1991, 262). The Princes Isles (T *Adalar*) have a considerable Jewish population, especially in the summer.

4.3. Even among its speakers, it is still somewhat difficult to find agreement concerning the name of the ethnic language of the Sephardic Jews in Turkey (for a discussion of the divergent terminology used by scholars, see Busse 1991 a). At present, the most commonly accepted self-designation by speakers of the language in Istanbul is *espanyol* ("Spanish"), or *cudyo* ("Jewish") which corresponds to T *Yahudice* (cf. Şaul 1983, 328, Malinowski 1986, 14; but cf. also Murphy 1986, 186). In formal writing, however, it is usually referred to as *judeo-espanyol* (< French), or *cudeo-espanyol* (cf. Benbanaste 1988, *passim*). This terminology has also been accepted to some degree in Turkish, where *Cudeo-İspanyolca* is used instead of *Yahudice* or *Yahudice İspanyolca* (a term also used by Galante in his Turkish writings). The use of the term *Ladino* (spelt *Lad'ino*; see 5.2.) is restricted to (mostly bilingual) editions of religious texts (cf. Mechoulam [1962]). The term *cudezmo* is apparently unfamiliar to the present generation (Malinowski 1982, 14).

4.4. The Jewish community of Istanbul, though predominantly Sephardic in outlook (ca. 95%, Murphy 1986, 180) has always contained a number of subdivisions. Thus, for canonical reasons, the Italian community, which had separated from the Sepharadim in 1866, continues to hold its own services. The Istanbul *Dönmes*, mostly descendants of immigrants from Salonica, have been linguistically assimilated to Turkish. However, endogamy still seems to be the rule and they keep a certain distance from Jews and Muslim Turks alike. Relations between the Sepharadim and the (mainly Yiddish-speaking) Ashkenazic Jews (whose number had considerably increased in the late 19th century) have long been characterized by mutual dislike (cf. Galante II, 219—220). Some resentment can still be felt today. The very small Karaite community (cf. 2.), which today numbers less than 100 members, continues to observe their own rites and traditions outside the authority and control of the Chief Rabbinate. Their ethnic language is a variety of Greek (Galante VIII, 99; Kuzgun 1993, 237).

5. Sociolinguistic situation

5.1. Unlike Greek and Armenian, JS has been traditionally held by its speakers (even monolingual ones) in very low esteem. By many, it is still regarded as a *"jargon"* (cf. Malinowski 1982, 16, Gilmer 1986, 29). This may reflect the hostile attitude of the teachers of the *Alliance*-schools; but one should also bear in mind that the language always had to compete with other languages, all of them more prestigious than JS: Hebrew as the liturgical language (which was also widely used for poetry), French as the language of Modernism and the first (or second) language of the upper classes, and Turkish as the official language and that of the dominant group.

5.2. For the translation of Hebrew texts, a specific variety of JS known as *Ladino* is still in use. Until the 19th century, most of the literature is in fact *Ladino*. Sticking slavishly to Hebrew syntax (*"Judéo-espagnol calque"* (Séphiha)), and having preserved certain archaic features, it could hardly serve as a model for a modern secular literary prose. The language used in the JS press, novel writing etc. which developed later, on the other hand, was strongly influenced by French patterns and has led to a variety of JS termed appropriately as *"judéo-fragnol"* by Séphiha (cf. Séphiha 1986, *passim*). This variety is still dominant in the articles published in JS by the last Jewish periodical left in Turkey, the weekly *Şalom*. As regards the spoken language, its different varieties reflected very much the prevailing social divisions of the community (for a systematic description, including the rabbinical variety with a strong Hebrew admixture, see Bunis 1976). The composite, but more Hispanic variety of JS remained the language spoken by the lower classes who used to mock the Gallicized speech of the French educated upper classes (*"frankeados"*; cf. Bunis 1982; Jerushalmi 1990, 35).

5.3. Turkish, though the official language, was far from being a dominant language in Istanbul until the middle of this century. Many speakers of JS (especially females) only had a very rudimentary knowledge of it. Furthermore, their Turkish was characterized by a very conspicuous accent which has long been ridiculed by the Turkish Shadow-theatre (*Karagöz*) and "Jewish Jokes" (*Yahudi Fıkra-*

ları). This accent can still be heard among speakers of the older generation (whereas speakers more proficient in Turkish may pronounce Turkish words in a more Turkish way). Interestingly enough, even monolingual speakers of Turkish retain an accent in terms of a peculiar sentence-melody (cf. Şaul 1983, 347, Jerushalmi 1990, 29).

6. Language political situation

6.1. The Sephardic community in Istanbul has experienced a double language shift in this century. Whereas the shift from JS to French was limited to a special section of the population, the subsequent shift to Turkish has affected the community as a whole (→ art. 187). Appeals to adopt Turkish have a long history which goes far beyond the Republican era. The *Vatandaş, Türkçe konuş!* ("Citizen, speak Turkish!") campaign starting in the late twenties met with hardly any resistance in the JS speaking community. It was supported wholeheartedly by certain institutions (cf. Farhi 1937) and by prominent members of the community. Two of them, Abraham Galante [Bodrumlu] (1880–1961), the eminent historian of the Jews of Turkey, and Munis Tekinalp (*alias* Moïse Cohen; 1883–1961), a supporter of the ideas of Turkish Nationalism, were particularly insistent upon comprehensive Turkification (cf. Landau 1984, 23). Although it is difficult to assess the community's reaction to their recommendations ("Think Turkish, speak Turkish, pray Turkish" etc.), these did in fact anticipate much of the course of things to come. Sephardic Jews not only adopted in great number Turkish family or even forenames after 1934 (on naming see also Gilmer 1986, 28), they also started to speak only in Turkish with their children who have become by now monolingual speakers of Turkish.

6.2. In the traditional education system of the community, JS had only served as a tool for the understanding of the sacred language, Hebrew, with which it shared the same alphabet. In the Jewish minority schools granted by the Treaty of Lausanne (of which only two have remained) instruction has been exclusively in Turkish (classes in Hebrew, however, are still offered). Many members of the community also send their children to State schools, whereas the wealthier continue to send them to foreign private schools (with English or French as the language of instruction).

6.3. In the absence of any institutional support in the form of schools, it is the synagogue which, besides the family, plays the most important role for the maintenance of the ethnic language. According to Séphiha, the position of JS is still undisputed in the Grand Rabbinate (Séphiha 1991, 79). Though standards in Hebrew have considerably declined, Turkish has still not become the liturgical language.

6.4. A particular aspect of "Turkification" is the adoption of Latin characters for JS. The Hebrew-based Raši-script (which faces similar problems in rendering the sounds of JS as the Arabic alphabet does for Turkish; cf. Kohring 1991) was replaced by the new alphabet from the early 30's onward (on the first spelling-system see Farhi 1937, 154). The Latin alphabet in its Turkish version (including certain spelling conventions) is now firmly established in publications in Turkey whereas the emigrant press in Israel uses a somewhat different system; ch (formerly tch) [tʃ], dj [dʒ] sh [ʃ] instead of ç, c, ş (cf. Kohring 1991, 99). After world war II, even Hebrew texts and prayer-books began to be published in Latin characters (cf. Mechoulam [1962]). Texts in *Ladino* are spelt in a slightly different way, by distinguishing, for example, between d and d' (for [ð]).

6.5. No serious attempts to standardize JS have been made by the Istanbul-community. Its speakers also sorely lack the most indispensable tools. Whereas Armenians and – to a lesser extent – Greeks used to publish a considerable number of grammars and bilingual dictionaries to facilitate the study of Turkish, none of these resources are available for JS. Since in the eyes of its speakers JS had become a specifically Jewish language, they very rarely resorted to Modern Spanish, and indeed long remained unaware of its very existence (cf. Şaul 1983, 327). It is vehemently rejected by some speakers even today (cf. Jerushalmi 1990, vi).

7. General contactlinguistic portrait

As a result of a centuries-old language contact, the lexicon of JS contains a large number of borrowings from Turkish. In the first version of the ethico-homiletical Bible commentary *Me'am Lo'ez* (18th c.) already, we find a considerable number of Turkish loanwards, mainly (but not exclusively) referring to material culture (foods and dishes, clothes, plants and animals, administrative terms etc. (cf. Wiesner 1981)). Some of the T borrowings in JS are genuine Turkish elements, whereas others came from other languages (even French) via Turkish (like *gazeta* "newspaper" (T *gazete*)) and form part of a common Levantine heritage. There are also adjectives (like the old Turkish loanwords *kolay* "easy" and *yuç* (< T *güç*) "difficult" (which later have been supplanted by the French borrowings *fasil* (cf. Spanish *fácil*) and *difisil* (or *defisil*)), adverbs (*yene* (T *yine*, *gene*) "once more", *mahsus* "expressly, on purpose", etc.), interjections (*ayde* (T *haydi*) "Go on!", *vah* (T *vah*) "What a shame!", etc.). In the spoken language, one encounters even whole sentences (curses, commands, protests, proverbs etc.; cf. Danon 1903—1904; 1913). Examples of code-switching can already be detected in humouristic dialogues published in the early 20th century. JS has also adopted a remarkably high number of Turkish verbs (with the ending -(d)ear), including derived (causative, passive) forms (cf. the list in Gilmer 1986, 91—100).

The status of these loans resembles very much that of T loanwords in other minority-languages, especially Greek (→ art. 188). Relatively few words occur in texts with a strongly Gallicized vocabulary. Many Turkish words can be avoided either by the use of synonyms from the Spanish stock or by drawing on the almost inexhaustible resources of the French language. Different forms may even be used for the same referent by the same speaker or writer: JS *köyes* (T *köy*) "villages" may thus be replaced by *vilajyos* (< F *village*) and the meaning of a sentence like "One should not interfere in government affairs" may be conveyed accordingly by *no kale mesklarse en kestiones* (< F *question*) *del governo* as well as by *no kale karişterearse* (< T *karıştırmak*) *en meseles* [< *mesele*] *del hukumat* (< *hükûmet*) (Jerushalmi 1990, v). In written JS, the frequency of T elements depends to a large extent on the genre. There are, of course, much more of them in humouristic literature and translations from Turkish than in newspaper articles or in novels translated from the French. Turkish words are more or less absent in texts in *Lad'ino*. In written JS, lexical instability has resulted in the curious practice of adding synonyms in parentheses to words supposed to be unfamiliar to the reader. We find this already in the 19th century. The synonyms provided were not always Turkish but the recent decline of JS and the increased proficiency of its speakers in T have led to an almost exclusive use of Turkish words in this context.

Turkish apparently had little if any impact on the phonetic system of JS. In spoken JS, Turkish words traditionally were adapted to the phonetics of JS. (The same is true for the variety of Turkish spoken by members of the old generation, termed "Judaeo-Turkish" (JT) for the purpose of this article). Certain loanwords seem to reflect older forms. But there may be also an influence of other contact languages (notably Greek). In general, the laws of Turkish vowel harmony are dealt with in JS (and JT) in a rather peculiar way. There is also the puzzling case of [y] and [œ] retained in certain borrowings from French (*enstrüksyon, doktör, jönes*) whereas the T rounded vowels /ö/, /ü/ are replaced by sounds close to them (e,o; i,u). T [ï] is replaced either by [u] or [i]. /h/ is dropped in Hebrew words as well as in borrowings from T (*cail* (< T *câhil*) "ignorant, unexperienced"; T palatal g [g'] is regularly replaced by [j]: cf. JS *yuç* (< T *güç*); JT *zenyin* (< T *zengin* "rich").

As far as nouns and adjectives are concerned, the Turkish elements are less consequently adapted to the structure of the language than in Greek. Some words have received Spanish feminine endings (*çanaka* (< T *çanak*) "pot"), and feminine forms exist for other borrowings (*muşteria* "(female) customer" (masc. *muşteri* (T *müşteri*)). Some T words ending in -a are treated like feminines: *munças paras* "a lot of money" (T *para* "money"), others obtain the diminutive suffixes (*-iko, -ito*; cf. Galanti 1948, 15). The majority of the borrowings, however, have not been incorporated in this way and form a sharp contrast with the Spanish elements. Many borrowings from T contain the suffixes *-ci* (*ezaci* (T *eczacı* [ɛz:a:dʒï]) "chemist", *kiraci* [k'ira:dʒi] (< *kira* JS/T "rent") "tenant"; *-li* (*Estanbolli, Istanbulli* "man from Istanbul" (fem. *Estanbolliya, Istanbulliya*) or *-lik*: *caillik* (< T *câhillik*) "ignorance, folly"). This suffix is sometimes also attached to Hebrew words: *sahallik* "foolishness" (< H *saḵal*) (cf. Galanti 1948, 15).

Calques have been a frequent phenomenon in JS (cf. Wagner 1954). In the following example from a novel by Eliya Karmona (1870–1931) (Karmona 1948, 88): *En esto eço tambyen Lui tyene un dediko* "Louis is also involved in this matter" (lit. "has a finger in it") reproduces the T expression (*bu işte*) *parmağı vardır*. JS *eço* corresponds semantically to T *iş* (1. work 2. business 3. affair). To this category also belong phraseological verbs formed with a noun and the verb *azer* "to do" (T *etmek*): cf. Bunis 1982, 60 (extract from the JS humouristical paper *El Djuguetón* "The Jestler"): ... *kere azer alay kon nozotros* "he wants to pull our legs" (= T *bizimle alay etmek istiyor*).

8. Critical evaluation of the sources and bibliography used

Although there has been a remarkable upsurge in Sephardic studies (mainly thanks to scholars living in the diaspora) during the last decades, relatively little attention has been devoted to the variety spoken in Istanbul since Wagner's description (Wagner 1914). The T elements in particular need to be analysed more thoroughly. The situation of the Jewish community (including their linguistic situation; cf. Farhi 1937, Séphiha 1973, Malinowski 1982) has been repeatedly studied since then and more surveys are expected to follow. Since JS, much like the *patois* and *langues régionales* in France, is a dying language, research will become increasingly difficult. The Sephardic community of Istanbul, struggling with the preservation of its cultural heritage, welcomes any interest showed for its ethnic language. But it cannot always meet the expectations of scholars in the field of JS studies. This is graphically illustrated by Séphiha commenting on his field work in 1970: "(...) enfant d'une famille émigrée de Constantinople en Europe vers 1913, notre judéo-espagnol nous parut plus près de ses sources que celui des Juifs de Turquie." (Séphiha 1991, 56)

9. Bibliography (selected)

Andrews, Peter Alford (Ed.) (1989): *Ethnic Groups in the Republic of Turkey*, Wiesbaden.

Benbanaste, Nesim (1988): *Örneklerle Türk Musevi Basının Tarihçesi* [History of the Jewish Press in Turkey with Examples], Istanbul.

Bunis, David M. (1982): "Types of nonregional variations in early Modern Eastern Spoken Judezmo". In: *International Journal of the Sociology of Language 37*, 41–69.

Busse, Winfried (Ed.) (1991): *Judenspanisch I*, [*Neue Romania 12*], Berlin.

Busse, Winfried (1991 a): "Zur Problematik des Judenspanischen". In: Busse (1991), 37–84.

Danon, Abraham (1903–1904): "Essai sur les vocables turcs dans le judéo-espagnol". In: *Keleti Szemle 4, 5*, 216–229, 111–126.

Danon, Abraham (1913): "Le turc dans le judéo-espagnol". In: *Revue Hispanique 29*, 5–12.

Epstein, Marc (1989): "The Jews in Turkey". In: Andrews (1989), 519–524.

Farhi, Gentille (1937): "La situation linguistique du Sephardite à Istanbul". In: *Hispanic Review 5*, 151–158.

Galante, Avram (1985): *Histoire des Juifs de Turquie*, 9 vols., Istanbul.

Galanti, Avram (1948): *Türkçenin İspanyolca üzerine teesiri* [The Turkish influence on Judaeo-Spanish], Istanbul.

Gilmer, Paul Gregory (1986): *Judeo-Spanish to Turkish: linguistic correlates of language death*, Ann Arbor, Mich. (Diss. University of Texas at Austin).

Jerushalmi, Isaak (1990): *From Ottoman Turkish to Ladino. The "Risâle-i Ahlâk" of Sadık Rifat Pasha*, Cincinnati.

Karmona, Eliya (1948): *Kazado por dolor* [A painful wedding] (Tk. title: *İztiraplı (sic) bir Evlenme. Musevice Roman*.) Gayus, Eliya (Ed.), Istanbul.

Kastoryano, Riva (1992): "From *millet* to community: the Jews of Istanbul". In: *Ottoman and Turkish Jewry. Community and Leadership*, Rodrigue, Aron (Ed.), Bloomington.

Kohring, Heinrich (1991): "Judenspanisch in hebräischer Schrift". In: Busse 1991, 95–170.

Kuzgun, Şaban (1993): *Hazar ve Karay Türkleri* [The Khazar and Karaite Turks], 2nd ed., Ankara.

Landau, Jacob M. (1984): *Tekinalp, Turkish Patriot 1883–1961*, Nederlands Historisch-Archaeologisch Instituut te Istanbul.

Malinowski, Arlene (1982): "A report on the status of Judeo-Spanish in Turkey". In: *International Journal of the Sociology of Language 37*, 7–23.

Mechoulam, David (1962): *La Agad'a de Pesah kon karakteres latinos. Ebreo i Lad'ino* [The Passover Haggada in Latin Characters. Hebrew and Ladino], Istanbul.

Murphy, Richard A. (1986): "Observations on language usage among bilingual communities in Istanbul". In: *Osmanlı Araştırmaları 5*, 175–193.

Şaul, Mahir (1983): "The mother tongue of the polyglot: Cosmopolitism and Nationalism among the Sepharadim of Istanbul." In: *Anthropological Linguistics 25/3*, 326–358.

Séphiha, Haïm Vidal (1973): "The present state of Judeo-Spanish in Turkey". In: *The American Sephardi 6*, 22−29.

Séphiha, Haïm Vidal (1986): *Le judéo-espagnol*, Paris.

Séphiha, Haïm Vidal (1991): *L'Agonie des Judéo-Espagnols*, 3rd edition, Paris.

Shaw, Stanford J. (1991): *The Jews of the Ottoman Empire and the Turkish Republic*, New York.

Wagner, Max Leopold (1914): *Beiträge zur Kenntis des Judenspanischen von Konstantinopel*, Vienna.

Wagner, Max Leopold (1954): "Calcos lingüísticos en el habla de los Sefarditas de Levante", *Homenaje a Fritz Krüger*, Tomo II, Mendoza, 269−281.

Wiesner, Christa (1981): *Jüdisch-Spanisches Glossar zum ME'AM LO'EZ des Iacob Kuli. Genesis und Exodus bis Teruma*, Hamburg.

Yetkin, Çetin (1992): *Türkiye'nin Devlet Yaşamında Yahudiler* [Jews in the Life of the Turkish State], Istanbul.

Johann Strauß, Freiburg i. Br. (Germany)

190. Türkisch−Armenisch

1. Geographie und Demographie
2. Territorialgeschichte und Staatsbildung
3. Politik, Wirtschaft und allgemeine kulturelle Situation
4. Statistik und Ethnoprofil
5. Soziolinguistische Lage
6. Sprachpolitische Lage
7. Allgemeines kontaktlinguistisches Porträt
8. Zur Forschungslage
9. Bibliographie (in Auswahl)

1. Geographie und Demographie

1.1. Die europäische Türkei ist in geographischer und historischer Hinsicht bereits in Artikel 187 allgemein behandelt worden. Auf diesem Hintergrund muß zunächst festgestellt werden, daß der größte Teil der Sprachkontakte zwischen Armeniern und Türken in den vergangenen Jahrhunderten in weiten Teilen der asiatischen Türkei (genauer: in Zentral- und Ostanatolien sowie in Kilikien und in Gebieten am Schwarzen Meer) stattgefunden hat, wo die Armenier seit dem Altertum einen beträchtlichen Bevölkerungsanteil gestellt haben. Erst mit politisch motivierten Flucht- und Wanderungsbewegungen breiteten sich die Armenier seit dem 6. Jahrhundert nach Westen aus (Charanis 1963, 13) und siedelten bereits am Ende des 12. Jahrhunderts auch in den europäischen Provinzen des byzantinischen Reiches (Charanis 1963, 55). Von einschneidender Wirkung auf die demographische Situation der Armenier war der Genozid durch die Jungtürken während des Ersten Weltkriegs (s. Kap. 2), der das ursprüngliche Bild des armenischen Siedlungsgebietes stark verändert hat, ohne daß allerdings die heutige Verteilung der in der Türkei verbliebenen armenischsprachigen Bevölkerung nach demographischen Maßstäben zuverlässig ermittelt werden könnte; verschiedene, z. T. stark voneinander abweichende Zahlen (zwischen 41 000 und 83 000) gibt Andrews (1989, 127 f). Heute dürfte die armenische Bevölkerung der europäischen Türkei auf das Stadtgebiet von Istanbul beschränkt sein und kann dort auf etwa 30 000 geschätzt werden (→ Sprachenkarte I).

2. Territorialgeschichte und Staatsbildung

2.1. Die Ethnogenese wie die Vorgeschichte der Armenier liegen im Dunkeln und werden in der Forschung kontrovers beurteilt. Nach einer Feststellung Herodots gelten die Armenier vielen Forschern als Verwandte der Phryger, während andere annehmen, daß die Armenier nahe einer in Anatolien angenommenen Urheimat der Indogermanen geblieben seien und damit als nahezu autochthon gelten müssen (vgl. z. B. Gamkrelidze/Ivanov 1984, 969). Klare Spuren vorhistorischer Beeinflussungen durch altkleinasiatische Völker zeigt das Armenische vor allem in lexikalischer Hinsicht (Džahukyan 1987, 417 ff).

2.2. Eine wechselvolle Geschichte brachte die Armenier zeitweise unter die Oberherrschaft von Persern, Griechen, Römern, Arabern und Mongolen, bis seit dem 11. Jahrhundert infolge des Eindringens turkmenischer Stämme nach Anatolien das Armenische mit dem Türkischen in Kontakt kam. Das gesprochene Armenische nahm in der Folgezeit zahlreiche Lehnwörter aus dem

Türkischen auf und hat auch, wenngleich in geringem Umfang, lexikalischen Einfluß auf regionale Sprachformen des Türkischen ausgeübt (vgl. Kap. 7.).

2.3. Einen folgenreichen Einschnitt in die Beziehungen zwischen Armeniern und Türken bewirkten die Massaker des 19. und 20. Jahrhunderts, in deren Verlauf ein großer Teil der autochthonen armenischen Bevölkerung vernichtet oder vertrieben wurde. Die ersten größeren Massaker fanden Mitte der neunziger Jahre des vergangenen Jahrhunderts statt und brachten ca. 200 000 Armeniern den Tod. Unter den „Jungtürken" ereigneten sich zuerst 1909 in Kilikien wieder Massaker an den Armeniern, dann führte der Genozid von 1915—1918 zum Tod von mehr als 1 Million Armeniern und zur Flucht von Hunderttausenden in den russisch beherrschten Teil Armeniens (vgl. Brentjes 1974, 9—15 und 197 f). Zahlreiche Armenier suchten auf dem Balkan Zuflucht, wo sie sich vor allem in Bulgarien und Rumänien, aber auch in Österreich-Ungarn und in Polen (dort bereits seit dem 11.—17. Jahrhundert, vgl. Hanusz 1889, 4) ansiedelten (Lynch 1901, 428, Goehlert 1886, Alem 1962, 49 ff). Quellen über den Genozid an den Armeniern erschließen beispielsweise Hofmann (1980) und Dadrian (1991 und 1994). Die aus den Verfolgungen resultierenden Wanderungsbewegungen der Armenier innerhalb der Türkei sind nur unzureichend untersucht und lassen lediglich die Feststellung einer allgemeinen demographischen Tendenz zu, nach der die armenische Landbevölkerung dazu neigt, nach Istanbul umzusiedeln (Libaridian 1979, 43).

3. Politik, Wirtschaft und allgemeine kulturelle Situation

Angaben zu der politischen und ökonomischen Situation der Armenier in der europäischen Türkei lassen sich gegenwärtig nur für Istanbul machen; über andere Gebiete liegen keine verläßlichen Daten vor. Die Situation der Armenier dort ist facettenreich und oft durch ein Spannungsverhältnis zwischen der türkisch-national orientierten Politik der Türkei einerseits und unterschiedlichen Strömungen innerhalb des armenischen politischen Spektrums gekennzeichnet, wobei besonders die extremistische *Armenische Geheimarmee zur Befreiung Armeniens* (ASALA) in den vergangenen 20 Jahren durch zahlreiche Anschläge in das Bewußtsein der Weltöffentlichkeit getreten ist. Dagegen ist der Alltag des armenischen Bevölkerungsteils überwiegend durch deren traditionell starke ökonomische Rolle bestimmt, die über den Handel hinaus auch die Entwicklung einer beachtlichen Intelligenz (Gelehrte, Ärzte, Künstler) ermöglicht hat (Strauß 1988, 261 f). Doch wird, wie Strauß (1988, 263 f) zeigt, die Loyalität der Armenier zum türkischen Staat auch heute noch türkischerseits immer wieder in Frage gestellt.

4. Statistik und Ethnoprofil

Zuverlässige statistische Angaben über die auf die türkischen Armenier bezogenen demographischen Gegebenheiten sind nicht verfügbar. Die publizierten Zahlen beruhen überwiegend auf Schätzungen, die eine große Spannweite zeigen. Es steht aber wohl außer Frage, daß die Bevölkerung Istanbuls nach wie vor einen annähernd umreißbaren Anteil an Armeniern umfaßt, wobei nach den Informationen von Murphy (1986, 178), der sich auf Zählungen des Armenischen Patriarchats in Istanbul beruft, etwa 30 000 Sprecher des Armenischen in dieser Stadt leben; weitere Zahlenangaben aus unterschiedlichen Quellen verzeichnen Andrews (1989, 127) und Anschütz (1989, 454 ff). Unklar bleibt dabei jedoch, wie groß der auf das europäische Stadtgebiet entfallende Anteil ist. Auch über die Vergangenheit sind zuverlässige Zahlen nicht verfügbar. So lassen sich hier auch nur Annäherungswerte geben, deren Genauigkeit nicht überprüft werden kann: Vor dem Ersten Weltkrieg betrug die Zahl der Armenier in der europäischen Türkei nach McCarthy (1983, 124) etwa 105 000. Dagegen nennt de Contenson (1913, 17) für die europäische Türkei eine Zahl von 250 000 nach „les plus récentes statistiques". Für 1927 gibt der türkische Zensus eine Anzahl von 53 273 (gregorianischen) Armeniern in den Provinzen der europäischen Türkei unter Einschluß von Istanbul an, wozu noch eine nicht bestimmbare Anzahl von Armeniern unter der katholischen (24 183) und protestantischen (4682) Bevölkerung zu zählen wäre (McCarthy 1983, 141, Anm. 22).

5. Soziolinguistische Lage

Die einzigen soziolinguistisch relevanten Daten zur Lage der Armenier in Istanbul stammen von R. A. Murphy, dessen globale Feststellungen über die relative Anzahl von Armeniern, die Armenisch als erste Sprache lernen und später auch lesen lernen, gewiß in allen Teilen Istanbuls Gültigkeit beanspruchen können: Im Vergleich zu Griechisch und Italienisch geht der Gebrauch des Armenischen schneller zugunsten des Türkischen zurück, und auch in der Alltagskommunikation verliert das Armenische an Boden, obwohl es etwa 30 armenische Schulen und mehrere Zeitungen gibt (vgl. Murphy 1986, 179).

6. Sprachpolitische Lage

Die gegenwärtige Sprachpolitik gegenüber den Armeniern ist gekennzeichnet durch Tolerierung des Gebrauchs der armenischen Sprache in Schulen und Druckwerken (vgl. zu letzterem Strauß 1988, 268, Anm. 42), wobei die Schriftsprache das besonders in Istanbul gepflegte Westarmenische (arm. *arewmtean hayerēn* oder *arevmtahayeren*) ist, das durch lautliche, morphologische und lexikalische Eigenheiten klar vom Ostarmenischen (arm. *arevelahayeren* oder *arewelean hayerēn*) der Republik Armenien und Persiens unterschieden ist. Beide Varianten der armenischen Schriftsprache sind in Gebrauch, wobei das Westarmenische und das in Persien benutzte Ostarmenische eine konservativere Orthographie als das in der Republik Armenien geschriebene und mehrfach orthographischen Reformen unterzogene Ostarmenische zeigen. Im liturgischen Bereich wird noch das Altarmenische verwendet.

7. Allgemeines kontaktlinguistisches Porträt

7.1. Die demographischen Veränderungen, die zu den hier einschlägigen Sprachkontakten geführt haben, sind oben in Kap. 2. beschrieben worden. Was nun das im europäischen Teil der Türkei gesprochene Armenische betrifft, so stellt der armenische Gelehrte H. Ačaṙyan (1909, 75) in seiner Klassifikation der armenischen Dialekte bereits fest, daß „dans la Turquie d'Europe la seule colonie arménienne qui n'ait pas perdu sa langue est celle de Rodosto [heute Tekirdağ] et de Malgara [Malkara], deux villes voisines. Leur parler n'est pas encore étudié (...)". Diese Bemerkung ist auf dem Hintergrund einer op. cit. S. 11 gegebenen Aufzählung der Siedlungsgebiete der Armenier, wo zur europäischen Türkei auch Konstantinopel gerechnet wird, nur eingeschränkt nachvollziehbar: Offenbar zählt der Verfasser die Istanbuler Armenier hier zum asiatischen Teil der Türkei. Das weitere Schicksal der armenischen Sprache in diesen Städten ist nicht dokumentiert, und auch der *Tübinger Atlas des Vorderen Orients* verzeichnet in seiner Karte „Ethnische Gruppen türkischer Nationalität 1960–1970" für dieses Gebiet keine Armenier mehr (Andrews 1987), doch ist dieser Befund wegen der Beschränkung der Karte auf den ländlichen Raum nur bedingt aussagekräftig.

7.2. Der armenische Dialekt von Istanbul ist von H. Ačaṙyan eingehender untersucht worden, wobei der Einfluß des Türkischen im Wortschatz mit 4200 Lehnwörtern beziffert wird (Ačaṙyan 1909, 5). Eine erste Beschreibung gibt der Verfasser 1909, 71 ff, freilich mit dem Hinweis darauf, daß dieser Dialekt, der die Grundlage der westarmenischen Literatursprache bildet, noch nicht wissenschaftlich untersucht worden sei. Die von ihm l. c. als bereits abgeschlossen bezeichnete Studie ist dann erst 1941 erschienen. Ein kurzer Abriß der Eigenheiten des Istanbuler Dialekts findet sich bei Grigoryan (1957, 298 ff) und in sehr geraffter Form bei Greppin/Khachaturian (1986, 155 ff). Weitergehende Einflüsse werden nicht diskutiert; syntaktische Übereinstimmungen zwischen dem Neuarmenischen und dem Türkischen (Ačaṙyan 1909, 8) lassen sich durch innersprachliche Entwicklung des Armenischen erklären (Pedersen 1906, 472), oder aber die Quelle des Einflusses läßt sich nicht genau genug ermitteln (Kusik'jan 1959, 142 f).

7.3. Die Diskussion von Fragen des Sprachkontakts zwischen Armenisch und Türkisch allgemein beschränkt sich sonst meist auf die Perspektive des türkischen Einflusses auf das Armenische (z. B. Ačaṙyan 1902, Schütz 1967) und ist in der Regel in den lexikologischen Kapiteln armenischer Dialektbeschreibungen anzutreffen (Hinweise auf einschlägige Arbeiten bei Džahukyan apud Greppin/Khachaturian 1986, 16). Doch gab es daneben schon früh Versuche, armenisches Lehngut im Türkischen zu identifizieren: H. Pedersen hat in seiner Abhandlung „Armenisch und die nachbarsprachen" den Versuch unternommen, „Armenische lehnwörter im Türkischen" (Pedersen 1906, 442–465) auf eine Zeit zu datieren, die „wohl um mehr als 1200 jahre älter als die Orchoninschriften" ist (1906, 443). Dieser Ansatz ist aus vielerlei

Gründen nicht haltbar und hat in der Forschungsgeschichte Kritik hervorgerufen, die z. T. aber selber gänzlich verfehlt ist, wie die von J. J. Karst (1911), der zu noch abenteuerlicheren, wahrhaft omnikomparatistischen Argumenten greift, wenn er für oberflächliche Ähnlichkeiten einer Reihe von Sprachen nicht Entlehnung, sondern einen „gemeinsamen turanischen Grundstock" für „das lexikalisch gemeinsame Element des Ural-Altaiischen, Armenischen und Hamitischen" in Anspruch nimmt (Karst 1911, 414).

7.4. Erst in jüngster Zeit sind weiterführende Arbeiten erschienen, die sich der Frage armenischen Lehngutes im Türkischen annehmen. Hier ist zwischen zwei Textgattungen zu unterscheiden, die dieser Problemstellung mit unterschiedlicher Intensität und ebenso unterschiedlichem Ertrag nachgehen. Zum einen handelt es sich um sprachgeschichtliche Abhandlungen von Autoren mit ausgeprägter armenologischer Kompetenz (z. B. Amiryan 1980, Pisowicz 1989, Bläsing 1992), zum anderen um Lexika des Türkischen oder von Varietäten des Türkischen, die etymologische Angaben enthalten und auf diesem Wege zur Dokumentation von Lehnbeziehungen zwischen Armenisch und Türkisch beitragen. Hierzu zählen Aktunç (1990) und das *Türkçe sözlük* (1988). Mit zahlreichen Mängeln behaftet und oft nicht wissenschaftlichen Ansprüchen genügend sind die Wörterbücher von Eyuboğlu (1988) und Gülensoy (1986).

7.5. Die lexikologischen Angaben in den zuletzt erwähnten Lexika lassen es bedauerlicherweise nicht zu, die Verwendung der armenischen Lehnwörter geographisch soweit einzugrenzen, daß sich ihre Relevanz für die Untersuchung der Kontaktbeziehungen zwischen den beiden Sprachen im europäischen Teil der Türkei mit der notwendigen Klarheit bestimmen ließe. Auch sind die durchweg globalen Hinweise auf die armenische Herkunft eines Wortes oft nicht ausreichend, um die dialektale Quelle einer Entlehnung identifizieren zu können. Als Beispiel diene etwa der Eintrag *ahbar* bei Aktunç (1990, s. v.), wo als Etymon armenisch *yeġpayr* „Bruder" angegeben wird. Semantisch ist die Beziehung zwischen Etymon und Lehnwort plausibel: *ahbar* wird als Anrede eines Mannes verwendet wie türk. *kardeşim* „mein Lieber", wörtlich „mein Bruder (bzw. Schwester)". Die lautliche Beziehung zwischen Etymon und Lehnwort ist aber nicht ohne weiteres klar und wird auch, der Natur des konsultierten Werkes entsprechend, nicht expliziert. Die altarmenische Ausgangsform *ełbayr* „Bruder" hat in den verschiedenen neuarmenischen Dialekten ein jeweils ganz unterschiedliches Schicksal erfahren, das insgesamt eine direkte Entlehnung einer Form *yeġpayr* als türk. *ahbar* ausschließt: Altarmen. *ełbayr* (aus indogerm. *$b^h r\bar{a}t\bar{e}r$, vgl. zur sprachgeschichtlichen Herleitung Schmitt 1981, 73; 78; das aus *r dissimilierte altarmenische velare oder velarisierte *l* ist in den neuarmen. Mundarten durchweg zu einem stimmhaften uvularen Frikativ geworden, der in bestimmten Positionen desonorisiert worden ist) findet sich in den neuarmenischen Dialekten überwiegend mit anlautendem *a* und stets mit desonorisierter uvularer Spirans *x*. Im Dialekt von Istanbul ist darüber hinaus der dem Uvular folgende labiale Plosiv eine Lenis, wie auch in den Dialekten von Akn, Aslanbeg und Sebastia; sonst findet sich gelegentlich auch eine Media aspirata (vgl. Ačaṙyan 1973 s. v. *ełbayr*); Grigoryan (1957, 301; 304) gibt das Wort für den Istanbuler Dialekt mit stimmloser, nichtaspirierter Fortis, was freilich der zutreffend als dichotomisch beschriebenen Verschlußlautopposition *Media* vs. *Tenuis aspirata* widerspricht (229). Greppin/Khachaturian (1986, 159) übernehmen, wohl von Ačaṙyan, unverständlicherweise die gleiche Schreibung (ebenso in der — nach Ačaṙyan — op. cit. p. 164, viert- u. drittletzte Zeile zitierten Textprobe); dagegen Ačaṙyan (1909, 72) über den Istanbuler Dialekt: „Il y a deux dégrés de consonnes: sonores et sourdes aspirées". Als Quelle von türk. *ahbar* liegt hier also der Istanbuler Stadtdialekt nahe. Die von Aktunç zitierte Form *yeġpayr* existiert demgegenüber so nicht. Selbst im insgesamt eher konservativen Ostarmenischen gilt *yexpayr* als orthoepisch (vgl. Łaragyulyan 1974, 197). — Problematisch bleiben etymologische Verknüpfungen der Art, die türk. *kavara* „Furz" (Aktunç s. v.) aus westarmen. *kagor* ⟨k'akor⟩ „Mist, Dung" herleiten, ohne die lautlichen wie semantischen Beziehungen zu klären.

7.6. Als beispielhaft auf dem Gebiet der Erforschung türkisch-armenischer Sprachkontakte ist jetzt die Arbeit von U. Bläsing (1992) anzusehen, in der der Autor von ihm selbst erhobenes Dialektmaterial aus dem Hemşin-Gebiet in der Nordost-Türkei diskutiert und dabei über 170 Wörter vermutlich armenischen Ursprungs präsentiert, die freilich zu einem erheblichen Teil lokal begrenzt sind. Auch andere, ähnlich angelegte Untersuchungen (Amiryan 1980, Pisowicz 1989) haben das traditionelle Siedlungsgebiet der Armenier in Anatolien zum Gegenstand.

8. Zur Forschungslage

Ebenso wie im Bereich der türkisch-armenischen Sprachkontakte sind auch die Kontakte zwischen dem (ausgestorbenen) Balkan-Armenischen und den umgebenden Sprachen (Rumänisch, Bulgarisch, Polnisch) bislang überwiegend nur im Hinblick auf die Beeinflussung der armenischen Mundarten durch die sie umgebenden Sprachen untersucht worden. Lediglich für das Rumänische (vgl. hierzu die umfangreiche Arbeit von Siruni (1968), wo freilich nur der Einfluß des Rumänischen auf das Armenische thematisiert wird) gibt es einen Hinweis auf den Einfluß des Armenischen in Lexikon und Onomastik (Poghirc 1977, 117). Sowohl für diese Sprachen wie für das Türkische muß die Sprachkontaktforschung im Hinblick auf das Armenische mit einer einschlägigen rezenten Feststellung von U. Bläsing (1992, 11) als ein dringendes Desiderat für die künftige Forschung angesehen werden: „Überhaupt ist zu bemerken, daß die armenischen Entlehnungen in Turksprachen noch in keiner Weise ausreichend aufgedeckt oder gar untersucht sind." Dies gilt in besonderem Maße für das Armenische in der europäischen Türkei.

9. Bibliographie (in Auswahl)

Ačaŕean [= Ačaŕyan], Hrač'ya (1902): T'urk'erênê p'oxaŕeal baŕer hayerêni mêj [Türkische Lehnwörter im Armenischen], Moskau/Vałaršapat.

Ačaŕyan, Hrač'ya (1941): „K'nnut'yun polsahay barbaŕi" [Untersuchung des armenischen Dialekts von Istanbul]. In: (V. M. Molotovi anvan Erevani petakan hamalsarani) Gitakan ašxatut'yunner 19, 19−250.

Ačaŕyan, Hrač'ya (1973): Hayeren armatakan baŕaran [Armenisches Wurzelwörterbuch], Bd. 2: E−K, Erevan.

Adjarian [= Ačaŕyan], Hrač'ya (1909): Classification des dialectes arméniens. [Bibliothèque de l'Ecole des Hautes Etudes, fasc. 173], Paris.

Aktunç, Hulki (1990): Türkçenin büyük argo sözlüğü (Tanıklarıyla) [Großes Argot-Wörterbuch des Türkischen], İstanbul.

Amiryan, Xač'ik (1980): „Hayerenic' p'oxaŕeal baŕer žamanakakic' t'urk'erenum" [Armenische Lehnwörter im heutigen Türkisch]. In: Haykakan SSH GA Lraber, 4−6, 81−87.

Andrews, Peter [Alford] (1987): Ethnische Gruppen türkischer Nationalität 1960−1970. Hg. vom Sonderforschungsbereich 19 „Tübinger Atlas des Vorderen Orients (TAVO)" der Universität Tübingen, Wiesbaden.

Andrews, Peter Alford (Ed.) (1989): Ethnic Groups in the Republic of Turkey. Beihefte zum Tübinger Atlas des Vorderen Orients, Reihe B, Nr. 60. Hg. im Auftrag des Sonderforschungsbereichs 19 von Heinz Gaube u. Wolfgang Röllig, Wiesbaden.

Anschütz, Helga (1989): „Christliche Gruppen in der Türkei". In: Andrews 1989, 454−468.

Bläsing, Uwe (1992): Armenisches Lehngut im Türkeitürkischen am Beispiel von Hemşin. [= Dutch Studies in Armenian Language and Literature, 2], Amsterdam/Atlanta, GA.

Brentjes, Burchard (1974): Drei Jahrtausende Armenien, Wien/München.

Charanis, Peter (1963): The Armenians in the Byzantine Empire, Calouste Gulbenkian Foundation Armenian Library, Lissabon.

Dadrian, Vahakn N. (1991): „Documentation of the Armenian Genocide in Turkish Sources". In: Genocide: A Critical Bibliographical Review, vol. 2, Charney, Israel W. (Ed.), London/New York, 86−138.

Dadrian, Vahakn N. (1994): „The Armenian Genocide in official Turkish records". Collected essays by Vahakn N. Dadrian. In: Journal of Political and Military Sociology, vol. 22, no. 1, Summer 1994.

Džahukyan, Gevorg Beglari (1987): Hayoc' lezvi patmut'yun; naxagrayin žamanakašrǰan [Geschichte der armenischen Sprache; der Zeitraum vor der Schriftlichkeit], Erevan.

Eyuboğlu, İsmet Zeki (1988): Türk dilinin etimoloji sözlüğü [Etymologisches Wörterbuch der türkischen Sprache], İstanbul.

Gamkrelidze, Tamaz Valerianovič/Ivanov, Vjačeslav Vsevolodovič (1984): Indoevropejskij jazyk i indoevropejcy [Das Indogermanische und die Indogermanen], 2 Bde., Tbilisi.

Greppin, John A[ird] C[outts]/Khachaturian [Xač'aturyan], Amalia (1986): A Handbook of Armenian Dialectology, Delmar/New York.

Grigoryan, Aharon V. (1957): Hay barbaŕagitut'yan dasənt'ac' [Lehrbuch der armenischen Dialektologie], Erevan.

Gülensoy, Tuncer (1986): Doğu anadolu osmanlıcası. Etimolojik sözlük denemesi [Das ostanatolische Osmanisch. Versuch eines etymologischen Wörterbuches], Ankara.

Hofmann, Tessa (Ed.) (1980): Der Völkermord an den Armeniern vor Gericht. Der Prozeß Talaat Pascha. Neuauflage der Ausgabe Berlin (Deutsche Verlagsgesellschaft für Politik und Geschichte) 1921. Hg. und eingeleitet von T. Hofmann im Auftrag der Gesellschaft für bedrohte Völker, Göttingen.

Karst, J. Josef (1911): „Zur ethnischen Stellung der Armenier". In: *Yušarjan grakan žołovacoy art'iw 100ameay yobelini hastatman mxit'arean miabanut'ean i Vienna (1811–1911)*. Huschardzan, Festschrift aus Anlaß des 100jährigen Bestandes der Mechitharisten-Kongregation in Wien (1811–1911), Wien, 399–431.

Kusik'jan, Iosif K. [= Kusikyan, Hovsep' K.] (1959): *Očerki istoričeskogo sintaksisa literaturnogo armjanskogo jazyka* [Abriß der historischen Syntax der armenischen Literatursprache], Moskau.

Łaragyulyan, T'ereza (1974): *Žamanakakic' hayereni ułłaxosut'yunə* [Die Orthoepie des Neuarmenischen], Erevan.

Libaridian, Gerald J. (1979): „Armenia and Armenians: A Divided Homeland and a Dispersed Nation". In: *Soviet Asian Ethnic Frontiers*, McCagg, Jr., William O./Silver, Brian D. (Eds.), New York, 26–60.

Murphy, Richard A. (1986): „Observations on language usage among bilingual communities in Istanbul". In: *Osmanlı Araştırmaları* [The Journal of Ottoman Studies] 5, 175–193.

Pedersen, Holger (1906): „Armenisch und die nachbarsprachen". In: *Zeitschrift für vergleichende Sprachforschung auf dem Gebiete der indogermanischen Sprachen* 39, 334–484.

Pisowicz, Andrzej (1989): „Die armenischen Entlehnungen in den türkischen Dialekten". In: *Folia Orientalia* (Krakau) 16, 123–129.

Poghirc, Cicerone (1977): „L'influence orientale sur la langue roumaine (Questions de méthode)". In: *Studia et Acta Orientalia* (Bukarest) 9, 108–127.

Schmitt, Rüdiger (1981): *Grammatik des Klassisch-Armenischen mit sprachvergleichenden Erläuterungen*. Innsbrucker Beiträge zur Sprachwissenschaft, Bd. 32, Innsbruck.

Schütz, Edmund (1967): „The Turkish loanwords in Simeon Lehaci's travel accounts". In: *Acta Orientalia Hungarica* 20, 307–324.

Siruni, Hakob Dj. (1968): „Considérations sur le dialecte arménien des pays roumains". In: *Studia et Acta Orientalia* (Bukarest) 7, 133–166.

Strauß, Johann (1988): „Die nichtmuslimischen Minderheiten in Istanbul". In: *Die Staaten Südosteuropas und die Osmanen*, Majer, H. G. (Ed.) [= Südosteuropa-Jahrbuch, 19], München, 255–269.

Türkçe sözlük [Türkisches Wörterbuch]. Yeni baskı [Neue Auflage] (1988). 2 Bde., Erken, H. (Ed.), Ankara.

Michael Job, Marburg (Deutschland)

191. Cyprus

1. Geography and demography
2. Territorial history and national development
3. Politics, economy, and general cultural and religious situation
4. Statistics and ethnoprofiles
5. Languages without contact in a divided society
6. Bibliography (selected)

1. Geography and demography

1.1. Geography

The island of Cyprus is situated in the north-eastern part of the Mediterranean Sea, 140 km from Syria to the east, 65 km from Turkey to the north, 400 km from Greece (Rhodos) to the west, 380 km from Egypt to the south and 200 km from Israel to the south-east.

The island covers an area of 9251 sq.km and is as such the third largest island in the Mediterranean. It is 225 km long and 97 km wide and has a coast-line of nearly 750 km.

Geologically, Cyprus is a rather young formation, constituted some 75 million years ago. Its main geo-morphological characteristics are determined by mountainfolding and faults, emergence and submergence of land in conjunction with changes in the sea-level, volcanic action, sedimentation as well as erosion.

The Cypriotic landscape shows great variation in spite of the small area. One can find high snow-covered mountain peaks as well as fertile plains and plateaus, small hills and sharp cliffs as well as valleys with meandering rivers and coastal plains and beaches.

The determinant features of the island, however, are the sharp Kyrania mountain range, along the northern coast, reaching an altitude of over 1000 metres and known in Greek as 'penta-dactylos', and the Troodos massif in the south-west rising close to 2000 metres.

1.2. Demography

Any demographic approach to Cyprus must take account of the political and military events of 1974 which resulted in the total separation of the two main population groups, Greeks and Turks, as well as considerable forced and/or induced migrations. According to the first and only census held in the Republic of Cyprus in 1960 (published in 1962), the population was composed of 449.991 Greeks, 104.350 Turks, and 23.274 Maronites and Armenians. It must be stressed that all figures other than these either do not cover the whole population or are extrapolations. Additionally, there are British military personnel and dependents, numbering some 10.000 persons, living on the two sovereign base areas of Akrotiri and Dhekelia.

The settlement structure of Cyprus is still of a rural nature, the degree of urbanization in 1973 being between 35 and 40 percent, with a slightly higher degree for the Turkish part of the population. Since 1974, due to the military action, the division of the country and the displacement of some 200.000 people as well as basic changes in the economic pattern, the demographic structure of Cyprus has dramatically changed.

The major towns are Nicosia (the divided capital), Limassol, Larnaca, Paphos (the tourist boom town) on the Greek side; Kyrenia, the only major town on the Turkish side. The once famous resort of Famagusta is now a semideserted ghost town on the ethnic divide.

The island has always counted small groups of Armenians, Jews and Arabs (mainly Maronites), whose numbers have increased considerably due to the population influx from Lebanon, starting in 1976 (→ Language Map I).

2. Territorial history and national development

From the dawn of history, the island of Cyprus was in the ambit of the great eastern empires, such as the Phenician (8th century BC), the Assyrian (7th century BC), the Egyptian (6th century BC) and the Persian (5th century BC).

Alexander the Great made Cyprus part of the Hellenic world in the 4th century BC. In the third century BC, it became a province of the Roman Empire and was christianized at a very early date. It remained under the authority of Rome until the 4th Century AD when it became part of the Eastern Roman Empire and was thus ruled from Byzantium. This era, which lasted until the 12th century, left a profound Greek and Christian orthodox imprint on the island. The expansion of the Arabic-Muslim world made the island quickly into a conflict zone and determined its importance as a maritime base and military support station. At the end of the 12th century, it was conquered by English participants in the Third Crusade. King Richard the Lionhearted sold the island to the Military Order of the Temple of Jerusalem, which for financial reasons transferred the rights to the French Lusignan dynasty. In 1196, the Lusignans were granted the title 'King of Cyprus' by the Holy Roman Emperor Henry VI. Under the Lusignans, the island went through a period of great economic and cultural prosperity, leaving some beautiful gothic monuments in the otherwise oriental landscape. The constant pressure from the Islamic surroundings, and also from Egypt, forced the Cypriot rulers to call in the help of the Venetian Republic, which took possession of the island. The Venetian administration ended on the eve of the collapse of the Byzantine Empire when it was conquered by the Turks in 1571. The Turkish governor started his administration with a census of the population, completed in 1571, which showed a population of about 100.000 persons, all Christians. Consequently, the Turkish authorities decreed an organised settlement of Turks into the sparsely populated areas. The main tension which had influenced Cypriot society for the previous three centuries was not linked to Christian-Islamic relations but mainly to a kind of brother fight between the Latin and Orthodox Christian churches, the former trying ruthlessly to sever the century-old ties of Cyprus with the Orthodox world. For three centuries, Cyprus remained part of the Ottoman Empire, under which the Christian population had a considerable amount of self-government through its religious structures under the Archbishop, in the framework of the 'millet' system (→ Art. 187). The Congress of Berlin in 1878 put Cyprus under the administration of the United Kingdom, the sovereignty remaining with Turkey, in return for a British promise to Turkey to come to its aid in the event of a Russian attack. This introduced a new protagonist − and his language − in the country.

In 1881, the British governor also organised a census of the population, which showed that out of a total population of 186.000, Turks constituted 46.389 persons and Christians 136.629 (this figure including, in addition to the Greek orthodox, 1920 Catholics, 212 Maronites, 154 Armenians and 691 protestants). The census also counted 69 Jews and 20 Gypsies. Due to the siding of Turkey with Germany, the United Kingdom formally annexed Cyprus in 1914 and installed a military administration. By virtue of the Treaty of Lausanne in 1923, Turkey relinquished all claims to Cyprus, which made it possible for Great Britain to elevate the island to the status of a crown colony in 1925. In the meantime, the independence and consolidation of the Kingdom of Greece, particularly the transfer by Great Britain of the Ionian Islands to Greece and the Unification of Crete with the mainland in 1905 (ratified in 1913), had a great impact on the Greek Cypriot population, which also wanted to be part of the Greek motherland, a movement which became known as 'Enosis'.

3. Politics, economy and general cultural and religious situation

The British rule over Cyprus restored the direct links between Cyprus and western Europe. It particularly gave the Greek majority, which consisted of over 80 percent of the population, hopes for a future integration into Greece, especially since the military importance of Cyprus was considerably reduced through the British control over Egypt and the opening of the Suez Canal. Already under British administration, a legislative assembly of eighteen members was introduced, consisting of six appointed British civil servants and twelve elected Cypriots. The elected members consisted of nine Greeks and three Turks, reflecting fairly well the population structure of the country. The British High Commissioner presided over the Assembly with a tie-breaking vote. This first political representative body contained the basic elements of the conflictual development of the island. From the outset, the Turkish members sided with the British appointees, continuously deadlocking the Assembly in a 9 to 9 vote, and thus in reality giving all the power to the High Commissioner. It was in this way that the High Commissioner discarded a Greek proposal for Enosis in the legislative Assembly on 29 July 1917. Slowly, the Greek population's conviction that the British colonial administration favoured the Turkish 'minority' gained momentum: they started a boycott of the Assembly and organised a so-called National Council under the leadership of the Greek-orthodox Etnarch. From that moment onwards, the resistance of the Greek Cypriot population to the British colonial administration would grow relentlessly and turned into covert military action, sabotage and terrorism, which in its turn compelled the British administration to engage in repressive measures. Until 1950, when Archbishop Makarios II, after an unofficial referendum in which the Greek population supported Enosis by 96 percent, brought the Cypriot question to the international forum, particularly the United Nations, Greece as well as Turkey had formally refrained from direct intervention. All this changed when the new Etnarch Makarios III took office in June 1950 and managed to have the Cypriot question placed on the agenda of the United Nations sixth session in the Third Committee, changing in the meantime the vocabulary from Enosis to self-determination. This forced Greece and Turkey to become the advocates of the respective population groups of the island. Inevitably and perhaps unconsciously, the people of Cyprus had relinquished the control over their own destiny, and the future of Cyprus was now to be decided in international and diplomatic conferences between the United Kingdom, Greece and Turkey. This meant a certain improvement for the defence of the Turkish Cypriot positions since their voice was hardly heard up to then, due to the overwhelming majority of Greeks in the official Cypriot structures. In 1957, the conviction grew on the Turkish side that if the Greek Cypriots were entitled to self-determination, the Turkish Cypriots had also to be granted this right. Since this seemed totally illusionary in view of the total mixture of the population patterns, the Turkish representatives introduced for the first time 'Taksim', meaning the division of the island in two parts. Since neither 'Enosis' nor 'Taksim' were options attainable without war, independence and neutralisation of Cyprus seemed to be the only issue left. In 1959, the United Kingdom, Turkey and Greece concluded the treaties of Zurich and London, which established the basic structure of the Republic Of Cyprus, combined with a Treaty of Guarantee between Turkey, Greece and the United Kingdom as well as a Treaty of Alliance between Turkey, Greece and Cyprus. On the basis of these three texts, independence was granted to Cyprus on 16 August 1960, under the Presidency of Archbishop Makarios III. Thus, the Cypriot population, Greeks as well as Turks, got a constitutional order drafted by foreign countries and on which they had never been able to express their adherence, nor even been asked their opinion.

The official colonial language, English, was replaced by Greek and Turkish and in all sections of government, administration and justice, separate positions for Greeks and Turks were created in a relationship conferring a slight advantage to the Turkish community in respect to the absolute population percentages. Although well-intentioned, the machinery established under the Constitution of 1960 was so complex that the way in which it worked gave rise to serious institutional difficulties which induced President Makarios in 1963 to propose amendments purportedly designed to improve the functioning of the institutions, but which to all intents and purposes in fact abrogated the basic agreements of Zurich and London. These proposals were rejected by the Turkish community and serious inter-communal clashes broke out throughout the island. These led to the first major regrouping of the population alongside ethnic divides in certain areas. Turkish officials withdrew from all established institutions and in 1964, the Greek side adopted a number of laws in the absence of the Turkish Cypriot representatives, thus fundamentally changing the nature of the Cypriot institutions, in violation of the Constitution. In the same year, the U.N. sent a military peace-keeping force to Cyprus. In the decade before the Turkish military action of 1974, the two communities slowly but inexorably began living separately, not only territorially and politically but also economically and socially, paving the way for the complete separation brought about by the events of July 1974.

Since that date, the Republic of Cyprus is divided by a military line, running from Famagusta in the east to Limnitis in the west dividing the capital of Nicosia, creating two quasi-homogeneous totally separated ethnic linguistic and religious communities, making of Cyprus probably the only multilingual island without language contact.

4. Statistics and ethnoprofiles

The ethnolinguistic profile of Cyprus today is the result not of a century-long historical process but of a radical military intervention and a demographic *état de fait* unrelated to the past. The present-day population of Cyprus is overwhelmingly composed of the Greek and Turkish communities, for which ethnic, linguistic, religious and national identity are amalgamated into two syncretic profiles divided by walls of mistrust, psychological barriers and mutual fears of insurmountable dimensions. On the fringes of this bipolar situation are found microscopic groups of Maronite Arabs and Armenians. This picture is completed by the British military personnel and dependents who, although not belonging to Cyprus in the political or legal sense of the word, through their presence certainly have contributed to a certain continuance of the functionality of the English language, lately further strengthened by the growing importance of tourism on the Greek side of the island. From a diachronic perspective, it is remarkable how stable the relative importance of the major population groups has been with a shift of approximately six percent to the benefit of the Greek community. The settlement pattern of pre-1963-1974 Cyprus has very precise historical origins. The Turkish settlers introduced after 1571 were not located at random on Greek-Cypriot property, but on the properties of the expelled French, Venetian and Genoese and of the expropriated Roman Catholic Church. Additionally, it was in the interest of the Turkish governor to distribute the Turkish inhabitants over all the island for security reasons. Consequently, there was no region on the island where the Turkish community constituted a majority. On the other hand, there was no region without a Turkish presence, so that one can truly speak of mixed population. The population pattern changes when one goes down to the village level where clear majorities can be distinguished. Out of 635 settlements, 329 can be called Greek, 117 Turkish and 126 of a mixed nature. For these settlements, the 1960 constitutional arrangement provided for a kind of parallel municipal structure for each community, copied on the national model. The tensions of 1963 destroyed these mixed communities and a limited migration took place. On the other hand, the abolition of English as the official language of the country seriously hampered the degree of communication between the two communities, since the number of Greek-Turkish bilinguals is extremely limited and the knowledge of English increasingly reduced to the ordinary level of a foreign language. It is important to note that there are also population changes which have no ethnic or linguistic connection but are the result of the normal tendencies to urbanisation and emigration from rural areas and small villages. Nevertheless, since the degree of urbanisation of the Turkish population was always slightly higher than that of the Greek population, and since the Turkish rural settlements were smaller than their Greek counterparts, the general phenomenon of 1960's urbanisation had a greater impact on the settlement pattern of the Turkish community.

In the decade preceding the military action of 1974, the Turks withdrew not only from the mixed villages, but also from the small purely Turkish villages if they were surrounded by larger Greek ones. These populations were first directed towards the nearest larger Turkish village and only in a second wave to the cities, particularly to the Turkish part of Nicosia. This created great unemployment and social distress among the Turkish population since they lost their agricultural livelihood. Thus appeared an ever-growing socio-economic gap in the development of the Turkish and Greek communities of which only the Turks were really aware, since a large number of them worked in Greek-controlled areas and since it was impossible for the Greeks to enter the Turkish enclaves. The division of the island following the military action of 1974 brought the most fertile and developed part of the country under Turkish control and concentrated the Greeks in the less developed south. Approximately 160.000 Greeks were displaced from north to south, barely compensated by the 45.000 Turks who left in the other direction. These two movements created two quasi ethno-linguistic and religious homogeneous areas, leaving a dwindling number of some 400 to 500 Greeks and Turks, mostly elderly people, in the respective other part of the country. They can not be called communities, but clusters of individuals, a possible exception being the 532 Greeks of the northeastern peninsula of Karpassia, who are the residual population of a community close to 8000. Most of them are very old people, living under great psychological, linguistic, cultural and religious constraint. There are no real community structures and only two elementary schools cater for this group, so that children are forced to attend secondary school in the south. Once reaching the age of 16 for boys and 18 for girls, they are not allowed to return to their home area. This reduces continuously the number of the community.

The two real minorities, Maronite Arabs and Armenians, find themselves each in one part of the country. The Armenians, being very urbanised, are mostly to be found in the southern cities of Limassol and Larnaca and essentially in the Greek part of Nicosia, where they have their own private schooling system, partly functioning in the Armenian language. The very tiny Maronite Arabic community numbering some 500 speakers is located in the northeastern villages of Kormakiti. All of the speakers are bilingual Greek-Arabic and illiterate in their Arabic dialect; some also have a basic knowledge of Turkish. No schooling or any other facility exists for this group.

Since no language other than Greek and Turkish in the respective areas is official and due to the polarised situation on the island, the pressure for assimilation on both groups is extremely strong. The Armenian group, with its economic strength and status as a Christian minority in a Christian environment, has evidently more prospects for survival than the extremely poor Christian Maronite Arab minority in the Islamic Turkish environment.

5. Languages without contact in a divided society

As mentioned earlier, the particular political situation of Cyprus today has as a consequence that except for the Maronite Arab and Armenian group, there are no other phenomena of language contact or conflict. Neither are there specific problems of language policy and planning. Indeed, one must consider both parts of the island as entirely monolingual in their structure and functioning. Moreover, the polarised and antinomic perception of the other group has eliminated any possibility or desire to learn the other community's language, such a desire being almost equated with treason. A clear feeling of superiority on the part of the Christian Greeks with respect to the 'Asiatic' and Islamic Turks permeates the perception of most Greek Cypriots. On the other hand, the latter are very aware of the fact that the Cypriot variant of the Greek language has a number of particularities which distinguish it from that of mainland Greece. This can induce a slight feeling of inferiority in the very nationalistic segment of the Greek Cypriotic population, but sometimes it is also used to argue for a particular identity for the Greek Cypriots within the larger Hellenic world. In the north, the arrival of tens of thousands of mainland Turkish settlers has also reinforced certain tendencies towards Turkish Cypriot particularism, so as to distinguish the original population from the newcomers.

These phenomena which can be observed on both sides of the divide may be the only remnant of a subconscious feeling of island identity on the part of the two 'big brothers'. Whether this will be sufficient to safeguard the existence of Cyprus as a state is doubtful. As was so pointly observed by Mr. A. Coste-Floret, a member of the European Parliament, who reported on the situation in Cyprus to the European Parliament in 1988: "There is no such thing as a Cypriot national sentiment, only a feeling of belonging to the Greek side in the south and a feeling of belonging to the Turkish side in the north (…) the more time passes, the more difficult it will be to bring together two populations now separated by an artificially hermetically sealed frontier."

6. Bibliography (selected)

Attalides, Michael (1979): *Cyprus, Nationalism and International Politics*, Edinburgh.

Baker, E. (1959): "The Settlement of Cyprus". In: *Political Quarterly 30*, 244–253.

Borg, Alexander (1985): *Cypriotic Arabic*, Stuttgart.

Catsiapis, Jean (1977): *Chypre, le Proche-Orient et les grandes Puissances*, Paris.

Coste-Floret, Alfred (1988): *Report on behalf of the Political Affairs Committee on the situation in Cyprus, European Parliament Session Document (1987–1988), Series A 2–317/87*, Luxemburg.

Cuco, Alfons (1992): *Demographic structure of the Cypriot Communities, Report for the Parliamentary Assembly of the Council of Europe*, Strasbourg.

Crouzet, François (1973): *Le Conflit de Chypre (1946–1959)*, Brussels.

de Vaumas, Etienne (1959): "La Repartition de la Population à Chypre et le Nouvel Etat Chypriote". In: *Revue de Geographie Alpine 47*, 457–530.

Dischler, Ludwig (1960): *Die Zypernfrage*, Francfort/Main.

Drury, M. P. (1981): "The Political Geography of Cyprus". In: *Change and Development in the Middle East*, London/New York, 289–304.

Emilianides, A. (1962): *Histoire de Chypre*, Paris.

Ertekun, Necati M. (1990): *The Status of the two peoples in Cyprus*, Nicosia.

Fernau, Frank W. (1964): "Zypern zwischen Griechen und Türken". In: *Aussenpolitik 15*, Stuttgart, 255–266.

Georghiades, A. (1963): *Die Zypernfrage*, Bonn.

Heinritz, G. (1986): *Bevölkerungs- und Siedlungsentwicklung*, Tübingen.

Hill, George F. (1940–1952): *A History of Cyprus*, 4 vol., Cambridge (UK).

Karouzis, George (1976): *Proposals for a solution to the Cyprus problem*, Nicosia.

Kolodny, Emile (1971): "Une Communauté insulaire en mediterranée orientale: Les Turcs de Chypre". In: *Revue de Geographie de Lyon 46*, 5–56.

Kyrnis, Costas P. (1985): *History of Cyprus*, Nicosia.

Melamid, A. (1956): "The Geographical Distribution of Communities in Cyprus". In: *Geographical Review 46*, 355–374.

Modinas, Polys (1987): *Chypre, le dur chemin de l'histoire*, Nicosia.

Nedjatigil, Zaim M. (1982): *The Cyprus Conflict, – A Lawyer's View*, Nicosia.

Ohr, Charles W.J. (1972): *Cyprus under British rule*, London.

Papaioannou, Ioannis (1984): *Politics in Cyprus between 1960 and 1981*, Nicosia.

Patrick, Richard A. (1976): *Political Geography and the Cyprus Conflict*, Waterloo (Canada).

Rossides, Z. (1957): *The problem of Cyprus*, Athens.

Seligman, A. (1956): *The Turkish People of Cyprus*, London.

Sonyel, Salahi R. (1991): *Settlers and refugees in Cyprus*, London.

Tenekides, George (1966): *Zypern – Jüngste Geschichte und politische Perspektiven*, Geneva.

Wolfe, James H. et al. (1987): *Zypern – Macht oder Land teilen?*, Intereg-Zeitfragen, Munich.

Yvo J. D. Peeters, Brussels (Belgium)

XV. Sprachkontakte in Mitteleuropa
Language Contacts in Central Europe
Contacts linguistiques en Europe Centrale

192. Poland

1. Demography
2. Geography, territorial history
3. Politics, economy and general cultural and religious situation
4. Statistics and ethnoprofiles
5. Sociolinguistic situation
6. Language political situation
7. Other minorities in contact with Polish
8. Evaluation of the sources and literature
9. Bibliography (selected)

Language contacts in present-day Poland involve ethnic groups whose linguistic, ethnic, national, and political status is varied and often lacks unambiguous definition. They take place in a rapidly changing political situation which exerts pervasive influence on the developments and processes occurring within particular groups. It is generally accepted that a major political and systemic transformation, which began in 1989, is still under way.

1. Demography

The most powerful determinants of the present geographic and demographic situation in Poland have been as follows: The Second World War (WW 2), the political decisions of "The Big Three" taken at the conferences in Yalta and Potsdam (1945), which determined the new political order in post-war Europe — new state borders, forced resettlement, migrations — and also the political system in post-war Poland. As a result of WW 2, Poland lost some 180,000 km^2 of its former territory in the east and gained about 110,000 km^2 in the west. The wartime loss of population was huge: only in 1978 did the population of Poland regain its 1939 level. In contrast to the pre-war period, however, the overwhelming majority of the population was now Polish. That was radically different from the traditional, pronouncedly heterogeneous ethnic structure of Polish society. Never since the 14th century had the percentage of non-Polish population within the state, ethnic, and cultural borders of Poland been so low. According to Ihnatowicz (Ihnatowicz 1979), during all periods for which numerical data are available, the percentage of non-Polish population varied between 30 and 60 per cent, depending on the period. The last census in Poland before WW 2 (1931) (according to the Concise Statistical Yearbook, 1937) indicated that over 30 per cent of the population did not speak Polish. Out of the total population of 31,915,800, there were 21,933,400 speakers of Polish; 3,222,000 of Ukrainian; 2,732,600 of Yiddish and Hebrew; 1,219,600 of Ruthenian; 989,900 of Belorussian; 741,000 of German; 138,000 of Russian; 878,600 inhabitants declared another language or no language at all, of which: 78,400 — Lithuanian, 31,300 Czech, and 708,200 — the "local" language.

Data on religious denominations differ from the linguistic data. Roman Catholic denomination was declared by 20,670,100 people; Greek Catholic by 3,336,200; Orthodox by 3,762,500; Protestant by 835,200; other Christian denominations by 145,400; Judaism by 3,113,900; other non-Christian denominations by 6,800; in 45,700 cases, no denomination was specified or no answer was given. The dramatic changes in the national/ethnic structure of the People's Republic of Poland justify the claim of the official statistics and propaganda that "in contrast to the pre-war period, Poland is now an ethnically homogeneous country." According to the PWN Publishers Great Encyclopaedia, minorities constitute between 1.5 and 2 per cent of the population of Poland (1960), which amounts to some 450,000 inhabitants, including: ca. 180,000 Ukrainians; ca. 170,000 Belorussians; ca. 30,000 Jews; ca. 20,000 Slovaks; ca. 20,000 Russians; ca. 10,000 Lithuanians; ca. 10,000 Greeks and Macedonians; ca. 3,000 Germans; ca. 2,000 Czechs.

The claim about the monoethnicity of Poland after WW 2 was not only an empirical statement — a simplified description of the status quo — but also a political tenet with a propaganda value. Accordingly, no questions were asked in post-war census questionnaires about people's language, religion, or nationality. The current estimates, indicating some 1.5 to 3 per cent of non-Polish population, point to a significant drop in the proportion of ethnic minorities within the present borders of Poland after WW 2.

1.1. Migrations

The scale, intensity, and social consequences of the migrations had no precedent in the history of Poland. Armies marched, civilians retreated, refugees fled the country, and, on top of it, people were deported and relocated on a massive scale (Kwilecki 1982: 39).

1.1.1. Migrations of the German population

Before WW 2, the German minority within Poland's borders comprised, according to the 1931 census, 741,000 people. In the territories taken over by Poland after WW 2, there had lived in 1939 8,860,000 people (including 395,000 in the Free City of Danzig) (Waszak 1959). According to German sources, their number was closer to 10 million. When the great wartime and post-WW 2 migrations were over, there remained within the Polish borders about one million indigenous native inhabitants (commonly referred to as autochthons) on the new Polish territories. Out of this number, some 800,000 remained in the Opole region and in the western part of the Upper Silesian Industrial Region. In the southern part of former East Prussia, there also remained another group of autochthonous population, the so-called Mazurians. According to the 1950 census, there were about 440,000 (55 per cent of the overall population) autochthons in Opole Silesia; 340,000 (15 per cent) in the Katowice district, and 196,000 (almost 29 per cent) in the Olsztyn district (Korbel 1977).

Making an allowance for the WW 2 casualties and those citizens of the Third Reich who declared Polish nationality and stayed in Poland, the number of Germans who left the territory of pre-WW 2 and post-WW 2 Poland can be estimated at seven million. About two thirds of these left Poland in the years 1944-1945. The wartime migration was essentially a general exodus, a flight from the advancing front. The second wave of the migration (1945–1947) was a period of forced deportations. Its objective was to expel all ethnic Germans from the parts of Poland formerly belonging to the Reich. Since these territories included regions (Upper Silesia, Mazuria) inhabited by an indigenous population of Polish origin which had been subjected to prolonged Germanization and had mixed with German settlers, the nationality question was solved by means of so-called "verification", officially completed by 1947 (the autochthonous inhabitants had to declare their nationality). All in all, it involved about a million persons in all the territories awarded to Poland (Korbel 1977: 31).

The total number of Germans who left Poland in the years 1945–1947 amounted to 2,214,000. Deportations of the German population continued, on a smaller scale, until April 1950. According to Polish statistics, the German population in Poland (excluding the autochthons) did not exceed 125,000 to 160,000 in 1950.

In the same year, there was launched a programme of so-called "reuniting families", which has been continued without interruption to this day. It gained momentum after 1956, leading to emigration of some 800,000 people (250,000 in the years 1950–1959, 200,000 in 1960–1972) to Germany. Initially, it was ethnic Germans who emigrated (the number of those who had stayed in Poland was officially estimated at ca. 4,000 in 1969–1970). Later on, however, large groups of the indigenous population of Upper Silesia and Mazuria followed in their footsteps. Such a state of affairs continued until 1989, after which the number of people declaring German nationality has increased sharply.

1.1.2. Migrations of the Ukrainian, Belorussian and Lithuanian population

The newly delineated borders of post-WW 2 Poland left in the Soviet Union, along with several million Poles, most of the Ruthenian and Lithuanian minorities which had lived in Poland before WW 2. Within the new borders of Poland, there remained about 600,000 Ukrainians, 150,000 Belorussians in eastern parts of the Białystok district, and 7,000 Lithuanians in the borderland villages northeast of the town of Suwałki (Maryański

1984: 112). The shifting of Poland's borders to the west and the idea of ethnic states in post-WW 2 Europe led to massive emigration of the Ukrainians — and, to a lesser degree, also the Belorussians and Lithuanians — to the Soviet Union. Their migration took on an organized form and was in principle voluntary, although in practice this was not always the case, in particular with the Ukrainian population. The organized resettlement continued between 1944 and 1946 and involved inhabitants of the Polish—Soviet borderland and the so-called Lemkian Wedge (the eastern part of the Polish Carpathians). All in all, 481,000 Ukrainians, 37,000 Belorussians and a very small group of Lithuanians left Poland for the USSR (Maryański 1984: 112).

In 1947, there started repressive displacement of the Ukrainian population that had stayed in Poland (including various Ruthenian ethnic groups, such as Lemkians, the Bojkos, and the inhabitants of Polesie). The deportations were executed in the course of the military "Vistula" operation (April—July 1947), aimed against the Ukrainian Insurrectionary Army (UPA), operating in the southeast corner of Poland. The UPA troops, of a strongly anti-communist orientation, embraced the ideology of the Ukrainian nationalist movements, which had been supported by Nazi Germany during WW 2. After WW 2, they refused to lay down their arms and continued armed resistance to both the Soviet and the Polish authorities. The deportations were meant to deprive the partisans of their foothold in the area.

The deportations included nearly all of the Ukrainian population, regardless of its actual links with the UPA troops. About 120,000 people were forcibly relocated, mostly to the northern and western territories of Poland, and became scattered in the process. In the vast majority of cases, the Ukrainians form just a fraction of the local population, usually ranging from 5 to 15 per cent.

The post-WW 2 migrations did not have any serious impact on the indigenous Belorussian and Lithuanian population, which mostly stayed where it was.

1.1.3. Migrations of the Polish population

In the north and west of Poland some 90 per cent of the population had been replaced. Among the settlers, there were ca. 1.5 million people of Polish origin, out of the total of ca. 2 million repatriates from the Soviet Union.

The situation of the Ukrainians in the northern and western territories was similar to that of the Poles relocated there from the USSR: both were pioneer settlers. Since a large proportion of the relocated Poles came from so-called Western Ukraine, which had been the scene of many bloody acts of violence during WW 2, the potential for conflict was obvious. In Opole Silesia, the indigenous population that had remained there after WW 2 constituted only 53.1 per cent of all the inhabitants in 1950. The others were newcomers who did not understand the specificity of the region and, for instance, often treated the autochthons as Germans. This gave rise to conflicts, covered up by the official propaganda (→ Language Map I).

2. Geography, territorial history

2.1. The two historical factors of greatest significance for the ethnic structure of Poland were (i) the eastward shift, observable since the 14th century, of the borders of the country, and (ii) the formation of a political union with the Grand Duchy of Lithuania (Union of Krewo in 1385, Union of Horodło in 1413, Union of Lublin in 1569). The retreat of the western border led to Germanization of the population of West Slavonic and Polish ethnic background; the expansion to the east, and in particular the political union with Lithuania resulted in Polonization of the Ruthenian and Lithuanian population in those areas. An important role in the socio-historical development of the country was played by language processes, in particular, the formation of the literary variety of Polish since the 16th century. The Polish nobility started to regard the Polish language and culture as the determinants of their identity.

In the 11th century, it became legally possible for Jews — expelled or driven out from other European countries — to settle in Poland. Jews lived within the ethnic and political borders of Poland until their extermination by the Nazis during the Holocaust.

Historically and geographically, four groups of ethnic minorities can be distinguished:

(1) Lithuanian, Belorussian and Ukrainian, whose links with Poland date back to the end of the 14th century, due to the union of the Kingdom of Poland with the Grand Duchy of Lithuania. Historically, the situation of these minorities was characterized by political, cultural, and economic domination of

the Polish element, which led to processes of linguistic Polonization. Geographically, the minorities in question are currently situated along the eastern border of Poland.

(2) Slovak and Czech, associated with the relatively stable southern border of Poland. The current border cuts through the historical area of Polish settlement, which extended into the territory of former Czechoslovakia. In this area, one can speak about two-way fluctuation of influence rather than ethnic domination. In terms of numbers, the Czechs and Slovaks are small groups, compared with the minorities living along the eastern and western borders.

(3) The western and northern borders of Poland were historically an area where the Polish, and, more generally, Slavonic element gradually gave way to the political, cultural, and economic domination of the Germans. The ethnic groups inhabiting the western and northern borderland include: (i) the German minority, consisting today mainly of descendants of the indigenous population, which used — historically Polish — Silesian dialects, and (ii) the Kashubs. The historical and linguistic processes going on in those areas were predominantly those of Germanization, although after WW 2, with the border shifted to the west, there occurred processes of Polonization, too.

(4) Minorities dispersed all over Poland. The historically most important one was the Jewish minority, which was almost totally exterminated by the Nazis during the Holocaust. Currently, the largest of the dispersed minorities is the Ukrainian one. Other minorities in this group include Gypsies (Romanies), Greeks and Macedonians (post-WW 2 political emigrés), and Russians.

2.1.1. The Lithuanian minority (10,000—13,000) is concentrated in the two borderland regions in the northeastern part of Poland, in the district of Suwałki. The Lithuanians live in the town of Puńsk (Lithuanian Pùnskas) and its environs, and in the former administrative region of Sejny, on Lake Gaładus̀. Their ancestors, who succeeded the former inhabitants, the Baltic tribe of Jatvingians, had lived in that wooded land since the 16th century. After WW 1, the presence of a Lithuanian minority in Poland resulted from the division of the ex-*guberniya* of Suwałki, with its ethnically mixed population, between the newly emerging states of Lithuania and Poland in 1919. Acute Polish—Lithuanian political tensions between the two world wars, and the impermeability of the Polish—Soviet border after WW 2 until recently, cut off the Polish Lithuanians from any language contacts with Lithuania. During the 19th century, Lithuanian dialects coexisted in the region with Belorussian ones; now they are surrounded by Polish dialects.

2.1.2. The Belorussian minority inhabits the eastern part of the Białystok district. This is the historical meeting-place of three groups of settlers: Polish (from Mazovia), Northern Ukrainian (Ruthenians living on the Bug River), and Belorussian (with a Lithuanian sub-component) from the lands on the Neman and Ros Rivers. It is a typical borderland area, without sharp ethnic and language boundaries. On the one hand, there is a Ruthenian—Polish border — or, rather, transition zone — running, roughly, from north to south between the Bug and the Czarna Hańcza Rivers, along the line defined by Białystok and Siemiatycze. On the other hand, there are isoglosses that generally follow the East—West direction, along the Narew River, and then take a turn to the south, along the southern edge of the Białowieża Woods. They separate Belorussian dialects from Northern-Ukrainian and mixed Ukrainian-Belorussian ones, which extend as far north as the Bug River. Larger-scale settlement in the Białystok region began relatively late, only in the 16th century.

2.1.3. The Ukrainian minority. Simplifying things a little, one can say that at the time the eastern border of Poland became delineated, the Ukrainian population (including the linguistically and ethnically distinct subgroup of the Lemkians and Bojkos) inhabited a several-dozen-kilometre-wide strip along that border, reaching as far north as the Bug and Narew Rivers, where it would begin to mix with the Belorussians. In the Carpathians, in the south of Poland, the Lemkian territory extended uninterruptedly all the way to Krynica and Muszyna in the west, while in the east, it bordered on the land of the Bojkos — the Bieszczady Mountains. As far as the areas of Polish—Ukrainian contacts are concerned, their penetration by the Polish element and its subsequent assimilation depended very much on the region. Generally speaking, the two populations did not tend to mix in the mountains (Beskid Niski, Bieszczady): ethnic borders were fairly clear-cut and almost no villages with a mixed population existed. In the submontane and lowland areas, on the other hand, the borderline was fuzzy, with a mixed population and language islands on both sides of the ethnic border, often at a considerable distance from it. In contrast, the Lemkians and Bojkos, shepherds in origin, maintained their ethnic separateness.

After the deportations of 1945−1947, no more than 20 or 30 thousand Ukrainians were left in the former districts of Kraków and Rzeszów (Maryański 1984). Some deportations of the Ukrainian population took place also in the district of Lublin. To the north of the Włodawka River, only a marginal number of inhabitants were relocated. The area to the south of the Włodawka, up to the foot of the Bieszczady, was repopulated with Polish settlers after the war. Resettlement in the mountains, on the other hand, proved much more difficult. In the areas of resettlement, the Polish population dominated the indigenous Ukrainians, who became assimilated to a greater extent than those living in the region of Włodawa and further to the north.

A small proportion of the Ukrainian population returned to their homeland after 1956. The total number of Ukrainians currently living in the territories they traditionally inhabited is estimated at between 50 and 60 thousand.

2.2. Territorial development and the evolution of national consciousness. Each of the minorities under discussion has its own history, interwoven with the history of the Polish-Lithuanian Republic (i. e., the Kingdom of Poland united with the Grand Duchy of Lithuania). Polonization proceeded through settlement and migrations. The nobility, educated strata, and city dwellers from those minorities generally underwent Polonization. The villages and the peasantry remained a domain of linguistically conservative elements (indigenous dialects). Of all the languages that came into contact with Polish (Lithuanian, Belorussian, Ukrainian), until the 18th century, only Belorussian had the status of an official language and was the language of legal documents in the Grand Duchy of Lithuania. It partly gave way to Latin, and then, to a greater degree, to Polish. Belorussian and Ukrainian, in addition to Old Church Slavonic, also had the status of religious and liturgical languages in the Orthodox and Greek Catholic Churches. In the Roman Catholic Church, the same functions were fulfilled by Latin and Polish. Generally speaking, the Poles and Lithuanians were Catholic, the Belorussians Orthodox, and the Ukrainians Greek Catholic. Having gradually lost its status as an official language, Belorussian remained in use as a spoken language, a rural dialect. The position of the Lithuanian language and the Ukrainian dialects was similar. After the partitions of Poland, beginning in 1795, and then in 1809, Belorussia, Lithuania, and the Eastern Ukraine were exposed to very strong Russification. Western Ukraine remained under Polish influence, combined with influence from German as the official language and the language of legal documents.

This situation was significantly changed only after WW 1, when Poland and Lithuania gained independence and Belorussia and Ukraine were partly incorporated into the Soviet Union, where they formed separate republics, and partly remained within the Polish borders.

In Polish−Lithuanian relations, the independence movement was marked by an unprecedented outburst of ethnic conflicts resulting from border disputes and the major controversy over the city of Vilna and the adjacent Polish-speaking areas. Diplomatic relations were established between Poland and Lithuania only in 1938, and private contacts of citizens of the two countries were severely restricted.

The developments after WW 1 did not provoke any major conflict between the Poles and the Belorussians. Such a conflict did occur, however, in the case of the Ukrainians. In the years 1918−1920, hostilities went on between Poland, Ukraine, and Soviet Russia. Apart from regular warfare, acts of insurgency were staged by both the Poles and the Ukrainians. The eventual outcome was as follows: Lvov, the capital city of Galicia, remained in Polish hands; the Ukrainians failed to establish an independent state; and the Polish−Soviet border was delineated along the river Zbruch.

During the period between the two world wars, the mounting, yet frustrated, ambitions of the Ukrainian nationalist movements, combined with the discrimination against the Ukrainians by the Polish government, resulted in a rise of anti-Polish terrorist activities (OUN, the Organization of Ukrainian

Nationalists). The Polish authorities responded with armed reprisals.

WW 2 led to a general intensification of ethnic conflicts. After 17 September, 1939, when Soviet troops invaded Poland in the aftermath of the Ribbentrop-Molotov Pact, Ukraine and Belorussia annexed so-called Western Ukraine and the district of Białystok, respectively. When Germany attacked the Soviet Union, Belorussia and Ukraine came under Nazi occupation, and Lithuania gained the status of a satellite state, controlled by the Third Reich. The Germans instigated nationalist movements in the areas under their occupation, especially in Ukraine, seeking military cooperation in their extermination programmes, aimed, among others, against the Poles. Polish resistance groups retaliated and staged equally bloody reprisals against the Ukrainian population. The Ukrainian underground army, of a nationalist, anti-communist and pro-German orientation, was defeated in post-WW 2 Poland only in 1947.

Polish—Lithuanian conflicts, then, date back to the first moments of independence in the 20th century; in Polish—Belorussian relationships, there are some conflicts on record, but none of them was ever particularly conspicuous; conflicts between the Poles and the Ukrainians span the entire history of their mutual relations, reaching their peak in the 20th century. Nevertheless, no serious Polish—Ukrainian conflicts have occurred in the post-WW 2 period.

2.3. Polish—Slovak and Polish—Czech ethnic contacts occur in the regions of Spisz, Orawa, Cieszyn Silesia, the environs of Racibórz and of Kudowa, and the Czech language islands in the vicinity of Piotrków Trybunalski.

The parts of Spisz and Orawa that lie within the present-day borders of Poland have an autochthonous population whose historical ancestors were Polish settlers. There are some 20,000 Slovaks living in those areas today, whose native ethnolect comprises the dialects — Polish by origin — of Spisz and Orawa. Most of the historical lands of Spisz and Orawa are located in present-day Slovakia. Into these areas came Polish settlers moving from the north, who encountered in both regions Slovak and German settlers advancing from the south. In the Middle Ages, both Spisz and Orawa were Hungarian provinces on the border with Poland. In the case of Orawa, this situation changed only in 1918, when Jabłonka and its environs were awarded to Poland. Spisz, on the other hand (or its northern part, called *Starostwo* [district] of Spisz), was pledged to Poland by the Hungarians in the 15th century. Never redeemed, it remained a Polish possession until 1769, when it was annexed by the Austrian Empire. After WW 1, Spisz became the site of a border dispute between Poland and Czechoslovakia. In 1920, its greater part was awarded to Czechoslovakia by way of international arbitration; Poland received just a small, northwestern part of the region. After the Nazi invasion, both Orawa and Spisz were incorporated in full into the Slovak state, controlled by the Germans. After WW 2, the borders of 1920 were restored.

In Cieszyn Silesia, the language border is situated on the Czech side.

The area to the south of Racibórz, along the border, is called the mixed-dialect zone. It comprises a cluster of dialects intermediate between Polish and Czech.

In the vicinity of Kudowa in Poland, there are several places where the Czech language is used by the local population. This area is called the Czech Corner. Before WW 2, it belonged to Germany. The Czech-speaking autochthons, of whom there were at one time about 5,500, perceived themselves mostly as Germans. After WW 2, the majority of them emigrated to Germany. The area was resettled by Poles, which led to the amalgamation of the Polish and Czech population, with the Polish element dominant.

In the present-day Piotrków Trybunalski district in the heartland of Poland, there are Czech language islands that date back to 18th-century Protestant religious emigration. The descendants of the emigrants have retained their language in their liturgy and in everyday life.

2.4. The German minority and the Kashubs. Both the contemporary German minority and the Kashubs inhabit those territories of present-day Poland where the Polish and West Slavonic population was gradually superseded over the centuries by German settlers advancing towards the east. Of all the Polish ethnic groups that came under German rule in the 14th century, only the inhabitants of Upper Silesia and, partly, Mazuria, have preserved until today their Polish dialect and ethnic specificity.

2.4.1. Upper Silesia is now inhabited partly by autochthons and partly by Polish settlers.

The indigenous population of Upper Silesia (30 per cent of which has declared German nationality since 1989) comprises descendants of the oldest Polish settlers (the tribes of Opolanie and Golęszyce), who mixed with German settlers over the centuries. From the beginning of the 14th century (the reign of King Casimir the Great), the region remained outside the Polish borders until the end of WW 1, when part of Upper Silesia was incorporated into Poland, as the result of a plebiscite and the armed struggle of Polish patriots (Silesian Uprisings). After WW 2 it became part of Poland. The inhabitants of Silesia identified themselves first of all with their region, rather than with their nationality. It was mostly outsiders who labelled the autochthons as belonging to one or another nationality. For Germans coming to Silesia, an autochthon was a Pole speaking so-called *Wasserpolnisch*; for many Poles who settled in the region after the war, the Silesians were Germans. The indigenous inhabitants remained under the influence of both Polish and German culture, and the choice of one's nationality was often dictated by external considerations.

Apart from Silesia, some autochthonous population, partly Germanized and partly bilingual (Polish/German), was to be found also in Mazuria after WW 2.

2.4.2. The Kashubs. Nowadays, the Kashub population (ca. 500,000) is concentrated in one area delimited by the Baltic coast in the north, the Vistula River on the east, the Piaśnica River on the west and the Brda River on the south. The area includes the Hel Peninsula and the Bay of Gdańsk and such towns as Puck, Wejherowo, Gdynia, Kartuzy and Kościerzyna.

Historically, the region belonged to that part of Pomerania which since 1466 had belonged to the Kingdom of Poland. The Kashub and West Slavonic language areas (including the Slovinian language) outside this territory remained under German rule since the 14th century and underwent complete Germanization.

During the first partition of Poland, from 1772 to WW 1, the Kashub region, annexed by Prussia, was exposed to Germanization. In 1920, it was returned to Poland. During WW 2 the Nazis strove to suppress the national identity of the Kashub population (people were forced to sign the *Volksliste* and had to serve in the *Wehrmacht*). After the war, the region was incorporated into Poland again.

Of all the ethnic groups discussed so far, only the Kashubs have never had a state to which they could turn for protection of their interests. Their ethnic and cultural specificity has always been based on community spirit and awareness of tradition. Towards the end of the 19th century, these traits were reinforced by conscious endeavours on behalf of the region's language and culture. These efforts reached their peak during the period between the world wars. No significant conflicts have ever been recorded in the history of Polish–Kashub relations.

3. Politics, economy and general cultural and religious situation

The national policy on ethnic minorities in post-WW 2 Poland was subordinated to the doctrine of the monoethnic character of Polish society after WW 2. At least four of the minorities living in Poland (Lithuanians, Ukrainians, Slovaks, Germans) had been involved to a greater or lesser degree in the war on the side of the enemy. The Ukrainians continued their armed struggle against Poland until 1947. The fear of the Germans after the five years of Nazi occupation was augmented by the memories of the role played by the German minority (so-called fifth column) during and before WW 2. The authorities adopted a repressive demographic policy, aimed especially against the German and Ukrainian minorities. As a result, research in this field was also hampered.

Officially, the subject of national minorities was more or less banned until the 1980s and was never mentioned in the media. However, it was allowed on a regional level and in small-circulation publications. The turning point was the year 1956, when the Ukrainians were allowed to open their own schools and form organizations. Most of the other minorities had already been granted similar rights, but only after 1956 did they begin to exercise them on a significant scale. The Germans' right to form organizations, to publish, and to establish schools was limited to territories outside Upper Silesia.

Ethnic policy in Upper Silesia was characterized by (i) repressiveness towards the Germans, and (ii) Polonization of the German-speaking and bilingual inhabitants, effected by means of depriving them of any opportunity to cultivate their language and the local tradition. After the verification — in many cases carried out by force — which was the condition on which the autochthons were allowed to stay in their native land, they were afraid to use German or stand up for their interests as a minority. This resulted in hidden conflicts, resentment, and a sense of ethnic oppression. For instance, those indigenous inhabitants of Silesia who initially spoke only German did not have in post-WW 2 Poland the right to hold onto this language as their mother tongue after having declared Polish nationality. Such a historical legacy combines nowadays with factors like (i) the economic superiority of Germany, a country with which many inhabitants of Silesia feel a bond of historically shared nationhood; (ii) the conviction that people of German nationality have better chances of fulfilling their aspirations; and (iii) the protectionist policy of Germany with regard to Silesia. All this has had a tremendous influence on nationality declarations since 1989.

Minorities in Poland pursue their own cultural and literary activities. The turning point in this area was also 1956 (the end of the Stalinist era in political life). After that date, new minority cultural and social organizations were formed (apart from those that already existed), which started their own periodicals. There were organized amateur theatres, choirs, instrumental ensembles, dance groups, folk song and dance groups, folk bands, poetry recitation groups, youth and children's ensembles, etc. Programmes for minorities appeared on local radio stations; regional museums were established; local publishing houses began to function, promoting literature in the ethnic languages.

However, these opportunities were not extended to the German minority in Upper Silesia. German organizations functioned in the cities of Wałbrzych, Wrocław, and Szczecin in the 1950s and 1960s. In the 1970s, their activity died out, as the members had emigrated to Germany. In Opole Silesia and the Katowice district, German social and cultural organizations have been proliferating only since 1989. In the 1980s, the issue of ethnic minorities in Poland was first taken up by the press and other media. Initially, it remained the domain of publications circulated illegally. The dominant theme of the ensuing discussion was the need to come to terms with the past. Old conflicts were unearthed, which was facilitated by the abolition of censorship in 1989. Foundations and other organizations (often cooperating closely with the Church) were established in order to support the minorities and promote openness and understanding among particular ethnic groups. In 1989, a representative of the Ukrainian minority was elected to the Sejm (Lower House of Parliament) on the Solidarity ticket. During the next parliamentary election of 1991, the organized German minority secured for itself eight seats in both houses of the parliament. This does not mean an elimination of all forms of conflict, prejudice, or hostile behaviour and the question of the loyalty of the newly-emerged German minority remains a legitimate concern not only in view of the past experience. On the other hand, it must be borne in mind that the repressive and conflict-prone policy toward the German minority pursued by post-WW 2 Poland in Upper Silesia since 1945 has left behind a legacy of distrust and frustration, not easy to overcome.

The German minority in Upper Silesia, the Slovak minority, and the Lithuanian minority are predominantly Roman Catholic, like the majority of Poles. Conflicts in the area of religion in post-WW 2 Poland have been mostly connected with the language of liturgy and sermons. Owing to the decisions of Polish ecclesiastical authorities in the past three years, the use of ethnic languages in liturgy has been extended, which has largely eliminated the conflicts. Unfortunately, however, new conflicts are arising, mostly about church buildings, that involve Greek Catholic and Orthodox communities. They demand that their churches, liquidated after the war and converted into Roman Catholic ones, should now be returned to them. Disputed ownership gives rise to conflicts and an escalation of ethnic tension. There are many cases, however, involving small churches in little towns, where an amicable settlement of the dispute is finally worked out.

4. Statistics and ethnoprofiles

Practically all ethnic minorities in Poland intermingle with the Polish population. Few self-contained, isolated areas with a homogeneous ethnic compositon exist in Poland today, in contrast with the situation before the war (e. g. in the areas inhabited by the Lemkians). The autochthonous minorities live mostly in the country, which is an environment that allows one to maintain an ethnic language and tradition more easily. One of the few exceptions is the town of Puńsk in the district of Suwałki, where, according to the mayor's information, 80 per cent of the inhabitants in 1989 were Lithuanian. In Puńsk, one can hear the Lithuanian language in the street or in stores. There still function an elementary school and a secondary school with Lithuanian as the language of instruction or as one of the subjects taught. This is similar to the situation in the town of Jabłonka in Orawa, where Slovaks constitute 50 per cent of the population. In Polish Spisz and Orawa, the shop signs and notice boards (but not traffic signs and place names) are bilingual.

In the area inhabited by the Belorussians, many live in the towns (Hajnówka, Sokółka, Białystok). However, ethnic Belorussians are less committed to using Belorussian (in its dialectal form) in their social contacts outside of the family.

Nowadays, national minorities in Poland are not prejudiced against intermarrying with Poles. This is true of all the minorities and leads to their constant amalgamation, and, consequently, assimilation and integration with the Polish population.

The ethnic languages are retained to a greater degree by the older generation (sometimes, although very rarely today, people remain monolingual; there are isolated cases in the Lithuanian, Belorussian and Lemkian areas). The young generation, which receives education and migrates to towns, often consciously reverts to the native language and tradition (cf. the sociological research carried out in ethnic Lemkian territories (Dziewierski 1992) and in Upper Silesia (Jacher 1993, Berlińska 1993)).

5. Sociolinguistic situation

Generally speaking, the situation of national minorities in Poland does not allow one to make a clear-cut distinction between bilingualism and diglossia without detailed sociolinguistic studies. No such studies have been carried out so far. Still, the dominant language throughout Poland is the general, standard variety of Polish, which comes into contact with dialectal, spoken varieties of ethnic languages and regional ethnolects. Polish is the official language and the language of external contacts: in town, in the street, or in stores; native ethnolects are used in private contacts, within the family or group, and are generally avoided in the presence of strangers. Apart from the language of the Kashubs, all the minority languages (German, Czech, Slovak, Ukrainian, Belorussian, Lithuanian) have the status of official languages in the neighbouring countries, but the degree to which their speakers in Poland come into contact with the standard form of each of the languages varies.

5.1. Lithuanian is represented in Poland by two dialects (those of Puńsk and Sejny), which belong to the southern group of Lithuanian dialects. It is used by Lithuanians living in Poland in unofficial situations and at home, in contrast with Polish as the official language. General Lithuanian is used in schools and in official contacts within the ethnic group.

5.2. Belorussian is represented first of all by dialectal varieties of the so-called "simple" language. The status of Belorussian as an official language is weak even in Belarus itself, where Russian is still the dominant language in towns, as the language of schools and offices.

5.3. Ukrainian is present in Poland in a whole range of varieties. The one that stands apart from the rest is the Lemkian ethnolect, which is identified as Ukrainian only by some speakers. In those regions from which the autochthonous population has not migrated, local dialects are in use (the region of Włodawa, mixed dialects in the area between the Bug and the Narew Rivers). The language of official contacts within groups and in schools is standard Ukrainian. There are literary works in Ukrainian written in Poland. Likewise, there are a Ukrainian press and many kinds of publications. Performances in Ukrainian, or the Lemkian dialect, are given by various folk ensembles, theatre groups, choirs, poetry readers, etc.

5.4. In Spisz and Orawa, where the native ethnolect comprises the local dialects of each region, different types of language contacts have developed. Slovak is first of all the language of religion, liturgy, school, and family contacts with Slovaks. The official language is still Polish, in its general variety.

5.5. In Opole Silesia, the native ethnolect is the Silesian dialect called by the Germans *Wasserpolnisch*, which remains in contact with general Polish. According to a 1990 study, 26 per cent of the autochthons have a very good or good command of German, while 19 per cent have no knowledge of it at all. Most of the people who know German belong to the older generation and once attended a German school. Recently, the popularity of German has increased, both among adults and the young generation, although sociological research indicates that the interest in that language is not as intense as it was expected to become (Berlińska 1993). Courses in German are offered, not only to the German minority, but to anyone who may be interested. There is an expanding network of libraries and reading rooms, where German press and literature are available. They are equipped with satellite TV, which allows the visitors to watch German programmes. Various folk ensembles, choirs, and glee clubs are organized. By popular demand, the use of German in churches and schools has been extended.

5.6. The Kashubs use various dialects, which are in contact mostly with Polish in its general and official varieties. The Kashub language has its written and literary varieties, cultivated by various regional cultural societies.

5.7. The language contacts of national minorities in Poland are not usually limited these days to the bilingual type. In most cases, there is a three-way relationship: local ethnolect (the dialect of the place); general standard variety of Polish; general variety of the minority's native tongue. Besides, neighbouring ethnolects interact with one another, which is particularly noticeable in regions where Ukrainian-Belorussian dialects are contiguous with Polish ones. Polish has the status of the dominant language. Speakers often avoid using their native ethnolect, and do so for a variety of reasons such as: reluctance to sound different from the dominating group (all ethnolects), political considerations and a repressive ethnic policy (German, Ukrainian), or negative stereotypes (German, Ukrainian; Lemkian dialect, avoided for fear of evoking associations with some negative stereotypes of a Ukrainian). Nowadays, sociologists observe a tendency, particularly among the young generation, to come out of such self-imposed isolation. People are no longer afraid to be different, to exhibit their own culture, and to use their language. Practically no separatist tendencies are observed; what can be seen is more aptly described as endeavours to overcome isolation. The interest in cross-ethnic contacts is mutual: it occurs also in the Polish population, both on a regional scale and globally. The strongly negative ethnic stereotypes that still exist function mostly among the old generation, although new stereotypes, of a much less negative type, also come into existence (cf. Jacher 1993, Dziewierski 1992), and in all regions, there exist local stereotypes that stem from ethnic differences. The new ethnic policy of the government, local-level administration, and church authorities is producing a change of attitudes and has had an impact on the situation of ethnic minorities, which are at the moment rethinking and redefining their place in society, their ethnic and national consciousness, their attitude towards the nation and the state, and towards their own language, tradition, and culture.

6. Language political situation

The first schools where minority languages were used became established soon after the end of WW 2. German, for instance, was the language of instruction in 136 primary schools in the school year 1953/1954. Such a state of affairs continued until 1956/1957. In the following year, the number of schools suddenly dropped to 45. The year 1962/1963 was the last year of functioning of German primary schools (2 schools with 48 pupils). In 1964, the statistical yearbook mentioned, for the last time, 18 pupils learning German as their native language (all these data come from the Concise Statistical Yearbook). The programme of reuniting families (started in 1956), under which Germans were allowed to leave Poland, resulted in a systematic decrease in the number of pupils and schools.

The first schools with Ukrainian as the language of instruction were established in 1956 (1956/1957 – 2 primary schools for 56 pupils, 1960/1961 – 6 primary schools for 283 pupils and 2 secondary schools for 143 pupils). Subsequently, the number of pupils and schools dropped steadily to zero. In 1981, there were 254 pupils of primary schools who learnt Ukrainian as their mother tongue. This drop in numbers is attributable to the dispersion of the Ukrainians, the lack of interest on the part of the pupils, and the fact that for some dialect-speaking Ukrainians the school meant the requirement to learn a language considerably different from their native ethnolect.

Ths situation of Belorussian, Lithuanian, and Slovak schools has always been fairly stable. The schools were quite numerous, and adequate to the needs (Belorussian — 67 primary schools for 4363 pupils and two secondary schools for 373 pupils in 1953/1954; Slovak — 33 primary schools for 2427 pupils and one secondary school for 86 pupils in 1953/1954). The number of schools with an ethnic language of instruction then started to decrease steadily. Pupils opted for lessons on their native language as just one of the subjects in an otherwise Polish-language school. The reason was the lack of the pupils' interest. This was a consequence of assimilation processes and the status of their native tongue, limited to informal contacts at home or within the group, as opposed to Polish. Instruction in one's native language did not allow one to continue education at university level and narrowed down the range of career opportunities.

7. Other minorities in contact with Polish

7.1. Jews. After WW 2, in mid-1946, the lists compiled by Jewish relief committees in Poland indicated 240,489 persons of Jewish origin. It is estimated that some 83,000 Jews had survived the war in the territory of Poland or in German concentration camps (the latter group comprised 35,959 persons). Many of the survivors had been sheltered by Polish families; many had fought in the resistance movement. The remaining part of the Jewish population in Poland in 1946 consisted mostly of people who had returned from the USSR. After 1956, when the Stalinist era was over, massive emigration of the Jews began. By 1959, their number in Poland had dropped to ca. 50,000 and kept decreasing. In 1968, there started a new wave of emigration of a political nature. By 1971, only ca. 15,000 Jews had remained in Poland, and subsequent estimates indicate even smaller numbers. At present, there is one bilingual (Yiddish/Polish) periodical published in Poland. There exists a Jewish Historical Institute, which publishes its materials in Polish. Besides, there are several cultural and social associations. Yiddish and Hebrew were the languages of instruction in 7 primary and 2 secondary schools (respectively, with 1,911 and 184 pupils) in the year 1954/1955. The last year for which the Concise Statistical Yearbook mentioned schools with Yiddish and Hebrew was 1963/1964. However, according to information from the press, it is once again possible to learn Hebrew in some schools in the year 1993/1994.

7.2. Gypsies (ca. 12,000). The first records of the presence in Poland of nomads from India date back fo 1419. The Polish Gypsies, like Jews, suffered ruthless extermination at the hands of the Nazis during WW 2. After WW 2, they were subjected to forced settlement. They use ethnolects of their own among themselves and Polish in external contacts. The Polish Gypsies form closed groups which resist penetration.

7.3. Greeks and Macedonians (ca. 10,000) in Poland are political émigrés from Greece (when the communist party was outlawed there in 1949) who settled in the western territories of Poland. They established a Wrocław-based Association of Political Refugees, and published a periodical in Greek. Gradually, they became assimilated. Schools offering instruction in Greek and Macedonian existed until 1967. In the year 1961/1962, there were 123 pupils who learnt their mother tongue at school. Some of the émigrés returned to Greece in the 1980s.

7.4. Russians (ca. 20,000). Very little data is available about this minority in Poland. For a short time they published a periodical in Russian, and they used to have their own Orthodox communes. Statistical yearbooks offer no information about schooling in Russian.

7.5. Armenians, Tartars, and Karaites do not constitute language minorities in Poland. They cultivate first of all their national and religious traditions. There exist, for instance, a Moslem Religious Assocation and a Karaite Religious Association.

8. Evaluation of the sources and literature

Studies on languages in contact in Poland have always focused on dialectological issues and followed the tradition of linguistic geography. Linguistic geography and Slavonic dialectology draw first of all on the works of Kazimierz Nitsch, Zdzisław Stieber, and Karol Dejna. Research carried out under the auspices of the Polish Academy of Sciences and in the form of independent projects has produced a number of linguistic atlases, which cover all the ethnic groups within the present borders of Poland. The theoretical foundation of Polish studies on languages in contact was laid, for the most part, by Z. Stieber, who discussed and classified in his works the types of language contacts conditioned by ethnic and territorial factors.

There are some fundamental differences between Polish and German scholars as far as, for instance, the Kashub ethnolect is concerned. In the Polish tradition, it has been treated as a dialect of Polish (from the Pomeranian group), while German writers accord to it the status of a separate language. Polish and German researchers differ also on matters of linguistic geography, such as the spatial distribution of German and Polish. The Polish point of view on this question was set out by Alfred Zaręba (1974). Other areas where the Polish and German views do not coincide include problems of demography, statistics, and the evaluation of the post-war migrations. But, of course, whenever minorities are concerned, conflicting interpretations of historical and social facts will inevitably occur. The developing modern sociolinguistics in Poland strives to address such issues.

9. Bibliography (selected)

Berlińska, Danuta (1993): "Śląskie nierówności" [Silesian inequalities]. In: *Dialog. Magazin für Deutsch–Polnische Verständigung 1*, 49–52.

Dziewierski, Marek/Pactwa, Bożena/Siewierski, Bogdan (1992): *Dylematy tożsamości* [The dilemma of identity], Katowice.

Ihnatowicz, Ireneusz/Mączak, Antoni/Zientara, Benedykt (1979): *Społeczeństwo polskie od X do XX wieku* [Polish society: 10th to 20th centuries], Warsaw.

Jacher, Władysław (Ed.) (1993): *Sytuacja społeczno-kulturowa mniejszości niemieckiej na Górnym Śląsku* [The socio-cultural situation of the German minority in Upper Silesia], Katowice.

Korbel, Jan (1977): *Wyjazdy i powroty. Migracje ludności w procesie normalizacji stosunków między Polską a RFN* [Leaving home, coming home: Migrations and the normalization of relations between Poland and the Federal Republic of Germany], Opole.

Kwilecki, Andrzej (1982): *Z pogranicza tematyki narodowej i międzynarodowej* [Between domestic and international problems], Warsaw.

Maryański, Andrzej (1984): *Migracje w świecie* [Migrations worldwide], Warsaw.

Rokoszowa, Jolanta (1989): "O mniejszościach narodowych w PRL" [National minorities in Poland]. In: *Język Polski 69*, 19–28.

Tomaszewski, Jerzy (1985): *Rzeczpospolita wielu narodów* [A republic of many nations], Warsaw.

Waszak, Stanisław (1959): "Liczba Niemców w Polsce w latach 1931–1959" [The size of the German population in Poland between 1931 and 1959]. In: *Przegląd Zachodni*, 318–349.

Zaręba, Alfred (1974): *Śląsk w świetle geografii językowej* [Silesia from the point of view of language geography], Wrocław.

Jolanta Rokoszowa, Cracow (Poland)

193. Polnisch–Deutsch

1. Geographie und Demographie
2. Geschichte
3. Politik, Wirtschaft und allgemeine kulturelle Lage
4. Statistik und Ethnoprofil
5. Soziolinguistische Lage
6. Sprachpolitische Lage
7. Allgemeines kontaktlinguistisches Porträt
8. Kritische Wertung der verwendeten Quellen und Literatur
9. Bibliographie (in Auswahl)

1. Geographie und Demographie

Nach den Angaben der Volkszählung von 1931 wohnten etwa 741 000 Deutsche in Polen, d. h. etwa 4% der gesamten Bevölkerung. Diese Zahl war direkt nach der Wiedererlangung der Unabhängigkeit durch Polen (1918) viel größer, man nimmt die Zahl von etwa 2 Mill. Deutschen an, doch in den Jahren von 1919 bis 1931 sank sie fast um eine Million;

die meisten Deutschen verließen die polnischen Westgebiete in den Jahren von 1919 bis 1922 (schätzungsweise über 700 000 Deutsche).

Während der deutschen Besatzung (1939—1945) wurden westliche und nördliche Teile Polens, die vor 1914 nicht zu Preußen gehörten, dem Dritten Reich eingegliedert. Das neue Gebiet zählte 10 Mill. Menschen; ab Ende 1939 begann eine systematische Deportation von Polen und Juden in das Generalgouvernement, d. h. in das besetzte polnische Restgebiet, das dem Deutschen Reich nicht eingegliedert wurde. Im Zuge dieser Deportation, die bis zum Frühjahr 1942 andauerte, wurden ungefähr eine halbe Million Polen zwangsevakuiert und rund 350 000 volksdeutsche Umsiedler aus dem Baltikum, aus Wolhynien, Bessarabien und der Bukowina in die eingegliederten Gebiete umgesiedelt. Die Eindeutschung der Ostgebiete versuchte man auch durch nominelle Eindeutschung, Eintragung in die sog. Deutsche Volksliste zu erreichen. Auf diese Weise wurden vor allem in Westpreußen Hunderttausende von Polen und Kaschuben zu Deutschen ernannt.

Die Aussiedlung von Polen und Ansiedlung von Volksdeutschen wurde teilweise auch auf das Generalgouvernement ausgedehnt. Nach der Zwangsevakuierung polnischer Bauern wurden im Distrikt Lublin (Kreis Zamość) 100 000 Volksdeutsche angesiedelt.

Nach dem Zweiten Weltkrieg kommt es zu einer Grenzverschiebung nach Westen. Polen erhält die deutschen Ostgebiete, in denen vor dem Krieg einschließlich der Freien Stadt Danzig etwa 9 Mill. Menschen lebten (die meisten von ihnen deutschsprachig, daneben auch Kaschuben, Masuren und Oberschlesier). Die genaue Zahl der Deutschen im Mai 1945 ist nicht bekannt, da viele Deutsche nach Westen flohen; laut polnischen Angaben betrug diese Zahl etwa 3,5 Mill. Menschen.

Ende 1946 erfolgte die Aussiedlung der deutschen Bevölkerung aus Polen — laut deutschen Quellen wurden ca. 12 Mill. Deutsche vertrieben —, so daß in Polen schätzungsweise 1,6 Mill. Deutsche geblieben sind. Durch die Aussiedlung in den fünfziger Jahren und die Übersiedlung in die Bundesrepublik in den siebziger und achtziger Jahren ging die Zahl der Deutschen auf 300 000 bis 500 000 zurück. Die meisten Deutschen wohnen in Oberschlesien, im Bezirk Oppeln, teilweise auch in den Bezirken Kattowitz und Tschenstochau. In den nördlichen Bezirken Polens wohnen zerstreut kleinere deutsche Gruppen.

2. Geschichte

Die deutsch-polnischen Sprachkontakte reichen in das 10. Jahrhundert zurück, in die Zeit der Christianisierung Polens, da deutsche Geistliche an der Christianisierung Polens stark beteiligt waren. Als Beginn der deutschen Kolonisation in Polen betrachtet man die Ansiedlung der deutschen Bauern durch das Zisterzienserkloster in Lubiąż (Leubus) aufgrund der Urkunde aus dem Jahre 1175. Die tatsächliche Ansiedlung der Bauern erfolgte jedoch erst 1202. Im 13. Jahrhundert kam es zu vielen Städtegründungen nach deutschem Recht, zunächst in Schlesien und Pommern, die nicht zum polnischen Staat gehörten. Die Ansiedlung der deutschen Siedler wurde durch schlesische und polnische Fürsten unterstützt, da das Land nach den Zerstörungen durch den Tatareneinfall von 1341 viele neue Arbeitskräfte brauchte. Die meisten deutschen Bauern und Bürger siedelten sich in Schlesien an, in Kleinpolen gab es zudem einige deutsche Städtegründungen, im Norden siedelte der Deutsche Orden deutsche Bürger und Bauern an, Pommern wurde im Mittelalter ebenfalls schrittweise vom Westen her von deutschen Siedlern kolonisiert.

Seit der zweiten Hälfte des 18. Jahrhunderts kamen viele protestantische Bauern nach Großpolen, ein starker Zustrom deutscher Siedler nach Polen erfolgte aber erst seit dem letzten Viertel des 18. Jahrhunderts, d. h. nach den Teilungen Polens, als Polen als selbständiger Staat zu existieren aufhörte. Seit 1772 gab es eine von Preußen und Österreich geförderte Ansiedlung deutscher Bürger und Bauern. Hinzu kommt die Verdrängung der polnischen Sprache aus der Schule, Verwaltung und Kirche, im preußischen Teil in stärkerem Maße als im zu Österreich gehörenden Teil Polens. Der obligatorische Unterricht in deutscher Sprache führte zum Bilingualismus in den ursprünglich ausschließlich polnischen Gebieten. Viele neue deutsche Siedlungen entstanden nicht nur im preußischen und österreichischen Teil Polens, sondern auch im russischen Teil um Lublin und Chełm (Cholm). Die deutschen Siedler stammten aus verschiedenen hochdeutschen Dialektgebieten. An der Weichselniederung und im Lubliner und Cholmer Land gab es ebenfalls niederdeutsche Siedler.

Nach der Entstehung des polnischen Staates 1918 gab es ebenfalls enge Kontakte zwischen dem Deutschen und Polnischen, da es in Polen einige geschlossene deutsche Sprachinseln gab, und im Westen viele Deutsche lebten. Der Zweite Weltkrieg und die deutsche Besetzung Polens führten wieder zu verstärkten Kontakten zwischen den beiden Sprachen. Nach der Niederlage des Dritten Reichs wurden die meisten Deutschen zwangsevakuiert, die übrigen Deutschen, die in Polen geblieben waren, waren einer intensiven Polonisierungspolitik ausgesetzt, so daß die heutige Zahl der Deutschen in Polen deutlich über der Zahl der offiziell Deutschsprachigen liegt, da viele Deutsche (vor allem die junge Generation) keine oder nur geringe Deutschkenntnisse haben.

3. Politik, Wirtschaft und allgemeine kulturelle Lage

Die allgemeine Situation der Deutschen in Polen nach dem Ersten Weltkrieg muß man im Rahmen der politischen Beziehungen zwischen Polen und der deutschen Minderheit einerseits und Deutschland und der deutschen Minderheit in Polen andererseits betrachten. Die Weimarer Republik (1918—1933) unterstützte finanziell die deutsche Minderheit in Polen und versuchte, sie als Instrument ihrer Außenpolitik zu betrachten, um in Zukunft eine Revision der Grenzen zu erreichen. Die finanzielle Hilfe für die Deutschen in Polen führte zu einer wirtschaftlichen Festigung des Besitzstandes der Deutschen in Polen. Es wurde nicht nur die Wirtschaft finanziell unterstützt, sondern auch die kulturelle und soziale Tätigkeit der deutschen Organisationen in Polen. Dank dieser finanziellen Mittel wurden deutsche Privatschulen und Theater gegründet und erhalten.

Nach der Machtergreifung durch Hitler (1933) wurden sozialdemokratische und katholische, dem polnischen Staat gegenüber loyale Organisationen der Deutschen in Polen durch die Nationalsozialisten bekämpft und aufgelöst; die nationalsozialistischen Ideen gewannen unter der deutschen Minderheit einen immer stärkeren Einfluß, insbesondere unter der deutschen Jugend. Der polnische Staat fühlte sich durch diese nationalsozialistische Tätigkeit der deutschen Organisationen in Polen stark bedroht.

Nach dem Zweiten Weltkrieg war die politische Situation für die deutsche Minderheit äußerst ungünstig; nach der zwangsweisen Aussiedlung der meisten Deutschen wurde die Existenz der deutschen Minderheit in Polen von der kommunistischen Regierung entschieden bestritten. Nach der herrschenden offiziellen Meinung gab es in Polen überhaupt keine nationalen Minderheiten. Lediglich in den Jahren von 1950 bis 1959 durften die Deutschen in Niederschlesien eigene Schulen, eine Kulturgesellschaft und eine deutschsprachige Zeitung unterhalten.

In Oberschlesien und im ehemaligen Ostpreußen durfte die deutsche Sprache nicht in Grund-, Ober- und Hochschulen unterrichtet werden. Der Gebrauch der deutschen Sprache war auch in der Öffentlichkeit untersagt. Erst seit der Entstehung einer demokratischen Regierung in Polen (1989) wird die deutsche Minderheit offiziell anerkannt; inzwischen haben die Deutschen in Polen eine breite Verbandsstruktur ausgebaut, die deutschen sozial-kulturellen Gesellschaften vereinigen z. Z. etwa 300 000 Mitglieder, die deutsche Minderheit ist mit einigen Abgeordneten im polnischen Sejm und einem Senator im Senat vertreten.

Die wirtschaftliche und soziale Lage der deutschen Minderheit ist schwer, aber sie unterscheidet sich nicht von der wirtschaftlichen Lage der übrigen Bevölkerung.

4. Statistik und Ethnoprofil

Nach den Angaben der Volkszählung von 1931 lebten in Polen 741 000 Deutsche, davon 91 000 Deutsche in Oberschlesien (7,0%), in Nord- und Westpolen — 297 000 Deutsche (9,6%), etwa 47 000 Deutsche in Wolhynien und etwa 295 000 Deutsche in Zentralpolen. Die deutschen Autoren betrachteten die Angaben der polnischen Volkszählungen im allgemeinen als viel zu niedrig und stellten ihnen ihre eigenen Schätzungen gegenüber. Ihre geschätzte Zahl der Deutschen in Polen weicht deutlich von den polnischen Angaben ab — besonders für Oberschlesien (polnische Volkszählung — 91 000 Deutsche in Oberschlesien; J. Czech — 350 000 Deutsche; die Gesamtzahl der Deutschen in Polen nach der Volkszählung von 1931 — 741 000 Deutsche, J. Czech — 1,16 Mill., W. Winkler — 1,7 Mill.).

Nach dem Zweiten Weltkrieg sind genaue Angaben über die Zahl der Deutschen in Polen nicht möglich, da es in den polnischen Volkszählungen keine Frage nach der Muttersprache bzw. nach der Nationalität gab. Die in den ehemaligen deutschen Ostgebieten wohnenden Deutschen wurden zwangsevakuiert; es wird angenommen, daß etwa 1,6 Mill. Deutsche in Polen geblieben sind, in den siebziger und achtziger Jahren siedelten etwa 800 000 Deutsche in die Bundesrepublik über. Die Zahl der heute in Polen lebenden Deutschen wird auf etwa 300 000 bis 500 000 geschätzt. Die meisten von ihnen wohnen in Oberschlesien, vor allem in der Woiwodschaft Oppeln/Opole, ein Teil in den Woiwodschaften Kattowitz/Katowice und Tschenstochau/Częstochowa. Im ehemaligen Ostpreußen leben etwa 5 000 Deutsche, und die Zahl der im Raum Stettin lebenden Deutschen wird ebenfalls auf etwa 5 000 geschätzt. Diese Zahlen decken sich nicht mit der Zahl der Deutschsprachigen, sie spiegeln nur die Zugehörigkeit zur deutschen Minderheit wider aufgrund der Entscheidung der Sprecher, die sich als Deutsche bekennen. Die Familiennamen geben ebenfalls keine Auskunft über die sprachliche Zugehörigkeit, da polnische Namen (Bartodziej, Brylka) bei den Deutschen vorkommen, und umgekehrt ein einsprachiger Pole einen deutschen Namen wie *Kohl* oder *Szulc* haben kann.

Ein relativ geschlossenes Gebiet, in dem die Deutschen leben, liegt in Oberschlesien, südlich von Oppeln, während im übrigen Gebiet die Deutschen zerstreut leben. Für den Großteil der in Oberschlesien lebenden Deutschen muß das sog. Wasserpolnische, d. h. die polnische schlesische Mundart als Muttersprache angesehen werden, denn es ist die Sprache, die zu Hause gesprochen wird (→ Art. 192, 2.4.1.).

5. Soziolinguistische Lage

Das Polnische war und bleibt weiterhin die Staatssprache, während das Deutsche eine von mehreren Minderheitensprachen war. Da die Deutschen vor dem Zweiten Weltkrieg meist in geschlossenen Sprachinseln lebten, gab es − vor allem in ländlicher Umgebung − z. T. noch deutsche Einsprachigkeit, die sich in der Kenntnis der Ortsmundart äußerte. Verschiedene Grade des Bilingualismus waren die Regel, wobei das Polnische als Zweitsprache in unterschiedlichem Grade beherrscht wurde, was Anlaß zu vielen Spötteleien auf beiden Seiten war. Vgl. z. B. die polnischen Redensarten: *włożył język pod niecki, umie mówić po niemiecku* (Er legt die Zunge unter das Becken und kann deutsch sprechen), *Niemcze, karaluchu, trzymaj język na łańcuchu* (Deutscher, du Küchenschabe, halte deine Zunge an der Kette). In manchen literarischen Werken wird ebenfalls die ungenügende Kenntnis des Polnischen bei den deutschen Sprechern in Polen polemisch geschildert (Brzezina 1989, 63). Durch das deutsche Schulwesen beherrschen die Deutschen neben der Ortsmundart auch die deutsche Standardsprache, so daß es eine weit verbreitete Triglossie gab.

Nach dem Zweiten Weltkrieg wird die Kenntnis der deutschen Sprache unter den Deutschen durch die intensive Polonisierungspolitik der Regierung stark zurückgedrängt; bei der älteren Generation kann man heutzutage vom Deutschen als Muttersprache sprechen, während die jüngere und junge Generation nur über geringe Deutschkenntnisse verfügt, so daß die deutsche Sprache unter den Deutschstämmigen zur Fremdsprache geworden ist.

6. Sprachpolitische Lage

Die sprachpolitische Lage der deutschen Minderheit im Vorkriegspolen war relativ günstig. Die Deutschen hatten dank der Unterstützung aus Deutschland viele eigene Elementarschulen und viele Gymnasien, der prozentuale Anteil der Schulen entsprach ungefähr dem prozentualen Anteil der deutschen Bevölkerung in Polen. Auch der Anteil der deutschen Presse mit 3,7% lag nur leicht unter dem Bevölkerungsanteil der deutschen Minderheit. Darüber hinaus gab es deutsche Theater in einigen polnischen Städten. Die meisten Deutschen waren Protestanten (etwa 70%), was sie von der katholischen oder russisch-orthodoxen und jüdischen Bevölkerung trennte. Die deutsche Minderheit war auch im polnischen Parlament vertreten.

Nach dem Zweiten Weltkrieg war die sprachpolitische Lage der deutschen Sprecher in Polen katastrophal. Lediglich in den Jahren von 1950 bis 1959 wurden die Deutschen in Niederschlesien als sprachliche Minderheit geduldet und konnten eigene Schulen unterhalten. In Oberschlesien dagegen wurden sie zwangspolonisiert, die Schreibweise ihrer Namen geändert. Erst seit 1990 erfolgt eine Wiederbelebung der deutschen Kulturtätigkeit, seit 1991 hat die deutsche Minderheit das

Recht, eigene Bildungs-, Kultur- und Religionseinrichtungen und -organisationen zu gründen und zu unterhalten.

Die Angehörigen der deutschen Minderheit haben wieder das Recht, die ethnische, kulturelle, sprachliche und religiöse Identität frei zum Ausdruck zu bringen und weiterzuentwickeln. Durch die Polonisierungspolitik ist die deutsche Sprache unter der deutschen Minderheit stark zurückgegangen. Für die junge Generation ist das Deutsche zu einer Fremdsprache geworden, die erst in der Schule erlernt wird. Der deutschsprachige Unterricht ist in der Schule z. Z. nicht möglich, erst seit 3 Jahren wird im Bezirk Oppeln versucht, die Kenntnis der deutschen Sprache zu beleben. Der Deutschunterricht wird ausgebaut, z. Z. gibt es aber in ganz Polen nur eine Schule in Warschau mit deutscher Unterrichtssprache (→ Art. 192, 5.5.).

Im Bistum Oppeln gibt es seit einiger Zeit zahlreiche katholische Kirchengemeinden mit einem Gottesdienst in deutscher Sprache. Es erscheint z. Z. nur eine zweisprachige Zeitung mit einer Auflage von 20 000 Exemplaren. Daneben erscheinen regional einige Informationsblätter der deutschen Minderheit. Von Radio Oppeln und Radio Kattowitz wird seit einiger Zeit ein deutschsprachiges Programm ausgestrahlt. Ein lokales Fernsehprogramm für die deutschen Sprecher wird vorbereitet.

7. Allgemeines kontaktlinguistisches Porträt

Der jahrhundertlange Sprachkontakt des Deutschen und Polnischen führte zu vielfachen Interferenzen und Transferenzen. Schon in der althochdeutschen (ahd.) Zeit sind einige deutsche Wörter ins Polnische entlehnt worden, z. B. *chwila* aus dem ahd. *(h)wila* (Weile), *mnich* aus dem ahd. *munich* (Mönch, lat. monachus), *myto* aus dem ahd. *muta* (Maut, lat. muta), *szlachta* aus dem ahd. *slahta* (Geschlecht), *żegnać* aus dem ahd. *seganon* (segnen). Aus der mittelhochdeutschen (mhd.) Zeit stammt eine größere Zahl deutscher Wörter im Polnischen, z. B. *barwa* aus dem mhd. *farve* (Farbe), *belka* aus dem mhd. *balke* (Balken), *blacha* aus dem mhd. *blech* (Blech), *cech* aus dem mhd. *zeche* (Zeche, Zunft), *cło* aus dem mhd. *zol* (Zoll), *folwark* aus dem mhd. *vorwerk*, *glejt* aus dem mhd. *geleite* (Geleit), *ratusz* aus dem mhd. *rathus* (Rathaus), *rynek* aus dem mhd. *rinc* (Ring), *smakować* aus dem mhd. *smecken* (schmecken).

Bei den älteren deutschen Entlehnungen im Polnischen wird darauf hingewiesen, daß viele deutsche Wörter über das Tschechische ins Polnische gelangt sind; manche Autoren heben die Vermittlerrolle des Tschechischen hervor, insbesondere bei den Entlehnungen aus dem Oberdeutschen (Kleczkowski), während andere Autoren diese vermittelnde Funktion als nicht hoch einschätzen (Kaestner, Czarnecki).

Die meisten deutschen Entlehnungen im Polnischen stammen aus der frühneuhochdeutschen und neuhochdeutschen Zeit. Sie beziehen sich auf Handel, Handwerk, Bauwesen, Verwaltung, Militärwesen und Seefahrt; Beispiele: *banknot* aus deutsch (dt.) *Banknote*, *dorsz* aus dt. *Dorsch*, *durszlak* aus dt. *Durchschlag*, *kartofel* aus dt. *Kartoffel*, *strych* aus dt. *Esterich*, *szuflada* aus dt. *Schublade*, *szyld* aus dt. *Schild*, *winszować* aus dt. *wünschen*, *zupa* aus dt. *Suppe*, u. a. m. Der Bilingualismus der deutschen Siedler bewirkt, daß das Polnische auch die deutschen Mundarten beeinflußt. Polnische lexikalische Integrate lassen sich in den deutschen Mundarten des ehemaligen Ostpreußens finden, z. B. *Bulwe* aus dem polnischen (poln.) *bulwa* (Knolle), *Pomager* aus dem poln. *pomagier* (Helfer), *Blott* aus dem poln. *błoto* (Kot, Sumpf). Im Preußischen Wörterbuch von Frischbier sind etwa 700 Lehnwörter polnischer Herkunft enthalten, die sich auf Landwirtschaft, Fischfang, Küche, Kleidung, Tiere, Pflanzen beziehen.

Viele lexikalische Integrate aus dem Polnischen findet man ebenfalls im Ostmitteldeutschen, insbesondere im Schlesischen (Bellmann, Eichler, Mitzka). Beispiele: *Bor(u)fke*, *Bar(u)fke* aus dem poln. *borówka* (Heidelbeere), *Pampuschen* aus dem poln. *papucie* (Hausschuhe), *Bulke* aus poln. *bułka* (Brötchen), *Komurke* aus *komórka* (kleine Kammer), *Kapuste* aus *kapusta* (Kohl), *Maline* aus *malina* (Himbeere), *Mauke* aus *mąka* (Brei aus Mehl), *Plauze* aus *płuca* (Lunge), *pomale* aus *pomału* (langsam), *Schüprine* aus *czupryna* (Haarschopf), *schißkojenne* aus *wszystko jedno* (einerlei, egal) u. a m.

Am stärksten ist das lexikalische Teilsystem beeinflußt, aber der Einfluß des Polnischen ist in der schlesischen Umgangssprache auch im phonetischen Bereich bemerkbar (Reiter 1960, 62 ff). Viele grammatische Besonderheiten des Deutschen in Oberschlesien gehen ebenfalls auf den Einfluß des Polnischen zurück. Polnische Einflüsse sieht man in der Satzgliedfolge, z. B. *Kamen die Gendarmen*, in der Ausklammerung von Adverbien:

Hab ihm gesagt gestern, oder in der Stellung des finiten Verbs im Nebensatz: *weil er hatte gestern keine Zeit*. Der häufigere Gebrauch der reflexiven Verben in Oberschlesien geht ebenfalls auf den Einfluß des Polnischen zurück: *sich spielen, sich gehen*. Es kann auch auf den von der deutschen Standardsprache abweichenden Gebrauch von Präpositionen, z. B. *auf einen Film, auf eine Vorstellung gehen*, hingewiesen werden.

Andererseits zeigte sich ein starker Einfluß des Deutschen in den Äußerungen der polnischen bilingualen Sprecher, z. B. der verstärkte Gebrauch des Personalpronomens beim Verb, fehlerhafter Gebrauch perfektiver und imperfektiver Verben, Fehler in der Rektion von Verben gehen auf den Einfluß des Deutschen auf das Polnische zurück (Pniewski, Tomaszewski, Trzaska).

Innerhalb der polnischen Dialekte zeigt die polnische schlesische Mundart den stärksten Einfluß des Deutschen. Polnische Sprecher in Oberschlesien waren vor dem Zweiten Weltkrieg einem starken Einfluß des Deutschen durch das Schulwesen und die Verwaltung ausgesetzt. Deshalb kennt die polnische schlesische Mundart viele deutsche Wörter, die weder in der polnischen Standardsprache noch in anderen polnischen Mundarten auftreten. Deutsche Wörter in der schlesischen Mundart betreffen vor allem den neueren Wortschatz aus dem Bereich des Bauwesens, Handwerks, Schulwesens und der Verwaltung. Deutsche Einflüsse im grammatischen Teilsystem betreffen vorwiegend den syntaktischen Bereich, insbesondere die Wortfolge; im morphologischen Bereich ist der deutsche Einfluß kaum bemerkbar. Im phonetischen Teilsystem zeigt sich der deutsche Einfluß auf die polnischen Mundartsprecher vor allem in der Substitution des polnischen präpalatalen /ś/ durch das koronale /ʃ/ und in der uvularen Realisierung des polnischen apikalen /r/, d. h. /r/ wird zu /R/.

Nach dem Zweiten Weltkrieg beeinflußt die polnische Sprache in stärkerem Maße das Deutsche der deutschen Sprecher in Polen. Der Einfluß des Deutschen auf das Polnische betrifft die deutsche Standardsprache, ihr Einfluß ist vor allem in lexikalischen Entlehnungen zu sehen.

8. Kritische Wertung der verwendeten Quellen und Literatur

In der linguistischen Literatur zu den deutsch-polnischen Sprachkontakten konzentriert man sich vorwiegend auf die Analyse der lexikalischen Entlehnungen in den beiden Kontaktsprachen (Mitzka, Czarnecki, Kaestner, Karszniewicz-Mazur, Eichler), phonologische und grammatische Einflüsse spielen dabei eine geringe Rolle. Die Behandlung der gegenseitigen Sprachkontakte war oft nicht frei von Werturteilen, insbesondere wenn die Autoren auf die soziale, politische und kulturelle Rolle der Deutschen im polnischen Sprachgebiet eingingen. Die nationalen Vorurteile führten deshalb oft zu polemischen Formulierungen auf beiden Seiten, was sich auf die Objektivität der wissenschaftlichen Darstellung negativ auswirkte.

9. Bibliographie (in Auswahl)

Born, Joachim/Dickgießer, Sylvia (1989): *Deutschsprachige Minderheiten. Ein Überblick über den Stand der Forschung für 27 Länder*, Mannheim.

Bellmann, Günter (1971): *Slavoteutonica. Lexikalische Untersuchungen zum slavisch-deutschen Sprachkontakt im Ostmitteldeutschen*, Berlin/New York.

Brzezina, Maria (1989): *Polszczyzna Niemców* [Das Polnische der Deutschen], Warschau/Krakau.

Czarnecki, Tomasz (1970): „Pośrednictwo czeskie w staropolskich pożyczkach z niemieckiego" [Tschechische Vermittlung bei den altpolnischen Entlehnungen aus dem Deutschen]. In: *Studia z Filologii Polskiej i Słowiańskiej*, 38—44.

Czech, Joseph (1932): *Bevölkerung Polens. Zahl und völkische Zusammensetzung*, Breslau.

Eichler, Ernst (1965): *Etymologisches Wörterbuch der slawischen Elemente im Ostmitteldeutschen*, Bautzen.

Frischbier, H. (1882): *Preußisches Wörterbuch*, Bd. 1—2, Berlin.

Hoffmann, Heinrich (1909): „Einfluß des Polnischen auf Aussprache, Schreibung und formale Gestaltung der deutschen Umgangssprache in Oberschlesien". In: *Zeitschrift für deutsche Mundarten*, 264—279.

Jungandreas, Wolfgang (1928): *Beiträge zur Erforschung der Besiedlung Schlesiens und zur Entstehungsgeschichte der schlesischen Mundart*, Breslau.

Kaczmarczyk, Zdzisław (1945): *Kolonizacja niemiecka na wschód od Odry* [Deutsche Kolonisation östlich der Oder], Posen.

Kaestner, Walter (1939): *Die deutschen Lehnwörter im Polnischen. I: Einleitung und Lautlehre*, Leipzig.

Karszniewicz-Mazur, Alicja (1989): *Zapożyczenia leksykalne ze źródła niemieckiego we współczesnej polcszyźnie* [Lexikalische Entlehnungen aus dem Deutschen im modernen Polnisch], Breslau.

Kleczkowski, Adam (1915): „Dialekty niemieckie w Polsce" [Die deutschen Dialekte in Polen]. In: *Encyklopedia polska*, Bd. III. Krakau, 387—394.

Mitzka, Walter (1962): *Schlesisches Wörterbuch.* Bd. *1, 2, 3,* Berlin.

Pniewski, Władysław (1927): „Błędy i właściwości językowe w zdaniach młodzieży polskiej w Gdańsku w świetle dialektów pomorskich i języka niemieckiego" [Fehler und sprachliche Eigentümlichkeiten in den Aufsätzen der polnischen Jugend in Danzig im Lichte der Dialekte Pommerns und der deutschen Sprache]. In: *Rocznik Gdański I,* 19−58.

Reiter, Norbert (1960): *Die deutsch−polnischen Sprachbeziehungen in Oberschlesien,* Berlin.

Siatkowski, Janusz (1983): „Polnische Interferenzen in deutschen Mundarten". In: *Die slawischen Sprachen,* Bd. 4, 119−131.

Stoliński, Zygmunt (1928): *Die deutsche Minderheit in Polen,* Warschau.

Tomaszewski, Adam (1927): „Błędy językowe uczniów szkół poznańskich" [Die sprachlichen Fehler der Schüler der Posener Schulen]. In: *Język Polski 12,* 45−52, 81−85.

Trzaska, Eugenjusz (1935): *Gwara i wpływy obce w języku uczniów śląskich* [Die Mundart und fremde Einflüsse in der Sprache der schlesischen Schüler], Katowitz.

Weinhold, Karl (1887): *Die Verbreitung und die Herkunft der Deutschen in Schlesien,* Leipzig.

Wiesinger, Peter (1983): „Deutsche Dialektgebiete außerhalb des deutschen Sprachgebiets: Mittel-, Südost- und Osteuropa". In: *Dialektologie, HSK Bd. 1.2.,* Besch, W./Knoop, U./Putschke, W./Wiegand, H. E. (Eds.), Berlin, 900−929.

Winkler, Wilhelm (1931): *Statistisches Handbuch der europäischen Nationalitäten,* Wien/Leipzig.

Józef Wiktorowicz, Warschau (Polen)

194. Polish−Kashubian

1. Geography and demography
2. History
3. Politics, economy and general cultural and religious situation
4. Statistics and ethnoprofile
5. Sociolinguistic situation
6. Language political situation
7. General contactlinguistic portrait
8. Evaluation of the sources and literature
9. Bibliography (selected)

1. Geography and demography

Most of the Kashubians in Poland live in their historical habitat Kashuby. It is bordered by the Vistula river in the East, by the Piaśnica river in the West, by the Brda river in the South and by the Baltic Sea in the North. After 1945 a number of Kashubians moved east- and westwards into the territory gained from Germany after the war (around Miastko, Bytów and Lębork), whereas earlier Kashuby stretched farther west and south.

Today the number of Kashubians is estimated at about 300,000 plus an additional 200,000 "half-Kashubians" (mixed married couples) (cf. Latoszek 1990). Mainly at the end of the 19th century Kashubians migrated in great numbers (about 130,000 in total) usually from south Kashuby to Germany, Canada, and the United States, where they are quite numerous, but also to Brazil, Australia and New Zealand (cf. Popowska-Taborska 1980, 21). After 1945 Germanized Slovincians and Kashubians from the area of Gniewino and Bytów emigrated to Germany (→ Language Map I).

2. History

Since the middle of the 10th century, Kashuby shared the history of Eastern Pomerania, which enjoyed considerable autonomy especially since the middle of the 11th century, and was ruled by its own dynasty in the second half of the 12th century. It became closely connected with Poland by the treaty of Kępno (1282). From 1309 to 1454, Pomerania was in the hands of the Teutonic Knights. Then it was incorporated into Poland. Between 1454 and 1637 the bordering areas of Bytów and Lębork were a Polish fiefdom in the possession of Western Pomeranian dukes, and from 1657 through 1772 they belonged to Brandenburg. After the first partition of Poland (1772), Kashuby found itself under Prussian rule. In 1918 most of the area still inhabited by Kashubians was returned to Poland. Following the 1939−1945 occupation Kashuby and the old territories in the west including those of Slovincians became part of Poland again.

The history of the Kashubians as the last Baltic West Slavonic tribe and their cultural and ethnic identity is closely tied with the history of Polish culture and language. The natural development of Kashuby towards political and ethnic unity collapsed at the turn of the 13th century with the invasion of the Teutonic Knights. Kashuby became the Slavonic—German border. The ties with Poland having lasted for hundreds of years and the struggle with Germanization in the 19th and 20th centuries strengthened the Kashubian sense of ethnic, regional and language identity. This was achieved by the efforts of Florian Ceynowa (1817—1881), Kashubian writers such as Hieronim Derdowski (1852—1902), Alexander Majkowski (1876—1938), Jan Karnowski (1886—1939), Alexander Labuda (1902—1981) and Jan Trepczyk (1907—1989). Since 1929, these efforts were further promoted by activities of regional organisations of the Kashubian-Pomeranian Association [Zrzeszenie Kaszubsko-Pomorskie, ZK-P, founded 1929], particularly since 1956.

3. Politics, economy and general cultural and religious situation

Kashuby has achieved neither political nor economic autonomy. Its economy is determined by its natural resources and thus restricted to agriculture, farming, forestry and fishing, as with, for example, the settlements on Hel Peninsula. Part of the population is employed in the shipyards and harbours of Gdańsk and Gdynia.

Culture, education and science in Kashuby have been enclosed in the framework of Polish structures and institutions. Although there has always been a tendency towards some cultural autonomy, only recently have some regional issues appeared in the school curriculum (cf. 6.). Kashubian cultural life has been developing under the influence of Christianity as well as Polish and German cultures. It has been described among others by Ceynowa 1866—1868 and Sychta 1967—1976. A most lively part of this culture is Kashubian fiction writing: especially dramas by Sychta, short stories by Anna Łajming and open air performances arranged by Paweł Szefka. The rich folk literature (fairytales, traditional stories, legends, proverbs, riddles) and folk music (songs, carols, couplets) have been preserved in the Kashubian magazines "Gryf", "Zrzesz Kaszëbskô", "Kaszëbë" and since 1963 in "Pomerania". They are published under the auspices of The Museum of Kashubian and Pomeranian Writing and Music in Wejherowo. The folklore tradition has also been cultivated by numerous regional dance and song groups, folk music bands, story-telling, song and reciting competitions. More material evidence of this culture is exhibited in "Skansen" museums (Kluki, Wdzydze) and other museums (Kartuzy, Puck, Hel, Wiele). It has partially survived in architecture and folk crafts such as pottery, plaiting, embroidery, amber-working, sculpturing and glasspainting.

The Kashubians are very religious and traditionally adhere to the Roman Catholic faith. The shrines of the Virgin Mary in Sianowo and Swarzewo are often frequented places of worship. The cloisters, e.g. in Oliwa, Kartuzy, Żarnowiec, Żukowo, are ancient religious centres. The town of Wejherowo is famous for its 17th century calvary; a younger one exists at Wiele.

4. Statistics and ethnoprofile

Kashuby is inhabited by 1.5 mln people, who use standard Polish in official or rather formal situations. In informal settings, they often use their native dialects in spoken language, i.e. mostly the local, native Kashubian dialects, but also the dialects brought in by migrants from central, southern or eastern Poland.

4.1. There are 500,000 speakers of Kashubian. In villages they constitute up to 90%, this number decreases in the cities, namely in the agglomeration of Gdańsk, Sopot, Gdynia and in the periphery of the ethnic area, where they amount to only 15%. However, only 300,000 Kashubians regularly use Kashubian in speaking and very few use it in writing (cf. 5.1.).

The Kashubians are mostly bilingual (cf. 5.2.). In the past, especially during the partitions (1772—1918), they were even trilingual speaking Kashubian at home and with neighbours, Polish in church (lessons in catechism, confessions) and German at school and in the office. They had also contact with the settlers speaking Plattdeutsch from the times of the Teutonic Knights.

4.2. The usually used ethnonyms are: *Kaszëbë*, Pol. *Kaszuby* [Kashuby], *Kaszëbi*, Pol. *Kaszubi* [Kashubians], *kaszëbskô mowa*, Pol. *kaszubska mowa* [the Kashubian speech]. In the past the name *kaszëbsko-słowińskô mowa*

[Kashubian-Slovincian speech] (Ceynowa since 1866) and *język pomorski* [Pomeranian language] (by S. Ramułt — cf. 5.1. — in 1893) were used. The internal linguistic and cultural differentiation of the Kashubians was stressed by the names of ethnic subgroups like, e. g., *Bylacy* (in the north-east) who pronounced *ł* as *l* e. g. *bél*, Pol. *był* 'he was' (this pronunciation is called *bylaczenie*), *Lesacy* (the middle-east) who speak their own dialect: *lesackô mowa*, *Gachy* (south-west): *gaskô mowa*, *Zaboraki* (south-east) who are also called *Krubanie*: *zaborskô* or *krubańskô mowa*. The extinct *Słowińcë* [Slovincians] (on Lake Gardno and Łebsko, north-west of Słupsk) used their own *słowińskô szprôka* [Slovincian dialect]. In *Kabatki* (in parishes Cecenowo and Główczyce, north-west of Lębork) also a separate dialect was used: *kabackô mowa*.

5. Sociolinguistic situation

Kashubian, regardless whether qualified by linguists as a dialect of Polish or as a separate language, remains a basic characteristic of Kashubians in importance rating almost as high as place of birth and their self-identification as Kashubians. Polish dialectologists (e. g. Kazimierz Nitsch, Zdzisław Stieber, Karol Dejna) regarded Kashubian as a Polish dialect (cf. Popowska-Taborska 1980, 67) and treated Kashubian texts as dialectal.

5.1. Kashubian is a branch of the historical Pomeranian dialects related to the dialects spoken in Wielkopolska and Mazowsze. Written Kashubian influenced by Polish writing emerged during the Reformation in Western Pomerania in the 16th to 18th centuries (for instance as writings by Szymon Krofey, Michał Mostnik, cf. Popowska-Taborska 1980, 47—52). Its further development was stopped by Germanization.

Only since F. Ceynowa's literary, scholarly, and public activity during the 19th century has the Kashubian language acquired a certain status:
1) that of a considerably different dialect of Polish. As such it has been rapidly developing over centuries (cf. 4.2.), and it relates to standard Polish similarly to the other Polish dialects.
2) the status of a means of communication purposefully cultivated for use in private as well as public writing (Popowska-Taborska 1988, 88). Ceynowa endeavoured a program aimed towards introduction of a Kashubian standard in grammar, pronunciation and spelling (Topolińska 1980, 189). It is based on relics of older Kashubian texts (Krofey, Mostnik), and the spirit of the 1848 Revolution. Ceynowa published his own literary works in Kashubian. Similarly he compiled treatises on Kashubian grammar, and published Kashubian texts alongside with their translations into other Slavic languages and German. The so-called Young Kashubians (A. Majkowski, J. Karnowski, etc.) and writers connected with the "Zrzesz Kaszëbskô" magazine (e. g., A. Labuda, J. Trepczyk) were influenced by Stefan Ramułt (1859—1913), who in turn was fascinated by Ceynowa and decidedly supported giving Kashubian the status of a full-fledged standard language. This idea was later accepted by the young Friedrich Lorentz (1870—1937) (cf. Popowska-Taborska 1980, 66 f). While Ceynowa tried to bestow the literary dignity of Kashubian on a single dialect, in the twentieth century attempts to standardize Kashubian, for instance by A. Majkowski, J. Karnowski, etc., mirror the tendency to establish a standard on an interdialect basis.

5.2. The Kashubians speaking Kashubian (cf. 4.1.) are either in the situation of bilingualism or diglossia. The latter comprises literary (standard) Kashubian on the one hand and the local Kashubian dialect on the other, and is even more frequent since an active knowledge of literary Kashubian is minimal.

5.3. In the compact Kashubian settlement, as many as 90% of the Kashubians speak (!) Kashubian (cf. 4.1.), with 60% of them using it mostly or even exclusively. It is mainly spoken by old people, housewives and farmers. The younger generation, especially pupils, students and educated people in the country avoid the application of Kashubian. Middle generation and workers use Kashubian as often as Polish. Kashubian is spoken mainly in informal situations in rural areas. It is less frequently used in the city and only occasionally in offices or institutions. It is used in the family between grandparents, parents and married couples. Socialization of the younger generation practically eliminates Kashubian in favour of Polish. Children often learn Kashubian from their schoolmates. About 50% of the Kashubian speakers are ashamed to use Kashubian outside their own social milieu in order not to reveal their rural origin, whereas speaking Polish suggests an urban life style and a higher social status.

6. Language political situation

The state pushed for assimilation of Kashubians by Germans during the partitions (1772–1918). However, after 1918 some autonomy of the Kashubians was recognized. Between 1945 and 1989 the state suppressed the regional culture and language of ethnic groups. The Kashubian cultural elite as well as the Kashubian-Pomeranian Association appreciate the ethnic values and kept trying to connect them with the Polish language and culture. These attempts are reflected in such slogans as: *Ni ma Kaszub bez Polonii, a bez Kaszub Polsci* [There are no Kashubians without Poland and no Poland without the Kashubians] (Derdowski in 1880) or *Jestem Kaszubą! Polska Matką moją!* [I am Kashubian! Poland is my Mother!] (Sędzicki in 1908). Members of the Kashubian-Pomeranian Association are aware that preservation of the Kashubian language equals preservation of the Kashubian ethnic and cultural identity. The Kashubians accepted a plan for regionalization of schooling (1981) aware of the problems connected with teaching literary Kashubian especially in its written form.

6.1. After WW 2 the unified Polish educational system was not concerned with regional education of Kashubians. Similarly Kashubians do not strive for all-Kashubian schools. Rather they want the regionalization of education with the aim of introducing a broad variety of school subjects. The realization of such a curriculum, however, encounters difficulties connected with a lack of trained teachers, teaching material and textbooks, although we should mention the pioneer work by Wosiak-Śliva/Cybulski 1992 and Gołąbek 1992. Lately it was attempted to introduce reading and writing in Kashubian at primary schools and as an optional language class at Gdańsk University.

6.2. Though occasionally and irregularly, Kashubian has been introduced into the liturgy in the form of readings, homilies, chosen prayers and songs, due to the initiative of Kashubian priests and churchgoers. This promotes its social prestige and strengthens its ethnic character. The text of the Holy Mass and Gospels (1992) have been translated by the priest Franciszek Grucza and the New Testament by Eugeniusz Gołąbek (1993). Religious songs are promoted by cassette recording. Nevertheless, there is a mixed reaction to these attempts.

6.3. There is a rich Kashubian writing (Ceynowa since 1843), fiction (Derdowski since 1880), and especially lyrical poetry and drama. Kashubian literature was presented in Neureiter 1973, 1978 and Drzeżdżon 1986. Nowadays also young people are writing and Kashubian literature has been translated into Polish, Lusatian, Bielorussian, Czech, German and French. There have been translations into Kashubian from German, Latavian, Polish and Latin. However, Kashubian literature has a rather limited influence, which is expressed by referring to it as "a literature without a reader".

6.4. Since the middle of the 19th century (Ceynowa) the standardization of literary Kashubian has been attempted, despite broad variation in spoken Kashubian. Consequently, the standardization of spelling is a complex issue, which has not been settled yet (cf. Breza/Treder 1974). There are only two bilingual dictionaries of literary Kashubian: Labuda 1981 and Trepczyk 1994. The grammar by Breza/Treder 1981 is only partially normative. Some writers pay particular attention to the proper selection of vocabulary, inflected form and sentence structures in order to avoid influences of standard Polish.

6.5. In mass media Kashubian is used only to a small degree: there is no exclusively Kashubian press (cf. 3.2.), and only some Kashubian articles appear in "Pomerania" and other non-periodical magazines. Similarly, there is no Kashubian TV or radio, except short infrequent informative programmes in which Kashubian is merely used for the recitation of poetry and prose; Kashubian tales, jokes, religious and other songs appear on cassettes. Literary and spoken Kashubian is promoted by theatrical groups (e. g. dramas by Sychta), singers, reciters and story-tellers (cf. 3.2.).

7. General contactlinguistic portrait

Spoken Kashubian differs clearly from inland Polish dialects as well as standard Polish, particularly by its phonetics, vocabulary and word-formation, less in inflection and syntax. Literary Kashubian is based on spoken language and analogies (evolutionary and genetic) as well as considerable differences with respect to standard Polish. The differences have been reinforced by conscious avoidance of convergent forms and a preference for archaic forms (cf. 7.1.−7.3.). Despite that, literary Kashubian is closer to Polish than to spoken northern and central Kashubian because of many loan-words from Polish (especially abstract words and terminology) and considerable similarities in syntax.

7.1. Synchronically spoken, nasal vowels (e. g. *zǫb* : *ząbë*, Pol. pronunciation *zomp* : *zemby* 'tooth : teeth') and depalatalization of proto-Slavonic *ě ≥ 'a* (e. g. *wierzec* : *wiara*, Pol. *wierzyć* : *wiara* 'to believe : belief') prove that Kashubian belongs to the West Slavonic languages. Features of archaic northern Kashubian show its relatedness to the West Lech languages (e. g. Polabian): 1. *'ar ≤ *ŕ̥*: *cwiardi*, Pol. *twardy* 'hard', 2. *åł ≤ *ḷ, ḷ̥*: *dåłgi, wåłk*, Pol. *długi* 'long', *wilk* 'wolf', 3. *TloT ≤ *TelT*: *młoc, płoc*, Pol. *mleć* 'grind', *pleć* 'to weed', 4. *TarT ≤ *TorT*: *warna*, Pol. *wrona* 'crow'. These connections are also suggested by free and variable stress as well as traces of an old quantitative opposition: *gádá* : *gadac* 'to tattle', *spiéwá* : *spiewac* 'to sing'. The medieval processes represent, among others, the connections with the eastern Lech language (Polish): *re-, je- ≤ ră-, jă-*: *rek, jerzmo*, Pol. *rak* 'crayfish', *jarzmo* 'yoke', and *-k, -c ≤ *-ъkъ, *-ьcь*: *kotk, ojc*, Pol. *kotek* 'little cat', *ojciec* 'father'. We can also mention a relic form: *z ≤ ʒ̓*: *jęza*, Pol. *jędza* 'shrew'. In Kashubian, like in other Polish dialects, long vowels *ā, ō, ē* changed into closed ones *á, ó, é*: *cál* 'inch', *dól* 'pit', *chléb* 'bread'. The following features are exclusively Kashubian: *i ≤ i̯ ≤ *ę* (non-depalatalized) (12th cent.): *trzisc*, Pol. *trząść* 'to shake'; *s, z, c, ʒ ≤ ś, ź, ć, ʒ̓* (after 12th cent.): *sedzec*, Pol. *siedzieć* 'to sit'; *ë ≤* (short) *ĭ, y̆, ŭ* (mid 17th cent.): *lës, bëc, dëch*, Pol. *lis* 'fox', *być* 'to be', *duch* 'spirit' or later *ć, ʒ̓ ≤ k, g̓*: *tacié nodzi*, Pol. *takie nogi* 'such legs' and *l ≤ ł*: *stól*, Pol. *stół* 'table'; the last one being restricted only to Bylacs and Slovincians (cf. 4.2.).

7.2. Nominal inflection is among other features characterized by: 1. north Kashubian archaic forms of Nom. sg. masc. of nouns as *kam(ë)* (beside such more recent forms as *kamień*, Pol. *kamień* 'stone') or preservation of *-ę* in Acc. sg. fem. of pronouns such as *ję*, *naszę* (beside *ją* 'her', *naszą* 'our', like as Polish); 2. later forms of adjectival inflection of nouns ending in *-ьje* as *kázanié* 'homily', *wieselé* 'wedding', so for instance Gen. sg., e. g. *wieselégo*, Dat. sg. *wieselému*, next to older forms Gen. *wiesela*, Dat. *wieseli*. Northern and central Kashubian has an ending *-ą (≤ -em)*: *bratą*, Pol. *bratem* 'with a brother' − in Instr. sg. masc.

Verb conjugation is mainly characterized by archaic forms: 1. present: *znaję, znajesz* (beside *znám, znász*, Pol. *znam, znasz* 'I, you know', 2. imperative: *niesë, robi* of archaic ending *-i/-ë* (beside *nies, rób*, Pol. *nieś, rób* 'carry it, do it'), 3. preterite: *znął jem, znął jes* etc. next to more recent forms *já, të znął*, Pol. *znałem, znałeś* 'I, you knew'. The dual ending *-ma, -ta* appears in the plural. The relic forms of the dual especially in pronouns have been preserved in Kashubian, e. g. *ma, naju, nama; wa, waju, wama*.

7.3. Kashubian word formation differs from standard Polish not so much in the repertoire of the derivational morphemes and procedures but rather in their distribution. Examples: *-ba*: *uczba*, Pol. *uczenie* 'learning', *-ę*: *celę*, Pol. *cielę* beside *cielak* 'calf', *-ica* (demineut. and femin.): *bardawica*, Pol. *brodawka* 'wart' and *warblëca* 'hen-sparrow', *-iszcze*: *grabliszcze*, Pol. *grablisko* 'big rake', *-ota*: *miłota*, Pol. *miłość* 'love', *-owac*: *pisowac*, Pol. *pisywać* 'to write', *-unk/-ënk*: *malënk*, Pol. *malowanie* 'painting' and *malowidło* 'picture', *ná-*: *nálepi*, Pol. *najlepiej* 'best'. The Kashubian has a great tendency towards hypocorism (especially in speaking to children) not only with nouns but also adjectives and adverbs, e. g. *daleczko* 'far', pronouns, e. g. *nick* 'nothing', numerals, e. g. *dwojiczko* 'two', and mainly verbs, e. g. *róbkac* 'to make'.

7.4. The genuinity of Kashubian vocabulary manifests itself in the preservation of many archaic forms (e. g. *jesorë* 'fish-bones', *kålp* 'sea swan', *nogawica* 'stocking') as well as in introduction of many Kashubian specific innovations (e. g. *sënówc* 'son-in-law', more recent *golëtka* 'safety-razor blade' *≤ żeletka*, *golëc* 'shave'; *kåłtón* 'tuft of matted hair' and 'mistletoe'). In the vocabulary the influence of standard Polish has been observable for centuries especially in administration, education, military, technical areas etc. where in Kashubian Polish words replace loan-words from German e. g. *powiat* − *kréz* 'district', *zeszit* − *heft* 'exercise-book', *armata* − *kanóna* 'cannon'. German loan-words constitute approx. 5% of the Kashubian vocabulary. Older loans come from Plattdeutsch (cf. 4.1.), more recent ones from literary German. Loan-words usually undergo phonetic and morphological assimilation, e. g. *czis* ≤ Germ. *Kies* 'grit'.

7.5. Kashubian syntax is still to be described but it already appears to be largely Polonized. German constructions are quite numerous as well, e. g. *zrobic czemu kuńc* cf. Germ. *ein Ende machen* 'to finish sth.'; German influence is reflected also in constructions with the word order, for instance the conjunction *ale* (Germ. *aber*) 'but': *to je ale dobré* : Germ. *es ist aber gut* 'how good it is', while in Polish it is *Ale to dobre*.

8. Evaluation of the sources and literature

The history and the present state of the Kashubian language including the discussion concerning its linguistic status is presented most comprehensively by Popowska-Taborska (1980) complemented by a long list of publications on the subject. Studies of the Kashubian literary language are fragmentary and mostly concerned with spelling. Sychta's *Dictionary* and *The Linguistic Atlas of the Kashubian and Neighbouring Dialects* (Stieber/Popowska-Taborska 1964) are the greatest achievements in the field of lexical studies, word formation and morphology including linguistic geography. An etymological dictionary (by W. Boryś and H. Popowska-Taborska) and a dictionary of the extinct Slovincian dialect (by Z. Sobierajski) are forthcoming. Kashubian collocations have been examined by Treder (1989). Less attention has been paid to issues of Kashubian inflection and least frequent have been studies of Kashubian syntax, whereas sociolinguistic research is rare (Latoszek 1990). Kashubian literature is published in Neureiter's and Drzeżdżon's textbooks (Neureiter 1978, Drzeżdżon 1986).

9. Bibliography (selected)

Boryś, Wiesław/Popowska-Taborska, Hanna (1994): *Słownik etymologiczny kaszubszczyny* [Etymological Dictionary of Kashubian], vol. I A–Č. Warsaw.

Breza, Edward/Treder, Jerzy (1981): *Gramatyka kaszubska. Zarys popularny* [Kashubian Grammar. An outline], Gdańsk.

Breza, Edward/Treder, Jerzy (Eds.) (1975): *Zasady pisowni kaszubskiej* [Principles of Kashubian Orthography], Gdańsk. Second edition 1984.

Ceynowa, Florian (1866–1868): *Skôrb kaszëbskosłowińsczi movë* [Outline of the Kashub-Slovincian Language], Swiecé.

Drzeżdżon, Jan (1986): *Współczesna literatura kaszubska 1945–1980* [Contemporary Kashubian Literature 1945–1980], Warsaw.

Gołąbek, Eugeniusz (1992): *Rozmówki kaszubskie* [Kashubian Phrase-book], Gdynia.

Labuda, Alexander (1981): *Słowôrz kaszëbsko-polsczi. Słownik polsko-kaszubski* [Kashub–Polish Dictionary. Polish-Kashubian Dictionary], Gdańsk.

Labuda, Gerard (1991): *O Kaszubach, o ich nazwie i ziemi zamieszkanie* [Kashubian People, their Name and Land], Gdynia.

Latoszek, Marek (Ed.) (1990): *Kaszubi, Monografia socjologiczna*, [Kashubs. A sociologic Study], Rzeszów.

Lorentz, Friedrich (1934): *Zarys etnografii kaszubskiej* [An outline of Kashubian Ethnography], Toruń.

Majewicz, Alfred F. (1987): "National minorities in Poland". In: *Bulletin of the Institute for the Study of North Euroasian Cultures, Hokkaido University*, 18, 279–300.

Neureiter, Ferdinand (1973): *Kaschubische Anthologie*, Munich.

Neureiter, Ferdinand (1978): *Geschichte der kaschubischen Literatur*, München. Second ed. 1991, Polish translation, Gdańsk 1982.

Popowska-Taborska, Hanna (1980): *Kaszubszczyzna. Zarys dziejów* [Kashubian. A Historical outline], Warsaw.

Popowska-Taborska, Hanna (1988): "Język czy dialekt? – raz jeszcze o statusie kaszubszczyzny" [A Language or a dialect? – the Status of Kashubian Reconsidered]. In: *Język Polski*, 28, 87–96.

Ramułt, Stefan (1893): *Słownik języka pomorskiego czyli kaszubskiego* [Handbook of the Pomoranian, i. e. Kashubian Language], Cracow.

Stieber, Zdzisław/Popowska-Taborksa, Hanna (Eds.) (1964–1978): *Atlas językowy kaszubszczyzny i dialektów sąsiednich* [Linguistic Atlas of Kashubian and Neighboring Dialects], Vol. I–XV, Wrocław.

Sychta, Bernard (1967–1976): *Słownik gwar kaszubskich na tle kultury ludowej* [Dictionary of the Kashubian Language based on Folklore Culture], vol. I–VII, Wrocław.

Topolińska, Zuzana (1974): *A Historical Phonology of the Kashubian Dialects of Polish*, The Hague/Paris.

Topolińska, Zuzana (1980): "Kashubian". In: *The Slavic Literary Languages*, Schenker A. M./Stankiewicz E. (Eds.), New Haven.

Treder, Jerzy (1989): *Frazeologia kaszubska a wierzenia i zwyczaje (na tle porównawczym)* [Kashubian Collocations, and Beliefs and Customs (a Comparative Study)], Wejherowo.

Trepczyk, Jan (1994): *Słownik polsko−kaszubski* [Polish−Kashubian Dictionary], vol. I−II, Treder, J. (Ed.), Gdańsk.

Wosiak-Śliwa, Róża/Cybulski, Marek (1992): *Kaszubski język literacki. Podręcznik dla lektoratów* [Kashubian Literary Language. A Textbook], Gdańsk.

Jerzy Treder, Gdansk (Poland)

195. Polish−Byelorussian

1. Geography and demography
2. History
3. Religion, social life and national identity
4. Sociolinguistic situation
5. Language political situation
6. General contactlinguistic portrait
7. Conclusion
8. Bibliography (selected)

1. Geography and demography

The Polish and Byelorussian languages in Poland influence each other mainly through their dialects. With a fairly broad and linguistically important strip of transient Byelorussian−Ukrainian dialects, the Mazovian and Podlasian dialects of Polish find themselves in direct territorial contiguity with the western periphery of the Byelorussian and Ukrainian dialects. The western line of this strip arches into the Polish territory south-westwards from the Augustów Canal crossing the rivers Biebrza, Supraśl, Narew, Nurzec, and finally reaching the river Bug (cf. map 195.1). It should be noted, however, that this line only marks the maximum spread of the Byelorussian dialects registered with speech samples of senior residents before 1960 and not the actual domain of dialect usage in communication. Already at that time the linguistic situation to the east of this area was not substantially uniform. There are villages where all the inhabitants, irrespective of their age, spoke either a Byelorussian or a transient to Ukrainian or a Ukrainian dialect in their daily life (at home and with neighbours), and villages where Byelorussian was spoken only by elderly people, while the rest of the population used a local variety of Polish. Between these two poles there certainly occurred intermediate cases (→ Language Map I).

2. History

The dialects of East Slavic type in Poland are highly differentiated since colonization of this territory varied with regard to space. The oldest stream of colonization dates back to the 14th, the youngest only to the 19th century (Wiśniewski 1964, 1980, 14 ff). The migration waves were of Polish-Mazovian [1] origin, Ukrainians from Bug and Brest (Breść) [2], Byelorussians from Niemen (town Grodno) [3], and Byelorussians from Wołkowysk [4], and finally "Jatvigians" and Lithuanians [5]. The oldest migration wave affected the area south of the Narew river and involved [1] and [2]. The area north-east from

1. Approximate western limit of East Slavic dialects. State as of 1960
2. Endings *-om*, *-ox*, in Dat., Loc. pl. type *val'om*, *val'ox*
3. Ending *-e*, (*-é*, *-ẏe͡, -ie*) in Gen. sg. f., non-palatalized stem
4. The western limit of sakanje, type *kup'aysa*
5. Ending *-ut* in 3. pl. type *id'ut*
6. The northern limit of depalatalization of consonants before [e], type *ov'es*, and nonstressed *ĕ* ≥ *i* type *pis'ok*
7. The southern limit of tsekanje and dzekanje: northern limit of pronoun *ś'ety* and palatalized [*ć*], type *xl'opeć*
8. Depalatalization of consonants of the type *xod'yty, rob'yty*

▨ Full akanje
▨ Partial akanje (auslaut excluded)
▨ Partial akanje (with irregular excluded)
▨ Traces of partial akanje
▨ Mazurenje

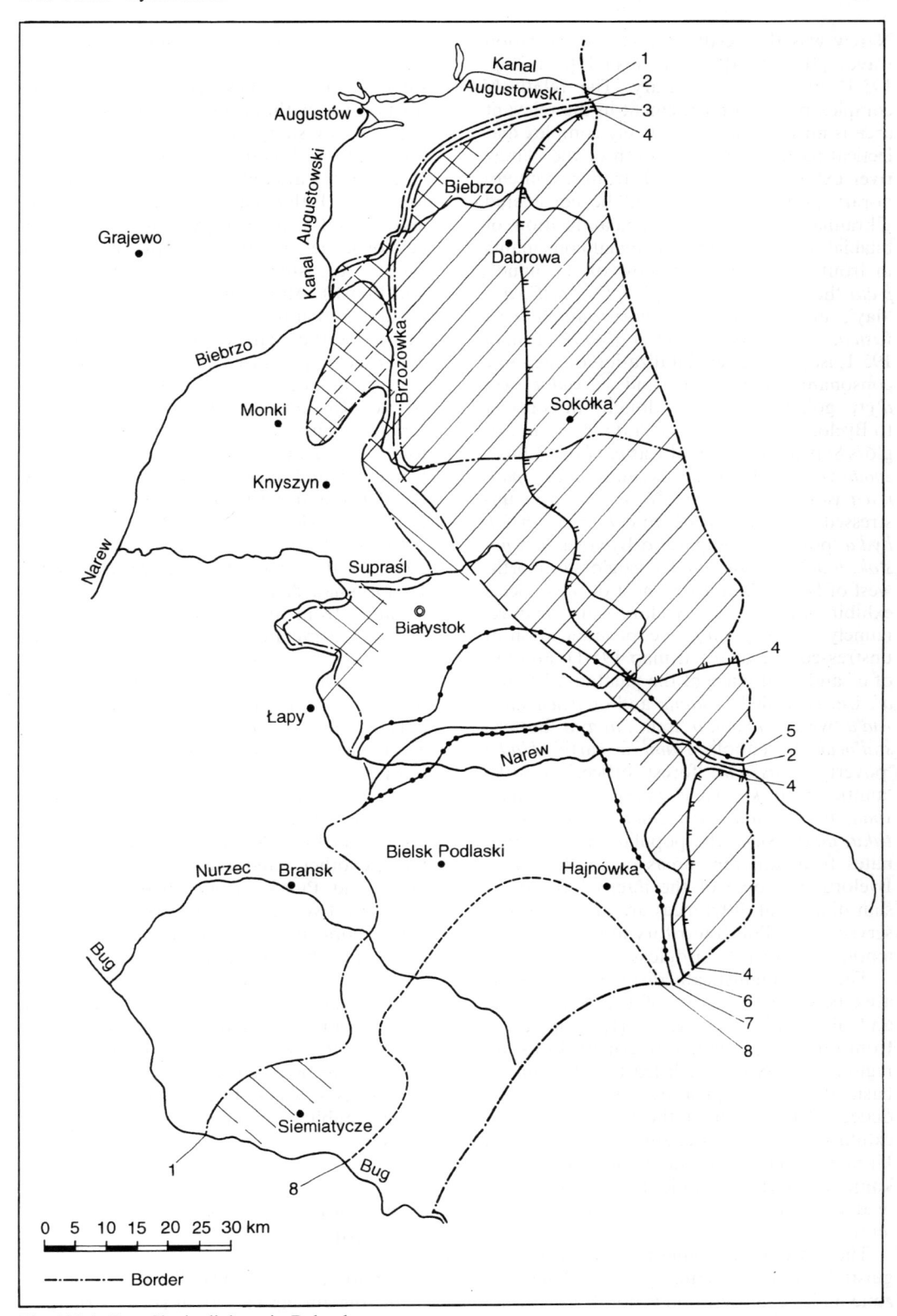

Fig. 195.1: East Slavic dialects in Poland

Narew was the destination of the migration waves [3] and [4] (partly also [1], cf. Fig. 195.1) in the 15th century. The relatively complex pattern of settlement in the relevant area is mirrored in its relatively complex dialectical pattern. Dialects south of the Narew river exhibit features which from a contemporary point of view would be considered Ukrainian, for instance depalatalization of bilabial, or labial and forelingual consonants in front of e: *žm'eńa* 'hollow of the hand', *p'eta* 'heel', *vesn'a* 'Spring', *tel"a* 'calf', *deń* 'day', in contrast to Byelorussian *žṁ'eńa, v́asn'a, c"al'a (v́esn'a, c"el'a), ʒ"eń* – cf. map 195.1, isogloss 6; depalatalization of the same consonants in front of *i* and *ie*: *xod'iti, xod'yty* 'go', *t̂iesto, t̂ýesto* 'dough', in contrast to Byelorussian *xaʒ"ic", c"'esta, c"'iesta*, isogloss 8; pronunciation of *c* as *ć, xl'opeć* 'boy', *spadn'yća* 'shirt', Byelorussian *xl'opec, spadn'ica* isogloss 7; change **ě > i* or *y* in unstressed positions: *pis'ok, pys'ok* 'sand', *bid'a, byd'a* 'poverty', compare to Byelorussian *p̀as'ok, b'ad'a, ṕes'ok, b'ed'a*, isogloss 6. Northwest of Narew/Białystok, most of the dialects exhibit the basic Byelorussian feature, namely *akanje, jakanje*, i.e. pronunciation of unstressed *o, e* as *a* (cf. map 195.1), and use of *c"* and *ʒ* in place of the palatalized *t'* and *d'*, i.e. so called *ciekanje* and/or *dzienkanje, vad'a* 'water', *małak'o* 'milk', *m'asła* 'butter', *stał'oček* 'footstool', *z"aml"a* 'earth', *b'ad'a* 'poverty', *l'as"ń'ik* 'forest officer'; *c"otka* 'auntie', *ʒ"ac"ka* 'uncle', comp. to Ukrainian *voda, mleko, stołoček, zemla, beda, lesnik; titka, ditko*. Since the population here originates from different areas of south eastern Byelorussia, some of the internal Byelorussian dialectical differences are also to be observed in the Polish territory in focus (for example cf. map 195.1 isogloss 2).

The least linguistically distinct region is the area between the curve of the Narew river and Białystok. Mazovians [1], population from Grodno [3] and southern Byelorussian regions [4] mixed, which led to a loss of the basic Byelorussian feature (akanje) of their dialect. The speech of the local population exhibits ciakanje, dziekanje (*c"eń, ʒ"eń*, cf. Ukrainian *teń, deń*) and simultaneously onkanje, i.e. lack of akanje, for example *vod'a* 'water', *kor'omysło* 'yoke' and not *vad'a, kar'omysla*.

The sense of belonging to a particular linguistic/national community in the dialectical zone under consideration is not decisively determined by linguistic criteria. Therefore, the Polish–Byelorussian linguistic contact can neither be adequately described without considering Baltic, and especially Lithuanian influence, nor without due attention to the absence of any sharp border-line between Byelorussian and Ukrainian dialects.

There is scattered – in the meantime Polonized – Lithuanian settlement east of Białystok and a more concentrated, nationally acknowledged Lithuanian community in the former Augustów district (vicinity of Sejny and Puńsk). Although the origin of the first group is rather uncertain, it is known that the earliest Lithuanian colonists were boyars who quickly polonized. Traces of the Lithuanian population and Polish–Lithuanian–(Byelo)-Russian language contact within the Grand Duchy of Lithuania can in general be found in personal names (Kondratiuk 1990), toponymy and micro-toponymy, and both in the Polish and the Byelorussian dialectal vocabularies (Kontratiuk 1985, Smułkowa 1963, 1969, 1981, Zdancewicz 1960, 1963, 1966, 1980). Some phonetic features of the Byelorussian dialects such as *ŋ* before *k* not resulting from the split of the nasals *žoŋka, k'išoŋka*, geminate simplification of the type *sać < ssać, bai̯'ica* instead of *bai̯'icca, treće < trecca, boi̯'iće, voda studni 'z studni'; ł < l* e.g. in *piłnawać, łnu* 'lnu' are interpreted as Lithuanisms (Glinka 1990). It is also assumed that Jatvingians, defeated in the 13th century, did not perish without traces. However, these are difficult to discover since in the course of time they mixed with the Slavic population (Kamiński 1955, Nalepa 1964, Hasiuk 1978). On the other hand the Lithuanians in the Sejny and Puńsk vicinity maintained their language (two different dialects: of kapsu and dzuku populations), which resulted in Lithuanian Polish bilingualism. The degree of competence in Polish, which obviously is their second language, varies depending on a number of psycho- and sociolinguistic factors (Kolis 1991, 107). Among themselves the Lithuanians use their own language in everyday life as well as in local administration and other public institutions including the church.

3. Religion, social life and national identity

The Catholic–Orthodox distinction plays a main role among factors of social structuration and consequently of social life in the area under consideration. This is reflected in the political stances of the respective population, and functions as the decisive factor of national identity.

Estimating the number of the Byelorussians in Poland is impeded by the want for statistic data as well as a rather unstable national self-identification of a part of the mixed population. Hence, the sources provide greatly varying data on the number of Byelorussians, ranging from 150,000 to 500,000. Recently this number appears not to exceed 200,000.

Intensive field research between 1957 and 1975 revealed that people most frequently defined their national identity on the basis of their religion rather than on the language they spoke. Thus, the population of Sokółka and Dąbrowa regions, who spoke a pure Byelorussian dialect, identified themselves as Poles because they were Catholic. The orthodox irrespective of their native language, be it Byelorussian or Ukrainian, categorized themselves with *my ruskaj wiery* (we are of the Russian creed), or often simply *ruskie* (Russians) as opposed to *polskie* (Catholics), or they identified themselves as Byelorussians. In order to correctly interpret this statement it needs to be considered that in contrast to English there is a distinction between *ruski* — Byelorussian and Ukrainian and *rosyjski* — Russian in Polish. Therefore, Russian here equals Orthodox. The other feature often used for national identification were the places of birth and residence, of being a native in the locality (*tutejszość* — nativeness), or both the traditional sense of belonging to the region or to some place of locality. The feature "nativeness" is often associated with the linguistic identity, even though the dialect is not termed "national" but opposed to Polish "simple speech": *my po prostu havorym, naša mova m'ešana, ni polska ni bełaruska* (we speak simply, our speech is mixed — neither Polish, nor Byelorussian). At the same time there is a general intelligibility of the local dialectal differences, which is shown explicitly in the popular saying *co wieś to inna pieśń* (a new village, a new song). Yet, the difference between the dialects is noticed by the population which is reflected by the ethnonym *xaxł'y, pa xaxł'acku hav'orać, xaxł'acka m'owa*, and the border-line of xaxł'ian (in fact Ukrainian) moves from north to south.

In recent years, the strength of the national consciousness of the population in the region has changed. Especially Byelorussian support for *Solidarność* (Solidarity), which was unanimously considered to be a purely Polish and thus Catholic organization, decreased as the activity of various nationally distinct Byelorussian and Ukrainian groups increased considerably after August 1989. An important role concerning the development of national identity in the region is being played by the Byelorussian intelligentsia and the association of Byelorussian students "BAS".

However, the process of establishing national consciousness in the territory considered has not been completed yet. The growth of the sense of Byelorussian national identity among younger students, born in rural areas, is balanced by the emergence of the Ukrainian national movement in the Bielsk Podlaski district. Occasionally even people who earlier referred to themselves as Byelorussians now identify themselves as Ukrainian. It should be noted that in the territory between the Bug and the Narew where (cf. 2.) transitional and Ukrainian dialects can be found, the sense of national identity of the Byelorussian is strongest. The largest group of students studying Byelorussian philology at Warsaw University comes from this very region and two Byelorussian lyceums in Bielsk Podlaski and Hajnówka had 630 pupils in the academic year 1991/1992. Although in the beginning the lyceums used Byelorussian exclusively as a language of instruction, they gradually shifted to Polish, though Byelorussian is still used in classes of Byelorussian language, literature and elementary history and geography lessons. The Byelorussian character of the schools has nevertheless been stressed by naming them after Bronisław Taraszkiewicz (1892—1938), an outstanding humanist, patriot and political leader, Byelorussian member of the Polish Parliament, and by observing national holidays and cultural traditions.

4. Sociolinguistic situation

The starting point of the sociolinguistic description of language contacts in the northeastern part of Poland should be a definition of the differences in the status of the contact languages and a distinct delimitation of their functions.

The Polish language in all its stylistic varieties enjoys the highest prestige as the language of public institutions, school, theatre, cinema and the various mass media. It is the language of social advance and provides a criterion for the individual's identification with the Polish speaking society.

The local variant of Polish is close to but not identical with the variant of Polish spoken in present-day Byelorussia and Lithuania (*Polszczyzna północnokresowa*) and standard Polish. The latter is spread through mass media and due to the cultural and educational influence from larger urban centres. This is effected not only by the bilingualism of the local population and the influence of administration language, but also by ethnic mingling of the earlier and new settlers in the villages, and is moreover promoted by the rather distinct Polish character of the majority population of cities and country towns in the region.

The Byelorussian dialectal speech remains the means of communication at home and among neighbours. It is considered to be simple and low, and not even respected by its speakers, who apart from using Polish in towns, offices, shops, hospitals, etc. even in their own villages speak Polish with newcomers, priests and teachers.

This classical distribution of functions is often broken by the interference of the local variant of Polish into family life mostly in the western parts of the Byelorussian dialectal area in Poland, where there is direct contact with the consolidated Polish region. The migration of population from rural districts to towns contributes to further linguistic polonization. This post-war tendency, common to Poland in general, was very great in the Białystok Region for the reason of a predominance of small farms and the decline of the agricultural sector.

In many villages the population now consists mostly of senior people whose children and grandchildren (especially the latter) visit the villages on holidays and vacation and are by now Polish-speaking.

There have been a number of attempts of the Byelorussian intelligentsia to enhance the prestige of the Byelorussian dialects and to promote the knowledge of the literary Byelorussian language by means of lectures, usage in spoken language and, in the first place, by publications on national and patriotic subjects including belletristic literature. "Niwa", a Byelorussian weekly magazine, has been issued in Białystok since 1956 (the last edition with 2,500 copies). Although the magazine has been aimed at the rural population, in the new political and social reality it started discussing a broader variety of political and historical issues and thus turned into a kind of tribune for the Byelorussian national minority in Poland in general.

It should, however, be noted that because of the great difference between the dialects, literary standard Byelorussian is not accepted by the speakers of the region as their national language, i. e. as their mother tongue. For example, even students of Byelorussian philology at Warsaw University, born in the region between the Bug and the Narew, use their own dialect in everyday life among themselves (as, for example, having a party) saying *a my po swojemu* (that is in our own language).

As a summary the sociolinguistic patterning of the north-eastern part of Poland has to be differentiated into:

(a) Polish monolinguals, who use either the non-Mazurian variant of Polish (č, ž, š do not change into c, z, s; the Sejny-Suwałki region) with a number of Byelorussian and Lithuanian interferences (the presence of the Byelorussian substratum in them has been shown by Zdancewicz (1966)), or the Polish Podlasian dialects in which the contact with Byelorussian has also left evident traces.
(b) Partially preserved Byelorussian monolingualism (senior population) with a passive knowledge of Polish.
(c) Lithuanian−Polish and Byelorussian−Polish bilinguals. The bilingualism exhibits a diglottic character, and Polish is represented by a wide variety of idiolects.
(d) Lithuanian−Polish and Byelorussian−Polish bilingualism of highly educated individuals. They are able to freely switch from one language to another. They use the common (standard) Polish with more or less distinct traces of the local variant.

5. Language political situation

Does a clearly established linguistic policy exist for the Białystok Region?

By linguistic policy, on the one hand a more or less pronounced state influence on the implementation of the minority rights with regard to educational development and cultural activity in the native language is understood, on the other, the development of social, political and educational organizations, whose activities are aimed at promoting the use of the native language.

It is obvious that with so complicated a phenomenon as the problem of national minorities, some of its aspects fall easy prey to neglect. However, a policy discriminating against the Byelorussian language has never been pursued in Poland.

The conditions for a development of primary and secondary Byelorussian education are being improved, also introducing Byelorussian philology (as a subject of university study in Poland in 1957). The state subsidizes the activities of the Byelorussian Social-Cultural Society, the weekly "Niwa", as well as other periodicals and publications, and numerous cultural events. For many years the Byelorussian dialects in Poland have been studied intensely, resulting in an atlas, several monographs, and numerous articles. Similarly, the history of colonizing the territory and its material and spiritual culture have been carefully investigated.

Byelorussians in Poland do speak the Byelorussian language, while Byelorussia itself underwent a wave of russification (→ art. 235). After World War II, two Byelorussian lyceums existed in the eastern part of the Białystok region, while in the capital of the Soviet Byelorussian Republic there was none. Furthermore, in the course of establishing the political independence of the Republic of Belarus, introduction of classes with Byelorussian as the language of instruction in many cases met with the strong opposition of the parents.

Despite all these pro-Byelorussian activities, the scope of Byelorussian communication is decreasing in Poland, mainly due to the prestige position of Polish and due to pragmatic regards of language users themselves. In the academic year 1991/1992, for instance, the Byelorussian language was taught to 2878 children in 44 schools and 2 school affiliations compared to 3033 children in 1990/1991 (*Niwa 4/91*, cf. 4.4.). This process is completely neglected by language policy, even though it is noticed and stressed by Byelorussians in Poland. However, the described development does not imply any Polish−Byelorussian conflict. Rather some symptoms of a conflict can be observed in connection with the increase of national consciousness in the southern part of the East Białystok region where the population (claiming Byelorussian nationality) speaks a dialect transitional to the Ukrainian type, and further, standard Ukrainian has begun to be taught (cf. 3.).

Polish and Byelorussian come into contact also in writing. Whereas the Polish language employs an adapted version of the Latin alphabet, Byelorussian uses a variant of the Cyrillic, so called *grazhdanka* (public [alphabet]).

The weekly "Niwa", calendars, scientific and artistic Byelorussian publications are printed in *grazhdanka* based on the orthographical rules used in Byelorussia. Several writings of a polemic nature, often anonymous and mostly from the time when "Solidarity" started its activity and during the martial law (1981−1983), were printed in Latin letters using rather phonetic orthography. It has been argued in favour of the use of the Latin alphabet for both practical reasons and the tradition of Byelorussian books being printed in Vilna (Vilnius) in Latin script (Smułkowa 1988 b, 305) in the beginning of the 20th century and the 1930's.

6. General contactlinguistic portrait

The language contacts in north-eastern Poland left permanent traces in the languages involved. Lithuanian features in the phonetic system of Byelorussian were already touched upon in (2.). Some Polish phonetic variants became permanent features of the Byelorussian dialects: in the western strip we find "mazurzenie", i. e., pronunciation *č, ž, š*, as *c, z, s*, e. g.: *cah'o, z'onka, x'oces*; but in contrast to Mazovian (Polish) the change *ž < ř* does not occur. In the respective position we find the East Slavic *r ≤ *ř*. So these dialects have *cas* 'time', *z'aba* 'frog', *v'ysła* 'she went outside' but *try, treba, brek* instead of *tšy, tš'eba, bžeg*, 'tree, necessary, bank'; we find Polish midlingual *ć, ź, ś* in the position of prepalatal *c", z", s"* especially in the speech of students. In the southern part of this zone the Polish influence prevented the Ukrainian depalatalization of **t'e ≥ te*, namely in villages in direct contact with Polish villages. Byelorussian and Polish anlaut *o-* and *je-* respectively is lexicalised and its distribution in words is not uniform throughout the region, e. g.: *i̯es'eń // 'os"eń, v'os"eń, i̯eʒ"'in // aʒ"'in, odin, i̯ez"'oro // 'oz'ero, v'ozero* 'lake' (Glinka et al. Eds. 1980, 58−60). The group opposition of Polish *dl* with Byelorussian *l* is lexicalised and words characterized by it exhibit differences in territorial distribution:

šydło : *šyło, mydło* : *myło, skrydło* : *kryło, krasidło* : *krasiło*; *krapidło* : *kropiło, matavidła* : *mataviła*, etc. (Atlas 1980, 126—131).

On the other hand the "melodiousness" of Polish in this region can be noticed, induced by strong dynamic stress and lengthening of the stressed vowels and a certain reduction of the unstressed, and in examples of a rather Byelorussian pronunciation, akanje occurs, e. g.: *stołečak*, *pagoda*, or examples of overcorrectness as an opposition to akanje, as general use of *rozowy* instead of *razowy* in the phrase *chleb rozowy* etc.

As regards other examples of interference it is necessary to mention:

— deviation in stress placement: *spodob'ał‿se, ʒ'e‿poʒ'ać‿śe*, Polish *spod'obał‿śe; ʒ'e‿po'ʒ'ać‿śe; ćepl'ej, davń'ej*, Polish *ć'eplei̯, d'avńei̯; ńe‿br'ał, ńe‿sxń'e*, Polish *ń'e‿brał, ń'e‿sxńe*; pob'’ił, *zab'’ił*, Polish *z'abił; i̯on'y, i̯eg'o*, Polish *'oni, i̯'ego*, etc.,
— hard *n* in names of the type *Za‿Gośćincem, Kačynsko*; *panstvo, tančyć*, Polish *ń, tańčyć*,
— voiced *v* in combination *tv, sv, cv, šv, tvoi̯, svoi̯, čvarty, švaġer*, etc., Polish *tf, sf, …, tfui̯, sfui̯, …*, etc.

Some interferences became stable and can be treated as systemic:

— The ending -*i* // -*y* of Nom. pl. of masculine and feminine nouns: *gości, Groʒ'i, Močudły*.
— Use of the Genitive instead of the Dative with the preposition *dla*, e. g. *powiedział dla pani*.
— Mutual use of the endings -*u*, -*owi* in Dative singular, e. g. *prosiaku, ogórku, chłopcowi*, Polish *prosiakowi, ogórkowi, chłopcu*.
— Wider distribution and higher frequency of the ending -*of* in Gen. pl. *Zaraśli, -of, Jamiski, -of*.
— Use of the full (strong) forms of pronouns: *mnie, jemu, jego*.
— Lack of *n*- in combinations of prepositional pronouns: *do‿j'ej, u‿j'ego, z'‿i̯'im*, (instead of *d'o‿ńei̯, u‿ńego, z'‿ńim*).
— Lack of personal ending in Past tense, this function being adopted by personal pronouns: *ja xoʒ'’ił, ty xoʒ'’ił, on xoʒ'’ił, my xoʒ'’ili, wy xoʒ'’ili, oni xoʒ'’ili* (instead of *xoʒ'’iłem, xoʒ'’ileś, x'oʒ'’ił; xoʒ'’iliśmy, xoʒ'’iliście, xoʒ'’ili*).
— Neutralization of the specific Polish gender opposition in Past Plural in the East Slavic manner: *mężczyzny, kobiety, dzieci xoʒ'’il'i* (comp. Polish *mężczyźni chodzili — kobiety, dzieci chodziły*).
— Irregularities in the use of reflexive forms resulting from the different distribution of the reflexive and nonreflexive verbs in the languages in contact.
— Excessive use of the particle *by*, as a result of a simultaneous realization of models of the Conditional of both languages: *i̯a by xc'ałby, žeb my pošli // pošl'ib*.

Furthermore, the influence of Polish on the Byelorussian dialects is most evident in the vocabulary. As the three most typical situations (Polonisms related to political and administrative life are left aside) can be mentioned:

(a) a Polish lexeme completely substitutes the Byelorussian one and is generally used: names of months, numerals from 11 to 19, *dzieńdobry, daleko, patelńa*, etc.
(b) a Polish lexeme is used alongside with its Byelorussian equivalent, e. g.: *garść* : *žmienia, klepisko* : *tok, stodoła* : *humno, kłunia* and other.
(c) a Polish lexeme is occasionally used in spoken Byelorussian, while normally its Byelorussian counterpart is used in the same or closely related meanings.

The borrowing of Polish wordstock is accompanied with a number of changes in the semantic fields of the native dialects, e. g.: the Byelorussian word *pasax* 'dowry' in contrast with the Polish loanword *wiano* ('dowry' in Polish), modifies its meaning in the dialects under study and means 'dowry in real things', while the borrowed word *vi̯eno* is used for 'dowry in cash'.

Interference of the languages is quite evident here and its results have taken extremely diverse forms in the toponymics and microtoponymics of the region. In the about 35,000 documented items collected in the north-eastern part of Poland between 1961 and 1970 it is possible to find, alongside with names of Polish, Byelorussian, Lithuanian and Ukrainian origin, numerous hybrid formations combining word-formation elements of different languages and exhibiting transitional dialectal features. For example: *Jeźužysko, Jeżerysko, Aźarysko, Ażerysko, Ozerysko, Ozarysko, Ożerysko, Ozerysko, Vozerysko*, etc. All of them use Polish -*isko* (the Byelorussian equivalent would be -*išče*), the West-Slavic anlaut *je*- is replaced by East-Slavic *o*- or *a*-, in some instances, Byelorussian palatalization contrasts Ukrainian non-palatalization of consonants (*z* in this particular case), and the prothetic *v-* under stress is a rather Byelorussian feature.

7. Conclusion

The problem of Polish−Byelorussian linguistic contact cannot be limited to the geographical overlapping of the variety of Polish−Mazovian dialects with the western periphery of the Byelorussian dialects within the borders of present-day Poland. Changes of the borderlines and migration of the population in different historical periods led to a constant mixing of the Polish, Byelorussian and Lithuanian population in the territory of Lithuania, Byelorussia, Poland and, to a certain extent, of Russia. This fact could but leave significant traces in the shape of linguistic features of the languages of the area. The results of the contacts range from mutual borrowing via mixing up the systems to assimilation. The latter stage is a long process, one phase of which is a rather seamless fusion of the languages in contact, namely when their speakers are in fact not able to differentiate between the system of their native language and the adopted one.

8. Bibliography (selected)

Barszczewska, Nina/Głuszkowska, Jadwiga et al. (1993): "Elementy bałtyckie i wschodniosłowiańskie w przygotowywanym słowniku nazw terenowych północno-wschodniej Polski" [Baltic and East-Slavic Elements in the Vocabulary of Microtoponyms in North-Eastern Poland]. In: *Acta Universitatis Lodziensis, Folia Linguistica* 27, 3−8.

Glinka, Stanisław/Obrębska-Jabłońska, Antonina/ Siatkowski, Janusz (Eds.) (1980): *Atlas gwar wschodnio-słowiańskich Białostocczyzny, I* [Atlas of East-Slavic Dialects of the Białystok Region), Wrocław.

Glinka, Stanisław (Ed.) (1988): *Atlas gwar wschodnio-słowiańskich Białostocczyzny, II* [Atlas of East-Slavic Dialects of the Białystok Region], Wrocław.

Glinka, Stanisław (1990): "Lituanizmy fonetyczne w gwarach białoruskich i polskich Białostocczyzny" [Phonetic Lithuanisms in Byelorussian and Polish Dialects of the Białystok Region]. In: *Bałtosłowiańskie związki językowe*, Kondratiuk, Michał (Ed.), Wrocław, 117−127.

Grek-Pabisowa, Iryda (1968): *Rosyjska gwara starowierców w województwach olsztyńskim i białostockim* [Russian Dialect of Old-believers in Olsztyn and Białystok Provinces], Wrocław.

Grek-Pabisowa, Iryda/Maryniakowa, Irena (1980): *Słownik gwary starowierców mieszkających w Polsce* [Vocabulary of the Old-believers living in Poland], Wrocław.

Hasiuk, Michał (1978): *Fonologia litewskiej gwary sejneńskiej* [Phonology of the Lithuanian Dialect in the Sejny Region], Poznań.

Kamiński, Aleksander (1955): *Jaćwież. Terytorium, ludność, stosunki gospodarcze i społeczne* [Yatvings. Territory, Population, Social and Economic Relations], Łódź.

Kolis, Nijola (1991): "Wybrane zagadnienia z fleksji polszczyzny Litwinów puńskich" [Some Problems of Flexion in Polish of Lithuanians from the Puńsk Region]. In: *Studia nad polszczyzną kresową*, Rieger, Janusz/Werenicz, Wiaczesław (Eds.), Wrocław, 107−129.

Kondratiuk, Michał (1985): *Elementy bałtyckie w toponimii i mikrotoponimii regionu białostockiego* [Baltic Elements in Toponymy and Microtoponymy of the Białystok Region], Wrocław.

Nalepa, Jan (1964): *Jaćwingowie. Nazwa i lokalizacja* [Yatvingians. Name and Location], Białystok.

Obrębska-Jabłońska, Antonina (Ed.) (1972): *Teksty gwarowe z Białostocczyzny z komentarzem językowym* [Dialectal Texts from the Białystok Region with a Lingual Glossary], Warsaw.

Smoczyński, Wojciech (1984): "Zapożyczenie słowiańskie w litewskiej gwarze puńskiej" [Slavic borrowings in the Lithuanian Puńsk dialect]. In: *Studia nad gwarami Białostocczyzny Morfologia i słownictwo*, Smułkowa, Elżbieta/Maryniakowa, Irena (Eds.), Warsaw, 179−221.

Smułkowa, Elżbieta (1963): "O białoruskim *g"ega* 'krzemień'. Przyczynek do zagadnienia substratu bałtyckiego w historii języków słowiańskich" [On the Byelorussian *g"ega* 'flint'. A Contribution to the Problem of Baltic Substrate in the History of Slavic Languages]. In: *Z polskich studiów slawistycznych* 2, 215−221.

Smułkowa, Elżbieta (1969): "Lituanizmy w białoruskim słownictwie rolniczym" [Lithuanisms in Byelorussian Agricultural Vocabulary]. In: *Lingua Posnaniensis* 14, 55−69.

Smułkowa, Elżbieta (1981): "K probleme belorusskich baltizmov. O statuse baltizmov v belorusskich govorach" [On the Problem of Baltisms in Byelorussian. Place of Baltisms in Byelorussian Dialects]. In: *Balto-slovjanskije Issledovanija AN SSSR, 1980*, Moscow, 203−214.

Smułkowa, Elżbieta (1968): *Słownictwo z zakresu uprawy roli w gwarach wschodniej Białostocczyzny na tle wschodniosłowiańskim* [Vocabulary of Agriculture in Dialects of the East Białystok Region against the East-Slavic Background], Wrocław.

Smułkowa, Elżbieta (1988): "Zagadnienie polskobiałorusko-litewskiej interferencji językowej na ziemiach północno-wschodniej Polski" [Problems of Polish−Byelorussian−Lithuanian Language Interference in north-east Poland]. In: *Z polskich studiów slawistycznych* 7, 395−405.

Smułkowa, Elżbieta (1990): "Problematyka badawcza polsko−białorusko−litewskiego pogranicza językowego" [Research Problems in the Polish−Byelorussian−Lithuanian Language Boundary]. In: *Studia nad Polszczyzną kresową*, Rieger, Janusz/Werenicz, Wiaczesław (Eds.), Wrocław, 151−164.

Smułkowa, Elżbieta (1992): "Pojęcie gwar przejściowych i mieszanych na polsko−białorusko−ukraińskim pograniczu językowym" [Understanding of Transition and Mixed Dialects in the Polish−Byelorussian−Ukrainian Lingual Borderland]. In: *Między Wschodem a Zachodem*, cz. IV, Zjawiska językowe na pograniczu polsko−ruskim, Bartmiński, Jerzy/Łesiów, Michał (Eds.), Lublin, 21−33.

Smułkowa, Elżbieta (1992): "Białorusko−polskie a białorusko−rosyjskie pogranicze językowe" [Byelorussian−Polish and Byelorussian−Russian Lingual Borderland]. In: *Słowiańskie pogranicza językowe*, Handke, Kwiryna (Ed.), Warsaw.

Smułkowa, Elżbieta/Kolis, Nijola (1992): "Polszczyzna dwujęzycznych Litwinów puńskich (wybrane zagadnienia)" [Polish of Lithuanian Bilinguals in the Puńsk Region (selected problems)]. In: *Słowiańsko−niesłowiańskie kontakty językowe*, Siatkowski, Janusz/Doliński, Ignacy (Eds.), Warsaw, 89−95.

Wiśniewski, Jerzy (1980): "Zarys dziejów osadnictwa na Białostocczyźnie" [Outline of the History of Colonization of the Białystok Region]. In: *Atlas gwar wschodniosłowiańskich Białostocczyzny* 1, Glinka, Stanisław et al. (Eds.), Wrocław, 14−27.

Zdancewicz, Tadeusz (1960): "Litewskie elementy słownikowe w gwarach polskich okolic Sejn" [Lithuanian Lexical Elements in Polish Dialects around Sejny]. In: *Lingua Posnaniensis* 8, 333−352.

Zdancewicz, Tadeusz (1963): "Litewskie i ruskie zasięgi słownikowe na Białostocczyźnie" [Scope of Lithuanian and Russian Vocabulary in the Białystok Region]. In: *Z polskich studiów slawistycznych* 2, 287−310.

Zdancewicz, Tadeusz (1964): "Wpływy litewskie i wschodniosłowiańskie w polskich gwarach pod Sejnami" [Lithuanian and East Slavic Influence on the Polish Dialects around Sejny]. In: *Acta Baltico-Slavica* 1, 227−246.

Zdancewicz, Tadeusz (1966): *Wpływy białoruskie w polskich gwarach pod Sejnami* [Byelorussian Influence on the Polish Dialects around Sejny], Poznań.

Zdancewicz, Tadeusz (1980): *Mazurzące gwary suwalskie* [Dialects of the Suwałki Region with Mazurian Features], Warsaw.

Zielińska, Anna (1991): "Cechy fonetyczne i fleksyjne polszczyzny staroobrzędowców rosyjskich z Wodziłek koło Suwałk" [Phonetical and Inflexional Features of Russian Old-Believers from Wodziłki at Sejny]. In: *Studia nad polszczyzną kresową*, Rieger, Janusz/Werenicz, Wiaczesław (Eds.), Wrocław, 131−153.

Elżbieta Smułkowa, Warsaw (Poland)

196. Polnisch−Litauisch

1. Geographie und Demographie
2. Geschichte
3. Politik, Wirtschaft und allgemeine kulturelle sowie religiöse Lage
4. Statistik und Ethnoprofil
5. Soziolinguistische Lage
6. Sprachpolitische Lage
7. Allgemeines kontaktlinguistisches Porträt
8. Kritische Wertung der verwendeten Quellen und Literatur
9. Bibliographie (in Auswahl)

1. Geographie und Demographie

Das Gebiet polnisch−litauischer Sprachkontakte liegt im nordöstlichen Teil Polens in der Woiwodschaft Suwałki. Im Süden wird es durch das Waldgebiet von Augustów, im Westen durch den Fluß Czarna Hańcza und im Norden und Osten durch die polnisch−litauische Staatsgrenze begrenzt.

Geographisch lassen sich drei Gebiete des synchronischen Sprachkontakts unterscheiden: (a) ein von Litauern bewohntes, geschlossenes Gebiet von ca. 40 km Länge und ca. 15 km Breite, das etwa 60 Dörfer der Gemeinden Puńsk, Sejny und Szypliszki umfaßt; es liegt direkt an der Staatsgrenze und wird im Nordwesten durch eine Linie begrenzt, die von Markiszki im Südosten über Żegary, Romanowce, Szlinokiemie, Romaniuki, Budzisko bis Jegliniec verläuft (Hasiuk 1978, 3 f; Garšva 1989, 32 f; Aleksaitė/Razmukaitė 1989, 79 f); (b) entlang der Staatsgrenze nördlich des Gebiets (a) liegende Dörfer, die durch die Linie Szypliszki, Rutka Tartak, Wiżajny, Bolcie begrenzt sind; in diesem Gebiet ließen sich noch bis vor kurzem Sprachkontakte verzeichnen, und litauischsprachige Personen sind dort vereinzelt anzutreffen; (c) Stadtgebiet von Suwałki und Sejny.

Die Angabe genauer demographischer Daten ist wegen des Nichtvorhandenseins offizieller Daten über nationale Minderheiten in Polen problematisch. In der Literatur werden unterschiedliche Zahlen angegeben. Danach schwankt die Zahl der Litauer in der Woiwodschaft Suwałki zwischen 9 und 15 Tausend. In ganz Polen beträgt sie ca. 30 Tausend (Garšva 1989, 36; Smoczyński 1981, 350; *Aušra* 1984/4, 7). Während des Zweiten Weltkriegs wurde fast die Hälfte der Einheimischen zur Auswanderung nach Litauen gezwungen. Nicht alle der in zwei Emigrationswellen (1940 und 1944—1948) Ausgewanderten kehrten zurück. Nach dem Zweiten Weltkrieg entstanden infolge politischer Migration litauische Gemeinden in vielen polnischen Großstädten. Die Erforschung der Nachkriegsmigrationen könnte neben weiteren interessanten Ergebnissen auch Aufschluß geben über das Verschwinden der Litauer aus der Gegend von Wiżajny, wo vor dem Krieg 25% der Einwohner Litauisch sprachen (Hasiuk 1978, 4); → Sprachenkarte I.

2. Geschichte

Bis zum Ende des 13. Jahrhunderts war die Suvalkija (Suwalszczyzna) ein Teil des den Jatvingern (Sudauer), einem baltischen Stamm, gehörenden Gebietes. 1283 wurden die Jatvinger endgültig vom Deutschritter Orden besiegt und die Restbevölkerung in das Samland umgesiedelt bzw. zur Flucht nach Litauen gezwungen (Kamiński 1953, 64 f). Nach 1410 und 1422 beginnt mit dem Ende des territorialen Streits zwischen dem Orden und Litauen zugunsten des letzteren eine systematische Umsiedlungsaktion von Litauern aus dem Großfürstentum. Noch seßhafte bzw. aus der Verbannung zurückgekehrte Jatvinger vermischten sich mit litauischen Siedlern aus Przełom, Olita (Alytus) und Merecz (Merkinė), und Russen aus Perstuń und Grodno (Wiśniewski 1963, 40 f). Zu ersten polnisch—litauischen Sprachkontakten kam es im südwestlichen Teil der Suvalkija, östlich der Czarna Hańcza, wo die beiden Siedlungswellen zusammentreffen und im ausgehenden 17. Jahrhundert polnische Siedlungen eine bedeutende Rolle spielen (Falk 1941, 17 f). In der Mitte des 16. Jahrhunderts kommen erstmals Polen in die Gegend von Sejny und Berzniki. Sie stammen aus Masurien und wurden von der Königin Bona Sforza zu Vermessungsarbeiten ins Land geholt. Die nächste polnische Einwanderungswelle ist mit der Gründung von Berzniki, Sejny und Puńsk (Ende des 16. Jahrhunderts) zu verzeichnen.

Nach der Seuche von 1710/1711, die die dortige Bevölkerung dezimierte, kommt es in einem großen Teil der Suvalkija zu Veränderungen in der sprachlichen Struktur und zum Verschwinden litauischer Elemente. Gegenwärtig lassen sich toponymische und sprachliche Elemente litauischen Ursprungs, vor allem in der Umgebung des Wigry-Sees, feststellen (Wiśniewski 1965, 85; Westfal 1946, 156 f; Falk 1941, 19).

Das von den Litauern bewohnte Gebiet nördlich der Seina (heute: Marycha) wird von polnischen Einflüssen kaum berührt. Weiterhin ist eine Regression des Litauischen am Ende des 19. und Anfang des 20. Jahrhunderts im Dreieck Sejny—Berzniki—Giby zu erwähnen. Nach einer kurzen zweisprachigen Periode entstehen in der ersten Hälfte des 20. Jahrhunderts in der Gegend von Szypliszki und Wiżajny polnische Mundarten auf dem litauischen Substrat.

3. Politik, Wirtschaft und allgemeine kulturelle sowie religiöse Lage

Nach dem Zweiten Weltkrieg wurde von der Regierung Polens die Idee eines ethnisch einheitlichen Staates propagiert. Nach der Wende von 1956 wurde den Litauern ermöglicht, unter staatlicher Kontrolle ihr eigenes Schulwesen und Kultur in eigener Sprache aufzubauen (Sław 1959, 166 f; *Aušra* 1981/3, 4 f).

Im Gebiet des polnisch—litauischen Sprachkontakts bilden Bauern die Mehrheit der Bewohner. So leben über 80% der Litauer in der Region Suwałki auf dem Lande (*Aušra* 1964/1, 2). Verglichen mit der Landwirtschaft in Ostpolen steht die litauische auf einem hohen Niveau. Auf kulturellem Gebiet ist Puńsk, die national einheitlichste litauische Gemeinde, führend: seit 1956 besteht ein litauisches Gymnasium. Unter der Schirmherrschaft des Hauses der Litauischen Kultur (tätig seit 1956), der Litauischen Kulturellen Gesellschaft (LVKD, tätig seit 1957) und der dortigen Schule sind Laientheater, Chöre, Tanzvereine, Musikkapellen tätig. Es werden Konzerte, literarische Abende, Vorträge und Sportwettkämpfe veranstaltet. 1981 wurde in Puńsk sogar eine wissenschaftliche Konferenz abgehalten (Makowski 1984, 329 f, Uździło 1987, 79 f). Neben der Herausgabe der *Aušra*, einer gesellschaftlich-kulturellen Zeitschrift (seit 1960), fördert die Litauische Kulturelle Gesellschaft (seit 1992 — *Lenkijos lietuvių draugija*) litauischsprachige Bücher und Zeitschriften. Seit 1992 sind zwei neue gesellschaftlich-kulturelle Vereine tätig: ein wieder ins Leben gerufener christlicher Verein aus der Vorkriegszeit — *Lietuvių šv. Kazimiero draugija*, und *Lenkijos lietuvių bendruomenė* (*Aušra* 1992/23, 2 f; 1992/24, 6 f). Weiterhin gibt es in Puńsk ein Heimatmuseum und ein ethnographisches Museum. Kulturelle Einrichtungen in Sejny hingegen sind ausschließlich auf die Pflege der polnischen Kultur ausgerichtet. Das gilt in noch größerem Maß für Suwałki.

Da Litauer und Polen größtenteils katholisch sind, werden dieselben Kirchen von beiden Nationen genutzt, was schon von jeher Anlaß zu Streitigkeiten gab (cf. 6.). Heute werden litauische Messen in Kirchen in Puńsk, Sejny, Smolany, Żegary und seit neustem einmal im Monat in Suwałki gelesen (Roch 1991, 18 f).

4. Statistik und Ethnoprofil

Die meisten der in diesem Kapitel auftauchenden Sachprobleme sind auf das Fehlen von offiziellen Daten und wissenschaftlichen Abhandlungen zu dieser Frage zurückzuführen. Auch wir müssen hier auf spärliche Daten zurückgreifen, die von Kazimieras Garšva (1989, 33 f) angegeben werden.

Im Gebiet (a) (cf. 1.) werden von Garšva 45 Dörfer mit einer Bevölkerung von 9000 Litauern erwähnt. 90–100% der Gesamtbevölkerung machen die Litauer in 18 Dörfern aus, 80–90% — in 5, 70–80% — in 6, 60–70% — in 4, 50–60% — in 4, 40–50% — in 3, 15–30% — in 2, 5–15% in einem, bis zu 5% in 2. Somit sind 40% der 45 Dörfer ethnisch einheitlich, und in 42% der Dörfer überwiegt die litauische Bevölkerung. Nur in 18% der Dörfer leben überwiegend Polen. Dennoch wird das Ethnoprofil dieser Region entscheidend durch drei Städte — Puńsk, Sejny und Suwałki — geprägt. 80% der Einwohner von Puńsk (ca. 1000 Einwohner) sind Litauer (*Aušra* 1992/15, 12; 1992/17, 16); in Sejny dagegen stellen die Litauer etwa 20% der Gesamtbevölkerung (ca. 5000 Einwohner) (*Aušra* 1990/1, 13; Garšva 1989, 34). Auf die Kritik, daß diese Zahlen zu niedrig seien (*Aušra* 1990/3, 32; 1990/5, 12), muß geantwortet werden, daß die genaue Zahl der litauischen Einwohner in Suwałki (ca. 60 000 Einwohner) schwer feststellbar ist. Ihre Zahl kann lediglich grob auf einige Prozent der Gesamtbevölkerung geschätzt werden. Einige ältere Litauischsprecher leben in der Gegend von Szypliszki und Wiżajny. Einige Litauer wohnen überdies in Dörfern, die an das Gebiet (a) grenzen, wo sie eine Minderheit in ansonsten überwiegend polnischen Dörfern darstellen (Zdancewicz 1963, 232). Zusammenfassend kann die betrachtete Region aus ethnolinguistischer Sicht in zwei Gebietstypen eingeteilt werden: (α) das geschlossene Gebiet (a) mit Puńsk als Zentrum, in dem das Litauische in Mundartform innerhalb der ethnischen Gruppe gebraucht wird, (β) Dörfer in der Nachbarschaft zum Gebiet (a), wo das Litauische nur zu Hause oder gar nicht gebraucht wird.

Im Gebiet mit polnisch-litauischem Sprachkontakt treten zwei Varietäten des Polnischen auf: die literarische Hochsprache in den Städten und die noch funktionierende nichtmasurische Mundart (*gwara niemazurząca*) in den Dörfern (Zdancewicz 1963, 232). Das litauischsprachige Gebiet kommt teilweise auch mit masurischen polnischen Mundarten (*polskie gwary mazurzące*) in Berührung (Zdancewicz 1980, 3 f). Die südlich der Linie Romaniuki–Wojczuliszki–Giełujsze ansässigen Litauer wiederum bedienen sich des Südhochlitauischen, das auch als westdzukische Mundart bezeichnet wird (*pietų aukštaičių bei vakarų dzūkų tarmė*). Die nördlich jener Linie ansässigen Litauer gebrauchen das Westhochlitauische, das auch Kauener Mundart bzw. Kapsu-Mundart genannt wird (*vakarų aukštaičių, kauniškių bei kapsų tarmė*). Die dzukische Mundart läßt sich ferner unterteilen in die Mundart von Sejny (*seiniškių*), die in acht Dörfern im südöstlichen Teil des Gebiets (a) gesprochen wird, und die Mundart von Puńsk (*punskiškių*), die von den meisten Litauern in jener Region gebraucht wird (Hasiuk 1978, 4 f). Die litauische Hochsprache wird hier von bestimmten gesellschaftlichen Kreisen gebraucht und hat verschiedene Funktionen.

5. Soziolinguistische Lage

Nach der Stewart'schen Einteilung (Schweizer 1977, 134 f) wird Polnisch als Standardsprache mit sämtlichen Merkmalen angesehen, das Litauische hingegen fungiert als nicht standardisierte Mundart, als lokale Sprache. Polnisch wird als offizielle Sprache, als Staatssprache verwendet und hat daher eine dominierende Stellung. Es wird von den hiesigen Polen und Litauern im öffentlichen, d. h. in Verwaltung, Büros und Behörden, sowie im politischen Leben gebraucht. Der Gebrauch von Polnisch überwiegt in Presse und Rundfunk, in Schule und Kirche sowie in Vereinen. Das Litauische hingegen fungiert als Gruppensprache, indem es nur von Angehörigen jener ethnischen Gruppe als Kommunikationsmittel gebraucht wird, und somit — im Verhältnis zum Polnischen — eine untergeordnete Stellung innehat. Das dortige Litauisch kann als Beispiel für klassische Diglossie Mundart—Hochsprache (literarische Sprache) angesehen werden. Während die Mundart zur Alltagskommunikation in der Gruppe gebraucht wird — von Bauern und Dorfbewohnern sowie einem Großteil der Stadtbewohner in Puńsk, Sejny, Suwałki —, erfüllt die Hochsprache kommunikative Funktionen in der Bildung (als Unterrichts- und Schriftsprache), dem gesellschaftspolitischen, literarisch-kulturellen und religiösen Leben und genießt damit höheres Ansehen. Sie wird auch häufiger in gebildeten, gesellschaftlich höher eingestuften Kreisen gebraucht — unter Lehrern, Journalisten, Beamten, Wissenschaftlern. Nicht immer wird die interne litauische Diglossie Mundart—Hochsprache mit dem Bilingualismus der Litauer verbunden. Besonders die ältere Generation in den Dörfern, die das Litauische nicht in der Schule gelernt hat, kann die Hochsprache nicht und ist nur der Mundart mächtig. Im Verhältnis zum Polnischen aber herrscht in dem für uns interessanten Gebiet der klassische Bilingualismus in Gestalt von *bilinguisme de promotion* vor. Durch Schulbildung und alltägliche Kontakte verfügen alle Litauer über eine mehr oder weniger große Kompetenz in Polnisch. Die Polen dagegen sind meistens monolingual. Außerdem kann in den in der litauischen Gesellschaft höher eingestuften Kreisen klassische Triglossie und Trilingualismus (Polnische—litauische Hochsprache—litauische Mundart) beobachtet werden.

Im Gebiet (a), wo das litauische Element überwiegt, spielt ein psychologischer Faktor, die sog. gesellschaftliche Kontrolle, in der Aufrechterhaltung der sprachlichen Stabilität eine bedeutende Rolle. Dieses Phänomen tritt auf dem Land auf, wo die Sprache in der Familie gemäß der Meinung der nächsten Umgebung (Nachbarn, Dorfbewohner) gewählt wird (Karaliūnas 1988, 10). Diese Kontrolle ist in den Nachbardörfern, wo das polnische Element überwiegt, und in den Städten (ausschließlich von Puńsk) weniger stark ausgeprägt. Oft wächst die einer bilingualen Generation folgende monolingual polnisch auf. Diese Entwicklung wird durch das unter den Polen verbreitete Stereotyp, das Litauische sei minderwertig oder lächerlich, gefördert. Werden bei Szypliszki die Litauer ironisch *klausiuki* (lit. klausyti — hören) und bei Sejny *saki-pasaki* (lit. sakyti — sprechen) genannt, und ein litauisches Mädchen wird pejorativ als *miergajka* (lit. mergaitė — Mädchen) bezeichnet. Die polnischen Wörter *Litwin* (Litauer) und *Litwinka* (Litauerin) besitzen sehr oft eine negative Konnotation. Die Animositäten kommen jedoch auch durch das Litauische *mozūrai* (Masuren) zum Ausdruck. Dennoch ist häufig zu beobachten, daß sich die Litauer im Ergebnis im erwähnten Übergangsgebiet und in den Städten ihrer Muttersprache schämen und sie verleugnen. Die Einsprachigkeit im Polnischen wird eindeutig auch durch Mischehen gefördert. In den Städten lassen sich Fälle von Intoleranz und Sprachkonflikten beobachten (*Aušra* 1991/11, 16; Sław 1959, 165 f).

6. Sprachpolitische Lage

Seit 1956 gibt es in der Region Suwałki ein Netz von litauischsprachigen Grundschulen und eine Oberschule (Żołędowski 1990, 218 f). Davon gebrauchen 5 Grundschulen und eine Oberschule das Litauische als Unterrichtssprache für fast alle Lehrfächer und in 7 polnischsprachigen Grundschulen wird nur als Lehrfach gelernt. Weiterhin ist ein litauischer Kindergarten vorhanden. 1990 lernten insgesamt 836 Schüler Litauisch.

Am 9. Dezember 1992 wurden die folgenden litauischen Forderungen vom Ausschuß des Sejms für Minderheitenfragen befürwortet: (1) Publikation von Schulbüchern für Litauisch und Geschichte, (2) Einrichtung neuer Schulen in Widugiery und Sejny, (3) Erstellen zweisprachiger Schulzeugnisse, (4) Genehmigung zweisprachiger Schulsiegel und -tafeln mit dem Namen der Schule (*Aušra* 1992/24, 30 f). Obwohl das als Zeichen für eine sich anbahnende Verbesserung in der Sprachpolitik angesehen werden kann, wurden weitere Forderungen der litauischen Minderheit nicht erfüllt, z. B. Vertretung in der lokalen Verwaltung in Sejny und in der Woiwodschaftsverwaltung in Suwałki, Anerkennung des Litauischen als zweite Amtssprache in den Gemeinden Sejny und Puńsk, Anbringen von zweisprachigen Orts- und Straßennamenschildern sowie Wegweisern in drei Gemeinden (cf. 1.), uneingeschränktes Recht auf die litauische Schreibweise von Namen und Vornamen (*Lituanica* 1991, 28).

Außer Schulbibliotheken verfügen auch einige öffentliche Büchereien über litauische Bücher in diesem Gebiet (*Aušra* 1976/4, 1). Das Haus der Litauischen Kultur in Puńsk ist die einzige öffentliche Einrichtung, die die vielseitigen Interessen der Litauer wahrnimmt. Daraus resultieren Forderungen der litauischen Bevölkerung, eine ähnliche Institution in Sejny ins Leben zu rufen (*Lituanica* 1991, 27 f). Neben *Aušra*, einer in Puńsk herausgegebenen kulturellen Zweiwochenzeitschrift, und einer sonntags ausgestrahlten, halbstündigen Rundfunksendung aus Białystok werden seit kurzem 26 Minuten lange Informationssendungen über Kurzwelle aus Warschau gesendet.

Nach fast vierzigjährigem Konflikt zwischen Gläubigen und konservativer Kirchenhierarchie um litauischsprachige Gottesdienste in Sejny, Smolany Żegary und sogar in Puńsk, haben die Litauer seit Anfang der achtziger Jahre uneingeschränkten Zugang zu Messen in ihrer Muttersprache. Vorher wurden trotz der Proteste der Litauer die Gottesdienste lange Zeit nur in Polnisch abgehalten. Vor kurzem entstand jedoch ein neuer Konflikt zwischen Gläubigen und Kirchenhierarchie um eine neue Pfarrkirche in Widugiery, der die Aufteilung der litauischen Gläubigen in den bisherigen Pfarrgemeinden Puńsk und Sejny betrifft (*Aušra* 1992/15, 5 f).

7. Allgemeines kontaktlinguistisches Porträt

Von den ca. 1700 slawischen Entlehnungen (auch aus dem Weißrussischen und Russischen) in der litauischen Mundart aus der Gegend von Puńsk bezeichnen die meisten Gegenstände im Haushalt und Bauernhof, Maschinen sowie Werkzeuge für Landwirtschaft und Handwerk, Futterpflanzen, Obstbäume, Gemüse und Tiere (Smoczyński 1984, 181 f). Weiterhin gibt es zahlreiche Entlehnungen in dem Teil des Wortschatzes, der mit Politik und Gesellschaft, mit Kirche und Religion, mit Wehrdienst, Verwaltung und städtischen Einrichtungen zusammenhängt. Bei den Verben lassen sich zwei Gruppen unterscheiden: (a) Bezeichnungen für psychische Zustände, z. B. *cakãvycis* 'ciekawić się' (neugierig sein), (b) Bezeichnungen für negativ gewertete Tätigkeiten, z. B. *krýbdzyc* 'krzywdzić' (Unrecht tun). Auch die meisten Adjektive bezeichnen negative Eigenschaften, z. B. *bridkùs* 'brzydki' (häßlich). Ebenso wurde ein großer Teil von hier obszön verwendeten Ausdrücken entlehnt. Die ältesten polnischen Entlehnungen sind mit christlicher Terminologie verbunden (seit dem 15. Jahrhundert), z. B. *apãštalas* 'apostoł' (Apostel), *gramnýčia* 'gromnica' (Weihkerze), u. a. (Zinkevičius 1989, 10). Manche Entlehnungen lassen sich mit der Abfolge der Siedlungswellen seit dem 16. Jahrhundert und mit dem dadurch verursachten Einfluß neuer kultureller Elemente (geistiger oder materieller Art) sowohl zeitlich als auch kausal erklären. Heute werden die meisten Polonismen aus Presse, Rundfunk, Fernsehen, Wissenschaft und Technik entlehnt.

In Entlehnungen lassen sich neue Phoneme feststellen. Im Vokalismus: (1 a) ein kurzes $|o|$ statt des einheimischen langen $|\bar{o}|$, z. B. *apònas* 'opona' (Autoreifen); (1 b) $|\varepsilon|$ nach harten Konsonanten, z. B. *tèčkè* 'teczka' (Mappe), auch im einheimischen Wortschatz nach entpalatalisierten Konsonanten, z. B. *lẽkc* 'lėkti' (fliegen) (Buch 1966, 33 f); (1 c) Varianten $|y|$ und $|\bar{y}|$ nach harten Konsonanten, z. B. *týpas* 'typ' (Typ), *pūstýnia* 'pustynia' (Wüste) (Hasiuk 1978, 9). Im Konsonantismus: (2 a) neue Verbindungen vom Typus $|c\ \mathfrak{z}\ \check{c}\ \mathfrak{\check{z}}\ s\ z\ \check{s}\ \check{z}\ r| + |\varepsilon|$ und $|l'| + |\varepsilon|, |j| + |\varepsilon|$, z. B. *procèsija* 'procesja' (Prozession), *čèkas* 'czek' (Scheck), *sèzonas* 'sezon' (Saison), *džèmas* 'dżem' (Jam); (2 b) Phoneme $|\check{c}\ \mathfrak{\check{z}}|$ stabilisieren sich vor einem Vokal, z. B. *čėsas* 'czas' (Zeit); (2 c) Phoneme $|z\ z'|$ stabilisieren sich vor einem stimmhaften Verschlußlaut, z. B. *ròzvodas* 'rozwód' (Scheidung), *lazeñkè* 'łazienka' (Badezimmer); (2 d) neue Phoneme $|f\ f'|$ und $|x\ x'|$ stabilisieren sich im Lautsystem, z. B: *fáinu* 'fajnie' (prima), *chlodnicà* 'chłodnica' (Kühlvorrichtung); (2 e) neue Konsonantengruppen stabilisieren sich im Anlaut, Inlaut und Auslaut: $|s| + T(R), |s|$ $\check{s}|\check{z}| + R, T + R$ (T – Verschlußlaut, R – Sonorlaut), die um Verbindungen mit *š*- und *z*- im Anlaut für den ersten und zweiten Typus sowie um Verbindungen mit *dm*-, *km*-, *gm*-, und *čv*- für den dritten Typus erweitert werden, z. B. *štakiẽtas* 'sztacheta' (Zaunlatte), *zdrodà* 'zdrada' (Verrat), *šrataĩ* 'śróty'

(Schrot), *znōkas* 'znak' (Zeichen), *dmukavà* 'dmuchawa' (Gebläse), *gmìnas* 'gmina' (Gemeinde), u. a. (Smoczyński 1984, 182 f). Man kann feststellen, daß die meisten beschriebenen phonetischen polnischen Entlehnungen schon seit langem in der dzukischen Mundart existieren. Jedoch sind manche Phänomene, wie z. B. die Entpalatalisierungserscheinung der Konsonanten vor den Vokalen |ε|, |y| bedeutend älter als die Entlehnung der neuen Phoneme |f f'| und |x x'|. Letzteres ist erst im letzten Jahrhundert eingetreten. So sprechen Angehörige der älteren Generation die Phoneme noch heute nicht aus.

Slawische Entlehnungen bekommen in der dzukischen Mundart die Flexionsendungen *-as*, *-a*, *-us* und werden in den ersten, zweiten und vierten Deklinationstyp einbezogen, z. B. *kvíetkas* 'kwiat' (Blume), *šobilià* 'szabla' (Säbel), *kavalíerius* 'kawaler' (Junggeselle). An die aus dem Polnischen entlehnten Verben wird das Suffix *-avoti* pol. *-ować* angehängt, z. B. *papìlniavoc* 'popilnować' (aufpassen). Das Präfix *da-* pol. *do-* ist in Verben weit verbreitet, z. B. *davažúoc* 'dojechać' (ans Ziel kommen). Diese Entlehnungen kann man als die am frühesten übernommenen betrachten. Eine Tendenz zur Verschiebung der Reflexivpartikel *-si-* pol. *się* von der Wortmitte ans Wortende läßt sich in letzter Zeit in der jüngeren Generation beobachten, z. B. lit. *nesijuõkia* → *nejuõkiasi* 'nie śmieje się' (er/sie lacht nicht). Der polnische Einfluß ist auch im Bereich der Syntax zu beobachten, z. B. *añ svecimõs dúonos iř peľẽ móka šeiminykáuc* 'na obcym chlebie i mysz umie gospodarzyć' (Sprichwort) (Jancza 1984, 114). Bei der Datumsangabe ist eine polnische Konstruktion üblich, z. B. lit. *saũsio pìrmą* → *pìrmo saũsio* 'pierwszego stycznia' (am ersten Januar). In der Syntax der dzukischen Mundart ist die Interferenz der polnischen Satzkonstruktionen ein wichtiger, gründliche Untersuchungen fordernder Prozeß, der seit Jahrhunderten bis heute andauert.

Schon seit dem 16. Jahrhundert wurden Entlehnungen aus dem Litauischen ins Polnische der Region Suwałki durch zahlreiche Besiedlungskontakte gefördert. Es scheint jedoch, daß der Einfluß des neuen litauischen Wortschatzes nach der Wiedergründung des polnischen Staates (1918) wesentlich geringer wurde. In der nichtmasurischen Mundart aus der Umgebung von Sejny lassen sich etwa 200 Entlehnungen aus dem Litauischen feststellen (Zdancewicz 1963, 237 ff; 1964, 231 ff). Sie beschränken sich zum einen auf spezifische Lebensbereiche, die von der literarischen Sprache kaum beeinflußt werden (Gołąbek 1990, 129 ff), und zum anderen auf expressive Euphemismen sowie Onomatopoetika. Ferner werden Eigennamen und Ortsnamen in großem Maße vom Litauischen beeinflußt. Seit den ersten polnisch–litauischen Sprachkontakten läßt sich auch eine Tendenz zur Slawisierung, hauptsächlich in der Wortbildung, feststellen. Litauische Suffixe wie z. B. *-utis*, *-anis* (*-onis*), *-inis*, *-ovis* (*-ovys*) werden durch slawische Suffixe *-uć*, *-aniec*, *-iniec*, *-uniec*, *-on'ec* ersetzt (Falk 1963, 87 ff; 1966, 3 ff; Otrębski 1963, 267 ff; Trypućko 1982, 17 f). Z. B. *Tripùtis* 'Trypućko', *Mazgùtis* 'Mozguć', *Eglìnė* 'Jegliniec', *Babõnys* 'Babańce', *Kreivìnis* 'Krejwiniec', *Butrimõnys* 'Butrymowce', *Sapackõnys* 'Sopoćkowce'. Heute hat dieser Prozeß jedoch keine große Bedeutung mehr.

Infolge der phonetischen Interferenz können in der polnischen nichtmasurischen Mundart folgende Änderungen beobachtet werden:
(1) Verschwinden von *h* im Anlaut, z. B. *andlować* 'handlować' (handeln), (2) palatalisierte Aussprache von *t'*, z. B. *putia* 'kura' (Henne), (3) diphthongierte oder labiale Aussprache von *o*, z. B. *duobra krŏwa* 'dobra krowa' (gute Kuh), (4) ein schwächer als in der Standardsprache vibriertes *r*, (5) Tendenz zur asynchronischen Palatalisierung von *p*, *b*, *f*, *v* vor Vokalen der hinteren Reihe, (6) labiodentales *l* statt des nichtsilbischen *u̯*, z. B. *łafka* ← *u̯afka* 'ławka' (Bank), (7) Aussprache von *ŋ* als Hinterzungenlaut vor *k*, *g*, z. B. *łoŋka* 'łąka' (Wiese), (8) Meiden von Doppelkonsonanten, z. B. *pana ana* 'panna Anna' (Fräulein Anna), (9) uneinheitliche, verlängerte Aussprache von betonten Vokalen, z. B. *bȳli* (sie waren), *bāba* (altes Weib) (Turska 1982, 89 ff; Glinka 1990, 125 f). Nur (6), (7), und (9) sind in der Sprache als Regionalzeichen übernommen worden, die übrigen sind heute bereits mit der Mundart im Verschwinden begriffen.

Im morphosyntaktischen Bereich haben sich polnische Mundarten des den litauischen Mundarten benachbarten Gebietes diminutive Suffixe mit der patronymischen Funktion *-uć*, *-uk* und *-un* (das letztere mit pejorativer Bedeutung) von litauischen Suffixen *-utis*, *-ukas*, *-ūnas* angeeignet, z. B.: *Korsakuć* 'syn Korsaka' (Sohn von Korsak), *Antuk* 'Antoni' (Anton), *kłyszun* 'mający krzywe nogi' lit. *klìšas* (jemand mit krummen Beinen). In der Syntax kommen litauische Satzkonstruktionen mit dem Participium praeteriti activi in unterschiedlichen Funktionen vor, z. B. *A gdzie ona poszetszy?* 'A gdzie ona poszła?' (Wo ist sie denn hin?), Satzkonstruktionen mit dem Agens im Genetivus und ohne Präposition, z. B. *I chfalił sie, ze nie pocienta myszof* 'I chwalił się, że nie pocieta przez myszy' (Und er war stolz darauf, daß sie von Mäusen nicht durchgeknabbert ist) (Zdancewicz 1964, 233 f). Es ist schwer zu bestimmen, zu welchem Zeitpunkt die genannten Erscheinungen erstmals aufgetreten sind, aber die syntaktische Interferenz scheint heute im Sprachkontakt aktuell zu sein.

8. Kritische Wertung der verwendeten Quellen und Literatur

Für die Erforschung der Geschichte der Region Suwałki ist das 1941 von K. O. Falk herausgegebene toponomastische Studium mit Nachbildungen der Quellen aus dem 16. Jahrhundert grundlegend (Wiśniewski 1963, 18 f). Die sogenannte schwedische Schule der Toponomastik legte den Grundstein für unzählige Arbeiten in der Onomastik, wobei besonders die von Falk, Buch, Nalepa, Otrębski, Zdancewicz und Kontratiuk zu nennen wären. Die Erforschung der Besiedlung des Gebietes nach dem Aussterben des Stammes der Jatvinger wurde von Wiśniewski betrieben. Die Studien von Zdancewicz leisten einen bedeutenden Beitrag zur Erforschung polnischer, weißrussischer und litauischer Mundarten; die von Buch, Hasiuk und Smoczyński zur Erforschung der litauischen Mundarten. Es muß mit Bedauern festgestellt werden, daß nur die Abhandlungen von Zdancewicz (1963; 1964) und von Smoczyński (1984) polnisch–litauische Sprachkontakte behandeln und auch da fast ausschließlich lexikalische Entlehnungen.

Obgleich die Quellen für die Genese der polnisch–litauischen Sprachkontakte als zufriedenstellend betrachtet werden können, so kann dies nicht für eine interlinguale Charakteristik im Bereich der Phonetik, Morphosyntax, Ethnolinguistik und Soziolinguistik der Kontaktsprachen behauptet werden. Bei der Darstellung der sprachlichen Interferenz wurde zum Teil auf die Arbeiten von Hasiuk (1970; 1980), Turska (1964; 1982), Glinka (1990) und Gołąbek (1990) zurückgegriffen. Ein großes Hindernis stellt das Nichtvorhandensein von Studien über die Kapsu-Mundart – Umgebung von Wiżajny sowie nichtmasurische polnische Mundarten dar.

Für die vorliegende Abhandlung wurde u. a. auf Arbeiten litauischer Forscher – u. a. Zinkevičius (1987; 1989) und Garšva (1989), und des deutschen Wissenschaftlers Prinz (1968) zurückgegriffen. Erwähnenswert ist auch die in Uppsala herausgegebene namenkundliche Abhandlung von Trypućko (1982). Die verwendeten Quellen zur Erforschung von demographischen, ethno- und soziolinguistischen Fragen und des Ethnoprofils müssen leider als unzulänglich betrachtet werden. Die einzige Ausnahme bildet die *Aušra*, in der viele aktuelle Berichte sowie Beiträge zur Erforschung der polnisch–litauischen Beziehungen zu finden sind.

9. Bibliographie (in Auswahl)

Aleksaitė, Irena/Razmukaitė, Marytė (1989): „Suvalkų vaivadijos lietuvių gyvenamų namų vardai" [Die Ortsnamen der von Litauern bewohnten Dörfer in der Woiwodschaft Suwałki]. In: *Kalbos kultūra 55*, 79–81.

Aušra (1960–1993): Lenkijos lietuvių leidinys [Litauische gesellschaftlich-kulturelle Zeitschrift], Sejny–Puńsk.

Buch, Tamara (1966): „Mundartliche Entpalatalisierungserscheinungen im Litauischen". In: *Acta Baltico-Slavica 3*, 33–36.

Falk, Knut O. (1941): *Wody wigierskie i huciańskie. Studium toponomastyczne* [Gewässer in der Gegend von Wigry und Huta. Toponomastische Studien], Uppsala.

Falk, Knut O. (1963): „Ze studiów nad slawizacją litewskich nazw miejscowych i osobowych. O wtórnej funkcji sufiksu -ec; o nazwach miejscowych na -ańce" [Aus den Studien zur Slawisierung litauischer Orts- und Personennamen. Über die sekundäre Funktion des Suffix -ec; über Ortsnamen mit Endung auf -ańce]. In: *Scando-Slavica 9*, 87–103.

Falk, Knut O. (1966): „O metodach slawizacji litewskich nazw osobowych i miejscowych. O genezie i rozpowszchnieniu nazw na -ańce" [Über Slawisierungsmethoden litauischer Personen- und Ortsnamen. Über Entstehung und Verbreitung der Ortsnamen mit Endung auf -ańce]. In: *Språkliga Bidrag 5/22*, 1–16.

Garšva, Kazimieras (1989): „Kalbinės situacijos raida pakraščių šnektose" [Die Entwicklung der Sprachsituation in den Peripheriemundarten]. In: *Lietuvių kalbotyros klausimai 28* (Kalbų ryšiai ir sąveikos), 12–38.

Garšva, Kazimieras/Stoskeliūnaitė, Birutė/Vaina, Juozas (1991): „Punsko šnektos skirtumų žodynas" [Das Wörterbuch der Besonderheiten der Mundart von Puńsk]. In: *Lietuvių kalbotyros klausimai 29*, 32–46.

Glinka, Stanisław (1990): „Lituanizmy fonetyczne w gwarach białoruskich i polskich Białostocczyzny" [Phonetische Lituanismen in den weißrussischen und polnischen Mundarten der Region Białystok]. In: *Prace Slawistyczne 81*, 117−127.

Gołąbek, Anna (1990): „Wpływy litewskie na polszczyznę okolic Puńska w zakresie nazw żywności" [Litauische Einflüsse auf das Polnische in der Gegend von Puńsk im Bereich der Lebensmittelnamen]. In: *Prace Slawistyczne 81*, 129−140.

Hasiuk, Michał (1970): „Die Ferndissimilation des k, g, in den litauischen Dialekten" In: *Donum Balticum*, Rūķe-Draviņa, V. (Ed.), Stockholm, 178−180.

Hasiuk, Michał (1978): *Fonologia litewskiej gwary sejneńskiej* [Phonologie der litauischen Mundart von Sejny], Posen.

Hasiuk, Michał (1980): „Depalatalization of consonants in the Lithuanian dialect of Sejny". In: *Lingua Posnaniensis 23*, 99−103.

Jancza, Maria (1984): „Wpływy słowiańskie w języku tekstów folklorystycznych ze wsi litewskich województwa suwalskiego" [Slawische Einflüsse in der Sprache der Heimatdichtung der litauischen Dörfer in der Woiwodschaft Suwałki]. In: *Studia nad gwarami Białostocczyzny*, Smułkowa, E./Martyniakowa, I. (Eds.), Warschau, 113−122.

Kamiński, Aleksander (1953): *Jaćwież. Terytorium, ludność, stosunki gospodarcze i społeczne* [Sudawien. Territorium, Bevölkerung, wirtschaftliche und gesellschaftliche Beziehungen], Łódź.

Karaliūnas, Simas (1988): „Bilingvizmo situacijos ir jų socialinė dinamika" [Bilinguale Situationen und ihre Sozialdynamik]. In: *Lietuvių kalbotyros klausimai 27*, 4−20.

Lituanica (1991): Pismo litewskiej społeczności w Polsce [Zeitschrift der litauischen Gesellschaft in Polen], Puńsk−Warszawa, I.

Makowski, Bronisław (1984): „Lituanistyczna sesja naukowa w Puńsku" [Lituanistische wissenschaftliche Konferenz in Puńsk]. In: *Acta Baltico-Slavica 16*, 329−331.

Otrębski, Jan (1963): „Slawizacja litewskich nazw wodnych i miejscowych" [Die Slawisierung litauischer Gewässer- und Ortsnamen]. In: *Z polskich studiów slawistycznych, Seria 2 Językoznawstwo* (*Prace na V. Międzynarodowy Kongres Slawistów w Sofii 1963*), Warschau, 267−286.

Prinz, Jürgen (1968): *Die Slavisierung baltischer und die Baltisierung slavischer Ortsnamen im Gebiet des ehemaligen Gouvernements Suwałki − Versuch der Entwicklung einer Theorie der Umsetzung von Ortsnamen am praktischen Beispiel*, Wiesbaden.

Roch, Jerzy (1991): „Pogoni półpoganie" [Die Halbheiden]. In: *Po prostu 4/50*, 18−20.

Schweizer, Aleksandr D. (1977): *Sovremennaja sociolingvistika* [Die zeitgenössische Soziolinguistik], Moskau.

Sław, Aleksander (1959): „Litwini w Sejnach. Przyczynek do problemu mniejszości narodowych w Polsce" [Die Litauer in Sejny. Beitrag zur Frage der Minderheiten in Polen]. In: *Nowe Drogi 1/115*, 163−172.

Smoczyński, Wojciech (1981): „Z badań nad gwarą litewską okolic Puńska. System samogłosek" [Aus den Untersuchungen zur litauischen Mundart von Puńsk. Das Vokalsystem]. In: *Rocznik Białostocki 14*, 349−371.

Smoczyński, Wojciech (1984): „Zapożyczenia słowiańskie w litewskiej gwarze puńskiej" [Die slawischen Entlehnungen in der litauischen Mundart von Puńsk]. In: *Studia nad gwarami Białostocczyzny*, Smułkowa, E./Martyniakowa, I. (Eds.), Warschau, 176−222.

Trypućko, Józef (1982): *O pewnym wypadku litewsko−polskiej interferencji językowej w zakresie onomastyki (lit. przyrostek -utis, pol. -uć)* [Über einen Fall litauisch−polnischer Sprachinterferenz im Bereich der Namenskunde (lit. Suffix -utis, pol. -uć)], Uppsala.

Turska, Halina (1964): „Wpływ substratu litewskiego na fleksję gwary polskiej" [Der Einfluß des litauischen Substrates auf die Flexion der polnischen Mundart]. In: *Sprawozdania z prac naukowych Wydziału Nauk Społecznych PAN 7/3 34*, Breslau, 22−28.

Turska, Halina (1982): „O powstaniu polskich obszarów językowych na Wileńszczyźnie" [Über die Entstehung polnischer Sprachgebiete im Wilnagebiet). In: *Studia nad polszczyzną kresową*, Rieger, J./Werenicz, W. (Eds.), Breslau, 19−121.

Uździło, Algiment (1987): „Działalność artystyczna zespołów pieśni i tańca oraz żywego słowa" [Die Kunsttätigkeit der Gesang- und Tanzvereine sowie lebende Worte]. In: *Kultura wsi puńskiej, Materiały konferencyjne*, Przychodzeń, Z. J. (Ed.), Warschau, 73−85.

Westfal, Stanisław (1946): „Lexical Elements of Baltic Origin in the Polish Dialect spoken near Lake Wigry Suwałki district, Poland". In: *The Slavonic and East European Review 24/63*, 156−159.

Wiśniewski, Jerzy (1963): „Dzieje osadnictwa w powiecie sejneńskim od XV do XIX wieku" [Die Besiedlungsgeschichte des Kreises Sejny vom 15. bis zum 19. Jahrhundert]. In: *Materiały do dziejów ziemi sejneńskiej*, Antoniewicz, J. (Ed.), Białystok, 9−222.

Wiśniewski, Jerzy (1965): „Dzieje osadnictwa w powiecie suwalskim od XV do połowy XVII wieku" [Die Besiedlungsgeschichte des Kreises Suwałki vom 15. bis zur Hälfte des 17. Jahrhunderts]. In: *Studia i materiały do dziejów Suwalszczyzny*, Antoniewicz, J. (Ed.), Białystok, 51−138.

Zdancewicz, Tadeusz (1963): „Gwary powiatu sejneńskiego na tle procesów osadniczych" [Mundarten des Kreises Sejny auf dem Hintergrund der Besiedlungsprozesse]. In: *Materiały do dziejów ziemi sejneńskiej*, Antoniewicz, J. (Ed.), Białystok, 231−266.

Zdancewicz, Tadeusz (1964): „Wpływy litewskie i wschodniosłowiańskie w polskich gwarach pod Sejnami" [Litauische und ostslawische Einflüsse in den polnischen Mundarten von Sejny]. In: *Acta Baltico-Slavica 1*, 227–246.

Zdancewicz, Tadeusz (1980): *Mazurzące gwary suwalskie* [Die masurischen Mundarten der Region Suwałki], Warschau/Posen.

Zinkevičius, Zigmas (1987): „Kitų baltų genčių įsiliejimas į lietuvių tautybę. Substrato reikšmė lietuvių tarmių formavimuisi" [Die Fusion der anderen baltischen Stämme zur litauischen Nation. Die Bedeutung des Substrats für die Entstehung der litauischen Mundarten]. In: *Lietuvių etnogenezė*, Volkaitė-Kulikauskienė, R. (Ed.), Vilnius, 212–236.

Zinkevičius, Zigmas (1989): „Seniausi lietuvių kalbiniai kontaktai su slavais" [Die ältesten Sprachkontakte der Litauer mit den Slawen]. In: *Lietuvių kalbotyros klausimai 28*, 4–11.

Żołędowski, Cezary (1990): „Szkolnictwo litewskie w Polsce" [Das litauische Schulwesen in Polen]. In: *Acta Baltico-Slavica 19*, 217–244.

Józef Marcinkiewicz, Posen (Polen)

197. Polish–Ukrainian

1. Geography and demography
2. History
3. Politics, economy and general cultural and religious situation
4. Statistics and ethnoprofiles
5. Sociolinguistic situation
6. Language political situation
7. General contactlinguistic portrait
8. Evaluation of the sources and literature
9. Bibliography (selected)

A synchronic analysis of language contacts between Polish and Ukrainian in the region of today's Poland concerns the language of the Ukrainian-speaking minority as well as the Polish dialects in the borderland with Ukraine. "Ukrainian" means either standard Ukrainian or Ukrainian dialect. "Rusyns" (= Ruthenians) is a former designation of Byelorussians and Ukrainians; nowadays it indicates a separate Ukrainian dialect with speakers living in the Carpathian mountains in Poland, Slovakia and Ukraine. The term "Lemkos" is used in Poland only.

1. Geography and demography

Up to 1945, Ukrainian dialects spread out along the contemporary eastern Polish border from the South up to Hajnówka and along the southern border up to the Poprad valley (with 3 villages further in the West). In the northern part of this territory, south of Hajnówka, there is an area of transitional Ukrainian–Byelorussian dialects; the southern belt is the region of Lemkos (Rusyns). There are only a few compact Ukrainian speaking areas and many mixed Polish–Ukrainian territories. Already before 1939 many Ukrainian-speaking villages along the Bug river were switching from the Ukrainian dialect to Polish, especially in the western part of the territory. In 1945, "Ukrainians and Rusyns" (483 000 persons) were repatriated to Ukraine. In 1947, the remainder of the Ukrainian-speaking population (about 150 000 persons) were resettled into new Polish territories in the north and west (Pudło 1992). Only in North Podlasie, people who were considered Byelorussians were not displaced. The deserted territories (except the infertile mountain grounds) were settled by Poles.

After 1956, a limited number of authorizations to return were issued – according to Pudło (1992) for 6000 families – to restricted areas only, mainly in the western Lemko region. According to Truchan (1990) about 20 000 people returned to Lublin province. In the 1980's, and especially after 1989 when all restrictions were lifted, only a few rather old people decided to return; the younger generation preferred to stay in their new settlements (Language Map I).

2. History

2.1. The territories near Przemyśl ("Przemyśl Gate") were settled by Poles and Ukrainians as early as in the 11th–14th c. Many changes of population were caused by Tartar and later by Cossack wars. The area on the Bug river was settled by Rusyns (Ukrainians) from the East and by Poles from the West (Czopek 1988, Nalepa 1991, Rieger 1977 and 1989). Generally up to the 20th c. the belt immediately along the Bug was Ukrainian with some Polish (Polonized) small cities and villages. Further west along this belt, the population was of a mixed character.

Ukrainians on the Bug river were Greek Catholics up to the partition of Poland (1795). In the territories acquired by Russia at that time (north of Hrubieszów) the Greek Catholic Church was eventually (in 1875) suppressed and the population was forced to convert to Orthodoxy. Only in 1905 were the descendants of Greek Catholics permitted to become Roman Catholics. Also in Galicia (after 1772, a part of the Austrian Empire), the Orthodox Church was spreading at the expense of Greek Catholicism, especially in 1918–1939 and after 1947. In 1947 the Greek Catholic Church was banned. Since 1956, Greek Catholic priests have semilegally celebrated services in Roman Catholic churches (Saładiak 1993). In 1989 the organisation and hierarchy of the Greek Catholic Church was restored. The minority of Ukrainian (and Lemkos) are Orthodox; after 1945 they could exercise their religion freely, though they were limited by the lack of a sufficient number of parishes and priests.

The introduction of Roman Catholicism into the Polish Ukrainian territories in 1905 strengthened Polonization tendencies along the Bug river since Roman Catholicism had been traditionally linked with Polish people and culture in the area. Nevertheless mutual Ukrainian–Polish language interferences date back to the 19th c. (Kość 1995) and earlier.

2.2. The first Ukrainian–Polish contacts had a rather local character. Not until the 16th–18th centuries did Ukrainian borrowings become numerous in Polish and no longer regionally restricted. Ukrainian also served as intermediary for the introduction of orientalisms into Polish, mostly from Turkish. The number of Ukrainian loans in Polish continued to grow in the 17th century. Polish romanticism (first half of the 19th century) introduced into the Polish standard new Ukrainian elements due to the influence of the poet Słowacki and the so-called "Ukrainian school" in Polish literature. In the 20th century until 1939, Polish was influenced by Ukrainian through Polish Lvov and writers born in the eastern Polish territories.

The strong influence of Polish on Ukrainian derives from the role of Polish as the state language and its status as the language of the upper and middle classes. Ukrainians studied at Polish universities. Many Ukrainian writers also wrote in Polish (Galatowski, Mohyła, Orlik, Smotrycki). Theological controversies between Orthodoxy and the Greek Catholic Church were debated not only in Church Slavonic, but also in Polish. The lexicon of Church Slavonic (= standard language of Ukrainian literature up to the 18th c.) and of *prosta mova* was largely Polish. Contemporary standard Ukrainian was shaped in the 19th c. under the considerable influence of writers connected with the Polish culture in Austrian Galicia (e. g. Ivan Franko, Vasyl Stefanyk, Ivan Wagilewicz-Wahylevych) and in the Russian part of Ukraine (Lesja Ukrainka, Mykhajlo Kocjubynśkyj). After 1918, Ukrainian was influenced by Polish within the Polish state. In the Soviet Ukraine of the 1920's, there were attempts to unify Kiev (Eastern) and Lvov (Western, "Polish") varieties of Ukrainian in one standard (esp. in vocabulary), but in the 1930's these attempts were replaced by a policy of Russification and by a campaign against "Gallicisms" similar to that against Polonisms (this campaign actually continued through the 1970's).

3. Politics, economy and general cultural and religious situation

After 1945 up to 1989, Ukrainians were deprived of any political representation in Poland. In 1989 they started with one member of parliament. The establishment of an independent Ukrainian state (1991) boosted the national activity of Ukrainians (cf. 4. and 6.). From the economic point of view, Ukrainians are in the same situation as Poles; their status depends on their region, education, etc.

Poles are Roman Catholics. The greater part of Ukrainian and Lemkos are Greek Catholics, while the minority is Orthodox. The Greek Catholic Church is Ukrainian; the Orthodox Church in Poland has Russian, Belorussian and Ukrainian members (see 2.1. and 6.). Since 1989, none of the churches is hampered in its activities. There are controversies among Greek Catholics and the Orthodox concerning churches taken away from the Greek Catholics after 1947.

4. Statistics and ethnoprofiles

There are no credible data concerning the number of Ukrainians (including Lemkos) in

Poland. Estimates range from 150 000 to 300 000 (Czech 1991). Kubijovych (1970) considered the number 300 000 cited by the Ukrainians as exaggerated. Uncertainty concerning the number of Ukrainians in Poland derives from these facts: Nationality of an individual is usually given by his/her declaration and many people of Ukrainian origin are without clear Ukrainian national consciousness; moreover the national self-identification of the population under study has not been researched for statistical purposes thoroughly enough; the tradition of "inheriting" religion and national affiliation — sons after father, daughters after mother — was broken; in many families the everyday language is Polish and the children see themselves as Poles, though the older generation speaks a Ukrainian dialect; during the period of the abolition of the Greek Catholic church (cf. 2.1.) many Ukrainians attended and baptized their children in Roman Catholic (i. e. "Polish") churches. (Nonetheless, Greek Catholics and Orthodox in most cases can be identified as Ukrainians (Lemkos)). The number of actual speakers of Ukrainian is almost certainly lower than the number of Ukrainians (Lemkos) by declaration.

As a result of the events of 1945—1947 and of the return of some of the displaced Ukrainians to their original territories, there are Ukrainian villages (and small areas with compact Ukrainian settlements) only in the northeastern part of the territory (in some districts, Ukrainians constitute 20—30% of the entire population). There are a few villages with an either mostly or significantly Ukrainian (Lemkian)-speaking population East of Przemyśl, in the Lemko region. The greater part of Ukrainians lives nowadays dispersed in new northern and western territories of Poland with concentrations in Masuria (Olsztyn region, 50 000—60 000 persons, 6% of the population), Pomerania (Koszalin and Szczecin regions), Lower Silesia (Wrocław and Zielona Góra regions; the Lemkos live mainly in Legnica, Wołów and Lubin districts) (cf. Kubijovych 1970, Pudło 1992).

The majority of Ukrainian-speaking people declare Ukrainian nationality. People in Northern Podlasie recognize themselves either as "here living people" or as Byelorussians (→ art. 195). Lemkos identify themselves either as Lemkos-Rusyns or Ukrainians. Boikos (speakers of a Ukrainian dialect) from the southeastern corner of Poland were resettled into Soviet Ukraine in 1945; the rest who were resettled with the neighbouring Lemkos in 1947 (see 1.) see themselves either as Lemkos or Ukrainians.

5. Sociolinguistic situation

The sociolinguistic situation of Ukrainian varies according to the percentage of Ukrainians in a given vicinity. Use of Ukrainian in its dialect form is limited to family, hamlet, village, to contacts among Ukrainians. Standard Ukrainian is generally limited either to the intelligentsia (including students) or to contacts with some Greek Catholic priests. Generally, standard Ukrainian has never been used in Poland as an official (administrative) language. Only in former Galicia was it a language of priests and was it taught in schools (except in some parts of the Lemko region). Up to 1918, the official language was Russian under Russian rule, German or Polish under Austrian rule. In the years 1918—1939, the official language was Polish. In 1939—1941 under Soviet occupation, the official language was Ukrainian (with Russian).

North of Włodawa, the Ukrainian dialect is still living among the older and middle generation (more so among the Orthodox population than among Catholics). As recently as the 1970's, there were old people who spoke only the Ukrainian dialect. Nevertheless the majority of the younger generation speaks only Polish. Even in compact Ukrainian areas, Polonization is advancing. Around Chełm and further south, there are very often only a few Ukrainian families in the village and in many of them Ukrainian is spoken only by a few persons of the oldest generation (Truchan 1990, Czyżewski 1994 et al.).

In the Lemko region the Ukrainian dialect is still used quite extensively, also by the young generation, and even in the villages with a quite small Lemko population. This dialect is the principal means of intervillage communication among Lemkos. In villages along main roads, the Polish population prevails; there the means of mutual communication between Lemkos and Poles is either standard Polish or dialectal Polish (it depends on age, the younger generation preferring standard Polish). The children attend Polish schools as well as additional courses in Ukrainian, or the "Rusyn language".

Today, all Ukrainians (and Lemkos) are bilingual. The younger generation speaks Polish as Poles do. As a result of study in Polish schools, they speak better Polish than Ukrainian in many cases, and very often Polish is their first language. According to (unpublished) research by Antonina Kłoskowska, the Ukrainian intelligentsia knows Polish culture and literature better than Ukrainian culture and literature.

After 1947 Ukrainians (Lemkos) avoided speaking Ukrainian in public because they were afraid of the consequences. Since 1989, this situation has changed (in the Przemyśl bazaar there are Poles who speak Ukrainian with people from Ukraine!). In North Podlasie, the use of the East-Slavic dialect is socially stigmatized as a symptom of provinciality, and the people have been ashamed of their "simple language" (*prosta mova*) in contacts with strangers.

6. Language political situation

The situation of Ukrainian before 1939 was better than in 1945–1952: there were Ukrainian schools; the Greek Catholic Church was Ukrainian; only in the Lemko region were there controversies among "old Rusyns" and the population which affiliated with Ukrainians. There were political and cultural organisations, newspapers and journals.

According to Czech (1993), there has been organized teaching of Ukrainian after World War II only since 1952. In 1952 there were 24 Ukrainian schools and classes with 487 students, in 1960 there were 9 Ukrainian schools and 147 Polish schools with Ukrainian courses with 3091 students; in 1989 there were 2 primary and 2 secondary Ukrainian schools, 56 establishments where Ukrainian was taught with only 1432 students. In 1993 there were 4 primary and 3 secondary Ukrainian schools, 83 establishments where Ukrainian was taught and 2539 students. It is characteristic that the number of students in these schools and courses has been growing since 1993. The Lemko milieu has been less interested in learning Ukrainian. In North Podlasie there are (Polish and) Byelorussian schools. The majority of Ukrainians (Lemkos) attend Polish schools.

The Ukrainian Social and Cultural Society was authorized in 1956. There were 3000 members (in 119 circles) in 1956; in 1989 the membership had grown to 7000. After 1989 the Society was transformed into Association of Ukrainians in Poland (67 000 members in 140 circles in 1993). Many new movements also emerged: Union of Lemkos in Poland (pro-Ukrainian, 450 members in 1993), Association of Ukrainians in Podlasie (300 members in 1993), scout movement (200 members in 1993), separatist Association of Lemkos, etc. (Pudło 1992, Czech 1993).

In 1956, a weekly, *Nashe Slovo* (Our Word), was founded (since 1959, it has been published with 1 page in Lemko dialect). Since 1957, *Ukrajins'kyj kalendar'* (Ukrainian Almanach) has been published. During the 1990's, the family of Ukrainian periodicals has been increasing: the monthly *Blahovist'*, the biweekly *Peremys'ki Dzwony*, etc. *Lemkivs'kyj kalendar* (Lemko Almanach) has been published only recently.

Since 1958–1959, there are Ukrainian radio programs in Olsztyn, Koszalin, Rzeszów, Lublin, Szczecin. Along the Ukrainian border, Ukrainian TV can be received. There are 21 Ukrainian folklore ensembles, mostly at schools and teaching establishments, well known ensembles as the Zhurawli (Cranes) and Lemkovyna (Lemko Land) among them. Each year there are 6 festivals and competitions of Ukrainian culture and folklore. Ukrainian organisations and their cultural activities (school, courses, schoolbooks, broadcasting) are sponsored by the State.

7. General contactlinguistic portrait

7.1. Both Polish and Ukrainian are Slavic languages. The former belongs to the West-Slavic, the latter to the East-Slavic languages. Generally, the morphological and syntactic systems (categories) are similar, though there are significant differences in forms, e. g. in the past tense person is indicated by endings in Polish (*byłem, byłeś, był*, etc.) and by pronouns in Ukrainian (*я був, ти був, він був* 'I, you, he/she was'). The Polish lexicon was influenced by Latin and West-European languages, the Ukrainian principally by Greek (through Church-Slavonic) and Turkic languages. In phonetics the main differences consist of soft consonants in Polish, e. g. *ʒeń, ćotka, ćixy* versus hard consonants before *e* and ancient *i* (changed into *y*) in Ukrainian, e. g. *den', teta, tyxyj* ('day', 'aunt', 'calm') and of the presence of nasal vowels (in various realisations), e. g. *vǫski', p'eńć* ('narrow', 'five') in Polish versus orals in Ukrainian, e. g. *uskyj, pjat'*.

Generally, standard Ukrainian in Poland is the same as in Ukraine, though it has fewer

Russisms than the Kiev variety. The knowledge of standard Ukrainian among Ukrainians in Poland was not under examination, but it is known that Polish interferences are very strong because there are limited possibilities to attend Ukrainian schools (classes, see 6.), and because in many cases Ukrainian is a second language. Contacts with Ukraine are improving the standard Ukrainian of the population only partly. There are no good contemporary Polish−Ukrainian and Ukrainian−Polish dictionaries.

Attempts to create a standard Rusyn (Lemko) language are still in the initial phase. Lemko literature is represented first of all by folklore; poetry, and short stories are rather poor. The Rusyn standard includes specific dialectal features, e. g. back *y* (in Cyrillic orthography ы: *сын* 'son', cf. Ukrainian *син*), "Slovak" forms like *кырвавый* 'bloody' (cf. Ukrainian *кривавий*), "Polish" endings in the present tense, e. g. *мам, маш, мат* 'I, you, have, he/she has' and "Slovak" ending in *маме* 'we have' (cf. Ukrainian *маю, маєш, має, маємо*), etc.

7.2. As a result of old contacts (see 2.2.) there are many Ukrainian elements in contemporary standard Polish and in dialects. Putting aside the stylistic use of Ukrainian elements in everyday language, one uses words like *ohydny* 'hideous', *rubaszny* 'coarse', *tuman* 'cloud; mist', *wertep* 'pathless tract', *hodować* 'to grow; to raise', *chata* 'peasant house', *klacz* 'mare', *czereśnia* 'cherry tree' et al. Many of them (also other borrowings, e. g. *loszę* 'foal') are known in the dialects far from the Polish−Ukrainian language border.

Many Ukrainian elements occur in Polish dialects with direct contacts (some of them grew up on the Ukrainian substratum), e. g. *hładyszka* 'clay pot', *sołoducha* 'soup made from flour'. In Subcarpathia there are loan words from the Lemko dialect, e. g. *chołosznie* 'wool pants', *gielatka* 'little barrel for a cheese' (of Rumanian origin), *odomasz* 'bargain drink' (of Hungarian origin, borrowed through Slovak). Due to "Valakh migrations" with Rumanian speaking shepherds, but with prevailing Ukrainian elements, these words (with toponyms like *Czerteż, Kotelnica*) are known further in the West.

Mutual influence in phonology and morphology in standard Ukrainian and Polish consists mostly in supporting internal tendencies. In Polish it concerns the change of [ó, é] into [u (= orthographic *ó*), e]. In morphology one can see the Ukrainian influence in changing old forms of 1. sg. pres. *depcę* 'I trample', *szepcę* 'I whisper' into *depczę, szepczę*, in the appearance of adjectives in *-eńki* (*maleńki*). In Polish dialects in contact with Ukrainian ones and in the language of the Poles resettled in 1945 to new Polish western and northern territories from Ukraine, one can observe the presence of "Ukrainian" soft *l'* (*l'ato*) and dental *ł* (*łan*), bilabial *w* (*ławka*) in place of common Polish *l, u* and *v* respectively.

7.3. Polish influence on Ukrainian was especially strong not only in Galicia (where there was a Polish cultural center in Lvov), but also in Volhynia and Podole (Podillja): there were many Polish villages (in Central Ukraine − under Soviet rule − up to 1935−1937 and in West Ukraine up to 1943−1945). Polish influence on West Ukrainian dialects was discussed by Dejna (1948), but there are no sufficient studies on the Central Ukrainian dialects.

Among Polish borrowings in Ukrainian dialects in Poland there are lexical items which are shared by standard Ukrainian (like *pan* 'man; master; lord', *bezpečnyj* 'safe', *micnyj* 'strong', *rada* 'council', *bryła* 'block; solid figure', *cukor* 'sugar', *ližko* 'bed'). Loanwords occurring less frequently in other Ukrainian dialects include *cały* 'whole', *cudnyj* 'wonderful', *dz'ura* 'hole', *necky* 'trough', *pec, p'ec* 'oven', *plontro* 'garret', *wendzonka* 'smoked bacon', *ogin* (*ohin*) 'tail', *pidgarla* 'dewlap'. In Ukrainian dialects in Poland occur the same Polish features as in some other West Ukrainian dialects: *l* (*lampa*), *u̯* (*u̯apa*), *v, f* (*u̯afka*), soft *ć ź ś* (*ćil̄yj, žat', śino* ∼ Ukrainian demisoft *c' z' s'*), *śc'* (*śćina* ∼ Ukrainian *st'ina*), more frequent *g* (*garnec*), sandhi (*deż buł* ∼ Ukrainian *des' buw*), *ł* can occur in front of a consonant (*osełka* ∼ Ukrainian *wk, u̯k*), I. sg. *z matom* (∼ Ukrainian *z mamoju*), L. sg. *f pol'u* (∼ Ukrainian *w pol'i*), praet. *robyv'im* (∼ Ukrainian *ja robyw*), fut. *budu robył* (∼ Ukrainian *budu robyty*) etc.; Polish suffixes *-aż, -dło* (*stolaż, vendz'idło* ∼ Ukrainian *stol'ar, vudyło*) entered into the dialectal system. In the western Ukraine, these features occur today mostly in the language of older generations. In Poland in villages where a Ukrainian-speaking population prevails the interferences are weaker, while in villages where the Ukrainian-speaking population constitutes a minority, especially in cities, the interferences are stronger.

8. Evaluation of the sources and literature

The literature on Polish–Ukrainian language contacts, esp. on their history, is abundant. The recent situation is presented in some monographs and papers on Ukrainian and Polish dialects. They focus mainly on the results of language contact, not on its process and sociolinguistic characteristics. There is not sufficient literature on the present situation of the Lemko region. There are very scanty and not satisfactory studies on the situation in the new Ukrainian (and Lemko) settlements. The description of the situation in villages near Przemyśl and in the Lemko region is based on the author's own field research.

Ukrainian and Polish dialectal texts from the borderland were published by Obrębska-Jabłońska (1972) and Czyżewski/Warchoł (in press). Ukrainian dialects are presented in atlases: Czyżewski (1986), Obrębska-Jabłońska (1980–1993), Rieger (1980–1991), Stieber (1956–1964). Polish dialects are presented in Małecki/Nitsch (1934), Nitsch/Karaś (1957–1970), Pelcowa (1985). There is a Lemko dictionary by Rieger (1995). For further bibliography see Czyżewski (1994), Rieger (1995), Sawaniewska-Mochowa in Rieger/Werenicz (vol. VI).

9. Bibliography (selected)

Bešta, Theodor (1971): "Z badań nad wschodniosłowiańskimi wpływami językowymi w polszczyźnie romantyków" [Studies on East Slavic Influence on the Polish Romantics Language]. In: *Łódzkie Towarzystwo Naukowe. Rozprawy Komisji Językowej 17*, 199–241.

Czech, Mirosław (Ed.) (1993): *Ukraińcy w Polsce 1989–1993. Kalendarium. Dokumenty. Informacje* [Ukrainians in Poland], Warsaw.

Czopek, Barbara (1988): *Nazwy miejscowe dawnej ziemi chełmskiej i bełskiej (w granicach dzisiejszego Państwa Polskiego)* [Place Names in the Ancient Chełm and Bełz Lands], Wrocław.

Czyżewski, Feliks (1986): *Altas gwar polskich i ukraińskich okolic Włodawy* [Atlas of Polish and Ukrainian Dialects near Włodawa], Lublin.

Czyżewski, Feliks (1994): *Fonetyka i fonologia gwar polskich i ukraińskich południowo-wschodniego Podlasia* [Phonetics and Phonology of Polish and Ukrainian Dialects in South East Podlasie region], Lublin.

Czyżewski, Feliks/Warchoł, Stefan (in press): *Polskie i ukraińskie teksty gwarowe z terenu wschodniej Lubelszczyzny* [Polish and Ukrainian Dialectal Texts from East Lublin Region], Lublin.

Dejna, Karol (1948): "Elementy polskie w gwarach zachodniomałoruskich" [Polish Elements in the West-Ukrainian Dialects]. In: *Język Polski 28*, 72–79.

Duć-Fajfer, Helena (1992): "Łemkowie w Polsce" [The Lemkos in Poland]. In: *Magury '91*, 11–30.

Kość, Józef (1995): "O kształtowaniu się gwar południowokresowych na terenie ziemi chełmskiej w XIX wieku" [On the Origin of the South-Eastern Polish in Chełm Land in the 19th c.]. In: Rieger/Werenicz, vol. VIII, 179–193.

Kubijovych, Volodymyr (1953): *Etnični hrupy Pivdenno-Zachidnoji Ukrajiny (Hałyčyny) na 1.I.1939*, Častyna I [Ethnic Groups of Galicia]. London/Munich/New York/Paris.

Kubijovych, Volodymyr (1970): "Pol'šča" [Poland]. In: *Encyklopedija Ukrajinoznavstva II-6*, Paris/New York.

Kuraszkiewicz, Władysław (1985): *Ruthenica. Studia z historycznej i współczesnej dialektologii wschodniosłowiańskiej* [Ruthenica. Studies on Ancient and Contemporary East Slavic Dialectology], Warsaw.

Kurzowa, Zofia (1985): *Polszczyzna Lwowa i Kresów południowo-wschodnich do 1939 r.* [The Polish Language of Lvov and South-Eastern Lands up to 1939], 2nd ed., Warsaw.

Lehr-Spławiński, Tadeusz (1928): "Wzajemne wpływy polsko-ruskie w dziedzinie językowej" [The Mutual Polish–Ukrainian Language Influences]. In: *Przegląd Współczesny XXIV*, 7, 249–266.

Łesiów, Michał (1958): "Polonizmy ukraińskiej gwary wsi Kolechowic" [Polonisms in the Ukrainian Dialect of Kolechowice]. In: *Język Polski 38*, 362–369.

Małecki, Antoni/Nitsch, Kazimierz (1934): *Atlas językowy polskiego Podkarpacia* [The Linguistic Atlas of the Polish Subcarpathia], Cracow.

Mazur, Jan (1976–1978): *Gwary okolic Biłgoraja* [Dialects near Biłgoraj] 1–2, Wrocław.

Minikowska, Teresa (1980): *Wyrazy ukraińskie w polszczyźnie literackiej XVI w* [Ukrainian Words in Polish Standard of the 16th c.], Warsaw.

Nalepa, Jerzy (1991): "Prapolski bastion toponimiczny w Bramie Przemyskiej i Lędzanie" [Proto-Polish Toponymic Bastion in the Przemyśl Gate and the Lędzanie Tribe]. In: *Onomastica 36*, 5–45.

Nitsch, Kazimierz/Karaś, Mieczysław (Eds.) (1957–1970): *Mały atlas gwar polskich* [A Little Atlas of Polish Dialects], vol. 1–13, Wrocław.

Obrębska-Jabłońska, Antonina (Ed.) (1972): *Teksty gwarowe z Białostocczyzny z komentarzem językowym* [Dialectal Texts from Białystok Region], Warsaw.

Obrębska-Jabłońska, Antonina et al. (Eds.) (1980–1993): *Atlas gwar wschodniosłowiańskich Bia-*

łostocczyzny [The Atlas of the East Slavic Dialects in Białystok Region]. Vol. I–III.

Pelcowa, Halina (1985): *Studia nad słownictwem gwarowym Lubelszczyzny* [Studies on Dialectal Vocabulary of the Lublin Region], vol. I, Lublin.

Pudło, Kazimierz (1992): "Dzieje Łemków po drugiej wojnie światowej (zarys problematyki)" [History of the Lemkos after World War II]. In: *Łemkowie w historii i kulturze Karpat*, Czajkowski, J. (Ed.), Rzeszów.

Rieger, Janusz (1977): *Imiennictwo ludności wiejskiej w ziemi sanockiej i przemyskiej w XV w.* [Peasants Anthroponymy in Sanok and Przemyśl Lands in the 15th c.], Wrocław.

Rieger, Janusz (Ed.) (1980–1991): *Atlas gwar bojkowskich* [Atlas of the Boiko Dialects], Vol. I–VII, Wrocław.

Rieger, Janusz (1989): "Kilka uwag o dawnej hydronimii w dorzeczu Sanu" [Some Remarks on the Ancient Hydronymy in San Basin]. In: *Hydronimia słowiańska*, Rymut K. (Ed.), Wrocław.

Rieger, Janusz (1993): "Język polski na Wschodzie" [The Polish Language East of Poland]. In: *Współczesny język polski (Encyklopedia kultury XX wieku, vol. 2)*, Bartmiński J. (Ed.), Wrocław.

Rieger, Janusz (1995): *Słownictwo i nazewnictwo łemkowskie* [Lemko Appellatives and Onomastics], Warsaw.

Rieger, Janusz/Werenicz, Wiaczesław (Eds.) (1982–1995): *Studia nad polszczyzną kresową* [Studies on the Polish Language East of Contemporary Poland]. Vol. I–VIII, Wrocław.

Saładiak, Andrzej (1993): *Pamiątki i zabytki kultury ukraińskiej w Polsce* [Souvenirs and Relics of Ukrainian Culture in Poland] Burchard Edition, Warsaw.

Shevelov, George Y. (1966): *Die ukrainische Schriftsprache 1798–1965. Ihre Entwicklung unter dem Einfluß der Dialekte*, Wiesbaden.

Stieber, Zdzisław (1956–1964): *Atlas językowy dawnej Łemkowszczyzny* [A Linguistic Atlas of the Ancient Lemko Land], Vol. I–VII, Łódź.

Truchan, Myroslav (1990): *Ukrajinci v Polšči pislja druhoji svitovoji vijny 1944–1984* [Ukrainians in Poland 1944–1984], New York.

Warchoł, Stefan (Ed.) (1989): *Interferencje językowe na różnych obszarach słowiańszczyzny* [Language Interferences in Different Slavic Areas], Lublin.

Janusz A. Rieger, Warsaw (Poland)

198. Polish–Slovak

1. Geography and demography
2. History
3. Politics, economy and general cultural and religious situation
4. Statistics
5. Sociolinguistic situation
6. Language political situation
7. General contactlinguistic situation
8. Critical evaluation of literature
9. Bibliography (selected)

1. Geography and demography

The Slovak minority is one of the less numerous minorities in Poland. Slovaks live in a compact zone in the Polish–Slovak borderland in Spisz and Orava (in Slovak *Spiš* and *Orava*). Some sources estimate the number of the Slovak population to be 20000. Precise statistics are lacking because no census in Poland since 1945 has distinguished nationalities.

2. History

The region of northern Spisz was colonized between the 13th and 16th centuries. Colonization was much more intensive from the Slovak than the Polish side. Colonization of Orava (Polish *Orawa*) took place later, mostly in the 16th and 17th centuries. German, Polish, Slovak and (in the 14th and 15th centuries also) Wallachian-Ukrainian immigrants took part in the colonization of Spisz, while Orava was colonized mostly by Poles and Slovaks.

Before 1918, Spisz and Orava were part of Upper Hungary, as was all of Slovakia. After World War I the newly created states – Poland and Czechoslovakia – could not agree on the border. Both sides presented historical-political and ethnic-cultural arguments. A plebiscite was planned but never held. Finally in July 1920, a board of ambassadors assigned two thirds of Spisz and half of Orava to Czechoslovakia. The remaining one third of Spisz and the other half of Orava became part of Poland. Poland did not recognize the Slovak minority after World War I and all citizens of Polish Spisz and Orava were considered Polish nationals. The educational system was Polish and the Slovak language lost ground to Polish. In the 1930's, even Slovak priests changed to Polish in their services.

In 1939, the whole of Spisz and Orava were annexed by the newly established Republic of Slovakia. A Slovak primary and secondary school system was organized. Polish priests were removed and Polish as the official language was replaced by Slovak. After World War II the annexed territories were returned to Poland and the 1920's border was re-established between Poland and Czechoslovakia.

3. Politics, economy and general cultural and religious situation

The economical situation of the Slovak and Polish population in Spisz and Orava has remained stable. Traditionally, the area has been agrarian, with farms of a medium size: between 5 and 15 hectares, divided into rather small lots. The farmers breed cattle, pigs and sheep. Agriculture has made technological advances during the last few years. Part of the population now works outside of agriculture, primarily in the shoe industry.

From the cultural or ethnographic point of view, the Slovak as well as Polish population of Orava and Spisz is part of a larger Carpathian cultural region, with its architectural and agricultural traditions as well as folklore, song, and art. Slovaks similarly as Poles are Catholics.

Slovaks were recognized as a national minority in Poland in 1947. Starting in 1947, a Slovak educational system has been renewed. The *Cultural Society of Czechs and Slovaks* was founded in 1957.

4. Statistics

The Polish parts of Spisz and Orava cover an area of 583 km^2 (14 villages in Spisz and 13 in Orava). The population of the entire area totals about 38 000. In statistics of 1880—1910, the entire population of the region was treated as Slovak. The Polish censuses of 1921 and 1931 regarded all these inhabitants as Poles (1921 — 29 800, 1931 — 19 200). The 1941 censuses of the Slovak Republic counted in Orava 16 614 Slovaks, 162 Poles and other nationalities, and in Spisz 9 361 Slovaks and 274 Poles and other nationalities. The results of the 1946 census have not been published. The Slovak authorities as well as the Cultural Society of Czechs and Slovaks in Poland estimate about 20 000 Slovak in Spisz and Orava.

There are certainly numerous sources of the differences in statistics. One of them is related to sociolinguistic issues: national consciousness of the population in Spisz and Orava does not necessarily coincide with linguistic differences. While the Goral dialect is structurally much closer to Polish than to Slovak (it is considered one of the Polish dialects), a native Goral speaker can and at different times also does declare Slovak nationality (Servátka 1987).

5. Sociolinguistic situation

The recent sociolinguistic situation of the area of Spisz and Orava has been decisively influenced by the dynamics of changing political circumstances. The core means of communication has always been the Goral dialect. Around the Goral dialect various multilingualisms have been centred. The various multilingual situations differ in principle in the languages involved as well as in the degree to which knowledge of these languages penetrates the Spisz and Orava community. Six major stages in the development of the sociolinguistic situation in Polish Spisz and Orava can be distinguished.

(1) Before 1918: Spisz (Orava)-Goral bilingualism. The main means of communication in Spisz and Orava was the highlander (Goral) dialect. The Slovak Spisz (Orava) dialect was used mainly in intergroup communication, i.e. in contacts of the Gorals with the Slovak Spisz and Orava population.

(2) Between 1918 and 1920. A new official language, namely standard Slovak, emerged on the sociolinguistic scene. Not all of the population was acquainted with it. Trilingualism (Goral dialect — Spisz (Orava) dialect of Slovak — standard Slovak) was only partial. Standard Slovak acquired some of the extragroup communicative functions in which the Spisz (Orava) dialect of Slovak had been used before. The spread of Standard Slovak was linked with the build-up of Slovak national consciousness in the community.

(3) Between 1920 and 1939. Polish became the official language. Despite the fact that Polish is structurally closer to the Goral dialect, its recognition as an official language partially contradicted Slovak national identification on the part of the Spisz and Orava population. Goral-Polish bilingualism was gradually established in the area. Polish ac-

quired the functions which had been fulfilled by the Slovak language. Slovak was preserved namely in Church, and later limited in its use even there.

(4) Between 1939 and 1945. Slovak returned as the official language and replaced Polish in that function. Slovak was restituted in schools and Church as well as in extra-group communication. The tradition of Goral-Slovak bilingualism known from the period of 1918—1920 was re-established.

(5) After 1945 and the restitution of the Czechoslovak—Polish border of 1920, Polish replaced Slovak in extra-group communication. The second wave of Goral-Polish bilingualism was launched. Nevertheless Goral-Slovak bilingualism persisted due to the existence of Slovak schools. The position of Slovak in the multilingual situation of Polish Spisz and Orava weakened.

(6) 1970's and beyond. The Slovak educational systems has lost ground. This reflects mainly on the linguistic competence of the younger generation in Slovak: it is diminishing despite the activities of the Cultural Society of Czechs and Slovaks, *Matica slovenská*, and the impact of Slovak mass media (radio and TV).

The six-stage development of the sociolinguistic situation reflects more or less directly on the distribution of Slovak-Goral bilingualism among generations of the Polish Spisz and Orava population today (Servátka 1987; numbers in the column of *Slovak-Goral bilinguals* give actually the percentage of speakers who are fluent in Slovak):

Table 198.1: Percentage of Slovak-Goral bilinguals

	age (in years)	% of Slovak-Goral bilinguals
1.	60—85	50— 60
2.	40—60	80—100
3.	30—40	30— 40
4.	10—30	0— 30

The oldest generation grew up in the Austria-Hungarian Empire (before 1918). The 40—60 age group reflects the period of restitution of Slovak as the official language after 1939. Finally, the rapid decrease in knowledge of Slovak in the youngest generation correlates with the sixth stage of sociolinguistic development in the area.

6. Language political situation

The status of the "Czechoslovak" minority in Poland was assured by a bilateral treaty between Poland and Czechoslovakia on April 23, 1925. The treaty guaranteed "Czechoslovakian" primary schools, and administration in the "Czechoslovak" language in the state bureaucracy as well as in the courts. However, in reality, these provisions were adhered to only in the case of Czechs in Wołyń. The Spisz and Orava Slovaks were considered by authorities Poles, or "Poles without Polish national identity". Use of Slovak in dealing with state institutions was permitted by a special ordinance for Spisz and Orava (October 15, 1920) only in cases when use of Polish would hamper prompt communication. In 1933, the so-called Jędrzejewicz school reform recommended use of students' "neighbour's language" in secondary school and lyceum. On the basis of this provision, Slovak and Czech were taught in the Nowy Targ Lyceum in 1933—1939. The main public domain where Slovak was used was the Church. Before 1925, Polish Spisz and Orava were part of the Spisz diocese. In 1925 the territory was incorporated into the Cracow archdiocese. The administrative change did not lead to the expulsion of Slovak priests from Polish Spisz and Orava, but it eventually contributed to a gradual replacement of Slovak priests with priests from Poland proper. Finally in the 1930's, the district office in Nowy Targ admonished rectors that religious services and chants should be held in Polish. The changes in the territorial organization of the Catholic church as well as the admonition by the district office contributed to the further shrinking of the territory where Slovak was in use.

Slovak regained its ground in Spisz and Orava during World War II when the entire Spisz and Orava territories were incorporated into the Republic of Slovakia and Slovak replaced Polish in all its public functions. The status of a national minority was guaranteed to the Slovak population in Poland by the Polish—Czechoslovak treaty in 1947.

Education in Slovak was provided in 33 schools (around 2500 pupils) in 1952—1953. In 1956—1957 the number of Slovak schools reached 50 with around 2100 students. Nevertheless in 1988—1989 there were only two Slovak primary schools with only 127 students, and Slovak language classes were held in an additional 20 primary schools (around 390 pupils) and in one secondary school

(6 students). In the 1988/1989 school year, the Slovak language was taught only as a non-compulsory subject in 23 primary schools, with enrolment totalling 532 pupils. A similar trend toward gradual reduction of the role of Slovak in the educational system in Polish Orava and Spisz can be detected also in the case of the secondary schools. Between 1951 and 1968, there was a secondary school (lyceum) with Slovak as the language of instruction in Jabłonka (Orava). At first the school had 67 students. In the school year 1965/1966 the number of students fell to 46 and in 1967/1968, the number further decreased to 21 students. Since then, Slovak has not been the language of instruction at the lyceum but only one of the subjects taught.

There are additional causes for the decline of Slovak education in Poland. First, it met difficulties because of the considerable structural gap between the local Goral dialect and standard Slovak. Second, teachers from Slovakia were gradually replaced by Polish teachers during the 1950's, a step which eventually lowered the standard of Slovak instruction (Servátka 1987). Finally, parents were pressured by school system supervisors (namely in Nowy Targ) not to pursue the education of their children in the Slovak language (Chalupec 1983, 12).

The *Cultural Society of Czechs and Slovaks* was established in 1957. It numbers over 3350 members, is divided into three main districts (Spisz, Orava and Zelov, with the Zelov district concerning mainly the Czech minority) and comprises 15 local groups in Spisz, 14 in Orava and one group in other localities (Cracow, Warsaw, Zelov, etc.). Since 1957, the *Cultural Society* publishes the monthly *Život* (3000 copies). Among other institutions crucial in preserving the ethnic distinctness of the Slovak minority the following institutions should be mentioned: 32 libraries, song and dance groups (*Niedzica* in Spisz, *Podskle* in Orava), folklore festivals, regional museums (in Czarna Góra and Zubrzyca Górna), and churches.

After the Slovak Republic was constituted as an independent state in January 1993, a Slovak Embassy was established in Warsaw. A Slovak cultural Center is to be founded as well. Since 1994, the TV studios in Cracow have been producing a program, *Our Own House*, which deals with issues of various national minorities in the region, the Slovak minority among them (others being the Lemko, Ukrainian, and Gypsy minorities).

7. General contactlinguistic situation

Polish as well as Slovak belongs to the West Slavic language family, but standard Slovak includes some south Slavic features which are absent in Polish.

The Slovak spoken in Polish Spisz and Orava is influenced mainly by the Goral dialects. Goral interferences can be found in its phonemics as well as in other linguistic strata.

Slovak speakers in Polish Spisz and Orava often preserve g, for instance *gospodarstveo* as in the Goral dialect (and Polish): *gospodarka*, whereas Slovak has h: *hospodárstvo*. There is a noticeable tendency among Slovak speakers in the Goral area not to preserve vowel quantity properly. Vowel quantity is phonologic in Slovak, unlike in the Goral dialect and in Polish. Speakers use short or half long vowels instead of the expected long ones; pronunciation of a particular word may vary in vowel quantity even in the speech of one individual. Regressive assimilation is common in Slovak, but Slovak speakers in Polish Spisz and Orava assimilate also progressively: groups *kv, tv, sv > kf, tf, sf*; thus /zlikfidovat, tfoj, sfet/ while Slovak preserves *kv, tv, sv* in all these instances. Slovak speakers in Poland tend to monophthongize diphthongs. They thus say /ńečo, d'et'a/, compared to Slovak *nieco* and *diet'a*.

A result of Goral influence is also *zaruceni* 'engaged'; cf. Goral *zarenčeńi* vs. standard Slovak *zasnúbeni*; similarly, Goral Slovak *sanokosene* 'haymaking, hay harvest' (*śanokošeńe // śé·ne zbiůrki* in the Goral dialect) vs. standard Slovak *senokosy*. The meaning of some words and morphemes is re-evaluated to meet the Goral pattern. In "Goral" Slovak *prispefki* does not mean *príspevky* (standard Slovak), i.e. contributions, but by analogy with Goral *pšiśpiefki*, 'sung insertions' (i.e. something that is sung — *śpiefki* — to something, *pri-*). Similarly the meaning of the prefix *vi-* is re-evaluated and used where standard Slovak would use the prefix *na-*: *viučili sa* thus means in the Slovak spoken in Polish Spisz and Orava the same as *naučili se* in standard Slovak. The corresponding expression in the Goral dialect is *vyucyć se*. The preposition *do* is used in Polish Spisz and Orava as it is usual in the Goral dialect (and in Polish as well), i.e. with the meaning of Slovak *k* 'towards': *vžal ih do seba, prišiel do krála* but *k sebe*, and *prišiel ku král'ovi* in standard Slovak (Servátka 1986 and 1988).

Influence is also exerted in the other direction, and Slovak elements appear in the Polish dialects spoken in the area of Spisz and Orava. Thus as a result of centuries-long contact, (*ŕ >) rz (ʳž) is replaced by r (as in Slovak): thus *trimać* and *kurić* (Slovak *trímat'*, *kúrit'*) instead of *trzymać* and *kurzyć // trzimać, kurzić*. Similarly, ńC is replaced by nC: *panski* (Slovak: *panský*), but Polish *pański*, and the "Slovak" initial stress replaces "Polish" penultimate stress in Spisz and Orava. Slovak inferences can be found also in phraseology and syntax. For example, *o dobrymu człowiekowi* where the dative ending -*owi* is used also in the locative, which is possible in Slovak but not in Polish: *o dobrém človekovi* or *o dobrém človeku* (Slovak) but only *o dobrym człowieku* (Polish). Slovak influence is assumed also in the case of some infinitive constructions: *widzoł go śedzeć, zostawieł go stoć*, instead of the expected participial construction in Polish (Slovak: *videl ho sediet', nechal ho stát'*, Polish: *widział go siedzącego, zostawił go stojącego*). Slovak origin is also ascribed to the verbal forms *idem, ideme, ńesem, ńeseme*; cf. Polish *idę, idziemy, niosę, niesiemy* and Slovak *idem, ideme, nesiem, nesieme*. Similarly in the imperative (first person plural), there is for instance *podźme, berme/bierme* in Spisz but *pójdziemy, bierzemy* in Polish and *pod'me, berme* in Slovak.

8. Critical evaluation of literature

Most of the earlier research on the linguistic situation in Spisz and Orava focused on defining the line separating the Polish and Slovak ethnic groups and on the dialectological map of the area. S. Czambel (1906) established that in northern Spisz, along the Poprad, Dunajec and Bialka rivers, the same dialects were spoken as in the neighbouring Podhala region, and listed features of this similarity. K. Nitsch (1921) dealt with the southern limits of the Polish state based on the Polish language. The actual topic of his interest was the "Polish population" in Austria-Hungary, i.e. the Goral ethnicum in this area (at the time all of Spisz and Orava were included in Northern Hungary, i.e. into the territory from which Slovakia was established as part of Czechoslovakia in 1918). The work by Z. Stieber (1929, 1934, 1938, 1945, 1950) has had considerable impact, mainly on M. Małecki. Results of Małecki's research on mutual influences of Polish and Slovak dialects in Spisz and Orava, on the gradual disappearance of Slovak features in the Polish part of Spisz and Orava, and on Polish features in the Slovak part of this territory have been summarized in Małecki 1933, 1938 and Małecki et al. 1934. From the Slovak perspective, the most controversial aspect seems to be Małecki's high estimates of the number of Poles living in the territory under study. The Goral ethnicum was counted as Poles; it is true that the Goral dialect exhibits Polish features, but the national consciousness before 1921 is believed by some linguists and ethnographers to have been rather Slovak (cf. 4. above).

Among Slovak dialectologists, J. Štolc (1937, 1938, 1939, 1974) must be mentioned. The Polish–Slovak border in Spisz and Orava is addressed by A. Bielovodsky, "Severné hranice Slovenska" (1946). A great deal of data on the "linguo-Polish" villages in Slovakia has been gathered by V. Vážný (1948). After World War II, linguistic issues concerning the Polish–Slovak borderland were addressed by Z. Gołąb (1955), E. Pawlowski (1956), and especially by Z. Sobierajski (1961, 1963, 1961–1978) and A. Zaręba (1961, 1968, 1990). Among the younger generation of linguists, A. Habovštiak (1954, 1961, 1979), J. Kriššáková (1982, 1984), M. Servátka (1986, 1987, 1990), and F. Sowa (1989) should be mentioned.

9. Bibliography (selected)

Bednarčík, Valentín (1990): "K otázke jazykového zatriedenia goralčiny na Slovensku" [Towards a linguistic classification of the Goral dialect in Slovakia]. In: *Život* 6, 8–9.

Bielovodský, Andrej (1946): *Severné hranice Slovenska* [The northern borders of Slovakia], Bratislava.

Bubak, Józef (1972): *Spiskie teksty gwarowe z obszaru Polski* [The Slovak texts from the Polish area], ZNUJ, Prace Językoznawcze 36, Cracow.

Bubak, Józef (1983): "Stav badań nad polskimi gwarami na Spiszu" [The state of studies on the Polish Spisz dialects]. In: *Język Polski* 63, 322–334.

Bubak, Józef (1987); "Polskie gwary spiskie" [Spisz Polish dialects]. In: *Polski Spisz. Prace ethnographiczne* 22, Biały Zb. (Ed.), 233–262.

Chalupec, Adam (1983): "Priestory slovenčiny" [Space for the Slovak Language]. In: *Život* 26, 12–13.

Czambel, Samuel (1906): "Slovenská reč a jej miesto v rodine slovanských jazykov. I. Osnovy a iný materiál rečový, 1. Vychodnoslovenské nárečie [The Slovak language and its place in the family of Slavic languages. I. Topics and other evidence. 1. The Eastern Slovak dialect], Turč. sv. Martin.

Gołąb, Zbigniew (1955): "O zróżnicowamniu wewnętrznym gwary podhalańskiej" [Internal differentiation of the Podhale dialect]. In: *Język Polski* 34, 85—111.

Habovštiak, Anton (1954): "Slovenská dialektológia v rokoch 1938—1953" [Slovak dialectology in the years 1938—1954]. In: *Jazykovedný časopis* 8, 69—107.

Habovštiak, Anton (1961): "Über die Ursachen der mundartlichen Differenzierung in Orava". In: *Studia Slavica*, 231—238.

Habovštiak, Anton (1979): "O jazykovom vývine na slovensko-poľskom pohraničí" [On the linguistic development in the Polish—Slovak borderland]. In: *Jazykovekný časopis* 30, 33—39.

Karaś, Mieczysław (1958): "Z problematyki gwar mieszanych i przejściowych" [Issues of transitional and mixed dialects]. In: *Język Polski* 38, 286—296.

Karaś, Mieczysław (1965): *Polskie dialekty Orawy. I. Fonologia i fonetyka* [The Polish dialects of Orava. I. Phonology and phonetics], Cracow.

Karaś, Mieczysław (1966): *Orawskie teksty gwarowe z obszaru Czechosłowacji* [Orava dialect texts from the area of Czechoslovakia], ZNUJ LXXIV, Prace Językoznawcze 8, Cracow.

Karaś, Mieczysław/Zaręba, Alfred (1964): *Orawskie teksty gwarowe z obszaru Polski* [Orava dialect texts from the Polish area], Cracow.

Krišsáková, Julia (1982): "O goralských nárečiach z aspektu slovensko-poľských jazykových kontaktov" [About highland dialects with respect to Polish—Slovak language contacts]. In: *Studia Academia Slovaca* 11, 235—249.

Krišsáková, Julia (1982): *Goralské nárečia (Odraz slovensko-polských jazykových kontaktov na fonologickej rovine). Autoreferát dizertácie na získanie vedeckej hodnosti kandidáta filologických vied* [Highland dialects (Polish—Slovak language contacts in phonology). Report for receiving the degree of candidate in philological sciences], Prague.

Krišsáková, Julia (1985): "Goralské nárečie vo svetle kolonizácii a teórie jazykových kontaktov" [The Goral dialect with respect to colonizations and the theory of language contacts]. In: *Slavica slovaca* 20, 165—177.

Krišsáková, Julia (1984): "O goralskom nareči z aspektu slovensko-poľských jazykových kontaktov" [On Goral dialects in regard to Slovak—Polish language contacts]. In: *Studia Academica Slovaca 11 — Papers presented on the XVII Summer Seminar of Slovak Language and Culture*, Mistrík, J. (Ed.), 235—249.

Małecki, Mieczysław (1928): *Archaizm podhalański (wraz w próbą wyznaczenia granic tego dialektu)* [The Podhale archaism (with attempt to reduce the borders of this dialect]. Monografie Polskich Cech Gwarowych nr 4, Cracow.

Małecki, Mieczysław (1933): "Do genezy gwar mieszanych i przejściowych (ze szczególnym wuzględnieniem granicy językowej polsko—czeskiej i polsko—słowackiej" [About the origin of the mixed and transitional dialects (with special respect to the Polish—Czech and Polish—Slovak language border)]. In: *Slavia Occidentalis* 12, 81—90.

Małecki, Mieczysław (1938): *Język polski na południe od Karpat* [The Polish language in the Southern Carpatians], Zakopane.

Małecki, Mieczysław/Nitsch, Kazimierz (1934): *Atlas językowy polskiego Podkarpacia* [The language atlas of the Polish Subcarpatian region], Cracow.

Nitsch, Kazimierz (1920): "Granice państwa a granice języka polskiego" [National boundaries and boundaries of the Polish language]. In: *Język Polski* 1, 97—101.

Nitsch, Kazimierz (1958): "Małopolska zmiana x w k lub f" [The Little Poland change of x into k or f]. In: *Wybór pism polonistycznych* 4, 305—343, Wrocław.

Pawłowski, Eugeniusz (1956): "O gwarze łapszańskiej" [The dialect of the village of Łapsze]. In: *Język Polski* 36, 21—27.

Servátka, Marián (1986): "Otázky jazykovej interferencie v slovenskom jazyku na Spiši v PLR" [Issues of interference in the Slovak language in Spiš in Poland]. In: *Studia Academica Slovaca 15 — Papers presented on the XXI Summer Seminar of Slovak Language and Culture*, Mistrík, J. (Ed.), 413—426.

Servátka, Marián (1987): "Goralsko-slovenský bilinguismus, resp. goralsko-spišsko-poľsko-slovenský multilinguismus" [Goral Slovak bilingualism, or Goral-Spiš—Polish—Slovak multilingualism]. In: *Studia Academica Slovaca 16 — Papers presented on the XVIII Summer Seminar of Slovak Language and Culture*, Mistrík, J. (Ed.), 385—395.

Servátka, Marián (1988): "Prvky jazykové interferencie v slovenskom jazyku na Spiši v PLR" [Interference in the Slovak language of Polish Spiš]. In: *Z česko—polských jazykových a literárních styků*, Petr, J. (Ed.), 137—145.

Sobierajski, Zenon (1961—1978): "Atlas polskich gwar spiskich na terenie Polski i Czechosłowacji" [Atlas of Polish Spisz dialects in the area of Poland and Czechoslovakia] vol. I—VI. Wrocław.

Sowa, Franciszek (1990): *System fonologiczny polskich gwar spiskich* [The phonological system of the Polish Spisz dialects]. Wrocław.

Stieber, Zdzisław (1929): "Ze studiów nad gwarami słowackimi południowego Spisza" [Studies on Slovak dialects of southern Spisz]. In: *Lud Słowiański* 1, 32—41.

Stieber, Zdzisław (1934): "Ze studiów nad dialektami wschodno-słowackimi" [On the Eastern-Slovak dialects]. In: *Lud Słowiański III*, 140—151.

Štolc, Jozef (1939): "Dialektologické členenie spišských nárečí" [Dialectological differentiation among Spisz dialects]. In: *Linguistica Slovaca I–II*, 191–207, Bratislava.

Štolc, Jozef (1978): "Slovensko-pol'ské jazykove pomedzie a jeho výskum" [The Slovak–Polish language borderland and its study]. In: *Jazykovedný časopis XXV*, 60–67.

Štolc, Jozef/Buffa, Ferdinand/Habovštiak, Anton (1968): *Atlas slovesného jazyka. I. Vokalizmus a konsonantizmus* [Altas of the Slovak language. I. Vocalism and consonantism]. Bratislava.

Vážný, Vaclav (1934): "Nářečí slovenska" [The dialects of Slovakia]. In: *Československá Vlastivěda, III*. Praha.

Vážný, Vaclav (1948): "Z mezislovanského jazykového zeměpisu. Příspěvky k dokumentární hodnotě díla: M. Małecki, K. Nitsch, Atlas języky polskiego Podkarpacia [On Slavic language geography. Contributions to the evaluation of "The language atlas of the polish Sub-Carpatian region" by M. Małecki and K. Nitsch]. Praha.

Zaręba, Alfred (1968): "Dialekty mieszane i przejściowe w ujęciu diachronicznym na przykładzie polsko-słowackiej gwary Hut i Borowego" [The mixed and transitional dialects from the diachronic perspective – an example of Polish–Slovak dialects of Huty and Borowe]. In: *Język Polski XLVIII*, 113–128.

Zaręba, Alfred (1974): "Ze zjawisk językowych na pograniczu polsko-słowackim" [On linguistic phenomena of the Polish–Slovak borderland]. In: *Slavica Slovaca 9*, 247–253.

Franciszek Sowa, Cracow (Poland)

199. Polnisch–Tschechisch

1. Geographie und Demographie
2. Wirtschaft und kulturelle sowie religiöse Lage
3. Statistik und Ethnoprofile
4. Soziolinguistische Situation
5. Sprachpolitische Lage
6. Allgemeines kontaktlinguistisches Porträt
7. Stand der polnisch–tschechischen Kontaktforschung
8. Bibliographie (in Auswahl)

1. Geographie und Demographie

1.1. Geographie

Die einst sehr regen tschechisch–polnischen Sprachkontakte sind gegenwärtig auf unmittelbare sprachliche Interferenzen in den tschechischen Mundarten auf polnischem Gebiet beschränkt. Diese Mundarten lassen sich hinsichtlich der in ihnen auftretenden Interferenzen in folgende drei Gruppen einteilen: (1) die Mundarten bei Kudowa (Bad Kudowa) und Strzelin (Strehlen), (2) Sprachinseln bei Łódź (Lodz), (3) lachische Mundarten im polnisch–tschechischen Grenzland bei Głubczyce (Leobschütz) und Racibórz (Ratibor). Der Sprachgebrauch ist nicht von tschechischem Nationalgefühl begleitet, was auch dazu führt, daß jegliche offiziellen statistischen Daten über diese Bevölkerung fehlen (→ Sprachenkarte J).

1.2. Demographie (einschließlich geschichtlicher Perspektive)

Die tschechische Besiedlung auf dem Territorium des heutigen Polen ist von unterschiedlichem Ursprung: bei Leobschütz und Ratibor ist es eine jahrhundertealte Nachbarschaft, bei Bad Kudowa handelt es sich um eine die ehemalige österreichisch–preußische Grenze überschreitende Enklave einer tschechischen Mundart des nordöstlichen Dialekttyps. Den Rest bilden die Mitte des 18. Jahrhunderts im preußischen Teil Schlesiens gegründeten und im Laufe der Zeit auf benachbarte Gebiete ausgeweiteten Siedlungen tschechischer religiöser Emigranten. Die tschechischen Mundarten bei Bad Kudowa und Strehlen unterlagen früher deutschen Einflüssen und traten erst nach dem Zweiten Weltkrieg in Kontakt mit dem Polnischen. Die Kolonien im Oppelner Schlesien und bei Syców haben noch vor dem Zweiten Weltkrieg Kontakte mit der dortigen polnischsprachigen Bevölkerung pflegen können, aber in der einschlägigen Literatur fehlt es an Informationen zu diesem Thema. Die Sprachinsel bei Lodz liegt seit ihrer Entstehung im Jahre 1802 in polnischsprachiger Umgebung (→ Sprachenkarte I).

2. Wirtschaft und kulturelle sowie religiöse Lage

Fast das ganze Grenzland bei Leobschütz und Ratibor war katholischer Konfession, mit Ausnahme der evangelischen Ortschaft Sciborzyce Wielkie (Stibořice, Steuberwitz). Auch bei Kudowa dominierte die katholische

Bevölkerung, und nur Straussenay bildete eine von den Nachkommen der Tschechischen Brüder gegründete Siedlung. In diesen Gebieten waren konfessionelle Gründe kein Hindernis für Kontakte mit der dortigen (polnischen und deutschen) Bevölkerung. In den Sprachinseln brachte die Zugehörigkeit der Nachkommen der tschechischen religiösen Emigranten zur reformierten evangelischen Kirche eine gewisse Isolation mit sich. Sie kam darin zum Ausdruck, daß keine Mischehen geschlossen wurden. Für den Erhalt der Mundart war diese Abgeschlossenheit allerdings entschieden förderlich. Nach dem Zweiten Weltkrieg war dieser Faktor weniger ausgeprägt. Wirtschaftlich war die tschechische Bevölkerung mit ihrer deutschen bzw. polnischen, später nur polnischen Umgebung verbunden. Bei Kudowa und in dem polnisch-lachischen Grenzgebiet wurden die früher regen Kontakte nach dem Zweiten Weltkrieg schwächer und brachen mit der Zeit fast völlig ab. Nach 1948 wurde die Staatsgrenze undurchlässiger, was stellenweise von Korrekturen des Grenzverlaufs sowie vom Fluraustausch begleitet war. Die grenznahe wirtschaftliche Zusammenarbeit wurde unterbrochen, und die gegenseitigen grenzüberschreitenden Besuche von Familienangehörigen wurden erschwert.

3. Statistik und Ethnoprofile

Die durch die Jahrhunderte hindurch bestehende, weitgehende Einheitlichkeit der tschechischsprachigen Gemeinschaften in allen drei Gruppen zerfiel erst im 20. Jahrhundert, besonders nach dem Zweiten Weltkrieg. In jeder der drei Gruppen sah die Situation anders aus.

In der ehemaligen Grafschaft Glatz im sog. „Böhmischen Winkel" wurde Anfang des 20. Jahrhunderts die Zahl der tschechischsprachigen Bewohner auf 5550 Personen geschätzt (Kubín 1913). Nach Gründung der Textilfabriken bei Bad Kudowa kam es zu wesentlichen Veränderungen der Bevölkerungsstruktur: ein Teil der Heimarbeiter fand Beschäftigung in den Fabriken, ein anderer Teil emigrierte in verschiedene Regionen Deutschlands; höhergelegene Ortschaften begannen sich zu entvölkern. Kurz vor dem Zweiten Weltkrieg benutzten in den Dörfern um Bad Kudowa mehr als 5000 Menschen Tschechisch als Alltagssprache.

Nach dem Zweiten Weltkrieg wurde ein Großteil der Autochthonen nach Deutschland ausgesiedelt oder siedelte selbst in die verschiedenen tschechischen Gebiete um. Zwischen 1954 und 1958 (Siatkowski 1962) wohnten dort noch etwa 500 tschechischsprachige Autochthone, vor allem in den Ortschaften Czermna (Německá/Velká Čermná, Groß Tscherbenay), Słone (Slané, Schlanay), Pstrążna (Stroužné, Straussenay), Bukowina (Bukovina, Bukowine) und Jakubowice (Jakubovice, Jakobowitz). Die Stadt Kudowa samt der eingemeindeten, früher selbständigen Ortschaften Zaksze (Zakš/Žakec, Sakisch) und Błażejów (Blažejov, Blasewei – heute Kudowa Górna), sowie Brzozowice (Březová, Brzezowie) und die jenseits des Hauptkamms des Heuscheuergebirges gelegene Ortschaft Ostra Góra (früher aus zwei Dörfern bestehend: Vostrá Hora – Scharfenberg und Nouzín – Naussenay) hatten nur wenige Einwohner, die die tschechische Sprache kannten.

Nach ca. 30 Jahren fanden sich 1988 bei Kudowa nur noch ca. 40 Autochthone (Siatkowski 1990), meist mit Verwandtschaft in Polen. Die Älteren waren gestorben, andere im Rahmen der Familienzusammenführung nach Deutschland und Tschechien emigriert. Die weiter entfernt von Kudowa gelegenen Dörfer waren teils völlig verschwunden, teils stark entvölkert. Es erfolgte ein Zuzug polnischer Siedler.

Die tschechische Siedlung bei Strehlen ist Mitte des 18. Jahrhunderts entstanden. Die aus dem tschechischen Nordosten stammenden religiösen Emigranten ließen sich in Strehlen nieder und gründeten auch die Siedlungen Husinec (Hussinetz, Gęsiniec bzw. Gęsino), später Poděbrady (Mehltheuer, Gościęcice) und Kuropatnik (Töppendorf) (Frinta 1913, Kubín 1931, Sliziński 1959). Vor dem Zweiten Weltkrieg lebten um Strehlen ca. 5000 Personen. Nach den Nachkriegsumsiedlungen nach Deutschland und Tschechien ging ihre Zahl auf ca. 600 zurück. Die einst kompakte tschechische Besiedlung wich einer gemischten, deutlich polnisch dominierten Bevölkerung. 1961, als Material für den Tschechischen Sprachatlas gesammelt wurde (Voráč/Jančák 1962), war die tschechische Mundart noch im Familienmilieu bei der alten und mittleren Generation erhalten. Bis heute wohnen bei Strehlen noch ca. 30 Autochthone, meist mit polnischen Siedlern verwandt.

Zwei weitere tschechische Siedlungen in Schlesien sind nach dem Zweiten Weltkrieg verschwunden. Das betrifft das Gebiet der im

Oppelner Schlesien gegründeten Ortschaften Grodziec, früher Grec (Bedřichův Hradec, Friedrichsgrätz), Lubienia (Lubín, Sacken) und Piotrówka (Petrovice, Petersgrätz) sowie die östlich von Syców gelegene Siedlung mit Tabor Wielki (Velký/Bedřichův Tábor, Friedrichstabor), Tabor Mały (Malý Tábor), Czermin (Čermín, Tschermine) und Weronikopole (Veronikopoli) (Frinta 1913).

Anders gestaltete sich die Entwicklung der im 19. Jahrhundert in polnischer Umgebung südlich von Lodz gegründeten tschechischen Siedlungen. 1802 haben die tschechischen Siedler aus der Gegend von Syców ein Gut in Zelów gekauft. Durch schnell steigende Geburtenrate und starken Zuzug entstanden im Gebiet um Zelów bald neue Siedlungen: Poździenice, Ignaców, Józefatów, Zelówek, Bujny, und um 1850 Kuców, von wo aus sich die tschechische Besiedlung auf Żłobnica, Folwark, Aleksandrów, Faustynów und Krzaki ausbreitete. Die ursprüngliche Kompaktheit der dort ansässigen Gemeinschaft wurde in gewissem Maße bereits nach dem Ersten Weltkrieg gestört, als ein Teil der Bewohner in die ehemalige Tschechoslowakei abwanderte. Allerdings waren die Tschechen in Zelów und Kuców bis zum Zweiten Weltkrieg in der Mehrheit. 1945—1946 emigrierten aus Zelów ca. 4500 Einwohner. Ebenso blieben nach dem Krieg nur 25 der 40 Familien in Kuców. Die zahlenmäßige Stärke der Sprachinsel von Zelów ging nach dem Krieg auf ca. 600 und der von Kuców auf ca. 200 Tschechen zurück (Vydra 1923, Dejna 1955, Wolska 1980). In letzter Zeit kam es aber zu Veränderungen, die das Fortbestehen dieser Mundart in der Zukunft gefährden. Durch die Ausweitung des Braunkohlentagebaus bei Bełchatów wurde das ganze Dorf Kuców geräumt, und die Bewohner zogen nach Bełchatów und Kleszczów um.

Im polnisch—tschechischen Grenzland bei Ratibor und Leobschütz blieb bis heute die lachische Mundart erhalten, die von der örtlichen Bevölkerung als mährische Mundart bezeichnet wird. Bis 1532 gehörten diese Gebiete zum Herzogtum Oppeln-Ratibor, regiert durch die Piasten-Herzöge und später bis 1742 durch die böhmischen Könige, bis sie — zusammen mit den südlich angrenzenden Gebieten des tschechischen Schlesien — Preußen angeschlossen wurden. Der ursprüngliche Sprachraum der lachischen Mundarten reichte wahrscheinlich weiter, aber größere Fortschritte machte dort die Germanisierung erst in der ersten Hälfte des 20. Jahrhunderts.

Auch die Grenze zwischen den lachischen und polnischen Mundarten hat sich dort in den 100—150 Jahren vor dem Zweiten Weltkrieg nicht verändert. Sie deckte sich ungefähr mit der Grenze des ehemaligen Bistums Olomouc/Olmütz. Im 20. Jahrhundert erreichte der Sprachraum des Lachischen in diesem Gebiet folgende Ortschaften: Branice Plur. (tschech. Branice Sing., dt. Branitz), Boboluszki (Bobolusky, Boblowitz), Wódka (Vodka, Hochkretscham), Chruścielów, früher auch Kraścielewo (Chrastělov, Krastillau), Nasiedle (Násilí, Nassiedel), Jakubowice (Jakubovice, Jakubowitz), Uciechowice (Utěchovice, Auchwitz), Wiechowice (Vechovice, Wehen), Ściborzyce Wielkie (Stibořice, Steuberwitz) und das nördlich von diesem Grenzstreifen gelegene Städtchen Baborów (Bavorov, Bauerwitz) in der Gegend von Leobschütz sowie Pietrowice Wielkie (Velké Petrovice, Groß Peterwitz), Samborowice, früher auch Szamarzowice (Šamařovice, Schammerwitz/Schammerau), Pietraszyn, früher auch Pietrzacin (Petřatin, Klein Peterwitz), Krzanowice, früher Krzenowice (Křenovice, Kranowitz/Kranstädt), Borucin/Borzucin (Bořutin, Borutin), Bolesław (Boleslav, Boleslau), Bieńkowice (Benkovice, B(i)enkowitz), Tworków (Tvorkov, Tvorkau/Tunskirch), Owsiszcze (Ovsiště, Owschütz), Nowa Wioska, früher Chałupki Owsiskie (Ovsišťké Chaloupky, Neudörfel) in der Gegend von Ratibor.

Nach dem Ersten Weltkrieg wurde der südliche Teil des Kreises Ratibor der ehemaligen Tschechoslowakei angegliedert und gelangte somit in den Einflußbereich der tschechischen Literatursprache, während der nördliche Teil innerhalb der Grenzen Deutschlands blieb und einer beschleunigten Gemanisierung ausgesetzt war. Nach dem Zweiten Weltkrieg ist es in den Polen zugefallenen lachischen Gebieten in der Gegend von Leobschütz und Ratibor zu weitgehenden Veränderungen gekommen. Unmittelbar nach dem Kriege war die dortige Bevölkerung zweisprachig, aber nur noch ältere Menschen bedienten sich der lachischen Mundart, während die Jugend ausschließlich deutsch sprach. Die lachischen Mundarten und deren polnische Nachbarmundarten haben in der älteren Generation ihren ursprünglichen Charakter noch bewahrt. Das beweisen auch die Ergebnisse von Feldforschungen, die Ende der 40er sowie in den 50er und 60er Jahren durchgeführt wurden (Dejna 1949, 1951, 1953, Teksty 1957, Skulina 1961,

1962a, 1962b, Laskowski 1966, 1971, Balhar 1968, Balhar/Jančák 1992). Nach 1945 standen die lachischen Mundarten unter dem Einfluß der polnischen Literatursprache, die sie aus der alltäglichen Kommunikation immer mehr zu verdrängen begann. In den Dörfern um Ratibor ist die Zahl der Autochthonen weitgehend gleich geblieben (nur in Groß Peterwitz erreicht die eingewanderte Bevölkerung jetzt beinahe 50%), jedoch kam es zu einer merklichen Entvölkerung infolge mehrerer Auswanderungswellen nach Deutschland. In der Gegend von Leobschütz wurde die autochthone Bevölkerung lachischer Ortschaften anfangs auch nicht ausgesiedelt. Die spätere Emigration hat jedoch dazu geführt, daß die Autochthonen dort nur noch einen geringen Bruchteil und die Umsiedler aus verschiedenen Gegenden Polens die Mehrheit der Einwohner ausmachen. Geblieben sind vor allem diejenigen Autochthonen, die in Verwandtschaftsbeziehungen zu den zugewanderten Polen stehen. Auch dort ist es zu einer merklichen Entvölkerung gekommen.

4. Soziolinguistische Situation

Infolge von Migration und geringerer Kontakte mit der Bevölkerung auf der tschechischen Seite der Grenze sowie fehlendem tschechischen Nationalgefühl kam es nach dem Zweiten Weltkrieg zu einer wesentlichen Veränderung der sprachlichen Situation, die sich in den drei Mundartengruppen unterschiedlich gestaltete: bei Bad Kudowa und Strehlen begann sich anstelle des früheren tschechisch−deutschen Bilinguismus ein tschechisch−polnisch−deutscher Trilinguismus bzw. tschechisch−polnischer Bilinguismus zu entwickeln, der je nach Familienbeziehungen, Alter und Berufsgruppe der Sprecher stark differierte. In den ehemals lachischen Gebieten bei Ratibor und Leobschütz wurde der ursprüngliche deutsch−lachische Bilinguismus durch den polnisch−deutschen Bilinguismus abgelöst. Im Falle dieser beiden dialektalen Gruppen kann in den letzten Jahren von einer einheitlichen tschechischen Mundart schon keine Rede mehr sein. Gegenwärtig besteht nur noch in der tschechischen Sprachinsel bei Lodz eine tschechische Gemeinschaft − wenn auch in beschränktem Maße.

5. Sprachpolitische Lage

In allen tschechischen Mundartgruppen auf polnischem Gebiet wird Tschechisch heute offiziell nicht gebraucht. Nirgends gibt es tschechische Schulen, Print- oder andere Medien; es besteht auch kein geschlossenes tschechisches Siedlungsgebiet, in dem eine tschechische Verwaltung funktionieren könnte. In Strehlen wurde die 1776 gegründete tschechische Schule 1870 durch eine deutsche ersetzt. Nach dem Zweiten Weltkrieg gab es bei Bad Kudowa und Strehlen einige Jahre lang tschechische Schulen, die dann durch polnische ersetzt wurden. In der Gegend von Leobschütz und Ratibor wurden die ehemals tschechischen Schulen bereits in der zweiten Hälfte des 19. Jahrhunderts durch deutsche ersetzt. Nach dem Zweiten Weltkrieg forderte niemand tschechische Schulen; erst seit einigen Jahren wird auf Verlangen der dort tätigen Organisation der deutschen Minderheit an den polnischen Schulen um Ratibor Deutsch als Pflichtfach unterrichtet.

Für die Erhaltung des Tschechischen in diesen Gebieten spielte auch die Kirche eine wesentliche Rolle. Die Emigranten haben ihre Religiosität weitestgehend bewahrt. Gegenwärtig ist Zelów ein wichtiges Zentrum der Nachkommen der einstigen Böhmischen Brüder. In der Ortskirche werden ständig Gottesdienste auf Polnisch zelebriert und tschechische Kirchenlieder gesungen. Der Priester aus Zelów ist gleichzeitig Verwalter der ehemaligen Gemeinden der reformierten evangelischen Kirche bei Strehlen und in Straussenay bei Bad Kudowa. In den lachischen Dörfern bei Leobschütz und Ratibor, in den ehemaligen Grenzen der Diözese Olmütz, sind tschechische Gottesdienste − obwohl allmählich durch deutsche verdrängt − in manchen Ortschaften zum Teil bis heute erhalten geblieben. In den einzelnen Ortschaften sah das jedoch sehr unterschiedlich aus. In der Gegend von Leobschütz hat das Deutsche mancherorts bereits zu Beginn des 20. Jahrhunderts das Tschechische verdrängt, aber in Nassiedel und Steuberwitz soll es sowohl vor als auch nach dem Krieg mährische Gottesdienste gegeben haben. In der Gegend von Ratibor blieb das Tschechische in der Kirche in der Regel bis in die Nazizeit hinein erhalten und wurde mancherorts in den ersten Nachkriegsjahren wieder eingeführt. Gottesdienste in tschechischer Sprache wurden um das Jahr 1952 endgültig eingestellt und administrativ durch polnische ersetzt. Etwas länger blieben tschechische Kirchenlieder sowie traditionelle Hochzeits- und Begräbnislieder erhalten. Jedoch konnte sich 1993 keiner meiner Informanten mehr daran erinnern. In der

Gegend von Ratibor werden seit einigen Jahren die Gottesdienste in der Kirche abwechselnd in Polnisch und in Deutsch abgehalten (Siatkowski 1994a).

Für den Fortbestand des Tschechischen in der Gegend von Bad Kudowa spielte die gut entwickelte Folklore auch eine wichtige Rolle. Sie wurde von begabten Volkserzählern während der *toulačky* genannten nachbarlichen Abendtreffen gepflegt (Kubín 1908, 1910, Jech 1959).

6. Allgemeines kontaktlinguistisches Porträt

Die historisch sehr vielfältigen tschechisch-polnischen Sprachkontakte waren anderer Art als die heutige unmittelbare mundartliche Interferenz. Die tschechische Literatursprache übte einen starken Einfluß auf das literarische Polnisch des 10.–16. Jahrhunderts aus (Siatkowski 1994b) und umgekehrt beeinflußte die polnische Sprache das Tschechische bei dessen Wiedergeburt im 19. Jahrhundert (Orłoś 1987). Gegenwärtig sind die literatursprachigen tschechisch–polnischen Einflüsse äußerst selten: neuerdings gebraucht man in verschiedenen polnischen Milieus die Bohemismen *spolegliwy* 'verläßlich', *styki* 'Beziehungen'. In den drei Typen der tschechischen Mundarten verlief die polnisch–tschechische Interferenz unterschiedlich.

Das Lachische als typische Übergangsmundart, vertreten in der Gegend von Leobschütz und Ratibor, wies konsequent auftretende sowohl tschechische (1) *trat, tlat – krava, hłava*, (2) Oralvokale anstelle der ursprünglichen Nasalvokale – *maso, huś*, (3) das Fehlen des Umlauts bei ursprünglichen *ě, e – suśet, ćetka*, (4) *h* anstelle des ursprünglichen *g – hrach, rohy*, (5) fehlende Palatalisierung von Lippenkonsonanten sowie von *s, z* vor dem alten *e – bereće, popeł, sestra*) als auch polnische Sprachmerkmale auf (1) das Fehlen der Vokalquantität, (2) die Wortbetonung auf der vorletzten Silbe, sowie in einem Teil der lachischen Mundarten: (3) der Übergang von *t', d'* zu *ć, ʒ – veʒeće*, (4) die Erhaltung der weichen *p', b', m', v* vor den alten *ě, ę, i – pata, hováźi*, (5) der Übergang der palatalisierten *s', z'* vor den alten *ě, i, ь* zu palatalen *ś, ź – huś, śeno, hroźba* u. a. m.). Ohne Zweifel mußte es dort seit jeher zu verschiedenen Interferenzerscheinungen kommen, z. B. in polnischen schlesischen Mundarten neben dem regelmäßig erhaltenen *g* auch das in Entlehnungen auftretende tschechische *h*, das in fester assimilierten Wörtern durch *ch* ersetzt wurde (*chledać, chruby*); andererseits gibt es in den lachischen Mundarten den *g*-Laut im polnischen Lehnwort *gorzałka*. Die noch kurz nach dem Krieg gut erhaltene lachische Mundart wird heute kaum mehr gesprochen (Siatkowski 1994a). In allen ursprünglich lachischen Ortschaften wird fast durchgehend polnisch gesprochen, in der Regel Standardsprache, nur einzelne mährische Worte und Formen werden eingeflochten. In jeder Äußerung werden die typischsten Merkmale des Lachischen durch polnische Formen ersetzt: (1) mit *trot, tlot – krova, vłosy*, (2) mit polnischen Fortsetzungen der Nasalvokale – *zajonc, język*, (3) mit Ablaut – *ḿasto, śostra*, (4) mit dem Konsonanten *g – głova*, (5) mit palatalen Konsonanten *ś, ź, ć, ʒ – śivy, śeʒeć* usw. Mehr mährische Elemente waren bei älteren Frauen zu finden, und zwar in Situationen, in denen mehrere Mundartkundige am Gespräch beteiligt waren.

In der Gegend von Bad Kudowa waren sich die Sprecher der tschechischen Gemeinschaft weitgehend keiner System- und Lexikentsprechungen zwischen dem Polnischen und Tschechischen bewußt. Die Informanten gebrauchten Formen des polnischen Systems, die sie für ihre eigenen hielten, z. B. *kroṷa, mnoho kruṷ* 'Kuh', 'viele Kühe' u. ä. m. Sie traten sporadisch auf und waren bei den einzelnen Informanten oft unterschiedlich ausgeprägt. Weiter verbreitet waren anfangs Entlehnungen im Wortschatzbereich der Verwaltung (*gmina* 'Gemeinde', *podátek* 'Steuer', *soltis* 'Dorfrichter, Dorfschulze') sowie häufiger gebrauchte Wörter (*robit* 'arbeiten', *list* 'Brief', *zauše* 'immer' usw.). Diese Entlehnungen wurden in der Regel phonetisch angeglichen durch die Beseitigung von Lauten, die der Mundart der Gegend von Bad Kudowa fremd waren, z. B. *lesniči* von poln. *leśniczy, vitečka* von *wycieczka, pjechotoṷ* von *piechotą*, u. ä. m. (Siatkowski 1962). Später war für alle charakteristisch: der häufige Schwund der Palatalkonsonanten *t', d', ń*, der Quantitätsschwund sowie zahlreiche lexikalische Polonismen, in denen die Konsonanten *ś, ź, ć, ʒ* durch *š, ž, č, ǯ* ersetzt waren (Siatkowski 1990).

Um Strehlen waren die neuen polnischen Einflüsse unmittelbar nach dem Kriege beschränkt auf den Wortschatz aus dem Bereich der Verwaltung und im Alltag besonders häufig vorkommender Wörter (*curka*

'Tochter', *ojtec* 'Vater', *musíme robit* 'wir müssen arbeiten'). Die ältere Generation unterlag noch keinen polnischen Einflüssen im Bereich der Phonetik (Betonung, Quantität, der Konsonant *ř*, poln. *ś, ź, ć, ʒ́* wurden ersetzt durch *s, z, t', d'* oder auch schon durch *š, ž, č, ǯ*), vgl. Voráč/Jančák 1962.

In letzter Zeit läßt sich um Bad Kudowa und Strehlen sowie im ehemaligen lachischen Mundartgebiet bei Ratibor und Leobschütz eine scheinbar regellose Mischsprache beobachten. Zur Bestimmung der sie beeinflussenden Faktoren erweist sich jedoch eine eingehendere soziologische Untersuchung als notwendig.

Unter den Bedingungen eines allgemeinen Bilinguismus ist es in der Mundart von Kucόw bei Lodz zu Interferenzen gekommen, die in den einzelnen Ebenen der Sprache unterschiedlich stark ausgeprägt sind (Dejna 1978—1990). In die tschechische Mundart von Kucόw ist eine sehr große Zahl von polnischen Lehnwörtern eingedrungen. Von den ca. 6000 Stichwörtern im Wörterbuch dieser Mundart kann für fast 2000 polnische Herkunft angenommen werden. In den Wortentlehnungen blieben zahlreiche polnische Merkmale erhalten wie (1) die Gruppen *trot, tlot* (*krul, chu̯opak*) und die Sonantenentwicklung (*sarna, peu̯ńa*), (2) die polnischen Fortsetzungen der Nasalvokale (*vuntroba, poremba*), (3) der Konsonant *ʒ* (*uroʒaj*), (4) der polnische Umlaut (*zavjas, ježoro*), (5) der Konsonant *g* (*gaʒina* 'Geflügel'), (6) weiche *ś, ź, ć, ʒ́* (*kośisko, teśćova, ʒ́eržava*), ersetzt auch durch *š, ž, č, ǯ* (*košarka, žrudło, mačora, spuǯelńa*) usw., (7) einige Merkmale der mittelpolnischen Mundarten wie *o ≤ å* (*modrok* 'Kornblume'), das sog. Masurieren (*vojcim* 'Stiefvater') u. a. m. Es kam auch zu phonologischen Interferenzen: (1) Schwund der phonologischen Vokallänge, (2) Ersetzen des frikativen *ř* durch *ž* (*š*), die sich aber von den ursprünglichen, „weicheren" *ž, š* (*žbet, pšyšli*) unterscheiden, (3) Übergang des *i* zu *y* nach harten *ž* (*š*) aus *ř* (*kšyš, žebžyna*), (4) Übergang der ursprünglichen Liquide *l* und *ł* zu *u̯* außer in der Stellung vor ursprünglichen *i* (*škou̯i* 'Schulen', *pou̯e* 'Feld' — *na poli* 'auf dem Feld'), (5) Herausbildung der Opposition *g : k* (*gu̯as* 'Felsstein' : *ku̯as* 'Ähre'), (6) Herausbildung der Opposition von harten und weichen Labialkonsonanten vor *i* (*mi* 'wir' : *ḿi* 'mir', *biu̯* '(er) war' : *ḃiu̯* '(er) schlug'). Im Bereich der Flexion lassen sich nur einige weiter verbreitete Erscheinungen der polnischen Interferenz anführen wie (1) der Gen. Plur. in der Funktion des Akk. Plur. belebter männlicher Substantive (*vid'eu̯ sem vojaku, sousedu̯*), (2) der Dat.-Loc. Sing. belebter männlicher Substantive auf *-ovi* (*k sousedovi, koňovi*), (3) Verallgemeinerung der Endungen im Imperativ Plur. auf *-ime, -ite* (*tahńime, tahńite*), (4) Ausweitung der in der Mundart von Kucόw vorhandenen Endungen unter dem Einfluß des Polnischen auch auf andere Deklinationstypen (z. B. Gen. Sing. auf *-u* in Substantiven mit weich auslautendem Stamm — *čaju, drobju*) u. a. m. Im Bereich der Wortbildung kam es zwar zu keiner Entlehnung von neuen Wortbildungselementen, wohl aber durch Wortentlehnungen aus dem Polnischen zu Frequenzänderungen einzelner Affixe, wie *-(i)je* (*parafije, religije*), *-isko* (*kośisko, pastvisko*) oder zu Distributionsänderungen wie z. B. *naučiteu̯* — tschech. *učitel, koležanka* — *kolegyně, amerikanski* — *americký* usw.

Trotz erheblicher Interferenz in Wortschatz, Phonetik und Phonologie sowie z. T. im grammatischen System blieb die Mundart von Kucόw bis in die letzten Jahre eine tschechische Mundart. Gut erhalten blieb das eigene grammatische und phonetische System mit charakteristischen mundartlichen Eigenschaften des tschechischen Nordostens.

7. Stand der polnisch—tschechischen Kontaktforschung

Die Fachliteratur über die tschechischen Mundarten auf dem heutigen Gebiet Polens ist sehr umfangreich. Sie umfaßt vor allem die inselhafte tschechische Besiedlung (Frinta 1913, Kubín 1931) und die Beschreibung der einzelnen Mundarten, wobei angestrebt wurde, möglichst die ältesten Formen zu erfassen und die polnisch—lachische Sprachgrenze sowie den Ursprung der lachischen Mundarten zu bestimmen (Stieber 1934, 1938, Havránek 1934, Dejna 1949, 1951, 1953, Skulina 1961—1962 u. a.). In dieser letzten Frage ist es nicht zur Annährung der Standpunkte der tschechischen und polnischen Sprachwissenschaftler gekommen. Vollständigere Informationen über die polnisch—tschechischen Interferenz gibt nur Dejna (1978—1990) für Kucόw an; für die anderen Gebiete gibt es nur fragmentarische Angaben (Siatkowski 1962, 1990, Voráč/Jančák 1962, Skulina 1961—1962, Balhar 1968). Die von mir 1993 um Ratibor und Leobschütz durchgeführten Untersuchungen und die Informationen des Konsistoriums der reformierten evangelischen Kirche in Warschau (Siatkowski 1994 a) ergaben, daß außer in der tschechischen Sprachinsel bei Lodz die übrigen tschechischen Mundarten kaum mehr gesprochen werden. Dadurch wird es auch unmöglich, die früher in ihnen abgelaufenen Interferenzprozesse genauer zu erforschen.

8. Bibliographie (in Auswahl)

Balhar, Jan (1968): „Lašská nářečí v marburském archivu" [Die lachischen Mundarten im Marburger Spracharchiv]. In: *Slezský sborník 66*, 494−510.

Balhar, Jan/Jančák, Pavel (1992): *Český jazykový atlas* [Der Tschechische Sprachatlas], Prag.

Dejna, Karol (1949): „Z najnowszej dialektologii śląskiej" [Aus der neuesten schlesischen Dialektologie]. In: *Język Polski 29*, 206−215.

Dejna, Karol (1951, 1953): *Polsko−laskie pogranicze językowe* [Das polnisch−lachische sprachliche Grenzland], I−II, Französische Zusammenfassung, Łódź.

Dejna, Karol (1955): „Gwara kuczowska na tle innych gwar czeskich" [Die Mundart von Kuców vor dem Hintergrund anderer tschechischer Mundarten]. In: *Rozprawy Komisji Językowej Łódzkiego Towarzystwa Naukowego (RKJ ŁTN) 3*, 5−30.

Dejna, Karol (1978): „Polskie elementy językowe w gwarze czeskiej wsi Kuców koło Bełchatowa" [Die polnischen sprachlichen Elemente in der tschechischen Mundart des Dorfes Kuców bei Bełchatów]. In: *Z polskich studiów slawistycznych 5*, 221−231.

Dejna, Karol (1981): „System fleksyjny gwary czeskiej mieszkańców Kucowa pod Bełchatowem" [Das Flexionssystem der tschechischen Mundart von Kuców bei Bełchatów]. In: *RKJ ŁTN 27*, 39−62.

Dejna, Karol (1983 a): „System fonetyczny i fonologiczny gwary czeskiej Kucowa pod Bełchatowem" [Das phonetische und phonologische System der tschechischen Mundart von Kuców bei Bełchatów]. In: *Studia z Filologii Polskiej i Słowiańskiej 21*, 165−176.

Dejna, Karol (1983 b): „Alternacje morfologiczne w gwarze mieszkańców Kucowa pod Bełchatowem" [Morphologische Alternationen in der Mundart der Bewohner von Kuców bei Bełchatów]. In: *RKJ ŁTN 28*, 11−20.

Dejna, Karol (1984): „Interferencje w mowie czeskiej mieszkańców Kucowa pod Bełchatowem wywołane kontaktami z językiem polskim" [Interferenzen in der tschechischen Sprache der Bewohner von Kuców bei Bełchatów infolge der Kontakte mit dem Polnischen]. In: *RKJ ŁTN 29*, 23−46.

Dejna, Karol (1985, 1987): „Geneza i struktura gwary czeskiej mieszkańców Kucowa pod Bełchatowem" [Genese und Struktur der tschechischen Mundart der Bewohner von Kuców bei Bełchatów]. In: *RKJ ŁTN 31*, 19−35; *33*, 29−36.

Dejna, Karol (1986): „Wyrazowe pożyczki z polszczyzny w gwarze czeskiej Kucowa pod Bełchatowem" [Wortentlehnungen aus dem Polnischen in der tschechischen Mundart von Kuców bei Bełchatów]. In: *RKJ ŁTN 32*, 67−71.

Dejna, Karol (1990 a): *Słownik gwary czeskiej mieszkańców Kucowa* [Wörterbuch der tschechischen Mundart der Bewohner von Kuców], Breslau.

Dejna, Karol (1990 b): „Słowotwórstwo sufiksalne gwary czeskiej okolic Kucowa" [Die suffixale Wortbildung der tschechischen Mundart in der Gegend von Kuców]. In: *RKJ ŁTN 35*, 19−68.

Frinta, Antonín (1913): „Čeština emigrantských osad v Prusku" [Die tschechische Sprache in den Auswanderersiedlungen in Preußen]. In: *Sborník filologický 4*, 207−231.

Havránek, Bohuslav (1934): „Nářečí česká" [Die tschechischen Mundarten]. In: *Československá vlastivěda 3: Jazyk*, Prag, 205−208, 211.

Jech, Jaromír (1959): *Lidová vyprávění z Kladska* [Glatzer Volksmärchen], Prag.

Kubín, Josef (1908, 1910): *Povídky kladské* [Glatzer Volksmärchen] I−II, Prag.

Kubín, Josef (1913): *Lidomluva Čechů kladských* [Die tschechische Mundart in der Grafschaft Glatz], Prag.

Kubín, Josef (1931): *České emigrantské osady v Pruském Slezsku. Čechové štrálští* [Die tschechischen Auswanderersiedlungen in Preußisch-Schlesien. Die Tschechen bei Strehlen], Prag.

Laskowski, Roman (1966, 1971): *Derywacja rzeczowników w dialektach laskich* [Die Ableitung der Substantive in den lachischen Mundarten] I−II, Französische Zusammenfassung, Breslau.

Siatkowski, Janusz (1962): *Dialekt czeski okolic Kudowy* [Der tschechische Dialekt der Umgebung von Kudowa] I−II, Breslau.

Siatkowski, Janusz (1990): „Obecna sytuacja językowa w okolicy Kudowy" [Die gegenwärtige sprachliche Situation in der Gegend von Kudowa]. In: *Tgolí chole Mêstró*, Lachmann, R., Lauhus, A., Lewandowski, T., Zelinsky, B. (Eds.), Köln−Wien, 117−123.

Siatkowski, Janusz (1994 a): „Polsko-czeskie kontakty językowe na terenie Polski" [Die polnisch−tschechischen Sprachkontakte auf dem Gebiet Polens]. In: *Prace Filologiczne 39*, 231−246.

Siatkowski, Janusz (1994 b): „Der Einfluß der tschechischen Sprache auf das Polnische". In: *Zeitschrift für Slawistik 39/2*, 261−269. Mit Besprechung der bisherigen Literatur.

Skulina, Josef (1961): „Lašské okrajové nářečí na Pštině a Odře" [Die periphere lachische Mundart an der Zinna und Oder]. In: *Slezský sborník 59*, 229−239.

Skulina, Josef (1962 a): „Glosa o lašském nářečí na území Polské lidové republiky" [Eine Glosse zur lachischen Mundart auf dem Gebiet der Volksrepublik Polen]. In: *Slavica Pragensia 4*, 593−598.

Skulina, Josef (1962 b): „Z problematiky vývoje nářečí na pomezí dvou blízce příbuzných jazyků" [Zu Problemen der Mundartenentwicklung im Grenzgebiet zweier eng verwandter Sprachen]. In: *Slezský sborník 60*, 232−236.

Stieber, Zdzisław (1934): *Geneza gwar laskich* [Die Genese der lachischen Mundarten], Krakau.

Stieber, Zdzisław (1938): *Sposoby powstawania słowiańskich gwar przejściowych* [Die Entstehungsarten der slawischen Übergangsmundarten]), Krakau.

Śliziński, Jerzy (1959): *Z działalności literackiej Braci Czeskish w Polsce* [Aus dem literarischen Wirken der Tschechischen Brüder in Polen], Breslau.

Teksty (1957): „Teksty gwarowe ze wsi Krzanowice w powiecie raciborskim" [Mundartliche Texte aus dem Dorf Kranowitz im Kreis Ratibor]. In: *Studia z Filologii Polskiej i Słowiańskiej 2*, 270−319.

Voráč, Jaroslav/Jančák, Pavel (1962): „K dnešnímu stavu nářečí střelínských Čechů v Polsku" [Zum heutigen Stand der tschechischen Mundart bei Strehlen in Polen]. In: *Slavica Pragensia 4*, 599−604.

Vydra, Bohumil (1923): „Z nářečí zelovských Čechů v Polsku" [Über die Mundart der Tschechen von Zelów in Polen]. In: *Pastrnkův sborník*, Prag, 142−157.

Wolska, Ilona (1980): „Fleksja rzeczowników gwary czeskiej Zelowa" [Die Flexion der Substantive in der tschechischen Mundart von Zelów]. In: *RKJ ŁTN 26*, 99−115.

Janusz Siatkowski, Warschau (Polen)

200. Tschechien

1. Geographie und Demographie
2. Territorialgeschichte und Staatsbildung
3. Politik, Wirtschaft und allgemeine kulturelle sowie religiöse Lage
4. Statistik und Ethnoprofile
5. Soziolinguistische Lage
6. Sprachpolitische Lage
7. Weitere Minderheiten und Kontaktsprachen
8. Zur Forschungslage
9. Bibliographie (in Auswahl)

1. Geographie und Demographie

1.1. Historisch-rechtlich betrachtet, setzt sich die Tschechische Republik (ČR), ein Staat mit einer Fläche von 78 864 km^2, aus drei Teilen zusammen: aus Böhmen (d. h. dem westlichen Teil), aus Mähren (dem östlichen Teil) und aus einem Teil von Schlesien (dem nordöstlichen Teil). Obwohl diese Teile keine politisch-verwaltungsmäßigen Einheiten darstellen, haben sie so viele spezifische kulturelle Wesenszüge (einschließlich der sprachlichen Spezifika), daß sie als gewissermaßen natürliche Entitäten wahrgenommen werden. Dazu trug gewiß auch die geographische Gliederung dieser Teile bei: während Böhmens Territorium von allen Seiten von Gebirgen umgeben ist, stellt Mähren mit seinen Tiefebenen ein in Richtung Österreich und des slowakischen Donaugebietes offenes Territorium dar.

1.2. Nach der letzten Volkszählung (3. 3. 1991) lebten auf dem Gebiet der ČR 10 302 215 Einwohner, die sich zu folgenden Nationalitäten bekannten: zur tschechischen 8 363 768 (81,2%), zur mährischen 1 362 313 (13,2%), zur slowakischen 314 877 (3,1%); die weiteren Nationalitäten sind mit weniger als 1% bzw. 0,5% vertreten: Polen (59 383), Deutsche (48 556), Schlesier (44 446), Roma (32 903), Ungarn (19 932), Ukrainer (8 220), Russen (5 062), Bulgaren (3 487), Griechen (3 379), Ruthenier (1 926), Rumänen (1 034), Sonstige (10 912), nicht Festgestellte (22 017). Die Nationalität der Bevölkerung wurde nicht auf der Grundlage der Muttersprache festgestellt, sondern auf deklarative Weise; man kann also nicht automatisch voraussetzen, daß ein Bürger, der diese oder jene Nationalität angab, zugleich auch Sprecher der entsprechenden Sprache ist. Die oben angeführte Klassifizierung der Nationalitäten reflektiert eine bestimmte Bewegung im Nationalitätenbewußtsein der Bevölkerung und ein offeneres Herangehen an die Nationalitätenprobleme seitens der Behörden. Anstelle der bisher angewendeten einheitlichen Kategorie *tschechische Nationalität* wurden drei Kategorien neu eingeführt: tschechische, mährische und schlesische Nationalität. Zu den weiteren Veränderungen gehört auch die Tatsache, daß man jetzt die ukrainische Nationalität in die ukrainische und die ruthenische unterteilt hat. Zum ersten Mal seit 1930 wurde auch die selbständige Nationalität der Roma festgestellt (Srb 1992).

1.3. Die aktuelle Bewegung größerer Bevölkerungsgruppen betrifft vor allem die Roma, die aus der Slowakei nach Böhmen migrieren (vgl. 7.1.). Aufgrund der Entscheidung der staatlichen Organe wurde die Zahl der vietnamesischen Werktätigen allmählich gesenkt; 1985 lebten hier 19 350 Gastarbeiter (Heroldová/Matějová 1987). Im Zusammenhang mit der Havarie des Atomkraftwerks Tschernobyl kam es 1991 zur staatlich gelenkten Remigration der sog. Wolhynien-Tschechen, die in den gefährdeten Gebieten der Ukraine lebten; in die ČR übersiedelten 893 (Valášková 1992); → Sprachenkarte K.

2. Territorialgeschichte und Staatsbildung

Unter dem Gesichtspunkt der weiteren Entwicklung der ethnischen Zusammensetzung der auf dem heutigen Territorium der ČR lebenden Bevölkerung ist die auf Initiative der tschechischen Herrscher im 12. und 13. Jahrhundert verlaufende sog. deutsche Kolonisation der bisher unbewohnten Wald- und Sumpfgebiete von grundlegender Bedeutung. Seit dieser Zeit koexistierten auf dem Territorium der heutigen ČR das tschechische und das deutsche Ethnikum. 1526 gelangten die Habsburger auf den böhmischen Thron; 1620 unterdrückten sie blutig den Aufstand des böhmischen Adels − es folgten die gewaltsame Rekatholisierung des Landes und eine definitive Übersiedelung des Staatsverwaltungszentrums von Prag nach Wien, die − namentlich zur Zeit der Aufklärung im 18. Jahrhundert − zur Dominanz des Deutschen in einigen Kommunikationsbereichen führte. Seit dem Ende des 18. Jahrhunderts bis in die sechziger Jahre des 19. Jahrhunderts verlief ein Prozeß, der traditionell *tschechische nationale Wiedergeburt* genannt wird; er war auf die Erringung einer größeren kulturellen und politischen Souveränität im Rahmen des Habsburger Reiches gerichtet und wurde von Anfang an auch als Wiedergeburt der tschechischen Sprache im Sinne der Erweiterung ihrer gesellschaftlichen Funktionen und Säuberung vom Einfluß des Deutschen verstanden. Die politischen Ambitionen der Tschechen wurden 1918 erfüllt, als die selbständige Tschechoslowakische Republik (Tschechoslowakei) als einer der Nachfolgestaaten der untergegangenen Habsburger Monarchie entstand. Die vielfältige Nationalitätenzusammensetzung der Tschechoslowakischen Republik war in der ganzen Zeit ihrer Existenz ein Spannungsherd und trug (im ganzen zweimal) entscheidend zu ihrem Untergang bei. Nach der Volkszählung des Jahres 1921 waren die einzelnen Nationalitäten wie folgt vertreten: die tschechische und slowakische 65,51% (im Sinne der Konzeption des einheitlichen tschechoslowakischen Volkes gemeinsam angeführt [vgl. 6.]), die deutsche 23,36%, die ungarische 5,57%, die ruthenische und russische 3,45%, die jüdische 1,35% (am Rande sei bemerkt, daß die Juden in den tschechischen Ländern zu dieser Zeit schon sprachlich assimiliert waren), die polnische 0,57%, die übrigen 0,2% (Fryščák 1978).

Einen Spannungsherd bildeten besonders die Beziehungen zwischen den Tschechen und Deutschen, den Tschechen und Slowaken und nicht zuletzt auch zwischen Slowaken und Ungarn. 1938 mußte auf der Grundlage des Münchener Abkommens die Tschechoslowakei umfangreiche Grenzgebiete, in denen das deutsche Ethnikum mehr als die Hälfte der Bevölkerung darstellte, an Deutschland abtreten. Das umstrittene Gebiet um Těšín (Teschin) in Schlesien fiel Polen zu. 1939 wurde Restböhmen und Mähren von Deutschland okkupiert und das sog. Protektorat ausgerufen. Die Slowakei schuf unter dem Patronat Hitlers den selbständigen slowakischen Staat und kämpfte an der Seite Deutschlands. Das Kriegsende bedeutete die Erneuerung der Tschechoslowakischen Republik (allerdings ohne die Karpaten-Ukraine). Eine grundlegende Änderung der ethnischen Zusammensetzung brachte besonders die Aussiedlung und Vertreibung der autochthonen deutschen Bevölkerung aus dem Grenzgebiet Böhmens und Mährens (an die drei Millionen Menschen) in den Jahren 1946 und 1947 auf der Grundlage der von den siegreichen Großmächten in Potsdam gefaßten Beschlüsse. Außerordentlich stark verringerte sich die Zahl der jüdischen Bevölkerung: von mehr als 160 000 Angehörigen dieser Gruppe (Angaben für die gesamte Tschechoslowakei) kehrten nach dem Krieg nicht ganz 20 000 zurück (als Folge der Judenverfolgung und der Emigration). Für die weitere Entwicklung der Tschechoslowakischen Republik waren die Beziehungen zwischen Tschechen und Slowaken entscheidend. Weder die Ideologie des proletarischen Internationalismus, den die kommunistische Partei (die entscheidende politische Kraft in den Jahren 1948−1989) propagierte, noch die föderative Gliederung des Staates (seit 1968 bzw. 1969 bestand die Tschechoslowakische Sozialistische Republik aus der Tschechischen Sozialistischen Republik und aus der Slowakischen Sozialistischen Republik), auch nicht die Errichtung eines neuen demokratischen Staates (seit 1989) waren imstande, die Bedingungen für ein harmonisches Zusammenleben der Tschechen und Slowaken zu schaffen. Ihr gemeinsamer Staat (seit 1990 offiziell Tschechische und Slowakische Föderative Republik genannt) wurde schließlich auf Entscheidung des tschechoslowakischen Parlaments aufgelöst − seit dem 1. 1. 1993 existieren die Tschechische Republik und die Slowakische Republik als zwei selbständige Staaten.

3. Politik, Wirtschaft und allgemeine kulturelle sowie religiöse Lage

3.1. Das gegenwärtige politische System der ČR knüpft an die demokratischen Traditionen der Tschechoslowakei aus den zwanziger und dreißiger Jahren und an die in der Tschechoslowakei nach dem Kollaps des kommunistischen Regimes 1989 aufgebaute pluralistische Demokratie an. Die deutliche pro-östliche politische Orientierung des kommunistischen Regimes (1948−1989) wurde schnell durch eine deutlich pro-westliche abgelöst.

3.2. Die ČR ist traditionell ein Industrieland. Ihr heutiges Territorium gehörte zu den industriell entwickeltsten Gebieten des Habsburger Reiches, ein sehr hohes wirtschaftliches Niveau hatte die Tschechoslowakische Republik auch in den zwanziger und dreißiger Jahren. Unter dem kommunistischen Regime wurde die Tschechoslowakei zwar oft als das wirtschaftlich am meisten entwickelte Land des sog. Ostblocks eingeschätzt, aber es blieb hinter dem Niveau der entwickelten westlichen Staaten ziemlich weit zurück.

3.3. Die häufigen Änderungen der politischen Systeme und der Staatsformationen auf dem Gebiet der heutigen ČR brachten mit sich, daß hier im Laufe des 20. Jahrhunderts die verschiedensten kulturellen Einflüsse (aus Österreich, Deutschland, den Vereinigten Staaten, Frankreich, Rußland bzw. der Sowjetunion) zur Geltung kamen. Diese globale kulturelle Atmosphäre illustriert auch gut die Entstehung und das Wirken der Prager sprachwissenschaftlichen Schule als gemeinsame Gedankenwelt der tschechischen, russischen, ukrainischen, deutschen u. a. Wissenschaftler.

3.4. Die Religiosität spielt traditionell im Leben der Bewohner Böhmens keine allzu große Rolle; stärker ist sie in Mähren ausgeprägt. Bei der Volkszählung 1991 führten 4 087 625 (39,7%) Einwohner an, ohne Konfession zu sein und bei 1 670 847 (16,2%) Befragten wurde keine konfessionelle Bindung festgestellt. Der größte Teil der Gläubigen bekannte sich dazu, römisch-katholisch zu sein (4 038 720).

4. Statistik und Ethnoprofile

4.1. Wie schon angeführt, leben in der ČR 314 877 Slowaken, d. h. 3,1% der Gesamtbevölkerung. Die Slowaken sind hier im Gegensatz zu der polnischen und deutschen Minderheit keine historische autochthone Minderheit; noch 1930 bekannten sich auf dem Gebiet der heutigen ČR nur 44 451 Einwohner (d. h. 0,4%) zur slowakischen Nationalität. Die Slowaken kamen in größerem Maßstab erst nach 1945 hierher, und zwar im Zusammenhang mit der organisierten Besiedlung der Grenzgebiete, die nach der Aussiedlung der Deutschen entvölkert waren sowie im Rahmen der Arbeitskräftewerbung für die Industriegebiete (Bergbau). Die 1961, 1970 und 1980 durchgeführten Volkszählungen wiesen eine ständig steigende Zahl von Slowaken auf. Die Abnahme der slowakischen Bevölkerung, die die Volkszählung 1991 aufweist (Unterschied zu 1980 mehr als 40 000 Personen) ist einerseits eine Folge der Assimilierung, andererseits die Folge der Tatsache, daß sich ein Teil der Roma nicht mehr zur slowakischen Nationalität bekannte, sondern die der Roma wählte. Die Angaben über die prozentuale Vertretung der Slowaken in der ČR ist nicht als Angabe über die Zahl der slowakisch Sprechenden zu verstehen. Forschungen in Nordböhmen, wo eine relativ hohe Konzentration der slowakischen Bevölkerung besteht, zeigten, daß 27,5% Slowaken Tschechisch als ihre Muttersprache ansehen (Sokolová 1991).

4.2. Zur polnischen Nationalität bekannten sich im Jahr 1991 59 383 Einwohner. Sie leben vor allem im historischen Schlesien (Gebiet von Těšín), in den Bezirken Karviná (Karwina) (23 780) und Frýdek-Místek (Friedek-Mistek) (20 707), daneben in einigen Diaspora in Nord- und Ostböhmen. Die höchste

Zahl der polnischen Minderheit lebte im Jahre 1910 auf dem Gebiet der heutigen ČR, nämlich 158 261 (laut sprachlichem Kriterium). Schon im nächsten Jahrzehnt ging die Zahl der Polen weit zurück (103 521), und zwar zum einen durch das Bekenntnis zu einer anderen Nationalität, zum anderen durch eine starke Emigrationswelle. Seit dieser Zeit sank die Zahl der Polen kontinuierlich bis auf den heutigen Stand. In den Jahren 1950—1980 assimilierten sich — vorwiegend zur tschechischen Nationalität — fast 33 600 Polen, was 46,2% ihrer Zahl aus dem Jahre 1950 ausmacht (Srb 1987). Die Erforschung der interethnischen Beziehungen im Gebiet von Ostrava (Ostrau) (Sokolová et al. 1985) zeigte, daß Polen beim Kontakt miteinander in 76,8% aller Fälle die polnische Sprache und zu 19,6% die tschechische Sprache benutzen, im Gespräch mit Angehörigen anderer Nationalitäten wählen sie zu 71,9% die tschechische Sprache und zu 22,5% die polnische Sprache (ein drittes Element, das hier noch im Spiel ist, ist das slowakische Ethnikum bzw. die slowakische Sprache; vgl. 5.2.).

4.3. Zur deutschen Nationalität bekannten sich 1991 48 556 Einwohner. Die meisten leben im Bezirk Sokolov (5 664), Karlovy Vary (Karlsbad) (3 781), Chomutov (Chomotau) (3 228), Teplice (Teplitz) (3 032), Děčín (Tetschen) (2 744), Liberec (Reichenberg) (2 085), Trutnov (Trautenau) (2 151), d. h. vor allem im nördlichen Grenzgebiet der ČR. Die stärkste Vertretung der Deutschen auf dem Gebiet der heutigen ČR ist im Jahre 1910 belegt (3 492 362); noch 1937 lebten hier 3 185 000. Mitte 1945 wurde infolge der Kriegsverluste und der Flucht der Deutschen auf dem Gebiet der heutigen ČR 2 809 000 deutsche Einwohner gezählt, so daß die deutsche Minderheit 26,3% der Population darstellte. Mitte 1947, nach der massiven Aussiedlung nach Deutschland, blieben auf dem Gebiet der heutigen ČR 180 000 Deutsche (2,1% der Population) (Srb 1988). Auch im Verlauf weiterer Jahrzehnte senkte sich ihre Zahl sehr rasch: 1950 (159 938), 1961 (134 143), 1970 (80 903), 1980 (58 211). Charakteristisch für die deutsche Bevölkerung ist eine sehr geringe Kinderzahl und ein hohes Maß an ökonomischer Einbindung (hauptsächlich in Arbeiterberufen). Personen weiblichen Geschlechts sind prozentual in der Überzahl und zwar in viel höherem Maße als bei den anderen Populationen, und 55% der deutschen Minderheit ist älter als 55 Jahre (Srb 1988). Die deutsche Aussiedlungsrate (nach Deutschland) ist hoch und die Assimilation ist sehr stark. Soziologische Forschungen in Nordböhmen belegten, daß 33% der Deutschen Tschechisch als Muttersprache ansehen (Sokolová 1991).

5. Soziolinguistische Lage

5.1. Zu den interessantesten Sprachkontakten auf dem Gebiet der ČR bzw. der ehemaligen Tschechoslowakei gehört der Kontakt zwischen Tschechisch und Slowakisch. Dieser Kontakt war immer dadurch determiniert, daß sich Tschechisch und Slowakisch strukturell sehr nahestanden. In der kommunikativen Praxis bedeutet das, daß ein Slowake und Tscheche, jeder in seiner Muttersprache, mit dem andern sprechen kann, und daß sie sich trotzdem gut untereinander verständigen können. Diese Tatsache, oft als passiver Bilinguismus bezeichnet (auch als Semikommunikation), war eines der bestimmenden Elemente der Sprach- und Nationalitätenpolitik der Tschechoslowakei (vgl. 6.1.). Zum verbalen Verhalten der Slowaken an Orten ihrer erhöhten Konzentration sind eine Reihe von soziologischen Forschungsarbeiten erstellt worden, die im Prinzip den allmählichen Übergang vom Slowakischen zum Tschechischen aufzeigten, und das nicht nur im Kontakt der Slowaken mit anderssprachigen Mitbürgern am Arbeitsplatz, sondern auch im Rahmen der Familienkommunikation: 20,8% Slowaken aus Nordböhmen (die sich zum Slowakischen als ihrer Muttersprache bekennen) führten an, daß sie in der Familie vorwiegend Tschechisch sprechen, 63,4% geben Tschechisch und Slowakisch an und nur 10,4% sprechen in der Familie vorwiegend Slowakisch (Sokolová 1991). Im Gebiet von Ostrava, in einem weiteren Gebiet, in dem eine hohe Konzentration von Slowaken besteht, ist die Orientierung hin zum Slowakischen zwar höher, trotzdem belegten die festgestellten Daten auch hier eine relativ schnelle sprachliche Assimilierung in Richtung Tschechisch. Hauptkommunikationsmittel ist hier Slowakisch bei 32,8% Slowaken (Sokolová 1992). Eine differenziertere soziolinguistische Untersuchung der Sprachkontakte zwischen Tschechen und Slowaken wurde nicht durchgeführt.

5.2. Zum Sprachkontakt des Tschechischen und Polnischen kommt es hauptsächlich im Gebiet von Ostrava, im Grenzgebiet zu Polen. Die tschechische Dialektologie spricht über dieses Territorium als das tschechisch-polnische Sprach-Grenzland bzw. über das Mundartgebiet des polnisch-tschechischen Mischstreifens. Weil es hier aber schon seit einer Reihe von Jahren auch eine bedeutende Konzentration von Slowaken (im Bezirk Karviná war der Anteil der Slowaken 1991 sogar genauso hoch wie der der Polen) gibt, kommt es zu Kontakten dreier Sprachen: des Tschechischen, Polnischen und Slowakischen (allerdings könnte man auch noch die Sprache der Roma und Ungarisch erwähnen). Diese Situation wurde bisher vorwiegend in der soziologischen Forschung untersucht; diese Untersuchungen zeigten z. B., daß die Polen viel stärker auf die Sprache ihres Ethnikums orientiert sind als die Slowaken; in den erforschten Sprachgemeinschaften orientierten sich ausschließlich oder fast ausschließlich auf ihre Muttersprache: 87,3% Tschechen, 60,9% Polen und 34,5% Slowaken (Sokolová et al. 1985). Einer der wichtigen Aspekte der Sprachsituation in diesem Gebiet ist auch der hohe Stellenwert der Mundart, besonders bei den Polen, bei denen sich deren Benutzung zwischen 24−72% bewegt, während die Tschechen wesentlich niedrigere Werte anführen (Sokolová et al. 1985). Die einzige umfangreichere soziolinguistische Arbeit, die sich mit diesem Gebiet befaßt, war vor allem der Kommunikation in den Eisenwerken von Třinec (Trzynietz) gewidmet (Davidová/Bogoczová/Jandová 1991).

5.3. Der Kontakt zwischen Tschechisch und Deutsch auf dem Gebiet der heutigen ČR hat eine lange Tradition. Schon seit dem 9. Jahrhundert kann man offensichtlich über tschechisch-deutsche Zweisprachigkeit sprechen (Skála 1977). Im Verlauf der folgenden Jahrhunderte änderten sich Status, Funktion und Prestige dieser zwei Sprachen in bedeutendem Maße und zwar in Abhängigkeit von der jeweiligen politischen und wirtschaftlichen Situation (vgl. 2., 4.3.). Zur synchronen Stellung des Deutschen in der ČR existieren nur einige wenige soziolinguistisch bzw. soziologisch orientierte Arbeiten. Diese zeigen, daß sich im Zeitraum von nicht ganz einer Generation die Funktion des Deutschen als Ethno-Identifikationsfaktor stark abschwächte: Während 1970 nur 7,2% Deutsche Tschechisch als ihre Muttersprache ansahen, waren es 1987 schon 33%. Im gleichen Jahr führten 8% der Deutschen (die sich zu Deutsch als ihrer Muttersprache bekannten) an, daß sie in der Familie vorwiegend Tschechisch sprechen; 79,8% führten Tschechisch und Deutsch an, und nur 5% sprechen in der Familie vorwiegend Deutsch (Sokolová 1991). Die linguistischen Studien untersuchen das verbale Verhalten etwas differenzierter (man arbeitet mindestens mit drei Klassifizierungsformen, z. B. deutscher Dialekt, Hochdeutsch, Tschechisch), die Generationszugehörigkeit wird jedoch als ausschlaggebender Faktor prinzipiell bestätigt: So z. B. benutzte im Egerland in den sechziger Jahren die älteste Generation der Deutschen den einheimischen Dialekt und die dialektal gefärbte Hochsprache, ebenso die mittlere Generation, die aber dazu noch das Tschechische benutzte, und die junge Generation sprach den Dialekt und Tschechisch (Povejšil 1975). Zwanzig Jahre später zeigte die Untersuchung in Jablonec (Gablonz) und Umgebung den teilweisen Rückgang der deutsch-tschechischen Zweisprachigkeit bei der mittleren Generation (selbstverständlich zugunsten des Tschechischen) und einen wesentlichen Rückgang in der jüngsten Generation; die älteste Generation benutzt im Familienkreis den deutschen Dialekt, aber in den übrigen Situationen schon das Tschechische (Bezděková 1988).

6. Sprachpolitische Lage

6.1. Die Sprachpolitik auf dem Gebiet der heutigen ČR änderte sich mit den wechselnden Staatsformen. Beachtenswert war unter diesem Aspekt die Entwicklung des legislativen Status des Slowakischen und dessen Konsequenzen. Die Entstehung der Tschechoslowakei 1918 war mit der Verkündung der Konzeption des einheitlichen tschechoslowakischen Volkes und zugleich der tschechoslowakischen Sprache verbunden, die zwei Formen aufweisen würde: die tschechische und die slowakische. Dieses legislative Konstrukt sollte unter anderem zur Annäherung beider Sprachen beitragen, in der Praxis aber bedeutete das manchmal die Verwischung der Spezifität des Slowakischen zugunsten des Tschechischen. Nach 1945 wurde die Konzeption der tschechoslowakischen Sprache aufgegeben, aber offiziell sprach man weiter von der Annäherung beider Sprachen. Die Nachkriegsentwicklung des tschechoslowakischen passiven Bilinguismus (vgl. 5.1.) reflektierte das Verfassungsgesetz von 1968 wie folgt: „Die tschechische und die slowakische Sprache werden gleichberechtigt bei der Proklamierung von Gesetzen und anderen allgemeingültigen wichtigen Vorschriften benutzt. Bei amtlichen Verhandlungen und im übrigen Kontakt mit den Bürgern werden beide Sprachen gleichberechtigt benutzt." Sowohl Tschechisch als auch Slowakisch hatten die Funktion eines übernationalen Verständigungsmittels. Man benutzte sie nicht nur in den tschechoslowakischen föderativen Institutionen wie dem Parlament, sondern auch in den Massenmedien (Fernsehen, Rundfunk); z. B. wechselten sich bei den Nachrichtensendungen oder Sportreportagen die tschechischen und slowakischen Moderatoren in regelmäßigen Intervallen ab.

Der entwickelte passive Bilinguismus und die staatliche Auffassung, daß das slowakische Volk keine Minderheit darstellt, führten allerdings dazu, daß die Slowaken auf dem Gebiet der ČR nicht ihr eigenes Schulwesen (mit Ausnahme von 1-2 Schulen im Ostrauer Gebiet) besaßen, was zu ihrer schnellen Assimilierung beitrug (den Ungarn, Polen, Ukrainern/Ruthenen und Deutschen, die den Minderheitenstatus besitzen, war seit 1968 das Recht auf Bildung in ihrer Sprache durch die Verfassung garantiert). Auf der anderen Seite aber muß man anführen, daß das Interesse der Slowaken an einem eigenen Schulwesen auf dem Gebiet der ČR verhältnismäßig gering war (vgl. 6.2.). Die Stellung der slowakischen Bevölkerung hat sich seit dem 1. 1. 1993 allerdings deutlich geändert – in der selbständigen ČR stellen sie jetzt eigentlich eine neue, mehr als 300 000 Personen zählende Minderheit dar.

6.2. Die Sprachpolitik in bezug auf das Polnische formierte sich im großen und ganzen in Übereinstimmung mit den verfassungsrechtlich garantierten Rechten.

Der polnischen Minderheit steht ein großes Netz von Schulen mit Polnisch als Unterrichtssprache zur Verfügung: in den Bezirken Karviná und Frýdek-Místek 42 Kindergärten, 29 Grundschulen und ein eigenes Gymnasium in Český Těšín (Stand 1983, vgl. Malá 1988). Die Zahl der Schulen sinkt aber: während 1970 69 Grundschulen mit Polnisch als Unterrichtssprache existierten, waren es 1985 nur noch 28 (Srb 1986 b). Die soziologische Forschung von 1983 zeigte, daß ein bedeutender Prozentsatz der Polen selbst (23,5%) Schulen mit Polnisch als Unterrichtssprache als nicht zweckmäßig ansieht (in der gleichen Studie sprachen sich 64,5% Slowaken negativ zur Zweckmäßigkeit von Schulen mit Slowakisch als Unterrichtssprache aus) (Malá 1988).

Fast die Hälfte der polnischen Erwachsenen ist im Polnischen Kulturverein organisiert (wirkt seit 1947). Es existiert eine polnische Lokalpresse, und es wird polnisch geschriebene Literatur regionaler Autoren herausgegeben. Eine bedeutende Rolle in der Entwicklung der polnischen Kultur spielen die polnischen Büchereien oder die polnische Abteilung in den Ortsbibliotheken beider Bezirke und auch die polnische Bühne des Theaters Těšín. Seit 1951 sendet der Rundfunk Ostrava kurze Programme in polnischer Sprache. Der Amtsverkehr ist zweisprachig; Ämter, verschiedene Institutionen, Geschäfte usw. benutzen zweisprachige, d. h. tschechische und polnische Aufschriften (Lotko 1994) (→ Art. 203).

6.3. Die Sprachpolitik bezüglich der Deutschen durchlief unterschiedliche Etappen. In den zwanziger und dreißiger Jahren hatten die Deutschen — ähnlich wie andere Minderheiten in der Tschechoslowakei — eine Reihe von sprachlichen und kulturellen Rechten. Diese galten schon in den Bezirken, in denen die entsprechende Minderheit zu 20% vertreten war. Die Deutschen besaßen ein ausgedehntes System von Grund-, Mittel- und Fachschulen und in Prag auch eine Universität.

Für die Sprachpolitik während der Okkupation unter Hitler war die gewaltsame Germanisierung typisch, die zu einer Bedrohung des tschechischen Volkes führen sollte (Malý 1991). Die Sprachpolitik hinsichtlich des Restes der Deutschen, die nach Kriegsende und nach der Aussiedlung der Mehrheit der deutschen Bevölkerung auf dem Gebiet der ČR verblieben, wurde durch die Kriegserfahrungen determiniert und korrespondierte mit der diskriminierenden Staatspolitik: die tschechoslowakische Staatsangehörigkeit erlangten alle Deutschen erst 1953 und den Rechtsstatus einer Minderheit erst 1968, d. h. acht Jahre später als die übrigen Minderheiten. Seit dieser Zeit hatten sie auch das Recht (verfassungsmäßig garantiert) auf Bildung in der Muttersprache, ohne daß jedoch eine Schule mit Deutsch als Unterrichtssprache entstanden wäre; Hauptargument war die Zerstreutheit der deutschen Bevölkerung und die fortgeschrittene Assimilierung in der jüngsten Generation. 1990 besuchten insgesamt lediglich 585 Schüler deutscher Nationalität (tschechische) Grundschulen (Vasiljev 1993).

Seit den sechziger Jahren wuchs unter der tschechischen Population das Interesse an

Deutsch als Fremdsprache. Deutsch gehörte gemeinsam mit Englisch (neben dem Pflichtfach Russisch) zu den meistunterrichteten Fremdsprachen. Das Interesse an Deutsch stieg nach dem Regimewechsel 1989 noch erheblich.

7. Weitere Minderheiten und Kontaktsprachen

7.1. Eine Sonderstellung nehmen die Roma bzw. deren Sprache in der ČR ein. Bei der Volkszählung 1991 bekannten sich zur Nationalität der Roma 32 903 Einwohner. Ihre Anzahl ist aber in der ČR zweifellos um vieles höher. Srb (1986a) führt an, daß allein im Zeitraum zwischen 1970 und 1980 in der ČR 28 308 Roma hinzugekommen sind und ihre Zahl sich damit auf 88 587 erhöht hat. Nach Schätzungen der Regierung waren es 1991 150 000—220 000. Die Roma kamen nach 1945 auf das Gebiet der heutigen ČR (viele „tschechische" Roma wurden während des Zweiten Weltkriegs in Konzentrationslagern ermordet). Die Roma-Bevölkerung der ČR ist stark urbanisiert, und zwar in höherem Maße als die übrige Population. 1980 gab es in der ČR zwölf Städte, in denen mehr als 1 000 Roma lebten (Srb 1986a). Die meisten leben in den Grenzstädten in Nordböhmen (z. B. Most (Brüx), Teplice, Ústí nad Labem (Aussig), Chomutov (Komotau)) und Nordmähren (Ostrava, Karviná). Ihre territoriale Verteilung korreliert stark mit der territorialen Distribution der Slowaken in der ČR und hängt ebenfalls wie bei den Slowaken mit der Grenzbesiedlung im Zeitraum nach der Aussiedlung der Deutschen zusammen. Unter dem kommunistischen Regime wurden den Roma verschiedene soziale Vorteile gewährt. Zugleich bemühte man sich um ihre Integration bzw. Assimilierung. Andererseits ist zu erwähnen, daß sich eine Reihe Roma mit dieser Assimilierung identifizierte und die Assimilierung ihres Ethnikums offen auch in den neuen gesellschaftlichen Bedingungen nach 1989 (→ Art. 239) propagiert.

Die Roma sind als zweisprachig zu charakterisieren. Unter sich benutzen sie das Romani, und im Kontakt mit der nicht zu den Roma gehörenden Bevölkerung bemühen sie sich, tschechisch resp. slowakisch zu sprechen. Bei der jüngsten Generation allerdings konnte man schon vor zwanzig Jahren eine erhöhte Benutzung des Tschechischen resp. des Slowakischen in der Kommunikation der Roma untereinander in der Öffentlichkeit, z. B. in der Schule, beobachten. Nach Hübschmannová (1976) hat das Tschechische der Roma den Charakter eines Ethnolekts. Auf allen sprachlichen und stilistischen Ebenen ist die Interferenz mit dem Romani zu spüren; in der Sprache der älteren Generation kann man auch lexikalische Einflüsse des Slowakischen finden. Beispiele und Kommentare aus der Studie von Hübschmannová (1976):

„my *domu* vůbec nevyprávíme romanes" (*domu* statt *doma*; khere — domů, doma: nach Hause, zu Hause; die Sprache der Roma unterscheidet nicht zwischen der Lokalbestimmung „wohin" und „wo") „kamaradim vic *českýma holkama*" (*českýma holkama* statt *s českýma holkama*; raklijenca — präpositionsloser Instrumental).

Andere Autoren charakterisieren das Tschechisch der Roma als Pidgin (bei der älteren Generation) oder als Kreol (bei den Kindern) (Neustupný 1992). Eine Reihe von Wörtern des Romani ist Bestandteil des tschechischen Argots.

Die Roma verfügen bis jetzt nicht über eine Schriftsprache. Sie besuchen tschechische Schulen; kürzlich wurden Versuche unternommen, das Romani als Hilfssprache in den Schulen einzuführen, um den Kindern der Roma den Schulanfang zu erleichtern. Im Alltagsleben nehmen die meisten Bewohner der ČR eine negative Haltung zu den Roma ein (vgl. Holšánová/Nekvapil 1995). Um die sprachliche und kulturelle Situation der Roma in der ČR kennenzulernen, sind besonders die Arbeiten von M. Hübschmannová wichtig. Sie ist auch Autorin des Lehrbuchs des Romani und Hauptautorin des Wörterbuchs Romani—Tschechisch.

7.2. Die Volkszählung von 1991 zeigte, daß in der ČR 19 932 Ungarn leben. Diese Minderheit wird nach der Entstehung der selbständigen ČR (1. 1. 1993) in hohem Maße als ein neues Phänomen aufgefaßt, denn im Rahmen der Tschechoslowakei konzentrierte sich die Aufmerksamkeit vor allem auf die mehr als eine halbe Million zählende ungarische Minderheit, die unter ganz anderen Bedingungen (kompakte Besiedlung) in der Südslowakei lebte (→ Art. 205). Die Ungarn gehören auf dem Territorium der ČR nicht zu den autochthonen Nationalitäten, aber immerhin gab es 1921 hier schon 7 049 (Migration aus der Slowakei und der Karpaten-Ukraine). Seit dieser Zeit weist die Zahl der Ungarn in der ČR eine leichte Steigerung auf. Sie leben zerstreut in allen Bezirken der ČR, besonders in den Industriegebieten im Westen und Norden Böhmens, im Norden Mährens (Bezirk Karviná) und selbstverständlich in Prag, dem kulturellen Mittelpunkt der ungarischen Bevölkerung in der ČR.

Soziologische Studien aus dem Jahre 1992 zeigen, daß mehr als zwei Drittel der befragten Ungarn in ihren Familien vorwiegend tschechisch sprechen (18,3% ungarisch und tschechisch und nur 12,9% vorwiegend ungarisch). 41,7% führten an, daß sie kein Interesse daran haben, ihre Kinder auf Ungarisch unterrichten zu lassen (26% haben Interesse, 32,3% haben keine Meinung dazu). Eine der Schlußfolgerungen der Studie war, daß die in der ČR lebenden Ungarn besser Tschechisch als Ungarisch sprechen. Die Studie zeigte auch, daß eine Reihe von Ungarn nicht möchte, daß man von ihrer ungarischen Nationalität weiß (Sadílek/Csémy 1993).

Die ungarische Bevölkerung hatte seit 1954 auf dem Territorium der ČR keine Kulturorganisation, in der sie sich auf der Grundlage der Nationalitätszugehörigkeit vereinen konnte. Erst nach dem Regimewechsel 1989 wurde der Bund der in der ČR lebenden Ungarn gegründet (1990). Dieser setzt auch die Herausgabe der ungarischen Presse durch und bemüht sich um ungarische Rundfunk- und Fernsehprogramme (Sadílek/Csémy 1993). Soziolinguistische Untersuchungen des Sprachverhaltens der Ungarn in der ČR gibt es bisher nicht.

7.3. Kurz noch zur Sprache der sich 1991 zur mährischen und schlesischen Nationalität bekennenden Bevölkerung: es geht – allerdings gewiß nicht ausnahmslos – um mährische oder schlesische Dialekte (Interdialekte) der tschechischen Nationalsprache (siehe Pallas 1970). Soziolinguistische Studien, die das neue Nationalitätsgefühl in Mähren und Schlesien reflektieren, existieren bislang nicht.

8. Zur Forschungslage

Die auf dem Gebiet der ČR bzw. der ehemaligen Tschechoslowakei bestehenden Sprachkontaktsituationen standen nicht im Vordergrund der tschechischen Sprachwissenschaft. Die soziolinguistisch orientierte Sprachwissenschaft war besonders mit den Problemen der Schriftsprache und der Sprachkultur beschäftigt. Die Problematik der Sprachkontakte konnte dann bei den Linguisten öfter mit der Problematik der Fremdwörter in der Schriftsprache (bzw. der verschiedenen Varietäten der tschechischen Sprache) zusammenfließen. So konnte es geschehen, daß heute überhaupt keine soziolinguistischen Studien des verbalen Verhaltens einer Reihe von Minderheiten (deren Aufzählung siehe 1.2.) existieren. Geradezu bestürzend ist zudem die Tatsache, daß selbst im Falle der mehr als 300 000 zählenden slowakischen Minderheit keine soliden Forschungen betrieben wurden. Man muß allerdings auch in Rechnung stellen, daß die Kommunikationspraxis einiger Minderheiten mit der übergeordneten politischen Problematik der nationalen Minderheiten zusammenhängt und diese in den verschiedenen Etappen in unterschiedlichem Maße tabuisiert wurde (Nekvapil 1995; Nekvapil/Neustupný im Druck).

9. Bibliographie (in Auswahl)

Bezděková, Eva (1988): „Deutsch als Muttersprache und Fremdsprache in Böhmen und Mähren". In: *Germanistische Mitteilungen 27*, 115–138.

Davidová, Dana/Bogoczová, Irena/Jandová, Eva (1991): *Využití jazyka při řízení pracovních kolektivů v ostravské průmyslové aglomeraci se zaměřením na zkoumání česko-slovensko-polské jazykové interference* [Zum Gebrauch der Sprache im Führungsbereich von Großbetrieben der Ostrauer Agglomeration, unter dem Aspekt der tschechisch-slowakisch-polnischen Interferenz], Ostrau.

Fryščák, Milan (1978): „The two official languages of Czechoslovakia". In: *Sociolinguistic problems in Czechoslovakia, Hungary, Romania and Yugoslavia* (= Folia Slavica, Vol. 1 No 3), Schmalstieg, William R./Magner, Thomas F. (Eds.), Columbus, Ohio, 343–352.

Heroldová, Iva/Matějová, Vlasta (1987): „Vietnamští pracující v českých zemích" [Die vietnamesischen Werktätigen in den böhmischen Ländern]. In: *Český lid 74*, 194–203.

Holšánová, Jana/Nekvapil, Jiří (1995): „Menschen 'fünfter Klasse': Reden über Abwesende in der Alltagskommunikation am Beispiel tschechischsprachiger Daten". In: *Nationale Selbst- und Fremdbilder im Gespräch*, Czyżewski, Marek/Gülich, Elisabeth/Hausendorf, Heiko/Kastner, Maria (Eds.), Opladen, 145–179.

Hübschmannová, Milena (1976): „K jazykové situaci Romů v ČSSR" [Soziolinguistische Lage des Romani in der Tschechoslowakei]. In: *Slovo a slovesnost 37*, 328–336.

Hübschmannová, Milena (1979): „Bilingualism among the Slovak Rom". In: *International journal of the sociology of language 19*, 33–49.

Lotko, Edvard (1994): "O jazykové komunikaci polské národnostní menšiny v České republice" [Zur Sprache der polnischen Minderheit in der ČR]. In: *Časopis pro moderní filologii 76*, 9−19.

Malá, Eva (1988): "Národnostní školství na Ostravsku" [Das Schulwesen der Nationalitäten im Ostrauer Gebiet]. In: *Slezský sborník 86*, 91−105.

Malý, Karel (1991): "Sprache − Recht und Staat in der tschechischen Vergangenheit". In: *Sprache − Recht − Geschichte*, Eckert, Joern/Hattenhauer, Hans (Eds.), Heidelberg, 257−281.

Národnostní složení obyvatelstva ČR (výsledky sčítání lidu, domů a bytů 1991) (1993) [Ethnische Zusammensetzung der Bevölkerung in der ČR. Ergebnisse der Volks-, Haus- und Wohnungszählung 1991] (= Zprávy a rozbory, řada 23, č. 2). Prag, Český statistický úřad.

Nekvapil, Jiří (1995): "Etnické menšiny a jejich jazyky na území České republiky" [Ethnische Minderheiten und ihre Sprachen auf dem Territorium der ČR]. In: *Přednášky z XXXVII, a XXXVIII, běhu LŠSS*. Univerzita Karlova, 17−31.

Nekvapil, Jiří/Neustupný, Jiří V. (im Druck): "Linguistic communities in the Czech Republic". In: *Linguistic minorities in Central and Eastern Europe*, Fenyvesi, Anna/Paulston, Christina Bratt/Peckham, Don (Eds.), Amsterdam/Philadelphia.

Nekvapil, Jiří/Ondrejovič, Slavo (1993): "Basic information on sociolinguistics in Ex-Czechoslovakia". In: *Sociolinguistica. Internationales Jahrbuch für Europäische Soziolinguistik 7*, 257−262.

Neustupný, Jiří V. (1992): *The Romani language and language management* (= CTS research report), Prag.

Pallas, Ladislav (1970): *Jazyková otázka a podmínky vytváření národního vědomí ve Slezsku* [Die Sprachenfrage und Voraussetzungen zur Bildung des Nationalbewußtseins in Schlesien], Ostrau.

Povejšil, Jaromír (1975): "Deutscher Dialekt und fremde Hochsprache bei zweisprachiger Bevölkerung". In: *Philologica Pragensia 18*, 100−110.

Předběžné výsledky (1991) *sčítání lidu, domů a bytů k 3. březnu 1991* [Vorläufige Ergebnisse der Volks-, Haus- und Wohnungszählung vom 3. März 1991], Prag.

Sadílek, Petr/Csémy, Tamás (1993): *Maďaři v České republice/Magyarok a Cseh Köztársaságban* [Ungarn in der Tschechischen Republik], Prag.

Skála, Emil (1977): "Vznik a vývoj česko-německého bilingvismu" [Die Entstehung und die Entwicklung des tschechisch-deutschen Bilinguismus]. In: *Slovo a slovesnost 38*, 197−207.

Sokolová, Gabriela (1985): "K některým otázkám bilingvismu v etnicky smíšených regionech ČSSR" [Zu einigen Problemen des Bilinguismus in den ethnisch gemischten Regionen der Tschechoslowakei]. In: *Sociológia 17*, 213−223.

Sokolová, Gabriela et al. (1985): "Nový výzkum interetnických vztahů na Ostravsku" [Die neue Untersuchung der Nationalitätenbeziehungen im Ostrauer Gebiet]. In: *Slezský sborník 83*, 1−24.

Sokolová, Gabriela (1991): "O jazykovém zaměření Slováků a Němců žijících v severních Čechách" [Zur sprachlichen Orientierung der Slowaken und der Deutschen im Gebiet Nordböhmen]. In: *Slezský sborník 89*, 172−180.

Sokolová, Gabriela (1992): "K jazykové orientaci Slováků v národnostně smíšených regionech České republiky" [Zur sprachlichen Orientierung der Slowaken in den ethnisch gemischten Regionen der Tschechischen Republik]. In: *Sociológia 24*, 89−93.

Srb, Vladimír (1986 a): "Koncentrace a urbanizace Cikánů v Československu" [Die Konzentration und Urbanisierung der Zigeuner in der Tschechoslowakei]. In: *Český lid 73*, 86−92.

Srb, Vladimír (1986 b): "Základní školy v Československu podle vyučovacího jazyka a národnosti žáků v letech 1970−1985" [Die Grundschulen in der Tschechoslowakei nach der Unterrichtssprache und nach der Nationalität der Schüler in den Jahren 1970−1985]. In: *Slezský sborník 84*, 253−263.

Srb, Vladimír (1987): "Demografický profil polské menšiny v Československu" [Das demographische Profil der polnischen Minderheit in der Tschechoslowakei]. In: *Český lid 74*, 151−165.

Srb, Vladimír (1988): "Demografický profil německé menšiny v Československu" [Das demographische Profil der deutschen Minderheit in der Tschechoslowakei]. In: *Český lid 75*, 29−42.

Srb, Vladimír (1992): "Předběžné výsledky sčítání lidu, domů a bytů v ČSFR 1991" [Vorläufige Ergebnisse der Volks-, Haus- und Wohnungszählung von 1991 in der Tschechoslowakei]. In: *Český lid 79*, 171−173.

Valášková, Naďa (1992): "K adaptaci současné reemigrační vlny Čechů z Ukrajiny" [Zur Adaptation der gegenwärtigen Remigrationswelle der Tschechen aus der Ukraine]. In: *Český lid 79*, 193−206.

Vasiljev, Ivo (1993): "Tschechoslowakei". In: *Sociolinguistica. Internationales Jahrbuch für Europäische Soziolinguistik 7*, 49−57.

Jiří Nekvapil, Prag (Tschechien)

201. Czech−Slovak

1. Geography and demography
2. History
3. Politics, economy and general cultural situation
4. Statistics and ethnoprofiles
5. Sociolinguistic situation
6. Language political situation
7. General contactlinguistic portrait
8. Development and contemporary state of the comparative study of Czech and Slovak
9. Bibliography (selected)

1. Geography and demography

1.1. According to the census of 1991, the population of the Czech Republic (CR) was 10,302,215, of whom 314,877 (3.1%) were of Slovak nationality. Slovaks are not evenly distributed across the territory of the CR. More than 3% live in two areas. The first is the whole border area with Germany, the former Sudetenland, mainly the regions of Sokolov (9.8%), Tachov (9.6%) and Cheb (8.9%) in western Bohemia, and the region of Český Krumlov (8.3%) in the southern part of Bohemia. The second area is the northern border region in Moravia, mainly in the vicinity of Karviná (8.3%). In other parts of the CR the percentage varies from 0.8 to 3.0% of the population (cf. Zeman 1995, 537).

1.2. The statistical data do not fully mirror the wide range of sociolinguistic relationships between Czechs and Slovaks. Nationality is determined on the basis of declaration: each inhabitant can choose his/her nationality according to his/her personal decision and feeling. Thus, the mother tongue of a Slovak is not necessarily the Slovak language. Furthermore, the statistical data in 1.1. include only those people of Slovak nationality who were domiciled in the CR. Not included were individuals with temporary residency in the CR, i. e., soldiers, students (in the CR for several years), etc.; → Language Map K.

2. History

Relations between the Czech and Slovak languages have been influenced by the historical development of both nations. In general, the political history of the two nations is different but their cultural history has many features in common.

2.1. At the beginning of this millennium the Czechs created the Czech kingdom. From 1526 till 1918, it was one of the lands of the Habsburg Monarchy. Slovakia was a part of Hungary till 1918.

The Czechoslovak Republic (CSR) (created in October 1918) was a multinational state, in which Czechs and Slovaks comprised 65% of the population. In 1939, the CSR was dissolved; the territory of the CR became a protectorate of Germany, and Slovakia was established as a separate state. After WW II the CSR was reestablished and lasted till 1992. On the 1st of January, 1993, the CSR was divided into two separate states: the Czech Republic and the Slovak Republic.

2.2. The cultural histories of both nations are similar and closely related. Linguistic as well as cultural contacts between Czechs and Slovaks have been uninterrupted, although their intensity and forms have been varied throughout their history.

The closeness of the cultural histories is facilitated by the genetic closeness of the Czech and Slovak languages (cf. Bělič et al. 1957, 5−10; Horálek 1968, 195−198). Czech and Slovak are very similar even today (cf. 7.1.) and both Czechs and Slovaks understand each other without difficulties (cf. 3.). Both languages belong to the West-Slavic languages and in this major group they form the Czech-Slovak subgroup. The genetic affinity underlies a structural affinity of the two languages, which are both inflective. Gradual differentiation of the Czech-Slovak subgroup started in the early 10th century. Standard (literary) Czech was established on the basis of the Central Bohemian dialect in the Middle Ages and its contemporary form is closely connected with the so-called National Revival in the late 18th and early 19th centuries. Standard (literary) Slovak arose in the middle of the 19th century on the basis of the Central Slovakia dialect. Before this (from the 15th century) Czech was used as the standard language (cultural idiom) in Slovakia (Czech was slightly modified for this purpose). This is the historical underpinning of the fact that the impact of the Czech language on Slovak has always been stronger than vice versa.

At the beginning of the existence of the CSR an idea of a "Czechoslovak" national language was conceived. The Czechoslovak language was assumed to exist in two variants, namely Czech and Slovak. The Czech variant was used as the official language in the CR and the Slovak variant in Slovakia. Actually, the Czech language gained a more important position to the detriment of the Slovak language since the latter, unlike the former, was not fully modernized, i. e. its means were not fully adequate to all language functions (→ art. 204, 209).

Even after 1945 the Czech language served as a model in dealing with issues of standard (literary) Slovak. There existed a tendency rather to bring the Slovak language closer to the Czech language than to separate them. This effort was most prominent in lexicology, especially in terminology (cf. Kuchař 1964, 1−9; → art. 209).

3. Politics, economy and general cultural situation

The establishment of the Federal Republic in the year 1968 further strengthened the "bilingual" situation in the CSR. In each of the republics the "home" language was used most, but at the same time the other language was used without any serious difficulties as well. A passive knowledge of the other language on the part of both Czechs and Slovaks was assumed (cf. 6.2.), and the language situation as a whole can be thus referred to as *passive bilingualism* (Czechs and Slovaks use in mutual communication their respective languages) (cf. Budovičová 1987, 159−160).

All the same, the position of Slovaks in the CR was special. There existed a thesis in official politics that Slovaks were one of the two constitutive nations of CSR. Nevertheless in the CR, Slovaks often found themselves indeed in a position of a minority nation; they did not have sufficient access to their own culture in their own language compared to other nationalities (cf. Zeman 1995).

4. Statistics and ethnoprofiles

A dramatic shift in the relationship between Czech and Slovak took place after 1945 when the national structure of the CSR changed. While before WW II, the most numerous was the German minority (3,22 million, i. e., 30.2% of all inhabitants) and only 44,451 people (0.4%) were of Slovak nationality, after the war Slovaks gradually grew into the largest non-Czech national group.

After 1945, most Germans mostly from the border areas of the CR were resettled to Germany; thus the biggest minority was reduced to some 160,000 (1.8%) in 1950. The scheme of a new settlement of the border area and subsequent rapid industrialization caused even larger shifting of inhabitants. By 1947, nearly 1.5 million people had moved to the border area, more than 170,000 (11%) out of this number from Slovakia. In 1950 the number of people of Slovak nationality rose to 258,025. The Slovaks have moved to and settled mostly in the areas where mainly German and Polish nationalities lived. Though Slovak immigration was not so extensive in later years, it was still relatively high (see table 201.1).

Table 201.1: Numbers of Slovaks living in the CR

year	total of inhabitants of the CR	total of Slovaks living in the CR	%
1950	8,896,133	258,025	2,9
1961	9,571,531	275,997	2,9
1970	9,807,697	320,998	3,3
1980	10,291,927	359,370	3,5
1991	10,302,215	314,877	3,1

Annual reports show even larger numbers of Slovaks living in the CR. This difference is partly due to their assimilation mostly among children and younger generations.

5. Sociolinguistic situation

There has been little attention paid to the language behaviour of Slovaks in the CR so far. Sociological research has focused first of all on the areas of the northern part of Moravia and the northern part of Bohemia, where most Slovaks live (cf. 1.1.). Nevertheless from this research already, some general conclusions can be drawn.

5.1. Slovaks use Czech and Slovak according to one of the following patterns:

5.1.1. Slovak speakers have not mastered Czech actively and therefore they use Slovak in the Czech environment. They attempt to imitate Czech speakers and for this reason they try to avoid typical Slovak phrases. Slovak words that are different from the Czech equivalents are either explained or substituted with Czech expressions. Czech lexical items are used purposefully to avoid misunderstanding. If the Slovak speakers have lived in the Czech environment for a longer period of time, some language items of their Slovak fade away and are substituted with Czech items. This gives rise to contact variants (language means that has been shaped by language contact) (cf. Bartáková 1986, 80−81).

5.1.2. Slovak speakers can speak Czech to a certain extent, but are not able to function in the frame of one code with confidence. Their language behaviour is a blend of Czech and Slovak. As the Czechs are used to the Slovak language due to indirect language contacts (cf. 6.1.) they do not accept this blending. Slovaks who try to speak Czech and make too many mistakes are asked to speak Slovak.

5.1.3. Slovak speakers can speak both languages, but in communication they prefer Slovak for various reasons.

5.1.4. Slovak speakers speak both languages and in communication they switch from one to the other. The switching can be uncontrolled (e. g., impact of emotions) or controlled (i. e. giving priority to a certain language according to communicational environment).

5.1.5. Slovak speakers use in their communication exclusively Czech.

5.2. The use of one or both languages depends on many factors that interact with each other. Among the most important ones are (cf. Sokolová 1985, 216−222):

5.2.1. The length and permanency of the stay of Slovaks in the CR. Slovaks who come to the CR only temporarily use mostly Slovak (see 5.1.1.). Slovaks who plan to stay in the CR permanently turn rather towards Czech. Their bilingualism depends on the length of their contact with the Czech environment: the longer in the CR, the more they gradually turn from Slovak to Czech in all situations.

5.2.2. Working place and family. At work, Slovaks use Czech in more than in one half of all the cases and one third of them use both languages. In a family, it is the nationality of the spouse and nationality of children that influences the choice of the language the most. With nationally mixed families communication is in Czech or in both languages. In homogeneous Slovak marriages the prevailing trend is communication in both languages. If a Slovak family uses only one language, then it is in accordance with the nationality of their children.

5.2.3. The choice of mother tongue of Slovaks. Typical consistency in mother tongue and nationality has been decreasing. Factors accelerating this situation are growing national heterogamy, education in Czech (cf. 5.2.4.), etc. The descendants of Slovak parents felt their mother tongue to be mostly Slovak; for the children of Czech-Slovak parents the mother tongue is in half of the cases Slovak and in half of the cases Czech. Slovaks with Czech mother tongue communicate mostly in Czech, people whose mother tongue is Slovak use Czech 60% of the time, both languages 30% of the time and Slovak 10% of the time (see Sokolová 1991, 175).

5.2.4. Slovaks who received their basic education in Slovak schools have Slovak as their mother tongue in more than 90% of the cases; most Slovaks who were educated in the Czech language environment (see 6.2.) consider Czech to be their mother tongue (Sokolová 1991, 175).

6. Language political situation

Due to tourism, trade and sport migration, direct language contacts between Czechs and Slovaks increased after 1945. But there existed places in the territory of the CR where Czechs were in close verbal contact with Slovaks: working places, universities, military environments where both languages were of command as well as of service, etc. In these places many new contact variants (see 5.1.1.) and lexical-loans from the other language arose.

6.1. The development of standard (literary) languages has not been significantly influenced by the aforementioned direct language contacts. They impacted more on local dialects (cf. 7.3.) and non-literary varieties (cf. 7.1.). Indirect language contacts and their various forms have been of crucial importance for the development of both literary languages.

Indirect language contacts were mediated by mass media communication. The use of Slovak had a special function in the CR: it did not primarily target Slovaks but it was supposed to help to prevent the raising of language barriers between Czechs and Slovaks.

Results of research show that the most effective were discourses which do not erect any linguistic barriers to communication, i. e. discourses which use means of expression which are parallel in both languages. That is why bilingualism is manifested mostly in news, sport and entertainment programmes on TV and radio. Both these media transmitted alternately in Czech and Slovak. A different situation arose in the perception of literary works, as the literary text is extremely difficult to understand due to richness of its language as well as due to the relatively low frequency and regional nature of language means used. Programmes of Slovak TV plays and films were the influential factor in this respect. In the early 80's also the number of foreign programmes dubbed in Slovak increased. The impact of Slovak cinematography was significantly less important.

The importance of written discourses on Czech-Slovak contacts has been considerably lower. Popular science magazines which used both languages in parallel had some possible influence on the development of bilingualism. Nevertheless the influence of newspapers was not extensive: for example, in 1991 only 14 Slovak daily papers were distributed in the CR, totaling only 4,439 copies (Nemcová – Ondrejovič 1992, 377). Also the influence of fiction has decreased. Translations were given priority, their number increasing in the 70's and 80's.

6.2. The development of passive bilingualism was brought about also by schools. In elementary and secondary schools classes have been given in Czech (the only exceptions were some secondary military schools). Teaching of the Slovak language was reduced to basic information about differences and comparison with Czech, and to the ability to read and understand written and spoken Slovak (cf. Hedvičáková 1985, 121–122). The goal has never been to master Slovak actively.

Courses at universities have been taught in both Czech and Slovak without regard to the location of the university. Only students of Czech studies were given a comparative description of Slovak in order to introduce the students to the structure, functions and stylistic differentiations of Slovak. University textbooks were often printed only in one language.

7. General contactlinguistic portrait

The most visible sign of the close synchronic relationship of the two languages is the fact that Slovaks and Czechs can understand each other without any difficulties. This intercomprehensibility is based on many structural similarities and coincidences of the two languages. Differences between them are smaller than between standard (literary) Czech and Silesian dialects (Sochová 1991, 124). Among the 500 most frequent words in both the languages, 230 (46%) are the same and 154 (30.8%) are in partial coincidence.

7.1. Similarities of Czech and Slovak prevail over differences. Both languages share many word stems as well as lexical (derivational) affixes. Very close to each other are also their morphological systems. On the other hand both languages exhibit particular features that distinguish them. For example, functional (stylistic) stratification of the two languages is different. Variation of Czech can be described in terms of structural varieties such as Standard (Literary) Czech, Colloquial Czech (a set of expressions appertaining to the colloquial style of Literary Czech, tolerant towards non-literary elements), Common Czech (a variety which is distinct from standard Czech and is not, more or less, regionally restricted; see Sgall/Hronek/Stich/Horecký 1992; Townsend 1990), interdialects and traditional territorial dialects. Within Slovak, there is no variety corresponding to Common Czech. Other varieties, for example slangs, have been developing in both languages nearly concurrently and many expressions in them are the same. Similar are in most instances the language of journalism, professional terminology, as well as the stylistically unmarked stock of the standard languages. On the other hand, fiction and spoken language encompass most of the differences between the two languages.

7.2. The nearly permanent contact of two related languages and an extensive bilingualism constituted suitable conditions for the rise of contact variants (see 5.1.1.). Most of them are of idiolectical character and their quality is determined by many psychological and social factors, on the length of the stay of the speaker in the Czech environment, on his/her education, etc. (cf. 5.2.).

7.2.1. Some contact variants can be detected in the speech of most or nearly all Slovaks of a certain social group and these variants are a part of their sociolect. Speakers use these variants to mirror the new environment more accurately. These features are most prominent in lexicon (*dělat'* – in Czech *dělat*, in Slovak *robit'*; *pres* – in Czech *přes*, in Slovak *cez*). Other contact variants could be found on the phonetic level (altered quality of sounds, i. e., not observing the quantity of vowels), partially in syntax (verbal valence, the choice of prepositions and conjunctions) and rarely in morphology and word derivation. Contact influence also supports those language items, the validity of which in their mother tongue is somehow restricted (cf. Hoffmannová/Müllerová 1993; Zeman 1987, 63; 1988, 174).

7.2.2. Contact Slovak variants penetrate Standard (Literary) Czech relatively infrequently. In most cases, they are represented by lexical items. They include words of the common spoken language (*rozlučka* – in Czech *rozloučení*, in Slovak *rozlúčka*), words of newspaper language (*středobod* – in Czech *těžiště*, in Slovak *stredobod*) as well as those that are used in literary style (*nepřestojně* – in Czech *neustále*, in Slovak *neprestojne*). Contact variants enlarge synonymity of the Standard (Literary) Czech lexicon (*dovolenka* – in Czech *dovolená*, in Slovak *dovolenka*).

Czech-Slovak contact can catalyze (initiate and/or support) certain grammatical processes in Czech. The contact seems to accelerate general simplifying of syntax, gradual use of accusative verb forms instead of genitive forms, decrease in the use of nominal forms of adjectives, increase of the use of compound forms, etc. (cf. Jedlička 1978, 86–90).

7.3. Dialects on the Czech-Slovak language border can be considered a result of the long-lasting direct contacts of the Czech and Slovak languages there are. In the territory of the CR they are represented by Moravian-Slovak dialects. In these dialects we can identify many features common to both the eastern part of the Czech language territory and to Slovak dialects (cf. Bělič 1972, 16–17).

8. Development and contemporary state of the comparative study of Czech and Slovak

8.1. The beginnings of Czech-Slovak comparative research can be found in the tradition of the Prague Linguistic School, whose interest in application of the comparative study of language systems (language teaching, translations) influenced the comparative approach to Czech and Slovak.

After the Slovak language was introduced as a study subject for bohemists and slavicists at Czech universities in 1953, Czech and Slovak linguists together worked out the textbook *Slovenština* (Bělič et al. 1957), which is still the only comparative description of Czech and Slovak. In the early 60's, Czech-Slovak comparative study was determined mainly by interests of translations of Slovak literature to Czech (cf. Jedlička 1961, 7–23).

The relationships between Czech and Slovak became a subject of discussion from the point of view of language policy in the early 60's as well (cf. Bělič/Doležel/Peciar (Eds.) 1962, 385–439; *Jazykovedné štúdie VII*). Results of this endeavour were later criticised and were not generally accepted. Especially the thesis on bringing Czech and Slovak closer together was later considered to be a symptom of a centralistic language policy. Nevertheless foundations of comparative study of both languages have been established and certain guidlines for language policy articulated.

8.2. A true, self-contained Czech-Slovak comparative study emerges in the early 70's. The wider linguistic context for these studies was set by the theory of communication, sociolinguistics and Slavic studies. The results concern various language strata and were published as theoretical articles in *Slavica Pragensia XVIII, XXV* and *XXX* (Rzounek (Ed.) 1975; Budovičová (Ed.) 1985; Budovičová (Ed.) 1989).

Two dictionaries are a product of the comparative endeavour in lexicology: a smaller *Slovensko-český slovník* (1967) by Ž. Gašparíková and A. Kamiš, and *Česko-slovenský slovník* (Horák et al. 1979), of more than 70,000 entries. A similar *Slovensko-český slovník* is forthcoming.

8.3. Sociolinguistic research on Czech-Slovak language contacts is in its initial stages. Some valuable sociolinguistic research focused on bilingualism in nationally mixed regions has been conducted (Sokolová 1985; 1991; Davidová/Bogoczová/Jandová 1991). Studies with the goal of compiling a list of contact variants in the speech of Slovaks living in the Czech milieu have been prepared as well (Hoffmannová/Müllerová 1993), but the major body of work remains to be done.

9. Bibliography (selected)

Bartáková, Jana (1986): "O jazykovej úrovni Slovákov žijúcich v českom prostredí" [On Language Standard of Slovaks Living in Czech Environment). In: *Kultúra slova 20*, 80–82.

Bělič, Jaromír (1972): *Nástin české dialektologie* [Outline of Czech Dialectology], Prague.

Bělič, Jaromír et al. (1957): *Slovenština* [The Slovak Language], Prague (6th edition 1980).

Bělič, Jaromír/Doležel, Lubomír/Peciar, Štefan (Eds.) (1962): *Problémy marxistické jazykovědy* [Issues of Marxistic Linguistics], Prague.

Budovičová, Viera (1987): "Literary Language in Contact. (A sociolinguistic Approach to the Relation between Slovak and Czech Today)". In: *Reader in Czech Sociolinguistics*, Chloupek, J./Nekvapil, J. (Eds.), Amsterdam/Philadelphia, 156–175.

Budovičová, Viera (Ed.) (1985): *Slavica Pragensia XXV. Česko-slovenské jazykovědné studie* [Studies in the Relationship between Czech and Slovak], Prague.

Budovičová, Viera (Ed.) (1989): *Slavica Pragensia XXX. Česko-slovenské jazykovědné studie II.* [Studies in the Relationship between Czech and Slovak II], Prague.

Davidová, Dana/Bogoczová, Irena/Jandová, Eva (1991): *Využití jazyka při řízení pracovních kolektivů v ostravské průmyslové aglomeraci se zaměřením na zkoumání česko-slovensko-polské jazykové interference* [The Use of Language in Management of Working Groups in the Ostrava Industrial and Urban Area with Special Attention to Czech-Slovak-Polish Interference], Ostrava.

Gašparíková, Želmíra/Kamiš, Adolf (1967): *Slovensko-český slovník* [The Slovak-Czech Dictionary], Prague.

Hedvičáková, Jaroslava (1985): "K historii vyučování slovenskému jazyku na českých školách" [A Contribution to the History of Teaching Slovak at Czech Schools]. In: *Filologické studie 13*, 113–122.

Hoffmannová, Jana/Müllerová, Olga (1993): "Die Interferenz des Tschechischen und Slowakischen in der gesprochenen Kommunikation". In: Sprache – Kommunikation – Informatik. Akten des 26. Linguistischen Kolloquiums, Darski, J./Vetulani, Z. (Eds.), Tübingen, 401–405.

Horák, Gejza (Ed.) (1979): *Česko-slovenský slovník* [Czech-Slovak Dictionary], Bratislava.

Horálek, Karel (1968): "Příbuzenství češtiny a slovenštiny" [Relatedness of Czech and Slovak]. In: *Naše řeč 51*, 193–199.

Jazykovedné štúdie VII. Spisovný jazyk (1963): [Linguistic Studies VII. Standard Language], Bratislava.

Jedlička, Alois (1961): "Jazyková problematika překladů ze slovenštiny do češtiny" [Issues in Translation from Slovak to Czech]. In: *Naše řeč 44*, 7–23.

Jedlička, Alois (1978): *Spisovný jazyk v současné komunikaci* [Standard Language in Present-day Communication], Prague.

Kuchař, Jaroslav (1964): "O koordinaci českého a slovenského názvosloví z hlediska teorie a praxe" [Coordination of Czech and Slovak Terminology from the Theoretical and Practical Point of View]. In: *Naše řeč 47*, 1–9.

Nemcová, Emília/Ondrejovič, Slavo (1992): "Regimewechsel, Medien und Semantik". In: *Regimewechsel, Demokratisierung und politische Kultur in Ost-Mitteleuropa*, Gerlich, P./Plusser, F./Ulram, P. A. (Eds.), Vienna/Cologne/Graz, 374–389.

Rzounek, Vítězslav (Ed.) (1975): *Slavica Pragensia 18.* Prague.

Sgall, Petr/Hronek, Jiří/Stich, Alexandr/Horecký, Ján (1992): *Variation in Language. (Code Switching in Czech as a Challenge for Sociolinguistics)*. Amsterdam/Philadelphia.

Sochová, Zdeňka (1991): "Blízké jazyky a konfrontační lexikografie" [Closely Related Languages and Comparative Lexicography]. In: *Naše řeč 74*, 124–131.

Sokolová, Gabriela (1985): "K některým otázkám bilingvismu v etnicky smíšených regionech ČSSR" [On Some Questions of Bilingualism in Ethnically Mixed Regions of the ČSSR]. In: *Sociológia 17*, 213–223.

Sokolová, Gabriela (1991): "O jazykovém zaměření Slováků a Němců žijících v severních Čechách (na základě sociologických výzkumů)" [Language Orientation of Slovaks and Germans living in the Northern Part of the Czech Republic (based on sociological research)]. In: *Slezský sborník 89*, 3/4, 172–180.

Townsend, Charles E. (1990): *A Description of Spoken Prague Czech*, Ohio.

Zeman, Jiří (1987): "K řečové komunikaci Čechů a Slováků v jednom sociálním prostředí" [Spoken Communication of Czechs and Slovaks in One Social Environment]. In: *Sborník přednášek z III. konference o slangu a argotu v Plzni 24.–27. ledna 1984*, Klimeš, L. (Ed.), Plzeň, 61–66.

Zeman, Jiří (1988): "K jazykovým kontaktům mezi češtinou a slovenštinou" [On Language Contacts between Czech and Slovak]. In: *Funkční lingvistika a dialektika. Linguistica XVIII/1*, Nekvapil, J./Šoltys, O. (Eds.), Prague, 172–175.

Zeman, Jiří (1995): "Ke vztahu češtiny a slovenštiny v České republice". [On the Relationship of Czech and Slovak Languages in the Czech Republic.] In: Innerslavischer und slavisch-deutscher Sprachvergleich. Beiträge zur Slavistik 27, Jelitte, H./Troškina, T. P. (Eds.), Francfort Main/Berlin/Bern/New York/Paris/Vienna, 523–537.

Jiří Zeman, Hradec Králové (Czechia)

202. Tschechisch—Deutsch

1. Geographie und Demographie
2. Geschichte
3. Politik, Wirtschaft und allgemeine kulturelle sowie religiöse Lage
4. Statistik und Ethnoprofile
5. Soziolinguistische Lage
6. Sprachpolitische Lage
7. Allgemeines kontaktlinguistisches Porträt
8. Kritische Wertung der verwendeten Quellen und Literatur
9. Bibliographie (in Auswahl)

1. Geographie und Demographie

Die Tschechische Republik besteht nach der Aufteilung der ehemaligen Tschechoslowakei (1993) aus den drei historischen Kronländern Böhmen, Mähren und einem Teil Schlesiens, in denen heute insgesamt fast 50 000 Deutsche (0,5%) leben, im ehemals deutschbesiedelten Grenzgebiet (Sudetenland), aber auch dort nicht als kompakte Siedlungsgruppe (→ Sprachenkarte K).

2. Geschichte

Größere Bedeutung gewann die deutsche Sprache in den Böhmischen Ländern im 13. Jahrhundert mit der sogenannten Ostkolonisation. Die Přemysliden-Herrscher, Klöster und auch einzelne Feudalherren holten in die nicht besonders dicht besiedelten Gebiete Siedler, die sich als Bauern, hauptsächlich jedoch als Handwerker und Bergleute sowohl in den Randgebieten von Böhmen und Mähren niederließen, als auch im Landesinneren, wo sich deutsche Sprachinseln bildeten.

In den neugegründeten Städten, die oft mit besonderen Privilegien ausgestattet wurden, bildete sich bald ein deutsches Patriziat. Am Hofe der Přemysliden war Deutsch als Sprache des Hochadels zugelassen, böhmische Herrscher waren Gönner deutscher Dichter, König Wenzel II. (1278—1305) schrieb selbst deutsche Minnelieder. Das enge Nebeneinander der beiden Sprachen und Kulturen läßt sich u. a. daran ermessen, daß zeitgleich um 1400 in Böhmen sowohl das hervorragende Werk der deutschen spätmittelalterlichen Literatur, der *Ackermann aus Böhmen*, entstand, als auch das thematisch verwandte tschechische Parallelstück *Tkadleček* (d. i. Weber). Durch die Hussitenkriege (1419—1436) wurde das Deutsche in Böhmen stark zurückgedrängt. Erst in der zweiten Hälfte des 16. und im 17. Jahrhundert kam es zu einem Wiedererstarken. Anfang des 17. Jahrhunderts waren die Deutschen in den Städten sogar so stark vertreten, daß die Stadtbehörden die Angelegenheiten deutscher Bürger auf deutsch erledigten, obwohl sie nach dem Stadtrecht verpflichtet waren, tschechisch zu amtieren. Mit der Sprachenfrage befaßte sich sogar der Böhmische Landtag, und 1615 erließ er ein Gesetz, nach dem Ausländer, die sich im Lande niederlassen wollten, Tschechischkenntnisse nachweisen mußten (Povejšil 1980, 7). Durch den Dreißigjährigen Krieg (1618—1648) und die Emigration tschechischer wie deutscher Protestanten verlor Böhmen die Hälfte der Einwohner. Durch Immigration deutschsprachiger Bevölkerung aus den benachbarten katholischen Regionen verschob sich die Sprachgrenze allmählich tief in das Landesinnere (Skála 1968a, 7—16). Seit Ende des 17. Jahrhunderts verlor Tschechisch als Sprache der gebildeten Kreise an Bedeutung, und Deutsch wurde fast allgemein zur Sprache der oberen Schichten.

Zu Beginn des 19. Jahrhunderts gab es drei sprachliche Bevölkerungsgruppen: Deutsche, Stockböhmen und zweisprachige Utraquisten meist tschechischer Herkunft. Tschechisch war die Sprache der Landbevölkerung und der unteren städtischen Schichten, Deutsch die der oberen Klassen, der Verwaltung und der Bildung. In der zweiten Hälfte des 19. Jahrhunderts emanzipierte sich das Tschechische vom Deutschen, und sein Funktionsbereich erweiterte sich ständig. Trotzdem „erhielt sich immer noch eine natürliche, d. h. nicht aus der Schule hervorgegangene Zweisprachigkeit, vor allem in jener kleinbürgerlichen Schicht, die dem utraquistischen Lager entstammte" (Trost 1980, 275). In den Städten herrschte noch lange „eine umfassende Zweisprachigkeit (...), die von einer mehr oder weniger vollkommenen Beherrschung des Deutschen bis zum geradebrechten sogenannten Kücheldeutsch reichte" (Trost 1965, 26). Das gepflegte Deutsch der Oberschicht in Prag genoß im 19. Jahrhundert in der österreichisch-ungarischen Monarchie den Ruf einer besonders reinen und gewählten Sprache, der allerdings im 20. Jahrhundert verlorenging. Das sogenannte Kleinseitner Deutsch (benannt nach dem Prager Stadtviertel, Kisch 1920, 276 ff) war dagegen ein von den tschechischen Volksschichten und z. T. im deutschen Kleinbürgertum gesprochenes Deutsch, dessen Grundlage das Vulgärösterreichische bildete und das mit tschechischer Phraseologie durchsetzt war (Trost 1965, 27). Jedoch gerade in der Zeit, in der das Deutsche auf vielen Gebieten seine Funktion einbüßte und durch das Tschechische ersetzt wurde, „entstand in Prag eine deutschsprachige Literatur vom höchsten Range" (Trost 1965, 39).

Nach ihrer Gründung (1918, → Art. 200, 2., 4.) lebten in der Tschechoslowakei etwas mehr als drei Millionen Deutsche, die damit die bedeutendste nationale Minderheit ausmachten. In den deutschsprachigen Regionen, d. h. vor allem im Grenzgebiet und den Sprachinseln, blieb das Deutsche eindeutig vorherrschend, und nicht nur dort genoß es als Amts- und Unterrichtssprache volle offizielle Anerkennung. Es existierte eine regionale wie überregionale deutsche Presse, deutsche Schulen, angefangen von den Elementarschulen bis hin zur deutschen Universität in Prag, und deutsche Theater. In den Städten des Grenzgebietes, die im 18. und 19. Jahrhundert rein deutschsprachig waren, siedelten sich — von den dort entstandenen Industrien angezogen — Tschechen an, die bald zweisprachig wurden. Vor 1945 gab es im Grenzgebiet kaum Tschechen, die nicht Deutsch gekonnt und gesprochen hätten. Dagegen besaß die deutschsprachige Bevölkerung kaum Tschechischkenntnisse. Erst in den 20er Jahren wurden, wie bei den Tschechen schon früher üblich, während der Ferien im Austausch Kinder nach Böhmen geschickt, um Tschechisch zu lernen.

Vor 1918 wie danach herrschte im Lande eine national und sprachlich gespannte Atmosphäre. Auf beiden Seiten wurden die beiden Kontaktsprachen oft unter dem nationalpolitischen Aspekt des Sprachkampfes betrachtet. Auf der tschechischen Seite entwickelte sich ein aggressiver Purismus, der mit ziemlich großem Erfolg deutsche Lehnwörter aus der Schriftsprache — nicht aber aus der Volks- bzw. Umgangssprache — beseitigte; auf der deutschen Seite hingegen entstand durch die Einstellung der Förderung des Deutschen durch den neuen Staat ein Gefühl der Benachteiligung. Die Situation änderte sich grundsätzlich mit der Errichtung des Protektorats Böhmen und Mähren (1939—1945), in dem nicht nur alle öffentlichen Aufschriften, Plakate, Urkunden usw., sondern sogar Ansagen im Rundfunk zweisprachig sein mußten, wie z. B. *Jetzt hören Sie Nachrichten. Teď uslyšíte zprávy*; *Das Orchester leitete XY. Orchestr řídil XY.*

Der Ausgang des Zweiten Weltkrieges und die daraus folgende Aussiedlung bzw. Vertreibung der deutschen Bevölkerung (1945—1947) brachte erneut eine weitgehende Veränderung des Verhältnisses Deutsch—Tschechisch. Von den über drei Millionen Deutschen blieben nur etwa 250 000 Menschen (Staněk 1993, 23), die sogenannte Antifaschisten oder Facharbeiter oder mit Tschechen verheiratete Deutsche waren. Von den Angehörigen der intellektuellen Schicht blieben nur sehr wenige.

3. Politik, Wirtschaft und allgemeine kulturelle sowie religiöse Lage

Das totalitäre Regime nach 1948 setzte die frühere restriktive Nationalitätenpolitik gegenüber den Deutschen intensiv und systematisch mit dem Ziel einer Assimilierung fort. Damit sollte verhindert werden, daß sich die im Lande verbliebenen Deutschen zu einer ethnischen Einheit formieren; sie wurden erst 1968 als nationale Minderheit anerkannt. Es durften zwar eine Vereinigung der Deutschen in der ČSFR, ein Wochenblatt, eine Prager deutsche Wanderbühne entstehen; diese hatten jedoch nur geringen Einfluß auf die deutsche Bevölkerung. Politisch und wirtschaftlich haben sich die Deutschen in die bestehenden Strukturen integriert; zivilisatorisch, kulturell und religiös (katholisch) standen sich beide Volksgruppen bereits seit Jahrhunderten nahe.

4. Statistik und Ethnoprofile

Nach 1947 sank die Zahl der Deutschen im Lande ständig. Der eine Grund dafür war der nachträgliche Aus- bzw. Umzug meistens in die Bundesrepublik Deutschland (besonders stark in der zweiten Hälfte der 60er Jahre), der andere das natürliche Ausscheiden der älteren und die Assimilation der jüngeren Generationen. Laut der zuletzt durchgeführten Volkszählung (1991) bekannten sich 48 556 Einwohner der Tschechischen Republik zur deutschen Nationalität (Staněk 1993, 197). Die meisten leben in den nord- und nordwestlichen Bezirken Trutnov (Trautenau), Liberec (Reichenberg), Děčín (Teschen), Teplice (Teplitz), Karlovy Vary (Karlsbad) und Sokolov (Falkenau). Noch Anfang der 60er

Jahre gab es in den genannten Bezirken einige Ortschaften, in denen sich die bodenständige deutsche Bevölkerung auf bis zu 40% belief (Skála 1977, 275). Heute findet man jedoch kaum einen Ort, in dem das deutsche Element zahlenmäßig, politisch oder gesellschaftlich relevant wäre. Man findet ebenso kaum Deutsche, die nicht Tschechisch könnten. In Nordböhmen gaben 1970 7,2% der Deutschen Tschechisch als ihre Muttersprache an, 1987 waren es in der jüngeren Generation bereits 33% (Sokolová 1991).

5. Soziolinguistische Lage

Noch vor etwa zwanzig Jahren war in Ortschaften, in denen eine größere deutsche Minderheit lebte, ein generationsbedingtes Sprachverhalten und Sprachspektrum feststellbar (cf. mundartliche Erhebungen in Nord- und Westböhmen durch Povejšil 1967; 1975; vgl. auch Staněk 1993, 131 ff). In solchen Ortschaften wurden drei Sprachen als Verständigungsmittel gebraucht: das Tschechische, das (mundartlich gefärbte) Hochdeutsch und der einheimische Dialekt. Das Tschechische galt als Amts- und Unterrichtssprache für Tschechen wie für Deutsche, für Tschechen natürlich auch als Sprache des täglichen Umgangs. An zweiter Stelle — was die Verbreitung und kommunikative Bedeutung betraf — stand der Dialekt. Er war das geläufigste Sprachmittel der deutschen Bevölkerung in Familie, im Freundeskreis, am Stammtisch und oft auch am Arbeitsplatz. Das Hochdeutsche war eher auf die passive Aufnahme von Informationen von außen her beschränkt, von Fernsehen, Rundfunk und Zeitung, und auf die Kommunikation mit Fremden.

Der Grad der Zwei- bzw. Dreisprachigkeit und die Kombination der Kodes waren und sind noch heute — trotz verminderter älterer Generation — je nach Altersgruppe verschieden. Die älteste Generation spricht meistens kein oder sehr dürftiges Tschechisch.

Die mittlere Generation beherrscht alle drei Kodes, wobei die Aussprache des Tschechischen, das erst nach 1945 gelernt wurde, durch einen eindeutig deutschen Akzent begleitet ist. Das äußert sich in der nicht einwandfreien Unterscheidung der stimmhaften und stimmlosen Konsonanten, in fehlerhaftem Gebrauch der Vokalquantität und Akzentsetzung und beim Verb in der Unsicherheit bei der Anwendung des Aspekts. Die jüngste Generation lernt als erste Sprache meist den Dialekt der Eltern bzw. Großeltern. Mit dem Schulalter kommt das Tschechische hinzu.

6. Sprachpolitische Lage

Heute ist die ehemals zweite Landessprache, von der noch gewisse Residuen in der ältesten Generation der tschechischen Bevölkerung haften bleiben, zu einer Fremdsprache, ähnlich dem Englischen oder Französischen, geworden. Allerdings bilden sich durch unmittelbare Nachbarschaft zu den deutschsprachigen Ländern, die Bildung grenzüberschreitender Regionen wie in Nordböhmen, im Böhmerwald und Südmähren sowie gemeinsame ökologische Interessen und Aktionen Zonen, in denen schon jetzt ein sich ausweitender menschlicher und natürlich auch sprachlicher Kontakt zu verzeichnen ist. Sowohl in der Politik als auch in Wirtschaft und Handel dieser Regionen ist wohl damit zu rechnen, daß das Deutsche im Gegensatz zu den anderen Fremdsprachen eine Sonderstellung einnehmen wird.

Elementare Deutschkenntnisse werden in der Schule und im für Erwachsene privat organisierten Fremdsprachenunterricht erworben. Eine „natürliche" Zweisprachigkeit ist eher die Ausnahme. Nach statistischen Angaben lernen an den Grundschulen 54% der Schüler Deutsch und 40% Englisch. An den Gymnasien muß das Verhältnis jedoch eher mit 33% zu 43% beschrieben werden (Houska 1992, 107).

Die beiden Gymnasien im südmährischen Znojmo (Znaim) (bilingual) und in Prag (österreichisch) sind mit deutschsprachigen Lehrkräften ausgestattet und können mit einem österreichischen Abitur bzw. in Österreich gültigen Abitur abgeschlossen werden. Es handelt sich dabei jedoch nicht um Minderheitsschulen, sondern um Institutionen, in denen die Schüler — überwiegend tschechische Muttersprachler — einwandfreie Deutschkenntnisse erwerben sollen. Auf dem gleichen Prinzip basieren auch die existierenden englischen und französischen Gymnasien.

Durch das Verfassungsgesetz von 1968 wurde das Recht der Deutschen auf Bildung in ihrer Muttersprache und auf die Verwendung ihrer Sprache im Amtsverkehr anerkannt. Jedoch wurden keine Grundschulen mit Deutsch als Unterrichtssprache errichtet mit der offiziellen Begründung, es gebe keine Ortschaften mit kompakter deutscher Besiedlung. Schülern aus deutschen Familien stand und steht in Regionen mit vereinzelt deutscher Besiedlung schon in der Grundschule fakultativer Deutschunterricht zur Verfügung, an dem oft auch Kinder aus tschechischen Familien teilnehmen (Staněk 1993, 132 ff). Z. Zt. ist die Errichtung weiterer Schulen mit Deutsch als Unterrichtssprache geplant (Šimečková 1992, 99).

In den letzten Jahren — namentlich nach der Wende im November 1989 — bahnt sich eine neue Art der deutsch-tschechischen Sprachkontakte an, die einen neuen Weg zur natürlichen Zweisprachigkeit der tschechischen Bevölkerung zumindest im Grenzgebiet darstellt.

Der Sprachkontakt wird vor allem durch folgende Faktoren bestimmt:

— Massentourismus und die damit verbundenen Dienstleistungen,
— deutsche und österreichische Firmen, die für ihre Niederlassungen zweisprachige einheimische Mitarbeiter benötigen,
— tschechische Pendler, die im deutschen Grenzgebiet arbeiten,
— deutschsprachige Werbung und Annoncen in der tschechischen Presse,
— die sich entwickelnde deutschsprachige Presse (z. B. das Wochenblatt „Prager Zeitung", das zweisprachige Monatsblatt „Český — Böhmen Expres"),
— deutschsprachiges Fernsehen aus dem deutschen Sprachraum,
— vermehrte kulturelle und gesellschaftliche Aktivitäten des Verbandes der Deutschen in Böhmen, Mähren und Schlesien und der (mit Hilfe deutscher Investitionen) errichteten Begegnungszentren in mehreren Städten, in denen bis zur Aussiedlung Deutsche lebten. Ihre Aufgabe besteht darin, den vereinzelt lebenden Deutschen eine Möglichkeit zur Begegnung zu bieten und Kontakte zwischen Deutschen und Tschechen sowie zwischen den im Lande verbliebenen und den nach 1945 ausgesiedelten Sudetendeutschen zu pflegen („Prager Zeitung" Nr. 49 vom 9. 12. 1993).

7. Allgemeines kontaktlinguistisches Porträt

In der Vergangenheit — bis etwa 1918 — war eindeutig Deutsch die dominierende Sprache. Das im folgenden gezeichnete Bild bezieht sich daher zum großen Teil auf das Vergangene und das bis heute Erhaltene, denn der gegenwärtige Kontakt hat — wie oben angedeutet — einen völlig anderen Charakter.

Es gab Versuche, bestimmte Erscheinungen des tschechischen Lautstandes mit der Kontaktsprache Deutsch zu erklären. Dabei handelt es sich namentlich um die Anfangsbetonung im Tschechischen, den Umlaut, der jedoch völlig anderer Natur ist als der im Deutschen, die Diphthongierung von langem *ý, ú > ej, ou* im Tschechischen und die von mittelhochdeutschem *î, û > ei, au* im Deutschen. Die neuere Forschung reagiert auf diese Versuche mit ernsten Einwänden (Komárek 1958, 149; Trost 1963, 29; Skála 1965; ders. 1991/92) und bezweifelt den Einfluß des Deutschen auf die lautliche Ebene des Tschechischen.

Durch den deutschen Einfluß wollte man auch den Verfall des Genitivs der Negation und des prädikativen Instrumentals im Tschechischen erklären, aber auch hier wurden Gegenargumente geäußert. Man kann mit ziemlicher Sicherheit behaupten, daß die lautliche wie die grammatische Struktur des Tschechischen vom Deutschen unberührt ist. Die Jahrhunderte währende Zweisprachigkeit in den Böhmischen Ländern vermochte weder die Deklination noch den verbalen Aspekt zu zerstören, noch das artikellose Tschechisch in eine Sprache mit Artikeln umzuwandeln (Trost 1963, 30). Für eindeutig erwiesen hält Trost (1965, 26) nur Einflüsse im Wortschatz und in der Phraseologie. „In der Schriftsprache handelte es sich überhaupt nicht um Lehnwörter, sondern um Lehnübersetzungen. Aber das Wesentliche ist hier nicht die Übereinstimmung in der Bezeichnungsweise, sondern der Umstand, daß Bezeichnungen derselben Bedeutungsstruktur vorhanden sind, d. h. eindeutige gegenseitige lexikalische Entsprechungen. (...) Ein tiefgreifender Einfluß des Deutschen aufs Tschechische in neuerer Zeit, außerhalb des lexikalischen Bereiches, läßt sich nicht fassen."

Deutsche Lehnwörter im heutigen Tschechisch wurden oftmals unter verschiedenen Aspekten in der Fachliteratur behandelt. Eine Auswahl aus diesem Wortgut bringt Skála (1968, 127, 141). Im 19. und Anfang des 20. Jahrhunderts bildeten sie noch einen eigentlich merkmallosen Bestandteil der tschechischen Umgangssprache. Es konnten sogar Sätze folgenden Typs (als Scherz) konstruiert werden: *Hausmajstrová pucuje na gonku fotrovi šláfrok*, d. h. 'Die Hausmeisterin putzt auf dem Gang Vaters Schlafrock'. „Grammatisch ist gegen diesen Satz nichts einzuwenden, nur sind fast alle lexikalischen Morpheme dem Deutschen entnommen" (Trost 1980, 276). Viele Wörter stammten aus dem Handwerkermilieu, dem des Militärs und des Staatsdienstes. Im Laufe der Stabilisierung der tschechischen Umgangssprache auf schriftsprachlicher Basis sank diese lexikalische Schicht in die niedere Umgangssprache und gewann das stilistische Merkmal des Saloppen, Familiären, evtl. des Abwertenden. Viele Ausdrücke, die noch in den 30er Jahren dieses Jahrhunderts im mündlichen Verkehr gebraucht wurden, sind der jetzigen jungen Generation nicht mehr bekannt, und sie bedient sich der tschechischen Ausdrücke.

Nicht alles ist jedoch im Schwinden begriffen. Es gibt Lehnwörter, die z. B. in tschechische bzw. mährische Volkslieder eingegangen sind (*šanovat* 'schonen', *kšírovat* 'den Pferden das Geschirr anlegen', *pucovat* 'putzen', *verbovat* 'junge Männer für den Militärdienst werben'), sie waren im Bänkelgesang enthalten (Trost 1961, 229), und auch im täglichen Umgang lassen sich Ausdrücke finden wie *kšeft, kšeftovat* 'Geschäft, Geschäfte machen' nicht immer auf eine saubere Weise, *nemá o tom ánunk* 'er hat keine Ahnung davon', *aušus* 'Ausschuß, minderwertige Ware', *trucovat* 'sich trotzig verhalten', *fajn* 'fein', und viele andere. Der Vergangenheit gehört auch der deutsch-tschechische Makkaronismus an. „Es konnte jedes geläufige deutsche Wort, tschechisch flektiert oder unflektiert, in die tschechische Rede eingefügt werden. Der Makkaronismus konnte in Sprachwechsel übergehen, die Utraquisten brachten deutsche Sätze oder Satzfolgen ein oder fielen im selben Gespräch aus der einen in die andere Sprache: a bißl deutsch, a bißl böhmisch" (Trost 1980, 276f). So auch im folgenden tschechisch-deutschen makkaronischen Volkslied, das der Verfasser dieses Textes in seiner frühen Jugend (ca. 1940) einen Dudelsackpfeifer aus Südböhmen singen hörte:

Můj zlatej Honzíčku	(Mein goldenes Hänschen)
was host tu kmocht	(was hast du gemacht)
já na tě čekala	(ich habe auf dich gewartet)
ti gonze Nocht	(die ganze Nacht)
já na tě čekala	(ich habe auf dich gewartet)
troumt hobs von dir	(ich habe von dir geträumt)
jak sem se vohlídla	(wie ich mich umgedreht habe)
tu schlofst bei mir	(du schläfst neben mir)

Die grammatische Struktur der beiden Sprachen ist hier völlig intakt.

Neue deutsche Lehnwörter finden nur selten Eingang ins heutige Tschechisch. Ziemlich geläufig ist z. B. *knäckebrot* geworden (ohne tschechisches Äquivalent), in letzter Zeit begegnet man öfters dem umgangssprachlichen Wort *kornšpic* 'žitná špička' (eine Art Salzhörnchen), das wohl auf das deutsche *Kornspitz/e/* zurückzuführen ist. In publizistischen Texten findet man den Ausdruck *sudetoněmecký landsmanšaft*, in dem das Substantiv maskulin ist. Aus einem älteren umgangssprachlichen Lehnwort *veksl* 'směnka' (Wechsel) ist neu die umgangssprachliche Bezeichnung *vekslák* entstanden für denjenigen, der ungesetzlich mit ausländischer Währung Geschäfte macht.

Nun stellt sich ganz folgerichtig auch die Frage, ob bzw. wie sich das Tschechische auf das Deutsche in den Böhmischen Ländern ausgewirkt hat. Der Einfluß des Tschechischen auf das Deutsche war weit geringer als umgekehrt. Es ist somit sicher übertrieben bzw. grob verallgemeinert, wenn Paul Eisner, ein bedeutender bilingualer Literat der Prager Kulturszene der 30er Jahre, schreibt: „So wurde das Prager Deutsch ... ein phonetisch slawisiertes, lexikalisch, syntaktisch, phraseologisch von Austriazismen, Bohemismen, Pragensismen durchsetztes Deutsch, bis zur gelegentlichen baren Unverständlichkeit für den Besucher aus dem Reich" (Eisner 1937, 46).

In dem „höherschichtigen" literarischen Deutsch (Beranek) findet man kaum Züge, die eindeutig auf tschechischen Einfluß zurückzuführen wären. In den deutschböhmischen Mundarten gab es zwar tschechische, aber oft regional beschränkte Lehnwörter, wie z. B. *Brabenzel/Wawrenze* 'Ameise' (mravenec, volkssprachlich brabenec), *Schmetten/ Schmeten* 'Sahne' (smetana), *Kapuste* 'Kohl' (kapusta), *Nusch* abwertend für 'Messer' (nůž), *Schwarken/Schkwarken* 'Grieben' (škvarky) (Schwarz 1958; Beranek 1970; Skála 1977, 261; Trost 1979, 247). In der sudetendeutschen Umgangssprache findet man neben vielen Lehnwörtern auch phraseologische Lehnübersetzungen wie z. B. *auf Schwämme gehen* 'Pilze suchen gehen' (jít na houby), *mir will sichs nicht* 'ich habe keine Lust' (nechce se mi), *du bist von Mehl* 'du bist mit Mehl beschmutzt' (jsi od mouky), *ich gehe mich ausbaden* 'ich gehe baden' (jdu se vykoupat), *sich heißen* (jmenovat se) (Beranek 1970, 22, 212, 214; Trost 1979, 246—247). Kennzeichnend für das sog. Böhmisch-Deutsch war die offene Aussprache der *e*-

Laute, *Säle* 'Seele', *ajnzigä Kronä* 'einzige Krone' (Trost 1979, 246), das Fehlen des obligatorischen Artikels, z. B. *Krojce von Friedhof* 'die Kreuze auf dem Friedhof', *wo sich abr Blic herkommt* 'woher aber der Blitz herkommt' (Fehr 1977, 136; Trost 1979, 247). Die Grundlage des Böhmisch-Deutschen, das in kleineren Städten der Böhmischen Länder mit deutscher Minderheit und tschechischer Mehrheit gesprochen wurde, bildete die „niedere österreichische Umgangssprache unter Einfluß des tschechischen Sprachmodells" (Trost 1979, 246).

8. Kritische Wertung der verwendeten Quellen und Literatur

Eine synthetische Darstellung der Kontakterscheinungen zwischen beiden Sprachen fehlt. Die unzähligen älteren wie neueren Teiluntersuchungen auf deutscher wie tschechischer Seite behandeln hauptsächlich Lehnwort- und toponomastische Fragen, wobei übereinstimmend das Tschechische die rezipierende Sprache ist (Rippl 1944; Beranek 1955, 1970; Schwarz 1958, 1954—1958; Trost 1964, 1969; Skála 1968). Neuere wichtige Beiträge zu dieser Thematik sind z. B. in Trost (1965, 1969) zu finden.

Wesentliches zu Formen des Sprachkontakts in zweisprachigen böhmischen Kleinstädten und speziell im Prag des ausgehenden 19. und der ersten Hälfte des 20. Jahrhunderts schreibt P. Trost (1963, 1965, 1979, 1980, 1981). Mit dem tschechisch-deutschen Sprachkontakt in den älteren Perioden und seinen späteren Nachwirkungen im Tschechischen befaßte sich E. Skála (1964, 1965, 1966, 1977), der kürzlich mit der These vom mitteleuropäischen (deutsch-tschechischen) Sprachbund von sich reden machte (1991/92, 1993). Den Sprachkontakt und die Funktionen des mehrschichtigen Deutschen und des Tschechischen im Nord- und Westböhmen der 60er—70er Jahre beschrieb J. Povejšil (1967, 1975).

9. Bibliographie (in Auswahl)

Beranek, Franz J. (1955): „Sudentendeutsche Umgangssprache". In: *Stifter-Jahrbuch IV*, Gräfelfing, 124—146.

Beranek, Franz J. (1970): *Atlas der sudetendeutschen Umgangssprache I*, München.

Eisner, Paul (1937): „Zwei Literaturen und ein Argot". In: *Prag heute*, Warschauer, F. (Ed.), Prag, 32—47.

Fehr, Götz (1977): *Fernkurs in Böhmisch*, Hamburg.

Kisch, Egon E. (1920): *Die Abenteuer in Prag*, Wien/Prag.

Komárek, Miroslav (1958): *Historická mluvnice česká I. Hláskosloví* [Tschechische historische Grammatik I, Lautlehre], Prag.

Povejšil, Jaromír (1967): „Dvojjazyčnost v západních Čechách" [Bilingualismus in Westböhmen]. In: *Slovo a slovesnost 28*, 431—434.

Povejšil, Jaromír (1975): „Deutscher Dialekt und fremde Hochsprache bei zweisprachiger Bevölkerung". In: *Philologica Pragensia 18*, 100—110.

Povejšil, Jaromír (1980): *Das Prager Deutsch des 17. und 18. Jahrhunderts*, Prag/Hamburg.

Povejšil, Jaromír (1987/88): „Die deutsche Sprache in der Tschechoslowakei". In: *brücken*, Germanistisches Jahrbuch DDR—ČSSR, Prag, 221—229.

Rippl, Eugen (1944): „Wege und Voraussetzungen einer deutsch-tschechischen Lehnwortkunde". In: *Slavia 18*.

Schwarz, Ernst (1958): „Probleme der sudetendeutschen Lehnwortgeographie". In: *Zeitschrift für Mundartforschung 26*, 128—150.

Schwarz, Ernst (1954—1958): *Sudetendeutscher Wortatlas*, München.

Skála, Emil (1964): „Die Entwicklung des Bilinguismus in der Tschechoslowakei vom 13. bis 18. Jahrhundert". In: *Paul-Braunes Beiträge* (Halle), 69—106.

Skála, Emil (1965): „Die Möglichkeit der Beeinflussung des alttschechischen phonologischen Systems durch das Mittelhochdeutsche". In: *Proceedings of the 5th International Congress of Phonetic Sciences*, Zwinger, E./Bethge, W. (Eds.), Basel/New York, 528—531.

Skála, Emil (1966): „Das Prager Deutsch". In: *Zeitschrift für deutsche Sprache 22*, 84—91.

Skála, Emil (1968): „Deutsche Lehnwörter in der heutigen tschechischen Umgangssprache". In: *Deutsch-tschechische Beziehungen im Bereich der Sprache und Kultur*, Havránek, B./Fischer, R. (Eds.), Berlin, 127—142.

Skála, Emil (1968a): „Die Entwicklung der Sprachgrenze in Böhmen von 1300 bis etwa 1650". In: *Acta univ. Carolinae — Germanistica Pragensia V*, 7—15.

Skála, Emil (1977): „Der deutsch-tschechische Bilinguismus". In: *Sprache der Gegenwart 41, Sprachwandel und Sprachgeschichtsschreibung im Deutschen*, Moser, H. et al. (Eds.), Düsseldorf, 260—279.

Skála, Emil (1991/92): „Deutsch und Tschechisch im mitteleuropäischen Sprachbund". In: *Brücken*, Berger, M./Krolop, K. (Eds.), Prag, 173—179.

Skála, Emil (1993): „Der Bilinguismus in Mitteleuropa: Die deutsch-tschechische Entwicklung". In:

Göttinger Beiträge zur Internationalen Übersetzungsforschung, Band 8, Teil 2, Übersetzen, Verstehen, Brücken bauen, Berlin, 766—774.

Sokolová, Gabriela (1991): „O jazykovém zaměření Slováků a Němců žijících v severních Čechách" [Zur sprachlichen Orientierung der Slowaken und der Deutschen in Nordböhmen]. In: *Slezský sborník 89,* 172—180.

Staněk, Tomáš (1993): *Německá menšina v českých zemích 1948—1989* [Die deutsche Minderheit in den Böhmischen Ländern], Prag.

Šimečková, Alena (1992): *O němčině pro Čechy* [Über das Deutsche für Tschechen], Prag.

Trost, Pavel (1961): „O germanismech v kramářských písních" [Über Germanismen im tschechischen Bänkelgesang]. In: *Václavkova Olomouc,* Dvořák, J./Kvapil, J. Š. (Eds.), Olmütz, 229—230.

Trost, Pavel (1962): „Das späte Prager Deutsch". In: *Acta univ. Carolinae — Germanistica Pragensia II,* 31—39.

Trost, Pavel (1963): „Německé vlivy na slovanské jazyky" [Deutscher Einfluß auf slawische Sprachen]. In: *Čs. přednášky pro V. mezinárodní sjezd slavistů v Sofii,* Havránek, B. et al. (Eds.), Prag, 29—30.

Trost, Pavel (1964): „Zur Problematik deutscher Lehnwörter im Tschechischen". In: *Wissenschaftliche Zeitschrift der E.-M.-Arndt-Universität Greifswald, Gesellschafts- und sprachwissenschaftliche Reihe 5,* 493—495.

Trost, Pavel (1965): „Deutsch-tschechische Zweisprachigkeit". In: *Deutsch-tschechische Beziehungen im Bereich der Sprache und Kultur 1,* Havránek, B./Fischer, R. (Eds.), Berlin, 21—28.

Trost, Pavel (1969): „Tschechisch-deutsche lexikalische Kongruenz". In: *Slawisch-deutsche Wechselbeziehungen in Sprache, Literatur und Kultur,* Krause, W./Stieber, Z./Bělič, J./Borkovskij, V. I. (Eds.), Berlin, 252—254.

Trost, Pavel (1979): „Böhmisch-Deutsch". In: *Zeitschrift für Dialektologie und Linguistik,* 246—248.

Trost, Pavel (1980): „Der tschechisch-deutsche Makkaronismus". In: *Wiener slawistischer Almanach 6,* 274—278.

Trost, Pavel (1981): „Die Mythen vom Prager Deutsch". In: *Zeitschrift für deutsche Philologie 100,* 381—390.

Jaromír Povejšil, Prag (Tschechien)

203. Tschechisch—Polnisch

1. Geographie und Demographie
2. Geschichte
3. Politik, Wirtschaft und allgemeine kulturelle sowie religiöse Lage
4. Statistik und Ethnoprofil
5. Soziolinguistische Lage
6. Sprachpolitische Lage
7. Allgemeines kontaktlinguistisches Porträt
8. Zur Forschungslage
9. Bibliographie (in Auswahl)

1. Geographie und Demographie

Laut Statistik aus dem Jahre 1991 leben auf dem Gebiet der Tschechischen und Slowakischen Republik 59 383 Polen. 43 479 davon sind Autochthone, die eine relativ kompakte polnische Minderheit im Grenzgebiet mit Polen bilden. Weitere etwa 18 000 Einwohner polnischer Nationalität leben verstreut in verschiedenen Orten der Tschechischen und der Slowakischen Republik. Die kompakte polnische Minderheit in der Tschechischen Republik hat ihren festen Siedlungsraum in den Grenzlandkreisen Karviná (Karwina) und Frýdek-Místek (Friedek-Mistek). Er wird von der einen Seite durch die Staatsgrenze und von der anderen durch die Verbindungslinie Lomná — Tyra — Řeka (Rzeka) — Komorní Lhotka (Kameral Ellgoth) — Hnojník — Třanovice (Trzanowitz) — Těrlicko — Bludovice (Blauendorf) — Petřvald (Peterswald) — Rychvald (Reichwalden) — Bohumín (Oderberg) begrenzt. Nach dem Namen des Grenzflusses Olše (polnisch Olza, deutsch Olsa) wird dieses Gebiet auch Śląsk Zaolziański bzw. Zaolzie auf Polnisch genannt. Sprachlich handelt es sich um das Gebiet der sog. Westteschner oder ostlachischen Dialekte.

Der prozentuale Anteil der polnischen Bevölkerung sinkt von der Staatsgrenze Richtung Westen. Die meisten Polen leben heute in einigen Ortschaften des südlichen, nichtindustriellen Teiles, weniger im industriellen Nordteil des Gebiets, sowie in den Städten Český Těšín (Teschen), Třinec (Trzynietz), Karviná (Karwina) und Havířov (→ Sprachenkarte K).

2. Geschichte

Die Frage nach der ethnischen Herkunft der polnischen Minderheit in der Teschner Region konnte bisher noch nicht endgültig beantwortet werden. Bis zum Ende des 13. Jahrhunderts breitete sich im Westteschner Gebiet ein mächtiges Waldgebiet aus, das am Ende des 13. und im 14. Jahrhundert von Siedlern aus Nordostmähren und dem Misteker Raum in Besitz genommen wurde. Die letzten Mitglieder der Piasten-Dynastie brachten auch deutsche Siedler ins Teschner Gebiet, vor allem Handwerker. Im Jahre 1327 wurde das schlesische Fürstentum der böhmischen Krone angeschlossen. Infolgedessen wurde im 15. und 16. Jahrhundert der Prozeß der Germanisierung Schlesiens durch die tschechische Sprache aufgehalten. Nach dem Breslauer Frieden (1742) wurde Schlesien zwischen Österreich (der Teschner Teil) und Preußen aufgeteilt. Der Einfluß des Deutschen als Staatssprache nahm zu. In der ersten Hälfte des 19. Jahrhunderts stießen die Wellen der polnischen und tschechischen nationalen Bewegungen aufeinander. Es entstanden polnische Zeitungen und Zeitschriften, die polnische Sprache wurde in einigen Schulen eingeführt, und als Kirchensprache verdrängte sie das Tschechische bzw. das Deutsche. Polnisch-tschechische Konflikte, die früher wegen des starken deutsch-slawischen Antagonismus fast bedeutungslos waren, erstarkten. Die „Gesellschaft zur Vervollkommnung in der polnischen Sprache" (Towarzystwo dla Wydoskonalenia w Języku Polskim) und später der „Kulturpolitische Verein zur Pflege des Schulwesens im Teschner Fürstentum" (Macierz Szkolna dla Księstwa Cieszyńskiego), ebenso wie eine Reihe weniger bedeutsamer kulturgesellschaftlicher, sportlicher und genossenschaftlicher Vereine bildeten die historische Grundlage für die Entstehung späterer kulturfördernder Organisationen. Bei politischen Konflikten zwischen dem polnischen und tschechischen Element kam die Tendenz auf, den örtlichen Dialekt als Politikum in der Bewegung der sog. Ślązaken auszunutzen. Unterschiede der Regionalsprache sowohl von der tschechischen als auch von der polnischen Schriftsprache wurden betont, und deshalb sollte das sog. „po našymu" bevorzugt werden. In Teschen entstand 1910 sogar ein „Komitee zur Pflege der Reinheit des schlesischen Dialekts" (Komitet dla utrzymania czystości dyalektu śląskiego), das die örtliche Mundart von deutschen Anleihen und Einflüssen des Polnischen säubern sollte.

Die sich infolge konkurrierender Machtansprüche verschärfenden Antagonismen wurden zeitweilig durch die Pariser Friedensbeschlüsse (1920) beigelegt, die das Teschner Gebiet zwischen Polen und der Tschechoslowakei aufteilten. Dieser Zustand war jedoch nicht von langer Dauer: Aufgrund des Drucks der polnischen Regierung mußte der tschechische Teil des Teschner Gebietes 1938 an Polen abgetreten werden. Während der deutschen Okkupation wurde der Kern des historischen Teschner Gebietes zum selbständigen Landkreis Teschen umgewandelt und unter deutsche Verwaltung gestellt. Die Indifferenz eines Teiles der slawischen Bevölkerung ermöglichte die Entfaltung der nazistischen Propaganda, deren Hauptziel die Festigung der deutschen Position in dem strategisch außerordentlich wichtigen Gebiet war. Auf der von den Nazis konstruierten gesellschaftlichen Rangliste standen die Polen ganz unten, etwas höher die Tschechen, danach die Eigentümer einzelner Volkslistengruppen und ganz oben die Deutschen. Nach dem Zweiten Weltkrieg wurde zwar der politisch-geographische Zustand des Jahres 1910 erneuert, die Streitigkeiten zwischen der polnischen und der tschechoslowakischen Regierung um das Teschner Gebiet hielten jedoch an. Erst der Vertrag von 1947 beendete sie.

3. Politik, Wirtschaft und allgemeine kulturelle sowie religiöse Lage

Der von Polen bewohnte tschechische Landstrich gehörte bereits zwischen den beiden Weltkriegen zu den industriell am besten entwickelten Regionen. Die meisten polnischen Bewohner arbeiteten in der Industrie, im Handwerk und im Bauwesen, in der Land- und Forstwirtschaft und im Dienstleistungsbereich. Der Vergleich der sozialen Struktur, der Qualifizierung und der Sozialstellung der tschechischen und der polnischen Bevölkerung weist dabei keine grundsätzlichen Unterschiede auf. Das Durchschnittsalter der polnischen Population ist höher als das der tschechischen, und der Unterschied wird noch stets größer. Weder ist eine Verbesserung der Altersstruktur, noch ein bedeutender Zuwachs der jüngsten Generation für die Zukunft zu erwarten. Dies kann durch den hohen Anteil der weiblichen Population sowie den Anstieg der Zahl der Mischehen erklärt werden (Zahradnik 1991).

Die Religion des national gemischten Gebietes ist ebenfalls gemischt, evangelisch oder katholisch. Beide Kirchen respektieren und unterstützen heute die nationalen Gefühle ihrer Mitglieder (Gottesdienste werden z. B. in der Regel in beiden Sprachen abgehalten).

Die Verfassung (1947) garantierte den Polen in der Tschechoslowakei das Recht auf Bildung in der Muttersprache, auf den Gebrauch der Muttersprache im amtlichen Verkehr und in Druckerzeugnissen. Dementsprechend wurde in den vergangenen Jahrzehnten auch die Unterstützung der nationalen Minderheiten angekündigt. Jedoch wurden die praktischen Aktivitäten der Minderheiten gedämpft und die Umsetzung der Verfassungsrechte durch komplizierte Bürokratie gehemmt: Das Prinzip der Zweisprachigkeit wurde nicht immer eingehalten, so z. B. Schulen mit polnischer Unterrichtssprache aufgelöst, bei Besetzung von Arbeitsplätzen Tschechen bevorzugt.

4. Statistik und Ethnoprofil

In der nationalen Struktur der Tschechoslowakei stieg nach 1945 der Anteil der tschechischen und slowakischen Bevölkerung deutlich an, während die Anteile der anderen Nationalitäten zurückgingen. Laut Statistik von 1950 lebten im relevanten Gebiet 59 005 Polen, 155 146 Tschechen, 4 388 Slowaken und keine Deutschen. In den letzten zehn Jahren ist die Zahl der polnischen Bewohner um mehr als 8000 gesunken. Die Polen machen heute lediglich 11,8% der Bevölkerung der Region aus. Nach der Statistik lebten die meisten Polen aus dem Landkreis Frýdek-Místek in dörflichen Gemeinschaften und nur 1,2% in größeren Städten. Im Landkreis Karviná lebten dagegen 68,9% der Polen in Städten.

Die Urbanisierung und der Zustrom der Bevölkerung anderer Nationalitäten ist wohl die Hauptursache für den ständigen Rückgang des Anteiles der polnischen Bevölkerung und das Fortschreiten der Assimilation, die am stärksten im Landkreis Karviná zu verzeichnen ist, weniger dagegen im Landkreis Frýdek-Místek. Damit wird die Tatsache bestätigt, daß Menschen, die in traditionellen Siedlungsgemeinschaften leben, mehr an die Kultur und Sprache der eigenen Nationalität gebunden und damit assimilatorischen Einflüssen weniger zugänglich sind als Sprecher in urbanen Gemeinschaften, besonders der jüngeren Generation. Das Nationalitätenklima ist in der letzten Zeit toleranter geworden.

Ein wichtiger ethnischer Umstand, der den Prozeß der natürlichen Assimilation beschleunigt und die zwischenethnischen Distanzen verringert, sind die Mischehen. Im besprochenen Gebiet gibt es weit mehr Mischehen als rein polnische Ehen. In den Mischehen überwiegt die Konstellation: Polin—Tscheche. Die nationale Heterogenität der Familien beschränkt sich nicht auf bestimmte Gesellschaftsgruppen, sondern ist zu einer allgemeinen gesellschaftlichen Erscheinung geworden. Die Angehörigen von Mischehen benutzen im Umgang meist beide Sprachen, was die örtliche Zweisprachigkeit fördert. Die Nationalität der Kinder aus gemischten Ehen wird überwiegend mit Tschechisch angegeben.

5. Soziolinguistische Lage

Auf dem untersuchten Gebiet werden folgende Kommunikationskodes benutzt: (a) der Westteschner Dialekt (strukturelle Ähnlichkeiten mit anderen polnischen Dialekten), (b) Hochtschechisch (mit umgangssprachlichen Elementen), (c) Hochpolnisch (vor allem die regionale umgangssprachliche Variante). Da die Sprecher die einzelnen, genetisch verwandten Sprachkodes meistens abwechselnd benutzen, kann man von kollektivem Bilinguismus sprechen.

Der örtliche Dialekt wird von der einheimischen Bevölkerung — ungeachtet ihres Alters, Bildungsgrades und ihrer sozialen Lage — oft als wichtigstes Kommunikationsmittel benutzt. Diese „Erhöhung" des örtlichen Dialekts zum primären Kommunikationsmittel anstelle einer höheren Sprachform hat bereits seine Tradition (vgl. 2.). Die Wahl eines bestimmten Kommunikationskodes beeinflussen mehrere sprachliche und gesellschaftliche Faktoren. Die Sprecher verfügen über eine bestimmte soziolinguistische Kompetenz, die sie entscheiden läßt, wann, wo, was, mit wem und wie gesprochen werden kann. Es lassen sich zwei Arten des Sprachumgangs unterscheiden: privater Umgang, in dem sich die Sprecher gleichrangig gegenüberstehen (Familie, Freundes- bzw. Arbeitskreis) und offizieller Umgang mit den unter- bzw. übergeordneten Rollen der Sprecher (Schule, Theater, Ämter, usw.). In der privaten Kommunikation überwiegt eindeutig der Westteschner Dialekt. In Mischehen wird allerdings häufig neben dem Dialekt auch tschechisch gesprochen. Nur ein geringer Teil der polnischen Bevölkerung (meist aus der Schicht der Intelligenz mit hochentwickeltem

Nationalbewußtsein) benutzt im alltäglichen Kontakt eine Variante des Hochpolnischen. In der schriftlichen Familienkommunikation und in der Religionspraxis wird das Polnische auch von der übrigen polnischen Bevölkerung benutzt. Der Dialekt überwiegt ebenfalls bei Arbeits- und Lokalkontakten (besonders bei älteren Leuten), wird aber langsam vom Tschechischen verdrängt. Der Sprecher entscheidet sich oft zwischen dem Dialekt und Tschechisch in Abhängigkeit von der Nationalität des Adressaten, mit dem er durch keine emotionalen Beziehungen verbunden ist, so daß die Anonymität steigt und das Tschechische als Sprache der nationalen Majorität expandiert. Im offiziellen Sprachkontakt bestimmen die Sprecher mit „höheren gesellschaftlichen Rollen" (Verkäufer, Beamter, Arzt) die Wahl der Sprache (initiatives Sprachverhalten), die anderen Sprecher passen sich meist an (reaktives Sprachverhalten). Im Gespräch mit dem Vorgesetzten wird der Dialekt nur von etwa einem Drittel der einheimischen Bevölkerung benutzt, das Polnische nur von 20% (Labocha 1988). In den Geschäften wird der Dialekt viel häufiger verwendet, Polnisch dafür nur ganz selten. In den Ämtern wird demgegenüber am häufigsten tschechisch gesprochen, nur die älteren Respondenten sprechen im Dialekt. Bei Gerichtsverhandlungen und in zentralen Ämtern wird fast ausschließlich Tschechisch gesprochen, da die Sprecher glauben, der Erfolg ihrer Angelegenheit sei von der Wahl des Sprachkodes abhängig. Auf diese Weise wächst der Einfluß der Staatssprache im offiziellen Sprachkontakt, und die sprachliche Dreierkonstellation: Dialekt − Tschechisch − Polnisch ändert sich zu einer Zweierkonstellation: Dialekt − Tschechisch. Die Benutzung des Dialekts oder des Polnischen im offiziellen Kontakt ist demnach als gezielter Ausdruck der nationalen Gesinnung der polnischen Bevölkerung zu werten. Im Wohnort kommunizieren manchmal auch die Sprecher im Dialekt, die sich als Tschechen verstehen bzw. die Zugehörigkeit zur mährischen oder schlesischen Nationalität angeben. Dieses Sprachverhalten mag ein Ausdruck von Lokalpatriotismus sein, aber ebenso der Abneigung gegen die Hochsprache oder des Bestrebens, sich sprachlich von der Umgebung nicht zu unterscheiden.

6. Sprachpolitische Lage

Im Siedlungsgebiet der polnischen Minderheit werden die Sprachrechte gewährleistet, indem z. B. in Ämtern, Institutionen, Geschäften usw. zweisprachige Schilder angebracht wurden. Das Prinzip der Zweisprachigkeit wird ebenfalls bei amtlichen Verhandlungen, Bekanntmachungen und Veröffentlichungen der Verwaltungsorgane befolgt und kontrolliert − trotzdem sind viele Polen davon überzeugt, daß es nicht eingehalten wird. Aufgrund der Ähnlichkeit der tschechischen und polnischen Sprache (bzw. des Dialekts) gelangt eine gewisse Anzahl der Respondenten (Madecka 1992) zu der pragmatischen Ansicht, die Zweisprachigkeit sei überflüssig, da die Polen Tschechisch verstünden. Negative Stellungnahmen zur Zweisprachigkeit resultieren ebenfalls aus der Verwechslung der nationalen und staatlichen Zugehörigkeit: So sind einige Tschechen der Meinung, die Polen sollten sich sprachlich anpassen, wenn sie in Tschechien leben.

Einen großen Einfluß auf das Kultur- und Sprachleben der nationalen Minderheiten übt das Schulwesen aus. Im untersuchten Gebiet existieren Kindergärten, Grund- und Mittelschulen (bzw. einige Klassen) mit Polnisch als Unterrichtssprache. Nach dem Zweiten Weltkrieg gab es die größte Schülerzahl in polnischen Grundschulen Anfang der 60er Jahre, als in 85 polnischen Grundschulen 8500 Schüler unterrichtet wurden. Bis zum Schuljahr 1980/81 ging die Zahl der polnischen Grundschulen auf 35 zurück, ebenso verringerte sich die Zahl der Schüler um 54%. Verursacht wird der andauernde Rückgang der Zahl der polnischen Schüler durch (a) die Verschlechterung der Altersstruktur der polnischen Population, (b) die niedrigere Natalität, (c) die wachsende Anzahl der Mischehen, (d) die ungünstige Ortslage der polnischen Schulen. Ein Teil der hiesigen polnischen Nachkriegsgeneration fühlt sich darüber hinaus weniger mit Polen verbunden und besteht deshalb nicht auf der Ausbildung ihrer Kinder in Polnisch. Das Niveau der tschechischen und polnischen Schulen ist etwa gleich. Für polnische Lehrer werden regelmäßig Kurse angeboten − sowohl im Inland als auch in Polen − um den Standard des Sprachunterrichts zu halten.

Das polnische Kulturleben ist gut organisiert: Mehr als die Hälfte der polnischen Population sind Mitglieder des „Polnischen Kultur- und Bildungsvereins" (Polski Związek Kulturalno-Oświatowy − PZKO, gegr. 1947). Vor allem das Bedürfnis nach gesellschaftlichem Zusammenhalt motiviert die Polen zum Vereinsleben. Das Kulturleben und die Sprache wird weiterhin von der örtlichen polnischen Presse beeinflußt (die Zeitung „Głos Ludu", das Monatsblatt „Zwrot", die Jugendzeitschriften für polnische Schulen „Jutrzenka" und „Ogniwo"). Fachzeitschriften werden aus Polen bezogen. Zwei Verlage geben die Werke der lokalen Autoren heraus: Das Profil in Ostrava (Ostrau) und der Verlag des PZKO in Böhmisch Teschen. Einige Regionalautoren publizieren auch in Polen. Populär sind: K. Piegza, J. Ondrusz, A. Wawrosz, W. Sikora, W. Przeczek u. a., regelmäßig erscheint der Schlesische Kalender (Kalendarz Śląski).

In Stadtbibliotheken beider Landkreise befinden sich polnische Abteilungen. Obgleich sich die Sprachbezogenheit eben bei der Wahl der belletristischen Lektüre am deutlichsten äußern müßte, lesen viele in Tschechien lebende Polen in beiden Sprachen. Seit 1951 sendet der Ostrauer Rundfunk polnische Nachrichten und Kulturprogramme, allerdings mit sehr begrenzten Sendezeiten. Deshalb wird auch polnischer Rundfunk gehört und das Programm des polnischen Fernsehens verfolgt, was die Polnischkenntnisse beider ethnischer Gruppen unterstützt. Es gibt eine professionelle polnische Bühne des Teschner Theaters und eine Reihe nicht-professioneller polnischer Schauspiel-, Tanz-, Folkloregruppen und Gesangsvereine. Das Konsumverhalten der Jugend, der Einfluß des Fernsehens, des Kinos und des Videos führen jedoch zu einem deutlichen Rückgang des Interesses an diesen künstlerischen Tätigkeiten.

7. Allgemeines kontaktlinguistisches Porträt

Die Westteschner Dialekte weisen auf allen Sprachebenen dominante polnische Strukturzeichen auf. Im folgenden soll zumindest eine Auswahl angegeben werden:

(1) Im Konsonantensystem gibt es im gesamten Gebiet die weichen Labiallaute *ṕ*, *b́*, *ḿ*, *f́*, *v́* im Gegensatz zu den harten; palatalisierte Phoneme *ś*, *ź*, *ć* im Gegensatz zu den unpalatalisierten; das Konsonantenpaar *ł* [u̯] – *l* (harte *l* – mittles *l*); die Phoneme *ʒ*, *ǯ*, *ǯ́*; das Phonem *g*; die Aussprache des Doppel-*n* (*Anna*, *kaḿynny*); die progressive Assimilation des Typs [tfardy, sfûj] (û – offenes *u*).

(2) Im Vokalsystem gibt es sieben nicht nasalierte Vokale *i*, *y*, *e*, *a*, *o*, *û*, *u* und zwei nasale Vokale *y̨*, *ų*. Die Vokale sind nur kurz, d. h. es gibt keinen phonologischen Gegensatz der kurzen und langen Vokale, wie im Tschechischen.

(3) Das ursprüngliche *l* nach den Labiallauten wird durch die Gruppe *eu̯* ersetzt, z. B. *peu̯ny*, *veu̯na* (tsch. *plný*, *vlna*). Das ursprüngliche *r̥* und *r̥'* wird durch *ar* ersetzt, z. B. *kark* (tsch. *krk*). Das *r̥'* kann phonetischer Umgebung nach durch *'yr*, *'er*, respektive *er*, z. B. *ćyrńi*, *serce* (tsch. *trní*, *srdce*) ersetzt werden.

(4) Die altertümlichen Gruppen *tort*, *tolt* werden durch *trot*, *tłot*, z. B. *groch*, *bu̯oto* (tsch. *hrách*, *bláto*) ersetzt.

(5) In der Deklination gibt es im Plural der Maskulina statt der Kategorie der belebten und unbelebten Substantive die Kategorie der persönlichen und unpersönlichen Substantive.

(6) Das Verhältnis zwischen der harten und weichen Deklination der Substantive ist hier ungefähr so wie in den mährischen Dialekten, z. B. *pole*, *bez pola* (tsch. *pole*, *bez pole*). Im 6. Sg. der weichen Deklination steht *-u*, z. B. *na biču*, *na sercu* (tsch. *na biči*, *na srdci*).

(7) Die Formen des 6. und 7. Sg. der Maskulina und Neutra der harten Deklination der Adjektive sind in der Mehrheit ausgeglichen, z. B. *o starym*, *ze starym* (tsch. *o starém*, *se starým*). Ähnlich auch die Formen der Genuspronomina.

(8) Im 7. Pl. aller Deklinationen ist die universale Endung *-ḿi*, *-aḿi*, z. B. *bŕegaḿi*, *gûraḿi* (tsch. *břehy*, *horami*); die Universalendung heißt auch im 3. Pl. (*-ûm*/*-um*) und im 6. Pl. (*-ach*), z. B. *ṕekořûm*, *gûrûm*, *sukńûm*, *o ṕekořach*, *gûrach*, *sukńach* (tsch. *pekařům*, *horám*, *sukním*, *o pekařích*, *horách*, *sukních*).

(9) Das Futur hat die Form *bedym čytou̯* und *bedym čytać*.

(10) Im gesamten Gebiet gibt es die Konstruktion mit Akkusativ des Typus *mûm dvûch synûf* (tsch. *mám dva syny*).

(11) Der Infinitiv erfüllt die Funktion des Satzkernes der Nebensätze, der durch die Konjunktionen *aby*, *coby*, *žeby* eingeleitet wird, z. B. *posu̯uchali, aby śe teš cośi doveźeć*.

(12) Der Wortakzent liegt auf der vorletzten Silbe und verbindet sich mit einem kräftigeren Unterschied zwischen den betonten und unbetonten Silben mehr als anderswo im tschechischen Sprachraum.

(13) Der Wortschatz hat ebenso einen schlesisch-polnischen Einschlag, jedoch mit vielen tschechischen Elementen. Manchmal wird angenommen (vor allem von tschechischer Seite), daß Wörter des Typus *fara*, *zbûr*, *starosta*, *obec*, *cesta*, *hûśle*, *patnost*, *devatnost*, *fau̯ešny*, *kohût*, *gumno*, *obarteł*, *sfořyń*, *oje*,

u͜ûnkoć, (u͜)otka ... in diesem Gebiet autochthon sind, und sich nicht anstelle der ursprünglichen polnischen Wörter im Laufe der Zeit einbürgerten. Durch die tschechischen lexikalischen Entlehnungen wurden die Strukturen des neuen phonetischen und morphologischen Systems erweitert. Dadurch kommt es zu einer allmählichen Modifizierung des einheimischen Systems, z. B. *hledać, hned(a), hrûm, chrûmy, metu͜a, perûn.*

Der Kontakt der engverwandten Sprachen (Dialekte) und der verbreitete Bilinguismus bilden in diesem Gebiet günstige Bedingungen für häufige Interferenzen auf der phonetischen, grammatischen und lexikalischen Ebene. In den tschechischen Äußerungen gehört zu den geläufigen Interferenzerscheinungen der Mangel an Vokallänge, die im Tschechischen phonologisch ist (*sraz* „Zusammentreffen" — *sráz* „Abhang"), und der grammatischen Bedeutungen (*učitele*, G. Sg. — *učitelé*, N. Pl.), und die progressive Assimilierung in den Gruppen *tv, sv, kv*, wenn keine Assimilierung im Tschechischen stattfindet. In der Schriftsprache der einheimischen Polen ist das mundartlich gebeugte *û* vielfach verbreitet, ebenso wie die mundartliche Aussprache der Nasale des Typus 1. Sg. [rob'ym, pracujym] und 3. Pl. [rob'ûm, pracujûm]. In Schriftäußerungen meiden die einheimischen Polen Halbsatzkonstruktionen, vor allem Partizipkonstruktionen, die im Gegensatz zu der westteschener Mundart und zum Tschechischen im Gegenwartspolnisch geläufig sind. Zu anderen syntaktischen Interferenzerscheinungen gehören: der Gebrauch der Satznegation auch in den Fällen, in denen ein Binnenpole eine Satzglied- oder lexikalische Negation benutzen würde, der Gebrauch des Akkusativs anstelle des Genetivs in verneinenden Sätzen, die Verbreitung der Verbvalenz und verschiedener Präpositionen aus einer Sprache (wo sie gebräuchlich sind) in die andere (wo sie ungebräuchlich sind) usw. (Lotko 1986, 131). Die häufigsten Interferenzen beider Sprachen gibt es auf der lexikalischen Ebene. Wir finden hunderte einheimische und fremde Wörter, die in beiden Sprachen identisch oder ähnlich sind, aber sie unterscheiden sich in der Bedeutung (manchmal auch in der Stilistik), z. B. tsch. *sklep* 'piwnica' — pol. *sklep* 'obchod', tsch. *sok* 'rywal' — pol. *sok* 'štáva'. Neben diesen „falschen Freunden des Übersetzers" gibt es Wörter, die in beiden Sprachen fast identisch oder ähnlich sind und auch in der Bedeutung übereinstimmen, sich aber stilistisch unterscheiden, z. B. pol. *grupa* 'skupina' — tsch. *grupa* (veraltet und umgangssprachlich), pol. *peron* 'nástupiště' — tsch. *peron* (umgangssprachlich). Zahlreiche entlehnte Substantive des weiblichen Genus im Tschechischen haben im Polnischen ihre Gegenpole, die in der Regel dem männlichen Genus angehören, z. B. tsch. *montáž* (fem.) — pol. *montaż* (mask.), tsch. *reportáž* (fem.) — pol. *reportaż* (mask.), tsch. *tramvaj* (fem.) — pol. *tramwaj* (mask.) (Lotko 1992, 168).

8. Zur Forschungslage

Die dialektologische Erforschung des tschechisch-polnischen Grenzgebietes wurde bereits im 19. Jahrhundert durch den polnischen Wissenschaftler Jan Bystroń (1885) begründet. Seine Forschungen bildeten die Grundlage für weitere Arbeiten (Nitsch 1909). Viel später wurde der tschechische Teil des Teschner Gebiets von tschechischen Dialektologen untersucht (Kellner 1946, 1949). Manche Resultate sind subjektiv zugunsten des Tschechischen manipuliert worden. Deshalb wurde diese Arbeit von polnischen Forschern kritisiert und ihre irreführende Bezeichnung „ostlachische Dialekte" abgelehnt (vgl. 1.). Die Erforschung der Ortsdialekte wurde mit der Frage des nationalen Bewußtseins bei Jaromír Bělič verbunden (Bělič 1972). Eine objektivere Sicht bietet Edvard Lotko (Lotko 1963). Der Erforschung der Materie dienen auch Einzelstudien, so z. B. zum Wortschatz des Dialekts (Basara 1975), zu Ortsnamen (Davídek 1945), zur phonologischen Struktur des Dialekts (Romportl 1958), zur Beziehung zwischen Sprache und Nationalbewußtsein (Pallas 1970), zur Geschichte des Tschechischen in Schlesien (Lamprecht 1967), zur Entwicklung des Dialekts (Raclavská 1992), zu Soziolekten und zur Jugendsprache (Téma 1958, 1966, Křístek 1956, Valíková 1971), zur Rolle des Polnischen im untersuchten Gebiet (Labocha 1988, Madecka 1992) usw.

Eingehende psycho- und soziolinguistische Untersuchungen der Sprachkontakte stehen erst am Anfang. Sie werden seit 1991 von der Arbeitsstelle für die Erforschung des polnischen Ethnikums der Universität Ostrau durchgeführt (Bogocz 1993). Zur Zeit konzentrieren sich die soziologischen Untersuchungen auf die gegenseitige Beeinflussung der ethnischen und nationalen Gesinnung der

Grenzgebietsbevölkerung. Die disparatesten Stellungnahmen zur Problematik des tschechisch-polnischen Grenzgebiets bieten Geschichtsstudien, die wesentlich häufiger als linguistische Untersuchungen von deutlichen nationalen Tendenzen geleitet und nicht selten von totalitären Ideologien der Vergangenheit beeinflußt sind. Andere Gesichtspunkte finden sich in Nachkriegspublikationen (Sokolová 1978, Grobelný 1977, Chlebowczyk 1949, Zahradnik 1991, 1992, Kadłubiec 1987 usw.).

9. Bibliographie (in Auswahl)

Basara, Jan (1975): *Słownictwo polskich gwar Śląska na terenie Czechosłowacji* [Wortschatz polnischer Dialekte auf dem Gebiet des tschechoslowakischen Teils Schlesiens], Breslau.

Bělič, Jaromír (1972): *Nástin české dialektologie* [Abriß der tschechischen Dialektologie], Prag.

Bogocz, Irena (1993): *Jazyková komunikace mládeže na dvojjazyčném územi ceshého Těšínska* (Jugendsprache im zweisprachigen tschechischen Teil des Teschner Gebietes), Ostrau.

Bystroń, Jan (1885): *O mowie polskiej w dorzeczu Stonawki i Łucyny w Księstwie Cieszyńskim* [Die polnische Sprache des Stonawka und Łucyna-Flußgebiets im Teschner Fürstentum], Krakau.

Davídek, Václav (1945): *O názvech a jménech Těšínska* [Ortsnamen und -bezeichnungen im Teschner Gebiet], Troppau.

Dejna, Karol (1953): „Gwary zachodnio-cieszyńskie w pracy czeskiego uczonego" [Westteschner Dialekte im Werk eines tschechischen Forschers]. In: *Zwrot 5*, 8–9.

Grobelný, Andělín (1977): „Nacistická národnostní politika a výkon okupačního práva na Těšínsku 1939–1945" [Nazistische Nationalitätenpolitik und die Ausübung des Okkupationsrechtes im Teschner Gebiet 1939–1945]. In: *Slezský sborník 75*, 23–38.

Chlebowczyk, Józef (1949): *Cieszyńskie szkice historyczne* [Abriß der Geschichte des Teschner Gebiets], Katowitz.

Jasiński, Zenon (1990): *Działalność kulturalno-oświatowa Polaków za Olzą (1920–1938)* [Kulturell-volksbildende Tätigkeit der Polen im Olsagebiet (1920–1938)], Oppeln.

Kadłubiec, Daniel (1987): *Uwarunkowanie cieszyńskiej kultury ludowej* [Wurzeln der Teschner Volkskultur], Teschen.

Kellner, Adolf (1946, 1949): *Východolašská nářeči* [Ostlachische Dialekte], 1. und 2. Teil, Brünn.

Křístek, Václav (1956): *Ostravská hornická mluva* [Ostrauer Bergmannsprache], Prag.

Labocha, Janina (1988): „Język polski na Śląsku Cieszyńskim w Czechosłowacji. Sytuacja językowa i jej perspektywy badawcze na tle uwarunkowań historycznych" [Das Polnische im tschechischen Teil des Teschner Gebiets. Die Sprachsituation und deren Forschungsperspektiven im historischen Kontext]. In: *Przegląd Polonijny 14*, 73–83.

Lamprecht, Arnošt (1967): *Dějiny českého jazyka ve Slezsku a na Ostravsku* [Geschichte der tschechischen Sprache in Schlesien und im Ostrauer Gebiet], Ostrau.

Lotko, Edvard (1963): „K problematice česko-polského jazykového pomezí" [Zur Problematik der tschechisch-polnischen Sprachgrenze]. In: *Slezský sborník 61*, 293–302.

Lotko, Edvard (1986): *Čeština a polština v překladatelské a tlumočnické praxi* [Tschechisch und Polnisch in der Übersetzungs- und Dolmetschpraxis], Ostrau.

Lotko, Edvard (1992): *Zrádná slova v polštině a češtině. Lexikologický pohled a slovník* [„Falsche Freunde des Übersetzers" im Polnischen und Tschechischen aus lexikologischer Sicht. Mit einem Wörterverzeichnis], Olmütz.

Madecka, Bożena (1992): „Zakres funkcjonowania języka polskiego" [Wirkungsbereich der polnischen Sprache]. In: *Zaolzie. Studia i materiały z dziejów społeczności polskiej w Czecho-Słowacji*, Gerlich, M. G./Kadłubiec, D. (Eds.), Katowitz.

Nitsch, Kazimierz (1909): *Dialekty polskie Śląska* [Polnische Dialekte Schlesiens], Krakau.

Pallas, Ladislav (1970): *Jazyková otázka a podmínky národního vědomí ve Slezsku* [Sprachproblematik und Bedingungen der Entwicklung des Nationalbewußtseins in Schlesien], Ostrau.

PZKO – *Polski Związek Kulturalno-Oświatowy* [Polnischer Kultur- und volksbildender Verein], Ostrau 1987.

Raclavská, Jana (1992): „Z dziejów polszczyzny cieszyńskiej" [Kapitel aus der Geschichte des Teschner Polnisch]. In: *Zaolzie. Studia i materiały z dziejów społeczności polskiej w Czecho-Słowacji*, Gerlich, M. G./Kadłubiec, D. (Eds.), Katowitz, 97–104.

Romportl, Milan (1958): *Zvuková stránka souvislé řeči v nářečích Těšínska* [Die phonetische Struktur des gesprochenen Idioms in den Dialekten des Teschner Gebiets], Ostrau.

Sokolová, Gabriela/Hernová, Šárka/Kozel, Jaroslav (Eds.) (1987): *Soudobé tendence vývoje národnosti v ČSSR* [Gegenwärtige Entwicklungstendenzen der Nationalitätenstruktur in der ČSSR], Prag.

Téma, Bedřich (1958): *Mluva hutníků na Bohumínsku a Karvínsku* [Sprache der Hüttenarbeiter in den Gebieten von Oderberg und Karwina], Prag.

Téma, Bedřich (1966): *Mluva studentů východního Těšínska* [Die Studentensprache des Ostteschner Gebiets], Prag.

Valíková, Dana (1971): *Běžně mluvený jazyk nejmladší generace města Havířova* [Umgangssprache der jüngsten Generation der Stadt Havirov], Prag.

Zahradník, Stanisław/Ryczkowski, Marek (Eds.) (1992): *Korzenie Zaolzia* [Wurzeln des Olsagebiets], Warschau/Prag/Trzynietz.

Zahradník, Stanisław (1991): *Struktura narodowościowa Zaolzia na podstawie spisów ludności 1880–1991* [Nationale Struktur des Olsagebiets nach den Volkszählungen von 1880–1991], Trzynietz.

Edvard Lotko, Olmütz (Tschechien)

204. Slowakei

1. Geographie und Demographie
2. Territorialgeschichte und Staatsbildung
3. Politik, Wirtschaft und allgemeine kulturelle sowie religiöse Lage
4. Statistik und Ethnoprofile
5. Soziolinguistische Lage
6. Sprachpolitische Lage
7. Weitere Minderheiten und Kontaktsprachen (Roma, Juden, Kroaten)
8. Zur Forschungslage
9. Bibliographie (in Auswahl)

1. Geographie und Demographie

1.1. Auf dem Gebiet der Slowakei (der Slowakischen Republik – SR) mit der Fläche von 49 014 km^2 lebten laut der letzten Volkszählung im Jahre 1991 5 268 935 Einwohner.

Die SR grenzt an fünf Staaten: im Osten an die Ukraine (98 km), im Norden an Polen (597 km), im Westen an die Tschechische Republik (265 km), im Südwesten an Österreich (127,7 km) und im Süden an Ungarn (697 km).

Die SR befindet sich im Raum der Westkarpaten, die einen Grenzbogen an der nördlichen Seite bilden. Sie besteht überwiegend – außer in den südlichen Teilen, wo sich die Donautiefebene und die Theißtiefebene befinden – aus Bergland. Mit der geographischen Öffnung des Landes nach Süden hängt auch die Vermischung der einheimischen Bevölkerung mit der Bevölkerung des Nachbarlandes Ungarn zusammen. Die Gebirgigkeit des nördlichen Landesteils ist verantwortlich für den geringen Einfluß aus dem nördlichen Nachbarland Polen. Die Gebirgigkeit des Landes bewirkte in der Vergangenheit auch eine bestimmte (sprachliche) Isolierung der Bevölkerung im Rahmen der einzelnen Bezirke, was sich in der Differenziertheit der slowakischen Dialekte widerspiegelt.

1.2. Die Hauptstadt der SR Bratislava (Preßburg), in den Jahren 1526–1784 auch die Hauptstadt des von den Türken unbesetzten Teils Ungarns und bis 1830 der Krönungsort der ungarischen Könige, hat heute 441 453 Einwohner (davon 91,1% Slowaken, 4,5% Ungarn, 2,3% Tschechen und 0,35% Deutsche). Sie liegt im südwestlichen Zipfel der Slowakei. Daneben zählt nur die Stadt Košice (Kaschau), im östlichen Teil des Landes gelegen, mit 234 000 Einwohnern (1991) mehr als 100 000 Einwohner.

Trotz des Wachstums der städtischen Bevölkerung in der SR beträgt der Anteil der Landbevölkerung 47%.

1.3. Laut der letzten Volkszählung aus dem Jahre 1991 sind von den 5 268 935 Einwohnern der SR 4 116 790 Slowaken (85,6%), 566 741 Ungarn (10,76%), 80 627 Roma (1,57%), 53 422 Tschechen (1,0%), 16 937 Ruthenen (0,32%), 13 847 Ukrainer (0,26%), 5629 Deutsche (0,10%), 3888 Mähren (0,08%) und 2969 Polen (0,06%). Darüber hinaus gibt es in geringem Umfang Einwohner der SR, die zur russischen (1624), schlesischen (1198), bulgarischen (1085), rumänischen (247), griechischen (45) und zu anderen (3684) Nationalitäten gehören. Die Minderheiten in der SR gehören – mit Ausnahme der Roma, Tschechen und Deutschen – zum grenznahen Typ der Minoritäten (sie werden vom Mutterland nur durch die Grenze getrennt). Es handelt sich vorwiegend um eine autochthone Bevölkerung. Als allochthon im strikten Sinne des Wortes kann man die Vietnamesen bezeichnen, deren Zahl (etwa 10 000) nach dem Jahre 1989 rapid gesunken ist, und die Kubaner, von denen sich jetzt fast keine mehr in der SR aufhalten.

1.4. In den letzten Jahren läßt sich in der Slowakei eine gewisse Migrationsmobilität beobachten (Landflucht). 30 000 Personen aus der Slowakei fahren täglich in die Tschechische Republik zur Arbeit (→ Art. 201). Es gibt eine geringe Migrationsbewegung der Bevölkerung — vor allem Ruthenen und Roma — in die Tschechische Republik (→ Sprachenkarte K).

2. Territorialgeschichte und Staatsbildung

2.1. Nach dem Untergang des Großmährischen Reiches Anfang des 10. Jahrhunderts wurden die Slowaken mit ihrem Gebiet in den ungarischen Vielvölkerstaat aufgenommen. Die Slowakei entwickelte sich im ungarischen Staat (Habsburgreich, Österreichisch-Ungarische Monarchie) bis 1918 als das Oberungarn („Felvidék").

2.2. Nach dem Zerfall der Österreichisch-Ungarischen Monarchie haben die Slowaken erstmals ihre Staatlichkeit (1918—1939) im Rahmen der Tschechoslowakischen Republik gewonnen; von 1938—1939 kommt es zu einer Autonomie. In den Jahren 1939—1945 existiert sie als selbständiger Staat, von 1945 bis 1992 als Bestandteil der Tschechoslowakei, ab 1968 schon als nationale Republik der Tschechoslowakischen sozialistischen Republik und nach dem Regimewechsel im Jahre 1989 der föderativen Republik. Seit dem 1. Januar 1993 ist die SR auf Grund eines Verfassungsgesetzes über die Teilung der Föderation (25. 11. 1992) ein selbständiger Staat.

2.3. Die Grenzen des Staates wurden bei den Friedensverhandlungen in Paris 1918—1920 bestimmt. Die nördliche Grenze der (Tscheho-)Slowakei mit Polen wurde von den historischen Grenzen des ehemaligen Ungarn abgeleitet, und im Grunde deckten sie sich mit den ethnischen Grenzen (→ Art. 207). Im Osten grenzte die Slowakei an Karpatenrußland, das bis 1946 Bestandteil der Tschechoslowakei war. Die Grenze mit Rußland wurde durch das Abkommen in St. Germaine festgelegt. Am kompliziertesten war aber die Bestimmung der Grenze zwischen Ungarn und der Slowakei, da es hier weder eine feste historische, noch eine ethnische Grenze gab. In Ungarn wurden die Grenzen der Slowakei nie festgelegt, obwohl es die Vertreter der Slowaken oft verlangten, z. B. in den „Forderungen des slowakischen Volkes" im Jahre 1848 und im „Memorandum des slowakischen Volkes" aus dem Jahre 1861. Es war dabei kaum möglich, sich auf die ungarischen Statistiken zu stützen, da in diesen Statistiken nicht die Nationalität, sondern die Kenntnis der ungarischen Sprache festgestellt wurde (vgl. dazu Očovský 1991). Am 21. Dezember 1918 wurde die Demarkationslinie festgesetzt, die das ethnische, wirtschaftliche und geographische (Flüsse) Prinzip berücksichtigt. Endgültig wurde die Grenze mit dem Abkommen von Trianon am 4. Juni 1920 festgelegt. Somit kamen 650 597 Ungarn zur Tschechoslowakei (nach der Volkszählung im Jahre 1921). Viele Slowaken (etwa 400 000) sind in Ungarn geblieben.

Außer in den Jahren 1938—1945, als die Slowakei aufgrund des Münchner Abkommens und der Wiener Arbitrage an Ungarn 10 390 km^2 mit 850 000 Einwohnern — davon 272 000 der slowakischen und der tschechischen Nationalität — abtreten mußte, gilt diese Grenze mit einer kleinen Korrektur am rechten Donauufer im sogenannten Bratislavaer Brückenkopf bis heute. Diese letzte Änderung wurde im Vertrag mit Ungarn im Jahre 1947 in Paris besiegelt.

3. Politik, Wirtschaft und allgemeine kulturelle sowie religiöse Lage

3.1. In der Österreichisch-Ungarischen Monarchie wurden die Slowaken national stark unterdrückt, besonders nach dem Österreichisch-Ungarischen Ausgleich 1867. Eine totale Madjarisierung des Schulwesens und der Kirche fand statt, die Idee eines einzigen ungarischen Volkes — des madjarischen — wurde durchgesetzt. Vor allem politische Gründe führten am Ende des Ersten Weltkrieges zur Gründung der Tschechoslowakischen Republik. Für sie galt die Doktrin des einen tschechoslowakischen Volkes und der einen tschechoslowakischen Sprache (→ Art. 209). Nur so konnte man die bunte nationale Palette „verstecken", die von der alten Monarchie geerbt wurde, und erreichen, daß das staatsbildende Volk die Zweidrittelmehrheit darstellte. Im Jahre 1921 gab es in der Tschechoslowakei 65,5% Angehörige des „tschechoslowakischen" Volkes, 23,4% Deutsche, 5,6% Ungarn, 3,4% Russen, 1,3% Juden, 0,6% Polen und 0,2% andere Nationalitäten. Die demokratische und liberale Innenpolitik des Staates, die sich durch Gesetze um Staatsintegrität bemühte, hatte positive Seiten (Unterstützung des nationalen Schulwesens und der Entwicklung der nationalen Kultur), aber auch negative. Während die tschechischen Länder modernisiert wurden, stagnierte die Wirtschaft der Slowakei. Die gefragten Stellen z. B. in der Staatsverwaltung, im Schulwesen usw., die nach dem Ausscheiden der ungarischen Beamten frei wurden, wurden durch Tschechen besetzt (von 1921 bis 1930 verdoppelte sich die Anzahl der tschechischen Einwohner von 72 000 auf 141 000 in der Slowakei, vgl. Bunčák 1990). In dieser Zeit sind aus der Slowakei 209 000 Menschen nach Amerika ausgewandert. Zugleich kam es aber zu einer sehr bedeutsamen Veränderung der Schul- und Bildungsbedingungen, und zwar auch dank der tschechischen Besiedler (Marsina et al. 1922, 192).

Die Minderheiten, die 44% der Bevölkerung bildeten, bekamen Schutz in der Verfassungsurkunde der Tschechoslowakei (§ 121 bzw. 122), laut derer die Gerichte und Behörden verpflichtet waren, in den Bezirken mit einer qualifizierten 20%igen ethnischen Minderheit mit Angehörigen einer Minderheit in deren Sprache zu verhandeln. In der Zeit des selbständigen Slowakischen Staates, der vor allem auf Wunsch von Hitlerdeutschland entstand (auch die Hlinka-Partei, die die Unzufriedenheit mit dem Prager Zentralismus ausnutzte, bemühte sich eigentlich nur um eine Autonomie im Rahmen der ČSR), hat das Slowakische Parlament im Jahre 1939 ein Verfassungsgesetz (§ 185) verabschiedet, in dem das Prinzip einer Reziprozität beschlossen wurde (die jeweilige Minderheit konnte nur so viele Rechte haben, wie die slowakische Minderheit im anderen Staat besaß). Die Verfassung aus dem Jahre 1948, die nach der Machtübernahme durch die kommunistische Partei entstand, garantierte nur einzelnen Personen Rechte, nicht den Minderheiten als solche. Die Prinzipien der Politik gegenüber Minderheiten als Gruppe wurden erst im Gesetz über die tschechoslowakische Föderation im Jahre 1968 festgelegt (entsprechende Repräsentation in den Vertretungsorganen, außerdem das Recht auf Ausbildung in ihrer Sprache, auf allseitige kulturelle Entwicklung, auf Benutzung ihrer Sprache im amtlichen Verkehr in den von ihnen bewohnten Regionen sowie das Recht auf Presse und Informationen in der Sprache der Minderheit).

In der SR wurde im Jahre 1990 das Gesetz über die slowakische Sprache als Amtssprache verabschiedet, nach dem die Minderheiten ihre Muttersprache im amtlichen Gebrauch (in den Gebieten mit mindestens 20%igem Minderheitenanteil) verwenden können. Die slowakische Verfassung von 1993, die auf einem nationalen Prinzip beruht, deklariert die slowakische Sprache als offizielle Staatssprache.

3.2. Die SR war traditionell ein Agrarland; nach dem Zweiten Weltkrieg kam es hier aber zu einer raschen Industrialisierung. Es wurde vor allem die Schwer- und Rüstungsindustrie aufgebaut, die hohe Ansprüche an die Rohstoff- und Energieversorgung stellte und die die Umwelt ökologisch belastete. Die schnelle Industrialisierung stand im Zusammenhang mit der Urbanisierung (in den fünfziger Jahren betrug der Anteil der städtischen Bevölkerung ein Drittel, Ende der siebziger Jahre fast die Hälfte der Population), während die Dorfstrukturen erhalten blieben. Nach dem Regimewechsel wurde die Rüstungsindustrie drastisch reduziert, und der vorwiegend auf die ehemalige Sowjetunion orientierte Handel mußte umgelenkt werden.

3.3. Das Bildungsniveau der Bevölkerung ist dank der tschechischen Unterstützung in den dreißiger Jahren und dank eines gut entwickelten Schulnetzes relativ hoch. Nach dem Bildungsindex der Bevölkerung stehen in der SR an erster Stelle die Tschechen, gefolgt von den Deutschen, Slowaken, Polen, Ungarn und Ruthenen-Ukrainern. Mit großem Abstand liegen die Roma (mit nur 56 Personen mit einer Hochschulausbildung) am Ende.

3.4. Die letzte Volkszählung (1991) hat die relativ starke Religiosität der Bevölkerung der SR bestätigt. Ohne Glauben sind nur 511 185, d. h. weniger als 10% der Bevölkerung. Die meisten sind römisch-katholischen Glaubens (3 179 201), gefolgt von protestantisch 413 384, griechisch-katholisch 179 623, orthodox 34 144 und tschechisch-hussitisch 618. In den vorigen Jahrhunderten gab es in der Slowakei einen größeren Anteil an protestantischer Bevölkerung; in der Geschichte kam es oft zu konfessionellen Auseinandersetzungen (z. B. in der Frage der Literatursprache, → Art. 209). Die Ruthenen haben sich als Nation auf der Basis des konfessionalistischen Prinzips konstituiert (vgl. 6.3.).

4. Statistik und Ethnoprofile

4.1. Unter den Minderheiten ist die größte die ungarische, die mit 566 741 Personen 10,76% der Bevölkerung der SR stellt. Sie bewohnt 13 Bezirke in der Südslowakei. Dominant ist sie vor allem in den Bezirken Dunajská Streda/Dunaszerdahely (87,9%) und Komárno/Komárom (Komorn) (71,7%). Außerdem lebt eine nicht unbedeutende Zahl in Bratislava und Košice (Kaschau). Für die ungarische Minderheit ist eine hohe Konzentration der ungarischen Bevölkerung in ländlichen Ortschaften, häufige ethnische Endogamie und die räumliche Nähe ihres Staates spezifisch. Die ungarische Minderheit bildet in der SR einen selbstsegregierenden Typus, was sich nicht nur in ihrer „großen sprachlichen Eingeschlossenheit" zeigt (die ungarische Sprache überwiegt in der Kommunikation in gemischten Gebieten), sondern auch in einer starken Betonung ihrer ethnischen Zugehörigkeit, in ihrem Verhältnis zu den nationalen Traditionen usw. (Zel'ová 1991 a, b). Nach eigener Bewertung beherrschen 64% der ungarischen Bevölkerung die slowakische Sprache gut, aber sie verwenden sie in den gemischten Regionen in der Kommunikation mit Slowaken nur dann, wenn die Slowaken nicht über Kenntnisse der ungarischen Sprache verfügen (21% Slowaken in den gemischten Regionen beherrschen die ungarische Sprache gut, 24% teilweise). Wie mehrere Untersuchungen zeigen, erwarten die Bürger ungarischer Nationalität von der Majoritätsbevölkerung in gemischten Gebieten eine größere Anpassungsbereitschaft als umgekehrt (Hübl 1990, Šoucová 1991a, Šutaj 1991 b, Zel'ová 1991 d).

4.2. Heute leben in der Slowakei 53 422 Bürger tschechischer Nationalität (1,0% der Bevölkerung) relativ zerstreut über das ganze Gebiet. Sie leben aber vorwiegend in großen Städten wie Bratislava und Kaschau und in Städten mit militärischen Schulen bzw. Garnisonen (Žilina (Sillein), Trenčín (Trentschin), Liptovský Mikuláš u. a.). Als Kommunikationsmittel verwenden sie vor allem die tschechische Sprache (nur in den gemischten Ehen überwiegt das Slowakische), und zwar nicht nur in der Familie. Aus Gründen der Verständlichkeit und aus „Gewohnheit" wird das Tschechische auch in der Kommunikation mit Slowaken verwendet.

4.3. Die Ergebnisse einer Untersuchung aus dem Jahre 1989 haben gezeigt, daß die ukrainisch-ruthenische Minderheit 0,73% der Bevölkerung bildet (Zel'ová 1991 b). Im Jahre 1991, bei der Möglichkeit, sich frei für die eigene Nationalität entscheiden zu können, rechneten sich zur ruthenischen Nationalität 0,32% und zur ukrainischen Nationalität 0,26% der Befragten, also insgesamt nur 0,58% der Population der SR. Der Rückgang der Ruthenen und Ukrainer, die zu 82% die vier ostslowakischen Bezirke bewohnen, ist offensichtlich (0,7% jährlich). Die Ursache liegt vor allem in der großen Zerstreuung (der Umzug in größere Städte – Kaschau und Prešov und in die Tschechische Republik) und an der niedrigen Endogamierate (mehr als die Hälfte hat einen slowakischen Partner). Auch die ungünstige Alterszusammensetzung, die gewaltsame Ukrainisierung und der Zwang zur orthodoxen Kirche in den fünfziger Jahren mögen Gründe für den Rückgang sein (Paukovič/Szedláková 1991, Šutaj 1991 b).

Außer dem Ethnonym *Russin* bzw. *Rusnak* wurde in der Vergangenheit die Bezeichnung *Karpatenrusse*, der *Ugrorusse*, der *Kleinrusse* verwendet. Heute setzt sich auch die Wortverbindung *Ruthene-Ukrainer* bzw. *Ukrainer-Ruthener* durch.

4.4. Heute rechnen sich zur deutschen Nationalität in der SR 5 629 Personen, davon geben 4 200 Personen Deutsch als ihre Muttersprache an. Sie besiedeln kein geschlossenes Gebiet, sondern leben zerstreut über das Land. In der Vergangenheit kamen viele Deutsche nach Bratislava und die Mittelslowakei. Zu den Zielen der deutschen Kolonisation gehörte aber vor allem Zips, die erste Region, die Deutsche überhaupt in Richtung Osten besiedelt haben. Im 14. Jahrhundert gab es in der Slowakei 250 000 Deutsche, was ein Viertel der Bevölkerung ausmachte. Bis 1945 waren es immer noch 130 000. Am Anfang dieses Jahrhunderts lebten in Bratislava auch Juden, deren Muttersprache Deutsch war (Jahn, 1971).

Die deutsche Bevölkerung hat eine äußerst ungünstige Altersstruktur: 48,2% sind über 60 Jahre. In der Slowakei wurden sie seit den dreißiger Jahren *Karpatendeutsche* bzw. auch *Slowakeideutsche* genannt.

4.5. Zur polnischen Nationalität rechnen sich in der SR ungefähr 3000 Einwohner, die sehr zerstreut leben (in Bratislava 494, in Poprad (Deutschendorf) 227, in Dolný Kubín 200, in Kaschau 200). Sie zeichnen sich durch einen hohen Frauenanteil und eine niedrige Geburtenrate aus, was zusammen mit einer Dekonzentration die Hauptursache ihrer schrittweisen Assimilierung (bis 1,06% jährlich) ist (vgl. Srb 1991, Servátka 1982).

5. Soziolinguistische Lage

5.1. Eine der Minderheiten, die Kommunikationsschwierigkeiten mit der Majoritätsbevölkerung der SR hat, ist die ungarische Minderheit. Die meisten Ungarn halten die Ausbildung ihrer Kinder in ihrer Muttersprache für die wichtigste Bedingung, um ihre Identität zu bewahren. Im Gegensatz dazu räumen fast alle ein, daß eine bessere Kenntnis der slowakischen Sprache (Ungarn beherrschen sie weniger als andere Minderheiten, Plichtová 1992) zur Verbesserung der Beziehungen und des Bildungsniveaus der ungarischen Minderheit beitragen könnte. Die gegenseitige Toleranz zwischen Ungarn und Slowaken ist dabei wesentlich höher in den gemischten Regionen als dort, wo weniger Ungarn leben (Zel'ová 1991 b, Ondrejovič 1992). Das Gesetz über die Amtssprache, nach dem die Verwendung des Ungarischen als Amtssprache in Gebieten mit einem höheren Anteil als 20% erlaubt ist, wird aber von beiden Nationalitäten prinzipiell anders empfunden: jeweils eher zugunsten der anderen Ethnie (Šoucová 1991 a).

5.2. Die Angehörigen der tschechischen Nationalität verwenden in der SR als Kommunikationsmittel fast ausschließlich das Tschechische. Dies ist durch die Ähnlichkeit zwischen der slowakischen und der tschechischen Sprache möglich. Jede Seite spricht ihre eigene Sprache, und die Kommunikation kann so ohne größere Störungen verlaufen (Semikommunikation Budovičová 1987).

In der neuen Situation ist der Druck der stärkeren Sprache auf die schwächere verschwunden, die Abwehr als ethnopsychologischer Faktor ist geschwächt (Dolník 1992). Die gemeinsamen Ausdrucksmittel des Slowakischen und des Tschechischen werden nicht mehr pauschal abgelehnt, sondern sie werden als Kontaktelemente eingeschätzt, die man stilistisch nutzen kann (vgl. Buzássyová/ Ondrejovič 1994). Einen Sonderfall der sprachlichen Kommunikation gibt es bis heute im Militär, wo eine tschecho-slowakische Mischform vorzufinden ist (vgl. dazu Zeman 1988).

5.3. Bis zu 47% der Ruthenen-Ukrainer sprechen in den Familien slowakisch, bzw. sie verwenden einen ostslowakischen Dialekt.

5.4. Die Kontaktsprache der deutschen Nationalität ist das Slowakische, nur in den Familien wird noch zum Teil Deutsch gesprochen. Einige Familien waren und sind immer noch zweisprachig bzw. auch dreisprachig, z. B. in Bratislava (außer slowakisch deutsch bzw. auch ungarisch); die Personen, die nach 1945 geboren wurden, sind vorwiegend einsprachig (Born/Dickgießer 1989).

5.5. Für die polnische Bevölkerung ist Zweisprachigkeit charakteristisch. In den einzelnen Regionen sprechen sie miteinander einen (slowakisierten) goralischen Dialekt, als Kontaktsprache werden aber das Slowakische bzw. die slowakischen Dialekte verwendet. Die slowakische Hochsprache beherrscht eher die mittlere und jüngere Generation (Buffa 1982). Ihr Zugehörigkeitsgefühl zur eigenen Nation ist relativ stark.

6. Sprachpolitische Lage

6.1. Nach der Entstehung der ČSR (1918) sind 650 597 Personen ungarischer Nationalität in die Slowakei gekommen. Ihre Adaptierung war trotz guter Bedingungen (Vertretung im Parlament, entwickeltes Schulwesen, kulturelle Organisationen, jedoch weniger Unterstützung im sozialen Bereich) kompliziert. Aus der Position der herrschenden Nation sind sie in die Position als Minderheit geraten. Ein Teil der ungarischen Repräsentanten verlangte den Anschluß großer Gebiete an Ungarn, was im Jahre 1938 auch geschah. Nach dem Krieg wurde ihnen (außer den Antifaschisten) die Staatsbürgerschaft entzogen. Es kam zu einem Austausch der Bevölkerung: Es wurden 80 000 Ungarn ausgesiedelt, in die Slowakei kamen 72 000 Slowaken zurück (vgl. Bobák 1982). Im Rahmen dieser Maßnahmen, die im Jahre 1948 beendet wurden, sind fast 20 000 Ungarn nach Böhmen ausgesiedelt worden, die später die tschechoslowakische Staatsbürgerschaft zurückbekamen. Das ungarische Schulwesen wurde wieder aufgebaut und ungarische Zeitschriften und Bücher veröffentlicht. Im Jahre 1949 wurde Czemadok (Kulturverein der ungarischen Arbeiter) gegründet. Heute hat die ungarische Bevölkerung die Möglichkeit, die Ausbildung in ihrer Muttersprache an 257 Grundschulen und an 18 Gymnasien (10 davon selbständig und 8 gemischt) und an weiteren Mittelschulen und Fachschulen zu absolvieren. In den letzten Jahren ist unter den Schülern ungarischer Nationalität die Tendenz gestiegen, sich für die Gymnasien mit

Slowakisch als Unterrichtssprache zu entscheiden (Gabzdilová 1991). Der slowakische Rundfunk sendet 34,4 Stunden in ungarischer Sprache, in der SR sind zwei ungarische Theater aktiv.

6.2. Die Basis der staatlichen Politik der 1. ČSR bildete die Theorie über die einheitliche tschechoslowakische Nation und tschechoslowakische Sprache. Das Verfassungsgesetz aus dem Jahre 1948 und vor allem aus dem Jahre 1968 erklärte das Tschechische und das Slowakische als gleichberechtigt. Beide Sprachen wurden wechselweise in den Massenmedien, vor allem in Nachrichten, Unterhaltungs- und Ausbildungsprogrammen verwendet. Seit dem 1. Januar 1993 ist in der Slowakei Slowakisch die Staatssprache. Das Tschechische hat sich aber trotzdem seinen Wirkungsbereich teilweise erhalten: Die slowakischen Rundfunk- und Fernsehanstalten übernehmen einige tschechische Programme. Wegen der großen Zerstreutheit der tschechischen Bevölkerung in der SR, aber auch aufgrund der Möglichkeit der slowakisch-tschechischen Semikommunikation, hat die tschechische Minderheit in der Slowakei keine eigenen Schulen.

6.3. Im Jahre 1952 wurden die Ruthenen für Ukrainer erklärt, und in den Jahren 1953/1954 wurden alle russischen Schulen in ukrainische umgewandelt. Die administrative Ukrainisierung ging einher mit dem Zwang, sich zur orthodoxen Kirche zu bekennen. Parallel wurde die griechisch-katholische Kirche der Ruthenen liquidiert. Ein Teil der Ruthenen-Ukrainer hat den orthodoxen Glauben nicht angenommen und ist zum römisch-katholischen Glauben übergewechselt. Dies führte in den meisten Fällen auch zur Selbstidentifizierung mit der slowakischen Nation. Die Ruthenen haben ihre ethnische Identität immer sehr eng mit der kirchlichen Identität verbunden. Jüngst kam es zur Stärkung des ruthenischen Bewußtseins durch die Aktivität proruthenisch orientierter Initiativen: ruthenische Zeitschriften werden herausgegeben, Vereine nach dem ethnischen Prinzip organisiert usw. Im Jahre 1991 fand in der Slowakei (in Medzilaborce) auch der Weltkongreß der Ruthenen statt. In der ruthenisch-ukrainischen Bevölkerung gibt es aber auch eine ukrainisch orientierte Bewegung (Zel'ová 1991, → Art. 208).

6.4. Die Deutschen erlangten im Jahre 1953 ihre Staatsbürgerschaft wieder, einen rechtlichen Schutz erhielten sie aber erst im Jahre 1968. Ähnlich wie die Tschechen und Polen haben sie wegen ihrer geringen Zahl und der großen Streuung keine eigenen Schulen. Die deutsche Sprache wird aber traditionell an den Mittelschulen und Gymnasien unterrichtet. Weiter gepflegt wird sie an den Lehrstühlen für Germanistik und Nordistik. Im Jahre 1969 entstand der Kulturverband der Bürger deutscher Nationalität in der ČSSR, in Bratislava wurde das Kulturzentrum der DDR errichtet, das 1992 zum Goethe-Institut umfunktioniert wurde.

6.5. Die verhältnismäßig schnelle Assimilierung der polnischen Bevölkerung, ihre kleine Anzahl und ihre Zweisprachigkeit haben zur Folge, daß die polnische Minderheit in der Slowakei keine eigenen Schulen hat. Hinsichtlich der Konfession unterscheidet sich diese Minderheit nicht von der anderen Bevölkerung.

7. Weitere Minderheiten und Kontaktsprachen (Roma, Juden, Kroaten)

7.1. Die demographischen Erhebungen zeigen, daß die Roma ungefähr 5% der Bevölkerung der SR stellen, obwohl sich selbst nur 1,53% zur Minderheit der Roma bekannt haben. Ihre Familien sind etwa viermal so groß wie eine slowakische Durchschnittsfamilie. In den unterschiedlichen Regionen der SR sind sie nicht gleichmäßig vertreten, sie bewohnen vor allem die Ostslowakei, was darauf zurückzuführen ist, daß sie sich in dieser Region zuerst niedergelassen haben (sie werden erstmals 1322 erwähnt).

Mit den Versuchen, die Roma der Lebensweise der Mehrheitsbevölkerung anzupassen, hat bereits Maria Theresia (1717–1780) mit Hilfe der sogenannten Regulation begonnen. Sie hat sogar versucht, sie völlig zu assimilieren (Verbot, ihre eigene Sprache zu verwenden, untereinander zu heiraten; ihre offizielle Bezeichnung war *Neubauer*). Dadurch hat man zwar ihre nicht-seßhafte Lebensweise eingeschränkt, aber es gelang nicht, sie in ein gesellschaftliches Leben einzugliedern. Nach dem Zweiten Weltkrieg hat die staatliche Politik gegenüber den Roma folgende Konzeptionen realisiert: (1) ihre soziale Assimilierung, (2) die geregelte Zerstreuung der Roma (seit 1965 vor allem von Orten mit hoher Konzentration in die tschechischen Länder),

(3) die Integration der Roma in die Gesellschaft (seit 1972). Im Jahre 1991 hat die Regierung neue politische Prinzipien für die Roma beschlossen: man erkannte ihren Status als ethnische Minderheit (Nationalität) an. Nach 1989 fingen die Roma an, ihre Ethnizität auch zu institutionalisieren. Es entstand eine ethnische Presse, bürgerliche und politische Gruppierungen stießen aber auf Schwierigkeiten als Folge ihrer historischen Entwicklung und der nicht eindeutigen ethnischen Zuordnung. Laut einer Untersuchung aus dem Jahre 1991 halten sich 37% für Roma, 28% für Zigeuner, 18% für Slowaken und 17% für Ungarn (Okáliová 1991).

Die Roma gehören in der Slowakei zu der am schlechtesten ausgebildeten Ethnie, sozial und beruflich sind sie homogen in den niedrigsten, unqualifizierten Berufen anzutreffen. Sie befinden sich in einem großen sozialen Abstand von der übrigen Bevölkerung. Einige von ihnen bemühen sich, sich der Mehrheitsbevölkerung anzupassen. Dabei distanzieren sie sich von ihrer ethnischen Herkunft, lehren ihren Kindern nicht die Romasprache, und sie lehnen traditionelle Bräuche ab. Diese Proassimilationstendenzen der Roma folgen aus dem Bemühen, einen vergleichbaren Lebensstandard mit entsprechendem sozialem Prestige zu erreichen. Innerhalb der politischen Bewegungen entstand sogar die „Partei zur Integration der Roma", deren Ziel es ist, „der möglichst schnellen Assimilierung der ethnischen Gruppe der Roma nachzuhelfen" (Bačová 1991).

Die Bevölkerung ist gegen die Roma vorwiegend negativ eingestellt. Es überwiegt eine feindliche Haltung (insgesamt 45%) gegenüber den Roma, eher freundlich bzw. eindeutig freundlich ist die Haltung nur bei 20% der Befragten (Koptová 1991). Laut einer anderen Untersuchung wünschen sich 45,2% der Befragten die Auswanderung der Roma aus der SR, und nur 4,7% würden die Roma als unmittelbare Nachbarn akzeptieren (Mann 1992). Der Grund für die negative Beziehung der Bevölkerungsmehrheit zu den Roma ist nicht nur in den sozialen Begünstigungen während des früheren Regimes zu suchen (z. B. bevorzugte Zuteilung der Wohnungen), sondern vor allem in ihrem asozialen Leben (hohe Kriminalitätsrate).

In der täglichen Kommunikation verwendet man für die Roma das Wort *Zigeuner* (bisher war das auch ihr offizielles Ethnonym).

Die Romasprache hat bisher keine entwickelte schriftliche oder gar stabilisierte Norm. Den slowakischen Romadialekt sprechen etwa 80% der Roma (Bačova 1991, 121). Die Romamundarten in der Slowakei enthalten auch einige Elemente der jeweiligen Region: in der Ostslowakei haben sie „ostslowakische" palatale Laute /ś/, /ź/, nur kurze Vokale, in der Südslowakei „ungarisches" enges /é/. Die Romasprache übernimmt lexikalische Mittel aus den jeweiligen Dialekten oder Minderheitensprachen und paßt sie sich formal an, z. B. durch die Endungen -*is* und -*os* (*dochtoris, učitelis, čilagos* — Arzt, Lehrer, Stern). Einige Wörter aus der Romasprache sind in den slowakischen Slang oder Argot übergegangen (*čaja, gadžo*).

Der Funktionsbereich der Romasprache ist relativ eng und wird immer kleiner. In den Familien wird bis zu 54% die Romasprache als Verständigungssprache verwendet, 38% sprechen slowakisch, 8% ungarisch und 1% eine andere Sprache. Eine niedrige Stufe der nationalen Selbstidentifizierung äußert sich auch darin, daß die Roma eine Verbreitung von Informationen über ihre Sprache und ihre Einführung in die Kindergärten und in die Grundschulen nicht für nötig halten.

7.2. Mitte des vorigen Jahrhunderts lebten im Ungarischen Reich 241 000 Juden. Ein Emanzipationsgesetz aus dem Jahre 1867 hat sie nicht als Nation bzw. Nationalität kategorisiert, sondern als Gruppe von Menschen, deren Integrationsbasis die religiöse Herkunft ist. Im Jahre 1868 wurde in Ungarn das Nationalitätengesetz verabschiedet, das die Existenz nur einer einheitlichen ungarischen (also madjarischen) Nation akzeptierte, während den anderen nichtmadjarischen Nationen nur stark reduzierte sprachliche und kulturelle Rechte zugesprochen wurden. Die Juden in der Slowakei hatten die Möglichkeit, sich entweder national der herrschenden madjarischen Nation zu assimilieren (wovon sie profitieren konnten) oder sich schrittweise der slowakischen Nation anzunähern, die damals einen Kampf gegen die madjarische Politik und für die Anerkennung ihrer Identität geführt hat. Der größte Teil der jüdischen Bevölkerung, die zu Zeiten der Jahrhundertwende auf dem Gebiet der Slowakei lebte, hat sich madjarisiert und wurde offiziell zur madjarischen Nationalität gezählt. Zur slowakischen Nation haben sich 4% der Juden gerechnet. Auch diese Tatsache führte zu gewissen slowakisch-jüdischen Spannungen. In der Zwischenkriegszeit formierte sich eine Bewegung ("Bund der slowakischen Juden"), die die Assimilierung an die slowakische Nation programmatisch forderte.

Heute registrieren die jüdischen Gemeinden etwa 3000 Juden. Mehrere Tausend Juden haben sich (nach den Verfolgungen und den faschistischen Vernichtungslagern während des Zweiten Weltkrieges und nach den Emigrationswellen in den Jahren 1945, 1948 und 1968) entweder an die slowakische Bevölkerung bzw. in den südlichen Bezirken an die ungarische vollständig assimiliert. Ihr Zugehörigkeitsgefühl wird eher von einem symbolischen Charakter geprägt und ist von der religiösen Zugehörigkeit und vor allem von den Traditionen von Kultur und Bräuchen abhängig (Kamenec 1991). Die eigene jüdische Sprache (Jiddisch) hat in diesem Jahrhundert in der SR keinen lebendigen Status mehr. Einige jiddische Wörter leben aber noch in den niedrigeren Sprachebenen des Slowakischen (*šlamastika, mešuge, chochmes*). Mehrere jüdische Familien sind zwei- bzw. dreisprachig (Slowakisch, Ungarisch, Deutsch).

7.3. Die Kroaten, die sich im 16. Jahrhundert in der Slowakei in etwa 80 Ortschaften niederließen (in 20 Ortschaften bildeten sie die Mehrheit), haben sich relativ schnell assimiliert. Heute leben sie noch in vier bis fünf Dörfern in der Westslowakei (in Devínska Nová Ves (Theben-Neudorf), Chorvátsky Grob (Kroatisch Eisgrub), Jarovce (Jarow) u. a.). Die slowakischen Kroaten sind in der älteren Generation zweisprachig, alle beherrschen das Slowakische gut. Die jüngere Generation ist schon einsprachig slowakisch. In letzter Zeit werden die kroatischen Traditionen wiederbelebt. Im Jahre 1990 entstand in Devínska Nová Ves (Theben-Neudorf) der „Kroatische Kulturverband" mit dem Ziel, die Entwicklung der nationalen Kultur, der Sprache und der Ausbildung zu unterstützen. Unter der kroatischen Bevölkerung beobachtet man eine sprachliche Renaissance: es werden Kontakte mit ihrer Heimat und mit anderen Kroaten, die in Ungarn, in Österreich und in Mähren leben, gepflegt. Eine besondere Rolle bei der Stärkung des Nationalbewußtseins spielt, so wie auch in der Vergangenheit, die (katholische) Kirche (Kučerová 1992).

8. Zur Forschungslage

8.1. Im Zuge der Volks-, Häuser- und Wohnungszählung aus dem Jahre 1991, aus der wir die neuesten Angaben über die nationale Zusammensetzung der Bevölkerung der SR entnehmen, wurden auch die Angaben zur jeweiligen Nationalität erhoben. Infolge eines nicht ausgeprägten ethnischen Bewußtseins unterscheiden sich die Resultate dieser Zählung nicht selten von den Ergebnissen anderer Quellen. Z. B. haben sich bei der Volkszählung 80 627 Menschen zur Romanationalität bekannt (d. h. 1,53% der Bürger), aber laut Angaben der Stadtämter der Staatsverwaltung aus dem Jahre 1989 lebten dort 253 943 Roma (also 4,8%), wobei in dieser Zählung nicht die Roma berücksichtigt werden, die auf einem der Mehrheitsbevölkerung entsprechenden Standard leben. Bei Untersuchungen über die kroatische Bevölkerung in der Slowakei (Kučerová 1992) rechneten sich in Chorvátsky Grob (Kroatisch Eisgrub) von den 1450 Einwohnern 1200 zu den Kroaten. Bei der letzten Volkszählung haben sich zur kroatischen Nationalität nur ganz wenige Personen bekannt.

8.2. Die Problematik der Minoritäten und der Minoritätensprachen ist in der Slowakei nicht genügend bearbeitet worden, sicher auch deswegen, weil dieses Thema in gewissem Maße tabuisiert wurde. Die umfangreichsten Untersuchungen hat das Gesellschaftliche Institut der Slowakischen Akademie der Wissenschaften in Kaschau durchgeführt. Die Einstellungen zu Minderheiten und nationalen Gruppen in der SR berücksichtigen vor allem die soziologischen Meinungsumfragen (1992). Die slowakische Dialektologie orientiert sich bei der Untersuchung ziemlich stark an der strukturellen Seite dieser Dialekte. Ein Desiderat wäre eine komplexe Untersuchung des verbalen und sozialen Verhaltens der einzelnen Mitglieder aller Nationalitäten in der Slowakei. Besonders wichtig in der aktuellen Situation wäre die Untersuchung der slowakisch-tschechischen und der slowakisch-ungarischen Beziehungen.

9. Bibliographie (in Auswahl)

Aktuálne problémy Česko-Slovenska (1992): [Aktuelle Probleme der Tschecho-Slowakei], Bratislava.

Bačová, Viera (1991): „Rómska minorita na Slovensku v súčasnosti" [Die Minderheit der Roma in der Slowakei heute]. In: *Paukovič 1991*, 118–131.

Bačová, Viera (1992): „Supporting and retarding factors of the Romanies' integration in the post-communist society of Slovakia". In: *Plichtová 1992*, 257—259.

Bobák, Ján (1982): „Výmena obyvateľstva medzi Československom a Maďarskom (1946—1948)" [Umsiedlung der Bürger zwischen der Tschechoslowakei und Ungarn (1946—1948)]. In: *Slováci v zahraničí 8*, 257—261.

Born, Joachim/Dickgießer, Sylvia (1989): *Deutschsprachige Minderheiten. Ein Überblick über den Stand der Forschung für 27 Länder*, Mannheim.

Buffa, Ferdinand (1976): „O vzájomných slovensko-poľských jazykových vplyvoch" [Zu den gegenseitigen slowakisch-polnischen Spracheinflüssen]. In: *Studia Academica Slovaca 5*, 33—48.

Budovičová, Viera (1987): „Semikomunikácia ako lingvistický problém" [Die Semikommunikation als ein linguistisches Problem]. In: *Studia Academica Slovaca 16*, 51—66.

Buzássyová, Klára/Ondrejovič, Slavo (1994): „Slowaki i Tschechi. Slowatskiy i tscheschsskiy jazyki. Etnosignifikativnyy, kulturologitscheskiy, psichologitschesskiy i sotsiologitscheskiy aspekty vzaimootnoschenija dvuch natsiy i ich jazykow" [Slowaken und Tschechen. Slowakische und tschechische Sprache. Ethnosignifikativer, psychologischer und soziologischer Aspekt der Beziehung der beiden Nationen und ihrer Sprachen]. In: *Jazyk — Kuľtura — Etnos*. Moskau, 113—140.

Dolník, Juraj (1992): „České slová v slovenčine" [Tschechische Wörter im Slowakischen]. In: *Studia Academica Slovaca 21*, 1—10.

Deák, Ladislav (1990): *Slovensko v politike Maďarska v r. 1938—1939* [Die Slowakei in der Politik Ungarns in den Jahren 1938—1939], Bratislava.

Doruľa, Ján (1977): *Slováci v dejinách jazykových vzťahov* [Die Slowaken in der Geschichte der Sprachkontakte], Bratislava.

Gabzdilová, Soňa (1992): „Schools in the Slovak Republic with instruction in the Hungarian language — present status". In: *Plichtová 1992*, 165—173.

Gawrecká, Marie (1989): „K národnostní otázce v ČSR v letech 1918—1938" [Zur Nationalfrage in der ČSR in den Jahren 1918—1938]. In: *Národnostní otázka v Československu (po roce 1918)*, Gawrecká, M./Malá, E. (Eds.), Troppau, 105—123.

Hübl, Milan (1990): „Postavení a problémy maďarské menšiny na Slovensku" [Die Stellung und die Probleme der ungarischen Minderheit in der Slowakei]. In: *Česi, Slováci a jejich sousedé*, Hübl, Milan, Prag, 105—123.

Hübschmannová, Milena (1979): „Bilingualismus among the Slovak Rom". In: *International journal of the sociology of language 19*, 33—49.

Jahn, Egbert Kurt (1971): *Die Deutschen in der Slowakei in den Jahren 1918—1929*, München/Wien.

Kamenec, Ivan (1992 a): „The problem of Jewish nationality in the modern Slovak history". In: *Plichtová 1992*, 247—249.

Kamenec, Ivan (1992 b): „Historická retrospektíva formovania židovskej národnosti v moderných slovenských dejinách" [Historischer Rückblick auf die Bildung der jüdischen Nationalität in der modernen slowakischen Geschichte]. In: *Sociológia 24*, 25—30.

Klimko, Ján (1980): *Vývoj územia Slovenska a utváranie jeho hraníc* [Die Entwicklung des slowakischen Territoriums und die Entstehung seiner Grenzen], Martin.

Kriššáková, Júlia (1984): „Goralské nárečia vo svetle kolonizácií a teória jazykových kontaktov" [Goralische Mundarten im Licht der Kolonisationen und die Theorie der Sprachkontakte]. In: *Slavica Slovaca 19*, 165—177.

Kučerová, Kveta (1992): „The Croatian minority in Slovakia". In: *Plichtová 1992*, 242—243.

Mann, Arne (1992): „The formation of the ethnic identity of the Romany in Slovakia". In: *Plichtová 1992*, 261—265.

Marsina, Richard/Čičaj, Viliam/Kováč, Dušan/Lipták, Ľubomír (1992): *Slovenské dejiny* [Slowakische Geschichte], Martin.

Okáliová, Dana (1991): „Slovenskí Romovia na začiatku 90. rokov" [Die slowakischen Roma am Anfang der neunziger Jahre]. In: *Paukovič 1991*, 136—151.

Ondrejovič, Slavo (1992): „K jazykovej situácii na Slovensku" [Zur Sprachsituation in der Slowakei]. In: *Studia Academica Slovaca 21*, 104—110.

Očovský, Štefan (1992): „Interpretation of statistical data on nationalities". In: *Plichtová 1992*, 94—100.

Paukovič, Vladimír (Ed.) (1991): *Etnické menšiny na Slovensku* [Ethnische Minderheiten in der Slowakei], Kaschau.

Paukovič, Vladimír/Szedláková, Lýdia (1991): „K problematike vývoja a postavenia rusínsko-ukrajinského etnika na Slovensku" [Zur Problematik der Entwicklung und Stellung der ruthenisch-ukrainischen Ethnie in der Slowakei]. In: *Paukovič 1991*, 129—134.

Plichtová, Jana (Ed.) (1992): *Minorities in Politics. Cultural and Language Rights*, Bratislava.

Plichtová, Jana (1992): „Bilingualism — yes or no?" In: *Plichtová 1992*, 159—164.

Sčítanie ľudu, domov a bytov 1991. Predbežné výsledky (1991) [Die Volks-, Häuser- und Wohnungszählung 1991. Vorläufige Ergebnisse], Bratislava.

Servátka, Marián (1987): „Goralsko-slovenský bilingvizmus, resp. goralsko-spišsko-poľsko-slovenský multilingvizmus" [Der goralisch-slowakische Bilinguismus, bzw. der goralisch-zipsisch-polnisch-slowakische Multilinguismus]. In: *Studia Academica Slovaca 16*, 385—395.

Sokolová, Gabriela (1987): *Soudobé tendence vývoje národností v ČSSR* [Die gegenwärtigen Tendenzen in der Entwicklung der Nationalitäten in der ČSSR], Prag.

Sokolová, Miloslava (1991): „Komunikatívna efektívnosť českých kontaktových javov v súčasnej slovenčine" [Die Kommunikationseffektivität der tschechischen Kontakterscheinungen in der gegenwärtigen slowakischen Sprache]. In: *Všeobecné a špecifické otázky jazykovej komunikácie II*, Odaloš, P./Patráš, V. (Eds.), Neusohl.

Srb, Vladimír (1986 a): „Koncentrace a urbanizace Cikánů v Československu" [Die Konzentration und Urbanisierung der Zigeuner in der Tschechoslowakei]. In: *Český lid 73*, 86−92.

Srb, Vladimír (1986 b): „Základní školy v Československu podle vyučovacího jazyka a národnosti žáků v letech 1970−1985" [Die Grundschulen in der Tschechoslowakei nach der Unterrichtssprache und nach der Nationalität der Schüler in den Jahren 1970−1985]. In: *Slezský sborník 84*, 253−263.

Srb, Vladimír (1987): „Demografický profil polské menšiny v Československu" [Das demographische Profil der polnischen Minderheit in der Tschechoslowakei]. In: *Český lid 74*, 151−167.

Šoucová, Dana (1991 a): „Občania maďarskej národnosti vo svetle výskumov verejnej mienky" [Die Bürger ungarischer Nationalität im Licht der Untersuchungen der öffentlichen Meinung]. In: *Paukovič 1991*, 31−42.

Šoucová, Dana (1991 b): „Obraz občana rusínsko-ukrajinskej národnosti podľa výskumu verejnej mienky" [Das Bild der Bürger ruthenisch-ukrainischer Nationalität anhand einer Meinungsumfrage]. In: *Paukovič 1991*, 65−71.

Šutaj, Štefan (1991): „Historický náčrt postavenia maďarskej menšiny na Slovensku" [Ein historischer Abriß über die Lage der ungarischen Minderheit in der Slowakei]. In: *Paukovič 1991*, 3−30.

Šutaj, Štefan (1992): „Changes of national identity in historical development". In: *Plichtová 1992*, 165−173.

Vasiliev, Ivo (1993): „Tschechoslowakei". In: *Sociolinguistica 7*, Tübingen.

Zeľová, Alena (1991 a): „Etnická identita maďarskej menšiny na Slovensku" [Die ethnische Identität der ungarischen Minderheit in der Slowakei]. In: *Paukovič 1991*, 43−53.

Zeľová, Alena (1991 b): „Etnická identita rusínsko-ukrajinskej menšiny na Slovensku" [Die ethnische Identität der ruthenisch-ukrainischen Minderheit in der Slowakei]. In: *Paukovič 1991*, 72−81.

Zeľová, Alena (1992): „The integration of the Hungarian minority in Slovakia − the language problem". In: *Plichtová 1992*, 155−158.

Zeman, Jiří (1988): „K jazykovým kontaktům mezi češtinou a slovenštinou" [Zu Sprachkontakten des Tschechischen und Slowakischen]. In: *Funkční lingvistika a dialektika*, Nekvapil, J./Šoltys, O. (Eds.), Prag.

Slavo Ondrejovič, Bratislava (Slowakei)

205. Slowakisch−Ungarisch

1. Geographie und Demographie
2. Geschichte
3. Politik, Wirtschaft und allgemeine kulturelle sowie religiöse Lage
4. Statistik und Ethnoprofile
5. Soziolinguistische Lage
6. Sprachpolitische Situation
7. Allgemeines kontaktlinguistisches Porträt
8. Kritische Wertung der verwendeten Quellen und Literatur
9. Bibliographie (in Auswahl)

1. Geographie und Demographie

Das ungarisch-slowakische Sprachgebiet (ca. 9000 km^2) erstreckt sich an der 550 km langen slowakisch-ungarischen Grenze. Aus geographischer Sicht wird sie gebildet durch die Donauebene, das Tal des Ipel, der Rimava und Slana und den südlichen Teil der ostslowakischen Ebene. Aus administrativer Sicht besteht dieses Gebiet aus 13 Kreisen (18 000 km^2). In diesen Kreisen bzw. in Bratislava (Preßburg) und in Košice (Kaschau) leben 99% der Ungarn in der Slowakei, davon in der südwestlichen Region bis zu 64%.

Die Migrationsbewegungen der Bevölkerung waren nach den Weltkriegen am stärksten. Die Migration führte nach 1948 in die Tschechei, später in die größeren Städte, besonders nach Preßburg und Kaschau.

Die Zahl der zur ungarischen Nationalitätengruppe gehörenden Bevölkerung sank stark in der ersten Hälfte des 20. Jahrhunderts: von 885 397 (30,3% der Gesamtbevölkerung der Slowakei) im Jahre 1910 auf 344 532 (10,3%) im Jahre 1950. Nach 1918 flohen ungefähr 100 000 Menschen nach Ungarn, in den Jahren 1945−1948 wurden 44 129 Personen in die Tschechei umgesiedelt (24 069 kehrten 1949 zurück) und mehr als 200 000

Ungarn wurden reslowakisiert (vgl. 4.1.1.). Im Rahmen eines Bevölkerungsaustausches wurden 89 600 Ungarn nach Ungarn umgesiedelt; an ihrer Stelle kamen 71 787 Slowaken (Kaplan 1990, 85–130, Šutaj 1990, 15–22). Seit den 50er Jahren steigt die absolute Zahl der Ungarn leicht an (Reslowakisanten bekennen sich erneut zur ungarischen Nationalität).

In den letzten 40 Jahren sinkt der natürliche Bevölkerungszuwachs in der Slowakei; bei der ungarischen Bevölkerung ist diese Tendenz noch deutlicher: 3,3 gegenüber 6,5 in den Jahren 1985–1990 (Očovský 1992, 100). Einer der Gründe ist die unterschiedliche Altersstruktur der Ungarn und Slowaken. Im Jahre 1991 waren 25,52% der slowakischen und 20,47% der ungarischen Bevölkerung im nichterwerbstätigen Alter (0–14) (Gyurqyik 1994, 107). Für Slowaken und auch für Ungarn ist eine Homogamie nach der Nationalität charakteristisch, aber bei den Ungarn steigt die Heterogamie; im Jahre 1991 wählten 17,8% der Ungarn Partner einer anderen Nationalität, besonders der slowakischen. Aus diesem Grund ist in der Südslowakei auch der Anteil an Mischehen bei Slowaken hoch (→ Sprachenkarte K).

2. Geschichte

Die ersten ungarischen Siedlungen entstanden auf dem derzeitigen ungarisch-slowakischen Sprachgebiet der Slowakei im 10. Jahrhundert. Die Region der heutigen Slowakei war bis 1918 integraler Bestandteil Großungarns, später der neuentstandenen Tschechoslowakei. Im Jahre 1938 wurde die Südslowakei (10 369 km²) nach dem Wiener Vertrag von Ungarn annektiert. Im Slowakischen Staat verblieben ca. 70 000 Einwohner ungarischer Nationalität. 1945 wurde das von Ungarn annektierte Gebiet der neu gegründeten Tschechoslowakei angegliedert.

Hinsichtlich der Entwicklung slowakisch-ungarischer interethnischer Beziehungen waren besonders folgende Zeiträume und Ereignisse wichtig:

(1) Ab dem 19. Jahrhundert verstärkte sich der nationale Emanzipationsprozeß der Slowaken; er stieß aber auf den Widerstand der regierenden Kreise Großungarns. Mit fortschreitender Urbanisierung und infolge der Magyarisierung beschleunigte sich die Assimilation der Slowaken.

(2) Die ungarische Regierung erkannte nach dem Ersten Weltkrieg die Teilung des ehemaligen Großungarns nicht an, sondern bemühte sich um eine Revision der Grenzen.
(3) Nach 1918 existierte auf dem ethnischen Gebiet der Ungarn eine zahlreiche tschechische Beamtenschaft. Im Rahmen einer Bodenreform bekamen in der Südslowakei slowakische und tschechische Grundbesitzer Boden zugeteilt. In den Jahren 1939–1945 kam es auch zu Konflikten zwischen der slowakischen Bevölkerung und den ungarischen Behörden.
(4) Nach dem Zweiten Weltkrieg ging die tschechoslowakische Politik vom Prinzip eines Nationalstaates der Tschechen und Slowaken aus und von einer kollektiven Schuld der Ungarn für die „Zerschlagung der Republik". Deshalb verloren in den Jahren 1945–1948 die Ungarn alle politischen und bürgerlichen Rechte.

3. Politik, Wirtschaft und allgemeine kulturelle sowie religiöse Lage

3.1. Die Slowaken in Großungarn wie auch die Ungarn in der Tschechoslowakei und in der Slowakei hatten – mit Ausnahme der Jahre 1948–1989 – eigene Parteien. Die Bevölkerung ungarischer Nationalität bevorzugt heute vier ungarische Parteien, besonders die Koalition der liberal-konservativ eingestellten Együttélés (Zusammenleben), der Ungarischen christdemokratischen Bewegung und der Ungarischen bürgerlichen Partei; die Koalition gewann in den Wahlen von 1994 10,18% der Stimmen und hat 17 Abgeordnete im Nationalrat der SR.

3.2. Das Gebiet der heutigen Südslowakei hatte immer landwirtschaftlichen Charakter; das Übergewicht des landwirtschaftlichen Sektors dauert weiterhin an – trotz der Erhöhung von Investitionen in der Industrie seit den 60er Jahren. Wegen des Mangels an Arbeitsplätzen am Wohnort ist ungefähr ein Fünftel der erwerbstätigen Bevölkerung außerhalb ihres Kreises beschäftigt (Sokolová 1987, 52). Nach wie vor ist ein überdurchschnittlicher Prozentsatz der ungarischen Bevölkerung in der Landwirtschaft und im Bauwesen tätig. In den südlichen Kreisen gibt es auch Unterschiede in der sozialen Stratifikation: Es gibt weniger Ungarn als Slowaken, die als Angestellte arbeiten

(1980 29,7% Ungarn gegenüber 50,7% Slowaken) (Paukovič 1990, 46—48).

3.3. Der provinzielle Charakter der Kultur in der heutigen Südslowakei verstärkte sich nach dem Ersten Weltkrieg durch den Exodus wesentlicher Teile der ungarischen Intelligenz. Nach dem Zweiten Weltkrieg wurde durch die Beseitigung der Mittelschicht auch die ungarische städtische Kultur aufgelöst, und die Literatur wurde nahezu das einzige Forum einer autonomen ungarischen Minderheitenkultur. Heute wird das kulturelle Leben in diesem Gebiet bestimmt durch ein verhältnismäßig geringes Bildungsniveau der Bevölkerung (im Jahre 1991 hatten 6,1% Slowaken, aber nur 2,9% Ungarn Hochschulbildung) und durch den ländlichen Charakter der Ansiedlungen. Im kulturellen Leben der Menschen sind besonders das Fernsehen und Formen von Laienkunst relevant. Es gibt zwei professionelle ungarische Theater in Komárno und Košice; die übrigen kulturellen Institutionen (Verlage) befinden sich in Bratislava.

3.4. Laut einer Volkszählung hat sich in diesem Jahrhundert die konfessionelle Zugehörigkeit nicht wesentlich geändert. Diese beträgt im Fall der Ungarn heute (im Vergleich mit gesamtslowakischen Daten): 64,9% (60,43%) römisch-katholisch; 11,4% calvinistisch; 2,2% (7,96%) evangelisch Augsburger Konfession; 1,4% (3,3%) griechisch-katholisch; 6,6% (9,7%) ohne Glaubensbekenntnis.

4. Statistik und Ethnoprofile

4.1. 1991 lebten auf dem Territorium der Slowakischen Republik 567 296 (10,8%) Personen ungarischer Nationalität, Ungarisch als Muttersprache haben 608 221 (11,5%) Personen angegeben. Was den Zusammenhang zwischen Nationalität, Muttersprache bzw. ethnischem Ursprung betrifft, sind folgende Momente relevant:

(1) Slowakische Experten bezweifeln die Ergebnisse der Volkszählung in Großungarn aus dem Jahre 1910 und sehen sie als eine Folge der Magyarisierung. Die sog. Reslowakisierung 1946—1948 ging ebenfalls von der These aus, daß die „Mehrheit der Bürger ungarischer Nationalität aus slowakischen Familien" stammt (Kaplan 1990, 116). Dadruch sollten jene mit slowakischen Vorfahren oder Slowakisch als Alltagssprache von ihrer ursprünglichen Nationalität überzeugt werden. Den Reslowaken wurden alle Rechte zuerkannt und sie wurden nicht in die Tschechei oder nach Ungarn umgesiedelt.

(2) Der Forschung zufolge ist sowohl für die slowakische als auch für die ungarische Bevölkerung ein hohes Maß an ethnischer Identität charakteristisch.

(3) 1991 haben in der Slowakei 75 901 Personen Roma als Nationalität angegeben; nach Schätzungen aber leben in der Slowakei etwa 250 000 Angehörige dieser Volksgruppe. 18% von ihnen fühlen sich als Slowaken und 17% als Ungarn. Dabei beherrschen die Roma in der Südslowakei auch die ungarische Sprache oder sehen sie als ihre Muttersprache an.

4.2. 1991 gab es auf dem Gebiet der Slowakei 551 Gemeinden mit einer mindestens 10%igen ungarischen Bevölkerung, davon ist in 176 Gemeinden ihr Anteil höher als 90%. In 435 Gemeinden mit mehr als 50% ungarischer Bevölkerung leben 77,7% aller Ungarn. Die Angehörigen dieser Minderheit leben heute hauptsächlich in kleineren Gemeinden; mehr als 10 000 Ungarn leben in Komárno (ung. Komárom, dt. Komorn), Bratislava (ung. Pozsony, dt. Preßburg), Dunajská Streda (ung. Dumasgerdahely), Nové Zámky (ung. Ėrsekujvár, dt. Neuhäusel), Košice (ung. Kassa, dt. Kaschau). In Städten mit über 50 000 Einwohnern ist ihr Anteil sehr gering: 5,8% gegenüber dem gesamtslowakischen Anteil von 25% (Gyurgyik 1994, 26).

5. Soziolinguistische Lage

5.1. Im Verlauf dieses Jahrhunderts hat sich der Funktions- und Anwendungsbereich der slowakischen Sprache erweitert. Parallel dazu verlor die ungarische Sprache ihre ursprüngliche Position. Heute besitzt sie in der Gesellschaft ein niedriges Prestige und wird wenig verwendet. Die dominierende Stellung der slowakischen Sprache unterstützen besonders diese Faktoren:

(1) Die ungarische Bevölkerung hat im gesamtstaatlichen Durchschnitt einen niedrigeren sozial-ökonomischen Status und ein niedrigeres Bildungsniveau.
(2) Die ungarische Sprache wird in der ungarischen Gemeinschaft überwiegend in der informellen Rede benutzt. Als Wissenschafts- und Amtssprache findet sie kaum Verwendung.

(3) Bis zu 72% der Slowaken und 63% der Ungarn meinen, daß für eine gesellschaftliche Arbeit die vollkommene Kenntnis der slowakischen Sprache Voraussetzung ist (Zel'ová 1992, 157).

5.2. Nach Befragungen führen Slowaken als positive Eigenschaft der Ungarn nationalen Stolz an; unter den negativen Eigenschaften treten am häufigsten Arroganz, Hochmut, Expansivität, Herrschsucht, Nationalismus, Chauvinismus, Aggressivität u. ä. auf. Slowaken aus sprachlich gemischten Gebieten haben dabei eine positivere Beziehung zu den Ungarn als Slowaken aus rein slowakischen Gebieten. Ungarn charakterisieren Slowaken als arbeitsam, bescheiden, anspruchslos. Als Eigenschaften nennen sie: Nationalismus, Chauvinismus, Alkoholismus und Neid (Rosová/Bútorová 1972, 178—179).

5.3. Nach neuesten Forschungen (Zel'ová 1992, 156—157) beherrschen mehr als 90% der Ungarn die slowakische Sprache; gleichzeitig beherrscht ungefähr die Hälfte der Slowaken aus den sprachlich gemischten Gebieten wenigstens teilweise die ungarische Sprache. Die Ungarn in der Slowakei zeichnen sich aus durch eine „hohe sprachliche Verschlossenheit" und einen großen Willen zum Erhalt ihrer Muttersprache. Aus diesem Grunde ist für die Mehrheit von ihnen Slowakisch die Zweitsprache, die sie sich erst in der Schule aneignen. Die Slowaken aus gemischten Gebieten eignen sich dagegen die ungarische Sprache spontan an.

5.4. Die Angehörigen der ungarischen Minderheit verwenden aktiv den örtlichen ungarischen Dialekt bzw. die regionalen Varianten der ungarischen Sprache und die slowakische Standardschriftsprache. Die ungarische Schriftsprache wird in den Schulen mit Ungarisch als Unterrichtssprache gelehrt; indes sind die Möglichkeiten ihrer Anwendung begrenzt. Im Rahmen der eigenen Sprachgemeinschaft werden Substandardvarianten der ungarischen Sprache in fast allen Kommunikationssituationen toleriert.

5.5. Zwischen Slowaken und Ungarn bzw. der ungarischen Bevölkerung und der Regierung bzw. den Behörden ist besonders die Auslegung und Einhaltung des Sprachgesetzes eine Quelle von Konflikten, insbesondere bei der Benutzung der ungarischen Sprache im Kontakt mit den Behörden, der zweisprachigen Bezeichnung von Gemeinden, Straßen und öffentlichen Gebäuden in Gemeinden mit ungarischer Bevölkerung.

6. Sprachpolitische Situation

6.1. Ungarn und die Tschechoslowakei haben sich als Nationalstaaten definiert, in denen den Angehörigen der Minderheiten neben allgemeinen bürgerlichen Rechten individuelle, sprachliche Rechte zuerkannt wurden. In der neuen Slowakischen Republik sind die Rechte der nationalen Minderheiten in der Verfassung verankert; die Verwendung der Minderheitensprachen regelt ein besonderes Sprachgesetz (vgl. 6.3.).

6.2. Zu Beginn dieses Jahrhunderts war mit Ausnahme von Volksschulen auf slowakischem ethnischem Gebiet das übrige Schulwesen ungarisch geprägt. Nach 1918 wurde die Zahl der Schulen mit ungarischer Unterrichtssprache reduziert. Im Schuljahr 1994/95 gab es ungarische Klassen in 299 Grundschulen, 25 mittleren Fachschulen, 19 Gymnasien und in 36 Berufsschulen mit Abitur. Auf Schulen und Klassen mit ungarischer Unterrichtssprache werden slowakische Sprache und Literatur als Pflichtfächer unterrichtet, auf mittleren Fachschulen werden Spezialfächer zweisprachig oder nur in slowakischer Sprache unterrichtet. Dabei besuchen 20% der Kinder ungarischer Nationalität slowakische Grundschulen und bis zu 60% slowakische mittlere Berufsschulen. An den Hochschulen ist Slowakisch Unterrichtssprache; eventuell wird teilweise für Studenten der Pädagogischen Fakultät in Nitra (ung. Nyitra, dt. Neutra) der Unterricht auf Ungarische erteilt.

6.3. Nach dem Sprachgesetz aus dem Jahre 1990 ist die Verwendung von Minderheitensprachen im mündlichen Kontakt mit Behörden erlaubt, falls in der betreffenden Gemeinde der Anteil der Minderheit an der Bevölkerung höher als 20% ist, wobei die Angestellten staatlicher und anderer Organe nicht verpflichtet sind, die Sprache der Minderheit zu beherrschen und zu verwenden. Im Gebiet der slowakisch-ungarischen Sprachgemeinschaft benutzten 1990 97% der Slowaken und 71% der Ungarn bei Behördengängen nur Slowakisch (Lanstyák 1991, 22).

6.4. Im öffentlichen Kontakt wird die Wahl der Sprache vor allem durch die nationale

Zusammensetzung der Bevölkerung der Gemeinde und den Charakter der Veranstaltung beeinflußt. In kleinen Gemeinden mit überwiegend ungarischer Bevölkerung wird gewöhnlich nur Ungarisch gesprochen. In Städten und in größeren Dörfern in der südwestlichen Slowakei werden öffentliche Veranstaltungen zweisprachig abgehalten, in den anderen Orten überwiegend slowakisch.

6.5. Im kirchlichen Leben wird die Verwendung der ungarischen Sprache durch den Mangel an Priestern, die die ungarische Sprache beherrschen, begrenzt. So sind z. B. in der katholischen Kirche von 250 Pfarreien mit ungarischen Gläubigen fast zwei Drittel unbesetzt. Ähnlich ist die Situation auch in der evangelischen Kirche. Zur reformierten calvinistischen Kirche bekennen sich vor allem Ungarn: von 204 mutterkirchlichen Körperschaften sind nur 29 slowakisch.

6.6. Zu Beginn des Jahrhunderts wurden Publikationen auf dem heutigen Gebiet der Slowakei überwiegend in ungarischer Sprache herausgegeben. Nach 1918 mußte ein großer Teil der ungarischen Zeitungen und Zeitschriften ihr Erscheinen einstellen. In den Zwischenkriegsjahren existierten von den 650 Periodika viele wegen finanzieller Probleme nur kurze Zeit. 1994 gab es in der Slowakei 1 Tageszeitung, 6 Wochen- und 12 Monatszeitschriften in ungarischer Sprache; 19 regionale Zeitschriften werden in zweisprachiger Übersetzung herausgegeben. Im slowakischen Rundfunk existierten seit 1928 Sendungen auf Ungarisch. 1994 wurden 40 Stunden wöchentlich in ungarischer Sprache (4% der gesamten Sendezeit) gesendet. Das slowakische Fernsehen sendet seit 1983 ein Nachrichtenmagazin in ungarischer Sprache (zweimal im Monat 35 Minuten, das entspricht ca. 0,4% der Sendezeit).

6.7. Das in der Slowakei gesprochene Ungarisch unterscheidet sich nicht wesentlich vom Standard-Ungarischen. Da die ungarischen Sprachwissenschaftler von der Idee einer einheitlichen ungarischen Sprache ausgingen, stuften sie die Neologismen, die hier unter dem Einfluß der slowakischen und tschechischen Sprache entstanden, als Fehler ein. Die geschriebene und gesprochene Form der ungarischen Sprache hat in der Slowakei bestimmte Züge einer Standardform; bisher fehlt jedoch die wissenschaftliche Beschreibung dieser regionalen Variante. In Schulen, Verlagen und Redaktionen werden in Ungarn herausgegebene Lehrbücher benutzt.

7. Allgemeines kontaktlinguistisches Porträt

Slowakisch und Ungarisch sind genetisch und typologisch unterschiedliche Sprachen, die sich jedoch seit dem 10. Jahrhundert nebeneinander in einem Staatsgebilde entwickelt haben. Viele Ähnlichkeiten in der Struktur können einerseits durch ihre gegenseitige Beeinflussung, andererseits durch den Einfluß anderer Sprachen dieser Region − besonders des Lateinischen und Deutschen − erklärt werden.

Während wir vor dem 18. Jahrhundert von einer gegenseitigen Beeinflussung dieser zwei Sprachen sprechen können bzw. von einem Übergewicht der ungarischen Sprache (vom 18.−19. Jh.), dominierte Slowakisch nach 1918 und besonders nach dem Zweiten Weltkrieg. Sein Einfluß zeigt sich einerseits direkt (z. B. Übernahme von Wörtern), andersseits indirekt darin, daß die Ungarn in der Slowakei von den synonymen Ausdrücken oder grammatischen Konstruktionen jene bevorzugen, die eine ähnliche formale und/oder semantische Struktur haben wie der äquivalente slowakische Ausdruck oder die jeweilige Konstruktion. Grundschüler mit slowakischer Unterrichtssprache verwenden in der Regel mehr Slowakismen als diejenigen, die eine ungarische Schule absolvierten. Die meisten Slowakismen entstehen spontan und werden im allgemeinen selten benutzt.

7.1. Was die Phonetik des Slowakischen und Ungarischen betrifft, so finden wir viele übereinstimmende Erscheinungen: die Konsonantensysteme sind in beiden Sprachen praktisch identisch; die Artikulierung der einzelnen Konsonanten ist ebenfalls ähnlich. Zwischen den vokalischen Systemen gibt es größere Differenzen. Die Kombinationsfähigkeiten der Phoneme sind etwas unterschiedlich. Im Bereich der suprasegmentalen Erscheinungen gibt es u. a. folgende Ähnlichkeiten: Die Betonung liegt in beiden Sprachen auf der ersten Silbe des Wortes (Prosodie); der melodische Verlauf der einzelnen Satztypen ist gleich. Interferenzen aus dem Bereich der Phonetik sind aus einigen benachbarten Dialekten bekannt, z. B. aus den ungarischen sog. palócen (Sulán 1963).

7.2. Die slowakische Sprache gehört aus typologischer Sicht zu den flektierenden Sprachen, die ungarische Sprache wiederum zu den agglutinierenden Sprachen. Hinsichtlich der gegenwärtigen Sprachkontakte sind folgende morphologische bzw. morphosyntaktische Eigenschaften der Sprachen relevant:

In der slowakischen Sprache gibt es eine grammatische Genus-Kategorie zur Bezeichnung von Namen. In der ungarischen Sprache wird dagegen das Genus von Lebewesen nur in bestimmten Fällen und lexikalisch ausgedrückt. Im Ungarischen wird nur im Falle typischer Frauenberufe durch das Suffix -*nő* unterschieden, ob es sich um einen Mann oder eine Frau handelt: *tanár* — *tanárnő* ('Lehrer' — 'Lehrerin'). In der Slowakei sind unter Einfluß der slowakischen Sprache auch diese Formen üblich: *fodrásznő* ('Friseuse'), *mérnöknő* ('Ingenieur'), *orvosnő* ('Ärztin'), *vezetőnő* ('Leiterin').

Die Nachahmung der Rektion der slowakischen Verben bzw. Substantive und Adjektive ist eher für die gesprochene Sprache charakteristisch. Als allgemein verbreitet sind zu qualifizieren: *megy valaki után* (sl. *íst' za niekým*, ung. *megy valakihez*, 'jmdn. amtlich besuchen'), *szobán lakik* (sl. *bývat' na izbe* — ung. *szobában lakik*, 'wohnen im Zimmer'), *kulcs a szobától* (sl. *kl'úče od izby* — ung. *a szoba kulcsa*, 'der Schlüssel von der Tür').

Im Ungarischen wird der Komparativ mit dem Suffix *-náll-nél* gebildet, im Dialekt auch mit dem Suffix *-tóll-től*. Das Äquivalent zur slowakischen Präposition *od* ist das Suffix *-tól* ..., welches von den Ungarn-Slowaken häufig verwendet wird.

In der ungarischen Konjugation sind zwei Systeme zu unterscheiden. Die Formen der Objekt-Konjugation beziehen sich auf ein im Satz genanntes oder rückweisendes Objekt, d. h. das Objekt wird durch das Personalsuffix „ersetzt". In einem slowakischen Satz dagegen muß das Objekt auftreten. Unter dem Einfluß der slowakischen Konstruktion akzeptieren die Ungarn in der Slowakei auch Sätze mit explizitem Objekt, z. B. *Tegnap láttalak téged a tévében* (sl. *Včera som t'a videl v televízii* — ung. *Tegnap láttalak a tévében*, 'Ich habe dich gestern im Fernsehen gesehen').

Eine wichtige Art der Wortbildung in der ungarischen Sprache ist die Bildung von Komposita. Die entsprechenden slowakischen Äquivalente sind oftmals attributive Konstruktionen. In ungarischen Texten in der Slowakei verwendet man statt der Komposita manchmal attributive Konstruktionen, z. B. *tanítók napja* (*Deň učitel'ov* — ung. *pedagógusnap*, 'Pädagogentag'.

7.3. Die meisten Interferenzen zwischen beiden Sprachen sind auf der lexikalischen Ebene zu beobachten.

Entlehnungen aus dem Slowakischen sind fast ausschließlich auf die gesprochene Sprache beschränkt. Die Ungarn in der Slowakei verwenden slowakische Namen von einigen Waren, z. B.: *horčica* (ung. *mustár* — 'Senf'), *párky* (ung. *virsli* — 'Würstchen'), ferner Wörter aus dem Gesundheitswesen, aus der Verwaltung und Wirtschaft, z. B. *sestra* (ung. *nővér*, 'Krankenschwester'), *ekonóm* (ung. *közgazda*, 'Ökonom'). Einige von diesen Entlehnungen galten schon als ungarische Wörter, z. B. aus dem sl. *žuvačka* (ung. *rágógumi*, 'Kaugummi') ist durch eine ungarische Derivationsform das Wort *zsuvi* entstanden.

In der slowakischen Sprache werden die Fremdwörter lateinischer (bzw. griechischer) Abstammung häufiger als im Ungarischen verwendet. In der Slowakei verbreiteten sich infolgedessen solche Fremdwörter (vor allem in der geschriebenen Sprache), die in Ungarn schon als veraltet galten oder eine andere Bedeutung haben, z. B. *rekreáció* (sl. *rekreácia*, ung. *üdülés*, 'Urlaub'), *poliklinika* (sl. *poliklinika*, ung. *rendelőintézet*, 'Poliklinik'). Diese Fremdwörter sind für ungarische Zeitungen in der Slowakei typisch.

Häufiger als die Lehnwörter kommen wörtliche Übersetzungen vor. So entstehen neue ungarische Wörter, z. B. *anyaszabadság* (sl. *materská dovolenka*, in Ungarn verwendet man die Abkürzung *gyes*, 'Karenzurlaub'). In den meisten Fällen bekommt jedoch ein schon existierendes Wort eine neue Bedeutung: z. B. *fal* (sl. *stena* — ung. *szekrénysor*, 'Schrankwand'), *kibeszélés* (sl. *výhovorka* — ung. *mentegetőzés, kifogás*, 'Ausrede').

Der Einfluß der slowakischen Sprache zeigt sich auch darin, daß Ungarn in der Slowakei von den Synonymen jene bevorzugen, die mit einem äquivalenten slowakischen Wort identisch sind, z. B. *Balkon* nennt man in Ungarn üblicherweise *erkély*, in der Slowakei *balkon* (sl. *balkón*); in Ungarn heißt 'Studentenheim' *kollégium*, in der Slowakei *internátus* (sl. *internát*).

7.4. Eine wissenschaftliche konfrontative Beschreibung dieser Sprachen ist noch nicht vorhanden; zur Verfügung stehen jedoch Fachbücher der einzelnen Sprachen. Es gibt auch mehrere kleinere zweisprachige Wörterbücher. Für Schulen mit ungarischer Unterrichtssprache existieren Lehrbücher der slowakischen Sprache, dagegen gibt es nur ein ungarisches Lehrbuch für Autodidakten.

In ungarischen Verlagen in der Slowakei werden Originalwerke ungarischer Schriftsteller aus der Slowakei (jährlich 10−15 Titel) und auch Übersetzungen aus dem Slowakischen herausgegeben; auch slowakische Verlage veröffentlichen Übersetzungen aus der ungarischen Literatur. Die Fachliteratur ist meist slowakisch; es gibt Lehrbücher (Übersetzungen aus dem Slowakischen und einige originale Literatur) und sprachwissenschaftliche Werke auf Ungarisch.

8. Kritische Wertung der verwendeten Quellen und Literatur

Für diesen Artikel wurden als Quellen offizielle statistische Daten bzw. Ergebnisse soziologischer Forschungen seit 1948 verwendet. Bei der Charakterisierung von Kontaktsprachen bzw. Interferenzen wurde von präskriptiven Grammatiken, Studien sowie Ergebnissen zu der soziolinguistischen Forschung bezüglich der Unterschiede von Varianten des Ungarischen in der Slowakei und in Ungarn ausgegangen.

Trotz einer langen Geschichte des Sprachkontaktes wurden bisher die gegenseitigen Einflüsse der slowakischen und ungarischen Sprache nicht detailliert wissenschaftlich erforscht. Nur einige Teilfragen des Sprachkontaktes wurden in der Vergangenheit z. B. bei Dorul'a (1977, 61−75), Gregor (1989, 141−195) und Sulán (1963, 253−265) untersucht. Zur Intensivierung des Slowakischunterrichts auf Schulen mit ungarischer Unterrichtssprache wurden in den 70er Jahren Forschungsprojekte zur konfrontativen Sprachbeschreibung begonnen, deren Ergebnisse in Fachzeitschriften und in einem Studienband (Sima 1978) publiziert wurden. Bei diesen Forschungen wurden jedoch Kontakterscheinungen bzw. Eigenschaften der ungarischen Sprachvarietät in der Slowakei kaum berücksichtigt. Die Ausarbeitung dieser Probleme ist das Hauptziel der soziolinguistischen Forschung.

9. Bibliographie (in Auswahl)

Dorul'a, Ján (1977): *Slováci v dejinách jazykových vzt'ahov* [Die Geschichte der Sprachkontakte der Slowaken], Bratislava.

Gregor, Ferenc (1989): „Magyar-szlovák nyelyi kapesolatok" [Ungarisch-slowakische Sprachkontakte]. In: *Nyelvünk a Duna-tájon*, Balász, J. (Ed.), Budapest.

Gyurgyik, László (1994): *Magyar mérleg* [Eine ungarische Bilanz], Bratislava.

Jakab, István (1983): *Nyelvünk és mi* [Aufsätze aus dem Bereich der Sprachkultur], Bratislava.

Kaplan, Karel (1990): *Pravda o Československu 1945−1948* [Die Wahrheit über die Tschechoslowakei 1945−1948], Prag.

Lanstyák, István (1991): „A szlovák nyelv árnyékában" [Im Schatten der slowakischen Sprache]. In: *Tanulmányok a határon túli kétnyelvűségről*, Kontra, M. (Ed.), Budapest.

Očovský, Štefan (1992): „Interpretation of statistical data on nationalities". In: *Minorities in politics*, Plichtová, J. (Ed.), Bratislava.

Paukovič, Vladimir (1990): „Základné sociálne a demografické charakteristiky mad'arskej národnostnej menšiny v Česko-slovensku" [Soziale und demographische Charakteristik der ungarischen Minderheit in der ČSSR]. In: *Vývoj a postavenie mad'arskej národnostnej menšiny na Slovensku po r. 1948*, Paukovič, V. et al., Kaschau.

Paukovič, Vladimír et al. (1990): *Vývoj a postavenie mad'arskej národnostnej menšiny na Slovensku po r. 1948* [Entwicklung und Lage der ungarischen Minderheit in der Slowakei nach 1948], Kaschau.

Plichtová, Jana (Ed.) (1992): *Minorities in Politics. Cultural and Language Rights*, Bratislava.

Rosova, Tatiana/Bútorová, Zora (1992): „Slovaks and Hungarians in Slovakia". In: *Minorities in politics*, Plichtová, J. (Ed.), Bratislava.

Sima, Ferenc (Ed.) (1978): *Z konfrontácie mad'arčiny a slovenčiny* [Ungarisch-slowakische konfrontative linguistische Studien], Bratislava.

Sokolová, Gabriela (1987): *Soudobé tendence vývoje národnosti v ČSSR* [Aktuelle Entwicklungstendenzen von Minderheiten in der ČSSR], Prag.

Sulán, Béla (1963): „A kétnyelvűség néhány kérdéséhez" [Zur Frage des Bilinguismus]. In: *Magyar Nyelv 59*, 253−265.

Šutaj, Štefan (1990): „Mad'arská otázka na Slovensku v rokoch 1948−1970" [Die ungarische Frage in der Slowakei in den Jahren 1948−1970]. In: *Vývoj a postavenie mad'arskej národnostnej menšiny na Slovensku po r. 1948*, Paukovič, V. et al., Kaschau.

Vígh, Károly (1992): *A szlovákiai magyarság sorsa* [Das Schicksal der Ungarn in der Slowakei], Budapest.

Zel'ová, Anna (1992): „The Integration of the Hungarian Minority in Slovakia − the Language Problem". In: *Minorities in politics*, Plichtová, J. (Ed.), Bratislava.

Gizella Szabómihály (Slowakei)

206. Slowakisch–Deutsch

1. Geographie und Demographie
2. Geschichte
3. Politik, Wirtschaft und allgemeine kulturelle sowie religiöse Lage
4. Statistik und Ethnoprofil
5. Soziolinguistische Lage
6. Sprachpolitische Lage
7. Allgemeines kontaktlinguistisches Porträt
8. Kritische Wertung der verwendeten Quellen und Literatur
9. Bibliographie (in Auswahl)

1. Geographie und Demographie

Bei der Volkszählung 1991 bekannten sich 5414 Bürger der Slowakischen Republik zur deutschen (dt.) Nationalität. 1921 waren sie mit 145 844 (4,9%) und 1930 mit 154 821 (4,65%) nach den Ungarn die zweitstärkste Minderheit, seit den 50er Jahren beträgt ihr Anteil nur 0,1% (Born/Dickgießer 1989, 217ff; Spetko 1991, 397 zählt 1950: 5979; 1970: 5328; 1980: 5121). Der drastische Rückgang ist eine Folge des Zweiten Weltkrieges. Von September 1944 bis Januar 1945 wurden auf Anordnung der Reichsbehörden ca. 120 000 Deutsche aus der Slowakei vor der heranrückenden Ostfront nach Österreich und in den Sudetengau evakuiert, die zumeist nicht mehr zurückkehrten. Gemäß Artikel 13 des Potsdamer Abkommens sowie des Beneš-Dekrets (Nr. 33), nach dem das Vermögen aller Deutschen beschlagnahmt wurde, sind bis zum 31. April 1946 weitere 32 450 aus der Slowakei abgeschoben worden. Die diskriminierende Politik zwischen 1945 und 1968 (erst 1953 wurde den Deutschen die Staatsbürgerschaft zuerkannt; die Anerkennung als Minderheit erfolgte 1968, was Polen, Ungarn und Ukrainern bereits 1960 per Verfassungsänderung eingeräumt worden war) führte neben weiteren Übersiedlungen zum beinahe völligen Verlust nationaler Identität (Sprachenkarte K).

2. Geschichte

Die Ansiedlung dt. Kolonisten im ursprünglich slawisch besiedelten Ober-Ungarn (→ Art. 204) setzt an der Wende vom 12. zum 13. Jahrhundert vom ostmitteldeutschen Raum her ein und wird bis ins 15. Jahrhundert aus schlesischen und bairisch-österreichischen Gebieten fortgeführt (Kuhn 1967, 20– 35). Die Einwanderer, die auf Einladung ungarischer Herrscher kamen, in den Urkunden „Gäste" genannt, ließen sich in den von Tataren entvölkerten Landstrichen nieder. Drei Regionen wurden zusammenhängend besiedelt: (a) Südwestslowakei (Zentrum: Preßburg/Bratislava), die an das geschlossene dt. Sprachgebiet Niederösterreichs angrenzt, (b) die Kremnitz-Deutsch-Probener Gruppe im westkarpatischen Bergbaugebiet, deren Sprache als „Pergstädterisch" bezeichnet wird, (c) unterhalb der Hohen Tatra das bekannteste dt. Siedlungsgebiet – die Zips, wo im Zuge eines langwierigen Prozesses wiederum drei Siedlungsräume entstanden: die mittlere Zips (Oberzips) mit den Zentren Leutschau/Levoča und Kesmark/Kežmarok; die nördliche Zips (Altlublau/Stará L'ubovňa und Pudlein/Podolínec), aus Schlesien besiedelt und bis zu Beginn des 14. Jahrhunderts zu Polen gehörig, sowie das Flußtal der Göllnitz/Gelnica (Unterzips bzw. Zipser Gründe) mit gleichnamigem Ort als Zentrum. Das 15. Jahrhundert war die Hoch-Zeit der dt. Besiedlung – 200 000–250 000 (ca. ein Viertel der Gesamtbevölkerung, vgl. Grothe 1943, 25). Aufgrund umfangreicher Rechte und der wirtschaftlichen wie politischen Reife und Organisiertheit verdrängten sie die slowakische (slow.) Bevölkerung auf Jahrhunderte aus wichtigen Lebensbereichen (Handel, Handwerk, Rechtsprechung). Das Deutsche wurde neben dem universalen Latein (bis 1848 Amtssprache) zur zweiten Amts- und inoffiziellen Staatssprache Ober-Ungarns. Der slowakisierende bzw. madjarisierende Prozeß setzte im schriftlichen Verkehr der Städte mit überwiegend slow. Bevölkerung allmählich Ende des 15. Jahrhunderts (Papsonová 1992) ein, in Gebieten mit dt. Besiedlung erst im 18. Jahrhundert, insbesondere nach dem österreichisch-ungarischen Ausgleich (1867). Bis 1918 zählten die Deutschen der Slowakei zu den ca. 2 Mio. Ungarndeutschen.

3. Politik, Wirtschaft und allgemeine kulturelle sowie religiöse Lage

Die heterogene Herkunft (landschaftlich wie sozial), die sich in Mundart (Ma.) und Konfession niederschlug, bedingte, daß die Deutschen in der Slowakei nach Gründung des tschechoslowakischen Staates (1918) kein Bewußtsein nationaler Zusammengehörigkeit ausprägten. Die Deutschen lebten in den überwiegend dreisprachigen Städten (Kaschau/Košice, Eperjes/Prešov, Bartfeld/Bardejov, Sillein/Žilina, Neutra/Nitra u. a.) und in der Diaspora. Zwischen den dt. Siedlungsräumen (keine kompakten Sprachinseln) bestanden kaum Kontakte. Die mehr auf Wien ausgerichteten Deutschen Preßburgs, der Südwestslowakei und des Hauerlandes (Mittelslowakei) waren römisch-katholisch, die bereits seit der Gegenreformation antihabsburgisch eingestellten Zipser evangelisch-lutherisch. Entsprechend der Gewerbestruktur waren zwei Drittel in der Land- und Forstwirtschaft, die übrigen im Bergbau, in Handel und Handwerk sowie in der Industrie tätig. Um 1930 ist bei den Deutschen eine deutliche Verlagerung zu registrieren (29,2% zu 57,6% Slowaken in der Landwirtschaft; 57,6% zu 18,8% Slowaken in Industrie und Gewerbe). Die städtische Bürgerschaft und Intelligenz (v. a. in Preßburg und in der Zips) war infolge systematischer Madjarisierung und ökonomischer Abhängigkeit zu großen Teilen assimiliert bzw. pro-ungarisch orientiert. Nach 1918 (die Verfassung der ČSR gewährte insgesamt bedeutende Minderheitenrechte) zeigte das dt. Bürgertum Preßburgs größere Bereitschaft zur Zusammenarbeit mit dem neuen Staat als die Zipser, die eher slow. Autonomiebestrebungen unterstützten bzw. bis in die 30er Jahre pro-ungarische Ambitionen hegten. Industrie und Gewerbe hatten schwer mit der böhmischen Konkurrenz zu kämpfen. Die 20er Jahre bringen engere Kontakte zu den national politisierten Sudetendeutschen, die v. a. über den „Deutschen Kulturverband in der ČSR" Einfluß ausübten. Die Entwicklung des dt. Schulwesens (von der Prager Regierung gefördert) wurde mehrheitlich von sudetendeutschen Lehrern getragen. Unter dem Einfluß völkisch-nationalistischer Orientierung der Sudetendeutschen entstand 1928 die „Karpatendeutsche Partei" (KdP), deren Name (ähnlich dem Begriff „sudetendeutsch") eine nationalpolitische Zusammengehörigkeit suggerieren sollte, die jedoch erst nach dem Anschluß Österreichs und der Sudetengebiete breiteren Zustrom (nun auch in der Zips) verzeichnen konnte; 1929 errang die KdP 18 000, 1935 28 000 Stimmen, ca. 30% der dt. Wähler. In der Slowakischen Republik (1939−1945) strebten die dt. Organisationen (v. a. die „Deutsche Partei") nach größerem gesamtgesellschaftlichem Einfluß. Im Mai 1944 wurden die Deutschen per Gesetz und zwischenstaatlicher Verträge von der slow. Regierung dem Dritten Reich und seinen Wehrverbänden überantwortet. Seit 1944 gab es keine dt. Bildungs- und Kultureinrichtungen, nur in Preßburg konnten bis in die Gegenwart deutschsprachige Gottesdienste beider Konfessionen aufrechterhalten werden. Die von Kollektivschuld aller Bürger dt. Nationalität ausgehenden völkerrechtswidrigen Beneš-Dekrete (Mai 1945) hatten nicht nur die Enteignung, sondern auch die wirtschaftliche und gesellschaftliche Ausgrenzung der verbliebenen Deutschen zur Folge. Bei der von parteipolitischen und ideologischen Prämissen geprägten Aufarbeitung des slowakischen Nationalaufstandes (nach seiner Ausrufung in Neusohl/Banská Bystrica, 29. 8. 1944, besetzte die Wehrmacht Teile des Landes) der Kriegs- und unmittelbaren Nachkriegszeit wurden die Verbrechen an der dt. Zivilbevölkerung in den Aufstandsgebieten (über 1000 Opfer in der Mittelslowakei), bei der Rückkehr aus den Sudetengebieten (das Massaker an der Schwedenschanze bei Prerau/Přerov, 19. 6. 1945) und in den Lagern, in denen Deutsche vor der Abschiebung interniert wurden, verschwiegen. Mit Ausnahme statistischer Angaben der Volkszählungen liegen nach 1945 keine das Leben, die Kultur, wirtschaftliche bzw. andere Aktivitäten der dt. Minderheit betreffenden Untersuchungen vor.

4. Statistik und Ethnoprofil

Um der nationalen Diskriminierung zu entgehen, wechselten nach 1945 viele Angehörige der dt. Minderheit zur herrschenden Nationalität. Die im Zusammenhang mit der Erforschung der Reliktmundarten in den 70er Jahren vorgenommenen Erhebungen (Valiska 1980; 1982) in den ursprünglich kompakt deutschbesiedelten Gebieten der Ostslowakei haben gezeigt, daß sich selbst in Gemeinden, in denen die Ortsmundart zumindest im privaten Umgang gebraucht wurde, bei der Volkszählung 1970 nur wenige Bürger zur dt. Nationalität bekannten. Daß ihre Zahl auch 1989 nicht wesentlich gestiegen ist, läßt sich v. a. auf zwei Tatbestände zurückführen: die Generation, die zwischen 1918 und 1945 dt. Schulen besuchte und neben der Mundart (Ma.) auch Hochdeutsch spricht, stirbt aus; die unter der andersprachigen Bevölkerung verstreute jüngere Generation ist sich, infolge der oktroyierten Assimilierung, ihrer Kultur und Herkunft kaum noch bewußt, bekennt sich demgemäß überwiegend zur slow. Nationalität. Die Mehrzahl der 5414 Deutschen (2469 Männer, 2945 Frauen) lebt verstreut in den ursprünglichen Siedlungsgebieten (Preßburg und Umgebung, Priwitz/Prievidza, Oberzips, Unterzips, Kaschau und Umgebung). Den höchsten Anteil weist die Altersgruppe 65—79 (1538) auf (50—54: 420, 55—59: 503, 60—64: 604); die übrigen sind im Alter 0—49. 2320 waren Rentner, 2343 ökonomisch aktive Personen, wobei die Sozialgruppen Angestellte (1290) und Arbeiter (678) am stärksten vertreten sind. 1127 besaßen Mittelschul- (Abitur), 595 Hochschulabschluß. 4189 gaben Deutsch, 925 Slowakisch, 155 Ungarisch, 65 Tschechisch, 15 Polnisch, 5 Romani als Muttersprache an. 4946 sind slow., 165 tschechische Staatsangehörige, 303 ohne Staatszugehörigkeit. Außer in Deutschland leben heute Karpatendeutsche in Österreich und Übersee (v. a. in Nordamerika), wo landsmannschaftliche Organisationen eine reichhaltige, vor allem auf die Pflege des Kulturgutes und die Aufarbeitung der jüngeren Vergangenheit konzentrierte Tätigkeit ausüben.

5. Soziolinguistische Lage

Die in unterschiedlichsten, auch innerhalb einer Gemeinde wechselnden Varianten und Varietäten der in der Slowakei noch gesprochenen dt. Mundarten (Maa.) (Reste der ursprünglich österreichischen Maa. bairischer Prägung der Südwestslowakei, der bairisch-ostmitteldeutschen Mischdialekte des Hauerlandes, der mitteldeutsch-schlesischen Maa. der Oberzips und des aus bairischen, zipserischen und schlesischen Elementen bestehenden Gemisches der Unterzips) befinden sich gegenwärtig in der letzten Phase ihrer Existenz. Die angeführten Angaben (s. 4.) zeigen, daß nicht alle Angehörigen der Ethnie eine Variante des Deutschen beherrschen. In den unmittelbar nach dem Krieg geborenen Altersgruppen wird die Ma. aktiv, z. T. jedoch nur passiv beherrscht. In Ausnahmefällen wurde der mittleren Generation die dt. Hochsprache gezielt vermittelt oder hat sie diese im Rahmen ihrer Ausbildung (Germanistikstudium, Studien und Aufenthalte im dt. Sprachraum) erlernt. Die Generation, die dt. Schulen besuchte, beherrscht neben der Ma. Hochdeutsch, oft auch Ungarisch, darüber hinaus die slow. Ma. des umliegenden Sprachareals und (je nach Bildungsgrad) auch die slow. Standardsprache. Die in Kombinationen anzutreffende Di- und Triglossie wird von Bi-, bei den Ältesten von Trilinguismus begleitet. Im offiziellen Umgang wird die allgemein besser beherrschte Sprache des überwiegenden Gebrauchs (Slow.) bevorzugt, die dann die kognitive und eigentliche kommunikative Funktion übernimmt, während die Ma. selten die Grenzen der Kontaktkommunikation (Familien- und Nachbarkontakt) überschreitet. Nur in Gemeinden mit höherem Anteil von Mundartsprechern (Metzenseifen/Medzev, Hopgarten/Chmeľnica) wird die Ma. auch in der Öffentlichkeit gesprochen. Im Zusammenhang mit dem neuerwachten Interesse am Erlernen der Sprache der Vorfahren (vgl. 6.) ist anzunehmen, daß der Gebrauch der dt. Standardsprache innerhalb der dt. Gemeinschaft aktiviert wird, während einzelne Reliktmaa. nur im Brauchtum Bestand haben werden. Mit Ausnahme der an die Sprachinseln grenzenden slow. Sprachareale wurde die Existenz der dt. Ethnie in der slow. Gesellschaft nach 1946 kaum wahrgenommen. So ist man sich z. B. bei der Verwendung der in der Ostslowakei geläufigen scherzhaften Bezeichnung „Mantake" (derjenige, der etwas nicht versteht; Mantaken, mantakisch — Benennung der Unterzipser und ihrer Ma.) der ursächlichen Bedeutung kaum bewußt. Ähnlich muß das von der ideologischen Propaganda der Nachkriegszeit präsentierte Bild des Deutschen als Feind nicht unbedingt auf die dt. Mitbürger übertragen worden sein. Gemäß der politischen Situation der letzten Jahrzehnte liegen in bezug auf Sprachkonflikte, Stereotypen und Images beider Kontaktsprachen keine Erkenntnisse vor. Der nach 1989 eingetretene politische Wandel, die in Medien präsentierten Diskussionen zur Nationalitätenpolitik sowie Aktivitäten der Ethnie selbst führen zu neuer Akzeptanz.

6. Sprachpolitische Lage

Die Situation nach 1945 war einerseits durch staatlich-regressive Maßnahmen, andererseits durch Identitätsverlust bzw. -verleugnung seitens der in der Slowakei verbliebenen Deutschen gekennzeichnet. Die dt. Sprache wurde seit Mitte der 50er Jahre in Konkurrenz zu Englisch und Französisch als 2. Fremdsprache an Schulen, Hochschulen, Universitäten gelehrt. Die germanistische Forschung wurde nach relativer Freizügigkeit in den 60er Jahren erneut reglementiert. Im Unterschied zu den Deutschen im tschechischen Teil (→ Art. 202) wurden selbst die bescheidenen Möglichkeiten kultureller Sammlung und Betätigung in der Slowakei kaum genutzt. 1989 erfuhr die Problematik der dt. Minderheit in ihrer historischen wie gegenwärtigen Dimension verstärkte Aufmerksamkeit und staatlicherseits vielfältige Unterstützung. 1990 konstituierte sich der „Karpatendeutsche Verein in der Slowakei" (KpV), der überparteilich für die Wiederentfaltung der beinahe versunkenen Identität und die Wahrung kultureller wie sozialer Interessen eintritt. Gemäß den Statuten liegt das Hauptaugenmerk des KpV in der Pflege und Kultivierung der Muttersprache. Angesichts der Tatsache, daß die jüngste Generation nur ausnahmsweise die dt. Sprache beherrscht, wurde in Zusammenarbeit mit bundesdeutschen Institutionen und dem slow. Schulministerium das „Schulprogramm 2000" ins Leben gerufen, wonach bilinguale Bildungseinrichtungen geplant sind. Im Schuljahr 1993/1994 wurde an 5 Grundschulen einzelner Regionen (vgl. 4.) jeweils eine 1. Klasse mit zweisprachigem Unterricht eröffnet, wobei 5 Lehrer aus deutschsprachigen Ländern zum Einsatz gelangen. Die nicht ausschließlich aus dt. Familien stammenden Kinder (1991 waren 491 jünger als 15 Jahre) werden so die dt. Sprache erlernen, in der auch andere Unterrichtsstoffe vermittelt werden; in diesen Orten sind zweisprachige Einrichtungen für Kinder im Entstehen begriffen. Da es an eigenen qualifizierten Lehrern sowie Lehrmitteln mangelt, ist man auf Unterstützung aus Österreich und Deutschland angewiesen. Ähnliche Schwierigkeiten zeigen sich bei den Bemühungen, in Gemeinden dt. Gottesdienste abzuhalten, lediglich bei besonderen Anlässen (Heimattreffen, Feiertagen) werden Messen von dt. bzw. österreichischen Geistlichen zelebriert. Seit 1992 verfügt der KpV über ein Organ („Karpatenblatt", monatlich, 2000—3000 Auflage). Über Aktivitäten informiert eine dt. Sendung des slow. Rundfunks für die Minderheit (wöchentlich ½ Stunde). Bei der Regierung besteht ein Minderheitenrat, in dem der KpV Sitz und Stimme hat.

7. Allgemeines kontaktlinguistisches Porträt

Das 800jährige Zusammenleben von Slowaken und Deutschen hat sowohl im Slow. als auch in den in der Slowakei gesprochenen dt. Maa. dauerhafte Spuren hinterlassen. Besonders auffällig ist die wechselseitige Beeinflussung des Wortschatzes.

7.1.1. Neben den das wirtschaftliche und öffentliche Leben bzw. ihre Organisation betreffenden Wörtern wurden auch viele mit Dingen und Erscheinungen des Alltagslebens zusammenhängende Benennungen ins Slow. integriert. Die Übernahme wurde auch von anderen außersprachlichen Faktoren begünstigt, so von der Migration bestimmter Sozialgruppen der einheimischen Bevölkerung (Handwerker, Kaufleute, Tagelöhner, Dienstpersonal, Militärdienst in der Armee der k. u. k. Monarchie), die aus der deutschsprachigen Umgebung oft spezielle Ausdrücke aus dem Bereich ihrer Erwerbstätigkeit und des gesellschaftlichen Lebens mitbrachten. Eine zahlenmäßig kleinere Gruppe Entlehnungen aus dem Deutschen ist zum festen Bestandteil der slow. Schriftsprache geworden (z. B. *cieľ* — Ziel, *plech* — Blech, *drôt* — Draht, *maštaľ* — Stall, ahd. marstal, *rytier* — Ritter), ihrer fremden Herkunft ist sich der Sprecher nicht bewußt. Eine besonders hohe Frequenz weisen Wörter dt. Herkunft v. a. in den einzelnen slow. Maa. bzw. in der Umgangssprache auf, wo sie — wie die lexikalischen Germanismen der Schriftsprache — als systemhafte Elemente und Basis für weitere Derivation fungieren. Neben den entlehnten, oft schon als Archaismen empfundenen Wörtern stehen meist einheimische Äquivalente. Was bei Angehörigen der älteren Generation üblicher Sprachgebrauch ist, wird von Jüngeren durch Neues ersetzt bzw. merkmalhaft (scherzhaft, pejorativ, abschätzig) verwendet. So stehen nebeneinander z. B. *bigľajs* Bügeleisen — *žehlička*, *šurc* Schürze — *zástera*, *šanovať* schonen — *šetriť*. Umgangssprachlichen Ausdrücken und Wortverbindungen kann man auch in der Belletristik und Presse begegnen, z. B. *robiť kšefty, kšeftovať* — Geschäfte machen, *nechať niekoho v štichu* — jdn. im Stich lassen, *fajront* Feierabend. Die umfangreichste Gruppe der Entlehnungen stellen Wörter aus dem Bereich des Handwerks. Die Mehrzahl der Entlehnungen kommt im ganzen Gebiet der Slowakei vor, bei anderen läßt sich der Verbreitungsbereich durch Isolexen abgrenzen (Habovštiak 1984). Besonders hohe kommunikative Kompetenz und Frequenz weisen diese Lexeme in den urspr. von Deutschen kompakter besiedelten Gebieten auf, in denen die Kontaktsituation bis ins 20. Jahrhundert aufrechterhalten blieb (eine vollständige Bestandsaufnahme liegt nicht vor). Die Mehrzahl der lexikalischen Entlehnungen dt. Herkunft im Slow. (über 70%) bilden die Substantive, etwa 20% die (oft von diesen erst sekundär abgeleiteten) Verben, den Rest die übrigen Wortarten, besonders Adjektive und Adverbien. Nicht selten handelt es sich dabei um in der dt. Schriftsprache nicht mehr existierende Formen und Bedeutungen, die die slow. Maa. bis in die Gegenwart konserviert haben.

7.1.2. Im Prozeß der eigentlichen Entlehnung unterliegen die lexikalischen Germanismen verschiedenen formalen Laut- und Systemveränderungen des Slow., wobei nicht alle Abweichungen, die die Lehnwörter gegenüber der dt. Schriftsprache aufweisen, Ergebnis der Adaptierung und Interferenz sind. Oft ist es lediglich die Beibehaltung der älteren (ahd., mhd.) bzw. Übernahme der in der jeweiligen dt. Ma. (bairisch, mitteldeutsch, schlesisch) bestehenden Lautung oder Form (Papsonová 1986). Da z. B. beide Sprachen über das gleiche Inventar der nicht umgelauteten Vokale verfügen (kein Grund zur Interferenz), sind auf diesen Vorgang Formen zurückzuführen, die gegenüber dem Hochdeutschen unterschiedliche Stammvokale aufweisen (*sporit'* — sparen, *ratovat'* — retten, *šuter* — Schotter, *šopa* — Schuppen, *šruba* — Schraube, *dišel* — Deichsel, *hamovat'* — hemmen). Bei der Delabialisierung der dem slow. Phonemsystem nicht immanenten gerundeten Vokale ist das Zusammenwirken der Adpatationsprozesse mit Eigentümlichkeiten der in der Slowakei gesprochenen dt. Maa. vorauszusetzen (*fedrovat'* — fördern, *vinšovat'* — wünschen), ähnlich bei der Jotierung der Diphthonge (*vercajk* — Werkzeug, *rajbat'* — reiben, waschen) beim Abfall des nebentonigen Vokals (*ksicht* — Gesicht, *hák* — Haken, mhd. hake, *cech* — Zeche, Zunft), der Palatalisierung (*koštovat'* — kosten) und der Adaptation (*štopkat'* — stopfen), weniger bei verschiedenen Assimilations- und Dissimilationsprozessen der Konsonanten, die in einzelnen slow. Maa. ein sehr unterschiedliches Bild zeigen. Nur die wenigen Entlehnungen der Schriftsprache werden in ihr Phonemsystem voll integriert. So wird z. B. der fallende dt. Diphthong durch steigende slow. Diphthonge substituiert (*krieda* — Kreide, *ciacha* — Zeichen, *fortiel'* — Vorteil), während er in den Maa. jotiert (*krajda, bl'ajvas* — Bleiweiß) oder durch einfachen Vokal ersetzt

wird (*štráf, štráfik* — Streifen) bzw. Varianten aufweist (*šiba* — Fensterscheibe/*šajba* — Scheibe, *lišta/lajsňa* — Leiste). Bei der morphologischen Integration werden die fremden Affixe durch einheimische ersetzt (*naštel'ovat'* — einstellen, *preštel'ovat'* — umstellen, *šnurovat'* — schnüren, *trafit'* — treffen) bzw. adaptiert (*blúza/blúzka* — Bluse, *mlynár* — Müller, *garbiar* — Gerber, *kufor* — Koffer, *cifra* — Ziffer, *štempel'* — Stempel, *fakl'a* — Fackel), nur resthaft haben sich in den Maa. urspr. Präfixe erhalten (*fartuch/firtuch/fertucha/fiertucha/fjertoch* — Vortuch, Fürtuch), die im Slowakischen nicht als solche empfunden werden. Die entlehnten urspr. Fem. wechseln nach dem e-Abfall zu den Mask. (s. o.), umgekehrt gehen die Mask., die ein -a annehmen, zu den Fem. (*šajta* — Scheit, *šachta* — Schacht) und werden wie die entlehnten Verben voll in das slow. Flexionssystem integriert (im Slow. gehen die meisten Mask. auf Konsonanten, Fem. auf -*a* aus). Auf syntaktischer Ebene macht sich der Einfluß des Deutschen im Slow. kaum bemerkbar.

7.2.1. Auch wenn in der ersten Etappe des Kontakts beider Sprachen weit mehr dt. Wörter ins Slow. kamen als umgekehrt, haben sich die Deutschen dem neuen Lebensniveau angepaßt und aus dem Slow. manche Ausdrücke übernommen, v. a. Benennungen aus dem Bereich des Brauchtums, der Haus- und Landwirtschaft. Über das Slow. gelangten in die dt. Inselmaa. Wörter aus dem Ungarischen sowie die mit der Almwirtschaft zusammenhängende Terminologie, übernommen von der im 14./15. Jahrhundert angesiedelten Bevölkerung ukrainisch-rumänischer Herkunft (Walachen). Die in der Westslowakei öfter belegten Bohemismen könnten über das Wienerische in den Preßburger Dialekt gekommen sein. In der Ober- und nördlichen Zips macht sich der Einfluß der dort gesprochenen polnischen Maa. (Goralen) stark bemerkbar. Nicht selten handelt es sich hierbei um Rückentlehnungen (*dupl'om* — doppelt, *groll/grulln* — Kartoffeln). Während die in den früheren Stadien des Kontakts entlehnten Lexeme den dt. Maa. noch phonologisch angepaßt und in das System eingegliedert wurden, werden in der letzten Phase der sozialen wie geistig-kulturellen Fusion mit der Staatssprache slow. Benennungen ohne jegliche Adaptation übernommen.

7.2.2. Auf die frühe Übernahme weisen Belege hin, die die Lautentwicklung der Muttersprache mitgemacht haben, wie z. B. Formen mit diphthongiertem slow. *ú* (*plautz* — pľúca, Lunge), mit Abfall des anlautenden *h* (*labotschllawatsche* — hlaváč, Schleie), mit palatalisiertem *s* (*schliegowitz* — slivovica, Pflaumenbrand, *schmetten* — smotana/smetana, Sahne), mit Beseitigung bzw. Vokalisierung des slow. silabischen *r* (*kiapl/kiäpl/kirpe/kürpel* — krpec, Bundschuh, *kretschen/kretschenhaus* — krčma, Wirtshaus). Die entlehnten Substantive bewahren meist die Genusverhältnisse der Ausgangssprache. Das auslautende -*a* der slow. Fem. wird zu -*e* (vgl. 7.1.2.), der Plural geht auf -*en*, -*n* aus (*dschabe* — žaba, Frosch). Die im Slow. frequentierten Diminutiva nehmen -*chen* an (*muschkelchen* — muška, Getreidekäfer), seltener sind dt. Ableitungssuffixe der Adjektiva zu finden (*pamelich/pumelich/pomali* — pomaly, langsam), öfter kommen hybride Komposita (*kurnštol* — kurín, Hühnerstall) und Lehnübersetzungen (*beisrchen* — sirôtka, Stiefmütterchen) vor. Infinitivendungen werden mit den Suffixen -*ein* (typisch für die zipserdt. Maa.), -*en*, -*n* gebildet. Infolge ihrer Entwicklung in slow. Nachbarschaft werden einerseits immer mehr Benennungen in die Inselmaa. aufgenommen, andererseits sind im System einzelner Maa. zunehmende Schwankungen und Störungen zu beobachten, die als eines der Merkmale ihres Untergangs charakterisiert werden können. Neben den phonetischen Varianten und Unregelmäßigkeiten gibt es bemerkenswerte Abweichungen in der Flexion (Deklination der Substantive und Pronomen, Komparation, Konjugation) und in der Syntax (die Wortstellung gleicht der des Slow., nur bei der ältesten Generation ist eine Tendenz zur Beibehaltung des prädikativen Satzrahmens festzustellen). Neben den ma. Ausdrücken erscheinen immer öfter slow. Äquivalente, die bei frequentierten Wortarten bevorzugt werden. Gegen die Slowakisierung der Maa., die bis jetzt nicht Gegenstand eingehender Forschung wurde, wehrt sich noch die älteste Generation; die mittlere, deren Sprache einen wesentlich höheren Prozentsatz von Slowakismen aufweist, empfindet die Ma. als Anachronismus (vgl. 4., 5.).

8. Kritische Wertung der verwendeten Quellen und Literatur

Entsprechend der Siedlungsgeschichte und späteren Stellung der Deutschen in Ober-Ungarn und der Slowakei existieren Deutungen der älteren wie neueren Forschungen zur Rolle der dt. Sprache und Kultur in jener Region. Die ältere wie gegenwärtige ungarische Historiographie behandelt Kultur und Entwicklung der Slowakei (inkl. der dort lebenden Deutschen) als Bestandteil der eigenen Nationalgeschichte. Zumindest nach 1918 studierte die dt. Jugend aus der Slowakei nicht mehr in Wien bzw. Budapest, sondern mehrheitlich an den dt. Hochschulen in Prag und Brünn. Das seit der Jahrhundertwende verstärkt einsetzende Interesse an Geschichte, Kultur und Sprache der dt. Siedler in der Slowakei ist demzufolge größtenteils deutschböhmisch initiiert und im Kontext volkskundlicher und völkischer Orientierung der an der Prager deutschen Universität wirkenden Professoren angeregt worden. Die in diesem Umfeld entstandenen Arbeiten sind nicht frei von Tendenzen, die Ergebnisse historischer und philologischer Untersuchungen für die Idee eines kulturbringenden Deutschtums zu interpretieren — so wird die Rolle der dt. Besiedlung beim Aufbau einer bodenständigen Kultur überbewertet. Nach 1945 erschienen vorerst populärwissenschaftliche Darstellungen zur Geschichte und Kultur. Zumeist waren die Autoren ehemals in der Region als Lehrer tätig gewesen, auch in diesen Arbeiten herrschen national motivierte Sichtweisen vor. In der Slowakei selbst bestand seitens der offiziösen Forschung kein Interesse an der Aufarbeitung dieses Kapitels eigener Geschichte. Erst seit den 60er Jahren ist die slow. Historiographie bemüht, den Anteil aller ethnischen Gruppen zu erforschen, wobei tendenziös-nationalistische Positionen früherer Untersuchungen kritisch hinterfragt werden. In diese Zeit fallen auch Neuansätze philologischer Forschung (linguistische Analysen mittelalterlicher Urkunden, Mundartforschung). Die zaghaften Ansätze slow. Forscher fanden nur geringen Wiederhall, zumal sie kaum über internationale Kontakte und Publikationsmöglichkeiten verfügten, wohingegen ausländische Wissenschaftler hervortraten (K. Mollay, C. J. Hutterer, S. Gárdonyi, I. T. Piirainen). Gegenwärtige Forschungen sind bemüht, die Sprachkontakte hinreichend darzustellen (Habovštiak 1987) und umfangreiche lexikographische Projekte zu realisieren (Habovštiak 1984; Peciar 1959 ff; Ripka 1980).

9. Bibliographie (in Auswahl)

Born, Joachim/Dickgießer, Sylvia (1989): *Deutschsprachige Minderheiten. Ein Überblick über den Stand der Forschung für 27 Länder*, Mannheim.

Grothe, Hugo (1943): *Das deutsche Volkstum in der Slowakei in Vergangenheit und Gegenwart*, München.

Habovštiak, Anton (1984): *Atlas slovenského jazyka. IV. Lexika* [Atlas der slowakischen Sprache. IV. Wortschatz], Bratislava.

Habovštiak, Anton (1987): „Zur Verbreitung von Wörtern deutschen Ursprungs in den slowakischen Dialekten". In: *Zeitschrift für Slawistik*, 212–229.

Hanika, Josef (1952): *Siedlungsgeschichte und Lautgeographie des deutschen Hauerlandes in der Mittelslowakei*, München.

Hutterer, Claus Jürgen (1968): „Mischung, Ausgleich und Überdachung in den deutschen Sprachinseln des Mittelalters". In· *Zeitschrift für Mundartforschung* 3–4, 339–405 (neu aufgelegt: Hutterer 1991, 87–92).

Hutterer, Claus Jürgen (1991): *Aufsätze zur deutschen Dialektologie*. Budapest.

Hutterer, Claus Jürgen (1995): „Über die mehrsprachige Konvergenz in der Entwicklung des Deutschen in der Zips". In: *Die Zips in der Kontinuität der Zeit*, Švorc, P. (Ed.), Prešov, 255–267.

Kováč, Dušan (1991): *Nemecko a nemecká menšina na Slovensku (1871–1945)* [Deutschland und die deutsche Minderheit in der Slowakei (1871–1945)], Bratislava.

Kuhn, Walter (1967): „Die deutsche Ostsiedlung". In: *Leistung und Schicksal*, Schulz, E. (Ed.), Köln/Graz, 20–35.

Lipold, Günter (1985): „Entwicklungen des Deutschen außerhalb des geschlossenen Sprachgebietes. I.: Ost- und Südeuropa". In: *Sprachgeschichte. Ein Handbuch zur Geschichte der deutschen Sprache und ihrer Erforschung. 2. Halbbd.*, Berlin/New York.

Lux, Julius (1961): *Wörterbuch der Mundart von Dobschau (Zips)*, Marburg.

Moser, Virgil (1929, 1951): *Frühneuhochdeutsche Grammatik, Bd. I/1; Bd. I/3*, Heidelberg.

Papsonová, Mária (1986): „Zum Prozeß der Übernahme von Wörtern deutscher Herkunft ins Slowakische". In: *Brücken. Germanistisches Jahrbuch DDR–ČSSR 1985/86*, 310–330.

Papsonová, Mária (1987): „Ergebnisse, Probleme und Aufgaben bei der Erforschung des Frühneuhochdeutschen in der Slowakei". In: *Zeitschrift für Germanistik 2*, 198–209.

Papsonová, Mária (1992): „Das Stadtrechtsbuch von Žilina und das Magdeburger Recht". In: *Brükken. Neue Folge*, 149–171.

Paul, Hermann/Moser, Hugo/Schröbler, Ingeborg (1975): *Mittelhochdeutsche Grammatik*, Tübingen.

Peciar, Štefan et al. (1959–1965): *Slovník slovenského jazyka I.–VI.* [Wörterbuch der slowakischen Sprache I.–VI.], Bratislava.

Piirainen, Ilpo Tapani/Papsonová, Mária (1992): *Das Recht der Spiš/Zips. Texte und Untersuchungen zum Frühneuhochdeutschen in der Slowakei*. 2 Bde., Oulu.

Ripka, Ivor et al. (1980): *Slovník slovenských nárečí. Ukážkový zväzok* [Wörterbuch der slowakischen Mundarten. Ein Musterband], Bratislava.

Ripka, Ivor (1993): „O slovensko-nemeckých interferenciách v nárečovej lexike" [Zu slowakisch-deutschen Interferenzen im Mundartwortschatz]. In: *Dialektologický zborník 3*, Bratislava.

Rudolf, Rainer (1991): *Die deutschen Lehn- und Fremdwörter in der slowakischen Sprache*, Wien.

Rudolf, Rainer/Ulreich, Eduard/Zimmermann, Fritz (1979): *Hauerland – Bergstädterland*, Wien.

Rudolf, Rainer/Ulreich, Eduard/Zimmermann, Fritz (1976, 1985): *Preßburger Land und Leute*, Wien.

Schwanzer, Viliam (1969): „Reste niederdeutscher Siedlungen in der Slowakei". In: *Jahrbuch des Vereins für niederdeutsche Sprachforschungen 92*, 104–115.

Schwanzer, Viliam (1976): „Nemecké slová v spisovnej a ľudovej slovenčine" [Deutsche Wörter in slowakischer Schrift- und Volkssprache]. In: *Studia Academica Slovaca 5*, 463–477.

Schwarz, Ernst (1935): *Sudetendeutsche Sprachräume*, München.

Spetko, Josef (1991): *Die Slowakei. Heimat der Völker*, Wien/München.

Steinacker, Ruprecht (1987): *Die Karpatendeutschen in der Slowakei* (Kulturelle Arbeitshefte 14), Bonn.

Valiska, Juraj (1967): *Die zipserdeutsche Mundart von Chmeľnica (Hopgarten)*, Bratislava.

Valiska, Juraj (1980): *Nemecké nárečie Dobšinej. Príspevok k výskumu zanikania nárečí enkláv* [Deutsche Mundart von Dobschau. Ein Beitrag zur Erforschung des Untergangs von Inselmundarten], Groß Steffelsdorf.

Valiska, Juraj (1982): *Nemecké nárečia horného Spiša. Príspevok k výskumu reliktných nárečí v pokročilom štádiu ich vývoja* [Deutsche Mundarten der Oberzips. Ein Beitrag zur Erforschung von Reliktmundarten im fortgeschritttenen Stadium ihrer Entwicklung], Altlublau.

Mária Papsonová, Prešov/Ivor Ripka, Bratislava (Slowakei)

207. Slowakisch—Polnisch

1. Geographie und Demographie
2. Geschichte
3. Politik, Wirtschaft und allgemeine kulturelle sowie religiöse Lage
4. Statistik und Ethnoprofil
5. Soziolinguistische Lage
6. Sprachpolitische Lage
7. Allgemeines kontaktlinguistisches Porträt
8. Zur Forschungslage
9. Bibliographie (in Auswahl)

1. Geographie und Demographie

Laut Volkszählung von 1991 hat die Slowakische Republik insgesamt 5 268 935 Einwohner, davon 2969 Personen polnischer Nationalität (→ Art. 204). Sie stellen nur 0,05% der Bevölkerung und gehören damit zu den kleinsten ethnischen Gruppen innerhalb der Slowakei. Insgesamt leben sie sehr zerstreut in verschiedenen Bezirken der West-, Mittel- und Ostslowakei, vorwiegend in den größeren Städten. Eine kleine Gruppe besiedelt bis heute auch die Dörfer im slowakisch-polnischen Grenzgebiet.

Die Slowakische Republik grenzt im Norden an Polen in einer Länge von 597 km. Die natürliche Grenze zwischen beiden Staaten bilden die Westkarpaten, die eine natürliche Sprachgrenze für Einflüsse des Polnischen auf das Slowakische darstellt (→ Sprachenkarte K).

2. Geschichte

Die nördliche Grenze der (Tschecho-)Slowakei mit Polen stimmt mit der historisch-ethnischen Grenze des ehemaligen Ungarn überein (die Slowakei war vom 10. Jh. bis 1918 ein nördlicher Bestandteil von Ungarn). In Friedensverhandlungen in Paris am 20. Juni 1920 wurde der Grenzverlauf abschließend festgelegt, wobei noch 13 Dörfer in der Zips und in Orava (Arva) polnisches Gebiet wurden (vgl. Klimko 1980).

An der Besiedlung der slowakisch-polnischen Grenzgebiete vom 13. bis zum 18. Jahrhundert waren Slowaken, Polen, Ukrainer und Deutsche beteiligt. In diesen Gebirgsregionen trafen verschiedene Ströme von Völkerwanderungen aufeinander. In Abhängigkeit von der Richtung der Besiedlung (Norden oder Süden) überwogen (in dem Gebiet, wo die goralische Mundart verbreitet ist) polnische oder slowakische Sprachelemente (Pavlík 1968, Krišsáková 1990). Heute kann man die goralischen Dialekte als slowakisch-polnische Grenzdialekte bezeichnen (Krišsáková 1990), deren Sprecher ein eher slowakisches Bewußtsein haben. „Die Bevölkerung dieser Gebiete sprach zwar einen Dialekt, der dem Polnischen näher als dem Slowakischen steht, allerdings hat sie immer ein slowakisches Nationalbewußtsein bewahrt" (Štolc 1974, 66).

3. Politik, Wirtschaft und allgemeine kulturelle sowie religiöse Lage

Alle Minderheiten in der Tschechoslowakei, die polnische eingeschlossen, waren durch die Verfassungsurkunde der Tschechoslowakischen Republik von 1922 rechtlich geschützt. So waren z. B. Beamte verpflichtet, in den Bezirken mit einer ethnischen Minderheit, deren Anteil mindestens 20% betrug, in deren Sprache zu sprechen. Die Politik gegenüber Minderheiten wurden im Gesetz von 1968 (die Verfassung aus dem Jahre 1948 garantierte die Rechte nur Personen) festgelegt. Demnach erhielten die Minderheiten das Recht, ihrer Anzahl entsprechend in den Vertretungsorganen mitzuwirken, sowie das Recht auf Ausbildung in ihrer Sprache und auf eine allseitige kulturelle Entwicklung. In der Slowakei wurde im Jahre 1990 „das Gesetz über die slowakische Sprache als Amtssprache" verabschiedet. Darin wird festgelegt, daß die Minderheiten ihre Sprache im amtlichen Gebrauch in den Gebieten mit mindestens 20%igem Minderheitenanteil wieder verwenden können. Dies galt wegen der geringen Sprecherzahl jedoch nicht für Polen. Diese Situation besteht auch in der unabhängigen slowakischen Republik fort.

In der Slowakei bildet die städtische Bevölkerung fast die Hälfte der Bevölkerung. Dieses Merkmal trifft auch für die Polen in der Slowakei zu. Die Ergebnisse der Volkszählung von 1991 bestätigen auch die relativ starke Religiosität der slowakischen Bevölkerung (Mehrheit römisch-katholisch). Dies gilt auch für die Polen in der Slowakei (91,1% Gläubige). Im Vergleich zu den Slowaken sind die Polen in der Kirche mehr engagiert (z. B. im kirchlichen Schulwesen). Auch das

Schulbildungsniveau der Polen in der Slowakei entspricht dem gesamtstaatlichen Durchschnitt. Sie absolvierten insgesamt mit 6,7% (Männer) bzw. 4,5% (Frauen) mehr Schuljahre im Vergleich zu anderen (Srb, 1987).

4. Statistik und Ethnoprofil

Seit 1910, als auf dem Gebiet der späteren Tschechoslowakei 158 261 Polen lebten, ist die Zahl der Polen drastisch zurückgegangen. In den darauf folgenden Jahrzehnten entwickelte sich der Anteil der polnischen Bevölkerung auf dem Gebiet der Slowakei wie folgt:
1921 — 6059 (0,20%)
1930 — 7023 (0,20%)
1950 — 1808 (0,05%)
1961 — 1012 (0,02%)
1970 — 1058 (0,02%)
1980 — 2053 (0,04%)
1991 — 1669 (0,05%)

Der Anteil von Frauen an der Gesamtbevölkerung übersteigt den der Männer bei weitem. Die polnischen Männer arbeiten vorwiegend in der Industrie, die Frauen im Schulwesen und in Geschäften.

Die Polen leben in der Slowakei sehr zerstreut, z. B. in Bratislava (Preßburg) 494, in Košice (Kaschau) 200, in Dolný Kubín 200, in Spišská Nová Ves (Neudorf) 99 usw. Sie sind nicht in bestimmten Wohngebieten überproportional konzentriert.

5. Soziolinguistische Lage

Für die Polen in der Slowakei ist Bilingualismus (slowakisch-polnisch) bzw. auch Trilingualismus (slowakisch-polnisch-„ostslowakisch") typisch. In den einzelnen Regionen, wo der goralische Dialekt verbreitet ist (Zips, Arva, Zamagurie), sprechen sie goralische Dialekte. Als Kontaktsprache verwenden sie aber das Slowakische bzw. die slowakischen Dialekte. Die slowakische Hochsprache beherrschen eher die mittlere und die jüngere Generation; alle sprechen den slowakischen Dialekt (Buffa 1980). Die in Städten lebenden Polen sprechen slowakisch; nur in den Familien wird noch teilweise Polnisch gesprochen.

Im Rahmen dieser Diglossie hat der goralische Dialekt ein ziemlich niedriges Prestige (Kriššáková 1984, 172—173). Slowakisch setzt sich auch immer mehr als Familiensprache in goralischen Gebieten durch.

6. Sprachpolitische Lage

Die verhältnismäßig schnelle Assimilation der polnischen Bevölkerung, ihr geringer Anteil an der Gesamtbevölkerung und ihr Bilingualismus machen es aus sprachpolitischer Sicht anscheinend überflüssig, daß sie in der Slowakei eigene Schulen haben. Sie haben auch keine eigenen Rundfunk- und Fernsehsendungen, Tageszeitungen und Zeitschriften. Sie lesen die polnische Presse, teilweise aus Polen, teilweise aus der Tschechischen Republik (vor allem Głos Ludu).

In Bratislava ist der polnische Kulturverband tätig; es stehen eine Bibliothek, ein Kinosaal und Ausstellungsräume zur Verfügung. Es werden dort Ausstellungen und auch polnische Abendkurse für die Bevölkerung organisiert. Diese Veranstaltungen sind ein Treffpunkt der in der Slowakei lebenden Polen.

7. Allgemeines kontaktlinguistisches Porträt

Beide Sprachen, Slowakisch und Polnisch, gehören zu den westslawischen Sprachen, obwohl der mittelslowakische Dialekt einige Gemeinsamkeiten mit den südslawischen Dialekten aufweist. Das phonologische System der heutigen polnischen Schriftsprache verfügt zusätzlich über die Nasal-Vokale /õ/ und /ẽ/ (orthographisch ą und ę), die im Slowakischen fehlen. Die polnischen Konsonanten weisen eine ausgeprägte Palatalisierungskorrelation und eine dreifache Gliederung der Zischlaute auf, die durch die Buchstabenverbindungen s-ś-sz, rz usw. gekennzeichnet sind (im Slowakischen gibt es nur eine zweifache Gliederung). Der Wortakzent liegt im Polnischen (fast) immer auf der vorletzten Silbe (im Slowakischen dagegen fast immer auf der ersten Silbe). Die polnische Morphologie zeigt einen im Bereich der Nominal- und Verbalflexion größeren Formenreichtum im Vergleich zum Slowakischen.

In der slowakischen Sprache ist die strenge Quantitätsopposition der Vokale besonders markant. Das „rhythmische Gesetz" bestimmt, daß zwei lange Silben (fast) nie aufeinander folgen dürfen. Die Wortbetonung fällt auf die erste Silbe. Das slowakische morphologische Paradigma ist im Vergleich zum Polnischen und Tschechischen einfacher und regelmäßiger (Novák 1984).

Polnisch besitzt mehr deutsche Lehnwörter als Slowakisch (z. B. *ślusarz—Schlosser*,

Wörter mit dem Suffix -unek, z. B. rachunek — Rechnung usw.).

Die Slowaken halten die polnische Sprache im Vergleich zu ihrer eigenen Sprache für weicher und sehr konsonantisch. Diese Einschätzung teilen auch die Polen. Im Polnischen gibt es 35 Konsonanten (87,5%), im Slowakischen 27 (60%). In den ostslowakischen Dialekten findet man einige polnische Wörter als Entlehnungen. Der Einfluß der slowakischen Sprache auf den goralischen Dialekt zeigt sich in der Vereinfachung der Formen (Krissáková 1985) und bezüglich des Polnischen in den Städten im Einfluß einiger lexikalischer Elemente slowakischer Herkunft (Servátka 1987). Detaillierte Untersuchungen in diesem Gebiet wurde mit J. Dudášová-Krissáková (1993) durchgeführt.

Den Einwohnern der Slowakei stehen verschiedene polnische Grammatiken und Wörterbücher zur Verfügung (Buffa/Ivaničková 1968, Buffa 1964, 1967, Stano/Buffa 1988 u. a.). Es gibt kein Slowakisch-Lehrbuch für Polen in der Slowakei.

8. Zur Forschungslage

Die Thematik „Polen in der Slowakei" ist bis jetzt nicht ausreichend erforscht worden. Neben der Fachliteratur über die slowakisch-polnischen goralischen Dialekte fehlen andere Quellen fast völlig, was vor allem auf die geringe Anzahl dieser Bevölkerung auf dem Gebiet der Slowakei zurückzuführen ist. In der wissenschaftlichen Forschung ist vor allem noch die Diskussion von Bedeutung, die die These von Z. Stieber (1929) ausgelöst hat. Seiner Meinung nach sind „die ostslowakischen Dialekte im Ursprung polnisch". Bei seiner Theorie stützte er sich auf die Formen *chłop, młodi* in den ostslowakischen Dialekten (anstatt *chlap, mladí*), die eine klare polnische Herkunft aufweisen. J. Stanislav (1935) hat aber bewiesen, daß es sich bei diesen Elementen um spätere Übernahmen fertiger lexikalischer Einheiten handelt. Dieser Meinung hat später (1950) auch Z. Stieber zugestimmt.

9. Bibliographie (in Auswahl)

Buffa, Ferdinand (1964, 1967): *Gramatika spisovnej poľštiny 1—3* [Grammatik der polnischen Schriftsprache], Bratislava.

Buffa, Ferdinand (1974): „O vzájomných slovensko-poľských jazykových vplyvoch" [Zu den gegenseitigen slowakisch-polnischen Spracheinflüssen]. In: *Studia Academica Slovaca 5*, 33—48.

Buffa, Ferdinand/Ivaničková, Halina (1968): *Učebnica poľštiny pre samoukov* [Das Lehrbuch des Polnischen für Autodidakten], Bratislava.

Doruľa, Ján (1977): *Slováci v dejinách jazykových vzťahov* [Die Slowaken in der Geschichte der Sprachkontakte], Bratislava.

Dudášová-Krissáková, Júlia (1993): *Goralské nárečia* [Goralische Mundarten], Bratislava.

Habovštiak, Anton (1979): „O jazykovom vývine na slovensko-poľskom pohraničí" [Zur Sprachentwicklung im slowakisch-polnischen Grenzgebiet]. In: *Jazykovedný časopis 30*, 33—39.

Klimko, Ján (1980): *Vývoj územia Slovenska a utváranie jeho hraníc* [Die Entwicklung des slowakischen Territoriums und die Entstehung seiner Grenzen], Martin.

Krissáková, Júlia (1984): „Goralské nárečia vo svetle kolonizácií a teória jazykových kontaktov" [Goralische Mundarten im Licht der Sprachkontakte]. In: *Slavica Slovaca 19*, 165—177.

Krissáková, Júlia (1988): „Zmeny v systéme laterál v goralských nárečiach z aspektu slovensko-poľských jazykových kontaktov" [Die Wandlungen im Lateralsystem in den goralischen Mundarten aus der Sicht der slowakisch-polnischen Sprachkontakte]. In: *Studia Linguistica Polono-Slovaca 1*, Jerzy Rymut (Ed.), Breslau/Warschau/Krakau/Danzig/Lodz, 29—35.

Krissáková, Júlia (1990): „Fonologický systém goralských nárečí z aspektu slovensko-poľských jazykových kontaktov" [Das phonologische System der goralischen Mundarten aus der Sicht der slowakisch-polnischen Kontakte]. In: *Studia linguistica Polono-Slovaca 2*, Milan Majtán (Ed.), Bratislava, 3—21.

Novák, Ľudovít (1984): „Aký jazyk je slovenčina" [Was für eine Sprache ist das Slowakische]. In: *Studia Academica Slovaca 13*, 389—411.

Pavlík, Emil (1968): „Poľské vplyvy a Spišská Magura" [Die polnischen Einflüsse und Zipser Magura]. In: *Spiš 2*, 101—124.

Sčítanie ľudu, domov a bytov 1991. Predbežné výsledky (1991) [Die Volks-, Häuser- und Wohnungszählung 1991. Vorläufige Ergebnisse], Bratislava.

Servátka, Marián (1986): „Otázky jazykovej interferencie v slovenskom jazyku na Spiši v PĽR" [Die Fragen der Sprachinterferenzen in der slowakischen Sprache in Zips in Polen]. In: *Studia Academica Slovaca 15*, 413—426.

Servátka, Marián (1987): „Goralsko-slovenský bilinguizmus, resp. goralsko-spišsko-poľsko-slovenský multilingvizmus" [Der goralisch-slowakische Bilinguismus, bzw. der goralisch-zipsisch-polnisch-slowakische Multilinguismus]. In: *Studia Academica Slovaca 16*, 385—395.

Servátka, Marián (1990): „Prejavy fonetickej interferencie v rámci slovensko-poľských jazykových kontaktov" [Die Manifestationen der phonetischen

Interferenz im Rahmen der slowakisch-polnischen Kontakte]. In: *Studia linguistica Polono-Slovaca 2*, Milan Majtán (Ed.), Bratislava, 22−35.

Sokolová, Gabriela (1987): *Soudobé tendence vývoje národností v ČSSR* [Die gegenwärtigen Tendenzen in der Entwicklung der Nationalitäten in der ČSSR], Prag.

Srb, Vladimír (1987): „Demografický profil polské menšiny v Československu" [Das demographische Profil der polnischen Minderheit in der Tschechoslowakei]. In: *Český lid 74*, 151−167.

Stanislav, Ján (1935): „Pôvod východoslovenských nárečí" [Der Ursprung der ostslowakischen Mundarten]. In: *Bratislava 9*, 51−89.

Stano, Matej/Buffa, Ferdinand (1988): *Poľsko-slovenský a slovensko-poľský slovník* [Polnisch-slowakisches und slowakisch-polnisches Wörterbuch], 3. Aufl., Bratislava.

Stieber, Zdzisław (1929): „Ze studiów nad gwarami słowackimi południowego Spisza" [Studien über die slowakischen Minderheiten in der Südzips]. In: *Lud słowiański 12*, 61−138.

Stieber, Zdzisław (1950): „Problém pôvodu východoslovenských nárečí" [Das Problem des Ursprungs der slowakischen Mundarten]. In: *Svojina 4*, 57−69.

Štolc, Jozef (1974): „Slovensko-poľské jazykové pomedzie a jeho výskum" [Das slowakisch-polnische Grenzgebiet − eine Untersuchung]. In: *Jazykovedný časopis 25*, 60−70.

*Slavo Ondrejovič/Sibyla Mislovičová,
Bratislava (Slowakei)*

208. Slowakisch−Ukrainisch

1. Geographie und Demographie
2. Geschichte
3. Politik, Wirtschaft und kulturelle sowie religiöse Situation
4. Statistik und Ethnoprofil
5. Soziolinguistische Situation
6. Sprachpolitische Situation
7. Allgemeines kontaktlinguistisches Porträt
8. Kritische Wertung der verwendeten Quellen und Literatur
9. Bibliographie (in Auswahl)

1. Geographie und Demographie

Die Ukrainer bewohnen das Gebiet der Nordostslowakei. Im Westen bildet der Fluß Poprad, im Norden und im Osten die Staatsgrenze zu Polen und zur Ukraine die Grenzlage der Region. Die südliche Grenze verläuft durch ein gemischtsprachiges slowakisch-ukrainisches Gebiet. An dieser Grenze liegen die Städte Snina, Humenné (Homenau), Prešov u. a.

Das von der ukrainischen Bevölkerung bewohnte Gebiet zählte zu den wirtschaftlich rückständigsten Agrarregionen des ehemaligen Ungarn, Österreich-Ungarns wie auch der ersten Tschechoslowakischen Republik (1918). Komplizierte sozial-ökonomische, geographische und ethnisch-kulturelle Verhältnisse verursachten die Migration bzw. Auswanderung der Bevölkerung. Seit der ersten offiziellen Volkszählung in Österreich-Ungarn im Jahre 1869 richteten sich die Hauptströme der arbeitsuchenden Auswanderer nach Übersee und in die Industrieländer Westeuropas. Nach den Schätzungen wanderten im Zeitraum von 1871−1914 etwa 650 000 Einwohner (einschließlich Ukrainer) aus der Slowakei aus. Nach dem Zweiten Weltkrieg besiedelten einige Tausend Ukrainer die nach der Abschiebung der Deutschen unbewohnten Grenzgebiete in Böhmen; 12 015 Menschen wurden in den Jahren 1946−1947 in die Ukraine repatriiert (Vanát 1985, 265), und ein beträchtlicher Teil der arbeitenden Bevölkerung zieht Jahre später in die Industriezentren der Tschechoslowakei. Der Rückgang der Migrationsbewegungen erfolgte in den letzten Jahrzehnten auf Grund des Aufschwungs der landwirtschaftlichen Großproduktion und des Dienstleistungswesens (→ Sprachenkarte K).

2. Geschichte

Die ersten Hinweise zur ostslawischen Besiedlung der südlichen Tiefebenen in der heutigen Ostslowakei sind in den Namen von Siedlungen wie z. B. Ruskov, Veľký Ruskov, Malý Ruskov und Gönczruska erhalten. Diese Orte wurden vermutlich spätestens im 11.−12. Jahrhundert gegründet (Varsik 1958, 143 f.), und die Umsiedler stellten das ostslawische Element des damaligen Kiewer Rus (im 9. Jh. bis zur ersten Hälfte des 13. Jh.) dar. Die ukrainische Sprachgemeinschaft bildete sich im 14.—17. Jahrhundert in den südwestlichen Gebieten des ehemaligen Kiewer Rus heraus. Für diese Gebiete hatte sich neben dem Namen Rus auch die Bezeichnung Ukraina eingebürgert (→ Art. 236). Intensiviert wird die Besiedlung des nördlichen Teiles des Südkarpatengebietes durch Ostslawen (Ukrainer) im 14. Jahrhundert in der Zeit der sog. walachischen Kolonisierung. Diese Besiedlung dauerte bis Ende des 16. Jahrhunderts bzw. der ersten Hälfte des 17. Jahrhunderts an. Die auf dem heutigen Gebiet der Ostslowakei angesiedelten Ukrainer betrieben Weide- und Landwirtschaft. Für die ukrainische Sprachgemeinschaft waren adlige und städtische Strukturen nicht typisch (Haraksim 1961, 14 ff). Die sozialen Mißstände führten zu Aufständen gegen die Feudalherren, sowie zu Flucht, Befehlsverweigerung und Räubereien. Religiös motivierte Unruhen entstanden durch den Druck der Feudalherren, orthodoxen Gläubigen den katholischen Glauben aufzuzwingen. Unter der Bedingung, daß sie den Papst als Oberhaupt der Kirche anerkannten, durften die Bekehrten ihren östlichen Gottesdienstritus, ihre kirchenslawische Sprache und die kanonischen Regeln der orthodoxen Kirche behalten. Ungeachtet des Widerstandes wurde 1646 neben der bestehenden orthodoxen die griechisch-katholische Konfession durchgesetzt. Diese Entwicklung fällt in die Zeit der Latinisierung, in der sich die Geistlichkeit ihrer Nationalität zu entfremden begann. Als Reaktion darauf ist das Streben eines Teiles der griechisch-katholischen Geistlichkeit am Ende des 18. Jahrhunderts zu sehen, das liturgische Kirchenslawische mit der lebendigen (Alltags-)Sprache gleichzusetzen und somit den Gebrauch des Kirchenslawischen als einer Schriftsprache der Ukrainer im Transkarpatenraum und der Ostslowakei zu begründen. Erst nach der Revolution von 1848 wird die Forderung nach Verwendung der lebenden Sprache an Stelle des Kirchenslawischen gestellt (vgl. 4.).

3. Politik, Wirtschaft und allgemeine kulturelle sowie religiöse Lage

Das ethnisch ukrainische Gebiet der Ostslowakei war bis 1945 der rückständigste Teil der Tschechoslowakischen Republik. Die Industrie war kaum entwickelt, ebenso rückständig war die Landwirtschaft. Der Lebensstandard sowie das Bildungsniveau der ukrainischen Bevölkerung lag weit unter dem gesamtstaatlichen Durchschnitt (Bajcura 1967, 135). In der Nachkriegszeit ändert sich das soziale und wirtschaftliche Gepräge der Region durch die schrittweise Industrialisierung und Investitionstätigkeit, wie z. B. im ehemaligen Bezirk Prešov in den Jahren 1949—1953: Investitionen in Höhe von 129 187 000 Kčs 1949 stiegen 1953 auf 335 841 000 (Bajcura 1967, 135). Der Aufschwung von Industrie und Landwirtschaft zeigte sich im zunehmenden Beschäftigungsgrad der Bevölkerung, dem Ansteigen des Lebensstandards und des allgemeinen Bildungsniveaus wie auch im Wandel der Sozialstruktur der Bevölkerung: Von insgesamt 419 100 Einwohnern des Bezirks Prešov waren 1949 3746, 1953 bereits 13 157 Menschen in der Industrie beschäftigt (Bajcura 1967, 137, 143). Es kam zu einer raschen Entwicklung der ukrainischen Schulen. Anfang der 50er Jahre entstanden in Prešov zwei Lehrerausbildungsstätten — die Höhere pädagogische Schule und die Pädagogische Hochschule. Später wurden die beiden Hochschulen in die Pavel Jozef Šafárik-Universität integriert (als philosophische und pädagogische Fakultäten), die u. a. Ukrainischlehrer sowie Fachleute für den Kulturbereich ausbildet und die Ukraine-Forschung organisiert. Von besonderer Tragweite für die Stärkung des Nationalbewußtseins und der nationalen Kultur war die Gründung des Ukrainischen Nationaltheaters (1945), des professionellen Ukrainischen Volksensembles (1956), des Museums der ukrainischen Kultur in Svidník (1950) und der Ukrainischen Redaktion des Tschechoslowakischen Rundfunks in Prešov (1945). Zu einem positiven Faktor in der Entwicklung des kulturellen und gesellschaftlichen Lebens der ukrainischen Bevölkerung sind die vom „Kulturverband der ukrainischen Werktätigen" (gegründet 1954) organisierten Volkskunstgruppen geworden. Erfolgreich ist ebenfalls die Tätigkeit des Prešover Verlags: Bis 1992 sind 465 künstlerische und wissenschaftliche Veröffentlichungen und ca. 1000 Lehrbücher erschienen.

Eine bedeutende Rolle in der Entwicklung von Kultur und Nation der Ukrainer spielten die griechisch-katholische Kirche und die orthodoxe Kirche. Die Restriktionen gegen die griechisch-katholische Kirche in der ČSR im Jahre 1950 sowie ihre Aufhebung nach 1968 führten in einigen Pfarrgemeinden zu offenen Auseinandersetzungen zwischen den Gläubigen. Der mit den Sprachfragen verbundene

Tab. 208.1: Einwohnerzahl der Ukrainer in drei ostslowakischen Komitaten laut offiziellen statistischen Angaben

Komitat / Jahr	1846	1870	1890	1900	1910	1921
Zemplin	92 934	59 738	31 036	34 836	39 083	51 543
Šariš	66 191	56 461	35 019	33 937	35 500	24 632
Zips	26 196	24 125	17 518	13 913	12 327	8 097
Insgesamt	187 321	140 324	83 573	82 666	89 910	84 272

Streit der beiden Konfessionen beschleunigte den Entnationalisierungsprozeß der ukrainischen Bevölkerung in der Ostslowakei.

4. Statistik und Ethnoprofil

4.1. Laut statistischen Angaben aus dem Jahre 1786 lebten in den ungarischen Nordkomitaten insgesamt 174 693 Ruthenen (Ukrainer): 84 844 in Zemplín, 45 300 in Šariš, 17 150 in der Zips (Spiš), 17 157 in Abau, 2591 in Gemer und 1249 in Torňa (Baran 1990, 7). Spätere statistische Angaben weisen eine abnehmende Zahl der ukrainischen Bevölkerung in den einzelnen Komitaten nach (Vanát 1973, 165) (Tabelle 208.1).

Im Vergleich zu 1921 bekannten sich als Ruthenen (Ukrainer) 84 272 Einwohner; bei der Volkszählung 1930 erhöhte sich ihre Zahl auf 90 824 (Mazúr 1974, 447). Auswanderung, innere Migration und verschiedene politische Umstände führen zu einem Rückgang der ukrainischen Bevölkerung in der Slowakei: 1961 – 35 411 Einwohner (ibid., 450), 1970 – 38 960, 1980 – 36 850 (Srb 1988, 70) und 1990 sind es 30 784 Einwohner (Výsledky 1991). In der damaligen ČSFR verzeichnet die offizielle Statistik 18 648 Ruthenen und 20 654 Ukrainer (insgesamt 39 302) (ibid.).

4.2. Für die ukrainische Bevölkerung in der Slowakei wurde die offizielle ethnische Bezeichnung Rusín verwendet (die Bevölkerung selbst nannte sich bereits seit dem 16. Jh. Rusnaky). In der Zeit der mitteleuropäischen Nationenbildung (18.–19. Jh.) strebten die Ruthenen im damaligen Ungarn eine Einheit mit den „Kleinrussen" (damalige offizielle Benennung der Ukrainer) an; dem Vorbild der Schriftsteller Galiziens folgend wurde die Alltags-Sprache (d. h. die ukrainischen Mundarten) im künstlerischen Schrifttum, in Schulen usw. verwendet. Die Vertreter der „nationalen" Ausrichtung (O. Duchnovyč, A. Kralickyj, O. Pavlovyč) waren bestrebt, eine Karpatenraum-Variante der ukrainischen Schriftsprache zu schaffen. Derartige Bemühungen scheiterten teilweise daran, daß bei bestimmten Teilen der Intellektuellen nach der Revolution von 1848 die Orientierung nach Moskau die Oberhand gewann, wobei das Russische als die Schriftsprache galt, während die Vertreter der „ruthenischen" Strömung (Strypskyj 1907, 15; Vološyn 1907) das sog. *Jazyčije*, ein Gemisch von ukrainischen Mundarten, Kirchenslawisch, Russisch und z. T. Ungarisch, gebrauchten. Der Sprachstreit nach 1848 wurde in der Zeit der ČSR (d. h. nach 1918) zunehmend stärker; manche qualitativen Änderungen innerhalb der einzelnen Sprachrichtungen sind allerdings eingetreten. Nach 1945 werden in der Region die beiden Schriftsprachen – das Russische und das Ukrainische – parallel verwendet. Das Nebeneinander der beiden Sprachen dauert bis 1953 an. Im selben Jahr wurde die ukrainische Schriftsprache als Unterrichtssprache in den Schulen und dem gesamten Kulturbereich der Ukrainer der Ostslowakei eingeführt. Ein bestimmter Teil der Intelligenz strebt seit 1989 die Kodifizierung der lokalen ukrainischen Mundarten bzw. des Interdialekts an. Die Kodifizierungsbemühungen um die Schaffung einer ruthenischen Schriftsprache (vgl. Paňko 1992, 17–21) gehen mit den Bestrebungen einher, die Identität einer spezifischen „ruthenischen Nation" zu sichern. Infolge dieser Bestrebungen flammten die gegenwärtigen Auseinandersetzungen um die Schriftsprache und die Nationalität der Angehörigen dieser Ethnie erneut auf. Die andauernden Zwistigkeiten haben v. a. auf das Schulwesen negative Auswirkungen, wo die ukrainische Unterrichtssprache durch das Slowakische ersetzt wird.

5. Soziolinguistische Situation

In der Vergangenheit wurden in den Schulen, der Literatur und der Publizistik das Russische, die „nationale" Sprache oder das sog. *Jazyčije* verwendet (vgl. 4.). In den übrigen Bereichen konnten sich die ungarische Schriftsprache, das Latein und später die slowakische Schriftsprache behaupten. Im Alltagsverkehr werden ukrainische Mundarten gesprochen, in Schulen, im Bereich der Kultur das schriftsprachliche Ukrainisch und im offiziellen Verkehr findet das schriftsprachliche Slowakisch seine Verwendung. Die slowakisch-ukrainische Zweisprachigkeit ist im Prinzip einseitig. Beide Sprachen beherrschen nur Ukrainer. Das Ukrainische als eine Sprache der nationalen Minderheit genießt im slowakisch-ukrainischen Bilinguismus ein geringeres gesellschaftliches Prestige, und in sozialer Hinsicht kommt sie ebenfalls weniger zur Geltung als das Slowakische. Die mittlere und die jüngere Generation der ukrainischen Bevölkerung beherrscht ukrainische Mundarten und größtenteils auch die ukrainische Schriftsprache, während die ältere Landbevölkerung Mundart spricht. Diejenigen Ukrainer, die ihre Ausbildung an den ehemaligen „moskauphilen" bzw. an den gegenwärtigen slowakischen Schulen erhielten, betrachten das Slowakische als ihre Schriftsprache.

6. Sprachpolitische Situation

Die ukrainische Minderheit in der Slowakei hat in der Vergangenheit eine sehr komplizierte Entwicklung durchlaufen. Mit der Gründung der Tschechoslowakischen Republik (1918) wurden für die nationale Entwicklung der ukrainischen Bevölkerung dennoch günstigere Bedingungen geschaffen. Die Verfassung der Tschechoslowakischen Republik erklärte das Recht aller Bürger, im privaten wie öffentlichen Bereich, in sämtlichen Veröffentlichungen u. dgl. eine Sprache ihrer Wahl zu verwenden und garantierte einen angemessenen Unterricht in der Muttersprache der Schulkinder (Art. 31 der 1921 Verfassung); diese Grundsätze blieben jedoch überwiegend nur Ankündigungen (Bajcura 1967, 24, 65). In der Tschechoslowakei der Nachkriegszeit waren die Rechte der Bürger ukrainischer wie auch anderer nationaler Minderheiten in der Verfassung vom 9. Mai nicht kodifiziert. Bereits am 1. März 1945 wurde indes der Ukrainische Nationalrat der Prjaševščina gegründet, der sich zum Ziel setzte, für nationale, kulturelle und soziale Rechte der Ukrainer in der ČSR einzutreten. Für die Durchsetzung dieser Ziele fehlten dem Rat jedoch die entsprechenden Rechtsgrundlagen. Spezielle, auf das Sichern einer freien Nationalitätenentfaltung ausgerichtete Gesetze standen bis zum Jahre 1960 noch aus. Die 1960 durchgeführte territoriale Verwaltungsreform und die anschließenden Änderungen der Bildungspolitik haben den Zerfallsprozeß des ukrainischen Schulsystems in Gang gesetzt. Innerhalb von 4 Jahren (1960–1963) gingen insgesamt 161 Schulen von der ukrainischen zur slowakischen Unterrichtssprache über (Vanát 1992, 11). Beschleunigt wurde dies auch durch die Aufhebung von einklassigen Schulen mit niedriger Schülerzahl in der 1.–5. Klasse. Diese Situation hat sich sogar nach 1989 nicht geändert. Die Verwendung der ukrainischen Schriftsprache ist in der Slowakischen Republik durch das Sprachgesetz von 1991 geregelt. In der Verwaltung sowie dem öffentlichen Verkehr wird ausschließlich das Slowakische verwendet. Es gibt mehrere Zeitschriften in ukrainisch: die Wochenzeitung „*Nove žyt't'a*", die Monatsschrift „*Družno vpered*", die Kinderzeitschrift „*Veselka*" und die literarisch-künstlerische und publizistische Zweimonatsschrift „*Dukl'a*".

Die gegenwärtige Verfassung der Slowakischen Republik garantiert jedem das Recht, über seine Nationalität frei zu entscheiden. Zugleich wird jegliche Beeinträchtigung dieser Entscheidungsfreiheit wie auch jede Art von Zwang, der auf Entnationalisierung abzielt, untersagt (Art. 12, Abs. 3).

7. Allgemeines kontaktlinguistisches Porträt

7.1. Bei Sprachkontakten in der Ostslowakei dominieren die Mundarten. Die Entwicklung der ukrainischen Mundarten dieser Region wird durch die Kontakte zu ostslowakischen und polnischen, in geringerem Maße auch zu ungarischen und rumänischen (walachischen) Mundarten markiert. Die Anfänge der ukrainisch-slowakischen und ukrainisch-polnischen Sprachkontakte reichen bis in das 13.–

14. Jahrhundert zurück. Ukrainische Mundarten standen im intensiven Kontakt zu den ostslowakischen. Es handelt sich dabei um Kontakte verwandter Mundarten, die jedoch zu den verschiedenen Sprachzweigen des Slawischen — nämlich West- und Ostslawisch — gehören.

Die Laut- und Formenlehre der ukrainischen Mundarten des Südkarpatenraums ist relativ gut (Verchratskyj 1899; Paňkevyč 1938; Latta 1991 u. a.), die slowakisch-ukrainischen sprachlichen Wechselwirkungen sind dagegen bislang nur unzureichend erforscht worden. Als phonetische und morphologische Erscheinungen des Slowakischen in ukrainischen Mundarten werden folgende Elemente betrachtet: (1) Der Typ *xblrbet, kblrve, hblrmit* (das bl ist dem russ. bl ähnlich) im westlichen Teil des ukrainischen Mundartareals, wo das *rъ* eine ähnliche Entwicklung erfuhr, wie es in slowakischen Mundarten der Fall war, vgl. *xerbet, kervi, hermi*. In den östlichen ukrainischen Mundarten wurde die Lautgruppe *rъ* zu *r + Vokal: xrebet, krovi* usw. (2) Die Existenz der Lautgruppen *trat, tlat (zdravia, zlato)* anstelle der Vollautformen (*zdorovia, zoloto*). Diese Erscheinung findet sich nur in geringer Zahl bei aus dem Slowakischen übernommenen Wörtern, weshalb sie für ukrainische Mundarten nicht typisch ist. (3) Das Suffix *-me* statt *-mo* in der 1. Pers. Pl. Präs.: *xodyme* statt *xodymo* (das y repräsentiert das ukr. и). (4) Die Endung *-ma, -ima* im Instr. Pl. der Pronomina und Adjektive (*tblma, dobrblma* statt *tblmy, dobrblmy*). (5) Das Präfix *da-* statt des ukrainischen *de-* in einigen Pronomina und Adverbien: *daxto, dakoly* statt *dexto, dekoly* u. a. (Stieber 1974, 478 f.). (6) Depalatalisierung von *š, ž* (*šbllo, žblto* statt *šylo, žyto*). (7) Die Formen *jeden* statt *odyn* (Paňkevyč 1938, 403). (8) Depalatalisierung von *d', t', ň, s', c'* im Wortauslaut in den Mundarten im Gebiet zwischen den Flüssen Ladomyrka und Poprad: *čel'ad, pjat, osin, dnes, zajac* gegenüber *čel'ad', pjat', osiň, dnes', zajac'* in den Mundarten östlich vom Fluß Ladomyrka. (9) Die Endung *-ox* im Gen. Pl. der maskulinen Substantive in den Mundarten westlich vom Fluß Laborec: *do xlopox, v doktorox, dvox vojakox* statt *do xlopiu̯, do doktoriu̯, dvox vojakiu̯* (Dzendzelivskyj 1973, 5 ff).

Einige Forscher untersuchen die Isoglossen gemeinsamer Erscheinungen in ukrainischen, ostslowakischen und polnischen Mundarten, ohne ihre Herkunft in Betracht zu ziehen. Aus einer Vielzahl von Gemeinsamkeiten auf lautlicher und morphologischer Ebene (Paňkevyč — 36 Züge, 1958, 173 ff; Dzendzelivskyj — 58 Züge, 1973, 5 ff) gehört nur ein geringer Teil zu den Systemerscheinungen der ukrainischen Mundarten (vgl. Beispiele 1, 3—9).

Slowakisch-ukrainische Sprachkontakte finden ihren Ausdruck am prägnantesten im Wortschatz der ukrainischen Mundarten. Stieber (1974, 479) zufolge gibt es sehr viele solcher Wörter, die sowohl aus dem Polnischen wie auch aus dem Slowakischen übernommen worden sein könnten. Dies belegt er durch folgende Beispiele: *pec, prypecok, jelen, jeden, teras, kel'o, povala, heu* usw., während er als typisch slowakisch die Formen *harda xvyl'a, tuni, dzecko, statok, hei, lem, hača, pal'unka* u. v. a. ansieht. Dzendzelivskyj (1969, 15—168) untersuchte 200 ukrainisch-polnisch-slowakische und 63 ukrainisch-slowakische Parallelen, wobei eine bedeutende Gruppe die Slowakismen bilden: *belavyj, blana, vec, hračka, kral', klanyca, lada, cmar, kutač* u. a. Als ukrainische Rückwirkungen auf die ostslowakischen Mundarten werden der Vokalwechsel *-o-* für das harte Jer, des weiteren die Formen *dobroho, dobromu* gegenüber den erwartbaren Formen *dobrého dobrému* (Krajčovič 1988, 31, 116) und die Endung *-ou* im Inst. Sg. fem. (Latta 1991, 170) betrachtet. Insgesamt ist festzustellen, daß der Einfluß des Ukrainischen auf die slowakischen Mundarten noch unzureichend untersucht wurde.

7.2. Die Kontakte zwischen ukrainischen und slowakischen Schriftsprachen entwickeln sich seit Ende der 20er Jahre mit der Verwendung der ukrainischen Schriftsprache. Interferenzerscheinungen treten vor allem im Wortschatz des Ukrainischen auf. Die Häufigkeit der Interferenzerscheinungen ist dabei in der Alltagssprache viel höher (Žluktenko 1966, 58). In der gesprochenen Form des Standardukrainischen gibt es eine beträchtliche Anzahl von Wörtern aus dem Slowakischen, beispielsweise *majetok* (ukr. *hospodarstvo*), *nabor* (ukr. *verbuvaňňa*), *konfekcia* (ukr. *hotovyj od'ah*), *cina* (ukr. *nahoroda*) u. a. m. In der geschriebenen Form kommt es zu bestimmten Übernahmen aus dem Slowakischen, so z. B. Wörter zum Benennen neuer Begriffe. Für die Sprache der Nachkriegszeit sind die Ausdrücke charakteristisch, die Neuerungen in verschiedenen Bereichen des damaligen gesellschaftlich-politischen, wirtschaftlichen und kulturellen Lebens benennen, z. B. Federal'ni zbory (slow. *Federálne zhromaždenie*), *krajovyj nacional'nyj komitet* (slow. *krajský národný výbor*), *mostarňa* (slow. *mostáreň*), *kul'turnyj dim* (slow. *kultúrny dom*, schriftsprachlich ukr. *budynok kul'tury*) u. ä.

In der Formenlehre geht es um den interparadigmatischen Ausgleich von *a*-Stämmen und *o*-Stämmen der Substantive (*sluhovi* statt *sluzi* im Dat. Sg.; *problemiv* statt *problem* im Gen. Pl., vgl. slow. *problémov*) wie auch um die Übernahme der slowakischen Verbpräfixe *vy-, z-, do-, u-*: vgl. *vymodel'uvaty, zharmonizuvaty, dorišyty, upriamyty* statt *model'uvaty, harmonizuvaty, rišaty* u. ä. (Štec 1969, 150).

Relativ hoch ist die Zahl von syntaktischen Interferenzen, die sich v. a. in Form von Modellnachahmungen des Slowakischen, in der Übernahme slowakischer präpositionaler und präpositionsloser Wortgruppenstrukturen, in einer slowakisch ausgeprägten Prädikat-Objekt-Kongruenz u. dgl. verdeutlichen, vgl. *zajty k dekanovi* statt *zajty do dekana, besida do form roboty* statt *besida pro formy roboty* u. a. m.

Beweise für eine lautliche Interferenz fehlen bisher. In beiden Mundarten, sowohl der ukrainischen als auch der slowakischen, aus denen die Übernahmen in das Standardukrainische erfolgen, sind gewisse wechselseitige Einflüsse zu beobachten, so z. B. das Vorkommen des sog. mittleren slowakischen *-l-* vor *-y (chodyly, buly/buli)*, eine schwächere Hervorhebung betonter Silben sowie der Einfluß der slowakischen Satzintonation auf das gesprochene Ukrainisch (Štec 1992, 35 ff).

Bei der Verwendung des schriftsprachlichen Ukrainischen in der Slowakei wird am Grundsatz der Normeinhaltung auf allen Sprachebenen festgehalten. Ausnahmen werden nur noch im Wortschatz zugelassen, wo es gilt, die Benennungen örtlicher Realien zu verwenden. Deshalb kommt hier sämtliche in der Ukraine verwendete linguistische Literatur zur Geltung: Ukrajinskyj pravopys, 2. Aufl. 1961, 3. Aufl. 1990; Slovnyk ukrajinskoji movy, 11 Bde., Kyjiv 1970−1980, die Grammatikdarstellungen der ukrainischen Schriftsprache wie auch Publikationen der künstlerischen und Fachliteratur.

8. Kritische Wertung der verwendeten Quellen und Literatur

Die Untersuchungen der slowakisch-ukrainischen Interferenzerscheinungen im Bereich der Mundarten wurden bislang im Grunde genommen auf die Lautlehre und nur z. T. auf den Wortschatz ausgerichtet. Eine Analyse der einzelnen Typen lexikalischer Interferenz in der Sprache nach 1945, d. h. in der Zeit der intensivsten Sprachkontakte, sowie Forschungen zur Syntax stehen noch aus. Gegenwärtig sind für die Forschung der slowakisch-ukrainischen wie ukrainisch-slowakischen Mundartkontakte gute materielle Voraussetzungen gegeben, vgl. u. a. den vierbändigen *Atlas slovenského jazyka* (Štolc/Buffa/Habovštiak, Eds., 1968−1984) und mehrere regionale Atlanten ukrainischer Mundarten.

Es wäre wünschenswert, die bisherigen Forschungen zu den slowakisch-ukrainischen Sprachkontakten fortzuführen wie auch weitere Gruppenforschungen unter Anwendung mehrerer Forschungsmethoden zu realisieren, die die Herkunft der einzelnen Interferenzerscheinungen feststellen könnten. Zu den aktuellen Vorhaben sind die Erforschung des slowakisch-ukrainischen Sprachgrenzgebietes und der Rückwirkungen der ukrainischen Mundarten auf die slowakischen zu zählen. Die Untersuchungen zur Problematik der slowakisch-ukrainischen Sprachkontakte, der slowakisch-ukrainischen Zweisprachigkeit und der Interferenz auf der Ebene der beiden Schriftsprachen befinden sich z. Z. in den Anfängen. Durchgeführt werden sie von den Mitarbeitern des „Lehrstuhls für ukrainische Sprache und Literatur" und des „Lehrstuhls für slowakische Sprache und Literatur" der „Pavel Jozef Šafárik-Universität" in Prešov.

9. Bibliographie (in Auswahl)

Bajcura, Ivan (1967): *Ukrajinská otázka v ČSSR* [Die ukrainische Frage in der ČSSR], Kaschau.

Baran, Oleksander (1990): *Narysy istorii Prjaševščyny* [Abriß der Geschichte von „Prjašivščyna"], Vinnipeg.

Dzendzelivskyj, Josyp (1973): *Dialektna vzajemodija ukrajinskoji movy z inšymy slovjanskymy v karpatskomu areali* [Dialekteinflüsse der ukrainischen Sprache und der slawischen Sprachen in der Karpaten-Region], Kiew.

Dzendzelivskyj, Josyp (1969): *Ukrajinsko-zachidnoslovjanski leksyčni paraleli* [Ukrainisch-westslawische lexikalische Parallelen], Kiew.

Haraksim, L'udovít (1961): *K sociálnym a kultúrnym dejinám Ukrajincov na Slovensku do roku 1867* [Zur Sozial- und Kulturgeschichte der Ukrainer in der Slowakei bis zum Jahre 1867], Bratislava.

Krajčovič, Rudolf (1988): *Vývin spisovného jazyka a dialektológia* [Die Entwicklung der Schriftsprache und die Dialektologie], Bratislava.

Latta, Vasyl' (1991): *Atlas ukrajinskych hovoriv Schidnoji Slovaččyny* [Atlas der ukrainischen Mundarten der Ostslowakei], Bratislava.

Latta, Vasyl' (1979–1981): „O klasifikacii ukrajinskich govorov" [Zur Klassifikation ukrainischer Mundarten]. In: *Naukovi zapysky*, Novak, M. (Ed.), Prjašiv, 119–130.

Mazúr, Emil (1974): „Národnostné zloženie" [Nationalitätenstruktur]. In: *Slovensko 3, L'ud, I. Čast'*, Plesník, P. a kol. (Eds.), Bratislava, 440–462.

Paňkevyč, Ivan (1958): „Do pytaňňa henezy ukrajinskych lemkivskych hovoriv" [Zur Herkunftsfrage der ukrainischen Lemkauer Mundarten]. In: *Slavjanskaja filologija. Sbornik statej* 2, Moskau, 164–199.

Paňkevyč, Ivan (1938): *Ukrajinski hovory Pidkarpatskoji Rusi i sumežnych oblastej* [Ukrainische Mundarten von Transkarpatien und den angrenzenden Gebieten], Prag.

Paňko, Jurij (1992): „Normy rusynskoho pravopisu" [Orthographienormen des Ruthenischen]. In: *Narodny novinky*, 17–21, 1–36, Prjašov.

Srb, Vladimír (1988): „Demografický profil ukrajinského obyvatel'stva v ČSFR" [Demographisches Profil der ukrainischen Bevölkerung in der ČSFR]. In: *Zpravodaj koordinované sítě vědeckých informací pro etnografii a folkloristiku* 6, Prag.

Stieber, Zdisław (1974): „Wpływ polski i słowacki na gwary Lemków" [Der polnische und slowakische Einfluß auf die Lemkauer Mundarten]. In: *Swiat językowy Słowian*, Warschau, 474–479.

Bileňkyj (Stripskyj Hijador) (1907): *Staršá ruska pismennost' na Ugorščyni* [Älteres russisches Schrifttum in Ungarn], Ungvar.

Štec, Mykola (1969): *Literaturna mova ukrajinciv Zakarpat't'a i Schidnoji Slovaččyny* [Literatursprache der Ukrainer in Transkarpatien und in der Ostslowakei], Bratislava.

Štec, Mykola (1992): „Funkcionuvaňňa ukrajinskoji literaturnoji movy v ČSFR" [Die Rolle der ukrainischen Literatursprache in der ČSFR]. In: *Dukl'a* 3, Prjašiv, 32–39.

Štolc, Jozef/Buffa, Ferdinand/Habovštiak, Anton (Eds.) (1968–1984): *Atlas slovenského jazyka* [Atlas der slowakischen Sprache], 4 Bde., Bratislava.

Ústava Československej republiky [Die Verfassung der Tschechoslowakischen Republik] (1921), Prag.

Vanat, Ivan/Ryčalka, Mychajlo/Čuma, Andrij (1992): *Do pytaň, pisl'avojennoho rozvytku, sučasnoho stanu ta perspektyv ukrajinskoho škil'nyctva v Slovaččyni* [Zu Fragen der Entwicklung des gegenwärtigen Standes sowie der Perspektiven des ukrainischen Schulwesens der Nachkriegszeit in der Slowakei], Prjašiv.

Vanat, Ivan (1979; 1985): *Narysy novitňoji istoriji ukrajinciv Schidnoji Slovaččyny. I. 1918–1938; II. 1938–1948* [Abriß der jüngsten Geschichte der Ukrainer der Ostslowakei], Bratislava.

Vanat, Ivan (1973): „Škil'na sprava na Prjaševščyni v period domjunchenskoji Čecho-Slovaččyny" [Das Schulwesen in der „Prjašivščyna" in der Tschechoslowakei vor dem Münchner Abkommen]. In: *Z mynuloho i sučasnoho ukrajinciv Čechoslovaččyny*, Rudlovčak, O. (Ed.), Bratislava, 159–195.

Varsík, Branislav (1958): „O pôvode a etymológii niektorých miestnych názvov na východnom Slovensku" [Zur Herkunft und Etymologie einiger Toponyma in der Ostslowakei]. In: *Sborník Filozofickej fakulty Univerzity Komenského* 9, Paulíny, E. (Ed.), Bratislava.

Verchratskýj, Ivan (1899; 1901–1902): *Znadoby dl'a piznaňňa uhorsko-ruskych hovoriv. T. I.–II.* [Quellen zum Studium der ungarisch-ruthenischen Mundarten]. In: *Zapysky Naukovoho tovarystva im. Ševčenka*, Bd. XXVII–XXX, Bd. XL, XLIV, XLV, Lemberg.

Vološin, Augustin (1907): *Gyakorlati Kisorosz (Ruthén) nyelvtan* [Praktische kleinrussische (ruthenische) Grammatik], Ungvar.

„Výsledky sčítania l'udu" [Ergebnisse der Volkszählung] (1991). In: *Pravda 151*, 2, Bratislava.

Zatovkaňuk, Mikolaš (1982): „K sociolingvističeskoj charakteristike slovacko-ukrajinskogo bilingvizma" [Zur soziolinguistischen Charakteristik des slowakisch-ukrainischen Bilinguismus]. In: *Bulletin ruského jazyka a literatury* 24, 33–56.

Žluktenko, Jurij (1966): *Movni kontakty* [Sprachkontakte], Kiew.

Mikuláš Štec, Prešov (Slowakei)

209. Slowakisch—Tschechisch

1. Geographie und Demographie
2. Geschichte
3. Politik, Wirtschaft und allgemeine kulturelle Lage
4. Statistik und Ethnoprofil
5. Soziolinguistische Lage
6. Sprachpolitische Lage
7. Allgemeines kontaktlinguistisches Porträt
8. Zur Forschungslage
9. Bibliographie (in Auswahl)

1. Geographie und Demographie

Die Slowakische Republik (SR) grenzt an die Tschechische Republik im Westen. Die gemeinsame Grenze der SR und der Tschechischen Republik ist 265 km lang. Auf dem Gebiet der Slowakischen Republik (Slowakei) leben laut Volkszählung vom Jahre 1991 5 274 335 Einwohner. 85,69% der Einwohner sind slowakischer Nationalität (4 519 328 Personen); die Zahl der Bürger tschechischer Nationalität (52 884 Personen) beträgt etwa 1% der Bevölkerung. Die Bürger tschechischer Nationalität bilden auf dem Gebiet der Slowakei keine geschlossene Enklave; sie leben relativ zerstreut über das ganze Gebiet, vorwiegend in großen Städten wie Bratislava (Preßburg; Hauptstadt der SR), Košice (Kaschau) bzw. in den Städten mit militärischen Garnisonen wie Prešov, Trenčín (Trentschin), Liptovský Mikuláš, Poprad u. a. (vgl. 4.); → Sprachenkarte K.

2. Geschichte

2.1. Archäologische Befunde beweisen, daß das heutige Gebiet der Slowakei im 5.—6. Jahrhundert von slawischen Stämmen nach und nach besiedelt wurde. Alte Namen einzelner, auf dem slowakischen Gebiet lebender Stämme blieben nicht erhalten. Im 1. Drittel des 9. Jahrhunderts entstand das erste gemeinsame Staatsgebilde der Vorfahren von Tschechen und Slowaken — das Großmährische Reich. Bei der Entwicklung der eigenständigen slowakischen und tschechischen Nationen und Sprachen spielten inner- und außersprachliche Faktoren eine Rolle. Die Entstehung des tschechischen (Ende des 9. Jh.s) und ungarischen (Anfang des 10. Jh.s) frühfeudalen Staates bot die äußeren Bedingungen für den Integrationsprozeß der tschechischen und slowakischen Nation. Die sprachlichen Phänomene, die als Ganzes für slowakische Mundarten kennzeichnend waren, wurden zu innersprachlichen ethnischen differenzierenden Merkmalen der slowakischen Sprache im Verhältnis zu anderen slawischen Sprachen. Das Slowakische weist im Vergleich zum Tschechischen z. B. folgende Unterschiede auf: für das Urslawische *dj* steht im Slowakischen *dž*, im Tschechischen *z* (*priadza—příze* Garn), für die Anlautgruppe *jь-* im Slowakischen *i-*, im Tschechischen *j-* oder *je-* (*idem, ihla — jdu, jehla* ich gehe, Nadel), für Lautgruppen *rъ, rь, lъ, lь* stehen im Slowakischen die silbischen *r̥, l̥*, im Tschechischen oft *re, le* (*krv, blcha — krev, blecha* Blut, Floh), im Slowakischen wurde nicht die Veränderung *r > ř* (*more—moře* Meer) und der Umlaut *ä > ě > e* (*duša, desat' — duše, deset* Seele, zehn) durchgeführt, u. a. m.

2.2. Nach dem Zerfall des Großmährischen Reiches besaßen die Slowaken lange Zeit kein eigenes politisches und kulturelles Zentrum als Ausgangspunkt für die weitere kulturelle und sprachliche Entwicklung. In dieser Hinsicht entstand in Böhmen eine günstigere Situation, indem Prag zu einem solchen Zentrum wurde. Mit dem politischen und wirtschaftlichen Aufschwung des tschechischen Staates hängt die Entwicklung der tschechischen Sprache zusammen, die auch in der Slowakei an Einfluß gewinnt. Tschechisch wird schon seit dem 14. Jahrhundert vor allem vom slowakischen Bürgertum gesprochen, das die Teilnahme an der Verwaltung der Städte anstrebt. Die tschechische Sprache konnte wegen ihrer Verständlichkeit von den Slowaken adaptiert und mannigfaltig slowakisiert werden. Ein Bild der Sprachkontakte und Interferenzen des Slowakischen und Tschechischen im 15.—18. Jahrhundert vermittelt das „Historisches Wörterbuch der slowakischen Sprache" (Majtán 1991, 1992). In der Epoche der Konstituierung moderner slawischer Sprachen (d. h. in der Zeit der sog. nationalen Wiedergeburt) war die tschechische Sprache bereits eine reiche, mit Traditionen aus dem 14. Jahrhundert. J. Dobrovskýs (1753—1829) Modell stützte sich auf eine gepflegte, klassische Sprache der älteren Epoche. Zur Anfangsphase der Wiedergeburt in der Slowakei gehört die breit konzipierte Kodifizierung der Schriftsprache durch A. Bernolák (1762—1813) in der 2. Hälfte des 18. Jahrhunderts. Einen neuen erfolgreichen

Schritt zur Kodifizierung der Schriftsprache machte die Generation von Ľ. Štúr (1815−1856). Ľ. Štúr sah den nationalen Geist vor allem im grammatischen Bau der Sprache, und deshalb widersetzte er sich nicht den lexikalischen Entlehnungen aus dem Tschechischen (insbesondere im Bereich des Fachwortschatzes).

Nach dem österreichisch-ungarischen Ausgleich (1867) verstärkte sich die Madjarisierung der anderen (besonders der slawischen) in Ungarn lebenden ethnischen Gruppen. Das slowakische Volk formierte und behauptete sich in Ungarn als eine moderne Nation trotz der Unterdrückungspolitik seitens der Ungarn. Zu Beginn des 20. Jahrhunderts waren die Slowaken entschlossen, zusammen mit den Tschechen einen freien Staat auf dem Prinzip der Selbstbestimmung zu bilden. Die Tschechoslowakei entstand im Herbst 1918 nach dem Zerfall der österreichisch-ungarischen Monarchie als einer der Nachfolgestaaten des Ersten Weltkrieges. Die Sprachbeziehungen und Kontakte des Slowakischen und Tschechischen nahmen in diesem neuen Staatsgebilde andere quantitative sowie qualitative Dimensionen an. Von 1939 bis 1945 existierte die Slowakei als ein selbständiger Staat. 1945−1992 war sie ein Bestandteil der Tschechoslowakei. Am 1. 1. 1993 entstanden auf verfassungsmäßigem Wege zwei selbständige Staaten, die Tschechische Republik und die Slowakische Republik.

3. Politik, Wirtschaft und allgemeine kulturelle Lage

Die Entwicklung der Tschechen und Slowaken im gemeinsamen Staat war nicht ausgewogen. Die Slowakei war 1918 im Vergleich zu Tschechien politisch und kulturell rückständiger; die Zahl der slowakischen Bevölkerung lag wesentlich niedriger, die Wirtschaftskraft und das Nationaleinkommen der Slowakei waren im Vergleich zu den tschechischen Ländern sehr niedrig. Ein Positivum im Vergleich zum vorherigen Zustand stellte die Existenz der demokratischen Rechte dar, die einen politischen und nationalen Aufschwung ermöglichten. Dank des Schulsystems stieg auch das allgemeine Bildungsniveau der Slowaken; es blieb jedoch noch lange im Schatten der entwickelten tschechischen Wissenschaft und Kultur.

Die Beziehungen zwischen den Tschechen und Slowaken wurden von der Staatsdoktrin des tschechoslowakischen Volkes und der tschechoslowakischen Sprache (vgl. 6.1.), die die Tschechen und Slowaken als „Zweige" einer Nation auffaßte (offiziell wurde diese Doktrin erst im Jahre 1945 nach dem Zweiten Weltkrieg aufgehoben) problematisiert. Die Geschichte des slowakischen Volkes und dessen Sprache wurde im Bildungssystem oft entstellt und einseitig präsentiert; hervorgehoben wurde vor allem das Fehlen herausragender Persönlichkeiten. Die Idee der Brüderschaft von Tschechen und Slowaken ging im Sinne des „Tschechoslowakismus" bis hin in die mythenhafte Beziehung zur Slowakei über. Stellenweise handelte es sich sogar um eine Bevormundung wie zwischen einem älteren und einem jüngeren Bruder, wodurch beide Völker in ihrer Beziehung als nicht gleichberechtigt festgelegt wurden (Lorenzová 1990, 232 f). Die neuesten soziologischen Ermittlungen bezeugen, daß Überbleibsel dieser Einstellungen bis heute überdauert haben.

4. Statistik und Ethnoprofil

4.1. Die ethnische Gemeinschaft der Slowaken wurde durch das gemeinsame Gebiet und die gemeinsame (mundartlich differenzierte) Sprache charakterisiert. In religiöser Hinsicht haben sie sich dem westeuropäischen Christentum angeschlossen. Laut Volkszählung von 1991 gehörten 3 187 383 Slowaken der römisch-katholischen, 419 987 der evangelischen, 178 733 der griechisch-katholischen und 34 376 der griechisch-orthodoxen Konfession an. Die Auffassung der ethnischen Gemeinschaft der Slowaken und der slowakischen Sprache ist, im Gegensatz zur tschechischen Gemeinschaft und Sprache, von der Tatsache determiniert, daß die Slowaken in der Vergangenheit nie in einem selbständigen Staatsgebilde lebten.

Das Slowakische und Tschechische sind zwei eigenständige Nationalsprachen, die sich in einer jahrhundertelangen kontinuierlichen Entwicklung herausgebildet und gefestigt haben. Es sind zwei eng verwandte westslawische Sprachen, die sich in einem unmittelbar angrenzenden mitteleuropäischen Kontaktraum und später in einem über 70 Jahre währenden gemeinsamen Staatsgebilde entwickelt haben. Die Verwandtschaft und gegenseitige Verständlichkeit des Slowakischen und Tschechischen finden in der Kommunikation der Tschechen und Slowaken untereinander ihren spezifischen Ausdruck. Beide Seiten gebrauchen ihre eigene Sprache, und die Kommunikation kommt ohne größere Schwierigkeiten zustande. Tschechen, die in der Slowakischen Republik leben, verwenden demzufolge als Verständigungsmittel überwiegend das Tschechische. Die konkrete Sprachsituation sowie weitere außersprachliche Faktoren (z. B. die mit der Ausbildung, dem Alter, der Dauer des Aufenthalts in der Slowakei u. ä. zusammenhängende Stufe der Beherrschung des Slowakischen) determinieren jedoch die Entstehung von mehreren Sprachkontaktformen.

4.2. Zur tschechischen Nationalität bekannten sich bei der letzten Volkszählung 52 884 Einwohner (23 874 Männer und 29 010 Frauen) der Slowakei. 6037 Personen zählten sich zur mährischen und 405 zur schlesischen Nationalität. Von der Gesamtzahl (52 884) hatten 37 544 Personen die Staatsbürgerschaft der Tschechischen Republik, 15 125 die der Slowakischen Republik, 215 Bürger führten keine Staatsangehörigkeit an. 45 630 in der Slowakei lebende Personen tschechischer Nationalität haben bei der Volkszählung das Tschechische, 6353 das Slowakische, 401 das Ungarische, 99 das Deutsche, 77 das Romani u. a. als ihre Muttersprache angegeben. Von den Altersgruppen ist bei den Angehörigen tschechischer Nationalität die der 40—44jährigen (5991 Personen) am stärksten vertreten. 11 804 Einwohner tschechischer Nationalität haben die Grundschule, 13 618 die Mittelschule mit Abitur absolviert, 8106 haben Hochschulabschluß. Eine Ausbildung in der tschechischen Sprache gab und gibt es in der Slowakei nicht.

4.3. Viele Tschechen haben sich in den letzten Jahren nach und nach in der Slowakei angesiedelt. Den Charakter einer Migration hat die Niederlassung tschechischer Protestanten auf dem Gebiet der Slowakei nach 1620 (ihre Nachkommen wurden mit der Zeit assimiliert) sowie die Ankunft der Tschechen (u. a. der Staatsbeamten) in der Slowakei nach der Gründung der Tschechoslowakei im Jahre 1918 angenommen. 1921 lebten z. B. in der Slowakei 72 000 Tschechen, 1930 waren es bereits 140 000.

5. Soziolinguistische Lage

Die Sprachsituation in der ČSFR (bis zum Jahresende 1992) wurde von der Spezifik der zwischensprachlichen Beziehungen und Kontakte gekennzeichnet. Tschechisch und Slowakisch als zwei selbständige und gleichberechtigte Sprachen erfüllten die Funktionen des gesellschaftlichen Kommunikationsmittels nicht nur auf dem Gebiet der jeweiligen nationalen Republik, sondern als Mittel der gesamtstaatlichen Kommunikation in föderativen Institutionen. Eine wichtige Rolle spielten die Massenmedien (Rundfunk, Fernsehen), für die der abwechselnde Gebrauch der tschechischen und slowakischen Sprache charakteristisch war, z. B. bei gesamtstaatlichen Veranstaltungen im Bereich Politik, Kultur und Sport wie auch bei einigen nationalen, tschechischen oder slowakischen Programmen. Dank der Medien wurden vor allem passive tschechisch-slowakische Sprachkontakte entwickelt. Die Sprecher beider Nationalsprachen können (auch bei aktiven Kontakten) Äußerungen in der anderen Sprache ohne weiteres verstehen, auch wenn sie nicht aktiv bilingual sind.

Von der Zweisprachigkeit wird auch die alltägliche Kommunikation in den Familien, Arbeitskollektiven u. ä. beeinflußt. In diesen Kommunikationssituationen entstehen sowohl im Tschechischen als auch im Slowakischen verschiedene Kontakt- und Interferenzerscheinungen. Grad und Umfang von Interferenzen zwischen Slowakisch und Tschechisch sind in den Äußerungen einzelner Sprecher unterschiedlich. Sie werden von der unterschiedlichen Sprachkenntnis, vom Typ der Persönlichkeit sowie ihrer psychischen Veranlagung, der gesamten Kommunikationssituation u. ä. determiniert. Die ständig bzw. langfristig in der Slowakei (nicht selten in Mischehen) lebenden Tschechen bedienen sich bei der Kommunikation mehrerer Sprachformen (vgl. Hoffmanová/Müllerová, 1993). Auch für die drei Grundmodelle ((a) die Tschechen beherrschen das Slowakische nicht aktiv, und in allen Situationen sprechen sie ausschließlich tschechisch; (b) sie beherrschen aktiv auch das Slowakische, und in der Kommunikation gebrauchen sie abwechselnd beide Sprachen; (c) sie beherrschen das Slowakische aktiv, und bei der Kommunikation mit Slowaken sprechen sie Slowakisch) sind verschiedene Interferenz- und Kontakterscheinungen charakteristisch (z. B. werden vor allem lexikalische Kontaktvarianten gebraucht).

6. Sprachpolitische Lage

Die Kontakte zwischen Slowakisch und Tschechisch haben im Laufe ihrer Entwicklung Veränderungen erfahren, wobei die jeweilige Sprachpolitik eine wichtige Rolle spielte. Die Slowaken setzten auch im Bereich der Sprachpolitik große Hoffnungen auf die Tschechoslowakische Republik, die im Jahre 1918 als gemeinsamer Staat der Tschechen und Slowaken entstand. Das Verfassungsgesetz vom 29. 2. 1920, in dem sprachliche Rechte festgelegt werden, legte jedoch fest, daß die offizielle Staatssprache der Republik die „tschechoslowakische" Sprache ist. Die Spannung zwischen der tschechoslowakischen Einheitstheorie (die stellenweise bis zur Negierung der Eigenständigkeit des slowakischen Volkes und der slowakischen Sprache in der slawischen Welt führte) und den slowakischen Differenzierungsbemühungen kennzeichnete das gesellschaftlich-kulturelle und politische Geschehen in den 20er und 30er Jahren. Den fiktiven Charakter einer einheitlichen tschechoslowakischen Nation und Sprache bewies Ľ. Novák (1935, 301—318), der überdies auch auf legislative Unstimmigkeiten in der Realisierung des betreffenden Gesetzes hingewiesen hatte. In der Slowakei wurde z. B. in slowakischer Sprache das Unterrichtsfach „Tschechoslowakisch", in Böhmen in tschechischer Sprache das Unterrichtsfach „Tschechisch" unterrichtet. Das slowakische kulturelle Leben ist auch von der Theorie der unzureichenden Ausdrucksmöglichkeiten der slowakischen Sprache im Bereich der Wissenschaft und Zivilisation beeinflußt worden. Häufig wurde die Meinung geäußert, daß sich die slowakische Sprache auf die schöngeistige Literatur beschränken sollte; die Wissenschaft sollte ausschließlich in tschechischer Sprache betrieben werden. Die Bemühungen um die tschechoslowakische Spracheinheit, die durch die Verdrängung der Eigenarten der slowakischen Schriftsprache und das starke Auftreten von (damals nicht den Charakter der Kontaktvarianten besitzenden) in Böhmen benutzten Wörtern in die schriftsprachliche Norm erreicht werden sollte, fanden ihren Ausdruck auch in der 1. Ausgabe der „Regeln der slowakischen Rechtschreibung" aus dem Jahre 1931.

Für „Sprachexperten" hielten sich auch politische Repräsentanten der sozialistischen Tschechoslowakei. Einen Aufschrei der Empörung löste ein Beitrag in der Rundfunkserie zum normgerechten Sprachgebrauch im Jahre 1975 aus: statt des slowakisierten Wortes *šupátko* (Schieber; nach der tschechischen Form *šoupátko*; das Suffix *-tko* ist in diesem Wortbildungstyp im Slowakischen nicht organisch) wurde das richtige slowakische Äquivalent *posúvač* empfohlen. Dieser „antitschechische" Ton des Beitrags mündete in der Verordnung, in den für die Öffentlichkeit bestimmten Sendungen nicht auf die Unterschiede zwischen dem Slowakischen und Tschechischen hinzuweisen. Es gab mehrere derartige Beispiele des politisch motivierten Dirigismus zur Annäherung des Tschechischen und Slowakischen (die Verordnungen zum Gebrauch des Adjektivs *dukelský* statt slow. *dukliansky*, des Lexems *dial'nica* statt *autostráda* u. a. m.).

7. Allgemeines kontaktlinguistisches Porträt

7.1. Der slawische Ursprung, die langzeitige parallele Entwicklung (in der Gruppe der westslawischen Sprachen) und gegenseitige Kontakte des Tschechischen und Slowakischen spiegeln sich auf allen Sprachebenen wider. Zu den ältesten Gemeinsamkeiten gehört die Entwicklung der urslawischen Lautgruppen *tolt, tort, telt, tert > tlat, trat, tlět, trět* (die sog. Metathese der Liquiden) in Wörtern wie *hlava*, tsch. *hlava* Kopf, *brada*, tsch. *brada* Kinn, *mlieko*, tsch. *mléko* Milch, *breza*, tsch. *bříza* Birke u. ä. Gemeinsam sind auch die Stabilisierung des Akzents auf der ersten Silbe, der Wechsel der urslawischen Intonations- in Quantitätsgegensätze, die Kontraktion, der Schwund und die Entwicklung von Jer, die Entwicklung einer reichen konsonantischen palatalen Korrelation, der Wechsel *g > h* u. a. m. Die älteste gemeinsame Entwicklungstendenz in der Morphologie ist der Zerfall des urslawischen Stammdeklinationssystems und die Entstehung eines Genussystems. In beiden Sprachen entwickelte sich die grammatische Kategorie der Belebtheit, es schwanden der Dual und einfache verbale Vergangenheitsformen (Imperfekt, Aorist). Der Satzbau weist in beiden Sprachen weitgehende Gemeinsamkeiten auf. Gemeinsam ist natürlich auch der ursprüngliche (ur-)slawische Kernwortschatz.

7.2. Zwischen dem Slowakischen und Tschechischen gibt es aber auch mehrere charakteristische Unterschiede. Typisch für die slowakische Sprache ist das Alternieren der langen und kurzen Silben (das sog. rhythmische Gesetz: zwei lange Silben dürfen nicht unmittelbar nacheinanderfolgen). Die tschechische Sprache hat nicht den Vokal *ä*, der in der slowakischen Schriftsprache für den urslawischen Nasalvokal nach Labialen (*mäso, pät' — maso, pět* Fleisch, fünf) steht. Die slowakische Sprache hat dagegen nicht den Vokal *ě*; dem tschechischen *ě* stehen *e* (*město — mesto* Stadt), *ä* (*pět — pät'*), mitunter *ie* (*někdo — niekto* jemand) gegenüber. Das Slowakische hat nicht den fallenden Diphthong *ou*, der im Tschechischen durch Diphthongierung *ú > ou* (*louka, moudrý — lúka, múdry* Wiese, weise) entstand. Das Tschechische hat wiederum keine steigenden Diphthonge vom Typ des slowakischen *ia* (*žák — žiak* Schüler), *ie* (*píseň—pieseň* Lied), *iu* (Akk. Sg. Fem. Adj. *cizí — cudziu* eine fremde /Frau/), *uo* (geschrieben *ô*; *můj, stůl — môj, stôl* mein, Tisch). Unter den slowakischen Konsonanten gibt es kein *ř*, dagegen hat das Tschechische kein palatalisiertes *l'* (slow. *riect', zver; l'an, žial' —* tsch. *říci, zvěř; len, žel;* sagen, Wild; Flachs, leider). In der Morphologie zeichnet sich das Slowakische im Vergleich zum Tschechischen durch eine größere Regelmäßigkeit in Paradigmen aus, was sich in einer größeren Ausgeglichenheit der morphologischen Basen, in einer ausgeprägteren Parallelität der harten und weichen Deklinations- und Konjugationstypen, in einigen Unterschieden im Synkretismus der Formen oder der ganzen Paradigmen äußert. Unterschiede sind auch in der Wortbildung festzustellen. Zur Bildung der Einwohnernamen dient im Slowakischen am häufigsten das Suffix *-čan*, demgegenüber stehen im Tschechischen die Suffixe *-an* oder *-ec* (z. B. *Bratislavčan — Bratislavan* der Bratislavaer). Dem tschechischen Suffix *-tko* in Werkzeugbenennungen steht im Slowakischen das Suffix *-dlo* (*strúhatko — strúhadlo* Spitzer) gegenüber. Im Slowakischen kommt der Typ der Vorgangssubstantive mit dem Suffix *-ná/-ená* (*kopaná, odbíjaná*) nicht vor; Äquivalente dafür sind ursprüngliche fremde Lexeme *futbal, volejbal*.

Unter kommunikativem Aspekt sind die bedeutendsten Differenzen die nichtparallelen Lexeme in beiden Sprachen. Ihr Repertoire wird in (zweisprachigen) Wörterbüchern registriert und in mehreren Beiträgen analysiert (vgl. 9.). Zu den markantesten und am häufigsten vorkommenden Differenzen im Tschechischen und Slowakischen gehören z. B. folgende Wörter: *brambory — zemiaky* Kartoffeln, *drůbež — hydina* Geflügel, *dělník — robotník* Arbeiter, *horník — baník* Bergmann, *hřebík — klinec* Nagel, *kartáč — kefa* Bürste, *kozel — cap* Ziegenbock, *kapesné — vreckové* Taschengeld, *knoflík — gombík* Knopf, *míč — lopta* Ball, *osel — somár* Esel, *tchán — svokor* Schwiegervater, *zed' — múr* Mauer, *žízeň — smäd* Durst usw. Es sind auch Lexeme, die im Tschechischen und Slowakischen in gleicher lautlicher (formaler) Form vorkommen, aber eine unterschiedliche (oft auch gegensätzliche) Bedeutung aufweisen. Sie werden auch als zwischensprachliche Homonyme oder sog. zweiseitige Ausdrücke bezeichnet. Es sind z. B. Lexeme *horký* (im Tschechischen heiß — im Slowakischen bitter), *chudý* (arm — nicht fettig; schlank), *kázeň* (Disziplin — Predigt), *špatný* (schlecht — häßlich) u. a. m. Spezifische Beziehungen entstehen bei solchen Lexemen, die darüber hinaus in einer der Kontaktsprachen (z. B. im Tschechischen) selbst homonym sind (Lexeme *pokoj, topit, zahájit* Zimmer/Ruhe, heizen/ertränken, eröffnen/einfrieden).

7.3. Bei den Analysen der gegenseitigen Beziehungen zwischen dem Tschechischen und Slowakischen wird manchmal auch die Existenz der sog. Kontaktsynonyme oder Kontaktneologismen vermutet (Budovičová 1985, 33). Es bestehen Unterschiede im Gebrauch, in der Bewertung sowie Einstellung zu Kontakterscheinungen. Kontaktvarianten des Typs *pilný — usilovný* fleißig, *drzý — bezočivý* frech, *kl'ud — pokoj* Ruhe, *jazdit' — viezt' sa* fahren, *jednanie — rokovanie* Verhandlung usw. verstehen und bewerten die Sprecher des Slowakischen ihrem Sprachbewußtsein entsprechend auf der breiten Skala vom grundsätzlichen Ablehnen (in der Theorie und Praxis) bis zu allgemeiner Akzeptanz bzw. nur in bestimmten stilistischen Funktionen (Buzássyová 1985).

8. Zur Forschungslage

Die neuesten Ergebnisse der Kontaktforschung des Tschechischen und Slowakischen (die nicht nur die Sprachproblematik, sondern auch einen breiteren Kontext der Nationalliteraturen und -kulturen betreffen) werden konzentriert dargestellt in mehreren Jahrgängen des Sammelbandes *Slavica Pragensia*, herausgegeben von der Karlsuniversität zu Prag. Die den Analysen und Interpretationen der slowakisch-tschechischen Kontakterscheinungen gewidmeten Arbeiten slowakischer Sprachwissenschaftler werden nur gelegentlich veröffentlicht. Charakteristisch für diese Arbeiten ist das Bemühen, bei der Erörterung der vielschichtigen Erscheinungen die unterschiedlichen psychologischen und historischen Erfahrungen beider Sprachgemeinschaften zu respektieren und sowohl die negativen als auch die positiven Folgen des Gebrauchs und des Fungierens der Kontaktvarianten in der slowakischen Sprache zu beschreiben. Eine adäquate Beschreibung der Beziehungen zwischen der tschechischen und slowakischen Sprache wurde durch eine Interpretation der Kontakterscheinungen ermöglicht, die die Stratifikation der Nationalsprache respektiert und die Sprach- (Kommunikations-)Gemeinschaft differenziert nach der regionalen, sozialen oder Generationszugehörigkeit sowie nach dem Kommunikationskontinuum untersucht.

Die Bedingungen der gegenseitigen Beziehungen und Kontakte des Tschechischen und Slowakischen werden modifiziert. Die Folgen dieses Wandels für die Kontakte zwischen den beiden Sprachen müssen noch untersucht werden.

9. Bibliographie (in Auswahl)

Blanár, Vincent (1986): „Kontinuitný alebo diskontuitný vývin slovenského jazyka?" [Kontinuität oder Diskontinuität in der Entwicklung der slowakischen Sprache?]. In: *Slovenská reč 51*, 196–207.

Budovičová, Viera (1985): „Z konfrontačného štúdia češtiny a slovenčiny. Československý model dvojjazyčnej komunikácie" [Konfrontative Studien zum Tschechischen und Slowakischen. Das tschechoslowakische Modell der zweisprachigen Kommunikation]. In: *Slavica Pragensia XXV*, 25–38.

Buzássyová, Klára (1985): „Kontaktové varianty a synonymá v slovenčine a v češtine [Kontaktvarianten und Synonyme im Slowakischen und Tschechischen]. In: *Jazykovedný časopis 44*, 92–107.

Dolník, Juraj (1992): „České slová v slovenčine" [Tschechische Wörter im Slowakischen]. In: *Studia Academica Slovaca 21*, 1–10.

Doruľa, Ján (1977): *Slováci v dejinách jazykových vzťahov* [Die Slowaken in der Geschichte der Sprachbeziehungen], Bratislava.

Gašparíková, Želmíra/Kamiš, Adolf (1967): *Slovensko-český slovník* [Slowakisch-tschechisches Wörterbuch], Prag.

Horák, Gejza (Ed.) (1979): *Česko-slovenský slovník* [Tschechisch-slowakisches Wörterbuch], Bratislava.

Hoffmanová, Jana/Müllerová, Olga (1993): „Interference češtiny a slovenštiny v mluvené komunikaci" [Interferenzen des Tschechischen und Slowakischen in der gesprochenen Kommunikation]. In: *Slavia 62*, 311–316.

Jedlička, Alois (1974): „Poznámky ke konfrontačnímu studiu češtiny a slovenštiny" [Bemerkungen zur konfrontativen Analyse des Tschechischen und Slowakischen]. In: *Jazykovedné štúdie 12*, 20–29.

Kačala, Ján/Pisárčiková, Mária (Eds.) (1987): *Krátky slovník slovenského jazyka* [Kurzes Wörterbuch der slowakischen Sprache], Bratislava.

Kačala, Ján et al. (Eds.) (1991): *Pravidlá slovenského pravopisu* [Regeln der slowakischen Orthographie], Bratislava.

Lorenzová, Helena (1990): „Mýtus Slovenska v české kultuře na přelomu 19. a 20. století" [Mythos der Slowakei in der tschechischen Kultur um die Wende des 19. und 20. Jh.]. In: *Kontexty českého a slovenského umenia*, Bakoš, J./Mojžišová, I. (Eds.), Bratislava, 232–239.

Majtán, Milan (Ed.) (1991–1992): *Historický slovník slovenského jazyka I–IV* [Historisches Wörterbuch der slowakischen Sprache], Bratislava.

Marsina, Richard/Čičaj, Viliam/Kováč, Dušan/Lipták, Ľubomír (1992): *Slovenské dejiny* [Slowakische Geschichte], Martin.

Marti, Roland (1993): „Slowakisch und Čechisch vs. Čechoslovakisch, Serbokroatisch vs. Kroatisch und Serbisch". In: *Slawistische Studien zum XI. Internationalen Slawistenkongreß in Pressburg/Bratislava*, Gutschmidt, K. et al. (Eds.), Köln/Weimar/Wien, 289–315.

Novák, Ľudovít (1935): *Jazykovedné glosy k československej otázke* [Sprachwissenschaftliche Glossen zur tschechoslowakischen Frage], Martin.

Pauliny, Eugen (1974): „Kontrastívna analýza slovenského a českého hláskoslovia" [Kontrastive Analyse der slowakischen und tschechischen Lautlehre]. In: *Studia Academica Slovaca 3*, 259–272.

Peciar, Štefan (1973): „Konfrontácia slovenčiny a češtiny" [Konfrontation des Tschechischen und Slowakischen]. In: *Studia Academica Slovaca 2*, 233–243.

Peciar, Štefan (Ed.) (1959–1968): *Slovník slovenského jazyka I–VI* [Wörterbuch der slowakischen Sprache], Bratislava.

Rehder, Peter (Ed.) (1991): *Einführung in die slavischen Sprachen*, Darmstadt.

Ripka, Ivor (1993): „Some Aspects of the Relationship between Czech and Slovak". In: *Varieties of Czech. Theory and Reality*, Eckert, E. (Ed.), Amsterdam/Atlanta, 276–285.

Ružička, Jozef (1970): *Spisovná slovenčina v Československu* [Die slowakische Schriftsprache in der Tschechoslowakei], Bratislava.

Sokolová, Miroslava (1991): „Komunikatívna efektívnosť českých kontaktových javov v súčasnej slovenčine" [Die Kommunikationseffektivität der tschechischen Kontakterscheinungen in der gegenwärtigen slowakischen Sprache]. In: *Všeobecné a špecifické otázky jazykovej komunikácie*, Odaloš, P./Patráš, V. (Eds.), Neusohl, 232–242.

Ivor Ripka, Bratislava (Slowakei)

210. Hungary

1. Geography and demography
2. Territorial history and national development
3. Politics, economy and general cultural and religious situation
4. Statistics and ethnoprofiles
5. Sociolinguistic situation
6. Language political situation
7. Presentation of language contact and contact languages
8. Critical evaluation of the sources and literature
9. Bibliography (selected)

A thorough introduction to the situation of Hungary's national minorities in the 1990s is impossible without taking into account the history of the Carpathian Basin, its often changing borders, and the Hungarian minorities in Hungary's neighboring countries.

A Mr. Csukás's life story, reported by The New York Times on January 25, 1993, encapsulates the shifting fortunes of Hungarians as well as other nationalities in the region. Born in 1918, Mr. Csukás was a citizen of Austria—Hungary. A few months later he became a citizen of Czechoslovakia, when Hungary lost substantial territory as a penalty for siding with Germany in WW I. When the Nazis dismembered Czechoslovakia in 1938, they gave a piece to Hungary, and Mr. Csukás became a Hungarian again. After WW II, the territory was restored to Czechoslovakia. On January 1, 1993 that country broke up, and Mr. Csukás took up his fifth citizenship, this time as a Slovak. Although he has been a citizen of five different countries, he has never left the narrow strip of villages along what is now the border between Hungary and Slovakia (→ Language Map L).

Similar stories of Romanians, Serbs or others could easily be cited. The fate of minority X in country Y in the Carpathian Basin is often influenced considerably by the fate of minority Y in country X. Sometimes even chain reactions occur, such as the attempted liquidation of the Hungarian minority in Czechoslovakia after WW II, which, in turn, influenced the fate of Hungary's German minority.

1. Geography and demography

Hungary is between the Slavic and the German worlds, in a region where Roman Catholicism, Protestantism and the Byzantine civilization meet. For a millenium before the First World War, historical Hungary extended over the central Danubian Basin. This region is also known as the Carpathian Basin because it is surrounded by the arc of the Carpathian mountains which begin at the Danube near Bratislava in the northwest and reach the river again at the Iron Gate in the southeast. Three sub-basins are distinguished: the Little Plain in western Hungary, the Great Plain east of the Danube and extending well beyond the Tisza river, and Transylvania in the east.

The original home of the Finno-Ugric peoples was in the region where the Volga and Kama rivers flow, west of the Ural mountains. Around 500 B.C. the ancestors of the Hungarians lived in what is today Bashkiria. In 895 the Hungarians, by now culturally Bulgar-Turkish but linguistically still Finno-Ugric, were driven by the nomadic Pechenegs from their temporary home near the Black Sea to the Carpathian Basin.

When the conquering Hungarians appeared in 896, "the plains between the Danube and the Tisza, as well as the northern steppe-like half of Transylvania, stood empty" (Makkai 1990, 7). The region west of the Danube was ruled by Slav dukes under Bavarian-German overlordship. The area south of the Maros river east of the Tisza was controlled by the Bulgarian tsar; and the region around Nyitra in the north belonged to the Moravian state. During the reign of King István I (St. Stephen; 997—1038) Hungary's transformation into a feudal monarchy was accomplished. István received his crown from Pope Sylvester II in the year 1000, and all Hungarians were converted, often by force, to Latin Christianity. Later King Ladislas I occupied Croatia, which became part of Hungary from the end of the 11th century.

2. Territorial history and national development

From its very beginning, Hungary was a multiethnic state. Side by side with the Magyar ruling nation lived other nationalities, rather peacefully until the 19th century. There were Slavs in the territory of today's Slovakia. The first Germans were monks, preachers, knights and craftsmen, who came to Hun-

Table 210.1: Population figures for Hungarians and non-Hungarians in historic Hungary (without Croatia-Slavonia), based on Dávid (1988, 343).

Year	H	R	S	S-C	Ru	G	Others	Total %	Thousands
1880	46.6	17.5	13.5	4.6	2.6	13.6	1.6	100.0	13,749
1910	54.5	16.1	10.7	3.6	2.5	10.4	2.2	100.0	18,264

Abbreviations: H = Hungarian, R = Romanian, S = Slovak, S-C = Serbo-Croatian, Ru = Ruthenian, G = German.

gary in the 11th century. More German settlers were invited after the Mongol invasion (1240–1242) devastated and depopulated a large part of the country. Following the battle of Mohács in 1526, the Ottoman Turks ruled the central part of Hungary for 150 years. A narrow western and northern strip became a Habsburg domain as the Hungarian crown became vacant and passed through inheritance to Ferdinand I (1526–1564). Created by the Turkish Sultan, the Principality of Transylvania enjoyed varying degrees of independence between 1541 and 1691. The Habsburg rule of Hungary lasted for almost four centuries. After the end of the 150 years of Turkish occupation, in the 17th and 18th centuries, the depopulated lands of the country were resettled through spontaneous migration of Serbs, Croats and Romanians, and later by massive population movement conducted by the Habsburgs, involving Swabian Germans as well as Slovaks, South Slavs, Ruthenes and others. Gypsies have lived in Hungary ever since the 15th century. Until the end of the 19th century the ruling Magyars constituted a minority in the multiethnic lands belonging to the Crown of St. István. "Magyar chauvinism and coercive assimilation, which were later to plague the Hungarian scene, did not exist before the nineteenth century" (Paikert 1967, 11).

The War of Independence (1848–49) was crushed by the Austrians with the aid of the Russian Tsar Nicholas I, and in 1867 a Compromise was worked out, which marked the beginning of Austria-Hungary, a monarchy with two independent nations (Austria and Hungary) but a joint army and some joint government, e. g. the foreign ministry. Croatia had almost total autonomy in her internal affairs.

According to Dávid (1988, 334), a leading Hungarian statistician, "Certain regions of historic Hungary were ethnically perhaps the most complex places in the world when census taking according to mother tongue began in the nineteenth century." The first ethnic census producing data on the basis of mother tongue took place in 1880. Table 210.1 presents the ethnic distribution of the population in 1880 and 1910, the year the last decennial census in historic Hungary was taken.

At that time the British historian R. W. Seton-Watson (1908/1972, 3) called Hungary "the most polyglot state in all Europe." Ten years later, in 1920, a linguistically rather homogeneous state came into being as a result of the partitioning of Hungary in the wake of the Peace Treaty of Trianon. When the Dual Monarchy collapsed after World War I, independent successor states were created around a shrunk Hungary: Czechoslovakia, Romania and Yugoslavia. Hungary lost about two-thirds of her territory and population to the successor states and millions of ethnic Hungarians became citizens of another country. Fig. 210.1 shows the country's old and new borders and the ethnic Hungarian population in 1920.

As one historian put it, "As a result of the territorial changes effected under the peace treaty the population of Hungary decreased to a figure considerably less than the actual number of Hungarians residing in Eastern Europe, while the population of Czechoslovakia, Romania and Yugoslavia became, in every case, considerably greater than the actual number of any of their respective national groups" (Kertész 1982, 48). Hungary's national minority population declined from 45.5 per cent in 1910 to 7.9 per cent in 1930.

Following WW I, jingo-nationalism at times went with military actions. After the short-lived Hungarian Soviet Republic in 1919, Romanian troops occupied Budapest and a major part of the country. The severe losses in territory and population lead to a revisionist foreign policy in the interwar

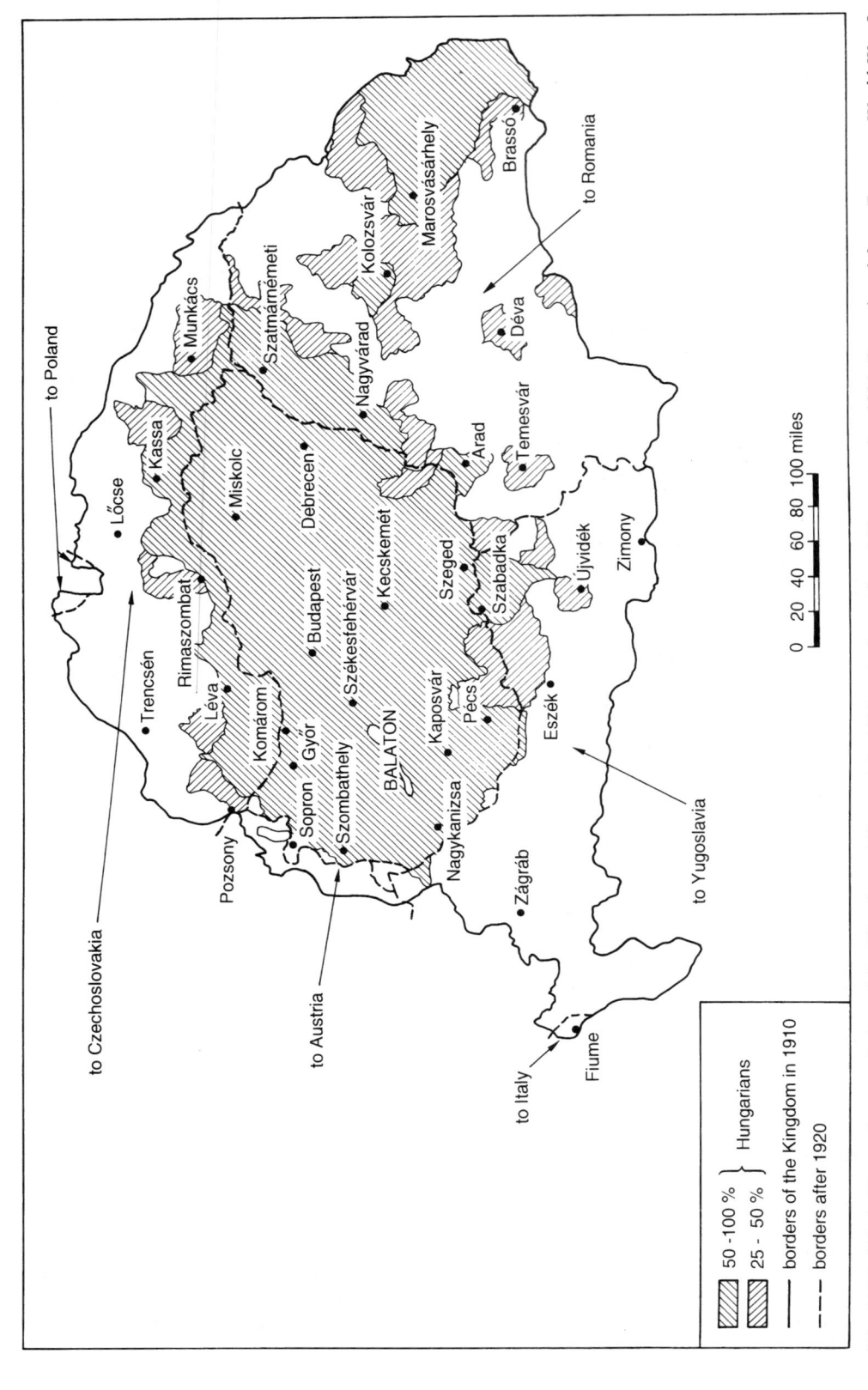

Fig. 210.1: Ethnic Hungarian population of the Kingdom of Hungary in 1910 and of partitioned Hungary after 1920. Reproduced from *Essays on World War I: total war and peacemaking, a case study on Trianon*, B. K. Király/Pastor/I. Sanders (Eds.), New York, 1982. Copyright by Atlantic Research and Publications.

years. With membership in the Axis Powers in WW II, Hungary regained some of its lost territories under the First and Second Vienna Awards (1938 and 1940) and as a result of independent military actions through 1942. When the Hungarians regained Southern Slovakia, Northern Transylvania and parts of Yugoslavia, their army brutalized Slovaks, Romanians and Serbs. By 1941 Hungary's nationalities increased to over 19 per cent.

The peace negotiations after WW II practically confirmed the state borders established after the First World War in 1920, and Hungary became a near-monolingual country.

After WW II, under the terms of the Potsdam Conference, about 200,000 Germans were expelled from Hungary to Germany (Kertész 1953, 205). Linked to this expulsion was the Hungaro-Slovak population exchange, whereby some 87,000 Hungarians were forced to leave Slovakia for Hungary and about 73,000 Slovaks went from Hungary to Slovakia without being forced (see Janics/Borsody 1982, Dávid 1988, 338). The properties of the German expellees were given to the Hungarians removed from Czechoslovakia and the Hungarian refugees from Bukovina. Predictably, this has resulted in bitter animosity between the remaining Germans and the resettled Hungarians, the repercussions of which are still felt to this day.

Under Communism (1948–1989), the nationality problems were largely swept under the rug. The prevailing ideology preached Leninist nationality policies, under which the problems and tensions would automatically cure themselves in both Hungary and her neighboring "brotherly socialist countries." Hungary's nationalities were said to have "the mission of bridge-building" between Hungary and the neighboring states (Aczél 1984). Partly in response to growing popular concern within Hungary for the fate of Hungarian minorities in neighboring countries, by 1989 – their final year – the Hungarian Communist party championed state support for language maintenance among Hungary's internal minorities. The aim was "to provide, on the international stage, the ethically unimpeachable model for what should be done for Hungarian minorities in Romania, Slovakia and other neighboring states" (Gal 1995, 96).

When Hungary was transformed from a single-party Communist dictatorship to a multi-party democracy in 1990, the nationality problems immediately surfaced, although their magnitude is not nearly comparable to those in Slovakia, Romania or the former Yugoslavia. The new, democratically elected parliament and government have passed legislation to dramatically improve the chances for minority language and culture maintenance (see 3.1.2. below).

3. Politics, economy, and general cultural and religious situation

3.1. Politics

3.1.1. Politics (1784–1990)

The Kingdom of Hungary was multinational ever since the Middle Ages. Emperor Joseph II of the Habsburg House issued a decree in 1784 which made German the official administrative language of Hungary, trying to supplant Latin which had been used for official transactions until that time. This measure contributed to the Hungarian literary revival and the movement to make Hungarian the official language of all authorities, courts, and schools, which happened in 1844. According to a contemporary report of an Englishman who travelled in Hungary

"The system so long and so ably followed up, of Germanizing Hungary, had succeeded to such a degree as to destroy to a considerable extent the feelings of nationality among the higher nobles: most of them were ignorant of the [Magyar] language; few of them took any interest in the affairs of Hungary [...] The restoration of the Hungarian language was therefore the First object. [...] [Count István] Széchenyi published several political works in the language, and Hungarian authorship has become fashionable. Among men it is now the medium of conversation; at public dinners, toasts and speeches in German would not be listened to" (Paget 1850/1971, Vol. I, 207–208).

Magyar nationalists, however, "failed to see why the linguistic claims of non-Magyars should be permitted to prevail in the public domain, or even locally at the village level" (Barany 1990, 204). Hungary's national minorities, the Germans, Slovaks, Ruthenes, Romanians, Croats and Serbs made up an absolute majority of the population.

Following the Compromise in 1867 and the creation of Austria-Hungary, when the nationality law 1868/XLIV was ratified, the law did not recognize the existence of separate nationalities. "The law was liberal only as far as the usage of languages was concerned" (Frank 1990, 255). The government supported voluntary Magyarization and used the school system to Magyarize the nationalities' intellectuals. Later Magyarization was pursued much more forcefully, but, according to Jeszenszky (1990, 270), "The emphasis on and gradual extension of Hungarian lessons in schools brought meager results. (In 1910 only 1.8 million of Hungary's 8.3 million non-Hungarians knew Hungarian.)" Hungarian chauvinist legislation resulted in a law to Magyarize place-names and people's names (1898), and the school laws called "Lex Apponyi", which made elementary education free, but used financial means to decrease the amount of non-Magyar-language teaching (1907).

With the exception of Austria, following the Trianon Treaty in 1920, Hungary became the most ethnically homogeneous successor state: 89.5 per cent of her population was Hungarian; the largest minority, Germans, amounted to 6.9 per cent (Hajdú/Nagy 1990, 314). Linguistic and demographic statistics show that the assimilation of minorities continued between the two World Wars (Karády 1990, 34). The complexity of assimilation is shown by a contemporary observation made in the mid-1930s, according to which "a paradoxical situation developed in that there were in Hungary at this time some communes where national minority schooling existed against the will of the ethnic group for whom it was designed" (Paikert 1953, 214−215).

After the expulsion of over 200,000 Germans and the Slovak-Hungarian population exchange which followed the Potsdam Conference, in 1948 the Hungarian government acknowledged the principle of equality for all nationalities. The Hungarian Communists gave up "the reactionary vision of Greater Hungary." In the words of Wagner (1988, 373), "No people in Central and Eastern Europe has ever made such a conciliatory gesture in renouncing its historic claims in order to establish − though unsuccessfully − a foundation for fruitful interethnic cooperation."

The 1949 Constitution of the Hungarian People's Republic declared that discrimination according to sex, denomination, or nationality was punishable by law, and all citizens were guaranteed equal opportunity of education in their mother tongue and the fostering of their national culture. The amended Constitution of 1989 of the Hungarian Republic declares that "The national and language minorities are under the protection of the Hungarian Republic. They have the right to take part collectively in public life, to foster their own culture, to use their mothertongue, to receive education in their mothertongue, and to use their personal names in their own language" (article 68, paragraph 2).

3.1.2. The Minorities Act (1993)

After about two years of preparation and debates, the draft of the "Act about the Rights of the National and Ethnic Minorities" was submitted to the Hungarian Parliament in the Fall of 1992. (The Hungarian terminological distinction between "national minority" and "ethnic minority" rests primarily on whether a minority has a "mother-country". Gypsies do not, hence they are called an ethnic minority; see 7.1.). The Act (*1993. évi LXXVII. törvény*) was passed in July 1993 and came into force three months later (see *Törvény*). A brief summary follows.

The Act applies to minorities who have lived in Hungary for at least a century, i. e. Armenians, Bulgarians, Croatians, Germans, Greeks, Gypsies, Poles, Romanians, Ruthenes, Serbs, Slovaks, Slovenes and Ukrainians. If at least 1,000 persons declare themselves to belong to a minority not listed in the Act, they may initiate legal procedures in order to become a recognized minority.

The personal names of individuals can be used in documents in non-Latin script, but in such cases a Hungarian version must also be used. Minority groups have the right to create their own schools using the minority language as the medium of instruction, or that and Hungarian.

Where and when local government elections result in over 50 per cent of the elected officials belonging to a minority, the said settlement has a minority local government. If more than 30 per cent of the elected local government officials belong to a minority, they are entitled to form a minority faction in the local government.

Teacher training for minorities is the national government's responsibility. Minority schools must also teach Hungarian.

Minority languages may be used by anybody, at any time, in any place. Members of parliament may also use their language in parliament. Local governments must also write their decrees and announcements in the minority language. In addition to Hungarian, forms and documents used must be made available in the minority language, and place-names and public signs can also be used in the minority's mother tongue.

3.2. Economic situation

The present-day socio-economic situation of Hungary's minorities has been largely defined by the egalitarian policies of the Communist era. A recent sociological investigation of Slovaks (Garami/Szántó 1991) has found minimal differences between that nationality and the majority Hungarian population.

Six hundred Slovaks between the ages of 50 and 60 were randomly selected in villages with a substantial Slovak population. (Thirty-four per cent of Hungarians live in cities. Slovaks, with 30 per cent, are much more urban than, for instance, Germans with 17 per cent.) A detailed comparison of the demographic, cultural and living conditions of the sample shows that Slovak villages are on a par with Hungarian villages of comparable size. The majority of the sample, 70 per cent, are unskilled or semi-skilled workers — a figure 10 per cent higher than that of the comparable Hungarian population. A discriminant analysis of all the socio-economic variables shows, however, that there is no difference between the Slovaks in the sample and the Hungarian control group (Garami/Szántó 1991, 29).

In absence of similar research about Germans, Southern Slavs and Romanians, one can only guess that their socio-economic situation may be largely similar to the Slovaks'. To the knowledge of this writer, no one has ever suggested that economic discrimination against Hungary's national minorities (Gypsies are a different issue, see 7.1. below) played any appreciable role during Communism.

3.3. Cultural situation

During the four decades of "mild assimilation" of Communism, organizations like The Democratic Association of Southern Slavs in Hungary (established in 1945) and similar associations of the Slovaks (1949), Romanians (1949) and Germans (1955) played an important part in fostering the nationalities' cultural life. Weekly journals as well as calendars such as *Narodni Kalendar, Náš Kalendár, Deutscher Kalender* and *Calendarul Nostru* were published and scores of nationality cultural groups toured the country disseminating their heritage.

After the collapse of Communism some cultural associations split up, e. g. Serbs and Croats formed independent organizations, a split which has also been followed by the transformation of the former Serbo-Croatian *gimnázium* in Budapest into a school with a Serbian and a Croatian track. Although political struggle affects some cultural organizations, e. g. that of the Germans, on the whole, the increasing cultural and material support provided by Germany is bound to have a beneficial effect. Support from some other neighboring countries is also forthcoming, for instance, in August 1992 the Slovak government decided to spend 1.7 million Crowns to establish a Slovak Cultural and Information Center in Békéscsaba.

According to a recent survey (Radó 1992, 138), out of 237 ethnically mixed villages and towns, nationality clubs operate in 75 localities, and nationality cultural associations are found in 95 settlements.

3.4. Religion

Considering religion to be a private affair of citizens, the Hungarian state keeps no statistics on religious affiliation. In a study of assimilation and schooling around 1900, Karady (1989, 287) illustrates the heavy interdependence of national and denominational groups some 90 years ago (table 210.2.)

Table 210.2: National and denominational distribution of Hungary's population around 1900 (Karady 1989, 287).

Denomination	% of the Hungarian population outside Croatia	Nationality
Jewish	5.0	Hungarian
Calvinist	14.4	Hungarian
Catholic	48.7	Hungarian German Slovak
Lutheran	7.5	Hungarian German Slovak
Greek Catholic and Greek Orthodox	11.0 13.1	mostly Romanian and Serbian

The last census to gather denominational data in the territory of present-day Hungary was taken in 1949. Roman Catholics constituted 67.8 per cent, Calvinists 21.9 per cent and Lutherans 5.2 per cent of a population of 9.2 million. Other denominations such as Greek Catholics numbered 2.7 per cent or less.

In the recent post-Communist years some ethnic-religious tensions have surfaced in Hungary. For instance, in August 1992 the president of the Association of Croatians in Hungary requested in an open letter that Cardinal Paskai, primate of the Hungarian Catholic Church, help stop the erosion of Croatian-Hungarian communities. The letter was prompted by the transfer of the Croatian-speaking parish priest from the small town of Kópháza.

4. Statistics and ethnoprofiles

Demographers at the Central Statistical Office agree that the size of a nationality in Hungary varies according to the questions asked in the census. The tendency is for the "nationality" figure to be the smallest, the "mother tongue" figure to be larger, and the largest figure is usually gained in answer to the question "what language other than your mother tongue do you speak?" The 1990 census defined "mother tongue" as that language which was learned first in childhood, which is usually used in the family, and which the person considers as her or his mother tongue.

According to the census of 1990, Hungarian is the mother tongue of 98.5 per cent of the country's population, while 97.8 per cent of the citizens claimed to be Hungarian by nationality. The country's total population is 10,375,000.

Slovaks (Hungarian *szlovák*, pejorative *tót*) constitute 0.1 per cent of the population. In the 1990 census 12,745 people claimed to be Slovak by mother tongue and 10,459 by nationality. Most Slovaks live in Békés, Komárom-Esztergom, and Pest counties.

Romanians (H *román*, pejorative *oláh*) number 8,730 by mother tongue, and 10,740 by nationality, totalling 0.1 per cent of the entire population. The largest numbers of Romanians live in Békés, Hajdú, and Pest counties.

Croatians (H *horvát*) are 17,577 by mother tongue, and 13,570 by nationality. Their larger communities are found in Baranya, Bács-Kiskún, Győr-Moson-Sopron, Vas, and Zala counties. They constitute 0.2 per cent of Hungary's population.

Serbs (H *szerb, rác*, a distinct group is called *bunyevác*) number 2,953 by mother tongue, and 2,905 by nationality. They mostly live in Pest, Békés, Bács-Kiskún and Csongrád counties and constitute less than 0.1 per cent of the population.

Slovenes (H *szlovén*) are also few in number: 2,627 by mother tongue, and 1,930 by nationality. Mostly located in Vas county, they constitute much less than 0.1 per cent.

Germans (H *német*, pejorative *sváb*) number 37,511 by mother tongue, and 30,824 by nationality. Baranya, Bács-Kiskún, Pest, and Tolna counties have the strongest German settlements. With 0.4 per cent of the population, they form the second largest minority in Hungary according to the census.

Gypsies (H *cigány*) number 48,072 by mother tongue, and 142,868 by nationality. Borsod-Abaúj-Zemplén and Szabolcs counties have the largest Gypsy population. By nationality figure they constitute 1.4 per cent of the people in Hungary.

A mixed category, "others", is formed by 22,079 people by mother tongue, and 19,640 by nationality, in all 0.2 per cent of the population. Among others, political and economic refugees from Bulgaria, Poland and Greece belong here.

A preliminary census of 463 nationality villages published in January 1991 allows a partial comparison of the changes from 1980 to 1990 of four minorities by nationality, mother tongue, and non-mother tongue spoken (table 210.3).

Table 210.3: Changes from 1980 to 1990 of four minorities.

	1990 (1980 = 100%)
Nationality:	
Slovak	107.1
Romanian	82.3
Yugoslav	91.4
German	331.7
Mother tongue:	
Slovak	77.8
Romanian	75.7
Yugoslav	76.2
German	114.8
Non-mother tongue spoken:	
Slovak	84.7
Romanian	184.7
Yugoslav	95.3
German	103.6

The most conspicuous differences are shown by the Germans: they increased by all three criteria and those claiming German as their nationality have grown more than three times. Speakers of Romanian have almost doubled. There are as yet no serious detailed studies of the reasons for the increases and decreases in these selected villages, where about three-fourths of Hungary's nationalities live.

An important caveat goes with all the above data: population exchanges, expulsions, and calling entire minorities collectively guilty after the two World Wars have all had an influence on census results. Therefore differences from one census to the next are due to a combination of real demographic changes and the minorities' fluctuating readiness to identify with the minority or the majority populations.

The federations of nationalities have their own estimates which show that some 200,000 to 220,000 Germans, 80,000 to 100,000 Southern Slavs, 100,000 to 110,000 Slovaks, and 20,000 to 25,000 Romanians live in Hungary (Lawson 1991, 790). However, such estimates are based on the demographically dubious notion of ancestry (Dávid 1993, 40–41).

The number of Gypsies and their mother-tongue figures have been debated for a long time. One sociolinguist estimates their number to be around 400,000, or 4 per cent of the country's population. A sociologist who has studied Gypsies for decades estimates that Gypsy children comprise about 8 per cent of the population in elementary schools. According to a linguistically dubious survey carried out in 1971, only about 21 per cent of the Gypsies were bilingual at that time. The bilinguals include Romāni-speakers (about 100,000), over half of whom speak the Lovari dialect, and the Boyash Gypsies (about 30,000), who speak certain dialects of Romanian.

5. Sociolinguistic situation

In a recent paper Patterson (1991, 120), an American anthropologist, suggests that "ethnicity in Hungary, at least in the case of its Romanian minority, is largely a matter of choice."

Although everything points to the high probability of Hungarian being considered the language of social prestige and economic advancement, few if any sociolinguistic studies have proved that point. The reason for this lacuna is the general lack of sociolinguistic research into bilingualism in Hungary.

Scholarly interest in the minority languages has been of the traditional dialectological kind. Borbély (1990) has studied the Romanian dialects in Hungary, Hutterer (1960) and Manherz (1977) the German dialects, and Stepanović (1986) the Serbian and Croatian dialects.

Nelde, Vandermeeren and Wölck (1991) is a sociolinguistic examination of German-Hungarian bilingualism in Pécs/Fünfkirchen carried out with educational aims, while Nelde (1990) contains some papers of sociolinguistic interest based on research before 1989.

In two highly original papers based on fieldwork in Bóly, southern Hungary, in 1987 and 1990, Gal (1993 and 1995) describes the symbolic associations of Hungarian and German, which are currently matters of denial, disagreement or dispute. Based on local images of the town's history and Bóly's experience of Cold War social cleavages, the current linguistic ideologies offer "a powerful, yet veiled criticism of state-socialism, one that innovatively re-evaluates the relative authority of German and Hungarian by recontextualizing the comparison between them to a pan-European political-economic field in which Hungarian, though the language of the state, is less powerful than German" (Gal 1995, 101).

In a sociological survey of language use in nationality-populated settlements, Radó (1992) reports on the public use of languages in various communicative situations. A study carried out in Pest County in 1989 found differences between the self-reported public use of nationality languages while, for instance, travelling on a train or bus among strangers. Seventeen per cent of the Germans and 5 per cent of the Slovaks studied reported that they never use their mother tongue on such occasions, but none of the Serbs and Croats did so.

A sociological study of Hungarian-Slovene bilingualism on both sides of the border, carried out in the mid-1980s, found that the use of Slovene in Hungary predominates within the nuclear and the extended family, while conversation with friends and schoolmates, as well as for shopping, tends to be bilingual. "15 per cent of the Slovenes living in Hungary replied that they had had dis-

Fig. 210.2

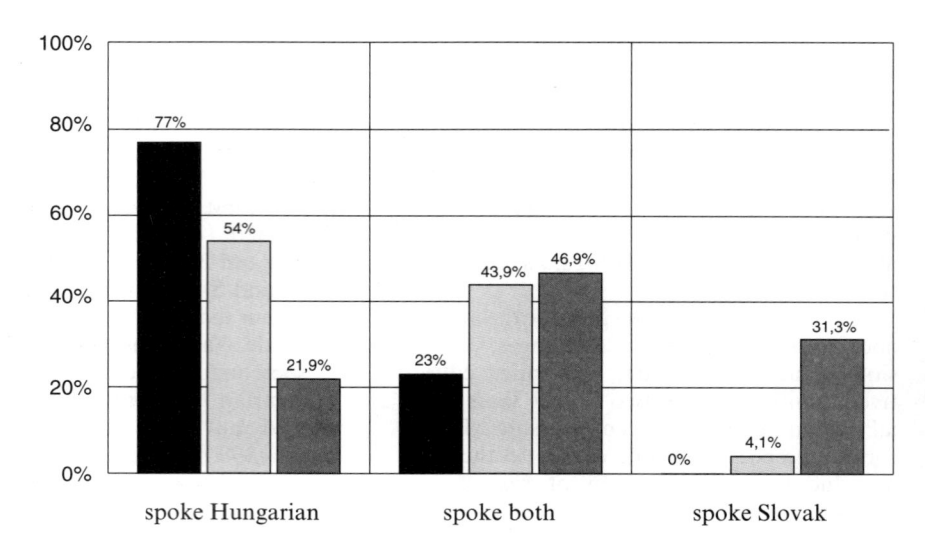

	spoke Hungarian	spoke both	spoke Slovak
Hungarian	77%	23%	0%
Mixed	54%	43,9%	4,1%
Slovak	21,9%	46,9%	31,3%

Language socialization background of parents: Hungarian, Mixed, Slovak

Fig. 210.2: Slovak parents' language socialization and their use of language to their young children. N = 600. Reproduced from Garami/Szántó (1991). Copyright by Társadalomkutatási Informatikai Egyesülés.

agreeable personal experiences when they had tried to use their mother tongue in the day-to-day business of living." (Joó 1991, 105).

It appears that the use of minority languages in the workplace is restricted to those employed in agriculture. In the administration of local governments, a clearcut functional differentiation is evident: in almost half of 107 settlements, local government offices use the nationality languages orally, but the same languages are hardly ever used in writing. In close to half of the churches, the language of service is Hungarian. In this respect Slovaks are the most Magyarized with 73 per cent of the services conducted in Hungarian, while the use of Romanian is reported in about half of the Romanian churches. The frequency of the use of German and Croatian is between that for Slovak and Romanian (Radó 1992, 140). Independent evidence for the little use of Slovak in church is furnished by Garami/Szántó (1991, 40) who found that over half of their 600-strong sample prays exclusively in Hungarian and only 11 per cent do so in Slovak.

Garami/Szántó (1991) provide some clear evidence of ongoing language shift among Slovaks. They studied eight villages in which, according to judgments of local council officials, the number of Slovaks was over 80 per cent. In the random sample used, the percentage of those who identified themselves as Slovak ranged from 5.1 to 89.9. On the basis of the subjects' parents' language use in the family and the subjects' use of Slovak or Hungarian among peers in childhood and in the schools attended, a language socialization space was created for six hundred 50-to-60-year-old Slovaks. Forty-four per cent of the sample have a Hungarian background, 23 per cent have mixed, and 33 per cent have a Slovak-language background.

Slightly less than 30 per cent of the children of the linguistically most Slovak parents have learned Slovak to native proficiency, and 70 per cent have deficient or no knowledge of Slovak. These findings — despite the obvious methodological differences — resemble Gal's (1979) study of language shift from Hungarian to German in Austria.

By and large little is known about the current sociolinguistic situation of Hungary's

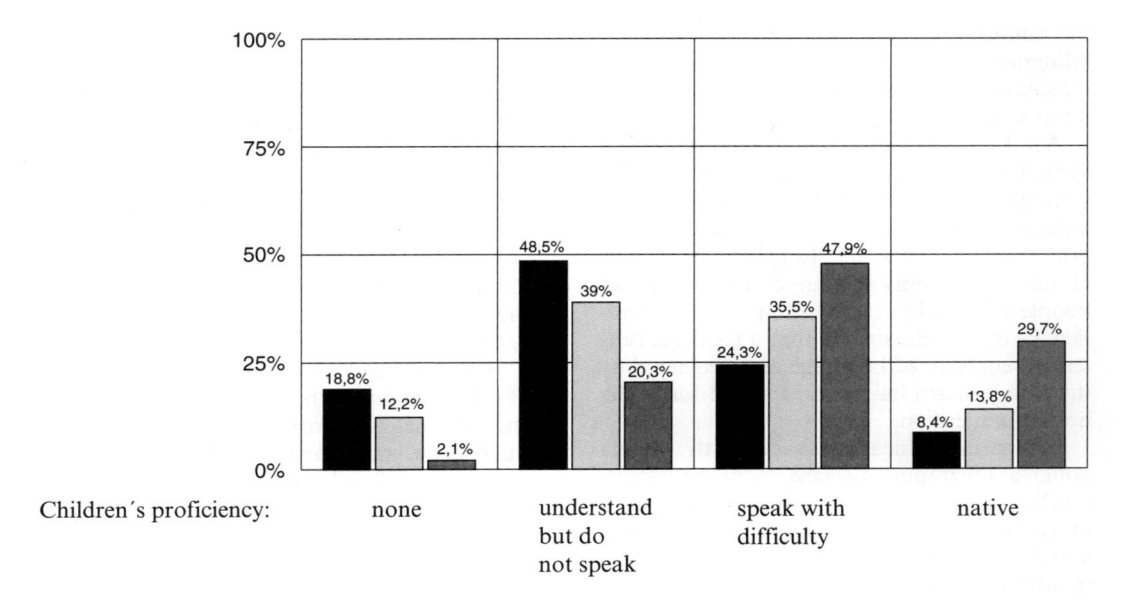

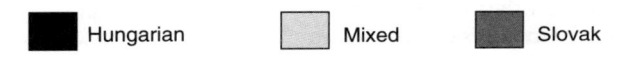

Fig. 210.3: Parents' language socialization and their children's proficiency in Slovak. N = 600. Reproduced from Garami/Szántó (1991). Copyright by Társadalomkutatási Informatikai Egyesülés.

national minorities. Their scattered settlements, a high degree of industrialization and urbanization are all conducive to language shift. Government efforts to check language shift and foster language maintenance, aided by increased contacts with the newly unified Germany, the newly separated Slovakia and other "mother countries", may bring about some changes in the future.

6. Language political situation

6.1. The language political situation

Deeply concerned for the rights of Hungarian minorities in neighboring countries, the government of the Hungarian Republic is vitally interested in fostering language maintenance among Hungary's national minorities. There is a broad consensus in Hungary that the *constitutional* position of the nationalities has been exemplary, but the extent to which the policies are realized in practice shows great variation.

On the basis of the recently passed Minorities Act (see 3.1.2. above), the language rights of nationalities in Hungary appear to be characterizable by a position somewhere between overt permission and promotion (see Skutnabb-Kangas 1990, 28).

Current political commitment towards minorities is reflected, for instance, by the 200 million Forints (US $2.5 million) allocated in the 1992 national budget for the operational costs of minority organizations, and the 90 million Forints (US $1.1 million) offered on a competitive basis for the support of minority cultural and educational activity.

6.2. Schools

During the coalition government in 1945–48, the national minorities tended to have schools in which instruction was provided through the medium of the nationality languages. There were, in addition, a number of Hungarian-language schools which also taught the minority languages. Minority language schooling increased until 1960, when the minority schools were officially renamed bilingual schools, thus putting an end to a system of education where the dominant medium was a nationality language.

Act I of 1985 on Education (enacted in September 1986) laid down as one of its basic principles that "the language of education at kindergartens and of education and instruction at schools shall be Hungarian as well as all national idioms spoken in the Hungarian People's Republic" (art. 7, chap. I). The significance of this consists in that a legal guarantee for equality of language as recognized by the Constitution has been provided for in the field of education.

Hungarian education is currently undergoing a revamping process from an almost totally government-controlled system to a more decentralized education. The outcome and how it will affect education for national minorities cannot yet be seen. Kontra/Székely (1993) characterized the educational scene in 1990 as follows:

There are three types of kindergartens for minority children: (1) mother tongue kindergartens provide 20–30 minutes of instruction in the nationality language every day, (2) bilingual kindergartens provide two days of mother tongue instruction a week, and (3) nationality kindergartens, which, since 1987, have provided education through the mother tongue for four days a week, and through Hungarian the fifth day. In 1989–90, ninety-five per cent of the 295 kindergartens for minority children were of type (1). Some form of kindergarten teaching through German, Romanian, Serbo-Croatian, Slovak or Slovene was provided for a total of 13,108 children.

General schools (for 6- to 14-year-olds) have also three kinds. In 1989–90, ninety-two per cent of the 43,300 pupils studying in a minority school were pupils of the type of school which provides no more than the teaching of the minority language and literature in the pupils' mother tongue, in four to six periods a week.

Secondary schools (for 15- to 18-year-olds) for minority students comprise (a) gimnáziums, and (b) vocational schools for kindergarten teachers, where singing, methods, teaching practicum and other subjects are taught through the mother tongue. In six minority gimnáziums a total of 600 students studied in 1989–90. Instruction in the gimnáziums is bilingual, with perhaps a slight domination of the minority language as the medium of teaching. An additional 350 German students received instruction through German in two other gimnáziums. Kindergarten teacher training was provided for 107 German, Serbo-Croatian and Slovak students.

Primary school teacher training began between 1946 and 1953 for the Yugoslav, Slovak and Romanian minorities, and in 1956 for the Germans. The task is shared between the Teacher Training Colleges in Szeged and Szombathely, and the University of Pécs.

A lack of qualified teachers in a number of schools is somewhat made up for by native speaking teachers from Germany, the former Yugoslavia, and Slovakia.

Gypsies (cf. 7.1. below) present a crucial problem, quite different from the other non-Magyar speakers. Almost without exception, bilingual Gypsy children are taught by monolingual Hungarian teachers in monolingual schools, in an educational milieu which does not much tolerate the linguistic and cultural differences which the Gypsy children bring to school. An almost total lack of qualified Gypsy teachers seems to be an unbreakable vicious circle. There is a great need for the elimination of the prevailing "elimination of the vernacular of Gypsies" attitude among policy-makers as well as those responsible for the implementation of policies.

6.3. Language planning

The *status* of nationality languages in Hungary will be probably elevated as a result of the new Minorities Act (cf. 3.1.2.). However, at least as important as the legal situation and government attitudes, are the relations between Hungary and the respective countries as perceived by the majority Hungarian population. The new political climate and the availability of German satellite TV programs are rapidly transforming German from a language to be forgotten to one that is symbolically perceived as more powerful than the state language, Hungarian (Gal 1995).

In other cases, whatever status planning may be undertaken in Hungary, the results may be very adversely affected by, for example, the ethnic cleansing in Slavonia and Serbia targeting also Hungarians or the extreme anti-Hungarian nationalism in Romania (see Gallagher 1992). In fact, Patterson (1991, 119) offers "embarrassment at being from an ethnic group whose native country persecutes its Hungarian minority" as one of four reasons for the loss of Romanian language and culture in Hungary.

As regards *corpus planning*, relatively much has been said about the conflict between the pupils' vernacular dialects and the literary languages taught in the schools. In the German town of Bóly, for example, the local dialect is clearly distinguished from the more general standard German learned in school. Satellite-transmitted German television has made the differences even more conspicuous, resulting in "a kind of folk comparative linguistics that distinguishes which stations (and thus regions) are 'easier to understand' and therefore 'closer to us'" (Gal 1995, 97). Although the differences between the local dialects and the respective standard varieties taught in schools are widely recognized, no thorough sociolinguistic studies of such differences have yet been conducted which may aid the educational process.

The major language planning task facing Hungary, however, is clearly related to Gypsy children's schooling. If Hungary is to break with her assimilationist educational policy for Gypsies (see 6.2. and 7.1.), a great amount of high-quality descriptive and sociolinguistic research has to be done in preparation for the writing of adequate teaching materials and the training of teachers. This is an enormous challenge; the success of vernacular education for bilingual Gypsies will be a litmus test of the success of the Minority Act.

6.4. The media

As of January 1993, Hungarian Radio broadcast a 30-minute program in each of five nationality languages (Croatian, German, Romanian, Serbian and Slovak) seven days a week. Once a week, Hungarian Television had a 25-minute program in each of these five languages plus in Slovenian. Gypsies also had 25 minutes allotted to a *Cigány Magazin* on television. At least one illegal radio station (*Tilos Rádió* 'Forbidden Radio') specialized in transmitting programs about ethnic diversity. How the electronic media scene will change when parliament passes the Media Act, which has been the source of a major domestic political crisis for years, is hard to tell.

7. Presentation of language contact and contact languages

7.1. Gypsy

According to the Encyclopedia of Human Rights (Lawson 1991, 791), "Recent decades have seen a considerable improvement in the material conditions of a significant part of [the Gypsy] population by comparison of the previously prevailing conditions of historical backwardness and marginality." Communist government programs covered such issues as improved housing (the liquidation of Gypsy shanties), education, health care, family planning etc. In the late 1980s the ratio of able-bodied males employed was about 85 per cent, conforming to that of non-Gypsy males. Female employment was at about 53 per cent, or 25 per cent below women's employment in Hungary. Primary school attendance improved dramatically, but many children repeat classes and are over-age. The ratio of those continuing their studies beyond the primary level, i. e. age 14, was very low, about 37 per cent, compared with 94 per cent of non-Gypsy children.

In 1961 the Central Committee of the ruling Communist Party decreed that Gypsies did not constitute a national minority. This laid the foundations of a policy which, disregarding differences in language and culture, treated Gypsies as nothing more than a social problem. Gypsies tend to be the poorest in Hungarian society, and poverty is viewed as a moral short-coming. The Hungarian word *cigány* is often used as a synonym for "criminality" in government discourse (Crowe 1991). In fact, it is only since January 1, 1990 that the Ministry of the Interior has banned the official use of the term *cigánybűnözés* 'Gypsy crime' in its documents. Current sentiments are illustrated by demands for "Gypsy-free zones" as well as skinhead attacks on Gypsies, which prompted the creation of a Gypsy Civilian Guard in late 1992.

The fact that Gypsies have been termed an ethnic minority in contradistinction to national minorities has had far-reaching consequences for their educational and linguistic treatment. While nobody has denied the right to mother-tongue education of the national minorities, most of the bilingual Gypsies have been denied the right to study in their non-Hungarian vernacular. During Communism, arguments for the denial included dialectal diversity, the lack of a standardized Romāni dialect for instruction, and the sparsity of teaching materials and qualified teachers. In the 1970s, some linguists and educators argued that Gypsy dialects had no more than about 1,200 lexical items, therefore Gypsy bilinguals could be successful academically only by giving up their mother tongue and assimilating to the majority culture. Sociolinguists like Réger investigated the linguistic aspects proper of the Gypsies' sociocultural deprivation, and thwarted the linguistically untenable views of Vekerdi (cf. Vekerdi 1988; Réger 1974, 1988, 1995).

Réger (1995) describes Gypsy-Hungarian bilingualism as bilingualism with diglossia à la Fishman. Romāni (or, in the case of the Boyash Gypsies, Romanian) is used for intragroup, mainly informal communication, while Hungarian serves the purpose of public communication. On special occasions, however, Romāni may be used for formal communication as well (see Stewart 1989).

In a recent paper on educational segregation, which is based on fieldwork conducted in 1985—86, Csongor writes the following:

"In none of the schools we studied did the Gypsy mother-tongue or bilingualism play a role in organizing classes. In only one case — in a day care center — did we meet a teacher who could understand and speak the children's vernacular. Teaching in the mother-tongue plays no role in the education of Gypsy children. Equally minimal is the success of teaching Hungarian.
We have heard about Gypsy audio cassettes and teaching materials. Their reception was problematic: teachers blamed either the Gypsy kids ('these children don't even know Gypsy') or the authors of the materials ('they don't know how Gypsies really speak.')" (Csongor 1991, 12)

In 1971 the proportion of Gypsy university graduates was 0.1 per cent, but of illiterates it was 40 per cent. By the end of 1992 unemployment in Hungary reached 10 per cent, but among Gypsies it was about 60 per cent. In this new situation, says Csalog (1992, 78), "the dreams of assimilation have vanished."

Important new developments have been taking place, however, since the fall of Communism in 1989. Gypsy journals have appeared and Gypsy intellectuals are publishing dictionaries, teaching materials and folklore anthologies in an effort to create Gypsy literature and help Gypsy literacy (for details and the problems generated by a mischosen transcription system see Réger 1995). They have also gained political representation unknown before: two Gypsies were elected to be members of the new parliament in 1990. The wording of article 45, paragraph 2 of the new Minority Act seems to grant the right from vernacular to bilingual education for Gypsies: "In order to decrease the educational disadvantages of the Gypsy minority, special educational conditions may be created." If bilingual educational programs are in fact implemented in future, the plight of the Hungarian Gypsy may be eased, at least in a linguistic-cultural sense.

The "Gypsy problem" is exacerbated by a "phalanx of prejudice" (cf. Crowe 1991, 120), which portrays Gypsies as unreliable, anti-social, even genetically prone to crime. This latter accusation has been made in the printed educational literature (cf. Csongor/Szuhay 1992, 239 for a brief review), and most recently by a writer-turned-politician, István Csurka (1992, 15—16). His ignorance in these matters earned him an invitation, printed in a national daily, to an introductory course in genetics from a professor in the University of Budapest (Fodor 1992).

7.2. Yiddish

Crowe (in Kovacs/Crowe 1985, 166—168) provides a succinct history of Hungary's Jewish community and its assimilation. Three decades ago Garvin (1965, 93) called Hungarian Yiddish, which belongs to the Western Yiddish dialects, "near-extinct". Interviewing Hungarian Yiddish speakers in New York City in 1943 and in 1959, he established five subdialect areas: Southwestern (northwest of Lake Balaton), South-Central (in and around Budapest), Northwestern (in Southwestern Slovakia), North-Central (from the city of Miskolc as far east as Šahy, Hungarian: Ipolyság, in Southern Slovakia), and Northeastern (around Kisvárda).

Hutterer (1965) is a phonology of Budapest Yiddish, based on tape recordings made in Budapest in 1960. The state of the language as obtained from the informants "reflects the usage before and at the turn of our century." He notes (1965, 143) that an analysis of Budapest Yiddish should consider "the Southwestern Yiddish basis; the Central Yiddish stratum; the influences of the local German dialects, the Viennese and literary German vernacular; and, at present, also the effect of the colloquial Hungarian language."

Whereas Yiddish is probably dead by now in Budapest, it has influenced some varieties of Budapest speech in intonation. It has been hypothesized by Kontra/Gósy (1987) that Hungarian-Americans, when speaking Hungarian with their American intonation, may evoke negative attitudes in those metropolitan Hungarians on whose ears the "sing-song Yiddish intonation" (cf. Weinreich 1956), equal to Budapest Yiddish intonation, grates.

8. Critical evaluation of the sources and literature

Historical sources with a focus on the minorities rather rarely offer unbiased views and objective treatment, although important exceptions exist. Propagandistic as it is, Kővágó (1981) is a major source for Communist policies. Kovacs/Crowe (1985) and Wagner (1988) are good short introductions written by westerners. Jointly authored by Hungarian and western scholars, Sugar (1990) contains plenty of information on the history of Hungarian minorities. Kertesz (1953) is a major source for the expulsion of Germans after WW II. Paikert's work (1953, 1967) furnishes probably the best description of the German-Hungarians between 1920 and 1945 as well as a detailed, excellent analysis of Hungarian national, linguistic, and educational policies in the same era. Janics/Borsody (1982) provides a meticulously documented history of the Slovak-Hungarian population exchange, completely unknown in the west before the book was published.

Karády (1990) is undoubtedly the best "historical-sociological sketch" of how Hungary has become a Hungarian-language country. Although limited in scope, the same author's 1989 paper is an excellent treatment of the denomination-cum-nationality scene around 1900.

The recent sociological studies, e.g. Garami/Szántó (1991), Joó (1991), Radó (1992), and the anthropological article by Patterson (1991) lack linguistic sophistication.

Vekerdi's views of the complex of Gypsy issues, succinctly summarized in his 1988 article, are countered by Réger's linguistically sound critique, published in the same year. Csongor/Szuhay (1992) is an excellent critical survey of research on Gypsies.

Based on considerable participant observation, Gal (1993) is pioneering in the study of linguistic attitudes and ideologies among Germans in Hungary. Finally, Sherwood's 1993 paper is essential reading for the understanding of the current Hungarian metalanguage on ethnicity.

8.1. Scientific and parascientific discussion on the international scene

Historians, politicians, journalists and amateur linguists all add to a noisy international discourse on ethnic problems within and outside Hungary. When Slovak writers accuse Hungary of the ethnocide of her Slovak minority (cited by Szarka 1992, 62–3), a rebuff points out the distortion and partial concealment from the public of historical facts (e.g. Janics 1992).

Despite the fact that the Hungarian government (and with a few exceptions all politicians) have been painstakingly avoiding any mention of changing borders, some propagandists and politicians in Romania and Slovakia rouse their constituents to the dangers of possible Hungarian aggression (see Baba 1992).

A curious border dispute emerged when Slovakia diverted the Danube at the Gabčikovo dam in the Fall of 1992: the Danube being the international border, the Hungarian prime minister considered this a violation of Hungary's territorial integrity (FBIS-EEU-92-246).

Ethnic persecution and violence have caused an influx of refugees into Hungary from Romania and the former Yugoslavia since 1987: in December 1992, an estimated 40,000 Yugoslav refugees were in Hungary (FBIS-EEU-92-246). A certain measure of anti-refugee sentiment, even among Romanian-Hungarians towards ethnic Romanian refugees (see Patterson 1991) on the one hand, and increasing levels of economic and cultural relations between Hungary and the unified Germany on the other hand, are some of the components which influence the climate for the national minorities in Hungary in the early 1990s.

9. Bibliography (selected)

1990. évi népszámlálás. A nemzetiségi népesség száma egyes községekben (1960–1990), Budapest, 1991.

1990. évi népszámlálás. Magyarország nemzetiségi adatai megyénként, Budapest, 1992.

Aczél, György (1984): "National minority rights: The law of socialism". In: *New Hungarian Quarterly 25/95*, 6–10.

Baba, Ivan (1992): "Frontiers and minorities: Interview with Ivan Baba". In: *East European Reporter 5/4*, 55–57.

Barany, George (1990): "The age of royal absolutism, 1790–1848". In: *A history of Hungary*, Sugar, P. (Ed.), Bloomington/Indianapolis, 174–208.

Borbély, Anna (1990): *Cercetări asupra graiurilor românesti din Ungaria: Chitigaz, Micherechi, Otlaka-Pusta*, Budapest.

Crowe, David (1991): "The Gypsies in Hungary". In: *The Gypsies of Eastern Europe*, D. Crowe/Kolsti, J. (Eds.), Armonk/London, 117–131.

Csalog, Zsolt (1992): "'We offer our love': Gypsies in Hungary". In: *New Hungarian Quarterly 33/127*, 70−80.

Csongor, Anna (1991): "Cigány osztályok Magyarországon: Szegregáció az általános iskolában". In: *Phralipe 10*, 9−15.

Csongor, Anna/Szuhay, Péter (1992): "Cigány kultúra, cigánykutatások". In: *BUKSZ 4*, 235−245.

Csurka, István (1992): "Néhány gondolat a rendszerváltozás két esztendeje és az MDF új programja kapcsán". In: *Magyar Fórum 4/34*, 9−16.

Dávid, Zoltán (1988): "The Hungarians and their neighbors, 1851−2000". In: *The Hungarians: A divided nation*, Borsody, S. (Ed.), New Haven, 333−345.

Dávid, Zoltán (1993): "A magyarországi nemzetiségek 1990-ben". In: *Valóság 10*, 34−42.

FBIS-EEU-92-246 = *Foreign Broadcast Information Service, East Europe*, 22 December 1992.

Fodor, András (1992): "Meghívom genetikai óráimra: Nyílt levél Csurka Istvánhoz". In: *Magyar Nemzet* 9 September, 14.

Frank, Tibor (1990): "Hungary and the Dual Monarchy, 1867−1890". In: *A history of Hungary*, Sugar, P. (Ed.), Bloomington/Indianapolis, 252−266.

Gal, Susan (1979): *Language shift*, New York.

Gal, Susan (1993): "Diversity and contestation in linguistic ideologies: German speakers in Hungary". In: *Language in Society 22*, 337−359.

Gal, Susan (1995): "Cultural bases of language use among German-speakers in Hungary". In: *International Journal of the Sociology of Language 111*, 93−102.

Gallagher, Tom (1992): "*Vatra Românească* and resurgent nationalism in Romania". In: *Ethnic and Racial Studies* 15, 570−598.

Garami, Erika/Szántó, János (1991). *Magyarországi szlovákok*. (Társadalomkutatási Informatikai Egyesülés, Gyorsjelentések 6.) Budapest.

Garvin, Paul L. (1965): "The dialect geography of Hungarian Yiddish". In: *The field of Yiddish, Second collection*, Weinreich, U. (Ed.), London/The Hague/Paris, 92−115.

Hajdú, Tibor/Nagy, Zsuzsa L. (1990): "Revolution, counterrevolution, consolidation". In: *A history of Hungary*, Sugar, P. (Ed.), Bloomington/Indianapolis, 295−318.

Hutterer, Miklós (1960): "A Dunántúli Középhegység németsége és a magyarországi német nyelvjáráskutatás problémái". In: *Magyar Nyelv 56*, 220−232.

Hutterer, C. J. (1965): "The phonology of Budapest Yiddish". In: *The field of Yiddish, Second collection*, Weinreich, U. (Ed.), London/The Hague/Paris, 116−146.

Janics, Kálmán/Borsody, Stephen (1982): *Czechoslovak policy and the Hungarian minority, 1945−1948*, New York.

Janics, Kálmán (1992): "Tudatlanság, felelőtlenség és dezinformálás". In: *Magyar Nemzet* 2 November, 1992, 7.

Jeszenszky, Géza (1990): "Hungary through World War I and the end of the Dual Monarchy". In: *A history of Hungary*, Sugar, P. (Ed.), Bloomington/Indianapolis, 267−294.

Joó, Rudolf (1991): "Slovenes in Hungary and Hungarians in Slovenia: ethnic and state identity". In: *Ethnic and Racial Studies 14*, 100−106.

Karady, Victor (1989): "Assimilation and schooling: national and denominational minorities in the universities of Budapest around 1900". In: *Hungary and European civilization*, Ránki, G. (Ed.), Budapest, 285−319.

Karády, Viktor (1990): "Egyenlőtlen elmagyarosodás, avagy hogyan vált Magyarország magyar nyelvű országgá?". In: *Századvég 2*, 5−37.

Kertesz, Stephen (1953): "The expulsion of the Germans from Hungary: A study in postwar diplomacy". In: *The Review of Politics 15*, 179−208.

Kertész, Stephen D. (1982): "The consequences of World War I: The effects on East Central Europe". In: *Essays on World War I: total war and peacemaking, a case study on Trianon*, Király, B. K./Pastor, P./Sanders, I. (Eds.), New York, 39−57.

Kontra, Miklós/Gósy, Mária (1987): "Interference in intonation: Notes on Hungarian-Americans". In: *The thirteenth LACUS forum, 1986*, Fleming, I. (Ed.), Lake Bluff, IL, 136−145.

Kontra, Miklós/Székely, András B. (1993): "Hungary". In: *Sociolinguistica 7*, 135−142.

Kovacs, Martin L./Crowe, David (1985): "National minorities in Hungary, 1919−1980". In: *Eastern European national minorities 1919−1980, A handbook*, Horak, S. M. (Ed.), Littleton, CO, 160−189.

Kővágó, László (1981): *Nemzetiségek a mai Magyarországon*, Budapest.

Lawson, Edward (1991): *Encyclopedia of human rights*, New York/Philadelphia/Washington/London.

Magyar Köztársaság alkotmánya. In: *Magyar Közlöny 74* (23 October, 1989).

Makkai, László (1990): "Hungary before the Hungarian conquest". In: *A history of Hungary*, Sugar, P. (Ed.), Bloomington/Indianapolis, 1−7.

Manherz, Karl (1977): *Sprachgeographie und Sprachsoziologie der deutschen Mundarten in Westungarn*, Budapest.

Nelde, Peter H. (Ed.), (1990): *Deutsch als Muttersprache in Ungarn*, Stuttgart.

Nelde, Peter H./Vandermeeren, Sonja/Wölck, Wolfgang (1991): *Interkulturelle Mehrsprachigkeit*, Bonn.

Paget, John (1850/1971): *Hungary and Transylvania, Volumes I & II*, Reprint edition, New York.

Paikert, G. C. (1953): "Hungary's national minority policies, 1920−1945". In: *The American Slavic and East European Review* 12, 201−218.

Paikert, G. C. (1967): *The Danube Swabians: German populations in Hungary, Rumania and Yugoslavia and Hitler's impact on their patterns*, The Hague.

Patterson, James G. (1991): "Hungary's disappearing Romanian minority". In: *East European Quarterly 25*, 117−123.

Radó, Péter (1992): "A nemzeti kisebbségek nyilvános nyelvhasználata Magyarországon". In: *Regio 3/2*, 135−146.

Réger Zita (1974): "Kétnyelvű cigánygyerekek az iskoláskor elején". In: *Valóság 1*, 50−62.

Réger, Zita (1988): "A cigány nyelv: kutatások és vitapontok". In: *Műhelymunkák a nyelvészet és társtudományai köréből 4*, 155−178.

Réger, Zita (1995): "The language of Gypsies in Hungary: An overview of researches". In: *International Journal of the Sociology of Language 111*, 79−91.

Réger, Zita/Berko Gleason, Jean (1991): "Romāni child-directed speech and children's language among Gypsies in Hungary". In: *Language in Society 20*, 601−617.

Seton-Watson, R. W. (1908/1972): *Racial problems in Hungary*, London. [1972 reprint, New York]

Sherwood, Peter (1993): "How to be a Hungarian. Some problems of meaning, reference and style in Hungarian discourse on ethnicity". In: *Studies in Cultural Interaction in Europe, East and West* 3, 23−33. University of Amsterdam.

Skutnabb-Kangas, Tove (1990): *Language, literacy and minorities. A Minority Rights Group Report*, London.

Spira, Thomas (1977): *German−Hungarian relations and the Swabian problem: from Károlyi to Gömbös, 1919−1936*, New York.

Stepanović, Predrag (1986): *A taxonomic description of the dialects of Serbs and Croats in Hungary*, Budapest.

Stewart, Michael (1989): " 'True speech': Song and the moral order of a Hungarian Vlach Gypsy community". In: *Man 24/1*, 79−101.

Szarka, László (1992): "A magyar kisebbségek Magyarország szomszédországi kapcsolataiban". In: *Regio 3/1*, 57−63.

Törvény. "1993. évi LXXVII. törvény a nemzeti és etnikai kisebbségek jogairól". In: *Magyar Közlöny 100* (22 July, 1993).

Vekerdi, József (1988): "The Gypsies and the Gypsy problem in Hungary". In: *Hungarian Studies Review 15/2*, 13−26.

Wagner, Francis S. (1988): "Ethnic minorities in Hungary since World War II". In: *Triumph in adversity*, Várdy, S. B./Várdy, A. H. (Eds.), New York, 367−387.

Weinreich, Uriel (1956): "Notes on the Yiddish rise-fall intonation contour". In: *For Roman Jakobson*, Halle, M. et al. (Eds.), The Hague, 633−643.

Miklós Kontra, Budapest (Hungary)

211. Ungarisch−Deutsch

1. Geographie und Demographie
2. Geschichte
3. Politik, Wirtschaft und kulturelle sowie religiöse Lage
4. Ethnoprofile
5. Soziolinguistische Lage
6. Sprachpolitische Lage
7. Allgemeines kontaktlinguistisches Porträt
8. Zur Forschungslage
9. Bibliographie (in Auswahl)

1. Geographie und Demographie

Obwohl die Angaben hinsichtlich der Zahl der Deutschen in Ungarn (im weiteren: Ungarndeutsche) relativ große Schwankungen zeigen, stellt diese Volksgruppe nach den Zigeunern die größte ethnische Minderheit der rund 10,5 Millionen Einwohner zählenden Ungarischen Republik dar (→ Sprachenkarte L).

Die mitunter erheblichen Diskrepanzen zwischen offiziellen Angaben und verschiedenen Schätzungen hinsichtlich der Zahl der Ungarndeutschen sind auf verschiedene Gründe zurückzuführen. Teils schwanken sie in Abhängigkeit von der jeweiligen politischen Situation bzw. der jeweils aktuellen Minderheitenpolitik, teils sind sie bedingt durch die konkrete Fragestellung. Bei dem ersten Zensus nach dem Zweiten Weltkrieg, 1949, wurden 2617(!) ungarndeutsche Bürger registriert; 1980 waren es 11 310; 1990 30 824 (aus: Történeti Statisztikai Idősorok [Historische Statistische Zeitfolgen] Bd. 1, S. 32 f. − Veröffentlichung des Ungarischen Statistischen Zentralamtes 1992). Nach ihrer Muttersprache befragt, gaben laut derselben Quelle 1980 31 231, 1990 37 511 Bürger Deutsch als Muttersprache an. Die Interessenvertretung der Ungarndeutschen bezifferte hingegen ihre Zahl im letzten Jahrzehnt stets auf 220 000.

Die Ungarndeutschen stellen in bestimmten Regionen des Landes teilweise noch immer einen relativ hohen Anteil an der Bevölkerung dar: in bestimmten Ortschaften der Branau (Baranya), in der Tolnau (Tolna), auch als Schwäbische Türkei bekannt, im Ofner Hügelland (Budai Hegyvidék), im Schildgebirge (Vértes), im Buchenwald (Bakony) und an der österreichischen Grenze um Ödenburg (Sopron), Güns (Kőszeg) und Steinamanger (Szombathely). Östlich der Donau, in der Großen Ungarischen Tiefebene (Alföld) gibt es weitere Dörfer mit einem bestimmten Anteil an ungarndeutschen Einwohnern (s. Karte 211.1).

Einvernehmen besteht darüber, daß für die Volksgruppe der Ungarndeutschen schon im ganzen 20. Jahrhundert eine starke Assimilierungstendenz charakteristisch war, die in ihren Wurzeln auf die ungarische Entwicklung im ausgehenden 19. Jahrhundert und um die Jahrhundertwende zurückgeht (vgl. 4. und 5.).

2. Geschichte

Der Sprachkontakt zwischen Ungarn und Deutschen besteht seit der Ungarischen Landnahme (896), d. h., seitdem das ungarische Volk im Karpatenbecken, in unmittelbarer Nachbarschaft zu dem deutschen Sprachraum, seßhaft geworden ist.

In der Gefolgschaft der Frau des ersten ungarischen Königs, Stephans des Hl. († 1038), Gisela von Bayern, zogen Adelige und Beamte, Priester, Soldaten und Handwerker in das junge Königreich auf dem Wege vom Heidentum zum Christentum. Am Ausbau und an der Stabilisierung des neuen Staates waren die deutschen „Gäste" — man nannte sie damals „hospes" — aktiv beteiligt. Die Kontakte waren in den folgenden Jahrhunderten stets relativ intensiv. So kam es zur Entstehung der ersten geschlossenen deutschen Siedlungen im damaligen Ungarn, größtenteils in Gebieten, die seit Ende des Ersten Weltkriegs außerhalb der Staatsgrenzen Ungarns liegen. Das deutsche Bürgertum war bereits zu Beginn des 14. Jahrhunderts zu einem wichtigen wirtschaftlichen und politischen Faktor geworden, da es den ungarischen König in seinem Kampf gegen die feudale Oligarchie unterstützte.

Die Kontakte sind in jenen Jahrhunderten nicht unidirektional geblieben. Schon sehr bald zogen wissensdurstige junge Ungarn an deutschsprachige Universitäten, wovon z. B. die Matrikeln der Wiener Universität zeugen: vom 14. bis Anfang des 17. Jahrhunderts hatten sich dort mehr als fünftausend Studenten aus dem damaligen Ungarn immatrikuliert. Auch fahrende junge Gesellen erlernten ihr Handwerk jahrhundertelang vielfach in deutschen Landen. Neben der bedeutenden gesellschaftlich-politischen Rolle vor allem des städtischen deutschen Bürgertums war es auch diesen Ungarn zu verdanken, daß das Deutsche, sowohl Sprache als auch Kulturgut, einen starken Einfluß auf die Entwicklung des Ungarischen ausübte. So wurden zahlreiche Urkunden in deutscher Sprache verfaßt: „Aus der Zeitspanne vom 14. Jahrhundert bis 1686 haben wir ein ziemlich reichhaltiges deutsches Schrifttum, darunter vom vierten Jahrzehnt des 16. Jahrhunderts an auch Drucke. (...) Die Textsorten reichen von den verschiedenen Gattungen der Kanzleipraxis und des praktischen Schrifttums der Bürger (Geschäftsbuch, Hausarzneibuch, Chronik usw.) bis zum Schöngeistigen" (Mollay 1986, 113). Nach Mollay ist die Zweisprachigkeit spätestens seit dem 16. Jahrhundert als wichtigste Quelle für Entlehnungen aus dem Deutschen anzusehen (Mollay 1982, 135 ff).

Die deutschen Kolonisten aus den Jahrhunderten bis zur Besetzung Ungarns durch die Türken haben sich im Laufe der Zeit weitgehend assimiliert. Im heutigen Ungarn sind es lediglich die Siedlungen entlang der österreichischen Grenze sowie das Dorf Großpilsen (Nagybörzsöny) nördlich der ungarischen Hauptstadt, die ihre Geschichte bis in die Jahrhunderte vor der Türkenbesetzung zurückverfolgen, ihre deutsche Muttersprache und Identität bis heute bewahrt haben.

Nach der rund 150jährigen Besetzung ausgedehnter Gebiete Ungarns durch die Türken (nach 1526 bis 1686) folgte die zweite Etappe der „Kolonisation", als in den entvölkerten Regionen vorwiegend deutsche Bauern angesiedelt wurden. Die Mehrheit der heutigen Ungarndeutschen verfolgt ihre Geschichte in der neuen Heimat bis ins 17.–18. Jahrhundert zurück, als die Ansiedlung ihrer Vorfahren in drei „Wellen" erfolgt war (Hutterer 1990, 51 f).

Bedingt durch die Zugehörigkeit Ungarns zum Reich der Habsburger bis 1918 verlagerte sich der Schwerpunkt der Kontakte zum Deutschen zunehmend auf den süddeutsch-österreichischen Raum mit der Folge, daß sich im späteren der Ausgleich der Mundarten auf bayrisch-österreichischer Grundlage vollzog (vgl. 7.).

Als wichtiger Einschnitt in der Geschichte der Ungarndeutschen ist der Zweite Weltkrieg mit all seinen Folgen hervorzuheben. Ungarndeutsche kämpften im Krieg in der ungarischen oder in der deutschen Armee; von der Zivilbevölkerung wurden zahlreiche Menschen, Frauen wie Männer, in die Sowjetunion zum Arbeitsdienst verschleppt, und viele starben in den Lagern durch Krankheit, Hungersnot und die harten Winter. Vom Januar 1946 bis 1950 erfolgte aufgrund des Potsdamer Abkommens die Aussiedlung der in Ungarn Verbliebenen, der aus dem Krieg oder dem Arbeitsdienst Zurückgekehrten. Diese Maßnahme erfaßte etwa 180 000 Menschen. So reduzierten Kriegsverluste, Flucht und Aussiedlung die Gesamtzahl der Ungarndeutschen auf die Hälfte (vgl. Bellér 1990, 42).

3. Politik, Wirtschaft und kulturelle sowie religiöse Lage

3.1. Politik

In der ungarischen Verfassung von 1949 waren Eigenständigkeit und Rechte der Minderheiten festgelegt, so das Recht auf Gebrauch und Pflege der Muttersprache, auf den schulischen Unterricht (in) der Muttersprache, auf Bewahrung und Pflege der eigenen Kultur. Die praktische Umsetzung erfolgte, bedingt durch die allgemeine politische Lage, zunächst eher zögernd, nach 1956 zunehmend mit größerer Effektivität. Bislang gilt der 1955 gegründete Verband der Ungarndeutschen als einzige offiziöse Interessenvertretung, die sich bemüht, mannigfaltige politische und kulturelle Aufgaben wahrzunehmen.

Im Zuge der tiefgreifenden gesellschaftlichen und politischen Umwälzungen wurde die ungarische Verfassung 1990 modifiziert, politische Rechte und Menschenrechte der Minderheiten bekräftigt. Es ist damit zu rechnen, daß das Ungarische Parlament 1993 ein neues Minderheitengesetz verabschiedet, von dem man sich eine positive Wirkung auf das Fortbestehen auch der Ungarndeutschen verspricht.

3.2. Wirtschaft

Die wirtschaftliche und allgemeine kulturelle Lage der Ungarndeutschen ist weitgehend dadurch bestimmt, daß sie zu einem relativ hohen Anteil nach wie vor in kleinen Dorfsiedlungen leben. Vor allem die jüngeren Generationen sind im Zuge der generell großen Mobilität in Städte oder deren Ballungsgebiete abgewandert und zu Industriearbeitern geworden. Eine nicht geringe Zahl schaffte durch entsprechende Ausbildung den Aufstieg in die Mittelklasse. Beide Entwicklungen führten in der Regel zur Zweisprachigkeit bzw. zum Sprachwechsel und damit zur zunehmenden Assimilation. Es existieren Angaben, nach denen dieser Prozeß bereits 80% der mittleren Generation erfaßt hat (vgl. Born/Dickgießer 1989, 232). Eine gegenläufige Tendenz — Besinnung auf Identität und Sprache — zeichnet sich in jüngster Zeit ab (vgl. Nelde/Vandermeeren/Wölck 1991, 119 f).

3.3. Kultur

Obwohl die Volksgruppe der heutigen Ungarndeutschen keine starke soziale Gliederung aufwies, bestand bis um die Jahrhundertwende auch eine intellektuelle Schicht und die entsprechende Kultur mit deutschen Wurzeln (vgl. 5.), die gesinnungsmäßig und sprachlich eher lose mit den handwerklich-bäuerlichen Schichten der Ungarndeutschen verbunden war und die sich durch die Magyarisierung in der ersten Hälfte des 20. Jahrhunderts auflöste.

Die noch erhaltenen Reste der traditionellen bäuerlichen Kultur werden in den meisten Regionen des Landes sorgfältig gepflegt. Zahlreiche Tanz- und Trachtengruppen, Chöre, Musikkapellen bemühen sich um die Neubelebung alter Sitten und Bräuche. Diese Aktivitäten, an denen sich auch die jüngeren Generationen beteiligen, fördern den Spracherhalt und stärken die eigene Identität. In Dorf- bzw. Heimatmuseen werden die noch erhaltenen Gegenstände des einstigen bäuerlichen Lebens und der verschiedensten, größtenteils bereits ausgestorbenen Berufe aufbewahrt.

Zum kulturellen Gesamtbild gehört die ungarndeutsche Gegenwartsliteratur, die „Anfang der siebziger Jahre — aus einem Zustand des Scheintodes — sozusagen mit Gewalt wieder ins Leben gerufen" wurde (Szabó 1992, 267). Die seither in beachtlicher Zahl, vor allem in Anthologien vorgelegten Werke beweisen, „daß Kultur im Minderheitendasein nicht unbedingt auf die folkloristische Fassade, auf Tanzen, Singen und höchstens etwas handwerkliche Tradition reduzierbar ist" (Szabó 1992, 268).

In der Medienlandschaft Ungarns sind die Ungarndeutschen eher bescheiden vertreten. Außer dem seit 1957 bestehenden Wochenblatt „Neue Zeitung" (Auflagenzahl: 4000) erscheint jährlich der „Deutsche Kalender". Radio Fünfkirchen (Pécs) strahlt seit 1956 täglich ein deutschsprachiges Programm aus (30 Minuten, am Wochenende 45 Minuten). Im UKW-Landesprogramm gibt es eine Sonntagssendung von weiteren 30 Minuten. Das Fernsehstudio Fünfkirchen sendet monatlich einmal in 30 Minuten das Programm „Unser Bildschirm". Die Programme sind inhaltlich und thematisch weitgehend dem Interesse der Ungarndeutschen angepaßt. Seit Mitte der 80er Jahre besteht in Szekszárd das Deutsche Theater. Sämtliche hier zitierten Angaben beziehen sich auf den Stand von 1992.

3.4. Religion

Da die katholischen Habsburger in erster Linie katholische Deutsche ansiedelten, sind die Ungarndeutschen überwiegend römisch-katholischen Glaubens, etwa ein Drittel evangelisch-lutherisch und kalvinistisch. Unabhängig von der konfessionellen Zugehörigkeit kann von einer vergleichsweise bewußten Pflege des Glaubens gesprochen werden: Kirche und Gebet sind eine Domäne, wo die älteren Generationen grundsätzlich noch ihre Muttersprache verwenden.

4. Ethnoprofile

Die Muttersprache der Mehrheit des Landes – das Ungarische – gehört zu den finno-ugrischen Sprachen, ist in Ostmitteleuropa die einzige Sprache dieser Sprachfamilie. Typologisch ist es eine vorwiegend agglutinierende Sprache. Es gilt als ein wichtiges Integrationsmerkmal der Ungarndeutschen als Gruppe, daß sie sich, mit Ausnahme der ältesten Generationen, die Mehrheitssprache angeeignet haben. So wird die deutsche Mundart – als Abbausprache – nur noch in bestimmten Domänen verwendet, und man kann bei den (erwachsenen) Ungarndeutschen von einer generellen Zweisprachigkeit ausgehen. Umgekehrt kommt es (als nicht typische Erscheinung) lediglich in Mischehen vor, daß nicht-ungarndeutsche Ehepartner die betreffende Mundart erlernen.

Während in der Hungarologie der deutsch-ungarische Sprachkontakt, insbesondere die lexikalische Entlehnung aus dem Deutschen, relativ gründlich erforscht ist, hat man in der ungarndeutschen Dialektologie der Frage des Sprachkontakts Ungarisch-Deutsch, dem Einfluß des Ungarischen auf die ungarndeutschen Mundarten, relativ wenig Aufmerksamkeit entgegengebracht. Der Einfluß der Mehrheitssprache ist in erster Linie im Wortschatz der Mundarten in Form von Entlehnungen nachzuweisen. Bezeichnungslücken, deren Zahl bereits in der Zwischenkriegszeit, insbesondere aber nach dem Zweiten Weltkrieg erheblich angestiegen war, deckte man vor allem durch die Übernahme ungarischer Wörter, weniger durch Lehnübersetzungen oder Lehnprägungen. Allerdings zeichnet sich diesbezüglich eine gewisse Veränderung ab, nachdem seit den 60er Jahren durch die verwandtschaftlichen Beziehungen die Kontakte vor allem zur Bundesrepublik intensiver geworden waren: Es tauchen zunehmend standardsprachliche lexikalische Elemente in den Mundarten auf. Andererseits dürfte mit dem Verlust bestimmter lexikalischer Entlehnungen aus dem Ungarischen zu rechnen sein: mit dem Verschwinden zahlreicher Einrichtungen des früheren politisch-ideologischen Gebildes hat sich auch ihre Bezeichnung erübrigt.

Durch die Ansiedlung von Szeklern und Ungarn vor allem aus der heutigen Slowakei in den ehemals überwiegend von Ungarndeutschen bewohnten Ortschaften nach dem Zweiten Weltkrieg kam es nach und nach zu einer ethnischen Mischung. Die in den 50er Jahren noch recht seltenen, wenn nicht undenkbaren Mischehen gehören heute zum Alltag.

5. Soziolinguistische Lage

Aus historischer Perspektive sind für die Entwicklung der Sprachkontakte grundsätzlich zwei Bereiche auseinanderzuhalten: (a) der Einfluß des Deutschen auf die ungarische Sprache durch die mehr oder minder ausgeprägte jahrhundertelange Zweisprachigkeit vor allem der Handwerker, des städtischen Bürgertums und des ungarischen Adels und (b) der Sprachgebrauch der zumeist in ländlichen Gebieten lebenden, ethnisch lange Zeit hindurch weitgehend homogenen und geschlossenen bäuerlichen Kolonisten aus dem 17. und 18. Jahrhundert.

Im Zuge der Entstehung einer ungarischen nationalen Identität entfaltete sich im 18. Jahrhundert das sog. „Hungarus"-Bewußtsein, mit der deutsch-ungarischen Zweisprachigkeit als Wesensmerkmal. Die deutsche Kultur im weitesten Sinn hatte Vorbildcharakter für die Schaffung der ungarischen nationalen Kultur — diese Rolle wäre ohne engste sprachliche Kontakte — d. h. ohne Entlehnungsprozesse — kaum denkbar gewesen. Der Einfluß der deutschen Sprache war vom Wortschatz der Wissenschaften über jenen des bürgerlichen Lebens bis in die Kunst gegenwärtig. Einen Eindruck über die Intensität der Kontakte vermitteln einige Daten: Es gab in Ungarn deutschsprachige Zeitschriften, z. B. den *Literarischen Anzeiger für Ungarn* (1797—1799), die *Zeitschrift von und für Ungarn* (1802—1804); ein ständiges deutsches Theater in Buda (Ofen) und Pest von 1787 bis 1889; eine deutschsprachige Tageszeitung, *Pester Lloyd* (1854—1944) bzw. nach 1956 bis etwa 1990 das Wochenblatt *Budapester Rundschau.*

Bei den bäuerlichen deutschen Kolonisten war die Zweisprachigkeit — bedingt durch die Lebensbedingungen — eher die Ausnahme als die Regel; Sprachkontakte entstanden — wenn überhaupt — vor allem in umgekehrter Richtung, als Einfluß des Ungarischen auf die deutschen Mundarten. Die gegenwärtige Lage ist durch eine Zwei- bzw. Dreisprachigkeit gekennzeichnet — mit geringfügigen generationsbedingten Unterschieden. Es ist dies eine spezifische Form des Sprachwechsels, von einem ungarndeutschen Dialekt zur Standardvarietät des Ungarischen, während die ungarndeutschen Kinder die deutsche Standardsprache in der Schule als Zweit- oder Drittsprache erlernen. Ihre Rolle als Kommunikationsmittel ist eher auf die Kontakte mit Ausländern beschränkt. Die deutsche Standardsprache erscheint noch in den Medien der Ungarndeutschen und bei der Ausübung der Religion.

Im Prestige der Mundart(kenntnisse) macht sich eine positive Entwicklung bemerkbar, insofern man sie als solide Grundlage für den Erwerb der deutschen Standardsprache betrachtet, deren Kenntnis wiederum für den wirtschaftlichen und sozialen Aufstieg, also das gesellschaftliche Prestige von Bedeutung ist. Herkömmlicherweise besteht für die gesamte deutsche Volksgruppe sowohl bei ihr selbst wie auch bei den Ungarn die Bezeichnung „Schwaben" (ung. „svábok"), obwohl sich das „schwäbische Element" auf höchstens 2% der Ungarndeutschen beläuft. Mehr oder weniger bewußt und konsequent unterscheidet man davon das nur mehr historisch relevante „deutsche Element", geprägt durch das städtische Bürgertum.

Der ungarischen Bezeichnung „svábok" haftet eine bestimmte Ambivalenz an, in der sich teilweise auch die Zwiespältigkeit des Image der Ungarndeutschen wiederspiegelt. Einerseits verbindet man mit der Bezeichnung bestimmte positive Werte wie Fleiß, Sparsamkeit und Ordnungsliebe, andererseits Pedanterie, Knauserigkeit und Kleinlichkeit. Während und nach dem Zweiten Weltkrieg wurde die negative Konnotation, aus verständlichen Gründen, noch verstärkt. Zur Entstehung und dem Weiterleben dieses Einheitsnamens vgl. Hutterer (1990, 69 ff). Der eher offizielle Sprachgebrauch signalisiert(e) mit der Bezeichnung „Ungarndeutsche" eine bewußte Abgrenzung den „Binnendeutschen/ Reichsdeutschen" gegenüber und die zweifache emotionelle Bindung der Mitglieder dieser Volksgruppe. Die durch den Nationalsozialismus und Ereignisse während des Zweiten Weltkriegs hervorgerufene emotionell negative Einstellung der Mehrheitsbevölkerung allem Deutschen gegenüber ist größtenteils überwunden. In jüngster Zeit zeichnen sich hinsichtlich des Image positive Entwicklungen ab, wobei der Einfluß Deutschlands als regionale (wirtschaftliche) Großmacht und die bereits traditionell guten Beziehungen der beiden Staaten sowie die (finanzielle) Förderung der Ungarndeutschen eine entscheidende Rolle spielen dürften.

6. Sprachpolitische Lage

Das Recht der Ungarndeutschen auf Gebrauch, Pflege und Unterricht ihrer Muttersprache ist im Grundgesetz der Republik Ungarn verankert (vgl. 3.). Dennoch gehen deklarierte Rechte und ihre Wahrnehmung im täglichen Leben mehr oder weniger auseinander. So ist den Ungarndeutschen z. B. prinzipiell die Möglichkeit nicht verwehrt, ihre Mundart in der Öffentlichkeit, im Verkehr mit (örtlichen) Behörden zu verwenden, doch vielerorts sind der Wahrnehmung dieser Möglichkeit durch den Mangel an entsprechenden Sprachkenntnissen der Kommunikationspartner Grenzen gesetzt. Nach einigen Jahren völliger Unterdrückung und Einschüchterung der in Ungarn verbliebenen ungarndeutschen Minderheit ist seit Ende der

50er Jahre vor allem im kulturpolitischen Bereich, so auch im Bildungswesen, eine gewiß langsame, doch grundsätzlich positive Entwicklung zu verzeichnen, die allerdings die negative Wirkung der Ereignisse unmittelbar nach dem Zweiten Weltkrieg nicht wettzumachen vermag.

Nach und nach wurde die Möglichkeit geschaffen, daß ungarndeutsche Kinder vom Vorschulalter bis zum Abitur Deutsch lernen. In Regionen mit einem relativ hohen Anteil von Ungarndeutschen wurde nicht nur die deutsche Sprache unterrichtet, sondern Deutsch wurde zur Unterrichtssprache. Verläßliche zahlenmäßige Angaben sind schwer zu ermitteln, da eine klare Trennung zwischen Deutsch als Fremdsprache und Deutsch als Mutter- bzw. Zweitsprache praktisch kaum möglich ist. Laut Angaben des Statistischen Zentralamtes nahmen im Schuljahr 1991/1992 am — nach ungarischem Wortgebrauch — „Minderheitenunterricht" (was den Unterricht der Sprache der Minderheiten bedeutet) in den Kindergärten 12 953 Kinder, in der achtklassigen Grundschule 35 463, in Gymnasien 754 Schüler teil. Getrennt wird die Zahl jener Kinder registriert, die selbständige Bildungseinrichtungen für die Minderheiten besuchen: 851 Kinder in deutschen Kindergärten, 2199 Schüler in Grundschulen, 944 in den insgesamt drei Gymnasien. Die Effektivität des Unterrichts leidet nach wie vor unter der teilweise noch immer fehlenden Infrastruktur, an dem Mangel an qualifizierten Lehrkräften, Lehrwerken, entsprechenden Curricula.

7. Allgemeines kontaktlinguistisches Porträt

Die Vielfalt der ungarndeutschen Mundarten kann in diesem Rahmen nur skizzenhaft dargestellt werden. Laut Hutterer „sind in Ungarn die hochdeutschen — also ober- und mitteldeutschen — Dialekte fast ausnahmslos vertreten. Größere Sprachräume bilden aber nur das Ostdonaubairische in Westungarn und im Ungarischen Mittelgebirge bzw. das Rheinfränkische in der „Schwäbischen Türkei" und in der Batschka. Ein schwäbischer Raum ist nur im Komitat Sathmar entstanden: davon liegen heute nur drei Dörfer in Ungarn." (Hutterer 1991, 271).

Im Hinblick auf die Charakteristika der Mundarten ist wichtig festzuhalten, daß es sich hier um Siedlungsmundarten handelt: sie sind in der neuen Heimat durch Verschmelzung ursprünglich verschiedener Dialekte und durch Ausgleich 1. bzw. 2. Stufe entstanden. In der ersten Etappe war es zur Entstehung einer homogenen Ortsmundart durch den Ausgleich der in der Dorfgemeinschaft vertretenen Mundarten gekommen. In der zweiten Etappe setzte eine weitere Integration benachbarter Ortsmundarten ebenfalls durch Ausgleich ein, wobei dieser Prozeß größere geographische Räume erfaßte. In typologischer Hinsicht geht es um Mischmundarten: Einander von vornherein nahestehende Mundarten wurden ausgeglichen, und das Ergebnis läßt sich unschwer jeweils als ungarndeutsche Variante eines binnendeutschen Dialekts identifizieren (bairisch, fränkisch, schwäbisch). Infolge mehrfacher Staffelungen und Überschichtungen bleibt eine in ihrem Umfang beschränkte Beschreibung notwendigerweise vereinfachend und auf die wesentlichsten Tendenzen beschränkt. Die tatsächliche Verteilung der verschiedenen Mundarten zeigt Abb. 211.1.

Man kann donaubairische (*ua*- und *ui*-) Mundarten, südbairische, schwäbische, ostfränkische, rheinfränkische sowie Mischmundarten unterscheiden. Die ostdonaubairische sog. *ui*-Mundart ist vertreten bei den Deutschen in Nordwestungarn sowie auch im Westabschnitt des Ungarischen Mittelgebirges (vgl. Hutterer 1991, 253 ff). Im Zusammenhang mit dem westungarischen Mundartraum wird jeweils darauf hingewiesen, daß die nahverwandte Wiener Umgangs- bzw. Verkehrssprache, ihre Betrachtung als sprachliche Norm, die Mundarten in ihrer Entwicklung mehr oder weniger stark beeinflußt hat. Die ostdonaubairische sog. *uv*-Mundart ist kennzeichnend für den gesamten Ostabschnitt des Ungarischen Mittelgebirges, sie ist aber auch im Westabschnitt vertreten. Ursprünglich fränkische und schwäbische Mundarten prägten ausgedehnte Regionen in Südosttransdanubien (Tolnau, Branau) sowie in der Nordbatschka. Laut Hutterer ging der Ausgleich zwischen Ortsmundarten aus verschiedenen Gründen hier etwas langsamer vor sich, und es war die mitteldeutsch-fränkische Volkssprache, die die ausgleichende Rolle spielte (Hutterer 1990, 63). Im Norden (Tolnau) war dabei ein hessischer, im Süden (Branau) ein spezifischer „fuldischer" Dialektraum entstanden. Für letztere Varietät sind u. a. eine starke Tendenz zur Diphthongierung sowie einige morphologische Merkmale, wie z. B. das Weglassen der Infini-

211. Ungarisch−Deutsch

○	donaubairische ua-Mundarten
△	donaubairische ui-Mundarten
■	südbairische Mundarten
□	schwäbische Mundarten
▽	ostfränkische Mundarten
●	rheinfränkische Mundarten
+	Mischmundart

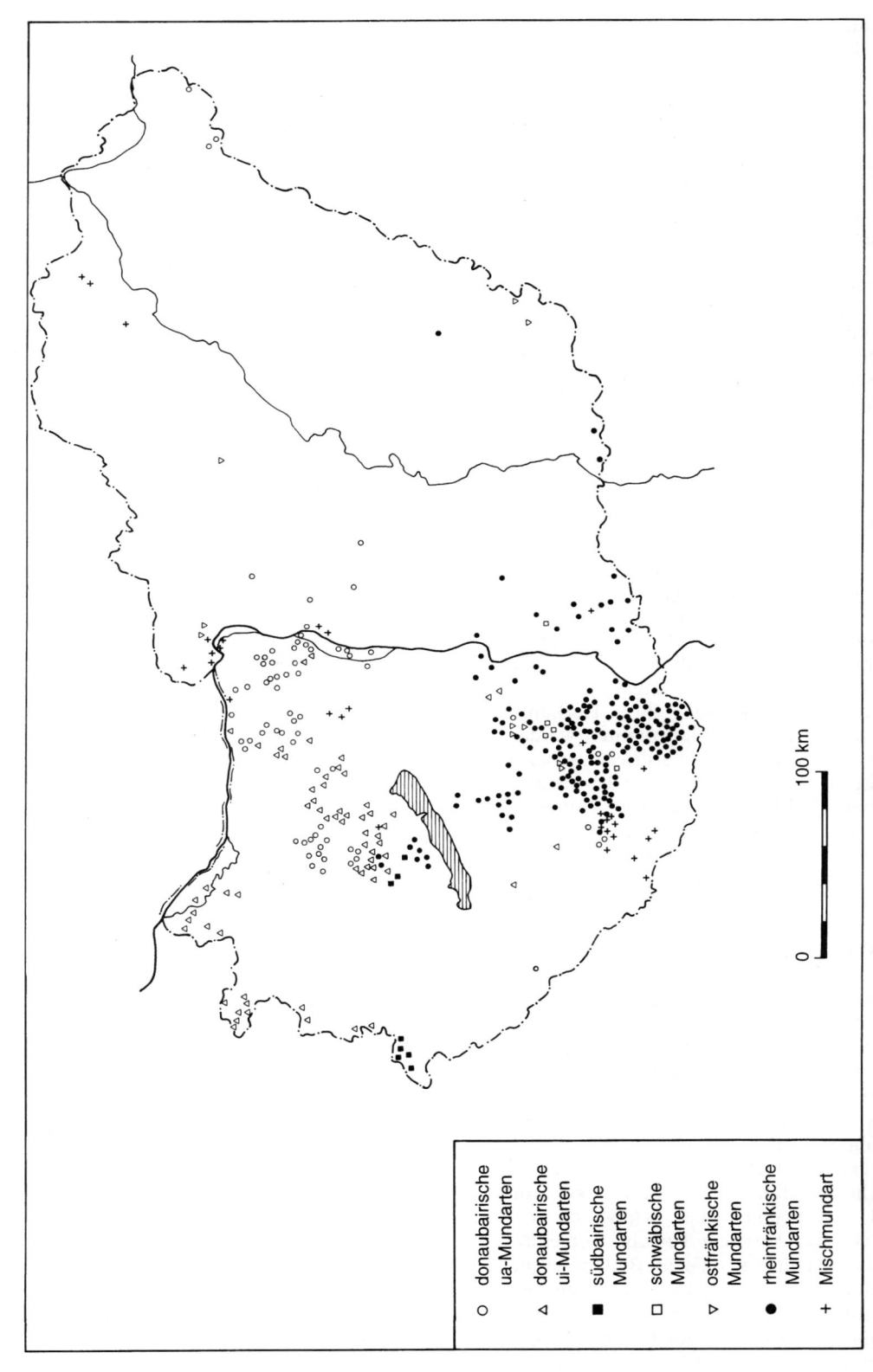

Abb. 211.1: Deutsche Mundarten in Ungarn

tivendung -en charakteristisch (vgl. Wild 1986). Der schwäbische Raum im Osten Ungarns (Sathmar) besteht in der heutigen Republik Ungarn aus drei Dörfern.

8. Zur Forschungslage

Die Fachliteratur erfaßt naturgemäß ein breites Spektrum an Aspekten, Fragen und Problemen. Thematisch lassen sich diese verschiedenen Bereichen zuordnen, von der Geschichtswissenschaft über Volkskunde und Literaturwissenschaft bis zur Linguistik.

In der Hungarologie werden die deutsch-ungarischen Sprachkontakte erforscht, wobei der Entlehnungsprozeß und die Integration deutschen Wortgutes in das Lexikon des Ungarischen im Mittelpunkt stehen. Als weiterer Schwerpunkt werden die literarischen Kontakte sowie die deutschsprachige Literatur in Ungarn untersucht. Die Literatur der Ungarndeutschen spielt in diesem Kontext eher nur am Rande eine Rolle.

Eine Fülle von wissenschaftlichen Publikationen ist der Dialektologie zuzuordnen, die eine Kontinuität von über 100 Jahren aufweisen kann. Sie bemühte sich um die Beschreibung der verschiedenen ungarndeutschen Dialekte, um die Klärung ihrer Herkunft, und erst in den letzten Jahrzehnten werden zunehmend auch soziolinguistische Aspekte einbezogen. Um die Erforschung der ungarndeutschen Dialekte und die deutsch-ungarischen Sprachkontakte haben sich schon immer vor allem Vertreter der ungarischen Germanistik bemüht. Die Forschungstätigkeit wurde im 20. Jahrhundert mit unterschiedlicher Intensität und teilweise unterschiedlicher Akzentuierung fortgesetzt, nicht völlig unabhängig von der jeweiligen historisch-politischen Lage. Dabei ist eine gewisse — traditionsbedingte — Einseitigkeit erkennbar: Man konzentrierte sich weitgehend auf die Erforschung der innersprachlichen, vor allem phonetisch-morphologischen Spezifika der Mundarten und schenkte z. B. dem Einfluß des Ungarischen weniger Aufmerksamkeit. Eine grundsätzlich positive Entwicklung wurde herbeigeführt durch die Tätigkeit von C. J. Hutterer und seiner Schule, die vor allem von K. Manherz bewußt fortgesetzt wird. In den mittlerweile in Budapest und Fünfkirchen entstandenen Forschungszentren wird auch den Fragen der Volkskultur der Ungarndeutschen reges Interesse entgegengebracht. Diplom- und Promotionsarbeiten zum Thema liegen bereits in großer Zahl vor; hinsichtlich der Inventarisierung und Beschreibung der noch vorhandenen deutschen Mundarten in Ungarn gibt es kaum noch „weiße Flecken". Unter der Leitung von K. Manherz wird seit 1981 mit bisher 6 Bänden die Reihe Ungarndeutsche Studien sowie die Beiträge zur Volkskunde der Ungarndeutschen herausgebracht. Ein authentisches Gesamtbild über Geschichte, Stand und Perspektiven der wissenschaftlichen Erforschung des Deutschtums in Ungarn vermittelt K. Manherz (1983). Von den ausländischen Experten seien stellvertretend für zahlreiche weitere Peter Nelde, Anton Schwob und Peter Wiesinger erwähnt.

9. Bibliographie (in Auswahl)

Bellér, Béla (1990): „Kurze Geschichte des Ungarndeutschtums". In: *Deutsch als Muttersprache in Ungarn*, Nelde, P. H. (Ed.), Stuttgart, 31−43.

Born, Joachim/Dickgießer, Sylvia (1989): *Deutschsprachige Minderheiten. Ein Überblick über den Stand der Forschung für 27 Länder*, Mannheim.

Hambuch, Wendelin (Ed.) (1988): *300 Jahre Zusammenleben. Aus der Geschichte der Ungarndeutschen* I−II, Budapest.

Horváth, Mária (1978): *Német elemek a 17. század magyar nyelvében* [Deutsche Elemente in der ungarischen Sprache des 17. Jahrhunderts], Budapest.

Hutterer, Claus Jürgen (1990): „Die deutsche Volksgruppe in Ungarn". In: *Deutsch als Muttersprache in Ungarn*, Nelde, P. H. (Ed.), Stuttgart, 45−75.

Hutterer, Claus Jürgen (1991): *Aufsätze zur deutschen Dialektologie*, Budapest.

Manherz, Karl (1983): „Zur wissenschaftlichen Erforschung des Deutschtums in Ungarn". In: *Deutsche Volksgruppen in Europa*, Pelka, R. (Ed.), Akademie Sankelmark, 79−104.

Manherz, Karl (1985): „Die ungarndeutschen Mundarten und ihre Erforschung in Ungarn". In: *Beiträge zur Volkskunde der Ungarndeutschen* 5, 27−38.

Mollay, Károly (1982): *Német-magyar nyelvi érintkezések a XVI. század végéig* [Deutsch-ungarische Sprachkontakte bis Ende des 16. Jahrhunderts], Budapest.

Mollay, Károly (1986): „Das Wörterbuch des Frühneuhochdeutschen in Ungarn". In: *Beiträge zur historischen Lexikographie*, Ágel, V./Paul, R./Szalai, L. (Eds.), Budapest, 111−122.

Nelde, Peter H./Vandermeeren, Sonja/Wölck, Wolfgang (1991): *Interkulturelle Mehrsprachigkeit. Eine kontaktlinguistische Umfrage in Fünfkirchen*, Bonn.

Szabó, János (1992): "Die ungarndeutsche Gegenwartsliteratur vor historischem Hintergrund". In: *Die deutsche Literaturgeschichte Ostmittel- und Südosteuropas von der Mitte des 19. Jahrhunderts bis heute. Forschungsschwerpunkte und Defizite*, Südostdeutsches Kulturwerk, München, 267—275.

Tarnói, László (1989): "Patriotismus und nationale Identität im Spiegel der deutschsprachigen Dichtung im Königreich Ungarn um 1800". In: *Berliner Beiträge zur Hungarologie* 4, 7—55.

Wild, Katharina (1985): "Sprachliche Situation und Sprachpflege. Zur Sprache der deutschen Volksgruppe in Ungarn". In: *Kolloquium zur Sprache und Sprachpflege der deutschen Bevölkerungsgruppen im Ausland. Referate und Auswahlbibliographie*, Ritter, A. (Ed.), Flensburg, 169—184.

Wild, Katalin (1986): *Untersuchungen zur Syntax der Konjunktionalsätze in der Bawazer (Babarc) deutschen Mundart*, Budapest.

Regina Hessky, Budapest (Ungarn)

212. Ungarisch—Serbokroatisch

1. Geographie und Demographie
2. Geschichte
3. Ethnoprofile
4. Soziokulturelle Rahmenbedingungen des Sprachkontakts
5. Allgemeines kontaktlinguistisches Porträt
6. Forschungsstand
7. Bibliographie (in Auswahl)

1. Geographie und Demographie

Demographische Erhebungen, die in Ungarn 1990 nach der Muttersprache durchgeführt wurden, ermittelten unter einer Gesamtbevölkerung von 10 374 823 einen Anteil von 23 157 bzw. 0,2% Südslaven, darunter 17 577 Kroaten und 2953 Serben — gegenüber einer magyarischen Mehrheit von 10 222 529 bzw. 98,5% (1990. évi népszámlálás). 1960 betrug der Anteil der Kroaten 25 262, der der Serben 4583. Solche, zahlenmäßig differierenden Angaben sind wenig aussagekräftig, da sich viele der Befragten offenbar nicht zu einer ethnischen Minderheit bzw. „Nationalität" bekennen (1980 waren dies insgesamt lediglich 1,22% der Bevölkerung, 1990 1,5%) (Takács 1989, 78). Das Bild wird auch dadurch verfälscht, daß bei den Erhebungen Muttersprache mit Nationalität gleichgesetzt wird, was nicht immer zutrifft, wurden doch z. B. im Komitat Baranya 1970 6343 Personen mit serbokroatischer Muttersprache, dagegen 8635 Personen ermittelt, die sich zu einer der südslavischen Nationalitäten zurechneten (Kővágó 1981, 26). Nach Schätzungen gibt es in Ungarn etwa 102 200 Südslaven, darunter 94 700 Kroaten und 7000 Serben (Sarosácz 1973, 369); Urosevics ermittelte 1969 in 11 ungarischen Komitaten und an 101 Orten 96 181 Südslaven: 85 294 Kroaten; 6400 Serben und 4487 Slowenen. Seit 1990 hat sich der Anteil der kroatischen und serbischen Muttersprachler mit ständigem Wohnsitz in Ungarn allerdings durch den Zustrom von Kriegsflüchtlingen aus dem ehemaligen Jugoslawien — ihre Zahl wird auf 30 000 geschätzt — wieder erhöht.

Verteilung der kroatischen und serbischen Wohnsitze in Ungarn: (A) Kroaten: (I) Sogenannte Bunjewazen (*Bunjevci, bunyevácok*) leben in der Gegend um Frankenstadt (Baja) und im Norden der Batschka (Bácska). Sie sind hierher wahrscheinlich im 17. Jahrhundert aus Dalmatien und der Herzegowina eingewandert; (II) die sogenannten Schokazen (*Šokci, sokácok*) sind im 16.—17. Jahrhundert aus Bosnien und der Herzegowina nach Südungarn eingewandert. Heute leben sie in Ortschaften des Komitats Branau (Baranya) um Fünfkirchen (Pécs), Siklós und im Komitat Batsch-Kleinkumanien (Bács-Kiskun) in der Gegend um Frankenstadt; (III) sogenannte Raitzische Kroaten leben in kleinen Ortschaften: Bátya, Dusnok, Érd, Ercsi und Tököl. (IV) Kroaten leben ferner entlang der Drave (Dráva/Drava) und an der Mur (Mura), um Nagykanizsa, Letenye und in der Schomodei (Somogy); (V) die sogenannten Gradischtschaner Kroaten (*Gradišćanski Hrvati/gradistyei horvátok*) sind im Zuge von Kolonisierungsmaßnahmen aus den adriatischen Küstenregionen nach Westungarn ausgewandert. Die meisten von ihnen leben heute im österreichischen Burgenland; in Ungarn finden wir sie um Ödenburg (Sopron), Wieselburg (Mosonmagyaróvár) und Steinamanger (Szombathely). (B) Serben leben (I) in Mohatsch (Mohács) und Umgebung, (II) in den südungarischen Komitaten Bekesch (Békés) und Csongrád (Deszk, Szőreg, Újszentiván, Magyarcsanád, Battonya und Segedin (Szeged)) sowie (III) im Komitat Pest und Umgebung (→ Sprachenkarte L).

Vor dem ersten Weltkrieg hatte das ungarische Kernland einen wesentlich höheren Anteil an kroatischer und serbischer Bevölkerung: 1910 gab es 198 700 kroatische und ca. 545 833 serbische Muttersprachler (Kővágó 1981, 7). Durch den Trianon-Vertrag (1920) wurden die von Serben bewohnten südungarischen Gebiete mit einem bedeutenden ungarischen Bevölkerungsanteil als Vojvodina in den neuen jugoslawischen Staat eingegliedert. In der Folgezeit wanderten weitere Serben aus Ungarn nach Jugoslawien.

2. Geschichte

2.1. Entstehung des Sprachkontakts

Was die Herkunft und den Siedlungsursprung der ungarländischen Südslaven, insbesondere der Kroaten und Slowenen, betrifft, werden diese in der wissenschaftlichen Literatur z. T. als Nachkommen jener slavischen Bevölkerung angesehen, die sich in den südungarischen Komitaten im 6.—7. Jahrhundert, also noch vor der ungarischen Landnahme, niedergelassen hatten (vgl. z. B. in Istorija naroda Jugoslavije I., 1953, 66). Die Ortsnamenkunde und archäologische Funde belegen südslavische Siedlungen in Westungarn; vgl. hierzu Orts- und Gewässernamen wie z. B. *Kanizsa* < *kněža* „Fürst-"; *Tapolca* < *toplica* „heißes Wasser", *Dombóvár* zu *dǫmbъ* „Eiche", *Balaton* < *blatьnъ* „schlammig" u. v. a. m. Die uns bekannten kroatischen und serbischen Siedlungen entstanden jedoch erst später. Die ungarischen Könige förderten im Interesse einer effektiveren Grenzverteidigung bereits im Mittelalter die Zuwanderung von Südslaven. Nach der Einnahme Serbiens, Bosniens und der Herzegowina durch die Osmanen drängte eine Flut serbischer und kroatischer Zuwanderer nach Ungarn. Die älteste serbische Siedlung wurde auf der Insel Csepel 1404 gegründet. Unter König Matthias Corvinus wurden viele Südslaven planmäßig angesiedelt: in der Gegend um Segedin, in der Branau (Baranya), in Tolnau (Tolna), Batschka (Bácska) und entlang der Donau bis hinauf nach Komorn (Komárom). Die Ansiedlung der westlichen Kroaten erfolgte schwerpunktmäßig zwischen 1520 und 1579 (in dieser Zeit ließen sich etwa 60 000—100 000 Kroaten in 189 Dörfern nieder). Doch auch danach wanderten Kroaten nach Ungarn. Die dritte südslavische Einwanderungswelle erreichte Ungarn zwischen 1687 und 1690, als die Osmanen schon weit auf den Balkan zurückgeschlagen wurden. Unter den Serben, die den Balkanfeldzug des österreichischen Kaisers unterstützten und sich vor der Rache der Osmanen fürchteten, verließen 37 000 bis 40 000 Familien unter der Führung ihres Ipeker Patriarchen Arsenije Crnojević (Čarnojević) ihre Heimat und flüchteten nach Ungarn. Später kehrten von ihnen einige in die osmanisch besetzte Heimat zurück, andere wanderten in die Ukraine aus.

2.2. Ungarn und Kroaten

Nach der Ermordung des kroatischen Königs Zvonimir (1089) fiel der ungarische König Ladislaus I. 1091 mit seinen Truppen in die nordkroatischen Gebiete ein. In weiteren Feldzügen drangen er und König Koloman (1095—1116) weiter nach Kroatien, Slawonien und Dalmatien vor. 1102 wurde zwischen dem ungarischen König und den kroatischen Ständen die „pacta conventa" abgeschlossen und durch sie eine Personalunion begründet. Koloman wurde in Jadera zum kroatischen König gekrönt. Die staatsrechtliche Bedeutung der „pacta conventa", deren Überlieferung erst ein Jahrhundert später einsetzte, war zwischen Ungarn und Kroatien bis in die Gegenwart hinein heftig umstritten. Nach kroatischer Auslegung sei die Personalunion unter gleichberechtigten Partnern entstanden, während die ungarische Historiographie Kroatiens untergeordnete Position im ungarischen Königreich unterstrich. In Zeiten gespannter ungarisch-kroatischer Beziehungen konnten die strittigen Punkte der „pacta conventa" kaum eine objektive Klärung erfahren. Erst nach Auflösung der Staatengemeinschaft trug u. a. Deér 1936 zur Versachlichung der Auseinandersetzungen bei: Er verwies auf den privatrechtlichen Charakter dieses Abkommens (die Personalunion), aus der sich erst nach und nach auch eine staatsrechtlich determinierte Staatengemeinschaft (eine Realunion) entwickelt habe.

Der größte Teil der dalmatinischen Küste befand sich nach Abschluß der „pacta conventa" nur zeitweise unter der ungarischen Krone; Nordwest- und Westkroatien sowie die nördlichen Teile der Küste standen indessen über acht Jahrhunderte lang in enger Verbindung zu Ungarn. Bereits im Mittelalter führte der ungarische König in Slawonien, Kroatien und Dalmatien eine Komitatsorganisation nach ungarischem Vorbild ein. In diesem Zusammenhang verbreiteten sich zahlreiche ungarische Begriffe des öffentlichen Lebens (vgl. hierzu 5.2.). Mit der Komitatsverwaltung wurde ein königlicher Oberbeamter, der *Banus*, beauftragt.

1356 befreiten sich die dalmatinischen Städte mit ungarischer Waffenhilfe von der venezianischen Herrschaft; 1358 begab sich Ragusa unter die Oberhoheit des ungarischen Königs (bis 1526).

Als Kroatien bis auf einen schmalen Streifen im Westen unter osmanische Herrschaft geriet, suchten viele Kroaten Schutz in Ungarn (s. oben unter 2.1.). Gegen Ende des 18. Jahrhunderts, mit aufkommendem Nationalbewußtsein der Kroaten, lockerten sich ihre Beziehungen zu den Ungarn. 1745, als einige Komitate zum Ausgleich dafür, daß das kroatische Gebiet zum Militärgrenzgebiet geworden war, nicht wieder an Ungarn, sondern an Kroatien angegliedert wurden, brachen die Kroaten Schritt für Schritt die Verbindungen zu den Ungarn ab. Die Magyarisierungspolitik verstärkte diesen Prozeß (vgl. hierzu 4.1.). Am 29. Oktober 1918 erklärte der kroatische Landtag die Verbindung mit Österreich-Ungarn für null und nichtig und verkündete den Anschluß Kroatiens an Jugoslawien.

2.3. Ungarn und Serben

Die serbisch-ungarischen Kontakte reichen bis in das 12. Jahrhundert zurück. Der serbische Despot war zugleich einer der reichsten Magnaten Ungarns; auch leisteten sich Serben und Ungarn gegenseitige Waffenhilfe gegen Byzanz. Nachdem die Serben infolge der osmanischen Eroberungswellen Südserbien verloren hatten und durch die Schlacht auf dem Amselfeld (Kosovo) (1389) schwer gezeichnet waren, stellten sie sich 1426 unter ungarische Schutzherrschaft. Seit dieser Zeit wanderten viele Serben nach Ungarn (vgl. oben unter 2.1.). Die Leopoldinischen Diplome von 1690 und 1695 sicherten den ungarländischen Serben weitgehende konfessionelle und verwaltungsmäßige Autonomie zu. Demgegenüber waren die ungarischen Stände bestrebt, auch bei ihnen die Komitatsverwaltung wiederherzustellen, was auf heftigen Widerspruch der Serben stieß. Angesichts dieser Konfrontation errichtete 1702 der Wiener Hof im Donau-Save- und im Theiß-Marosch-Gebiet die Militärgrenze und entzog sie der ungarischen Komitatsverwaltung.

Im 18. Jahrhundert lag fast der gesamte Donauhandel in den Händen serbischer Kaufleute. Aus ihren Reihen rekrutierte sich jene Intelligenz, die zu Wegbereitern der serbischen nationalen Wiedergeburt wurden (vgl. 3.3.).

1849 wurden das Banat (Bánát) und die Batschka (Bácska) von Ungarn abgetrennt und zu selbständigen serbischen Vojevodschaften unter Österreich (mit Sitz der Regierung in Temeschburg [Temesvár]) deklariert, aber schon 1860 wurde die Vojvodina (Vajdaság) wieder von den Ungarn einverleibt. Das ungarische Gesetz über die Gleichberechtigung aller Nationalitäten von 1867/68 hatte für die Serben nur in Bezug auf freie Religionsausübung Relevanz. Von einer politischen Mitbestimmung waren sie ausgeschlossen (vgl. auch 4.1.). Mit fortschreitender Magyarisierung zogen sich die Serben aus dem Zentrum Ungarns schrittweise zurück. 1864 verlagerte sich das serbische literarische Zentrum (vgl. auch 3.3.) von Pest und Buda nach Neusatz (Novi Sad), und in den 80er Jahren wurde Belgrad kulturelles Zentrum der Serben. Nun begann die Südwanderung der ungarländischen Serben und ihre Abkehr von den Ungarn, die durch die Abtrennung der Vojvodina im Trianon-Vertrag (1920) besiegelt wurde (vgl. auch 1.1.).

3. Ethnoprofile

3.1. Die Etymologie des Ethnonyms *Bunjevac* (ung. *bunyevác*) ist ungeklärt. Unklar ist auch die Bezeichnung Schokazen (*Šokac*, *sokác*); vielleicht hängt er mit dt. *Sachse* als einer im Mittelalter für die unter der serbischen Bevölkerung lebenden Nichtserben üblichen Bezeichnung zusammen.

Die ungarische Lautung der Bezeichnung *Hrvat*: *horvát* wurde von ungarischer Seite in Zeiten der Magyarisierungswelle häufig herabsetzend gebraucht: *Horvát nem ember* „Ein Kroate ist kein Mensch" (vgl. Klaić 1966). Ebenso wurde von ungarischer Seite *rác* „Rascianus, Raize" zeitweise pejorativ zur Bezeichnung von Serben verwendet.

3.2. Bis in die Gegenwart leben Kroaten und Serben in Ungarn in voneinander getrennten Siedlungen. 1955/56 waren 85% von ihnen in der Landwirtschaft beschäftigt (Kővágó 1981, 117). Seit 1945 hatten sie einen gemeinsamen Interessen- und Kulturverband: den Demokratischen Verband der Ungarländischen Südslaven, eine gemeinsame Presse sowie Rundfunk- und Fernsehanstalten. In den Kindergärten, Volksschulen und Gymnasien wurde Serbokroatisch unterrichtet. In Fünfkirchen wurde eine serbokroatische Redaktion des ungarischen Fernsehens gebildet, die zunächst einmal monatlich Sendungen in serbokroatischer Sprache ausstrahlte. Gegenwärtig wird die Trennung dieser Gemeinsamkeiten vorangetrieben (vgl. hierzu auch unter 4.2.).

Die ungarländischen Kroaten sprechen verschiedene kroatische Mundarten: die Bunjewazen und Schokazen eine der kroatischen Literatursprache näherstehende Mundart; die Kroaten in Westungarn das Čakavische, das auf eine eigene geschriebene Literatur zurückgreifen kann (vgl. Hadrovics 1974), an der Mur das Kajkavische. Durch ihre römisch-katholische Konfessionszugehörigkeit begünstigt, adaptierten die ungarländischen Kroaten zahlreiche ungarische Elemente der Alltagskultur und integrierten sie in ihre eigene — so im Bereich des Bauens und Wohnens und in der Kleidung, bis zu einem gewissen Grade auch in Brauchtum und Volksdichtung (hierzu u. a. Kerecsényi 1982).

Die ungarländischen Serben sind serbisch-orthodox. Ihr kirchliches und kulturelles Zentrum, zu dem auch ein Museum gehört, befindet sich in St. André (Szentendre, Sentadreja/Sveti Andrija). Von hier aus werden sie von einem serbischen Bischof betreut. Durch die aktive Tätigkeit der serbischen Kirche in der Pflege tradierter serbischer Kultur konnten die ungarländischen Serben ihre kulturelle Eigenständigkeit in Liedgut, Brauchtum und Volksdichtung in hohem Maße bewahren (hierzu u. a. Kiss 1988).

Volkskundler des 19. und 20. Jahrhunderts (Margalits 1896—1899, Róheim 1925, Vujicsics 1957 u. a.) stellten zahlreiche Interferenzen in der Volkskultur (vor allem in Liedgut und Volksglauben) der Ungarn und der ungarländischen Südslaven fest. Im epischen Liedgut der Südslaven haben ungarische historische Persönlichkeiten und Begebenheiten, die sich mit dem Abwehrkampf gegen die Osmanen verbinden, einen festen Platz. In ihm wird die Schicksalsgemeinschaft von Ungarn und Südslaven in der Zeit der osmanischen Fremdherrschaft thematisiert. Auch in der Hochliteratur, etwa in der kroatischen Dichtung des 17. Jahrhunderts, ist die Erinnerung daran bewahrt. Enge Wechselbeziehungen bestanden zwischen Ungarn einerseits, Kroaten und Serben andererseits bis zum 19. Jahrhundert auch in der Hochliteratur. Die epischen Zehnsilbenverse (*deseteac*) der serbischen Volksdichtung, die sog. Serbus-Manier, fand auch Eingang in die ungarische Dichtung. Enge Verbindungen bestanden im 19. Jahrhundert zwischen ungarischen und serbischen Literaten. Der Serbe Jovan Jovanović Zmaj orientierte sich z. B. an seinem ungarischen Dichterkollegen Sándor Petőfi; er pflegte auch enge Kontakte zu János Arany u. a., war Mitglied der ungarischen Kisfaludy-Dichtergesellschaft. An Mór Jókai und Kálmán Mikszáth orientierte sich der 1824 in St. André geborene Jakov Ignjatović (hierzu ausführlich u. a. Pot 1993; Szerbek és magyarok a Duna mentén 1983, 1987).

3.3. Eine der ältesten Siedlungen der Serben an der Donau ist St. André. Die hier von serbischen Kaufleuten errichtete Kirche, die ihr besonderes Gepräge durch das Zusammentreffen von serbischem Kirchenzeremoniell und österreichisch-ungarischem Barockstil erhalten hat, erinnert an die einstigen wohlhabenden serbischen Kaufleute und die Intelligenz in Ungarn, aus deren Reihen die Wegbereiter der serbischen Nationalbewegung, wie z. B. Dositej Obradović (1739—1811), hervorgegangen sind. Zu materiellem Wohlstand gelangt, ließen die ungarländischen Serben ihre Söhne in Ofen (Buda), Wien, Berlin und Kiew studieren. In Ofen und Pest befand sich ihr geistiges Zentrum: 10% der Pester Einwohnerschaft zu Beginn des 19. Jahrhunderts waren Serben, und auch in Buda war ihre Zahl hoch. 1826 gründeten sie in Pest die *Matica Srpska*, ihren ersten literarischen Verein. Seit 1795 wurde in Ofen eine serbische Druckerei betrieben.

4. Soziokulturelle Rahmenbedingungen des Sprachkontakts

4.1. Die von Josef II. 1785 durchgeführte Volkszählung, die in Ungarn unter 8 Mio. Einwohnern nur 2,32 Mio. Ungarn ermittelte, bewog den vorwiegend ungarischen Adel dazu, aus nicht-magyarischen Bewohnern Magyaren zu machen. Samuel Décsi proklamierte 1790 die Notwendigkeit der Verbreitung der ungarischen Sprache im Lande, und auch Ludwig Kossuth, der Führer des ungarischen Aufstandes von 1848/49, bekannte sich zu diesem Ziel. 1791 wurde das erste ungarische Sprachengesetz erlassen, und ihm folgten viele weitere. In ihnen wurde ein immer größerer Anwendungsbereich des Ungarischen fixiert. Ungarisch sollte als Pflichtfach an den Schulen, als Sprache im offiziellen Schriftverkehr, bei Gericht und auf dem Landtag durchgesetzt werden. Den nicht Ungarisch sprechenden Beamten wurde eine Frist gesetzt, die ungarische Sprache zu erlernen. In einige Komitaten wurde angeordnet, Firmenschilder in ungarischer Sprache anzubringen und die Buchführung auf Ungarisch vorzunehmen. Sogar in den Zünften sollte man sich des Ungarischen bedienen. Ferner wurde in vielen Gegenden verfügt, daß nur Ungarisch sprechende Notare und Geistliche ihr Amt ausüben dürften. Predigten sollten Ungarisch gehalten und Matrikel Ungarisch geführt werden.

Die Kroaten, die darin einen Angriff auf ihre Autonomie sahen, forderten die Einführung des Kroatischen als offizielle Landessprache. Nun unternahmen sie intensive Anstrengungen zur Entwicklung der kroatischen Sprache und Literatur. Der Illyrismus Gajs verband mit kultureller Erneuerungsarbeit das Ziel der Schaffung eines selbständigen kroatischen Staates innerhalb Ungarns, dann seit Mitte der 40er Jahre eines großen südslavischen Staates. 1849 wurden die ungarischen Sprachengesetze teilweise rückgängig gemacht. 1868 wurden durch den Ausgleich zwischen Ungarn und Kroaten die beiden Völker als gleichberechtigte Partner anerkannt. Als dann von ungarischer Seite in den 80er Jahren die Magyarisierungspolitik erneut aufgenommen wurde (Pflicht zur Erlernung des Ungarischen durch die nichtungarischen Nationalitäten, besonders durch Staatsbeamte und Lehrer; Schaffung ungarischer Kulturvereine), um aus nichtungarischen Staatsbürgern überzeugte Ungarn zu machen, empfanden die Südslaven dies als offene Vertragsverletzung.

Die Serben in Südungarn befanden sich insofern in einer etwas günstigeren Position, als sie zum großen Teil im Militärgrenzgebiet ansässig waren, zu dem der ungarische Komitatsadel weniger Zugriff hatte, ferner dadurch, daß sich die orthodoxe Kirche der direkten Einflußnahme durch die Ungarn entziehen konnte. Dennoch versuchten die Ungarn, auch bei den Serben die ungarische Sprache durchzusetzen. Sie verboten u. a. die serbischen Kalender. Die Serben reagierten mit ebenso starkem Unwillen; sie forderten Gleichstellung bei der Besetzung von Beamtenstellen, die Errichtung serbischer Schulen und eines unabhängigen Gebietes Vojvodina. Seit Beginn der 40er Jahre entwickelte Garašanin ein Gegenstück zu Gajs illyrischen Plänen: die Vereinigung aller Südslaven unter serbischer Führung. Diesen Plan unterstützten viele Serben in Ungarn. Vergeblich forderten sie 1848 Autonomie und nationale Gleichberechtigung. Die Nationalitätenpolitik Ungarns löste unter ihnen einen immer aktiveren Widerstand aus und beschleunigte die südslavischen Einigungsbestrebungen.

4.2. Die ungarische Verfassung von 1949 sichert den ethnischen Minderheiten volle Gleichberechtigung, den Gebrauch der Muttersprache in Schulen und vor Behörden sowie die Pflege der nationalen Kultur zu. Sie enthält jedoch keine Bestimmungen zu kollektiven Rechten der Minderheiten. Im Europa-Rat wurde im Februar 1993 ein Entwurf eines neuen ungarischen Minderheitengesetzes eingebracht, der auch Gemeinschaftsrechte enthält.

Bereits 1946 wurde von ungarischer Seite zur Pflege der serbokroatischen Muttersprache eine serbokroatische Lehrerbildungsinstitution in Fünfkirchen gegründet, die vier Jahre später um ein Gymnasium erweitert wurde und ihre Tätigkeit nach Budapest verlagerte. 1960/61 wurden für die nationalen Minderheiten zweisprachige Schulen eingerichtet, um deren Kompetenz in der jeweiligen Muttersprache zu verbessern. 1979/1980 gab es in Ungarn zwar 28 serbokroatische Kinderheime, aber nur 6 zweisprachige Schulen mit 44 Schülergruppen bzw. 499 Schülern und 45 Muttersprachen-Lehrern; 1 Gymnasium mit 6 Schülergruppen bzw. 127 Schülern und 11 Lehrern. Darüber hinaus betrieben die Südslaven Ungarns 1977 29 Klubs, 22 Gesangs-, 40 Musik-, 40 Tanz- und 12 Theatervereine (Kővágó 1981, 181ff). Wöchentlich ist in Ungarn die kroatische Zeitschrift *Hrvatski glasnik* und die serbische Zeitung *Srpske narodne novine* erhältlich; sie sind an die Stelle der früheren gemeinsamen Zeitschrift *Narodne novine* getreten. In ihnen wird die Leserschaft über die kulturelle Situation in Kroatien und Serbien sowie über spezifische Themen der ungarländischen Südslaven informiert. Das ungarische Fernsehen strahlt gegenwärtig wöchentlich, der Kossuth-Sender täglich einmal, getrennte Sendungen für die ungarländischen Kroaten und Serben aus.

5. Allgemeines kontaktlinguistisches Porträt

5.1. Südslavische Elemente des Ungarischen datieren vor allem aus der Landnahmezeit und der Symbiose zwischen Ungarn und den hier bereits ansässigen Pannonoslaven, unter denen es auch Südslaven gab (vgl. hierzu auch 2.1.). Die ungarischen Einwanderer, Hirtennomaden mit einer militärisch begabten Führungsspitze, fanden in ihrer neuen Heimat bereits christianisierte Slaven vor, die auf verhältnismäßig entwickeltem Niveau Viehzucht, Ackerbau und Hausgewerbe betrieben und außerdem über eine differenzierte Sozialorganisation verfügten. Die ungarisch-südslavische Symbiose dieser Zeit bezeugen zahlreiche, zum ungarischen Grundwortschatz gehörende slavische Lehnwörter: Bezeichnungen des offiziellen Lebens, des christlichen Glaubens, des Ackerbaus, der Viehzucht und des Handwerks, der Wochentage, der Pflanzen- und Tierwelt sowie des häuslichen Lebens; vgl. z. B. *király* „König" < *kraljь*; *udvar* „Hof" < *dvorъ*, *szent* „heilig" < slaw. *svętъ*; *barázda* „Furche" < *brazda*; *csütörtök* „Donnerstag" < *četvьrtъkъ*; *család* „Familie" < *čeljadь*, *kasza* „Sense" < *kosa*; *bolha* „Floh" < *blъcha*; *vacsora* „Abendessen" < *večera* u. a. Häufig ist es angesichts des weit zurückliegenden Zeitpunkts der Entlehnung jedoch unmöglich, die genaue Quelle dieser Wörter anzugeben.

Auf südslavisches Muster wird auch die ungarische Zählweise von 10 aufwärts zurückgeführt, vgl. ungarisch *tiz-en-egy* „eins auf zehn" (entsprechend serbokroatisch *jedanaest* „elf"; allerdings geht im Slavischen der Einer der Zehn voraus), ferner die Bildung des Superlativs im Ungarischen, vgl. ungarisch *leg-nagyobb* „größter", serbokroatisch *naj-veći* „ds." Bei genauerer Betrachtung ist einiges festzustellen, was Ungarisch mit Serbokroatisch verbindet und einer näheren Untersuchung bedarf: so z. B. die Bildung des ungarischen Futurs mit *fog-* „greifen, fassen, anfangen" und des serbokroatischen Futurs mit Hilfe von *uzeti* „nehmen", einem Derivat von *jęti*, ebenso die Bildung des ungarischen Konditionalis mit Hilfe von *volna*, einer Suppletivform zu *lenni* „sein"; *hol dolgoztam volna?* „wo hätte ich gearbeitet?" gegenüber serbokroatisch *gde bih radio?* „ds.".

5.2. Ungarische Elemente im Serbokroatischen

Im Rahmen des ungarischen Königreiches waren auf kroatischem Gebiet seit dem Mittelalter zahlreiche ungarische Bezeichnungen der Verwaltung, Rechtsprechung und des christlichen Glaubens gebräuchlich; u. a. kroatisch *hatar* ~ *kotar* „Grenze" < ung. *határ*; *meja* ~ *medja*; *vārmedja*, *varmeđa* „Komitat" < ung. *megye*, *vármegye*; *vároš* „Stadt" < *város*; *šereg* „Truppe" < ung. *sereg*; *birov* „Richter" < ung. *bíró*; *jeršek* „Erzbischof" < ung. *érsek* (Schubert 1982; Hadrovics 1985). Auch das in Kroatien im Mittelalter gebräuchliche Latein enthält ungarische Elemente (Hadrovics 1969). Die ungarische Rechtschreibung hatte auch für die kroatische Rechtschreibung Gültigkeit, und zwar auf kajkavischem wie auf čakavischem, vom glagolitischen oder italienischen Schreibsystem nicht beeinflußten Gebiet. Hier schrieb man entsprechend *danasz* (für *danas*), *gozpodin* (für *gospodin*), *imas* (für *imaš*) usw.

Früheste Spuren des Ungarischen in der Sprache südungarischer Serben traten in der zweiten Hälfte des 17. Jahrhunderts in Erscheinung. Diese beziehen sich nicht auf das öffentliche, sondern auf das private Alltagsleben und verbreiteten sich im Rahmen des Neben- und Miteinanders von Ungarn und Serben: vgl. serb. *fijóka* „Schubfach" < ung. *fiók*; *gàzda* „Hausherr, Wirt, reicher Bauer" < *gazda*; *kècelja* „Schürze" < *kecel*, *köcölye*; *čobanja* „Wasserbehälter" < ung. *csobány* usw. Aus der Vojvodina verbreiteten sich viele von ihnen auch in das übrige Serbien.

Eine ganze Reihe von Magyarismen verbreitete sich im gesamten serbokroatischen Sprachgebiet; so z. B. ung. *szoba* „Zimmer" > serb., kroat. *soba*; ung. *gazda* „Wirt" > serb., kroat. *gazda*; *város* „Stadt" > serb., kroat. *varaš* ~ *vároš*, *vāroš* und v. a. Auch Lehnprägungen finden sich, vor allem im Kroatischen, wie z. B. *dotičnost* „Zuständigkeit, Befugnis" zu ung. *illet* „betreffen, berühren" (Nyomárkay 1989).

Seit 1945 setzte unter den ungarländischen Kroaten und Serben ein stetiger Prozeß der sprachlichen Assimilation an ihre ungarische Umgebung ein, die zu einer asymmetrischen Zwei-, häufig auch Dreisprachigkeit führte. Das Ungarische ist dabei als die im Beruf und in der Alltagskommunikation verwendete Sprache die dominierende — insbesondere bei jenen Kindern der ungarländischen Serben und Kroaten, die ungarische Schulen und Universitäten besuchen. Die kroatische bzw. serbische Muttersprache findet nur im privaten Bereich Anwendung. Häufig — insbesondere bei älteren Menschen — ist die Kompetenz beider Sprachen unzureichend. In allen

Fällen aber geht mit der Zwei- bzw. Dreisprachigkeit auch eine Mischsprachigkeit einher, die dadurch gekennzeichnet ist, daß an die Stelle muttersprachlicher Bezeichnungen Magyarismen treten: so z. B. anstelle von *čaj* „Tee": *teja* zu ung. *tea*; anstelle von *grudnjak* „Büstenhalter" *meltartoka* zu ung. *melltartó*; statt *m(j)esečna karta* „Monatskarte" *berlet* zu ung. *bérlet* usw. Solche Bezeichnungen werden in erster Linie in der gesprochenen Sprache verwendet.

Die Zweisprachigkeit entwickelte sich zur Dreisprachigkeit dadurch, daß ein Großteil der ungarländischen Südslaven von Hause aus eine lokale Mundart und nicht die jeweilige Literatursprache kennt, letztere jedoch sekundär an Schulen, in Bildungsinstitutionen, durch Zeitung, Rundfunk und Fersehen vermittelt bekommt. Stepanović (1986) beschreibt einen solchen Prozeß bei jenen serbischen und kroatischen Grenzbewohnern, die regelmäßig Rundfunk- und Fernsehsendungen aus Serbien bzw. Kroatien empfangen.

Aus dieser Situation der „Mischsprachigkeit" erklären sich die Bemühungen der Bildungs- und Kulturinstitutionen der Nationalitäten, ferner auch der Kulturpolitiker Ungarns, sowohl die regionale Sprache und Kultur, als auch die normierte serbische bzw. kroatische Schriftsprache unter den Südslaven Ungarns zu fördern und zu verbreiten.

6. Forschungsstand

Die erste wissenschaftliche Analyse der slavischen Elemente des Ungarischen ist mit dem Namen Franz Miklosichs (Miklosich 1871) verbunden. Nach ihm befaßten sich auch ungarische Slavisten (Oszkar Asbóth; János Melich) zu Beginn des 20. Jahrhunderts mit diesem Thema. Umfassend wurde es jedoch von István Kniezsa 1955 bearbeitet.

Zu Teilaspekten der ungarischen Elemente des Kroatischen und Serbischen erschien u. a. 1936 István Kniezsas Beitrag zu den ungarischen Einflüssen in der kroatisch-kajkavischen christlichen Terminologie. Danach beschäftigte sich vor allem László Hadrovics zwischen 1938 und 1974 mit verschiedenen Themen der ungarisch-kroatischen Kultur- und Sprachbeziehungen (in Arbeiten zur kajkavischen Literatur, zum südslavischen Trojaroman, zur Sprache der Burgenländischen Kroaten, zur Orthographie der kroatischen protestantischen Druckwerke des 16. Jahrhunderts, zu onomastischen Fragen der ungarisch-südslavischen Symbiose u. a.). 1985 verfaßte er eine Gesamtdarstellung der ungarischen Elemente im Serbokroatischen. Zu diesem Thema arbeiteten auch Schubert 1982 und Nyomárkay 1984. Wichtige Hinweise hierzu finden sich ferner bei Popović 1960.

Ausführlich mit der Geschichte der ungarländischen Südslaven beschäftigt sich Urosevics 1969. Ihre sprachliche Situation beschreibt Stepanović 1986. Mokuter (1975) und Kővágó (1981) beleuchten die soziokulturelle Situation der kroatischen und serbischen Minderheit im heutigen Ungarn. Umfassendere Erhebungen hierzu stehen allerdings noch aus.

Auch Ethnologen widmeten sich den in Ungarn lebenden Kroaten und Serben; sie interessieren sich für die tradierten und in der ungarischen Umgebung adaptierten Formen ihrer tradierten Kultur (u. a. Kerecsényi 1982 und Kiss 1988).

7. Bibliographie (in Auswahl)

1990. évi népszámlálás (1992) [Volkszählung vom Jahre 1990]. Magyarország nemzetiségi adatai megyénként [Angaben über die Nationalitäten Ungarns nach Komitaten]. Központi Statisztikai Hivatal, Budapest.

Deér, József (1936): „Die Anfänge der ungarisch-kroatischen Staatsgemeinschaft". In: *Archivum Europae Centro-Orientalis II*, 5—45.

Djordjević, Dimitrije: „Die Serben". In: *Die Habsburgermonarchie 1848—1918*, Band III: Wandruszka, A./Urbanitsch, P. (Eds.), Die Völker des Reiches, 1. Teilband, Wien, 734—774.

Hadrovics, László (1938): „Ungarische Helden in den Dramen des Junije Palmotić". In: *Archivum Europae Centro-Orientalis IV*, 515—522.

Hadrovics, László (1941): „Ungarn und die Kroaten". In: *Ungarische Jahrbücher 21*, 136—172.

Hadrovics, László (1969): „Mađarski elementi u srednjovjekovnom latinitetu Hrvatske" [Ung. Elemente in der mittelalterlichen Latinität Kroatiens]. In: *Starina 54*, Zagreb.

Hadrovics, László (1974): *Schrifttum und Sprache der burgenländischen Kroaten im 18. und 19. Jahrhundert*, Wien.

Hadrovics, László (1985): *Ungarische Elemente im Serbokroatischen*, Wien.

Istorija naroda Jugoslavije (1953) [Geschichte der Völker Jugoslawiens], Band I., Zagreb.

Jireček, Constantin (1911—1918): *Geschichte der Serben*. 2 Bde, Gotha.

Kann, Robert A. (^{2}1964): *Das Nationalitätenproblem der Habsburgermonarchie. I. Band: Das Reich und die Völker*, Graz/Köln, hier 239—264; 287— 298.

Kerecsényi, Edit (1982): *Povijest i materijalna kultura pomurskih Hrvata* [Geschichte und materielle Kultur der Kroaten an der Mur], Budapest.

Kiss, Mária (1988): *Délszláv szokások a Duna mentén* [Südslavische Bräuche entlang der Donau], Budapest.

Klaić, Bratoljub (1966): *Veliki rječnik stranih riječi, izraza i kratica* [Großes Wörterbuch der fremden Wörter, Ausdrücke und Abkürzungen], Zagreb.

Kniezsa, István (1936): „Magyar hatás a kaj-horvát keresztény terminológiában" [Ung. Einfluß auf die kaj-kroatische christliche Terminologie]. In: *Nyelvtudományi Közlemények* L, 191—199.

Kniezsa, István (^{2}1974): *A magyar nyelv szláv jövevényszavai* [Die slavischen Lehnwörter der ungarischen Sprache]. 2 Bde, Budapest.

Kővágó, László (1981): *Nemzetiségek a mai Magyarországon* [Nationalitäten im heutigen Ungarn], Budapest.

Miklosich, Franz (1871): *Die slavischen Elemente im Magyarischen*, Wien. (Denkschriften der Kaiserlichen Akademie der Wissenschaften in Wien, Philologisch-historische Klasse, Bd. 21.).

Mokuter, Iván (1975): *Nemzetiségi iskola — anyanyelvi nevelés* [Nationalitätenschule — Muttersprachenbildung]. Pädagogisches Landesinstitut, Budapest.

Nyomárkay, István (1984): *Strane riječi u hrvatskosrpskom (srpskohrvatskom) jeziku* [Fremdwörter in der kroatoserbischen (serbokroatischen) Sprache], Budapest.

Nyomárkay, István (1989): „A magyar és a szerbhorvát nyelv kapcsolata" [Beziehungen zwischen der ungarischen und der serbokroatischen Sprache]. In: Nyelvünk a Duna-tájon [Unsere Sprache in der Donau-Gegend], Red.: Balázs, János, Budapest.

Popović, Ivan (1960): *Geschichte der serbokroatischen Sprache* (Bibliotheca Slavica). Wiesbaden, insbes. 41—43; 216—222; 602—604.

Pot, Ištvan (1993): *Srpsko-madarski kulturni odnosi u XIX. veku* [Serbisch-ungarische Kulturbeziehungen im 19. Jh.], Neusatz.

Sarosácz, György (1973): „Magyarország délszláv nemzetiségei" [Die südslavischen Nationalitäten Ungarns]. In: *Népi kultúra — Népi társadalom* [Volkskultur — Volksgesellschaft]. Red. Ortutay, Gyula (Jahrbuch der Forschungsgruppe für Volkskunde der Ungarischen Akademie der Wissenschaften VII.), Budapest.

Šišić, Ferdinand von (1917): *Geschichte der Kroaten I* (bis 1102), Zagreb.

Sós, Ágnes Cs. (1973): *Die slawische Bevölkerung Westungarns im 9. Jahrhundert*, München.

Stepanović, Predrag (1986): *A taxonomic Description of the Dialects of Serbs and Croats in Hungary*, Budapest.

Suppan, Arnold (1980): „Die Kroaten". In: *Die Habsburgermonarchie 1848—1918*, Wandruszka, A./Urbanitsch, P. (Eds.), Band III: Die Völker des Reiches, 1. Teilband, Wien, 626—733.

Szerbek és magyarok a Duna mentén (1983, 1987) [Serben und Ungarn entlang der Donau] I. 1848—1849, Red.: Bona, G., Budapest 1983; II. 1858—1867, Red.: Fried, I., Budapest 1987.

Takács, Imre (1989): „Die gegenwärtige Nationalitätenpolitik in Ungarn". In: *Südosteuropa-Mitteilungen 29*, 76—81.

Schubert, Gabriella (1982): *Ungarische Einflüsse in der Terminologie des öffentlichen Lebens der Nachbarsprachen*, Berlin.

Urosevics, Danilo (1969): *A magyaroroszági délszlávok története* [Geschichte der ungarländischen Südslaven], Budapest.

István Nyomárkay, Budapest (Ungarn)
Gabriella Schubert, Berlin (Deutschland)

213. Ungarisch—Slowenisch

1. Geographie und Demographie
2. Geschichte
3. Ethnoprofile
4. Sprachpolitische Lage
5. Zweisprachigkeit der Slowenen
6. Allgemeines kontaktlinguistisches Porträt
7. Bibliographie (in Auswahl)

1. Geographie und Demographie

1.1. Geographie

Im heutigen Ungarn lebt im Komitat Eisenburg (Vas), südlich von St. Gotthard (Szentgotthárd) und des Flusses Raab (Rába), in einem durch die österreichische und die slowenische Grenze umschlossenen, zipfelförmigen Gebiet eine zahlenmäßig kleine slowenische Minderheit. Dieses Gebiet, früher als „Wenden-", heute als „Slowenen-Region" bezeichnet, gehört zur geograpisch-ethnographischen Region „Örség" [Wart] — benannt nach den hier befindlichen Grenzwachen des Mittelalters — bzw. zur Hügellandschaft „Eisenburg-Sala (Vas-Zala)" (Mukicsné 1974, 87 ff). Die von den Slowenen bewohnte Region beträgt 92 km². Im Norden ist sie flach; im Westen und Süden erstreckt sich eine 260–400 m hohe Hügellandschaft mit tonhaltigem Boden, die vom Geröll der Flüsse Raab und Mur übersät ist. Der Boden ist hier häufig sauer und kalkarm. Zum größeren Teil gibt es hier Waldboden, zum kleineren Schwemmland. In dieser Region mischt sich alpines mit pannonischem Klima. Es ist das regenreichste und sonnenscheinärmste Gebiet Ungarns (Durchschnittstemperatur 16 °C), das von Wäldern, Wiesen und Rasenflächen bedeckt ist, jedoch für den Anbau vieler Kulturpflanzen keine günstigen Voraussetzungen bietet (Zelenay 1987, 447).

Die „Wenden-Region" besteht aus 9 Siedlungen in 7 Gemeinden, südlich von St. Gotthard (Szentgotthárd): Windischdorf (Rábatótfalu, Slovénska Vés) – seit 1984 gehört es verwaltungsmäßig zu St. Gotthard; Unterzemming (Alsószölnök, Dólnji Seník); Steffelsdorf (Apátistvánfalva, Stévanovci); Permise (Vérica); Ritkaháza (Rítkovci) – die beiden letzteren sind seit 1951 unter dem Namen Kétvölgy vereinigt; Újbalázsfalva (früher Börgölin), seit 1937 an Steffelsdorf angeschlossen; Oberzemming (Felsőszölnök, Górnji Seník); Orfalu (Ándovci); → Sprachenkarte L.

1.2. Demographie

Die konkrete Zahl der in Ungarn lebenden Slowenen ist nicht genau feststellbar; viele von ihnen besitzen keine klare Vorstellung von ihrer Zuordnung zu einer Ethnie und haben sich bei statistischen Erhebungen nicht als Slowenen bezeichnet: 1980 waren es lediglich 1731; 1990 1930 Personen, die sich als Slowenen ausgaben. Ganz andere Ergebnisse erzielte die Zählung nach der Muttersprache: Als slowenische Muttersprachler bezeichneten sich 1970 4205, 1980 3142 und 1990 2627 Personen. In den slowenischen Siedlungen des Raab-Gebietes lebten nach Zählungen im Jahre 1980 2715, im Jahre 1990 1453 Personen mit slowenischer Muttersprache. Es wird angenommen, daß es im Jahre 1980 4287 Personen, im Jahre 1990 4193 Personen mit slowenischer Muttersprache in Ungarn gab (Klinger 1992, 12). Überwiegend siedeln sie im Raab-Gebiet, jedoch leben in geringer Zahl Slowenen auch außerhalb des Komitats Eisenburg, in 12 weiteren Komitaten.

Die Slowenen-Region ist ein im Komitat Eisenburg wirtschaftlich unterentwickeltes Gebiet. Zwar hatte es zeitweilig eine relative Überbevölkerung aufzuweisen, bot aber für eine landwirtschaftliche Nutzung wenig günstige natürliche Voraussetzungen. Dies führte zu Abwanderungswellen und einem kontinuierlichen Rückgang der Bevölkerungszahlen. Diese Tendenz hält auch in der Gegenwart an; seit den 60er Jahren wandern immer mehr arbeitsfähige Männer in die Städte ab, um sich ihren Unterhalt als Industriearbeiter zu verdienen (Zelenay 1987, 452 f).

2. Geschichte

Die Slowenen haben ihre heutigen Wohnsitze nördlich der Save offenbar schon zur Zeit der frühesten Einwanderung der Südslaven nach dem Balkan eingenommen – für die Altertümlichkeit des Slowenischen sprechen einige Ortsnamen mit einer sehr altertümlichen slavischen Lautgestalt (z. B. *Soča, Logatec, Ptuj*). In Niederpannonien befand sich ein slowenisches Reich, das auch nach dem heutigen Ungarn hineinreichte (hierzu u. a. Šuman 1881, 1–183; Gruden/Mal I–II; Kos 1955). Von 869 bis 874 residierte der slowenische Fürst Kocelj in Blatograd am südwestlichen Zipfel des Plattensees (Balaton), in der Gegend des heutigen Zalavár. Das ungarische Hydronym *Balaton* geht auf südslav. *blatьnъ* „schlammig, sumpfig" zurück, das mit dem sumpfigen, morastigen Ufer des Sees zusammenhängt und auch in dem deutschen Namen der Residenzstadt Koceljs *Mosapurg* (= Morastburg, Sumpfburg) zum Ausdruck kommt (hierzu Popović 1960, 113). 874 wurde Kocelj abgesetzt, und die Slowenen gerieten unter fränkische Oberhoheit. Mit der ungarischen Landnahme (896–900) verschwand unter der ungarischen Herrschaft die selbständige slowenische Kolonisation in der pannonischen Ebene, zum anderen brach die territoriale Verbindung zwischen den West- und den Südslaven im mittleren Donaugebiet ab.

Es ist nicht ganz klar, welcher Zusammenhang zwischen den pannonischen Slowenen der Landnahmezeit und den heutigen Slowenen des Mur- sowie des Raab-Gebiets besteht. Nach Király (1978, 128) seien diese Gebiete noch lange Zeit nach der Landnahme unbewohnt gewesen. Die Slowenen seien während der Landnahme in die Steiermark und nach Kroatien geflohen, und später, in friedlicheren Zeiten, hierher zurückgekehrt – nach Grafenauer (1955, 62) im 12. Jahrhundert. Die Vorfahren der Bewohner von Steffelsdorf (Apátistvánfalva, Stévanovci), Orfalu (Ándovci), Szakonyfalu und Windischdorf (Rábatótfalu, Slovénska Vés) wurden von den Zisterziensern aus der benachbarten Steiermark und dem Murgebiet angesiedelt. Oberzemming (Felsőszölnök, Górnji Seník), Unterzemming (Alsószölnök, Dólnji Seník) und Kétvölgy gehörten seit dem 15. Jahrhundert zum Familienbesitz der Battyanys in Dobra (heute Neuhaus, Österreich) (Székely 1987, 516). Bis zum Trianon-Vertrag (1920) bildeten die Slowenen des heutigen Ungarn mit jenen des Murgebietes eine Einheit innerhalb der Grenzen des historischen Ungarn (zwischen den Flüssen Raab und Mur). Sie waren von ihren Landsleuten jenseits der Grenzen sprachlich wie kulturell isoliert und lebten zudem bereits seit dem Mittelalter mit Ungarn zusammen, später auch mit (bajuwarisch-österreichischen) Deutschen und Südslawen, besonders Kaj-Kroaten.

Infolge ihrer Absonderung verfügten die ungarischen Slowenen erst relativ spät über ein eigenes Schrifttum. Dabei handelte es sich in erster Linie um kirchliche Texte, Liederbücher, Gebetsbücher und erbauliche Kalender- und Lehrbücher. Aus der 2. Hälfte des 17. Jahrhunderts stammt ein im ungarländisch-slowenischen Dialekt verfaßtes Bußgebet *molitv e pokore* (Hadrovics 1956). Der Bischof von Steinamanger Szily förderte gegen Ende des 18. Jahrhunderts die Abfassung und Verbreitung slowenischer Glaubens- und Schulbücher. Die erste slowenische Zeitschrift unter dem Titel „Prijatel" wurde 1875—1879 von Augusztics in Budapest herausgegeben.

Durch den Trianon-Vertrag gerieten die im Murgebiet (Pomurje) lebenden Slowenen und auch die hier in kompakten Siedlungen lebenden Ungarn in das „Königreich der Serben, Kroaten und Slowenen" (Kraljevina SHS). Der kleinere Teil, das Raab-Gebiet (Porabje), verblieb innerhalb der Grenzen Ungarns.

3. Ethnoprofile

Bis Ende des 18. Jahrhunderts bezeichneten die Ungarn die ungarischen Slowenen wie auch andere südslavische Minderheiten auf ungarischem Gebiet, die Kaj-Kroaten und die Slowaken, mit dem Kollektivbegriff *tót*; diese Bezeichnung besaß eine pejorative Konnotation. Das Ethnonym *szlovén* erschien im Ungarischen (als deutsches Lehnwort) erst zu Beginn des 19. Jahrhunderts; davor nannte man die Slowenen — ebenfalls abwertend — *vendek* (Pl.). *vend* wird für den ungarischen Slowenen auch heute noch, jedoch in neutraler Konnotation, verwendet.

Die Alltagskultur der ungarischen Slowenen weist mit jener der Ungarn im südwestlichen Teil des Landes große Ähnlichkeiten auf — etwa in der Siedlungsweise, in der Wohnkultur (Flechtwerkhäuser; rechtwinklige Anordnung von Wohn- und Wirtschaftsräumen und in der Kleidungsgestaltung).

Eine besondere Relevanz für die slowenische Volksdichtung hat die ungarische historische Persönlichkeit des König Matthias (1443—1490). Matthias war ein sehr volkstümlicher König. In seinem schier unbesiegbaren „schwarzen Heer" dienten auch Slowenen neben anderen Südslaven. Infolge der engen Beziehungen des Hauses Hunyadi zum slowenischen Grafen Cilli wurde die Gestalt des Matthias bei den Slowenen außerordentlich populär; sie identifizierten sich mit ihm genauso wie die Südslaven mit Marko Kraljević. König Matthias ist in den Volksmärchen, Sagen, Liedern und Balladen der Slowenen weit mehr als ein üblicher historischer Held; er erhebt sich in mythische Höhen. Matthias entwickelte sich zum idealen Vertreter slowenischer Wesensart, mit all ihren Tugenden und Fehlern. In der Volksdichtung berichten die Gedichte im Balladenton von der Heirat des Matthias: *Ženidba Matjaša kralja*, über seine osmanische Gefangenschaft: *Matjaš v vozi turski*, über seinen Tod: *Matjašova smert* und über seine Höllenfahrt: *Kralj Matjaš peklom*. In den Sagen ergrünt der dürre Baum, wenn Matthias nach dem Endkampf seinen Schild daran hängt, zum Zeichen des ewigen Friedens, denn Kralj Matjaž ist der für Recht und Glauben kämpfende Retter der Christenheit.

4. Sprachpolitische Lage

In der Verfassung der Republik Ungarn ist die Gleichberechtigung aller Staatsbürger, aller Sprachen und Kulturen der in Ungarn ansässigen ethnischen Minderheiten garantiert (Arday 1987, 436).

In administrativer Hinsicht leiten örtliche Selbstverwaltungen und zwei Kreisnotariate von Steffelsdorf und Unterzemming die slowenischen Gemeinden. St. Gotthard ist das wissenschaftliche, kulturelle und politische Zentrum des Raab-Gebietes; hier hat der Verband der Slowenen Ungarns seinen Sitz. Er entfaltet seine Tätigkeit auf der Grundlage der durch die ungarische Verfassung garantierten Minderheitenrechte, ferner im Rahmen eines zwischen Ungarn und Slowenien abgeschlossenen Nationalitätenvertrages. In St. Gotthard erscheint die slowenische Wochenzeitschrift „Porabje". Das regionale Hörfunkprogramm bietet wöchentlich eine 30minütige Sendung für die slowenische Minderheit; im zweiten ungarischen Fernsehprogramm gibt es jeden Samstag vormittag eine Sendung für sie.

Der ungarische Staat ist um den Erhalt der ungarischen Slowenen bemüht. In einem in Vorbereitung befindlichen Nationalitätengesetz sollen sie mit einer noch höheren Gebietsautonomie (u. a. in wirtschaftl. Hinsicht) ausgestattet werden. In den 80er Jahren begann der zweisprachige Unterricht in den Grundschulen der Gemeinden. In Steinamanger, an der Pädagogischen Hochschule „Dániel Berzsenyi", befindet sich ein Lehrstuhl für slowenische Sprache und Literatur; hier werden seit 1980 slowenische Lehrer und Wissenschaftler ausgebildet.

5. Zweisprachigkeit der Slowenen

Die ungarischen Slowenen sind heute zweisprachig; im öffentlichen Leben kommunizieren sie ungarisch. Allerdings kommt es unter den älteren, in tradierten bäuerlichen Sozialorganisationen und in Abgeschiedenheit lebenden Leuten oft vor, daß sie das Ungarische mit vielen Fehlern sprechen. Gleichzeitig weicht aber auch die örtliche Sprachvariante der Slowenen stark von der slowenischen Standardsprache ab. Pável beobachtete hier beispielsweise 1909 (88) die Bewahrung des Nasalvokals (so in *glandálo* „Spiegel" gegenüber slowen. *gledálo, kondravi, -a, -o* „Kraus" — altbulg. *kǫdrjavъ*). Die starke Abweichung der in Ungarn gesprochenen slowenischen Mundart von der slowenischen Standardsprache bringt Schwierigkeiten im Bildungswesen der ungarischen Slowenen mit sich, denn die Schulbücher sind in der Standardsprache geschrieben. Die Kinder in der Schule aber müssen gleichzeitig die örtliche Variante und die Standardsprache erlernen. Dies erfordert von den Lehrern, daß sie beide Sprachvarianten auf einem hohen Niveau beherrschen müssen. Um diese Kompetenz auch bei Erwachsenen zu pflegen, verwendet die Wochenzeitschrift „Porabje" zur Hälfte die örtliche Variante, zur Hälfte den Standard des Slowenischen. Genau genommen müssen sich ungarische Slowenen um die Kompetenz in drei Sprachstandards bemühen, was in vielen Fällen zur Folge hat, daß sich die Sprecher auf die lokale Variante und das Ungarische — jeweils in Abhängigkeit von ihrer Schulbildung — beschränken.

Die lokale Variante kann sich ebenfalls auf eine standardisierte schriftliche Basis berufen, die von den ungarischen Slowenen — unabhängig von den Slowenen jenseits der Mur — zu Beginn des 18. Jahrhunderts geschaffen wurde (Király 1978, 135; Zorko 1980, 175). Sie entstand im Zusammenhang mit der Verbreitung religiöser Literatur und von Schulbüchern, die in ungarischen Druckereien (Raab, Güns, Ödenburg, Preßburg, Steinamanger) gedruckt wurden und sich der ungarischen Orthographie bedienten. In ihnen sind *s* als *sz* oder *z*, *š* als *c*, *nj* als *ny* wiedergegeben. Entsprechend lautet der Titel eines in Ödenburg 1797 erschienenen Gebetsbuches: *Molitvi, na sztári szlovenszki jezik obnyene ino na haszek slovenskoga národa vo dane.* Als syntaktische Eigentümlichkeit zeigen diese Texte unter dem Einfluß des Ungarischen den regelmäßigen Gebrauch des bestimmten und unbestimmten Artikels: *te cslovik, te szad, edno milosztivno lusztvo.*

Bis heute ist die lokale slowenische Sprachvariante im Hinblick auf ihre soziale Wertigkeit gegenüber dem Ungarischen in einer sehr ungünstigen Lage, die sich mit fortschreitender Assimilation an die ungarischsprachige Umgebung noch verstärkt.

6. Allgemeines kontaktlinguistisches Porträt

6.1. Ungarische Elemente des Slowenischen

Im Laufe des ungarisch-slowenischen Zusammenlebens entlehnten die Slowenen zahlreiche ungarische Begriffe aus verschiedenen Bereichen des offiziellen Lebens (vgl. z. B. *bíróv* „Richter" zu ung. *bíró*, *gyiléš* „Versammlung" zu ung. *gyűlés*), des Wirtschaftslebens (z. B. *bériš ~ béroš* „Knecht" zu ung. *béres*; *váma* „Zoll" zu ung. *vám*; *bouta* „Laden" zu ung. *bolt*), aber auch des religiösen und privaten Lebens (z. B. *püčpek* „Bischof" zu ung. *püspök*; *baja* „Unglück" zu ung. *baj*; *beteg ~ betežan* „krank" zu ung. *beteg*). Auch im Slowenischen außerhalb der Grenzen des historischen Ungarn ist die Zahl der ungarischen Lehnwörter relativ groß (hierzu u. a. Schubert 1982).

Während das Ungarn-Slowenische in früheren Zeiten das übernommene ungarische Lehnwort durch die Anfügung slavischer Endungen dem eigenen Formensystem anpaßte (vgl. *baja*; *bouta*), werden Magyarismen in der Gegenwart auch endungslos übernommen; so z. B. *čempe* „Kachel" (*csempe*); *butor* (*bútor*); *lakaš* (*lakás*); *elnök* (*elnök*) usw. Verben werden ebenso mit ihren ungarischen Suffixen übernommen; lediglich in der Mundart von Oberzemming (Felsőszölnök, Górnji Seník) werden sie mit dem slavischen Suffix *-vate* versehen: z. B. *lakni-vate* „wohnen" (zu ung. *lakni*) (Emberšić 1991, 112 ff).

Abweichend zur slowenischen Literatursprache kennen die ungarischen Slowenen unter ungarischem Einfluß palatale labiale Vokale mittlerer und hoher Zungenlage (*ö*, *ü*), ebenso ein *å* tiefer Zungenlage statt des illabialen *a* (vgl. ebda., 170 f). Auch im Konsonantensystem hat sich das Slowenische des Raab-Gebietes der örtlichen Variante des Ungarischen angenähert; das standardsprachliche *lj* erscheint hier in depalatalisierter Form: z. B. *vola* „Wille" statt *volja*; *bole* „besser" statt *bolje*; *kole* „er schneidet" statt *kolje* usw. Eine solche Depalatalisierungstendenz zeigt allerdings auch die ungarische Mundart dieses Gebietes; vgl. u. 6.2. Zu den Eigentümlichkeiten des ungarischen Slowenisch gehört ferner die Umlautung von standardsprachlichem *j* zu *dj* im Anlaut vor einem Vokal bzw. im Inlaut nach stimmhaften Konsonanten; vgl. *djájce* „Ei" statt *jajce*; *djá* „ich" statt *ja* usw. (hierzu Asbóth 1908, 14 ff).

Auf den ständigen Kontakt mit dem Ungarischen sind möglicherweise einige Veränderungen in Morphologie und Syntax des ungarischen Slowenisch zurückzuführen. Sie betreffen (1) (a) Vereinfachungen des Genussystems (unter dem Einfluß fehlender Genuskategorien im Ungarischen) bzw. den Genuswechsel von Maskulina und Neutra zu Feminina und (b) Genusschwankungen im Gebrauch der Verbalendungen der Vergangenheitsform; so sagt eine weibliche Person *Ge sa büulbiu* (statt *bila*) *v cérkvi* „Ich war in der Kirche"; (2) eine dem Ungarischen angeglichene Wortfolge; vgl. *Ge tö den* wörtlich „Ich auch gehe" für slowenisch standardsprachlich *Tudi jaz grem* „Auch ich gehe".

6.2. Slowenische Elemente des Ungarischen

Mit slowenischen Einflüssen auf das Ungarische muß für die Zeit nach der ungarischen Landnahme gerechnet werden, allerdings ist es angesichts der weit zurückliegenden Entlehnungszeit und des hohen Ähnlichkeitsgrades im Wortschatz der südslavischen Sprachen oft unmöglich, die genaue Quelle der einst entlehnten Wörter zu ermitteln. Zu ihnen gehören Begriffe wie z. B. *király* „König" < slav. *kraljь*, *szent* „heilig" < *svętъ*, *paraszt* „Bauer" < *prostъ* „einfach, gemein" u. v. a. m. Sie können aus verschiedenen slavischen bzw. südslavischen Sprachen und Mundarten entlehnt worden sein, u. a. auch aus der kajkavischen Mundart des Kroatischen. Es erscheint daher problematisch, slowenische Einflüsse in der betrachteten Kontaktzone isoliert zu betrachten. Im regionalen ungarischen Wortschatz finden sich allerdings verschiedene Slavismen, die sehr wahrscheinlich Entlehnungen aus dem Slowenischen darstellen: *gelencsér* ~ *gerencsér* ~ *gölöncsér* „Töpfer"; *szalados* „ein süßer Kuchen aus Weizenkeimen" < *szalad + os*; *ragya* ~ *rogya* „Rostkrankheit"; *berezna* ~ *brázna* „Ackerfurche"; *szelence* „Lieder"; *paszita* „Taufschmaus" usw. (Szabó 1980, 43 ff; Molnár 1988, 207 f).

Die nach dem 16. Jahrhundert eingetretene Depalatalisierung des palatalen *l* in ungarischen Mundarten dieses Gebiets dürfte sich unter dem Einfluß der hier gesprochenen südslav. Idiome entwickelt haben; vgl. ung. *foló* < *folyó* „Fluß"; *goló* < *golyó* „Kugel" usw. (hierzu Szabó 1991, 205). Ebenso sind auch die hier vorkommenden Abweichungen von der „Vokalharmonie" zu begründen: vgl. *kertnál* „beim Garten" statt *kertnél*; *firho* „sich verheiraten" statt *férjhez*; *kapáve* „mit der Hacke" statt *kapával* usw.

7. Bibliographie (in Auswahl)

Arday, Lajos (1987): „A nemzetiségi politika és a nemzetiségi jogok rendszerének néhány fontosabb vonása Magyarországon" [Einige Grundzüge des nationalitätenpolitischen und -rechtlichen Systems in Ungarn]. In: *Magyarok és szlovének*, 433–446.

Asbóth, Oszkár (1908): „A *j > gy* változás a hazai szlovének nyelvében és a dunántúli magyar nyelvjárásokban" [Der Lautwandel *j > gy* in der Sprache der ungarischen Slowenen und in den transdanubischen ung. Mundarten]. In: *Értekezések a Nyelv- és Széptudományok köréből*, 463–522.

Embersics, Erzsébet (1988): „Znacilnosti gornjeseniskega narečja" [Eigenschaften der Oberzemminger Mundart]. In: *Nemzetközi Szalvisztikai Napok III*, Steinamanger, 169–177.

Emberšič, Elizabeta (1991): „Madžerske beseda v gornjeseniskem narečju" [Ungarische Wörter in der Oberzemminger Mundart]. In: *Nemzetközi szlavisztikai Napok IV*, Steinamanger, 111–120.

Grafenauer, Bogo (1955): *Zgodovina slovenskega naroda II* [Geschichte des Slowenentums], Laibach.

Grafenauer, Ivan (1951): *Slovenske pripovedke o kralju Matjažu* [Slowenische Sagen von Matthias Corvinus]. Slovenska Akademija znan. i umetn. Razred za filološke in liter. vede, dela 4., Inst. za slovensko narodopisje 1.), Laibach.

Gruden, J./Mal, J. (I: 1910–1916; II: 1928–1939): *Zgodovina slovenskega naroda* [Geschichte des slowenischen Volkes] I, Celovec; II, Celje.

Győri-Nagy, Sándor (1987): „Kétnyelvűség-dinamika Felsőszölnökön" [Zweisprachigkeitsdynamik in Oberzemming]. In: *Magyarok és szlovének*, Budapest, 543–570.

Hadrovics, László (1956): „Ein Bußgebet der ungarländischen Slowenen aus dem 17. Jahrhundert". In: *Studia Slavica* 2, 388–394.

Király, Péter (1978): „Beiträge zur slowenischen Mundart in Ungarn". In: *Hungaro-Slavica 1978. VIII. Internationaler Kongreß der Slawisten Zagreb*, Hadrovics, L./Hollós, A. (Eds.).

Klinger, András (1992): „A nemzetiségi statisztika Európában és Magyarországon" [Die Nationalitätenstatistik in Europa und in Ungarn]. In: *Magyar Tudományos Akadémia Demográfiai Bizottsága. Nemzetiségi Staisztikai Konferencia*, Budapest.

Kniezsa, István (1938): *Magyarország népei a XI. században* [Die Völker Ungarns im 11. Jahrhundert], Budapest.

Kniezsa, István (1974): *A magyar nyelv szláv jövevényszavai* [Slawische Lehnwörter der ungarischen Sprache], Budapest.

Kos, M. (1955): *Zgodovina Slovencev od naselitve do petnajstega stoletja* [Geschichte der Slowenen von ihrer Niederlassung bis zum 15. Jahrhundert], Laibach.

KSH 1990. évi népszámlálás. A nemzetiségi népesség száma egyes községekben 1960–1990 [Volkszählung 1990. Die Zahl der Nationalitätenbevölkerung in den einzelnen Gemeinden 1960–1990], Zentrales Statistisches Amt, Budapest 1991.

Melich, János (1925–1929): *A honfoglaláskori Magyarország* [Ungarn zur Zeit der Landnahme], Budapest.

Molnár, Zoltán Miklós (1988): „A Magyar Nyelvjárások Atlasza szlovén vonatkozású elemeinek kérdéséhez" [Zur Frage der slowenischen Elemente im Atlas der Ungarischen Mundarten]. In: *Nemzetközi szlavisztikai Napok III*, Steinamanger, 107–209.

Mukicsné Kozár, Mária (1984): *Szlovénvidék. A szlovén etnikai terület néprajzi topográfiája XX. század* [Das Slowenengebiet. Ethnographische Topographie des slowenischen Gebietes. 20. Jahrhundert], Laibach/Steinamanger, 78–225.

Pável, Ágost (1909): *A vashidegkúti szlovén nyelvjárás hangtana* [Lautlehre der slowenischen Mundart von Vashidegkút], Budapest.

Pável, Ágost (1917): *A Hunyadiak a délszláv népköltészetben* [Die Hunyadis in der südslawischen Volksdichtung], Steinamanger.

Pável, Ágost (1942): *Mátyás király és a szlovének* [König Matthias und die Slowenen], Fünfkirchen.

Popović, Ivan (1960): *Geschichte der serbokroatischen Sprache* (Bibliotheca Slavica), Wiesbaden.

Schubert, Gabriella (1981): „Ungarn und Slowenen". In: *Zeitschrift für Balkanologie XVII/1*, 82–88.

Schubert, Gabriella (1982): *Ungarische Einflüsse in der Terminologie des öffentlichen Lebens der Nachbarsprachen* (Osteuropa-Institut an der Freien Universität Berlin, Balkanologische Veröffentlichungen 7), Berlin.

Šuman, Josef (1881): *Die Slowenen* (Die Völker Österreich-Ungarns. Ethnographische und culturhistorische Schilderungen X), Wien/Teschen.

Szabó, Géza (1980): „A nyelvi kontaktus kutatásának néhány kérdése a nyugati magyar nyelvjárásokban" [Zu einigen Fragen des Sprachkontaktes in den westungarischen Dialekten]. In: *A Szombathelyi Tanárképző Főiskola Tudományos Közleményei II.*, Steinamanger, 37–54.

Szabó, Géza (1991): *A magyar-déli szláv nyelvi kapcsolatok tükröződése a nyugati típusú nyelvjárásainkban* [Wiederspiegelung der ungarisch-südslawischen Sprachkontakte in unseren Mundarten westlichen Typs]. In: *Nemzetközi szlavisztikai napokk IV*, Steinamanger, 203–205.

Székely, Bertalan (1987): *Oktatás kultúra, közművelődés és tömegkommunikáció a magyarországi szlovén nemzetiség körében* [Unterricht, Kultur, Bildungswesen und Massenmedien in Kreisen des Slowenentums in Ungarn]. In: *Magyarok és szlovének*, Budapest, 500–542.

Zelenay, Anna (1987): „A földrajzi, gazdasági, társadalmi és demográfiai viszonyok a Rába-vidéken" [Geschichte, wirtschaftliche, gesellschaftliche und demographische Lage im Raab-Gebiet]. In: *Magyarok és szlovének*, Budapest, 447–469.

Zorko, Zinka (1980): „Govor vasi Stevanovci v Porabju" [Die Sprache von Steffelsdorf im Raab-Gebiet]. In: *Az együttműködés 10 éve. A Szombathelyi Tanárképző Főiskola és a Mariborsi pedagógiai akadémia tudományos ülésszaka*, Steinamanger, 156–178.

Gabriella Schubert, Berlin (Deutschland)
Géza Szabo, Steinamanger (Ungarn)

214. Ungarisch−Slowakisch

1. Geographie und Demographie
2. Geschichte
3. Ethnoprofile
4. Soziokulturelle Rahmenbedingungen des Sprachkontakts
5. Allgemeines kontaktlinguistisches Porträt
6. Folgen des Sprachkontakts
7. Forschungsstand
8. Bibliographie (in Auswahl)

1. Geographie und Demographie

Im heutigen Ungarn können drei größere, relativ geschlossene slowakische Siedlungsgebiete hervorgehoben werden: (a) in der südöstlichen Tiefebene, in den Komitaten Bekesch (Békés) und Csongrád die ehemaligen Marktflecken Békéscsabe, Beren (Mezőberény), Szarvas, Tótkomlós; (b) in Transdanubien, im Pilis-Gebirge (Pest; Komorn/Komárom; Gran) die Siedlungen Pilisszentkereszt, Piliscsév, Pilisszántó, Kesztölc und (c) in dem nordungarischen Mittelgebirge Mátra, Bükk und Zemplin (Zemplén) (Komitat Naurad/Nógrád/Novohrad). Darüber hinaus leben Slowaken verstreut über das Land in nicht zusammenhängenden Gebieten oder in kleineren Sprachinseln.

Die slowakischen Siedlungsgebiete in Ungarn entstanden in der ersten Hälfte des 18. Jahrhunderts im Norden des Landes und dehnten sich später nach Süden aus (vgl. dazu unter 2.). 1880 wurden 213 249 Slowaken in Ungarn gezählt; diese Zahl war bis 1930 um mehr als die Hälfte auf 104 809 gesunken. Im Zuge des zwischen der Tschechoslowakei und Ungarn 1946−1947 durchgeführten Bevölkerungsaustausches migrierten über 73 000 Slowaken aus Ungarn in die Tschechoslowakei. Dadurch verloren mehrere Ortschaften 40−80% ihrer slowakischen Einwohnerschaft; hier ließen sich ungarische Einwanderer aus der Slowakei nieder. In jüngster Vergangenheit löste die ungarische Wirtschaftsreform von 1965 auch unter der slowakischen Bevölkerung eine Binnenmigration in die urbanen Zentren aus. Heute wird die Zahl der ungarischen Slowaken auf 70 000−100 000 geschätzt. 1990 wurden in Ungarn allerdings nur knapp 13 000 slowakische Muttersprachler gezählt (→ Sprachenkarte L).

2. Geschichte

Im 9. Jahrhundert entstand durch Vereinigung des Fürstentums Nitra (im Gebiet der heutigen Slowakei) mit dem Mährischen Reich das Großmährische Reich. Bereits zu dieser Zeit wurde unter der hier lebenden slavischen Bevölkerung durch die Slavenapostel Kyrill und Method das Christentum verbreitet. Die magyarische Landnahme bedeutete ein einschneidendes Ereignis für die Slaven Pannoniens und des Großmährischen Reiches: Die Magyaren keilten sich in die kompakte slavische Besiedlung dieses Gebietes ein und trennten die West- von den Südslaven. Mitte des 10. Jahrhunderts zerstörten sie das Großmährische Reich und besetzten einen Teil des Fürstentums Nitra (auf dem rechten Donauufer) und brachten bis zum Ende des 11. Jahrhunderts auch die übrigen Teile des slawischen Siedlungsgebietes in ihre Gewalt. Zwar fehlt es an schriftlichen Belegen aus dem 10. und 11. Jahrhundert, doch kann angenommen werden, daß Slowaken und Ungarn im nördlichen und nordwestlichen Teil des Landes bereits zu diesem Zeitpunkt zusammenlebten. Viele slowakische, stadtähnliche Handels- und Bergbausiedlungen wurden im 12. Jahrhundert durch deutsche und wallonische Bergleute und Handwerker besiedelt (Stoob 1977, 192 ff). Die Nutzung der Bodenschätze und der Salzabbau intensivierte im 12. Jahrhundert die Zuwanderung von Bergleuten. Die Ortsbezeichnung *de Banya* (1240) im slowakischen Erzgebirge deutet darauf hin, daß die Bergwerksverwaltung in ungarischer Hand lag (vgl. ung. *bánya* „Bergwerk"). Nachdem das slowakische Siedlungsgebiet im 13. Jahrhundert durch Tataren und Kumanen verwüstet wurde, brachte das 14. Jahrhundert eine Belebung der west- und ostslowakischen Städte mit sich. Demgegenüber verarmte die slowakische Bauernschaft immer mehr; dies führte 1514 zu dem Bauernaufstand unter dem ungarischen Bauernführer György Dózsa, an dem auch slowakische Bauern beteiligt waren. Nach dessen Niederwerfung und der Einführung der Leibeigenschaft verstärkten sich die Konflikte zwischen Slowaken einerseits und Ungarn sowie Deutschen andererseits. Diesen Zwistigkeiten bereitete der Ansturm der Osmanen ein Ende. Nach 1526 bzw. der Einnahme des größten Teils von Ungarn durch die Osmanen wurde die Slowakei ein Zufluchtsort flüchtender Ungarn, Kroaten und Rumänen. Mit der Gründung ungarischer Niederlassungen in der Slowakei wurden viele ungarische Bezeichnungen des städtischen Lebens, des Militärs, sozialer Gegebenheiten, aber auch des Alltagslebens ins Slowakische entlehnt (vgl. unter 6.).

Nach Abzug der osmanischen Besatzung setzte das Zurückfluten jener Ungarn ein, die früher vor den Osmanen nach Norden geflüchtet waren; zur selben Zeit setzte unter der slowakischen Bevölkerung (Leibeigenen, Kleinadligen) aus wirtschaftlichen, demographischen (Überbevölkerung im 16.–17. Jahrhundert) und konfessionellen Gründen (Verfolgung der Lutheraner) eine Südwanderung ein, und zwar nicht nur aus den benachbarten Ebenen, sondern auch aus entfernteren Gebieten wie den Komitaten Arwa (Orava, Árva), Zips (Szepes), Liptau (Liptó), Trentschin (Trenčín, Trencsén) und Neutra (Nitra, Nyitra). Bereits Ende des 17. Jahrhunderts entstanden die neuen Siedlungen Acsa (Komitat Pest), Bánk (Komitat Nauraden, Domoszló (Komitat Hewesch) und Balassagyarmat. Auf die erste Siedlerwelle von 1690 bis 1711 folgten weitere verstärkte Einwanderungswellen zwischen 1711 und 1740 sowie 1740 und 1780 (Manga 1972, 282 f). Zunächst spielte sich die Migration hauptsächlich im Gebiet der Komitate Naurad (Nógrád) und Hont ab; in einigen Fällen wirkte sie sich auch auf die Komitate Pest und Hewesch aus. Von hier aus wanderten viele Slowaken weiter südwärts, bis in Komitate jenseits der Theiß.

Im 19. Jahrhundert verschärften sich die nationalen Rivalitäten im Kaiserreich. Die Slowaken als eine der kleinsten Volksgruppen waren bis zum Ende des 18. Jahrhunderts politisch wie kulturell in starkem Maße ungarischen Einflüssen ausgesetzt. Sie forderten nun die Selbstverwaltung innerhalb Ungarns, teils auch völligen Separatismus und Vereinigung mit den Tschechen (vgl. hierzu unter 4.). 1918 entstand die erste Tschechoslowakische Republik. Der Friedensvertrag von Trianon (1920) besiegelte die Abtrennung der Slowakei von Ungarn mit einem bedeutenden ungarischen Bevölkerungsanteil.

3. Ethnoprofile

Slowaken wurden von den Ungarn häufig mit dem Namen *tót* versehen. Bis etwa 1800 diente dieser Name zur Bezeichnung der Slawen allgemein, danach lediglich der Slowaken. Er hatte eine negative, abwertende Konnotation. Im Zusammenhang mit der Magyarisierungswelle (vgl. unter 4.) verbreitete sich die Aussage: *Tót nem ember* „Ein Slowake ist kein Mensch". Nach der Auflösung der Österreichisch-Ungarischen Monarchie wurde das Ethnonym *tót* allerdings in den Hintergrund gedrängt.

Im ländlichen Alltagsleben in den slowakischen Sprachinseln hatte das Zusammenleben von Slowaken und Ungarn indessen eine ganz andere Qualität. Während des 18. und 19. Jahrhunderts wurde die slowakische Minderheit in Ungarn zwar in starkem Maße an die ungarische Mehrheit assimiliert, doch geschah in mehrheitlich slowakischen Gebieten auch das Umgekehrte, d. h. die Slowakisierung von Ungarn, so z. B. in Weinhied (Bánhida), Oroszlány und Vértesszőlős im Komorner Komitat (Komárom), in Gemeinden des Pilisch-Gebirges oder in Csernye im Komitat Wesprim (Veszprém) (Manga 1972, 293 f).

Durch das Zusammenleben von Slowaken und Ungarn entwickelten sich viele Gemeinsamkeiten in Volksdichtung, Volksmusik, Volksepik, Volksglauben und Brauchtum. So verbreitete sich z. B. die Pilischer Sage von den während der Osmanenherrschaft zerstörten Kirchenruinen unter Ungarn wie Slowaken, ebenso auch mittelalterliche Legenden, Liedmotive, Marienballaden u. a. Die Gemeinsamkeiten in der Volksmusik stellte Béla Bartók in seinen vergleichenden Forschungen zur Volksmusik des pannonischen Raumes heraus.

Der größte Teil der im 18. Jahrhundert nach Ungarn gewanderten Slowaken gehörte dem Bauernstand an. In den slowakischen Dörfern beschäftigte man sich vorzugsweise mit Weinbau, in Pilisszentlélek mit der Kalkbrennerei; sonst bestritten die slowakischen Bewohner ihren Lebensunterhalt mit Korbflechten, Steinschlagen und Tagelöhnerarbeiten. Ein nicht unbedeutender Teil von ihnen lebte bereits im 19. Jahrhundert in Bergwerkssiedlungen in Transdanubien und in der Umgebung von Großstädten. Der Kohlenbergbau wurde nach dem Ersten Weltkrieg zur Haupterwerbsquelle mehrerer slowakischer Gemeinden (Manga 1972, 291 ff). Nach 1945 wurden durch den tschechoslowakisch-ungarischen Bevölkerungsaustausch (s. auch unter 1.) geschlossene slowakische Gemeinden in Ungarn aufgelöst; es änderte sich die soziale und berufliche Struktur der ungarischen Slowaken. Zwischen 1945 und 1975 migrierten aus Tótkomlós (Komitat Bekesch/Békés, mit 12 000 Einwohnern) 120 Familien nach Budapest. 1955 waren noch 66% der ungarischen Slowaken Bauern, während 25% Arbeiter, 3% Intellektuelle waren und 6% unter die Kategorie „Sonstige" fielen. 1980 bot sich ein verändertes sozioprofessionelles Bild: 58,4% der Slowaken waren Arbeiter, 26,4% Bauern, 12,6% Intellektuelle, 2,6% Kaufleute und Handwerker.

Heute pflegen die ungarischen Slowaken ihre Kultur teils in folklorisierter Form: in Chören, Tanzgruppen, Volksmusikgruppen usw., teils in Institutionen der Elitekultur. Es gibt slowakische Klubs und Muttersprachzirkel, in denen die slowakische Umgangssprache gepflegt wird.

Etwa zwei Drittel der ungarischen Slowaken ist evangelischer, knapp ein Drittel römisch-katholischer und ein kleiner Teil griechisch-katholischer Konfessionszugehörigkeit. Innerhalb der ungarischen Kirchenorganisation gibt es keine selbständige slowakische Kirchenorganisation. Nur in wenigen slowakischen Gemeinden ist das Slowakische (in katholischen) bzw. das Tschechische (in evangelischen Gemeinden) die Kirchensprache.

4. Soziokulturelle Rahmenbedingungen des Sprachkontakts

Bis zum Ende des 18. Jahrhunderts waren die Slowaken innerhalb der Habsburgermonarchie als eine der kleinsten Volksgruppen, die keine nennenswerte nationale politische Vergangenheit oder einen national bewußten Adel aufzuweisen hatten, auch in geistig-kultureller Hinsicht stark ungarischen Einflüssen ausgesetzt (Kann 1964, 274ff). Um die Wende des 18. zum 19. Jahrhundert trat die slowakische Nationalbewegung verstärkt hervor. Ján Kollár (1793−1852) und Paul J. Šafařík (1795−1861) traten für die tschechisch-slowakische Einigungsbewegung ein. Der Wiener Hof unterstützte zunächst die slowakische Wiedergeburtsbewegung, um dem wachsenden ungarischen Einfluß Einhalt zu gebieten, doch änderte dies auch nach der Niederwerfung der ungarischen Revolution von 1848 an der Lage der slowakischen Bevölkerung wenig. Die Magyarisierung im politischen und kulturellen Leben war in den innerungarischen slowakischen Sprachinseln noch viel intensiver als im historischen Oberungarn, wo die Slowaken kompakt siedelten. Die Unterdrückung der nationalen Rechte nahm nach 1867 zu. Nachdem in Volksschulen Ungarisch Pflichtunterrichtssprache war, die slowakischen Gymnasien geschlossen, die zentralen slowakischen Kulturinstitutionen aufgelöst und die slowakischen Zeitungen einer strengen Zensur unterworfen worden waren, war der Wille zur Vereinigung mit den Tschechen in der Slowakei nicht mehr aufzuhalten.

Im sozialistischen Ungarn kam die erste slowakische Organisation auf Landesebene bereits 1945 zustande. Die „Antifaschistische Front der Slawen in Ungarn" wurde von Slowaken und Serben gegründet, doch schieden letztere 1946 aus der Organisation aus. 1948 entstand der „Demokratische Verband der Slowaken in Ungarn". Zunächst verstand er sich als Kulturverband, ab 1948 aber auch als wirtschaftlicher und politischer Interessenverband der ungarischen Slowaken. 1951 wurde er von offiziell-ungarischer Seite aufgelöst. Zwar wurde 1951 ein tschechoslowakisch-ungarisches Kulturabkommen unterzeichnet, so daß die ungarischen Slowaken über staatliche Organisationen bzw. über die „Matica Slovenska" Beziehungen zur Slowakei unterhielten, doch wurden in Ungarn erst 1990/1991 erneut slowakische Verbände ins Leben gerufen: der „Verband der Ungarischen Slowaken"; der „Jugendverband der Ungarischen Slowaken"; die „Freie Organisation der Slowaken"; der „Verein der Slowakischen Schriftsteller" in Ungarn sowie das „Slowakische Folkloreensemble".

Nach der Abtrennung der Slowakei von Ungarn geriet die sprachliche Entwicklung der in Ungarn verbliebenen Slowaken in eine Inselsituation. Zwar wurde nach 1945 das slowakische Schulnetz stufenweise ausgebaut. 1949 wurden fünf regionale Grundschulen mit Internaten gegründet. Zunächst an 40, dann an 70 Orten wurde die slowakische Sprache als fakultatives Unterrichtsfach eingeführt. Dennoch gerieten die örtlichen Dialekte in eine umfassende Krise und wurden mehr und mehr in den Hintergrund gedrängt. Der Sprachwechsel zum Ungarischen setzte in einigen slowakischen Ortschaften bereits in den 40er und 50er Jahren, häufig innerhalb einer Familie, ein. Seit den 60er Jahren ist das Ungarische hier nicht nur Amtssprache, sondern auch die gemeinsame Kommunikationsbasis. Dazu haben wirtschaftliche und politische Veränderungen, Binnenmigrationen (vgl. oben unter 3.) bzw. Auflösung bisheriger Gemeinschaften und Mischehen, aber auch restriktive bildungspolitische Maßnahmen von staatlicher Seite beigetragen. 1961 wurden fünf slowakische Schulen mit Muttersprachunterricht in zweisprachige Schulen umorganisiert.

Seit etwa zwei Jahrzehnten kennen die Schulkinder die örtliche Mundart höchstens passiv; sie bemühen sich nur noch selten darum, sie zu erlernen. In der Schule wird die slowakische Literatursprache gelehrt, Kinder und Jugendliche kommunizieren untereinander jedoch ausschließlich auf ungarisch.

Eine seit 1985 veränderte ungarische Bildungspolitik will dieser Tendenz entgegenwirken und den slowakischen Muttersprachenunterricht an Grund- und Mittelschulen fördern. In Budapest und Békéscsaba gibt es zwei slowakische Gymnasien; in Budapest werden slowakische Kindergärtnerinnen ausgebildet; in Gran (Esztergom), Békéscsaba und Szarvas werden slowakische Lehrer und Kindergärtnerinnen, in Segedin (Szeged) und Budapest Lehrer ausgebildet.

Das in Ungarn seit dem 20. Oktober 1993 geltende Minderheitengesetz sichert den Minderheiten in Ungarn eine breite Verwaltungs-, Bildungs- und Unterrichtsautonomie sowie den Gebrauch der Muttersprache in allen Lebenssphären zu. Letzteres hat jedoch für die Praxis immer weniger Relevanz. Seit der politischen Wende in Ungarn (1989) wird westlichen Sprachen überall, auch unter der slowakischen Minderheit, der Vorrang eingeräumt. Während 1988 noch 7637 Kinder in 76 Grundschulen das Slowakische erlernten, waren es 1992 nur noch 5527.

Wöchentlich wird im ungarischen Fernsehen eine 30minütige Sendung in slowakischer Sprache ausgestrahlt; täglich gibt es eine 30minütige slowakische Rundfunksendung und ein zweieinhalbstündiges regionales Rundfunkprogramm für die südliche Tiefebene. Seit 1957 erscheint die slowakische Wochenzeitung *Ludové noviny*. Der Verband der ungarischen Slowaken gibt einen eigenen Jahreskalender „Naš kalendár" heraus; in Békéscsaba erscheint der „Čabiansky kalendár".

5. Allgemeines kontaktlinguistisches Porträt

Die Slowaken in Ungarn sprechen verschiedene slowakische Mundarten: die mittelslowakische Variante wird in der südöstlichen Tiefebene, zwischen Donau und Theiß, im Komitat Nauraden, die westslowakische in Transdanubien und die ostslowakische in Zemplin (Zemplén) und teilweise im Bükk-Gebirge gesprochen. Die Unterschiede mundartlicher wie auch lokal-kultureller Natur sind auch heute noch spürbar. Es haben sich jedoch infolge der slowakischen Binnenmigrationen in neu gegründeten Siedlungen mit Sprechern verschiedener Dialekte auch zahlreiche neue Mischmundarten herausgebildet. Nur an wenigen Orten wie z. B. im transdanubischen Pilisch-Gebirge konnte sich eine rein-westslowakische Mundart erhalten (Gregor 1975); ebenso blieb das Ostslowakische in Ostungarn, im Zemplin-Gebirge, bewahrt.

6. Folgen des Sprachkontakts

Zu den ältesten Magyarismen des Slowakischen zählen Verwaltungs- und Rechtstermini, die in den ersten slowakischen Texten des 15. Jahrhunderts belegt sind, jedoch bei den Slowaken bereits seit den frühesten Zeiten der ungarischen Herrschaft bekannt gewesen sein dürften; zu ihnen zählen *varmed'a* „Komitat" (ung. *vármegye*); *chotár* „Grenze" (ung. *határ*); *vidék ~ vidiek* „Landschaft, Landkreis" (ung. *vidék*); *išpán* „Gespan" (ung. *ispán*); auch die ung. Grafenbezeichnung *gróf* ist bereits Mitte des 15. Jahrhunderts belegt. Im 16. Jahrhundert, als von den vor den Osmanen flüchtenden Ungarn neue ungarische Niederlassungen in der Slowakei gegründet wurden, verbreiteten sich viele ung. Bezeichnungen des städtischen Lebens im Slowakischen: u. a. *város* „Stadt" (slk. *varoš*), *polgár* „Bürger" (slk. *polgar*); *kamarás* „Kämmerer" (slk. *komoraš*); *porkoláb* „Burggraf" (slk. *porkoláb*), ferner, im Zusammenhang mit der militärischen Bedeutung der ungarischen Husarenregimenter, Bezeichnungen wie ung. *sátor* „Zelt" (slk. *šátor ~ šiator*, 1614), *sereg* „Truppe" (slk. *šarag ~ šereg*), *huszár* „Husar" (slk. *husar*, ab 1533) sowie Begriffe des Feudalwesens; z. B. ung. *élés* „eine Art Naturalabgabe" (slk. *ileš ~ jileš*); *örök* „Erbsitz" (slk. *irek ~ urek ~ orek*) (hierzu Schubert 1982).

Zu Magyarismen des 16.—18. Jahrhunderts gehören neben Begriffen des Hirtenwesens und der Landwirtschaft wie *gazda* „Hirt"; *bojtár* „Hirtenjunge"; auch Berufsbezeichnungen wie *varga* „Schuhmacher", *inas* „Lehrling" und Begriffe des Handels wie *vásárbíró* „Marktrichter".

Die slowakischen Neusiedler des 18. Jahrhunderts erlernten auf ungarischem Boden schon sehr bald das Ungarische, wie auch die unter ihnen lebenden Ungarn sich das Slowakische mehr oder minder aneigneten. In diesem Zusammenhang wurden zahlreiche ungarische Bezeichnungen des täglichen Lebens im Slowakischen gebräuchlich; so z. B. slk. *lenča* „Linse" (ung. lencse); *rizkaša* „Reisbrei" (ung. *rizskása*); *paplon* „Bettdecke" (ung. *paplan*); *sersám* „Werkzeug" (ung. *szerszám*); *ištenem* „mein Gott" (ung. *istenem*). Zu neueren Entlehnungen gehören z. B. *kalaus* „Schaffner" (ung. *kalauz*); *mošogatou* „Abwaschbecken" (ung. *mosogató*); *rendir* „Polizist" (ung. *rendőr*).

In den Dialekten der ungarischen Slowaken ist der Wortschatz in noch stärkerem Maße mit Magyarismen durchsetzt − in erster Linie betreffen sie Substantive und in geringerem Maße Verben. In den letzten zwei Jahrzehnten mischen slowakische Dialektsprecher auch schon ganze Sätze oder Satzteile des Ungarischen mit dem Slowakischen. In ihrer Alltagskommunikation können drei Tendenzen beobachtet werden: (a) die Älteren haben Schwierigkeiten im Gebrauch spezifischer Formen des Ungarischen wie der subjektiven und objektiven Verbkonjugationen; (b) die meisten Sprecher benutzen ungarische Lehnwörter als einen organischen Teil der slowakischen Sprache und spüren ihre Fremdheit nicht und (c) in der Sprache der jüngeren Generation macht sich die Phonetik der ungarischen Sprache, vor allem bei den tiefen Vokalen, bemerkbar.

7. Forschungsstand

Die ersten Arbeiten über die slowakischen Mundarten in Ungarn wurden von slowakischen Linguisten verfaßt (Štolc, Ondruš). Spätere ungarische Arbeiten waren darum bemüht, den Charakter dieser Mundarten in den Gesamtzusammenhang des slowakischen Mundartsystems einzuordnen (Gregor 1985, Sipos 1967). Im Rahmen der Aufarbeitung der slawischen Mundarten Ungarns ist ein Atlas der slowakischen Mundarten Ungarns erstellt worden. Mit der Vermischung der Mundarten und deren soziolinguistischen Hintergründen haben sich Király und Sipos beschäftigt (beide Arbeiten liegen nur als Manuskript vor). Soziolinguistische Aspekte sind auch in soziologisch-ethnographischen bzw. kulturanthropologischen Arbeiten über die Slowaken Ungarns enthalten (z. B. Gyivicsán 1993). Mit ungarisch-slowakischen Sprachkontakten beschäftigt sich seit längerem Ferenc Gregor. Seine Arbeiten dazu sind in den in Budapest erscheinenden Bänden der „Studia Slavica" sowie als Monographien erschienen.

8. Bibliographie (in Auswahl)

Fügedi, Erik-Gregor/Ferenc-Király, Péter (1993): *Atlas slovenských nareči − Atlas der slowakischen Mundarten in Ungarn* (slowakisch-deutsch) mit 235 Karten, Budapest.

Gregor, Ferenc (1975): *Der slowakische Dialekt von Pilisszántó*, Budapest.

Gregor, Ferenc (1985): *Die alte ungarische und slowakische Bergbauterminologie mit ihren deutschen Bezügen*, Budapest.

Gyivicsán, Anna (1992): „Fundbericht über eine nationale Minderheit: Die Slowaken in Ungarn". In: *Minderheitenfragen in Südosteuropa*, 187−197.

Gyivicsán, Anna (1992): „Ethnopsychische und psycholinguistische Motivation der zweisprachigen Kultur". In: *Szlavisztikai tanulmányok* [Slawistische Studien], Nyomárkay, I. (Ed.), Budapest.

Gyivicsán, Anna (1993): *Anyanyelv, kultura, közösseg. A magyarországi szlovákok* [Muttersprache, Kultur, Gemeinschaft. Die ungarischen Slowaken], Budapest.

Kann, Robert A. (1964): *Das Nationalitätenproblem der Habsburgermonarchie*. I. Band: Das Reich und die Völker, 2. Aufl., Graz/Köln.

Király, Péter (1962): „Beiträge zur Frage der Mundartmischung". In: *Studia Slavica* (Budapest) VIII. B. 1−4. N. 339−377.

Király, Péter (1972): *A nyelvkeveredés. A magyarországi szláv nyelvjárások tanulságai*. Kezirat [Die Sprachmischung. Erkenntnisse aus den ungarisch-slawischen Mundarten. Manuskript]. (Bibliothek der Akademie der Wissenschaften) D 5625.

Manga, János (1982): „Die Slowaken in Ungarn. Slowakische Siedlungen in den 17. und 18. Jahrhunderten". In: *Acta Ethnographica Academiae Scientiarum Hingaricae* 21, Budapest, 279−316.

Ondrus, Pavel (1956): *Stredoslovenské nárečia v Madarskej ľudovej republike* [Mittelslowakische Mundarten in Ungarn], Bratislava.

Schubert, Gabriella (1982): *Ungarische Einflüsse in der Terminologie des öffentlichen Lebens der Nachbarsprachen*. (Osteuropa-Institut an der Freien Universität Berlin, Balkanologische Veröffentlichungen 7), Berlin.

Sipos, István (1958): *Geschichte der slowakischen Mundarten der Huta- und Hámor-Gemeinden des Bükk-Gebirges*, Budapest.

Sipos, ‚István (1967): *A nyelvi együtteles fejlődési szakaszai s tapasztalatai*. Kézirat [Entwicklungsstufen und Erfahrungen des sprachlichen Zusammenlebens. Manuskript] (Bibliothek der Akademie der Wissenschaften) D 3509.

Štolc, Jozef (1949): *Narecie troch slovenskych ostrovov v Maďarsku* [Mundart von drei slowakischen Inseln in Ungarn], Bratislava.

Stoob, Heinz (1977): „Die mittelalterliche Städtebildung im Karpatenbogen". In: *Die mittelalterliche Städtebildung im südöstlichen Europa.* (Städteforschung. Veröffentlichungen des Instituts für vergleichende Städtegeschichte in Münster, hg. v. H. Stoob, Reihe A: Darstellungen, Band 4). Köln/Wien.

Anna Gyivicsán, Budapest (Ungarn)
Gabriella Schubert, Berlin (Deutschland)

215. Hungarian−Romanian

1. Geography and demography
2. History
3. Politics, economy and general cultural situation
4. Statistics
5. Sociolinguistic situation
6. Language political situation
7. General contactlinguistic portrait
8. Conclusion
9. Bibliography (selected)

Throughout this paper 'Hungarian Romanian' (HR hereafter) refers only to the Romanian minority that has been living in Hungary for several centuries. This article does not discuss either those Romanians who have come to Hungary in the last few decades or the Boyash Romany (Romanian speaking Gypsies) (cf. Réger 1988).

1. Geography and demography

Hungarian Romanians today live in nearly twenty settlements near the Hungarian-Romanian border, in the three southeastern counties of Hungary: Békés, Hajdú-Bihar, and Csongrád (→ Language Map 2). Hungarian Romanians constitute a numerical majority relative to the inhabitants of other ethnic groups in only two of these: Méhkerék (90%) and Kétegyháza (65%). The cultural center of Hungarian Romanians is Gyula.

2. History

The ancestors of the HRs came to Hungary in several waves from the area (in present-day Romania) bounded by the Crişul-Repede, Crişul-Negru, and Mureş rivers. Most of them settled between 1700 and 1750, after the Turks were expelled from Hungary. The settlers came to the new country in the hope of a better life. The settlements were established with ethnic minorities living separately. This helped the new communities become accustomed to the new conditions (Márkus 1936, 82) and as a result they retained their old habits, life style, and ethnic identity for centuries.

3. Politics, economy and general cultural situation

Prior to the Second World War most HRs were involved in agriculture. Following the Communist takeover, collectivization eliminated small village farms, causing the break up of closely-knit village communities all over the country. Today, most HRs work on collective farms or as skilled laborers. Some are clerks or professionals.

From the time of HR settlement, HRs worshiped in a separate Orthodox Church. In these churches religious services were and are still held in Romanian. Today, in three villages there is also a Baptist Romanian community, with Hungarian dominant bilingual religious services. In Hajdú-Bihar county most HRs practice Greek Catholicism. Until the beginning of this century religious services were held in Romanian, but today they are exlusively in Hungarian.

Currently there are twelve kindergartens where Romanian courses are offered 2−4 hours a week. The HRs have six minority elementary schools with some courses in Romanian. In particular, Romanian language and literature are taught in Romanian, while the other subjects are taught predominantly in Hungarian. There are also six Hungarian elementary schools where Romanian language and literature are taught. The HRs also have a secondary school in Gyula, the only secondary school where Romanian is taught in Hungary. At the highest levels of education, there are three colleges and one university where Romanian is taught as a major.

The Association of HRs is the highest organ of representation of HR interests. It was founded in 1948 along with the first postwar HR weekly paper in Hungary. Schoolbook publishers have supported publications of Hungarian minorities, including HRs. Since 1976, approximately 30 books have been published in Romanian. Hungarian Radio has been broadcasting minority programs since 1980. Currently it offers a 30 minute Romanian program every day. The Hungarian Television has been offering ethnic broadcasting since 1982. Recently it established a weekly 25-minute program in Romanian.

Since the 1980s local cultural associations have been established in eleven settlements. Their task is to reinforce Romanian ethnic identity and cultivate Romanian language and culture. In 1991, a research group was also formed, with the aim of carrying out systematic research on the Romanian community in Hungary.

During the local elections in the autumn of 1990 one mayor was elected from the HR minority. In the local self-government bodies in villages, 25 members of the HR minority were elected. There are no HRs among the members of the Hungarian Parliament. The Office of National and Ethnic Minorities, created by the Hungarian Government in 1990, also has a HR representative.

4. Statistics

The 1990 census counted 10,740 Romanians living in Hungary, but the Association of HRs estimates the count at about 20,000 to 25,000.

5. Sociolinguistic situation

Currently the majority of HRs are Hungarian-Romanian bilinguals. They speak their mother tongue, which is a local variant of Romanian, and Hungarian (also a local variant). A minor part of the community, mainly the younger generation, can be considered Hungarian monolingual. In the case of the HRs, bilingualism can be considered a transitory state between Romanian and Hungarian monolingualism.

5.1. Bilingualism and the sociolinguistic situation

Bilingualism among HRs results from the postwar border modifications of 1920. After the Second World War the process of bilingualism was advanced by the radical postwar social changes. These changes have caused the isolation of the HRs to dissolve. Since the 50s, the HRs have established stronger contact with the Hungarian majority (Hungarian workplaces, mixed marriages, etc.), and have modified their attitudes and emotions towards their own Romanian minority culture and language.

The attitude of Hungarians towards the HR minority and their language is mostly neutral or negative. Negative feelings have erupted on occasion due to political events of this century (e. g. 'Speak Hungarian if you eat Hungarian bread!' − after 1920, around 1940 and in the 50s). Since 1989, negative incidents against HR institutions have occurred sporadically in reaction to ethnic discrimination against Hungarians living in Romania.

At different times in the 20th century, HRs have reacted differently to the occasional negative feelings and expression of the Hungarians. Between the two World Wars, the assimilationist tendencies on the part of the Hungarian majority elicited an emotion of solidarity (cf. Gal 1991) in the Romanian minority, causing an increase in loyalty towards their minority language. Following the Second World War, HR minority solidarity and loyalty towards their own minority group decreased. They favored Hungarian more and more over Romanian. This behavior is currently widespread among the middle-aged and especially the younger generation.

The prestige of Romanian language variants spoken in Hungary is low among the Romanians of Romania. The former communist regime of Romania considered 'Romanian' all those people who lived within the Romanian borders and labeled 'not Romanian' those who lived outside these borders. Nevertheless definite and rapid changes have been occurring in the attitudes toward Romanians outside Romania in the last few years. The interest in HRs is beginning to increase in Romania.

5.2. Description of bilingualism and language use

Among HRs, virtually all are dominant in one language or the other. The majority of the oldest generation and a small part of the middle-aged generation can be considered Romanian dominant bilinguals, while the Hungarian dominant bilinguals belong mainly to the younger generations. Ambilingual speakers (cf. Halliday 1968) are found mainly among the intellectuals in the HR community.

Neither the Romanian language variants nor the Hungarian language can be assigned clearly distinguishable functions which would justify characterizing the situation as one of diglossia (Ferguson 1971). The use of the two languages differs on the basis of the age of the speaker. It displays two different symbol-systems rather than two different functions. Romanian variants symbolize the past, the hard peasant life, backwardness, and lack of education. Hungarian symbolizes the present and the future, that is, modern life, educational opportunities and careers. The two languages have become languages of two generations, Romanian being the language of the older, Hungarian the language of the younger generation (cf. Patterson 1991).

The Romanian language of the HRs is used in conversations within family, between friends and neighbors, during Orthodox religious services, at meetings with Romanian relatives, and in Romanian language classes. Except for conversations before and after Orthodox religious services, however, the dominant language (spoken by more than 50 percent of the interlocutors) is Hungarian. In other places in the community (e. g. shops, doctor's waiting-rooms, the Mayor's Office, local workplaces) Hungarian is used with very few exceptions (e. g. when an older person who does not speak Hungarian well is helped at an official place by a minority member working there). Outside the local settlements where the HRs live Hungarian is the only language used. Thus HRs speak Hungarian more often than their mother tongue.

The choice of the Romanian language also is determined by the interlocutor: 'I know that he/she speaks Romanian better so I am also speaking Romanian' or 'I know that he/she likes me to speak Romanian'. Hungarian is widely used by HRs amongst themselves as well, although its occurrence is strongly dependent on the subject matter (professional topic, official matter), the place and the audience. In the presence of a person who does not speak Romanian only Hungarian is used due to politeness considerations.

6. Language political situation

Currently the declared political view in Hungary, as opposed to that of the 50s, is to support minorities in using their languages in as wide a circle of communication as possible. The realization of this view is, however, very difficult. On the one hand, few if any doctors, lawyers, officials, clerks, etc., speak Romanian. On the other hand, HRs do not possess the linguistic repertoire needed to conduct official business in Romanian. Very few HRs speak a variety of Romanian close to Standard Romanian, in addition to their local Romanian dialect. A Standard HR variant is used in the institutions of the HRs, school classes, broadcasting, and Orthodox church services (cf. 7.2.3).

7. General contactlinguistic portrait

The Romanian language variants in Hungary vary from settlement to settlement. Even within a particular town or village one can find dialect differences between speakers.

7.1. Between-settlement variation

Romanian language variants can be classified into two major groups. The first group includes the variants spoken in the villages of Békés (with just one exception) and Csongrád counties, while the other group includes the variants of all minority villages in Hajdú-Bihar, and that of Méhkerék (Békés county). Apart from several phonetic and lexical differences the most significant difference between the two dialect groups is seen in the divergent form of the conjunctive (să/și) (Cosma 1985).

In villages where HRs are in the majority, language assimilation to Hungarian is weaker, and conversely, in settlements where HRs constitute a smaller proportion of the inhabitants (in the towns and in Hajdú-Bihar where the Greek Catholic churches were Magyarized) assimilation to Hungarian is stronger.

7.2. Within-settlement variation

Within the settlements several local Romanian language variants have traditionally been spoken. These show variability along a dimension having at one pole Standard Romanian and at the opposite an archaic local variant. Focusing on the extent of divergence from Standard Romanian three main variant types can be differentiated.

7.2.1. The first is the archaic local Romanian variant that has best preserved age-old features of the Crișean region dialect. Such characteristics include the phoneme variants of [ẹ], [ọ], [t'], [d'], [n'], and numerous phonetic changes causing divergencies from the Standard, for example, [e] > [ă] *merg* > *mărg* ('I go'); [i] > [î] *ziuă* > *zîuă* ('day'); [ĝ] > [j] *ger* > *jer* ('freezing'). Also typical are countless words of Hungarian origin that are completely integrated phonetically and morphologically into Romanian, for example, *bet'ag* (from *beteg* 'ill') or *lipid'eu̯* (from *lepedő* 'sheet') (Borbély, 1990). There are also phonetically not integrated lexical items borrowed from Hungarian which use phonemes not present in Standard Romanian (such as 'ö' and 'ü'). These archaic variants can be found most consistently in the speech of those over 70 who have not completed more than three years of schooling.

7.2.2. The second main variant type is basically an archaic local Romanian variant which borrowed some elements from Standard Romanian. Such examples are (i) the occasional dental (t, d, n) and labial (p, b, m) articulation of stops instead of the archaic palatalised ones; (ii) the [ẹ] > [e] phonetic adjustment to the standard variant: *mẹre* > *mere* ('apples'); (iii) the replacement of words of Hungarian origin with their Standard Romanian counterparts (e. g. *gară* instead of *ștațiie* 'railway station'; *sfat* instead of *tọnaî* 'local authority'; *colectivă* instead of *colhoz* 'agricultural co-operative'). This variety can also be characterized by the pronunciation of certain Standard Romanian variants according to the local language variant, like *perfẹct* instead of *perfect* 'fluent (in language)' or *jermană* instead of *germană* 'German'. This variant occurs mainly among the 40–70 year olds who have not completed more than 8 grades, and who have a stronger than average sense of Romanian ethnic identity. This variant has been developed through conscious efforts and is used in conversations with minority intellectuals and relatives living in Romania. In conversations with other members of the minority community these speakers use an archaic local variant.

7.2.3. The third variant is Standard HR which is closest to Standard Romanian. It can be differentiated from Standard Romanian on the basis of certain grammatical forms (in particular grammatical agreement and conjugation), smaller vocabulary, slower rate of speech, and in some cases stress and intonation. Standard HR is a learned variant developed through the systematic replacement of dialectal elements of an archaic local variant (the mother tongue) with the corresponding elements of Standard Romanian. The minority institutions that teach Romanian have played a significant role in the creation of this variant. It is spoken only by people under 50 (except for older Orthodox priests) who have studied Romanian language and literature in secondary school and/or at the university. These people all speak one of the local variants as well.

7.3. Hungarian language influences

The influence of Hungarian is evident at all levels (phonemes, lexemes, stress changes, etc.) in HR language variants. Most frequent are Hungarian loan-words (e. g. *mozdonyvezető* 'engine-driver') and loan translations (e. g. *hazafelé* > *cătăcasă* 'to home'), while rarer forms are loan-blends and semantic borrowings (about these phenomena cf. Haugen 1950; Kontra 1990, 99–101; Bartha 1992). Loan-words are predominantly nouns (common names, personal names, and names of settlements). Very characteristic in the HR variants is the use of Hungarian verb prefixes (for example Standard Romanian *se suie (pe cal)* ('get on the horse') becomes *să suie sus (pă cal)* ('get on the horse') in HR dialects because of the influence of Hungarian *Felül (a lóra) (fel-* 'on').

8. Conclusion

The main point of this article is that HR bilingualism has developed as a result of political (border shift) and economic (collectivization) changes, as well as the linguistic situation (many HR varieties with no widespread use of Standard HR). It is expected that HR bilingualism will decrease, and that HRs will become Hungarian monolinguals within some decades.

9. Bibliography (selected)

Bartha, Csilla (1992): "A nyelvek közötti érintkezés univerzáléi" [The universals of language contact]. In: *Emlékkönyv. Rácz Endre hetvenedik születésnapjára*, Kozocsa, Sandor Géza/Laczkó, Krisztina (Eds.), Budapest, 19–28.

Borbély, Anna (1990): *Cercetări asupra graiurilor românești din Ungaria* [Research on Romanian dialects in Hungary], Budapest.

Cosma, M. (1985): "Situaţia limbii noastre materne" [The state of our mother tongue]. In: *Timpuri*, Gyula, 25−34.

Ferguson, Charles A. (1971): "Diglossia". In: *Language structure and language use*, Dil, Anwars (Ed.), Stanford.

Gal, Susan (1991): "Kódváltás és öntudat" [Codeswitching and consciousness in the European periphery]. In: *Tanulmányok a határainkon túli kétnyelvűségről*, Kontra, M. (Ed.), Budapest, 123−157.

Halliday, Michael A. K. (1968): "The users and uses of language". In: *Readings in the sociology of language*, Fishman, J.A. (Ed.), The Hague/Paris.

Haugen, Einar (1950): "The analysis of linguistic borrowing". In: *Language 26*, 210−231.

Kontra, Miklós (1990): *Fejezetek a South Bend-i magyar nyelvhasználatból* [The Hungarian Language as Spoken in South Bend, Indiana], Budapest.

Márkus, György (Ed.) (1936): *Békés-vármegye* [County of Békés], Budapest.

Patterson, G. James (1991): "Hungary's disappearing Romanian minority". In: *East European Quarterly XXV, 1*, 117−123.

Réger, Zita (1988): "A cigány nyelv: Kutatások és vitapontok" [Romany: Research and points at issue]. In: *Műhelymunkák a nyelvészet és társadalomtudományai köréből*, IV. MTA Nyelvtudományi Intézete, 155−175.

Anna Borbély, Budapest (Hungary)

216. Deutschland

1. Geographie und Demographie
2. Territorialgeschichte und Staatsbildung
3. Politik, Wirtschaft und allgemeine kulturelle sowie religiöse Lage
4. Statistik und Ethnoprofile
5. Soziolinguistische Lage
6. Sprachpolitische Lage
7. Andere Sprachkontakte: Immigranten in Deutschland
8. Kritische Wertung der verwendeten Quellen und Literatur
9. Bibliographie (in Auswahl)

1. Geographie und Demographie

1.1. Geographische Bedingungen

Deutschland liegt in der Mitte Europas. Im Norden bilden Meere, die Nord- und die Ostsee, eine natürliche Grenze, im Süden der Gebirgszug der Alpen. Die östlichen und westlichen Grenzen werden dagegen von Flüssen (Oder, Neiße, Rhein) oder von Mittelgebirgen gebildet (Erzgebirge, Böhmerwald u. a.), oder sie stellen keine natürlichen Hindernisse dar. In diesem Raum, in dem heute die deutsche Sprache dominant ist, haben sich Siedlungsgebiete sowie Sprach- und politische Grenzen im Laufe der Jahrhunderte wiederholt verschoben. Die Folge ist, daß politische Grenzen oft nicht mit den Sprachgrenzen zusammenfielen und zusammenfallen. So schließt das deutsche Sprachgebiet auch die benachbarten (ganz oder teilweise) deutschsprachigen Staaten ein: Österreich, Deutsche Schweiz, Liechtenstein, Luxemburg. Auch in den meisten anderen angrenzenden Staaten wird Deutsch (oder ein deutscher Dialekt) von Minderheiten gesprochen: Dänemark, Belgien, Frankreich, Italien, Slowakei, Tschechien, Polen (→ Sprachenkarte M).

Sprachkontaktgebiete waren und sind vor allem die östlichen und die westlichen Grenzbereiche sowie das Land zwischen Nord- und Ostsee. Hier gab es Zonen, in denen jahrhundertelang verschiedensprachige Bevölkerungsgruppen nebeneinander lebten, teilweise gab und gibt es auch Zwei- und Mehrsprachigkeit. Einige dieser Bevölkerungsgruppen haben sich in Resten bis heute erhalten. In Deutschland sind dies die Sorben im Osten, die Ostfriesen im Nordwesten und die Nordfriesen und Dänen im Norden. Sie bilden die Grundlage für den heutigen autochthonen Sprachkontakt.

1.2. Demographische Charakteristik

Zur Zeit leben in Deutschland ca. 80 Mio Menschen auf einer Fläche von 356 000 km². Mit einer Bevölkerungsdichte von etwa 225 Ew./km² gehört Deutschland zu den am dichtesten besiedelten Ländern in Europa. Die einzelnen Regionen sind unterschiedlich dicht besiedelt, der Norden weniger dicht als die Mitte und der Süden. Stärker industriell geprägte Ballungsgebiete sind das Ruhrgebiet, das Rhein-Main- und das Rhein-Neckar-Gebiet, das mitteldeutsche Industriegebiet, die Gebiete um Großstädte wie Berlin, München, Stuttgart u. a. Wie in anderen Ländern auch sind städtische Siedlungen in den letzten Jahrzehnten stark angewachsen. Dieser Trend hat inzwischen nachgelassen. Neue Wohngebiete entstehen vorwiegend an den Rändern der Städte, viele Menschen siedeln sich in kleineren Gemeinden an.

Die Altersstruktur der deutschen Bevölkerung ist, wie in vielen Industrieländern, durch eine Zunahme der älteren Jahrgänge gekennzeichnet. Die gegenwärtige Altersstruktur der deutschen Bevölkerung reicht deshalb nicht mehr aus, die Größe der arbeitsfähigen Bevölkerungsgruppen konstant zu halten. Die Differenz zwischen Todesfällen und Geburten liegt gegenwärtig etwa bei 300 000 jährlich. Einen Ausgleich schaffen die Immigranten, unter denen jüngere Altersgruppen, in den letzten Jahren auch Kinder, stärker vertreten sind.

In Deutschland leben heute etwa 6,5 Mio Ausländer. Das sind mehr als 8% der Bevölkerung. Die stärkste Gruppe unter ihnen bilden die Türken, gefolgt von Immigranten aus dem ehemaligen Jugoslawien und von Italienern, außerdem Griechen und Spanier. In den ostdeutschen Bundesländern bilden Vietnamesen und Polen die stärksten Gruppen. Die Verteilung der Ausländer auf die einzelnen Bundesländer ist unterschiedlich. Ihr Anteil ist in Industriegebieten höher. Bezogen auf die Gesamtbevölkerung, ist der Ausländeranteil in Berlin am höchsten, relativ hoch aber auch in Baden-Württemberg.

Die hohe Zahl der Arbeitsimmigranten hat zu besonderen Sprachkontakt-Problemen geführt (vgl. dazu Punkt 7.).

In jüngerer Zeit ist unter den Immigranten der Anteil deutschstämmiger Aussiedler stark gestiegen, hinzu kommen Flüchtlinge aus Krisengebieten und Asylbewerber. Seit Bestehen der Bundesrepublik sind insgesamt ca. 3 Mio deutschstämmige Aussiedler aus osteuropäischen Ländern (ehemalige Sowjetunion, Rumänien, Polen u. a.) aufgenommen worden. Sprachkontakt-Probleme ergaben und ergeben sich mit ihnen insofern, als ein größerer Teil von ihnen nicht die deutsche Standard-(Hoch-)Sprache beherrscht, sondern nur einen deutschen Dialekt, und dieser oft nur in eng begrenzten Bereichen anwendbar ist.

Gegen Ende des Zweiten Weltkrieges sind zahlreiche Deutsche aus osteuropäischen Ländern nach Deutschland geflüchtet. Im Gefolge der im Potsdamer Abkommen (1945) von den Siegermächten festgelegten Abtrennung deutscher Gebiete im Osten (Sudetengebiet, Schlesien, Teile der Mark Brandenburg, Hinterpommern, Ost- und Westpreußen) sind in den Jahren nach 1945 mindestens 11 Mio Deutsche ausgesiedelt worden. Von ihnen wurden 3,5 Mio in Ostdeutschland und 8,5 Mio in Westdeutschland ansässig.

Eine noch anhaltende innerdeutsche Migration hat von 1945 bis heute schätzungsweise 5 Mio Menschen aus den östlichen in die westlichen Landesteile geführt. Dies waren insbesondere Deutsche, die die sowjetische Besatzungszone und später die DDR verließen. Aber auch nach der Vereinigung hält die Übersiedlung Deutscher von Ost nach West an.

Die starke Migration von Deutschen seit 1945 hatte Auswirkungen auf die regionale Gliederung des deutschen Sprachraumes. In Dialektgebieten wurden Sprecher anderer Dialekte ansässig, die Ausbildung von großräumigeren Umgangssprachen, insbesondere im Umkreis der Städte und in Ballungsgebieten, wurde gefördert. Aber auch auf die Kontaktsprachen innerhalb des deutschen Sprachraumes hatte diese Migration einen Einfluß. So wurden z. B. im Gebiet der Sorben, die nach dem Krieg auf dem Land teilweise noch die Bevölkerungsmehrheit bildeten, zahlreiche Umsiedler ansässig, die Zahl der Deutschsprachigen wuchs also beträchtlich. Später gab es dann noch einmal einen Zuzug von Arbeitskräften in die Gebiete der Braunkohlenförderung und -industrie.

2. Territorialgeschichte und Staatsbildung

2.1. Vorgeschichte

Eine kurze Betrachtung der Vorgeschichte ist insofern wichtig, als sich relativ früh bestimmte Voraussetzungen dafür ausbildeten, daß einzelne Stammessprachen die Grundlage für das spätere Deutsch werden konnten und daß sich spezifische Nachbarschaftsverhältnisse zu anderen Sprachen entwickelten.

In der Jungsteinzeit und der Bronzezeit besiedelten sog. prägermanische Stämme Teile Norddeutschlands sowie Dänemark und Südschweden. Später breiteten sie sich über das nördliche Mitteleuropa aus, im Westen bis zur Ems und zum Rhein, im Osten teilweise bis zur Weichsel. Ein Teil der späteren germ. Stämme (Sueben, Semnonen, Burgunder u. a.) verließ im 2. und 1. Jahrhundert v. Chr. die Wohngebiete im Nordwesten und Norden und besiedelte Süd- und Westdeutschland. So zogen Kimbern und Teutonen an den Nieder- und Mittelrhein, auch bis in das von Kelten bewohnte Gallien. Suebische Stämme wanderten aus dem Elbe-Gebiet in das keltische Rhein-Main-Gebiet. Andere (Semnonen) zogen aus dem Elbe-Havel-Gebiet durch Thüringen nach Süddeutschland. Im Zentrum des noch verbliebenen germ. Siedlungsgebietes bildeten sich die Stammesverbände der Sachsen und der Franken.

Durch die Wanderungen und Zusammenschlüsse breiteten sich elbgerm. und rheinweser-germ. Dialekte, die Zweige der westgerm. Gruppe bildeten, in großen Teilen Mitteleuropas aus. Insbesondere auf der Basis der elbgerm. Dialekte entstand später die deutsche Sprache.

Nachbarn der germ. Stämme waren im Osten baltische und slawische Stämme, im Süden und Westen Kelten, im Süden teilweise auch italische Stämme. Im Norden grenzten die westgerm. Dialekte an die nordgermanischen. Innerhalb des Westgermanischen wird zwischen Nordsee-, Weser-Rhein- und Elbgermanisch unterschieden. Zum Nordseegerm. wird neben dem Angelsächsischen u. a. das Friesische gerechnet.

Zwischen den Sprachen der germanischen und der nicht-germanischen Stämme gibt es eine Reihe von Übereinstimmungen in der Grammatik und im Wortschatz, die teils auf eine gemeinsame Grundlage, teils auf frühen Sprachkontakt zurückgehen, was im einzelnen aber oft nicht zu entscheiden ist. Beispiele sind etwa die Parallelen von ahd. *ambahti* 'Amt', got. *andbahts* 'Diener' und lat.-kelt. *ambactus* 'Diener' oder von germ. *tūna* 'befestigte Siedlung' (nhd. *Zaun*) und gall. *dunum* (engl. *town* 'Stadt'). Eine germ.-ital. Parallele ist etwa lat. *collus (collum)* und got./ahd. *hals* 'Hals'. Germ.-balt.-slaw. Parallelen sind got. *reiks* 'Herrscher', und apreuß. *rīks* 'Reich', *rikijs* 'Herrscher' oder lit. *kunigas* und ahd. *chuning* 'König' oder got. *hlaifs*, ahd. *hleib* 'Laib Brot' und russ. хлеб (chleb) 'Brot'. — Keltischen Ursprungs sind zahlreiche Fluß- und Gebirgsnamen in Deutschland (Rhein, Donau, Main, Neckar, Weser, Elbe u. a.; Taunus, Hunsrück u. a.). Die deutsch-slawischen Sprachkontakte sind verschiedenen Zeiten zuzuordnen. Der ältesten Schicht folgten frühe Einflüsse auf ostdeutsche Dialekte, slawische Ortsnamen sind von deutschen Siedlern vielfach übernommen worden. In das Hochdeutsche eingegangen sind zahlreiche Wörter, die im späten Mittelalter aus slawischen Sprachen entlehnt wurden (*Grenze, Gurke, Jauche, Peitsche, Quark, Säbel, Schmetterling*).

Im Merowingerreich, das den größten Teil des heutigen Frankreich einschloß, hatten sich enge Beziehungen zwischen den Franken im Nordosten und den benachbarten Galloromanen herausgebildet. Es bestand ein Sprachgegensatz zwischen dem germ. Fränkischen und dem Welschen (nach der keltischen Stammesbezeichnung *Volcae*). Daneben gab es einen Gegensatz zwischen der Verwaltungssprache Latein und der als „deutsch" (*Þeudisk*, althochdeutsch *diutisc*) bezeichneten Volkssprache. Als die ursprüngliche Stammes- und Sprachbezeichnung „fränkisch" später einen anderen politischen Inhalt bekam, setzte sich „deutsch" als Bezeichnung für die Sprache der germ. Stämme im östlichen Teil des Frankenreiches durch, das im Osten (Elbe-Saale, Böhmerwald) an die slawischen Stämme grenzte, also nicht mehr nur die Franken als Stamm einschloß. Später wurde „deutsch" dann auch auf die politischen Verhältnisse in diesem Raum bezogen.

2.2. Entwicklung des Sprachgebietes

Im Westen bildeten sich, abgesehen von einer Übergangszone, bald relativ feste politische Grenzen zwischen einer deutsch- und einer romanischsprachigen Bevölkerung heraus (Aufteilung des Karolingerreiches). In der Übergangszone (Flandern, Brabant, Luxemburg, Lothringen, Elsaß) fällt allerdings bis heute die politische Grenze nicht mit der Sprachgrenze zusammen. Politische Grenzen haben sich hier im Laufe der Geschichte auch mehrfach verändert.

Der Osten und Norden des heutigen Sprachgebietes war nach dem Wegzug der germ. Stämme nur noch dünn besiedelt. Wie aber u. a. aus der Übernahme germ. Orts- und Gewässernamen durch Slawen hervorgeht (so sind etwa Spree und Havel germanischen Ursprungs), müssen Reste der germ. Stämme ständig hier ansässig gewesen sein. Zwischen dem 6. und 9. Jahrhundert drangen slawische Stämme aus der Weichselgegend und aus Böhmen in das Gebiet ein (Obodriten und Wilzen im Norden, Heveller, Sorben, Lusizi und Milzener in der Mitte). Einzelne slaw. Siedlungen gab es aber auch bis nach Ost-Holstein, Thüringen und Nordost-Bayern. Es gab Bündnisse zwischen slaw. Stämmen und Franken und auch Mischsiedlungen im fränkischen Gebiet. Und im ostelbischen Gebiet, das zum Kernland der Herausbildung germ. Stämme gehört hatte, siedelten

Slawen und Reste der germ. Stämme nebeneinander.

Seit der Zeit der Ottonen begann eine umfangreiche und über mehrere Jahrhunderte andauernde Eroberungs- und Besiedlungsbewegung nach Osten, die teils durchaus friedlich, teils aber auch gewaltsam war. Zunächst wurden westslaw. Gebiete östl. von Elbe, Saale und Böhmerwald in das Ottonenreich eingegliedert. Dem folgte eine bäuerliche und städtebürgerliche Besiedlung, die von den alten Stammesgebieten und den Niederlanden ausging und schon im 12. und 13. Jahrhundert bis Ostpreußen und Schlesien drang. Sprachlich gab es offenbar weithin ein Nebeneinander von deutschen und slawischen Dialekten, das einen jahrhundertelangen Sprachkontakt mit zahlreichen gegenseitigen Beeinflussungen einschloß. Mit der Zunahme deutscher Siedler und der Festigung deutscher politischer Einheiten vermischte sich die slawische Bevölkerung teilweise mit der deutschen. Die slawischen Dialekte wurden immer mehr zurückgedrängt. Dagegen wurden slawische Ortsnamen zu einem großen Teil von deutschen Siedlern übernommen bzw. umgebildet (Berlin, Potsdam, Schwerin, Güstrow). Zahlreiche slaw. Wörter wurden in ostmitteldeutsche Dialekte aufgenommen, etwa *Kummet* 'Halsjoch', *graupeln* 'hageln', *Krabaze* 'Auswurf', *dalli* 'schnell' (poln. *dalej*), oder *Plauze, Plinse, Schaluppe, Kaschemme*. Die westslaw. Dialekte sind jedoch weitgehend untergegangen (wie z. B. das Polabische) oder wurden auf kleine Restgebiete zurückgedrängt. Zu letzteren gehören das Sorbische in Deutschland oder das Kaschubische und das Masurische im heutigen Polen.

Infolge des Zusammenkommens deutschsprachiger Siedler aus unterschiedlichen Dialektgebieten war die dialektale Gliederung im ostmitteldeutschen Raum weniger stark als in den „alten" Gebieten. Die Ausbildung einer einheitlichen deutschen Sprachnorm wurde, nach neueren Auffassungen, jedoch wesentlich über die Verbreitung von schriftlichen Traditionen vorangetrieben. Erst im 19. Jahrhundert galt die Schriftnorm dann auch als Vorbild für das gesprochene Deutsch.

Preußen und später das Deutsche Reich haben sich vorübergehend große Teile des slawischen Sprachgebietes (Polen, Tschechei), aber auch des dänischen (Nordschleswig) eingegliedert. Diese Eingliederungen wurden nach dem Ersten Weltkrieg und endgültig nach dem Zweiten Weltkrieg wieder rückgängig gemacht. Nach dem Zweiten Weltkrieg (Potsdamer Abkommen) wurden auch bis dahin vorwiegend deutschsprachige Gebiete abgetrennt.

In historischer Sicht war auch das Niederdeutsche eine selbständige Sprache innerhalb des deutschen Sprachgebietes. Es besaß überregionale Geltung und konnte eine längere schriftsprachliche Tradition ausbilden. Das Niederdeutsche hat im wesentlichen den germ. Konsonantenbestand erhalten; es wurde nicht von der sog. 2. Lautverschiebung erfaßt und unterscheidet sich dadurch von allen anderen (hoch- und oberdeutschen) Dialekten und von der Hochsprache. Auch besaß es in seiner Frühzeit (als Altsächsisch) noch Gemeinsamkeiten mit dem Nordseegermanischen. Später näherte sich das Niederdeutsche dem Hochdeutschen an. Der Untergang der mittelniederdeutschen Literatursprache ist vor allem auf die hochdeutsch geprägte Reformation und den Niedergang der Hanse zurückzuführen. Heute ist „Niederdeutsch" eine Sammelbezeichnung für norddeutsche Dialekte.

2.3. Bildung des deutschen Staates

Die Staatsbildung begann im 9. und 10. Jahrhundert, nachdem 843 der Karolingerstaat in ein westfränkisches, ein ostfränkisches und ein Mittelreich zerfallen war und eine selbständige Entwicklung des östlichen Teils des Frankenreiches, in dem mehrere deutschsprachige Herzogtümer in einen lockeren Verband getreten waren, einsetzte. Eine Zentralgewalt bestand jedoch zunächst kaum. Sie bildete sich erst im Verlauf von Jahrhunderten äußerst langsam heraus. Es gab keine Hauptstadt, Könige und Kaiser wechselten ihre Regierungsorte. Außerdem waren ihre Herrschaftsgebiete, nicht zuletzt wegen der angestrebten Krönung durch den Papst (Heiliges Römisches Reich Deutscher Nation), oft so groß, daß sie kaum noch regierbar waren. Sie gingen auch weit über das deutsche Sprachgebiet hinaus (z. B. Böhmen, Norditalien). Die eigentliche Macht ging deshalb von meist kleineren Staatsgebilden aus. Die daraus folgende starke regionale Gliederung gibt der kulturellen und sprachlichen Entwicklung in Deutschland bis heute ihr Gepräge.

Der 30jährige Krieg (1618–1648) brachte Verwüstungen, eine beträchtliche Entvölkerung und eine weitere Schwächung der zentralen Gewalt. In der Folge des Krieges wurden Gebiete an Frankreich und Schweden abgetreten; die Schweiz und die Niederlande schieden aus dem Reichsverband aus.

Deutschland existierte, im Unterschied zu den meisten Nachbarländern, nur noch in einer Vielzahl kleiner Staaten. Weitere Gebiete wurden nach der Französischen Revolution abgetrennt. Auf dem Höhepunkt der „Kleinstaaterei" gab es bis zu 200 einzelne, meist kleine, mehr oder weniger selbständige Staaten. Für lange Zeit bestand die Einheit Deutschlands mehr ideell als politisch und wirtschaftlich.

Nach dem Sieg über Napoleon wurde auf dem Wiener Kongreß (1814/15) die Bildung des Deutschen Bundes beschlossen, eines losen Zusammenschlusses der souveränen Einzelstaaten. 1834 wurde mit dem Deutschen Zollverein von 18 deutschen Einzelstaaten unter der Führung Preußens ein einheitlicher Binnenmarkt geschaffen. Im Deutsch-Dänischen Krieg (1864) erzwangen Preußen und Österreich von Dänemark die Abtretung Schleswigs. Mit dem militärischen Sieg Preußens über Österreich (1866) wurde der Kampf um die Vorherrschaft in Deutschland zugunsten Preußens entschieden. Der Deutsche Bund wurde wieder aufgelöst, an seine Stelle trat der Norddeutsche Bund, dem Österreich nicht mehr angehörte. Preußen, das sich in mehreren Etappen auch große Teile Polens eingegliedert hatte (Polnische Teilungen), arbeitete nun auf eine Staatsbildung unter seiner Führung hin. Der franz. Widerstand gegen einen solchen Zentralstaat wurde im Krieg 1870/71 gebrochen; Elsaß-Lothringen kam zu Deutschland. Der preußische König wurde zum deutschen Kaiser ausgerufen. Berlin wurde Hauptstadt. Damit begann die Zeit des Deutschen Reiches, zunächst unter dem Kaiser, dann als (Weimarer) Republik und schließlich als nationalsozialistische Diktatur.

Nach dem Ersten Weltkrieg wurden die im Westen, Osten und Norden Deutschlands eingegliederten Gebiete wieder abgetrennt. Mit dem Sieg der Alliierten über den Hitlerfaschismus (1945) endete faktisch die Existenz des Deutschen Reiches. Nun wurden auch die Gebiete östlich von Oder und Neiße abgetrennt, und das verbleibende Gebiet wurde in vier Besatzungszonen und Berlin aufgeteilt. Aus den drei westlichen Zonen entstand 1949 die BRD, kurz darauf aus der östlichen Zone die DDR. Während der mehr als vierzigjährigen Existenz zweier deutscher Staaten, die verschiedenen politischen Systemen angehörten, entwickelten sich beide Teile wirtschaftlich, politisch und in den darauf aufbauenden Lebensformen recht unterschiedlich. Dies fand auch in der deutschen Sprache mit zahlreichen neuen Wörtern, neuen Bedeutungen und für die verschiedenen Lebensformen charakteristischen Redeweisen seinen Niederschlag. Dennoch war die Einheitlichkeit der deutschen Sprache durch diese Entwicklungen nie in Frage gestellt. 1989 mußte die kommunistische Regierung der DDR unter dem Druck der Bevölkerung zurücktreten. Nach einer kurzen Zwischenzeit trat die DDR 1990 der BRD bei. Seitdem existiert Deutschland wieder als ein einheitlicher Staat.

2.4. Nationalbewußtsein und Sprachbewußtsein

Das Vorhandensein einer einheitlichen Sprache (Nationalsprache) wird gewöhnlich als wichtiges oder sogar entscheidendes Merkmal einer Nation angesehen. (Wobei ein und dieselbe Sprache selbstverständlich auch von verschiedenen Nationen, mindestens von verschiedenen Staatsnationen − im Unterschied zu sog. Kulturnationen − gesprochen werden kann.) Zum Nationalbewußtsein gehört deshalb auch, daß sich die Angehörigen einer Nation der Tatsache einer sie zusammenhaltenden Sprache bewußt sind und daß sie ihr bestimmte positive Werte zuschreiben. In Zeiten, in denen die Einheit der Nation eher ideell und kulturell als politisch und wirtschaftlich realisiert ist, aber auch in Zeiten der Auseinandersetzung mit benachbarten Nationen, gewinnt die Sprache einen besonderen Stellenwert für die Entwicklung des Nationalbewußtseins. Sie wird zu einem Symbol, mit dessen Hilfe Identifizierungen und Abgrenzungen definiert werden können.

Für die öffentliche Bewertung von Sprachkontakten, aber auch für die Begründung von Sprachpolitik des Staates (vgl. dazu 3.4.), ist dies insofern wichtig, als das Hochwerten der eigenen Sprache beinahe notwendig mit einem Abwerten fremder Sprachen verbunden ist und unter bestimmten Bedingungen auch Formen der Bekämpfung und der Unterdrückung von fremden Sprachen als gerechtfertigt erscheinen läßt.

Die einfachste und augenfälligste Form dieses Verhaltens gegenüber fremden Sprachen ist das Bewußtmachen von sog. Fremdwörtern. Fremdwörter gibt es in jeder Sprache; mit der Intensität von Sprachkontakten − ganz gleich, ob ihre Umstände friedlich oder eher unfriedlich sind − wächst in der Regel auch die Zahl von einseitig oder zweiseitig übernommenen Wörtern und von Entlehnungen verschiedenster Art. Ihr Anteil kann in bestimmten Verwendungsbereichen einer Sprache so groß werden, daß sie der Öffentlichkeit auffallen und der Ruf, sie doch zu vermeiden und durch eigene Wörter zu ersetzen, eine gewisse Berechtigung erlangt. In Deutschland begannen solche Prozesse seit dem 17. Jahrhundert markantere Formen anzunehmen, als Krieg das Land zerstörte und der Zusammenhalt der Nation einen Tiefstand erreichte. Sprachgesellschaften wie etwa die bereits 1617 in Weimar gegründete „Fruchtbringende Gesellschaft" setzten sich die Reinigung der Sprache zum Ziel. Auch die 1700 nach einem Plan von Leibniz gegründete „Preußische Societät der Wissenschaften" wollte gegen „Mischmasch" und „Unkenntlichkeit" der Sprache kämpfen und deren Reinheit erhalten. Gegenstand der Reinigungsbemühungen waren vornehmlich Wörter französischer und allgemein romanischer Herkunft.

Die eigene Sprache kann auch dadurch aufgewertet werden, daß man ihre Gleichwertigkeit mit anderen Sprachen, eher aber noch ihre Überlegenheit erklärt. Entsprechende Argumentationen können damit beginnen, daß die Aufmerksamkeit auf Ausdrucksmöglichkeiten der eigenen Sprache gelenkt wird, daß ihr etwa die gleiche Kraft, Geschmeidigkeit, ja Eleganz zum Ausdruck von Poesie und Wissenschaft zugeschrieben wird wie entwickelteren Nachbarsprachen oder den Sprachen der Antike. Die Argumentationen können aber auch andere, die Überlegenheit der eigenen Sprache und ihrer Sprecher begründende Wertsysteme heranziehen.

Als es in Deutschland darum ging, eine einheitliche nationalsprachliche Norm durchzusetzen, als sich die Nationalliteratur herausbildete und als schließlich im 19. Jahrhundert eine neue Etappe in der Entwicklung des Nationalbewußtseins begann, spielten solche Argumentationen eine wichtige Rolle. So sah Johann Gottfried Herder die Überlegenheit der deutschen Sprache auch darin, daß sie sich mit anderen Sprachen nicht vermischt hätte, und er hob die Beherrschbarkeit anderer Völker durch eine „ausgebildetere", also überlegene Sprache hervor. Von Ernst Moritz Arndt gibt es eine Schrift „Über Volkshaß und den Gebrauch einer fremden Sprache", in der er sich gegen die Übernahme von Fremdem wendet. Andere Werte des Deutschen (oder der „Muttersprache"), die vor allem im 19. Jahrhundert beschworen wurden, waren Reinheit, Klarheit, Deutlichkeit, Wehrhaftigkeit, Gefühlsreichtum, Geborgenheit usw.

Nach der Reichsgründung 1871 (und der Gründung des Deutschen Sprachvereins 1885) nahm das Hochwerten der deutschen Sprache aggressivere Züge an. Deutsch war Weltsprache geworden und sollte entsprechend beachtet werden. Deutschsprachige Minderheiten im Ausland wollte man nicht so behandelt sehen wie man die anderssprachigen Minderheiten im eigenen Land behandelte. In der Zeit des Nationalsozialismus wurden die Förderung der deutschen Sprache im Ausland und das Eintreten für das — in einigen Fällen eingeschränkte — Recht auf Muttersprache auch in die beginnende Kriegspropaganda einbezogen.

Heute ist das Verhältnis der Deutschen zu ihrer Sprache weitgehend entemotionalisiert. Für die Öffentlichkeit ist es kein vorrangiges Thema mehr. Das hat aber auch zur Folge, daß die Existenz von Kontaktsprachen innerhalb Deutschlands den meisten Deutschen kaum bewußt ist. Und in bezug auf „fremde" Sprachen wirken im Hintergrund zahlreiche Stereotype und Vorurteile weiter: welche Sprachen besonders ehrlich, besonders schwierig (also fremd), besonders häßlich klingend (also unangenehm) usw. sind. Da Sprachkontakte immer soziale Beziehungen zwischen Sprechern darstellen, sind die in einer Gemeinschaft verbreiteten Einstellungen eine wichtige Bedingung für die Entwicklung des Sprachkontakts.

3. Politik, Wirtschaft und allgemeine kulturelle sowie religiöse Lage

3.1. Politischer Aufbau

Die Bundesrepublik Deutschland ist ein demokratischer und sozialer Rechtsstaat. Sie ist nach dem föderalen Prinzip organisiert und besteht aus 16 Ländern, die über jeweils eigene Regierungsorgane verfügen. Das föderale Prinzip hat die deutsche Geschichte zum Hintergrund, aber die heutigen Bundesländer entsprechen nur zum kleineren Teil den früheren Einzelstaaten. Politischer Leitrahmen des gesamten Staates ist das Grundgesetz. Entsprechend dem Prinzip der Gewaltenteilung nehmen voneinander unabhängige Organe die Funktionen des Staates wahr. Staatsoberhaupt ist der Bundespräsident. Das Parlament ist der für vier Jahre gewählte Bundestag, in dem gegenwärtig 5 Parteien vertreten sind (CDU/CSU und SPD als stärkste). Die Vertretung der Länder bildet den Bundesrat, der an der Gesetzgebung mitwirkt. Bundeskanzler und Bundesminister bilden die Bundesregierung. Das Bundesverfassungsgericht wacht über die Einhaltung des Grundgesetzes.

3.2. Wirtschaft

Deutschland gehört zu den führenden Industrieländern. Das Wirtschaftssystem hat sich seit 1945 zu einer „sozialen Marktwirtschaft" entwickelt: Markt, private Initiative und Wettbewerb bilden die Grundlagen, gleichzeitig ist die Wirtschaft aber bestimmten sozialen Bindungen unterworfen. Der Staat schafft bestimmte Rahmenbedingungen, er unterbindet Wettbewerbsbeschränkungen, kann einige Bereiche partiell aus dem marktwirtschaftlichen System herausnehmen (Landwirtschaft, Verkehrswesen, Steinkohle u. a.), gewährt soziale Unterstützungen, kontrolliert bestimmte Berufe, verzichtet aber zu einem großen Teil auf Eingriffe in Preis- und Lohnbildung. Der Arbeitsmarkt wird weitgehend durch die Sozialpartner und ihre Organisationen, Gewerkschaften und Arbeitgeberverbände, geregelt. Die Arbeitslosigkeit ist in den letzten Jahren teilweise beträchtlich gestiegen. Arbeitslose sind durch eine gesetzliche Arbeitslosenversicherung in einem gewissen Umfang gesichert (Arbeitslosengeld, Arbeitsförderung).

Stark entwickelte Industrien sind: Maschinenbau, Stahl- und chemische Industrie, Autoindustrie, Feinmechanik/Optik, elektrotechnische Industrie, Verbrauchsgüterindustrien. Rohstoffe müssen zum größeren Teil importiert werden. Produktion und Beschäftigung verlagern sich von der Landwirtschaft über Industrie und Handwerk zum Dienstleistungsbereich. Die Landwirtschaft deckt etwa 80% des Inlandbedarfs an Nahrungsmitteln. Sie war bisher von staatlichen Unterstützungen abhängig.

3.3. Kultur

Der späte Zusammenschluß zu einem einheitlichen Nationalstaat und der föderale Charakter sind im Bereich der Kultur bis heute am stärksten spürbar. Es gibt mehrere kulturelle Zentren: Berlin, Frankfurt, Hamburg, Köln, München, Leipzig, Dresden. Auch viele mittlere und kleinere Städte sind kulturell bedeutsam. Kultur und Bildung liegen im wesentlichen in der Hand der Länder.

3.4. Religion

Im Grundgesetz sind die Freiheit des Glaubens und die ungestörte Religionsausübung gewährleistet. Seit der Weimarer Reichsverfassung von 1919 gibt es eine weitgehende Trennung von Staat und Kirche. Es gibt also keine Staatskirche. Andererseits sind die Kirchen aber auch keine privaten Vereinigungen. Sie sind öffentlich-rechtliche Körperschaften, die in einem partnerschaftlichen Verhältnis zum Staat stehen und vom Staat unterstützt werden. Dieses Verhältnis ist nicht nur durch die Verfassung, sondern auch durch Konkordate und Verträge geregelt. Bei der Regierung gibt es Kirchenbevollmächtigte; der Staat zahlt Geld an die Kirchen; diese erheben mit Hilfe des Staates Geld von ihren Mitgliedern.

85% der Bevölkerung (alte Bundesrepublik Deutschland) bekennen sich zu einer der christlichen Konfessionen, in den ostdeutschen Ländern etwas weniger. Insgesamt gibt es etwa 30 Mio evangelische Christen, davon sind jedoch nur etwa 2 Mio Kirchgänger. Die katholische Kirche hat 26,7 Mio Mitglieder, von denen weniger als 6 Mio Kirchgänger sind.

Rheinland-Pfalz, das Saarland und Bayern sind mehrheitlich katholisch, in Baden-Württemberg und Nordrhein-Westfalen sind beide Konfessionen gleichstark, die anderen Länder, insbesondere die ostdeutschen, sind überwiegend evangelisch. Die heutige Verteilung der Konfessionen hat ihren Ursprung im Zeitalter der Reformation und der Gegenreformation.

Zum Islam bekennen sich in Deutschland mehr als 2 Mio (vorwiegend Türken). Weitere kleinere Religionsgemeinschaften sind: jüdische Gemeinden (über 34 000 Mitglieder), sowie Methodisten, Mennoniten, Baptisten und die Griechisch-orthodoxe Kirche.

3.5. Sprachpolitik

Sprachpolitik kann auf verschiedene Gegenstände gerichtet sein. Sie kann erstens Maßnahmen zur Förderung einer der Varietäten einer Sprache zum Inhalt haben, gewöhnlich des Standards (Hochsprache). Sie verwirklicht sich dann als Normierung (Kodifizierung) sowie als Organisation und Ausrichtung des Muttersprachunterrichts. Zweitens kann sie Maßnahmen zur Verbreitung, Förderung und Unterstützung vor allem einer Standardsprache im Ausland zum Inhalt haben. Dies ist die Aufgabe auswärtiger Kulturpolitik. Drittens schließlich kann sich Sprachpolitik auf die Behandlung von Minderheitensprachen, von mit der offiziellen Staatssprache nicht identischen Kontaktsprachen beziehen. Dies ist gewöhnlich ein Teil der Innenpolitik.

(1) Entscheidender Inhalt von varietätenbezogener Sprachpolitik ist die Hinführung zur Standardsprache im Schulunterricht. Das ist für den mündlichen Standard deshalb erforderlich, weil die Kinder zunächst im allgemeinen eine mehr oder weniger regional gefärbte Redeweise erwerben. Besonders wichtig ist aber die Hinführung zum schriftlichen Standard, der ja von Schulanfängern überhaupt noch nicht beherrscht wird. Diese Hinführung wird durch die jeweilige Schulgesetzgebung geregelt. Die erforderlichen personellen Voraussetzungen werden an Universitäten und an speziellen Lehrerbildungseinrichtungen geschaffen. In Deutschland hat der Staat die Aufsicht über den gesamten Bereich, wobei es auf der Ebene der Bundesländer verschiedene Modifikationen gibt.

Bei der Hinführung zur Standardsprache ergeben sich folgende Probleme: Je nach der Stelle, die der Muttersprachunterricht im System der Unterrichtsfächer einnimmt, und in Übereinstimmung mit seinen besonderen inhaltlichen Ausrichtungen, kann ein Ausleseverfahren installiert werden, das Kindern mit höherer standardsprachlicher Kompetenz Vorteile für den Schulabschluß und für die spätere berufliche Entwicklung verschafft. Gewöhnlich ist die standardsprachliche Kompetenz in Familien aus unteren Schichten geringer. Besonders ungünstig ist die Situation für ausländische Kinder, in deren Familien nicht oder wenig Deutsch gesprochen wird. Sie erwerben die deutsche Sprache vor allem im Kontakt mit deutschen Kindern sowie in der Schule. Die Furcht vor ungünstigeren Bedingungen in der Schule ist in vielen Fällen auch der Grund dafür, daß Kontaktsprachen (und auch Dialekte) in der Familie nur eingeschränkt verwendet werden, daß mit den Kindern möglichst im Standard oder in einer standardnahen Varietät gesprochen wird.

Als Maßnahmen zur Reduzierung solcher Probleme wurden vorgeschlagen: eine stärkere Verbindung des Deutschunterrichts mit den Lebenswelten, aus denen die Kinder kommen; die Zulassung dialektaler Redeweisen; eine weniger strenge Zensierung von standardsprachlichen Fehlern; Unterricht in nicht-standardsprachlichen Varietäten bzw. in Kontaktsprachen. — In den 70er Jahren setzte auf diesem Gebiet der Schul- und Sprachpolitik eine gewisse Liberalisierung ein. Heute ist eher eine Rückkehr zur höheren Bewertung standardsprachlicher Richtigkeit zu beobachten.

(2) Die Verbreitung und Förderung des Deutschen im Ausland ist für Deutschland erst seit der Reichsgründung eine Aufgabe. Die Sprache erweist sich als ein Mittel, mit dem man Kultur und Ideen tranportieren kann. Dies und die Kenntnis der Sprache schaffen Voraussetzungen für eine verbesserte wirtschaftliche und politische Zusammenarbeit. Ein anderer Aspekt ist das Aufrechterhalten von Kontakten zu deutschsprachigen Bevölkerungsgruppen im Ausland. Man erkannte bald, daß hier Potentiale für eine Umsetzung der jeweiligen auswärtigen Politik bestehen. Deshalb wurde diese Form der Sprachpolitik entweder durch staatliche oder vom Staat unterstützte Institutionen wahrgenommen. Praktisch verwirklicht wird sie heute über zwischenstaatliche Kulturabkommen, über das Goethe-Institut mit seinen Zweigstellen in zahlreichen Ländern, über den Deutschen Akademischen Austauschdienst, das Institut für Auslandsbeziehungen und andere. Vermittlungsformen sind insbesondere Sprachkurse, der Austausch von Personen, die Organisation von Ausstellungen. (Vgl. dazu Ammon 1989.)

(3) Sprachpolitik, die sich auf Kontaktsprachen innerhalb des eigenen Staates richtet, schließt insbesondere ein: Verbot oder bloße Duldung dieser Sprachen (mit unterschiedlichen Konsequenzen, mindestens einer Benachteiligung im sozialen Aufstieg und in der Mitwirkung am politischen Leben) oder ihre gleichberechtigte Behandlung (z. B. im offiziellen Verkehr) bzw. die Einschränkung auf bestimmte Kommunikationsbereiche (z. B. auf die Familie), die Förderung von Schriftlichkeit (z. B. durch eigene Zeitungen); die Ausstrahlung von speziellen Sendungen im Rundfunk und im Fernsehen; die Möglichkeit des Unterrichts in der eigenen Sprache oder den Zwang zum Erlernen der dominanten Staatssprache.

In der deutschen Sprachpolitik überwogen in der Vergangenheit restriktive oder repressive Maßnahmen oder eine nur duldende statt einer fördernden Haltung. Erst in der Weimarer Reichsverfassung (1919) wurde festgelegt, daß die „fremdsprachigen Volksteile des Reiches" im Gebrauch ihrer Muttersprache nicht „beeinträchtigt" werden dürfen. Die eigentlich notwendige Förderung wurde erst nach dem Zweiten Weltkrieg möglich.

Ein besonderes Kapitel dieser Form von Sprachpolitik ist die Behandlung von nichtdeutschen Sprachen in Gebieten, die vorübergehend annektiert oder besetzt waren. Preußen verfolgte zu Beginn des 19. Jahrhunderts noch eine relativ liberale Politik gegenüber dem Polnischen in dem von ihm annektierten Teil Polens, ebenso auch gegenüber dem Wallonischen (Malmedy). In der Zeit vor der Reichsgründung und danach verfolgte es aber eine immer härtere Politik. Deutsch wurde als die alleinige Amtssprache eingeführt, der muttersprachliche Unterricht wurde reduziert bzw. abgeschafft. Ähnlich wurde auch das Dänische in Schleswig behandelt, das im Deutsch-Dänischen Krieg (1864) wieder in den Besitz Preußens gekommen war. (Vgl. dazu Pabst 1980.)

Das nationalsozialistische Deutschland verschärfte noch die Unterdrückung nichtdeutscher, insbesondere slawischer Sprachen. Mit der radikalen Reduzierung des muttersprachlichen Unterrichts sollten ganze Völker, darunter auch die Sorben, auf die Stufe von Arbeitssklaven zurückgedrängt werden.

4. Statistik und Ethnoprofile

4.1. Allgemeines

Gebiete autochthonen Sprachkontakts sind in Deutschland vornehmlich die Ränder des Sprachraumes. Diese Gebiete waren auch in besonderem Maße von Veränderungen in den politischen Herrschaftsverhältnissen betroffen, die teilweise die Form von mehr oder weniger gewaltsamen Eingliederungen und Annexionen hatten. Die Folge war dann eine Zurückdrängung oder auch Unterdrückung der nicht-deutschen Sprachen. Sie wurden isoliert, büßten durch die Beschränkung auf bestimmte Verwendungsbereiche an kommunikativem Wert ein, und die Zahl der aktiven Sprecher ging zurück. Zugehörigkeit zu unterschiedlichen politischen Strukturen, Randlage und Isolierung bewirkten, daß sich die anderssprachigen Restgruppen kaum zu geschlossenen Kommunikationsgemeinschaften entwickeln konnten. Die Ausbildung einheitlicher Sprachnormen wurde auf diese Weise behindert, eine starke Differenzierung in kleinräumige Dialekte blieb erhalten oder wurde noch verstärkt.

Auch für die dominante deutsche Sprache hat sich erst relativ spät eine mehr oder weniger einheitliche Norm durchgesetzt. Ebenso ist ihre dialektale und regionale Gliederung bis heute stark. Selbst innerhalb der einheitlichen Norm ist immer noch das österreichische Deutsch als besondere (nationale) Variante mit Eigenheiten in der Aussprache, aber auch im Wortschatz und in der Grammatik zu unterscheiden. Dennoch war Deutsch für die autochthonen Kontaktsprachen immer eine mächtige dominante Sprache, die heute für mehr als 100 Mio Menschen Muttersprache und im größten Teil des deutschen Sprachraums einzige Staatssprache ist.

In den folgenden Abschnitten werden nur allgemeine Angaben über Statistik und Ethnoprofile der Kontaktsprachen gemacht. Für Details wird auf die nachfolgenden Artikel zu den Sprachpaaren verwiesen.

4.2. Dänisch

Schleswig war seit eh und je eine Übergangszone zwischen nord- und westgermanischen (bzw. verschiedenen westgerm.) und später dänischen, deutschen und friesischen Dialekten. Dementsprechend lebten hier Stämme, die zu den Nordseegermanen (Angeln, Sachsen, Friesen u. a.) und den Nordgermanen (Dänen) gerechnet werden, auf einem relativ engen Raum zusammen. Südlich davon siedelten elbgerman. Stämme. In diesem Raum wurde Plattdeutsch, *Süderjütisch* (als dänischer Dialekt), Nordfriesisch und dann auch Hochdeutsch und *Reichsdänisch* gesprochen. Schon im Mittelalter setzte eine noch nicht abgeschlossene Süd-Nord-Bewegung ein, die Süderjütisch durch Plattdeutsch abzulösen begann. Die Bewegung dürfte an der jetzigen Landesgrenze einen Abschluß finden. Die wechselnde Zugehörigkeit Schleswigs (bzw. Nord-Schleswigs) zu Dänemark oder Deutschland verband sich mit einer gegen die jeweils andere Sprache gerichteten Sprachpolitik, ohne daß jedoch in Nord-Schleswig Deutsch und in Süd-Schleswig Dänisch durchgesetzt werden konnten (→ Art. 217). Für die heutige Zeit wird die Volkszugehörigkeit eher ethnisch und kulturell als sprachlich definiert. Ergebnisse aus Volkzählungen liegen nicht vor.

4.3. Nord- und Ostfriesisch

Sprachgeschichtlich gehört Friesisch zum Westgerm. und nimmt eine Stellung zwischen Deutsch und Englisch ein. Heute umfaßt es drei Dialektgruppen, von denen zwei in Deutschland verbreitet sind: *Nordfriesisch* (an der Westküste von Schleswig-Holstein und auf den vorgelagerten Inseln) wird von etwa 9 000—10 000 Menschen aktiv gesprochen, die Zahl der passiven Sprecher ist etwa doppelt so hoch (→ Art. 218 und 219). *Ostfriesisch* (im Saterland, zu Niedersachsen gehörig) wird von etwa 2000 Menschen gesprochen (→ Art. 220). Insbesondere das Nordfriesische ist dialektal stark untergliedert, die Unterschiede zwischen den einzelnen Dialekten (Inseln und Festland) sind relativ groß.

Die dritte und größte Gruppe des Friesischen bildet das Westfriesische, das in der niederländischen Provinz Friesland von ca. 400 000 Menschen gesprochen wird und hier regionale Amtssprache ist (→ Art. 140). Von den beiden anderen Dialektgruppen ist das Westfriesische, das auch eine städtische Varietät kennt, sprachlich relativ stark unterschieden. Dennoch gibt es ein gesamtfriesisches Zusammengehörigkeitsgefühl. Alle Sprecher des Friesischen haben eine Zweitsprache: Niederländisch oder Deutsch.

4.4. Sorbisch

Die Sorben, ein westslawisches Volk, besiedelten im frühen Mittelalter einen großen Teil des mitteldeutschen Raumes (→ Art. 221). Sie wurden früh germanisiert. Ein Rest blieb in der Lausitz ansässig und siedelte später auch im Spreewald (südöstlich von Berlin). Die einzelnen Teile des (späteren) Siedlungsgebietes waren historisch unterschiedlichen politischen Strukturen ein- oder angegliedert: Böhmen, Brandenburg, Meißen, später Sachsen und Preußen. Dies trug dazu bei, daß das Sorbische eine starke dialektale Gliederung beibehielt. Nach dem Zweiten Weltkrieg wurde die Zahl der Sorben mit 100 000 angegeben. Gegenwärtig bekennen sich noch ca. 50 000 als Sorben, weitere 20 000 beherrschen die sorbische Sprache. Das sind etwa 12% der Gesamtbevölkerung in diesem Gebiet.

5. Soziolinguistische Lage

5.1. Einschränkung der Verwendungsbereiche

Dominierte Sprachen werden, ähnlich wie Dialekte, häufig auf bestimmte Verwendungsbereiche (Domänen) eingeschränkt. Sie erlangen nicht den Zugang zu allen, insbesondere den offiziellen Kommunikationssituationen, weil dominante und überregionale Sprachen diesen Bereich von vornherein besetzthalten, oder sie verlieren den Zugang, weil sie in der Konkurrenz mit einer anderen Sprache unterliegen. Ihr Rückzugsgebiet ist in der Regel die Kommunikation in der Kleingruppe (Dorfgemeinschaft, Freizeitgruppen) oder in der Familie, oft auch noch auf die ältere Generation beschränkt.

Das *Sorbische* wurde lange Zeit für die Kommunikation innerhalb der Dorfgemeinschaften verwendet. Hier bildeten die Sorben noch lange Zeit die Bevölkerungsmehrheit. Die Zugehörigkeit ihres Siedlungsgebietes zu verschiedenen Staatsterritorien führte auch zu konfessionellen Unterschieden. Im südlichen Gebiet hatte sich die Reformation nicht durchgesetzt, so daß ein Teil der Sorben katholisch blieb. Daraus entstand ein gewisses Interesse an überregionalen Varietäten, die in der Kirche verwendet werden konnten. Es bildeten sich zwei Schriftnormen, *Ober-* und *Niedersorbisch*, aus. Die auf dieser Grundlage entstehenden schriftlichen Traditionen öffneten dem Sorbischen auch Zugang zu weiteren Kommunikationsbereichen. Dennoch blieb der mündliche Gebrauch des Sorbischen bis heute vornehmlich auf die Dorfgemeinschaft beschränkt, weniger wird es schon am Arbeitsplatz gesprochen, wo der Kontakt mit deutschsprachigen Sprechern zunahm und das Sorbische allmählich zurückgedrängt wurde. Auch als es nach 1945 mit dem Deutschen teilweise gleichgestellt wurde, konnte sich sein Verwendungsbereich nur bedingt erweitern. Die Schriftnorm wird auch heute eher passiv beherrscht.

Auch das *Nord-* und *Ostfriesische* sind Sprachen, die vornehmlich in der Familie und in Kleingruppen Verwendung finden. Schriftliche Traditionen sind hier weniger ausgeprägt. Das Bewußtsein für das Nordfriesische ist auf den Inseln stärker entwickelt als auf dem Festland, wo die Randlage durch verkehrsmäßige Erschließung aufgehoben ist. Auch die Abgrenzung gegenüber den Touristen mag auf den Inseln zu einer Stärkung des Sprachbewußtseins beigetragen haben. Versuche, Friesisch zu unterrichten, wurden auf den Inseln positiver aufgenommen als auf dem Festland. Hier wird, wie in anderen Diglossie-Gebieten auch, die weniger verbreitete Sprache als hinderlich für schulisches und berufliches Fortkommen angesehen. Deshalb sprechen die Eltern zwar noch untereinander Friesisch, mit ihren Kindern aber bereits Hochdeutsch.

5.2. Soziale Charakteristik der Sprecher

Der Beschränkung auf bestimmte Verwendungsbereiche entspricht eine charakteristische soziale Zusammensetzung der Sprecher.

Die dominierten Sprachen werden eher von der Land- als der Stadtbevölkerung bzw. von sozial niederen Schichten der Stadtbevölkerung gesprochen. So war *Süderjütisch* eine Sprache der Bauern und niederer städtischer Schichten. Ebenso war *Dänisch* in Südschleswig eine Sprache der Unterprivilegierten. Die Sprecher des *Nordfriesischen* auf dem Festland gehören heute vor allem der Arbeiterklasse und der unteren Mittelschicht an. Für das *Sorbische* dürfte die Situation auf Grund der weitaus größeren Sprecherzahl und der Förderung in den letzten Jahrzehnten geringfügig anders sein. In der Vergangenheit hatten die Sorben kaum Zugang zu den Städten, ein sorbisches Bürgertum entwickelte sich nicht.

5.3. Zwei- und Mehrsprachigkeit

Zwei- und Mehrsprachigkeit entstehen z. B. dann, wenn eine andere als die Muttersprache offizielle oder Prestige-Sprache ist. In dieser Situation ist Zweisprachigkeit in der Regel einseitig: eine Minderheit oder eine dominierte Bevölkerungsgruppe muß Kompetenz in einer weiteren, der dominanten Sprache erwerben, nicht umgekehrt. Dies belastet die meist ohnehin schwierige soziale Lage von Minderheiten noch zusätzlich.

So bildeten die *Sorben* zwar außerhalb der Städte noch lange die Bevölkerungsmehrheit, in einigen katholischen Landgemeinden ist dies auch heute noch der Fall, Deutsch war aber in den meisten offiziellen Situationen die einzig zugelassene Sprache. Wer am öffentlichen und überregionalen Leben teilhaben wollte, mußte das Deutsche erlernen. Heute beherrschen fast alle Sorben auch die deutsche Schriftsprache. In der mündlichen Kommunikation verwenden Deutsche und Sorben die jeweiligen deutschen Umgangssprachen (Ostsächsich, Brandenburgisch-Berlinisch). — Ähnlich ist die Situation auch in bezug auf das *Friesische*.

5.4. Sprachkonflikte

Sprachkonflikte entstehen häufig dann, wenn eine Sprachpolitik (vgl. 3.4.) gewaltsam durchzusetzen versucht wird oder wenn Sprachkontakte ideologisiert werden. Gewaltsame Sprachpolitik bedeutet vor allem die Verletzung des Rechts auf Muttersprache und hat die Zerstörung der ethnischen Identität, die Verweigerung oder Verkürzung politischer Rechte sowie die Verhinderung oder Einschränkung des sozialen Aufstiegs zur Folge. Die Ideologisierung von Sprachkontakten (vgl. 2.4.) schafft das Klima, in dem Sprachpolitik realisiert wird, sie trägt auch dazu bei, gewaltsame Sprachpolitik zu rechtfertigen.

Sprachkonflikte in diesem Sinne hat es historisch in bezug auf das *Dänische* in Schleswig gegeben, das vor allem unter der preußischen Herrschaft unterdrückt wurde. — Schärfer noch waren die Konflikte in bezug auf das *Sorbische*. Sie erstreckten sich auch über einen längeren Zeitraum und waren Teil der deutschen Politik gegenüber slawischen Sprachen generell. Das Sorbische wurde lange Zeit, vor allem im Kaiserreich, diskriminiert, der Schulunterricht war reduziert, im nationalsozialistischen Deutschland wurde das Sorbische verboten. — Heute sind die Konflikte weitgehend überwunden. Es gibt eine Koexistenz mit dem Deutschen, allerdings ist die Zahl der aktiven Sprecher der dominierten Sprachen inzwischen weiter zurückgegangen.

6. Sprachpolitische Lage

6.1. Allgemeines

Wenn repressive Sprachpolitik in Deutschland der Vergangenheit angehört, dann ist zu fragen, wie weit heute Kontaktsprachen als offizielle oder gar gleichberechtigte Sprachen zugelassen sind, ob und in welchem Umfang sie an den Schulen unterrichtet werden, ob und auf welche Weise ihre Schriftlichkeit gefördert wird, wie die lokale Verwaltung in den betreffenden Gebieten organisiert ist, ob die Medien Beiträge in den Kontaktsprachen bringen und in welchem Umfang sie Gegenstand wissenschaftlicher Forschung sind.

Heute erfahren alle Kontaktsprachen innerhalb Deutschlands gewisse Förderungen. Aber auch ihre Sprecher haben sich zu Gesellschaften und Vereinen zusammengefunden, die sich um die Wiederbelebung oder Wiedereinführung der Sprachen bemühen. Das Zusammengehörigkeitsgefühl stärkt sich. Auch in den Verfassungen wird nicht mehr nur die Duldung (Nicht-Beeinträchtigung) garantiert, sondern auch die Förderung. Dennoch werden eher bewahrende als wiederbelebende Effekte erreicht. Das Gewicht des Deutschen ist zu groß. Die Sprecher der Kontaktsprachen teilen sich ihre Siedlungsgebiete mit immer mehr Deutschsprachigen. Sie werden zu Minderheiten, die ihre Sprache nur noch in der seltener werdenden Kommunikation untereinander verwenden können.

Schließlich stehen auch die für eine Wieder- oder gar Neubelebung erforderlichen beträchtlichen finanziellen Mittel nicht zur Verfügung. Damit wird aber auch die gleichberechtigte Behandlung der Kontaktsprachen weitgehend zu einer Illusion.

6.2. Friesisch (Nordfriesisch)

Friesisch ist in den betreffenden Gebieten keine offizielle Sprache. In den Medien ist Friesisch mit Sendungen und Beiträgen relativ schwach vertreten. An den Schulen werden 2 Wochenstunden Friesisch gegeben, die allerdings bestenfalls zu einer passiven Beherrschung der Sprache führen. Es gibt ein friesisches Schrifttum, aber keine eigentliche Standardisierung des schriftlichen Gebrauchs. An der Pädagogischen Hochschule Flensburg existiert ein Lehrstuhl für die Didaktik des Friesischen. Mit einer Dokumentation der friesischen Dialekte ist die Nordfriesische Wörterbuchstelle an der Universität Kiel befaßt (→ Art. 218).

6.3. Sorbisch

Sorbisch war lange Zeit eine unterdrückte Sprache. Erst nach der Reichsverfassung von 1919 durften die Sorben — wie andere „fremdsprachige Volksteile" auch — „nicht im Gebrauch ihrer Muttersprache beim Unterricht sowie bei der inneren Verwaltung und Rechtspflege beeinträchtigt werden". In der Wirklichkeit sah dies freilich anders aus. Die Staatspolitik setzte sich vor allem die Förderung des „Deutschtums" in den sorbischen Gebieten zum Ziel. Im nationalsozialistischen Deutschland wurde das Sorbische verboten, und es gab einen Plan, die Sorben in das von Deutschland okkupierte Böhmen und Mähren umzusiedeln. Die erste Verfassung der DDR (1949) schloß sich im Wortlaut weitgehend an die Weimarer Verfassung an, neben den Ausschluß von Behinderung trat nun aber die Verpflichtung des Staates zur Förderung. In der zweiten Verfassung der DDR (1968) sowie in späteren Versionen wurde auf eine konkrete Formulierung der Rechte der Sorben verzichtet, dafür war aber von Bürgern „sorbischer Nationalität" die Rede. Dies bedeutete eine explizite Anerkennung der sorbischen Nationalität und damit eine gewisse Gleichstellung der Sorben mit den Deutschen, wenigstens auf kulturellem und bildungspolitischem Gebiet.

1912 war die Domowina als Bund Lausitzer Sorben gegründet worden. Sie nahm nach dem Zweiten Weltkrieg eine gewisse Vertretung sorbischer Interessen gegenüber dem Staat wahr. Eine sorbische Verwaltung gab und gibt es jedoch nicht, auch nicht auf lokaler Ebene. Sorben sind natürlich in den örtlichen Organen vertreten. Offiziell wird eine gewisse Zweisprachigkeit dokumentiert (Ortsnamen, Bezeichnung von Institutionen u. a.).

Bald nach dem Zweiten Weltkrieg wurde der Sorbisch-Unterricht eingeführt. 1946 wurde in Bautzen ein Sorbisches Institut für Lehrerbildung gegründet. In vielen Schulen wird die sorbische Sprache mit mehreren Wochenstunden unterrichtet. Allerdings ist Sorbisch fakultatives Fach. Daneben gibt es auch Schulen, in denen Sorbisch Unterrichtssprache ist. Ende der 80er Jahre nahmen 4700 Schüler am Sorbischunterricht teil, 1300 besuchten Schulen mit sorbischer Unterrichtssprache. Dies hat bewirkt, daß heute auch zahlreiche jüngere Menschen das Sorbische zumindest passiv beherrschen.

Die sorbische Schrifttradition hat es ermöglicht, daß eine sorbische Literatur (Belletristik) entstehen konnte. Es gibt auch zahlreiche Übersetzungen aus anderen Sprachen, erschienen meist im Domowina-Verlag. Die Sorben verfügen über ein umfangreicheres Pressewesen. Anknüpfend an die Zeit vor dem Faschismus begannen in den Nachkriegsjahren Tageszeitungen sowie kulturpolitische und religiöse Wochen- und Monatszeitschriften zu erscheinen. Es gab Sendungen in sorbischer Sprache und sorbische Stücke im Theater.

Entsprechend entwickelt ist auch die wissenschaftliche Beschäftigung mit dem Sorbischen. Sorbische Sprachwissenschaftler gab es schon im 19. Jahrhundert. Nach dem Zweiten Weltkrieg wurde an der Universität Leipzig ein Institut für Sorabistik gegründet, 1951 das Institut für sorbische Volksforschung in Bautzen, das zur Akademie der Wissenschaften gehörte. Dies ermöglichte eine gründliche Erforschung der sorbischen Sprache und ihrer Dialekte. Es entstand ein Sorbischer Sprachatlas, 1981 wurde der 1. Band einer Grammatik der obersorbischen Schriftsprache der Gegenwart vorgelegt, mit einem Deutsch-obersorbischen Wörterbuch wurde begonnen.

All dies hat viel zur Wiederbelebung und Bewahrung des Sorbischen und zur Stärkung des Nationalbewußtseins der Sorben beigetragen. Infolge der zunehmenden Industrialisierung der Lausitz (Braunkohle) und des damit verbundenen Zustroms deutscher Bevölkerung war der allmähliche Rückgang des Sorbischen aber nicht aufzuhalten (→ Art. 221).

7. Andere Sprachkontakte: Immigranten in Deutschland

7.1. Emigranten und Immigranten

Seit Jahrhunderten sind große Bevölkerungsgruppen, die insgesamt viele Millionen ausmachen, aus Deutschland ausgewandert. Auswanderungswellen fallen in der Regel mit Zeiten besonderer Not und Unterdrückung zusammen. Das gilt insbesondere für den Anfang und die Mitte des 19. Jahrhunderts, aber auch für die Zeit nach den beiden Weltkriegen oder für die Zeit des Faschismus. Gründe für die Auswanderung aus Deutschland waren dementsprechend: wirtschaftliche Not, politische, religiöse und rassische Verfolgung, daneben aber auch die Anwerbung zur Ansiedlung. Die Auswanderer kamen faktisch aus allen Gebieten Deutschlands, in besonderem Maße aus West-, Süd- und Mitteldeutschland. Zielländer waren z. B.: bereits mit dem 12. Jahrhundert beginnend das spätere Rumänien, früh aber auch schon Rußland und Ungarn, im 19. Jahrhundert vor allem die USA, aber auch Argentinien, Australien, Brasilien, Chile, Israel, Kanada, Mexiko, Paraguay u. a. In all diesen Ländern gibt es bis heute starke deutschstämmige Minderheiten, die teilweise die Millionengrenze übersteigen. Viele von ihnen bzw. ihrer Nachfahren haben die deutsche Sprache (oder einen deutschen Dialekt) bewahrt. Einige dieser deutschsprachigen Bevölkerungsgruppen werden in anderen Kapiteln behandelt (vgl. dazu aber auch Born/Dickgießer 1989).

Andererseits waren Teile Deutschlands schon früh das Ziel von Einwanderern. So war Preußen (insbesondere die Mark Brandenburg) immer auch ein Einwanderungsland. Politische und ökonomische Gründe trafen hier zusammen, um Ausländer (französische Hugenotten, Böhmen, Holländer u. a.) in das unterentwickelte und dünn besiedelte Land zu holen. In der Zeit des wirtschaftlichen Aufschwungs Ende des 19. Jahrhunderts strömten neben Arbeitern aus den östlichen Landesteilen auch zahlreiche Osteuropäer (vor allem Polen) in die entstehenden Industriezentren Ost-, Mittel- und Westdeutschlands.

7.2. Immigration nach dem Zweiten Weltkrieg

In allen Industrieländern Europas entstand nach dem Zweiten Weltkrieg ein großer Bedarf an Arbeitskräften. An der Peripherie, besonders in Süd- und Südosteuropa, gab es einen Überschuß an Arbeitskräften, die Arbeitslosigkeit stieg. Deshalb setzte in den 60er Jahren eine Wanderung in die industriellen Zentren ein. 1973 gab es in der Bundesrepublik Deutschland 2,7 Mio ausländische Arbeitnehmer, vorwiegend aus der Türkei, dem damaligen Jugoslawien, Italien und Griechenland. Sie trugen beträchtlich zum wirtschaftlichen Aufschwung bei, während nur ein kleiner Teil der erarbeiteten Werte in die Heimatländer zurückfloß, die dort entstandenen Probleme also kaum gelöst werden konnten. Ein großer Teil der ausländischen Arbeitnehmer war von deutschen Betrieben angeworben worden. Sie brachten, da ein längerer Aufenthalt in Deutschland vorgesehen war, häufig ihre Familien mit oder holten sie nach. Arbeit fanden sie damals vor allem in der Industrie und im Dienstleistungsgewerbe. Eine spezielle Ausbildung war oft nicht erforderlich, kürzere Anlernzeiten genügten. Der sozialen Herkunft nach kamen die Arbeitsimmigranten deshalb überwiegend aus der Unterschicht oder der unteren Mittelschicht. Heute lebt die Mehrheit von ihnen bereits länger als 10 Jahre in Deutschland, der größere Teil der ausländischen Kinder ist hier geboren.

Der Zustrom von Arbeitsimmigranten war nicht gleichmäßig. Nachdem die Anwerbung beschränkt worden war, ging die Zahl in den späten 70er und den 80er Jahren etwas zurück. 1989 lebten aber immerhin 4,8 Mio Ausländer (mit Familienangehörigen) in der Bundesrepublik. Inzwischen steigt die Zahl wieder an. Immigranten kommen heute in größerem Umfang aus osteuropäischen Ländern. Unter ihnen hat die Zahl der Flüchtlinge und Asylbewerber aus Krisengebieten stark zugenommen (Rumänien, ehemaliges Jugoslawien, Türkei, Bulgarien, Iran, Afghanistan u. a.). Eine große Gruppe bilden auch deutschstämmige Aussiedler aus Osteuropa, vor allem aus der ehemaligen Sowjetunion, aber auch aus Rumänien und Polen. 1990 kamen fast 400 000, 1991 noch 222 000. Ihre Einwanderung wird vom Staat gefördert. Die deutsche Sprache beherrschen die Aussiedler oft nur in einem geringeren Umfang.

In der DDR war die Zahl der ausländischen Arbeitnehmer und Immigranten wesentlich geringer. 1989 gab es dort etwas mehr als 190 000 Ausländer. Die größte Gruppe unter ihnen bildeten Vietnamesen, gefolgt von Polen, Russen, Ungarn, Mosambikanern, Kubanern u. a. Sie waren zum größeren Teil auf der Grundlage bilateraler staatlicher Verträge für eine befristete Zeit als Arbeitskräfte oder zur Ausbildung in die DDR gekommen. Nur in wenigen Fällen haben sie ihre Familien mitgebracht oder nachgeholt. Ihre Integration war relativ gering. Nach dem Beitritt der DDR zur BRD sind viele von ihnen mit Schwierigkeiten konfrontiert, weil die alten Verträge nicht mehr bestehen und Sonderregelungen schwer zu erreichen sind.

7.3. Deutsche Ausländerpolitik

Die deutsche Ausländerpolitik ist zwiespältig. Einerseits gibt es nach wie vor ein Interesse an Arbeitskräften für bestimmte, meist schwere und weniger gut bezahlte Tätigkeiten. Hinzu kommt, daß die Altersstruktur der deutschen Bevölkerung (Verschiebung des Verhältnisses zwischen Rentenempfängern und arbeitender Bevölkerung) auf längere Sicht nur dann ausgeglichen werden kann, wenn es einen Ausländeranteil mindestens in der jetzigen Größenordnung und in der jetzigen Zusammensetzung (jüngere Arbeiter und Kinder) gibt. Andererseits gibt es ein Interesse, den Zustrom von Ausländern zu kontrollieren, der angesichts der weltweiten Zunahme von politischen und ökonomischen Krisenregionen und des Wegfalls von Grenzen stärkeren Veränderungen unterworfen ist.

So gewährt das erstmals 1965 beschlossene Ausländergesetz − das sich in manchen Punkten an das von 1938 anlehnt − nur eine bedingte aufenthaltsrechtliche Sicherheit, die durch die Erneuerung des Gesetzes 1991 teilweise noch weiter eingeschränkt wurde. Es macht eine Unterscheidung zwischen der Aufenthaltserlaubnis und der Aufenthaltsberechtigung. Die Aufenthaltserlaubnis wird zunächst nur befristet und gebunden an eine bestimmte Berufstätigkeit in einem bestimmten Betrieb erteilt. Eine unbefristete Aufenthaltserlaubnis setzt voraus, daß die befristete bereits 5 Jahre bestanden hat, daß sie nicht mehr an einen bestimmten Betrieb gebunden ist, daß die deutsche Sprache mündlich beherrscht wird und ausreichender Wohnraum vorhanden ist. Eine Aufenthaltsberechtigung wird dann erteilt, wenn seit 8 Jahren eine Aufenthaltserlaubnis besteht, der Lebensunterhalt aus eigener Erwerbstätigkeit gesichert werden kann und mindestens 60 Monate lang Beiträge zur gesetzlichen Rentenversicherung gezahlt wurden. Die Familie kann dann nachziehen, wenn der ausländische Arbeitnehmer die Aufenthaltserlaubnis besitzt und den Lebensunterhalt der Familienangehörigen bestreiten kann.

Eine Einbürgerung setzt neben anderem voraus, daß die bisherige Staatsangehörigkeit aufgegeben wird. Es gibt in Deutschland keine doppelte Staatsangehörigkeit.

Diese Einschränkungen bedeuten für einen großen Teil der Ausländer in Deutschland, daß sie sich nicht frei auf dem Arbeitsmarkt bewegen können. In Zeiten steigender Arbeitslosigkeit sind sie deshalb besonders gefährdet. Von politischer Mitverantwortung sind sie weitgehend ausgeschlossen. Ihre sozialen Aufstiegschancen sind begrenzt, die soziale Integration ist erschwert und ihre Ghettoisierung begünstigt.

In jüngerer Zeit ist die Zahl der Asylbewerber stark gestiegen (1991 kamen ca. 250 000). Schwierigkeiten traten in bezug auf die Entscheidung über Asylanträge auf. Die anzuerkennenden Gründe und das Bearbeitungsverfahren werden teilweise bis heute zwischen den Parteien und in der Bevölkerung kontrovers diskutiert. Die gegenwärtigen Regelungen erlauben eine schnelle Zurückweisung, wenn bestimmte Bedingungen nicht erfüllt sind (wenn Asylbewerber z. B. aus einem Land oder über ein Land einreisen, in dem es − nach Meinung des deutschen Gesetzgebers − keine politische Verfolgung gibt). Die Zahl der entstehenden Zweifelsfälle ist groß. Solange keine europäische Lösung gefunden ist, belasten die bestehenden Regelungen teilweise die Nachbarländer Deutschlands, insbesondere die östlichen.

7.4. Sprachprobleme der Immigranten

Seßhaftwerden und soziale Integration sind gesetzlich an die Beherrschung der deutschen Sprache gebunden. Dies wird zu einem besonderen Problem, wenn die Familien mit- oder nachziehen. In der Regel wird dann zu Hause die mitgebrachte Muttersprache gesprochen. Am Arbeitsplatz wird, je nach den kommunikativen Notwendigkeiten, eine dem Deutschen angenäherte Sprache (Lernervarietät) gesprochen. In der Schule lernen und sprechen die Kinder natürlich Formen der deutschen Standardsprache. Soweit die Frauen nicht berufstätig sind, kommen sie mit dem Deutschen weniger in Kontakt. Insgesamt erfolgt das Erlernen der deutschen Sprache für die ältere und mittlere Generation eher auf „natürlichem" Wege, für die jüngere verstärkt auch über den Unterricht. Dem entspricht der Grad der Sprachbeherrschung, der erreicht werden kann. Für die jüngere Generation bedeutet dies, daß sie im idealen Fall *in* zwei Kulturen aufwächst, realistischer ist aber, daß sie *zwischen* zwei Kulturen aufwächst. Daraus ergeben sich ungünstigere Bedingungen für das Hineinwachsen in jede der Kulturen. Auch später Eingereiste haben deutliche Nachteile in ihrer beruflichen Entwicklung.

Die Schwierigkeiten, auf die ausländische Arbeitnehmer und ihre Kinder beim Erlernen der deutschen Sprache stießen, haben in den 70er Jahren zahlreiche sprachwissenschaftliche Forschungsprojekte entstehen lassen. Sie beschäftigten sich mit den spezifischen Bedingungen des Erlernens, mit häufigen Fehlern, mit sprachlichen und kulturellen Interferenzen. Es wurden Vorschläge gemacht, wie Sprachlehrgänge unter den verschiedenen Bedingungen organisiert sein müßten. Diese Forschungsprojekte haben wesentlich dazu beigetragen, daß Sprachkontakte nicht mehr nur als ein Problem der Grenzregionen gesehen wurden. Ebenso haben sie die Festigung des Faches „Deutsch als Fremdsprache" gefördert und nicht zuletzt die sprachliche Integration ausländischer Bürger in Deutschland. Dennoch kann man nicht sagen, daß die Probleme bereits gelöst oder sämtlich auf dem Weg der Lösung sind.

In jüngster Zeit ziehen Sprachprobleme von Aussiedlern verstärkt das Interesse von Sprachwissenschaftlern auf sich. Diese Probleme sind insofern spezifisch, als die emotionale Verbundenheit mit der Sprache des Herkunftslandes (z. B. Russisch) weniger eng ist. Andererseits kann diese Sprache aber die am besten beherrschte sein und die Kenntnis der deutschen Standardsprache ähnlich gering wie bei den Arbeitsimmigranten der vorangegangenen Zeit.

8. Kritische Wertung der verwendeten Quellen und Literatur

Eine ins Detail gehende kritische Wertung erscheint hier weder notwendig noch sinnvoll, zumal die Literaturverweise zum Teil nur einen exemplarischen Charakter haben und in einem Überblicksartikel auch nicht alles belegt werden kann. Stattdessen sollen einige Anmerkungen die Orte von Strittigem und die Richtung von Vorbehalten skizzieren.

8.1. Zahlen

Wieviele Sprecher eine Kontaktsprache hat, kann man meist eher schätzen als zählen. Selbst wenn man zählt, ist man unsicher, ab wann jemand eine Sprache mehr aktiv oder mehr passiv beherrscht und von welchen Motiven seine Antworten bestimmt sein könnten. Die Größe von Bevölkerungsgruppen ist Änderungen unterworfen. Auch Können und Selbsteinschätzungen von Individuen ändern sich. Umfassende Aufnahmen der Kommunikation repräsentativer Bevölkerungsgruppen, die solche Unsicherheiten ausgleichen könnten, sind praktisch kaum realisierbar, ihre Auswertung wäre es ebensowenig. Deshalb sind Sprecherzahlen immer als Näherungswerte zu betrachten. Das gilt aber in gewisser Weise auch für alle anderen Zahlen, wenn Zählkriterien schwer bestimmbar oder die gezählten Objekte in ständiger Bewegung sind (Einwohner-, Emigranten-, Immigrantenu. a. Zahlen).

8.2. Perspektiven

Sachverhalte können in der Regel aus unterschiedlichen Perspektiven heraus dargestellt werden. Der unmittelbar Betroffene wird — völlig zu Recht — das Dominiertsein der eigenen Sprache mit ganz anderen Erfahrungen und auch Wünschen verbinden als der Berichterstatter, für den die Erfahrungen anderer zu bloßen Zahlen geronnen sind und der vielleicht noch darum bemüht ist, so etwas wie eine die verschiedenen Seiten berücksichtigende Gesamtperspektive zu etablieren. Die Bedingungen für das Überleben kleinerer Kontaktsprachen sind in unserer Zeit jedenfalls ungünstig — auch wenn es gelegentlich Perspektiven gibt, die ein optimistischeres Bild entstehen lassen.

8.3. Disproportionen

Daß im eigenen Land nicht-deutsche Sprachen gesprochen und häufig auch geschrieben werden, nehmen die meisten Deutschen, wenn es sich um Immigrantensprachen handelt, als etwas Normales wahr, vielleicht als etwas Exotisches, schlimmstenfalls als etwas Bedrohliches. Die autochthonen Kontaktsprachen nehmen sie dagegen eher als etwas bislang Unbekanntes, beinahe Folkloristisches wahr. Die Probleme, mit denen anderssprachige Sprecher in deutscher Umgebung konfrontiert sind, bleiben mehr oder weniger unreflektiert. Über deutsche Sprachpolitik der Vergangenheit (aber auch der Gegenwart) ist kaum etwas bekannt. Daß nach dem Beitritt der DDR nun auch die Sorben (wieder) zu Deutschland gehören, muß erst verarbeitet werden.

8.4. Deutsche und Ausländer

Deutschland war zu fast allen Zeiten entweder Auswanderungs- oder Einwanderungsland — auch wenn diese Begriffe jüngeren Datums sind. Das deutsche Volk hat, ähnlich wie andere Völker auch, sein heutiges Gesicht durch das allmähliche Zusammenwachsen mit Gruppen anderer Völker bekommen. Sprachkontakte und Zweisprachigkeit waren die selbstverständliche Begleitung dieses Zusammenwachsens, ganz gleich, ob es in Mitteleuropa oder anderswo stattfand. Im Laufe der jüngeren Geschichte dürfte Deutschland insgesamt mehr Auswanderer als Einwanderer gehabt haben, auch wenn sich gegenwärtig das Verhältnis wandelt. Sicher war Deutschland früher weniger dicht besiedelt, aber es war nicht so entwickelt und nicht so reich.

9. Bibliographie (in Auswahl)

Ammon, Ulrich (1989): „Zur Geschichte der Sprachverbreitungspolitik der Bundesrepublik Deutschland von den Anfängen bis 1985". In: *Deutsche Sprache* 3, 229−263.

Atlas zur Geschichte, hrsg. vom Zentralinstitut für Geschichte der Akademie der Wissenschaften der DDR. 2 Bände. VEB Hermann Haack, Geographisch-Kartographische Anstalt Gotha/Leipzig 1973 und 1975.

Besch, Werner (1988): „Standardisierungsprozesse im deutschen Sprachraum". In: *Sociolinguistica* 2, 186−208.

Born, Joachim/Dickgießer, Sylvia (1989): *Deutschsprachige Minderheiten. Ein Überblick über den Stand der Forschung für 27 Länder*, Mannheim.

Dittmar, Norbert (1978): „Die soziale und rechtliche Diskriminierung von Arbeitsimmigranten in der Bundesrepublik". In: *Sprache und Kultur: Studien zur Diglossie, Gastarbeiterproblematik und kulturellen Integration*, Kühlwein, W./Radden, G. (Eds.), Tübingen, 123−160.

Faßke, Helmut (1993): „Zweisprachigkeit in der Lausitz". In: *Sociolinguistica* 7, 71−78.

The Frisian Language, o. J., hrsg. von der Provinz-Verwaltung Friesland.

Gernentz, Hans J. (1980): *Niederdeutsch − gestern und heute*, Rostock.

Herrmann, Joachim (Ed.) (1986): *Welt der Slawen. Geschichte, Gesellschaft, Kultur*, Jena/Berlin.

Hübner, Emil/Rohlfs, Horst-Henneck (1993): *Jahrbuch der Bundesrepublik Deutschland 1992/93*, München.

Hyldgaard-Jensen, Karl (1980): „Die Begegnung des Dänischen und des Deutschen in Schleswig". In: *Sprachkontakt und Sprachkonflikt*, Nelde, P. H. (Ed.), Wiesbaden, 237−241.

Krahe, Hans (1956): *Germanische Sprachwissenschaft. I. Einleitung und Lautlehre*, Berlin.

Krüger, Bruno (Ed.) (1976/1983): *Die Germanen. Geschichte und Kultur der germanischen Stämme in Mitteleuropa*, 2 Bände, Berlin.

Lötzsch, Ronald (1989): „Förderung und Erforschung des Sorbischen in der Deutschen Demokratischen Republik". In: *Zeitschrift für Phonetik, Sprachwissenschaft und Kommunikationsforschung*, Bd. 42, 4, 452−461.

Pabst, Klaus (1980): „Das preußische Geschäftssprachengesetz von 1876 − Sprachwechsel nationaler Minderheiten als Mittel politischer Integration". In: *Sprachkontakt und Sprachkonflikt*, Nelde, P. H. (Ed.), Wiesbaden, 191−200.

v. Polenz, Peter (1978, 9. Aufl.): *Geschichte der deutschen Sprache*, Berlin/New York.

Rosenkranz, Heinz (1985): „Bodenständige sorbische Relikte in Thüringen". In: *Wiss. Zeitschrift der Friedrich-Schiller-Universität Jena, Gesellschaftswiss. Reihe*, 34/1, 11−20.

Schildt, Joachim (1976): *Abriß der Geschichte der deutschen Sprache*, Berlin.

Schuster-Šewc, Heinz (1992): „Zur schriftsprachlichen Entwicklung im Bereich des Sorbischen". In: *Sociolinguistica* 6, 65−83.

Søndergaard, Bent (1980): „Vom Sprachenkampf zur sprachlichen Koexistenz im deutsch-dänischen Grenzraum". In: *Sprachkontakt und Spachkonflikt*, Nelde, P. H. (Ed.), Wiesbaden, 297−305.

Tatsachen über Deutschland. Die Bundesrepublik Deutschland. Gütersloh, 6. Aufl. 1989.

Walker, Alastair (1980): „Some factors concerning the decline of the North Frisian tongue". In: *Sprachkontakt und Sprachkonflikt*, Nelde, P. H. (Ed.), Wiesbaden, 453−460.

Wolfdietrich Hartung, Berlin (Deutschland)

217. Deutsch–Dänisch

1. Geographie und Demographie
2. Geschichte
3. Politik und allgemeine kulturelle Lage
4. Statistik
5. Soziolinguistische Lage
6. Sprachpolitische Lage
7. Allgemeines kontaktlinguistisches Porträt
8. Kritische Wertung
9. Bibliographie (in Auswahl)

1. Geographie und Demographie

1.1. Der geographische Rahmen

Auf deutschem Gebiet ist die dänische Minderheit im nördlichsten Teil des Bundeslandes Schleswig-Holstein beheimatet, der auf deutsch „Landesteil Schleswig" und auf dänisch „Sydslesvig" genannt wird. Diese Landschaft erstreckt sich von der Eider im Süden (der Grenze zwischen Schleswig und Holstein) bis zur Staatsgrenze zwischen der Bundesrepublik Deutschland und dem Königreich Dänemark im Norden. Wie in der dänischen Bezeichnung ausgedrückt, handelt es sich um den südlichen Teil der Landschaft Schleswig, dessen nördlicher Teil, Nordschleswig (oder „Sønderjylland") zu Dänemark gehört (→ Art. 218); → Sprachenkarte M.

Das Gebiet Südschleswig umfaßt ca. 5000 qkm, die Einwohnerzahl beträgt ca. 575 000. Die Bevölkerungszahl geht seit einigen Jahren zurück, da Abwanderungsbewegungen in andere Teile der Bundesrepublik zu verzeichnen sind, die vor dem Hintergrund der vergleichsweise wenig ausgeprägten wirtschaftlichen und industriellen Entwicklung und der überdurchschnittlichen Arbeitslosigkeit zu sehen sind. Von dieser Entwicklung ist auch die dänische Minderheit betroffen, der viele Handwerker und Arbeiter angehören.

1.2. Der demographische Rahmen

Es ist mit großen Schwierigkeiten verbunden, die Anzahl der Mitglieder dieser Minorität zu bestimmen, die im gesamten Landesteil, besonders aber im nördlichsten Teil anzutreffen sind. Dies ist darauf zurückzuführen, daß keine öffentliche Registrierung der Mitglieder der Minderheit stattfindet, ebensowenig verfügt die Minderheit selbst über ein zentrales Register ihrer Mitglieder. Eine solche Kategorisierung würde auch dadurch erschwert, daß die Minderheit keine präzisen Kriterien für die Zugehörigkeit zur Minorität vorgibt, sondern das Prinzip der Selbstdefinition anwendet: Jeder, der sich der Minderheit zugehörig fühlt, gehört ihr an. Ein solches Prinzip ist jedoch wissenschaftlich nicht anwendbar, da es als diffus und subjektiv aufzufassen ist.

Oft wird von der Minderheit angeführt, daß sie aus ca. 50 000 Mitgliedern bestehe, von denen einige dem Nordfriesenverband „Nationale Friiske" angehören, die mit der dänischen Minderheit zusammenarbeitet (→ Art. 218). Auf diese Weise käme man zu dem Resultat, daß die Minderheit knapp 10% der Bevölkerung Südschleswigs ausmachte. Diese Zahl erscheint jedoch kaum realistisch; wendet man traditionelle wissenschaftliche Kriterien für die Definition der Zugehörigkeit zu einer nationalen Minderheit an, wäre anzunehmen, daß sich diese Zahl ganz beträchtlich verringern würde. (Unter 3. werden Zahlenangaben genannt, die die Größenordnung der Minorität illustrieren können.) Insgesamt ist die Grenze zwischen Minorität und Majorität in vielen Gebieten fließend, und die Minderheit selbst sieht offenbar nicht die Notwendigkeit einer begrifflichen Klärung.

Nicht nur der Aspekt des Zahlenmaterials sorgt für Probleme in der Beschreibung der dänischen Minderheit in Südschleswig, sondern auch eine so grundlegende Fragestellung wie: Was macht im Grunde die typische Eigenheit dieser Minderheit aus, die sie von der Mehrheit in der Bevölkerung unterscheidet? Negativ ausgedrückt kann festgestellt werden, daß es sich nicht um eine eigentliche ethnische Minderheit handelt, da keine nachweisbaren ethnischen Unterschiede zwischen „Schleswigern" in Norddeutschland und „Jüten" in Süddänemark bestehen. Außerdem ist festzustellen, daß es sich nicht um eine eigentliche sprachlich-kulturelle Minderheit in dem Sinne handelt, daß eine tiefe Vertrautheit mit der dänischen Sprache und Kultur als kennzeichnend für diese Gruppe generell angesehen werden könnte. Noch weniger läßt sich behaupten, daß die Mitglieder der Minderheit im allgemeinen eine andere Haussprache als die Majorität hätten (vgl. Kap. 4).

Es stößt also auf große Schwierigkeiten, deutliche äußere, d. h. diagnostizierbare Unterschiede zwischen Minorität und Majorität festzustellen. Die Zugehörigkeit zur Minderheit ist in höherem Maße durch „innere" als durch „äußere" Faktoren bestimmt. Mitunter wird der Begriff der „Gesinnungsminderheit" als Schlüsselwort für eine solche Charakteristik verwendet, indem als konstituierendes Element der Minderheit eine prodänische, emotional fundierte Haltung postuliert wird. Von einem wissenschaftlichen Standpunkt aus betrachtet ist diese Definition jedoch unbefriedigend, weil es ihr an Bestimmtheit fehlt. Daher ist anzunehmen, daß die prodänische Einstellung ein breites Spektrum an Haltungen von einem unverbindlichen Interesse bis zur engagierten Überzeugung aufweisen und sich daher auch auf höchst unterschiedliche Weise äußern kann. Auf diese Weise wird die Minderheit zu einer unbestimmten und unstrukturierten Größe.

2. Geschichte

2.1. Die historischen Voraussetzungen für den Sprachkontakt

Die historischen Voraussetzungen für das Bestehen der dänischen Minderheit in der jetzigen Form wurden mit der Errichtung der neuen Staatsgrenze zwischen Dänemark und Deutschland (d. h. Preußen) im Jahre 1920 geschaffen. Die Grenzziehung geht auf das Ergebnis einer Volksabstimmung zurück, deren Prinzipien nicht unumstritten sind, da Deutschland vor dem Hintergrund seiner Kriegsniederlage keinen Einfluß auf die Konzeption der Abstimmung hatte.

1920 entstand im Grenzland eine ganz neue staatspolitische Situation, indem die bislang geschichtlich zusammengehörende Landschaft Schleswig geteilt wurde, als Nordschleswig Dänemark und Südschleswig Preußen/Deutschland angegliedert wurden. Das deutsch-dänische Problem ist jedoch wesentlich älteren Datums, und das Verhältnis komplizierte sich durch Grenzverlegungen. Von 1864, d. h. dem zweiten schleswigschen Krieg, der von Preußen und Österreich gewonnen wurde, bis 1920 verlief die deutsch-dänische Grenze an der Königsau, was bedeutete, daß sowohl Nord- als auch Südschleswig Preußen einverleibt waren. Vom ersten schleswigschen Krieg (1848—1851), der von Dänemark gewonnen wurde, bis 1864 wurde von dänischer Seite versucht, Schleswig von Holstein zu lösen und stärker an das dänische Königreich anzubinden.

Vom Mittelalter bis zur Mitte des 19. Jahrhunderts hatte Schleswig einen Sonderstatus gehabt, indem es ein besonderes Herzogtum mit dem dänischen König als Herzog und in gemeinsamer Regierung mit dem südlich gelegenen Holstein darstellte, das eine rein deutschsprachige Bevölkerung aufwies.

2.2. Die drei Kontaktsprachen

Diese notdürftige Skizze der sehr komplizierten historischen und politischen Verhältnisse ist als Verständnishintergrund für den entstehenden Kontakt der drei ursprünglichen Sprachen und ihr Verhältnis zueinander in diesem Gebiet unbedingt erforderlich: die deutsche Sprache (hier als Niederdeutsch/Plattdeutsch), die dänische Sprache (als dänischer Dialekt „Sønderjysk") und die nordfriesische Sprache (→ Art. 218). Schematisch vereinfacht stellt sich die Bewegung der Sprachen wie folgt dar: Aus westlicher Richtung drangen Friesen in das Gebiet, aus dem Süden kamen niederdeutsch sprechende Sachsen und aus dem Norden „sønderjysk" sprechende Jüten. Im Gebiet nördlich der Eider stießen die beiden letztgenannten Gruppen vermutlich erst im Laufe des Mittelalters aufeinander, da es sich um ein nur schwer landwirtschaftlich nutzbares Gebiet handelte, das, wie die Ortsnamen dokumentieren, spät besiedelt wurde. Traditionell wird davon ausgegangen, daß die ursprüngliche Sprachgrenze zwischen Dänisch und Deutsch sich von Husum im Süden über die Stadt Schleswig bis zur Eckernförder Bucht zog, die Verwendung der Bezeichnung „Sprachgrenze" scheint dabei nicht korrekt — der Begriff „Sprachkontaktzone" ist dem Sachverhalt eher angemessen. Von dänischer Seite besteht die beliebte Vorstellung, daß die „Sprachgrenze" mit der später historisch-politisch bedeutsamen Eidergrenze zwischen Schleswig und Holstein zusammenfiel, die Analyse der Ortsnamen belegt aber, daß die südlich gelegenen Teile Südschleswig von deutschsprachigen Einwanderern kolonisiert wurden. Hierin besteht eine Grundvoraussetzung für das Verständnis der Sprachentwicklung dieses Gebietes in den folgenden Jahrhunderten.

Vermutlich kann man erst im späten Mittelalter von einem direkten Sprachkontakt zwischen Dänisch und Deutsch in größerem Umfang ausgehen, ein Kontakt, der zwei wesentliche Folgen hatte: Zum einen entwickelte sich eine frühe Zweisprachigkeit/Mehrsprachigkeit in einigen Teilen der Bevölkerung, ausgehend von den südlichen Handelsstädten Husum und Schleswig, nicht zuletzt mit Rücksichtnahme auf die Dominanz des Plattdeutschen in Holstein und Norddeutschland allgemein. Zum anderen setzte eine allmähliche Verschiebung von der dänischen („sønderjysk") zur deutschen (plattdeutschen, in der späteren Phase hochdeutschen) Umgangssprache ein. Das Resultat war jedoch kein reines Plattdeutsch (wie in Holstein), sondern eine Mischssprache, die stark durch den Kontakt zum „Sønderjysk" geprägt war. Bock benannte diese Sprache bereits 1933 als „Niederdeutsch auf dänischem Substrat". In gleicher Weise wurde „Sønderjysk" so sehr durch den Kontakt mit dem Deutschen beeinflußt, daß es das Prädikat „ein unästhetisches Patois" erhielt (vgl. Søndergaard 1980 a, 299).

Dieser Prozeß der Sprachverschiebung in Form einer von Süden nach Norden verlaufenden Bewegung findet kontinuierlich vom Spätmittelalter bis heute statt, er ist bisher nicht abgeschlossen, da es immer noch Menschen im Landesteil gibt, deren Tradition, „Sønderjysk" zu sprechen, ungebrochen ist, doch handelt es sich um vergleichsweise alte Menschen, die im nördlichsten Gebiet in der Nähe der heutigen Staatsgrenze leben. Mit ihren Kindern und Enkeln sprechen diese Menschen durchgehend deutsch, weshalb „Sønderjysk" als tägliche Umgangssprache bald aussterben wird. Bezeichnenderweise war „Sønderjysk" immer ein nationalpolitisch neutraler Sprachcode, der sowohl von der Minorität als auch der Majorität verwendet wurde. Diese Sprache signalisiert also keine prodänische Haltung.

Auf diese Weise hat der Sprachwechsel von der dänischen zur deutschen Umgangssprache viele Jahrhunderte in Anspruch genommen, obwohl es sich um ein sehr begrenztes Gebiet handelt, in dem der Abstand zur ursprünglichen „Sprachgrenze" und zur Staatsgrenze nur ca. 50—60 km beträgt. Das langsame Voranschreiten der Entwicklung ist nicht durch eine bewußte Sprachloyalität dem ursprünglichen Sprachcode gegenüber zu erklären, sondern ist eher die Folge eines sprachlichen Konservatismus in ländlichen Gebieten mit geringer geographischer und sozialer Mobilität.

Betrachtet man den Sprachwechsel und die Mehrsprachigkeit in diesem Gebiet in historischer Perspektive, entdeckt man folgendes Muster:

(1) Zwischen Stadt und Land herrschte ein gegensätzliches Verhältnis: In den Städten war der Bedarf für Mehrsprachigkeit größer, und hier setzte der Sprachwechsel ein, während die Landgebiete monolingual „sønderjysk" sprechend verblieben.

(2) Der Süd-Nord-Gegensatz kam zum Tragen: Je südlicher, desto ausgeprägter war die deutsche Sprache, je nördlicher, desto häufiger die Verwendung der dänischen Sprache.
(3) Eine soziale Gegensätzlichkeit war wirksam: Es waren die niedrigeren sozialen Schichten, die an „Sønderjysk" als Haussprache festhielten. Die privilegierten Schichten sprachen deutsch. Damit gerät der Begriff des sozialen Prestiges in den Vordergrund.
(4) Das gegensätzliche Verhältnis von Kultur- und Umgangssprache spielte eine entscheidende Rolle, indem Deutsch diejenige Sprache war, die alle Formen der „Hochkultur" vermittelte, während „Sønderjysk", das bis zur Mitte des 19. Jahrhunderts ohne Verbindung zum Reichsdänischen war, sich nicht über das Niveau der täglichen Umgangssprache hinaus entwickelte.

Nachdem das Plattdeutsche als offizielle Sprache dem Hochdeutschen gewichen war, führte die sprachliche Situation dazu, daß sich eine Diskrepanz zwischen der offiziellen hochdeutschen Sprache und den „Volkssprachen" („Sønderjysk", Plattdeutsch, Nordfriesisch) entwickelte. Die Bevölkerung hatte diese Situation wohl kaum als unnatürlich empfunden, und vor Beginn des 19. Jahrhunderts hat es anscheinend keine Veranlassung zu Sprachkonflikten gegeben, primär, weil der sprachliche und der nationale Aspekt noch nicht miteinander verknüpft waren. Sprache war schlichtweg Kommunikationsmittel, und Mehrsprachigkeit galt als nützlich. Sprache verfügte nicht über eine symbolische Funktion.

Mitte des 19. Jahrhunderts setzte der direkte Sprachenkampf zwischen Dänisch und Deutsch ein, wobei die Impulse hierzu nicht aus der Region selbst stammten, sondern der Konflikt durch störendes Eingreifen von außen, nämlich durch die Initiative der dänischen Regierung verursacht wurde. Ihr Eingreifen wurde mit der Zielsetzung begründet, daß in Schleswigs „dänischer Periode" zwischen den beiden schleswigschen Kriegen (1851—1864) eine geographische Übereinstimmung von Volkssprache („Sønderjysk") und der neuen offiziellen Sprache (Reichsdänisch) hergestellt werden sollte. Diese Zielsetzung spiegelte in ihrer Sichtweise des Verhältnisses von „Muttersprache" und „Nationalsprache" eine romantische Ideologie wider, eine Haltung, die eine Verkennung der vorherigen Haltung zur Sprache in der gesamten Region bedeutete. Das Entscheidende war bislang nicht gewesen, ob man dänisch oder deutsch sprach, sondern ob man sich dem dänischen König gegenüber loyal verhielt.

Die Forschung hat nachweisen können, daß das eigentliche Motiv für den Sprachenkampf ein anderes als das offiziell verkündete war: Man wollte nicht nur den Sprachverlagerungsprozeß von der dänischen zur deutschen Umgangssprache aufhalten, sondern auch einige der verlorengegangenen Gebiete redanisieren. Der bittere Sprachenkampf schlug fehl, weil er — zu einem sehr späten Zeitpunkt — ein unnatürlicher Versuch war, einen jahrhundertealten, freiwilligen Sprachverschiebungsprozeß zu bremsen, und dies mit Hilfe einer fremden offiziellen Sprache (Reichsdänisch), die bislang in diesem Gebiet keine Rolle gespielt hatte. Die Sprachverschiebung setzte sich mit der ihr eigenen inneren Dynamik fort, auch nachdem das Gebiet nach 1864 unter preußische Herrschaft gekommen war.

Nach der Grenzziehung von 1920 ist man sprachenpolitisch zum Zustand vor dem Sprachenkampf zurückgekehrt, d. h. man überläßt den Vorgang der allmählichen Sprachverlagerung dem freien Spiel der Kräfte. Diese Entwicklung wird dazu führen, daß die Staatsgrenze und die Grenze für Deutsch als Umgangssprache bald identisch sein werden.

Zusammenfassend läßt sich sagen, daß die Entwicklung der Sprachverhältnisse im Grenzland als dreiphasiger Verlauf angesehen werden kann: von der sprachlichen Koexistenz zum Sprachenkampf mit anschließender Rückkehr zur Koexistenz der Sprachen, wobei sich in den letzten 70 Jahren eine deutliche Entemotionalisierung der Einstellung zum Verhältnis der Sprachen durchgesetzt hat.

3. Politik und allgemeine kulturelle Lage

3.1. Die Rechtsgrundlage

Die Rechtsgrundlage, die das Verhältnis von Majorität und Minorität regelt, ist in den sog. Bonn-Kopenhagener Erklärungen von 1955 formuliert. Allgemein wird diese Erklärung als ausreichendes Instrument angesehen, um die Rechte der Minderheiten wahren und schützen zu können — ihre praktische Umsetzung hat zu großen Konflikten bisher keinen Anlaß gegeben. Die Erklärung verwahrt sich gegen die Diskriminierung der Minderheit und will das Recht der freien politischen und kulturellen Entfaltung sichern:

„(Die Angehörigen der dänischen Minderheit haben) (...) das Recht auf gleiche Behandlung, nach dem niemand wegen seiner Abstammung, seiner Sprache, seiner Herkunft oder seiner politischen Anschauung benachteiligt oder bevorzugt werden darf." (Becker-Christensen 1992, 29). Wichtig ist auch die Bestätigung des sog. „Gesinnungsprinzips", damit einhergehend, daß bestimmte äußere Kriterien, z. B. die Sprachbeherrschung nicht erfüllt zu sein brauchen, sofern sich jemand als der Minorität zugehörig betrachtet: „Das Bekenntnis zum dänischen Volkstum und zur dänischen Kultur ist frei und darf von Amts wegen nicht bestritten oder nachgeprüft werden." (ibid.). Dies verhindert, daß die Behörden „Gesinnungskontrollen" vornehmen könnten. Eine solche Bestimmung liegt der Selbstdefinition zugrunde: Die Minderheit besteht aus denjenigen Personen, die sich selbst zur Minderheit rechnen.

In der neuen Schleswig-Holsteinischen Verfassung von 1990 wird präzisiert, daß nicht nur das Bundesland, sondern auch die lokalen Behörden dazu verpflichtet sind, sowohl die dänische als auch die friesische Minderheit des Landesteils ökonomisch zu unterstützen und ihre Aktivitäten zu fördern. Dies wird als entscheidender Schritt im Rahmen der finanziellen Gleichstellung in Relation zur Majorität angesehen, aber das Gesetz ist erst seit so kurzer Zeit in Kraft, daß noch nicht abzuschätzen ist, wie groß seine Durchschlagskraft in der praktischen Umsetzung sein wird.

In Zusammenarbeit mit den Friesen und Sorben versuchte die dänische Minderheit, einen Minderheitenschutz im neuen deutschen Grundgesetz zu verankern.

3.2. Politische und kulturelle Lage

Innerhalb des skizzierten Rahmens entfaltet die dänische Minderheit umfassende Aktivitäten unterschiedlichster Art, da sie über ein Netzwerk politischer, kultureller, pädagogischer und sozialer Vereinigungen verfügt. Einige Beispiele sollen hier näher erläutert werden:

Politisch ist die Minderheit im Südschleswigschen Wählerverband organisiert (SSW), der nur einen Repräsentanten im Kieler Landtag hat, in der Realität aber über einen größeren Einfluß verfügt. Die Partei erhielt bei der letzten Landtagswahl 1992 ca. 28 000 Stimmen, bei den früheren Wahlen lagen die Zahlen der Stimmen zwischen 20 000 und 26 000, die Zahl registrierter Minderheitsmitglieder beträgt jedoch nur ca. 5000. Bei den

Kommunalwahlen der letzten beiden Jahrzehnte lag die Zahl der Stimmen zwischen 21 000 und 29 000. Bei der letzten Wahl 1990 lag die Zahl der Stimmen bei etwa 23 000, wodurch die Partei 109 Repräsentanten im lokalpolitischen Bereich erhielt. Die kulturelle Hauptorganisation nennt sich „Sydslesvigsk Forening", der zwischen 17 000 und 18 000 Mitglieder angehören. Dieser Verein leistet kulturelle und humanitäre Arbeit. Kirchliche Aktivitäten entfalten sich unter der Schirmherrschaft von „Dansk Kirke i Sydslesvig" mit ca. 6500 Mitgliedern.

Die Jugendarbeit, die dem Sport eine zentrale Stellung einräumt, wird von „Sydslesvigs danske Ungdomsforeninger" mit ca. 11 800 Mitgliedern wahrgenommen.

4. Statistik

Über die Sprachverwendung im Kontaktgebiet liegen (innerhalb der Minorität und der Majorität) keine umfassenden statistischen Untersuchungen vor, eine vor 20 Jahren veröffentlichte Untersuchung kann aber in der Tendenz verdeutlichen, von wem welche Sprache in welchen Situationen verwendet wird (Petersen 1975). Die Anwendung der Codes in einer Population von 800−900 Personen in einem Dorf in Südschleswig wird in einem Sprachgebiet untersucht, in dem sämtliche fünf Codes des Landesteiles vorzufinden sind.

Die Untersuchung kommt zu folgendem Resultat:

- 99% können Hochdeutsch verstehen und sprechen,
- 86% können Plattdeutsch verstehen und 70% können es sprechen,
- 45% können Sønderjysk verstehen und 32% können es sprechen,
- 15% können Reichsdänisch verstehen und 9% können es sprechen,
- 9% können Nordfriesisch verstehen und 4% können es sprechen.

Aus dem Zahlenmaterial wird ersichtlich, daß lediglich die drei erstgenannten Sprachen eine bedeutende Rolle als umgangssprachliche Codes einnehmen. Das Verhältnis der Codes zur Altersverteilung ist aber uneinheitlich, und in der heutigen Situation vermutlich noch unausgewogener, da „Sønderjysk" vornehmlich mit der ältesten Bevölkerungshälfte assoziiert werden kann, weil in den 30er und 40er Jahren ein radikaler Rückgang als Haussprache zu verzeichnen war. Aber auch das Plattdeutsche hat keine so starke Stellung wie häufig angenommen wird. 24% der Eltern sprachen 1973 plattdeutsch mit ihren Kindern, während nur 15% „Sønderjysk" verwendeten. Gerade in den Familien fand ein auffälliger Sprachwechsel statt, indem die ursprünglichen Umgangssprachen Plattdeutsch und „Sønderjysk" ausstarben, weil die Eltern diese Codes nicht mehr automatisch an ihre Kinder weitergaben, sondern durch Hochdeutsch ersetzten.

Diese Untersuchung unterstreicht eine klare Entwicklungstendenz für die Umgangssprachen in ganz Südschleswig: den Wechsel von der Mehrsprachigkeit zur Einsprachigkeit. „Sønderjysk" ist als lebendige Umgangssprache zum Tode verurteilt. Auch das Plattdeutsche ist eine bedrohte Sprache. Die Tendenz stimmt mit der rückläufigen Entwicklung des „Sønderjysk" überein, aber der Prozeß findet mit zeitlicher Verschiebung statt.

Obwohl Südschleswig insgesamt in überschaubarer Zukunft im Hinblick auf die Umgangssprache monolingual sein dürfte, ist dies nicht unbedingt gleichbedeutend damit, daß die passiven Kenntnisse der vier Minoritätssprachen verschwinden − von einer lebendigen Mehrsprachigkeit kann allerdings nicht mehr die Rede sein.

5. Soziolinguistische Lage

Die Existenz einer recht umfassenden dänischen Minderheit in Südschleswig geht nicht mit einer starken Stellung des Dänischen als lebendiger Minoritätssprache einher, welches darauf zurückzuführen ist, daß die Minorität primär keine sprachlich-kulturelle Minderheit ist (vgl. Kap. 1.). Dänisch ist daher in höherem Maße die offizielle Sprache der Minderheit, d. h. eher eine symbolische Sprache als die reelle und freiwillig angewandte Sprache der Kommunikation. Als solche hat die Sprache bei den Mitgliedern in leitender Position eine hohe Priorität, wogegen sie bei den Mitgliedern an der Basis keinen hohen Stellenwert einnimmt. Nicht wenige Personen, die traditionell zur Minderheit gezählt werden, sind daher nicht in der Lage, dänisch zu sprechen, z. B. die Eltern vieler Kinder, die dänische Kindergärten oder Schulen besuchen.

Vor diesem Hintergrund ist es nachvollziehbar, daß die dänische Sprache primär nicht in den Familien vermittelt, entwickelt und gefördert wird, sondern in den kulturellen Einrichtungen wie Kindergärten, Schulen,

Bibliotheken, Kirchen. Es scheint berechtigt, die dänische Sprache in diesem Umfeld insgesamt als Institutionssprache zu bezeichnen. Bezeichnenderweise hat die Tatsache, daß viele Südschleswiger in den letzten 50 Jahren eine dänische Minderheitsschule besucht haben, keinen meßbaren Effekt auf die Ausbreitung des Dänischen als Haussprache gehabt. Das Reichsdänische war nie natürliche Haussprache vieler aus Südschleswig stammender Personen, und der aussterbende Dialekt „Sønderjysk" ist nie sprachliches Kennzeichen einer prodänischen Haltung gewesen.

Eine derartige Verteilung der Sprachcodes bei bilingualen Personen kann als wenig fruchtbar bezeichnet werden. Deshalb sind Minderheitsangehörige auf oberster Ebene mit dieser Situation nicht zufrieden — daher werden mitunter Initiativen zur Förderung und häufigeren Anwendung der dänischen Umgangssprache ergriffen, z. B. auch im privaten Bereich, aber diese Aktionen mit der Strategie „Sprich Dänisch, wo und wann immer es möglich ist" zeigen anscheinend keinen langfristigen Effekt. Im Hinblick auf die Wahl ihrer täglichen Umgangssprache verhält sich die Minderheit so selbstbewußt, daß sie sich keinem Druck aussetzen läßt. Daher scheint es auch unmöglich, die aktuelle Verteilung der Codes zu ändern, um so mehr, weil es keine historische Begründbarkeit für ein solches Vorgehen gibt. Ein solches Eingreifen würde als unnatürlich empfunden werden.

6. Sprachpolitische Lage

Die Sprachenpolitik der Majorität gegenüber der Minorität ist in den erwähnten Bonn-Kopenhagener Erklärungen festgelegt: „Angehörige der dänischen Minderheit und ihre Organisationen dürfen am Gebrauch der gewünschten Sprache in Wort und Schrift nicht behindert werden. Der Gebrauch der dänischen Sprache vor den Gerichten und Verwaltungsbehörden bestimmt sich nach den diesbezüglichen gesetzlichen Vorschriften." (Becker-Christensen 1992, 29). Anders ausgedrückt: Die Behörden mischen sich nicht in die interne Sprachverwendung der Minderheit ein. In der Praxis werden oft sowohl Dänisch und Deutsch verwendet, z. B. bei politischen Zusammenkünften oder anderen nach außen gerichteten Aktivitäten, mit Rücksicht auf die Teilnehmer, die kein Dänisch können. Auf der anderen Seite haben die Mitglieder der Minderheit keinen Anspruch darauf, sich auf dänisch in mündlicher oder schriftlicher Form an die Behörden wenden zu können, da Schleswig-Holstein wie die gesamte Bundesrepublik ein offiziell einsprachiges Land ist. Eine solche Möglichkeit hätte wohl auch eher symbolische als praktische Bedeutung, weil alle aus Südschleswig stammenden Minderheitsmitglieder Deutsch beherrschen und Dänisch selten als Erstsprache gelernt haben. Zwischenzeitlich hat es jedoch Initiativen gegeben, auch von seiten der Majorität, Dänisch einen offizielleren Status in Flensburg, der Hauptstadt Südschleswigs, zu verleihen, ein solcher Vorstoß erscheint aber wenig realistisch, nicht nur aus praktischen, sondern auch aus ideologischen Gründen, da derartige Umsetzungsversuche tradierte, latent vorhandene deutsch-dänische Gegensätzlichkeiten wiederbeleben könnten. Daß diese Stadt nichtsdestotrotz in bestimmten Sektoren, z. B. in Handel und Dienstleistung, auch im öffentlichen Bereich einen gewissen Grad von Zweisprachigkeit aufweist, ist primär nicht der Existenz der Minderheit, sondern den vielen grenzüberschreitenden Kontakten zu Dänemark zu verdanken.

Die Intention der Sprachenpolitik der Minderheit kann also wie folgt zusammengefaßt werden: In erster Linie geht es darum, die Anwendung und Ausbreitung der dänischen Sprache innerhalb der Minderheit zu fördern.

Da die dänische Minderheit in Südschleswig also primär keine sprachliche Minorität darstellt, wird die Vermittlung der Dänischkenntnisse vornehmlich auch nicht in den Familien der Mitglieder geleistet. Diese Aufgabe übernehmen Kindergärten und Schulen. Ohne diese zentrale Vermittlung von Sprach- und Kulturkenntnissen durch diese pädagogischen Einrichtungen wäre die Existenz der dänischen Minderheit in der jetzigen Form undenkbar. Es erscheint also nicht unberechtigt, die von Kindergärten und Schulen geleistete Arbeit als den erfolgreichsten Bestandteil der dänischen Aktivitäten in Südschleswig zu sehen.

Die Minderheitenschulen werden von ca. 5200 Schülerinnen und Schülern besucht, in den dänischen Kindergärten befinden sich ca. 1900 Kinder. Die Minderheit verfügt über ein voll ausgebautes alternatives Schulsystem zu den deutschen Schulen (und Kindergärten), welches den Verbleib einer Schülerin/eines Schülers von der Kindergartenzeit (mit 3 Jahren) bis zum deutsch-dänischen Abitur an dem eigenen Gymnasium der Minderheit ermöglicht und ihr/ihm die Studienzugangsberechtigung für beide Länder gewährt. Die maximale Verweildauer für eine Schülerin/einen Schüler in diesem Bildungssystem beträgt 16 Jahre, welches eine kontinuierliche sprachlich-kulturelle Beeinflussung ermöglicht. Es ist jedoch zu bedenken, daß die am Ende erreichte sprachliche und kulturelle Kompetenz mitunter recht begrenzt erscheint, sofern der Einfluß nur von seiten der Institution erfolgt, d. h. daß Familie und privater Umgangskreis keinen Beitrag leisten können und auf diese Weise eine doppelseitige Einflußnahme unterbleibt.

7. Allgemeines kontaktlinguistisches Porträt

7.1. Allgemein

Generell läßt sich sagen, daß sich sowohl im mündlichen als auch im schriftlichen Ausdruck der Südschleswiger Dänen so markante Abweichungen von der reichsdänischen Norm feststellen lassen, daß diese Personen sprachlich nicht als „richtige" Dänen identifiziert werden. Ihre Sprache wird — wenn auch in unterschiedlichem Maße — Züge einer Sprachbildung in einer bilingualen Kontaktsituation aufweisen, in der das Deutsche dominiert. Sie ist als dänische „Kreolsprache" auf deutschem Substrat beschrieben worden (Braunmüller 1991). In Dänemark herrscht allgemein ein geringes Wissen über die Bedingungen dieser Sprache und daher mitunter auch eine recht geringe Toleranz ihr gegenüber.

Viele Mitglieder der Minderheit haben außerdem eine hohe Kompetenz im Deutschen. Im idiomatischen Bereich ist es jedoch schwierig, Interferenzen aus dem Dänischen völlig zu vermeiden, welches wiederum zu negativen Reaktionen von seiten der monolingualen Deutschen führen kann.

7.2. Phonetische, morphologische, syntaktische und lexikalische Charakteristika

Es gibt nur eine umfassende phonetische, morphologische, syntaktische und lexikalische Analyse der in Südschleswig gesprochenen dänischen Sprache („Sydslesvigdansk"), in der bilinguale Südschleswiger mit Reichsdänen kommunizieren (Søndergaard 1985a).

In der Produktion des im Verhältnis zum Deutschen stärker differenzierten Lautsystems sind die Abweichungen vom Reichsdänischen nicht sehr groß. Die morphologische Struktur des Dänischen im Vergleich zum Deutschen ist einfach, hier treten im Südschleswiger Dänisch nur marginale Abweichungen vom Reichsdänischen auf.

Innerhalb der gleichermaßen einfachen dänischen Syntax treten nur wenige markante Abweichungen in Erscheinung.

Es läßt sich zusammenfassend feststellen, daß die lautlichen und grammatikalischen Abweichungen in quantitativer und qualitativer Hinsicht weniger ausgeprägt sind als die Abweichungen im lexikalischen Bereich, wobei zum Teil ein Code-Wechsel stattfindet oder sich Interferenzen einstellen. Bei einigen Personen, die nur begrenzte Möglichkeit haben, Dänisch im Alltag zu verwenden, sind Interferenzen stark ausgeprägt.

7.3. Dänisch als Schriftsprache

Es liegen nur wenige Untersuchungen des Südschleswiger Dänisch als Schriftsprache in den Bereichen Sachprosa und Fiktion vor, aber die Sprachverwendung der zweisprachigen Tageszeitung „Flensborg Avis" wurde in einer Untersuchung behandelt (Søndergaard 1991). Das wichtigste Ergebnis besteht darin, daß die angewandte Variante des Dänischen klar von der reichsdänischen Norm abweicht. Am deutlichsten tritt dies im Hinblick auf den Code-Wechsel hervor, nicht zuletzt in den Fällen, in denen direkte Äquivalente in der dänischen Sprache fehlen, vornehmlich dadurch, daß die deutsche Gesellschaft in vielen Bereichen anders als die dänische strukturiert ist. Aber auch bei den Interferenzen, besonders im Bereich von Wortschatz und Syntax, treten die Abweichungen in so deutlicher Weise auf, daß man von einer schleichenden Vermischung beider Codes sprechen kann. Es besteht hiermit die Gefahr, daß der angewandte Code einer fortschreitenden „Pidginisierung" zum Opfer fällt, weil bei einigen Journalisten ein sprachliches Bewußtsein bei ihrer Entscheidung fehlt, was unter „echtem Dänisch" und „echtem Deutsch" zu verstehen ist. Einige dieser Abweichungen können als typische „Sydslesvigianismer" bezeichnet werden, oft ist ihre Existenzberechtigung nicht zu bezweifeln, andere erscheinen dagegen überflüssig. Es sollte zur Klärung gebracht werden, welches sprachliche Ideal eine solche zweisprachige Zeitung verfolgt.

Es kann überhaupt zur Verwunderung Anlaß geben, daß die sprachlichen Normprobleme des Südschleswiger Dänisch so selten diskutiert werden. Stillschweigend wird vorausgesetzt, daß die reichsdänischen Normen auch hier Geltung haben, obwohl die Praxis zeigt, daß dies für die meisten eine deutliche Überforderung ist. Von pädagogischer Seite wird z. B. eingeräumt, daß die Ansprüche der Sprachrichtigkeit, die in den Schulen verfolgt werden, unrealistisch sind. Es wäre wünschenswert, daß das Südschleswiger Dänisch als eine selbständige, bilinguale Variante des Dänischen anerkannt würde, die unter ganz anderen Bedingungen entstanden ist als das Reichsdänische — dann müßten jedoch spezielle sprachliche Normen festgelegt werden.

Es liegt eine im Südschleswiger Dänisch verfaßte Belletristik vor, die angesichts der Tatsache, daß sie von einer Minderheit hervorgebracht wird, die nicht vornehmlich sprachlich zu fassen ist, einen nicht unbeträchtlichen Umfang erreicht hat. Mehrere der in Dänisch schreibenden Verfasser haben Deutsch als Erstsprache.

Sprachlich kommt die Andersartigkeit der Literatur Südschleswigs im Vergleich zur reichsdänischen Literatur in dreierlei Hinsicht zum Ausdruck: (1) Archaisierung, die vermutlich durch die geographische Isolation der Südschleswiger Dänen zu erklären ist und die dazu führt, daß sprachliche Neuschöpfungen aus dem „Mutterland" nur langsam hierher vordringen, (2) viele und zudem klare Interferenzen aus dem Deutschen, besonders im Bereich des Wortschatzes und der Syntax, (3) Code-Wechsel vom Dänischen zum Deutschen, wobei deutsche Begriffe ohne dänische Entsprechung unübersetzt gelassen werden, oder wobei deutschsprachige fiktive Figuren sporadisch, aber durchaus nicht konsequent deutsch sprechen.

8. Kritische Wertung

In den vorangegangenen Kapiteln wurde eine komplexe Sprachkontaktsituation des Deutschen und Dänischen auf dem historischen „Kampfplatz" beider Länder analysiert. Die gegenwärtige Situation kompliziert sich dadurch, daß die Minoritätssprache an eine Minderheit mit einer so spezifischen Struktur geknüpft ist, daß sie kaum mit einer anderen Minderheit völlig vergleichbar ist.

Generell scheint der Zugang einer freien und kritischen Forschung zu dieser Minderheit recht schwierig zu sein. Dies gilt vermutlich in besonderem Maße für das für die Minorität lebenswichtige pädagogische Gebiet. Vor diesem Hintergrund ist es nicht verwunderlich, daß keine Forschung auf hohem, fachwissenschaftlichem Niveau vorliegt, die sich der Untersuchung der Minderheit als gegenwärtigem Phänomen widmet. (Dagegen gibt es eine reiche und qualifizierte wissenschaftliche Literatur zu historischen Aspekten dieser Problematik.) Die bisherige Forschung, z. B. die linguistische und die pädagogische, ist einem ganz kleinen Personenkreis zu verdanken. Quantitativ ist sie nicht sehr umfassend, und die theoretische Grundlage ist oft spärlich, da das Hauptgewicht häufig auf einer systematisierenden Beschreibung der Phänomene liegt. Ein Teil der Forschungsliteratur ist von Nicht-Fachleuten verfaßt und wirkt daher aus wissenschaftlicher Sicht unbefriedigend.

9. Bibliographie (in Auswahl)

Andresen, Sigfred/Sørensen, Viggo (1989): „Fra den yderste forpost mod syd — det danske sprog i Læk". In: *Ord og sag* 9, 20—29.

Becker-Christensen, Henrik (1992): *The Danish-German Minority Arrangement — a Model for Others?*, Apenrade.

Bjerrum, Anders (1963): „Den dansk-tyske sproggrænse i middelalderen". In: *Namn och Bygd* 50, 182—192.

Bock, Karl N. (1933): *Niederdeutsch auf dänischem Substrat*, Kopenhagen.

Bracker, Jochen (1972—1973): „Die dänische Sprachpolitik 1850—1864 und die Bevölkerung Mittelschleswigs". In: *Zeitschrift der Gesellschaft für Schleswig-Holsteinische Geschichte* 97 u. 98.

Braunmüller, Kurt (1991): „Sydslesvigdansk — et interferenssprog?" In: *3. møde om udforskningen af dansk sprog*, Kunøe, M./Larsen, E. V. (Eds.), Århus, 55—62.

Byram, Michael S. (1979): *Das Phänomen der Zweisprachigkeit. Theoretische Betrachtungen unter besonderer Berücksichtigung des deutsch-dänischen Grenzraums*, Birkerød.

Byram, Michael S. (1981): „Minority Schools in the Former Duchy of Schleswig". In: *Journal of Multilingual and Multicultural Development* 3, 175—182.

Christophersen, Hans (1979): „Det danske sprog i Sydslesvig". In: *Mål og mæle* 2, 8—16.

Dänisches Generalsekretariat (1970): „Die dänische Volksgruppe in Südschleswig". In: *Handbuch der europäischen Volksgruppen*, Straka, M. (Ed.), Wien.

Dyhr, Mogens/Zint, Ingeborg (1985): „Vorüberlegungen zu einem Projekt 'Sprachvarianten in Flensburg'". In: *Kopenhagener Beiträge zur germanistischen Linguistik* 23, 91—104.

Engsnap, Knud B. (1987): „Dansk i Sydslesvig (Mit dt. Zusammenfassung v. A. B. Hattesen)".

In: *Sprachkontaktforschung im deutsch-dänischen Grenzgebiet*, Institut für Regionale Forschung und Information (Ed.), Flensburg/Apenrade, 47—57.

Hattesen, Anni B. (1988): *The Danish Language in Primary Education in Sydslesvig, Schleswig-Holstein, Federal Republic of Germany*, Ljouwert/Leeuwarden.

Pedersen, Karen M. (1984): *Mødet mellem sprogene i den dansk-tyske grænseregion. En bibliografi*, Apenrade.

Pedersen, Karen M. (1991): „Dansk i Sydslesvig". In: *Det danske sprogs status år 2001*, Normann Jørgensen, J. (Ed.), Kopenhagen.

Pedersen, Karen M. (1991): *Det danske og det tyske mindretal i dag — set i et sprogligt perspektiv*, Apenrade.

Petersen, Søren R. (1975): *Dansk eller tysk?*, Flensburg.

Selk, Paul (1937): *Die sprachlichen Verhältnisse im deutsch-dänischen Sprachgebiet südlich der Grenze*, Flensburg.

Selk, Paul (1950): „Der Sprachwandel in Schleswig — eine Kulturbewegung". In: *Aus Schleswig-Holsteins Geschichte und Gegenwart*, Hähnsen, F. et al. (Eds.), Neumünster.

Stenz, Christian (1977): *Grænselandets sprog*, Grænseforeningens årbog.

Søndergaard, Bent (1980a): „Vom Sprachenkampf zur sprachlichen Koexistenz im deutsch-dänischen Grenzraum". In: *Sprachkontakt und Sprachkonflikt*, Nelde, P. H. (Ed.), Wiesbaden, 297—305.

Søndergaard, Bent (1980b): *Die Anfänge der bilingualen Forschung im deutsch-dänischen Grenzgebiet. Eine Bibliographie* (Text auf Dänisch, Deutsch und Englisch), Kopenhagen.

Søndergaard, Bent (1981): „The Fight for Survival: Danish as a Living Minority Language South of the German Border". In: *Minority Languages Today*, Haugen, E. et al. (Eds.), Edinburgh, 138—143.

Søndergaard, Bent (1984a): „Code Switching in Bilingual Speech". In: *Nordic Linguistic Bulletin* 8 (1/2), 5—9.

Søndergaard, Bent (1984b): „Language Contact in the German-Danish Border Region: the Problems of Interference". In: *Scandinavian Language Contacts*, Ureland, P. S./Clarkson, I. (Eds.), Cambridge, 221—229.

Søndergaard, Bent (1985a): „Bidrag til en karakteristik af sydslesvigdansk". In: *Dansk Folkemål* 27, 5—23.

Søndergaard, Bent (1985b): „Interferenz und Kontrastierung im Spracherwerb". In: *Arbeiten zur Skandinavistik*, Beck, H. (Ed.), Frankfurt/Main, 359—366.

Søndergaard, Bent (1987): „Om sprogtvang i en bilingual kontekst (with an English summary)". In: *Aspects of Multilingualism*, Wande, E. et al. (Eds.), Uppsala, 201—208.

Søndergaard, Bent (1990): „Kampen for en egen identitet — en linie gennem sydslesvigdansk litteratur". In: *Nordica* 7, 109—134.

Søndergaard, Bent (1991): „Om sproglig 'urenhed' i en dansksproget avis — set i et finlandssvensk perspektiv". In: *Språkbruk* 4, 14—17.

Søndergaard, Bent (1992a): „Om sproglig 'anderledeshed' som kendetegn på minoritetslitteratur". In: *Danske Studier*, 129—134.

Søndergaard, Bent (1992b): „The Problem of Pedagogy versus Ideology". In: *European Models of Bilingual Education*, Baetens Beardsmore, Hugo (Ed.), Clevedon/Avon.

Thomas, Ceinwen H. (1954): *The Return of a Language. An Experiment in the Revival of Danish in South Slesvig*, Cardiff.

Bent Søndergaard, Flensburg (Deutschland)

218. Deutsch—Nordfriesisch

1. Geographie und Demographie
2. Geschichte
3. Politik und Wirtschaft
4. Statistik und Ethnoprofil
5. Soziolinguistische Lage
6. Sprachpolitische Lage
7. Allgemeines kontaktlinguistisches Porträt
8. Kritische Wertung
9. Bibliographie (in Auswahl)

1. Geographie und Demographie

'Nordfriesisch' (Ndfr.) steht im folgenden als Sammelbegriff für alle ndfr. Idiome. Diese werden auf den Inseln Sylt, Föhr, Amrum und Helgoland sowie an der Westküste Schleswig-Holsteins (Wiedingharde, Bökingharde, Karrharde, Goesharde mit den Halligen) gesprochen (→ Sprachenkarte M). Durch Sturmfluten im 14. und 17. Jahrhundert ist das ursprüngliche ndfr. Sprachgebiet erheblich reduziert worden. Im 19. und 20. Jahrhundert kam es zu einer bedeutenden Auswanderung nach Übersee. Schätzungsweise etwa 9000 oder 6% der Einwohner des Kreises Nordfriesland haben noch aktive Kompetenz eines ndfr. Idioms.

2. Geschichte

2.1. Ethnogenese

Die Nordfriesen sind im frühen Mittelalter aus dem friesischen Stammland zwischen Ijsselmeer und Weser eingewandert. Die Inseln wurden um 700, das Festland und die Halligen etwa 200–300 Jahre später besiedelt. Ndfr. und Südjütisch sind die einzigen autochthonen Sprachen dieser Region. Auf die gesamte Sprachkontaktsituation im schleswigschen Raum, an der auch Niederdeutsch (Nd.) und Dänisch Anteil haben (Århammar 1976, 55 ff; 1984, 930 ff, Wilts 1978, 149 ff, Nickelsen 1982, 17 ff), kann im vorgegebenen Rahmen nicht eingegangen werden.

2.2. Entstehung des Sprachkontakts

Das Hochdeutsche (Hd.) fungierte vom 17. Jahrhundert an als Schrift-, Schul- und Kirchensprache, jedoch ohne die ndfr. Umgangssprache zu beeinflussen (Nickelsen 1982, 37 ff). Erst die verkehrstechnische Erschließung und die Zentralisierung der Verwaltung Ende des 19. Jahrhunderts brachten einen Zustrom hd. sprechender Ortsfremder in die entlegene Region. Seit dem Anfang des 20. Jahrhunderts führte der Badebetrieb ebenfalls zu einer starken Zuwanderung und längerfristig zur sozio-ökonomischen Umschichtung der ndfr. Gesellschaft.

3. Politik und Wirtschaft

Mit der Annexion Schleswigs durch Preußen setzte eine energische Eindeutschungspolitik ein, die mit Unterbrechungen fast hundert Jahre dauern sollte. Die Friesen, die sich auf keinen Staat ihres Volkstums außerhalb der Grenzen der Bundesrepublik stützen können, erlangten somit nie den völkerrechtlichen Status einer nationalen Minderheit. Die Verfassung von Schleswig-Holstein bestätigt erst seit 1990 ausdrücklich den „Anspruch auf Schutz und Förderung" der ndfr. Volksgruppe. Die Wirtschaftsstruktur des Kreises zeichnet sich durch das besondere Gewicht des Dienstleistungssektors vor allem im Bereich des Fremdenverkehrs aus. Landwirtschaft und Fischerei sind demgegenüber von geringerer Bedeutung.

4. Statistik und Ethnoprofil

4.1. Sprecherzahlen

Es gibt keine amtliche Statistik der aktuellen Sprecherzahl. Vorhandene Statistiken (vgl. hierzu Walker 1978, 130 ff, Kööp 1991, 150 ff) sind z. T. veraltet und umfassen nur jeweils eine Mda. oder Mda.gruppe. Die folgenden Zahlen aus der Periode 1970–1988 gründen sich auf eine Erhebung in den Schulen sowie auf Schätzungen von Ortskundigen (Kööp 1991, 74 ff, 150 ff): Goesharden mit Halligen: 535; Bökingharde mit Karrharde: 2680; Wiedingharde: 1300; Festland insgesamt: 4515. Sylt: 1500; Föhr: 1600; Amrum: 600; Helgoland: 800; Inseln insgesamt: 4500. Gesamtes Sprachgebiet: ca. 9000 Sprecher mit aktiver Kompetenz. Die Zahl der Sprecher mit passiver Kompetenz wird auf etwa 20 000 geschätzt. Einwandfrei im System stehen nur noch einige wenige Sprecher im vorgerückten Alter; es gibt schätzungsweise nur ein paar Dutzend friesischsprachige Vorschulkinder.

4.2. Sprachnamen

Nur die Festlandsfriesen nennen ihre Sprache 'Friesisch' (je nach Mda. *Freesk, Frasch, Freesch, Fräisch*). Die Insulaner benennen sie nach der jeweiligen Insel: *Sölring, Fering, Öömrang* und *Halunder.*

4.3. Ethnolinguistische Lage

Die ndfr. Idiome sind im frühen Mittelalter aus dem sog. nordseegermanischen Sprachverband hervorgegangen und nur indirekt mit dem Hd. verwandt. Sie gliedern sich in zwei Hauptgruppen: Insel- und Festlandsfriesisch (einschließlich der Halligen) mit je drei Untergruppen. Sprecher einer Inselmundart können sich nur mit Schwierigkeit mit Sprechern anderer Inselmundarten oder mit den Festlandsfriesen auf friesisch verständigen; auf dem Festland ist die regionale Variation geringer. Alle Sprecher des Friesischen beherrschen auch das Hoch- und meist (zumindest passiv) auch das Niederdeutsche. Abgesehen von Westerland-Föhr und der Gemeinde Risum-Lindholm auf dem Festland gibt es keine geschlossenen friesischen Sprachgemeinschaften mehr. Zunehmend wird die Sprache nicht mehr an die jüngste Generation weitergegeben.

5. Soziolinguistische Lage

5.1. Status

Die ndfr. Idiome werden von den Sprachträgern nicht als Subvarietäten einer Hochsprache, sondern das jeweils eigene Idiom wird als 'das' Friesische schlechthin verstanden (Nickelsen 1982, 41 ff). Ein sprachpolitisch oder ideologisch begründetes Sprachbewußtsein ist dagegen kaum vorhanden. Auf dem Festland wurde das Ndfr. lange als 'Tagelöhnersprache' betrachtet, auf den Inseln wird es jedoch von der autochthonen Mittelschicht getragen und genießt als Symbol der eigenen Identität hohes Ansehen.

5.2. Diglossie

Noch in den dreißiger Jahren bestand eine relativ stabile hd.-ndfr. diglossische Situation, in der das Ndfr. als Haus- und Familiensprache sowie als Ortsmundart, das Hd. als Hochsprache fungierte. Daneben nahm das Niederdeutsche die Stellung einer überregionalen Verkehrssprache ein. Durch den Rückzug auf das Private und Lokale konnte das Ndfr. lange die direkte Konfrontation mit dem übergeordneten Hd. vermeiden (Nickelsen 1982, 41 ff). Diese Situation verändert sich seit dem zweiten Weltkrieg grundlegend: Das Hd. drängt zunehmend auch in den umgangssprachlichen Bereich ein. Der Gebrauch des Ndfr. nimmt ab, nicht nur, weil die Zahl der Sprecher abnimmt, sondern auch, weil die friesischen Sprechsituationen im Zuge der sozioökonomischen Veränderungen auf der Makroebene immer seltener werden.

5.3. Sprachwechsel und Spracherhalt

Der Kontaktverlauf äußert sich in Form eines unaufhaltsamen Sprachwechsels zugunsten des Hd. (Kööp 1991, 150 f). Dieser wird von der Mehrsprachigkeit der Sprecher begünstigt. Während er sich anfänglich vom Ndfr. zum Nd. vollzog, findet seit dem zweiten Weltkrieg ein direkter Übergang vom Ndfr. zum Hd. statt (Århammar 1976, 63). Diese Entwicklungen müssen im Gesamtrahmen der Verdrängung der Regionalsprachen (Ndfr., Nd., Südjütisch) im ndfr. Raum gesehen werden (Wilts 1978, 149 ff). Die folgenden Zahlen vermitteln ein Bild der steten Rückentwicklung des Ndfr. im gesamten Sprachgebiet: 1890: 17 859; 1927: 14 148 (ohne Helgoland); 1954: 12 000 (geschätzte Zahl) (Kööp 1991, 150). Gleichzeitig lassen sich spracherhaltende Bestrebungen beobachten. Für diese bilden jedoch Faktoren wie niedrige Sprecherzahl, ethnische Streulage, spärliche Verschriftlichung und starke Migration eine denkbar ungünstige Ausgangslage. Zudem herrscht in der Sprachgemeinschaft weitverbreitetes Desinteresse im kulturellen Bereich und eine durch die Medien geförderte Ausrichtung auf modische, überregionale Leitbilder (Kööp 1991, 147).

5.4. Sprachkonflikt

Der deutsch-dänische Gegensatz im Grenzland hat lange in die ndfr.-hd. Kontaktsituation hineingewirkt (Steensen 1986, 150 ff). Er hat zu einer Spaltung der Nordfriesen in zwei Lager geführt: Während die „nationalen Friesen" Anlehnung an die dänische Minderheit suchen und die Sprache als Symbol der eigenen Identität sehen, betrachten die „deutschgesinnten" Friesen sich als „deutschen Stamm" und das Ndfr. als „eine deutsche Sprache". Hierdurch wurde die Entstehung einer eigenständigen friesischen Sprachbewegung verhindert.

6. Sprachpolitische Lage

6.1. Sprachpolitik

1987 debattierte der schleswig-holsteinische Landtag erstmals über einen Bericht zur Sprache und Kultur der Friesen. Seit 1988 besteht ein Gremium für Fragen der friesischen Bevölkerungsgruppe mit dem Ziel, „die friesische Sprache, Bildung und Kultur zu pflegen und zu fördern".

6.2. Schule

Über ein eigenes Schulwesen verfügen die Nordfriesen nicht. Z. Zt. wird an allen Schulen des ndfr. Sprachgebiets in der Regel im 3. und 4. Schuljahr 2 Wochenstunden Friesischunterricht erteilt, und zwar als freiwilliges Wahlfach. 1989 nahmen 944 Schülerinnen und Schüler am Friesischunterricht teil. Mehr als eine begrenzte passive Kompetenz kann jedoch nicht erzielt werden. 1988 konnten die Friesen die Einrichtung eines Lehrstuhls des Friesischen und seiner Didaktik an der Pädagogischen Hochschule Flensburg durchsetzen. Von diesem werden entscheidende Initiativen im Bereich der Didaktisierung erwartet.

6.3. Öffentlichkeit

Im öffentlichen Leben hat das Ndfr. nie eine Rolle gespielt. In den Behörden ist Hd. die einzige zugelassene Sprache. Einige Standesämter lassen Trauungen auf ndfr. zu. Gelegentlich werden Gottesdienste auf friesisch gehalten. In einigen Gemeinden, vor allem auf den Inseln, gibt es friesischsprachige Straßenschilder.

6.4. Medien

In den Medien ist das Ndfr. nur spärlich vertreten: In den ndfr. Lokalblättern sowie in einigen regionalen Zeitschriften finden sich vereinzelt fries. Texte. In Risum-Lindholm sowie auf Föhr und Amrum erscheinen als Privatinitiativen sporadisch friesischsprachige Lokalblätter. Seit 1989 sendet der NDR einmal wöchentlich ein Programm auf hd. von 5–10 Minuten über ndfr. Kulturleben, in dem auch kurze aktuelle Mitteilungen auf ndfr. vorkommen.

6.5. Standardisierung

Eine gesamtndfr. Standardisierung ist wegen der großen Heterogenität der ndfr. Idiome nicht möglich. Im Rahmen der lexikographischen Erschließung des Ndfr. mußte jedoch eine gewisse Normierung der schriftlichen Form erfolgen (Sjölin 1990, 510). Ein schwieriges Problem ist hierbei die Ableitung von Sprachnormen aus dem aktuellen, meist sehr schwankenden Sprachgebrauch. Die Verschriftlichung vermag jedoch an und für sich die gesprochene Sprache kaum zu beeinflussen.

6.6. Orthographie

Es ist nicht möglich, die vielen sehr unterschiedlichen ndfr. Phonemsysteme in einer uniformen Orthographie unterzubringen. Abgesehen vom Sylterfriesischen, das eine gefestigte orthographische Norm besitzt, haben sich bei den meisten Idiomen die verschiedensten orthographischen Systeme in schneller Folge abgelöst. Während anfänglich eine Schreibweise in Anlehnung an die dt. Rechtschreibung angewandt wurde, ist man seit 1945 vielfach bemüht, den Abstand des ndfr. Schriftbildes zum Hd. zu vergrößern (Århammar 1976, 75 f).

7. Allgemeines kontaktlinguistisches Porträt

Unter 'Hd.' ist hier ggf. auch die mit nd. Elementen durchsetzte schleswigsche Variante der hd. Umgangssprache zu verstehen. Charakteristisch für die ndfr. Idiome sind, neben einer stark vereinfachten Flexionsmorphologie, die vielen unterschiedlichen, reich ausgebildeten Phonemsysteme. Insbesondere der Vokalismus unterscheidet sich durch eingreifende Neuerungen radikal von dem der übrigen germ. Sprachen (vgl. z. B. *fask* 'Fisch', *iirwe* 'erben', *üülj* 'alt', *reeg* 'Rücken', *lise* 'leiden', *liise* 'lösen', *kluuse* 'Kleider'). Das Lexikon zeigt selbst im zentralen Wortschatz starken nd. und nordischen Einfluß. Die so gut wie ausschließliche Realisationsform der ndfr. Idiome ist die mündliche.

7.1. Nordfriesische Interferenzen

Ndfr. Interferenzen im Hd. sind selten; sie treten praktisch nur auf der phonetischen Ebene und bei der ältesten Generation auf, wie z. B. die Aussprache von ⟨rch⟩ als [rx] in z. B. 'Kirche', oder die durchgehend stimmlose Aussprache des /s/ durch die älteste Generation der Sylter (Willkommen 1991, 100, 139).

7.2. Hochdeutsche Interferenzen im Nordfriesischen

Obwohl einige Entwicklungen sich auch als systeminterne Vereinfachungen deuten lassen, ist auf allen Ebenen die allgemeine Tendenz zur Angleichung an das jeweilige hd. System unverkennbar.

7.2.1. Phonetische Interferenz

Die auffälligsten Erscheinungen sind der durchgehende Ersatz des apikalen [r] bei der jüngeren Generation durch das uvulare oder velare [R] sowie die stimmhafte Realisation des /s/ entsprechend der Regelung im Hd. Als Beispiele für weitere Angleichungen an das Hd. können angeführt werden: Die alveolare, labialisierte Realisation des ursprünglich stark palatalen /ʃ/ oder die Entstehung eines kombinatorischen Allophons [ç] zum Phonem /x/ im Föhrerfriesischen: Statt liich /li:x/ 'niedrig' wird [li:ç] gesprochen (Walker 1990, 414, Willkommen 1991, 121, 139 f, 142, Parker 1993, 78 f, 91 ff).

7.2.2. Phonologische Interferenz

In den Vokalsystemen der Ndfr. Idiome tritt oft Zusammenfall der halbgeschlossenen mit der halboffenen Reihe ein: So hat z. B. im Sylterfriesischen raaki 'treffen' (urspr. /rɔ:ki/) nunmehr denselben Vokal /o:/ wie rooki 'rauchen' (Willkommen 1991, 91 ff). Durch solche Entwicklungen werden vierstufige Systeme durch dreistufige ersetzt (Århammar 1990/1991, 23 ff). Als Beispiel für Vereinfachungen im Konsonantensystem können Tendenzen zur Aufhebung der Opposition palatal : alveolar bei den Dentalen genannt werden (Walker 1990, 415, Parker 1993, 79 f, 93 f). Århammar (1984, 937) und Parker (1993, 87 f) registrieren im Föhrerfriesischen außerdem eine Tendenz zur Aufhebung der Distinktion stimmhaft – stimmlos im Wortauslaut in Anlehnung an die hd. Auslautverhärtung.

7.2.3. Morphologische Interferenz

Im Bereich der Nominalflexion tritt oft Genuswechsel in Analogie zu den entsprechenden hd. Wörtern auf (Parker 1993, 112). Gesamtndfr. sind Vereinfachungen im Pronominalsystem: So kongruiert im Föhrerfries. ursprünglich das Poss. Pron. Sing. in Genus mit seinem Bezugswort (*man kai* 'mein Schlüssel', *min hüs* 'mein Haus'). Dieses System wird zunehmend aufgegeben zugunsten der Einheitsformen *min, din, sin* in allen Genera (Walker 1990, 417, Parker 1993, 130 ff; weitere Beispiele bei Århammar 1984, 937).

7.2.4. Lexikalische und semantisch-syntaktische Interferenz

Der ndfr. Sprecher muß häufig auf hd. Interaktionsmuster zurückgreifen, weil eine bestimmte Kategorie von Sprechhandlungen im Bereich des Ndfr. normalerweise nicht vorkommt oder weil er die entsprechenden ndfr. Interaktionsmuster nicht (mehr) beherrscht. Dabei werden die in den Kommunikationsabläufen eingebetteten Äußerungen als hd. präterminale Ketten Lexem für Lexem bzw. Morphem für Morphem mehr oder weniger vollständig ins Friesische umgesetzt (Sjölin 1993; zahlreiche Beispiele bei Århammar 1984, 934 ff). Diese Ausdrücke können sowohl im bestehenden System voll integriert sein, als auch jederzeit beliebig ad hoc gebildet werden. Voraussetzung ist die Kenntnis des Sprechers der Korrespondenzen der beiden Sprachen im Bereich der Lautung, der Morphemik und der Lexik. Durch diese Entwicklung werden die eigenständigen ndfr. lexikalischen und semantisch-syntaktischen Strukturen nach und nach durch mechanische Umsetzungen verdrängt. Kompetenz des Ndfr. setzt m. a. W. Kompetenz des Hd. voraus.

7.3. Grammatiken, Lehrbücher, Lexika, Belletristik

Die einschlägigen Titel verzeichnet seit 1970 das vom 'Nordfriesischen Institut' in Bredstedt herausgegebene 'Nordfriesische Jahrbuch'. Eine Bibliographie des ndfr. Schrifttums (außer Sylt und Helgoland) bietet Joldrichsen (1988, 1990).

8. Kritische Wertung

8.1. Philologie und Linguistik

Bis in die jüngste Vergangenheit dominierte bei der Erforschung des Ndfr. die historische Wortforschung. Deswegen fehlen noch heute weitgehend nicht nur moderne, systematische Beschreibungen der ndfr. Idiome, sondern auch empirisch fundierte Untersuchungen der Verwendung der Kontaktsprachen in Kommunikationssituationen sowie über die Auswirkung des Kontakts auf ihre Struktur. An der Nordfriesischen Wörterbuchstelle der Universität Kiel sind intensive Bemühungen im Gange, die nordfr. Idiome auf allen Ebenen noch möglichst adäquat zu dokumentieren.

8.2. Sprachpflege und Sprachforschung

Die regionale parawissenschaftliche Sprach- und Kulturarbeit in Nordfriesland erfolgt vorwiegend in traditionellen historisch-philologischen Kategorien; primäre Zielgruppe sind die Angehörigen der deutschsprachigen Bildungsschicht. Rezeption und systematische Verwertung der Ergebnisse der Sprachforschung, insbesondere im Bereich der Kontaktlinguistik, hat bislang kaum stattgefunden. Daher fehlt die Einsicht in die Dynamik des Kontaktverlaufs.

9. Bibliographie (in Auswahl)

Århammar, Nils Rudolf (1976): „Historisch-soziolinguistische Aspekte der nordfriesischen Mehrsprachigkeit". In: *Nordfriesisches Jahrbuch 12*, 55—76.

Århammar, Nils Rudolf (1984): „Friesisch/Deutsch". In: *Sprachgeschichte I*, Besch, W. et al. (Eds.), Berlin/New York, 930—938.

Århammar, Nils Rudolf (1990/1991): „Didaktische Aspekte der jüngsten Vereinfachung des Mooringer Vokalsystems". In: *Nordfriesisches Jahrbuch 26/27*, 23—33.

Joldrichsen, Anke (1988—1990): *Bibliographie des nordfriesischen Schrifttums von 1661 bis 1969*, I, II, Amsterdam/Kiel.

Kööp, Karl-Peter (1991): *Sprachentwicklung und Sprachsituation in der Nordergoesharde*, Bredstedt.

Nickelsen, Hans Christian (1982): *Das Sprachbewußtsein der Nordfriesen in der Zeit vom 16. bis ins 19. Jahrhundert*, Bredstedt.

Parker, Timothy Scott (1993): *Modern North Frisian and North German*, Amsterdam/Kiel.

Sjölin, Bo (1990): „Lexikographie im Dienste der Spracherhaltung". In: *Budalex '88 Proceedings*, Budapest, 507—516.

Sjölin, Bo (1993): „Goes it to wash? Über Routine und Sprachverfall im Friesischen". In: *Us Wurk, 42*, 69—79.

Steensen, Thomas (1986): *Die friesische Bewegung in Nordfriesland im 19. und 20. Jahrhundert*, Kiel.

Walker, Alistair Gilbert Howard (1978): „Nordfriesisch — eine sterbende Sprache?" In: *Sprachkontakte im Nordseegebiet*, Ureland, P. S. (Ed.), Tübingen, 129—148.

Walker, Alistair Gilbert Howard (1990): „Nordfriesland als Sprachkontaktraum". In: *Germanistische Linguistik 101/103*, 407—423.

Willkommen, Dirk (1991): *Sölring. Phonologie des nordfriesischen Dialekts der Insel Sylt*, Amsterdam/Kiel.

Wilts, Ommo (1978): „Dänisch, Nordfriesisch, Hoch- und Niederdeutsch in Schleswig-Holstein". In: *Sprachkontakte im Nordseegebiet*, Ureland, P. S. (Ed.), Tübingen, 149—166.

Bo Sjölin, Kiel (Deutschland)

219. Dänisch—Nordfriesisch

1. Geographie
2. Geschichte
3. Politik
4. Statistik und Ethnoprofil
5. Soziolinguistische Lage
6. Sprachpolitische Lage
7. Allgemeines kontaktlinguistisches Porträt
8. Kritische Wertung
9. Bibliographie (in Auswahl)

1. Geographie

Die 1920 gezogene deutsch-dänische Staatsgrenze teilte das alte Herzogtum Schleswig in zwei Teile: Südlich der Grenze entstand der Landesteil Schleswig bzw. Südschleswig und nördlich der Grenze Nordschleswig bzw. Sønderjylland (jeweils die von deutscher bzw. dänischer Seite benutzten Bezeichnungen für diese Gebiete).

Das Nordfriesische wird an der Westküste des Landesteils Schleswig von der deutsch-dänischen Staatsgrenze bis südlich der Stadt Bredstedt sowie auf den vorgelagerten Inseln Sylt, Föhr, Amrum und Helgoland und auf den Halligen gesprochen. Im 19. und 20. Jahrhundert wanderten viele Bewohner vor allem der Inseln Föhr und Amrum nach Amerika aus (Sievers 1989; Pauseback 1995).

Unter dem Begriff „Dänisch" muß zwischen der dänischen Mundart „Jütisch" und der dänischen Hochsprache „Reichsdänisch" unterschieden werden. In Nordschleswig ist das Jütische weit verbreitet. Südlich der Grenze wird es nur in einem schmalen Streifen entlang der Grenze gesprochen. Das Reichsdänische ist die Sprache der dänischen Minderheit im Landesteil Schleswig und die Amtssprache in Dänemark (→ Sprachenkarte M).

2. Geschichte

Die Friesen haben von ihrem Stammland an der Südküste der Nordsee aus im 8. Jahrhundert die nordfriesischen Geestinseln und vermutlich den westlichen Teil Eiderstedts sowie einige Teile des Festlandes besiedelt. Etwa 200—300 Jahre später erfolgte die weitere Besiedlung des Festlands und der Halligen.

Das Jütische expandierte in der Wikingerzeit von Jütland in südlicher Richtung bis zur Eiderlinie. Im Mittelalter erfolgte eine leichte Expansion des Friesischen in das angrenzende jütische Sprachgebiet hinein. Im übrigen scheinen das Friesische und das Jütische jahrhundertelang friedlich nebeneinander existiert zu haben.

Der friesisch-dänische Sprachkontakt ist aus verschiedenen Anlässen erfolgt und hat bis in die jüngste Vergangenheit hinein gewirkt (Århammar 1966, 302 f; Wilts 1978): (i) Die Besiedlung der Geestinseln führte zu einer Assimilierung der dort kurz zuvor eingewanderten Jüten. (ii) Nach der Besiedlung des Festlands war der friesische Sprachraum bis in das 20. Jahrhundert hinein im Osten von jütischen Mundarten eingefaßt. (iii) Im Mittelalter war das Dänische teilweise Hoch- und Verkehrssprache in Nordfriesland, bis es vom Mittelniederdeutschen abgelöst wurde. (iv) In einigen Dörfern des nördlichen Festlandes entstand eine friesisch-jütisch-niederdeutsche Mehrsprachigkeit. (v) Auf Grund der Teilnahme eines großen Teils der männlichen Inselbevölkerungen am Walfischfang im 17. bis 19. Jahrhundert kamen zahlreiche jütische Knechte als Aushilfskräfte auf die Inseln. (vi) Die Insel Sylt war bis zum Bau des Hindenburg-Damms 1927 nur über das dänische Sprachgebiet zu erreichen. (vii) Nach dem Zweiten Weltkrieg begann die dänische Minderheit Schulen im friesischen Sprachgebiet zu errichten.

3. Politik

Der dänischen Minderheit wurde zusammen mit den Nordfriesen 1949 in der sogenannten „Kieler Erklärung" bestimmte Rechte eingeräumt. Diese wurden 1955 in den Bonn-Kopenhagener Erklärungen erweitert, allerdings diesmal ohne Berücksichtigung der Friesen. In der Schleswig-Holsteinischen Landessatzung von 1949 hieß es in Artikel V: „Das Bekenntnis zu einer nationalen Minderheit ist frei". Dies bezog sich lediglich auf die dänische Minderheit. Die neue, 1990 in Kraft getretene Landesverfassung Schleswig-Holsteins erweiterte den Artikel V und stellte die dänische Minderheit und die friesische Volksgruppe gleich: „Die nationale dänische Minderheit und die friesische Volksgruppe haben Anspruch auf Schutz und Förderung".

4. Statistik und Ethnoprofil

Ca. 8000—10 000 Personen sprechen in Nordfriesland friesisch und schätzungsweise weitere 20 000 verstehen es. Die Inselfriesen bezeichnen ihre Sprache nicht als „friesisch", sondern nennen sie nach der jeweiligen Insel. Auf dem Festland wird dagegen die dialektale Variante des Grundbegriffs „Friesisch" verwandt. Um eine übergeordnete Bezeichnung einzuführen, die keine Einzelmundart bevorzugen sollte, wurde die künstliche Form „Friisk" geprägt.

Durch den Zuzug auswärtiger Arbeitskräfte etwa aus den Niederlanden auf die Inseln Nordstrand und Pellworm infolge der Sturmflut 1634 oder im Zuge des Baus der Süd-Nord-Eisenbahn Ende des 19. Jahrhunderts sind viele Fremde nach Nordfriesland gekommen, die auch ihre Spuren in der Sprachlandschaft hinterlassen haben. Seit dem Zweiten Weltkrieg sind in diesem Zusammenhang die Flüchtlinge aus dem Osten, der Ausbau der Nordseebäder und die militärischen Standorte von Bedeutung gewesen (Walker 1990, 409 f).

Das Jütische (Sønderjysk) wird südlich der Grenze von ca. 3000 Personen gesprochen. Eine Kompetenz im Jütischen ist in nationalpolitischer Hinsicht wertneutral und wird nur in der Familie oder Nachbarschaft erworben (Laur 1978).

Das Dänische (Rigsdansk) ist ein Hauptmerkmal der durch den ganzen Landesteil Schleswig verstreuten dänischen Minderheit und wird von ca. 50 000 Personen gesprochen. Für viele Mitglieder der dänischen Minderheit ist Dänisch eine Zweitsprache.

5. Soziolinguistische Lage

In Nordfriesland existieren fünf Sprachvarietäten nebeneinander: Die zwei Standardsprachen Hochdeutsch und Dänisch und die drei Nicht-Standardsprachen Friesisch, Niederdeutsch und Jütisch.

Das Hochdeutsche ist die Amtssprache. Das Friesische besteht aus neun z. T. stark abweichenden Hauptmundarten, deren Gebrauch weitgehend auf den familiären Bereich und die nähere Umgebung beschränkt ist. Friesisch gilt allgemein als eigenständige Sprache.

Neben seinen Funktionen als Erst- und Familiensprache ist das Niederdeutsche auch eine regionale Verkehrssprache, u. a. bei Sprechern unterschiedlicher friesischer Mundarten (Stellmacher 1981, 1987). Die Diskussion um den Status des Niederdeutschen als Sprache oder Dialekt hat im Zusammenhang mit der „Europäischen Charta für Regional- oder Minderheitensprachen" des Europarats an Aktualität gewonnen.

Das Jütische ist auf den familiären Bereich und nähere Umgebung beschränkt. Die Bezeichnung „Kartoffeldänisch" spiegelt das niedrige Ansehen des Jütischen wider.

Bei den drei Nicht-Standardsprachen läßt sich ein fortschreitender Sprachwechsel feststellen.

Der Mitte des 19. Jahrhunderts ausgebrochene deutsch-dänische Konflikt verhinderte die Entstehung einer eigenständigen friesischen Bewegung und führte im Zusammenhang mit den Volksabstimmungen des Jahres 1920 zu einer Teilung in „deutsch-" und „dänischgesinnte" Friesen. Diese besteht heute noch durch die Existenz zweier nordfriesischer Vereine: Der „Nordfriesische Verein" und die „Foriining for nationale Friiske" (Steensen 1986, 116 ff). Der Konflikt hat jedoch inzwischen stark nachgelassen.

Der „Nordfriesische Verein" sieht das Friesische eingebettet im deutschen Kulturkreis und faßt die Friesen als eine Volksgruppe auf. Die „Foriining for nationale Friiske" betrachtet die Friesen als ein eigenständiges Volk mit dem Status einer nationalen Minderheit, das enge Verbindungen zu Skandinavien unterhält. Diese Auseinandersetzung spiegelt sich z. B. in der friesischen Orthographie wider. Das Graphem ⟨å⟩ wird z. T. als „dänisches" Graphem abgelehnt und die Groß- bzw. Kleinschreibung von Substantiven richtet sich z. T. ebenfalls nach nationalpolitischen Gesichtspunkten.

Alle Personen in Nordfriesland, die nicht das Hochdeutsche als Muttersprache haben, sind mindestens zweisprachig. Dreisprachigkeit ist aber weitverbreitet und Viersprachigkeit kommt vor. Die frühere stabile Diglossie ist einer instabilen Diglossie gewichen, indem das Hochdeutsche verschiedene dem Friesischen vorbehaltene Domänen unterwandert hat. Im Gegenzug versucht das Friesische heute in hochsprachliche Domänen einzudringen. Bei der dänischen Minderheit scheint das Dänische eher eine Institutions- als eine Familiensprache zu sein (Pedersen 1991, 179 f).

6. Sprachpolitische Lage

Seit etwa Mitte der 70er Jahre erlebt das Friesische einen Aufschwung. 1987 brachte erstmals der Schleswig-Holsteinische Landtag einen Bericht über das Friesische heraus, der fortan einmal pro Legislaturperiode erscheinen soll. 1988 wurde ein „Gremium für Fragen der friesischen Bevölkerungsgruppe im Lande Schleswig-Holstein" beim Schleswig-Holsteinischen Landtag eingerichtet. Nach Aufnahme der Friesen 1990 in die neue Landesverfassung hat sich die finanzielle Förderung des Friesischen gebessert. Das Friesische dürfte als Minderheitssprache in die „Europäische Charta" des Europarates aufgenommen werden.

Friesisch wird in fast allen Schulen des Sprachgebietes unterrichtet. Im Schuljahr 1992/1993 erhielten 1071 Schüler Friesischunterricht an 33 Schulen, eine oder zwei Stunden wöchentlich. Seit August 1991 wird an zwei Kindergärten Friesisch angeboten. An der Universität Kiel und der Bildungswissenschaftlichen Hochschule Flensburg, Universität bestehen seit 1978 bzw. 1988 Lehrstühle für Friesisch (Walker 1993, 40 f).

In der Verwaltung gilt das Hochdeutsche als Amts- und Schriftsprache. Friesisch wird jedoch gelegentlich in mündlichen Verhandlungen (Sitzungen, Trauungen usw.) gebraucht.

Durch Straßen- und Hausnamen, Theater- und Chorauführungen, Friesenabende und die Einrichtung friesischer Kulturzentren ist das Friesische in der Öffentlichkeit vertreten. Eine Diskussion über die Einführung friesisch-hochdeutscher Ortsnamenschilder wurde durch die Überlegung erschwert, daß die Ortsnamenschilder in bestimmten Fällen viersprachig (hochdeutsch-friesisch-dänisch-niederdeutsch) sein sollten.

In den Medien ist Friesisch mit sporadischen Beiträgen in den örtlichen Zeitungen und Zeitschriften sowie in einigen privat herausgegebenen Blättern vertreten. Im Radio gibt es eine fünfminütige Sendung wöchentlich auf friesisch. Es werden gelegentlich friesische Gottesdienste geboten.

Die meisten friesischen Mundarten verfügen inzwischen über eine genormte Orthographie und Wörterbücher (Århammar 1990). Die schriftliche Beherrschung des Friesischen ist jedoch nur schwach verbreitet.

Das Jütische erfährt fast keine Unterstützung. Es erscheinen lediglich vereinzelte Zeitungsartikel und Schriften in einer inoffiziellen Orthographie. Eine Theatergruppe spielt jütische Stücke.

Die dänische Minderheit ist durch den Abgeordneten des „Südschleswigschen Wählerverbandes" (SSW) im Schleswig-Holsteinischen Landtag vertreten. Der Landtag legt seit 1986 einmal in der Legislaturperiode einen Bericht über die Arbeit der dänischen Minderheit vor.

Die dänische Minderheit hat ein vollständig ausgebautes Kindergarten- und Schulsystem (53 Schulen und 5.239 Schüler im Jahre 1991), einen eigenen Jugendverband, ein eigenes Bibliothekswesen und Gesundheitssystem sowie eine eigene Kirche und Zeitung (Dansk Generalsekretariat 1991). Eine finanzielle Förderung bekommt die dänische Minderheit sowohl aus Kiel als auch aus Dänemark.

7. Allgemeines kontaktlinguistisches Porträt

Das Friesische gehört der nordseegermanischen Sprachgruppe an und hat eine stark vereinfachte Flexionsmorphologie. Zu den augenfälligsten Merkmalen gehört der starke nordische Einschlag.

Das Jütische ist eine dänische Mundart und gehört somit zum Nordgermanischen. Einige Merkmale weisen ihm jedoch eine Brückenfunktion zwischen Nord- und Westgermanisch zu, z. B. der vorangestellte Artikel bei Substantiven (Nielsen 1959, 42).

Der jütische Einfluß ist am stärksten im Norden des friesischen Sprachgebietes sichtbar und nimmt in südlicher Richtung an Bedeutung ab. Dies kann mit einer Verdrängung durch das Niederdeutsche zusammenhängen (Åhammar 1966). Durch das Jütische beeinflußte Lautentwicklungen sind im Osten am stärksten vertreten und nehmen in westlicher Richtung ab (Hofmann 1956, 95 ff).

Mögliche jütische Interferenzen im Friesischen im phonetisch-phonologischen Bereich sind etwa in der Wiedingharde die Neutralisierung des Merkmals Stimmhaftigkeit bei den Phonemen /s/ und /z/ im An- und teilweise Inlaut und die Stützung des Phonembündels /sk/ < afr. sk in den Dörfern, in denen Jütisch noch gesprochen wird, z. B. Rodenäs *skäp* < afr. *skip* „Schiff", sonst auf dem Festland *schap* u. ä.

In der nordfriesischen Lexik gibt es 300—400 Wörter dänischen Ursprungs, von denen jeweils etwa 100 nur auf dem Festland oder auf den Inseln vorkommen. Diese können wiederum in ältere und neuere Lehnwörter und nach Sachgebiet eingeteilt werden. Beispiele für ältere Lehnwörter sind: (Gesellschaft und Brauch) *lii* „mieten", *jül* „Weihnachten", *bradlep* „Hochzeit"; (Haushalt) *doord* „Frühstück", *wiis* „sengen"; (Landwirtschaft) *lääs* „Fuder", *gris* „Ferkel" (Åhammar 1966, 310 f). Beispiele für jüngere Lehnwörter sind: *gääsling* < dän. *gjæsling* „Gänseküken", *harw* < dän. *harv* „Egge" (Löfstedt 1931, 210—214).

Weitere wichtige Felder der Entlehnung sind Orts-, Flur- und Personennamen, z. B. *Nebel*, *Niebüll*, *Nieblum* mit dem dänischen Ortsnamenelement *-bøl* < adän. *bøle* „Wohnstätte, Einzelhof".

In der jüngeren Zeit werden reichsdänische Lehnwörter über eine Verschriftlichung des Friesischen im Zuge des Sprachausbaus übernommen. Um eine Übermacht des Hochdeutschen bei der Bildung von Neologismen zu verhindern, werden Beispiele aus dem Dänischen herangezogen, z. B. *foriining* < dän. *forening* „Verein", *grünleede* < dän. *grundlægge* „gründen" (Åhammar 1988, 704).

Die Frage von friesischen Entlehnungen im Jütischen ist bislang kaum behandelt worden. Faltings hat neuerdings 30—35 Flurnamenelemente in den jütischen Mundarten gefunden, die wahrscheinlich friesischer Herkunft sind (Faltings 1993). Hofmann (1956, 103 f) zitiert Beispiele, die von einer friesischen Überlegenheit in der Viehzucht und Heugewinnung zu zeugen scheinen, aber Faltings (1983, 304 ff) kann nachweisen, daß selbst auf diesen Gebieten manches aus dem Dänischen entlehnt worden ist.

Als Übersichten dienen Åhammar (1990) für friesische Grammatiken, Lehrbücher usw., Joldrichsen (1988, 1990) für nordfriesisches Schrifttum (außer Sylt und Helgoland) und Nyberg (1987) für Jütisch.

8. Kritische Wertung

In der bisherigen Forschung des dänischen Einflusses überwiegt die historische Wortforschung (Åhammar 1992, 48—57). Wünschenswert wäre eine Ausdehnung dieses Gebietes auf die Suche nach friesischem Lehnwortgut im Jütischen, die vielleicht mehr über das Verhältnis zwischen diesen zwei Sprachen aussagen könnte.

Wichtig wäre auch ein gesamtsprachlicher Ansatz, der alle in Nordfriesland befindlichen sprachlichen Varietäten auf Gemeinsamkeiten auf den verschiedenen sprachlichen Ebenen hin untersucht, der zu der These der partiellen gemeinsamen Grundlage beitragen könnte (Walker 1990, 413 f). Dieser Ansatz könnte den traditionellen, eher einsprachig ausgerichteten Ansatz gut ergänzen.

9. Bibliographie (in Auswahl)

Åhammar, Nils (1966): „Nordische Lehnwörter und lexikalische Stützung im Nordfriesischen". In: *Nordfriesisches Jahrbuch*, N.F. 2, 302—316.

Åhammar, Nils (1988): „Zum lexikalischen Ausbau des Nordfriesischen vom 16. Jahrhundert bis zur Gegenwart." In: *Deutscher Wortschatz. Lexikologische Studien*, Munske, H. H./Polenz, P. v./Reichmann, O./Hildebrandt, R. (Eds.), Berlin/New York, 687—726.

Åhammar, Nils (1990): „At Nuurdfresk jister, daaling an maaren. Das Nordfriesische gestern (1978), heute (1989) und morgen (2000)". In: *Friesen heute*, Steensen, Th./Walker, A. (Eds.), Bräist/Bredstedt, 15—30.

Åhammar, Nils (1992): „Om danske låneord i nordfrisisk". In: *Ord & Sag 12*, 46—65.

Dansk Generalsekretariat (1991): *Südschleswig — der Landesteil und die dänische Volksgruppe*, [Flensburg].

Faltings, Volkert F. (1983): *Die Terminologie der älteren Weidewirtschaft auf den nordfriesischen Inseln Föhr und Amrum*, Bräist/Bredstedt.

Faltings, Volkert F. (1993): „Nordfriesische Elemente in der Toponymie südjütischer Dialekte". In: *Namn och Bygd 81*, 91—113.

Hofmann, Dietrich (1956): „Probleme der nordfriesischen Dialektforschung". In: *Zeitschrift für Mundartforschung 24*, 78—112.

Joldrichsen, Anke (1988, 1990): *Bibliographie des nordfriesischen Schrifttums von 1661 bis 1969*. I, II., Kiel/Amsterdam.

Laur, Wolfgang (1978): „Nationale Minderheiten und Sprachgruppen im deutsch-dänischen Grenzgebiet". In: *Language Problems and Language Planning 2*, 17—26.

Löfstedt, Ernst (1931): *Nordfriesische Dialektstudien. Die nordfriesische Mundart des Dorfes Ockholm und der Halligen II*, Lund.

Nielsen, Niels. Å. (1959): *De jyske Dialekter*, Kopenhagen.

Nyberg, Magda (1987): "Sønderjysk nördlich und südlich der Grenze". In: *Sprachkontaktforschung im deutsch-dänischen Grenzgebiet*, Flensburg/Apenrade, 6−27.

Pauseback, Paul-Heinz (1995): *Aufbruch in eine neue Welt*, Bräist/Bredstedt.

Pedersen, Karen M. (1991): "Intentions and Innovations in Minority Language Education". In: *European Lesser Used Languages in Primary Education*, Sikma, J./Gorter, D. (Eds.), Ljouwert/Leeuwarden, 179−188.

Präsident des Schleswig-Holsteinischen Landtages (Ed.) (1986): *Bericht zur Arbeit der Minderheiten*, Kiel.

Präsident des Schleswig-Holsteinischen Landtages (Ed.) (1987): *Bericht zur Sprache und Kultur des friesischen Bevölkerungsteils*, Kiel.

Präsidentin des Schleswig-Holsteinischen Landtages (Ed.) (1992): *Bericht zur Arbeit der Minderheiten und der friesischen Volksgruppe für die 12. Legislaturperiode (1988−1992)*, Kiel.

Sievers, Kai D. (1989): "Auswanderung aus Nordfriesland im 19. und 20. Jahrhundert". In: *Friesenkongreß auf Föhr, 12.-15. Mai 1988*, Kongreßbericht, Friesenrat (Ed.), Bräist/Bredstedt, 27−42.

Steensen, Thomas (1986): *Die friesische Bewegung in Nordfriesland im 19. und 20. Jahrhundert (1879−1945)*, Neumünster.

Stellmacher, Dieter (1981): *Niederdeutsch. Formen und Forschungen*, Tübingen.

Stellmacher, Dieter (1987): *Wer spricht Platt?* Zur Lage des Niederdeutschen heute, Leer.

Walker, Alastair G. H. (1990): "Nordfriesland als Sprachkontaktraum". In: *Germanistische Linguistik 101−103*, 407−426.

Walker, Alastair G. H. (1993): "An educational project promoting bilingualism and biculturalism in two North Frisian communities". In: *Bilingual education in Friesland*, Zondag, K. (Ed.), Ljouwert/Leeuwarden, 39−51.

Wilts, Ommo (1978): "Dänisch, Nordfriesisch, Hoch- und Niederdeutsch in Schleswig-Holstein". In: *Sprachkontakte im Nordseegebiet*, Ureland, P. S. (Ed.), Tübingen, 149−166.

Alastair Walker, Kiel (Deutschland)

220. Deutsch−Ostfriesisch

1. Geographie
2. Geschichte
3. Politik, Wirtschaft und allgemeine kulturelle Lage
4. Statistik
5. Soziolinguistische Lage
6. Sprachpolitische Lage
7. Interferenz
8. Zur Forschungslage
9. Bibliographie (in Auswahl)

1. Geographie

Das Saterland ist eine selbständige Gemeinde im äußersten Nordwesten des Landkreises Cloppenburg; es grenzt im Norden und Westen an die Landkreise Leer und Emsland. Die Gemeinde liegt ca. 30 km östlich der ostfriesischen Stadt Leer und umfaßt die drei Dörfer Strücklingen, Ramsloh und Scharrel mit den angrenzenden Bauerschaften. Die Ortschaften Sedelsberg und Neuscharrel können nicht mehr zum eigentlich Saterland gerechnet werden, da sich in diesen Dörfern kaum noch Friesischsprachige befinden. Das Saterland war bis zum Beginn des 19. Jahrhunderts dem allgemeinen Verkehr kaum zugänglich. Auf dem Landwege konnte man ins Saterland nur eindringen, wenn die das ganze Gebiet umschließenden Moore gefroren waren. Der Verkehr mit der Außenwelt fand hauptsächlich auf der Sater-Ems statt, die das auf einem 15 km langen und bis zu 4 km breiten Sandrücken gelegene Saterland von Süden nach Norden durchfließt und bei Barßel in die Leda mündet (→ Sprachenkarte M).

2. Geschichte

Man nimmt an, daß das Saterland in vorgeschichtlicher Zeit nur dünn besiedelt und infolge der abgeschlossenen Lage nur schwer bewohnbar war. Die friesische Landnahme im Saterland fällt in die Zeit zw. 1000 und 1500, als heftige Sturmfluten die friesische Nordseeküste wiederholt heimsuchten. Infolge dieser Naturkatastrophen begannen heimatlos gewordene Friesen, die vorwiegend aus dem Küstenraum des westlichen Ostfrieslands und des Groningerlandes stammten, sich in der das Saterland und einen großen Teil des Hümmlings umfassenden Tecklenburger Grafschaft Sögel (*Comitia Sygeltra*) niederzulassen. Im Saterland überlagerten sie die relativ kleine westfälische Bevölkerung und zwangen ihr ihre Sprache, eine emsfriesische Mundart des Altostfriesischen (Altostfr.), auf, deren heutige Form noch viel Ähnlichkeit mit den inzwischen ausgestorbenen friesischen Dialekten des Harlingerlandes und der Insel Wangerooge zeigt. Das Saterland war von 1400 bis 1800 dem Bistum Münster unterstellt. Im Jahre 1803 wurde das Saterland dem Großherzogtum Oldenburg einverleibt, und nach den Befreiungskriegen Oldenburg wieder zugesprochen. Im Zusammenhang mit dem 1933 erlassenen Vereinfachungsgesetz wurde auch in diesem Jahr die Oldenburgische Verwaltungsreform durchgeführt. Die Gemeinden Neuscharrel, Scharrel, Ramsloh und Strücklingen wurden aufgelöst; Neuscharrel, Scharrel und Ramsloh wurden zu einer neuen Gemeinde Saterland vereinigt, und Strücklingen wurde in die Gemeinde Barßel eingegliedert. Nach 1945 wurden die Gemeinden Neuscharrel, Scharrel, Ramsloh und Strücklingen wieder selbständig. Diese vier Gemeinden wurden 1974 wieder aufgelöst, und während sich Neuscharrel für den Anschluß an Friesoythe entschied, wurden die drei alten friesischsprachigen Gemeinden zur Gemeinde Saterland zusammengeschlossen. Die Gemeinde hat zur Zeit 10 000 Einwohner, von denen immer noch 1500 bis 2000 Ostfriesisch oder Saterfriesisch (Sfrs.), wie wir es im folgenden nennen werden, sprechen.

3. Politik, Wirtschaft und allgemeine kulturelle Lage

3.1. Politik

Obwohl die Saterfriesen zw. 1400 und 1430 politische Beziehungen zu Ostfriesland unterhielten und das Saterland im Mittelalter ausdrücklich unter den sieben friesischen Seelanden genannt wird, haben die Saterfriesen bereits im 15. Jahrhundert den Bischof von Münster als ihren Landesherrn anerkannt. Die heutige überwiegend katholische Bevölkerung ist politisch konservativ, und das bürgerlich-konservative Lager erfreut sich einer komfortablen Mehrheit.

3.2. Wirtschaft

Bis ins 19. Jahrhundert hinein arbeiteten die Saterfriesen fast ausschließlich als Bauern, Torfgräber, Handwerker und Schiffer. Im heutigen Saterland gibt es mehrere mittelständische Betriebe und zwei Großbetriebe, so daß mindestens ein Teil der nicht in der Landwirtschaft tätigen Bevölkerung innerhalb des Saterlandes Arbeit finden kann.

3.3. Kultur

Von einem friesischen Volksbewußtsein bei den Saterfriesen, wie wir es bei den West-, Ost- und Nordfriesen finden, kann keine Rede sein. Wenn ein Saterfriese von *do Fräizen* spricht, dann meint er die niederdeutsch sprechenden Ostfriesen, seine nächsten Nachbarn. Kulturelle Veranstaltungen im Saterland — plattdeutsches (nicht saterfriesisches!) Theater, Gesangvereine, Trachten- und Tanzgruppen — unterscheiden sich kaum von ähnlichen Vorstellungen in den umliegenden niederdeutschen (nd.) Gebieten. Erst in jüngster Zeit haben sich die Saterfriesen als Ostfriesen mit den Nord- und Westfriesen zusammengeschlossen, um sich gemeinsam auf europäischer Ebene für gesetzliche Maßnahmen zur Erhaltung und Pflege der friesischen Sprache und Kultur einzusetzen.

4. Statistik

Nach den wissenschaftlich durchgeführten statistischen Erhebungen von Kollmann (1891), Matuszak (1951) und Drees (1971) und den Schätzungen von Hoche (1800), Hettema/Posthumus (1836), Minssen (1846), Bröring (1897/1901) und Heuer (1913) schwankte die Sprecherzahl in den Jahren 1800 bis 1950 zw. 2000 und 3000. Heute darf man von einer aktiven Sprecherzahl von 1500 bis 2000 ausgehen, von denen fast alle ebenfalls das Nd. und das Hd. beherrschen. Diesen höchstens 2000 Sprachfriesen stehen ca. 8000 Einwohner der Gemeinde Saterland gegenüber, die Hd. und häufig auch noch Nd., aber kein Sfrs. sprechen.

5. Soziolinguistische Lage

5.1. Fremde Einflüsse

Um 1850 sprachen mindestens 85% der Bevölkerung des Saterlandes das Sfrs. Nd. und das damals im ländlichen nordwestdt. Raum als Umgangssprache immer noch verhältnismäßig seltene Hd. sprach man mit fremden Händlern und Kaufleuten, aber die Alltagssprache blieb Friesisch. Mit der Gründung der nahegelegenen Fehndörfer im Zusammenhang mit der Urbarmachung der umliegenden Moore und infolge des Zuzugs von annähernd 2000 Ostvertriebenen nach dem

Zweiten Weltkrieg siedelten sich immer mehr Fremde im Saterland an. Im Jahre 1950 war die sfrs. Sprecherzahl auf 50% gesunken und heute beträgt sie nicht mehr als 20% der Gesamtbevölkerung der Gemeinde.

5.2. Saterfriesisch als Haussprache

Die Erschließung des Gebietes und der Anschluß an das überregionale Verkehrsnetz machten Hd. und/oder Nd. in zunehmendem Maße zu Arbeitssprachen. Nur bei Landwirten und Handwerkern konkurriert das Nd. noch mit dem Sfrs. Sonst hat sich Hd. überall im Saterland als Arbeitssprache durchgesetzt.

5.3. Schulängste der Eltern

Es wird, rein statistisch gesehen, immer seltener, daß ein(e) friesischsprachige(r) Einwohner(in) des Saterlandes eine(n) Ehepartner(in) findet, der/die ebenfalls das Sfrs. als Muttersprache beherrscht, und selbst wenn eine solche Ehe zustande kommt, sprechen die Eheleute, wenn sie Eltern werden, aus Angst vor Schulproblemen meistens nur Hd. mit den Kindern. Wenn die Eltern nach der Einschulung der Kinder das Sfrs. nachträglich als Haussprache einführen wollen, dann müssen sie häufig erleben, daß die Kinder auf deutsch antworten und sich weigern, aktive sfrs. Sprachkenntnisse zu erwerben.

5.4. Saterfriesisch/niederdeutsch/hochdeutsche Mischehen

Wenn die nd. oder hd. sprechende Frau ins Haus kommt, so wird der Gatte gezwungen, mit ihr Hd. oder Nd. zu reden. Die evtl. im Hause wohnende Schwiegermutter mag Sfrs. mit der Schwiegertochter sprechen; sie antwortet auf nd. oder hd., also in einer Sprache, welche die Schwiegermutter ohne weiteres verstehen und sprechen kann, denn es ist leider besonders einfach, dem dreisprachigen (Sfrs., Nd., Hd.) Saterfriesen eine Sprache aufzuzwingen, die er ohnehin versteht und spricht. In den meisten Fällen lernt die fremde Schwiegertochter Sfrs. verstehen, aber die aus solchen Ehen stammenden Kinder haben als Muttersprache fast immer Hd.

6. Sprachpolitische Lage

Das Sfrs. ist nirgendwo im Saterland Arbeits-, Amts- oder Kirchensprache. Es wird sporadisch an den Schulen und in den Kindergärten in freiwilligen Arbeitsgemeinschaften unterrichtet, und es gibt einen Kursus Sfrs. als Fremdsprache an der Volkshochschule im Saterland. Es gibt keine Standard-Rechtschreibung, obwohl eine wissenschaftliche Lautschrift mit festen orthographischen Regeln entwickelt worden ist; sie wird in diesem Beitrag verwendet.

7. Interferenz

7.1. Phonetik und Phonologie

Das vokalische Phoneminventar des Sfrs. besteht aus acht (8) Kurzmonophthongen und dreizehn (13) Halblang- und Langmonophthongen, von denen die geschlossenen Halblangvokale [i.] (*Sliek* 'Schlick'; [u.] (*kuut* 'kurz'); [y.] (*Tüüt* 'Haarknoten') und die offenen Langvokale [ɔ:] (*moakje* 'machen') und [œ:] (*Gööte* 'Gosse, Rinne') in betonter Stellung in der deutschen Hochlautung nicht vorkommen. Von den sechzehn Diphthongen kommen nur [ai] (*Bail* 'Bügel'); [au] (*Hauk* 'Habicht') und [ɔʏ:] (*Moite* 'Mühe') im Dt. vor. Die Konsonanten g (im Sfrs. ein stimmhafter Reibelaut wie nordndl. g), anlautendes stimmhaftes s (sfrs. *säike* 'suchen', [w] (wie engl. w; sfrs. *leeuwe* 'glauben') und die Konsonantenverbindung [sx] (sfrs. *schäärp* 'scharf') sind dem Dt. fremd. Die vom Hd. stark abweichende Aussprache bietet dem Lernenden (und Lehrenden) erhebliche Schwierigkeiten.

7.2. Morphologie

Die Formen des bestimmten *Artikels* sind *die* (*dän*), *ju*, *dät*; *do* 'der, die das; die'. Lediglich das Maskulinum zeigt einen Akkusativ *dän*. Der unbestimmte Artikel lautet *en*. Eine seltene feminine Form *ne*, die vor Adj. vorkommt, ist wohl unter nd. Einfluß entstanden. Das sfrs. *Substantiv* bleibt im Sg. gewöhnlich unverändert. Die gebräuchlichste Pluralendung ist -e, Substantive auf -e bilden den Plural meistens auf -n: *die Wäänt,-e* 'der Junge,-n'; *ju Bloume,-n* 'die Blume,-n'. Das *Adjektiv* erhält die Endungen -e, -(e)n und -ø. Der Komparativ endet auf -e, der Superlativ auf -ste. Im Gegensatz zum Dt. zeigen viele einsilbige Adjektive keinen Umlaut, sondern eine Kürzung des Stammvokals im Komparativ und gelegentlich im Superlativ: *klouk, klokker, kloukste/klokste* 'klug, klüger, klügste'. Die *Personalpronomen* sind: *iek, mie* 'ich, mir/mich'; *du, die* 'du, dir/dich'; *hie, him* 'er, ihm/ihn'; *ju, hier* 'sie, ihr/sie'; *et* 'es'; *wie, uus* 'wir, uns'; *jie, jou* 'ihr, euch'; *jo/do, him/do* 'sie, ihnen/sie'. Neben *hie, him; ju, hier* und *jo, him* gibt es die unbetonten Formen *er, ne; ze, ze*. Das *Tempussystem* des Sfrs. unterscheidet sich nicht von dem des Dt. Im Gegensatz zum Dt. jedoch sind die für das Afrs. kennzeichnenden zwei Klassen der Verben auf *-e* (sfrs. *teeuwe*, afrs. *teva* 'warten') und *-je* (sfrs. *moakje/maakje*, afrs. *makia* 'machen') im Sfrs. erhalten. Jüngere Sprecher neigen dazu, allen schwachen Verben die Endung *-je* anzuhängen.

7.3. Interferenz

Das Sfrs. hat kaum Einfluß auf den dt. Sprachgebrauch des Saterfriesen. Für das Sfrs. sowie für das Nd. typische, ins Dt. übernommene syntaktische Konstruktionen (hd. *da weiß ich nichts von*/nd. *dor weet ik nix van*/sfrs. *deer weet iek niks fon*; hd. *paßt auf, Kinder, und geht nirgends bei*/nd. *paast up, Kinner, un gaht nargends bi*/sfrs. *paasjet ap, Bäidene, un gunget nargends bie*) sind der allgemeinen nd. Substratwirkung in der norddt. Umgangssprache und keinem spezifisch sfrs. Einfluß zuzuschreiben. Die meisten Einwohner des Saterlandes, ob friesischsprachig oder nicht, sprechen gutes Hd. Das Hd. beeinflußt das Sfrs. vor allem im lexikalischen Bereich. Alte sfrs. Wörter, die zum Grundwortschatz der ältesten Sprecher gehören, gehen bei den nach 1930 Geborenen allmählich verloren: dt. *Blüte* statt sfrs. *Blossem*; nd. *Slöätel* statt sfrs. *Kai, Koai*; dt. *Sarg*/nd. *Dodenkist(e)* statt sfrs. *Huusholt*; nd. *möie/mööie* statt sfrs. *würich*; dt. *Masern* statt sfrs. *Mezel*.

7.4. Grammatiken, Lehrbücher, Lexika

Da das Sfrs. keine Schriftsprache ist, gibt es keine präskriptiven Grammatiken. Die Wörterbücher, Grammatiken und Textsammlungen von Siebs (1893, 1901, 1934; veraltet, aber für die Sprachentwicklung wertvoll), Matuszak (1951), Kramer (1964, 1982, 1992) und Fort (1980, 1985, 1990) bieten eine Übersicht über die Grammatik des Sfrs. und die für die Kommunikation verhältnismäßig geringfügigen, aber doch auffallenden Unterschiede zw. den Mundarten von Ramsloh, Scharrel und Strücklingen/Utende.

8. Zur Forschungslage

Es gibt viele Arbeiten über das Saterland, aber nur wenige, die sich intensiv mit dessen Sprache beschäftigen. Das älteste sfrs. Wörterverzeichnis stammt aus M. Dettens *Reisebemerkungen* (1794). Ein Bild der früheren Isolation der Saterfriesen und ihrer Sprache liefert J. G. Hoche (1800). Der älteste uns überlieferte sfrs. Text (1812), eine Übersetzung des Gleichnisses vom verlorenen Sohn, 1987 von J. Möller im Osnabrücker Staatsarchiv entdeckt, wurde 1988 von M. C. Fort mit Kommentar herausgegeben. Eine bis auf einige Ausnahmen zuverlässige Wörterliste enthält N. Westendorps *Over de Saterlanders* (1820), eine Kurzbeschreibung des täglichen Lebens im Saterland. Die erste breit angelegte systematische Analyse des Sfrs. stammt von dem Theologen und Sprachwissenschaftler J. F. Minssen, der 1846 im Saterland forschte und zwischen 1847 und 1854 seine Ergebnisse veröffentlichte. Die übrigen lange verschollenen Aufzeichnungen aus Minssens Nachlaß wurden 1964 und 1970 von P. Kramer und der *Fryske Akademy* herausgegeben. Theodor Siebs (1862−1941), der bedeutendste Friesist seiner Zeit, behandelt die Phonologie und Morphologie des Sfrs. in seiner *Geschichte der friesischen Sprache* (2. Aufl., 1901) und in mehreren Aufsätzen zur sfrs. Volkskunde. Eher volkskundlich-kulturgeschichtlich als linguistisch wertvoll ist J. Brörings (1867−1948) *Das Saterland*, denn der in Damme (Oldbg.) geborene, aber im Saterland aufgewachsene Bröring besaß nur mittelmäßige sfrs. Sprachkenntnisse. Die erste systematische Untersuchung des sfrs. Wortschatzes nach J. F. Minssen lieferte H. Matuszak in einer Bonner Dissertation, in der er das Sfrs. mit den umliegenden Mundarten von Leer, Lorup (Emsland) und Friesoythe vergleicht. P. Kramer veröffentlichte 1964 die Textsammlung *Dät Ooldenhuus*, 1982 die Kurzgrammatik *Kute Seelter Sproakleere* und 1992 den ersten Band (A−F) seines *Näi Seelter Woudebouk*. M. C. Fort gab in Zusammenarbeit mit H. Dumstorf ein *Saterfriesisches Wörterbuch* (1980) heraus. Forts Textsammlungen *Saterfriesisches Volksleben* (1985) und *Saterfriesische Stimmen* (1990) bieten volkskundliche Texte mit dt. Übersetzung, eine Skizze der sfrs. Geschichte und einen ausführlichen Forschungsbericht mit Bibliographie.

9. Bibliographie (in Auswahl)

Bröring, Julius (1897−1901): *Das Saterland: Eine Darstellung von Land, Leben und Leuten in Wort und Bild.* 2. Teil, Oldenburg.

Drees, Jan (1973): „Anmerkungen zum Gebrauch der saterfriesischen Sprache im Jahre 1971." In: *Friesisches Jahrbuch*, 159−170.

Fort, Marron C. (1980): *Saterfriesisches Wörterbuch mit einer grammatischen Übersicht.* Unter Mitarbeit von Hermann Dumstorf, Hamburg.

Fort, Marron C. (1990): *Saterfriesische Stimmen,* Rhauderfehn.

Fort, Marron C. (1985): *Saterfriesisches Volksleben,* Rhauderfehn.

Fort, Marron C. (1988): „Die ferläddene Súun: der bisher älteste saterfriesische Text." In: *Jahrbuch für das Oldenburger Münsterland,* 25–33.

Fort, Marron C. (1990): „Nicolaas Westendorp: Over de Saterlanders." In: *Jahrbuch für das Oldenburger Münsterland,* 151–159.

Groustra, G. R. (1976): „Was geschieht in Seelterlound?" In: *Nordfriesland* 9, 180–182.

Hettema, M./Posthumus, R. R. (1974): *Onze Reis naar Sagelterland,* Franeker: 1836; Nachdr. Leer: Schuster, 1974.

Heuer, J. (1913): „Die Sprache des Saterlandes." In: *Heimatkunde des Herzogtums Oldenburg,* Oldenburgischer Landeslehrerverein (Ed.), Bremen, 469–477.

Hoche, Johann Gottfried (1800): *Reise durch Osnabrück und Niedermünster in das Saterland, Ostfriesland und Groningen,* Bremen.

Janssen, Hans (1937): *Die Gliederung der Mundarten Ostfrieslands und der angrenzenden Gebiete,* Marburg.

Kollmann, Paul (1891): „Der Umfang des friesischen Sprachgebietes im Großherzogtum Oldenburg." In: *Zeitschrift des Vereins für Volkskunde* 1, 377–403.

Kramer, Pyt (1964): *Dät Ooldenhuus.* Unter Mitarbeit von Hermann Janssen, Rhauderfehn.

Kramer, Pyt (1982): *Kute Seelter Sproakleere,* Rhauderfehn.

Kramer, Pyt (1992): *Näi Seelter Woudebouk,* Elst.

Matuszak, Hans (1951): „Die saterfriesischen Mundarten von Ramsloh, Scharrel und Strücklingen inmitten des niederdeutschen Sprachraums." Diss. Bonn.

M. D. (= Mauritz Detten), Professor (1798): „Reisebeschreibung über das Niederstift Münster im Jahre 1794." In: *Neues fortgesetztes Westphälisches Magazin* 4, 386–416.

Minssen, Johann Friedrich F. (1854): „Mittheilungen aus dem Saterlande." Friesisches Archiv, Bd. 2, 135–227.

Minssen, Johann Friedrich F. (1970): *Mitteilungen aus dem Saterlande,* Kramer, P. (Ed.), Leeuwarden: Fryske Akademy Bde. 2 (1965)/3.

Siebs, Theodor (1893): „Das Saterland: Ein Beitrag zur deutschen Volkskunde." In: *Zeitschrift des Vereins für Volkskunde* 3, Heft 3/4, 239–278; 373–410.

Siebs, Theodor (1901): „Geschichte der friesischen Sprache." In: *Grundriß der germanischen Philologie,* Paul, H. (Ed.) 2. Aufl. Straßburg, S. 1152–1464.

Siebs, Theodor (1934): „Zur friesischen Volkskunde des Saterl." In: *Volkskundliche Gaben,* Berlin/Leipzig.

Marron C. Fort, Oldenburg (Deutschland)

221. Deutsch–Sorbisch

1. Geographie und Herkunft
2. Geschichte
3. Politik, Wirtschaft und allgemeine kulturelle sowie religiöse Lage
4. Statistik und Ethnoprofile
5. Soziolinguistische Lage
6. Sprachpolitische Lage
7. Deutsch-sorbische Interferenz
8. Deutsch-sorbische Kontaktforschung
9. Bibliographie (in Auswahl)

1. Geographie und Herkunft

1.1. Sorbisch – in älterer, der Eigenbezeichnung *serbski* nicht entsprechender Benennung auch Wendisch – ist eine in der Lausitz gesprochene westslawische Sprache. Ihre Träger, die Sorben, sind die Nachfahren jener slawischen Stämme, die im 6./7. Jahrhundert nördlich des Lausitzer und des Erzgebirges das Land zwischen Bober und Queis im Osten und der Saale im Westen besiedelten. Die Grenze zwischen den sorbischen und den polabischen Stämmen im Norden verlief entlang der Pleiske, südlich von Frankfurt/Oder über Fürstenwalde nach Köpenick, von hier in Richtung Baruth–Dahme und schwenkte am Niederen Fläming entlang über Jüterbog – Zerbst – Burg in Höhe von Magdeburg zur Elbe. Während die ersten fränkischen Quellen nur von den Surbi (631) oder Sorabi (806) sprechen und diese an der mittleren Elbe bzw. im Saale-Elbe-Bereich lokalisieren (s. Kurze 1895, 61; 121), werden seit Mitte des 9. Jahrhunderts einzelne Stämme genannt, darunter die Milzener, Lusizer und Sprewanen an der Spree.

1.2. Die sorbischen Stämme hatten bereits früh Kontakt zum fränkischen Feudalstaat, unter dessen Botmäßigkeit sie gerieten. Als letzte wurden die Milzener 1003 durch Heinrich II. besiegt. Die andauernden Feldzüge der sorbischen Stämme hatten die Entwicklung ihrer Stammesorganisationen gehemmt. Sie haben aber zur ethnischen Integration geführt, sichtbar in der Übernahme des Stammesnamens Serby (lat. Surbi, Sorabi) auch durch die Lusizer und Milzener.

2. Geschichte

2.1. Die endgültige Unterwerfung der sorbischen Stämme leitete im 11. Jahrhundert die deutsche Herrschaft und Territorienbildung zwischen Saale und Bober/Queis ein. War bisher die Tributzahlung die überwiegende Form der Abhängigkeit, so begann nun die Herausbildung von feudalen Grundherrschaften. Einer dünnen deutschen Herrschaftsschicht stand im 11. Jahrhundert die fast ausschließlich slawische Landbevölkerung gegenüber. Ihr Anteil an der Gesamtbevölkerung betrug etwa neun Zehntel.

2.2. Seit der Mitte des 12. Jahrhunderts kam es zu einem starken Zuzug deutscher Bauern, Handwerker und Kaufleute in die wenig besiedelten sorbischen Gebiete. Doch auch slawische Bauern wurden in den Landesausbau einbezogen. Vom Umfang ihrer Teilnahme zeugt die große Zahl von sorbischen Ortsnamen, die durch ihre Wurzel auf Wald- und Brandrodung hinweisen. Der Zuzug deutscher Siedler, ihr wirtschaftliches Übergewicht sowie die missionierende Tätigkeit der im sorbischen Altsiedelland gegründeten Klöster, Bistümer und Kirchen führte alsbald zur Assimilation der sorbischen Bevölkerung. Sie war in den Territorien westlich der Elbe etwa um 1500 abgeschlossen, während in den östlichen Gebieten die sorbische Bevölkerung beträchtlich zunahm.

2.3. Einen entscheidenden Einfluß auf die Veränderung der ethnischen und sprachlichen Verhältnisse im Altsiedelgebiet der Sorben hatten die Städte. Die sorbische Bevölkerung war zwar prinzipiell bürgerrechtsfähig, ihrem Aufstiegswillen waren jedoch Schranken gesetzt. Die patrizische Oberschicht solcher Städte war bestrebt, zur Bewahrung ihrer Vormachtstellung die Zunahme des sorbischen Bürgeranteils und dessen sozialen Aufstieg abzuwehren. So erhöhte die Stadt Kamenz 1518 einseitig das von Sorben zu entrichtende Bürgerrechtsgeld um das Vierfache des für Deutsche üblichen. In die Ordnungen der Gilden und Zünfte wurden Bestimmungen aufgenommen, die die „Wenden" als Zunftgenossen ausschlossen und vom Zunftheischenden den Nachweis deutscher Geburt verlangten. „Wendisch", „Wende" wurde im Bewußtsein des deutschen Bürgertums zum Synonym für minderwertig, unehelich, asozial und – da sich die Sorben gegen Benachteiligung und Unterdrückung zur Wehr setzten – für halsstarrig, niedrig, betrügerisch.

2.4. Zu Beginn des 16. Jahrhunderts bildeten nur noch das Markgraftum Niederlausitz von der Queis im Osten bis über die Dahme im Westen sowie das Bautzener Land des oberlausitzer Markgraftums von der Neiße im Osten bis zur Großen Röder und Schwarzen Elster im Westen ein relativ geschlossenes sorbisches Sprachgebiet. In Resten hat sich ein sorbischer Bevölkerungsanteil zu jener Zeit noch im Elbtal (um Pirna und Meißen), zwischen Elbe und Mulde (um Eilenburg und Wurzen) sowie beiderseits der Elbe um Wittenberg erhalten (s. Brankatschk/Mětšk 1977, Karte).

Selbst in dem noch verbliebenen sorbischen Kerngebiet war die weitere Entwicklung des sorbischen Ethnos stark eingeschränkt. Es war in mehrere feudalstaatliche Territorien geteilt, in denen die Sorben – außer im Markgraftum Niederlausitz – jeweils eine Minderheit darstellten und auch weiterhin der Assimilation ausgesetzt waren. Der Dreißigjährige Krieg und seine Folgen bewirkten einen absoluten Rückgang der sorbischen Bevölkerung um annähernd 50% (s. Brankatschk/Mětšk 1977, 224). 1667 ordnete der brandenburgische Kurfürst die Konfiskation und Vernichtung jeglichen sorbischen Schrifttums, das Verbot der sorbischen Sprache in Kirche und Schule sowie die Ausweisung der sorbischen Geistlichen aus dem Wendischen Distrikt der Kurmark an (vgl. Mětšk 1965, 122 ff). Ein Jahr später folgte das Lübbener Oberkonsistorium mit einer ähnlichen Verordnung (s. Mětšk 1981, 42; 86). Ein in begrenzter Form sich bildendes sorbisches Bürgertum wirkte einer raschen Germanisierung entgegen. Bereits 1514 gründete der aus Sommerfeld stammende sorbische Humanist Jan Rak ein als Universitas Serborum bezeichnetes Gymnasium in Cottbus. Zur Zeit Luthers studierten allein an der Wittenberger Universität 40 junge Sorben, bis zum Ende des 16. Jahrhunderts weitere

147. Seit 1539 wurde an der Frankfurter Viadrina eine größere Zahl sorbischer Studenten ordiniert. Hier wurden, nachweislich bis 1656, über ein Jahrhundert lang sorbische Sprachübungen abgehalten. Von dieser Bürgerschicht getragen, begann sich mit und nach der Reformation ein sorbisches Schrifttum zu entwickeln. Bereits 1548 beendete Miklawš Jakubica die Übersetzung des Neuen Testaments. 1574 erschien das erste gedruckte sorbische Buch, die Übersetzung des Lutherischen Katechismus ins Niedersorbische von Albin Moller, 1595 folgte dessen Übersetzung ins Obersorbische von Wenzeslaus Warichius (s. Jenč 1954, 30 ff). Eine ausgeprägt germanisatorische Sprachenpolitik setzte erst mit der territorialen Neuordnung nach dem Wiener Kongreß ein, der den sorbischen Siedlungsraum auf Preußen und Sachsen aufteilte. Die Verbreitung der deutschen Sprache durch staatliche Maßnahmen − Verringerung oder Liquidierung des sorbischen Unterrichts (s. Kunze 1977, 119), Reduzierung des Gebrauchs des Sorbischen in der Kirche − führte zur Zweisprachigkeit der sorbischen Bevölkerung, die an der Schwelle zum 20. Jahrhundert im wesentlichen erreicht war. Gesetzliche Schutzbestimmungen der Weimarer Republik, von denen das Sorbische kaum profitieren konnte, wurden im NS-Staat aufgehoben. 1937/1938 wurden alle sorbischen kulturellen und wirtschaftlichen Vereinigungen, Organisationen und Institutionen aufgelöst, der Gebrauch des Sorbischen in der Öffentlichkeit verboten, aus dem Sorbischen stammende Ortsnamen durch deutsche ersetzt (→ Sprachenkarte M).

3. Politik, Wirtschaft und allgemeine kulturelle sowie religiöse Lage

3.1. Auch nach 1945 hielten sich die auf das Sorbische wirkenden Faktoren durchaus nicht die Waage. Unter den das Sorbische fördernden Umständen ist zu nennen:

(a) Die Schaffung rechtlicher Garantien für die Gleichstellung der Sorben durch das „Gesetz zur Wahrung der Rechte der sorbischen Bevölkerung". Dieses garantierte den Unterricht in sorbischer Sprache, die Gleichstellung des Sorbischen in der Öffentlichkeit, vor Gericht und in der Verwaltung, kulturelle Autonomie der Sorben durch die Bildung eines eigenen Kultur- und Volksbildungsamtes sowie die Pflege der sorbischen Kultur durch Bereitstellung von finanziellen Mitteln aus dem Staatshaushalt.
(b) Die Gründung von Institutionen zur Durchsetzung der politischen und kulturellen Interessen der Sorben. 1946 nahm ein sorbisches Lehrerbildungsinstitut seine Tätigkeit auf, dem folgte die Einrichtung der sorbischen Gymnasien in Bautzen (1947) und Cottbus (1951). Ebenfalls 1947 begannen mit der Herausgabe der sorbischen Zeitung *Nowa doba* und belletristischer Literatur ein sorbischer Verlag und eine Druckerei ihre Tätigkeit. In den 50er Jahren folgten weitere Gründungen von Institutionen zur Pflege der sorbischen Sprache und Kultur: des Instituts für sorbische Volksforschung in Bautzen und des Instituts für Sorabistik in Leipzig (1951), des sorbischen Volkstheaters (1948), des Staatlichen Ensembles für sorbische Volkskultur (1952), des Hauses für sorbische Laienkunst (1952), zweier sorbischer Sprachschulen für Erwachsenenqualifizierung und der Arbeitsstelle für sorbische Schulen. Seit 1948 werden auch Rundfunksendungen in sorbischer Sprache ausgestrahlt, gegenwärtig mit einer Sendezeit von 16 Wochenstunden.

3.2. Der Ausbau einer sorbischen kulturellen Infrastruktur konnte dennoch den weiteren Fortgang der Assimilation nicht aufhalten. Der massenhafte Zustrom deutscher Bevölkerung nach 1945 aus Schlesien, den Sudeten und aus Ungarn senkte den Anteil der Sorben an der Gesamtzahl der Bevölkerung in der Lausitz erheblich. Eine Folge davon war, daß die sorbische Sprache im Prinzip ihre Rolle als Kommunikationsmittel der örtlichen Gemeinschaft verlor. Außerdem stieg die Zahl der deutsch-sorbischen Mischehen, die in der Regel zum Sprachwechsel in der nächsten Generation führte. Der Ausbau insbesondere der Braunkohleindustrie bewirkt den weiteren Zugang deutscher Bevölkerung, die Devastierung sorbischer Dörfer und die Umsiedlung ihrer Bewohner in die Städte, was in den meisten Fällen ebenfalls zum Sprachwechsel führte. Die bäuerliche Bevölkerung, der wesentliche Träger der sorbischen Sprache, nahm durch die Bildung von landwirtschaftlichen Produktionsgenossenschaften merklich ab. Ihr Anteil war 1987 auf 13,9% gegenüber noch 40,7% im Jahre 1956 zurückgegangen (s. Förster 1991, 40 f). Die gemeinsame Arbeit mit deutschsprachigen Mitgliedern der Genossenschaft verdrängte die sorbische Sprache auch aus der Sphäre der landwirtschaftlichen Produktion.

Das öffentliche Leben ist fast ausschließlich deutschsprachig geprägt. Die Verwaltungsakte aller Dienststellen werden durch den Gebrauch der deutschen Sprache vermittelt, die Sendungen der elektronischen Medien vornehmlich in deutscher Sprache empfangen. Erst seit 1992 sendet der Ostdeutsche Rundfunk Brandenburg monatlich eine halbe Stunde ein Fernsehprogramm in sorbischer Sprache.

3.3. Die Mehrheit der sorbischen Bevölkerung ist — sofern kirchlich gebunden — evangelischer Konfession. Die landeskirchlichen Behörden waren insbesondere seit der politischen Neuordnung nach dem Wiener Kongreß entscheidende Stützen einer planmäßigen Germanisierung. Freiwerdende Pfarrstellen wurden nicht mehr mit sorbischen Geistlichen besetzt, der sorbische Gottesdienst durch einen deutsch-sorbischen abgelöst. Gegenwärtig sind von 56 Pfarrstellen evangelischer Kirchgemeinden mit sorbischem Bevölkerungsanteil nur 4, davon nur eine in der Niederlausitz, mit einem die sorbische Sprache beherrschenden Geistlichen besetzt.

Der Anteil der Sorben katholischer Konfession ist mit annähernd 20% an der Gesamtzahl der sorbischen Bevölkerung relativ gering. Die 9 katholischen Parochien bilden ein geschlossenes Areal im Dreieck zwischen den Städten Bautzen—Kamenz—Hoyerswerda. Hier hat sich durch die sprachfördernde Haltung der katholische Kirche das Sorbische bis in die Gegenwart fast ungefährdet erhalten. Gefördert durch das Bautzener Domkapitel, wurde die Priesterschaft, ohne Ausnahme Sorben, in Prag ausgebildet. Hier bestand bis 1927 das durch ein Legat der Brüder Šiman 1706 errichtete Lausitzer Seminar, das sich bald zu einer bedeutenden Pflegestätte der sorbischen Sprache und Kultur entwickelte (s. Jenč 1954, 193 ff).

4. Statistik und Ethnoprofile

4.1. Die ethnolinguistische Situation des Sorbischen ist vor allem bestimmt durch die absolute Zahl seiner Sprecher sowie durch deren quantitatives Verhältnis zu den Angehörigen der deutschen Sprachgemeinschaft. Statistisch gesicherte Angaben zur gegenwärtigen Zahl der Sorben bzw. der das Sorbische sprechenden Personen liegen nicht vor. Ältere Erhebungen widersprechen sich oft in ihrem Ergebnis. Eine neuere Hochrechnung läßt eine Zahl von annähernd 50 000 als Sorben sich bekennender bzw. von 70 000 die sorbische Sprache beherrschender Personen, das sind ca. 12% der Gesamtbevölkerung in den als deutsch-sorbisches Gebiet bezeichneten Kreisen, als der Wirklichkeit nahe erscheinen (s. Elle 1991, 24). Die Mehrheit bilden die Sorben nur in den Orten mit überwiegend katholischer Bevölkerung (s. 3.3.), in denen ihr Anteil bis zu 90% erreicht.

4.2. Seit dem Ausgang des vergangenen Jahrhunderts ist die sorbische Bevölkerung im wesentlichen zweisprachig. Die Beherrschung des Sorbischen ist unter der mitwohnenden deutschen Bevölkerung eine Ausnahme. Während der Sorbe die deutsche Sprache in allen Kommunikationssituationen benutzt, ist Sorbisch primär das Kommunikationsmittel in der Familie, in der Dorfgemeinschaft, schon weniger am Arbeitsplatz. Er bedient sich dabei seines sorbischen Ortsdialekts, die Kenntnis der schriftsprachlichen Norm ist passiv und im wesentlichen beschränkt auf die Fähigkeit, literatursprachliche Texte zu rezipieren. Die deutsche Schriftsprache dagegen beherrschen alle zweisprachigen Sorben in dem Maße, der der Bildungsstufe des einzelnen entspricht und der relativ wenige Interferenzen des Sorbischen aufweist (s. Michalk 1968, 21 ff).

5. Soziolinguistische Lage

5.1. Eine Besonderheit des Sorbischen ist dessen kleinräumige dialektale Differenzierung mit einer Kernlandschaft im Süden und einer solchen im Norden (s. Faßke 1968, 193 f) sowie die darauf beruhende, durch historische Umstände bedingte Existenz von zwei schriftsprachlichen Normen, dem Obersorbischen und dem Niedersorbischen. In einer schmalen Kontaktzone zwischen der Ober- und Niederlausitz überlappen sich die Geltungsbereiche beider. Hier sind auch diglossieähnliche Verhältnisse entstanden. Die Dialekte dieses Grenzraumes stehen der niedersorbischen Schriftsprache näher, liegen aber in der Oberlausitz, in der durch Kirche und Schule die obersorbische Schriftsprache gepflegt wird.

Standardisierungsgrad und Funktionsbreite der beiden sorbischen Schriftsprachen sind ungleich. Das Obersorbische ist aufgrund reicherer schriftsprachlicher Tradition und einer größeren Sprecherzahl sowohl strukturell gut ausgebaut als auch — obgleich in den Anwendungsbereichen eingeschränkt — polyfunktional. Der Gebrauch der sorbischen Schriftsprachen ist in allen Sphären begrenzt, er ist noch am häufigsten in der Sphäre der Bildung, er ist kaum üblich in der Verwaltung (vgl. Faßke 1982, 29 ff).

5.2. Die Zweisprachigkeit der Sorben und die Praxis zweier Sprachen in der Lausitz führten zu sowohl interlingualen als auch interethnischen Sprachkonflikten. Der interlinguale Konflikt besteht in der ungenügenden Kenntnis der schriftsprachlichen Norm des Sorbischen, die die Differenz zum Dialekt nicht überbrücken kann und dadurch das Verhältnis zur Schriftsprache belastet. In Dialekträumen mit größerer Distanz zur Schriftsprache führt dieser Konflikt selbst zur terminologischen Unterscheidung: Schriftsprache = Sorbisch, eigener Dialekt = Wendisch. Ein Ergebnis dieses Widerspruchs ist die Minderbewertung der eigenen Sprechweise und damit der Verzicht auf das Sorbische überhaupt. Diese Minderbewertung wird durch interethnische Sprachkonfliktssituationen noch verschärft. Die wechselseitige deutsch-sorbische Interferenz beeinflußt sowohl das Sorbische als auch das Deutsche im Munde des zweisprachigen Sorben. Nicht zuletzt auch dies ist die Quelle auch heute noch anzutreffender antisorbischer Haltungen, die sich in diskriminierenden Wertungen der sorbischen Sprache, im „guten Rat" zu ihrer Aufgabe, manchmal auch in der Abwehr ihres Gebrauchs, äußert.

6. Sprachpolitische Lage

6.1. Die staatliche Sprachenpolitik war in der Vergangenheit primär auf die Durchsetzung des Deutschen und die Zurückdrängung des Sorbischen ausgerichtet (s. 2.4.). Veränderungen traten nach dem Ende des Zweiten Weltkriegs und mit der Gründung der DDR ein. Diese setzte die mit dem sächsischen „Gesetz zur Wahrung der Rechte der sorbischen Bevölkerung" und der entsprechenden brandenburgischen Verordnung rechtlich fixierte Anerkennung des Sorbischen und dessen staatliche Förderung fort. Bereits mit Wiederaufnahme des Schulunterrichts im Herbst 1945 wurde, zunächst nur in der sächsischen Oberlausitz, in Schulen mit mehrheitlich sorbischen Kindern sorbischsprachiger Unterricht, in den übrigen Schulen Sorbisch als Unterrichtsfach eingeführt. Die Teilnahme am sorbischen Sprachunterricht war freiwillig, doch beteiligten sich an ihm nicht selten geschlossene Klassen. Im Schuljahr 1961/1962 betrug die am sorbischen Sprachunterricht teilnehmende Schülerzahl bereits knapp 11 800. Die ministerielle Anordnung zur Regelung der Schulverhältnisse im sorbischen Sprachgebiet vom April 1952 sanktionierte die bisherige Praxis, führte offiziell die Unterscheidung von A-Schulen (mit sorbischer Unterrichtssprache) und B-Schulen (mit sorbischem Sprachunterricht) ein, ließ jedoch Sorbisch als Unterrichtssprache uneingeschränkt nur in der Unterstufe zu. In den mathematisch-naturkundlichen Fächern sollte der Unterricht zunehmend in deutscher Sprache geführt werden. Die 7. Durchführungsbestimmung zum Schulgesetz der DDR vom April 1964, die den Sorbischunterricht weiter einschränkte und sachliche Entscheidungshilfen für die Elternschaft nicht zuließ, minderte die Zahl der Teilnehmer am sorbischen Sprachunterricht sprunghaft, sie fiel auf insgesamt 3 250 im Schuljahr 1964/1965. Erst nach korrigierter Neufassung dieser Bestimmungen 1968 stieg die Teilnehmerzahl allmählich auf 6 000 im Schuljahr 1988/1989, fiel jedoch wegen fehlender schulpolitischer Entscheidungen nach der Vereinigung erneut, so in den B-Schulen im Schuljahr 1990/1991 um 30% auf 3 300, im Schuljahr 1991/1992 auf 2 785.

6.2. Die sorbische Sprachpflege war auf die Überwindung der noch bestehenden graphischen, orthographischen und grammatischen Differenzen der beiden konfessionell gebundenen Gebrauchsweisen der obersorbischen Schriftsprache gerichtet. Zwar hatte die wissenschaftliche Gesellschaft Maćica Serbska im vergangenen Jahrhundert eine einheitliche Norm des Obersorbischen kodifiziert (s. Faßke 1984, 870 ff), doch benutzten evangelische und katholische Autoren weiterhin unterschiedliche (ortho)graphische Systeme. Seit 1945 ist die durch die Maćia Serbska gesetzte Norm verbindlich. Versuche, auch die ober- und niedersorbische Schriftsprache einander anzunähern, blieben erfolglos und wurden aufgegeben, nur wenige Kompromißvorschläge konnten sich durchsetzen: wortanlautendes kh im Obersorbischen wurde durch ch (os. *khory* > *chory* 'krank' wie ns. *chory*), prothetisches h im Niedersorbischen durch w (ns. *humyś* > *wumyś* 'abwaschen' wie os. *wumyć*) ersetzt. In ihrer Anfangsphase waren die Grundpositionen der bewußten sorbischen Sprachpflege und Sprachreform in Abwehr des Interferenzdrucks des Deutschen stark puristisch geprägt. Die Entwicklung von Lehrmaterialien, Grammatiken und Wörterbüchern sowie die relativ umfangreiche sorbischsprachige Buch- und Zeitschriftenproduktion (im Zeitraum 1948—1987 erschienen außer Zeitungen und Zeitschriften mehr als 2700 sorbische Bücher, vgl. Nowusch 1988, 125) haben zu einem hohen Standardisierungsgrad des Obersorbischen, weniger des Niedersorbischen geführt.

7. Deutsch-sorbische Interferenz

7.1. Der Einfluß des Deutschen auf das Sorbische ist durch den bereits 1000 Jahre währenden Kontakt natürlich. Mundart und Umgangssprache stehen diesem praktisch unbegrenzt offen, doch auch die Schriftsprache kann sich ihm nicht entziehen. Besonders das Lexikon ist davon betroffen, das in seinem Bestand eine große Zahl von Entlehnungen aus dem Deutschen enthält, darunter nicht wenige bereits aus dem Alt- bzw. Mittelhochdeutschen übernommene (s. Bielfeldt 1933, XXII ff). Das Niedersorbische ist zudem vom Niederdeutschen beeinflußt worden, wie *dupiś* 'taufen' < mnd. *dōpen*, *lidowaś* 'leiden' < mnd. *līden* u. a. belegen. Der größte Teil dieser älteren Entlehnungsschicht, auch der aus dem Frühneuhochdeutschen stammende (z. B. os. *hasa*/ns. *gasa* < nhd. *Gasse*, ns. *bom* < nhd. dial. *bōm*), hat auch Eingang in die Schriftsprache gefunden, während jüngere Entlehnungen aus dem Neuhochdeutschen, als solche leicht erkennbar, in die Schriftsprache meist nicht aufgenommen oder durch den Einfluß des Purismus aus ihr verdrängt wurden.

Auch in der Wortbildung ist Einfluß des Deutschen feststellbar. Er ist bezeugt durch die Spiegelübersetzung von Komposita des Typs *ryćer/kubło — Ritter/gut*, *doma/pytać — heim/suchen*, *smerć/chory — tod/krank* sowie durch Lehnprägungen, in denen ein deutsches Verbalpräfix durch ein bedeutungsnahes sorbisches Adverb ersetzt wird, vgl. *aufnehmen — horje brać*, *einfahren — nutř wozyć*, *herausnehmen — won brać* etc. Im grammatischen Bau des Sorbischen hat sich das Deutsche im Verlust des präpositionslosen Instrumentals (*z ruku dźěłać — mit der Hand abeiten*), in der Nachahmung deutscher Konstruktionen vom Typ *geschenkt kriegen/bekommen* zu sorb. *darjene krydnyć/dostać* (s. Lötzsch 1990, 360 ff) oder in der synthetischen Bildungsweise des Futurs perfektiver Verben mittels Futurformen des Hilfsverbs *być* (*ich werde aufschreiben — budu napisać* statt *napišu*) ausgewirkt. Im Lautstand des Sorbischen ist Einfluß des Deutschen weniger bemerkbar. Der Einfluß des Deutschen auf Satzstruktur und Wortfolge, Tempusgebrauch und Verbalaspekt ist selbst in der Literatur nachweisbar.

7.2. Der deutsch-sorbische Sprachkontakt hat auch im Deutschen seine Spuren hinterlassen, als Reliktwörter in obersächsisch-thüringischen Mundarten, von denen manche, wie *Grenze*, *Peitsche*, *Karausche*, *Preiselbeere* u. a. in der deutschen Hochsprache Geltung erlangt haben, in der stark vom Sorbischen geprägten Herausbildung des Deutschen in der Lausitz, dem Neulausitzischen (s. Bellmann 1961, 63). Die Wirkung des Sorbischen auf das Neulausitzische zeigt sich vor allem in der Aufhebung der Vokallängen, der weitgehenden Bewahrung der stimmhaften Qualität anlautender Lenes, der Lenisierung von Fortes vor Sonoren und in zahlreichen Lehnübersetzungen. Der deutsch-sorbischen sprachlichen Interferenz in beiden Richtungen sind Michalk/Protze (1967 und 1974) nachgegangen.

7.3. Die Masse der sorbischen Bevölkerung ist heute im Umgang mit der deutschen Sprache geübter als im schriftlichen Gebrauch des Sorbischen. Dies gilt in besonderem Maße für die Sorben der Niederlausitz. Im Niedersorbischen erscheinen lediglich eine Wochenzeitung und nur wenige Bücher. Günstiger liegen die Verhältnisse im Bereich des Obersorbischen. Hier erscheinen eine Tageszeitung (*Serbske Nowiny*), die kulturpolitische Monatsschrift *Rozhlad*, die kirchlichen Wochenblätter *Pomhaj Bóh* und *Katolski Posoł*, die pädagogische Fachzeitschrift *Serbska šula* sowie belletristische Literatur in größerer Zahl. Selbst wissenschaftliche und populärwissenschaftliche Sachprosa zur Sorabistik erscheint in obersorbischer Schriftsprache.

8. Deutsch-sorbische Kontaktforschung

8.1. Der deutsch-sorbische Sprachkontakt hat bisher wenig Aufmerksamkeit gefunden. Die meisten Forscher auf diesem Gebiet

(Bielfeldt 1933; v. Polenz 1963; Schönfeld 1963; Eichler 1965; Bellmann 1971) befassen sich mit den Folgen der deutsch-sorbischen Interferenz, die sich als Reliktwortgut im Deutschen bzw. als Lehnwörter im Sorbischen niedergeschlagen haben. Erst in neuerer Zeit sind Fragen aufgenommen worden, die das aktuelle Verhältnis von deutscher und sorbischer Sprache in der Lausitz sowie die Bedingungen, den Umfang und die Mechanismen der Beeinflussung des Sorbischen durch das Deutsche zu klären suchen. Michalk (1968, 102 f) wendet sich gegen die These von Ščerba (1926, 12), der zweisprachige Sorbe gebrauche nur *eine* Sprache in zwei verschiedenen Ausdrucksweisen ('une langue a deux modes d'expression') bzw. *eine* Sprache als Mischung zweier Systemteile ('langue mixte a deux termes'). Er weist dagegen nach, daß es eine solche Gleichung der Elemente und Strukturen beider Sprachen trotz wechselseitigen Transfers nicht gibt. Zum einen werden trotz intensiver wechselseitiger Beeinflussung nicht alle semantischen Merkmale sprachlicher Zeichen aufgehoben oder angeglichen (die Opposition *hić — chodźić* bleibt bewahrt, obgleich im Deutschen deren Bedeutungen allein durch *gehen* abgedeckt werden), zum anderen wird das System der Sprache A unter dem Einfluß der Sprache B zwar affiziert und umstrukturiert, doch das Ergebnis dieser Beeinflussung ist nicht die Identität der Systeme A und B. Die Kürzung der Langvokale im Neulausitzischen führt nicht zur Aufhebung der Quantitätsopposition. Die Länge wird lediglich zum fakultativen Merkmal: *ratən* = 1. 'Ratten', 2. 'Raten', *rātən* = 'Raten' (nicht 'Ratten'). Lötzsch (1991, 323) stellt als strukturelle Voraussetzung von Interferenz im Bereich der Morphologie die semantische Identifizierbarkeit von grammatischen Morphemen in kontaktierenden Sprachen heraus, wodurch Formen des Typs *budy napisać = werde aufschreiben, darjene dóstać = geschenkt bekommen, z ruku dźěłać = mit der Hand arbeiten* u. ä. erklärt werden können. Zur materiellen Entlehnung von grammatischen Morphemen, sowohl von Suffixen als auch von freien Morphemen, kommt es nur in Ausnahmefällen (vgl. *bity wordować — geschlagen werden*), doch auch dann ohne völlige Deckungsgleichheit: *wordować* 'werden' wird zur Futurbildung nicht gebraucht (*werde schreiben = budu pisać*, jedoch nicht *worduju pisać).

9. Bibliographie (in Auswahl)

Bellmann, Günter (1961): *Mundart und Umgangssprache in der Oberlausitz*, Marburg.

Bellmann, Günter (1971): *Slavotheutonica*, Berlin/New York.

Bielfeldt, Hans-Holm (1933): *Die deutschen Lehnwörter im Obersorbischen*, Leipzig.

Brankatschk, Jan/Mětšk, Frido (1977): *Geschichte der Sorben, Bd. 1, Von den Anfängen bis 1789*, Bautzen.

Eichler, Ernst (1965): *Etymologisches Wörterbuch der slawischen Elemente im Ostmitteldeutschen*, Bautzen.

Elle, Ludwig (1991): „Die Sorben in der Statistik". In: *Die Sorben in Deutschland*, Bautzen.

Faßke, Helmut (1968): "Serbski rěčny atlas a jeho problematika". In: *Beiträge zur sorbischen Sprachwissenschaft*, Bautzen.

Faßke, Helmut (1982): „Serbska spisowna rěč a komunikaciske sfery jeje wužiwanja". In: *Język literacki i jego warianty* (= Prace komisji słowianoznawstwa, 43), Breslau/Warschau/Krakau.

Faßke, Helmut (1984): „Zur Herausbildung einer einheitlichen Graphik und Orthographie des Obersorbischen im 19. Jahrhundert". In: *Zeitschrift für Slawistik XXIX*, 6, 870—876.

Förster, Frank (1979): „Die Berufstätigenstruktur des deutsch-sorbischen Gebiets von 1971". In: *Lětopis* (Jahresschrift des Instituts für sorbische Volksforschung), Reihe C, Nr. 22, 53—63.

Förster, Frank (1986): „Die Bevölkerungsstruktur des deutsch-sorbischen Gebiets von 1981". In: *Lětopis* (Jahresschrift des Instituts für sorbische Volksforschung), Reihe C, Nr. 29, 2—23.

Förster, Frank (1991): „Siedlungsgebiet, Kriterium und Struktur der Sorben ausgangs der 80er Jahre". In: *Lětopis* (Jahresschrift des Instituts für sorbische Volksforschung), Reihe C, Nr. 34, 36—42.

Jenč, Rudolf (1954): *Stawizny serbskeho pismowstwa*, Teil I, Bautzen.

Kunze, Peter (1977): *Die preußische Sorbenpolitik 1815—1847*, Bautzen.

Kurze, Friedrich (1895): *Monumenta Germaniae historia, scriptores rerum Germanicarum in usum scholarum*, Hannover.

Lehmann, Rudolf (1930): *Geschichte des Wendentums in der Niederlausitz bis 1815*, Langensalza.

Lötzsch, Ronald (1990): „Grammatische Interferenz und ihre historischen Voraussetzungen". In: *Sprache in der sozialen und kulturellen Entwicklung* (= Abhandlungen der Sächsischen Akademie der Wissenschaften zu Leipzig), Berlin.

Lötzsch, Ronald (1991): „Strukturelle Voraussetzungen für morphologische Interferenzen zwischen nicht nahverwandten Sprachen". In: *Zeitschrift für Phonetik, Sprachwissenschaft und Kommunikationsforschung* 44, Berlin.

Mětšk, Frido (1965): *Der Kurmärkisch-wendische Distrikt*, Bautzen.

Mětšk, Frido (1981): *Studien zur Geschichte sorbisch-deutscher Kulturbeziehungen*, Bautzen.

Michałk, Frido (1968): „Přinošk ke kwantifikaciji rěčneje interferency". In: *Beiträge zur sorbischen Sprachwissenschaft*, Bautzen.

Michalk, Siegfried/Protze, Helmut (1967): *Studien zur sprachlichen Interferenz, I, Deutsch-sorbische Dialekttexte aus Nochten, Kreis Weißwasser*, Bautzen.

Michalk, Siegfried/Protze, Helmut (1974): *Studien zur sprachlichen Interferenz, II, Deutsch-sorbische Dialekttexte aus Radibor, Kreis Bautzen*, Bautzen.

Nowusch, Hans (1988): *Die Gleichberechtigung der Bürger sorbischer Nationalität in der DDR — verwirklichtes Menschenrecht*, Bautzen.

v. Polenz, Peter (1963): „Slawische Lehnwörter im Thüringisch-Obersächsischen". In: *Deutsche Wortforschung in europäischen Bezügen*, Bd. 2, Gießen.

Schönfeld, Helmut (1963): *Slawische Lehnwörter in den deutschen Mundarten östlich der unteren Saale*, Berlin.

Schuster-Šewc, Heinz (1967): *Sorbische Sprachdenkmäler, 16.–18. Jahrhundert*, Bautzen.

Ščerba, Lev Vladimirovič (1926): „Sur la notion de mélange des langues". In: *Jafetičeskij sbornik IV*.

Helmut Faßke, Bautzen (Deutschland)

222. Österreich

1. Geographie und Demographie
2. Territorialgeschichte und Staatsbildung
3. Politik, Wirtschaft und allgemeine kulturelle sowie religiöse Lage
4. Statistik und Ethnoprofile
5. Soziolinguistische Lage
6. Sprachpolitische Lage
7. Sprachkontakte
8. Kritische Wertung der verwendeten Quellen und Literatur
9. Bibliographie (in Auswahl)

1. Geographie und Demographie

Österreich ist ein Kleinstaat in Mittteleuropa, hauptsächlich in den Ostalpen gelegen, im Nordosten in den Böhmerwald und im Osten in die Pannonische Tiefebene hineinreichend. Österreich liegt am Schnittpunkt der europäischen Hauptverkehrswege, linguistisch betrachtet darüber hinaus auch am Schnittpunkt der drei großen europäischen Sprachfamilien: selbst als deutschsprachiges Land zur germanischen Sprachfamilie gehörend, grenzt es im Süden an den romanischen, im Nordosten und Südosten an den slawischen Bereich und ferner noch im Osten an das (finno-ugrische) Ungarische. Es hat demnach außer deutschen auch italienische, rätoromanische, slowenische, ungarische, slowakische und tschechische Nachbarn. Österreich ist ein republikanischer Bundesstaat, bestehend aus 9 Bundesländern. Die zwei Kammern des Parlaments sind der Nationalrat mit 183 und der Bundesrat mit 63 Abgeordneten; das Staatsoberhaupt ist der direkt vom Volk gewählte Bundespräsident (→ Sprachenkarte N).

Österreich umfaßt 83 856 qkm mit (1991) 7,8 Mill. Einwohnern (davon 542 000 Ausländer). Die Österreicher sind zu 99% deutschsprachig, lediglich 80 384 Personen (mit österreichischer Staatsbürgerschaft) gaben bei der Volkzählung 1991 an, eine der Minderheitensprachen (Kroatisch, Slowenisch, Tschechisch, Ungarisch, Slowakisch oder Romanes) als Umgangssprache zu gebrauchen (genaue Zahlen s. 4). Die österreichische Bundeshauptstadt ist Wien mit über 1,5 Mill. Einwohnern; Wien ist gleichzeitig auch ein eigenes Bundesland. In ihrem Selbstverständnis sind die Österreicher trotz ihrer deutschen Sprache politisch gesehen keine Deutschen, sondern sie bilden eine Nation, die historisch aus der (negativen) Erfahrung des „Anschlusses" an Nazi-Deutschland von 1938 und der 1945 wiederhergestellten Eigenstaatlichkeit entstanden ist. Entscheidend war hier der Wille der Mehrheit der Österreicher, in einem unabhängigen Staat zu leben, daher repräsentieren sie eine „Willensnation" (Bruckmann 1989, 145), die als „eine mit dem Heimatgedanken eng verknüpfte, unkomplizierte, positive Staatsgesinnung, unterstützt durch politischen Realismus, erstarkt und (...) gefestigt" (Zöllner 1988, 96) zu betrachten ist. Historisch gesehen sind die deutschsprachigen Österreicher größtenteils Baiern, nur im Tiroler Lechtal und Vorarlberg Alemannen.

2. Territorialgeschichte und Staatsbildung

2.1. Österreich allgemein

In Stichworten sei die allgemeine österreichische Geschichte wie folgt skizziert. Zur Römerzeit gehörte der größte Teil des heutigen Österreich zur Provinz Noricum, bloß der äußerste Westen (Vorarlberg und Teile von Tirol) und Osten (Wiener Becken und Burgenland) war ein Teil der benachbarten Provinzen Raetien und Pannonien. In der Völkerwanderungszeit herrschten vorübergehend mehrere germanische Stämme über den ostalpinen Raum, ab 500 n.Chr. siedeln Alemannen im nördlichen Vorarlberg, während sich sonst noch die keltoromanische Bevölkerung halten kann, insbesondere im südlichen Vorarlberg und in Tirol (am längsten offensichtlich in Kals/Osttirol, bis ins 13. Jahrhundert), was durch zahlreiche Ortsnamen romanischer Herkunft unterstrichen wird (vgl. u. a. Finsterwalder 1990). Um 530 siedeln Baiern (Bajuwaren) im Alpenland, in Nordtirol und Salzburg und sind ab 650 auch in Südtirol anzutreffen. Im Osten herrschen ab 570 die Awaren und die von ihnen abhängigen slawischen Stämme (vgl. 2.1.). Demnach finden wir in diesen Gebieten Ortsnamen slawischer Herkunft (vgl. u. a. Kronsteiner 1973, 1974 u. 1976). Von Altbayern her langsame, zumeist friedliche Kolonisation und Christianisierung, im Kampf gegen die Awaren wird östlich der Enns die „Awarische Mark" (karolingische Ostmark) errichtet; dieses Gebiet wird später als „Bairische Ostmark" nach dem Zurückdrängen der Ungarn (955, erstmals urkundlich 972 genannt) wiedererrichtet; allerdings ist der Name „Ostmark" im deutschen Sprachgebiet jener Zeit nicht nachweisbar (vgl. Zöllner 1988, 15). 976 werden die Babenberger Markgrafen dieses Gebietes, das nun die Keimzelle Österreichs wird und bis heute in den Namen der beiden Bundesländer Ober- und Nieder*österreich* weiterlebt. Der Name *Österreich* wird als *Ostarrîchi* in einer Schenkungsurkunde, betreffend Besitztümer in Neuhofen an der Ybbs, datiert mit dem 1.11.996, zum ersten Mal urkundlich erwähnt. Diese Bezeichnung ist wörtlich mit „Ost-Reich" zu übersetzen, meinte aber den östlich gelegenen „Bereich" einer Herrschaft oder Landschaft (vgl. Zöllner 1988, 11). Der Name wurde vorwiegend im juridisch-administrativen Schrifttum verwendet, in der Dichtung wird der Name *Osterlant* bevorzugt.

Im gleichen Jahr (976) wird das Herzogtum Kärnten errichtet; sein Vorläufer war das karantanische Fürstentum, das im 8. Jahrhundert unter bairische Oberhoheit gekommen war, als Fürst Boruth, von den Awaren bedrängt, den Baiernherzog Odilo zu Hilfe rief. Der Slawenfürst hatte seinen Sitz an einem Ort namens *Carantum* (aus dem Kelt., „Fels", heute *Karnburg*) auf einer felsigen Terrasse am Fuße des *Mons Carantanus* (heute *Ulrichsberg*) am Rande des Zollfeldes, das als historische Kernlandschaft des heutigen Bundeslandes Kärnten zu betrachten ist. Beim Fürstenstein zu Karnburg fand die feierliche Herzogseinsetzung statt, die in den Quellen des 13./14. Jahrhunderts beschrieben wird, denen zufolge ein Edling (der „Herzogbauer"), nachdem er als Repräsentant des Volkes den neuen Fürsten „in windischer Rede" auf seine Eignung zum Herrscher und auf seinen christlichen Glauben geprüft hat, dem Herzog symbolisch die Herrschaft übertrug, indem er den Stein freigab. Die Herkunft dieser Zeremonie ist unklar, dennoch widerspiegelt sie die Integration des Kärntner Slowenentums, was auch in mehreren Ortsnamen rund um den Fürstenstein und Herzogstuhl zum Ausdruck kommt. Das Dorf, in dem der „Herzogbauer" seinen Wohnsitz hatte, heißt *Blasendorf*, slow. *Blažna* oder *Važnja ves*, d. i. „Dorf des *blag* (des Richters, Verwalters, Edlings"; vgl. Pohl 1991, 153 mit Lit.).

Österreich wird unter dem Babenberger Markgrafen Heinrich II. Jasomirgott im Jahre 1156 zum Herzogtum. Nach dem Aussterben der Babenberger bemächtigt sich Ottokar II. Přemysl, König von Böhmen, vorübergehend Österreichs (auch der Steiermark, Kärntens und Krains), doch 1282 erhalten die Habsburger Österreich und die Steiermark, 1335 Kärnten und Krain und 1363 Tirol; es entsteht das „Haus Österreich" (vgl. Zöllner 1988, 37ff). Dieser Territorialbegriff wurde nach und nach auf den ganzen habsburgischen Machtbereich ausgedehnt, nicht aber auf die Länder der ungarischen Krone, die die Habsburger 1516 erworben hatten. In der ersten Hälfte des 19. Jahrhunderts wurde allerdings der Habsburgische Gesamtstaat oft als „Österreichischer Kaiserstaat" oder „Österreichische Monarchie" genannt. Nach dem (unfreiwilligen) Ausscheiden Österreichs aus dem Deutschen Bund (1866) und dem „Ausgleich" mit Ungarn (1867) kam es zur Bildung der Österreichisch-Ungarischen Monarchie, einer Doppelmonarchie, welche aus dem Kaisertum Österreich und dem Königreich Ungarn bestand, zwei unabhängigen und gleichberechtigten Staaten, die durch die Person des Herrschers, durch gemeinsame Außenpolitik, Finanzverwaltung und Landesverteidigung miteinander jedoch eng verbunden waren und die den Ersten Weltkrieg nicht überleben sollten (vgl. 2.3.).

2.2. Die Slawen in Österreich

Die heutigen Kärntner Slowenen gehören zu den Einwohnern Österreichs mit der längsten Siedlungskontinuität. Sie sind die Nachkommen der „Alpenslawen", mit welchem Terminus die ältesten slawischen Bewohner Österreichs zu bezeichnen sind (vgl. Kronsteiner 1976, 5). Das frühmittelalterliche Österreich ist gekennzeichnet durch die Raumbegriffe *partes sclavanorum* und *partes baiovariorum*, dazu kommt im Süden noch eine *regio carantanorum vel sclavorum* (ebda. 7.), also das Gebiet des slawischen Stammes der Karantanen, als deren Herrscher die *Conversio Bagoariorum et Carantanorum* Boruth und dessen Sippe nennt (Wolfram 1979, 41 f, 73 ff, bes. 75 f). Das alte Karantanien umfaßte nicht bloß das heutige Kärnten, sondern ist im wesentlichen als Nachfolger der spätantiken Provinz Noricum Mediterraneum zu betrachten (etwa das heutige Kärnten, Osttirol und die Steiermark umfassend). Die Baiern selbst sind eine Stammesneubildung auf germanischer und keltoromanischer Grundlage im Zuge der Ausdehnung der fränkischen Herrschaft auf den Alpenraum.

Die frühmittelalterliche Zweiteilung Österreichs in ein bairisches und slawisches Gebiet besagt nicht, beide Teile wären geschlossene slawische bzw. bairische Siedlungsräume gewesen. Vielmehr war deren Gebiet mit Gruppen romanischer und romanisierter Restbevölkerung durchsetzt. Auf Grund der Toponymie läßt sich eindeutig zeigen, daß Baiern und Slawen keineswegs in menschenleere Räume eingedrungen sind, sondern daß Kontakte mit einer romanischen Vorbevölkerung stattgefunden haben. Nur so findet die Tatsache eine Erklärung, daß *vor*slawisches[-bairisches] Namengut bis heute weiterlebt.

Das im Frühmittelalter slawisch besiedelte Gebiet Österreichs umfaßte etwa das heutige Kärnten, Osttirol, den Salzburger Lungau sowie Niederösterreich mit Teilen von Oberösterreich und die Steiermark. Die Westgrenze verlief also ungefähr entlang des Alpenhauptkammes von Südosten nach Nordwesten und folgte im Alpenvorland der Enns, doch reichen slawische Siedlungen bis in Traunviertel und Salzkammergut hinein (Kronsteiner 1980).

Typisch alpenslawische Lautungen begegnen uns im ältesten Namenmaterial, z. B. Bewahrung der (sonst „westslaw.") *dl*-Gruppen, z. B. ON *Matschiedl* (slow. *Močidlo*) im Gailtal (so noch heute mundartlich), aber slow. *Selo* „Zell" (bei Ebenthal), *Sele* „Zell (Pfarre)" (urslaw. **sedlo* „Dorf"), oder alpenslaw. **k̑* für urslaw. **tj*, slow. *č*, z. B. ON *Radweg* (aus **Radovike*) slow. *Radoviče* (vgl. Pohl 1982, 7 u. 9; Ramovš 1924, 194 u. 266 f). Mitunter lassen sich im Namenmaterial auch dialektale Besonderheiten im Alpenslawischen bzw. Frühslowenischen ausmachen wie z. B. das Fehlen der *j*-Prothese in Osttirol und Oberkärnten (ON *Arnig* und *Amlach*, BN *Auernig* zu slaw. *(j)avor* „Ahorn", *(j)ama* „Grube") oder Wiedergabe des slaw. Suffixes *išče* in Oberkärnten und Osttirol als *schk*/*sk* (z. B. ON *Trasischk* aus **stražišče* „Wachtturm", *Plasischk* u. *Plasisk* aus **plazišče* zu *plaz* „Lawine"), in Unterkärnten aber als *st* (älter *št*, z. B. ON *Gassarest* aus **kozarišče* „Ort der Ziegenhirten").

Im gemischtsprachigen Gebiet Kärntens läßt sich aus der Lautgestalt der entlehnten Ortsnamen oft die ungefähre Zeit der Übernahme aus dem Slowenischen ins Deutsche und umgekehrt feststellen: z. B. zeigt *Reifnitz* die deutsche Diphthongierung, muß also vor 1300 entlehnt sein im Gegensatz zum jüngeren *Ribnitza* (beide aus slow. *Ribnica* „Fischbach"), oder slow. *Pliberk* „Bleiburg" muß noch vor 1300 aus dt. *Pliburch* (so urkundl. 1128) entlehnt worden sein im Gegensatz zum jüngeren *Slovenji Plajberg* „Windisch Bleiberg" (weitere Beispiele mit Lit. vgl. Pohl 1992a, 7−9 u. 31).

2.3. Der Zerfall der Österreichisch-Ungarischen Monarchie

Die Umstände, die zum Untergang der Doppelmonarchie geführt haben, sind allgemein bekannt. Die historischen Länder des Vielvölkerstaates stimmten vielfach mit den Siedlungsgebieten seiner Nationalitäten nicht überein, was in polyethnischen Gebieten zu Spannungen und ungelösten administrativen Problemen und letztlich zu einer vom Nationalitätenkampf beherrschten politischen Dauerkrise führte (1894−1914, vgl. Zöllner 1974, 427 ff). Die Donaumonarchie hatte zuletzt (1910) insgesamt ca. 51,4 Mill. Einwohner, die Reichshaupt- und Residenzstadt Wien etwas über 2 Mill. Einwohner (und erreichte um 1916 mit 2,24 Mill. ihren Höchststand). In der österreichischen Reichshälfte stellten die Deutschen mit 35,6% und in der ungarischen Reichshälfte die Magyaren mit 48,1% nur die relative Mehrheit. Die stärksten Nationalitäten in Österreich waren neben den Deutschen die Tschechen mit 23%, Polen mit 17,8%, Ruthenen (Ukrainer) mit 12,6% und Slowenen mit 4,5%, in Ungarn neben den Magyaren die „Serbo-Kroaten" und Rumänen mit je 14,1%, Deutschen mit 9,8% und Slowaken mit 9,4%. Die Hauptstadt Wien war jedoch ganz überwiegend deutschsprachig, was von ihrer großen assimilatorischen Kraft zeugt, obwohl zwei Drittel der Zuwanderer aus tschechischen Bezirken stammten (Zöllner 1974, 443 f); man schätzt, daß 1910 in Wien 100 000 – 500 000 Personen Tschechen waren (s. 3.3.).

Am 28. Oktober 1918 wird in Prag die unabhängige ČSR (Tschechoslowakische Republik) proklamiert, am 29. Oktober erklärt der Agramer Nationalrat der Serben, Kroaten und Slowenen das staatsrechtliche Verhältnis der südslawischen Gebiete zur Monarchie für gelöst (er schließt sich am 1.12. mit dem Königreich Serbien und Montenegro zum SHS-Königreich zusammen) und am 16.11.1918 wird die Ungarische Republik (vorübergehend) ausgerufen, aber schon am 17.10. hatten die Ungarn als Reaktion auf das Kaiserliche Manifest an die Völker der Monarchie, das die Umgestaltung der österreichischen Reichshälfte in einen föderativen Staat vorsah, ihre Selbständigkeit erklärt. Somit war Österreich-Ungarn zerfallen, der deutschösterreichische Reststaat bestand zunächst aus 7 historischen Ländern und war hinsichtlich seiner definitiven Grenzen ein Produkt der Willkür der Sieger (vgl. Zöllner 1974, 493).

2.4. Die Entstehung der Republik Österreich

Am 12. November 1918 proklamierte die provisorische Nationalversammlung die Republik Deutschösterreich, an die sich auch diejenigen deutschen Gebiete anschließen wollten, die außerhalb der 7 historischen Länder, die dann die Erste Republik bilden sollten, lagen. Schließlich verblieben bei Österreich die Länder Nieder- und Oberösterreich, die Steiermark, Salzburg, Tirol, Kärnten (vgl. 2.5.1.) und – losgelöst von der Innsbrucker Statthalterei – Vorarlberg. Allerdings haben manche von ihnen Teile ihres Gebietes an die Nachfolge- bzw. Siegerstaaten abtreten müssen, v. a. Südtirol und die Südsteiermark. Als 8. Bundesland wurde 1920 auf Grund der neuen Verfassung Wien vorgesehen (vollzogen erst 1922); zum 9. Bundesland wurde das Burgenland (ursprünglich zu Ungarn gehörig, vgl. 2.5.2.). Die provisorische Nationalversammlung hatte zwar (gleichzeitig mit der Ausrufung der Republik) einstimmig den Anschluß an das Deutsche Reich verkündet, doch wurde dieser im Artikel 88 des Friedensvertrages von St. Germain verboten (vgl. Zöllner 1974, 499). Durch die Volksabstimmung vom 10. Oktober 1920 blieb das südliche Kärnten bei Österreich.

Die österreichischen Minderheiten – sie sind im Friedensvertrag in den Artikeln 62 f, 66–88 ausdrücklich erwähnt – sind ein Erbe aus der Österreichisch-Ungarischen Monarchie. Sie genießen seit den Anfängen der Republik Österreich einen gesetzlich festgelegten Volksgruppenschutz (vgl. Fischer 1980, 241 f sowie Veiter 1970). Auf Grund der Volkszählung von 1923 lebten in Österreich damals rund 50 000 Tschechen, 35 000 Slowenen, 43 000 Kroaten, 12 000 Ungarn sowie 1500 Slowaken.

2.5. Die besondere Entwicklung in Kärnten und im Burgenland

2.5.1. Kärnten

Die Geschichte der Kärntner Slowenen beginnt Ende des 6. Jahrhunderts mit dem Vordringen der Alpenslawen in die Ostalpen und im 8. Jahrhundert mit der Gründung des alpenslawischen Fürstentums Karantanien (vgl. 2.1. u. 2.2.). Seit Beginn der Landesgeschichte kommt es in Kärnten (seit 976 Herzogtum) zu einer Durchmischung der Bevölkerung. Es ist das österreichische Bundesland mit der längsten historischen Tradition; ein Teil seiner Einwohner, nämlich die Kärntner Slowenen, können auf die längste Siedlungskontinuität im Lande zurückblicken. Die Einbeziehung des Landes in das Frankenreich, später Ostfränkisches Reich, bedeutete das Einströmen von deutschen Siedlern und es wurde der Grundstein für den ethnischen und sprachlichen Dualismus gelegt, der bis heute anhält und zu einer Verflechtung beider Sprachvölker und deren Kulturen geführt hat. Die historische deutsch-slowenische Sprachgrenze des 19. Jahrhunderts dürfte bereits seit Ende des Mittelalters bestanden haben. Bis ins 19. Jahrhundert spielte jedoch die ethnische Zugehörigkeit nur eine untergeordnete Rolle. Erst der aufkeimende Nationalismus des 19. Jahrhunderts führte zu einem politischen und nationalen Erwachen der Völker und somit zu einem gemeinsamen Bewußtsein aller Slowenen, das sich u. a. in der Forderung niederschlug, alle slowenischen Länder Österreichs administrativ zu einem eigenen Kronland zusammenzufassen, was allerdings eine Teilung Kärntens entlang der Sprachgrenze bedeutet hätte (und überhaupt eine Zerstückelung der historisch gewachsenen Länder), wogegen sich auch führende Kärntner Slowenen aussprachen (z. B. der Abgeordnete zum Kärntner Landtag Dr. M. Rulitz, vgl. Wadl 1990, 12 u. Bogataj 1989, 51 f). Auch bezüglich des Schulwesens herrschte im 19. Jahrhundert unter den Kärntner Slowenen keine Übereinstimmung: ein Teil befürwortete Schulen mit slowenischer Unterrichtssprache, die seit 1855 in kirchlichen Händen lagen; aber schon 1869 wurde das Schulwesen im Rahmen der Gemeindeselbstverwaltung neu organisiert, wodurch insbesondere die sogenannte *utraquistische* Schule zum Zug kam, die die Beherrschung der deutschen Sprache förderte, was durchaus dem Wunsche der Mehrheit der Eltern entsprach (vgl. Wadl 1990, 13 u. 16 sowie die Monographie Kurz 1990). Es bildeten sich also Ende des 19. Jahrhunderts zwei Lager unter den Kärntner Slowenen heraus, ein (minoritäres) nationales und ein (majoritäres) deutschfreundliches, was dann für den Ausgang der Volksabstimmung vom 10. 10. 1920 entscheidend war.

Nach dem Zusammenbruch der Österreichisch-Ungarischen Monarchie und dem Entstehen neuer Staaten stellte sich das Problem der Grenzziehung zwischen Österreich und dem SHS-Staat (ab 1929 „Jugoslawien"). Der slowenische Nationalrat in Laibach reklamierte das gesamte slowenische Gebiet Kärntens für den neuen Staat, wogegen seitens der Bevölkerung bewaffneter Widerstand geleistet wurde. Nach dem „Abwehrkampf" (1918—1919) und zähen diplomatischen Verhandlungen wurde in den Friedensverträgen für das umstrittene Gebiet eine Abstimmung festgelegt. In diesem Gebiet (es umfaßt rund ⅔ des historischen Siedlungsgebietes der Kärntner Slowenen) hatten bei der Volkszählung von 1910 68,6% Slowenisch als Umgangssprache angegeben; trotzdem sprachen sich 59% bei der Volksabstimmung am 10. Oktober 1920 für Österreich aus. Es müssen also außer den 31,4% Deutschsprachigen auch 27,6% Slowenischsprachige (das sind ca. 40% aller stimmberechtigten Kärntner Slowenen) für Österreich gestimmt haben, was auf eine politische Spaltung innerhalb der Kärntner Slowenen hinweist und reichen Konfliktstoff bis in die Gegenwart liefert. Übrigens haben auch einige Hundert Personen, die 1910 Deutsch als Umgangssprache angegeben haben, für Jugoslawien gestimmt (Zahlen bei Wadl 1990, 178 f). Alles zusammen zeigt, daß aus den Daten zur *Umgangssprache* keine genauen Angaben zur *ethnischen Zugehörigkeit* zu gewinnen sind.

Nach der Volksabstimmung von 1920 wurde die Kluft zwischen denen, die für Österreich gestimmt haben, und denen, die dem SHS-Königreich ihre Stimme gaben, größer, also zwischen „Nationalslowenen" und „deutsch orientierten Slowenen (oder Windischen)". Letztere — von den Nationalslowenen als „Abtrünnige", „traurige, in jeder Hinsicht demoralisierte Renegatenfiguren" (vgl. Wutte 1927, 1) diskreditiert — lehnten sich politisch noch mehr als zuvor an die deutschen Parteien an und wurden von diesen als „heimattreue Slowenen" bzw. „Windische" vereinnahmt. Das politische Klima in Kärnten war von 1920 bis 1938 in nationaler Hinsicht sehr gespannt, was sich u. a. dadurch manifestierte, daß die Nationalslowenen auf kein Verständnis für ihre Haltung stießen und ein besonderes Statut für kulturelle Autonomie nicht zustandekam, u. a. auch deshalb, weil jedes Zugeständnis gegenüber den Slowenen in Österreich auch (auf Grund des Prinzips der Reziprozität) Zugeständnisse für die Deutschen in Jugoslawien nach sich hätte ziehen müssen, woran man in Jugoslawien kaum interessiert war (vgl. Einspieler 1980, 32).

Nach der Okkupation Österreichs und dem „Anschluß" ans Deutsche Reich verhielt sich das NS-Regime zunächst zwiespältig den Kärntner Slowenen gegenüber: einerseits wurde (wohl aus Rücksicht auf die deutsche Minderheit in Jugoslawien, zu dem man an guten Beziehungen interessiert war) Wohlwollen demonstriert, andererseits wurden Schritt für Schritt kontinuierlich die nationalen Entfaltungsmöglichkeiten eingeschränkt (z. B. Einschränkung des Schulunterrichts in slowenischer Sprache, Versetzung von Slowenen in rein deutsche Gebiete außerhalb Kärntens usw.). Im Stillen wurden aber bereits Richtlinien für die Germanisierung der Slowenen vorbereitet, die dann nach dem Überfall Hitlers auf Jugoslawien (1941) im gesamten slowenischen Siedlungsgebiet, soweit es unter deutschem Zugriff war, brutal exekutiert wurden (vgl. v. a. Bogataj 1989, 79 ff). Für Kärnten bedeutete dies die Aussiedlung von über 1000 Personen, was auch bei der deutschen Bevölkerung und der Wehrmacht Bestürzung hervorrief (vgl. Walzl 1991). Diese Aktionen trugen aber wesentlich dazu bei, daß sich ein bewaffneter Widerstand der Kärntner Slowenen gegen die NS-Machthaber in Verbindung mit Partisanengruppen in Krain und der Südsteiermark formierte, der seinerseits wieder Repressalien der deutschen Truppen (v. a. der SS) nach sich zog.

Auch nach 1945 war das Verhältnis zwischen Mehrheits- und Minderheitsbevölkerung weiter gespannt. Jugoslawischen Gebietsansprüchen steuerte man mit einem relativ großzügigen Schulwesen (mit obligatem Deutsch- *und* Slowenischunterricht im ganzen gemischtsprachigen Gebiet) entgegen; doch noch 1947 forderte Jugoslawien die Abtretung „Südkärntens", ein Wunsch, der letztlich durch den Bruch zwischen Tito und Stalin unerfüllbar geworden war und zuletzt durch den Staatsvertrag von 1955 jede Grundlage verlor. Die darin verbrieften Rechte für die Kärntner Slowenen wurden allerdings nur sehr zögerlich verwirklicht (→ Art. 223). Doch die neu entstandene Lage nach dem Sturz der kommunistischen Herrschaft und der Unabhängigkeitserklärung Sloweniens 1991 hat bereits eine neue Qualität in den Beziehungen zwischen den Volksgruppen in Kärnten eingeleitet.

2.5.2. Burgenland

Das Burgenland ist das jüngste österreichische Bundesland, im Rahmen der Österreichisch-Ungarischen Monarchie war es ein Teil von Ungarn. Sein Name wurde nach den vier westungarischen Komitaten *Wieselburg* (Moson), *Ödenburg* (Sopron), *Eisenburg* (Vas) und *Preßburg* (ungar. Pozsony bzw. slowak. Bratislava) gebildet. Das Komitat Preßburg war übrigens zur Gänze der neugegründeten ČSR zugesprochen worden; keine einzige Komitatshauptstadt liegt auf heute österreichischem Gebiet. Zur Hauptstadt wurde Eisenstadt (ungar. *Kismarton*, kroat. *Željezno*) auf Grund eines Entscheides der burgenländischen Bürgermeister erklärt.

Nach dem Zusammenbruch Österreich-Ungarns wurde in Mattersburg am 7.12.1918 eine „Republik Heinzenland" ausgerufen, die seitens des ungarischen Militärs unterdrückt wurde. Allerdings vertrat die österreichische Friedensdelegation in St. Germain die Ansprüche auf das überwiegend deutschsprachige „Deutschwestungarn" mit Erfolg, so daß schließlich das gesamte Gebiet (inklusive Ödenburg) Österreich in den Friedensverträgen von St. Germain und Trianon zugesprochen wurde. Die Abtretung des Gebietes hätte gleichzeitig mit der Ratifizierung des ungarischen Friedensvertrages erfolgen sollen, die jedoch durch innenpolitische Wirren hinausgeschoben wurde. Aber auch ungarische Freischärler widersetzten sich den Verträgen. Durch italienische Vermittlung wurde entgegen den Friedensverträgen für Ödenburg und Umgebung − dem einzigen Gebiet mit einem stärkeren ungarischen Bevölkerungsanteil − eine Volksabstimmung festgelegt, durch die dieses Gebiet an Ungarn fiel; das übrige Burgenland kam dann endgültig (als 9. Bundesland) im Jahr 1921 zu Österreich (vgl. Zöllner 1974, 496−498).

Die deutsche Besiedlung des heutigen Burgenlandes begann ab 1076 unter Kaiser Heinrich IV. (1056−1106), Ungarn wurden ab dem 12. Jahrhundert als Grenzwächter angesiedelt; doch als Folge der Änderung der Wehrverfassung und der Errichtung starker Grenzburgen wurden diese Ungarn größtenteils absorbiert, einige Inseln blieben aber bestehen wie die 1327 wiedererrichtete „Wart" der ungarischen Grenzwächter zwischen den Burgen Bernstein und Güssing sowie die mittelburgenländischen Orte Ober-, Mittel- und Unterpullendorf sowie Großmutschen. In Ober- und Mittelpullendorf konnte sich das ungarische Element bis heute halten.

Zu einer gravierenden Veränderung der Bevölkerungsverhältnisse des heutigen Burgenlandes kam es, als die Türken nach Ungarn und weiter bis Wien (1529) vordrangen. Schon vorher hatten die westungarischen Gebiete unter der Pest (1408/09) und durch die Grenzkriege zwischen Kaiser Friedrich III. (1440−1493) und Matthias Corvinus (1458−1490) gelitten. Es kam im 16. Jahrhundert zu mehreren Siedlungsströmen ins heutige Burgenland: einerseits wanderten ungarische Siedler ein, andererseits kamen kroatische Flüchtlinge ins Land, wobei auch die Tatsache eine Rolle spielte, daß die meisten ungarischen Magnatengeschlechter Besitzungen sowohl in Kroatien und Slawonien als auch in Westungarn hatten und daher ihre Untertanen nach den Bedürfnissen der Zeit von den einen Gütern auf die anderen übersiedeln konnten. Auf diese Weise kam es zu jenen Bevölkerungsverhältnissen, die das Burgenland prägen. Noch vor dem Ersten Weltkrieg betrug der Anteil der Ungarisch sprechenden Einwohner 25%, bei der ungarischen Volkszählung 1920 waren es 25 000 Personen, aber schon 1923, bei der ersten österreichischen Volkszählung, nur mehr 15 000; die Hauptsiedlungszentren der Ungarn waren (und sind es z. T. auch heute noch) Oberwart und Unterwart, Ober- und Mittelpullendorf bzw. der Seewinkel. Diese drei Sprachinseln stellten 1920 44% der burgenländischen Magyaren; sonst hatten v. a. die Marktgemeinden einen höheren Anteil, der allerdings die 30%-Marke nirgendwo überschritt. Nach 1921 ist der Anteil der Magyaren an der Bevölkerung von Österreichs jüngstem Bundesland rapide gesunken (vgl. Gutleb/Unkart 1990, 42 f, Hödl 1989, 72 und → Art. 225).

Zur Entwicklung der burgenländischen Kroaten: sie sind seit 1515 auf Grund ihrer Namen nachweisbar, ihre Einwanderung dauert bis in die 80er Jahre des 16. Jahrhunderts an (vgl. Hadrovics 1974, 16 f mit Lit. u. Quellen). Auf Grund des dialektologischen Befundes läßt sich mit einiger Sicherheit sagen, daß ihre Vorfahren aus der Lika, aus dem Küstenland zwischen Senj und Obrovac, aus der Gegend zwischen Otočac und der Kupa sowie aus Westslawonien stammen. Ihre Zahl betrug 1910 rund 44 000 und ist zunächst langsam, nach dem Zweiten Weltkrieg aber schneller auf weniger als die Hälfte ihres ursprünglichen Standes zurückgegangen (durch Assimilation und Binnenwanderung bzw. Pendeln v. a. nach Wien und Graz).

3. Politik, Wirtschaft und allgemeine kulturelle sowie religiöse Lage

3.1. Slowenen: → Art. 223

3.2. Kroaten: → Art. 224

3.3. Tschechen (und Slowaken)

Die Wiener Tschechen (und Slowaken) sind die Nachkommen von Einwanderern in der zweiten Hälfte des 19. Jahrhunderts aus den Gebieten der späteren ČSR nach Wien im Zuge von Landflucht und Industrialisierung. Charakteristisch für sie waren Berufsgruppen wie Handwerker (Schneider, Schuster, Tischler), (Bau- und Ziegelei-)Arbeiter sowie Dienstpersonal (in adeligen und bürgerlichen Häusern); darüber hinaus gab es auch Schüler, Lehrlinge, Studenten und Militärpersonen. Man vermutet, daß Anfang unseres Jahrhunderts rund 10% der Einwohner Wiens (Hödl 1989, 74), nach anderen Schätzungen 250 000 von ca. 2 Mill. (so Fischer 1989, 24) Tschechen waren (andere Autoren sprechen von 400—500 000, vgl. Steinhauser 1978, 5 u. Henke 1988, 146), die sich bei der Volkszählung 1910 aber nur z. T. zu ihrer Sprachzugehörigkeit bekannt haben (nämlich 98 461 Personen lt. amtlichen Ergebnissen). Als Ursachen werden dafür angegeben: eine zu schwache tschechische Mittel- und Oberschicht, das Überwiegen ökonomischen Drucks über nationale Bindungen sowie geringes nationales Prestige (Fischer 1989, 26). Obwohl die Tschechen ein reiches und vielfältiges Vereins-, Schul- und Bildungswesen auf- und ausgebaut hatten, fehlte es dem tschechischen Nationalismus in Wien an Integrationskraft. Dazu kam das gespannte deutsch-tschechische Verhältnis in Böhmen und Mähren, wo auch die national-emanzipatorischen Prozesse widersprüchlich verliefen und durch Spaltung in den eigenen Reihen gekennzeichnet waren (vgl. Fischer 1989, 26 f).

Nach dem Ende der Monarchie und der Gründung der ČSR als eigener Staat im Jahr 1918 kam es zu einer Rückwanderungswelle (ca. 105 000 Personen, darunter viele Akademiker und Beamte), doch wurden bei der Volkszählung 1923 immer noch ca. 50 000 Tschechen gezählt (größtenteils Arbeiter, Gewerbetreibende und kleine Kaufleute). Das rege Vereinsleben sowie private und öffentliche Schulwesen bestand jedoch weiter, bis die NS-Ära diesem ein schnelles Ende bereitete, was die Zahl der Personen, die sich zu ihrer nationalen und sprachlichen Identität bekannten, sprunghaft sinken ließ. 1951 wurden in Wien offiziell nur mehr 3438 Tschechen und 102 Slowaken gezählt — ein Tiefpunkt: Spätfolge der NS-Unterdrückung und unmittelbare Folge der 1948 im „Mutterland" eingetretenen politischen Veränderungen (Etablierung der kommun. Herrschaft). Dazu kam noch eine Auswanderungswelle nach 1945 (mindestens 10 000 Personen), der eine Rückwanderungs- bzw. Emigrationswelle nach 1948 folgte, die die Minderheit aber — wie auch jene des Jahres 1968 — nicht spürbar stärkte. Bei der Volkszählung 1961 wurde deren Zahl überhaupt nicht ermittelt (erst wieder ab 1971).

Die Spaltung der tschechischen Minderheit in Wien in einen kommunistischen und einen demokratisch-pluralistischen Verband trug ebenfalls das Seine zum Schwund der tschechischen Volksgruppe bei. Heute unterhält der Schulverein „Komenský" noch einen Kindergarten, eine Volks- und Hauptschule (in Wien-Landstraße), die rund 200 Kinder besuchen. Außerdem existiert noch ein Kulturverein, der die alten Traditionen pflegt. Zusammenfassend muß festgestellt werden, daß die Wiener Tschechen und Slowaken den mit Abstand größten Substanz- und Identitätsverlust erlitten haben (vgl. weiteres Hödl 1989, 73 f; Fischer 1989, 24 ff). — Ihrem religiösen Bekenntnis nach sind die meisten Tschechen und Slowaken römisch-katholisch und verfügen über eine eigene Vereinskirche auf dem Rennweg in Wien (Henke 1988, 153). Im wirtschaftlichen Leben spielen sie keine besondere, eigenständige Rolle.

3.4. Ungarn (Magyaren): → Art. 225 sowie Gutleb/Unkart 1990, 42 ff

3.5. „Zigeuner": Roma und Sinti (und Lovara)

Die in Österreich lebenden (vermutlich) 6 000 — 10 000 „Zigeuner" (eine geschätzte, genauer nicht zu belegende Zahl: vgl. Henke 1988; 165, Gronemeyer/Rakelmann 1988, 207; Baumgartner 1987, 48) empfinden diesen Namen als Schimpfwort: daher hat sich in der Literatur die Bezeichnung „Roma und Sinti" eingebürgert. Die bei weitem größte Gruppe sind die *Roma*, deren Sprache *Romanis* in die österreichische Volkszählung Eingang gefunden hat (122 Personen, davon 93 im Burgenland — eine zweifellos viel zu niedrige Zahl). Die bedeutendste Gruppe der Roma ist die des Burgenlandes (vermischt mit Lovara-Angehörigen): einst (1927) insgesamt über 7000 Personen, heute nur noch knapp 700 (Baumgartner 1987, 48); die übrigen sind den NS-Verfolgungen zum Opfer gefallen, z. T. sind Überlebende nach dem Zweiten Weltkrieg abgewandert, hauptsächlich nach Wien und Schwechat. Der Schwerpunkt der *Lovara* ist heute Wien; sie haben sich z. T. im Wiener Geschäftsleben etablieren können (Antiquitäten-, Teppichhandel und im Umfeld des Reitsportes); aus Wiener Lovara-Familien sind zahlreiche international bekannte Musiker hervorgegangen. *Roma* und *Lovara* sind aus Ungarn eingewandert und lebten im seinerzeitigen Westungarn und heutigen Burgenland seit Maria Theresia; dort sind sie zwangsangesiedelt und mit Grundbesitz ausgestattet worden. Hingegen sind die *Sinti* (ca. 500 Personen) aus Deutschland eingewandert, zum Großteil vor dem Ersten Weltkrieg; sie leben z. T. in Wien und in den westlichen Bundesländern (Baumgartner 1987, 48) sowie in Kärnten und der Steiermark (Heinschink 1978, 8). Dazu kommen noch jüngere Einwanderungsgruppen (z. B. die *Yerli* aus Makedonien, sie sind als Gastarbeiter tätig). Viele der in Österreich lebenden „Zigeuner" sind Ausländer (wie z. B. die Yerli) oder staatenlos (v. a. Sinti-Familien).

Auf dem Gebiet des heutigen Österreich leben Roma und Sinti seit dem 16. Jahrhundert, werden in Urkunden jedoch schon früher erwähnt. Im 19. Jahrhundert lebten auf dem heutigen Gebiet des Burgenlandes rund 3000 „Zigeuner", die hauptsächlich als Nagelschmiede, Rastelbinder und Musiker sowie als Landarbeiter ihren Lebensunterhalt bestritten, wobei sie meist von der Grundherrschaft abhängig waren. Sie lebten ursprünglich nicht in „Ghettos", sondern unter den anderen Einwohnern der Dörfer, was zur vollständigen Assimilation vieler Familien führte. In der zweiten Hälfte des 19. Jahrhunderts kam es zu einem massenhaften Zuzug „deutscher Zigeuner". So entstanden die Zigeunerkolonien am Rande der Dörfer auf Gemeindegrund, wobei in manchen Orten die Zahl der „Zigeuner" größer wurde als die der einheimischen Bevölkerung. Die größte Konzentration von Roma gab es bis in die Zwischenkriegszeit im Gerichtsbezirk Oberwart (ca. 8% der Bevölkerung). — Eine weitere Einwanderungswelle war die der Lovara ins heutige Nordburgenland (nach 1880).

Die heutige wirtschaftliche Lage der „Zigeuner" ist alles andere als günstig; dazu kommt, daß sie bis 1992 in Österreich nicht als Volksgruppe anerkannt waren. Das soll sich jetzt ändern, indem sie im Sinne des Volksgruppengesetzes die gleichen Rechte erhalten sollen, wie sie Kroaten, Slowenen, Ungarn und Tschechen bereits besitzen (Europa Ethnica 50, 1993, 64). Indem sie meist über keine abgeschlossene Schul- oder Berufsausbildung verfügen, ist es für sie besonders schwer, Arbeit zu finden. Auf Grund von Sprach- und anderen Schwierigkeiten, die in einer vom Durchschnittsösterreicher grundverschiedenen Sozialisation begründet sind, werden die Kinder meist in die Sonderschule abgeschoben. Das wiederum führt dazu, daß viele „Zigeuner" ihre Herkunft verleugnen (insbesondere in Wien), was ihnen allerdings den Weg zu regelmäßiger Beschäftigung auf dem Arbeitsmarkt erleichtert (sie geben sich dabei oft als „Jugoslawen" aus). Sonst bleibt nur der Antiquitäten- und Altwarenhandel oder Tätigkeiten in Randzonen des Wirtschaftslebens bis hin zur Hehlerei (vgl. Baumgartner 1987, 49). Das ist ihrem Image bei der Mehrheitsbevölkerung nicht dienlich und fördert Vorurteile, worunter sie immer schon zu leiden hatten, indem sie seit jeher im besten Falle geduldet waren, meist jedoch ausgegrenzt wurden – bis hin zu ihrer Deportation und Ermordung Anfang der 40er Jahre durch die Nationalsozialisten. Nur wenige „Zigeuner" (hauptsächlich einige Geschäftsleute aus der Lovara-Gruppe sowie Musiker und Künstler, höchstens einige Hundert Personen) haben ein relativ hohes Einkommen, die meisten sind jedoch am unteren Ende der Einkommensskala zu finden (vgl. Baumgartner 1987, 50). Die Folge davon ist die Flucht in die Anonymität der Großstadt, die ihre totale Assimilation bedeutet und im Falle von Eheschließungen mit „Weißen" zur Verleugnung der „Zigeunerverwandtschaft", mit der man nichts mehr zu tun haben will, führt. Somit sind die österreichischen „Zigeuner" eine schwindende Volksgruppe, wie auch ihre Siedlungen im Burgenland langsam aussterben.

Sprachlich zerfallen sie in drei Gruppen (Dialekte, nach Heinschink 1978, 8):

(1) Romani (oder ungarischer Zigeunerdialekt): hauptsächlich im Burgenland;
(2) Lovari (Lovara-Dialekt, ein Vlah-Dialekt): im Burgenland und in Wien;
(3) Sinti: im Raum Wien, Linz, Kärnten und Steiermarkt.

In der österreichischen Volkszählung von 1991 scheint nur „Romani" auf. – Religiös haben sie sich immer an ihre Umgebung angepaßt, doch ist ihre ganze Kultur vielschichtig, verschiedener Herkunft und variablen Alters. – Allgemein zu den „Zigeunern" vgl. die Monographie von Gronemeyer/Rakelmann 1988 und → Art. 239.

3.6. Juden

Jede Aufzählung der österreichischen Volksgruppen ohne Erwähnung der religiösen Minderheit der Juden, wäre unvollständig. Grundsätzlich handelt es sich bei ihnen um eine von ihrer Religion her konstituierte Gemeinschaft, die sich in Österreich sowohl der Sprachen der Monarchie als auch – v. a. im Osten – einer eigenen Sprache, des Jiddischen, bediente, das sich hauptsächlich auf oberdeutscher (bairisch-böhmischer) Grundlage infolge der sozial-kulturellen Isolierung des Judentums seit dem 12./13. Jahrhundert herausgebildet hat (→ Art. 238). Die spätmittelalterliche Siedlungsbewegung (Flucht) in den Osten (v. a. ins Polen der Jagellonen) führte zum Entstehen zweier großer Dialekte, West- und Ostjiddisch. Trotz des deutschen Grundcharakters des Jiddischen, das sich zu einer Schrift- und Literatursprache entwickelt hat, ist es zu einer selbständigen Sprache geworden, angereichert mit hebräisch-aramäischen Elementen (v. a. im Wortschatz) und mit slawischem Sprachgut (v. a. Syntax und Phraseologie).

Der Massenmord der Nationalsozialisten an den Juden (an dem auch sehr viele Österreicher beteiligt waren) hat zu einem starken Rückgang auch der Sprecher des Jiddischen geführt: sprachen vor dem Zweiten Weltkrieg rund 5 Mill. Personen Jiddisch, sind es heute nur noch ca. 700 000. Die Zahl der „Jidden" (= jiddischsprechende Juden) ist in Österreich nie statistisch erhoben worden; laut Volkszählung von 1910 gab es in Wien zwar ca. 175 000 „Israeliten" nach der Religion, aber keine „Jidden" nach der Sprache. Der österreichische Ethnograph Baron von Czoernig (1856, 54 u. 60) rechnete die Juden zwar zu den (sic!) „asiatischen Sprachstämmen", gibt aber keine sprachlichen Daten an. Er begnügt sich mit der Feststellung, daß „sie sich (...) der Mehrzahl nach der deutschen, (...) slavischen, magyarischen und italienischen Landessprache bedienen." – Bis 1938 hatte die Israelitische Kultusgemeinde in Wien rund 180 000 Mitglieder, heute sind es nur noch 6000 (bzw. 9000–10 000 inkl. Zuwanderer aus der ehemaligen Sowjetunion). Die Gesamtzahl der Personen jüdischen Glaubens mit österreichischer Staatsbürgerschaft dürfte 7500 nicht übersteigen. – Lit.: Henke 1988, 171 ff; Haarmann 1975, 358; Landmann 1964.

4. Statistik und Ethnoprofile

Zu den Ethnoprofilen der Kontaktsprachen vgl. die Angaben unter 3.2.–3.5. – Die statistischen Daten sind aus der Tabelle ablesbar; sie beruhen auf der Volkszählung 1991 und geben die Angaben nach der *Umgangssprache* österreichischer Staatsbürger (auch in Kombination mit Deutsch) wieder.

Bei den Slowenen Kärntens scheint der von Volkszählung zu Volkszählung zu beobachten gewesene Schwund gestoppt zu sein; 1991 haben nur noch 900 Personen „Windisch" angegeben, dies bedeutet, daß die Zahl der „bewußten" Slowenischsprachigen in den letzten 10 Jahren mit ca. 14 000 Personen

Tab. 222.1: Statistik der nichtdeutschsprachigen Minderheiten Österreichs

Österreich gesamt 1991	80 384
Kroatisch	29 596
Slowenisch[1]	20 191
Ungarisch	19 638
Tschechisch	9 822
Slowakisch	1 015
Romani	122

Zum Vergleich	1910	1934	1951[2]	1981
Kroatisch	44 243	41 392	31 182	22 113
Slowenisch	74 210	26 300	19 976	18 640
Ungarisch	26 570	10 055	5 566	12 043
Tschechisch	} 119 447	{ 32 274	3 817	5 101
Slowakisch		835	301	?

	1991	1981	1971	1939	1910
Burgenland					
Kroatisch	19 109	18 648	24 332	36 482	43 633
Ungarisch	4 973	4 025	5 447	8 346	26 225
Romani	93	?	?	(ca. 7000)	?
Kärnten					
Slowenisch[1]	14 850	16 552[3]	20 972[3]	43 179	66 463
Steiermark					
Slowenisch	1 697	893	1 684	4 460	5 744
Wien					
Tschechisch	6 429	4 106	6 528	52 275	98 461
Slowenisch	1 832	624	507	?	1 118
Kroatisch	6 604	2 557	2 316	?	377[4]
Ungarisch	8 930	5 683	6 099	?	205
Slowakisch	619	?	317[5]	3 973	?
Romani	22	?	?	?	?

Anmerkungen:
1. inklusive „Windisch"
2. ohne Kombination „Deutsch-X"
3. davon 14 204 ohne „Windisch" (1981) bzw. 17 011 (1971)
4. „Serbisch-Kroatisch"
5. nach der *Sprachenerhebung* 1976

gleich geblieben ist. Im Bezirk Völkermarkt sprachen 17% slowenisch, in drei weiteren Bezirken zwischen 1% und 7%; die Gemeinde Zell liegt weiter mit über 90% an der Spitze gefolgt von Globasnitz mit über 50%; weitere 6 Gemeinden haben mehr als 20% Slowenischsprachige (Angaben nach Wiener Zeitung, 10. 9. 1992).

5. Soziolinguistische Lage

Dazu wurden bereits sub 3. zahlreiche Angaben gemacht, so daß hier nur eine kurze Zusammenfassung erfolgt. Am günstigsten scheint – soziolinguistisch gesehen – die Lage für das Slowenische in Kärnten zu sein, da die gemischtsprachige Region Kärntens an das slowenische Staatsgebiet grenzt und die Kenntnis des Slowenischen die Wirtschaftsbeziehungen zwischen beiden Ländern stützt und dabei auch eine Rolle spielt. Trotzdem ist innerhalb Kärntens (und auch den gemischtsprachigen Grenzgemeinden in der Steiermark) allein das Deutsche dominant, da nur dieses *alle* Funktionen im privaten und öffentlichen Leben erfüllen kann und auch von allen Angehörigen der Minderheiten mit österreichischer Staatsbürgerschaft beherrscht wird. Das Slowenische hat mit den anderen Minderheitensprachen (d. h. mit dem Kroatischen und Ungarischen) gemein, daß es zwar hauptsächlich nur innerhalb der Minderheit zugehörigen oder nahestehenden Kreisen im täglichen Leben gebraucht wird (und auch hier vorwiegend als Haus-, Familien- und Vereinssprache), daß aber doch zumindest das Kroatische und Slowenische über eine oft unterschätzte gesellschaftliche Reichweite verfügen, die über Familie und Vereine hinausgeht, insbes. als Kirchensprache und in einigen Gemeinden als Alltagssprache, z. T. auch auf Ebene des Gemeinderates (vgl. Holzer/Münz 1993). Dies alles trifft allerdings nicht auf das Romanes zu, da viele junge Roma den Gebrauch dieser Sprache ablehnen (Baumgartner 1987, 49). Auch die Lage der Tschechen in Wien ist nicht günstig; das für Slowenen, Kroaten und Ungarn Mögliche ist für sie unerreichbar, ganz abgesehen davon, daß sie oft als *Böhm'* (ausgesprochen [pɛm]) Ziel des Spottes sind, was die Assimilation als Flucht vor der Diskriminierung fördert (vgl. Henke 1988, 153 f).

Empirische Untersuchungen zum Stellenwert des Slowenischen und Kroatischen in der Gesellschaft geben recht interessante Details. Folgende Daten sind zusammengestellt nach Filla/Flaschberger/Pachner/Reiterer 1982. Bewußte Kroaten und Slowenen sehen sich als Angehörige einer eigenen Kultur, Assimilanten neigen dazu, diese eher zu leugnen oder zumindest zu verdrängen, insbesondere die sogenannten „Windischen" in Kärnten (bei solchen Feststellungen wird aber meist übersehen, daß in Kärnten — anders als im Burgenland — die kulturellen Unterschiede zwischen Mehrheit und Minderheit minimal sind). In Kärnten stehe die private Sphäre auch im kulturellen Leben im Vordergrund, denn man könne „Slowene nur in der Familie sein". In wichtigen Berufen werde das Kroatische im Burgenland mehr gebraucht als das Slowenische in Kärnten (wogegen allerdings der Einwand zu erheben ist, daß der Einkaufstourismus aus Slowenien den Gebrauch des Slowenischen im Geschäftsleben eher fördert und es einen entwickelten slowenischen Wirtschaftssektor gibt). Wirtschaftliche Faktoren würden von Slowenen höher eingeschätzt, sie verfügen über politische Organisationen und eigene Genossenschaften, hingegen haben die Organisationen der Kroaten eher kulturellen Charakter. Daher kämen die Spannungen zwischen Mehrheit und Minderheit in Kärnten deutlicher zum Vorschein als etwa im Burgenland, wo sich Konflikte vielfach — von parteipolitischen Gegensätzen überlagert — eher innerhalb der Minderheit abspielen. Abschließend muß man nüchtern feststellen, daß die soziolinguistische Lage der Sprachen der Minderheiten in Österreich eher *ungünstig* ist.

6. Sprachpolitische Lage

Sprachpolitisch dominant ist in Österreich das Deutsche als Staats- und Amtssprache; Minderheitensprachen sind nur zusätzlich zum Deutschen als Amtssprache bei *lokalen* Behörden (nicht aber bei *Bundesbehörden*) zugelassen; darüber hinaus auch als Unterrichtssprachen in einigen gemischtsprachigen Regionen und eigens für Angehörige der Minderheit eingerichteten öffentlichen Schulen. In der Realität trifft dies — in der Reihenfolge des Umfanges — für das Slowenische in Kärnten und das Kroatische und Ungarische im Burgenland zu.

Grundlage aller Gesetze für die Sprachen der kroatischen und slowenischen Minderheit in Österreich ist der Artikel 7 des Österreichischen Staatsvertrages von 1955, der den Anspruch auf Elementarunterricht in der jeweiligen Sprache, eine verhältnismäßige Anzahl von Mittelschulen, die Verwendung als Amtssprache und zweisprachige topographische Aufschriften garantiert. Das Volksgruppengesetz von 1976 ist eine Art Ergänzung, in mancher Hinsicht auch Interpretation und bis zu einem gewissen Grad sogar Einschränkung der Bestimmungen des Staatsvertrages (schärfer: „verfassungs- und völkerrechtswidrig", so Hödl 1989, 157).

Zum Slowenischen sei kurz festgestellt, daß es in Kärnten ein entwickeltes zweisprachiges Pflichtschulwesen gibt, ein slowenisches Gymnasium und eine Handelsakademie in Klagenfurt, Amtssprachenregelungen und (allerdings in einem beschränkten Umfang) auch topographische Aufschriften. Im Burgenland ist die Lage für die kroatische Minderheit weniger günstig: Kroatisch ist nur Unterrichtsgegenstand mit wenigen Wochenstunden; nur 1044 (1986/87) bzw. 1240 (1990) Schüler werden an 28 Volksschulen in irgendeiner Weise in Kroatisch unterrichtet — oder 5% aller Schüler (zum Vergleich: in 62 Schulen Kärntens haben über 20% aller Schüler zweisprachigen Unterricht). Dazu kommen noch je 4 Hauptschulen mit „Kroatisch als Freigegenstand" bzw. im Schulversuch „mit besonderer Berücksichtigung von Kroatisch"; allerdings wurde 1992 in Oberwart ein Volksgruppen-Gymnasium („Pannonisches Gymnasium") eingerichtet, mit kroatischer und ungarischer Unterrichtssprache in zwei Parallelklassen, beginnend mit der 5. Schulstufe. Ferner werden an einigen (Haupt- und Höheren) Schulen des mittleren und nördlichen Burgenlandes Kroatisch und Ungarisch als Fremdsprachen angeboten. Zweisprachige topographische Aufschriften gibt es bisher im Burgenland nur ganz wenige (z. B. in Frankenau/Frakanava). — Gesetzestexte und nähere Angaben s. Gutleb/Unkart 1990, 60 bzw. 180 ff sowie 41 ff bzw. 161 ff bzw. Bundeskanzleramt 1977.

Obwohl die Rechte der Ungarn im Staatsvertrag nicht ausdrücklich erwähnt werden, wurden die durch das Volksgruppengesetz festgelegten Schutzbestimmungen für die kroatische Minderheit im Burgenland auch den Ungarn zuerkannt. Es gibt zwei Volksschulen in zwei Gemeinden mit ca. 50 Schülern mit zweisprachigem Unterricht (ähnlich wie bei den Kroaten), ferner zwei Hauptschulen mit „Ungarisch als alternativem Pflichtgegenstand". Daneben gibt es ein reges Kulturleben, ein zweimonatlich erscheinendes Periodikum und wöchentliche Radiosendungen (Gutleb/Unkart 1990, 46—49).

Auch die tschechische Minderheit wird im Staatsvertrag nicht erwähnt. Ein auf Privatinitiative beruhendes Schulwesen unterhält der „Komenský-Schulverein" in Wien-Landstraße (Kindergarten, Volks- und Hauptschule) mit ca. 200 Kindern. Dazu kommen mehrere Kultur- und Sportvereine sowie eine Wochenzeitung (Henke 1988, 152, Hödl 1989, 74).

Die Sprache der Roma und Sinti — Romani — hat nie den Status einer Schulsprache erreicht, ein Interesse daran besteht nicht (Baumgartner 1987, 49). Ob die Anerkennung der Roma und Sinti als Volksgruppe 1992 durch einstimmigen Beschluß des Österreichischen Nationalrates (im Sinne des Volksgruppengesetzes von 1976) etwas bewirken wird, bleibt abzuwarten.

7. Sprachkontakte

7.1. Österreichisches Deutsch

Dem Sprachkontakt zwischen Deutsch einerseits und Slowenisch, Kroatisch und Ungarisch andererseits sind eigene Kapitel gewidmet. Doch hier ist auch der Platz, auf einige durch Sprachkontakt hervorgerufene Besonderheiten der österreichischen Variante des Standarddeutschen einzugehen. Das österreichische Deutsch bildet zwar keine absolute Einheit, sondern weist vielmehr sowohl eine innere Schichtung als auch verschiedenartige Beziehungen zu den anderen süddeutschen Varietäten auf (vgl. Walla 1992, 174). Allzu sehr ist man geneigt, was für Wien typisch ist, für ganz Österreich anzunehmen. Doch Wien war in der Geschichte die Drehscheibe, über die viel Sprachgut aus den anderen Sprachen der Österreichisch-Ungarischen Monarchie ins österreichische Deutsch gelangt ist (z. B. *Powidl* aus dem Tschechischen, *Palatschinken* aus dem Ungarischen), und über Wien sind auch viele „binnendeutsche" Ausdrücke in Österreich „eingebürgert" worden (z. B. *Tischler* gegenüber bairisch *Schreiner*).

Der Sprachkontakt auf der Ebene der österreichischen Variante des Standarddeutschen macht sich *nur* im Wortschatz und in einigen (allerdings umgangssprachlichen) Redewendungen bemerkbar. Einige Beispiele, aus dem Italienischen: *Stampiglie* „Stempel(gerät)", *Krida* „fahrlässig oder betrügerisch herbeigeführte Zahlungsunfähigkeit", *Fisole* „grüne Bohne"; aus dem Ungarischen: *Fogosch* „Zander", *Schinakel* „Ruderboot, kleines Boot", *Palatschinke* „Pfannkuchen" (eig. ungar.-rumän. Mischform); aus slawischen Sprachen: *Klobasse* „Selchwurst", *Kolatsche* „eine Mehlspeise", *Powidl* „Pflaumenmus" (alle Beispiele nach Ebner 1988, 165—169). Eine solche Liste läßt sich mit Hilfe des „Duden" beliebig fortsetzen, z. B. *Jause* (slowen.) „Zwischenmahlzeit, Brotzeit" (nur Ost- und Südösterreich, im Westen aus dem Romanischen *Marende*), *Brimsen* (slowak.) „ein Schafkäse" usw.

Die österreichische Variante des Standarddeutschen, die auch Besonderheiten in der Aussprache (Lipold 1988) und der Grammatik (Tatzreiter 1988) aufweist, wird vom „Binnendeutschen" (dem Sprachgebrauch der Bundesrepublik Deutschland) immer mehr zurückgedrängt. In Zeitungs- und Rundfunkmeldungen kann man ein Überhandnehmen „deutschländischer" (so Möcker 1992, 249) Ausdrücke beobachten, wie z. B. *Junge, Jungs* (statt *Knabe/Bub, Bursche(n)*), *Treppenhaus* (statt *Stiegenhaus*), *Tomate* (statt *Paradeiser*), auch amtssprachlich: z. B. *Fleischer* statt *Fleischhauer*, *das Gehalt* statt (früher in den österreichischen Gesetzestexten) *der Gehalt*. Im Rundfunk („heterozentrischer Aussprachekult": Pollak 1992, 155) *die Fünf* statt *der Fünfer*, Aussprache von *zwanzig*, *Essig* zunehmend *-ich* [iç], gewöhnlich jedoch [ik]. Zu diesem Problemkreis vgl. v. a. Wiesinger 1988 und zuletzt Pollak 1992 sowie Möcker 1992. Die Vernachlässigung der österreichischen Variante des Standarddeutschen steht im Widerspruch zum gefestigten österreichischen Nationalbewußtsein und wirft Probleme auf, die von Politikern nicht (vgl. Möcker 1992, 236) und von Germanisten kaum (vgl. Pollak 1992, 155) wahrgenommen werden.

7.2. Tschechisch−Deutsch

Der Wiener Großstadtdialekt, aber auch die Umgangs- und Verkehrssprache der Hauptstadt ist vom Tschechischen nachhaltig beeinflußt worden, wobei der Höhepunkt heute längst überschritten ist. Mit dem Aussterben der vor dem Ersten Weltkrieg aus den Ländern der Böhmischen Krone eingewanderten Personen schwinden auch viele tschechische Ausdrücke, was ich auch selbst konstatieren kann: viel Sprachgut, das in den 50er und 60er Jahren unseres Jahrhunderts noch üblich war, ist heute nur mehr selten zu hören. Dazu kommt, daß in den letzten 30−40 Jahren vornehmlich deutschsprachige Österreicher nach Wien zugezogen sind, so daß auch eine Verschiebung der Struktur der Wiener Bevölkerung hinsichtlich ihrer Herkunft eingetreten ist, wobei die Gesamtbevölkerung zurückgegangen ist (von ca. 1,7 auf ca. 1,5 Mill. Einwohner).

An Veränderungen im phonologischen System der Wiener Mundart werden dem Tschechischen zugeschrieben:
(1) die Monophthongierung der Diphthonge /ai/ und /au/ zu [æ:] und [ɔ:] sowie /oi/ zu [œ:] in der Umgangssprache, zu [æ:] im Dialekt;
(2) der Verlust des geschlossenen *e* und *o*;
(3) Verschiebung der Drucksilbengrenze (ähnlich der Kärntner Dehnung: → Art. 223, 7.1.);
(4) Verlust der (fürs Mittelbairische sonst so typischen) Nasalvokale; und (5) gerolltes *r* (nach Steinhauser 1978, 11 ff).

(ad 1) Wurde erstmals vom Wiener Anglisten Luick (1904, 37 u. 76) beobachtet. Diese Monophthongierung tritt mehrmals in tschechischer und magyarischer Nachbarschaft auf (vgl. Kranzmayer 1956, 49). Beispiele: [tsæ:t] "Zeit", [hɔ:s] "Haus", (mundartlich) [læ:t] (bzw. umgangssprachlich) [lœ:tɛ] "Leute".

(ad 2) Es gibt phonologisch nur ein *e* bzw. *o*, die phonetisch − wie im Tschechischen − offen artikuliert werden (vgl. Kranzmayer 1953, 211 ff).

(ad 3) Die Verschiebung der Drucksilbengrenze in Fällen wie *of-fen*, *wis-sen*, *Masch-[sch]en* zu *o-ffm*, *wi-ssn*, *Ma-sch[sch]n* führt zu einer Längung des Vokals, die allerdings nicht so deutlich ausfällt wie bei der Kärntner Dehnung. Doch in expressiver Rede können die Vokale mehr gedehnt werden: z. B. [de:s kɔ: ma jɔ: nɛt wi:sn] "das kann man ja nicht wissen", auch vor Plosiven wie z. B. *in dɛərə hi:tn* "in dieser Hütte" usw.

(ad 4) Das Tschechische kennt keine Nasalvokale, das Mittelbairische (auch "Donaubairisch" genannt) jedoch sehr wohl, auf welchem Boden Wien liegt. Da der 1942 zuerst beobachtete Verlust der Nasalvokale nur in Wien, zunächst nicht in der Umgebung (erst jetzt scheint er sich auszubreiten) auftrat, ist tschechischer Einfluß wahrscheinlich. Tschechen sprachen Wörter wie [gẽ:] "gehen", [a'lã:] "allein" und [hĩ:] "hin" entweder [gɛ:n], [a'lain] und [hi:n] oder der Mundart angenähert, aber ohne Nasalierung, [gɛ:], [a'la:] und [hi:] aus, was sich dann offensichtlich ausbreiten und durchsetzen konnte (vgl. Steinhauser 1978, 20 f).

(ad 5) Diese Erscheinung ist m. E. heute rezessiv, aber in früherer Aussprache wurde offensichtlich nach tschechischer Manier das *r* auch dort deutlich artikuliert, wo es sonst der *r*-Vokalisierung unterliegt (erstmals von Steinhauser im Jahre 1913 beobachtet), z. B. [gɔ:nər] "Gauner", [blɛ:dər hu:nd] "blöder Hund" mit deutlich artikuliertem wortschließenden *-r* (Steinhauser 1978, 21 f). − Auch das Wiener "Vorstadt-*L*" (etwa [ł], insbesondere im Wort- und Silbenauslaut) ist vielfach auf tschechischen Einfluß zurückgeführt worden, doch im Auslaut ist dieses *l* im Zuge der mittelbairischen *l*-Vokalisierung zunächst geschwunden und erst nachträglich unter hochsprachlichem Einfluß restituiert worden, eben als [ł], z. B. *weil* basilektal [vœi], umgangssprachlich [vɛ:ł]. Doch das tschechische *l* ist dem standarddeutschen *l* ähnlich (aus slawistischer Sicht ein "mittleres *l*"). Nach Kranzmayer (1956, 119) ist das Wiener *l* "postdental in bestimmten Gesellschaftsschichten".

Umstritten ist der tschechische Ursprung von wienerisch "setzen wir sich" (statt "...uns"); vergleichbare Erscheinungen kommen auch in anderen deutschen Mundarten vor (vgl. die

ausführliche Diskussion bei Steinhauser 1978, 23−31). Sonst umfaßt der tschechische Einfluß insbesondere den Wortschatz, wobei sich zwei Gruppen unterscheiden lassen:
(1) schriftsprachliche Lehnwörter (die größtenteils auch außerhalb von Wien verstanden werden und z. T. auch außerhalb Österreichs);
(2) mundartliche, z. T. umgangssprachliche (in jedem Fall aber nicht schriftsprachliche) Lehnwörter.

Steinhauser (1978, 105 ff) nimmt noch eine dritte Gruppe „altösterreichischer" (also nur in Österreich gebräuchlicher) Lehnwörter an; ich habe sie sub (1) eingereiht.

Von der Semantik her handelt es sich bei diesem Lehngut um Bezeichnung von Tieren, Pflanzen, Speisen, Musik und Tanz, aus dem Fuhrwesen, einige Ausdrücke aus der Sprache der staatlichen Verwaltung und des Militärs sowie einige durch das Tschechische vermittelte russische Ausdrücke (darunter auch Ethnonyme). Einige Beispiele hierzu (in Klammer die entsprechende tschechische Quelle).

(ad 1) *Zeisig* (čížek), *Stieglitz* (stehlec, stehlík), *Zobel* (sobol aus russ. *sobol'*), *Kürschner* (krzno), *Preiselbeere* (bruslina), *Reizker* (ryzek), *Kren* „Meerrettich" (chřen, křen), *Polka* (půlka), *Kummet* (chomout), *Polák* „Pole" (Polák), *Powidl* „Zwetschkenmus" (povidla), *Kolátsche, G-* „eine Mehlspeise" (koláče), *Sliwowitz* (slivovice), *Ainetze* „Gabeldeichsel" (ojnice) usw.
(ad 2) *Strizzi* „Zuhälter" (strýc „Onkel"), *schetzkojedno* „alles eins" (všecko jedno), *pomáli* „langsam" (po málu), Mischformen wie *Feschak* „Schönling" (fesch + tschech. *-ák*), *Böhmak* (alt) „tschechischer Dickkopf" (*Böhme* + *-ák*), davon *böhmakeln* „mit tschechischem Akzent deutsch sprechen".

Ferner sind viele der Wiener Familiennamen tschechischer Herkunft (vgl. Repp 1960 bzw. 1974).

7.3. Einige Bemerkungen zum Romanes

Die Sprache der „Zigeuner" hat keine erkennbaren Spuren im österreichischen Deutsch hinterlassen, doch hat das Deutsche ihre Sprache beeinflußt, wobei ähnliche Erscheinungen zu beobachten sind wie auch bei anderen Sprachen der Minderheiten in Österreich, so z. B. Calques nach Vorbild deutscher Komposita, z. B. *avri asav* „spotten" (= „aus+lachen"), *palal dav* „nach-geben" (Lovara-Dialekt); *upre dela* „auf-geben (eine Schulaufgabe)" (Romanes im Burgenland).

Auch wenn „Zigeuner" deutsch sprechen (insbesondere bei älteren Personen), kommt es zu Interferenzen, z. B. *fahren wir uns auf den Markt* nach Lovari *žas amenge po piaco*, *ich gehe mir spazieren* nach Lovari *žav mange te phirav* (*žav* 1.Psg.Kond., *žas* 1.Ppl.Kond.; *mange* „mir", *amenge* „uns/Dpl." − eine Art *dativus ethicus*).

Beispiele nach Heinschink 1978, 10 f und Knobloch 1953, 30 ff.

8. Kritische Wertung der verwendeten Quellen und Literatur

Der Sprachkontakt als Triebfeder des Sprachwandels in den bairischen Mundarten Österreichs ist bereits relativ früh erkannt worden: es sei hier auf die Arbeiten von Schuchardt 1883 oder Lessiak 1910 bzw. 1983 verwiesen. Auch Gesamtdarstellungen (wie Kranzmayer 1956) und Einzeldarstellungen (z. B. Hornung 1964; Lessiak 1903) berücksichtigen den mannigfaltigen Sprachkontakt. Eine umfassende Monographie zum Sprachkontakt in Österreich ist allerdings m. W. bisher nicht geschrieben worden; doch zu den meisten Einzelsprachen liegen umfassende Darstellungen vor (zum Slowenischen: Hafner/Prunč 1982 ff, Neweklowsky 1990, Pohl 1992 b; zum Kroatischen: Neweklowsky 1978, Hadrovics 1974; zum Tschechischen: Steinhauser 1978 usw.).

Ein Problem sui generis ist die Darstellung der Minderheiten in Österreich an sich. Die offiziellen Darstellungen der Minderheitenproblematik in Österreich − sowohl vom Bundeskanzleramt als auch von den Landesregierungen herausgegeben − vermitteln ein recht günstiges Bild über die Minderheiten in Österreich (z. B. Gutleb/Unkart 1990; Bundeskanzleramt 1977). Darstellungen von seiten der Minderheiten geben naturgemäß meist ein recht düsteres Bild (z. B. Malle o. J. [1973?]), wenn sie auch oft staatsloyale Kooperationsbereitschaft erkennen lassen (z. B. Bogataj 1989). Die der österreichischen Minderheitenpolitik gegenüber kritisch eingestellte Literatur beruht nur z. T. auf fundierten Untersuchungen (z. B. Flaschberger/Reiterer 1980). Oft gleitet sie zu sehr in die Politikwissenschaft und allgemeine Gesellschaftskritik ab und begibt sich damit in die Niederungen der Tagespolitik (z. B. Fischer 1980). Das trifft leider auf viele Publikationen zu, die in ihrem Selbstverständnis als Anwälte der Minderheiten auftreten, aber gegenüber der Mehrheit nicht die richtigen Worte finden (wie z. B. Hödl 1989), wie überdies auch Wissenschaft und Politik nicht immer die richtigen Worte gegenüber den Minderheiten finden. Allerdings hat Österreich — und das muß unumwunden festgestellt werden — die aus dem Staatsvertrag von 1955 abzuleitenden Rechte der Minderheiten nur sehr zögerlich (z. B. wurde das Volksgruppen-Gymnasium im burgenländischen Oberwart erst 1992 eingerichtet) und auch nicht in vollem Umfang (z. B. zweisprachige topographische Aufschriften) verwirklicht. Somit hatte die beharrliche Kritik an der österreichischen Minderheitenpolitik durchaus ihre Berechtigung, wobei manches Positive (z. B. die finanzielle Förderung von Vereinen durch die Bundesregierung: für slowenische Vereine im Jahre 1992 nach Presseberichten ca. 22 Millionen Schilling) in den Hintergrund trat.

Trotz mancher Auffassungsunterschiede kann man aber dennoch feststellen, daß die österreichische Wissenschaft sich darüber einig ist, daß die Minderheiten ein konstitutives Element des modernen Österreich sind. Denn Österreich hat auf seinem Weg ins 20. Jahrhundert mehrere schwierige Stationen durchlaufen, deren entscheidende jene der Habsburger-Monarchie war, nach deren Untergang sich das verbleibende „Deutschösterreich" 1918 als unglücklicher Kleinstaat wiedersah, der erst nach 1945 zu sich selbst gefunden und ein neues (politisch nicht-deutsches) Selbstbewußtsein entwickelt hat, in dem die Minderheiten als ein bereicherndes Element und wertvolles Erbe aus früherer Zeit ihren Platz haben.

9. Bibliographie (in Auswahl)

Baumgartner, Gerhard (1987): „Sinti und Roma in Österreich". In: *Pogrom* (Zeitschrift für bedrohte Völker) 18, Nr. 130, 47—50.

Bogataj, Mirko (1989): *Die Kärntner Slowenen*, Klagenfurt/Wien.

Bruckmann, Gerhart (1989): *Österreicher, wer bist du? Versuch einer Orientierung*, Wien.

Bundeskanzleramt (1977): *Die rechtliche Stellung der Volksgruppen in Österreich. Eine Dokumentation*, Wien.

Czoernig, Carl (1856): *Die Vertheilung der Voelkerstaemme und deren Gruppen in der Oesterreichischen Monarchie*, Wien. Nachgedruckt in: *Die slawischen Sprachen* (Salzburg) 15 (1988), 79—139.

Ebner, Jakob (1988): „Wörter und Wendungen des österreichischen Deutsch". In: Wiesinger, 99—187.

Einspieler, Valentin (1980): *Verhandlungen über die der slowenischen Minderheit angebotene Kulturautonomie 1925—1930. Beitrag zur Geschichte der Slowenen in Kärnten*, Klagenfurt.

Filla, Wilhelm/Flaschberger, Ludwig/Pachner, Franz/Reiterer, Albert F. (1982): *Am Rande Österreichs. Ein Beitrag zur Soziologie der österreichischen Volksgruppen*, Wien.

Finsterwalder, Karl (1990): *Tiroler Familiennamenkunde*, Innsbruck.

Fischer, Gero (1980): *Das Slowenische in Kärnten. Eine Studie zur Sprachenpolitik*, Wien/Klagenfurt.

Fischer, Gero (1989): „Die Situation der österreichischen sprachlichen und ethnischen Minderheiten und ihre Bedingungen für die Entwicklung interethnischer Beziehungen". In: *Grazer linguistische Studien* 31, 17—31.

Flaschberger, Ludwig/Reiterer, Albert F. (1980): *Der tägliche Abwehrkampf. Kärntens Slowenen*, Wien.

Gronemeyer, Reimer/Rakelmann, Georgia A. (1988): *Die Zigeuner. Reisende in Europa*, Köln.

Gutleb, Angelika/Unkart, Ralf (Red.) (1990): *Die Minderheiten im Alpen-Adria-Raum*. Arbeitsgemeinschaft Alpen-Adria, Klagenfurt.

Haarmann, Harald (1975): *Soziologie und Politik der Sprachen Europas*, München.

Hadrovics, László (1974): *Schrifttum und Sprache der Burgenländischen Kroaten im 18. und 19. Jahrhundert*, Wien/Budapest.

Hafner, Stanislaus/Prunč, Erich (1982 ff): *Thesaurus der slowenischen Volkssprache in Kärnten*, Wien (I 1982, II 1987, III 1992, IV 1994).

Heinschink, Mozes (1978): „La langue tsigane parlée en Autriche et en Yougoslavie". In: *Revue des Etudes Tsiganes* 1, 8—11.

Henke, Reinhold (1988): *Leben lassen ist nicht genug. Minderheiten in Österreich*, Wien.

Hödl, Günther (Red.) (1989): *Bericht der Arbeitsgruppe „Lage und Perspektiven der Volksgruppen in Österreich". Mit einem statistischen Ergänzungsheft*, Wien.

Holzer, Werner/Münz, Rainer (Eds.) (1993): *Trendwende. Sprache und Ethnizität im Burgenland*, Wien.

Hornung, Maria (1964): *Mundartkunde Osttirols*, Wien.

Kärntner Landesarchiv (1990): *Der 10. Oktober 1920. Kärntens Tag der Selbstbestimmung. Vorgeschichte — Ereignisse — Analysen*, Klagenfurt.

Knobloch, Johann (1953): „Romani-Texte aus dem Burgenland". In: *Burgenländische Forschungen* 24, 1—97.

Kranzmayer, Eberhard (1953): „Lautwandlungen und Lautverschiebungen im gegenwärtigen Wienerischen". In: *Zeitschrift für Mundartforschung* 21, 197—239.

Kranzmayer, Eberhard (1956): *Historische Lautgeographie des gesamtbairischen Dialektraumes*, Wien.

Kronsteiner, Otto (1973): „Die slawischen geographischen Namen Österreichs". In: *Österreichische Namenforschung* 1973/2, 32–58.

Kronsteiner, Otto (1974): „Kartographische Darstellung der Grenzen zwischen dem West- und Südslawischen auf österreichischem Gebiet". In: *Österreichische Namenforschung* 1974/1, 10–18.

Kronsteiner, Otto (1976): „Die frühmittelalterlichen Sprach- und Besiedlungsverhältnisse Österreichs aus namenkundlicher Sicht". In: *Österreichische Namenforschung* 1976/2, 5–24.

Kronsteiner, Otto (1980): „Die slawischen Ortsnamen in Oberösterreich". In: *Baiern und Slawen in Oberösterreich*, Holter, K. (Red.), Linz, 211–228.

Kurz, Maria (1990): *Zur Lage der Slowenen in Kärnten. Der Streit um die Volksschule in Kärnten (1867–1914)*, Klagenfurt.

Landmann, Salcia (1964): *Jiddisch. Abenteuer einer Sprache*, München.

Lessiak, Primus (1903): „Die Mundart von Pernegg in Kärnten". In: *Beiträge zur Geschichte der Deutschen Sprache und Literatur* 28, 1–227.

Lessiak, Primus (1910): „Alpendeutsche und Alpenslawen in ihren sprachlichen Beziehungen". In: *Germanisch-romanische Monatsschrift* 2, 274–288.

Lessiak, Primus (1983): Nachdruck von Lessiak 1910 in: *Die Wiener Dialektologische Schule*, Wiesinger, P. (Ed.), Wien, 249–263.

Lipold, Günter (1988): „Die österreichische Variante der deutschen Standardaussprache". In: Wiesinger 31–54.

Luick, Karl (1904): *Deutsche Lautlehre – Mit besonderer Berücksichtigung der Sprechweise Wiens und der österreichischen Alpenländer*, Leipzig/Wien.

Malle, Augustin (Red.) (o. J. |1973|): *Die Slovenen in Kärnten – Slovenci na Koroškem. Gegenwärtige Probleme der Kärntner Slovenen – Sodobni problemi koroških Slovencev*, Ferlach/Borovlje.

Möcker, Hermann (1992): „Aprikosenklöße? – Nein, danke! „Österreichisches" Deutsch – „Deutschländisches" Deutsch". In: *Österreich in Geschichte und Literatur* 36, 236–249.

Neweklowsky, Gerhard (1978): *Die kroatischen Dialekte des Burgenlandes und der angrenzenden Gebiete*, Wien.

Neweklowsky, Gerhart (1990): „Kärntner Deutsch aus slawistischer Sicht: zum deutsch-slowenischen Sprachbund in Kärnten". In: Germanistische Linguistik 101–103, 477–500.

Pohl, Heinz Dieter (1982): „Einleitung". In: *Die slowenischen Namen Kärntens*, Kronsteiner, O. (Ed.), Österreichische Namenforschung, Sonderreihe 1, 5–43.

Pohl, Heinz Dieter (1991): „Die Bedeutung des Slowenischen für die Dialektologie und Onomastik Kärntens (und Osttirols)". In: *Die slawischen Sprachen* 27, 147–163.

Pohl, Heinz Dieter (1992a): „Kärnten – Deutsche und slowenische Namen". In: *Österreichische Namenforschung* 20, 1–88.

Pohl, Heinz Dieter (1992b): „Die Bedeutung des Slowenischen für die Deutsch-Kärntner Mundart". In: *Dialekte im Wandel*, Weiss, A. (Ed.), Göppingen, 157–169.

Pollak, Wolfgang (1992): *Was halten die Österreicher von ihrem Deutsch? Eine sprachpolitische und soziosemiotische Analyse der sprachlichen Identität der Österreicher*, Wien.

Ramovš, Fran (1924): *Historična gramatika slovenskega jezika II. Konzonantizem*, Laibach.

Repp, Friedrich (1960): „Slawische Familiennamen in Wien". In: *Polizei-Jahrbuch*, Wien, 169–178.

Repp, Friedrich (1974): Nachdruck von Repp 1960 in: *Österreichische Namenforschung* 1974/2, 41–49.

Scheuringer, Hermann (1992): „Deutsches Volk und deutsche Sprache". In: *Österreich in Geschichte und Literatur* 36, 162–173.

Schuchardt, Hugo (1883): *Slawo-deutsches und Slawo-italienisches. Dem Herrn Franz von Miklosich zum 20. Nov. 1883*. Graz [1884].

Steinhauser, Walter (1978): *Slawisches im Wienerischen*, Wien.

Tatzreiter, Herbert (1988): „Besonderheiten in der Morphologie der deutschen Sprache in Österreich". In: Wiesinger, 71–98.

Veiter, Theodor (1970): *Das Recht der Volksgruppen und Minderheiten in Österreich*, Wien.

Wadl, Wilhelm (1990): „Zur Entwicklung des Nationalitätenkonfliktes in Kärnten bis zum Jahre 1918 – historische Voraussetzungen". „Die Kärntner Volksabstimmung. Vorbereitung – Ablauf – Ergebnisanalyse – Nachwirkungen". In: *Kärntner Landesarchiv* 1990, 9–23 u. 165–198.

Walla, Fred (1992): „Vatersprache Deutsch: Überlegungen zur Sprache des Österreichers". In: *Österreich in Geschichte und Literatur* 36, 173–181.

Walzl, Werner (1991): „Reaktionen auf die Aussiedlung von Kärntner Slowenen". In: *Carinthia* I 181, 453–464.

Wiesinger Peter (Ed.) (1988): *Das österreichische Deutsch*, Wien.

Wolfram, Herwig (1979): *Conversio Bagoariorum et Carantanorum. Das Weißbuch der Salzburger Kirche über die erfolgreiche Mission in Karantanien und Pannonien*, Wien/Köln/Graz.

Wutte, Martin (1927): *Deutsch – Windisch – Slowenisch*, Klagenfurt.

Zöllner, Erich (1974): *Geschichte Österreichs*, Wien.

Zöllner, Erich (1988): *Der Österreichbegriff. Formen und Wandlungen in der Geschichte*, Wien.

Heinz Dieter Pohl, Klagenfurt (Österreich)

223. Deutsch−Slowenisch

1. Geographie und Demographie
2. Geschichte
3. Politik, Wirtschaft und allgemeine kulturelle sowie religiöse Lage
4. Statistik und Ethnoprofil
5. Soziolinguistische Lage
6. Sprachpolitische Lage
7. Allgemeines kontaktlinguistisches Porträt
8. Zu Forschungsgeschichte und Literatur
9. Bibliographie (in Auswahl)

1. Geographie und Demographie

Deutsch-slowenische Sprachkontakte finden im österreichischen Bundesland Kärnten seit vielen Jahrhunderten statt (s. 2.). Seit Beginn der Landesgeschichte, als das Herzogtum Kärnten (976) errichtet wurde, sind sowohl Slowenen als auch Deutsche autochthone Bevölkerung; allerdings breitet sich das Deutsche bis zum heutigen Tage auf Kosten des Slowenischen aus. Auf der Ebene der alltäglichen Umgangssprache und der Mundarten beruht die Beeinflussung der beiden Sprachen durchaus auf Gegenseitigkeit, wenngleich das Einwirken des Deutschen auf das Slowenische weitaus stärker ist bzw. in den letzten Jahrzehnten noch zugenommen hat, nicht zuletzt eine Folge der Prädominanz der deutschen Sprache bzw. ihres höheren Prestiges.

Das Bundesland Kärnten (slow. *Koroška*) umfaßt 9533 km² mit ca. (1991) 552 000 Einwohnern; seine Hauptstadt ist Klagenfurt (slow. *Celovec*) mit rund 90 000 Einwohnern. Es grenzt im Westen an (Ost-)Tirol, im Norden an Salzburg und die Steiermark, die auch im Osten eine gemeinsame Grenze mit Kärnten hat. Im Süden sind Italien und Slowenien (bis 1991 Jugoslawien) die Nachbarländer. Kärnten ist ein Becken- und Durchgangsland, das „alpine Drauland" (so Paschinger 1937, 5), vom Hochgebirge umschlossen; es bildet eine geographische Einheit. Seit es 1335 Habsburgischer Besitz geworden ist, hat sich seine Fläche nur mehr unwesentlich geändert (→ Sprachenkarte N).

Das historische Siedlungsgebiet der Slowenen in Kärnten war ein zusammenhängendes Areal, das einen breiten Streifen bildete und rund ein Viertel der Landesfläche bedeckte. In diesem Gebiet stellten sie − wenn man von den beiden großen Städten Klagenfurt und Villach absieht − den Hauptanteil der Bevölkerung, unter der bäuerlichen Bevölkerung nahezu 100%. Nach Czoernig (1857, 27, 74 und 77) verlief die deutsch-slowenische Sprachgrenze wie folgt (von Westen nach Osten): Malborghet − Möderndorf/Hermagor − Wasserscheide Gail/Drau − Villach − Zauchen − Dellach (bei Feldkirchen) − Moosburg − Nußberg − Galling − St. Donat − St. Sebastian − St. Gregorn (bei Klein-St. Veit) − Schmieddorf − Wölfnitz/Saualpe − Pustritz − Granitztal − Eis-Ruden (an der Drau) − Lavamünd (wobei die genannten Orte noch größtenteils im deutschsprachigen Gebiet liegen). Damals standen ca. 96 000 Slowenen ca. 223 000 Deutschen gegenüber; im Jahre 1910 betrug das Verhältnis ca. 74 000 zu ca. 300 000; heute geben nur noch ca. 15 000 Personen (das sind weniger als 3% der Einwohner Kärntens) Slowenisch als *Umgangssprache* an, eine Zahl, die den wahren Verhältnissen nicht ganz entspricht. Heute kann man auch von keinem geschlossenen slowenischen Siedlungsgebiet mehr sprechen, sondern nur von einem gemischtsprachigen Gebiet, das durch Sprachwechsel (Assimilation) zu einem solchen geworden ist. In den Gemeinden mit slowenischem Bevölkerungsanteil schwankt dessen Prozentsatz zwischen einigen Prozent (z. B. Magdalensberg 1,3%) und 95% (so Zell/Sele), im gesamten gemischtsprachigen Gebiet dürfte der Anteil slowenischsprachiger Personen bei 13% liegen (berechnet nach Gutleb/Unkart 1990, 163 u. 176).

Die Siedlungssituation der Kärntner Slowenen wird oft als Streulage inmitten einer deutschsprachigen Mehrheit bezeichnet (so Gutleb/Unkart 1990, 162), was zwar dem Status quo entspricht, aber der historischen Entwicklung nicht gerecht wird, handelt es sich doch beim slowenischen Sprachgebiet um ein durch Sprachwechsel (Assimilation) entstandenes Rückzugsgebiet. Insgesamt trifft für das Areal des deutsch-slowenischen Sprachkontakts der Begriff „gemischtsprachiges Gebiet" am ehesten zu (→ Art. 222).

2. Geschichte

Die Geschichte der slowenischen Volksgruppe in Kärnten wird im Zusammenhang mit der gesamtösterreichischen in Art. 222 abgehandelt.

3. Politik, Wirtschaft und allgemeine kulturelle sowie religiöse Lage

Kärnten ist eines der 9 Bundesländer der Republik Österreich. Nach der derzeit gültigen Verfassung hat der Landtag 36 Abgeordnete. Seit 1945 ist es keiner slowenischen wahlwerbenden Gruppe gelungen, einen Sitz im Kärntner Landtag zu erringen, jedoch wurden Slowenen in Gemeinderäte gewählt (1985 waren es 44, zu denen noch einige weitere auf Listen von ÖVP und SPÖ kamen, vgl. Bogataj 1989, 317 u. Gutleb/Unkart 1990, 165); diese sind im „Klub slowenischer Gemeinderäte" organisiert, die meisten von ihnen auf der „Kärntner Einheitsliste/Koroška Enotna Lista" (KEL).

In wirtschaftlicher Hinsicht gehören die slowenischen Gebiete Kärntens zu den strukturschwachen Regionen, die auch heute noch stark agrarisch geprägt sind (16% aller Slowenen leben von der Landwirtschaft, aber nur 6,5% der Deutschen). Insgesamt waren laut Volkszählung 1981 im gemischtsprachigen Gebiet 81% der Beschäftigten als Pendler einzustufen; von den Slowenen pendeln 72%, meist nach Klagenfurt und Villach (Zahlen nach Bogataj 1989, 326). Allerdings verfügen die Slowenen über ein gut entwickeltes Genossenschaftswesen, seit 1989 gibt es auch einen Slowenischen Wirtschaftsverband. Slowenische Gewerbebetriebe sind größtenteils Transport- und Einzelhandelsunternehmen sowie im Fremdenverkehrsbereich anzutreffen, v. a. letzterer trägt zum wirtschaftlichen Aufschwung des gemischtsprachigen Gebietes bei.

Im Bildungswesen bestehen keine gravierenden Unterschiede zwischen Deutschen und Slowenen, letztere weisen jedoch eine höhere Akademikerquote auf, wie überhaupt die Bildung der etwa 30—35jährigen Angehörigen der Minderheit überdurchschnittlich gut ist (Bogataj 1989, 326 f; Gutleb/Unkart 1990, 169), nicht zuletzt eine positive Folge des Schulwesens; im gemischtsprachigen Gebiet (und seit 1989 auch in Klagenfurt) wird Unterricht sowohl in slowenischer als auch deutscher Sprache angeboten; die Schüler, die zum zweisprachigen Unterricht angemeldet sind, erhalten Unterricht zu gleichen Teilen in beiden Sprachen. Die Anmeldungen sind in den letzten Jahren wieder leicht angestiegen und liegen in 62 Schulen bei etwa 22%, woraus folgt, daß nicht nur Kinder von Slowenen am slowenischen Unterricht teilnehmen. Seit dem Schuljahr 1976/1977 besuchen an ca. 15 Hauptschulen rund 350 Schüler slowenischen Sprachunterricht (Gutleb/Unkart 1990, 167). Im Jahre 1957 wurde in Klagenfurt das Gymnasium für Slowenen gegründet, aus dem bis 1992 über 1000 Absolventen hervorgegangen sind. 1992 nahm auch eine slowenische Handelsakademie, ebenfalls in Klagenfurt, ihre Tätigkeit auf. An der 1970 gegründeten Hochschule für Bildungswissenschaften, heute Universität Klagenfurt, gibt es seit 1973 Slowenistik als Studienfach mit z. T. auch slowenischsprachigen Lehrveranstaltungen.

Die beiden slowenischen Zentralverbände „Rat der Kärntner Slowenen (Christlicher Kulturverband)" und „Zentralverband slowenischer Organisationen (Slowenischer Kulturverband)" geben je eine Wochenzeitung heraus („Naš Tednik" bzw. „Slovenski vestnik"), daneben erscheint noch eine ganze Reihe weiterer periodischer Druckschriften (vgl. Bogataj 1989, 328 ff). Der Hermagoras-Verlag (Klagenfurt) ist einer der ältesten Verlage Kärntens und hat schon mehr als 17 Millionen Bücher herausgegeben. Im Rundfunk (Landesstudio Kärnten in Klagenfurt) wird täglich 50 Minuten (Mo.—Sa. 18.10—19.00, So. 6.30—7.00 u. 18.10—18.30 Uhr) in slowenisch gesendet; am Sonntag gibt es seit Mitte 1989 ein halbstündiges slowenisches Fernsehprogramm („Dober dan, Koroška", 13.00—13.30 Uhr). Darüber hinaus ist in den meisten Gebieten mit gemischtsprachiger Bevölkerung Hörfunk und Fernsehen aus der Republik Slowenien zu empfangen (auch über Kabel).

Die Kärntner Slowenen sind — von wenigen Ausnahmen abgesehen — nach ihrem religiösen Bekenntnis Katholiken. Die katholische Kirche hat im Laufe der Jahrhunderte durch ihre Bildungsarbeit die slowenische Volksgruppe in ihrer kulturellen Entwicklung maßgeblich mitgeformt (vgl. Bogataj 1989, 183 ff), und auch heute noch spielt sie im Leben der Minderheit eine tragende Rolle. Auch zum friedlichen Zusammenleben der beiden Sprachvölker Kärntens hat die Kirche einen bedeutenden Beitrag geleistet. In der 3. Session der Kärntner Diözesan-Synode vom 26./27. 10. 1972 wurde das zukunftsweisende Dokument „Das Zusammenleben der Deutschen und Slowenen in der Kirche Kärntens" verabschiedet. Der deutsch-slowenische Koordinationsausschuß der Diözese Gurk gibt regelmäßig Sammelbände mit dem Titel „Das gemeinsame Kärnten — Skupna Koroška" heraus (so z. B. Waldstein/Inzko 1991). — Der

Vollständigkeit halber sei erwähnt, daß es auch protestantische Slowenen (Augsburger Bekenntnis) gibt, und zwar ist der zweisprachige Ortsteil der Gemeinde Arnoldstein *Agoritschach* (slow. *Zagoriče*) mit seinen rund 700 Einwohnern rein evangelisch (vgl. Bogataj 1989, 189).

4. Statistik und Ethnoprofil

Die Mehrheitsbevölkerung in Kärnten wird meist „deutsch", auch „Deutschkärntner", bezeichnet, die Slowenen werden heute ebenfalls „Slowenen" oder genauer „Kärntner Slowenen" genannt. Früher wurden die Slowenen im Deutschen „Windische" genannt, dann war „windisch" und „slowenisch" synonym, wobei „windisch" immer mehr eine spezielle, teils pejorative Nebenbedeutung erhalten hat. In der nationalpolitischen Auseinandersetzung in der ersten Hälfte unseres Jahrhunderts wurde *slowenisch* als „nationalslowenisch, sich zum Slowenentum bekennend", *windisch* als „slowenischsprachig, nicht nationalbewußt, politisch zum Deutschtum tendierend usw." aufgefaßt (vgl. Wutte 1927; Pohl 1990 a, 118 ff). Noch heute gibt es eine (allerdings politisch und statistisch nicht ins Gewicht fallende) kleine Gruppe von „Windischen", Personen slowenischer Abstammung mit überwiegend deutscher Schulbildung. Da in den statistischen Erhebungen noch immer *windisch* neben *slowenisch* geführt wird, sind die „Windischen" als besondere Gruppe präsent, wenn auch ihre Existenz wissenschaftlich nicht nachgewiesen werden kann (vgl. u. a. Goebl 1988, 858 f; Dressler 1974, 245). Auf Slowenisch werden die Deutschen *nemci*, sie selbst *slovenci*, auch *koroški slovenci*, die „Windischen" *vindišarji* (in der wissenschaftlichen Literatur) oder *nemčurji* (d. i. „Deutschtümler", umgangssprachlich und in der politischen Auseinandersetzung) genannt. Unter *Windisch* wird im deutschen Sprachgebrauch (v. a. in der Germanistik bis vor nicht allzu langer Zeit) auch „volkstümliches, mundartliches Slowenisch aus Kärnten" im Gegensatz zu der auf den Krainer Mundarten beruhenden *slowenischen Schrift-* und *Literatursprache* verstanden; diese Sichtweise läßt die historische Bedeutung des Begriffes außer Acht, nämlich daß *windisch* und *slowenisch* synonym waren, auch wenn Slowenen deutsch schrieben (man denke an Gutsmanns „Deutsch-windisches Wörterbuch" aus dem Jahre 1789 oder Dajnkos „Lehrbuch der windischen Sprache" aus dem Jahre 1824). Heute hat *Windisch* in der deutschen Umgangssprache vielfach auch die Bedeutung „schlechtes Deutsch".

Nach den statistischen Angaben der Volkszählung 1991 bekannten sich 14 580 Personen, das sind weniger als 3% der Gesamtbevölkerung Kärntens, ausdrücklich als slowenisch- oder „windisch"-sprechend auf Grund der Frage nach der *Umgangssprache*. Die tatsächliche Zahl der slowenischsprachigen Kärntner liegt freilich weit höher und wird auf ca. 50 000 geschätzt (so Bogataj 1989, 287).

Das Slowenische in Kärnten wird traditionell vier Dialekten zugeordnet, die zu einer allerdings auch (nach Italien und Slowenien hineinreichenden) „Kärntner Gruppe" (Koroška skupina) zusammengefaßt werden (vgl. Ramovš 1957; Fischer 1980, 91; Logar 1975, 107 ff):

(1) Gailtaler Dialekt/Ziljsko narečje
(2) Rosentaler Dialekt/Rožansko narečje
(3) Jauntaler Dialekt/Podjunsko narečje
(4) Remschenig- oder Obir-Dialekt/Remšeniško narečje.

5. Soziolinguistische Lage

Trotz einer ganzen Reihe von minderheitenfreundlichen administrativen Maßnahmen auf Grund des Artikels 7 des „Staatsvertrages" aus dem Jahre 1955 (vgl. Gutleb/Unkart 1990, 180), des Volksgruppengesetzes 1976 (vgl. ebda. 180 f) und einiger Verordnungen der österreichischen Bundesregierung (vgl. ebda. 184 ff) spielt die slowenische Sprache im öffentlichen Leben Kärntens ein Schattendasein, wenn auch grundsätzlich ihre Lage ungleich besser ist als die des Kroatischen im Burgenland (→ Art. 224). Die Ursachen dafür sind vielfältig, in erster Linie dürfte es daran liegen, daß zwar nahezu alle Slowenen von Kindheit an auch die deutsche Sprache beherrschen, umgekehrt aber die deutschen Kärntner in den rein deutschen Gebieten und in den Ballungszentren kaum, in den gemischtsprachigen Gebieten nur z. T. über Slowenischkenntnisse verfügen. Die bei der deutschsprachigen, z. T. slowenischstämmigen Bevölkerung (insbesondere der älteren Generation) vorhandenen Vorurteile spielen hier eine nicht zu unterschätzende Rolle; auch der kleine slowenische Sprachraum mit ca. 2,2 Mill. Menschen liefert nur geringen Anreiz, die Sprache zu erlernen bzw. zu gebrauchen. Wenn sich auch in der jüngeren und mittleren Generation die Einstellung zur slowenischen Sprache wandelt und sie wieder als zweite Landessprache auf mehr Akzeptanz stößt, ist derzeit noch kein Ansteigen ihres Gebrauchs im öffentlichen Leben festzustellen. Slowenische Aufschriften im gemischtsprachigen Gebiet beschränken sich zumeist auf *Ljudska šola* „Volksschule" oder *Gasilski dom* „Feuerwehrhaus" bzw. private Aufschriften wie *Gostilna* „Gasthaus" oder *Trgovina* „Kaufhaus, Geschäft"; topographische Bezeichnungen in slowenischer Sprache sind nur in einem geringen Umfang (in den Bezirken Völkermarkt und Klagenfurt-Land) auf Grund der Straßenverkehrsordnung auf Ortstafeln und einigen Wegweisern angebracht worden (in 9 Gemeinden von insgesamt 30 in Frage kommenden). Jedoch ist der Gebrauch des Slowenischen als Amtssprache zusätzlich zum Deutschen bei 13 Gemeindebehörden und Gendarmerieposten und den zuständigen Bezirksgerichten und 63 Regionalbehörden (wie Bezirkshauptmannschaften und Amt der Kärntner Landesregierung) zulässig (vgl. Gutleb/Unkart 178; zur Verwendung des Slowenischen in der amtlichen Kartographie vgl. Jordan 1988 u. 1992). Es wird auch in Gemeinderatssitzungen z. T. slowenisch gesprochen, überwiegend z. B. in Zell/Sele.

Trotzdem muß man abschließend feststellen, daß die slowenische Sprache in Kärnten v. a. im privaten und familiären Bereich und in den slowenischen Genossenschaften (17), Sparkassen (27) und Vereinen (ca. 80) verwendet wird. Von einer echten Gleichberechtigung (und mitunter sogar Bevorzugung) kann man nur im kirchlichen Bereich sprechen. Dementsprechend werden bei Befragungen nach der Verwendung der slowenischen Sprache außerhalb der Familie am meisten die mit der Religionsausübung verbundenen sprachlichen Ausdrucksformen genannt (54,4%), dann folgt der Nachbar (54,1%); Briefträger und Arbeitskollegen werden schon deutlich weniger genannt (29,2% bzw. 29,4%), am wenigsten spricht man slowenisch mit dem Chef (11,6%) und dem Gendarmen (10,3%; vgl. Flaschberger/Reiterer 1980, 809).

6. Sprachpolitische Lage

Zum Schulwesen s. o. sub 3., zum Gebrauch des Slowenischen im öffentlichen Leben sub 3. (Rundfunk und Fernsehen) und sub 5. (Amtssprachenregelung u. dgl.). — Anders als bei den burgenländischen Kroaten (→ Art. 224) wurde von den Kärntner Slowenen immer die allen Slowenen gemeinsame Schriftsprache verwendet.

7. Allgemeines kontaktlinguistisches Porträt

In Kärnten erfolgt der Sprachkontakt sowohl vom Deutschen zum Slowenischen als auch vom Slowenischen zum Deutschen, in beiden Fällen hauptsächlich auf der Ebene der Verkehrs- und täglichen Umgangssprache, die Dialekte miteinschließend. Auf der Ebene der Schriftsprache war der deutsche Einfluß auf das Slowenische sehr groß, wurde aber durch sprachplanerische Maßnahmen zurückgedrängt („Slawisierung", „Archaisierung", „Purismus", vgl. Lenček 1982, 271; Bezlaj 1967, 9 ff). Die slowenische Volkssprache weist auch außerhalb Kärntens einen starken deutschen Einfluß auf (vgl. Kranzmayer 1944 u. Striedter-Temps 1963), der allerdings durch den Wegfall der entsprechenden Rahmenbedingungen (d. h. durch die Vertreibung und Aussiedlung der Deutschen nach 1945) rezessiv ist.

7.1. Slowenisch-deutscher Sprachkontakt

Die (ehemalige, s. o. sub 1.) deutsch-slowenische Sprachgrenze teilt das Gebiet der deutschen Mittelkärntner Dialekte in zwei Varianten (Pohl 1992, 157 f): in die zentrale, nördliche und westliche, bäuerlich geprägte Mundart (deren Kennzeichen die Diphthonge *ea oa* in Wörtern wie *roat, gean, schean, groas/greaser* „rot, gehen, schön, groß/größer" sowie altertümliche Wortformen wie *å:he* „hinunter", *fertn* „voriges Jahr" sind) und in eine südliche, städtisch geprägte Mundart (die *ro:t, ge:n, sche:n, gro:s/gre:ser* spricht bzw. *å:we, fu:rigs Jå:r* sagt). Für diese „Südmittelkärntner" Mundart, die sich von den Städten aus über das ursprünglich rein slowenische bäuerliche Gebiet ausgebreitet hat, sind zahlreiche Erscheinungen typisch, die auf slowenische Einflüsse schließen lassen — die Folge von Sprachkontakt.

Daß slowenisch-deutscher Sprachkontakt historisch gesehen großräumiger anzusetzen ist als heute, zeigt u. a. die „Kärntner Dehnung" (nach der in Kärntner Mundart *Wiese(n)/wissen, Ofen/offen* gleich lauten, nämlich [wi:sn], [o:fn]), die Folge einer bereits vor mehreren hundert Jahren eingetretenen phonologischen Interferenz (vgl. Pohl 1992, 16 ff; Neweklowsky 1990, 486 f mit Lit.). Auch der Wortschatz zeigt dies: so gibt es in Oberkärnten und Osttirol Reliktwörter slowenischer Herkunft, die es weiter östlich heute nicht mehr gibt (z. B. *Koprits* „ein Almkraut" von slow. *koperc* „Fenchel", *Puaklat* „vorderer Teil der Heufuhre" von slow. *pod* „unter" + *klet* „Haufen", *Topanits* „ein Gebäck" zu slow. *topel* „warm", vgl. slowak. *topenica*; vgl. Pohl 1989 a, 254 u. 256 bzw. 1992, 166). Es gibt auch gemeinbairische Lehnwörter wie *Paier* „Quecke" (slow. *pirje*) und *Jause* (slow. *južina* „Mittagessen", welche Bedeutung das deutsche Wort heute noch im Lesachtal hat), die keineswegs auf Kärnten beschränkt sind (vgl. Pohl 1989 a, 254 u. 257 bzw. 1992, 165).

Die Folgen des Sprachkontaktes machen sich auf allen Ebenen des Sprachsystems bemerkbar. So entspricht die Deutschkärntner Aussprache von (z. B.) *Villach/Villacher* bezüglich des *ch* ziemlich genau der slowenischen von (z. B.) slow. *suh/suha* „trocken" (vgl. Neweklowsky 1989, 207 f). Ferner haben die zentralen Mittelkärntner deutschen und die Kärntner slowenischen Mundarten eine Verlagerung der Artikulation in den hinteren Bereich der Mundhöhle gemeinsam: im Slowenischen zeigt sich dies am Übergang von *k/g* zu *q/h*, im Deutschen in einer mehr hinteren Artikulation von *k*, *kh* und *g*, in beiden Sprachen bei *d*, *t* und *r* (Neweklowsky 1989, 205).

Im Bereich der Satzlehre fällt auf, daß im Südmittelkärntner Bereich (auch in den Städten Klagenfurt und Villach) das Pronomen *es* in Sätzen wie *re:gnet* „es regnet", *schnaip(t)* „es schneit", *hait wår khålt* „heute war es kalt" fehlt, mit anderen Worten: die slowenische Konstruktion (*dežuje, sneži, danes je bilo mrzlo*) wird nachgeahmt (Neweklowsky 1990, 488 f). Ferner ist im gleichen Gebiet *mir mitn Frantse* „wir mit Franz" statt „ich und Franz" zu beobachten — ebenfalls auf Grund eines slowenischen Musters (Neweklowsky 1985, 35 f). Häufig ist das Verbum an den Anfang des Satzes gerückt, insbesondere im Dialog, bei Antworten u. dgl., z. B. *khum i glaich* „ich komme gleich", *khumt/khimp a schon* „er kommt schon", *saint se schon untawe:gs* „sie sind schon unterwegs" usw. Initialstellung des Verbs ist auch im Slowenischen sehr weit verbreitet; dadurch, daß das Pronominalsubjekt (*ich, du* ...) meist wegfällt, steht rein statistisch das Verb noch häufiger am Satzanfang, als es ihm wortfolgetheoretisch eigentlich zukommt. Das hat nun auch seine Auswirkungen auf das Kärntner Deutsch (vgl. Pohl 1992, 162). Auffällig ist auch der adverbiale Gebrauch von *nichts* [niks] im Sinne von „nicht" (als Negation), was genau dem slow. *nič* entspricht (vgl. Neweklowsky 1990, 491): z. B. *er is niks då*: „er ist nicht da", (a) *khumst hait niks tsu uns?* „kommst du heute nicht zu uns?".

Beim Sprachkontakt spielen die Lehnbeziehungen die größte Rolle. Bisher wurden rund 180 slowenische Lehnwörter in der Fachliteratur gesammelt (Pohl 1989 b, 77 ff, 1989 a/1990 b). Dazu kommen noch mehrere Mischformen wie z. B. *Plerénke* „weinerliches Kind" (zu dt. *plärren* mit slow. Wortbildung) oder *Kaischleka(r)* „Keuschler, Bewohner einer Keusche" (vgl. Pohl 1992, 164). Von den ca. 180 Lehnwörtern sind heute noch 46% regional in bäuerlicher Mundart üblich, 24% sind heute schon unverständlich, aber immerhin 16% sind allgemein in der Kärntner deutschen Umgangssprache gebräuchlich (Beispiele s. u.).

Wie eng der Sprachkontakt war, zeigt sich u. a. darin, daß auch deutsche Lehnwörter im Slowenischen ins Deutsche rückentlehnt wurden, wie z. B. *Patsche* „Eber" (slow. *pačej* von dt. *Bock*, Pohl 1989 a, 258, 1992, 165), *Maischl* „Netzlaibchen" (slow. *majželj* zu bair. *Maisen* „Schnitte", vgl. Pohl 1989 a, 258; Striedter-Temps 1963, 174), *Schwachta* „Sippschaft (abwertend)" (slow. ma. *złahta* „Verwandtschaft" zu dt. *Ge-schlecht*, vgl. Pohl 1989 a, 258; Kranzmayer 1944, 37 f).

Als weitere Beispiele für slowenische Lehnwörter im Kärntner Deutsch seien genannt (s. a. Pohl 1992, 164 ff; sie sind in der Umgangssprache des Kärntner Zentralraumes allgemein üblich): *Kopa(r)* „Dille" (slow. *koper*), *Moidú:sch* „meiner Seel'!" (slow. *moji duši*), *Sa:saka* „Verhacktes (aus Speck als Brotaufstrich)" (slow. *zaseka*), *Jaukh* „Föhn" (slow. *jug* „Süden"), *Tschoja* „Eichelhäher" (slow. *šoja*), *Štrankalan* „Fisolen, grüne Bohnen" (slow. *strok* „Hülse, Schote", aus **strank-*), *Potítsn* „Potitze (ein Kuchen)" (slow. *potica*), *Pogátschn* „ein Weißbrot" (slow. *pogača*), *tswi:ln* „schreien, jammern (von Kleinkindern)" (slow. *cviliti*), *Tschatsch* „Plunder" (slow. *čača*).

Soziolinguistisch kann man die slowenischen Lehnwörter im Kärntner Deutsch in zwei Gruppen teilen (vgl. Pohl 1992, 166 f):

(1) *ad hoc*-Entlehnungen: Wörter, die unter den Bedingungen der Zweisprachigkeit Zitatwörter geworden sind, dazu gehören einige Bezeichnungen von Speisen und aus der bäuerlichen Sphäre.

(2) allgemein-umgangssprachliche Entlehnungen: Wörter, die dem Sprachschatz der allgemeinen Kärntner Umgangssprache (zumindest des Zentralraumes) angehören bzw. in der lokalen (bäuerlichen) Mundart allgemein üblich sind.

Zu Ortsnamen → Art. 222.

7.2. Deutsch-slowenischer Sprachkontakt

Trotz zahlreicher deutsch-slowenischer Interferenzerscheinungen und eines sich auf allen Ebenen des Sprachsystems manifestierenden deutschen Einflusses sind die typisch slowenischen Sprachstrukturen als solche intakt geblieben (z. B. Flexion, Dual usw.). Viele der im folgenden genannten Erscheinungen kommen auch außerhalb Kärntens vor. — Auf konvergente phonologische Entwicklungen wurde bereits sub 7.1. hingewiesen, weiteres Material bieten Neweklowsky 1990, 483 ff; Lessiak 1983, 253 = 1910, 278. Zur Lautsubstitution in den Lehnbeziehungen vgl. u. a. Striedter-Temps 1963, 1 ff; auch in Kranzmayer 1944 finden sich zahlreiche Hinweise.

Einflüsse im grammatischen System der slowenischen Mundarten sind in der Flexion weniger, v. a. aber in Wortbildung und -folge häufig zu beobachten. Zunächst ist der Artikel zu nennen: bestimmter Artikel *ta* (auch *tə, tɛ, ti*) mit z. T. anderer Funktion als im Deutschen (vgl. Isačenko 1939, 89 f und Prunč 1979, 7); unbestimmter Artikel *en, ena, eno* (z. B. Zell/Sele *an* usw., Obir-Dialekt *hən* usw.), z. B. *je to sám tî húdə dúh* „er ist selbst der böse Geist" (Isačenko 1939, 90), *mɔ́:ja ta stà:ra mú:za* „mein alter Arbeitshut", *hən bù:rən pà:wər* „ein armer Bauer" (Karničar 1990, 63); wie im Kärntner Deutsch ist der unbestimmte Artikel auch im Plural möglich: *anî qŕajncɜ̀ pŕawələ* (etwa) „gewisse Krainer erzählten" (Isačenko 1939, 91), *hənɛ pèa:trɛd šì:lingu* (etwa) „ungefähr 50 Schilling" (Karničar 1990, 63). In der älteren slowenischen Schriftsprache wurde der Artikel auch geschrieben, z. B. Trubar *„Ta perui deil tiga nouiga Testamenta"* (= der erste Teil des Neuen Testaments).

In der Flexion ist aus dem Deutschen das Element *-n-* (über Entlehnungen) eingedrungen, z. B. *nudl* „Nudel", pl. *nudlni* (Lessiak 1983, 253 = 1910, 278), *bù:rštsè:məl* (m.!), Gsg. *-əlna* „Wurstsemmel", detto *sɔ́:xən, -xna* „Sache" (Karničar 1990, 64); vgl. auch Bildungen wie *Pri Joklnu* „Beim Jokl" (= Bierjokl, Gasthaus in Klagenfurt) oder bei Hofnamen, z. B. *pər Qə́rlna* „beim Karl", *pər ər-*

nêjclnə „beim Arneitzel" (Feinig 1958, 10 Nr. 21 u. 58 Nr. 139). Im älteren Dialekt auch Umlauterscheinungen, z. B. in Lehnwörtern *ajnfɔl* „Einfall", pl. *ajnfelə*, z. T. auch in slawischen Wörtern, z. B. *kezəca = kozica*, Diminutiv zu *koza* „Ziege" (vgl. Lessiak 1983, 253 = 1910, 278).

In der verbalen Wortbildung gibt es zahlreiche Lehnpräfixe, wie z. B. *bek-* „weg-" (z. B. *bek iti* „weggehen"; Hafner/Prunč 1982, 95 ff insgesamt 19 Zusammensetzungen) oder *co-* (*cu:-, cuə-*) „zu-" (z. B. *co pustiti* „zulassen"; Hafner/Prunč 1987, 41 ff insgesamt 39 Zusammensetzungen), auch Nachbildungen (Calques) wie *gor iti* „hinaufgehen", *dol iti* „hinuntergehen" (allgemein umgangssprachlich; weitere Beispiele bei Karničar 1990, 139 f u. 150). Ferner geläufig Bildungen wie *pərglihat* (slow. *pri* + dt. *gleichen*) „vergleichen" (Andrej 1980, 30), in anderen Wortarten z. B. *c mɔw* „zu wenig" (dt. *zu* + slow. *mal*) oder *c weik* „zu groß" (dt. *zu* + slow. *velik*, Andrej 1980, 30).

Die deutschen Substantiva werden größtenteils nicht in ihrem grammatischen Geschlecht, sondern nach morphologischen Kriterien integriert, z. B. *čȉŕfat* m. (aus *Kirchfahrt*), da auf Konsonant endend, aber *fȁŕba* f. (aus *Farbe*), da auf Vokal endend (vgl. Isačenko 1939, 93); *-e* wird oft als Pluralmorph aufgefaßt, z. B. *w Kwè:laχ* „im Quelle[kauf]haus]", *na tà:nkštè:laχ* „an der Tankstelle" (Lpl., Karničar 1990, 64). Wenn Slowenen deutsch sprechen, wird oft das grammatische Geschlecht des Lehnwortes im Slowenischen ins Deutsche tranferiert, wie z. B. *da Ra:dl* (m.) „(der) Fahrrad", *da Fasl* (m.) „(der) Faß" (vgl. Andrej 1980, 26 und v. a. Prunč 1979, 17 ff), doch viele Abweichungen im Kärntner Deutsch sind gemeinbairisch (z. B. *da Pentsí:n* „(der) Benzin", *da Te:n* „(der) Tenne", daher ist die Frage des slowenischen Einflusses von Fall zu Fall zu prüfen. — Bemerkenswert erscheint, daß dt. *-ung* nicht der oben skizzierten Regel folgt, sondern durch *-inga* (f.) substituiert wird, z. B. *basinga* „Fassung", *beringa* „Währung" (Hafner/Prunč 1982, 86 u. 109), *cajt-inga, -unga, -ejnga* (f. sg.), *-enge* (f. pl.) „Zeitung" (Hafner/Prunč 1987, 6 f).

Oft ist die Wortfolge vom Deutschen beeinflußt, z. B. *qədər pa maw câjta je* „wenn dann etwas Zeit ist" (Auxiliare *je* am Satzende wie im Deutschen, vgl. Sturm-Schnabl 1973, 180), *wčè:ra j bŕɛst wən bè:w* „gestern ist die Frist aus gewesen" (Karničar 1990, 64), oder es wird unter den Bedingungen der

Zweisprachigkeit überhaupt die deutsche Phraseologie nachgeahmt, z. B. *qə̀dər snȋəχ prɔ̀w wę̂lqə sem prída* (wörtlich) „wenn Schnee recht viel daher kommt" (vgl. Sturm-Schnabl 1973, 181), *ję̀s hŕeam lȋəč* (wörtlich, dt. ma.) „ich gehe liegen" (Isačenko 1939, 132). Wie im Zusammenhang mit den Lehnwörtern auch eine „Lehnphraseologie" entsteht, zeigen folgende Beispiele: *jas sm̩ knɔp pr ka:sə* „ich bin knapp bei Kasse", *motor jə ha:slaufaw* „der Motor ist heißgelaufen" (Andrej 1980, 31), *ən ję na tǫ́ fərbǫ̂ltər šǫ́w, da sə patrȋp tərštę́lala* „Und der Verwalter ist darauf eingegangen, daß sie den Betrieb eingestellt haben" (Isačenko 1939, 132).

Daß beim Lehnwortschatz zwischen Lehnwort und Zitatwort nur schwer unterschieden werden kann, darauf hat schon Isačenko (1939, 124 ff) hingewiesen und es so formuliert (Isačenko 1939, 146): „Von Lehnwörtern gilt, daß sie, infolge der weitgehenden Zweisprachigkeit, zunächst als 'Zitatwörter' eindringen, sodaß die alte Form neben dem Zitatwort bestehen bleibt (*cajt* neben *čas* „Zeit"). Oft besteht keinerlei Notwendigkeit der Entlehnung, da der Begriff in der Mundart einen alten ererbten Namen trägt. Die Zweisprachigkeit läßt aber den Sprechenden gar nicht dessen gewahr werden, daß er eigentlich ein fremdes Wort verwendet hat, weil er bei seinem ebenfalls zweisprachigen Gesprächspartner das Verständnis des Zitatwortes aus der anderen Sprache voraussetzen kann. So ist es nicht immer leicht, eine genaue Grenze zwischen assimilierten Lehnwörtern und noch nicht angeglichenen Zitatwörtern zu ziehen." Die Häufigkeit solcher Zitatwörter ist u. a. im „Thesaurus" leicht feststellbar (vgl. Hafner/Prunč 1982 ff); in jeder slowenischen Mundartaufnahme kommen sie vor.

7.3. Gemeinsame Züge aus dem Romanischen

Die romanische Nachbarschaft hat einen Einfluß sowohl auf das Slowenische als auch auf das Bairische ausgeübt, der sich im Sprachkontakt potenziert hat. Systematische Untersuchungen liegen hier noch nicht vor. Gemeinsame Calques sind z. B. dt. ma. *Auswart*, slow. ma. *vigred* „Frühling" (vgl. furlan. *inšude*, Umbildung von roman. **exitus*) oder dt. ma. *Unterdå':ch*, slow. *podstrešje* „Dachboden" (vgl. furlan. *sotèt* von roman. *subtum tectum*), gemeinsame Lehnwörter z. B. dt. ma. *tschentschen* „nörgeln, räsonieren", slow. *čančati* „klatschen, plaudern" (vgl. ladin. *čan-čar* „reden, sprechen") oder dt. ma. *Fra:tn*, slow. *frata* „Holzschlag" (vgl. furlan. *fràte* „entholzte Stelle"; weitere Beispiele Pohl 1992, 167). Aus dem Bereich der Morphologie sei u. a. auf den Superlativ hingewiesen, der in beiden Kontaktsprachen nach dem Muster „Artikel + Komparativ" gebildet wird, z. B. slow. ma. *tə stá:riš* (wörtlich) „der ältere" (solche Bildungen waren einst im Bairischen gang und gäbe, sind aber heute selten geworden).

8. Zu Forschungsgeschichte und Literatur

Der Sprachkontakt in Kärnten und das Fortschreiten der Ausdehnung des Deutschen auf Kosten des Slowenischen ist schon in jener Zeit beobachtet worden, als die Lage für letzteres noch weitaus günstiger war als heute, nämlich in der ersten Hälfte des 19. Jahrhunderts durch Urban Jarnik in seinen „Andeutungen über Kärntens Germanisierung. Ein philologisch statistischer Versuch" (1826 in der Zeitschrift „Carinthia"). Die erste umfangreiche (germanistische) Studie zum wechselseitigen Sprachkontakt ist Lessiak 1910. Seit damals ist keine Publikation zu deutschen oder slowenischen Mundarten Kärntens ohne Bezug auf Interferenzen bzw. Sprachkontakt (z. B. Isačenko 1939 oder Kranzmayer 1944) zu nennen. In den letzten Jahren hat in bezug auf Kärnten zuerst die slowenische, dann auch die deutsche dialektologische Forschung einen großen Aufschwung erfahren. Man denke hier v. a. an das große Unternehmen Hafner/Prunč 1982 ff oder an Monographien wie Karničar 1990. Es war auch ein Slawist, der die erste neue Studie zur Rolle des Slowenischen in der Kärntner Sprachlandschaft vorgelegt hat (Neweklowsky 1985) und von einem „deutsch-slowenischen Sprachbund" spricht (Neweklowsky 1990). In meinen eigenen Arbeiten bin ich bestrebt, die regionale Ausdehnung des slowenischen Einflusses auf die Kärntner Volkssprache festzustellen und diesen möglichst vollständig zu erfassen und zu dokumentieren (v. a. Pohl 1989 a, 1990 b u. 1992).

9. Bibliographie (in Auswahl)

Andrej, Johann (1980): *Untersuchungen zur Zweisprachigkeit in Griffen und Umgebung*, Graz (Hausarbeit, unveröffentlicht).

Bezlaj, France (1967): *Eseji o slovenskem jeziku*, Laibach.

Bogataj, Mirko (1989): *Die Kärntner Slowenen*, Klagenfurt/Wien.

Czoernig, Carl v. (1857): *Ethnographie der österreichischen Monarchie*, Bd. I/1., Wien.

Dressler, Wolfgang (1974): „Minderheitssprachen als Spannungsfaktoren". In: *Wissenschaft und Weltbild 27*, 243−252.

Feinig, Anton (1958): *Die Namen der Bauernhöfe im Bereich der einstigen Grundherrschaft Hollenburg in Kärnten*, Wien (Dissertation).

Fischer, Gero (1980): *Das Slowenische in Kärnten. Eine Studie zur Sprachpolitik*, Wien.

Flaschberger, Ludwig/Reiterer, Albert F. (1980): *Der tägliche Abwehrkampf. Kärntens Slowenen*, Wien.

Goebl, Hans (1988): „Forschungsethische Probleme". In: *Soziolinguistics/Soziolinguistik*, Ammon, U./Dittmar, N./Mattheier, K. D. (Eds.), vol. II, Berlin/New York, 855−866.

Gutleb, Angelika/Unkart, Ralf (Red.) (1990): *Die Minderheiten im Alpen-Adria-Raum*, Arbeitsgemeinschaft Alpen-Adria, Klagenfurt.

Hafner, Stanislaus/Prunč, Erich (1982 ff): *Thesaurus der slowenischen Volkssprache in Kärnten*, Wien (I 1982, II 1987, III 1992, IV 1994).

Isačenko, Alexander V. (1939): *Narečje vasi Sele na Rožu*, Laibach.

Jordan, Peter (1988): *Möglichkeiten einer stärkeren Berücksichtigung slowenischer Ortsnamen in den heutigen amtlichen topographischen Karten Österreichs*, Wien.

Jordan, Peter (1992): „Slowenische Ortsnamen in den amtlichen topographischen Karten Österreichs. Heutiger Zustand und Vorschläge zu seiner Verbesserung". In: *Österreichische Namenforschung 20*, 89−105.

Karničar, Ludwig K. (1990): *Der Obir-Dialekt in Kärnten. Die Mundart von Ebriach/Obirsko*, Wien.

Kranzmayer, Eberhard (1944): *Die deutschen Lehnwörter in der slowenischen Volkssprache*, Laibach.

Lenček, Rado (1982): *The Structure and History of the Slovene Language*, Columbus/Ohio.

Lessiak, Primus (1910): „Alpendeutsche und Alpenslawen in ihren sprachlichen Beziehungen". In: *Germanisch-romanische Monatsschrift 2*, 274−288.

Lessiak 1983 = Nachdruck von Lessiak 1910. In: *Die Wiener Dialektologische Schule*, Wiesinger, P. (Ed.), Wien, 249−263.

Logar, Tine (1975): *Slovenska narečja*, Laibach.

Neweklowsky, Gerhard (1985): „Slowenische Elemente im Kärntner Deutsch". In: *Die Brücke* (Klagenfurt) 1985/3, 33−38.

Neweklowsky, Gerhard (1989): „Slowenisch und Deutsch in Kärnten. Phonetische Gemeinsamkeiten". In: *Zbornik razprav iz slovanskega jezikoslovja Tinetu Logarju ob sedemdesetletnici*, Laibach, 203−211.

Neweklowsky, Gerhard (1990): „Kärntner Deutsch aus slawistischer Sicht: zum deutsch-slowenischen Sprachbund in Kärnten". In: *Germanistische Linguistik 101−103*, 477−500.

Paschinger, Viktor (1937): *Landeskunde von Kärnten*, Klagenfurt.

Pohl, Heinz Dieter (1989 a): „Slovenske (in slovanske) izposojenke v nemškem jeziku Koroške". In: *Slavistična revija 37*, 253−262.

Pohl, Heinz Dieter (1989 b): *Kleine Kärntner Mundartkunde mit Wörterbuch*, Klagenfurt.

Pohl, Heinz Dieter (1990 a): „Die Slowenen in Kärnten. Zum 70. Jahrestag der Volksabstimmung in Kärnten vom 10. Oktober 1920". In: *Die slawischen Sprachen 21*, 115−140 (mit Karte).

Pohl 1990 b = Pohl 1989 a (Fortsetzung). *Slavistična revija 38*, 101−104.

Pohl, Heinz Dieter (1992): „Die Bedeutung des Slowenischen für die Deutsch-Kärntner Mundart". In: *Dialekte im Wandel*, Weiss, A. (Ed.), Göppingen, 157−169.

Prunč, Erich (1979): *Zum Problem sprachlicher Interferenzen im bilingualen Gebiet in Kärnten*, Klagenfurt.

Ramovš, Fran (1957): *Karta slovenskih narečij v priročni izdaji*, Laibach.

Striedter-Temps, Hildegard (1963): *Deutsche Lehnwörter im Slowenischen*, Berlin/Wiesbaden.

Sturm-Schnabel, Stanislava Katharina (1973): *Die slovenischen Mundarten und Mundartreste im Klagenfurter Becken*, Wien (Dissertation).

Waldstein, Ernst/Inzko, Valentin (1991): *Das gemeinsame Kärnten − Skupna Koroška 11*, Klagenfurt.

Wutte, Martin (1927): *Deutsch − Windisch − Slowenisch*, Klagenfurt.

Heinz Dieter Pohl, Klagenfurt (Österreich)

224. Deutsch−Kroatisch

1. Geographie und Demographie
2. Geschichte
3. Politik, Wirtschaft und allgemeine kulturelle sowie religiöse Lage
4. Statistik und Ethnoprofil
5. Soziolinguistische Lage
6. Sprachpolitische Lage
7. Allgemeines kontaktlinguistisches Porträt
8. Kritische Wertung der verwendeten Quellen und Literatur
9. Bibliographie (in Auswahl)

1. Geographie und Demographie

Kroatisch-deutsche Sprachkontakte finden im heutigen Bundesland Burgenland (Bgld.), wo eine seit dem 16. Jahrhundert ansässige kroatische Bevölkerung lebt, statt, darüberhinaus auch in Wien, wo viele Kroaten des Bgld.es das Zentrum ihrer Lebensinteressen gefunden haben. Unter dem Terminus „burgenländisch-kroatisch" wird in der wissenschaftlichen Literatur aber nicht nur die Sprache der im Bgld. lebenden Kroaten verstanden, sondern auch die Sprache aller seit den Migrationen des 16. Jahrhunderts ins ehemalige Westungarn, nach Südmähren und nach Niederösterreich gekommenen Kroaten, da sie eine deutliche sprachliche Einheit bilden (Neweklowsky 1978, 19 f). Die heutigen Überreste dieser einst mächtigen Einsiedlung befinden sich vor allem im Bgld., ferner entlang der burgenländisch-ungarischen Grenze in Westungarn (um Sopron/Ödenburg und Szombathely/Steinamanger) und in der Nähe von Bratislava/Preßburg. Die Kroaten in Südmähren (drei Dörfer in der Nähe von Drnholec/Dürnholz) sind nach dem Zweiten Weltkrieg ausgesiedelt worden, so daß diese Siedlungen nicht mehr als kroatisch (kr.) bezeichnet werden können (Breu 1974).

Das Bundesland Bgld. umfaßt 3965 km² mit über 270 000 Einwohnern. Es grenzt im Osten an Ungarn, im Süden an Slowenien, im Norden an die Slowakei und im Westen an Niederösterreich und die Steiermark, seine Hauptstadt ist Eisenstadt (kr. Željezno). Der Norden des Landes wird von der fruchtbaren Ebene um den Neusiedlersee eingenommen, der Süden ist wald-, obst- und weinreiches Hügelland. Seine Nord-Süd-Ausdehnung beträgt fast 200 km, seine durchschnittliche Breite nur 30 km. Die Bevölkerung setzt sich aus Deutschen, Kroaten, Ungarn und Zigeunern zusammen (→ Sprachenkarte N).

Die Kroaten bilden heute kein zusammenhängendes Siedlungsgebiet, sondern siedeln über mehrere Bezirke des Bgld.es verstreut. Dialektologisch werden sie nach Neweklowsky (1978, 346 f) in folgende Gruppen geteilt: (a) die „Haci" und „Poljanci" in den Bezirken Neusiedl am See, Eisenstadt und Mattersburg, sowie die „Dolinci" im Bezirk Oberpullendorf, (b) die Mundart von Weingraben im Bezirk Oberpullendorf, (c) die Čakaver des südlichen Bgld.es (Bezirk Güssing), (d) die „Štoji" und „Vlahi" in den Bezirken Oberwart und Güssing. Die Gruppen (a)−(c) gehören dem čakavischen Dialekt an, die Gruppe (d) dem štokavischen, wobei dieses Štokavische den čakavischen Mundarten des Bgld.es aber ziemlich nahe steht.

2. Geschichte

Die deutsche Besiedlung des heutigen Bgld.es erfolgte größtenteils ab 1076 unter Kaiser Heinrich IV. (1056−1106) mit Kolonisten aus Oberfranken, die Ungarn wurden etwa im 12. Jahrhundert als Grenzwächter angesiedelt.

Die Besiedlung von Teilen des ehemaligen Westungarn, Niederösterreichs und Südmährens durch Kroaten ist als Teil der großen Wanderbewegungen, die durch das Vordringen der Türken auf die Balkanhalbinsel seit dem 14. Jahrhundert vor sich gingen, zu verstehen. Die Voraussetzungen für die Aufnahme von Siedlern in der neuen Heimat waren gegeben durch die Entvölkerung weiter Landstriche im Zuge der Pest 1408/09, durch die Grenzkriege zwischen Kaiser Friedrich III. und dem Ungarnkönig Matthias Corvinus und schließlich durch die Vorstöße der Türken nach Niederösterreich (Wien 1529) und Westungarn (Güns 1532).

Ein wichtiger Faktor für die Neubesiedlung war die Tatsache, daß die meisten ungarischen Magnatengeschlechter Besitzungen sowohl in Kroatien und Slawonien als auch in Westungarn hatten. Auf diese Weise konnten sie ihre kroatischen Untertanen in Westungarn ansiedeln. Ihrem Beispiel folgten auch Grundherren in Niederösterreich. So kam es zu organisierten Bauernwanderungen. Ein kleiner Teil der Einwanderer, die sog. „Vlahi" des Bezirks Oberwart, waren vermutlich Hirten und Viehzüchter (vgl. Prickler 1984).

Die Einwanderung in die neue Heimat begann zwischen 1493 (Schlacht auf dem Krbavafeld) und 1515. In diesem Jahr sind die ersten kroatischen Familiennamen in der Herrschaft Eisenstadt bezeugt. Es ist auch ungefähr bekannt, woher die Zuwanderer stammten: aus der Lika, aus dem Küstenland zwischen Senj und Obrovac, aus der Gegend zwischen Otočac und dem Fluß Kupa und, ferner, aus Westslawonien. — Nach dem Fall der Festung Kostajnica 1556 eroberten die Türken die Gebiete zwischen den Flüssen Kupa und Una, so daß es zu einem mächtigen Siedlerstrom von dort kam. Die Migration hörte im Verlauf des 16. Jahrhunderts allmählich auf (Ujević 1934, 8f).

Das Bgld. kam als administrative Einheit 1921 ohne Volksabstimmung zu Österreich; sein Name wurde nach den ungarischen Komitaten Wieselburg (Moson), Ödenburg (Sopron) und Eisenburg (Vas) gebildet. Zwischen 1938 und 1945 war es zwischen Niederösterreich (Niederdonau) und der Steiermark aufgeteilt.

3. Politik, Wirtschaft und allgemeine kulturelle sowie religiöse Lage

Das Bgld. bildet eines der neun Bundesländer der Bundesrepublik Österreich. Nach der Verfassung 1981 hat sein Landtag 36 Abgeordnete, die Landesregierung sieben Mitglieder; an ihrer Spitze steht der Landeshauptmann. Die Minderheiten haben keine eigenen Vertreter im Landtag oder in der Landesregierung.

Wirtschaftlich steht das Bgld. im Vergleich der österreichischen Bundesländer an letzter Stelle; es ist am stärksten agrarisch geprägt, wobei Kleinbetriebe vorherrschen (Getreide, Mais, Zuckerrüben, Obst, Wein). Die Viehzucht spielt eine geringere Rolle, die Industrie ist traditionell (Textil, Lebensmittel, Zucker). Bedeutsam auch für das Leben der Minderheitensprachen ist die Tatsache, daß 28% der arbeitenden Bevölkerung in andere Bundesländer (vor allem nach Wien) auspendeln.

Die ältesten schriftlichen Aufzeichnungen der Burgenländer Kroaten finden sich in einem lateinischen gedruckten Missale von 1501 (Klingenbacher Missale). Deutsche Eintragungen aus den Jahren 1502 bis 1518 bestätigen, daß Klingenbach zu jener Zeit noch ein deutschsprachiges Dorf gewesen sein muß. Das letzte Blatt enthält kroatische Eintragungen, und zwar in lateinischer, kyrillischer und glagolitischer Schrift (Facsimile in Vlasits 1986, 257). Es wird dort das Jahr 1561 erwähnt, was darauf hinweist, daß es in den sechziger Jahren des 16. Jahrhunderts bereits Kroaten in Klingenbach gab. — Die ersten gedruckten Bücher der Kroaten sind zwei Sammlungen von geistlichen Liedern (*Duševne pesne*), 1609 und 1611, von Grgur Pythiraeus-Mekinić.

Erst im 18. Jahrhundert begann eine kontinuierliche literarische Tradition: Gedruckt wurden die Evangelien, ein Lektionar, Katechismen. Eine wichtige Rolle in der Geschichte des Buchdrucks spielten die Franziskaner. So erschienen unter ihrer Obhut in der zweiten Hälfte des 18. und der ersten Hälfte des 19. Jahrhunderts noch eine ganze Reihe von Gebetbüchern. Die genannten Werke sind Ausdruck einer bescheidenen literarischen Tätigkeit. Dennoch war sie von größter Bedeutung für die Burgenländer Kroaten: ihre Sprache und Orthographie besaßen Vorbildwirkung. Nach dem ausschließlich geistlichen Schrifttum des 18. Jahrhunderts erschienen Anfang des 19. Jahrhunderts die ersten Bücher weltlichen Charakters, und zwar ein Kalender und eine Schulfibel (Hadrovics 1974, 19—39). Der Ungarnslowene Jožef Ficko, der den größten Teil seines Lebens unter Kroaten verbrachte, übte einen großen Einfluß auf die weitere Entwicklung der Schriftsprache aus. Nach der Mitte des Jahrhunderts sind die ersten Annäherungen der Schriftsprache der Burgenländer Kroaten an die Schriftsprache in Kroatien („Illyrische Bewegung") zu beobachten (Benčić 1972, 16ff).

Erst gegen Ende des 19. Jahrhunderts traten die ersten Dichter auf, allen voran Mate Meršić-Miloradić aus Frankenau/Frakanava, der eine sehr klare und volkstümliche Sprache schrieb. In der Zwischenkriegszeit wuchs die literarische Produktion an, es entstanden auch immer mehr Prosawerke (z. B. Ignaz Horvat). In dieser Zeit kam es auch zu Kontroversen in der Frage, ob man im Burgenland die kroatische Schriftsprache einführen solle oder nicht (Weilguni 1984). Eine Gesamtbibliographie des kroatischen Schrifttums bis 1921 ist von Kuzmich (1992) zusammengestellt worden.

Von Beginn ihrer Ansiedlung an besaßen die Kroaten das Recht, ihre Pfarrer selbst zu wählen. Dadurch wurde das kroatische Wort in allen Funktionen, die in die Domäne der Kirche fielen, gesichert. Dort, wo die Kroaten in der Minderheit waren und ihre Sprache nicht durch die Kirche gestützt war, wurden sie bald assimiliert. Der Protestantismus fand unter ihnen keine Anhänger, der Katholizismus wurde zum nationalen Element. Es ist kein Zufall, daß fast alle Schriftsteller des 19. Jahrhunderts, aber auch viele Autoren des 20. Jahrhunderts, Geistliche waren oder sind.

Durch die Bildung des Bgld.es ergab sich die Notwendigkeit einer Neuorganisierung in kirchlich-administrativer Hinsicht. Die kirchliche Verwaltung erfolgte zunächst von Wien aus, bis 1960 eine eigene Diözese Bgld. geschaffen wurde. Die kroatischen und gemischtsprachigen Gemeinden sind heute alle mit kroatischen Priestern besetzt (Stubić 1983, 97, 105). Seit 1946 erscheint regelmäßig eine Kirchenzeitung („Crikveni glasnik"). Es besteht eine Übersetzung des Neuen Testaments (1952), auch Teile des Alten Testaments liegen bereits übersetzt vor.

Die Kroaten haben ihre kulturellen Vereinigungen, unter denen die wichtigste der 1929 gegründete Kroatische Kulturverein ist. Zu nennen ist auch der Kroatische Akademikerklub, um den sich die Studenten in Wien scharen. Seit 1984 besteht eine Volkshochschule der Burgenländer Kroaten. Darüber hinaus gibt es zahlreiche Tamburizza-, Folklore- und Laienspielgruppen.

4. Statistik und Ethnoprofil

Die im Bgld. ansässigen Deutschen werden meist als *Heanzen* (*Hienzen*, *Heinzen*) bezeichnet, was wohl auf den Namen Heinz/Heinrich zurückgeht. Die Kroaten werden vielfach (eher verächtlich) „Wasserkroaten" („-krabaten") genannt, eine Bezeichnung, die etymologisch nicht klar ist, volksetymologisch mit *Wasser* (Donau, Neusiedlersee) oder *Bosnien* (Bosna-Kroaten) in Verbindung gebracht wird. Die Kroaten bezeichnen die Deutschsprachigen als *Nimci* „Deutsche", ihre Sprache als *nimški* „deutsch"; sie selbst nennen sich *Hrvati* „Kroaten", zum Unterschied von den *Hrvaćani* „Bewohner Kroatiens", ihre Sprache *hrvatski* „kroatisch", vielfach aber auch bloß *naš*, *naški*, *po našu* „unsere, auf unsere Art".

Nach den Angaben der Volkszählung 1981 bekannten sich 18 762 Personen als Kroaten, das sind 7% der burgenländischen Bevölkerung (Burgenland 1990, 44). Die Zahl der Kroaten hat seit der Schaffung des Bundeslandes Bgld. ständig abgenommen (1923 wurden noch über 42 000 gezählt). Die vorläufigen Ergebnisse der Volkszählung 1991 zeigen aber wieder eine leichte Erhöhung ihrer Zahl, nämlich 19 400 (s. die Wochenzeitung „Hrvatske Novine" vom 27. XI. 1992). Die Ergebnisse früherer Volkszählungen findet man in Breu 1970 (175–181), Schreiner 1983 (224), Geosits 1986 (354 ff), Burgenland 1990 (44).

5. Soziolinguistische Lage

Eine vollwertige, polyvalente Standardsprache ist in Österreich nur das Deutsche, das *alle* Funktionen im öffentlichen und privaten Leben erfüllen kann. Die Minderheitensprachen können dies nicht oder nur eingeschränkt. Dabei befinden sich die Kroaten in einer besonders schwierigen Situation, da ihre Sprache von der in der Republik Kroatien verwendeten kroatischen Standardsprache verschieden ist. Das Kroatische im Bgld. hat sich seit dem 18. Jahrhundert kontinuierlich entwickelt, und zwar ohne Kontakt zu seinem Herkunftsland, auf der Grundlage des čakavischen, ikavisch-ekavischen Dialekts, während die Schriftsprache in Kroatien erst viel später (ab den 30er Jahren des 19. Jahrhunderts) und auf der Basis des štokavischen Ostherzegowina-Dialekts entstanden ist, der als Basis für eine gemeinsame Schriftsprache der Kroaten und Serben dienen konnte.

Alle Kroaten des Bgld.es sprechen auch deutsch. Wir haben es daher mit einem kollektiven, einseitig gerichteten, natürlichen Bilingualismus zu tun. In der Vergangenheit (bis 1921) war die Staats- und Schulsprache Ungarisch, so daß die Kroaten meist dreisprachig und die Deutschen vielfach zweisprachig waren.

Buranits u. a. (1993, 165–169) berichten über eine Untersuchung zur Einstellung der Burgenländer Kroaten gegenüber ihrem Ortsdialekt, ihrer Schriftsprache und dem Deutschen in Form eines Polaritätsprofils. Die Dorfdialekte erzielten die besten Werte in bezug auf Ästhetik und Intimität, die Schriftsprache in bezug auf Modernität und Regelmäßigkeit, die deutsche Sprache aber in bezug auf Nützlichkeit. In der Untersuchung werden auch regionale Unterschiede besprochen und kommentiert.

Sprachkonflikte spielen sich im Bgld. eher innerhalb der kroatischen Volksgruppe ab als zwischen Deutschen und Kroaten, wobei es meist um die Frage der Bewahrung oder Aufgabe der kroatischen Sprache geht.

6. Sprachpolitische Lage

Der Anspruch auf Elementarunterricht in kroatischer Sprache sowie auf eine verhältnismäßige Anzahl von Gymnasien, ferner die Verwendung des Kroatischen als Amtssprache zusätzlich zum Deutschen sind im Artikel 7 des Österreichischen Staatsvertrags von 1955 garantiert. Die dort ebenfalls erwähnten zweisprachigen topographischen Aufschriften sind bis heute nicht verwirklicht worden.

Die Schulsprachenregelung hat ihre gesetzliche Grundlage im Landesschulgesetz von 1937. Danach ist Kroatisch dann Unterrichtssprache, wenn nach der jeweils letzten Volkszählung 70% der Schulgemeinde der Minderheit angehören; bei 30–70% sind die Schulen gemischtsprachig, bei unter 30% ist Kroatisch Freigegenstand.

In Wirklichkeit gibt es nirgends kroatische Schulen. Unterrichtssprache ist überall Deutsch, Kroatisch nur Unterrichtsgegenstand mit mehr oder weniger Wochenstunden. Die Zahl der kroatischen Kinder hat sich in den letzten Jahren drastisch vermindert. Nach den Daten, die wir „Hrvatske Novine" (20. 2. 1987) entnehmen können, besuchten im Schuljahr 1986/1987 1044 Schüler kroatischer Muttersprache die Pflichtschulen des Bgld.es (nach den Angaben in „Burgenland" 1990, 47, beträgt ihre Zahl rund 1240). In demselben Schuljahr gab es im Bgld. 28 Schulen, an denen in irgendeiner Form Kroatisch unterrichtet wurde. Insgesamt sind etwa 5% aller Schüler an den Schulen des Bgld.es Kroaten. Diese Zahl ist jedenfalls niedriger als es dem Anteil der Kroaten an der Gesamtbevölkerung des Bgld.es entsprechen würde, ein Hinweis darauf, daß nicht mehr alle Kinder kroatischer Eltern auch die kroatische Sprache erlernen. Eines der größten Probleme in diesem Zusammenhang sind die Kindergärten, da in den meisten von ihnen ausschließlich deutsch gesprochen wird. Erst im Schuljahr 1992/93 kam es in Oberwart zur Gründung eines mehrsprachigen Bundesgymnasiums, in dem Kroatisch und Ungarisch ein besonderer Platz zukommt. Freilich ist dies kein rein kroatisches Gymnasium.

1947 näherte man die Orthographie weiter an die der kroatischen Schriftsprache an, z. B. bei der Schreibung des ehemaligen *Jat* als *ije*, *je* und *i* (vorher hatte man *e* und *i* geschrieben) oder bei der Schreibung des auslautenden *-o* (früher *-l*) (vgl. Benčić 1972, 26). Trotz aller Reformversuche ist die Grundlage der Schriftsprache der Burgenländer Kroaten der čakavische Dialekt geblieben, wie er im nördlichen und mittleren Bgld., also in der Mehrzahl der Dörfer, gesprochen wird.

Heute spielt das gedruckte Wort eine wichtige Rolle, vor allem die Wochenzeitung „Hrvatske Novine" (von 1923–1942 und wieder seit 1960), ferner der alljährliche Kalender „Gradišće" mit literarischen und populärwissenschaftlichen Beiträgen sowie die Bücher, die der Kroatische Presseverein herausgibt. (Übersicht über alle Periodika in Benčić 1985).

Seit den 70er Jahren ist es zu sprachlichen Normierungsbestrebungen in Zusammenarbeit zwischen der Burgenländischen Landesregierung, dem Institut für Slawistik der Universität Wien und dem Zagreber „Zavod za jezik" (Institut für Sprache) gekommen, da eine entsprechende Institution der Burgenländer Kroaten selbst fehlt. Als Resultat sind zwei Wörterbücher (Benčić et al. 1982, 1991), die heute als Norm betrachtet werden und weite Anwendung finden, entstanden. Die burgenländischen Kroaten haben nämlich eingesehen, daß die einzige Chance des Überlebens ihrer Sprache in Österreich darin besteht, daß sie ihre eigene, seit Jahrhunderten gewachsene Schriftsprache – in einer überregionalen Form, die man freilich erst erlernen muß, aber die doch den Mundarten nahe steht – pflegt, weil die kroatische Schriftsprache einfach zu andersartig und zu schwer zu erlernen ist.

Die burgenländische-kroatische Schriftsprache steht seit 1979 in Gebrauch bei Radio Bgld. (Radio Zagreb sendet seit vielen Jahren für die Burgenländer Kroaten in deren Sprache). Aus sehr bescheidenen Anfängen haben sich diese Sendungen dahingehend entwickelt, daß man heute die kroatische Sprache mehrmals täglich hören kann. Es werden Nachrichten, Kulturprogramme, Kindersendungen, Wunschkonzerte u. a. gesendet. Seit 1989 hat das Kroatische einmal wöchentlich auch das regionale Fernsehen erobert.

7. Allgemeines kontaktlinguistisches Porträt

Im Bgld. gehen der Sprachkontakt und damit die Transferenzen nur in eine Richtung, nämlich vom Deutschen (aber auch Ungarischen) zum Kroatischen. Die Ursachen dafür liegen in der Sprachinselsituation des Kroatischen und dem höheren Prestige der Umgebungssprachen. Die deutsch-kroatischen Kontakte im Bgld. müßten im größeren Kontext Ostösterreich-Westungarn-Slowakei betrachtet werden, da es Erscheinungen gibt, die im Sinne von Sprachbundphänomenen weit über das Bgld. hinausgehen. (Neweklowsky 1978, 28—56, 1984, 4—12).

7.1. Phonetische Interferenzerscheinungen

Phonetische Interferenzerscheinungen sind hauptsächlich in der gesprochenen Sprache zu beobachten.

Charakteristisch für die deutschen und kroatischen Dialekte des Bgld.es ist die Dehnung der Vokale in der letzten, betonten oder einzigen Silbe eines Wortes z. B. dt. *fi:š* < *Fisch*, aber Pl. *fiš*, kr. *bra:t* < *brat*, Pl. *brati* „Bruder", *ota:c* < *otac* „Vater".

Die Mehrzahl der kroatischen Mundarten des Bgld.es besitzt musikalischen Akzent, d. h. auf langen Vokalen werden zwei Toneme unterschieden, z. B. *ljù:di* N.pl. ~ *ljú:di* Gen.pl. „Leute". Die Tatsache, daß im gesamten südlichen Bgld. solche Intonationsoppositionen nicht bestehen, kann auf deutsch-kroatische Interferenz zurückgeführt werden. Auch andere Erscheinungen im prosodischen System wie der Verlust der Unterscheidung unbetonter Längen und Kürzen oder Vokaldehnungen, die allerdings nur kleinräumig oder individuell bekannt sind, gehen auf Konto des Deutschen.

Ein auffälliges Merkmal beider Sprachen ist die Neutralisierung der Stimmbeteiligungskorrelation der Obstruenten an der Wortgrenze. Während am Satzende nur stimmlose Obstruenten stehen, geht die Richtung der Neutralisierung innerhalb der Äußerung zur Stimmhaftigkeit, wann immer der erste Laut (Vokal, Sonant, Obstruent) stimmhaft ist, z. B. dt. *vo:z va:z i:* „was weiß ich", kr. *otadz i mat* < *otac* „Vater und Mutter", *jedinajz let* < *jedinajs* „elf Jahre", *srdid nastal* < *srdit* „wurde zornig", *jednodž zdavno* < *jednoč* „vor langer Zeit"; vor stimmlosen Obstruenten: *je vrak sidil* < *vrag* „der Teufel saß". Diese Art der Neutralisierung ist sonst in serbokroatischen Dialekten nicht bekannt (sie kommt andererseits im Ungarischen und Slowakischen vor).

Ein weiteres Beispiel ist der Übergang von /l'/ in /j/ in manchen kroatischen Mundarten, entweder in allen oder nur in bestimmten Positionen, z. B. *judi* < *ljudi* „Leute", *nedija* < *nedilja* „Sonntag". Würden wir die kroatischen Dialekte des Bgld.es isoliert betrachten, könnten wir sie mit denjenigen Dialekten Kroatiens verbinden, in denen diese Erscheinung ebenfalls anzutreffen ist (Dalmatien, Istrien). Da weder in den deutschen noch in den westungarischen Dialekten ein Phonem /l'/ existiert, kann man den Verlust dieses Phonems ohne weiteres durch Unterdifferenzierung nach dem Vorbild der Sprachen der Umgebung erklären. Ähnliches gilt für den Verlust des Phonems /t'/, das in Einzelmundarten in /č/ übergeht, z. B. *not'* (geschrieben *noć*) > *noč* „Nacht" (häufig in der Kindersprache).

Die Bewahrung des Phonems /χ/ gilt als typisch für den čakavischen Dialekt. Im Bgld. hat sich die Situation insoweit geändert, als [χ] im Wortauslaut und im Wortanlaut vor Sonant ersatzlos geschwunden ist, z. B. *krù:* < *kruχ* „Brot", *rú:ška* < *χruška* „Birne", und daß in den übrigen Positionen /χ/ zwei Allophone, [h] und [χ], besitzt: vor Vokalen das erste, nach Vokalen das zweite, z. B. *hiža* „Zimmer", *meχko* „weich". Da eine solche Verteilung genau der Verteilung in den deutschen Mundarten des Bgld.es (Laky 1937, 127 f, Kranzmayer 1956, 102) entspricht, ist wohl das Deutsche für die Veränderungen verantwortlich zu machen.

7.2. Grammatik

Durch den Einfluß der Nachbarsprachen können zwei Tendenzen beobachtet werden: (a) die Bewahrung von Archaismen, die sich sonst im Kroatischen und Serbischen anders weiterentwickelt haben, und (b) die Bildung von Neuerungen nach dem Muster der Kontaktsprachen Deutsch und Ungarisch.

Zum ersten Typ gehört z. B. die Bewahrung der Unterscheidung von Orts- und Richtungsadverbien. Beispiele: *odzgor(a)* „oben" ~ *gori(ka)* „hinauf, herauf", *odzdol(a)* „unten" ~ *doli(ka)* „hinunter, herunter", *nutr(a)* „innen" ~ *nutri* „hinein" (vgl. schriftspr. *gore* „oben" und „hinauf, herauf"). Ein anderes Beispiel ist die gute Bewahrung der Opposition zwischen bestimmten und unbestimmten Adjektiven, die im wesentlichen der Funktion des bestimmten und unbestimmten Artikels im Deutschen (und Ungarischen) entspricht. Die Opposition manifestiert sich vor allem in prosodischen Merkmalen, z. B. *lí:pa divuójka* „das schöne Mädchen" ~ *lî:pa divuójka* „ein schönes Mädchen" (Intonation), *tànka* ~ *tankà:* „dünn" (Akzentstelle). Obwohl sich das Kroatische in Kontakt mit Artikelsprachen befindet, hat sich kein bestimmter Artikel herausgebildet. Andererseits wird das Zahlwort *(j)edan* „ein" häufig in der Funktion des unbestimmten Artikels gebraucht.

Ein Beispiel für den zweiten Typ ist der Verlust des Possessivpronomens *svoj* „mein, dein, sein, etc.", das sich wie das lat. *suus* auf das Subjekt des Satzes bezieht, zugunsten der Pronomina *moj* „mein", *tvoj* „dein", *njegov* „sein", *nje* „ihr", usw. Oft werden beide Formen nebeneinander gebraucht, z. B. *povidala je majka o nje čudnovitom ozdravljenju, o nje nevolji i žukom putu, o iskanju muža i svoje dice* „die Mutter erzählte von ihrer wunderbaren Heilung, von ihrer Krankheit und ihrem bitteren Weg, von der Suche nach dem Gatten und ihren Kindern". Alle Possessivpronomina beziehen sich auf das Subjekt „die Mutter", dennoch finden wir im kroatischen Text zweimal *nje* und einmal *svoj* „ihr".

7.3. Lexik und Semantik

In der gesprochenen Sprache sind die deutschen Entlehnungen sehr zahlreich. Der einfachste Fall lexikalischer Entlehnung ist die Übernahme von Lautfolgen (Lexemen) aus einer Sprache in die andere, sei es zur Bezeichnung von neuen Begriffen oder aus anderen Gründen (Handwerk, Technik, Verwaltung). Die Wörter werden dabei gewöhnlich morphologisch und auch wortbildungsmäßig adaptiert. Einige Beispiele: *šostar* „Schuster", *šnajdar* „Schneider", *pumpa* „Pumpe", *šprica* „Spritze", *cukar (cukr)* „Zucker", dazu *cukrka* „Zuckerrübe", *farba* „Farbe", *farnik* „Pfarrer", *flajsik* (undeklinierbar) „fleißig", *gvišan* „gewiß, sicher", *herati seljerati se* „sich irren", *jerbati* „erben", etc. Ähnlich auch Übernahmen aus dem Ungarischen (→ Art. 212 und 225). In der gesprochenen Sprache sind Lehnwörter aus dem Deutschen wie auch ad-hoc-Entlehnungen häufig, z. B. *facajgati* „verzeihen", *fajfa* „Pfeife", *fajnast* „fein", *fajtl* „Feitel, Taschenmesser", *fajvergar* „Feuerwehrmann", *farcokt* „verzagt", *farcvajvljan* „verzweifelt", *fardinst* „Verdienst", *farhoftati* „verhaften", *farmeng* „Vermögen" etc. etc. (Neweklowsky 1989, sub F; vgl. auch Koschat 1978, 137—143, zu älteren Entlehnungen Neweklowsky 1987, 12 ff).

Sehr typisch sind Lehnprägungen nach deutschem Muster, die schon in der älteren Literatur der Bgld.er Kroaten vorhanden sind. Einige Beispiele nach Hadrovics 1984 (435—440): *na klinac obisiti* „an den Nagel hängen", *krače potegnuti* „den kürzeren ziehen", *na dugu klup odvlačiti* „auf die lange Bank schieben", *k srcu zeti* „zu Herzen nehmen". Sehr charakteristisch ist der Gebrauch von Adverbien als Verbalpräfixe nach deutschem Vorbild, wobei aber auch der ungarische Einfluß nicht zu vernachlässigen ist (Hadrovics 1974, 183—187, 436 f): *najper dojti* „vorkommen, scheinen", *najper štati* „vorlesen", *nuter zeti* „einnehmen", *prik dati* „übergeben", *van stati* „ausstehen", *van zgledati* „aussehen", etc.

8. Kritische Wertung der verwendeten Quellen und Literatur

Die Phänomene des deutsch-kroatischen Sprachkontakts im Bgld. wurden bisher ausschließlich von der Slawistik untersucht. Neben dem deutsch-kroatischen Sprachkontakt besteht auch ungarisch-kroatischer Kontakt. Über Kontakte in der umgekehrten Richtung, nämlich vom Kroatischen zum Deutschen, ist mir aus der Literatur nichts bekannt. Auch die oben angeschnittenen Sprachkontakte Ostösterreich-Westungarn-Teile der Slowakei sind bisher noch nicht erforscht, ja noch nicht einmal als Problem gesehen worden. Die Geschichte der Erforschung der deutsch-kroatischen Sprachkontakte im Bgld. ist daher gleichbedeutend mit der Geschichte der Erforschung der kroatischen Sprache im Bgld. Die ältesten Bemerkungen über deutsch-kroatische Interferenzen findet man bei Csaplovics (1828, 25 ff). Im Laufe des 19. Jahrhunderts ist eine Reihe von Reisebeschreibungen, die sich mit den Kroaten unseres Raumes beschäftigen, entstanden, bei denen allerdings wenig über Sprache gesagt wird. Sehr ausgiebig und kompetent beschäftigt sich Hadrovics (1974) mit der Sprache des Schrifttums, wobei er die vollständige Grammatik einschließlich Syntax und Wortschatz bearbeitet. Deutsch-kroatische Sprachkontakte werden bes. SS. 432—440 besprochen. Die erste vollständige dialektologische Beschreibung, Klassifizierung und Einordnung der kroatischen Dialekte stammt von Neweklowsky (1978); er geht auf die Geschichte der Erforschung der Dialekte (21—24) und speziell auf Interferenzerscheinungen (28—56) ein. Mit der Frage der Sprachkontakte befaßten sich auch Koschat (1978), und Tornow (1992). Quellen für die Feststellung von Entlehnungen aus dem Deutschen sind Dialektwörterbücher wie Koschat (1978, 183—298), Palkovits (1987), Tornow (1989), Neweklowsky (1989), aber auch die schon zitierten modernen normativen Wörterbücher. Die Erforschung der kroatischen Dialekte des Bgld.es war in den letzten beiden Jahrzehnten außerordentlich erfolgreich. Es wurden auch große Fortschritte in Richtung auf eine polyvalente normierte Standardsprache gemacht.

Die kontaktlinguistische Erforschung steht noch in ihren Anfängen. Ansätze gibt es bei Koszogovits (1984); ein umfangreicheres Projekt ist das oben erwähnte von Buranits et al. 1993.

Ansonsten sind Geographie, Siedlungsgeschichte, Volksgruppenpolitik, Sprache, Literatur und Volkskunde der Burgenländer Kroaten in einer ganzen Reihe von Publikationen ausgezeichnet dokumentiert (Breu 1970, Geosits 1986, Neweklowsky und Gaál 1991, Schreiner 1983, Vasilev 1966, et al.).

9. Bibliographie (in Auswahl)

Benčić, Nikola (1972): „Abriß der geschichtlichen Entwicklung der burgenländisch-kroatischen Schriftsprache". In: *Wiener slavistisches Jahrbuch 17*, 15—28.

Benčić, Nikola (1985): *Novine i časopisi Gradišćanskih Hrvatov*, Željezno.

Benčić, Nikola et al. (1982): *Deutsch-burgenländischkroatisch-kroatisches Wörterbuch*, Eisenstadt/Zagreb.

Benčić, Nikola, et al. (1991): *Burgenländischkroatisch-kroatisch-deutsches Wörterbuch*, Zagreb/Eisenstadt.

Breu, Josef (1970): *Die Kroatensiedlung im Burgenland und den anschließenden Gebieten*, Wien.

Breu, Josef (1974): „Karta IV-Karte IV". In: *Symposion croaticon*, Palkovits, F. (Ed.) Beč/Wien.

Buranits, Josef F./Csenar, Manfred/Dressler, Wolfgang U./Palatin, Jandre (1993): „Sprache und Bewußtsein. Das Image des Kroatischen bei den burgenländischen Kroaten". In: *Trendwende? Sprache und Ethnizität im Burgenland*, Holzer, Werner/Münz, Rainer (Eds.), Wien, 155—176.

„Burgenland" (1990): In: *Die Minderheiten im Alpe-Adria-Raum. Deutsche Fassung*, Land Kärnten (Ed.), Klagenfurt, 39—67.

Csaplovics, Johann von (1828): *Kroaten und Wenden in Ungarn*, Preßburg.

Geosits, Stefan (Ed.) (1986): *Die burgenländischen Kroaten im Wandel der Zeiten*, Wien.

Hadrovics, László (1974): *Schrifttum und Sprache der burgenländischen Kroaten im 18. und 19. Jahrhundert*, Wien/Budapest.

Koschat, Helene (1978): *Die čakavische Mundart von Baumgarten im Burgenland*. Wien.

Koszogovits, Helga (1984): *Sprachbewußtsein und Alltagskultur bei den Kroaten des südlichen Burgenlandes*, Wien (ungedr. Diss.).

Kranzmayer, Eberhard (1956): *Historische Lautgeographie des gesamtbairischen Dialektraumes*. Mit 27 Laut- und 4 Hilfskarten, Wien.

Kuzmich, Ludwig (1992): *Kulturhistorische Aspekte der burgenlandkroatischen Druckwerke bis 1921 mit einer primären Bibliographie*, Eisenstadt.

Laky, A. (1937): *Lautlehre der Mundarten des Pinkatales*, Wien (ungedr. Diss.).

Neweklowsky, Gerhard (1978): *Die kroatischen Dialekte des Burgenlandes und der angrenzenden Gebiete*, Wien.

Neweklowsky, Gerhard (1984): „Investigating Burgenland-Croatian Dialects". In: *Melbourne Slavonic Studies 18*, 1—14.

Neweklowsky, Gerhard (1987): „Lexikalische Übereinstimmungen im nordwestlichen Südslawischen". In: *Slavistična revija 3*, 3—16 und 187—209.

Neweklowsky, Gerhard (1989): *Der kroatische Dialekt von Stinatz. Wörterbuch*, Wien.

Neweklowsky, Gerhard/Gaál, Károly (1991): *Kroatische Märchen und Totenklagen aus Stinatz im Burgenland*, Zagreb.

Palkovits, Elisabeth (1987): *Wortschatz des Burgenländischkroatischen. Mit einem Vorwort von J. Hamm*, Wien.

Prickler, Harald (1984): „Die burgenländischen Walachensiedlungen und ihre „Freiheiten"". In: *Österreichische Osthefte 26*, 246—272.

Schreiner, Bela (1983): *Das Schicksal der burgenländischen Kroaten durch 450 Jahre — Sudbina gradišćanskih Hrvatov kroz 450 ljet*, Eisenstadt.

Stubić, Leo (1983): „Die Bedeutung der katholischen Kirche für die burgenländischen Kroaten". In: Schreiner 1983, 89—107.

Tornow, Siegfried (1971): *Die Herkunft der kroatischen Vlahen des südlichen Burgenlandes*, Berlin.

Tornow, Siegfried (1989): *Burgenlandkroatisches Dialektwörterbuch. Die vlahischen Ortschaften*, Berlin.

Tornow, Siegfried (1992): „Etappen des Sprachenwechsels beim Übergang vom Kroatischen zum Deutschen im Burgenland". In: *Zeitschrift für Slawistik 37*, 248—251.

Ujević, Mate (1934): *Gradišćanski Hrvati*. 2. Auflage, Zagreb.

Vasilev, Christo (1966): „Die heutige čakavische Schriftsprache der Burgenland-Kroaten". In: *Ost und West. Aufsätze zur Slavischen Philologie*, Wiesbaden, 189—233.

Vlasits, Josef (1986): „Die Sprache der burgenländischen Kroaten". In: *Geosits 1986*, 254—267.

Weilguni, Werner (1984): *Die Diskussion um die Standardsprache bei den Burgenländerkroaten*, Wien (ungedr. Diss.).

Gerhard Neweklowsky, Klagenfurt (Österreich)

225. Deutsch−Ungarisch

1. Geographie und Demographie
2. Geschichte
3. Politik, Wirtschaft und allgemeine kulturelle sowie religiöse Lage
4. Statistik und Ethnoprofil
5. Soziolinguistische Lage
6. Sprachpolitische Lage
7. Allgemeines kontaktlinguistisches Porträt
8. Zum Stand der Forschung über Ungarisch und Deutsch im Burgenland
9. Bibliographie (in Auswahl)

1. Geographie und Demographie

Zur Geographie und Demographie des Burgenlandes → Art. 224

2. Geschichte

2.1. Regional- und Landesgeschichte des Burgenlandes
→ Art. 222 und 224

2.2. Ethnogenese und soziale Struktur der ungarischen Sprachgruppe im Burgenland

Die ungarische Besiedlung des heutigen Burgenlandes erfolgte vor ca. 900 Jahren. Ungarische Wehrbauern wurden von den ungarischen Landesfürsten in diesem Gebiet als Grenzwächter angesiedelt (Triber 1977). Nach dem Ausbau der Komitatsburgen im 12. Jahrhundert wurde der Großteil dieser Siedlungen wieder verlassen (Filla et al. 1982, 47). Eine Ausnahme bildeten die Siedlungen der Oberen Wart im südlichen Burgenland (Oberwart/Felsőör, Unterwart/Alsóőr, Siget i. d. Wart/Őrisziget) und Oberpullendorf/Felsőpulya bzw. Mitterpullendorf/Középpulya im mittleren Burgenland. Die Nachkommen der kleinadeligen ungarischen Freibauern bilden bis heute den Kern der ungarischen Sprachgruppe im Burgenland.

Ab dem frühen 18. Jahrhundert entwickelten sich auf den entstehenden Großmeierhöfen entlang der heutigen österreichisch-ungarischen Grenze weitere geschlossene ungarische Siedlungsgebiete, insbesondere im Gebiet des Seewinkels und auf dem Heideboden im nördlichen Burgenland. Die v. a in der zweiten Hälfte des 19. Jahrhunderts aus der Gegend von Kapuvár und aus Ostungarn angesiedelten Landarbeiter bzw. Lohnknechte (*berés*) und Angestellten der adeligen Gutsbesitzer bildeten auf den Meierhöfen ein sozial und sprachlich isoliertes ungarischsprachiges Kollektiv. Die ungarischen Meierhofarbeiter rangierten innerhalb der ungarischsprachigen Gesellschaft auf der untersten Stufe der sozialen Hierarchie. An deren Spitze standen die ungarischen Magnatenfamilien (Esterházy, Draskovich, Batthyány, Pálffy, Erdödy u. a.) als Angehörige der Hocharistokratie. Zwar verloren diese Herrschaftsfamilien nach 1921 ihre politische Macht, ihre ökonomische, soziale und kulturelle Dominanz blieb jedoch bis in die heutige Zeit weitgehend unangetastet.

Eine weitere bedeutende Gruppe der Ungarn im westungarischen Grenzgebiet bildeten Beamte des öffentlichen Dienstes, der katholische und evangelische Klerus, Angehörige freier Berufe sowie Handels- und Gewerbetreibende. In ungarischen Schulen ausgebildet und vor allem nach 1867 („Ausgleich" zwischen Österreich und Ungarn) im national-ungarischen Geist erzogen, hatten sich viele unter ihnen, die aus nicht-ungarischen Familien stammten, erst zur ungarischen Sprache assimiliert und als „Magyaronen" ein Zugehörigkeitsgefühl zur ungarischen Volksgruppe entwickelt. Viele von ihnen siedelten nach 1921 nach Ungarn über. Eine durch ihren jüdischen Glauben innerhalb der Ungarischsprachigen isolierte Gruppe bildeten bis 1938 die zum Großteil den „Magyaronen" zuzurechnenden jüdischen Angehörigen freier Berufe, Gewerbetreibenden und Industriellen (Gold 1970, Baumgartner 1989, 76).

Auch unter den Industrie- und Bergarbeitern waren die Ungarn vertreten. Schließlich sprach ein großer Teil der 8.000 vor 1938 im Burgenland lebenden Roma Ungarisch, besonders jene in Oberwart und Unterwart (Baumgartner 1989, 76); → Sprachenkarte N.

3. Politik, Wirtschaft und allgemeine kulturelle sowie religiöse Lage

3.1. Politik

Das Verhältnis der Kontaktsprachen Deutsch und Ungarisch im westungarischen Raum bzw. im Burgenland war immer von den jeweiligen innenpolitischen Verhältnissen geprägt. In der ersten Hälfte des 19. Jahrhunderts zielten Maßnahmen der ungarischen Komitatsbehörden im Bereich der Schulverwaltung auf die Verwendung von Ungarisch, auch in Schulen außerhalb des ungarischen Siedlungsgebietes. Nach einer Phase der massiven Zurückdrängung der ungarischen bzw. Aufwertung der deutschen Sprache in Schule und Verwaltung (1849—1867) setzte nach dem „Ausgleich" von 1867 zwischen Österreich und Ungarn eine offensive Politik der Magyarisierung ein, die mit der Einführung des ungarischen Schulgesetzes im Jahre 1907 (Lex Apponyi) ihren Höhepunkt erreichte (Baumgartner 1993, 218). Mit dem Anschluß des Burgenlandes an Österreich im Jahr 1921 änderte sich die Situation erneut. Die Zwischenkriegszeit war von einer stark anti-magyarischen und deutsch-nationalen Stimmung gekennzeichnet.

Die österreichische Verfassung von 1920 erhob Deutsch zur alleinigen Staatssprache. Daran änderte sich auch nach dem Anschluß des *de facto* mehrsprachigen Burgenlandes nichts. Die Verwendung von Ungarisch als Kirchensprache und als Unterrichtssprache im konfessionellen Schulwesen wurde nach 1921 zwar beibehalten, die weiterführenden Schulen in ungarischer Sprache jedoch relativ rasch geschlossen. Gemeinderatsprotokolle aus den 20er und 30er Jahren belegen, daß die Minderheitensprachen in überwiegend ungarischen bzw. kroatischen Gemeinden in der ersten Republik noch als innere Amtssprachen verwendet werden konnten. In den öffentlichen Schulen und bei den Landesbehörden wurde hingegen nach 1921 Deutsch als einzige Unterrichts- bzw. Amtssprache forciert. Den mehrheitlich ungarischen Gemeinden blieb die wenig attraktive Wahl zwischen einer selbstfinanzierten konfessionellen Volksschule mit eigener Unterrichtssprache oder der Umwandlung in eine öffentliche Schule mit Deutsch als erster oder sogar einziger Sprache. Erst das vom katholisch-autoritären Ständestaat (1934—1938) erlassene Minderheitenschulgesetz von 1937 schuf Voraussetzungen für die Bestellung und Besoldung ungarischsprachiger Volksschullehrer. Es trat allerdings erst 1945 in Kraft.

Nach dem Anschluß Österreichs an Deutschland (1938) verschlechterte sich die Situation der Minderheiten (vgl. 4.). Auch nach 1945 geschah im Burgenland lange Zeit wenig zum Schutz der ethnischen Minderheiten. Selbst die Verankerung der Minderheitenrechte im österreichischen Staatsvertrag von 1955 änderte daran nicht viel. Ungarn und Roma kamen in diesem Vertragswerk übrigens gar nicht vor.

Die Schulgesetze von 1962 verringerten sogar die Verwendung des Ungarischen und Kroatischen im Unterricht. Die Volksschulzeit wurde von acht auf vier Jahre verkürzt und stattdessen Hauptschulen für 10- bis 14jährige errichtet, die nicht unter das Minderheitenschulgesetz fielen. Das Volksgruppengesetz von 1976 bewirkte für die Ungarn eine gewisse Besserstellung. Sie wurden erstmals als Volksgruppe anerkannt.

3.2. Wirtschaft
(vgl. Pkt. 2. und 5.)

3.3. Kultur und Religion

Die ungarischen Siedlungen im Burgenland bildeten bzw. bilden keineswegs kulturell isolierte Exklaven. Volksmärchen, Liedgut, Tänze und Brauchtum weisen deutliche Parallelen zur Kultur der umliegenden nicht-ungarischsprachigen Orte auf. Der Csárdás ist im Burgenland zwar nur bei den Ungarn der Oberen Wart anzutreffen, für die Tanzkultur der burgenländischen Ungarn, die genauso wie die deutschsprachige Mehrheit die jeweiligen Modetänze übernehmen, ist dieser jedoch keineswegs repräsentativ (Gaál 1977, 325). Andererseits sind bzw. waren in bezug auf die meisten Kulturerscheinungen auch Besonderheiten bei den Burgenland-Ungarn auszumachen (eigene Trachten, Volkstänze, spezifisch ungarische Speisen usw.). Deutliche Unterschiede zwischen der Kultur der Ungarn im Südburgenland und den übrigen Bevölkerungsgruppen gibt es v. a. in der Siedlungsform („Sippensiedlung"; Gaál 1977).

Heute gehören die Ungarischsprachigen drei Glaubensrichtungen an: der römisch-katholischen Kirche (Unterwart, mittleres Burgenland), der evangelisch-lutherischen Kirche (Siget i. d. Wart) und der calvinistisch-reformierten Kirche (Oberwart). Bis 1938 hatte es auch unter den burgenländischen Juden eine große Gruppe Ungarischsprechender gegeben (vgl. Pkt. 2.).

4. Statistik und Ethnoprofil

4.1. Ungarisch in den Volkszählungen

In der Volkszählung 1991 gaben 4.973 Burgenländer — das entspricht 1.9% der burgenländischen Wohnbevölkerung mit österreichischer Staatsbürgerschaft — Ungarisch (zum Großteil in Kombination mit Deutsch) als *Umgangssprache* an. Einschließlich der ausländischen Bevölkerung verwenden insgesamt 6.763 Personen im Burgenland Ungarisch (ÖSTAT 1993). Nur Deutsch als Umgangssprache sprechen laut Volkszählung 1991 239.097 Burgenländer (darunter 237.516 Österreicher; = 90.3%). 19.460 (darunter 19.109 Österreicher; = 7.3%) gaben Kroatisch (einschließlich der Kombination mit Deutsch) als Umgangssprache an.

Im Burgenland sank der Anteil der autochthonen ungarischen Volksgruppe an der burgenländischen bzw. deutsch-westungarischen Bevölkerung im Laufe des 20. Jahrhunderts von 9.1% (1910) auf 1.5% (1981). Erst die Volkszählung 1991 markiert eine Trendumkehr (vgl. Tab. 225.1).

Tab. 225.1: Ungarisch in den Volkszählungen (Quellen: ÖSTAT 1993, Münz 1989).

Jahr	absolut	% der Wohnbevölkerung des Burgenlandes
1910	26.225	9.1
1920	24.930	8.4
1923	14.931	5.2
1934	10.442	3.5
1939	8.346	2.9
1951	5.251	1.9
1961	5.629	2.1
1971	5.447	2.0
1981	4.025	1.5
1991	4.973	1.8

Die ungarische Volkszählung von 1910 weist über 26.000 Personen mit ungarischer Muttersprache aus. Zu starken Rückgängen der ungarischen Bevölkerung kam es unmittelbar nach der Angliederung des Burgenlandes an Österreich und in den 20er Jahren. Ausschlaggebend dafür waren eine einsetzende Rück- bzw. Abwanderung ungarischer Beamter, Eisenbahner und Militärangehöriger, Gutsverwalter sowie anti-österreichisch gesinnter Angehöriger der Intelligenz nach Ungarn, die Abwanderung vieler ungarischer Meierhofarbeiter in die angrenzenden Industrieregionen Niederösterreichs und nach Wien (Suppan 1983, 82) sowie die Auswanderung nach Übersee in den 20er Jahren. Die antimagyarische Stimmung und die auf eine Germanisierung des Burgenlandes abzielenden schulpolitischen Maßnahmen des NS-Regimes trugen bis 1945 wesentlich zum Rückgang des Bekenntnisses zur ungarischen Sprache bei. Nach Kriegsende blieb der Anteil der burgenländisch-ungarischen Bevölkerung trotz sozioökonomischem Wandel im großen und ganzen konstant. Die Volkszählung von 1961 ergab aufgrund des Zuzugs von Flüchtlingen aus Ungarn (1956/57) sogar einen leichten Anstieg. Nur zwischen den Volkszählungen 1971 und 1981 war ein deutlicher Rückgang des Ungarischen als Umgangssprache zu verzeichnen.

4.2. Ungarisch-Kenntnisse im Burgenland

Die effektive Kenntnis der Volksgruppensprachen Ungarisch und Kroatisch ist im heutigen Burgenland deutlich weiter verbreitet, als dies die Volkszählungsergebnisse 1991 vermuten lassen. Dies zeigt eine Zusatzerhebung zum Mikrozensus 1990 bzw. eine Nacherhebung 1991 zu Sprachkenntnissen und -verwendung im Burgenland (Holzer/Münz 1993, 19).

Von den etwas über 270.000 Burgenländern sprechen oder verstehen über 16.700 Personen (6.1%) Ungarisch, mehr als 24.000 Personen (9.0%) sprechen oder verstehen Kroatisch. Nur Deutsch sprechen rund 232.000 Personen bzw. 84.9% der Landesbevölkerung (vgl. Tab. 225.2).

Tab. 225.2: Sprachkenntnisse im Burgenland 1990/91 (Quellen: Mikrozensus 1990, Holzer/Münz 1993).

Sprachkenntnisse	absolut	in %
nur Deutsch	231.893	84.9
auch Ungarisch	16.737	6.1
auch Kroatisch	24.459	9.0

Von den Burgenländern mit Ungarisch-Kenntnissen beherrschen fast 14.500 die Sprache *aktiv*; 2.300 haben bloß *passive* Kenntisse. Fast 2.000 Burgenländer sprechen oder verstehen sowohl Ungarisch als auch Kroatisch. Ein Teil dieser Ungarischsprachigen ist nicht der ethnischen Gruppe der Burgenland-Ungarn im engeren Sinn zuzurechnen. Viele Angehörige der älteren Generation mit nicht-ungarischer Muttersprache lernten Ungarisch in der Volksschule, pendelten in der Zwischenkriegszeit auch an weiterführende Schulen in Westungarn, ohne sich selbst je der ungarischen Sprachgruppe im Burgenland zugehörig zu fühlen. Für einen hohen Anteil der vor 1930 Geborenen mit Ungarisch-Kenntnissen (1991: 23% aller Personen mit Ungarisch-Kenntnissen) spielt Ungarisch weder in privaten noch in öffentlichen Lebensbereichen eine Rolle.

4.3. Aktuelle räumliche Verteilung der ungarischen Sprachgruppe im Burgenland

Die wichtigsten Wohngebiete der ungarischen Sprachgruppe liegen heute im südlichen (Oberwart, Unterwart, Sziget i. d. Wart) und mittleren (Oberpullendorf, Mitterpullendorf) Burgenland. Mit 66% burgenländisch-ungarischer Bevölkerung ist Unterwart heute die einzige mehrheitlich von Ungarn bewohnte Gemeinde des Burgenlandes. Im nördlichen Burgenland lebt in der Landeshauptstadt Eisenstadt ein über dem Landesdurchschnitt (Volkszählung 1991) liegender Anteil an Ungarischsprachigen. Im Bezirk Neusiedl verteilen sich die Ungarischsprachigen, in erster Linie Nachkommen der ungarischen Meierhofarbeiter, im wesentlichen auf sechs Gemeinden. Die höchsten relativen Anteile der Ungarn an der Ortsbevölkerung weisen dort Frauenkirchen (Boldogasszony) und Andau im Seewinkel (Mosonbánfalva) sowie Parndorf (Pandrof) nördlich des Neusiedler Sees auf.

5. Soziolinguistische Lage

5.1. Status des Ungarischen im Burgenland

Das Prestige der ungarischen Sprache in Deutsch-Westungarn bzw. im Burgenland war immer eng mit dem sozialen Status ihrer Sprecher verbunden. Für Angehörige und Nachkommen der ungarischen Adelsfamilien, aber auch für etliche Kinder und Enkel von „Magyaronen" blieb das Ungarische bis heute Teil ihres elitären Selbstbewußtseins. Angesichts der realen gesellschaftlichen und politischen Verhältnisse im modernen Burgenland ist dies bei vielen allerdings nur mehr nostalgische Erinnerung und Symbol ihrer früheren gesellschaftlichen Stellung.

Bis zum Ende der Ersten Republik (1938) konnten die Nachkommen des ungarischen Kleinadels als ehemals mit Privilegien ausgestatteter freier Stand größtenteil ihr tradiertes ständisch-lokales und sprachliches Selbstbewußtsein erhalten. Die Abschaffung der ungarischen Unterrichtssprache durch das NS-Regime (1938–1945) konnte diese Identität erstmals in hohem Maß erschüttern. Dazu kam, daß sich durch Erbteilung und Entagrarisierung die ökonomische Situation der einst wirtschaftlich gutgestellten Bauern der Oberen Wart und im mittleren Burgenland in der Zweiten Republik verschlechterte. Viele waren zu Nebenerwerbslandwirten geworden. Für die jüngere, sozial mobilere Generation war Ungarisch zu einer im Alltag „nutzlosen" Sprache geworden. Die deutsche Sprache gewann deutlich an Prestige, sie versprach ökonomischen und sozialen Erfolg. Dieses neue Bewußtsein verstärkte die seit der Abschaffung des konfessionellen ungarischen Schulwesens durch die Nationalsozialisten einsetzende Bilingualisierung dieser Gemeinden. In ihrer 1974 durchgeführten Feldforschung zum Sprachwechsel in Oberwart stellt Gál (1977) fest, daß junge zweisprachige Eltern darauf bedacht sind, daß ihre Kinder ein von ungarischen Einflüssen restlos bereinigtes Deutsch lernen.

Wesentlich früher — schon in den 20er und 30er Jahren — hatte der Sprachwechsel der nordburgenländischen Meierhofarbeiter eingesetzt. Dieser von der deutschsprachigen Umwelt isolierten, sozial deklassierten Schicht erschien die eigene ungarische Muttersprache mehrheitlich als Stigma. Sozialer Aufstieg schien etlichen nur über Assimilierung, vielfach auch durch Abwanderung oder Pendeln in industrielle Ballungsräume möglich.

5.2. Aktuelle soziale Struktur der Ungarischsprachigen

Die Gruppe der Burgenländer, die Ungarisch sprechen oder zumindest verstehen (vgl. 4.), ist im Durchschnitt deutlich älter als die Gruppe der Nur-Deutschsprachigen. Für die soziale Struktur bedeutet dies, daß es unter den Ungarischsprachigen deutlich mehr Rentner gibt, als unter den Nur-Deutschsprachigen. Unterrepräsentiert sind im Gegensatz dazu Personen im Haupterwerbsalter, Schüler, Studenten, Kinder im Vorschulalter. Im Vergleich zur deutschen Sprachgruppe sind Ungarischsprachige in etwas höherem Ausmaß als Beamte, im Dienstleistungssektor und als an- und ungelernte Arbeiter beschäftigt. In der zwischen 1950 und 1975 geborenen Generation zeigt sich bei den Ungarischsprachigen ein überdurchschnittlicher Maturanten- und Akademikeranteil.

5.3. Aktuelle soziale Funktion des Ungarischen im Burgenland

Von den ca. 12.000 über 10jährigen Burgenländern, die der ungarischen Sprachgruppe im weiteren Sinn zuzurechnen sind (vgl. 4.), spielt nur mehr für die Hälfte die ungarische Sprache (auch) in öffentlichen Lebensbereichen (Gemeinde, Kirche oder Arbeitsplatz) eine Rolle. Während die ungarische Sprache im Bezirk Neusiedl fast nur noch im privaten Lebensbereich Verwendung findet, wird diese in den Bezirken Oberwart und Oberpullendorf von der überwiegenden Mehrheit der Ungarischsprachigen auch im öffentlichen Leben gesprochen. Im Arbeits- und Wirtschaftsleben ist seit 1989 eine zunehmende Bedeutung der ungarischen Sprache für die Erwerbstätigen des Burgenlandes festzustellen.

Vier von zehn verheirateten bzw. in Lebensgemeinschaft lebenden Ungarischsprachigen leben mit einem Partner zusammen, der kein Ungarisch versteht. Der Anteil der gemischtsprachigen Ehen korreliert eindeutig mit dem Alter: die Jüngeren leben wesentlich häufiger in gemischtsprachigen Ehen als die Älteren. Das Ausmaß an Homogamie hängt in erster Linie von der Stärke der Sprachgruppen in den einzelnen Ortschaften ab. 15% der Ungarischsprachigen verwenden in Gesprächen mit dem Partner nur Deutsch, auch wenn beide Ungarisch verstehen.

Nur die Hälfte der ungarischsprachigen Mütter bzw. Väter spricht mit ihren Kindern häufig oder zeitweise Ungarisch. Entscheidend dafür ist in erster Linie, ob beide Eltern zweisprachig sind oder nur ein Elternteil die Minderheitensprache beherrscht.

Die ungarischsprachigen Burgenländer konsumieren Medien in ihrer eigenen Sprache viel weniger intensiv als die deutschsprachige Mehrheit. Die mäßige Inanspruchnahme ungarischer ORF-Sendungen ist auf das geringe Angebot zurückzuführen (keine tägliche Sendeleiste). Ein Teil der Sprachgruppe konsumiert stattdessen regelmäßig die in Ungarn produzierten und ausgestrahlten Radio- und Fernsehprogramme (Holzer/Münz 1993).

6. Sprachpolitische Lage

Trotz oder vielleicht gerade wegen ihrer bedrohten Existenz haben die Ungarn, Kroaten und Roma im Burgenland wesentlich weniger Minderheitenrechte als etwa die Deutsch-Tiroler und Ladiner in der Provinz Bozen. Wenn sie in ein anderes Bundesland übersiedeln, gehen ungarische und kroatische Burgenländer überdies ihrer Minderheitenrechte verlustig, da diese laut Staatsvertrag (1955) und dem österreichischen Volksgruppengesetz (1976) nur im „historischen Siedlungsgebiet" gelten, also territorial begrenzt sind. Im Gegensatz zu Belgien oder zur Schweiz achten die Bundesbehörden in Wien nicht auf die Rekrutierung einer Mindestquote von Beamten mit ungarischer bzw. kroatischer, slowenischer oder tschechischer Muttersprache. Erst die 80er Jahre brachten sowohl auf der Ebene des kollektiven Bewußtseins als auch in der Bewertung der Minderheitensprachen eine Trendwende. Das Ende der kommunistischen Herrschaft in den Nachbarländern und die Öffnung der Grenzen haben dazu nicht unwesentlich beigetragen. Seit 1984 sendet der ORF Lokalprogramme in ungarischer Sprache. 1987 wurde Ungarisch erstmals als Unterrichtsfach im Gymnasium Oberpullendorf eingerichtet („Pannonisches Gymnasium"). Daneben gibt es heute sechs weitere höhere Schulen, in denen Ungarisch als Frei- oder (Wahl-)Pflichtgegenstand angeboten wird. 1992 folgte schließlich die Eröffnung des „Zweisprachigen Bundesgymnasiums" in Oberwart mit Ungarisch/Deutsch bzw. Kroatisch/Deutsch als Unterrichtssprache. In den Hauptschulen Oberwart und Oberpullendorf gibt es Schulversuche mit Ungarisch als Pflichtgegenstand, an acht weiteren Hauptschulen wird Ungarisch als Freigegenstand angeboten. Nur noch in zwei (Siget i. d. Wart und Unterwart) der ehemals (bis 1938) zehn Volksschulen wird Ungarisch als Pflichtgegenstand unterrichtet. An den zweisprachigen Volksschulen in Oberwart und Oberpullendorf wird Ungarisch ebenso wie in sieben weiteren Volksschulen lediglich als Freigegenstand angeboten. In den Kindergärten der ungarischen Orte der Oberen Wart sowie in Oberpullendorf wird Ungarisch zusätzlich zu Deutsch verwendet, von einer zweisprachigen Erziehung der Kinder kann jedoch in den wenigsten Fällen gesprochen werden. Eine Ausbildung zum Ungarisch-Lehrer ist im Burgenland nicht möglich (Kaiser 1993).

Seit 1989 wird aus österreichischer Sicht die Kenntnis sogenannter Ostsprachen positiver bewertet. Die völlige Normalisierung der Beziehungen zu Ungarn erleichtert die Kontakte zu den benachbarten Ungarn und bietet ungarischsprachigen Burgenländern bessere Erwerbschancen (vgl. Pkt. 5.). Da die Generation der nach 1960 geborenen Ungarischsprachigen allerdings in der Regel lediglich den lokalen Dialekt beherrscht (Baumgartner 1993, 231), ist die Vermittlung ungarischer Hochsprachkenntisse in weiterführenden Schulen in diesem Zusammenhang von besonderer Bedeutung.

Die Ungarn im Burgenland verfügen seit 1968 über einen gemeinsamen Kulturverein

("Burgenlandi Magyar Kultúregyesület"). Auf dessen Initiative konstituierte sich 1979 — als erster der gesetzlich vorgesehenen Beiräte — der ungarische Volksgruppenbeirat. Dessen Aktivitäten blieben allerdings angesichts äußerst beschränkter finanzieller Mittel und durch die Kontroverse um den Status der ungarischen Emigranten des 20. Jahrhunderts eingeschränkt. Die burgenländischen Ungarn wollten bis 1992 die überwiegend in Wien und anderen größeren Städten lebenden ungarischen Emigranten nicht als Teil ihrer Minderheit anerkennen.

Neben den Aktivitäten des Kulturvereins und den zweisprachigen Volksschulen in Unterwart und Siget i. d. Wart tragen die Kirchen wesentlich zum Erhalt der ungarischen Sprachgruppe im Burgenland bei.

Hinweise auf den Willen zur Selbstbehauptung als Gruppe gibt die Bereitschaft der Eltern, die eigene Mutter- bzw. Familiensprache an die Kinder weiterzugeben. Dies tun nur vier von zehn (45%) nach 1954 geborene ungarischsprachige Mütter bzw. Väter (Holzer/Münz 1993, 84).

7. Allgemeines kontaktlinguistisches Porträt

7.1. Der burgenländisch-deutsche Dialekt

Ungarisch war jahrhundertelang Sprache der Eliten und 1867–1921 Staatssprache im heutigen Burgenland. Dennoch nahm die burgenländisch-deutsche Umgangssprache relativ wenige ungarische Sprachelemente auf. Dies sind z. B. Ausdrücke und Redewendungen wie *bieresch* „Lohnknecht", *die mas(ch)ik Seitn* „die andere Seite", *Bokantsch* „Schnürschuh" (Baumgartner 1993, 230), besonders aber Ausrufe, Namen und persönliche Anreden (Gál 1977, 314).

7.2. Der burgenländisch-ungarische Dialekt

In den ungarischen Dialekten der bereits seit über 800 Jahren, besonders seit der Belagerung von Köszeg/Güns durch die Türken im 16. Jahrhundert (Imre 1977, 305), vom ungarischen Sprachgebiet im Osten isolierten ehemaligen Grenzwächtersiedlungen der Oberen Wart haben sich bis heute Charakteristika der ungarischen Gemeinsprache des 16. Jahrhunderts erhalten. Anderseits hat das Burgenländisch-Ungarische, das immer von der deutschen Mehrheitssprache umgeben war, neue Wörter und Wendungen aus dem Deutschen übernommen.

Die nachstehenden Beispiele, die die Besonderheiten des burgenländisch-ungarischen Dialekts der Oberen Wart — genauer der Mundart der Gemeinde Oberwart — dokumentieren, entstammen, wenn nicht anders ausgewiesen, dem Beitrag Samu Imres „Der ungarische Dialekt der Oberen Wart" (Imre 1977).

Die wichtigsten, das Lautsystem betreffenden Unterschiede zwischen dem Dialekt der Oberen Wart und der ungarischen Hochsprache sind:

— Anstelle langer Vokale *ó, ö, é* häufig die Diphthonge *uo, üö, ië*: *juo* „gut" *kiëz* „Hand" statt *jó, kéz*.

— Statt *e* ist v. a. in deutschen Lehnwörtern oft *ëe* bzw. *ie* zu hören: *rëen* „Bratpfanne, Reindl".

— Vor das *e* des Demonstrativpronomens *ez* und des Verbalpräfixes *el* tritt ein *j*-Laut: *jerre* „entlang", *jeladom* „ich verkaufe es" statt *erre, eladom*.

— Die deutlichsten Erkennungszeichen des Ungarischen in der Stadt Oberwart sind die Verwendung von *cs* bzw. *dzs* anstelle von *ty* bzw. *gy*: *bácsám* „mein älterer Bruder", *ádzs* „Bett" statt *bátyám, ágy*. In Unterwart und Siget i. d. Wart hört man diese Aussprache dagegen überhaupt nicht.

— Der Laut *i* tritt häufig anstelle des hochsprachlichen *e* auf: *kefi* „Bürste" statt *kefe*.

— Statt *o* hört man oft *a* und umgekehrt.

Was die Wortbildung betrifft, wird anstatt *-dos/-des/-dös* mehr das Suffix *-doz/-döz* verwendet: *fogdoz* „er faßt an", *lögdöz* „er stößt an". Das Kausativsuffix *-tat/-tet* der ungarischen Hochsprache wird in einigen Fällen mit *-at/et* gebildet: *ropagat* „er knabbert". Im ungarischen Dialekt der Oberen Wart absolut unbekannt ist das Suffix *-val/-vel* („mit"). Es wird durch die alte Form *-ve* bzw. *-je* ersetzt. Hier heißt es: *autóve megyek* „ich fahre mit dem Auto" und nicht: *autóval megyek* (Baumgartner 1993, 231). Unterschiede gibt es auch hinsichtlich der besitzanzeigenden Personalendungen der Mehrzahl, die z. B. statt mit *-l/aim* mit *-iëk* gebildet werden: *liányokiëk* „meine Töchter".

In bezug auf die Lexik sind im ungarischen Dialekt sowohl archaische Formen des Ungarischen (*eves* „eiterig", *hiëb* „Dachboden", *keszkönyüö* „Tuch, Handtuch") als auch Eigenkreationen der Oberen Wart (*vastagborsuo* „Bohnenzuspeise", *szülessíg* „Viehfutter", *kelep* „Sensenhammer") zu finden.

Besonderes Kennzeichen des burgenländisch-ungarischen Dialekts ist das hohe Ausmaß an deutschen Lehnwörtern. Diese Übernahme verstärkte sich als Folge der Bilingualisierung der ehemals einsprachig-ungarischen Dörfer gegen Ende der 30er Jahre. Die bäuerliche Lebensform trat immer mehr in den Hintergrund. Für viele Errungenschaften und Gegenstände des modernen Lebens mußten neue Begriffe gefunden werden. In der Regel geschah dies dadurch, daß deutsche Wörter mit ungarischen Suffixen versehen in die ungarische Umgangssprache übernommen wurden (Imre 1977, 311). Zwar hatte auch die ungarische Standardsprache im Laufe ihrer Entwicklung viele Wörter aus dem österreichischen Deutschen entlehnt und assimiliert. Imre hat allerdings nachgewiesen, daß in das Ungarische der Oberen Wart eine beträchtliche Anzahl von deutschen Lehnwörtern eingegangen ist, die nicht über die ungarische Hochsprache entlehnt wurden (in der sie z. T. gar nicht vorkommen), sondern aus den benachbarten deutschen Dialekten des Südburgenlandes stammen. Diese Tendenz verstärkte sich auch durch die neue geopolitische Situation nach dem Zweiten Weltkrieg, als die Verbindung mit Ungarn durch den Eisernen Vorhang für Jahrzehnte unterbrochen worden war.

Am häufigsten wurden Verben und Substantiva aus dem Deutschen entlehnt, andere Wortarten dagegen relativ selten. Fast alle Verben erhalten das Suffix -l: *foarul* „fahren" (Burgenländisch-Deutsch: „foan") oder *pittül* „bitten". Die mit Abstand häufigsten deutschen Lehnwörter sind Substantiva. Diese nehmen sehr oft die Endungen -li oder -ni an: *flëkkëli* „Fleckerl", *vinkli* „Winkel", *rëntni* „Rente". Nach ihrer häufigsten semantischen Herkunft können sie in folgende Gruppen zusammengefaßt werden (Imre 1977, 312): Speise- und Getränkenamen (*prëzbuost* „Preßwurst", *foarfëlli* „Foafl" = „Teigflocke", *krahëlli* „Kracherl" = „Brause"), Früchte (*hëcsësëlli* „Hetscherl" = „Hagebutte"), Kleidung (*suorc* „Schurz"), Hausgeräte, Werkzeuge, landwirtschaftliche Geräte (*ëszcajg* „Esszaig" = „Eßzeug", *vájdling* „Waidling" = „große Schüssel", *siërhokli* „Schirhaggl" = „Schürhaken"), in den Jahren der Modernisierung entstandene Bezeichnungen für Maschinen, Institutionen, Behörden, Berufe usw.

7.3. Deutsch-ungarische Zweisprachigkeit im heutigen Burgenland

Heute ist die gesamte ungarischsprachige Bevölkerung des Burgenlandes auch deutschsprachig. Neben dem lokalen ungarischen Dialekt oder der ungarischen Hochsprache beherrschen sie auch den burgenländisch-deutschen Dialekt und/oder die deutsche Hochsprache. Außer der Dialekt- und Hochsprachvariante der beiden Sprachen ist im Oberwarter Raum das sogenannte „Pidgin"-Ungarisch weitverbreitet, eine durch extreme Entlehnung deutscher Strukturen und Lexeme gekennzeichnete Varietät (Gál 1977, 314; Baumgartner 1993, 230). Insgesamt umfassen die sprachlichen Ressourcen der zweisprachigen burgenländisch-ungarischen Bevölkerung somit fünf Kategorien:

1. österreichische Variante der deutschen Hochsprache,
2. burgenländisch-deutsche Dialekte,
3. „Pidgin"-Ungarisch mit deutschen Elementen,
4. burgenländisch-ungarische Dialekte,
5. ungarische Hochsprache.

(Gál 1977, Baumgartner 1993).

Die Zweisprachigkeit der ungarischsprachigen Bevölkerung im Burgenland unterscheidet sich dabei je nach Generationszugehörigkeit und sozialen Merkmalen deutlich:

— Die Generation der vor 1921 Geborenen beherrscht neben dem lokalen ungarischen Dialekt auch die in der Schule erlernte ungarische Hochsprache. Ihre Deutsch-Kenntnisse reichen jedoch meist über den örtlichen Dialekt nicht hinaus.

— Die Gruppe der „Magyaronen" (vgl. Pkt. 2.) verfügt in der Regel über Kenntnisse sowohl des ungarischen als auch des deutschen Standards und der burgenländisch-deutschen Mundart.

— Die mittlere Generation (vor 1960 geboren) beherrscht häufig alle fünf Formen der deutsch-ungarischen Zweisprachigkeit, während in der jüngsten Generation (nach 1960 geboren), die häufig keinen Ungarisch-Unterricht mehr hatte, Kentisse der ungarischen Hochsprache kaum vorhanden sind.

— Die Gruppe der nach 1945, 1956 und 1989 aus Ungarn und Siebenbürgen Eingewanderten spricht vor allem die ungarische und die deutsche Hochsprache (Baumgartner 1993, 230) sowie Dialekte ihrer Herkunftsregion.

8. Zum Stand der Forschung über Ungarisch und Deutsch im Burgenland

Die sprachwissenschaftliche Forschung zum Ungarischen und zum Sprachkontakt zwischen Deutsch und Ungarisch im Burgenland beschränkt sich im wesentlichen auf die ungarischen Siedlungen der Oberen Wart. Zu Fragen der Oberwarter ungarischen Mundart sind von Imre (neben der in Pkt. 7. zitierten Arbeit, Imre 1977) auch eine Monographie (Imre 1971) sowie ein Dialektwörterbuch (Imre 1973) erschienen. Eine Bibliographie zu den Dialekten in der Umgebung von Oberwart bis zum Jahre 1949 findet sich in Benkö/Lörincze 1961. In ihrer 1974 durchgeführten Feldstudie erforschte Susan Gál (Gál 1977 und 1979) Sprachgebrauch und Sprachwechsel der ungarischen Bevölkerung in Oberwart sowie deren Einstellung zur deutschen und ungarischen Sprache. In dem Sammelband „Die Obere Wart", herausgegeben von Ladislaus Triber (1977) zum Gedenken an die Wiedererrichtung der Oberen Wart im Jahre 1327, finden sich neben den oben erwähnten Beiträgen von Imre und Gál eine Reihe von Arbeiten zu Geschichte und Volkskultur der Ungarn im Oberwarter Raum.

Zu Kenntnis, aktueller privater und öffentlicher Verwendung sowie zur Weitergabe des Ungarischen im Burgenland liegt seit kurzem eine umfassende empirische Studie vor (Holzer/Münz 1993). Die derzeitige Verwendung von Ungarisch als Umgangssprache bzw. das Bekenntnis zum Ungarischen dokumentiert die Volkszählung von 1991.

9. Bibliographie (in Auswahl)

Baumgartner, Gerhard (1989): „Idevalósi vagyok – Einer, der hierher gehört. Zur Identität der ungarischen Sprachgruppe des Burgenlandes". In: *Identität und Lebenswelt. Ethnische, religiöse und kulturelle Vielfalt im Burgenland*, Baumgartner, G./Müllner, E./Münz, R. (Eds.), Eisenstadt, 69–84.

Baumgartner, Gerhard (1993): „Prolegomena zum Sprachverhalten ungarischsprachiger Burgenländer". In: *Trendwende? Sprache und Ethnizität im Burgenland*, Holzer, W./Münz, R. (Eds.), Wien, 215–235.

Benkö, Loránd/Lörincze, Lajos (1961): *Magyar nyelvjárási bibliográfia (1817–1949)* [Ungarische Mundartenbibliographie], Budapest.

Filla, Wilhelm/Flaschberger, Ludwig/Pachner, Franz/Reiterer, Albert F. (1982): *Am Rande Österreichs. Ein Beitrag zur Soziologie der österreichischen Volksgruppen*, Wien.

Gaál, Károly (1977): „Zur Volkskultur der Magyaren in der Wart". In: *Die Obere Wart*, Triber, L. (Ed.), Oberwart, 325–350.

Gaál, Károly (1985): *Kire marad a kiskömön. Wer erbt das Jankerl?*, Steinamanger.

Gál, Susan (1977): „Der Gebrauch der deutschen und ungarischen Sprache in Oberwart". In: *Die Obere Wart*, Triber, L. (Ed.), Oberwart, 313–324.

Gál, Susan (1979): *Language Shift. Social Determinants of Linguistic Change in Bilingual Austria*, New York.

Gold, Hugo (1970): *Gedenkbuch der untergegangenen Judengemeinden des Burgenlandes*, Tel Aviv.

Holzer, Werner/Münz, Rainer (Eds.) (1993): *Trendwende? Sprache und Ethnizität im Burgenland*, Wien.

Imre, Samu (1971): *A felsőőri nyelvjárás* [Die Oberwarter Mundart], Budapest.

Imre, Samu (1973): *Felsőőri tájszótár* [Oberwarter Dialektwörterbuch], Budapest.

Imre, Samu (1977): „Der ungarische Dialekt der Oberen Wart". In: *Die Obere Wart*, Triber, L. (Ed.), Oberwart.

Kaiser, Andrea (1993): „Zweisprachige Erziehung in Kindergarten und Schule". In: *Trendwende? Sprache und Ethnizität im Burgenland*, Holzer, W./Münz, R. (Eds.), Wien, 243–266.

Münz, Rainer (1989): „Zwischen Assimilation und Selbstbehauptung. Sprachgruppen und Minderheitenpolitik im Vergleich". In: *Identität und Lebenswelt. Ethnische, religiöse und kulturelle Vielfalt im Burgenland*, Baumgartner, G./Müllner, E./Münz, R. (Eds.), Eisenstadt, 24–45.

ÖSTAT(1993): Volkszählung 1991 (Arbeitstabellen).

Suppan, Arnold (1983): *Die österreichischen Volksgruppen. Tendenzen ihrer gesellschaftlichen Entwicklung im 20. Jahrhundert*, Wien.

Szeberényi, Ludwig (1986): *Die ungarische Volksgruppe im Burgenland und ihr Volksgruppenbeirat*, Wien.

Triber, Ladislaus (Ed.) (1977): *Die Obere Wart*, Oberwart.

Werner Holzer, Wien (Österreich)
Rainer Münz, Berlin (Deutschland)

226. Schweiz

1. Geographie und Demographie
2. Geschichte und Staatsbildung
3. Politik, Wirtschaft und allgemeine kulturelle sowie religiöse Lage
4. Statistik
5. Soziolinguistische Lage
6. Sprachpolitische Lage
7. Nichtlandessprachen als Kontaktsprachen
8. Zur Forschungslage
9. Bibliographie (in Auswahl)

1. Geographie und Demographie

Die Schweiz ist ein in der Mitte Westeuropas zwischen Deutschland, Frankreich, Italien und Österreich liegender Kleinstaat mit einer Ausdehnung von rund 350 km von Westen nach Osten und 220 km von Norden nach Süden. Geographisch läßt sich die Schweiz in fünf Hauptregionen gliedern: in Jura, Mittelland, Voralpen, Alpen und Alpensüdseite. Den zentralen Teil des Landes bildet die gebirgige Alpenregion mit den für die europäischen Nord-Süd-Verkehrswege wichtigen Alpenübergängen und den Quellgebieten der Flüsse Rhône, Rhein, Inn und Ticino. Die Alpen nehmen gut 40% der Fläche des Landes (Gesamtfläche rd. 41 000 km²) ein, sind aber nur sehr dünn besiedelt (Bundesamt 1992, 79 ff; Schweizer Lexikon 1991, 649 ff).

Der größte Teil der Bevölkerung wohnt im Mittelland in Städten und Agglomerationsregionen. Trotz der alpinen Regionen ist die Schweiz ein dicht besiedeltes Land (Bevölkerungsdichte 1990: 165 Einw./km²). Die Bevölkerung der Schweiz hat sich im Laufe des 20. Jahrhunderts mehr als verdoppelt, wobei das Bevölkerungswachstum in den einzelnen Regionen unterschiedlich verlief, je nach deren wirtschaftlicher Entwicklung und Struktur. Den größten Zuwachs zeigen in den letzten Jahrzehnten Vororts- und Agglomerationsgemeinden von Städten. Der stark zunehmende Verstädterungsprozeß zeigt sich nicht zuletzt darin, daß 1990 über zwei Drittel der Bevölkerung in städtischen Agglomerationen lebten. 1980 waren es noch knapp 62% der Bevölkerung gewesen. Nach einem Rückgang in den siebziger Jahren hat die ausländische Wohnbevölkerung in den achtziger Jahren wieder zugenommen: 1990 betrug der Anteil der ausländischen Wohnbevölkerung 18,1%. Kennzeichen der Bevölkerungsentwicklung ist auch eine allmähliche Zunahme der älteren Wohnbevölkerung (14,4% der Bevölkerung waren 1990 älter als 65 Jahre). 1990 wies die Schweiz eine Wohnbevölkerung von rund 6,8 Millionen auf (Bundesamt 1992, 35 ff; Geschichte 1986, 741 ff, 878 ff).

2. Geschichte und Staatsbildung

2.1. Zur Geschichte der Schweizerischen Eidgenossenschaft

Der Beginn der schweiz. Eidgenossenschaft liegt in Bündnissystemen des 13. Jahrhunderts, besonders im Bund der späteren Kantone Uri, Schwyz und Unterwalden, ländlicher Gebiete im zentralen Alpenraum, aber auch in Bünden der Reichsstädte Zürich und Bern. Diese Bündnissysteme schlossen sich im 14. Jahrhundert zu einem festeren Bündnisgeflecht zusammen. Der eidgenössische Bund, in dem Länder und Städte gleichberechtigte Partner waren, kontrollierte zentrale Alpenpässe und einen wichtigen West-Ost-Verkehrsweg und war bald so attraktiv, daß sich ihm weitere Städte und Gebiete anschlossen. Eine Rolle spielte dabei auch der Widerstand gegen österreichisch-habsburgische Hegemoniebestrebungen. Die Eidgenossenschaft, die ein besonderes militärisches Ansehen genoß, betrieb zunächst eine aktive, expansive Außenpolitik (ausgebautes Söldnerwesen). Nach militärischen Niederlagen in Norditalien zu Beginn des 16. Jahrhunderts beschränkte sie sich weitgehend auf eine neutrale Außenpolitik.

Innerhalb der Schweiz kam es im Laufe ihrer Entwicklung zu Stadt-Land-Konflikten (Eidgenössische Bauernkriege, Tendenz zur Aristokratisierung der Gesellschaft im 17. Jahrhundert) wie zu konfessionellen Spaltungen, die jedoch nicht zum Auseinanderbrechen der Eidgenossenschaft führten. Am Ende des 18. Jahrhunderts wurde die Ordnung der alten Eidgenossenschaft unter französischem Druck zerstört und 1798 wurde für einige Jahre die zentralistische Helvetische Republik errichtet. Wegen des Widerstands gegen eine zentralistische Lösung mußte bald wieder ein föderalistischer Staat eingerichtet werden, wobei ehemalige Untertanengebiete zu selbständigen Kantonen wurden. Endgültig festgelegt wurde diese territoriale Neuordnung der Kantone 1815 auf dem Wiener Kongreß, der auch eine erneute völkerrechtliche Anerkennung der schweiz. Neutralität brachte.

Das 19. Jahrhundert steht im Zeichen der teilweise auch konfessionell gefärbten Auseinandersetzungen zwischen liberalen (im Gegensatz zum übrigen Europa seit dem 1. Drittel des 19. Jahrhunderts dominierend) und konservativen Kräften. Nachdem sich in einem religiös bedingten Bürgerkrieg („Sonderbundskrieg") die Liberalen durchgesetzt hatten, wurde 1848 mit einer neuen Verfassung der heutige schweiz. Bundesstaat geschaffen. Dessen weitere Geschichte ist gekennzeichnet durch den allmählichen Wandel von einer agrarisch geprägten Gesellschaft über einen Industriestaat zu einem Dienstleistungsstaat (Geschichte 1986; Schweizer Lexikon 1991, 671 ff).

2.2. Sprachgrenzen und Sprachgebiete im Laufe der schweizerischen Geschichte

Das Gebiet der heutigen Schweiz war auf Grund seiner Lage und Topographie schon immer Grenz- und Überschneidungsraum unterschiedlicher Sprachgruppen. In vorrömischer Zeit waren es das Gallo-Keltische im Westen sowie das Rätische im Osten, die dann in der Folge der römischen Herrschaft romanisiert wurden. Seit dem 5. Jahrhundert n.Chr. kam schließlich mit dem allmählichen Vordringen der Alemannen von Norden her das Germanische hinzu. Im Laufe der Sprachgeschichte des Gebiets kam es dabei sowohl zur Germanisierung ursprünglich romanischer wie zur allerdings merklich kleineren Romanisierung germanischer Sprecher.

Sprachgrenzen spielten in der Geschichte der Eidgenossenschaft immer eine Rolle, so daß auch vom „bestimmenden Sprachgrenzdasein der Schweiz" gesprochen wird (Sonderegger 1991, 13). Eigentliche (allerdings noch nicht geschlossen verlaufende) deutschromanische Sprachgrenzen lassen sich seit dem Frühmittelalter nachweisen. Im Westen und Süden stehen die Sprachgrenzen zwischen dem Deutschen (Dt.) und dem Französischen (Frz.) bzw. zwischen dem Dt. und dem Italienischen (It.) und damit die entsprechenden Sprachgebiete seit dem Spätmittelalter mehr oder weniger fest. Zu späteren, kleineren Verschiebungen der dt.-frz. Sprachgrenze kam es in den Kantonen Wallis (Vorrücken der frz. Sprache), Freiburg (Verdeutschung des Gebiets um Murten) und Bern (Entwicklung der Stadt Biel von einer dt.-sprachigen zu einer zweisprachigen Stadt) (Zimmerli 1899, 100 ff). Dagegen ist die dt.-rätoromanische (rtr.) Sprachgrenze im Südosten des Landes weit weniger stabil geblieben, das Gebiet des Rtr. ist gerade in den letzten hundert Jahren stark zurückgegangen (Holtus 1989, 863 ff; Kraas 1992, 127 ff; Viletta 1978, 388 f, 413).

Die alte Eidgenossenschaft war im wesentlichen dt.-sprachig bestimmt. Bei der Gründung der schweiz. Eidgenossenschaft spielte also das sprachliche Element keine Rolle. Vollmitglieder des Bundes waren nur dt.-sprachige Gebiete oder das zweisprachige Freiburg, dessen Oberschicht im 15. und 16. Jahrhundert aber eine aktive Germanisierungspolitik betrieb. Die anderssprachigen Gebiete der Eidgenossenschaft waren Untertanengebiete dt.-sprachiger Kantone. Diese bedienten sich im Verkehr mit ihren Untertanen deren Sprache. Zum mehrsprachigen Staat wurde die Schweiz erst am Ende des 18. Jahrhunderts mit der Errichtung der Helvetischen Republik (2.1.), die eine Gleichberechtigung aller Bürger brachte, was in der Schweiz entgegen der einheitssprachlichen Tendenz Frankreichs zu einer Gleichstellung der Sprachen führte. Staatsrechtlich verankert wurde die Mehrsprachigkeit der Schweiz in der Bundesverfassung von 1848, in deren Artikel 109 festgehalten wird: „Die drei Hauptsprachen der Schweiz, die deutsche, französische und italienische, sind Nationalsprachen des Bundes." Ein entsprechender Verfassungsartikel findet sich auch in den späteren, revidierten Bundesverfassungen, wobei die Schweiz 1938 mit der Anerkennung des Rtr. als vierter Landessprache ein offiziell viersprachiger Staat wurde (6.1.); → Sprachenkarte O.

Im Laufe des 19. Jahrhunderts bauten die frz.-sprachigen Kantone ein ausgeprägtes schweiz. Nationalbewußtsein auf (Müller 1977; Kreis 1987). Im Ersten Weltkrieg nahmen die verschiedenen Sprachgruppen jeweils für die entsprechenden Sprachnationen verbal Partei. Das Verhalten der dt.-freundlichen Armeeführung verstärkte diesen „Graben" zwischen der dt.- und der frz.-sprachigen Schweiz noch. Allerdings führte dieser „Graben" nicht zum Auseinanderbrechen der Schweiz, sondern konnte nach und nach überbrückt werden, nicht zuletzt durch die integrierende Funktion der Mundart für die dt.-schweiz. und die gesamtschweiz. Bevölkerung (Abgrenzung gegen Deutschland). Sprachfragen bildeten in der ersten Hälfte dieses Jahrhunderts Gegenstand polemischer Auseinandersetzungen zwischen Sprachpflegern der dt. und der frz. Schweiz; dabei ging es um sprachliche Hegemonieansprüche im anderen Sprachgebiet (z. B. frz. Anschriften im dt.-sprachigen Bern), den Mundartgebrauch der Deutschschweizer, die Bekämpfung des *français fédéral* (schlechtes Frz. unter dt. und schweizerdt. Einfluß) (Du Bois 1984). In letzter Zeit sind Unterschiede zwischen der dt.-sprachigen und der frz.-sprachigen Schweiz — die it. und die rtr. Schweiz werden bei den Diskussionen um Gegensätze zwischen den Sprachgruppen weniger beachtet — wieder vermehrt zum politischen Thema geworden.

Die Sprachgrenzen in der Schweiz fallen kaum mit politischen Grenzen (die Staatsgrenze ist nur selten Sprachgrenze und nur wenige Kantonsgrenzen sind auch Sprachgrenzen) oder konfessionellen Grenzen zusammen. (Zum hist. Hintergrund der schweiz. Mehrsprachigkeit cf. Haas 1982 b; 1994; McRae 1983, 39 ff; Sonderegger 1981; 1985, 1875 ff; 1991; Weibel 1986, 223 ff).

3. Politik, Wirtschaft und allgemeine kulturelle sowie religiöse Lage

Das schweiz. politische System weist eine ausgeprägt föderalistische Struktur auf mit 26 Kantonen (eigentliche Teilrepubliken des föderalistischen Staatenbundes) und rund 3000 Gemeinden, die über weitgehende Autonomie gegenüber dem Bundesstaat verfügen. So kennt die Schweiz eine dreigeteilte Steuerhoheit, Schul-, Erziehungs- und Gesundheitswesen sind Angelegenheit der Kantone, zudem besitzen Kantone und Gemeinden große Zuständigkeiten im Polizei- und Gerichtswesen. Dadurch daß etwa Bildung und Kulturförderung in erster Linie Angelegenheit der Kantone sind, gibt es kein gesamtschweiz. Unterrichtsministerium, sondern nur freiwillige Kooperationsvereinbarungen der Kantone für das Bildungswesen. Weitere bestimmende Kennzeichen der schweiz. Politik sind neben dem ausgeprägten Föderalismus die stark ausgebaute direkte Demokratie —

Mehrmals im Jahr wird an der Urne über politische Sachgeschäfte abgestimmt, und zwar auf allen föderalistischen Ebenen. Zudem verfügen die Stimmbürger über das Recht, sogenannte „Volksinitiativen" zu lancieren und gegen bestimmte Beschlüsse von Parlament und Regierung das Referendum zu ergreifen.

— und die Ausrichtung auf Konkordanzpolitik —

Das politische System ist nicht als Konkurrenzdemokratie mit einer deutlichen Trennung zwischen einer Regierungspartei und einer starken Oppositionspartei organisiert. Vielmehr bilden die vier großen Parteien des Landes, drei bürgerliche und eine sozialdemokratische, seit Ende der fünfziger Jahre eine Koalitionsregierung. Das konkordanzdemokratische Prinzip ist nicht nur auf nationaler, sondern auch auf kantonaler und kommunaler Ebene zu finden. In vielen Kantons- und v. a. in Gemeinderegierungen sind zudem neben Mitgliedern der vier großen Parteien noch einzelne Mitglieder kleinerer politischer Gruppierungen vertreten. Das auf Konkordanzdemokratie ausgerichtete System ist nicht unumstritten und wird bei politischen Streitfällen zunehmend in Frage gestellt, besonders was die Regierungsbeteiligung der Sozialdemokraten betrifft, hat sich aber bis heute gehalten.

Diese Merkmale haben zu einem stabilen, stark auf Kompromisse und Absprachen ausgerichteten politischen System geführt, in dem sich Änderungen nur langsam und allmählich durchsetzen können (in der Schweiz sind Frauen erst seit 1971 stimm- und wahlberechtigt). Das Beharrungsvermögen der direkten Demokratie zeigt sich auch in der stark von alten Neutralitätsvorstellungen und föderalistischem Abseitsstehen geprägten Außenpolitik: so haben die Schweizer Stimmberechtigten 1986 den Beitritt zur UNO und 1992 den Beitritt zum Europäischen Wirtschaftsraum EWR abgelehnt — trotz vielfältiger internationaler Wirtschaftsbeziehungen. Ein föderalistisch organisierter Kleinstaat ist in besonderem Maße darauf angewiesen, daß Einzelne gleichzeitig zahlreiche Funktionen ausüben, daß etwa Politik zu einem großen Teil nebenamtlich ausgeübt wird. Das führt in der Schweiz zu einem weitreichenden Milizsystem und damit zu einer starken Verflechtung von Politik, Wirtschaft, Militär und Gesellschaft. (Wehling 1988, Riklin 1983, Klöti 1984, Germann/Weibel 1986).

Die Schweiz gehört vom statistischen Volkseinkommen her gesehen in die Gruppe der führenden Industrienationen. Die Schweizer Wirtschaft erlebte in der Zeit nach dem Zweiten Weltkrieg bis in die siebziger Jahre hinein ein markantes Wachstum verbunden mit einem Wandel hin zu einer hochindustrialisierten Dienstleistungsgesellschaft. In der Mitte der siebziger Jahre erfolgte ein starker konjunktureller Einbruch, der nur deshalb nicht zu hohen Arbeitslosenzahlen führte, weil der Abbau von Arbeitsplätzen zur Hauptsache ausländische Arbeitskräfte traf, welche zu einem großen Teil zur Rückwanderung in ihre Heimatländer gezwungen waren. Dagegen ist in der zweiten großen, 1991 beginnenden Rezessionsphase die Arbeitslosigkeit auf ein für Schweizer Verhältnisse hohes Maß von landesweit gegen 5% angestiegen. Die wirtschaftliche Entwicklung hat sich nicht im ganzen Land gleichmäßig vollzogen. Dominantes Zentrum der schweiz. Volkswirtschaft ist der Wirtschaftsraum und Finanzplatz Zürich. Weil neben Zürich noch weitere wirtschaftlich wichtige Zentren in der Dt.-schweiz liegen, werden die anderssprachigen Landesteile von ihr wirtschaftlich dominiert. Das zeigt sich sogar gelegentlich in der Werbung, die in der Regel aus dem Dt. ins Frz. und It. übersetzt wird, was nicht immer mit der nötigen Sorgfalt geschieht (Bund schweiz. Werbeagenturen 1986). (Bundesamt 1992, 105 ff; Geschichte 1986, 827 ff).

Die beiden großen Konfessionsgruppen sind die römisch-katholische und die evangelisch-reformierte Kirche. Die Schweiz ist nicht in geschlossene konfessionelle Gebiete gegliedert, wenn es auch Regionen und Kantone gibt, die überwiegend katholisch resp. protestantisch sind. Die Grenzen zwischen katholischen und protestantischen Gebieten fallen nicht mit Sprachgrenzen zusammen. Weil die Kirchenhoheit bei den Kantonen liegt, ist das Verhältnis zwischen Kirche und Staat recht unterschiedlich geregelt. Das Zahlenverhältnis zwischen den Konfessionsgruppen hat sich in den letzten Jahrzehnten geändert: waren zu Beginn des Jahrhunderts 57,8% der Bevölkerung protestantisch, so sinkt v. a. immigrationsbedingt seit 1930 der Anteil der Protestanten zugunsten der Katholiken und anderer Konfessionen. 1990 bezeichneten sich 40% der Bevölkerung (47,3% der schweiz. Bevölkerung) als evangelisch-reformiert, 46,1% (43,3%) als römisch-katholisch, 5% als Angehörige anderer Konfessionen und 7,4% als konfessionslos. Im Laufe der achtziger Jahre hat v. a. der Anteil ostkirchlich-orthodoxer Gruppierungen (1%) und der Mohammedaner (2,2%) zugenommen. Gestiegen ist auch der Anteil der Konfessionslosen, wobei sich hier deutliche regionale Unterschiede zeigen: während in den Berggebieten und ländlichen Regionen ihr Anteil gering ist, sind es in den Städten beträchtliche Gruppen; am größten ist ihr Anteil in der Stadt Basel, wo ein Drittel der Bevölkerung angibt, keiner Kirche oder Religionsgemeinschaft anzugehören (Bundesamt 1992, 353; 1993, 354 f; Campiche 1992).

Das kulturelle Leben ist einerseits stark von regionalen Traditionen geprägt, was die Herausbildung einer vielgestaltigen Volkskultur ermöglicht hat; andererseits sind die einzelnen Sprachregionen, was institutionalisierte Kultur (Massenmedien, Literatur, Theater, etc.) betrifft, stark auf die angrenzenden großen Sprach- und Kulturräume Deutschland, Frankreich und Italien ausgerichtet. So werden die nationalen Rundfunk- und Fernsehprogramme zwar von einer Gesellschaft getragen, aber die drei Fernsehprogramme (dt., frz. und it.) und die Rundfunkprogramme in den drei Sprachen werden nicht zentral, sondern in den jeweiligen Sprachregionen produziert und unterscheiden sich hinsichtlich Gestaltung und Themensetzung deutlich voneinander. Es gibt Bemühungen, den Kulturkontakt zwischen den verschiedenen Sprachregionen zu intensivieren, etwa durch die Förderung von Übersetzungen literarischer Werke oder dadurch, daß das vor kurzem gegründete Schweiz. Literaturarchiv die vier Literaturen der Schweiz betont. Beim „sprachabhängigen Kulturbereich" ist es v. a. das Gebiet des Films, wo der Kulturkontakt recht gut funktioniert.

4. Statistik

4.1. Zur schweizerischen Sprachstatistik

Die schweiz. Sprachstatistik ist nicht sehr gut ausgebaut; es läßt sich gar von „rather incomplete statistical data" (McRae 1983, 66) sprechen. Regelmäßig erfaßt wird die *Muttersprache* der Bevölkerung seit 1850 im Rahmen der im Zehnjahresrhythmus durchgeführten Volkszählungen. Die zur Ermittlung der Muttersprache verwendete Fragestellung war verschiedentlich Gegenstand der Kritik, so wurde etwa der Rückgang des Anteils Dt.-sprachiger bei der Zählung um 1900 (Abb. 229.1) auf eine Änderung der Formulierung der frz. Frage zurückgeführt (Müller 1977, 17 ff). Der größte Mangel der amtlichen schweiz. Sprachstatistik ist der, daß bis vor kurzem keine Angaben zur Zwei- oder Mehrspachigkeit der Bevölkerung und zu ihren Sprachkenntnissen erhoben worden sind. Gefragt wurde allein nach der Muttersprache, die umschrieben wurde als „die Sprache, in der man denkt und die man am besten beherrscht" (Bundesamt 1991, 322). Erst mit dem Mikrozensus von 1988 und der Volkszählung von 1990 sind die Fragen zur Sprache ausgebaut worden in Richtung Erfassung von Zweisprachigkeit (neben der *Mutterspra-*

Tab. 226.1: Entwicklung der Wohnbevölkerung nach Sprachgruppen (Hauptsprache) in absoluten Zahlen und in Prozent. Angaben zur gesamten Wohnbevölkerung im Normaldruck, Angaben zur *Schweizer* Bevölkerung *kursiv* (für die Zeit vor 1910 liegen keine Zahlen zu dieser Unterscheidung vor).

Jahr	Gesamtbevölkerung	Deutsch	in%	Französisch	in %	Italienisch	in %	Rätoromanisch	in%	Andere Sprachen	in%
1888	2 917 754	2 082 855	71.4	634 855	21.8	155 130	5.3	38 357	1.3	6 557	0.2
1900	3 315 443	2 312 949	69.8	730 917	22.0	221 182	6.7	38 651	1.2	11 744	0.4
1910	3 753 293	2 594 186	69.1	793 264	21.1	302 578	8.1	40 234	1.1	23 031	0.6
	3 201 282	*2 326 138*	*72.7*	*708 650*	*22.1*	*125 336*	*3.9*	*39 349*	*1.2*	*1 809*	*0.1*
1920	3 880 320	2 750 622	70.9	824 320	21.2	238 544	6.1	42 940	1.1	23 894	0.6
	3 477 935	*2 540 101*	*73.0*	*753 644*	*21.7*	*138 118*	*4.0*	*42 010*	*1.2*	*4 062*	*0.1*
1930	4 066 400	2 924 313	71.9	831 097	20.4	242 034	6.0	44 158	1.1	24 798	0.6
	3 710 878	*2 735 134*	*73.7*	*778 998*	*21.0*	*148 654*	*4.0*	*43 372*	*1.2*	*4 720*	*0.1*
1941	4 265 703	3 097 060	72.6	884 669	20.7	220 530	5.2	46 456	1.1	16 988	0.4
	4 042 149	*2 987 185*	*73.9*	*844 230*	*20.9*	*158 690*	*3.9*	*45 653*	*1.1*	*6 391*	*0.2*
1950	4 714 992	3 399 636	72.1	956 889	20.3	278 651	5.9	48 862	1.0	30 954	0.7
	4 429 546	*3 285 333*	*74.2*	*912 141*	*20.6*	*175 193*	*4.0*	*47 979*	*1.1*	*8 900*	*0.2*
1960	5 429 061	3 765 203	69.3	1 025 450	18.9	514 306	9.5	49 823	0.9	74 279	1.4
	4 844 322	*3 604 452*	*74.4*	*979 630*	*20.2*	*198 278*	*4.1*	*49 208*	*1.0*	*12 754*	*0.3*
1970	6 269 783	4 071 289	64.9	1 134 010	18.1	743 760	11.9	50 339	0.8	270 385	4.3
	5 189 707	*3 864 684*	*74.5*	*1 045 091*	*20.1*	*207 557*	*4.0*	*49 455*	*1.0*	*22 920*	*0.4*
1980	6 365 960	4 140 901	65.0	1 172 502	18.4	622 226	9.8	51 128	0.8	379 203	6.0
	5 420 986	*3 986 955*	*73.5*	*1 088 223*	*20.1*	*241 758*	*4.5*	*50 238*	*0.9*	*53 812*	*1.0*
1990	6 873 687	4 374 694	63.6	1 321 695	19.2	524 116	7.6	39 632	0.6	613 550	8.9
	5 628 255	*4 131 027*	*73.4*	*1 155 683*	*20.5*	*229 090*	*4.1*	*38 454*	*0.7*	*74 001*	*1.3*

che/*Hauptsprache* auch Fragen zur *Umgangssprache* im Alltag und zur Verwendung des *Dialekts*). Neben der amtlichen Statistik finden sich sprachstatistische Angaben auch in vereinzelten publizistischen Meinungsumfragen zu Sprachthemen oder in Auswertungen wissenschaftlicher Erhebungen (Bickel/ Schläpfer 1994; Schläpfer et al. 1991). Die Sprachstatistik stellt auch die Sprachgebiete fest, wobei jede Gemeinde entsprechend der Muttersprache der Mehrheit oder einer wichtigen Minderheit der Bevölkerung einem Sprachgebiet zugeteilt wird; Enklaven werden in der Regel dem sie umgebenden Sprachgebiet zugeordnet (Bundesamt 1991, 322 ff; Kraas 1992, 36 ff; McRae 1983, 49 ff; Müller 1977, 17 ff; Viletta 1978, 70 ff).

4.2. Die Verteilung der Sprachgruppen

Zwischen den vier Landessprachen bestehen recht unterschiedliche Größenverhältnisse: knapp zwei Drittel der Gesamtbevölkerung resp. knapp drei Viertel der Schweizer Bevölkerung sind dt.-sprachig: die Dt.-sprachigen dominieren also die anderen Sprachgruppen bei weitem; die Frz.sprachigen bilden mit rund einem Fünftel der (gesamten wie der schweiz.) Bevölkerung eine bedeutende Minderheit; wesentlich kleiner ist mit einem Anteil von 8 resp. 4% die Gruppe der It.-sprachigen und noch einmal eine Größenordnung kleiner ist die rtr. Sprachgruppe mit einem Anteil von weniger als einem Prozent (Tabelle 226.1 und 226.2). Die Größenverhältnisse zwischen den verschiedenen Sprachgruppen sind in diesem Jahrhundert innerhalb der schweiz. Bevölkerung einigermaßen stabil geblieben; einzig das Rtr. ist tendenziell im Rückgang begriffen. Verschiebungen im Verhältnis der Sprachgruppen ergaben sich dagegen innerhalb der Gesamtbevölkerung. So ist die markante Zunahme des Anteils It.-sprachiger im Laufe der fünfziger und sechziger Jahre und dessen allmähliche Abnahme seit den siebziger Jahren auf Zuwanderungs- resp. Rückwanderungsbewegungen it. Arbeitskräfte zurückzuführen. Entsprechendes gilt für die stetige, besonders in den letzten Jahrzehnten stark ansteigende Zunahme des Anteils von Sprechern einer Nichtlandessprache. Unter diesen sind u. a. Spanisch, Portugiesisch, Englisch, Türkisch und slawische Sprachen (v. a. Serbokroatisch) stark vertreten. Sprecher dieser Sprachen finden

Tab. 226.2: Gegenwärtige Verteilung der Sprachgruppen in der Schweiz (Darstellung der Wohnbevölkerung nach Hauptsprache und Staatszugehörigkeit gemäß den Ergebnissen der Eidgenössischen Volkszählung 1990). Die Sprachen sind, soweit genauer spezifiziert, entsprechend des Umfangs ihrer Verbreitung in der gesamten Wohnbevölkerung angeordnet, wobei die vier *Landessprachen kursiv* gedruckt sind.

Sprache	gesamte Bevölkerung	in %	Schweizer Bevölkerung	in %	ausländische Bevölkerung	in %
Deutsch	*4 374 694*	*63.64*	*4 131 027*	*73.40*	*243 667*	*19.56*
Französisch	*1 321 695*	*19.23*	*1 155 683*	*20.53*	*166 012*	*13.33*
Italienisch	*524 116*	*7.62*	*229 090*	*4.07*	*295 026*	*23.69*
Slawische Spr.	128 093	1.86	10 628	0.19	117 465	9.43
Spanisch	116 818	1.70	13 162	0.23	103 656	8.32
Portugiesisch	93 753	1.36	4 857	0.09	88 896	7.14
Türkische Spr.	61 320	0.89	764	0.01	60 556	4.86
Englisch	60 786	0.88	22 985	0.41	37 801	3.04
Rätoromanisch	*39 632*	*0.58*	*38 454*	*0.68*	*1 178*	*0.09*
Weit. europ. Spr.	79 735	1.16	12 866	0.23	66 869	5.37
Andere Sprachen	73 045	1.06	8 739	0.16	54 306	5.16

sich in erster Linie in Städten, mit Abstand am meisten in Genf, wo rund ein Fünftel der Bevölkerung eine Nichtlandessprache als Muttersprache hat.

Das Rtr. wird im Südosten der Schweiz in Teilen des Kantons Graubünden gesprochen; It. im Süden, im Kanton Tessin und in einigen Tälern des Kantons Graubünden; das frz. Sprachgebiet liegt im Westen, während das dt. Sprachgebiet daran anschließend den zentralen Raum, den Norden und Osten der Schweiz umfaßt; → Sprachenkarte O.

4.3. Mehrsprachigkeit der Bevölkerung

Der ungenügenden statistischen Erfassung der schweiz. Zwei- oder Mehrsprachigkeit wegen (4.1.) lassen sich nur ein paar Angaben machen. In der mehrsprachigen Schweiz wächst der größte Teil der (schweiz.) Bevölkerung einsprachig auf: nur ein Achtel der schweiz. Bevölkerung ist mehrsprachig aufgewachsen in dem Sinne, daß vor der Schulzeit eine zweite Sprache erworben wurde. Mehrsprachige Herkunft ist nicht in allen Sprachgruppen gleich häufig anzutreffen, sie ist vielmehr umgekehrt proportional zur Größe der Sprachgruppen verteilt: während mehr als ein Viertel der Rtr. mehrsprachig aufgewachsen sind, trifft dies nur für ein knappes Achtel der Dt.-sprachigen zu und die Werte der It.- und Frz.-sprachigen liegen dazwischen (Bundesamt 1991, 322 ff). Wenn mehrsprachige Herkunft nicht indirekt erschlossen, sondern direkt nach Mehrsprachigkeit gefragt wird, liegen die Werte viel niedriger, besonders bei der dt.-sprachigen Mehrheit: im Durchschnitt bezeichnen sich gut 6% der Schweizer als mehrsprachig, von den Dt.-sprachigen noch knapp 5%; die häufigste Sprachkonstellation ist Dt./Frz., gefolgt von Dt./It. (Dürmüller 1991a, 117f; Bickel/Schläpfer 1994, 247 ff). Ein ähnliches Verhältnis von Sprachgruppengröße und Mehrsprachigkeitsanteil zeigt sich bei der funktionellen Mehrsprachigkeit, das heißt der Frage nach der Verwendung mehrerer Sprachen im Alltag (Tabelle 226.3): je geringer die Sprachgruppe desto weniger Sprechende kommen im Alltag allein mit dieser Sprache aus. Das gilt in besonderem Maße für Sprechende von Nichtlandessprachen, die größtenteils gezwungen sind, sich im Alltag auch einer ortsüblichen Sprache bedienen zu müssen.

Obwohl nur ein kleiner Teil der schweiz. Bevölkerung mehrsprachig aufwächst oder im Alltag mehrsprachig kommunizieren muß — die Rtr. sind gewissermaßen die einzigen mehrsprachigen Schweizer —, erwirbt doch

Tab. 226.3: Ein- und Mehrsprachigkeit der Wohnbevölkerung, gestützt auf Fragen zur Umgangssprache, d. h. Fragen nach den Sprachen, die im Alltag verwendet werden (Ergebnisse der Daten der Volkszählung 1990).

Umgangssprache	gesamte Bevölkerung	Einsprachigkeit	in %	Mehrsprachigkeit	in %
Deutsch	4 951 280	3 237 615	65.39	1 713 665	34.61
Französisch	2 268 499	985 428	43.44	1 283 071	56.56
Italienisch	998 187	269 886	27.04	728 301	72.96
Rätoromanisch	62 353	15 782	20.25	49 724	79.75
Englisch	761 760	12 629	2.07	745 978	97.93
Übrige Sprachen	769 173	126 053	16.39	643 120	83.61

der größte Teil in der Schule Kenntnisse anderer Sprachen (6.3.). Der Grad dieser Bildungsmehrsprachigkeit ist recht unterschiedlich. Trotz aller bildungspolitischen Ziele gibt es Schweizer, die keine Kenntnisse in einer anderen Landessprache erworben haben und sich teilweise auch als einsprachig bezeichnen. Auf die Zahl dieser Einsprachigen lassen sich nur einige Hinweise aus Rekrutenbefragungen finden, bei denen über ein Zehntel der Befragten angab, keine Fremdsprachenkenntnisse erworben zu haben. Ihr Anteil ist bei Angehörigen der beiden großen Sprachgruppen Dt. und Frz. bedeutend höher als bei den der kleinen Sprachgruppen It. und Rtr. Zudem zeigen sich auch innerhalb einer Sprachregion deutliche Unterschiede zwischen einzelnen Kantonen. Ein Fünftel der dt.- und frz.-sprachigen Schweizer und ein Drittel der it.-sprachigen Schweizer kann als gebildet dreisprachig, ein Zwanzigstel der dt.- und frz.-sprachigen und ein Viertel der it.-sprachigen als gebildet viersprachig (drei Landessprachen und Englisch) bezeichnet werden. Kenntnisse aller vier Landessprachen sind praktisch nur bei rtr. Sprechern zu finden (Bundesamt 1992, 351 f; Dürmüller 1991 a, 126 ff; Bickel/Schläpfer 1994, 209 ff; zur Sprachbeherrschung Jugendlicher in zweisprachigen Städten Kolde 1981, 302 ff).

5. Soziolinguistische Lage

5.1. Sprachsituation in den Sprachregionen

Die vier Sprachregionen unterscheiden sich beträchtlich voneinander, was soziolinguistische Variablen, wie Verhältnis von Standardsprache und Mundart, Sprachformengebrauch, dialektale Variation oder Einstellungen zu Sprachnorm und Sprachgebrauch, betrifft (Haas 1988 a, 1370 ff).

Kennzeichen der Dt.-schweizer Sprachsituation ist ein klares Nebeneinander der zwei Sprachformen Mundart und Hochdt., in dem die Mundarten wesentliche Domänen innehaben. Obwohl die Dt.-schweizer Sprachsituation eines der Beispiele zur Erläuterung des klassischen Diglossiebegriffs ist, läßt sie sich damit nicht treffend erfassen. Die Sprachformenwahl ist in erster Linie situativ-medial und auch rezeptions-/produktionsbezogen bestimmt: gesprochen wird generell Mundart außer in bestimmten formellen Situationen (z. B. Vorlesung, Nachrichten), geschrieben wird Standardsprache; gelesen und auch viel gehört (Massenmedien) wird Standardsprache, die erst in der Schule erworben wird. Diese „Zweisprachigkeit in der einen (deutschen) Sprache" (Sieber/Sitta 1986, 34) läßt sich mit dem Begriff *mediale Diglossie* (Kolde 1981, 65—76; Haas 1988 b) charakterisieren. Die Sprachsituation in Deutschland unterscheidet sich grundlegend von der in der Dt.-schweiz, was sich an der Grenze zu Deutschland — wo beidseits der Grenze gleiche Dialekträume zu finden sind, die Landesgrenze sich jedoch als „pragmatische Sprachgrenze" (Ris 1979, 51) bemerkbar macht (Löffler 1987; Schifferle 1990) — sowie an den für sie oft unerwarteten Erfahrungen dt. Migranten mit dem Dt.-schweizer Sprachverhalten (Koller 1992) zeigt. Die generelle Tendenz zu informellerem Sprachgebrauch, zur Abwendung von rein schriftsprachlich geprägten Normen und zu Verschiebungen des Kommunikationsverhaltens in Richtung vermehrter

Mündlichkeit wirkt sich in einer Situation medialer Diglossie als Vordringen der Mundart in weitere Domänen (z. B. Predigt) aus. Das führt zu Verständigungsproblemen und Irritationen der anderen Sprachgruppen, da diese in der Schule Hochdt. lernen und dann feststellen müssen, daß sie damit in der Dt.-schweiz nicht problemlos kommunizieren können. In sprachpolitischen Diskussionen wird der Mundartgebrauch der Dt.-schweiz denn auch oft als Hauptgrund für Verständigungsschwierigkeiten zwischen der dt. und der frz. Schweiz dargestellt. Die Mundarten der Dt.-schweiz werden als *Schweizerdt.* bezeichnet, eine zusammenfassende Bezeichnung, die eine nichtexistierende Einheitlichkeit suggeriert, zeichnen sie sich doch durch eine große Vielfalt und beträchtliche Unterschiede voneinander aus (Hotzenköcherle 1984). Bei allen Ausgleichs- und Angleichungstendenzen, die innerhalb der Mundarten festzustellen sind, läßt sich keine Entwicklung zu einem Einheitsschweizerdt. feststellen, wenn auch die mediale Diglossie einer bildungsbürgerlichen Sprachkritik die Möglichkeit gibt, gleich zweifach den Sprachverfall zu beklagen, nämlich den der Hochsprachkompetenz wie den der reinen Mundart (Haas 1986; 1992). Das schweiz. Hdt. unterscheidet sich vom bundesdt. Standard; schon in der Aussprache, v. a. aber im Bereich des Wortschatzes, wo sich zahlreiche Helvetismen finden und frz. Einfluß bemerkbar macht (Schilling 1970). (Zur schweiz. Norm des Hochdt. Kaiser 1969/1970; Meyer 1989; Haas 1982a, 113 ff).

Im Gegensatz zu den anderen Sprachregionen spielen die Mundarten in der frz.-sprachigen Schweiz keine Rolle; sind sie doch als Folge der starren monozentrischen Norm des Frz. (vor allem in den protestant. Kantonen) nahezu ausgestorben. Die Orientierung an der zentralistischen Pariser Norm setzte im 16. Jahrhundert schon vor der Reformation ein, so daß im 19. Jahrhundert kaum mehr Mundart (*patois*) gesprochen wurde. Das Schweizer Frz. ist eine regionale Variante des Frz., die sich durch eine Reihe archaischer Züge und Regionalwortschatz auszeichnet. Die Besonderheiten des schweiz. Frz. sind entgegen verbreiteter Meinung in der Westschweiz weniger auf dt. und schweizerdt. Einfluß zurückzuführen, sondern auf die Randlage und die politische Unabhängigkeit von Frankreich. Der umgekehrte Einfluß des Frz. auf das Dt. ist bei weitem bedeutender, was mit dem hohen Prestige, das das Frz. landesweit genießt, zu tun hat. Im Gegensatz zu den historischen Mundarten ist das Schweizer Frz. schlecht erforscht, mittlerweile gibt es immerhin Zusammenstellungen schweiz. Regionalausdrücke (z. B. Pidoux 1984). Einige Helvetismen sind auch von normsetzenden Instanzen Frankreichs anerkannt worden, was wohl nicht zuletzt mit einem Wandel der rigiden frz. Sprachnorm zu tun hat. (Zum Schweizer Frz. und der Sprachsituation in der Westschweiz cf. Schmitt 1990; Knecht 1982 und → Art. 228). Die in den Schulen immer noch vorherrschende Überbetonung des Normcharakters der Sprache wirkt sich auf die Sprachkultur und Spracheinstellungen aus. Diese Einstellungen werden auch auf andere Sprachen angewendet, was zu Verkennung der Deutschschweizer Sprachsituation führt. Vor dem Hintergund solcher Spracheinstellungen erscheint der bevorzugte Gebrauch der Dialekte als verderbte, ungrammatische Sprechweise neben dem eigentlichen, korrekten Standarddeutsch, dem *bon allemand* (Christen 1991; Lüdi/Py 1994, 145 ff; Lüdi/Papaloizos/De Pietro 1989/90, 285; Windisch 1992, 445 ff).

Die Sprachsituation in der it. Schweiz war bis vor ein paar Jahrzehnten derjenigen in der dt. Schweiz vergleichbar, hat sich aber durch eine ständige Domänenausweitung der Standardsprache gegensätzlich entwickelt. Die Abwendung von den Dialekten ist verbunden mit einer stärkeren Regionalisierung der it. Standardsprache, eine Entwicklung, die sich nicht auf die it. Schweiz beschränkt, sondern im ganzen lombardischen Sprachraum festzustellen ist. Allerdings sind Dialektkenntnisse und Funktionsverteilung des Dialekts in der it. Schweiz immer noch größer als in Italien: in der it. Schweiz finden sich also teilweise drei Register nebeneinander. Im It. der it. Schweiz sind deutliche dt.-sprachige Einflüsse bemerkbar, wobei es sich weniger um direkte Entlehnungen, sondern v. a. um Lehnbedeutungen und Lehnbildungen und um einige morphosyntaktische Eigenheiten (Präpositionen, Adjektivstellung) handelt. In Teilen der it. Schweiz leben große Gruppen Dt.-sprachiger, die in einigen Orten mehr als die Hälfte der Bevölkerung ausmachen. Es handelt sich allerdings v. a. um kleinere Orte, konzentriert auf zwei touristisch relevante Gebiete; ein knappes Zehntel der Bevölkerung der it. Schweiz ist dt.-sprachig − meist ältere Leute. Das It. spielt auch außerhalb der it.-sprachigen Schweiz eine große Rolle als Sprache der it. Migranten (7.2.). (Berruto/

Burger 1985; 1987; Bianconi 1980; 1989, 230 ff; 1994; Lurati 1982; 1988; 1992 und → Art. 229).

Das Rtr. weist nicht nur die kleinste Sprecherzahl auf, es ist auch die einzige Sprache ohne geschlossenes, einigermaßen stabiles Sprachgebiet, ohne städtisches Zentrum, ohne Anschluß an eine angrenzende Sprachnation und ohne überdachende Standardsprache. Unter der Bezeichnung Rtr. werden verschiedene romanische Mundarten mit fünf regionalen Schreibsprachen („Idiome") zusammengefaßt, die heute noch in drei voneinander getrennten Zonen des Kantons Graubünden gesprochen werden. Daß sich bis vor kurzem kein Vorschlag zur Schaffung einer Einheitssprache durchsetzen konnte, ist eine Folge des beschränkten Geltungsbereichs einer rtr. Standardsprache und der sehr kleinräumigen Sprachloyalität der Rtr.: Fremdsprachenkenntnisse (It. und v. a. Dt.) waren und sind wichtiger als ein gemeinsamer rtr. Standard, so daß, wenn der regionale Standard nicht verwendet werden kann, lieber gleich auf Dt. umgestellt wird. Für die Präsenz des Rtr. auf nationaler Ebene ist in einer Dienstleistungsgesellschaft die Existenz eines rtr. Standards wichtig. Der jüngste Versuch zur Schaffung einer Einheitssprache, das *Rumantsch grischun* (Schmid 1982; 1989; Darms 1989, 849 ff), scheint nun eine gewisse Aussicht auf Erfolg zu haben, wohl nicht zuletzt wegen des linguistisch fundierten wie behutsamen Vorgehens: Rumantsch Grischun ist als Ausgleichssprache konzipiert, an der alle fünf rtr. Sprachen („Idiome") beteiligt sind und die für alle Rtr. ohne großen Aufwand verständlich sein soll. Zudem ermöglicht das Rumantsch Grischun die für eine Kleinsprache wichtige Bildung von Neologismen. Ob sich dieser Standard gegen den durchaus auch vorhandenen Widerstand (Kraas 1992, 288 ff) durchsetzen wird, bleibt abzuwarten; zur Zeit stagniert sein Vormarsch eher. Für die rtr. Sprachgruppe ist Zwei- und Mehrsprachigkeit Alltag, bedingt durch die wirtschaftlichen Gegebenheiten und die Situation des Rtr. sowie die Zuwanderung von Dt.-sprachigen (Kristol 1989; Billigmeier 1983, 284 ff; Cathomas 1977; Holtus 1989; Lutz/Arquint 1982; Viletta 1984).

5.2. Kontaktbereiche und -situationen

Als Folge der durch das Territorialitätsprinzip (6.1.) gegebenen Einteilung der Schweiz in verschiedene Sprachregionen lebt, abgesehen von den Rtr., ein Großteil der Bevölkerung einsprachig. Die schweiz. Mehrsprachigkeit ist für sie höchstens im Hintergrund präsent durch mehrsprachige amtliche Veröffentlichungen und Dokumente, durch mehrsprachige Beschriftung vieler Produkte oder durch gelegentlichen Kontakt mit anderssprachigen Schweizern. Für die innerschweiz. Kommunikation zwischen anderssprachigen Schweizern wird ein partnersprachbezogenes „Modell Schweiz" propagiert: Jeder spricht in seiner Sprache und wird von den anderen verstanden (EDK 1987, 99 f). Dieses Modell funktioniert allerdings nur in einigen institutionalisierten Kommunikationskontexten für die Dt.- und Frz.-sprachigen einigermaßen, während die It.- und Rtr.-sprachigen gezwungen sind, Dt. oder Frz. zu sprechen.

Mehrsprachigkeits- und Sprachkontaktsituationen finden wir (außerhalb des rtr. Gebietes und der Dt.-Hochburgen im Tessin) in Zonen entlang der dt.-frz. Sprachgrenze und in den nahe dieser Sprachgrenze gelegenen, zweisprachigen Städten Freiburg/Fribourg und Biel/Bienne. In Einzelfällen ergeben sich diese Situationen durch (temporäre) Bildungsmigration, interne Migration oder zweisprachige Partnerschaften. Nicht ganz außer acht gelassen werden darf, daß es auch in der Dt.-schweiz durch die Situation der medialen Diglossie und die Vielfalt der Mundarten gewisse Sprachkontaktsituationen gibt; bei einigen schwerer verständlichen Kleinraumdialekten haben sich bestimmte Anpassungsmuster für den Kontakt mit Sprechern anderer Mundarten herausgebildet (Ris 1979, 51 ff; Schnidrig 1986).

Über die komplexen und differenzierten Verhältnisse in der Kontaktzone entlang der dt.-frz. Sprachgrenze, wo (besonders im Kanton Fribourg) die unterschiedlichsten Formen zweisprachiger Gemeinwesen zu finden sind, informiert die umfassende Studie alltäglicher Mehrsprachigkeit von Windisch (Windisch 1992; s. auch Mäder/Froidevaux 1992), eine etwas ältere umfangreiche Studie hat sich mit der Situation in den zweisprachigen Städten befaßt (Kolde 1981). Auf nationaler Ebene richtet sich die Wahrnehmung v. a. auf die Konfliktfälle an der Sprachgrenze. Bei einer Betrachtung des alltäglichen Geschehens in den Gemeinwesen entlang der Sprachgrenze zeigt sich, daß bei allen Problemen und Konflikten die Beziehungen zwischen den Sprachgemeinschaften insgesamt doch durch ein „climat de bonne volonté qui règne" (Windisch 1992, 502) gekennzeichnet sind. Dazu tragen z. B. symbolische Handlungen der

Vertreter der Sprachmehrheit gegenüber der Sprachminderheit viel bei. Bei zweisprachigen Paaren in diesen Sprachgrenzzonen erweist sich Frz. tendenziell als die starke Sprache, und zwar unabhängig davon, ob es die Sprache des Mannes oder der Frau ist (Brohy 1992, 290 f).

Erschwerend wirkt sich in den Sprachgrenzzonen wie in allen anderen Sprachkontaktsituationen gelegentlich die Tatsache aus, daß der Zweisprachigkeit, der Zugehörigkeit zu zwei Sprach- und Kulturgemeinschaften, eigentlich kein Wert beigemessen wird und bestimmte Erscheinungsformen der Mehrsprachigkeit eher negativ bewertet werden. So wird alternierende Verwendung zweier Sprachen (z. B. *code-switching*) oft als mangelnde Sprachbeherrschung aufgefaßt. Es zeigt sich auch, daß Zweisprachigkeit zu einem Großteil außerhalb der Schule erworben wird (Brohy 1992, 295), ein Hinweis darauf, daß die Schule gerade in Sprachkontaktzonen mehr zur Förderung der Zweisprachigkeit leisten könnte. Eine höhere Bewertung der Zweisprachigkeit könnte das Leben in Sprachkontaktsituationen durchaus erleichtern. Dies gilt nicht zuletzt auch für interne Migranten, die durch den Wechsel in ein anderes Sprachgebiet zu tiefgreifenden Änderungen ihrer sozialen Verhaltensweisen und v. a. ihres Sprachverhaltens und ihrer Sprachvorstellungen gezwungen sind, auch wenn sie im gleichen Land bleiben. Die interne Migration und ihre Auswirkungen auf das alltägliche Sprachverhalten sind erst in den achtziger Jahren eingehender erforscht worden (De Pietro et al. 1989/90; Franceschini et al. 1989/90; Lüdi 1981; Lüdi/Py 1984; 1989/90; 1994). In die wirtschaftlich dominierende Dt.-schweiz ziehen anteilmäßig mehr Einwohner anderer Sprachgebiete als Dt.-schweizer in diese; aber in allen Sprachregionen wohnt eine beträchtliche Zahl Dt.-schweizer bedingt durch das zahlenmäßige Übergewicht dieser Sprachgruppe. In der frz. Schweiz assimilieren sich die Dt.-schweizer schnell und leicht, in den anderen Sprachregionen ist ihre Anpassungsbereitschaft geringer. Die frz.-sprachigen Schweizer weisen in der dt. Schweiz eher ein sprachbewahrendes Verhalten auf.

Die innerschweiz. Bildungsmigration ist recht einseitig ausgerichtet. Dadurch daß es in der it. Schweiz keine Universität gibt, sind it.-sprachige Schweizer gezwungen, entsprechende Ausbildungen in der dt. oder frz. Schweiz zu absolvieren, sofern sie in der Schweiz studieren wollen; fast die Hälfte studiert in Zürich. In der Dt.-schweiz existiert eine Tradition des *Welschlandjahres*, eines temporären Aufenthalts junger Dt.-schweizerinnen nach der Schulzeit (meist) bei einer Familie in der frz. Schweiz mit dem Ziel der Verbesserung ihrer Frz.-kenntnisse. Allerdings zeigt sich, daß in erster Linie die Erfahrung des Lebens in der „Fremde" diese Aufenthalte prägt und der Sprach- und Kulturkontakt eher nebensächlich ist (Gyr 1989, 418 ff; 1992; Hess et al. 1989/90). Ein entsprechendes *Dt.-schweizjahr* gibt es nicht.

6. Sprachpolitische Lage

6.1. Sprachpolitik und Sprachenrecht

Die schweiz. Sprachpolitik beruht auf zwei Prinzipien: dem Personalitätsprinzip (Sprachenfreiheit) und dem Territorialitätsprinzip. Die Sprachenfreiheit, die nur als ungeschriebenes, implizit durch die Rechtsprechung bestätigtes Verfassungsrecht anerkannt ist, wird in zweierlei Hinsicht eingeschränkt: durch den Verfassungsartikel über die „Nationalsprachen" (jeder kann sich in seiner Muttersprache an die eidgenössischen Behörden wenden, sofern sie eine *Landessprache* ist) und das Territorialitätsprinzip. Dieses gibt den Kantonen die Sprachhoheit, d. h. die Kantone haben das Recht, für ihr gesamtes Territorium eine (gegebenenfalls mehrere) *Amtssprache* festzulegen. Wer in einen anderssprachigen Teil der Schweiz übersiedelt, muß sich also im Verkehr mit den lokalen Behörden der dortigen Amtssprache bedienen und seine Kinder werden (in öffentlichen Schulen) in dieser Sprache unterrichtet. Das Territorialitätsprinzip gilt als Garant für die Erhaltung der Sprachgebiete. Im Kanton Graubünden ist die Sprachhoheit den Gemeinden übertragen, was als Grund für den Rückgang des rtr. Sprachgebiets angesehen wird, haben doch viele Gemeinden ihre Amtssprache gewechselt. Das Territorialitätsprinzip bringt auch Probleme: so ist umstritten, wie rigide es auszulegen sei, ob eher als politische Maxime oder als Rechtsgrundsatz; umstritten ist auch seine Anwendung in Sprachgrenzzonen, wo tatsächlich zu fragen ist, ob in sprachlichen Kontaktzonen nicht vermehrt mehrsprachige Lösungen zugelassen werden sollten. Die verschiedenen Sprachregionen werden nicht durch Bundesrecht festgelegt und haben auch keine politische Funktion. Zwei Verfassungsbestimmungen gehen auf sprachliche Fragen ein, daneben gibt es aber kein eigentliches schweiz. Sprachenrecht; viele Regelungen sind Gewohnheitsrecht (Viletta 1978, 175 ff; 1983, 111 ff; Weibel 1986, 227 ff).

Schwerpunkt der offiziellen Sprachpolitik der letzten Jahre waren die Bemühungen um die Revision des sogenannten „Sprachenartikels" der Bundesverfassung (Art. 116). Die entsprechenden Arbeiten und Diskussionen zeichnen sich nicht unbedingt durch linguistische Fundierung aus, etwa bei der Beschreibung der Dt.-schweizer Sprachsituation (Hengartner 1991); zwar sind linguistische Materialien bereitgestellt worden (Eidg. Dep. des Innern 1989 b), die wurden aber im Schlußbericht der zuständigen Expertenkommission (Eidg. Dep. des Innern 1989 a) und in der Vorlage der Regierung für das Parlament (Botschaft 1991) nur teilweise angemessen berücksichtigt. Im Entwurf des neuen Artikels sind sowohl die Sprachenfreiheit wie der Schutz der Sprachgebiete explizit erwähnt. Diese Festschreibungen führten zu Auseinandersetzungen v. a. zwischen dt.- und frz.-sprachigen Parlamentariern, weshalb sie im Laufe der verschiedenen parlamentarischen Beratungen gestrichen wurden. Der neue Sprachenartikel wird sich somit auf die Förderung des Rtr. (und des It. im Kanton Tessin) konzentrieren, so daß in der Verfassung keine Regelung der sprachpolitischen Kernbereiche und auch keine Förderung der Zweisprachigkeit festgeschrieben sein wird.

Der Mehrsprachigkeit des Landes muß auch in der nationalen Politik und der zentralen Bundesverwaltung Rechnung getragen werden. Bei der Wahl eines Mitglieds der siebenköpfigen Landesregierung gilt es, neben parteipolitischen, regionalen, religiösen auch sprachliche Faktoren zu berücksichtigen. Im Parlament könnten alle drei Amtssprachen verwendet werden; *de facto* zeigt sich aber, daß das It. kaum benutzt wird; es wird auch nur in Dt. und Frz. simultan übersetzt. Bei der Bildung parlamentarischer Kommissionen wird versucht, dem Sprachenproporz Genüge zu leisten. In der hauptsächlich im dt.-sprachigen Bern domizilierten Bundesverwaltung sind insgesamt die Sprachgruppen einigermaßen entsprechend ihrem Anteil an der Gesamtbevölkerung vertreten. Allerdings zeigen sich beträchtliche Unterschiede zwischen den verschiedenen Departementen. Auch ist die Leitung wichtiger Bundesämter (Ministerialbehörden) eher in den Händen von Dt.-schweizern. Von Bundesbeamten werden ausreichende Kenntnisse in mindestens zwei Landessprachen verlangt. Trotzdem finden sich unter den dt.- und frz.-sprachigen Beamten zahlreiche einsprachige. *De facto* ist die Bundesverwaltung aufgrund wenig verbreiteter It.-kenntnisse nur zweisprachig (Eidg. Personalamt 1980; 1989; Hauck 1990; 1993, McRae 126 ff; Weibel 1986, 254 ff; Widmer 1986). Bei der Erarbeitung von Gesetzen und Verordnungen dominiert das Dt., werden diese doch zum überwiegenden Teil auf dt. verfaßt und anschließend ins Frz. und It. übersetzt. Um Texte vermehrt auch in den anderen Sprachen redigieren zu können, ist vor kurzer Zeit die Koredaktion der Gesetze eingeführt worden, bei der in einer gemischtsprachigen Kommission die dt. und die frz. Fassung eines Gesetzes gleichzeitig redigiert werden (Caussignac/Kettiger 1991; Hauck 1993, 153 ff).

6.2. Sprachpolitische Problem- und Konfliktsituationen

Die Schweiz gilt als mehrsprachiger Staat mit erstaunlich wenig Sprachkonflikten. Gründe dafür liegen in der historischen Entwicklung, der föderalistischen Struktur und der Tatsache, daß sich politische, konfessionelle und teilweise auch wirtschaftliche Grenzen nicht mit den Sprachgrenzen decken (McRae 1983, 229 ff; Weilenmann 1925). Die Sprachsituation der Deutschschweiz mit ihrer medialen Diglossie bietet Konfliktstoff wie auch konfliktverhindernde Elemente, ist doch durch sie die größte Sprachgemeinschaft weniger eine geschlossene, homogene Gruppe und gleichzeitig auch an Sprachanpassung gewöhnt (Haas 1988 a, 1377). Daß sich Sprachkonflikte auch in der Schweiz finden, zeigen sprachpolitische Diskussionen über die Erhaltung des Rtr. oder die Angst der it.-sprachigen Schweiz vor dem Verlust ihrer *Italianità*. Die sprachpolitische Auseinandersetzung wird v. a. von den nicht immer gleich stark beachteten Unterschieden zwischen der dt. und der frz. Sprachgruppe geprägt. Seitdem vor kurzem (Dez. 1992) in einer Volksabstimmung der Beitritt zum EWR abgelehnt worden ist, wobei die frz.-sprachigen Kantone diesem Beitritt kompakt zugestimmt haben, sind diese Gegensätze wieder vermehrt in den Brennpunkt öffentlichen Interesses gerückt, ist der sogenannte sprachliche „Graben" zwischen Dt.- und Welschschweiz wieder ein Thema politischer Diskussion. Die Fixierung des öffentlichen Augenmerks auf diese Sprachgruppengegensätze führt oft dazu, daß die beträchtlichen Unterschiede innerhalb einer Sprachgemeinschaft übersehen werden. So steht bei Wahlen und Abstimmungen das abweichende Abstimmungsverhalten der frz. und der dt. Schweiz im Mittelpunkt der Berichterstattung, wobei weniger beachtet wird, daß nur in wenigen Fällen die Mehrheit der frz. Kantone anders stimmt als die dt.-sprachigen und daß v. a. neben sprachlicher Zugehörigkeit auch noch andere Gegensätze (konfessionelle, Stadt-Land, Berggebiet-Mittelland) bestimmend sind (Windisch 1992, 376 ff). Im Rahmen der Diskussionen über Unterschiede zwischen der dt. und der frz. Schweiz wird die Dt.-schweizer Sprachsituation oft zum Thema, wobei sich zeigt, daß führende Sprachpolitiker die Situation der medialen Diglossie vielfach verkennen und dementsprechende Kritik äußern und Vorschläge anbringen. Interessant ist, daß junge Frz.-Schweizer die mediale Diglossie der Dt.-schweiz als viel geringeres Problem einschätzen als die Sprachpolitik (Schläpfer et al. 1991, 249 f).

Einer der heftigsten innenpolitischen Konflikte der Nachkriegszeit, der Jurakonflikt, der 1979 zur Abtrennung eines Gebiets vom Kanton Bern und zur Gründung des Kantons Jura führte, scheint zu einem wesentlichen Teil sprachlich bedingt zu sein. Das geht darauf zurück, daß die frz.-sprachigen Separatisten eine sprachethnische Ideologie vertraten, und zwar mit einer für Schweizer Verhältnisse unüblichen Vehemenz. Daß die sprachlichen Unterschiede allein nicht ausreichender Grund zur Trennung waren, zeigt sich daran, daß die neuen, in mehreren Volksabstimmungen bestimmten Kantonsgrenzen nicht entlang der Sprachgrenze, sondern entlang von konfessionellen, historischen und parteipolitischen Grenzen verlaufen (McRae 1983, 185 ff; Weibel 1986, 231 ff u. 256 ff).

An der dt.-frz. Sprachgrenze finden sich noch andere Konfliktsituationen, etwa im Kanton Fribourg (Boschung 1989; Brohy 1992, 32 ff; Windisch 1992, 33 ff). Der Sprachgrenzverlauf auf dem Gebiet dieses Kantons ist äußerst kompliziert (Brohy 1992, 39 f; Mäder/Froidevaux 1992, 525). Die Sprachsituation wird zudem noch dadurch bestimmt, daß die gesamthelvetisch dominierenden Dt.-sprachigen im Kanton Fribourg eine Minderheit gegenüber einer frz.-sprachigen Mehrheit bilden. In letzter Zeit sind viele Dt.-sprachige in den Kanton gezogen, weil einige Dt.-schweizer Firmen hier Niederlassungen eröffnet haben; z. B. auch in der frz.-sprachigen Gemeinde Marly. Dort kam es zu einem Streit um den Schulbesuch dt.-sprachiger Kinder und damit um die Striktheit der Auslegung des Territorialitätsprinzips (Fleiner-Gerster 1991; Windisch 1992, 417 ff).

6.3. Sprachunterricht

Der größte Teil der (schweiz.) Bevölkerung wächst einsprachig auf und erwirbt Zweitsprachkenntnisse in der Schule (McRae 1983, 147 ff). Als erste Fremdsprache wird eine Landessprache unterrichtet: in der frz. Schweiz Dt., in der it. und dt. Schweiz Frz. mit Ausnahme des an das it. Sprachgebiet angrenzenden Kantons Uri, in dem seit kurzem It. als erste Fremdsprache unterrichtet wird. Die zweite Fremdsprache ist in der dt. und frz. Schweiz meist Englisch, in der it. Schweiz Dt. In der Schule werden zur Hauptsache die beiden großen Landessprachen Frz. und Dt. sowie die internationale Verkehrssprache Englisch und nur in viel geringerem Umfang die dritte Landessprache, das It., gelehrt. Seit einigen Jahren wird die Förderung des It.-unterrichts, zumindest einer Verstehenskompetenz, propagiert (EDK 1987, 130 ff). Es gibt allerdings wegen der kantonalen Bildungshoheit keine koordinierte Schweizer Bildungspolitik, sondern 26 verschiedene Schulsysteme, so daß sich über Beginn, Umfang und Gestaltung des Fremdsprachenunterrichts kaum generelle Aussagen machen lassen. Erstaunlicherweise spielt die Schweiz praktisch keine Rolle auf dem Gebiet der Fremdsprachdidaktik (Haas 1988 a, 1370). Auch um Förderung der Didaktik der für das „Schweizer Modell" eigentlich besonders wichtigen Verstehenskompetenz hat man sich erst in den letzten Jahren bemüht. In der Schweiz findet sich zwar eine der wenigen zweisprachigen Universitäten Europas (Fribourg/Freiburg), aber es existieren, abgesehen von der rtr. Schweiz, weder eine Tradition zwei- oder mehrsprachiger Ausbildung noch entsprechend umfassende Unterrichtsversuche (z. B. Immersion); erst in letzter Zeit sind Projekte für mehrsprachige Ausbildungsgänge, für welche die Schweiz prädestiniert wäre, vorgelegt worden (Watts/Andres 1990; Heller 1990; Keller 1990; Stotz/Andres 1990). Die Realisierung entsprechender Versuche und Ausbildungsgänge wird von Vertretern einer strikten Auslegung des Territorialitätsprinzips bekämpft. Die Unterrichtssprache wird im Interesse der sprachlichen Assimilation durch das Territorialitätsprinzip bestimmt, wobei sich in einigen Fällen Fragen nach der Rigidität der Auslegung stellen (Fleiner-Gerster

1991, 98 ff; Viletta 1978, 342 ff). Eine, teilweise umstrittene, Ausnahme bildet die frz. Schule in der Landeshauptstadt Bern, weil hier viele frz.-sprachige Beamte mit ihren Familien leben. Es gibt gewissen Zusatzunterricht für Kinder ausländischer Immigranten, aber praktisch keine Zusatzangebote für Kinder interner Migranten, so daß z. B. in der Dt.-schweiz lebende Schüler frz.-sprachiger Herkunft fast ausnahmslos den normalen, für Dt.-sprachige konzipierten, Frz.-unterricht besuchen.

Die Situation der medialen Diglossie in der Dt.-schweiz stellt besondere Anforderungen an den Erstsprachunterricht, weil die aktive mündliche Hochdt.-Kompetenz erst in der Schule erworben wird und deshalb auch die informelle Mündlichkeit gefördert werden sollte (Sieber/Sitta 1986). Es stellt sich auch die sprachpolitisch umstrittene Frage, ob nicht in den anderssprachigen Regionen eine gewisse Hörverstehenskompetenz für schweizer-dt. Dialekte vermittelt werden sollte (EDK 1987, 110 ff).

7. Nichtlandessprachen als Kontaktsprachen

7.1. Englisch in der Schweiz

Englisch wird in der Schule weniger lang und weniger intensiv unterrichtet, es ist bestenfalls die zweite Fremdsprache, trotzdem gibt es eine Reihe (jüngerer) Schweizer v. a. aus der frz. und der dt. Schweiz, die angeben, bei einer allfälligen Kommunikation mit anderssprachigen Schweizern vorzugsweise Englisch anstelle der gelernten Landessprache zu verwenden. Vorschläge, Englisch als erste Fremdsprache lernen zu lassen oder zumindest den Englischunterricht auszubauen, finden bei Befragungen große Zustimmung. In einigen wirtschaftlichen und wissenschaftlichen Bereichen mit ausgeprägtem Gebrauch englischer Fachsprache ist die Verwendung von Englisch in der innerschweiz. Kommunikation üblich. Dies sind Anzeichen eines beginnenden Statuswandels des Englischen in der Schweiz von einer Fremdsprache zu einer internen Verständigungssprache und damit der Abwendung von einem partnerbezogenen Kommunikationsmodell zwischen den Sprachgruppen zu einem Verkehrssprachenmodell. Die offizielle Sprachpolitik sieht diese Tendenz eher als Gefahr für die schweiz. Sprachkultur (Botschaft 1991, 319; Eidg. Dep. des Innern 1989 a, 61 f, 134). Der mögliche Statuswandel des Englischen wird durch eine Reihe von Faktoren begünstigt: Status des Englischen als Weltsprache, Wichtigkeit englischer Fachsprache in vielen beruflichen Bereichen, Präsenz des Englischen im schweiz. Alltag (Werbung, Musik), kulturelle Ausrichtung auf den angloamerikanischen Kulturraum (Musik, Film, Nahrungsverhalten), größere Motivation zum Erwerb und Gebrauch dieser Sprache. Englisch ist zudem keine Landessprache und damit gewissermaßen sprachenpolitisch neutral. Diese Faktoren sind weiterhin gegeben, so daß anzunehmen ist, daß die Bedeutung des Englischen noch zunehmen wird (Dürmüller 1986; 1991 a; 1991 b; 1994).

7.2. Migrantensprachen

Die einzelnen Sprachgebiete sind keineswegs mehr so homogen wie dies der Idee des Territorialitätsprinzips zugrundeliegt. Sie sind als Folge der Einwanderung ausländischer Arbeitskräfte (von den Kaderleuten aus Deutschland Ende des 19. Jahrhunderts und in der Zwischenkriegszeit über die Arbeitskräfte aus Italien seit den fünfziger Jahren, später aus Spanien und Portugal und im letzten Jahrzehnt aus Ex-Jugoslawien und der Türkei) insbesondere in den städtischen Agglomerationen längst mehrsprachig und auch multikulturell geworden. Das hat mittlerweile sogar die offizielle Sprachpolitik erkannt (Botschaft 1991, 317 ff). Prinzipiell wird erwartet, daß sich auch ausländische Immigranten sprachlich assimilieren, wobei dies in sehr unterschiedlichem Maße gefördert wird. Bei Erwachsenen beschränkt sich das Sprachlernen in der Regel auf den ungesteuerten Spracherwerb. Für Kinder werden gewisse Zusatzkurse zum Erwerb einer Landessprache angeboten. Erst seit Mitte der achtziger Jahre werden Kurse in heimatlicher Sprache und Kultur stärker in das Unterrichtssystem integriert (Allemann-Ghionda 1993; Eidg. Dep. des Innern 1989 b, 89 ff; Gretler 1989).

Von besonderer Bedeutung ist das It.; in der dt. (und teilweise auch in der frz.) Schweiz dient It., genauer gesagt eine pidginisierte Form des It., als *lingua franca* der Immigranten, und zwar nicht nur bei Immigranten mit romanischem Sprachhintergrund. Ein Teil der Einwanderer erwirbt sogar zunächst It.- und erst danach Dt.-kenntnisse. Daß It. zur *lingua franca* der Einwanderer geworden ist, geht darauf zurück, daß die it. Einwanderer die am längsten ansässige und immer noch die größte Migrantengruppe sind, auch wenn die Einwanderung der letzten Jahre hauptsächlich aus anderen Ländern erfolgte (Berruto 1991; Lüdi/Py 1984, 29 f; Meyer-Sabino 1992, 869).

8. Zur Forschungslage

Darstellungen und Untersuchungen zur Situation der viersprachigen Schweiz gibt es aus verschiedensten Bereichen: juristische (Viletta 1978), juristisch-politische (Eidg. Dep. des Innern 1989 a), historische (Weilenmann 1925; Du Bois 1983), politologische (Weibel 1986), soziologische (McRae 1983) und auch einige sprachwissenschaftliche (kompakt und umfassend: Haas 1988 a; Schläpfer 1982; Bickel/Schläpfer 1994). Bei den meisten linguistischen Arbeiten zur Schweizer Sprachsituation steht nicht die gesamte Situation, sondern ein bestimmter Aspekt im Vordergrund; besondere Beachtung fanden neben der historischen Entwicklung der viersprachigen Schweiz (z. B. Sonderegger 1981; 1991; Zimmerli 1891 ff), die Sprachsituation der Dt.-schweiz (z. B. Schwarzenbach 1969; Haas 1986; 1988 b; Sieber/Sitta 1984; 1986; Sonderegger 1985) und die Situation des Rtr., die schon in Weinreichs Arbeit über Kontaktlinguistik besonders berücksichtigt worden ist (z. B. Billigmeier 1983; Cathomas 1977; Kristol 1984; Weinreich 1953). Erst in letzter Zeit ist das Augenmerk der Forschung vermehrt auf die Auswirkungen und das Funktionieren der Mehrsprachigkeit im Alltag, an der Sprachgrenze und bei internen Migranten, gelegt worden (Brohy 1992; Lüdi 1981; Lüdi/Py 1989/90; 1994; Windisch 1992). Daß ein Bewußtsein für die Erforschung der konkreten Auswirkungen und der alltäglichen Probleme der Mehrsprachigkeit gewachsen ist, zeigt sich auch an der Gründung eines Forschungszentrums für Mehrsprachigkeit (Werlen 1991).

Das sprachpolitisch bedeutendste Vorhaben der letzten Jahre, die Reform der sprachenpolitischen Verfassungsgrundlagen (s. 6.1.), wurde auf Anregung rtr. Sprachpolitiker in Angriff genommen. Die öffentliche sprachpolitische Diskussion beschäftigt sich aber zur Hauptsache mit dem Verhältnis der dt. und frz. Schweiz (s. 6.2.), wobei sprachliche Fragen oft eher der äußerliche Anlaß zu Auseinandersetzungen über die Beziehungen der dt. und der frz. Schweiz bilden. Auffällig ist, daß gerade führende Sprachpolitiker sich relativ wenig um sprachliche Fakten oder die effektive Sprachsituation kümmern und linguistisch fundierte Stimmen kaum Gehör finden.

9. Bibliographie (in Auswahl)

Albrecht, Urs/Schneider, Christian (1990): „Brauchen wir einen neuen Sprachenartikel?" In: *Gesetzgebung heute*, H. 3, 47−68.

Allemann-Ghionda, Cristina (1993): *Schulung von Migrantenkindern und interkulturelle Erziehung in der Praxis des schweizerischen Bildungswesens: Eine Übersicht über Innovationen*, Bern.

Andres, Franz (1990): „Language relations in multilingual Switzerland". In: *Multilingua 9*, 11−45.

Berruto, Gaetano (1984): „Appunti sull'italiano elvetico". In: *Studi linguistici italiani 10*, 76−108.

Berruto, Gaetano (1991): „Fremdarbeiteritalienisch: fenomeni di pidginizzazione dell'italiano nella Svizzera tedesca". In: *Rivista di Linguistica*, 3, 333−367.

Berruto, Gaetano/Burger, Harald (1985): „Aspetti del contatto fra italiano e tedesco in Ticino". In: *Archivio storico ticinese 26*, H. 101, 29−76.

Berruto, Gaetano/Burger, Harald (1987): „Aspekte des Sprachkontaktes Italienisch-Deutsch im Tessin". In: *Linguistische Berichte 111*, 367−380.

Bianconi, Sandro (1980): *Lingua matrigna. Italiano e dialetto nella Svizzera italiana*, Bologna.

Bianconi, Sandro (1989): *I due linguaggi. Storia Linguistica della Lombardia svizzera dal '400 ai nostri giorni*, Bellinzona.

Bianconi, Sandro (Ed.) (1994): *Lingue nel Ticino. Un'indagine qualitativa e statistica*, Locarno.

Bickel, Hans/Schläpfer, Robert (Eds.) (1994): *Mehrsprachigkeit − eine Herausforderung*, Aarau etc.

Billigmeier, Robert H. (1983): *Land und Volk der Rätoromanen. Eine Kultur- und Sprachgeschichte*, übers. v. Morlang, W., Frauenfeld.

Boschung, Peter (1989): *Die freiburgische Sprachenfrage*, Freiburg i.Üe.

Botschaft (1991): „Botschaft über die Revision des Sprachenartikels der Bundesverfassung (Art. 116 BV)". In: *Bundesblatt*, Bd. II, H. 18, 309−346.

Brohy, Claudine (1992): *Das Sprachverhalten zweisprachiger Paare und Familien. In Fribourg/Freiburg (Schweiz)*, Freiburg i.Üe.

Bund Schweizerischer Werbeagenturen (1986) (Ed.): *Werbung in einem mehrsprachigen Land / La publicité dans un pays multilingue*, Freiburg i.Üe.

Bundesamt für Statistik (Ed.) (1991) ff: *Statistisches Jahrbuch der Schweiz 1992 ff*, Zürich.

Camartin, Iso (1982): „Die Beziehungen zwischen den schweizerischen Sprachregionen". In: *Die vier-*

sprachige Schweiz, Schläpfer, R. (Ed.), Zürich, 301−351.

Campiche, Roland (1992): „Von der religiösen Identität als Vorschrift zur religiösen Identität als Konstruktion". In: *Handbuch der schweizerischen Volkskultur*, Hugger, P. (Ed.), 3 Bde., Zürich, Bd. 3, 1443−1470.

Cathomas, Bernard (1977): *Erkundungen zur Zweisprachigkeit der Rätoromanen. Eine soziolinguistische und pragmatische Leitstudie*, Bern.

Caussignac, Gerard/Kettiger, Daniel (1991): „Rédaction parallèle au Canton de Berne/Koredaktion im Kanton Bern". In: *Gesetzgebung heute*, H. 3, 78−87.

Centlivres, Pierre (1986): „L'identité régionale: langage et pratiques. Approche ethnologique, Suisse romande et Tessin". In: *Regionale Identität und Perspektiven: fünf sozialwissenschaftliche Ansätze*, Centlivres, P. et al. (Eds.), Bern, 77−126.

Christen, Helen (1991): „'...also schon mal die Grammatik ist nicht da...' Erfahrungen aus drei Semestern Lehrtätigkeit in alemannischer Dialektologie an der Universität Genf". In: *Bulletin CILA 54*, 147−158.

Darms, Georges (1989): „Bündnerromanisch. Sprachnormierung und Standardsprache". In: *Lexikon der Romanistischen Linguistik*, Bd. III, Tübingen, 827−853.

Decurtins, Alexi (1981): „Zum deutschen Sprachgut im Bündnerromanischen. Sprachkontakt in diachronischer Sicht". In: *Kulturelle und sprachliche Minderheiten in Europa. Aspekte d. europ. Ethnolinguistik*, Ureland, P.S. (Ed.), Tübingen, 111−137.

De Pietro, Jean-François/Lüdi, Georges/Papaloizos, Lilli (1989/90): „Une communauté francophone en milieu germanophone: Identité linguistique et réseaux de sociabilité dans la ville de Bâle". In: *Langage et société 50/51*, 93−115.

Diekmann, Erwin (1980): „Deutsch-Surselvische Interferenzprobleme im Bündner-Romanischen". In: *Sprachkontakt und Sprachkonflikt*, Nelde, P.H. (Ed.), Wiesbaden, 53−62.

Du Bois, Pierre (Ed.) (1983): *Union et divisions des Suisses. Les relations entre Alémaniques, Romands et Tessinois aux XIXe et XXe siècles*, Lausanne.

Du Bois, Pierre (1984): „Welsch, Deutsch, Schweizerdeutsch. Der 'Unterschied des Idioms'". In: *Schweizer Monatshefte 64*, 793−804.

Dürmüller, Urs (1986): „The Status of English in multilingual Switzerland". In: *Bulletin CILA 44*, 7−38.

Dürmüller, Urs (1991 a): „Swiss Multilingualism and International Communication". In: *Sociolinguistica 5*, 111−159.

Dürmüller, Urs (1991 b): „The Changing Status of English in Switzerland". In: *Status Change of Languages*, Ammon, U./Hellinger, M. (Eds.), Berlin, 355−370.

Dürrmüller, Urs (1994): „Multi-Lingual talk or English only? The Swiss experience." In: *Sociolinguistica 8*, 44−64.

EDK (Schweizerische Konferenz der kantonalen Erziehungsdirektoren) (1987): *Herausforderung Schweiz. Materialien zur Förderung des Unterrichts in den Landessprachen*, Bern.

Eidg. Departement des Innern (Ed.) (1989 a): *Zustand und Zukunft der viersprachigen Schweiz. Abklärungen, Vorschläge und Empfehlungen einer Arbeitsgruppe des Eidgenössischen Departements des Innern*, Bern.

Eidg. Departement des Innern (Ed.) (1989 b): *Materialienband zum Schlussbericht der Arbeitsgruppe zur Revision von Artikel 116 der Bundesverfassung*, Bern.

Eidg. Personalamt (Ed.) (1980): *Kolloquium. Die Mehrsprachigkeit der Schweiz in Staat und Verwaltung. Heute und Morgen*, Montreux.

Eidg. Personalamt (Ed.) (1989): *Die Landessprachen in der Bundesverwaltung*, Bern.

Eisner, Manuel/Fux, Beat (Eds.) (1992): *Politische Sprache in der Schweiz. Konflikt und Konsens*, Zürich/Köln 1992.

Fleiner-Gerster, Thomas (1991): „Das sprachliche Territorialitätsprinzip in gemischtsprachigen Gebieten". In: *Gesetzgebung heute*, H. 1, 93−107.

Franceschini, Rita/Müller, Myriam/Schmid, Stephan (1984): „Comportamento linguistico e competenze dell'italiano in immigrati di seconda generazione: un'indagine a Zurigo". In: *Rivista italiana di dialettologia 8*, 41−72.

Franceschini, Rita/Oesch-Serra, Cecielia/Py, Bernard (1989/90): „Ruptures et reconstitutions discursives du sens en situation de migration". In: *Langage et société 50/51*, 117−131.

Germann, Raimund E./Weibel, Ernest (Eds.) (1986): *Handbuch politisches System der Schweiz, Band 3 Föderalismus*, Bern.

Geschichte (1986): *Geschichte der Schweiz und der Schweizer*, unter d. wiss. Betreuung d. Comité pour une Nouvelle Histoire de la Suisse, red. v. Mesmer, B., Basel/Frankfurt a. M.

Ghirlanda, Elio (1991): „La politica delle lingue in Svizzera vista da un ticinese". In: *Gesetzgebung heute*, H. 1, 27−44.

Gretler, Armin (Ed.) (1989): *Etre migrant. Approches des problèmes socio-culturels et linguistiques des enfants migrants en Suisse*, 2. erw. Aufl., Bern/Frankfurt a. M.

Gyr, Ueli (1989): *Lektion fürs Leben. Welschlandaufenthalte als traditionelle Bildungs-, Erziehungs- und Übergangsmuster*, Zürich.

Gyr, Ueli (1992): „Welschlandaufenthalte als Übergangs- und Kontaktmuster". In: *Handbuch der schweizerischen Volkskultur*, Hugger, P. (Ed.) (1992), 3 Bde., Zürich, Bd. 2, 119−128.

Haas, Walter (1982 a): "Die deutschsprachige Schweiz". In: *Die viersprachige Schweiz*, Schläpfer, R. (Ed.), Zürich, 71–160.

Haas, Walter (1982 b): "Sprachgeschichtliche Grundlagen". In: *Die viersprachige Schweiz*, Schläpfer, R. (Ed.), Zürich, 21–70.

Haas, Walter (1986): "Der beredte Deutschschweizer oder die Hollandisierung des Hinterwäldlers". In: *Das Deutsch der Schweizer. Zur Sprach- und Literatursituation der Schweiz*, Löffler, H. (Ed.), Aarau etc., 41–59.

Haas, Walter (1988 a): "Art. 153 Schweiz". In: *Sociolinguistics/Soziolinguistik. Ein internationales Handbuch zur Wissenschaft von Sprache und Gesellschaft*, Ammon, U. et al. (Eds.), 2 Halbbd., Berlin/New York, 1365–1383.

Haas, Walter (1988 b): "Die Verwendung von Mundart und Standardsprache in der deutschsprachigen Schweiz". In: *Niederdeutsch und Zweisprachigkeit*, Bremen, 35–48.

Haas, Walter (1992): "Reine Mundart". In: *Verborum Amor. Studien zur Geschichte und Kunst der deutschen Sprache. Festschrift für Stefan Sonderegger*, Burger, H. et al. (Eds.), Berlin/New York, 578–610.

Haas, Walter (1994): "Zur Rezeption der deutschen Hochsprache in der Schweiz.". In: *Sprachstandardisierung*, Lüdi, G. (Ed.), Freiburg i. Üe.

Hauck, Werner (1990): "Aktuelle Probleme der Mehrsprachigkeit in der schweizerischen Bundesverwaltung". In: *Mehrsprachigkeit im Rechtsleben*, Bozen, 93–97.

Hauck, Werner (1993): "Die Amtssprachen der Schweiz – Anspruch und Wirklichkeit". In: *Deutsch als Verkehrssprache in Europa*, Born, J./Stickel, G., Berlin/New York, 147–163.

Hegnauer, Cyril (1947): *Das Sprachenrecht der Schweiz*, Zürich.

Hegnauer, Cyril (1990): "Das Gerichtssprachenrecht der Schweiz". In: *Mehrsprachigkeit im Rechtsleben*, Bozen, 4–25.

Heller, Monica (1990): "French immersion in Canada: a model for Switzerland?" In: *Multilingua 9*, 67–85.

Hengartner, Thomas (1991): "Die Revision des Sprachenartikels der Bundesverfassung und des Schweizers Deutsch". In: *Gesetzgebung heute*, H. 1, 69–92.

Hess, Beatrice/Nadai, Eva/Stucki, Brigitte (1989/1990): "Begegnungen über den Röstigraben: Kulturkontakt in der Schweiz am Beispiel des Welschlandjahres". In: *Ethnologica Helvetica 13/14*, 255–268.

Holtus, Günter (1989): "Bündnerromanisch. Externe Sprachgeschichte". In: *Lexikon der Romanistischen Linguistik*, Bd. III, Tübingen, 854–871.

Hotzenköcherle, Rudolf (1984): *Die Sprachlandschaften der deutschen Schweiz*, Aarau etc.

Hugger, Paul (Ed.) (1992): *Handbuch der schweizerischen Volkskultur*, 3 Bde., Zürich.

Jeanneret, René (Ed.) (1991): *700 ans de contacts linguistiques en Suisse*. Numéro spécial pour le 700ème anniversaire de la Confédération Helvétique, *Bulletin CILA 54*.

Kaiser, Stephan (1969/70): *Die Besonderheiten der deutschen Schriftsprache in der Schweiz. Bd. 1 Wortgut und Wortgebrauch, Bd. 2 Wortbildung und Satzbildung*, Mannheim etc.

Keller, Peter (1990): "Legal aspects of language choice in schools: possibilities and limits for language immersion programs in Switzerland". In: *Multilingua 9*, 105–112.

Klöti, Ulrich (1984): *Handbuch politisches System der Schweiz, Band 2 Strukturen und Prozesse*, Bern.

Knecht, Pierre (1982): "Die französischsprachige Schweiz". In: *Die viersprachige Schweiz*, Schläpfer, R. (Ed.), Zürich, 161–209.

Kolde, Gottfried (1980): "Vergleichende Untersuchungen des Sprachverhaltens und der Spracheinstellungen von Jugendlichen in zwei gemischtsprachigen Schweizer Städten". In: *Sprachkontakt und Sprachkonflikt*, Nelde, P.H. (Ed.), Wiesbaden, 243–253.

Kolde, Gottfried (1981): *Sprachkontakte in gemischtsprachigen Städten. Vergleichende Untersuchungen über Voraussetzungen und Formen sprachlicher Interaktion verschiedensprachiger Jugendlicher in den Schweizer Städten Biel/Bienne und Fribourg/Freiburg i. Üe.*, Wiesbaden.

Kolde, Gottfried (1986): "Einige aktuelle sprach- und sprachenpolitische Probleme in der viersprachigen Schweiz". In: *Muttersprache 86*, 58–68.

Kolde, Gottfried (1988): "Language Contact and Bilingualism in Switzerland". In: *International Handbook of Bilingualism and Bilingual Education*, Paulston, Ch. P. (Ed.), New York etc., 515–537.

Koller, Werner (1992): *Deutsche in der Deutschschweiz. Eine sprachsoziologische Untersuchung*, Aarau etc.

Kraas, Frauke (1992): *Die Rätoromanen Graubündens. Peripherisierung einer Minorität*, Stuttgart.

Kreis, Georg (1987): "Die besseren Patrioten. Nationale Idee und regionale Identität in der französischen Schweiz vor 1914". In: *Auf dem Weg zu einer schweizerischen Identität 1848–1914*, Capitani, F. de/Germann, G. (Eds.), Freiburg/Fribourg, 55–75.

Kreis, Georg (1992): "Die Frage der nationalen Identität". In: *Handbuch der schweizerischen Volkskultur*, Hugger, P. (Ed.) (1992), 3 Bde., Zürich, Bd. 2, 781–799.

Kristol, Andres Max (1984): *Sprachkontakt und Mehrsprachigkeit in Bivio (Graubünden). Linguistische Bestandsaufnahme in einer siebensprachigen Dorfgemeinschaft*, Bern.

Kristol, Andres Max (1989): „Bündnerromanisch. Soziolinguistik". In: *Lexikon der Romanistischen Linguistik*, Bd. III, Tübingen, 813−827.

Löffler, Heiner (Ed.) (1989): *Das Deutsch der Schweizer. Zur Sprach- und Literatursituation der Schweiz*, Aarau.

Löffler, Heinrich (1987): „Landesgrenze als Sprachgrenze im alemannischen Dreiländereck". In: *Sprachspiegel 43*, 73−81 und 109−115.

Löffler, Heinrich (1989): „Die Frage nach dem landesspezifischen Gesprächsstil − oder die Schweizer Art zu diskutieren". In: *Dialoganalyse*, Weigand, E./Hundsnurscher, F. (Eds.), Tübingen, Bd. 2, 207−221.

Lüdi, Georges (1981): „Migration interne et intégration linguistique en Suisse. Vers une étude de la diglossie intrafamiliale dans un état multilingue basé sur le principe territorial". In: *Etre migrant*, Gretler, A. (Ed.), Bern, 127−137.

Lüdi, Georges (1985): „Zur Methodologie der Interpretation der Rede von Zweisprachigen über ihre Sprachenwahl". In: *Methoden der Kontaktlinguistik*, Nelde, P.H. (Ed.), Bonn, 105−118.

Lüdi, Georges (1990): „Naturalisation et dialectes". In: *Devenir suisse. Adhésion et diversité culturelle des étrangers en Suisse*, Centlivres, P. (Ed.), Genf, 229−242.

Lüdi, Georges/Py, Bernard (1984): *Zweisprachig durch Migration. Einführung in die Erforschung der Mehrsprachigkeit am Beispiel zweier Zuwanderergruppen in Neuenburg (Schweiz)*, Tübingen.

Lüdi, Georges/Py, Bernard (1989/90): „La Suisse: un laboratoire pour l'étude de la dynamique des langues en contact". In: *Langage et société 50/51*, 87−91.

Lüdi, Georges/Py, Bernard (Eds.) (1994): *Fremdsprachig im eigenen Land. Wenn Binnenwanderer in der Schweiz das Sprachgebiet wechseln und wie sie darüber reden*, Basel/Frankfurt a. M.

Lüdi, Georges/Papaloizos, Lilli/De Pietro, François (1989/90): „Etranger dans son propre pays: Dimensions linguistiques de la migration interne en Suisse". In: *Ethnologica Helvetica 13/14*, 269−297.

Lurati, Ottavio (1976): *Dialetto e italiano regionale nella Svizzera Italiana*, Lugano.

Lurati, Ottavio (1982): „Die sprachliche Situation der Südschweiz". In: *Die viersprachige Schweiz*, Schläpfer, R. (Ed.), Zürich, 211−252.

Lurati, Ottavio (1988): „Italienisch: Areallinguistik III. Lombardei und Tessin". In: *Lexikon der Romanistischen Linguistik*, Tübingen, Bd. IV, 485−516.

Lurati, Ottavio (1992): „Schwierig ist es, Schweizer italienischer Kultur zu sein". In: *Handbuch der schweizerischen Volkskultur*, Hugger, P. (Ed.) (1992), 3 Bde., Zürich, Bd. 2, 801−809.

Lutz, Florentin/Arquint, Jachen C. (1982): „Die rätoromanische Schweiz". In: *Die viersprachige Schweiz*, Schläpfer, R. (Ed.), Zürich, 253−300.

Mäder, Denise/Froidevaux, Didier (1992): „Meyriez: ein Bild der sprachlichen Koexistenz im Kanton Freiburg". In. *Handbuch der schweizerischen Volkskultur*, Hugger, P. (Ed.) (1992), 3 Bde., Zürich, Bd. 2, 525−530.

McRae, Kenneth D. (1983): *Conflict and compromise in multilingual societies. Switzerland*, Waterloo, Ontario.

Meyer, Kurt (1989): *Wie sagt man in der Schweiz? Wörterbuch der schweizerischen Besonderheiten*, Mannheim.

Meyer-Sabino, Giovanna (1992): „Ethnische Minderheiten: Fremdarbeiter zwischen Akkulturation und Integration". In: *Handbuch der schweizerischen Volkskultur*, Hugger, P. (Ed.) (1992), 3 Bde., Zürich, Bd. 2, 859−886.

Müller, Hans-Peter (1977): *Die schweizerische Sprachenfrage vor 1914. Eine historische Untersuchung über das Verhältnis zwischen Deutsch und Welsch bis zum Ersten Weltkrieg*, Wiesbaden.

Nay, Giusep (1991): „La posiziun dal rumantsch sco linguatg giudizial". In: *Gesetzgebung heute*, H.1, 9−26.

Pache, Véronique (1989/90): „Les associations portugaises de Suisse ou l'image d'une Suisse méconnue". In: *Ethnologica Helvetica 13/14*, 339−354.

Pidoux, Edmond (1984): *Le langage des Romands*, Lausanne.

Ramseier, Markus (1988): *Mundart und Standardsprache im Radio der deutschen und rätoromanischen Schweiz. Sprachform, Sprach- und Sprechstil im Vergleich*, Aarau.

Ratti, Remigio/Bianconi, Sandro/Ceschi, Raffaelo (1993): *Tessin − eine offene Region*, Basel.

Redard, Françoise/Jeanneret, René/Métral, Pierre (Eds.) (1982): *Le Schwyzertütsch 5ᵉ langue nationale? Bulletin CILA 33*.

Riklin, Alois (Ed.) (1983): *Handbuch politisches System der Schweiz. Band 1 Grundlagen*, Bern.

Ris, Roland (1979): „Dialekte und Einheitssprache in der deutschen Schweiz". In: *International Journal of the Sociology of Language 21*, 41−61.

Ris, Roland (1987): „Die Ausbildung eines sprachlich-kulturellen Bewusstseins in der deutschen Schweiz 1890−1914 (mit besonderer Berücksichtigung des Kantons Bern)". In: *Auf dem Weg zu einer schweizerischen Identität 1848−1914*, de Capitani, F./Germann, G. (Eds.), Freiburg, 353−380.

Rossinelli, Michel (1991): „Protection des minorités linguistiques helvétiques et révision de l'article 116 de la Constitution fédérale". In: *Gesetzgebung heute*, H.1, 45−68.

Rovere, Giovanni (1974): *Aspetti sociolinguistici dell'emigrazione italiana in Svizzera*, Basel.

Rupp, Heinz (1989): „Die deutsche Sprache in der deutschsprachigen Schweiz". In: *Jahrbuch für Internationale Germanistik 21*, 26−37.

Schäppi, Peter (1971): *Der Schutz sprachlicher und konfessioneller Minderheiten im Recht von Bund und Kantonen*, Zürich.

Schifferle, Hans-Peter (1990): „Badisches und schweizerisches Alemannisch am Hochrhein". In: *Germanistische Linguistik 101–103*, 315–340.

Schilling, Rudolf (1970): *Romanische Elemente im Schweizerhochdeutschen*, Mannheim etc.

Schläpfer, Robert (1982) (Ed.): *Die viersprachige Schweiz*, Zürich.

Schläpfer, Robert/Gutzwiler, Jürg/Schmid, Beat (1991): *Das Spannungsfeld zwischen Mundart und Standardsprache in der deutschen Schweiz. Spracheinstellungen junger Deutsch- und Welschschweizer. Eine Auswertung der Pädagogischen Rekrutenprüfungen 1985*, Aarau.

Schmid, Heinrich (1982): *Richtlinien für die Gestaltung einer gesamtbündnerromanischen Schriftsprache, Rumantsch Grischun*, Chur.

Schmid, Heinrich (1989): *Eine einheitliche Schriftsprache: Luxus oder Notwendigkeit? Zum Problem der überregionalen Normierung bei Kleinsprachen. Erfahrungen in Graubünden*, San Martin de Tor (Südtirol, Ladinien).

Schmid, Stephan (1989): „L'italiano degli svizzeri tedeschi". In: *Italiano & Oltre 4*, 138–141, 237–240.

Schmitt, Christian (1990): „Frankophonie III. Regionale Varianten des Französischen in Europa II.c) Schweiz". In: *Lexikon der Romanistischen Linguistik*, Bd. V, 1, Tübingen, 726–732.

Schneider, Christian (1992): „Koredaktion von Gesetzestexten des Bundes". In: *Gesetzgebung heute*, H.3, 83–90.

Schnidrig, Kurt (1986): *Das Dusseln. Ein Subsidiärdialekt im Deutschwallis*, Bern.

Schwarzenbach, Rudolf (1969): *Die Stellung der Mundart in der deutschsprachigen Schweiz. Studien zum Sprachbrauch der Gegenwart*, Frauenfeld.

Schweizer Lexikon (1991) ff: *Schweizer Lexikon. 91. In sechs Bänden*, Luzern.

Seidelmann, Erich (1989): „Der Hochrhein als Sprachgrenze". In: *Dialektgeographie und Dialektologie. Festschrift für Günter Bellmann*, Marburg 1989, 75–88.

Sieber, Peter/Sitta, Horst (1984): „Schweizerdeutsch zwischen Dialekt und Sprache". In: *Kwartalnik Neofilologiczny 31*, 3–40.

Sieber, Peter/Sitta, Horst (1986): *Mundart und Standardsprache als Problem der Schule*, Aarau.

Solèr, Clau (1983): *Sprachgebrauch und Sprachwandel. Eine theoretische Faktorenanalyse und die Pragmatik der Sprachbehandlung bei den Rätoromanen von Lumbrein*, Zürich.

Solèr, Clau/Ebneter, Theodor (1988): *Romanisch im Domleschg*, Zürich.

Sonderegger, Stefan (1981): *Die viersprachige Schweiz zwischen Geschichte und Zukunft*. Aulavorträge 12 der Hochschule für Wirtschafts- und Sozialwissenschaften, St. Gallen.

Sonderegger, Stefan (1985): „Die Entwicklung des Verhältnisses von Standardsprache und Mundarten in der deutschen Schweiz". In: *Sprachgeschichte. Ein Handbuch zur Geschichte der deutschen Sprache und ihrer Erforschung*, Besch, W. et al. (Eds.) 2 Halbbd., Berlin/New York 1985, 1873–1939.

Sonderegger, Stefan (1991): „Die Schweiz als Sprachgrenzland. Eine historisch-typologische Standortbestimmung". In: *Zeitschrift für Literaturwissenschaft und Linguistik 83*, 13–39.

Stäuble, Antonio (Ed.) (1989): *Lingua e letteratura italiana in Svizzera*, Bellinzona.

Stern, Otto (1988): „Divergence and Convergence of Dialect and Standard from the Perspective of the Language Learner. Standard language acquisition by the Swiss-German dialect speaking child". In: *Variation and Convergence. Studies in Social Dialectology*, Auer, P./Luzio, A. di (Eds.), Berlin/New York, 134–156.

Stotz, Daniel/Andres, Franz (1990): „Problems in Developing Bilingual Education Programs in Switzerland". In: *Multilingua 9*, 113–136.

Stricker, Hans (1987): „Romanisch und Deutsch im Schanfigg (GR)". In: *Vox Romanica 45*, 55–82.

UFM/Universitäres Forschungszentrum für Mehrsprachigkeit (1992 a): *Zweisprachigkeit im Kanton Bern. Umfrage unter politischen MandatsträgerInnen des Kantons Bern*, Bern/Brig.

UFM/Universitäres Forschungszentrum für Mehrsprachigkeit (1992 b): *Zweisprachigkeit im Kanton Wallis. Eine Politikerbefragung*, Brig/Bern.

Viletta, Rudolf (1978): *Abhandlungen zum Sprachenrecht mit besonderer Berücksichtigung des Rechts der Gemeinden des Kantons Graubünden, Bd. I, Grundlagen des Sprachenrechts*, Zürich 1978.

Viletta, Rudolf (1981): „Die Regelung der Beziehungen zwischen den schweizerischen Sprachgemeinschaften". In: *Bulletin CILA 33*, 42–72.

Viletta, Rudolf (1983): „Untersuchungen zur Mehrsprachigkeit in der Schweiz unter besonderer Berücksichtigung des Rätoromanischen". In: *Mehrsprachigkeit/Multilingualism*, Nelde, P. H. (Ed.), Bonn, 107–146.

Viletta, Rudolf (1984): „Die Rätoromanen, ethnopolitisches Gewissen der Schweiz". In: *Spracherwerb, Sprachkontakt, Sprachkonflikt*, Oksaar, E. (Ed.), Berlin/New York, 142–166.

Vouga, Jean-Pierre (Ed.) (1990/91): *La Suisse face à ses langues/Die Schweiz im Spiegel ihrer Sprachen*, Aarau.

Watts, Richard James/Andres, Franz (Eds.) (1990): *Zweisprachig durch die Schule. Französisch und Deutsch als Unterrichtssprache. Le bilinguisme à travers l'école*, Bern.

Weber, Daniel Erich (1984). *Sprach- und Mundartpflege in der deutschsprachigen Schweiz. Sprachnorm und Sprachdidaktik im zweisprachformigen Staat*, Frauenfeld.

Wehling, Hans Georg (Ed.) (1988): *Die Schweiz*, Stuttgart etc.

Weibel, Ernest (1986): „Les rapports entre les groupes linguistiques". In: *Handbuch politisches System der Schweiz, Band 3 Föderalismus*, Germann, R.E./Weibel E. (Eds.), Bern, 221—263.

Weibel, Ernest (1988): „Sprachgruppen und Sprachprobleme in der Schweiz. Konflikte und Konfliktregelungsmodelle". In: *Die Schweiz*, Wehling, H.-G. (Ed.), Stuttgart, 79—99.

Weilenmann, Hermann (1925): *Die vielsprachige Schweiz. Eine Lösung des Nationalitätenproblems*, Basel.

Weinreich, Uriel (1953): *Languages in contact. Findings and Problems*, New York 1953.

Werlen, Iwar (1985): „Dialektsprechen in mehrdialektalen Gesellschaften am Beispiel des südlichen Deutschland und der deutschen Schweiz". In: *Kontroversen, alte und neue*, Schöne, A. (Ed.), Tübingen, Bd. 4, 279—297.

Werlen, Iwar (1988): „Swiss German Dialects and Swiss Standard High German". In: *Variation and Convergence. Studies in Social Dialectology*, Auer, P./Luzio, A. di (Eds.), Berlin/New York, 93—123.

Werlen, Iwar (1991): „Gründung eines Forschungszentrums für Mehrsprachigkeit". In: *Gesetzgebung heute*, H.1, 148—150.

Widmer, Jean (1986): *Rapporto sulle condizioni de lavoro degli agenti dell'administrazione federale a Berne, secondo la loro lingua materna*, Bern.

Willi, Urs/Solèr, Clau (1990): „Der rätoromanisch-deutsche Sprachkontakt in Graubünden". In: *Germanistische Linguistik* 101—103, 445—475.

Windisch, Uli et al. (1992): *Les relations quotidiennes entre romands et suisses allemands. Les cantons bilingues de Fribourg et du Valais*, 2 tomes, Lausanne.

Wunderli, Peter (1968): „Deutsch und Italienisch im Tessin". In: *Vox Romanica 27*, 299—318.

Zimmerli, Jacob (1891/1895/1899): *Die deutsch-französische Sprachgrenze in der Schweiz*, 3 Bde., Basel/Genf.

Jürg Niederhauser, Bern (Schweiz)

227. Deutsche Schweiz

1. Geographie und Demographie
2. Territorial- und Staatsbildung
3. Politik, Wirtschaft und allgemeine kulturelle sowie religiöse Lage
4. Statistik und Ethnoprofile
5. Soziolinguistische Lage
6. Sprachpolitische Lage
7. Sprachkontakte, Kontaktsprachen
8. Kritische Wertung der verwendeten Quellen
9. Bibliographie (in Auswahl)

1. Geographie und Demographie

Die Geographie und Demographie der gesamten Schweiz ist im Artikel 226 ausführlich dargestellt. Hier werden nur noch einige Merkmale herausgehoben, die für die sprachliche Situation der Deutschschweiz kennzeichnend sind. Die deutsche Schweiz umfaßt geographisch die Mitte der Schweiz und bildet die bei weitem größte Sprachregion mit ca. 4,37 Millionen deutschsprechenden Einwohnern in 18 deutschen und den drei gemischtsprachigen Kantonen Bern/Berne, Freiburg/Fribourg und Wallis/Valais.

2. Territorial- und Staatsbildung

Die heutige Prädominanz des (Schweizer)-Deutschen ist nicht nur durch den größten Anteil an Sprechern (65%), sondern auch durch die historische Entwicklung der Eidgenossenschaft bedingt. Die Urkantone und die frühe Eidgenossenschaft waren deutschsprachig. Die französischen und italienischen Gebiete bildeten bis zur „Helvetischen Republik" (zur Zeit der napoleonischen Kriege 1798—1802) sogenannte Untertanengebiete.

3. Politik, Wirtschaft und allgemeine kulturelle sowie religiöse Lage

Die deutsche Schweiz hat Teil an allen geographischen und wirtschaftlichen Gegebenheiten, die auch die Gesamtschweiz kennzeichnen: am Mittelland mit Industrie, Dienstleistungen und Groß-Landwirtschaft, der Voralpenzone mit Gras- und Viehwirtschaft und an der unwirtlichen Hochgebirgszone. Auch die großen Städte und Agglomerationen: Zürich, Basel, Bern, Luzern, St.Gallen und die meisten Universitäten und

Hochschulen liegen in der Deutschschweiz. Die beiden großen christlichen Konfessionen sind in der Deutschschweiz gleichmäßig vertreten, wobei in den Städten Basel, Zürich und Bern die Reformierten leicht überwiegen.

Territoriale Kontakte zu gleichsprachigen Nachbarstaaten hat die Deutschschweiz auf einer Gesamtlänge von ca. 580 km (!): bei Basel und südwestlich davon auf einer Länge von nur ca. 30 km zum französischen, alemannisch sprechenden Territorium des südlichen Elsaß, nach Norden und Osten 346 km zu Deutschland (Baden-Württemberg) hin; auf einer Länge von 165 km teilt die Schweiz die Grenze mit Österreich und mit Liechtenstein auf 41 km. Im äußersten Osten, im Münstertal (Val Müstair), grenzt die Schweiz noch einige Kilometer an das deutschsprachige Südtirol (Italien). An Italien stößt die Deutschsprachige Schweiz im Südteil Graubündens (Splügen, Bergell, Bernina); doch kann man nicht eigentlich von einer territorialen Kontaktzone sprechen, da die Grenze auf den Alpenkämmen verläuft und es sich auf Deutschschweizer Seite im Grunde um rätoromanisches, zumindest gemischtsprachiges Sprachgebiet handelt. Auf ähnliche Weise kann man im Puschlav (Poschiavo) nur in schematischer Hinsicht von deutsch-italienischen Kontaktzonen sprechen, so auch zwischen dem Kanton Uri und dem Tessin, welche durch das Gotthardmassiv zwar getrennt, mit der Gotthard-Paßstraße und den beiden Tunnels jedoch verbunden sind. Dabei ist ungewiß, ob sich an politischen Grenzen (Landesgrenzen) oder an geographischen Hindernissen wie Gebirgszügen, Grenzflüssen und Grenzseen (Rhein, Genfersee, Bodensee) in bezug auf die Sprache eher Kontakt- oder doch eher Distanzphänomene herausbilden. Es scheint so, als ob alte Saumpfade über das Gebirge oder Bootsverkehr über den See sprachliche Kontakte mehr gefördert haben, als dies durch die heutigen modernen Verkehrsadern wie Autobahnen, Eisenbahnen, Paßstraßen und Tunnels geschieht. Was die ausländische Nachbarschaft betrifft, so stößt die Deutschschweiz über den größten Teil ihrer Außenlinie an ebenfalls deutschsprachige Gebiete Alemanniens: an das Elsässische, das Badische und das Oberschwäbische (in Baden-Württemberg), das zum „Niederalemannischen" gehört, an das Vorarlbergische (ebenfalls niederalemannisch) und Liechtensteinische (Ostschweizerisch) und im äußersten Osten an das Südtirolische (Bairische).

Die inländische Sprachgrenze zwischen der Deutschschweiz und der (französischen) Westschweiz verläuft mitten durch die Kantone Bern, Freiburg und Wallis. Nur zwischen den Kantonen Solothurn und dem Jura ist die Kantonsgrenze ein Stück weit identisch mit der deutsch-französischen Sprachgrenze (→ Sprachenkarte O).

Die Sprachgrenzen fallen also praktisch nirgends mit politischen Grenzen zusammen, weder nach außen zu den Nachbarstaaten hin noch im Innern: keine Landesgrenze ist eine sprachliche Außengrenze und keine Kantonsgrenze ist — bis auf das Stück Solothurn/Jura — eine binnenschweizerische Sprachgrenze. Die Landesgrenzen zu den gleichsprachigen Nachbarn in Frankreich, Deutschland und Österreich stellen allerdings seit einiger Zeit eine „pragmatische Sprachgrenze" dar (s. unten Kap. 7).

4. Statistik und Ethnoprofile

(Die folgenden Angaben stammen zur Hauptsache aus der Teilveröffentlichung der Volkszählung 1990, s. Bundesamt für Statistik 1993 und 1993a, 351 ff sowie Schläpfer 1991). Die Zahl der Deutschsprechenden in der Schweiz betrug 1990 4,37 Mio = 63,6% (1980: 4,14 Mio = 65%); französisch sprachen 1,3 Mio = 19,2%, italienisch 0,52 Mio = 7,6% und rätoromanisch 0,039 Mio = 0,58%.

Trotz des strengen Territorialprinzips, welches besagt, daß auf einem Gemeinde- oder Kantons(teil)gebiet nur eine Sprache als Schul- und Amtssprache gelten darf, sind besonders die Deutschschweizer Städte und Kantone nicht zu 100% deutschsprachig. In Basel-Stadt sprachen 1990 „nur" 78% deutsch, 2,7% französisch und 6,4% italienisch. Als Umgangssprache wird Französisch jedoch von 20% der Bevölkerung Basels angegeben, das Italienische als Umgangssprache (UGSp) mit 14,6%. Für den Kanton Baselland gelten folgende Zahlen: 86% Deutsch (1,7% Französisch [UGSp 18,7%]; 4,6% Italienisch [UGSp 12,3%]). Kanton Zürich: 82% Deutsch, 1,5% Französisch [UGSp 15,5%]; 5,8% Italienisch [UGSp 14,8%]. Auch die französischen Kantone sind nicht rein französischsprachig: in Genf geben nur 70% an, französisch zu sprechen; 5,4% deutsch [UGSp 12,9%]; 5,2% italienisch [UGSp 12,2%]. Selbst der Kanton Jura hat nur 87% französischsprachige Einwohner (deutsch sprechen: 4,7% [UGSp 14,6%]).

Interessant ist der Anteil des Englischen als „Umgangssprache" neben der Deutschschweizer Muttersprache: in Zürich 16,4%, in Basel-Stadt 15,3%, in Basselland 15,2%, in Zug (!) 15,7%, in Bern nur 10,4%, im Aargau 11,3%, im Waadtland 11,5% und in Genf 17%. Gesamtschweizerisch wurde 1990 das Englische als mögliche Umgangssprache mit 11% angegeben (vgl. auch Kap. 6). Die fremden wie auch einheimischen sprachlichen Minderheiten haben kein Anrecht auf öffentlichen Unterricht in ihrer Sprache oder Berücksichtigung bei den Ämtern und Behörden, wenngleich sie doch Anlaß sind für eine funktionale Zweisprachigkeit im öffentlichen Bereich.

Der hohe Anteil an italienischsprachigen Einwohnern in der Deutschschweiz wird durch die dauernde Anwesenheit italienischer Gastarbeiter begründet. Die „Gäste" profitieren noch vom Privileg, eine der Schweizer Landessprachen zu sprechen.

Der Anteil der Dialektsprecher unter der deutschsprachigen Bevölkerung der Schweiz wurde 1990 mit 96% angegeben. Umgekehrt gaben 66,4% der Deutschschweizer an, überhaupt nie hochdeutsch, sondern immer nur schweizerdeutsch zu sprechen. In den welschen, d. h. französischsprachigen Kantonen liegt der Anteil der Dialektsprechenden unter den deutschsprachigen Einwohnern nur bei etwa 50%. Dies kommt daher, daß in den französischen Kantonen und im Tessin unter den Deutschsprachigen sehr viele Bundesdeutsche sind, die aus beruflichen Gründen dort wohnen oder ihren Alterssitz aufgeschlagen haben (Tessin). In den Westschweizer Kantonen liegt der *Patois*-Anteil zum Vergleich bei 2% und im Tessin der *dialetto* bei 17,5%. Neben den schon genannten sprachlichen Minderheiten sind in der Schweiz noch folgende Sprachen mit meßbaren Sprecheranteilen vertreten: Englisch 0,06 Mio = 0,88%; Spanisch 0,116 Mio = 1,7%; Portugiesisch 0,093 Mio = 1,36%; Slavische Sprachen 0,12 Mio = 1,86%; Türkisch 0,061 Mio = 0,89%.

Aus der Statistik geht hervor, daß das Deutsche, d. h. der Deutschschweizer Dialekt, gesamtschweizerisch betrachtet eine dominante Rolle sowohl gegenüber den anderssprachigen Landesteilen als auch gegenüber den gleichsprachigen ausländischen Nachbarn spielt. Trotz der sprachlichen Vielfalt der Schweiz wird das Schweizerdeutsch von außen wie von innen als das beherrschende Sprachmerkmal der Gesamtschweiz angesehen.

5. Soziolinguistische Lage

Der soziolektale Charakter der in Kontakt stehenden Sprachen in der Deutschschweiz ist einerseits bestimmt durch den binnenländischen Kontakt des Deutschen mit den übrigen Landessprachen (Französisch, Italienisch, Rätoromanisch) und auf der anderen Seite durch die Kontakte mit dem gleichsprachigen Ausland (vgl. Löffler 1994 a).

Die Kontaktprobleme, welche die anderssprachigen Landsleute und die gleichsprachigen Ausländer mit dem Schweizerdeutschen haben, sind weniger von der Varianz innerhalb des Schweizerdeutschen als vielmehr von der sogenannten Diglossie verursacht.

Es ist ein soziolinguistisches Merkmal der deutschen Schweiz, daß im Gebrauch von Dialekt und Schriftsprache (Diglossie) vordergründig keine sozialen Unterschiede festzustellen sind. Der Direktor und der Arbeiter reden gleichermaßen Dialekt und verwenden beim Schreiben und in feierlicher Rede bzw. zum Sprechen mit Fremden die Schriftsprache. Zu dieser weitverbreiteten These gehört auch, daß kein soziales Gefälle zwischen den Sprachregionen besteht, und daß es auch bei den französischsprechenden Westschweizern keine durch sprachliche Unterschiede (Soziolekte) symbolisierten sozialen Hierarchien gibt. Das gilt in gleicher Weise auch für die italienischsprechenden Tessiner.

So wie die Tatsache des Dialektsprechens alle Deutschschweizer über jegliche sozialen Unterschiede hinweg verbindet, so überdeckt die Tatsache des Schweizerseins alle sprachlichen und sozialen Unterschiede zwischen Welschen, Tessinern, Rätoromanen und Deutschschweizern. Von dieser soziolektalen Neutralität der drei bzw. vier Landessprachen profitieren die italienischen Gastarbeiter, indem sie eine allseits geschätzte Landessprache beherrschen (s. auch oben Kap. 4).

In der Nordwestschweiz sind die elsässischen Büroangestellten und Verkäuferinnen aus dem benachbarten Frankreich wegen ihrer Mehrsprachigkeit (Elsässisch-Alemannisch; Französisch und Schriftdeutsch, teilweise auch Englisch) wohl angesehen. Sie vermitteln dem ausländischen Besucher den Eindruck, in der Deutschschweiz seien die meisten Leute mehrsprachig.

Wie aus der Rekrutenbefragung des Jahres 1985 (Schläpfer 1991) hervorgeht, bezeichnen sich nur gerade 3,4% der deutschen Rekruten, 9,3% der französischen, 8,4% der Tessiner und 17,7% der Rätoromanischsprechenden als mehrsprachig. Interessant ist, daß die Mehrsprachigkeit entlang der innerschweizerischen Sprachgrenze nicht besonders ausgeprägt ist. Mehrsprachigkeit ist unter geographischem Gesichtspunkt eher in städtischen Gebieten anzutreffen (Schläpfer 1991, 19).

Die binnenländische Mehrsprachigkeit ist in der Schweiz weder eine Folge der Sprachpolitik noch an eine soziale Hierarchie gebunden. Die Verteilung der Sprachen und Varietäten richtet sich in der Regel nach praktisch-kommunikativen Bedürfnissen. Diese werden gesteuert von der Mobilität, der Sprachloyalität und dem gegenseitigen Ansehen bzw. der Wertschätzung der Landessprachen untereinander.

Die Rekrutenbefragung aus dem Jahre 1985 und Zusatzerhebungen bei Schweizerbürgern und -bürgerinnen zu den „Sprachen in der Schweiz" kann hierzu einige soziolinguistisch interessante Angaben beisteuern (Schläpfer 1991): die persönliche Mobilität zwischen den Sprachregionen ist bei den befragten jungen Leuten unterschiedlich ausgeprägt: in der französischen Schweiz leben über 10% Deutschschweizer; in der Deutschschweiz aber nur 1,9% Westschweizer. Im italienischen Tessin leben 12,3% Deutschschweizer, in der Deutschschweiz nur 1,1% Tessiner. Was die Sprachloyalität betrifft, so wurde folgendes festgestellt: die Deutschschweizer zeigen die stärkste Sprachloyalität gegenüber ihrem Wohnort − wohl auf Grund des lokalen Dialekts. Die Westschweizer fühlen sich eher dem Sprachgebiet zugehörig, die Tessiner hingegen mehr dem italienischen Kulturraum. Die Deutschschweizer andererseits fühlen sich am wenigsten mit dem gesamtdeutschen Kulturraum verbunden. Eine Folge davon ist, daß hochdeutschsprechende Personen in der Deutschschweiz nicht in sehr hohem Ansehen stehen, obwohl sie eigentlich die am weitesten verbreitete Landessprache Deutsch sprechen. Da sie aber nicht das typische Erkennungsmerkmal der Deutschschweizer besitzen, nämlich die mediale Diglossie Dialekt − Schriftsprache, gelten sie eher als sprachliche Außenseiter. An der Spitze der Sozialpyramide sind jedoch Ausnahmen zu beobachten: der Professor, der Theaterintendant oder der Spitzentrainer dürfen hochdeutsch sprechen. Die vom Amt und der Funktion verlangte Autorität wird durch die H-Varietät (*high-level-language*, vgl. Löffler 1994, 79f) Hochdeutsch oder Standardsprache positiv verstärkt.

Während die Deutschschweizer ohne weiteres in der Westschweiz oder im Tessin wohnen möchten, gilt dies nicht ebenso für die Welschen und Tessiner. Die Tessiner könnten sich hingegen gut in der Westschweiz vorstellen, die Westschweizer eigentlich eher nur bei sich zu Hause oder allenfalls im Tessin. In der gegenseitigen Wertschätzung finden sich die Deutschschweizer in einer einseitigen Sympathiebeziehung zu ihren welschen und italienischen Landsleuten: 80% der Deutschschweizer finden die Welschen und Tessiner sympathisch, die Westschweizer hingegen tun dies den Deutschschweizern gegenüber nur mit 47%, die Tessiner gar nur mit 39%.

Zur Frage einer Kommunikationssprache mit anderssprachigen Landsleuten (*lingua franca* oder Ausgleichssprache) wurde folgendes ermittelt: die Deutschschweizer sprechen mit den Welschen gerne französisch (48%), mit den Tessinern aber nur zu 17% italienisch, zu 42% hingegen schweizerdeutsch. Mit den Rätoromanen sprechen alle anderen die eigene Sprache oder haben gar keine Kontakte. Die Westschweizer sprechen mit den Deutschschweizern lieber französisch, d. h. ihre eigene Sprache (47%) und mit den Tessinern ebenfalls (51%). Die Tessiner sprechen mit den Deutschschweizern zu 46% deutsch, mit den Westschweizern zu 77% französisch. Dies paßt zu der Tatsache, daß die Deutsch- und Westschweizer des Italienischen eben nur zu einem geringen Teil mächtig sind.

Die Deutschschweizer hegen also nicht nur Sympathie gegenüber den Westschweizern, sie gehen auch auf deren Sprache ein. Noch mehr tun dies gezwungenermaßen die Tessiner, die mit anderen Landsleuten kaum einmal die eigene Sprache sprechen können. Die Westschweizer hingegen sind ihrer Sprache am meisten treu, nur zu 30% bzw. 14% geben sie an, mit andern deutsch bzw. italienisch zu reden. Für den Fall, daß der andere die eigene Sprache nicht versteht, würden die Deutschschweizer zu 53% französisch, zu 27% italienisch parlieren bzw. zu 21 oder 27% englisch. Die Westschweizer würden auch zu 57% deutsch, zu 24% italienisch oder notfalls zu 11 bzw. 18% englisch reden. Die Italiener möchten zu 50% deutsch, zu 88% französisch, nicht aber englisch (!) reden.

Auch hier ergibt sich für die Deutschschweizer wiederum die größte Flexibilität, insbesondere wenn auch das Englische mitberücksichtigt wird. Zur Beliebtheit und Verbreitung des Englischen mag neben einem allgemeinen Trend noch die Tatsache beitragen, daß seit der Zeit des Zweiten Weltkrieges die Spielfilme in den Schweizer Kinos im allgemeinen nicht synchronisiert sind. Die Filme werden in der Originalsprache mit Untertiteln gezeigt. Hierdurch entsteht eine positive Einstellung gegenüber den fremden Sprachen, insbesondere auch dem Englischen. Gleichzeitig wird aber auch die Aversion gegen die binnendeutsche Umgangssprache genährt, die in der (bundes)deutschen Filmsynchronisationssprache eine besonders unsympathische Variante zeigt, in der alle wenig geschätzten Unarten des „preußischen" Jargons vorkommen.

6. Sprachpolitische Lage

In der Deutschschweiz gelten, basierend auf dem Artikel 116 der Bundesverfassung, dieselben sprachpolitischen Grundbedingungen wie in der gesamten Schweiz. Für die sprachliche Zugehörigkeit gilt das Territorialprinzip, das heißt: an einem Ort und in einer Gegend gilt jeweils nur eine Landessprache als offizielle Schul- und Amtssprache. Dadurch ist also das „Territorium" des Deutschen konstitutionell geschützt.

Der Verlauf der Sprachgrenze ist daher sehr scharf. Es gibt auf der einen Seite Gemeinden mit weit überwiegendem Anteil an Französischsprechenden und auf der andern Seite Gemeinden mit großer Mehrheit an Deutschsprachigen, aber keine allmählichen Übergänge. In den Jahren von 1950 bis 1980 ist entlang der Sprachgrenzen keine merkliche Bevölkerungsverschiebung festzustellen (Eidgenössisches Departement des Inneren 1989; Schläpfer 1991, 6—9).

Dank dem Territorialprinzip hat das Deutsche (als Schriftsprache und als Dialekt) keine eigentliche Konkurrenz durch eine der übrigen Landessprachen. Lediglich in den gemischtsprachigen Gemeinden Graubündens, wo Rätoromanisch als Amtssprache gilt, steht das Deutsche in direktem Wettstreit mit dem Rumantsch. Die romanischsprechende Bevölkerung ist jedoch ausnahmslos bilingue, d. h. zweisprachig. Dies gilt umgekehrt nicht für die deutschsprechende Bevölkerung Graubündens. Der Konkurrenzkampf zwischen Schweizerdeutsch und Rätoromanisch scheint zugunsten des Deutschen auszugehen. Es ist eine Frage der Zeit, bis die Zweisprachigkeit der Rätoromanen von einer deutschen Einsprachigkeit abgelöst wird. Intensive staatliche Fördermaßnahmen und die Einführung einer einheitlichen Schriftsprache werden diesen Prozeß nicht aufhalten, sondern nur verzögern (→ Art. 230). In einigen Parlamenten ist Schriftdeutsch noch offizielle Geschäfts- und Verhandlungssprache, so im National- und Ständerat (Bundesparlament) in Bern und besonders in den zweisprachigen Kantonsparlamenten von Bern, Fribourg und dem Wallis. In andern Parlamenten wie z. B. in Basel-Stadt wird Schriftdeutsch neben dem Schweizerdeutschen als Option gewahrt.

Als Schulsprache ist in der Deutschschweiz nach kantonalen Gesetzen und Verordnungen das Schriftdeutsche vorgesehen. Nur die manuellen und musischen Fächer sind davon ausgenommen. In Wirklichkeit wird jedoch auch in den Kern- und Sprachfächern ein Großteil des Unterrichts auf Schweizerdeutsch abgehalten. Die Diglossie ist auch in der Schule so etabliert, daß die Schriftsprache sich mehr und mehr auf das Schreiben und das Lesen von Geschriebenem beschränkt.

Für die Schulfremdsprachen gilt gesamtschweizerisch die Regelung, daß als erste Fremdsprache jeweils die „zweite Landessprache" noch vor dem Englischen zu erlernen sei. 85% der deutschen Rekruten geben an, Französisch gelernt zu haben, die Westschweizer ihrerseits haben mit 83% Deutsch gelernt, die Italiener im Tessin zu 71% Deutsch und 95% Französisch. Das Deutsche und Französische nehmen unter den „zweiten Landessprachen" in der Schule also einen gleichen Rang ein. Hingegen wird Italienisch in der Deutschschweiz nur mit 14%, in der Westschweiz nur mit 9% als Schulfremdsprache gelernt. Englisch wird in allen Landesteilen von 40 bis 55% der Jungen als Schulfremdsprache gelernt (Schläpfer 1991, 14).

Die Verwendung von Schweizerdeutsch und Schriftdeutsch in den Medien ist nicht gesetzlich geregelt. In der Praxis wird in allen Printmedien (Zeitungen) ausnahmslos Schriftdeutsch geschrieben. In Radio und Fernsehen wird die Sprachwahl den Redaktoren und Moderatoren überlassen. Lokalradios verwenden verständlicherweise das lokale Idiom (Orts- oder Regionaldialekt). Beim „Landessender" Radio DRS ist man nach einer Periode fast ausschließlicher Dialektalität seit kurzem wieder vermehrt zur Schriftsprache zurückgekehrt. Im Kulturprogramm von DRS 2 wird seit 1991 wieder Schriftdeutsch verwendet (Neue Zürcher Zeitung vom 16.8.1993).

7. Sprachkontakte, Kontaktsprachen

Wie bei der soziolinguistischen Charakterisierung müssen auch die kontaktsprachlichen Phänomene selbst wiederum unterschieden werden in solche, die sich entlang der sprachlichen Außengrenzen bilden und in solche, die sich im Landesinnern durch funktionale Kontakte ergeben.

Die Sprachkontakt-Phänomene an der Sprach-Außengrenze gegen Deutschland resultieren aus dem Aufeinandertreffen zweier unterschiedlicher Sprachverwendungszonen (s. „pragmatische Sprachgrenze": R. Ris 1979): die Verwendung von Dialekt und Hochsprache ist in der Deutschschweiz und im badischen Nachbarland unterschiedlich verteilt. Insbesondere gibt es in Deutschland die zwischen Hochsprache und Mundart angesiedelte Umgangssprache (Löffler 1988; Löffler 1988 a). Diese hat in der Schweiz keine Entsprechung und wird deshalb als typisch deutsch empfunden und wenig geschätzt (s. auch Kap. 5).

Ein anderes Kontaktphänomen in der Deutschschweiz ist ebenfalls auf der pragmatischen Ebene angesiedelt. Es besteht gegenüber den deutschen Nachbarn eine Unsicherheit in der Verwendung von Schriftsprache und Dialekt. Es ist nicht gewiß, welches sprachliche Register der deutschen Umgangssprache (vgl. Löffler 1987, 80 ff) auf Deutschschweizer Seite entspricht. Die Folge ist, daß man in Situationen noch immer Hochdeutsch redet, wo in Deutschland schon längst die Umgangssprache adäquat wäre.

Ein weiteres geographisches Kontaktphänomen entsteht durch die Einstrahlung der deutschen Medien Radio und Fernsehen in einen breiten Grenzgürtel der deutschen Schweiz. Dieses Faktum ist älter als die durch den Satelliten-Empfang neuerdings geöffneten Kommunikationsgrenzen. Dies führt bei vielen Deutschschweizern, auch bei Kindern und Jugendlichen, zu einer passiven Kompetenz gegenüber der gesprochenen Hochsprache (Umgangssprache) oder dem Moderatorendeutsch der Jugendmusiksendungen von SWF 3 und „Schwarzwaldradio". Dies macht sich beim Lese- und Schreibunterricht in der Primarschule als Vorteil bemerkbar. Ein drittes (spiegelverkehrtes) Kontaktphänomen sind die Helvetismen in der Deutschschweiz. Darunter versteht man Wörter und Wendungen des Schweizerhochdeutschen, die nur in der Schweiz gelten und somit typisch sind für die Deutschschweizer Variante der deutschen Standardsprache. Es sind terminologisch gesehen keine eigentlichen Substandards, sondern regionale Varianten der deutschen Standardnorm. Ein Musterbeispiel hierfür sind die französischen Fremdwörter im Bahn- und Postwesen: *Perron, Kondukteur, Coupé, Billet, Coupon, Chargé*, etc. Gegenüber den bundesdeutschen Staatsbetrieben kommt hier eine sprachliche und administrative Selbständigkeit zum Ausdruck.

Eine sprachliche Untersuchung der amtlichen Telefon- und Kursbücher in den ehemals vier deutschsprachigen Ländern Bundesrepublik, DDR, Österreich und Schweiz vom Jahre 1985 hatte ergeben, daß die beiden damaligen deutschen Staaten und Österreich zusammen eine weitgehende post- und bahnterminologische Gemeinschaft bilden, die Schweizer Telefon- und Kursbücher hingegen viersprachig abgefaßt sind (deutsch, französisch, italienisch und englisch) und im deutschen Teil einen von den andern Ländern abweichenden Sprachgebrauch zeigen (Löffler 1987, 112 ff).

Bei einem Teil der Helvetismen im Schweizerhochdeutschen liegt der Grund in der schweizerischen Verfassungswirklichkeit und den Formen der Demokratie und des Parlamentarismus (*Referendumsdemokratie, Volksinitiative, Initiativbegehren, fakultatives Referendum, Volksrechte, Stimmbürger, Souverän, föderalistisch* usw.: vgl. Meyer 1989). Eine wichtige binnenkommunikative Funkton vieler Helvetismen liegt darin, daß sie ohne Übersetzung in den andern Sprachen verstehbar sind: z. B. *Velo* (statt Fahrrad), *Pneu* (statt Auto-Reifen), *Garage* (statt Werkstatt), *Car* (für Bus), *Referendum, Alpentransversale, PTT, Telecom, Swissnet, Swissmetro, Detaillierungsgrad* und viele andere. So ist auch das Suffix *-ation (Deklaration, Identifikation, Personifikation)* häufiger als das deutsche *-ierung (Deklarierung, Identifizierung, Personifizierung)*, weil die Entsprechungen in den beiden andern Sprachen (Frz. und It.) ebenfalls auf *-ation* oder *-azione* gehen.

Der sprachliche Kontakt zur Westschweiz entlang der Sprachgrenze ist minimal. Er führt auf keiner Seite, also auch nicht in der Deutschschweiz, zu einer Mehrsprachigkeit, eher zur Bereitschaft der Deutschschweizer, mit den Westschweizern Schulfranzösisch zu sprechen. Die Möglichkeit, in einem Welschlandjahr das Schweizerfranzösisch zu erlernen, bis vor einigen Jahren noch sehr beliebt für junge Deutschschweizerinnen, ist aus der Mode gekommen. Begegnungen auf Gemeinde- oder Schulebene haben eher Seltenheitswert und gleichen, wenn sie einmal stattfinden, in ihrem Charakter den Städtepartnerschaften oder Schüleraustauschprogrammen, wie sie sonst zwischen verschiedensprachigen Ländern organisiert werden (Lüdi/Py 1991). Ein weiteres Kontaktphänomen indirekter Art sind die gegenseitigen Exonyme. Darunter versteht man nicht so sehr die Doppelbenennungen von größeren Ortschaften durch deren Bewohner selbst: Biel/Bienne, Fribourg/Freiburg, sondern das Phänomen, daß Orte und Städte von außen, also vom andern Sprachgebiet her, anders benannt werden als von den Einheimischen: vgl. *Mailand — Milano; Venedig — Venezia, Rom — Roma* usw. In der Schweiz haben fast alle größeren Orte landesübliche Exonyme: *Délémont* heißt deutsch *Delsberg*, *Basel* französisch *Bâle* und italienisch *Basilea*, *Genève* deutsch *Genf* und italienisch *Ginevra*, *Zürich* französisch *Zurich* und italienisch *Zurigo*.

In geringerem Maße gilt dies auch für Ortsnamen im Tessin: *Bellenz* wäre die deutsche Version für *Bellinzona*, doch werden die deutschen Exonyme im Tessin kaum gebraucht, hingegen in umgekehrter Richtung sehr wohl: *Basilea, Ginevra, Zurigo*. Auch im Rätoromanischen tragen viele Orte neben dem heimischen Namen noch Exonyme, z. B. rätoromanisch *Mustér* — „deutsch" *Disentis* — oder: *Müstair* — deutsch: *Münster*.

Exonymische Doppelnamigkeit ist ein sehr altes Phänomen der „Sprachen im Kontakt" und läßt vielerlei Rückschlüsse zu auf extralinguistische Verhältnisse wie alte Stammes- und Siedlungsgrenzen, Verkehrsräume, Bevölkerungsanteile, Wirtschaftsverhältnisse u. a. (Sonderegger 1983 und 1991).

Zum Rätoromanischen hin gibt es im übrigen keine scharfe Sprachgrenze. Die Kontaktphänomene sind daher auch eigener Natur. Alle Rätoromanischsprechenden beherrschen neuerdings (seit etwa 1950) auch Schweizerdeutsch (Bündnerisch), nicht jedoch umgekehrt (s. oben Kap. 5). Nur im Namenbereich gefällt sich die Deutschschweizer Gesellschaft darin, neben den schon genannten Exonymen auch die exotisch-heimeligen Original-Namen wie *Ftan, S-chanf, S-charl, Segl* (für dt. *Sils Maria*) oder *Schlarigna* (für dt. *Celerina*) zu gebrauchen (vgl. Löffler 1987a und 1988b, 166f). Das klingt exquisit, und gleichzeitig wird der Eindruck erweckt, man täte etwas für die rätoromanische Sprache, die es vor dem Untergang zu retten gilt. So führt auch das Radio DRS (= „Radio der deutschen und rätoromanischen Schweiz") diese Minderheitensprache nicht nur im Titel, sondern nimmt sich auch im Programm ihrer an. Und viele Deutschschweizer behaupten, Rätoromanisch einigermaßen zu verstehen, wenn im Deutschschweizer Fernsehprogramm das Wort zum Sonntag mit „cars spectaturs" eingeleitet wird. Im übrigen zeigen die Rekrutenbefragungen, daß man zu rätoromanisch-sprechenden Landsleuten keine Kontakte pflegt, so daß eigentliche Kontaktphänomene über die angedeuteten hinaus nicht auftreten (s. oben Kap.5).

Eine andere binnenländische Sprachkontaktfolge, die sich aus der Mehrsprachigkeit des Landes ergibt, aber nicht zu den Sprachgrenzphänomenen gehört, ist die Dreisprachigkeit im öffentlichen Bereich oder bei sprach-überregionalen Institutionen z. B. bei der Bahn (SBB), bei der Post (PTT), den Großbanken oder bei landesweit arbeitenden Großverteilern (Migros, Coop, und anderen Warenhausketten). So sind die meisten Warenpackungen dreisprachig beschriftet: *Milch — lait — latte; Käse — fromage — formaggio* oder *Butterzopf — Tresse au beurre — Treccia al burro; Heringfilets in Tomatensauce — Filet de hareng en sauce tomate — Filetti d'aringa in salsa di pomodoro* und ermöglichen tägliche Sprachkurse am Eßtisch. Daß Gebrauchsanleitungen für technische Geräte mehrsprachig abgefaßt sind, ebenso wie die Beipackzettel bei Medikamenten, mag zwar neuerdings auch für nichtschweizerische Verbraucher im europäischen Rahmen nichts besonderes mehr sein. In der Schweiz hat dies im institutionellen und direktiven Bereich jedoch bereits eine längere Tradition und führt zu einer eingeschränkten passiven Mehrsprachigkeit bei den Verbrauchern.

Im öffentlichen Bereich des Rechts und der Verordnungen wirkt sich die Mehrsprachigkeit in der Weise aus, daß bundesweit geltende Texte in jeder Sprache so verfaßt sein müssen, daß sie formal und inhaltlich identisch sind. In der Praxis geht man so vor, daß man eine meist deutsche oder auch französische Muster-Vorlage erstellt, von der aus man sinngleiche Übersetzungen in die jeweils anderen Sprachen anfertigt. Dies ist der Grund, weshalb die deutsche Rechtsprache in der Schweiz nur in eingeschränktem Maße die Merkmale der binnendeutschen Verwaltungssprache (Nominalismen, Funktionsverbgefüge, komplizierte Satzkonstruktionen) zeigt. Die deutsche Rechtsprache in der Schweiz wirkt dank dem Zwang zur adäquaten Übersetzbarkeit in zwei andere Sprachen einfacher und klarer als in Deutschland.

Die Folge der mehrsprachigen Öffentlichkeit, die weniger aus den grenznahen Kontakten resultiert als vielmehr auf einer gemeinsamen mehrsprachigen Verfassungswirklichkeit beruht, führt zu einem allgemeinen innergesellschaftlichen Sprachausgleich. Auf die deutsche Schweiz bezogen ist folgendes festzustellen: (1) Die Deutschschweizer sind in bezug auf die zweite Landessprache Französisch und auf das Englische als *lingua franca* relativ mobil. (2) Das Schweizerhochdeutsche – eigentlich eine Variante der gesamtdeutschen Standardsprache – hat unter allen regionalen Subvarianten des Deutschen (gemeint sind das österreichische oder bayerische Hochdeutsch) das auffälligste Eigengepräge. (3) Die zunehmende Distanz zur gesprochenen Standardsprache in Deutschland wird kommunikativ kompensiert durch die überdurchschnittliche Kompetenz in zwei anderen Weltsprachen, dem Französischen und dem Englischen.

Als ein negatives Kontaktphänomen zwischen der Deutschschweiz und der Westschweiz kann die Tatsache angesehen werden, daß in der Westschweiz in der Schule das Schriftdeutsche nach (bundes)deutschen Lehrbüchern als zweite Landessprache gelernt wird. Man lernt also nicht die Umgangsvariante der zweiten Landessprache, das wäre nämlich Schweizerdeutsch, sondern die Weltsprachen-Variante „Standarddeutsch". Dies führt zwar zu einem verminderten Kontakt mit den Deutschschweizer Nachbarn, hält hingegen die kommunikative Türe zu einer Welt- und Kultursprache offen.

Die Kontakte zwischen den Sprachen in der Schweiz sind also gerade so intensiv wie nötig, um die gemeinsamen Verfassungsstrukturen auszufüllen. Sie sind angesichts der institutionellen oder offiziellen Vierschigkeit jedoch andererseits gering und spiegeln damit die verfassungsgemäße Autonomie von Kantonen und Gemeinden wider, die zu einem Teil auf Unvergleichlichkeit der politischen Einheiten, d. h. im Grunde auf Kontaktlosigkeit beruht.

Es sind die vielfältigen Anziehungs- und Abstoßungskräfte, die einen Gleichgewichtszustand herbeiführen, der den Zusammenhalt von Unvergleichlichem garantiert und den Gedanken eines sprachlich bedingten Separatismus oder Anschlusses an den jeweils größeren Sprachnachbarn eigentlich verhindert.

8. Kritische Wertung der verwendeten Quellen

Quellen für die Statistik und Demographie sind die Auswertungen der Volkszählungen, die einen relativ hohen Gültigkeitsgrad haben, wenngleich man mit nur gerade zwei Fragen (nach der Muttersprache und der Umgangssprache) auskommen mußte (Bundesamt für Statistik 1993).

Eine wichtige und in ihrer Art kaum zu wiederholende Datenbeschaffungsaktion war die Rekrutenbefragung vom Jahre 1985 (Schläpfer 1991). Hier wurden mit einem detaillierten Fragebogen die Sprachlichkeit, das Sprachgefühl und die Identitäts- und Loyalitätsprobleme eines ganzen männlichen Jahrgangs erhoben und ausgewertet.

Neben diesen harten Daten gibt es im Zusammenhang mit dem Thema „Viersprachige Schweiz" auch einige Mythen: so z. B., daß alle Schweizer einander mehr oder weniger verstehen, wenn sie in ihrer Muttersprache reden, oder daß die Deutschweizer alle Variationen des Schweizerdeutschen ohne weiteres verstehen, daß über 70% der Deutschschweizer angeblich französisch können – oder daß der größte Teil der Schweizer zwei- oder gar dreisprachig sei. Auch wenn man die Sprachwirklichkeit dieser Mythen entkleidet, bleibt für die Besonderheit der Schweizer Sprach- und Sprachkontaktverhältnisse noch recht viel Interessantes übrig. Daß die Deutschschweiz dabei in der Mitte steht, hat nicht nur geographische, sondern vor allem auch historische Gründe.

9. Bibliographie (in Auswahl)

Bickel, Hans/Schläpfer, Robert (Eds.) (1994): *Mehrsprachigkeit – eine Herausforderung.* Aarau/Frankfurt a. M./Salzburg.

Bundesamt für Statistik (Ed.) (1993): *Pressemitteilung 31/93. Neue Vielfalt der Sprachen und Konfessionen in der Schweiz.* Bern.

Bundesamt für Statistik (Ed.) (1993): *Statistisches Jahrbuch der Schweiz 1994.* Zürich.

Eidgenössisches Departement des Inneren (Ed.) (1989): *Materialienband zum Schlußbericht der Arbeitsgruppe zur Revision von Artikel 116 der Bundesverfassung.* Bern.

Löffler, Heinrich (1987): Landesgrenze als Sprachgrenze im alemannischen Dreiländereck. In: *Sprachspiegel 43,* 73–81 und 109–115.

Löffler, Heinrich (1987a): „Official Standardization and Actual Usage of Place Names in a Trilingual Country such as Switzerland". In: *Logos 1/2*

(1985), Windhoek, Namibia, 121–125 (Third Congress of the Names Society of Southern Africa, Windhoek 1985).

Löffler, Heinrich (1988): „Gemeinsame Sprache in unterschiedlichem Gebrauch. Zum Verhältnis Dialekt-Standardsprache im Badischen und in der Schweiz". In: *L'Allemand en Alsace. Die deutsche Sprache im Elsaß.* Actes du Colloque de Strasbourg des 28–30 novembre 1985 réunis par Adrien Finck et Marthe Philipp, Straßburg, 111–126.

Löffler, Heinrich (1988a): „Dialekt – Schule – Öffentlichkeit im alemannischen Sprachgebiet". In: *Die historische Landschaft zwischen Lech und Vogesen. Forschungen und Fragen zur gesamtalemannischen Geschichte*, Pankraz, F./Sick, W.D. (Eds.), Augsburg, 187–202.

Löffler, Heinrich (1988b): „Names and Regional resp. National Identity in a Plurilingual Country such as Switzerland" (4th Congress of the Names Society of Southern Africa, Stellenbosch Sept. 1987). In: *Nomina Africana Vol. 2 No. 1*, 159–170.

Löffler, Heinrich (1994): *Germanistische Soziolinguistik*. 2. Aufl. Berlin.

Löffler, Heinrich (1994a): „Zur Sprachsituation in der Schweiz". In: *Germanistische Mitteilungen (Brüssel) 39*, 75–92.

Lüdi, Georges/Py, Bernard (1991): *Binnenwanderung und Sprachkontakte in der Schweiz. Vom Wechseln der Sprache und vom Sprechen darüber.* Basel.

Meyer, Kurt (1989): *Wie sagt man in der Schweiz? Wörterbuch der Schweizerischen Besonderheiten.* Mannheim.

Ris, Roland (1979): „Dialekte und Einheitssprache in der deutschen Schweiz". In: *International Journal of the Sociology of Language 21*, 41–61.

Sonderegger, Stefan (1983): „Grundsätzliches zum Methodischen zur namengeschichtlichen Interferenzforschung". In: *Zwischen den Sprachen*, Haubrichs, W./Ramge, H. (Eds.), Saarbrücken, 25–57.

Sonderegger, Stefan (1991): „Die Schweiz als Sprachgrenzland. Eine historisch-typologische Standortbestimmung". In: *Zeitschrift für Literaturwissenschaft und Linguistik 83*, 13–39.

Schläpfer, Robert (1991): *Sprachen in der Schweiz.* Basel.

Heinrich Löffler, Basel (Schweiz)

228. Suisse romande

1. Géographie et démographie
2. Histoire territoriale et formation de la Confédération helvétique
3. Economie et culture
4. Langues en contact
5. Situation sociolinguistique
6. Droit et politique linguistiques en Suisse romande
7. Références, discussions, approches contradictoires
8. Bibliographie (sélective)

1. Géographie et démographie

1.1. On appelle Suisse romande (SR) la partie du territoire de la Confédération helvétique où la langue française jouit du statut de langue officielle. Ce territoire qui forme un espace continu n'est pas régi par une structure politique propre (voir fig. 228.1). Il est composé de 4 cantons entièrement francophones (Genève, Jura [à l'exception de la commune germanophone d'Ederswiler], Neuchâtel, Vaud) et s'étend également sur 3 autres cantons (Berne, Fribourg, Valais) qui comportent une partie francophone à côté d'une partie germanophone. De ces derniers, Fribourg et Valais, sont majoritaires francophones à ⅔, tandis que dans Berne, la partie francophone ne représente que 6–7% de la population du canton. A cet espace institutionnellement monolingue il convient d'ajouter un territoire officiellement bilingue: il s'agit du district de Bienne (Berne), situé sur la limite linguistique et qui comporte deux communes: Biel/Bienne et Evilard/Leubringen avec un pourcentage francophone d'environ 40% sur un total de 55 000 habitants.

Dans l'ensemble, la population francophone résidant en Suisse romande s'élève à près de 1,5 million de personnes, ainsi réparties par cantons: Vaud 36%, Genève 21%, Valais 12%, Fribourg 11%, Neuchâtel 11%, Jura 5%, Berne 4% (→ carte linguistique O).

1.2. On voit d'emblée apparaître un trait significatif de la distribution géographique du français en Suisse: il n'y a de contiguïté qu'avec le territoire germanophone, au détriment de voisinages avec les autres langues latines de Suisse: italien, rhéto-roman (Camartin 1985). Cette situation, qui est la conséquence lointaine de la coupure du territoire lati-

228. Suisse romande

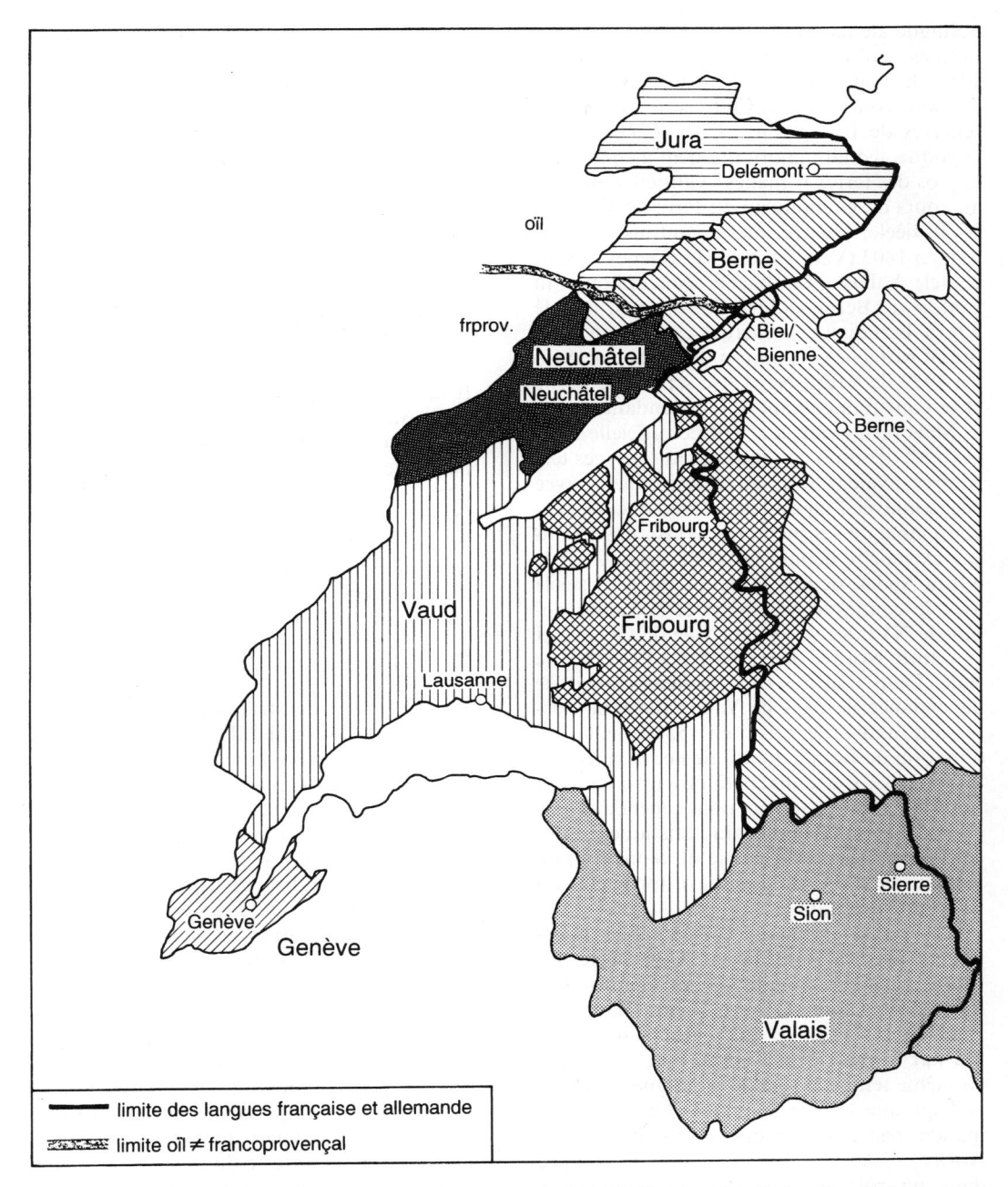

Fig. 228.1: Géographie des cantons de la Suisse romande (avec indication des limites linguistiques entre français et allemand et entre langue d'oïl et francoprovençal).

nophone par l'arrivée des Alamans à la fin de l'Empire romain, va renforcer la position privilégiée du contact linguistique français-allemand/alémanique, déjà très forte en raison du poids démographique majoritaire à plus de ⅔ de l'allemand en Suisse.

2. Histoire territoriale et formation de la Confédération helvétique

2.1. Depuis 1291, date de sa fondation, jusqu'à la fin de l'Ancien Régime, la Confédération suisse était une entité pratiquement monolingue alémanique. Des sept cantons mentionnés, seul Fribourg en faisait partie depuis 1481. Il avait prêté main forte à Berne lors de son conflit avec Charles le Téméraire (guerres de Bourgogne 1474−1477). Mais à l'époque, il était majoritairement alémanique, le gros des terres romanes ayant été annexées au cours de la conquête du Pays de Vaud au XVIe siècle. Quatre autres cantons y entrèrent en 1803 (Vaud) et en 1815 (Genève, Neuchâtel, Valais). La partie francophone du canton de Berne («Jura Sud», aussi appelé «Jura bernois») et l'actuel canton du Jura furent rattachés au canton de Berne en 1815. En 1979, le «Jura Nord» se sépara de Berne et se constitua en canton indépendant.

Mais bien avant leur entrée officielle dans la Confédération en tant que cantons, ces territoires avaient tous eu certains liens avec elle, soit avec l'un ou l'autre, soit encore avec l'ensemble de ses membres. Ainsi, des alliances existaient depuis le XIVe siècle avec le «Jura Sud», depuis le début du XVe siècle avec le comté de Neuchâtel et le Valais, depuis le XVIe siècle avec la ville de Genève et le «Jura Nord» dépendant de l'Evêché de Bâle. Dans d'autres cas, les liens étaient de dépendance: le pays de Vaud, ancienne possession savoyarde, passa en 1536 sous la domination de Berne, dont il demeura sujet jusqu'en 1798. Cette diversité et leur commune tradition 'française' ne doit cependant pas cacher une importante caractéristique: toutes ces terres avaient fait partie du Saint Empire Romain et n'ont donc jamais appartenu au Royaume de France.

Des bouleversements considérables intervinrent avec la Réforme au XVIe siècle. La future Suisse romande devint majoritairement protestante (Genève, «Jura bernois», Neuchâtel, Vaud), ce qui renforça son identité par rapport à la France, mais consolida en même temps le rôle de la langue française en tant que langue standard. La Suisse romande restée catholique (Fribourg, «Jura Nord», Valais) se vit désormais cantonnée dans un rôle mineur, tout en conservant, dans le cas de Fribourg et Valais, des affinités politiques non négligeables avec la partie de la Suisse alémanique qui était restée catholique.

A l'époque napoléonienne, enfin, la Suisse romande connut, comme le reste de la Suisse, la période la plus agitée de son histoire. Alors que le pays tout entier était satellisé par la France, certains de ses territoires, comme le Jura Nord et Sud, Genève et le Valais se virent même annexés à la France et ne recouvrèrent leur indépendance qu'avec la chute du Premier Empire.

2.2. A cette histoire politique relativement riche correspond une histoire linguistique peu mouvementée (Haas 1985). La configuration du domaine linguistique a en effet peu changé au cours des siècles. Quelques zones anciennement romanes ont été germanisées (rive gauche du Lac de Bienne [Berne], région de Morat [Fribourg], distr. de Loèche [Valais]), mais le domaine roman a également regagné du terrain qu'il avait perdu (Valais central). Il faut aussi souligner que ni la domination bernoise sur le Pays de Vaud pendant plus de deux siècles et demi, ni le statut de principauté de Prusse de Neuchâtel pendant plus d'un siècle (1707−1815) n'eurent de conséquences linguistiques: aussi bien Berne que la Prusse étaient culturellement francophiles et ne tentèrent à aucun moment de germaniser ces provinces.

3. Economie et culture

3.1. L'absence de structures administratives propres à la SR rend difficile l'observation de 'son' activité économique et financière. Les statistiques sont cantonales et fédérales et ne reflètent que partiellement une vie économique 'romande'. Certaines inégalités entre régions linguistiques sont cependant dues en premier lieu à la disproportion géographique et démographique entre des minorités latines numériquement faibles et une majorité alémanique très consistante.

Depuis les années 70, le discours minoritaire romand, autrefois occupé principalement par la défense de la langue et de la culture française, s'est emparé du domaine économique en mettant vigoureusement en cause l'attitude 'impérialiste' des milieux économiques alémaniques, accusés de volonté de domination sur le reste du pays. Ce n'est pas la distribution du revenu national par tête, très équilibré entre la Suisse romande et la Suisse alémanique, qui est la cause principale du mécontentement, mais bien plus la dépendance incontestable de l'économie romande des centres de décision alémaniques. Ainsi, sur les 100 premières sociétés ayant leur siège en Suisse en 1993, 83 sont domiciliées en Suisse alémanique et seulement 16 en Suisse romande (Büchi 1993). Par ailleurs, Zurich contrôle en Suisse romande 736 entreprises avec plus de 15 000 employés, tandis que la Suisse romande ne contrôle à Zurich que 195 entreprises avec moins de 4 500 employés. La vulnérabilité de l'économie romande apparaît assez nettement à travers les taux comparés de chômage, avec une moyenne romande de 7% contre 3,5% en Suisse alémanique.

Une très nette spécificité romande dans la géographie des attitudes s'est manifestée à propos de l'intégration européenne. Le vote de 1992 sur l'adhésion à l'« Espace économique européen » a été très significatif à cet égard. Alors que les Romands ont voté massivement en faveur de l'adhésion, le vote majoritairement négatif des Alémaniques a fait capoter la ratification, même si l'antagonisme entre les communautés linguistiques est nuancé par le vote positif des principales villes alémaniques.

Ces frustrations sont aggravées par l'impuissance avec laquelle les Romands assistent au renforcement d'un obstacle déjà ancien à la communication avec la majorité. D'un poids plus lourd que la limite des langues elle-même pèse aujourd'hui la frontière pragmatique entre une Suisse alémanique qui cultive ses dialectes et une Suisse romande attachée au culte du 'bon français'. Un contraste qui est devenu un véritable contentieux à la suite de la récente expansion de l'usage du dialecte alémanique dans des domaines qui restaient traditionnellement réservés à l'allemand standard (surtout dans la radio et la télévision).

3.2. Mais dans le domaine de l'éducation et de la culture, la Suisse romande est loin d'occuper le rôle de parent pauvre. Sur un total de 8 Universités, 3 sont entièrement romandes (Genève, Lausanne, Neuchâtel) et une quatrième (Fribourg) est bilingue allemand-français. Une des deux Ecoles polytechniques fédérales est romande (Lausanne) et une extension romande du Musée national actuellement concentré à Zurich est en préparation.

Son paysage médiatique n'est pas non plus celui d'une province délaissée. Deux chaînes nationales de radio (RSR 1 et 2) et une chaîne nationale de télévision (TSR) bénéficient d'une clé de répartition des redevances très favorable. La presse écrite, très enracinée dans les traditions locales et cantonales, disposait, jusqu'à il y a peu de temps, de plusieurs dizaines de titres de quotidiens. Des concentrations récentes en ont réduit le nombre, mais il reste plus d'une douzaine d'organes à audience cantonale et pluri-cantonale.

Ce n'est qu'en 1991 qu'a été lancé le premier quotidien sans étiquette cantonale avec une claire ambition d'atteindre le public romand dans son ensemble.

La présence, sur un marché relativement restreint, de nombreuses maisons d'édition témoigne d'une longue tradition d'activité dans ce secteur. Faute de rentabilité suffisante, elles deviennent cependant de plus en plus dépendantes de subventions.

4. Langues en contact

4.1. En Suisse romande, le monolinguisme de fait, même dans les cantons à cheval sur le français et l'allemand, a été une constante tout au long de l'histoire et l'est encore largement aujourd'hui. Les relations entre les citoyens des cantons romands (ou les collectivités publiques romandes) et l'administration fédérale se déroulent en français. Cet unilinguisme francophone peut d'ailleurs compter sur d'ardents partisans. Par exemple, les modestes projets d'enseignement bilingue qui se font jour ici et là le long de la frontière linguistique doivent faire face à de fortes résistances: toute officialisation d'une autre langue — même nationale comme l'allemand — est perçue par beaucoup de gens comme une atteinte au moins virtuelle d'une part à la position du français en Suisse (on craint un rétrécissement du territoire francophone), d'autre part à l'identité culturelle de la Suisse romande (au *Romandie*) (cette identité repose donc largement, dans cette optique, sur la préservation de l'unilinguisme francophone). La réalité se distingue toutefois très nettement de l'officialité et des représentations collectives.

4.1.1. D'abord, à l'échelle géographique de la fin du XXe siècle, le territoire de la Suisse romande est si petit qu'il est difficile d'y vivre et d'y travailler sans traverser plus ou moins régulièrement des frontières linguistiques. Si Genève (la ville située le plus à l'ouest de la Suisse romande) n'est qu'à trois heures de train de Zurich (la capitale économique du pays), le trajet Lausanne—Berne dure une heure dix, et Neuchâtel n'est qu'à une heure et demie de Bâle. A l'échelle d'un grand pays européen, Neuchâtel pourrait être la banlieue de Berne. Trois villes sont bilingues: Bienne/Biel, Fribourg/Freiburg et Sierre/Siders. Dans l'ensemble, les contacts entre francophones et germanophones sont donc relativement fréquents. Il est vrai qu'il est plus facile pour un francophone de s'exprimer dans sa propre langue lorsqu'il se trouve à Berne ou à Bâle que pour un germanophone d'utiliser sa langue à Genève ou Neuchâtel: les Alémaniques ont la réputation d'être plus ouverts à l'apprentissage du français que l'inverse. Par ailleurs, l'allemand standard enseigné dans les écoles est fort différent des dialectes alémaniques omniprésents dans la communication orale, et n'est donc que partiellement utile aux Romands qui se déplacent en Suisse alémanique.

4.1.2. Ensuite, les données fournies par l'Office fédéral de la statistique (basées sur le recensement fédéral de 1990) montrent que la population de la Romandie est loin de présenter l'homogénéité linguistique qu'on a l'habitude de lui reconnaître. C'est ainsi que la proportion de personnes qui se déclarent francophones varie entre 70,4% et 87,8% selon les cantons. C'est dire qu'entre 12,2% et 29,6% des habitants de ces régions ne considèrent pas le français comme leur première langue.

4.1.3. Il faut aussi tenir compte qu'une partie importante de la population romande est plurilingue. Beaucoup de personnes, tout en se considérant comme francophones (en ce sens qu'elles considèrent le français comme leur langue première du point de vue des usages qu'elles en font) pratiquent régulièrement une langue autre que le français. C'est le cas en particulier des immigrés de deuxième ou troisième génération.

Les trois villes bilingues constituent un cas spécial en ce sens que le français et l'allemand y cohabitent dans la vie quotidienne. Cette situation ne soulève pas de difficultés particulières (Kolde 1981, Windisch 1992). A Bienne, les francophones constituent 30,7% de la population, à Fribourg 58,4% et à Sierre 67,7%.

4.2. Les langues (autres que le français) les plus parlées sont l'allemand (Al), l'italien (I), l'espagnol (E), le portugais (P), les langues slaves (S) et l'anglais (An). On constate que l'allemand est considéré comme langue première par 2,5 à 14% de la population des régions officiellement francophones (on trouvera des précisions dans le tableau récapitulatif ci-dessous). Pour l'italien, les chiffres varient entre 1,3 et 5,3%, pour l'espagnol entre 1,1 et 5,4%, pour le portugais entre 1,3 et 4,8%, pour les langues slaves entre 0,5 et 1,2% et pour l'anglais entre 0,2 et 3,3%.

Une remarque enfin sur le romanche. Cette langue, bien que nationale, est très peu représentée: sa part n'atteint 1% dans aucun des cantons romands.

Tableau 228.1: Distribution, pour 1990, des principales langues déclarées premières en pourcentage. Ces chiffres prennent en compte les cantons unilingues (Genève, Neuchâtel, Vaud) et les régions francophones des cantons bilingues (Berne, Fribourg, Valais; à l'exclusion des villes bilingues Bienne, Fribourg et Sierre).

	F	Al	I	E	P	S	An
Berne	77,2	14,0	3,9	1,5	1,3	0,5	0,3
Fribourg	84,6	7,2	1,3	1,1	3,2	0,6	0,4
Genève	70,4	5,5	5,3	5,4	4,8	1,2	3,3
Jura	87,8	4,8	2,5	2,2	0,8	0,5	0,2
Neuchâtel	80,2	5,2	4,8	2,0	4,5	0,5	0,8
Vaud	77,1	6,0	4,4	3,4	3,5	1,1	1,8
Valais	77,7	2,5	3,8	1,9	4,8	1,0	1,0

Dans l'interprétation de ces chiffres, il est important de tenir compte du fait que, en vertu du principe de territorialité des langues, les enfants des familles d'origine allophone sont systématiquement scolarisés en français et que cette langue devient rapidement principale pour beaucoup d'entre eux. Plus généralement, une partie importante des personnes qui déclarent le français comme langue première utilisent par ailleurs d'autres langues dans leur vie quotidienne. Par exemple, une étude partielle (Lüdi/Py 1993) montre qu'en ville de Neuchâtel 6% des habitants déclarent que l'allemand est leur langue principale; cependant 11% l'utilisent en famille et 10% sur leur lieu de travail. Neuchâtel ne constituant pas un cas particulier d'un point de vue sociolinguistique, on peut en conclure que l'importance quantitative des contacts de langues est sensiblement plus grande que ne le laissent penser les chiffres présentés dans le tableau ci-dessus.

4.3. Avant la diffusion du français comme langue de conversation, les habitants employaient (comme c'est le cas aujourd'hui encore en Suisse alémanique) des dialectes — de type francoprovençal pour Fribourg, Genève,

« Jura Sud » (district de Neuveville), Neuchâtel, Valais et Vaud, et de type oïlique pour le « Jura Nord » et les deux autres districts du « Jura Sud ».

Vu la distance linguistique non négligeable entre ces dialectes (ou patois) et le français, consolidée par l'absence de toute forme de continuum, des phénomènes de contact entre systèmes différents se sont produits constamment pendant toute la période de transition où le français a progressivement absorbé des domaines auparavant réservés aux dialectes, soit pendant la phase de bilinguisme patois/français qui a duré du XVIIe jusqu'à la première moitié du XXe siècle. Ce processus a laissé de nombreuses traces aussi bien dans la substance du français que des patois. Alors que ces derniers ont été massivement francisés au cours de la dernière phase de leur emploi (Marzys 1971), le français a emprunté aux dialectes une série de traits phonétiques, morpho-syntaxiques et surtout lexicaux. En phonétique, on peut noter la prononciation du suffixe -ée [e:j] comme dans *coulée* [kule:j] avec la conservation de la longueur vocalique due au patois [kola:jə]. Un exemple morpho-syntaxique d'origine dialectale se trouve dans l'emploi de *vouloir* comme auxiliaire du futur: *il veut pleuvoir* 'il va pleuvoir'. Parmi les nombreux dialectalismes du lexique, un exemple frappant est fourni par *chotte* n. f., 'abri', du patois ['ʃɔta], avec un épaississement du S- latin initial (SŬSTA) qui ne se produit qu'en patois.

Mais en dépit de la différence des substrats dialectaux – francoprovençal et oïlique – on n'observe pas de différences marquées entre un français régional du domaine d'oïl et un français régional de type francoprovençal.

En revanche, c'est l'intensité des contacts historiques entre le Jura (Sud et Nord) et la Suisse alémanique qui a donné au français régional jurassien un profil spécifique, caractérisé par l'importance relative des germanismes lexicaux, et dû à l'existence d'un bilinguisme non négligeable au cours des 150 dernières années. Ils sont souvent très faciles à identifier grâce à la conservation de groupes consonantiques initiaux inadmissibles en français standard: *schneuquer* 'fouiller', *schmoutser* 'embrasser', etc.

Globalement, l'influence de l'adstrat germanique a été traditionnellement surévaluée pour la Suisse romande, comme d'ailleurs en Belgique et au Canada. De nombreux dialectalismes ont été pris pour des emprunts à l'allemand, comme *il est loin* pour 'il est parti', qui ne vient pas de l'allemand *er ist weg*, mais en patois [l ɜ vja]. C'est aussi le cas d'archaïsmes français comme *lui aider* qui ne vient pas de *ihm helfen*. Car les spécificités du français en Suisse romande ne sauraient être mises seulement sur le compte des interférences, que ce soit avec le substrat ou avec l'adstrat. Les écarts sont également dus aux nombreux archaïsmes conservés, ainsi qu'à un nombre relativement restreint d'innovations.

Dans l'ensemble, le français de Suisse romande ne se distingue pas fondamentalement de celui qui est parlé en France ou en Belgique (Knecht 1985). Comme dans ces pays, le respect des normes académiques est d'ailleurs considéré très généralement comme une marque essentielle de culture et de distinction, encore qu'il semble régner une certaine ambiguïté dans les attitudes des Romands face aux régionalismes (Bayard/Jolivet 1984, Singy 1989, De Pietro 1995, Lüdi/Py 1993).

5. Situation sociolinguistique

5.1. Parmi les langues autres que le français, il convient d'abord de distinguer d'une part les langues nationales (allemand, italien et romanche), d'autre part les langues étrangères. Les langues nationales ont par définition un statut privilégié. Cette distinction est toutefois assez formelle, surtout s'agissant du romanche. En fait, seul l'allemand en bénéficie d'une certaine manière, et jusqu'à un certain point seulement: son enseignement est obligatoire dans l'ensemble des différents systèmes scolaires romands. Sa connaissance est un atout professionnel dans la mesure où la vie économique ne connaît guère les frontières linguistiques internes. Beaucoup d'offres d'emploi exigent une certaine connaissance de l'allemand. Dans les rencontres de travail réunissant des personnes issues de régions linguistiques différentes, l'usage veut que chacun s'exprime dans sa propre langue et fasse l'effort de comprendre celle des autres. Cet usage vaut cependant plus pour le français et l'allemand que pour l'italien. En revanche, les enfants germanophones établis en Suisse romande ne jouissent pas de cours spéciaux de langue et de culture allemandes – et ceci contrairement aux immigrés de langue italienne, espagnole, et portugaise entre autres. Mais au moins, les germanophones et italophones ont accès aux médias alémaniques et tessinois (journaux, radio, télévision), ce qui signifie qu'ils reçoivent, s'ils le désirent, des informations dans leur langue sur ce qui se passe en Suisse. Enfin, ils peuvent utiliser leur langue pour communiquer avec les représentants de l'administration fédérale à Berne et pour prendre connaissance des documents officiels d'origine fédérale. En revanche, la communication avec les administrations et autres institutions cantonales et communales (si importante dans un pays fédéraliste comme la Suisse) se fait obligatoirement en français.

5.2. Une seconde distinction doit être établie entre, d'une part, les langues utilisées au sein de communautés immigrées dotées d'une organisation assise sur des traditions relativement anciennes, et, d'autre part, les langues introduites plus récemment, représentées par des locuteurs réalisant des séjours plus brefs, parfois au gré des événements politiques des pays d'origine, ou plus simplement pour des raisons professionnelles. Le premier groupe est représenté par l'allemand, l'italien, l'espagnol et (dans une moindre mesure) le portugais. Les usagers de ces langues connaissent une vie associative assez riche, développent des activités culturelles, politiques, syndicales ou religieuses, envoient leurs enfants à des cours de langue et culture organisés dans le cadre des écoles locales par l'ambassade de leur pays d'origine (à l'exception notable et paradoxale des germanophones). Les élèves qui préparent le baccalauréat peuvent choisir l'italien ou (dans certains établissements) l'espagnol comme seconde langue étrangère (après l'allemand, qui est toujours obligatoire). Le second groupe contient l'ensemble des autres langues.

5.3. Il est encore possible de classer les langues autres que le français en fonction des chances qu'elles ont de pouvoir être utilisées dans la communication entre Romands et alloglottes. Si l'on prend comme critère de diffusion les programmes scolaires, l'allemand occupe en principe la première place puisque son enseignement est obligatoire dans toutes les filières scolaires. Tout Romand est censé posséder des connaissances d'allemand au moins élémentaires. L'anglais est, lui aussi, bien placé. Même si son apprentissage n'est pas obligatoire, une très grande partie de la population scolaire en a acquis des connaissances. En Suisse comme ailleurs, la musique anglo-saxonne joue un rôle important dans la diffusion et le prestige de cette langue (Murphy 1990). L'italien et surtout l'espagnol ne sont enseignés qu'à une minorité d'élèves. Le portugais et les langues slaves ne figurent pas dans les programmes scolaires, sinon de façon très marginale.

5.4. Dans une situation de contact, le statut d'une langue dépend aussi des attitudes dont elle est l'objet de la part des groupes sociaux utilisant d'autres langues. Une étude partielle a été réalisée sur ce thème auprès de lycéens neuchâtelois (Apothéloz/Bysaeth 1981). Les sujets devaient évaluer un groupe de langues au moyen d'adjectifs portant sur trois aspects: esthétique, utilité et accessibilité de ces langues. C'est l'anglais qui est le mieux évalué, et ceci sous les trois aspects. L'allemand standard est apprécié sur le seul plan de l'utilité. L'italien et l'espagnol sont bien considérés sous les aspects de l'esthétique et de l'accessibilité. Le dialecte alémanique obtient de mauvais résultats sous les trois aspects. Il serait cependant imprudent de généraliser ces conclusions à l'ensemble des régions et des groupes sociaux constituant la Romandie.

5.5. Le statut social des membres des différents groupes linguistiques permet aussi de situer les langues les unes par rapport aux autres. L'italien, l'espagnol et le portugais sont avant tout les langues de l'immigration ouvrière. L'allemand n'est pas marqué socialement et se retrouve dans toutes les couches de la population. En revanche, les anglophones sont souvent des cadres d'entreprises étrangères ou des fonctionnaires internationaux. Par ailleurs, comme le reste de la Suisse et de l'Europe, la Suisse romande accueille depuis quelques années — avec un statut de demandeurs d'asile — un nombre relativement important de locuteurs de langues très diverses. Cette population est par nature instable, et les langues représentées varient fortement dans le temps.

6. Droit et politique linguistiques en Suisse romande

6.1. Les constitutions des cantons entièrement francophones Genève, Neuchâtel et Vaud restent silencieuses sur l'usage du français comme seule langue officielle. C'est un fait considéré comme allant de soi. Seule la constitution de la jeune République et Canton du Jura de 1977 précise que le français y est 'langue nationale et officielle' (art. 3).

6.2. Dans les trois cantons partiellement francophones Berne, Fribourg et Valais, la question linguistique est réglée de manière diverse. La constitution de Berne reconnaît l'allemand et le français comme 'langues nationales', fixe la géographie de leur emploi officiel, notamment le français pour les trois districts du 'Jura bernois' et l'allemand et le français pour le district de Bienne (art. 6), tout en garantissant 'la liberté de la langue' (art. 15). Dans Fribourg, la constitution reconnaît également le principe de territorialité (art. 21), tandis que la constitution du Valais ne prescrit que 'l'égalité de traitement entre les deux langues' dans 'la législation et dans l'administration' (art. 12). Bien que non spécifiée dans les textes, la territorialité des langues est pratiquement appliquée au Valais, où six districts sont considérés comme francophones. Mais grâce à son statut non contraignant, les villes de Sierre (proche de la limite des langues) et de Sion (en all. Sitten, capitale du canton) abritent chacune une école publique de langue allemande.

En revanche, dans Fribourg, le régime constitutionnel de la territorialité, non corrigé par une disposition sur l'existence de zones bilingues (comme dans Berne), conduit à la non-reconnaissance officielle des importantes minorités de langue allemande dans la ville de Fribourg et dans une série de petites communes situées dans les districts du Lac et de la Sarine, à l'ouest de la frontière linguistique officielle (Actes de l'Institut national genevois 1988).

6.3. De tout temps, le principe de territorialité avait paru être la seule garantie de protection pour les minorités linguistiques suisses. La Suisse romande en a tiré incontestablement des bénéfices en préservant un acquis qui aurait pu être menacé. Aussi, dans le débat parlementaire de 1993 sur une nouvelle version de l'article 116 de la Constitution fédérale concernant les langues, les représentants de la Suisse romande ont-ils plaidé majoritairement pour une mention explicite de ce principe qui jusqu'à maintenant relevait de la coutume.

7. Références, discussions, approches contradictoires

7.1 La plupart des travaux partent du principe que la Suisse romande est une région francophone unilingue et monoglossique, étant bien entendu que les anciens patois ne sont plus pratiqués que par une infime minorité de personnes. Dès lors la notion de contact de langue se réduit à deux problématiques:

7.1.1. La frontière linguistique. Les recherches se concentrent alors sur les déplacements historiques de la frontière entre français et allemand, dans une perspective géographique (Sonderegger 1966–1967) ou démographique.

7.1.2. L'influence de l'allemand sur le français parlé en Suisse romande. La chasse aux germanismes réels ou supposés est un passe-temps apprécié des personnes qui se targuent de parler *le bon français*.

7.2. Sans nécessairement s'écarter de la prémisse unilingue et monoglossique, d'autres travaux s'intéressent aux villes de Bienne, Fribourg et Sierre, dans lesquelles le bilinguisme français-allemand est un fait social reconnu (Kolde 1981, Windisch 1992).

7.3. La diffusion des langues parlées par les immigrés arrivés massivement en Suisse dans les années soixante a d'abord été appréhendée comme un obstacle à l'intégration sociale et scolaire. La tâche des enseignants et des chercheurs a consisté dès lors à créer des moyens pédagogiques permettant aux immigrés (et surtout à leurs enfants) d'apprendre le mieux possible le français. Ce n'est que dans un deuxième temps que la langue d'origine des immigrés, en même temps que leur culture, a été prise en considération (Gretler et al. 1981) et que, du même coup, leur situation sociolinguistique a été pensée en terme de bilinguisme (Lüdi/Py 1986).

7.4. Une autre approche consiste à étudier le bilinguisme des personnes qui franchissent la frontière linguistique entre la Suisse romande et la Suisse alémanique. Dans la mesure où ces personnes, bien qu'établies à Bâle, Berne ou Zurich, ont gardé des liens étroits avec leur langue et leur région d'origine, leur situation fait en effet partie du phénomène général des contacts de langues (Lüdi/Py 1993).

8. Bibliographie (sélective)

Actes de l'Institut national genevois (1988): *Mois suisse. Les rapports entre les différentes communautés linguistiques de quelques cantons plurilingues Fri-*

bourg – *Valais* – *Tessin* – *Grisons. 4 cantons* – *4 conférences-débats*, Genève.

Apothéloz, Denis/Bysaeth, Léo (1981): «Attitudes linguistiques. Résultat d'une enquête». In: *Travaux neuchâtelois de linguistique 2*, 60–90.

Bayard, Catherine/Jolivet, Rémi (1984): «Les Vaudois devant la norme». In: *Le Français moderne 3–4*, 151–158.

Le bilinguisme dans le canton de Berne. Une enquête auprès des politiciens bernois (1992): Brigue–Berne, Centre universitaire de recherche sur le plurilinguisme.

Le bilinguisme dans le canton du Valais. Une enquête auprès des politiciens valaisans (1992): Brigue–Berne, Centre universitaire de recherche sur le plurilinguisme.

Büchi, Christophe (1993): «Der Geisterjet – eine Phantasie». In: *Neue Zürcher Zeitung, Folio*, n° 8.

Camartin, Iso (1985): «Les relations entre les quatre régions linguistiques». In: Schläpfer, R. (Ed.) *La Suisse aux quatre langues*, Genève 251–292.

Département fédéral de l'Intérieur (1989): *Le quadrilinguisme en Suisse – présent et futur*, Berne.

De Pietro, Jean-François (1995): «Francophone ou Romand? Qualité de la langue et identité linguistique en situation minoritaire». In: Eloy, J.-M. (Ed.), *La qualité de la langue? Le cas du français*, 223–250.

Gretler, Armin et al. (1981): *Etre migrant*, Berne.

Haas, Walter (1985): «Histoire linguistique de la Suisse»: In: Schläpfer, R. (Ed.), *La Suisse aux quatre langues*, Genève 21–64.

Haas, Walter (1988): «Schweiz». In: *Sociolinguistics/Soziolinguistik*. Ammon, U./Dittmar, N./Mattheier, K. (Eds.), Berlin/New York, vol. 2, 1365–1382.

Knecht, Pierre (1985): «La Suisse romande». In: *La Suisse aux quatre langues*, Schläpfer, R. (Ed.), 125–169.

Kolde, Gottfried (1981): *Sprachkontakte in gemischtsprachigen Städten*, Wiesbaden.

Lüdi, Georges/Py, Bernard (1986): *Etre bilingue*, Berne.

Lüdi, Georges/Py, Bernard (1993): *Changement de langage, langage du changement. Aspects linguistiques de la migration interne en Suisse*, Lausanne.

Marzys, Zygmunt (1971): «Les emprunts au français dans les patois». In: *Actes du Colloque de dialectologie francoprovençale, Neuchâtel, 23–27 septembre 1969*, Marzys, Z. (Ed.), Neuchâtel/Genève, 173–188.

Murphy, Tim (1990): *Song and music in language learning. An analysis of pop song lyrics and the use of song and music in teaching English to speakers of other languages*, Berne.

Singy, Pascal (1989): «Français régional et fonction comme signum social». In: *Bulletin de la Section de Linguistique de la Faculté des Lettres de l'Université de Lausanne* 10, 17–102.

Sonderegger, Stefan (1966–1967): «Die Ausbildung der deutsch-romanischen Sprachgrenze in der Schweiz im Mittelalter». In: *Rheinische Vierteljahresblätter 31*, 223–290.

Windisch, Uli et al. (1992): *Les relations quotidiennes entre Romands et Suisses allemands: Les cantons bilingues de Fribourg et du Valais*, Lausanne.

Pierre Knecht/Bernard Py, Neuchâtel (Suisse)

229. Suisse italienne

1. Géographie et démographie
2. Histoire et formation du Canton du Tessin
3. Politique, économie et situation culturelle
4. Statistiques
5. Situation sociolinguistique
6. Etat de la politique linguistique
7. Portrait général des contacts linguistiques
8. Bibliographie (sélective)

1. Géographie et démographie

La «République et Canton du Tessin», dénomination officielle du canton méridional de la Suisse, compte (selon le recensement fédéral de 1990) environ 280 000 habitants, dont 83% sont de langue et de culture italienne. Sur le plan de la vie quotidienne et au vu de la problématique envisagée ici, il n'est pas sans intérêt de noter que l'organisation spatiale est caractérisée par les courtes distances à parcourir pour rejoindre les centres des principales régions adjacentes comme Milan (à 70 kilomètres de Lugano), ou Zurich (à 200 kilomètres de Bellinzona, chef-lieu du canton).

Le tableau démographique est caractérisé par un taux de croissance naturelle oscillant autour de 0% (1980–1990). L'accroissement de la population est dû essentiellement à l'immigration.

2. Histoire et formation du Canton du Tessin

2.1. Histoire

En restreignant l'histoire tessinoise à quelques dates fondamentales pour l'évolution de la langue et de ses contacts, il faut mentionner l'année 1803, qui marque l'entrée du Tessin dans la Confédération suisse, l'année 1884, quand le Tessin se distancie de la Lombardie en devenant diocèse autonome, et 1882, année de l'achèvement du tunnel du Saint-Gothard, permettant le rapprochement du Tessin et de la Suisse alémanique, avec des conséquences considérables sur la mobilité de la population.

Les premiers contacts du Tessin avec ses voisins du Nord commencent à se produire dès le XVe siècle (Bianconi 1989, Lurati 1992a, 147−148). Après une longue appartenance à la Lombardie, à partir de 1512 le Tessin se trouve dans le champ de gravitation de la ligue des cantons suisses (période des bailliages, 1513−1798), pour devenir enfin canton indépendant (1798) avec les révolutions de la fin du XVIIIe siècle. Mais l'impact sur la langue de cette « administration » gérée par les « landfogti » (= *Landvögte*) suisses est, tout compte fait, négligeable, vu qu'il ne s'agissait ni d'une occupation militaire ni d'une vraie domination. Le Tessin continuait à s'orienter vers les modèles lombards et rien ne permet de supposer la formation d'une conscience communautaire suisse-italienne (Lurati 1992a, 152−153, 157). Il faudra attendre jusque vers 1840 pour avoir, avec la publication de *La Svizzera Italiana* de Stefano Franscini, une sorte de sanction officielle de la particularité identitaire de la Suisse italienne, que ce soit par rapport à la Lombardie ou par rapport au reste de la Confédération helvétique.

2.2. Le quadrilinguisme suisse: un modèle à revoir?

La Suisse, un modèle d'un Etat plurilingue et pluriculturel? L'égalité des langues nationales étant garantie par la Constitution au moins depuis 1938, les élections des représentants au gouvernement helvétique devant tenir compte non pas exclusivement des couleurs politiques, mais également de la provenance culturelle et linguistique des candidats, le respect du plurilinguisme helvétique paraît en effet un pilier fondamental à la préservation de la cohésion nationale.

Qu'en est-il du point de vue de la Suisse italienne, « politiquement minoritaire en Suisse et culturellement marginale par rapport à l'Italie » (telle est la description que l'on trouve souvent dans des prises de position tessinoises)? Qu'en est-il de ces « fossés linguistiques » proclamés régulièrement par les médias? D'où provient le grand nombre de motions et d'initiatives promues au sein du parlement suisse visant à la protection ou à la promotion des minorités linguistiques? Le fait que l'on soit en train depuis quelques années de travailler à la révision de l'article 116 de la Constitution qui sert de base à la politique linguistique helvétique, est de toute façon un indice assez clair d'un certain malaise, ressenti surtout par les minorités. Les petits groupes linguistiques ne semblent plus longtemps disposés à soutenir le lieu commun d'une Suisse quadrilingue, qui en réalité ne renvoie à rien d'autre qu'à la simple reconnaissance juridique de quatre langues nationales. En tenant compte des forces réelles des langues présentes sur le territoire helvétique, seuls l'allemand et le français peuvent prétendre au statut de « langues complètes ». A côté du romanche, inexistant sur le plan national, à l'italien a été réservée l'étiquette de la « cosa a metà », de la chose à moitié (Dipartimento federale dell'interno 1989, 270); cf. également le titre provocateur de H. R. Dörig/Ch. Reichenau (éd. 1982), *2½-sprachige Schweiz*, Disentis (→ carte linguistique O).

3. Politique, économie et situation culturelle

Les dernières décennies du XIXe siècle sont marquées − entre autres à cause de l'ouverture du Gothard, de la politique centraliste de la Confédération et de la création d'une frontière douanière vers le sud − par un éloignement majeur envers la Lombardie, et par l'établissement de liens plus étroits sur les plans politique, économique et social avec la Confédération suisse. C'est dans ce contexte historique de passage, de recherche d'une identité propre, que se pose pour la première fois le problème d'une identité linguistique et culturelle.

Le mouvement vers la Confédération se précise pendant la première moitié du XXe siècle pour déboucher, dans les années cinquante et surtout les années soixante, sur une transformation accélérée qui touchera tous les secteurs de la vie quotidienne tessinoise. Les transformations rapides dans l'économie ne restent pas sans conséquences sur la démographie et des domaines tels que les attitudes et les mentalités. Aujourd'hui, le Tessin se veut «région ouverte», que ce soit vers le reste de la Suisse, vers l'Italie, ou l'Europe. Pourtant, cette ouverture déclarée dans des publications récentes telles que *Il Ticino regione aperta* (Ratti et al. 1990), *Ticino, Svizzera, Europa* (Fidinam 1991), n'est pas exempte d'une certaine crainte de perdre sa propre identité. Minorité depuis toujours, le Tessin vit donc de très près les tensions qui peuvent se créer entre l'universalisation ou uniformisation planétaire (selon le point de vue) de la vie quotidienne et la volonté de préserver une identité régionale particulière. Dans ce cadre forcément dynamique et contradictoire, certes difficile et parfois douloureux pour ceux qui y vivent, entre ouverture et conservation, entre minorité menacée (p. ex. par la prétendue germanisation du Tessin) et communauté cosmopolite (p. ex. à travers des manifestations culturelles comme le festival international du film à Locarno), il n'est pas surprenant de trouver, comme réponse à l'ouverture européenne prônée par les hommes politiques, les intellectuels et les milieux économiques, un refus très clair du Tessin de voter l'adhésion à l'espace économique européen (61,5% de non, 38,5% de oui). Voici le commentaire du *Corriere del Ticino*, le jour suivant les votations (7. 12. 1992): «On craignait de devenir moins Suisses et d'être plus insérés dans la réalité italienne».

Les contradictions se poursuivent également au niveau des analyses. Ratti et al. (1990, 17) témoignent d'un certain optimisme et d'une très grande confiance dans les possibilités du Tessin: «Accettata la sfida della modernità (...) spariscono gli atteggiamenti di chiusura, non si chiede più allo Stato di provvedere alla difesa etnica o linguistica». Ailleurs, dans le rapport sur le quadrilinguisme suisse rédigé par un groupe d'experts en vue de la révision de l'article constitutionnel sur les langues (Dipartimento federale dell'interno 1989, 248−254), on continue à signaler une culture régionale en difficulté et une langue italienne, tout compte fait, en position subalterne et pas toujours sur un pied d'égalité par rapport aux autres langues de la Confédération.

4. Statistiques

Sur le plan national, les Suisses italiens reçoivent l'appui de nombreux immigrés italiens, ce qui fait que les italophones représentaient en 1990 7,6% de la population résidant en Suisse. Les oscillations dans les chiffres concernant les italophones en Suisse sont dues au flux migratoire. Si l'on ne considère que la population suisse, les quatre groupes linguistiques se révèlent assez stables; pour les statistiques concernant la distribution des langues dans tout le territoire suisse → art. 226.

En regardant de plus près la présence des langues dans la réalité tessinoise, les données pour 1990 se présentent de la manière suivante: italien 82,8% (83,9% en 1980), allemand 9,8% (11,1%), français 1,9% (1,9%), romanche 0,1% (0,2%), langues autres que nationales 5,4% (2,9%) (Office fédéral de la statistique 1993).

Avec 280 000 habitants, le Tessin ne constitue que 4% de la population résidant en Suisse. Se trouvant donc en nette position minoritaire, il est certes remarquable que la Confédération suisse ait réussi à faire respecter et à protéger sur le plan juridique et institutionnel ce nombre restreint de locuteurs italophones. Rappelons seulement que la Suisse italienne possède une des trois chaînes de télévision suisses et une station radiophonique (avec trois programmes). Même si la cohabitation linguistique ne sort pas indemne de certaines tensions et de quelques malentendus, la paix linguistique n'a jamais été mise en cause.

Les quatre vallées des Grisons de langue italienne représentent un cas particulier. Si la Mesolcina et le val Calanca peuvent profiter de leurs contacts avec le Tessin, le val Poschiavo et la Bregaglia se trouvent topographiquement isolés soit par rapport aux Grisons soit par rapport au Tessin. Presque tous les journaux distribués étant en allemand, et les jeunes étant pratiquement obligés de quitter la vallée et d'aller à Coire ou dans d'autres régions germanophones pour leur formation scolaire et professionnelle, la population italophone du val Poschiavo et de la Bregaglia vit une forte pression économique et culturelle germanophone. Pour la Bregaglia, le dernier recensement confirme clairement une évolution en cours depuis longtemps, à savoir la régression progressive de l'italien, processus soutenu par toute une série de facteurs tels que l'émigration de la main d'œuvre, la dénatalité, le vieillissement de la population, la faiblesse économique. Menacées depuis toujours, il n'est pas surprenant que ces communautés aient développé une forte tendance vers une politique linguistique « interventionniste » et parfois puriste; pour des exemples cf. Lurati (1989 a, 167).

5. Situation sociolinguistique

5.1. La cohabitation entre les groupes linguistiques

Du point de vue de la Suisse italienne, le débat sur la cohabitation entre les différents groupes linguistiques s'aligne traditionnellement sur les rapports avec la Suisse alémanique. Les points principaux sont d'un côté la pression exercée par l'allemand en tant que langue dominante dans la vie publique confédérale, et de l'autre la présence non éphémère de germanophones au Tessin. Quant à ce dernier aspect, des analyses plus attentives des influences des communautés germanophones sur l'italien aboutissent à des conclusions moins dramatiques et plus souples que dans le passé. La grande majorité des germanophones (monolingues) résidant au Tessin sont des retraités, ou des personnes peu désireuses de participer à la vie économique et culturelle tessinoise. Leur impact linguistique est donc beaucoup moins fort que ce à quoi on pourrait s'attendre en ne tenant compte que des chiffres statistiques bruts. Si l'italien recule devant l'allemand, c'est avant tout là où l'on cède aux besoins et aux lois de l'économie et du tourisme de masse. Ajoutons que depuis le recensement de 1980 la présence germanophone a diminué de 1,3%.

De nouvelles recherches ont permis d'affiner nos connaissances sur les communautés plurilingues. C'est ainsi que Windisch (1992) a réussi à démontrer de façon convaincante que le long des frontières linguistiques (franco-allemandes), c'est-à-dire dans les régions traditionnellement bilingues, la coexistence entre les différents groupes est vécue de façon pragmatique et peu problématique. Windisch (1992, 2. 502): « En premier lieu, il faut rappeler l'énorme fossé entre la mise en scène médiatique de quelques situations conflictuelles dans une ou deux communes et le grand nombre de communes qui ont trouvé des modalités originales et particulièrement intéressantes pour gérer quotidiennement les relations intercommunautaires, mais dont on ne parle pour ainsi dire jamais ». Le malaise souvent signalé semble donc dans la plupart des cas un sentiment alimenté par ceux qui ne sont guère concernés directement et n'est donc pas exempt d'une certaine idéologie conservatrice.

De même, le recensement de 1990 contraint à revoir nos vues concernant la germanisation du Tessin. La plupart des germanophones présents sur le territoire tessinois semblent effectivement être plurilingues, et seule une infime minorité (2−3% de toute la population tessinoise) parlerait exclusivement allemand. Des informations plus précises sur la diffusion du bilinguisme sont attendues de la part d'un groupe de chercheurs actuellement en train d'évaluer de plus près les données fournies pour la première fois par le dernier recensement populaire.

L'analyse la plus approfondie sur la prétendue germanisation linguistique du Tessin reste à l'état actuel de la recherche le travail résumé dans Berruto/Burger (1985). On y trouve confirmé que l'impact linguistique de la présence alloglotte germanophone est plutôt marginal. Il ressort que l'influence majeure de l'allemand sur l'italien est attribuable à des facteurs exogènes (Berruto/Burger 1985, 62), c'est-à-dire au fait de vivre dans un Etat fédéral plurilingue où la partie germanophone est nettement la plus dominante.

Les raisons de la prétendue germanisation du Tessin, qui pourtant continue à préoccuper les gens, sont donc moins à chercher dans la présence alloglotte sur le territoire tessinois que dans la situation particulière suisse, où la plupart des grands centres de décision, soit en politique, soit dans le secteur économique, sont situés en Suisse alémanique. A lire les dernières analyses (Ratti et al. 1990; Generali in Fidinam 1991, 89 ss.), cette situation a profondément changé dans les dernières années, le secteur tertiaire devenant de plus en plus indépendant face au reste de la Confédération. On commence par exemple à reconnaître une « culture bancaire tessinoise », avec un esprit sensiblement différent des entreprises mères situées de l'autre côté du Saint-Gothard. C'est d'ailleurs cet esprit particulier qui assurerait le succès des banques tessinoises auprès de leur clientèle, essentiellement italienne. Telle est la conclusion de la partie consacrée à l'économie dans Ratti et al. (1990, 160−270). Le modèle de ce qui a été appelé « economia a rimorchio » (c'est-à-dire dépendante de la Suisse alémanique) tend donc, au moins dans le troisième secteur, à être remplacé par des comportements plus autonomes et par une confiance croissante dans les particularités offertes par l'espace économique tessinois.

Bien que la germanisation soit à relativiser, que ce soit sur le plan quantitatif ou qualitatif, le rapport avec la Suisse alémanique et avec la langue allemande (et le dialecte suisse allemand) continue à donner lieu dans les médias (les linguistes sont généralement plus optimistes) à des discussions animées et des prises de positions plutôt polémiques. Un des problèmes est constitué par l'afflux des touristes (le plus souvent d'origine suisse), germanophones pour la plupart, et dont on déplore surtout l'arrogance, en ce sens qu'ils imposent l'usage de l'allemand et rechignent à s'adapter aux besoins communicatifs des indigènes italophones. Le tourisme de masse est d'ailleurs un phénomène peu propice à la rencontre des personnes et à l'échange culturel. Il contribue, au contraire, à alimenter des stéréotypes et des clichés sans aucune base historique; cf. les extraits d'interviews de jeunes Tessinois dans Ratti et al. (1990, 315—316). La situation ne change guère si l'on regarde de plus près ce que l'on aime définir comme Etat plurilingue et pluriculturel. Si, du côté de la majorité suisse-alémanique, les problèmes inhérents à cette cohabitation culturelle ne semblent guère perçus (à part peut-être une reconnaissance, à vrai dire superficielle, du «Roesti-Graben», terme qui postule un fossé culturel et linguistique entre la Suisse alémanique et la Suisse romande), les minorités sont évidemment beaucoup plus sensibles et n'hésitent pas à signaler ce qu'il y a de fallacieux dans le plurilinguisme et le pluriculturalisme helvétique. Ainsi Lurati (1989 a, 171): «Colpisce constatare quante difficoltà abbiano le diverse regioni a mettersi nella 'pelle' degli altri. Ogni regione culturale vive spesso ignorando praticamente le altre: è desolante vedere la mancanza di conoscenze reciproche: lacune prontamente colmate dagli eterostereotipi, dai pregiudizi. Le nostre quattro culture vivono gomito a gomito l'una accanto all'altra, non convivono. Al più vi è 'coesistenza pacifica', non certo convivenza. Si vive a compartimenti stagni, in una notevole non informazione e indifferenza verso quanto avviene fuori della propria regione».

5.2. Attitudes et identités

La question des langues en contact renvoie toujours à d'autres entités plus vastes, telle que l'identité culturelle régionale, définie en général négativement par rapport aux communautés adjacentes. En polarisant la multiplicité des discours qui s'enchevêtrent sur ce sujet, il est possible de distinguer, pour la Suisse italienne, trois attitudes en partie corrélées avec des situations politiques, économiques et culturelles spécifiques: l'insistance sur l'italianité, sur l'helvéticité, et enfin, nouvelle proposition promue ces dernières années surtout par les économistes, proclamant le «Tessin région ouverte». Un aperçu historique de la prédominance de l'une ou de l'autre attitude est fourni par Ratti et al. (1990, 16 ss.).

La revendication de l'italianité est mise en évidence dans les premières décennies du XXe siècle, afin de faire face à la prétendue menace provenant de la Suisse alémanique, accusée par certains groupes d'intellectuels de «germaniser» le Tessin et de conduire une politique d'expropriation foncière. Sous la pression du fascisme, les attitudes glissent progressivement vers la revendication d'une helvéticité plus marquée, jusqu'à devenir partie intégrante de la «défense spirituelle» qui commençait à s'établir dans toute la Suisse pour répondre aux bouleversements politiques et idéologiques qui touchaient l'Europe environnante.

Après un revirement vers une attitude conservatrice, caractérisée par une politique culturelle qui, dans l'immédiat après-guerre, relance le thème de la défense de l'italianité, on passe graduellement, non pas sans des moments d'incertitude, vers ce qui a été défini comme «Ticino regione aperta», programme où, semble-t-il, l'opposition *italianité* vs. *helvéticité* s'annule dans l'acceptation et la valorisation équilibrée des deux dimensions et auxquelles s'ajoute évidemment la préoccupation de participer à une ouverture internationale. Il est difficile pourtant de capter ce que pensent la population et surtout les jeunes. «Ticino regione aperta» reste pour le moment un projet nourri par les intellectuels et les milieux économiques et culturels.

Très variée, et de toute façon difficile à quantifier, est la gamme des positions des jeunes interrogés (dans le cadre d'une recherche sur l'identité régionale et nationale; Bianconi/Patocchi in Ratti et al. 1990, 271—325) sur leurs sentiments d'appartenance. Une attitude «tessinocentrique» réunit essentiellement deux groupes, l'un conservateur, qui veut le Tessin différent de la Suisse et de l'Italie, l'autre innovateur par son ouverture internationale. C'est dans le cadre de ce deuxième groupe qu'a été formulée la métaphore linguistique du bilinguisme «dialecte (tessinois) – anglais». Une deuxième position, plutôt helvétocentrique, connaît également tout un éventail de variations. On y retrouve les stéréotypes répandus dans toute la Suisse qui, face à l'Italie, s'expriment en termes de couples antonymes tels que *ordine* vs. *caos*, *pulizia* vs. *sporcizia*, *efficienza* vs. *disorganizzazione*, etc. Plus modérés sont ceux qui, sans renoncer à mettre en évidence la particularité de l'italianité tessinoise, soulignent l'importance des liens et des contacts avec l'Italie du Nord. Il est cependant frappant que, s'interrogeant sur les contenus de leur identité helvétique, les jeunes ne fassent davantage recours à des «valeurs idéales», mais qu'ils utilisent les stéréotypes les plus courants et véhiculés par la société tels que *sûreté*, *bien-être économique*, *ordre*, *efficacité*, *beauté du paysage*, etc.

Quelle est l'influence de ces attitudes sur l'emploi des langues? La corrélation ne s'établit pas à travers une simple analogie et l'équivalence souvent posée entre plurilinguisme et pluriculturalisme se révèle une formule trop vague et trop simplificatrice. En réalité, bien qu'il y ait des convergences, les deux concepts tendent à s'articuler selon des axes différents. La définition culturelle, ou la recherche d'une identité culturelle régionale, se fait à l'aide de toute une série de critères dont la langue n'est qu'un exemple. Tandis que la langue italienne apparaît comme trait pertinent dans la délimitation identitaire envers la Suisse alémanique, le même élément langue ne fonctionne plus comme critère de démarcation pour la définition des rapports avec l'Italie, si ce n'est par le recours au dialecte local. Bien que le Tessin partage quotidiennement la culture italienne, à travers les médias, la mode, l'alimentation, etc., des lieux communs et des préjugés continuent à persister, produisant des sentiments d'hostilité qui peuvent même se transformer en refus des Italiens (voir Bianconi 1980; Ratti et al. 1990, 39; Lurati 1992 b, 728–731).

Un autre problème est celui de la gestion du plurilinguisme helvétique, habituellement cité comme garant d'une ouverture mentale et d'un enrichissement culturel. Bien plus pragmatiques sont les appréciations faites par les gens qui jour après jour sont obligés de vivre le trilinguisme helvétique, dont ils perçoivent surtout le côté problématique. L'impression que l'on en retire n'est guère celle d'une ouverture multiculturelle, mais celle d'une situation de malaise où l'existence de plusieurs langues sur un même territoire est considérée souvent comme un obstacle. Le bi- ou plurilinguisme est accepté comme une nécessité, comme le poids désormais indispensable pour réussir dans le marché du travail. La discussion toujours actuelle et régulièrement renouvelée sur l'utilité de l'apprentissage du français et de l'allemand est un témoignage significatif de cette perception de la part de la minorité tessinoise. Voici la controverse telle qu'elle transparaît d'un récent éditorial d'un journal tessinois: «Gli svizzeri italiani hanno sempre messo l'apprendimento delle lingue nazionali in cima ai loro pensieri. Per ragioni economiche e politiche, sia perché il tedesco e il francese erano (e sono) le lingue del pane, sia perché occorreva testimoniare, giorno dopo giorno, l'attaccamento alla patria. Imparare le altre lingue era sì uno sforzo, ma anche un atto di fede. Ma tanto sacrificio è davvero giustificato, soprattutto quando è a senso unico? (...) Perché non privilegiare l'inglese a scapito di una lingua nazionale?» (Cooperazione n. 36, 9. 9. 1993, 3); cf. également Forni (1993) qui discute les difficultés liées à l'apprentissage de «trop de langues».

6. Etat de la politique linguistique

Pendant des siècles, la Confédération était de fait un Etat monolingue, caractérisé par l'allemand. Ce n'est qu'à la fin du XVIIIe siècle et surtout pendant le XIXe siècle que la Suisse reconnaît d'abord au français puis à l'italien un statut paritaire au sein des autorités exécutives et législatives. Dès la Constitution fédérale de 1848, l'italien est considéré «langue nationale», de même que l'allemand et le français. En 1938 le romanche est proclamé quatrième langue nationale, les trois autres étant promues «langues officielles» («Amtssprachen») de la Confédération. A cette réglementation juridique s'ajoutent deux principes fondamentaux, celui du «principe de territorialité» et celui de la «liberté de la langue» (cf. Schläpfer 1982 et Dipartimento federale dell'interno 1989). Le principe de territorialité devrait assurer l'homogénéité et la vitalité des quatres langues dans les diverses régions linguistiques. Ce principe, une des pièces de résistance dans la politique linguistique suisse, a été remis en question ces dernières années par des voix de plus en plus nombreuses, surtout parmi les minorités comme les Tessinois et les Romanches, qui soulignent son insuffisance et son manque d'efficacité.

Si un des buts du principe de territorialité est de protéger les minorités linguistiques, sa mise en œuvre par le Tribunal fédéral a été dans la plupart des cas défavorable aux minorités (Dipartimento federale dell'interno 1989, 187). Le principe de territorialité, stricto sensu, ne protège une communauté linguistique qu'aussi longtemps qu'elle est majoritaire sur son propre territoire, mais empêche sa promotion en situation alloglotte. Un des effets juridiques qui en découlent pour les minorités en dehors de leur territoire est l'assimilation à la langue et à la culture majoritaire. Sur le plan juridique, une application rigide et formaliste (telle qu'elle a été pratiquée dans le passé par le Tribunal fédéral) a empêché notamment la création d'écoles bilingues et une intégration raisonnable de la langue maternelle dans la formation scolaire; cf. Lüdi (1993).

Le principe de territorialité se base essentiellement sur la conception (traditionnelle) d'une langue ou d'une communauté linguistique comme étant liée à un territoire spécifique, et ne tient absolument pas compte d'une des conséquences qui caractérise les sociétés modernes, celle de la mobilité des personnes; pour les conflits qui peuvent naître entre le principe de la liberté de langue et celui de territorialité dans une société marquée par l'immigration et la migration interne, cf. p. ex. Dipartimento federale dell'interno (1989, 202 ss.) et les commentaires dans *Gesetzgebung heute* 1 (1991).

Une des principales limites du principe de territorialité se trouve donc dans son esprit «conservateur» et se révèle par là un instrument peu adapté pour mettre en place une politique linguistique capable de satisfaire les exigences des minorités, toujours plus nombreuses dans un pays tout compte fait de migrants (voir notamment Lüdi/Py et al. 1995). Des critiques à ce même principe s'élèvent aujourd'hui chez les chercheurs qui sont actuellement en train de revoir le cadre sociolinguistique suisse sur la base des données du recensement de 1990 (voir p. ex. *Le Nouveau Quotidien* 31. 8. 1993, 19). La découverte d'un très haut taux de plurilingues et d'une présence considérable par exemple du français dans des villes telles que Bâle, Berne et Zurich, met en doute l'image traditionnelle d'un territoire linguistique homogène, avec des frontières bien définies. De plus en plus, on insiste sur les effets négatifs du principe de territorialité, en signalant par exemple qu'il empêche ceux qui se trouvent, pour de multiples raisons (immigration, migration interne), dans une situation d'alloglottes, de bénéficier d'une éducation qui intègre leur langue maternelle. Bref, le principe de territorialité est devenu un obstacle pour ce qui pourrait être une des rares «ressources naturelles» de la Suisse, à savoir le développement du bi- et plurilinguisme. Malheureusement, les débats actuellement en cours dans les parlements suisses (1993) ne permettent pas d'espérer de grands changements en matière de politique linguistique.

Au Tessin, on déplore surtout la régression de la langue italienne dans la vie quotidienne du reste du pays et surtout dans les écoles d'outre-Gothard (Dipartimento federale dell'interno 1989, XIII, 52−53, 251−252, 282−283). C'est dans ce contexte socio-politique que se situe une proposition du Département Fédéral de l'Intérieur, alors dirigé par le Tessinois Flavio Cotti, et de la Conférence suisse des directeurs de l'Instruction publique (1992), visant à introduire dans le nouveau règlement de maturité qu'on est actuellement en train de discuter en Suisse (1993), un article selon lequel l'enseignement d'une troisième langue nationale (l'italien pour la Suisse alémanique et romande) deviendrait obligatoire pendant deux années. Pourtant, si les autres propositions concernant la réforme de la maturité ont été bien accueillies par la majorité des institutions consultées, l'enseignement de la troisième langue nationale a été vivement critiqué par la presque totalité des instances interpellées.

Bien que «langue officielle», l'italien reste dans une position peu confortable quant à sa diffusion sur le plan national. Un point souvent souligné est le décalage entre les droits garantis par la loi et ses applications réelles. Bien que les fonctionnaires fédéraux de langue maternelle italienne aient le droit d'utiliser leur langue, ils n'usent pratiquement pas de ce droit, persuadés de ne pas être compris. Quant aux documents officiels publiés par la Confédération, la majorité des textes italiens ne sont que des traductions de l'allemand.

Des difficultés se rencontrent également dans la tentative de renforcement de la position de la langue et culture italienne à l'aide d'une plus étroite collaboration avec l'Italie; voir p. ex. les difficultés des écrivains tessinois à publier en Italie et y être reconnus (Lurati 1992 a, 170 s.). Il est tout à fait compréhensible qu'une communauté de moins de

300 000 habitants n'ait qu'une position fragile face à 55 millions d'Italiens qui par ailleurs sont confrontés à des problèmes d'ordre politique et social beaucoup plus graves.

7. Portrait général des contacts linguistiques

A quels problèmes linguistiques le Tessin est-il confronté à l'intérieur d'un Etat plurilingue et confédéral comme la Suisse? Il y a d'abord, pour commencer par l'aspect le moins problématique, ce qui a été appelé «l'italien fédéral» ou «l'italien helvétique» (Berruto 1984). Répondant aux besoins spécifiques de la réalité suisse, ses particularités linguistiques s'appliquent normalement aux autres langues nationales et constituent souvent des «parallélismes trilingues» ou «quadrilingues»; pour des exemples cf. Berruto (1984), Lurati (1989a), Bianconi (1989), Petralli (1990), Spiess (1993). L'italien se trouve généralement dans une situation passive, c'est-à-dire qu'il accepte et adapte à ses propres besoins linguistiques des données provenant de l'extérieur. La quantité négligeable d'emprunts non adaptés illustre soit la capacité d'adaptation d'un système linguistique dynamique et bien vivant, soit la volonté des sujets parlants de sauvegarder la base structurale de leur langue maternelle. Les emprunts non adaptés — qui sont d'ailleurs très souvent des noms de produits typiquement suisses tels que *Fleischkäse, Landjäger, Zwieback* — proviennent plus fréquemment, phénomène compréhensible vu la parenté structurale des langues, du français: *à côté, agraffe* préféré à *Büroklammer* (tandis qu'en Italie on parle plutôt de *graffetta*), *éclair, buvette*. Il semble également que l'italien régional tessinois soit moins ouvert que l'italien d'Italie aux emprunts non adaptés anglais.

Les influences linguistiques de l'allemand et du français vont évidemment au-delà des contacts administratifs et bureaucratiques et touchent tous les secteurs de la vie quotidienne. Par exemple: c'est probablement de la culture alémanique que le Tessin a hérité le geste et l'expression *jemandem die Daumen drücken*, penser à quelqu'un pour qu'il réussisse (par ex. avant des examens). Mais face à l'allemand, le tessinois garde toute son autonomie en traduisant librement cette locution par *tenere i pugni*, phraséologisme inconnu en Italie (cf. également romand *tenir les pouces à quelqu'un*).

Un autre fait ne reste pas sans influence sur la structure linguistique de l'italien au Tessin, à savoir l'absence d'un centre universitaire (le dernier projet ayant été refusé en votation populaire en 1986). Contraints à assurer leur formation dans des Universités germanophones ou francophones, une bonne partie des étudiants contribuent à ce qui a été appelé «italiano di riporto», un italien fortement imprégné d'éléments lexicaux allemands ou français, qui, élaboré dans les centres de formation transalpins, reviennent au Tessin (Berruto/Burger 1985, 71−72). Ceci explique partiellement la présence considérable de germanismes dans la presse tessinoise, une présence qui va au-delà du lexique et touche également des plans structuraux tels que l'usage des prépositions, ou la formation et l'ordre des mots (cf. l'analyse dans Berruto/Burger 1985, 63−70).

Quelle est la position de l'italien du Tessin face à l'italien d'Italie? La recherche linguistique italienne ne découvre qu'avec retard les italiens régionaux comme objet d'étude. A côté d'une recherche traditionnelle toscocentrique, les régions linguistiques étaient laissées aux dialectologues. Bien que certains chercheurs aient signalé dès les années soixante (à commencer par G. B. Pellegrini) l'existence d'un italien régional, ce n'est que dans les années quatre-vingt que les italiens régionaux obtiennent l'attention qui leur est due de la part de la recherche italienne (cf. Cortelazzo/Mioni 1990 et Bruni 1992). Il est vrai que même le Tessin a vécu, surtout dans les années trente, des tendances puristes et toscocentriques. Aspirant à l'italianisation, les écoles s'efforçaient de bannir tout ce qui semblait dialectal ou régional. Peu à peu le Tessin a renoncé à ces tendances puristes en adoptant dans les dernières décennies une position «endonormative» (Lurati 1992a, 143), c'est-à-dire une norme qui s'oriente selon les besoins internes de la communauté. Ce processus d'émancipation a permis l'apparition de phénomènes régionaux qui vont bien au-delà de l'«italien helvétique» dont nous avons parlé. Cette tendance peut être illustrée, par exemple, par la diffusion croissante des emprunts, même dans des cas où l'italien d'Italie fournirait une solution, mais où l'on n'hésite pas à adopter une variante régionale: it. rég. *comanda* vs. it. *ordinazione*, it. rég. *termopompa* vs. it. *pompa a calore*, it. rég. *nota* vs. it. *voto*, it. rég. *aver il formato per un certo posto* vs. it. *aver la stoffa/la statura*, it. rég. *sussidi a innaffiatoio* vs. it. *sussidi a pioggia*, it. rég. *conduttore* vs. it. *controllore/ bigliettaio*, it. rég. *profilarsi* vs. it. *farsi valere/ mettersi in evidenza*, etc.

L'autonomie tessinoise face à la norme italienne ne doit pourtant pas cacher une autre tendance, celle d'une dérégionalisation de l'italien tessinois. On observe auprès des jeunes la disparition des particularités intonatives et phonologiques régionales, remplacées par une variante neutre, tendanciellement proche d'un italien septentrional standardisé et suprarégional (Lurati 1992 c, 808; Bianconi-Patocchi in Ratti et al. 1990, 303 ss.). On peut constater les mêmes tendances à la dérégionalisation sur les plans morphologique, syntaxique et lexical.

8. Bibliographie (sélective)

Andres, Franz (1990): « Language relations in multilingual Switzerland ». In: *Multilingua* 9, 11–45.

Berruto, Gaetano (1984): « Appunti sull'italiano elvetico ». In: *Studi linguistici italiani* 10, 76–108.

Berruto, Gaetano/Burger, Harald (1985): « Aspetti del contatto fra italiano e tedesco in Ticino ». In: *Archivio storico ticinese* 101, 29–76.

Bianconi, Sandro (1980): *La lingua matrigna. Italiano e dialetto nella Svizzera Italiana*, Bologne.

Bianconi, Sandro (1989): *I due linguaggi. Storia linguistica della Lombardia svizzera dal '400 ai nostri giorni*, Bellinzona.

Bianconi, Sandro (Ed.) (1994): *Lingue nel Ticino. Un'indagine qualitativa e statistica*, Locarno.

Bianconi, Sandro/Gianocca, Cristina (1994): *Plurilinguismo nella Svizzera italiana. Le lingue nella Svizzera italiana secondo il censimento federale della popolazione del 1990*, Bellinzona.

Bruni, Francesco (Ed.) (1992): *L'italiano nelle regioni. Lingua nazionale e identità regionali*, Turin.

Cortelazzo, Michele A./Mioni Alberto M. (Eds.) (1990): *L'italiano regionale. Atti del XVIII congresso internazionale di studi della SLI*, Rome.

Dipartimento federale dell'interno (Ed.) (1989): *Quadrilinguismo svizzero – presente e futuro. Analisi, proposte e raccomandazioni di un gruppo di lavoro del Dipartimento federale dell'interno*, Berne.

Fidinam Fiduciaria (Ed.) (1991): *Ticino, Svizzera, Europa. Rapporti tra cultura, storia e contemporaneità*, Bellinzona.

Forni, Mario (1993): « Forse le lingue sono troppe ». In: *Italiano & oltre* 8, 35–39.

Grin, François (1993): « Ein Bundesamt für Sprachen. Für eine aktive Sprachpolitik ». In: *Schweizer Monatshefte* 7/8, 571–587.

Lüdi, Georges (1993): « Suisse ». In: *Mehrsprachigkeitskonzepte in den Schulen Europas = Sociolinguistica* 7, Ammon, U./Mattheier, K. J./Nelde, P. H. (Eds.), 32–48.

Lüdi, Georges/Py, Bernard et al. (1995): *Changement de langage et langage du changement. Aspects linguistiques de la migration interne en Suisse*, Lausanne (éd. allemande: Bâle et Francfort/Main 1994).

Lurati, Ottavio (1976): *Dialetto e italiano regionale nella Svizzera italiana*, Lugano.

Lurati, Ottavio (1989 a): « Tra neologia di calco e identità progettuale: le sfide agli Svizzeri italiani d'oggi ». In: *Lingua e letteratura italiana in Svizzera*, Stäuble, Antonio (Ed.), Bellinzona, 161–177.

Lurati, Ottavio (1989 b): « Italienische Schweiz, wohin? ». In: *Schweizer Monatshefte* 69, 35–52.

Lurati, Ottavio (1992 a): « Il Canton Ticino ». In: Bruni (Ed.) (1992), 143–177.

Lurati, Ottavio (1992 b): « Modi di vita oggi. Note dalle Svizzera italiana ». In: *La Svizzera. Vita e cultura popolare*, Hugger, Paul (Ed.), Bellinzona, 2, 721–747 (éd. allemande: Zurich, éd. française: Lausanne).

Lurati, Ottavio (1992 c): « Diventa difficile essere svizzeri di cultura italiana ». In: *La Svizzera. Vita e cultura popolare*, Hugger, Paul (Ed.), Bellinzona 2, 801–809.

Office fédéral de la statistique (1993): *Recensement fédéral de la population 1990. Langues et religions*, Berne.

Petralli, Alessio (1990): *L'italiano in un cantone. Le parole dell'italiano regionale ticinese in prospettiva sociolinguistica*, Milan.

Ratti, Remigio/Ceschi, Raffaello/Bianconi, Sandro (Eds.) (1990): *Il Ticino regione aperta. Problemi e significati sotto il profilo dell'identità regionale e nazionale*, Locarno.

Schläpfer, Robert (Ed.) (1982): *Die viersprachige Schweiz*, Zurich/Cologne.

Spiess, Federico (1993): « Veri e falsi tedeschismi nell'italiano regionale della Svizzera italiana ». In: *Actes du XXe Congrès International de Linguistique et Philologie Romanes*, Hilty, Gerold (Ed.), Tübingen/Bâle, 3, 627–640.

Windisch, Uli et al. (1992): *Les relations quotidiennes entre Romands et Suisses allemands. Les cantons bilingues de Fribourg et du Valais*, Lausanne.

Marco Bischofsberger, Bâle (Suisse)

230. Rätoromanische Schweiz

1. Geographie und Demographie
2. Geschichte
3. Politik und religiöse Lage
4. Statistik und Ethnoprofile
5. Soziolinguistische Lage
6. Sprachpolitische Lage
7. Allgemeines kontaktlinguistisches Porträt
8. Quellenlage und Forschung
9. Bibliographie (in Auswahl)

1. Geographie und Demographie

1.1. Einleitende Bemerkung und Terminologie

Im Unterschied zu großen Sprachen in Kontakt mit einem Kerngebiet und einer Kontaktzone steht beim Bündnerromanischen nicht nur das ganze Gebiet direkt in Kontakt mit der Dominanzsprache, sondern „die Sprachgrenze hat sich in die Menschen [hinein] verschoben", wie Catrina (1983, 247) die Definition von U. Weinreich ergänzt, und beeinflußt zunehmend auch die Sprachform (vgl. 7.2). In diesem Beitrag wird der Begriff *Bündnerromanisch*, Brm. und adj. brm., gleichwertig mit *Romanisch* bzw. *romanisch* verwendet und bezeichnet die gesprochenen romanischen Idiome (vgl. 4.1) sowie das Romanische gegenüber dem Deutschen. Die Beispiele werden in der gesamtbündnerromanischen Schriftsprache *Rumantsch grischun* (rg) notiert.

1.2. Geographie

Das brm. Sprachgebiet liegt im Kanton Graubünden mit 173 890 Einw. (1990) und einer Fläche von 7 106 km² im südöstlichen Teil der Schweizer Alpen und umfaßt abgelegene Talschaften der Flußsysteme des Rheins und des Inns. Die tieferliegende Verbindungsplatte im Norden (Churer Rheintal) wurde im 15. Jahrhundert verdeutscht, so daß keine sprachliche Verbindung mehr zwischen den verschiedenen Talschaften und auch kein gemeinsames städtisches Zentrum existieren. Aufgrund einer relativen Stabilität während der letzten Jahrhunderte von der Reformation bis tief ins 19. Jahrhundert hinein nennt man die Gebiete mit mehr als 50% Romanischsprechern um 1860 „traditionelles Sprachgebiet", das aber keinen Rechtsschutz genießt.

1.3. Demographie und Migration

Die bisherige Praxis der Volkzählung mit der Erfassung der *Muttersprache* als jener Sprache, in der man denkt und die man am besten beherrscht, ist für die Zählung zweisprachiger Menschen mit starker Domänenorientierung nicht brauchbar, ja sogar „leichtfertig" (Nelde 1984, 168). Erstmals wurde bei der Volkszählung von 1990 nach der *Hauptsprache* (nur eine Sprachangabe zulässig) und nach der *Umgangssprache* (Mehrfachnennung möglich) gefragt. Damit entfällt der emotional befrachtete Begriff *Muttersprache*, der gleichzeitig zur Bezeichnung der Erstlernsprache bei abgewanderten brm. Personen in deutscher Umgebung diente. Verkehrs- oder Dominanzsprache ist Brm. nur im eigentlichen Sprachgebiet.

Das heutige brm. Gebiet gehörte in der Vergangenheit zum Auswanderungsgebiet der Alpen allgemein. Neben der saisonalen Auswanderung mit jährlichem Urlaub in der Heimat war der lebenslange Aufenthalt in fremden Ländern von großer Bedeutung. Ihm folgte nicht selten nach erfolgreichem Berufsleben die Rückkehr in die Heimat. Diese Heimkehrer haben besonders am Ende des 19. Jahrhunderts und zu Beginn des 20. Jahrhunderts die brm. Renaissance stark unterstützt, aber auch das Engadinische stark italienisch beeinflußt (vgl. Diekmann 1982, 535—549).

Die heutige Abwanderung führt in die Wirtschaftszentren außerhalb des brm. Gebietes, besonders nach Zürich und Chur (50 Stellen beim Radio, Fernsehen und bei der Lia rumantscha mit Brm. als Berufsqualifikation), und innerhalb des brm. Gebietes in die Tourismus- und Regionalzentren, die trotz der Zuwanderung von brm. Sprachangehörigen allmählich durch eine zusätzliche nichtbrm. Zuwanderung und durch endogenen Sprachwechsel verdeutscht werden. Den Abwanderungsgebieten fehlt es zunehmend an aktiver Bevölkerung. Die Folge davon ist eine Überalterung mit geringem Nachwuchs, wie Kraas (1992, 181 f) belegt. 40,9% der brm. Bevölkerung hält sich zwar in der Diaspora auf, doch nimmt ihr Einfluß auf die brm. Sprachgruppe aufgrund ihres zunehmenden Organisierungsgrades zu (→ Sprachenkarte O).

2. Geschichte

2.1. Geschichte als Regionalgeschichte

Seit dem ausgehenden Mittelalter hat man es zu tun mit der Geschichte der gemischtsprachlichen Drei Bünde und den Gerichtsgemeinden als wirtschaftlichen und politischen Einheiten. Neben der Frontgermanisierung von Norden her verdeutschte die Walsereinwanderung im 13.–14. Jahrhundert inselartig höhere Regionen und auch die brm. bevölkerten tieferen Täler. Die Situation mit zwei Sprachen in Kontakt führte allmählich zu einem Monolinguismus mit größeren zusammenhängenden deutschen Gebieten neben deutschen Inseln innerhalb der brm. Gebiete. Auch während der Reformation bedeutete die Sprache kein Kriterium für den Konfessionsverbleib oder -wechsel. Hingegen haben Reformation und Gegenreformation sich stark der Volkssprache und im besonderen auch des Brm. als Werkzeug angenommen. Die geistlichen Eliten an Rhein und Inn übersetzten ihre religiösen Schriften jeweils ins regionale Brm. und begründeten damit die Schreibtradition der Schriftidiome (vgl. 4.1). Die kleinräumig nebeneinander lebenden Sprachgruppen bildeten weniger einen Plurilinguismus als vielmehr ein Nebeneinander von drei Sprachen (Brm., Deutsch der Alemannen und Walser und Italienisch) mit klarer Domänentrennung und wenig Berührungspunkten. Diese Isolation ist erst durch die verkehrsbedingte Mobilität, die zunehmenden wirtschaftlichen Einflüsse (Handel, Arbeitsmigration und Tourismus), die Zentralisierung und die vollständige Ausrichtung auf die Deutschschweiz seit Beginn des 19. Jahrhunderts in der Form eines permanenten Sprachkontaktes ersetzt worden.

2.2. Bewußtwerdung der Kontaktsituation

Die Linguisten haben früh erkannt, daß exogene Elemente als Transferenzen oder als Lehnübersetzungen im Brm. vorhanden waren, aber der Prozeß des Sprachkontaktes, der synchronen Interferenzen, wurde kaum thematisiert. Das diffuse Bild des Sprachkontaktes kommt besonders in der häufig vertretenen Ansicht zum Vorschein, daß die Schule und somit das Standarddeutsche der gefährlichste Gegner des Brm. seien, obwohl der tägliche Kontakt völlig auf das Alemannische ausgerichtet ist. Die Mehrsprachigkeit und deren unterschiedliche Bedeutsamkeit wird durch die direkt beteiligten Romanisch- und Italienischsprecher in sozialkommunikativer Weise erlebt. Sie sehen sich gegenüber dem Deutschen:

- wirtschaftlich mit ihrer angestammten Sprache im Nachteil,
- sozial ohne Prestige, weil sie eine fremde Verständigungssprache lernen mußten,
- wegen ihrer besonderen Aussprache des Deutschen verspottet (stigmatisiert).

2.3. Gruppenbewußtsein

Ausländische Beispiele haben am Ende des 19. Jahrhunderts die brm. Intellektuellen dazu bewogen, auch ihrerseits die Existenz einer brm. Nation zu postulieren. Markantester Ausdruck dafür sind die zahlreichen Gründungen von Sprachvereinigungen. Der weitere Schritt zu einer brm. Ethnie als „Menschengruppe mit gemeinsamer Abstammung, Stammesüberlieferung und Wir-Bewußtsein" (Höfer 1988, 134, zit. nach Kraas 1992, 32) erfolgte nur zeitweise und in abgeschwächter Form. Zuviele der üblicherweise erforderlichen Kriterien wie „Sprache, Recht, Siedlung, Religion und Kultur" (Hofer 1988, 134, zit. nach Kraas 1992, 32) treffen speziell für die brm. Bevölkerung nicht zu oder erfassen Graubünden oder die Alpenbevölkerung im allgemeinen. Bezüglich der Religion und der Parteizugehörigkeit ist die Affinität zwischen den Sprechern verschiedener Sprachen größer als innerhalb der Brm. Die regionale bzw. nur auf das eigene Idiom bezogene Identitätsbildung ist schwach. Zum Deutschen besteht eine größere Sprachloyalität als zu den anderen brm. Idiomen (5.1). Es findet auch keine Ethniebildung statt, da keine generalisierte Akzeptanz einer führenden Dachsprache besteht (vgl. 5.2) und auch der Wille zu einer einheitlichen Front gegenüber anti-brm. Hindernissen (vgl. 6.1), ja sogar gegenüber der dem Brm. entgegengebrachten Mißachtung, fehlt.

3. Politik und religiöse Lage

3.1. Politisches System

Die Schweiz ist ein föderatives System von relativ autonomen Kantonen; die Kantone bestehen aus Gemeinden, wobei speziell in Graubünden die Gemeinden völlige kulturelle und sprachliche Autonomie (freie Wahl der Schul- und der Amtssprache) besitzen.

Das Brm. ist auf Bundesebene seit 1938 eine „Nationalsprache" ohne amtssprachliche Funktion. Erst seit 1986 gibt der Bund wichtige Texte im Brm. (rg) heraus. Im Kanton Graubünden ist das Brm. (Sursilvan und Vallader) zusammen mit dem Italienischen und Deutschen verfassungsmäßig „Amtssprache" in den folgenden Bereichen:

- bei Wahlen und Abstimmungen
- vor Gericht
- in den Gesetzestexten
- in anderen Texten, Dokumenten, Personalausweisen (teilweise).

Der Kanton Graubünden anerkennt in seinen Grundschulen die folgenden Unterrichtssprachen und stellt dafür die entsprechenden Lehrmittel zur Verfügung: Deutsch, Italienisch, Sursilvan, Sutsilvan, Surmiran, Putér und Vallader; diese Sprachen bzw. Sprachformen wurden auch früher für den Romanischunterricht am kantonalen Gymnasium, am Lehrerseminar und an der kantonalen Frauenschule anerkannt (vgl. 5.4).

3.2. Religion

In Graubünden existiert keine Korrelation zwischen Deutsch und Romanisch einerseits sowie den Konfessionen andererseits (47% reformiert, 53% katholisch), wohl aber eine Beziehung zwischen den Konfessionen und den fünf historischen Idiomen:

kath.: Sursilvan, Surmiran
ref.: Sursilvan (teilweise), Sutsilvan, Puter und Vallader (Kraas 1992, 198 f).

Die konfessionelle Orientierung hat die Idiome voneinander distanziert bzw. deren Vereinheitlichung verhindert.

4. Statistik und Ethnoprofile

4.1. Die Sprachen im Kontakt

Die Volkszählung von 1990 (vgl. 1.3) liefert folgende Resultate:

Tab. 230.1: Sprachenverteilung in Graubünden

	Hauptsprache	Umgangssprache
Deutsch in GR	113 611	141 828
Italienisch in GR	19 190	38 447
Romanisch in GR	29 679	39 777
Brm. in der Schweiz	39 632	62 353

Davon lebten im brm. Sprachgebiet nach Idiomen (1980, hochgerechnet):

Sursilvan 16 854
Sutsilvan   1 245
Surmiran   2 954
Puter   3 615
Vallader   5 547

4.2. Sprachformen im Kontakt

Die dominante Komponente stellt die deutsche Sprache mit ihren Erscheinungsformen *Standarddeutsch* und *Bündnerdeutsch* dar. Letzteres ist eine alemannische Mundart, die aus dem Churer Rheintalischen und aus dem Walserischen besteht, die beide aber in dialektologischer Hinsicht relativ stark voneinander abweichen (vgl. Willi/Solèr 1990, 448 f). Die in der Schweiz besonders im 20. Jahrhundert stark ausgeprägte Diglossie zwischen Standard- und Bündnerdeutsch führt bei den Bündnerromanen dazu, daß sie — vor allem seit dem Ersten Weltkrieg — neben dem Brm. eine Hochsprache und einen Dialekt lernen und verwenden müssen.

Das Brm. als Einzelsprache existiert nicht, sondern repräsentiert einen Oberbegriff für zahlreiche Ortsdialekte, die ihrerseits von fünf Schriftidiomen überdacht sind. Dazu kommt seit 1982 das *Rumantsch grischun* (rg) als Kompromißschriftsprache. Das Italienische (lombardische Dialekte und Standard) in Poschiavo, in der Val Bregaglia und in der Val Mesocco und Calanca ist topographisch von den übrigen Sprachgebieten abgetrennt und präsentiert sich für die Deutsch- und Romanischbündner als Fremdsprache mit wenigen innerbündnerischen Sprachkontakten.

4.3. Zur Namensproblematik (Glottonymie)

Die Romanischsprecher bezeichnen ihre Sprache nach außen als *romontsch/rumantsch*; in Graubünden als *romontsch* (Rheinischbünden) und als *(rumantsch) ladin* (Engadin); isolierte Mundarten haben eigene Namen (*Bargunsegner* für Bravuogn, *Jauer* für Val Müstair). Wertend sind Bezeichnungen wie *mumma romontscha* „romanische Mutter" (positiv), aber auch *Kuhspanisch, Geröllhaldenenglisch, Bauernlatein* (negativ) oder das historische *Kauderwelsch*. Zur Glottonymie- und Terminologiediskussion siehe Kattenbusch (1985, 5—16).

5. Soziolinguistische Lage

5.1. Status und Funktion

Der Status einer Sprache wird durch ihren sozialen Stellenwert und durch ihre Verwendung bestimmt. Auch das Brm. muß primär aufgrund seiner Kommunikationsfähigkeit

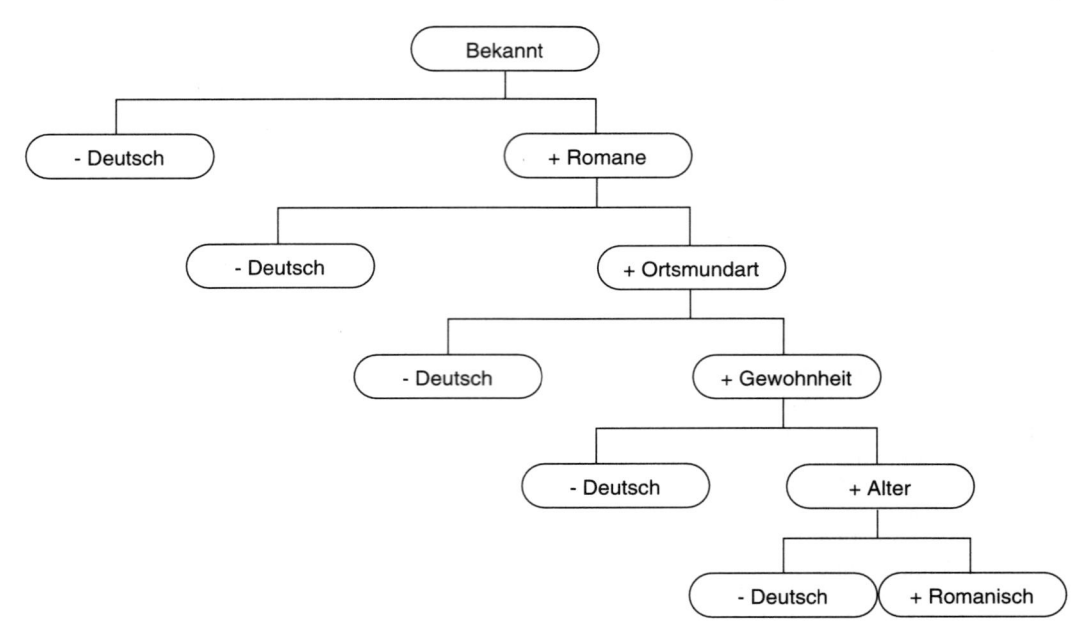

```
                          ┌─────────┐
                          │ Bekannt │
                          └────┬────┘
                   ┌───────────┴───────────┐
              ┌─────────┐              ┌─────────┐
              │- Deutsch│              │+ Romane │
              └─────────┘              └────┬────┘
                              ┌──────────────┴──────────────┐
                         ┌─────────┐                 ┌──────────────┐
                         │- Deutsch│                 │+ Ortsmundart │
                         └─────────┘                 └──────┬───────┘
                                          ┌──────────────────┴──────────────┐
                                     ┌─────────┐                    ┌──────────────┐
                                     │- Deutsch│                    │ + Gewohnheit │
                                     └─────────┘                    └──────┬───────┘
                                                       ┌──────────────────┴────────────┐
                                                  ┌─────────┐                    ┌─────────┐
                                                  │- Deutsch│                    │ + Alter │
                                                  └─────────┘                    └────┬────┘
                                                                         ┌──────────────┴──────────────┐
                                                                    ┌─────────┐               ┌──────────────┐
                                                                    │- Deutsch│               │ + Romanisch  │
                                                                    └─────────┘               └──────────────┘
```

Abb. 230.1: Strategie der Sprachwahl

beurteilt werden. Wertende Begriffe wie Liebe zur Muttersprache oder Identitätsinhalt sind dabei nur zweitrangig. Bilinguale Sprecher wählen diejenige Sprache, die ihnen den direkten Erfolg garantiert. Solèr (1983, 103) listet die Bedingungen bezüglich des Partners auf, die erfüllt sein müssen, damit ein Romanischsprecher Brm. verwendet (s. Abb. 230.1).

Sprecher mit einer soliden brm. Sprachpraxis verwenden mit Partnern eines benachbarten Idioms sicher Brm. und sogar im Kontakt mit den entferntesten Idiomen (Sursilvan — Vallader und umgekehrt) ihr Idiom; durchschnittliche Romanischsprecher sind weniger souverän und verwenden nur in ihrer eigenen Region Brm. Die abnehmende Bereitschaft, außerhalb der eigenen Ortsmundart Brm. zu verwenden, weist auf den abnehmenden Status der betroffenen Sprache aus der Sicht der Sprachverwender hin.

5.2. Attitüde und Identität

Camartin (1985, 67) faßt wohl eine längere Periode der brm. Sprachidentität zusammen, wenn er schreibt: „Die Identität des Sprechers wandelt sich seiner angestammten Sprache gegenüber, wenn er entdeckt, wie wenig weit er mit ihr kommt". Das Brm. steht im Kraftfeld dieser ökonomischen Sicht und auch des Folklorismus vieler Diasporabewohner. Es genießt als Sprache einer beliebten Ferienregion und als Minderheitensprache bei den Auswärtigen ein gewisses Prestige und wird daher gerne in der Werbung verwendet:

— *Steak quarta lingua*
— *turta rumantscha*
— *rätoromanische Orgelmusik.*

Dieses folkloristische Bild ist auch von den Romanen selber übernommen worden, obwohl es oft im Kontrast zur effektiven Sprachverwendung steht. Eine allgemeine Identität gibt es nicht, sondern „es besteht eine starke sentimentale Bindung der Bevölkerung der Surselva und des Engadins [und auch aller anderer Gegenden] an ihre jeweilige Schriftsprache" (Kristol 1989, 814), obwohl z. T. große Unterschiede zur im mündlichen Verkehr verwendeten Ortsmundart bestehen.

Der rückwärtsgewandte regionale Partikularismus führte 1991 zu einer Petition aus der Surselva an den schweizerischen Bundesrat, die verlangte, daß die neue Schriftsprache *Rumantsch grischun* nicht weiter verwendet werden dürfe, obwohl die Petenten gleichzeitig ihre Liebe zum Brm. beschworen.

5.3. Konflikte und Lösungsansätze

Das populär vorherrschende Sprachenstereotyp sowie die eingeschränkte Funktion des

Brm. bilden einen starken Kontrast zu einer modernen funktionalistischen Sprachauffassung mit:
- einer Standardform (rg) des Brm. über den Ortsmundarten (Diglossie)
- wichtigen Domänen für das Brm. (koordinierter Bilinguismus)
- territorialer Integrität (Territorialitätsprinzip) vor individueller Sprachfreiheit (in der schweiz. Bundesverfassung verankert).

Wichtig wäre die Entmystifizierung des mehr als 100jährigen *Muttersprachen*begriffs und ein weitgehend rationaler Umgang mit den Begriffen *Bilinguismus*, *Sprachwandel* und *Nützlichkeit* der Sprache (Cathomas 1984, 10 f). Zusammengefaßt lautet die Frage, ob die romanische Gemeinschaft bereit ist, heute einen Strukturwandel vorzunehmen und die überlieferte romanische Sprache anzupassen (korpuslinguistisch wie auch im funktionalen Einsatz), oder ob die Sprache in ihrer überkommenen Gestalt und mit ihren alten Funktionen bewahrt werden soll und solcherart sicher vergehen wird, weil die gesellschaftliche Strukturänderung sie als anachronistisch obsolet werden läßt.

5.4. Bilinguismus und Diglossie

Bilingual interagieren nur die Bündnerromanen und die Italophonen Graubündens, und zwar partnergesteuert (vgl. 5.1) und kaum themenbedingt. Der diglossische Bilinguismus beginnt im Kindesalter (s. Tabelle 230.2).

In der Sprachdiaspora lernen die Kinder gewöhnlich nur mündlich Brm., und zwar mit Bezug auf die Domänen der Familie. Die Zuwanderung und die Exogamie (beinahe die Hälfte der Ehen sind gemischtsprachig: Osswald 1988, 66) führen bei den Romanischsprechern zu hoher Deutschkompetenz, in deren Folge das Brm. zur Zweitsprache werden kann.

6. Sprachpolitische Lage

6.1. Sprachpolitik

Wie Haarmann (1975, 92) schreibt, „[sind] Sprachregelung und Sprachgesetzgebung äußere Zeichen dafür, wie sich die Regierung eines Staates zu den verschiedenen Sprachgemeinschaften in ihrem Land stellt". Die brm. Minderheit innerhalb eines mehrsprachigen Kantons und Landes wird eindeutig fremdbestimmt. Dies zeigt sich auch in den Entscheidungen des Bundes mit der Anerkennung des

Tab. 230.2: Phasen der Spracherlernung (Willi/Solèr 1990, 456, erweitert)

Alter Jahre	Brm.	Dt.
0–3	Ortsdialekt in der Familie	Schwdt. mit dt. Kindern
4–7		Schwdt. audiovisuell
8–10	Schriftidiom als Unterrichtssprache	Standarddt. aus Kinderliteratur
11–13	Fach in der Schule (2 Std./W + 1 Fach auf Brm.)	Standarddt. als Schulfach
14–20	Fach in den Mittelschulen und am Lehrerseminar (+ 1 Fach auf Brm.)	Fach und Unterrichtssprache in Berufs- und Mittelschule
20+	Studienfach an Universitäten	voll ausgebaute Sprache

Brm. als *Nationalsprache* 1938 (politischer Akt ohne weiterführende *amtssprachliche* Konsequenz) oder in der Praxis des Kantons Graubünden, je nach Anwendungsgebieten überhaupt kein Brm. oder nur zwei der fünf Idiome zu verwenden und damit bedeutende Bereiche für das Brm. auszuschließen. Eine weitere Ungerechtigkeit besteht darin, daß die kantonale Standeskanzlei die Übersetzungen, die Herausgabe der Rechtsbücher, des Amtsblattes und Teile des Unterrichts an kantonalen Schulen in it. und brm. Sprache den betreffenden Sprachgemeinschaften gesondert verrechnet. Damit wird *de facto* Graubünden zum deutschsprachigen Kanton erklärt.

6.2. Schulsprache und Medienangebot

Die Gemeinden können autonom zwischen brm. (jeweils eines der fünf Idiome, vgl. 3.1) Grundschule (1.–6. Klasse Brm. als Unterrichtssprache mit Deutsch als Fach vom 4. Schuljahr an, vgl. 5.4) oder deutscher Grundschule mit ev. brm. Unterricht (2 Std./Woche) entscheiden. Die Zahlenverhältnisse (Osswald 1988, 103 f) sagen kaum etwas über die bilinguale Problematik in Ortschaften aus, wo die Schule zu einem brm. Inselbetrieb in deutscher Umgebung wird (betrifft untere Surselva, Oberengadin) und eine ungewohnte

Domänenverteilung mit schwachen Romanischkenntnissen in dominant deutschsprachiger Schulsituation entsteht. Im Medienbereich nimmt das Brm. mit Zeitungen von lediglich regionaler Bedeutung (2 erscheinen zweimal, 2 einmal wöchentlich) neben der dominanten deutschen Tagespresse eine marginale Stellung ein. Das Radio rumantsch mit ca. 7 Std. Programm pro Tag wird durch drei weitere deutschsprachige Sendeketten im 24-Stunden Betrieb ergänzt. Das brm. Fernsehen sendet innerhalb des deutschen Fernsehens DRS ca. 30 Min. brm. Beiträge pro Woche.

6.3. Standardisierung

Die Standardisierung und Normierung der fünf brm. Idiome wurde von den jeweiligen Wörterbuch- und Grammatikverfassern zwar in gegenseitiger Absprache vorgenommen, doch können auch kleinste Änderungen gelegentlich zu größeren Streitereien oder sogar zu schismatischer Gruppenbildung innerhalb einer Region führen (vgl. Darms 1989, 847 ff). Die aufgestellten Normen erhalten offiziellen (Schul-)Charakter durch ihre Anerkennung von seiten der kantonalen Regierung.

7. Allgemeines kontaktlinguistisches Porträt

7.1. Variation innerhalb des Bündnerromanischen

Die fünf Schriftidiome, jeweils bestehend aus der Summe der jeweiligen Ortsdialekte, unterscheiden sich trotz der grundlegenden linguistischen Ähnlichkeit doch in der Morphosyntax, Syntax und Lexik voneinander. Das kann eine spontane, gegenseitige Verständigung verhindern (vgl. 5.1). Die Unterschiede zwischen Sursilvan und Vallader erweisen sich je nach Auffassung als wesentlich bzw. unwesentlich (s. Tabelle 230.3).

Differenzen im lexikalischen Bereich beruhen oft auf unterschiedlichen Geosynonymen.

7.2. Deutsch-romanischer Sprachkontakt

7.2.1. Phonetik

Von deutschen Phonemen interferieren nur die im Surselvischen, Sutselvischen und Surmiranischen unbekannten [y, ø] und das generell im Brm. unbekannte [ç] (Tabelle 230.4).

Die zwei affrizierten brm. Phoneme [tɕ], [tʃ] mit wenigen eindimensionalen Oppositionen

Tab. 230.3: Unterschiede zwischen Sursilvan und Vallader

Sursilvan	Vallader	deutsche Bedeutung
in cavagl vegl	*ün chavagl vegl*	ein altes Pferd
il cavagl ei vegls	*il chavagl es vegl*	das Pferd ist alt
jeu vegn a salidar	*eu salüdarà*	ich werde grüßen
jeu selavel	*eu am lav*	ich wasche mich
jeu hai salidau ellas	*eu n'ha salüdà ad ellas, eu tillas n'ha salüdadas*	ich habe sie begrüßt
Els han buca bia raps a disposiziun	*Els nun han a disposiziun blers raps*	sie haben nicht viel Geld zur Verfügung

Tab. 230.4: Deutsche vs. bündnerromanische Phoneme

deutsche Phoneme		brm. Phoneme	
[y]	*ü*berhaupt Gülle	[ɪ]	*i*berhà
[ø]	Knödel	[e]	gh*e*lla
		[e]	can*e*del
[ç]	Ar*ch*itekt	[h]	ar*h*itect

(Solèr 1995) werden von brm. Sprechern zunehmend zu [tʃ] vereinfacht.

Aus Sprachökonomie reduzieren jüngere Brm. zunehmend [λ] zu [j], so wie die sekundären Romanischsprecher, die dafür selten auch [l] verwenden (Tabelle 230.5).

Tab. 230.5: Traditionelle vs. heutige Aussprache

trad. Aussprache	heutige Aussprache	
taglier [taλɪər]	> [tɪər]	„Teller"
glina [λɪnɑ]	> [jnɑ]	„Mond"
bigl [bɪλ]	> [bej]	„Trog"

Erst die sich anschließenden Reduktionen der unbetonten Silben führen zu stärkerer Homonymie, z. B. im Sutselvischen:

230. Rätoromanische Schweiz

[tɪər] = *taglier* „Teller" = *tagliear* „schneiden" = *tier* „bei" und „Tier" (Solèr 1991, 163).

7.2.2. Morphosyntax

Das Augmentativmorphem *u-* aus alemannischem *u-, uu-* in *uplaschair* „Riesenfreude" oder brm. Endungen an deutschen Verbalstämmen bei *sibar* < sieben, *rasar* < rasen (fällt zusammen mit brm. *rasar* „ausbreiten") sowie Zehn-er > *diescher* „zehn Rappen-Stück" sind Zufallsbildungen und als solche kaum produktiv (Solèr 1995).

7.2.3. Syntaktische Interferenzen

Markant ist die brm. Unterdifferenzierung der deutschen Präpositionen mit gleichzeitig konkreter und übertragener Bedeutung (Tabelle 230.6).

Tab. 230.6: Konkreter vs. figurativer Sinn

Brm. Form	Dt. Redewendung
vegnir sut la glieud sut „unterhalb"	unters Volk kommen
il clom suenter agid suenter „nach, darnach"	der Ruf nach Hilfe
vesi giu da las uras giu „herunter, herab"	von der Zeit abgesehen

Derartige Interferenzen des Brm. sind als Systemwechsel zum Deutschen hin zu betrachten. Solche Bildungen entsprechen dem Ascolischen Prinzip der „materia romana e spirito tedesco".

Auch die brm. Wortstellung wird oft der deutschen angepaßt (Tabelle 230.7).

7.2.4. Lexikon

Früher aus Purismus bekämpfte Entlehnungen sind später als Transferenzen aufgrund ihrer Assimilation exemplarisch dargestellt worden. Durch die völlige Beherrschung des Deutschen von seiten der Brm.-Sprecher sind lexikalische Entlehnungen im Brm. generell und in allen Bereichen anzutreffen (vgl. Solèr 1991, 157 f).

7.3. Romanisch-deutscher Sprachkontakt

Gemäß Willi/Solèr (1990, 461 f) sonorisieren Romanischsprecher beim Deutschsprechen intervokalische Konsonanten [s] > [z], [ʃ] >

Tab. 230.7: Deutsch kontaminierte Wortstellung

brm. korrekt		brm. kontaminiert		deutsch
trimma masauna	×	masauna trimma	−	mittelmäßiges Rind
betg discurrer pli	×	betg pli discurrer	−	nicht mehr reden
pon pajar quai	×	pon quai pajar	−	können das bezahlen
hai tratg enturn els	× ×	hai els tratg enturn	− ×	habe sie herumgezogen

[ʒ], aspirieren velare Plosivlaute [k] > [kh], reduzieren teilweise [ç] > [h] und berücksichtigen bei Vokalen nur deren Qualität und nicht deren Quantität (letztere ist im Brm. phonologisch nicht relevant).

Dativ und Akkusativ werden analog zum Brm. nicht unterschieden. Reflexiva und das unpers. *es* können entfallen in: *man getraut (sich) nicht; hier ist (es) schön*. Bildungen wie *Sie kommt mit seiner* (statt: *ihrer*) *Schwester* < *sia sora; ein Lied für* (statt: *auf*) *deutsch* < *per tudestg* sind allerdings als Zufallsinterferenzen selten, denn gemäß Cathomas (1977, 167) „[unterscheiden] sich Zweisprachige insgesamt nicht auffallend von den [deutschen] Einsprachigen".

7.4. Sprachwechsel

Die Zunahme der deutschen Kontaktsituationen sowie deren hohe Intensität (Dominanzsprache) hat aus brm. Sprechern mit dt. Sprachkenntnissen ausgeglichene Bilinguale gemacht, deren brm. Syntaxstrukturen sehr stark vom Deutschen beeinflußt sind (vgl. 7.2.3). Zahlreich sind aber auch primär brm. Sprecher mit Dominanzsprache Deutsch, die aber nur eine geringe brm. Kompetenz in beschränkten, traditionell-häuslichen Domänen besitzen.

8. Quellenlage und Forschung

Die korpuslinguistische Erforschung und Darstellung der einzelnen brm. Idiome kann sich auf zahlreiche Monographien, qualitativ hochwertige Standardwerke (wie das historische Wörterbuch DRG) und viel Quellenmaterial stützen. Neuere thematische Untersuchungen betreffen die Sprachkompetenz bilingualer Romanen (Cathomas 1977), den Sprachwandel und -wechsel bei unterschiedlichen Sprachzuständen (Solèr 1983) und gesamthaft eine plurilinguale Gemeinschaft im Wandel (Kristol 1984). Das Forschungsprogramm „Zweisprachigkeit am Hinterrhein", von den Forschungen U. Weinreichs inspiriert, liefert neben den detaillierten Analysen beider Sprachen in den Bänden über das Brm. Einsichten in spezielle Kontaktsituationen (z. B. Solèr 1991).

9. Bibliographie (in Auswahl)

Camartin, Iso (1985): *Nichts als Worte? Ein Plädoyer für Kleinsprachen*, Zürich.

Cathomas, Bernard (1977): *Erkundungen zur Zweisprachigkeit der Rätoromanen*, Bern.

Cathomas, Bernard (1984): „Minderheiten in der Selbstbesinnung und Selbstbestimmung". In: *Ladinia 8*, 5–15.

Catrina, Werner (1983): *Die Rätoromanen zwischen Resignation und Aufbruch*, Zürich.

Darms, Georges (1989): „Sprachnormierung und Standardsprache". In: *Lexikon der Romanistischen Linguistik III*, Holtus, G./Metzeltin, M./Schmitt, C. (Eds.), Tübingen, 827–853.

Diekmann, Erwin (1982): „Italienisches Wortgut im Engadinischen vermittelt durch sozio-ökonomische Wanderbewegungen". In: *Beiträge zur allgemeinen, indogermanischen und romanischen Sprachwissenschaft*, Winkelmann, O./Baisch, M. (Eds.), Bern, 535–549.

DRG = Planta von, Robert et al. (Eds.) (1939 ff): *Dicziunari rumantsch grischun*, Chur.

Gross, Manfred/Cathomas, Bernard (1992): *Il rumantsch. Das Rätoromanische*, Chur.

Haarmann, Harald (1975): *Soziologie und Politik der Sprachen Europas*, München.

Kattenbusch, Dieter (1988). „Rätoromanisch oder Ladinisch". In: *Ladinia 12*, 5–16.

Kraas, Frauke (1992): *Die Rätoromanen Graubündens*, Stuttgart.

Kristol, Andres M. (1984): *Sprachkontakt und Mehrsprachigkeit in Bivio (Graubünden)*, Bern.

Kristol, Andres M. (1989): „Soziolinguistik". In: *Lexikon der Romanistischen Linguistik III*, Holtus, G./Metzeltin, M./Schmitt, C. (Eds.), Tübingen, 813–826.

Nelde, Peter H. (1984): „Sprachökologische Überlegungen am Beispiel Altbelgiens". In: *Spracherwerb – Sprachkontakt – Sprachkonflikt*, Oksaar, E. (Ed.), Berlin/New York, 167–179.

Osswald, Sylvia E. (1988): *Stabilitätsmindernde Faktoren bei einer sprachlichen Minderheit. Die Rätoromanen in Graubünden*, Hannover.

Solèr, Clau (1983). *Sprachgebrauch und Sprachwandel*, Zürich.

Solèr, Clau (1991): *Romanisch im Schams*, Zürich.

Solèr, Clau (1995): „Sprachwandel und Sprachwechsel bei ausgeglichenem Bilinguismus". In: *Verhandlungen des Internationalen Dialektologenkongresses Bamberg 1990*, Viereck, W. (Ed.), ZDL-Beiheft, Stuttgart, 263–275.

Weinreich, Uriel (1977): *Sprachen in Kontakt*, München.

Willi, Urs/Solèr, Clau (1990): „Der rätoromanisch-deutsche Sprachkontakt in Graubünden". In: *Grenzdialekte*, Kremer, L./Niebaum, H. (Eds.), Germanistische Linguistik 101–103, Hildesheim, 445–475.

Clau Solèr, Chur (Schweiz)

XVI. Sprachkontakte in den westlichen GUS-Staaten und im Baltikum
Language Contacts in the Western States of the CIS and the Balticum
Contacts linguistiques dans les Etats occidentaux de la CEI et dans les Etats baltiques

231. Die westlichen GUS-Staaten

1. Geographie und Demographie
2. Territorialgeschichte und Staatsbildung
3. Politik, Wirtschaft und allgemeine kulturelle sowie religiöse Lage
4. Statistik und Ethnoprofile
5. Soziolinguistische Lage
6. Die Sprachkontaktsituation in Rußland im Vergleich
7. Mehrsprachigkeit als Interaktionspotential – Perspektiven für die Zukunft
8. Bibliographie (in Auswahl)

1. Geographie und Demographie

Nach der Auflösung der Sowjetunion Ende 1991 hat sich die politische Landschaft in der Westregion ihres europäischen Teils durch die Konstituierung neuer Nationalstaaten entscheidend gewandelt. Die früheren Sowjetrepubliken (Estnische SSR, Lettische SSR, Litauische SSR, Weißrussische SSR, Ukrainische SSR, Moldauische SSR) sind seit Herbst 1991 selbständige Staaten. Die Änderung des politischen Status hat grundsätzliche Veränderungen der Sprachenverhältnisse in diesen Ländern bewirkt.

Die Westregion der ehemaligen Sowjetunion ist seit vielen Jahrhunderten eine interkulturelle Kontaktzone (s. Bruk/Apenčenko 1964, 16 f), und Mehrsprachigkeit war für die Bevölkerung dieser Gebiete bereits charakteristisch, bevor das Moskowiterreich seine Grenzen ins Baltikum, nach Weißrußland, in die Ukraine und nach Moldawien ausdehnte (Haarmann 1992 b, 24 ff). Die in der Westregion verbreiteten Sprachen gehören verschiedenen sprachgenetischen Gruppierungen an. Das Estnische und Liwische (in Lettland) sind finno-ugrische Sprachen und Vertreter der ostseefinnischen Gruppe. Nahverwandte Sprachen sind das Finnische und Ingrische (im benachbarten Ingermanland). Zur finnougrischen Sprachfamilie gehört auch die Sprache der ungarischen Minderheit im äußersten Westen der Ukraine (Karpatenukraine). Das Lettische und Litauische sind indoeuropäische Sprachen, und zwar die einzigen lebenden Vertreter der baltischen Gruppe. Zu den slawischen Sprachen der Westregion gehören das Russische, Weißrussische, Ukrainische, Polnische sowie die Sprachen nationaler Minderheiten in der Ukraine wie das Slowakische, Bulgarische u. a. Die Angehörigen der Titularnation Moldawiens sprechen Rumänisch, eine romanische Sprache (→ Art. 237). In der Westregion leben auch Angehörige ethnischer Gruppen, die Turksprachen sprechen, und zwar Tatarisch, Gagausisch und Karaimisch. Andere Minderheitensprachen sind Deutsch, Jiddisch, Albanisch, Griechisch (Haarmann 1979 b).

Das Russische ist die einzige Schriftsprache mit interregionaler Bedeutung in der gesamten Westregion. Als Faktor der Sprachkontakte wirkte das Russische auf die Regionalsprachen in seinen verschiedenen Varianten, in gesprochener und geschriebener Form.

Entsprechend der heutigen ethnopolitischen Differenzierung des Großraums variieren die ethnodemographischen Verhältnisse in den fünf multinationalen Staaten teilweise erheblich. Der nationalstaatliche Charakter trifft am ehesten auf Litauen zu, in dem 80,1% Litauer leben. Am wenigsten nationalstaatlich sind die Verhältnisse in Lettland, wo die Angehörigen der Titularnation lediglich 51,8% der Landesbevölkerung ausmachen (→ Sprachenkarte P).

2. Territorialgeschichte und Staatsbildung

Bereits zu Beginn der zwanziger Jahre brach mit der Diskussion über die Frage der administrativen Neugliederung des sowjetischen Territoriums der Konflikt zwischen Lenin und Stalin auf. Während Lenin die Schaffung selbständiger nichtrussischer Sowjetrepubliken forderte, um der Gefahr antirussischer Ressentiments auszuweichen, trat Stalin (mit Kamenev und Manuilsky) für eine unitarische Lösung mit autonomen Regionen für Nichtrussen in einer von Russen dominierten sowjetischen Föderation ein (Smith 1992, 5). Die seit 1922 tatsächlich durchgeführte Reform entsprach einem Kompromiß. Für die nichtrussischen Nationalitäten richtete man administrative Territorien verschiedenen Typs ein, außerhalb Rußland sogenannte S(ozialistische) S(owjet) R(epubliken) (= S.S.R.) für verschiedene Titularnationalitäten (z. B. für Weißrussen, Ukrainer, Armenier, Usbeken, u. a.), innerhalb der Russischen Föderation (Russische S.F.S.R.) autonome Regionen (A.S.S.R.) und nationale Kreise (russ. *nacional'nye okrugi*).

Die frühen zwanziger Jahre in der UdSSR sind gekennzeichnet durch eine liberale Sprachplanung, die auf die faktische Ausweitung der sozialen Funktionen und auf die prestigemäßige Aufwertung nichtrussischer Sprachen abzielte. Diese Liberalisierungsphase basiert auf den ideologischen Richtlinien der Leninschen Demokratisierung der Nationalitätenpolitik. Das wichtigste Medium für die Kodifizierung neuer und der Reform alter Schriftsprachen war die Lateinschrift, die von Lenin als Symbol der „Revolution im Osten" bezeichnet wurde. Hinter dem Schlagwort stand der Wunsch des Anschlusses sowjetischer Sprachen an den Standard der Schriftlichkeit Westeuropas. Eine ähnliche, wenn auch ideologisch abweichende Orientierung an westeuropäischen Standards zeigt der Kurs der türkischen Sprachpolitik. Die Umstellung von der arabischen auf die lateinische Schrift zur Schreibung des Türkischen Ende der zwanziger Jahre war ebenfalls ein Symbol gesellschaftlicher Modernisierung.

Die zweite Phase der sowjetischen Sprachpolitik entfaltet sich erst gegen Ende der zwanziger Jahre. Der sich in einigen Regionen bis in die dreißiger Jahre hinziehende Prozeß der Umstellung von der lateinischen auf die kyrillische Schrift illustriert die Hinwendung in der Sprachpolitik zu einem unitarischen Kurs, der einem Trend nach größerer Vereinheitlichung des Sprachgebrauchs folgt. Diese zweite Phase der Sprachpolitik ist der konkrete Ausdruck einer von Stalin praktizierten Politik der bürokratischen Zentralisierung. Parallel mit der Kyrillisierung der Schriftsysteme nichtrussischer Sprachen (Isaev 1979, 236ff) wird auch der Schulunterricht in russischer Sprache stärker ausgebaut. Die Zahl der Unterrichtssprachen war in den fünfziger Jahren im Vergleich zur Situation Anfang der dreißiger Jahre deutlich reduzierter (Lewis 1972, 184). Das Besondere an den Umwälzungen der sowjetischen Sprachenpolitik und deren Neuorientierung unter Stalin ist der Umstand, daß die Zwei-Phasen-Entwicklung offiziell nie sanktioniert worden ist. Nach ideologischer sowjetischer Lesart hat es eine Abweichung von den Leninschen Prinzipien der Nationalitäten- und Sprachenpolitik nie gegeben.

Im Sinn der Leninschen Demokratisierung der Nationalitätenpolitik wurden in den zwanziger Jahren Anstrengungen unternommen, bei der Konsolidierung des schriftsprachlichen Standards des Weißrussischen und Ukrainischen möglichst auf Abstand gegenüber dem Russischen zu achten. In jener Zeit wurden einheimische Wortschöpfungen ebenso wie eine regionalsprachliche Phraseologie bevorzugt. Das geschriebene Russisch nahm zwar damals bereits einen breiten Raum im öffentlichen Leben der slawischen Westregion ein, die einheimischen Schriftsprachen fanden aber Verwendung auf allen Ebenen, und besonders im Schulwesen setzten sie sich durch.

Die Folgeerscheinungen des von Stalin durchgesetzten Zentralismuskonzepts waren eine zunehmende Sowjetisierung des Alltagslebens und eine Russifizierung des Sprachgebrauchs. Seit Mitte der dreißiger Jahre schrieb man in Weißrußland ein vom Russischen überformtes Weißrussisch (Wexler 1992, 44), seit Ende der dreißiger Jahre in der Ukraine ein russifiziertes Ukrainisch. Im Ausbildungssektor wurde das Russische zunehmend bevorzugt, vor allem in den höheren Klassen.

Seit den siebziger Jahren allerdings stagnierte die Russifizierung in manchen Domänen, unter anderem deshalb, weil der Funktionsbereich des Russischen bereits damals saturiert war. Seit den frühen siebziger Jahren hat sich beispielsweise der Trend der Druckproduktion auf ungefähr gleichbleibendem Niveau stabilisiert (*Narodnoe obrazovanie* 1989, 376 ff, 387, 392). Die durchschnittliche Jahresproduktion von Büchern lag beispielsweise im Zeitraum zwischen 1970 und 1988 bei 60.000−65.000 Einzeltiteln. Im Jahre 1988 erschienen 76,6% aller sowjetischen Buchtitel in russischer Sprache, lediglich 2,2% in Ukrainisch und 0,5% in Weißrussisch. Im Baltikum war das Litauische mit 2,7% vertreten, auf das Estnische entfielen 1,6%, auf das Lettische 1,2%. In der Druckproduktion der Zeitschriften zeichnet sich eine ähnliche Dominanz des Russischen ab. Von der Gesamtzahl aller Titel für 1988 entfielen 84,6% auf das Russische (gegenüber 1,9% für das Ukrainische, 0,7% für das Weißrussische, 2,1% für das Litauische, 1,3% für das Lettische und 1,5% für das Estnische). Im Bereich der Zeitungsproduktion offenbaren sich folgende Proportionen: 65,7% in russischer Sprache gegenüber 14,7% in Ukrainisch, 1,5% in Weißrussisch, 1,3% in Litauisch, 0,8% in Lettisch und 0,4% in Estnisch.

Vergleicht man die Druckproduktion des Weißrussischen und Ukrainischen mit der der Sprachen im Baltikum, so stellen sich erhebliche Disproportionen heraus. Für die große Sprachgemeinschaft der Ukrainer wurden pro Einzelleser weniger Bücher und Zeitschriften in der Muttersprache gedruckt als vergleichsweise für die viel kleinere litauische Sprachgemeinschaft. Lediglich im Bereich des Zeitungswesens verschieben sich die Proportionen in Abhängigkeit von der größeren Leserzahl zugunsten des Ukrainischen.

Die soziokulturelle Situation der Sprachen im Balitkum weicht auch in mancher anderer Hinsicht von der in den slawischen Westgebieten und in anderen Regionen ab. Beispielsweise werden seit Jahrhunderten die Sprachen des Baltikums in Lateinschrift geschrieben, und daran hat die sowjetische Sprachplanung auch nach 1940 nichts geändert. Anders als im Fall kleinerer finno-ugrischer Sprachen in der Wolgaregion oder zahlreicher kaukasischer Sprachen, deren lexikalische Modernisierung ausschließlich vom Russischen abhängt, verfügen das Estnische, Litauische und Lettische über einen historisch gewachsenen, vom Russischen unabhängigen Kulturwortschatz, dessen Herkunft größtenteils auf die gleichen westlichen Quellen wie im Fall des Russischen ausgerichtet ist, das Deutsche und Französische. Dies betrifft vor allem den umfangreichen Bestand an Internationalismen (z. B. russ. *socializm* 'Sozialismus' oder *filosofija* 'Philosophie' im Verhältnis zu estn. *sotsialism* oder *filosofia*; zum politischen und wissenschaftlichen Wortschatz des Estnischen s. Päll 1977, 167 f).

Die Zahl der direkt entlehnten Russismen nach 1940 im Litauischen, Lettischen und Estnischen ist gering. Größer ist die Zahl der lehngeprägten Sowjetismen, also einheimische Wortschöpfungen nach russischem Muster (z. B. estn. *insener-keemik* 'Chemieingenieur' nach russ. *inžener-chimik*, lit. *brigados generolas* 'Brigadegeneral' nach russ. *general brigady*). In sowjetischer Zeit ist auch die Bedeutung einheimischer Termini russifiziert worden, indem sich der Sprachgebrauch dem des Russischen anpaßte (z. B. lett. *draugs*, lit. *draugas* 'Freund' in Beziehung zu russ. *drug*; lett. *laudis*, lit. *liáudis* 'Leute, Volk' in Beziehung zu russ. *ljudi*). Mit der Auflösung der sozialistischen Gesellschaftsordnung und dem Abbau ihrer Institutionen verschwand auch der sowjetisch-sozialistische Wortschatz aus dem öffentlichen und privaten Sprachgebrauch.

3. Politik, Wirtschaft und allgemeine kulturelle sowie religiöse Lage

Entscheidend für die Veränderung der sprachlichen Verhältnisse in der Westregion war die Konstituierung selbständiger Nationalstaaten im Herbst 1991 und die nominelle Auflösung der Sowjetunion Ende 1991.

Die Westregion, deren Planwirtschaft bis 1991 im wesentlichen auf den Warenaustausch mit Rußland festgelegt war, steuert seither auf die Marktwirtschaft westeuropäischer Prägung zu. Am rasantesten ist die Umstellung in den baltischen Staaten verlaufen, insbesondere in Estland, das enge Wirtschaftskontakte mit Finnland unterhält. Angesichts der teilweise sehr unterschiedlichen politischen Interessenlage der in der ehemaligen Westregion entstandenen Staaten ist deren wirtschaftliche Kooperation bislang wenig entwickelt. Der Lebensstandard in den baltischen Regionen war schon in sowjetischer Zeit höher als in Weißrußland und in der Ukraine. Moldawien war und ist die vergleichsweise ärmste Region.

Eine Neuerung im öffentlichen Leben der neuen Staaten ist die wiederbelebte Rolle der kirchlichen Institutionen. Die während der sowjetischen Periode verdeckte Religiosität artikuliert sich erneut im Glaubensbekenntnis der Menschen und ihrer Zugehörigkeit zu den verschiedenen Konfessionen. Der Protestantismus lutherischer Prägung überwiegt in Estland und Lettland, kleinere Gruppen von Lutheranern gibt es auch in Litauen und Weißrussland. Der Katholizismus ist anteilmäßig am stärksten in Litauen vertreten, rund 70% der Bevölkerung bekennen sich zu diesem Glauben. Es gibt in allen Staaten der Westregion russisch-orthodoxe Christen, in Weißrussland und in der Ukraine sind deren Anteile aber vergleichsweise größer als in den anderen Regionen, in Weißrussland sind die orthodoxen Christen sogar in der Mehrheit (ca. 60%). Die meisten Ukrainer gehören der griechisch-katholischen (unitarischen) Glaubensrichtung an. In Moldawien überwiegt der Anteil der rumänisch-orthodoxen Bevölkerung.

Die staatliche Souveränität hatte unmittelbare und einschneidende Veränderungen im politischen Status der Regionalsprachen zur Folge. Die früher bestehende amtliche Zweisprachigkeit ist aufgehoben. Die Nationalsprachen der Titularnationen fungieren seit Anfang 1992 nominell als Staatssprachen ihrer Länder (d. h. Estnisch in Estland, Lettisch in Lettland, Litauisch in Litauen, Weißrussisch in Weißrußland und Ukrainisch in der Ukraine). Faktisch hatten diese Sprachen schon seit Ende der achtziger Jahre das Russische immer mehr zurückgedrängt, obwohl man in der Bürokratie bis heute nicht völlig darauf verzichten kann. In Weißrußland ist das Russische im Mai 1995 wieder als zweite Amtssprache zugelassen worden. Das Russische hat auch seinen bevorzugten Status im Ausbildungswesen verloren. Zwar bleibt Russisch Unterrichtsfach neben dem Englischen und anderen Sprachen im Fremdsprachenprogramm der Schulen, als Unterrichtsmedium aber hat es seine frühere Rolle an die Nationalsprache abgegeben.

Der Übergang von der national-russischen Zweisprachigkeit zum nationalsprachlichen Monolingualismus im öffentlichen Leben hat den Status der Schriftlichkeit geändert. Im Baltikum erforderte diese Statusänderung keine Umstellung der schriftsprachlichen Normen der dort verwendeten Abstandsprachen des Russischen. Die estnische, lettische und litauische Schriftsprache haben lediglich ihr sowjetisches Couleur, ihre sozialistische Lexik und ihre teilweise vom Russischen überformte Phraseologie abgestreift. In den slawischen Gebieten der Westregion dagegen war die Folge der Statusänderung auch eine Umstellung im Schriftstandard der Nationalsprachen. In der Ukraine hat man sich an den Schriftstandard der „Ukrainisierungs"-periode angelehnt. Die weißrussische Schriftsprache macht derzeit einen tiefgreifenden Wandel durch, nämlich um sich zu entrussifizieren und einen Standard zu re-adaptieren, der sich in den zwanziger Jahren gefestigt hatte, d. h. einen „klassischen" Standard, dessen Syntax, Lexik und Stilvariationen sich im wesentlichen unabhängig vom russischen Patronat entfalten. Nach Expertenmeinung hängt die Konsolidierung des „klassischen" weißrussischen Standards davon ab, mit welcher Konsequenz das Russische in Weißrußland vom Schriftsprachengebrauch ausgeschlossen wird (Wexler 1992, 49).

Das Russische hat seine ehemalige Funktion als All-Unions-Sprache der Sowjetunion in den Regionen verloren. In den baltischen Staaten wird den meisten Russen derzeit sogar die Staatsbürgerschaft vorenthalten. Die wesentlichen Modalitäten für deren Vergabe sind ein langjähriger bleibender Aufenthalt im Staatsgebiet sowie der Nachweis von Kenntnissen der Landessprache. Beispielsweise müssen in Estland Nicht-Esten zur Erlangung der Staatsbürgerschaft nachweisen, daß sie Estnisch verstehen, amtliche Formulare ausfüllen und sich auf Estnisch verständlich machen können (→ Art. 232). Die von sowjetischen Gesellschaftsplanern propagierte national-russische Zweisprachigkeit der Nicht-Russen ist umgeschlagen in eine nationalstaatliche Haltung, nach der die Umstellung vom russischen Monolingualismus auf Varianten der russisch-nationalsprachlichen (d. h. russisch-estnischen, russisch-litauischen u. a.) Zweisprachigkeit von den Russen gefordert wird. Gleichzeitig wird durch diese Umstellung Druck auf diejenigen Nicht-Russen ausgeübt, bei denen sich bereits früher ein Wechsel zum Russischen vollzogen hat und die gar nicht mehr die Sprache ihrer Nationalität sprechen. Dies gilt nach dem Stand von 1979 (*Čislennost'* 1984) für 7,2 Mill. Ukrainer, 2,4 Mill. Weißrussen, 69 280 Letten, 47 140 Litauer und 46 280 Esten mit russischer Muttersprache. Diese nicht-russischen Assimilanten sind nach ihrer Abstammung Angehörige der regionalen Titularnation, sie gehören jedoch sprachlich zur Gruppe der russischen Minderheit.

Die Lage der nicht-russischen Minderheiten in den neuen Nationalstaaten, die seit jeher an Mehrsprachigkeit gewöhnt sind, ist wesentlich günstiger als die in ihrem Mono-

Tab. 231.1: Tendenzen des Sprachwechsels und der Zweitsprachenattraktion bei den Minderheiten in der Ukraine (nach Haarmann 1979 b)

Niveau der Quoten	Primärsprachenbereich			Zweitsprachenbereich	
	Primärsprachliche Resistenz	Russische Primärsprache	Ukrainische Primärsprache	Russische Zweitsprache	Ukrainische Zweitsprache
bis 10%	Griechen	Slovaken Rumänen Ungarn	Rumänen Albaner Bulgaren Griechen Ungarn	–	Bulgaren Rumänen Albaner
10%–20%	Polen	Polen	Slovaken	–	Ungarn
20%–30%	–	Tschechen Bulgaren	Tschechen	Rumänen Ungarn	Griechen
30%–40%	–	–	–	Slovaken Polen	–
40%–50%	Tschechen	Albaner	–	Tschechen	Polen Tschechen Slovaken
50%–60%	Albaner Slovaken	–	–	–	–
60%–70%	Rumänen	–	Polen	–	–
70%–80%	Bulgaren	–	–	Albaner Bulgaren Griechen	–
80%–90%	–	–	–	–	–
über 90%	Ungarn	Griechen	–	–	–

lingualismus isolierten Russen. Die Finnen in Estland sprechen seit jeher auch Estnisch, die Liwen Lettisch, viele Polen in Litauen beherrschen das Litauische. Diejenigen Minderheitengruppen, die außer über russische Zweitsprachenkenntnisse auch über landessprachliche Drittsprachenkenntnisse verfügen, werden ebenfalls in den slawischen Gebieten der Westregion am ehesten teilhaben am öffentlichen Leben der neuen Nationalstaaten.

Varianten der national-weißrussischen oder national-ukrainischen Zweisprachigkeit der Minderheiten, die noch bis vor kurzem zu den „auslaufenden Modellen" der sowjetischen Gesellschaftsplanung gehörten, werden derzeit prestigemäßig hoch gewertet. Die ethnostatistischen Tendenzen, die sich in den siebziger Jahren zugunsten der national-russischen und zu ungunsten der national-ukrainischen Zweisprachigkeit in der Ukraine abzeichneten (Tabelle 231.1), werden sich in den kommenden Jahren voraussichtlich umkehren. Diese Entwicklung wird teilweise überflügelt von Tendenzen zum Sprachwechsel bei der Folgegeneration der Minderheiten, womit sich die älteren Strukturen der Zweisprachigkeit im Monolingualismus auflösen werden.

4. Statistik und Ethnoprofile

Die demographischen Strukturen aller Anrainerstaaten Rußlands sind heutzutage durch erhebliche russische Bevölkerungsanteile charakterisiert. Der Zustrom russischer Migranten in die Westregion hat insbesondere in den siebziger und achtziger Jahren zugenommen (Arutjunjan et al. 1992, 28 ff). Die meisten Russen außerhalb Rußlands leben in der Ukraine, wo 11,356 Mill. (1989) Angehörige dieser ethnischen Gruppe (entsprechend 20,3% der Landesbevölkerung) beheimatet sind. An zweiter Stelle steht Weißrußland mit seiner russischen Bevölkerungsgruppe (1,342 Mill., entsprechend einem Anteil von 12%). Lettland ist der Staat mit anteilmäßig den meisten Russen (33,8%). Die kleinste regionale russische Minderheitengruppe (0,344 Mill.) ist in Litauen beheimatet, wo die Russen 8,6% der Landesbevölkerung ausmachen. Die Russen leben überwiegend in den Städten, insbesondere in den industriellen Ballungsgebieten. Dort liegt ihr Anteil auch über dem Landesdurchschnitt. Die Anteile der Russen an der Bevölkerung der Hauptstädte der ehemaligen Sowjetrepubliken lagen deutlich über dem Landesdurchschnitt. Beispielsweise machte nach dem Census von 1970

(*Itogi* 1973) der Anteil der Russen an der Bevölkerung der Weißrussischen SSR 10,4% aus. In der Hauptstadt Minsk betrug der Anteil der Russen dagegen 23,3%.

Der situationelle Druck des Russischen, der sich außer durch die Präsenz russischer Bevölkerungsgruppen in nichtrussischen Gebieten auch durch die amtliche Rolle der All-Unions-Sprache, ihre Bedeutung in Wirtschaft und Wissenschaft sowie als wichtige Komponente in der zweisprachigen Schulausbildung aufgebaut hatte, war in sowjetischer Zeit das wichtigste Korrektiv für das Niveau der Spracherhaltung in den nichtrussischen Sprachgemeinschaften. Nach den Angaben des letzten sowjetischen Census von 1989 (*Social'noe razvitie* 1991) ergab sich folgende Rangfolge für die Erhaltung regionaler Muttersprachen bei den größeren Nationalitäten: Litauer (97,7%), Esten (95,5%), Letten (94,8%), Moldauer (91,6%), Ukrainer (81,1%), Weißrussen (70,9%). Die Quoten für Spracherhaltung bei den Minderheiten (abgesehen von den Russen, die überall die höchste muttersprachliche Resistenz zeigen) in der Westregion liegen in der Regel unter dem Durchschnitt für die Titularnation, z. B. Gagausen in Moldawien: 87,5%, Bulgaren in der Ukraine: 68,2%, Polen in Weißrußland: 30,5%.

In den Staaten der Westregion leben Tataren (1989: 86 900 in der Ukraine, 12 400 in Weißrußland, 4 800 in Lettland, 4 000 in Estland, u. a.), Armenier (1989: 54 200 in der Ukraine, 3 000 in Lettland, 2 800 in Moldawien, u. a.), Georgier (1989: 23 500 in der Ukraine, 1 400 in Lettland, u. a.) und andere Nichtrussen. Das Russische war für diese Binnenmigranten und ihre Nachkommen bis zur Auflösung der Sowjetunion das wichtigste Kommunikationsmedium im Kontakt mit Nichtrussen und Russen in der Westregion. Heutzutage ist deren kommunikative Mobilität stark begrenzt, falls sie nicht auch die jeweilige Staatssprache beherrschen.

In den neuen Staaten der Westregion sind auch Angehörige der Nationalitäten aus den westlichen (und nördlichen) Anrainerländern (ethnische Außengruppen) beheimatet. In Estland gehören die Finnen zu den zahlenmäßig bedeutenderen Minderheiten. Auf den großen estnischen Inseln lebt noch eine kleine Gruppe von Schwedisch-Sprachigen. Die zweitstärkste Minderheit in Litauen sind die Polen mit 0,258 Mill. Polen leben auch in Weißrußland (0,418 Mill.) und in der Ukraine (0,219 Mill.). Die ungarische Bevölkerung in der Karpatenukraine ist eine Grenzlandminderheit, bei den übrigen Minderheiten (z. B. Rumänen, Slowaken, Tschechen, Bulgaren, Griechen, Deutsche) handelt es sich um Streugruppen (Haarmann 1979 b: 12 f, 122 ff). Angehörige der neuen Staatsnationen leben als Grenzlandminderheiten in größerer Zahl in Polen, u. zw. Ukrainer (0,18 Mill.) sowie Weißrussen (0,17 Mill.). In der Slowakei gibt es eine ukrainische Minderheit (47 000).

Die Kontakte dieser Sprachen untereinander sind jeweils geprägt durch spezifische sprachökologische Bedingungen. Das Russische stand wegen seiner Rolle als All-Unions-Sprache der Sowjetunion mit den Sprechern aller anderen Sprachen der Region im Kontakt (s. 2). Die Kontakte des Estnischen als nichtverwandter Abstandsprache zum Russischen unterscheiden sich qualitativ deutlich von denen des Weißrussischen, das zum nahverwandten Russisch im Verhältnis einer Nur-Ausbausprache steht. Die Verhältnisse werden komplexer, wenn man die Kontaktdynamik der regionalen Landessprachen (und neuen Staatssprachen) mit einbezieht, die ihrerseits im Kontakt sowohl zum Russischen als auch zu den Minderheitensprachen stehen (z. B. ukrainisch-russische sowie ukrainisch-polnische, ukrainisch-deutsche und andere Kontakte).

Am komplexesten sind die Sprachkontakte der Minderheiten, die zumeist in einem mehrsprachigen Kontaktmilieu leben. Für die in Weißrußland lebenden Polen beispielsweise ist das Ukrainische wie auch das Russische für die Alltagskommunikation von Bedeutung. Bei den Minderheiten sind auch die meisten Zweit- und Drittsprachenkenntnisse verbreitet. Während nur ein verschwindend kleiner Teil der russischen Bevölkerung irgendeine andere Sprache außer Russisch beherrscht, sind Zwei- und Mehrsprachigkeit bei den Minderheiten die Regel. Ein Beispiel für die sprachliche Mobilität bei den Angehörigen von Minderheiten sind die Sprachverhältnisse der Zigeuner, deren Mehrsprachigkeit in der Karpatenukraine außer dem Romani als Muttersprache das Ungarische (dieses auch in Primärsprachenfunktion), Ukrainische und Russische als Zweit- und Drittsprachen einschließt (vgl. Haarmann 1979 c, 191 ff, 1986, 49 ff).

5. Soziolinguistische Lage

Der Schlüssel zum Verständnis der Kontaktrolle des Russischen in der Westregion sowie der von den sowjetischen Ideologen betriebenen kulturellen und sprachlichen Fusion zwischen nichtrussischen Nationalkulturen mit dem russischen ethnischen Komplex liegt im Mechanismus der national-russischen Zweisprachigkeit (russ. *nacional'no-russkoe dvujazyčie*; Deşeriev 1973a).

Wenn die „Annäherung zwischen den Nationalsprachen und -kulturen" (russ. *sbliženie nacional'nych jazykov i nacional'nych kul'tur*) und deren Fusion in einer „sowjetischen sozialistischen Nation" (russ. *soveckaja socialističeskaja nacija*) das Fernziel der sowjetischen Nationalitätenpolitik war, dann sollte die national-russische Zweisprachigkeit als Instrument dienen, um dieses Ziel zu erreichen. Formen der national-russischen Zweisprachigkeit gab es bereits vor der Revolution von 1917 in vielen Teilen Rußlands (z. B. bei den finnisch-ugrischen Völkerschaften in der Wolgaregion, in Weißrußland und in der Ukraine). Die Wahl der Zweisprachigkeit als bewußtes Mittel der gesellschaftlichen Integration und als Instrument zur Durchsetzung des sprachpolitischen Zentralismus sind aber erst späteren Datums. Bereits zu Stalins Lebzeiten wurde die Migration von Russen in die Industriegebiete und städtischen Zentren außerhalb Rußlands gefördert, wo die russische Bevölkerung bis in die jüngste Vergangenheit als Motor für die regionale Zweisprachigkeit und als Kristallisationspunkt für die Russifizierung fungierte (Haarmann 1992a, 115 ff).

Statistisch läßt sich die Entwicklung der national-russischen Zweisprachigkeit bis zum Census von 1989 (*Social'noe razvitie* 1991) verfolgen, obwohl dessen Ergebnisse unvollständig und nur auszugsweise veröffentlicht worden sind. Als generelle Beobachtung bestätigt sich eine Zunahme der Anteile für die russische Zweitsprachenkomponente, während gleichzeitig die Assimilationsraten zugenommen hatten (vgl. *Itogi* 1973, *Čislennost'* 1984, *Social'noje razvitie* 1991). Im europäischen Teil der Sowjetunion gab es zur Zeit des Census von 1970 nur eine Region, wo russische Zweitsprachenkenntnisse ebenfalls nur mäßig verbreitet waren: das Baltikum. Dort wurden die niedrigsten Raten für Russisch als Zweitsprache bei Esten (30,3%) und Litauern (36,4%) ermittelt. Im stärker russifizierten Lettland lag der Durchschnittswert immerhin bei 47,3%. Die Verbreitung russischer Zweitsprachenkenntnisse zeigte eine relativ hohe Rate in Weißrußland (60,4%), eine deutlich niedrigere Quote aber in der Ukraine (42,3%).

Im städtischen Milieu waren die Bedingungen der Alltagsinteraktion bereits in den siebziger Jahren durch ein hohes Maß an russischer Zweitsprachenattraktion gekennzeichnet. Die russische Zweitsprachenkomponente war bei der weißrussischen Stadtbevölkerung mit 76,6% am stärksten vertreten. Bei allen anderen Nationalitäten lagen die Quoten deutlich niedriger (vgl. ukrainische Stadtbev.: 61,7%, lettische Stadtbev.: 55,0%, litauische Stadtbev.: 53,0%, estnische Stadtbev.: 39,0%). Die männlichen Stadtbewohner besaßen anteilmäßig mehr russische Zweitsprachenkenntnisse als die Frauen (z. B. 65,4% : 58,6% in der Ukraine, 58,6% : 47,8% in Litauen), was ohne weiteres als ein Zeichen für eine zumeist berufsbedingte divergente Geschlechtsspezifik der kommunikativen Mobilität zu deuten ist.

Die national-russische Zweisprachigkeit wurde vor allem im Ausbildungswesen etabliert (Deşeriev 1973a, 26 ff). Der situationelle Druck des Russischen in der Rolle der im außerfamiliären und im schulischen Milieu erworbenen Zweitsprache korrelierte seit den siebziger Jahren mit einer entsprechenden Assimilationsdynamik. Dies bedeutet, daß in den Bevölkerungsgruppen mit hoher russischer Zweitsprachenquote auch die Assimilationsraten relativ hoch liegen. Von den hier verglichenen Gruppen weist die weißrussische Bevölkerung nicht nur die stärkste russische Zweitsprachenmobilität (s. o.), sondern auch die stärkste Assimilation auf. Bei insgesamt 19,4% (1970), 25,4% (1979) bzw. 28,5% (1989) der Weißrussen hatte sich ein Sprachwechsel zum Russischen als Primärsprache vollzogen. Diese Nichtrussen hatten also ihre nationale Muttersprache (d. h. Weißrussisch) nicht mehr im familiären Milieu als erste Sprache erworben.

Die Assimilationsrate der Ukrainer lag bei 14,3% (1970), 17,1% (1979) bzw. 18,8% (1989). Die Völker im Baltikum zeigen für diesen Zeitraum ein hohes Niveau an Spracherhaltung, die Quoten für den Sprachwechsel zum Russischen beliefen sich bei den Litauern auf 2,1% (1970), 1,6% (1979) bzw. 1,8% (1989), bei den Esten auf 4,5% (1970), 4,5% (1979) bzw. 4,4% (1989) und bei den Letten auf 4,8% (1979), 4,8% (1979) bzw. 5,0% (1989). Die Vergleichsdaten zeigen, daß sich die Tendenz zum Sprachwechsel in Weißrußland und in der Ukraine zwischen 1970 und 1989 verstärkt hat, während sich das Niveau der Spracherhaltung im Baltikum nur unwesentlich verändert hat oder stagnierte.

Sprachwechsel war ein von der Sowjetideologie bewußt eingeplanter Prozeß. Der Übergang zum Russischen wurde von Ideologen nicht „Assimilation" (russ. *assimiljacija*) oder „Russifikation" (russ. *russifikacija*) genannt, sondern als Wechsel zur „zweiten Muttersprache" (russ. *vtoroj rodnoj jazyk*) bezeichnet. Mit dieser Bezeichnung wich man nicht nur negativen Wertungen des Assimilationsprozesses aus, sondern der Übergang zur Sprache der allgemeinen Sowjetkultur wurde auch positiv gedeutet. Mit der positiven Bewertung dieser Form des Sprachwechsels korrelierte zweifellos der praktische Nutzeffekt einer Beherrschung des Russischen als Primärsprache für die kommunikativen Belange der Sozialkontakte und der Arbeitswelt. Viele nichtrussische Sowjetbürger dürften im Sprachwechsel zum Russischen auch unabhängig von der Propaganda die positiven Aspekte gesehen haben.

Abgesehen von der indirekten Wirkung der national-russischen Zweisprachigkeit für die Verstärkung assimilatorischer Trends gab es ein direktes Mittel zur Stimulation des Sprachwechsels, nämlich interethnische Familienbindungen. Als Motor des Internationalismus waren gemischte Ehen (russ. *nacional'no-smešannye braki*) ein beliebtes Thema der sowjetischen Soziologie und Ethnographie (Kozlov 1975, 227 ff; über die Entwicklung der gemischten Ehen als gesellschaftspolitischer Faktor bis in die achtziger Jahre s. Arutjunjan et al. 1992, 191 ff). In Familien mit Ehepartnern verschiedener nationaler Zugehörigkeit überwog in der Regel das Russische als Heimsprache, so daß auch der Spracherwerb der Kinder meistens an diesem Medium orientiert blieb. Vor allem in interkulturellen und multilingualen Kontaktgebieten spielten interethnische Familienbindungen eine wichtige Rolle für den Sprachwechselprozeß zum Russischen (Lewis 1972, 117 ff). In der Westregion der Sowjetunion korrelieren Zahlen für gemischte Ehen mit Quoten für die Primär- und Zweitsprachenattraktion des Russischen. In Litauen machte der Anteil der gemischten Ehen nach dem Stand von 1970 nur 9,6% aus, in Estland 13,6%. Weitaus höhere Anteile wurden für Lettland (21,0%) und die slawischen Gebiete (Weißrußland: 16,6%, Ukraine: 19,7%) ausgewiesen. In Lettland waren die meisten gemischten Ehen solche zwischen Letten und Russen oder Ukrainern (Cholmogorov 1970, 86 ff).

Die Kombination einer regionalen Nationalsprache im Primärsprachenstatus mit dem Russischen im Zweitsprachenstatus war in sowjetischer Zeit die wichtigste und gleichzeitig am weitesten verbreitete Variante der Zweisprachigkeit. In bestimmten Regionen der Sowjetunion gab es auch Varianten der Zweisprachigkeit ohne Beteiligung des Russischen (z. B. finnisch-estnische Zweisprachigkeit der finnischen Minderheit in Estland, liwisch-lettische Zweisprachigkeit der Liwen in Lettland, deutsch-litauische Zweisprachigkeit der deutschen Minderheit in Litauen, polnisch-weißrussische Zweisprachigkeit der polnischen Minderheit in Weißrußland, slowakisch-ukrainische Zweisprachigkeit der slowakischen Minderheit in der Ukraine). Während solche Varianten in sowjetischer Zeit nur marginale Bedeutung hatten, stellen sie in den neuen Nationalstaaten heute den Prototyp der Zweisprachigkeit bei den regionalen Minderheiten dar.

6. Die Sprachkontaktsituation in Rußland im Vergleich

Die Russische SFSR (Sozialistische Föderative Sowjetrepublik) gehörte bis Ende 1991 administrativ zur Sowjetunion. Ihr rechtspolitischer Nachfolger ist die souveräne Republik Rußland (russ. *Rossija*), ein Territorium mit multinationaler Bevölkerung (s. Tabelle 231.2). Nach den Erhebungen der letzten sowjetischen Volkszählung von 1989 (*Social'noe razvitie* 1991) sind 82,6% der Bevölkerung Rußlands ethnische Russen. In den meisten Nachfolgestaaten der Sowjetunion, d. h. in den früheren Sowjetrepubliken, sind die Mehrheiten der jeweiligen regionalen Titularnationen geringer als im Fall Rußlands. Die Proportionen der Multinationalität dort ähneln denen in Aserbaidschan, wo 82,7% der Landesbevölkerung Aserbaidschaner sind. Lediglich in Armenien liegt der prozentuale Anteil der Titularnation mit 93,3% deutlich über dem Durchschnitt Rußlands. Die meisten Russen und Nichtrussen leben im europäischen Teil Rußlands.

Die größten nichtrussischen Bevölkerungsgruppen in diesem Großraum sind die Tataren (Wolga- bzw. Kasantataren) mit mehr als 5 Mio. und die Ukrainer mit mehr als 4 Mio. Rußland ist der einzige Staat Europas mit interkontinentaler Ausdehnung. Zu seiner Bevölkerung gehören Menschen der unterschiedlichsten rassischen Herkunft (Euro-

Tab. 231.2: Eckwerte zur ethnischen Zusammensetzung der Bevölkerung Rußlands (nach *Social'noe razvitie* 1991)

Ethnische Gruppe	Angehörige (Stand: 1989)	Anteil an der Landesbevölkerung	Niveau der Erhaltung der Muttersprache
Russen	119.866.000	82,6%	99,8%
Tataren	5.522.000	4,6%	83,2%
Ukrainer	4.363.000	3,6%	81,1%
Tschuwaschen	1.774.000	1,2%	76,5%
Baschkiren	1.345.000	weniger als 1%	72,3%
Weißrussen	1.206.000	weniger als 1%	70,9%
Mordwinen	1.073.000	weniger als 1%	67,1%
Tschetschenen	899.000	weniger als 1%	98,1%
Deutsche	842.300	weniger als 1%	48,8%
Mari	644.000	weniger als 1%	80,8%
Awaren	544.000	weniger als 1%	97,2%
aschkenasische Juden	537.000	weniger als 1%	11,1%
Burjaten	417.000	weniger als 1%	86,3%
Osseten	402.000	weniger als 1%	87,0%
Jakuten	380.000	weniger als 1%	93,8%
u. a.			

pide, Uralide, Mongolide, u. a.; Uibopuu 1988, 45 ff), die Sprachen ganz verschiedener genetischer Affiliation sprechen (s. Comrie 1981 als Gesamtüberblick, Vinogradov 1966 zu den indoeuropäischen Sprachen, Baskakov 1966 zu den türkischen Sprachen, Lytkin 1966 zu den uralischen Sprachen, Bokarev/Lomtatidze 1967 zu den kaukasischen Sprachen, Skorik 1968 zu den mongolischen, tungusischen und paläosibirischen Sprachen), und die Angehörige der unterschiedlichsten religiösen Gemeinschaften sind (Christen verschiedener Konfession, Muslime, Animisten, Judaisten). Der letztere Aspekt der religiösen Bindung wurde in sowjetischer Zeit zugunsten eines angeblich weitverbreiteten, propagandistisch geförderten Atheismus verschwiegen.

Dort wo das moderne Rußland an andere Territorien der ehemaligen Sowjetunion angrenzt, leben Nichtrussen in größerer Zahl (s. Bruk/Apenčenko 1964, 14f, 18f, 23). Dabei handelt es sich zumeist um Angehörige von Nationen, die nach dem Zerfall der Sowjetunion Eigenstaatlichkeit erlangt haben. Die heutigen Minderheiten Rußlands lassen sich fünf Kategorien zuordnen:

(1) Autochthone Minderheiten mit regionaler politisch-kultureller Autonomie (z. B. Tataren in Tatarstan, Burjat-Mongolen in Burjatien, Kalmüken in der Kalmükischen Republik/Chalm-Tangsch);
(2) Autochthone Minderheiten ohne politische Autonomie (z. B. Eskimo oder Tschuktschen in Ostsibiren, Taten im nördlichen Kaukasus, Ischoren im Gebiet St. Petersburg);
(3) Alte nationale Minderheiten mit politischer Autonomie (z. B. aschkenasische Juden mit ihrer autonomen Region im Fernen Osten; für die Deutschen ist die Wiedereinrichtung der Wolgaregion in Planung);
(4) Alte nationale Minderheiten ohne politische Autonomie (z. B. Griechen im nördlichen Kaukasus);
(5) Neue nationale Minderheiten mit bis heute ungeklärtem politisch-kulturellem Status (z. B. Esten, Letten, Ukrainer, Georgier, Armenier, Usbeken u. a.).

Der Status des Russischen in Rußland hat sich zwar nominell, nicht aber faktisch verändert. In der sowjetischen Periode übernahm das Russische die Rolle einer All-Unions-Sprache (russ. *vsesojuznyj jazyk*), womit die interregionale Verfügbarkeit dieses Kommunikationsmediums für die Interaktion zwischen den Völkern der Sowjetunion hervorgehoben wurde. Das Selbstwertgefühl der Russisch-Sprachigen, wozu russische Muttersprachler, nichtrussische Assimilanten und Sprecher des Russischen als Zweitsprache gehören, wurde durch das Attribut „erhaben" (russ. *velikij*) unterstrichen, das man in der politischen Propaganda zur Kennzeichnung des Russischen bevorzugte. Faktisch füllte das Russische damals schon die Funktionen einer Staatssprache (russ. *gosudarstvennyj jazyk*) aus, obwohl sich die Sowjetideologen permanent bemühten, die Faktizität dieses Status zu negieren und zu verschleiern. Stattdessen wurde die Gleichrangigkeit der Sprachen in der sowjetischen Union propagiert. Im modernen Rußland ist der Status des Russischen als Staatssprache auch nominell bestätigt worden, was einer Anpassung der offiziellen Terminologie an die sprachpolitischen Realitäten im Lande entspricht.

Für die meisten der in Rußland beheimateten Nichtrussen (1989: 27,2 Mio.) ist das Russische eine im Berufs- wie Alltagsleben vertraute und vielerorts unverzichtbare Zweitsprache. Während die von der sowjetischen Sprachplanung propagierte national-russische Zweisprachigkeit mit einer nichtrussischen Sprache als Primärsprache und dem Russischen als Zweitsprachenkomponente in der West- und Südregion sowie in Mittelasien vorrangig ein ideologisches Mittel war, den Zusammenhalt der inneren Kolonien der Sowjetunion zu gewährleisten, entsprach dieses Kommunikationsmodell innerhalb Rußlands seit jeher den natürlichen Gegebenheiten. Nichtrussen lernen vielerorts schon im Vorschulalter Russisch, und dieses Medium dient auch über die Schulausbildung hinaus als bevorzugte Umgangs- und Schriftsprache. Trotz der prestigemäßigen Aufwertung und Modernisierung der Regionalsprachen (z. B. des Tatarischen, Baschkirischen oder Kalmükischen) in der Welle des aufstrebenden Lokalpatriotismus nichtrussischer Regionen ist und bleibt das Russische der einzige Garant für die kommunikative Mobilität der Bevölkerung Rußlands.

Obwohl die generelle Tendenz der Kulturpolitik heute die einer Abwendung und Überwindung von sowjetischen Institutionen ist, gibt es daneben das reale Erbgut der sozialistischen Epoche, das gleichsam stillschweigend übernommen wird. Hierzu gehören die zahlreichen Standardsprachen der größeren und kleineren Völker Rußlands, die von den sowjetischen Sprachplanern normiert worden sind (s. Lewis 1972, 154 ff zur Geschichte der Standardisierung). Bei aller Kritik an den Widersprüchen und totalitären Zügen der sowjetischen Sprachplanung dürfen deren effektive Errungenschaften bei der Verschriftung, Normierung und Modernisierung der nichtrussischen Sprachen nicht übersehen werden (s. Haarmann 1993, 303 ff zu einer Gesamteinschätzung der sowjetischen Sprachenpolitik). Das sprachpolitische Erbe des Sowjetismus wird auch weiterhin im Schriftsprachenpotential Rußlands tradiert, wozu außer dem Russischen mehr als 40 regionale Schriftmedien gehören (Tabelle 231.3).

Zum Erbe aus der sowjetischen Periode gehören auch die geschlechter- sowie milieuspezifische Verteilung russischer Sprachkenntnisse und die Varianzstrukturen der Spracherhaltung in den nichtrussischen Sprachgemeinschaften. Die Verteilung russischer Sprachkenntisse ist ebenso wie die Erhaltung nichtrussischer Muttersprachen milieugebunden. Als Ergebnis soziodemographischer und ethnostatistischer Analysen zur Mehrsprachigkeit in der Sowjetunion (s. Haarmann 1986, 119 ff und 1991, 195 ff) lassen sich einige empirisch-allgemeine Feststellungen über die Sprachverteilung treffen:

(a) Die nichtrussischen Muttersprachen werden von der weiblichen Bevölkerung besser bewahrt als von der männlichen. In bezug auf die Tendenz zum Sprachwechsel (d. h. den Übergang zum Russischen im Generationenwechsel) gilt, daß sich Männer bereitwilliger assimilieren als Frauen.

(b) Die nichtrussischen Muttersprachen werden von der Landbevölkerung besser bewahrt als von der Bevölkerung im Kontaktmilieu. Die Assimilation ist entsprechend bei der Stadtbevölkerung stärker als im ländlichen Siedlungsmilieu.

(c) Die Verteilung von Kenntnissen des Russischen im Zweitsprachenstatus zeigt ähnliche Proportionen wie der Assimilationsprozeß. Die männliche Bevölkerung der meisten nichtrussischen Sprachgemeinschaften besitzt mehr Zweitsprachenkenntnisse des Russischen als die weibliche Bevölkerung. Die Attraktion des Russischen ist gleichzeitig im urbanen Kontaktmilieu stärker als auf dem Lande.

(d) In der Verteilung von Kenntissen der (nichtrussischen) Primär- und russischen Zweitsprache sind vier Grundtypen von Zweisprachigkeit zu unterscheiden, die sich im Hinblick auf die Korrelation von Primär- und Zweitsprachenniveau voneinander unterscheiden (s. Haarmann 1986, 125 ff zur Typologie). Je höher das Niveau der Spracherhaltung, je geringer der kommunikative Druck des Russischen, und umgekehrt.

Ganz anders ist die Situation des Russischen und sein Verhältnis zu den Regionalsprachen in den neuen souveränen Staaten mit mehrheitlich nichtrussischer Bevölkerung. Jenseits der Grenzen des modernen Rußland hat das Russische seine faktische Staatssprachenfunktion sowie seine nomi-

Tab. 231.3: Schriftreform im europäischen Teil der ehemaligen Sowjetunion

Schriftmedium	Kyrillisches Alphabet	Lateinisches Alphabet	Anderes Alphabet
Russisch	+	−	−
Ukrainisch	+	−	−
Weißrussisch	+	−	−
Litauisch	−	+	−
Lettisch	−	+	−
Estnisch	−	+	−
Armenisch	−	−	armenisches Alphabet
Georgisch	−	−	georgisches Alphabet
Aissor	−	−	Estrangelo
Moldauisch	1930−1933 seit 1937 1957 (Reform)	1924−1929 1933−1937 seit 1989	−
Tatarisch	seit 1939	1928−1938	bis 1927 arabisches Alphabet
Baschkirisch	seit 1940	1929−1939	bis 1929 arabisches Alphabet
Tschuwaschisch	+	−	−
Mordwinisch (Mokscha-Mordwinisch)	1947 (Reform) 1957 (Reform)	−	−
Mordwinisch (Erza-Mordwinisch)	1928 (Reform)	−	−
Tscheremissisch (Wiesentscheremissisch)	1938 (Reform)	−	−
Tscheremissisch (Bergtscheremissisch)	1938 (Reform)	−	−
Wotjakisch	bis 1932 seit 1939	1932−1938	−
Syrjänisch (Komi-Syrjänisch)	bis 1931 seit 1939	1932−1938	−
Syrjänisch (Komi-Permjakisch)	1921−1931 seit 1939	1932−1938	−
Kalmükisch	1924−1930 seit 1938	1931−1937	bis 1924 zaja-panditisches Alphabet
Ossetisch	seit den vierziger Jahren des 19. Jhs.	−	−
Adygeisch	seit 1937	1927−1936	bis 1927 arabisches Alphabet
Abchasisch	seit 1954	1928−1938	bis 1928 arabisches Alphabet 1938−1953 georgisches Alphabet
Tschetschenisch	seit 1938	1928−1938	bis 1927 arabisches Alphabet
Jurakisch	seit 1938	1931−1937	−
Gagausisch	seit 1957	−	−
Karaimisch	−	bis 1939	bis 1939 hebräisches Alphabet
Liwisch	−	1921−1939	−
Karelisch	1939−1940	1931−1939 seit 1989	−
Wepsisch	−	1931−1937 seit 1989	−
Ingrisch	−	1935−1937	−
Jiddisch	−	−	hebräisches Alphabet
Romani	−	30er Jahre	−
Polnisch	−	nach 1945 in Litauen und in der Ukraine	−
Ungarisch	−	nach 1945 in Transkarpatien	−
Finnisch	−	nach 1945 in Sowjet-Karelien	−
Samisch (Kildin-Dialekt)	seit 1984	−	−

nelle Rolle als eine den sozialistischen Internationalismus fördernde Zweitsprache in den nichtrussischen Territorien der ehemaligen Sowjetunion (mit Ausnahme Weißrußlands) eingebüßt. Dies gilt für die neuen Staaten der Westregion (s. 5) ebenso wie für die Südregion (Kaukasus) und den Großraum des früheren sowjetischen Mittelasien. Im Kaukasus fungieren die Nationalsprachen der neuen Staaten als Staatssprachen (d. h. Armenisch, Aserbaidschanisch, Georgisch). Das Russische ist die einzige Sprache der Südregion, die von der Mehrheit der Kaukasier, Indoeuropäer und Türken (d. h. turksprachlichen Völkern wie Aserbaidschanern, Kumüken oder Balkaren) verstanden und im interethnischen Kontakt benutzt wird. Trotz seiner interaktiven Funktionen, die sich im multinationalen Kontaktmilieu des Kaukasus in Jahrzehnten bewährt hatten, besitzt das Russische dort keinen offiziellen Status mehr.

Ähnliches gilt für das ehemalige Sowjetasien, wo die Nationalsprachen der Titularnationen Kasachstans, Usbekistans, Turkmeniens, Kirgisiens und Tadschikistans zu Staatssprachen avanciert sind. Die Umstellung der Administration auf die Landessprachen, die in sowjetischer Zeit neben dem Russischen bestenfalls eine Statistenrolle im amtlichen Bereich gespielt hatten, verläuft nicht problemlos. Faktisch ist man weiterhin auf das Russische, zumindest für eine Übergangszeit, angewiesen.

In der Westregion, in der Südregion und in den modernen mittelasiatischen Staaten leben insgesamt mehr als 25 Mio. Russen. Deren sprachlicher, kultureller und politischer Minderheitenstatus ist bislang ungeklärt. Nach den Chinesen sind die Russen heutzutage das Volk mit dem größten Anteil an Minderheiten außerhalb des Mutterlandes.

7. Mehrsprachigkeit als Interaktionspotential — Perspektiven für die Zukunft

Wenn auch die russische Bevölkerung derzeit eine Übergangsphase erlebt, die den Abbau ihrer früheren sozialen Vorrangstellung und das Risiko bedeuten, sich antirussischen Ressentiments im Kreis der neuen nicht-russischen Majoritäten auszusetzen, weicht ihr Minderheitenstatus dennoch faktisch von dem anderer Minderheiten ab. In allen Staaten der Westregion sind die Russen nach der Titularnation die stärkste Bevölkerungsgruppe. Insofern wird ihre Sprache auch in der Minderheitenpolitik der Nationalstaaten eine besondere Beachtung finden müssen. Außerdem ist das Russische (zweite) Muttersprache für Millionen von nicht-russischen Assimilanten geworden. Weiterhin ist Russisch das einzige vertraute Kommunikationsmedium mit internationaler Reichweite, d. h. es kann potentiell zur zwischenstaatlichen Verständigung (z. B. im Kontakt der baltischen Staaten untereinander), innerhalb der Westregion (z. B. im Kontakt Litauens mit Weißrußland) sowie im Kontakt mit Rußland und den übrigen Regionen der ehemaligen Sowjetunion fungieren.

Die Konsolidierung des nationalstaatlichen Ausbildungswesens auf der Basis des nationalsprachlichen Mediums (z. B. Estnisch in Estland als ausschließliche Unterrichtssprache) hat Einbußen für das Russische und seine Verbreitung gebracht, die in der Zukunft nicht wieder ausgeglichen werden. Das Russische wird zwar auch weiterhin — über den Fremdsprachenunterricht mit Russisch als Wahlfach — ein integrativer Bestandteil der kommunikativen Mobilität bei der nicht-russischen Bevölkerung bleiben, seine ehemalige Bedeutung ist aber bereits drastisch zurückgegangen. Englisch ist die erste Fremdsprache und das vormals verbindliche Russisch muß derzeit mit anderen Fremdspachen wie Deutsch und Französisch konkurrieren.

Die radikale Umstellung der sprachpolitischen Organisation in der Westregion, die auf den Ausschluß des Russischen im öffentlichen Sektor und auf den Abbau dieser Sprache im Ausbildungswesen abzielt, wird zwar aus der Stimmung des revitalisierten regionalen Nationalismus heraus verständlich, diese nationalsprachliche Tendenz unterminiert aber faktisch das Interaktionspotential, über das die Bevölkerung in der Westregion mit ihrer während der sowjetischen Periode entwickelten national-russischen Zweisprachigkeit verfügt. Es stellt sich die Frage, ob Sprachkenntnisse (in diesem Fall des Russischen) nicht zu wertvoll sind, als daß man sie politischen Interessen opfern sollte.

8. Bibliographie (in Auswahl)

Achunzjanov, E. M. et al. (1987): „Russkij jazyk — odin iz osnovnych istočnikov razvitija i obogoščenija jazykov narodov SSSR" [Das Russische — eine der grundlegenden Quellen für die Entwicklung und Bereicherung der Sprachen der Völker der UdSSR]. In: *Deśeriev*, 85–99.

Ager, Dennis/Muskens, George/Wright, Sue (Eds.) (1993): *Language Education for Intercultural Communication*, Clevedon/Philadelphia/Adelaide.

Arutjunjan, J. V. et al. (Eds.) (1992): *Russkie. Etnosociologičeskie očerki* [Die Russen. Ethnosoziologischer Abriß], Moskau.

Baskakov, N. A. (Ed.) (1966): *Jazyki narodov SSSR II: Tjurkskie jazyki* [Die Sprachen der Völker der UdSSR II: Turksprachen], Moskau.

Baskakov, N. A. (Ed.): (1969): *Osnovnye processy vnutristrukturnogo razvitija tjurkskich, finno-ugorskich i mongol'skich jazykov* [Grundlegende Prozesse der innerstrukturellen Entwicklung türkischer, finnisch-ugrischer und mongolischer Sprachen], Moskau.

Bátori, István (1980): *Russen und Finnougrier. Kontakt der Völker und Kontakt der Sprachen*, Wiesbaden.

Beloded, Ivan Konstantinovič/Deśeriev, J. D. (Eds.) (1977): *Naučno-techničeskaja revoljucija i funkcionirovanie jazykov mira* [Die wissenschaftlich-technische Revolution und die Funktionstüchtigkeit der Sprachen der Welt], Moskau.

Bokarev, E. A./Lomtatidze, K. V. (Eds.) (1967): *Jazyki narodov SSSR IV: Iberijsko-kavkazskie jazyki* [Die Sprachen der Völker der UdSSR IV: Iberischkaukasische Sprachen], Moskau.

Bromlej, J. V. (Ed.) (1988): *Narody mira. Istoriko-etnografičeskij spravočnik* [Die Völker der Welt. Ein historisch-ethnographisches Nachschlagewerk], Moskau.

Bruk, S. I./Apenčenko, V. S. (1964): *Atlas narodov mira* [Atlas der Völker der Welt], Moskau.

Carrère d'Encausse, Hélène (1979): *Risse im roten Imperium. Das Nationalitätenproblem in der Sowjetunion*, Wien.

Cholmogorov, A. I. (1970): *Internacional'nye čerty sovetskich nacij* [Internationalistische Wesenszüge der sowjetischen Nationen], Moskau.

Čislennost' i sostav naselenija SSSR. Po dannym Vsesojuznoj perepisi naselenija 1979 goda [Zahl und Zusammensetzung der Bevölkerung der UdSSR. Nach den Daten der All-Unions-Volkszählung von 1979] (1984), Moskau.

Comrie, Bernard (1981): *The Languages of the Soviet Union*, Cambridge.

Deśeriev, J. D. (1987a): „Vlijanie russkogo jazyka na jazyki narodov SSSR i razvitie obščego leksičeskogo fonda" [Der Einfluß der russischen Sprache auf die Sprachen der Völker der UdSSR und die Entwicklung einer allgemeinen lexikalischen Grundlage]. In: *Deśeriev* (Ed.), 31–62.

Deśeriev, J. D. (Ed.) (1973a): *Razvitie nacional'no-russkogo dvujazyčija* [Die Entwicklung der national-russischen Zweisprachigkeit], Moskau.

Deśeriev, J. D. (Ed.) (1973b): *Vnutristrukturnoe razvitie staropis'mennych jazykov* [Die innerstrukturelle Entwicklung der alten Schriftsprachen], Moskau.

Deśeriev, J. D. (Ed.) (1987b): *Vzaimovlijanie i vzaimoobogoščenie jazykov narodov SSSR* [Lehnbeziehung und Bereicherung der Sprachen der Völker der UdSSR durch Entlehnung], Moskau.

Haarmann, Harald (1979a): *Elemente einer Soziologie der kleinen Sprachen Europas, Bd. 2: Studien zur Multilingualismusforschung und Ausbaukomparatistik*, Hamburg.

Haarmann, Harald (1979b): *Quantitative Aspekte des Multilingualismus*, Hamburg.

Haarmann, Harald (1979c): *Spracherhaltung und Sprachwechsel als Probleme der interlingualen Soziolinguistik*, Hamburg.

Haarmann, Harald (1979d): *Multilinguale Kommunikationsstrukturen*, Tübingen.

Haarmann, Harald (1985): „The Impact of Group Bilingualism in the Soviet Union". In: *Kreindler* (Ed.), 313–344.

Haarmann, Harald (1986): *Language in Ethnicity. A View of Basic Ecological Relations*, Berlin.

Haarmann, Harald (1992a): „Measures to Increase the Importance of Russian Within and Outside the Soviet Union – A Case of Covert Language-Spread Policy (A Historical Outline)". In: *International Journal of the Sociology of Language* 95, 109–129.

Haarmann, Harald (1992b): „Historical Trends of Cultural Evolution Among the Non-Russian Languages in the European Part of the Former Soviet Union". In: *Sociolinguistica* 6, 11–41.

Haarmann, Harald (1993): *Die Sprachenwelt Europas. Geschichte und Zukunft der Sprachnationen zwischen Atlantik und Ural*, Frankfurt/New York.

Itogi vsesojuznoj perepisi naselenija 1970 goda, t. IV [Ergebnisse der All-Unions-Volkszählung des Jahres 1970] (1973), Moskau.

Kask, A. (1969): „Estonskij jazyk" [Das Estnische]. In: *Baskakov*, 268–301.

Kask, A. (1975): „Estonskij jazyk'» [Das Estnische]. In: *Lytkin* et al., 167–202.

Knowles, Frances (1993): „From USSR to CIS and Beyond: Visceral Politics vis-à-vis Ethnolinguistic Realities". In: *Ager* et al., 131–158.

Kozlov, Viktor Ivanovič (1975): *Nacional'nosti SSSR* [Die Nationalitäten der UdSSR], Moskau.

Kreindler, Isabelle T. (Ed.) (1985): *Sociolinguistic Perspectives on Soviet National Languages. Their Past, Present and Future*, Berlin/New York/Amsterdam.

Kruopas, J. et al. (1973): „Litovskij jazyk" [Das Litauische]. In: *Deśeriev* (Ed.), 101–162.

Lewis, E. Glyn (1972): *Multilingualism in the Soviet Union. Aspects of Language Policy and Its Implementation*, Den Haag/Paris.

Lytkin, V. I. (Ed.) (1966): *Jazyki narodov SSSR III: Finno-ugorskie i samodijskie jazyki* [Die Sprachen der Völker der UdSSR III: Finnisch-ugrische und samojedische Sprachen], Moskau.

Lytkin, V. I. et al. (Eds.) (1975): *Osnovy finno-ugorskogo jazykoznanija. Pribaltijsko-finskie, saamskij i mordovskie jazyki* [Grundlagen der finnisch-ugrischen Sprachwissenschaft. Ostseefinnische Sprachen. Lappisch und mordwinische Sprachen], Moskau.

Michal'čenko, V. J. (1973): „Uslovija litovsko-russkogo dvujazyčija" [Bedingungen der litauisch-russischen Zweisprachigkeit]. In: *Dešeriev* (Ed.), 54–71.

Narodnoe obrazovanie i kul'tura v SSSR. Statističeskij sbornik [Volksbildung und Kultur in der UdSSR. Ein statistisches Sammelwerk] (1989), Moskau.

Päll, E. N. (1977): „Funkcionirovanie estonskogo jazyka kak jazyka nauki" [Das Funktionieren des Estnischen als Sprache der Wissenschaft]. In: *Beloded/Dešeriev* (Eds.), 164–171.

Raun, Toivo U. (1985): „Language Development and Policy in Estonia". In: *Kreindler* (Ed.), 13–35.

Selickaja, I. A. (1973): „Uslovija estonsko-russkogo dvujazyčija" [Bedingungen der estnisch-russischen Zweisprachigkeit]. In: *Dešeriev* (Ed.), 72–85.

Shamshur, Oleg V./Izhevskaya, Tatiana I. (1993): „Multilingual Education as a Factor of Interethnic Relations: The Case of the Ukraine". In: *Ager* et al., 159–167.

Skorik, P. J. (Ed.) (1968): *Jazyki narodov SSSR V: Mongol'skie, tunguso-man'čžurskie i paleoaziatskie jazyki* [Die Sprachen der Völker der UdSSR V: Mongolische, tungusisch-mandschurische und paläosibirische Sprachen], Leningrad.

Smith, Graham (Ed.) (1992): *The Nationalities Question in the Soviet Union*, London/New York (3. Aufl.).

Social'noe razvitie SSSR 1989 – Statističeskij sbornik [Die soziale Entwicklung der UdSSR 1989 – Ein statistisches Sammelwerk] (1991), Moskau.

Solchanyk, R. (1985): „Language Politics in the Ukraine". In: *Kreindler* (Ed.), 57–105.

Uibopuu, Valev (1988): *Finnougrierna och deras språk. Kapitel om de finsk-ugriska folkens förflutna och nutid* [Die Finno-Ugrier und ihre Sprachen. Abhandlung über die Vergangenheit und Gegenwart der finnisch-ugrischen Völker], Lund.

Vinogradov, V. V. (1945): *Velikij russkij jazyk* [Die erhabene russische Sprache], Moskau.

Vinogradov, V. V. (Ed.) (1966): *Jazyki narodov SSSR I: Indoevropejskie jazyki* [Die indoeuropäischen Sprachen], Moskau.

Wexler, Paul (1985): „Belorussification, Russification and Polonization. Trends in the Belorussian Language 1890–1982". In: *Kreindler* (Ed.), 37–56.

Wexler, Paul (1992): „Diglossia et schizoglossia perpetua – The Fate of the Belorussian Language". In: *Sociolinguistica* 6, 42–51.

Harald Haarmann, Helsinki (Finnland)

232. Estonia

1. Geography and demography
2. Territorial history and national development
3. Politics, economy and general cultural and religious situation
4. Statistics and ethnoprofiles
5. Language political situation
6. Conclusion
7. Bibliography (selected)

1. Geography and demography

The Republic of Estonia is situated on the eastern coast of the Baltic Sea. The area of Estonia is 45.226 sq.km. To the north and to the west, Estonia has the Baltic Sea; in the east it shares a mainland frontier with Russia and in the south with Latvia. The population is 1.506 million (January 1, 1994), ethnic Estonians comprising 64% of the population. Immediately following the Soviet occupation in 1940, continuous immigration from all over the Soviet Union began at the instigation and encouragement of Moscow, eventually resulting in the influx of 1.4 million immigrants, of whom 0.8 million left. As a result, the number of non-Estonians grew from 23 thousand (2.7%) in 1945 to 602 thousand (38.5%) in 1989.

The number of Estonians, which was reduced through mass deportations to Siberia (1941, 1949), imprisonment and executions, as well as through refugee flows to the west in 1944 and human losses in World War II (WW II), has never reached the pre-war level again.

According to the 1989 census the population of Estonia was 1.565 million comprising 121 different nationalities. Of non-Estonians, 61% were first-generation immigrants, ca 20% second-generation immigrants, 15%

third-generation immigrants; 4% were indigenous ethnic groups.

The official language is Estonian. About 18% of non-Estonians speak Estonian. Due to the significant immigrant Russian-speaking community formed during the occupation, besides Estonian in unofficial communication also Russian is widely used (→ Language Map P).

2. Territorial history and national development

2.1. History up to 1940
2.1.1. Politics

Estonians, a Finno-Ugric people, have lived in their present habitat since the 3rd millennium B.C. In the early 13th century the Estonian lands were subjugated by the State of the Teutonic Order, except for the Setu territory in South-East Estonia which was under the Principality of Pskov. In the middle of the 16th century the Estonian territory was divided between Poland, Denmark, Sweden and the Principality of Moscow. Since 1629 Estonia was ruled by the Swedish Kingdom. The Great Northern War left Estonia as the possession of the tsarist Russian Empire for almost two centuries: 1721—1918.

After the October Revolution in Russia, the Estonian national state was founded (21 February 1918). On 17 June 1940, the Soviet Union annexed Estonia, and on 6 August 1940, Estonia was incorporated into the Soviet Union. The Soviet occupation lasted until Estonia reestablished its sovereignty on 20 Aug. 1991.

The major immigration flows into Estonia have always accompanied and followed wars: in the 13th century mainly Germans and Danes; in the 16th—17th centuries Swedes; in the 18th—19th centuries Russians. Despite these migrations, up to the beginning of the Soviet occupation in 1940, the population of the Estonian territory was ethnically quite homogeneous. It was only after the Great Northern War, in the 17th century, that the proportion of non-Estonians reached the level of about 15% (representing about a dozen different peoples).

2.1.2. Standardization of the Estonian language

The name Estonian (Est. *eesti*, Lat. *aesti*) was introduced into the Estonian literary language from German or Swedish in the 17th century. In popular usage, however, the words *eestlane* and *eesti keel* (Estonian for the nationality and the language, respectively) were accepted only in the second half of the 19th century. Before that Estonians had referred to themselves as the "country people" and to their language as the "country language".

In medieval times the language used in the municipal administration was Baltic German, based on Low German (Niederdeutsch); clergy used Latin for their sacred routines; the language of the land supervisor depended on the language of the conquerors, i.e. (Low) German, Swedish, Russian, and in some places Danish and Polish.

The history of the Estonian literary language can be traced back to the 16th century when the first longer Estonian texts originate. The 17th century saw the emergence of two literary languages: the North Estonian, or Tallinn literary language and the South Estonian, or Tartu literary language. The role of the South Estonian literary language began to wane in the 18th century in conjunction with the publication of the Bible in North Estonian (1739). In the first half of the 19th century the foreign-flavoured language of religious literature was gradually superseded by more popular usage, which also acquired secular functions. The second half of the 19th century was a time of unification in the national literature; textbooks and periodicals were also published. The first four decades of the 20th century may be identified as the era of normalization of the literary language; it acquired some strong puristic features. According to the Constitution Estonian has become the national language. Its usage was fixed in the Language Law of 1934 and corresponding language regulations.

2.1.3. Minorities

Between WW I and WW II Estonian minorities (Russians, Germans, Swedes, Jews) enjoyed ample cultural autonomy. According to the 1934 census, the ethnic composition of the population of Estonia was as follows: 992,000 (88%) Estonians, 92,000 (8%) Russians, 16,300 (1.5%) Germans, 7,600 (0.7%) Swedes, and 4,400 (0.4%) Jews. Most non-Estonians were bilingual. The majority of the largest minority i.e. Russians lived in rural areas, the most "Russian" areas being the town of Narva (29.7%), the territories east of Narva, and the Petseri region. In Tallinn the percentage of Russians was 5.7%. Other major ethnic groups, Germans and Jews, lived in towns, Swedes in the Estonian coastal region and islands. In response to an appeal from Hitler, most Germans left Estonia in October 1939.

2.2. History 1940—1988
2.2.1. World War II

Following the Soviet-German Non-Aggression Pact and its Secret Protocol (the Molotov—Ribbentrop Pact), the Soviet Union occupied Estonia in June 1940 and proclaimed it a part of the Soviet Union as the Estonian Soviet Socialist Republic on 6 August 1940. These measures entailed disastrous changes in the population, including its ethnic composition: mass deportation (over 10,000 people) and imprisonment of the autochthonous inhabitants (about 7,000), and the first influx of colonists.

World War II overrode Estonia twice. Germany conquered Estonia in 1941, and in 1944 the country was again occupied by the Soviet Union. At the end of 1941 Estonia was claimed by the Germans to be *judenfrei*. In 1943, 85% of the Swedes left for Sweden, in accordance with a German-Swedish treaty. In 1944, before the arrival of the Soviet army, 70,000 Estonians fled to Sweden and Germany. Many factors contributed to the further decrease in the Estonian population: war damages, mobilization for war duty by both Soviet and German forces, losses in direct military actions, evacuation to the Soviet Union, the transfer of Estonian territory to Russia in 1945 (ca 1500 sq.km). By 1945, the Estonian population had decreased by one-fifth (i.e. by 200,000) to 831,000.

2.2.2. Soviet Occupation

In the years 1945—50, while natural increase was only 8,700, 170,000 non-Estonians settled permanently in Estonia, over 90 per cent of them in towns. Their reasons for moving to Estonia were: a better standard of living (there was famine in Russia); organized recruitment (construction work, oil industry); positions in certain strategic areas where Estonians were not trusted, e.g. navigation and aviation, the railways, communications etc. The oppression of Estonians continued, a reaction to which was the guerilla movement known as the "forest brothers". Several mass arrests and deportations of Estonians to other regions of the Soviet Union took place (altogether ca 50,000 between 1945 and 1949). In March 1949 over 20,000 Estonians were deported to the Far East and Siberia, the majority women and children. During the occupation immigrants settled mainly in: 1) the town of Narva (its resettlement by Estonians was restricted in the post-war years); 2) Sillamäe, an area closed to Estonians because of uranium mining and processing; 3) the Kohtla-Järve oil-shale mines; 4) the country's capital, Tallinn (large Russian factories and Soviet bases), and 5) the submarine base Paldiski. In connection with the building of large Soviet Air Force bases, the linguistic situation changed drastically in Tartu, Tapa, Haapsalu and Pärnu. After the 1960s, migration diminished, but until the end of the 1980's, the number of new-comers exceeded those leaving by 8—900 per year.

The total immigration during the Soviet occupation was 1.4 million, emigration 0.8 million. As the number of Estonians did not reach the pre-WWII level, being less than a million, their proportion of the population dropped from 97.3 in 1945 to 61.5 in 1989.

2.2.3. Language policy

The decrease of functional as well as regional areas where the Estonian language was used was accompanied by a rapid rise of the status of Russian. A Russian-speaking network of plants, factories, offices, institutions and service bureaus as well as entertainment facilities and residence areas was put into place, with a full-scale Russian education system, including higher education and vocational schools. As a result a Russian-speaking environment in Estonia was created with no contacts with Estonians or the Estonian language, effectively hindering any possible integration. Nevertheless, the Estonian language was maintained, Estonian education preserved and research on Estonian in the Institute of Language and Literature conducted. An Orthographical Dictionary was published in 1960 (second edition 1976). A number of terminological committees worked in various professional and technical fields. For many years a National Orthographical Committee operated.

During the post-war period, Estonian was discriminated against in the curriculum, not only in Russian schools, but also in Estonian educational institutions. To retain the obligatory status of the Estonian language and literature in Estonian schools, Estonian-based "national" schools were prolonged by one year as compared to the Russian-based schools. For other linguistic groups, using one's native language in education was not allowed; their education was mostly in Russian (exceptionally in Estonian). Instruction of Russian had become a political issue. An enhancement of the quantity as well as quality of instruction of Russian in schools with Estonian as language of instruction, even at the expense of other subjects, had become a matter of government decrees and protocols.

The teaching of Russian received a considerable amount of additional material support that enabled the authorities to raise the salaries of Russian language teachers and to reduce the number of students in the Russian language classes by dividing them into parallel groups. The Estonian-based schools were required to teach Russian as a "second native language", whereas the curricula of the Russian-based schools contained little practical Estonian and no Estonian history or geography whatsoever. Due to the unbalanced education system, two separate linguistic communities developed, whose mutual understanding was deficient both linguistically and culturally.

2.2.4. Russian Influence on Estonian

Russian interference phenomena beginning in 1940 have been studied by Mati Hint (1990). These may be observed on lexical, grammatical and phonetic levels. The lexical interferences have reflected the changes in the society, the main areas of loan words being in ideological and economic spheres (*kolhoos, perestroika*) or neologisms (*sputnik*). Ideologically directed semantic shifts were also significant, e. g. *national language* meaning non-Russian autochthonous language in the Soviet Union, *foreign languages* as opposed to *Soviet languages*, etc. Loan idioms and compound words from Russian came into use (*ööpäevaringselt*; cf. R. *kruglosutočno*).

In the grammar Russian language structures were borrowed and became productive afterwards, like the expanding usage of reflexive verbs (*probleem lahendub* for *lahendatakse*), negation (*ei saa jätta märkimata* for *tuleb märkida*), plurale tantum (*rahad* for *raha*, cf. R. *dengi*), preposition instead of postposition (*läbi eelarve* for *eelarve kaudu*), word order, etc. The interference phenomena on the phonetic level have been dealt with by Ilse Lehiste.

3. Politics, economy and general cultural and religious situation

Influenced by *perestroika* and *glasnost*, the Supreme Council of the Estonian SSR passed the Declaration of Sovereignty (16 November 1988), and superseded Estonian laws over Soviet ones. The Estonian language was declared the official state language in Estonia by a Constitutional amendment of December 6, 1988. After the failure of the coup of August 1991 in Moscow and the restoration of Estonian independence the Estonian Government introduced a normalization programme:

(1) Financial help for those who want to repatriate (according to opinion polls, up to 15% of non-Estonians).
(2) Governmental funding for activities promoting integration (e. g. Estonian language learning; 2/3 of non-Estonian population has demonstrated their interest).
(3) Financial help for minorities in order to preserve their language and culture.

The level of repatriation has been significant. The main factors hindering it are Russia's indifference and devastating economic situation in the CIS countries. Net migration in Estonia (immigration − emigration) is strongly negative: 1990 ... −4000; 1991 ... −8000; 1992 ... −35,000; 1993 ... 14,000. Reasons for emigration vary: the rapid change of social environment and restructuring of the economy, erection of country borders between families and their relatives, regulations which govern obtaining Estonian citizenship (see below). In the case of Ukrainians and Byelorussians another factor seems to be relevant, namely a search for their ethnic roots and national identity.

As for the other two programmes, the government as well the international community are providing considerable funds for Estonian and minority language courses, minority language radio programmes, etc.

The dichotomous structure of the Estonian society is reflected also in its religious situation. The most influential church at present is the Estonian Evangelical Lutheran Church. Second in influence is the Russian Orthodox Church (Apostolic Orthodox Church). The latter uses two languages in its services, namely Russian (amongst the Russian population, the church is subordinated to the Patriarch of Moscow), and Estonian (the independent church affiliated with the Patriarch of Constantinople).

Among the major normalization problems is the issue of Estonian citizenship. The current citizenship regulations derive from the 1920 Tartu Peace Treaty between Estonia and Russia and from the 1938 Law on Citizenship which introduced the *jus sanguinis* principle. Those individuals who do not qualify for Estonian citizenship on the basis of these two legal norms can obtain it through a naturalization process which requires 2 + 1 years of residency in Estonia and a basic knowledge of Estonian. According to the Law on Estonian Language Requirements for Applicants for Citizenship (1993), one must have a basic listening comprehension, be able to hold a conversation on everyday topics, read and provide a short summary of news and reports, and be able to complete simple written exercises, such as filling out personal applications, composing a curriculum vitae, writing an address on an envelope, writing an application for study or employment, writing a letter of authorization and filling out standard forms. It also provides special examination guidelines for persons born before January 1, 1930, and for disabled persons. The citizenship issue has caused tension because the half-a-million immigrant community in Estonia lost its citizenship. They did not meet the requirements for Estonian citizenship and, since the successor of the USSR, the CIS, decided to change the naturalization laws from *jus sanguinis* to *jus soli*, thus depriving citizens of the former Soviet Union of their previous citizenship, the Russian immigrants in Estonia remained stranded without any citizenship whatsoever.

Russia considers the immigrant community a Russian minority and accuses Estonia of minority discrimination. There have been numerous human rights missions to Estonia (16 since the restoration of independence); none of them have found any gross or systematic violation of human rights.

4. Statistics and ethnoprofiles

According to the 1989 census, the ethnic composition of Estonia (altogether 121 ethnicities) was as follows: 963,000 Estonians (61,5%), 475,000 Russians, 48,000 Ukrainians, 28,000 Belorussians, 16,600 Finns, 4,600 Jews, 4,000 Tartars, 3,500 Latvians and 3,000 Poles, and other smaller groups. Only two of these ethnic groups – Estonians and Russians – had largely retained their mother tongue. A third of Estonians could speak Russian, which was a compulsory school subject, while only 15% of Russians were bilingual in Russian and Estonian. These were mainly local indigenous Russians. Of the other minorities, 40% spoke their native language, 52% were Russified, approximately 8% spoke Estonian. The lack of education in native languages of these minorities has resulted in an underdeveloped sense of ethnic identity, which hinders their cultural recovery.

The 1989 census also reveals the following immigration pattern:

(1) Most non-Estonians are first-generation immigrants with social and family ties outside Estonia. About 95% among them are 45 years old or younger.
(2) The second-generation immigrants fail to follow the socialization patterns of the local population and join the Russian language community.
(3) Contacts between immigrants and the Estonian population are marginal (different workplaces, cultural habits, small number of mixed marriages). Though immigration was put under control with the Law on Immigration in 1990 and the Law on Aliens in 1993, the influence of this social pattern will last long. The non-Estonian sector of the population is mainly concentrated in towns (91% of all non-Estonians), the principal concentrations (for 80% of all aliens) being in six major Estonian towns: Tallinn, Tartu, Narva, Kohtla-Järve, Pärnu, Sillamäe.

The contact languages used by these diverse nationalities were Estonian (mainly in the country) and Russian (mainly in towns). Apart from their mother tongue, 31.3% of the population (490,000 people) have a command of another language. For most people the second language is Russian (77% of bilinguals), followed by Estonian (18%). The frequency of other languages in the role of a second language is below 1 per cent.

5. Language political situation

Though the Language Law (passed on January 18, 1989) describes Estonian as the sole official language, in principle it requires Estonian-Russian bilingualism of holders of certain jobs. To reach the required proficiency level (in most cases 800 words are sufficient) four years are provided since the proficiency requirements are effective starting February 1, 1993. In order to coordinate the teaching of Estonian to Russian adults, a special office, the Estonian Language Center, was founded on March 13, 1989.

After the 1990 elections a number of steps were taken in order to restore the status of the Estonian language in society. In August 1990 the Estonian Government decided to repeal all acts which discriminated against the use of Estonian. On 23 November 1990, the National Language Board was established. It monitors the usage of Estonian as the native as well as the second language, and supports and regulates minority language usage among the adult population. The primary function of the Board is to elaborate language policy and language planning strategies, organize, supervise, and analyse the implementation of the Language Law, to improve language teaching methods, to supervise normative terminological and onomastic work, and to pursue sociolinguistic studies. Thanks to positive political developments the social status of Estonian has risen, and its range of use has widened.

In the 1992/1993 schoolyear there were 553 Estonian schools, 108 Russian schools and 28 mixed schools (some Estonian, some Russian classes). Besides these there were 5 minority language (Swedish, Jewish, etc.) schools operating in Estonia.

6. Conclusion

During the pre-WW II period, sociolinguistic research was minimal and connected nearly exclusively with issues of lexicon, particularly with influences of other languages on the Estonian lexicon, and with etymology. Vivid purist debates took place in the 1920's and 1930's. During the Soviet occupation, sociolinguistic research was restrained to confirmation of ideological postulates. Worth mentioning is the most thoroughly studied national-Russian bilingualism. Some of the results obtained in this study proved to be of significant scientific value. Contrastive language studies formed another popular area of study. A special group of studies focused on the language of Estonians in diaspora: Estonian-Russian in the Caucasus and in St. Petersburg, Estonian-Swedish in Sweden, Estonian-English.

With *perestroika* and the disintegration of the Soviet Union, language policy, language planning and language rights have become topics of the day. Nowadays, contactlinguistic research is conducted in the research department of the National League Board (language planning, language rights) and by contactlinguists working in the Estonian Language Institute (contrastive studies, ethnolinguistics).

7. Bibliography (selected)

Grin, François (1991): "The Estonian Language Law: Presentation with Comments". In: *Language Problems and Language Planning*, Vol. 15, 191–201.

Hilkes, Peter (1990): "The Estonian SSR as an Example of Soviet School reform in the 1980s". In: *Regional identity under Soviet rule: The case of the Baltic States*, Hackettstown, N.J., 249–266.

Hint, Mati (1990): "Russian influences in the Estonian language". In: *Congressus septimus Internationalis Fenno-Ugristarum 1A Sessiones Plenares*, Keresztes, L./Matissah, S. (Eds.), Debrecen, 87–104.

Kreindler, Isabelle (1990): "Baltic Area Languages in the Soviet Union: A Sociolinguistic Perspective". In: *Regional identity under Soviet rule: The case of the Baltic States*, Hackettstown, N.J., 233–248.

Raag, Raimo (1982): *Lexical Characteristics in Swedish Estonian*, Uppsala.

Rannut, Mart (1991): "Beyond Linguistic Policy: The Soviet Union versus Estonia." In: *Rolig-papir* 48/91, 23–52.

Rannut, Mart (1990): "Linguistic Policy in the Soviet Union". In: *Multi-Linguism, Self-Organisation, and Ethnicity*, Vol. 3, 437–447.

Rannut, Mart/Eek, Arvo (1991): "Legal Protection of Threatened Language. The Lesser Used Languages-Assimilating Newcomers". In: *Proceedings of the Conference held af Carmarthen*, Dafis, Llinos (Ed.), 71–87.

Sinilind, Sirje [pseudonym of Juhan Talve] (1985): *Viro ja Venäjä. Havaintoja Neuvostoliiton kansallisuus-politiikasta Virossa 1940–1984* [Estonia and Russia. Observations on the Soviet national policy in Estonia 1940–1984], Alea-Kirja, Jyväskylä.

Taagepera, Rein (1990): "Who Assimilates Whom? – The World and the Baltic Region". In: *Regional identity under Soviet rule: The case of the Baltic States,* Hackettstown, N.J., 137–150.

Uibopuu, Henn-Jüri (1981): "The legislation of the ESSR. Preservation of national identity or russification?" In: *Osteuroparecht*, 247–262.

Viikberg, Jüri (1990): "The Siberian Estonians and language policy". In: *Fourth Int. Conference on Minority Languages*: Western and Eastern European Papers, D. Gorter/J. F. Hoenstra/L. G. Jausma/J. Ytsma (Eds.), Philadelphia, 175–186.

Mart Rannut, Tallinn (Estonia)

233. Latvia

1. Geography and demography
2. Territorial history and national development
3. Politics, economy and general cultural and religious situation
4. Statistics and ethnoprofiles
5. Sociolinguistic situation
6. Language political situation
7. Linguistic interferences of contact languages
8. Conclusion
9. Bibliography (selection)

1. Geography and demography

The Republic of Latvia lies on the western edge of the East European plain, and comprises a territory of 64.000 km². Latvia borders with Estonia (in the North), Russia (in the East), Byelorussia (in the South East), Lithuania (in the South). Latvia has a marine border with Sweden. The population of Latvia is 2.6 million, including 1.4 million ethnic Latvians. About 200.000 Latvians live abroad (USA, Germany, Sweden, Russia, etc.). Latvians have always had direct contacts with other languages and cultures: with Livonian (the only autochthonous language except Latvian in this territory), Estonian, Lithuanian, Byelorussian, Russian as neighbouring languages, with Polish, Swedish, German, and Latin as languages of cultural exchange and official languages. As a result interference in all language strata, especially in lexicon, and mutual influences in ethnography can be observed.

The first data about the population of Latvia have been available since the 18th century. There were 873.000 inhabitants: 89.8% Latvians, 6.5% Germans, 1.1% Jews, 0.8% Poles, 0.6% Russians, 0.3% Livs (Dunsdorfs 1972, 306). Since the period of the Northern War (1700–1721) the number of Russians in Latvia has constantly increased. – There have been several waves of migration during the last 60 years. In 1939 more than 60000 Germans left Latvia for Germany. After the annexation of the Republic of Latvia by the USSR more than 50.000 Latvians were deported to Siberia and Northern parts of the USSR (June 1941). This fact determined the mass emigration in 1944 when 120.000 Latvians, fearing further repression, left Latvia for Western countries. The second mass deportation (55.000 Latvians) came in March 1949 (Krastiņš, Mežgailis, Šmulders 1991). As a result of the industrialization of Latvia and the ensuing process of migration the number of Russian-speaking people has increased almost 5 times while the number of Latvians has diminished. Latvians have become a minority in six of the seven largest cities; in the capital, Riga, there are only 34% Latvians (Latvijas ... 1991, 9ff). The population in the 20th century has developed as shown in table 233.1:

Table 233.1: Development of the population in the 20th century (Vēbers (Ed.) 1992, 4)

Year	1935		1989	
Nationality	Number	%	Number	%
Total (000's)	1905.9	100.0	2657.0	100.0
Latvians	1467.0	77.0	1396.1	52.2
Russians	168.3	8.8	902.3	34.0
Byelorussians	26.8	1.4	117.2	4.4
Ukrainians	1.8	0.1	89.3	3.4
Poles	48.6	2.5	59.7	2.2
Lithuanians	22.8	1.2	34.1	1.3
Jews	93.4	4.9	16.3	0.6
Gipsies	3.8	0.2	7.2	0.3
Estonians	6.9	0.4	3.2	0.1
Germans	62.1	3.3	2.9	0.1
Others	4.4	0.2	28.7	1.1

Only since the reestablishment of the independence of the Republic of Latvia (1991) has there been no increase in immigration. A special program has been initiated to facilitate the return of the Latvians from the Western countries and Russia to prevent a precarious demographic future for Latvians in their native country (→ Language Map P).

2. Territorial history and national development

The Latvian language belongs to the Baltic group of Indo-European languages. Ancient

Baltic tribes gave rise to the Latvian nation and language in the 10–12th century AD. Three dialects are distinguished in Latvian: Tamian, High Latvian, which developed a written form, and the Central dialect which forms the basis of the literary language. The first written monuments date back as far as the 16th century, when Latvian orthography was shaped on the basis of German. The advantageous geographical position of Latvia ensured economical and cultural connections with other countries. Since the 10th century rivalry between major powers for the influence over the territory of Latvia took place. After the destruction of the state-like formations of ancient Latvians (12th–13th century) the territory was incorporated into other countries (Germany, Sweden, Poland). After the Northern war (1700–1721) Latvia came under Russian control but German influence (the privileges of German landlords, the German language in state affairs, Lutheran religion, etc.) were still preserved. Since then Latvian language and culture developed within the context of the coexistence and rivalry of German and Russian elements (Rūķe-Draviņa 1977). One of the most critical periods for Latvians was the end of the 19th century and the beginning of the 20th, when Russification tendencies strengthened considerably. Latvian had no official status; its functions were reduced to the minimum. Only Russian and German were the languages of secondary education, of all governing state bodies, of the courts. But Latvia at the end of the 19th century was consolidated as a nation, a national literature had developed significantly, and strong national tendencies were on the rise. The national intelligentsia promoted the enrichment and the development of the Latvian language to make it functionally comparable with the languages of other European nations. When a favourable international situation allowed the establishment of an independent Republic of Latvia (November 18, 1918), the legal status of Latvian became one of the most important issues of domestic policy. Several Language Laws were adopted; the first decrees and laws (1918, 1921) tried to strengthen the position of Latvian besides German and Russian, and from 1932 Latvian had the legal status of the only official state language. The Latvian language was firmly standardized and covered all the functions of the official state language to a full extent.

In 1940 as a result of the Molotov-Ribbentrop Pact (1939), the Republic of Latvia lost its sovereignty and was incorporated into the USSR. Since then major ethnodemographic changes have taken place. On May 4, 1990, Latvia declared its intent to become an independent state, and on August 21, 1991, the independence of the Republic of Latvia was reestablished.

3. Politics, economy and general cultural and religious situation

The Republic of Latvia is a democratic multiparty parliamentary state. On June 6, 1993, the first free elections of parliament took place, and the Constitution of the Republic of Latvia (1922) was renewed.

Since the 19th century the capital, Riga, has become an important industrial centre; due to its advantageous geographical position Latvia has a developed network of transport communications and trade connections. In the 1920s and 1930s its agricultural production was high. During the short period of independence Latvia became a well-developed country with high living standards and a dynamic cultural life, e.g. Latvia occupied the first place in Europe as to its per capita number of students and the second place as to the number of published books per capita. During the Soviet period (1940–1990) the normal proportions of national economics were distorted by forced industrial development. Now the Latvian economy is undergoing a reconstruction.

There is no state religion in the Republic of Latvia. There were 779 parishes in 1993: 282 Lutheran, 109 Catholic, 94 Russian Orthodox, 54 Old Ritualist, 68 Baptist, 33 7th-Day Adventist, 5 Judaic, etc. Freedom of religion is guaranteed by the Constitution.

4. Statistics and ethnoprofiles

Latvians constitute only 52% of the total population in Latvia. Although Latvia is historically a multi-ethnic region, it is now the only Baltic state whose indigenous population is losing its majority (cf. 1.). The retention rates for Latvian as a mother tongue are high but there are increased percentages of Latvians who claim Russian as their second language. Knowledge of Russian among Latvians is reported as follows:

Table 233.2: Knowledge of Russian among Latvians (Čislennost' 1984, 71; Narodnoe [...] 1991, 77)

Year	Latvian as native language	Russian as second language
1970	95.2%	45.1%
1979	94.9%	56.7%
1989	94.8%	64.4%

The Russians, constituting 34% the total population, can be divided into two groups: those whose ancestors have lived in Latvia since the 17–18th centuries as inhabitants of the colonies of Old Ritualists in the Eastern part of Latvia, and those who immigrated after WW II from the USSR. The first group is as a rule bilingual. As to the second group, according to the most recent poll, Latvian is spoken and written fluently by 7%, 28% can speak the language, 53% understand some phrases and 10% do not speak a word. 72% of Russians living in Latvia plan to apply for Latvian citizenship; there are requirements of state language skills for naturalization.

The Livs (Finno-Ugric language group) had common territory and close economic ties with the Latvians from the 10th–11th centuries and processes of assimilation took place. At the beginning of the 20th century there were only 200–400 Livs, all of them bilingual. Only about 15 people can speak Livonian fluently at present. There is a Livonian cultural heritage association. Special protection is provided to the ethnographic and cultural heritage of the Livs. In the Language Law of the Republic of Latvia the rights of the Livs as native inhabitants of Latvia are specially protected.

Byelorussians and Ukrainians constitute 4.4% and 3.4% of the total population, respectively. 69% Ukrainians and 81% Byelorussians were not born in Latvia and moved there after WW II from the USSR. The policy toward these nations during the Soviet period can be characterized largely as one of Russification and assimilation, and this is also reflected in Latvia. For the majority of representatives of all the largest minorities — Ukrainians, Byelorussians, Poles, Jews — the native language is Russian. For 64% of Lithuanians the native language is Lithuanian, for 24% Latvian; for 50% of Estonians the native language is Estonian, for 24% Latvian; for 85% of Gipsies the native language is Romani, for 10% Latvian.

In the 1920s–1930s there were a set of minority cultural institutions and schools. Education took place in 7 languages in Latvia; in the 1930s 29.9% of all elementary schools and 14.4% of the high schools belonged to the minorities. During the Soviet period this system was destroyed. Under the influence of Soviet ideology *homo sovieticus* was being shaped. As a consequence, several generations of non-Russian minorites in Latvia have lost their native language. After the reestablishment of the independent Republic of Latvia more than 20 national cultural heritage associations were founded and minority schools and language classes were organized.

5. Sociolinguistic situation

The sociolinguistic situation in the Republic of Latvia is quite complicated due to the considerable ethnodemographic shifts during the Soviet period. The Latvian language has enjoyed the status of official state language since 1988; the Language Law was adopted in 1989. According to the 1989 census, Latvian language skills are posessed by: 21.1% Russians, 15.5% Byelorussians, 8.9% Ukrainians, 22.8% Poles, 40.3% Lithuanians, 27% Jews, 52.3% Gipsies. 95% representatives of other nationalities, among them 64.4% Latvians, know Russian (Vēbers (Ed.) 1992, 6). From 1989, when the Language Law was adopted, until 1992, when it came into force, non-Latvians were offered free language tuition during regular working hours. Numerous Latvian language instruction programs have been instituted, a number of self-taught textbooks were published, but the response has been tepid. The main reason seems to be a psychological one: a negative attitude toward the independence of Latvia among non-Latvians in general and the neglect of languages other than Russian is the worst legacy of the Soviet period yet to be dealt with.

The most significant and extensive research concerning the language situation in Latvia was performed in 1987. It found that in 7 functionally essential spheres (industry, agriculture, transport and communications, public service, culture, sciences and education) the situation is to be characterized as asymmetric bilingualism. The Latvian language functioned as a component of Latvian-Russian bilingualism against the background of the widespread Russian language. Almost exclusively the Russian language functioned in the administrative apparatus on the state level (the language of the Supreme Soviet and Council of Ministers was as a rule Russian), in big enterprises and in numerous local offices, to say nothing of such branches like shipping, railway transport, aviation and military spheres. At schools more lessons were allotted to Russian than to Latvian; moreover, Latvian was not mandatory at Russian schools. Although the claim of absolute legal equality of languages in the Soviet Union was upheld during the last decades, there has been a marked decrease in the use of Latvian (Blinkena 1994/95). Its consequences are being felt to the present day.

6. Language political situation

The changes in Soviet domestic policy paved the way for the rise of popular movements in favour of the independence of Latvia. In 1988 an active movement of all the Baltic peoples for full language rights began. On October 6, 1988, the Latvian language regained its status as state language. On May 5, 1989, the new Language Law was adopted. As the Republic of Latvia restored its independence, some amendments to this Law were adopted.

The Republic of Latvia Language Law determines the place of Latvian and other languages in the national economy and in social life, it declares the right of language preference and the protection of minority languages. All institutions must use Latvian, the official State language, in conducting their affairs, and in all documents related to the conduct of their affairs, as well as in their correspondence with addressees within Latvia. At conferences, meetings, etc., a speaker has the freedom to use the language of his/her choice, but in government and administrative bodies the language used to conduct affairs is Latvian. Individuals who do not know Latvian may upon agreement use any other language. In this case, the organizer must provide a translation into Latvian, even it is requested by only one participant of a meeting.

To ensure the revival of Latvian in social life where almost only Russian has functioned up to the present, employees of those State institutions whose professional responsibilities include contacts with the general public or who perform office work shall be subjected to the official state language certification regardless of their nationality if they have not undergone their instruction in Latvian (Official State Language Proficiency Certification Regulation, 1992).

In all educational institutions with a language of instruction other than Latvian, the Latvian language is taught. Persons who graduate from secondary, specialized and vocational secondary schools and from universities must take an examination in Latvian. The necessary language proficiency level is determined and language instruction is ensured by the State Ministry of Education. The State finances the instruction of Latvian at State-owned institutions and organizes the production of the necessary educational resources.

To put into practice the demands of the Latvia Language Law regarding the usage of Latvian in place names, titles of enterprises and organizations, public information and advertising, and business and commerce, special regulations have been worked out (Regulations On the Official State Language Usage in Titles and Information, 1992). The Republic of Latvia Place Names Commission was established to promote preservation and precise usage of historical place names. Official and shortened versions of enterprises' names shall be created and introduced in the State language in conformity with the demands of normative orthography of the Latvian literary language. In all the documents first and last names of persons shall be written in accordance with the accepted rules of Latvian spelling.

The official State language status of Latvian does not affect the constitutional rights of residents of other nationalities to use their native language or other languages, specifically in national culture heritage associations and religious institutions. With the reestablishment of independence the schools of national minorities were renewed. In the school year 1991/92, 892 state-financed schools were functioning in Latvia, of which 554 were Latvian, 208 Russian, 126 co-educational schools for Latvians and Russians, 3 Polish, 1 Ukrainian, 1 Estonian, 1 Lithuanian, and 1 Jewish (Russian is the language of instruction; both Yiddish and Hebrew are taught).

To govern the observance of the Language Law and other resolutions pertaining to language issues, the State Language Inspection Board was established (Regulations of the Republic of Latvia Official State Language Inspection Board, 1992). All the activities in language policy in Latvia are supervised by the State Language Centre of the Council of Ministers in co-operation with the Latvian Language Institute of the Latvian Academy of Sciences, the Official State Language Consultation Service and other institutions.

7. Linguistic interferences of contact languages

The proximity of different peoples, wars, migration and other processes have found their reflection in the Latvian language. Linguistic interferences have taken place throughout all the history of Latvian.

Latvian and Russian have long traditions of territorial and functional contacts. There are common Balto-Slavic lexical strata and also common features in phonetics, derivational system and grammar. The first direct borrowings from Slavic date back to the 9th—12th centuries when close trade contacts were established. (*svēts* 'holy' < *святой*, *grāmata* 'book' < *грамота*, *grēks* 'sin' < *грех*). When Latvia came under German control earlier close contacts with Russia stopped. The next period of Russian influence was at the end of the 19th century when Russification tendencies were experienced, but the linguistic impact of Russian was blocked by German to a great extent. From the beginning of the Soviet era contacts with Russian grew extensively. In vocabulary, loan translations became widespread (*teicamnieks* 'excellent pupil' < *отличник*, *piecgade* < 'five-year period' < *пятилетка*).

Through Russian many international words (*aerosols* 'spray' < *аэрозоль*, *kibernētika* 'cybernetics' < *кибернетика*) and regionalisms (*stepe* 'steppe' < *степь*, *taiga* 'taiga' < *тайга*) came into Latvian. Direct loans in Standard Latvian were limited (*boļševiks* 'communist, Bolshevik' < *большевик*, *kolhozs* 'collective farm' < *колхоз*, *sputņiks* 'satellite' < *спутник*) because Latvian normative sources have always recommended dropping a Russian loan if a Latvian word existed or could be found. There were numerous direct Russian borrowings in Latvian slang (*hatņiks* 'home party' < *хатник*, *korešs* 'friend' < *кореш*) and in spoken Latvian (*kurtka* 'jacket' < *куртка*, *samosvals* 'lorry' < *самосвал*). — Syntax and phraseology are two areas in which the influence of Russian appears as a consequence of the massive amount of translation. Word-for-word translations lead to syntactical errors and Russicisms (*par cik — par tik* 'as — as' < *поскольку — поскольку*, *gramáta lasás* 'the book is read', lit. 'the book reads' < *книга читается*, *bút pie sevis* 'to be in one's room', lit. 'to be at oneself' < *быть у себя*). Nevertheless, in the Soviet period when the social functions of Latvian were considerably reduced, the linguistic impact of Russian was not as great as it might appear. Latvian retained its traditional alphabet. Phonological changes have also been minimal (e. g. palatalization in Russian proper names *T'ihonovs*, *Vlad'imirs* — there are no palatals *t'* and *d'* in the phonological system of the Latvian language). That was largely due to activities of Latvian linguists in preserving the purity of Latvian (Drízule, Gerentović 1987). The impact of Latvian on Russian in Latvia has also been observed since 1816 when the first Russian newspaper in Latvia was published. There are some lexical borrowings (*rinda* 'queue' < *рында*, *šlipse* 'tie' < *шлипса*) as well as Lettonisms in word order and syntactic constructions (Semenova 1973).

The influence of German on Latvian is assumed to have started in the 12th century when German and Latvian were spoken in a unified community. Due to the dominant position of German language and culture there were a considerable number of borrowings in various spheres (from Middle Low German at first) (*zāģis* 'saw' < Middle Low German *sage*, German *Säge*, *niere* 'kidney' < MLG *nére*, G. *Niere*, *spēle* 'play' < MLG *spel(e)*, G. *Spiel*, *slikts* 'bad' < MLG *slicht*, G. *schlecht*). Later centuries brought mainly High German influence (*kleita* 'dress' < G. *Kleid*, *loze* 'lot' < G. *Los*). German influence was slowed to some extent in the second half of the 19th century due to the puristic tendencies of the Latvian intelligentsia. In the 20th century, appearance of new German loanwords has been scarce. The total number of German loanwords is about 3000 (Sehwers 1936); at present many of them are out of active use.

There have also been direct loans as well as influences in grammar, phraseology and semantics from neighbouring languages: Lithuanian (*ģimene* 'family' < Lit. *giminé* 'clan', *veikals* 'shop' < Lit. *veikalas* 'activity'), Livonian or Estonian (*puķe* 'flower' < Liv., Est. *putk*, *sēne* 'mushroom' < Liv. *sén*, Est. *seen*, *vai* 'or' < Liv. *voi* or Est. coll. *vai*), but the neighbouring languages were more influenced by Latvian.

There were mainly indirect contacts with Western languages. There are approximately 2500 words from the Romance languages (including Latin) but most of them are indirect loans mediated through German or Russian and Polish. The first English loanwords in Latvian appeared at the end of the 18th century when limited direct contacts between Latvian and English in the sphere of seatrade were established. Close contacts with the English-speaking countries in the 1920s–1930s contributed to the growth of English lexical influence. After a short respite, the process of borrowing intensified, especially in terminology. By the 1980s about 1500 English loanwords had been identified in Latvian (Baldunčiks 1989). Due to the orientation toward the West, there was a marked intensification of the process of borrowing in the 1990s.

8. Conclusion

In the Soviet period in Latvia, as in the whole of the USSR, language conflicts were never mentioned. Officially the view was held that there was a true bilingualism and the privileged position of Russian did not contradict with the claim of absolute equality of languages in the Soviet Union. Latvians experienced a shrinking of the area of use of Latvian, but an open defence of the Latvian language could have been classified as a political offence. Language conflicts were growing under the surface and only from time to time broke out in everyday situations.

The loss of independence, though it was only for a twenty-year duration, was never accepted as legitimate by Latvians; among the several symbols of national identity language was identified as the most important. The process of regaining Latvian language rights was peaceful and tolerant. The period of implementation of the language Law was 3 years. The process has provoked statements alleging discrimination against non-users of Latvian. There have been claims that language requirements for naturalization infringe the rights of the Russian speaking population. Several expert commissions from the EC and the UN worked in Latvia in 1992–1993. They found that language policy in Latvia does not contradict democratic principles and that the requirement of state language skills is a normal phenomenon in a civilized world.

There have been many public discussions on language issues in Latvia. The unwillingness of the Russian-speaking population to learn and use Latvian seems to be supported by factors inherited from Soviet ideology. Its neglecting attitude toward languages other than Russian was grounded in the widespread "theory" of the so-called objective inevitability of merging of languages and supported by comparison of the quality of languages in favour of Russian. Individuals therefore cannot be blamed. They arrived in Latvia without any thought of the Baltic states being anything but another Russian province, and were told that the Russians had liberated Latvia and helped the Latvians to overcome their backwardness. When the actual historical facts came to light in the late 1980s, and the independence of Latvia was restored, the new status of Russian was hard to accept for them. On the other hand, the Latvians cannot be blamed for wishing to preserve their language in a land which is the only corner of the world where this language can survive. Demands for Russian as a second official state language in Latvia seem to be dangerous for the existence of Latvian in the present sociolinguistic situation: asymmetrical bilingualism would continue and the Russian-speaking population would still remain monolingual.

The sociolinguistic situation in the Baltic states and in Latvia particularly is hardly comparable with any other multilingual region of the world (Druviete (Ed.) 1995). The minority-majority problem is very complicated in the Latvian case. It seems that to equate the status of Russians in Latvia with that of minorities in other societies is to ignore compelling historical facts. The main issue is how the basic needs of the Russian-speaking population can be integrated with the legitimate national needs of the Latvians. The present policy gives ground for optimism that a loyal citizenry from a nationally diverse population will be created, that all the rights of minorities will be preserved, and that ancient and well-preserved Latvian will not be extinct.

9. Bibliography (selection)

Baldunčiks, Juris (1989): *Anglicismi latviešu valodā*, [Anglicisms in the Latvian language], Riga.

Bergmane, Anna/Blinkena, Aina (1986): *Latviešu rakstības attīstība* [The development of writing in Latvia], Riga.

Blinkena, Aina (1994/1995): "The Latvian Language: Some Problems of its Existence and Development". In: *Acta de langue française et de linguistique. Terminology and LSP Linguistics.* vol. 7/8, 463−469, Halifax.

Čislennost' i sostav naseleniya SSSR [Number and composition of the population of the USSR] (1984), Moscow.

Drīzule, Viktorija A./Gerentović, Viktorija V. (1987): *Latyśsko-russkoe dvujazyćie. Kratkij obzor i bibliografićeskij ukazatel'* [The Latvian-Russian bilingualism. A short review and bibliography], Riga.

Druviete, Ina (Ed.) (1995): *The Language Situation in Latvia, Sociolinguistic Survey. − Part 1. Language Use and Attitudes among Minorities in Latvia*, Riga.

Dunsdorfs, Edgars (1972): *Latvijas vēsture* [The History of Latvia], Stockholm.

Endzelīns, Jānis (1922): *Lettische Grammatik*, Riga.

Grabis, Rūdolfs (ed.) (1959, 1962): *Mūsdienu latviešu literārās valodas gramatika* [The grammar of the contemporary standard Latvian language] I−II, Rīga.

Krastiņš Oļģerts/Mežgailis, Bruno/Šmulders, Modris (1991): *Latvijas iedzīvotāji. Statistikas izziņas* [The population of Latvia. Statistical information], Rīga.

Latvian Research. An International Evaluation (1992), Copenhagen.

Latvijas valsts statistikas komiteja/State Committee of Statistics (1991): *1989 gada tautas skaitīšanas rezultāti* [Results of the 1989 census], Riga.

Narodnoe xozyaistvo SSSR v 1990 godu [National economy of the USSR in 1990] (1991), Moscow.

Official State Language Proficiency Certification Regulation. May 25, 1992, Riga.

Regulations of the Republic of Latvia Official State Language Inspection Board, July 22, 1992, Riga.

Regulations On the Official State Language Usage in Titles and Information. November 4, 1992, Riga.

Republic of Latvia Law on Additions to the Latvia Code on Administrative Violations Concerning the Official State Language Issues. July 1, 1992, Riga.

Republic of Latvia Language Law. March 31, 1992, Riga.

Rūķe-Draviņa, Velta (1977): *The Standardization Process in Latvian. 16th Century to the Present*, Stockholm.

Sehwers, Johan (1936): *Sprachlich-kulturhistorische Untersuchungen vornehmlich über den deutschen Einfluß im Lettischen*, Leipzig.

Semenova, Mariya (1973): *Russko-latyśskie yayykovye svyazi* [Russian Latvian language contacts], Riga.

Vēbers, Elmārs (Ed.) (1992): *The Ethnic Situation in Latvia Today*, Riga.

Ina Druviete, Riga (Latvia)

234. Lithuania

1. Geography and demography
2. Territorial history and national development
3. Political, economic, general cultural and religious situation
4. Statistics and ethnoprofiles
5. Sociolinguistic situation
6. Language political situation
7. Language contact
8. Critical evaluation of the sources and literature used
9. Bibliography (selected)

1. Geography and demography

The territory of the Republic of Lithuania is a lowland, lying at an average sea level of 100 m, and constitutes the western part of the great East European plain. The total area of Lithuania encompasses 65,200 sq. km.

Today the population of Lithuania is 3,751,000. The majority (69%) reside in towns, the largest of which are Vilnius, Kaunas, Klaipėda, Šiauliai and Panevėžys. The proportion of urban and rural inhabitants changed radically during Soviet rule, because the pre-war Lithuanian Republic was an agricultural country. Two causes were responsible for this internal migration: the expropriation of private lands and the accelerated growth of industry.

109 ethnic groups live in Lithuania, only 14 of them comprising more than 1,000 people. Lithuanians constitute the majority (4/5) of the total population. There are some ethnic minorities which have lived in Lithuania since ancient times, e. g.: Poles, Jews, Tatars, Karaites, Latvians, Germans, and a small number of Russians (Kobeckaitė et al. 1992, 3 f). The majority of Russians, Byelorussians and Ukrainians moved in from the former USSR after World War 2 (WW 2) as colo-

nists replacing the more than 350,000 Lithuanians who had been deported to Siberia and other parts of Soviet Russia (1944–1953) or had lost their lives during the post-war guerilla war (1944–1952). Later, a new wave of colonists, primarily Russian-speaking, came to build the nuclear power plant and several large industrial enterprises (→ Language Map P).

2. Territorial history and national development

Lithuania has never included all Lithuanian ethnic areas since the formation of the Lithuanian state in the middle of the 13th century. The south-western territories shortly after were occupied by the Teutonic Order. On the basis of these territories, Lithuania Minor emerged in East Prussia in the 16th century. There, under the influence of the Reformation, a distinctive Lithuanian culture and written language developed. After the end of the 15th century, the Lithuanian ethnic areas began to shrink, mostly under the pressure of Slavs from the south and south-east.

The Grand Duchy of Lithuania (13th–18th centuries) was a multiethnic state famed for its laws tolerant of all its ethnic minorities. Initially the nobility of Lithuania adopted the Byzantine culture of the Eastern Slavs; later they succumbed to Polish influence, especially after 1569, when a federal union with Poland was formed.

After the complete collapse of the Commonwealth of Lithuania and Poland at the end of the 18th century, the greater part of Lithuania was annexed by the Russian Empire. Because of the strict anti-Lithuanian policy carried out by the Tsarist government since the end of the 19th century the percentage of Lithuanians living in the territory decreased from 62% (1897) to 52% (1914). This figure increased significantly (to 68%) after WW 1 because the ethnic minorities residing in Lithuania decreased more than Lithuanians had during the war (Zinkevičius 1993, 139 ff).

The year 1918 saw the proclamation of an independent Lithuanian Republic, free of all previous ties with Poland and Russia. The territory of 88,000 sq. km corresponding more or less to the ethnic area was assigned to the Republic of Lithuania by international treaties (Budreckis 1985, 584 f). However, in 1920, the Polish army annexed Vilnius and the territory surrounding it, comprising nearly a third of Lithuania. In 1939, the Germans annexed the Klaipėda region, while the Soviet Union helped to return Vilnius and a part of its territory to Lithuania forcing Lithuania to sign a "treaty of friendship". The Molotov-Ribbentrop pact (23. 08. 1939) and its secret protocols destroyed the independent Lithuanian state, which was annexed by the Soviet Union (1940–1990). Mass repression, deportations, repatriations, emigrations and the post-war colonial policy changed the ratio of ethnic minorities significantly. On the one hand, the number of Jews diminished ten times; that of the Germans, eight times; of the Poles, two times; on the other hand, the number of Russians increased four times, and the number of Lithuanians had increased to 79% by 1959 (Zinkevičius 1993, 234 ff).

After WW 2, Lithuania was forcibly incorporated into the USSR as one of its republics, defined by the borders of 1940 with the returned Klaipėda region. Some tens of thousands of authochthonous Lithuanians remained outside the territory of Lithuania, in Poland, Byelorussia, Russia (Kaliningrad region) and Latvia. The independence of Lithuania was reestablished on 11. 03. 1990.

3. Political, economic, general cultural and religious situation

The Republic of Lithuania is a parliamentary state with a democratically elected Parliament (Seimas), Government and President. The policy of the young state, which is seeking its own place in Europe and the world, is based on developing friendly relations with all states, especially its neighbours, and on the respect of human rights.

Lithuania is an industrial-agrarian state. Its economy is now suffering from a great depression caused by the transition from a planned to a market economy, as well as from public to private property.

Culturally Lithuania belongs to Western Europe, with which it has old cultural and religious ties (dating from the 13th century). Lithuania is a Catholic country located farthest to the north-east of Europe among Orthodox and Protestant countries. The Roman Catholic Church has 666 religious communities and 3 theological seminaries in Lithuania. About 160 religious communities belong to the Russian Old and Orthodox Believers, the Lutherans, and other churches (cf. Kobeckaitė et al. 1992, 30 f).

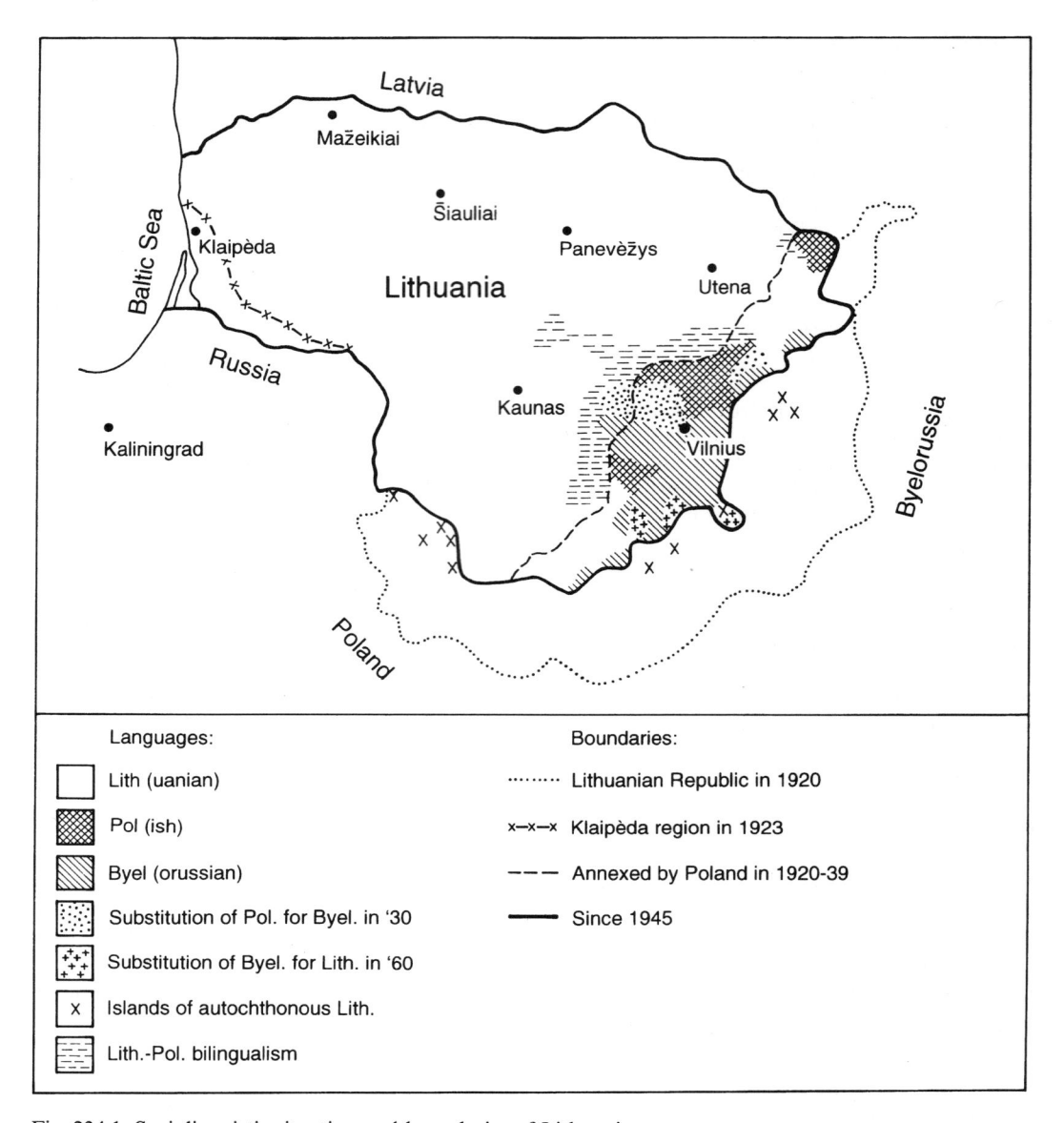

Fig. 234.1: Sociolinguistic situation and boundaries of Lithuania

4. Statistics and ethnoprofiles

4.1. During the Soviet regime, only Lithuanian, Russian and Polish were permitted at schools as languages of instruction, as well as in the mass media.

4.1.1. Nearly 80% of the total population consider Lithuanian (lietùvių kalbà) to be their native language. Lithuanians occupy the greater part of Lithuania with the exception of the south-east and the eastern fringes of the country, where Slavic nationalities and languages predominate.

4.1.2. Russian (Lith. rùsų kalbà) is the second language as measured by the number of native speakers in Lithuania. Almost all Russians (96%), constituting 9% (344,000) of the total population, consider Russian their native language. Nearly one half of the Ukrainians, Byelorussians, and Germans, and one third of the Jews, as well as a small percentage of Poles and other minorities, declare Russian as their mother tongue as well (all statistical figures on §§ 4.1−4.2 see in Kobeckaitė et al. 1992, 3−9, 17). Russian speakers thus might constitute 12−13% of the total population.

4.1.3. Polish (Lith. *lénkų kalbà*) is used as a home language (i. e. it is confined to communication at home, among family members) by about a third of the people of Polish nationality, constituting 7% (258,000) of the total population. Polish-speaking Poles live in Vilnius (18% of the population of the city), in the countryside to the north-east of Vilnius, in the district of Trakai and in the north-eastern fringes of the country. The majority of these people speak a local Polish sociolect (they say they speak *po prostemu*, i. e. "simply"), which is to be viewed as a variant of literary Polish formed on the basis of Lithuanian and, here and there, of a Byelorussian substratum. As a language of the Catholic confession, Polish is used in almost all of south-eastern Lithuania, where the majority of the people of Polish nationality live.

4.2. All other languages were used only at home as vernaculars during the Soviet regime. We shall point out only those which are important from the point of view of contact linguistics.

4.2.1. Byelorussian or, more precisely, a dialect of Byelorussian (Lith. *gùdų/baltarùsių kalbà*), is spoken in villages and small towns located to the south, north-west and northeast of Vilnius, as well as in the district of Šalčininkai. Generally, Byelorussian speakers call themselves *tuteishy*, i. e. "locals", and say they speak *po prostu*, i. e. "simply" (Budreckis 1985, 640 f). Typologically the same phenomenon is observed in the region of Klaipėda, where the population, under German rule since the 13th century, call themselves *šišioniškiai* ("locals").

The national consciousness of the majority of Byelorussian speakers was formed on the basis of Catholicism, which came from Poland and was therefore interpreted as Polish. That is why the people identify their "simple" language as Polish although structurally it is a Byelorussian dialect.

4.2.2. Tatars, numbering about 4,000, live in several villages in the district of Vilnius and generally speak Byelorussian and Polish (sometimes Lithuanian as well).

4.2.3. Ukrainians (44,000) are mostly newcomers who settled in towns, especially in Vilnius. About half of them consider Russian to be their native language.

4.2.4. The Jews were one of the most important ethnic groups in Lithuania from the 14th century on. Before WW 2, there was a vibrant Jewish presence in Lithuania (Jews constituted about 8% of the total population), and Vilnius used to be referred to as the second Jerusalem. The majority of Lithuanian Jews considered and still consider Yiddish (*litvišer jidiš*; Lith. *žỹdų kalbà*) as their native language, while the Jewish newcomers from the neighbouring Slavic countries generally speak Russian as their mother tongue. Jewish schools, which were widespread before WW 2, were not allowed by the Soviets. After 1990, the education of Jews was reestablished on the basis of Modern Hebrew rather than Yiddish because most schoolchildren were going to leave Lithuania. Today, about 8,000 Jews live in Lithuania, and this figure is decreasing every year.

4.2.5. Latvian (*latviešu valoda*, Lith. *lātvių kalbà*) is spoken by about 4,000 Latvians living mostly in the northern part of Lithuania, where active contacts with the Lithuanian dialects take place.

4.2.6. A specific variant of Romani influenced by Lithuanian, Byelorussian and Polish (*litóuska romá*, Lith. *čigõnų kalbà*) is used by 3,000 Gipsies living in Lithuania.

4.2.7. Only half of the 2,000 Germans living mostly in western and southern Lithuania consider German (Lith. *vókiečių kalbà*) to be their native language. German has had a limited influence on dialectal and Standard Lithuanian.

4.2.8. The Karaites, an ethnic minority of Jewish faith, still live in the old Lithuanian capital Trakai and speak their own language (Lith. *karaĩmų kalbà*). This language is an archaic form of Turkic influenced by Lithuanian at the level of vocabulary. Today, 269 Karaites live in Lithuania.

5. Sociolinguistic situation

5.1. The Lithuanian language is the national official standard enshrined in the present Constitution (1988, ratified in 1992) as the only state language. Until 1990, Lithuanian was one of the latent bilingualism components in the Soviet Union, and the number of Lithuanian-Russian bilinguals increased. Until 1990, Russian gradually relegated Lithuanian to the status of a minority language.

This could be observed in situations when on public occasions native Lithuanians switched to Russian even if there was only one Russian speaker among them. This phenomenon was characteristic of the inhabitants of large cities and of those from the south-eastern parts of Lithuania. In general, only Lithuanians in rural areas are Lithuanian monolingual or show a low degree of Lithuanian-Russian bilingualism. Recently Russian has been receding due to a functional expansion of Lithuanian.

5.2.1. A sociolinguistically particular situation is found in the south-east of Lithuania. Part of the population there identify themselves as Poles and usually speak Byelorussian or Polish. Nevertheless, their grandparents or even parents used to speak Lithuanian, a result of historical and political circumstances. At first, i. e. from the end of the 19th to the beginning of the 20th century, they were taught to be Poles even if they did not speak Polish; later, during the Polish occupation in 1920−1939, they were taught to consider Poland to be their motherland. They referred to themselves as "the inhabitants of this land". During the Soviet era they quite naturally became Soviet oriented.

The Lithuanian language thus does not enjoy the same social prestige in south-eastern Lithuania as elsewhere. Almost every Polish or Byelorussian speaker, identifying himself as a Pole, does not speak Lithuanian and, apart from elderly people, speaks Russian on official occasions and Polish or Byelorussian at home. Even pupils in Polish schools used to speak Russian during breaks. Nevertheless, there have been some recent changes: the prestige of the Polish language has been growing rapidly, with the Russian language receding. Thus, in the early 1990's, Polish could have become a basis of the Polish-Lithuanian national and linguistic conflicts, which were perceived by Lithuanians as inspired by the Moscow leadership. The conflicts also became an issue of negotiation of the Polish and Lithuanian governments.

5.2.2. One of the most obvious manifestations of Lithuanian nationalism was the consolidation of the Lithuanian language as the official language of the Republic of Lithuania. Most recent Russian-speaking immigrants have found it difficult to see Lithuanian-Russian bilingualism disappear. But open conflict on the basis of language is no longer observed.

Beginning in 1995, non-Lithuanian speakers will be bound by law to learn the state language if they wish to get a job in civil service or state enterprises. Generally, the law has been accepted as a needed measure, and non-Lithuanian speakers have even begun to attend Lithuanian language courses.

5.2.3. The smaller ethnic minorities speak their own languages at home, but they use the language of their neighbours, e. g. Polish or Byelorussian, in everyday communication with them. On other occasions they use both Lithuanian and Russian, the latter being more prestigious. This pattern of language use is characteristic of Jews, Karaites, Tatars, etc.

5.3. The phenomenon of intralingual diglossia is characteristic of both Lithuanian and Polish speakers. The Lithuanian language has two variants, i. e. the standard form and the territorial or urban dialects. As the standard form is more prestigious, it stimulates the levelling of dialects, to the extent that they are found to be merging. These processes are spreading rapidly since the standard language is the only medium used in the educational system and in the mass media. The merging of the western dialects is, however, slower because they differ from the standard form to a much higher degree than the others. Standard Lithuanian is based on the western *Aukštaičiai* dialect located to the south-west of Kaunas.

The Poles use spoken Polish, which is quite remote from its standard form. Only those leaving Polish schools try to use standard Polish while communicating with Polish speakers.

6. Language political situation

6.1. Soviet language policy resulted in replacing national languages in many socially prestigious areas by Russian (→ art. 231). That is why the present language policy of Lithuania sets forth the following tasks: (1) to return the Lithuanian language to all spheres of social life; (2) to codify the powerful wave of new terms and words; (3) to create conditions for non-Lithuanian speakers to learn the state language; (4) to protect the languages of the ethnic minorities. The language policy has been regulated by the Language Law (1990) and the Ethnic Minorities Law (1991). Special state departments and institutions, such as the State Language Inspection, the Nationalities Department, and the Lithuanian Language Teaching Centre have been established. The Lithuanian Language Committee (established in 1977) was established by law and has now acquired state status. Official language proficiency certification has also been instituted.

6.2. The present situation of language policy has been occasioned by Lithuanian-Russian bilingualism, which has been widespread throughout all spheres of social life for the past fifty years (Dini 1993, 234−236). The Russian language was used in government and administration to a greater extent than anywhere else. All possible ways of introducing the Russian language into public life were used. More and more programmes and films in Russian were shown on TV.

The educational system was able to withstand the pressure. Lithuanian children attended only Lithuanian schools. There were Russian and Polish schools according to the number of Russian or Polish speakers. Children of other ethnic minorities used to choose schools in accordance with the languages they spoke in their local areas. The system of mixed schools was created in order to encourage children to speak Russian. In the 1970's, the number of Polish schools began to decrease to the advantage of the Russian ones. The opposite process has been taking place in recent years. Due to the growing prestige of Lithuanian and Polish the children of ethnic minorities are being sent to Lithuanian and Polish schools respectively, even if they cannot speak those languages.

According to the Ethnic Minorities Law (1991) Russian, together with other languages of minorities, was given a legal basis to become a regional language of ethnic minorities living compactly in administrative-territorial units for the purposes of the local government bodies; at the court one is permitted to request an interpreter.

Lithuanian radio and TV broadcasting includes also programmes in Russian, Polish, Byelorussian, Ukrainian (the first two are daily programmes, the others weekly); newspapers and magazines are also published in these languages as well as in Yiddish and German. Four Lithuanian newspapers are reviewed weekly in Russian and two in Polish. Books are printed also in Russian and Polish. There are Russian and Polish theatres and numerous public and cultural organizations founded on an ethnic basis.

The church was greatly devastated in Lithuania during the last fifty years. Though less attended, the Catholic Church has remained throughout the country. It uses Lithuanian or Polish in its services according to the language of parishioners. Byelorussian Catholics use Polish in the church; Russian Old and Orthodox Believers use Russian. There are almost no worship houses of Jews, Tatars, Karaites and Germans left. A revival of the ethnic minorities' religions has been taking place since 1990.

7. Language contact

7.1 Changes in Lithuanian standard usage are caused mainly by internal factors with the Russian language playing an active role. (The influence of the Lithuanian language on Russian is insignificant; sometimes the insertion of Lithuanian words is observed). One of the most obvious changes on the phonetic and phonological level is the progressive neutralization of the short/long vowel opposition, especially in inflections. The palatalization of consonant groups before front vowels is becoming less strictly defined (cf. Grumadienė/Stundžia 1987). Changes on the morphological and morphosyntactic level concern the verb system to a great extent. The participle, the gerund and verbal constructions are receding due to the overlapping of noun or pronoun constructions: *jis vaikščiojo lietui lyjant* 'he walked when it rained', i. e. dat. sg. + gerund. is replaced with *jis vaikščiojo, kai lijo lietus*, i. e. a nom. sg. + verb past. indef. construction. The compound tenses are being simplified: *aš esu apie tai rašęs* 'I have written about that' is often changed to *aš rašiau apie tai* 'I wrote about that'. The declension system is being simplified: some case endings of less productive stems are being replaced by one of the more productive types.

The level of syntax is more influenced by contemporary language contact than phonetic or morphological ones. Lithuanian verb government is being replaced with Russian-type verb government, e. g. *atstovauti Seimui* 'to represent Parliament' (inf. + dat.) becomes *atstovauti Seimą* (inf. + acc.). A similar situation is observed in prepositional constructions. Vocabulary (and semantics) is influenced by Russian mostly through word-formation patterns and calques (for details on issues of this paragraph cf. Ambrazas 1967).

7.2. The Polish language emerged in Lithuania on a Lithuanian (occasionally a Byelorussian) substratum, so even now its articulatory basis resembles Lithuanian more than Polish. Many Lithuanian morphological and syntactic features are still preserved (participial constructions, the inflections of the 3rd person, etc.). Some vocabulary was taken from Lithuanian and adapted grammatically without being translated. The same is characteristic of some proper nouns, too (cf. Čekman 1982; Zinkevičius 1993, 114 ff).

Almost the same features are characteristic of the Byelorussian dialect, though it is usually considered superstratic, the Polish language being considered adstratic.

8. Critical evaluation of the sources and literature used

8.1. The problem of Lithuanian-Russian bilingualism is usually viewed from one of two perspectives, "Russian" or "Lithuanian". Publications on both points of view are not very numerous (cf. Karaliūnas 1983), even since the major political changes in 1990. The main drawback of present publications is that they are based on sociolinguistic investigations carried out on a very small scale.

8.2. The influence of internal and external factors on the development of present-day Lithuanian is discussed very cautiously; this is especially true concerning internal factors. Lately synchronic analysis has been carried out for some territorial dialects and urban sociolects of Lithuanian from the sociolinguistic viewpoint including analysis of language contacts.

8.3. Discussions on language policy erupted in 1988. The promotion of Lithuanian to the status of official language was warmly supported by Lithuanians while Russian speakers would have preferred Lithuanian-Russian bilingualism and recognition of Russian and Lithuanian as two official state languages.
Discussions on the relationship of the Lithuanian and Polish languages and the respective nations, as well as their genesis, have had quite a different character. Very often they remain deadlocked on issues of Polish-Lithuanian history. The Lithuanian-Polish conflict between the Polish cultivated Lithuanian nobility and the local people with growing Lithuanian national awareness dates back to the national-liberation movement of 1863. Scholars of both countries are unable to rid themselves of stereotypes by which both nations perceive each other. What results is a lack of communication. The Symposium on Lithuania-Poland relations held in 1992 in Vilnius was virtually ignored by Polish scholars. Similarly symposiums held in Poland usually invite Lithuanian politicians but not scholars.

The problems of the origins of Poles and the languages they use (Polish and Byelorussian) are not widely discussed in Lithuania at present. By contrast, the concept of "Polonized Lithuanians" is actively and aggressively discussed in Poland. Lithuanian scholars address the issue as one of peripheral Lithuanian dialects. In studies of this kind, solutions to the problems of a Lithuanian language substratum and to former ethnic boundaries of Lithuania are based on linguistic observations. The mechanism of the spread of Polish and Byelorussian has been described in detail by the Polish linguist Halina Turska (1939). Only in 1989 was a survey of the sociolinguistic situation in present-day south-east Lithuania made again (cf. Čekmonas/Grumadienė 1993). Research into the Byelorussian dialect used in Lithuania is being carried out, but to a very small extent, as is also the case with the Polish language in Lithuania (Čekman 1983).

8.4. There are few studies about the Jews (Lemchenas 1970), Germans and the other smaller ethnic minorities (cf. Gerullis 1932; Kryczyński 1938). A revival of interest in these problems can be seen. Recently a discussion of the fate of the "East Prussia" inhabitants started in Germany.

9. Bibliography (selected)

Ambrazas, Vytautas (Ed.) (1967): *Lietuvių kalba tarybiniais metais* [The Lithuanian language in the Soviet period], Vilnius.

Budreckis, Algirdas M. (Ed.) (1985): *Eastern Lithuania*, Chicago.

Čekman, Valerij (1982): "K sociolingvističeskoj xarakteristike pol'skix govorov belorussko-litovskogo pograničja" [On the sociolinguistic characteristic of Polish dialects of the Byelorussian-Polish border]. In: *Studia nad polszczyzną kresową 1*, 123–138.

Čekmonas, Valerijus/Grumadienė, Laima (1993): "Rytų Lietuvos kalbų paplitimo žemėlapis" [Map of the linguistic situation in East Lithuania]. In: *Lietuvos rytai*, Garšva, K./Grumadienė, L. (Eds.), Vilnius, 132–136.

Dini, Pietro U. (1993): "Le lingue baltiche fra il II e il III millennio D.C.". In: *Mille anni di storia linguistica europea*, Banfi, E. (Ed.), Firenze, 197–254.

Gerullis, Georg (1932): "Muttersprache und Zweisprachigkeit in einem preussisch-litauischen Dorf". In: *Studi Baltici 2*, 59–67.

Grumadienė, Laima/Stundžia, Bonifacas (1987): "Dinamika oppozicij slogovyx intonacij v fonologičeskix sistemax dialektnoj i gorodskoj reči" [Dynamics of the oppositions of accents in the phonological systems of dialectal and urban speech]. In: *Proceedings XIth ICPhS 5*, 95–98.

Karaliūnas, Simas (1983): "Respublikos lingvosocialinės situacijos charakteristika" [Characterization of the linguosocial situation of the Republic]. In: *Lietuvių kalbotyros klausimai 23*, 4–45.

Kobeckaitė, Halina et al. (Eds.) (1992): *National minorities in Lithuania*, Vilnius.

Kryczyński, Stanisław (1938): *Tatarzy Litewscy* [Lithuanian Tatars], Warsaw.

Lemchenas, Chackelis (1970): *Lietuvių kalbos įtaka Lietuvos žydų tarmei. Lietuviškieji skoliniai* [Influence of Lithuanian on the dialect of Lithuanian Jews. The Lithuanian borrowings], Vilnius.

Turska, Halina (1939): *O powstaniu polskich obszarów językowych na Wileńszczyznie* [On the origin of the Polish language areas in the Vilnius region], Vilnius.

Zinkevičius, Zigmas (1993): *Rytų Lietuva praeityje ir dabar* [East Lithuania. Past and present], Vilnius.

*Laima Grumadienė/
Bonifacas Stundžia, Vilnius (Lithuania)*

235. Byelorussia

1. Geography and demography
2. Territorial history and national development
3. Politics, economy, and general cultural and religious situation
4. Statistics and ethnoprofiles
5. Sociolinguistic situation
6. Language political situation
7. General contactlinguistic portrait
8. Critical evaluation of the sources and literature used
9. Bibliography (selected)

1. Geography and demography

The Republic of Belarus (Byelorussia, Belorussia) (207,600 km) borders Russia, Latvia, Lithuania, Poland, and Ukraine. Its six provinces and the capital Mensk (Minsk) are populated by 10.1 million people, 78 percent of whom are Belarusans. More than two million Belarusans lived in other Soviet republics in 1989, an additional 170–300.000 in Poland and a million in other parts of the world. The most numerous minorities are Russians, Poles, Ukrainians and Jews. The percentages for the various national groups have varied during this century due to changing territory, World War II and Soviet policies (→ Language Map P).

2. Territorial history and national development

Originally inhabited by Baltic tribes, the area of today's Republic of Belarus was gradually populated by East Slavic tribes during the 4th to 8th centuries AD. In the 10th and 11th centuries the area became a part of Kievan Rus. When the Mongol/Tatar rulers took advantage of the feudal disruption of the 12th and 13th centuries, Belarus remained outside their tribute area, and in the 14th century became part of the Lithuanian Grand Duchy. Approximately two thirds of the inhabitants of this state were Slavs. Church Slavic, which gradually developed local, Belarusan characteristics, was adopted as the official language of the Grand Duchy.

The 14th century personal union between Poland and the Lithuanian Grand Duchy opened the state to Catholicism. The 1569 Lublin treaty united Poland and the Grand Duchy in *Rzecz Pospolita Polska*. Polonization increased among the gentry, Latin and Polish (P) were used in administration, and by 1697 Belarusan (BR) was banned from the courts and offices (Vakar 1956, 62). Religious rivalries resulted in the Brest Union of 1596 and the establishment of the Uniate Church, whereby part of the Orthodox accepted the supreme authority of the Pope. Animosities increased during the 17th century, and the Uniate Church, standing between Catholic and Orthodox, had the chance of becoming a national symbol of Belarus.

From the partitions of Poland to the 1917 revolution, the area was part of the Russian (R) Empire. As a result of the P uprising of 1831 the Catholic Church was restricted, the Uniate Church banned and the use of the vernacular prohibited. The name Belorussija was replaced with *Severo-Zapadnyj kraj* (Northwest District). The 1863 uprising led to the exchange of P for R in education, administration and the courts. The gentry converted to Orthodoxy, 30,000 in 1865–66 alone (Vakar 1956, 74). The Belarusan dialects were considered to be dialects of Great Russia.

The second half of the 19th century marked the first sparks of a national consciousness. Research in archeology, linguistics and ethnology resulted in strengthening national consciousness. Kastus Kalinowski, who published the first BR newspaper (*Mužyčaja praŭda*), later became a national symbol. The 1897 census reported that more than five million people in the Northwestern District claimed their language to be BR. The early 20th century saw the founding of the Belorussian Socialist *Hramada* in 1903 in St. Petersburg, while the 1905 revolution led to the recognition of BR and a prominent role for the Hramada newspaper *Naša Niva* (Our Field). A BR Democratic Republic was proclaimed in 1918 but dissolved as a result of the P invasion in the following year.

In 1921 the Treaty of Riga divided the country between Poland and Soviet Russia, the eastern territory becoming part of the Belarusan SSR, proclaimed in 1919. With Russian cessions in 1924 and 1926, the population totalled five million. Soviet policy in the 1920s led to a rapid Belarusification of the Republic. A number of national institutions were established, including an academy, a university, colleges, museums, schools, newspapers etc. R was banned from the educational and administrative systems, but the armed forces as well as the police mostly remained under R control (Vakar 1956, 142). The minorities were granted extensive rights concerning education, publications and cultural organizations. In 1924 Belarusan, Russian, Polish and Yiddish were declared to be of equal status.

From 1929 onwards the picture changed considerably. Belarus lost most of the national Communists and a major part of the national intelligentsia due to Stalinist purges. The changes also affected minority culture. In the 1930s Russification began including a linguistic policy "in order to bring the national idiom close to the Russian standard" put forward in 1934 (Vakar 1956, 153). In 1938 Russian became compulsory in the schools. Pro-Soviet sentiments nourished by the Polonization efforts in Polish West Belarus quickly vanished after the Soviet annexation in 1939.

During WW II and the purges connected with it, about one quarter of the population perished, including about 80 percent of the Jews.

3. Politics, economy, and general cultural and religious situation

Glasnost and *perestrojka* came late to the conservatively governed Belarusan republic. The Chernobyl catastrophe in 1986 and the 1988 discovery of the mass graves of the victims of the Stalin era in Kurapaty were turning points with regard to public opinion. Policy changes were, however, very slow and mostly concerned a more national Communism. The failed August coup in Moscow led to the Declaration of Independence on August 26, 1991. The Communist Party was banned and the national and democratic forces gained ground, but power remained in the hands of the old *nomenclatura*. The policy can be characterized by rather gradual changes, the expressed goal being a democratic and neutral country.

After the devastating WW II, the post-war period has involved very rapid industrialization and urbanization of the country and large-scale social changes for the BR people. Industry was, and is, strongly dependent on raw material and fuel from other parts of the former USSR. This interdependence is also evident in exports. The natural resources of the country are modest. The economy has declined since 1989 and is now due to slow change in a deep crisis.

Culturally the republic became very "Sovietized" in the post-WW II period. This also included a preference for (Soviet) Russian culture and language. Being granted no cultural or language rights the situation was unfavourable for the minorities. Polish was used in the Catholic Church, which survived with a very restricted status. The situation for the Orthodox Church, which had its center in Moscow, was somewhat better, but far from ideal. Recently both churches have been revitalized. The Orthodox Church has been renamed as the Belarusan Orthodox Church with Filaret as its head. The Catholic Church has reestablished many churches. The Uniate Church has returned from exile but is still small, and its adherents are mostly from the BR intelligentsia who sees it as a national church (cf. 2.).

4. Statistics and ethnoprofiles

Table 235.1 lists the figures concerning the major nationalities in the Belorusan SSR and their mother tongues stated by the last Soviet census in 1989.

Language and nationality do not coincide, which is a situation typical for the Soviet republics. Russians were favourable towards their own language. A huge percentage of Belarusans state Russian as their mother tongue. When assimilating linguistically, minorities shift to R, not BR. Only the Poles deviate in this respect. As many as 64% gave BR as their mother tongue. P organizations believe that the number of Poles in the 1989 census is too small and should amount to at least 600.000. Russians and Jews mainly live in towns and cities, Poles in the western parts of the country, and Ukrainians in the south.

The ethnic profiles of the various nationalities levelled out in the post-war period, when regardless of nationality at least on the surface ethnic identity was substituted by "Soviet" identity. The most conspicuous cultural differences in Belarus are not ethnic but religious. The Catholic-Orthodox dichotomy has survived and does not coincide with the P-BR ethnic division. There are approximately two million Catholics in Belarus but only 418.000 Poles. Another cultural difference is derived from the east-west division, the former area with a long Soviet tradition and the latter with a Polish past.

5. Sociolinguistic situation

Due to the complicated history of the area and Russification in the post-war period, all languages in today's Belarus could be considered minority languages.

5.1. Russian and Belarus

The Belarusans were easy prey for Russification policy. Firstly, the BR national consciousness was not fully developed since the Belarusification period in the 1920s was too short and the repressions and WW II annihilated most of the newly establishing intelligentsia (cf. Bankowski-Züllig 1991, 322). Secondly, in the period between the wars, BR society was still rural, and towns and cities were inhabited by a non-BR majority. Rapid post-war industrialization and urbanization

Table 235.1: Distribution of population of Belarusan SSR according to nationalities and their languages (1989). Column 2 lists the size of the population for the various nationalities, column 3 the percentage of the total population of all nationalities, column 4 the fraction (in percent) of the population which consider themselves to have the same mother tongue as their nationality, columns 5–7 the fraction of the population mastering a second language. (Source: *Vestnik statistiki* 1990, 11)

Nationality	Population	Percentage of all	Mother tongue	Second language		
				Russian	Belarusan	Other
Belarusans	7,897,781	77.8	80.2	60.4	9.5	0.1
Russians	1,341,055	13.2	97.7	1.8	24.5	1.6
Poles	417,648	4.1	13.3	44.7	17.8	0.3
Ukrainians	290,368	2.9	45.3	41.4	10.5	16.7
Jews	111,789	1.1	7.6	8.6	27.6	8.5
Tatars	12,352	0.12	25.7	40.3	10.8	12.4
Gypsies/Roma	10,762	0.11	82.7	69.0	4.3	5.8
Azerbaijanians	6,634	0.06	69.2	56.7	5.4	8.7
Lithuanians	7,589	0.07	57.7	47.7	19.4	11.6
Moldovians	5,348	0.05	57.9	54.9	5.7	14.0
Others	47,922	0.47	–	–	–	–
All nationalities	10,149,248	100.0	77.7	50.8	12.0	1.0

converted the Belarusans into town- and city-dwellers, while at the same time due to Russification the towns became R-speaking. Thirdly, the existence of some feeling of kinship between Belarusans and Russians facilitated the Russification process, as did the close relationship of the two languages (Bankowski-Züllig 1991, 322). The Belarusans, who migrated in such numbers from the countryside, may have perceived Russian as their literary language rather than as a different language.

The results of Russification were striking. In the 1980s the language of administration and political life was R, urban education took place almost exclusively in R schools, higher education was almost exclusively in R, the language of the massmedia was more R than BR, the language of belletristics was to a great extent R (in 1984, 95.3% of the printed pages were in R), and of the 15 theatres only 3 used BR (*Listy da Harbačova*). The BR language held thus a very clear minority position, and BR culture was on the verge of becoming a folkloristic reserve.

The linguistic situation was thus a rather typical case of diglossia with R as the dominant language. The drive for R-BR bilingualism was an important part of the Russification policy. The 1989 census shows that this policy was indeed effective: 89.7% of the Belarusans spoke R either as their mother tongue or a second language, as did 90.1% of the Ukrainians, 67.3% of the Poles and 98.6% of the Jews (Cutting 1992, 201). Knowledge of R was especially extensive in towns and cities. Thus, from the point of view of their mother tongue the majority of the BR population are BR-R bilinguals, but functionally they must be considered R-BR bilinguals (Lukašanec 1989, 23). Some of the population is trilingual, i.e. minority language — BR — R.

The similarity between R and BR has led to a wide variety of interference phenomena (see for example Mixnevič (Ed.) 1985). There are probably very few bilingual Belarusans who speak both languages without interference (cf. 7.).

The BR literary language also had a limited position in the countryside and was at best the language of instruction even though in many schools R was gaining ground. The BR literary language was also to be found in journals and newspapers as well as programmes on the radio and sometimes television. However, in the family and for informal communication the local dialect or a mixed R-BR language was most common. R was the language of administration, meetings, hospitals, etc. and usually culture as well. The spoken R was very seldom a pure literary spoken Russian.

5.2. Polish

WW II left Belarus with a substantial P minority with no minority rights. In 1959 the number of Poles was 539,000 (6.7%), in 1970, 383,000 (4.5%), in 1979, 403,000 (4.2%) and in 1989, 417,000 (4.1%) (Urban & Zaprudnik 1993, 112). The use of P was restricted to the family, the few functioning Catholic churches (Dzwonkowski 1992, 104) and the reading of prayer-books (Dobrynin 1992, 3). The statistics show a low knowledge of P in the last decades. In 1970 only 13.1% of the Poles declared P as their mother tongue, in 1979, 7.8% and in 1989, 13.3%. The majority of the Poles (64%) considered BR as their first language (Cutting 1992, 198), but a growing number state R to be their mother tongue (4.0% in 1959 and 22.6% in 1989).

The low percentage of Poles having P as their mother tongue may be explained by a whole series of factors (Kurzowa 1992, 127—129): (1) The persecutions and deportations during the war watered down the P milieu in Belarus; (2) The repatriations of Poles (1944—48 and 1956—58) removed the nationally most conscious part of the P population; (3) The P language had no official functions in society, e. g. no schools etc. (4) A probable factor is the fact that the overwhelming majority of today's Poles in Belarus are descendants of Polonized autochthonous inhabitants of Belarus; (5) A fifth factor may be the tradition of equating Catholicism and Polishness.

In the villages with P population, Polish is very often only spoken by elderly people, who were educated in Polish schools in the interwar years. The knowledge of the language is rather restricted in the young generation. Otherwise the *prosta mowa*, i.e. BR dialect, is used. In some villages P is not spoken at all, but it is remembered in prayers and in Polish songs.

5.3. Yiddish

The Jews in Belarus were not granted any cultural rights after WW II. As a result of the Holocaust, they lacked the security of dense settlements. The official attitude was primarily anti-Zionist, and some outright anti-Semitism was tolerated. Without any opportunity to use the language or to organize cultural or religious life on the surface their life resembled that of other citizens. Since the 1970s, emigration to Israel and other countries has drained the group of many of its most conscious members which led to rapid Russification. In 1989 Yiddish was the mother tongue of only 7.6% of the remaining 111,789 Jews, while R accounted for 90.0%.

6. Language political situation

6.1. Belarus and Russian

On January 26, 1990 the Law on Languages was adopted in the Belarusan SSR. This law granted BR the status of the state language of the republic. It came into force on September 1, 1990 and was followed up by a governmental programme for the development of BR and other languages on September 20, 1990. R is explicitly mentioned. A re-Belarusification is anticipated, but is expected to take some time, 3 to 10 years.

For both objective and subjective reasons the Belarusification will remain a relatively slow process (Bieder 1992, 147—8). Thus R is still often the language of politics even in the parliament. One group of deputies would like to see R as the second state language, but such proposals are opposed by BR patriots, who state that BR needs to be defended by a language law.

Changes are visible in the school system. According to recent statistics 3,141 of 4,953 schools used BR during the school year 1992/93, 397 R, and 1,415 both languages (*Nastaŭnickaja hazeta*, Dec. 25, 1992). In the same year, 68.5% of the pupils in the first grade were educated in BR, compared to 28.9% only two years ago. In higher education the switch to BR comes first in the humanities and then in the political sciences, while the natural sciences are still seldom taught in BR. Even for future teachers of BR, part of the lectures are still in R.

Television now has a BR channel, which, however, TV-viewers consider inferior to the Russian programmes from Moscow and St. Petersburg. The BR channel has fewer resources and is still rather unprofessional. Even if the reporters use BR, the replies in interviews are often in R. BR radio has a better standard. In 1987, 31 of a total of 110 journals were published in BR, while of the 215 newspapers 130 were BR and 80 R. The total circulation of the BR newspapers was 1.7 million copies, whereas the Russian newspapers had a total exceeding 3.5 million (Bieder 1992, 155—6). The proportions may have changed somewhat, but the R newspapers appear to have retained their position. However, a number of journals and newspapers represent the BR renaissance (Bieder 1992, 156). The change in the mass media is more a change in quality than quantity. The same could probably be said for *belles-lettres*. Many works forbidden or suppressed earlier are now available. Prose and poetry glorifying the mother tongue may be found (Bieder 1992, 158). Theatre and film are still primarily in R. Only 4 out of 18 theatres use BR and the film-studio Belarus' film has not yet produced any films in BR (Bieder 1992, 156—7). The Catholic Church uses predominantly P; the Orthodox Church, Church Slavic and R. Although the Belarusification of church language is a strong desideratum of the BR patriots, it progresses slowly and meets with resistance.

The Belarusification discussion also concerns the substance of the language. Orthography appears to be an important issue. The opposition now often uses the *taraškevica* (a phonetically based orthography by Branislaŭ Taraškevič in the 1920s) whereas official Belarus still sticks to the *narkomaŭka* (an orthography designed in the 1930s to bring BR closer to R). There are even advocates of the Latin script. The BR nationalists call for a thorough cleansing of the language of Russian elements. The limited use of BR in the post-war period has led to a lack of fully developed terminologies. Another much-discussed problem is the naming of towns, villages, streets, places, etc. (Bieder 1992, 148—9).

6.2. Polish

The rights of the minorities were clearly expressed in the Law on Languages in Belarus and subsequent documents, as well as in the Law of the Republic of Belarus on National Minorities in the Republic of Belarus from November 11, 1992. Though short (containing only twelve articles), the Minority Law provides the minorites with the legal protection necessary. The changed official attitude has revitalized the life of the minorities. Major activities are exhibited by Poles and Jews.

The first P society came into existence in Hrodna (Harodna) in 1988. Since 1990 the numerous P societies are connected in an umbrella organization, the Union of Poles in Belarus (*Związek Polaków na Białorusi*). The Union publishes a newspaper *Głos znad Niemna* (The Voice from Nemen) and a journal *Magazyn Polski* (The Polish Magazine). The P societies support a stronger P identity by teaching P to those Poles who do not know the language. According to official statistics, P was taught to about 10,000 pupils in more than 200 schools in Brest, Hrodna, Mensk, and Vicebsk provinces, as well as in the capital (*Nastaŭnickaja hazeta*, October 31, 1992). Ten first grade classes had been started with P as the language of instruction, and five manuals for beginners had been published. Since 1990 the Hrodna University has a Polish faculty and hundreds of young people have been sent to Poland for their studies. A Centre for Polish Culture is being built in Hrodna, and a Polish People's University (*Polski Uniwersytet Ludowy*) with courses such as P history is established in Minsk and Brest. The use of P on television and radio is limited to a few minutes per month or week in local broadcasts in Mensk and Hrodna. The P revival and P education are supported by organizations from Poland. The P revival is often combined with the return of the Catholic Church. The new priests usually come from Poland and, thus, use P.

6.3. Yiddish

Jewish life is also being revitalized in Belarus. About a hundred organizations of various types are found throughout Belarus. Their umbrella organization *Belorusskoe Ob"edinenie Evrejskix Organizacij i Obščin* (The Belarusan Association of Jewish Organizations and Communities) publishes the R language newspaper "Aviv" (Spring). The Union of Jewish Youth and Students also produces a small R language newspaper *Evrejskie Novosti* (Jewish News). Furthermore, organizations from abroad are active. The Jewish organizations frequently have contacts with their counterparts in other countries. At least a small number of synagogues have been established in Mensk, Homel, Brest and Yicebsk.

One of the most important tasks of the Jewish organizations is to revive the Jewish culture of the less orthodox Jews. Special activities for children and teenagers have high priority. Hebrew is taught (often with the help of teachers from Israel) not only to those who intend to emigrate. At least 8 Sunday schools exist, the one in Mahiljou attended by 250 pupils. Hebrew is also taught in many language circles. Yiddish is considered mostly a matter of the past, although a Sunday course in Yiddish exists in Mensk with about 25 participants, mostly elderly and middle-aged, and some non-Jews.

7. General contactlinguistic portrait

BR is closely related to both R and P. The BR dialects and literary language have been very open to influence from both languages. From the Middle Ages up to the 20th century, Western culture was introduced through P, being the language of culture and administration. After the divisions of Poland and especially after the P uprising in 1863, the influence of R was felt even stronger. After the period of Belarusification in the 1920s and 30s, Russification gathered momentum and intensified in the post-WW II-period. In spite of the Russification, many words of P origin still belong to the neutral vocabulary of BR.

The linguistic situation in post-war Belarus with R as the dominant language has brought about many interference phenomena. The close similarity in phonetic and grammatical structure as well as in vocabulary has not only strengthened the forces of interference, but also rendered it into a reciprocal feature of both languages. A result of both Russification and the proximity of the two languages is the *trasjanka* (meaning 'mixed cattlefood', Bieder 1992, 152), a "creole" which mixes elements from both languages. The proximity of the languages makes any such mixing intelligible. The *trasjanka* thus varies from person to person. Consequently a description of *trasjanka* would to a large extent be a description of the language use of individuals, of idiolects. The R of Belarusans (cf. Mixnevič 1985) shows slightly more regularity with regard to interference, which might justify calling the R of Belarus a specific variant of R. Even speakers with a good command of R morphology, syntax and vocabulary very often keep traits of BR pronunciation.

The impact of R on BR is felt on every level. Because it is controlled and premeditated, written BR has a slightly better position. Spoken BR is heavily influenced by R. Spoken literary BR has been restricted to very few areas and a spoken norm has had little chance of being more widely accepted. Spoken BR has normally been dialectal. The return of BR to more areas of public life has slightly changed the situation but reportedly there are still very few who can speak BR without interference from R. The number of Russianisms is highly idiosyncratic.

8. Critical evaluation of the sources and literature used

Sociolinguistic research on Belarus is scarce both inside and outside the republic. Language contacts between BR and other Slavic languages, especially R, have, however, been discussed in the framework of both historical-comparative and contrastive research. The official insistance on bilingualism made the study of R-BR language relations and R-BR bilingualism feasible. With regard to national-R bilingualism, these studies had to adopt the official point of view but can nevertheless be interesting because of the material used. The book *Russkij jazyk v Belorussii* (The Russian Language in Belarus, 1985) edited by A. A. Mixnevič represents a substantial shift towards more contemporary sociolinguistic research on Belarus. Outside the Soviet Union only a small number of studies on the linguistic situation in Belarus have been carried out. Poland has been an exception, due to the BR minority there and the numerous Polish minority in Belarus and other Soviet republics.

Due to the rapid changes in Belarus in the last years, interest in the country has grown and many shorter, usually well-documented, articles have been published in the West (Zaprudnik 1989, Clem 1990, Urban/Zaprudnik 1993, etc.). Most of them also touch upon the revival of the BR language and culture. Some of them give shorter accounts of BR history and the development of national consciousness. The latter is dealt with especially by Čakvin/Tereškovič (1990) and Guthier (1977). A few articles are devoted to the problems of language policy and the BR rebirth (Bankowski-Züllig 1991, Maldsis 1992, and Bieder 1991 and 1992). In many articles there is, however, a tendency to equate the BR national and cultural revival and democratization. Most studies on BR history are either nationalistically or Socialist/Communistically biased. Vakar (1956), however, seems to be almost unbiased.

9. Biobliography (selected)

Aviv [Spring]: Newspaper for *Belorusskoe ob"edinenie evrejskix organizacij i obščin, izrailskaja associacija "Geser Alija"*, Minsk.

Banowski-Züllig, Monika (1991): "Perestrojka und Sprachpolitik. Der Fall Weissrussland". In: *Schweizer Monatshefte für Politik, Wirtschaft und Kultur*, April, 318–328.

Bieder, Hermann (1992): "Die erste und zweite Wiedergeburt der weissrussischen Sprache und Kultur". In: *Georg Mayer zum 60. Geburtstag*, Bieber, U./Woldan, A. (Eds.), München, 405–451.

Bieder, Hermann (1992): "Die gegenwärtige sprach- und kulturpolitische Entwicklung in Weissrussland". In: *Die Welt der Slaven. Jahrgang XXXVII, 1 + 2, N.F. XVI, 1 + 2*, 142–168.

Čakvin, I. V./Tereškovič, P. V. (1990): "Iz istorii stanovlenija nacional'nogo samosoznanija belorusov (XIV – načalo XX v.)" [Topics in history of establishing national self-consciousness of Belorussians (14th through early 20th centuries)]. In: *Sovetskaja etnografija 6*, 42–54.

Clem, Ralph S. (1990): "Belorussians". In: *The Nationalities Question in the Soviet Union*, Smith, G. (Ed.) London/New York, 109–122.

Cutting, Marion (1992): "Vitryssland". In: *Gamla och nya stater. Det upplösta sovjetimperiet*, Gustavsson, S./Svanberg, I. (Eds.), Stockholm, 188–204.

Dobrynin, M. (1992): "Język polski na Białorusi" [The Polish language in Belarus]. In: *Głos znad Niemna*, April 15–30.

Dzwonkowski, Roman (1992): "Stan badań nad historią Kościoła i życiem religijnym katolików obrządku łacińskiego v ZSRR (1917–1990)". [The state of the research on the history of the Catholic Church and of the religious life of Catholics of Latin rite in the USSR]. In: Kubiak et al. (Eds.), 103–118.

Głos znad Niemna. Pismo Związku Polaków na Białorusi [The Voice from Nemen. Newspaper of the Union of Poles in Belarus], Minsk.

Guthier, Steven L. (1977): "The Belorussians: National Identification and Assimilations 1897–1970". In: *Soviet studies 29, 1. January*, and *2. April 40–48, 207–283*.

Kurzowa, Zofia (1992): "Język polski na kresach wschodnich po II wojnie światowej" [The Polish language in the Eastern border region after WW II]. In: Kubiak et al. (Eds.), 127–132.

Listy da Harbačova or *Letters to Gorbachev* (1987). The Association of Byelorussians in Great Britain, London.

Lukašanec, A. (1989): "Da xaraktarystyki dvuxmoŭja u BSSR" [To the characterization of bilingualism in the BSSR]. In: *Belaruskaja linhvistyka 36*, 18–23.

Maldsis, Adam (1992): "Die Wiedererstehung der Belorussischen Nation aus ihrem historischen und kulturellen Erbe". In: *Osteuropa*, 42. Jahrgang, Heft 4, 310–318.

Mixnevič, A. (Ed.) (1985): *Russkij jazyk v Belorussii* [Russian in Belarus], AN Belorusskoj SSR, Minsk.

Hieronim Kubiak et al. (Eds.) (1992): *Mniejszości Polskie i Polonia w ZSRR* [Polish minorities and Poles in the USSR]. Uniwersytet Jagielloński, Instytut Badań Polonijnych, Wrocław/Warsaw/Cracow.

Nastaŭnickaja hazeta [Teachers' Journal], Mensk.

Urban, Michael/Zaprudnik, Jan (1993): "Belarus: a long road to nationhood". In: *Nation and politics in the Soviet successor states*, Bremmer, I./Taras, R. (Eds.), Cambridge, 99–120.

Vakar, Nicholas P. (1956): *Belorussia. The Making of a Nation. A Case Study*, Cambridge, Massachusetts.

Wexler, Paul (1974): *Purism and Language. A Study in Modern Ukrainian and Belorussian Nationalism (1840–1907)*. Bloomington.

Zaprudnik, Jan (1989): "Belorussian Reawakening". In: *Problems of Communism, July–August*, 36–52.

Sven Gustavsson, Uppsala (Sweden)

236. Ukraine

1. Géographie et démographie
2. Histoire
3. Politique, économie et situations culturelle et religieuse en général
4. Statistiques
5. Situation sociolinguistique
6. Etat de la politique linguistique
7. Contacts des langues
8. Examen critique de la bibliographie
9. Bibliographie (sélective)

1. Géographie et démographie

L'Ukraine est un jeune Etat indépendant créé dans le processus de désagrégation de l'URSS en 1991. Ayant une superficie de 603 700 km², l'Ukraine est délimitée au nord par la Biélorussie, au nord et à l'est par la Russie, au sud-ouest par la Moldavie, par la Roumanie et à l'ouest par la Pologne, la Slovaquie, et la Hongrie.

L'Ukraine est une des Républiques les plus développées et les plus peuplées de l'ex-URSS. En 1989, la population de la République s'élevait à 51 499 000 habitants, la population urbaine étant de 66,6% (en 1913 de 19%). Après la deuxième guerre mondiale, un tiers des bourgs s'étaient formés et la migration active de la population a eu lieu, y compris celle de l'Ukraine. Le taux le plus élevé de la population urbaine se trouve dans les régions de l'Est et du Sud-Est de l'Ukraine. Dans la plupart des régions centrales et occidentales, la population est majoritairement villageoise. La densité de population des différentes régions de l'Ukraine est très inégale. La région de Poliessie et quelques régions du Sud sont relativement dépeuplées (→ carte linguistique P).

2. Histoire

La situation contemporaine ethnique et linguistique est le reflet, dans une certaine mesure, de l'histoire de la formation de l'Ukraine depuis l'époque de la Russie de Kiev. La particularité de l'histoire de l'Ukraine est due au fait qu'après le déclin de la Russie de Kiev (XIIIe siècle) ses terres ont fait partie d'Etats différents. La plupart d'entre eux se sont trouvés sous la domination de la Lituanie et de la Pologne (XIVe siècle); la Transcarpathie fut conquise par la Hongrie (XIe–XIIIe siècles), la Bucovine du Nord par la Principauté Moldave (XIVe siècle). Au XVIIe siècle, à la suite de l'accroissement du rôle politique et culturel des territoires de l'Ukraine Centrale, il y eut des possibilités de transformer l'Ukraine en Etat indépendant. Mais ces possibilités ne furent pas réalisées: les territoires situés sur la rive gauche du Dniepr et la région de Kiev sont passés sous le protectorat de la Russie, et l'Ukraine de la rive droite est restée sous le protectorat de la Pologne. A la fin du XVIIIe siècle, la Russie a assujetti aussi la plus grande partie de l'Ukraine de la rive droite. La réunification finale des terres ukrainiennes eut lieu en 1939–1940, quand l'Ukraine faisait partie de l'URSS. On y a rattaché les territoires de l'Ukraine occidentale, la Transcarpathie, la Bucovine du Nord et la Bessarabie. L'état arriéré des terres ukrainiennes entraîna la limitation des droits des Ukrainiens à leur langue et à leur culture natales, déterminant la nouvelle répartition des rôles sociaux des langues en contact.

L'époque du gouvernement polonais-lituanien a été caractérisée par une lutte simultanée de tendances innovatrices et conservatrices dans la langue ukrainienne. Selon la tradition, elle est restée la deuxième langue des documents concernant les territoires ukrainiens. Le latin devint langue officielle, remplacé depuis par le polonais dans cette fonction. La division des terres ukrainiennes entre la Russie et la Pologne a déterminé l'accroissement du rôle de la langue polonaise en Ukraine occidentale. Dès la deuxième moitié du XVIe siècle la langue ukrainienne tomba en désuétude et survécut uniquement comme langue de l'église.

La limitation des fonctions de la langue ukrainienne s'effectua différemment dans les territoires qui faisaient partie de la Russie. Le russe a été reconnu comme la seule langue officielle de l'Empire russe. Cette politique officialisée par la législation [voir la circulaire du ministre Valouyev (1863) et l'oukase d'Emsk (1876)] a rendu impossible l'utilisation de la langue ukrainienne dans la presse, dans les sciences, dans les écoles et les institutions. Les belles-lettres sont devenues la principale source du développement l'ukrainien standard.

Dès 1917 l'Ukraine entame une nouvelle période de son développement territorial et national. En janvier 1918, fut proclamée la République Ukrainienne Populaire. Mais cet Etat indépendant ne dura pas longtemps. Sous la pression des Bolcheviks et surtout à la suite d'une intervention militaire de la part de la Russie, l'Ukraine perd son indépendance et dès 1922 elle fait partie de l'URSS comme République d'Union. En 1939–1940 les territoires de l'Ukraine Occidentale, la Bessarabie et la Bucovine du Nord sont rattachés à l'Ukraine. En 1954, la Crimée passe de la Fédération Russe à l'Ukraine.

3. Politique, économie et situations culturelle et religieuse en général

En 1991, l'Ukraine a proclamé son indépendance. Le nouvel Etat indépendant a commencé à formuler de nouveaux principes économiques qui prévoyaient la dénationalisation et la privatisation de la propriété sociale. Evidemment, ces changements ont déterminé la révision des postulats idéologiques du passé et ont entraîné la transition d'un régime politique totalitaire à la démocratie, activant l'aspiration des peuples de l'Ukraine à l'auto-détermination nationale et linguistique. Une des marques caractéristiques de la vie spirituelle contemporaine de l'Ukraine est l'accroissement du rôle de l'église. Les citoyens de l'Ukraine sont de plus en plus nombreux à renier l'athéisme imposé par l'idéologie communiste et à s'adonner à la pratique religieuse.

En particulier, l'on constate que de 1991 à janvier 1993, le nombre des communautés religieuses est passé de 10 810 à 14 038. 31 nouvelles associations religieuses ont vu le jour comptant 184 communautés. D'après le nombre des paroissiens et leur diffusion dans toutes les régions de l'Ukraine, l'orthodoxie est prédominante. Elle est confessée par l'Eglise Orthodoxe Ukrainienne (5590 communautés), l'Eglise Orthodoxe Ukrainienne (Patriarcat de Kiev) (963 communautés), l'Eglise Orthodoxe Ukrainienne Autocratique (800 communautés), l'Eglise Orthodoxe Russe des Vieux Croyants (45 communautés), etc. Les Eglises ci-dessus n'ont pas de différences canoniques et se distinguent seulement par la langue de l'office et aussi par leur diffusion dans les différentes régions de l'Ukraine. L'Eglise Orthodoxe Ukrainienne emploie le vieux-slave et le russe; l'Eglise Orthodoxe Ukrainienne (Patriarcat de Kiev), le vieux-slave et l'ukrainien; l'Eglise Orthodoxe Ukrainienne Autocratique, présente aussi à l'Ouest du pays, utilise uniquement l'ukrainien; l'Eglise Orthodoxe Russe des Vieux Croyants, répandue davantage dans les régions du Sud, le vieux-slave. A l'Ouest de l'Ukraine, les Eglises catholiques – Grecque et Romaine – sont assez bien représentées, comptant 2807 et 517 communautés respectivement. Ces dernières utilisent, selon l'appartenance nationale des paroissiens, l'ukrainien, le polonais ou le russe. On peut citer parmi les religions les plus répandues sur le territoire de l'Ukraine aussi différents courants du protestantisme. Les communautés juives (52), présentes sur tout le territoire, et aussi celles des musulmans (42), localisées au Sud de l'Ukraine et surtout en Crimée, sont considérablement moins répandues.

4. Statistiques

Le recensement de la population de 1989 a identifié, sur le sol de la République, 88 ethnies. Les Ukrainiens représentent une ethnie prédominante dans toutes les régions de l'Ukraine (sauf la Crimée). Ils constituent les trois quarts de la population générale de l'Ukraine (37,4 millions) et peuplent d'une façon particulièrement compacte les régions centrales et la plupart des régions occidentales. La deuxième des grandes ethnies de l'Ukraine sont les Russes (11,3 millions). Ils sont aussi répandus sur le territoire entier, en particulier à l'est et au sud (Crimée, régions de Vorochylovgrad (Lougansk), Zaporogié, Donetzk, Khar'kov) et dans les villes.

Viennent ensuite les Juifs (486 mille) et les Biélorusses (440 mille), qui habitent surtout les villes. Les zones d'habitation compacte des Biélorusses se trouvent en Poliessie. Les Polonais (219 mille) sont assez largement établis en Ukraine, mais la plupart d'entre eux habitent les régions de Jytomir, Khmelnitzkiy, Vinnitza, Volyn, Lvov et Ternopol. D'autres grands groupes ethniques ont leurs foyers principalement dans les régions frontalières. Parmi eux, il y a les Moldaves (324 mille), les Bulgares (233 mille), les Hongrois (163 mille), les Roumains (135 mille), les Grecs (99 mille), et les Tatars (87 mille). Le nombre des Tatars de Crimée s'accroît très vite, vu qu'ils retournent dans leur patrie historique d'où ils ont été déportés vers l'Asie Centrale en 1944. En comparaison avec l'année 1979 leur nombre s'est accru; en 1989 ils sont au nombre de 44 mille.

Le recensement de l'année 1989 a révélé, en Ukraine, l'existence de 88 langues. Mais la grande majorité de ces langues restent seulement des symboles pour les consciences nationales respectives et ne servent pas à la communication. Seulement 22 langues possèdent des fonctions communicatives plus ou moins considérables. D'après le nombre des locuteurs, les plus répandues sont les langues indoeuropéennes (en particulier d'origine slave; nous indiquons entre parenthèses le nombre de personnes qui ont reconnu chaque langue comme leur langue maternelle): ukrainien (33,2 millions), russe (17,0 millions), biélorusse (155,7 mille), bulgare (161,7 mille), polonais (27,0 mille), tchèque (3,2 mille), slovaque (2,8 mille), roumain (= moldave: 336,7 mille), yiddish (34,5 mille), allemand (8,8 mille), albanais (1,8 mille), grec (roméen et ourome: 18,2 mille considèrent la langue de leur nationalité − roméenne ou ourome − comme langue maternelle; les recensements de 1989 ne distinguent pas les Ouromes des Grecs-Roméens), le tsigane (28,0 mille), l'arménien (29,9 mille). La famille turque est représentée par le tatar (42,4 mille), le tatar de Crimée (40,5 mille), le caraïme (131 personnes), le crymchake (142 personnes), le gagaouse (25,4 mille), et le tchouvache (8,6 mille); la famille finno-hongroise compte le hongrois (155,9 mille) et l'estonien (1,3 mille); la famille sémitique la langue assyrienne (1,2 mille).

5. Situation sociolinguistique

Parmi les langues de l'Ukraine, il y a deux langues absolument prédominantes qui déterminent la situation linguistique entière: l'*ukrainien*, ayant depuis 1989 le rang de langue d'Etat, et le *russe*. Elles sont utilisées sur le territoire entier de la République et dans toutes les situations communicatives. Malgré le rang plus élevé de la langue ukrainienne et aussi la prépondérance du nombre des habitants qui la considèrent comme langue maternelle, dans les villes de l'Ukraine et dans les régions de l'Est et du Sud, le russe conserve une certaine valeur fonctionnelle et communicative. Des recherches sur la compétence linguistique des Ukrainiens (auprès de ceux qui considèrent la langue ukrainienne comme leur langue maternelle), ont démontré nettement la nature de la pratique linguistique diglossique à fin des années 1980. Parmi les 2257 témoins interrogés, la distribution des situations communicatives est la suivante: voir le tabl. 236.1.

Les restrictions sensibles de l'usage fonctionnel de la langue ukrainienne et la propagande du rôle exclusif de la langue russe dans l'ex-URSS renforcent l'idée du rang social inférieur de la langue ukrainienne. C'est pourquoi le bilinguisme ukrainien-russe, qui dominait en Ukraine, porte les traits de la diglossie. En fait il s'agit d'un processus de substitution de la langue maternelle (c'est-à-dire de l'ukrainien) par le russe. A cause de l'abolition de la langue ukrainienne dans l'éducation supérieure, la grande majorité de la population russophone ne la maîtrise pas.

Les autres langues indigènes de l'Ukraine conservent toute leur valeur communicative à l'intérieur de leurs foyers. Conformément au nombre de leurs locuteurs, on distingue toute une gamme de domaines communicatifs des langues. Le *tatar* de Crimée possède le plus haut rang, parce qu'il est reconnu avec l'ukrainien et le russe comme la langue officielle de la République Autonome de Crimée. Pourtant ce rang exprime avant tout la reconnaissance politique du droit du peuple tatar de Crimée à sa patrie historique. La lan-

Tableau 236.1: Aspects communicatifs de la diglossie entre ukrainien et russe

Le type de communication	Ukr. %	Rus. %	Ukr.-Rus. %	Sans réponse %
Avec les enfants d'âge préscolaire	75,2	14,3	1,4	9
Avec les enfants d'âge scolaire	71,6	15,3	1,9	10,9
Avec l'époux ou l'épouse	67,7	13,5	1,8	17,1
Avec les parents	86,4	9,1	2,4	2,1
Avec les amis	71,6	18,1	9,5	0,9
Avec les voisins	74,5	15,1	9,7	0,7
Avec les collègues	62	21,1	6,9	9,9
Avec les subordonnés	56,3	18,4	3,4	21,8
Avec les chefs	57,1	27,3	3,3	12,3
Le discours à la réunion	53,2	36,5	3,5	6,6
Avec le vendeur	56,4	32,7	6,4	4,4
Au transport	54,4	34,8	6,2	4,6
Au cinéma, au théâtre	55,9	33	5,3	5,8
Avec le médecin	54,6	37,1	5,2	3,1
Avec l'instituteur des enfants	53,4	24,6	3,5	18,3

gue tatare de Crimée, à cause d'une standardisation insuffisante et de l'absence d'écoles tatares en Crimée, est employée principalement dans la communication orale. Dans une certaine mesure, elle est utilisée dans la presse, à la radio, à la télé et à l'église. Mais c'est la langue russe qui occupe le premier rang en Crimée.

La langue *roumaine* est langue officielle dans les zones d'habitation compacte des Moldaves et des Roumains (Bucovine). En 1991, elle a obtenu le rang de langue officielle locale. Comme langue standardisée, elle s'emploie largement dans toutes les sphères de communication: dans la vie courante comme dans la production. En 1991, des enquêtes sociolinguistiques ont montré que parmi 140 Roumains interrogés (région de Tchernovtsy) 36,4% emploient la langue roumaine en famille, 89,2% dans la communication avec les connaissances, 83,5% dans le cadre professionnel. La grande utilité linguistique du roumain est liée à l'existence, dans la région de Tchernovtsy, d'un ample réseau d'écoles avec enseignement en roumain (en 1992, en Ukraine, 120 écoles fonctionnaient avec 30 mille élèves), et à l'existence d'une presse écrite quotidienne et périodique et de mass media parlés électroniques. L'emploi de la langue roumaine dans les églises est devenu le facteur de sa sauvegarde. Près de la moitié des Moldaves et des Roumains sont bilingues. Le bilinguisme roumain-russe est prédominant: en 1989, 55,6% des Moldaves et 50,3% des Roumains ont une connaissance suffisante du russe.

La langue *hongroise* se caractérise aussi par l'usage courant dans les zones d'habitation compacte des Hongrois (Transcarpathie). D'après les données d'une enquête sociolinguistique de 1991 (83 informants), elle s'emploie à 97,6% dans la communication familiale, à 80,7% dans la communication amicale, à 72,3% dans la communication professionnelle avec les collègues. Ce qui distingue les Hongrois, c'est leur haut niveau de conscience linguistique: 95,5% des Hongrois considèrent leur idiome comme langue maternelle. C'est le deuxième niveau après les Russes (98,3%). Tout comme les Moldaves et les Roumains, près de la moitié des Hongrois se déclarent bilingues: 42,7% ont déclaré leur connaissance du russe comme suffisante.

Contrairement aux langues roumaine et hongroise, l'usage actif de la langue *polonaise*, qui pendant longtemps était la langue d'Etat, a sensiblement diminué: seulement 12,5% des Polonais l'ont reconnue comme langue maternelle. Parmi les facteurs qui contribuent à la déperdition de la langue des Polonais, il faut noter avant tout l'exiguïté des foyers des Polonais, la diminution quantitative des écoles polonaises et les oppressions nationales et politiques sous Staline. Les zones d'établissement les plus considérables des Polonais se trouvent dans les régions de Jytomir, Vinnitza et Lvov. L'on y trouve des écoles nationales et un grand nombre de Groupes volontaires qui se dédient à l'étude du polonais. La langue polonaise s'emploie avec le latin dans les églises catholiques. Tous ces facteurs concourent au maintien de la langue polonaise dans la communication courante et favorisent la sauvegarde de sa standardisation.

Quant aux *Biélorusses* et aux *Juifs*, leur dissémination territoriale a contribué à une atrophie graduelle des acquis de l'usage de la langue ethnique même dans la communication familiale. Le *yiddish* se défend comme langue littéraire et, sporadiquement, dans les journaux juifs. Il s'emploie aussi au cours des cérémonies religieuses et comme une des langues des associations culturelles juives. L'amplification progressive des locuteurs de l'*hébreu* est un phénomène récent. L'hébreu est notamment employé dans les écoles juives (en 1992, celles-ci étaient au nombre de 5).

Les enquêtes sociolinguistiques sur quelques foyers isolés des *Biélorusses* (Poliessie) ont mis en évidence une très forte interférence du côté de la langue ukrainienne. Les habitants de ces zones qualifient eux-mêmes leur langue de *mélange biélorusse-ukrainien*. C'est ainsi que les réponses des locuteurs à propos de leur langue expriment plutôt une *conscience ethnique* que leurs véritables *connaissances linguistiques*. L'absence de la standardisation du biélorusse est liée dans une mesure considérable à l'absence d'écoles et de périodiques nationaux. Hors des zones de l'établissement compact, les Biélorusses gravitent vers la langue russe.

Citons encore une autre ethnie qui est presque deux fois moins grande que les Biélorusses, à savoir les *Bulgares* (232,8 mille) qui possèdent leurs zones d'établissement compact dans les régions d'Odessa et de Zaporojyé. Malgré l'absence d'écoles, ces zones sont mieux protégées contre l'influence du russe. Les Bulgares emploient largement leur langue dans la famille, dans la communication avec les amis et avec les collègues sur le lieu de travail. D'après des enquêtes sociolinguistiques effectués en 1991 (161 informants), il s'agit de, respectivement, 95%, 91,3%, 71,4%.

Les langues des plus petites ethnies se trouvent dans quelques localités isolées. Le *tchèque* à la Volyn; le *slovaque* en Transcarpathie; le *tsigane* en Transcarpathie, en Crimée, dans la région d'Odessa; le *tatar*, *l'ourome*, le *roméen*, *l'assyrien* dans la région de Donetsk; le *caraïme* en Crimée, dans les régions d'Odessa et de Volyn; le *gagaouse* dans la région d'Odessa. A cause de l'absence d'établissements scolaires, toutes ces langues se limitent à l'usage familial. Cependant, ces derniers temps, on assiste à la revitalisation de quelques-unes d'entre elles. En particulier, dans les zones de l'établissement compact on a créé des groupes facultatifs pour l'étude de la langue *grecque* moderne (27 groupes), du *slovaque* (7 groupes) et du *tchèque* (4 groupes). Ainsi, les principaux problèmes de la situation linguistique actuelle en Ukraine sont: l'insuffisance des connaissances d'ukrainien d'un nombre considérable des habitants ukrainiens pour les besoins de la communication officielle, la prépondérance du russe dans la communication dans les villes, l'élaboration insuffisante des langues des petites ethnies de l'Ukraine.

6. Etat de la politique linguistique

La situation actuelle des langues est déterminée par la collision de la vieille politique linguistique pratiquée jadis en URSS et de celle mise en œuvre en 1989 dans l'Ukraine devenue indépendante. La politique menée en URSS était pleine de contradictions. Au début, le renoncement au russe comme langue officielle a favorisé le développement des fonctions sociales des langues des différents peuples de la Russie. En particulier au XXe siècle, la langue ukrainienne a formé et développé tous les styles nécessaires pour subvenir aux besoins sociaux. Le développement des langues des ethnies indigènes de l'Ukraine fut particulièrement efficace en 1925–1932. Pendant cette période, pour garantir le droit à la langue nationale aux Ukrainiens on a déclaré obligatoire la connaissance de la langue ukrainienne pour les salariés; le nombre des écoles et des instituts assurant l'enseignement en langue ukrainienne s'est rapidement accru, l'édition de la presse et des livres ukrainiens s'est activée, la terminologie scientifique ukrainienne s'est formée. Simultanément on a prêté plus d'attention à d'autres ethnies: dans certaines régions l'on assista à l'introduction d'autres langues régionales utilisées parallèlement à l'ukrainien; on a ouvert une maison d'édition publiant des livres dans les langues des différents peuples de l'Ukraine; on a instauré des écoles assurant l'enseignement des langues nationales (telles le polonais, le moldave, le hongrois, le bulgare, l'hébreu, l'allemand, le grec, l'arménien, le tchèque, l'assyrien).

En 1933, la politique linguistique change. Sous la devise de la lutte contre le nationalisme local, le pouvoir moscovite a déclenché des répressions massives contre l'intelligentsia, accompagnées d'une réduction des programmes précédents nationaux et culturels, et de la suppression des écoles, à l'exception des écoles russes et ukrainiennes.

L'exaspération de l'idéologie de l'intégration des nations et la glorification du rôle de la langue russe ont déterminé le rétrécissement graduel des fonctions sociales de la langue ukrainienne, ainsi que la tendance à la disparition des langues des autres ethnies. La langue russe devient dominante dans l'éducation supérieure, obtient dans la conscience de nombreux habitants de la République le rang de la langue la plus prestigieuse. En même temps, la langue ukrainienne, se transforme en langue de second rang, sans prestige, provinciale. Cette situation linguistique a contribué à l'adoption de la Loi sur les langues en 1989. Par sa conception, la Loi garantit à tous les citoyens le droit à la langue et à la culture nationale et, en même temps, sanctionne la priorité du développement de la langue ukrainienne et son officialisation comme langue d'Etat.

L'analyse de la politique linguistique actuelle révèle des changements sensibles dans la sphère administrative et des affaires publiques. Le rôle de la langue ukrainienne s'est considérablement accru dans l'éducation supérieure, et on s'apprête à officialiser l'ukrainien aussi dans les domaines scientifique et technique. Le prestige de la connaissance de la langue ukrainienne a visiblement augmenté. En particulier, cela a contribué à l'accroissement rapide du nombre des écoles avec l'enseignement en ukrainien. En 1992, il y avait 15,4 mille écoles avec 3,1 millions d'élèves. Les écoles avec l'enseignement en russe étaient au nombre de 4 mille (2,4 millions d'élèves). En plus, il existait 1318 écoles, où on enseignait en ukrainien comme en russe (262 mille élèves). Le nombre des écoles pour d'autres ethnies a considérablement augmenté: leur nombre s'élevait à 350 (55 mille élèves).

Cependant, la rapidité du changement des habitudes linguistiques des habitants de l'Ukraine ne correspond pas aux délais prévus par la Loi. Ce fait est lié à de nombreux facteurs: la crise économique en Ukraine, l'absence des ressources nécessaires au travail culturel et scolaire. Enfin, il faut citer la mauvaise volonté de la part des habitants quant au changement de leurs habitudes linguistiques. Cela se manifeste surtout dans les fréquentes revendications visant à officialiser, en Ukraine, *deux* langues: le russe *et* l'ukrainien. Celles-ci sont formulées surtout dans les régions du Sud et de l'Est de l'Ukraine.

7. Contacts des langues

La situation linguistique contemporaine en Ukraine est riche en contacts linguistiques, qui sont très variés quant à leur manifestation. Ils accusent l'influence de forces extra-linguistiques aussi bien qu'intralinguistiques. Le petit nombre des locuteurs de telle ou telle langue, leur diffusion, l'absence d'écoles avec l'enseignement en langue maternelle provoquent une forte influence des langues ukrainienne et russe. L'influence du russe joue un rôle décisif à l'Est et au Sud de l'Ukraine. La force de l'influence des langues dominantes (ukrainien et russe) sur d'autres langues est en relation directe avec l'affinité génétique des langues en contact. En particulier, dans les villages biélorusses de la région de Rovno, la symbiose des éléments des langues ukrainienne et biélorusse est très forte. L'influence réciproque de l'ukrainien et du russe est moins considérable. L'influence de la langue ukrainienne sur le russe est plus sensible aux niveaux phonétique et lexical. Les violations des normes phonétiques de la langue russe sont avant tout liées à une réduction des voyelles dans les syllabes inaccentuées, à la prononciation du son [h] au lieu de [g] et aussi à de légères variations dans l'intonation des phrases. On remarque ces interférences dans le langage courant de la plupart des locuteurs de la langue russe. Les violations des normes lexicales, dues à l'emprunt du lexique et de la phraséologie ukrainiens et aussi à des contaminations sémantiques, dépendent du niveau d'instruction des locuteurs. Au contraire, l'influence de la langue russe sur l'ukrainien est observée avant tout au niveau du lexique et de la dérivation. Un nombre considérable d'emprunts russes a envahi le lexique ukrainien. A l'étape actuelle, caractérisée par une élévation du rôle social de l'ukrainien, on constate une tendance vers le refoulement des russismes, surtout dans le domaine de la terminologie scientifique et de la technique.

8. Examen critique de la bibliographie

En Ukraine, la sociolinguistique a commencé à se développer dans les années soixante de notre siècle. Les conditions politiques existant à cette époque ont laissé une empreinte visible sur le contenu et la tendance des recherches sociolinguistiques: elles ont provoqué le caractère tendancieux de la présentation du matériel et ont transformé la sociolinguistique en moyen de soutien de la politique et de l'idéologie officielles. Le trait caractéristique de la sociolinguistique dans les années 60−80 a été un dogmatisme militant, une attention exclusive à l'élaboration insuffisante de la langue, l'occultation des faits réels de la situation linguistique en Ukraine et la limitation de la base empirique aux seules données des recensements de la population. Les tentatives d'éclaircir les processus de la russification, de la restriction progressive des fonctions de l'ukrainien et d'autres langues, ont provoqué des persécutions de la part des autorités soviétiques. Depuis la deuxième moitié des années 80, la sociolinguistique en Ukraine s'émancipe peu à peu des entraves antérieures et cherche à s'enrichir de nouvelles directions et méthodes de recherche.

9. Bibliographie (sélective)

Britsyn, Victor M. (1981): "Movna sytuacia v USSR i actual'ni pytann'a rosvytku sociolingvistyčnych dosližen" [La situation linguistique en URSS et les questions actuelles du développement des recherches sociolinguistiques]. In: *Funkcionuvann'a i rosvytok sučasnych slovjans'kych mov*, Kiev, 4−24.

Černyšova Tat'jana N. (1958): *Novogrečeskij govor sel Primorskogo (Urzufa) i Jalty, Pervomajskogo rajona, Stalinskoj oblasti* [Le parler grec moderne des villages Primorskoye (Ourzouf) et Yalta du district Pervomayskiy de la région de Stalino], Kiev.

Čislennost i sostav naselenia SSSR: Po materialam Vsesoiuznoj perepisi naselenia 1979 goda [La quantité et la composition de la population de l'URSS. D'après les matériaux du recensement de l'Union entière de 1979] (1993), Moscou.

Ermolenko, Svitlana/Kolesnyk, Grygorij/Lenec' Kateryna (Eds.) (1977): *Mova i čas* [La langue et le temps], Kiev.

Garkavec, Alexandr N. (1981): "O proischoždenii i klasifikacii urumunskich govorov Severnogo Priazov'ja" [Sur l'origine et la classification des parlers ouromes de la région de l'Azov du Nord]. In: *Sovetskaja tjurkologija* 2, 46−58.

Ižakevič, Galina P./Britsyn, Victor M./Bulachov Michail G. (Eds.) (1981): *Funkcionirovanie russkogo jazyka v blizkorodstvennom jazykovom okruženii* [Le fonctionnement de la langue russe dans l'entourage de ses langues sœurs], Kiev.

Javorskaja Galina M./Tkačenko Orest B./Žluktenko Jurij A. (1992): "Sociolinguistika" [La sociolinguistique]. In: *Metodologičeskie osnovy novych napravlenij v mirovom jazykoznanii*, Jermolenko, S. C./Žluktenko J. A./Linnik, Tat'jana G. (Eds.), Kiev, 16−139.

Narodnoe gospodarstvo Ukrains'koi RSR v 1990 roci: Statystyčnyi ščoričnik [L'économie nationale de la RSS d'Ukraine en 1991, L'annuaire statistique] (1992), Kiev.

Naulko, Vsevold (1966): *Etničnyi sklad naseleni'a Ukrains'koi RSR: Statystyko-kartografične doslidženn'a* [La composition ethnique de la population de la RSS d'Ukraine: Une recherche statistico − cartographique], Kiev.

Nesterova, Svetlana L./Nikolajev, Michail N. (1987): "Osobennosti rasprostranenija dvujazyčija i mnogojazyčija v etnokontaktnoj zone" [Les particularités de l'extension du bilinguisme et du plurilinguisme dans les zones de contact ethnique. In: *Ukrainsko − moldavskije etnokul'turnyje vzaimnosv'azi v period socializma*, Kiev, 262−283.

Orlov, Anatolij V. (1986): "Projavlenije etničnosti v sovremennom razvitii duchovnoj sfery bytovoj kultury" [La manifestation de l'ethnicité dans le développement contemporain de la sphère spirituelle de la culture de la vie quotidienne]. In: *Etničeskie processy v SSSR i SŠA. Materialy sovetsko amerikanskogo simpoziuma*, Moscou, 130−141.

Popescu, Ivan (1992): "Aspecte sociolingvistice ale funcţionării limbilor în actuala regiune Cernăuţi" [Les aspects sociolinguistiques du fonctionnement des langues de la région de Cernăuţi. In: *Ţara Fagilor*, 93−97.

Rusanivs'kyj, Vitalij M. (1985): Džerela rozvytku schidnoslovjans'kych mov [Les sources du développement des langues littéraires des Slaves de l'Est], Kiev.

Rusanivs'kyj, Vitalij M. (1989): "Prognostyčni funkcii sociolingvistyky" [Les fonctions de pronostics de la sociolinguistique]. In: *Movoznavstvo* 1, 3−10.

Victor M. Britsyn, Kiev (Ukraine)

237. Moldawien

1. Geographie und Demographie
2. Territorialgeschichte und Staatsbildung
3. Politik, Wirtschaft und allgemeine kulturelle sowie religiöse Lage
4. Statistik und Ethnoprofile
5. Soziolinguistische Lage
6. Sprachpolitische Lage
7. Sprachkontakte und die Rolle lexikalischer Innovation
8. Bibliographie (in Auswahl)

1. Geographie und Demographie

Moldawien, der südlichste der modernen Nationalstaaten in der Westregion der ehemaligen Sowjetunion (→ Art. 231) und südwestlicher Nachbarstaat der Ukraine, umfaßt die historische Landschaft Bessarabien zwischen Prut und Dnestr sowie Gebiete östlich dieses Flusses (Transnistrien). Die Landfläche Moldawiens ist nur wenig kleiner als die Baden-Württembergs. Dieses Areal bildet kulturell wie sprachlich eine Brücke zwischen der Romanität im Westen (rumänische Kulturregion) und den slawischen Regionen im Osten (ukrainische und russische Kulturregion), und zwar wegen der Multikulturalität und Mehrsprachigkeit seiner Bevölkerung (s. Abb. 237.1). Die romanische Bevölkerung des Landes spricht Moldauisch, eine regionale Variante des Rumänischen, das auf beiden Seiten der rumänisch-moldauischen (der ehemaligen rumänisch-sowjetischen) Grenze verbreitet ist. Der Schriftstandard des Rumänischen in Moldawien wich aber jahrzehntelang von dem im benachbarten Rumänien ab, so daß eine Zeitlang mit der politischen auch eine sprachliche Trennung aufrechterhalten wurde. Heutzutage fungiert dieselbe Sprache westlich und östlich der Grenze Moldawiens mit Rumänien als Staatssprache mit den politischen Zentren Bukarest und Chişinău.

Außer Moldauern leben Angehörige slawischer Völker in Moldawien und zwar Russen, Ukrainer und Bulgaren. Die Bulgaren sind eine Grenzlandminderheit, die im Süden, beiderseits der moldauisch-ukrainischen Staatsgrenze lebt. Die Zahl der Bulgaren auf ukrainischer Seite (1989, 233 800) ist größer als die in Moldawien (1989, 88 400). Eine andere Grenzlandminderheit sind die Gagausen. Diese leben in Nachbarschaft der Bulgaren im Süden. Auf ukrainischer Seite wohnen die Gagausen inmitten der Siedlungszone der bulgarischen Minderheit. Ihre Zahl in der Ukraine (1989, 32 000) ist bedeutend kleiner als in Moldawien (→ Sprachenkarte P).

2. Territorialgeschichte und Staatsbildung

Bessarabien war im 19. Jahrhundert ein unbedeutendes Gouvernement im äußersten Südwesten des Zarenreiches. Das Bildungsniveau der damaligen romanischen Bevölkerung lag weit unter dem Durchschnitt der Bevölkerung im europäischen Teil Rußlands. Nach der ersten russischen Volkszählung von 1897 konnten nur 22,2% der Moldauer lesen und schreiben (gegenüber 32,0% in Weißrußland oder 54,2% in Litauen). Dabei besagte das Minimumkriterium des Census für Literalität lediglich, daß die Person in der Lage sein mußte, ihren Namen zu schreiben. Kulturell war Bessarabien eine Provinz, und für den Ausbau eines rumänischsprachigen Schulwesens unternahm die zaristische Verwaltung wenig. Die wohlhabenderen Familien schickten ihre Kinder ohnehin in russische Schulen, um ihnen die Möglichkeit zu sozialem Aufstieg in russischem Milieu zu ermöglichen (Weigand 1904, 20).

Der politische Anschluß des größten Teils Bessarabiens an Rumänien war im wesentlichen die Folge einer rumänischen militärischen Intervention des Jahres 1918, und weniger Ausdruck des Willens der Moldauer zum Zusammenschluß mit den übrigen Rumänen (Kramer 1980, 136 f).

Zwischen 1924 und 1940 bestand die Moldauische A(utonome) S(ozialistische) S(owjet-) R(epublik) als Teil der Ukrainischen SSR. Verwaltungszentrum im moldauischen Grenzland war zunächst Balta im Nordosten, seit 1928 Birzulav im Zentrum und seit 1929 Tiraspol' am Dnestr. Nach dem Anschluß Bessarabiens an die Sowjetunion (1940) wurde Moldawien der Status einer Sowjetrepublik zugesprochen und diese Region als Moldauische SSR benannt. Als Hauptstadt der Region wurde Kišinëv (mold. Chişinău) gewählt (1940/41, seit 1944). Die offizielle Benennung als Moldauische SSR hatte Bestand bis Mai 1991, als die Region in „Moldawien" (rum. *Moldova*) umbenannt wurde.

Das Regionalparlament in Chişinău schlug Ende der achtziger Jahre — dem Beispiel der

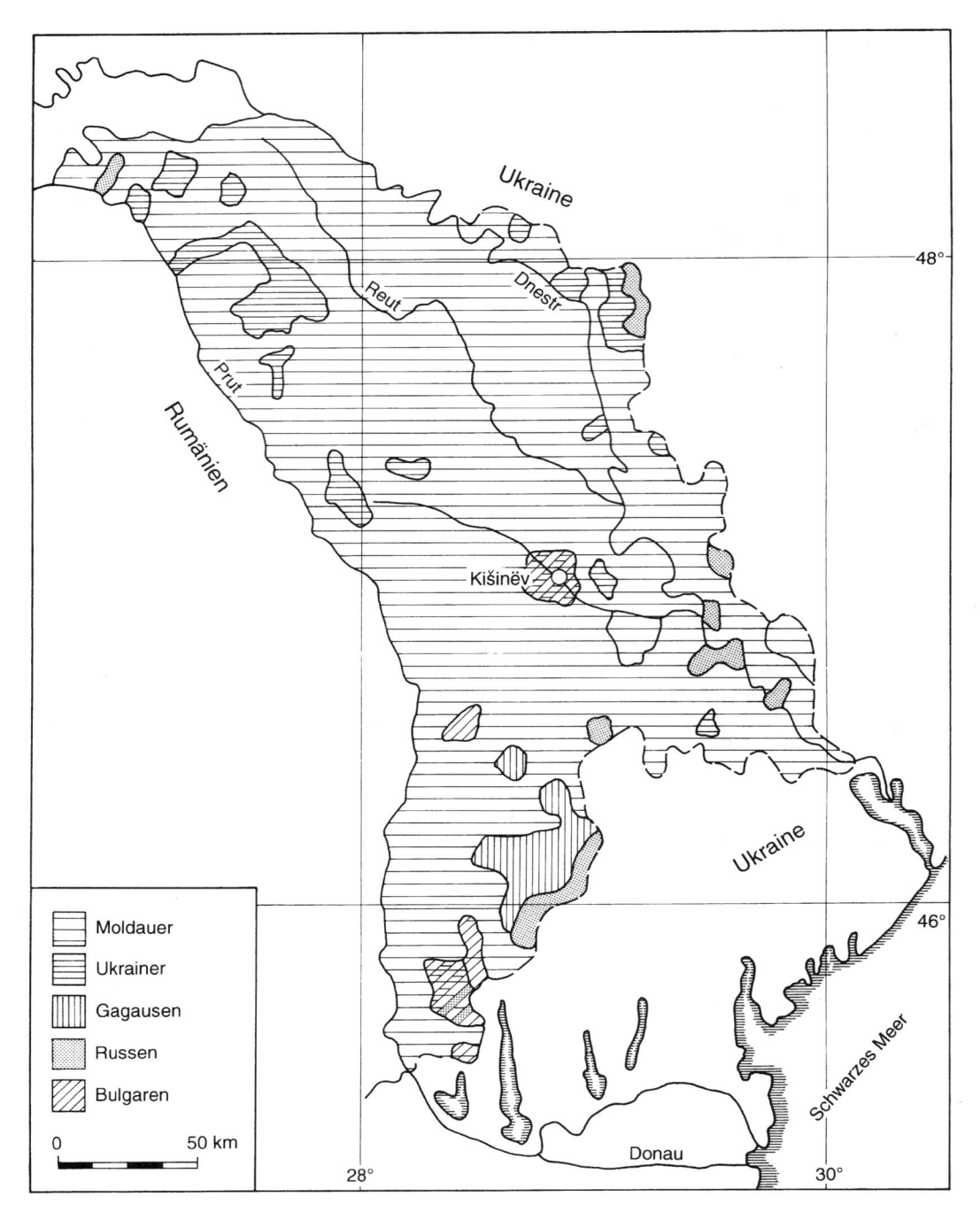

Abb. 237.1: Die ethnische Differenzierung der Bevölkerung Moldawiens (Haarmann 1978, 80)

baltischen Republiken folgend — einen nationalen Kurs ein, der auf die Erweiterung der Regionalautonomie auf dem Weg zur Eigenstaatlichkeit abzielte. Am 23.6.1990 gab das Parlament eine Souveränitätserklärung ab. Dagegen stellten sich die Vertreter der russischen Bevölkerung, die eine Verschlechterung ihres soziopolitischen Status befürchteten.

Als Moldawien mit der Unabhängigkeitserklärung vom 27.8.1991 faktisch seine Souveränität erlangte, brach der Interessengegensatz zwischen Moldauern und Russen zum offenen Konflikt auf. Beide Gruppen sind seit 1992 in einen lokalen Bürgerkrieg verstrickt.

3. Politik, Wirtschaft und allgemeine kulturelle sowie religiöse Lage

Die Umstellung von der Plan- zur Marktwirtschaft hat zu einer Verschlechterung der Versorgungslage und zu einem Rückgang der industriellen sowie landwirtschaftlichen Produktion geführt. Für die Bevölkerung Moldawiens, das seit jeher zu den ärmsten Regionen im europäischen Teil des Sowjetstaates gehörte, bedeuten die Einbußen in der Produktion, daß rund 50% (1991) der Erwerbstätigen auf einem Niveau unterhalb der Armutsgrenze leben. Die Verteilung des Bruttosozialprodukts auf die ethnischen Gruppen ist extrem ungleichgewichtig. Die fortschrittlichste Region sind die fünf Bezirke in Transnistrien (Region östlich des Flusses Dnestr), wo die metallverarbeitende Industrie konzentriert ist. Dieses Gebiet ist hauptsächlich von Russen bewohnt, die das Gros der Erwerbstätigen im städtischen Milieu stellen.

Die am 2.9.1990 proklamierte Dnestr-Republik erklärte sich nach dem Referendum vom 1.12.1991 für unabhängig. Diese politische Loslösung von Moldawien ist vom Parlament in Chişinău nicht anerkannt worden. Der bewaffnete Konflikt zwischen den transnistrischen Russen, die die Kontrolle über die Industrieregion nicht an Nichtrussen abgeben wollen, und den Moldauern ist vielleicht nur vordergründig wirtschaftlich motiviert. Es spielen sicher auch antislawische Ressentiments auf Seiten der romanischen Bevölkerung eine Rolle, die sich seit jeher von den im allgemeinen sozial besser gestellten Russen zurückgesetzt fühlen. In der Auseinandersetzung finden beide Gruppen ihre Verbündeten, die Russen in Transnistrien werden militärisch von den Russen in Rußland unterstützt, der Nachschub für die moldauische Armee kommt aus Rumänien. Ähnlich konfliktbeladen ist das politische Verhältnis Moldawiens zu seiner Südregion Gagausien, die seit dem 26.10.1990 über ihr eigenes Parlament verfügt. Die am 19.8.1990 erklärte und im Referendum vom 1.12.1991 bestätigte Unabhängigkeit ist von der moldauischen Regierung nicht anerkannt worden.

Die meisten Moldauer sprechen Russisch als Zweitsprache. Russisch ist auch als Kontaktsprache zwischen Moldauern und Gagausen wichtiger als das Rumänische. Konfessionell gehören Moldauer wie Gagausen zur selben Gruppe, zur rumänisch-orthodoxen Kirche. Der ethnische Gegensatz von Moldauern und Russen dagegen spiegelt sich auch in der konfessionellen Spaltung zwischen Rumänisch-Orthodoxen und Russisch-Orthodoxen.

4. Statistik und Ethnoprofile

Moldawien hat 4.335.000 Einwohner (1989), davon 2.795.000, i. e. 63,9% rumänischsprachige Moldauer, 600.000, i. e. 13,8% Ukrainer, 562.000, i. e. 12,8% Russen, 153.500 Gagausen, 88.400 Bulgaren, 65.700 Juden, 19.600 Weißrussen, 11.600 Zigeuner u. a. (*Social'noe razvitie* 1991). Die Bevölkerung ist in den vergangenen Jahrzehnten rasant angewachsen (vgl. 1970: 3,569 Mill., 1979: 3,950 Mill., 1989: 4,335 Mill.), d. h. zwischen 1970 und 1989 um 21,5%. Obwohl die Moldauer die Majorität der Bevölkerung Moldawiens (1989: 63,9%) ausmachen, ist ihr Anteil in den vergangenen Jahrzehnten trotz hoher Geburtenraten leicht gesunken. Im Jahre 1970 betrug der Anteil der Moldauer noch 64,6%. Der Anteil der russischen Bevölkerung ist angestiegen (von 1970: 11,6% auf 1989: 12,8%), der Anteil der ukrainischen Minderheit im selben Zeitraum gesunken (von 1970: 14,2% auf 1989: 13,8%).

Die russische Bevölkerung konzentriert sich hauptsächlich in den Industriegebieten östlich des Dnestr. Im Süden des Landes leben die Gagausen, ein Turkvolk, dessen Angehörige auch jenseits der Grenze in dem zur Ukraine gehörenden Gebiet Odessa siedeln. Der Bevölkerungsanteil der Gagausen ist in Moldawien konstant geblieben, d. h. seit den siebziger Jahren macht er 3,5% aus.

Die in sowjetischer Zeit aufrechterhaltene Differenzierung zwischen den Moldauern (russ. *moldavane*) als einer sowjetischen Nationalität und den Rumänen (russ. *rumyny*) als einem davon verschiedenen Volk begründete sich im wesentlichen ideologisch. Die Trennung in zwei ethnische Gruppen sollte einerseits den territorialen Anspruch des Sowjetstaates auf Moldawien legitimieren, andererseits dem Bewußtsein sprachlich-kultureller Zusammengehörigkeit beiderseits der sowjetmoldauisch-rumänischen Grenze den

Nährboden entziehen. Dementsprechend wurden von den sowjetischen Linguisten auch zwei romanische Sprachen unterschieden: Rumänisch und Moldauisch (Šišmarev 1952). Die kyrillische Schrift des Moldau-Rumänischen, die jahrzehntelang verwendet wurde, war für die Sowjetideologie ein wichtiges Mittel der Abgrenzung gegenüber der in Lateinschrift geschriebenen Nachbarsprache. Die Trennung der romanischen Bevölkerung in zwei nationale Gruppen fand ihren Niederschlag auch in der Behandlung der Ethnien in der Sowjetunion selbst. In der Ethnographie sowjetischer Völker wurde zwischen einheimischen Moldauern und Rumänen als nationaler Minderheit unterschieden (cf. Bruk/Apenčenko 1964, 17 für die Grenzlandminderheiten in der Ukraine). Ebenfalls im sowjetischen Census (z. B. *Itogi* 1973, 152 ff) wird für die multinationale Bevölkerung der Ukraine zwischen Moldauern und Rumänen unterschieden. Es scheint, daß sich bei manchen Moldauern — auch unabhängig von der ideologischen Überformung der öffentlichen Meinung — ein Regionalbewußtsein entwickelt hat, dessen Abstandnahme zum Rumänentum in etwa den Stellenwert hat wie das Bayerisch-Sein zum Deutschtum.

Während für die sowjetische Nationalitäten- und Sprachenpolitik diese Trennung immer grundlegend geblieben ist, hat man seit den sechziger Jahren in vielen rumänischen Publikationen demgegenüber die Zusammengehörigkeit betont. Nachdem die früheren ideologischen Barrieren gefallen sind, hat sich die sprachliche Gemeinsamkeit von Moldauern und Rumänen in deren Selbstbekenntnis artikuliert (Eyal 1992, 131 f). Die Annahme der lateinischen Graphie und der standardsprachlichen Normen des benachbarten Rumänisch für den Sprachgebrauch in Moldawien ist ein konkreter Ausdruck dieser Identitätsfindung.

5. Soziolinguistische Lage

Das sowjetische Modell der national-russischen Zweisprachigkeit (→ Art. 231) kam auch in Moldawien zur Anwendung. Die moldauische Bevölkerung war trotz eines funktionierenden muttersprachlichen Schulunterrichts vom Russischen als Hauptmedium in den höheren Ausbildungsstufen abhängig. Das Niveau der Spracherhaltung ist bei den Moldauern nicht nur sehr hoch, sondern es ist auch trotz einer sich verstärkenden assimilatorischen Dynamik des Russischen im vergangenen Jahrzehnt nur unwesentlich gesunken (vgl. 1970: 97,7% — 1979: 96,5% — 1989: 91,6%). Diese Quoten gehören zu den höchsten in der Westregion der Ex-Sowjetunion. Lediglich bei den Esten und Litauern liegen die Raten für Spracherhaltung über 95%. Im städtischen Milieu ist das Russische als Zweitsprache doppelt so stark verbreitet wie auf dem Lande.

Das Sprachverhalten der slawischen Bevölkerung in Moldawien war bis vor wenigen Jahren bestimmt durch die allgemeine national-russische Zweisprachigkeit. Die russische Bevölkerung war größtenteils einsprachig, da das Russische die wichtigste interethnische Kontaktsprache war. Lediglich 10,7% (1979) der in Moldawien lebenden Russen beherrschten Rumänisch als Zweitsprache. Die Angehörigen der ukrainischen und weißrussischen Minderheit in Moldawien bevorzugten eindeutig das Russische als Zweitsprache. Die Zahl der Ukrainer mit russischen Zweitsprachenkenntnissen war 1979 mehr als dreimal so groß wie die derjenigen, die auch Rumänisch sprachen. Das Sprachverhalten der Gagausen ähnelt dem der Ukrainer und Weißrussen. Die meisten sprechen Russisch als Zweitsprache, ein kleinerer Teil beherrscht auch Rumänisch. Dies betrifft vor allem die Generationen, deren Vertreter vor 1940 in rumänische Schulen gingen.

Mehrsprachigkeit ist nur bei einem kleineren Teil der erwähnten, überwiegend zweisprachigen Minderheitengruppen verbreitet, wohingegen die Beherrschung mehrerer (d. h. von drei oder sogar vier) Sprachen charakteristisch für die kommunikative Mobilität der in der Diaspora lebenden Juden und Zigeuner Moldawiens ist. Von den 1979 insgesamt 26.533 Juden (33,1%), die sich nicht assimiliert hatten und in der Hauptsache Jiddisch als Primärsprache sprachen, beherrschten 24.333 (d. h. 91,7%) Russisch als Zweitsprache und 11.920 (d. h. 44,9%) Rumänisch als Drittsprache (*Čislennost'* 1984, 128 f). Von der Gesamtzahl aller Juden in Moldawien (1979: 80.127) hatte sich der überwiegende Teil bereits assimiliert, die meisten (52.996) an das Russische, die wenigsten (426) an das Rumänische. Für die Zigeuner andererseits ist das Rumänische als Kontaktsprache wichtiger als das Russische, und zwar sowohl vom Standpunkt des Sprachwechsels (1970: 17,8% Assimilanten mit rumänischer gegenüber 2,0% mit russischer Primärsprache) als auch nach dem Kriterium der Zweitsprachenattraktion (1970: 46,3% Zigeuner mit rumän. gegenüber 27,3% mit russ. Zweitsprachenkenntnissen). Bei der Landbevölkerung divergierten die Proportionen noch deutlicher (1970: 60,3% Zigeuner mit rumän. gegenüber 19,8% mit russ. Zweitsprache); (Haarmann 1979 b, 64, 163).

6. Sprachpolitische Lage

Die Konsolidierung der Normen für eine moldau-rumänische Standardsprache war vielleicht das ambitionierteste, widersprüchlichste und gleichzeitig das vom politisch-ideologischen Standpunkt aus betrachtet brisanteste aller Projekte der sowjetischen Sprachplanung im europäischen Teil der Sowjetunion (Haarmann 1978, 247 ff). Während das Rumänische in Bessarabien bis 1917 von den meisten Gebildeten als unkultivierter Jargon der Landbevölkerung betrachtet worden war, bemühten sich die Sprachplaner im sowjetischen Teil Moldawiens um die Anhebung des soziokulturellen Niveaus der lokalen Mundart zu dem einer modernen Ansprüchen genügenden Schriftsprache.

Die Normierung der moldauischen Standardsprache, deren vom Rumänischen abweichende Eigenbezeichnung (vgl. mold. *limba moldovenjaskă*/russ. *moldavskij jazyk* 'moldauische Sprache' gegenüber rum. *limba română*/russ. *rumynskij jazyk* 'rumänische Sprache') bereits die Intention der sowjetischen Sprachplaner signalisierte, diese „sowjetische" Sprachform gegen die des Nachbarlandes abzusetzen, vollzog sich in unterschiedlichen Phasen (Heitmann 1965). Äußeres Kennzeichen des soziokulturellen Abstands gegenüber dem Rumänischen in Rumänien war der Gebrauch der kyrillischen Schrift für das Moldauische. Schon vor 1918 war die romanische Sprachvariante Bessarabiens, wenn auch selten, in Kyrillica geschrieben worden (Boršč 1966). Das erste Planungsmodell einer moldauischen Schriftsprache zwischen 1924 und 1929 allerdings basiert auf der Lateinschrift (Tabelle 237.1), die damals in der gesamten Sowjetunion das Hauptmedium der Orthographiereform war (Isaev 1979, 59 ff).

Anders als im Fall der übrigen sowjetischen Schriftsprachen, die im Verlauf der dreißiger Jahre endgültig von der lateinischen auf die kyrillische Graphie umgestellt wurden (z. B. Tatarisch, Wotjakisch, Kalmükisch; → Art. 231), kehrten die moldauischen Sprachplaner 1933 noch einmal zur Lateinschrift zurück. Von 1937 schließlich bis zum Jahre 1989 wurde das Moldauische kontinuierlich in kyrillischer Schrift geschrieben.

Der graphischen Differenzierung entsprach allerdings eine unterschiedliche soziokulturelle Ausrichtung des Rumänischen beiderseits der Grenze. Zwar wurden 1957 die Normen des Schriftmoldauischen denen des Schriftrumänischen im Westen weitgehend angeglichen (Kramer 1980, 146 ff), es blieben aber dennoch Unterschiede in der stilistischen Verwendung der Standardsprache sowie in der Phraseologie. Der Sprachgebrauch des Moldauischen wirkte auf so manchen Rumänen in Rumänien fremdartig. Bis 1989 bestand die Situation einer bizentrischen Hochsprache mit einem westlichen Kulturareal (Rumänien und das Zentrum Bukarest) und einem östlichen Kulturareal (Moldauische SSR und das Zentrum Kišinëv), wobei die gesprochenen Mundarten im Westen und Osten jeweils von einem Schriftmedium in divergierender Graphie überdacht wurden. Die Schwankungen des Schriftsystems fanden vor 1957 ihre Parallele in unterschiedlichen Orientierungen der dialektalen Basis der Schriftsprache sowie ihrer lexikalischen Strukturen.

Drei Grundtendenzen konkurrierten in chronologischer Abfolge miteinander, eine Annäherung an die rumänische Schriftsprache (z. B. 1924−1929, 1933−1937, 1957−1989), eine Abstandnahme gegenüber dem Rumänischen und Orientierung an lokalmundartlicher Spezifik (z. B. 1930−1933, 1937−1950) und eine Hervorhebung der sowjetischen soziokulturellen Bindungen durch die Betonung des slawischen (insbesondere russischen) Lehnwortschatzes für die Standardsprache (z. B. 1937−1950). Der Trend zur Abstandnahme gegenüber dem Schriftrumänischen in Rumänien deckte sich dabei periodisch mit dem Trend zur Betonung des slawischen Kulturerbes, wie in den Jahren zwischen 1937 und 1950.

Als besonders schwierig stellte es sich heraus, die Alternative einer sowohl vom Rumänischen als auch vom Russischen unabhängigen Sprachplanung zu verwirklichen. Am konsequentesten verfolgt wurde dieser Trend zwischen 1930 und 1933. Diese Periode in der Geschichte der moldauischen Schriftsprache ist geprägt durch den Einfluß von L. A. Madan. Charakteristisch für den Madanismus waren Neologismen auf der Basis des Erbwortschatzes und der einheimischen Wortbil-

Tab. 237.1: Periodisierung der sowjetischen Sprachplanung und charakteristische Merkmale der moldauischen Standardsprache (Haarmann 1978, 259 f)

	Normierung der Graphie/Orthographiereform	Normierung der Schriftsprache (Grammatische Struktur/ Dialektale Basis)	Lexik/Fachterminologische Normierung
1924–1929	lateinisches Alphabet	starke Anlehnung an die rumänische Schriftsprache bei gleichzeitiger Betonung von Unterschieden („romanophile Tendenz"; vgl. Heitmann 1965. 110 f)	Adaption des rumänischen Kulturwortschatzes sowie der Fachterminologien
1930–1933	kyrillisches Alphabet	bewußte Abstandnahme von der rumänischen Schriftsprache sowie Loslösung vom rumänischen Kulturerbe; vgl. Grammatik (1930) von L. A. Madan (sog. Madanismus; vgl. Heitmann 1965. 111 f); dialektale Basis ist die Mundart des Bezirks Orhei	Ablehnung lateinischer, französischer sowie russischer Neologismen; stattdessen Betonung von Eigenprägungen auf der Basis des moldauischen Erbwortschatzes
1933–1937	lateinisches Alphabet	leichte Anlehnung an die rumänische Schriftsprache („Latinisierungsphase"; vgl. Heitmann 1965. 112 f)	Anlehnung an die lexikalischen Normen der rumänischen Schriftsprache
seit 1937	kyrillisches Alphabet	starke Dialektalisierung (концепцие вулгаризатоаре 'Vulgarisierungskonzeption' von I. D. Čobanu; vgl. Heitmann 1965. 112 ff)	Vermeidung vor allem von Latinismen; Ersetzung durch slavische Lehnwörter (russ. Neologismen) oder durch Eigenprägungen; Ausmerzen von Dialektalismen, die vom Madanismus propagiert wurden
1957	kyrillisches Alphabet	Konsolidierung der schriftsprachlichen Normen auf der Basis der Mundart von Kišinëv mit leichter Anlehnung an die rumänische Schriftsprache (vgl. Heitmann 1965. 114 ff)	Fortsetzung der Entrumänisierungstendenz; kompromißhafte Teilanlehnung an die lexikalischen Normen der rumänischen Schriftsprache
seit 1989	lateinisches Alphabet	rumänischer Schriftstandard	Entsowjetisierung lexikalischer Strukturen

dung. In jener Zeit sind neue Termini entstanden, durch die ältere Elemente des rumänischen Kulturwortschatzes oder des russischen Lehnwortschatzes ersetzt werden sollten (z. B. mold. *kelduro-mesuretor* 'Thermometer' für rum. *termometru*). Nach 1937 haben die Sprachplaner solche künstlichen Innovationen, die ohnehin nicht populär wurden, wie überhaupt den Madanismus als planerischen Trend aufgegeben.

Die andere autochthone Sprache mit eigener Schriftkultur in Moldawien ist das Gagausische (Pokrovskaja 1969). Ein nach seinem Umfang bescheidenes Schrifttum in Gagausisch entstand in der Zeit zwischen 1910 und 1938. Dabei handelt es sich um Übersetzungen religiöser Schriften, die vom Episkopat in Chişinău verbreitet wurden. Bis 1918 wurden diese in russischem Alphabet, danach in Lateinschrift aufgezeichnet. Zu den wenigen Projekten der sowjetischen Sprachplanung in der Nachkriegszeit gehörte auch die Normierung des Gagausischen. Nach anfänglichen Experimenten Ende der vierziger Jahre wurde im Juli 1957 das Planungsprojekt einer gagausischen Schriftsprache vom Obersten Sowjet der Moldauischen SSR etabliert. Die schriftsprachlichen Normen wurden auf der Basis der zentralen Mundart konsolidiert, mit einigen Anleihen an die südliche Mundart.

Basis des Schriftsystems ist die Kyrillica, deren Zeichenbestand um zunächst drei Sonderzeichen (und zwar ä, ö und y) erweitert wurde (*Pravila orfografii* 1958). Später wurde noch das Zeichen ж [ž] aus der kyrillischen Graphie des Moldau-Rumänischen adaptiert. Die neue gagausische Schriftsprache fand auch Eingang in den Schulunterricht. Der muttersprachliche Unterricht wurde in der Primar- und Sekundarstufe gefördert, die höhere Schulausbildung blieb allerdings weiterhin dem Medium des Russischen vorbehalten.

In gagausischer Sprache wurden vor allem Bücher für den schulischen Bedarf gedruckt, auch einzelne Broschüren über folkloristische Themen. Für praktische sowie wissenschaftliche Zwecke entstanden verschiedene Handbücher (z. B. Gajdarzi et al. 1973, Gucul et al. 1975). Als Schriftsprache hat sich das Gagausische in sowjetischer Zeit weder gegen das Moldauische noch gegen das Russische durchsetzen können. Das Russische besitzt heutzutage keinen Prestigewert mehr im Süden Moldawiens, und das Gagausische übernimmt in der Regionalverwaltung sogar amtliche Funktionen.

7. Sprachkontakte und die Rolle lexikalischer Innovation

7.1. Der moldau-rumänische Dialekt teilt mit dem Dakorumänischen in Rumänien die wesentlichen Strukturen von romanischem Erb- und slawischem Lehnwortschatz (Korletjanu 1987, 190 f). Auch der moderne Kulturwortschatz ist in seinen Grundzügen einheitlich. Dabei sind die Quellen im Rumänischen Rumäniens andere als in Moldawien. Während das Deutsche und Französische im vergangenen Jahrhundert als Bildungssprachen direkt auf das Rumänische in Rumänien einwirkten, gelangten die betreffenden Kulturwörter über den Umweg russischer Vermittlung ins Moldau-Rumänische (z. B. *abzac* 'Absatz (Text)', *banket* 'Bankett', *konstruktiv* 'konstruktiv'). Dies gilt auch für die modernen Internationalismen, die im Rumänischen direkt aus westlichen Sprachen adaptiert, im Moldau-Rumänischen indirekt über das Russische entlehnt worden sind (z. B. *motel* 'Motel', *peniciline* 'Penizillin', *reaktor* 'Reaktor').

Die gesellschaftlichen Gegensätze zwischen dem sozialistischen Moldawien und dem „bourgeoisen" Rumänien vor 1940 spiegelten sich auch im Wortschatz. Während die moldau-rumänische Terminologie bereits seit den zwanziger Jahren Sowjetismen verwendete (z. B. *kolchoz* 'Kolchose', *komisar* 'Kommissar (politisch)', *kolektivizm* 'Kollektivismus'), entwickelten sich die lexikalischen Strukturen sozialistisch-kommunistischer Prägung im westlichen Rumänien erst nach 1944. Seit Kriegsende ist die Entwicklung der Lexik auf beiden Seiten der Grenze im wesentlichen gleichartig verlaufen. In den vergangenen Jahrzehnten wurde vor allem der politisch-gesellschaftliche und wissenschaftliche Wortschatz von Sowjetismen geprägt. Hierzu gehören unter anderem zahlreiche Lehnprägungen nach russischem Muster (z. B. *antipartinik* 'jemand, der gegen die Parteiinteressen handelt', *apolitizm* 'a-politisches Verhalten, politisches Desinteresse', *aseleniza* 'in eine Mondumlaufbahn einschwenken (vom Raumschiff)'.

In Entsprechung der Veränderungen in der sozialen Berufswelt wurden nach dem Krieg weibliche Formen für viele Berufsbezeichnungen verwendet, wo diese vorher unüblich oder unbekannt waren (z. B. *inžiner* 'Ingenieur' : *inžinere* 'Ingenieurin', *žurnalist* 'Journalist' : *žurnaliste* 'Journalistin', *traktorist* 'Traktorfahrer' : *traktoriste* 'Traktoristin') (Korletjanu et al. 1973, 187 ff). Seit Ende der achtziger Jahre wurde die sozialistisch geprägte Terminologie bewußt abgeschwächt. Diese Schicht des rumänischen Wortschatzes ist heute historisch. Stattdessen werden der Kulturwortschatz insbesondere französischer Provenienz und die einheimische latinisierende Terminologie reaktiviert.

In den achtziger Jahren wurde die Wechselseitigkeit der Einflüsse im Rahmen der national-russischen Sprachkontakte betont (Dešeriev 1987). Unter anderem werden auch einige Moldowanismen als Beispiele angeführt, die ihren Weg bis in die russische Literatursprache gefunden haben; z. B. *brynza* 'Schafskäse', *papuša* 'Bündel Tabakblätter', *cigejka* 'Schafsfell'. Größer ist die Zahl der Moldowanismen in den russischen Mundarten Moldawiens, wo unter anderem moldau-rumänische Termini in der Sprache des Weinanbaus, der Viehhaltung und Weidekultur, der regionalen Gastronomie und im Bauwesen zu finden sind (Korletjanu et al. 1987, 192 f, 200 f). Die Kontakte der Moldauer und Ukrainer haben sich seit dem vergangenen Jahrhundert auch sprachlich ausgewirkt. Das Moldau-Rumänische hat die lokalen Mundarten des Ukrainischen im moldauisch-ukrainischen Grenzland beeinflußt, wo Angehörige beider ethnischer Gruppen im ländlichen Milieu in Siedlungsnachbarschaft leben (Beloded 1969, 279 ff).

7.2. Den entscheidenden Durchbruch zu ihrer „Naturalisierung" erlebte die moldauische Standardsprache im Sommer 1989, als das Parlament in Kišinëv beschloß, die Kyrillica aufzugeben und die Lateinschrift wieder einzuführen. Dies war ein deutliches Signal zur Solidarisierung mit der rumänischen Sprachgemeinschaft. Die orthographischen Normen des Rumänischen in Moldawien folgen seither denen des Schriftrumänischen in Rumänien. Der von Sowjetismen überformte Wortschatz des Moldau-Rumänischen wurde abgebaut, und der Sprachgebrauch hat sich den lexikalischen Wandlungen im übrigen rumänischen Sprachgebiet angepaßt.

Das Verhältnis von Rumänisch und Russisch hat sich drastisch verändert. Bis gegen Ende der achtziger Jahre war das Russische die bevorzugte interne (d. h. innerhalb der Region) und externe (d. h. im Kontakt mit der übrigen Sowjetunion) Verwaltungssprache der Moldauischen SSR. Im Bereich der Schriftkultur dominierte das Russische in den höheren Stufen der Ausbildung sowie in der Druckproduktion im Hinblick auf die Vielzahl an Buch- und Zeitschriftentiteln sowie der Zeitungsorgane. Nach der Auflage lagen die Anteile der russisch-sprachigen Druckproduktion zwar niedriger als die in rumänischer Sprache, allerdings höher als das Niveau der Verbreitung russischer Sprachkenntnisse (Haarmann 1978, 312 ff). Die sowjetisch geprägte Zweisprachigkeit im Amtsverkehr und in der Schriftkultur Moldawiens ist praktisch zusammengebrochen. Das Russische besitzt keinen amtlichen Status mehr, als Schriftsprache wird es nicht mehr bevorzugt, und als Minderheitensprache wird es prestigemäßig geringer bewertet als vergleichsweise das autochthone Gagausisch.

8. Bibliographie (in Auswahl)

Baskakov, N. A. (Ed.) (1969): *Osnovnye processy vnutristrukturnogo razvitija tjurkskich, finno-ugorskich i mongol'skich jazykov* [Grundlegende Prozesse der innerstrukturellen Entwicklung türkischer, finnisch-ugrischer und mongolischer Sprachen], Moskau.

Beloded, Ivan Konstantinovič (1969): *Razvitie jazykov socialističeskich nacii SSSR* [Die Entwicklung der Sprachen der sozialistischen Nationen der UdSSR], Kiew.

Borodina, M. A./Guryčeva, M. S. (Eds.) (1966): *Metody sravnitel'no-sopostavitel'nogo izučenija sovremennych romanskich jazykov* [Methoden der vergleichend-kontrastiven Erforschung der modernen romanischen Sprachen], Moskau.

Boršč, Anton T. (1966): „K voprosu o slavjanskom pis'me v Moldavii" [Zur Frage der slawischen Schrift in Moldawien]. In: *Borodina/Guryčeva* (Eds.) 1966, 326—334.

Boršč, Anton T. et al. (1977): *Dikcionar eksplikativ al limbij moldovenešt'* [Erklärendes Wörterbuch der moldauischen Sprache], vol. 1, Kišinëv.

Bruk, S. I./Apenčenko, V. S. (Eds.) (1964): *Atlas narodov mira* [Atlas der Völker der Welt], Moskau.

Čislennost' (1984): *Čislennost' i sostav naselenija SSSR. Po dannym Vsesojuznoj perepisi naselenija 1979 goda* [Zahl und Zusammensetzung der Bevölkerung der UdSSR. Nach den Daten der All-Unions-Volkszählung von 1979], Moskau.

Dešeriev, J. D. (Ed.) (1973): *Vnutristrukturnoe razvitie staropis'mennych jazykov* [Die innerstrukturelle Entwicklung der alten Schriftsprachen], Moskau.

Dešeriev, J. D. (Ed.) (1987): *Vzaimovlijanie i vzaimoobogoščenie jazykov narodov SSSR* [Lehnbeziehung und die Bereicherung der Sprachen der Völker der UdSSR durch Entlehnung], Moskau.

Dešeriev, J. D./Tumanjan, E. G. (Eds.) (1980): *Vzaimootnošenie razvitija nacional'nych jazykov i nacional'nych kul'tur* [Lehnbeziehungen in der Entwicklung der Nationalsprachen und Nationalkulturen], Moskau.

Eyal, Jonathan (1992): „Moldavians". In: *Smith*, 123—141.

Gabinskij, Mark Aleksandrovič (1980): *Grammatičeskoe var'irovanie v moldavskom jazyke* [Grammatische Varietät in der moldauischen Sprache], Kišinëv.

Gajdarzi, G. A. et al. (Eds.) (1973): *Gagauzsko-russko-moldavskij slovar'* [Gagausisch-russisch-moldauisches Wörterbuch], Moskau.

Gucul, L. A. et al. (Eds.) (1975): *Moldavskoe sovetskoe jazykoznanie (1924—1974)* [Moldauisch-sowjetische Sprachwissenschaft (1924—1974)], Kišinëv.

Haarmann, Harald (1978): *Balkanlinguistik (2): Studien zur interlingualen Soziolinguistik des Moldauischen*, Tübingen.

Haarmann, Harald (1979 a): *Multilinguale Kommunikationsstrukturen. Spracherhaltung und Sprachwechsel bei den romanischen Siedlungsgruppen in der Ukrainischen SSR und anderen Sowjetrepubliken*, Tübingen.

Haarmann, Harald (1979 b); *Spracherhaltung und Sprachwechsel als Probleme der interlingualen So-*

ziolinguistik. Studien zur Mehrsprachigkeit der Zigeuner in der Sowjetunion, Hamburg.

Haarmann, Harald (1984): „Zur Gruppenmehrsprachigkeit in der Sowjetunion". In: *Jachnow*, 560–577.

Heitmann, Klaus (1965): „Rumänische Sprache und Literatur in Bessarabien und Transnistrien". In: *Zeitschrift für romanische Philologie* 81, 109–156.

Isaev, Magomet Izmajlovič (1979): *Jazykovoe stroitel'stvo v SSSR* [Der sprachliche Aufbau in der UdSSR], Moskau.

Itogi (1973): *Itogi vsesojuznoj perepisi naselenija 1970 goda. t. IV* [Ergebnisse der All-Unions-Volkszählung des Jahres 1970], Moskau.

Jachnow, Helmut (Ed.) (1984): *Handbuch des Russisten. Sprachwissenschaft und angrenzende Disziplinen*, Wiesbaden.

Korletjanu, N. G. et al. (1973): „Moldavskij jazyk" [Das Moldauische]. In: *Dešeriev*, 163–221.

Korletjanu, N. G. (1987): „Svidetel'stva mnogovekovych jazykovych vzaimosvjazej (k diachronno-sinchronnoj traktovke moldavsko-russkich vzaimootnošenij)" [Zeugnisse der jahrhundertelangen sprachlichen Lehnbeziehungen (zur diachronisch-synchronischen Erläuterung der moldauisch-russischen Lehnbeziehungen)]: In: *Dešeriev*, 190–202.

Kramer, Johannes (1980): „Das Moldauische". In: *Balkan-Archiv/Neue Folge* 5, 125–155.

Narodnoe obrazovanie (1989): *Narodnoe obrazovanie i kul'tura v SSSR. Statističeskij sbornik* [Volksbildung und Kultur in der UdSSR. Ein statistisches Sammelwerk], Moskau.

Pokrovskaja, L. A. (1969): „Gagauzskij jazyk" [Das Gagausische]. In: *Baskakov*, 211–235.

Pravila orfografii gagauzskogo jazyka (1958), Kišinëv.

Raevskij, N./Gabinskij, M. (Eds.) (1978): *Skurt dikcionar etimoložik al limbij moldovenešt'* [Kurzes etymologisches Wörterbuch der moldauischen Sprache], Kišinëv.

Romano-slavjanskie jazykovye otnošenija i paralleli [Romanisch-slawische Sprachkontakte und Parallelen] (1978), Kišenëv.

Šišmarev, V. F. (1952): „Romanskie jazyki Jugovostočnoj Evropy i nacional'nyj jazyk Moldavskoj SSR" [Die romanischen Sprachen Südosteuropas und die Nationalsprache in der Moldauischen SSR]. In: *Voprosy jazykoznanija* 1, 80–106.

Smith, G. (Ed.) (1992): *The Nationalities Question in the Soviet Union*, London/New York (3. Aufl.).

Social'noe razvitie (1991): *Social'noe razvitie SSSR 1989 – Statističeskij sbornik* [Die soziale Entwicklung der UdSSR 1989 – Ein statistisches Sammelwerk], Moskau.

Weigand, Gustav (1904): *Die Dialekte der Bukowina und Bessarabiens*, Leipzig.

Harald Haarmann, Helsinki (Finnland)

XVII. Sprachkontakte des Jiddischen und Romani
Language Contacts of Yiddish and Romani
Contacts linguistiques du Yiddish et du Romani

238. Jiddisch

1. Geographie und Demographie
2. Geschichte
3. Politik gegenüber dem Jiddischen und seinen Sprechern im 20. Jahrhundert
4. Statistik und Ethnoprofil
5. Sprachpolitische Lage
6. Charakteristik des jiddischen Sprachsystems im Vergleich zu dem seiner Kontaktsprachen
7. Kritische Wertung der verwendeten Literatur
8. Bibliographie (in Auswahl)

1. Geographie und Demographie

1.1. Das ursprüngliche *Verbreitungsgebiet* des Jiddischen deckt sich im wesentlichen mit dem mittelalterlichen polnischen Staat. Dieser umfaßte seit der Vereinigung mit Litauen im Jahre 1387 auch einen Teil Lettlands, Weißrußland und fast die ganze Ukraine.

Die seit dem 13. Jahrhundert aus Deutschland nach Polen ausgewanderte, als Ausgangsform des späteren Jiddischen sog. *Jüdisch-Deutsch* sprechende und sich in ihrem hebräischsprachigen Schrifttum auch *Aškenazim* ('Deutsche') nennende jüdische Bevölkerung konzentrierte sich dabei in den Städten, wo sie insbesondere in Kleinstädten, dem berühmten jüdischen „Štetl", oft die Mehrheit stellte. Die ländlichen Gebiete waren vorwiegend von Polen, Litauern, Weißrussen und Ukrainern bewohnt.

An dieser Verbreitung änderte sich auch nach den 1772, 1793 und 1795 vorgenommenen Teilungen Polens kaum etwas, da es im zaristischen Rußland, an das der größte Teil des polnischen Staatsgebiets gefallen war, Juden bei Strafe verboten war, sich außerhalb des ursprünglich zu Polen gehörenden Territoriums niederzulassen. Lediglich Juden mit Hochschulbildung, die zu erlangen nur wenigen vergönnt war, und Juden, die 25 Jahre in der Zarenarmee gedient hatten, erhielten eine Aufenthaltserlaubnis. Von Rußland, aber auch von Galizien, das 1772 zu Österreich gekommen war, breitete sich Jiddisch in die östlichen Gebiete der Habsburgermonarchie sowie in die rumänischsprachigen Fürstentümer Moldau und Walachei aus. Auch in Preußen entstand eine, wenn auch bald weitgehend assimilierte Diaspora. Zu einer weiteren Verbreitung dieser Sprache kam es im letzten Viertel des 19. Jahrhunderts, als nach vom Regime inspirierten Pogromen Hunderttausende Juden Rußland verließen und nach Amerika, Palästina, Westeuropa, Australien und nach Südafrika auswanderten.

1.2. Über die *Anzahl der Jiddischsprecher* gibt es nur Schätzungen. Für den Beginn dieses Jahrhunderts nennt Birnbaum (1918, 5f) 11 bis 12 Millionen. Diese verteilten sich auf Westrußland (bis zu einer Linie Finnischer Meerbusen—Asowsches Meer): über 7 Millionen; Österreich-Ungarn (Galizien, Bukowina, Nordostungarn): 1,5 bis 2 Millionen; Rumänien: über 250 000; USA: über 2 Millionen (allein New York über eine Million); Großbritannien: 250 000; Palästina, Argentinien und Kanada je etwa 100 000. Der Rest entfiel danach auf die „Hauptstädte Mittel- und Westeuropas, auf Südafrika, sowie andere außereuropäische und europäische Gebiete". Dem Völkermord der Nazis an den Juden fielen annähernd 6 Millionen Menschen zum Opfer, von denen die Mehrheit Sprecher des Jiddischen waren. Für die Gegenwart wird von ca. 5—6 Millionen ausgegangen, die das Jiddische zumindest als Zweitsprache noch beherrschen. Fal'kovič (1966, 599) gibt 4 Millionen an. Die meisten von ihnen entfallen auf die USA und Israel. In Polen hatten sich nach dem Zweiten Weltkrieg etwa 30 000 Juden, die den Genozid überlebt hatten, wieder angesiedelt. Die Mehrzahl verließ jedoch seit dem Ende der sechziger Jahre wegen wieder auflebender antisemitischer Tendenzen das Land.

In der UdSSR gaben 1989 bei der letzten Volkszählung von 1 376 910 Personen, die sich als Aschkenasim deklarierten, 11,1% Jiddisch als Muttersprache an. Das wären 152 837 Personen. Die tatsächliche Zahl der Jiddischsprecher auf dem Gebiet der Ex-UdSSR ist jedoch wahrscheinlich wesentlich höher. So hatten z. B. bei der vorletzten Volkszählung von 1979 neben 257 813 Muttersprachlern 96 898 Juden die „Sprache der eigenen Nationalität" als Zweitsprache angegeben. Bei dieser Volkszählung waren jedoch die nicht-aschkenasischen Juden nicht gesondert ausgewiesen worden. Deren Anzahl ist zwar gering (1989: Bergjuden − 19 516, georgische Juden − 16 123, mittelasiatische Juden − 36 568, Krymtschaken − 1559), der Anteil der Muttersprachler bei ihnen jedoch wesentlich höher als bei den Aschkenasim (Bergjuden mit Tatisch − 73,2% = 14 286, georgische Juden mit Georgisch − 90,7% = 14 624, mittelasiatische Juden mit „Judenpersisch" − 64,6% = 23 623, Krymtschaken mit Krimtatarisch − 38,4% = 599), so daß ihr Anteil an der Gesamtzahl der sowjetischen Juden, die die Sprache ihrer Nationalität als Muttersprache angaben, mit 53 132 etwa ein Viertel ausmacht. Die 1979 von 96 898 sowjetischen Juden als Zweitsprache angegebene „jüdische Sprache" dürfte also in den meisten Fällen Jiddisch gewesen sein. Inzwischen hat jedoch die gerade in den achtziger Jahren verstärkte Emigration sowjetischer Juden in besonders starkem Maße die Aschkenasim erfaßt (1979 1 761 724; 1989 − 1 376 910, ein Rückgang auf 78,2%). Demgegenüber ist bei den Nichtaschkenasim mit Ausnahme der Krymtschaken sogar ein beträchtlicher Zuwachs zu verzeichnen (Bergjuden: 1979 − 9 389, 1989 − 19 516, Zuwachs − 208%; Georgische Juden: 1979 − 8 455, 1989 − 16 123, Zuwachs − 190,7%; mittelasiatische Juden: 1979 − 28 308, 1989 − 36 583, Zuwachs − 129,2%; Krymtschaken: 1979 − 3 000, 1989 − 1 559, Rückgang − 52%). Diesen erstaunlichen Zuwachs erklärt Kupovecki (1990, 131) damit, daß 1979 die Angabe „Sprache der eigenen Nationalität" von Zählern irrtümlich als Jiddisch gewertet wurde. Mit bestimmten Dunkelziffern hinsichtlich der Angaben über die Mutter- bzw. Zweitsprache ist daher auch bei den Aschkenasim zu rechnen. Außerdem gaben 1989 29,2% (= 402 058 Personen) der Aschkenasim an, neben der Sprache der eigenen Nationalität bzw. Russisch eine weitere Sprache der Sowjetunion zu beherrschen. Angesichts des hohen Grades ihrer Russifizierung (1979 − 83,3%, für 1989 waren entsprechende Angaben bisher nicht zugänglich) könnte dabei teilweise auch Jiddisch gemeint sein; → Sprachenkarte P.

2. Geschichte

2.1. In welchem Maße sich die Aschkenasim, solange sie in *Deutschland* lebten, in ihre deutschsprachige christliche Umgebung integrierten, läßt sich mit Sicherheit nicht mehr feststellen. Ihre wirtschaftliche und soziale Integration muß jedoch ziemlich weitgehend gewesen sein, denn sonst wäre es nicht zur Übernahme des Deutschen als Umgangssprache gekommen. Andererseits verhinderte der religiöse und kulturelle Gegensatz offenkundig eine vollständige Einbeziehung in das deutsche Ethnos, denn anders ließe sich die vornehmlich in gesellschaftlichen Krisensituationen immer wieder aufflammende Judenfeindschaft und Judenverfolgung (z. B. seit 1096 im Gefolge der Kreuzzüge, dann 1347/1348 wegen einer Pestepidemie) kaum erklären. Die Interpretation der religiösen und kulturellen Andersartigkeit der deutschen Juden als Zugehörigkeit zu einem besonderen Ethnos spielte auch in der Folgezeit noch eine Rolle und war wohl eine der Ursachen für die Wiederbelebung eines militanten Antisemitismus im 19. Jahrhundert und für die Passivität der meisten Deutschen gegenüber dem nazistischen Genozid an den Juden. So formulierte z. B. Friedrich (1784, unpaginierte Vorrede): „Es ist eine Schande (...), daß wir Christen eine *Nation* (Kursivierung von mir − R. L.), mit welcher wir täglich umgehen, und Verkehr haben, nicht verstehen sollen, so bald sie unter einander ihre jüdischdeutsche Sprache anstimmen, da sie doch unsere Muttersprache selbst sprechen". Die sprachliche Integration unterliegt also für Friedrich, obwohl er jüdisch-deutsche Eigenheiten ausdrücklich hervorhebt, keinerlei Zweifel. Sie ist auch durch die Sprachbezeichnung *Teutsch* in mit hebräischen Buchstaben geschriebenen jüdisch-deutschen Texten mehrfach bezeugt. So enthält das Titelblatt des Erstdrucks des Schmuelbuches von 1543/ 1544 die in hebräischer Schrift gedruckte Formulierung „das buch schmuel in teutscher sprach" (Simon 1988, 50 f). In hebräischsprachigen Texten kommt die Bezeichnung *lešón aškenáz* (wörtlich 'Sprache Deutschlands') vor. Sollte ihre Spezifik hervorgehoben werden, wurde die Sprache der deutschen Juden auch *Jüdisch-Deutsch* oder *Ivre-Deutsch* genannt (*ivre* aus dem Hebräischen übernommene Bezeichnung der hebräischen Sprache).

Die Kenntnis des Hebräisch-Aramäischen dürfte bei den deutschen Juden im Mittelalter weiter verbreitet gewesen sein als die Beherrschung des Lateinischen bei deutschen Christen. Während Latein dem Klerus und wenigen Gelehrten vorbehalten blieb, war das Hebräisch-Aramäische für Juden nicht nur Sakralsprache, sondern diente ihnen als Sprache der schriftlichen Kommunikation schlechthin. Schon die Aneignung des *lešón kodéš*, der „heiligen Sprache", durch ausnahmslos alle Knaben bereits im zartesten Alter unterschied sich wesentlich von der Erlernung des Lateinischen in christlichen Schulen. Da es jüdische Bauern praktisch nicht gab, und Juden vornehmlich im Handel und Finanzwesen beschäftigt waren, war der Anteil der Analphabeten zumindest unter der männlichen jüdischen Bevölkerung viel geringer als bei den Christen.

2.2. Es ist bis heute noch nicht geklärt, warum die nach *Polen* ausgewanderten Aschkenasim sich sprachlich nicht der Bevölkerungsmehrheit ihrer neuen Heimat anpaßten, sondern zäh an ihrer jüdisch-deutschen, sich allmählich zum Jiddischen verselbständigenden Muttersprache festhielten. Möglicherweise spielte dabei eine Rolle, daß der polnische Staat, die *Rzeczpospolita Polska*, schon während der jüdischen Einwanderung ein Vielvölkerstaat war. Der Adel und im eigentlichen polnischen Siedlungsgebiet auch die Mehrheit der Bauernschaft waren polnischsprechende Katholiken. In Litauen, in der Ukraine und in Weißrußland wurde zwar der Adel mehr oder weniger vollständig polonisiert, die Bauern aber blieben bei ihrer ostbaltischen bzw. ostslavischen Muttersprache. Die sich als polnisch-litauische Untertanen allmählich zu besonderen Ethnien entwickelnden und sich auch sprachlich immer mehr vom Russischen entfernenden Weißrussen und Ukrainer behielten außerdem mehrheitlich ihre orthodoxe Konfession. Die Städte besaßen meist eine unterschiedlich gemischte Bevölkerung, zu der auch ein christliches deutsches Element gehörte, mit dem die die gleiche Sprache sprechenden Juden möglicherweise engere Kontakte unterhielten.

Dennoch konnte kein Zweifel darüber bestehen, daß mit den einwandernden Aschkenasim ein weiteres Ethnos mit nichtslavischer und nichtbaltischer Sprache ins Land kam. Die dominierende Eigenbezeichnung der Aschkenasim *Jude/Jüde/Jide* (slavisch *Žid*, litauisch *Žydas*) mußte hier so von allem Anfang an den Charakter eines Ethnonyms, das davon abgeleitete Adjektiv *jidiš* auch die Bedeutung einer Sprachbezeichnung annehmen. Nicht zuletzt wegen ihrer vorwiegenden Tätigkeit als Händler und Handwerker waren die polnischen Juden gezwungen, sich die Sprachen ihrer slavischen Landsleute anzueignen. Dies waren vor allem das Polnische als Sprache des Hofes und des Adels sowie (neben dem Latein) der katholischen Kirche, seit 1696 alleinige offizielle Sprache der *Rzeczpospolita*. Im Osten des Landes mußten sie außerdem zur Verständigung mit den weißrussischen und ukrainischen Bauern deren Dialekte erlernen. Unklar bleibt, in welchem Maße auch das Litauische als Viert- oder Fünftsprache (nach Hebräisch-Aramäisch und Polnisch bzw. auch Weißrussisch oder Ukrainisch) von Juden in der Kommunikation mit Litauern eine Rolle spielte. Einerseits ist es wenig wahrscheinlich, daß die Verständigung mit den litauischen Bauern, die kaum Polnisch und allenfalls im Grenzgebiet ein wenig Weißrussisch gesprochen haben dürften, anders als in ihrer Muttersprache erfolgte. Andererseits gibt es im jiddischen Wortschatz bei hochgradiger Slavisierung keinerlei Spuren eines litauischen Einflusses. Die meisten jüdischen Männer waren jedenfalls schon aus wirtschaftlichen Gründen zur Mehrsprachigkeit gezwungen. Die daraus resultierende nachhaltige Einwirkung des Slavischen auf die jüdisch-deutschen Dialekte war ein wesentlicher Faktor bei der Weiterentwicklung des Jüdisch-Deutschen zur selbständigen jiddischen Sprache.

Auch das Hebräisch-Aramäische erlangte als Schriftsprache, insbesondere als Sprache des Kultes, als *lošn kójdeš*, wie es nunmehr in aschkenasischer Aussprache genannt wurde, im Osten eine noch größere Bedeutung als vorher in Deutschland, wie das Aufblühen des Schrifttums in dieser Sprache bezeugt. Zur slavischen Komponente des Jiddischen kam zusätzlich eine semitische, die ebenfalls nicht auf den Wortschatz beschränkt blieb.

2.3. Bei der Aufteilung Polens zwischen Rußland, Österreich-Ungarn und Preußen am Ende des 18. Jahrhunderts kam der gesamte mehrheitlich nicht polnisch besiedelte Teil, nämlich Litauen mit Lettgallen, Weißrußland und die Ukraine mit Ausnahme Galiziens, zu Rußland. Nach dem Wiener Kongreß (1815) folgte außerdem der größte Teil des eigentlichen polnischen Gebietes. Damit wurde die Mehrheit der Jiddischsprecher zu Untertanen des russischen Imperiums und zum Objekt der restriktiven zaristischen Sprachpolitik sowie regimeinspirierter antijüdischer Pogrome. Außerdem hatte dies *de facto* eine weitergehende Isolierung des Jiddischen von seiner deutschen Grundlage zur Folge, obwohl die jiddischsprachigen Juden von der zaristischen Bürokratie auch zu „Deutschen mosaischen Glaubens" deklariert wurden. Lebensnotwendig wurde nun für die meisten Männer die Beherrschung der russischen Staatssprache, neben der lediglich in den zu Beginn des 18. Jahrhunderts von Rußland annektierten, vorher schwedischen Ostsee-Gouvernements Kurland, Livland und Estland das Deutsche und im autonomen, 1809 von Schweden zu Rußland gekommenen Großfürstentum Finnland das Schwedische und seit 1883 auch das Finnische einen offiziellen Status besaßen. Wie noch zu zeigen ist, wurde die Eigenart des Jiddischen letztendlich vom Russischen entscheidend geprägt.

In Preußen überwog demgegenüber die Tendenz zur Germanisierung der Jiddischsprecher, die sich am Ende auch weitgehend durchsetzte, obgleich bestimmte Traditionen der Pflege des Jiddischen, namentlich in Berlin, wo 1925 das *Jüdische Wissenschaftliche Institut* (abgekürzt JIWO) gegründet wurde, bis zur Machtergreifung der Nazis Bestand hatten. Unterstützt wurden diese Bestrebungen durch Zuwanderung von Jiddischsprechern aus dem Osten.

In Österreich-Ungarn gab es einerseits angesichts der Dominanz des Deutschen als wichtigster Sprache ebenfalls die Tendenz zur Assimilierung, andererseits begünstigte die zunehmende Gleichstellung auch anderer Sprachen des k. u. k. Vielvölkerstaates den sog. „Jiddischismus", d. h. die Bemühungen um die Anerkennung des Jiddischen als der nationalen Sprache der nichtassimilierten aschkenasischen Juden. Diese Bestrebungen gipfelten schließlich 1908 in der Sprachkonferenz von Czernowitz, auf der dieser Status für das Jiddische proklamiert wurde. Daß dabei auch Vorstellungen von den Jiddischsprechern als einem besonderen jüdischen Ethnos bei aller Anerkennung der Zusammengehörigkeit des gesamten Judentums eine Rolle spielten, verdeutlichen besonders prägnant die Ausführungen eines der Hauptinitiatoren der Konferenz, des Wiener Juristen Dr. Nathan Birnbaum, des Vaters des späteren berühmten Jiddisten Salomo Birnbaum. Er sagte: „Nicht die Sprache macht das Volk, sondern das Volk die Sprache. Viele Völker haben fremde Sprachen übernommen und für sich eingerichtet, zu ihrer eigenen gemacht, mit ihrem Geist erfüllt. Und das Jüdische ist obendrein mehr als übernommenes Deutsch. Es ist eine Sprachmischung, wie etwa das Englische eine darstellt, und daher eine ganz neu erzeugte und *eigene* Sprache der Erzeuger (...). Es besitzt wohl niemand den Mut, der englischen Sprache den einheitlichen Charakter abzusprechen, wiewohl ihre germanischen, romanischen und keltischen Elemente ebenso erkennbar nebeneinander stehen, wie im Jüdischen die deutschen, hebräischen und slavischen. Aber Englisch ist die Sprache eines mächtigen Volkes, man fürchtet sich lächerlich zu machen, wenn man ihren einheitlichen Geist und damit eigentlich die Existenz des englischen Volkes in Frage zieht. Bei den Ostjuden sieht einem nicht die ganze Welt auf die Finger; im Gegenteil, da der großen Allgemeinheit die ostjüdischen Verhältnisse ziemlich unbekannt sind, kann man munter drauflossündigen (...). Ungehindert kann man die Tatsachen totschlagen und einem einheitlichen Volke, wie es die Ostjuden sicherlich vorstellen, seine von ihm gesprochene eigentümliche Sprache als *seine* absprechen. Diese Sprache ist noch vogelfrei. Jeder Ideologe kann kommen und ableugnen, was für den realistischen Beobachter unleugbar ist (...)." (zitiert nach Kohan 1991, 4 f).

Die von Birnbaum beschworene Einheit des *ostjüdischen* Volkes beinhaltete enge Kontakte über die russisch-österreichische Grenze hinweg, und die von ihm erwähnten slavischen Elemente des Jiddischen schlossen die russische Komponente mit ein. Zur Stärkung des Widerstands in Österreich-Ungarn wirkender „Jiddischisten" gegen die Bestrebungen assimilationsbereiter Verfechter der jüdischen Aufklärung, der sog. Haskalá (jiddisch *haskóle*), die jiddische Sprache zum minderwertigen „Jargon" zu stempeln, trug auch bei, daß bei den Jiddischsprechern Rußlands die Assimilationsbereitschaft verständlicherweise noch viel geringer ausgeprägt war als in der k. u. k. Monarchie. Ging es doch dort unbestreitbar um die Aufgabe der Muttersprache, des *máme-lošn*, während hier das Argument, es handle sich lediglich um die Übernahme der höchsten Existenzform der eigenen Sprache, bei oberflächlichem Herangehen nicht ganz von der Hand zu weisen war. Nicht unerwähnt bleiben darf in diesem Zusammenhang auch der Einsatz der bündisch organisierten jüdischen sozialistischen Arbeiterbewegung für das Jiddische.

Mit der Emigration größerer Gruppen jiddischsprachiger Aschkenasim aus Rußland und Österreich-Ungarn wurde die zwar noch nicht kodifizierte, aber dennoch im Schrifttum verwendete und damit relativ stabilisierte Sprache nach Westeuropa und Übersee verpflanzt, wo sie in kompakteren jüdischen Siedlungszentren in nur geringfügig modifizierter Gestalt bis zum heutigen Tag zumindest Zweitsprache ist. Der Assimilationsdruck war in der Diaspora, selbst in solchen Zentren wie New York und Israel, natürlich wesentlich stärker als im Entstehungs- und ursprünglichen Verbreitungsgebiet.

3. Politik gegenüber dem Jiddischen und seinen Sprechern im 20. Jahrhundert

3.1. Einen tiefen Einschnitt in der *Situation* der osteuropäischen Aschkenasim *bis zum Beginn der dreißiger Jahre* stellt der Erste Weltkrieg und sein Ausgang dar. Der zu Rußland gehörende Teil ihres Siedlungsgebietes wurde 1914/1915 bis zu einer Linie Riga, Daugavpils (Dünaburg), Minsk von den Mittelmächten besetzt. Die wilhelminischen und k. u. k. Militärbehörden waren bestrebt, die jüdische Bevölkerung unter Berufung auf die sprachliche Verwandtschaft zur Kollaboration zu ermuntern. Selbst zeitgenössische Wörterbuchpublikationen in Deutschland (z. B. Strack 1916) atmen diesen Geist. Die Ergebnisse waren angesichts der verstärkten Repressalien gegen die Juden im nichtbesetzten größeren Teil Rußlands allerdings bescheiden.

Zu einschneidenden Veränderungen kam es nach der Niederlage der Mittelmächte und nach dem Zerfall des zaristischen Rußlands und der k. u. k. Monarchie. Während des Krieges zwischen den Bolschewiki, die im November 1917 im nicht besetzten Teil Rußlands die Macht an sich rissen, und deren in- und ausländischen Gegnern kam es insbesondere in der Ukraine zu Massakern an Juden, die beschuldigt wurden, auf der Seite des neuen Regimes zu stehen.

Tatsache war, daß die sowjetischen Behörden überall, wo sie die Macht behaupten konnten, also in Rußland, im größeren östlichen Teil von Weißrußland und der Ukraine, die Juden als eigenständige Nationalität anerkannten und die sie diskriminierenden Bestimmungen abschafften. Dies betraf in erster Linie den *txum-hamójšev*, wie die jiddische Bezeichnung lautete, die Siedlungsgrenze, östlich und nördlich von der sich Juden ohne spezielle Erlaubnis nicht aufhalten durften. Die unentgeltliche Nutzung des nunmehr verstaatlichten Bodens war selbstverständlich auch Juden gestattet. Viele jüdische Handwerker und arbeitslose Proletarier aus der nach Weltkrieg und Bürgerkriegswirren am Boden liegenden Industrie machten davon Gebrauch und gründeten landwirtschaftliche Kolonien. Darüber hinaus nahmen auch die Aschkenasim überall dort, wo sie kompakt siedelten, das durch die Sowjetmacht proklamierte Recht auf nationale Selbstverwaltung in Anspruch. Namentlich in der Ukraine entstanden zahlreiche jüdische nationale Kreise, in denen das Jiddische erstmals in der Geschichte dieser Sprache einen offiziellen Status erhielt. Es entstand ein staatliches Schulwesen mit jiddischer Unterrichtssprache. In Instituten der Akademien der Wissenschaften der Ukraine und Weißrußlands wurden jiddistische Abteilungen eingerichtet, in denen sich Sprachwissenschaftler der Kodifizierung von Orthographie und Grammatik, der Erfassung des jiddischen Wortschatzes sowie der Erforschung der jiddischen Dialekte widmeten. Entsprechende staatliche Einrichtungen sorgten für die Umsetzung im Schulwesen, in den zahlreichen staatlichen und Laientheatern sowie im zum Zwecke der kommunistischen Propaganda und Agitation großzügig ausgebauten Pressewesen. In Moskau erschien seit 1919 die für die Belange der gesamten Sowjetunion bestimmte Tageszeitung *der emes* ('Die Wahrheit').

Der Preis für diese positive Entwicklung war neben der wirtschaftlichen Knebelung im Gefolge der Liquidierung auch des kleinsten privaten Gewerbes eine zunehmend unerträglichere ideologische Indoktrinierung sowie eine immer rigorosere Beschneidung der religiösen Freiheiten.

Auch außerhalb der Sowjetunion wurde der Spielraum für die Entfaltung der jiddischsprachigen Kultur und der Jiddistik nach der Befreiung von der Zarenherrschaft größer. Die relativ große Freiheit, die das Judentum und der „Jiddischismus" in Österreich genossen, wurde nun von Galizien aus auf das wiedererstandene Polen übertragen. Wilna (Vilnius), das von 1920 bis 1939 zu Polen gehörte, wurde zum „Jerusalem des Nordens". Hierher wurde bald nach seiner Gründung das *Jüdische Wissenschaftliche Institut* verlegt, das ähnliche Ziele verfolgte wie die entsprechenden staatlichen Einrichtungen in der Sowjetunion. Auch in Polen bestanden bis zum Zweiten Weltkrieg ein hochentwickeltes Pressewesen (allein in Warschau erschienen sechs Tageszeitungen) sowie nicht weniger als 36 Berufs- und Laientheater. Getragen wurden das dichte Netz jiddischsprachiger kultureller Einrichtungen hier nicht vom Staat, sondern von privaten jüdischen, vor allem religiösen Einrichtungen. Auch der in der Sowjetunion bald nach dem Oktoberumsturz liquidierte, in Polen jedoch weiterbestehende „Bund" beteiligte sich an diesen Aktivitäten (Kühn-Ludewig 1992, 1 ff).

Etwa vergleichbar war die Lage des Jiddischen und seiner Sprecher auch im Baltikum und in den meisten Nachfolgestaaten der k. u. k. Monarchie sowie in jüdischen Ansiedlungen in Westeuropa und Übersee. Zu nennen ist in erster Linie New York.

3.2. Bei allen Unterschieden im Charakter des *Antisemitismus* der beiden totalitären Regime, des *deutschen Nationalsozialismus* und des *Stalinismus*, ist beiden eine antijüdische Politik mit verheerenden Auswirkungen auf die Verbreitung des Jiddischen gemein.

Während die Nationalsozialisten über ihre von Rassenwahn geprägte Judenfeindschaft von allem Anfang an niemanden im Zweifel ließen, so daß der von ihnen während des Zweiten Weltkrieges praktizierte Völkermord niemanden zu verwundern brauchte, gingen die Stalinisten subtiler vor.

Jede von Stalins Handlangern unternommene antijüdische Maßnahme erfolgte entweder ohne jede propagandistische Begleitmusik oder wurde mit verlogenen Parolen als gegen irgendwelche Kategorien von „Volksfeinden" gerichtet, ohne jeden Bezug zum Judentum, hingestellt. Offen antisemitische Agitation wurde in der Sowjetunion erst mit Gorbatschows Glasnost wieder möglich und verstärkte sich nach dem Zerfall der UdSSR in einigen von deren Nachfolgestaaten, nicht zuletzt in Rußland. Die judenfeindliche Komponente von Stalins Politik trat auch nicht sofort in Erscheinung, nachdem es ihm etwa 1929 gelungen war, alle Konkurrenten im Kampf um die Macht auszuschalten und die kommunistische Partei und den Staatsapparat der Sowjetunion seiner uneingeschränkten Kontrolle zu unterwerfen. Nicht wenige seiner Komplizen und Henker waren selbst Juden (z. B. Lázar Kaganóvič, Mitglied des Politbüros/Präsidiums der KPdSU bis 1957, oder Génrix Jágoda, Chef des NKWD während der ersten Phase blutiger Säuberungen 1934—1936), was die Verschleierung des antijüdischen Charakters seiner Politik zusätzlich begünstigte.

Die erste größere, letztendlich gegen die Interessen der Juden gerichtete Aktion wurde sogar mit großem propagandistischen Aufwand als projüdische Maßnahme verherrlicht. Es handelte sich dabei um die 1934 erfolgte Gründung des sog. *Jüdischen Autonomen Gebiets* im Fernen Osten der Sowjetunion, in den Sumpfniederungen des Amurgebiets, wo Juden nie gelebt hatten. Es gelang zwar, einige Zehntausend Juden zur Umsiedlung in diese unwirtliche Gegend zu veranlassen, doch im Grund war es eine Farce, eine Verhöhnung des im gleichen Zusammenhang erneut lauthals verkündeten Rechts auf Selbstbestimmung. Verschwiegen wurde dabei, daß gleichzeitig die in echter Inanspruchnahme dieses Rechts in den zwanziger Jahren entstandenen jüdischen nationalen Kreise liquidiert wurden, die in der sog. „Stalinschen Verfassung" von 1936 nicht mehr vorgesehen waren. Die Zeitung *der emes* wurde 1938, auf dem Höhepunkt von Stalins mörderischen Säuberungen, über Nacht ohne jede Angabe von Gründen eingestellt.

Antijüdische Maßnahmen mehrten sich im Zuge der Vorbereitung und der nachfolgenden Realisierung des Hitler-Stalin-Paktes. So sollen bis 1939 nahezu alle jüdischen Kultureinrichtungen und alle 750 Schulen mit jiddischer Unterrichtssprache geschlossen worden sein (Rapoport 1992, 72 f). Unter den Millionen, die 1940/1941 aus den auf Grund des Geheimabkommens mit Hitler von der Sowjetunion annektierten Gebieten deportiert wurden, befanden sich überproportional viele Juden. Da Nachrichten über die Greuel, die die SS an den polnischen Juden verübte, in der UdSSR im Interesse der „sowjetisch-deutschen Freundschaft" systematisch unterdrückt wurden, ahnten viele sowjetische Juden nicht, was sie erwartete, als Deutschland 1941 die Sowjetunion überfiel. Danach wurde das Ausmaß der Massaker an den sowjetischen Juden verschwiegen, ihre besondere Gefährdung bei den Evakuierungsmaßnahmen ignoriert. Zwei Millionen wurden Opfer des Völkermords.

Erst 1942 kam es zu einer Änderung dieser Politik. Mit dem „Jüdischen Antifaschistischen Komitee" (JAK), dessen Vorsitz der weltberühmte Schauspieler Michoels übernahm, wurde eine Organisation geschaffen, deren Hauptaufgabe darin bestand, das internationale Judentum zur Unterstützung der Verteidigungsanstrengungen der UdSSR im Krieg gegen Deutschland und dessen Satelliten zu mobilisieren. Nun endlich fand die Aufklärung über den Massenmord der Nazis an den Juden Eingang in die Medien. Zu diesem Zwecke durfte auch wieder eine jiddische Zeitung erscheinen, die diesmal *ejnikajt* ('Einigkeit') hieß. Im Grunde handelte es sich wieder um eine mit vielen Zugeständnissen an stalinistische Dogmen und Praktiken zu erkaufende Neuauflage der doppelzüngigen Politik gegenüber den Juden. Ihr wahrer Charakter trat 1948 zutage, als Stalin unter dem Vorwand der angeblichen Aufdeckung eines „Spionagerings" im JAK sowie des Kampfes gegen „Kosmopolitismus" sämtliche nach dem Kriege wiedergegründeten jüdischen kulturellen und wissenschaftlichen Einrichtungen liquidieren, Hunderte prominenter jüdischer Intellektueller, darunter die bedeutendsten jiddischschreibenden Literaten, verhaften und viele von ihnen hinrichten (Michoels' Ermordung wurde als Autounfall kaschiert) sowie Zehntausende weiterer Juden in die Lager verschleppen ließ. Von da an war bis 1956 jedwede Veröffentlichung in jiddischer Sprache verboten. Lediglich das Amtsblatt des „Jüdischen Autonomen Gebiets" durfte weiter teilweise auch in Jiddisch erscheinen. Vor weitergehenden, bereits geplanten Repressalien rettete die sowjetischen Juden der Tod des Diktators im Jahre 1953.

3.3. Die *gegenwärtige Situation* des Jiddischen ist noch immer von den Auswirkungen des nazistischen Völkermords und der stalinistischen Unterdrückungspolitik geprägt. Das Verbot jiddischsprachiger Veröffentlichungen blieb in der UdSSR acht Jahre lang bestehen. Erst nach der Entlarvung der Verbrechen Stalins durch Chruschtschow auf dem 20. Parteitag der KPdSU 1956, wobei seine antijüdischen Aktionen verschwiegen wurden, durften wieder Bücher in jiddischer Sprache gedruckt werden. Von 1961 bis 1991 erschien in Moskau die Literaturzeitschrift *sovetiš hejmland* ('Sowjetheimat'), die auch sprachwissenschaftliche Beiträge sowie Lehrmaterial veröffentlichte. Ansonsten kommt die Jiddistik in Rußland nach dem (teilweise gewaltsamen) Tod ihrer namhaftesten Vertreter nur sehr zögernd wieder in Gang. In Moskau existiert seit einiger Zeit eine staatlich anerkannte jüdische Universität, an der es auch die Fachrichtung Jiddistik gibt. In Minsk (Weißrußland) wird ernsthaft die Neueinrichtung eines Lehrstuhls für Jiddistik an der Universität angestrebt. Etwas besser ist die Situation in der Ukraine, wo es Neugründungen jiddistischer Einrichtungen in der Akademie der Wissenschaften gibt. Seit 1992 erscheint in Moskau als Fortsetzung von *sovetiš hejmland* — ohne dessen bis gegen das Ende der achtziger Jahre beibehaltene ideologische Einseitigkeit — die Zeitschrift *di jidiše gas* ('die jüdische Gasse'), an der jiddischschreibende Autoren aus allen Nachfolgestaaten der UdSSR mitarbeiten. In diesen entstanden in den letzten Jahren jüdische Kulturorganisationen, die enge Kontakte zu analogen Gesellschaften in Israel oder den USA unterhalten, von denen sie angesichts ihrer beklagenswerten finanziellen Situation auch materiell unterstützt werden.

Im Zusammenhang damit leben gewisse Tendenzen einer verächtlichen Einstellung zum angeblich minderwertigen „Jargon" wieder auf. Eine Rolle spielt dabei auch der erschreckend hohe Grad der Russifizierung, der angesichts der Nichtzulassung des Jiddischen im Schulunterricht, und zwar auch nicht als Unterrichtsfach, seit 1939 nicht zu verwundern braucht.

Nicht einmal das „Jüdische Autonome Gebiet" bildet dabei eine Ausnahme. Von seinen 8 887 jüdischen Bewohnern (4,2 % der Gesamtbevölkerung des Gebiets, 0,65 % der sowjetischen Aschkenasim!) gaben lediglich 11,7 % Jiddisch als Muttersprache und 6,5 % als Zweitsprache an. Von den Angehörigen der in der Statistik ausgewiesenen 46 Nationalitäten, auf die sich die übrigen 205 198 Einwohner des Gebiets verteilten, behaupteten lediglich jeweils 0,01 % der Russen und Ukrainer, 0,05 % der Weißrussen, 0,1 % der Moldauer und 0,5 % der Polen, Jiddisch zu sprechen. Andererseits entfalten viele jüdische Organisationen Aktivitäten, um jüngeren Menschen die Erlernung der Sprache ihrer Vorfahren zu ermöglichen. Die seit der Lockerung und schließlichen Beseitigung der Ausreiseverbote in den achtziger Jahren progressiv zunehmende Emigration osteuropäischer Juden nach Israel, Westeuropa und den USA vermindert zwar die Zahl der Sprecher des Jiddischen in dessen Ursprungsländern und vergrößert die Gefahr ihrer Assimilierung, führt aber andererseits auch teilweise zur Stärkung der Position des Jiddischen in der Neuen Heimat mit noch nicht abzusehenden Konsequenzen. Zentrum der Pflege des Jiddischen und jiddistischer Aktivitäten bleibt New York, wo das noch rechtzeitig vor Ausbruch des Zweiten Weltkriegs von Wilna dorthin verlagerte *Jüdische Wissenschaftliche Institut* (nunmehr YIWO) seine fruchtbare Tätigkeit — nicht zuletzt zur Kodifizierung und Propagierung der jiddischen Standardsprache — mit Erfolg fortsetzt und u. a. die linguistische Zeitschrift *di jidiše šprax* herausgibt.

4. Statistik und Ethnoprofil

4.1. *Hebräisch* und *Aramäisch* als die ersten Kontaktsprachen des Jiddischen hatten bereits in dessen Vorgeschichte in Deutschland den Charakter spezifischen Kommunikationszwecken vorbehaltener Zweitsprachen vor allem der männlichen Aschkenasim. Darüber hinaus bestanden teilweise Kontakte zu jüdischen Sprechern dieser Sprachen mit anderer als jüdisch-deutscher Muttersprache. Deren Aussprache der semitischen Idiome dürfte sich dabei von der aschkenasischen wesentlich unterschieden haben.

Dies war insbesondere der Fall, als sich in der zionistischen Bewegung die sefardische Aussprache des Ivrith durchsetzte. Diese Konstellation ist im Prinzip bis zum heutigen Tage erhalten. Mit der weitgehenden Russifizierung der osteuropäischen Aschkenasim geht allerdings auch ein nahezu vollständiger Verlust der Kenntnis des Hebräisch-Aramäischen einher. In der Gegenwart sind Jiddischsprecher vor allem in Israel mit Ivrith als der offiziellen Sprache dieses Staates konfrontiert.

4.2. *Slavische Sprachen*, und zwar *Polnisch, Ukrainisch, Weißrussisch* und *Russisch*, sind neben dem Hebräisch-Aramäischen die wichtigsten Kontaktsprachen des Jiddischen. Da diese in anderen Artikeln ausführlicher behandelt werden, beschränkt sich ihre Darstellung hier im wesentlichen auf ihre Beziehungen zum Jiddischen.

4.2.1. Das westslavische *Polnische* spielte in der Entwicklung des Jiddischen als die erste slavische Kontaktsprache eine große Rolle. Es war damals die Sprache der polnischen Völkerschaft und der herrschenden Schicht der Rzeczpospolita. Als deren offizielle Sprache war sie relativ früh kodifiziert. Ihre Dialektgrundlage ist nicht mehr eindeutig zu ermitteln. Gegenwärtig ist Polnisch die Muttersprache von ca. 35 Millionen Menschen. In der Sowjetunion bekannten sich 1989 1 126 137 Personen zur polnischen Nationalität, von denen 30,4% Polnisch als Muttersprache angaben.

Inwiefern Polnisch in der Gegenwart noch eine Rolle als Zweit- oder sogar Erstsprache von Jiddischsprechern eine Rolle spielt, läßt sich nur schwer ermitteln. In Polen leben kaum noch Juden. Die letzten sowjetischen Volkszählungen enthalten keinerlei Angaben über die Verwendung des Polnischen durch Nichtpolen, da diese Sprache nirgends mehr einen offiziellen Status besaß. Denkbar sind jiddisch-polnische Kontakte in den USA, wo größere Gruppen von Einwanderern aus Polen leben, die teilweise auch noch Polnisch sprechen.

4.2.2. *Ukrainisch* und *Weißrussisch* befanden sich im Prozeß der Herausbildung des Jiddischen selbst noch im Prozeß der Differenzierung vom Russischen und voneinander. Zur Ausbildung von Standardsprachen kam es erst während des 19. Jahrhunderts, zur endgültigen Kodifizierung erst im 20. Jahrhundert. Jüdische Handwerker und Händler verwendeten bei der Kommunikation mit ukrainischen und weißrussischen Kunden und Geschäftspartnern deren Dialekte.

Bei der Volkszählung 1989 bekannten sich in der UdSSR 44 135 989 Menschen (in der Ukraine — 37 370 368) zur ukrainischen Nationalität, von denen 81,1% (in der Ukraine — 87,7%) Ukrainisch als Muttersprache angaben. Weißrussen wurden 10 030 441 (in Weißrußland — 7 897 781) gezählt. Die Angaben zur Muttersprache betrugen 70,9% (in Weißrußland — 80,2%).

In Weißrußland und der Ukraine sprachen nach eigenen Angaben 1989 27,6% bzw. 46,5% der dort lebenden Juden trotz ihrer hochgradigen Russifizierung auch Weißrussisch bzw. Ukrainisch. Seit der Verselbständigung der beiden Republiken im Jahre 1991 dürfte dieser Anteil rapide angestiegen sein. Jiddisch als Muttersprache gaben demgegenüber nur 7,6 bzw. 7,1% an. Allerdings dürften die 8,5 bzw. 4,7% in Weißrußland bzw. in der Ukraine lebenden Juden, die die Beherrschung einer weiteren Sprache der Sowjetunion angaben, damit teilweise auch Jiddisch gemeint haben.

4.2.3. Das *Russische* ist seit den Teilungen Polens zur wichtigsten Kontaktsprache des

Jiddischen in Osteuropa geworden. Es ist die Muttersprache von 99,8% der in der Statistik von 1989 für die UdSSR ausgewiesenen 145 071 550 Russen. Darüber hinaus hatten 1979 noch über 16 Millionen Angehörige anderer Nationalitäten Russisch als Muttersprache angegeben. Diese Rolle dürfte es auch bei jüdischen Emigranten aus der UdSSR und deren Nochfolgestaaten noch für längere Zeit behalten. Schon 1979 gaben 83,3% der sowjetischen Juden als Muttersprache Russisch an. Sie standen damit an der Spitze aller in der Statistik ausgewiesenen sowjetischen Nationalitäten. Lediglich solche kleinen Völkerschaften wie die 546 Seelen zählenden Aleuten, die Kamtschadalen mit 1370 Angehörigen oder die Giljaken mit 4 397 kamen mit 81,5, 75,4 bzw. 69,1% in ihre Nähe. Selbst die Deutschen folgten mit 42,6% in weitem Abstand.

5. Sprachpolitische Lage

5.1. Grundlage des *Jiddischen* ist das Jüdisch-Deutsche. Auch diese Sprache fand, ungeachtet der Funktion des Hebräisch-Aramäischen als traditioneller Schriftsprache aller Juden, ganz gleich welche Sprache sie im Alltag gebrauchten, schon früh Anwendung im Schrifttum. Diese Literatur mit vorwiegend biblischem oder folkloristischem Inhalt war vor allem zur Erbauung und Unterhaltung der Frauen bestimmt, die des Hebräisch-Aramäischen nur ausnahmsweise mächtig waren. Da auch die jüdischen Autoren an einer möglichst weiten Verbreitung ihrer Werke interessiert waren, verfaßten sie diese in einer Sprachform, in der eng Mundartliches vermieden wurde. Diese Tendenz verstärkte sich nach der Einführung des Buchdrucks. Ostjüdische Verleger waren natürlich daran interessiert, ihren Produkten auch bei den im deutschen Sprachgebiet verbliebenen Glaubensgenossen noch einen gewissen Absatz zu sichern, und deshalb bemüht, den Abstand der von ihnen verwendeten Sprache zum Deutschen der alten Heimat nicht allzu groß werden zu lassen. Auf die Dauer war dies jedoch nicht durchzuhalten. Denn das sich zum Jiddischen entwickelnde Jüdisch-Deutsche der osteuropäischen Aschkenasim entfernte sich nicht zuletzt infolge des massiven slavischen Einflusses immer mehr von seiner Grundlage. Schließlich mußten sich selbst die Vertreter der jüdischen Aufklärung, die eigentlich für die Verwendung des Hebräischen bzw. des Polnischen oder Russischen im Schrifttum eintraten, in ihren Schriften der Volkssprache mit allen ihren Slavismen und Hebraismen bedienen, wollten sie von ihren potentiellen Lesern überhaupt verstanden werden. Auf diese Weise wurde seit dem ausgehenden 18. Jahrhundert allmählich der Boden für die Entstehung der modernen jiddischen Literatur vorbereitet. Diese schufen dann die Klassiker Méndele Mójxer Sfórim (eigentlich Šólem-Jánkev Abramóvič, 1836–1917), Jícxok Lejb Pérec (1852–1915) und Šólem Aléjxem (eigentlich Šólem Rabinóvič, 1859–1916). Es ging dabei auch darum, eine Sprachnorm zu finden und durchzusetzen, die für Sprecher aller jiddischen Dialekte akzeptabel war.

Nachdem sich bereits im Jüdisch-Deutschen Ausgleichsprozesse vollzogen hatten, die weitergingen als die partielle gegenseitige Annäherung der von den weniger mobilen Nichtjuden gesprochenen Mundarten, entstanden im Osten neue Mischdialekte. Im Entstehungsgebiet des Jiddischen werden im wesentlichen drei Hauptdialekte unterschieden: (1) Nordostjiddisch, gesprochen in Litauen, Lettland und Weißrußland (diese Region wird jiddisch auch *lite*, ihre jüdischen Bewohner *litvakes* oder *litvákes*, ihr jiddischer Dialekt *litviš* genannt), (2) Zentraljiddisch im eigentlichen Polen, in der Ostslowakei und Ostungarn sowie in der Karpatenukraine und (3) Südostjiddisch in der Ukraine, der Bukowina und Moldawien. Die Unterschiede betreffen sowohl den Wortschatz als auch Phonetik und Grammatik. Das Zentraljiddische bewahrt z. B. im wesentlichen die in den übrigen Dialekten aufgegebene phonologische Quantität der Vokale. Im Litwischen wird westgermanisches /a/ in bestimmten Positionen zu /o/ und langes /ō/ unterschiedlicher Provenienz diphthongiert zu /ej/, /u/ bleibt unverändert. In den anderen beiden Dialekten entsprechen diesen Vokalen /u/, /oj/ und /i/. Die Entsprechungen für *Tag, Brot, Auge* (über ostmitteldeutsches *ōge*), *Hund* sind also im Litwischen — *tog, brejt, ejg, hunt*, in den anderen Dialekten — *tug, brojt, ojg, hint*. Zentraljiddisch zeichnet sich u. a. durch den Wandel von langem /ē/ unterschiedlicher Herkunft zu /aj/ aus, während die anderen beiden Dialekte dafür /ej/ haben, z. B. in *kajt* 'Kette', *bajn* 'Knochen' bzw. *kejt, bejn*. Eine Besonderheit des Südostjiddischen ist der Ausfall von anlautendem /h/ (*ant* aus *hant* 'Hand').

In grammatischer Hinsicht neigt das Litwische zum Verlust des Neutrums. Während die anderen Dialekte wie im Deutschen z. B. *dos ferd, dos bux* haben, heißt es im Litwischen *der ferd, der bux* ('das Pferd', 'das Buch').

Wie alle von Juden im Schrifttum verwendeten Sprachen wird auch Jiddisch, wie vorher schon Jüdisch-Deutsch, mit hebräischen Buchstaben von rechts nach links geschrieben. Großbuchstaben gibt es nicht, ursprünglich auch keine Vokalbuchstaben. Es bedurfte einer langen Entwicklung, bis schließlich eine im wesentlichen phonemische Schreibung gefunden wurde, die der tatsächlichen Aussprache der deutschen und slavischen Elemente des Jiddischen weitgehend gerecht wurde. Die nachstehende Beschreibung dient gleichzeitig zur Illustrierung der im weiteren verwendeten Transkription, die den für eine populäre Wiedergabe jiddischer Texte gedachten Empfehlungen von Blum (1992, 1 ff) nicht folgt.

Zur Bezeichnung der Vokale dienen dabei Buchstaben mit ursprünglich konsonantischem Lautwert, teilweise in Verbindung mit im traditionellen Hebräischunterricht in didaktischer Funktion verwendeten diakritischen Zeichen. Die in den meisten jiddischen Mundarten vorhandenen 5 Vokale werden dabei folgendermaßen wiedergegeben: /a/ mit א (jiddische Bezeichnung des Buchstabens -*álef*, diente im Hebräischen ursprünglich zur Wiedergabe des Kehlkopfverschlußlautes; אזא *azá* 'so ein'); /o/ mit אָ (*kómec-álef, kómec* Name für diakritisches ָ; אָן *on* 'an' oder 'ohne', האָר *hor* 'Haar'); /e/ mit ע (*ájen*, diente im Hebräischen ursprünglich zur Wiedergabe eines spirantischen Kehllauts; עלטער *élter* '(das) Alter' oder 'älter'); /u/ mit ו (*vov*, im Hebräischen ursprünglich Graphem für unsilbiges *u*; vor ו und י, neben וו mit einem links von ו stehenden Punkt [*melúpn-vov*]; טוונג *túung* 'Handlung', צוווּקס *cúvuks* 'Zuwachs', בורזשוי *buržúj* 'Bourgeois'); /i/ mit י (*jud*, im Hebräischen ursprünglich Graphem für unsilbiges *i*; neben Vokalen, Diphthong und /j/ zur Unterscheidung von diesem mit einem Punkt unter dem *jud*; מיר *mir* 'mir', קי *ki* 'Kühe', לעגיאָן *legión* 'Legion', מאַיס *mais* 'Mais', ייד *jid* 'Jude'). Zur Wiedergabe der Diphthonge /aj/, /ej/, /oj/ dienen die Digraphen ײַ (*cvej judn mit a pasex, pasex* — Name für diakritisches ַ; דרײַ *draj* 'drei'), ײ (*cvej judn*; קײן *kejn* 'kein'), וי (*vov-júd*; אזוי *azój* 'so'):. Zur Signalisierung der vokalischen bzw. (vor י) diphthongischen Aussprache von ו und י im Wortanlaut wird davor *štumer alef* geschrieben (אום *um* 'um', אויך *ojx* 'auch', איר *ihr* 'ihr', אײ *ej* 'Ei', אײַז *ajz* 'Eis').

Zur Wiedergabe der meisten Konsonanten wird jeweils ein hebräischer Buchstabe verwendet, und zwar (in der Reihenfolge des lateinischen Alphabets) für: /b/ — ב (*bejs*; באָבע *bóbe* 'Großmutter'); /c/ (Affrikate /ts/) — צ (*cádek*; צאַצקע *cácke* 'Spielzeug'), am Wortende ץ (*langer cadek*; קאַץ *kac* 'Katze'); /d/ — ד (*daled*; דודקע *dúdke* 'Pfeife'); /f/ — פֿ (*fej*; פֿעפֿער *féfer* 'Pfeffer'), am Wortende ף (*langer fej*; שאָף *šof* 'Schaf'); /g/ — ג (*giml*; געגנט *gegnt* 'Gegend'), /h/ (im Jiddischen ein stimmhafter Spirant, der auch vor /l/, /n/, /r/ ausgesprochen wird) — ה (*hej*; האַנט *hant* 'Hand', הליבע *hlíbe* 'Batzen', 'Brocken', הנידע *hníde* 'Nisse', הראַב *hrab* 'Hainbuche'); /j/ — י (*jud*; יאַר *jar* 'Schlucht', יאָר *jor* 'Jahr', יויך *jojx* 'Suppe'); /k/ — ק (*kuf*; קוק *kuk* 'Blick'); /l/ — ל (*lámed*; לעלע *léle* 'Insektenpuppe'); /m/ — מ (*mem*; מאַמע *máme* 'Mutter'), am Wortende ם (*šlos-mem*; אום *um* 'um'); /n/ — נ (*nun*; נודנע *núdne* 'langweilig'), am Wortende ן (*langer nun*; אײן *ejn* 'ein'); /p/ — פ (*pej*; פאַפ *pap* 'Kleister'); /r/ — ר (*rejš*; רער *rer* 'Röhre'); /s/ — ס (*sámex*; סאָסנע *sósne* 'Föhre'); /š/ — ש (*šin*; שישקע *šíške* 'Zapfen'); /t/ — ט (*tes*; טאַטע *táte* 'Vater'); /v/ — וו (*cvej vovn*; וועווערקע *véverke* 'Eichhörnchen'); /x/ („ach-Laut" auch in der Umgebung vorderer Vokale bzw. nach den Vibranten /r/, /l/) — כ (*xof*; באם *xam* 'Flegel', ביכער *bíxer* 'Bücher'), am Wortende ך (*langer xof*, דורך *durx* 'durch'); /z/ — ז (*zájen*; זי *zi* 'sie', איז *iz* 'ist'). Der stimmhafte Zischlaut /ž/ wird mit dem Digraphen זש (*zájen-šin*; זשאַבע *žábe* 'Frosch', סאַזשע *sáže* 'Ruß') wiedergegeben, die Affrikate /dž/ mit dem Trigraphen דזש (דזשאַז *džaz* 'Jazz').

Die hier charakterisierte Schreibung der deutschen und slavischen Komponente des Jiddischen entspricht dem 1930 nach langer Diskussion per Dekret in der Sowjetunion eingeführten und in „di jidiše gas" bislang beibehaltenen Usus (im folgenden — *SU-Norm*). Die von YIWO praktizierte Norm unterscheidet sich jedoch kaum davon. Hinsichtlich der Phonem-Graphem-Relation betrifft sie eigentlich nur die Schreibung von /a/, das hier mit „pasex-alef", also mit אַ, wiedergegeben wird, sowie von /f/ im An- und Inlaut, wo über dem פ ein Strich geschrieben wird. Eine andere Besonderheit der YIWO-Orthographie ist die Verwendung des *štumen alef* auch nach Präfixen (z. B. באַאומרויקן *baúmruikn* 'beunruhigen' statt באומרויקן, פאראייביקן *faréjbikn* 'verewigen' statt פארייביקן), die nach SU-Norm unzulässige zweimalige Schreibung ein und desselben Konsonanten im Auslaut eines Präfixes und Wurzelanlaut (z. B. אָננעמען *ónnemen* 'annehmen', statt אָנעמען, אָפּפֿראָוועןֿ *óppraven* 'feiern' statt אָפֿראָוועןֿ, פֿאַרדרוקןֿ *farrúkn* 'verriegeln', statt פֿאַרוקן. Weitere Unterschiede betreffen die Schreibung einiger Affixe und Präpositionen. So wird das zur Bildung weiblicher Personenbezeichnungen verwendete Suffix -in in der YIWO-Orthographie ausgeschrieben (לערערין *lérerin*), während die SU-Norm die reale Aussprache zugrunde legt (לערערן *lérern*). Nach der YIWO-Orthographie gilt die Schreibung אויף sowohl für die normalerweise unbetonte Präposition 'auf' (אויף דער וואַנט *ojf der vant* 'an der Wand') als auch für das stets betonte Präfix 'auf-' (אויפֿבלי *ójfbli* 'Aufblühen'), die SU-Norm unterscheidet zwischen אַף *af* (אַף דער וואַנט *af der vant*) und אוף- *uf-* (אופֿבלי *úfbli*). Inzwischen wurde in *sovetiš hejmland* hinsichtlich der Schreibung von *ojf(-)/ af/ uf-* Kompromißbereitschaft signalisiert. Der Präposition *bei* entspricht nach der YIWO-Norm בײ (*baj*), nach SU-Norm בא (*ba*). Nicht nur um Unterschiede in der Schreibung, sondern auch in der Aussprache handelt es sich bei dem deutschem *-keit* entsprechenden Suffix, das nach YIWO-Norm ־קייט (*-kejt*), nach SU-Norm ־קײט (*-kajt*) geschrieben wird. Schließlich wird *au* griechischer oder lateinischer Provenienz in Internationalismen unterschiedlich wiedergegeben. Nach der YIWO-Norm entspricht ihm וי (*oj*), nach SU-Norm meist או (*av*), z. B. in dem Präfix *Auto-/auto-* אויטאָ־ (*ojto-*), bzw. ־אַוטאָ (*avto-*) oder אויגוסט *ojgúst* 'August', אויטאָריטעט *ojtorität* 'Autorität', אַסטראָנויט *astronójt* 'Astronaut' bzw. אַװגוסט *ávgust*, אַװטאָריטעט *avtorität*, קאָסמאָנאַװט *kosmonávt*, doch אוידיטאָריע *ojditórje* 'Auditorium' bzw. אַודיטאָריע *auditórje* (vgl. *аудитория*) oder einheitliches קאַװקאַז *kavkáz* 'Kaukasus'.

Nicht kodifiziert ist bis zum heutigen Tage die Aussprache. Sprecher der nichtlitwischen Dialekte lesen z. B. אָ als /u/ und ו als /i/. Ebenso können die Digraphen ײ, ײַ, ױ je nach Dialekt unterschiedlich ausgesprochen werden (ײַ z. B. als /aj/ oder /a/, ױ- als /oj/ oder /ej/). Selbst in der Bühnenaussprache sind solche Unterschiede noch bemerkbar.

Dem Fehlen einer einheitlichen Orthoepie ist es möglicherweise zuzuschreiben, daß der in der Diskussion vor der sowjetischen Orthographiereform von 1930 gemachte Vorschlag, die drei Diphthonge phonetisch mit אַי, עי, אָי wiederzugeben, nicht akzeptiert wurde.

Zu einer weit ernsteren, da auch ideologisch belasteten Frage wurde die Schreibung der Hebraismen. Für sie wurde die traditionelle Schreibweise beibehalten, obwohl sich ihre Aussprache im Jiddischen grundlegend verändert hatte. So war der Akzent um eine Silbe zum Wortanfang verschoben, die meisten unbetonten Vokale zu einer Art Schwa reduziert, /ā/ war zu /o/, /e/ und /o/ in offener Silbe zu /ej/ und /oj/ geworden. Der im Hebräischen mit dem Buchstaben ת wiedergegebene t-Laut wurde wie /s/ ausgesprochen. Die hebräischen Wörter mit der Bedeutung 'Mond', 'Bursche', 'Feind', 'Sabbat', 'Grab', deren traditionelle Schreibung לבנה, בחר, שׂנא, שבת, קבר gewöhnlich mit *lebanā*, *bāḥûr*, *śoné*, *šabbāt*, *keber* transkribiert wird, lauten z. B. *levóne*, *bóxer*, *sójne*, *šábes*, *kéjver*. Die traditionelle Schreibung der Hebraismen impliziert u. a. die Verwendung von Buchstaben bzw. mit spezifischen diakritischen Zeichen versehener Varianten von Buchstaben, die bei der Schreibung der germanischen und slavischen Elemente nicht vorkommen. Es sind dies: כּ (*kof*), שׂ (*sin*), ת (*sov*), תּ (*tov*), בֿ (*vejs*), ח (*xes*), mit denen neben den bereits angeführten und in „Germanismen" und Slavismen ausschließlich verwendeten Graphemen die Phoneme /k/, /s/, /t/, /v/ und /x/ wiedergegeben werden.

Wer das Hebräisch-Aramäische sowieso beherrschte, hatte damit keine Probleme. Schwerer hatten es die Frauen, die normalerweise kein Hebräisch konnten, sowie unabhängig vom Geschlecht die jüdischen Arbeiter, Handwerker und Kleinhändler, deren ausgedehnter Arbeitstag ihnen kaum Zeit zur Beschäftigung mit dem „lošn kojdeš" ließ.

In der Sowjetunion, wo religiöse Tabus mit der Stabilisierung des neuen Regimes nach 1917 nicht mehr galten, wurde deshalb im Rahmen der sog. „Kulturrevolution" eine Vereinfachung der jiddischen Orthographie auch hinsichtlich der Hebraismen angestrebt. Die 1930 dekretierte Reform sah schließlich auch deren „farjidišung", d. h. ihre phonetische Schreibung vor. Die angeführten Beispiele für eine völlig veränderte Aussprache *levóne*, *boxer* usw. werden nach SU-Norm folgendermaßen geschrieben: באָכער, לעוואָנע, קייוער, שאַבעס, סוינע. Einige Abstriche von einer konsequent phonemischen Schreibweise wurden dennoch konzediert, um Morphemzusammenhänge zu verdeutlichen, z. B. in זקיינים *zkéjnim*, Plural von זאָקן *zokn* 'Greis', ebenso in der Ableitung זקיינע *zkéjne* 'Greisin'. Auch in den jiddischen Entsprechungen für *Feier-*

tag bzw. *Jom Kippur*, die auf hebräisches יו̇ם טוב (*jom toḇ* 'guter Tag') bzw. יום כיפור (*jom kippúr* 'Tag der Vergebung') zurückgehen und *jóntev* bzw. *joŋkíper* gesprochen werden, also das Phonem /n/ enthalten, wird מ (/m/) geschrieben (אָמטעוו, יאָמקיפער).

Orthodoxen Juden mußte eine solche Schreibweise als Blasphemie erscheinen. Da der Hebräischunterricht rigoros unterbunden wurde, war die Mehrheit der jüngeren sowjetischen Aschkenasim bald nicht mehr imstande, außerhalb der UdSSR erschienene Texte ohne Schwierigkeiten zu verstehen, was allerdings angesichts des inzwischen errichteten „Eisernen Vorhangs" ohnehin ohne größere Bedeutung war.

Nunmehr sind Bestrebungen zur Lockerung der SU-Norm im Gange. In Nr. 3/1993 von *di jidiše gas* veröffentlichte deren Redaktion eine Erklärung (S. 147), nach der künftig beide Normen zugelassen sind. Hebraismen in traditioneller Schreibung soll in Klammern ihre „farjidišung", nach SU-Norm geschriebenen Wörtern die traditionelle Schreibweise beigegeben werden.

Hinsichtlich der Kodifizierung des Wortschatzes, insbesondere der Schaffung von Fachterminologien, gab es im 19. Jahrhundert zeitweilig Bestrebungen, die entstehende jiddische Standardsprache maximal an das Deutsche anzulehnen. Dies führte zur Entlehnung zahlreicher Wörter, die sich in ihrer Lautform von echt jiddischen unterscheiden. Vgl. z. B. *ójfgabe* 'Aufgabe' mit *gob* 'Gabe'. Von ersterem ist lediglich das Präfix „verjiddischt", die Wurzel an ihrem Vokalismus (*a* statt *o*) dagegen eindeutig als deutsche Entlehnung erkennbar und die Endung -*e* völlig unjiddisch. Letzteres ist dagegen die reguläre jiddische Entsprechung zu deutschem *Gabe*. Ähnlich zu werten sind die jiddischen Äquivalente von *Frage*: *frage* (f.) und *freg* (m.). Einen weitergehenden „dajčmerizm" lehnte die Mehrheit der Schriftsteller und Sprachwissenschaftler jedoch ab. Der „Ausbau" basierte infolgedessen zu einem beträchtlichen Teil auf Internationalismen, die, wie ihre Form, nicht zuletzt Genus und Akzent, verraten, über das Russische entlehnt wurden. Vgl. z. B. die Maskulina *barák*, *etáž*, *fakultét*, *front*, *instrumént*, *kabinét*, *komitét*, *komód*, *konvért* 'Kuvert', *miljón*, *portrét*, *protokól*, *sezón*, *signál*, *telefón*, *žurnál*, deren deutsche Entsprechungen ausnahmslos Feminina oder Neutra sind, mit den russischen Maskulina барáк, этáж, факультéт, фронт, инструмéнт, кабинéт, комитéт, комóд, конвéрт, миллиóн, портрéт, протокóл, сезóн, сигнáл, телефóн, журнáл. Femininen wie *probléme*, *prográm*, *sistém* entsprechen im Russischen ebenfalls Feminina (проблéма, прогрáмма, систéма), im Deutschen hingegen Neutra. Auch Lehnübersetzungen nach russischem Muster sind häufig: z. B. *iberrajs* 'Pause', 'Unterbrechung' (wörtlich 'Durchriß' von *iberrajsn* 'durchreißen'; vgl. russisches перерыв von перерывáть 'durchreißen') oder *hinterojgler* 'Fernstudent' (vgl. russisches заóчник: Präfix за- 'hinter' + óч- [palatalisierte Wurzel ок- von óко 'Auge'] + -ник [Suffix zur Bildung von Bezeichnungen männlicher Personen wie jiddisches -*ler*]).

5.2. Die Orthographie des *Hebräisch-Aramäischen* war lange vor der Entstehung des Jiddischen kodifiziert und wurde beibehalten, als sich seine Aussprache (d. h. des „lešon kodeš") bei den Aschkenasim in vielfacher Hinsicht wesentlich veränderte. Sein Wortschatz blieb beschränkt, der eigentliche „Sprachausbau" erfolgte erst im 19. und 20. Jahrhundert mit der Entwicklung des Neuhebräischen, insbesondere aber seit der Entstehung und dem Aufschwung der zionistischen Bewegung bzw. nach dessen Etablierung als Staatssprache von Israel (Grande 1963, 3 ff).

5.3. Da für die Schreibung des Jiddischen einerseits und der mit ihm in Kontakt stehenden *slavischen* Sprachen andererseits völlig verschiedene Schriftsysteme verwendet werden, die sich gegenseitig nicht beeinflußt haben, sollen hier lediglich die allgemeinsten Grundlagen ihrer Verschriftung und ihres „Sprachausbaus" kurz charakterisiert werden.

5.3.1. Bei der *Verschriftung* der slavischen Sprachen spielte die Konfession eine entscheidende Rolle. Katholiken schreiben lateinisch, Orthodoxe kyrillisch. Seit der Entstehung eines *polnischen* Schrifttums im 14. Jahrhundert wird die Lateinschrift angewandt. Für spezifische Laute wurden schon früh diakritische Zeichen (für die im Polnischen bewahrten slavischen Nasalvokale z. B. die Grapheme ą, ę; zur Kennzeichnung der Palatalität von Konsonanten außer vor Vokalen, wo *i* diese Funktion hat, ein Strich über dem Buchstaben: ń, ć, ś, ź; zur Wiedergabe von /ž/ — ż, zur Kennzeichnung des heute meist als unsilbiges *u* ausgesprochenen velaren *l* — ł) oder Digraphen eingeführt (für /č/, /š/ — cz, sz).

Die drei aus dem Altrussischen hervorgegangenen *ostslavischen* Sprachen werden mit der unter Peter dem Großen (1672—1725) reformierten kyrillischen Schrift geschrieben, die mit dem Nachteil behaftet ist, daß sie in den meisten Positionen kein besonderes Graphem für /j/ hat. Das weißrussische und ukrainische Alphabet besitzt für /i/ nach palatalen Konsonanten außerdem den lateinischen Buchstaben *i*, das ukrainische darüber hinaus für die Verbindung /j/ + /i/ — *ï*. Die Orthographie ist weitgehend phonemisch mit erheblichen Konzessionen an eine morphemische Schreibung. Für die Vokalphoneme /a/, /o/, /e/, /u/ gibt es jeweils zwei Buchstaben (*а — я, о — ё* [statt *ё* wird meist *е* geschrieben], *э — е, у — ю*), von denen der eine (*я, ё, е, ю*) nach palatalen Konsonanten steht bzw. die Verbindung des entsprechenden Vokals mit davorstehendem /j/ wiedergibt. Hinsichtlich der Schreibung von /i/ unterscheiden sich die drei Sprachen. Im Russischen steht nach palatalen bzw. nach ursprünglich palatalen Konsonanten mit Ausnahme von /c/ sowie im Anlaut *и*, das in bestimmten Fällen auch die Verbindung von /j/ + /i/ wiedergibt, sonst *ы*. Im Weißrussischen entspricht dem *i* und *ы*, im Ukrainischen *i*, *ï* (s. o.) und *и*. In bestimmten Positionen, insbesondere im Morphemauslaut, wird /j/ in allen drei Sprachen mit *й* wiedergegeben. Vor Konsonanten und im Auslaut wird die Palatalität von Konsonanten mit dem sog. Weichheitszeichen *ь* markiert.

5.3.2. Der *Ausbau des Wortschatzes* der slavischen Kontaktsprachen des Jiddischen repräsentiert drei Typen.

Für das *Polnische* als offizielle Sprache einer einstigen europäischen Großmacht sind vor allem mittel- und westeuropäische (tschechische, deutsche, französische) Einflüsse charakteristisch, die mit großer Unbefangenheit rezipiert wurden. Selbst in der Standardsprache „wimmelt" es z. B. von Germanismen, und sogar die Wortbildung bleibt davon nicht unberührt.

Die aus der Verschmelzung der Umgangssprache von Moskau und dem Kirchenslavischen hervorgegangene russische Standardsprache ist demgegenüber, insbesondere was den abstrakten Wortschatz betrifft, hochgradig von letzterem geprägt. Auch der Morphologie hat das Kirchenslavische seinen Stempel aufgedrückt. Das archaische Partizipialsystem z. B. ist durchweg nichtrussischen Ursprungs.

Weißrussisch und *Ukrainisch* verdanken ihre Entstehung der Isolierung vom Russischen nach der Eroberung der westlichen Gebiete der durch den Mongoleneinfall geschwächten Kiewer Rus' durch das Großfürstentum Litauen. Bis zur Union mit Polen (1387) bildeten die orthodoxen Ostslaven die Bevölkerungsmehrheit des Großfürstentums, und ihr Russischkirchenslavisch war dessen offizielle Sprache. Die Entwicklung des Wortschatzes ihrer Dialekte war dann nachhaltig vom Polnischen geprägt. Da die Kodifizierung eigener Standardsprachen bei Weißrussen und Ukrainern erst nach den Teilungen Polens unter der Dominanz des Russischen begann, richtete sich der Purismus gegen dieses und nicht gegen die Polonismen, die sich insbesondere im Ukrainischen keineswegs auf die Lexik beschränken.

6. Charakteristik des jiddischen Sprachsystems im Vergleich zu dem seiner Kontaktsprachen

6.1. Da der *Phonembestand* bereits im Zusammenhang mit der Orthographie behandelt wurde, sei hier nur auf die Besonderheiten verwiesen, die das Jiddische dem Einfluß der slavischen Kontaktsprachen verdankt.

Das *Vokalsystem* der in dieser Hinsicht auf dem Litwischen und dem Südostjiddischen basierenden jiddischen Standardsprache mit seinen fünf Phonemen entspricht genau dem ostslavischen System. Charakteristisch ist insbesondere der Verlust der phonologischen Quantität. Auch in bezug auf die offene Aussprache von /o/ und /e/ stimmt das Jiddische mit allen vier Kontaktsprachen überein.

Auch das *Konsonantensystem* weist bedeutende Gemeinsamkeiten mit den slavischen Systemen auf. Lediglich die für das Polnische, Russische und Weißrussische charakteristische Palatalisierung ursprünglich aller Konsonanten vor vorderen Vokalen, die später durch die partielle (im Russischen) bzw. vollständige Verhärtung der Zischlaute, im Weißrussischen auch von /r'/, teilweise wieder eingeschränkt wurde, fehlt im Jiddischen. Mit dem Ukrainischen stimmt es insofern überein, daß ursprüngliches /e/ und /i/ keine Palatalisierung bewirkt. Phonologische Relevanz der Palatalitätsopposition gibt es in Entlehnungen, insbesondere bei dem Paar /l/ : /l'/; vgl. *mol* 'Mole' : *mol'* 'Motte' (vgl. russisches *мол : моль*). In der Schrift wird die Palatalität allerdings nur vor Vokalen bezeichnet, vgl. *rezoljúcje* 'Resolution' : *kultúr* 'Kultur' (= russisch *резолюция* : *культура*). Der in Vorbereitung der sowjetischen Orthographiereform gemachte Vorschlag, die Palatalität in Entlehnungen aus dem Russischen durchwegs mit Apostroph zu kennzeichnen, wurde nicht akzeptiert (Šlosberg 1990, 136).

Als phonetische Auswirkungen des slavischen Einflusses sind zu werten: die nichtaspirierte Aussprache der stimmlosen Klusile; die velarisierte Aussprache von nichtpalatalem /l/; die Bewahrung des Verschlusses in der Verbindung ŋg (vgl. *ziŋgen* mit deutschem *singen*). Die stimmhafte Artikulierung des /h/ teilt das Jiddische mit dem Weißrussischen und Ukrainischen, wo sich dieses Phonem aus /g/ entwickelt hat, ebenso seine Bewahrung vor /l/, /n/, /r/ (vgl. *hlíbe* 'Batzen', 'Brokken', *hníde* 'Nisse', *hréčke* 'Buchweizen', *hrízen* 'nagen', *hrúbe* 'Ofen' mit ukrainischem *глиба*, *гнида*, *гречка*, *гризти*, *груба*. Die Wiederherstellung der Stimmhaftigkeit auslautender Klusile entspricht dem slavischen Stand bei Beginn der Einwirkung auf das Jüdisch-Deutsche (Weinreich 1963). Heute ist er nur im Ukrainischen bewahrt.

6.2. Die Darstellung des Ausdrucks der *grammatischen Kategorien* und der *Formenbildung* beschränkt sich im wesentlichen auf die Komponenten, in denen Einwirkung der Kontaktsprachen sichtbar wird.

6.2.1. *Nomina* besitzen die Kategorien des Genus, Numerus und Kasus sowie der Determiniertheit. Das Jiddische hat mit Ausnahme des litwischen Dialekts die Genera Maskulinum, Femininum und Neutrum. Hinsichtlich des Verlustes des Neutrums im Litwischen vermutet Simon (1988, 151) Einfluß des Litauischen, in dem dieses Genus nur noch in Relikten bei movierten Pronomina und Adjektiven existiert. Der Annahme einer so weitgehenden grammatischen Interferenz steht jedoch das Fehlen jedweder Spuren eines litauischen Einflusses im Wortschatz entgegen. Das Standardjiddische stimmt hinsichtlich des Genus der Substantive germanischer Provenienz im großen und ganzen mit dem Deutschen überein. Abweichungen betreffen u. a. Personenbezeichnungen, bei denen im Jiddischen eine stärkere Tendenz zur Übereinstimmung mit dem natürlichen Geschlecht besteht. So werden z. B. *dos vajb, dos mejdl* in der Regel mit *zi* pronominalisiert wie russisches *жена, девушка* mit *она*, polnisches *żona, dziewczynka* mit *ona*. Es gibt jedoch eine ganze Reihe von Substantiven germanischer Herkunft, deren Genus nicht mit dem heutigen Deutschen, sondern mit dem ihrer slavischen Äquivalente übereinstimmt. Hier kann nicht ausgeschlossen werden, daß der Genuswechsel bzw. sein Ausbleiben in den Fällen, in denen er in der Entwicklung des Deutschen eintrat, vom Slavischen beeinflußt wurde. Vgl. z. B. *di bord, di lid, di fel, di bret, di prajz, di por; dos veš* einerseits mit deutschem *der Bart, das Lied, das Fell, das Brett, der Preis, das Paar; die Wäsche*, andererseits mit russischem *борода, песня, шкура, доска, цена, пара* (alle Feminina); *бельё* (Neutrum), die angeführten jiddischen Feminina außerdem mit polnischem *broda, piosenka, skóra, deska, cena, para* (ebenfalls alle Feminina).

Auch hinsichtlich des Funktionierens der Numeruskategorie unterscheiden sich Jiddisch und Deutsch kaum. Dennoch fällt auf, daß Klassen von Gegenständen, die im Slavischen ausschließlich oder vorwiegend als Kollektiva aufgefaßt und durch Singularia tantum ausgedrückt werden, im Jiddischen genaue Entsprechungen haben, während das Deutsche für das einzelne Element der Klasse eine Bezeichnung besitzt, die sowohl im Singular als auch im Plural vorkommt. Vgl. z. B. *(dos) gevér, (di) kartófl* (Singularia tantum) einerseits mit deutschem *Waffe, Kartoffel* (Singulative, die Singular und Plural aufweisen), andererseits mit russischem *оружие, картошка/картофель* (Singularia tantum), ersteres auch mit polnischem *broń* (Singulare tantum). Umgekehrt lassen sich im Jiddischen wie im Slavischen von Stoffbezeichnungen, die im Deutschen Singularia tantum sind bzw. nur selten in stilistischer Funktion einen Plural zulassen, Pluralformen bilden, um eine große Menge auszudrücken. Vgl. z. B. *šnéjen* (Plural zu *šnej*) oder *néplen* (Plural zu *nepl*) einerseits mit deutschem *Schnee* (Singulare tantum) und *Nebel* (im neutralen Stil Singulare tantum), andererseits mit russischem *снега* 'Schneemassen' (Plural von *снег*), *туманы* 'dichter Nebel' (Plural von *туман*). Schließlich können im Jiddischen wie im Slavischen bestimmte Gegenstände ausschließlich durch Pluralia tantum bezeichnet werden, denen im Deutschen ein Substantiv entspricht, das auch im Singular gebraucht wird. Vgl. z. B. *(di) briln* 'Brille' (Plurale tantum) mit russischem *очки* und polnischem *okulary* (beide Plurale tantum).

Bei der Bildung der Pluralformen tritt der nachhaltige Einfluß des Hebräisch-Aramäischen zutage. Nicht nur maskuline Entlehnungen aus dem Hebräischen wie *gíber* 'starker Mann', *nign* 'Melodie', *xójdeš* 'Monat', *séjfer* '(hebräischsprachiges) Buch' und viele andere bilden den Plural mit dem hebräischen Suffix *-im* (meist mit Alternationen im Stammvokalismus: *gibójrim, nigúnim, xadóšim, sfórim*). Auch Substantive deutscher Herkunft wie *pójer* 'Bauer', *dóktor* 'Arzt', *kéjser* 'Kaiser', *nar* 'Narr' weisen eine solche Pluralbildung auf (*pójerim, doktójrim, kejsórim* oder *kisríim, naróním*). Bei *lign* 'Lüge' ist sie (*ligúnim*) fakultativ neben *ligns*. Die außerordentlich produktive Pluralendung *-es* dürfte auf hebräisches *-ot* (ות-) zurückgehen. Von Paaren wie *nesíe* 'Reise' — *nesíes* (aus hebräischem נסיעה *nesiáh* — נסיעות *nesiót*) wurde sie übertragen auf Feminina mit der Endung *-e* wie *dáme* 'Dame' — *dámes, sóve* 'Eule' (aus dem Slavischen) — *sóves* sowie auf aus dem Slavischen entlehnte Maskulina vom Typ *zéjde* 'Großvater' — *zéjdes, sibirják* 'Sibirier' — *sibirjákes, lížnik* 'Skiläufer' — *lížnikes, snop* 'Garbe' — *snópes* und viele andere.

Die Kasus sind Nominativ, Dativ, Akkusativ und Possessiv. Sie werden nur teilweise formal unterschieden, und zwar — abgesehen von den Personalpronomina *mir* 'wir' und *ir* 'ihr' (Dativ und Akkusativ *undz* bzw. *ajx*) und ganz seltenenen Fällen beim Possessiv — ausschließlich im Singular.

Ausgedrückt werden die Kasusformen mit Ausnahme ganz weniger Lexeme nicht am Substantiv selbst, sondern am bestimmten Artikel und/oder kongruierenden Adjektiv oder Pronomen. Im Maskulinum fallen dabei Dativ und Akkusativ zusammen, während im Femininum und Neutrum der Akkusativ dem Nominativ entspricht. Die attributive Verbindung *der guter man* z. B. nimmt im Dativ/Akkusativ die Form *dem gutn man* an, von *di gute froj* oder *dos gute kind* wäre der Dativ *der guter froj* bzw. *dem gutn kind*. Ausnahmen bilden die Personenbezeichnungen *táte* 'Vater', *zéjde* 'Großvater', *jid* 'Jude', *menč* 'Mensch', *rébe* 'jüdischer Lehrer'; *máme* 'Mutter', *bóbe* 'Großmutter', *múme* 'Tante', deren Dativ (bei Feminina) bzw. Dativ und Akkusativ (bei Maskulina) die Endung *-n* annimmt, wobei im Maskulinum auslautendes *-e* ausfällt. Die entsprechenden Formen lauten somit: *dem tatn, zejdn, jidn, menčn, rebn; der mamen, boben, mumen*. Die Possessivpronomina *majn, dajn, zajn, ir, úndzer, ájer, zéjer* 'ihr (Plural)' bleiben direkt vor dem Beziehungswort unverändert, bilden aber einen Plural (*majn bux — majne bixer, zejer kind — zejere kinder*); der unbestimmte Artikel *a* (vor Vokal *an*) und der Negativartikel *kejn* sind unveränderlich. Als Pronomen mit der Bedeutung 'niemand' wird *kéjner* wie ein Adjektiv dekliniert, und der Dativ/Akkusativ des Maskulinums lautet *kejnem* (auf Diphthong, betonten Vokal und *-m* auslautende Adjektive haben statt *-n* die Endung *-en*, auf *-n* auslautende sowie *naj* 'neu' und *genój* 'genau' die Endung *-em*, z. B. *krúmen, kléjnem, nájem*). Die Pronomina *ver* 'wer', *émecer* 'jemand', *ále* 'alle' haben die Dativ/Akkusativ-Form *vémen, émecn, álemen*. Alle drei Kasusformen — abgesehen vom Possessiv — werden lediglich bei den Personalpronomina *ix* und *du* unterschieden, deren Dativ und Akkusativ *mir, mix* bzw. *dir, dix* lauten.

Der Possessiv wird fast ausschließlich von Personenbezeichnungen bzw. von auf Personen verweisenden Pronomina, insofern diese nicht mit einem besonderen Possessivpronomen korrespondieren, gebildet, und zwar mit der Endung *-s* (nach *s, z, š, č: -es*), die, soweit ein entsprechender Kasus formal unterschieden wird, an den Dativ antritt. In Nominalgruppen erhält nur das letzte Wort diese Endung. Von den angeführten Nomina bzw. Nominalgruppen lauten die Possessivformen dementsprechend: *dem guten mans, der guter frojs, dem guten kinds* (Plural: *die gute manens, frojens, kinders*); *dem tatns, zejdns, jidns, menčns, rebns; der mames, bobes, mumes; vemens, emecns, alemens*. Es ergibt sich also eine interessante Übereinstimmung mit dem Slavischen, in dem von Substantiven, die Personen bezeichnen, und nur von diesen, neben dem Genitiv eine besondere Possessivform, die sog. Possessivadjektive, abgeleitet werden können. Mit der Possessivform des Jiddischen haben diese außerdem gemein, daß sie im neutralen Stil normalerweise vorangestellt werden und daß ihre Verwendung nicht obligatorisch die Bestimmtheit des regierenden Gliedes signalisiert. Vgl. z. B. *Vaters Buch* (= *das Buch des Vaters*) mit im Jiddischen möglichem *dem tatns a bux* 'ein Buch von Vater/des Vaters' (wörtlich „Vaters ein Buch") sowie dessen russischem Äquivalent одна папина книга (wörtlich „ein Vaters Buch"). Die gleiche semantische Übereinstimmung zwischen dem Jiddischen und Russischen zeigt sich bei der Verwendung der Possessivpronomina. Vgl. z. B. *majner a frajnt* bzw. *a frajnt majner* 'ein Freund von mir', 'einer meiner Freunde' (wörtlich „meiner ein Freund", „ein Freund meiner") mit один мой друг (wörtlich „ein mein Freund"). Die nicht obligatorische

Bestimmtheit des regierenden Gliedes in attributiven Verbindungen mit einem Possessivpronomen ermöglicht somit auch die zusätzliche Verwendung des bestimmten Artikels wie in *der frajnt majner*. Bei aller partiellen Übereinstimmung zwischen dem Jiddischen und Slavischen dürfen dabei die wesentlichen Unterschiede zwischen den beiden Systemen hinsichtlich Bildung und Verwendung der Possessivformen nicht übersehen werden.

Diese bestehen vor allem darin, daß im Jiddischen bei aller Seltenheit vom Plural abgeleiteter Possessivformen diese doch grundsätzlich möglich sind. Außerdem wird im slavischen Possessivadjektiv Kasus, Genus und Numerus des Beziehungswortes ausgedrückt, während die jiddische Possessivform in dieser Hinsicht unveränderlich ist. Das in der Possessivform stehende Substantiv kann im Jiddischen ohne weiteres durch Attribute ergänzt werden, was in den slavischen Kontaktsprachen praktisch nicht mehr vorkommt. Schließlich kann die Possessivform im Jiddischen auch von fast allen Klassen von Pronomina gebildet werden, während das russische Possessivadjektiv fast nur noch von zur *a*-Deklination gehörenden Eigennamen und einigen Verwandtschaftsbezeichnungen wie *Маша* 'Mascha', *Миша* 'Mischa', *Ваня* 'Wanja', *папа* 'Papa', *мама* 'Mama', *дядя* 'Onkel', *тетя* 'Tante' usw. ableitbar ist.

6.2.2. Annäherungen an das Slavische zeigen sich auch im System der *Adjektive*. Die deutsche Gegenwartssprache kennt bekanntlich sog. schwache und starke Adjektivformen, von denen erstere nach einem Artikel oder Pronomen mit ausgeprägter (sog. starker) Kasusform, letztere in allen anderen Fällen verwendet werden. Daneben gibt es eine endungslose Form, die im neutralen Stil fast ausschließlich prädikativ, als Supplement oder adverbial gebraucht wird. Im Jiddischen ist die Unterscheidung starker und schwacher Adjektivformen aufgegeben worden. Im Maskulinum und Femininum hat sich eine einheitliche Deklination herausgebildet, in der sich je nach Kasus entweder die starke oder die schwache Form durchgesetzt hat (s. o.). Im Neutrum ist diese Flexion auf die Position nach dem bestimmten Artikel und nach flektierten Pronomina beschränkt, während nach dem unbestimmten Artikel unabhängig vom Kasus vor dem Substantiv (bei dieser Wortfolge auch nach nichtflektierten Pronomina) die unveränderte Stammform (*a / majn gut kind*) und nach dem Substantiv eine mit dem unbestimmten Artikel kombinierte Form mit der Endung -*s* (*a kind a guts*) Verwendung findet.

Während im Deutschen die flektierten Formen nur relativ selten prädikativ gebraucht werden, geschieht dies im Jiddischen ungemein häufig, und zwar nach den Regeln der normativen Grammatik (Fal'kovič 1966, 609) immer dann, wenn ein relativ stabiles Merkmal prädiziert werden soll. Die Opposition *er iz a gezúnter* — *er iz gezúnt* entspricht also genau der Verwendung der sog. Lang- und Kurzform des Adjektivs im Russischen, vgl. *он здоро́вый — он здоро́в*. Im Deutschen steht das Adjektiv auch in prädikativ-attributiver Funktion sowie bei Nachstellung des Attributs in der Kurzform. Für das Jiddische ist in diesen Positionen die Verwendung der flektierten Formen charakteristisch (*er drejt zix arum ... a drimlendiker un fojler* 'Er treibt sich ... herum, verschlafen und faul'; *an orem mit odern, dike vi štrik* 'ein Arm mit Adern, dick wie Stricke'), so wie für das Russische die der Langformen (vgl. *Он шляется ..., заспанный и ленивый; рука с жилами, толстыми как веревки*).

Schließlich ist festzustellen, daß aus dem Slavischen entlehnte Adjektive mit der Endung -*e* (vgl. *núdne* 'langweilig', *chitre* 'durchtrieben', *dámske* 'Damen-' mit russischem *нудный, хитрый, дамский; vátove* oder *vatóve* 'wattiert' mit polnischem *watowy*) auch in attributiver Funktion unflektiert gebraucht werden können.

In besonders starkem Maße tritt slavischer Einfluß in der Komparation zutage. Neben den wie im Deutschen mit den Suffixen -*er* bzw. -*st* synthetisch gebildeten und vielfach Umlaut aufweisenden Komparativ- und Superlativformen (*alt — élter — éltster*) werden ungemein häufig auch analytisch mittels *mer* 'mehr' bzw. *sáme* (vgl. russisches *самый*) gebildete Formen (*mer alt, mer elter* bzw. *der same alter, der same eltster*) gebraucht. Diese Bildungen entsprechen genau den russischen vom Typ *более стар(ый)* (umgangssprachlich auch *более старе́е), самый старый / ста́рший* (ausführlicher Lötzsch 1974). Da im Falle des Superlativs sogar eine materielle Entlehnung vorliegt, kann an ihrem interferenzbedingten Charakter keinerlei Zweifel bestehen.

6.2.3. Slavischer Einfluß zeigt sich auch im *Pronominalsystem*. Wie im Slavischen ist sowohl das betonte Reflexivpronomen *zix* (vgl. russisches *себя*, polnisches *siebie*) als auch die aus ihm hervorgegangene graphisch in der Regel nicht unterschiedene reduzierte Form, die als polysemes Verbalmorphem fungiert (vgl. russisches -ся, polnisches *się*), nicht auf die 3. Person beschränkt.

Als Demonstrativpronomen zum Ausdruck der hic-Deixis dient am häufigsten *der, di, dos*, verstärkt durch die direkt aus dem Slavischen entlehnte Partikel *o(t)* (vgl. ukrainisches und weißrussisches от, russisches вот) — *ot der* 'dieser'. Dabei werden die beiden Varianten (*o* und *ot*) in der Emphase oft miteinander kombiniert: *ot der-o* 'dieser hier'. Zum Ausdruck der ille-Deixis kann die ebenfalls aus dem Slavischen übernommene Partikel *on* verwendet werden: *on der* 'jener', *on der-o* 'der dort'.

Wie im Russischen kann emphatische Deixis auch durch Verbindung einer deiktischen Partikel mit dem Interrogativ- bzw. Relativpronomen ausgedrückt werden: *ot ver* 'der da', *ot vos* 'folgendes' (vgl. вот кто, вот что).

Auch das reich entwickelte System der jiddischen Indefinitpronomina offenbart slavischen Einfluß. In der Bedeutung der russischen Bildungen mit -нибудь (ukrainisch -небудь, weißrussisch -небудзь) werden am häufigsten Verbindungen der Interrogativstämme mit *-(s')nit-iz* verwendet, die eine analoge Struktur aufweisen: *ver-(s')nit-iz* 'irgendwer', 'irgend jemand', *vos-(s')nit-iz* 'irgend etwas', *velxer-(s')nit-iz* 'irgendeiner'. Neben diesem Typ, der in allen drei ostslavischen Sprachen vorkommt, ist eine Variante in Gebrauch, die nur im Ukrainischen eine Parallele zu haben scheint. Sie enthält statt *-s'nit-iz*: *-es-iz* (*ver-es-iz, vos-es-iz*, vgl. ukrainisches хтобудь, що-будь). Ein anderer semantischer Typ enthält das aus dem Ukrainischen bzw. Weißrussischen entlehnte Morphem *abi* (vgl. ukrainisch абu, weißrussisch абы). Diese Pronomina haben eine leicht abwertende Bedeutung, weswegen sie meist negiert gebraucht werden: *majn mame iz nit abiver* 'Meine Mutter ist nicht irgendwer'.

6.2.4. Sehr zahlreich sind Spuren slavischen Einflusses im Verbalsystem. Das Tempussystem stellt gewissermaßen eine Kontamination des russischen und polnischen Systems dar. Mit jenem hat es ein Iterativpräteritum (*flegt šrajbn* 'pflegte schreiben') gemeinsam, mit diesem ein nur selten gebrauchtes Plusquamperfektum (*hot gehat gešribn* 'hatte geschrieben'). Die bei grammatischer Interferenz festzustellende Tendenz der Kontaktsprachen zur Übereinstimmung hinsichtlich synthetischer bzw. analytischer Bildungsweise (Lötzsch 1991, 41) wird beim jiddischen Präteritum durchbrochen. Dieses kennt ausschließlich analytische, mit den Hilfsverben *hobn* und *zajn* gebildete Formen (*hot gešribn, iz gekumen*), während dieses Tempus heute sowohl im Russischen (писал, пришел) als auch im Polnischen (pisał, przyszedł) einen eindeutig synthetischen Charakter aufweist. Im Jüdisch-Deutschen, dessen Grundlage trotz mitteldeutschem *kop* 'Kopf', *šepn* 'schöpfen', *ferd* 'Pferd' maßgeblich oberdeutsch geprägt ist, war der Verlust des synthetischen Imperfekts zweifellos schon weit fortgeschritten, als seine Sprecher mit dem Slavischen in Berührung kamen. Einen ähnlichen Stand hatte die Verdrängung des synthetischen Imperfekts und Aorists durch das mit dem Hilfsverb *byti* 'sein' und der sog. *l*-Form gebildete Perfekt (*pisal jestь* 'hat geschrieben' [wörtlich „geschrieben habender ist"]) zu diesem Zeitpunkt im Polnischen und Ostslavischen erreicht. So konnte dieses Tempus, das seinen analytischen Charakter noch nicht völlig eingebüßt hatte, nicht nur semantisch und hinsichtlich seiner Frequenz als nahezu einziges Vergangenheitstempus, sondern auch formal mit dem jiddischen Perfekt identifiziert werden. Die Gleichsetzung wurde auch dann noch beibehalten, als sich das polnische und ostslavische Präteritum zu einer synthetischen Form weiterentwickelten. Mit russischem Einfluß könnte es zusammenhängen, daß sich im Jiddischen ein aus Formen des Hilfsverbstammes *fleg-* und dem Infinitiv bestehendes Iterativpräteritum herausgebildet hat. Im 18. Jahrhundert, als sich die Sprecher des Jiddischen das Russische aneignen mußten, waren die heute kaum noch gebräuchlichen Formen des Typs пи́сывал, да́вивал, едал, пивал 'pflegte zu schreiben, zu geben, zu essen, zu trinken' in dieser Sprache noch äußerst häufig. Das viel seltener als im Deutschen gebrauchte Plusquamperfekt besteht aus dem Präteritum von *hobn* (*hot gehat*) oder *zajn* (*iz geven*) und dem Partizip II. Die Distribution sollte die gleiche sein wie im Präteritum (*hot gehat gešribn*, aber *iz geven gekumen*). Häufig werden jedoch auch abweichende Formen des Präteritums der Hilfsverben (*iz gehat* bzw. *hot geven*) gebraucht. Diese Unsicherheit könnte damit zusammenhängen, daß die slavischen Kontaktsprachen, die überhaupt noch ein Plusquamperfekt besitzen, nämlich Polnisch, Ukrainisch und Weißrussisch, dieses nur mit einem Hilfsverb, nämlich *być* bzw. *бути, быць*, bilden.

Das Jiddische weist Ansätze zur Herausbildung eines Aspektsystems auf. Auch der formale Ausdruck der potentiellen Aspektformen ähnelt dem der slavischen Kontaktsprachen. So hat das Präfix *on-* in *onšrajbn* nicht die Bedeutung *an-* in deutschem *anschreiben*, sondern entspricht slavischem *na-* in polnischem *napisać*, russischem *написать*, signalisiert also den perfektiven Aspekt. Verwendet werden solche Formen insbesondere zum Ausdruck der Vorzeitigkeit in Kontexten wie *Wenn er den Brief geschrieben hat/geschrieben haben wird, schickt er ihn ab/wird er ihn abschicken*. Vgl. *ven er vet onšrajbn dem briv, vet er im avekšikn* mit polnischem *Kiedy napisze ten list, wyśle go* oder russischem *Когда он напишет письмо, он его отправит*. Die perfekten Futurformen sind hier in allen drei Sprachen obligatorisch. Während jedoch das polnische und ostslavische Aspektsystem analytische Futurformen nur im imperfekten Aspekt zuläßt (*będzie pisał*, aber *napisze*, *будет писать*, aber *напишет*), kennt das Jiddische für das mit dem Hilfsverbstamm *ve(l)-* (*vel, vest, vet, veln* usw.) zu bildende analytische Futur keine Aspektbeschränkungen (*vet onšrajbn* wie *vet šrajbn*).

Auffällige Übereinstimmungen zwischen dem Jiddischen und den slavischen Kontaktsprachen gibt es auch im System des Genus verbi. Die erwähnte Identifizierung von *zix*, das in allen drei Personen verwendet werden kann, mit polnischem *się* und ostslavischem *-ся* bewirkt, daß einerseits mit *zix* gebildete Passivformen auch mit nichtmodaler Bedeutung gebraucht werden können (*dos hojz bojt zix* 'Das Haus wird gebaut', vgl. russisches *дом строится*, polnisches *dom buduje się*) und andererseits wie im Deutschen mit dem Hilfsverb *vern* gebildete Passivformen auch modale Bedeutung haben können (*dos vert derklert* 'das erklärt sich'). Daß in nichtmodaler Bedeutung *bojt zix* und *vert gebojt* synonym sind, führt zur Synonymie auch in modaler Funktion. Während in deutschen Konstruktionen vom Typ *hier lebt/arbeitet es sich gut* der Ausdruck des Agens unmöglich ist, nimmt er im Jiddischen wie im Slavischen die Form des Dativs an. Vgl. *im lebt/arbet zix do gut* mit russischem *ему тут хорошо живется/работается*.

6.3. Das jiddische Wortbildungssystem weist sogar eine Fülle materieller Entlehnungen aus dem Slavischen auf. Allein zur Bildung von Bezeichnungen weiblicher Personen bzw. Tiere (*-ixe*) wurden nicht weniger als fünf Suffixe übernommen. Es sind dies: *-nice, -ke, -še, -ínje, -ixe* (russisch und polnisch *-ница/-nica, -ка/ka*, russisch außerdem: *-ша, -иня, -уха*). Diese Suffixe sind so produktiv geworden, daß sie zur Ableitung von Stämmen verwendet werden, deren slavische Äquivalente andere Suffixe erhalten. Vgl. z. B. einerseits *grafinje* 'Gräfin', *hózixe* 'Häsin' mit den hinsichtlich der Bildungsweise genau entsprechenden russischen Pendants *графиня, зайчиха* und andererseits *kejserínje* 'Kaiserin', 'Zarin', *vólfixe* 'Wölfin', *léjbixe* 'Löwin' mit *царица, императрица, волчица, львица*.

Den im Jiddischen ursprünglich ebenso wie im Deutschen uneingeschränkt bildbaren Komposita stehen im Slavischen meist Wortverbindungen gegenüber. Insbesondere gilt dies für den Typ *Kuhmilch*, *Pferdeschwanz* (russisch *коровье молоко, конский хвост*). Unter slavischem Einfluß beginnen solche Verbindungen auch im Jiddischen zu dominieren, so daß Beziehungsadjektive ableitbar werden, die im Deutschen absolut undenkbar sind, z. B. *kien* in *kiene milx* oder *férdiš* in *férdišer ek* 'Pferdeschwanz'.

Auf eine weitergehende Darstellung des jiddischen Wortbildungssystems muß hier verzichtet werden (ausführlicher Lötzsch 1992).

6.4. Hinsichtlich der jiddischen Syntax kann hier nur angemerkt werden, daß sich die Wortstellung stark verändert hat. Die Zweitstellung des finiten Teils des Prädikats ist zwar nicht nur im normalen Aussagesatz bewahrt, sondern bleibt auch in der Satzfrage erhalten, da die entlehnte Fragepartikel *ci* (vgl. weißrussisches *ці*) diese Wortstellung ermöglicht (z. B. *du kumst fun šul. — ci kumstu fun šul?* 'Du kommst aus der Schule. — Kommst du aus der Schule?). Doch ist die für das Deutsche charakteristische Rahmenkonstruktion und die Endstellung des finiten Teils des Prädikats im Nebensatz nahezu vollständig aufgegeben worden, wie folgendes Beispiel zeigt: *an óremer melámed, a šlímazl, iz gegángen afn jaríd cu kojfn zix a cig ... dos vajb zajns hot im ópgemolt akurát, viazój a cig zet ojs, vórem zi hot dox gevúst, az er iz a šlímazl* 'Ein armer jüdischer Lehrer, ein Unglücksrabe, ist auf den Markt gegangen, um sich eine Ziege zu kaufen ... Sein Weib hat ihm genau beschrieben, wie eine Ziege aussieht, denn sie wußte doch, daß er ein Unglücksrabe ist'.

7. Kritische Wertung der verwendeten Literatur

Als Jiddisch wird hier die in der Jiddistik traditionell als Ostjiddisch bezeichnete westgermanische Sprache verstanden, die sich seit dem 13. Jahrhundert in Polen entwickelte, wohin größere Gruppen sog. Jüdisch-Deutsch sprechender Juden auswanderten, als sie in Deutschland wegen ihres Glaubens zunehmend diskriminiert und verfolgt wurden. Als Schriftsprache diente ihnen das Hebräisch-Aramäische, insbesondere als Sprache der jüdischen Religion, aber auch bei der Kommunikation mit Glaubensgenossen, die sich ansonsten anderer Sprachen bedienten. Zumindest viele Männer müssen das Hebräisch-Aramäische bis zu einem Grade beherrscht haben, so daß auch der Wortschatz ihrer deutschen Alltagssprache semitische Elemente aufnahm. Insbesondere mit der Religion und dem Handel zusammenhängende Begriffe wurden mit semitischen Entlehnungen bezeichnet. Dieses Idiom deswegen als eine vom Deutschen verschiedene, als Westjiddisch bezeichnete Sprache anzusehen, wie dies insbesondere Salomo Birnbaum und Max Weinreich postulierten und wie es seitdem in der traditionellen Jiddistik üblich ist, erscheint nicht gerechtfertigt, wie Bettina Simon (1988, passim) überzeugend nachgewiesen hat.

8. Bibliographie (in Auswahl)

Birnbaum, Salomo (1918): *Praktische Grammatik der jiddischen Sprache für den Selbstunterricht. Mit Lesestücken und einem Wörterbuch*, Wien/Leipzig.

Blum, Jost G. (1992): „Zur Transkription des Standardjiddischen". In: *Jiddistik-Mitteilungen 7*, 1–30.

falkovič, elje (1929): *gramatik far dervaksene*, Moskau.

falkovič, elje (1940): *jidiš*, Moskau.

Фалькович, Э. М. [Fal'kovič, É. M.] (1966): „Еврейский язык (идиш) [Evrejskij jazyk (idiš): Die jüdische Sprache (Jiddisch)]". In: *Языки народов СССР* [Jazyki narodov SSSR: *Die Sprachen der Völker der UdSSR*] Moskau, 599–629.

Фалькович, Э. Fal'kovič, É.] (1984): „О языке идиш [O jazyke idiš: Über die jiddische Sprache]". In: *Русско-еврейский (идиш) словарь* [Russko-evrejskij (idiš) slovar': *Russisch-jüdisches (jiddisches) Wörterbuch*], Moskau, 666–720.

Friedrich, C. W. (1784): *Unterricht in der Judensprache und Schrift zum Gebrauch für Gelehrte und Ungelehrte*, Prenzlau (Zitiert nach: Simon 1988).

Гранде, Б. М. [Grande, B. M.] (1963): *Иврит-русский словарь* [Ivrit-russkij slovar': Iwrith-russisches Wörterbuch], Moskau.

jofe, j. a. (1927–1928): „der slavišer element in jidiš". In: *pinkes I*, 235–256, II, 296–312.

kagorov, j. (1926): „di grund-stixie fun jidišn sintaksis". In: *filologiše šriften*. landoj-bux, Wilna, 425–428.

Kohan, David (1991): „Über den „Schmendrekismus" und seine mannigfaltigen Begleiterscheinungen". In: *Jiddistik-Mitteilungen 5*, 1–6.

Kühn-Ludewig, Maria (1992): „Zur Kulturarbeit des Bund". In: *Jiddistik-Mitteilungen 8*, 1–6.

kupovecki, mark (1990): „jidiš – dos mame-lošn fun 150 tojznt sovetiše jidn". In: *sovetiš hejmland* H. 3, 131.

Lötzsch, Ronald (1974): „Slawische Elemente in der grammatischen Struktur des Jiddischen". In: *Zeitschrift für Slawistik 19*, 446–459.

Lötzsch, Ronald (1991): „Strukturelle Voraussetzungen für morphologische Interferenz bei Kontakten zwischen nicht nahverwandten Sprachen". In: *Zeitschrift für Phonetik, Sprachwissenschaft und Kommunikationsforschung 44*, 311–324.

Lötzsch, Ronald (1992): „Slawische Elemente in Wortbildung und Grammatik des Jiddischen". In: *Słowiańsko-niesłowiańskie kontakty językowe*, Warschau, 97–104.

mark, judl (1978): *gramatik fun der jidišer klalšprax*, New York.

Rapoport, Louis (1992): *Hammer, Sichel, Davidstern. Judenverfolgungen in der Sowjetunion*, Berlin.

rejzn, zalmen (1924): „gramatišer min in jidiš". In: *jidiše filologje I*, Warschau, 11–22, 180–192, 303–322.

Simon, Bettina (1988): *Jiddische Sprachgeschichte. Versuch einer neuen Grundlegung*, Leipzig.

Strack, Hermann (1916): *Jüdisches Wörterbuch*, Leipzig.

šlosberg, b. (1930): „der jidišer ojslejg in ratnfarband". In: *der ejnhajtlexer jidišer ojslejg. materialn un projektn cu der ortografišer konferenc fun jivo*, Wilna. Nachdruck in: *sovetiš hejmland* 1990/7, 134–140.

vajnrajx, maks (1973): *gešixte fun der jidišer šprax*, New York, 2 Bde.

vejnger, m. (1913): *jidišer sintaksis*, Warschau.

vejnger, m. (1925): *foršt jidiše dialektn. program farn materjaln-klojber*, Minsk.

vejnger, m. (1929): *jidiše dialektologje*, Minsk.

vejnger, m. (1928): „šprachvisnšaft un ojslejg". In: *jidiše ortografie, projektn un materialn*, Kiew (zitiert nach: *sovetiš hejmland* 1990/7, 134).

vejnger, m./zarecki, a. (1926): *praktiše jidiše gramatik far lerers un študentn*, Moskau.

Weinreich, Uriel (1949): *College Yiddish*, New York.

Weinreich, Uriel (1963): „Four riddles in bilingual dialectology". In: *American Contributions to the Fifth International Congress of Slavists*. Sofia 1963, Den Haag, 85–109.

Weinreich, Uriel (1968): *Modern English–Yiddish, Yiddish–English Dictionary*, New York.

zarecki, ajzik (1927): *grajzn un sfejkes. kapitlen stilistiše gramatik*, Kiew.

zarecki, ajzik (1929): „vegn jidišer ortoepje". In: *di jidiše šprax*, Moskau, 3, 16. Nachdruck in: *sovetiš hejmland* 1991/6, 122–126.

zarecki, ajzik (1929–1931): *kurs fun jidišer šprax*, Charkow.

zarecki, ajzik (1931): *jidiše ortografje*, Moskau/Charkov/Minsk.

Ronald Lötzsch, Leipzig (Deutschland)

239. Romani

1. Verbreitung der Roma in Europa
2. Von Indien nach Europa
3. Roma-Kultur, Wirtschaft und Politik
4. Zigeuner – Roma – Romani
5. Soziolinguistische Lage des Romani
6. Sprachpolitische Entwicklungen
7. Das Romani und die Kontaktsprachen
8. Zur Forschungslage
9. Bibliographie (in Auswahl)

1. Verbreitung der Roma in Europa

Zigeuner oder – nach ihrer Eigenbezeichnung – *Roma* leben heute in fast allen Ländern des europäischen Kontinents, die meisten in Südosteuropa. Seit dem 19. Jahrhundert sind zahlreiche Gruppen nach Nord- und Südamerika, auch nach Südafrika und Australien ausgewandert. Bezüglich der Größe der Gesamtethnie bzw. ihrer Vertreter in einzelnen Staaten stehen kaum verläßliche Quellen zur Verfügung, da praktisch alle Angaben auf Schätzungen beruhen. Die Ergebnisse staatlicher Erhebungen sind aus mehreren Gründen unzuverlässig: sei es, weil die Roma als ethnische Gruppe nicht gesondert aufgeführt werden, sei es, weil sie sich – etwa aus Angst vor Repressionen – nicht als Roma zu erkennen geben, sei es, weil verschiedene Zuordnungsoptionen bestehen, wie dies der Fall des ehemaligen Jugoslawien in besonders deutlicher Weise zeigt. Beim Zensus von 1981 ließen sich 168.197 Personen als Roma registrieren, während ein weitaus größerer Teil sich als „Jugoslawen", „Moslems" oder auch Türken, Albaner, Serben deklarierte oder von der Möglichkeit, keine Angaben über die ethnische Zugehörigkeit zu machen, Gebrauch gemacht hat. Nach Angaben von Roma-Interessenvertretungen beläuft sich die Anzahl der Roma in Ex-Jugoslawien auf 650.000–1 Million, mit einem deutlichen Schwerpunkt in Serbien, dem Kosovo und Makedonien. Die folgenden, aus verschiedenen jüngeren Quellen zusammengestellten Daten sollen auch zur Veranschaulichung der *Spannweite* der Angaben dienen: Rumänien: 500.000–3 Millionen; Bulgarien: 500.000–800.000; Ungarn: 500.000–600.000; Griechenland: 50.000–100.000; Tschechien: 100.000; Slovakei: 350.000–600.000; Spanien: 250.000–1 Million; Albanien: ca. 50.000; Deutschland: ca. 50.000; Frankreich: 80.000–200.000; Großbritannien: ca. 50.000; GUS: 250.000. In einzelnen Ländern Südosteuropas machen die Roma bis zu 10% der Gesamtbevölkerung aus. Weltweit wird die Größe der Ethnie auf 10 Millionen geschätzt. Die demographischen Verhältnisse unterliegen neuerdings Verschiebungen von statistisch noch kaum erfaßbarem Ausmaß: zunächst die Wirtschaftskrise im Jugoslawien der 80er Jahre, dann die mit dem Aufbrechen nationaler Zwistigkeiten verbundenen politischen Umwälzungen in Osteuropa haben neue Migrationsbewegungen der Roma besonders nach Mitteleuropa ausgelöst.

2. Von Indien nach Europa

Die Roma haben ihre indische Heimat vermutlich zwischen dem 6. und dem 9. Jahrhundert verlassen; über die Gründe für den Exodus gibt es verschiedene Hypothesen, die jedoch mangels historischer Zeugnisse allesamt dem Spekulativen oder gar Mythischen verhaftet bleiben. Die Analyse der historisch-linguistischen Beziehungen zwischen dem Romani und den indo-arischen Sprachen bietet Evidenz für Migrationen der Roma schon im indischen Raum (vgl. Turner 1926). Nachdem J. Rüdiger und H. Grellman schon 1782 bzw. 1783 unabhängig voneinander die Verbindung zwischen dem Romani und indischen Sprachen erkannt hatten und der Indogermanist F. A. Pott (1844—45) die Verwandtschaft auf eine breite wissenschaftliche Grundlage gestellt hatte, konnte F. Miklosich (1872—82) aus den Lehnwortschichten des Romani die Migrationsroute der Zigeuner erschließen: die Vorfahren der heute in Europa siedelnden Zigeuner sind durch persisches und armenisches Sprachgebiet gezogen, bevor sie im 11. Jahrhundert das Territorium des Byzantinischen Reiches erreichten, um sich nach einem längeren Verbleib in griechischsprachigen Gebieten seit dem 13. Jahrhundert über den Balkan und schließlich ganz Europa auszubreiten.

Die frühen, teils noch unsicheren historischen Quellen gehen auf das 11. Jahrhundert zurück (vgl. Soulis 1961). Seit dem 14. Jahrhundert mehren sich in ganz Europa die Quellen, die Aufschluß über die Geschichte der Roma geben: 1362 ist ihre Anwesenheit in Ragusa (Dubrovnik) bezeugt, 1407 in Hildesheim, 1420 in Brüssel, 1422 in Bologna; die ersten Zeugnisse aus Skandinavien und Großbritannien stammen vom Beginn des 16. Jahrhunderts. Anfänglich als vermeintliche Pilger über einen kurzen Zeitraum toleriert, stellt sich die Geschichte der Roma in den folgenden Jahrhunderten als eine Geschichte der Verfolgung und Diskriminierung dar, deren Kulmination die versuchte Ausrottung der Ethnie im nationalsozialistischen Deutschland und den von ihm abhängigen Ländern war (vgl. Kenrick/Puxon 1972).

Bedeutend, auch für das Verständnis der großen Migrationswellen der Zigeuner seit der zweiten Hälfte des 19. Jahrhunderts, ist die jahrhundertelang während Leibeigenschaft im Gebiet des heutigen Rumänien. Die erste schriftliche Urkunde über Roma in der Walachei von 1382 berichtet über den Verkauf von Zigeunersklaven. Seitdem lebten Zigeuner in den Donaufürstentümern als Leibeigene im Besitz des Staates, der Kirche oder einzelner Bojaren. Erst 1856 wurde die Leibeigenschaft in den Fürstentümern der Moldau und Walachei endgültig abgeschafft.

Seit ihrer Ankunft in einem Europa der überwiegend seßhaften Populationen hat die Nicht-Seßhaftigkeit der Roma ihr Image bis heute geprägt, auch dort, wo es längst von der Realität überholt worden ist und Roma seit Jahrzehnten, manchmal seit Jahrhunderten, an einem Ort bzw. in einem Land ansässig sind. Die Geschichte der Sprache und der Kultur der Roma muß auf dem Hintergrund der jahrhundertelangen Migrationen auch als die Geschichte interethnischer Beziehungen verstanden werden, oftmals mit sich kurzfristig abwechselnden Kontaktkulturen und Kontaktsprachen.

3. Roma-Kultur, Wirtschaft und Politik

Über die Unterschiede zwischen einzelnen Roma-Gruppen innerhalb eines Staates und über Landesgrenzen hinweg bestehen Ähnlichkeiten, auf die sich nach Jahrhunderten der Trennung einzelner Gruppen voneinander ein „Wir-Bewußtsein" gründet, das die Einheit der Ethnie konstituiert. Versuche, die Gemeinsamkeiten mit wenigen Worten zu umreißen, sind wegen der Mannigfaltigkeit der kulturellen Manifestationen dazu verurteilt, nur einen Ausschnitt der Realität zu geben. Zur besseren Orientierung sei darum auf die im Literaturverzeichnis aufgeführten Bibliographien verwiesen.

Zu den Stereotypen über die Zigeuner gehört, daß sie jeweils die Religion der „Gastvölker" annehmen, und bei näherem Hinsehen bestätigt sich auch tatsächlich, daß die Konfessionen der Roma mit denen der jeweiligen Majoritätsbevölkerung übereinstimmen. Religionswechsel wie auch religiöser Synkretismus sind heute vor allem in Gebieten mit gemischter christlicher und islamischer Population (Makedonien, Kosovo, Bulgarien, Thrazien) häufig anzutreffen. Die alle Lebensbereiche der Roma durchziehende Religiosität, die sich kaum je in vorgegebene Institutionen fügt, hat zu zahlreichen Thesen über den indischen Ursprung einzelner Riten und Glaubenselemente geführt. Doch über eine gemeinsame „Urreligion" der Zigeuner, deren Spuren nach jahrhundertelangen Anpassungsprozessen in Reinlichkeitsriten, der Verehrung weiblicher Gottheiten, Ahnenkult oder auch der Kunst des Wahrsagens gesucht werden, gibt es mehr Spekulationen denn gesicherte Erkenntnisse.

In der Sozialorganisation der Roma, besonders für den Zusammenhalt der einzelnen Gruppe, spielt das Berufsleben eine zentrale Rolle. Die althergebrachten Berufe wurden und werden z. T. bis heute oft in der Gruppe ausgeübt und von Generation zu Generation tradiert. Besonders für die in Südosteuropa ausgeübten produzierenden Handwerke ist zum einen eine starke Spezialisierung, zum anderen eine große Flexibilität in der Anpassung an veränderte Bedürfnisse des Marktes charakteristisch. Das oft zu den ältesten Berufen der Roma gerechnete Schmiedehandwerk ist in einer fast unüberschaubaren Anzahl von Spezialisierungen anzutreffen; von längst nicht mehr ausgeübten Handwerken zeugen oft nur die Gruppenbezeichnungen (vgl. 4.2). Wenngleich viele der traditionell von Zigeunern ausgeübten Handwerke und Berufe, die übrigens gleichermaßen Folge und Ursache nomadischer Lebensweise waren, aufgrund veränderter wirtschaftlicher Bedingungen ausgestorben oder im Schwinden begriffen sind, verdienen viele Roma bis heute ihren Lebensunterhalt durch überlieferte Gewerbe wie Schaustellerei, Hausiererei und Handel, als Musiker, als Saisonarbeiter bei Ernteeinsätzen, darüberhinaus aber auch zunehmend in gewöhnlich nicht mit „Zigeunern" assoziierten Berufssparten wie denen des Industriearbeiters oder des Akademikers.

Der Beginn der organisierten Roma-Nationalbewegung wird von G. Puxon (1979) auf ein Treffen im württembergischen Cannstatt im Jahre 1878 datiert, doch bleiben die politischen Anstrengungen bis zum Ende des Zweiten Weltkriegs eher sporadisch und zusammenhanglos. Seit den 50er Jahren wurden weltweit Zusammenschlüsse gegründet, die zum einen das Ziel hatten, die Bürgerrechte für Roma zu erstreiten (in Deutschland ging es vor allem um Wiedergutmachung für die Opfer des Nazi-Regimes), zum anderen auf Anerkennung als nationale Minderheiten drängten. Ein Höhepunkt in der Koordinierung der nationalen Bewegungen war der 1. Internationale Roma-Kongreß 1971 in London. Die in der Folge des zweiten Kongresses, Genf 1978, gegründete Internationale Roma-Union beantragte die Mitgliedschaft in der UNO und wurde am 28.2.1979 als nicht-staatliche Organisation mit beratendem Status in die UNO aufgenommen.

4. Zigeuner – Roma – Romani

4.1. Roma und Gadže

Das Wort *Roma*, die Eigenbezeichnung der meisten europäischen Zigeuner, wird aus alt- bzw. mittelindisch *ḍomba* hergeleitet, wo es die Mitglieder einer Kaste von Musikern bezeichnet. Etymologisch verwandt ist hindi *ḍom* gleicher Bedeutung. In den Dialekten der Roma wird bei den Begriffen für Mann/ Ehemann, Frau/Ehefrau, Junge/Sohn und Mädchen/Tochter konsequent unterschieden, ob es sich um Mitglieder der eigenen oder einer fremden Ethnie handelt: so bezeichnen *rom* „Mann" (pl. *roma*) und *romni* „Frau" (pl. *romnja*) gleichzeitig die Zugehörigkeit zur Ethnie der Roma in Abgrenzung zu den Nicht-Zigeunern. Für diese stehen neben dem wohl am weitesten verbreiteten *gadžo* (mask. sg.) Begriffe wie *xalo, das, balamo* zur Verfügung. Desgleichen werden *čhavo* „Junge" und *čhaj* „Mädchen" für Mitglieder der Roma-Ethnie in Unterscheidung zu *raklo* und *rakli* verwendet.

Die *in-group* Bezeichnungen *rom, romni, čhavo, čhaj* sind bei allen Zigeunergruppen bekannt und gebräuchlich, ausgenommen jenen, die die Sprache gewechselt haben (s. 4.4, 5). Die Roma nennen ihre Sprache *romani čhib* („Roma-Sprache"); in anderssprachlichen Kontexten wird neben *Romani* oft das Adverb *romanes* in substantivierter Form („das Romanes") als Sprachbezeichnung verwendet.

4.2. Gruppen- und Stammesnamen

Die sich in ständiger Entwicklung befindliche Sozialorganisation der Zigeuner (s. Münzel 1981) hat eine unüberschaubare Anzahl von Stammes- und Sippenbezeichnungen hervorgebracht: unter den seit dem 15. Jahrhundert in Mitteleuropa ansässigen Zigeunern ist vor allem in Deutschland der Name *Sinte/Sinti* verbreitet, ein Wort unklarer Herkunft, dessen versuchte Herleitung aus *Sindh* etymologisch nicht stichhaltig ist. Auch die Sinte nennen ihre Sprache *romani čhib*. In der Slovakei und in Slovenien siedeln Gruppen, die man aufgrund sprachlicher Merkmale zu den Sinte stellen könnte, bei denen jedoch der Name *Sinte* nicht bekannt ist. Den Sinte sprachlich nahe verwandte Gruppen in Frankreich und Italien nennen sich *Manuš* („Menschen"). Daneben ist der vor allem als Eigenbezeichnung der spanischen Roma bekannte Name *Kale* („Schwarze") auch für Mitteleuropa belegt; in England und z. T. Frankreich nennen sich die Roma *Romaničal*.

In Südosteuropa trifft man auf Gruppennamen, die aus Berufsbezeichnungen (kontaktsprachlicher Herkunft) entstanden sind, und die beibehalten wurden, nachdem die entsprechenden Tätigkeiten an Bedeutung verloren haben oder ganz aufgegeben wurden, so z. B. *Kalderaš* (rumän.) „Kesselflicker", *Ursarja* (rumän.) „Bärenführer", *Bugurdži* (türk.) „Bohrermacher", *Kovačja* (slav.) „Schmiede", *Džambazja* (türk.) „Viehhändler, Gaukler", *Grebenarja* (slav.) „Kammacher", u. v. a. m. Auch Spottnamen haben sich zu Eigenbezeichnungen entwickelt: so nennt sich eine Untergruppe der in Serbien lebenden Kalderaš *Khanjarja* „Hühnerdiebe" (zu Romani *khajni* „Huhn"), und eine über die Türkei nach Griechenland eingewanderte Gruppe führt den Namen *Kalpazea* (< türk. *kalpazan* „Falschmünzer") — die Bedeutung in der Herkunftssprache ist in Vergessenheit geraten. Eigen- und Fremdbezeichnungen der Roma-Gruppen untereinander weichen oft voneinander ab, besonders wenn die Gruppen nicht in unmittelbarer Nachbarschaft leben. Oft gibt es für eine Gruppe verschiedene Bezeichnungen und umgekehrt trifft man gelegentlich auf den gleichen Eigennamen bei Gruppen mit stark divergierenden Dialekten: so im Fall der Bugurdži im Kosovo und einer anderen Gruppe gleichen Namens in Bulgarien.

4.3. Fremdbezeichnungen

Bei der seßhaften Bevölkerung waren für die Roma von alters her verschiedene Namen geläufig: auf dem Balkan und in Osteuropa sind die zu griech. Ἀθίγγανος/Τσιγγάνος zu stellenden Bezeichnungen wie slav. *cigan(in)*, rumän. *țigan*, dann auch deutsch *Zigeuner* usw. verbreitet. Die Herkunft des Wortes wird in dem Namen der in Phrygien beheimateten religiösen Sekte der *Athinganoi* vermutet. Zwar gibt es keinen Anhaltspunkt dafür, daß die Sekte zu dem Zeitpunkt des Eintreffens der Roma in Byzanz noch existierte, doch rechnet man damit, daß die bei der Bevölkerung noch vorhandene Kenntnis ihrer rituellen und magischen Praktiken zu einer Übertragung des Namens auf die neu eingetroffenen Roma geführt hat, da diese ähnliche Kulthandlungen praktizierten (Miklosich IV, 1874, 62; Starr 1936, 103; Soulis 1961, 146). Weite Verbreitung haben die nach der vermeintlichen (oder vorgeblichen) Herkunft der Roma aus *Ägypten* geprägten Bezeichnungen wie griech. Γύφτος (<Αἰγύπτιος) (vgl. Georgakas 1942), ital. *gitano*, engl. *gypsy* u. a. gefunden. In ähnlicher Weise wurden die Roma in den ersten urkundlichen Erwähnungen in Mitteleuropa nach den Ländern ihrer vermuteten oder ihrer unmittelbaren Herkunft mit den Namen *Tataren* (in Skandinavien bis heute gebräuchlich), *Sarazenen*, *Äthioper*, *Böhmen* (in Frankreich), *Hunnen* u. a. belegt.

Das ursprünglich als Ethnikon verwendete Wort *Zigeuner* hat unter dem Eindruck der Nicht-Seßhaftigkeit der Roma verschiedene Bedeutungswandel erfahren: einmal ist es zu einem Synonym für „Landstreicher", „Herumtreiber" u. ä. geworden, daneben ist es als Begriff für Nomaden unabhängig von der ethnischen Zugehörigkeit generalisiert worden. Als Reaktion auf die häufig mit dem Begriff verbundenen pejorativen Konnotationen sind die rezenten Versuche zu verstehen, das Wort *Zigeuner* und entsprechende Fremdbezeichnungen durch die Eigenbezeichnung *Rom(a)*" zu ersetzen. Dabei werden in den jeweiligen Kontaktsprachen unterschiedliche Adaptationspraktiken verwendet, die in jedem Fall die komplizierten Regelungen des Romani (s. 4.1) negligieren, indem das Wort *rom* bzw. die Pluralform *roma* undifferenziert nach Geschlecht und Alter des Bezeichneten verwendet werden.

Der Name *Zigeuner*, der in Deutschland bis in die 70er Jahre in den Bezeichnungen von Sinte/Roma-Verbänden gebräuchlich war, wird heute vehement abgelehnt; statt dessen wird *Sinte und Roma* verwendet, womit auch eine Abgrenzung zwischen den seit Jahrhunderten in Mitteleuropa lebenden Zigeunern mit der in-group-Bezeichnung *Sinte*, und anderen, seit dem vorigen Jahrhundert eingewanderten Gruppen sprachlich zementiert wird. Die Sprachregelungen haben bislang noch die größten Erfolge im Behördendeutsch gezeigt, wo sie durch administrative Maßnahmen durchsetzbar sind. In inoffiziellen Diskursen der Roma regelt sich die Distribution von *Sinte/Roma* vs. *Zigeuner* gewöhnlich danach, ob Romani oder Deutsch gesprochen wird. In Südosteuropa scheinen insgesamt weniger Bedenken gegenüber den Bezeichnungen *ciganin* etc. zu bestehen, allerdings zeichnen sich auch hier Tendenzen zur Verallgemeinerung von *Roma* für *in-group* wie *out-group* Kontexte ab. In Griechenland wiederum ist, sowohl bei den Roma selbst als auch bei den Griechen, die Bezeichnung τσιγγάνος mit eher positiven Konnotationen verbunden gegenüber dem als abwertend empfundenen γύφτος, welches allerdings bei sprachlich assimilierten Gruppen als *in-group* Bezeichnung fungiert.

4.4. Zigeuner und Romani-Dialekte

Die ethnische Zugehörigkeit der Zigeuner ist kaum in Termini der genetischen Abstammung determinierbar, da die jahrhundertelange Koexistenz mit anderen Völkern immer wieder zu Mischungen geführt hat. Da im Ergebnis von Sprachwechsel (vgl. 5) nicht alle Zigeuner Europas einen auf das Indische zurückführbaren Romani-Dialekt als Muttersprache sprechen (und daher auch den ingroup Namen *Roma* nicht kennen), kann auch die Sprache nicht als entscheidendes Kriterium zur Bestimmung der Ethnizität fungieren. Die Anzahl der Sprecher von Romani-Dialekten ist nicht identisch mit der Zahl der Zigeuner.

Die Gruppen, bei denen die Tradierung des Romani als Muttersprache bis heute intakt ist, sprechen zahlreiche Dialekte oder Varianten, die sich bei allen divergenten Entwicklungen auf eine bis zum Eintreffen in Europa relativ homogene Sprachform zurückführen lassen.

Nicht zu den muttersprachlich tradierten Dialekten gehören die „Mischdialekte", auch „Para-Romani" genannt (vgl. Bakker/Cortiade 1991), deren Lexikon zwar zum Großteil aus dem Romani stammt, die aber im übrigen die voreuropäischen Strukturen aufgegeben und durch die Grammatik der jeweiligen Kontaktsprache ersetzt haben. Solche Dialekte sind wiederholt unter dem Einfluß typologisch unterschiedlicher Sprachen entstanden: am besten dokumentiert sind das *Angloromani* mit englischer, *Caló* mit spanischer, das *Lomavren* mit armenischer Grammatik; weiter das *Basque-Romani* aus Romani-Lexikon mit baskischer, das *Norwegische* mit norwegischer Grammatik u. a. Die Mischdialekte sind ihrer Funktion nach Gruppen- oder Sondersprachen vergleichbar; der wichtigste Unterschied zu diesen besteht in der durch die ethnische Zugehörigkeit der Sprecher (oder eines Teils der Sprecher) determinierten Herkunft des lexikalischen Bestandes. Die Genese der Mischdialekte — die im folgenden nicht berücksichtigt werden — kann nicht als abschließend geklärt gelten.

Aufgrund sprachlicher Zusammenhänge wird eine historische Verwandtschaft zwischen den europäischen Roma und Gruppen in Kleinasien postuliert. Die Gegenüberstellung des Romani mit den Dialekten der armenischen (Gruppenname: *Boša*; Dialektbezeichnung: *Lomavren*) und der syrischen Zigeuner (Gruppenname: *Nawar/Nuri*; Dialektbezeichnung: *Domari*) hat zu einer Dreiteilung in „Lom", „Dom" und „Rom" geführt, nach dem Reflex des indischen Zerebrallauts *ḍ* als *l* im Dialekt der armenischen, *d* im Dialekt der syrischen Zigeuner bzw. *r* in den europäischen Zigeunerdialekten. Nach dem Reflex der Mediae Aspiratae als Tenuis Aspiratae im Lomavren und Romani und einfacher Mediae im Dialekt der Nuri unterscheidet man (nach dem Wort für „Schwester") die *Phen-* und *Ben-* Gruppe (Sampson 1923). Für die europäischen Dialekte wird nach einem Vorschlag von Gilliat-Smith (1915/16) bis heute oft mit einer Zweigliederung in „Vlach-" und „Nicht-Vlach-Dialekte" gerechnet, wobei unter Vlach-Dialekten diejenigen verstanden werden, die während der Jahrhunderte der Leibeigenschaft in den Donaufürstentümern durch das Rumänische beeinflußt wurden und während dieser Zeit gemeinsame Entwicklungen durchgemacht haben. Unter den Nicht-Vlach-Dialekten werden dann sehr heterogene Varianten wie mitteleuropäische Sinte-Dialekte und südbalkanische Dialekte zusammengefaßt. Trotz vieler Unzulänglichkeiten hat sich diese Zweiteilung, besonders im Hinblick auf diachrone Zusammenhänge, bewährt. Darüber hinaus sind viele detailliertere Gliederungen vorgeschlagen worden. So hat schon Miklosich (1872—82) mit 13 Dialekten gerechnet — völlig verfehlt, wie man heute weiß. Alle bisherigen Gliederungsversuche kranken zum einen an theoretischen und terminologischen Insuffizienzen, vor allem aber an der mangelnden Dokumentation von Einzeldialekten. Wenn Münzel (1981, 24) das „Dilemma beim Durcheinander der Stammesnamen und -abgrenzungen" dahingehend resümiert, daß „200 Jahre Zigeunerforschung (...) keine Ordnung in die Stämme haben bringen können", so gilt eben dies auch für die Dialekte. Eine Gliederung der in Europa beheimateten Zigeunergruppen und ihrer Dialekte, ohnehin kompliziert durch die große Anzahl von Stammes- und Sippenbezeichnungen, von ingroup und out-group Namen, wird durch unterschiedliche, oft nicht spezifizierte Referenzkonventionen in der Literatur zusätzlich erschwert.

5. Soziolinguistische Lage des Romani

Da die Roma als Minderheit(en) in allen über den Familienkontext hinausgehenden sozialen Bereichen auf den Umgang mit der Majoritätsbevölkerung angewiesen sind, sind sie in der Regel zwei- oder mehrsprachig; der Gebrauch des Romani ist auf die Gruppe/Familie beschränkt. Als Sprache ohne Schrifttradition genießt das Romani bei den Völkern, unter denen die Zigeuner leben, nur geringes

Prestige, was oft in pejorativen Äußerungen von Romani-Sprechern über ihre Muttersprache reflektiert wird.

Zahlreiche Gruppen von Zigeunern haben in der Vergangenheit die Sprache gewechselt, ohne darüber das Bewußtsein ihrer ethnischen Zugehörigkeit verloren zu haben. Nicht nur in Rumänien, auch in Bulgarien, Griechenland, Serbien und Ungarn leben heute Zigeuner, die Rumänisch als Muttersprache sprechen; der einzige linguistische Hinweis auf die aufgegebene Sprache ist das Wort *cigan* in der Bedeutung „Mann/Ehemann" (vgl. 4.4). Die zweite Sprache, die von Zigeunergruppen in Südosteuropa als Primärsprache gebraucht wird, ist das Türkische (Gruppen in Rumänien, Bulgarien, Makedonien, Griechenland). Außerdem gibt es überall Zigeuner, die das Romani zugunsten der Sprache der staatstragenden Völker aufgegeben haben – so sprechen in Ungarn etwa siebzig Prozent der Zigeuner Ungarisch, zehn Prozent Rumänisch und nur zwanzig Prozent verschiedene Romani-Dialekte als Muttersprache.

Wo die muttersprachliche Tradierung des Romani intakt ist, ist die Sprache auch ein wichtiger gruppenstabilisierender und identitätsstiftender Faktor; die zahlreichen Fälle von Sprachwechsel, die nicht an Integration oder gar Assimilation gekoppelt sind, zeigen, daß das Romani nicht das alleinige Konstitutiv der Roma-Ethnizität ist.

6. Sprachpolitische Entwicklungen

Der Anteil der Analphabeten unter den Zigeunern liegt in allen Ländern Europas weit über dem der Majoritätsbevölkerung. Die Alphabetisierung der Roma findet überall in der Sprache der Majoritätsbevölkerung statt; erst seit Mitte der achtziger Jahre wird Romani in einigen Ländern als Wahlfach an staatlichen Schulen unterrichtet (Schweden, Ungarn, Kosovo). Seit dem politischen Wandel in Osteuropa sind die sprachpolitischen Forderungen der Roma-Organisationen – Schulunterricht in der Staatssprache und Romani – verstärkt ins Blickfeld der Behörden und der Öffentlichkeit gerückt. Die internen sprachpolitischen Auseinandersetzungen der Roma-Organisationen sind von den Fragen im Zusammenhang mit der Schaffung einer literarischen Standardform bestimmt: die Diskussion bewegt sich um linguistische Fragen, zu deren Klärung zunächst Einheit über das Geltungsgebiet einer zu schaffenden Norm (regional beschränkt oder Ausgleichsnorm für Dialekte innerhalb von Staatsgrenzen, über Staatsgrenzen hinweg) zu erzielen ist. Hier gibt es, in theoretischer wie praktischer Hinsicht, eine Vielzahl sehr unterschiedlicher, oftmals kontroverser Ansätze, deren Koordination in der jüngsten Zeit allenthalben in überregionalen Gremien zur Debatte steht.

7. Das Romani und die Kontaktsprachen

7.1. Skizze der Romani-Dialekte

Die Mehrzahl der Unterschiede zwischen den europäischen Romani-Dialekten läßt sich auf divergente Entwicklungen, die erst im europäischen Raum eingesetzt haben, zurückführen; darunter handelt es sich bei einem Großteil um einzeldialektalen, kontaktsprachlich induzierten Wandel. Das allen Dialekten gemeinsame Lexikon setzt sich zusammen aus indischem Wortgut, sowie einer persischen, armenischen, griechischen und – in geringerem Umfang – slawischen Lehnwortschicht. Das voreuropäische Lexikon besteht, den Bestand aller Dialekte zusammengerechnet, aus maximal 600 Wörtern (Wurzeln), die einzeldialektal unterschiedlich gut erhalten sind. Lehnwörter aus den verschiedenen europäischen Kontaktsprachen gehören zum festen, muttersprachlich tradierten Bestandteil der einzelnen Dialekte.

Der Grundstock an grammatischen Kategorien des Romani ist dialektal durch Verluste und/oder Innovationen verändert. Die Symbolisierung der grammatischen Funktionen erfolgt mit Hilfe flektierender und agglutinierender Mittel. Auf dem Hintergrund des Maximalbestandes der europäischen Romanidialekte läßt sich das Kategoriengefüge wie folgt ansetzen:

Im Nominalbereich sind Genus durch Maskulin und Feminin, Numerus durch Singular und Plural sowie Kasus durch Nominativ, Akkusativ (Obliquus), Vokativ, Dativ, Lokativ, Instrumental, Ablativ und Genitiv vertreten. Definitheit wird durch einen präponierten Artikel (mask. *o*, fem. *eli*) ausgedrückt, als indefiniter Artikel fungiert das Numerale *(j)ekh* „eins".

Im Nominativ, Akkusativ und Vokativ haben Kasus und Numerus kombiniert symbolisierte Endungen, vgl. nom. sg. *phral* „Bruder", *phen* „Schwester" – akk. sg. *phrales*, *phenja* – akk. pl. *phralen*, *phenen* – vok. sg.

phrala!, *phene!* Die sogenannten „sekundären" Kasus — Dativ, Lokativ, Ablativ, Instrumental und der possessive Genitiv — haben für Singular und Plural die gleichen Suffixe (mit morphophonologischen Alternationen). Diese treten an die Akkusativausgänge, vgl. (jeweils sg. u. pl.): dat. *phrales-ke/phralen-ge, phenja-ke/phenen-ge*; lok. *phrales-te/phralen-de, phenja-te/phenen-de*; abl. *phrales-tar/phralen-dar, phenja-tar/phenen-dar*; instr. *phrale(s)-sa/phralen-ca, phenja-sa/phenen-ca*; gen. *phrales-ko/phralen-go, phenja-ko/phenen-go*. Diese durch die Agglutination von Postpositionen entstandenen Kasusmarker treten z. T. auch als Präpositionen auf, vgl. abl. *phrales-tar* vs. *tar o phral*. Dialektale Abweichungen betreffen vor allem den Ersatz der durch Suffigierung gebildeten Kasus durch Präpositionalphrasen, vgl. instr. *e phralesa* „mit dem Bruder", abl. *e phralestar* „von dem Bruder" vs. *met u phral* und *fon u phral* in Sinte-Dialekten mit aus dem Deutschen entlehnten Präpositionen für „mit" und „von". Gemeinsam ist den Dialekten die Belebtheitskategorie, die durch morphosyntaktische Mittel ausgedrückt wird: Das direkte Objekt steht bei Belebten im Akkusativ, bei Unbelebten im Nominativ. Die Unbelebten verwenden die Obliquusmarkierung als Basis für die „sekundären" Kasus, vgl. *phral* — akk. *phrales* — dat. *phrales-ke* gegen *vast* „Hand" (Nominativ und Kasus des direkten Objektes) — dat. *vastes-ke*.

Im Verbalbereich finden sich neben Person (1—3) und Numerus (Singular, Plural), das Tempus mit den Kategorialgliedern Präsens, Präteritum sowie — allerdings nicht allgemein erhalten — Imperfekt und Plusquamperfekt, außerdem ein Futur mit dialektal unterschiedlichen, oft periphrastischen Ausdrücken. Das Genus Verbi setzt sich aus synthetisch gebildeten Gliedern Aktiv und Medio-Passiv zusammen; konkurrierend zum Medio-Passiv haben viele Dialekte einen periphrastischen Ausdruck aus Aktiv und Reflexivpronomen. Der Modus wird durch Indikativ und Imperativ sowie einen periphrastischen Konjunktiv aus der Partikel *te* + Indikativ repräsentiert. Beim Konditional sind die dialektalen Abweichungen beachtlich, gewöhnlich wird das Imperfekt zu seinem Ausdruck verwendet. An infiniten Verbformen sind zu nennen das passivische Partizip und, nur dialektal noch produktiv, das Gerundium. Auffällig ist der allgemeine Verlust des Infinitivs, der wie die Futurbildung mit einer aus dem Verb „wünschen, wollen" verkürzten Partikel (s. 7.2.4), die periphrastische Komparativbildung (s. 7.2.3) und die Ausbildung eines definiten Artikels in Zusammenhang mit dem Griechischen bzw. den Balkansprachen gebracht wird. Bei der in mittel- und osteuropäischen Romani-Dialekten anzutreffenden Verwendung der 3. Person Singular (seltener der 2. Singular oder der 3. Plural) mit der Konjunktivpartikel *te* in Infinitivfunktion dürfte es sich um eine jüngere Entwicklung handeln.

Beim Verb sind Person und Numerus kombiniert symbolisiert, wobei es zwei Reihen von Ausgängen für Präsens und Präteritum gibt, vgl. für „machen": präs. *ker-av, -es, -el, -as, -en, -en*, prät. *ker-d-em/ker-d-jom, -an, -as, -am, -en, -e*. Imperfekt und Plusquamperfekt werden u. a. in Vlach-Dialekten durch Anfügen von *-as* (< *sas* „war" 3. Sg.), im makedonischen Arli durch *-sine* („war") an Präs. und Prät. gebildet, vgl. für die 1. Sg.: *kerav/kerava* „ich mache" → Imperf. *kerav-as/kerava-sine*; Prät. *kerdem/kerdjom* → Plqpf. *kerdem-as/kerdjom-sine*.

7.2. Interferenzen

Das Romani ist vermutlich immer eine *dominierte* Sprache gewesen; sein Verhältnis zu den jeweiligen Kontaktsprachen war und ist nie bilateral, sondern stets asymmetrisch. Als „Gebersprache" tritt das Romani nur durch die lexikalische Beeinflussung von Sondersprachen und Argots auf. Demgegenüber umfaßt der Einfluß auf das Romani auch Phonetik, Morphologie und Syntax; aus der Phänomenologie der kontakt-induzierten Sprachwandelprozesse werden im Folgenden nur solche, die einen größeren dialektalen Verbreitungsgrad haben oder die einen beträchtlichen Einfluß auf ererbte Strukturen ausgeübt haben, ausgewählt.

7.2.1. Lexikalische Entlehnungen, Lehnübersetzungen

Der Bilinguismus der Romani-Sprecher führt dazu, daß zum lexikalischen Ausbau der Dialekte in erster Linie auf Entlehnungen aus den Kontaktsprachen zurückgegriffen wird und die vorhandenen Möglichkeiten der Wortbildung ungenutzt bleiben. Lexikalische Entlehnung ist nicht grundsätzlich gleichzusetzen mit Erweiterung des muttersprachlich tradierten Wortschatzes, da Lehnwörter aus der aktuellen oft solche aus ehemaligen Kontaktsprachen ersetzen; in geringerem Umfang führt sie auch zum Abbau von Lexemen aus dem gemeinsamen (voreuropäischen) Wort-bestand. Der hohe Anteil rezenter Lehnwörter in Romani-Diskursen und die Fähigkeit der Sprecher, mühelos von einer Sprache zur anderen zu wechseln, führt nicht zu einem permanenten code-switching, da Lehnwörter nach einem festen Adaptationsmechanismus integriert werden (vgl. Boretzky 1989), welcher in der frühen Kontaktphase Romani-Griechisch, d. h. vor dem endgültigen Auseinanderbrechen in Einzeldialekte, entstanden ist. Durch Unterschiede in der Betonung sowie in den Ausgängen (s. 7.2.3) sind voreuropäische Lexeme grundsätzlich von späteren Entlehnungen abgrenzbar; dialektal ist diese Unterscheidung durch Akzentverschiebungen teilweise aufgehoben. Bei aus der aktuellen Kontaktsprache stammenden Lexemen ist kaum zu entscheiden, ob es sich um ad-hoc Entlehnungen oder um ein muttersprachlich erlerntes Wort handelt.

Der Lexemtransfer wird durch Lehnübersetzung und Lehnübertragung ergänzt, wobei die einzelnen Dialekte in unterschiedlichem Maß Gebrauch von diesen Mitteln machen. Die deutschen Sinte-Dialekte z. B. haben Verfahren für die Übersetzung deutscher präfigierter Verben entwickelt, wobei es von der semantischen Transparenz abhängt, ob die deutschen Komposita als ganzes entlehnt oder analysiert und übersetzt werden, vgl. *ruferau an* und *karau an* (*kar-* „rufen") „ich rufe an" vs. *čhinau tele* (*čhin-* „schneiden") „ich schneide ab" und *asau vi* (*as-* „lachen") „ich lache aus" mit den ursprünglichen Adverbien *tele* „unten" und *vi* „draußen" als standardisierter Übersetzung für deutsch „ab-" und „aus-".

7.2.2. Phonetik

Die Divergenzen in den Lautsystemen der Romani-Dialekte lassen sich durchweg als Ergebnis der Annäherung an die Systeme der Kontaktsprachen deuten. Der kontaktsprachliche Einfluß betrifft vor allem die phonetische Realisierung: mit Lehnwörtern entlehnte Phoneme bleiben meist auf diese beschränkt. Für direkten Phonemtransfer mit Ausweitung der Distribution auf Erbwörter gibt es insgesamt nur wenige Beispiele. So kommen z. B. in Vlach-Dialekten die zentralisierten Vokale [ɪ] und [ə] des Rumänischen nicht nur in entlehnten Lexemen, sondern auch in Erbwörtern vor (Boretzky 1991); mitteleuropäische Romani-Dialekte haben zu dem Fünfvokalsystem /a e i o u/ sekundär eine Quantitätenopposition entwickelt.

Das Konsonantensystem der Romani-Dialekte unterscheidet sich von den europäischen Sprachen durch die Bewahrung der Opposition von Aspirierten und Nicht-Aspirierten (*p:ph, k:kh, t:th* sowie *č:čh*), welche trotz geringer funktionaler Belastung nur in minimalem Umfang beeinträchtigt ist. Als Beispiel der phonetischen Angleichung des Konsonantensystems seien die unterschiedlichen Ergebnisse der Velarenpalatalisierung in Untermundarten des Gurbet genannt: *k d* sind in Serbien zu *ć dź*, im Kosovo zu *č dž* und in Makedonien zu *kj gj* geworden; nur die unter dialektal albanischem Einfluß (Kosovo) eingetretene Entwicklung hat auch zu Veränderungen der Phonemdistribution geführt: *č dž* < *k g* sind vor vorderen Vokalen mit alten *č dž* zusammengefallen, so daß *k:č, dž:g* in dieser Position komplementär verteilt sind.

7.2.3. Morphementlehnung

Von den Morphemen, die in den Romani-Dialekten zur Lehnwortadaptation verwendet werden, stammen die meisten aus dem Griechischen; z. T. ist mit einer Überlagerung von griechischem und slawischem oder rumänischem Einfluß zu rechnen. Die ältesten Lehnwörter, die die hier zu besprechenden Adaptationsmorpheme aufweisen, sind in allen Dialekten Gräzismen; in der Folge sind die Ausgänge bei Lehnwörtern aus den späteren Kontaktsprachen verallgemeinert worden. Maskuline Lehnwörter enden auf unbetontes *-os/-o* und/oder *-is/-i* (gegen betontes *-ó* oder *-K[ons]* bei voreuropäischen Lexemen). Die *s*-haltigen Ausgänge sind unschwer auf griechische Maskulina auf *-os* und *-is* zurückzuführen, bei *-o/-i* ist mit Herkunft aus griechischen Neutra auf *-o* und *-i* zu rechnen; für Dialekte mit Schwund von *-s* kommt auch *-o -i* < *-os -is* in Betracht. Manche Dialekte weisen beide Endungstypen auf, in anderen haben sich entweder die *s*-haltigen oder *s*-losen Ausgänge durchgesetzt, bei Gräzismen unabhängig vom Wortausgang in der Herkunftssprache, vgl. *kokalos* < κόκαλο im rumänischen Ursaritischen gegen *kokalo* im Kalderaš-Dialekt. Die Pluralausgänge weisen dialektal größere Vielfalt auf: man findet *-ida* im bulgarischen Drindari, *-urja* im Kalderaš, *-o(v)ja* im Sofioter Erli, worin jeweils Verbindungen aus griech. -ίδες, rumän. -*uri* bzw. slaw. -*ove* mit dem Romani-Pluralmorphem *-a* zu erkennen sind. Das Pluralmorphem *-i* zu Maskulina auf *-os/-o* in mitteleuropäischen Dialekten kann auf griech. -οι [i] oder — da die entsprechenden Dialekte auch starke slawische Einflüsse aufweisen — auf die slawische Pluralendung -i zurückgeführt werden. Als Feminina adaptierte Lehnwörter gehen auf unbetontes -a aus, für das außer dem Griechischen auch Slawisch und Rumänisch als Herkunftssprachen in Betracht kommen. Das entsprechende Pluralzeichen ist einzeldialektal -es, zweifellos aus dem Griechischen stammend, oder -e; letzteres entweder durch s-Schwund < -es oder rumänischer bzw. südslawischer (serbischer/kroatischer) Herkunft.

Auch Verben werden mit Hilfe griechischer Verbalmorpheme entlehnt, an die die Romani-Personalendungen treten (z. T. unter Einfügung der indigenen Transitiv/Intransitivmorpheme -ar- und -av-). In Südosteuropa sind drei Typen vertreten: Vlach-Dialekte verwenden -V[oc]s-ar- (-isar- osar-), das auf den sigmatischen Aoriststamm griechischer Verben zurückgeht; im bulgarischen und makedonischen Raum ist -Vz- (-iz-, -oz-) mehrfach belegbar (aus griech. Verben auf -ίζω); weiterhin -Vn- (-in-, -on-) aus griechischen Verben auf [ino] (-ίνω, -ύνω, -είνω) und [ono] (-ώνω), das auch in slovakischen, südpolnischen und z. T. in Sinte-Dialekten vertreten ist. Schon bei griechischen Etyma sind die Adaptationsmorpheme unabhängig von der Form des Verbs in der Herkunftssprache generalisiert worden, vgl. die Varianten kun-iz-el — kun-in-el — kun-is-ar-el < κουνῶ (aor. κούνισα) „schaukeln" und ir-iz-el — ir-in-el — (j)ir-is-ar-el < griech. γυρίζω (aor. γύρισα); aus anderen Sprachen entlehnte Verben wurden später nach den dialektal etablierten Mustern adaptiert, vgl. škur-iz-av — škur-in-av — škur-is-ar-av < alb. shkruan „schreiben", misl-iz-av — misl-in-av — misl-is-ar-av < slaw. misliti „denken". Nicht geklärt ist, ob die scharf abgegrenzte Distribution der Adaptationsmorpheme das Ergebnis späterer („nach-griechischer"), einzeldialektaler Verallgemeinerungen ist, oder ob sie auf den Beginn der dialektalen Zersplitterung des Romani in der Kontaktphase Romani-Griechisch deutet.

Die übrigen Beispiele für die Entlehnung gebundener grammatischer Morpheme stammen überwiegend aus der Wortbildung. Entlehnungen aus dem Griechischen mit übereinzeldialektaler Verbreitung sind das Partizipmorphem -me(n) (< -μένος), -to zur Bildung von Ordinal- aus Kardinalzahlen, sowie das Adjektivsuffix -(i)tiko/ -itko/ -tko/ -icko (dialektale Varianten) aus -ίτικο. Diminutivsuffixe, Suffixe zur Bildung von Verbalnomina und Abstrakta sowie Nomina Agentis sind aus verschiedenen Sprachen entlehnt worden. Als historische Faustregel, von der synchron allerdings zahlreiche Abweichungen zu verzeichnen sind, gilt, daß sich ererbte (voreuropäische) Morpheme mit ererbten Lexemen, entlehnte Morpheme mit entlehnten Lexemen verbinden: vgl. für das Kalderaš javi-mos „Benachrichtigung" (zu serb. javiti „benachrichtigen" mit -mos < griech. -ιμο/ -μος) gegen pi-pel pi-mos „Trinken, Getränk" (romani pi- „trinken"); einmal mit dem Suffix -(i)pe < altind. -tvana, dann mit entlehntem -mos.

Ein vereinzeltes Beispiel für die Entlehnung von Flexionsmorphologie findet sich in slovenischen Sinte-Dialekten: hier werden im Präsensparadigma der Verben die Pluralendungen aus dem Slovenischen entlehnt: vgl. für die Kopula sja-mo „wir sind", sja-te „ihr seid", sja-jo „sie sind" gegen die weiter gebräuchlichen Formen sjam, sjan, si.

In den Romanidialekten Südosteuropas ist die alte Komparativbildung auf -eder weitestgehend durch periphrastische Ausdrücke mit entlehnten Steigerungspartikeln ersetzt worden: vgl. bar-eder „größer" vs. maj-baro/po-baro/daha-baro „dass.". Das aus dem Rumänischen stammende maj (mai) wird im Kalderaš und anderen rumänisch beeinflußten Dialekten verwendet; die slawische Komparativpartikel po findet man in makedonischen und bulgarischen Romanidialekten. Türkisch daha „noch", in der Herkunftssprache ein in Komparativkonstruktionen häufig zum Ausdruck der Emphase gebrauchtes Element, ist in Romani-Dialekten im Einflußbereich des Türkischen (regional in Makedonien, Kosovo, Bulgarien) als Komparativmarker interpretiert worden. Einen Hinweis auf die historische Übergangsstufe von dem synthetischen zum periphrastischen Ausdruck findet man in der Doppelmarkierung des Komparativs vom Typ maj-bar-eder.

In Varianten des Gurbet-Dialekts im Kosovo und in Makedonien wird mit der aus dem Albanischen entlehnten Partikel tuj (schriftsprachl. duke) und dem Präsens ein Gerundium gebildet, das funktional dem alten Gerundium auf -indos/-indoj entspricht und dieses weitgehend verdrängt hat: vgl. avel rovindos „er kommt weinend" vs. avel tuj rovol „idem".

Die Liste der Morphementlehnungen läßt sich bei Heranziehung regionaler Dialekte und Varianten um einiges erweitern: auf den Einzeldialekt bezogen bleibt der Transfer grammatischer Morpheme aber stets auf wenige Fälle beschränkt. Frequentiell bedeutender scheint die Nachbildung grammatischer Ausdrücke ohne direkten Morphemtranfer zu sein (s. 7.2.4).

7.2.4. Morphosyntax

Während in mitteleuropäischen Dialekten das einfache oder das um -*a* erweiterte Präsens mit futurischer Bedeutung verwendet werden kann, steht in Romani-Dialekten Südosteuropas die Partikel *ka(m)* oder *ma* + Präsens zum Ausdruck des Futurs. *ka* ist eine Verkürzung aus dem Verb *kamav* „wünschen, lieben", während *ma* eine Kurzform von *mangav* „wünschen, wollen" zu sein scheint; möglicherweise handelt es sich aber gleichfalls um eine Verkürzung aus *kamav* (mit Abfall der ersten Silbe). Diese Konstruktion entspricht dem Typus der balkanischen Kontaktsprachen, welche das Futur aus einer vom Verb „wollen" verkürzten Partikel und dem Präsens bilden. Der zweite auf dem Balkan verbreitete Typ ist das Futur mit „haben", welches ursprünglich debitiv-nezessitive Bedeutung hatte. Das Romani besitzt kein Verb für „haben"; Possession wird durch die 3.Person Singular + Akkusativ für den Besitzer ausgedrückt; vgl. *si man/si tut* „ich habe/du hast" (wörtl. „ist mich/dich"). Im Bulgarischen und Makedonischen sind wollen- und haben-Futur auf die bejahte und negierte Form des Verbs verteilt: in den Romani-Kontaktdialekten findet sich die gleiche Verteilung: vgl. *ka/ma džav* „ich werde gehen" (< „ich will gehen") — *naj ma te džav* „ich werde nicht gehen" (< „ich habe nicht zu gehen").

Unter dem Einfluß des Griechischen wird im Dialekt der Kalpazea in der Protasis irrealer Konditionalsätze das Imperfekt, in der Apodosis die Futurpartikel mit dem Imperfekt gebraucht: vgl. *te phenesas ... — ka avelas* und griech. άν έλεγες ... — θά ερχόταν „wenn du ... gesagt hättest — wäre er gekommen".

Die morphosyntaktischen Einflüsse sind in der Regel jeweils auf Einzeldialekte beschränkt. Sie sind weniger augenfällig als direkter Morphemtransfer und haben daher in Deskriptionen des Romani nur wenig Beachtung gefunden.

8. Zur Forschungslage

Die Roma-Forschung (auch: „Tsiganologie") kann bis heute eine fast unüberschaubare Anzahl von Veröffentlichungen aufweisen (s. die Bibliographien von Binns 1982, Black 1914, German 1930 und Hohmann 1992). Unter den Autoren linguistischer Publikationen rangieren seit dem vorigen Jahrhundert neben namhaften Sprachwissenschaftlern — Indogermanisten wie F.A. Pott und Franz Miklosich, Indologen wie Turner — auch zahlreiche Laien, deren Arbeiten teilweise bis heute für die Romani-Linguistik von hohem Wert sind, während andere bestenfalls nur mehr dokumentarischen Wert für die Geschichte der Diziplin haben. So haben viele Autoren in die Beschreibung bestimmter Einzeldialekte von ihren Vorgängern bei anderen Dialekten aufgezeichnetes Material eingearbeitet, ohne dies immer deutlich zu machen. Andere — auch jüngere — Arbeiten fallen dadurch unangenehm auf, daß sie unter dem Anspruch, eine vermeintliche „Standardform" zu erfassen, willkürliche Normierungen vornehmen, ohne daß die zugrundeliegenden Dialekte und/oder Dialektvarianten deskriptiv erfaßt wären. Aus der Vielzahl der Publikationen seien als beispielhaft die detaillierten Dialektbeschreibungen von Sampson (1926) und Gjerdman/Ljungberg (1963) zitiert.

Ein dringendes Desiderat der Romani-Linguistik liegt weiterhin auf der deskriptiven Ebene, besonders im Hinblick auf die Beschreibung von in ihrer Existenz bedrohten Dialekten, worunter solche Dialekte verstanden seien, die von der jüngeren Sprechergeneration nicht mehr weitertradiert werden.

9. Bibliographie (in Auswahl)

Bakker, Peter/Cortiade, Marcel (Eds.) (1991): *In the Margin of Romani. Gypsy Languages in Contact*, Amsterdam.

Binns, Dennis (1982): *Gypsy Bibliography*, Manchester.

Black, George F. (1914): *A Gypsy Bibliography*, London.

Boretzky, Norbert (1989): „Zum Interferenzverhalten des Romani". In: *Zeitschrift für Phonetik, Sprachwissenschaft und Kommunikationsforschung 42*, 357—374.

Boretzky, Norbert (1991): „Contact-induced sound change". In: *Diachronica 8, 1*, 1—15.

Boretzky, Norbert (1994): *Romani. Grammatik des Kalderaš-Dialekts mit Texten und Glossar* (= Osteuropa-Institut der Freien Universität Berlin. Balkanologische Veröffentlichungen. Band 24), Berlin, Wiesbaden.

German, A. B. (1930): *Bibliografija o Cyganach*, Moskau.

Georgakas, D. (1942): „Über das Ethnikon 'gyphtos'". In: *Glotta 29*, 156–161.

Gilliat-Smith, Bernard (1915–16): „Report on the Gypsy tribes of North-East Bulgaria". In: *Journal of the Gypsy Lore Society, N. S. 9, Teil 1:* 1–54; *Teil 2:* 65–109.

Gjerdman, Olof/Ljungberg, Erik (1963): *The Language of the Swedish Coppersmith Gipsy Johan Dimitri Taikon*, Falköping.

Grellmann, Heinrich M.S. (1783): *Historischer Versuch über die Zigeuner*, Göttingen.

Gronemeyer, Reimer/Rakelmann, Georgia A. (Eds.) (1988): *Die Zigeuner. Reisende in Europa*, Köln.

Hancock, Ian (1987): *The Pariah Syndrome. An Account of Gypsy Slavery and Persecution*, Ann Arbor.

Hancock, Ian (1988): „The Development of Romani Linguistics". In: *Languages and Cultures. Studies in Honor of Edgar C. Polomé*, Jazyeri, A./Winter, W. (Eds.), Den Haag.

Hohmann, Joachim S. (1992): *Neue deutsche Zigeunerbibliographie. Unter Berücksichtigung aller Jahrgänge des „Journal of the Gypsy Lore Society"*, Frankfurt a. Main/Berlin/Bern/New York/Paris/Wien.

Kenrick, Donald/Puxon, Grattan (1972): *The Destiny of Europe's Gypsies*, London.

Miklosich, Franz (1872–1882): „Über die Mundarten und die Wanderungen der Zigeuner Europas". Teil I – XII. In: *Denkschriften der philosophisch-historischen Classe der kaiserlichen Akademie der Wissenschaften* [Wien], 21–23, 25–27, 30–31.

Münzel, Mark (1981): „Zigeuner und Nation". In: *Kumpania und Kontrolle. Moderne Behinderungen zigeunerischen Lebens*, Münzel, M./Streck, B. (Eds.), Gießen.

Pott, August Friedrich (1844/45): *Die Zigeuner in Europa und Asien. Ethnographisch-linguistische Untersuchung vornehmlich ihrer Herkunft und Sprache.* Teil I u. II, Halle/Leipzig 1965[2].

Puxon, Grattan (1979): „Einhundert Jahre Nationalbewegung der Zigeuner". In: Zülch.

Rüdiger, Johann C.C. (1782): *Von der Sprache und Herkunft der Zigeuner aus Indien*, Göttingen (Nachdruck: Hamburg 1990).

Sampson, John (1923): „On the origin and the Early Migrations of the Gypsies". In: *Journal of the Gypsy Lore Society, 3rd S. 2*, 156–169.

Sampson, John (1926): *The Dialect of the Gypsies of Wales*, Oxford (1968[2]).

Soulis, George S. (1961): „The Gypsies in the Byzantine Empire and the Balkans in the Late Middle Ages". In: *Dumbarton Oaks Papers 15*, 144–165.

Starr, Joshua (1936): „An Eastern Christian Sect: The Athinganoi". In: *Harvard Theological Review 29, 2*, 93–106.

Turner R. (1926): „The Position of Romani in Indo-Aryan". In: *Journal of the Gypsy Lore Society*, 145–188.

Vossen, Rüdiger (1983): *Zigeuner. Roma, Sinti, Gitanos, Gypsies. Zwischen Romantisierung und Verfolgung. Katalog zur Ausstellung des Hamburgischen Museums für Völkerkunde*, Frankfurt.

Zülch, Tilman (Ed.) (1979): *In Auschwitz vergast – bis heute verfolgt. Zur Situation der Roma in Deutschland und Europa*, Reinbek.

Birgit Igla, Sofia (Bulgarien)

Sprachenkarten

Einleitende Bemerkungen

1. Die in der Folge präsentierten 16 Sprachenkarten enthalten vorwiegend *ethnolinguistisch* relevante Informationen. Dies bedeutet, daß vorrangig nur solche Idiome kartiert werden, die in den Augen ihrer Sprecher den Status von symbolisch und sozial distinkten Entitäten haben. Derartige „volkslinguistisch" relevante Klassifikationen können – wie man weiß – von jenen der Fachlinguistik gelegentlich differieren. Signifikativ für diesen Unterschied ist die Karte G (Ex-Jugoslawien), wo anstelle der nach 1991 sozial und sprachpolitisch obsolet gewordenen Sprache *Serbokroatisch* nunmehr die Sprachen *Kroatisch, Bosnisch* und *Serbisch* (gemeinsam mit ihren Sprechern – also den *Kroaten, „Muslimen", Serben* und *Montenegrinern*) vermerkt sind. Diese sprecherzentrierte Perspektive wird gelegentlich auch „emisch" genannt.

Besonderes Augenmerk wurde auf die Kartierung mehrsprachiger Situationen gelegt, ohne daß es dabei möglich gewesen wäre, die damit verbundenen vielfältigen Mischungs- und Koexistenzformen hinreichend genau darzustellen.

2. Die technische Herstellung der Karten erfolgte nach den Skizzen bzw. Angaben der Kartenautoren durch den Regensburger Kartographen Herbert Kneidl, wobei der für Kartenproduktion zuständige Herausgeber um die weitestgehende inhaltlich-thematische und kartographisch-technische Vereinheitlichung aller 16 Karten bemüht war. Die Herausgeber sind Herrn Kneidl für seine kompetente und geduldige Arbeit zu besonderem Dank verpflichtet.

In kartentechnischer Hinsicht wurden Flächenfarben, Schraffuren und Punktraster verwendet, oft in Kombination, um örtliche Mehrsprachigkeiten zu markieren. Die Kartierung erfolgte meist absolut; auf die differenzierte Darstellung *örtlicher* (bzw. *regionaler*) Sprachmischungsverhältnisse mußte verzichtet werden.

3. Spezielle Probleme ergeben sich bei der Darstellung der mehrsprachigen Topo- und Choronymik. Um den Intentionen dieses dem Kontakt von Sprachen gewidmeten Handbuchs weitestgehend zu entsprechen, wurde folgende Lösung gewählt: prinzipiell werden *innerhalb* des Titularstaates einer Karte die Ortsnamen (Toponyme) und Länder- bzw. Landschaftsnamen (Choronyme) in ihrer *endonymen* Form angegeben. Dabei wird freilich vorausgesetzt, daß der betreffende Staat nur *eine* dominante Hauptsprache besitzt.

Neben diesen Endonymen werden fallweise zusätzlich vermerkt:

1) in Klammern: Namen in der Sprache einer heute oder in unmittelbarer Vergangenheit dort lebenden Minderheit,
2) nach Schrägstrich: kooffizielle Namen in der Sprache einer autochthonen Minderheit nach heutiger Rechtslage.

Beispiel: So findet man auf der Karte N (Österreich) neben den deutschen Namen der Städte *Villach* und *Klagenfurt* (die beide für die slowenische Minderheit Kärntens von großer Bedeutung sind) in Klammern die slowenischen Namensformen *Beljak* und *Celovec*. Dagegen ist die östlich von *Klagenfurt (Celovec)* liegende Stadt *Bleiburg* in der Form *Bleiburg/Pliberk* eingetragen, weil das Slowenische ebendort einen besonderen

Rechtsstatus hat. Ähnliches gilt z. B. für die amtliche Zweinamigkeit in Südtirol (siehe dazu die Karte F−Italien, aber auch die Karten N−Österreich oder O−Schweiz).

Außerhalb des Gebietes des Titularstaates einer Karte werden ebenso die jeweiligen *Endonyme* verwendet. Doch werden diesen Endonymen fallweise noch Exonyme aus der Sprache des betreffenden Titularstaates in Klammern beigegeben, sofern diese Exonyme heute noch gebräuchlich sind.

Beispiel: Auf der Karte M (Deutschland) findet man in Dänemark unter dem dänischen Endonym *København* das deutsche Exonym *Kopenhagen* oder in Belgien (Wallonien) unter dem französischen Endonym *Liège* das deutsche Exonym *Lüttich*. Das niederländische Exonym *Luik* findet man dagegen auf der Karte C (Benelux).

Allerdings ist es schwierig, dieses Prinzip durchgängig auch dann anzuwenden, wenn es sich um Karten mit mehreren Titularstaaten bzw. -sprachen handelt, wie dies für die Karten A (Skandinavien), C (Benelux), E (Spanien und Portugal), G (Ex-Jugoslawien und Albanien), H (Rumänien und Bulgarien), I (Griechenland und europäische Türkei), K (Tschechien und Slowakei), O (Schweiz, mit vier Nationalsprachen) und P (westlicher Teil des europäischen Rußland) zutrifft. In diesen Fällen werden zur Unterscheidung der mehrfachen Namengebung *verschiedene Schriftarten* bzw. *hochgestellte Zahlen* eingesetzt, die der Numerierung der Sprachen in der Kartenlegende entsprechen.

Die extensive Berücksichtigung der *standpunktbezogenen Exonymie* schien gerade aus der Perspektive der *Kontakt*linguistik besonders angebracht zu sein.

4. Die Redaktion einiger Karten stellte die Kartenautoren vor besondere Herausforderungen, da die benutzbaren Quellen ungenau, widersprüchlich und fallweise überhaupt inexistent waren. Zudem entstand manchmal der Eindruck, daß es inopportun sei, ethno- und kontaktlinguistische Sachverhalte kartographisch festzuhalten: dies betraf vor allem die Karte I (Griechenland).

Für zahlreiche Ratschläge und Hinweise danken die Herausgeber den Herren Emanuele Banfi (Trient, Italien), Hermann Bieder (Salzburg), Josef Breu (Wien), Walter Breu (Konstanz), Wolfgang Dahmen (Jena), Panayote Dimitras (Kifisia, Griechenland), Peter Hill (Canberra, Australien), Peter Jordan (Wien), Klaus Kreiser (Bamberg), Max Demeter Peyfuss (Wien), Hans-Jürgen Sasse (Köln) und Ulrich Theissen (Salzburg).

5. Hinsichtlich der benützten Fachliteratur sei auf die anschließende Bibliographie verwiesen. *Allgemeine* und *kartographiespezifische Informationen* zum Thema „Sprachen- und Völkerkarten" findet man bei Arnberger 1966, Dörflinger 1990, Eckert 1925, Fischer 1991, Hassinger 1941, Krallert 1961, im Lexikon von Kretschmer/Dörflinger/Wawrik 1986, bei Meynen 1938, Ormeling 1983 und Peeters/Williams 1993. *Exemplarische Kartenrealisierungen* liegen in Breu 1989, Jordan 1992, Jordan/Schappelwein 1993 und in den Atlanten von Magocsi 1993 sowie Moseley/Asher 1994 vor. Zur *politischen Prekarietät* von Sprachen- und Völkerkarten geben Bonfante 1959, Dörflinger 1990, Fischer 1991, Krallert 1961, Meynen 1938, Staatswissenschaftliches Institut 1942 und Wilkinson 1951 Auskunft.

Linguistic Maps

Preliminaries

1. The following 16 linguistic maps are based principally on ethnolinguistic data, and therefore include mostly only those languages that, because of their symbolic and social status in the minds of their speakers, constitute autonomous linguistic entities. Such classifications made by speakers may of course differ from those of professional linguists. Map G (former Yugoslavia), for example, shows "Croatian," "Bosnian," and "Serbian" (and their respective speakers, i. e., *Croats, Muslims, Serbs*, and *Montenegrins*) rather than the linguistic entity "Serbo-Croatian" that has been socially and glottopolitically obsolete since 1991. Such a method of classification based on speakers' perceptions is frequently termed an "emic" perspective.

The authors and editors of the section on cartography have taken particular care to assure that the maps accurately depict multilingual contexts. Nonetheless, various limitations of a technical nature have prevented us from including certain details of the checkered landscape of language contact in Europe.

2. The technical production of these maps was overseen by the cartographer Herbert Kneidl (Regensburg). Map sketches furnished by the various authors were first thematically and formally standardized by the individual editors and then sent to Mr. Kneidl, whose competent work and painstaking efforts are gratefully acknowledged by the Handbook editors.

Multilingual situations are represented on the maps by means of different colors, hatching, and shading of varying intensity, often in combinations to indicate local multilingualism. Each language corresponds to a single color, with the result that complex *local* and *regional* multilingual situations could not always be depicted.

3. Certain problems arose in the toponymic and mapping procedures involving multilingual situations. In accord with the comparatist approach used in this Handbook on language contact, we have adopted the following principle: *within* the territory of the subject country of a given linguistic map, toponyms and mapping terms are represented in their *endonymic* form, which evidently assumes that the country represented on such a map has a single national language.

In addition to endonymic terms, the following are included:

1) in parentheses, names cited in local or regional minority languages in use currently or in the recent past;
2) following a slash, co-official names cited in local or regional minority languages in accordance with their current legal status.

Example: Map N (Austria) shows, in addition to the German toponyms *Villach* and *Klagenfurt* (both of which have certain social implications for the Slovene minority in Carinthia), the Slovene forms in parentheses *Beljak* and *Celovec*. On the other hand, the bilingual toponymy of the city of *Bleiburg/Pliberk* east of *Klagenfurt (Celovec)* is indicated by means of a slash between the German and Slovene names, reflecting the particular legal status of Slovene in that region. This procedure applies as well to, among others, the official bilingual toponymy of the Southern Tyrol (see Maps F−Italy, N−Austria, and O−Switzerland).

The same *endonymic method* applies as well to territories situated *outside of* a map's subject country. In this instance, endonymic terms are accompanied by the *exonym* in parentheses corresponding to the language of the subject country, whenever such an exonym is still in use.

Example: Map M (Germany) shows, in Denmark, the German exonym *Kopenhagen* below the Danish endonym *København*. The same procedure is used in the case of French-speaking Belgium (Wallonia), where the German exonym *Lüttich* is given below the French endonym *Liège*. Similarly, the Dutch exonym *Luik* is cited on Map C (Benelux).

There are obvious problems in the application of this procedure to maps representing two (or several) subject countries — and accordingly, languages — such as Maps A (Scandinavia), C (Benelux), E (Spain and Portugal), G (former Yugoslavia and Albania), H (Romania and Bulgaria), I (Greece and European Turkey), K (Czechia and Slovakia), O (Switzerland, with 4 national languages), and P (the western part of European Russia). In these instances, *different characters* and *superscript numbers* are employed, as explained in the map legends. Viewed overall, our approach involving a *relational exonymy* appears unquestionably to be in line with the comparatist and contrastive objectives of this Handbook of *contact* linguistics.

4. Some of the linguistic maps presented particular difficulties caused by incorrect, contradictory, or even inexistent empirical data. We were faced with serious reservations concerning the representation of certain current ethnic and ethnolinguistic situations, notably in the preparation of Map I (Greece and European Turkey).

We have received the advice and support of a number of international cartography specialists and wish to express to them our heartfelt gratitude. We would like especially to thank Emanuele Banfi (Trent, Italy), Hermann Bieder (Salzburg), Josef Breu (Vienna), Walter Breu (Constance), Wolfgang Dahmen (Jena), Panayote Dimitras (Kifisia, Greece), Peter Hill (Canberra, Australia), Peter Jordan (Vienna), Klaus Kreiser (Bamberg), Max Demeter Peyfuss (Vienna), Hans-Jürgen Sasse (Cologne), and Ulrich Theissen (Salzburg).

5. For specialized bibliography, see Paragraph 6. For *general* and *cartographic information*, see Arnberger 1966, Dörflinger 1990, Eckert 1925, Fischer 1991, Hassinger 1941, Krallert 1961, Kretschmer/Dörflinger/Wawrik (Lexicon) 1986, Meynen 1938, Ormeling 1983, and Peeters/Williams 1993. The following excellent *cartographic representations* may well serve as models: Breu 1989, Jordan 1992, Jordan/Schappelwein 1993, Magocsi 1993, and Moseley/Asher (Atlas) 1994. For the *political implications* of mapping languages and peoples, see Bonfante 1959, Dörflinger 1990, Fischer 1991, Krallert 1961, Meynen 1938, Staatswissenschaftliches Institut 1942, and Wilkinson 1951.

Cartes linguistiques

Remarques préliminaires

1. Les informations répertoriées dans les 16 cartes linguistiques ci-jointes sont avant tout d'ordre ethnolinguistique. Ceci signifie que − en règle générale − seuls ont été mis en carte des idiomes qui, aux yeux de leurs locuteurs et de leur point de vue symbolique et social, constituent des entités linguistiques autonomes. Il est bien connu que de telles classifications populaires peuvent diverger de celles des linguistes de métier. La carte G (relative à l'ex-Yougoslavie) en fournit un exemple significatif. C'est qu'à la place de l'entité linguistique «serbocroate» − devenue obsolète depuis 1991 du point de vue social et glottopolitique − y figurent désormais les trois langues «croate», «bosniaque» et «serbe» (avec, respectivement, leurs locuteurs, à savoir les *Croates*, les *Musulmans*, les *Serbes* et les *Monténégrins*). Précisons que la considération du point de vue classificatoire des locuteurs est souvent appelée «perspective émique».

Le souci des éditeurs et des auteurs des cartes respectives visait surtout à assurer une bonne mise en carte des contextes plurilingues. Ceci n'empêche que, pour des raisons techniques variées, beaucoup de particularités du paysage bigarré des contacts linguistiques européens ont dû être négligées.

2. La réalisation technique des cartes linguistiques se trouvait sous la responsabilité de Herbert Kneidl, cartographe à Ratisbonne (Regensburg). Les croquis établis par les différents auteurs de cartes ont d'abord été uniformisés du point de vue thématique et formel par les soins de l'éditeur responsable. Ils ont ensuite été remis à M. Kneidl envers qui d'ailleurs les éditeurs de ce manuel sont redevables de son travail engagé et patient.

La symbolisation cartographique des situations plurilingues a été effectuée à l'aide de plages en couleurs, de hachures et de figurés en grisés de grain plus ou moins fin. La représentation cartographique des différentes langues obéit au principe «une langue = une couleur» et néglige par conséquent la visualisation graduée de multilinguismes *locaux* ou *régionaux* complexes.

3. La toponymie et la choronymie plurilingues ont soulevé un certain nombre de problèmes. En accord avec l'orientation comparatiste de ce manuel dédié au contact des langues, nous avons adopté le principe suivant: *à l'intérieur* du territoire d'un Etat titulaire d'une carte linguistique particulière, les toponymes et les choronymes sont représentés dans leur forme *endonyme*. Evidemment ce principe suppose que tel Etat titulaire d'une carte linguistique ne dispose que d'une seule langue nationale.

A côté des endonymes l'on trouve en outre:

1) entre parenthèses: les noms d'une langue minoritaire locale ou régionale encore en usage soit de nos jours soit dans le passé récent.
2) derrière un trait oblique: les noms (co)officiels d'une langue minoritaire locale ou régionale jouissant, de nos jours, d'un statut juridique particulier.

Exemple: sur la carte N (Autriche) le lecteur trouvera, à côté des toponymes allemands des villes de *Villach* et *Klagenfurt* (ayant toutes les deux une certaine importance sociale pour la minorité slovène de Carinthie) et entre parenthèses, les formes slovènes *Beljak* et *Celovec*. La toponymie bilingue de la ville de *Bleiburg/Pliberk* par contre, située à l'Est de *Klagenfurt (Celovec)*, est marquée par le recours au trait oblique entre le nom allemand et le nom slovène du fait que le slovène y jouit d'un statut juridique particulier. La même remarque vaut, entre autres, pour la toponymie bilingue officielle du Tyrol du Sud (voir les cartes F—Italie, N—Autriche et O—Suisse).

L'*endonymie générale* vaut également pour les territoires situés *en dehors* de l'Etat titulaire d'une carte linguistique donnée. Les endonymes respectifs y sont d'ailleurs accompagnés, toujours entre parenthèses, d'un *exonyme* appartenant à la langue de l'Etat titulaire de la carte linguistique en question, là où cet exonyme est de nos jours encore en usage.

Exemple: sur la carte M (Allemagne) l'on trouve, au Danemark, au-dessous de l'endonyme danois *København*, l'exonyme allemand *Kopenhagen*. La même chose vaut pour la Belgique francophone (Wallonie) où l'on trouve l'exonyme allemand *Lüttich* au-dessous de l'endonyme français *Liège*. L'exonyme néerlandais *Luik* par contre peut être répertorié sur la carte C (Bénélux).

Evidemment il est difficile d'appliquer ce principe à des cartes réprésentant deux (ou plusieurs) Etats (et partant langues) titulaires telles que les cartes A (Scandinavie), C (Bénélux), E (Espagne et Portugal), G (ex-Yougoslavie et Albanie), H (Roumanie et Bulgarie), I (Grèce et Turquie d'Europe), K (Tchéquie et Slovaquie), O (Suisse, avec 4 langues nationales) et P (partie occidentale de la Russie européenne). Dans ce cas, le lecteur trouvera des *caractères différents* et des *chiffres mis en puissance* après les toponymes respectifs tels qu'ils figurent dans les légendes des cartes.

La considération générale de l'*exonymie relationnelle* cadre, sans aucun doute, fort bien avec les objectifs comparatistes et contrastifs de ce manuel sur la linguistique de *contact*.

4. La rédaction de quelques-unes de nos cartes linguistiques a posé des problèmes particuliers dus surtout à la déficience ou carrément à l'inexistence d'une documentation empirique appropriée. Quelquefois nous nous sommes heurtés à de sérieuses réserves face à la mise en carte de situations ethniques ou ethnolinguistiques actuelles: ces réserves concernaient surtout la carte I (Grèce et Turquie d'Europe).

Comme nos travaux cartographiques ont profité des conseils et de l'appui d'un certain nombre de spécialistes internationaux, nous leur exprimons ici notre profonde gratitude; en particulier il s'agit de MM. Emanuele Banfi (Trente, Italie), Hermann Bieder (Salzbourg), Josef Breu (Vienne), Walter Breu (Constance), Wolfgang Dahmen (Jéna), Panayote Dimitras (Kifisia, Grèce), Peter Hill (Canberra, Australie), Peter Jordan (Vienne), Klaus Kreiser (Bamberg), Max Demeter Peyfuss (Vienne), Hans-Jürgen Sasse (Cologne) et Ulrich Theissen (Salzbourg).

5. Quant à la bibliographie spécialisée en la matière nous renvoyons au paragraphe 6. Pour des *renseignements généraux* et d'ordre *cartographique* voir les contributions de Arnberger 1966, Dörflinger 1990, Eckert 1925, Fischer 1991, Hassinger 1941, Krallert 1961, le lexique de Kretschmer/Dörflinger/Wawrik 1986, Meynen 1938, Ormeling 1983 et Peeters/Williams 1993. Les ouvrages suivants constituent d'excellentes *réalisations cartographiques* et peuvent donc servir de modèle: Breu 1989, Jordan 1992, Jordan/Schappelwein 1993 et les atlas de Magocsi 1993 et de Moseley/Asher 1994. Pour les *implications politiques* de la mise en carte de langues et de peuples cf. Bonfante 1959, Dörflinger 1990, Fischer 1991, Krallert 1961, Meynen 1938, Staatswissenschaftliches Institut 1942 et Wilkinson 1951.

6. Bibliographie (in Auswahl)
Bibliography (selected)
Bibliographie (sélective)

Arnberger, Erik (1966): *Handbuch der thematischen Kartographie*, Wien (94–101: Karten über Volkstum und Sprache).

Bonfante, Giulio (1959): „Le carte linguistiche d'Europa". In: *Annali di ricerche e studi di geografia* (Genova) 15, 49–66.

Breton, Roland (1976): *Géographie des langues*, Paris.

Breu, Josef (1989): *Atlas der Donauländer, Karte 231: Sprachenverteilung (1:2 Mill.)*, Wien (mit Kommentarblatt).

Dörflinger, Johannes (1990): „Sprachen- und Völkerkarten des mitteleuropäischen Raumes vom 18. Jahrhundert bis in die 2. Hälfte des 19. Jahrhunderts". In: *4. kartographiehistorisches Kolloquium* (Karlsruhe 1988), Scharfe, W./Musall, H./Neumann, J. (Eds.): Berlin, 183–195.

Eckert, M. (1925): *Die Kartenwissenschaft. Forschungen und Grundlagen zu einer Kartographie als Wissenschaft*, Berlin/Leipzig, 2 vol. (vol. 2: 430–478).

Fischer, Holger (1991): „Karten zur räumlichen Verteilung der Nationalitäten in Ungarn. Darstellungsmöglichkeiten und Grenzen ihrer Interpretation am Beispiel von ungarischen Nationalitätenkarten des 19. und 20. Jahrhunderts". In: *Aspekte ethnischer Identität. Ergebnisse des Forschungsprojektes „Deutsche und Magyaren als nationale Minderheiten im Donauraum"*, Hösch, E./Seewann, G. (Eds.), München, 325–393.

Hassinger, H. (1941): „Bemerkungen über Entwicklung und Methode von Sprachen- und Völkerkarten". In: *Wissenschaft und Volkstumskampf. Festschrift für Erich Gierach zum 60. Geburtstag*, Oberdorffer, K./Schier, B./Wostry, W. (Eds.), Reichenberg, 47–62.

Jordan, Peter (1992): *Ethnische Struktur Südosteuropas um 1992 (1:1,5 Mill.)*, Wien (mit Begleittext von Gešev, G. et alii, 88 pp., deutsch und englisch).

Jordan, Peter/Schappelwein, Karl (1993): *Ethnische Struktur des östlichen Europas und Kaukasiens um 1990 (1:6 Mill.)*, Wien (mit Begleittext von Tarhov, S./Jordan, P., 90 pp., deutsch und englisch).

Krallert, Wilfried (1961): „Methodische Probleme der Völker- und Sprachenkarten dargestellt an Beispielen über Ost- und Südosteuropa". In: *Internationales Jahrbuch für Kartographie* 1, 99–118.

Kretschmer, Ingrid (1975): „Ethnologische Atlanten in Europa, ihre Entwicklung und ihr Beitrag an die Thematische Kartographie". In: *Internationales Jahrbuch für Kartographie* 15, 55–90.

Kretschmer, Ingrid/Dörflinger, Johannes/Wawrik, Friedrich (Eds.) (1986): *Lexikon der Geschichte der Kartographie von den Anfängen bis zum Ersten Weltkrieg*, Wien, 2 vol.

Magocsi, Paul Robert (1993): *Historical Atlas of East Central Europe*, Seattle/London.

Meynen, E. (1938): „Volks- und Sprachenkarten Mitteleuropas". In: *Deutsches Archiv für Landes- und Volksforschung* 2, 240–262, 963–1011.

Moseley, Christopher/Asher, R. E. (1994): *Atlas of the World's Languages*, London.

Ormeling, Ferdinand Jan (1983): *Minority Toponyms on Maps. The Rendering of Linguistic Minority Toponyms on Topographic Maps of Western Europe*, Utrecht.

Peeters, Yvo/Williams, Colin H. (Eds.) (1993): *The Cartographic Representation of Linguistic Data*, Staffordshire University.

Staatswissenschaftliches Institut (Ed.) (1942): *Rumänische ethnographische Landkarten und ihre Kritik*, Budapest.

Wilkinson, Henry Robert (1951): *Maps and Politics. A Review of the Ethnographic Cartography of Macedonia*, Liverpool.

A. Sprachenkarte von Nordeuropa (Skandinavien und Island)

1. Kartenthema

Autochthone Sprachen und deren räumliche Verzahnung; → Art. 116–130.

2. Kartierungstechnik

Fächenfarbe, Farbschraffuren variabler Dicke, Punkt- und Linienraster in Schwarzweiß, Signierung von Flächenfarben mittels Buchstaben, zwei Detailausschnitte (Island, Faröer).

Im einzelnen:
Farbflächen für die großen Sprachgebiete; Raster für Mischlagen mit Mehrsprachigkeit: Samisch-Norwegisch/Schwedisch an der skandinavischen Gebirgskette und in Finnland (Schwedisch-Finnisch); Schraffur für die Triglossie (Norwegisch-Samisch-Finnisch) an den nordnorwegischen Fjords mit Punktsignaturen für besondere Zentren der dortigen finnischsprachigen „kväner"; auch Schraffur für die Di- und Triglossie der Nordfriesen, Südjütländer und (Nieder)Deutschen in Südschleswig.

3. Kommentar des Kartenautors

Die autochthonen Sprachen Skandinaviens wurden kartiert: Isländisch und Färöisch (Inselnordisch); *Bokmål* und *Nynorsk* in Norwegen und ihre Mischlagen mit Samisch (LpN) und Finnisch (*kväner*) an der skandinavischen Gebirgskette und im nördlichen Fjordgebiet; Schwedisch und die ähnliche Mischlage mit Samisch (LpS und LpN) weiter östlich der Gebirgskette sowie mit Finnisch (fiT) im Norden; Finnisch und die Mischlage mit Samisch (LpN, LpI) in Nord-Finnland sowie mit Schwedisch an der Ostsee, auf den Åland-Inseln und am Finnischen Meerbusen im Süden; Dänisch und die Mischlage mit Deutsch in Nord-Schleswig; Südjütisch und die Mischlage mit Friesisch, Niederdeutsch und Hochdeutsch in Süd-Schleswig.

4. Benützte Quellen

Aikio, Marjut/Lindgren, Riitta (1985): „Map of Finnish-speaking places and northern Finnish areas". In: *Forskningsnytt* 1985 (Karte 45).

Aikio, Marjut (1984): „The position and use of the Same Language: historical, contemporary and future perspectives". In: *Second International Conference on Minority Languages.* Molde, B./Sharp, D. (Eds.). *Journal of Multilingual and Multicultural Development 5,* 277–291.

Aikio, Marjut (1988): *Saamelaiset kielenvaihdon kierteessä.* Kieli sosiologinen tutkimus viiden saamelaikylän kielenvaihdosta 1910– 1980, Helsinki.

Korkiasaari, Juhani (1989): *Suomalaiset maailmalla,* Turku.

Aarseth, Bjørn (1989): *Grenser i Sameland.* In: Samiske samlinger, vol. XIII, Oslo.

Allardt, Erik/Starck, Christian (1981): *Språkgränser och samhällsstruktur.* Finlandssvenskarna i ett iäinförande perspektiv, Lund.

Devik, Bjørn (1980): *Sameskolen i Havika 1910–1951.* Et tidsskifte sørsamernes kulturreisning (*Tromsø Museums skrifter* 16), Tromsø (Karte der südsamischen Siedlungen auch in Ottar Nr. 116–117: 14–15).

Eyram, Michael (1986): *Minority Education and Ethnic Survival. Case Study of a German School in Denmark.* Clevedon (Map 3, S. 22).

Fernandez, M. M. Jocelyne (1982): *Le finnois parlé par les sames bilingues d'Utsjokiohcejohka (Laponie finlandaise): Structures contrastives, syntaxiques, discursives.* Paris.

Finlandssvensk rapport, Nr. 20 (1990): *Finlandssvenskarna 1990. En statistik översikt.* Helsinki.

Die Finnlandschweden (1986). Broschüre, Svenska litteratursällskapet i Finland und Svenska Finlands Folkting (Ed.), Helsinki.

Finlandssvensk rapport (1981): *En statistik rapport om finlandssvenskarna Nr. 2*, Helsinki.

Friis, A. (1888): *Etnografisk kart.* Christiana.

Hansegård, Nils-Erik (1978): *The Transition of the Jukkasjärvi Lapps from Nomadism to Settled Life and Farming* (Studia Ethnographica Upsaliensia, XXXIX) Uppsala (Karte auf S. 9).

Hormia, Osmo (1970): *Finska dialekter.* Stockholm (Karte 1, 51).

Korhonen, Mikko (1967): *Die Konjugation im Lappischen. Morphologisch-historische Untersuchung.* I. Die finiten Formkategorien. Helsinki.

Larsen, Nils-Erik (1984): „Statistical investigations of language death in a North Frisian community". In: Ureland/Clarkson, 191–220 (Map 1, 192).

Manker, Ernst (1947): *De svenska fjällapparna.* Stockholm.

Niemi, Einar (1978): „Den finske kolonisasjon av Nordkalotten – forløp og årsaker". In: *Ottar* 103 (Karten 64–67).

Samerätt och sameting (1989). In: *Statens offentliga utredningar* 1989: 41, Figur 7, S. 175.

Selk, Paul (1986): *Die sprachlichen Verhältnisse im deutsch-dänischen Sprachgebiet südlich der Grenze.* Hamburg.

Slotte, Peter (1992): „Svenska dialekter och svensk dialektforskning i Finland". In: *Selskab for Nordisk Filologi Årsberetning 1990–91.* Kopenhagen, 52–63.

Sydslesvig – der Landesteil und die dänische Volksgruppe (1988): Dansk Generalsekretariat (Ed.), Kopenhagen (Karte: 24).

Sondergaard, Bent (1984): „Language contact in the German-Danish border region: the problems of interference". In: Ureland/Clarkson, 221–229 (Map I: 222).

Straka, Manfred (1970): *Handbuch der europäischen Volksgruppen.* Wien.

Straka, Manfred (1978): Völker und Sprachen Europas unter besonderer Berücksichtigung der Volksgruppen. Graz.

Ureland, P. Sture (1987): „Language Contact Research in Northern Scandinavia". In: *Third International Conference on Minority Languages.* MacEoin, Gearóid, Ahlquist, Anders/OhAodha, Donnacha (Eds.). General Papers. *Journal of Multilingual and Multicultural Development, Vol. 8:* 43–73.

Ureland, P. Sture/Clarkson, Iain (Eds.) (1984): *Scandinavian Language Contacts.* Cambridge.

Wande, Erling (1982): „Finska språket i Sverige". In: *Kulturfonden för Sverige och Finland.* Stockholm, 40–73.

Wande, Erling/Winsa, Birger (1992): „Attitudes and bilingual behaviour in the Torne Valley". In: *Proceedings from the International Conference on the Maintenance and Loss of Minority Languages.* Nordwijkerhout, 1–29.

Winsa, Birger (1991): *Östligt eller västligt? Det äldsta ordförrådet i gällivarefinskan och tornedalsfinskan.* Stockholm.

5. Persönliche Recherchen

Durch eigene Reisen im Norden und persönliche Kontakte mit Samen und Finnen und Dialektologen in Schweden und Norwegen konnte mit Hilfe der Sekundärliteratur ein zuverlässiges Bild der Verbreitung der Samisch- und Finnischsprachigen im norwegischen und schwedischen Gebirgs- und Fjordgebiet entworfen werden.

Per Sture Ureland, Mannheim (Deutschland)

A. Sprachenkarte von Nordeuropa (Skandinavien und Island)

— — — Sprachgrenze zwischen Samisch einerseits und Norwegisch, Schwedisch und Finnisch andererseits, wo Samisch praktisch überall eine Minderheitensprache ist und wo die Samen zwei- oder dreisprachig sind.

- - - - - Grenze zwischen Varietäten des Samischen, z.B. LpS (Südsamisch), LpP (Pitesamisch), LpT (Torniosamisch) oder LpN (Nordsamisch).

+ + + Sprachgrenze zwischen dem geschlossenen schwedischsprachigen Gebiet und Finnisch (fiT) in Nordschweden.

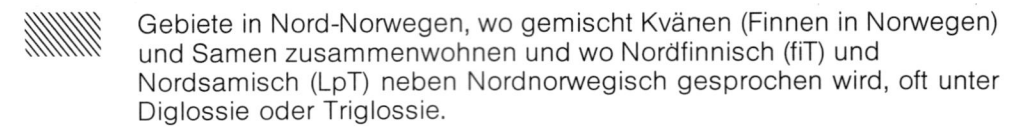

▨ Gebiete in Nord-Norwegen, wo gemischt Kvänen (Finnen in Norwegen) und Samen zusammenwohnen und wo Nordfinnisch (fiT) und Nordsamisch (LpT) neben Nordnorwegisch gesprochen wird, oft unter Diglossie oder Triglossie.

☰ Gebiete in Nord-Norwegen und Nordfinnland, wo Nordsamisch (LpN) oder Inarisamisch (LpI) oder Skoltsamisch (LpSk) neben Norwegisch und Finnisch unter Diglossie oder Triglossie gesprochen wird.

▨ Nordfriesisch zusammen mit Südjütisch und Niederdeutsch/Hochdeutsch unter Diglossie oder Triglossie.

┊┊┊┊┊ Deutsch (Nieder- oder Hochdeutsch) in Nordschleswig.

- - - - - Südjütisch südlich der dänisch-deutschen Grenze in Schleswig

o Vier deutschsprachige Städte in Nordschleswig [Tønder (Tondern)], Åbenrå (Apenrade), Sønderborg (Sonderburg) und Haderslev (Hadersleben) wo Diglossie oder Triglossie mit Niederdeutsch/Hochdeutsch vorkommt.

(●)
 1 Orte und Gebiete in Nord-Norwegen, wo "Kvänen" (Finnischsprachige in Norwegen) gemischt mit Samischsprachigen und Norwegischsprachigen in größerer Anzahl wohnen.

Westliche Kvänendialekte
1 das Lyngenfjord-Gebiet
2 das Nordreisa-Gebiet am Kvænangenfjord
3 das Kvænangenfjord-Gebiet
4 das Altafjord-Gebiet

Porsanger Kvänendialekte
5 das Lachselv-Gebiet am Porsangenfjord
6 das Børselv-Gebiet am Porsangenfjord

Östliche Kvänendialekte
7 das Tanaelv-Gebiet am Tanafjord
8 das Neiden-Gebiet zwischen Finnmark und Nord-Finnland
9 das Pasviktal-Gebiet an der Grenze zu Rußland
10 das Vadsø-Gebiet am Varangerfjord
11 das Vardø-Gebiet am Varangerfjord

Abkürzungen:

LpN	Nordsamisch	**LpUm**	Umesamisch
LpFio	Fjordsamisch	**LpS**	Südsamisch
LpT	Torniosamisch	**LpI**	Inarisamisch
LpL	Lulesamisch	**LpSk**	Skoltsamisch
LpP	Pitesamisch	**fiT**	Tornio-Finnisch

Nordeuropa – Sprachen

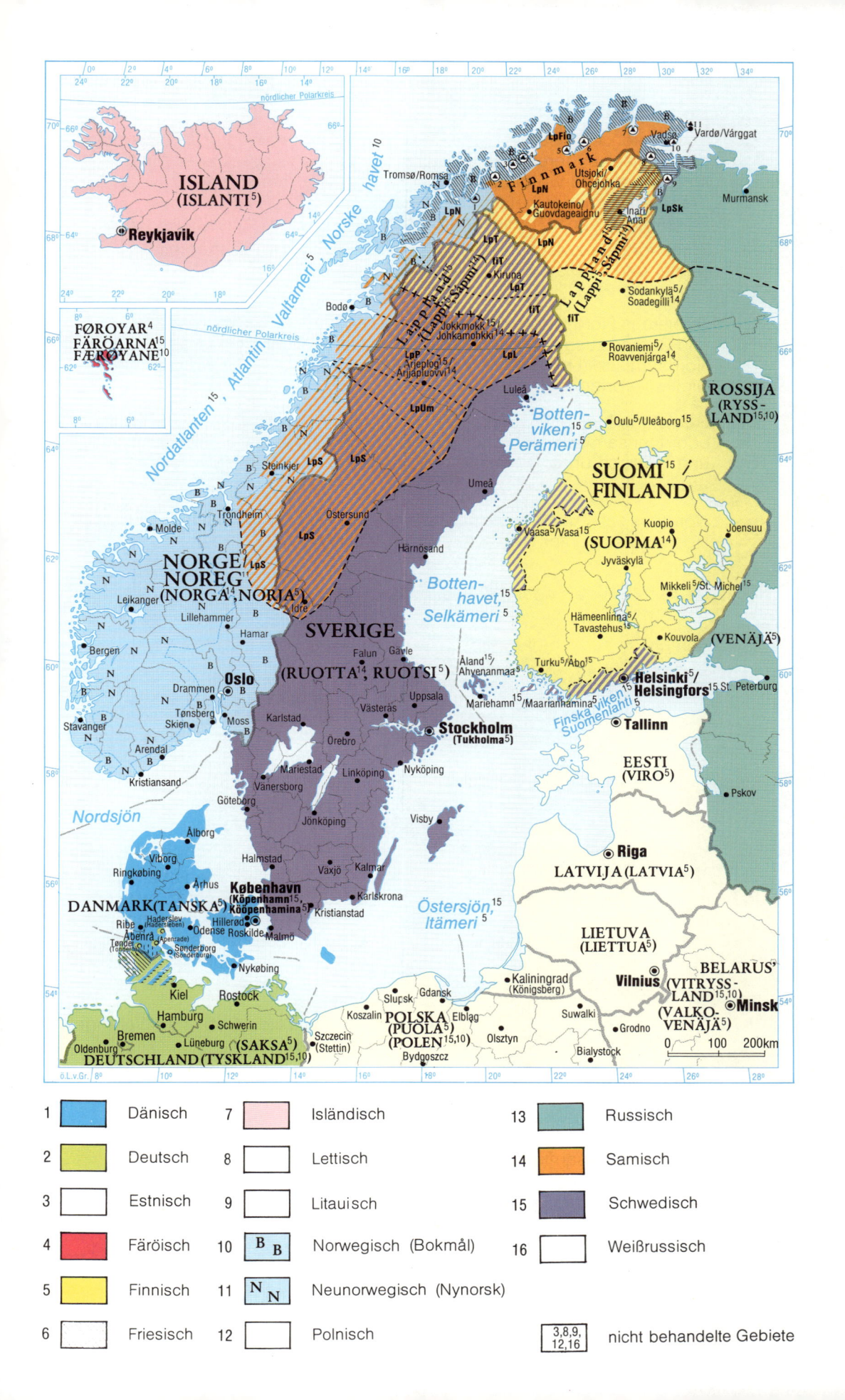

Legende

Nr.	Farbe	Sprache
1	blau	Dänisch
2	hellgrün	Deutsch
3		Estnisch
4	rot	Färöisch
5	gelb	Finnisch
6		Friesisch
7	rosa	Isländisch
8		Lettisch
9		Litauisch
10	B B	Norwegisch (Bokmål)
11	N N	Neunorwegisch (Nynorsk)
12		Polnisch
13	grün	Russisch
14	orange	Samisch
15	violett	Schwedisch
16		Weißrussisch
3,8,9,12,16		nicht behandelte Gebiete

Länder und Städte (Auswahl)

- **ISLAND (ISLANTI⁵)** – Reykjavík
- **FØROYAR⁴ / FÄRÖARNA¹⁵ / FÆRØYANE¹⁰**
- **NORGE / NOREG (NORGA⁴, NORJA⁵)** – Oslo, Bergen, Stavanger, Kristiansand, Arendal, Tønsberg, Skien, Drammen, Moss, Hamar, Lillehammer, Leikanger, Molde, Trondheim, Steinkjer, Bodø, Tromsø/Romsa, Vadsø, Vardø/Várggat
- **SVERIGE (RUOTTA¹⁴, RUOTSI⁵)** – Stockholm (Tukholma⁵), Göteborg, Malmö, Uppsala, Västerås, Örebro, Linköping, Jönköping, Norrköping, Karlstad, Falun, Gävle, Mariestad, Vänersborg, Halmstad, Växjö, Kalmar, Kristianstad, Karlskrona, Visby, Umeå, Luleå, Östersund, Härnösand
- **SUOMI / FINLAND (SUOPMA¹⁴)** – Helsinki⁵/Helsingfors¹⁵, Turku⁵/Åbo¹⁵, Vaasa⁵/Vasa¹⁵, Oulu⁵/Uleåborg¹⁵, Kuopio, Joensuu, Jyväskylä, Mikkeli⁵/St. Michel¹⁵, Hämeenlinna⁵/Tavastehus¹⁵, Kouvola, Rovaniemi⁵/Roavvenjárga¹⁴, Sodankylä⁵/Soadegilli¹⁴, Inari/Anár, Utsjoki/Ohcejohka, Kautokeino/Guovdageaidnu, Åland¹⁵/Ahvenanmaa, Mariehamn¹⁵/Maarianhamina⁵
- **DANMARK (TANSKA)** – København (Køpenhamn¹⁵, Kööpenhamina), Århus, Ålborg, Viborg, Ringkøbing, Ribe, Tønder (Tondern), Åbenrå (Apenrade), Haderslev (Hadersleben), Sønderborg (Sonderburg), Odense, Roskilde, Hillerød, Nykøbing
- **DEUTSCHLAND (TYSKLAND¹⁵,¹⁰) (SAKSA⁵)** – Hamburg, Bremen, Oldenburg, Kiel, Lübeck, Rostock, Schwerin, Hamburg, Lüneburg
- **POLSKA (PUOLA⁵, POLEN¹⁵,¹⁰)** – Gdańsk, Elbląg, Słupsk, Koszalin, Szczecin (Stettin), Suwałki, Olsztyn, Białystok, Bydgoszcz, Kaliningrad (Königsberg)
- **EESTI (VIRO⁵)** – Tallinn, Pskov
- **LATVIJA (LATVIA⁵)** – Riga
- **LIETUVA (LIETTUA⁵)** – Vilnius
- **BELARUS' (VITRYSSLAND¹⁵,¹⁰, VALKOVENÄJÄ⁵)** – Minsk
- **ROSSIJA (RYSSLAND¹⁵,¹⁰, VENÄJÄ⁵)** – Murmansk, St. Peterburg

Gewässer

- Norske havet¹⁰ / Valtameri⁵ / Atlanttimeri⁵
- Nordatlanten¹⁵
- Nordsjön
- Bottenviken, Perämeri
- Bottenhavet, Selkämeri⁵
- Finska viken, Suomenlahti
- Östersjön¹⁵, Itämeri⁵

Regionen

- Finnmark (LpN)
- Lappland / Lapi (Lappi⁵, Sápmi¹⁴) – LpT, LpN, LpS, LpSk, LpFi, LpP, LpL, LpUm

B. Sprachenkarte von Großbritannien und Irland

1. Kartenthema

Autochthone und allochthone Sprachen sowie deren räumliche Verteilung; → Art. 131–134.

2. Kartierungstechnik

Flächenfarben, Farbschraffuren variabler Dicke, Kreissegmentdiagramme in Schwarzweiß, ein Detailausschnitt (Kanalinseln).

3. Kommentar des Kartenautors

Nach dem Aussterben des Cornish im Südwesten Englands und des Manx auf der Isle of Man besteht autochthoner Kontakt des Englischen nur noch mit dem Walisischen in Wales, dem Gälischen im Nordwesten Schottlands und dem Irischen in der Gaeltacht Irlands. In all diesen Fällen zeigt die Karte auf der Basis neuerer Statistiken und Untersuchungen den jeweiligen Anteil und die Verbreitung der Sprecher der keltischen Sprachen. Diachrone Vergleiche zeigen in allen Fällen einen stetigen Rückgang dieser bereits heute fast ausschließlich bilingualen Sprecher, am ausgeprägtesten in Schottland, deutlich ebenso in Irland und relativ schwächer noch in Wales.

In England selbst besteht Sprachkontakt vorrangig mit allochthonen Gruppen, Einwanderern aus den ehemaligen Kolonien und deren Nachkommen. Die Kreisdiagramme zeigen für England und Wales die relative Stärke der wichtigsten Ethnien sowie den prozentualen Anteil Angehöriger ethnischer Minoritäten insgesamt an der Bevölkerung der Region.

Auf den Kanalinseln hat im Laufe des letzten Jahrhunderts das Englische das Französische verdrängt. Es existieren noch kleinere, im Rückgrang begriffene und durchwegs bilinguale Sprachgemeinschaften des älteren französischen Patois.

3.1. England

Die demographischen Anteile ethnischer Minoritäten werden in Form von Tortendiagrammen zu einzelnen Regionen dargestellt. Für insgesamt 12 Regionen Großbritanniens zeigen die jeweils linken Diagramme den Anteil ethnischer Minoritäten an der Gesamtbevölkerung der Region, die rechten Diagramme dagegen dessen Aufteilung auf verschiedene ethnische Gruppen. Verhältnismäßig große Minderheitengruppen findet man demnach vor allem im Großraum von London, aber auch in den West Midlands; erkennbar werden auch Tendenzen der Konzentration bestimmter Ethnien in einzelnen Regionen, so etwa der Zuwanderer von den Westindischen Inseln in London und den südlicheren Teilen Englands, oder der Pakistani im Großraum Glasgow und den nördlichen Teilen Englands, während bei anderen ethnischen Gruppen, wie bei den Chinesen oder, mit Einschränkungen, auch bei den Indern geringere regionale Unterschiede zu vermerken sind. Den Kreisdiagrammen liegen folgende Rohdaten für 1986/87 (basierend auf einer stichprobengestützten Fortschreibung der Volkszählung von 1981) zugrunde (siehe nächste Seite).

3.2. Wales

Die Flächenschraffuren zeigen den Anteil der walischsprachigen Bevölkerung in verschiedenen Regionen.

Quelle: Lewis 1981.

3.3. Schottland

Die Flächenschraffuren zeigen den Anteil der gälischsprachigen Bevölkerung in verschiedenen Regionen.

Quelle: MacKinnon 1991, 522.

3.4. Irland

Die strichlierte Linie und die schraffierten Gebiete zeigen Lage und Ausdehnung des offiziell gälischsprachigen Gebiets („Gaeltacht") nach der Festlegung der *Gaeltacht Commission* von 1956. Tatsächlich wird jedoch auch innerhalb dieses Gebiets überwiegend oder ausschließlich Englisch gesprochen. Das tatsächlich noch in allen Altersgruppen vorwiegend irischsprachige Gebiet („Fior-Ghaeltacht") beschränkt sich auf äußerst kleine Gebiete in den westlichen Küstenregionen der Counties Donegal, Mayo, Galway, und Kerry; auch die faktisch noch teilweise irischsprachige Übergangszone („Breac-Ghaeltacht") nimmt nach neueren Untersuchungen nur mehr einen kleineren Teil des offiziellen Gaeltacht ein.

Quelle: Hindley 1990, 32, 64, 77, 87, 106, 116, 123 und 129.

Tabelle: Anteil ethnischer Minoritäten an der Bevölkerung in verschiedenen Regionen Großbritanniens, 1986−88

	W.I.	Af.	I.	P.	B.	Ch.	Ar.	M.	O.	Aemg	Emp
North	4	1	12	34	16	10	4	14	4	100	1.4
Yorkshire and Humbershire	12	2	22	42	3	4	3	10	3	100	4.2
East Midlands	10	1	56	10	2	4	1	11	4	100	4.0
East Anglia	8	2	15	26	1	11	0	23	13	100	2.1
Greater London	26	7	30	7	5	5	3	9	8	100	16.6
Remainder of South East	12	3	29	16	5	7	3	17	9	100	2.9
South West	25	4	20	2	3	12	5	23	6	100	1.2
West Midlands	22	1	39	22	5	1	1	7	2	100	7.3
North West	11	4	25	33	2	5	3	12	4	100	3.6
Wales	9	4	15	15	3	10	14	27	3	100	1.2
Central Clydeside Conurbation	0	0	10	62	2	10	10	5	1	100	1.5
Remainder of Scotland	5	13	13	8	2	10	11	26	12	100	0.5

W.I. = West Indian
Af. = African
I. = Indian
P. = Pakistani
B. = Bangladeshi
Ch. = Chinese
Ar. = Arab
M. = Mixed
O. = Other
Aemg. = All ethnic minority groups
Emp = Ethnic minority population as %

Quelle: Haskey 1991, 27

3.5. Kanalinseln

Aufgrund politischer und wirtschaftlicher Faktoren sind die Kanalinseln in der jüngeren Vergangenheit zu einem fast ausschließlich englischsprachigen Gebiet geworden; Sprecher des früher dort heimischen französischen Patois findet man nur noch als kleine Minderheiten, vor allem in der älteren Generation.

Geschätzter Anteil von Sprechern des französischen Patois an der jeweiligen Inselbevölkerung:

Insel		Dialekt	Sprecherzahl	Bevölkerungsanteil
engl.	franz.			
Guernsey	Guernesey	Guernesiais	6.000	11%
Jersey	Jersey	Jèrriais	10.000	13–14%
Sark	Sercq	Sercquiais	60	10%
Alderney	Aurigny	Auregnais	—	

Quelle: Ramisch 1989, 52−53.

4. Benützte Quellen

Lewis, E. Glyn (1981): *Bilingualism and Bilingual Education*, Oxford.

Haskey, John (1991): „The Ethnic Minority Populations Resident in Private Households − Estimates by County and Metropolitan District of England and Wales". In: *Population Trends* 63, 22−35 (hier: 27).

Hindley, R. (1990): *The Death of the Irish Language. A Qualified Obituary*, London, New York (hier v. a. SS. 32, 64, 77, 87, 106, 116, 123, 129 und passim).

MacKinnon, Kenneth (1991): „Language-Maintenance and Viability in Contemporary Gaelic Communities: Skye and the Western Isles today". In: *Language Contact in the British Isles. Proceedings of the Eight International Symposium on Language Contact in Europe* (Douglas, Isle of Man, 1988), Ureland, P. Sture/Broderick, George (Eds.), Tübingen 522.

Ramisch, Heinrich (1989): *The Variation of English in Guernsey/Channel Islands*, Frankfurt et al., 52−53.

Edgar Schneider, Regensburg (Deutschland)

1990 B. Sprachenkarte von Großbritannien und Irland

SPRACHKONTAKTE in GROSSBRITANNIEN: 1986-1988

Gesamtbevölkerung von North: 3.042.000
davon 1,4% ethnische Minoritäten = 42.000

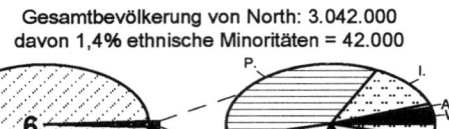

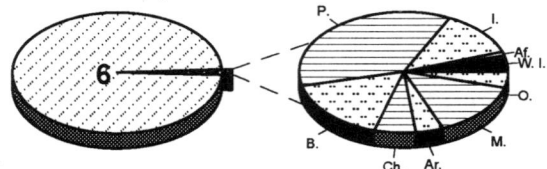

Gesamtbevölkerung von Yorkshire and Humberside: 4.847.000
davon 4,2% ethnische Minoritäten = 205.000

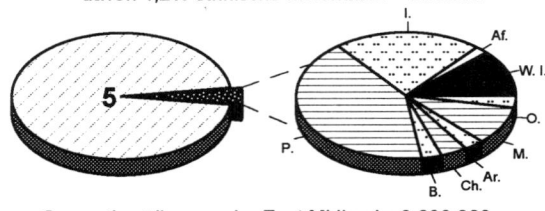

Gesamtbevölkerung der East Midlands: 3.899.000
davon 4% ethnische Minoritäten = 157.000

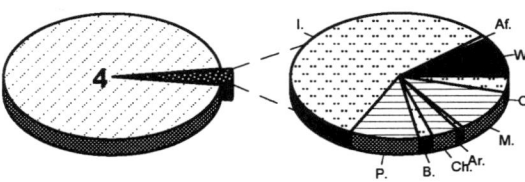

Gesamtbevölkerung von East Anglia: 1.982.000
davon 2,2% ethnische Minoritäten = 41.000

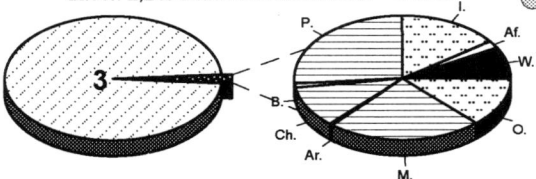

Gesamtbevölkerung des Remainder of South East: 10.358.000
davon 2,9% ethnische Minoritäten = 295.000

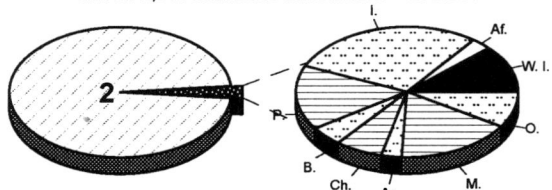

Gesamtbevölkerung von Greater London: 6.640.000
davon 16,6% ethnische Minoritäten = 1.100.000

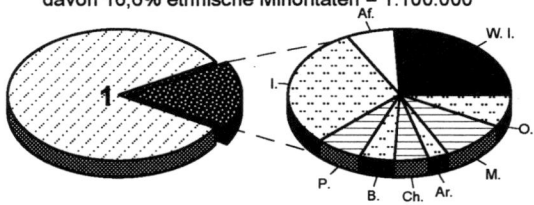

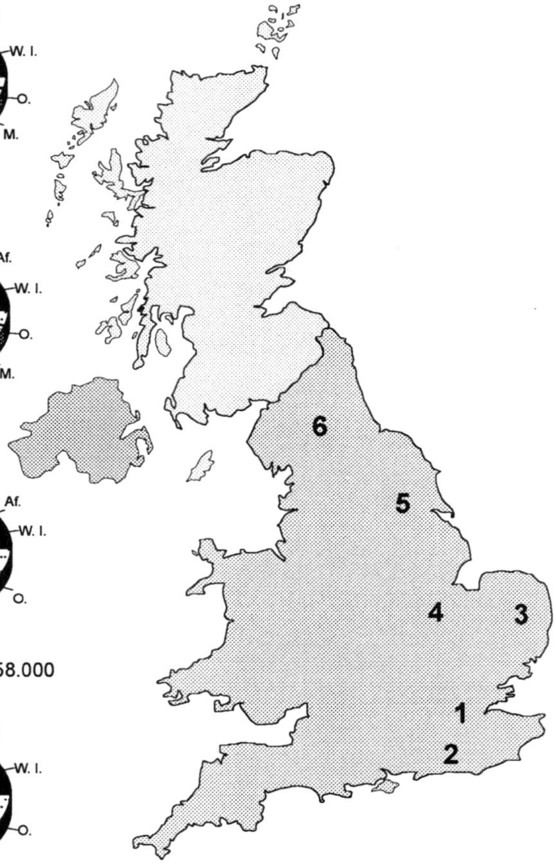

Af. =	African		I. =	Indian
Ar. =	Arab		M. =	Mixed
B. =	Bangladeshi		O. =	Other
Ch. =	Chinese		P. =	Pakistani
		W. I. = West Indian		

B. Sprachenkarte von Großbritannien und Irland

SPRACHKONTAKTE in GROSSBRITANNIEN: 1986-1988

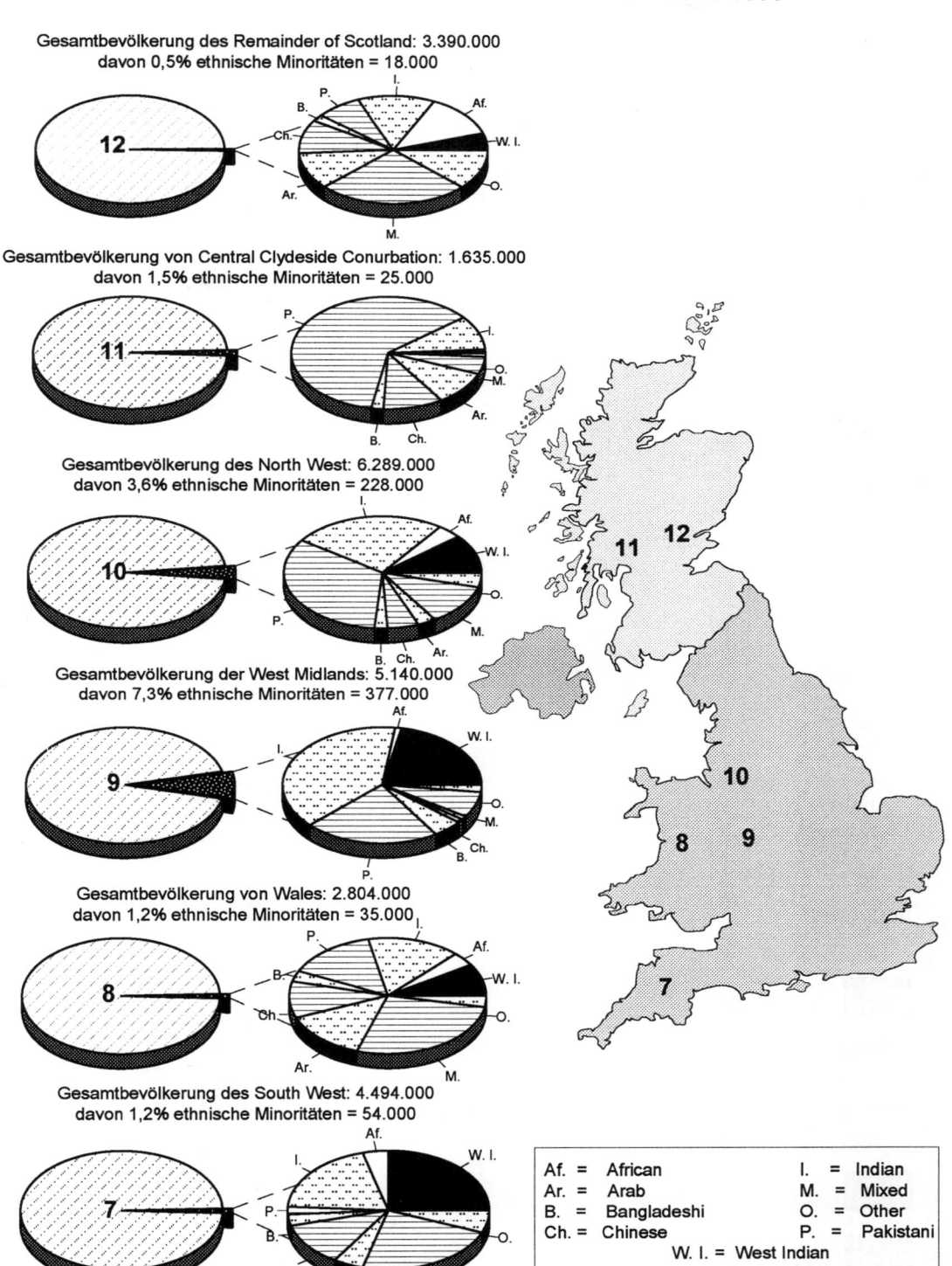

Gesamtbevölkerung des Remainder of Scotland: 3.390.000
davon 0,5% ethnische Minoritäten = 18.000

Gesamtbevölkerung von Central Clydeside Conurbation: 1.635.000
davon 1,5% ethnische Minoritäten = 25.000

Gesamtbevölkerung des North West: 6.289.000
davon 3,6% ethnische Minoritäten = 228.000

Gesamtbevölkerung der West Midlands: 5.140.000
davon 7,3% ethnische Minoritäten = 377.000

Gesamtbevölkerung von Wales: 2.804.000
davon 1,2% ethnische Minoritäten = 35.000

Gesamtbevölkerung des South West: 4.494.000
davon 1,2% ethnische Minoritäten = 54.000

Af. =	African	I. =	Indian
Ar. =	Arab	M. =	Mixed
B. =	Bangladeshi	O. =	Other
Ch. =	Chinese	P. =	Pakistani
	W. I. = West Indian		

EDV-Kartographie: Heide Marie Pamminger (Salzburg)

1992 B. Sprachenkarte von Großbritannien und Irland

Legende:

1 ▮ Englisch

2 ▮ Französisch

3 ▮ Irisch/Gälisch

4 ▮ Schottisch/Gälisch

5 ▮ Walisisch

.... Sprachgrenze:
Irisch/Gälisch- Englisch

B. Sprachenkarte von Großbritannien und Irland   1993

C. Language Map of the Benelux (Belgium, Netherlands, Luxemburg)

1. What has been mapped?

a. Indigenous languages (Dutch, Frisian, French, German, Luxemburg),
b. The most important non-indigenous minority groups; → Art. 135–141.

2. Cartographic Techniques Used

The techniques used come from your handbook cartographers. These means can be indicated in the standard way.

Secondly, pie charts have been added for presenting quantitative information on minority groups in places with more than 100 000 inhabitants in the Netherlands and Belgium; the Luxemburg figures relate to Luxemburg country.

Language areas distinguished within the Benelux by colours, rasters, etc.:

- Frisian language area
- Luxemburg language area
- German language area
- French language area with protected status for German
- French language area with protected status for Dutch and German
- French language area
- Brussels-capital bilingual area
- French language area with protected status for Dutch
- Dutch language area with protected status for French.

3. Additional Remarks of the Author

Non-indigenous minority groups, defined on the basis of nationality ('foreigners') and country of origin; information is presented in pie chart format.

For all places in the Netherlands and Belgium with more than 100 000 inhabitants figures on the most important (= larger) non-indigenous minority groups are given. The figures for Luxemburg relate to Luxemburg country.

For all three countries figures are given on the basis of nationality, which gives the so-called category of *'foreigners'*.

In addition, information is available for the four large cities of the Netherlands, for which figures are available for the Surinamese and Antillian group (they have (most of the times) the Dutch nationality; they can be distinguished by information on country of origin). These figures are given in a separate category: *'minority groups'*.

Groups distinguished:

- Netherlands   Turkey, Morocco, European countries, other countries, Surinam, Netherlands Antilles
- Belgium   Turkey, Morocco, Italy, EC countries, other countries
- Luxemburg   Portugal, Italy, other countries

All informations are related to 1991 (as close as possible).

4. Bibliography (Sources)

Aunger, E. A. (1993): "Regional, national and official languages in Belgium". In: *International Journal of the Sociology of Language* 104, 31–48.

Deprez, K./Wynants, A. (1989): "Voeren/ Fourons". In: *Historische Sprachkonflikte*, Nelde, P. H. (Ed.), Bonn, 95–105.

Jansma, L. G./Jelsma, G. H. (1987): "Language, language borders, and social class". In: *International Journal of the Sociology of Language* 64, 21–35.

Roelandt, Th./Roijen, J./Veenmann, J. (1992): *Minderheden in Nederland. Statistisch Vademecum 1992*, The Hague.

Nationaal Instituut voor de Statistiek (NIS) (1992): *Algemene volks- en woningtelling. Deel 1 B, Bevolkingscijfers: leeftijd, geslacht, nationaliteit per gemeente 1992*, Brussels.

Service central de la statistique et des études économiques (STATEC) (1992): *Annuaire statistique du Grant-Duché de Luxembourg*, Luxemburg.

Vandeputte, O./Vincent, T./Hermans, T. (1981): *Dutch. The language of twenty million Dutch and Flemish people*, Rekkem.

Roeland van Hout, Tilburg (Netherlands)

C. Language Map of the Benelux (Belgium, Netherlands, Luxemburg)

FOREIGNERS IN DUTCH CITIES

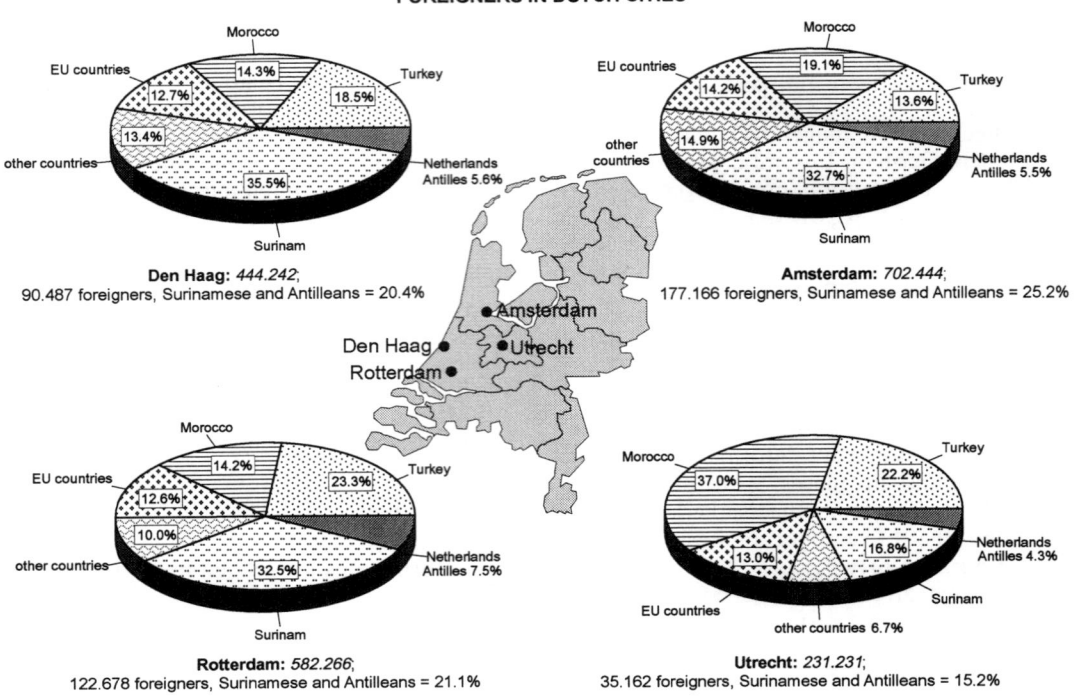

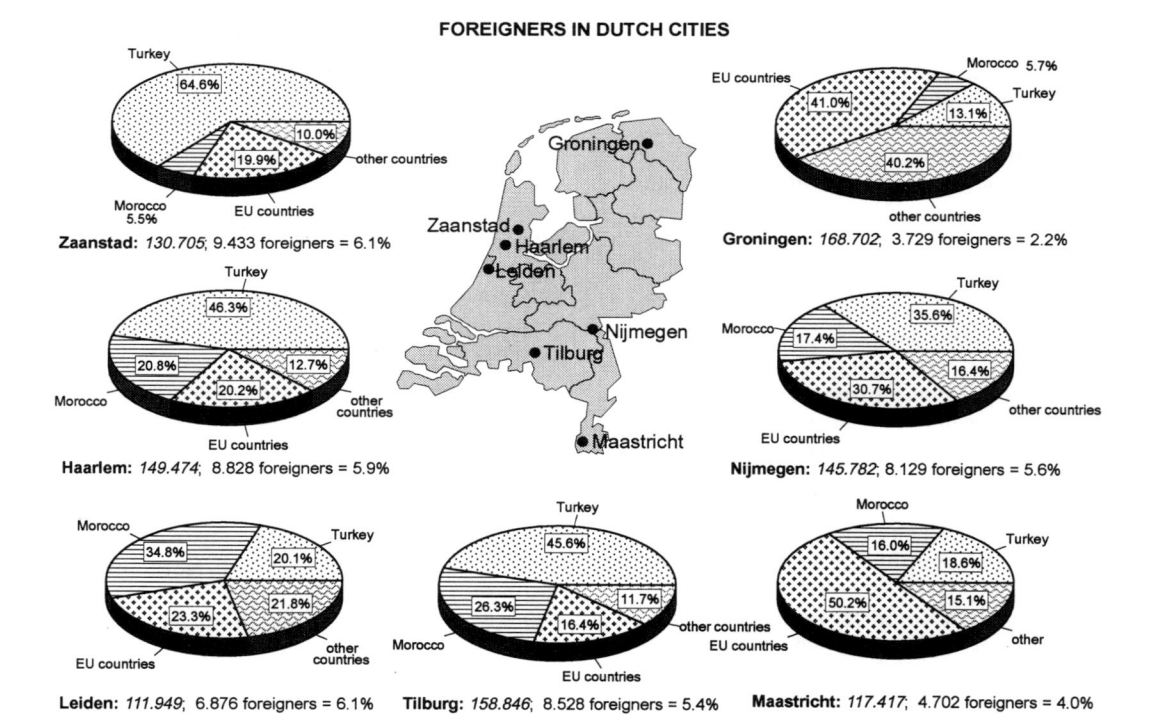

Den Haag: *444.242*;
90.487 foreigners, Surinamese and Antilleans = 20.4%
- Morocco 14.3%
- Turkey 18.5%
- Netherlands Antilles 5.6%
- Surinam 35.5%
- other countries 13.4%
- EU countries 12.7%

Amsterdam: *702.444*;
177.166 foreigners, Surinamese and Antilleans = 25.2%
- Morocco 19.1%
- Turkey 13.6%
- Netherlands Antilles 5.5%
- Surinam 32.7%
- other countries 14.9%
- EU countries 14.2%

Rotterdam: *582.266*;
122.678 foreigners, Surinamese and Antilleans = 21.1%
- Morocco 14.2%
- Turkey 23.3%
- Netherlands Antilles 7.5%
- Surinam 32.5%
- other countries 10.0%
- EU countries 12.6%

Utrecht: *231.231*;
35.162 foreigners, Surinamese and Antilleans = 15.2%
- Morocco 37.0%
- Turkey 22.2%
- Netherlands Antilles 4.3%
- Surinam 16.8%
- other countries 6.7%
- EU countries 13.0%

FOREIGNERS IN DUTCH CITIES

Zaanstad: *130.705*; 9.433 foreigners = 6.1%
- Turkey 64.6%
- other countries 10.0%
- EU countries 19.9%
- Morocco 5.5%

Groningen: *168.702*; 3.729 foreigners = 2.2%
- Morocco 5.7%
- Turkey 13.1%
- other countries 40.2%
- EU countries 41.0%

Haarlem: *149.474*; 8.828 foreigners = 5.9%
- Turkey 46.3%
- other countries 12.7%
- EU countries 20.2%
- Morocco 20.8%

Nijmegen: *145.782*; 8.129 foreigners = 5.6%
- Turkey 35.6%
- other countries 16.4%
- EU countries 30.7%
- Morocco 17.4%

Leiden: *111.949*; 6.876 foreigners = 6.1%
- Morocco 34.8%
- Turkey 20.1%
- other countries 21.8%
- EU countries 23.3%

Tilburg: *158.846*; 8.528 foreigners = 5.4%
- Turkey 45.6%
- other countries 11.7%
- EU countries 16.4%
- Morocco 26.3%

Maastricht: *117.417*; 4.702 foreigners = 4.0%
- Morocco 16.0%
- Turkey 18.6%
- other 15.1%
- EU countries 50.2%

C. Language Map of the Benelux (Belgium, Netherlands, Luxemburg)

FOREIGNERS IN DUTCH CITIES

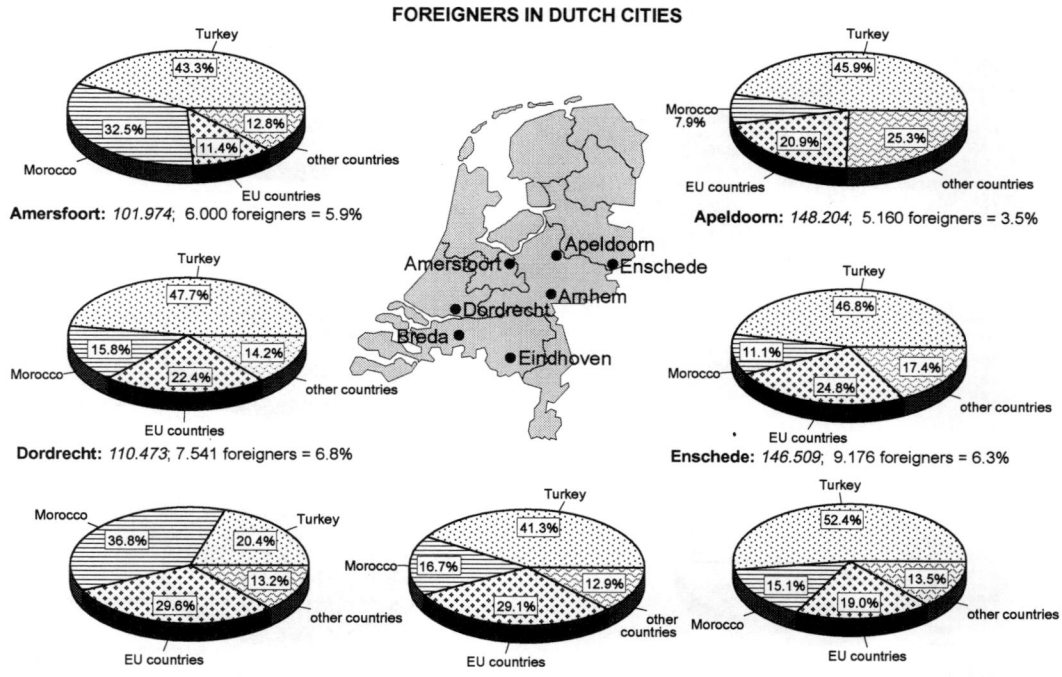

Amersfoort pie chart: Turkey 43.3%, Morocco 32.5%, EU countries 11.4%, other countries 12.8%
Amersfoort: *101.974*; 6.000 foreigners = 5.9%

Apeldoorn pie chart: Turkey 45.9%, Morocco 7.9%, EU countries 20.9%, other countries 25.3%
Apeldoorn: *148.204*; 5.160 foreigners = 3.5%

Dordrecht pie chart: Turkey 47.7%, Morocco 15.8%, EU countries 22.4%, other countries 14.2%
Dordrecht: *110.473*; 7.541 foreigners = 6.8%

Enschede pie chart: Turkey 46.8%, Morocco 11.1%, EU countries 24.8%, other countries 17.4%
Enschede: *146.509*; 9.176 foreigners = 6.3%

Breda pie chart: Morocco 36.8%, Turkey 20.4%, EU countries 29.6%, other countries 13.2%
Breda: *124.794*; 6.685 foreigners = 5.4%

Eindhoven pie chart: Turkey 41.3%, Morocco 16.7%, EU countries 29.1%, other countries 12.9%
Eindhoven: *192.895*; 12.088 foreigners = 5.9%

Arnhem pie chart: Turkey 52.4%, Morocco 15.1%, EU countries 19.0%, other countries 13.5%
Arnhem: *131.703*; 8.960 foreigners = 6.8%

Cities shown on map: Amersfoort, Apeldoorn, Enschede, Arnhem, Dordrecht, Breda, Eindhoven

FOREIGNERS IN THE COUNTRY OF LUXEMBURG

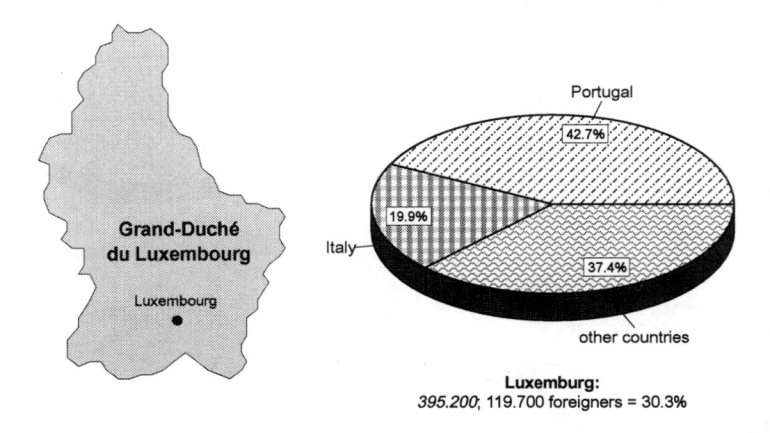

Grand-Duché du Luxembourg — Luxembourg

Luxemburg pie chart: Portugal 42.7%, Italy 19.9%, other countries 37.4%
Luxemburg:
395.200; 119.700 foreigners = 30.3%

C. Language Map of the Benelux (Belgium, Netherlands, Luxemburg)

FOREIGNERS IN BELGIAN CITIES

Antwerpen: *486.875*; 53.018 foreigners = 10.9%
- Morocco 36.6%
- Turkey 12.2%
- other countries 20.6%
- EU countries 28.3%
- Italy 2.3%

Brussel/Bruxelles: *960.324*; 274.590 foreigners = 28.6%
- Morocco 28.5%
- Turkey 7.8%
- other countries 17.9%
- EU countries 34.1%
- Italy 11.7%

Gent: *230.446*; 16.650 foreigners = 7.2%
- Turkey 48.5%
- other countries 21.0%
- EU countries 19.2%
- Italy 2.0%
- Morocco 9.3%

Charleroi: *206.928*; 38.224 foreigners = 18.5%
- Morocco 6.9%
- Turkey 10.6%
- other countries 8.2%
- EU countries 13.7%
- Italy 60.6%

FOREIGNERS IN BELGIAN CITIES

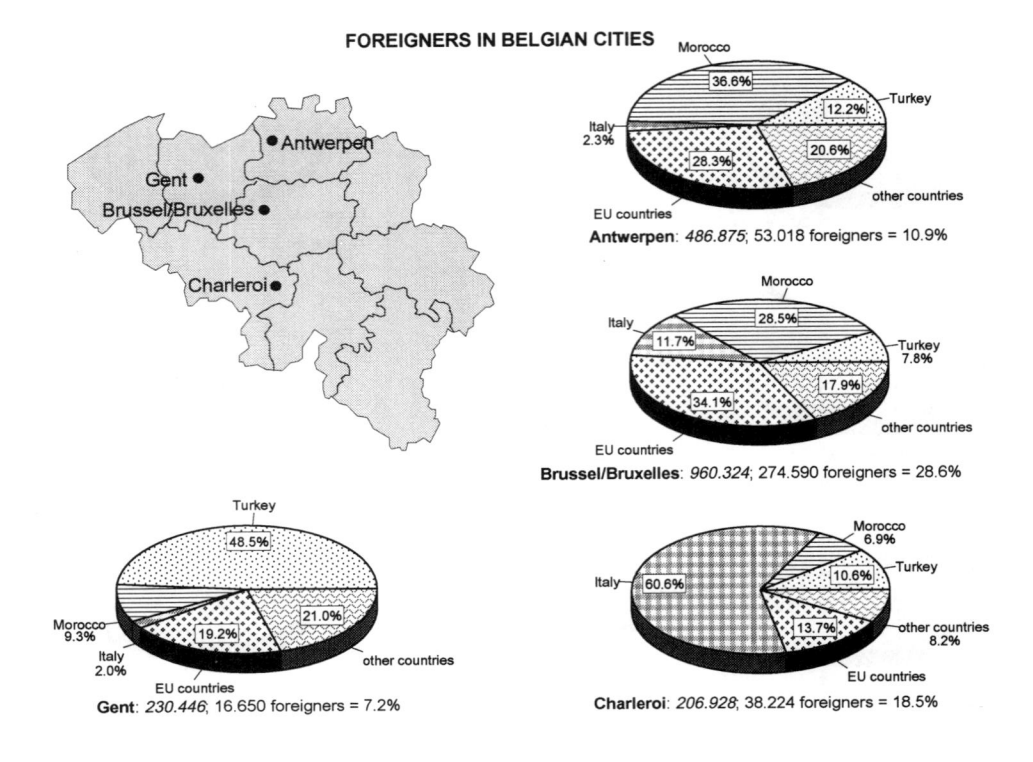

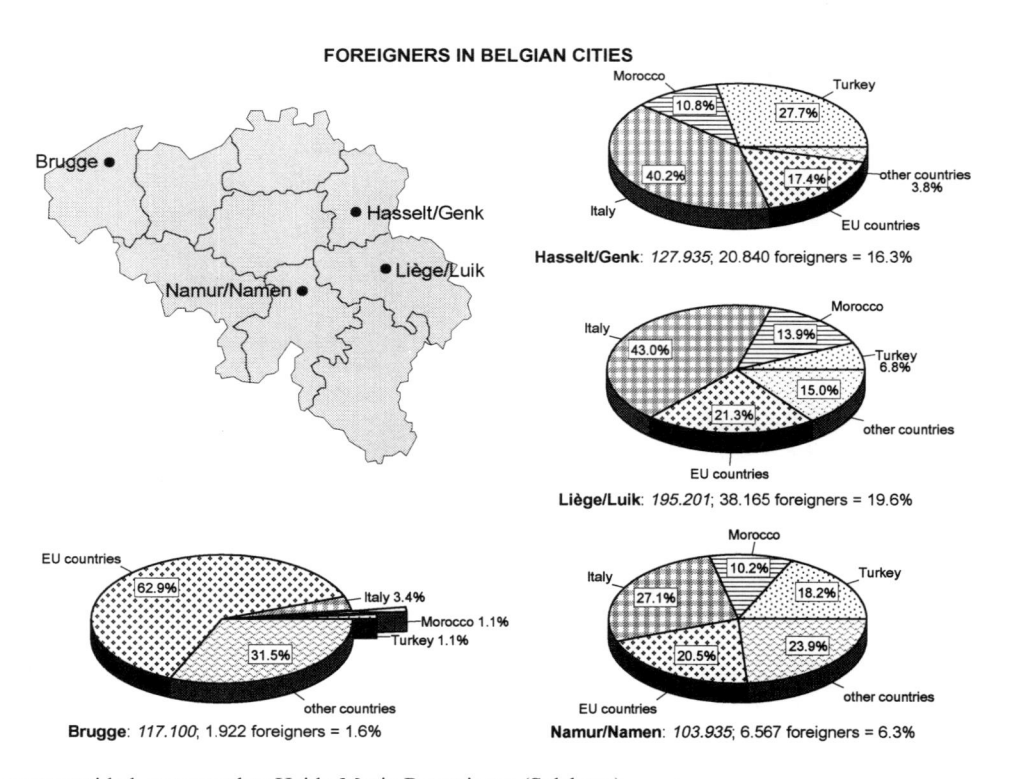

Hasselt/Genk: *127.935*; 20.840 foreigners = 16.3%
- Morocco 10.8%
- Turkey 27.7%
- other countries 3.8%
- EU countries 17.4%
- Italy 40.2%

Liège/Luik: *195.201*; 38.165 foreigners = 19.6%
- Morocco 13.9%
- Turkey 6.8%
- other countries 15.0%
- EU countries 21.3%
- Italy 43.0%

Brugge: *117.100*; 1.922 foreigners = 1.6%
- EU countries 62.9%
- Italy 3.4%
- Morocco 1.1%
- Turkey 1.1%
- other countries 31.5%

Namur/Namen: *103.935*; 6.567 foreigners = 6.3%
- Morocco 10.2%
- Turkey 18.2%
- other countries 23.9%
- EU countries 20.5%
- Italy 27.1%

Computer aided cartography: Heide Marie Pamminger (Salzburg)

C. Language Map of the Benelux (Belgium, Netherlands, Luxemburg)

Legend:

1 Dutch
2 French
3 Frisian
4 German
5 Luxemburgish ("Lëtzebuergisch")

French language area with protected status for German
French language area with protected status for Dutch
Dutch language area with protected status for French
German language area with protected status for French

Three Old-Belgian bilingual areas (French-German):

A Old-Belgium North (around Montzen[4])
B OLd-Belgium Centre (around Bocholz[4], Beho[2])
C Old-Belgium South (around Arel[4], Arlon[2])

C. Language Map of the Benelux (Belgium, Netherlands, Luxemburg) 2001

D. Sprachenkarte von Frankreich

1. Kartenthema

Autochthone und allochthone Sprachen sowie deren räumliche Verteilung; → Art. 142–150.

2. Kartierungstechnik

Flächenfarben, Farbschraffuren variabler Dicke, Buchstabensignaturen zur Markierung allochthoner Sprachen (v. a. in Städten), fünf Detailausschnitte (Baskenland, Bretagne, Westhoek, Elsaß-Lothringen, Korsika), Graurasterdiagramme.

3. Kommentar des Kartenautors

3.1. Autochthone Sprachen

3.1.1. Sprachgrenzen

Die Sprachgrenzen der vorliegenden Karte sind weitgehend konventionelle Abgrenzungen, deren Bedeutung von Fall zu Fall verschieden ist. Die Zuweisung eines geographischen Punktes zu einem Sprachgebiet setzt nämlich eine sprachsystematische und eine soziolinguistische Entscheidung voraus.

Die an dem betreffenden Punkt gesprochene Varietät muß typologisch eindeutig einer bestimmten Sprache zuweisbar sein. Diese Voraussetzung ist dann nicht gegeben, wenn genetisch eng verwandte Sprachen allmählich ineinander übergehen wie Französisch und Okzitanisch im *Croissant*. Es muß ferner geklärt sein, welche Merkmale einer Sprechergruppe im Hinblick auf ihren Anteil an der Ortsbevölkerung, Altersstruktur, Herkunft, Sprachkompetenz und -gebrauch usw. Voraussetzung für die Zuweisung zu einem Sprachgebiet sind. Da entsprechende soziolinguistische Untersuchungen großen Stils fehlen (vgl. aber zum Bretonischen die methodisch hochinteressante Studie von Wiliams/Ambrose 1988), werden Sprachgrenzen vielfach zu konventionellen Symbolen. Es entstehen Linien, die festgelegt wurden, als es noch viele monolinguale Sprecher der Regionalsprachen gab, und die weiter „benützt" werden, obwohl ungeklärt ist, welche sprachliche Realität sie heute abgrenzen.

a) Bretonisch: Standardlinie bei Sébillot 1886; nach Panier 1942 Westverschiebung; teilweise noch weiter westlich liegende Linie bei Timm 1983, 445 – Der Detailausschnitt enthält die Sébillot-Linie und die Rückzugslinie nach Panier 1942/Timm 1983.
b) Niederländisch: Grenze nach *ALEPic* 1989; Karte mit niederländischen bzw. französischen Dominanzzonen für 1970 bei Vanneste 1982, 28.
c) Deutsch: Grenze nach *ALEA* 1969 und *ALELG* 1977.
d) Baskisch: Grenze nach Séguy 1952, 386.
e) Katalanisch: Grenze nach Guiter 1973, 82.
f) Okzitanisch: Maßgebend für den Westen und das Zentrum: Tourtoulon/Bringuier 1876; darauf basieren Ronjat 1930, 14–21 (durchgehende Schraffierung) und Fontan 1969, 165–168 (unterbrochene Schraffierung); Untersuchungen zum Ostteil: Escoffier 1958, Tuaillon 1972. Wissenschaftsgeschichtliche Aufarbeitung bei Brun-Trigaud 1990.

3.1.2. Sprecherzahlen

Die meisten Angaben sind grobe Schätzungen, da es keine repräsentativen Daten gibt, außer Volkszählungen bis 1962 für das Elsaß und INSEE-Umfragen für das Elsaß 1979 sowie Korsika 1982. Außerdem werden in unterschiedlichem Maße auch Sprecher ohne Vollkompetenz berücksichtigt. – Die %-Werte beziehen sich auf die Gesamtbevölkerung der Territorien der Regionalsprachen. Da die großen Städte, außer im Elsaß (Strasbourg 1979: 64% Dialektkenntnis), weitgehend französisiert sind, liegen die Werte für die ländlichen Gebiete höher.

a) Bretonisch: Ständige Sprecher: 240/386 T., Gelegenheitssprecher 685 T. = 44% (Kuter 1989, 75; Gwegen 1975, 55 f).
b) Niederländisch: 150 T. (Pottier 1968, 1159); 70–120 T. (Wood 1960, 108); 60–100 T. (Röhrig 1987, 10 f); 40–100 T. (Sansen 1988, 185).
c) Deutsch: In Lothringen 10 T. (*Langue dominante* 1982, 84) bis 40 T. (48% in Thionville, 90% in Sarrebourg; Giordan 1984, 43). – Elsaß (Hartweg 1988, 40, 48): Volkszählung 1962: 1,3 Mio. (85%); INSEE 1979: ca. 1 Mio., d. h. etwa 75% der über 15jährigen. – Starker Gebrauchsverlust bei der mittleren Generation und der Jugend: Während 84–88% der über 45jährigen den Dialekt verwenden, tun das 57–74% der Gymnasiasten untereinander nie.

d) Baskisch: ca. 80 T., d. h. etwa 30% der Bevölkerung; in Hasparren Kenntnis bei 53% der 20jährigen (Rolssenn 1985, 41).

e) Katalanisch: 170 T. (Pottier 1968, 1155); 100 T., rd. 30% (Tozzi 1984, 53).

f) Okzitanisch: Starke Diskrepanz der Zahlen (Zusammenstellung bei Kremnitz 1981, 12 f.). Vollsprecher ca. 1−2 Mio., rd. 10%; nur Verstehen: 4−10 Mio.

h) Korsisch: 60−80 T., rd. 25% (Tozzi 1984, 57); INSEE-Umfrage 1982: 150 T. (86% der Einheimischen, 1 Viertel der Ausländer; Marcellesi 1988, 818 f).

3.2. Nichtterritorialsprachen (allochthone Sprachen)

Da wegen des Fehlens von Sprachfragen bei den Volkszählungen der Nationalität ein ho-

3.2.1.3. Jiddisch, Judenarabisch, Judenspanisch: Das Westjiddische der alteingesessenen, meist aus dem Elsaß stammenden französischen Juden hat kaum noch Sprecher: „A l'heure présente, cette langue se meurt" (Rafael 1988, 320). Durch die Einwanderung nach dem 1. Weltkrieg entstand eine (ost)jiddische Sprachgruppe; in den 60er Jahren Immigration aus Nordafrika. − Jüdische Bevölkerung Frankreichs: 500−600 T., davon 200 T. Ostjuden (Ertel 1988, 348), 150 T. Judenaraber, 80 T. Sefarden (Sephiha 1988, 305). Sprecher des Jiddischen: 60−80 T. Erstsprachler, 150 T. Muttersprachler (Ertel 1988, 332). Bensimon/Pergola 1986, 279−301 präzisieren die Sprachkenntnis für Paris und die anderen Städte mit mehr als 10 T. jüdischen Einwohnern.

Sprachkenntnisse (in % der jüdischen Bevölkerung)

	Paris	Marseille	Lyon	Nice	Toulouse	Strasbourg
Jiddisch	15	1,4	9	3	3	18
Judenar.	12,4	7	9	12	18	8
Judensp.	3,1	−	3	5	1	−

her Wert als Sprachindiz zukommt, und die Einbürgerung von Immigranten mit der 2. in Frankreich geborenen Generation weitgehend abgeschlossen ist, richtet sich die Einteilung nach Zeit und Dauer der Einwanderungsbewegungen.

3.2.1. Sprachgruppen mit fast ausschließlich französischer Nationalität.

3.2.1.1. Zigeunersprachen/Romani: Die Zahl der Zigeuner ist nur grob abschätzbar: 150−200 T. − Über Kenntnis und Gebrauch der verschiedenen Varietäten gibt es keine Untersuchungen (Williams 1988, 404).

3.2.1.2. Armenisch: Als Folge der Einwanderungswelle in den 20er Jahren gibt es ca. 250−350 T. Franzosen armenischer Abstammung. Verbreitung: Paris 120 T.; Raum Lyon/Saint-Etienne/Valence/Grenoble: 60 T. (Dédéyan 1982, 640f). − Sprachverwendung: Schon bei der 1. in Frankreich geborenen Generation Dominanz des Französischen, bei der 2. Generation „disparition quasi totale de l'arménien parlé dans la vie quotidienne" (Andesian/Hovanessian 1988, 69).

Daraus ergeben sich für den Raum Paris (268 T.) folgende Sprecherzahlen: Jiddisch: 40 T., Judenarabisch: 33 T., Judenspanisch: 8 T. Kommentar zum Zusammenhang von Sprachkenntnis und Lebensalter: „parmi les moins de 25 ans la coinnaissance des langues juives non-hébraïques a pratiquement disparu" (ib. 286).

3.2.1.4. Polnisch: Starke polnische Einwanderung in den 20er Jahren: 1931 ca. 0,5 Mio., 1936: 19% aller Ausländer. Starke Konzentration im Norden und in Lothringen. − Sprachgebrauch: Bei der 2. in Frankreich geborenen Generation ist Französisch generell Erstsprache, Jüngere verstehen Polnisch meist nicht mehr (Ponty/Masiewicz 1988, 272); unmittelbar nach dem 2. Weltkrieg war Polnisch, je nach Beruf, noch bei 16−45% Familiensprache (Girard/Stoetzel 1953, 78).

3.2.1.5. Französische Kreolsprachen: Mehr als 300 T. Personen aus den D.O.M., insbes. Guadeloupe, leben in Frankreich (Tessonneau 1988, 167). − Über den Sprachgebrauch der Erwachsenen liegen keine Angaben vor. Bei den Kindern von Kreolsprechern scheint die Sprache der Eltern schneller zu schwinden als bei anderen Immigrantengruppen (Heredia-Deprez 1989, 78).

3.2.2. Kontinuierliche Immigration

3.2.2.1. Italiener: Schon 1882 113 T.; stärkste Immigrantengruppe zwischen 1900 und 1960; 1931: 808 T., 1936: 33% aller Ausländer (*Quid 1993*, 613 f). Konzentration im Osten, Südosten, Garonnebecken. Die Zahl der Italienischstämmigen wird auf mehr als 3 Mio. geschätzt (Véglianté 1988, 239). − Schnelle sprachliche Assimilation: Schon die 1. in Frankreich geborene Generation hat gewöhnlich keine aktive Sprachkompetenz mehr (Véglianté 1988, 258). Auch nach Girard/Stoetzel (1953, 244−246) geringerer Grad von Sprachbewahrung als bei den Polen: Familiensprache bei 8−32%.

3.2.2.2. Spanier: Bereits starke Immigration zwischen den Kriegen. 1921: 255 T., mit starker Konzentration im Südwesten: über 50% in 7 Departements. 1939 flüchteten 500 T. Spanier nach Frankreich. Heutige Siedlungsschwerpunkte: Ile-de-France, Languedoc-Roussillon, Rhône-Alpes. − Hoher Grad an Sprachbewahrung und -weitergabe (Taboada Leonetti 1988, 194−200).

3.2.3. Einwanderung nach dem 2. Weltkrieg

Bei jüngeren Immigrationswellen können die statistischen Daten über die ausländische Wohnbevölkerung und die Einbürgerungen herangezogen werden, um die annähernde Anzahl der Sprecher einer bestimmten Sprache festzustellen.

3.2.3.1. Umfang der ausländischen und von Ausländern abstammenden Bevölkerung (*Recensement 1982*, 18, 20; *Quid 1993*, 613 ff): Die Volkszählungsdaten der letzten 2 Jahrzehnte zeigen nur geringe Veränderungen, d. h. Zuzug und Einbürgerungen halten sich in etwa die Waage. Anzahl der Ausländer 1975: 3,4 Mio., 1982: 3,7 Mio., 1990: 3,6 Mio. Diese Zahlen gelten als Unterschätzungen, die des Innenministeriums (1990: 4,5 Mio.) als Überschätzung. Man kann für die 80er Jahre also von rd. 4 Mio. Ausländern ausgehen. Als Sprecher von Immigrationssprachen müssen aber auch eingebürgerte Ausländer gelten: 1990 ca. 1,8 Mio. Insgesamt kommt man also auf rd. 5,5−6 Mio. Personen ausländischer Herkunft. Da die Sprachbewahrung teilweise bis in die 2. in Frankreich geborene Generation reicht, sind auch Franzosen mit einem ausländischen Eltern- oder Großelternteil zu berücksichtigen. Die umsichtige Schätzung von Tribalat (1991, 56), bei der nur die Nachkommen eingewanderter Frauen gerechnet werden, kommt zu einem indirekten Bevölkerungszuwachs durch Immigration (1. und 2. in Frankreich geborene Generation), von 5,8−6,9 Mio.; d. h. daß wenigstens 11 Mio., also 1 Fünftel der Gesamtbevölkerung Frankreichs, Ausländer sind, es waren, oder Kinder bzw. Enkel von Ausländerinnen sind.

3.2.3.2. Große Sprachgruppen

Übersicht (in Tausend, nach *Recensement 1982*, 20)

	1946	1962	1982	1982 + Einbürgerungen
Polen	423	177	65	225
Spanier	302	442	321	596
Italiener	451	629	334	752
Portugiesen	22	50	765	835
Algerier Marokkaner Tunesier	40	410	1416	1589

a) Arabischsprecher: Mit 1.5 Mio. größte Sprachgruppe; abzüglich Berberischsprecher und zuzüglich Harkis ca. 2 Mio. Muttersprachler. − Äußerst schneller Sprachverlust: Bereits bei der 1. in Frankreich geborenen Generation hoher Anteil von Französischmonolingualen (je nach Alter 20−40%; Jerab 1988, 31, 39).

b) Portugiesen: Hoher Anteil von Familienmigration, starker Kontakt zur Heimat; deshalb Familiensprache meist Portugiesisch; die Kinder untereinander sprechen überwiegend französisch (Villanova 1988, 286).

3.2.4. Kleinere oder durch die Nationalitätenstatistik nicht erfaßbare Sprachgruppen

a) Berberisch: 500−600 T. Personen mit berberischer Muttersprache. Starker Sprachverlust bei den in Frankreich geborenen Jugendlichen: Mehr als die Hälfte hat keine aktive Sprachkompetenz (Chaker 1988, 152).

b) Sprachen des ehemaligen Jugoslawien: ca. 100 T. potentielle Sprecher. − Schon bei der 1. in Frankreich geborenen Generation viel-

fach nur passive Kenntnis der Sprache der Eltern (Morokvašić 1988, 322).
c) Sprachen Südostasiens: Der größte Teil der ca. 48 T. Kambodschaner ist kmerophon; die ca. 35—50 T. Laoten sprechen meist Lao; bei beiden Sprachgruppen schon bei der 1. in Frankreich geborenen Generation starker Sprachverlust (Choron-Baix 1988, 117; Simon-Barouh 1988 b, 102 f).
Vietnamesisch: Die Immigranten der 1. Jahrhunderthälfte und die Umsiedler nach dem Indochinakrieg haben die Sprache gut bewahrt (Simon Barouh 1988a, 92). Seit 1975 ca. 32 T. vietnamesischsprechende Flüchtlinge.
Chinesisch: ca. 40 T. Chinesischsprecher aus Indochina; starke Konzentration in Paris: XIIIe, XXe, XVIIIe Arrondissement. Das Chinesische bleibt Familiensprache (Hassoun 1988, 139 ff).

3.2.5. Geographische Verbreitung

Die ausländische Bevölkerung konzentriert sich vor allem in den Großstädten: 70% in Städten über 100 T. Einwohner (Gesamtbevölkerung: 40%). Starke regionale Unterschiede: Während der Ausländeranteil für ganz Frankreich bei 6,8% liegt, beträgt er in der Ile-de-France 13%, in Paris 17%. Die Extreme bei den Großstädten mit 110—150 T. Einwohnern: Roubaix 19,3%, Le Mans 3,3% (Ogden 1989, 55).

Ebenso herrscht „much variability by nationality" (Ogden 1989, 54—56): Der Anteil der Immigranten aus den Maghrebländern an der ausländischen Bevölkerung (Durchschnitt: 38,5%) beträgt in Clermont-Ferrand 20%, in Paris 29,5%, in Marseille 69%, in Toulon 72%. In der Ile-de-France leben 18,5% der Italiener, 26,7% der Spanier, 34,5% der Nordafrikaner, 44% der Portugiesen.

Ungleichmäßig ist auch die Verteilung auf die Stadtviertel: In Marseille konzentrieren sich die Ausländer im Zentrum und Norden, in Paris im Nordosten und Westen (Ogden 1989, 57).

4. Benutzte Quellen

ALEA = Beyer, E./Matzen, R. (1969): *Atlas linguistique et ethnographique de l'Alsace*, vol. I, Paris.

ALELG = Philipp, M./Bothorel, A./Levieuge, G. (1977): *Atlas linguistique et ethnographique de la Lorraine germanophone*, vol. I, Paris.

ALEPic = Carton, F./Lebègue, M. (1989): *Atlas linguistique et ethnographique picard*, Paris.

Andesian, S./Hovanessian, M. (1988): „L'arménien. Langue rescapée d'un génocide". In: Vermes II, 60—84.

Bensimon, D./Pergola, S. della (1986): *La population juive de France: socio-démographie et identité*, Paris.

Brun-Trigaud, G. (1990): *Le croissant: le concept et le mot. Contribution à l'histoire de la dialectologie française au XIXe siècle*, Lyon.

Chaker, S. (1988): „Le berbère. Une langue occultée, en exil". In: Vermes II, 145—164.

Choron-Baix, C. (1988): „Le Lao. Une langue ethnique dominante". In: Vermes II, 112—119.

Dédéyan, G. (1982): *Histoire des Arméniens*, Toulouse.

Ertel, R. (1988): „Le yiddish. Entre élection et interdit". In: Vermes I, 332—359.

Escoffier, S. (1958): *La recontre de la langue d'oil, de la langue d'oc et du francoprovençal entre Loire et Allier. Limites phonétiques et morphologiques*, Paris.

Fontan, F. (1969): „La nation occitane, ses frontières, ses régions". In: *Humanitas ethnica: Menschenwürde, Recht und Gemeinschaft. Festschrift für Th. Veiter*, Riedl, F. H. (Ed.), Wien—Stuttgart, 159—182.

Giordan, H. (Dir.) (1984): *Par les langues de France*, Paris.

Girard, A./Stoetzel, J. (1953): *Français et immigrés. I. L'attitude française. L'adaptation des Italiens et des Polonais*, Paris.

Guiter, H. (1973): „Atlas et frontières linguistiques". In: *Les dialectes romans de France à la lumière des atlas régionaux*, Paris, 61—109.

Gwegen, J. (1975): *La langue bretonne face à ses oppresseurs*, Quimper.

Hartweg, G. (1988): „L'alsacien. Un dialecte allemand tabou". In: Vermes I, 33—86.

Hassoun, J.-P. (1988): „Le chinois. Une langue d'émigrés". In: Vermes II, 132—144.

Heredia-Deprez, Ch. de (1989): „Le plurilinguisme des enfants à Paris". In: *Revue Européenne des Migrations Internationales* 5, 71—87.

Jerab, N. (1988): „L'arabe des maghrébins. Une langue, des langues". In: Vermes II, 31−59.

Kremnitz, G. (1981): *Das Okzitanische. Sprachgeschichte und Soziologie*, Tübingen.

Kuter, L. (1989): „Breton vs. French: Language and the opposition of political, economic, social, and cultural values". In: *Investigating obsolescence. Studies in language contraction and death*, Dorian, N. C. (Ed.), Cambridge, 75−89.

Langue dominante, langues dominées, 1982.

Lequin, Y. (Dir.) (1988): *La mosaïque France. Histoire des étrangers et de l'immigration*, Paris.

Marcellesi, J. B. (1988): „Korsisch: Soziolinguistik". In: *Lexikon der Romanistischen Linguistik* IV, Holtus, G./Metzeltin, M./Schmitt, Ch. (Eds.), Tübingen, 809−820.

Morokvašić, M. (1988): „Le serbocroate et les autres langues yougoslaves. Des langues qui s'effacent". In: Vermes II, 317−338.

Noin, D. et al. (1984): *Atlas des Parisiens*, Paris.

Ogden, Ph. E. (1989): „International migration in the nineteenth and twentieth centuries". In: *Migrants in modern France*, Ogden, Ph. E./White, P. E. (Eds.), London, 34−59.

Panier, R. (1942): „Les limites actuelles de la langue bretonne. Leur évolution depuis 1886". In: *Le Français Moderne* 10, 97−115.

Ponty, J./Masiewicz, A. (1988): „Le polonais. Immigrés depuis trois générations". In: Vermes II, 263−282.

Pottier, B. (1968): „La situation linguistique en France". In: *Le langage*, Martinet A. (Ed.), Paris, 1144−1161.

Quid 1993 = Frémy, D./Frémy, M. (1992): *Quid 1993*, Paris.

Rafael, F. (1988): „Le «jeddish-daitch» des Juifs d'Alsace: une langue qui se meurt". In: Vermes I, 318−331.

Recensement général de la population de 1982: les étrangers (1984), Paris.

Rimani, S. (1988): *Les Tunisiens de France. Une forte concentration parisienne*, Paris.

Röhrig, J. W. (1987): *Die Sprachkontaktsituation im Westhoek: Studien zum Bilinguismus und zur Diglossie im französisch-belgischen Grenzraum*, Gerbrunn bei Würzburg.

Rolssenn, B. (1985): *Das Euskara−Das Baskische: Überlebenskampf einer kleinen Sprache und Kultur. Eine soziolinguistische Untersuchung der Situation des Baskischen in Frankreich*, Diss. Frankfurt.

Ronjat, J. (1930): *Grammaire istorique des parlers provençaux modernes, I.*, Montpellier.

Sansen, J. (1988): „Le flamand. Une langue-frontière mal connue". In: Vermes I, 169−187.

Sébillot, F. (1886): „La langue bretonne: Limites et statistique". In: *Revue d'ethnographie*, 1−29.

Séguy, J. (1952): „Basque et gascon dans l'Atlas Linguistique de la Gascogne". In: *Orbis* 1, 385−391.

Sephiha, A. (1988): „Le judéo-espagnol: une langue sans interlocuteurs. Le judéo-arabe: le parler d'une communauté". In: Vermes I, 305−317.

Simon-Barouh, J. (1988): „Le vietnamien. Rapatriés et réfugiés". In: Vermes II, 89−97. (= 1988 a)

−: „Le Kmer. Une langue nationale". In: Vermes II, 98−111. (= 1988 b)

Taboada Leonetti, J. (1988): „L'espagnol. Langue nationale de référence". In: Vermes II, 194−217.

Taboada Leonetti, J./Guillon, M. (1987): *Les immigrés des beaux quartiers. La communauté espagnole dans le XVIe*, Paris.

Tessonneau, A. (1988): „Le créole en métropole. Point d'ancrage de l'identité". In: Vermes II, 165−193.

Timm, L. A. (1983): „The shifting linguistic frontier in Brittany". In: *Essays in honour of Ch. F. Hockett*, Agard B. et al. (Eds.), Leiden, 443−457.

Tourtoulon, Ch. de/Bringuier, O. (1876): „Rapport sur la limite géographique de la langue d'oc et de la langue d'oïl". In: *Archives des missions scientifiques et littéraires*, 3ème série, 3, 545−605.

Tribalat, M. (Dir.) (1991): *Cent ans d'immigration, étrangers d'hier, Français d'aujourd'hui. Apport démographique, dynamique familiale et économique de l'immigration étrangère*, Paris.

Tozzi, M. (1984): *Apprendre et vivre sa langue*, Paris.

Tuaillon, G. (1972): „Le francoprovençal: progrès d'une définition". In: *Travaux de Linguistique et de Littérature* 10/1, 293−339.

Vanneste, A. M. S. (1982): „Le français et le flamand en Flandre française: Essai sur le recul de la frontière linguistique". In: *Sprachen im Kontakt*, Caudmont, J. (Ed.), Tübingen, 17−35.

Végliante, J.-C. (1988): „L'italien. Une italophonie honteuse". In: Vermes II, 234−262.

Vermès, G. (1988): *Vingt-cinq communautés linguistiques de la France*, 2 vol., Paris.

Villanova, R. de (1988): „Le portugais. Une langue qui se ressource en circulant". In: Vermes II, 283−300.

Williams, P. (1988): „Langue tsigane. Le jeu « romanès »". In: Vermes I, 381−413.

Williams, C. H./Ambrose, J. E.: „On measuring language border areas". In: *Language in geographic context*, Williams C. H. (Ed.), Clevedon 1988.

Wood, R. E. (1980): „Language maintenance and external support: The case of the French Flemings". In: *International Journal of the Sociology of Language* 25, 107−119.

Josef Felixberger, Regensburg (Deutschland)

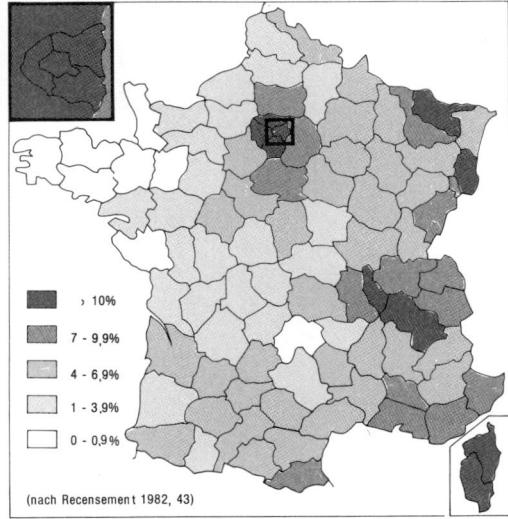

D. Sprachenkarte von Frankreich

Legende (Karte 1):
- > 10%
- 7 - 9,9%
- 4 - 6,9%
- 1 - 3,9%
- 0 - 0,9%

(nach Recensement 1982, 43)

Anteil der Ausländer an der Gesamtbevölkerung Frankreichs nach Départements

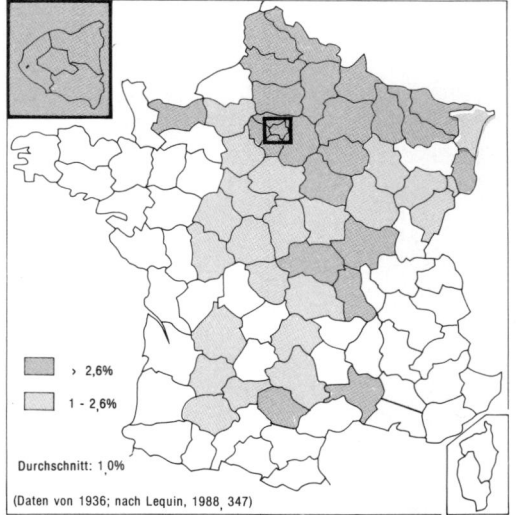

Legende (Karte 2):
- > 2,6%
- 1 - 2,6%

Durchschnitt: 1,0%

(Daten von 1936; nach Lequin, 1988, 347)

Anteil der Polen an der Gesamtbevölkerung nach Départements

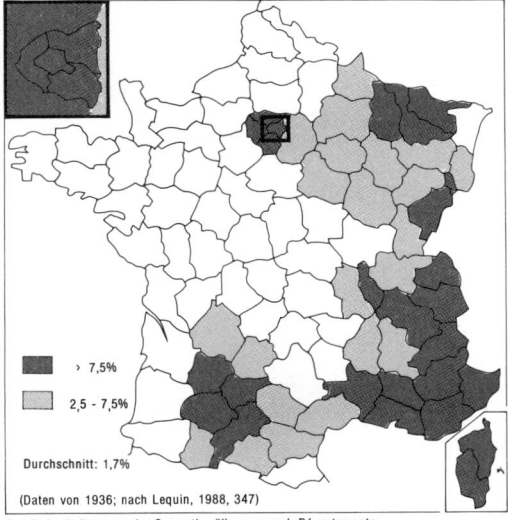

Legende (Karte 3):
- > 7,5%
- 2,5 - 7,5%

Durchschnitt: 1,7%

(Daten von 1936; nach Lequin, 1988, 347)

Anteil der Italiener an der Gesamtbevölkerung nach Départements

Legende (Karte 4):
- Algerier > 1,8% (Durchschnitt: 1,5%)
- Portugiesen > 1,8% (Durchschnitt: 1,4%)

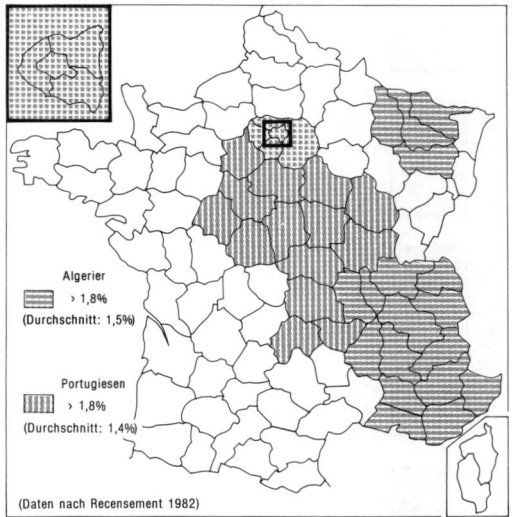

(Daten nach Recensement 1982)

Anteil der Algerier und Portugiesen an der Gesamtbevölkerung nach Regionen

Legende (Karte 5): 4,1 - 7,9 | 2,7 - 4,0 | 1,9 - 2,6 | 0,8 - 1,8 | 0,2 - 0,7%

Anteil der Spanier an der Gesamtbevölkerung von Paris nach Quartiers
(Daten von 1975; nach Noin et al. 1984, 24)

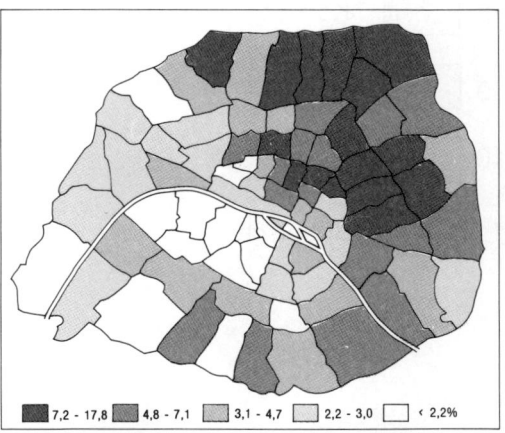

Legende (Karte 6): 7,2 - 17,8 | 4,8 - 7,1 | 3,1 - 4,7 | 2,2 - 3,0 | < 2,2%

Anteil der Nordafrikaner an der Gesamtbevölkerung von Paris nach Quartiers
(Daten von 1982; nach Rimani 1988, 79)

D. Sprachenkarte von Frankreich

Legende:

1   Baskisch
2   Bretonisch
3   Deutsch
4   Englisch
5   Französisch
6   Italienisch
7   Katalanisch
8   Korsisch
9   Niederländisch
10   Okzitanisch
11   Spanisch

Sprachen in Streulage:

A   Armenisch
G   Genuesisch
J   Jiddisch
Ja   Judenarabisch
Js   Judenspanisch

D. Sprachenkarte von Frankreich 2011

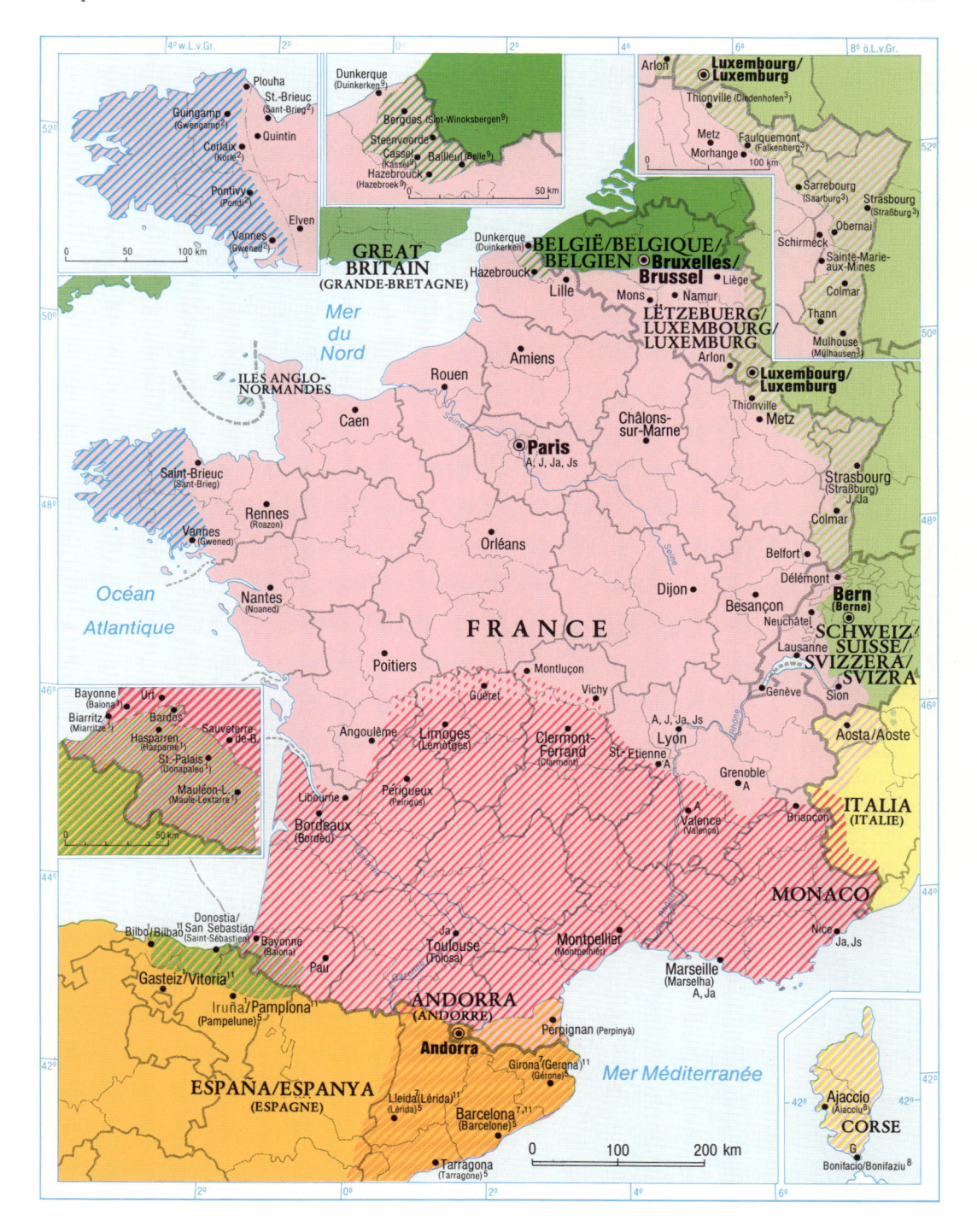

E. Sprachenkarte von Spanien und Portugal

1. Kartenthema

Autochthone Sprachen (unter Einschluß von in Ausbau befindlichen Regionalsprachen) und deren räumliche Verteilung; → Art. 151–155.

2. Kartierungstechnik

Flächenfarben, Farbschraffuren variabler Dicke, Punktraster in Schwarzweiß, zwei Detailausschnitte (Azoren; Madeira, Kanarische Inseln).

3. Kommentar des Kartenautors

3.1. Portugal

Einsprachiger Staat mit Portugiesisch als Amts- und Landessprache; mehr als 95% der Bevölkerung port. Muttersprachler. Sprachgrenze entlang der Staatsgrenze zu Spanien; einige kleine zweisprachige Grenzzonen, insbesondere um Olivenza/Olivença (1801 an Spanien abgetreten) und Miranda (im Mittelalter von Léon aus besiedelt). Sprachgeographisch wird das Portugiesische in die Varietäten Nordportugiesisch sowie Zentral- und Südportugiesisch gegliedert.

Das portugiesische Staatsgebiet (einschließlich Inselregionen Madeira und Azoren) ist sprachlich sehr einheitlich und ohne minderheitensprachliche Regionen.

Allochthone Sprachgruppen: Nach der Volkszählung 1981 betrug die ausländische Wohnbevölkerung 108 Tsd. (1,1%), davon die Hälfte aus dem portugiesischsprachigen Afrika und Brasilien; die stärksten alloglotten Nationalitäten waren Franzosen (12 Tsd.) und Spanier (8 Tsd.). Ein politisches Sprachproblem mit den alloglotten Gruppen besteht nicht.

3.2. Spanien

Dominant einsprachiger Staat mit regionaler Zweisprachigkeit. Spanisch alleinige Amtssprache des Gesamtstaates und in elf Autonomen Gemeinschaften; in sechs Autonomen Gemeinschaften Kooffizialität Spanisch – Regionalsprache (Galicisch/Baskisch/Katalanisch).

Etwa 80% der Bevölkerung span. Muttersprachler, praktisch 100% mit Spanischkompetenz – es gibt heute keine monolingualen Muttersprachler der drei Regionalsprachen.

3.2.1. Spanisch

Sprachlich einheitliches Kerngebiet in der Nordmitte Spaniens sowie im Zentrum und Süden (einschließlich Kanarische Inseln und nordafrikanische Exklaven Ceuta, Melilla). Sprachgeographisch gegliedert in eine südliche Varietät (Andalusisch) und eine nördlich-zentrale (Kastilisch); zum Galicischen und Katalanischen sprachliche Übergangszonen (Asturisch-Leonesisch bzw. Aragonesisch). Die romanische Sprachgrenze des Spanischen wird nach sprachhistorischen Kriterien (Diphthongierung von lat. ĕ, ŏ) festgelegt: maßgebend hierzu Karte „España dialectal" in Menéndez Pidal 1904 und Karte 4 „Areas de las lenguas peninsulares" in ALPI 1962 (Datenerhebung 1931–1936).

3.2.2. Galicisch

Sprachgebiet: Galicien sowie Weststreifen (Franxa) von Asturien und Kastilien-León. Sprachgrenze zum Asturisch-Leonesischen und Nordport. dialektal fließend (Kontinuum), nach sprachhistorischen Kriterien festgelegt; sprachsoziologisch eindeutige Trennung zum Port. wegen der Diglossie Galicisch–Spanisch.

Status und Sprecherzahl: Ko-Amtssprache in Galicien; in der Franxa nicht offizialisiert. Nach der Volkszählung 1991 können in Galicien 87% der Bevölkerung Galicisch sprechen; 50% verwenden es normalerweise, 36% gelegentlich, 8% nie (6% keine Angabe).

3.2.3. Baskisch

Sprachgebiet: (Nördliches) Baskenland und Nordnavarra. Die Sprachgrenze – wegen der typologischen Verschiedenheit kann es zwischen Baskisch und Spanisch keine sprachliche Übergangszone geben – wird nach dem unteren Grenzwert (hier 20% auf Gemeindeebene) des baskischen Bevölkerungsanteils festgelegt.

Status und Sprecherzahl: Ko-Amtssprache im Baskenland und (eingeschränkt) in Nordnavarra. Nach der Volkszählung 1991 können im Baskenland 27% der Bevölkerung Baskisch sprechen und 46% verstehen; keinerlei Kenntnis haben 54% – sprachstatistisch ist also Baskisch im Baskenland die Sprache einer Minderheit.

3.2.4. Katalanisch

Sprachgebiet: Katalonien, Ost-Valencia, Balearen sowie Oststreifen (Franja) von Aragón. Grenze zum Aragonesischen fließend

(Dialektkontinuum), nach sprachhistorischen Kriterien festgelegt; ansonsten historische Grenze zum spanischen (kastilischen) Siedlungsraum. Sprachgeographisch geringe Differenzierung, allerdings wird im Sprachgruppenbewußtsein der Eigenwert der valenzianischen und balearischen Varietät betont.

Status und Sprecherzahl: Ko-Amtssprache in den Autonomen Gemeinschaften Katalonien, Valencia, Balearen; in der Franja nicht offizialisiert. In Andorra ist Katalanisch Staatssprache.

Katalanischkompetenz (Daten nach Volkszählung 1986)

	Katalonien	Valencia	Balearen
Sprechen	66%	51%	72%
Verstehen	90%	83%	90%

Über Sprachgebrauch und Muttersprache liegen keine Volkszählungsdaten vor.

3.2.5. Allochthone Sprachen

Nach der Volkszählung 1991 betrug die ausländische Wohnbevölkerung Spaniens 408 Tsd. (1,04%), darunter 60 Tsd. aus dem spanischsprachigen Ausland. Die stärksten alloglotten Nationalitäten waren Briten (78 Tsd.), Deutsche (45 Tsd.) und Portugiesen (33 Tsd.); ein sprachpolitisches Problem mit den alloglotten Gruppen gibt es nicht.

4. Benützte Quellen

ALPI = Atlas Lingüístico de la Península Ibérica, vol. I: Fonética 1, Madrid 1962.

Berschin, Helmut/Fernández-Sevilla, Julio/Felixberger, Josef (1995): Die spanische Sprache. Verbreitung, Geschichte, Struktur, 2. Aufl., München.

Boléo, Manuel de Paiva/Silva, M. H. Santos (1974): O 'Mapa dos dialectos e falares de Portugal continental' (1962). In: Boléo, M. de Paiva: Estudos de linguística portuguesa e românica, vol. I, 1: Dialectologia e história da língua, Coimbra, 309–352.

Menéndez Pidal, Ramón (1982): Manual de gramática histórica española (^{1}1904), Madrid.

Metzeltin, Michael/Winkelmann, Otto (1992): Sprachkarte „Die Sprachgebiete auf der Iberischen Halbinsel". In: Holtus, G./Metzeltin, M./Schmitt, Ch. (Eds.): Lexikon der Romanistischen Linguistik, vol. VI, 1: Aragonesisch/Navarresisch, Spanisch, Asturianisch/Leonesisch, Tübingen.

Sigüan, Miguel (1992): España plurilingue, Madrid.

Helmut Berschin, Gießen (Deutschland)

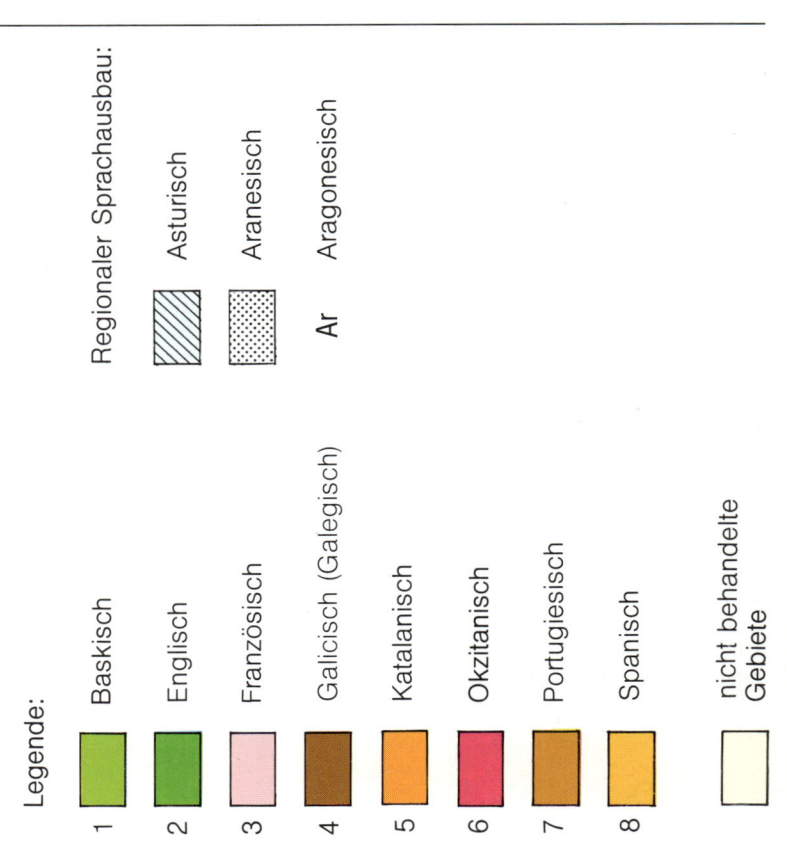

E. Sprachenkarte von Spanien und Portugal

F. Sprachenkarte von Italien und Malta

1. Kartenthema

Autochthone Sprachen und deren räumliche Verteilung; → Art. 156−167.

2. Kartierungstechnik

Flächenfarben, Farbschraffuren variabler Dicke, Buchstabensignaturen zur Markierung von sehr kleinräumig implantierten Minderheitensprachen, zwei Detailausschnitte (Malta und Friaul).

3. Kommentar des Kartenautors

3.1. Albanisch

Eingemeindete Orte, die früher selbständig waren, sind nicht einzeln aufgeführt.

Abruzzen-Molise
1. Campomarino, 2. Montecilfone, 3. Portocannone, 4. Ururi, 5. Villa Badessa;

Apulien
1. Casalvecchio di Puglia, 2. Chieuti, 3. S. Marzano di S. Giuseppe;

Basilicata
1. Barile, 2. Ginestra, 3. Maschito, 4. S. Costantino A., 5. S. Paolo A.;

Kalabrien
1. Acquaformosa, 2. Andalí, 3. Caraffa, 4. Carfizzi, 5. Castroregio, 6. Cerzeto, 7. Civita, 8. Falconara, 9. Firmo, 10. Frascineto, 11. Lungro, 12. Marcedusa, 13. Mongrassano, 14. Pallagorio, 15. Plataci, 16. S. Basile, 17. S. Benedetto Ullano, 18. S. Caterina A., 19. S. Cosmo A., 20. S. Demetrio Corone, 21. S. Giorgio A., 22. S. Martino di Finita, 23. S. Nicola dell'Alto, 24. S. Sofia d'Epiro, 25. Spezzano A., 26. Vaccarizzo A., 27. Vena (di Maida);

Kampanien
1. Greci

Sizilien
1. Contessa Entellina, 2. Piana degli Albanesi, 3. S. Cristina Gela;

Quelle: Birken-Silverman 1992

3.2. Deutsch

3.2.1. *Südtirol*: 67,99% dt., 27,65% it., 4,36% lad., Gesamtbevölkerung: 422 851; (Quelle: Landesinstitut für Statistik 1992. Gemeinden mit mehrheitlich italienischsprachiger Bevölkerung: Bozen/Bolzano 72,59%, Branzoll/Bronzolo 59,96%, Leifers/Laives 69,34%, Salurn/Salorno 61,31%, Pfatten/Vadena 57,87%; Gemeinden mit einem italienischen Bevölkerungsanteil von 25−50%: Brenner/Brennero 29,23%, Brixen/Bressanone 27,03%, Kurtinig a. d. Weinstraße/Cortina s. s. d.v. 30,67%, Neumarkt/Egna 38,71%, Franzensfeste/Fortezza 44,11%, Meran/Merano 49,01%, Auer/Ora 30,10%, Burgstall/Postal 28,38%.

3.2.2. Sprachinseln: Val d'Aosta (Aostatal), Piemont, Trentino, Veneto, Friuli-Venezia Giulia

a) *Val d'Aosta*: Walsersiedlungen (Sprache „Ditsch") Gressoney-La-Trinité, Gressoney-Saint-Jean (1990 zusammen ca. 1000 E.), Issime (1990 365 E.);

b) *Piemont*: Sesiatal (Alagna, Rima, Rimella), Anzascatal (Macugnaga, hier kennt die Jugend die Mundart kaum noch);

c) *Trentino*: Fersental (Palai, St. Felix, St. Franz, Gereut, Eichleit); Lusern (1981: 401 von 415 E. = 96,6%; 1993 noch 375 E.);

d) *Veneto*
− Tredici Comuni (Prov. Verona): 1971 noch 2,2% Sprecher (nur noch Giazza: 257 von 563 Einwohnern = 45,6%);
− Sette Comuni (Prov. Vicenza): 1981 noch 1,2% Sprecher (nur noch Roana mit Mezzaselva: 227 von 3597 E. = 6,3%);
− Sappada (Pladen);

e) *Friuli-Venezia Giulia*
Timau (Tischelwang), Sauris (Zahre).

Quellen: Bellinello 1989, Wurzer 1977.

3.3. Frankoprovenzalisch

1. *Val d'Aosta*: Autonomiestatut; offizielle Sprachen Französisch, Italienisch, ca. 120 000 E., 80 000 Emigranten in Paris. Schätzungen über den frankophonen Anteil der Bev. schwanken zwischen 20 und 70%;

2. *Piemont*: Alpentäler nordwestlich von Turin: Val di Susa (ca. 10 000 Sprecher, ≈ 23% der Bevölkerung), Val Soana (990 Sprecher, ≈ 59%), (Val Cenischia 990 Sprecher, ≈ 58%) sowie in weiteren Tälern, insgesamt rund 22 000 Sprecher

(≈ 28% der ansässigen Bevölkerung) (1982), Telmon.
3. *Apulien* (Prov. Foggia): Faeto, Celle San Vito ca. 1000−1200 Sprecher (cf. Kattenbusch, 1982).

3.4. Griechisch

Kalabrien (Prov. Reggio Calabria)
Nur in Chorio di Rogudi / Chorio tu Roghudiu (700 E.) und Gallicianò (350 E.) wird üblicherweise Griechisch gesprochen; in Bova / Vua (Bova Superiore 2000 E.) nur von Erwachsenen. In Condofuri und Amendolea / Amiddalia nur noch wenige alte Leute, die gr. verstehen und sprechen.

Quelle: Karanastasis 1972.

Apulien (Prov. Lecce)
1. Calimera
2. Sternatia
3. Martano
4. Zollino
5. Castrignano dei Greci
6. Corigliano d'Otranto
Praktisch ausgestorben ist das Gr. in Martignano, Soleto und Melpignano.

Quelle: Profili 1983.

Sprecherzahl nach Karananstasis 1972: Calimera (7000 E.), Sternatia (4000), Corigliano (5000), Martignano (2000), Zollino (3000); in Martano ca. ⅓ von 9000 Einwohnern; Sprecherzahl nach Spano 1965: Sternatia 74,9%, Corigliano 71,1%, Martano 59,8%, Zollino 59,4%, Martignano 56,8%, Castrignano dei Greci 52,4%, Calimera 51,5%, Melpignano 17,4%, Soleto 11%.

3.5. Katalanisch

Sizilien (Provinz Sassari)
Alghero 45 000 E., davon ca. 45% Katalanischsprecher.

3.6. Kroatisch

Molise
1. Acquaviva Collecroce (Zivavoda Brdodokriz/Kruč), 2. San Felice del Molise (Sti Filič), 3. Montemitro (Mundimitar). Von den 2449 E. (1981) rund 2000 Kroatischsprecher.

3.7. Provenzalisch

1. *Piemont* (Prov. Torino): Chisonetal, Pellicetal;
2. *Kalabrien* (Prov. Cosenza): Guardia Piemontese ca. 500 Sprecher.

3.8. Rätoromanisch

a) (Sella-)Ladinisch (aufgrund Selbsteinschätzung und linguistischer Kriterien): Gadertal, Gröden, Fassa, Buchenstein, Ampezzo, ca. 30 000 Sprecher;
b) Comelianisch (linguistische Kriterien; geringes Sprachbewußtsein): Candide, Casada, Comèlico, Costa, Costalisoio, Costalta, Danta, Dosoledo, Pàdola, Santo Stefano, Valle; ca. 10 000 Sprecher;
c) Friaulisch (vorwiegend linguistische Kriterien): Friuli-Venezia Giulia außer Timau (Tischelwang), Sauris (Zahre), beide dt.; Kanaltal Deutsch/Slowenisch/Friaulisch/Italienisch; Grado, Triest, Monfalcone venezisch; Grenzgebiet zu Slowenien slowenisch; Erto (ladinisch);
im Westen der Region sowie im Südosten des Veneto friaulisch-venezische Übergangszone;
in den größeren Städten Friauls sowie in deren näherer Umgebung immer stärkere Verbreitung einer venezischen Koine als Basilekt.

Quellen: Frau 1984, LRL 3 (1989) (Artikel 210−217; 563−645; Karte, XIX), Steinicke 1992.

3.9. Sardisch

Ganz Sardinien außer Alghero (L'Alguer: Katalanisch), Carloforte und Calasetta (genuesische Sprachinseln; L = Ligurisch).
Das Sassaresische und das Galluresische im Norden der Insel sind stark vom Korsischen beeinflußt.

Quelle: Virdis 1988.

3.10. Slovenisch

Region Friuli-Venezia Giulia: in den Provinzen Trieste (ca. 8%), Gorizia (ca. 12%) und Udine (ca. 28%), insgesamt rund 50 000 Sprecher. Zahlen basieren auf Volkszählungen, werden aber sowohl von der Mehrheitsbevölkerung angezweifelt. Keine sicheren Daten über konkrete Sprecherzahlen, da bei der ital. Volkszählung nach der Muttersprache, nicht nach der Gebrauchssprache gefragt wird. Neben Standardslovenisch zahlreiche Mundarten. Mehrheitlich slovenische Gemeinden:
− Prov. Udine: Resia/Rezija, Taipana/Tipana, Lusévera/Brdo;
− Prov. Gorizia: S. Floriano del Collio/Števerjan, Savogna d'Isonzo/Sovodnje ob Soči, Doberdò del Lago/Doerdob;

– Prov. Trieste: Sgonico/Zgoník, Monrupino/Repentabor, S. Dorligo della Valle/ Dolina.

Quelle: Arbeitsgemeinschaft 1990, Clauss 1982, 357 ff.

3.11. Norditalienische Dialekte in Süditalien und Sardinien

Sizilien
San Fratello (Prov. Messina), Sperlinga, Nicosia, Piazza Armerina, Aidone (Prov. Enna); S = dialetti settentrionali (norditalienische Dialekte).

Basilicata (Prov. Potenza):
1. Tito, Picerno, Pignola, z. T. Potenza; Dialekte weisen galloitalienische Züge auf. (cf. Rohlfs, 1931);
2. Nemoli, Rivello, San Constantino, Trecchina; Dialekte weisen galloitalienische Züge auf; cf. Rohlfs, 1941);
S = dialetti settentrionali (norditalienische Dialekte).

3.12. Malta

Die bodenständige maltesische Sprache ist semitischen Ursprungs. Das Maltesische wurde 1934 als Amtssprache anerkannt. Bis dahin waren Englisch und Italienisch − und davor Italienisch − offizielle Amtssprachen. Heute sind Englisch und Maltesisch die Amtssprachen. Prozentsatz der Einsprachigen (sowohl Englisch als auch Maltesisch) unter 5%. Personen mit Italienisch-Kenntnissen noch in der älteren Generation. In jüngerer Zeit Einflüsse des Italienischen (besonders unter Jugendlichen) durch das italienische Fernsehen, das auf Malta empfangen werden kann.

Sliema weist eine starke englischsprachige Minderheit auf; dort größter Prozentsatz englischsprachiger Muttersprachler (ca. 10%).

4. Benützte Quellen

Arbeitsgemeinschaft Alpen-Adria (Ed.) (1990): *Die Minderheiten im Alpen-Adria-Raum*, Klagenfurt.

Bellinello, Pier Francesco (1989): „Le colonie dei 'Cimbri' in Italia". In: *Le minoranze etniche e linguistiche. Atti del 2° Congresso Internazionale* (Piana degl Albanesi, 1988), Palermo, 751−776.

Birken-Silverman, Gabriele (1992): „Phasen des Rückgangs einer Sprache am Beispiel des Albanischen in Italien". In: *Zeitschrift für Balkanologie* 28, 1−22.

Clauss, Jan Ulrich (1982): *Sprachminderheiten in den EG-Staaten am Beispiel von acht Fallstudien aus Italien und Belgien*, Badia Fiesolana, Florenz (hier: 357 ff).

Frau, Giovanni (1984): *I dialetti del Friuli*, Udine.

Karanastasis, A. (1972): „Lo stato in cui si trovano oggi i dialetti neogreci dell'Italia meridionale". In: *Bilinguismo e diglossia in Italia*, Pisa, 23−27.

Kattenbusch, Dieter (1982): *Das Frankoprovenzalische in Süditalien*, Tübingen.

Landesinstitut für Statistik der Autonomen Provinz Bozen/Südtirol (Ed.) (1992): *Statistisches Jahrbuch für Südtirol*, Bozen.

LRL: *Lexikon der romanistischen Linguistik*, Holtus, G./Metzeltin, M./Schmitt, Chr. (Eds.), Tübingen 1988 ff.

Profili, Olga (1983): Le parler grico de Corigliano d'Otranto, Grenoble (Thèse d'Université).

Rohlfs, Gerhard (1931): „Galloitalienische Sprachkolonien in der Basilikata". In: *Zeitschrift für romanische Philologie* 51, 249−279.

Rohlfs, Gerhard (1941): „Galloitalienische Sprachkolonien am Golf von Policastro (Lukanien)". In: *Zeitschrift für romanische Philologie* 61, 79−113.

Spano, B. (1965): *La grecità bizantina e i suoi riflessi geografici nell'Italia meridionale e insulare*, Pisa.

Steinicke, E. (1992): „Das viersprachige Kanaltal − seine ethnographische Sonderstellung im Friulanischen Gebirge". In: *Europa Ethnica* 4 (N. F.) 185−204.

Telmon, Tullio (1982): *Sociologia della comunicazione*, Turin.

Virdis, Maurizio (1988): „Sardisch. Areallinguistik. Sardo. Aree linguistiche". In: *LRL* 4, 897−913 (hier: 905, Karte).

Wurzer, Bernhard (1977): *Die deutschen Sprachinseln in Oberitalien*, Bozen.

Dieter Kattenbusch, Gießen (Deutschland)

F. Sprachenkarte von Italien und Malta

Legende:

1. Albanisch
2. Deutsch
3. Englisch (auf Malta)
4. Französisch (incl. Frankoprovenzalisch)
5. Griechisch
6. Italienisch
7. Katalanisch (auf Sardinien)
8. Korsisch
9. Kroatisch
10. Maltesisch
11. Provenzalisch (Alpinokzitanisch)
12. Rätoromanisch
    Bündnerromanisch
    (Sella-)Ladinisch
    Comelianisch
    Friaulisch
13. Sardisch
    Sassaresisch und Galluresisch
14. Slowenisch

nicht behandelte Gebiete

Streusiedlungen:

s s Norditalienische Dialekte in Süditalien, Sardinien, Sizilien und Korsika

Zimbern:

VII Sieben Gemeinden (Veneto)

XIII Dreizehn Gemeinden (Veneto)

F. Sprachenkarte von Italien und Malta

G. Sprachenkarte von Slowenien, Kroatien, Bosnien-Herzegowina, Jugoslawien (Serbien und Montenegro), Makedonien und Albanien

1. Kartenthema

Autochthone Sprachen und deren räumliche Verteilung (Stand: 1991, vor dem Zerfall Jugoslawiens); → Art. 168–173.

2. Kartierungstechnik

Flächenfarben, Farbschraffuren variabler Dicke, Buchstabensignaturen zur Markierung räumlich diffus verteilter Ethnien.

3. Kommentar des Kartenautors

Die Kartierung betrifft Sprachen und deren Sprecher (im Falle des Serbokroatischen wurde zwischen Serben, Kroaten und Moslems unterschieden) auf Grund von absoluten Mehrheiten; Mischlagen erscheinen schraffiert.

4. Benützte Quellen

Jordan, Peter/Kelnhofer, Fritz (Eds.) (1993): *Atlas Ost- und Südosteuropa 2.5–0.1: Ethnische Struktur des östlichen Europas und Kaukasiens um 1990.* Wien.

Popović, Ivan (1960): *Geschichte der serbokroatischen Sprache.* Wiesbaden.

Pohl, Heinz Dieter (1991–1992): „Zur Geschichte und zur Unabhängigkeit Sloweniens und Kroatien. Hintergründe und historische Daten zum Zerfall Jugoslawiens". In: *Klagenfurter Beiträge zur Sprachwissenschaft* 17–18, 5–60.

Enciklopedija Slovenije, Laibach: Lexikonartikel „Jugoslavija".

Heinz Dieter Pohl, Klagenfurt (Österreich)

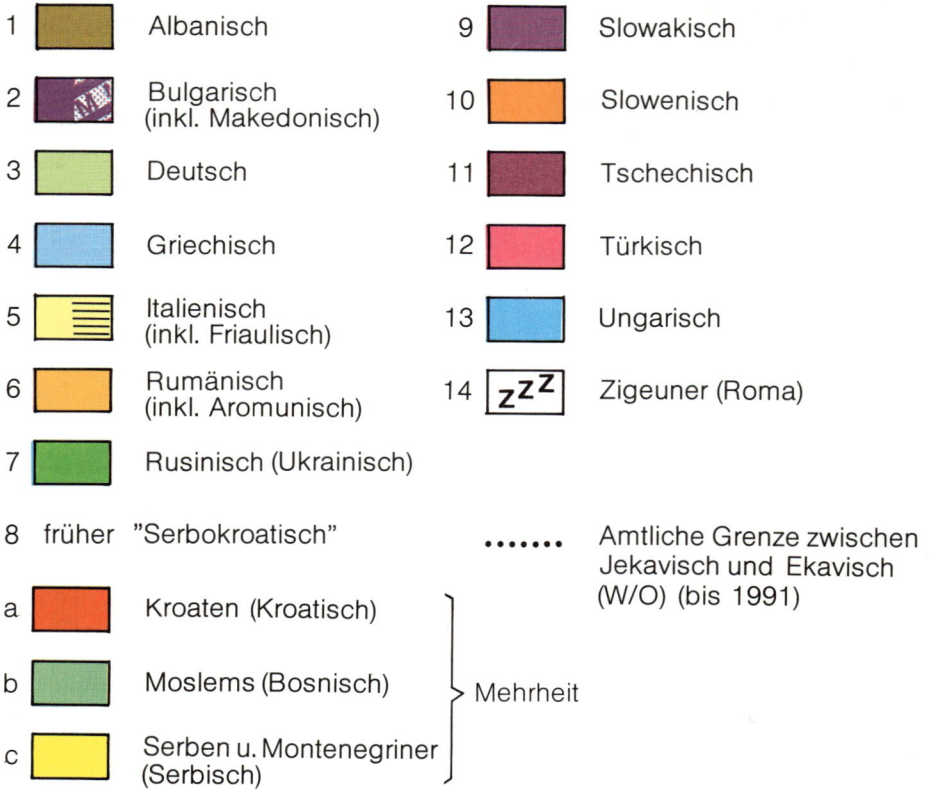

G. Sprachenkarte von Slowenien, Kroatien, Bosnien, Jugoslawien, Makedonien und Albanien

Legende: (Stand nach 1.1.1991)

1	Albanisch	9		Slowakisch
2	Bulgarisch (inkl. Makedonisch)	10		Slowenisch
3	Deutsch	11		Tschechisch
4	Griechisch	12		Türkisch
5	Italienisch (inkl. Friaulisch)	13		Ungarisch
6	Rumänisch (inkl. Aromunisch)	14		Zigeuner (Roma)
7	Rusinisch (Ukrainisch)			

8 früher "Serbokroatisch"

a Kroaten (Kroatisch) ⎫
b Moslems (Bosnisch) ⎬ Mehrheit
c Serben u. Montenegriner (Serbisch) ⎭

······· Amtliche Grenze zwischen Jekavisch und Ekavisch (W/O) (bis 1991)

G. Sprachenkarte von Slowenien, Kroatien, Bosnien, Jugoslawien, Makedonien und Albanien

H. Sprachenkarte von Rumänien und Bulgarien

1. Kartenthema

Autochthone Sprachen und deren räumliche Verzahnung; → Art. 174−180.

2. Kartierungstechnik

Flächenfarben, Farbschraffuren variabler Dicke, Symbolsignaturen zur Markierung ethnischer Streulagen.

3. Kommentar des Kartenautors

3.1. Rumänien

Über Stärke und Entwicklung der Minderheiten in Rumänien geben die in etwas unregelmäßigen Abständen 1948, 1956, 1966, 1977 und 1992 durchgeführten Volkszählungen (*Recensămînt*) eine zuverlässige Auskunft, was jedoch kleinere Verzerrungen oder Manipulationen nicht ausschließt, z. B. 1977 die Differenzierung: *Deutsche, Schwaben, Sachsen*. Die Angaben zur Muttersprache und Nationalität differieren bis auf spezifische Fälle (Juden und Zigeuner geben nicht immer *Jiddisch* bzw. *Romani* an) geringfügig. Die geographische Verteilung der 16 erfaßten Minderheiten (*Ungarn, Deutsche, Zigeuner, Ukrainer, Russen, Türken, Serben, Tataren, Slowaken, Bulgaren, Juden, Kroaten, Tschechen, Polen, Griechen, Armenier*) läßt sich bis auf die Ebene der Verwaltungsbezirke (*Județ*) exakt verfolgen. Größere Konzentrationen geben einen ersten Hinweis auf geschlossene Minderheitensiedlungen, die seit 1971 offiziell nur noch den rumänischen Namen tragen dürfen. Weitere Präzisierungen geben die historischen Untersuchungen, die freilich nicht mehr in allen Fällen aktuell sind. Bei *Zigeunern, Juden, Griechen* und *Armeniern* handelt es sich vorwiegend um Stadtbewohner. Die verschiedenen Gruppen von Slaven (0,3−0,02%) wohnen nur in den Grenzgebieten kompakt. Von der allgemeinen prozentualen und numerischen Abnahme der Minderheiten durch Abwanderung (s. Pfeile) weichen nur *Zigeuner, Ukrainer, Russen, Türken* und *Tataren* signifikant ab.

3.2. Bulgarien

Die Ergebnisse der jüngsten, sehr komplexen Volkszählung (Prebrojavane) von 1992 liegen noch nicht vor, so daß die Karte von älteren, sowohl hinsichtlich der Anzahl wie auch der exakten geographischen Verteilung der Minderheiten unbefriedigenden Daten ausgeht. Mit den Ergebnissen der Zählungen von 1956 und 1965 werden die letzten amtlichen Angaben gemacht, danach ist man wegen der Ende der 50er Jahre einsetzenden assimilatorischen Politik auf Schätzungen und Hochrechnungen angewiesen. Problematischer als im Falle Rumäniens ist die Abgrenzung zwischen Nationalität, Religion und Sprache. Grundlage für die Karte ist primär die Muttersprachlichkeit. Die Religionszugehörigkeit kann zu einer abweichenden nationalen Zuordnung führen, z. B. sprechen die muslimischen *Pomaken* Bulgarisch, hingegen die christlichen *Gagauzen* eine Turksprache und die *Zigeuner* je nach Religion Bulgarisch, Türkisch oder Rumänisch. Ein Sonderproblem stellen die *Makedonier* dar: sprachlich liegt ein Dialektkontinuum vor, das sich nicht an aktuellen Staatsgrenzen orientiert, politisch werden die Zahlen einmal in der einen (1956: 187 789) oder anderen Richtung (1965: 9632) manipuliert. Je nach politischem Standpunkt ist dann Makedonien Teil des bulgarischen bzw. der Bezirk Blagoevgrad (Pirinmakedonien) Teil des makedonischen Sprachgebiets.

Die *Türken* sind mit 8−10% die bedeutendste sprachliche Minderheit, die in zwei größeren Gebieten kompakt siedelte und dort zahlenmäßig sogar die Bulgaren übertraf: Im Nordosten zwischen Razgrad, Šumen und Dobrič sowie im Südosten im Bezirk Kărdžali. Diese und andere Gebiete verließ ein beträchtlicher Teil von ihnen in verschiedenen Auswanderungswellen (1950/1, 1970−74, ab 1989). Nach 1990 gab es kurzfristig eine Rückwanderung, da die Türkei dem gewaltigen Zustrom (etwa 300 000) nicht gewachsen war. Die restlichen Sprachgruppen (*Armenier, Russen, Griechen, Juden, Tataren, Rumänen, Deutsche, Serben, Tschechen, Ungarn, Karatschanen, Albaner, Aromunen*) rangieren zwischen 0,25−0,01%. Erheblich gewachsen ist sicherlich der Anteil der Zigeuner, zuletzt mit 1,81% angegeben. Im Norden und Nordosten gibt es noch relativ geschlossene Siedlungen von Tataren, Russen und Rumänen, während die anderen Gruppen überwiegend in Städten wohnen.

4. Benützte Quellen

4.1. Rumänien

Quellenwerke sind die veröffentlichten Ergebnisse der Volkszählungen — die neuesten Zahlen sind enthalten in *Recensămîntul populaţiei şi locuinţelor 1992. Rezultate preliminare. Conferinţa de presă. Comisia Naţională pentru Statistică.* Bucureşti, 29. Mai 1992 [Die Zählung der Bevölkerung und Wohnungen 1992. Vorläufige Resultate] — sowie die statistischen Jahrbücher für Rumänien (*Anuarul statistic al RSR* …). Diese Quellen bilden die Grundlage für die zahlreichen Untersuchungen zu den Minderheiten in Rumänien, von denen folgende Karten und Literaturangaben enthalten: Joó, R. (1988): *Report on the situation of the Hungarian minority in Rumania prepared for the Hungarian Democratic Forum*, Budapest; Schöpflin, G. (1979): *Les hongrois de Roumanie*, Paris (= Groupement pour les droits de minorités, Rapport Nr. B); Steinke, Klaus (1977): „Les minorités hongroise et allemande de Roumanie". In: *Recherches sociologiques* 1, 1977, 51—74; Wagner, E. (1977): *Historisch-statistisches Ortsnamenbuch für Siebenbürgen*, Köln.

4.2. Bulgarien

Detaillierte Angaben zu Wohnsitzen von Minderheiten in der östlichen Hälfte Bulgariens machen die ersten beiden Kommentarbände des Bulgarischen Dialektatlasses (*Bălgarski dialekten atlas*, Sofia 1964, 1966). Aktuell ist noch: Troebst, St. (1990): „Nationale Minderheiten". In: *Südosteuropa-Handbuch, Bulgarien, vol. VI*, Grothusen, K.-D. (Ed.), Göttingen.

Klaus Steinke, Erlangen (Deutschland)

Legende:

1. Albanisch
2. Bulgarisch (inkl. Makedonisch)
3. Deutsch
4. Griechisch
5. Rumänisch
6. Russisch
7. Serbisch
8. Türkisch
9. Ukrainisch
10. Ungarisch

nicht behandelte Gebiete

Streusiedlungen:

- ▼ Bulgaren
- ★ Gagausen
- ⬢ Kroaten
- ⊙ Polen
- ● Rumänen (Aromunisch)
- ■ Russen
- ⬟ Serben
- ▲ Slowaken
- × Tataren
- ▲ Tschechen
- ○ Türken
- ▼ Ukrainer

H. Sprachenkarte von Rumänien und Bulgarien

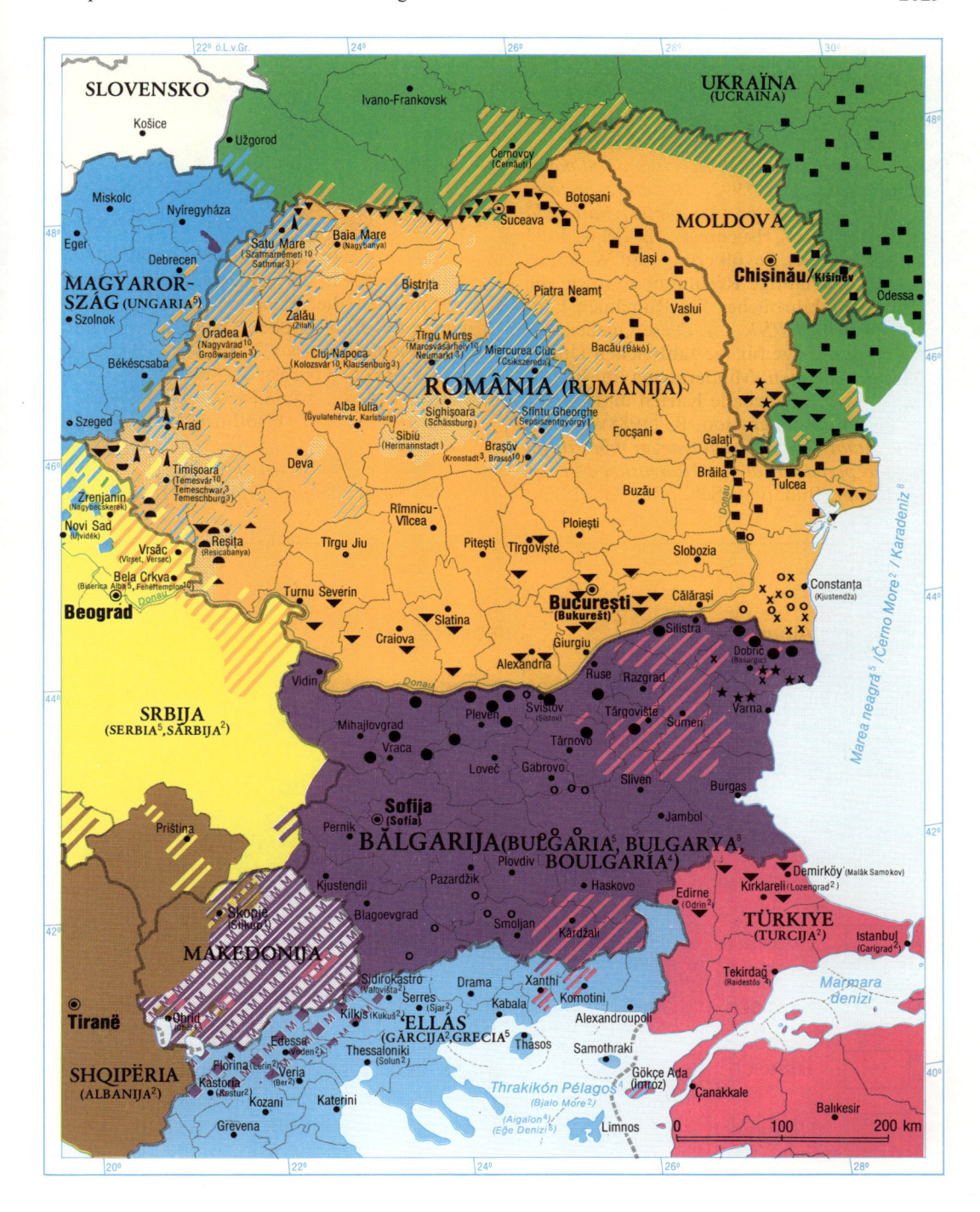

I. Sprachenkarte von Griechenland, Zypern und der europäischen Türkei

1. Kartenthema

Autochthone Sprachen und deren räumliche Verzahnung; auch Berücksichtigung allochthoner Sprachgruppen; → Art. 181–191.

2. Kartierungstechnik

Flächenfarben, Farbschraffuren variabler Dicke, Symbolsignaturen (Buchstaben) zur Markierung punktuell oder diffus implantierter Sprachen bzw. Ethnien, ein Detailausschnitt (Zypern).

3. Kommentar des Kartenautors

3.1. Zur Wiedergabe griechischer Wörter

Anders als die *Transliteration*, deren Anliegen die exakte Rekonstruierbarkeit der jeweiligen Buchstabenabfolge in der Ausgangssprache ist, strebt die hier aus praktischen Gründen bevorzugte *Transkription* eine möglichst getreue lautliche Wiedergabe der griechischen Bezeichnungen in der Zielsprache an. Zur Kennzeichnung von nicht zum deutschen Laut- bzw. Grapheminventar gehörenden Konsonanten wurde *dh* für [ð], *th* für [θ] sowie *gh* für [γ] verwendet. Die übrigen Zeichen entsprechen im wesentlichen ihrem deutschen Wert, wobei allerdings zu beachten ist, daß die Plosive nicht aspiriert werden, dafür aber vor „hellen" Vokalen (e, i) eine leicht palatalisierte Artikulation gebräuchlich ist. Des weiteren richtet sich die Aussprache von *ch* (griech. χ) nach dem folgenden und nicht, wie im Deutschen, nach dem vorhergehenden Vokal: Vor „hellen" Vokalen (e, i) lautet *ch* [ç], vor dunklen Vokalen und vor nichtpalatalisierten Konsonanten [x]. Die Vokale sind halboffen und halblang (keine phonematisch relevante Opposition Öffnungsgrad–Länge: e [ɛ], o [ɔ]. Progressive Assimilation der Plosive ist üblich: *nt* [nd, d], *mp* [m̩b, b], *gk* [ŋg, g].

3.2. Gestaltung der Karte

Die Karte markiert das *wahrscheinliche* Sprachverhalten, also nicht notwendigerweise auch das ethnische, religiöse oder Stammesbewußtsein. Als Minimalkriterium wurde dabei das *passive* Sprachverständnis angenommen, was insbesondere in den arvanitischen Zonen bei der jüngeren Sprechergeneration das Maximum der Sprachkompetenz ausmacht. Im aromunischen Kerngebiet (Pindosgebirge) ist in der Regel aber gleichzeitig noch eine aktive mündliche Sprachkompetenz anzutreffen; gleiches gilt für die turkophonen Regionen, wo letztere zunehmend mit einer schriftlichen Kompetenz im Türkeitürkischen einhergeht — obwohl die 50%-Schwelle beim Analphabetismus (bei der Gesamtbev. dagegen < 10%) noch nicht unterschritten wird (Eteria jia ta dhikeomata ton mionotiton 1992, 5).

Die dichte Schraffur bezeichnet alloglosse Zonen mit ca. 35–65% Allophonen (meist eher unter als über 50%, nur bei den Thrakientürken oft deutlich über 50%), die weite Schraffur eine Präsenz von ca. 15–35% Allophonen. Kleinere Streugruppen werden mit den entsprechenden Buchstabensiglen markiert.

Angesichts eines für eine differenzierte synchrone Dokumentation des Sprachgebrauchs insbesondere der nichtmuslimischen Gruppen nur sehr bruchstückhaften Datenmaterials — eine löbliche Ausnahme ist die Erhebung von Ciampi (1985) — mußte öfters „extra-" bzw. „interpoliert" werden, d. h. an Hand siedlungs- und wirtschaftsgeographischer Faktoren die gegenwärtige Konsistenz des Sprachgebietes geschätzt werden. Für den im Einzugsgebiet von Groß-Athen liegenden Teil Ostattikas wurde etwa aufgrund der starken Zuwanderung eine Erosion des arvanitischen Sprachgebietes angenommen. Bei der Kennzeichnung der turkophonen Zonen konnte angesichts der hier weitgehenden Koinzidenz von Sprach- und Stimmverhalten (Ausnahme: slavophone muslimische Pomaken) auf die von Dhodhos (1994) dokumentierten Wahlergebnisse der Minderheitenpartei „Empistosini" (Vertrauen) zurückgegriffen werden.

Fast alle arvanitischen, aromunischen und slavischen Allophonen sind zweisprachig, wobei die Minderheitensprache in der Regel die Rolle der L-Variante einnimmt. Vor allem im aromunischen Bereich ist jedoch das Minderheitenidiom nicht nur Heim- und Herdsprache, sondern dient mitunter auch als orales Kommunikationsmedium auf lokaler Ebene (Dorfplatz, Kaffeehaus usw.).

3.3. Zahlenangaben
(für Griechenland bis auf die Muslime grobe Schätzungen, z. T. widersprüchlich)

Griechenland: Turkophone Muslime: < 120 000, Pomaken (slavophone Muslime) ca. 35 000, Aromunischsprachige ca. 50 000 – 120 000, Slavophone Orthodoxe ca. 50 000 – 100 000, Albanischsprachige (Arvaniten) ca. 30 000 – 100 000;

Türkei: Gräkophone Orthodoxe: Istanbul ca. 2500, Imbros ca. 350, Tenedos ca. 40; gräkophone Muslime ca. 10 000; kurdischsprachige Gruppen: Istanbul/kleinasiatisches Küstengebiet ca. 700 000 – 1 200 000; Armenier: Istanbul ca. 35 000;

Zypern: Griechen ca. 600 000, Türken ca. 130 000 (einschl. Zuwanderer), Armenier ca. 4000 – 5000 (im griech. Teil).

4. Benützte Quellen

Aggelopulos, Ath. (1979): „Population Distribution of Greece Today according to Language National Consciousness and Religion". In: *Balkan Studies* 20, 123 – 135 [gibt den offiziösen griechischen Standpunkt wieder].

Alexandris, Alexis (1983): *The Greek Minority of Istanbul and Greek-Turkish Relations 1918 – 1974*, Athen.

Alexandris, Alexis (1990): „Imbros and Tenedos: A Study in Turkish Attitudes Toward Two Ethnic Greek Island Communities Since 1923". In: *Journal of the Hellenic Diaspora* 7, 10 – 19.

Andrews, Peter Alford (1983): *Ethnic Groups in the Republic of Turkey*, Wiesbaden.

Bornträger, Ekkehard W. (1994): „Die Konstantinopelgriechen in der türkischen Republik". In: *Europa Ethnica* 51, 1 – 15.

Bornträger, Ekkehard W. (1996): „Die griechische Volksgruppe auf Imbros und Tenedos". In: *Europa Ethnica* 53, 21 – 28.

Ciampi, Gabriele (1985): „Le sedi dei greci arvaniti". In: *Rivista geografica italiana* 92, 75 – 116.

Dahmen, Wolfgang/Kramer, Johannes (1985): *Aromunischer Sprachatlas* 1, Hamburg.

Daum, Nicolaus/Hofwiler, Roland (1992): „Mazedonien". In: *Pogrom* 165, 14 – 31 [hauptsächlich über Griechisch-Mazedonien, u. a. mit Interviews und Rundgesprächen unter Beteiligung von Slavomazedoniern aus Griechenland].

Dhodhos, Dimosthenis Ch. (1994): *Eklojiki jeoghrafia ton mionotiton [Wahlgeographie der Minderheiten]*, Athen.

Dimitras, Panayote (1992): „Minorités linguistiques en Grèce". In: *Les minorités en Europe*, Giordan, H. (Ed.), Paris, 301 – 321 [kritische Bestandsaufnahme mit den entsprechenden Volkszählungsergebnissen von 1928 u. 1951].

Eteria jia to dhikeomata ton mionotiton [Gesellschaft für die Rechte der Minderheiten, griechische Abteilung der Minority Rights Group, London] (1992): *Mionotites stin Elladha [Minderheiten in Griechenland]*, Athen.

Grulich, Rudolf (1977): „Die türkische Minderheit in Griechenland". In: *Materialia Turcica* 3, 83 – 88.

Härtel, Hans Joachim (1993): „Die muslimische Minorität in Griechenland". In: *Der ruhelose Balkan*, Weithmann, M. (Ed.), München, 214 – 217.

Hill, Peter (1989): *The Macedonians in Australia*, Canberra.

Hill, Peter (1993): „National Minorities in Europe". In: *Journal of Intercultural Studies* 14, 33 – 48.

Helsinki Watch/Human Rights Watch (Ed.) (1992): *Denying Human Rights and Ethnic Identity: The Greeks of Turkey*, Washington.

Helsinki Watch/Human Rights Watch (Ed.) (1992): *Destruction de l'identité ethnique: Les Turcs de Grèce*, Washington.

Kitis, Eliza (1993): „Greece". In: *Sociolinguistica* 7, 119 – 134 [offiziöser griechischer Standpunkt].

Kowallik, Sabine/Kramer, Johannes (Eds.) (1993): *Romanojudaica*, Gerbrunn bei Würzburg.

Krüger, Eberhard (1984): *Die Siedlungsnamen Griechisch-Makedoniens nach amtlichen Verzeichnissen und Kartenwerken*, Berlin.

Lazarou, Achille G. (1986): *L'aroumain et ses rapports avec le grec*, Saloniki.

Lithoxou, Dhimitris (1992): *Mionotika zitimata ke ethniki sinidhisi stin Elladha [Minderheitenfragen und Nationalbewußtsein in Griechenland]*, Athen [kritische, von nationalistischen Einseitigkeiten freie diachronische Darstellung].

Meinardus, Roland: „Die griechisch-türkische Minderheitenfrage". In: *Orient* 26, 48—61.

Saramandu, Nicolae (1988): „Harta graiurilor aromâne și meglenoromâne din peninsula balcanica". In: *SCL Studi și cercetarii lingvistice* 39, 225—245.

Sarides, Emmanuel (1987): *Ethnische Minderheit und zwischenstaatliches Streitobjekt: Die Pomaken in Nordgriechenland*, Berlin.

Sasse, Hans Jürgen (1991): *Arvanitika. Die albanischen Sprachreste in Griechenland 1*, Wiesbaden.

Trudgill, P./Tzavaras, G. A. (1977): „Why Albanian Greeks are not Albanians: Language Shift in Attica and Biotia". In: *Language, Ethnicity and Intergroup Relations*, Giles, H. (Ed.), 171—184.

Briefliche Mitteilung von Hill, Peter (Canberra) vom 18. 2. 1994 und Kartenskizze zur slavischen Bevölkerung Mazedoniens, übermittelt von Nelde, Peter H. (Brüssel).

*Ekkehard W. Bornträger,
Freiburg im Üchtland (Schweiz)*

I. Sprachenkarte von Griechenland, Zypern und der europäischen Türkei

Legende:

1 ▮ Albaner, Arvaniten
2 ▮ Aromunen, Megleniten
3 ▮ Bulgaren, Makedonier (= slavophone Orthodoxe)
4 ▮ Griechen (Hellenen)
5 ▦ Muslime
6 ▮ Serben
7 ▮ Türken

Streusiedlungen:

A Albaner, Arvaniten
AM Armenier
AR Aromunen
B, M Bulgaren, Makedonier
Bo Bosnier (slavophone Orthodoxe)
E Engländer (auf Zypern)
G Griechen (Hellenen)
K Kurden
LD Ladinosprecher
MA Maroniten
P* Pomaken (slavophone Muslime)
T Türken

* muslimischen Glaubens
( ) Flüchtlinge

I. Sprachenkarte von Griechenland, Zypern und der europäischen Türkei

J. Sprachenkarte von Polen

1. Kartenthema

Autochthone Sprachen und deren räumliche Verteilung; → Art. 192−199.

2. Kartierungstechnik

Flächenfarben, Farbschraffuren variabler Dicke, Symbolsignaturen zur Markierung diffuser Implantierungen von Sprachen bzw. deren Sprechern, Punktraster in Schwarzweiß.

3. Kommentar des Kartenautors

a) Information der Polnischen Botschaft Köln im Februar 1993:
Bevölkerung 38 Mio., davon 1−1,5 Mio. anderer Volkszugehörigkeit (2,6−3,9%).

Schätzungen:
Ukrainer	ca. 300 000: Masuren, Pomorze, Schlesien, SO-Polen
Weißrussen	ca. 200−250 000: östl. Wojewodschaft Białystok an der Grenze zu Weißrußland
Litauer	ca. 20−25 000: Hälfte im NO der Wojewodschaft Suwałki, sonst Wrocław, Szczecin, Słupsk, Gdańsk, Bydgoszcz
Deutsche	ca. 150−250 000: 85% Schlesien, sonst Pommern, Ermland, Masuren
Slowaken	ca. 25 000: Spisz, Orawa (Wojewodschaft Nowy Sącz); 22 Grundschulen
Juden	15 000
Griechen und Mazedonier	4500
Tschechen	ca. 3000

Sonst Russen, Tataren, Karaimen und Ormianen, Zigeuner u. a.

Ukrainische Grundschulen: in Biały Bór, Bartoszyce, Banie Mazurskie; Ukrainische Lizeen: Legnice, Górowie Iławeckie (Masuren), Biały Bór (Pom.)

Deutsche Minderheitenorganisationen seit 1989 besonders in den Wojewodschaften Katowice, Opole, Częstochowa, Biskupiec (Mas.), Gdańsk, Toruń, Poznań, Elbląg, Olsztyn, Szczytno, Ostróda, Szczecin, Radom, Wałbrzych, Jelenia Góra, Wrocław (dt. Kattowitz, Oppeln, Tschenstochau, Bischofsburg, Danzig, Thorn, Posen, Elbing, Allenstein, Ortelsburg, Osterode, Stettin, Radom, Waldenburg, Hirschberg, Breslau).

b) Nach Grulich-Pulte 1975 gelten für Polen fogende Zahlen:
Bevölkerung	33 Mio.
Deutsche	750 000
Ukrainer	800 000
Weißrussen	200 000
Slowaken	30 000
Litauer	10 000
Tschechen	6 000

Ferner Kaschuben, Tataren, Karaimen, Tschechen.

Welchen Status Grulichs Zahlen haben, ist schwer einzuschätzen; auffallend ist die große Differenz zu obigen Zahlen für Deutsche und Ukrainer: zwar sind seit den 70er Jahren sehr viele Deutsche in die BR Deutschland ausgesiedelt worden, trotzdem werden auch heute Zahlen von 5−600 000 Deutschen in Polen genannt. Die Abweichungen hinsichtlich der Ukrainer sind mir nicht erklärlich.

Die *Kaschuben*, die 1772 bis 1920 im preußisch-deutschen Staat das Deutsche als 'Dachsprache' benützten, aber im 19. und beginnenden 20. Jh. eine kaschubische Standardsprache anstrebten, die (auch heute noch) hauptsächlich literarisch gebraucht wurde (wird), werden im heutigen polnischen Staat sprachlich und ethnisch als Polen mit besonderem Dialekt und anderen Eigenheiten behandelt, insofern auch nicht als Minderheit erfaßt. Linguistisch ist ihre Sprache der Rest des weitgehend verschwundenen Pomoranischen, das im Rahmen des 'Lechitischen' mit dem Polnischen eng verwandt, aber nicht identisch ist.

4. Benützte Quellen

Borzyszkowski, Józef (1993): „Die Kaschuben − ihre Geschichte und Gegenwart". In: *Europa Ethnica* 50, 39−50 [unzuverlässig].

Grulich, Rudolf/Pulte, Peter (1975): *Nationale Minderheiten in Europa*, Opladen.

Informacja na temat mniejszości narodowych w Polsce [Informationen zum Thema nationaler Minderheiten in Polen], 12 S. DIN A 4 (Typoskript).

Popowska-Taborska, Hanna (1980): *Kaszubszczyzna. Zarys dziejów* [Das Kaschubentum. Geschichtlicher Abriß], Warschau.

Rokoszowa, Jolanta: „Poland" (→ Art. 192).

Tomaszewski, J. (1991): *Mniejszości w Polsce XX wieku* [Minderheiten im Polen des 20. Jahrhunderts], Warschau.

Topolińska, Zuzanna (1974): *A Historical Phonology of the Kashubian Dialects of Polish*, Den Haag/Paris.

Baldur Panzer, Heidelberg (Deutschland)

Legende:

1. Deutsch
2. Kaschubisch
3. Litauisch
4. Polnisch
5. Russisch
6. Slowakisch
7. Sorbisch
8. Tschechisch
9. Ukrainisch
10. Ungarisch
11. Weißrussisch
12. Roma (Zigeuner)

nicht behandelte Gebiete

J. Sprachenkarte von Polen

K. Sprachenkarte Tschechiens und der Slowakei

1. Kartenthema

Muttersprache und Nationalität (Stand 1980); gemeindeweise Darstellung; → Art. 200−209.

2. Kartierungstechnik

Farbflächen; geschlossene Landdarstellung (einschließlich spärlich besiedelter Gebirgs-, Wald- und Moorgebiete, jedoch ohne größere Seeflächen).

3. Kommentar des Kartenautors

Mischlagen schraffiert (unter flächenproportionaler Berücksichtigung des jeweiligen Gemeindegebietes).

4. Benützte Quellen

Breu, Josef/Duschanek, Michael (1989): „Sprachenverteilung". In: *Atlas der Donauländer*, Wien, 231 [Karte].

Michael Duschanek, Wien (Österreich)

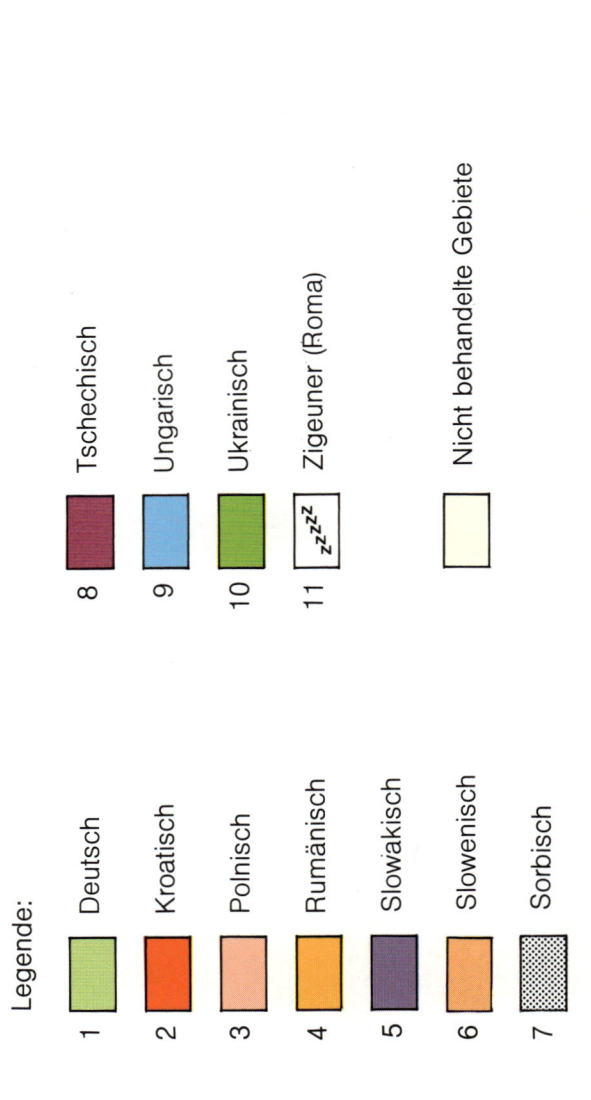

K. Sprachenkarte Tschechiens und der Slowakei

Legende:

1 Deutsch
2 Kroatisch
3 Polnisch
4 Rumänisch
5 Slowakisch
6 Slowenisch
7 Sorbisch
8 Tschechisch
9 Ungarisch
10 Ukrainisch
11 Zigeuner (Roma)

Nicht behandelte Gebiete

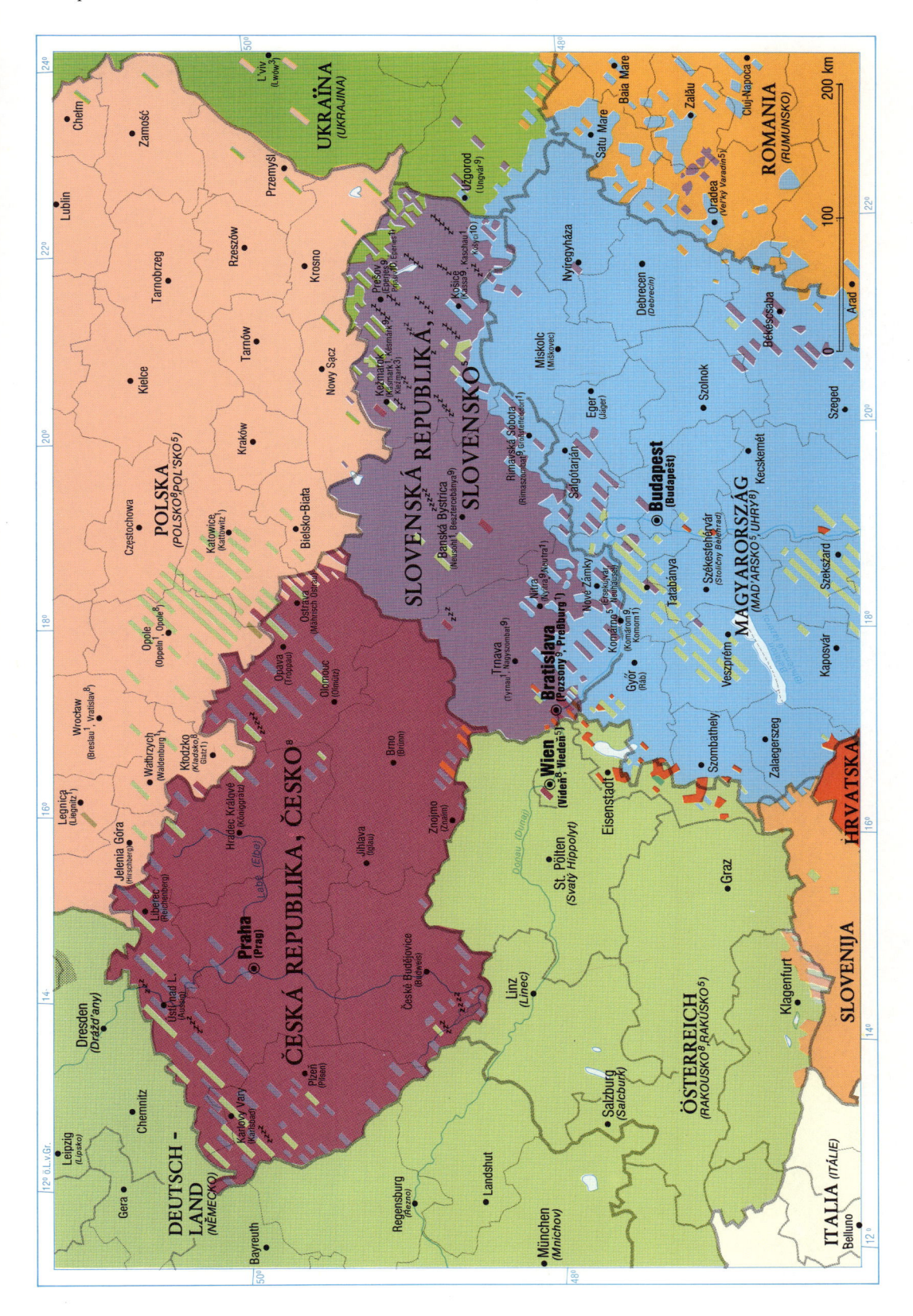

K. Sprachenkarte Tschechiens und der Slowakei

L. Sprachenkarte von Ungarn

1. Kartenthema

Muttersprache und Nationalität (Stand 1980); Darstellung nach Gemeinden und Ortschaften; → Art. 210−215.

2. Kartierungstechnik

Farbflächen, geschlossene Landdarstellung (einschließlich öder Berg-, Sumpf- und Moorgebiete, jedoch ohne größere Seeflächen).

3. Kommentar des Kartenautors

Mischlagen schraffiert unter flächenproportionaler Berücksichtigung des jeweiligen Gemeindegebietes).

Zwischen 1960 und 1990 wurden bei vier Volkszählungen nach verschiedensten Modellen die Minderheitensprachen erhoben. Als Ergebnis zeigte sich ein für ungarische Verhältnisse typisches sprunghaftes Auf-und-Ab der Sprachgruppenzugehörigkeitsbekenntnisse. Gefragt wurde nach Nationalität (Volksgruppe), Muttersprache, Zweitsprache (Minderheitensprache) sowie „Nationalitätenkulturinteresse−Zugehörigkeit". Aus den jeweils zwei besten Werten daraus wurde ein Mittelwert erhoben und kartiert.

4. Benützte Quellen

Breu, Josef/Duschanek, Michael (1989): „Sprachenverteilung". In: *Atlas der Donauländer*, Wien, 231 [Karte].

Központi statisztikai hivatal (1992): *1990. Évi népszámlálás: Magyarország nemzetiségi adatai megyénként. A mindenkori államigazgatási beosztás szerint (1870−1990)* [Statistisches Zentralamt (1992): Volkszählung 1990: ungarische Nationalitätenstatistik nach Komitaten. Jeweilige Verwaltungseinteilung laut Zählung (1870−1990)], Budapest.

Központi statisztikai hivatal (1991): *1990. Évi népszámlálás: A nemzetiségi népesség szama egyes községekben (1960−1990)* [Statistisches Zentralamt (1991): Volkszählung 1990: Nationalitätenbevölkerung − Anzahl einzeln nach Gemeinden (1960−1990)], Budapest.

Michael Duschanek, Wien (Österreich)

Legende:

1 Deutsch
2 Kroatisch
3 Rumänisch
4 Serbisch
5 Slowakisch
6 Slowenisch
7 Tschechisch
8 Ukrainisch
9 Ungarisch
10 Zigeuner (Roma)

Nicht behandelte Gebiete

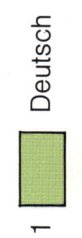

Streusiedlungen:

B Bunjewatzen (katholische Serben)
S Schokatzen (katholische Serben)
U Uskoken (griechisch-katholische Kroaten)

L. Sprachenkarte von Ungarn

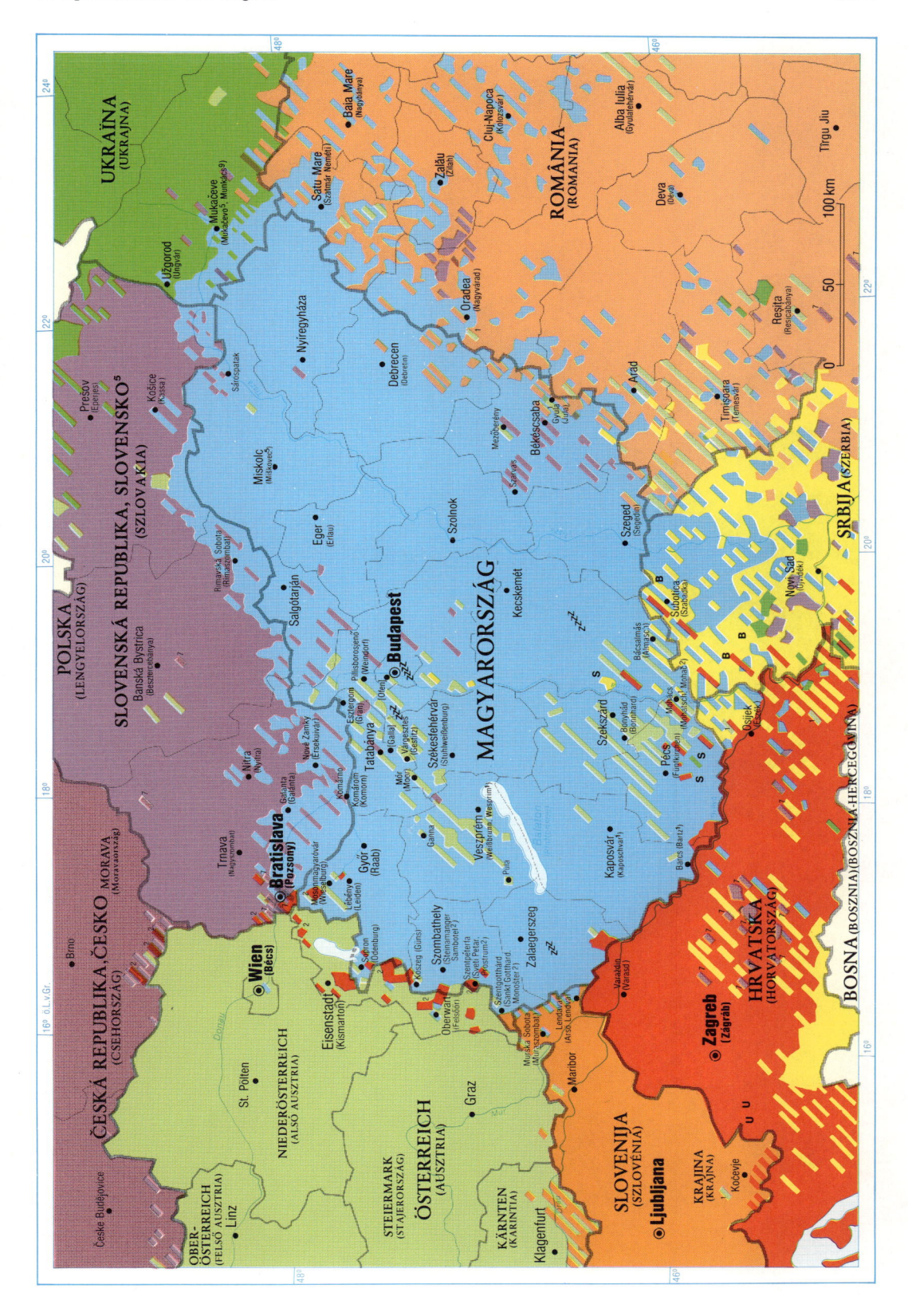

M. Sprachenkarte von Deutschland

1. Kartenthema

Autochthone und allochthone Sprachen sowie deren räumliche Verteilung; → Art. 216−221.

2. Kartierungstechnik

Flächenfarben, Farbschraffuren variabler Dicke, Punktraster und Strichraster in Schwarzweiß, ein Detailausschnitt (Lausitzer Sorbisch), Kreissegmentdiagramme.

3. Kommentar des Kartenautors

3.1. Die dänische Minderheit in Schleswig-Holstein

Im Landesteil Schleswig ('Südschleswig') nördlich der Eider leben nach Haarmann 1975 3500 (= 35 000?), nach einer Broschüre der *Dansk Skoleforening for Sydslesvig* 1990 ca. 50 000 Angehörige der (autochthonen) dänischen Volksgruppe. Da sie kein kompaktes Gebiet bewohnt und sprachlich nicht manifest wird (durchgehende Zwei- oder Dreisprachigkeit: dänisch, niederdeutsch, hochdeutsch), ist ihre genaue Anzahl und Verbreitung schwer zu ermitteln, zumal es sich großenteils auch um Bekenntnisdänen mit entsprechender Familientradition handelt. Anhaltspunkte geben das Wahlverhalten und der Schulbesuch: auf den SSW (Südschleswigscher Wählerverband, Partei der dänischen Minderheit) entfielen bei der Landtagswahl 1988 26 643 = 1,7% der abgegebenen Stimmen. An öffentlichen und privaten allgemeinbildenden Schulen nahmen im Schuljahr 1992/3 204 Haupt., 1905 Realschüler, 226 Gymnasiasten mit Dänisch als Fremdsprache = 2335 Schüler am fremdsprachigen Dänischunterricht teil, an den privaten Schulen der dänischen Minderheit (1990: 53 sowie 62 Kindergärten) mit dänischer Unterrichtssprache nahmen 1990 5171 (5257), 1992 5270 Schüler teil, davon allein 2262 in der Stadt Flensburg (s. beil. Karte!). Hierbei ist aber wohl zu berücksichtigen, daß am 31. 12. 1989 auch 5081 Personen dänischer Staatsangehörigkeit in SH gemeldet waren, die sicher auch z. T. dänische Schulen besuchen, u. a. viele Lehrer dieser Schulen bzw. ihre Kinder. Außer in Flensburg, wo durch starken Grenzverkehr eine Sondersituation herrscht, läuft gewöhnlich die Kommunikation zwischen Dänen und Deutschen auf Hoch- oder Niederdeutsch. Zu bedenken ist auch, daß die ca. 10 500 Nordfriesen (Haarmann 1975) (Bredstedt, nordfr. Inseln) z. T. ihre kulturellen und politischen Belange durch die dänische Minderheit und ihre Organisationen vertreten sehen.

3.2. Die sorbische Minderheit in Deutschland
(Niedersorbisch in Brandenburg, Obersorbisch in Sachsen)

Nach dem von der *Maćica Serbska* durch Jan Mahling und Martin Völkel 1991 in Bautzen herausgegebenen Bänden „Die Sorben in Deutschland" gab es 1987 67 000 Sorbisch-Sprecher in der Lausitz, aber nur 45 000 Personen mit sorbischer nationaler Selbstidentifikation (Elle 1991, 24). H. Faßke schätzt (1991, 28) die Zahl der „die sorbische Sprache beherrschenden Personen" auf „etwa 70 000". Die Schulverhältnisse werden von L. Budar dort auf S. 62 zusammengefaßt, wonach (1991) ca. 1400 Schüler am sorbischen Muttersprachunterricht, ca. 4000 am sorbischen Sprachunterricht in der gesamten Lausitz teilnehmen. Die Bevölkerungsverhältnisse vom 16. Jh. bis heute sind skizziert bei Marti in Europa Ethnica 49 (1992), S. 25.

3.3. Ausländer in Deutschland (Stand 31. 12. 1992)

AUSLÄNDER in DEUTSCHLAND am 31.12.1992
gesamt: 6.495.792

Herkunft nach Kontinenten

Europa

82,62%

9,23%

Afrika   Amerika   Asien
Australien   Staatenlos/
                              ungeklärt

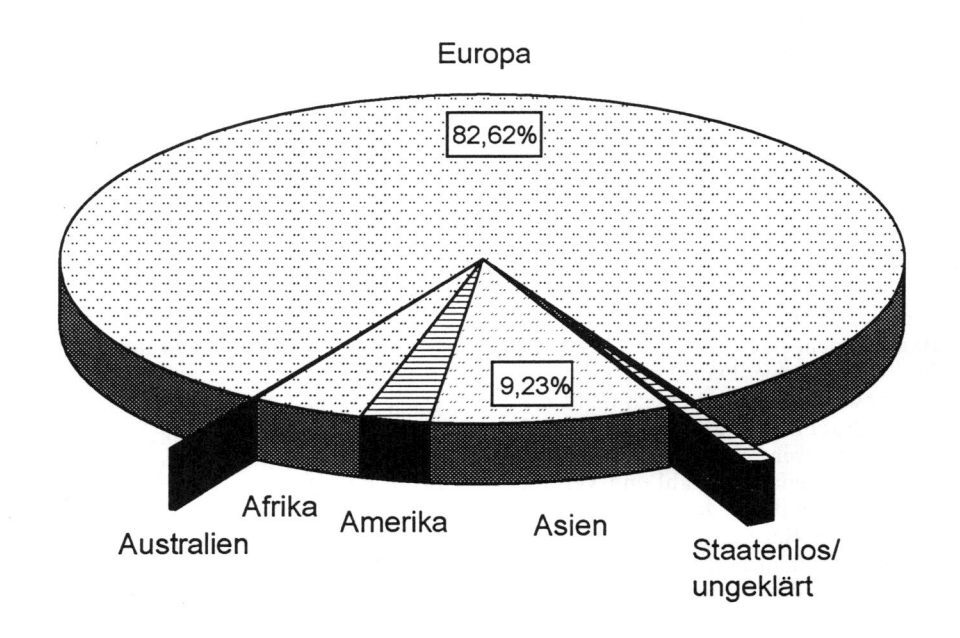

| Afrika - 4,37% | Australien und Ozeanien - 0,14% |
| Amerika - 2,60% | Staatenlos/ungeklärt - 1,04% |

Ausländer am 31. 12. 1922 in Deutschland
Herkunft nach Kontinenten

Nr.	Kontinent	Anzahl	in %
1	Europa	5.367.074	82,62%
2	Asien	599.519	9,23%
3	Afrika	283.949	4,37%
4	Amerika	168.811	2,60%
5	Australien und Ozeanien	9.124	0,14%

Nr.	Kontinent	Anzahl	in %
6	Staatenlos/ ungeklärt/ ohne Angabe	67.315	1.04%
	Ausländer insgesamt	6.495.792	100%

M. Sprachenkarte von Deutschland

AUSLÄNDER in DEUTSCHLAND am 31.12.1992
gesamt: 6.495.792

Verteilung nach Staatsangehörigkeit

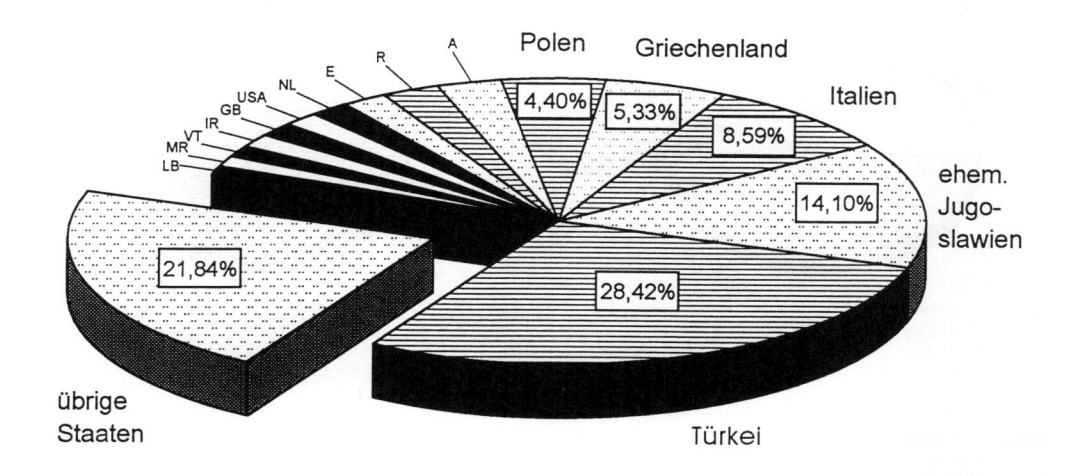

- Polen 4,40%
- Griechenland 5,33%
- Italien 8,59%
- ehem. Jugoslawien 14,10%
- Türkei 28,42%
- übrige Staaten 21,84%

A = Österreich (2,85%)		GR = Griechenland (5,33%)	MR = Marokko (1,24%)		USA = Ver. Staaten (1,61%)	
E = Spanien (2,06%)		IR = Iran (1,53%)	NL = Niederlande (1,75%)		VT = Vietnam (1,32%)	
GB = Großbritannien (1,59%)		LB = Libanon (0,82%)	R = Rumänien (2,58%)			

Ausländer am 31. 12. 1992 in Deutschland
Verteilung nach der Staatsangehörigkeit

Nr.	Staatsangehörigkeit	Anzahl	in %
1	Griechenland	345.902	5,33%
2	Großbritannien und Nordirland	103.499	1,59%
3	Italien	557.709	8,59%
4	Niederlande	113.552	1,75%
5	Spanien	133.847	2,06%
6	ehem. Jugoslawien	915.636	14,10%
7	Österreich	185.276	2,85%
8	Polen	285.553	4,40%
9	Rumänien	167.327	2,58%
10	Türkei	1.845.945	28,42%

Nr.	Staatsangehörigkeit	Anzahl	in %
11	Marokko	80.278	1,24%
12	Vereinigte Staaten	104.368	1,68%
13	Iran	99.069	1,53%
14	Libanon	53.469	0,82%
15	Vietnam	85.656	1,32%
	Summe 1–15	5.077.086	78,19%
16	Übrige Staaten	1.418.706	21,81%
	Ausländer insgesamt	6.495.792	100%

AUSLÄNDER IN DEUTSCHLAND am 31.12.1992
gesamt: 6.495.792

Verteilung auf einzelne Bundesländer

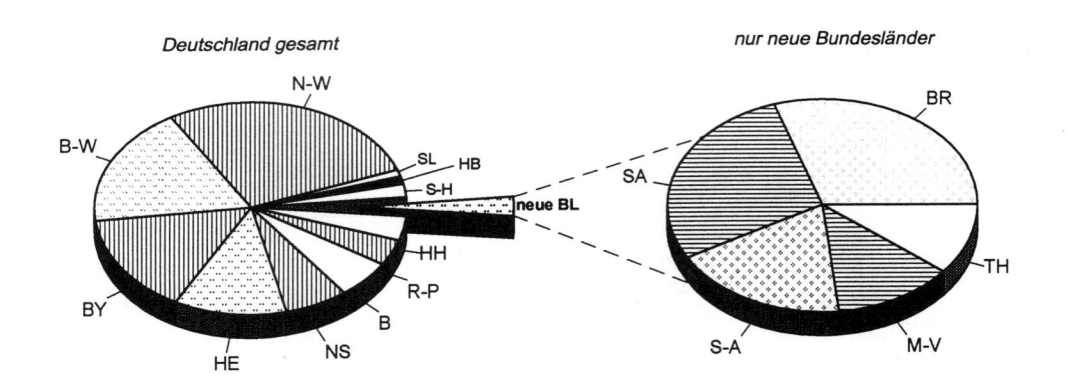

Deutschland gesamt — *nur neue Bundesländer*

alte Bundesländer: 97,01 %
N-W = Nordrhein-Westfalen (27,90%)
B-W = Baden-Württemberg (18,33%)
BY = Bayern (15,27%)
H = Hessen (11,48%)
NS = Niedersachsen (6,56%)

B = Berlin (5,89%)
R-P = Rheinland-Pfalz (3,99%)
HH = Hamburg (3,63%)
S-H = Schleswig-Holstein 1,94%
HB = Bremen (1,17%)
S = Saarland (1,05%)

neue BL = neue Bundesländer: 2,99%
BR = Brandenburg (29,79%)
SA = Sachsen (28,37%)
S-A = Sachsen-Anhalt (18,53%)
M-V = Mecklenburg-Vorpommern (12,55%)
TH = Thüringen (10,76%)

EDV-Kartographie: Heide Marie Pamminger (Salzburg)

Ausländer am 31. 12. 1992 in Deutschland
Verteilung auf Bundesländer

Bundesländer	Anzahl	in %
Baden-Württemberg	1.190.785	23%
Bayern	991.859	15,2%
Berlin	382.792	5,9%
Brandenburg	54.545	0,8%
Bremen	75.731	1,1%
Hamburg	235.474	3,6%
Hessen	745.570	11,5%
Mecklenburg-Vorpommern	22.975	0,35%
Niedersachsen	425.801	6,7%
Nordrhein-Westfalen	1.812.264	27,8%

Bundesländer	Anzahl	in %
Rheinland-Pfalz	258.888	4,0%
Saarland	68.237	1,1%
Sachsen	51.393	0,8%
Sachsen-Anhalt	33.929	0,5%
Schleswig-Holstein	125.850	1,9%
Thüringen	19.699	0,3%
alte Bundesländer	*6.313.251*	*97,01%*
neue Bundesländer	*182.541*	*2,99%*
Deutschland gesamt	6.495.792	100%

4. Benützte Quellen

4.1. Dänisch (und Sprecher)

Dansk Skoleforening for Sydslesvig (Ed.) (1990): *Danske skoler of Børnehaver i Sydslesvig. Dänische Schulen und Kindergärten in Südschleswig.* Broschüre, Flensburg.

Dansk Skoleforening for Sydslesvig (1993): Beretning over Skoleforeningens virksomhed i skoleåret 1991—2 ved skoledirektør Hans Andresen. Årsberetning 68, Flensburg.

Haarmann, Harald (1975): Soziologie und Politik der Sprachen Europas, München.

Statistische Berichte des Statistischen Landesamtes Schleswig-Holstein A I 4 — S/89 (ausgegeben am 4. 7. 1990 sowie 430 a-0792 für Fremdsprachen- bzw. Dänischunterricht 1991/2 und 1992/3).

4.2. Sorbisch (und Sprecher)

Budar, L. (1991): „Zum sorbischen Schulwesen". In: *Die Sorben in Deutschland.* Maćica Serbska (Ed.), Bautzen, 59—63.

Elle, L. (1991): „Die Sorben in der Statistik". In: ibid., 21—25.

Ders. (1992): „Zur aktuellen Sprachsituation der Lausitzer Sorben". In: *Europa Ethnica* 49, 1—12.

Faßke, H. (1991): „Sorbische Sprache". In: ibid., 27—32.

Marti, R. (1992): „Die Sorben — Prüfstein und Experimentierfeld für Nationalitätenpolitik". In: *Europa Ethnica* 49, 13—36.

4.3. Ausländer in Deutschland

Volkszählungsresultate vom 31. 12. 1992.

Baldur Panzer, Heidelberg (Deutschland)

Legende:

1 ▪ Dänisch
 ▪ Dänische Volksgruppe in Deutschland (Gebiete mit dänischen Schulen)
2 ▪ Deutsch
 ▪ Deutsche Volksgruppe in Dänemark (Gebiete mit deutschen Kultureinrichtungen)
3 Friesisch
 ▪ Nordfriesisch (in D)
 ▪ Westfriesisch (in NL)
 ▪ Ostfriesisch (Saterland, in D)
4 ▪ Französisch
5 ▪ Italienisch
6 ▪ Lëtzebuergisch
7 ▪ Niederländisch

8 ▪ Polnisch
9 ▪ Rätoromanisch
 ▪ Bündnerromanisch
 ▪ Dolomitenladinisch
 ▪ Friaulisch
10 ▪ Slowakisch
11 ▪ Slowenisch
12 Sorbisch
 ▪ ≤ 25%
 ▪ > 25%
13 ▪ Tschechisch

▪ nicht behandelte Gebiete

M. Sprachenkarte von Deutschland 2055

N. Sprachenkarte von Österreich

1. Kartenthema

Autochthone Sprachen und deren räumliche Verteilung; → Art. 222−225.

2. Kartierungstechnik

Flächenfarben, Farbschraffuren mit variabler Dicke, Punktraster.

3. Kommentar des Kartenautors

In den österreichischen Volkszählungen wird seit den Zeiten der Monarchie die „Umgangssprache" der Bevölkerung erhoben: diese ist mehrheitlich Deutsch. Auf der Karte sind auch diejenigen Gebiete Österreichs angegeben, in denen eine andere Sprache als Deutsch als Umgangssprache angegeben wurde, einschließlich Doppelnennungen (also Kombinationen, z. B. Deutsch-Slowenisch). „Windisch" wurde als „Slowenisch" gerechnet.

Bezugszeitpunkt: 1991 (Volkszählung).

4. Benützte Quellen

Gutleb, Angelika/Unkart, Ralf (Eds.) (1990): *Die Minderheiten im Alpen-Adria-Raum.* Deutsche Fassung. Klagenfurt.

Neweklowsky, Gerhard (1969): „Die kroatischen Mundarten im Burgenland. Überblick". In: *Wiener slavistisches Jahrbuch* 15, 94−115.

Malle, Augustin (Ed) (o. J. [1992]): *Die Slowenen in Kärnten/Slovenci na Koroškem.* Ferlach/Borovlje.

Heinz-Dieter Pohl, Klagenfurt (Österreich)

N. Sprachenkarte von Österreich

Legende:

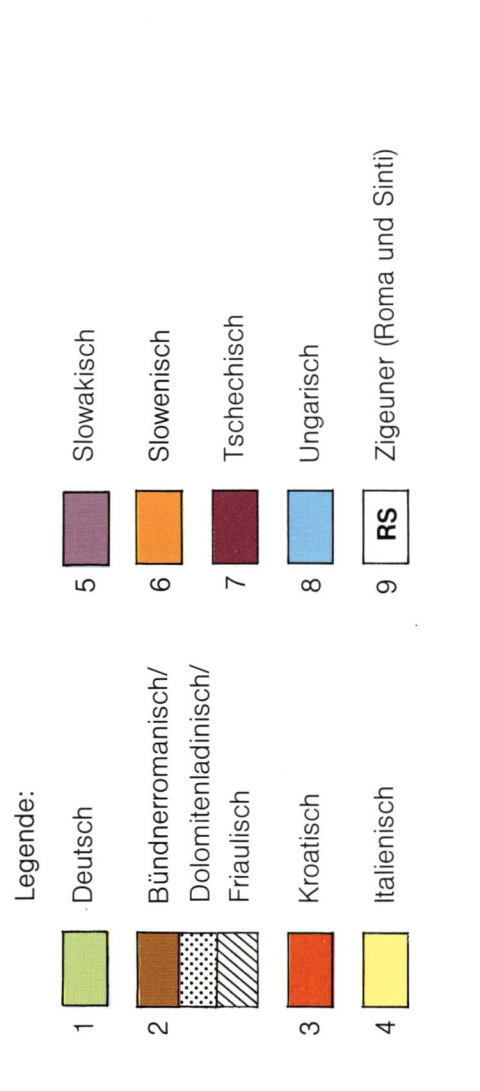

1. Deutsch
2. Bündnerromanisch/ Dolomitenladinisch/ Friaulisch
3. Kroatisch
4. Italienisch
5. Slowakisch
6. Slowenisch
7. Tschechisch
8. Ungarisch
9. Zigeuner (Roma und Sinti) — RS

Detailkarte A

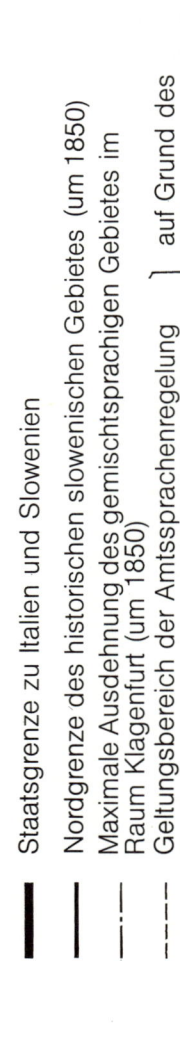

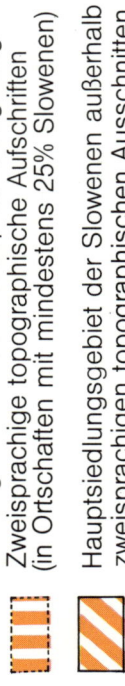

- Staatsgrenze zu Italien und Slowenien
- Nordgrenze des historischen slowenischen Gebietes (um 1850)
- Maximale Ausdehnung des gemischtsprachigen Gebietes im Raum Klagenfurt (um 1850)
- Geltungsbereich der Amtssprachenregelung ⎫
- Zweisprachige topographische Aufschriften (in Ortschaften mit mindestens 25% Slowenen) ⎬ auf Grund des Volksgruppengesetzes von 1977
- Hauptsiedlungsgebiet der Slowenen außerhalb des Gebietes mit zweisprachigen topographischen Ausschnitten (1951 noch über 20%)

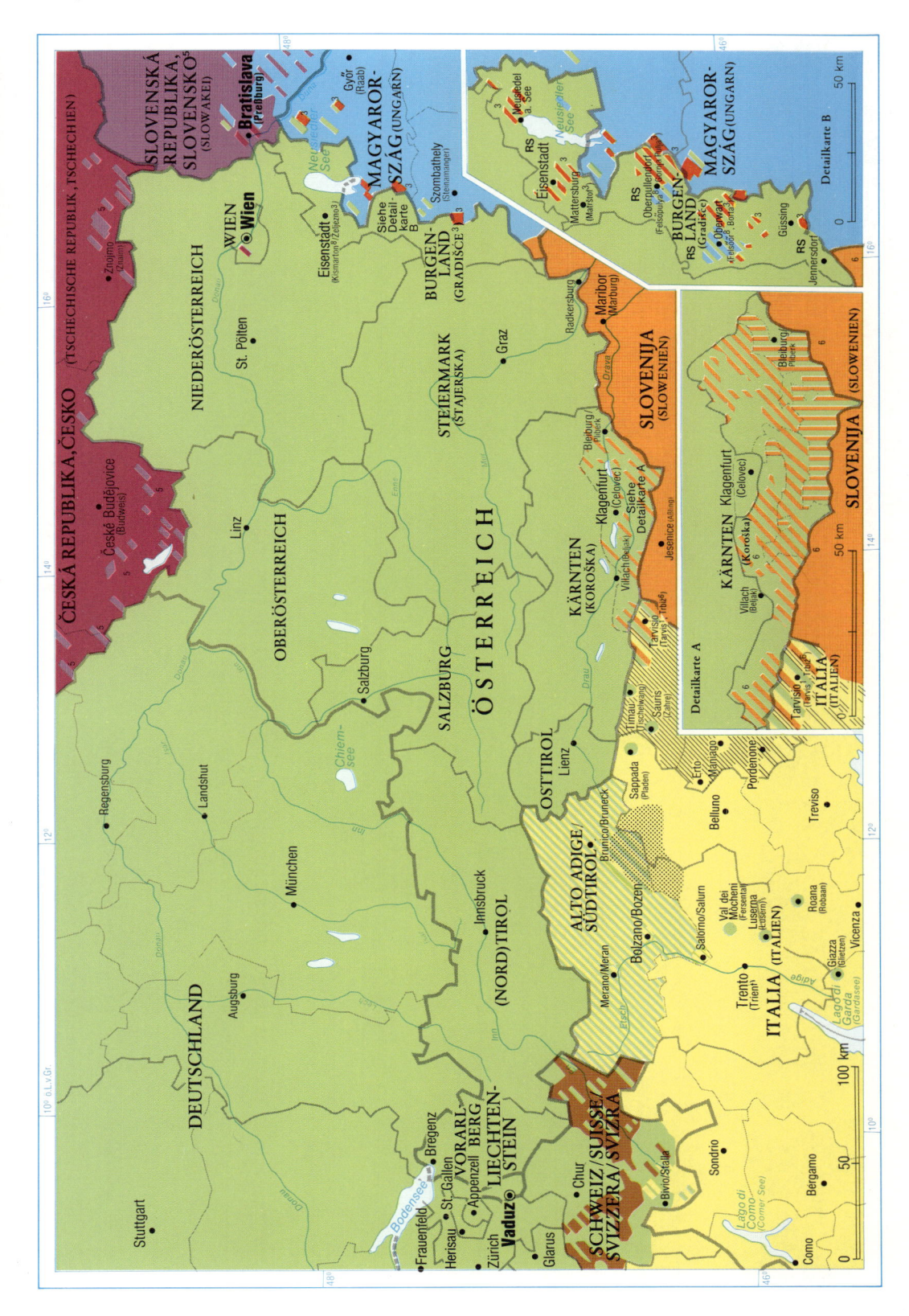

N. Sprachenkarte von Österreich

O. Sprachenkarte der Schweiz

1. Kartenthema

Muttersprache der Schweizer (Stand 1990); gemeindeweise Darstellung; → Art. 226—230.

2. Kartierungstechnik

Farbflächen, geschlossene Landdarstellung (einschließlich Hochgebirge, jedoch ohne größere Seeflächen).

3. Kommentar des Kartenautors

Mischlagen schraffiert (unter flächenproportionaler Berücksichtigung des jeweiligen Gemeindegebietes).

4. Benützte Quellen

Bundesamt für Statistik, Bern (1982): *Ergebnisse der Volkszählung 1980: Wohnbevölkerung der Kantone nach Muttersprache. — EDV-Sonderauswertung nach Kantonen, Gemeinden, getrennt nach Schweizern und Ausländern*, Bern.

Bundesamt für Statistik, Bern (1993 f.): *Ergebnisse der Volkszählung 1990: Wohnbevölkerung nach Gemeinden und Hauptsprache*, Bern.

Michael Duschanek, Wien (Österreich)

O. Sprachenkarte der Schweiz

Legende:

1 Deutsch
2 Französisch
3 Italienisch
4 Rätoromanisch (Bündnerromanisch)

O. Sprachenkarte der Schweiz

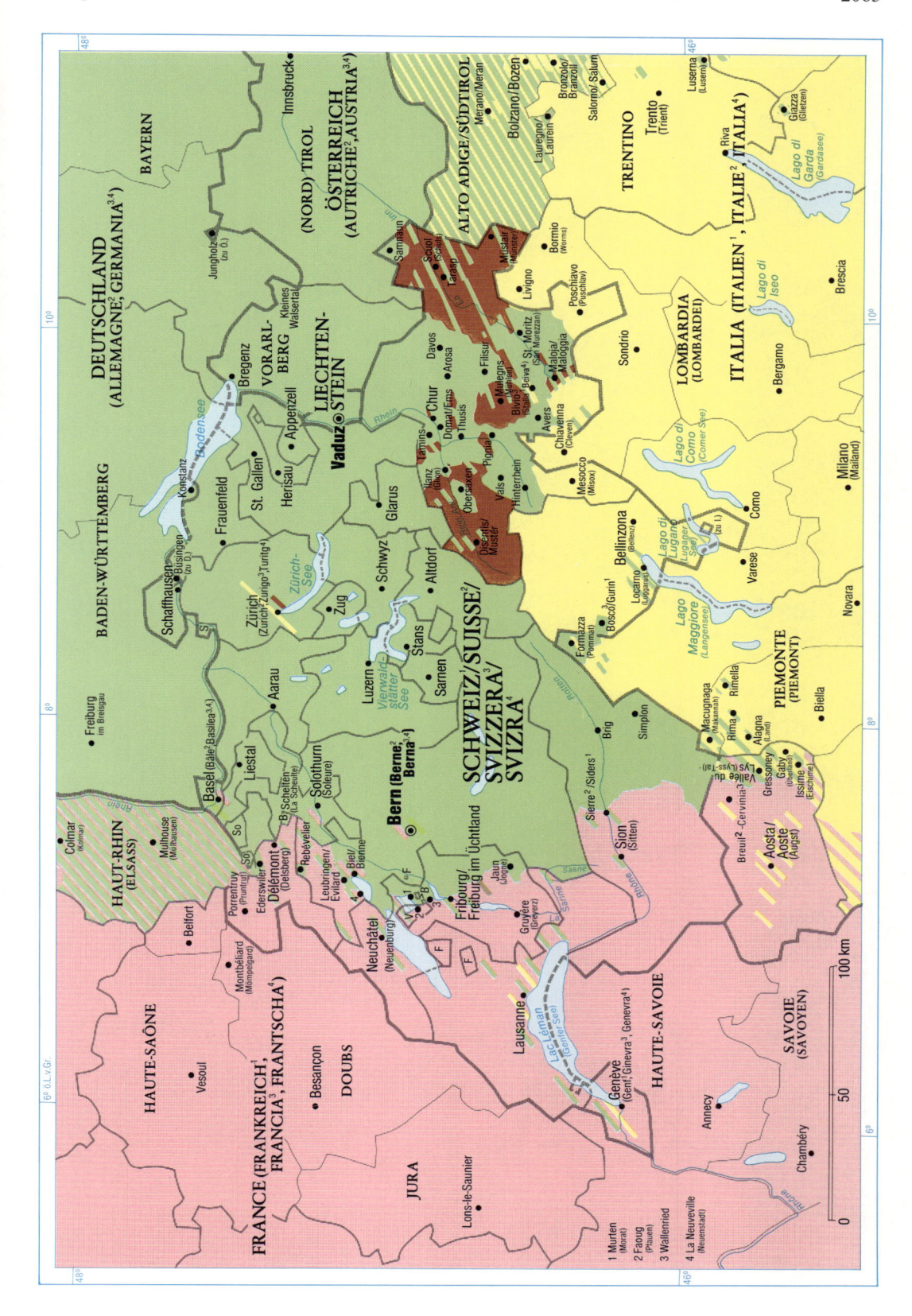

P. Sprachenkarte von Weißrußland, der Ukraine, dem westlichen Teil des europäischen Rußland und der baltischen Staaten (Litauen, Lettland, Estland)

1. Kartenthema

Autochthone Sprachen und deren räumliche Verzahnung; → Art. 231–237.

2. Kartierungstechnik

Flächenfarben, Balken, Raster, Farbschraffuren mit variabler Dicke, *Schrägschrift* bei Topo- und Choronymen (meist zwischen Klammern) außerhalb der Ukraine: *ukrainisch*; gerade Schrift bei Topo- und Choronymen (meist zwischen Klammern) außerhalb Rußlands: russisch.

3. Kommentar des Kartenautors

Kartiert wurden im Prinzip Sprachen, doch teilweise (gilt für die Staaten außerhalb der ehemaligen Sowjetunion) nicht auf der Basis der *Sprachen-*, sondern der *Nationalitäten*statistik. Dabei wurden örtliche Mehrheiten unter Zuhilfenahme relativ großmaßstäbiger ethnischer und Sprachenkarten topographisch (nicht auf statistische oder Verwaltungseinheiten bezogen) umgrenzt und durch Flächenfarben bezeichnet. Örtliche Minderheiten sind durch Balkung kenntlich gemacht, wobei außerhalb der großen Städte die Dichte der Balkung dem jeweiligen Anteil der Minderheit etwa proportional ist. In Gebieten mit sehr kleinen und verstreuten Sprachminderheiten steht ein Balken (ohne Bezug zur wirklichen topographischen Verteilung) ungefähr in der Mitte des Gebiets. In großen Städten konnte das Vorhandensein von Sprachminderheiten wegen des kleinen Kartenmaßstabs nur durch die unproportionale Anhäufung von Balken zum Ausdruck gebracht werden. Die Flächenfarben für Sprachmehrheiten in Weißrußland (Belarus'), der Ukraine und Moldawien (Moldova), die zu mehr als 50% das Russische als Zweitsprache verwenden, sind mit einem (hellblauen) Strichraster überzogen.
Bezugszeit 1989–1992.

4. Benützte Quellen

Breu, Josef (1989): „Sprachenverteilung" (1: 2 000 000). In: *Atlas der Donauländer*, Österreichisches Ost- und Südosteuropa-Institut (Ed.), Wien, 231.

Eberhardt, Piotr (1993): „Liczbenosć i rozmieszczenie ludności polskiej na bialorusi w XX wieku" [Zahl und Verteilung polnischer Bevölkerung in Weißrußland im 20. Jahrhundert]. In: *Czasopismo geograficzne* 64, 143–183.

Glavnoe upravlenie geodezii i kartografii pri Sovete Ministrov SSSR (Ed.) (1967): *Atlas Leningradskoj oblasti* [Atlas der Region Leningrad], Moskau.

Glavnoe upravlenie geodezii i kartografii pri Sovete Ministrov SSSR (Ed.) (1985): *Atlas SSSR*, Moskau.

Gosudarstvennyj komitet SSSR po statistike (Ed.) (1990): *Nacional'nyi sostav naselenija SSSR po dannym vsesojuznoy perepisi naselenija 1989 g* [Nationale Struktur der Bevölkerung der UdSSR nach Daten der unionsweiten Volkszählung des Jahres 1989], Moskau 1990.

Jordan, Peter (1993): „Nationalitäten in Südosteuropa (1: 5 000 000)". In: *Österreichischer Unterstufenatlas*, Hölzel, E. (Ed.), 4. verb. Aufl. der Neubearbeitung 1989, Wien, 169.

Lietuvos TSR valstybinis plano komitetas/ Lietuvos TSR aukstojo ir specialiojo vidurinio mokslo ministerija (Eds.) (1981): *Lietuvos TSR Atlasas*, Moskau.

MAPA LTD (Ed.) (1992): *Atlas Ukrainci shìdna dìaspora* [Atlas der ukrainischen östlichen Diaspora], Kiew.

Mežs, Ilmars (1992): *The Ethnic Structure in the Urban Population of Latvia*, Riga.

Nacionalen statističeski institut (Ed.) (1994): *Resultati ot prebrojavane n a naselenieto* [Resultate der Volkszählung], Sofia.

România, Comisia naţională pentru statistică (Ed.) (1992): *Recensămîntul populaţiei şi locuinţelor din 7 ianuarie 1992. Rezutate preliminare* [Zählung der Bevölkerung und der Wohnungen vom 7. Jänner 1992. Vorläufige Ergebnisse], Bukarest.

Suomen Maantieteellinen Seura/Helsingin Yliopiston Maantieteen laitos (Eds.) (1960): *Suomen Kartasto* [Atlas von Finnland], Helsinki.

Peter Jordan, Wien (Österreich)

P. Sprachenkarte von Weißrußland, der Ukraine, Westrußland und dem Baltikum

Legende:

1	■	Abchasisch	13	■	Lettisch
2	■	Adygeisch	14	■	Litauisch
3	■	Albanisch	15	■	Polnisch
4	■	Armenisch	16	■	Rumänisch
5	■	Bulgarisch	17	■	Russisch
6	■	Deutsch	18	■	Schwedisch
7	■	Estnisch	19	■	Slowakisch
8	■	Finnisch	20	■	Tatarisch
9	■	Gagausisch	21	■	Türkisch
10	■	Georgisch	22	■	Ukrainisch
11	■	Griechisch	23	■	Ungarisch
12	■	Karelisch	24	■	Weißrussisch

Russische Exonyme: recte
Ukrainische Exonyme: kursiv

P. Sprachenkarte von Weißrußland, der Ukraine, Westrußland und dem Baltikum

Autorenregister / Index of Authors / Index des auteurs

Vorbemerkung

Das Autorenregister enthält alle im Text und in den Bibliographien der Handbuchartikel genannten Namen von wissenschaftlichen Autoren (fallweise auch Institutionen) und markanten Einzelpersönlichkeiten aus Geschichte, Politik und Wissenschaft. Bei letzteren wurden die Regierungs- bzw. Lebensdaten in Klammern vermerkt.

Die Schreibweise der Namen richtet sich im Prinzip nach jener der Handbuchartikel bzw. der dazugehörenden Bibliographie. Offenkundige Fehler wurden allerdings – soweit diese erkennbar waren – korrigiert. Namen mit *van, de* (etc.) wurden in der Regel unter *V* bzw. *D* (etc.) vermerkt. Im Zweifel wurde nach den Angaben der Auswahlbibliographien alphabetisiert. Zu einigen wenigen Namen gibt es Mehrfacheinträge.

Die meisten Vornamen wurden abgekürzt; wo sie beibehalten wurden, dienen sie vorwiegend zur Unterscheidung von homographischen Familiennamen.

Die Reihenfolge ist streng alphabetisch. Diakritika wurden beim Alphabetisieren nicht berücksichtigt: daher gilt: a = ä, o = ö, u = ü, æ = ae etc., bzw. c = ć oder č, f = þ, s = ś, ş, š etc.

Die Zahlen hinter den Namen beziehen sich auf die fortlaufende Paginierung der beiden Teilbände des Handbuchs.

Die Herausgeber sind Heide Marie Pamminger (Universität Salzburg) für ihren hingebungsvollen und überaus kompetenten Einsatz bei der Erstellung des Autorenregisters zu großem Dank verpflichtet.

Introductory

The Index of Authors lists the names of the scholars and scientists cited in the Handbook articles and corresponding bibliographies. It also includes the names of some personalities of distinction in history, politics or science, along with their term of office or their year of birth and death added in parentheses.

The spelling of the names generally follows that of the Handbook text and corresponding bibliographies. In the rare instance of an obvious error in the text this was corrected in the Index. Names including *van, de* (etc.) are usually listed under *V* and *D*, respectively. When in doubt, the alphabetic order of the particular selected bibliography was observed. For a few cases there are multiple entries.

Most first names are abbreviated to initials. Complete forms have been maintained when necessary to distinguish between persons with identical last names.

Names are listed in strict alphabetic order: diacritics have not been taken into consideration, i. e. a is equivalent to ä, o = ö, u = ü, æ = ae etc., c = ć or č, f = þ, s = ś, ş, š etc.

Numbers after names refer to the (continuous) pagination of the two Handbook volumes.

The editors owe a very special debt of gratitude to Heide Marie Pamminger of the University of Salzburg for her expert assistance in the preparation of the Index of Authors.

Remarque préliminaire

Cet index contient les noms de tous les auteurs (ou institutions) scientifiques ainsi que ceux de quelques personnages historiques et de personnalités scientifiques de renom, cités tant dans les articles que dans les bibliographies (sélectives) y ayant trait. Les noms des personnages historiques sont accompagnés de leurs dates biographiques (concernant soit leur vie soit la durée de leur activité politique).

Nous avons tâché de conserver l'orthographe originale utilisée par les auteurs bien que, dans certains cas, d'évidentes erreurs aient dû être corrigées. Les noms précédés de *van, de* (etc.) ont été répertoriés le plus souvent sous *V, D* (etc.). En cas de doute, l'insertion alphabétique a été réalisée sur le modèle de la bibliographie (sélective) respective. Rares sont les noms qui ont été répertoriés plus d'une fois.

Les prénoms ont été dans leur quasi-majorité abrégés; seuls ont été conservés ceux qui servent à la différenciation de noms d'auteurs homographes.

L'ordre est strictement alphabétique. Les signes diacritiques n'ont pas été pris en considération; il en résulte les correspondances suivantes: a = ä, o = ö, u = ü, æ = ae etc., respectivement c = ć ou č, f = þ, s = ś, ş, š etc.

Les chiffres répertoriés derrière les noms d'auteurs se réfèrent à la numérotation de pages continue des deux tomes de ce volume.

Les éditeurs tiennent à remercier cordialement Mme Heide Marie Pamminger (Université de Salzbourg) qui, animée d'une ténacité et d'une compétence informatique inégalables, a mené à bien l'établissement de l'index des auteurs.

A

Aarseth, Bjorn 961, 1981
Aasen, Ivar 950. 952
Abboud, P. F. 394, 397
Abdulaziz, M. M. H. 723, 895, 899
Abelson, R. P. 694, 700
Abler, R. F. 74, 75
Aboud, F. E. 39
Abrahams, R. D. 547, 548
Abrams, D. 41, 42, 43, 44, 45, 46, 47, 48
Abramson, Harold 1106
Ačaṙean, H. (= Ačaṙyan, H.) 1574, 1575, 1576
Achard, Pierre 679, 683, 907, 911
Achunzjanov, E. M. 1898
Ackermann, I. 96
Aclan, Z. G. 481
Acquaviva, Sabino 1215, 1220, 1221
Aczél, György 1711, 1721
Adams, M. J. 181, 192, 629, 633
Adegbija, E. 689, 691
Adler, M. K. 255
Adler, Patricia A. 754, 760
Adler, Peter 754, 760
Adler, Winfried 1333, 1336
Adorno, Theodor 208
af Trampe, P. 11
Afendras, Evangelos A. 452, 456, 457
Afolayan, A. 83, 88, 489, 491
Africa, H. 489, 491, 492
Ağacanoğlu, Adnan 1024, 1031
Agar, M. H. 748
Agard, B. 2007
Agard, F. B. 1260
Ågel, V. 1730
Ager, Dennis 419, 1899, 1900

Ageron, Ch.-R. 194, 199
Aggelopulos, Ath 2032
Agheyisi, R. 696, 699, 700
Agostiniani, L. 641
Agustín Ozamiz, J. 356
Åhammar, Nils 1784, 1785
Aikio, Marjut 575, 576, 722, 723, 947, 948, 962, 963, 965, 1019, 1981
Aikio, Samuli 1019
Airila, Martti 992
Aitchison, Jean 102, 103, 137
Aitchison, John 1081, 1087
Aizpurua, X. 775, 776
'Aipolo, A. 721, 724
Ajzen, I. 692, 693, 694, 700
Akinnaso, F. 142, 143
Akiwowo, A. 79
Aktouf, O. 412, 413
Aktunç, Hulki 1557, 1559, 1575, 1576
Alatis, J. E. 130, 243, 525, 633, 714, 912, 1544
Albano Leoni, Federico 1328, 1329, 1382
Alberco, W. L. 898, 899
Albert, M. L. 15, 20, 37, 40, 87, 88, 236, 243, 585, 604, 605, 642, 658
Albrecht, G. 181, 187, 190, 319
Albrecht, J. 513
Albrecht, Urs 1849
Alderson, J. Ch. 507
Aleemi, J. 7, 8, 380, 384
Aleksaitė, Irena 1614, 1620
Alemany, R. 1309
Alessio, Giovanni 1217, 1221, 1367, 1370
Alexander, N. 904, 905
Alexandris, Alexander 1523, 1555, 1557, 1559, 1560, 1561, 1562, 1563, 1565

Alexandris, Alexis 2032
Alexics, György 1485
Alexieva, Afrodita 1512, 1514
Alexiou, M. 891, 892
Alfaro, R. J. 4, 8
Alfonsi, Tommaso 1207, 1213
Alfonso X el Sabio (1252–1284) 1286
Algeo, J. 127, 129
Alhaug, Gulbrand 1494, 1495
Alibert, Louis 1192, 1193, 1194
Aliotti, N. C. 35, 40
Alisjahbana, S. T. 840, 896, 900
Alladina, Safder 190, 331, 332, 1060, 1073, 1074
Allardt, Erik 78, 79, 208, 348, 350, 351, 356, 1014, 1981
Allemann-Ghionda, Cristina 1848, 1849
Allen, P. 475, 481
Allendorf, S. 291, 293
Alleyne, M. C. 53, 54, 55, 656, 657
Allières, Jacques 1268, 1269
Allman, W. F. 297, 309
Allport, G. W. 208, 692, 700
Alonso Estravís, Isaac 1293, 1294
Alonso, A. 612, 623
Alonso, W. 834, 840
Altenberg, E. P. 375, 377
Althaus, H. 584
Altimari, Francesco 1375
Altoma, S. J. 393, 397
Altube, Severo 1267, 1268
Altuna, P. 1268
Altwerger, B. 88
Alvar, Manuel 612, 623, 695, 700, 1283, 1284
Alvarez, C. 587, 589, 592
Alvarez, Rosario 1293, 1294
Alvarez-Pereyre, Frank 683, 789, 795

Ambrazas, V. 1918
Ambrose, J. E. 2003, 2008
Ambrose, John 66, 67, 68, 69, 74, 216, 218, 1259
Ameka, Felix 134, 137, 138
Amian, Werner 1142
Amin, Samir 190
Amiryan, X. 1575, 1576
Ammann, Jakob 313
Ammon, Ulrich 109, 175, 176, 177, 179, 193, 217, 218, 244, 255, 256, 266, 270, 282, 283, 319, 320, 369, 370, 384, 398, 399, 418, 419, 423, 425, 426, 456, 464, 540, 608, 623, 640, 641, 674, 691, 701, 702, 708, 724, 749, 763, 787, 804, 810, 818, 819, 825, 833, 853, 854, 855, 856, 857, 861, 864, 886, 895, 900, 901, 911, 1129, 1151, 1171, 1399, 1405, 1760, 1768, 1820, 1850, 1851, 1870, 1878
Anastasiadis, G. I. 1523
Anatole, Christian 1194
Andersen, R. W. 289, 293, 521, 523, 563, 566, 567, 582, 584, 585, 661, 666
Anderson, B. 76, 79, 185, 191, 402, 404, 587, 592, 923, 928
Anderson, E. A. 452, 456
Anderson, O. 733, 735, 737
Anderson, R. 116, 327, 629, 633
Andersson, P. 278, 283, 385,
Andersson, Th. 370, 373, 377, 583, 584, 605
Andesian, S. 1183, 1186, 2004, 2006
André, Robert 1107, 1121
Andreassen, Irene 965
Andrej, Johann 1818, 1819
Andres, Franz 1847, 1849, 1853, 1878
Andresen, Sigfred 1776
Andrews, Peter Alford 1556, 1559, 1562, 1565, 1566, 1571, 1572, 1573, 1574, 1576, 2032
Andriotis, Nicholas P. 1513, 1514, 1522, 1523, 1549
Androussou, A. 1182, 1186
Angelopoulos, Athanasios 1533, 1539
Anghie, A. 360, 362
Angogo, R. 895, 900
Anić, Vladimir 1433
Anschütz, Helga 1573, 1576
Anschütz, S. R. 819
Anselmi, G. 466, 471
Anton, Th. 869, 870
Antonić, Ivana 1410, 1415
Antoniewicz, J. 1621
Antonijević, Dragoslav 1511, 1514

Antonovska, Svetlana 1449
Anttila, R. 98, 103, 545, 546, 548
Anttonen, Marjut 963, 965
Apalategi, J. 353, 356
Apenčenko, V. S. 1887, 1895, 1899, 1936, 1940
Apothéloz, Denis 1868, 1870
Appadurai, A. 748
Appel, René 8, 112, 115, 116, 131, 137, 574, 576, 586, 592, 599, 600, 605, 755, 760, 836, 840, 1150
Aquilina, Joseph 1401, 1403, 1405
Aracil, Lluís Vicent 238, 239, 243, 249, 250, 255, 353, 356, 802, 803, 1298, 1301
Aravantinos, Panajotis 1523
Arbeitsgruppe Bielefelder Soziologen 760, 797, 803
Arcelo, A. A. 898, 900
Archambault, A. 439, 443
Ard, J. 562, 565, 566
Arday, Lajos 1740, 1742
Ardouin, P. 281, 283
Ares Vázquez, M. C. 1293, 1294
Argamendi, J. 494, 500
Argemí, Aureli 351, 352, 355, 356, 357
Argente, Joan A. 141, 143, 1300, 1301
Arguelles, M. 1119, 1121
Argüeso, M. Angeles 1303, 1309
Argyle, M. 419
Århammar, Nils Rudolf 1778, 1779, 1780, 1781
Aristoteles 233
Armengaud, André 1194
Armstrong, C. A. J. 1124, 1129
Árnason, Kristján 1056, 1057
Arnau, Joaquim 1301
Arnaud, N. 79
Arnberg, L. 7, 8, 380, 382, 383, 384
Arnberger, Erik 1974, 1976, 1978, 1979
Arndt, Ernst Moritz (1769−1860) 154
Aronson, Howard 1491, 1494
Aronsson, Kjell-Åke 981
Aronstein, Ph. 146, 151
Arquint, Jachen C. 1844, 1852
Artigal, J. M. 83, 88, 293, 469, 470, 471
Arutjunjan, J. V. 1891, 1894, 1899
Arutjunov, S. A. 843, 852
Arvinte, Vasile 1468, 1469, 1475, 1476
Arza Arza, Neves 1292, 1295
Asante, M. K. 41, 42, 43, 44, 45, 47, 928

Asbóth, Oszkár 1737, 1742
Ascoli, Graziadio Isaia 2, 176, 179, 613, 623, 1335, 1336, 1370, 1371, 1377, 1381, 1388, 1392
Asenova, Petya 1514, 1549, 1553, 1554
Asensio, Eugenio 1276, 1283
Ash, S. 810
Ashby, E. 670, 674
Asher, J. J. 7, 8, 88
Asher, R. E. 75, 666, 1974, 1976, 1978, 1979
Asiwaju, A. I. 199
Asmuth, B. 149, 152
Asp, Erkki 1019
Aster, R. 760, 761, 763
Asuncion-Landé, Nobleza C. 897, 900
Atanasov, Petar 1446, 1449
Atatürk, Kemal Pascha (1881−1938) 344, 619
Atlas Narodov Mira 74
Attalides, Michael 1582
Atten, Alain 1159, 1171
Atteslander, P. 738, 743
Atwood, M. 95, 96
Atxa, Jesus 1307, 1309
Au, K. H. 631, 634, 636
Aubert, J.-F. 355, 356
Aubert, Vilhelm 961
Auburger, Leopold 635, 640
Auer, Peter 16, 20, 55, 241, 243, 322, 326, 452, 456, 588, 592, 596, 605, 755, 760, 761, 762, 801, 803, 804, 925, 926, 928, 929, 1853, 1854
Auerbach, E. 273, 282
Aufhauser, E. 1397
Augustus (30 v. Chr.−14 n. Chr.) 1272
Aune, R. K. 335, 340
Aunger, E. A. 78, 79, 1995
Aurelian (214−275) 1479
Aurousseau, M. 445, 449
Auroux, Sylvain 50, 55, 676, 683
Aurouze, Joseph 1193, 1194
Aurrekoetxea, Gotzon 1268, 1309
Austin, Jane 139, 142, 143
Austin, Robert 1454, 1458
Austin, W. C. 48
av Skarði, Jóhannes 1045, 1049
Averof, Evangelos A. 1519, 1523
Axtell, R. E. 304, 309
Azevedo Filho, Leodegário A. de 1314, 1316
Azevedo Maia, Clarinda de 1315, 1316
Azkarate, Miren 1308, 1309

B

Baba, Ivan 1721
Babić, Stjepan 1433
Babin, Radomir 1411, 1415

Babitch, R. 785, 787
Babu, N. 35, 40
Baccon Bouvet, Clelia 1347, 1349
Bach, A. 270
Bacher, Josef 1356
Bacher, Nikolaus (→ Rü, Micurá de) 1388
Bachmeier, Peter 1506, 1509
Back, M. 533, 540
Back, Otto 445, 448, 449, 887
Backstrom, Ch. 735, 737
Backus, A. 322, 326, 598, 605
Bačová, Viera 1675, 1676
Bade, K. J. 8, 180, 181, 185, 188, 191, 192
Badia i Margarit, Antoni 1282, 1283, 1300, 1301
Bæk Simonsen, Jørgen 1022, 1027, 1031
Baer, G. 181, 191
Baetens Beardsmore, Hugo 8, 9, 12, 39, 84, 88, 234, 236, 239, 243, 292, 293, 294, 366, 369, 404, 453, 456, 466, 468, 469, 470, 471, 472, 473, 494, 500, 595, 790, 795, 1114, 1119, 1122, 1126, 1127, 1129, 1777
Baggioni, D. 49, 50, 52, 55
Bähr, Dieter 1095, 1096
Bahrick, H. 567, 576
Bailey, C.-J. 658
Bailey, N. 562, 566
Bailey, R. 900, 901, 908, 909, 911
Bain, B. 803, 842
Baisch, M. 1886
Bajčev, Bojan 1491, 1494
Bajcura, Ivan 1696, 1698, 1700
Baker, Colin 8, 9, 81, 83, 84, 86, 88, 466, 471, 472, 696, 700, 1061, 1064, 1067, 1068, 1069, 1072, 1074, 1075
Baker, E. 1582
Baker, K. 632, 633
Baker, Ph. 644, 648
Baker, R. G. 429, 430
Bakhtin, M. M. 747, 748
Bakker, M. 1151
Bakker, Peter 793, 795, 1965, 1970
Bakoš, J. 1707
Bakos, Ferenc 1468, 1469, 1486
Bal, Willy 1112, 1122
Balász, J. 1684
Balcou, Jean 1259, 1260
Bald, W.-D. 910, 913, 1317
Baldauf, Richard 423, 426, 857
Baldinger, Kurt 1316
Baldunčiks, Juris 1911
Balhar, Jan 1637, 1639, 1640
Balibar, Renée 178, 179, 210, 217, 878, 890, 892, 1173, 1186

Balkan, L. 34, 38
Ball, M. 14, 20, 452, 456
Bally, C. 146, 147, 152, 548, 874, 877, 878
Bamgbose, A. 426, 430, 670, 674, 831, 832
Banarlı, Nihat Sami 1557, 1559
Banfi, Emanuele 1327, 1328, 1919, 1974, 1976, 1978
Banowski-Züllig, Monika 1925
Banton, M. 208
Banyeres, J. 355, 356
Baraby, A.-M. 794, 795
Bar-Adon, A. 903, 905
Barakat, R. A. 309
Baran, Oleksander 1697, 1700
Baranow, Ulrich 5, 9
Barany, George 1711, 1721
Baratta, Mario von 1399, 1405, 1459, 1462, 1469
Barba, Vasile 1533, 1539
Barbara, A. 380, 384, 388, 389, 390
Barber, C. 798, 803
Bardovi-Harlig, K. 563, 566
Barentsen, A. 1415
Barić, Eugenija 1412, 1415, 1440, 1441
Barker, G. 798, 803
Barkin, F. 88
Barnade, P. 437
Barnes, J. A. 810
Barnett, George A. 432, 433, 434, 435, 437, 438
Barnouw, D. 96
Barrera i Vidal, A. 861, 864
Barringer, F. 402, 404
Barry, B. 200, 202
Barry, Ch. 131, 132, 137
Barszczewska, Nina 1613
Bartáková, Jana 1652, 1654
Barth, E. 146, 152
Barth, F. 206, 208
Barth, R. 623
Bartha, Csilla 1752
Barthel, D. L. 319
Barthes, R. 301, 309
Bartholy, Heike 1402, 1405
Bartmiński, Jerzy 1614, 1628
Bartsch, Renate 464, 610
Baruch, Kalmi 1441
Barzilay, M. 375, 378
Basara, Jan 1667, 1668
Baskakov, N. A. 1895, 1899, 1940, 1941
Basso, K. 749, 792, 795
Bassola, Péter 370
Bastardas, Albert 442, 444, 1114, 1122, 1281, 1283, 1299, 1301
Bastide, R. 50, 51, 55
Bates, E. 289, 294
Bátori, István 1899
Batowski, H. 449

Battiste, M. 793, 794, 795
Battisti, Carlo 1217, 1221, 1367, 1370, 1396
Baudement, T. 833
Baudou, Evert 976
Baudouin de Courtenay, Jean (1845−1929) 882, 886, 1361
Bauer, O. 155, 159, 246, 247, 255
Baugh, John 711, 713, 714
Baum, R. 513, 878
Bauman, J. J. 664, 665, 666
Bauman, R. 170, 174, 409, 413, 747, 748, 750, 760, 788, 789, 790, 795, 796 1543
Baumann, K.-D. 513
Baumgartner, Gerhard 1804, 1805, 1807, 1808, 1811, 1828, 1829, 1832, 1833, 1834, 1835
Baumgärtner, K. 266, 270
Bausani, A. 881, 886
Bausch, Karl Richard 369, 416, 419, 512, 513
Bausch, Karl-Heinz 8, 9, 755, 760
Bausinger, Hermann 270
Bautista, M. L. S. 898, 899, 900
Bayard, Catherine 1867, 1870
Bayer, J. M. 74, 79, 80, 215, 217, 218
Bazin, L. 107, 108, 1532
Beach, Hugh 981
Bean, F. 867, 870
Beattie, G. 438
Beattie, K. W. 432, 437
Beaufays, Jean 1142, 1143
Beauregard, Yves 596, 605
Beauvillain, C. 125, 129
Bec, Pierre 177, 179, 613, 623, 1188, 1192, 1193, 1194
Bechert, Johannes 144, 152, 255, 750, 760, 815, 818, 1328
Beck, H. 1357
Becker, A. 132, 137
Becker, H. 751, 755, 760
Becker, J. D. 126, 127, 129
Becker, K. 621, 623
Becker-Christensen, Henrik 1036, 1041, 1772, 1774, 1776
Beckers, Hartmut 1142
Beckwith, Lillian 1094, 1096
Becquelin-Monod, A. 790, 795
Becquet, Ch. 154, 159
Bédard, A. 386, 390
Bédard, E. 878, 832
Bednarčík, V. 1632
Beebe, L. 336, 337, 340, 500, 523
Beer, W. R. 76, 78, 79, 80, 350, 351
Beheydt, Ludo 1119, 1122
Beier, R. 511, 513, 515
Beinke, Ch. 874, 878

Bélanger, M. 787
Belardi, Walter 1396
Bělić, Jaromír 1650, 1654, 1655, 1662, 1667, 1668
Bell, A. 336, 340, 428, 430, 724
Bell, D. 204, 206, 208
Bell, N. 48, 325, 326
Bellenger, L. 419
Bellér, Béla 1725, 1730
Bellin, W. 380, 384
Bellinello, Pier Francesco 1328, 1329, 2017, 2019
Bellmann, Günter 5, 9, 1598, 1599, 1795, 1796, 1853
Bellucci Maffei, P. 641
Beloded, Ivan K. 1899, 1900, 1940
Belson, W. A. 728, 732
Benattig, R. 325, 326
Benavides, A. 501
Benbanaste, Nesim 1556, 1558, 1559, 1567, 1568, 1571
Benčić, Nikola 1822, 1824, 1827
Bender, H. S. 316, 319, 396, 397
Bender, K. H. 880
Bender, Rainer J. 1409, 1415
Benediktsson, Hreinn 1056, 1057
Benedini, Paola 641
Beneke, Jürgen 418, 419, 510, 513
Beneš, E. 152, 256
Benet, Josep 1277, 1284
Bengtsson, S. 874, 878
Beniak, E. 374, 377, 378, 591, 593, 765, 770, 786, 787
Benincà, Paola 1396
Benkö, Loránd 1835
Bennett, J. R. 146, 152
Bennett, Scott E. 1014
Benninghaus, H. 727, 732
Benrath, Josef 1130, 1133, 1136
Bensimon, D. 388, 390, 2004, 2006
Bentahila, A. 6, 9, 595, 600, 605, 695, 699, 700
Bentler, P. M. 694, 700
Benton, R. 904, 905
Benveniste, E. 406, 413
Benzécri, J.-P. 780, 786
Ben-Zeev, S. 33, 34, 38
Beran, H. 359, 362
Beranek, Franz J. 1660, 1661
Bérard, Jean 1511, 1514
Berend, N. 399, 815, 816, 818, 819
Beretta, A. 516, 524
Bereznak, Catherine 666
Berg, Guy 1171
Berg, M. E. van den 335, 336, 340
Berg-Ehlers, L. 149, 152
Bergel, Hans 1471, 1476
Bergemann, N. 420, 421

Berger, Ch. R. 335, 340
Berger, H. 753, 760
Berger, K. 880
Berger, M. 1661
Berger, Maria Renate 1259
Berger, Marianne R. 453, 456, 695, 700
Bergeron, G. 831, 832
Bergeron, L. 96
Berghe, P. L. van den 208
Bergmane, Anna 1911
Bergmann, J. 415, 419
Bergmans, B. 352, 356
Bergmans, Bernhard 1116, 1122, 1132, 1136
Bergroth, Hugo 1014
Bergsland, Knut 938, 947, 961, 981
Berić, V. 1416
Berko Gleason, Jean 582, 585, 1723
Berk-Seligson, S. 605
Berlińska, Danuta 1594
Berlin, B. 127, 129
Berlin, I. 200, 201, 202
Berman, J. J. 41, 46, 47
Bernabé, J. 53, 55
Bernadó, D. 802, 803
Bernal Berna, Chesús Gregorio 1194
Bernardó, Domènec 1201
Bernhard, J. 310
Bernini, Giuliano 321, 326, 1151
Berns, J. B. 1151, 1152
Bernstein, Basil 248, 255, 710, 713
Bernstein, S. R. 1504
Berrendonner, Alain 872, 878, 1217, 1221
Berruto, Gaetano 322, 323, 326, 1204, 1213, 1214, 1221, 1326, 1329, 1334, 1337, 1843, 1849, 1873, 1877, 1878
Berschin, Helmut 1312, 1316, 2014
Bert, Paul 1349
Bertels, L. 189, 191
Bertelson, P. 629, 633
Bertha, Alfred 1137, 1138, 1139, 1142
Berthelsen, Christian 1053, 1054
Bertić, Ivan 1441, 1442
Bertoldi, Maria B. 1356
Besch, Werner 175, 176, 177, 179, 258, 261, 266, 270, 271, 816, 818, 819, 1239, 1240, 1357, 1600, 1768, 1781, 1853
Bešta, Theodor 1627
Betcke, P. 855, 856, 857
Bétemps, Alexis 1333, 1337
Bethge, W. 1661
Bethlen, Gabór (1613–1629) 1480

Bettoni, C. 570, 576
Betz, Werner 4, 9, 548, 872, 878
Beukema, F. 1151
Bevin, J. H. 311
Beyer, E. 2006
Beyer, Ernest 1239
Bezděková, Eva 1645, 1648
Béziers, M. 246, 256
Bezlaj, France 1816, 1820
Bhardwaj, M. 521, 524
Bhatia, T. K. 910, 912
Bhatt, R. M. 895, 900
Bialystok, E. 35, 38, 40, 243, 605, 606, 609, 631, 633
Bianconi, Sandro 1844, 1849, 1852, 1871, 1874, 1875, 1877, 1878
Biber, Dušan 1423
Bichel, Ulf 270
Bickel, Hans 1840, 1841, 1842, 1849, 1861
Bickerton, D. 123, 521, 524, 649, 651, 653, 655, 657, 790
Bidwell, Charles E. 1514
Bieber, Ursula 1925
Bieder, Hermann 1923, 1924, 1925
Bielfeldt, Hans-Holm 1795, 1796
Bielovodskýő, Andrej 1632
Biemer, P. P. 732, 743, 744
Bierbach, Ch. 451, 453, 456
Billiez, Jacqueline 322, 326, 1183, 1184, 1186
Billigmeier, Robert H. 904, 906, 1844, 1849
Binns, Dennis 1970
Birch, A. 359, 362
Birkenfeld, H. 189, 191
Birken-Silverman, Gabriele 1328, 1329, 1371, 1373, 1375, 1376, 1396, 2017, 2019
Birnbaum, H. 1565
Birnbaum, N. 903, 906
Birnbaum, Salomo 1942, 1945, 1960
Birren, J. 585
Biscaretti di Ruffia, P. 163, 168
Bischoff, Heinrich 1134, 1136
Bischofsberger, Marco 1878
Bishop, G. F. 732, 739, 743
Bister, Helga 1126, 1129
Bjerrum, Anders 1776
Björklund, Kaj 1014
Black, George F. 1970
Black, J. W. 333, 340
Blake, C. A. 928
Blanár, Vincent 1707
Blanc, André 1459, 1469
Blanc, H. 394, 397
Blanc, Michel 32, 33, 36, 37, 38, 39, 44, 45, 46, 48, 82, 83, 84, 86, 88, 234, 235, 236, 244, 256, 776, 787, 790, 794, 795

Blanchet, Philippe 1194
Blanke, D. 881, 883, 884, 885, 886
Blas, José Luis 1300, 1301
Blasco Ferrer, Eduardo 1377, 1380, 1381, 1383
Bläsing, Uwe 1575, 1576
Blaunstein, A. P. 168
Bless, H. 742, 744
Bliesener, U. 416, 419
Blinkena, Aina 1909, 1911, 1912
Bliss, Alan 1106
Bloch, J. 394, 397
Blom, Jan-Petter 141, 142, 143, 595, 596, 597, 605, 710, 713, 801, 803, 810
Blommaert, Jan 587, 592, 928
Bloomfield, L. 169, 174, 234, 243, 365, 369, 392, 397, 542, 543, 548, 559, 560, 566, 586, 592, 656, 657
Blouet, Brian 1399, 1405
Blum, Jost G. 1951, 1960
Blumer, H. 756, 757, 760
Blum-Kulka, S. 14, 20, 55, 56, 143, 464, 925, 928
Boas, F. 50, 51, 55, 789, 794
Boase, Roger 1274, 1284
Bobák, Jan 1673, 1677
Bochmann, Klaus 832, 1328, 1329
Bochner, St. 419, 464, 929
Bock, Karl N. 1771, 1776
Bock, P. 925, 929
Bodenhausen, G. V. 731, 732
Bodi, L. 245, 457
Bodine, A. 720, 724
Bodnarckij, M. C. 449
Boeglin, B. 860, 864
Boehm, Max Hildebert 155, 159, 717, 719
Boeschoten, Hendrik 125, 129, 321, 322, 326, 580, 585, 595, 600, 604, 605, 1150, 1151
Boeschoten, Riki van 1549
Boev, Emil 1506, 1509
Boev, P. 1511, 1514
Bogaards, P. 507
Bogaert, E. 419
Bogas, Evangelos 1531
Bogataj, Mirko 1801, 1802, 1810, 1811, 1814, 1815, 1820
Bogdain, K. 384
Bogdanović, Dimitrije 1409, 1415
Bogoczová, Irena 1645, 1648, 1654, 1655, 1667, 1668
Böhme, G. 180, 191
Böhmer, E. 813, 818
Bohnsack, R. 760
Bohrnstedt, G. W. 728, 732
Boissevain, J. 810, 811
Boisvert, J. 439, 444

Boivert, Georges 1316
Boix, Emili 1301, 1302
Bojadžiev, Todor 1491, 1494, 1495, 1503, 1552, 1554
Bojadschi, Michael G. 1536, 1539
Bojsen, Else 1028, 1031
Bokarev, E. A. 1895, 1899
Boléo, Manuel de Paiva 2014
Bolinger, D. 708
Bolitho, A. R. 512, 514
Boller, F. 245
Bologna, Piero 1349
Bolognari, Mario 1375
Boltanski, L. 683
Bolten, J. 512, 514
Bolton, K. 924, 929, 930
Bolton, S. 507
Bombaci, A. 1532
Bona, G. 1738
Bonaparte, Louis-Lucien (1813–1891) 1268, 1303
Bond, Ch. F. jr. 309
Bond, M. H. 695, 702
Bond, R. N. 336, 342
Bondis, M. 309
Bonfante, Giulio 1974, 1976, 1978, 1979
Bongaerts, Th. 6, 11
Bonifacio, P. S. 897, 900
Bonin, D. 217
Bonini, Giuseppe Fausto 1324, 1329
Bonnot, J. F. 683
Bonser, R. N. 309
Bonß, W. 752, 760
Borbély, Anna 1715, 1721, 1752, 1753
Borcia, Ion 1475, 1476
Borden, G. A. 301, 309
Boretzky, Norbert 539, 1968, 1970
Borg, Albert 1400, 1401, 1405
Borg, Alexander 1405, 1582
Borg, Joseph 1405
Borges, Naír Odete de Câmara 1316
Borghi, M. 1121, 1122
Borin, Lars 1007
Born, Joachim 384, 396, 397, 857, 1389, 1390, 1396, 1599, 1673, 1677, 1685, 1690, 1725, 1730, 1765, 1768, 1851
Bornträger, Ekkehard W. 1329, 1523, 2032, 2033
Borodina, M. A. 1940
Boršč, Anton T. 1937, 1940
Borsody, Stephen 1711, 1721, 1722
Bortoni, Stella Maris 484, 491
Bortoni-Ricardo, Stella Maris 808, 809, 810
Bortz, J. 730, 732

Boruth, Fürst 1798
Borý, Wiesław 1605
Borzeix, A. 410, 412, 413
Borzyszkowski, J. 2037
Boschung, Peter 1847, 1849
Bossong, Georg 75, 624
Bot, Kees de 18, 20, 21, 22, 245, 327, 375, 377, 567, 577, 579, 580, 582, 583, 584, 585, 1151
Bothorel, Arlette 1240, 2006
Bothorel-Witz, Arlette 678, 683, 1239
Bott, E. 806, 807, 810
Böttcher, W. 854, 857
Bottomley, G. 463, 464
Bouda, Karl 1268
Boudart, Marina 1121, 1122, 1123
Boudart, Michel 1122
Bouderbala, N. 195, 199
Bourdieu, Pierre 239, 243, 282, 463, 464, 590, 592, 597, 679, 680, 682, 683, 747, 748, 827, 832, 924, 929
Bourgain, D. 680, 683
Bourgeois, H. 1250
Bourgeois-Gielen, Hélène 1129
Bourhis, Richard Y. 42, 43, 44, 47, 48, 326, 334, 336, 337, 339, 340, 341, 433, 437, 572, 573, 577, 596, 606, 696, 700
Boutet, Josiane 243, 326, 327, 1186, 1187
Bouvier, Jean Claude 683, 1349
Boves, Th. L. L. 334, 340
Bowe, H. 416, 419
Bowen, J. D. 561, 567, 609
Bowen, M. 860, 864
Bowerman, M. 521, 524
Boyd, M. 388, 390
Boyd, Sally 17, 20, 370, 373, 377, 575, 576, 580, 583, 584, 600, 602, 605, 992
Boyd-Barrett, Oliver 426, 429, 430, 431
Boyer, Henri 256, 676, 678, 680, 681, 683, 717, 719, 1193, 1194
Bracker, Jochen 1776
Bradac, J. J. 48, 334, 335, 340, 341
Bradburn, N. M. 726, 729, 730, 732, 733, 738, 741, 743, 744
Bradean-Ebinger, Nelu 1007
Braga, G. 81, 405, 691, 802, 803
Brailsford, Henry 1488, 1495
Branch, Michael 1007
Brand, J. A. 79
Brankatschk, Jan 1791, 1796
Brann, Conrad M. B. 256, 272, 277, 282
Brass, P. R. 76, 78, 79, 396, 397, 404
Bratanic, M. 852

Brătianu, G. I. 1479, 1486
Braude, Benjamin 1555, 1559, 1565
Brauer-Figueiredo, M. Fátima V. 1316
Braun, P. 4, 9
Braunmüller, Kurt 614, 623, 755, 760, 1775, 1776
Brborić, Branislav 1410, 1415
Breakwell, G. 48
Breckler, S. J. 700
Bree, Cor van 1152
Breedlove, D. 129
Breen, Richard 1099, 1106
Brehm, J. W. 694, 700
Breitborde. L. B. 801, 802, 803, 804, 810
Breivik, L. E. 578
Brekel, H. 592
Bremer, K. 54, 55
Bremmer, I. 1926
Brend, R. M. 129
Brendemoen, Bernt 1558, 1559
Brennan, Eileen M. 784, 786
Brennan, John S. 784, 786
Brenndörfer, Johann 1476
Brenneis, D. 143
Brenner, M. 745, 748
Brentjes, Burchard 1573, 1576
Brent-Palmer, C. 35, 38, 787
Brenzinger, Matthias 571, 576
Brès, J. 238, 243
Breton, Roland 65, 68, 74, 154, 159, 216, 217, 1979
Breu, Josef 450, 1821, 1823, 1827, 1974, 1976, 1978, 1979, 2041, 2045, 2065
Breu, Walter 1364, 1366, 1376, 1974, 1976, 1978
Brewer, W. F. 633
Breza, Edward 1603, 1605
Brigaglia, Manlio 1377, 1381
Briggs, Charles L. 746, 747, 748, 750, 789, 790, 795
Briggs, V. M. jr. 188, 191
Bright, William 56, 640, 753, 754, 759, 760, 761, 762, 770, 841, 879, 1450, 1495
Brilmayer, L. 362
Brincat, Joseph M. 1401, 1405
Bringuier, O. 2003, 2007
Brink, Lars 1022, 1023, 1028, 1031
Brinton, D. M. 293, 294
Brislin, R. W. 309, 929
Britsyn, Victor M. 1932
Britto, F. 394, 397
Brix, E. 93, 96
Broca, Paul 50, 1268
Broch, Ingvild 945, 947, 948
Broch, Olaf 338, 340, 945, 947
Broeder, Peter 16, 20, 55, 132, 137, 372, 377, 519, 524, 1150, 1151

Brohy, Claudine 280, 282, 695, 700, 1845, 1847, 1849
Bromberger, Ch. 51, 55
Bromlej, J. V. 223, 232, 843, 852, 1899
Broncato, P. 128, 129
Bronckart, J.-P. 233, 243, 876, 880
Brøndal, Viggo 2
Bröring, Julius 1787, 1789
Broudic, François 1259
Brown, D. 76, 77, 79,
Brown, P. 650, 658,
Brown, R. 561, 566, 710, 714
Brozović, Dalibor 640, 1433, 1435, 1437, 1438, 1439, 1441, 1442
Bruce, B. C. 633
Brüch, Josef 878
Bruch, Robert 1169, 1171
Bruck, M. 500
Bruckmann, Gerhart 1797, 1811
Brudner, L. 695, 700
Brugmans, Hendrik 1109, 1111, 1122
Bruguera, Jordi 1282, 1284, 1299, 1301
Bruk, S. I. 1887, 1895, 1899, 1936, 1940
Brumfit, C. 841
Brun, Auguste 1193, 1194
Brun-Trigaud, Guylaine 176, 179, 2003, 2006
Bruna Rosso, Pietro A. 1347, 1349
Bruneau, T. 303, 310
Brunetti, C. 356
Bruni, Francesco 1214, 1221, 1222, 1343, 1877, 1878
Brunn, St. 69, 74
Brunner, Georg 1469
Brunner, R. 232, 233
Brunot, Ferdinand 1186
Bruun, Inger 1020, 1024, 1025, 1026, 1031
Bryssinck, René 1122
Brzezina, Maria 1597, 1599
Bubak, Józef 1632
Bucak, S. 670, 675
Buch, Tamara 1618, 1620
Buchanan, A. 362
Buchheit, Lee 362
Buchheit, Robert H. 396, 397
Buchholz, Oda 1457, 1458
Büchi, Christophe 1864, 1870
Buck, K. 512, 514
Budai-Deleanu, Ion 1485, 1486
Budar, L. 2049, 2053
Budovičová, Viera 1651, 1654, 1655, 1673, 1677, 1706, 1707
Budreckis, Algirdas M. 1913, 1915, 1918
Buffa, Ferdinand 1673, 1677, 1693, 1694, 1695, 1700, 1701

Bugarski, Ranko 105, 108, 829, 830, 832, 1415, 1423, 1450, 1451
Bugge, Aage 1053, 1054
Buhlmann, R. 511, 512, 514
Bulicke, I. 396, 397
Bull, Tove 944, 947, 948, 956, 965
Buller, D. B. 335, 340
Bungard, W. 752, 760
Bungarten, Theo 417, 419, 420, 421, 857
Bunis, David M. 1523, 1568, 1571
Buranits, Josef 1823, 1827
Burckhart, S. 622, 623
Burger, Harald 1844, 1849, 1851, 1873, 1877, 1878
Burger, Peter 1129
Burgess, G. W. 451, 457,
Burgess, R. G. 751, 754, 760, 761
Burkert, W. 221, 232
Burnaby, B. 390, 795
Burridge, K. 398
Burrow, T. 102, 103
Burt, M. K. 285, 294, 519, 524, 561, 562, 566
Buson, Ornella 1352, 1356
Busse, Winfried 1568, 1571
Butler, T. 1495
Butt Philip, Allan 1080, 1087
Butters, N. 62
Butzkamm, Wolfgang 466, 472
Buzássyová, Klára 1673, 1677, 1706, 1707
Bybee, Joan L. 533, 540
Byram, Michael 84, 85, 88, 466, 467, 472, 755, 760, 761, 1038, 1039, 1041, 1042, 1776
Byrne, D. 43, 46, 48
Byrne, F. 658
Byrne, J. L. 43, 44, 46, 48
Byrnes, H. 749
Byron, Janet I. 1448, 1449, 1458
Bysaeth, Léo 1868, 1870
Bystroń, Jan 1667, 1668

C

C.I.E.M.E.N 356
Çabej, Eqrem 1376
Cachia, Mons Lewrenz 1405
Cadiot, Pierre 322, 326
Cadzow, John F. 1469
Caferoğlu, Ahmet 1527, 1532
Cajot, José 1138, 1142, 1143, 1150, 1151
Čakvin, I. V. 1925
Calafiore, Giovanni 1396
Calame-Griaule, G. 50, 51, 55
Caldwell, J. 466, 472

Callan, V. J. 17, 20, 334, 340
Callebaut, Bruno 1252
Calogeropoulos-Stratis, S. 358, 362
Calsamiglia, Helena 1301
Calvet, Louis-Jean 190, 191, 195, 196, 197, 199, 256, 430, 669, 674, 790, 795, 827, 829, 832, 839, 840, 878, 889, 892, 1245, 1250
Camaj, Martin 1376
Camartin, Iso 1849, 1862, 1870, 1882, 1886
Cameron, D. 724
Camilleri, Antoinette 1405
Camões, Luís de (1524−1580) 1312
Campbell, C. G. 419
Campbell, D. T. 693, 694, 695, 700
Campbell, Lyle 99, 100, 101, 102, 103, , 659, 660, 661, 662, 666
Campiche, Roland 1839, 1850
Campion, A. 616, 623
Candaugh, D. 789, 796
Canetti, Elias 96
Cantineau, J. 394, 397
Capdevielle, Marie-Monique 1263, 1268
Capidan, Theodor 1517, 1523, 1538, 1539
Capitani, F. de 1851, 1852
Capitant, H. 324, 326
Capotorti, F. 163, 168, 359, 362, 668, 673, 674
Capraro, Giuseppe 1352, 1356
Capurro, R. 510, 514
Caput, J. P. 874, 878
Caracausi, Girolamo 1371, 1523
Carageani, Gheorghe 1538, 1539
Caragiu Marioţeanu, Matilda 1537, 1538, 1539
Caramazza, A. 37, 38
Caravolas, J.-A. 282
Carayol, M. 655, 657
Cardús, Salvador 1296, 1297, 1301
Carey, S. T. 39
Carisse, C. 380, 384, 389, 390
Çark, Rh. Y. 1555, 1559
Carlevaro, T. 886
Carlock, E. K. 770
Carlsmith, J. M. 30, 31
Carrère d'Encausse, Hélène 1899
Carrithers, M. 760, 761
Carroll, J. B. 507
Carroll, M. 137
Carroll, S. 499, 501
Carrozza, Paolo 1329, 1375
Carruba, O. 1151
Carsaniga, G. 461, 464
Carstensen, B. 4, 9

Carta Raspi, Raimondo 1377, 1381
Cartagena, N. 615, 623
Carter, Harold 1081, 1087
Carton, Fernand 1176, 1186, 1242, 1245, 1246, 1247, 1248, 1249, 1250, 1252, 2006
Cartwright, D. 70, 74, 217
Casagrande, J. B. 573, 577
Casanova, Emili 1301
Cashmore, E. E. 204, 206, 208
Casse, P. 924, 925, 929
Cassel, C.-M. 735, 737
Cassese, A. 362
Cassidy, F. G. 656, 657
Cassoni, Mauro 1367, 1370
Castellan, Georges 1469
Castillo, F. Bonilla 492
Castles, St. 180, 191
Castonguay, Charles 374, 377, 380, 381, 384, 386, 390
Čašule, Vanga 1503
Catani, M. 456
Catford, John C. 1089, 1096
Cathomas, Bernard 1844, 1849, 1850, 1883, 1885, 1886
Catrina, Werner 1879, 1886
Catsiapis, Jean 1582
Caudmont, Jean 1252, 2008
Caussignac, Gerard 1846, 1850
Cavalli-Sforza, L. L. 223, 232
Cavilla Ote, Manuel 1283, 1284
Cazden, C. B. 841
Ceauşescu, Nicolae (1918−1989) 1461
Cebulu, R. 181, 191
Ceccaldi, Mathieu 1210, 1213, 1217, 1221
Cecić, Ivo 1442
Cedergren, H. 770
Čekman, Valerij 1918
Čekmonas, Valerijus 1918, 1919
Celan, Paul 97
Centlivres, Pierre 1850, 1852
Cerdà, Ramon 1300, 1301
Cerexhe, E. 354, 356
Cerlogne, Jean-Baptiste 1334, 1336, 1337
Černyšova, T. N. 1932
Certeau, Michel de 278, 282, 1186, 1243, 1245, 1250
Cerwenka, E. J. 311
Ceschi, Raffaelo 1852, 1878
Ceynowa, Florian 1601, 1602, 1603, 1605
Chabot, J.-L. 200, 202
Chacón, Rafael 1286, 1294
Chafe, Wallace L. 666, 711, 714
Chaica, E. 129
Chaker, S. 1181, 1186, 2005, 2006
Chakraborty, R. 180, 191
Chalupec, Adam 1631, 1632

Chambers, J. K. 64, 74, 176, 179
Chamoiseau, P. 55
Champagne, M. 33, 38, 369
Chanlat, A. 412, 413
Chanlatte, J. 656, 657
Chapelle, J. 62
Chapman, M. 203, 206, 209
Charlemagne (768−814) 1229, 1332
Charles le Chauve (823−877) 1224
Charles le Téméraire (1467−1477) 1864
Charles VI (1711−1740) 1358
Charles, F. 523
Charney, Israel W. 1576
Charry, Eddy 1150, 1151
Chasiotis, Ioannis K. 1515, 1516, 1523
Chaudenson, R. 53, 55, 256, 649, 650, 651, 652, 653, 654, 655, 657, 790, 830, 832
Chaudhuri, A. 735, 737
Chave, E. J. 702
Cheetham, J. 868, 870
Chein, I. 694, 700
Chen John, T. S. 620, 623
Chenal, Aimé 1336, 1337
Cherpillod, A. 450
Cherubim, Dieter 539
Chesanow, N. 299, 309
Cheshire, Jenny 19, 20, 270, 334, 341, 722, 724, 895, 899,900, 901, 908, 912, 1149, 1151
Cheval, J.-J. 428, 430
Chiasson-Lavoie, M. 683
Chiellino, Carmine 1329
Child, I. L. 236, 243
Chimombo, M. 33, 38
Ching, P. S. 593
Chiocchetti, Fabio 1396
Chiorboli, Jean 1175, 1186, 1204, 1213, 1214, 1218, 1219, 1220, 1221, 1222
Chirac, J. 878
Chirol, L. 873, 878
Chiti-Batelli, A. 159
Chlebowczyk, Józef 1668
Chloupek, J. 1655
Chmilar, P. 633
Choi, Y. 437
Cholmogorov, A. I. 1894, 1899
Chomba, B. 675
Chomsky, Noam 13, 20, 56, 285, 289, 294, 518, 519, 524, 561, 566, 669, 674
Choron-Baix, C. 2006
Christ, Hannelore 270
Christ, Herbert 369, 416, 419, 507, 514
Christen, Helen 1843, 1850
Christian, D. 495, 500
Christie, P. 787

Christie, W. 103
Christmann, H. H. 876, 878
Christoforidis, Konstantinos 1522, 1523
Christophersen, Hans 1776
Christophory, Jules 1162, 1165, 1166, 1171
Chua, K. F. 419
Chu-Chang, M. 632, 633
Chumak-Horbatsch, R. 452, 456
Ciampi, Gabriele 2031, 2032
Čičaj, Viliam 1707
Cichocki, Wladyslaw 780, 785, 787
Cichon, Peter 1192, 1194
Cicourel, A. V. 29, 31, 745, 746, 747, 748, 749
Cierbide Martinena, R. 1268
Cihac, Alexandre de 1485, 1486
Cioffi-Revilla, C. 426, 438
Cipolla, C. M. 428, 430
Civelli, M. 691
Civil, M. 105, 108
Claes, L. 62, 78, 79
Claeys, P.-H. 404
Clahsen, H. 285, 287, 292, 294, 520, 521, 522, 523, 524
Clair, R. St. 548
Clark, H. H. 432, 437, 739, 743
Clark, L. F. 744
Clark, M. S. 732, 744
Clark, W. A. 181, 191
Clarkson, Iain 549, 1316, 1777, 1982
Clasen, C.-P. 316, 319
Claudi, U. 533, 534, 537, 540
Clausén, Ulla 1047, 1048
Clauss, Jan Ulrich 1329, 1377, 1381, 2019
Claussen, D. 180, 191
Claut, H. 181, 192
Clem, Ralph S. 1925
Clément, R. 44, 46, 48, 596, 433, 437, 605, 680, 683
Clercq, Martine de 96, 459, 463, 464
Clifford, J. 587, 592, 760, 761
Cline, T. 87, 88
Clivio, Gianrenzo 1349
Clogg, Richard 1561, 1563, 1565
Cloonan, J. 869, 870
Cluver, August D. de 891, 892
Clyne, Michael 4, 6, 9, 14, 16, 18, 20, 21, 22, 96, 110, 113, 115, 116, 190, 191, 323, 324, 326, 371, 377, 452, 454, 456, 464, 547, 548, 567, 571, 577, 578, 580, 584, 593, 594, 595, 599, 600, 601, 604, 605, 606, 640, 721, 722, 723, 724, 725, 750, 755, 761, 812, 816, 818, 853, 857, 868, 870, 895, 900, 901, 926, 927, 929, 1442

Clyne, P. R. 749
Coates, J. 721, 724
Cobarrubias, J. 667, 673, 674, 1122
Cobb, W. J. 749
Cobreros Mendazona, E. 352, 356
Cochran, M. 810
Cochran, W. G. 735, 737
Cohen, Andrew. D. 582, 584, 585
Cohen, Antony. 929
Cohen, D. 616, 623
Cohen, E. 335, 338, 340
Cohen, N. J. 59, 62
Cohen, Raymond 297, 309
Cohen, Robert 81, 88
Cohen, Roberta 866, 870
Cohen, Ronald 865, 870
Cole, M. 710, 714, 925, 929
Cole, P. 143, 420, 770
Coleman, H. 841, 857
Collet, B. 386, 390
Collet, P. 310
Collin, H. 209
Collinder, Björn 981
Collinge, N. E. 648
Collins, R. 429, 430
Colombani, Ignaziu 1207, 1209, 1213
Colomina, Jordi 1301
Colón, Germà 1282, 1284, 1299, 1300, 1301, 1302
Colotti, Mariateresa 1369, 1370, 1371
Comet, R. 355, 356
Comiti, Jean-Marie 1208, 1213
Comrie, Bernard 548, 619, 623, 624, 895, 900, 1895, 1899
Condon, J. C. 302, 309, 929
Conev, Benjo 1507, 1509
Confiant, R. 55
Conklin, N. F. 170, 172, 174
Connor, U. 14, 20
Connor, W. 76, 77, 79, 208
Conrad, A. W. 433, 437, 459
Conseil de l'Europe 282, 506, 507
Constantinesco, L. J. 159
Constantino, E. 896, 897, 900
Contini, Michel 1377, 1381
Contu, G. 352, 356
Converse, J. M. 726, 732, 739, 740, 743
Conwan, W. 795
Cook, V. 558, 566
Cook-Gumperz, J. 143, 718, 719, 755, 761
Cooley, C. H. 24, 29, 31
Cooper, R. L. 16, 20, 88, 175, 335, 338, 340, 379, 397, 398, 399, 432, 433, 437, 472, 492, 584, 586, 588, 592, 634, 724,

776, 787, 828, 830, 831, 832, 865, 866, 868, 870, 887, 888, 892, 907, 912
Coornaert, Emile 1243, 1250
Cope, B. 88
Corbea, Andrei 1476, 1477
Corbeil, J.-C. 827, 830, 832
Corder, S. P. 15, 20, 113, 116, 171, 174, 515, 520, 524, 561, 562, 566, 648
Corgnier, Giselle 1334, 1337
Cornagliotti, Anna 1349
Cornejo, R. 38
Cornett, Andreas P. 1033, 1041
Cornips, Leonie 1150, 1151
Coromines, Joan 1301, 1302
Cortelazzo, Manlio 556, 558, 1366, 1398, 1523
Cortelazzo, Michele A. 1877, 1878
Cortes y Vásquez, L. 1316
Cortiade, Marcel 1965, 1970
Corvalán, G. 487, 491
Coseriu, Eugenio 89, 96, 148, 152, 527, 529, 530, 534, 535, 536, 539, 540, 1275, 1279, 1280, 1284
Cosma, M. 1751, 1753
Cosnier, J. 243
Cossu, Antonio 1377, 1381
Costa, Elisabeth 1119, 1122
Coste-Floret, Alfred 1582
Couderc, Yves 252, 256, 802, 803, 1193, 1194
Coulmas, Florian 19, 20, 89, 96, 104, 106, 108, 109, 134, 137, 191, 216, 217, 218, 239, 243, 256, 464, 793, 795, 832, 833, 845, 852, 858, 860, 862, 864, 878, 892, 928, 929, 1074
Coupland, J. 333, 334, 340, 341, 579, 584
Coupland, Niklas 41, 42, 43, 44, 45, 46, 47, 48, 326, 333, 334, 336, 338, 339, 340, 341, 759, 761, 1087
Courthiade, Marcel 1457, 1458
Coutelle, Louis 1523
Couturat, L. 883, 884, 886
Covell, M. 78, 79, 400, 403, 404
Coveri, Lorenzo 1379, 1381
Cowan, Jane K. 1544, 1549
Cox, E. P. 740, 743
Craffonara, Lois 1356, 1385, 1396, 1398
Craft, A. 1072, 1074
Craig, C. 173, 174, 662, 663, 666
Craig, J. A. 929
Craig, R. 138, 143
Creider, C. 296, 309
Cremer, R. D. 839, 840
Cremona, A. 1403, 1405
Cresswell, R 51, 55

Criper, C. 520, 524
Crocker, J. 46, 48
Croft, K. 21
Crookes, G. 516, 524
Crosby, A. W. 645, 648
Crosby, C. 37, 39, 137
Crößmann-Osterloh, Helga 1464, 1468, 1469, 1474, 1475, 1476
Crouzet, François 1582
Crowe, David 1719, 1720, 1721, 1722
Crowley, T. 722, 723, 724
Crown, C. L. 336, 340
Crozier, M. 405, 413
Crutchfield, R. S. 739, 743
Cruz, B. R. 632, 634
Crvenkovski, D. 1503
Crystal, D. 147, 152, 908, 912
Csalog, Zsolt 1720, 1722
Csaplovics, Johann von 1826, 1827
Csémy, Tamás 1648, 1649
Csenar, Manfred 1827
Csongor, Anna 1720, 1721, 1722
Csurka, István 1720, 1722
Cuco, Alfons 1582
Culioli, A. 677, 681, 683
Čuma, Andrij 1701
Cumming, A. 388, 390
Cummins, Jim 15, 19, 20, 35, 36, 38, 83, 85, 86, 87, 88, 218, 236, 243, 291, 292, 293, 294, 295, 321, 325, 326, 367, 369, 465, 469, 472, 475, 477, 479, 480, 481, 484, 485, 491, 493, 494, 500, 501, 624, 626, 627, 631, 633, 673, 675, 691, 871
Cunha, C. 617, 623
Curran, J. 431
Curtius, E. R. 90, 91, 96
Cutsumbis, M. N. 1523
Cutting, Marion 1922, 1925
Cvetkovski, Victor 1503
Cybulski, Marek 1603, 1606
Cyert, R. M. 405, 413
Cyr, André 414
Cyr, Danielle 794, 795, 796
Czambel, Samuel 1632
Czarnecki, Tomasz 1598, 1599
Czech, Joseph 1596, 1599
Czech, Mirosław 1625, 1627
Cziko, G. 84, 88, 498, 500
Czoernig, Carl von 1805, 1811, 1813, 1820
Czopek, Barbara 1622, 1627
Czyżewski, Feliks 1624, 1627
Czyżewski, Marek 1648

D

Dabène, Louis 322, 325, 326, 327, 1183, 1184, 1186
Dadder, R. 929
Dadrian, V. N. 1573, 1576
Dafis, Llinos 1905
Dahmen, Wolfgang 1171, 1172, 1317, 1382, 1470, 1536, 1538, 1539, 1974, 1976, 1978, 2032
Dahrendorf, Rudolf 415, 419
Dalanoi, G. 202
Dalbera-Stefanaggi, Marie-José 1214, 1220, 1221
Dale, I. R. H. 104, 109
Dalleggio, Eugène 1529, 1532
Dammann, R. 752, 761
Danan, M. 429, 430
D'Andrea, D. 582, 585
Danesi, M. 83, 85, 88, 477, 480
D'Anfton, L. 1122
Daniel, V. 57
Danon, Abraham 1570, 1571
Daoust, Denise 210, 217, 830, 832
Dapit, Roberto 1361
Darbelnet, Jean 146, 153
Darcy, N. T. 34, 38
Darms, Georges 1844, 1850, 1884, 1886
Darnell, R. 683
Darski, J. 1655
Darwin, Charles (1809–1882) 2
DasGupta, J. 76, 78, 79, 400, 404, 578, 585, 690, 691,839, 840
Dauby, J. 1242, 1248, 1249, 1250
Daum, Nicolaus 2032
Dauses, A. 539
Dauzat, Albert 1259
Dávid, Zoltán 1709, 1711, 1715, 1722, 1723
Davídek, Václav 1667, 1668
Davidová, Dana 1645, 1648, 1654, 1655
Davies, Alan 520, 524
Davies, Eirlys 6, 9, 595, 600, 605
Davies, Evelyn 14, 22, 868, 871
Davies, John 352, 356, 1076, 1079, 1080, 1087
Davies, Maureen 363
Davis, J. A. 739, 743
Davis, Kingsley 191
Davis, Patricia 868, 871
Davy, D. 147, 152
Dawkins, R. M. 101, 103, 1523
de Gaulle, Ch. (1890–1970) 159
de Marchi, Bruna 1340, 1342, 1343, 1353, 1354, 1356
de Pietro, Pierre François 1843, 1845, 1850, 1852, 1867, 1870
de Robillard, D. 832
de Rota y Monter, F. 472
de Rougemont, D. 160
de Vincenz, A. 5, 12
Deák, Ladislav 1677
Dean, L. F. 917, 920
Deane, Seamus 1105, 1106
Debes, Hans Jacob 1048
DeBose, Ch. F. 595, 606
Debrock, Mark 1114, 1122
DeCamp, D. 252, 256, 655, 657
Decaux, A. 889, 893
Decker, Jacques de 1110, 1122
Declara, J. 1391, 1397
Decurtins, Alexi 1850
Dédéyan, G. 2004, 2006
Deér, József 1732, 1737
DeFrancis, J. 104, 109
Dejna, Karol 1594, 1602, 1626, 1627, 1636, 1639, 1640, 1668
Del Piano, Lorenzo 1376, 1381
Del Puente, Patrizia 1366
Del Toso, Luciana 1340, 1343
Delabastita, D. 429, 430
Delamotte-Legrand, R. 81, 88
Deleeck, Herman 1110, 1114, 1122
Della Peruta, Franco 1329
Dell'Agata, Giuseppe 1494, 1495
Delrieu, J. 325, 326
Demandt, A. 186, 191
Demarchi, F. 893
Deming, W. E. 735, 736, 737
Demoor, M. 1152
Demos, V. 395, 398
Deneckere, Marcel 1124, 1129
Deniau, X. 863, 864
Denis, M.-N. 381, 385
Denison, Norman 1353, 1356
Densham, J. 691
Deny, J. 1532
Denzin, N. K. 754, 756, 757, 759, 761
Deprez, Kas 69, 74, 452, 456, 699, 700, 1115, 1120, 1122, 1139, 1142, 1143, 1151, 1157, 1995
Deroy, L. 4, 9
Derville, Alain 1243, 1250
Déry, R. 408, 413
Descartes, René (1596–1650) 2
Deschanel, E. 873, 878
Dešeriev, J. D. 1893, 1899, 1900, 1939, 1940, 1941
Desgrouais, J. 1267, 1268
Desnickaja, Agniia V. 1494, 1495
Desrochers, A. 38, 40
Dessemontet, F. 355, 356
DeStefano, J. S. 431, 433, 435, 437
Detrez, Raymond 1458, 1550
Dettori, Antonietta 1379, 1381
Deuchar, M. 721, 724
Deutsch, B. 741, 744
Deutsch, Karl W. 64, 74, 76, 79
Deutschmann, Olaf 878
DeVault, M. L. 747, 749
Devellioğlu, Fuat 1532

Devereux, G. 752, 761
Devetak, Silvo 208, 209, 1423
Devik, B. 1981
de Vriendt, Seraphim 88
de Wachter, W. 78, 79
Dewandre, N. 202
Dewey, J. 694, 700
Dewulf, H. 1151
Di Iorio, Francesco 1337
Di Luzio, A. 55, 755, 760, 761, 762, 926, 928, 929
Dias, Jorge 1314, 1316
Díaz Borque, J. M. 1295
Diaz, R. M. 6, 9, 34, 35, 38, 39, 603, 606
Dickason, O. P. 791, 793, 795
Dickgießer, Sylvia 397, 1599, 1673, 1677, 1685, 1690, 1725, 1730, 1765, 1768
Diebold, R. 369
Diehl-Zelonkina, N. 420
Diekmann, Erwin 1850, 1879, 1886
Diercks, Willy 755, 760, 1041
Dietrich, R. 521, 524
Díez, Miguel 1284
Dijkstra, W. 738, 743
Dil, Anwars 803, 1753
Dillman, D. A. 731, 732, 739, 740, 741, 742, 743
Dimitras, Panayote 1974, 1976, 1978, 2032
Dimitrescu, Florica 1468, 1469
Dimitrovski, Todor 1503
Dimock, E. C. 912
Dine, P. 853, 857
Dinekov, Petur 1494, 1495
Dini, Pietro U. 1917, 1919
Diringer, D. 104, 109
Dirven, René 416, 418, 419, 691
Dischler, Ludwig 1582
DiSciullo, A.-M. 115, 116, 595, 600, 606
Dissanayake, W. 911, 912
Dittmann, J. 270
Dittmar, Norbert 55, 179, 193, 244, 248, 255, 256, 285, 292, 294, 320, 321, 326, 372, 377, 384, 398, 399, 456, 540, 623, 641, 674, 691, 710, 714, 724, 749, 754, 761, 763, 801, 803, 804, 810, 811, 818, 819, 825, 833, 901, 911, 924, 929, 930, 1171, 1330, 1405, 1768, 1820, 1870
Dittrich, E. J. 189, 191, 208
Dixon, R. M. W. 571, 577
Dizikirikis, G. S. 1563, 1565
Dizikirikis, Jakovos 1529, 1531, 1532
Djité, P. G. 863, 864, 895, 900
Djordjević, Dimitrije 1550, 1551, 1554, 1737

Doany, N. 437
Dobrynin, M. 1922, 1925
Dodos, Dimosthenis Ch. 2031, 2032
Dodson, C. 367, 369, 465, 466, 472
Doege, Immo 1041
Doerfer, Gerhard 1507, 1509
Dofny, A. 79
Doise, W. 336, 340
Doležel, L. 146, 152, 1495
Doliński, Ignacy 1614
Dolník, Juraj 1673, 1677, 1707
Dolphin, C. Z. 305, 309
Domingue, N. 546, 548
Dominique, J. 278, 282
Donald, M. 220, 232
Doob, L. W. 694, 700
Doornaert, Mia 1120, 1122
Döpke, S. 14, 20, 380, 383, 384
Doppagne, Albert 1126, 1129, 1159, 1170, 1171
Dörflinger, Johannes 1974, 1976, 1978, 1979
Doria, Mario 1361, 1362
Dorian, Nancy C. 18, 20, 113, 116, 171, 174, 376, 377, 387, 390, 391, 567, 568, 573, 577, 578, 580, 581, 584, 586, 590, 591, 592, 593, 598, 606, 661, 662, 663, 665, 666, 779, 787, 802, 803, 1542, 1543, 2007
Dorion, H. 554
Doron, E. 600, 604, 606
Doruľa, Ján 1677, 1684, 1694, 1707
Douaud, P. C. 764, 770
Dow, J. R. 218, 319, 323, 326
Downing, B. T. 868, 869, 870
Downing, J. 624, 631, 633
Dowty, D. R. 607
Doyle, A. B. 33, 38, 368, 369
D'Oyley, V. 491, 492
Draja, A. M. S. 464
Draye, Hendrik 1111, 1122, 1123, 1129
Drees, Jan 1787, 1789
Dreschel, E. J. 796
Drescher, H. W. 641, 1157
Dressler, Wolfgang U. 18, 20, 113, 116, 375, 377, 533, 540, 586, 590, 591, 592, 667, 674, 1259, 1815, 1820, 1827
Drettas, Georges 1545, 1548, 1549
Driedger, L. 764, 770
Drízule, V. A. 1910, 1912
Drummond, G. 437
Drury, M. P. 1582
Druviete, Ina 1911, 1912
Drzeżdżon, Jan 1603, 1605
Du Bois, Pierre 1838, 1849, 1850
Dua, H. R. 462, 464, 895, 900

Duc Goninaz, M. 886
Duć-Fajfer, Helena 1627
Duchesne, L. 384
Duchhardt, H. 186, 191
Dudášová-Krišśáková, Júlia 1694
Dudok, Daniel 1412, 1413, 1415
Duerr, H. P. 752, 761
Dufour, M. 409, 413
Dular, Janez 1423
Dulay, H. C. 285, 294, 519, 524, 561, 562, 566
Duličenko, A. D. 884, 886, 1366
Dumont, P. 197, 199
Dunăre, Nicolae 1481, 1486
Duncan, Perry 1495
Duncan, St. 306, 309
Dundes, Alan 1542, 1543
Dunsdorfs, Edgars 1906, 1912
Dupas, Georges 1246, 1248, 1250
Duran, R. P. 606, 607, 608, 609
Duranti, A. 143
Duridanov, Ivan 1497
Durkheim, Emil 25, 27, 31
Dürmüller, Urs 1841, 1842, 1848, 1850
Duschanek, Michael 2041, 2045, 2061
Duškova, L. 560, 566
Dutton, Th. E. 643, 644, 648
Duvosquel, Jean-Marie 1242, 1250
Dvořák, J. 1662
Dweik, B. 770
Dyck, C. J. 313, 314, 319
Dyhr, Mogens 1776
Džahukyan, G. B. 1572, 1574, 1576
Dzendzelivskyj, Josyp 1699, 1700
Dziewierski, Marek 1591, 1592, 1594
Dzwonkowski, Roman 1922, 1925

E

Eakins, B. W. 305, 309
Eakins, R. G. 305, 309
Eastman, C. A. 14, 20, 606, 608, 895, 900
Eben-Ezra, S. 132, 138
Eberenz, Rolf 1276, 1284
Eberhardt, Piotr 2065
Eble, C. 127, 129, 548
Ebner, Jakob 1808, 1811
Echenique Elizondo, Maria T. 1284
Echtermeyer, K. 512, 514
Eckert, E. 1707
Eckert, Joern 1649

Eckert, M. 1974, 1976, 1978, 1979
Eckert, P. 248, 256, 588, 592, 721, 724, 802, 803
Eckman, F. 521, 524, 565, 566
Eckmann, Janos 1529, 1532
Eco, Umberto 460
Edelman, G. 85, 88
Edelsky, C. 87, 88
Edmonston, B. 867, 870
Edwards, D. G. 294
Edwards, John 44, 45, 48, 570, 576, 577, 586, 704, 705, 706, 707, 708, 716, 717, 718, 719
Edwards, O. M. 1079
Edwards, Viv 190, 331, 332, 810, 1060, 1073, 1074
Edwards, Walter 810
Eek, Arvo 1905
Egede, Paul 1053, 1054
Egger, Kurt 280, 282, 380, 381, 382, 383, 384, 385, 1351, 1352, 1355, 1356, 1357
Eggers, A. 513
Eggers, D. 513
Eggs, Ekkehard 1259
Egli, M. 235, 243
Ehlich, Konrad 14, 20, 21, 190, 191, 193, 923, 924, 929, 931
Eibl-Eibesfeldt, Irenäus 180, 191, 309
Eichhoff, Jürgen 4, 9, 262, 270
Eichinger, Ludwig M. 92, 96, 97
Eichler, Ernst 554, 1598, 1599, 1796
Eidheim, Harald 960, 961
Eilers, R. E. 33, 38
Einspieler, Valentin 1801, 1811
Eiríksson, Eyvindur 1057
Eisenburger, Eduard 1478, 1486
Eisenstein, E. L. 428, 430
Eiser, J. R. 48, 692, 694, 701
Eisermann, Felix 1351, 1356
Eisner, Manuel 1850
Eisner, Michael 360, 362
Eisner, Paul 1660, 1661
Ejerhed, E. 9, 371, 377
Ejskjær, Inger 1023, 1031
Ekman, P. 296, 304, 306, 307, 309, 310
Ekstrand, L. 35, 38
Elbiad, M. 895, 900
Elcock, William Denis 1274, 1284
Eleonora d'Arborea (1362−1403) 1377
Elia, Sílvio 1314, 1316
Eliade, I. 873, 878
Elías-Olivares, L. 378, 379
Eliasson, Stig 595, 600, 606
Elizarenkova, R. Y. 635, 640
Elklit, J. 1041
Elle, Ludwig 1793, 1796, 2049, 2053

Ellena, A. 893
Ellis, N. 62
Ellis, Rod 15, 20, 292, 294, 515, 516, 522, 524, 663, 666, 1030, 1031
Ellul, S. 366, 369
Eloy, Jean-Michel 828, 833, 1870
Eloy, S. V. 335, 340
Elteto, Louis J. 1469
Elwert, W. Theodor 366, 369, 1391, 1396, 1397, 1468, 1469
Emberšičs, Elizabeta 1742
Embleton, S. M. 638, 640
Emeneau, M. B. 103, 889, 893
Emilianides, A. 1582
Eminov, Ali 1492, 1493, 1495, 1496, 1501, 1503, 1506, 1509, 1510
Emmans, K. 420, 855, 857
Emmer, P. C. 186, 191
Endzelīns, J. 1912
Eneholm, Gerhard 1511, 1514
Engberg-Pedersen, Elisabeth 1027, 1031
Engelbrekt, Kjell 1454, 1458, 1489, 1490, 1495
Engle, P. L 491, 632, 633
Engsnap, Knud B. 1776
Enkvist, N. E. 148, 152
Ennaji, M. 197, 199, 600, 606, 895, 900
Enninger, Werner 144, 312, 316, 317, 318, 319, 398, 751, 758, 759, 761, 925, 930
Epstein, A. L. 208
Epstein, I. 9, 13, 20, 246, 256
Epstein, Marc 1566, 1571
Eraly, A. 405, 408, 413
Erben, J. 876, 878
Erdmann, U. 15, 20
Erdos, P. 731, 732
Erfurt, Jürgen 826, 833
Erickson, F. 142, 143, 749, 750, 755, 761, 923, 929
Eriksen, Knut-Einar 964, 965
Eriksen, Lars H. 1041
Eriksson, Riitta 976, 992
Erimer, K. 1509
Ermacora, Felix 217, 352, 356, 363, 849, 852, 1356
Ermolenko, Svitlana 1932
Ernst, Gerhard 876, 878
Ertekun, Necati M. 1582
Ertel, R. 1179, 1187, 2004, 2006
Ervin, S. M. 37, 38, 124, 129, 235, 243, 432, 437
Ervin-Tripp, Susan 28, 31, 695, 701
Esarte-Sarries, V. 466, 472
Escobar, Alberto M. 770
Escobedo, T. H. 7, 9
Escoffier, Simone 177, 179, 1336, 1337, 2003, 2006

Escure, G. 656, 657, 722, 723, 724
Esman, M. J. 79, 80, 208
Espenshade, E. B. 75
Esselborn, K. 96
Esser, E. 743, 751, 761, 763
Esser, H. 189, 191, 208, 311, 319, 761
Estel, B. 185, 191
Etiemble, R. 872, 874, 875, 878
Ettmayer, Karl von 1349, 1395, 1397
Ettori, Fernand 1203, 1207, 1208, 1213
Etxebarria, Maitena 1308, 1309
Etxeberria, P. 1268
Etxepare, Bernard 1268
Eusko, Jaurlaritza 1284
Exarchos, Giorgis S. 1523
Extra, Guus 56, 320, 321, 323, 325, 326, 372, 378, 471, 472, 578, 850, 852, 931, 976, 1150, 1151, 1157, 1495
Eyal, Jonathan 1936, 1940
Eyram, Michael 1981
Eysenck, M. W. 138
Eyuboğlu, I. Z. 1575, 1576
Ezzaki, A. 632, 634

F

Fabbro, F. 375, 378
Faber, Helm von 512, 514
Faerch, C. 241, 243
Færch, Claus 1029, 1031
Fagoo, Arthur 1245, 1250
Falc'hun, François 1259
Falcone, Giuseppe 1370, 1371
Fal'ković, Ě. M. (= falković, elje) 1960
Falk, Knut O. 1615, 1619, 1620
Falkenberg, Johannes 960, 961
Falkenstein, A. 105, 109
Faltings, Volkert F. 1785
Fan, S. K. 835, 840
Fanfani, M. L. 872, 878
Fanshel, D. 749
Fantini, A. E. 6, 9, 366, 369, 380, 384
Fantuzzi, Ch. 516, 524
Farhi, Gentille 1569, 1571
Farrell, Th. 711, 714
Fase, W. 20, 567, 577, 578, 580, 584
Fasold, Ralph 586, 592, 639, 640, 702, 721, 724, 785, 787, 811, 1028, 1031
Faßke, Helmut 1768, 1793, 1794, 1796, 1797, 2049, 2053
Fattier-Thomas, D. 657
Faulbaum, F. 741, 744
Faulseit, D. 147, 152

Fausel, E. 5, 9
Favaro, Graziella 1328, 1329
Fayol, H. 405, 413
Fazio, R. H. 695, 701, 702
Fazzini Giovannucci, Elisabetta 1352, 1353, 1356
Fearns, A. 511, 512, 514
Fehr, Götz 1661
Feinig, Anton 1818, 1820
Feitsma, Anthonia 1156, 1157
Feixó Cid, Xosé C. 1293, 1294
Feldman, J. J. 749
Feldstein, St. 333, 335, 336, 340, 342
Felix, Sascha W. 7, 9, 292, 294, 466, 472
Felixberger, Josef 2008, 2014
Fellman, J. 903, 906
Fellmann, A. 579, 584
Fenech, Edward 1405, 1406
Fenoglio, Irène 683, 684
Fenton, Alexander 1095, 1096
Fenyvesi, Anna 1649
Ferenc-Király, Péter 1748
Ferguson, Charles A. 6, 9, 16, 20, 22, 82, 88, 113, 116, 173, 174, 237, 243, 244, 246, 247, 248, 249, 250, 253, 255, 256, 266, 270, 283, 369, 372, 378, 392, 395, 398, 441, 444, 453, 456, 518, 524, 578, 585, 587, 628, 633, 635, 638, 640, 678, 684, 691, 695, 701, 710, 714, 770, 797, 803, 839, 840, 1329, 1401, 1406, 1751, 1753
Fernández de Heredia, F. J. de 277, 282, 457, 555, 558
Fernández Rodríguez, Mauro A. 1294
Fernandez, M. M. Jocelyne 1981
Fernández, Mauro 1291, 1294
Fernández-Sevilla, Julio 2014
Fernau, Frank W. 1582
Ferrara, K. 334, 340
Ferrer i Gironès, Francesco 1284
Ferro Ruibal, Xesús 1406
Ferry, J.-M. 202
Festinger, L. 28, 31
Fetterman, D. M. 754, 755, 757, 759, 761
Feyry, M. 874, 878
Fichte, Johann Gottlieb (1762−1814) 154, 155, 159, 202
Fiederlein, S. L. 867, 870
Fiedler, K. 744
Fiedler, Wilfried 1457, 1458
Fielder, Grace 1491, 1495, 1496
Filipova-Bajrova, Marija 1553, 1554
Filipovic, Rudolf 3, 546, 548, 852
Filippi, Paul 1208, 1213

Fill, A. 852
Filla, Wilhelm 1807, 1811, 1828, 1835
Fillenbaum, S. 61, 62, 706, 708
Fillmore, Charles 134, 137, 140, 143
Fillmore, L. W. 285, 294
Finck, Adrien 96, 1235
Fine, John 1503
Fink, E. L. 4, 434, 435, 438
Finka, B. 1433
Finkenstaedt, Thomas 505, 507
Finnäs, Fjalar 381, 384, 773, 775, 776, 1014
Finsterwalder, Karl 1798, 1811
Fiorini, Stanley 1405
Firchow, Evelyn S. 548
Fischer, C. 810
Fischer, Gero 1800, 1803, 1804, 1810, 1811, 1815, 1820
Fischer, H. 761, 763
Fischer, Holger 1974, 1976, 1978, 1979
Fischer, R. 1661, 1662
Fishbein, M. 692, 693, 694, 700, 701
Fisher, A. B. 300, 309
Fishman, Joshua A. 3, 6, 7, 9, 16, 17, 20, 21, 25, 31, 42, 45, 47, 48, 76, 79, 169, 170, 174, 179, 199, 237, 240, 243, 244, 248, 249, 252, 255, 256, 266, 270, 283, 292, 294, 323, 326, 369, 379, 392, 394, 398, 399, 404, 432, 433, 437, 451, 453, 455, 456, 465, 470, 472, 481, 483, 484, 485, 491, 567, 568, 572, 574, 577, 578, 580, 584, 585, 586, 587, 588, 589, 592, 595, 606, 618, 623, 628, 630, 631, 633, 635, 640, 664, 665, 666, 667, 668, 674, 678, 680, 683, 684, 685, 686, 687, 691, 695, 696, 697, 699, 700, 701, 702, 709, 714, 719, 721, 723, 724, 725, 776, 787, 790, 796, 797, 798, 799, 800, 801, 802, 803, 804, 818, 828, 833, 839, 840, 841, 864, 890, 893, 902, 903, 904, 905, 906, 929, 1114, 1120, 1122, 1129, 1157, 1324, 1329, 1450
Fisiak, Jaček 3, 103, 137, 559, 566
Fisz, M. 735, 737
Fitouri, Ch. 196, 199
Fitzpatrick, F. 1071, 1074
Fjalldal, Magnús 1057
Flanker, A. 1433
Flannery, R. 720, 724
Flanz, G. H. 168
Flasaquier, M. 325, 326, 327
Flaschberger, Ludwig 1807, 1810, 1811, 1816, 1820, 1835

Flatrès, Pierre 1254, 1259
Flege, J. E. 288, 289, 291, 294
Fleiner-Gerster, Thomas 1847, 1850
Fleischer, Wolfgang 146, 149, 152
Fleming, I. 1722
Flere, S. 208
Fletcher, B. A. 374, 378
Flick, U. 757, 761
Flikeid, K. 786, 787
Floc'h, Guillaume 1259
Flodell, G. 575, 577
Flora, Radu 1413, 1415
Florea, Ion A. 1474, 1476
Flores, B. 88
Florina, Aridea 1549
Fluck, H. R. 508, 512, 513, 514
Fluehr-Lobban, C. 794, 796
Flydal, L. 148, 152
Flynn, S. 520, 524
Fodor, András 1720, 1722
Fodor, I. 108, 833, 1106
Foerste, W. 5, 9
Foley, W. A. 113, 116, 134, 137
Foltys, Ch. 556, 557, 558
Fontaine, José 1143
Fontan, F. 154, 156, 158, 159, 2003, 2006
Fontana, Josef 1356, 1397
Fonteyn, Guido 1143
Foresti, Fabio 641
Forni, Mario 1875, 1878
Forrest-Pressley, D. L. 38,633
Þorsteinsson, Björn 1055, 1058
Förster, Frank 1792, 1796
Forster, L. 90, 92, 93, 96, 458, 459, 464
Forster, P. G. 886
Fort, Marron C. 1789, 1790
Fortescue, Michael 1054
Foster, B. 4, 9
Foster, Ch. R. 156, 159
Foster, J. L. 479, 480
Foster, L. 891, 893
Fosty, A. 861, 864
Foucault, Michel 746, 749
Fougstedt, Gunnar 1014
Foulcher, K. 464
Fourikis, Petros A. 1522, 1523
Fourquet, Jean 270
Fowler, F. J. 742, 743
Fowler, R. 749
Fox, J. J. 170, 174
Fraenkel, E. 1496, 1503, 1504
Þráinsson, Björn 1057
Francard, Michel 1121, 1122
Francescato, Giuseppe 275, 282, 380, 384, 640, 1338, 1339, 1340, 1341, 1342, 1343, 1351, 1355, 1356
Franceschini, Rita 1845, 1850
Franchi, L. 163, 168

Francioni, Federico 1376, 1381
Francis, D. 793, 796
Francis, E. K. 204, 206, 207, 209
Franco, Francisco (1892–1975) 1277, 1297
François, F. 81, 88
Frank, H. 885, 886
Frank, Tibor 1711, 1722
Frankenberg, R. 759, 761
Franklyne-Stokes, A. 302, 309
Franz Joseph I. (1848–1916) 1480
Franz, E. 870
Franz, K. 181, 191
Fraser, C. 341
Fraser, I. 551, 554
Frau, Giovanni 1329, 1338, 1341, 1343, 2018, 2019
Fred, B. 666
Freddi, Giovanni 1329
Frederickson, N. 87, 88
Fredstedt, E. 755, 761
Freed, B. F. 18, 21, 567, 578, 579, 584, 585
Freedman, J. L. 30, 31
Freesemann, H. 608
Frei, E. J. 897, 900
Freitag, U. 415, 420
Frémy, D. 2007
Frémy, M. 2007
French, J. W. 373, 374, 391, 392, 393, 395, 396, 400, 401, 402, 405, 426, 427, 428, 429, 430, 432, 433, 434, 435, 436, 437
Frendo, Henry 1402, 1406
Freudenstein, R. 419, 512, 514, 585
Frey, J. 393, 398, 798, 803
Frick, D. 811
Frideres, J. 695, 701
Fried, C. 209
Fried, I. 1738
Friedberg, E. 405, 413
Friedman, Victor A. 1414, 1415, 1443, 1444, 1445, 1449, 1450, 1451, 1489, 1495, 1498, 1499, 1503, 1504
Friedrich III. (1440–1493) 1802, 1821
Friedrich, C. J. 77, 79, 398, 403, 404
Friedrich, C. W. 1943, 1960
Friedrichs, J. 452, 456, 751, 752, 753, 761
Fries, D. 872, 878
Friesen, W. V. 296, 304, 309, 310
Friis, A. 1981
Frijhoff, J. Willem 1128, 1129
Frinta, A. 1635, 1636, 1639, 1640
Frischbier, H. 1598, 1599
Frith, U. 243
Fröhlich, Harald 1163, 1166, 1171, 1172

Froidevaux, Didier 1844, 1847, 1852
Fryščák, Milan 1642, 1648
Fthenakis, W. 292, 293, 294
Fügedi, Erik-Gregor 1748
Fugger, B. 876, 878
Fuglsang-Damgaard, Ad 1054
Fülei-Szántó, E. 415, 420
Fundació Jaume Bofill 353, 356
Furer, J.-J. 355, 356
Furet, F. 96, 274, 282
Furikis, Petros A. 1543
Furlani, Silvio 1329
Furnham, A. 929
Fusina, Jacques 1214, 1221
Füves, Ödön 1523
Fux, Beat 1850

G

Gaál, Károly 1827, 1829, 1835
Gabanyi, Anneli Ute 1486
Gabinskij, Mark A. 1940, 1941
Gabler, Siegfried 737
Gabzdilová, S. 1674, 1677
Gaj, Ljudevit 1426
Gajdarzi, G. A. 1939, 1940
Gal, Susan 16, 21, 141, 143, 173, 174, 387, 390, 456, 572, 574, 576, 577, 581, 584, 586, 587, 588, 590, 591, 592, 593, 596, 597, 598, 606, 663, 666, 710, 714, 722, 724, 747, 749, 785, 787, 801, 802, 803, 804, 808, 809, 810, 1711, 1715, 1716, 1718, 1719, 1721, 1722, 1750, 1753, 1831, 1833, 1834, 1835
Gălăbov, I. 1450, 1467, 1469
Galante, Avram 1568, 1569, 1570, 1571
Gáldi, László 147, 152, 1479, 1485, 1486
Galileo, Galileo (1600–1649) 2
Galinsky, H. 4, 9
Gallagher, Tom 1718, 1722
Gallois, C. 17, 20, 334, 340
Galtung, J. 926, 929
Gambier, Yves 1014
Gamkrelidze, T. V. 1572, 1576
Gamulescu, Dorin 1413, 1415
Gandarillas, Maria A. 1303, 1309
Gašparíková, Želmíra 1654, 1655
Garagorri, Xabier 1305, 1309
Garami, Erika 1713, 1716, 1721, 1722, 1723
Garavini, Fausta 1194
García Arias, Xaver Luís 1283, 1284
García Cancela, Xermán 1293, 1295

García Macho, Maria Lourdes 1119, 1122
García Negro, M. Pilar 354, 356, 1287, 1294
García, Constantino 1284, 1293, 1294
García, E. 606
García, Ofelia 457
Garcia, R. 7, 8
García-Sevilla, Ll. 353, 356
Gardès-Madray, F. 238, 243
Gardette, P. 177, 179, 180
Gardin, Bernard 56, 1174, 1187, 1259
Gardner, Richard. C. 7, 9, 38, 433, 437, 497, 500, 582, 584, 585, 695, 701, 706, 708
Gardner, Robert 523, 524
Gardner-Chloros, Pénélope 243, 244, 451, 456, 595, 598, 600, 603, 606, 754, 755, 761, 1239
Gardy, Philippe 252, 253, 255, 256, 684, 685, 691, 802, 804, 1177, 1187, 1191, 1194
Garfinkel, H. 754, 761
Garibaldi, Giuseppe (1807–1882) 1319
Garkavec, Alexandr N. 1932
Garmendia, Maria 775, 776, 904, 906
Garrett, M. F. 604, 606
Gartner, Theodor 1387, 1390, 1397
Garšva, Kazimieras 1614, 1615, 1616, 1620
Garvin, Paul L. 56, 152, 173, 174, 640, 1720, 1722
Gary Waller, T. 38
Garzon, S. 172, 173, 174
Gasaitéar na hÉireann 450
Gasca Queirazza, Giuliano 1349
Gascon, J. 833
Gaski, H. 460, 464
Gass, Susan 524, 525, 562, 565, 566, 567
Gasser, M. 519, 524
Gaube, Heinz 1576
Gauger, H.-M. 615, 623
Gauthier-Darley, M. 147, 152
Gavin, W. J. 33, 38
Gawrecká, Marie 1677
Gay, G. 547, 548
Gayus, Eliya 1571
Gazetteer of conventional names 450
Gazetteer of geographical names of undersea features 450
Gazzero, V. 368, 369
Geagea, Christea 1538, 1539
Gebhardt, Karl 873, 878, 1193, 1194
Geel, A. E. 419, 420
Geerts, Guido 401, 404, 760, 761, 925, 929

Geertz, Clifford 750, 760, 761
Geibel, E. 865, 870
Geiser, S. 316, 317, 319
Gelas, N. 243
Gelb, I. J. 105, 109
Gelder, Beatrice de 132, 137
Gellner, E. 73, 74, 200, 202, 209, 347, 350
Genc, Lajoš 1412, 1415
Genčev, Nikolaj 1511, 1514
Gendron, J.-D. 275, 283
Generalitat de Catalunya 439, 442, 444
Genesee, Fred 19, 21, 35, 38, 291, 293, 294, 474, 475, 477, 480, 481, 493, 494, 495, 496, 497, 498, 499, 500, 501, 596, 606, 632, 633
Genishi, C. 603, 606
Genova, Angelo 1364, 1366
Genre, Arturo 1344, 1345, 1349
Georgakas, D. 1964, 1971
George, H. V. 561, 566
Georghiades, A. 1582
Georgiadis, Pavlos 1531, 1532, 1563, 1564, 1565
Georgiev, Vladimir 1450, 1497
Georgieva, Elena 1494, 1495
Geosits, Stefan 1823, 1827
Gerentović, V. V. 1910, 1912
Gerlich, M. G. 1668
Gerlich, P. 1655
Germain, C. 276, 282
German, A. B. 1970, 1971
Germann, G. 1851, 1852
Germann, Raimund E. 1838, 1850, 1854
Gernentz, Hans J. 1768
Geronimi, Dominique Antoine 1207, 1213, 1216, 1217, 1222
Gerritsen, Marinel 533, 539, 540
Gertner, M. H. 724
Gerullis, Georg 1918, 1919
Geschiere, Louis 1122
Gesemann, Wolfgang 1450
Geyer, C.-F. 927, 929
Geyer, Inge 1356
Ghermani, Dionisie 1481, 1485, 1486
Ghirlanda, Elio 1850
Giacalone Ramat, Anna 321, 326, 595, 600, 606, 1151, 1327, 1328, 1329
Giacobbe, J. 235, 244, 326
Giacomo, Mathée 1174, 1187
Giacomo-Marcellesi, Mathée 1221
Giambelli, Rodolfo 1328, 1329
Gibbons, J. 570, 576, 595, 606, 754, 761, 810
Gibson, M. A. 476, 480
Gielen, U. P. 842
Giersch, H. 188, 191

Giesbers, Herman 6, 9, 1149, 1150, 1151
Giesecke, M. 90, 96
Giesen, B. 92, 96, 97
Giffinger, R. 1397
Giglioli, P. 174
Gilbert, G. G. 9, 607, 656, 657, 658
Giles, Howard 8, 9, 17, 21, 41, 42, 43, 44, 45, 46, 47, 48, 132, 138, 173, 174, 302, 309, 323, 326, 333, 334, 335, 336, 337, 339, 340, 341, 342, 432, 437, 455, 456, 523, 570, 572, 573, 576, 577, 579, 584, 694, 701, 702, 704, 708, 759, 761, 1524, 2033
Gill, J. 388, 390
Gilliat-Smith, Bernard 1965, 1971
Gilliat-Smith, Petulengro 1494, 1495
Gillies, William 1096
Gillmeister, H. 876, 878
Gillmore, P. 631, 633
Gilman, A. 710, 714
Gilman, S. L. 227, 232
Gilmer, Paul Gregory 1566, 1568, 1569, 1570, 1571
Gimbel, J. 10, 464, 1025, 1026, 1029, 1030, 1031, 1032
Gimeno, Francesc 1301, 1302
Gingràs, R. C. 599, 606
Giochalas, Titos 1523
Giordan, Henri 201, 202, 218, 345, 350, 351, 356, 357, 893, 1175, 1187, 1191, 1194, 1329, 2003, 2006, 2032
Girard, A. 2004, 2005, 2006
Girard, D. 50, 62
Girardet, R. 200, 201, 202
Girin, J. 409, 413
Girji O. S., Davvi 961
Girke, W. 247, 256
Girtler, Roland 752, 754, 761
Gíslason, Gylfi Th. 1055, 1057
Gíslason, I. 1056, 1057
Givón, T. 139, 140, 143, 521, 524, 531, 536, 537, 539, 540
Gjerdman, Olof 1970, 1971
Gjidara, M. 363
Gjinari, Jorgii 1541, 1543
Glaser, B. G. 756, 757, 761
Glaser, Elivra 1376
Glass, D. 895, 900
Glatthorn, A. 631, 633
Glazer, N. 189, 191, 203, 205, 207, 208, 209
Gleich, Utta von 484, 485, 488, 491, 758, 761, 768, 769, 770
Gleitman, L. 294, 591, 593
Glinert, L. 838, 840, 896, 900
Glinka, St. 1608, 1611, 1613, 1614, 1619, 1620

Gloy, K. 877, 879
Glück, Helmut 857
Głuszkowska, Jadwiga 1613
Glyn, L. E. 465, 472
Gnutzmann, Claus 512, 513, 514, 853, 857
Goddard, H. H. 364, 369
Goebl, Hans 175, 177, 178, 179, 233, 244, 277, 280, 282, 635, 637, 638, 640, 716, 719, 760, 762, 820, 825, 894, 900, 1211, 1221, 1316, 1383, 1397, 1815, 1820
Goel, B. S. 488, 492
Goenawan, M. 464
Goethe, Johann Wolfgang von (1749−1832) 7
Goffin, R. 839, 840
Goffman, E. 29, 31, 747, 749, 754
Göhring, H. 929
Gökbilgin, T. 1532
Gołob, Z. 1446, 1447, 1449, 1450, 1487, 1494, 1495, 1632, 1633
Gołobek, Anna 1619, 1620, 1621
Gołobek, Eugeniusz 1603, 1605
Gold, Hugo 1828, 1835
Goldblatt, H. 894, 900, 901
Golden, B. 885, 886
Goldman, K. 301, 310
Goldstein, T. 388, 390, 721, 724
Goldstrom, J. M. 428, 430
Goltschnigg, D. 94, 96
Goltschnigg, G. 1477
Gómez Piñro, Francisco 1303, 1309
Gommans, P. 375, 377, 584
Gonçalves, Carlos Lélis de Câmara 1315, 1316
Gonzales Seoane, Ernesto 1295
Gonzales, A. B. FSC 898, 899, 900
Gonzalez, N. 716, 720
González-Anleo, Juan 1302
González Blasco, Pedro 1302
González González, Manuel 1284, 1293
González Ollé, Fernando 1276, 1284
Gonzo, S. 580, 582, 584
Goodchild, M. F. 70, 71, 74
Goodenough, W. 929
Goodman, J. 295
Goody, E. N. 749
Goody, J. 792, 796
Goodz, N. S. 32, 34, 38
Goossens, Jan 270, 1136, 1143
Gordon, A. I. 384
Gordon, D. C. 344, 345, 350, 872, 875, 879
Görlach, Manfred 607, 900, 901, 908, 909, 911

Gorter, Durk 336, 341, 575, 576, 577, 776, 904, 906, 1154, 1156, 1157, 1786, 1905
Gorter, T. R. 420, 835, 841, 855, 857
Görtz, B. 872, 873, 879
Göschel, Joachim 270
Gósy, Mária 1720, 1722
Gosy, Miklos 336, 341
Gottfried von Straßburg (ca. 1210) 1229
Gottzmann, Carola L. 94, 96
Goudailler, Jean-Pierre 876, 879
Govaert, S. 354, 357
Gowan, J. C. 35, 40
Goyheneche, Eugène 1268
Grabis, R. 1912
Graefen, G. 926, 929
Graeh, F. 152
Grafenauer, Bogo 1739, 1743
Grafenauer, Ivan 1743
Grafman, J. 245
Grainger, J. 125, 130
Grammont, M. 7, 9, 34, 38
Gramsci, A. 922, 927, 929, 930
Graña Núñez, Xosé 1295
Grande, B. M. 1953, 1960
Grandguillaume, Gilbert 199, 895, 900
Grannes, Alf 1491, 1494, 1495, 1509
Granovetter, M. 808, 810
Grant, William 1089, 1096
Grassi, Corrado 1336, 1337, 1348, 1349
Grathoff, R. 191
Gratz, D. L. 316, 317, 319
Grau, R. 353, 357
Greco, Anna R. 1349
Green, D. W. 37, 38
Green, Jerald R. 296, 310
Green, John N. 611, 624, 641, 1284, 1285, 1295, 1381, 1382
Green, L. 76, 78, 80
Greenberg, J. H. 536, 537, 539, 540, 634
Greenfield, L. 433, 437, 800, 803, 804
Greenwald, A. G. 700
Greenwood, D. J. 349, 350
Gregersen, Frans 1028, 1032
Gregg, K. 516, 518, 524, 525
Grégoire, A. 652, 657
Gregor, Ferenc 1684, 1747, 1748
Gregorio, G. de 5, 9
Gregory, D. 75
Gregory, M. J. 148, 152
Grek-Pabisowa, Iryda 1613
Grellmann, Heinrich M. S. 1971
Grendel, M. 582, 583, 585
Grenier, P. 476, 481
Greppin, J. A. 1574, 1575, 1576
Gretler, Armin 326, 1848, 1850, 1852, 1869, 1870

Greven, H. 439, 444
Grice, H. P. 140, 143, 420
Griefenow-Mewis, C. 895, 900
Griera, Antoni 1282, 1284
Grießhaber, W. 927, 929
Grigoryan, A. V. 1574, 1575, 1576
Grillo, R. D. 590, 593
Grimm, Jacob 154, 155, 260, 812, 818
Grimm, Wilhelm 812, 818
Grimshaw, A. D. 745, 749, 801, 802, 804
Grimstad, K. 548
Grin, François 211, 215, 217, 236, 244, 439, 443, 444, 1878, 1905
Grise, J.-B. 413
Griset, Ilia 1349
Grobelný, A. 1668
Gromacki, J. P. 360, 363
Grønbech, K. 1532
Grondal, G. 1119, 1122
Gronemeyer, Reimer 1804, 1805, 1811, 1971
Groot, A. M. B. de 131, 132, 137
Grootaers, L. 6, 9, 1119, 1122
Grosjean, François 6, 9, 13, 21, 36, 38, 125, 130, 137, 234, 235, 236, 240, 242, 244, 256, 321, 322, 326, 384, 604, 605, 606, 631, 633
Gross, B. 792, 796
Gross, F. 798, 804
Gross, Manfred 1886
Großjohann, Wilfried 1399, 1406
Grossman, Robin. E. 607
Grossmann, Maria 1380, 1382
Grossmann, Rudolf 4, 9
Grothe, Hugo 1685, 1691
Grothusen, K.-D. 1469, 1470, 1509, 1510, 1559
Groustra, G. R. 1790
Groves, R. 730, 732, 742, 743, 744
Gruber, Alfons 1356
Gruber, Alfred 96
Gruber, F. 593
Gruden, J. 1739, 1743
Gruenais, M.-P. 832
Grulich, Rudolf 2032, 2037
Grumadienė, Laima 1917, 1918, 1919
Grumet, Joanne 1450
Grundström, Harald 981
Gruzinski, S. 232
Gsell, Otto 1392, 1395, 1397
Guarnerio, Pier E. 1380, 1382
Gubert, Renzo 1323, 1329, 1351, 1352, 1356
Gucul, L. A. 1939, 1940

Gudykunst, W. B. 41, 42, 43, 44, 45, 46, 47, 48, 929
Guerend, J. P. 384
Guespin, Louis 677, 683, 828, 830, 833, 1209, 1213
Guillet (Sieur de la Guilletière) 555, 558
Guillon, M. 2007
Guiraud, Pierre 146, 152, 872, 879, 1246, 1251
Guiter, H. 2003, 2006
Gülensoy, Tuncer 1575, 1576
Gülich, Elisabeth 1648
Gumbrecht, H. U. 97
Gumperz, John 3, 6, 9, 13, 14, 21, 50, 51, 52, 53, 55, 56, 139, 141, 142, 143, 169, 170, 174, 239, 240, 243, 244, 247, 248, 256, 324, 326, 396, 398, 437, 454, 455, 456, 586, 588, 593, 595, 596, 597, 598, 599, 605, 606, 607, 701, 710, 713, 718, 719, 747, 750, 754, 756, 760, 762, 789, 790, 796, 797, 799, 801, 803, 804, 809, 810, 925, 926, 929, 930, 1186, 1187
Gundersen, Dag 956
Gunew, S. 464
Gunnarsson, L. 810
Gunnermark, E. 74
Günter, H. 833
Gunther, G. 208, 209
Günthner, S. 926, 930
Gupta, A. F. 924, 930
Gupta, R. S. 912
Gurevitch, M. 431
Gurny, R. 325, 326
Gürtler, Karin G. 399
Gurvitch, G. 55
Guryčeva, M. S. 1940
Gusejnov, M. M. 220, 232
Gustavsson, Sven 1925, 1926
Guthier, Steven L. 1925
Guthrie, J. P. 631, 634
Guthrie, L. F. 625, 633
Gutleb, Angelika 1803, 1804, 1808, 1810, 1811, 1813, 1814, 1815, 1816, 1820, 2057
Gutschmidt, K. 1707
Guttman, L. 697, 701, 785, 787
Guttorm, Eino 1018
Guttorm, Hans Aslak 1018
Guttorm, Inga 1019
Gutzwiler, Jürg 1853
Guy, G. R. 810
Guzzetta, Antonino 1376
Gwegen, J. 2003, 2006
Győrffy, György 1480, 1486
Győri-Nagy, Sándor 1743
Gyarmathi, Sámuel 2
Gyivicsán, Anna 1748, 1749
Gyllin, Roger 1494, 1495
Gyr, Ueli 1845, 1850

Gysseling, Maurits 1124, 1129, 1242, 1251, 1252
Gyurgyik, László 1680, 1684

H

Haan, Germ de 1157
Haarhoff, Th. J. 273, 282
Haarmann, Harald 209, 221, 223, 229, 232, 233, 249, 256, 344, 347, 350, 619, 620, 623, 635, 638, 640, 642, 790, 796, 831, 833, 843, 844, 848, 851, 852, 854, 857, 860, 864, 1387, 1397, 1805, 1811, 1883, 1886, 1887, 1892, 1893, 1896, 1899, 1900, 1937, 1940, 1941, 2049, 2053
Haas, Walter 892, 1838, 1842, 1843, 1846, 1847, 1849, 1851, 1864, 1870
Haase, Martin 1268
Haastrup, Kirsten 1031
Habel, F. P. 352, 357
Haberland, Hartmut 372, 377, 1028, 1032
Habermas, Jürgen 510, 514, 749
Habovštiak, Anton 1632, 1633, 1634, 1688, 1690, 1691, 1694, 1700, 1701
Hadrian (117–138 n. Chr.) 1272
Hadrovics, László 1734, 1736, 1737, 1740, 1743, 1803, 1810, 1811, 1822, 1826, 1827
Hadžiefendić, R. 1438, 1439, 1440, 1441, 1442
Haebler, Klaus 1519, 1522, 1523
Haedo, F. D. de 557, 558
Haeseryn, René 1119, 1122
Hafner, Stanislaus 1810, 1811, 1818, 1819, 1820
Hagège, Claude 50, 56, 108, 201, 202, 385, 390, 676, 683, 828, 833, 879, 1106
Hagemann, K. 418, 421
Hagen, Anton M. 582, 585, 1149, 1150, 1151
Hagström, Björn 1047, 1048, 1049
Hähnsen, F. 1777
Hajdú, Tibor 1712, 1714, 1722
Hájek, J. 735, 737
Hakuta, K. 34, 39, 479, 480, 580, 582, 585, 630, 631, 633
Hale, J. R. 1129
Hale, K. 587, 593, 659, 666
Halén, Harry 1007
Halink, Ruud 1246, 1251
Hall, Ch. J. 531, 540
Hall, E. T. 303, 305, 310, 925, 930
Hall, G. M. 652

Hall, M. R. 310
Hall, Robert A. jr. 649, 657, 877, 879
Hall, W. S. 625, 633
Halldórsson, Halldór 1056, 1057
Halle, M. 1723
Hallek, C. 853, 857
Haller, M. 203, 205, 206, 207, 209
Halliday, Michael A. K. 126, 146, 148, 152, 652, 657, 1751, 1753
Hämäläinen, Pekka K. 1007, 1014
Hamans, Camiel 1150, 1151
Hambuch, Wendelin 1730
Hamel, Rainer Enrique 453, 456, 671, 674
Hamers, Josiane 32, 33, 34, 35, 36, 37, 38, 39, 40, 44, 45, 46, 48, 82, 83, 84, 86, 88, 234, 235, 236, 244, 256, 776, 787, 790, 795
Hamm, J. 1827
Hammacher, S. 181, 191
Hammer, Ole 1020, 1024, 1025, 1026, 1031, 1032
Hammond, P. 50, 56
Hamp, Eric P. 101, 103, 1443, 1447, 1450, 1457, 1458, 1494, 1495, 1541, 1543
Hancock, Ian 331, 332, 895, 900, 1059, 1074, 1971
Handelskammer Hamburg 854, 857
Handke, Kwiryna 1614
Handke, P. 94, 96
Handler, R. 904, 906
Hanf, Th. 360, 361, 363
Hanika, Josef 1691
Hankey Wax, R. 751, 755, 760
Hanks, W. F. 747, 749
Hannah, J. 615, 624
Hannan, D. 1106
Hannappel, H. 270
Hannick, Christian 256, 1523
Hannum, H. 358, 360, 363
Hanse, Joseph 1114, 1122, 1126, 1129
Hansegård, Nils-Erik 4, 256, 487, 492, 984, 986, 981, 992, 1981
Hansen, Erik 7, 10, 464, 1028, 1032
Hansen, G. 181, 191
Hansen, M. H. 735, 737
Hanson, I. A. 629, 633
Happel, Stephen K. 1459, 1469
Haraksim, L. 1696, 1700
Harder, A. 540
Harding, E. 383, 384
Hare, D. R. 757, 763
Haritschelhar, Jean 1268, 1303, 1304, 1309

Harkins, J. 134, 137
Harley, B. 475, 481, 497, 498, 500, 501
Harlow, R. 721, 724, 725
Harman, L. D. 455, 456, 810
Harris, R. J. 130, 131, 137,309
Harris, T. K. 372, 373, 378
Harris, W. 811
Harrison, G. 380, 384
Harrison, Ph. A. 296, 310
Härtel, Hans Joachim 2032
Hartig, Matthias 24, 28, 31, 392, 398, 931
Hartl, Hans 1469
Hartmann, Claudia 1165, 1169, 1171
Hartung, Wolfdietrich 1768
Hartweg, Frédéric 396, 398, 1232, 1237, 1239, 1240
Hartweg, G. 2003, 2006
Harviainen, Tapani 1007
Harwood, J. 339, 341
Haselhuber, J. 860, 861, 864
Hasenau, M. 674
Hasiuk, M. 1608, 1613, 1614, 1615, 1616, 1618, 1620, 1621
Haskey, John 1989, 1993
Hasselbrink, Gustav 981
Hasselmo, N. 6, 9, 280, 282, 548, 594, 599, 607
Hassinger, H. 1974, 1976, 1978, 1979
Hassoun, J.-P. 452, 457, 1180, 1187, 2006
Hatch, E. 6, 10, 295, 516, 524
Hattenhauer, Hans 1649
Hattesen, Anni B. 1776, 1777
Hatton, T. J. 188, 191
Hattox, Ralph S. 1559, 1565
Hatz, G. 1397
Hatzfeld, H. 147, 152
Haubrichs, Walter 1862
Hauck, Werner 1846, 1851
Haudricourt, A. G. 51, 56
Haugen, Einar 3, 4, 10, 12, 15, 17, 21, 51, 56, 110, 112, 116, 123, 124, 125, 130, 178, 179, 234, 236, 244, 248, 256, 365, 366, 367, 368, 369, 392, 395, 398, 541, 543, 544, 545, 548, 572, 574, 577, 580, 585, 586, 593, 594, 601, 607, 666, 695, 701, 710, 714, 722, 724, 750, 762, 764, 770, 798, 804, 815, 818, 828, 833, 839, 841, 842, 879, 956, 1120, 1122, 1157, 1752, 1753, 1777
Haupenthal, R. 881, 886, 887
Hauschild, Th. 755, 763
Hausendorf, Heiko 1648
Haust, Jean 176, 179, 1119, 1122
Haut Conseil de la Francophonie 863, 864

Havelka, J. 37, 39, 137
Havránek, Bohuslav 146, 148, 152, 251, 256, 1639, 1640, 1661, 1662
Havu, J. 354, 357
Hawkesworth, Celia 832, 1450, 1451
Hawkey, R. H. 512, 514
Hawkins, A. 540
Hawkins, E. 420
Hawkins, F. 867, 870
Hazai, György 1506, 1507, 1509, 1510, 1559
Head, S. W. 426, 430
Heath, J. 98, 99, 103, 111, 112, 116, 574, 577, 600, 602, 607
Heath, S. B. 396, 398, 400, 404, 710, 714, 755, 762
Hébert, R. 475, 481
Hécart, G. A. J. 1242, 1251
Hechter, M. 77, 78, 79, 80, 207, 209
Heckmann, F. 209
Hedvičáková, Jaroslava 1653, 1655
Hegnauer, Cyril 1851
Héguy, Txomin 1261, 1263, 1268
Hegyi, O 618, 623
Heidelberger Forschungsprojekt „Pidgin-Deutsch" 762
Heilmann, Luigi 1396, 1397
Heindrichs, W. 514
Heine, Bernd 533, 534, 537, 540, 571, 576
Heinelt, H. 868, 870
Heinrich II. Jasomirgott (1141−1177) 1798
Heinrich IV. (1056−1106) 1802, 1821
Heinritz, G. 1582
Heinschink, Mozes 1804, 1805, 1810, 1811
Heinz, S. 1397
Heisler, B. S. 865, 870
Heisler, M. O. 209
Heitmann, Klaus 1470, 1471, 1476, 1477, 1937, 1941
Helander, E. 10, 575, 577
Helander, Kaisa Rautio 965
Hélias, Pierre-Jakez 1256, 1257, 1259
Heller, Karin 1357, 1397, 1398
Heller, Monica 6, 10, 21, 22, 53, 56, 117, 142, 143, 218, 242, 243, 244, 373, 378, 388, 389, 390, 391, 451, 455, 456, 457, 476, 481, 541, 546, 548, 549, 577, 578, 588, 593, 595, 597, 598, 605, 606, 607, 608, 609, 752, 755, 762, 787, 810, 833, 1847, 1851
Hellgardt, H. 233
Hellinger, M. 217, 218, 319, 886, 900, 901, 1129, 1850

Henderson, C. R. 810
Henderson, J. S. 794, 795
Hendrick, C. 732, 744
Hengartner, Thomas 1846, 1851
Henke, Reinhold 1803, 1804, 1805, 1807, 1808, 1811
Henkes, Th. 563, 566
Henley, N. 724
Henne, H. 584
Henning, C. 295
Henninger, Thomas 1554
Henriksen, Carol 1032
Henripin, J. 386, 391, 772, 773, 774, 775, 776
Henríquez Salido, Maria de Carmo 1314, 1316
Henrysson, Inger 9
Henrysson, Jan 371, 377
Henschel, H. 879
Hensel, G. 96
Henwood, K. 334, 340
Heraclides, A. 360, 363
Herasimchuk, E. 784, 787
Héraud, Guy 154, 156, 157, 158, 159, 160, 211, 212, 217, 244, 361, 363, 1134, 1136
Herbert, R. 608
Herberts, Kjell 19, 21, 460, 463, 464
Herculano de Carvalho, José G. 1314, 1316
Herder, Johann Gottfried (1744−1803) 76, 93, 154, 233, 671, 921, 924, 930
Hérédia, Christine de 322, 326, 1185, 1187
Hérédia-Deprez, Christine de 752, 758, 762, 2005, 2006
Herget, W. 319
Hering, Gunnar 246, 256, 1523, 1525
Heritage, J. 139, 143
Herman, S. R. 696, 701
Hermans, Michel 1139, 1143
Hermans, T. 1995
Hermida, Carme 1287, 1295
Hernandez-Chavez, E. 607
Hernová, Šárka 1668
Heroldová, Iva 1642, 1648
Herrero Valeiro, Mário J. 1293, 1295
Herrlitz, Wolfgang 417, 418, 420
Herrmann, Joachim 1768
Herskovits, M.-J. 51, 56
Hertel, M. 416, 420
Herzog, M. 713, 714
Hess, Beatrice 1845, 1851
Hessky, Regina 1731
Hess-Lüttich, Ernest W. B. 20, 146, 152
Hettema, M. 1787, 1790
Heuer, J. 1787, 1790
Heugh, K. 486, 492

Hewitt, R. 754, 762
Hewstone, M. 48, 732
Heyd, U. 619, 623
Hicky, T. 332
Hiebert, E. 633
Highfield, A. 117, 138, 652, 657, 658
Highfield, J. 1129
Hildebrandt, N. 694, 701
Hildebrandt, R. 1473, 1474, 1477, 1785
Hilkes, Peter 1905
Hill, George F. 1582
Hill, J. H. 232, 573, 576, 577, 586, 587, 588, 591, 593, 595, 598, 600, 602, 607, 660, 661, 662, 663, 666, 722, 747, 749, 754, 762
Hill, K. C. 57, 232, 576, 577, 586, 587, 588, 591, 593, 595, 600, 602, 607, 662, 666, 747, 749, 754
Hill, P. B. 743, 751, 763
Hill, Peter 1523, 1974, 1976, 1978, 2032, 2033
Hiltsch, B. 878
Hilty, Gerold 244, 1878
Hinderling, Robert 755, 762
Hindley, Reg 893, 1105, 1106, 1987, 1989
Hinds, J. 14, 21
Hinnenkamp, V. 648, 924, 925, 930
Hinskens, Frans 1150, 1151
Hint, Mati 1903, 1905
Hipp, H. 95, 96
Hippler, Hans-J. 729, 731, 732, 733, 738, 739, 740, 741, 743, 744
Hirataka, F. 900
Hirokawa, R. Y. 297, 310
Hirsch, Ernst 1349
Hjelmslev, L. 5, 654, 657
Ho, Mian Liao 22
Hobbs, J. R. 748
Hoberg, R. 508, 509, 510, 514
Hobsbawm, E. J. 76, 80, 201, 202, 668, 675
Hoche, Johann-Gottfried 1787, 1789, 1790
Hock, H. H. 534, 540
Hockett, Charles F. 149, 152, 169, 174, 2007
Hodge, B. 749
Hodgson, R. 706, 708
Hödl, Günther 1803, 1804, 1807, 1808, 1811
Höeg, Carsten 1514
Hoekstra, Jarich 1157
Hoenstra, J. F. 1905
Hof, B. 188, 191
Hofbauer, C. L. 749
Hoffer, Bates L. 297, 310, 547, 548, 549

Hoffet, F. 158, 159
Hoffmann, Ch. 567, 577
Hoffmann, Fernand 1164, 1166, 1168, 1169, 1170, 1171, 1172
Hoffmann, Heinrich 1599
Hoffmann, L. 508, 512, 514
Hoffmann-Nowotny, H.-J. 181, 182, 191
Hoffmannová, Jana 1654, 1655, 1704, 1707
Hoffmeister, Walter 1240
Hoffmeyer-Zlotnik, J. H. P. 761, 762
Hoffner, D. 310
Hofmann, Dietrich 1784, 1785
Hofmann, Tessa 1573, 1576
Hofstede, G. 190, 191
Hofwiler, Roland 2032
Hogg, M. A. 41, 42, 43, 44, 45, 46, 47, 48
Høgmo, Asle 960
Hohmann, Joachim S. 1970, 1971
Hoinville, G. 743
Højrup, Th. 810
Holden, N. 439, 444
Holden, S. 512, 514
Holland, D. 930
Hollander, E. P. 28, 31
Hollós, A. 1743
Hollqvist, H. 854, 855, 857
Holm, J. A. 607, 645, 648, 649, 657
Holm, K. 739, 743, 770
Holmberg, Veikko 1019
Holmen, Anne 7, 10, 20, 458, 460, 464, 1023, 1028, 1029, 1030, 1031, 1032, 1042
Holmes, Janet 21, 22, 432, 437, 696, 701, 721, 723, 724, 725
Holmes, R. 435, 438
Holmquist, J. C. 722, 724
Holobow, Naomi 481, 499, 501
Holobow, Walter 498, 500
Holšánová, Jana 1647, 1648
Holt, R. F. 464
Holter, K. 1812
Holtus, Günter 177, 178, 179, 244, 257, 326, 558, 623, 624, 642, 876, 879, 880, 1193, 1194, 1221, 1222, 1284, 1295, 1317, 1329, 1343, 1381, 1382, 1383, 1397, 1398, 1406, 1469, 1470, 1837, 1844, 1851, 1886, 2007, 2014, 2019
Holzer, Werner 1807, 1811, 1827, 1830, 1832, 1833, 1835
Holzschuh, H. 270
Homans, G. C. 43, 46, 48
Homburg, T. 562, 566
Hommes, Brigitte 1167, 1168, 1170, 1171
Honess, T. 48
Honey, J. 277, 282

Hongkai, S. 900
Hook, David 1284
Hope, T. E. 548, 872, 879
Hopf, Ch. 761, 762
Höpken, Wolfgang 1509
Hoppenbrouwers, Cor 1150, 1151
Hopper, R. 432, 437
Horák, Gejza 1654, 1655, 1707
Horak, St. M. 1458, 1722
Horálek, Karel 146, 152, 1650, 1655
Horecký, Ján 1653, 1655
Hormats, R. D. 188, 192
Hormia, Osmo 1981
Horn, D. 815, 818
Hornberger, N. H. 235, 244, 624, 633
Hornby, P. A. 38, 39, 244
Hornung, Herwig 1356
Hornung, Maria 1352, 1353, 1356, 1810, 1811
Horowitz, D. L. 76, 77, 80, 694, 701
Horsch, J. 316, 319
Horst, P. 787
Horvath, B. 722, 724
Horváth, Mária 1730
Hösch, Edgar 1461, 1469
Höskuldur, Þráinsson 1057, 1058
Hostert, H. 468, 472
Hostetler, J. A. 314, 315, 319, 392, 398
Hotzenköcherle, Rudolf 1843, 1851
Houdremont, Alphonse 1166, 1171
Hough, G. 149, 152
Houghton, C. 82, 88
Houis, M. 51, 56, 253, 256
House, J. 14, 20, 401, 415, 461, 464, 928
Housen, Alex 84, 88, 470, 472, 525
Houwer, Annick de 6, 10, 14, 20, 290, 291, 294, 452, 457
Hovanessian, M. 452, 457, 1183, 1186, 2004, 2006
Hovelacques 50
Hovland, C. I. 692, 693, 695, 696, 700, 702
Howatt, A. P. R. 520, 524
Howe, J. 789, 790, 796, 807
Howell, W. J. 427, 430
Hronek, J. 1653, 1655
Huang, X. 104, 109
Huber, Manfred 1461, 1469
Hübl, Milan 1672, 1677
Hübner, Emil 1768
Hübner, P. 743
Hübschmannová, Milena 1647, 1648, 1677
Huck, Dominique 81, 88, 678, 683

Hudabiunigg, I. 189, 191
Hudelson, S. 88
Hudler, Ingeborg 1476
Hudson, Alan 256, 453, 457
Hudson, Richard 170, 174, 430, 721, 724
Huebner, P. 648, 658
Huebner, T. 523
Huerta-Macías 603
Huffines, M. L. 375, 378, 395, 398, 574, 578, 662, 663, 666
Hugger, Paul 1850, 1851, 1852, 1878
Huguet, J. 353, 357
Hulk, A. 1151
Hull, C. L. 692, 701
Hull, Geoffrey 1406
Hüllen, W. 16, 21, 369
Huls, Erica 1150, 1152, 1251
Humbley, J. 81, 88
Humboldt, Wilhelm von (1767−1835) 95, 154, 264, 267, 534, 789, 921
Hume, I. 1075
Hummel, K. M. 37, 39, 125, 130
Humphreys, Humphrey Ll. 1259
Hunfalvy, Pál 1485, 1486
Hünnemeyer, F. 534, 537, 540
Hunt, H. 606
Hurch, B. 1268
Hurrelmann, K. 762
Hursh-César, G. 735, 737
Hurwitz, W. N. 735, 737
Husband, Ch. 41, 44, 45, 46, 48
Huss, Leena M. 992
Hutchinson, T. 512, 514
Huter, J. 315
Hutnik, N. 189, 192, 204, 206, 207, 209
Hutterer, Claus Jürgen 812, 813, 814, 815, 816, 818, 1690, 1691, 1722, 1724, 1727, 1728, 1730
Hutterer, Miklós 1715, 1720, 1722
Huxley, R. 295
Huys, Bernard 1110, 1122
Huyse, L. 401, 404
Hyldgaard-Jensen, Karl 514, 857, 1768
Hyltenstam, Kenneth 236, 244, 295, 369, 375, 378, 567, 569, 577, 578, 607, 992, 1030, 1031, 1032
Hyman, H. 745, 749
Hymes, Del H. 3, 9, 10, 14, 15, 21, 49, 50, 51, 52, 56, 116, 139, 143, 169, 171, 174, 432, 437, 586, 590, 593, 605, 606, 607, 649, 652, 657, 658, 667, 675, 701, 702, 711, 713, 714, 747, 749, 750, 753, 754, 759, 762, 789, 790, 792, 796, 803, 810

I

Ianco-Worrall, A. D. 7, 10, 132, 137
Ide, S. 14, 21, 931
Igla, Birgit 1494, 1495, 1510, 1971
Ihnatowicz, Ireneusz 1583, 1594
Ilchev, Ivan 1490, 1495
Ilievski, Petar H. 1443, 1450
Illyés, Elemér 1463, 1466, 1469
Imedadze, N. V. 34, 39
Imhoff, G. 478, 481
Imre, Samu 1833, 1834, 1835
Ineichen, Gustav 1215, 1216, 1220, 1221, 1222
Inglehart, R. R. 76
Ingram, E. 95
Innerhofer, Josef 1356
Inoue, F. 400, 404, 783, 787
Instruktion für die Schreibweise geographischer Namen 450
Intxausti, J. 616, 623
Inzko, Valentin 1814, 1820
Ioannou, K. 1549
Iordan, I. 873, 879
Isačenko, Alexander V. 1818, 1819, 1820
Isaev, Magomet I. 1888, 1937, 1941
Isaković, Alija 1438, 1439, 1440, 1441, 1442
Ishii, S. 303, 310
Ising, E. 894, 901
Ismajli, Rexhep 1449, 1450
Issacs, H. R. 80
Ithurria, Etienne 1263, 1267, 1268
Itkonen, Erkki 221, 232, 981, 1019
Itkonen, T. I. 1019
Ivănescu, G. 1467, 1469
Ivaničková, Halina 1694
Ivanoff, J. 52, 56
Ivanoski, Orde 1504
Ivanov, Jordan 1549
Ivanov, V. V. 1572, 1576
Ivarsson, J. 430
Ivić, Pavle 394, 398, 1362, 1366, 1433, 1437, 1441, 1442
Ivir, Vladimir 548, 1451
Iwersen, Philipp 1041
İz, F. 1532
Ižakević, Galina 1932
Izhevskaya, Tatiana I. 1900
Izzo, S. M. 132, 137

J

Jaakkola, Magdalena 348, 350, 992, 1007
Jaberg, Karl 1348, 1349
Jabine, Th. B. 738, 743
Jaccard, J. 694, 701
Jacher, W. 1591, 1592, 1594
Jachnow, Helmut 247, 256, 1941
Jachomowski, Dirk 1472, 1476
Jackson, B. E. 305, 309
Jackson, D. D. 311
Jackson, J. 170, 173, 174,
Jackson, Kenneth 1091, 1096
Jackson, Marvin 1459, 1469
Jacob, J. E. 79, 80, 344, 345, 350, 351, 400, 402, 404
Jacobs, B. 523, 524
Jacobsen, Mads A. 1045, 1048
Jacobsen, Maryanne 707, 708
Jacobson, R. 6, 10, 600, 604, 606, 607, 608, 896, 901
Jacobson, Th. 437
Jäger, K. H. 695, 701
Jäger, Siegfried 873, 877, 879
Jahn, Egbert Kurt 1672, 1677
Jahr, Ernst Håkon 138, 548, 578, 939, 942, 944, 945, 946, 947, 948, 956
Jakab, István 1684
Jakobovits, L. A. 132, 137, 432, 437, 695, 701
Jakobson, Roman 102, 103, 285, 294, 1723
Jamaldin bin Najor Din 420
Jambu, M. 780, 785, 787
James, H. 219, 232
Jančák, Pavel 1635, 1637, 1639, 1640, 1641
Jancza, Maria 1619, 1621
Jandová, Eva 1645, 1648, 1654, 1655
Janics, Kálmán 1711, 1721, 1722
Janković, Srđan 1437, 1441, 1442
Jansma, L. G. 1995
Janssen, Hans 1790
Janssen, Hermann 1790
Jardel, J.-P. 246, 247, 256
Jaritz, G. 192
Jašar-Nasteva, Olivera 1445, 1449, 1450
Jäschke, Gotthard 1561, 1565
Jasiński, Zenon 1668
Jaspaert, Koen 17, 18, 20, 21, 85, 88, 567, 577, 578, 581, 584, 585, 1114, 1115, 1122, 1150, 1151
Jauréguiberry, Francis 1263, 1268
Jausma, L. G. 1905
Javorskaja, Galina M. 1932
Jazyeri, A. 1971
Jeanneret, René 167, 168, 1851, 1852
Jech, J. 1638, 1640
Jedig, H. 815, 816, 818
Jedlička, Alois 1654, 1655, 1707
Jeggle, U. 752, 753, 758, 762
Jelavich, Barbara 1488, 1495, 1554
Jelavich, Charles 1554
Jelitte, H. 1655
Jelsma, Gjalt H. 1157, 1995
Jenč, Rudolf 1792, 1793, 1796
Jenkins, S. 866, 867, 870
Jenniges, Hubert 1132, 1133, 1134, 1136, 1142
Jensen, A. 710, 711, 714
Jensen, H. 620, 623
Jerab, N. 2005, 2007
Jermolenko, S. C. 1932
Jernsletten, Johan 1019
Jernsletten, Nils 947, 948, 961
Jernudd, Björn H. 423, 426, 691, 830, 833, 839, 841, 842, 857
Jerushalmi, Isaak 1568, 1569, 1570, 1571
Jespersen, O. 542, 548, 657, 720, 724, 881, 886
Jeszenszky, Géza 1712, 1722
Jetne, Kjellaug 947, 948
Jilbert, K. 88
Jireček, Constantin 1737
Job, Michael 1577
Jobe, J. B. 738, 743
Jochalas, Titos 1523
Jochnowitz, G. 178, 179
jofe, j. a. 1960
Johanson, Lars 1510
Johnson, H. G. 296, 310
Johnson, J. D. 432, 437
Johnson, K. 500
Johnson, M. 432, 437
Johnson, P. 43, 44, 45, 47, 48, 185, 192, 334, 335, 341, 455, 456, 694, 701
Johnson, Sahnny 296, 310
Johnson, Sally 695, 701
Johnson-Weiner, K. M. 218, 864
Johnston, M. 522, 525, 721, 723, 724
Johnston, R. J. 75
Joldrichsen, Anke 1781, 1785
Jolibert, A. 420
Jolivet, Rémi 1867, 1870
Joly, D. 327
Jonekeit, S. 380, 382, 383, 384
Jones, S. 397, 398
Jong, E. D. de 380, 382, 383, 384
Jonke, Ljudevit 1433
Jonkman, Reitze J. 1157
Jónsson, Baldur 1057
Jónsson, Bergsteinn 1055, 1058
Jónsson, Jón H. 1057
Jónsson, S. 1058
Joó, Rudolf 1716, 1721, 1722
Joos, M. 798, 804
Jordan, Peter 1816, 1820, 1974, 1976, 1978, 1979, 2023, 2065

Jordens, P. 583, 585
Jorgensen, D. L. 752, 753, 759, 762
Jørgensen, Jens N. 7, 10, 20, 464, 1022, 1025, 1026, 1028, 1029, 1032
Joscelyne, T. A. 429, 430
Joseph, Brian D. 1449, 1450, 1494, 1495
Joseph, J. E. 279, 282, 586, 589, 593, 638, 640, 675, 732, 746, 749, 829, 833, 857, 872, 879
Joshi, A. 600, 604, 607
Jouve, E. 355, 357, 362, 363
Jowell, R. 743
Joy, R. 386, 391
Jucquois, Guy 1119, 1122
Jud, Jakob 1348
Juhász, J. 4, 10
Julia, Dominique 1186, 1250
Jumuga, Margareta-Sigrid 1474, 1476
Jungandreas, Wolfgang 1599
Junttila, Jorid Hjulstad 947, 948, 965
Junyent, C. 354, 357
Jupp, T. C. 14, 22, 142, 143, 868, 871, 930
Jurdant, B. 787
Jürgens, H. 229, 233
Just Jeppesen, Kirsten 1025, 1026, 1032
Just, R. 204, 205, 209
Juta, C. J. 904, 906
Jysk Ordbog 1032

K

Kaase, M. 737, 743
Kabasonov, Staiko 1504
Kačala, Ján 1707
Kachru, Braj B. 19, 21, 152, 277, 282, 485, 486, 492, 895, 901, 906, 907, 908, 909, 910, 911, 912, 913
Kachru, Y. 909, 912
Kaczmarczyk, Z. 1599
Kadłubiec, Daniel 1668
Kadar-Hoffmann, G. 290, 291, 294
Kadelbach, A. 316, 319
Kaestner, Walter 1598, 1599
kagorov, J. 1960
Kahane, Henry 256, 555, 556, 558, 833, 838, 841, 907, 912, 1532
Kahane, Renée 256, 555, 556, 558, 838, 841, 907, 912, 1532
Kahn, R. 730, 732
Kaiser, Andrea 381, 382, 384, 1832, 1835
Kaiser, Stephan 1843, 1851

Kakuk, Zsuzsanna 1507, 1509, 1510
Kalantsis, M. 85, 88
Kalema, J. 675
Kalin, R. 38
Kälin, W. 186, 192
Kallmeyer, Werner 451, 454, 456, 457, 458, 816, 818
Kalogjera, Damir 548, 1451
Kalpaka, A. 180, 192
Kalsbeek, W. D. 736, 737
Kalton, G. 726, 732
Kalverkämper, H. 513
Kamenec, Ivan 1676, 1677
Kamiński, Aleksander 1608, 1613, 1615, 1621
Kamiš, Adolf 1654, 1655
Kampasakalís, D. J. 1554
Kampmann, Jan 1023, 1032
Kandiah, T. 394, 398, 895, 901
Kann, Robert A. 155, 160, 1482, 1486, 1737, 1746, 1748
Kanter, A. de 632, 633
Kapanga, A. M. 464
Kapesh, A. 794, 795, 796
Kapferer, B. 810
Kaplan, Karel 1679, 1680, 1684
Kaplan, R. B. 14, 20, 21, 836, 841, 926, 930
Kaplitza, G. 766, 770
Kapoor, J. M. 492
Kapoor, K. 912
Kappel, G. 417, 420
Kapsomenos, Stavros G. 1370, 1371
Karaś, M. 1627, 1633
Karadžić, Vuk 1408, 1439
Karady, Victor 1712, 1713, 1721, 1722, 1723
Karagiannis, C. 464
Karakasidou, Anastasia 1523, 1549
Karaliūnas, Simas 1617, 1621, 1918, 1919
Karanastasis, Anastasios 1323, 1329, 1368, 1369, 1370, 1371, 1523, 2018, 2019
Karatzas, Stavros C. 1370, 1371
Kardam, F. 608
Kardel, Harboe 1041
Kardiner, Abram 1110, 1122
Kretu, T. 673, 675
Karl V. (1519−1556) 1399
Karl VI. (1711−1740) 1472
Karlsson, Fred 1007
Karmasin, F. 737, 739, 740, 741, 743
Karmasin, H. 737, 739, 740, 741, 743
Karmona, Eliya 1571
Karničar, Ludwig K. 1818, 1819, 1820
Karouzis, George 1582

Karp, I. 746, 749
Karpat, Kemal 1491, 1493, 1495
Karst, J. Josef 1575, 1577
Karsten, T. E. 548
Karszniewicz-Mazur, Alicja 1599
Karttunen, L. 607
Kašić, Jovan 1433
Kask, A. 1899
Kasparian, S. 776, 783, 787
Kasper, Gabriele 13, 14, 20, 21, 55, 56, 241, 243
Kastner, Maria 1648
Kastoryano, Riva 1567, 1571
Katičić, Radoslav 1433, 1494, 1495
Katovsky, D. 592
Katsougiannis, Tilemachos M. 1523
Kattenbusch, Dieter 1328, 1329, 1330, 1397, 1881, 1886, 2018, 2019
Kaufman, T. 54, 57, 103, 112, 116, 117, 121, 333, 338, 339, 342, 538, 539, 540, 586, 593, 602, 609, 790
Kaufmann, G. 816, 818
Kausen, R. 232
Kavalliotis, Theodorus 1523
Kazazis, Kostas 1563, 1564, 1565
Kazinczy, F. von 10
Keatley, C. W. 125, 130, 131, 132, 137
Kebir, S. 927, 930
Keep, L. 475, 481
Keesing, Robert 644, 648
Keesing, Roger M. 141, 144
Kegel, G. F. 384
Keiler, A. R. 103
Keim, Inke 759, 762
Keiser, R. 416, 420
Keleş, R. 1554, 1559
Keller, Hans-Erich 1336, 1337
Keller, Peter 1847, 1851
Keller, R. 526, 528, 529, 530, 531, 533, 534, 535, 536, 540
Kellerer, H. 734, 737
Kellerman, Ahron 433, 437
Kellerman, Eric 517, 521, 524, 561, 562, 564, 566
Kelley, B. 1260
Kelley, H. H. 48
Kellner, Adolf 1667, 1668
Kelly, A. 137
Kelly, L. G. 10, 11, 20, 81, 82, 276, 282
Kelly, R. J. 343, 351
Kelnhofer, Fritz 2023
Kelp, Helmut 1471, 1474, 1476
Kelz, Heinrich P. 515
Kelz, R. J. 509, 510, 512, 513, 514, 515
Kendall, J. R. 632, 633, 746, 749

Kendi, Erich 1462, 1463, 1465, 1466, 1469, 1478, 1483, 1486
Kendon, A. 309, 311
Kennedy, Ch. 512, 514
Kenrick, Donald 74, 1493, 1495, 1962, 1971
Keramopoullos, Antonios 1539
Kerbrat-Orecchioni, C. 243
Kerecsényi, Edit 1734, 1737, 1738
Keresztes, L. 1905
Kerkofs, Jan 1123
Kern, Rudolf 366, 369, 1133, 1135, 1136, 1142, 1143
Kertesz, Stephen 1709, 1711, 1721, 1722
Kets de Vries, M. F. R. 405, 410, 413
Kettiger, Daniel 1846, 1850
Key, M. R. 309
Keyes, Ch. F. 209
Khachaturian, A. 1574, 1575, 1576
Khan, S. A. 721, 724, 867, 870
Khlief, Bud B. 78, 80, 430, 1157
Khubchandani, L. M. 83, 88, 105, 109, 895, 901
Kielhöfer, Bernd 367, 369, 380, 382, 383, 384
Kim, Ch.-W. 896, 901
Kim, Y. Y 41, 42, 43, 44, 45, 46, 47, 48, 303, 310, 929
Kimple, J. 695, 699, 701
Kincaid, D. L. 310, 433, 438
King, B. T. 700
King, M. L. 130
King, R. 188, 192
Kin-Kong Lam, D. 363
Kinzer, St. 869, 870
Kiparsky, P. 342, 350
Király, B. K. 1722,
Király, Péter 1739, 1741, 1743, 1748
Kirch, M. S. 5, 10
Kirkness, Alan 872, 874, 879
Kirsch, W. 854, 857
Kirsner, K. 125, 130
Kisch, Egon 1656, 1661
Kisch, Gustav 1476
Kiselinovski, Stojan 1501, 1502, 1503, 1504, 1549
Kish, Leslie 727, 732, 735, 737
Kiss, Lajos 450
Kiss, Mária 1734, 1737, 1738
Kitis, Eliza 2032
Kjolseth, R. 257
Klaassen, L. H. 433, 437
Klaić, Bratoljub 1733, 1738
Klann-Delius, G. 720, 721, 724
Klaster-Ungureanu, Grete 1473, 1476
Klatter-Folmer, Jetske 1251
Klavans, J. L. 600, 607

Kleczkowski, Adam 1598, 1599
Klee, C. A. 371, 378
Kleff, H.-G. 192
Klein, E. 532, 540
Klein, Karl K. 818, 1471, 1473, 1476
Klein, Samuelis 1486
Klein, Wolfgang 285, 292, 294, 321, 326, 515, 516, 517, 520, 521, 524, 930
Klein-Braley, Christiane 507
Kleineidam, H. 856, 857, 864
Kleinmann, H. 563, 566
Kleinschmidt, Samuel 1053, 1054
Kleinschmitt, E. 513, 514
Kleivan, Inge 460, 464, 1050, 1054
Klemenčić, Mladen 1442
Klimeš, L. 1655
Klimko, Ján 1677, 1692, 1694
Klinge, Matti 1007
Klinger, András 1739, 1743
Klingler, Cynthia 35, 38, 603, 606
Klingler, Th. 651, 657
Klinkenberg, J.-M. 149
Kloepfer, Rudolf 257, 880
Klopčić, Vera 1423
Kloskowska, A. 191
Kloss, Heinz 4, 6, 10, 17, 18, 21, 89, 94, 97, 156, 160, 169, 174, 178, 179, 210, 212, 217, 248, 249, 252, 256, 277, 281, 282, 392, 395, 398, 571, 578, 580, 581, 585, 634, 635, 636, 637, 638, 639, 640, 641, 669, 675, 816, 817, 818, 819, 828, 852, 888, 893, 894, 900, 901, 1164, 1171, 1193, 1211, 1213, 1329, 1402, 1403, 1405, 1406
Klöti, Ulrich 1838, 1851
Klövekorn, Martin 1014
Kluckhohn, C. 930
Kluge, F. 398
Knapp, K. 143, 144, 417, 420, 925, 930
Knapp-Potthoff, A. 144, 925, 930
Knappert, J. 397, 398
Knäuper, B. 744
Knecht, Pierre 1843, 1851, 1867, 1870
Kneidl, Herbert 1973, 1975, 1977, 1240
Kniezsa, István 1737, 1738, 1743
Kniffka, Hannes 825
Knight, D. 363
Knobloch, Johann 1471, 1477, 1810, 1811
Knoke, D. 728, 732
Knoop, Ulrich 175, 176, 177, 179, 270,1600

Knowles, Frances 1899
Kočar, Meri R. 1558, 1559
Kočev, Ivan 1552, 1554
Kobeckaité, Halina 1912, 1913, 1915, 1919
Koch, S. 700
Kochen, M. 437
Kochman, Th. 923, 930
Köckeis-Stangl, E. 757, 762
Kocks, A. 416, 420
Kocsis, Károly 1478, 1479, 1480, 1486
Koefoed, Geert 1151
Koenig, O. 180, 191
Koepeci, Béla 1486
Koepf, P. 869, 870
Koerner, K. 789, 790, 796
Kofman, E. 69, 74
Kofos, Evangelos 1546, 1549
Kohan, David 1945, 1960
Kohl, Christine von 1411, 1415
Kohli, M. 25, 31
Kohls, J. 472
Kohn, H. 716, 717, 719
Kohring, Heinrich 1569, 1571
Kokot, W. 192
Kolb, H. 3, 4, 10, 11
Kolde, Gottfried 696, 697, 698, 701, 1851, 1866, 1869
Kolder, M. 420
Kolers, P. A. 37, 39, 132, 137, 607
Kolesnyk, Grygorij 1932
Kolinsky, R. 130
Kolis, Nijola 1608, 1613, 1614
Koller, Werner 146, 152, 1842, 1851
Kollmann, Peter 1787, 1790
Kolodny, Emile 1582
Kolsti, J. 1721
Koltsidas, Antones 1539
Komárek, Miroslav 1659, 1661
Kondosopoulos, Nikolaos 1550
Kondratiuk, M. 1608, 1613
Koneski, Blazhe 1449, 1450, 1503
König, E. 1157
König, R. 743, 751, 752, 762
König, Walter 1473, 1477
Königs, F. G. 853, 857
Konstantakopoulou, Aggeliki 1523
Konstantinidis, Alexandros 1563, 1565
Konstantinov, Yulian 1494, 1495, 1496
Kontra, Miklós 336, 341, 1684, 1718, 1720, 1722, 1723, 1752, 1753
Kontzi, Reinhold 2, 10, 1404, 1406
Koo, J. H. 310
Koole, T. 190, 192, 925, 928, 930

Koolwijk, J. von 726, 732
Kööp, Karl-Peter 1778, 1779, 1781
Koop, W. 417, 420
Kopp, B. 921, 930
Köppe, R. 603, 607
Korać, Stanko 1433
Korazim, J. 868, 870
Korbel, Jan 1584, 1594
Korhonen, Mikko 1007, 1981
Korhonen, Olavi 981
Korkiasaari, Jouni 963, 965
Korletjanu, N. G. 1939, 1941
Körner, H. 192
Korobar, Pero 1504
Korte, H. 8, 10
Korubin, Blagoja 1449, 1450
Korzenny, F. 436, 438
Kos, M. 1739, 1743
Kość, Józef 1623, 1627
Koschat, Helene 1826, 1827
Koselleck, R. 96
Koskinen, Arja 963, 964, 965
Kostanick, Huey Louis 1551, 1554
Kosteski, Nikola 1444, 1449, 1450
Kotthoff, H. 930
Kotzé, Ernst F. 492
Kotzian, Ortfried 1472, 1477
Koufis, Pavlos 1549
Koukkidis, Konstantinos 1522, 1531, 1532, 1564, 1565
Koulouriotis, Anastasios I. 1522, 1523
Kouwenberg, S. 122, 123
Kováč, Dušan 1677, 1691, 1707
Kovačec, August 1410, 1416, 1433, 1436, 1437, 1438, 1439, 1440, 1441, 1442
Kovacs, Martin L. 1720, 1721, 1722
Kővágó, László 1721, 1722, 1731, 1732, 1733, 1735, 1737, 1738
Kowallik, Sabine 2032
Kowalski, Tadeusz 1506, 1507, 1508, 1510, 1528, 1532
Kozel, Jaroslav 1668
Kozlov, Viktor I. 1894, 1899
Kozocsa, Sandor Géza 1752
Kraas, Frauke 1837, 1840, 1844, 1851, 1879, 1880, 1881, 1886
Krag, H. L. 344, 350
Krahe, Hans 1768
Krallert, Wilfried 1974, 1976, 1978, 1979
Králové, Hradec 1655
Kramer, Christina 1496, 1503, 1504
Kramer, Johannes 1133, 1136, 1164, 1166, 1170, 1171, 1172, 1351, 1355, 1356, 1388, 1397, 1467, 1469, 1533, 1535, 1538, 1539, 1933, 1937, 1941, 2032
Kramer, Pyt 1789, 1790
Kramer, W. 857
Kranzmayer, Eberhard 4, 10, 1356, 1809, 1810, 1811, 1812, 1816, 1817, 1818, 1819, 1820, 1825, 1827
Krashen, St. 84, 85, 87, 88, 89, 365, 369, 516, 518, 524, 562, 566
Krastiņš, O. 1906, 1912
Kraus, J. 152
Kraus, Sidney 297, 310
Krause, W. 1662
Krauss, Michael 659, 660, 666, 708
Krauss, Robert 334, 341
Kraybill, D, B. 319
Krech, Dieter 739, 743
Krefeld, Thomas 1465, 1469
Kreindler, Isabelle T. 1899, 1900, 1905
Kreis, Georg 1837, 1851
Kreiser, Klaus 1555, 1559, 1974, 1976, 1978
Kremer, D. 1469
Kremer, Ludger 1150, 1151, 1886
Kremnitz, Georg 211, 217, 226, 232, 237, 238, 244, 249, 251, 252, 256, 257, 613, 623, 641, 802, 804, 893, 1188, 1189, 1190, 1193, 1194, 1195, 1201, 1402, 1405, 1406, 2004, 2007
Kreppner, K. 753, 762
Kress, G. 749
Kretschmer, Ingrid 1974, 1976, 1978, 1979
Kretschmer, W. 218, 232
Krier, Fernande 1404, 1406
Kriššáková, J. 1632, 1633, 1677, 1692, 1693, 1694
Křístek, Václav 1668
Kristol, Andres Max 1844, 1849, 1851, 1852, 1882, 1886
Kritz, M. M. 188, 192
Kriz, J. 751, 753, 762
Kroeber, A. L. 51, 930
Kroll, J. F. 131, 137
Krolop, Kurt 1661
Kromnow, A. 836, 841
Kroner, Michael 1471, 1477
Kronsteiner, Otto 445, 450, 1798, 1799, 1812
Kroon, Sjaak 17, 18, 20, 21, 567, 577, 578, 581, 584, 585, 1151
Kroskrity, P. 746, 749
Krug, W. 735, 737
Krüger, Bruno 1768
Krüger, Eberhard 2032
Krüger, Fritz 1316, 1572
Krüger, G. 97
Krumm, H. J. 369
Kruopas, J. 1899
Krupa, Victor 634
Krusche, D. 925, 930
Kruskal, W. 733, 734, 737
Kryczyński, St. 1918, 1919
Kubat, D. 865, 870
Kubiak, H. 1925, 1926
Kubijovych, Volodymyr 1624, 1627
Kubín, Josef 1635, 1638, 1639, 1640
Kučerová, Kveta 1676, 1677
Kuchař, Jaroslav 1651, 1655
Kuen, Heinrich 1391, 1396, 1397
Kühebacher, Egon 450, 554, 1356
Kuhl, P. K. 290, 294
Kühlwein, Wolfgang 21, 930, 1768
Kühn, G. 147, 152
Kuhn, H. 5, 10
Kuhn, Walter 815, 819, 1685, 1691
Kühnel, Horst 1471, 1477
Kühn-Ludewig, Maria 1947, 1960
Kuhs, K. 292, 294
Kulick, D. 572, 578, 589, 593, 646, 648, 722, 724
Kumatani, A. 896, 901
Kunøe, M. 1776
Kunz, G. 735, 737
Kunze, Peter 1792, 1796
Kuo, E. C. Y. 452, 456, 457
Kupinsky, B. 629, 633
Kupovecki, Mark 1943, 1960
Kuraszkiewicz, W. 1627
Kürschner, W. 886
Kurz, Maria 1801, 1812
Kurz, U. 24, 31, 392, 398
Kurze, Friedrich 1790, 1796
Kurzowa, Zofia 1627, 1922, 1925
Kusik'jan, Iosif K. (= Kusikyan, Hovsep K.) 1574, 1577
Kuter, L. 391, 2003, 2007
Kutscher, E. Y. 616, 623
Kutschker, M. 854, 857
Kuvlesky, W. P. 722, 725
Kuzgun, Ş. 1568, 1571
Kuzmich, Ludwig 1822, 1827
Kvapil, J. S. 1662
Kwilecki, Andrzej 1584, 1594
Kwok, H. 929, 930
Kyrnis, Costas P. 1582

L

La Villemarqué, Théodore Hersart de (1815–1895) 1257, 1259

Labba, Per S. 1019
Laberge, S. 650, 658, 683
Labocha, J. 1665, 1667, 1668
Labov, William F. 21, 139, 144, 169, 170, 171, 172, 173, 174, 248, 252, 257, 334, 341, 393, 398, 534, 535, 540, 545, 547, 548, 572, 578, 651, 657, 677, 679, 683, 695, 701, 704, 709, 710, 713, 714, 721, 724, 749, 757, 762, 790, 797, 808, 811, 838, 841
Labrie, Normand 64, 74, 79, 80, 213, 214, 217, 218, 464, 765, 770, 810, 811, 829, 831, 833, 861, 864, 890, 893
Labuda, Alexander 1601, 1602, 1603, 1605
Labuda, Gerard 1605
Lach, F. H. 399
Lachapelle, R. 386, 391, 772, 773, 774, 775, 776
Lachmann, R. 1640
Laczkó, Krisztina 1752
Ladd, P. 331, 332, 1060, 1074
Ladefoged, P. 587, 593, 708
Ladin, Wolfgang 686, 691, 1240
Ladmiral, Jean R. 420
Lado, R. 13, 21, 51, 56, 504, 507, 518, 524, 559, 560, 561, 566
Ladusaw, W. 130, 137
Lafitte, Pierre 1268, 1269
Lafon, René 1268
Lafont, R. 154, 156, 160, 196, 199, 207, 227, 232, 251, 252, 253, 255, 256, 257, 353, 357, 420, 678, 683, 684, 685, 691, 802, 804, 893, 1177, 1187, 1191, 1194, 1209, 1213
Laforge, L. 69, 73, 74
LaFrance, M. 335, 341
Lagercrantz, Eliel 981
Lagman, H. 5, 10
Lainio, Jarmo 8, 10, 376, 378, 575, 578, 992, 1005, 1007
Laitin, D. D. 76, 78, 80, 397, 398, 401, 404, 587, 588, 593
Lajeunesse, G. 633
Lakoff, G. 137
Laky, A. 1825, 1827
Lalleman, Josien A. 1150, 1151
Lallukka, S. 774, 776
LaLonde, R. N. 433, 437, 582, 584
Lambert, J. 429, 430
Lambert, R. D. 18, 21, 567, 578, 579, 584, 585, 666
Lambert, Wallace E. 15, 21, 34, 36, 37, 39, 40, 61, 62, 132, 137, 291, 295, 337, 340, 367, 369, 370, 432, 437, 474, 476, 477, 480, 481, 486, 491, 492, 495, 496, 497, 498, 499, 500, 501, 603, 608, 632, 633, 667, 675, 692, 694, 695, 698, 701, 706, 708
Lambourne, A. D. 429, 430
Lamendella, J. 58, 62
Lamnek, S. 752, 753, 756, 762
Lamprecht, A. 1667, 1668
Lamuela, Xavier 357, 890, 891, 893
Lance, D. M. 599, 607
Landau, Jacob M. 1569, 1571
Landi, Addolorata 1366
Landmann, Salcia 1805, 1812
Lane, H. 285, 294
Lang, Franz 1471, 1477
Lang, H. 181, 192
Lang, J. 176, 179
Lange, L. 692, 701
Lange, W. 416, 420
Langenbacher, J. 876, 879
Langgård, Per 1050, 1054
Langohr, Jozef 1122
Lanham, L. W. 901
Lanstyák, István 1681, 1684
Lanthaler, Franz 270, 1355, 1356, 1357
Lanzen, Ch. 21
Lapesa, Rafael 1271, 1272, 1275, 1276, 1284
Lapide, P. E. 393, 398
LaPiere, R. T. 693, 695, 701
Lapierre, J.-W. 160, 210, 217, 399, 402, 404
Lapierre, L. 405, 413
Lapiower, Alain 1110, 1122
Lapkin, Susan 19, 22, 84, 89, 465, 473, 474, 475, 481, 496, 501
Laponce, J. A. 65, 74, 76, 79, 80, 211, 212, 215, 217, 218, 401, 404, 422, 426, 431, 433, 438
Laporte, Dominique 878, 890, 892, 1186
Laporte, Pierre-E. 442, 444
Laprade, R. 396, 398
Laragyulyan, T. 1575, 1577
Large, Andrew 839, 841, 884, 886
Large, J. 418, 420
Larner, M. 810
Laroussi, Foued 196, 198, 199, 1175, 1184, 1187
Larrañaga, Iñaki 1306, 1309
Larsen, E. V. 1776
Larsen, K. 337, 341
Larsen, Nils-Erik 1982
Larsen-Freeman, D. 515, 516, 517, 522, 523, 524
Laskaridou, A. D. 1563, 1565
Laskowski, Roman 1637, 1640
Lasnik, H. 606, 609
Latiegui, V. de 621, 623
Latoszek, Marek 1600, 1605
Latta, Vasyl' 1699, 1701
Laube, Gustav 1388, 1398
Lauffer, H. 3, 4, 10, 11
Lauhus, A. 1640
Laur, Wolfgang 1783, 1785
Laurén, Christer 19, 69, 74, 293, 294, 380, 384
Laurent, B. 363
Lausberg, H. 874, 879
Lautman, F. 388, 390
Lavinio, Cristina 1377, 1379, 1382
Lawson, Edward 1715, 1719, 1722
Laycock, D. C. 647, 648
Layton-Henry, Z. 188, 192
Lázaro Carreter, F. 558
Lazarou, Achille G. 1524, 2032
Lazarsfeld, P. F. 739, 743
Le Berre, Yves 1259, 1260
Le Cornec, J. 873, 879
Le Dû, Jean 1259, 1260
Le Floc'h, Jean-Louis 1259
Le Gallo, Yves 1259, 1260
Le Guern, M. 1217, 1221
Le Lannou, Maurice 1376, 1382
Le Page, Robert 54, 56, 170, 175, 180, 235, 238, 244, 324, 326, 588, 593, 643, 648, 656, 657, 713, 714, 776, 784, 785, 787, 811
Leau, L. 883, 886
Leavitt, R. 794, 796
Lebègue, Maurice 1242, 1246, 1250, 1252, 2006
Lebrun, N. 292, 293, 294, 468, 471, 472
Lebrun, Yves 7, 11, 132, 138
Leca, J. 200, 203
Leclerc, J. 442, 444
Lee, A. 419
Lee, H.-B. 896, 901
Lee, Jennifer 113, 116
Lee, Joseph 1099, 1106
Lee, V. J. 175
Leech, G. 139, 144
Leets, L. 8, 9, 48, 326, 339, 341
Leewen, E. van 509, 510, 514
Lefebvre, Anne 1175, 1176, 1187
Lefèbvre, Claire 147, 152, 652, 656, 657
Lefèbvre, Gilles 657
Lefevre, Jacques A. 683
Legère, Karsten 492
Leggewie, C. 924, 930
Legrand, Francine-Claire 1110, 1122
Lehiste, I. 98, 103, 132, 137
Lehmann, Ch. 533, 537, 540
Lehmann, Rudolf 1796
Lehmann, Wilfried P. 545, 548, 714

Lehmkuhl, Gerd 226, 233
Lehmkuhl, Ulrike 233
Lehr-Spławiński, Tadeusz 1627
Leibniz, Gottfried Wilhelm (1646–1716) 69, 74
Leinonen, Marja 1007
Leisi, Ernst 301, 310
Leisi, Ilse 301, 310
Leite de Vasconcelos, José 1314, 1316, 1317
Leman, J. 84, 85, 88, 467, 468, 472
Lemarchand-Unger, Brigitte 1260
Lemberg, Hans 1469
Lemchenas, Chackelis 1918, 1919
Lemmens, G. 85, 88
Lenček, Rado 1816, 1820
Lenec', Kateryna 1932
Lengyel, Z. 370
Lénine, V. I. 157, 828
Lenneberg, E. H. 7, 10, 285, 289, 290, 294, 365, 370, 704, 708
Lenoble, J. 202
Lentacker, Firmin 1241, 1251
Leonardy, Ernst 1110, 1122
Leopold, W. F. 6, 7, 10, 32, 33, 39, 285, 290, 294, 364, 366, 370, 380, 384, 421
LePoire, B. A. 335, 340
Lequin, Y. 2007
Lerat, P. 879
Lerner, D. 64, 74, 431
Łesiów, Michal 1614, 1627
Leskien, A. 2
Lessiak, Primus 1810, 1812, 1818, 1819, 1820
Lessler, J. 736, 737
Leveau, R. 188, 192
Levelt, W. J. M. 584, 585, 604, 607
Levi, M. 78, 80
Lévi, P. 4, 10
Levieuge, Guy 1240, 2006
Levin, M. D. 233
Levinson, St. 138, 140, 144
Levi-Strauss, C. 26, 31
Lévy, Laurette 388, 389, 390, 391
Levy, Paul M. G. 1111, 1123, 1240
Lewandowski, Theo 1640
Lewin, M. 751, 752, 762
Lewis, Bernard 1555, 1559, 1565
Lewis, E. Glyn 482, 492, 695, 702, 834, 838, 841, 1888, 1894, 1896, 1899, 1987, 1989
Lewis, G. J. 834, 841
Lewis, G. L. 121, 123
Lewis, P. 866, 870
Lewy, Ernst 2

Leydi, Roberto 1329
Leyens, J.-P. 334, 340
Leyer, E. M. 189, 192
Leyk, J. 885, 886
Lhande, Pierre 1268, 1269
Li, Charles N. 540
Li, Wei (→ Wei, Li) 597, 598, 607
Lian, H. M. M. 901, 908, 912
Lian, K. F. 209
Libal, Wolfgang 1411, 1415
Libaridian, Gerald J. 1573, 1577
Liebaers, Herman 1110, 1123
Lieberman, J. 705, 708
Liebermann, Ph. 294
Lieberson, Stanley 209, 380, 381, 384, 387, 391, 588, 593, 722, 724, 781, 787
Lieberson, Stephen 16, 21
Liebkind, Karmela 44, 45, 48, 1014
Liebmann, E. 40
Liedtke, W. W. 35, 39
Lienau, Cay 1524
Lijphart, A. 76, 77, 80, 81, 209, 404
Likert, R. 697, 702
Lill, Rudolf 1329
Lim, L. L. 188, 192
Lin, J.-S. 765, 770
Lin, N. 810, 811
Lindgren, Anna-Riitta 947, 948, 962, 963, 965, 966, 1019, 1981
Lindholm, Kathryn J. 33, 39, 40, 493, 479, 481, 494, 501
Lindner, R. 752, 762
Linell, P. 336, 341
Linguistic Minorities Project 171, 174, 585, 721, 724
Linhart, D. 410, 412, 413
Link-Heer, U. 97
Linnik, T. G. 1932
Linton, Ralph 51, 56, 1110, 1123
Lipold, Günter 1691, 1808, 1812
Lippi-Green, R. L. 810, 811
Lipski, J. M. 105, 109, 607
Lipták, L. 1677, 1707
List, Friedrich 667, 675
List, Pia 417, 420
Liste des exonymes français d'Europe 450
Lithoxoos, Dhimitris 1545, 1547, 1550
Lithoxou, Dhimitris 2032
Ljungberg, Erik 1970, 1971
Llamzon, T. 900
Lo Bianco, Joseph 853, 857, 869, 871
Lobin, G. 886
Lockhart, R. S. 130
Lockwood, D. G. 129
Lodge, R. A. 872, 879

Loeb Adler, L. 842
Löffler, Heinrich 258, 259, 260, 265, 270, 382, 384, 754, 762, 814, 819, 1842, 1851, 1852, 1856, 1857, 1859, 1860, 1861, 1862
Lofland, John 759, 762
Lofland, Lyn H. 759, 762
Löfstedt, Ernst 1785
Loftus, E. F. 738, 743
Logar, Tine 1815, 1820
Lohman, A. 868, 870
Loi Corvetto, Ines 1214, 1222, 1329, 1377, 1379, 1381, 1382
Løland, Ståle 1025, 1032
Loman, Bengt 992
Lomtatidze, K. V. 1895, 1899
Long, M. H. 289, 290, 291, 294, 515, 516, 517, 518, 522, 523, 524
Looms. P. O. 855, 856, 857
López García, Angel 1277, 1284
López Martínez, M. Sol 1292, 1295
López Muñoz, Daniel 1295
Lopez, C. 897, 901
Lorentz, Friedrich 1602, 1605
Lorentz, Ove 947, 948
Lorenz, E. B. 499, 501
Lorenzo, Ramón 1294, 1317
Lorenzová, Helena 1703, 1707
Lörincze, Lajos 1835
Lorwin, Val 1129
Lothaire (795–855) 1224
Lotko, Edvard 1646, 1649, 1667, 1668, 1669
Lötzsch, Ronald 1768, 1795, 1796, 1957, 1958, 1959, 1960, 1961
Lou, Ch. 104, 109
Louden, M. L. 814, 816, 819
Loughlin, J. 79, 80
Louis le Germanique (817–843) 1224
Louis XIV (1643–1715) 1240
Loulidi, R. 396, 398
Lourie, M. A. 170, 172, 174
Loveday, L. J. 895, 901
Lowenberg, P. H. 912
Lowi, Th. J. 76
Lowry, H. W. 1559, 1565
Lowy, E. G. 724
Lück, H. E. 752, 760
Luckel, Frédéric 1240
Luckmann, Theodor 270, 801, 802, 803, 804
Lucy, J. A. 50, 51, 56, 749
Ludanyi, Andrew 1469
Lüdi, Georges 53, 56, 234, 235, 237, 238, 239, 240, 241, 242, 243, 244, 245, 257, 322, 323, 324, 325, 326, 327, 456, 457, 595, 762, 895, 901, 1185,

1187, 1843, 1845, 1849, 1850, 1851, 1852, 1860, 1862, 1866, 1867, 1869, 1870, 1876, 1878
Lüdtke, Helmut 526, 527, 529, 530, 531, 532, 533, 534, 535, 536, 537, 538, 540, 751, 761, 880, 1218, 1222, 1275, 1284
Lüdtke, Jens 1281, 1282, 1284
Ludwig, O. 833
Lugan, J. C. 893
Luick, Karl 1809, 1812
Lük, Albina 1423
Lukas, J. 217
Lukašanec, A. 1922, 1925
Lummer, H. 180, 191
Lund, J. 1022, 1028, 1031, 1032
Lunden, Sverdrup S. 945, 946, 948
Lundén, Th. 69, 74, 349, 350
Lunt, Horace 929, 1443, 1447, 1449, 1450, 1492, 1495, 1498, 1499, 1501, 1503, 1504
Lurati, Ottavio 396, 398, 1844, 1852, 1871, 1873, 1874, 1875, 1876, 1877, 1878
Lüschen, G. 735, 737
Lüsebrink, Claire 92, 96
Lüsebrink, Hans-Jürgen 91, 97
Luther, Martin (1483−1532) 346
Lutterer, I. 553, 554
Lutz, Florentin 1844, 1852
Lux, Julius 1691
Luyken, Georg-Michael 429, 430
Luyken, Michaela 618, 621, 623
Luzio, A. di 1853, 1854
Lyberg, L. E. 732, 743
Lyngbye, Hans C. 1048
Lynge, Kristoffer 1054
Lyon, D. W. 871
Lyons, John J. 50, 56, 294, 325, 326, 327, 837, 841
Lytkin, V. I. 1895, 1899, 1900

M

Ma, Roxanna 388, 432, 437, 440, 462, 584, 614, 651, 724, 776, 784, 787
Maag, G. 741, 744
Maas, Utz 247, 253, 257, 828, 830, 833
Mabille, X. 403, 404
MacCana, Proinsias 1105, 1106
MacDonald, Donald A. 1095, 1096
MacGrianna, S. 1106
Machado, José Pedro 1317
Machan, T. W. 912
Macht, K. 415, 416, 421
MacIver, D. N. 209
Mack, M. 37, 39
Mackay, John 433, 438

Mackay, Ronald 512, 514
Mackenzie, Frazer 4
Mackey, William F. 3, 10, 15, 68, 69, 75, 82, 83, 89, 124, 217, 271, 272, 274, 275, 276, 277, 278, 279, 280, 281, 282, 283, 381, 382, 384, 385, 391, 392, 398, 401, 404, 463, 464, 465, 472, 481, 492, 548, 635, 641, 700, 703, 708, 798, 804, 844, 845, 852, 1123
MacKinnon, G. E. 38, 633
MacKinnon, Kenneth M. 331, 332, 685, 691, 887, 893, 1065, 1069, 1074, 1091, 1096, 1097, 1987, 1989
Mackridge, Peter 1563, 1565
MacLeod, Iseabail 1095, 1096
Macnamara, John 137, 604, 607, 695, 702
MacNeill, W. 181, 192
MacPherson, J. 582, 584
Macrea, D. 1467, 1469
Mączak, Antoni 1594
Madden, C. 524, 525, 562, 566
Madecka, B. 1665, 1667, 1668
Mäder, Denise 1844, 1847, 1852
Mader, L. 831, 833
Madera, Mónica 175
Madow, W. G. 735, 737
Madray, F. 1187
Maeckelberghe, Frank 1243, 1244, 1251
Mæhlum, Brit 945, 948
Magdu, Lia 1413, 1416
Magenau, Doris 5, 10, 1170, 1172
Magga, O. H. 673, 675
Magkriotis, Jiannis 2032
Magnan, M. 439, 443
Magner, Thomas F. 1648
Magosci, Paul Robert 1493, 1494, 1495, 1974, 1976, 1978, 1979
Mahecha, N. R. 375, 378
Maher, Cindy 495, 500
Maher, Juliane 652, 657
Mahmood, Cynthia 1157
Mahmoud, A. 309
Maidhof, Adam 1532
Maingueneau, D. 406, 413
Mair, Walter N. 1398
Majer, H. G. 1577
Majewicz, Alfred F. 1605
Major, B. 46, 48
Major, R. C. 373, 374, 378
Majtán, Milan 1694, 1695, 1702, 1707
Makkai, László 1708, 1722
Makowski, B. 1615, 1621
Mal, J. 1739, 1743
Malá, Eva 1646, 1649, 1677
Malblanc, A. 146, 152

Maldsis, Adam 1925
Małecki, Antoni 1627, 1632
Małecki, M. 1633, 1634
Malinowski, Arlene 1567, 1568, 1571
Malinowski, B. 25, 26, 31, 750, 762, 921, 930
Malkiel, Y. 714
Malle, Augustin 1810, 1812, 2057
Mallia-Milanes, Victor 1405, 1406
Malý, Karel 1636, 1646, 1649
Mályusz, E. 1486
Mancini, P. S. 156, 160
Mańczak, W. 135, 136, 137
Mandelbaum, D. 725
Mândrescu, Simion C. 1477
Manes, B. 675
Manes, J. 457, 458, 691, 709, 714, 818
Manessy, Gabriel 651, 653, 658
Manessy-Guitton, Jacqueline 54, 56
Manga, János 1745, 1748
Mangion, Giovanni 1401, 1402, 1406
Manherz, Karl 818, 1715, 1722, 1730
Manker, Ernst 1982
Mann, Arne 1675, 1677, 1683
Manoliu-Manea, M. 635, 641
Manousakas, Manousos I. 1524
Manov, Atanas I. 1491, 1495
Mantou, Reine 1243, 1251
Marçais, W. 246, 247, 257
Marcato, Carla 1342, 1343, 1344
Marcellesi, Jean-Baptiste 49, 56, 177, 178, 179, 198, 199, 677, 683, 828, 830, 833, 1173, 1175, 1187, 1209, 1211, 1213, 1220, 1221, 1222, 1259, 2004, 2007
March, J. G. 405, 413
Marchetti, Giuseppe 1342, 1343
Marchetti, L. F. 1218, 1222
Marchetti, Pascal 1207, 1209, 1210, 1212, 1213, 1216, 1217, 1218, 1220, 1222
Marchio, Fernando 1329
Marcinkiewicz, Józef 1622
Marconot, J. L. 676, 680, 683
Marcus, George 760, 761
Marcus, Melvin 74, 75
Mardaga, P. 683
Maretić, Tomo 1433
Maretzky, Th. W. 380, 385
Margaritis, Apostolos 1517, 1524
Margue, Paul 1159, 1172
Marí, Isidor 352, 357, 1297, 1299, 1302
Maria Theresia (1740−1780) 1359, 1472

Markhof, Wolfgang 1191, 1192, 1194
Márkus, G. 1749, 1753
Marleau, L. 430
Mar-Molinero, C. 79, 80, 215, 217
Marouzeau, J. 147, 152
Marques Balsa, Casimiro 1113, 1123
Marriott, H. 14, 21, 835, 841
Marsá, Francisco 1300, 1302
Marsden, P. V. 810, 811
Marsh, David 417, 420
Marsh, Philip 310
Marshall, B. 865, 868, 869, 871
Marshall, D. F. 840, 864
Marshall, M. 651, 655, 658
Marsina, Richard 1671, 1677, 1707
Marteel, Jean-Louis 1119, 1123, 1245, 1251
Martel, Claude 1349
Martens, K. 384
Marti, Roland 1192, 1707, 2049, 2053
Martial (43−104 n. Chr.) 1272
Martin, Harry J. 337, 341
Martin, Helmut 620, 623
Martin, Jean-Baptiste 1335, 1337, 1349
Martin, John 561, 567
Martin, Leonhard 728, 733, 738, 744
Martin, Philip L. 188, 192
Martin, R. 875, 879
Martin-Jones, Marilyn 466, 472, 801, 802, 804, 1067, 1074
Martinet, André 56, 62, 253, 257, 527, 533, 540, 623, 624, 877, 879, 880, 2007
Martínez, Gerard 1297, 1302
Martinez-Brawley, E. 173, 174
Martins, E. 10
Martinsen, H. 375, 378
Martinussen, Bente 947, 948
Márton, Gyula 1464, 1468, 1469, 1485, 1486
Martyniakowa, I. 1621
Maryański, A. 1584, 1585, 1587, 1594
Maryniakowa, Irena 1613
Marzys, Zygmunt 1337, 1867, 1870
Masagara, N. N. 395, 398
Masanao, T. 415, 420
Masayesva, L. 666
Mäsch, N. 293, 294, 471, 472
Masica, C. P. 834, 841
Masiewicz, A. 1182, 1187, 2004, 2007
Mason, D. 209
Massajoli, Pierleone 1347, 1349
Massey, J. T. 732

Mateene, K. 670, 675
Matějová, Vlasta 1642, 1648
Mather, James Y. 1096
Mathesius, V. 3, 10
Mathiot, Madeleine 130, 173, 174, 640
Matissah, S. 1905
Matras, Christian 1045, 1048, 1049
Matsumoto, D. 304, 310
Matsumoto, M. 296, 310
Matteis, Mario de 7
Mattheier, Klaus J. 179, 189, 192, 193, 244, 249, 255, 256, 257, 260, 271, 283, 320, 344, 350, 366, 370, 382, 384, 398, 399, 420, 456, 540, 623, 641, 674, 691, 724, 749, 763, 804, 810, 813, 814, 816, 818, 819, 825, 833, 901, 911, 1405, 1171, 1820, 1870, 1878
Matthias Corvinus (1458−1490) 1802, 1821
Matuszak, Hans 1787, 1789, 1790
Matzel, Klaus 1352, 1353, 1356
Matzen, Raymond 1239, 1240, 2006
Maurais, Jean 74, 210, 217, 352, 357, 439, 442, 444, 830, 832, 878, 1284, 1309
Maurel, B. 658
Maurenbrecher, Th. 192, 453, 457
Mauri, Marco 1328, 1329
Mauviel, M. 789, 796
Mavrogordatos, George Th. 1547, 1550
Mayer, H. 881, 885, 886
Mayer, K. 775, 776
Mayer, P. 805, 811
Mayer, T. 185, 191
Mayer-Kress, G. 533, 540
Mayntz, R. 738, 743
Mayo, E. 405, 413
Mayr, G. von 734, 737
Mayrhofer, M. 882, 886
Mazrui, A. A. 911, 912
Mazúr, Emil 1697, 1701
Mazur, Jan 1627
Mazzini, Giuseppe (1805−1872) 1319
Mazzon, Gabriella 1400, 1401, 1402, 1406
Mbangwana, P. 462, 464
Mc Harris, D. 721, 723, 725
McArthur, Tom 1094, 1095, 1096
McCagg, William O. Jr. 1577
McCall, G. J. 44, 48
McCarthy, Justin 1554, 1559, 1565
McClosky, H. 236, 244

McClure, E. 596, 599, 603, 607, 666
McClure, J. Derrick R. 1095, 1096
McConnell, Grant D. 69, 73, 74, 275, 277, 281, 282, 283, 636, 641
McConwell, P. 574, 578
McCormack, W. C. 10
McDermott, J. F. 380, 385
McDonald, Maryon 203, 205, 209, 387, 391, 598, 607, 1260
McEntegart, D. 784, 785, 787
McGee, R. 363
McGilly, C. 481
McGinnies, E. 700
McGroarty, Mary E. 870, 871
McIntosh, A. 148, 152
McKenzie, D. 451, 457
McKinnon, K. 802, 804
McKirnan, D. J. 48
McLaughlin, A. 628, 634
McLaughlin, B. 6, 7, 10, 32, 40, 85, 86, 89, 292, 293, 294, 465, 472, 485, 486, 492, 515, 516, 517, 518, 525
McLaughlin, M. L. 48, 341, 438
McNeill, D. 285, 294
McRae, Kenneth D. 8, 10, 64, 74, 75, 76, 80, 210, 211, 215, 218, 361, 363, 396, 398, 399, 400, 401, 402, 403, 404, 827, 833, 1014, 1114, 1116, 1117, 1119, 1123, 1838, 1839, 1840, 1846, 1847, 1849, 1852
McWhinney, B. 289, 294
Mežgailis, Bruno 1906, 1912
Mežs, Ilmars 2065
Meade, R. D. 39
Meadows, M. 428, 430
Mecheln, R. D. 691
Mechoulam, David 1568, 1569, 1571
Međeši, Helena 1411, 1416
Medicine, B. 722, 724
Meert, Hypoliet 1128, 1129
Meeus, Boudewijn 257, 1112, 1123
Meeuwis, M. 141, 143, 144
Meid, Wolfgang 1397, 1398
Meier, V. 181, 192
Meillet, Antoine 2, 9, 654, 658
Meinardus, Roland 1562, 1565, 2033
Meinefeld, W. 693, 702
Meisel, Jürgen M. 291, 294, 295, 321, 327, 522, 523, 524, 603, 607
Meissner, B. 1469
Meissner, D. M. 188, 192
Melamid, A. 1582
Melich, János 1737, 1743
Melis, Guido 1376, 1380, 1382

Melis, Ludo 177, 180
Melotti, Umberto 1329
Mendelsohn, S. 61, 62
Mendes da Luz, Maria Albertina 1285
Menéndez Pidal, Ramón 1272, 1273, 1275, 1284, 2013, 2014
Menis, Gian Carlo 1338, 1343
Menn, L. 116
Mennonite Encyclopedia 319
Meny, I. 1381
Méo, G. di 181, 192
Meraner, Rudolf 1355, 1356
Mercier, P. 49, 51, 56
Mercurio Gregorini, Rimedia 1379, 1382
Merk, V. 417, 420
Merkelbach, V. 270
Merkens, H. 759, 760, 762
Mermet, Gérard 1317
Merrifield, D. F. 512, 514
Merritt, R. L. 426, 438
Mertz, E. 574, 578, 589, 593, 749
Mesmer, B. 1850
Messing, E. E. L. 416, 420
Messner, Dieter 1313, 1315, 1317, 1397, 1398
Met, M. 499, 501
Métral, Jean-Pierre 167, 168, 1852
Mětšk, Frido 1791, 1796, 1797
Metternich, Wenzel Fürst (1773–1859) 358
Metzeltin, Michael 179, 244, 257, 326, 556, 558, 623, 624, 642, 879, 880, 1193, 1194, 1221, 1222, 1284, 1295, 1317, 1329, 1343, 1381, 1382, 1383, 1397, 1398, 1406, 1469, 1470, 1886, 2007, 2014, 2019
Mey, J. L. 831, 833
Meyer, Gustav 1522, 1524, 1531, 1532
Meyer, Kurt 1843, 1852, 1859, 1862
Meyerhoff, M. 336, 341
Meyer-Lübke, Wilhelm 1269, 1370, 1377, 1382
Meyer-Sabino, Giovanna 1849, 1852
Meyn, M. 186, 192
Meynen, E. 1974, 1976, 1978, 1979
Michael, Jan 1284
Michaels, E. 428, 430
Michailidis, Evangelos 1524
Michal'čenko, V. J. 1900
Michałk, Frido 1797
Michalk, Siegfried 1793, 1795, 1796, 1797
Michel, G. 147, 149, 152
Michelena, Luis 1308, 1309

Mićović, Veljko 1410, 1416
Miemois, Karl-Johan 1014
Mifsud, Manwel 1405
Migliorini, Bruno 1222
Mijavec, Marija 1412, 1416
Mikes, Melanie 485, 492, 1411, 1415, 1416, 1423
Miklosich, Franz 1522, 1524, 1737, 1738, 1962, 1964, 1965, 1970, 1971
Milán, W. G. 724
Milardo, R. M. 806, 811
Miles, R. 672, 675
Milgrim, N. 842
Milian i Massana, Antoni 357
Miljan, Toivo 1014
Miller, Casey 245
Miller, Christopher 119, 124, 599, 602, 779, 786, 787
Miller, Danny 405, 410, 413
Miller, Davis 202
Miller, Herman 405
Miller, J. L. 604, 605
Miller, Roy Andrew 615, 623
Millon, G. 394, 398
Milović, J. M. 1416
Milroy, James 586, 593, 597, 608, 710, 807, 808, 809, 1060, 1074
Milroy, Lesley 16, 21, 123, 170, 173, 174, 238, 244, 322, 327, 576, 578, 586, 593, 595, 597, 605, 607, 608, 710, 807, 808, 809, 811, 893
Minikowska, Teresa 1627
Minova-G'urkova, Liljana 1497
Minssen, Johann Friedrich F. 1787, 1789, 1790
Mintzberg, H. 408, 409, 413
Mioni, Alberto M. 798, 801, 804, 1355, 1357, 1877, 1878
Miranda, R. V. 394, 397, 398
Mirčev, Dimitar 1444, 1450
Mirčev, Kiril 1507, 1510, 1512, 1514
Miron, Paul 1470
Mishler, E. G. 745, 746, 749
Misirkov, Krste P. 1497, 1499, 1504
Mislovičová, Sibyla 1695
Mistrúk, J. 1633
Mitchell, Ch. 867, 871
Mitchell, J.C. 805, 806, 807, 809, 810, 811
Mitchell, T. F. 399
Mithun, M. 663, 666
Mitkos, Evthymios 1522, 1524
Mitten, R. 712, 713, 714
Mittner, M. 56
Mitzka, Walter 1598, 1599, 1600
Mixnevič, A. 1922, 1924, 1925, 1926
Mladenov, Maksim S. 1495, 1497, 1500, 1504, 1549, 1550

Moahanty, A. K. 40
Moberg, Lena 976
Möcker, Hermann 1808, 1809, 1812
Modeen, Tore 1014
Modiano, N. 484, 487, 492
Modinas, Polys 1582
Moelleken, Melita A. 768, 769, 770
Moelleken, Wolfgang W. 393, 395, 396, 399, 768, 769, 770
Moermann, M. 925, 930
Moffatt, S. 811
Moguš, Milan 1433
Mohanty, A. K. 35, 36, 40
Möhn, D. 511, 512, 513, 514
Mojžišová, I. 1707
Mokuter, Iván 1737, 1738
Molbæk Hansen, Peter 1023, 1032
Molde, Bert 1981
Moldenhawer, Bolette 1032
Molenaar, N. J. 740, 743
Moll, Francese de Borja 1300, 1302
Mollay, Károly 1724, 1730
Mollov, Riza 1508, 1509, 1510
Mollova, Mefküre 1507, 1508, 1509, 1510
Molnár, Zoltán Miklós 1742, 1743
Molony, C. 11
Monaco, R. 358, 363
Mondéjar, José 1275, 1283, 1284
Monteagudo Romero, Henrique 1280, 1284, 1285, 1286, 1289, 1293, 1294, 1295
Monteil, V. 618, 623
Montes Giraldo, J. J. 639, 641
Montgomery, Michael 1095, 1096
Monti Civelli, E. 81, 405
Montoya, B. 1300, 1301, 1302
Moorcroft, R. 582, 585
Moore, N. 132, 137
Morais, J. 130
Morales, Francisco 1277, 1284
Moreau de Saint-Méry, F.-L.-E. 658
Morgan, Adam J. 731, 732
Morgan, J. 143, 420
Morgan, Raleigh J. 655, 658
Morgana, Silvia 1339, 1342, 1343
Moriani, Roberto 1347, 1349
Morin, Estelle 351, 357
Morin, Françoise 413
Morison, S. 479, 481
Morlang, W. 1849
Mörner, M. 186, 191
Morokvašić, M. 2006, 2007
Morosi, Giuseppe 1344, 1348, 1349, 1370, 1371, 1380, 1382

Morottaja, Matti 1019
Morris, Ch. 139, 140, 144
Morris, D. 296, 310
Morrison, F. 498, 501
Mosel, U. 646, 648
Moseley, Christopher 75, 1974, 1976, 1978, 1979
Moser, Ch. A. 726, 732
Moser, Hans 1355, 1357
Moser, Hugo 874, 877, 879, 1661, 1691
Moser, Virgil 1691
Moskos, Ch. 1524
Mosnikoff, Jouni 1019
Mosteller, F. 733, 734, 737
Mot, Ludo de 856, 857
Mougeon, Raymond 373, 374, 377, 378, 386, 391, 591, 593, 765, 770, 786, 787
Mounin, G. 50, 56
Moura Santos, Maria José de 1314, 1317
Moureau-Martini, U. 420
Mow International Research Team 414
Mowrer, O. H. 288, 295
Moyer, M. 598, 608
Moynihan, D. P. 189, 191, 208, 209
Mpiris, Kostas 1524
Mpogkas, Evangelos 1524
Mufwene, S. 608, 654, 658
Mühlhäusler, Peter 113, 116, 117, 235, 239, 244, 292, 295, 571, 578, 642, 643, 645, 647, 648, 649, 650, 652, 653, 654, 658, 670, 675, 790, 889, 893, 895, 901, 923, 930
Mujika Urdangarin, Luis-Maria 1269
Mukicsné Kozár, Mária 1743
Mulac, A. 48, 334, 341
Mulder, J. 763
Muljačić, Žarko 635, 636, 637, 638, 639, 641, 642, 894, 901, 1211, 1213, 1222, 1366, 1398
Mullard, Ch. 672, 675
Müller, Bernd-Dietrich 420, 930
Müller, Bodo 873, 875, 879, 1336, 1337
Muller, Germain 1235
Müller, Hans-Peter 1837, 1839, 1840, 1852
Müller, Klaus E. 222, 233
Müller, Kurt E. 401, 404
Müller, Myriam 1850
Müller, N. 10, 289, 295
Müller, W. C. 152
Müller, Wulf 878
Müllerová, Olga 1654, 1655, 1704, 1707
Müllner, E. 1835
Municio, Ingegerd 992

Munske, Horst Haider 262, 271, 1785
Münstermann, Henk 1150, 1151
Muntaner, R. 555, 558
Munteanu, Romul 1471, 1475, 1477
Muntzel, M. 659, 660, 661, 662, 666
Münz, Rainer 1807, 1811, 1827, 1830, 1832, 1833, 1835
Münzel, Mark 1963, 1965, 1971
Murchison, C. 700
Murdock, G. 51, 56
Murphy, A. B. 69, 75, 79, 401, 404
Murphy, Richard A. 1556, 1559, 1562, 1563, 1565, 1568, 1571, 1573, 1574, 1577
Murphy, Tim 1868, 1870
Murray, James A. H. 1089, 1096
Murrell, M. 7, 10
Murru Corriga, Giannetta 1380, 1382
Musa, M. 429, 430, 838, 841
Muschinsky, Lars J. 1032
Muskens, George 1899
Mussafia, Adolfo 1349
Mussolini, Benito (1883–1945) 1202, 1399
Muylaert, W. 429, 430
Muysken, Pieter 8, 112, 115, 116, 117, 119, 123, 124, 131, 136, 137, 138, 574, 576, 586, 592, 595, 599, 600, 605, 606, 607, 608, 658, 755, 760, 786, 787, 836, 840, 1151
Myers-Scotton, C. (→ Scotton, C. M.) 6, 10, 13, 21, 115, 117, 118, 119, 123, 142, 144, 240, 242, 243, 244, 322, 327, 595, 599, 600, 601, 602, 603, 604, 605, 695, 702, 801, 802, 804
Myhill, J. 810
Mylonas, George E. 1551, 1554
Mytton, G. 426, 430

N

Nadai, Eva 1851
Nader, L. 695, 702
Nadkarni, M. V. 122, 123
Nagel, J. 404
Nagy, Zsuzsa 1712, 1722
Nail, N. 270
Nairn, T. 76, 77, 80
Nalepa, Jan 1608, 1613
Nalepa, Jerzy 1620, 1622, 1627
Nam, Ch. B. 188, 192
Namier, L. B. 903, 906
Nandris, O. 619, 623
Naotsuka, R. 930
Napoleon, Bonaparte (1769–1821) 1399

Nas, G. L. J. 131, 137
Nash, M. 203, 209
Nash-Webber, B. 129
Natale, M. 334, 341
Natchev, Eija 992
Naulko, V. 1932
Navaza Blanco, Gonzalo 1293, 1295
Nay, Giusep 1852
Naylor, Kenneth E. 1446, 1450
Nazzi, Gianni 1342, 1343
Nebel, Jeanne J. 1471, 1477
Nećak Lük, Albina (→ Lük, Albina) 1423, 1424
Nedjatigil, Zaim M. 1582
Neill, Deborah 14, 20, 452, 456
Neisser, U. 582, 585
Nekvapil, Jiři 1647, 1648, 1649, 1655, 1678
Nelde, Peter Hans 5, 8, 10, 11, 12, 13, 16, 17, 18, 21, 39, 64, 69, 74, 75, 79, 80, 96, 213, 218, 239, 244, 257, 271, 283, 295, 299, 310, 350, 363, 368, 369, 370, 384, 385, 391, 398, 399, 404, 425, 430, 452, 456, 457, 458, 464, 507, 546, 548, 611, 624, 642, 691, 702, 750, 755, 761, 762, 763, 764, 770, 776, 787, 788, 790, 796, 827, 833, 836, 841, 852, 857, 924, 930, 931, 936, 1122, 1123, 1130, 1133, 1134, 1135, 1136, 1141, 1142, 1143, 1316, 1382, 1396, 1469, 1477, 1539, 1715, 1722, 1725, 1730, 1768, 1777, 1850, 1851, 1852, 1853, 1878, 1879, 1886, 1995, 2033
Nelli, René 1189, 1194
Nelson, C. 909, 910, 912
Nelson, J. 172, 175
Nelson, K. E. 39
Nelson. L. D. 35, 39
Nemcová, Emília 1653, 1655
Németh, György 1506, 1507, 1508, 1509, 1510
Nemser, W. 292, 295, 515, 520, 525
Neönipapa, W. H. 450
Neri, Pierino 1363, 1364, 1366
Nesheim, A. 944, 947, 948
Nesi, Annalisa 1214, 1215, 1220, 1221, 1222
Nesterova, Svetlana L. 1932
Nestorescu, Virgil 1491, 1494, 1495, 1496
Neto, Serafin da Silva 617, 624
Neubert, Albrecht 918, 920
Neumann, I. 655, 658
Neureiter, Ferdinand 1603, 1605
Neustupný, J. V. 14, 15, 21, 300, 305, 310, 834, 835, 841, 1647, 1648, 1649

Newbrook, M. 486, 492
Neweklowsky, Gerhard 1416, 1810, 1812, 1817, 1818, 1819, 1820, 1821, 1825, 1826, 1827, 2057
Newman, S. 77, 78, 80
Newmark, E. 928
Newmeyer, F. 116, 137, 592, 810, 811
Newton, Brian 1512, 1514, 1564, 1565
Ney, Karin 1474, 1476, 1477
Ngugi-wa Thiong'o 675, 908, 909, 911, 912
Nicholls II, W. L. 732
Nichols, P. C. 376, 378, 403
Nickel, G. 11, 512, 514
Nickel, Klaus P. 1019
Nickelsen, Hans-Christian 1778, 1779, 1781
Nicolae, Octavian 1476, 1477
Nicolaisen, Wilhelm F. H. 550, 554
Niculescu, Alexandre 718, 719, 720, 1460, 1469
Nida, E. A. 915, 920
Niebaum, Hermann 1886
Niederhauser, Jürg 419, 420, 1854
Niedzielski, Henry Z. 376, 378, 571, 578
Niedzielski, Nancy 342, 336, 341
Niehaus-Lohberg, E. 417, 418, 420
Nielsen, Frederik 203, 206, 209, 1054
Nielsen, Konrad 981
Nielsen, Niels A. 1784, 1785
Niemann, M. 751, 763
Niemi, Einar 961, 962, 964, 965, 966, 1982
Nierenberg, G. I. 420
Nikolaev, Rada 1490, 1491, 1492, 1493, 1496, 1502, 1504
Nikolajev, Michail N. 1932
Nikol'skij, L. B. 640, 642
Nikov, Peter 1511, 1514
Ninio, A. 629, 634
Ninyoles, Rafael Lluis 238, 239, 244, 250, 251, 257, 802, 803, 804, 1191, 1195
Nishisato, S. 780, 787
Nissen, Hans J. 1040, 1041
Nitsch, Kazimierz 1594, 1602, 1627, 1632, 1633, 1634, 1667, 1668
Nixdorff, H. 755, 763
Niyi, Ajirotutu 142, 143
Noble, Gres 88
Noblit, George W. 757, 763
Noël, D. 679, 684
Noelle-Neumann, Elisabeth 727, 732, 738, 740, 743, 744

Noels, K. A. 44, 46, 48
Noia Campos, M. Camino 1294, 1295
Noin, D. 2007
Noor Al-Deen, H. 437
Nootens, Johan 430, 431, 432
Noppeney, Marcel 1170, 1172
Nord, Ch. 385, 386, 405, 409, 410, 412, 460, 462, 464
Nordberg, Bengt 976
Nordeng, H. 375, 378
Nordenstam, N. 338, 341
Norman, Marjatta 963, 964, 965, 966
Noro, H. 384, 452, 457
North, B. 506, 507
Nortier, J. 574, 578, 595, 600, 603, 608
Nothnagel, D. 419
Nourney, M. 735, 737
Novák, Ľudovít 1693, 1694, 1705, 1707
Novak, M. 1701
Novak Lukanovič, Sonja 1423
Nowusch, Hans 1795, 1797
Noyau, C. 521, 524
Nuijtens, Emiel 1149, 1151
Nunan, D. 525
Nunberg, G. 403, 404
Nuolijärvi, Pirkko 1007
Nurmio, Yrjö 1007
Nussbaum, H. 295
Nyberg, Magda 1785, 1786
Nyomárkay, István 1736, 1737, 1738, 1748

O

Ó Baoill, Dónall 1106
Ó Cuív, B. 708
Ó Danachair, C. 707, 708
Ó Gadhra, N. 78, 80
Ó Gliasáin, Micheál 1106
Ó Muirithe, Diarmaid 1106
Ó Murchú, M. 1106
Ó Riagáin, Pádraig 1106
Oakes, P. J. 48
Oaklely, A. 749
Oakley, Stewart 1022, 1032
O'Barr, W. M. 76, 80
Obidinski, E. E. 209
Obler, Jean 77, 80
Obler, L. K. 15, 20, 37, 40, 87, 88, 116, 236, 243, 244, 295, 369, 375, 378, 585, 604, 605, 607, 608
Obrębska-Jabłońska, Antonina 1613, 1627
Obura, Anna P. 484, 492
Ochoa, E. M. 1303, 1309
Ochs, E. 143, 144, 714, 755, 763
Ockers, Luc 429, 431

Očovský, Štefan 1670, 1677, 1679, 1684
Odaloš, P. 1678, 1707
Odili, Herzog 1798
Odlin, T. 521, 525
Odysseus 180
Oesch-Serra, Cecielia 1850
Oeter, St. 360, 363
Ogata, S. 188, 192
Ogbu, J. U. 476, 480, 481
Ogden, Ph. E. 834, 841, 2006, 2007
Ohama, R. 927, 930
Ohlsson, Stig Örjan 1025, 1032
Öhmann, Emil 4, 10
Ohr, Charles W. J. 1582
Okáliová, Dana 1675, 1677
Okoh, N. 35, 40
Oksaar, Els 3, 4, 5, 6, 7, 10, 11, 12, 14, 21, 22, 234, 244, 257, 325, 327, 364, 366, 367, 369, 370, 423, 426, 466, 473, 501, 507, 759, 763, 925, 930, 1853, 1886
Okuka, Milos 1410, 1416
Olesky, W. 14, 22
Olivesi, Claude 203
Olivieria, Omar S. 432, 437
Oller, D. K. 33, 38
Oller, J. M. 507, 563, 564, 566
Olmi, Massimo 1326, 1328, 1329
Olsen, C. Chr. 346, 350
Olshtain, E. 143, 375, 378, 582, 585
Olson, D. R. 631, 634
Olson, J. 74, 75
Olsson, G. 73, 75
Olzack, S. 209
Omar, Adrian 309
Omar, Asmah Haji 395, 399, 896, 901
Omari, Anila 1414, 1416
Ondrejovič, Slavo 1649, 1653, 1655, 1673, 1677, 1678, 1695
Ondrus, Pavel 1748
Oñederra, M. L. 1268
O'Neil, W. A. 548
Ong, W. 711, 714
Onu, L. 619, 624
Oomen, T. K. 209
Oprea, Ioan 1472, 1477
Orioles, Vincenzo 1343
Orjala, P. 656, 658
Orletti, F. 1327, 1329
Orlov, A. V. 1932
Ormeling, Ferdinand Jan 66, 67, 75, 450, 1974, 1976, 1978, 1979
Ornstein, Jacob 548, 609, 700
Orožen, Martina 1423
Orr, E. W. 711, 714
Ortmanns, K. P. 5, 11
Ortseifen, K. 319

Osa, E. 1307, 1309
Osgood, Charles E. 37, 38, 124, 129, 132, 235, 243, 432, 437, 692, 698, 702
O'Shaughnessy, M. 310
Osherson, D. 606, 609
Osman, M. M. 233
Osswald, Sylvia E. 1883, 1886
Østberg, Kristian 961, 966
O'Sullivan, P. 188, 192
Otanes, F. 900
Otheguy, R. 457
Otrębski, Jan 1619, 1620, 1621
Ott, K. A. 874, 879
Ott, W. 737, 743
Ottokar II. Přemysl (1252−1278) 1798
Ottósson, Kjartan G. 1056, 1058
Ouane, A. 691
Oud-de Glas, M. 857
Overbeke, Maurits van 11
Oyama, S. 291, 295
Ozamiz, J. A. 1309
Ozouf, J. 274, 282

P

Pabst, Klaus 1131, 1133, 1134, 1136, 1137, 1143, 1761, 1768
Pache, Véronique 1852
Pachner, Franz 1807, 1811
Pactwa, B. 1594
Padilla, A. M. 33, 34, 35, 38, 39, 40
Padilla, K. A. 603, 606
Padilla, R. V. 492, 501
Paech, N. 184, 192
Paganelli, J. 1219, 1222
Paget, John 1711, 1723
Paikert, G. C. 1709, 1712, 1721, 1723
Pais, J. 1382
Paivio, A. 38, 40, 132, 138
Pala, Pietro 1376, 1382
Paladin, Livio 1359, 1362
Palatin, Jandre 1827
Palešutski, Kastadin 1497
Palkovits, Elisabeth 1826, 1827
Palkovits, F. 1827
Päll, E. N. 1889, 1900
Palla, Luciana 1398
Pallas, Ladislav 1648, 1649, 1667, 1668
Pallis, A. Alexandros 1560, 1565
Palmeira, W. 499, 501
Palmer, J. D. 512, 514
Palmer, M. T. 437
Palomba, G. 1380, 1382
Pálsson, G. 1056, 1058
Pálsson, Heimir 1057, 1058
Pamp, Bengt 976
Pan, B. 582, 585
Pan, Ch. 217, 352, 356
Paňkevyč, Ivan 1699, 1701
Paňko, Jurij 1697, 1701
Pandit, I. 608
Pandit, P. P. 395, 397, 399
Paneth, Ph. 903, 906
Panier, R. 2003, 2007
Pankraz, F. 1862
Panoff, F. 796
Panoff, M. 789, 792, 796
Panzer, Baldur 2038, 2053
Paoli, M. 641
Paoli, Pasquale (Pascal) (1725−1807) 1202
Pap, Leo 1315, 1317
Papademetriou, D. G. 188, 192
Papadhopoulos, Anthymos 1532, 1550
Papadrianos, Ioannis A. 1524
Papahagi, Tache 1538, 1539
Papaioannou, Ioannis 1582
Papaloizos, Lilli 1843, 1850, 1852
Papazeses, Demetrios T. 1539
Pappageotes, G. C. 1514
Papsonová, M. 1685, 1689, 1691
Paracelsus 2
Paradis, Michel 7, 11, 40, 59, 60, 62, 132, 138, 236, 237, 245, 604, 608
Parajuli, P. 279, 283
Parasher, S. V. 689, 691
Parasnis, I. 39
Paredes, A. 747, 749, 789, 790, 792, 796, 1543
Paredis, M. 391
Park, R. E. 451, 457
Parker, Timothy Scott 1780, 1781
Parlangèli, Oronzo 1368, 1370, 1371
Parodi, T. 291, 295
Parovel, Paolo 1360, 1362
Parry-Williams, Thomas H. 1096
Parsons, T. 29, 31
Pascasio, E. M. 899, 901
Paschinger, Viktor 1813, 1820
Pascu, George 1522, 1524
Pascu, Štefan 1479, 1486
Passel, J. 867, 870
Pastor, P. 1722
Patella, V. 722, 725
Paterson, H. O. 209
Patráš, V. 1678, 1707
Patrick, Richard A. 1582
Patry, J.-L. 751, 763
Pattanayak, D. P. 40, 74, 79, 80, 215, 217, 218, 488, 492, 670, 671, 675
Patterson, James G. 1715, 1718, 1721, 1723, 1751, 1753
Pattnaik, K. 35, 40
Pauchant, T. C. 413
Paufler, Hans-Diether 1317
Pauković, Vladimir 1672, 1676, 1677, 1678, 1680, 1684
Paul, D. N. 790, 793, 796
Paul, Hermann 2, 3, 11, 529, 534, 540, 1790
Paul, R. 1730
Pauliny, Eugen 1701, 1707
Paulston, Christina 8, 11, 78, 80, 88, 89, 483, 484, 485, 491, 492, 575, 578, 580, 585, 630, 631, 634, 1649, 1851
Paunonen, Heikki 1007, 1008, 1013
Pauseback, Paul-Heinz 1782, 1786
Pautasso, Mariella 1326, 1329
Pauwels, Anne 238, 245, 453, 457, 721, 722, 723, 725, 816, 817, 819
Pável, A. 1741, 1743
Pavlík, Emil 1692, 1694
Pavlovitch, M. 6, 11
Pawłowski, Eugeniusz 1633
Pawley, A. 126, 127
Payne, A. 338, 341
Payne, St. 740, 743
Payrató, Lluís 141, 143, 1300, 1301, 1302
Peal, E. 34, 40, 291, 295, 367, 370, 608
Peciar, Štefan 1690, 1691, 1707
Peckham, Don 1649
Pedersen, Holger 541, 548, 1574, 1577
Pedersen, Karen M. 761, 1041, 1042, 1777, 1784, 1786
Pedersen, P. 929
Pée, Willem 1242, 1244, 1250, 1251, 1252
Peeters, Constant H. 1128, 1129
Peeters, Yvo J. D. 64, 73, 75, 361, 363, 1582, 1974, 1976, 1978, 1979
Pehrsen, Robert 981
Peitgen, H.-O. 229, 233
Pelcowa, Halina 1627, 1628
Pelka, R. 512, 514
Pellegrini, Giovan Battista 1328, 1329, 1362, 1370, 1388, 1391, 1397, 1398
Peltz, R. 377, 378
Pendovski, Branko 1503
Penfield, J. 725
Penfield, W. P. 37, 40, 365, 370, 604, 608
Penn, William 313, 315
Penny, R. 548
Pennycook, A. 911, 912
Péntek, János 1464, 1468, 1469, 1485, 1486
Pentzopoulos, Dimitri 1516, 1524

Perdue, Clive 241, 245, 321, 326, 327, 372, 378, 521, 524, 525, 1150, 1151
Perecman, E. 375, 378, 608
Pergola, S. della 2004, 2006
Périgaud, J. 388, 391
Perini, Nereo 1328, 1330, 1343, 1344
Pernot, Hubert 1370, 1371
Pernstich, Karin 1355, 1357
Peroche, Gregory 1434, 1442
Péronnet, L. 785, 787
Perrenoud, Ph. 876, 880
Perron, Piero 1347, 1349
Perrow, Ch. 405, 414
Perry, Duncan M. 1454, 1458
Persoons, Yves 452, 456, 695, 698, 702
Petek-Salom, G. 1183, 1187
Peterlini, Oskar 1354, 1357
Peters, B. G. 868, 871
Petersen, Robert 1052, 1054
Petersen, U. 539
Petit, Jean 1228, 1237, 1239, 1240
Petr, J. 1633
Petralli, Alessio 1877, 1878
Petrov, Petur 1496
Petrović, Dragoljub 1433
Petrović, Ruža 1445, 1450
Petrovic, R. 381, 384
Petrovici, Emil 1468, 1469
Pettifer, James 1453, 1458
Peura, Markku 673, 675, 992
Peuser, G. 514
Peyfuss, Max Demeter 1524, 1533, 1534, 1536, 1539, 1974, 1976, 1978
Peytard, J. 676, 680, 681, 683, 684
Pfaff, Carol W. 7, 11, 373, 378, 453, 457, 521, 525, 595, 599, 603, 604, 608, 609
Pfeiffer, K. L. 4, 97
Pfeiffer, Waldemar 513, 514, 853, 857
Pfister, Charles 1233, 1240
Pfleger, M. 867, 871
Philipp, Marthe 1239, 1240, 2006
Philippe d'Iribarne 412
Philippe, B. 885, 886
Philippe, C. 388, 391
Philipps, Eugène 1235, 1240
Philips, S. U. 607, 724
Philipsen, G. 789, 796
Phillips, D. L. 737, 743
Phillipson, Robert 19, 22, 217, 280, 283, 428, 431, 464, 489, 492, 667, 670, 673, 674, 675, 685, 691, 839, 841, 908, 910, 911, 912, 1031, 1032
Phlipponeau, C. 787

Photiadis, Kostas 1525, 1532
Piazza, A. 223, 232
Pic, François 1195
Picchio, R. 894, 901
Pick, H. L. 333, 341
Pickles, J. 72, 75
Pidoux, Edmond 1843, 1852
Pienemann, M. 294, 522, 523, 524, 525
Pieper, A. 820, 825
Pierson, N. 433, 437
Pietro di, Robert J. 11
Pietro, J.-F. de 241, 243
Piette, B. 354, 356, 380, 384
Piette, Jean R. F. 1096
Piirainen, I. T. 1690, 1691
Pilch, Herbert 11
Pimpaneau, J. 620, 624
Pineda, P. B. P. 898, 899, 901
Pinto, Vivian 1494, 1496
Pirak, Anita 981
Piromalli, Antonio 1328, 1330
Pisani, Vittorio 2, 1349
Pisárčiková, Mária 1707
Pisowicz, A. 1575, 1576, 1577
Pittau, Massimo 1377, 1379, 1382
Pivetta, Marie-Louise 1119, 1123
Pižurica, Mato 1414, 1416
Pizzorusso, Alessandro 1328, 1330
Plangg, Guntram A. 1397, 1398
Plank, Pieter van der 1157
Planta, Robert von 1886
Platiel, S. 1181, 1187
Plato 1, 407
Platt, J. T. 19, 22, 457, 908, 909, 912
Pleines, J. 189, 192
Plesník, P. 1701
Pletschette, Nikolas 1170, 1172
Plichtová, Jana 675, 1673, 1677, 1678, 1684
Pline le Jeune (62–113) 273
Pluka, M. 1442
Plusser, F. 1655
Pniewski, W. 1599, 1600
Poche, Bernard 1121, 1123
Poel, Kris van de 379
Poesmans, D. 430
Poghirc, Cicerone 1576, 1577
Pogorelec, Breda 1423
Pohl, Heinz Dieter 1798, 1799, 1810, 1812, 1815, 1816, 1817, 1819, 1820, 2023, 2057
Pohl, Jacques 1115, 1123, 1125, 1129
Pointner, H. 181, 191
Poirier, J. 50, 56, 385, 391
Pokorny, Jules 2
Pokrovskaja, L. A. 1938, 1941
Polakovič, St. 159, 160
Polenz, Peter von 872, 874, 877, 879, 1768, 1785, 1796, 1797

Polich, E. 495, 500
Polivanov, E. 13, 22
Pollak, Wolfgang 1809, 1812
Polome, Edgar C. 379, 534, 540
Pong, S. 597, 607
Pönisch, H. 419
Pons, Teofilo 1347, 1349
Pons-Ridler, S. 218
Ponty, J. 1182, 1185, 1187, 2004, 2007
Pool, J. 64, 76, 78, 80, 399, 400, 401, 404, 405
Popescu, Ivan 1932
Poplack, Shana 13, 22, 113, 115, 117, 118, 119, 123, 124, 125, 130, 141, 144, 242, 245, 373, 378, 455, 457, 546, 548, 595, 598, 599, 601, 602, 603, 608, 609, 779, 780, 784, 786, 787
Poplin, D. 169, 175
Popović, Ivan 1414, 1415, 1416, 1737, 1738, 1739, 1743, 2023
Popovic, Zvonimir 992
Popovski, T. 1546, 1547, 1550, 1454, 1458
Popowska-Taborska, Hanna 1600, 1602, 1605, 2038
Popp, H. 192
Porru, Vissentu 1378, 1382
Porst, Rolf 739, 742, 743, 744
Porter, R. E. 298, 305, 309, 310, 311
Porter, R. P. 477, 478, 481
Portes, A. 869, 871
Posner, Rebecca 611, 624, 641, 1284, 1285, 1295, 1381, 1382
Posner, Roland 15, 22
Posthumus, R. R. 1787, 1790
Pot, I. 1734, 1738
Pott, August Friedrich (1802–1887) 1970, 1971
Potter, J. 138, 144
Pottier, B. 2003, 2004, 2007
Potts, L. 188, 192
Poulet, Denise 1243, 1246, 1247, 1248, 1249, 1250, 1251
Poulisse, N. 6, 11
Poulsen, Jóhan H. W. 346, 350, 1047, 1048
Poulton, Hugh 1453, 1454, 1456, 1458, 1493, 1494, 1496, 1500, 1501, 1504, 1550
Povejšil, Jaromir 1645, 1649, 1656, 1658, 1661, 1662
Powdermaker, H. 751, 763
Powell, I. V. 647, 648, 665, 666
Powesland, P. F. 42, 48, 334, 337, 340, 576, 577
Poyart, N. 1126, 1129
Poyatos, F. 296, 297, 301, 310, 311, 549
Poynting, S. 88
Pranjić, K. 1433

Pratkanis, R. 700
Pred, A. 73, 75
Pree, M. de 405, 408, 413
Preiswerk, R. 675
Prešov, Mária Papsonová 1691
Press, V. 187, 192
Pressat, R. 773, 776
Presser, St. 695, 697, 702, 729, 732, 738, 739, 740, 741, 743, 744
Preston, D. R. 171, 174, 175, 333, 335, 337, 341, 522, 525, 801, 804
Preston, M. S. 37, 40
Pribichevich, Stoyan 1504
Price, G. 718, 720
Prickler, Harald 1821, 1827
Pride, J. 19, 21, 22
Primo de Rivera, Miguel (1870−1930) 1297
Prinz, Jürgen 1620, 1621
Priscian (ca. 500−550 n. Chr.) 1
Procacci, Giuliano 1319, 1330
Prode, J. B. 310
Profili, Olga 1328, 1330, 1370, 1371, 2018, 2019
Prosser, M. H. 925, 930
Protze, Helmut 1795, 1797
Prudent, L. F. 246, 253, 257, 652, 658
Prunč, Erich 1810, 1811, 1818, 1819, 1820
Pryce, W. T. R. 1061, 1074, 1075, 1078, 1087
Przychodzeń, Z. J. 1621
Psathas, G. 438
Psichari, Jean 246, 247, 256, 257, 678
Pudło, Kazimierz 1622, 1624, 1625, 1628
Puech, G. 1217, 1221
Pueyo, Miquel 1301, 1302
Pugh, Anthony 175, 430, 431, 432
Pugliese Carratelli, G. 104, 109
Puhvel, J. 21
Puig Salellas, Josep Maria 1298, 1302
Pulinckx, Raymond 1110, 1123
Pulte, Peter 2037
Pupier, P. 168
Pupovac, Milorad 1433
Puru Shotam, N. 452, 457
Puşcariu, Sextil 1479, 1484, 1486
Püschel, Ulrich 147, 152
Putschke, Wolfgang 270, 1600
Pütz, Martin 21, 691
Putzer, Oskar 1357
Puxon, Grattan 1962, 1963, 1971
Py, Bernard 39, 236, 240, 241, 242, 244, 245, 321, 322, 326, 327, 579, 585, 762, 1843, 1845, 1849, 1850, 1852, 1860, 1862, 1866, 1867, 1869, 1870, 1876, 1878
Pye, L. W. 76, 80

Q

Quasthoff, Uta 699, 702
Quattrocchi, Luigi 1357
Quilis, A. 321, 327
Quinn, N. 930
Quintilian (ca. 40−ca. 115 n. Chr.) 1, 7, 1272
Quirk, R. 839, 841, 910, 912
Qvigstad, Just K. 947, 948, 981

R

Raag, Raimo 1905
Raats, U. 507
Raclavská, Jana 1667, 1668
Radatz, H.-I. 613, 624
Radden, G. 1768
Radeva, Vasilika 1495
Radó, Péter 1713, 1715, 1716, 1721, 1723
Radovanović, M. 1416
Radtke, Edgar 1382, 1469
Radtke, F.-O. 189, 191, 208
Rădulescu, I. E. 1485, 1486
Radvaň, Šiližská 1684
Raevskij, N. 1941
Rafael, F. 2004, 2007
Raffaele, S. 725
Raffler-Engel, Walburga von 296, 297, 298, 299, 304, 305, 308, 309, 310, 311, 547, 548, 549
Raith, Joachim 318, 319, 320, 762, 763, 801, 804, 813, 817, 819, 936
Raitz, W. 270
Rakelmann, Georgia A. 1804, 1805, 1811, 1971
Rall, Dietrich 512, 514
Ram, T. 907, 911, 912
Ramat, Paolo 1216, 1222
Ramers, K. H. 295
Ramey, D. R. 477, 478, 481
Ramge, Hans 1862
Ramirez, J. D. 477, 478, 481
Ramisch, Heinrich 1096, 1988, 1989
Ramon, Oriol 357
Ramovš, Fran 1361, 1362, 1799, 1812, 1815, 1820
Rampton, M. B. H. 598, 608
Ramseier, Markus 271, 1852
Ramsey, S. 298, 302, 310
Ramułt, Stefan 1602, 1605
Ranard, D. A. 867, 871

Ránki, G. 1722
Rannut, Mart 675, 1905
Rao, A. 184, 192
Rapoport, Louis 1947, 1960
Rapp, M. 760
Räsänen, Martti 1527, 1528, 1532
Rasinski, K. A. 728, 729, 733
Rasmussen, Chr. 1054
Rasmussen, G. 418, 421
Rasmussen, Petur M. 1048, 1053
Rat, M. 873, 879
Ratajski, L. 450
Rathmayr, R. 417, 420
Ratti, Remigio 1852, 1872, 1873, 1874, 1875, 1878
Rattunde, E. 876, 878, 879, 880
Rauhut, F. 921, 931
Raun, Toivo U. 1900
Ravem, R. 7, 11
Raven, P. H. 129
Ravenstein, Ernest G. 1089, 1096
Raybould, W. H. 1064, 1075, 1081, 1085, 1087
Razmukaitė, M. 1614, 1620
Rebuffot, J. 172, 175, 474, 481
Récatas, B. 1535, 1539
Recoura, G. 558
Redard, Françoise 167, 168, 1852
Redder, A. 92, 97, 925, 926, 927, 929, 930, 931
Redfield, R. 51, 56
Regan, D. T. 695, 702
Réger, Zita 1720, 1721, 1723, 1749, 1753
Regueira, Xosé Luís 1293, 1294, 1295
Reh, M. 534, 537, 540
Rehbein, Jochen 189, 192, 925, 926, 927, 929, 930, 931
Rehder, Peter 1407, 1415, 1416, 1451, 1458, 1707
Rei, Fernández Francisco 1285, 1288, 1293, 1294, 1295
Reich, H. H. 270
Reichenkron, Günter 1366, 1485, 1486
Reicher, S. D. 48
Reichertz, J. 759, 763
Reichman, R. 138, 144
Reichmann, Oskar 1240, 1785
Reid, E. 1071, 1074
Reif, L. 416, 417, 421
Rein, Kurt 314, 315, 316, 320, 393, 395, 399, 819, 1464, 1468, 1469, 1471, 1472, 1473, 1474, 1476, 1477
Reinecke, J. F. 645, 648, 651, 658
Reinheimer-Ripeanu, S. 1496
Reinhold, Carl Heinrich Theodor 1522, 1524

Reinmar von Hagenau (1160−1210) 1229
Reisdoerfer, Joseph 1166, 1168, 1172
Reissman, Catherine K. 747, 749
Reist, Hans 313
Reiter, Norbert 5, 1376, 1524, 1527, 1598, 1600
Reiterer, Albert F. 1807, 1810, 1811, 1816, 1820, 1835
Reixach, M. 451, 456, 457
rejzn, zalmen 1960
Remacle, L. 176, 180
Renan, E. 156, 160
Renner, Karl (1870−1950) 155, 160, 361, 362, 363
Renucci, J. 354, 357
Repp, Friedrich 1810, 1812
Reres, Demetri 1372
Rešetar, Milan 1362, 1363, 1366
Reuschel, W. 895, 900
Reuter, E. 417, 421
Reuter, Mikael 1014
Reuther, Tilmann 1366
Revel, Jacques 278, 282, 1186, 1250
Rex, J. 209, 327
Rey, Micheline 132, 138
Rey-von Allmen, Micheline 327
Reyes, R. 599, 608
Reynolds, A. G. 35, 39, 40
Rezende Matias, Fátima de 1317
Rezsohazy, Rudolphe 1111, 1123
Rial, J. 79, 80, 349, 351
Rialle, G. de 50
Rice, F. A. 257, 839, 841
Rice, R. E. 433, 434, 437, 438, 658
Richards, W. D. Jr. 11, 433, 438
Richebuono, Bepe 1390, 1398
Richmond, A. D. 209
Richter, Gisela 1474, 1477
Rickard, P. 549
Rickford, J. R. 175, 338, 341, 655, 656, 658, 770, 811
Ridder, Paul de 1109, 1122
Riding, A. 866, 871
Ridler, N. B. 218
Riedl, F. H. 2006
Riedmann, Gerhard 1355, 1357
Rieger, Janusz A. 1613, 1614, 1621, 1622, 1627, 1628
Riesel, E. 146, 147, 148, 149, 152
Riesz, J. 97
Rieu, B. 802, 803
Rigaux, F. 360, 363
Riggins, H. R. 427, 430, 431
Riggs, Fred 1113, 1123
Rigiru, Lopigna 1217, 1222
Riguet, M. 196, 199
Riklin, Alois 1838, 1852
Riley, D. 810

Riley, Ph. 383, 384
Rimani, S. 2007
Rindler Schjerve, Rosita 802, 804, 1328, 1330, 1353, 1357, 1377, 1379, 1381, 1382, 1383
Ringbom, H. 521, 525, 563, 564, 566, 567
Ringger, K. 1397
Ripka, Ivor 1690, 1691, 1707
Rippl, Eugen 1661
Rips, L. J. 729, 732
Ris, Roland 1842, 1844, 1852, 1859, 1862
Rissel, Dorothy 125, 130
Risteski, Stojan 1447, 1450
Ristovski, B. 1503, 1504
Ritchie, W. 910, 912
Ritter, Alexander 97, 1731
Rivier d'Arc, H. 188, 192
Rizzi, Elena 641
Robert, H. 749
Robert-Jones, Philippe 1110, 1123
Roberts, Catrin 77, 81, 685, 691
Roberts, Celia 14, 22, 55, 143, 685, 691, 868, 871, 930
Roberts, L. R. 37, 40, 365, 370, 608
Roberts, Mary 723, 725
Roberts, Murat H. 3, 11
Robertson, B. 770
Robins, R. H. 50, 56, 576, 577
Robinson, W. P. 41, 42, 43, 44, 45, 47, 48, 437
Roch, Jerzy 1616, 1621
Roche, N. 862, 864
Rockhill, K. 388, 391
Rodrigue, Aron 1571
Rodríguez Neira, Modesto A. 1292, 1294, 1295
Rodríguez Yáñez, X. P. 1294, 1295
Rodríguez, F. 354, 357
Roeder, Ph. G. 78, 80
Roelandt, Th. 1995
Rogers, E. M. 433, 438
Rogge, Waltraud 1190, 1192, 1195
Rogowski, R. 80, 81, 206, 207, 209, 1157
Rohlfs, Gerhard 1216, 1217, 1219, 1222, 1269, 1367, 1369, 1370, 1371, 1524, 2019
Rohlfs, Horst-Henneck 1768
Rohr, Rupprecht 1376, 1396, 1539
Rohrer, J. 85, 89
Röhrig, Johannes W. 1243, 1251, 2003, 2007
Rohweder, Jürgen 1041, 1042
Roijen, J. 1995
Rojo, Guillermo 1291, 1295
Rokkan, St. 64, 75, 79, 80, 342, 345, 346, 351

Rokoszowa, Jolanta 1594, 2038
Röll, W. 906, 912
Rolph, E. S. 869, 871
Rolshoven, Jürgen 1534, 1539
Rolssenn, B. 2004, 2007
Roltenburg, R. 763
Romaine, Suzanne 11, 19, 22, 87, 89, 112, 115, 116, 117, 171, 174, 175, 243, 245, 292, 295, 366, 367, 368, 370, 486, 492, 586, 593, 595, 599, 609, 643, 647, 648, 649, 650, 651, 655, 656, 658, 695, 702, 713, 714, 724, 725, 787, 790, 811
Roman, J. 200, 202, 203
Romanello, M. T. 722, 725
Romani, G. 1216, 1222
Romportl, Milan 1667, 1668
Rondeau, Guy 840, 841
Rongoni, Giocondo 1329
Ronjat, Jules 7, 11, 32, 33, 40, 291, 295, 364, 366, 370, 384, 1188, 1193, 1195, 2003, 2007
Ronzevalle, P. Louis 1531, 1532, 1563, 1564, 1565
Rooij, J. de 105, 109, 1129
Roosens, A. 401, 405
Roosens, Eugeen 1113, 1123
Rosaldo, M. 143, 144
Rosalio, Maria Rita 1441, 1442
Rosamani, Enrico 1361, 1362
Rosen, H. 171, 175
Rosenberg, M. J. 692, 693, 695, 696, 702
Rosenberg, Peter 817, 819
Rosenfield, I. 85, 89
Rosenkranz, Heinz 1768
Rosetti, Alexandru 1496
Rosier, P. 904, 906
Rosling, Marianne 1025, 1032
Rosova, Tatiana 1684
Ross, J. A. 46, 48
Ross, St. 336, 341
Rossebastiano Bart, Alda 1336, 1337
Rossera, F. 434, 438
Rossi, P. H. 743
Rossi-Landi, F. 444
Rossi-Taibbi, Giuseppe 1370, 1371
Rossides, Z. 1582
Rossinelli, Michel 213, 218, 1852
Rossing, C. 375, 377, 584
Rössler, G. 1396
Rossos, Andrew 1499, 1504
Rost-Roth, M. 924, 931
Rotaetxe, Karmele 1303, 1305, 1306, 1308, 1309
Rotar, Janez 1424
Roth, K.-H. 188, 192
Roth, P. A. 760, 761, 763
Rother, Klaus 1373, 1376
Roulet, E. 648

Rouquette, Rémy 1191, 1195
Rousseau, C. 358, 363
Rousseau, Jean- Jacques (1712–1778) 154, 157, 160
Rousso-Lenoïr, F. 357
Rovere, Giovanni 1852
Rowley, Antony R. 1357
Rowston, G. 429, 430
Roy, P. 492
Rü, Micurá de (→ Bacher, Nikolaus) 1388
Rubagumya, C. M. 670, 675, 685, 691
Rubal Rodríguez, Xosé 1292, 1295
Rubin, J. 690, 691, 831, 833, 839, 841
Rucktäschel, Annemarie 879
Rüdiger, Johann C. C. 1962, 1971
Rudin, Catherine 1492, 1496, 1501, 1503, 1506, 1509, 1510
Rudlovčak, O. 1701
Rudolf, Rainer 1691, 1700
Rudolph, J. R. Jr. 79, 80, 405
Ruf, W. 188, 192
Ruggiero, G. 725
Ruiter, Jan J. de 1150, 1151
Ruiz Olabuenaga, J. L. 356, 1309
Ruíz Velasco, E. 492
Rūķe-Draviņa, Velta 6, 7, 11, 37, 40, 1621, 1907, 1912
Rumbaut, R. G. 869, 871
Rumpler, Helmut 1424
Rumsey, A. 135, 138
Runblom, H. 8, 12
Runggaldier, Heidi 1398
Ruong, Israel 981
Rupel, Dimitrij 1424
Rupp, Heinz 1852
Rusanivs'kyj, V. M. 1932
Rusanov, Valeri 1494, 1496
Russell, J. 702, 721, 725, 810, 811
Rustow, D. 403, 405
Rusu, Valeriu 1539
Rutherford, W. E. 517, 524, 525, 563, 566, 567, 657
Ruys, Manu 1125, 1129
Ružička, Jozef 1707
Ryčalka, Mychajlo 1701
Ryan, E. B. 35, 38, 43, 45, 48, 132, 138, 570, 577, 631, 633, 694, 701, 702, 706, 708
Ryckeboer, Hugo 1243, 1245, 1246, 1250, 1251, 1252
Rzounek, V. 1654, 1655

S

Sabater, E. 179, 180
Sabatier, R.-R. 194, 199
Sabban, Annette 1094, 1095, 1096
Sabín, Angel 1284
Sadílek, Petr 1649
Saenger, H. R. 431
Saer, D. 364, 370
Safran, W. 401, 403, 405
Sagarin, E. 343, 351
Sager, J. C. 840, 841
Sagisaka, Y. 294
Saifullah-Khan 41, 44, 45, 46, 48
Saini, S. K. 488, 492
Saint Robert, Ph. de 873, 879
Saint-Jacques, B. 48, 106, 109
Saitz, R. L. 296, 311
Sakaguchi, A. 881, 883, 885, 886
Sakamoto, N. 930
Sala, M. 539, 540
Saładiak, A. 1623, 1628
Salaville, Sévérien 1529, 1532
Salazar, A. de Oliveira (1889–1970) 1311
Salazar, M. S. 897, 901
Salimbeni, Fulvio 1338, 1343
Salmon, Gilbert-Lucien 1239, 1240
Salmon, Joe 13, 22
Salmons, J. 5, 11, 819
Salomon, L. 27, 31
Salt, J. 181, 192, 331, 332
Saltarelli, M. 580, 582, 584
Saltveit, Laurits 938, 948
Salverda de Grave, J. J. 1124, 1129
Salvi, Sergio 156, 160, 1328, 1330, 1359, 1360, 1362, 1376, 1380, 1382
Salvioni, Carlo 1349
Samarin, W. J. 320, 395, 398, 399
Sammallahti, Pekka 981, 999, 1004, 1005, 1018, 1019
Sammut, Frans 1402, 1406
Samovar, L. A. 298, 305, 309, 310, 311
Sampson, John 1965, 1970, 1971
Sampson, R. 872, 879
San, L. J. 607
Sánchez Carrión, José M. 1269, 1306, 1309
Sanders, I. 1722
Sanders, W. 146, 152
Sandfeld, Kristian 549, 1411, 1415, 1416, 1449, 1451, 1468, 1469, 1494, 1496, 1552, 1554
Sandig, Barbara 147, 149, 152
Sandkühler, H. J. 192
Sandlund, Tom 1014
Sandvei, Marius 938, 948
Sanguin, André-Louis 1398
Sankoff, D. 113, 117, 118, 119, 123, 124, 125, 130, 196, 199, 242, 245, 595, 599, 602, 609, 770, 776, 779, 784, 786, 787, 810, 811

Sankoff, G. 16, 22, 588, 593, 650, 653, 658
Sanna, Antonio 1377, 1378, 1380, 1382
Sansen, J. 1245, 1250, 1251, 2003, 2007
Santamarina, Antón 1280, 1284, 1288, 1289, 1293, 1295, 1317
Santangelo, A. 300, 311
Santiago-Santiago, I. 483, 484, 492
Santos Silva, M. H. 2014
Santos, L. K. 897, 901
Santos, R. G. 548
Sapienza, A. 409, 414
Sapir, Edward 50, 51, 55, 56, 101, 103, 343, 351, 542, 544, 546, 549, 720, 725
Sapon, St. M. 507
Saralegui, Carmen 1283, 1284
Saramandu, Nicolae 1464, 1469, 1537, 1538, 1539, 2033
Sarantis, Theodoros K. P. 1524
Sarathy, R. 439, 440, 444
Sarides, Emmanuel 2033
Sarmiento, R. 879
Särndal, C.-E. 735, 737
Sarosácz, György 1731, 1738
Sarris, Neoklis 1561, 1562, 1565
Sarton, G. 278, 283
Sasse, Hans-Jürgen 660, 666, 1522, 1524, 1542, 1544, 1974, 1976, 1978, 2033
Šatava, L. 668, 675
Sato, Ch. 521, 525
Satta, Antonio 1380, 1381, 1382
Saucier, J. F. 384
Sauerwein, Friedrich 1515, 1524
Şaul, Mahir 1556, 1557, 1558, 1559, 1568, 1569, 1571
Saunders, G. W. 14, 22, 291, 295, 366, 368, 370, 380, 381, 382, 383, 384, 385
Saupe, D. 229, 233
Saussure, Ferdinand de 542, 548, 639, 642, 706, 708
Sauvageot, A. 876, 879
Sauzet, P. 257, 893
Savard, Jean-Guy 79, 281, 283, 404
Savas, T. 608
Saville-Troike, M. 51, 56, 171, 175, 658, 722, 725, 750, 753, 755, 763
Savolainen, Maija 992
Saxalber, Annemarie 270
Saxalber-Tetter, Annemarie 1356, 1357
Sayers, D. 480
Scaglione, A. 894, 900, 901
Scalco, Laura 1343, 1344
Ščerba, Lev V. 1796, 1797
Schaar, J. H. 236, 244

Schachter, J. 520, 525, 562, 563, 566, 567
Schaie, W. 585
Schaller, Helmut Wilhelm 1450, 1468, 1469, 1495
Schank, R. C. 129
Schappelwein, Karl 1974, 1976, 1978, 1979
Schäppi, Peter 1853
Schärer, Martin R. 1137, 1143
Schaus, Emile 1169, 1172
Scheel, H. 1532
Scheffler, W. 218
Schegloff, E. A. 432, 438
Schenker, A. M. 1496, 1605
Scherer, Anton 1472, 1477
Scherer, K. R. 341
Scheuch, E. K. 737, 738, 743
Scheuring, B. 741, 744
Scheuringer, Hermann 1812
Schiavi Fachin, Silvana 1342, 1344
Schickele, René (1883–1940) 1225, 1232, 1235, 1239, 1240
Schieffelin, B. 710, 714, 749
Schifferle, Hans-Peter 1842, 1853
Schiffman, H. F. 396, 399
Schiffrin, Deborah 138, 139, 144, 409, 414, 592, 811
Schildt, Joachim 1768
Schiller, U. 695, 701
Schilling, Rudolf 1843, 1853
Schirmunski, V. M. 812, 819
Schlachter, Wolfgang 981
Schläpfer, Robert 271, 398, 1840, 1841, 1842, 1847, 1849, 1850, 1851, 1852, 1853, 1855, 1856, 1857, 1858, 1861, 1862, 1870, 1875, 1878
Schleicher, August (1821–1868) 2, 11
Schlesinger, A. Jr. 477, 481
Schleyer, W. 510, 514
Schlieben-Lange, Brigitte 96, 97, 1190, 1195, 1330
Schlobinski, Peter 189, 192, 695, 702, 754, 763, 810, 811
Schlösser, Rainer 1539
Schmalstieg, William 1648
Schmid, Beat 1853
Schmid, Heinrich 1844, 1853
Schmid, Stephan 1850, 1853
Schmidt, Annette 18, 22, 113, 117, 137, 138, 568, 571, 573, 578, 586, 590, 591, 593, 810, 811
Schmidt, G. 1397
Schmidt-Mackey, I. 280, 283
Schmidt-Radefeldt, Jürgen 540, 1315, 1317
Schmidt-Rohr, G. 798, 804
Schmied, J. 489, 492, 689, 691

Schmitt, Christian 179, 244, 326, 558, 623, 624, 642, 872, 873, 874, 875, 876, 877, 879, 880, 1193, 1194, 1221, 1222, 1284, 1295, 1317, 1329, 1337, 1343, 1381, 1382, 1383, 1397, 1398, 1406, 1465, 1469, 1470, 1843, 1853, 1886, 2007, 2014, 2019
Schmitt, E. H. 176, 177, 180
Schmitt, Ludwig E. 1476
Schmitt, Rüdiger 1575, 1577
Schmitz, C. A. 931
Schmöe, F. 857
Schneider, Christian 1849, 1853
Schneider, Edgar 1989
Schneiderman, E. 770
Schnell, R. 737, 739, 740, 743, 751, 763
Schnidrig, Kurt 1844, 1853
Schober, M. F. 739, 743
Schoeni, G. 876, 880
Scholtmeijer, Harry 1150, 1151
Schöne, A. 1854
Schönfeld, Helmut 1796, 1797
Schönfelder, K.-H. 2, 3, 4, 11
Schöni, G. 243
Schooling, St. 395, 399, 810, 811
Schorer, H. 735, 737
Schott, S. 734, 737
Schottmann, H. 4, 11
Schramm, Gottfried 1469
Schramm, W. 426, 431
Schreiber, Wilfried E. 1463, 1469
Schreiner, Bela 1823, 1827
Schreuder, R. 585
Schrijver, Reginald de 1108, 1122
Schröbler, Ingeborg 1691
Schröder, H. 14, 22, 417, 421, 929
Schröder, K. 416, 421
Schrøder, Kim 440, 444
Schroeder, Klaus-Henning 1467, 1469
Schrøter, Johan H. 1046, 1049
Schubert, Gabriella 1468, 1470, 1479, 1481, 1483, 1485, 1486, 1736, 1737, 1738, 1741, 1743, 1747, 1748, 1749
Schubert, K. 647, 886
Schuchardt, Hugo 2, 3, 6, 11, 557, 558, 882, 886, 906, 912, 1269, 1810, 1812
Schüle, Ernest 1336, 1337
Schüle, Rose-Claire 1337
Schullerus, A. 1476
Schultz, J. 142, 143
Schultz-Lorentzen, C. W. 1053, 1054
Schulz, E. 1691
Schulze, H. 233, 245
Schulze, R. 763
Schuman, H. 695, 697, 702, 729, 732, 738, 739, 741, 743, 744

Schumann, J. H. 54, 56, 57, 285, 290, 295, 523, 524, 525, 563, 567
Schuppenhauer, C. 266, 271
Schurig, Dorothea 1315, 1317
Schuster-Šewc, Heinz 1768, 1797
Schütz, A. 926, 931
Schütz, Edmund 1574, 1577
Schütze, F. 751, 754, 756, 757, 763, 797, 801, 804
Schwanenflugel, Paula J. 132, 138
Schwanzer, Viliam 1691
Schwarz, D. 8, 11
Schwarz, Ernst 1660, 1661, 1691
Schwarz, Norbert 729, 731, 732, 733, 738, 739, 740, 741, 742, 743, 744
Schwarze, Ch. 873, 880
Schwarzenbach, Rudolf 1849, 1853
Schweda-Nicholson, N. 405, 869, 871
Schweizer, Aleksandr 1616, 1621
Schweizer, M. 192
Schweizer, T. 192, 755, 757, 763
Schwob, Anton 94, 96, 97, 1472, 1477
Schwörer, E. 647, 649
Sciriha, Lydia 1400, 1405
Scognamillo, Giovanni 1557, 1559
Scollon, Ronald 572, 578, 586, 593, 790, 796
Scollon, Suzanne 572, 578, 586, 593, 790, 796
Scott, C.T. 912
Scott, J. 633, 811
Scott, Sheridan 35, 40
Scott, Stan 1370, 1371
Scotton, C. M. (→ Myers-Scotton, C.) 42, 48, 115, 117, 455, 457, 546, 549, 595, 596, 602, 604, 608, 609
Scovel, Th. 285, 289, 295
Scribner, N. 710, 714
Scribner, S. 925, 929
Searle, J. 139, 142, 144
Sears, D. O. 30, 31
Sebba, M. 598, 609
Sebeok, Thomas A. 56, 129, 714, 900, 901, 1543
Sébillot, F. 2003, 2007
Sébillot, Paul 1260
Sechehaye, C. A. 548, 652, 658
Secord, P. G. 749
Secretariat for Language Policy 471, 473
Seewann, Gerhard 208, 1407, 1409, 1416, 1486
Segalowitz, N. 33, 38, 369
Segui, J. 130
Séguy, Jean 175, 180, 1193, 1195, 1268, 1269, 2003, 2007

Sehwers, Johan 1910, 1912
Seidelmann, Erich 1853
Seigel, G. M. 333
Seiler, Hans Jakob 4
Seip, Didrik A. 938, 948
Sekulić, Ante 1407, 1416
Selby, H. A. 749
Selickaja, I. A. 1900
Seliger, H. W. 371, 377, 378, 515, 525, 579, 584, 585, 590, 593
Seligman, A. 1582
Selinker, L. 54, 57, 113, 117, 515, 516, 517, 520, 525, 562, 566, 567
Seliščev, Afanasi M. 1457, 1458
Seliščev, Matreevič M. 1496, 1497
Selk, Paul 1777, 1982
Selkirk, 5th Earl of 1089, 1096
Seltig, M. 336, 341
Semenova, Mariya 1910, 1912
Semin, G. 744
Senelle, Robert 354, 357
Sennett, R. 409, 414
Sephiha, A. 1178, 1187, 2004, 2007
Séphiha, Haïm Vidal 1557, 1558, 1559, 1560, 1566, 1568, 1569, 1571, 1572
Seppolla, Bjomar 966
Sepstrup, P. 429, 431
Serow, W. J. 188, 192
Serracino-Inglot, Erint 1403, 1406
Servan-Schreiber, Jean-Jacques 412, 414
Servátka, Marián 1629, 1630, 1631, 1632, 1633, 1672, 1677, 1694
Seton-Watson, R. W. 1709, 1723
Sgall, Petr 1653, 1655
Shamshur, Oleg V. 1900
Shangriladze, Kot K. 1450
Shapiro, Michael C. 393, 396, 399, 842
Shapson, L. R. 633
Shapson, S. M. 491, 492, 633
Sharp, Derrick 1981
Sharwood-Smith, M. 518, 525, 566, 567, 583, 585, 605, 609
Shaw, Stanford J. 1555, 1556, 1558, 1559, 1560, 1566, 1567, 1568, 1572
Shaw, W. D. 690, 691
Sheard, J. A. 917, 920
Sheffield, J. R. 485, 492
Shenton, H. N. 424, 426
Sherwood, Peter 1721, 1723
Sherzer, Joel 170, 174, 409, 413, 593, 760, 788, 789, 790, 795, 796
Shevell, St. K. 729, 732

Shevelov, George Y. 1628
Shibatani, M. 615, 624
Shimakawa, Y, 298, 310
Shinn, H. K. 901
Shirai, Y. 516, 524
Shohamy, E. 515, 525
Sholl, A. 131, 137
Shopen, T. 666
Shortreed, I. 336, 341
Shreve, G. M. 918, 920
Shrivastava, P. 407, 414
Shryock, H. 772, 773, 776
Shuken, Cynthia R. 1095, 1096
Shultz, J. 749, 923, 929
Shuteriqi, D. S. 1494, 1496
Shuy, Roger W. 337, 341, 342, 625, 634, 657, 658, 702, 822, 825
Siatkowski, Janusz 1600, 1613, 1614, 1635, 1638, 1639, 1640, 1641
Sibayan, Bonifacio P. 897, 898, 899, 900, 901
Sick, W. D. 1862
Sieben, Cees 1260
Siebenborn, E. 871, 880
Sieber, Peter 271, 1842, 1848, 1849, 1853
Siebs, Theodor 1789, 1790
Siedentop, L. 202
Siegel, G. M. 341
Siegel, Jacob 772, 773, 776
Siegel, Jeff 333, 336, 341
Sievers, J. 450
Sievers, Kai D. 1782, 1786
Siewierski, Bogdan 1594
Sieyès, E, J. (1748−1836) 154, 157, 160
Sifianou, M. 432, 438
Siguan, Miguel 7, 11, 245, 322, 326, 327, 381, 383, 385, 464, 465, 473, 687, 691, 1305, 1309, 2014
Sikma, Jantsje A. 1157, 1786
Silva-Corvalán, C. 590, 661, 666
Silver, Brian D. 1577
Silverstein, M. 589, 593, 746, 747, 749
Sima, Ferenc 1684
Simard, L. 43, 48, 334, 335, 341
Šimečková, Alena 1659, 1662
Simeonov, Boris 1494, 1496, 1514
Simmel, G. 23, 27, 28, 31
Simões de Silva Lopes, Ana Maria 1317
Simon, Bettina 1943, 1955, 1960
Simon, F. 29, 31
Simon, H. A. 405, 414
Simon, J. L. 188, 193
Simon, P. 416, 421
Simon, Philippe 1250
Simon-Barouh, J. 2006, 2007

Simonot, M. 55
Simonov, Simon 1493, 1496
Simons, Ph. J. 146, 152
Simonyi, Siegmund 1486
Simpson, E. 458, 464
Simpson, J. M. Y. 666
Sin Ching, P. 811
Sinclair, A. 336, 340
Sinclair-de Zwaart, H. 288, 295
Singer, Rudolf 1404, 1406
Singh, Rajenda 112, 115, 116, 595, 600, 606
Singleton, David 364, 370
Singy, Pascal 1867, 1870
Sinilind, Sirje 1905
Sion, Georges 1110, 1123
Šipka, M. 1442
Sipos, István 1748
Sirén, Ulla 976, 992
Sirotković, J. 1442
Siruni, Hakob D. 1576, 1577
Šišić, Ferdinand von 1738
Šišmarev, V. F. 1936, 1941
Siti Rohaini, K. 419
Sitta, Horst 1842, 1848, 1849, 1853
Sixirei Paredes, Carlos 1285, 1295
Sjoholm, K. 562, 567
Sjölin, Bo 1780, 1781, 1782
Skála, Emil 1645, 1649, 1656, 1658, 1659, 1660, 1661
Skanderbeg, Gjergji Kastriota (ca. 1405−1468) 1372
Skautrup, Peter 1028, 1032
Skehan, P. 523, 525
Škiljan, Dubravko 1433
Skinner, B. F. 288, 295, 561, 566
Šklifov, Blagoj 1549, 1550
Sköld, Tryggve 942, 948, 981
Skorik, P. J. 1895, 1900
Skubic, Mitja 1362
Skudlik, S. 423, 426, 857
Skulina, Josef 1636, 1639, 1640, 1641
Skutnabb-Kangas, Tove 35, 40, 89, 217, 236, 245, 280, 283, 292, 295, 465, 473, 489, 492, 631, 634, 667, 670, 673, 674, 675, 691, 836, 841, 871, 992, 1032, 1717, 1723
Slade, D. 88
Slaughter, H. 499, 501
Sław, Aleksander 1615, 1617, 1621
Ślizinski, Jerzy 1635, 1641
Slobin, D. I. 14, 22, 132, 138, 289, 295, 521, 524, 525
Šlosberg, b. 1955, 1960
Slotte, Peter 1982
Sly, D. F. 188, 192
Smalley, B. 1129
Smith, A. D. S. 203, 204, 209, 718, 720

Smith, A. L. 925, 931
Smith, D. M. 75, 652, 658
Smith, Graham 1888, 1900, 1925, 1940, 1941
Smith, L. E. 691, 909, 910, 912, 931
Smith, Marilyn C. 130
Smith, Michael 519, 525
Smith, Philip M. 437, 721, 725
Smitherman, G. 710, 711, 713, 714
Smoczyński, W. 1613, 1615, 1618, 1619, 1620, 1621
Smolicz, J. J. 17, 22, 572, 573, 578, 668, 675, 721, 723, 725
Smułkowa, Elżbieta 1608, 1611, 1613, 1614, 1621
Šmulders, Modris 1906, 1912
Sneck, S. 432, 438
Snow, C. E. 629, 634, 841
Snow, M. A. 294
Snyder, E. 657
SOAS 75
Sobierajski, Zenon 1605, 1632, 1633
Sobrero, Alberto A. 722, 725, 1326, 1330
Sochová, Z. 1653, 1655
Socor, Vladimir 1483, 1486
Söderbergh, R. 7, 11
Söderholm, Eira 965, 966
Soffietti, J. P. 7, 11
Sokolik, M. E. 519, 525
Sokolova, B. B. 1494, 1496
Sokolová, Gabriela 1643, 1644, 1645, 1649, 1652, 1654, 1655, 1658, 1662, 1668, 1677, 1679, 1684, 1695
Sokolová, Miroslava 1678, 1707
Solà, D. F. 485, 492
Solà, Joan 1299, 1300, 1301, 1302
Solano, Francesco 1376
Solans, Henri 1197, 1201
Solbakk, Aage 1019
Solchanyk, R. 1900
Sole, Leonardo 1379, 1382
Solé, Y. 722, 725
Solèr, Clau 1853, 1854, 1881, 1882, 1883, 1884, 1885, 1886
Solis, F. G. 375, 379
Sollors, W. 94, 97
Solta, Georg Renatus 1468, 1470
Šoltys, O. 1655, 1678
Sommer, G. 571, 576
Sommerfelt, A. 11
Sonderegger, Stefan 1240, 1837, 1838, 1849, 1851, 1853, 1860, 1862, 1869, 1870
Søndergaard, Bent 1038, 1039, 1041, 1042, 1048, 1049, 1768, 1771, 1775, 1777, 1982
Sonner, A. 294

Sonntag, Selma K. 76, 77, 78, 80, 81, 400, 401, 402, 403, 404, 405
Sonyel, Salahi R. 1582
Soravia, Giulio 1326, 1330
Sorensen, A. P. 720, 725
Sørensen, Viggo 1776
Sós, A. C. 1738
Šoucová, Dana 1672, 1673, 1678
Soulis, George S. 1962, 1964, 1971
Sourisseaux, A. L. J. 420, 421
Southworth, F. C. 1170, 1172
Sowa, Franciszek 1632, 1633, 1634
Sowell, Th. 327, 332
Sowinski, Bernhard 147, 152
Spada, N. 371, 379
Spano, Benito 1323, 1330, 1367, 1370, 1371, 2018, 2019
Spano, Giovanni 1378, 1382, 1383
Sparhawk, C. M. 296, 311
Speckart, G. 694, 700
Speitel, Hans-Henning 1089, 1096
Spence, N. C. 1059, 1074
Spencer, H. 31, 25, 692, 702
Spencer, J. William 759, 763
Spencer, John 148, 152
Sperber, D. 50, 57
Spetko, Josef 1685, 1691
Spiecker-Salazar, M. 897, 901
Spiess, Federico 1877, 1878
Spiewok, W. 147, 152
Spillner, Bernd 146, 149, 153, 755, 758, 763, 930, 931
Spindler, Sylvane 1239
Spira, Thomas 1723
Spiro, R. J. 633
Spolsky, Bernard 7, 11, 80, 81, 88, 89, 376, 379, 398, 472, 485, 492, 516, 517, 525, 630, 631, 634, 675, 691
Spoo, Caspar-Matthias 1168
Spradley, J. P. 756, 759, 763
Spratt, J. E. 632, 634
Sprenger, R. 1415
Sprissler, M. 514
Squire, L. R. 62
Srb, Vladimír 1642, 1644, 1646, 1647, 1649, 1672, 1678, 1693, 1695, 1697, 1701
Sreberny-Mohammadi, A. 429, 431
Sridhar, Kamal K. 909, 910, 913
Sridhar, S. N. 485, 486, 492, 910, 913
Srivastava, R. N. 395, 399, 488, 492
St. Clair, R. N. 310, 694, 701, 708
Stackelberg, J. von 423, 426

Staczek, John J. 1302
Stadtler, K. 740, 744
Stagl, J. 757, 763
Stahlke, H. F. W. 152
Stairs, A. 476, 481
Stalin, Josef (1879−1953) 156, 160, 401, 851, 1802
Stamatoski, Trajko 1503
Stammler, Wolfgang 320
Staněk, Tomáṱ 1657, 1658, 1659, 1662
Stanford, L. M. 765, 770
Stanislav, Ján 1694, 1695
Stankiewicz, Edward 1440, 1442, 1496, 1605
Stankov, Valentin 1495
Stanley, M. 495, 500, 507
Stano, Matej 1694, 1695
Starck, Christian 1014, 1981
Stark, O. 188, 193
Starke, G. 152
Starr, Joshua 1964, 1971
Stassen, Albert 1143
Stäuble, Antonio 1853, 1878
Stavenhagen, R. 202, 203
Stavrianos, Leften S. 1504
Štec, Mikuláš (= Mykola) 1700, 1701
Stedje, A. 11
Steele, S. 607, 724
Steensen, Thomas 1779, 1782, 1783, 1785, 1786
Steenwijk, Han 1362
Steever, S. B. 608
Stefan Dušan der Mächtige (1346−1355) 1408, 1452, 1545
Ştefănescu, Ştefan 1486
Steger, Hugo 243, 266, 270, 283
Steiger, Arnald 1285
Stein, D. 533, 539, 540
Steinacker, Ruprecht 1691
Steinberg, J. B. 871
Steiner, J. 77, 80
Steinhauser, Walter 1803, 1809, 1810, 1812
Steinicke, Ernst 1330, 1352, 1354, 1357, 2018, 2019
Steinig, W. 417, 421
Steininger, R. 78, 80
Steinke, Klaus 2028
Stella, Angelo 1329
Stellmacher, Dieter 1783, 1786
Stenbaek, M. A. 427, 431
Stene, A. 4, 11
Stenger, H. 735, 737
Stenz, Christian 1777
Stepanović, Predrag 1715, 1723, 1737, 1738
Stephan IV. Báthory (1571−1586) 1480
Stephan, F. F. 736, 737
Stephens, J. 432, 438

Stephens, M. 8, 12
Stergar, Janez 1423
Stern, C. 7, 12, 285, 295
Stern, Otto 1853
Stern, W. 7, 12, 285, 295
Sternberg, E. 835, 841
Stetkevych, J. 618, 624
Steuerwald, Karl 619, 624, 1557, 1560
Steven, B. 1495
Stevens, F. 498, 501
Stevenson, Patrick 79, 80, 215, 217
Stewart, Michael 1720, 1723
Stewart, W. A. 248, 257, 392, 393, 399, 654, 658, 836, 841, 893
Stich, Alexandr 1653, 1655
Stickel, Gerhard 857, 1851
Stieber, Z. 1594, 1602, 1605, 1627, 1628, 1632, 1633, 1639, 1641, 1662, 1694, 1695, 1699, 1701
Stienen, A. 239, 245, 323, 327
Stierlin, H. 25, 29, 31
Stimm, Helmut 878, 879, 1397
Stockley, D. 891, 893
Stockwell, R. 561, 567
Stoetzel, J. 2004, 2005, 2006
Stojkov, Stojan 1504
Stojkov, Stojko 1496
Štolc, Jozef 1412, 1416, 1632, 1634, 1692, 1695, 1700, 1701, 1748, 1749
Stölting, Wilfried 11, 378, 380, 382, 385
Stölting-Richert, Wilfried 189, 193, 320, 755, 763
Stolz, Benjamin 1450, 1495
Stolz, Otto 1357, 1388, 1398
Stolz, T. 218, 319, 527, 530, 533, 537, 539, 540
Stone, G. 880, 1495
Stone, J. 209
Stone, R. M. 4, 12
Stoob, Heinz 1744, 1749
Storti, G. 299, 311
Stošić, D. 1554
Stouffer, S. A. 701
Strabon (58 v. Chr.-25 n. Chr.) 1272
Strack, F. 728, 729, 731, 732, 733, 738, 739, 741, 744
Strack, Hermann 1960
Straf, M. L. 738, 743
Straka, G. 180
Straka, Manfred 1041, 1776, 1982
Strange, W. 294
Stranj, P. 354, 357
Strašimir, Dimitrov 1504
Strassoldo, Raimondo 892, 893, 1340, 1342, 1344

Strauss, A. L. 756, 757, 761
Strauss, D. 641, 1157
Strauß, Johann 1560, 1565, 1572, 1573, 1574, 1577
Streck, B. 1971
Streeck, J. 925, 931
Street, R. L. Jr. 336, 341
Strehaljuk, Vaso 1436, 1438, 1439, 1442
Strelka, J. P. 97
Strevens, P. 148, 152, 839, 841
Stricker, Hans 1853
Striedter-Temps, Hildegard 1816, 1817, 1818, 1820
Strine, J. 869, 870
Stroebe, W. 732
Stroh, Cornelia 1240
Strohmeyer, F. 146, 153
Stroop, J. R. 37, 40
Stroops, Jan 1151
Strosetzki, Ch. 880, 1316
Stroud, Christopher 236, 244, 375, 378, 567, 569, 576, 578
Strubell (i Trueta), Miquel 904, 906, 1280, 1281, 1285, 1297, 1302
Štrukelj, Inka 1423, 1424
Stubbs, Michael 81, 89, 138, 144, 428, 431, 1070, 1074
Stubić, Leo 1823, 1827
Stucki, Brigitte 1851
Stückrath, J. 270
Studemund, M. 1524
Stundžia, Bonifacas 1917, 1919
Sturm-Schnabel, Stanislava Katharina 1820
Stutterheim, Ch. von 924, 929
Subirats, Marina 1298, 1302
Sudman, S. 726, 727, 730, 732, 733, 738, 741, 743, 744
Suetonius, Caius-Tranquillus (ca. 75 − ca. 160) 826, 833
Sugar, P. 1721, 1722
Sulán, Béla 1682, 1684
Sulzby, E. 634
Šuman, Josef 1739, 1743
Sumpf, J. 147, 153
Sun, S.-L. 385, 437
Suppan, Arnold 1424, 1738, 1830, 1835
Sureja, Jusuf 1414, 1415
Sussex, R. 138
Susskind, Nathan 394, 399
Šutaj, Štefan 1672, 1678, 1679, 1684
Sutcliffe, D. 595, 609
Suttles, G. 451, 457
Suttner, Ernst Chr. 1462, 1470
Sutton, P. 691
Suzuki, Y. 300, 311
Svabo, Jens Christian 1044, 1049
Svalastoga, Kaare 1042
Svanberg, Ingvar 8, 12, 976, 1925

Svavrarsdóttir, Ásta 1058
Švejcer, A. D. 640, 642
Svonni, M. 575, 578
Švorc, P. 1691
Swadesh, M. 343, 351, 586, 593, 660, 666
Swain, Merril 19, 22, 33, 34, 40, 84, 85, 88, 89, 291, 294, 295, 465, 471, 472, 473, 474, 475, 481, 496, 498, 499, 500, 501, 518, 525
Swamy, Gopal 328, 332
Swamy, Gurushi 834, 841
Swann, J. 175
Swing, Elisabeth 1118, 1123
Swinney, M. 479, 480
Sychta, Bernard 1601, 1603, 1605
Sylvain, C. 654, 658
Symeonidis, Charalambos 1522, 1524, 1527, 1531, 1532
Szabó, Ádám T. 1486
Szabó, Géza 1742, 1743
Szabó, János 1725, 1726, 1731
Szabómihály, Gizella 1684
Szalai, L. 1730
Szántó, János 1713, 1716, 1721, 1722, 1723
Szarka, László 1721, 1723
Szeberényi, Ludwig 1835
Szegedi, Edith 1482, 1486
Székely, András B. 1718, 1722
Székely, Bertalan 1740, 1743
Szewczyk, J. 450
Szuhay, Péter 1720, 1721, 1722

T

Taagepera, Rein 1905
Taboada Leonetti, J. 1182, 1187, 2005, 2007
Tabory, Ephraim 173, 175
Tabory, Mala 173, 175, 363
Tabouret-Keller, André 52, 54, 55, 56, 57, 175, 180, 235, 238, 244, 253, 257, 324, 326, 571, 578, 581, 588, 593, 643, 656, 713, 714, 787, 801, 804, 811, 1020, 1032, 1240
Tadadjeu, M. 484, 485, 492
Taeldeman, Johan 1150, 1151
Taeschner, Traute 6, 12, 14, 22, 33, 34, 40, 125, 130, 291, 295, 366, 367, 370, 380, 383, 385, 603, 609
Tagliante, Ch. 504, 507
Tagliavini, Carlo 1485, 1486
Taguieff, P.-A. 202
Tahitu, Egbertus 1150, 1152
Taillemite, E. 658
Tajfel, H. 17, 22, 41, 42, 43, 44, 48, 334, 340, 573, 578, 694, 702

Takács, Imre 1731, 1738
Talal, H. B. 867, 870
Talmon, Alberto 1349
Talmy, L. 136, 137, 138, 143
Tamas, André 1458
Tamás, Lajos 1479, 1485, 1486
Tan, Y. Ph. 452, 457
Tanasković, Darko 1448, 1451
Tandefelt, Marika 571, 575, 578, 999, 1005, 1014
Tanguy, Bernard 1259
Tannen, Deborah 130, 138, 144, 609, 711, 714, 723, 725, 790, 796
Tansley, P. 1072, 1074
Tanur, J. M. 738, 743
Tanz, C. 607, 724
Taras, R. 1926
Tarhov, S. 1979
Tarkianen, Kari 992
Tarnói, László 1731
Tarone, C. 522, 525
Tasić, N. 1554
Tassin, M. 1119, 1123
Tatzreiter, Herbert 1808, 1812
Tauli, V. 839, 841, 872, 880, 881, 883, 887
Tax, S. 56
Taylor, A. R. 174
Taylor, B. 1284
Taylor, D. M. 46, 48, 326, 334, 335, 341, 404, 433, 437
Taylor, F. W. 405, 414
Taylor, H. 572, 573, 577
Taylor, Monica J. 1062, 1068, 1074, 1075
Taylor, T. J. 139, 144, 675, 749, 795, 796, 829, 833
Teale, W. 634
Tees, R. 289, 295
Tekavčić, Pavao 1216, 1222
Telmon, Tullio 1330, 1331, 1333, 1335, 1336, 1337, 1345, 1346, 1349, 1387, 1388, 1389, 1398, 2018, 2019
Téma, B. 1667, 1668
Tempesta, Immacolata 1326, 1330
ten Thije, J. 190, 192, 925, 928, 930
Téné, D. 616, 624
Tenekides, George 1582
ter Heide, H. 181, 191
Tereškovič, P. V. 1925
Terpstra, V. 439, 440, 444
Terracini, Benvenuto 1348, 1349
Terrell, T. 84, 89
Terreros y Pando, E. 557, 558
Tesch, G. 3, 4, 5, 12
Tessonneau, A. 1181, 1187, 2004, 2007
Tetzchner, St. von 378
Teulat, Roger 1195

Teyssier, Paul 615, 624, 1311, 1314, 1315, 1317
Thakerar, J. N. 334, 341
Thayer, L. 420
Theissen, Ulrich 1974, 1976, 1978
Thelander, Mats 976
Thévenot, J. 873, 880
Thibaut, J. W. 48
Thiel, M. 608
Thiers, Jacques 677, 680, 681, 684, 1204, 1205, 1207, 1208, 1209, 1212, 1213, 1214, 1220, 1221, 1222
Thiéry, Ch. 365, 370
Thill, G. 1159, 1172
Thogmartin, C. 426
Thomas, Alan 341
Thomas, Alexander 418, 421
Thomas, Barry 185, 192
Thomas, Ceinwein H. 1777
Thomas, George 992
Thomas, Jacqueline M. C. 789, 796
Thomas, Jenny 14, 22
Thomas, W. 385
Thomasius 2
Thomason, S. G. 54, 57, 98, 99, 102, 103, 112, 116, 117, 121, 124, 333, 338, 339, 342, 538, 539, 540, 586, 593, 602, 609, 790
Thomassen, Arnfinnur 1048, 1049
Thompson, R. J. 79, 80, 405
Thompson, R. W. 654, 658, 895, 901
Thomson, D. 666
Thomson, Derick S. 1089, 1091, 1096
Thomson, R. L. 1061, 1075
Thornberry, P. 363
Thorndell, Ch. 605
Thorne, B. 724
Thrul, R. 294
Thual, François 1464, 1470
Thun, Harald 1285
Thurow, J. 11
Thurston, W. 649
Thurstone, L. L. 697, 702
Thussu, D. K. 430
Tickoo, M. L. 910, 913
Tielemans, M. 1415
Tiersma, Pieter 1156, 1157
Tietz, M. 880, 1397
Tietze, Andreas 1509, 1510, 1522, 1524, 1527, 1531, 1532
Tiittula, L. 417, 421
Tiktin, H. 1470
Tilander, Gunnar 1276, 1285
Tillery, K. H. 868, 869, 870
Timm, L. A. 2003, 2007
Timm, Leonora A. 391, 588, 593, 599, 609, 1260

Timm, Lois A. 816, 819
Tindall, D. B. 433, 438
Tingbjörn, G. 867, 871
Tiryakian, E. A. 80, 81, 206, 209, 1157
Tito, Josip Broz (1892–1980) 1802
Titone, Renzo 7, 12, 465, 473, 516, 525
Titunik, I. R. 1495
Titze, M. 232
Tkačenko, Orest B. 1932
Toda, E. 1380, 1383
Todd, L. 895, 901
Todisco, Enrico 1327, 1330
Toft, Gösta 1041, 1042
Togan, Z. V. 1532
Tohkura, Y. 294
Tola, Salvatore 1377, 1383
Tollefson, James W. 80, 829, 833, 865, 866, 871, 911, 913, 1446, 1451
Tomasi, E. 450
Tómasson, T. 1056, 1058
Tomaszewski, Adam 1599, 1600
Tomaszewski, Jerzy 1594, 2038
Tomić, Olga M. 1449, 1451
Tomlin, R. 521, 525
Tondi, Domenicano 1370, 1371
Toniolo, S. 450
Tonkin, E. 203, 205, 209
Tonkin, H. 218, 864
Tönnies, F. 25, 31
Topolińska, Zuzanna 1602, 1605, 2038
Toporišič, J. 1424
Toporov, V. N. 635, 640
Tornow, Siegfried 1826, 1827
Torrance, A. P. 35, 40
Torres, L. 453, 457
Torvinen, Taimi 1007
Tosi, A. 467, 473
Toukomaa, P. 35, 40, 89, 236, 245, 292, 295
Touraine, A. 78, 81
Tourangeau, R. 728, 729, 733, 738, 743, 744
Tournier, André 1268, 1269
Tourtoulon, Ch. de 2003, 2007
Toury, P. 429, 431
Toussaint, Maurice 1240
Tovar, Antonio 1271, 1285
Tovey, Hilary 1099, 1106
Townsend, Charles E. 1653, 1655
Townsend, Erica W. 1450
Tozzi, M. 2004, 2007
Trabant, J. 97
Tracy, K. 138, 143
Trajan (98–117 n. Chr.) 1272
Trapman, H. 585
Traugott, E. C. 537, 540
Trausch, Gérard 1159, 1172

Treder, Jerzy 1603, 1605, 1606
Treffers, Jeanine 451, 455, 457
Treffers-Daller, Jeanine 595, 598, 601, 602, 609
Treiber-Netoliczka, Luise 1481, 1486
Treinen, Jean Michel 1169, 1172
Tremblay, M.-A. 230, 233, 404, 773, 776
Trepczyk, Jan 1601, 1602, 1603, 1606
Trew, T. 749
Triandis, H. C. 692, 702
Tribalat, M. 2005, 2007
Triber, L. 1828, 1835
Troebst, Stefan 1468, 1470, 1505, 1506, 1510
Troike, R. 87, 89, 548, 632, 634
Troškina, T. P. 1655
Trost, Pavel 1656, 1657, 1659, 1660, 1661, 1662
Troxel, Luan 1489, 1493, 1496
Troy, J. 722, 725
Truchan, Myroslav 1622, 1624, 1628
Truchot, C. 707, 708, 833, 860, 861, 864
Trudgill, Peter 5, 15, 64, 74, 75, 176, 179, 333, 337, 338, 339, 341, 342, 394, 399, 590, 593, 615, 624, 704, 707, 708, 711, 714, 720, 725, 939, 945, 948, 1073, 1074, 1075, 1120, 1121, 1123, 1524, 2033
Trueba, H. T. 483, 492, 631, 634
Tryjarski, Edward 1509, 1510
Tryon, D. 648, 649
Trypućko, Józef 1619, 1620, 1621
Trzaska, Eugenjusz 1599, 1600
Tse, J. K.-P. 838, 841
Tsitsipis, Lukas D. 587, 588, 591, 593, 1521, 1522, 1524, 1540, 1541, 1542, 1543, 1544
Tsokalidou, R. 723, 725
Tsopanakis, Agapitos 1369, 1370, 1371, 1522, 1524
T'sou, B. 453, 457
Tsunoda, M. 426
Tuaillon, Gaston 1175, 1176, 1177, 1187, 1335, 1336, 1337, 1349, 2003, 2007
Tucker, G. R. 474, 477, 480, 481, 484, 492, 496, 501, 632, 633, 667, 675
Tuğlacı, Pars 1556, 1557, 1560
Tulving, E. 138
Tumanjan, E. G. 1940
Tumin, M. M. 26, 31
Turčan, Jaroslav 1411, 1416
Turczynski, Emanuel 1471, 1477
Turi, Johan 981
Turi, Joseph-G. 163, 168, 218

Türkay, Kaya 1558, 1560
Turner, G. W. 147, 153
Turner, John C. 41, 42, 43, 44, 46, 47, 48, 512, 514
Turner, P. 38
Turner, R. 1961, 1970, 1971
Turska, Halina 1619, 1620, 1621, 1918, 1919
Tusón, Amparo (Empar) 1300, 1301, 1302
Tuttle, Edward F. 1377, 1381
Txillardegi, P. 1269, 1308, 1309
Tydén, Mattias 976
Tyler, E. B. 921, 931
Tzavaras, G. A. 2033
Tzelgov, J. 132, 138
Tzitzilis, Christos 1522, 1525, 1527, 1528, 1531, 1532

U

Ua Conchubhair, P. E. S. 1106
Uffelmann, I. 91, 97
Ugrinova, Rada 1502, 1504
Uhlenbeck, E. M. 576, 577
Uhlik, Rade 1441, 1442
Uibopuu, Henn-Jüri 1905
Uibopuu, Valev 1895, 1900
Ujević, Mate 1822, 1827
Ulich, D. 762
Ulijn, J. M. 835, 841, 855, 857
Ulram, P. A. 1655
Ulreich, Eduard 1691
UNESCO 295, 322, 326, 327, 482, 484, 492, 668, 674, 691
Unger, K. 188, 193
Unkart, Ralf 1803, 1804, 1808, 1810, 1811, 1813, 1814, 1815, 1816, 1820, 2057
UNO 326, 328, 332
Urban, G. 589, 593
Urban, Michael 1922, 1925, 1926
Urbanitsch, P. 1737, 1738
Ureland, P. Sture 371, 379, 549, 702, 770, 947, 948, 1260, 1316, 1356, 1376, 1397, 1469, 1777, 1782, 1786, 1850, 1982, 1989
Uribe Villegas, O. 257
Urla, J. 587, 589, 593
Urosevics, Danilo 1731, 1737, 1738
Urwin, D. W. 64, 75, 79, 80, 342, 345, 346, 351
Uth, Manfred 1040, 1042
Uździlo, Algiment 1621

V

Vachek, J. 152, 256
Vafiadou, Valasia 1513, 1514
Vago, R. M. 377, 378, 579, 584, 585, 590, 593

Vaiana, M. 871
Vaid, J. 39, 130, 237, 245
Vaillancourt, F. 439, 444
Vajda, G. M. 90, 91, 93, 97
Vajnrajx, Maks 1960
Vakalopoulos, Apostolos E. 1525
Vakar, Nicholas P. 1919, 1920, 1925, 1926
Valášková, N. 1642, 1649
Valdes, G. 596, 609
Valdes-Fallis, G. 725
Valdman, Albert 117, 138, 579, 585, 652, 653, 655, 656, 657, 658
Valentin, Hugo 1386, 1398
Valentini, Erwin 1398
Valette, R. M. 504, 507
Valíková, Dana 1667, 1669
Valiska, Juraj 1686, 1691
Valjavec, Fritz 1471, 1477
Valkhoff, Marius 1246, 1251
Vallée, F. G. 16, 20
Vallen, Ton 1150, 1151
Vallverdú, Francesc 249, 251, 257, 802, 804, 1301, 1302
Valois, Daniel 374, 377, 378
Valois, Denis 765, 770
van Belle, William 1114, 1122
van Boeschoten, Joost A. 1150, 1152
van Bree, Cor 1150, 1152
van de Craen, Pete 89, 700, 755, 763, 1124, 1129
van de Graaf, Jacques 755, 758, 763
van de Poel, Kris 379
van de Velde, Marc 419
van den Bulck, J. 403, 405
van den Steene, W. 1143
van der Auwera, Johan 1157
van der Elst, G. 270
van der Merwe, I. 63, 75
van der Wijst, P. 421
van der Zouwen, J. 738, 743
van Deth, Jean-Pierre 860, 862, 864
van Deyck, Rika 180
van Dijk, Toon 138, 143, 712, 714, 796
van Dyck, Ruth 361, 363
van Eerde, John A. 1260
van Els, Theo 18, 21, 22, 245, 327, 579, 584, 585, 857, 1151
van Gemert, L. 421
van Goethem, Herman 1245, 1251
van Hemel, Hedwig 1246, 1251
van Hoecke, Willy 1247, 1250, 1251, 1252
van Hout, Roland 18, 21, 119, 123, 786, 787, 1150, 1151, 1152, 1157, 1995

van Ingen, F. 93, 97
van Leuwensteijn, J. A. 1151, 1152
van Overbeke, Maurits 6, 14, 22, 246, 256, 391, 399
van Reenen, Pieter 1252
van Reenen-Stein, Karin 1252
van Rijn, Gerard 1260
van Schendelen, M. P. 78, 81
van Scherpenzee, Marianne 1150, 1152
Vanat, Ivan 1701
Vance, T. J. 607
Vandenberghe, Roxane 1250, 1251
Vandenbroeke, Chris 1241, 1251
Vandeputte, O. 1995
Vandermeeren, Sonja 370, 695, 699, 702, 763, 765, 770, 924, 930, 1140, 1143, 1715, 1722, 1725, 1730
Vandeweyer, L. 179, 180
Vanelli, Laura 1342, 1344, 1398
Vanneste, A. M. S. 2003, 2008
Vanneste, Alex 452, 458, 1244, 1252
Vanneufville, Eric 1242, 1252
Vanniarajan, D. 609
Várdy, A. H. 1723
Várdy, S. B. 1723
Vargiu, Luciano 1376, 1383
Varon, Matilda 1496
Varro, G. 389, 391
Varsík, Branislav 1701
Vasa, Gustav 993
Vasić, V. 1416
Vasilev, Christo 1827
Vasiljev, Ivo 1646, 1649, 1678
Vasmer, Max 1553, 1554
Vasseur, M.-Th. 55
Vatasescu, C. 1457, 1458
Vater, Heinz 295
Vatikiotis-Bateson, E. 294
Vaumas, Etienne de 1582
Vautherin, Raymond 1336, 1337
Vážný, Vaclav 1632, 1634
Vázquez Cuesta, Pilar 1276, 1285, 1286, 1295
Vēbers, Elmrs 1906, 1908, 1912
Vedovelli, Massimo 1327, 1330
Veenmann, J. 1995
Vegezzi-Ruscalla, Giovenale 1347, 1349
Véglianté, J.-C. 1182, 1187, 2005, 2008
Veiga Martínez, Daniel 1292, 1295
Veit, W. 245, 457
Veiter, Theodor 157, 160, 1800, 1812, 2006
Veith, W. H. 271, 317, 318, 320
Vejnger, M. 1960
Vekerdi, József 1720, 1721, 1723
Velčeva, Borjana 1497
Velkovska, Vera 1443, 1445, 1451
Veltman, Calvin J. 381, 385, 386, 390, 402, 405, 836, 841
Vendryes, J. 101, 103
Venediktov, Grigorij 1494, 1496, 1498, 1503, 1504
Veny, Joan 1296, 1300, 1301, 1302
Verbeke, C. A. 839, 841
Verchratskyj, Ivan 1699, 1701
Verdoodt, Albert 80, 257, 402, 404, 405, 638, 642, 1112, 1114, 1119, 1121, 1123, 1134, 1135, 1136
Verhoeven, G. 105, 109
Verhoeven, Ludwig 125, 129, 235, 245, 320, 321, 322, 323, 325, 326, 471, 472, 578, 580, 585, 595, 604, 605, 626, 627, 630, 634, 850, 852, 976, 1150, 1151, 1152, 1157, 1495
Verivaki, M. 721, 723, 725
Verjans, Pierre 1139, 1143
Verlinde, S. 177, 180
Vermeer, Anne 634, 1150, 1152
Vermeire, Antoine 419
Vermes, Geneviève 178, 179, 180, 243, 320, 326, 327, 893, 1186, 1187, 1201, 1251, 2008, 2009, 2011
Vernant, J.-P. 221, 233
Vernez, G. 869, 871
Véronique, Daniel 57
Verougstraete, I. 402, 405
Verschueren, Johan 140, 141, 144, 587, 592, 928
Verzeichnis der Exonyme 450
Vestergaard, T. 440, 444
Vetulani, Z. 1655
Vial, Salvador 1299, 1302
Videgain, Charles 1268, 1269
Videnov, Mixail 1491, 1494, 1496
Vidoeski, B. 1449, 1450
Vidov, B. 1364, 1366
Viereck, Wolfgang 701, 910, 913, 1095, 1096, 1097, 1317, 1886
Vígh, Károly 1684
Vigneault, R. 79, 404
Vignetta, Andrea 1347, 1349
Vignoli, G. 1220, 1222
Vihman, M. 603, 609
Viikberg, Jüri 1905
Vikør, Lars S. 948, 956, 1007, 1014, 1025, 1032
Vila, Xavier. F. 1302
Vildomec, V. 2, 3, 12, 257
Viletta, Rudolf 160, 213, 218, 355, 357, 1837, 1840, 1844, 1846, 1848, 1849, 1853
Villanova, R. de 1182, 1187, 2005, 2008
Villanueva, Maria Dolores 1303, 1309
Villares, Ramón 1286, 1295
Villasante, L. 621, 624
Villehardouin, G. de (ca. 1150-ca. 1212) 555, 558
Vinay, J.-P. 146, 153
Vince, Zlatko 1433, 1437, 1439, 1442
Vincent, T. 1995
Vincenz, A. de 12
Vinogradov, V. V. 1895, 1900
Vinokur, G. 549
Virdis, Maurizio 1330, 1381, 1383, 2018, 2019
Virginia, L. 1260
Vittorio Emanuele II. (1861–1878) 1319
Vlasits, Josef 1822, 1827
Vöő, István 1464, 1468, 1469, 1485, 1486
Voegelin, C.-F. 590
Voegelin, F.-M. 590
Vogler, Bernard 1240
Vogt, H. 99, 103
Vogt, R. 886
Volkaitė-Kulikauskienė, R. 1622
Vollmer, H. 504, 507
Voloshinov, V. N. 747, 750
Vološin, Augustin 1701
Volterra, V. 33, 34, 40, 367, 370, 603, 609
Voortman, Berber 1150, 1152
Voráč, Jaroslav 1641
Vospernik, R. 97
Voß, J. 608
Vossen, Rüdiger 1971
Vouga, Jean-Pierre 1853
Vousten, Rob 1150, 1152
Voyé, Liliane 1111, 1123
Vreese, Willem de 1128, 1129
Vriendt, Marie Jeanne de 931
Vries, Jan de 16, 20, 325, 326, 771, 774, 775, 776, 777, 787, 1124, 1129, 1150, 1151, 1152
Vryonis, S. 1565
Vuorela, Katri 1007
Vydra, Bohumil 1636, 1641

W

Wacke, A. 237, 245
Wacker, H. 5, 12
Wadl, Wilhelm 1801, 1812
Wag, A. v. d. 437
Wagenaar, S. 433, 437
Wagner, D. 632, 634
Wagner, Francis S. 1712, 1721, 1723
Wagner, J. 417, 420
Wagner, Max Leopold 1377, 1378, 1383, 1525, 1570, 1571, 1572

Wagner, R. 1477
Wagner, S. 476, 481
Wahren, H.-K. 421
Waksberg, J. 732
Walcott, Derek 460
Wald, Alfred 1150, 1152
Wald, P. 680, 681, 683, 684
Waldstein, Ernst 1814, 1820
Wales, R. 294
Walker, Alastair 384, 1041, 1768, 1778, 1780, 1781, 1782, 1783, 1784, 1785, 1786
Walker, Antonio G. 188, 192
Walker, C. A. 608
Walker, John 1089, 1096
Walla, Fred 1808, 1812
Wallace, A. F. C. 174
Waller, T. G. 633
Wallman, Sandra 204, 209
Walsh, J. 301, 311
Walter, Henriette 1177, 1187, 1263, 1269
Walzl, Werner 1802, 1812
Wande, Erling 378, 976, 992, 1007, 1982
Wandruszka, Adam 1329, 1737, 1738
Wandruszka, Mario 257, 266, 271, 502, 507, 880
Wandruszka, Ulrich 1397
Wandt, Karl-Heinz 319, 751, 758, 759, 761, 763
Wangermée, Robert 1110, 1123
Wanner, E. 294, 591, 593
Warchoł, Stefan 1627, 1628
Wardhaugh, Ronald 75, 78, 81, 396, 399, 586, 593, 894, 901
Warner, S. 499, 501
Warschauer, F. 1661
Wartburg, Walther von 2, 1242, 1246, 1251, 1252
Washabaugh, W. 648
Waszak, St. 1584, 1594
Watahomigie, L. 664, 665, 666
Waters, A. 512, 514
Watson, I. 33, 40
Watson, J. B. 692, 702
Watson, J. L. 925, 931
Watson, L. 219, 233
Watson, M. E. 209
Watts, M. J. 72, 73, 75
Watts, Richard James 21, 216, 218, 924, 925, 931, 1847, 1853
Watzlawick, Paul 299, 311
Wawrik, Friedrich 1974, 1976, 1978, 1979
Wayne, H. 906
Weathersby, E. K. 603, 606
Webb, E. J. 752, 763
Webb, J. T. 333, 342
Webber, Jude 906, 1302
Weber, Daniel Erich 1854

Weber, E. 348, 351, 893
Weber, Heidi K. 22, 901, 904, 908, 912
Weber, Heinrich 152
Weber, M. H. 1179, 1187
Weber, Max 23, 31
Weber, Peter 770, 1123, 1310, 1317
Weber Egli, Daniela 380, 382, 385, 1351, 1357
Weber-Kellermann, I. 1486
Weckmann, André 94, 96, 1235, 1240
Weczerka, Hugo 1471, 1477
Weekes, A. J. 787
Weeks, F. 839, 841
Wegener, B. 741, 744
Wehling, Hans Georg 1838, 1854
Wei, Li (→ Li, Wei) 238, 244, 588, 593, 811
Weibel, Ernest 1838, 1846, 1847, 1849, 1850, 1854
Weick, K. 408, 414
Weifert, Ladislaus 1414, 1416
Weigand, Gustav 1458, 1476, 1522, 1525, 1533, 1534, 1536, 1539, 1547, 1550, 1933, 1941
Weigel, H. 618, 624
Weijnen, Antoon 271, 1112, 1123, 1246, 1247, 1248, 1250, 1252
Weilbacher, W. 439, 444
Weilenmann, Hermann 1846, 1849, 1854
Weiler, F. 180, 191
Weilguni, Werner 1822, 1827
Weill, C. 247, 257
Weiner, M. 395, 398, 426, 431, 444
Weingarten, E. 761, 762
Weinhold, Karl 1600
Weinreich, Uriel 3, 4, 5, 6, 12, 22, 49, 50, 51, 52, 53, 54, 55, 57, 59, 62, 76, 81, 98, 100, 102, 103, 109, 110, 111, 112, 116, 117, 120, 124, 125, 130, 131, 138, 141, 144, 235, 245, 246, 257, 320, 333, 342, 392, 399, 541, 544, 545, 549, 558, 567, 586, 593, 609, 709, 713, 714, 715, 716, 717, 718, 720, 722, 725, 750, 763, 772, 776, 790, 797, 798, 804, 815, 819, 828, 833, 842, 872, 880, 893, 901, 1314, 1317, 1720, 1722, 1723, 1849, 1854, 1879, 1886, 1955, 1960, 1961
Weinrich, Harald 90, 92, 93, 96, 97, 425, 426, 508, 514, 682, 684, 874, 880
Weinstein, B. 79, 399, 404, 405, 433, 438

Weisgerber, Bernd 261, 269, 271
Weisgerber, Jean 1110, 1123
Weisgerber, Leo 260, 263, 271
Weiss, Andreas 1812, 1820
Weiss, Andreas von 3, 12
Weiß, R. 853, 854, 856, 857
Weissberg, R. 299, 311
Weithmann, M. 2032
Weitling, Günter 1042
Welkowitz, J. 335, 336, 340, 342
Weller, F.-R. 505, 507
Weller, G. 375, 379
Weller, R. 513
Wellman, B. 433, 438
Wells, G. 629, 634
Wells, John C. 1095, 1096
Wells, M. 82, 88
Weltens, B. 18, 21, 22, 236, 245, 321, 327, 579, 581, 582, 583, 584, 585, 1151
Wen-Shing, T. 380, 385
Wenning, N. 181, 191
Wentz, J. 599, 603, 607
Werenicz, W. 1613, 1614, 1621, 1627, 1628
Werker, J. 289, 295
Werlen, Erika 754, 758, 763, 764
Werlen, Iwar 213, 218, 266, 271, 759, 764, 901, 1849, 1854
Werner, Ormar 540
Werner, R. 1469
Werth, M. 192
Wesche, M. B. 33, 40, 294
Wesprim, Zsolt Lengyel 370
Wessén, E. 4, 12
West, John F. 1043, 1049
Westfal, St. 1615, 1621
Westoby, A. 420
Westwood, A. 373, 378
Wetherell, M. 48, 138, 144
Wettinger, Godfrey 1401, 1406
Wexler, Paul 227, 233, 248, 257, 834, 842, 1888, 1890, 1900, 1926
Weydt, H. 152
Wheeler, S. 373, 378
Wherritt, I. 716, 720
Whinnom, K. 651, 654, 658
Whitaker, Ian 981
White, C. L. 204, 209
White, D. 695, 700
White, L. 518, 520, 525, 565, 567
White, P. E. 2007
Whitney, W. D. 2, 112, 117
Whyte, William. F. 765, 770, 930
Wiśniewski, Jerzy 1606, 1614, 1615, 1620, 1621
Wicker, A. 694, 702
Widmer, Jean 1846, 1854
Wieczerkowski, Wilhelm 1040, 1041, 1042
Wieden, W. 292, 295

Wiegand, Herbert Ernst 270, 584, 1600
Wieken-Mayser, M. 732
Wierlacher, Anton 514, 515, 925, 929, 931
Wierzbicka, Anna 14, 22, 134, 138
Wieser, J. 507, 509, 514
Wiesinger, Peter 271, 812, 813, 814, 818, 819, 1357, 1600, 1809, 1811, 1812, 1820
Wiesner, Christa 1570, 1572
Wiggen, Geirr 948, 957
Wikemann, E. 903, 906
Wiklund, K. B. 981
Wiktorowicz, Józef 1600
Wild, Beate 1535, 1539
Wild, Katharina 1730, 1731
Wildgen, Wolfgang 144, 152, 750, 760, 815, 818, 1328
Wilkins, David P. 117, 138
Wilkinson, Henry Robert 1974, 1976, 1978, 1979
Wilkinson, I. 633
Willemyns, Roland 211, 218, 700, 1124, 1125, 1126, 1127, 1129, 1245, 1252
Willes, M. J. 839, 840
Willi, Urs 1854, 1881, 1883, 1885, 1886
Williams, Colin H. 63, 64, 66, 67, 68, 69, 70, 73, 74, 75, 79, 80, 213, 216, 217, 218, 283, 575, 578, 686, 691, 722, 725, 776, 1061, 1064, 1074, 1075, 1076, 1078, 1080, 1081, 1085, 1087, 1088, 1259, 1974, 1976, 1978, 1979, 2003, 2008
Williams, F. 713
Williams, Glanmor 1077, 1087
Williams, Glyn 76, 77, 81, 391, 638, 642, 684, 685, 686, 691, 802, 804, 865, 866, 871, 1079, 1087
Williams, Gwyn A. 1087
Williams, P. 1179, 1187, 2004, 2008
Williamson, J. G. 188, 191
Williamson, Robert C. 1260
Willig, A. 632, 634
Willkommen, Dirk 1038, 1041, 1042, 1780, 1782
Wilpert, C. 327
Wilson, J. 757, 764
Wilson, K. 917, 920
Wilson, M. 762
Wilson, R. 607
Wilson, Th. P. 757, 764
Wilson, W. 358
Wilts, Ommo 1778, 1779, 1782, 1786
Wimmer, E. 876, 878
Wind, Bartina H. 1126, 1129

Windisch, Uli 8, 12, 540, 1843, 1844, 1847, 1849, 1854, 1866, 1869, 1870, 1873, 1878
Winford, D. 170, 175
Winkelmann, Otto 372, 379, 874, 880, 1283, 1285, 1469, 1886, 2014
Winnifrith, Tom J. 1455, 1456, 1458, 1493, 1494, 1496
Winsa, Birger 992, 1982
Winter, Alexandre 1211, 1213
Winter, K. 96
Winter, S. 514
Winter, Werner 134, 135, 136, 138, 397, 1971
Winzer, F. 185, 193
Wirth, L. 451, 458
Wis, M. 4, 12
Withers, Charles W. J. 72, 75, 1061, 1075, 1091, 1096, 1097
Witte, B. de 210, 217, 355, 356, 861, 864
Witte, Els 8, 12, 1298, 1302
Witzel, A. 753, 756, 764
Wodak(-Leodolter), Ruth 18, 20, 586, 590, 592, 712, 713, 714, 1259, 1379, 1383
Wode, Henning 7, 12, 235, 245, 257, 284, 285, 286, 288, 289, 290, 291, 292, 293, 295, 517, 525
Woehrling, J. 168, 211, 217, 218
Woelfel, J. 434, 435, 437, 438
Wölck, Wolfgang 124, 125, 129, 130, 172, 175, 370, 453, 458, 695, 702, 759, 763, 764, 765, 767, 768, 769, 770, 924, 930, 1094, 1096, 1715, 1722, 1725, 1730
Woldan, Alois 1925
Wolf, H. J. 880
Wolf, Johann 1473, 1477
Wolf, L. 873, 880
Wolf, M. 239, 245, 323, 327
Wolf, Preben 1042
Wolfe, James H. 1582
Wolff, H. 2, 176, 180, 695, 702
Wolfgang, A. 298, 311, 492
Wolfram, Herwig 1799, 1812
Wolfram, W. 335, 342
Wolfsgruber, Karl 1390, 1398
Wolfson, J. 675
Wolfson, N. 457, 458, 691, 709, 714, 757, 764, 818
Woll, Dieter 1317
Wolska, Ilona 1636, 1641
Wood, D. 67, 68, 75
Wood, R. E. 2003, 2008
Wood, Ralph C. 317, 320
Wood, Richard 1245, 1252
Woodhouse, Christopher M. 1551, 1554
Woodward, M. 76, 80

Woolard, Kathryn A. 142, 144, 336, 342, 400, 405, 455, 458, 574, 575, 576, 578, 587, 589, 590, 591, 593, 597, 609, 747, 749, 750, 811, 906, 1301, 1302
Woolford, E. 115, 117, 595, 600, 609, 648
Worchel, S. 48
Worth, D. 1495
Wosiak-Śliwa, R. 1606
Woudstra, E. 421
Wretman, J. H. 735, 737
Wright, E. N. 476, 481
Wright, J. D. 743
Wright, Roger 1275, 1285
Wright, Sue 1899
Wu, J.-J. M. 35, 40
Wunderli, Peter 878, 1854
Wurm, St. A. 10, 648, 649
Wurzel, Wolfgang U. 533, 540
Wurzer, Bernhard 814, 819, 1330, 1357, 2017, 2019
Wüster, Erwin 881, 887
Wutte, Martin 1801, 1812, 1815, 1820
Wyer, R. S. 731, 732
Wylie, L. 296, 311
Wynants, Armel 363, 1139, 1140, 1141, 1142, 1143, 1995
Wynne, R. 304, 311

X

Xove Ferreiro, Xosé 1293, 1295

Y

Yaeger-Dror, M. 336, 342
Yamamoto, A. 664, 665, 666
Yanabu, A. 106, 109
Yang, K.-S. 695, 702
Yardley, K. 48
Yatrakis, P. 433, 438
Yeager, J. 412, 414
Yeni-Komshian, G. 37, 38
Yetkin, C. 1567, 1572
Yinger, M. 209
Ylönen, S. 513, 515
Young, D. 489, 492
Young, L. 48
Yousef, F. 929
Youssi, A. 393, 399
Ytsma, Johannes 1156, 1157, 1905
Yu, A. 835, 842
Yuen, S. D. 478, 481
Yum, J. O. 338, 342
Yvia-Croce, Hyacinthe 1217, 1218, 1222
Yzermann, N. 513, 515

Z

Zaborski, B. 64, 75
Zach, Krista 1463, 1464, 1470
Zafrani, H. 616, 623
Zahradník, St. 1669
Zaimov, Jordan 1450, 1545, 1550
Zanna, H. 695, 701
Zapf, W. 415, 419
Zappert, L. T. 632, 634
Zaprudnik, Jan 1922, 1925, 1926
Zaręba, Alfred 1594, 1632, 1633, 1634
Zarecki, Ajzik 1960, 1961
Zarjevski, Y. 866, 867, 871
Zatovkaňuk, M. 1701
Zawadowski, L. 5, 12
Zdancewicz, Tadeusz 1608, 1610, 1614, 1616, 1619, 1620, 1621, 1622
Zeh, Jürgen 1041, 1042
Zelenay, Anna 1739, 1743
Zelger, Peter 1357
Zelinsky, B. 1640
Zelinsky, W. 64, 69, 75
Zel'ová, Anna 1672, 1673, 1674, 1678, 1681, 1684
Zeman, Jiři 1650, 1651, 1654, 1655, 1673, 1678
Zempel, S. 458, 464
Zentella, A. 596, 609
Žerov, Stojan 1495
Zervudacki, C. 454, 458
Zhou, M. 869, 871
Ziahosseiny, S. 563, 564, 566
Zielińska, Anna 1614
Zientara, B. 1594
Zimmerli, Jacob 1837, 1849, 1854
Zimmermann, Fritz 1691
Zimmermann, P. 925, 931
Zinkevičius, Zigmas 1618, 1620, 1622, 1913, 1918, 1919
Zinnes, D. A. 426, 438
Zinovieff, Maurice 1464, 1470
Zinsli, Paul 1353, 1357
Zint, Ingeborg 1776
Zlotnik, H. 188, 192
Žluktenko, Jurij A. 1699, 1701, 1932
Zobl, H. 11, 521, 525, 560, 563, 567
Zolberg, A. R. 76, 77, 81
Żołędowski, Cezary 1622
Zöllner, Erich 1797, 1798, 1799, 1800, 1802, 1812
Zondag, Koen 396, 399, 471, 473, 1156, 1157
Zorc, R. D. 221, 233
Zorko, Zinka 1741, 1743
Zuber 243
Zubiri, I. 624
Zubrzycki, J. 138
Zuengler, J. 689, 691
Zülch, Tilman 1971
Zurif, E. B. 37, 38, 604, 609
Zwicky, A. M. 607
Zwinger, E. 1661
Zwolinski, P. 450

Sachregister / Topical Index / Index des matières

Vorbemerkung

Das Sachregister enthält dreierlei Einträge:
1) wissenschaftliche Begriffe aus den 239 Einzelartikeln und den Kommentaren der 16 Sprachenkarten des Handbuchs,
2) für einen Gutteil dieser originalsprachlichen (d. h. deutschen, englischen oder französischen) Begriffe Verweise in den jeweils beiden anderen Sprachen,
3) Ortsnamen, die sich vor allem auf die 16 Sprachkarten am Ende des zweiten Halbbandes beziehen.

Ad 2) Die Lemmata der Verweise sind *kursiv* gedruckt. Aufgabe der Verweise ist es, einen Leser, der nicht alle drei Sprachen des Handbuchs gleichermaßen beherrscht, bei der Benützung des Sachregisters zu unterstützen.

Ad 3) Bei den Ortsnamen wurde besonders auf eine praktikable Dokumentation der *Mehr*namigkeit (d. h. von *Endo*nymen und *Exo*nymen) geachtet. Die überwiegende Mehrzahl der im Sachregister erfaßten Namen stammt von den 16 Sprachenkarten des Handbuchs. Daher ist die im Sachregister aufscheinende Mehrnamigkeit nicht exhaustiv, sondern verbleibt nur im Rahmen dessen, was auf den 16 Sprachenkarten dokumentiert ist. So enthält das Sachregister für das deutsche Endonym *Wien* zwar die mitteleuropäischen Exonyme *Bécs* (ung.), *Vídeň* (tsch.), *Viedeň* (slw.) und *Wiedeń* (pln.), nicht aber die westeuropäischen Exonyme *Vienna* (eng.) oder *Vienne* (frz.), da diese auf keiner der 16 Sprachenkarten aufscheinen.

Die Reihenfolge ist streng alphabetisch. Diakritika wurden beim Alphabetisieren nicht berücksichtigt: daher gilt: a = ä, o = ö, u = ü, æ = ae etc., bzw. c = ć oder č, f = þ, s = ś, ş, š etc.

Die Zahlen hinter den Sachbegriffen und Namen beziehen sich auf die fortlaufende Paginierung der beiden Teilbände des Handbuchs.

Die Herausgeber sind Heide Marie Pamminger und Susanne Oleinek (Universität Salzburg) für ihren hingebungsvollen und überaus kompetenten Einsatz bei der Erstellung des Sachregisters zu großem Dank verpflichtet.

Introductory

The Topical Index lists three types of entries:
1) scientific concepts mentioned in the 239 individual articles and in the comments of the 16 language maps of the Handbook,
2) references in the other two languages for the majority of the terms in the original (English, French, German) articles, and
3) place names, especially those occurring in the 16 language maps of vol. II.

Ad 1) The terms of the references appear in *italics*, in order to assist readers who are not multilingual in the use of the index.

Ad 2) In listing the place names some attention has been paid to the recognition of *poly*nomy. Since the majority of names listed in the Index corresponds to the 16 language maps of the Handbook the *poly*nomous listing is incomplete. Entries are limited to the names on the maps. Accordingly, the Topical Index lists against the German endonym *Wien* the Central European exonyms *Bécs* (ung.), *Vídeň* (tsch.), *Viedeň* (slw.) and *Wiedeń* (pln.), and omits the Western European exonyms *Vienna* (eng.) or *Vienne* (frz.) which do not figure on any of the 16 language maps.

Names are listed in strict alphabetic order: diacritics have not been taken into consideration, i. e. a is equivalent to ä, o = ö, u = ü, æ = ae etc., c = ć or č, f = þ, s = ś, ş, š etc.

Numbers after scientific concepts and names refer to the (continuous) pagination of the two Handbook volumes.

The editors owe a very special debt of gratitude to Heide Marie Pamminger and Susanne Oleinek of the University of Salzburg for her expert assistance in the preparation of the Topical Index.

Remarque préliminaire

L'index des matières contient trois sortes d'entrées:
1) des concepts scientifiques relatifs aux 239 articles et aux commentaires des 16 cartes linguistiques de ce manuel,
2) des renvois trilingues (*allemand* → anglais, français; *anglais* → allemand, français; *français* → allemand, anglais) relatifs à de nombreux concepts scientifiques répertoriés dans l'index des matières dans la langue originale (allemand, anglais ou français),
3) des toponymes (noms de lieu) dont la plupart figurent sur les 16 cartes linguistiques à la fin du second tome.

Ad 2) L'objectif des renvois dont les entrées sont en caractères *italiques* est de rendre plus aisé l'usage de ce manuel à des lecteurs ne disposant pas de la pleine maîtrise de l'allemand, de l'anglais et du français.

Ad 3) Quant aux toponymes, il nous semblait important d'en saisir la *poly*nomie (c.-à-d. la coexistence d'*endo*nymes et d'*exo*nymes) répertoriée sur les 16 cartes linguistiques de ce manuel et de la présenter dans une documentation d'un accès facile. Comme l'écrasante majorité des exonymes répertoriés dans l'index des matières se réfère uniquement aux cartes linguistiques, l'information exonymique de l'index ne saurait être exhaustive. C'est ainsi que pour l'endonyme allemand *Wien* (capitale de l'Autriche), le lecteur trouvera, dans l'index, les exonymes centre-européens *Bécs* (ung.), *Vídeň* (tsch.), *Viedeň* (slw.) et *Wiedeń* (pln.) mais non pas les exonymes ouest-européens *Vienna* (eng.) ou *Vienne* (frz.) puisque ces derniers ne figurent sur aucune des 16 cartes linguistiques du manuel.

L'ordre est strictement alphabétique. Les signes diacritiques n'ont pas été pris en considération; il en résulte les correspondances suivantes: a = ä, o = ö, u = ü, æ = ae etc., respectivement c = ć ou č, f = þ, s = ś, ş, š etc.

Les chiffres répertoriés derrière les concepts scientifiques et les toponymes se réfèrent à la numérotation de pages continue des deux tomes de ce volume.

Les éditeurs tiennent à remercier cordialement Mesdames Heide Marie Pamminger et Susanne Oleinek (Université de Salzbourg) qui, animées d'une ténacité et d'une compétence informatique inégalables, ont mené à bien l'établissement de l'index des matières.

Abkürzungen / Abbreviations / Sigles

	Deutsch	English	Français
alb.	Albanisch	Albanian	albanais
arb.	Arabisch	Arabic	arabe
ast.	Asturisch	Asturian	asturien
bkm.	Norwegisch:Bokmål	Norwegian:Bokmål	norvégien:Bokmål
blg.	Bulgarisch	Bulgarian	bulgare
brt.	Bretonisch	Breton	breton
bsk.	Baskisch	Basque	basque
bsn.	Bosnisch	Bosnian	bosniaque
dän.	Dänisch	Danish	danois
dt.	Deutsch	German	allemand
eng.	Englisch	English	anglais
est.	Estnisch	Estonian	estonien
far.	Färöisch	Faroese	féroien

fin.	Finnisch	Finnish	finnois
frl.	Friulanisch	Friulian	frioulan
frs.	Friesisch	Frisian	frison
frz.	Französisch	French	français
gal.	Galegisch/Galicisch	Galician	galicien
gr.	Griechisch	Greek	grec
ir.	Irisch	Irish	irlandais
it.	Italienisch	Italian	italien
kat.	Katalanisch	Catalan	catalan
krs.	Korsisch	Corsican	corse
krt.	Kroatisch	Croatian	croate
lit.	Litauisch	Lithuanian	lituanien
ltt.	Lettisch	Latvian	letton
lux.	Lëtzebuergisch/Luxemburgisch	Luxemburgish	luxembourgeois
mak.	Makedonisch	Macedonian	macédonien
mal.	Maltesisch	Maltese	maltais
ndl.	Niederländisch	Dutch	néerlandais
nyn.	Norwegisch:Nynorsk	Norwegian:Nynorsk	norvégien:Nynorsk
okz.	Okzitanisch	Occitan	occitan
pln.	Polnisch	Polish	polonais
rss.	Russisch	Russian	russe
rtr.	Rätoromanisch	Rhaeto-Romance	rhéto-roman
rum.	Rumänisch	Romanian (Rumanian)	roumain
sam.	Samisch	Sa(a)mi	sami
slk.	Slowakisch	Slovak	slovaque
slw.	Slowenisch	Slovenian	slovène
sor.	Sorbisch	Sorbian	sorabe
sp.	Spanisch	Spanish	espagnol
srb.	Serbisch	Serbian	serbe
swd.	Schwedisch	Swedish	suédois
trk.	Türkisch	Turkish	turc
tsch.	Tschechisch	Czech	tchèque
ukr.	Ukrainisch	Ukrainian	ukrainien
ung.	Ungarisch	Hungarian	hongrois
wrs.	Weißrussisch	B(y)elorussian	biélorusse

A

Aachen (dt.) → Aix-la-Chapelle (frz.), Aken (ndl.) 2001
Aarlen (ndl.) → Arel (dt.), Arlon (frz.) 2001
abduction 533
Åbenrå (dän.) → Apenrade (dt.) 2055
Abgrenzungsstrategie 222
Åbo (swd.) → Turku (fin.) 1985
aboriginal language 428
Abruzzo-Molise 1371
Abstand, kultureller − → distance culturelle
Abstandsprache 277
Abstandsprache → langue par distanciation
Académie Celtique (1804−1814) 1258
accent mobile 1226
accent musical 1228
accommodation theory 334, 573
Accord Gruber-De Gasperi (1946) → Gruber-De Gasperi-Abkommen (1946)

Accords d'Osimo (1975) 1358
Accords de Latran (1929) 1360
acculturation 51, 907, 909 f
accuracy (s. tests) 506
Achse Berlin-Rom 1320
Acquaviva Collecroce (it.) → Zivavoda Brdodokriz (krt.) 1323, 1363, 2021, 2025
acquisition 61, 603
− simultanée 32
morphological − 372
acrolect 643
acrolecte 277, 655
Actes de l'Amérique du Nord Britannique (1867) 214
active bilingualism 971, 989
active vocabulary 582
ad hoc-Entlehnung 1817, 1826
adaption of names, phonological − 550
additive bilingual education 493
Adhrianupoli (gr.) → Edirne (trk.) 2035
administrative language → langue administrative
Adstrat 1271, 1313, 1320, 1374

adstrate 2
advertising → publicité
− *campaign* → campagne publicitaire
− industry 301
affichage commercial 163
affichage public 163
affix 109
African American English 710
Afrikaans 167, 489
Afrique 91, 247, 484, 688
− du Nord 1196
− Noire 1178, 1181
Afrique du Sud → South Africa, Südafrika
agglomération urbaine 450
agglutinating languages 110
Agordino 1391
Ähnlichkeit → similarity
Ahvenanmaa (fin.) → Åland (swd.) 1985
Aiacciu (krs.) → Ajaccio (it.) 2011, 2021
Aigaîon (gr.) → Eǧe Denizi (trk.) 2029
Aix-la-Chapelle (frz.) → Aachen (dt.), Aken (ndl.) 2001

Ajaccio (it.) → Aiacciu (krs.) 2011, 2021
Ajii Saranta (gr.) → Sarandë (alb.) 2035
Aken (ndl.) → Aachen (dt.), Aix-la-Chapelle (frz.) 2001
Akkademja tal-Malti 1402
Akkomodation 28
Akkulturation 290, 319
Alacant (kat.) → Alicante (sp.) 2015
Alagna (it.) → Land (dt.)2021; Olen (dt.) 2021, 2063
Alamans 1863
Alamans → Alemannen
Åland (swd.) → Ahvenanmaa (fin.) 1985
Alanen 1273
Alava 1303
Alba Iulia (rum.) → Karlsburg (dt.) 2029; Gyulafehérvár (ung.) 2029, 2047
albanais → Albanisch
albanais-aroumain 1457
albanais-grec 1457
albanais-macédonien 1457
Albanais 1436, 1453 f, 1455 f
Albanais → Albaner
Albaner 1407, 1409 f, 1515
Albaner → Albanais
Albania 66, 332
Albanía (gr.) → Shqipëria (alb.) 2035
Albanian 1026, 1030 f, 1417, 1425, 1427, 1429, 1443, 1444, 1445, 1446 ff, 1490,
– Alphabet Conference 1444
Albania → Albanie, Albanien
Albanian → Albanais, Albanisch, Albaner
Albanie 1451–1458
Albanie → Albania, Albanien
Albanien → Albania
albanien → Albanian, Albaner, Albanisch
Albanien 1961
Albanija (blg., bsn., krt., srb.) → Shqipëria (alb.) 2025, 2029
Albanisch 1320, 1371, 1410 f, 1414
Albanisch → Albanian, albanien
Albanisch-Serbokroatisch 1411, 1414
Alberta 773
Alcobaça 1312
Alcyoniadi (1992) 1368
Alderney (eng.) → Aurigny (frz.) 1993
alémanique 1333
alémanique → alemannisch
Alemannen 1797, 1837
Alemannen → Alamans
Alemannien 1855

alemannisch 1163, 1226
alemannisch → alémanique
Alexandhrupoli (gr.) → Dedeağaç (trk.) 2035
Algarve 1275, 1310
Algeria 329
Algérie → Algeria
Algerien → Algeria
Alghero (it.) 194, 1323, 1377, 1381 → L'Alguer (kat.) 352, 2021
Algonquien 793
Alicante (sp.) → Alacant (kat.) 2015
aliénation 158, 196, 212, 1191
aljamía 1274
Alleanza Nazionale 1320
Allemagne 155, 202, 386, 453
– wilhelminienne 1225
Allemagne (frz.) → Deutschland (dt.), Germania (it., rtr.) 2063
allemand 1110, 1174, 1222, 1866
– standard 1866
allemand → Deutsch, German
– *alsacien* → Elsässer Deutsch
– *autrichien* → Deutsch, österreichisches –
allemand-français 60
Allemands 1437, 1439
Allemands → Deutsche, Germans
Allenstein (dt.) → Olsztyn (pln.) 2039
Allgäu 1224
allocation of funds → Mittelallokation
allochthon 894
allochthonous, allochtone → allochthon
allogeni 1384, 1388
allomorphs 109
Allonymie 444
Alltagssprache 259
Almasca (krt.) → Bácsalmás (ung.) 2047
Alpenhauptkamm 1799
Alpenslawen 1799
alphabet, Cyrillic – → Schrift, kyrillische –
alphabet, latin-cyrillic – → Schrift, lateinisch-kyrillische –
alphabétisation 254, 890, 894
alphabétisation → Alphabetisierung, literacy
Alphabetisierung 894
Alphabetisierung → literacy
alphabets, Latin and Cyrillic – → écriture latine et cyrillique
Alpinokzitanisch 1323
Alsace 69, 1174, 1224
Alsace-Lorraine 1223
Alsacian → Elsässer
alsacien 199

alsacien → Elsässer
Alsatian German → Elsässer Deutsch
Alsó Ausztria (ung.) → Niederösterreich (dt.) 2047
Alsóőr → Unterwart
Altaic Turkish 344
Altamische 316
Altbelgien 1130, 1134
Altbelgien-Mitte 1130
Altbelgien-Mitte → Vieille-Belgique-Centre
Altbelgien-Nord 1130, 1136
Altbelgien-Nord → Vieille-Belgique-Nord
Altbelgien-Süd 1130
Altbelgien-Süd → Vieille-Belgique-Sud
alternance
– codique 53
– de langue 1184
– des codes 33, 460
– des langues 57
– *de codes* → code-switching, Kodewechsel
– *linguistique* → Sprachmischung
Althochdeutsch 1226
Altkirchenslawisch, Altbulgarisch → Church Slavic, Old Church Slavonic
Altnorwegisch → Old Norse
Alto Adige (it.) → Südtirol (dt.) 94, 381, 447, 1318, 1320, 1350, 2059, 2063
Altostfriesisch 1787
Amalgamierung 230
aménagement linguistique 462, 828 f, 834 f, 839, 856, 865, 876, 882, 905, 1438
aménagement linguistique → language policy, Sprachenpolitik, Sprachplanung
American 305
– Finnish 662
– Revolution 400
Amerika 1270, 1942
Amerikanische Revolution → American Revolution
Amérique Centrale → Mittelamerika
Amérique du Sud → Südamerika
Amisch 314
Amish 189, 392
Amohostos (gr.) → Gazi Magusa (trk.) 2035
Ampezzo 1323
Amsterdam 1146
Amtssprache 843, 854 f, 898, 1138, 1169, 1385, 1400, 1761 f, 1829, 1845, 1858, 1881
Amtssprache → langue officielle, official language

Anabaptisten 312
analogie 167
analphabètes 1367
analyse
 - de la conversation 925
 - du texte 462
 - littéraire 461
 - *contrastive* → contrastive analysis
 - *contrastive appliquée* → Applied Contrastive Analysis
 - *de la conversation* → Konversationsanalyse
 - *des réseaux* → network analysis
 - *en composantes principales* → principal component analysis
 - *factorielle* → factor analysis
Analyse, angewandte kontrastive - → Applied Contrastive Analysis
Analyse, kontrastive - → contrastive analysis
analysis of variance 785
Anár (sam.) → Inari (fin.) 1985
Ancien Régime 1261
Andalusien 1272
Andorra (kat., sp.) → Andorre (frz.) 1198, 2011
Andorre (frz.) → Andorra (kat., sp.) 1198, 2011
anglais 167, 1866, 1868
anglais → Englisch
 - langue seconde (ALS) 473
 - comme langue de specialité 840
 - *comme langue de spécialité* → English for special purposes
 - *comme langue officielle* → Englisch als offizielle Sprache
anglais-espagnol 33
anglicisme 873 f
anglicization 1061
anglicization → Anglisierung
Anglisierung 897, 1089
Anglisierung → anglicization
Anglizismus 425, 873 f
Anglo-Canadian 43
anglophone 386
Anglophonie 195
Angola 1311, 1312
anomalie 167
anomie 77
Anschluß (1938, Österreich) 1829
answer, closed - → *Antwort, geschlossene* -
anthropologie 49
 - culturelle 50, 921
 - linguistique 49
 - *culturelle* → Kulturanthropologie
antideutsche Einstellung 1137

Antillians 1144
Antisemitismus 1947
Antwerp → Anvers
Antwerpen (dt., ndl.) → Anvers (frz.) 1113, 2001
Antwort, geschlossene - 729
Anvers (frz.) 1113 → Antwerpen (dt., ndl.) 2001
Aorist 1958
Aosta (it.) 349 → Augst (dt.) 2063; Aoste (frz.) 2011, 2063
Aosta Valley → Aostatal, Vallée d'Aoste, Augst
Aostatal 1318
Aostatal → Val d'Aosta, Vallée d'Aoste
Aoste (frz.) → Augst (dt.) 2063; Aosta (it.) 2011, 2063
Apartheid 490
apartheid linguistique 215
Apenrade (dt.) → Åbenrå (dän.) 2055
aphasia 375
Aphasie 236
appartenance ethnique 455
appartenance sociale 455
Applied Contrastive Analysis 559
apprentissage 61
approche monothétique 177
approche polythétique 177
appropriation des langues étrangères 54
aptitude test → test d'aptitude
Apulien 1323, 1371
Aquileia 1358
Aquitaine 1189
Aquitains 1260
arabe 198, 247, 616, 1180, 1377
arabe → Arabic, Arabisch
Araber 1399
Arabes 304, 1296
Arabic 392, 975, 1026 f
arabisation 197
Arabisch 91, 320
Arabisch → arabe, Arabic
Aragon 352, 1202, 1275, 1296
Aragonesisch 1275
Aramäisch 1949
Arb(ë)reshe 1373
Arbeitsimmigrant 1754, 1765, 1767
Arbeitsimmigration 924
Arbeitsmarkt 188
Arbeitsmigration 95, 320
Arbeitssprache → langue de travail, working language
Archaismen 1163, 1825
Ardeal (Siebenbürgen) 1478
Ardeal (Siebenbürgen) → Erdély, Siebenbürgen, Transsylvanie
Ardennes 1107
area symbols 67

areal diffusion: phonological, phonetic - 98, 102
Arealkontakt 1276
Arel 214
Arel (dt.) → Arlon (frz.) 2001; Aarlen (ndl.)
Arel → Arlon
Areler Land 1130
Arfé-Resolution 932
Argel (sp.) → El-Djesaïr (arb.) 2015
Argelia (sp.) → Djazaïrijja (arb.) 2015
Arjeplog (swd.) → Árjjapluovvi (sam.) 1985
Arjirokastro (gr.) → Gjirokastër (alb.) 2035
Árjjapluovvi (sam.) → Arjeplog (swd.) 1985
Arlon (frz.) 1161 → Arel (dt.), Aarlen (ndl.) 214, 2001
Armenier → Arméniens
Armenian 1498, 1490, 1554 ff, 1555 f, 1558 f, 1569, 1578, 1581
Armenian → Arménien, Armenisch
Armenian-French 783
Armenians → Arméniens, Armenier
arménien 273, 1183
arménien → Armenisch
Arménien 325
Arméniens 1455, 1593
Arméniens → Armenier
Armenier 232, 1463, 1572 ff
Armenisch 320, 1520, 1574
Armenisch → Arménien
Armoricains 1254
armorique 1173
Arnheim (dt.) → Arnhem (ndl.) 2001, 2055
Arnhem (ndl.) → Arnheim (dt.) 2001, 2055
Aromanian 1443, 1445 f, 1447 f
Aromanian → Aromunen, Aromunisch, aroumain, Valaque, Vlach, Vlah language, Wallachian
Aromunen 1515, 1516 ff, 1520, 1533 – 1537
Aromunisch 1516 f, 1518 f, 1535, 1536
Aromunisch → Aromanian, aroumain
Aromunisch-Bulgarisch 1537
Aromunisch-Mazedonisch 1537
aroumain 254, 1456
Aroumain → Aromanian, Aromunen, Aromunisch, Valaque, Vlach, Vlah language, Wallachian
Arras (frz.) → Atrecht (ndl.) 2001

Arső Lendva (ung.) → Lendava (krt.) 2047
articulation des langues 527
artifactural communication 301, 302
Artois 1242
Aruba 1144
Arumanian (eng.) → Aromanian (eng.)
Arvaniten 1519
Arvanites 1541 f
Arvanítika 1540−1542
Arvanitisch 1518, 1520 f
Aschkenasim 1943
Ashkenazic Jews 1566, 1568
Asiago (it.) → Sleghe (dt.) 2021
Aškenazim 1942
Aßling (dt.) → Jesenice (slw.) 2059
Aspektsystem 1959
Assimilanten 1807
assimilation 390, 984, 987, 1029, 1712 f, 1720, 1751
− linguistic 854, 889, 986
 linguistic − → Sprachanpassung, Sprachassimilation
− *linguistique* → language assimilation, Sprachanpassung, sprachliche Assimilation
Assimilation (Assimilierung) 381, 1034, 1039, 1135, 1725, 1800, 1813
Assimilationspolitik 1482
Assimilationsprozeß 687, 817
Association pour le Bilinguisme en Classe dès la Maternelle (ABCM, 1990) 1239
Asturer 1272
Astipalea (gr.) → Stampalia (gr.) 2035
Asturians → Asturer
Asturie-León 1275
Asturiens → Asturer
Asylanten 225, 869
Asylanten → asylum seekers
Asylbewerber 1754, 1765 f
asylum seeker → Asylanten
asylum seekers 869
Athina (gr.) → Atina (trk.) 2035
Äthiopien → Ethiopia
Atina (trk.) → Athina (gr.) 2035
Atlantikcharta (14.8.1941) → Charte Atlantique (14/8/1941)
Atlantin Valtameri (fin.) → Norske havet (bkm.), Nordatlanten (swd.), 1985
Atlas Linguarum Europae (ALE) 260
Atrecht (ndl.) → Arras (frz.) 2001
attitude 906, 911, 1750
attitude → Einstellung
− idéologique, linguistique 1003, 1048, 1213, 1306
− *and behavior* → Einstellung und Verhalten
− *et comportement* → Einstellung und Verhalten
− linguistique → language attitude, Sprachattitüde, Spracheinstellung
− *research* → Einstellungsforschung
Attitüde 30, 1400
attractiveness 706
Attraktivität → attractiveness
attrition → décrochage
Aubel-Klause 1136
Aufklärung → Lumières
aufzeichnen 759
Augst (dt.) → Aoste (frz.), Aosta (it.) 2063
Aurigny (frz.) → Alderney (eng.) 1993
Ausbau 1210
 -sprache 277, 893 f
 -*dialekt* → dialecte en voie d'élaboration
 -*sprache* → langue par élaboration
Ausbildungsniveau → education level
Ausgangssprache 913 f
Ausgangssprache → langue de départ
Ausgleich (1867, Österreich-Ungarn) 1798, 1829
Ausgleichsmundart 1472
Ausgleichsprozesse 1950
Ausgleichssprache 1857
Ausgleichstendenzen 1843
Ausrottung 1962
Außenmundart, dachlose − → dialecte exposé
Außensprachinsel 813
Aussiedler 181, 868, 1754, 1765
Aussiedler → expelled Germans
Aussig (dt.) → Ústí nad L. (tsch.) 2043
Australasian English 722
Austria (eng., it., pln., rtr.) 330, 588, 1427 → Österreich (dt.) 229, 1350, 1797, 2021, 2039, 2063; Autriche (frz.) 2063; Austria (it., rtr.) 2021, 2063;
Austria-Hungary → Autriche-Hongrie
Austrian Empire → Österreichischer Kaiserstaat
Austrian Monarchy → Österreichische Monarchie
Austrija (krt.) → Österreich (dt.), Avstrija (slw.) 229, 1350, 1797, 2025
Austro-Hungarian Monarchy → Österreichisch›ungarische Monarchie

Auswertung → évaluation
Ausztria (ung.) → Österreich (dt.) 229, 1350, 1797, 2047
autochthon 771, 894, 932
autochthonous groups 342
autochthonousness 350
autochthons 342
autochtone 351, 891, 894, 932
autodétermination 157, 357, 360
auto-détermination → Selbstbestimmung, self›determination
Autogenese 285
Autonome Ungarische Region 1483
Autonomie 1320, 1354, 1355
Autonomiestatut (Südtirol, 1948) 1350
auto-odi 239, 1191, 1198, 1298
auto-odi → Selbsthaß
Autriche (frz.) 354, 387 → Österreich (dt.) 229, 1350, 1797, 2063, Austria (it., rtr.)
Autriche-Hongrie 155, 202
Auvergne 1188, 1189
Avlona (gr.) → Vlorë (alb.) 2035
Avstrija (slw.) → Österreich (dt.), Austrija (krt.) 229, 1350, 1797, 2025,
Awaren 1798

B

Babenberger 1798
baby talk 1327
Babylonier 232
Bacău (rum.) → Bákó (ung.) 2029
backwardness 1751
Bácsalmás (ung.) → Almasca (krt.) 2047
badiot 1387
Baetica 1272
Baia Mare (rum.) → Nagybánya (ung.) 2029, 2047
Baiern 1797
Baile Atha Cliath (ir.) → Dublin (eng.) 1993
Bailleul (frz.) 1241 → Belle (ndl.) 2011
Baiona (bsk.) → Bayonne (frz.) 1261, 2011, 2015
Bairisch 26, 259
Bairische Ostmark 1798
Bairisch-österreichisch 1226
Bajuwaren 1383, 1798
Bákó (ung.) → Bacău (rum.) 2029
balanced bilingual → bilingue équilibré
Balaton (ung.) → Blatenské jazero (slk.) 2043
Baléares 352, 1198, 1296

Bâle → Basel
Bălgarija (blg.) → Bugarska (bsn., krt., srb.); Boulgaría (gr.) 2029/ Bulgaría (gr.) 2035; 2025; Bulgaria (rum.) 2029; Bolgarija (rss.) 2067; Bulgarya (trk.) 2029, 2035; Bolgarija, Bolharija (ukr.) 2067
Balkan league 1494
Balkan War, Second − (1913) 1443
Balkan Wars (1912/13) 1488, 1554 f, 1566
Balkan Wars (1912/13) → Guerres balkaniques (1912/13)
balkanisation 360
Balkankriege (1912/13) 1408, 1533, 1550 f
Balkankriege (1912/13) → Balkan Wars (1912/13), Guerres balkaniques (1912/13)
Balkan-Sprachbund 1448 f, 1459, 1494, 1496 f, 1507, 1537
Balkan-league → union linguistique balkanique
Balkan-Sprachbund → union linguistique balkanique
Baltijs'ke more (ukr.) → Baltijskoe more (rss.) 2067
Baltijskoe more (rss.) → Baltijs'ke more (ukr.) 2067
bambara 198
Banat 155, 1478
Banater Schwaben 1471
Bangladesh 161, 331
Banská Bystrica (slk.) → Neusohl (dt.) 2043, Besztercebánya (ung.) 2043, 2047
Bantu-Sprache 489
Baptistes → Täufer
baragouiner 1255
Barbarian Migrations → Völkerwanderung
barbarisme 1300
Barcelona (kat., sp.) → Barcelone (frz.) 451, 1198, 2011
Barcelone (frz.) 451, 1198 → Barcelona (kat., sp.) 2011
Bardonnèche 1332
Bargunsegner 1881
barrière linguistique 873 f, 881
barrière linguistique → Sprachbarriere
bas-allemand 1115
bas-allemand → Low German, Niederdeutsch, Plattdeutsch
Bas-Rhin 1224
bas-sorabe → Niedersorbisch
Basargic (rum.) → Dobrič (blg.) 2029
bascophone → euskaldun
base language 600

base language → langue de base
Basel 1855
Basilea → Basel
basilecte 277, 655
Basilicata 1318
Basissprache → langue de base
Baskenland 1270
Baskenland → Pays Basque
Baskisch 293
Baskisch → Basque, euskara
Basque 344, 349, 350, 352, 616, 1260, 1261, 1303
basque → Baskisch, euskara
Basque Country → Pays Basque
Batalha 1312
batu 1262
Bauernlatein 1881
Bautzen (dt.) → Budyšin (pln.) 2039; Budyšin (sor.) 2055
Bavaria → Baiern
Bavarian → Bairisch, Bayrisch
bavarois → Bairisch, Bayrisch
Bavière → Baiern
Bayonne (frz.) 1261 → Baiona (bsk.) 2011, 2015
Bayrisch 26
Bécs (ung.) → Wien (dt.) 1797, 1800, 2047; Wiedeń (pln.) 2039; Viedeň (slk.) 2043; Vídeň (tsch.) 2043
Befragtenverhalten 731
Befragung → interviewing schriftliche − 738
Befragungsmodus 728
Befragungstyp 727
Behaviorismus 692
behaviorist view of language 560
Beho (frz.) 214 → Bocholz (dt.) 2001
Beiva (rtr.) → Stalla (dt.), Bivio (it.) 2063
Bela Crkva (srb.) → Biserica Albă (rum.), Fehértemplon (ung.) 2029
Bela Woda (sor.) → Weißwasser (dt.) 2055
Belarus' (wrs.) → Valkovenäjä (fin.), Białoruś (pln.) 2039; Belorussija (rss.) 2067; Vitryssland (swd.) 1985; Bilorusija (ukr.) 2067
Belfast 807
België (ndl.) → Belgien (dt.) 1158; Belgique (frz.) 2001, 2011, 2055
Belgien (dt.) 1158 → Belgique (frz.), België (ndl.) 2001, 2011, 2055
Belgier 1159
Belgique (frz.) 162, 195, 202, 211, 354, 1107 → Belgien (dt.) 1158; België (ndl.) 2001, 2011, 2055

Belgique → Belgien, Belgium
Belgisch Beschaafd 1125
Belgische Revolution (1839) 1161, 1167
Belgium 69, 77, 207
Belgium → Belgien, Belgique
Belgizismen 1125
Belize creole 785
Beljak (slw.) → Villach (dt.) 1241, 2059
Belle (ndl.) → Bailleul (frz.) 2011
Bellenz (dt.) → Bellinzona (it.) 2063
belles-lettres 458
Bellinzona 1870
Bellinzona (it.) → Bellenz (dt.) 2063
Belluno 1338
Belorussia → Weißrußland, Belarus'
Belorussian 1583, 1587, 1591
Belorussian → Byelorussian, Weißrussisch
Belorussija (rss.) 2067 → Valkovenäjä (fin.), Białoruś (pln.) 2039; Vitryssland (swd.) 1985; Bilorusija (ukr.) 2067; Belarus' (wrs.)
Belostok (rss.) → Białystok (pln.) 2067
Benečija 1358
Benečija → Slavia friulana, Slavia veneta
Beneška Slovenija 1358
Bengali 1066
beobachtende Teilnahme 751
Beobachterparadox 823
Ber (blg.) → Veria (gr.) 2029
Berber 1145
berbère 198, 1180
Berberisch 320, 324
Bergen (ndl.) → Mons (frz.) 2001
Bergjuden 1943
Berg-Karabach 220
Bergell → Bregaglia
Bergues (frz.) → Sint-Winoksbergen (ndl.) 2011
Bergues 1241
Berliner Kongreß 1461
Berliner Kongreß (1878) → Congress of Berlin (1878)
Bern (dt.) 1836, 1855, 2021, 2063 → Berne (frz.) 1854, 1862, 2011, 2063; Berna (it., rtr.) 2021, 2063
Berna (it.; rtr.) 2021, 2063, → Bern (dt.) 2011, 2063; Berne (frz.) 1854, 1862, 2063
Berne (frz.) 1854, 1862, 2011, 2063 → Bern (dt.) 2021, 2063; Berna (it., rtr.) 2063
bertsulari 1261

Berufsethik 820
Berufssprache 259
Besztercebánya (ung.) → Neusohl (dt.) 2043, Banská Bystrica (slk.) 2043, 2047
Betriebe, multinationale − 852 f
Betriebsidentität 854 f
Bewertung → évaluation
Bezugssprache → langue de référence
Białoruś (pln.) → Belarus' (wrs.) 2039
Białystok (pln.) → Belostok (rss.) 2067
Biarritz (frz.) → Miarritze (bsk.) 2011
bias 745
Biel (Bienne) 1837
Biel → Bienne
biélorusse − ukrainien 1930
Biélorussie → Weißrußland
biélorusse → Belorussian, Byelorussian, Weißrussisch
Bienne 1862
Bienne → Biel
bigestural dictionary 299
Bikulturalismus 316
Bilbao (sp.) → Bilbo (bsk.) 2011, 2015
Bilbo (bsk.) → Bilbao (sp.) 2011, 2015
Bildungsmigration 1845
Bildungssprache 510, 896
bilingual, Bilingual
− Communication Network 432
− community 142
− competence 603
− education 1069, 1421
− English 1068
− fiction 458
− mind 131
− schools 1718
bilinguale Diglossie 801
bilingualism 339
bilingualism → bilinguisme, Zweisprachigkeit
− Byelorussian-Polish 1610
− in Ireland 1101
− Lithuanian-Polish 1607, 1610
− of Kashubians 1602
Bilingualismus 266, 1473
Bilingualität 234
bilingualité
− additive 36
− consécutive 32
− précoce 32
− simultanée 32
− soustractive 36
bilingue
− composé 37
− coordonné 37
− équilibré 32

bilinguisme 212, 246, 1114, 1243, 1250, 1306, 1334, 1342, 1512, 1867, 1869
bilinguisme → bilingualism, Zweisprachigkeit
− institutionnalisé 354
− passif 1299
− précoce 58
− *actif* → active bilingualism
− *fonctionnel* → functional bilingualism
− *précoce* → Zweisprachigkeit im Kleinkindesalter
Bilinguismus 1164, 1272, 1372
biliteracy 1067
biliterate 628
Bilorusija (ukr.) → Belorussija (rss.), Belarus' (wrs.) 2067
Bilts 1154
Binnenmigration 1746
Binnensprachinsel 813
Binnenwanderung 187
Biscaye 1303
Biserica Albă (rum.) → Bela Crkva (srb.), Fehértemplon (ung.) 2029
Bislama 722
Bistum Brixen 1385
Bistum Säben 1385
Bivio (it.) → Stalla (dt.) 2059, 2063; Beiva (rtr.)
Bjalo More (blg.) → Thrakikón pélagos (gr.) 2029
Black English 69, 710
Black Sea → Mer Noire
Blatenské jazero (slk.) → Balaton (ung.) 2043
Bleiburg (dt.) → Pliberk (slw.) 2059
Bocholz (dt.) 1130 → Beho (frz.) 214, 2001
Bodensee 1855
body rhythm 298
Bohême → Bohemia
Bohemia 553
Böhmen → Bohemia, Bohême
Boikos 1624
Bokmål 937 f, 975
Bolchen (dt.) → Boulay (frz.) 2001
Bolivian Quechua 786
Bolgarija (rss.) → Bălgarija (blg.), Bolgar ja (ukr.) 2067
Bolgarija/Bolharija (ukr.) → Bălgarija (blg.), Bolgarija (rss.) 2067
Bologne 1962
Bolshevik Revolution 400
Bolzano (it.) → Bozen (dt.) 2021, 2055, 2059, 2063
Bonifacio (it.) → Bonifaziu (krs.) 2011
Bonifaziu (krs.) → Bonifacio (it.) 2011

Bonnhard (dt.) → Bonyhád (ung.) 2047
Bonorva 1379
Bonyhád (ung.) → Bonnhard (dt.) 2047
Bordeaux (frz.) → Bordèu (okz.) 2011
border 69
Bordèu (okz.) → Bordeaux (frz.) 2011
Bormio (it.) → Worms (dt.) 2063
borrowability 786
borrowed (phonological) rule 100 f
borrowed sounds 99 f
borrowing 124 f, 373, 541, 599, 839
− hierarchies 112, 114
− of grammatical morphemes 112
− of semantic space 136
− scale 112
− phonological − 102
− syntactic − 121 f
borrowing → emprunt
borrowings → Lehnwörter
Borta (krt.) → Oberwart (dt.), Felsőőr (ung.) 572, 1821, 1828, 2059
Bosco (it.) → Gurin (dt.) 2063
Bosna (bsn.) → Bosznia, Bosznia-Hercegovina (ung.) 2047
Bosna i Hercegovina (bsn.; krt.; srb.) → Bosna in Hercegovina (slw.) 2025
Bosna in Hercegovina (slw.) → Bosna i Hercegovina (bsn., krt., srb.) 2025
Bosnia → Bosnie
Bosniaken 226
Bosniaken → Bosnians
Bosnian → Bosnisch
Bosnians 348
bosniaque 1438
bosniaque → Bosnisch
Bosnie 362
Bosnie-Herzégovine 1434 ff
Bosnien 226
Bosnien-Herzegowina → Bosnie-Herzégovine
Bosnien → Bosnie
Bosnier → Bosnians
Bosnisch 1410
Bosznia, Bosznia-Hercegovina (ung.) → Bosna (bosn.) 2047
Bottenhavet (swd.) → Selkämeri (fin.) 1985
Bottenviken (swd.) → Perämeri (fin.) 1985
Boulay (frz.) → Bolchen (dt.) 2001
Boulgaría/Bulgaría (gr.) → Bălgarija (blg.), Bulgaria (rum.), Bulgarya (trk.) 2029

Boulogne → Bologne
Boulonnais 1242
bound morpheme 109
boundary 169, 171, 431
boundary, social − → Grenze, soziale
Bova (Uva) 1323
− Superiore 1367
Bozcaada (trk.) → Tenedhos (gr.) 2035
Bozen (dt.) → Bolzano (it.) 2021, 2055, 2059, 2063
Brabant 1137
brach 1388
Branzoll (dt.) → Bronzolo (it.) 2063
Brasilien → Brazil
Braşov (rum.) → Kronstadt (dt.), Brassó (ung.) 2029
Brassó (ung.) → Kronstadt (dt.), Braşov (rum.)2029
Bratislava (slk.) 1821 → Preßburg (dt.) 2043, 2059; Poszony (ung.) 2043
Brazil 330
Bregaglia 1872
Brésil → Brazil
Breslau (dt.) → Wrocław (pln.) 2039, 2043; Vratislav (tsch.) 2043
Brest (rss.; wrs.) 2067 → Brześć (pln.) 2039; Brèst (wrs.) 2067
Brèst (wrs.) → Brześć (pln.) 2039; Brest (rss.; wrs.) 2067
Bretagne 178, 387
− bretonnante 1252
Breton 178, 194, 344, 1252
Breuil (frz.) → Cervinia (it.) 2063
bridge link 432
Briga Alta 1344
British India 328
British Sign Language 1060
Brittany 69
Brittany → Bretagne
Brixen 1383
Brno (tsch.) → Brünn (dt.) 2043
Bromberg (dt.) → Bydgoszcz (pln.) 2039
Bronzolo (it.) → Branzoll (dt.) 2063
Bruges (frz.) → Brügge (dt.), Brugge (ndl.) 2001
Brugge (ndl.) → Brügge (dt.), Bruges (frz.) 2001
Brügge (dt.) → Bruges (frz.), Brugge (ndl.) 2001
Bruneck (dt.) → Brunico (it.) 2059
Brunico (it.) → Bruneck (dt.) 2059
Brünn (dt.) → Brno (tsch.) 2043

Brüssel (dt.) 1137, 1962 → Bruxelles (frz.) 2001; Brussel (ndl.)
Brussel (ndl.) → Brüssel (dt.) 2001; Bruxelles (frz.) 2001, 2011
Brussels (eng.)→ Bruxelles, Brussel, Brüssel
Bruxelles 451, 1107 (frz.) → Brüssel (dt.) 2001; Brussel (ndl.) 2001, 2011
bruxellois 1115
Brythonic 1060
Brześć (pln.) 2039 → Brest (rss., wrs.) 2039, 2067; Brèst (wrs.) 2067
Bucarest → Bukarest
Bucureşti (rum.) → Bukurešt (blg.) 2029; Buharest, Bucharest (rss.) 2067; Bukurešt (ukr.) 2067
Buchenstein 1323, 1383
Buchenstein (dt.) → Livinallongo (it.), Fodóm (rtr.)
Buchstabenschrift 263
Bucovina → Bukowina
Buda → Budapest, Ofen, Pest
Budapest (ung.) → Budimpešta (bsn., krt., slw., srb.) 2025; Budapešt (slk.) 2043
Budapest → Ofen, Pest
Budapešt (slk.) → Budapest (ung.) 2043
Budimpešta (bsn.; krt.; slw.; srb.) → Budimpešta (krt., slw., srb.); Budapest (ung.) 2025
Buddhism 394
Budweis (dt.) → České Budějovice (tsch.) 2043, 2055, 2059
Budyšin (pln.; sor.) → Bautzen (dt.) 2039
Buffalo 454
Bugarska (bsn.; krt.; srb.) → Bălgarija (blg.) 2025
Buharest, Bucharest (rss.) → Bucureşti (rum.) 2029; Bukarešt (ukr.) 2067
Bukarešt (blg.; ukr.) → Bucureşti (rum.) 2029; Buharest, Bucharest (rss.) 2067
Bukarest 1478
Bukowina 1471
-deutsche 1471
bulgare 1930
Bulgare-Grec 1510−1514
Bulgaren 1407, 1409 f, 1463, 1505, 1515, 1550 ff
Bulgares 1437
Bulgares → Bulgaren
Bulgaria (eng.) 1487−1496
Bulgaría/Boulgaría 2035 (gr.) → Bălgarija (blg.), Bugarska

(bsn., krt., srb.); Bulgaria (rum.) 2029; 2025; Bulgarya (trk.) 2035
Bulgaria (rum.) 2029 → Bălgarija (blg.), Boulgaría (gr.), Bulgarya (trk.) 2029
Bulgarian 1427, 1490, 1491 f, 1498, 1501, 1555
Bulgarian → bulgare
Bulgarian-Macedonian 1492, 1498−1504
Bulgarians → Bulgaren, bulgare
Bulgarien 1459, 1961
Bulgarisch 1552
Bulgarisch-Mazedonisch 1496
Bulgarisch-Türkisch 1504−1510
Bulgars 1554
Bulgarya (trk.) → Bălgarija (blg.) 2029, 2035; Boulgaría (gr.) 2029 / Bulgaría (gr.) 2035; Bulgaria (rum.) 2029
Bündnerdeutsch 1881
Bündnerromanisch 1879
Bunjewatzen 1407, 1409 f
burden of bilingualism 1045
Bureau Européen pour les langues moins répandues 932, 1342
Bureau Européen pour les langues moins répandues → Europäisches Büro für Sprachminderheiten
Bureau Régional pour l'Ethnologie et la Linguistique (BREL), Vallée d'Aoste 1334
Burgenland (dt.) 1804, 1821 → Gradišće (krt.) 2059
Burgenlandi Magyar Kultúregyesület 1833
Burgenländisch-Kroatisch 1821
Burgurdži 1963
Burma 328
Bush Negroes (Maroons) 1145
Bwrdd yr Iaith Gymraeg (the Welsh Language Board) 1086
Bydgoszcz (pln.) → Bromberg (dt.) 2039
Byelorussian 1584ff, 1591, 1622, 1919−1926
Byelorussian → Belorussian, Weißrussisch
Byelorussian-Ukrainian transient dialects 1606
Byzantins 1202, 1376

C

Caerdydd (ir.) → Cardiff (eng.) 1993
Cagliari 1377
Caipira 808
Čakavisch 1734, 1736, 1821, 1823, 1825

Calabre 1345
Calabria 300
calandreta 1191
Calasette 1323
Calimera 1366
calque 1300, 1810, 1819
calque → calquing, loan translation, loanword
calques syntaxiques 1361
calquing 663
calvinisme 1111
calviniste 1189
calvinistisch-reformiert 1829
Calway (eng.) → Ghaillimh (ir.) 1993
campagne publicitaire 441
campidanien (campidanese) 1378
Campobasso 1363
Canada 83, 202, 211, 386
Canadian 343
Cantabrer 1272
Canton de Tessin 1870
canton suisse 213
Cantonese 336, 1148
Capétiens 1254
Capodistria (it.) → Koper (slw.) 2025
Cardiff (eng.) → Caerdydd (ir.) 1993
carélien → Karelian
caretaker function 376
Carghese (Corse) 194
Carigrad (blg.) → Istanbul (trk.) 2029
Carinthia → Kärnten
Carinthie → Kärnten
Carloforte 1323
Carniens 1337
Carta de Logu (1359) 1377
cartes → maps
cartography 65
case study → Fallstudie, étude de cas
Cassel (frz.) 1241 → Kassel (ndl.) 2011
Castilian 336, 345
castillan 612, 1196
castillan-basque 469
castrapo 1294
Castrignano dei Greci 1366
CAT → Communication Accommodation Theory
catalan 1174, 1195, 1211, 1296, 1379
catalan → Katalanisch
Catalan 255, 350, 400, 442, 613, 717
catalanisation 1299
catalanophone 1198
Catalogne 161, 352, 469, 1296
Catalogne → Catalunya (kat.), Cataluña (sp.)
– française 1197

– Nord 352, 1296
Catalonia → Catalogne (frz.)
Cataluña (sp.) → Catalunya (kat.) 2015
Catalunya (kat.) → Cataluña (sp.) 2015
Catholic 395
catholique 1189
Caucasian 302, 307
Čedad (slw.) → Cividale (it.) 2021
CEI → GUS
Celle 1322
Celovec (slw.) → Klagenfurt (dt.) 1813, 2025, 2059
Celtes 1337, 1358
Celtic 1060
– expansion 342
celtique 1252
Celtique → Celtic, Celts
Celts 1097
census 402, 774, 957, 1004, 1015, 1714
census → Volkszählung, Zensus
Central America → Mittelamerika
Central Europe → Mitteleuropa
Central Old Belgium → Altbelgien-Mitte
Centre
– d'Etudes francoprovençales, Vallée d'Aoste 1334
– de Recherche Bretonne et Celtique 1256
– de Recherche et d'Etudes Catalanes (Perpignan) 1200
– de recherche sur le plurilinguisme (Bruxelles) → Forschungsstelle für Mehrsprachigkeit (Brüssel)
Čerkasi, Čerkasy (ukr.) → Čerkassy (rss.) 2067
Čerkassy (rss.) → Čerkasi, Čerkasy (ukr.) 2067
Černigiv, Černihiv (ukr.) → Černigov (rss.) 2067
Černigov (rss.) → Černigiv, Černihiv (ukr.) 2067
Černivci (ukr.) → Černovcy (rss.) 2067
Černo More (blg.) → Karadeniz (trk.), Marea Neagră (rum.) 2029
Černovcy (rss.) → Černivci (ukr.) 2067
Cervinia (it.) → Breuil (frz.) 2063
Česká Republika, Česko (tsch.) → Tschechien, Tschechische Republik (dt.) 2055, 205; Czechy (pln.) 2039; Csehország (ung.) 2047
České Budějovice (tsch.) → Budweis (dt.) 2043; 2055, 2059

Çesme (trk.) → Krini (gr.) 2035
Ceuta 1271
Chakavian 1431
champenois 1115
change through contact → changement par „contact"
change, dynamic → Wandel, dynamischer
changement
– de code 1342
– linguistique 526, 826f, 836, 902, 904f
– linguistique, cause du – 533
– par „contact" 538
– *de langue* → alternance des langues, language shift, Sprachwechsel
– *linguistique* → language change, linguistic change
Chaos-Theorie 844
chaos-theory → théorie du chaos
chapurrado 1294
Charte
– Atlantique (14/8/1941) 359
– canadienne des droits et libertés (1982) 214
– de la langue française (1977) 211, 214, 442, 826f
– de la langue française du Québec 410
– des Nations Unies 359
– européenne des langues régionales ou minoritaires (1992) 216, 932, 936
chauvinisme 200
– linguistique 847
– *linguistique* → Sprachchauvinismus
Chiavenna (it.) → Cleven (dt.) 2063
Chicano 28
child bilingualism → bilinguisme précoce, Zweisprachigkeit im Kleinkindesalter
child language → Kindersprache
China 328
Chinese 302, 305, 307, 308, 344, 1144
Chinese – English 809
chinois 167, 280, 1180
chinois → Chinese
Chişinău (rum.) → Kišinev (blg.) 2029; Kišiněv (rss.) 2067; Kišiniv, Kyšyniv (ukr.) 2067
Chociebuż (pln.) → Cottbus (dt.), Chośebuz (sor.) 2039
choix
– linguistique 847
– linguistique → language choice, Sprachwahl
– *multiple* → Mehrfachnennung
Chorio 1367

Chośebuz (sor.) → Cottbus (dt.) 2039, 2055; Chociebuź (pln.) 2039
chronemics 301
Chronolekt 259
Chur (dt.) 1879 → Coira (it.) 2021
Church Slavic 1489, 1498, 1623, 1919
Church Slavic → Kirchenslawisch
Chypre 216
Cimbri 1353
Cimbri → Zimbern
circulaire Savary (1982) 1175, 1191, 1245
CIS → GUS
Cividale (it.) → Čedad (slw.) 2021
Clape Cultural Acuilee 1342
Clarmont (okz.) → Clermont-Ferrand (frz.) 2011
cleansing, ethnic − → Säuberung, ethnische −
Clermont-Ferrand (frz.) → Clarmont (okz.) 2011
Cleven (dt.) → Chiavenna (it.) 2063
Cluj-Napoca (rum.) 1463 → Klausenburg (dt.) 1463, 1478, 2029; Kolozsvár (ung.) 2029, 2047
cluster analysis 784
clustering 565
Coblence (frz.) → Koblenz (dt.) 2001
cocktail chatter 302
code
− d'éthique 794
− -alternation 798
− -breaking strategy 629
− -mixing 3f, 1375
− -switching 4, 6f, 42, 113, 115, 116, 117f, 119, 141f, 145, 191, 242, 322, 373, 455, 543, 574, 594, 663, 723, 754, 779, 801, 809−976, 991, 1250, 1375, 1379
− *-mixing* → Sprachmischung
− *-switching* → alternance codique, alternance de langue, alternance des codes, Kodewechsel
codes, alternance de − 33, 460
codes, mélange de − 33
Codeselektion 16
codification 251, 827, 890, 894, 910, 1293, 1491
codification → Kodifizierung
coding 778
cognate 562
cognitive
− developement 631

− factors 41
− maps 298
− processes 125, 129
− processes (in lexical contact) 125, 129
− semantics and contact semantics 137
− unit 47
cognitivism 521
coherence, paradigmatic − 120
cohérence 462
cohésion 201, 462
cohort estimation 774
coiffure linguistique 634
Coimbra 1312
Coira (it.) → Chur (dt.) 1879, 2021
Colle S. Lucia 1383
Colmar (frz.) 1223 → Kolmar (dt.) 2063
Cologne (frz.) → Köln (dt.) 2001; Keulen (ndl.)
colonial language → Kolonialsprache
colonialism 672
colonialisme 838
colonization 193, 196, 336
Comelianisch 1323
Comer See (dt.) → Lago di Como (it.) 2059, 2063
Comines (frz.)/Komen (ndl.) 213, 1242
Comino 1399
comique 718
Comitau Limba Sarda (1977 f) 1381
Common Gaelic 1088
communauté
− de parole 51
− langagière 859, 861
− linguistique 210, 679
− *Européenne* → EG (Europäische Gemeinschaft)
− *linguistique* → language community, speech community, Sprachgemeinschaft
communication 431
− -Accommodation Theory 42, 332, 335
− -matrix 170
 nonverbal − 296, 547
− non-verbale 925
communication
 non verbal − → Kommunikation, nonverbale −
− *non-verbale* → communication, nonverbal − ; Kommunikation, nonverbale −
− *interculturelle* → intercultural communication
 special − → Fachkommunikation
communicative

− competence 590, 747
− *competence* → compétence communicative
− *style theory* → kommunikative Stiltheorie
Community-Profile 759
community profile → profil de la communauté
compensatory strategies 372
competence 706
− grammatical − 590
 communicative − → kommunikative Kompetenz
 pragmatic − → compétence pragmatique
compétence 252
− communicative 845 f
− pragmatique 54
− *communicative* → kommunikative Kompetenz
− *linguistique* → language competence
complexification 650
comportement langagier 276, 1185
compound bilingual 131, 432
compound bilingual → bilingue composé
compréhension auditive → Hörverstehen
compréhension lecturaire → Leseverstehen
comprehension, listening − → Hörverstehen
Computer Aided Mapping 64
Computer im Befragungsprozeß 732
Computer-Kartographie → Computer Aided Mapping
Comtat Venaissin 1189
Comté de Barcelone → Grafschaft Barcelona
Comté de Toulouse 1173
Comtes de Toulouse 1189
Comunidad Autónoma Vasca 1303, 1304
Comunidad Valenciana (sp.) → País Valencià (kat.) 2015
conceptual structure 132
Concile de Tours (813) 273
Concours Cerlogne 1334
Condofuri 1367
confédéralisme 360
Confédération Germanique → Deutscher Bund
Confédération helvétique 213, 355, 1862
Confédération suisse 1871, 1872
Conférence de Versailles (1919) 358
configurationalité 1308
conflation, phonological − 135
conflict

latent — 1011
communicative — → Kommunikationskonflikt
— *model* → Konfliktmodell
conflit
— linguistique 246, 249, 1191, 1298, 1306, 1044
— normatif 609
— *linguistique* → Sprachkonflikt
Congrès de Berlin (1878) 1452
Congrès de Vienne (1815) 358, 1108
Congress of Berlin (1878) 1488, 1578
Coni 1344
connaissance de langues étrangères → Fremdsprachenkenntnis
connaissance opérationnelle 502
connectionist models (of SLA) 518
conscience
— linguistique 675, 1369
— métalinguistique 35
— *linguistique* → language awareness, Sprachbewußtsein
— *nationale* → Nationalbewußtsein
consciousness, national — → Nationalbewußtsein
consecutive interpretation 860
consecutive interpretation → interprétation consécutive
Conseil de l'Europe 356, 359
Conseil des langues régionales endogènes 1115
consensus model → Konsensmodell
consonantisme 1264, 1265
Constanţa (rum.) → Kjustendža (blg.) 2029
Constitution
— de la République Italienne (1947) 1359
— espagnole (1978) 1298, 1303
— fédérale (1848, Suisse) 1875
Constitution of (the): 161
— Belgium 400
— India 400
— Japan 400
— Spain 400
— Switzerland 400
— United States 400
constraint on intrasentential codeswitching 113
constraints on code-switching 141 f
constraints on morphemic transfer 111 f
contact
— euro-amérindien 793
— linguistics, history 1—8
— morphology 110, 112, 116

— morphology and current morphological theory 116
— pidgin vs. L$_2$ pidgin 122
—, psychological aspects 131 f
— semantics 130, 136 f
—, socio-cultural aspects 133 f
— English → Kontaktenglisch
— *language* → Kontaktsprache
— *linguistics* → Kontaktlinguistik
— *linguistique* → Sprachkontakt
contact-induced linguistic variety 113
contact-induced simplification 113
context of acquisition → contexte d'appropriation
context of usage → contexte d'utilisation
contexte d'appropriation 57
contexte d'utilisation 59
contextual analysis 72
contextualization cues 142
contingency table 779
continuing education 860
continuum post-créole 655
contrastive analysis 518, 559
contrastive linguistics and language contact 3
Convention sur les droits fondamentaux des groupes ethniques européens (1993) 217
convergence 332
syntactic — 602
conversation analysis → analyse de la conversation, Konversationsanalyse
conversion linguistique 1243
cooficialisation 1292
co-officialité 1298
coordinate bilingual 131
coordinate bilingual → bilingue coordonné
Corcaigh (ir.) → Cork (eng.) 1993
Corée → Korea
core values 573
Corigliano d'Otranto 1323, 1366
Cork (eng.) → Corcaigh (ir.) 1993
Corlaix (frz.) → Korle (brt.) 2011
Cornish 349, 1059
Cornouaille 1253
Cornwall → Cornouaille
corporate identity → Betriebsidentität
corporatism 403
corpus 1377
— planning 904, 1719
— *planning* → Korpusplanung, planification du corpus
correspondance analysis 780

corsancese 1208, 1209
Corse
— du Nord 1216
— du Sud 1216
corse-italien 1214
Corse (frz.) 179, 1173, 1201, 1214 → Corsica (it.) 2021
Corsica (it.) 2021 → Corse (frz.) 179, 1173, 1201, 1214, 2021
Corsican → corse
Corsicans 344
Cortina d'Ampezzo 1383
Cospicua (Bormla) 1401
cost-benefit analysis 866
cost-benefit analysis → Kosten-Nutzen-Analyse
Côte d'Ivoire 198
Côtes-du-Nord 1254
Cottbus (dt.) → Chociebuź (pln.) 2039; Chóśebuz (sor.) 2039, 2055
Coumboscuro 1346
Council of Europe → Conseil de l'Europe
counter-identity 204
couple 385
— endogame 385
— exogame 388
Cour Internationale de Justice 167
covert
— deviation 300
— factor 298
— linguistic prestige 711
— prestige 707
Cratital 1371, 1373
création ethno-lexicale 1186
creative construction 519, 561
creole 3, 122 f, 330, 338
creole → créole, Kreol, Kreolsprache, langue créole
créole 197, 1211
— à base française (CBF) 650
— de la Guyane 655
— endogène 651
— exogène 651
— louisianais 650
creoles 834
créolisation 53, 539, 649
creolization 643
Creolle → créole, Kreol, Kreolsprache, langue créole
creuset → melting pot
critique littéraire → Literaturwissenschaft
Crna Gora (bsn., krt, srb.) → Mali i Zi (alb.) 2025
croate 1183, 1437
croate/Croates → Kroatisch, Kroaten
Croates 1434, 1435
Croatia 1424 ff
Croatian 348, 1713 ff, 1719

Croatian → croate, Kroaten, Kroatisch
Croatian-Albanian 1427, 1429
Croatian-Bošnjak 1428 f
Croatian-Czech 1427 f, 1429
Croatian-German 1428 f
Croatian-Hungarian 1429 f
Croatian-Istria-Romanian 1428
Croatian-Italian 1429
Croatian-Romani 1428 f
Croatian-Ruthenian 1428 f
Croatian-Serbian 1428 f, 1430 ff
Croatian-Slovak 1428 f
Croatian-Slovenian 1428 f
Croatian-Ukrainian 1429
Croatie → Croatia
Croats 1417 f, 1425 ff
cross-linguistic influence 562
Csángós 1478, 1479, 1481
Csárdás 1830
Csehország (ung.) → Česká Republika, Česko (tsch.) 2047
Csíkszereda (ung.) → Miercurea-Ciuc (rum.) 2029
cudezmo 1568
cuius regio, eius lingua 362
cuius regio, eius religio 313, 361
cultivation linguistique 836, 876
cultural
 − imperialism 428, 911
 − klutz 299
 − transition zones 70
 − *anthropology* → anthropologie culturelle, Kulturanthropologie
 − *imperialism* → impérialisme culturel
culture loyality 718
culturème 466, 612
Cuneo (it.) → Coni (frz.)
Cuncolta Naziunale 1202
Curaçao 1144
Cymdeithas yr Iaith Gymraeg (The Welsh Language Society) 1080
Cymru (ir.) → Wales (eng.) 1993
Cyprus 329, 1577−1582
Cyrillic − Latin script 1448
Czech 1425, 1427, 1429, 1583, 1584, 1586, 1588
Czech → Tchèque, Tschechisch
Czech − German 553
Czech − Slovak 1650−1655
Czechia → Tschechien
Czechoslovak language 1650 f
Czechy (pln.) → Tschechische Republik, Tschechien (dt.) 1641−1649, 2055, 2059; Česká Republika, Česko (tsch.) 2039
Częstochowa (pln.) → Tschenstochau (dt.) 2039

D

Dachsprache → langue-toit
Dacia 1459
DaDa-Bewegung 92
Dakien 1459, 1479
Dakien → Dacia, Dazien
Damão 1311
Dänemark (dt.) → Danmark (dän.) 2055, Denmark (eng.) 345
Dania (pln.) → Danmark (dän.) 2039
Dänisch 1761, 1763, 1778 f
Danish 346, 427, 937 f, 949 f, 972, 975, 1056
Danish → Dänisch
Danmark (dän.) → Dänemark (dt.) 2055; Tanska (fin.) 1985; Dania (pln.) 2039
danois 179
danois → Dänisch
Dano-Norwegian 938 f, 954, 956, 1025
Danzig (dt.) → Gdaňsk (pln.) 2039
data
 − analysis 776
 − management 778
 − reliability 778
 − − *collection* → Datenerhebung
 − quantitative − 777
Daten
 − -analyse 728
 − -erhebung 730
 − -treue 823
 − *-analyse* → data analysis
Daugavpils 1946
Dazien 230
DDR (Deutsche Demokratische Republik) 449
dead language → langue morte
Debrecen (ung.) → Debreţin (rum.) 2047; Debrecín (slk.) 2043
Debrecín (slk.) → Debrecen (ung.) 2043
Debreţin (rum.) → Debrecen (ung.) 2047
Déclaration
 − des droits des personnes appartenant à des minorités nationales ou ethniques, religieuses et linguistiques (1992) 216
 − Universelle des Droits collectifs des Peuples (1990) 360
 − Universelle des Droits de l'Homme 168, 355
décodage 37
décolonisation 193, 359, 828 f, 895
décolonisation → Entkolonialisierung

decolonization → Entkolonialisierung
décréolisation 655
Decreto de Nueva Planta (1714) 1297
décrochage 475
Dedeağaç (trk.) → Alexandhrupoli (gr.) 2035
défense de la langue 201
defense strategy (endangered languages) 650 f
déficiences linguistiques 87
deficit hypothesis 710
Defizit, sprachliches − 322
dégalicisation 1291
degeneration 587
degree of integration 807
degree of structural and syntagmatic integration 112
Deixis 1958
Délémont (frz.) → Delsberg (dt.) 2063
Delsberg (dt.) → Délémont (frz.) 2063
Demeter 221
demi-langue 636
Demirköy (trk.) → Malăk Samokov (blg.) 2029
demographic balancing equation 772
demographic process 773
demographics 302
demography 771
demolinguistics 774
dénationalisation → Entnationalisierung
denationalization → Entnationalisierung
dénazification 1226
Denmark (eng.) 345
dénomination de la langue 612
density 806
Département Ourthe 1137
Départements et Territoires d'Outre-Mer 1178, 1181
Deportation 1463
Designgewichtung 736
Deutsch, deutsch 91, 287, 316, 424, 1130, 1134, 1136, 1320, 1350, 1470, 1682, 1813, 1821, 1828, 1830, 1837, 1840, 1841, 1945
Deutsch, deutsch → allemand, German
 − als Fachsprache 513
 -kärntner 1815
 − -Österreich (1918) 1811
 österreichisches − 1808, 1834
 -schweiz 323, 1842, 1854
 -sprachig 1134
 -sprachige Gemeinschaft 1132
 -tiroler Dialekt 1390
 -tümler 1815

- -*Lothringen* → Lorraine thioise
- -*schweiz* → Suisse alémanique
Deutsch-Italienisch 381
Deutsch-Kroatisch 1821
Deutsch-Serbokroatisch 1411, 1413 f
Deutsch-Slowenisch 1813
Deutsch-Ungarisch 1828
Deutsche 1351, 1462, 1594 ff, 1598, 1642, 1644, 1656 ff, 1663, 1669 ff, 1674, 1800
Deutsche → Allemands, Germans
- Schweiz 1854
Deutscher Bund 1161, 1798
Deutscher Sprachatlas (DSA) 260
Deutscher Sprachverein 874
Deutschland (dt.) 1943, 1961 → Allemagne (frz.) 2063; Germania (it., rtr.) 2063; Duitsland (ndl.) 2001; Niemcy (pln.) 2039, Německo (tsch.) 2043
Deutschlisch 425, 855
Deuxième Guerre Mondiale (1939–1945) 358
Deva (rum.) → Déva (ung.) 2047
Déva (ung.) → Deva (rum.) 2047
devanagari 280
development, cognitive – → kognitive Entwicklung
développement
- bilinguistique 32
- cognitif 34
- linguistique 839
- métalinguistique 35
- *cognitif* → kognitive Entwicklung, cognitive developement
- *linguistique* → language development
diachronie 526
dialect 671
dialect → Mundart
- borrowing 543
- continuum 338
  roofed – → dialecte couvert
  roofless – → dialecte exposé
dialecte 636
dialecte (patois) → Mundart
- couvert 636
- en voie d'élaboration 636
- exposé 636
dialectes alémaniques 1868
dialectologie 176
dialectométrie 177, 635
dialectophonie 1238
Dialekt 686
Dialekt → dialecte
Dialekt-Renaissance 266
Dialektometrie → dialectométrie
diamorph 110
Diaspora 229, 1946

Dichte → density
dictionaries → Wörterbücher
dictionnaires → Wörterbücher
Didaktik 268
didaktisches Exonym 448
Diedenhofen (dt.) → Thionville (frz.) 2001, 2011, 2055
Diedenhofen (dt.) → Thionville (frz.)
Diekirch 1158
différence 248
differentiation, functional – → funktionale Differenzierung
diffusability of morphemes 111
diffused sound change 101
diffusion linguistique 826 f, 887, 904
diffusion linguistique → language spread
Digest of On-Flight Origin and Destination (OFOD) 435
diglosia de adscripción 1291
diglossia 6, 344, 392, 587, 986, 1044, 1045, 1050, 1146, 1430, 1491, 1519, 1558, 1602, 1720, 1751
- *bilingual* – → bilinguale Diglossie
diglossie 452, 678, 718, 923, 1114, 1204, 1243, 1256, 1306, 1334, 1348, 1368, 1380, 1438
- bulgaro-greque 1512
- conflictuelle 1291
Diglossie 90, 145, 237, 245, 266, 316, 323, 797, 923, 1164, 1314, 1323, 1372, 1401, 1473, 1762, 1779, 1783 f, 1846, 1856, 1883
- mediale – 1842, 1847
- vs. Zweisprachigkeit 16 f
- mit Bilingualismus 237
- ohne Bilingualismus 237
- -Theorie 684
Digraphie 104
dimension, spatial – 65
Dimotiki 246, 1519, 1543, 1547, 1563
Dinomie 316
dinymie → Zweinamigkeit
Dionisia 1368
diplomacy 297
diplomatic signalling 297
Diplomatie → diplomacy
direct (phonological) diffusion 99
directionalité 530
discountinous vs complete (language) change 1542 f
discours 406
- de l'organisation 409
- épilinguistique 1203
- identitaire 1205
- interculturel 928

- politique 409
- revendicatif 1256
discourse 138 f
- analysis 138 f
- analysis and contact linguistics 141 f
- type 709
  intercultural – → Diskurs, interkultureller –
discoursive hegemony 748
discrimination linguistique → linguistic discrimination
discriminatory discourse 712
Diskriminierung 1772
Diskurs, interkultureller – 928
Diskursstrategie → stratégie discursive
dissimilarity 564
distance
- culturelle 454
- interlinguistique 634, 280
- linguistique 176, 1112, 1867
- psychologique 87
- sociale 87
  cultural – → distance culturelle
  linguistic – → écart linguistique
distanciation 1212
Distinktheitsbewußtsein 817
„distinctness" of Quebec 401
Diu 1311
divergence linguistique 336, 808, 877
divergence linguistique → Sprachendivergenz
Diwan (1951) 1256
Djazaïrijja (arb.) → Argelia (sp. 2015
Dnepropetrovsk (rss.) → Dnipropetrovs'k (ukr.) 2067
Dnipropetrovs'k (ukr.) → Dnepropetrovsk (rss.) 2067
Dobrič (blg.) → Basargic (rum.) 2029
docimologie 503
Dolinci 1821
DOM–TOM → Départements et Territoires d'Outre-Mer
domain of language use → Sprachverhaltensdomäne
domain of necessity 707
domaine linguistique 891, 898
Domäne 240, 898, 1351, 1373, 1400
Domänenkonstrukt 802
Domänenspezifik 1165
dominant group 207
dominant language → langue dominante
dominante Sprache 228, 231
dominante Sprache → langue dominante

Dominanz des Englischen 424
Dominanzsprache 1885
Domowina 1764
Donapaleu (bsk.) → St.-Palais (frz.) 2011
Donau (dt.) → Duna (ung.) 2059
Donaufürstentümer 1459
Doneck (rss.) → Donec'k (ukr.) 2067
Donec'k (ukr.) → Doneck (rss.) 2067
Donostia (bsk.) → Saint-Sébastien (frz.) 1303, 2011
Doppelimmersion → double immersion
Doppelnamen 447
Doppelnamigkeit 1860
doublage → dubbing
double codage 38
double immersion 495
doublet 541
Drážďany (tsch.) → Dresden (dt.) 2043
Drei Bünde 1880
Dreisprachigkeit 1163
 asymmetrische — 1736
Dreizehn Gemeinden 1352, 1353
Dreizehn Gemeinden → Tredici Comuni
Dresden (dt.) → Drezno (pln.) 2039; Drážďany (tsch.) 2043
dress code 302
Drezno (pln.) → Dresden (dt.) 2039; Drážďany (tsch.) 2043
driemol lëtzebuergesch 1161
Drittes Reich → Troisième Reich
droit
 — à la langue 163, 164
 — à l'autodétermination 357
 — à l'indépendance 358
 — collectif 359
 — de récession 358
 — individuel 359
 — linguistique 160
droits fondamentaux 161, 166
 — humains 833, 866, 870
 — linguistiques 891, 861
 — *humains* → human rights
 — *linguistiques* → language rights, linguistic rights
DRS (Radio der Dt. und Rätorom. Schweiz) 1860
dubbing 429
Dublette → doublet
Dublin (eng.) → Baile Atha Cliath (ir.) 1993
Dubrovnik (bsn.; krt.; srb.) → Ragusa (it.) 1962, 2021, 2025
Duché de Carinthie (976s.) → Herzogtum Kärnten (ab 976)
Duché de Savoie 1344

Duinkerken (ndl.) → Dünkirchen (dt.) 2001; Dunkerque (frz.) 1241, 2001, 2011
Duchy of Carinthia (976f) → Herzogtum Kärnten (ab 976)
Duitsland (ndl.) → Deutschland (dt.) 2001
Duna (ung.) → Donau (dt.) 2059
Dünaburg → Daugavpils
Dunkerque (frz.) 1241 → Dünkirchen (dt.) 2001; Duinkerken (ndl.) 2001, 2011
dunkhards → Tunker
Dünkirchen (dt.) → Dunkerque (frz.), 1241; Duinkerken (ndl.) 2001
Düsseldorf (dt.) → Dusseldorp (ndl.) 2001
Dusseldorp (ndl.) → Düsseldorf (dt.) 2001
Dutch 336, 345, 372, 1152
Dutch → Niederländisch
 — Antilles 1144
 — East Indies 1144
Dutch-West Frisian 1152
dyadic conversation 432
Dynamik 324
dynamique 826f
Dynastie
 — Avis 1311
 — Bragança 1311
 — Burgund 1310
Džambazja 1964

E

early (child) multilingualism 7
early immersion 494
early immersion → immersion précoce
East
 — Africa 328
 — Germany 329
 — Sutherland Gaelic 663
Eastern Tyrol → Osttirol
écart linguistique 280
échantillon 765
échantillon → Stichprobe
 — aléatoire 766
 — aléatoire préstratifié 767
 — en fonction des quotas 767
 — représentatif 766
 — stratifié non proportionnel 766
 — *aléatoire* → Zufallsstichprobe
échantillonnage 767
échantillonnage → sampling, Stichprobenauswahl
échelle implicationnelle 655
échelle implicationnelle → implicational scale
école élémentaire → Volksschule

Ecole Européenne 470
écoles bilingues → bilingual schools
ecolinguistics 65
écologie linguistique, écolinguistique → Ökologie der Sprache, Sprachökologie, Ökolinguistik
écologie urbaine 451
ecology of language, ecolinguistics → Ökologie der Sprache, Sprachökologie, Ökolinguistik
economic strength (of a language) → ökonomische Stärke (einer Sprache)
économie → Wirtschaft
économie de la langue 439
économie morphologique 1266
economy → Wirtschaft
Ecosse 387
Ecosse → Schottland, Scotland
écriture 537, 618
écriture → Schrift
 — arabe 619
 — chinoise 619
 — cyrillique 619
 — gothique 620
 — latine et cyrillique 1437
 — *chinoise* → Schrift, chinesische —
 — *cunéiforme* → Keilschrift
 — *cyrillique* → Schrift, kyrillische —
Edessa/Edhessa (gr.) → Voden (blg.; mak) 2025, 2029, 2035
Edirne (trk.) → Odrin (blg.) 2029; Adhrianupoli (gr.) 2035
education level 581
education, intercultural — → *éducation interculturelle*
educational linguistics → éducation linguistique
educational psychology → psychopédagogie
éducation
 — bilingue 82
 — bilingue faible 83
 — bilingue forte 83
 — interculturelle 463
 — linguistique 81
 — multilingue, Etats-Unis/Canada 473
 — permanente 860
 — plurilingue, Europe 465
 — plurilingue, théories 465
 — trilingue, Luxembourg 468
 — *permanente* → continuing education
Eesti (est.) → Viro (fin.) 1985, Estonija (rss., ukr.) 2067
EG (Europäische Gemeinschaft) 415

égalité des langues 1871
Eğe Denizi (trk.) → Aigaîon (gr.) 2029
Eger (ung.) → Erlau (dt.) 2047; Jáger (slk.) 2043
Ehe, gemischtsprachige – → mariage linguistiquement mixte
Ehen, gemischtsprachige – 381
Eide, Straßburger – *(842)* → Serments de Strasbourg (842)
Eidgenossenschaft 1836
Eidgenossenschaft → Confédération helvétique
Eignungstest → test d'aptitude
eine Person – eine Sprache 364, 383
Einfachnennung 739
Eingeborene 823
Einheit, kognitive – → cognitive unit
Einheitssprache 261
Einnamigkeit 446
einsprachig → unilingue
Einsprachigkeit 1842
Einsprachigkeit, regionale – → regional unilingualism
Einstellung 30, 1134
– und Verhalten 693
Einstellungsforschung 692
Eire (ir.) → Ireland (eng.) 1993
Eischime (dt.) → Issime (frz.) 1333, 1353, 2021, 2063
Eis Sprooch 1162
Eisenburg 1822
Eisenstadt (dt.) 1821, 2047 → Željezno (krt.) 2059, Kismarton (ung.) 2047, 2059
Eisteddfod 1084
Eivissa (kat.) → Ibiza (sp.) 2015
Ekavian 1431
Ekavian → Ekavisch
Ekavisch 1410, 1823
elaborated and restricted code 710
élaboration linguistique 634, 1211
élaboration → Ausbau
Elbing (dt.) → Elbląg (pln.) 2039
Elbląg (pln.) → Elbing (dt.) 2039
El-Djesaïr (arb.) → Argel (sp.) 2015
Elfenbeinküste → Côte d'Ivoire
elimination of sounds, contact induced – 100
ELIT → ethnolinguistic identity theory
elite 77
Elláda/Elladha/Ellas/Hellás (gr.) → Gărcija (blg.); Grčka (bsn., krt., srb.) 2025; Grecia (rum.) 2029; Yunanistan (trk.) 2035
Elsässer 381
– Deutsch 685

Elsaß (dt.) → Haut-Rhin (frz.) 1224, 2063
Elsaß → Alsace
embedded language 601
emblem 306, 547
emblematic switching 119
Emigranten 366
Emigration 1310
emmagasiner 61
Empire
– Carolingien 1224
– ottoman 202
– romain 272, 1296, 1863
– tsariste 202
– d'Autriche → Österreichischer Kaiserstaat
– *romain* → Roman Empire
emprunt 195, 271, 281, 839, 886, 871, 916, 1185, 1236, 1336, 1877
emprunt → borrowing
– lexical 1246, 1247, 1299, 1361
– linguistique 195
emprunts → Lehnwörter
enaciados 1274
encodage 37
encoding → encodage
enculturation 303
endangered language 587, 659
Endogamie 317
endogen 288
endonormatif 1220, 1877
endonormative standard 486
Endonym 445
Engadin 1882
Englisch 287, 1089, 1400, 1841, 1847, 1856
Englisch → anglais, Englisch
– als offizielle Sprache 688
– in Indien 689
   maltesisches – 1401
– als Zweitsprache → anglais langue seconde (ALS)
Englisch-Deutsch 364
Englisch-Gälisch 1088
English 308, 316, 343, 345, 938, 950, 991, 1006, 1026 f, 1045, 1050, 1056, 1057, 1059, 1076, 1098, 1569
English → anglais, Englisch
– for special purposes 840
– *as a Second Language (ESL)* → anglais langue seconde (ALS)
– *as official language* → Englisch als offizielle Sprache
– *for special purposes (ESP)* → Anglais comme langue de specialité
„English only" movement 401, 713
English-French 597
English-Russian 946

English-Spanish 784
English-Swedish 602
English-Welsh 1075
Enlightment → Lumières
Enneberg 1384
Ennerberger Schulstreit (1873–1895) 1384, 1390
enquête → survey
– *orale* → mündliche Umfrage
enseignement
– public obligatoire 274
– *de(s) langues de spécialité* → Fachsprachenunterricht
– *des langues étrangères* → Fremdsprachenunterricht
Entemotionalisierung 1758, 1772
Entente littéraire de Vienne (Bečki književni dogovor, 1850) 1437
enterprise, „ailing" → entreprise „pathologique"
Entfremdung → aliénation
Entkolonialisierung 895
Entkolonialisierung → décolonisation
Entlehnung 871, 1474, 1748, 1785, 1826
Entlehnung → borrowing, emprunt
   phonologische – → borrowing, phonological
   semantische – → semantic borrowing, semantic loan
   syntaktische – → borrowing, syntactic
Entnationalisierung 1350
Entnazifizierung → dénazification
entreprise „pathologique" 410
entreprises multinationales 852 f
Entstehung von Kreolsprachen → genèse de créoles
Entwicklung, kognitive – → cognitive developement, développement cognitif
environmental factors → Umweltfaktoren
Eperies (dt.) → Prešov (slk.), Prjašiv (ukr.) 2043; Eperjes (ung.)
Eperjes (ung.) Eperies (dt.), Prešov (slk.) 2043, 2047; Prjašiv (ukr.) 2043
épilinguisme 677, 1203
episodic memory 132
equal opportunity laws 834
equivalence constraint 373, 599
equivalent constituent order constraint 118
Erdély 1478
Erdély → Ardeal, Siebenbürgen, Transilvania, Transilvanien, Transsylvanie

Erhebungsverfahren 751
Erklärung, Allgemeine – der
  Menschenrechte → Déclaration Universelle des Droits de l'Homme
Erlau (dt.) → Eger (ung.) 2047
Erlernen → apprentissage
error analysis 559
Érsekújvár (ung.) → Neuhäusel (dt.) 2043; Nové Zámky (slk.) 2043, 2047
Erster Balkankrieg (1912) → First Balkan War (1912)
Erstsprache → langue première
Erstspracherwerb 268
Erwachsenensprache 259
Erwerb → acquisition
Erziehung, interkulturelle – → éducation interculturelle
Erziehung, zweisprachige – → bilingual education
Erziehungspsychologie → psychopédagogie
Espagne (frz.) → Espanya (kat.), España (sp.) 2011
Espagne (frz.) → Spanien (dt.); Spain (eng.)
espagnol 615, 1182, 1296, 1285, 1303, 1866
espagnol → Spanisch, Spanish
espagnol-basque 1303
espagnol-catalan 1296
espagnol-galicien 1285
España (sp.) → Espagne (frz.), Espanya (kat.) 2011
Espanya (kat.) → Espagne (frz.), España (sp.) 2011
Esperanto 647
Estland 1945
Estnisch → Estonian
Estonia 348, 1900–1905
Estonia → Estland
Estonian 993, 1901
Estonija (rss., ukr.) → Eesti (est.) 2067
Estremadura 1275
Eszék (ung.) → Osijek (krt.) 2047
Esztergom (ung.) → Gran (dt.) 2047
ETA → Euskadi Ta Askatasuna
Etat
Etat → Staat, State
– italien unifié 1380
– multilingue 211
– plurilingue 1877
– plurinational 355
– républicain français 353
– souverain 158
– unitaire bilingue 454
– disparate 158
Etat-Nation 253, 276, 278, 611
Etats-Unis 212

Etats-Unis → United States, USA
ethics → Ethik
Ethik 819
Ethiopia 332
ethnic
– cleansing 207, 837, 1718
– consciousness 204
– group 206
– *identity* → identité ethnique
– *membership* → appartenance ethnique
– *poetry* → ethnopoésie
ethnic(al) cleansing → purification ethnique
ethnicité 716
ethnicity 203
Ethnie 203, 791, 1962
ethnische
– Identität 1763
– *Identität* → identité ethnique
– *Säuberung* → ethnic cleansing, purification ethnique
Ethnizität 219, 318
ethno-lexical 1186
ethnocentricity 298
ethnocentrism 208
ethnocide 1721
ethnocide → Völkermord
Ethnogenese 1114, 1459
ethnographic method 575
ethnographie 788
– de la communication 51
– du contact 790
Ethnographie der Kommunikation 750
ethnography of communication 139
ethnography of communicaiton → ethnographie de la communication
ethnography of speaking 754
ethnoïde Nation 156
ethnolecte 454, 944
Ethnolekt 965
ethnolinguistic
– identity 44, 77
– identity theory 44
– vitality 43
ethnolinguistique 51, 788
ethnologie
– du langage 788
– naïve 792
ethnomethodology 139
ethnonyme 555
ethnopoésie 460
ethnoprofile 1153
Ethos des Forschers 821
étude de cas 769
étude de cas → Fallstudie
Eupen 1108
Eupener Land 1133
Eurocentres 506

eurocrates (Eurokraten) 861
eurocrats 861
EUROMOSAIC 935
Europäer 224
Europäische Charta 932, 936
Europäische Gemeinschaft → EG (Europäische Gemeinschaft)
Europäisches Büro für Sprachminderheiten 932
Europäisches Büro für Sprachminderheiten → Bureau Européen pour les langues moins répandues
Europäismus 876
Europarat → Conseil de l'Europe
Europaschule → Ecole Européenne
Europaschulen 293
Europe centrale → Mitteleuropa
European
– Science Foundation 1150
– *Bureau for Lesser Used Languages (EBLUL)* → Bureau Européen pour les langues moins répandues, Europäisches Büro für Sprachminderheiten
– *Chart* → Europäische Charta
– *Community* → EG (Europäische Gemeinschaft)
– *School* → Ecole Européenne
européanocentrisme 360
Euskadi (bsk.) → País Vasco (sp.) 2015
Euskadi 70
Euskadi Ta Askatasuna 1303
Euskadie-Nord 1188
Euskal Herria 1303
euskaldun 1305
euskaldunberri 1305
Euskaldunon egunkaria 1307
Euskaltzaindia/Académie de la Langue Basque (1918 s.) 1307
euskara 352, 1260, 1305
evaluation of immersion programs 495
evaluation of literacy programs 632
évaluation 467, 470, 471, 474, 479, 495, 503, 505, 632
– des compétences langagières 503
– des programmes bilingues 479
– des programmes d'immersion 474
– du plurilinguisme individuel 505
– du Projet Foyer 467
– externe 471
– interne 470
– intra-système 471
evangelisch-lutherisch 1829

evangelisch-reformiert 1839
Evolutionstheorie 285
(Ex-)Jugoslawien 1159
exchange network 806
Exogamie 380, 385, 1008, 1011
exolecte 277
exolingual 242
exonormatif 1220
Exonym 445
  vermitteltes – 449
exonyme 1860
expansion fonctionnelle des créoles 652
expelled Germans 868
expressive (affective) symbolism and phonemic borrowing 100
expulsion 1712
expulsion → Vertreibung
extermination → Ausrottung
extinction of languages 659
extra-linguistic framing 569
Extremadura 1313

F

Fachenglisch → Anglais comme langue de spécialité, English for special purposes
Fachkommunikation 510
Fachsprache 259, 508, 886
Fachsprache → langue de spécialité
Fachsprachenerwerb 509
Fachsprachenunterricht 507
Fachterminologie 262, 509
Fachwortschatz 509
facial expression 299, 301, 303, 307
facteur extra-scolaire 469
factor analysis 784
factor interpretation 783
Faeto 1322
faits suprasegmentaux 1265
Faktoren, kognitive – → cognitive factors
Faktorenanalyse 844
Faktorenanalyse → factor analysis
falares fronteiriços 1314
Fallstudie 753
Fallstudie → étude de cas
Falkenberg (dt.) → Faulquemont (frz.) 2011
false friend 110
Familie, zweisprachige – 379
Familienzweisprachigkeit 1351
Faoug (frz.) → Pfauen (dt.) 2063
farjidišung 1952
Faroese 339, 346
Färöarna (swd.) → Færøyene (bkm.), Føroyar (far.) 1985
Färöisch → Faroese

Færøyene (bkm.) → Färöarna (swd.), Føroyar (far.) 1985
Farsi 1026
Faschismus 180, 1355, 1350
fascian 1388
Fassa 1323, 1383
Fassaner → fascian
Faulquemont (frz.) → Falkenberg (dt.) 2011
faux ami → false friend
federalism 401
Fehértemplon (ung.) → Biserica Albă (rum.) 2029; Bela Crkva (srb.)
fédéralisme 360
Fehleranalyse → error analysis
Feldarbeit 752
Feldforschung 752
Félibrige 1190
Felső Ausztria (ung.) → Oberösterreich (dt.) 2047
Felsőőr (ung.) → Oberwart (dt.) 572, 1821, 1828, 2047, 2059;Borta (krt.) 2059
Felsőpulya (ung.) → Oberpullendorf (dt.) 1803, 1828; Gornja Pulja (krt.) 2059
Fennomania 996
Fennomanics 996f
Fernsehen → television
féroien → Faroese
Fersental (dt.) 1353 → Val dei Mòcheni (it.) 2059
Fertigkeiten → habiletés
fiction → belles-lettres
fiction, bilingual – → bilingual fiction
field research → Feldforschung
fieldwork 824
fieldwork → Feldarbeit
Fiji 328, 336
Filippupoli (gr.) → Plovdiv (blg.) 2035
Finistère 1254
Finland (eng.; swd.) 69, 329, 330, 348 → Suomi (fin.) 1985, 2067; Finljandija (rss., ukr.) 2067; Suopma (sam.) 1985
Finlande 354
Finljandija (rss.) → Finland (eng., swd.), Suomi (fin.) 2067; Finljandija (ukr.)
Finljandija (ukr.) → Finland (eng., swd.), Suomi (fin.), Finljandija (rss.) 2067
Finnen → Finns
Finnisch 977f
Finnisch-Norwegisch 963
Finnisch-Samisch 963
Finnisch-Schwedisch 381, 447
Finnish 346, 938f, 953, 967, 971f
Finnish → Finnisch

Finnish-Norwegian 944
Finnish-Russian 1002
Finnish-Swedish 562, 967, 974
Finnish-Turkish 1001
Finnland 1945
Finnland (dt.) → Finland (eng.; swd.)
Finnmark 957f, 962f
finnois, Finnois → Finnisch, Finns
Finno-Ugric 343, 344
Finns 78
Finska viken (swd.) → Suomenlahti (fin.) 1985
First Balkan War (1912) 1443
first generation immigrants 721
first language → langue première
first-order network 806
Fiume (it.) → Rijeka (slw.) 2025
flamand 354, 1109, 1174, 1241
flamand, Flamand → Flämisch, Flame
flamandophone 1243
Flame 698, 1132
flamingant 1241
flamingant → flämischgesinnt
Flämisch 1124
Flämische Bewegung 1125
flämischgesinnt 1140
Flandern 1124
Flandern → Flanders, Flandre
Flanders 401
Flandre 1107, 1174, 1240
Flandre, Flandres → Flanders, Flandern
flandricisme 1248
Fleming → Flame
Flemings 349
Flemish 78, 336
Flemish → Flämisch, flamand
Flemish-Wallon 70
Florina (gr.) → Lerin (blg.) 2025, 2029, 2035; Lerin (mak.) 2035
Flüchtling 1754, 1765, 1783
FMC → free morpheme constraint
Föderalisierung 1135
Föderalismus 1838
Föderalismus → federalism
fodóm 1388
Fodóm (rtr.) → Buchenstein (dt.), Livinallongo (it.)
Fodóm 1383
folk spirit 949
fonctionnement diglossique 252
fonctions cognitives 86
fonctions langagières 86
Fondation Charles-Plisnier 154
foreign language
 – *knowledge* → Fremdsprachenkenntnis
 – *learning* → appropriation des langues étrangères

– *teaching* → Fremdsprachenunterricht
foreign word vs. loanword 4
foreigner talk 113, 127, 755
forensic linguistics → forensische Linguistik
forensische Linguistik 151, 825
Forez 1330
Formazza (it.) 1353 → Pommat (dt.) 2021, 2063
Formulierung, transkodische – 242
Føroyar (far.) → Færøyene (bkm.), Färöarna (swd.)1985
Forschungsethik 819
Forschungsstelle für Mehrsprachigkeit (Brüssel) 1135
Forum Iulii 1337
fossé linguistique 1871
fossilisation 517
Fossilisierung 910
fossilization 910
Fourons 213, 765, 1136
Fourons → Voeren, Vuren
Frage, geschlossene – 739
Frage, halboffene – 739
Fragebogen 727
Fragebogen → questionnaire
– -erstellung 737
Fragenreihenfolge 741
Fragensukzession 741
frame analysis 29
Frame semantics 134
français 167, 178, 274, 1188, 1195, 1201, 1222, 1240, 1252, 1260, 1330
français, Français → Französisch, Franzose, French
– bruxellois 60
– comme lingua franca 459
– fédéral 1838
– populaire 1177
– régional 1177, 1193, 1204, 1248, 1264
– standard du Québec 476
français-allemand 1222
français-basque 1260
français-breton 1252
français-catalan 1195
français-corse 1201
français-néerlandais 1240
français-occitan 1188
France (frz.) 202, 212, 329, 344, 386, 1172, 1202 → Frankreich (dt.) 1961, 2055; Francia (it.) 2021; Francia (sp.) 2015;
Franche-Comté 1330
Francia (it., sp.) → France (frz.) 202, 212, 329, 344, 386, 1172, 1202, 1961, 2015, 2021
francique 1242
francique → Fränkisch
– mosellan 1226

francisation 1173, 1196, 1214, 1243
francisation → Französisierung
francitan 252, 1193
francophone 386, 1186, 1862
francophonie 195, 475, 827
francoprovençal 176, 1173, 1188, 1330, 1866, 1867
francorse 1208
Franglais 425, 855, 874, 876
Franja d'Aragón 1297
Franja de Ponent 352, 1296
Fränkisch 259
Frankoprovenzalisch 1322
Frankreich (dt.) → France (frz.) 202, 212, 329, 344, 386, 1172, 1202, 1961, 2055
Franzose 1159
Französisch 91, 424, 1123, 1130, 1137, 1837, 1840, 1841, 1858
Französisch → français, French Schweizer – 1843
Französisch-Deutsch 364, 1130
Französisch-Niederländisch 1127
Französisch-Okzitanisch 684
Französische Revolution 1311
Französische Revolution → Révolution française
Französisierung 1139
Frassilongo (it.) → Gereut (dt.) 2021
Frauensprache 259
free morpheme constraint 113, 115, 599
Freiburg im Üchtland (dt.) 1837, 1847, 1854, 2063 → Fribourg (frz.) 2063; Friburgo (it.) 2021
Freigrafschaft → Franche-Comté
Freistaat Triest (1947–1954) 1325
Fremdsprachenerwerb → appropriation des langues étrangères
Fremdsprachenkenntnis 416
Fremdsprachenunterricht 509, 824, 1847
Fremdverstehen 757
Fremdwort 1757, 873 f
Fremdwort → mot étranger
– *vs. Lehnwort* → foreign word vs. loanword
French 330, 343, 669, 707, 956, 975, 1556 ff, 1567 ff
French → français, Franzose, Französisch
– Revolution 345, 400
– *based creole* → créole à base française (CBF)
– *Revolution* → Französische Revolution, Révolution française
French-Arabic 602

French-Canadian 43
French-Dutch 400, 581
French-English 373, 783
French-English-Micmac 785
fréquence d'utilisation 60
frequency distribution 778
frequency of usage → fréquence d'utilisation
frequency table 779
Friaul → Frioul
Friaulisch 1322
Friaulisch → frioulan
Fribourg (frz.) 1862 → Freiburg im Üchtland (dt.) 1837, 1847, 1854, 2063; Friburgo (it.) 2021
Friburgo (it.) → Freiburg im Üchtland (dt.) 1837, 1847, 1854, 2063; Fribourg (frz.) 2021
Frieden von Rijswijk (1697) 313
Frieden von Trianon (1919/20) 1480
Friedensvertrag von Bukarest (1913) 1551
Friedensvertrag von Saint-Germain (1919) 1320, 1350
Friesisch 270, 1761 ff, 1772
Friesland 1144, 1152
Frioul 1337, 1358
Frioul-Vénétie Julienne 1357
frioulan 1337, 1360
frioulanité 1343
Frisia Magna 1153
Frisian 78, 336, 1145, 1153
Frisian → Friesisch
Frisian freedom 1153
frison → Friesisch
Frison du Nord → Nordfriesisch
Friuli → Frioul
Friuli-Venezia Giulia 1325, 1337
Friuli-Venezia-Giulia → Frioul-Vénétie Julienne
Friulian → frioulan
Fronte di Liberazione Naziunale di a Corsica 1202
frontière → border, boundary
– linguistique 175, 201, 215, 354, 386, 827, 1242, 1258, 1869, 1873
– pragmatique 1865
– ˙linguistique → language boundary, Sprachgrenze
Frysk Nasjonale Partij 1154
Fryske Akademy 1155, 1156
Fryslân → Friesland
functional
– bilingualism 971, 1003
– competence 496
– load 661
– proficiency 493
functionalism 521
functions, cognitive – → fonctions cognitives

Fünfkirchen (dt.) → Pécs (ung.) 2047
Funktion 1400
funktionale Differenzierung 798
funktionale Pragmatik 927
funktionale Zweisprachigkeit → functional bilingualism
Funktionalistik 146
Funktionalstil, Funktionalstilistik 146, 147 f
Funktionen, kognitive — → fonctions cognitives
Fursil 1383, 1391
fusional languages 110
Futhark 396

G

Gaby (frz.) → Überland (dt.) 2063
Gadertal (Val Badia) 1323, 1355, 1383
Gadjé (= non Tsigane) 1179
Gadjé → Gadže
Gadže 1963
Gaelic 78, 173, 345, 349, 427, 1061
Gaelic → Gälisch
Gaelic League 1099
Gaelic-English 550
gaélique → Gaelic
Gaeltacht 1099
Gaeltachtai 72
gagaouze 1930
Gagausen (in Moldawien) 1505 f
Gagausisch 1506
Gagausisch → gagaouze
Gagauz 1491
Gagauz language → gagaouze
Gagaouzes (en Moldavie) → Gagausen (in Moldawien)
Gailtaler Dialekt 1815
Galanta (slk.) → Galánta (ung.) 2047
Galánta (ung.) → Galanta (slk.) 2047
Galegisch → Galician
Galego-Portugiesisch 1313
Galicia (gal.) → Galice (frz.) 1285; Galiza (gal.), Galicia (sp.) 2015
Galicia (sp.) → Galice (frz.) 1285; Galiza (gal.) 2015
Galician 589, 1270
Galicien, Galizien (E) → Galice, Galicia, Galiza
galicien 1285
Galicien 1310
Galicien → Galician
Galileo System 434
Gälisch 230, 1088, 1092
Gälisch → Gaelic

Galiza (gal.) → Galice (frz.) 1285; Galicia (gal.), Galicia (sp.) 2015
Galizien (PL) 1942
Gallia Lugdunensis 1332
gallicisme 873 f
Gallizismus 873 f, 1125
gallo 1176, 1255
gallo-italien 1331
gallo-roman 1173
gallois 466
gallois → Gälisch, Walisisch, Welsh
Gallura 1377
Galluresisch 1323
gallurien (gallurese) 1378
game theory 78
Gand (frz.) → Gent (dt., ndl.) 2001
Gărcija (blg.) → Ellás (gr.), Grecia (rum.) 2029
Gardasee (dt.) → Lago di Garda (it.) 2059, 2063
Gascogne 1261
gascon 1190, 1260
Gastarbeiter 366
Gastarbeiter → travailleur migrant
-deutsch 453
-literatur 95
Gasteiz (bsk.) 1305 → Vitoria (sp.) 1305, 2011, 2015
Gasteiz → Victoria
Gastwort → guest-word
Gaugaz (in Moldavia) → Gagausen (in Moldawien)
Gaule 1173, 1242
Gazi Magusa (trk.) → Amohostos (gr.) 2035
Gdańsk (pln.) → Danzig (dt.) 2039
GDR (German Democratic Republic) → DDR (Deutsche Demokratische Republik)
Gebärdensprache → sign language
Gebietsautonomie 1741
Gebrauchsfrequenz → fréquence d'utilisation
Gebrauchskontext → contexte d'utilisation
Gedächtnis, zweisprachiges — → mémoire bilingue
Gedicht, mehrsprachiges — → poème polyglotte
Geg, gegisch → guègue
Gegs 1445
gelet 394
Gemeinschaftsprofil → Community-Profile, profil de la communauté
gemischte Rede 367
Gemmenich 1136

genderlect 720
Generation, dritte — (G 3) 321
Generation, zweite — (G 2) 321
genèse de créoles 653
Gênes 1202, 1377
genetics → Genetik
Genetik 223
génétique → Genetik
Genève (frz.) 1862 → Genf (dt.) 2063; Ginevra (it.) 2021, 2063; Genevra (rtr.) 2063
Genevra (rtr.) → Genf (dt.), Genève (frz.) 1862; Ginevra (it.) 2063
Genf (dt.) → Genève (frz.) 1862, Ginevra (it.), Genevra (rtr.) 2063
Genfer Konvention 186
Genfer See (dt.) 1855 → Lac Léman (frz.) 2063
génocide linguistique → linguistic genocide
génos 203
Genova (it.) → Gênes (frz.)
Gent (dt., ndl.) → Gand (frz.)
Genozid 231 f, 1942
Genozid, linguistischer — → linguistic genocide
Genua (dt.) → Gênes (frz.)
Genus verbi 1959
Geographic Information Systems (GIS) 70
géographie des mots → word geography
géographie des peuples 210
geography 63
geolinguistics 63
géopolitique 216
Geosynonyme 1884
Gereut (dt.) → Frassilongo (it.) 2021
Gerichtshof, Internationaler — → Cour Internationale de Justice
German 950, 955 f, 975, 1002, 1006, 1009, 1013, 1056, 1583, 1592, 1708 f, 1711, 1713 ff
German → allemand, Deutsch
— *Confederation* → Deutscher Bund
— *Empire* → Saint Empire Romain
— *for special purposes* → Deutsch als Fachsprache
Austrian — → Deutsch, österreichisches —
German-Dutch 583
German-English 375
German-Hungarian 808
Germania 1159
Germania (it.) → Deutschland (dt.), Allemagne (frz.), Germania (rtr.) 2063

Germania (rtr.) → Deutschland (dt.), Allemagne (frz.), Germania (it.) 2063
Germanic 343
germanique 179, 1226, 1357
germanisation 1872, 1874
Germanisierung 1819
germanisme 874, 1867
Germanismus 874, 1954
germanophone 1222
Germans 1419 f, 1422, 1490, 1584, 1586 ff, 1600 f, 1603, 1651
Germans → Allemands, Deutsche
expelled − → Aussiedler
Germany 329
Germany → Allemagne, Deutschland
Geröllhaldenenglisch 1881
Gerona (sp.) → Gérone (frz.) 2011; Girona (kat.) 2011, 2015
Gérone (frz.) → Girona (kat.), Gerona (sp.) 2011, 2015
Geschlecht und Sprache → sex and language
geschlossener Hof (maso chiuso) 1386
geschriebene Sprache → written language
gesellschaftlicher Bilingualismus 799
Gesellschaftstyp 25
Gesinnungsminderheit 1033 f, 1770, 1772
gesprochene Sprache → spoken language
gesticulations 298
Gestitz (dt.) → Várgesztes (ung.) 2047
gesture 296, 547
Gewichtung 736
Ghaillimh (ir.) → Calway (eng.) 1993
Gherdëina 1383, 1387
Giazza (it.) 1352 → Glietzen (dt.) 2059, 2063 / Ljetzan (dt.) 2021
Gibraltar 1270
Ginevra (it.) → Genf (dt.) 2063; Genève (frz.) 1862, 2021, 2063; Genevra (rtr.) 2063;
Giordan-report 345
Gipsies → Romani
Gipsy 1487, 1490, 1492 f
Girid (trk.) → Kriti (gr.) 2035
Girona (kat.) → Gérone (frz.) 2011; Gerona (sp.) 2011, 2015;
Gironde 1188
Gjirokastër (alb.) → Arjirokastro (gr.) 2035

glagolitische Schrift 1822
Glasgow 1065
Glasnost 1947
Glatz (dt.) → Klodzko (pln.), Kladsko (tsch.) 2043
Glietzen (dt.) → Ljetzan (dt.) 2021; Giazza (it.) 1352, 2059, 2063
Glion (rtr.) → Ilanz (dt.) 2063
Glossendichtung 90
Glottolekt 259
glottonyme 555
Glottonymie 1881
Glottonymie → dénomination de la langue
glottophagie 190, 790, 827, 1210, 1212
glottophagie → linguistic cannibalism
glottopolitique 197, 677, 829, 1195, 1211, 1219, 1245
glottopolitique → language policy
glottotomie 716, 1133
glottotomie → linguistic cleavage, language segregation
Goa 1311
Goidelic 1060
Gökçeada (trk.) → Imvros (gr.) 2035
Golden Bull 2
Goral dialect 1629−1632
Gorica (slw.) → Gurize (frl.) 2021; Gorizia (it.) 1323, 1337, 1357, 2021, 2025
Gorice (frz.) → Gorizia (it.)
Gorizia (it.) 1323, 1337, 1357 → Gurize (frl.) 2021; Gorica (slw.) 2021, 2025
Gornja Pulja (krt.) → Oberpullendorf (dt.), Felsőpulya (ung.) 1803, 1828, 2059
Görz 1320
Görz (dt.) → Gorizia (it.)
Gorzów Wielkopolski (pln.) → Landsberg (dt.) 2039
Gouvernement Basque 1306
Gouvernement de Vichy 1174
Gozo 1399
grabar 1558
Gradec (slw.) → Graz (dt.) 2025
Gradišće (krt.) → Burgenland (dt.) 1804, 1821, 2059
Grado 1338
Grafschaft Barcelona 1275
Grafschaft Toulouse → Comté de Toulouse
grammaire universelle → Universal Grammar
grammaticalisation 537
grammaticality 600
grammaticalization 123
Grammatik, mentale − 242
Gran (dt.) → Esztergom (ung.) 2047

Granada 1275
Grande-Bretagne (frz.) → Great-Britain (eng.) 207, 338, 1059, 2011
Grande-Grèce 193
Grandes invasions → Völkerwanderung
Graphie 1375
Graubünden 447, 1841, 1858, 1879
graue Literatur 424
Graz (dt.) → Gradec (slw.) 2025
grazhdanka 1611
Gräzismus 871
Grčka (bsn., krt., srb.) → Gărcija (blg.) 2025; Ellása / Hellás (gr.)
Great Britain (eng.) 207, 338, 1059 → Grande-Bretagne (frz.) 2011
Grebenarja 1964
grec 272, 1182, 1366, 1455 f, 1930
− de Calabre 1367
− salentin 1367
grec-macédonien 1544−1550
grecanico 1367
Grecia (rum.) → Gărcija (blg.) 2029; Ellás (gr.)
Grèce 1452 f
Greci 1372
grécophones 1367
grecs slavophones (bulgarophones) 1544
Grecs 193, 1453, 1544 f
Greece 329, 330
Greece (eng.) → Grèce (frz.)
Greek 395, 1427, 1443, 1489, 1490, 1554 ff, 1558 f, 1569, 1578−1581, 1584, 1593
Greek-Albanian 1540−1544
Greek-Arabic 1579
Greek-Arvanítika 1541−1543
Greeks → Grecs
Greenlandic 426
Greenlandish 346
Grenze 181
Grenze → border, boundary soziale − 23
Grenzgürtel-Methode 66
Grenzmarkierung 222
Greschoney (dt.) → Gressoney-la-Trinité (frz.) 1322, 1333, 1353, 2021
Gressoney-la-Trinité (frz.) 1322, 1333 → Greschoney (dt.) 2021
Gressoney-Saint-Jean 1322, 1333
Grevenmacher 1158
Greyerz (dt.) → Gruyère (frz.) 2063
gríco (gríko) 1367
Grieche 1463, 1515, 1519, 1550 ff

Griechen → Grecs
Griechenland 1515−1525
Griechenland → Grèce
Griechentum 180
Griechisch 316, 1271, 1322, 1519, 1521
Griechisch-Albanisch 1517
Griechisch-Aromunisch 1532−1539
Griechisch-Bulgarisch 1517, 1550−1554
Griechisch-Türkisch 1525−1532
Grisons 213, 1872
Grisons → Graubünden
Gröden 1323, 1355, 1383
Gröden → Gherdëina
groenlandais → Greenlandic
Grodk (sor.) → Spremberg (dt.) 2055
Grodna, Hrodna (wrs.) → Grodno (rss.) 2067
Grodno (rss.) → Grodna, Hrodna (wrs.) 2067
Groningen 1145
Grönländisch → Greenlandic
Großbritannien 1961, 1962
Großbritannien → Great Britain
Großgriechenland → Grande-Grèce
Großstadt → agglomération urbaine
Großsteffelsdorf (dt.) 1478 → Rimavská Sobota (slk.) 2043; Rimaszombat (ung.)
Großwardein (dt.) → Oradea (rum.), Nagyvárad (ung.) 2029, 2047
group identity 706
groupe
− autochtone 351
− dominé 351
− ethnique 211, 358
− linguistique 211
Gruber-De Gasperi-Abkommen (1946) 1325
Grünberg (dt.) → Zielona Góra (pln.) 2039
Grundgesamtheit 727, 733
Gruppe 182
Gruppenbildung 222
Gruyère (frz.) → Greyerz (dt.) 2063
Guarani 487
Guardia Marina 1344
Guardia Piemontese 1323, 1344
guègue 1453, 1455
Guernesey (frz.) → Guernsey (eng.) 1993
Guernsey (eng.) → Guernesey (frz.) 1993
Guerre de Succession d'Espagne (1701−1714) 1297
Guerre froide 358

Guerre Mondiale, Première − 246
Guerre Mondiale, Seconde − (1939−1945) → World War, Second − (1939−1945)
Guerres balkaniques (1912/13) 1452, 1560, 1545
Guerres balkaniques (1912/13) → Balkan Wars (1912/13)
guerres carlistes 1303
guest-word 604
guest-worker → Gastarbeiter
Guinea-Bissau 1312
Guingamp (frz.) → Gwengamp (brt.) 2011
Guipuzcoa 1303
Gümülçine (trk.) → Komotini (gr.) 2035
Güns (dt.) → Kőszeg (ung.) 2047
Guovdageaidnu (sam.) → Kautokeino (bkm.) 1985
Gurin (dt.) → Bosco (it.) 2063
Gurize (frl.) → Gorizia (it.), Gorica (slw.) 1323, 1337, 1357, 2021
GUS 1961
Guyana 328
Gwalarn 1257
Gwened (brt.) → Vannes (frz.) 1253, 2011
Gwengamp (brt.) → Guingamp (frz.) 2011
Gymnasium, Pannonisches − 1808, 1832
Győr (ung.) → Raab(dt.) 2047, 2059; Ráb (slk.) 2043
Gypsies → Roma, Roms, Sinte/ Sinti, Tsiganes, Zigeuner
gypsy 1557, 1579, 1593, 1631, 1714 f, 1718 f
Gypsy-Hungarian 1720
Gyula (ung.) → Jula (rum.) 2047
Gyulafehérvár (ung.) → Karlsburg (dt.) 2029; Alba Iulia (rum.) 2029, 2047

H

H (variété haute) 239, 247, 262, 266
habiletés 504
hablas fronterizas 1314
Habsbourg 1159, 1224
Habsburger 1311, 1480
Haci 1821
Hadersleben (dt.) → Haderslev (dän.) 1985, 2055
Haderslev (dän.) → Hadersleben (dt.) 1985, 2055
Hainaut 1241
haine de soi 251
haine de soi → Selbsthaß

Haïti 656
Hakka-Chinese 1146
Halbsprache → demi-langue
Halbsprachiger → semi-speaker
Halbsprachigkeit 368, 487
doppelte − 236, 321, 325
Halbsprachigkeit → semilinguisme
half-open question → Frage, halboffene −
Halvdan Koht 941 f
Hämeenlinna (fin.) → Tavastehus (swd.) 1985
Hamina 967
Handelssprache → language of commerce, langue du commerce
Haparanda 987
haptics 301
Har'kov, Char'kov (rss.) → Harkiv, Charkiv (ukr.) 2067
Harkiv, Charkiv (ukr.) → Har'kov, Char'kov (rss.) 2067
Harlem (New York) 454
Harmoniemodell 684
Haskalá 1945
Hasparren (frz.) → Hazparne (bsk.) 2011
Hauptkomponentenanalyse → principal component analysis
Hauptsprache 1840, 1879
Haute-Bretagne 1252
Haut-Rhin (frz.) 1224 → Elsaß (dt.) 2063
haut-sorabe → Obersorbisch
Hawai 338
Hazebroek (ndl.) → Hazebrouck (frz.) 2001, 2011
Hazebrouck (frz.) → Hazebroek (ndl.) 2001, 2011
Hazparne (bsk.) → Hasparren (frz.) 2011
heathenism 204
Hebräer 232
Hebräisch 225, 316, 1949
Hebräisch → Hebrew
Hebräisch-Aramäisch 1944
hebräische Buchstaben 1943
hébreu 616, 1930
Hebrew 347, 394, 664, 1567 ff, 1583, 1593
Heidelberger Projekt 754
Heidentum → heathenism
Heiliger Sava 1408
Heiliges Römisches Reich → Saint Empire Romain
Heimatbestimmung 816
Heimatvertriebener 30
Hel'sinki, Chel'sinki (rss.) → Helsinki (fin.), Helsingfors (swd.) 2067
Helsingfors (swd.) → Helsinki (fin.) 1985, 2067; Hel'sinki, Chel'sinki (rss.) 2067

Helsinki (fin.) → Hel'sinki, Chel'-sinki (rss.) 2067; Helsingfors (swd.) 1985, 2067
helvéticité 1874
Helvetische Republik (1789−1814) 1836, 1854
Helvetismus 1843, 1859
Hemisphäre, linke − → hémisphère gauche
Hemisphäre, rechte − → hémisphère droit
hemisphere, left − → hémisphère gauche
hemisphere, right − → hémisphère droit
hémisphère droit 61
hémisphère gauche 61
Hennegau → Hainaut
heritage language 494
Herkunftsfrage 1476
Hermagoras-Verlag (Klagenfurt) 1814
Hermannstadt (dt.) → Sibiu (rum.) 2029
Herzogtum Kärnten (ab 976) 1813
Het Reuzekoor 1245
hiérarchisation 361
hierarchy of part of speech categories 112
Highland English → Hochlandenglisch
Highland Line → Hochlandlinie
Highlands 1088
Hilfsschulsprachen 898
Hilfssprache, internationale − → international auxiliary language
Hindi 400, 488, 689, 1145
Hinduism 394
Hirschberg (dt.) → Jelenia Góra (pln.) 2039, 2043
Hispanic American 307
Hispanisierung 897
hispanisme 874
hispano-américain 477
Hispanogoten 1273
historical linguistics and language contact 2
historical linguistics and phonemic borrowing 102
hmong 1180
Hoch
 -alemannisch 1223
 -deutsch, bayerisches − 1861
 -deutsch, österreichisches − 1861
 -landenglisch 1095
 -landlinie 1089
 -sprache 1355
 -stufe 1473
Holland 1143
Holländer 1159

Holländische Antillen → Dutch Antilles
home language 482, 774
homo erectus 220
homo sapiens 220, 286, 289
homogenization 206
Homophonie 882
homophonous diamorph 110
Hong Kong 338, 1146
Hongrois 1437
hongrois 387, 1929
hongrois → Ungarisch
Horvátország (ung.) → Hrvatska (krt.) 2047
Hörverstehen 511
host society 207
Hoyerswerda (dt.) → Wojerecy (sor.) 2055
Hradec Králové (tsch.) → Königgrätz (dt.) 2043
Hrvaška (slw.) → Hrvatska (bsn., krt., srb.) 2025
Hrvatska (bsn.) → Hrvatska (krt., srb.), Hrvaška (slw.) 2025
Hrvatska (krt.) → Hrvatska (bsn., srb.) 2025; Hrvaška (slw.), Horvátország (ung.) 2047
Hrvatska (srb.) → Hrvatska (bsn., krt.), Hrvaška (slw.) 2025
Hrvatske Novine 1824
Hugenotten 186
human rights 866, 870
human rights → droits humains
Humanwissenschaften 222
Hungarian 336, 993, 1444
Hungarian → hongrois, Ungarisch
Hungarian-German 572, 588, 596
Hungarian-Slovene 1715
Hungarians 1417, 1419 f, 1425, 1427, 1429
Hungarians → Ungarn
Hungarismen 1483
Hungarologie 1730
Hutterer 189, 315 f
Hutterer → Hutterites
Hutterites 393
H-Varietät → H (variété haute)
H-variety → H (variété haute)
hybrid 543
hybridation linguistique 1217
hypercorrection 643, 679, 1217
Hyperkorrektur 1396
hyperlecte 277
hypothèse
 − d'indépendance 37
 − d'interdépendance 37
 − du commutateur simple 37
 − monogénétique (créolisation) 654

 − substratophile (créolisation) 654
 − universaliste (créolisation) 653

I

Iberisch 1272
Iberische Halbinsel 1270
Iberische Halbinsel → Péninsule Ibérique
Ibiza (sp.) → Eivissa (kat.) 2015
Icelandic 346, 1044
identification 205, 264
Identität 183, 189, 218, 204, 279, 324, 1162, 1183
 ethnische − 1374
 sprachliche − 323
Identitätstheorie, ethnolinguistische − 694
Identitätsverlust 236
identité
 − culturelle 200, 1875
 − ethnique 717
 − multiple 455, 909
identity, national − 426
Idiolekt 259
Ideologie 243, 690
idéologie → Ideologie
 − diglossique 1211
 − linguistique 1198
 − métalinguistique 1214
Ideologisierung 1763
ideology → Ideologie
Idiome, rätoromanische − 1844, 1880
Iekavian 1430
Iglau (dt.) → Jihlava (tsch.) 2043
Ijekavian → Iekavian
ijekavien → Iekavian 1437 f
IJsselmeerpolders 1150
ikastola 1262, 1304
Ikavian → ikavien
ikavien 1437
Ikavisch 1823
Ikavisch → ikavien
il-Belt Valletta (mal.) → Valletta (it.) 1399, 2021
il-Birgu (mal.) → Vittoriosa (it.) 2021
Ilanz (dt.) → Glion (rtr.) 2063
Ile-de-France 1173
Ille-et-Vilaine 1254
Illes Balears (kat.) → Islas Baleares (sp.) 2015
Illyres 1358
Illyric renaissance 1426
Illyricum 1374
Illyrische Bewegung 1822
ilôt linguistique 715
îlot linguistique → language island, Sprachinsel

immersion
— bidirectionnelle 479
— delayed — 495
— late — 495
— moyenne 474
— partial — 494, 837
— partielle 837
— précoce 474
— programme 1102
— tardive 474
— teachers 493
— bidirectionnelle → two-way bilingual immersion
— delayed — → immersion moyenne
— late — → immersion, late —
— partial — → immersion partielle
— partielle → immersion, partial
— précoce → early immersion
— program → programme d'immersion
— tardive → immersion tardive
Immersion 239, 293, 1847
— frühe — → early immersion, immersion précoce
— mittlere — → immersion moyenne
— späte — → immersion, late —
Immersionsmodell 486
Immersionsprogramm → programme d'immersion
Immersionsunterricht 1384
immigrant men 721
immigrant women 721
Immigrantenfamilie 379
immigration 1178
immigrés 1868
impérialisme
— culturel 911
— linguistique 908
— culturel → cultural imperialism
— linguistique → linguistic imperialism
implicational scale 785
implicational scale → échelle implicationnelle
Implikationsskala → échelle implicationnelle, implicational scale
Imvros (gr.) → Gökçeada (trk.) 2035
inadequacy of acquisition 590
Inari (fin.) → Anár (sam.) 1985
Inari Saami 1016, 1019
Inde 83, 362
Indefinitpronomina 1958
independency hypothesis → hypothèse d'indépendance
index of fusion 110
index of synthesis 110
India 78, 331

India → Inde
Indian language → Indianersprache
Indianersprache 487
Indians 343
Indien 488, 689, 1961
Indien → Inde
indirect (phonological) diffusion and phonemic borrowing 99
individuation sociolinguistique 1211
Indochine 195
Indo-Dutch 1147
indominant language → langue indominante; Sprache, indominante —
indominante Sprache → langue indominante
industrialization and language 1077
infant bilingualism → bilingualité précoce
infix 109
inflection 109
Informant 821
Informantendatenschutz 823
Informantenschutz 823
information processing in bilingual children 625
in-glossia 249
Inn 1836, 1879
input model 518
Inquisition 1345
Inselenglisch 1094
Institut
— Basque de l'Administration Publique 1307
— Culturel Basque 1263
— d'Estudis Catalans 1198
— d'Etudes Occitanes 1190
institutional multilingualism 861, 864
instrumentalism 77
Insular Scots 1093
integration index 808
intégrité territoriale 359
Intelligenztests 364
interaction 506
interactionist model 520
interactive network 806
Interaktion 318
intercode 277
intercompréhension 176
intercultural
— communication 134, 1029
— counseling 297
interculturalité 922 f
interdependency 626
interdependency hypothesis → hypothèse d'interdépendance
Interdependenzhypothese 485
interest group 403
interference 3, 4, 5, 6 f, 518, 550, 558, 580, 1018

— vs. integration 124
— phonetic — 98
interférence 33, 59, 271, 538, 1235, 1246, 1263, 1300, 1369
Interferenz 15, 145, 287, 980, 1040, 1392, 1396, 1403, 1404, 1474, 1767, 1775 f, 1789, 1780 f, 1795 f, 1825, 1885, 1955
-forschung 1355
— pragmatische — → pragmatic interference
— semantische — → semantic interference
intergroup communication 1045
intergroup salience 44
Interkulturalität 922 f
interlangage → interlanguage
interlanguage 516, 910, 1029
— model 520
interlangue 54, 277, 504
Interlinearversion 914
Interlingua 884
interlingual identification 110
interlinguale Stilunterschiede 150
interlinguale Variation 845
Interlinguistik 881
intermediary language 906
intermediary language → langue intermédiaire
internal
— colonialism 79, 207
— migration 772
— prestige 706
international auxiliary language 647
Internationale Roma-Union 1963
Internationaler Roma-Kongreß (1971, London) 1963
internationalism 546
Internationalismen 1953
interpersonal distance 305
interprétation
— consécutive 860
— simultanée 860
— consécutive → consecutive interpretation
— simultanée → simultanous interpretation
interpreter 302
Intertextualität 919
intertextualité 919
intertolérance 1221
inter-utterance code switching 603
interval data 777
interview
— discourse 746
— format 746
— mode → Befragungsmodus
— process → Erhebungsverfahren

- *structure* → Strukturiertheit der Befragung
- *type* → Befragungstyp
- *written* – → Befragung, schriftliche –

interviewing 744
intimate borrowing 543
intra-sentential switching 599
intralinguale Variation 845
Inuit 427, 476, 1049, 1050
inuktitut 280
inuktitut-anglais 476
inuktitut-français 476
Ioannina (gr.) → Janinë (alb.) 2035
Iparralde (Pays basque nord) 1188, 1260
IQ-tests → Intelligenztests
ir-Rabat (mal.) → Victoria (it.) 2021
Iran 344
Iraq 344
Ireland 329, 1097
Ireland (eng.) → Eire (ir.) 1993
Ireland's census 1099
Irisch 446
Irish 396, 427, 664, 1065, 1098, 1102
- language policy 1103
- speaking areas 1102
- medium education 1101
Irish-English 1105
irlandais → Irisch
Irlande 161, 201
Irlande du Nord → Northern Ireland
Irmandades da Fala 1288
irrédentisme 216
Iruña (bsk.) → Pampelune (frz.) 2011; Pamplona (sp.) 2011, 2015
Iskeçe (trk.) → Xanthi (gr.) 2035
Islam 397
Island (bkm.) → Islanti (finn.), Island (swd.) 1985
Island (swd.) → Islanti (finn.), Island (bkm.) 1985
Island English → Inselenglisch
islandais → Icelandic
Isländisch → Icelandic
Islanti (fin.) → Island (bkm., swd.) 1985
Islas Baleares (sp.) → Illes Balears (kat.) 2015
Isle of Man 1062
isogloss 66, 177
isolat homogène 794
isolation language 110
isolierter Dialekt 686
Israel 1946
Israelit 1805
Israelitische Kultusgemeinde (Wien) 1805

Issime (frz.) 1333, 1353 → Eischime (dt.) 2021, 2063
Istanbul (trk.) → Carigrad (blg.) 2029; Konstantinupoli (gr.) 2035
Istitut cultural ladin „Majon di Fascegn" (1975 f) 1384
Istitut cultural ladin „Micurá de Rü" (1977 f) 1384
Istitut pedagogic ladin (1987 f) 1384
Italia (it.) → Italija (bsn., krt., slw., srb.) 2025; Italien (dt.)1318, 1350, 1436 ff, 2055, 2059, 2063; Italie (frz.) 2011, 2063; Italia (rtr.) 2063; Itálie (tsch.) 2034
Italian 956
Italian-German 596
italianisation 1342, 1877
italianisme 874
Italianismus 874
italianité 1214, 1220, 1874
italiano
- pidginizzato 1327
- popolare 1374
- regionale bolzanino 1355
Italians 296, 1417, 1420, 1425, 1427 ff
Italie 202
Italie (frz.) → Italien (dt.) 2063; Italia (it.) 2011, 2063; Italia (rtr.) 2063
Itálie (tsch.) → Italia (it.) 2034
italien 613, 1182, 1214, 1337, 1344, 1357, 1366, 1379, 1862, 1866, 2103
italien → Italian
- de Bosnie-Herzégovine 1436, 1438 f
- fédéral 1877
- helvétique 1877
- régional 1343, 1877
- tessinois 1878
Italien (dt.) 1318, 1350, 1436 ff → Italie (frz.) 2063; Italia (it., rtr.) 2055, 2059, 2063
italien-français (francoprovençal) 1330
italien-frioulan 1337
italien-grec 1367
italien-occitan 1344
italien-slovène 1357
Italiener 1159, 1351
Italiener → Italians
Italienisch 91, 320, 1350, 1363, 1371, 1402, 1837, 1840, 1841
Italienisch → Italian
Italienisch-Albanisch 1371
Italienisch-Deutsch 1350
Italienisch-Kroatisch 1363
Italiens → Italians
Italija (bsn., krt., slw., srb.) → Italia (it.) 2025

Itämeri (fin.) → Östersjön (swd.) 1985
Iterative Proportional Fitting 736
Iterativpräteritum 1958
Iulium Carnicum 1338
Ivano-Frankivs'k (ukr.) → Ivano-Frankovsk (rss.) 2067
Ivano-Frankovsk (rss.) → Ivano-Frankivs'k (ukr.) 2067
Ivory Coast → Côte d'Ivoire
Ivre-Deutsch 1944
Ivrith 1949
Izmir (trk.) → Smirni (gr.) 2035

J

Jacobin 353
Jadransko more (bsn., krt., srb.) → Jadransko morje (slw.) 2025
Jadransko morje (slw.) → Jadransko more (bsn., krt., srb.) 2025
Jáger (slk.) → Eger (ung.) 2043
Jakobiner → Jacobin
Jakobsweg (Santiago de Compostela) 185
Janinë (alb.) → Ioannina (gr.) 2035
Japan 299 f, 328
Japaner 224
Japaner → Japanese
Japanese 301, 303, 307 f, 336
japanese, Japanisch → japonais, Japaner
Japlisch 425, 855
Japon → Japan
japonais 280
jargon 259, 644, 650
Jauer 1881
Jaun (dt.) → Jogne (frz.) 2063
Jauntaler Dialekt 1815
Jazyčije 1697 f
Jekavian → Jekavisch
jekavien → Jekavisch
Jekavisch 1410
Jelenia Góra (pln.) → Hirschberg (dt.) 2039, 2043
Jersey (eng.) → Jersey (frz.) 1993
Jersey (frz.) → Jersey (eng.) 1993
Jesenice (slw.) → Aßling (dt.) 2059
Jews 296, 1427, 1443, 1490, 1578, 1584 f, 1593
Jidde 1805
Jiddisch 95, 225, 1805, 1942
Jiddisch → Yiddish
Jiddischismus 1946
Jiddistik 1959
Jihlava (tsch.) → Iglau (dt.) 2043
Jogne (frz.) → Jaun (dt.) 2063

Johanniterorden 1399
Johkamohkki (sam.) → Jokkmokk (swd.) 1985
Jokkmokk (swd.) → Johkamohkki (sam.) 1985
Jude 291, 1463, 1519, 1670, 1672, 1674 ff, 1805, 1828
Juden → Jews
Judenspanisch 1519
Judenspanisch → Judeo-Spanish
Judentum 180
Judenverfolgung 1943
judéo-arabe 1178
judéo-espagnol 1178, 1437 f, 1440 f
judéo-espagnol → Judeo-Spanish
judeo-español 1274
judéo-fragnol 1558, 1568
Judeo-Spanish 372, 1556 ff, 1568 f
judéos 1274
Judezmo 1443
judgement, linguistic — → jugement linguistique
judicat d'Arborea 1377
Jüdisch-Deutsch 1942, 1944
Jüdisches Antifaschistisches Komitee 1947
Jüdisches Autonomes Gebiet 1947
Jüdisches Wissenschaftliches Institut 1945, 1949
jugement linguistique 680
Jugendsprache 259
Jugoslawen 1407, 1409
Jugoslawen → Yougoslaves
Jugoslawien 1407 ff, 1961
Jugoslawien → SHS-Staat, Yougoslavie, Yugoslavia
Juifs 1113, 1455
Juifs → Jews
Jula (rum.) → Gyula (ung.) 2047
Jura 1330, 1863
Jura → République et Canton du Jura
— Conflict 396
-konflikt 1847
— Nord 1864
— Sud 1864

K

Kaale 1000
kachoube → Kashub (Kashubian)
Kaikavian 1431
Kajkavisch 1734, 1736 f
Kalabrien 1322, 1323, 1371
Kalabrien → Calabria
Kalabro-Albaner 1373
Kalderaš 1963
Kale 1963

Kalevala 996
Kaliningrad (rss.) → Königsberg (dt.) 1985, 2039; Królewiec (pln.) 2039
Kalisch (dt.) → Kalisz (pln.) 2039
Kalisz (pln.) → Kalisch (dt.) 2039
Kalter Krieg → Guerre froide
Kamenz (dt.) → Kamjenc (sor.) 2055
Kamjenc (sor.) → Kamenz (dt.) 2055
Kampanien 1371
Kanada → Canada
Kanal 4, Wales → Sianel Pedwar Cumru (S4C)
Kanaltal (dt.) 1352, 1354 → Val Canale (it.) 2021
Kanarische Inseln 1270
Kantone 1836
Kapetinger → Capétiens
Kapverdische Inseln 1312
Karadeniz (trk.) → Černo More (blg.), Marea Neagră (rum.) 2029
Karaites 1566, 1568, 1593
karamanli 1561 f
Karamanlidika (Karamanli) 1515, 1529
Karantanen 1799
Karantani 1417
Karantania 1417
Karantanien 1798
Karelian 993, 1003
Karelien 228
Karelisch → Karelian
Karintia (ung.) → Kärnten (dt.) 1354, 1798, 1805, 1813, 2047
Karlistenkriege → guerres carlistes
Karlovy Vary (tsch.) → Karlsbad (dt.) 2043
Karlsbad (dt.) → Karlovy Vary (tsch.) 2043
Karlsburg (dt.) → Alba Iulia (rum.), Gyulafehérvár (ung.) 2029
Kärnten (dt.) 1354, 1798, 1805, 1813 → Koroška (slw.) 2059; Karintia (ung.) 2047
Kärntner Slowenen 1799, 1815
Karolingerreich → Empire Carolingien
Karten → maps
Karthager 1271
Kartographie → cartography
Kasachstan 229
Kaschau (dt.) → Košice (slk.), Košyci (ukr.) Kassa (ung.) 2043
Kaschubisch → Kashub (Kashubian)

Kashub (Kashubian) 1586, 1588 f, 1592, 1594, 1600–1602
Käsmark (dt.) → Kiežmark (pln.), Kežmarok (slk.), Késmárk (ung.), 2043
Kassa (ung.) → Kaschau (dt.) 2043; Košice (slk.) 2043, 2047; Košyci (ukr.) 2043
Kassel (ndl.) → Cassel (frz.) 1241, 2011
Kastilisch 1276
Kastilisch → Castilian
Kastoria (gr.) → Kostur (blg.) 2029, 2035; Kostur (mak.) 2035
Katalanisch 293, 686, 1323
Katalanisch → Catalan
Katalonien 1270, 1275
Katalonien → Catalogne
katharevousa (katharévousa), katharevusa (katharévusa), katharavousa 246, 1543, 1547, 1558, 1562 ff
Katholiken 1953
katholisch 1165
katholisch → Catholic
Katowice (pln.) → Kattowitz (dt.) 2039, 2043
Kattowitz (dt.) → Katowice (pln.) 2039, 2043
Kauderwelsch 1881
Kautokeino (bkm.) → Guovdageaidnu (sam.) 1985
kawlata 1401
Kazan 1001
Kea (gr.) → Tzia (gr.) 2035
Keenan-Report (1880) 1402
Keilschrift 105
Kelten → Celts
Keltisch → Celtic
Keltismus 1272
keltoromanisch 1798
Kenya 162
Kerkira (trk.) → Korfuz (alb.), Korfu (gr.) 2035
Kernekwek (Cornish) 1059
Kernwerte → „core values"
Késmárk (ung.) → Käsmark (dt.), Kežmarok (slk.), Kiežmark (pln.) 2043
Kežmarok (slk.) → Käsmark (dt.), Kiežmark (pln.), Késmárk (ung.) 2043
Keulen (ndl.) → Köln (dt.), Cologne (frz.) 2001
khmer 1180
Kibris (trk.) → Kipros (gr.) 2035
Kiev (rss.) → Kiïv, Kyjiv (ukr.) 2067
Kiewer Rus 1954
Kiežmark (pln.) → Käsmark (dt.), Kežmarok (slk.), Késmárk (ung.) 2043

Kiïv, Kyjiv (ukr.) → Kiev (rss.) 2067
Kilkis (gr.) → Kuku– (blg.) 2029, 2035; Kukuš (mak.) 2035
Killilea-Resolution 932
Kindersprache 259
Kindestaufe 312
kinesic atlas 296
kinesics 301, 306
Kipros (gr.) → Kibris (trk.) 2035
Kirchenslawisch 231, 1697, 1954
Kirchensprache 1138
Kırklareli (trk.) → Lozengrad (blg.) 2029
Kišinev (blg.) → Chişinău (rum.) 2029
Kišiněv (rss.) → Chişinău (rum.), Kišiniv, Kyšyniv (ukr.) 2067
Kišiniv, Kyšyniv (ukr.) → Kišiněv (rss.), Chişinău (rum.) 2067
Kismarton (ung.) → Eisenstadt (dt.) 2047; Željezno (krt.) 2059
Kiswahili 395
Kjustendža (blg.) → Constanţa (rum.) 2029
Kladsko (tsch.) → Glatz (dt.), Klodzko (pln.) 2043
Klagenfurt (dt.) 1813 → Celovec (slw.) 2025, 2059
Klausenburg (dt.) 1463, 1478 → Cluj-Napoca (rum.), Kolozsvár (ung.) 2029
Kleingruppe → petit groupe
Kleinrussen 1697
Klingenbacher Missale 1822
Klodzko (pln.) → Glatz (dt.), Kladsko (tsch.) 2043
knowledge, operational – → connaissance opérationnelle
København (dän.) → Kopenhagen (dt.) 2055; Kööpenhamina (fin.), Köpenhamn (swd.) 1985
Koblenz (dt.) → Coblence (frz.) 2001
Kodemischung → code-mixing
Kodewechsel 15, 16, 980 f, 1775 f
Kodewechsel → alternance codique, alternance des codes, code-switching
Kodieren → coding
Kodierung → encodage
Kodifizierung 894
Kodifizierung → codification
kognitive Entwicklung 367
Kognitivismus → cognitivism
Kohärenz → cohérence
Kohäsion → cohésion
Koiné 1164, 1339, 1341
Kolmar (dt.) → Colmar (frz.) 1223, 2063

Köln (dt.) → Cologne (frz.), Keulen (ndl.) 2001
Kolonialismus → colonialism
Kolonialismus 186
Kolonialsprache 483
Kolozsvár (ung.) → Klausenburg (dt.) 1463, 1478, 2029; Cluj-Napoca (rum.) 1463, 2029, 2047
Komárno (slk.) → Komorn (dt.), Komárom (ung.) 2043, 2047
Komárom (ung.) → Komorn (dt.) Komárno (slk.) 2043, 2047
Koménsky-Schulverein (Wien) 1808
komisch → comique
Kommitee voor Frans-Vlaanderen 1246
Kommunikation 241
Kommunikation → communication
  interkulturelle – 190
  nonverbale – 925
  interkulturelle – → intercultural communication
  nichtverbale – → communication, nonverbal –
  nonverbale – → communication non-verbale
Kommunikationsbruch 928
Kommunikationskonflikt 417
kommunikative Stiltheorie 149 f
Komorn (dt.) → Komárno (slk.), Komárom (ung.) 2043, 2047
Komotini (gr.) → Gümülçine (trk.) 2035
Kompetenz 241, 322
Kompetenz → competence
  kommunikative – 1038, 845 f
  mehrsprachige – 235
  grammatische – → competence, grammatical –
  kommunikative – → compétence communicative
Komplexitätsreduktion 30
Konferenz von Lausanne (1923) 1551
Konfession 223
Konflikt 1401, 1763, 1779, 1783, 1794, 1844
Konfliktmodell 684
Konglomeration 231
Königgrätz (dt.) → Hradec Králové (tsch.) 2043
Königreich Italien 1384
Königsberg (dt.) → Królewiec (pln.) 2039; Kaliningrad (rss.) 1985, 2039
Konkani 394
Konsekutivdolmetschen → consecutive interpretation, interprétation consécutive

Konsensmodell 686
Konsonantismus → consonantisme
Konstantinupoli (gr.) → Istanbul (trk.) 2035
Kontaktenglisch 1094
Kontaktlinguistik 15 f
  –, Gegenstandsbereich 12 f
  –, Hauptforschungsfragen 13 f
  –, Hinblick auf Stilphänomene 144 f
  –, Paradigmata 18
  –, psycholinguistische und neurolinguistische Fragen 14 f
  –, soziolinguistische Fragen 15 f
  –, *Geschichte* → contact linguistics, history
Kontaktsprache 539
Kontakttyp 27
Kontamination 1885
Kontexteffekt 741
Kontinentalwestgermanisch 1133
Kontinuitätstheorie 1479
Kontinuum 258
Konvergenz → convergence
  syntaktische – → convergence, syntactic –
Konversationsanalyse 925
Konversationsanalyse → analyse de la conversation
Kööpenhamina (fin.) → København (dän.), Kopenhagen (dt.), Köpenhamn (swd.) 1985, 2055
Köpenhamn (swd.) → København (dän.), Kopenhagen (dt.), Kööpenhamina (fin.) 1985, 2055
Koper (slw.) → Capodistria (it.) 2025
Korea 328
Korean 343
Korfu (gr.) → Korfuz (alb.) 2025, 2035; Krf (bsn., krt., srb.) 2025; Kerkira (trk.) 2025, 2035
Korfuz (alb.) → Krf (bsn., krt., srb.) 2025; Korfu (gr.), Kerkira (trk.) 2025, 2035
Korle (brt.) → Corlaix (frz.) 2011
Koroška (slw.) → Kärnten (dt.) 1354, 1798, 1805, 1813, 2047, 2059
Korpusplanung 896
Korpusplanung → corpus planning, planification du corpus
Korrespondenzsprachen 854 f
Korsisch 230
Korsisch → Corse
Kosadası (trk.) → Kos (gr.) 2035
Kos (gr.) → Kosadası (trk.) 2035

Košice (slk.) → Kaschau (dt.) 2043; Kassa (ung.) 2043, 2047; Košyci (ukr.) 2043
Köslin (dt.) → Koszalin (pln.) 2039
Kosovë (alb.) → Kosovo (srb.) 1407ff, 1451ff. 2035
Kosovo (srb.) 1407ff, 1451ff → Kosovë (alb.) 2035
Kosten-Nutzen-Analyse 866
Kosten-Nutzen-Analyse → cost-benefit analysis
Kostur (blg.; mak.) → Kastoría (gr.) 2029, 2035
Košyci (ukr.) → Kaschau (dt.), Košice (slk.), Kassa (ung.) 2043
Koszalin (pln.) → Köslin (dt.) 2039
Kőszeg (ung.) → Güns (dt.) 2047
Kovačja 1963
Krain 1798
Krajina (slw.) 1425f, 1430 → Krajna (ung.) 2047
Krajna (ung.) → Krajina (slw.) 1425f, 1430, 2047
Krautwalsch 1388
Kreol 145, 1647
Kreol → creole, créole
Kreolisch 320
Kreolisierung → créolisation
Kreolsprache 190, 881, 895
Kreolsprache → langue créole
Kreolsprachen → creoles, langues créoles
Krf (bsn., krt., srb.) → Korfuz (alb.), Korfu (gr.) 2025
Krimtataren 232
Krimtatarisch 1943
Krini (gr.) → Çesme (trk.) 2035
Kriti (gr.) → Girid (trk.) 2035
Kroaten 1407ff, 1463, 1674, 1676, 1821
Kroaten → Croates
Kroatien → Croatia
Kroatisch 1323, 1363, 1806, 1821, 1830
Kroatisch → croate
Kroatischer Kulturverein 1823
Królewiec (pln.) → Königsberg (dt.), Kaliningrad (rss.) 2039
Kronstadt (dt.) → Brașov (rum.), Brassó (ung.) 2029
Kronstadt 1478
Krymtschaken 1943
Kuhspanisch 1881
Kukuš (blg.; mak.) → Kilkis (gr.) 2029, 2035
Kuijpers-Resolution 932
Kultur
 -anthropologie 921
 -theorie 925
 -kampf 923
 -kritik 921
 -muster 224
 -nation 847
 -anthropologie → anthropologie culturelle
 -imperialismus → cultural imperialism, impérialisme culturel
 -loyalität → culture loyalty
kulturelle Autonomie 1792
kulturelle Hegemonie 922
Kulturem → culturème
künstliche Zweisprachigkeit 382
kurde → Kurdish
Kurdes 254
Kurdisch 321
Kurdisch → Kurdish
Kurdish 344, 670, 1024f, 1030f
Kurds 343, 1144
Kurland 1945
Küstenland 1320
Kven 943, 961f
Kyrillica 226
Kyrn 1214

L

L (variété basse) 247
l-Isla (mal.) 1401 → Senglea (it.) 2021
L-Varietät 239, 262, 266
L-Varietät → L (variété basse)
L-variety → L (variété basse)
L_1 236
L_1 development 496
L_1-Erwerb 291
L_2 236
L_2 skills 496
L_2-Erwerb 291
La Alamedilla 1314
labor migration → Arbeitsmigration
Lac Léman (frz.) → Genfer See (dt.) 1855, 2063
ladin 1387, 1881
 − dolomitan 1389
Ladiner 1351
Ladiner → Ladins
Ladinia → Ladinien
Ladinian → ladin
Ladinians → Ladins
Ladinien 1383
Ladinisch 1323, 1355
Ladinisch → ladin
Ladino 1487, 1558, 1568f
Ladins 1386
Laestadian 972, 985
Laestadianisch 962f, 978
L'Alguer (kat.) 352 → Alghero (it.) 194, 1323, 1377, 1381, 2021
Lago di Como (it.) → Comer See (dt.) 2059, 2063
Lago di Garda (it.) → Gardasee (dt.) 2059, 2063
Lago di Lugano (it.) → Luganer See (dt.) 2063
Lago Maggiore (it.) → Langensee (dt.) 2063
La Jonica (1968ff.) 1368
Lallans (Scots) 1066
Land (dt.) → Olen (dt.) 2021; Alagna (it.) 2021, 2063
Landessprache 1837, 1858
Landflucht 187
landfogti (Landvögte) 1871
Landsberg (dt.) → Gorzów Wielkopolski (pln.) 2039
Landsmål 940, 949
La Neuveville (frz.) → Neuenstadt (dt.) 2063
langage
 − de programmation 881
 − enfantin → Kindersprache
 − scientifique → Wissenschaftssprache
Langensee (dt.) → Lago Maggiore (it.) 2063
Langobards 1358
language
 − assimilation 630
 − attitude 173, 784, 1069
 − attrition 579, 902, 904f, 943
 − awareness 571
 − boundary 69
 − census 774, 1081
 − change 371
 − choice 782, 808
 − community 771
 − competence 573
 − cultivation 836, 1013, 1045
 − death 113, 312, 339, 580, 587, 659, 667
 − development 839
 − extinction 375
 − island 1008
 − law 401
 − loss 374, 568, 579, 902, 904f
 − loyalty 173, 902, 1025
 − maintenance 312, 395, 567, 581, 630, 807, 902, 904f
 − maintenance factors, ambivalent − 571
 − maintenance factors, demographic − 573
 − maintenance factors, institutional support 573
 − maintenance factors, stable − 571
 − maintenance factors, status − 573
 − maintenance project 665
 − mixing 373, 594
 − national − 345, 672
 − obsolence 587
 − of commerce 906

- of wider communication 483, 704
- planning 64, 344, 834 f, 839, 865, 905, 1048, 1718 f
- polarization 838
- policy 8, 713, 861, 865, 1044, 1056, 1057, 1101, 1904 f, 1909 f, 1916 f
- preservation 375
- proficiency 371
- reinforcement 902 f
- religious − 392
- retention 567
- revitalization 664
- revival 718
- revival project 664
- rights 861
- segregation 630
- shift 312, 374, 568, 586, 772, 808, 836, 902, 904 f, 943, 947, 986, 989, 1010, 1019, 1068, 1078, 1098, 1716
- simplification 134
- split 1431
- spread 904, 943
- standardization 1431
- *attitude* → Sprachattitüde, Spracheinstellung
- *attitude research, methods of* − → Spracheinstellungsforschung, Methoden der −
- *awareness* → conscience linguistique, Sprachbewußtsein
- *barrier* → barrière linguistique, Sprachbarriere
- *boundary* → frontière linguistique, limite linguistique, Sprachgrenze
- *chauvinism* → chauvinisme linguistique, Sprachchauvinismus
- *choice* → choix linguistique, Sprachwahl
- *community* → communauté linguistique, Sprachgemeinschaft
- *conflict* → conflit linguistique, Sprachkonflikt
- *contact* → Sprachkontakt
- *cultivation* → cultivation linguistique, Sprachpflege
- *developement* → développement linguistique
- *distance* → distance interlinguistique, distance linguistique
- *divergence* → divergence linguistique, Sprachendivergenz
- *domain* → domaine linguistique
- *elaboration* → élaboration linguistique
- *ethnology* → ethnologie du langage
- *for special purposes* → Fachsprache, langue de spécialité
- *functions* → fonctions langagières
- *island* → ilôt linguistique
- *label* → dénomination de la langue
- *legislation* → législation linguistique, Sprachengesetzgebung, Sprachgesetzgebung
- *loss* → Sprachverlust
- *loyality* → loyauté linguistique, Sprachloyalität
- *maintenance* → maintien de langue, maintien linguistique, Sprachbewahrung, Spracherhalt
- *of commerce* → langue du commerce
- *of instruction* → Unterrichtssprache
- *planning* → aménagement linguistique, planification linguistique, Sprachplanung
- *policy* → politique linguistique, Sprachenpolitik, Sprachpolitik
- regional − → Regionalsprache
- *revival* → revivification linguistique
- *rights* → droits linguistiques
- *shift* → changement linguistique, Sprachwechsel
- *spread* → diffusion linguistique
- *use* → usage linguistique
- *variation* → sprachliche Variation, Sprachvariation, variation linguistique
- written − → Schriftsprache
language-learner 517
language-use pattern 782
lingua geral (Port.) 558
langue
- administrative 406
- cible 913 f
- commune 162
- congénère 635
- créole 527, 834, 881, 895
- d'oc 1173
- d'oïl 1173
- de base 650
- de culture 272
- de départ 913 f
- de France 1220
- de référence 636
- de spécialité 886
- de travail 890
- dominante 388
- dominée 252
- du commerce 906
- du foyer 272
- du travail 839, 858 f
- d'usage 166
- endogène 1119
- éteinte 527
- ethnique 272
- exogène 1119
- franque 556
- indominante 847, 850
- intermédiaire 906
- maternelle 166, 276
- minoritaire 469
- mixte 792
- mondiale 858
- monocentrique 614
- morte 527
- moyenne 639
- nationale 1876
- officielle 276, 843, 854 f, 858, 861 f, 890, 898, 1115
- ou dialecte 639
- par distanciation 636
- par élaboration 636
- pluricentrique 895
- polycentrique 614
- polynomique 1211
- préférée 466
- première 271, 887
- propre 161, 1298
- régionale 847, 850, 1175
- régionale 924, 932
- seconde 271, 882, 887, 889 f
- standard 834
- -toit 637
- universelle 881
- véhiculaire 272, 889, 895
- vernaculaire 272
- *auxiliaire internationale* → international auxiliary language
- *cible* → target language (TL), Zielsprache
- *créole* → Kreolsprache
- *d'enseignement* → Unterrichtssprache
- *de contact* → Kontaktsprache
- *de départ* → Ausgangssprache
- *de publication* → Publikationssprache
- *de spécialité* → Fachsprache
- *d'élaboration* → Ausbausprache
- *du commerce* → language of commerce
- *du travail* → working language
- *écrite* → Schriftsprache, written language
- *indienne* → Indianersprache
- *indominante* → Sprache, indominante −
- *intermédiaire* → intermediary language
- *littéraire* → Literatursprache
- *maternelle* → mother tongue

- *minoritaire* → minority language
- *mixte* → Mischsprache
- *mondiale* → world language
- *officielle* → Amtssprache, official language
- *régionale* → Regionalsprache
- *religieuse* → language, religious –
- *seconde* → L₂, Zweitsprache
- *standard* → standard language
- *universelle* → Universalsprache

Languedoc-Roussillon 1188
langues créoles → creoles
langues slaves 1866
Langzeitgedächtnis → long term memory
lao 1180
Lapons → Lappen, Sa(a)mi
Lappen 221
Lappen → Lapps, Sa(a)mi
Lappi (fin.) → Sápmi (sam.), Lappland (swd.) 1985
Lappland (swd.) → Lappi (fin.), Sápmi (sam.) 1985
Lapps 343
Lapps → Lappen, Sa(a)mi
La Scheulte (frz.) → Schelten (dt.) 2063
Latein 1124, 1685, 1756, 1736, 1944
Lateinisch 90, 316, 1682
latéralisation cérébrale 57
Latin 253, 938, 973, 995, 998, 1286, 1587
Latin → Latein
Latini 1372
latinisme 874
Latinismus 874
Latinität 180
Latvia (fin.) 348, 1906–1912 → Latvija (ltt.) 1985
Latvian-Estonian 1910
Latvian-German 1910
Latvian-Lithuanian 1910
Latvian-Livonian 1910
Latvian-Russian 1908 f, 1910
Latvija (ltt.; ukr.) → Latvia (fin.) 348, 1906–1912, 1985; Latvija (ukr.) 2067
laughter 307
Lauregno (it.) → Laurein (dt.) 2063
Laurein (dt.) → Lauregno (it.) 2063
Lausanne (frz.) → Losanna (it.) 2021
Layout (eines Fragebogens) 742
learnability 565
learning → apprentissage
– environment 517

– path 563
– rate 562
Lebensalter 289
Lébény (ung.) → Leiden (dt.) 2047
Lechtal (Tirol) 1797
Leeuwarden (ndl.) → Ljouwert (frs.) 2001
Lefkoşa (trk.) → Lefkosia (gr.) 2035
Lefkosia (gr.) → Lefkoşa (trk.) 2035
Lega Nord 1320
législation linguistique 160, 843
législation linguistique → Sprachengesetzgebung, Sprachgesetzgebung
Legnica (pln.) → Liegnitz (dt.) 2039, 2043
Lehn
-elemente 242
-phraseologie 1819
-prägung 1391, 1726, 1826
-übersetzung 1128, 1391, 1726
-wörter 886, 873 f, 916, 1128, 1385, 1391, 1817, 1834
-wortschatz 1819
-wortschicht 1364
-*übersetzung* → calquing, loan translation
-*wort* → loanword
-*wort vs. Lehnbildung* → loanword vs. loanformation
Lehrmaterial 512
Leibeigenschaft 1962
Leiden(dt.) → Lébény (ung.) 2047
Leipzig (dt.) → Lipsko (tsch.) 2043
Lemkian (Lemko language) 1590 ff, 1624, 1626
Lemkos (Rusyns) 1622 ff, 1631
Lemòtges (okz.) → Limoges (frz.) 2011
Lendava (krt.) → Arsó Lendva (ung.) 2047
Lengyelország (ung.) → Polska (pln.) 2047
Léonais → Leonesisch
Leonese → Leonesisch
leonesisch 1314
Lérida (frz.; sp.) → Lleida (kat.) 2011, 2015
Lerin (blg.; mak.) → Florina (gr.) 2025, 2029, 2035
Lernbarkeit 288
Lerneffekt 823
Lerngeschwindigkeit 289
Lernpsychologie → psychology of learning
Leseunterricht → reading instruction

Leseverstehen 511
lessón kodé– 1944
Leszno (pln.) → Lissa (dt.) 2039
Lettland → Latvia
Lettonie → Latvia
Lëtzebuerg (lux.) → Luxemburg (dt.) 2001, 2011, 2055, Luxembourg (frz.)
Lëtzebuerger Däitsch 1162
Letzeburgisch 265, 1161
Leuven → Löwen
level of representation 565
Lex Apponyi (1907) 1482
lexical
– acquisition 372
– borrowing, constraints on – 119
– root 109
– unit formation 127 f
lexicon → Lexik, Lexikon
approaches to – 126 f
lexifier language 642
Lexik 1375
Lexik → lexicon, approaches to –
lexikalische Zugehörigkeit 445
Lexikon 1404
lexique 1219, 1236, 1264, 1267, 1346
lexique → Lexik, Lexikon
– de spécialité → Fachwortschatz
Lia rumantscha 1879
Liban 362
Liberalism 76
Libération (1944) 1174
Liberec (tsch.) → Reichenberg (dt.) 2043
liberté de la langue 213
Liège (frz.) 1158 → Lüttich (dt.) 1137, 2011, 2055; Luik (ndl.) 2001
Liegnitz (dt.) → Legnica (pln.) 2039, 2043
Liettua (fin.) 1985 → Litwa (pln.) 2039; Litva (rss.) 2067; Litva, Lytva (ukr.) 2067
Lietuva (lit.) → Liettua (fin.) 1985; Litwa (pln.) 2039; Litva (rss.) 2067; Litva, Lytva (ukr.) 2067
Ligurien 1318
Lika 1822
Likert-Skala 697
Lille (frz.) → Rijsel (ndl.) 2001
Limbourg 1108
Limburg 1137, 1145
Limerick (eng.) → Luimneach (ir.) 1993
limite linguistique 1255
Limoges (frz.) → Lemòtges (okz.) 2011
Limousin 1188, 1189

Linec (tsch.) → Linz (dt.) 2043
line symbol 66
linear code switching constraints 599
LINGUA 932
lingua
- franca 210, 238, 323, 418, 429, 482, 554, 649, 834, 855, 896, 899, 904, 910, 973, 975, 988, 1420f, 1848, 1857,
- sacra 972
- -guida 1341
linguicide 667, 827
 cause of − 669
linguicism 667
linguistic
- accommodation 332, 865, 867f
- adaption 866
- area (diffusion area, Sprachbund) 99
- autonomy 402
- awareness 1014
- cannibalism 669
- change 721, 808
- cleavage 76
- competence 142
- discrimination 709
- division 711
- domination 590
- elitism 711
- genocide 668
- hierarchy 428
- identity 173
- ideology 589
- imperialism 428, 908
- interference 3, 4, 5, 6f
- minority 667
- pluralism 863
- prejudice 712
- purism 864
- repertoire 1751
- rights 672
- sign 131
- stereotype 711
- symbolism 588
- transfer 552
- uniformity 347
- unity 347
- *anthropology* → anthropologie linguistique
- *assimilation* → assimilation linguistique, sprachliche Assimilation
- *environment* → sprachliche Umgebung
- *imperialism* → impérialisme linguistique
- *island* → Sprachinsel
- *purism* → Sprachpurismus
- *stereotype* → stéréotype linguistique
- *transfer* → sprachlicher Transfer, transfert linguistique

linguistique
- anthropologique 49
- créologique 177
- interne 255
- politique 830
- scolaire 81
- *de contact* → Kontaktlinguistik
- *de contact, historique* → contact linguistics, history
Linguo-Kognition 288
link language 483
Linz (dt.) → Linec (tsch.) 2043
Lippowaner 1463
lips 304, 307
Lipsko (tsch.) → Leipzig (dt.) 2043
Lisbon → Lissabon
Lisbonne → Lissabon
Lissa (dt.) → Leszno (pln.) 2039
Lissabon 1310
Litauen 1944
Litauen → Lithuania
Litauer → Lithuanians
literacy 625, 670
literacy → Schriftlichkeit, scripturalité, Alphabetisierung
- instruction models 628
- needs 628
- policies 630
- program 624
literalisation → Alphabetisierung
literary criticism → Literaturwissenschaft
literary language → Literatursprache
Literatur
- der Minderheiten 94
- sprache 89
- wissenschaft 89
 schöne − → belles-lettres
 zweisprachige − → bilingual fiction
Lithuania 348, 1912−1919
Lithuanian-Polish 1918
Lithuanian-Russian 1916ff
Lithuanians 183, 1584ff, 1587, 1589ff, 1591, 1606f, 1613
littéralité → Schriftlichkeit
littérature beur 95
littérature dans l'enseignement 463
littérature grise → „graue Literatur"
Little Russians → Kleinrussen
Lituanie → Lithuania
Lituaniens → Lithuanians
Litva (rss.) → Lietuva (lit.); Litva, Lytva (ukr.) 2067
Litva, Lytva (ukr.) → Lietuva (lit.), Litva (rss.) 2067
Litwa (pln.) → Lietuva (lit.) 2039

Litwisch 1955
Livinallongo 1323, 1383
Livinallongo (it.) → Buchenstein (dt.), Fodóm (rtr.)
Livland 1945
Livonian 993
Ljetzan (dt.) → Glietzen (dt.) 2021, 2059, 2063; Giazza (it.) 2021
Lleida (kat.) → Lérida (frz.) 2011; Lérida (sp.) 2011, 2015
Ljouwert (frs.) → Leeuwarden (ndl.) 2001
Ljublin (rss.) → Lublin (pln.) 2067
loan
- -blend 543
- displacement 544
- homonym 544
- -shift 543
- synonym 544
- translation 543, 1028, 1752
- -word vs. loanformation 4f
- -word 541
Locarno (it.) → Luggarus (dt.) 2063
locuteur primaire 1190
logistic regression 786
Logosphere Programme 70
logoudorien (logudorese) 1377, 1378
loi, Loi
- de Base de Normalisation de l'Utilisation du Basque 1307
- de Grammont 34
- de Normalisation Linguistique (1983) 1292
- Deixonne (1951) 1174, 1191, 1245, 1256, 1263
- sur les langues officielles (1969) (1988) 211, 214, 831
- Toubon 717
linguistique → language law
Loire 1228
lois, Lois
- de Normalisation Linguistique (1983, 1986) 1298
- scolaires de Jules Ferry 1175, 1196
Lombardei (dt.) 1318 → Lombardia (it.) 2063
Lombardia (it.) → Lombardei (dt.) 1318, 2063
Lombardie 1871
Lombardie (frz.) → Lombardei (dt.), Lombardia (it.)
Lombards 1338
Lombardy (eng.) → Lombardei (dt.), Lombardie (frz.)
Lombert 1388
Londoner Vertrag (1839) 1161
long term memory 625
looseknit network 807

lorrain 1115
Lorraine 1174, 1224
— thioise 1224
lošn kójdeš 1944
Losanna (it.) → Lausanne (frz.) 2021
loss of vocabulary 582
Lothringen → Lorraine
lothringisch → lorrain
Louisiana creole → créole louisianais
Lovara 1804
Low German 396, 938 f, 975, 1028
Low German → bas-allemand, Niederdeutsch, Plattdeutsch
Löwen 1137
Lower Sorbian → Niedersorbisch
Lowland Scots 1093
Lowlands 1088
Loyalität 368, 1141
Loyalitätskonflikt 1035
loyality 1146
loyauté linguistique 715, 893, 902
loyauté linguistique → language loyality, Sprachloyalität
Lozengrad (blg.) → Kırklareli (trk.) 2029
Lugano 1870
Lübbenau (dt.) → Lubnjow (sor.) 2055
Lublin (pln.) → Ljublin (rss.) 2067
Lubnjow (sor.) → Lübbenau (dt.) 2055
Lucerna (it.) → Luzern (dt.) 2021
Luck (rss.) → Luc'k (ukr.) 2067
Luc'k (ukr.) → Luck (rss.) 2067
Luganer See (dt.) → Lago di Lugano (it.) 2063
Lugansk (rss.) → Lugans'k, Luhans'k (ukr.) 2067
Lugans'k, Luhans'k (ukr.) → Lugansk (rss.) 2067
Lugdunum (Lyon) 1332
Luggarus (dt.) → Locarno (it.) 2063
Luik (ndl.) → Lüttich (dt.) 1137, 2001; Liège (frz.) 1158, 2001, 2055
Luimneach (ir.) → Limerick (eng.) 1993
Luiseño 663
Lumières 358
Lungro 1373
Lusern (dt.) 1322, 1352 → Luserna (it.) 2021, 2059, 2063
Luserna (it.) → Lusern (dt.) 1322, 1352, 2021, 2059, 2063
Lusiadas 1312
Lutheran Reformation 345

Lutherans 395
lutte des langues 610
Lüttich (dt.) 1137 → Liège (frz.) 2001. 2055; Luik (ndl.) 2001
Luxembourg (frz.) 330, 1108 → Luxemburg (dt.), Lëtzebuerg (lux.), 265, 270, 1133, 1158, 2001, 2011, 2055
Luxemburg (dt.) 265, 270, 1133, 1158 → Luxembourg (frz.), Lëtzebuerg (lux.), 330, 1108, 2001, 2011, 2055
Luxemburg (Großherzogtum) 1158
luxemburgeois-allemand-français 468
Luxemburger Deutsch 1171
Luxemburger Französisch 1170
Luxemburgisch 1162
Luxuslehnwörter 1392
Luzern (dt.) → Lucerna (it.) 2021
L'viv (ukr.) → Lwów (pln.) 2039, 2043, L'vov (rss.) 2067
L'vov (rss.) → L'viv (ukr.) 2067
LWC → language of wider communication
Lwów (pln.) → L'viv (ukr.) 2039, 2043
lydien 273
Lyss-Tal (dt.) → Vallée du Lys (frz.) 2063

M

Maarianhamina (fin.) → Mariehamn (swd.) 1985
Maas → Meuse
Maastricht (ndl.) 1145 → Maestricht (frz.) 2001
Maastrichter Verträge (1992) 1161
Macao 1311
maccaronic poetry → makkaronische Dichtung
Macedo-Bulgarian language 1498
Macédoine 1544
Macédoine → Macedonia
Macedonia 66, 1026, 1030 f, 1442 ff, 1444, 1488, 1498 f, 1501,
Macedonia → Macédoine
Macedonian 1417, 1425, 1427 f, 1445 ff, 1490, 1496 f, 1584, 1593
Macedonian → macédonien, Makedonisch
Macedonian Greek 1448 f
Macedonian-Albanian 1447
Macedonian-Bulgarian 1444
Macedonian-Serbo-Croatian 1444, 1446, 1448 f

Macedonian-Turkish 1447 ff
Macedonian-Vlah 1448 f
Macedonians → Macédoniens, Makedonier
macédonien 1547 f
macédonien → Macedonian
Macédoniens 1436, 1453 f, 1545, 1546 f
machine translation 429, 647
Macomer, bataille de — (1478) 1377
macrosociolinguistique 888
Macugnaga (it.) → z' Makanà / Makannah (dt.) 2021, 2063
Mađarska (bsn.; krt.; srb.) → Madžarska (slw.); Magyarország (ung.) 2025
Mad'arsko (slk.) → Uhry (tsch.), Magyaroroszág (ung.) 2043
Madžarska (slw.) → Mađarska (bsn., krt., srb.); Magyarország (ung.) 2025
Maestricht (frz.) → Maastricht (ndl.) 1145, 2001
mafia 1367
Maghreb 195, 197, 1178
Maghrebịa (arb.) → Marruecos (sp.) 2015
Maghrebinisch 1401
Magilëŭ, Mahilëu (wrs.) → Mogilëv (rss.) 2067
Magna Graecia 300
Magna Graecia → Grande-Grèce
Magnaten 1828
Magyaren 1800
Magyarisierung 1733, 1745 f, 1735
Magyarization 1712
Magyaronen 1828, 1831, 1834
Magyarország (ung.) → Mađarska (bsn., srb., krt.) 2025; Ungarn (dt.) 1407, 1409 ff, 1462, 1642, 1647, 1669 ff, 1685, 1808, 1961, 2059; Węgry (pln.) 2039; Ungaria (rum.) 2029; Mad'arsko (slk.) 2043; Madžarska (slw.) 2025; Uhry (tsch.) 2043
Mährisch Ostrau (dt.) → Ostrava (tsch.) 2043
Mailand (dt.) → Milan (frz.) 1870; Milano (it.) 2063
mainstream culture 1031
maintenance 339
maintien
— de langue 715
— linguistique 902, 904 f
— de (la) langue → language maintenance, Sprachbewahrung, Spracherhalt
majority bilingualism 1430
majority language 7
Majorque (Mallorca) 1296

Makannah (dt.) → z' Makanà / Makannah (dt.) 2021, 2063; Macugnaga (it.) 2021, 2063
Makedonien → Macedonia, Macédoine
Makedonier 1407, 1409 f, 1550, 1552
Makedonier → Macédoniens
Makedonija (bsn.; krt.; srb.) → Maqedonia (alb.) 2025
makedonisch → macédonien
Makedonisch 1550
makkaronische Dichtung 90
makrosoziolinguistisch 240
Malăk Samokov (blg.) → Demirköy (trk.) 2029
Malay 1148
Malaysia 328, 338
Mali 198
Mali i Zi (alb.) → Crna Gora (bsn., krt., srb.) 2025
Malinche 232
Malmédy 213, 1108
Malta 1399
maltais → Maltesisch
Malte 161
Maltese → Maltesisch
 — English 1401
Maltesisch 1399
máme-lošn 1945
mandarin 452
Manià (frl.) → Maniago (it.) 2021
Maniago (it.) → Manià (frl.) 2021
Männersprache 259
männliche Rollen → rôle des hommes
Manu— 1963
Manx 349, 1062
maps 67
Maqedonia (alb.) → Makedonija (bsn., krt., srb.) 2025
Maramureş 1478
Marano 1339
Marburg (dt.) → Maribor (slw.) 2059
Marche Hispanique 1296
Marea Neagră (rum.) → Černo More (blg.), Karadeniz (trk.) 2029
Marebbe (it.) → Enneberg (dt.)
marèo 1387
Mareo/marèo (rtr.) → Enneberg (dt.)
Marginalität 93
Mari 228
mariage linguistiquement mixte 385
Maribor (slw.) → Marburg (dt.) 2059
Mariehamn (swd.) → Maarianhamina (fin.) 1985

markedness 113, 122, 661
marketing 439
Markiertheit → markedness
Markierung, transkodische — 241
Markierungen 322
Marktwirtschaft 853
Marmarosch → Maramureş
Mar Mediterráneo (sp.) → Mar Mediterrània (kat.) 2015
Mar Mediterrània (kat.) → Mar Mediterráneo (sp.) 2015
Maroc → Morocco
Marokko 1270
Marokko → Morocco
Maronite Arabs 1578 f, 1581
Maroons (Bush Negroes) 1145
Marosvásárhely (ung.) → Neumarkt (dt.) 1483, Tîrgu-Mureş (rum.) 2029
marque transcodique 53
marque transcodique → Markierung, transkodische —
Marquisat de Saluces 1344
marriage, linguistically mixed — → Ehen, gemischtsprachige —; mariage linguistiquement mixte
Marruecos (sp.) → Maghrebja (arb.) 2015
Marseille (frz.) → Marselha (okz.) 2011
Marselha (okz.) → Marseille (frz.) 2011
Martano 1323
Martignano 1366
Märtyrer 317
Marxism 76
maschinelle Übersetzung → machine translation
mass media 205, 426, 432, 1292
Massenmedien 323
Massenwanderung 187
match, qualitative — → Übereinstimmung, qualitative —
match, quantitative — → Übereinstimmung, quantitave —
matched-guise technique 698
materia romana con ispirito tedesco 1392
Matrix Language Frame (MLF) 600
Matrix Language Hypotheses 115, 118
Matrštof (krt.) → Mattersburg (dt.) 2059
Mattersburg (dt.) → Matrštof (krt.) 2059
Maule-Lextarre (bsk.) → Mauléon-L. (frz.) 2011
Mauléon-L. (frz.) → Maule-Lextarre (bsk.) 2011
Mauritius 328

Mazedonien → Macedonia
Mazedonier → Macédoniens
Mazedonisch → Macedonian
Mazovian dialect 1606
Mazovians 1606 f
mécanisme mnésique 58
media (in Ireland) 1104
médias 1299
Medien 1166
Mediterranean → Méditerranée
Méditerranée 193
Mehrfachnennung 739
Mehrheitssprache → majority language
Mehrnamigkeit 444
Mehrsprachigkeit 14 f, 16, 17, 19, 144 f, 233, 284, 321, 1842
Mehrsprachigkeit → multilingualism, plurilinguisme
 individuelle — 234, 895
 institutionelle — 234
 kollektive — 237
 soziale — 234
 territoriale — 234
 frühe — von Kindern → early (child) multilingualism
 institutionalisierte — → institutional multilingualism
Mehrsprachigkeitsmodelle, Dritte Welt 481
Meinungsfrage 729
Melanesian Pidgin English 644
mélange
 — des codes bulgaro-grec 1513 f
 — *de codes* → code-mixing
 — *linguistique* → language mixing
Melbourne 452
Melilla 1271
melting pot 687, 970
membership in the language community 772
mémoire
 — bilingue 37
 — déclarative 58
 — implicite 58
 — procédurale 59
Mémorandum de Londres (1954) 1358
memory, bilingual — → mémoire bilingue
men's roles → rôle des hommes
Mennoniten 291
Mennonites 393
Menschenrechte → droits humains, human rights
mental lexicon 132
Mentalismus 692
mentalist model 519
Mer du Nord → North Sea
Mer Noire 193
Meran (dt.) → Merano (it.) 2059, 2063

Merano (it.) → Meran (dt.) 2059, 2063
MERCATOR 933 f
Mesocco (it.) → Misox (dt.) 2063
mésolecte 655, 1339
message 466
meta-analysis 632
metadiscoursive practice 747
metalinguistic consciousness → conscience métalinguistique
metalinguistisches Bewußtsein → conscience métalinguistique
metaphor 135
metaphorical switching 595
metonymy 135
metropolitan area → agglomération urbaine
Meuse 1107
Mexicano-Spanish 598
Mexico → Mexiko
Mexiko 487
Mexique → Mexiko
Miarritze (bsk.) → Biarritz (frz.) 2011
Micmac 793
microlecte 277
microsociolinguistique 888
Middle Ages → Moyen Age
Middle East → Moyen-Orient
„middle" languages 393
Middle Norwegian 938
Midi-Pyrénées 1189
Midilli (trk.) → Mitilini (gr.) 2035
Miercurea-Ciuc (rum.) → Csíkszereda (ung.) 2029
Migrant 320 f, 322
migrant → Arbeitsimmigrant
 – *worker* → travailleur migrant
Migrantensprache 1848
migration 327, 773, 836, 865
 – économique 450
 – politique 450
 – *worker* → Arbeitsimmigrant
Migration 180, 320, 1326, 1961
 affluente – 183
 religiöse – 311
Migrationsthese 1459
Mikkeli (fin.) → St. Michel (swd.) 1985
Mikolaïv, Mykolajiv (ukr.) → Nikolaev (rss.) 2067
mikrosoziolinguistisch 240
Mikrozensus 1839
Milano (it.) → Mailand (dt.) 2063; Milan (frz.) 1870
millet 1435, 1443, 1488 f, 1533, 1555 f, 1560 f, 1566
Milton 459
Minderheit → minorité, minority
Minderheit, sprachliche – 269
Minderheiten-
 -gesetz (1868, Ungarn) 1482

 -schutz 848 f
 -*schutz* → protection des minorités
 -*sprache* → langue minoritaire, minority language
minimum de distance structurale 637
Minnesänger 1229
minorisation des langues 279
Minoritätensprachen in Rußland 1896 ff
minorité 358
minorité → minority
 – ethnique 165
 – immigrée 467
 – linguistique 165
 – nationale 165
 – *linguistique* → linguistic minority, Minderheit, sprachliche –
 – *nationale* → national minority
minorities
 – in Croatia 1427 ff
 – in European Turkey 1556 f
 – in Macedonia 1443, 1445
 – in Slovenia 1419 ff
minority 348
minority → minorité
 – bilingualism 1430
 – language 7
 – language (in the media) 427
 – languages in Britain 1067
 – languages in European Turkey 1558 f
 – media 427
 – *language* → langue minoritaire
 linguistic – → Minderheit, sprachliche
 – *protection* → Minderheitenschutz, protection des minorités
Minsk (rss., wrs.) 1946, 2067
Miranda, Terra de – 1314
mirandês 1314
mirror-image-Technik 699
Misch-
 -dichtung 90
 -rede 1393
 -sprache 1403
 -varietät 317
 -*sprache* → langue mixte
Mishari 1001
Miskolc (ung.) → Miškovec (slk.) 2043, 2047
Miškovec (slk.) → Miskolc (ung.) 2043, 2047
Misox (dt.) → Mesocco (it.) 2063
missionaries 395
Mittelallokation 821
Mittel-
 -amerika 487
 -europa 1961

 -hochdeutsch 1226
 -*alter* → Moyen Age
 -*meer* → Méditerranée
Mittlerer Osten → Moyen-Orient
Mitilini (gr.) → Midilli (trk.) 2035)
mitwohnende Nationalitäten 1482
mixed
 – language 546, 644
 – semantic systems 131
 – *language* → langue mixte, Mischsprache
 – *speech* → gemischte Rede
mixilinguisme 1342
Mnichov (tsch.) → München (dt.) 2043
Mobilität 416, 1130
Mòcheni 1353
Modane 1332
modèle de conflit → Konfliktmodell
modèle socio-cognitif 36
modernisation linguistique 1308
modernisation theory 64
modernismo 1312
modularity theory 123
Moena 1383
moenat 1388
Moeskroen → Mouscron
Mogilëv (rss.) → Mag lëu, Mahilëu (wrs.) 2067
Mohač (krt.) → Mohatsch (dt.) 1480, Mohács (ung.) 2047
Mohács (ung.) → Mohatsch (dt.), Mohač (krt.) 1480, 2047
Mohatsch (dt.) 1480 → Mohač (krt.), Mohács (ung.) 2047
mohawk 476, 663
Moldau 1460, 1478, 1962
Moldauisch 1937–1939
Moldauisch-Gagausisch 1938 f
Moldauisch-Rumänisch 1938 f
Moldauisch-Russisch 1937, 1939 f
moldave → Moldauisch
Moldavia → Moldawien
Moldavian → Moldauisch
Moldavie → Moldawien
Moldavija (rss.; ukr.) → Moldova (rum.), Moldavija (ukr.) 1458, 2067
Moldawien 230, 1458, 1933–1941
Moldova (rum.) 1458 → Moldavija (rss., ukr.) 2067
Molise 1318, 1323, 1363
 -kroatisch 1363
 -slaven 1363
Moluccans 1144
Mömpelgard (dt.) → Montbéliard (frz.) 2063

Monarchie austro-hongroise →
  Österreichisch-ungarische
  Monarchie
Monarchie autrichienne → Österreichische Monarchie
Monfalcone 1339
monogenetic hypothesis (creolization) → hypothèse monogénétique (créolisation)
monogenetische Hypothese (Kreolisierung) → hypothèse monogénétique (créolisation)
monoglossique 1869
monolingualism 1447
monolingue → unilingue
monomorphemic (word) 110
mononymie → Einnamigkeit
Mons (frz.) → Bergen (ndl.) 2001
Monošter (krt.) → Sankt Gotthard (dt.), Szentgotthárd (ung.) 2047
Montbéliard (frz.) → Mömpelgard (dt.) 2063
Montemitro 1363
Montenegriner 1407, 1409 f
Monténégrins 1417, 1425, 1427, 1436, 1453
Montenegrins, Monténégrins → Montenegriner
Montenegro 1407 ff
Monténégro → Montenegro
Montpelhièr (okz.) → Montpellier (frz.) 2011
Montpellier (frz.) → Montpelhièr (okz.) 2011
Montreal 172, 334
Montzen 1108, 1137
Montzener Land 1130, 1133
Moor (dt.) → Mór (ung.) 2047
Mór (ung.) → Moor (dt.) 2047
Morat (dt.) → Murten (frz.) 2063
Morava (tsch.) → Moravaország (ung.) 2047
Moravaország (ung.) → Morava (tsch.) 2047
Morbihan 1252
Mordwinen 228
Moresnet 1137
moriscos 1274
Moroccan Colloquial Arabic 602
Moroccans 1144
Morocco 329
moros 1274
Morphem, freies − → morpheme, free −
Morphem, gebundes − → bound morpheme
morpheme 109
  free − 109
  − order 561
  − structure 7

Morpheme-Order Principle 115
morphologie 1336, 1347
Morphologie 1818
Morphosyntax 1365, 1374, 1404, 1885
morphosyntaxe 1216, 1264, 1265
mortalité → mortality
Morze Bałtyckie (pln.) → Ostsee (dt.) 2039
mortality 773
Mosel → Moselle
  -fränkisch 1133, 1169, 1223
  -fränkisch → francique mosellan
Moselle 1224
Moslems 1145
Mosonmagyaróvár (ung.) → Wieselburg (dt.) 1822, 2047
mot étranger 873 f
mother tongue 169, 772
Mouscron 213, 1240
mouth movements 301
mouvement autonomiste néosarde 1380
mouvement nationaliste 200
movements 296
Movimento Friuli 1339
Moyen Age 273
Moyen-Orient 195
Mozambique 195, 1311
mozárabes 1274
mudéjares 1274
Muggia 1339
Mühlen (dt.) → Mulegns (rtr.) 2063
Mukačeve (ukr.) → Mukačevo (slk.), Munkács (ung.) 2047
Mukačevo (slk.) → Mukačeve (ukr.), Munkács (ung.) 2047
Mülhausen (dt.) 1223 → Mulhouse (frz.) 2011, 2055, 2063
Mulhouse (frz.) → Mülhausen (dt.) 1223, 2011, 2055, 2063
Mulegns (rtr.) → Mühlen (dt.) 2063
multi-ethnic 206
multi-identity 909
multicultural society 205
multiculturalism 7, 970
Multidimensional Model 522
multidimensional scaling (MDS) 434
multilingualism 1 f, 5 f, 8,
multilinguism → multilingualism, plurilinguisme
  − in Macedonia 1447
  personal − → Mehrsprachigkeit, individuelle −
multilinguisme 254
  − extensif 440
  − intensif 441
multilingualisme → Mehrsprachigkeit

multinationals → Betriebe, multinationale − ; entreprises multinationales
multiple choice → Mehrfachnennung
multiple regression 786
multiplexity 806
multivariate description 780
mumma romontscha 1881
München (dt.) → Mnichov (tsch.) 2043
Mundart 258, 1355, 1842
Mundart → dialect
  -insel 814
  -theater 1133
  überdachte − → dialecte couvert
mündliche Befragung 738
mündliche Umfrage 730
Mündlichkeit → oralité
Munkács (ung.) → Mukačevo (slk.), Mukačeve (ukr.) 2047
Munster (ndl.) → Münster (D, dt.) 2001
Münster (CH, dt.) → Müstair (rtr.) 2063
Münster (D, dt.) → Munster (ndl.) 2001
Muntenien 1479
Muntese 1216
Muraszombat (ung.) → Murska Sobota (krt.) 2047
Murcia 1275
Murska Sobota (krt.) → Muraszombat (ung.) 2047
Murten (frz.) → Morat (dt.) 2063
Muslime 1407, 1409 f, 1516
Muslims 1425, 1427 f, 1446
Müstair (rtr.) → Münster (CH, dt.) 2063
Musulmans 1435 ff
Muttersprache 267, 1839, 1879
Muttersprache → mother tongue
Muttersprachenhochstufe 1473
Muvimentu Corsu per l'Autodeterminazione 1202
Mythologie, griechische − 221
Mythos 220

N

na našu 1363
naš jezik 1363
Nagybánya (ung.) → Baia Mare (rum.) 2029, 2047
Nagybecskerek (ung.) → Zrenjanin (srb.) 2029
Nagyszombat (ung.) → Trnava (slk.) 2043, 2047; Tyrnau (dt.) 2043

Nagyvárad (ung.) → Großwardein (dt.) 1478, 2029; Oradea (rum.) 2029, 2047
Nahsprache 264
name translation 550
Namen (ndl.) → Namur (frz.) 2001
Namen, geographische — 445
Namenskunde → onomastics
Namensübersetzung → name translation
names, geographic — → Namen, geographische —
Namibia 419, 489
naming patterns 127 f
Namur (frz.) → Namen (ndl.) 2001
Nantes (frz.) → Noaned (brt.) 2011
narratologie 462
nation 154, 203, 205
— building 426
— de volonté 156 f
— ethnique 156
national, National
— Language Policy 713
— languages and literacy institute 837
— minority 674
-bewußtsein 1809
nationale Identität 93
nationale Minderheit → national minority
nationalism 858
nationalisme 200, 716, 858
nationaliste 1202
Nationalitätengesetz (1868, Ungarn) 1461
nationalization 206
National-
-literatur 92
-sozialismus 1947
-sprache 92, 484, 1169, 1400, 1837, 1880
-staat 688
-stolz 225
-*staat* → Etat-Nation
nations 355, 358
Nations Unies 167 f, 358
nation-state 75, 206, 347, 587, 671
nation-state → Etat-Nation
natives → Eingeborene
Nativismus 180, 318
nativization 909
nativization of verbs 115
Natural Semantic Metalanguage (NSM) 134
Navarre 1303, 1307
ndrangheta 1367
Nederlanden (ndl.) → Niederlande (dt.) 2055
néerlandais → néerlandais 1110, 1240

néerlandais → Dutch, Niederländisch
néerlandais-français 467
Negation 286
negative transfer 559
Německo (tsch.) → Deutschland (dt.) 2043
néobascophone → euskaldunberri
neologism 1006, 1045, 1048, 1051, 1053, 1056, 1057
Netherlands 330, 1143, 1153
Netherlands → Pays-Bas
network
network → Netzwerk
— analysis 805
— electronic — 858
— link 808
— model 431
— strength scale 807
Network of Researchers on Code Switching and Language Contact 595
Netzwerk 317, 318, 322, 799
-konzept 802
-*analyse* → network analysis
Netzwerke, elektronische — → networks, electronic —
Neu-Guinea → New Guinea
Neubelgien 1131
Neuchâtel (frz.) 1330, 1862 → Neuenburg (dt.) 2055, 2063
Neuenburg (dt.) → Neuchâtel (frz.) 1330, 1862, 2055, 2063
Neuenstadt (dt.) → La Neuveville (frz.) 2063
Neuhäusel (dt.) → Nové Zámky (slk.), Érsekújvár (ung.) 2043
Neuhochdeutsch 1228
Neumarkt (dt.) 1483 → Tîrgu-Mureș (rum.), Marosvásárhely (ung.) 2029
Neurolinguistik 236
neurologie 57
Neusohl (dt.) → Banská Bystrica (slk.), Besztercebánya (ung.) 2043
Neustrukturierung → restructuration
Neutra (dt.) → Nitra (slk.), Nyitra (ung.) 2043
neutrale Sprache 489
new-ethnicity 718
New Guinea 589
New Testament 204
New York 172, 296, 1946
Newrican 453
Nice (frz.) → Nizza (it.) 2021
Nichtstichprobenfehler 736
Niederalemannisch 1223, 1855
Niederdeutsch 1756, 1770, 1778 f, 1782 ff, 1787 ff
Niederdeutsch → bas-allemand, Low German

Niederlande (dt.) → Pays-Bas (frz.) 1111; Nederlanden (ndl.) 2055
Niederländisch 91, 1123, 1136, 1762
Niederländisch → Dutch, néerlandais
Niederländisch-Deutsch 1136
Niederländisch-Französisch 1123
niederländisch-französische Sprachgrenze 699
Niederösterreich (dt.) → Alsó Ausztria (ung.) 2047
Niedersorbisch 1762, 1792, 1794 f
Niemcy (pln.) → Deutschland (dt.) 2039
Nigeria 429
Nigéria 83
Nijmegen (ndl.) 1149 → Nimwegen (dt.) 2001
Nikolaev (rss.) → Mikolaïv, Mykolajiv (ukr.) 2067
Nimègue (frz.) → Nijmegen (ndl.)
Nimwegen (dt.) → Nijmegen (ndl.) 1149, 2001
Nitra (slk.) → Neutra (dt.) 2043; Nyitra (ung.) 2043, 2047
niveau d'éducation → education level
Nizza (it.) → Nice (frz.) 2021
Noaned (brt.) → Nantes (frz.) 2011
nom de lieu → place name, toponyme
nomadism 834
Nomadismus 183 f
non verbal communication → communication non-verbale
nonce borrowing 601
Nonconformists 1079
nonverbal codes 300
Nordatlanten (swd.) → Norske havet (bkm.) 1985, Atlantin Valtameri (fin.)
Nordfriesisch 1034, 1761 ff, 1770 f, 1773, 1787
Nordirland → Northern Ireland
Nordsee → North Sea
Noreg (nyn.) → Norge (bkm.), Norja (fin.), Norga (sam.) 1985
Noregs Mållage 953
Norga (sam.) → Norge (bkm.), Norja (fin.), Noreg (nyn.) 1985
Norge (bkm.) → Norja (fin.), Noreg (nyn.), Norga (sam.) 1985
Noricum 1798
Norja (fin.) → Norge (bkm.), Noreg (nyn.), Norga (sam.) 1985

norm
- enforcement mechanism 806
- *conflict* → conflit normatif
  ethic – → Norm, ethische –
Norm
- der Bezugsgruppe 696
  ethische – 822
  -konflikt 486
normalisation 211, 250, 279, 442, 826f, 1191, 1217
Normalisierung 239
normalité 281
normalització lingüística 1298
Normandie 1177
Normannen 1399
normativisation 251, 1192
norme 609, 678
- américaine 615
- britannique 615
- italienne 1878
- lexicale 617
- linguistique 442
- morphosyntaxique 616
- phonétique 613
- *subjective* → subjektive Norm
- -étalon 610
Normenkonflikt → conflit normatif
normes 281
Normierung 263
Norske havet (bkm.) → Atlantin Valtameri (fin.), Nordatlanten (swd.) 1985
North
- Saami 1016, 1019
- Sea 1153
- *Frisian* → Nordfriesisch
- *Old Belgium* → Altbelgien-Nord
Northern Ireland 1062
norvégien → Norwegian
Norwegian 338, 948f, 972, 974f, 1018, 1019, 1025, 1044
Norwegian-Swedish 975
Norwegisch 978
Norwegisch → Norwegian
Nouvelle-Guinée → New Guinea
Nové Zámky (slk.) → Neuhäusel (dt.) 2043; Érsekújvár (ung.) 2043, 2047
Novi Sad (bsn.; krt.; srb.) → Újvidék (ung.) 2025, 2029, 2047
NS-Deutschland 1161
Nueva Planta (1714) 1297
Nullmorphem → zero morpheme
numerische Skala 740
Numeruskategorie 1955
nuorese 1378
Nyitra (ung.) → Neutra (dt.) 2043; Nitra (slk.) 2043, 2047
Nynorsk 937f, 975

O

Oath of Strasbourg (842) → Serments de Strasbourg (842)
Oberösterreich (dt.) → Felső Ausztria (ung.) 2047
Oberpullendorf (dt.) 1803, 1828 → Gornja Pulja (krt.) 2059; Felsőpulya (ung.)
Obersorbisch 1762, 1793ff
Oberwart (dt.) 572, 1821, 1828 → Borta (krt.) 2059; Felsőőr (ung.) 2047, 2059
Oberwart
Obir-Dialekt 1815
observation participante → participant observation, teilnehmende Beobachtung
Observatori Sociolingüístic del Pirineu Català (Perpinyà, Perpignan) 1200, 1201
observer's paradox → Beobachterparadox
observing participation → beobachtende Teilnahme
occitan 274, 680, 1173, 1188, 1211, 1344, 1345
Occitan, Occitanian → occitan
Occitania → Occitanie
Occitanie 1189
occitaniste 78
Occitans 255
Oceano Atlântico (pg.) → Océano Atlántico (sp.) 2015
Océano Atlántico (sp.) → Oceano Atlântico (pg.) 2015
Occupation 1257
Ödenburg (dt.) 1822 → Sopron (ung.) 1821, 2047
Odesa (ukr.) → Odessa (rss.) 2067
Odessa (rss.) → Odesa (ukr.) 2067
Odrin (blg.) → Edirne (trk.) 2029
Ofen 1480, 1481
Ofen (dt.) → Pest, Budapest (ung.)
offene Antwort 729
offene Frage 739
official language 400, 671, 686, 775, 858, 861f
official language → Amtssprache, langue officielle
oghjincu 1205
Ohcejohka (sam.) → Utsjoki (fin.) 1985
Ohër (alb.) → Ohrid (mak.) 2029
Ohrid (mak.) → Ohër (alb.) 2029
oïlique 1867
Ojibwa 793
Ökolekt 259
Ökolinguistik 750

Ökolinguistik → ecolinguistics
Ökologie der Sprache 750
ökonomische Stärke (einer Sprache) 418
Okzitanen → Occitans
Okzitanien → Occitanie
Okzitanien 227
Okzitanisch → occitan
Old Belgium → Altbelgien
Old Church Slavonic 1587
Old East Frisian → Altostfriesisch
Old Norse 937f, 1022, 1044
Olen (dt.) → Land (dt.) 2021, Alagna (it.)
Olivenza 1315
Olmütz (dt.) → Olomouc (tsch.) 2043
Olomouc (tsch.) → Olmütz (dt.) 2043
Olsztyn (pln.) → Allenstein (dt.) 2039
onomastics 549
onomastique → onomastics
Ontario 389
- French 591, 782
ONU 194
Opava (tsch.) → Troppau (dt.) 2043
open answer → offene Antwort
open question → offene Frage
Operation Principles 521
Operationalisierung 727
opinion question → Meinungsfrage
Opole (pln., tsch.) → Oppeln (dt.) 2039, 2043
Oppeln (dt.) → Opole (pln.) 2039, 2043; Opole (tsch.) 2043
oppression of minority languages 670
Oradea (rum.) → Großwardein (dt.) 1478, 2029; Vel'ký Varadín (slk.) 2043; Nagyvárad (ung.) 2029, 2047
oral survey → mündliche Umfrage
oralité 610
orality → oralité
ordinal data 777
ordinal measurement 777
ordre des mots 1266
organisation
- composée 59
- coordonnée 59
- neurofonctionnelle 61
- subordonnée 59
Organisation Mondiale de la Santé 167
Orientals 307
origin of creoles → genèse de créoles

Oristano 1379
Őrisziget (ung.) → Siget in der Wart (dt.)
Orthodoxe 1953
orthographe 621
- française 622
- grecque 622
Orthographie 104, 107f, 151
Orthographie → orthographe
-reform 895
orthography → orthographe
Ortsmundart 1728
Ortsname → place name
Ortsnamen → toponymes
Osgood's semantic differential technique 132
Osmanen 1480
Osijek (krt.) → Eszék (ung.) 2047
Osman-Türkisch - Bulgarisch 1507
Ostafrika → East Africa
Ostdeutschland (DDR) → East Germany
Österreich (dt.) 229, 1350, 1797 → Autriche (frz.) 2063; Austria (it., rtr.); Austrija (bsn., krt., srb.) 2025; 2021, 2063; Austria (pln.) 2039; Austria (ung.) 1797, 2047; Rakúsko (slk.) 2034; Avstrija (slw.) 2025; Rakousko (tsch.), Ausztria (ung.) 2047
Österreich-Ungarn → Autriche-Hongrie
Österreichisch-ungarische Monarchie 1798
Österreichische Monarchie 1798
Österreichischer Kaiserstaat 1798
Östersjön (swd.) → Itämeri (fin.) 1985
Ostfränkisch 1226
Ostfriesisch 1761 f
Ostmark 1798
Ostrava (tsch.) → Mährisch Ostrau (dt.) 2043
Ostsee (dt.) → Morze Bałtyckie (pln.) 2039
Osttirol 1799
Oulu (fin.) → Uleåborg (swd.) 1985
out-glossia 249
overdifferentiation 544
overlapping communities 171
overproduction 563
overt deviationism 300
Oviedo (sp.) → Uviéu (ast.) 2015

P

Paar → couple
paganisme → heathenism
Pagliera 1363
País Valencià (kat.) → Comunidad Valenciana (sp.) 2015
País Vasco (sp.) → Euskadi (bsk.) 2015
Paix d'Utrecht (1714) 1377
Paix de Nimègues (1713) 1240
Paket (Südtirol, 1972) 1354, 1384
Pakistan 331
Palästina 1942
Palatalisierung 1385
Pali 231
Palmanova (it.) → Palme (frl.) 2021
Palme (frl.) → Palmanova (it.) 2021
Pampelune (frz.) 1303 → Iruña (bsk.), Pamplona (sp.) 2011
Pamplona (sp.) → Iruña (bsk.) 2011, 2015; Pampelune (frz.) 1303, 2011
Paname 167
Panjabi 1026f, 1030
Pannonien 1798
pantomine 299
Papua New Guinea 572
paradigm
  formalist - 139
  functionalist - 139
Paradigma
  qualitatives - 752
  quantitatives - 751
paradox of the Gaeltacht 707
Paraguay 487
parallélismes trilingues 1877
parameter theory 123
parameters 519
parenté génétique 248
Parijs (ndl.) → Paris (frz.) 1173, 1177, 2001
Paris (frz.) 1173, 1177 → Parijs (ndl.) 2001
Pariser Vertrag (1946) 1350, 1354
Parlement Européen 356, 359, 1220
parler bilingue 53
parler mixte → gemischte Rede
Parliamentary Translation Office (Irish) 1104
Parti d'Action Sarde (Partito Sardo d'Azione) 1381
participant observation 575
participant observation → teilnehmende Beobachtung
participation 171
Partido Galeguista 1288
Partito Popolare Italiano 1320
Pas-de-Calais 1240, 1241
Pasigraphie 881, 883 f
passeport des langues 506
passive
- bilingualism 1651, 1653
- vocabulary 582
- Zweisprachigkeit 1646
- bilingualism → passive Zweisprachigkeit
patois 347, 686, 1190, 1334, 1335, 1345, 1856, 1867
Patriarcat d'Aquilée 1359
Patriarcat d'Aquileia 1338
Patriarches d'Aquileia 1338
patriotisme 200
patrons culturels 50
patterns of language choice 571
patterns, cultural - → patrons culturels
Pays Basque 161, 469, 1267
Pays Basque → Euskal Herria
Pays Catalans 1296
Pays de Bade 1224
Pays de Galles 201
Pays Valencien 352, 1296
Pays-Bas 1111
Pays-Bas (frz.) → Niederlande (dt.), Netherlands (eng.)
Pečuj (bsn., krt., srb.) → Pécs (ung.) 2025
Pécs (ung.) → Fünfkirchen (dt.) 2047; Pečuj (bsn., krt., srb.) 2025
pédagogie 81
Peirigús (okz.) → Périgueux (frz.) 2011
Pendeln 184
Pendlertum 1830
Péninsule Ibérique 1286, 1296
Péninsule Ibérique → Iberische Halbinsel
Pennsylvania 229, 313
- German 375, 392, 663
-deutsche 316
Perämeri (fin.) → Bottenviken (swd.) 1985
perception of language distance 564
Peremyšl' (ukr.) → Przemyśl (pln.), Peremyšl' (rss.) 2067
Peremyšl' (rss.) → Przemyśl (pln.), Peremysl' (ukr.), 2067
performance, communicative - 846
Performanz, kommunikative - 846
Périgueux (frz.) → Peirigús (okz.) 2011
période prélinguistique 32
Perpignan (frz.) → Perpinyà (okz.) 1195, 2011, 2015
Perpinyà (okz.) → Perpignan (frz.)1195, 2011, 2015
Perpinyà → Perpignan
Personalitätsprinzip 1845
Personalprinzip 447
Personenbestandsaufnahme (Luxemburg, 1941) 1161, 1168

personnes cibles 766
perte de la langue → language loss
perte de vocabulaire → loss of vocabulary
Pest 1481
Pest → Buda, Ofen (dt.), Budapest (ung.)
petit groupe 388
Pfalz 313, 314
phanariotes 1560 f
phatic communication 302
Pfauen (dt.) → Faoug (frz.) 2063
Phéniciens → Phönizier
Phocéens 1202
Phoenicians → Phönizier
phoneme substitution 98
phonemic foreignization 101
Phonetik 1374
phonétique 1263, 1347
Phönizier 1271, 1399
phonologie 1216, 1235, 1263, 1308, 1336
phonotactics 98, 99, 101
phrygien 273
Phylogenese 285
Piana degli Albanesi 1373
picard 1115, 1175, 1243
picard → Pikardisch
picardisation 1246
pidgin, Pidgin 3, 15, 122 f, 134, 338, 545, 1647
– afro-portugais 654
– creole 646
– English 376
– German 372
– Maltese 1401
pidginisation 453, 650
pidginisation → pidginization
Pidginisierung 292, 1775
Pidginisierung → pidginization
pidginization 113, 642
Pidginsprache 881
Piemont (dt.) → Piemonte (it.) 2063
Piemont 1322
piémontais 1331, 1333, 1345
Piemonte (it.) → Piemont (dt.) 2063
Pignerol 1344
Pikardisch 1123
Piła (pln.) → Schneidemühl (dt.) 2039
Pilgerschaft 184
Pilisborosjenő (ung.) → Weindorf (dt.) 2047
Pilsen (dt.) → Plzeň (tsch.) 2043, 2055
Pirin (Macedonia) 1487, 1491, 1498 ff, 1544
Pise 1202, 1377
pivot language 429, 647
place name 553, 836

place names → toponymes
Pladen (dt.) → Sappada (it.) 1352, 1353, 2021, 2059
Plaid Genedlaethol Cymru (The Welsh National Party) 1080
planification
– du corpus 828 f, 896, 904
– du statut 638, 828 f, 904
– linguistique 251, 828 f, 887
– *du corpus* → corpus planning, Korpusplanung
– *du statut* → status planning
– *linguistique* → language planning
Plantagenêts 1254
Plastizität 365
Plattdeutsch 1034, 1761, 1770 f, 1773, 1787
Pléiade 1177
Pliberk (slw.) → Bleiburg (dt.) 2059
Plovdiv (blg.) → Filippupoli (gr.) 2035
pluralism, linguistic – → pluralisme linguistique
pluralisme linguistique 863
pluralisme linguistique → linguistic pluralism
pluricentric languages → langue pluricentrique
pluriculturalisme 1874
plurilektal 1372
plurilinguisme 199
– helvétique 1871, 1874
– individuel 501, 895
– institutionalisé 861, 864
– officiel 361
– *individuel* → Mehrsprachigkeit, individuelle –
– *institutionalisé* → institutional multilingualism
Plurilinguismus 1390
plurizentrische Sprache → langue pluricentrique
Plzeň (tsch.) → Pilsen (dt.) 2043, 2055
Po 1344
Podjunsko narečje → Jauntaler Dialekt
Podlasian dialect of Polish 1606, 1610
poem, multilingual – → poème polyglotte
poème polyglotte 458
Pogrome 1945
point symbols 66
Pola (it.) → Pula (bsn., krt., srb.), Pulj (slw.) 2025
Poland 1583–1594
polarisation linguistique 838
polarisation linguistique → language polarization
Polarisierung 1141

sprachliche – → polarisation linguistique
polarization, language – → polarisation linguistique
Polen (bkm., dt., swd.) 1463, 1643 f, 1662 ff, 1669 ff, 1685, 1942 → Puola (fin.) 1985; Polska (pln.) 1985, 2039, 2055
Poles → Polen
Poles 1427, 1583, 1585, 1587 f, 1651
Polish 376, 1583, 1591, 1916, 1920, 1922 ff
Polish → Polnisch
Polish-Byelorussian 1606
Polish-Kashubian 1600–1606
Polish-Slovak 1628–1634
Polish-Ukrainian 1622–1628
politeness rules 299
political
– aspects of names 553
– live (in Wales) 1079
– party 401
– science 75
politics 399
politique linguistique 163, 212, 253, 717, 830, 861, 865, 1306, 1334, 1875, 1930 f
politique linguistique → Sprachpolitik
Politologie → political science
Poljanci 1821
Polnisch 320, 1687, 1944, 1949
Polnisch → Polish
Polnisch-Deutsch 1594–1600
Polnisch-Litauisch 1614–1622
Polnisch-Tschechisch 1634–1641
polonais, Polonais → Polen, Polish
polonais 1182, 1436 ff, 1927, 1929 f
Polonais de Bosnie-Herzégovine 1436 ff
Polonian 453
Pol'ša (russ.) → Polska (pln.), Pol'šča (ukr.) 2067
Pol'šča (ukr.) → Polska (pln.), Pol'ša (russ.) 2067
Polska (pln.) → Polen (bkm, swd.) 1985; Polen (dt.) 2039, 2055; Puola (fin.) 1985; Pol'ša (russ.) 2067; Pol'sko (slk.) 2043; Pol'šča (ukr.) 2067; Lengyelország (ung.) 2047; Polsko (tsch.) 2043
Polyglossie 237
polymorphemic word 110
polymorphisme phonétique 1369
polynomie 1220
polynomique 1211
polyphonie discursive 790
Polysemie 882
polysynthetic language 110

Pomaken 1504, 1506, 1519, 1522, 1526
Pomaks 1490, 1493
Pomaks → Pomaken
Pomaques → Pomaken
Pommat (dt.) → Formazza (it.) 1353, 2021, 2063
Pomoranian dialects 1602
Pondi (brt.) → Pontivy (frz.) 2011
Pontafel (dt.) → Pontebba (it.), Tablja (slw.) 2021
Pontebba (it.) → Pontafel (dt.), Tablja (slw.) 2021
Ponte Novu (1769) 1202
Pontivy (frz.) → Pondi (brt.) 2011
pop-rock catalan 1299
popular speech → Volkssprache
population cible 768
Pordenon (frl.) → Pordenone (it.) 1337, 2021
Pordenone (it.) 1337 → Pordenon (frl.) 2021
Porrentruy (frz.) → Pruntrut (dt.) 2063
portfolio 506
portmanteau 110
Portogruaro 1338
portugais 615, 1182, 1866
portugais brésilien 617
Portugal 195, 328, 345, 1310
Portugiesen 1159
Portugiesisch 320, 1310, 1841
Portugiesisch → portugais
  brasilianisches — → portugais brésilien
Portuguese 330, 345
Portuguese → portugais
  Brazilian — → portugais brésilien
Poschiavo (it.) 1855 → Puschlav (dt.) 2063
Posen (dt.) → Poznán (pln.) 2039
positive transfer 559
Posrexurdimento 1287
post-creole continuum → continuum post-créole
posture 305
Poszony (ung.) → Preßburg (dt.), Bratislava (slk.) 2043
power 703
power differential 568
Poznán (pln.) → Posen (dt.) 2039
Präfix → prefix
Prag (dt.) → Praha (tsch.) 2043, 2055
Praga (pln.) → Praha (tsch.) 2039
Prager Schule → Prague School
pragmatic interference 134

pragmatic mode of communication 521
pragmatics 139 f, 296
  functional — → funktionale Pragmatik, pragmatique fonctionnelle
Pragmatik, funktionale — → pragmatique fonctionnelle
pragmatique fonctionnelle 927
pragmatique fonctionnelle → funktionale Pragmatik
Prague School 3
Praha (tsch.) → Prag (dt.) 2043, 2055; Praga (pln.) 2039
pratique langagière 1183
prefix 109
prejudice 208, 709
préjugé → prejudice, Stereotype, Vorurteil
préjugé linguistique → linguistic prejudice
Première Guerre Balkanique (1912) → First Balkan War (1912)
Prešov (slk.) → Eperies (dt.) 2043; Prjašiv (ukr.) 2043; Eperjes (ung.) 2043, 2047
Preßburg (dt.) 1821 → Bratislava (slk.) 1821, 2043, 2059; Poszony (ung.) 2043
prestige 251, 255, 324, 703, 1831
  – form 721
Prestige 26
  -wert 26
  -abstand 26
  -unterschied 26
Pretest 727
Preußen 1945
Preußen → Prusse
primacy effect 740
Primärsozialisation 1372
primary school → Volksschule
primordialism 77
principal component analysis 784
principe
  – de personnalité 210
  – de territorialité 163, 210, 1876
  – *de territorialité* → territorial principle
principle of government 115 f
Printmedien (Zeitungen) 1858
Prishtinë (alb.) → Priština (bsn., krt., slw.) 2025; Priština (srb.) 2035
Priština (bsn., krt., srb.) → Prishtinë (alb.), Priština (krt., srb.) 2025, 2035
privileged witness → témoin privilégié
privilegierter Zeuge → témoin privilégié

Privilegium Andreanum (1224) 1479
Prjašiv (ukr.) → Eperies (dt.), Prešov (slk.), Eperjes (ung.) 2043, 2047
processing → traitement
processing models of code switching 604
processus d'assimilation → Assimilationsprozeß
processus publicitaire 439
Produktion 415
professional ethics → Berufsethik
profil
  – de la communauté 764
  – ethnique 1113, 1190, 1297
  – ethnographique 764
Profil, ethnographisches — → profil ethnographique
profile, ethnographic — → profil ethnographique
programme
  – 'bivalent' 83
  – d'enseignement minoritaire 477
  – d'immersion 83, 469
  – d'immersion en français 474
  – de submersion 83
  – de transition bilingue 477
  – ségrégationniste 83
  – séparatiste 83
  – transitoire 83
programmes bilingues 476
Programmiersprache 881
Programmiersprache → langage de programmation
programming language → langage de programmation
prohibition (on the mixing of morphologies within the word) 113
Projet Foyer 85, 467
pronoms indéfinis → Indefinitpronomina
Proporzbestimmungen 1354
prosemics 301, 305
Prostrum (krt.) → Sveti Petar (slw.), Szentpéterfa (ung.) 2047
protection des minorités 848 f
protection des minorités → Minderheitenschutz
Protestant 344
Protestant vs. Catholic (Irish) 1062
Protestanten 1472
Protestants 396
provençal 1190, 1333
Provence-Côte d'Azur 1189
Provenzalisch 1323
Provinz Bozen 1325
Provinz Trient 1325
proxemics 301, 305

Prozesse, kognitive — → cognitive processes
Pruntrut (dt.) → Porrentruy (frz.) 2063
Prusse 1864
Przemyśl (pln.) → Peremyšl' (rss.), Peremysl' (ukr.) 2067
psychologie 31
— of learning 558
psychopédagogie 465
psychotypology, learner's — 564
publicité 438
Publikationssprache 423
publishing language → Publikationssprache
Puerto Rican 723
Puerto Rico 335
Puertorikanisch → Puerto Rican
Pula (bsn., krt., srb.) → Pola (it.), Pulj (slw.) 2025
Pulj (slw.) → Pola (it.) 2025
Punjabi 43
Punktsymbole → point symbols
Puola (fin.) → Polen (bkm., dt., swd.), Polska (pln.) 1985
purification
— ethnique 360, 362
— linguistique 165
purisme (linguistique) 276, 717, 864, 872
Purismus 872, 1128, 1393, 1885
puriste 1877
Puschlav (dt.) → Poschiavo (it.) 1855, 2063
Pyrenäen 1270
Pyrenäen → Pyrénées
-frieden (1659) 1159
Pyrénées 1303
-Atlantiques 1188, 1260
-Orientales 1189, 1195, 1296

Q

qeltu 394
qualitative data 777
Quartier
— allemand 1159, 1167
— wallon 1159, 1167
quasi-population 771
Quatorze Points 358
Quebec 57, 201, 330, 335, 343, 407, 473, 773
Québec → Quebec
Quechua 371, 396
questione della lingua 718
question
closed — → Frage, geschlossene —
— order → Fragenreihenfolge
— sequence → Fragensukzession
questionnaire 680
questionnaire → Fragebogen

— design → Fragebogenerstellung
quiet behavior 298
Quileute 665
quota sample → échantillon en fonction des quotas
Quotenstichprobe → échantillon en fonction des quotas

R

Raab (dt.) → Győr (ung.) 2047, 2059
Ráb (slk.) → Győr (ung.) 2043
race 205
racine, lexicale — → root, lexical —
radio, Radio
— Cymru (Welsh-medium radio) 1084
— libres 428
— transmission 426
— Uylenspiegel 1245
— *der Dt. und Rätorom. Schweiz* → DRS
Ragusa (it.) → Dubrovnik (bsn., srb., krt.) 2021, 2025
Raidestós (blg.) → Tekirdağ (trk.) 2029
Rakousko (tsch.) → Österreich (dt.) 229, 1350, 1797; Rakúsko (slk.) 2034
Rakúsko (slk.) → Österreich (dt.) 229, 1350, 1797; Rakousko (tsch.) 2034
Rama language 173
random sample → échantillon aléatoire, Zufallsstichprobe
Randstad 1143
range 506
— *or scope of a survey* → Reichweite einer Umfrage
scalar — → Reichweite einer Skala
Rangordnung der Sprachen 423
Rapport
— Capotorti (1979) 163, 359
— Giordan (1982) 198, 1175, 1191
— Ramirez 477
Rasse → race
Rassenhaß 226
Rassenwahn 1947
Rat der Kärntner Slowenen 1814
Ratgeber 383
Rätien 1798
ratio data 777
rational choice theory 78
rationalization 669
Rätoromanisch 270, 447, 1837, 1840, 1841, 1858

Rätoromanisch → rhéto-roman
Rätoromanische Schweiz 1879
RDA (République Démocratique Allemande) → DDR (Deutsche Demokratische Republik)
reading comprehesion → Leseverstehen
reading instruction 627
Real Academia Epañola (seit 1713) 1276
réalité
— administrative 410
— cognitive 412
— construite 407
— organisationnelle 408
— sociale 412
re-analysis, morphological — 553
reborrowing 544
recatalanisation 1199
Received Pronounciation (RP) 615
recency effect 740
recensement → Volkszählung, Zensus
— *linguistique* → census, language census
recessive language 591
recoding 778
Reconquista 1273, 1312
Redhestos (gr.) → Tekirdağ (trk.) 2035
reduction, morphological — 661
réfection savante 1217
referee design 428
reference group norm → Norm der Bezugsgruppe
reference language → langue de référence
Reformation 186, 1879
Reformation → Réforme
Réforme 1224, 1345
refugee → Flüchtling
réfugié → Flüchtling
Regensburg (dt.) → Řezno (tsch.) 2043
régiolecte 178
Regiolekt 261
regional
— unilingualism 402
— variety 376
— *language* → langue régionale
régionalisme 360
Regionalsprache 484, 847, 850, 924, 932
Regionalsprache → langue régionale
Register 147 f, 394
-theorie 146
regression analysis 436
régulation linguistique 827
Reiche, germanische — 1273

Reichenberg (dt.) → Liberec (tsch.) 2043
Reichsdänisch 1034 ff, 1761, 1771 ff, 1782 f
Reichsland Elsaß-Lothringen 1225
Reichweite
— einer Skala 741
— einer Umfrage 735
  kommunikative — 239
reinterpretation of distinctions 545
Rekrutenbefragung 1861
relation écologique 790
relearning 583
relexification 120, 136, 591, 642
reliability 745
religion 391 f
relinguification 905
Remšeniško narečje (slw.) → Obir-Dialekt, Remschenig-Dialekt (dt.)
Remschenig-Dialekt 1815
renegados 1274
Rennes (frz.) → Roazon (brt.) 2011
Repertoire 236
répertoire linguistique 389, 460
repidginisation 652
Repräsentation, semantische — → semantic representation
repräsentative Methode 734
Repräsentativität 733, 755
  qualitative — 735
représentation 680
representativeness → Repräsentativität
représentativité → Repräsentativität
Repubblica Sociale Italiana 1320
Republik Österreich 1800
République
— de Venise 1338
— et Canton du Jura 1868
— et Canton du Tessin 1870
Research Center on Multilingualism (Brussels) → Forschungsstelle für Mehrsprachigkeit (Brüssel)
research ethics → Forschungsethik
réseau → Netzwerk
— électronique 858
— linguistique 888, 891
— électronique → networks, electronic —
reshapedness → Umgestaltetheit
Resia 1323
Resicabánya (ung.) → Reşiţa (rum.) 2029, 2047
résistance linguistique 353
Reşiţa (rum.) → Resicabánya (ung.) 2029, 2047

resource mobilization theory 78
respondent behavior → Befragtenverhalten
responsabilité linguistique 680
ressemblance 177
restructuration 654
restructuring 376
restructuring → restructuration
resyntactization 122
revernacularization 903
reverse substitution 544
revitalisation → revitalization, Wiederbelebung
— de langue → language revitalization
revitalization 376, 983, 985, 988
revitalization → Wiederbelebung
revival movement 664
revivalisme 717
revivaliste 718
revivification linguistique 717
Révolution
— française 154, 202, 254, 278, 1174, 1224
— américaine → American Revolution
— *française* → Französische Revolution
Rexurdimento 1287, 1313
Rezija → Resia
Řezno (tsch.) → Regensburg (dt.) 2043
Rhaeto-Romance → Rätoromanisch, rhéto-roman, Romanisch, romontsch, rumantsch
Rhein 1836, 1855, 1879
Rheinfränkisch 1223
Rheinischer Fächer 1228
rhéto-roman 178, 1862
rhéto-roman → Rätoromanisch, Romanisch, romontsch, rumantsch
Rhin → Rhein
Rhine → Rhein
Rhodhos (gr.) → Rodosadası (trk.) 2035
Rhône 1188, 1836
Ribe (dän.) → Ripen (dt.) 2055
Richtungsadverbien 1825
Riforma Gentile (1923) 1360
Riga (ltt.) → Riga (rss.) 1946, 2067
Rijeka (slw.) → Fiume (it.) 2025
Rijsel (ndl.) → Lille (frz.) 2001
Riksmål 940, 951, 953 f
Rimaszombat (ung.) → Großsteffelsdorf (dt.) 2043; Rimavská Sobota (slk.) 2043, 2047
Rimavská Sobota (slk.) → Großsteffelsdorf (dt.) 2043; Rimaszombat (ung.) 2043, 2047
Rio de Onor 1314
Ripen (dt.) → Ribe (dän.) 2055

Ripuarisch 1163
Risorgimento 155
Rivne (ukr.) → Rovno (rss.) 2067
Rjašiv, Žešuv (ukr.) → Rzeszów (pln.) 2067
Roana (it.) 1352 → Robaan (dt.) 2021, 2059
Roavvenjárga (sam.) → Rovaniemi (fin.) 1985
Roazon (brt.) → Rennes (frz.) 2011
Robaan (dt.) → Roana (it.) 1352, 2021, 2059
Roccaforte 1367
Rochudi 1367
Rodosadası (trk.) → Rhodhos (gr.) 2035
Rois Catholiques 1286
rôle des femmes 388
rôle des hommes 388
role relation → Rollenbeziehung
role system → Rollensystem
Rollenbeweglichkeit 799
Rollenbeziehung 798
Rollensystem 28
Roma 1407, 1409 ff, 1643, 1647, 1462, 1669 ff, 1674 ff, 1680, 1804, 1828, 1961
Roma in Italien 1326
Romains 193, 1202, 1254
roman 179, 1357
Roman conquest 342
Roman Empire 342
Roman Empire → Empire romain
romance 1274
Romandie 1865
Romandie → Suisse romande, Westschweiz
Romanes 1810, 1963
Romani 339, 938, 1006, 1326, 1420, 1444, 1446 ff, 1498, 1506, 1715, 1719 f, 1804, 1806, 1961
Romani → Roma, Romasprache, Tsiganes
romani čhib 1963
Romaničal 1963
Romania 1159, 1229
— submersa 1374
România (rum.) → Rumănija (blg.) 2029; Rumunija (bsn., krt., srb.) 2025; Rumunia (pln.) 2039; Rumynija (rss.) 2067; Rumunsko (slk.) 2043; Rumunija (ukr.) 2067; Romania (ung.) 2047
Romanian 1709, 1713 ff, 1718 ff
Romanian → roumain
Romanians 1417, 1425, 1427 f, 1490, 1493 f
Romanies 1427 f, 1429

romanisation 272
Romanisch 1819
Romanisch-Deutsch 1885
Romanisprache → Romanes
Romanität 230
Romans 304
Romasprache 1675
Romasprache → Romani, Romanes
Romaunsh → Rätoromanisch, rhéto-roman, Romanisch, romontsch, rumantsch
Römer → Romains, Romans
Römer 1318, 1350
Römisches Recht 234, 1310
Römisches Reich → Empire romain, Roman Empire
römisch-katholisch 1462, 1829, 1839
römisch-orthodox 1462
romontsch 1881
romontsch → rumantsch, rhéto-roman, , Romanisch
Roms → Roma, Romani
Roms 1443, 1446
roofing → coiffure linguistique
− *language* → langue-toit
root, lexical − 109
roots 203
Rosija (ukr.) → Rossija (rss.) 2067
Rossija (rss., wrs.) → Venäjä (fin.) 1985; Ryssland (swd.); Rosija (ukr.) 2067
Rosentaler Dialekt 1815
Rösti-Graben 1874
roumain 719, 1929
roumain, Roumain → Romanian, Rumäne
Roussillon 1174
Rovaniemi (fin.) → Roavvenjárga (sam.) 1985
Rovno (rss.) → Rivne (ukr.) 2067
Royaume de France 1864
Royaume Uni → United Kingdom
Rožansko narečje (slw.) → Rosentaler Dialekt (dt.)
Rückständigkeit → backwardness
Rückwanderung 181, 1803
Rudi-Carell-Modell 418
Rumänen 1407, 1409 f, 1935 f
Rumänen → Romanians
Rumanian (eng.) → Romanian (eng.)
Rumänien 230, 1458, 1478, 1961
Rumänija (blg.) → România (rum.) 2029
Rumänisch 1470, 1478,
Rumänisch → Romanian, roumain
Rumänisch-Deutsch 1470
Rumänisch-Serbokroatisch 1411, 1413
Rumänisch-Ungarisch 1478
rumantsch 1881
rumantsch → romontsch, rhéto-roman, Romanisch
Rumantsch grischun 1844, 1879, 1881
Rumunia (pln.) → România (rum.) 2039
Rumunija (bsn., krt., srb., ukr.) → Rumynija (rss.) 2067; România (rum.), 2025
Rumunsko (slk.) → România (rum.) 2043
Rumynija (rss.) → România (rum.), Rumunija (ukr.) 2067
Ruotsi (sam.) → Ruotta (fin.), Sverige (swd.) 1985
Ruotta (fin.) → Ruotsi (sam.), Sverige (swd.) 1985
rural 1289
− migration 327
Rusinisch (Ruthenisch)-Serbokroatisch 1411 f
russe → Russian, Russisch
Russen 1463, 1670, 1672, 1935
− in den westlichen GUS-Staaten 1891 f
Russenorsk 938 f
Russes 1437
Russia → Rußland
Russian 344, 938 f, 996, 1001 f, 1006, 1009, 1013, 1427, 1490, 1498, 1583, 1584, 1593, 1916
Russian → Russisch
Russian-Estonian 1902 f, 1904
Russian-Byelorussian/ Belorus 1920 f, 1923 ff
Russians (in Latvia) 1907 f, 1911
Russians → Russen
Russie → Rußland
Russisch 231, 1618, 1697 f, 1949
Russisch → Russian
− in den westlichen GUS-Staaten 1889 ff, 1898
− in Rußland 1895
Rußland 1894−1898, 1942
-deutsche 316
Rusyns/Ruthenians 1622, 1624, 1626
Ruthenen 1407, 1409 ff, 1436 f, 1439, 1463,1670 f, 1673 f, 1697, 1800
Ruthenen → Rusyns/Ruthenians
ruthène 1436 f, 1440
ruthène → Ruthenian
Ruthènes → Ruthenen, Rusyns/ Ruthenians
Ruthenian 1425, 1427, 1583, 1584 f, 1709
Ruthenians → Ruthenen, Rusyns/Ruthenians
Ruthenisch → ruthène, Ruthenian
Ryssland (swd.) → Venäjä (fin.), Rossija (wrs.) 1985
Rzeczpospolita Polska 1643 f
Rzeszów (pln.) → Rjašiv, Žešuv (ukr.) 2067 1944

S

Sa(a)mi 937 f, 967 f, 970 f, 993, 999, 1004 f
Sa(a)mi → Lappen, Lapps, Samisch
Saarbrücken (dt.) → Sarrebruck (frz.) 2001
Saarbuckenheim (dt.) → Sarre-Union (frz.) 2001
Saarburg (dt.) → Sarrebourg (frz.) 2001, 2011
Saargemünd (dt.) → Sarreguemines (frz.) 2001
Sachprosa 1403
Sachsen (Siebenbürgen) 1471
Sächsisch 26, 259
Sacile 1338
Saint-Brieuc (frz.) → Sant-Brieg (brt.) 2011
Saint Empire Romain 1864
Saint-Gothard 1871
Saint-Jacques-de-Compostelle 1285
Saint-Jacques-de-Compostelle → Santiago de Compostela
Saint-Omer 1243
Saint-Sébastien (frz.) 1303 → Donostia (bsk.) 2011
Sakralsprache 318
Saksa (finn.) → Tyskland (bkm.), Tyskland (swd.) 1985
Säkularisierung (1803) 1384
Salcburk (tsch.) → Salzburg (dt.) 2043
Salente 1366
salience 563
Salorno (it.) → Salurn (dt.) 1322, 2059, 2063
Saluces 1344
Salurn (dt.) 1322 → Salorno (it.) 2059, 2063
Saluzzo (it.) → Saluces (frz.)
Salzburg (dt.) → Salcburk (tsch.) 2043
Salzkammergut 1799
Sambotel (krt.) → Steinamanger (dt.) 1821, 2059; Szombathely (ung.) 2047
Same-Átnam 977
Sameting 971
Sami 343, 371, 953
sami, Sami → Lappen, Lapps, sa(a)mi, Samisch

Samisch 961, 965
Samnorsk 950
sample → échantillon, Stichprobe
— *selection* → Stichprobenauswahl
representative — → échantillon représentatif
sampling 809
sampling → échantillonnage
— *theory* → Stichprobentheorie
San Antioco (Sardaigne) 1377, 1381
San Felice de Molise 1363
Sankt Gotthard (dt.) → Monošter (krt.), Szentgotthárd (ung.) 2047
San Marino 1318
San Murezzan (rtr.) → St. Moritz (dt.) 2063
San Pietro (Sardaigne) 1377, 1381
Sanskrit 231, 393
Sant-Brieg (brt.) → Saint-Brieuc (frz.) 2011
Santiago de Compostela 1275
Santiago de Compostela → Saint-Jacques-de-Compostelle
Santorini (gr.) → Thira (gr.) 2035
São Tomé 1312
Sapir-Whorf-Hypothese 422
Sápmi (sam.) → Lappi (fin.), Lappland (swd.) 1985
Sappada (it.) 1322, 1353 → Pladen (dt.) 2021, 2059
Sarandë (alb.) → Ajii Saranta (gr.) 2035
Sărbija (blg.) → Serbia (rum.), Srbija (srb.) 2029
Sardaigne 194, 352, 1214, 1376
sarde 1379
Sardinia → Sardaigne
Sardinien 1318
Sardinien → Sardaigne
Sardisch 1323
Sark (eng.) → Sercq (frz.) 1993
Sarre-Union (frz.) → Saarbukkenheim (dt.) 2001
Sarrebourg (frz.) → Saarburg (dt.) 2001, 2011
Sarrebruck (frz.) → Saarbrücken (dt.) 2001
Sarreguemines (frz.) Saargemünd (dt.) 2001
Sassaresisch 1323
sassarien (sassarese) 1377, 1378
satellisation 1211, 1212
Saterland 1786 ff
Sathmar (dt.) 1478 → Satu-Mare (rum.); Szatmárnémeti (ung.) 2029

Satu-Mare (rum.) → Sathmar (dt.) 1478; Szatmárnémeti (ung.) 2029, 2047
Säuberung, ethnische — 837
Säuberung, ethnische — → purification ethnique
saudosismo 1312
Sauris (it.) 1322, 1339, 1353 → Zahre (dt.) 2021, 2059
Savoie (frz.) 1344 → Savoyen (dt.) 2063
Savoyen (dt.) → Savoie (frz.) 1344, 2063
Saxon → Sächsisch
scale
— of adaptability 544
— of adoptability 112
— of receptivity 544
scales 67
scalogramme de Guttman 767
scapegoat 208
Schallperzeption 289
Schäßburg (dt.) → Sighișoara (rum.) 2029
Schätzung, repräsentative — 736
Schelten (dt.) → La Scheulte (frz.) 2063
schiavone 1364
Schirmeck 1226
Schleifton, südniederfränkischer — 1142
Schleitheimer Glaubensbekenntnis (1527) 312
Schmelztiegel → melting pot
Schneidemühl (dt.) → Piła (pln.) 2039
Schottland 230, 1088
Schottland → Ecosse, Scotland
Schrift 104, 108
Schrift → écriture
-deutsch 1858
— und politische Grenzen 104
— und Religion 104
chinesische — 106
kyrillische — 1953, 1954
lateinisch-kyrillische — 1883
-lichkeit 235
-losigkeit 220
-reform 105, 107
-sprache 261
-system 194, 105, 108
lateinische und kyrillische — → écriture latine et cyrillique
-*lichkeit* → scripturalité
-*reform* → *writing system reform*
-*system* → writing system
Schule 293
paritätische — 1385
Schulen
mehrsprachige — 239, 325
zweisprachige — 239

Schuls (dt.) → Scuol (rtr.) 2063
Schulsprache 293, 1138, 1858, 1883
Schulsprachregion 369
Schutzfunktion 30
Schwaben (Banat) 1471
Schwaben (Ungarn) 270
Schwäbisch (Banat) 1472
Schwarzes Meer → Mer Noire
Schweden (dt.) → Sverige (swd.) 2055
Schweden (dt.) → Sweden (eng.)
Schwedisch 293, 1945
Schwedisch → Swedish
Schweiz (dt.) 229, 1836 → Suisse (frz.) Svizzera (it., rtr.) 2021, 2011, 2055, 2059, 2063
Schweiz → Confédération helvétique, Suisse, Switzerland
Schweizer Brüder 312
Schweizerdeutsch 317, 1843, 1854, 1856, 1858
Schweizerhochdeutsch 1843, 1861
Schwyz 1836
Schwyzertütsch 234, 265
science politique → political science
scientific language → Wissenschaftssprache
Scotland 550, 1061
Scotland → Ecosse, Schottland
script
Latin-Cyrillic — 1427, 1429 f, 1431
Arabic — → écriture arabe
Chinese — → écriture chinoise; Schrift, chinesische
Cyrillic — → écriture cyrillique
gothic — → écriture gothique
scripta 1339
scripturalité 610
Scuol (rtr.) → Schuls (dt.) 2063
second generation immigrants 722
second language → langue seconde, Zweitsprache
— acquisition 7, 113, 515
— immersion programs 493
— learning 136
— *acquisition* → Zweitsprach(en)erwerb
Second World War (1939–1945) → Deuxième Guerre Mondiale, Seconde Guerre Mondiale (1939–1945)
Seconde Guerre Mondiale (1939–1945) 216
sécurité linguistique 680
Sedentarität 183
sédimentation 827
Segedin (bsn., krt., rum., srb.) → Szeged (ung.) 2025, 2047

ségrégation linguistique → language segregation
Selânik (trk.) → Solun (blg., mak.), Thessaloniki (gr.) 2035
Selbstbestimmung 686
Selbstbestimmung → autodétermination, self-determination
-srecht → droit à l'autodétermination
Selbsthaß 227, 239
Selbsthaß → auto-odi, haine de soi
self government 360
self-categorization 42
self-determination 671
self-determination → autodétermination, Selbstbestimmung
self-hatred → auto-odi, haine de soi
Selkämeri (fin.) → Bottenhavet (swd.) 1985
Sellamassiv 1383
semantic
— adaption 135
— borrowing 135
— broadening 135
— conflation 135
— constraints on borrowing 135 f
— decomposition 133
— differential scale 784
— interference 131, 134
— loan 543
— memory 132 f
— narrowing 135
— priming technique 132
— representation 130, 131, 132
— unpacking 134
semantics (as dimension of semiosis) 139 f
semantisches Differential 698
semi-dialect 146
Semikommunikation 1673
semilanguage → demi-langue
semilingualism → Halbsprachigkeit
semilinguisme 35
semilinguisme → Halbsprachigkeit
Seminario dos Estudos Galegos (1923 f) 1288
semiotics 301
semi-speaker 568, 590, 662
Senftenberg (dt.) → Zły Komorow (sor.) 2055
Senglea (it.) 1401 → l-Isla (mal.) 2021
Separation 230
Sephardic Jews 1554 ff, 1566, 1568 f
Sephardic Jews → Sephardim
Sephardim 1437
sephardische Juden → Sephardic Jews

Sepharditen → Sephardim
Sepsiszentgyörgy (ung.) → Sfîntu Gheorghe (rum.) 2029
serbe 1183, 1438, 1439
serbe → Serbian
serbocroate 1437
Serben 1463, 1407 ff, 1515
Serben → Serben, Serbs
Serbes 1434 ff, 1439
Serbes → Serbs, Serben
Serbia (alb., rum.) → Sărbija (blg.); Srbija (bsn., krt., srb.) 2025, 2029
Serbia (eng.) → Serbien (dt.)
Serbian 1713 ff, 1719
Serbie (frz.) → Serbien (dt.)
Serbien 1407 ff
Serbien und Montenegro (Königreich) 1800
Serbisch 1410 f
Serbisch → Serbian
serbo-croate → Serbo-Croatian, serbocroate
Serbo-Croatian 1024, 1026, 1030, 1031, 1444, 1709, 1713, 1718
Serbo-Kroaten 1800
Serbokroatisch → Serbo-Croatian, serbocroate
Serbokroatisch — Schrift 1410
Serbs 348, 1417 f, 1420, 1425 ff, 1443
Serbs → Serben, Serbian
Sercq (frz.) → Sark (eng.) 1993
Serments de Strasbourg (842) 1224, 1229, 1243
Serres (gr.) → Skar (blg.) 2029
Seßhaftigkeit 183
Seßhaftigkeit → Sedentarität
Sette Comuni 1322
Sette Comuni → Sieben Gemeinden
sex and language 720
Sfîntu Gheorghe (rum.) → Sepsiszentgyörgy (ung.) 2029
shibboleths 1336
Shkup (alb.) → Skopje (blg.) 2029
Shqipëria (alb.) → Albanija (blg.) 2029; Albanija (bsn., krt., srb.) 2025; Albanía (gr.) 2035;
SHS-Staat 1800
Sianel Pedwar Cumru (S4C) 1084
Sibiu (rum.) → Hermannstadt (dt.) 2029
Siders (dt.) → Sierre (frz.) 1869, 2063
Sidirokastro (gr.) → Vatovista (blg.) 2029
Sieben Gemeinden 1352, 1353
Sieben Gemeinden → Sette Comuni

Siebenbürgen 1471, 1478
Siebenbürgen → Ardeal, Erdély, Transilvania, Transsylvanie
Siebenbürger Sachsen 1471
Siebenbürger Schule 1461
Siebenbürgisch-Deutsch 94
Siedlungsmundart 1728
Sierre (frz.) 1869 → Siders (dt.) 2063
Siget in der Wart 1828
Sighișoara (rum.) → Schäßburg (dt.) 2029
sign 139 f
— language 1027
Sikhs 395
Sikulo-Albaner 1373
Simferopol' (rss., ukr.) → Simferopol' (ukr.) 2067
similarity 564
simplification 374, 591
— *linguistique* → language simplification
grammatical — 122
Simplifizierung, grammatische — → simplification, grammatical —
Simultandolmetschen → interprétation simultanée, simultaneous interpretation
simultaneous
— bilingual acquisition 603
— interpretation 860
— *acquisition* → acquisition simultanée
— *interpretation* → interprétation simultanée
Singapore → Singapour
Singapour 162, 452
Single European Act 402
single switch theory → hypothèse du commutateur simple
Sinte/Sinti 1462, 1804, 1963
Sint-Winoksbergen (ndl.) → Bergues (frz.) 2011
Sion (frz.) 1869 → Sitten (dt.) 2063
Sippenaken 1137
Sistov (rum.) → Svistov (blg.) 2029
Sitten (dt.) → Sion (frz.) 1869, 2063
situational interference 6
Six-Year Primary Program (SYPP) 490
Sizilien 1399
Skalen 740
Skalogramm von Guttman 697
Skandinavien 1962
Skar (blg.) → Serres (gr.) 2029
skill productif 504
skills → habiletés
Skolt Saami 1016, 1019
Skopia (gr.) → Skopje (blg.), Üsküp (trk.) 2035

Skopje (blg., mak.) → Shkup (alb.) 2029; Skoplje (bsn., krt., srb.) 2025; Skopia (gr.), Üsküp (trk.) 2035
Skoplje (bsn., krt., srb.) → Skopje (mak.) 2025
Slang 259
slave 1357
Slavia friulana 1358
Slavia friulana → Benečija, Beneška, Slovenija
Slavia veneta 1358
Slavia veneta → Beneška Slovenija
Slavic 343
Slavisierung 1944
Slavismus 872
slavo 1363
Slavonia → Slawonien
Slavonie 1425, 1434
Slavonie → Slawonien
Slawen 1798
Slawonien 1413
Slawonien → Slavonie
Sleghe (dt.) → Asiago (it.) 2021
Sliema 1401
Sliema Jargon 1401
Sligeach (ir.) → Sligo (eng.) 1993
Sligo (eng.) → Sligeach (ir.) 1993
Slovak 1425, 1427 ff, 1584, 1586, 1588 ff, 1591, 1709, 1013 f, 1716 ff
Slovak → slovaque, Slowake, Slowakisch
Slovakia → Slowakei
Slovakisch → Slovak, Slovaque
slovaque → Slovak, Slowake, Slowakisch
slovaque 1436 f, 1930
Slovaques 1436 f
Slovaques → Slowaken
Slovaquie → Slowakei
Slovene 1714 f, 1718 f
Slovene-German 1417 f, 1420, 1422
Slovene-Hungarian 1417 ff
Slovene-Italian 1417, 1420 ff
Slovene-Serbo-Croatian 1417, 1419 ff
Slovenen → Slowenen, Windische
Slovenes 1417
slovène 354, 1357
slovène → Slovene
Slovènes 1436
Slovènes → Slovenes
slovènes, Slovènes → Slowenen, Windische
Slovenia (it.) → Slovenija (slw.) 2021
Slovenia 1416 ff
Slovenian 1444
Slovenian → Slowenisch, Slovènes

Slovenians 1425, 1427 f
Slovenians → Slowenen, Slovènes, Windische
Slovénie → Slovenia
Slovenija (slw.) → Slowenien (dt.) 2055, 2059; Slovenia (it.) 2021; Szlovénia (ung.) 2047
Slovenisch → Slovene, slovènes, Slowenisch
Slovensko (slk.) → Slowakei (dt.) 1669–1678, 1961, 2059; Słowacja (pln.) 2039; Szlovakia (ung.) 2047
Slovincians 1600
Słowacja (pln.) → Slovensko (swk.) 2039
Slowakei (dt.) 1669–1678, 1961 → Slovensko (slk.) 2059
Slowaken 1407, 1409 f, 1463, 1642 ff, 1664, 1669, 1671 f, 1803
Slowaken → Slovaques
Slowakisch 1671, 1674, 1806
Slowakisch → Slovak, slovaque
Slowakisch-Deutsch 1685–1691
Slowakisch-Polnisch 1692–1695
Slowakisch-Serbokroatisch 1411 ff
Slowakisch-Tschechisch 1702–1707
Slowakisch-Ukrainisch 1695–1701
Slowakisch-Ungarisch 1678–1684
Slowenen 226, 1408 ff, 1800
Slowenen → Slovenes, Slovènes, Windische
Slowenien (dt.) → Slovenija (slw.) 2055, 2059
Slowenien (dt.) → Slovenia (eng.)
Slowenisch 1323, 1354, 1806, 1813
Slowinzen → Slovincians
Słupsk (pln.) → Stolp (dt.) 2039
small group dynamics 46
Smirni (gr.) → Izmir (trk.) 2035
Soađegilli (sam.) → Sodankylä (fin.) 1985
social
 — aspects of code switching 596
 — correlates of language shift 588
 — dialect 547
 — function 587
 — identity 572
 — identity theory (SIT) 41
 — network 805, 991
 — psychology of language 41
 — ressources 170
 — *membership* → appartenance sociale
sociaux-démocrates autrichiens 155

Società Filologica Friulana 1342
societal bilingualism → gesellschaftlicher Bilingualismus
société primitive 793
society, type of — → Gesellschaftstyp
sociogram 431
sociolect 1056
sociolecte 406
sociolinguistics, interactional — 139
sociolinguistique 248
sociologie des langues 1300
sociology of language → Sprachsoziologie
sociostylistique 455
Sodankylä (fin.) → Soađegilli (sam.) 1985
Sofia (rum.) → Sofija (blg.) 2029
Sofia (gr.) → Sofija (blg.) 2035
Sofija (blg.) → Sofía (gr.) 2035; Sofia (rum.) 2029
soins langagiers → language cultivation, Sprachpflege
Soleure (frz.) → Solothurn (dt.) 2063
Solidarität 222
 mechanische — 25
 organische — 25
solidarity 576, 588, 706, 807
Solombala-English 946
Solothurn (dt.) → Soleure (frz.) 2063
Solun (blg., mak.) → Thessaloniki (gr.) 2025, 2029, 2035; Solun (mak.) 2035; Selânik (trk.) 2035
Somali 221
Somalia 332
sondage → Meinungsfrage
Sønderborg (dän.) → Sonderburg (dt.) 1985, 2055
Sonderburg (dt.) → Sønderborg (dän.) 1985, 2055
Sonderbundskrieg (1847, Schweiz) 1837
Sønderjysk 1033 ff, 1770 f, 1773 f, 1783
Sondersprache 259
Sonderstatut (1948) 1384
Sopron (ung.) 1821 → Ödenburg (dt.) 1822, 2047
sorabe → Sorbisch, Wendisch
Sorbian → Sorbisch, Wendisch
Sorbisch 1762 ff, 1767
Sorbisch → Wendisch
souletin 1264
sous-échantillonnage 769
sous-représentation 769
sous-titre → sub-titling
South
 — Africa 45, 328
 — Tyroleans 349

- Italy 298
- *Africa* → Südafrika
- *America* → Südamerika
- *Old Belgium* → Altbelgien-Süd
- *Tyrol* → Südtirol, Tyrol du Sud

souveraineté du peuple 157
Soviet Union 332, 348
Soviet Union → Union Soviétique
soziale Integration 1766
Sozialisation 290
Sozialstatus 25
Soziolekt 259
Soziolinguistik vs. Sprachsoziologie 16
Soziologie 23
Spain 328, 330
Spalato (it.) → Split (bsn., krt., srb.) 2021, 2025
Spanien 1270, 1310
Spanien → Spain (eng.), Espagne (frz.), Espanya (kat.), España (sp.)
Spanier 1159
Spanisch 487, 1270, 1841
Spanisch → espagnol, Spanish
Spanischer Erbfolgekrieg 1159
Spanischer Erfolgekrieg (1701–1714) → Guerre de Succession d'Espagne (1701–1714)
Spanish 172, 343, 975
Spanish → espagnol, Spanisch
- in the U. S. 582
- -Habsburg Empire 1144
- -immersion programs 494
Spanish – English 373, 599
späte Immersion → immersion tardive
spatiale, dimension – → dimension, spatial –
special
- *language learning* → Fachsprachenerwerb
- *terminology* → Fachterminologie
- *vocabulary* → Fachwortschatz

speech
- accommodation 173
- -accommodation theory (SAT) 43
- act (theory) 139, 142 f
- community 141, 143, 169, 859, 861
- *act theory* → Sprechakttheorie
- *community* → communauté de parole, communauté langagière

speichern → emmagasiner
Spezialisierung 221

Spieltheorie → game theory
Split (bsn., krt., srb.) → Spalato (it.) 2021, 2025
spoken language 309
Spontanentlehnung 242
Sprach-
-anpassung 854
-assimilation 816
-attitüde 692, 1374
-ausbau 1393, 1953
-barriere 873 f, 881
-beherrschung 1772
-bewahrung, Spracherhalt 381
-bewußtsein 93, 1385
-bund 339, 927, 1460
-chauvinismus 225, 847
-einstellung 692, 1141
-einstellung und Sprachverhalten 695
-einstellungsforschung, Methoden der – 696
-einstellung-Sprachverhaltens-Modell 696
-erhalt 1779
-erwerb 284
-erwerbstypen 284
-fähigkeit 285
-gebrauch 267
-gebrauch, diglossischer – 323
-gemeinschaft 169, 801, 813
-geograph 260
-gesetzgebung 687
-grenze 1124, 1755
-grenze, pragmatische – 1842, 1855
-grenzfestlegung (1962, Belgien) 1140
-gruppe 1351
-halbinsel 814
-insel 812, 1352, 1746
-inseln, südbairische – 1353
-kolonie 812
-konferenz von Czernowitz (1908) 1945
-konflikt 684, 1389
-kontakt vs. Sprachenkontakt 145 f
-kontakt 1141
-kontakt, graphischer – 104, 105 f
-kontinuum 1125
-kultur 1848
-kurs 509
-lehrer 509
-lenkung 238
-lernfähigkeit 285
-lernspanne 289
-loyalität 893, 1355, 1857
-mischung 145
-ökologie 750
-ökonomie 1884

-pflege 876, 1128, 1781, 1794 f
-planung 18 f, 448, 856, 876, 882
-planung der UdSSR 1888 f, 1893
-politik 1757, 1759 ff, 1763, 1767
-politik, zaristische – 1945
-purismus 107
-reform 1795
-reinigung 261
-repertoire 323
-soziologie 799
-tod 1353
-variation 843 f, 845, 1163
-verfall 1353
-vergleich 917
-verhaltensdomäne 796
-verlagerung 1772
-verlust 902, 904 f
-verschiebung 1771 f
-verwirrung 233
-wahl 802, 847, 1882
-wechsel 15, 16, 17, 228, 238, 1727, 1746, 1771, 1773, 1779, 1879, 1885, 1893 f
-abbau → language attrition
-abstand → distance interlinguistique, distance linguistique, écart linguistique
-anpassung → assimilation linguistique
-anthropologie → anthropologie linguistique
-assimilierung → language assimilation
-ausbau → élaboration linguistique
-ausrottung → extinction of languages, language extinction
-barriere → barrière linguistique
-bewahrung → language preservation, language retention
-bewußtsein → conscience linguistique, language awareness, linguistic awareness
-chauvinismus → chauvinisme linguistique
-diskriminierung → linguistic discrimination
-domäne → domaine linguistique
-einstellung → language attitude
-entwicklung → développement linguistique, language development
-erhalt → language maintenance, maintien de langue, maintien linguistique

-*erwerbskontext* → contexte d'appropriation
-*erziehung* → éducation linguistique
-*funktionen* → fonctions langagières
-*gebrauch* → usage linguistique
-*gemeinschaft* → communauté langagière, communauté linguistique, language community
-*gesetz* → language law
-*gesetzgebung* → législation linguistique
-*grenze* → frontière linguistique, language boundary, limite linguistique
-*imperialismus* → impérialisme linguistique, linguistic imperialism
-*insel* → îlôt linguistique, language island
-*kompetenz* → language competence
-*konflikt* → conflit linguistique
-*loyalität* → language loyality, loyauté linguistique
-*minderheit* → linguistic minority
-*mischung* → language mixing
-*pflege* → cultivation linguistique, language cultivation
-*planung* → aménagement linguistique, language planning, planification linguistique
-*pluralismus* → linguistic pluralism, pluralisme linguistique
-*purismus* → purisme (linguistique)
-*politik* → language policy, politique linguistique
-*spaltung* → linguistic cleavage, glottotomie
-*standardisierung* → language standardization
-*stereotyp* → stéréotype linguistique
-*symbolik* → linguistic symbolism
-*tod* → language death
-*trennung* → language segregation, glottotomie
-*urteil* → jugement linguistique
-*variation* → variation linguistique
-*verbreitung* → diffusion linguistique, language spread
-*vereinfachung* → language simplification
-*verfall* → language obsolence
-*verlust* → language loss
-*wahl* → choix linguistique, language choice
-*wandel* → language change, linguistic change
-*wandel, kontaktinduzierter* - → changement linguistique par „contact"
-*wechsel* → alternance des langues, changement linguistique, language shift
-*wiederbelebung* → language revitalization
-*wissenschaft, kontrastive -- und Sprachkontakt* → contrastive linguistics and language contact
-*zensus, -zählung* → language census
Sprache, gefährdete -- → endangered language
Sprache, indominante -- 228, 231, 847, 850
Sprachen
-- der westlichen GUS-Staaten 1887
plurizentrische -- 895
agglutinierende -- → agglutinating languages
Sprachen-
-dekret (1784, Joseph II.) 1481
-divergenz 877
-freiheit 1130, 1846
-gesetzgebung 843
-kampf 1124, 1772
-politik 15, 19, 1774, 1794
-proporz 1846
-streit 1402
-wahl 240
-*divergenz* → divergence linguistique
-*freiheit* → liberté de la langue
-*fresserei (Glottophagie)* → linguistic cannibalism
-*kampf* → lutte des langues
-*recht* → linguistic rights
-*rechte* → droits linguistiques, language rights
-*spaltung* → glottotomie, linguistic cleavage
sprachliche
-- Assimilation 986
-- Umgebung 445
-- Variation 15
-- *Polarisierung* → language polarization
sprachlicher
-- Darwinismus 1035
-- Konservatismus 1771
-- Transfer 873 f

Sprechakttheorie 925, 927
Sprechakt(theorie) → speech act (theory)
Sprecherbiographie 265
Sprechergemeinschaft → communauté de parole
Spremberg (dt.) → Grodk (sor.) 2055
Srbija (bsn., krt., srb.) 2025 → Serbia (alb.), Sărbija (blg.) 2029; Serbia (rum.) 2029; Szerbia (ung.) 2047
Sri Lanka 328
St Lucia Creole 784
St. Michel (swd.) → Mikkeli (fin.) 1985
St. Moritz (dt.) → San Murezzan (rtr.) 2063
St. Pölten (dt.) → Svatý Hippolyt (tsch.) 2043
St-Brieuc 1253
St-Jean-de-Luz 1261
St-Palais (frz.) → Donapaleu (bsk.) 2011
St-Vith 1108
Staat → Etat
Staatsvertrag (1955, Österreich) 1807, 1815, 1832
stabile Diglossie 801
stabilisation 650
Stajerország (ung.) → Steiermark (dt.) 1798, 2047
Štajerska (krt.) → Steiermark (dt.) 1798, 2059
Stalla (dt.) → Bivio (it.) 2059, 2063; Beiva (rtr.) 2063
Stalinismus 1947
Stamm → stem
Stampalia (gr.) → Astipalea (gr.) 2035
standard
-- discourse 712
-- language 345, 834, 1491
-- variety 376
-- *language* → langue standard
Standard
-- Scottish English 1089
-kroatisch 1364
-sprache 1842
-deutsch 1808, 1861, 1881
-*deutsch* → allemand standard
-*sprache* → langue standard, standard language
-*variante* → standard variety
standardisation 162, 251, 279, 718, 889, 910, 1147
standardisation linguistique → language standardization
standardisiertes Interview 738
standardization 345, 428, 910
-- of Irish 1104
Ständestaat (1934−1938, Österreich) 1829

State 203, 205, 826f
State → Etat, State
statistical tools 777
Statistik 735
stato-nations 157
status, Status
 − and function (pidgins) 646
 − planning 904, 1718
 − *planning* → planification du statut
 -planung → planification du statut, status planning
Statut d'Autonomie de Galice (1980) 1292
statut social 1290
Stedfrysk 1154
Steiermark (dt.) 1798 → Štajerska (krt.) 2059; Stajerország (ung.) 2047
Steinamanger (dt.) → Sambotel (krt.) 2047; Szombathely (ung.) 1821, 2047, 2059
stem 109
Sterblichkeit → mortality
Stereotype 337, 699
stéréotype linguistique 678
Stereotypen 1481, 1962
stéréotypes → Vorurteile
stereotyping 208
Sternatia 1323, 1366
Stettin (dt.) → Szczecin (pln.) 1985, 2039, 2055
Stichprobe 726, 733
Stichprobe → échantillon
 repräsentative − → échantillon représentatif
Stichproben-
  -auswahl 727
  -theorie 735
  -ziehung → sampling
stigma 703
Stigmatisierung 1165
stigmatization 669
Stil
 − und Entlehnung 150f
 − und Übersetzung 151
 manuelinischer − 1312
  -mischung 151
Stilistik 146f
stocks and flows 771
Stockholm (swd.) → Tukholma (fin.) 1985, Stokgol'm (rss.), Stokhol'm (ukr.) 2067;
Štoje 1821
Štokavian 1425
Štokavian → štokavien
štokavien 1437f
Štokavisch 1821
Štokavisch → Štokavian, štokavien
Stokgol'm (rss.) → Stockholm (swd.), Stokhol'm (ukr.) 2067
Stokhol'm (ukr.) → Stokgol'm (rss.), Stockholm (swd.), 2067

Stoličny Belehrad (slk.) → Székesfehérvár (ung.) 2043
Stolp (dt.) → Słupsk (pln.) 2039
storing → emmagasiner
Strasbourg (frz.) 1174, 1223 → Straßburg (dt.) 2011, 2055
Straßburg (dt.) → Strasbourg (frz.) 1174, 1223, 2011, 2055
stratégie de neutralité 455
stratégie discursive 461
Strategie, repräsentative − 735
structural constraints on code switching 115
structure administrative 408
structured observation → strukturierte Beobachtung
strukturelle Zugehörigkeit 445
Strukturen, semantische − 1404
strukturierte Beobachtung 751
Strukturiertheit der Befragung 738
Struthof 1226
Stuhlweißenburg (dt.) → Székesfehérvár (ung.) 2047
Svatý Hippolyt (tsch.) → St. Pölten (dt.) 2043
stylistic shrinkage 662
stylistics, functional − → Funktionalstil, Funktionalstilistik
Styria (eng.) → Steiermark (dt.)
Styrie (frz.) → Steiermark (dt.)
subject → Versuchsperson (VP)
 − *protection* → Informantenschutz
subjective norm → subjektive Norm
subjektive Norm 693
Submersionsprogramm 486
subordinate language 591
subordinative bilingual 131
Subotica (srb.) → Szabadka (ung.) 2047
substitution 211, 250
substrat, Substrat 145, 1271, 1374
 − dialectal 1867
 − lexical 1247
 − neuronal 60
substrate theory 2
Substrathypothese (Kreolisierung) → hypothèse substratophile (créolisation)
substratum 393, 644
 phonological phenomena of − 102
 − *hypothesis (creolization)* → hypothèse substratophile (créolisation)
sub-titling 429
subtraktiver Bilingualismus 382
Südafrika 489, 1942
Südafrika → South Africa
Südamerika 487

Süddanubien 1479
süddeutsche Varietäten 1808
Süderjütisch 1034f, 1761, 1763, 1778f, 1782ff,
Südfränkisch 1223
Südtirol (dt.) 94, 381, 447, 1318, 1320, 1350 → Alto Adige (it.) 2059, 2063
Südtirol (dt.) → Tyrol du Sud (frz.)
Südtiroler → South Tyroleans
Südtiroler Volkspartei 1320, 1385
sudtyrolien 352
Sueben 1273, 1313
Suède → Sweden
suédois → Schwedisch, Swedish
Suisse (frz.) 155, 211, 212 → Schweiz (dt.) 229, 1836; Svizzera (it.), Svizra (rtr.), 2011, 2021, 2055, 2059, 2063
Suisse (frz.) → Confédération helvétique, Schweiz (dt.), Switzerland (eng.)
 − alémanique 441, 1224, 1865, 1866, 1873
 − italienne 1870
 − romande 1862
 − *romande* → Westschweiz
suitability of immersion 499
sujet → Versuchsperson (VP)
sumérien 272
Sumi, Sumy (ukr.) → Sumy (rss.) 2067
Summer Institute of Linguistics 899
sun-language theory 1558
Suomenlahti (fin.) → Finska viken (swd.) 1985
Suomi (fin.) → Finljandija (rss., ukr.) 2067; Suopma (sam.)1985; Finland (swd.) 1985, 2067
Suopma (sam.) → Suomi (fin.), Finland (swd.) 1985
Superstrat 145
superstrat germanique 1242, 1247
superstrate 2
suprafix 109
Surinamese 1144
Surmiranisch 1884
Surselva 1882
Sursilvan 1882, 1884
survey 575
 written − → Umfrage, schriftliche −
Suse (Susa) 1330, 1344
Sutselvisch 1884
Švecija (rss., ukr.) → Sverige (swd.) 2067
Svekomanics 996, 998
Sverige (swd.) → Schweden (dt.) 2055; Ruotta (fin.), Švecija

(rss., ukr.) 2067; Ruotsi (sam.) 1985
Sveti Petar (slw.) → Prostrum (krt.), Szentpéterfa (ung.) 2047
Svistov (blg.) → Sistov (rum.) 2029
Svizra (rtr.) → Schweiz (dt.) 229, 1836; Suisse (frz.) 155, 211, 212; Svizzera (it.,) 2011, 2021, 2055, 2059, 2063
Svizzera (it.) → Schweiz (dt.) 229, 1836, Suisse (frz.) 155, 211, 212, Svizra (rtr.) 2011, 2021, 2055, 2059, 2063
Svizzera italiana 1871
Svizzera italiana → Suisse italienne
Swahili 91
Sweden 330, 338, 345, 348
Swedish 343, 346, 938, 942, 993 f, 1018, 1019, 1025, 1031
Swedish → Schwedisch
Swedish-Finnish 774
Switzerland 77, 207
Switzerland → Schweiz, Suisse, Svizzera, Confédération helvétique, Confédération suisse
symbole 1256
symbolic
 − effect 587
 − integration 170
 − value 662
symbolisme linguistique → linguistic symbolism
Symbolwert → symbolic value
synchronisieren → dubbing
Synkretismus 1962
Synode de Chanforan (1532) 1345
syntactic
 − mode of communication 521
 − reduction 661
 − substitution 544
syntagmatic coherence 120
syntax 139 f
syntaxe 1218, 1336
System Morpheme Principle 115
System, grammatisches − 1818
système
 − limbique 58
 − neurofonctionnel 60
 − *graphique* → writing system
systemic constraints 112
systemic equivalence 112
Systemwechsel 1885
Szabadka (ung.) → Subotica (srb.) 2047
Szatmárnémeti (ung.) → Sathmar (dt.) 1478, Satu Mare (rum.) 2029, 2047
Szczecin (pln.) → Stettin (dt.) 1985, 2039, 2055

Szeged (ung.) → Segedin (bsn., krt., srb.) 2025; Segedin (rum.) 2047
Székesfehérvár (ung.) → Stuhlweißenburg (dt.) 2047; Stoličný Belehrad (slk.) 2043
Szekler 1478, 1479
Szentgotthárd (ung.) → Sankt Gotthard (dt.), Monošter (krt.) 2047
Szentpéterfa (ung.) → Prostrum (krt.), Sveti Petar (slw.) 2047
Szerbia (ung.) → Srbija (srb.) 2047
Szlovakia (ung.) → Slovensko (slk.) 2047
Szlovénia (ung.) → Slovenija (slw.) 2047
Szombathely (ung.) → Steinamanger (dt.), Sambotel (kroat.), 1821, 2047, 2059

T

Taalbuto 1156
Tablja (slw.) → Pontafel (dt.), Pontebba (it.) 2021
tagarinos 1274
Taglisch 899
Taiap 572, 589
Taiwanese 336
Talian 1388
Tallin (rss.) → Tallinn (est.) 2067
Tamil 394, 1027
Tanska (fin.) → Danmark (dän.) 1985
target
 − language (TL) 336, 515
 − *language* → langue cible, Zielsprache
 − *population* → population cible
Tarragona (kat., sp.) → Tarragone (frz.) 2011
Tarragone (frz.) → Tarragona (kat., sp.) 2011
Tartar 1001, 1463, 1928
Tarvis (dt.) 1354 → Tarvisio (it.) 1354; Trbiž (slw.) 2021, 2059
Tarvisio (it.) → Tarvis (dt.), Trbiž (slw.) 2021, 2059
Tatar → Tartar
Tataren → Tatars
Tatars 1490, 1593
Tatisch 1943
Täufer 312, 316
 -bewegung 312
tautological addition 551
Tavastehus (swd.) → Hämeenlinna (fin.) 1985
taxonomie numérique 177
tây bôi 653
Tchèque 1436 f, 1930

tchèque, Tchèque → Czech, Tschechisch, Tschechen
Tchéquie → Tschechien
tea ceremony 304
teaching materials → Lehrmaterial
teaching models of special language instruction → Unterrichtsmodelle des Fachsprachenunterrichts
teaching of languages for special purposes → Fachsprachenunterricht
Technolekt 259
Tegaere Toegaen 1245
Teilimmersion → immersion, partial −; immersion partielle
teilnehmende Beobachtung 750, 1036
teilnehmende Beobachtung → beobachtende Teilnahme, participant observation
Tekirdağ (trk.) → Raidestós (blg.) 2029; Redhestos (gr.) 2035
telecommunication 432
telefonische Befragung 738
telefonische Umfrage 730
Telefonkommunikation 418
telephone
 − conversation 432
 − *interview* → telefonische Befragung
 − *survey* → telefonische Umfrage
television 429
Temeschburg (dt.) → Temeschwar (dt.), Timişoara (rum.), Temesvár (ung.), 1471, 2029
Temesvár (ung.) → Temeschburg (dt.) 1471, 2029; Temeschwar (dt.) 2029; Timişoara (rum.) 2029, 2047
Temeschwar (dt.) → Temeschburg (dt.) 1471, Timişoara (rum.), Temesvár (ung.) 2029
témoin privilégié 769, 936
témoins privilégiés → Zeugen, privilegierte −
tendance 50
Tenedhos (gr.) → Bozcaada (trk.) 2035
terminologie 839
Terminologie 509
terminology 839
Ternopil' (ukr.) → Ternopol' (rss.) 2067
Ternopol' (rss.) → Ternopil' (ukr.) 2067
territoire 210
territorial approach 64
territorial principle 402, 1070
Territorialitätsprinzip 1125, 1132, 1845, 1855, 1847

Territorialitätsprinzip → principe de territorialité
territorialité 210, 827, 861, 1869
– linguistique 361
territoriality 348, 861, 1004
Territorialprinzip → territorial principle
Territorium 182
Tessin 163, 1841, 1844, 1870
Tessin → République et Canton du Tessin, Ticino
tessinois 1867
test
– d'aptitude 504
– de contrôle 504
– de langue 501
– de niveau 504
– de plurilinguisme 501
– de progrès 504
– standardisé 503
Tetraglossie 1164
Text-
  -produktion 508
  -rezeption 508
  -sorten 423
  -analyse → analyse du texte
Thai 336
Thailand 335
theoretical sampling 756
Theorie der zweifachen Monolingualität 365
théorie
– de l'identité 455
– de la gestion 409
– de la traduction 461
– du chaos 844
– *d'accommodation* → accommodation theory
– *de la diglossie* → Diglossie-Theorie
– *des jeux* → game theory
– *du chaos* → Chaos-Theorie
theory of consociational democracy 77
theory of diglossia → Diglossie-Theorie
thèse
– archaïsante 1367
– dorique 1367
– modernisante 1367
Thessaloniki (gr.) → Solun (blg.) 2025, 2029, 2035; Solun (mak.) 2035; Selânik (trk.) 2035
Thionville (frz.) → Diedenhofen (dt.) 2001, 2011, 2055
Thionville 1223
thiois 1242
Thira (gr.) → Santorini (gr.) 2035
Thorn (dt.) → Toruń (pln.) 2039
Thrace 1488, 1550 f, 1554 f, 1560, 1566

Thrace → Thrakien (Griechenland)
Thrakien (Griechenland) 1525
Thrakien → Thrace
Thrakikón pélagos (gr.) → Bjalo More (blg.) 2029
Three Languages Formula 488
Three Level Sample 759
Thurstone-Skala 697
Ticino 1836
Ticino → République et Canton du Tessin, Tessin
Tiefstufe 1473
Timau (it.) 1322, 1339, 1353 → Tischelwang (dt.) 2021, 2059
Timişoara (rum.) 2025 → Timišvar (bsn., krt., srb.) 2025; Temeschburg (dt.) 1471; Temeschwar (dt.) 2029; Temesvár (ung.) 2029, 2047
Timišvar (bsn., krt., srb.) → Timişoara (rum.) 2025
Timor 1312
Tirana (bsn., krt., srb.) → Tiranë (alb.) 2025
Tiranë (alb.) → Tirana (bsn., krt., srb.) 2025
Tîrgu-Mureş (rum.) → Marosvásárhely (ung.), Neumarkt (dt.) 1483, 2029
Tirol 1384, 1798
Tischelwang (dt.) → Timau (it.) 1322, 1339, 1353, 2021, 2059
Tiwa-English 785
Tiwi 376
Tok Pisin 572, 589, 650
Tolmezzo (it.) → Tumieč (frl.) 2021
Tolosa (okz.) → Toulouse (frz.) 2011
Tønder (dän.) → Tondern (dt.) 1985
Tondern (dt.) → Tønder (dän.) 1985
Tonem 1825
topic avoidance 662
topographische Aufschriften 1811, 1816
toponyme → place name
toponymes 836, 1199
toponymie 179
Toponymik 444
toponymy 553
Tornedal 961, 964, 967 f, 982
Toruń (pln.) → Thorn (dt.) 2039
toscan → Tuscan
Tosk 1445, 1541
Tosk → tosque
Toskanisch → Tuscan
Toskisch → Tosk
tosque 1453, 1455
tosque → Tosk
Total Design Method 742

Total Physical Response 84
tote Sprache → langue morte
touching behavior 305
Toulouse (frz.) → Tolosa (okz.) 2011
Tour de Babel 791
Tourcoing 1240
Tower of Babel → Tour de Babel, Turmbau zu Babel
traducteur → Übersetzer
traduction 461, 840, 860
traduction → translation
– automatique → machine translation
trait linguistique 176
Traité → Frieden, Friedensvertrag, Paix, Treaty, Vertrag,
– de Berlin (1878) 1545
– de Bucarest (1913) 1511, 1544, 1545
– de Lausanne (1923) 1546, 1560 ff
– de Londres 1452
– de Neuilly (1919) 1545
– de St-Germain (1919) 155
– de Verdun (843) 1107
– de Versailles (1768) 1202
– de Westphalie (1648) 1224
– des Pyrénées (1659) 1196
traitement 60
– de l'information 36
traits-list approach 51
transcription rules → Umschriftregeln
transfer 374, 518
– in biliteracy training 626
morphemic (morphological)
– 110, 116
– of bound grammatical morphemes 112
– of full grammatical paradigm 112
Transfer 287
Transfer → transference
  sprachlicher – → transfert linguistique
transference 3, 58
Transferenz 15
transfert → transference
– de langue 196
– linguistique 386, 873 f
– *linguistique* → sprachlicher Transfer
Transilvania 1478
Transilvanien 1458
Transilvanismus 1482
transitional dialects (Ukrainien-Byelorussian) 1622
transitional literacy instruction 632
transkodisch 240, 322
Transkription 1951
translation 840, 860

translation → traduction
  morphological – of names 550
  – *theory* → théorie de la traduction
translator → Übersetzer
transmigrant → Umsiedler
Transmigration 189
transmigration → Umsiedlung
trans-national identity 705
transparency of the form-meaning relationship 113
transport system 1078
transportation 435
Transsylvanie 155
Transylvania → Ardeal, Erdély, Siebenbürgen, Transsylvanie
Traunviertel (Oberösterreich) 1799
travailleur migrant 453
Trbiž (slw.) → Tarvis (dt.) 1354, Tarvisio (it.) 2021, 2059
Treaty → Frieden, Friedensvertrag, Paix, Traité, Vertrag
  – of Bucharest (1913) 1499
  – of Lausanne (1923) 1555, 1558, 1567, 1579
  – of Neuilly (1919) 1487, 1498
  – of Santo Stefano (1878) 1488
  – of Sèvres (1919) 1444, 1555
Tredici Comuni 1322
Tredici Comuni → Dreizehn Gemeinden
tremblement de terre de 1976 (Frioul) 1339, 1341
Trentino 1322
  – Alto Adige 349
  – Tiroler Etschland 1384
Trento (it.) → Trient (dt.) 2059, 2063
Treuga Dei 185
Trèves (frz.) → Trier (dt.) 2001
Triangulation 757
Trient (dt.) → Trento (it.) 2059, 2063
Trier (dt.) → Trèves (frz.) 2001
Triest → Trieste
Trieste (it.) 1338, 1339, 1357, 1359 → Trst (slw.) 2021, 2025
triglossia 393
Triglossie 963, 1164, 1401
trilinguale Kompetenz 1038
trilingualism → Trilingualismus
  asymetrical – → Dreisprachigkeit, asymmetrische –
Trilingualismus 1617
trilinguisme → Dreisprachigkeit
  – helvétique 1875
  – *asymétrique* → Dreisprachigkeit, asymmetrische –
Trinidad 328

Trnava (slk.) → Tyrnau (dt.) 2043; Nagyszombat (ung.) 2043, 2047
Troisième Reich 1225
Troppau (dt.) → Opava (tsch.) 2043
Trst (slw.) → Trieste (it.) 1338, 1339, 1357, 1359, 2021, 2025
troubadour → Minnesänger
Tscheche, Tschechisch → Tchèque, Czech
Tschechen 1463, 1642f, 1669, 1672f, 1803
Tschechien, Tschechische Republik 1641–1649, 2055, 2059
Tschechisch 1673f, 1682, 1687, 1746
Tschechisch → Czech, Tchèque
Tschechische Republik, Tschechien (dt.) 1641–1649 → Česká Republika, Česko (tsch.) 2055, 2059
Tschechisch-Deutsch 1645, 1646, 1656–1662, 1809
Tschechisch-Polnisch 1644ff, 1662–1669
Tschechisch-Slowakisch 1644f
Tschechoslowakisch-Ungarisch 1743
Tschechoslowakische Republik 1800
tschechoslowakische Sprache 1645, 1670, 1674, 1703–1706
Tschenstochau (dt.) → Częstochowa (pln.) 2039
tsigane 178, 1179
tsigane → gypsy
Tsiganes 1436ff, 1439, 1455
Tsiganes → Gipsy, Roma, Romani, Roms, Sinte/Sinti, Zigeuner
Tukholma (fin.) → Stockholm (swd.) 1985
Tumiéč (frl.) → Tolmezzo (it.) 2021
Tunesia 329
Tunesien 1399
Tunisie 193
Tunker 314
turc → Türkisch
Turc-grec 1560–1565
Turcija (blg.) → Türkiye (trk.) 2029
Turcs 453, 1183, 1434, 1437, 1545
Turcs → Türken, Turks
Turdetaner 1272
Turin 1330
turinois 1333
Türkei 225
  europäische – → Turkey, European –

Türken 321, 1407ff, 1463, 1504f, 1506, 1525f, 1516, 1519
Türken → Turcs, Turks
Turkey 329
  European – 1554–1560
Turkía (gr.) → Türkiye (trk.) 2035
Türkisch 1520, 1526, 1841
  – in Griechenland 1526
  – in Bulgarien 1506f
Türkisch-Armenisch 1572–1577
Türkisch-Serbokroatisch 1411, 1414f
Turkish 372, 401, 670, 1024f, 1028f, 1444, 1446ff, 1498, 1501, 1556ff, 1568f, 1579, 1623
Turkish → Türkisch
Turkish-Dutch 626
Turkish-German 603
Turkish-Judeo-Spanish 1566–1572
Türkiye (trk.) → Turcija (blg.) 2029; Turkía (gr.) 2035
Turks 344, 1144, 1427, 1445ff, 1490, 1554ff, 1578–1581
Turks → Turcs
Turku (fin.) → Åbo (swd.) 1985
Turmbau zu Babel 233
Turmbau zu Babel → Tour de Babel
Tuscan 346
two-way bilingual immersion 494
two-way immersion → immersion bidirectionnelle
typological similarity (of pidgins) 645
typologie de l'éducation bilingue 82
Typologie der Zweisprachigkeit 367
Tyrnau (dt.) → Trnava (slk.), Nagyszombat (ung.), 2043
Tyrol du Sud 354
Tyrol du Sud → Südtirol
Tyrol oriental → Osttirol
Tyroliens du Sud → South Tyroleans
Tyskland (bkm., swd.) → Saksa (fin.) 1985
Tzia (gr.) → Kea (gr.) 2035

U

U. S. English 403
Überdachung → coiffure linguistique, langue-toit
Übereinstimmung
  qualitative – 738
  quantitave – 738

Überfremdung 28, 876
Überland (dt.) → Gaby (frz.) 2063
Übersetzer 94
Übersetzung → traduction, translation
Übersetzungstheorie → théorie de la traduction
Ucraina (rum.) → Ukraïna (ukr.) 2029
Udin (frl.) → Udine (it.) 1337, 1357, 2021
Udine (it.) 1337, 1357 → Udin (frl.) 2021; Viden (slw.) 2025
UdSSR 1943
Uhry (tsch.) → Maďarsko (slk.), Magyaroroszág (ung.) 2043
Újvidék (ung.) → Novi Sad (bsn., krt.srb.) 2025, 2029, 2047
Ukraïna, Ukrajina (ukr.) → Ukrajina (pln.) 2043; Ukraina (rss.) 2067; Ucraina (rum.) 2029; Ukrajna (ung.) 2047
Ukraine 1458, 1926–1932, 1944
Ukrainer 1409, 1463, 1669, 1671, 1673 f, 1685
Ukrainian 1587, 1591 f
Ukrainians 1425, 1429, 1583 ff, 1587, 1589 f, 1609, 1623 ff, 1631
ukrainien-russe 1928
Ukrainiens 1436 ff
Ukrainisch 1949
Ukrainisch-Polnisch 1698
Ukrajina (pln.) → Ukraïna (ukr.) 2043
Ukrajna (ung.) → Ukraïna (ukr.) 2047
Uleåborg (swd.) → Oulu (fin.) 1985
Umbrien 1318
Umfrage 726
Umfrage → survey
 schriftliche – 730
Umgangssprache 258, 1355, 1805, 1815, 1835, 1840, 1855, 1879
Umgestaltetheit 636
Umschriftregeln 107
Umsiedler 1754
Umsiedlung 311, 1463
Umsiedlung → Transmigration
Umweltfaktoren 842, 843, 844
Unähnlichkeit → dissimilarity
underdifferentiation 544
under-representation → sous-représentation
under-sampling → sous-échantillonnage
UNESCO 167
Ungaria (rum.) → Magyarország (ung.) 2029

Ungarisch 1478, 1687, 1828
Ungarisch → hongrois
Ungarisch-Deutsch 1726
Ungarisch-Serbokroatisch 1411
Ungarn (dt.) 1407, 1409 ff, 1462, 1642, 1647, 1669 ff, 1685, 1808, 1961 → Magyarország (ung.) 2059
Ungarn → Hongrois
Ungvár (ung.) → Užgorod (ukr.) 2043, 2047
unilingue 1869
unilinguisme officiel 163
Union
 – Autonomista Ladina 1386
 – des Grecs de l'Italie méridionale 1368
 – Européenne 354
 – Generela di Ladins dla Dolomites 1384
 – linguistique balkanique 1512
 – Soviétique 212
 – Valdôtaine 1322
 – *linguistique balkanique* → Balkan-Sprachbund
Unione di u Populu Corsu 1202
United Kingdom 330, 331
United States 172, 299 f, 336, 343
United States → Etats-Unis
Universal
 – Grammar 519, 565
 -grammatik 285, 289
 -sprache 881
 – *hypothesis (creolization)* → hypothèse universaliste (créolisation)
 – *language* → langue universelle, Universalsprache
 -*sprache* → langue universelle
Université de Corse (Corte/ Corti) 1214
unmarked language 596
UNO → ONU
Unternehmen, multinationale – → entreprises multinationales
Unterrichtsmodelle des Fachsprachenunterrichts 510
Unterrichtssprache 483, 1829, 1881
Unterschichtsprache 896
Untertanengebiete 1854
Untertitel → sub-titling
Unterwalden 1836
Unterwart 1828
Upper Sorbian → Obersorbisch
urban
 – migration 327
 – way of life 451
 – *ecology* → écologie urbaine
urbanization index 808
Urdd Gobaith Cymru (Welsh League of Youth) 1079

Urdialekt 317
Urdu 1027, 1030, 1145
Urheimat (der Siebenbürger) 1476, 1479
Uri 1836
Urkantone 1854
Ursarja 1963
URSS 202
Urt-Departement 1137
USA 418
usage linguistique 827
Üsküp (trk.) → Skopje (blg.), Skopia (gr.) 2035
Ústí nad L. (tsch.) → Aussig (dt.) 2043
usure 531
Uto-Aztecan 588
Utsjoki (fin.) → Ohcejohka (sam.) 1985
utterance (in context) 140 f
Uviéu (ast.) → Oviedo (sp.) 2015
Užgorod (ukr.) → Ungvár (ung.) 2043, 2047

V

Vaasa (fin.) → Vasa (swd.) 1985
Val
 – Canale (it.) → Kanaltal (dt.) 1352, 1354, 2021
 – Chisone 1344
 – d'Ala 1331
 – d'Aosta 1322
 – d'Aran (frz.) → Vall d'Aran (kat.), Valle de Arán (sp.) 2015
 – de Viù 1331
 – dei Mòcheni (it.) → Fersental (dt.) 1353, 2059
 – Grana 1344
 – Grande 1331
 – Natisone 1339
 – Pellice 1344, 1345
 – Resia 1339
 – Sangone 1331
 – Soana 1331
 – Varaita 1344
 – *Canale* → Kanaltal
 – *d'Aosta* → Vallée d'Aoste, Aostatal
 – *di Fassa* → Fassa
 – *Gardena* → Gröden
Valachians → Wallachians, Valaques, Vlachen
Valachie → Walachei
Valais 1862
Valais → Wallis
Valaques 1454 f, 1544
Valaques → Vlachen, Walachen
Valença (okz.) → Valence (F, frz.) 2011
Valence (F, frz.) → Valença (okz.) 2011

Valence (E, frz.) 1198, 1296 → València (kat.), Valencia (sp.) 2015
Valencia (sp.) → Valence (F, frz.) 1198, 1296; València (kat.) 2015
València (kat.) → Valence (E, frz.) 1198, 1296; Valencia (sp.) 2015
valencien 352
valeur
 − identitaire 454
 − symbolique 389, 454, 680
 − *symbolique* → symbolic value
valide (gültig) 738
validity 745
Valkovenäjä (fin.) → Vitryssland (swd.), Belarus' (wrs.) 1985
Vall d'Aran (kat.) → Val d'Aran (frz.), Valle de Arán (sp.) 2015
Vallader 1882, 1884
Valle de Arán (sp.) → Val d'Aran (frz.), Vall d'Aran (kat.) 2015
Valle dei Mòcheni → Fersental
Valle di Fèrsina → Fersental
Vallée d'Aoste 1330, 1333
Vallée d'Aoste → Aostatal, Val d'Aosta, Augst
Vallée de Résia 1361
Vallée du Lys (frz.) → Lyss-Tal (dt.) 2063
Valletta (it.) 1399 → il-Belt Valletta (mal.) 2021
valorisaton du passé 201
Vandalen 1273
Vandales 1202, 1376
Vannes (frz.) 1253 → Gwened (brt.) 2011
Varaždin (krt.) → Varasd (ung.) 2047
Varasd (ung.) → Varaždin (krt.) 2047
Vardø (bkm.) → Várggát (sam.) 1985
Várgesztes (ung.) → Gestitz (dt.) 2047
Várggát (sam.) → Vardø (bkm.) 1985
Variable Competence Model 522
Variablenmatrix 845
variables, description of − 779
variation 287, 526
 − linguistique 826f, 843f, 845
 − *linguistique* → Sprachvariation
variationist model 522
Variationsmodell → variationist model
Varšava (rss., ukr.) → Warszawa (pln.) 2067
Vas → Eisenburg

Vasa (swd.) → Vaasa (fin.) 1985
Vatikan 1318
Vatovista (blg.) → Sidirokastro (gr.) 2029
Vaud 1330, 1862
Vaudois 1345
Vaupés Indians 173
Vel'ký Varadín (slk.) → Oradea (rum.) 2043
Venäjä (fin.) → Ryssland (swd.), Rossija (wrs.) 1985
Venetia et Histria 1338
Venezia 1338
Venezia → Venise
Venezien 1318
Venise 1338
Venise → Venezia
Vepsian 993
Vepsisch → Vepsian
Verarbeitung → traitement
verbal pause 302
verbal repertoire 170
verbale Wortbildung 1818
verbalisierte Skala 740
Verbannung 185
Vereinfachung → simplification
Vereinigte Staaten → Etats-Unis, USA
Verfassung → Constitution
Verhalten 1134
 -sbericht 729
Veria (gr.) → Ber (blg.) 2029
Verkehr → transportation
Verkehrssprache 895
Verkehrssprache → langue véhiculaire
Verkehrssprachenmodell 1848
Vermittlungssprache → intermediary language, langue intermédiaire
vernaculaire → Volkssprache
vernacular 671
 − form 721
Vernakular 482
Versailler Friedensvertrag (1919) 1131
Verschriftung 1953
Verseczn (ung.) → Vîrşet (rum.), Vršac (srb.) 2029
Verstehenskompetenz 1847, 1848
Versuchsobjekt 821
Versuchsperson (VP) 822
Vertrag → Traité, Treaty, Frieden, Friedensvertrag, Paix
 − von Bukarest (1913) 1533
 − von Lausanne (1923) 1521
 − von Osimo (1975) 1325
 − von San Stefano (1878) 1551
Vertreibung 311
Vertreibung → expulsion
Verwaltungssprache → langue administrative
Verwandtschaft, genetische − → parenté génétique

Veszprém (ung.) → Weißbrunn (dt.) 2047
viaggianti 1327
Vicebsk (wrs.) → Vitebsk (rss.) 2067
Vichy 1257
Victoria (it.) → ir-Rabat (mal.) 2021
Viden (slw.) → Udine (it.) 1337, 1357, 2025
Vídeň (tsch.) → Wien (dt.) 1797, 1800; Viedeň (slk.) 2043
Viedeň (slk.) → Wien (dt.) 1797, 1800; Vídeň (tsch.) 2043
Vieille-Belgique → Altbelgien
Vieille-Belgique-Centre 214
Vieille-Belgique-Centre → Altbelgien-Mitte
Vieille-Belgique-Nord 213
Vieille-Belgique-Nord → Altbelgien-Nord
Vieille-Belgique-Sud 214
Vieille-Belgique-Sud → Altbelgien-Süd
Vienna Agreement 1431
Vienna Agreement → Entente littéraire de Vienne (Bečki književni dogovor, 1850)
vietnamien 1179
vieux norvégien → Old Norse
vieux Slavon, vieux bulgare → Church Slavic, Kirchenslawisch, Old Church Slavonic
vigilance métalinguistique 679
Vikings 195, 342
Villach (dt.) 1814 → Beljak (slw.) 2059
Vilnius (lit.) → Vil'njus (rss.) 2067, Wilno (pln.) 2039
Vilnius (lit.) → Wilna (dt.)
Vil'njus (rss.) → Vilnius (lit.) 2039, 2067
Vinnica (rss.) → Vinnicja (ukr.) 2067
Vinnicja (ukr.) → Vinnica (rss.) 2067
Viro (fin.) → Eesti (est.) 1985
Vîrşet (rum.) → Vršac (srb.), Verseczn (ung.), 2029
visions 309
Vitebsk (rss.) → Vicebsk (wrs.) 2067
Vitoria (sp.) 1305 → Gasteiz (bsk.) 1305, 2011, 2015
Vitryssland (swd.) → Valkovenäjä (fin.), Belarus' (wrs.), 1985
Vittoriosa (it.) 1401 → il-Birgu (mal.) 2021
Vlachen 1459
Vlachen → Valaques, Walachen, Wallachians
Vlachs 1490, 1493

Vlah language 1444 f, 1446 ff
Vlah language → Aromunisch, Aromanian
Vlahi 1821
Vlahs → Valaques, Walachen, Wallachians
Vlorë (alb.) → Avlona (gr.) 2035
vocabulaire actif → active vocabulary
vocabulaire passif → passive vocabulary
vocalisme 1369
Voden (blg., mak.) → Edessa (gr.) 2025, 2029 / Edhessa (gr.) 2035
Voeren 403
Voeren → Fourons, Vuren
Vojvodina 1407 ff, 1425
Vojvodine 1434
Volk-
    -sgruppengesetz (1976, Österreich) 1815
    -sinsel 812
    -sschule 1832
    -ssprache 90
    -szählung 1354, 1839, 1840, 1841, 1943
    -*sgeist* → folk spirit
    -*ssouveränität* → souveraineté du peuple
    -*ssprache* → vernacular
    -*szählung (Zensus)* → census
Völkermord 1942, 1947
Völkermord → ethnocide
Völkerwanderung 181, 186
Vorarlberg 1224, 1797
vorrömische Sprache 1271
Vorurteil → prejudice, Stereotype
    sprachliches − → linguistic prejudice
Vorurteile 225, 1805
Votian 993
Votisch → Votian
Vršac (srb.) → Vîrşet (rum.), Verseczn (ung.) 2029
Vratislav (tsch.) → Breslau (dt.), Wrocław (pln.) 2043
Vuren 1136
Vuren → Voeren

W

Waadt → Vaud
Walachei 1460, 1962
Walachen 1407, 1409 f, 1516, 1518, 1520
Walachen → Aromunen, Valaques, Vlachen
Wałbrzych (pln.) → Waldenburg (dt.) 2039, 2043
Waldenburg (dt.) → Wałbrzych (pln.) 2039, 2043

Waldenser → Vaudois
Wales (eng.) → Cymru (ir.) 1993
Wales 69, 1060, 1075
Wales → Pays de Galles
Walisisch 686
Walisisch → gallois, Welsh
Walisisch − Englisch 364
Wallachia → Walachei
Wallachians 1427
Wallachians → Aromunen, Valaques, Vlachen, Walachen
Wallis 1837, 1854
Wallis → Valais
wallon 336, 354, 1109
− liégeois 176
Wallonia 401
Wallonie → Wallonia
Wallonien 1133
Wallonien → Wallonia
Wallonisch 1138
wallonischgesinnt 1139, 1140
Wallons 349
Walser 1322, 1333, 1352, 1353
Wandel, dynamischer − 29
Wanderarbeit 184
Wandertheorie 1479
War of the Spanish Succession (1701−1714) → Guerre de Succession d'Espagne (1701−1714)
Warlpiri 428
Warszawa (pln.) → Varšava (rss., ukr.) 2067
Wasserkroaten 1823
Wasserpolnisch 1589, 1592
weed metaphor 646
Węgry (pln.) → Magyarország (ung.) 2039
weibliche Rollen → rôle des femmes
weighting → Gewichtung
Weindorf (dt.) → Pilisborosjenő (ung.) 2047
Weißbrunn (dt.) → Veszprém (ung.) 2047
Weißrussisch 1618, 1949
Weißrussisch → Belorussian, Byelorussian
Weißrußland 226, 1944
Weißwasser (dt.) → Bela Woda (sor.) 2055
Welkenraedt 1108
Welkenraedt → Welkenrat
Welkenrat 1137
Welkenrat → Welkenraedt
Welsche 1856
Welschlandjahr 1845
Welschschweiz → Suisse romande, Westschweiz
Welsh 336, 345, 427, 1060, 1076
Welsh → gallois, Walisisch
− Language Acts 1070
− Language Board 1082

− -medium education 1081
− -medium publishing 1083
Weltbevölkerung 182
Welthilfssprache 881
Weltkrieg, Erster − (1914−1918) → Guerre Mondiale, Première − (1914−1918)
Weltkrieg, Zweiter − (1939−1945) → World War, Second − (1939−1945)
Weltsprache → langue mondiale, world language
Wende, pragmatische − 266
Wendisch 1790 f, 1794
Wendisch → Sorbisch
Werbekampagne → campagne publicitaire
Werbung → publicité
West
− Africa 338
− Frisian 1152
− Indies 330
    -europa 1942
    -fälischer Friede (1648) 313
    -friesisch 1762, 1787
    -goten 1273, 1313
    -schweiz 1856
Wiedeń (pln.) → Wien (dt.) 1797, 1800, 2039; Viedeň (slk.) 2043; Vídeň (tsch.), Bécs (ung.) 2047
Wiederbelebung → revitalization
Wiederbelebung 1763 f
Wiedertaufe 312
Wien (dt.) 1797, 1800 → Wiedeń (pln.) 2039, Viedeň (slk.) 2043; Vídeň (tsch.), Bécs (ung.) 2047
Wiener Becken 1798
Wiener Kongreß (1815) 1159, 1167
Wiener Kongreß (1815) → Congrès de Vienne (1815)
Wiener Schiedsspruch (1940) 1482
Wieselburg (dt.) 1822 → Mosonmagyaróvár (ung.) 2047
Wikinger → Vikings
Willensnation 1797
Wilna (dt.) 1946 → Vilnius (lit.) 2039, 2067
Wilno (pln.) → Wilna (dt.) 1946; Vilnius (lit.) 2039, 2067
Windische 1805, 1806, 1815
Wirtschaft 414
    -ssprache 511, 875
Wissenschaftssprache 259, 422, 508
witnesses, privileged − → Zeugen, privilegierte −
Wojerecy (sor.) → Hoyerswerda (dt.) 2055

Wojwodina → Vojvodina
women's roles → rôle des femmes
word
– association test 132
– coinage 663
– decoding 625
– geography 66
– *of foreign origin* → mot étranger
– *order* → ordre des mots
words with mixed morphologies 115
working language 839, 858 f
working language → langue de travail, langue du travail
world, World
– Englishes 911
– language 858
– War, Second – (1939–1945) 1146
– *language* → langue mondiale
– *War, First – (1914–1918)* → Guerre Mondiale, Première – (1914–1918)
Worms (dt.) → Bormio (it.) 2063
Wortatlas der deutschen Umgangssprache 262
Wortbildung 262, 1959
Wörterbücher 1403
Wortschatz
  aktiver – → active vocabulary
  passiver – → passive vocabulary
  -verlust → loss of vocabulary
Wortschrift 263
Wortstellung 1394, 1959
Wortstellung → ordre des mots
writing → écriture, Schrift
– system 396
– *system* → Schriftsystem
– *system reform* → Schriftreform
  cuneiform – → Keilschrift
written language 629
Wrocław (pln.) → Breslau (dt.) 2039, 2043; Vratislav (tsch.) 2043
Wurzel, lexikalische – → root, lexical –

X

Xalma 1314
Xanthi (gr.) → Iskeçe (trk.) 2035
Xenismus 871, 874, 876
Xhosa 805

Y

Yerli 1804
Yiddish 178, 347, 377, 394, 664, 1001, 1006, 1556, 1568, 1583, 1593, 1720, 1920, 1922, 1924, 1179, 1930
Yiddish, yiddish → Jiddisch
YIWO-Norm 1952
YIWO-Orthographie 1952
Yoruba 490
Yougoslaves 1434, 1436
Yougoslaves → Jugoslawen
Yougoslavia → Yougoslavie
Yougoslavie 202, 215, 1452 f
Yougoslavie → Jugoslawien, Yugoslavia
Yougoslavs → Yougoslaves, Jugoslawen
Yugoslavia 329, 1418, 1420, 1423
Yugoslavia → Jugoslawien
Yugoslavs → Jugoslawen, Yougoslaves
Yunanistan (trk.) → Elladha (Ellas) (gr.) 2035

Z

z' Makanà / Makannah (dt.) → Macugnaga (it.) 2021
Zadar (bsn., krt., srb.) 1320 → Zara (it.) 2021, 2025
Zágráb (ung.) → Zagreb (krt.) 2047
Zagreb (krt.) → Zágráb (ung.) 2047
Zahre (dt.) 1322, 1352, 1353 → Sauris (it.) 1322, 1352, 1353, 2021, 2059
Zalău (rum.) → Zilah (ung.) 2029, 2047
Zaporižžja (ukr.) → Zaporož'e (rss.) 2067
Zaporož'e (rss.) → Zaporižžja (ukr.) 2067
Zara (it.) → Zadar (bsn., krt., srb.) 2021, 2025
Zeichen → sign
Željezno (krt.) → Eisenstadt (dt.) 1821, 2047; Kismarton (ung.) 2047, 2059
Zensus 1723
Zent Ladina Dolomites 1384
Zentralverband slowenischer Organisationen 1814
zero morpheme 110
zero vs. overt morpheme in transfer 112
„zerreißende" Zweisprachigkeit 486
Zeugen, privilegierte – 936
Zielgruppe → population cible
Zielona Góra (pln.) → Grünberg (dt.) 2039
Zielsprache 913 f
Zielsprache → langue cible, target language (TL)
Zigeuner 232, 1504 f, 1675, 1804, 1961
Zigeuner → Gipsy, gypsy, Roma, Romani, Roms, Sinte/Sinti, Tsiganes
Zilah (ung.) → Zalău (rum.) 2029, 2047
Ziljsko narečje (slw.) → Gailtaler Dialekt (dt.)
Zimbern 1353
Zingari 1326
Zips 1471
Zitatwort 1819
Zivavoda Brdodokriz (krt.) → Acquaviva Collecroce (it.) 1323, 1363, 2021, 2025
Zły Komorow (sor.) → Senftenberg (dt.) 2055
Znaim (dt.) → Znojmo (tsch.) 2043, 2059
Znojmo (tsch.) → Znaim (dt.) 2043, 2059
Zoldo 1391
Zrenjanin (srb.) → Nagybecskerek (ung.) 2029
Zufallsstichprobe 735
Zufallsstichprobe → échantillon aléatoire
Zugehörigkeit, ethnische – → appartenance ethnique
Zugehörigkeit, etymologische – 446
Zugehörigkeit, soziale → appartenance sociale
Zuidersee 1150
zuilen 78
Zulu 490
Zürcher Reformation 312
Zurich 1870
Zürich 1836, 1855
Zürich → Zurich
Zweinamigkeit 447
zweisprachige Erziehung → éducation bilingue
zweisprachige Schulen → bilingual schools
Zweisprachigkeit 14 f, 16, 17, 19, 321, 1665
Zweisprachigkeit → bilinguisme, bilingualism
– im Kleinkindesalter 366
– in Moldawien 1936 f
  additive – 236
  asymmetrische – 235
  national-russische – 1893 f
  -sprüfung 1352
  symmetrische – 235
  additive – → bilingualité additive

aktive – → active bilingualism
frühe – → bilinguisme précoce
-sprogramme → programmes bilingues
Zweiter Weltkrieg 1402
Zweiter Weltkrieg → Deuxième Guerre Mondiale (1939–1945)
Zweitsprache 882
Zweitsprache → L$_2$, langue seconde
Zweitsprach(en)erwerb 15, 145
Zweitsprachendidaktik 1474
Zweitsprachenimmersion → second language immersion programs
Zweitspracherwerb → second language acquisition, second language learning
Zweitspracherwerb, gesteuerter – 321
Zwinglianer 316
Zwischensprache → interlanguage
Zypern → Cyprus